EDUCATIONAL RANKINGS
ANNUAL

ISSN 0077-4472

EDUCATIONAL RANKINGS
A N N U A L

Over 4400 Rankings and Lists on Education, Compiled from Educational and General Interest Published Sources

2002

- Reputation
- Faculty Publications
- Tuition Rates
- Library Facilities
- Test Scores
- Alumni Achievement
- Faculty Salaries
- Admissions Selectivity

Lynn C. Hattendorf Westney
Editor

GALE GROUP
THOMSON LEARNING

Detroit • New York • San Diego • San Francisco
Boston • New Haven, Conn. • Waterville, Maine
London • Munich

Lynn C. Hattendorf Westney, *Editor*

Gale Group Staff

Kathleen E. Maki Potts, *Coordinating Editor*

Venus Little, *Manager, Database Applications, Technical Support Services*
Magdalena Cureton-Streicher, *Programmer/Analyst*

Evi Seoud, *Assitant Production Manager*
NeKita McKee, *Buyer*

Mike Logusz, *Graphic Artist*

While every effort has been made to ensure the reliability of the information presented in this publication, the Gale Group does not guarantee the accuracy of the data contained herein. The Gale Group accepts no payment for listing; and inclusion in the publication of any organization, agency, institution, publication, service, or individual does not imply endorsement of the editors or publisher.

Errors brought to the attention of the publisher and verified to the satisfaction of the publisher will be corrected in future editions.

This publication is a creative work fully protected by all applicable copyright laws, as well as by misappropriation, trade secret, unfair competition, and other applicable laws. The authors and editors of this work have added value to the underlying factual materials herein through one or more of the following: unique and original selection, coordination, expression, arrangement, and classification of the information.

The Gale Group will vigorously defend all of its rights in this publication.

© 2002 Gale Group, Inc.
27500 Drake Rd.
Farmington Hills, MI 48331-3535

All rights reserved including the right to reproduce in whole or in part in any form.

ISBN 0-7876-3452-2
ISSN 0077-4472

Printed in the United States of America
Published in the United States by the Gale Group
Gale Group and Design is a trademark used herein under license

This edition of *Educational Rankings Annual* is dedicated to my dear husband, Robert (Bob) J. Westney.

Contents

Introduction ix

Sample Entry xiv

Outline of Contents xv

Educational Rankings 1

Index 533

Introduction

- What were the average 2001 tuition and fees for students in public 4-year colleges? How do they compare with those of private 4-year colleges?
- What public 2-year college had the highest 2001 in-state tuition and fees? Which had the lowest?
- What is the world share of Japan's published science and social science papers for 1996-2000?
- What were the top five countries in terms of total spending per student in 1997? What countries were the lowest?
- What were the top 10 career-related web sites?
- According to *Syllabus* magazine, what are the top education web sites for educators interested in technology?
- What is the percentage by state of high school freshmen who go on to college soon after graduation?
- What are the fastest-growing women's and men's college sports?
- What countries grant the most annual leave days for their employees?
- What are the top five high-impact U.S. universities ranked by average citations per published paper in the field of management?
- What universities contributed the greatest number of published papers to the field of chemistry?
- What were the top 10 most-cited scientific research articles published from 1990-1998 and cited through December 1999?
- What were the best audiobooks of 2000 according to *Library Journal*?
- According to *U.S. News and World Report*, what are the top-ranked law school programs in environmental law and health law?
- What is the most selective preparatory school in Chicago?
- What higher education institutions employ the most full-time Hispanic faculty?
- What universities grant the most Masters degrees in journalism and mass communication?
- What are the top 10 issues impacting school administrators?
- In the fields of macroeconomics and microeconomics, what are the top-ranked journals by citation impact?
- What books were chosen by *Library Journal* as the best reference sources of 2000?
- In 2001, what was the average price for physics periodicals?

These and thousands of other questions about the field of education are answered in the 2002 edition of *Educational Rankings Annual*.

ERA Fills the Gap for Students, Parents, Librarians, and Educators

Educational Rankings Annual (*ERA*) is published in response to the enormous concerns expressed by students, parents, teachers, librarians, guidance counselors, educational administrators, and others for reliable rankings based on intellectually defensible criteria. Rankings are used in assisting students, parents, and others to find information about the quality of education at all levels. Administrators of libraries and educational institutions use rankings to defend budgets, justify new positions, obtain government funding, recruit students and faculty through rankings publicity, and attract philanthropic support. Primary, secondary, and preparatory schools; junior colleges; school districts; colleges and universities; departments, disciplines, and programs; college guides; financial aid; test scores; and admission rates—all these topics and more are contained in *ERA*.

ERA's Origins in RQ

A series of articles in the Spring issues of the American Library Association journal *RQ* (Lynn C. Hattendorf, "College and University Rankings: An Annotated Bibliography of Analysis, Criticism, and Evaluation," Parts 1-5, vols. 25-29, 1986-1990) identified and evaluated rankings sources in the area of higher education. *ERA* is responding to the concerns that have been expressed at all levels of the educational hierarchy by including educational lists from school district ratings through doctoral work and by including the actual rankings that address all aspects and all facets of education.

ERA Lists Rankings from a Wide Variety of Reputable Sources

"The public wants *anything* that will rate and compare colleges," stated R. Miles Uhrig, director of admissions at Tufts University (Deidre Carmody, "Picking College Guides: No Easy Task," *New York Times*, December 2, 1987, v. 137, p. 19). Hattendorf created the *RQ* ranking series to ensure that the public does not receive *just anything* and the Gale Group conceived *ERA* to respond in a responsible manner to the demands for accurate, comprehensive, reliable, and timely information about ratings and rankings in all areas of the educational arena.

Rankings information appears randomly and in diverse publications ranging from newspapers and popular magazines to books, college guides, scholarly journals, and government publications. The lack of organization and consolidation makes it problematic and often impossible to identify educational rankings at all, not to mention in a timely manner. Rankings published in newspapers and popular magazines have the potential to reach the greatest number of users even though better rankings data may be available in scholarly journals which are published for a limited audience.

Educational Rankings Annual is a selective reference source. It does not include rankings publications which have received extensive negative criticism by rankings experts or that fall short of Gale's high standards for its publications. If a source is missing that you think should be included, please write to the editor or the Gale Group.

Rankings Methodologies

Compiling educational rankings is a complex process because they attempt to measure quality. While business rankings are compiled on simple objective measures such as company or industry assets, billings, sales, and other quantifiable and measurable statistics, educational rankings are based primarily on more complex measures such as academic reputation, citation analysis, the publication productivity of faculty, peer evaluations or perceptions, distinguished alumni, student achievement in later life, admissions selectivity, application rates, test scores, tuition, faculty salaries, library and computer facilities—none of which precisely reflects the educational quality being offered by institutions. These methods serve only as indicators—they are not measuring devices.

Arguments appear throughout the literature for and against each of the major ranking methodologies: 1) reputational rankings; 2) citation analysis; 3) faculty research and publication productivity; and 4) statistical rankings. (For a fascinating history of rankings research and for detailed information about the types of educational rankings methodologies, see David S. Webster, *Academic Quality Rankings of American Colleges and Universities*, Springfield, IL: Charles C. Thomas, 1986.)

The four major educational ranking methodologies are briefly summarized as follows:

> 1. Reputational Rankings
> Reputational rankings are derived from the opinions of college and university presidents, deans, department chairpersons, senior scholars, and others who are in a position to know who are the most influential and prolific scholars in a field or which are the highest-quality academic institutions. These studies are based on the subjective opinions of select groups of people.

2. Citation Analysis
Citation analysis is a method of assessing the influence and intellectual importance of research over time, and thus, of assessing individual departments and institutions—the more citations the higher the rank order of a department when it is compared with departments from other institutions. In order for citation analysis to reflect accurate measures of objectivity and fairness, it is necessary to adjust for the presence of self-citations (sometimes the only citations to individual works are from their respective authors), and to adjust for collaborative writing (often only the first author is counted even though other authors may have contributed equally or more). Citation indexes do not distinguish between good, neutral, or bad citations.

3. Faculty Productivity
The research and publication productivity of faculty is measured by counting the number of publications an individual scholar has published during a particular period. The more publications faculty members have, the higher the rankings of themselves, their departments, and their disciplines—depending on what variables are being used to compile the rankings or to create comparisons. While many arguments have been made against these types of studies because they measure the quantity of the faculty's research, not necessarily their quality or teaching, the counter argument is that faculty who perform research on a continuing and prolific basis will stay current with the latest developments in their fields. This, in turn, should make them better teachers, but that is not always the case. Quantity and quality do not necessarily go hand-in-hand. Nevertheless, the highest-ranked institutions in most areas also have tenured faculty who are prolific scholars in the areas of research and publication.

4. Statistical Rankings
Numerical lists and rankings derived from such arbitrary information as the colleges with the highest endowments, the largest library facilities, the most selective admissions rates, etc., are interesting, but what do they actually reveal about educational quality? While the statistics are often significant in themselves, there is the danger that too much importance will be attached to them in measuring the overall quality of education offered by those institutions.

ERA Gives the User a Variety of Rankings to Study

There is NO individual ranking in any area of education that should be considered THE definitive ranking. Rankings change and vary over time according to environmental factors (when application rates decrease, even "selective" colleges will lower their admissions standards in order to fill their vacancies) and according to what is being ranked and how the ranking is compiled. All rankings in the educational arena should be examined and compared with other available studies; they should not be judged in a vacuum. People should derive their own conclusions about the integrity and intellectual worth of individual rankings based on their own personal and comparative evaluations of the sources and methodologies that have been used.

ERA Presents Current and Classic Rankings

Because of the complexity of devising research methodologies and the prohibitive length of time it takes to conduct surveys, compile results, submit them for publication, and ultimately get the results published, most educational rankings do not appear on an annual or timely basis. Many one-of-a-kind rankings studies often span decades. For example, the "Often-Cited Papers Appearing in the *American Journal of Physics*, 1945-90;" the "Most Frequently-Cited Law Reviews and Legal Periodicals, 1924-1986;" the "Most Frequently-Cited Clinical Dermatology Articles, 1945-1990;" and the Franklin and Marshall Rankings of Private Undergraduate Colleges and Universities Producing the Most Ph.D.s in various disciplines, 1920-1990, are examples of these stand-alone studies. The value of this genre of rankings research increases over time because these studies are unique, retrospective, and comprehensive. Studies that examine individual facets of education over long periods of time often suggest important implications that should not be ignored by future researchers. Much remains to be accomplished by contemporary rankings researchers who should be building upon existing research.

New rankings for individual subject areas do not appear every year. In fact, often only one ranking may be available for a discipline during an entire decade, and no rankings currently exist for many educational areas. Rankings often generate discussion and comment in the professional literature, but these responses may not appear until years after the publication of the original research. Because of this time lag and because of the comprehensive nature of some studies, *ERA* includes both retrospective studies that remain valuable and important in rankings research, as well as current lists and rankings. In fact, about 800 entries from *ERA 2001* have been included in this new volume either because no recent research has been done to update those rankings or because those rankings remain classics, even though more recent rankings may also be included. Earlier rankings can be identified and traced through the references and bibliographic citations which appear in the bibliographies of the sources of rankings included in *ERA*.

Rankings from online and electronic (nonprint) journals are included.

More Than Rankings

A number of publications address problems and methodologies in compiling educational rankings. Some discuss highly regarded schools and programs without providing actual numerical rankings. Nonetheless, they are important sources that extend and enhance the value of numerical rankings and serve to illuminate areas that have not been sufficiently addressed elsewhere. These types of publications, which critique or respond to previously published rankings, have been included as Related Information entries and immediately follow entries with rankings. All are listed under appropriate subject categories derived from those of the Educational Resources Information Center (ERIC).

Index Is a Tool in Itself

ERA's expanded index not only lists the schools, programs, states, and other items ranked, but also ties the descriptive entry titles to what is being ranked. For example, when you look up Oberlin College you will find the entry title "Private, 4-year undergraduate colleges and universities producing the most Ph.D.s in all fields of study, 1920-1990," plus its corresponding entry number, in addition to various other listings ranking Oberlin. Thus, the index provides a quick look at the areas in which the school that interests you is being ranked.

One-Stop Source

ERA is a one-stop source of rankings information which includes not just source citations, but also the actual rankings. It should be the first source one turns to when attempting to identify rankings for a particular area of education or when looking for rankings information on education in general. Its scope is largely American although Canadian and other international studies are included when deemed relevant.

With the number of jobs requiring a college degree increasing and the cost of getting that degree rising annually, the search for "the right college" has become a more complicated process than it has been in the years past. The editorial staff of the Gale Group has conceived this *Educational Rankings Annual* to assist all users who have questions about the quality of education.

Suggestions Are Welcome

Comments and suggestions for *ERA* are always welcome and can be addressed:

Educational Rankings Annual
The Gale Group
27500 Drake Road
Farmington Hills, MI 48331-3535

Lynn C. Hattendorf Westney, Associate Professor
The University of Illinois at Chicago
The Richard J. Daley Library

Sample Entry

Below is a sample showing the typical format of an *Educational Rankings Annual* entry. Each numbered item is explained in the paragraph with the corresponding number.

---

❶ ★ 1 ★
❷ **Colleges with the highest number of freshmen Merit Scholars, 2000**
❸ **Ranking basis/background:** Determined by *The Chronicle* from an alphabetical listing appearing in the National Merit Scholarship Corp.'s 1999-2000 annual report. A total of 8,170 Merit Scholars enrolled in the fall of 2000; 4,674 at 233 private colleges and universities and 3,496 at 148 public institutions.
  ❹ **Remarks:** Original Source: National Merit Scholarship Corporation. ❺ **Number listed:** 85

❻
1. Harvard University, with 382 scholars
2. Unversity of California, Berkeley, 246
3. University of Texas, Austin, 245
4. Stanford University, 209
5. Yale University, 191
6. University of Florida, 166
7. Rice University, 162
8. University of Chicago, 151
9. Massachusetts Institute of Technology, 148
10. University of Southern California, 148

❼ **Source:** "2001 Freshman Merit Scholars," *The Chronicle of Higher Education* 47: A48 (January 16, 2001).

---

❶ Sequential entry number.
❷ Ranking title: A descriptive phrase, identifying the contents of the list cited. These titles may be taken verbatim from the original source, or, if need be, assigned by the editor to better categorize the list.
❸ Ranking basis/background: Indicates the criteria that establish the hierarchy, with specifics of dates and units of measure, if given.
❹ Remarks: Provides additional details relating to the list from the source material.
❺ Number listed: Notes the number of listees in the ranking source.
❻ Ranking: The complete or partial (if extensive) ranking. Discrepancies in format of names cited (Wharton School of Business or University of Pennsylvania, Wharton School of Business) reflect diversity in sources.
❼ Source: Gives complete bibliographic details. For periodical articles, notes article title, authors, title of periodical, volume number, inclusive pages, and date. For books, lists publisher as well.

Outline of Contents

Entry categories for *Educational Rankings Annual* can be identified by scanning the Outline of Contents. The category headings are based on ERIC descriptors.

A

Academic Achievement
Accounting Programs *See:* Business Administration—Accounting; Business Administration, Graduate—Accounting
Achievement Tests—Schools, Elementary & Secondary *See also:* College Entrance Examinations
ACT *See:* College Entrance Examinations
Advanced Placement Tests
Aerospace Engineering *See:* Engineering—Aerospace; Engineering, Graduate—Aerospace
African Americans *See:* Black Americans
Agricultural Education
Agriculture
Alcohol Education *See:* Substance Abuse and Education
American Indians—Enrollment, College
Anthropology
Anthropology, Graduate
Anthropology Periodicals
Archaeology
Architecture
Architecture, Graduate
Art
Art History, Graduate
Artificial Intelligence
Arts & Humanities—Federal Aid
Associate Degrees *See:* Degrees (Academic)
Astronomy
Astronomy, Graduate
Athletics
Athletics—Colleges & Universities
Athletics—Colleges & Universities—Baseball
Athletics—Colleges & Universities—Basketball
Athletics—Colleges & Universities—Football
Athletics—Elementary & Secondary Schools

B

Basic Skills Tests *See:* Achievement Tests—Schools, Elementary & Secondary
Biological Science Periodicals
Biological Sciences
Biological Sciences—International
Biology
Biology, Graduate
Biology, Graduate—Cellular/Molecular
Biology, Graduate—Microbiology

Biomedical Engineering *See:* Engineering, Graduate—Biomedical
Biostatistics *See:* Mathematics, Graduate—Statistics
Black Americans
Black Colleges and Universities
Black Students—Financial Aid
Blacks—Enrollment, College
Boarding Schools *See:* Schools, Elementary & Secondary; Schools, Secondary
Books *See also:* Censorship; Libraries
Books, Children and Young Adult
Books, Reference
Business Administration
Business Administration—Accounting *See also:* Business Administration, Graduate—Accounting
Business Administration—Finance *See also:* Business Administration, Graduate—Finance
Business Administration, Graduate
Business Administration, Graduate—Accounting *See also:* Business Administration—Accounting
Business Administration, Graduate—Finance *See also:* Business Administration—Finance
Business Administration, Graduate—General Management
Business Administration, Graduate—Insurance *See also:* Business Administration—Insurance
Business Administration, Graduate—International
Business Administration, Graduate—Manufacturing *See also:* Business Administration—Manufacturing
Business Administration, Graduate—Marketing *See also:* Business Administration—Marketing
Business Administration, Graduate—Quantitative Analysis
Business Administration, Graduate—Technology Management *See also:* Business Administration—Technology Management
Business Administration—Insurance *See also:* Business Administration, Graduate—Insurance
Business Administration—International
Business Administration—Manufacturing *See also:* Business Administration, Graduate—Manufacturing

Business Administration—Marketing *See also:* Business Administration, Graduate—Marketing; Business Periodicals
Business Administration—Technology Management *See also:* Business Administration, Graduate—Technology Management
Business Periodicals *See also:* Economics and Business Periodicals; Real Estate Periodicals
Business Schools (College) *See:* Business Administration; Business Administration, Graduate

C

Campus Crime
Careers
Cellular Biology, Graduate *See:* Biology, Graduate—Cellular/Molecular
Censorship
Chemical Engineering *See:* Engineering—Chemical; Engineering, Graduate—Chemical
Chemistry
Chemistry, Graduate
Chemistry Periodicals
Civil Engineering *See:* Engineering—Civil; Engineering, Graduate—Civil
Civil Rights—Federal Aid
Classical Studies, Graduate
College Administration
College Administration, Minority
College Admission
College Admission—Tests *See:* College Entrance Examinations
College Bookstores
College Choice
College Enrollment *See also:* American Indians—Enrollment, College; Blacks—Enrollment, College; College Students; Disabilities—Enrollment of Students; Foreign Students—Enrollment, College; Hispanic Americans—Enrollment, College; Minority Groups—Enrollment, College
College Enrollment—Illinois
College Entrance Examinations
College Faculty
College Faculty, Minority
College Graduates *See also:* Degrees (Academic); Doctoral Degrees
College Guides
College Life

College Presidents *See:* College Administration; Salaries—Colleges & Universities
College Students
College Students, Graduate *See:* Graduate Students
Colleges & Universities *See also:* Black Colleges and Universities; Two-Year Colleges
Colleges & Universities—Canada
Colleges & Universities—Enrollment *See:* American Indians—Enrollment, College; Blacks—Enrollment, College; College Enrollment; Disabilities—Enrollment of Students; Foreign Students—Enrollment, College; Hispanic Americans—Enrollment, College; Minority Groups—Enrollment, College
Colleges & Universities—Financial Support & Expenditures *See also:* Research & Development Funding; Research Funding
Colleges & Universities—Honors Programs
Colleges & Universities, Liberal Arts
Colleges & Universities, Liberal Arts—Middle Western States
Colleges & Universities, Liberal Arts—Northeastern States
Colleges & Universities, Liberal Arts—Southern States
Colleges & Universities, Liberal Arts—Student Costs
Colleges & Universities, Liberal Arts—Tuition *See:* Colleges & Universities, Liberal Arts—Student Costs
Colleges & Universities, Liberal Arts—Western States
Colleges & Universities—Middle Western States
Colleges & Universities—Northern States
Colleges & Universities—Research *See:* Research & Development Funding; Research Funding
Colleges & Universities—Revenue *See:* Colleges & Universities—Financial Support & Expenditures
Colleges & Universities—Selection *See:* College Choice; Evaluation Criteria & Methodologies
Colleges & Universities, Small—Student Costs
Colleges & Universities—Southern States
Colleges & Universities—Speciality
Colleges & Universities—State Aid *See:* Colleges & Universities—Financial Support & Expenditures

xv

OUTLINE OF CONTENTS

Educational Rankings Annual • 2002

Colleges & Universities—Student Costs See also: Colleges & Universities, Liberal Arts—Student Costs; Colleges & Universities, Small—Student Costs
Colleges & Universities—Student Costs—Alabama
Colleges & Universities—Student Costs—Alaska
Colleges & Universities—Student Costs—Arizona
Colleges & Universities—Student Costs—Arkansas
Colleges & Universities—Student Costs—California
Colleges & Universities—Student Costs—Colorado
Colleges & Universities—Student Costs—Connecticut
Colleges & Universities—Student Costs—Delaware
Colleges & Universities—Student Costs—District of Columbia
Colleges & Universities—Student Costs—Florida
Colleges & Universities—Student Costs—Georgia
Colleges & Universities—Student Costs—Hawaii
Colleges & Universities—Student Costs—Idaho
Colleges & Universities—Student Costs—Illinois
Colleges & Universities—Student Costs—Indiana
Colleges & Universities—Student Costs—Iowa
Colleges & Universities—Student Costs—Kansas
Colleges & Universities—Student Costs—Kentucky
Colleges & Universities—Student Costs—Louisiana
Colleges & Universities—Student Costs—Maine
Colleges & Universities—Student Costs—Maryland
Colleges & Universities—Student Costs—Massachusetts
Colleges & Universities—Student Costs—Michigan
Colleges & Universities—Student Costs—Minnesota
Colleges & Universities—Student Costs—Mississippi
Colleges & Universities—Student Costs—Missouri
Colleges & Universities—Student Costs—Montana
Colleges & Universities—Student Costs—Nebraska
Colleges & Universities—Student Costs—Nevada
Colleges & Universities—Student Costs—New Hampshire
Colleges & Universities—Student Costs—New Jersey
Colleges & Universities—Student Costs—New Mexico
Colleges & Universities—Student Costs—New York
Colleges & Universities—Student Costs—North Carolina
Colleges & Universities—Student Costs—North Dakota
Colleges & Universities—Student Costs—Ohio
Colleges & Universities—Student Costs—Oklahoma
Colleges & Universities—Student Costs—Oregon
Colleges & Universities—Student Costs—Pennsylvania
Colleges & Universities—Student Costs—Puerto Rico
Colleges & Universities—Student Costs—Rhode Island
Colleges & Universities—Student Costs—South Carolina

Colleges & Universities—Student Costs—South Dakota
Colleges & Universities—Student Costs—Tennessee
Colleges & Universities—Student Costs—Texas
Colleges & Universities—Student Costs—Utah
Colleges & Universities—Student Costs—Vermont
Colleges & Universities—Student Costs—Virginia
Colleges & Universities—Student Costs—Washington
Colleges & Universities—Student Costs—West Virginia
Colleges & Universities—Student Costs—Wisconsin
Colleges & Universities—Student Costs—Wyoming
Colleges & Universities—Tuition See: Colleges & Universities—Student Costs
Colleges & Universities—Western States
Colleges, Junior See: Two-Year Colleges
Communication See: Data Communications—North America; Mass Media; Speech Communication
Community Colleges See: Two-Year Colleges
Comparative Literature, Graduate
Competency Tests for Students See: Achievement Tests—Schools, Elementary & Secondary; College Entrance Examinations
Computer Engineering See: Engineering—Computer; Engineering, Graduate—Computer
Computer Science See also: Data Communications—North America
Computer Science, Graduate See also: Engineering, Graduate—Computer
Computer Software
Computer Uses at Home
Computer Uses in Education See also: Distance Education
Consumer Research See: Business Administration, Graduate—Marketing; Business Administration—Marketing
Cooking Instruction
Criminal Justice See also: Law Enforcement
Crystallography

D

Data Communications—North America See also: Computer Science
Default Rate on Student Loans See: Loan Repayment
Degrees (Academic) See also: Doctoral Degrees; Degrees (Academic)—Minority Groups
Degrees (Academic)—Minority Groups
Degrees (Professional)
Demography
Dentistry
Dermatology
Diploma Mills See: Degrees (Academic)
Disabilities—Enrollment of Students
Disabilities—Federal Aid
Disabilities, Learning See: Learning Disabilities
Disadvantaged—Federal Aid
Distance Education See also: Computer Uses in Education
Doctoral Degrees See also: Degrees (Academic); specific discipline or program, graduate, e.g. Art History, Graduate

Doctoral Students See: Graduate Students
Dropouts
Drug Education See: Substance Abuse and Education

E

Early Admission, College See: College Admission
Early Parenthood See: Teen Pregnancy
Earth Science
Earth Science, Graduate
Econometrics See: Economics
Economics
Economics and Business Periodicals See also: Real Estate Periodicals
Economics, Graduate
Economics, Graduate—Canada
Economics—Real Estate See: Real Estate
Education See also: Higher Education; School Districts & School Systems; Schools, Elementary & Secondary; Teacher Education
Education—Financial Support See also: Colleges & Universities—Financial Support & Expenditures; Expenditures per Pupil; Schools, Elementary & Secondary—Revenue
Education—International
Education Periodicals
Education, Schools of See: Teacher Education
Educational Finance See: Colleges & Universities—Financial Support & Expenditures; Education—Financial Support; Expenditures per Pupil; Schools, Elementary & Secondary—Revenue
Electrical Engineering See: Engineering—Electrical/Electronic; Engineering, Graduate—Electrical/Electronic
Empirical Sciences See: Physical Sciences, Graduate
Employment
Employment Opportunities
Employment Outlook
Employment Potential
Endowment, College See: Colleges & Universities—Financial Support & Expenditures
Engineering
Engineering—Aeronautical See also: Engineering, Graduate—Aeronautical
Engineering—Aerospace See also: Engineering, Graduate—Aerospace
Engineering—Chemical See also: Engineering, Graduate—Chemical
Engineering—Civil See also: Engineering, Graduate—Civil
Engineering—Computer See also: Engineering, Graduate—Computer
Engineering—Electrical/Electronic See also: Engineering, Graduate—Electrical/Electronic
Engineering—Environmental See also: Engineering, Graduate—Environmental
Engineering, Graduate
Engineering, Graduate—Aeronautical See also: Engineering—Aeronautical
Engineering, Graduate—Aerospace See also: Engineering—Aerospace
Engineering, Graduate—Agricultural
Engineering, Graduate—Biochemical
Engineering, Graduate—Biomedical
Engineering, Graduate—Chemical See also: Engineering—Chemical

Engineering, Graduate—Civil See also: Engineering—Civil
Engineering, Graduate—Computer See also: Engineering—Computer
Engineering, Graduate—Electrical/Electronic See also: Engineering—Electrical/Electronic
Engineering, Graduate—Environmental See also: Engineering—Environmental
Engineering, Graduate—Industrial See also: Engineering—Industrial
Engineering, Graduate—Marine See also: Engineering—Marine
Engineering, Graduate—Materials/Metallurgical See also: Engineering—Materials/Metallurgical
Engineering, Graduate—Mechanical See also: Engineering—Mechanical
Engineering, Graduate—Nuclear See also: Engineering—Nuclear
Engineering, Graduate—Petroleum See also: Engineering—Petroleum
Engineering—Industrial See also: Engineering, Graduate—Industrial
Engineering—Marine See also: Engineering, Graduate—Marine
Engineering—Materials/Metallurgical See also: Engineering, Graduate—Materials/Metallurgical
Engineering—Mechanical See also: Engineering, Graduate—Mechanical
Engineering—Nuclear See also: Engineering, Graduate—Nuclear
Engineering—Petroleum See also: Engineering, Graduate—Petroleum
English ACT or SAT Scores See: College Entrance Examinations
English Language and Literature See also: Theatre Arts
English Language and Literature, Graduate
Enrollment, College See: American Indians—Enrollment, College; Blacks—Enrollment, College; College Enrollment; Disabilities—Enrollment of Students; Foreign Students—Enrollment, College; Hispanic Americans—Enrollment, College; Minority Groups—Enrollment, College
Enrollment, School See: Disabilities—Enrollment of Students; School Enrollment
Entomology
Environmental Education
Environmental Engineering See: Engineering—Environmental; Engineering, Graduate—Environmental
Ethnic Groups See under headings of particular groups
Evaluation Criteria & Methodologies See also: specific discipline or program, e.g. Political Science
Evaluation Criteria & Methodologies—Bibliographies
Evaluation Criteria & Methodologies—Institutions See also: College Choice; Colleges & Universities
Evaluation Criteria & Methodologies—Peers See also: specific discipline or program, e.g. Political Science
Evaluation Criteria & Methodologies—Programs (Academic) See also: specific discipline or program, e.g. Political Science

xvi

Educational Rankings Annual • 2002 — OUTLINE OF CONTENTS

Evaluation of Periodicals *See:* Periodicals; specific subject periodicals, e.g. Anthropology Periodicals
Expenditures per Pupil

F

Faculty *See:* College Faculty; Teachers, Elementary and Secondary
Faculty-Student Ratio *See:* Schools, Elementary & Secondary—Teacher-Student Ratio
Federal Aid
Federal Aid to Education *See:* Colleges & Universities—Financial Support & Expenditures; Education—Financial Support; Expenditures per Pupil; Schools, Elementary & Secondary—Revenue; specific subject—federal aid, e.g. Disabilities—Federal Aid; Student Financial Aid
Federal Aid to the Disadvantaged *See:* Disadvantaged—Federal Aid
Federal Aid to the Handicapped *See:* Disabilities—Federal Aid
Federal Grants in Research *See:* Research Funding; Research & Development Funding; Scientific & Technological Research & Development Funding; Scientific & Technological Research Funding
Federal Student Grants *See:* Student Financial Aid
Film *See:* Motion Pictures
Film Studies *See:* Mass Media
Finance *See:* Business Administration—Finance; Business Administration, Graduate—Finance
Financial Aid to Students *See:* Student Financial Aid
Football *See:* Athletics
Foreign Countries
Foreign Language Programs *See:* Language Programs
Foreign Students—Enrollment, College
Foreign Study
Foundations (Institutions) *See:* Philanthropic Foundations
French Language and Literature, Graduate
Freshmen, College *See:* College Students
Fundraising, College *See:* Colleges & Universities—Financial Support & Expenditures

G

Geography
Geography, Graduate
Geology *See also:* Earth Science
Geology, Graduate *See also:* Earth Science, Graduate
Geology Periodicals
Geophysics Periodicals *See:* Physics Periodicals
Geoscience *See:* Earth Science, Graduate
German Language and Literature, Graduate
GMAT
Graduate Degrees *See:* Degrees (Academic); Doctoral Degrees
Graduate Education (General) *See also:* specific discipline or program, graduate, e.g. Art History, Graduate
Graduate Schools *See:* Colleges & Universities

Graduate Students *See also:* Graduate Education (General); specific discipline or program, graduate, e.g. Art History, Graduate
Graduates, College *See:* College Graduates; Degrees (Academic); Doctoral Degrees; Salaries—College Graduates
Graduates, High-School *See:* Schools, Secondary—Graduates
Graduation Rates—College *See:* College Graduates
Grants, Federal *See:* Research Funding; Research & Development Funding; Scientific & Technological Research & Development Funding; Scientific & Technological Research Funding; specific subject—federal aid, e.g. Disabilities—Federal Aid; Student Financial Aid
Graphic Arts *See:* Art

H

Handicapped *See:* Disabilities—Enrollment of Students; Disabilities—Federal Aid
Health
Health—Federal Aid
Health, Graduate
High School Dropouts *See:* Dropouts
High Schools *See:* Schools, Secondary
Higher Education
Higher Education—Financial Support *See:* Colleges & Universities—Financial Support & Expenditures
Higher Education Institutions *See:* Black Colleges and Universities; Colleges & Universities; Two-Year Colleges
Hispanic Americans—Enrollment, College
History
History, Graduate
Home Schooling
Homework
Hotel and Restaurant Management
Human Resources
Human Resources, Graduate

I

Income *See also:* Salaries—College Graduates; Salaries—Colleges & Universities; Salaries—Schools, Elementary & Secondary
Industrial Organization *See:* Economics
Information Science *See:* Library Science
Information Systems
Institutional Evaluation *See:* Evaluation Criteria & Methodologies—Institutions
Insurance *See:* Business Administration, Graduate—Insurance; Business Administration—Insurance
International Business *See:* Business Administration
International Economics *See:* Economics
International Relations *See:* Political Science
Internet
Internships
Interpersonal Communication *See:* Speech Communication

J

Journalism *See:* Mass Media—Journalism

Junior Colleges *See:* Two-Year Colleges

L

Labor Economics *See:* Economics
Language Programs
Language Programs, Graduate *See also:* English Language and Literature; French Language and Literature, Graduate; German Language and Literature, Graduate; Spanish Language and Literature, Graduate
Law
Law Enforcement *See also:* Criminal Justice
Law Schools
Law Schools—Students
Learning Disabilities
Lecturers, College *See:* College Faculty; Salaries—Colleges & Universities
Liberal Arts *See also:* specific discipline or program, e.g. English Language and Literature
Liberal-Arts Colleges *See:* Colleges & Universities, Liberal Arts
Liberal Arts, Graduate *See also:* specific discipline or program, graduate, e.g. English Language and Literature, Graduate
Libraries
Libraries, Law
Libraries, Public
Libraries, Research—North America
Library Science
Library Science Periodicals
Life Sciences *See:* Biological Sciences
Linguistics
Linguistics, Graduate
Literacy
Literary Criticism
Loan Repayment

M

Macroeconomics *See:* Economics
Management Courses (Credit) *See:* Business Administration
Management Information Systems
Management Science *See:* Business Administration
Marketing *See:* Business Administration, Graduate—Marketing; Business Administration—Marketing
Mass Media
Mass Media, Graduate
Mass Media—Journalism
Materials/Metallurgical Engineering *See:* Engineering, Graduate—Materials/Metallurgical; Engineering—Materials/Metallurgical
Mathematical ACT or SAT Scores *See:* College Entrance Examinations
Mathematics
Mathematics Achievement
Mathematics, Graduate
Mathematics, Graduate—Statistics
Mathematics Periodicals
Mathematics—Statistics
Measurement *See:* Evaluation Criteria & Methodologies
Mechanical Engineering *See:* Engineering, Graduate—Mechanical; Engineering—Mechanical
Medical Centers
Medical Periodicals
Medical Schools
Medical Schools—Enrollment
Medicine
Merit Scholarships *See:* Student Financial Aid

Metallurgical Engineering *See:* Engineering, Graduate—Materials/Metallurgical; Engineering—Materials/Metallurgical
Microbiology *See:* Biology, Graduate—Microbiology
Microeconomics *See:* Economics
Military Schools
Minority Groups—Enrollment, College
Molecular Biology *See:* Biology, Graduate—Cellular/Molecular
Motion Pictures
Music *See also:* Opera
Music, Graduate

N

Natural Science ACT Scores *See:* College Entrance Examinations
Newspapers
Nuclear Engineering *See:* Engineering, Graduate—Nuclear
Nursing
Nursing—Graduate
Nutrition

O

Oceanography *See:* Earth Science
Opera *See also:* Music
Optics
Oral Interpretation *See:* Speech Communication
Organizations
Organizational Communication *See:* Speech Communication
Organizational Theory and Behavior *See:* Business Administration

P

Peer Evaluation *See:* Evaluation Criteria & Methodologies—Peers
Periodicals *See also:* specific subject periodicals, e.g. Anthropology Periodicals
Petroleum Engineering *See:* Engineering, Graduate—Petroleum; Engineering—Petroleum
Pharmacy
Pharmacy, Graduate
Ph.D. *See:* Doctoral Degrees
Philanthropic Foundations
Philosophy, Graduate
Physical Sciences, Graduate *See also:* Chemistry, Graduate; Earth Science, Graduate; Engineering, Graduate; Physics, Graduate
Physics
Physics, Graduate
Physics Periodicals
Physiology, Graduate
Playwrighting *See:* Theatre Arts
Political Candidates
Political Science
Political Science, Graduate
Political Science Periodicals
Preparatory Schools *See:* Schools, Secondary
Private Schools *See:* Schools, Elementary & Secondary; Schools, Secondary
Professional Associations
Psychiatry
Psychology
Psychology, Graduate
Psychology Periodicals
Public Address *See:* Speech Communication
Public Affairs *See:* Political Science
Public Schools *See:* Schools, Elementary & Secondary; Schools, Secondary
Publishing

xvii

OUTLINE OF CONTENTS

Q

Quality Ratings *See:* Evaluation Criteria & Methodologies

R

Real Estate
Real Estate Periodicals
Religion, Graduate
Research & Development
Research & Development Funding *See also:* Scientific & Technological Research Funding
Research Funding *See also:* Research & Development Funding; Scientific & Technological Research & Development Funding; Scientific & Technological Research Funding; specific discipline or program, e.g. Political Science
Research Universities—Salaries *See:* Salaries—Colleges & Universities
Retailing *See:* Business Administration, Graduate—Marketing; Business Administration—Marketing
Rhetoric *See:* Speech Communication

S

Salaries
Salaries—College Graduates
Salaries—Colleges & Universities
Salaries—Colleges & Universities, Faculty
Salaries—High School Graduates
Salaries—Schools, Elementary & Secondary
SAT *See:* College Entrance Examinations
Scholarships *See:* Student Financial Aid
School Administration
School Districts & School Systems
School Districts & School Systems—Chicago Metropolitan Area
School Districts & School Systems—Enrollment *See:* School Enrollment
School Districts & School Systems—Illinois

School Enrollment *See also:* Disabilities—Enrollment of Students
School Facilities
School Systems *See:* School Districts & School Systems
Schools, Elementary & Secondary *See also:* Schools, Secondary
Schools, Elementary & Secondary—Enrollment *See:* School Enrollment
Schools, Elementary & Secondary—Financial Support *See:* Schools, Elementary & Secondary—Revenue
Schools, Elementary & Secondary—International
Schools, Elementary & Secondary—Revenue *See also:* Expenditures per Pupil
Schools, Elementary & Secondary—Students
Schools, Elementary & Secondary—Teacher-Student Ratio
Schools, Elementary & Secondary—Teachers *See:* Teachers, Elementary and Secondary; Salaries—Schools, Elementary & Secondary
Schools, Elementary & Secondary—Tests *See:* Achievement Tests—Schools, Elementary & Secondary; Advanced Placement Tests
Schools, Private *See:* Schools, Elementary & Secondary; Schools, Secondary
Schools, Secondary
Schools, Secondary—Graduates
Schools of Education *See:* Teacher Education
Science Periodicals
Sciences *See also:* specific science, e.g. Chemistry
Sciences—Australia
Sciences, Graduate *See also:* Physical Sciences, Graduate; specific science, graduate, e.g. Chemistry, Graduate
Sciences—Great Britain
Sciences—International
Scientific & Technological Research & Development Funding
Scientific & Technological Research Funding
Skiing *See:* Athletics
Social Sciences Periodicals
Social Work, Graduate
Sociology

Sociology, Graduate
Sociology Periodicals
Spanish Language and Literature, Graduate
Spectroscopy
Speech Communication *See also:* Mass Media
Speech Communication—Women
Sports *See:* Athletics
Stafford Loans *See:* Loan Repayment; Student Financial Aid
State Aid to Education *See:* Colleges & Universities—Financial Support & Expenditures; Schools, Elementary & Secondary—Revenue; Scientific & Technological Research & Development Funding; Student Financial Aid
Statistics *See:* Mathematics, Graduate—Statistics; Mathematics—Statistics
Student Costs *See:* Colleges & Universities, Liberal Arts—Student Costs; Colleges & Universities—Student Costs
Student Financial Aid
Student Financial Aid—Blacks *See:* Black Students—Financial Aid
Student Financial Aid—Repayment on Loans *See:* Loan Repayment
Student-Teacher Ratio *See:* Schools, Elementary & Secondary—Teacher-Student Ratio
Student Tests *See:* Achievement Tests—Schools, Elementary & Secondary; College Entrance Examinations
Substance Abuse and Education

T

Teacher Behavior
Teacher Education
Teacher Education, Graduate
Teacher-Student Ratio *See:* Schools, Elementary & Secondary—Teacher-Student Ratio
Teachers, College *See:* College Faculty
Teachers, Elementary and Secondary
Teachers, Elementary and Secondary—Salaries *See:* Salaries—Schools, Elementary & Secondary
Technical Communication

Technological Research Funding *See:* Scientific & Technological Research & Development Funding
Technology
Technology Management *See:* Business Administration—Technology Management
Teen Pregnancy
Tests for College Admission *See:* College Entrance Examinations
Tests for Student Competency *See:* Achievement Tests—Schools, Elementary & Secondary; Advanced Placement Tests; College Entrance Examinations
Textiles
Theatre Arts
Tuition, College *See:* Colleges & Universities, Liberal Arts—Student Costs; Colleges & Universities—Student Costs
Tuition Savings Plans
Two-Year Colleges
Two-Year Colleges—Administration *See:* College Administration
Two-Year Colleges—Enrollment *See:* College Enrollment
Two-Year Colleges—Salaries *See:* Salaries—Colleges & Universities

U

Undergraduate Education *See:* Colleges & Universities
Universities *See:* Colleges & Universities
Urban Economics *See:* Economics; Real Estate

V

Veterans' Educational Benefits *See:* Student Financial Aid
Veterinary—Animal Health
Violence

W

Women Executives
Women's Studies

Educational Rankings Annual

ACADEMIC ACHIEVEMENT

★1★
Academic achievement comparison of 12th graders, 1998
Ranking basis/background: Ranking of U.S. 12th graders compared to other developed countries.
Remarks: Original source: Education Trust; Education Dept.; Census Bureau. **Number listed:** 3.
    Math, U.S. ranked 19th out of 21 developed countries
    Science, 16th out of 21
    Graduation rates, 17th out of 29
Source: Symonds, William C., "How to Fix America's Schools," *Business Week*, 3724: 66-72, (March 19, 2001).

★2★
All-USA College Academic First Team, 2001
Ranking basis/background: Outstanding undergraduates in all disciplines ranging in age from 19 to 44. **Number listed:** 20.
    Sarah Airey, Virginia Tech (Major: Computer engineering)
    Marshawn Evans, Texas Christian University (Political science)
    Erin Cline, Belmont University (Philosophy)
    D. Matthew Baugh, Duke University (International development and health)
    Annina Burns, Pennsylvania State University (Nutrition, media studies)
    Christine Garton, University of Kansas (Business administration, French)
    Shannon Kishel, Denison University (Environmental studies)
    Matthew Huenerfauth, University of Delaware (Computer and information science)
    Han Kang, University of California, Irvine (Biological sciences, international studies)
    Pooja Kumar, Duke University (Health policy and social values)
    Grace MacDowell-Boyer, Southern Utah University (Psychology)
    Kira Martin, University of Alabama, Birmingham (International studies, French)
    Lance Relland, University of California, Riverside (Biomedical sciences)
    Lillian Pierce, Princeton University (Math)
    Skelly McCay, Loyola University (Philosophy)
    Peter Love, West Virginia University (Political science, finance)
    Philip Roessler, Indiana University (Political science)
    Kevin Schwartz, Harvard University (Government)
    Carl Tape, Carleton College (Physics, geology)
    Brian Skotko, Duke University (Biological anthropology, anatomy)
Source: "All-USA College Academic Teams," *USA Today*, February 15, 2001, Section D, pp. 1-1D.

★3★
All-USA College Academic Second Team, 2001
Ranking basis/background: Outstanding undergraduates in all disciplines ranging in age from 19 to 44. **Number listed:** 20.
    Lisa Ahrens, Iowa State University (Major: Agronomy, agriculture business)
    Sean Bennett, Harvard University (Cognitive neuroscience)
    Kara Calvert, University of Wyoming (Business administration)
    Stefani Carter, University of Texas, Austin (Government, news and public affairs)
    Jason Grissom, North Carolina State University (Statistics, political science, multidisciplinary studies)
    Pranav Gupta, University of Pennsylvania (Finance, computer science)
    Clifford Haugen, University of Pennsylvania (Environmental risk management, environmental systems engineering)
    Sunit Jariwala, Rutgers University (Molecular biology, biochemistry)
    Niuniu Ji, Case Western Reserve University (Systems engineering)
    Erez Lieberman, Princeton University (mathematics)
    Robert Luo, Harvard University (History, science, East Asian studies)
    Brooke Manning, University of Vermont (Psychology)
    Haley Naik, University of Illinois, Chicago (Biochemistry)
    Heather O'Hara, Carleton College (Studio art)
    Michael Sosso, Arizona State University (Economics, political science)
    Timothy Strabbing, United States Naval Academy (Political science)
    Alan Trammell, Wake Forest University (German, economics)
    Dana Wallace, University of Richmond (Biology, economics)
    Dorothy Weiss, Harvard University (Cognitive neuroscience)
    Charles Wu, University of Chicago (Economics)
Source: "All-USA College Academic Teams," *USA Today*, February 15, 2001, Section D, pp. 1-1D.

★4★
All-USA College Academic Third Team, 2001
Ranking basis/background: Outstanding undergraduates in all disciplines ranging in age from 19 to 44. **Number listed:** 20.
    Mark Bradshaw, University of Kansas (Major: American studies)
    Xavier Corona, University of California, Berkeley (Peace and conflict studies, Chicano studies)
    Brian Dassler, University of Florida (English)
    Hetal Doshi, Emory University (Economics, political science)
    Nicholas Fitzkee, Carnegie Mellon University (Computational physics)
    Lipika Goyal, University of Pennsylvania (Biological basis of behavior)
    Kristian Hargadon, Hampden-Sydney College (Biology)
    Trina Hofreiter, New College of the University of South Florida (Environmental science)
    Peter Huskey, University of North Carolina, Asheville (Chemistry)
    Noah Knauf, University of Arizona (Management information systems, operations management)
    Duarte Machado, Trinity College (Neuroscience)
    Amit Malhotra, Johns Hopkins University (Biomedical engineering)
    Scott Martin, Furman University (Math, political science)

ACCOUNTING PROGRAMS

Sarah Mast, University of Southern California (Public relations)
Christina McElderry, College of St. Catherine (Urban policy, sociology, women's studies)
Kirk Pak, University of California, Irvine (Neurobiology)
Mathew Parker, University of South Carolina (Computer engineering)
Jessica Posner, Wake Forest University (History)
Grishma Shah, Rutgers University (Political science)
Kay Yeung, University of Arizona (Medical technology)

Source: "All-USA College Academic Teams," *USA Today*, February 15, 2001, Section D, pp. 1-1D.

★5★
Colleges with the highest number of freshman Merit Scholars, 2000

Ranking basis/background: Determined by The *Chronicle* from an alphabetical listing appearing in the National Merit Scholarship Corp.'s, 1999-2000 annual report. A total of 8,170 Merit Scholars enrolled in the fall of 2000; 4,674 at 233 private colleges and universities and 3,496 at 148 public institutions. **Number listed:** 85.

1. Harvard University, with 382 scholars
2. University of California, Berkeley, 246
3. University of Texas, Austin, 245
4. Stanford University, 209
5. Yale University, 191
6. University of Florida, 166
7. Rice University, 162
8. University of Chicago, 151
9. Massachusetts Institute of Technology, 148
10. University of Southern California, 148
11. Texas A&M University, 142
12. Washington University (MO), 141
13. University of North Carolina, Chapel Hill, 137
14. University of Oklahoma, 132
15. New York University, 130
16. Arizona State University, 119
17. University of Kansas, 116
18. Brigham Young University, 115
19. Iowa State University, 113
20. Ohio State University, 110

Source: "2000 Freshman Merit Scholars," *The Chronicle of Higher Education*, 47: A48, (January 16, 2001).

★6★
Comparison of 8th grade science achievement scores, U.S. and worldwide, 1999

Ranking basis/background: Average science achievement score. Average international score is 488. Average U.S. score is 515. **Remarks:** Original source: International Study Center at Boston College. **Number listed:** 9.

1. Naperville School District No. 203, Illinois, with 584
2. Chinese Taipei, 569
3. Singapore, 568
4. First in the World Consortium, Illinois, 565
5. Michigan Invitational Group, 563
6. Academy School District No. 20, Colorado, 559
7. Hungary, 552
8. Japan, 550
9. Republic of Korea, 549

Source: "Where Sci Flies," *U.S. News & World Report*, 130: 11, (April 16, 2001).

★7★
Eighth grade students' proficiency

Ranking basis/background: Percentage of 8th grade students proficient for their grade level according to the 1998 National Assessment of Educational Progress. **Remarks:** Original source: Education Trust; Education Dept.; Census Bureau. **Number listed:** 3.

Reading, with 33%
Writing, 27%
Math, 24%

Source: Symonds, William C., "How to Fix America's Schools," *Business Week*, 3724: 66-72, (March 19, 2001).

★8★
Historically black institutions with the highest number of National Achievement Scholars, 1998

Ranking basis/background: Total number of scholars enrolled at each institution. **Remarks:** Original source: ACT Testing. **Number listed:** 9.

1. Howard University, with 59 scholars
2. Florida A&M University, 58
3. Spelman College, 17
4. Xavier University (LA), 6
5. Morehouse College, 5
6. North Carolina A&T State University, 3
7. Fisk University, 1
7. Fort Valley State College, 1
7. Lincoln University, 1

Source: Roach, Ronald, "Special Report: Minority Student Recruitment & Retention," *Black Issues in Higher Education*, 17: 36-46, (October 26, 2000).

★9★
U.S. universities enrolling the most National Achievement Scholars, 1994

Ranking basis/background: Total number of scholars enrolled at each institution. **Remarks:** Original source: ACT Testing. **Number listed:** 7.

1. Harvard University, with 75 scholars
2. Florida A&M University, 54
3. Howard University, 43
4. Yale University, 33
5. Massachusetts Institute of Technology, 22
5. University of Florida, 22
5. University of Virginia, 22

Source: Roach, Ronald, "Special Report: Minority Student Recruitment & Retention," *Black Issues in Higher Education*, 17: 36-46, (October 26, 2000).

★10★
U.S. universities enrolling the most National Achievement Scholars, 1995

Ranking basis/background: Total number of scholars enrolled at each institution. **Remarks:** Original source: ACT Testing. **Number listed:** 5.

1. Florida A&M University, with 59 scholars
2. Harvard University, 57
3. Howard University, 43
4. University of Oklahoma, 29
5. Stanford University, 23

Source: Roach, Ronald, "Special Report: Minority Student Recruitment & Retention," *Black Issues in Higher Education*, 17: 36-46, (October 26, 2000).

Educational Rankings Annual • 2002

★11★
U.S. universities enrolling the most National Achievement Scholars, 1996

Ranking basis/background: Total number of scholars enrolled at each institution. **Remarks:** Original source: ACT Testing. **Number listed:** 5.

1. Howard University, with 70 scholars
2. Harvard University, 69
3. Florida A&M University, 51
4. Yale University, 28
5. University of Virginia, 23

Source: Roach, Ronald, "Special Report: Minority Student Recruitment & Retention," *Black Issues in Higher Education*, 17: 36-46, (October 26, 2000).

★12★
U.S. universities enrolling the most National Achievement Scholars, 1997

Ranking basis/background: Total number of scholars enrolled at each institution. **Remarks:** Original source: ACT Testing. **Number listed:** 5.

1. Florida A&M University, with 73 scholars
2. Harvard University, 58
3. Howard University, 43
4. University of Florida, 38
5. Stanford University, 31

Source: Roach, Ronald, "Special Report: Minority Student Recruitment & Retention," *Black Issues in Higher Education*, 17: 36-46, (October 26, 2000).

★13★
U.S. universities enrolling the most National Achievement Scholars, 1998

Ranking basis/background: Total number of scholars enrolled at each institution. **Remarks:** Original source: ACT Testing. **Number listed:** 5.

1. Harvard University, with 63 scholars
2. Howard University, 59
3. Florida A&M University, 58
4. University of Florida, 24
5. Princeton University, 22

Source: Roach, Ronald, "Special Report: Minority Student Recruitment & Retention," *Black Issues in Higher Education*, 17: 36-46, (October 26, 2000).

ACCOUNTING PROGRAMS
See: **Business Administration–Accounting Business Administration, Graduate–Accounting**

ACHIEVEMENT TESTS–SCHOOLS, ELEMENTARY & SECONDARY
See also: **College Entrance Examinations**

★14★
Eight grade science achievement scores from selected countries, 1999

Ranking basis/background: Average achievement score received for each country from results of the Third International Mathematics and Science Study. International average score is 488. **Number listed:** 28.

1. Taiwan, with 569
2. Singapore, 568
3. Hungary, 552
4. Japan, 550
5. South Korea, 549

6. Netherlands, 545
7. Australia, 540
8. Czech Republic, 539
9. England, 538
10. Finland, 535
11. Canada, 533
12. Russia, 529
13. Bulgaria, 518
14. United States, 515
15. New Zealand, 510
16. Italy, 493
17. Lithuania, 488
18. Thailand, 482
19. Romania, 472
20. Israel, 468
21. Jordan, 450
22. Iran, 448
23. Indonesia, 435
24. Turkey, 433
25. Tunisia, 430
26. Chile, 420
27. Philippines, 345
28. South Africa, 243

Source: Holden, Constance, "Asia Stays on Top, U.S. in Middle in New Global Rankings," *Science*, 290: 6, (December 8, 2000).

★15★
Illinois elementary schools with the highest 5th grade writing scores

Ranking basis/background: Average 5th grade writing scores. Maximum score is 32. **Remarks:** Original source: Sun-Times research. **Number listed:** 10.

1. Edgebrook Elementary School (Chicago), with an average score of 29.06
2. Skinner Elementary School (Chicago), 28.90
3. Elm Elementary School (Burr Ridge), 28.77
4. Central Elementary School (Riverside), 28.66
5. El Sierra Elementary School (Downers Grove), 28.63
6. Edison Gifted Elementary School (Chicago), 28.61
7. Longfellow Elementary School (Wheaton), 28.39
8. Wayne Thomas Elementary School (Highland Park), 28.24
9. Palos East Elementary School (Palos Heights), 27.96
10. Winston Campus Elementary School (Palatine), 27.93

Source: "School Report Card 2000," *Chicago Sun-Times*, November 1, 2000, pp. 1R-22R.

★16★
Illinois elementary schools with the highest ISAT scores in reading and math

Ranking basis/background: Percentile of percentage of students statewide scoring the same as or worse than the average student. Only schools that tested at least two grades (3rd, 5th or 8th) were included. **Remarks:** Original source: Sun-Times research. **Number listed:** 10.

1. Decatur Classical Elementary School (Chicago), with a percentile of 94.8
2. Washington Gifted Elementary School (Peoria), 94.5
3. Edison Elementary Regional Gifted Center (Chicago), 92.2
4. Lenart Elementary Regional Gifted Center (Chicago), 92.1
5. Nettle Creek Elementary School (Morris), 91.1
6. Keller Elementary Gifted Magnet (Chicago), 89.4
7. Skinner Elementary School (Chicago), 89.4
8. Lexington Elementary School (Lexington), 88.1
9. Hollywood Elementary School (Brookfield), 87.1
10. Field Park Elementary School (Western Springs), 86.7

Source: "School Report Card 2000," *Chicago Sun-Times*, November 1, 2000, pp. 1R-22R.

★17★
Illinois schools with the highest 7th grade science scores

Ranking basis/background: Average science scores from schools in the six county area. **Remarks:** Original source: Sun-Times research. **Number listed:** 10.

1. Lenart Gifted (Chicago), with 184.78
2. Edison Gifted Elementary School (Chicago), 184.28
3. Young Magnet (Chicago), 183.29
4. Keller Gifted (Chicago), 175.21
5. Wilmette Junior High School (Wilmette), 174.91
6. Roosevelt Middle School (River Forest), 173.96
7. Kenwood Academy High School (Chicago), 173.83
8. Marie Murphy Middle School (Wilmette), 173.75
9. Washburne Junior High (Winnetka), 172.59
10. Lincoln Junior High (Chicago), 172.49

Source: "School Report Card 2000," *Chicago Sun-Times*, November 1, 2000, pp. 1R-22R.

★18★
Illinois suburban elementary schools with the highest ISAT scores in reading and math

Ranking basis/background: Percentile of percentage of students statewide scoring the same as or worse than the average student. Only schools that tested at least two grades (3rd, 5th or 8th) were included. **Remarks:** Original source: Sun-Times research. **Number listed:** 10.

1. Hollywood Elementary School (Brookfield), with a percentile of 87.1
2. Field Park Elementary School (Western Springs), 86.7
3. Meadow Glens Elementary School (Naperville), 85.5
4. Prospect Elementary School (Clarendon Hills), 85.5
5. Joseph Sears Elementary School (Kenilworth), 84.9
5. Madison Elementary School (Hinsdale), 84.9
7. Monroe Elementary School (Hinsdale), 84.6
8. Highlands Elementary School (Naperville), 84.4
9. Central Elementary School (Glencoe), 84.1
9. Greeley Elementary School (Winnetka), 84.1

Source: "School Report Card 2000," *Chicago Sun-Times*, November 1, 2000, pp. 1R-22R.

★19★
Math achievement test comparison

Ranking basis/background: Difference from average score from a sample of the world's 4th graders tested in math in 1995 and 8th graders tested in 1999. **Remarks:** Original source: National Center for Education Statistics. **Number listed:** 17.

1. Singapore, with a difference from average score of 73 for 4th grade in 1995; 80 for 8th graders in 1999
2. Republic of Korea, 63; 63
3. Hong Kong, 40; 58
4. Japan, 50; 55
5. Netherlands, 32; 16
6. Hungary, 4; 8
7. Canada, 12 below; 7
8. Slovenia, 8; 6
9. Australia, 0; 1
10. Czech Republic, 23; 4 below
11. Latvia, 18 below; 19 below
12. United States, 0; 22 below
13. England, 33 below; 28 below
14. New Zealand, 48 below; 33 below
15. Italy, 7 below; 39 below
16. Cyprus, 42 below; 48 below
17. Iran, 130 below; 102 below

Source: "The Stark Facts of College Stalking," *U.S. News & World Report*, 130: 14, (February 12, 2001).

ACT
See: **College Entrance Examinations**

ADVANCED PLACEMENT TESTS

★20★
Advanced placement averages for African Americans, by gender, 2000

Ranking basis/background: Advanced placement averages based on a maximum score of 5. **Number listed:** 2.

Men, with 2.25
Women, 2.12

Source: "Disparities & Gaps in America," *Black Issues in Higher Education*, 18: 28-29, (March 1, 2001).

★21★
Advanced placement averages for Asian Americans, by gender, 2000

Ranking basis/background: Advanced placement averages based on a maximum score of 5. **Number listed:** 2.

Men, with 3.14
Women, 2.99

Source: "Disparities & Gaps in America," *Black Issues in Higher Education*, 18: 28-29, (March 1, 2001).

★22★
Advanced placement averages for Hispanic Americans, by gender, 2000

Ranking basis/background: Advanced placement averages based on a maximum score of 5. **Number listed:** 2.

Men, with 3.09
Women, 3.08

ADVANCED PLACEMENT TESTS

Source: "Disparities & Gaps in America," *Black Issues in Higher Education*, 18: 28-29, (March 1, 2001).

★23★
Advanced placement averages for Mexican Americans, by gender, 2000

Ranking basis/background: Advanced placement averages based on a maximum score of 5. **Number listed:** 2.
  Men, with 2.71
  Women, 2.81

Source: "Disparities & Gaps in America," *Black Issues in Higher Education*, 18: 28-29, (March 1, 2001).

★24★
Advanced placement averages for Native Americans, by gender, 2000

Ranking basis/background: Advanced placement averages based on a maximum score of 5. **Number listed:** 2.
  Men, with 2.76
  Women, 2.5

Source: "Disparities & Gaps in America," *Black Issues in Higher Education*, 18: 28-29, (March 1, 2001).

★25★
Advanced placement averages for Puerto Ricans, by gender, 2000

Ranking basis/background: Advanced placement averages based on a maximum score of 5. **Number listed:** 2.
  Men, with 2.81
  Women, 2.85

Source: "Disparities & Gaps in America," *Black Issues in Higher Education*, 18: 28-29, (March 1, 2001).

★26★
Advanced placement averages for white Americans, by gender, 2000

Ranking basis/background: Advanced placement averages based on a maximum score of 5. **Number listed:** 2.
  Men, with 3.17
  Women, 2.97

Source: "Disparities & Gaps in America," *Black Issues in Higher Education*, 18: 28-29, (March 1, 2001).

★27★
Number of Advanced Placement Exams administered to African Americans, 1998-2000

Ranking basis/background: Total AP exams administered. **Remarks:** Original source: The College Board. **Number listed:** 3.
  1998, with 38,859
  1999, 45,725
  2000, 53,136

Source: "Special Report: Minority Student Recruitment & Retention," *Black Issues in Higher Education*, 17: 34-35, (October 26, 2000).

★28★
Number of Advanced Placement Exams administered to Asian Americans, 1998-2000

Ranking basis/background: Total AP exams administered. **Remarks:** Original source: The College Board. **Number listed:** 3.
  1998, with 127,633
  1999, 145,654
  2000, 167,490

Source: "Special Report: Minority Student Recruitment & Retention," *Black Issues in Higher Education*, 17: 34-35, (October 26, 2000).

★29★
Number of Advanced Placement Exams administered to Hispanic Americans, 1998-2000

Ranking basis/background: Total AP exams administered. **Remarks:** Original source: The College Board. **Number listed:** 3.
  1998, with 76,960
  1999, 93,079
  2000, 112,559

Source: "Special Report: Minority Student Recruitment & Retention," *Black Issues in Higher Education*, 17: 34-35, (October 26, 2000).

★30★
Number of Advanced Placement Exams taken by African Americans, by subject, 2000

Ranking basis/background: Total AP exams taken by African American students for each subject. **Remarks:** Original source: The College Board. **Number listed:** 32.
  U.S. history, with 9,112
  Art history, 310
  Studio art-drawing, 238
  Studio art-general, 360
  Biology, 3,859
  Chemistry, 1,850
  Computer science A, 552
  Computer science AB, 107
  Economics micro, 622
  Economics macro, 806
  English language, 6,019
  English literature, 10,047
  Environmental science, 662
  European history, 1,873
  French language, 671
  French literature, 69
  German literature, 44
  U.S. government and politics, 3,053
  Government and politics comp., 382
  International English language, 0
  Latin virgil, 116
  Latin literature, 90
  Calculus AB, 5,480
  Calculus BC, 614
  Music theory, 239
  Physics B, 915
  Physics C mech, 336
  Physics B E&M, 111
  Psychology, 1,705
  Spanish language, 1,548
  Spanish literature, 102
  Statistics, 1,244

Source: "Special Report: Minority Student Recruitment & Retention," *Black Issues in Higher Education*, 17: 34-35, (October 26, 2000).

★31★
Number of Advanced Placement Exams taken by Asian Americans, by subject, 2000

Ranking basis/background: Total AP exams taken by Asian American students for each subject. **Remarks:** Original source: The College Board. **Number listed:** 32.
  U.S. history, with 21,760
  Art history, 1,579
  Studio art-drawing, 445
  Studio art-general, 826
  Biology, 13,785
  Chemistry, 10,255
  Computer science A, 2,870
  Computer science AB, 1,630
  Economics micro, 3,259
  Economics macro, 4,094
  English language, 11,881
  English literature, 18,073
  Environmental science, 1,638
  European history, 7,097
  French language, 1,659
  French literature, 167
  German literature, 247
  U.S. government and politics, 8,795
  Government and politics comp., 1,061
  International English language, 1
  Latin virgil, 397
  Latin literature, 259
  Calculus AB, 20,280
  Calculus BC, 8,506
  Music theory, 595
  Physics B, 5,707
  Physics C mech, 3,349
  Physics B E&M, 1,770
  Psychology, 4,124
  Spanish language, 5,181
  Spanish literature, 378
  Statistics, 5,822

Source: "Special Report: Minority Student Recruitment & Retention," *Black Issues in Higher Education*, 17: 34-35, (October 26, 2000).

★32★
Number of Advanced Placement Exams taken by Hispanic Americans, by subject, 2000

Ranking basis/background: Total AP exams taken by Hispanic American students for each subject. **Remarks:** Original source: The College Board. **Number listed:** 32.
  U.S. history, with 12,678
  Art history, 762
  Studio art-drawing, 438
  Studio art-general, 785
  Biology, 5,104
  Chemistry, 2,480
  Computer science A, 644
  Computer science AB, 178
  Economics micro, 1,118
  Economics macro, 1,948
  English language, 10,786
  English literature, 12,847
  Environmental science, 1,148
  European history, 3,265
  French language, 1,086
  French literature, 100
  German literature, 100
  U.S. government and politics, 5,701
  Government and politics comp., 474
  International English language, 0
  Latin virgil, 74
  Latin literature, 46
  Calculus AB, 7,617
  Calculus BC, 1,136
  Music theory, 264
  Physics B, 1,541
  Physics C mech, 644
  Physics B E&M, 217
  Psychology, 1,992
  Spanish language, 29,514
  Spanish literature, 6,150
  Statistics, 1,722

★33★
Number of African American 9th or 10th graders taking Advanced Placement Exams, 1998-2000

Ranking basis/background: Total AP exams taken. **Remarks:** Original source: The College Board. **Number listed:** 3.
- 1998, with 1,391
- 1999, 1,733
- 2000, 2,112

Source: "Special Report: Minority Student Recruitment & Retention," *Black Issues in Higher Education*, 17: 34-35, (October 26, 2000).

★34★
Number of African American 11th graders taking Advanced Placement Exams, 1998-2000

Ranking basis/background: Total AP exams taken. **Remarks:** Original source: The College Board. **Number listed:** 3.
- 1998, with 10,015
- 1999, 11,558
- 2000, 13,622

Source: "Special Report: Minority Student Recruitment & Retention," *Black Issues in Higher Education*, 17: 34-35, (October 26, 2000).

★35★
Number of African American 12th graders taking Advanced Placement Exams, 1998-2000

Ranking basis/background: Total AP exams taken. **Remarks:** Original source: The College Board. **Number listed:** 3.
- 1998, with 15,085
- 1999, 16,942
- 2000, 19,469

Source: "Special Report: Minority Student Recruitment & Retention," *Black Issues in Higher Education*, 17: 34-35, (October 26, 2000).

★36★
Number of African American students who took 3-5 Advanced Placement Exams, 1998-2000

Ranking basis/background: Total number of students taking 3-5 AP exams each year. **Remarks:** Original source: The College Board. **Number listed:** 3.
- 1998, with 13,654
- 1999, 15,814
- 2000, 17,954

Source: "Special Report: Minority Student Recruitment & Retention," *Black Issues in Higher Education*, 17: 34-35, (October 26, 2000).

★37★
Number of Asian American students taking 3-5 Advanced Placement Exams, 1998-2000

Ranking basis/background: Total number of students taking 3-5 AP exams each year. **Remarks:** Original source: The College Board. **Number listed:** 3.
- 1998, with 84,614
- 1999, 94,715
- 2000, 108,868

Source: "Special Report: Minority Student Recruitment & Retention," *Black Issues in Higher Education*, 17: 34-35, (October 26, 2000).

★38★
Number of Hispanic American 9th and 10th graders taking Advanced Placement Exams, 1998-2000

Ranking basis/background: Total number of Hispanic American students taking AP exams. **Remarks:** Original source: The College Board. **Number listed:** 3.
- 1998, with 6,088
- 1999, 7,270
- 2000, 8,822

Source: "Special Report: Minority Student Recruitment & Retention," *Black Issues in Higher Education*, 17: 34-35, (October 26, 2000).

★39★
Number of Hispanic American 11th graders taking Advanced Placement Exams, 1998-2000

Ranking basis/background: Total number of Hispanic American students taking AP exams. **Remarks:** Original source: The College Board. **Number listed:** 3.
- 1998, with 21,069
- 1999, 25,408
- 2000, 30,279

Source: "Special Report: Minority Student Recruitment & Retention," *Black Issues in Higher Education*, 17: 34-35, (October 26, 2000).

★40★
Number of Hispanic American 12th graders taking Advanced Placement Exams, 1998-2000

Ranking basis/background: Total number of Hispanic American students taking AP exams. **Remarks:** Original source: The College Board. **Number listed:** 3.
- 1998, with 25,240
- 1999, 28,501
- 2000, 33,641

Source: "Special Report: Minority Student Recruitment & Retention," *Black Issues in Higher Education*, 17: 34-35, (October 26, 2000).

★41★
Number of Hispanic American students taking 3-5 Advanced Placement Exams, 1998-2000

Ranking basis/background: Total number of Hispanic American students taking 3-5 AP exams. **Remarks:** Original source: The College Board. **Number listed:** 3.
- 1998, with 45,827
- 1999, 53,400
- 2000, 62,918

Source: "Special Report: Minority Student Recruitment & Retention," *Black Issues in Higher Education*, 17: 34-35, (October 26, 2000).

★42★
Percentage of Advanced Placement Exams taken, by race ethnicity, 2000

Ranking basis/background: Ethnic percentages of AP exam takers. **Remarks:** Original source: The College Board. **Number listed:** 4.
1. White, with 67%
2. Non-Black minority, 22%
3. African American, 5%
4. Other, 6%

Source: "Special Report: Minority Student Recruitment & Retention," *Black Issues in Higher Education*, 17: 34-35, (October 26, 2000).

★43★
Total number of African American students taking Advanced Placement Exams, 1998-2000

Ranking basis/background: Total number of African American students taking AP exams each year. **Remarks:** Original source: The College Board. **Number listed:** 3.
- 1998, with 27,054
- 1999, 31,023
- 2000, 36,158

Source: "Special Report: Minority Student Recruitment & Retention," *Black Issues in Higher Education*, 17: 34-35, (October 26, 2000).

★44★
Total number of Asian American 9th and 10th graders taking Advanced Placement Exams, 1998-2000

Ranking basis/background: Total number of Asian American students taking AP exams each year. **Remarks:** Original source: The College Board. **Number listed:** 3.
- 1998, with 6,822
- 1999, 7,918
- 2000, 9,355

Source: "Special Report: Minority Student Recruitment & Retention," *Black Issues in Higher Education*, 17: 34-35, (October 26, 2000).

★45★
Total number of Asian American 11th graders taking Advanced Placement Exams, 1998-2000

Ranking basis/background: Total number of Asian American students taking AP exams each year. **Remarks:** Original source: The College Board. **Number listed:** 3.
- 1998, with 26,276
- 1999, 29,659
- 2000, 33,628

Source: "Special Report: Minority Student Recruitment & Retention," *Black Issues in Higher Education*, 17: 34-35, (October 26, 2000).

★46★
Total number of Asian American 12 graders taking Advanced Placement Exams, 1998-2000

Ranking basis/background: Total number of Asian American students taking AP exams each year. **Remarks:** Original source: The College Board. **Number listed:** 3.
- 1998, with 34,176
- 1999, 37,182
- 2000, 41,538

Source: "Special Report: Minority Student Recruitment & Retention," *Black Issues in Higher Education*, 17: 34-35, (October 26, 2000).

★47★
Total number of Asian American students taking Advanced Placement Exams, 1998-2000

Ranking basis/background: Total number of Asian American students taking AP exams each year. **Remarks:** Original source: The College Board. **Number listed:** 3.

1998, with 68,109
1999, 75,875
2000, 85,756

Source: "Special Report: Minority Student Recruitment & Retention," *Black Issues in Higher Education*, 17: 34-35, (October 26, 2000).

★48★
Total number of Hispanic American students taking Advanced Placement Exams, 1998-2000

Ranking basis/background: Total number of Hispanic American students taking AP exams each year. **Remarks:** Original source: The College Board. **Number listed:** 3.
  1998, with 53,627
  1999, 62,853
  2000, 74,852

Source: "Special Report: Minority Student Recruitment & Retention," *Black Issues in Higher Education*, 17: 34-35, (October 26, 2000).

AEROSPACE ENGINEERING
See: Engineering–Aerospace Engineering, Graduate–Aerospace

AFRICAN AMERICANS
See: **Black Americans**

AGRICULTURAL EDUCATION

★49★
Australian universities with the greatest impact in agricultural sciences, 1993-97

Ranking basis/background: For each university, total number of citations divided by number of published articles during the same time period. **Remarks:** Original source: *National Science Indicators on Diskette, 1981-97* **Number listed:** 5.
1. University of Melbourne, with 19.85 citations per paper; 270 total papers
2. Institute of Advanced Studies, 16.12; 130
3. Monash University, 15.09; 77
4. Australian National University, 12.99; 167
5. La Trobe University, 8.38; 85

Source: "Australia: High-Impact Universities in Agricultural Sciences, 1993-97," *What's Hot*, July 13, 1998.

AGRICULTURE

★50★
Agriculture journals by citation impact, 1981-96

Ranking basis/background: For each journal, total number of citations divided by number of published articles during the same time period. **Remarks:** Original source: ISI's *Journal Citation Reports* and *Journal Performance Indicators on Diskette*. **Number listed:** 10.
1. *Advances in Agronomy*, with 17.44 citations per paper
2. *Pesticides Monitoring Journal*, 15.21
3. *Agriculture and Environment*, 10.40
4. *Agro-Ecosystems*, 9.09
5. *Agricultural Meteorology*, 8.11
6. *Agricultural and Biological Chemistry*, 7.60
7. *Journal of Agriculture and Food Chemistry*, 7.55
8. *Hilgardia*, 7.50
9. *Agronomy Journal*, 7.28
10. *Agricultural and Forest Meteorology*, 6.45

Source: "Journals Ranked by Impact: Agriculture," *Institute for Scientific Information: What's Hot*, February 17, 1998.

★51★
Agriculture journals by citation impact, 1981-99

Ranking basis/background: Impact factor calculated by taking the number of current citations to source items published and dividing it by the number of articles published in the journal during that time period. **Number listed:** 10.
1. *Advances in Agronomy*, with a 21.17 impact factor
2. *Pesticides Monitoring Journal*, 16.32
3. *Theoretical and Applied Genetics*, 13.67
4. *Agriculture and Environment*, 11.49
5. *Agro-Ecosystems*, 11.34
6. *Hilgardia*, 9.72
7. *Agricultural Meteorology*, 9.52
8. *Agricultural and Biological Chemistry*, 9.24
9. *Agronomy Journal*, 8.91
10. *Agricultural and Forest Meteorology*, 8.75

Source: "Journals Ranked by Impact: Agriculture," *What's Hot in Research* (http://www.isinet.com/isi/hot/research) *Institute for Scientific Information*, January 29, 2001.

★52★
Agriculture journals by citation impact, 1992-96

Ranking basis/background: For each journal, total number of citations divided by number of published articles during the same time period. **Remarks:** Original source: ISI's *Journal Citation Reports* and *Journal Performance Indicators on Diskette*. **Number listed:** 10.
1. *Agricultural and Biological Chemistry*, with 4.09 citations per paper
2. *Advances in Agronomy*, 3.43
3. *Agricultural and Forest Meteorology*, 3.15
4. *Journal of Agriculture and Food Chemistry*, 2.93
5. *Netherlands Journal of Plant Pathology*, 2.54
6. *Plant and Soil*, 2.20
7. *Journal of Economic Entomology*, 2.17
8. *Pesticide Science*, 2.07
9. *Australian Journal of Agricultural Research*, 2.05
10. *Bioscience, Biotechnology and Biochemistry*, 1.96

Source: "Journals Ranked by Impact: Agriculture," *Institute for Scientific Information: What's Hot*, February 17, 1998.

★53★
Agriculture journals by citation impact, 1995-99

Ranking basis/background: Impact factor calculated by taking the number of current citations to source items published and dividing it by the number of articles published in the journal during that time period. **Number listed:** 10.
1. *Advances in Agronomy*, with a 5.21 impact factor
2. *Theoretical and Applied Genetics*, 4.76
3. *Plant and Soil*, 3.44
4. *Agricultural and Forest Meteorology*, 3.19
5. *Journal of Agriculture and Food Chemistry*, 2.95
6. *Biological Control*, 2.39
7. *European Journal of Plant Pathology*, 2.37
8. *American Journal of Enology and Viticulture*, 2.29
9. *Apidologie*, 2.28
10. *Bioscience, Biotechnology and Biochemistry*, 2.21

Source: "Journals Ranked by Impact: Agriculture," *What's Hot in Research* (http://www.isinet.com/isi/hot/research) *Institute for Scientific Information*, January 29, 2001.

★54★
Agriculture journals by citation impact, 1999

Ranking basis/background: Impact factor calculated by taking the number of current citations to source items published and dividing it by the number of articles published in the journal during that time period. **Number listed:** 10.
1. *Molecular Breeding*, with a 2.79 impact factor
2. *Advances in Agronomy*, 2.10
3. *Theoretical and Applied Genetics*, 2.08
4. *Agricultural and Forest Meteorology*, 1.47
5. *Journal of Agriculture and Food Chemistry*, 1.45
6. *American Potato Journal*, 1.44
7. *Apidologie*, 1.33
8. *Plant and Soil*, 1.28
9. *Biological Control*, 1.27
10. *Weed Science*, 1.41

Source: "Journals Ranked by Impact: Agriculture," *What's Hot in Research* (http://www.isinet.com/isi/hot/research) *Institute for Scientific Information*, January 29, 2001.

★55★
Top recruiters for agribusiness jobs for 2000-01 bachelor's degree recipients

Ranking basis/background: Projected number of college hires from on-campus recruitment for 2000-01. **Remarks:** Numbers reflect total expected hires, not just African American projected hires. **Number listed:** 1.
1. Parker Hannifin, with 10 projected hires

Source: "The Top 100 Employers and the Majors in Demand for the Class of 2001," *The Black Collegian*, 31: 19-35, (February 2001).

★56★
Trends in U.S. Department of Agriculture grants, 1991 through 2000

Ranking basis/background: Total number of grants awarded by the National Research Initiative, a U.S. Department of Agriculture program, for each year. **Number listed:** 10.
  1991, with 2,713 grants
  1992, 2,911
  1993, 2,893
  1994, 3,517
  1995, 3,169
  1996, 3,010
  1997, 2,772
  1998, 2,559
  1999, 2,719
  2000, 2,759

Source: Southwick, Ron, "Is an Agriculture-Research Effort Dying on the Vine?," *The Chronicle of Higher Education*, 46: A23-A24, (August 18, 2000).

★57★
U.S. universities publishing the most papers in the fields of agriculture/agronomy, 1994-98

Ranking basis/background: Total number of papers published from each university. **Remarks:** Original source: University Science Indicators on Diskette, 1981-97. **Number listed:** 5.
1. University of California, Davis, with 363 papers
2. Iowa State University, 353
3. University of Florida, 344
4. University of Nebraska, 309
5. University of Minnesota, 275

Source: "Agriculture/Agronomy: Most Prolific U.S. Universities, 1994-98," *What's Hot in Research* (http://www.isinet.com/hot/research) *Institute for Scientific Information*, April 17, 2000.

ALCOHOL EDUCATION
See: **Substance Abuse and Education**

AMERICAN INDIANS–ENROLLMENT, COLLEGE

Related Information

★58★
Pavel, Michael, et. al., "American Indians and Alaska Natives in Postsecondary Education, NCES 98-291," *National Center for Education Statistics*, October 1998.
Remarks: Examines American Indian and Alaska Native demographics, access to and enrollment in postsecondary institutions, high school performance, degree completions, receipt and use of financial aid, national statistics and a historical view of tribal colleges.

ANTHROPOLOGY

★59★
Radcliffe Institute for Advanced Study fellowship recipient in the field of social anthropology, 2000-01

Ranking basis/background: Recipient and institutional affiliation of the Radcliffe Institute for Advanced study fellowship for pursuit of advanced work across a wide range of academic disciplines, professions, and creative arts. **Number listed:** 1.
   Kathleen Coll, Stanford University
Source: "The Radcliffe Institute for Advanced Study," *The Chronicle of Higher Education*, 46: A59, (June 2, 2000).

★60★
Radcliffe Institute for Advanced Study fellowship recipients in the field of anthropology, 2000-01

Ranking basis/background: Recipient and institutional affiliation of the Radcliffe Institute for Advanced study fellowship for pursuit of advanced work across a wide range of academic disciplines, professions, and creative arts. **Number listed:** 2.
   Mary Catherine Bateson, George Mason University
   Purnima Mankekar, Stanford University
Source: "The Radcliffe Institute for Advanced Study," *The Chronicle of Higher Education*, 46: A59, (June 2, 2000).

ANTHROPOLOGY, GRADUATE

★61★
Most effective anthropology research-doctorate programs as evaluated by the National Research Council

Ranking basis/background: From a survey of nearly 8,000 faculty members conducted in the spring of 1993. Respondents were asked to rate programs in their field on "effectiveness of program in educating research scholars/scientists." **Remarks:** See *Chronicle* article for more details. Scores of 3.5-5.0 indicate "extremely effective;" 2.5-3.49 "reasonably effective;" 1.5-2.49 "minimally effective;" and 0.0-1.49 "not effective." Programs also ranked by "scholarly quality of program faculty." **Number listed:** 69.
1. University of Michigan, with an effectiveness rating of 4.40
2. University of Chicago, 4.19
3. University of California, Berkeley, 3.93
4. University of Pennsylvania, 3.68
5. Harvard University, 3.67
6. Stanford University, 3.63
7. University of Arizona, 3.60
8. University of California, Los Angeles, 3.50
9. University of Illinois, Urbana-Champaign, 3.47
10. Johns Hopkins University, 3.44

Source: "Rankings of Research-Doctorate Programs in 41 Disciplines at 274 Institutions," *The Chronicle of Higher Education* 42: A21-A30 (September 21, 1995).

★62★
Top anthropology research-doctorate programs as evaluated by the National Research Council

Ranking basis/background: From a survey of nearly 8,000 faculty members conducted in the spring of 1993. Respondents were asked to rate programs in their field on "scholarly quality of program faculty." When more than one program had the samescore, the council averaged the rank order and gave each program the same rank number (if three programs tied for the top position, each received a rank of 2). **Remarks:** See *Chronicle* article for more details. Scores of 4.01 and above indicate "distinguished;" 3.0-4.0 "strong;" 2.51-3.0 "good;" 2.0-2.5 "adequate;" 1.0-1.99 "marginal;" and 0.0-0.99 "not sufficient for doctoral education." Programs also ranked by "effectiveness of program in educating research scholars/scientists." **Number listed:** 69.

1. University of Michigan, with a quality rating of 4.77
1. University of Chicago, 4.77
3. University of California, Berkeley, 4.51
4. Harvard University, 4.43
5. University of Arizona, 4.11
6. University of Pennsylvania, 3.94
7. Stanford University, 3.71
8. Yale University, 3.67
8. University of California, Los Angeles, 3.67
8. University of California, San Diego, 3.67
11. University of Florida, 3.65
12. University of Texas, Austin, 3.62
13. New York University, 3.60
14. University of Illinois, Urbana-Champaign, 3.59
15. University of California, Davis, 3.51

Source: "Rankings of Research-Doctorate Programs in 41 Disciplines at 274 Institutions," *The Chronicle of Higher Education* 42: A21-A30 (September 21, 1995).

ANTHROPOLOGY PERIODICALS

★63★
Anthropology journals by citation impact, 1991-98

Ranking basis/background: Impact factor calculated by taking the number of current citations to source items published and dividing it by the number of articles published in the journal during that time period. **Number listed:** 10.
1. *Yearbook of Physical Anthropology*, with a 14.48 impact factor
2. *Annual Review of Anthropology*, 10.50
3. *American Journal of Physical Anthropology*, 9.53
4. *Journal of Human Evolution*, 8.75
5. *Culture, Medicine and Psychiatry*, 7.79
6. *Current Anthropology*, 7.69
7. *Journal of Anthropology and Archaeology*, 7.55
8. *Social Networks*, 6.76
9. *American Ethnologist*, 6.73
10. *Man*, 6.09

Source: "Journals Ranked by Impact: Anthropology," *What's Hot in Research* (http://www.isinet.com/isi/hot/research) *Institute for Scientific Information*, July 3, 2000.

★64★
Anthropology journals by citation impact, 1994-98

Ranking basis/background: Impact factor calculated by taking the number of current citations to source items published and dividing it by the number of articles published in the journal during that time period. **Number listed:** 10.
1. *Yearbook of Physical Anthropology*, with a 3.79 impact factor
2. *Journal of Human Evolution*, 3.39
3. *Human Nature: An Interdisciplinary Biosocial Perspective*, 3.11
4. *American Journal of Physical Anthropology*, 3.01
5. *Current Anthropology*, 2.77
6. *Annual Review of Anthropology*, 2.71
7. *Man*, 2.30
8. *American Anthropologist*, 2.20
9. *American Antiquity*, 1.95
10. *Culture, Medicine and Psychiatry*, 1.94

ARCHAEOLOGY

Source: "Journals Ranked by Impact: Anthropology," *What's Hot in Research* (http://www.isinet.com/isi/hot/research) Institute for Scientific Information, July 3, 2000.

★65★
Anthropology journals by citation impact, 1998

Ranking basis/background: Impact factor calculated by taking the number of current citations to source items published and dividing it by the number of articles published in the journal during that time period. **Number listed:** 10.
1. *American Journal of Physical Anthropology*, with a 1.75 impact factor
2. *Current Anthropology*, 1.60
3. *Journal of Human Evolution*, 1.58
4. *Yearbook of Physical Anthropology*, 1.47
5. *Human Nature: An Interdisciplinary Biosocial Perspective*, 1.29
6. *Medical Anthropology Quarterly*, 1.09
7. *American Ethnologist*, 1.01
8. *American Antiquity*, 0.99
9. *Cultural Anthropology*, 0.95
10. *Annual Review of Anthropology*, 0.93

Source: "Journals Ranked by Impact: Anthropology," *What's Hot in Research* (http://www.isinet.com/isi/hot/research) Institute for Scientific Information, July 3, 2000.

ARCHAEOLOGY

★66★
U.S. universities publishing the most papers in the field of archaeology, 1994-98

Ranking basis/background: Total number of papers published from each university. **Remarks:** Original source: University Science Indicators on Diskette, 1981-97. **Number listed:** 5.
1. University of Arizona, with 44 papers
2. Arizona State University, 40
3. University of California, Berkeley, 38
4. University of Pennsylvania, 34
5. Harvard University, 32

Source: "Archaeology: Most Prolific U.S. Universities, 1994-98," *What's Hot in Research* (http://www.isinet.com/hot/research) Institute for Scientific Information, January 10, 2000.

ARCHITECTURE

★67★
Radcliffe Institute for Advanced Study fellowship recipient in the field of architectural history, 2000-01

Ranking basis/background: Recipient and institutional affiliation of the Radcliffe Institute for Advanced study fellowship for pursuit of advanced work across a wide range of academic disciplines, professions, and creative arts. **Number listed:** 1.
   Nancy Stieber, University of Massachusetts, Boston

Source: "The Radcliffe Institute for Advanced Study," *The Chronicle of Higher Education*, 46: A59, (June 2, 2000).

★68★
Top recruiters for architecture jobs for 2000-01 bachelor's degree recipients

Ranking basis/background: Projected number of college hires from on-campus recruitment for 2000-01. **Remarks:** Numbers reflect total expected hires, not just African American projected hires. **Number listed:** 1.
1. U.S. Air Force (Active Duty Hires), with 5 projected hires

Source: "The Top 100 Employers and the Majors in Demand for the Class of 2001," *The Black Collegian*, 31: 19-35, (February 2001).

★69★
Top recruiters for Naval architecture jobs for 2000-01 bachelor's degree recipients

Ranking basis/background: Projected number of college hires from on-campus recruitment for 2000-01. **Remarks:** Numbers reflect total expected hires, not just African American projected hires. **Number listed:** 1.
1. Ingalls Shipbuilding, with 10 projected hires

Source: "The Top 100 Employers and the Majors in Demand for the Class of 2001," *The Black Collegian*, 31: 19-35, (February 2001).

★70★
U.S. universities publishing the most papers in the fields of art and architecture, 1994-98

Ranking basis/background: Total number of papers published from each university. **Remarks:** Original source: University Science Indicators on Diskette, 1981-97. **Number listed:** 5.
1. Columbia University, with 97 papers
2. Harvard University, 87
3. New York University, 70
4. University of California, Berkeley, 51
5. Yale University, 48

Source: "Art & Architecture: Most Prolific U.S. Universities, 1994-98," *What's Hot in Research* (http://www.isinet.com/hot/research) Institute for Scientific Information, March 20, 2000.

Related Information

★71★
Polo, Marco Louis, "Ten Schools," *The Canadian Architect*, May 1998, pp. 24-29.
   Remarks: Discusses the assessment and upgrade of Canadian architecture schools, and surveys programs at ten Canadian schools of architecture with full professional accreditation.

ARCHITECTURE, GRADUATE

★72★
Top recruiters for Naval architecture jobs for 2000-01 master's degree recipients

Ranking basis/background: Projected number of college hires from on-campus recruitment for 2000-01. **Remarks:** Numbers reflect total expected hires, not just African American projected hires. **Number listed:** 1.
1. Ingalls Shipbuilding, with 5 projected hires

Source: "The Top 100 Employers and the Majors in Demand for the Class of 2001," *The Black Collegian*, 31: 19-35, (February 2001).

ART

★73★
Best living artists

Ranking basis/background: Alphabetical list by name of the best living artists as chosen by museum directors, curators, and art critics from around the world. **Number listed:** 10.
   Matthew Barney
   Louise Bourgeois
   Jasper Johns
   Ilya Kabakov
   Agnes Martin
   Bruce Nauman
   Sigmar Polke
   Gerhard Richter
   Cindy Sherman
   Jeff Wall

Source: Pollack, Barbara, "The 10 Best Living Artists," *ARTnews*, 98: 137-147, (December 1999).

★74★
Canada's best performing artists of the 20th century

Ranking basis/background: Most significant creators and works from a number of areas, selected by *Maclean's* critics and an art historian. Not listed in order of importance. **Number listed:** 15.
   Guy Lombardo
   Oscar Peterson
   Jon Vickers
   Glenn Gould
   Paul Anka
   Gordon Lightfoot
   Leonard Cohen
   Joni Mitchell
   Neil Young
   Anne Murray
   Gilles Vigneault
   Karen Kain
   Robert Lepage
   Benn Heppner
   Celine Dion

Source: Bemrose, John, "Best of the Century," *Maclean's*, 113: 241-246, (January 1, 2000).

★75★
Canada's best visual artists of the 20th century

Ranking basis/background: Most significant creators and works from a number of areas, selected by *Maclean's* critics and an art historian. Not listed in order of importance. **Number listed:** 15.
   Emily Carr (1871-1945) painter
   Tom Thomson (1877-1917) painter
   David Milne (1882-1953) painter
   Lawren Harris (1895-1970)
   Paul-Emile Borduas (1905-1960) painter
   Jack Bush (1909-1977) painter
   Michael Snow (1929-) film
   Joyce Wieland (1931-1998)
   Jana Sterbak (1955-) sculptor
   Stan Douglas (1960-) film

Source: Bemrose, John, "Best of the Century," *Maclean's*, 113: 241-246, (January 1, 2000).

★76★
Highly influential artists of the 20th century

Ranking basis/background: As compiled by *ARTnews* editors, art critics, scholars, and curators asked to evaluate each artist's legacy. List is alphabetical. **Number listed:** 25.

- Joseph Beuys, born in Kleve, Germany (1921-1986)
- Louise Bourgeois, Paris, France (1911-)
- Constantin Brancusi, Pestisani, Romania (1876-1957)
- Salvador Dali, Figueras, Spain (1904-1989)
- Donald Judd, Excelsior Springs, Missouri (1928-1994)
- Vasily Kandinsky, Moscow, Russia (1866-1944)
- Le Corbusier, La-Chaux-de-Fonds, Switzerland (1887-1965)
- Kazimir Malevich, Kiev, Russia (1878-1935)
- Man Ray, Philadelphia, Pennsylvania (1890-1977)
- Henri Matisse, Le Cateau-Cambresis, Picardy (1869-1954)
- Claude Monet, Paris, France (1840-1926)
- Bruce Nauman, Fort Wayne, Indiana (1941-)
- Nam June Paik, Seoul, South Korea (1932-)
- Pablo Picasso, Malaga, Spain (1881-1973)
- Jackson Pollock, Cody, Wyoming (1912-1956)
- Robert Rauschenberg, Port Arthur, Texas (1925-)
- Cindy Sherman, Glen Ridge, New Jersey (1954-)
- Robert Smithson, Passaic, New Jersey (1938-1973)
- Alfred Stieglitz, Hoboken, New Jersey (1864-1946)
- Andy Warhol, Pittsburgh, Pennsylvania (1928-1987)
- Frank Lloyd Wright, Richland Center, Wisconsin (1867-1959)

Source: Cembalest, Robin, et. al., "The Century's 25 Most Influential Artists," *ARTnews*, May 1999, pp. 126-152.

★77★
Most influential African American entertainers

Ranking basis/background: Alphabetical listing compiled by the DuSable Museum of African American History. **Number listed:** 19.

- Marian Anderson, classical music
- Louis Armstrong, jazz
- Harry Belafonte, recordings/Broadway/television
- Diahann Carroll, Broadway/film/TV
- Nat "King" Cole, recordings/TV
- Bill Cosby, television
- Miles Davis, jazz
- Edward "Duke" Ellington, composer/recordings
- Ella Fitzgerald, jazz/recordings
- Aretha Franklin, recordings
- Billie Holiday, jazz
- Lena Horne, film/music/Broadway
- Spike Lee, film
- Oscar Micheaux, film
- Arthur Mitchell, dance
- Sidney Poitier, film
- Leontyne Price, classical music
- Paul Robeson, film/Broadway
- Stevie Wonder, composer/recordings

Source: Moffett, Nancy, "Voices of Power," *Chicago Sun-Times*, February 2, 2000, p. 39.

★78★
Most influential African Americans in the arts

Ranking basis/background: Alphabetical listing compiled by the DuSable Museum of African American History. **Number listed:** 14.

- Maya Angelou, author
- James Baldwin, author
- Amiri Baraka, poet
- Gwendolyn Brooks, poet
- Alex Haley, author
- Lorraine Hansberry, playwright
- Langston Hughes, author-poet
- Richard Hunt, sculptor
- Zora Neale Hurston, author
- Toni Morrison, author
- Susan Taylor, editor
- Alice Walker, author
- August Wilson, playwright
- Richard Wright, author

Source: Moffett, Nancy, "Voices of Power," *Chicago Sun-Times*, February 2, 2000, p. 39.

★79★
Radcliffe Institute for Advanced Study fellowship recipients in the field of visual arts, 2000-01

Ranking basis/background: Recipient and institutional affiliation of the Radcliffe Institute for Advanced study fellowship for pursuit of advanced work across a wide range of academic disciplines, professions, and creative arts. **Number listed:** 3.

- Alison Crocetta, Alfred University
- Colleen Kiely, Massachusetts College of Art
- Ann Messner, Pratt Institute

Source: "The Radcliffe Institute for Advanced Study," *The Chronicle of Higher Education*, 46: A59, (June 2, 2000).

★80★
Top recruiters for art jobs for 2000-01 bachelor's degree recipients

Ranking basis/background: Projected number of college hires from on-campus recruitment for 2000-01. **Remarks:** Numbers reflect total expected hires, not just African American projected hires. **Number listed:** 4.

1. Houghton Mifflin, with 15 projected hires
2. Sherwin-Williams, 10
3. General Motors, 5
4. Henrico County Public Schools, 4

Source: "The Top 100 Employers and the Majors in Demand for the Class of 2001," *The Black Collegian*, 31: 19-35, (February 2001).

★81★
Top recruiters for art jobs for 2000-01 master's degree recipients

Ranking basis/background: Projected number of college hires from on-campus recruitment for 2000-01. **Remarks:** Numbers reflect total expected hires, not just African American projected hires. **Number listed:** 2.

1. Houghton Mifflin, with 5 projected hires
2. Henrico County Public Schools, 1

Source: "The Top 100 Employers and the Majors in Demand for the Class of 2001," *The Black Collegian*, 31: 19-35, (February 2001).

Related Information

★82★
"American Artist 2001 Art School Directory," *American Artist*, 65: 74-94, (March 2001).
Remarks: Provides an alphabetical list of art workshops, schools, colleges, and universities in the U.S. and abroad. Includes contact information and limited program descriptions.

★83★
Liu, Robert K., "Connecting Links: New York Jewelry Schools," *Ornament*, 23: 56-61, (Autumn 1999).
Remarks: Overviews three New York jewelry schools.

★84★
"The 2000 Edition: North American Guide to Schools, Internships and Recruitment," *Animation Magazine*, 14: 31-32, (January 2000).
Remarks: Provides information on U.S. schools that offer programs and internships in animation, and a director of recruitment companies in North American relating to animation.

★85★
"Ceramics Education Directory," *American Ceramics*, January 1998, pp. 48-49.
Remarks: Provides information on U.S. art schools that offer ceramics education.

★86★
"Art Schools," *Artweek*, January 1998, pp. 23-31.
Remarks: Provides information on midwestern U.S. schools that offer undergraduate and graduate degrees in art. Includes details of areas of emphasis, current tuition fees, special facilities or equipment, and average student-to-instructor ratios.

★87★
Doherty, M. Stephen, "The Water Street Atelier and Other Center of Classical Art," *American Artist*, August 1998, pp. 68-70.
Remarks: Describes the Water Street Atelier in Brooklyn, New York, a new art school set up by artist Jacob Waters to offer classical art training unavailable in most art schools.

★88★
"Design Sourcebook 2001 (Vol. 47 11 Article Special Issue)," *ID*, December 2000, pp. 22-127.
Remarks: Provides directories of design schools, design associations, professional services, stock photography agencies, material supply firms, and sources for graphic design, product design, packaging design, environments design, interactive media design, and computer hardware design.

★89★
"Design School Roundup: the ABCs," *TCI*, October 1998, pp. 70-71.
Remarks: Provides information on U.S. schools that offer theater-related undergraduate and graduate programs. Includes a number of course locations and their costs, contact addresses, phone numbers, fax numbers and e-mail addressees.

★90★
"How I Got Into College: A Guide to Design Schools and Their Requirements (for degrees in theatre design)," *TCI*, October 1997, p. 44.

ART HISTORY, GRADUATE

Remarks: Provides information on U.S. schools that offer graduate programs in theater design and technology, or both. Includes guidelines for admission and finance, program details, noted faculty and alumni, and tuition rates.

ART HISTORY, GRADUATE

★91★
Most effective art history research-doctorate programs as evaluated by the National Research Council

Ranking basis/background: From a survey of nearly 8,000 faculty members conducted in the spring of 1993. Respondents were asked to rate programs in their field on "effectiveness of program in educating research scholars/scientists." **Remarks:** See *Chronicle* article for more details. Scores of 3.5-5.0 indicate "extremely effective;" 2.5-3.49 "reasonably effective;" 1.5-2.49 "minimally effective;" and 0.0-1.49 "not effective." Programs also ranked by "scholarly quality of program faculty." **Number listed:** 38.

1. Yale University, with an effectiveness rating of 4.29
2. New York University, 4.32
3. Columbia University, 4.29
4. University of California, Berkeley, 4.18
5. Harvard University, 4.11
6. Princeton University, 3.78
7. University of Michigan, 3.58
8. Northwestern University, 3.57
9. University of Pennsylvania, 3.51
10. University of Chicago, 3.49

Source: "Rankings of Research-Doctorate Programs in 41 Disciplines at 274 Institutions," *The Chronicle of Higher Education* 42: A21-A30 (September 21, 1995).

★92★
Radcliffe Institute for Advanced Study fellowship recipient in the field of art history, 2000-01

Ranking basis/background: Recipient and institutional affiliation of the Radcliffe Institute for Advanced study fellowship for pursuit of advanced work across a wide range of academic disciplines, professions, and creative arts. **Number listed:** 1.

Martha Buskirk, Montserrat College of Art

Source: "The Radcliffe Institute for Advanced Study," *The Chronicle of Higher Education*, 46: A59, (June 2, 2000).

★93★
Top art history research-doctorate programs as evaluated by the National Research Council

Ranking basis/background: From a survey of nearly 8,000 faculty members conducted in the spring of 1993. Respondents were asked to rate programs in their field on "scholarly quality of program faculty." When more than one program had the samescore, the council averaged the rank order and gave each program the same rank number (if three programs tied for the top position, each received a rank of 2). **Remarks:** See *Chronicle* article for more details. Scores of 4.01 and above indicate "distinguished;" 3.0-4.0 "strong;" 2.51-3.0 "good;" 2.0-2.5 "adequate;" 1.0-1.99 "marginal;" and 0.0-0.99 "not sufficient for doctoral education." Programs also ranked by "effectiveness of program in educating research scholars/scientists." **Number listed:** 38.

1. Columbia University, with a quality rating of 4.79
1. New York University, 4.79
3. University of California, Berkeley, 4.67
4. Harvard University, 4.49
5. Yale University, 4.44
6. Princeton University, 4.04
7. Johns Hopkins University, 3.93
8. Northwestern University, 3.83
9. University of Pennsylvania, 3.80
10. University of Chicago, 3.74
11. University of Michigan, 3.71
12. City University of New York, Graduate School and University Center, 3.60
13. University of California, Los Angeles, 3.52
14. Stanford University, 3.49
15. University of Delaware, 3.40

Source: "Rankings of Research-Doctorate Programs in 41 Disciplines at 274 Institutions," *The Chronicle of Higher Education* 42: A21-A30 (September 21, 1995).

ARTIFICIAL INTELLIGENCE

★94★
Artificial intelligence journals by citation impact, 1981-99

Ranking basis/background: Impact factor calculated by taking the number of current citations to source items published and dividing it by the number of articles published in the journal during that time period. **Number listed:** 10.

1. *Artificial Intelligence*, with a 20.08 impact factor
2. *IEEE Transactions on Pattern Analysis*, 19.98
3. *Neural Networks*, 12.23
4. *International Journal of Computer Vision*, 11.07
5. *Machine Learning*, 8.74
6. *IEEE Transactions of Neural Networks*, 7.97
7. *Neural Computation*, 7.91
8. *Knowledge Acquisition*, 7.29
9. *Cognitive Brain Research*, 6.56
10. *Chemometrics and Intelligent Laboratory Systems*, 6.44

Source: "Journals Ranked by Impact: Artificial Intelligence," *What's Hot in Research* (http://www.isinet.com/isi/hot/research) Institute for Scientific Information.

★95★
Artificial intelligence journals by citation impact, 1995-99

Ranking basis/background: Impact factor calculated by taking the number of current citations to source items published and dividing it by the number of articles published in the journal during that time period. **Number listed:** 10.

1. *Knowledge Acquisition*, with a 5.40 impact factor
2. *Cognitive Brain Research*, 4.75
3. *Neural Computation*, 4.15
4. *Network: Computation in Neural Systems*, 3.56
5. *IEEE Transactions on Pattern Analysis*, 3.47
6. *IEEE Transactions on Fuzzy Systems*, 3.46
7. *International Journal of Computer Vision*, 3.26
8. *Machine Learning*, 3.06
9. *Chemometrics and Intelligent Laboratory Systems*, 2.88
10. *Artificial Intelligence*, 2.87

Source: "Journals Ranked by Impact: Artificial Intelligence," *What's Hot in Research* (http://www.isinet.com/isi/hot/research) Institute for Scientific Information.

★96★
Artificial intelligence journals by citation impact, 1999

Ranking basis/background: Impact factor calculated by taking the number of current citations to source items published and dividing it by the number of articles published in the journal during that time period. **Number listed:** 10.

1. *Neural Computation*, with a 2.83 impact factor
2. *Data Mining and Knowledge Discovery*, 2.55
3. *Cognitive Brain Research*, 2.33
4. *Machine Learning*, 2.19
5. *Atificial Intelligence*, 1.95
6. *IEEE Transactions on Pattern Analysis*, 1.88
7. *AI Magazine*, 1.71
8. *Chemometrics and Intelligent Laboratory Systems*, 1.66
9. *International Journal of Computer Vision*, 1.65
10. *IEEE Transactions on Fuzzy Systems*, 1.60

Source: "Journals Ranked by Impact: Artificial Intelligence," *What's Hot in Research* (http://www.isinet.com/isi/hot/research) Institute for Scientific Information.

★97★
Artificial intelligence journals with the greatest impact measure, 1981-98

Ranking basis/background: Citations-per-paper impact score is the total citations to a journal's published papers divided by total number of papers the journal has published over an eighteen year period. **Remarks:** Original source: *Journal Citation Reports* and *Journal Performance Indicators on Diskette*. **Number listed:** 10.

1. *Artificial Intelligence*, with an impact score of 19.20
2. *IEEE Transactions on Pattern Analysis and Machine Intelligence*, 18.21
3. *Neural Networks*, 11.48
4. *International Journal of Computer Vision*, 9.90
5. *Machine Learning*, 7.17

6. *IEEE Transactions on Neural Networks*, 6.93
7. *Neural Computation*, 6.52
8. *Chemometrics and Intelligent Laboratory Systems*, 6.12
9. *Knowledge Acquisition*, 6.03
10. *Pattern Recognition*, 5.15

Source: "Journals Ranked by Impact: Artificial Intelligence," *What's Hot in Research* (http://www.isinet.com/hot/research) Institute for Scientific Information, February 28, 2000.

★98★

Artificial intelligence journals with the greatest impact measure, 1994-98

Ranking basis/background: Citations-per-paper impact score is the total citations to a journal's published papers divided by total number of papers the journal has published over a five year period. **Remarks:** Original source: *Journal Citation Reports* and Journal Performance Indicators on Diskette. **Number listed:** 10.

1. *Cognitive Brain Research*, with an impact score of 5.09
2. *Neural Computation*, 4.23
3. *Knowledge Acquisition*, 3.42
4. *Chemometrics and Intelligent Laboratory Systems*, 3.19
5. *IEEE Transactions on Neural Networks*, 3.12
6. *IEEE Transactions on Fuzzy Systems*, 3.10
7. *International Journal of Computer Vision*, 3.06
8. *Network-Neural Computations*, 2.98
9. *Artificial Intelligence*, 2.85
10. *IEEE Transactions on Pattern Analysis and Machine Intelligence*, 2.80

Source: "Journals Ranked by Impact: Artificial Intelligence," *What's Hot in Research* (http://www.isinet.com/hot/research) Institute for Scientific Information, February 28, 2000.

★99★

Artificial intelligence journals with the greatest impact measure, 1998

Ranking basis/background: Ratio of citations and recent citable items published. **Remarks:** Original source: *Journal Citation Reports* and Journal Performance Indicators on Diskette. **Number listed:** 10.

1. *Cognitive Brain Research*, with a ratio of 2.76
2. *Neural Computation*, 2.07
3. *Chemometrics and Intelligent Laboratory Systems*, 1.75
4. *AI Magazine*, 1.62
5. *Artificial Intelligence*, 1.61
6. *IEEE Transactions on Pattern Analysis and Machine Intelligence*, 1.42
7. *Network-Neural Computations*, 1.33
8. *International Journal of Computer Vision*, 1.29
9. *IEEE Transactions on Neural Networks*, 1.28
10. *Knowledge Engineering Review*, 1.27

Source: "Journals Ranked by Impact: Artificial Intelligence," *What's Hot in Research* (http://www.isinet.com/hot/research) Institute for Scientific Information, February 28, 2000.

★100★

U.S. universities publishing the most papers in the field of artificial intelligence, 1995-99

Ranking basis/background: Number of papers published in the field of artificial intelligence, robotics, and automatic control over a five-year period, and percent of field based on each university's percentage of the 26,603 papers entered in the ISI database from ISI-indexed artificial-intelligence journals. **Number listed:** 6.

1. Massachusetts Institute of Technology, with 324 papers, 1.22% of field
2. Carnegie Mellon University, 276, 1.04%
3. University of California, Berkeley, 248, 0.93%
3. University of Maryland, College Park, 247, 0.93%
5. University of Michigan, Ann Arbor, 228, 0.86%
6. Caltech, 210, 0.79%

Source: "Artificial Intelligence: Most Prolific U.S. Universities, 1995-99," *What's Hot in Research* (http://www.isinet.com/isi/hot/research) Institute for Scientific Information, January 22, 2001.

ARTS & HUMANITIES–FEDERAL AID

★101★

Proposed fiscal 2002 appropriations for arts and humanities

Ranking basis/background: Based on the U.S. government's proposed fiscal 2002 appropriations for arts and humanities. **Number listed:** 12.

National Endowment for the Humanities: Research and education programs, with $24,594,000
NEH: Public and enterprise programs, $12,560,000
NEH: State programs, $30,593,000
NEH: Preservation and access programs, $18,288,000
NEH: Regional Humanities Centers, $1,186,000
NEH: Challenge grants, $10,436,000
NEH: Treasury matching grants, $4,000,000
National Endowment for the Arts, $105,200,000
Institute of Museum and Library Services: Office of Museum Services, $24,899,000
Institute of Museum and Library Services: Office of Library Services, $168,078,000
National Archives and Records Administration, $244,247,000
National Historical Publications and Records Commission, $4,436,000

Source: "Bush's Fiscal 2002 Budget Plan for Higher Education and Science," *The Chronicle of Higher Education*, 47: A36-A37, (April 20, 2001).

ASSOCIATE DEGREES
See: **Degrees (Academic)**

ASTRONOMY

★102★

Astronomy and astrophysics journals by citation impact, 1981-99

Ranking basis/background: Impact factor calculated by taking the number of current citations to source items published and dividing it by the number of articles published in the journal during that time period. **Number listed:** 10.

1. *Annual Review of Astronomy and Astrophysics*, with a 93.22 impact factor
2. *Astrophysical Journal Supplement Series*, 38.45
3. *Annual Review of Earth and Planetary Science*, 34.25
4. *Astronomy and Astrophysics Review*, 33.15
5. *Astrophysical Journal*, 23.50
6. *Astronomical Journal*, 17.62
7. *Journal of Geophysical Research-Space Physics*, 16.79
8. *Monthly Notices of the Royal Astronomy Society*, 16.47
9. *Journal of Geophysical Research, Section D-Atmospheres*, 16.19
10. *Icarus*, 14.92

Source: "Journals Ranked by Impact: Astronomy & Astrophysics," *What's Hot in Research* (http://www.isinet.com/isi/hot/research) Institute for Scientific Information, September 11, 2000.

★103★

Astronomy and astrophysics journals by citation impact, 1995-99

Ranking basis/background: Impact factor calculated by taking the number of current citations to source items published and dividing it by the number of articles published in the journal during that time period. **Number listed:** 10.

1. *Annual Review of Astronomy and Astrophysics*, with a 29.22 impact factor
2. *Astronomy and Astrophysics Review*, 14.27
3. *Astrophysical Journal Supplement Series*, 13.20
4. *Annual Review of Earth and Planetary Science*, 10.00
5. *Astrophysical Journal*, 9.62
6. *Astronomical Journal*, 7.64
7. *Monthly Notices of the Royal Astronomy Society*, 6.54
8. *Journal of Geophysical Research, Section D-Atmospheres*, 6.43
9. *Journal of Geophysical Research-Solid Earth*, 6.05
10. *Astronomy & Astrophysics*, 5.60

Source: "Journals Ranked by Impact: Astronomy & Astrophysics," *What's Hot in Research* (http://www.isinet.com/isi/hot/research) Institute for Scientific Information, September 11, 2000.

★104★

Astronomy and astrophysics journals by citation impact, 1999

Ranking basis/background: Impact factor calculated by taking the number of current citations to source items published and dividing it by the number of articles published in the journal during that time period. **Number listed:** 10.

1. *Annual Review of Astronomy and Astrophysics*, with a 15.07 impact factor
2. *Annual Review of Earth and Planetary Science*, 5.33
3. *Monthly Notices of the Royal Astronomy Society*, 4.55

4. *Astrophysical Journal Supplement Series*, 3.75
5. *New Astronomy*, 2.95
6. *Astronomical Journal*, 2.88
7. *Astroparticle Physics*, 2.81
8. *Icarus*, 2.80
9. *Solar Physics*, 2.76
10. *Astrophysical Journal*, 2.54

Source: "Journals Ranked by Impact: Astronomy & Astrophysics," *What's Hot in Research* (http://www.isinet.com/isi/hot/research) *Institute for Scientific Information*, September 11, 2000.

★105★
Astronomy and astrophysics journals by impact factor, 1981 to 1998

Ranking basis/background: Current citations to journal's published papers divided by total papers published over an 18-year period. **Remarks:** Original source: *Journal Citation Reports* and *Journal Performances Indicators on Diskette*. **Number listed:** 10.
1. *Annual Review of Astronomy and Astrophysics*, with 84.48
2. *Astrophysical Journal Supplement Series*, 35.71
3. *Annual Review of Earth and Planetary Science*, 32.05
4. *Astronomy and Astrophysics Review*, 31.42
5. *Astrophysical Journal*, 22.51
6. *Journal of Geophysical Research-Space Physics*, 16.18
7. *Astronomical Journal*, 16.17
8. *Monthly Notices of the Royal Astronomy Society*, 15.43
9. *Journal of Geophysical Research, Section D-Atmospheres*, 15.10
10. *Icarus: International Journal of Solar System Studies*, 13.97

Source: "Journals Ranked by Impact: Astronomy & Astrophysics," *What's Hot in Research*, http://www.isinet.com/whatshot/whatshot.html, Institute for Scientific Information (April 26, 1999).

★106★
Astronomy and astrophysics journals by impact factor, 1994 to 1998

Ranking basis/background: Current citations to a journal's published papers divided by total papers published over the past five years. **Remarks:** Original source: *Journal Citation Reports* and *Journal Performances Indicators on Diskette*. **Number listed:** 10.
1. *Annual Review of Astronomy and Astrophysics*, with 24.96
2. *Astronomy and Astrophysics Review*, 16.86
3. *Astrophysical Journal Supplement Series*, 11.80
4. *Annual Review of Earth and Planetary Science*, 9.83
5. *Astrophysical Journal*, 8.74
6. *Astronomical Journal*, 6.59
7. *Publications of the Astronomical Society of Japan*, 6.05
8. *Journal of Geophysical Research, Section D – Atmospheres*, 5.97
9. *Journal of Geophysical Research-Solid Earth*, 5.92
10. *Monthly Notices of the Royal Astronomy Society*, 5.74

Source: "Journals Ranked by Impact: Astronomy & Astrophysics," *What's Hot in Research*, http://www.isinet.com/whatshot/whatshot.html, Institute for Scientific Information (April 26, 1999).

★107★
Astronomy degrees awarded at master's-granting institutions, by type of degree, 1998-99

Ranking basis/background: Number of astronomy degrees awarded at each level. **Number listed:** 2.
Bachelors, with 8
Masters, 7

Source: Nicholson, Starr and Patrick J. Mulvey, "Roster of Astronomy Departments with Enrollment and Degree Data, 1999," *AIP: American Institute of Physics Report*, August 2000.

★108★
Astronomy degrees awarded at Ph.D.-granting institutions, by type of degree, 1998-99

Ranking basis/background: Number of astronomy degrees awarded at each level. **Number listed:** 4.
Bachelors, with 134
Masters, 16
Masters enroute, 62
Ph.D., 88

Source: Nicholson, Starr and Patrick J. Mulvey, "Roster of Astronomy Departments with Enrollment and Degree Data, 1999," *AIP: American Institute of Physics Report*, August 2000.

★109★
Radcliffe Institute for Advanced Study fellowship recipient in the field of astronomy, 2000-01

Ranking basis/background: Recipient and institutional affiliation of the Radcliffe Institute for Advanced study fellowship for pursuit of advanced work across a wide range of academic disciplines, professions, and creative arts. **Number listed:** 1.
Kim McLeod, Wellesley College

Source: "The Radcliffe Institute for Advanced Study," *The Chronicle of Higher Education*, 46: A59, (June 2, 2000).

ASTRONOMY, GRADUATE

★110★
First-year astronomy graduate students, by citizenship, 1997-98

Ranking basis/background: Percentage of U.S. and foreign first-year physics graduate students. **Number listed:** 2.
U.S., with 70%
Foreign, 30%

Source: Mulvey, Patrick J. and Casey Langer, "1998 Graduate Student Report: First-Year Students," *AIP: American Institute of Physics Report*, November 2000.

★111★
First-year astronomy graduate students, by gender, 1997-98

Ranking basis/background: Percentage of male and female first-year physics graduate students. **Number listed:** 2.
Men, with 74%
Women, 25%

Source: Mulvey, Patrick J. and Casey Langer, "1998 Graduate Student Report: First-Year Students," *AIP: American Institute of Physics Report*, November 2000.

★112★
First-year astronomy graduate students from the U.S., by age, 1997-98

Ranking basis/background: Percentage of first-year physics graduate students from the U.S. in each age group. **Number listed:** 3.
23 or younger, with 58%
24-25, 24%
26 or older, 18%

Source: Mulvey, Patrick J. and Casey Langer, "1998 Graduate Student Report: First-Year Students," *AIP: American Institute of Physics Report*, November 2000.

★113★
Foreign first-year astronomy graduate students, by age, 1997-98

Ranking basis/background: Percentage of foreign first-year physics graduate students in each age group. **Number listed:** 3.
23 or younger, with 20%
24-25, 30%
26 or older, 50%

Source: Mulvey, Patrick J. and Casey Langer, "1998 Graduate Student Report: First-Year Students," *AIP: American Institute of Physics Report*, November 2000.

ATHLETICS

Related Information

★114★
"The Ultimate Driving School," *U.S News & World Report* 113: 9 (December 21, 1992).
Remarks: Brief details on courses for the Skip Barber Racing School, the world's largest car racing school.

★115★
Tunstall, Jim, "National Classtime: Umpire School: The First Step to the Big Leagues," *Chicago Tribune Magazine*, April 5, 1992, p. 14-20.
Remarks: A case study of the Brinkman-Froemming Umpire School in Cocoa Beach, Florida.

ATHLETICS–COLLEGES & UNIVERSITIES

★116★
Adjusted admission advantage for college athletes, 1999

Ranking basis/background: Percent of adjusted admission advantage for men and women in three student categories. From a survey of 30 selective colleges and universities. **Remarks:** Original source: The Game of Life. **Number listed:** 3.
Minorities, with 18% men; 20% women
Legacies, 25%; 24%
Athletes, 48%; 53%

Source: Maszak-Szegedy, Marianne, "Winning the 'Game of Life,'" *U.S. News & World Report*, 130: 42, (January 29, 2001).

ATHLETICS—COLLEGES & UNIVERSITIES

★117★
African American college athletics administrators and staff, by gender, 1999-2000

Ranking basis/background: Total number of African American men and women in each administrative or staff position. **Remarks:** Original source: NCAA. **Number listed:** 5.

- Assistant athletics director, with 75 men; 27 women
- Compliance coordinator, 51; 44
- Academic advisor, 126; 83
- Graduate assistant, 86; 33
- Intern, 35; 33

Source: Suggs, Welch, "Top Posts in Sports Programs Still Tend to Go to White Men," *The Chronicle of Higher Education*, 46: A53-A54, (June 2, 2000).

★118★
African American college athletics head coaches, by gender, 1999-2000

Ranking basis/background: Total number of African American men and women in each head coach position. **Remarks:** Original source: NCAA. **Number listed:** 5.

- Football, with 44 men; 0 women
- Men's basketball, 154; 0
- Women's basketball, 37; 64
- All men's teams, 570; 20
- All women's teams, 374; 224

Source: Suggs, Welch, "Top Posts in Sports Programs Still Tend to Go to White Men," *The Chronicle of Higher Education*, 46: A53-A54, (June 2, 2000).

★119★
African American college athletics senior administrators, by gender, 1999-2000

Ranking basis/background: Total number of African American men and women in each senior administrator position. **Remarks:** Original source: NCAA. **Number listed:** 5.

- Athletics director, with 61 men; 10 women
- Associate athletics director, 40; 23
- Senior woman administrator, 0; 71
- Business manager, 31; 22
- Faculty athletics representative, 54; 11

Source: Suggs, Welch, "Top Posts in Sports Programs Still Tend to Go to White Men," *The Chronicle of Higher Education*, 46: A53-A54, (June 2, 2000).

★120★
Coaches winning the most NCAA tournaments

Ranking basis/background: Number of tournament wins through 2000. **Number listed:** 10.

1. Dean Smith with 27 tournament wins
2. Bob Knight, 24
3. Denny Crum, 23
4. Lute Olson, 21
5. John Thompson, 20
5. Jim Boeheim, 20
5. Adolph Rupp, 20
8. Mike Kryzewski, 16
8. John Wooden, 16
10. Jerry Tarkanian, 14

Source: *The World Almanac and Book of Facts 2001*, World Almanac Books, 2001.

★121★
College athletics administrators and staff, by gender, 1999-2000

Ranking basis/background: Total number men and women in each administrative or staff position. **Remarks:** Original source: NCAA. **Number listed:** 5.

- Assistant athletics director, with 781 men; 369 women
- Compliance coordinator, 360; 327
- Academic advisor, 329; 388
- Graduate assistant, 720; 485
- Intern, 243; 180

Source: Suggs, Welch, "Top Posts in Sports Programs Still Tend to Go to White Men," *The Chronicle of Higher Education*, 46: A53-A54, (June 2, 2000).

★122★
College athletics head coaches, by gender, 1999-2000

Ranking basis/background: Total number of men and women in each head coach position. **Remarks:** Original source: NCAA. **Number listed:** 5.

- Football, with 532 men; 0 women
- Men's basketball, 766; 0
- Women's basketball, 330; 509
- All men's teams, 6,540; 230
- All women's teams, 4,015; 3,064

Source: Suggs, Welch, "Top Posts in Sports Programs Still Tend to Go to White Men," *The Chronicle of Higher Education*, 46: A53-A54, (June 2, 2000).

★123★
College athletics senior administrators, by gender, 1999-2000

Ranking basis/background: Total number of men and women in each senior administrator position. **Remarks:** Original source: NCAA. **Number listed:** 5.

- Athletics director, with 746 men; 159 women
- Associate athletics director, 523; 295
- Senior woman administrator, 6; 723
- Business manager, 254; 218
- Faculty athletics representative, 682; 201

Source: Suggs, Welch, "Top Posts in Sports Programs Still Tend to Go to White Men," *The Chronicle of Higher Education*, 46: A53-A54, (June 2, 2000).

★124★
College sports officials, by race, 1999-2000

Ranking basis/background: Percentage of sports officials at NCAA colleges for each race. Total sports officials tallied is 19,124. **Remarks:** Original source: NCAA. **Number listed:** 3.

1. White, with 87.7%
2. African American, 8.7%
3. Other minorities, 3.5%

Source: Suggs, Welch, "Top Posts in Sports Programs Still Tend to Go to White Men," *The Chronicle of Higher Education*, 46: A53-A54, (June 2, 2000).

★125★
Comparison of GPA percentile rank of athletes for selected years

Ranking basis/background: GPA percentile rank of high-profile athletes, lower-profile athletes, and students at large in selected years. From a survey of 30 selective colleges and universities. **Remarks:** Original source: The Game of Life. **Number listed:** 3.

- 1951, with an average GPA of 45 for high-profile athletes; 50 for lower-profile athletes; and 47 for students at large
- 1976, 33; 44; 49
- 1989, 25; 40; 49

Source: Maszak-Szegedy, Marianne, "Winning the 'Game of Life'," *U.S. News & World Report*, 130: 42, (January 29, 2001).

★126★
Division I-A all-time coaching victories

Ranking basis/background: Number of wins over the last 10 years, including bowl games. **Number listed:** 35.

1. Paul "Bear" Bryant, with 323 wins
2. Glenn "Pop" Warner, 319
3. Joe Paterno, 317
4. Amos Alonzo Stagg, 314
5. Bobby Bowden, 304
6. Tom Osborne, 255
7. LaVell Edwards, 251
8. Woody Hayes, 238
9. Bo Schembechler, 234
10. Hayden Fry, 232

Source: *The World Almanac and Book of Facts 2001*, World Almanac Books, 2001.

★127★
Division I-A all-time percentage leaders

Ranking basis/background: Number of wins over the last 10 years, including bowl games. Ties are computed as half won and half lost. **Number listed:** 25.

1. University of Michigan, with 796 wins
2. University of Notre Dame, 767
3. University of Nebraska, 743
4. University of Texas, 735
5. University of Alabama, 735
6. Penn State University, 734
7. Ohio State University, 716
8. University of Southern California, 699
9. University of Oklahoma, 689

Source: *The World Almanac and Book of Facts 2001*, World Almanac Books, 2001.

★128★
Division I all-time winningest college teams

Ranking basis/background: Number of wins and percentage through the 1999-2000 season. **Number listed:** 20.

1. University of Kentucky, with 1,771 wins; .764 percentage
2. University of North Carolina, 1,555; .738
3. University of Nevada, Las Vegas, 870; .726
4. University of Kansas, 1,712; .700
5. University of California, Los Angeles, 1,466; .698
6. St. John's University (NY), 1,607; .690
7. Syracuse University, 1,524; .682
8. Duke University, 1,614; .680
9. University of Western Kentucky, 1,390; .664
10. University of Arkansas, 1,334; .657

ATHLETICS—COLLEGES & UNIVERSITIES

Source: *The World Almanac and Book of Facts 2001*, World Almanac Books, 2001.

★129★
Division I women's career high scorers

Ranking basis/background: Ranked by average. Total points also given. **Number listed:** 10.
1. Patricia Hoskins, Mississippi Valley State, with 3,122 points; an average of 28.4
2. Sandra Hodge, New Orleans, 2,860; 26.7
3. Lorri Bauman, Drake, 3,115; 26.0
4. Andrea Congreaves, Mercer, 2,796; 25.9
5. Cindy Blodgett, Maine, 3,005; 25.5
6. Valorie Whiteside, Appalachian State, 2,944; 25.4
7. Joyce Walker, LSU, 2,906; 24.8
8. Tarcha Hollis, Gambling, 2,058; 24.2
9. Korie Hlede, Dusquesne, 2,631; 24.1
10. Karen Pelphrey, Marshall, 2,746; 24.1

Source: *The World Almanac and Book of Facts 2001*, World Almanac Books, 2001.

★130★
Fastest growing men's collegiate athletics teams

Ranking basis/background: Number of teams in 1998-99 and the percentage of change in total teams since 1981-82. **Remarks:** Original source: General Accounting Office. **Number listed:** 5.
1. Equestrian, with 33 teams in 1998-99; a 1,550% change since 1981-82
2. Sailing, 22; 47%
3. Rowing, 70; 46%
4. Lacrosse, 197; 43%
5. Soccer, 879; 18%

Source: "Water Polo, Anyone?," *U.S. News & World Report*, 130: 10, (March 26, 2001).

★131★
Fastest growing women's collegiate athletics teams

Ranking basis/background: Number of teams in 1998-99 and the percentage of change in total teams since 1981-82. **Remarks:** Original source: General Accounting Office. **Number listed:** 5.
1. Water polo, with 37 teams in 1998-99; a 3,600% change since 1981-82
2. Soccer, 926; 1,058%
3. Equestrian, 41; 486%
4. Golf, 402; 222%
5. Rowing, 122; 184%

Source: "Water Polo, Anyone?," *U.S. News & World Report*, 130: 10, (March 26, 2001).

★132★
Minority college athletics administrators and staff, by gender, 1999-2000

Ranking basis/background: Total number of minority men and women in each administrative or staff position, excluding African Americans. **Remarks:** Original source: NCAA. **Number listed:** 5.

    Assistant athletics director, with 18 men; 13 women
    Compliance coordinator, 12; 10
    Academic advisor, 17; 19
    Graduate assistant, 25; 12
    Intern, 15; 7

Source: Suggs, Welch, "Top Posts in Sports Programs Still Tend to Go to White Men," *The Chronicle of Higher Education*, 46: A53-A54, (June 2, 2000).

★133★
Minority college athletics head coaches, by gender, 1999-2000

Ranking basis/background: Total number of minority men and women in each head coach position, excluding African Americans. **Remarks:** Original source: NCAA. **Number listed:** 5.

    Football, with 5 men; 0 women
    Men's basketball, 12; 0
    Women's basketball, 8; 5
    All men's teams, 209; 11
    All women's teams, 182; 59

Source: Suggs, Welch, "Top Posts in Sports Programs Still Tend to Go to White Men," *The Chronicle of Higher Education*, 46: A53-A54, (June 2, 2000).

★134★
Minority college athletics senior administrators, by gender, 1999-2000

Ranking basis/background: Total number of minority men and women in each senior administrator position, excluding African Americans. **Remarks:** Original source: NCAA. **Number listed:** 5.

    Athletics director, with 17 men; 2 women
    Associate athletics director, 9; 6
    Senior woman administrator, 4; 15
    Business manager, 12; 14
    Faculty athletics representative, 22; 4

Source: Suggs, Welch, "Top Posts in Sports Programs Still Tend to Go to White Men," *The Chronicle of Higher Education*, 46: A53-A54, (June 2, 2000).

★135★
NCAA Division I ski teams with the most championships

Ranking basis/background: Number of team championships. **Remarks:** Original source: NCAA. **Number listed:** 6.
1. University of Colorado, with 15 team championships
1. University of Denver, 15
3. University of Utah, 9
4. University of Vermont, 5
5. Dartmouth College, 2
5. University of Wyoming, 2

Source: Horrow, Ellen J. and Adrienne Lewis, "Colleges Set to Ski for Title," *USA Today*, March 8, 2001, Section C, p. 1C.

★136★
NCAA Division I women's swimming teams with the most individual championships

Ranking basis/background: Number of individual championships including relays. **Remarks:** Original source: NCAA. **Number listed:** 5.
1. Stanford University, with 102 championships
2. University of Florida, 79
3. University of Texas, 63
4. Southern Methodist University, 24
5. University of Georgia, 18

Source: Horrow, Ellen J. and Adrienne Lewis, "Women's Swimmers Hit The Mark," *USA Today*, March 15, 2001, Section C, p. 1C.

★137★
NCAA men's gymnastics teams with the most individual champions

Ranking basis/background: Number of individual champions. **Remarks:** Original source: NCAA. **Number listed:** 5.
1. Penn State University, with 44
2. University of Illinois, 42
2. University of Nebraska, 42
4. University of California, Los Angeles, 28
5. University of Southern California, 24

Source: Horrow, Ellen J. and Sam Ward, "Penn State Vaults to the Top," *USA Today*, April 6, 2001, Section C, p. 1C.

★138★
Percentage of African American athletic administrators at NCAA Division I institutions, 1999

Ranking basis/background: Percentage of African Americans employees in each position during 1999 and percent change from 1995. **Remarks:** Original source: NCAA. **Number listed:** 6.

    Director of athletics with 7.5% in 1999; a 2.6% decrease from 1995
    Associate director of athletics, 7.6%; 1.5% decrease
    Assistant director of athletics, 9.9%; 0.4% decrease
    Senior woman administrator, 11.0%; 2.6% decrease
    Academic advisor, 24.0%; 1.2%
    Overall, 10.1%; 1.1%

Source: Greenlee, Craig T., "NCAA Report Finds Little Diversity in Sports Administration," *Black Issues in Higher Education*, 17: 16-17, (June 22, 2000).

★139★
Percentage of African American athletic administrators at NCAA Division II institutions, 1999

Ranking basis/background: Percentage of African Americans employed in each position during 1999 and percent change from 1995. **Remarks:** Original source: NCAA. **Number listed:** 6.

    Director of athletics, with 11.0% in 1999; a 0.2% change from 1995
    Associate director of athletics, 7.3%; 2.5% decrease
    Assistant director of athletics, 6.4%; 0.9% decrease
    Senior woman administrator, 11.4%; 5.7% decrease
    Academic advisor, 15.3%; 0.2%
    Overall, 9.9%; 1.5% decrease

Source: Greenlee, Craig T., "NCAA Report Finds Little Diversity in Sports Administration," *Black Issues in Higher Education*, 17: 16-17, (June 22, 2000).

★140★
Percentage of African American athletic administrators at NCAA Division III institutions, 1999

Ranking basis/background: Percentage of African Americans employed in each position during 1999 and percent change from 1995. **Remarks:** Original source: NCAA. **Number listed:** 6.

    Director of athletics, with 4.2% in 1999; a 0.8% change from 1995
    Associate director of athletics, 4.3%; 1.4%
    Assistant director of athletics, 4.3%; 1.8% decrease
    Senior woman administrator, 4.5%; 2.2%
    Academic advisor, 12.5%; 2.0%

Overall, 4.6%; 0.6%
Source: Greenlee, Craig T., "NCAA Report Finds Little Diversity in Sports Administration," *Black Issues in Higher Education*, 17: 16-17, (June 22, 2000).

★141★
Proportion of female nonresident aliens involved in collegiate athletics, 1998-99

Ranking basis/background: Figures for total undergraduates and nonresident aliens involved in collegiate sports and the proportion nonresident aliens comprise of all undergraduates. **Remarks:** Original source: NCAA. **Number listed:** 4.
- Basketball players, with 3,938 undergraduates involved; 190 nonresident aliens (a proportion of 4.8%)
- Cross-country/track and field athletes, 5,438; 390 (7.2%)
- Athletes in other sports, 19,690; 1,397 (7.1%)
- All female athletes, 29,239; 1,990 (6.8%)

Source: Suggs, Welch, "As More Coaches Recruit Foreign Talent, All-Americans Aren't Always American," *The Chronicle of Higher Education*, 47: A50-A51, (April 6, 2001).

★142★
Proportion of male nonresident aliens involved in collegiate athletics, 1998-99

Ranking basis/background: Figures for total undergraduates and nonresident aliens involved in collegiate sports and the proportion nonresident aliens comprise of all undergraduates. **Remarks:** Original source: NCAA. **Number listed:** 5.
- Basketball players, with 3,712 undergraduate involved; 237 nonresident aliens (a proportion of 6.4%)
- Baseball players, 5,950; 91 (1.5%)
- Cross-country/track and field athletes, 4,498; 395 (8.8%)
- Football players, 14,592; 101 (0.7%)
- Athletes in other sports, 11,520; 1,692 (14.7%)
- All male athletes, 40,329; 2,509 (6.2%)

Source: Suggs, Welch, "As More Coaches Recruit Foreign Talent, All-Americans Aren't Always American," *The Chronicle of Higher Education*, 47: A50-A51, (April 6, 2001).

★143★
Selected financial data for NCAA Division I-A institutions, 1998-99

Ranking basis/background: Figures for average revenue, expenses, and net, from a report compiled by Daniel L. Fulks of Transylvania University. **Remarks:** Original source: NCAA. **Number listed:** 3.
- Average revenue, with $20,000,000
- Average expenses, $20,000,000
- Average net, $0

Source: Suggs, Welch, "Gap Grows Between the Haves and Have-Nots in College Sports," *The Chronicle of Higher Education*, 47: A73, (November 17, 2000).

★144★
Selected financial data for NCAA Division I-AA institutions, 1998-99

Ranking basis/background: Figures for average revenue, expenses, and net, from a report compiled by Daniel L. Fulks of Transylvania University. **Remarks:** Original source: NCAA. **Number listed:** 3.
- Average revenue, with $3,200,000
- Average expenses, $5,400,000
- Average net, negative $2,200,000

Source: Suggs, Welch, "Gap Grows Between the Haves and Have-Nots in College Sports," *The Chronicle of Higher Education*, 47: A73, (November 17, 2000).

★145★
Selected financial data for NCAA Division I-AAA institutions, 1998-99

Ranking basis/background: Figures for average revenue, expenses, and net, from a report compiled by Daniel L. Fulks of Transylvania University. **Remarks:** Original source: NCAA. **Number listed:** 3.
- Average revenue, with $2,200,000
- Average expenses, $4,700,000
- Average net, negative $2,500,000

Source: Suggs, Welch, "Gap Grows Between the Haves and Have-Nots in College Sports," *The Chronicle of Higher Education*, 47: A73, (November 17, 2000).

★146★
Selected financial data for NCAA Division II institutions (with football), 1998-99

Ranking basis/background: Figures for average revenue, expenses, and net, from a report compiled by Daniel L. Fulks of Transylvania University. **Remarks:** Original source: NCAA. **Number listed:** 3.
- Average revenue, with $800,000
- Average expenses, $1,900,000
- Average net, negative $1,000,000

Source: Suggs, Welch, "Gap Grows Between the Haves and Have-Nots in College Sports," *The Chronicle of Higher Education*, 47: A73, (November 17, 2000).

★147★
Selected financial data for NCAA Division II institutions (without football), 1998-99

Ranking basis/background: Figures for average revenue, expenses, and net, from a report compiled by Daniel L. Fulks of Transylvania University. **Remarks:** Original source: NCAA. **Number listed:** 3.
- Average revenue, with $500,000
- Average expenses, $1,400,000
- Average net, negative $900,000

Source: Suggs, Welch, "Gap Grows Between the Haves and Have-Nots in College Sports," *The Chronicle of Higher Education*, 47: A73, (November 17, 2000).

★148★
U.S. colleges and universities with the most alumni in the LPGA

Ranking basis/background: Number of alumni in the LPGA. **Remarks:** Original source: LPGA. **Number listed:** 5.
1. Arizona State University, with 15 alumni
2. Furman University, 10
2. University of Texas, 10
4. University of Georgia, 9
5. University of Arizona, 8

Source: Horrow, Ellen J. and Marcy E. Mullins, "Women's Swimmers Hit The Mark," *USA Today*, February 22, 2001, Section C, p. 1C.

★149★
Women's Division I track and field programs with the most outdoor championships

Ranking basis/background: Total number of team and individual wins between 1987 and 1997. **Remarks:** Original source: NCAA. **Number listed:** 5.
1. Louisiana State University, with 11 team wins; 38 individual wins; and 49 total
2. University of Texas, 3; 26; 29
3. University of California, Los Angeles, 2; 25; 27
4. University of Wisconsin, 0; 18; 18
5. University of Nebraska, 0; 16; 16

Source: Horrow, Ellen J. and Marcy E. Mullins, "LSU Women Look to Run Up Totals," *USA Today*, June 1, 2000, Section C, p. 1C.

Related Information

★150★
Kadupski, Charlie, *Official Athletic College Guide: Soccer, 11th ed.*, The Sport Source, 2000.
Remarks: Gives coaches, parents, and student athletes information about college soccer programs such as contact information, coach's names, academic facts, and an "athletic profile" of the institution.

★151★
Kadupski, Charlie, *Official Athletic College Guide: Softball, 11th ed.*, The Sport Source, 2001.
Remarks: Gives coaches, parents, and student athletes information about college softball programs such as contact information, coach's names, academic facts, and an "athletic profile" of the institution.

★152★
Brown, Gerry and Michael Morrison, editors, *The 2001 ESPN Information Please Sports Almanac*, Hyperion/ESPN Books, 2000.
Remarks: Collection of college football, college basketball, and NCAA sports statistics and rankings.

ATHLETICS–COLLEGES & UNIVERSITIES–BASEBALL

Related Information

★153★
Kadupski, Charlie, *Official Athletic College Guide: Baseball, 7th ed.*, The Sport Source, 2000.
Remarks: Gives coaches, parents, and student athletes information about 1400 college baseball programs such as contact information, coach's names, academic facts, and an "athletic profile" of the institution.

ATHLETICS–COLLEGES & UNIVERSITIES–BASKETBALL

★154★
Division I NCAA men's basketball players with the highest tournament scores

Ranking basis/background: Career points in the Division I men's tournament. **Number listed:** 5.
1. Christian Laettner, Duke University, with 407 points
2. Elvin Hayes, University of Houston, 358
3. Danny Manning, University of Kansas, 328
4. Oscar Robertson, University of Cincinnati, 324
5. Glen Rice, University of Michigan, 308

Source: Horrow, Ellen J. and Marcy E. Mullins, "Laettner Lit Up in the Tournament," *USA Today*, March 20, 2001, Section C, p. 1C.

★155★
NCAA Division I female basketball scoring leaders

Ranking basis/background: Career scores. **Remarks:** Original source: NCAA **Number listed:** 5.
1. Chamique Holdsclaw, University of Tennessee, with 479
2. Bridgette Gordon, University of Tennessee, 388
3. Cheryl Miller, University of Southern California, 333
3. Janice Lawrence, Louisiana Tech, 333
5. Penny Toler, San Diego State/Long Beach State, 291

Source: Horrow, Ellen J. and Adrienne Lewis, "Holdsclaw Holds Tournament Record," *USA Today*, March 21, 2001, Section C, p. 1C.

★156★
NCAA Division I women's basketball teams with the best scoring margin

Ranking basis/background: Team and opponent scores and scoring margin. **Remarks:** Original source: NCAA. **Number listed:** 5.
1. University of Connecticut (1995), with 89.5 Team; 56.3 Opponent; a margin of 33.2
2. Louisiana Tech (1982), 87.3; 54.3; 33.0
2. Louisiana Tech (1990), 86.5; 53.5; 33.0
4. Louisiana Tech (1996), 86.4; 53.5; 32.9
5. Old Dominion University (1997), 84.4; 52.4; 32.0

Source: Horrow, Ellen J. and Robert W. Ahrens, "Huskies Have Huge Scoring Margin," *USA Today*, March 2, 2001, Section C, p. 1C.

★157★
Women's basketball teams with the most appearances in the Final Four

Ranking basis/background: Number of appearances in the Final Four basketball championships. **Number listed:** 5.
1. University of Tennessee (final appearance in 2000), with 12
2. Louisiana Tech (1999), 11
3. Stanford University (1997), 6
4. University of Connecticut (2001), 5
4. University of Georgia (1999), 5

Source: Horrow, Ellen J. and Sam Ward, "Huskies Make Final Four a Habit," *USA Today*, March 29, 2001, Section C, p. 1C.

ATHLETICS–COLLEGES & UNIVERSITIES–FOOTBALL

★158★
Longest field goals in college football

Ranking basis/background: Longest field goals, in yards, kicked in college football over the past 10 years. **Remarks:** Original source: NCAA. **Number listed:** 4.
1. Martin Gramatica, Kansas State University (1998), with 65 yards
2. Bill Gramatica, South Florida University (2000), 63
3. Jason Hanson, Washington State University (1991), 62
3. Terance Kitchens, Texas A&M University (1999), 62

Source: Horrow, Ellen J. and Alejandro Gonzalez, "Gramatica Brothers Get a Kick Out of Records," *USA Today*, December 1, 2000, Section C, p. 1C.

★159★
U.S. colleges and universities with the highest average football attendance, 1996-99

Ranking basis/background: Average attendance at football games from 1996 through 1999. **Remarks:** Original source: Chronicle reporting and the NCAA. **Number listed:** 16.
1. University of Michigan, Ann Arbor (Big Ten conference), with an average attendance of 108,543
2. University of Tennessee, Knoxville (Southeastern), 106,444
3. Pennsylvania State University, University Park (Big Ten), 96,568
4. Ohio State University (Big Ten), 93,010
5. University of Florida (Southeastern), 85,415
6. University of Georgia (Southeastern), 83,351
7. Auburn University (Southeastern), 81,950
8. Louisiana State University, Baton Rouge (Southeastern), 79,622
9. University of South Carolina, Columbia (Southeastern), 78,139
10. Florida State University (Atlantic Coast), 77,931

Source: Suggs, Welch, "Football's Have-Nots Contemplate Their Place in the NCAA," *The Chronicle of Higher Education*, 46: A47-A48, (June 30, 2000).

★160★
U.S. colleges and universities with the lowest average football attendance, 1996-99

Ranking basis/background: Average attendance at football games from 1996 through 1999. **Remarks:** Original source: Chronicle reporting and the NCAA. **Number listed:** 16.
1. University of Akron (Mid-American conference), with an average attendance of 8,418
2. Kent State University (Mid-American), 11,379
3. Eastern Michigan University (Mid-American), 11,389
4. San Jose State University (Western Athletic), 11,765
5. Middle Tennessee State University (Sun Belt), 12,072
6. Northern Illinois University (Mid-American), 12,601
7. New Mexico State University (Sun Belt), 12,767
8. Temple University (Big East), 12,779
9. Bowling Green State University (Mid-American), 12,972
10. State University of New York, Buffalo (Mid-American), 13,545

Source: Suggs, Welch, "Football's Have-Nots Contemplate Their Place in the NCAA," *The Chronicle of Higher Education*, 46: A47-A48, (June 30, 2000).

ATHLETICS–ELEMENTARY & SECONDARY SCHOOLS

★161★
All-America boys' high school basketball 1st team, 2001

Ranking basis/background: Players chosen by college coaches, scouts, and recruiters from around the country. **Remarks:** Article ranks players in the first through fourth teams. **Number listed:** 10.
- Eddy Curry, Thornwood High School (South Holland, IL)
- Dajuan Wagner, Camden High School (Camden, NJ)
- Kelvin Torbert, Northwestern-Edison High School (Flint, MI)
- Tyson Chandler, Dominguez High School (Compton, CA)
- Kwame Brown, Glynn Academy (Brunswick, GA)
- De Sagana Diop, Oak Hill Academy (Mouth of Wilson, VA)
- Ousmane Cisse, St. Jude High School (Montgomery, AL)
- Rick Rickert, Duluth East High School (Duluth, MN)
- David Lee, Chaminade High School (St. Louis, MO)
- David Harrison, Brentwood Academy (Brentwood, TN)

Source: O'Shea, Michael, "Meet Parade's All-America High School Boys Basketball Team," *Parade Magazine*, April 1, 2001, pp. 20-21.

★162★
All-America boys' high school basketball 2nd team, 2001

Ranking basis/background: Players chosen by college coaches, scouts, and recruiters from around the country. **Remarks:** Article ranks players in the first through fourth teams. **Number listed:** 10.
- Julius Hodge, St. Raymond High School (Bronx, NY)
- Jawad Williams, St. Edward High School (Lakewood, OH)
- Aaron Miles, Jefferson High School (Portland, OR)
- Wayne Simien, Leavenworth High School (Leavenworth, KS)
- James White, Hargrave Military Academy (Chatham, VA)
- LeBron James, St. Vincent-St. Mary High School (Akron, OH)
- Shavlik Randolph, Broughton High School (Raleigh, NC)
- Cedric Bozeman, Mater Dei High School (Santa Ana, CA)

T.J. Ford, Willowridge High School (Houston, TX)
John Allen, Coatesville High School (Coatesville, PA)

Source: O'Shea, Michael, "Meet Parade's All-America High School Boys Basketball Team," *Parade Magazine*, April 1, 2001, pp. 20-21.

★163★
All-America boys' high school basketball 3rd team, 2001

Ranking basis/background: Players chosen by college coaches, scouts, and recruiters from around the country. **Remarks:** Article ranks players in the first through fourth teams. **Number listed:** 10.

Maurice Williams, Murah High School (Jackson, MS)
Carlas Hurt, Moore Traditional High School (Louisville, KY)
Josh Childress, Mayfair High School (Lakewood, CA)
Billy Edelin, Oak Hill Academy (Mouth of Wilson, VA)
Pierre Pierce, Westmont High School (Westmont, IL)
Rashaad Carruth, Oak Hill Academy (Mouth of Wilson, VA)
Raymond Felton, Latta High School (Latta, SC)
Anthony Richardson, Leesville Road High School (Raleigh, NC)
Anthony Roberson, Saginaw High School (Saginaw, MI)
Jamal Sampson, Mater Dei High School (Santa Ana, CA)

Source: O'Shea, Michael, "Meet Parade's All-America High School Boys Basketball Team," *Parade Magazine*, April 1, 2001, pp. 20-21.

★164★
All-America boys' high school basketball 4th team, 2001

Ranking basis/background: Players chosen by college coaches, scouts, and recruiters from around the country. **Remarks:** Article ranks players in the first through fourth teams. **Number listed:** 10.

Chris Thomas, Pike High School (Indianapolis, IN)
Earnest Shelton, White Station High School (Memphis, TN)
Alan Anderson, DeLaSalle High School (Minneapolis, MN)
Channing Frye, St. Mary's High School (Phoenix, AZ)
Travis Diener, Goodrich High School (Fond du Lac, WI)
Quemont Greer, Berkshire School (Homestead, FL)
Rashad McCants, New Hampton School (New Hampton, NH)
Levi Watkins, Montrose Christian High School (Rockville, MD)
Shelden Williams, Midwest City High School (Midwest City, OK)
Chuck Hayes, Modesto Christian High School (Modesto, CA)

Source: O'Shea, Michael, "Meet Parade's All-America High School Boys Basketball Team," *Parade Magazine*, April 1, 2001, pp. 20-21.

★165★
All-America boys' high school soccer team defenders, 2001

Ranking basis/background: Players chosen by college coaches, scouts, and recruiters from around the country. **Number listed:** 11.

Ryan Cochrane, Portland, OR, Senior
Jordan Harvey, Mission Viejo, CA, Junior
C.J. Klaas, Cherry Valley, IL, Senior
Chad Marshall, Riverside, CA, Junior
Gray Griffin, Huntersville, NC, Junior
David Chun, Irvine, CA, Junior
Chris Lancos, Belford, NJ, Junior
Hunter Freeman, Allen, TX, Sophomore
Chefik Simo, Plano, TX, Junior
Carlos Parra, Germantown, MD, Junior
Daniel Bills, Thornton, CO, Senior

Source: O'Shea, Michael, "Meet Parade's All-America High School Boys Soccer Team," *Parade Magazine*, March 11, 2001, pp. 8-9.

★166★
All-America boys' high school soccer team forwards, 2001

Ranking basis/background: Players chosen by college coaches, scouts, and recruiters from around the country. **Number listed:** 14.

Edward Johnson, Bunnell, FL, Junior
Devin Barclay, Annapolis, MD, Junior
Brett Wiesner, Brookfield, WI, Senior
Michael Magee, Long Grove, IL, Sophomore
Paul Johnson, Princeton, NJ, Junior
Josh Villalobos, Fayetteville, NC, Sophomore
Wesley Kirk, Bloomington, NJ, Senior
Adam Stuller, Wilmington, DL, Senior
Dwayne Jones, New Orleans, LA, Junior
Kyle McMorrow, Waterville, ME, Senior
Jeff (J.D.) Johnston, Portage, MI, Senior
Sasha Gotsmanov, Woodbury, MN, Senior
David Maier, Broadview Heights, OH, Senior
Zachary Tobin, North Kingston, RI, Junior

Source: O'Shea, Michael, "Meet Parade's All-America High School Boys Soccer Team," *Parade Magazine*, March 11, 2001, pp. 8-9.

★167★
All-America boys' high school soccer team goalkeepers, 2001

Ranking basis/background: Players chosen by college coaches, scouts, and recruiters from around the country. **Number listed:** 3.

Steve Cronin, Fair Oaks, CA, Senior
Adam Schuerman, Brrokfield, WI, Junior
Ford Williams, Raleigh, NC, Junior

Source: O'Shea, Michael, "Meet Parade's All-America High School Boys Soccer Team," *Parade Magazine*, March 11, 2001, pp. 8-9.

★168★
All-America boys' high school soccer team midfielders, 2001

Ranking basis/background: Players chosen by college coaches, scouts, and recruiters from around the country. **Number listed:** 17.

Santino Quaranta, Baltimore, MD, Junior
Ned Grabavoy, New Lenox, IL, Senior
Paul Dolinsky, Carmel, IN, Senior
Justin Mapp, Brandon, MS, Sophomore
Ricardo Clark, Jonesboro, GA, Senior
Michael Enfield, Ventura, CA, Senior
Craig Capano, Hyde Park, NY, Sophomore
Jordan Stone, Allen, TX, Junior
David Johnson, Riverside, CA, Junior
Brian Devlin, Philadelphia, PA, Junior
Bryan Hinkle, Fredericksburg, VA, Senior
John Hayden, Louisville, KY, Junior
Adam Zenor, Cedar Rapids, IA, Senior
Victor Krasij, Avon, CT, Senior
Michael Amersley, St. Louis, MO, Senior
Ross Vaillancourt, Bedford, NH, Junior
Christopher Corcoran, Marshfield, MS, Senior

Source: O'Shea, Michael, "Meet Parade's All-America High School Boys Soccer Team," *Parade Magazine*, March 11, 2001, pp. 8-9.

★169★
All-America boys' high school soccer team player of the year, 2001

Ranking basis/background: Players chosen by college coaches, scouts, and recruiters from around the country. **Number listed:** 1.

Steve Cronin, Fair Oaks, CA, Senior

Source: O'Shea, Michael, "Meet Parade's All-America High School Boys Soccer Team," *Parade Magazine*, March 11, 2001, pp. 8-9.

★170★
All-America girls' high school basketball 1st team, 2001

Ranking basis/background: Players chosen by college coaches, scouts, and recruiters from around the country. **Number listed:** 10.

Cappie Pondexter, Marshall High School (Chicago, IL)
Shyra Ely, Ben Davis High School (Indianapolis, IN)
Shanna Zolman, Wawasee High School (Syracuse, IN)
Ashley Earley, Briarcrest Christian High School (Memphis, TN)
Clare Droesch, Christ the King High School (Middle Village, NY)
Loree Moore, Narbonne High School (Harbor City, CA)
Katie Robinette, Community High School (South Sioux City, NE)
Jacqueline Batteast, Washington High School (South Bend, IN)
Seimone Augustus, Capital High School (Baton Rouge, LA)
Shawntinice Polk, Hanford High School (Hanford, CA)

Source: O'Shea, Michael, "Meet Parade's All-America High School Girls Basketball Team," *Parade*, April 15, 2001, pp. 14-16.

★171★
All-America girls' high school basketball 2nd team, 2001

Ranking basis/background: Players chosen by college coaches, scouts, and recruiters from around the country. **Number listed:** 10.

Sandora Irvin, Fort Lauderdale High School (Fort Lauderdale, FL)
Ann Strother, Highlands Ranch High School (Highlands Ranch, CO)
Monique Currie, The Bullis School (Potomac, MD)
Gillian Goring, Germantown Academy (Fort Washington, PA)
Courtney Young, Buena High School (Ventura, CA)
Wynter Whitley, Holy Innocents Episcopal High School (Atlanta, GA)

ATHLETICS—ELEMENTARY & SECONDARY SCHOOLS

Julie Sailer, Council Rock High School (Newtown, PA)
Teresa Borton, West Valley High School (Yakima, WA)
Mistie Bass, Parker High School (Janesville, WI)
Tabitha Pool, Huron High School (Ann Arbor, MI)

Source: O'Shea, Michael, "Meet Parade's All-America High School Girls Basketball Team," *Parade*, April 15, 2001, pp. 14-16.

★172★
All-America girls' high school basketball 3rd team, 2001

Ranking basis/background: Players chosen by college coaches, scouts, and recruiters from around the country. **Number listed:** 10.

Chelsea Newton, Carroll High School (Monroe, LA)
Bethany LeSueur, Garden City High School (Garden City, NY)
T'Nae Theil, Weatherford High School (Weatherford, TX)
Angelina Williams, George Washington High School (Chicago, IL)
Katy Flecky, Highlands Ranch High School (Highlands Ranch, CO)
Michelle Munoz, Mason High School (Mason, OH)
Nicole Wolff, Walpole High School (Walpole, MA)
Erin Grant, Mansfield High School (Arlington, TX)
Genesis Choice, Maynard Evans High School (Orlando, FL)
Elizabeth Dancause, Nashua High School (Nashua, NH)

Source: O'Shea, Michael, "Meet Parade's All-America High School Girls Basketball Team," *Parade*, April 15, 2001, pp. 14-16.

★173★
All-America girls' high school basketball 4th team, 2001

Ranking basis/background: Players chosen by college coaches, scouts, and recruiters from around the country. **Number listed:** 10.

Kristen O'Neill, Meadowdale High School (Lynnwood, WA)
Tan White, Tupelo High School (Tupelo, MS)
Kelly Greathouse, Buena High School (Ventura, CA)
Danielle Cheesman, Mountain View High School (Orem, UT)
Erica Smith, Palestine-Wheatley High School (Palestine, AR)
Cisti Greenwalt, Clovis High School (Clovis, NM)
Tanisha Wright, West Mifflin High School (West Mifflin, PA)
Heather Schreiber, Windthorst High School (Windthorst, TX)
Chelsea Domenico, Horizon High School (Thornton, CO)
Jenni Dant, Stevenson High School (Lincolnshire, IL)

Source: O'Shea, Michael, "Meet Parade's All-America High School Girls Basketball Team," *Parade*, April 15, 2001, pp. 14-16.

★174★
All-America girls' high school soccer team defenders, 2001

Ranking basis/background: Players chosen by college coaches, scouts, and recruiters from around the country. **Number listed:** 11.

Jessica Ballweg, Metuchen, NJ, Senior
Amy Steadman, Brevard, NC, Sophomore
Hayley Hunt, San Marino, CA, Junior
Holly Azevedo, Folsom, CA, Senior
Jamie Fabrizio, Carmel, IN, Senior
Stephanie Ebner, Taylorsville, UT, Junior
Katie Bunch, St. Louis, MO, Senior
Amy Fazio, Alamo, CA, Senior
Christine Sinak, St. Louis, MO, Senior
Kathryn Beal, Alexandria, VA, Senior
Sarah Elnicky, Rochester, NY, Senior

Source: O'Shea, Michael, "Meet Parade's All-America High School Girls Soccer Team," *Parade Magazine*, February 18, 2001, pp. 12-13.

★175★
All-America girls' high school soccer team forwards, 2001

Ranking basis/background: Players chosen by college coaches, scouts, and recruiters from around the country. **Number listed:** 12.

Natalie Sanderson, Ventura, CA, Senior
Mary McDowell, Lakewood, CO, Senior
Robynn Anne Morrell, Plymouth, MI, Senior
Kristen Weiss, Brecksville, OH, Junior
Linsay Tarpley, Kalamazoo, MI, Junior
Katie Rivera, Mission Viejo, CA, Junior
Taline Tahmassian, Great Falls, VA, Senior
Lindsay Gusick, Livonia, MI, Senior
Kelly McDonald, Littleton, CO, Senior
Kelly Wilson, Odessa, TX, Senior
Keeley Dowling, Carmel, IN, Senior
Katie McGregor, Simsbury, CT, Junior

Source: O'Shea, Michael, "Meet Parade's All-America High School Girls Soccer Team," *Parade Magazine*, February 18, 2001, pp. 12-13.

★176★
All-America girls' high school soccer team goalkeepers, 2001

Ranking basis/background: Players chosen by college coaches, scouts, and recruiters from around the country. **Number listed:** 3.

Ashlyn Harris, Satellite Beach, FL, Freshmen
Kim Bingham, San Ramon, CA, Sophomore
Alexandra Gagarin, Austin, TX, Senior

Source: O'Shea, Michael, "Meet Parade's All-America High School Girls Soccer Team," *Parade Magazine*, February 18, 2001, pp. 12-13.

★177★
All-America girls' high school soccer team midfielders, 2001

Ranking basis/background: Players chosen by college coaches, scouts, and recruiters from around the country. **Number listed:** 13.

Sara Randolph, Cincinnati, OH, Senior
Nicole Breger, Sterling Heights, MI, Senior
Leslie Osborne, Menomonee Falls, WI, Senior
Christine Johnson, Irvine, CA, Senior
Lori Chalupny, Chesterfield, MO, Junior
Noelle Keselica, Gaithersburg, MD, Junior
Sarah Huffman, Flower Mound, TX, Junior
Carli Lloyd, Delran, NJ, Senior
Stacy Lindstrom, Laguna Niguel, CA, Sophomore
Kim Francis, Richboro, PA, Senior
Ashley Casas, Mission Viejo, CA, Senior
Kayla Lockaby, Hamilton, OH, Senior
Sue Flamini, Crandord, NJ, Senior

Source: O'Shea, Michael, "Meet Parade's All-America High School Girls Soccer Team," *Parade Magazine*, February 18, 2001, pp. 12-13.

★178★
All-America girls' high school soccer team player of the year, 2001

Ranking basis/background: Players chosen by college coaches, scouts, and recruiters from around the country. **Number listed:** 1.

Natalie Sanderson

Source: O'Shea, Michael, "Meet Parade's All-America High School Girls Soccer Team," *Parade Magazine*, February 18, 2001, pp. 12-13.

★179★
All-American boy's high school football all-purpose players, 2000

Ranking basis/background: Players selected by college coaches and recruiters, professional scouts, and representatives of football organizations. **Number listed:** 4.

Bryan Randall, Bruton High School (Williamsburg, VA)
Michael Bell, Tolleson Union High School (Tolleson, AZ)
Matt Ware, Loyola High School (Los Angeles, CA)
Dontrel Moore, Roswell High School (Roswell, NM)

Source: O'Shea, Michael, "Meet Parade's All-America High School Football Team," *Parade Magazine*, January 28, 2001, pp. 8-10.

★180★
All-American boy's high school football defensive backs, 2000

Ranking basis/background: Players selected by college coaches and recruiters, professional scouts, and representatives of football organizations. **Number listed:** 3.

Ernest Shazor, Martin Luther King Jr. High School (Detroit, MI)
Antrel Rolle, South Dade High School (Homestead, FL)
Ahmad Carroll, Douglass High School (Atlanta, GA)

Source: O'Shea, Michael, "Meet Parade's All-America High School Football Team," *Parade Magazine*, January 28, 2001, pp. 8-10.

★181★
All-American boy's high school football kicker, 2000

Ranking basis/background: Players selected by college coaches and recruiters, professional scouts, and representatives of football organizations. **Number listed:** 1.

Joe Rheem, Wichita Collegiate High School (Wichita, KS)

Source: O'Shea, Michael, "Meet Parade's All-America High School Football Team," *Parade Magazine*, January 28, 2001, pp. 8-10.

★182★
All-American boy's high school football linebackers, 2000

Ranking basis/background: Players selected by college coaches and recruiters, professional scouts, and representatives of football organizations.
Number listed: 8.
- Michael-Jordan Craven, La Quinta High School (La Quinta, CA)
- Kevin Simon, De La Salle High School (Concord, CA)
- LaMarcus Rowell, Opelike High School (Opelika, AL)
- Leon Williams, Canarsie High School (Brooklyn, NY)
- Derrick Johnson, Waco High School (Waco, TX)
- Jeb Heckeba, Harding Academy (Searcy, AR)
- Marvin Simmons, Long Beach Polytechnic High School (Long Beach, CA)
- Chauncy Davis, Auburndale High School (Auburndale, FL)

Source: O'Shea, Michael, "Meet Parade's All-America High School Football Team," *Parade Magazine*, January 28, 2001, pp. 8-10.

★183★
All-American boy's high school football linemen, 2000

Ranking basis/background: Players selected by college coaches and recruiters, professional scouts, and representatives of football organizations.
Number listed: 18.
- Blake Larsen, Atlantic High School (Atlantic, IA)
- Shaun Cody, Los Altos High School (Hacienda Heights, CA)
- Tommie Harris, Ellison High School (Killeen, TX)
- Charles Rush, Cathedral Preparatory High School (Erie, PA)
- Lorenzo Alexander, St. Mary's High School (Berkeley, CA)
- Jami Hightower, Jacksonville High School (Jacksonville, TX)
- Anttaj Hawthorne, Hamden High School (Hamden, CT)
- Ben Wilderson, Hemphill High School (Hemphill, TX)
- Mark LeVoir, Eden Prairie High School (Eden Prairie, MN)
- Zachary Giles, Marshfield High School (Marshfield, MA)
- Shawn Andrews, Camden Fairview High School (Camden, AR)
- Chris Spencer, Madison Central High School (Madison, MS)
- Jocques Dumas, Asheboro High School (Asheboro, NC)
- Orien Harris, Newark High School (Newark, DE)
- Titus Adams, Creighton Preparatory High School (Omaha, NE)
- Robert Taylor, Oak Creek High School (Oak Tree, WI)
- Dan Stevenson, Barrington High School (Barrington, IL)
- Jared Helming, Kickapoo High School (Springfield, MO)

Source: O'Shea, Michael, "Meet Parade's All-America High School Football Team," *Parade Magazine*, January 28, 2001, pp. 8-10.

★184★
All-American boy's high school football quarterbacks, 2000

Ranking basis/background: Players selected by college coaches and recruiters, professional scouts, and representatives of football organizations.
Number listed: 7.
- Joe Mauer, Cretin-Derham Hall (St. Paul, MN)
- Matt Leinart, Mater Dei High School (Santa Ana, CA)
- D.J. Shockley, North Clayton High School (College Park, GA)
- Ingle Martin, Montgomery Bell Academy (Nashville, TN)
- Brent Rawls, Evandel Christian Academy (Shreveport, LA)
- Kellen Clemens, Burns High School (Burns, OR)
- Justin Holland, Bear Creek High School (Lakewood, CO)

Source: O'Shea, Michael, "Meet Parade's All-America High School Football Team," *Parade Magazine*, January 28, 2001, pp. 8-10.

★185★
All-American boy's high school football receivers, 2000

Ranking basis/background: Players selected by college coaches and recruiters, professional scouts, and representatives of football organizations.
Number listed: 6.
- Roscoe Crosby, Union High School (Union, SC)
- Marcus Spears, Southern Laboratory High School (Baton Rouge, LA)
- Reggie Williams, Lakes High School (Lakewood, WA)
- Charles Frederick, Pope John Paul II High School (Boca Raton, FL)
- Jerome Janet, Union High School (Tulsa, OK)
- Michael Clayton, Christian Life High School (Baton Rouge, LA)

Source: O'Shea, Michael, "Meet Parade's All-America High School Football Team," *Parade Magazine*, January 28, 2001, pp. 8-10.

★186★
All-American boy's high school football running backs, 2000

Ranking basis/background: Players selected by college coaches and recruiters, professional scouts, and representatives of football organizations.
Number listed: 10.
- Tyler Ebell, Ventura High School (Ventura, CA)
- Cedric Benson, Robert E. Lee High School (Midland, TX)
- Carnell Williams, Etowah High School (Attalla, AL)
- Kelly Baraka, Northern High School (Portage, MI)
- Jabari Davis, Tucker High School (Tucker, GA)
- Kevin Jones, Cardinal O'Hara High School (Springfield, PA)
- Frank Gore, Coral Gables High School (Coral Gables, FL)
- Cedric Houston, Clarendon High School (Clarendon, AR)
- Eric Shelton, Bryan Station High School (Lexington, KY)
- Maurice Hall, Brookhaven High School (Columbus, OH)

Source: O'Shea, Michael, "Meet Parade's All-America High School Football Team," *Parade Magazine*, January 28, 2001, pp. 8-10.

★187★
All-American boy's high school football team, 2000

Ranking basis/background: Players selected by college coaches and recruiters, professional scouts, and representatives of football organizations.
Number listed: 8.
- Joe Mauer, Quaterback
- Tyler Ebell, Running Back
- Roscoe Crosby, Receiver
- Blake Larsen, Lineman
- Jordan Craven, Linebacker
- Ernest Shazor, Defensive Back
- Bryan Randall, All-Purpose Player
- Joe Rheem, Kicker

Source: O'Shea, Michael, "Meet Parade's All-America High School Football Team," *Parade Magazine*, January 28, 2001, pp. 8-10.

BASIC SKILLS TESTS
See: Achievement Tests–Schools, Elementary & Secondary

BIOLOGICAL SCIENCE PERIODICALS

★188★
Soil science journals by citation impact, 1981-99

Ranking basis/background: Impact factor calculated by taking the number of current citations to source items published and dividing it by the number of articles published in the journal during that time period. **Number listed:** 10.
1. *Journal of Soil Science*, with a 17.63 impact factor
2. *Soil Science Society of America Journal*, 13.34
3. *Soil Biology & Biochemistry*, 12.10
4. *Clays & Clay Minerals*, 11.39
5. *Plant and Soil*, 8.49
6. *Soil Science*, 7.97
7. *Australian Journal of Soil Science*, 7.85
8. *Biology and Fertility of Soils*, 7.36
9. *Geoderma*, 7.24
10. *Canadian Journal of Soil Science*, 7.18

Source: "Journals Ranked by Impact: Soil Science," *What's Hot in Research (http://www.isinet.com/isi/hot/research) Institute for Scientific Information*, November 6, 2000.

★189★
Soil science journals by citation impact, 1995-99

Ranking basis/background: Impact factor calculated by taking the number of current citations to source items published and dividing it by the number of articles published in the journal during that time period. **Number listed:** 10.
1. *European Journal of Soil Science*, with a 4.38 impact factor
2. *Plant and Soil*, 3.44
3. *Soil Science Society of America Journal*, 3.35
4. *Soil Biology & Biochemistry*, 3.30

BIOLOGICAL SCIENCES

5. *Clays & Clay Minerals*, 3.03
6. *Biology and Fertility of Soils*, 2.62
7. *Soil Science*, 2.58
8. *Geoderma*, 2.25
9. *Australian Journal of Soil Science*, 2.15
10. *Journal of Soil and Water Conservation*, 1.82

Source: "Journals Ranked by Impact: Soil Science," *What's Hot in Research* (http://www.isinet.com/isi/hot/research) *Institute for Scientific Information*, November 6, 2000.

★190★
Soil science journals by citation impact, 1999

Ranking basis/background: Impact factor calculated by taking the number of current citations to source items published and dividing it by the number of articles published in the journal during that time period. **Number listed:** 10.

1. *Soil Science Society of America Journal*, with a 1.60 impact factor
2. *Soil Biology & Biochemistry*, 1.49
3. *European Journal of Soil Science*, 1.44
4. *Clays & Clay Minerals*, 1.41
5. *Soil Use & Management*, 1.31
6. *Plant and Soil*, 1.28
7. *Biology and Fertility of Soils*, 1.27
8. *Soil Science*, 1.16
9. *Geoderma*, 1.13
10. *Applications in Soil Ecology*, 1.00

Source: "Journals Ranked by Impact: Soil Science," *What's Hot in Research* (http://www.isinet.com/isi/hot/research) *Institute for Scientific Information*, November 6, 2000.

BIOLOGICAL SCIENCES

★191★
Journals with the highest impact factor in the field of neuroscience, 1981-96

Ranking basis/background: Impact factor is calculated as a ratio between citations and recent citable items published. **Remarks:** Original source: ISI's *Journal Citation Reports* and *Journal Performance Indicators on Diskette*. **Number listed:** 10.

1. *Annual Review of Neuroscience*, with an impact factor of 124.44
2. *Brain Research Review*, 72.53
3. *Neuron*, 56.65
4. *Trends in Neuroscience*, 49.05
5. *Progress in Neurobiology*, 36.60
6. *Annals of Neurology*, 34.72
7. *International Review of Neurobiology*, 33.51
8. *Brain*, 28.99
9. *Journal of Cerebral Blood Flow*, 28.43
10. *Journal of Comparative Neurology*, 27.82

Source: "Journals Ranked by Impact: Neuroscience," *What's Hot*, April 13, 1998.

★192★
Private, 4-year undergraduate colleges and universities producing the most Ph.D.'s in the life sciences, 1920-1990

Ranking basis/background: Number of doctoral degrees granted to graduates of 914 private, 4-year U.S. undergraduate colleges and universities. Medical, law, and other professional, non-doctoral degrees are not included. **Remarks:** Original source: Office of Scientific and Engineering Personnel of the National Research Council. Report contains 50 other tables detailing the distribution of doctoral recipients by field of study over various time frames. **Number listed:** 350.

1. Oberlin College, with 481 Ph.D.'s
2. Swarthmore College, 325
3. Pomona College, 313
4. Mount Holyoke College, 297
5. Carleton College, 286
6. Wellesley College, 275
7. Barnard College, 268
8. Smith College, 262
9. Reed College, 259
9. Philadelphia College of Pharmacy and Science, 259
11. DePauw University, 233
12. Amherst College, 227
13. St. Olaf College, 224
14. Bucknell University, 220
15. Wesleyan University, 215
16. Vassar College, 207
17. Earlham College, 198
18. Union College, 196
19. College of Wooster, 195
20. Antioch College, 194

Source: *Baccalaureate Origins of Doctorate Recipients*, 7th ed., Franklin & Marshall College, March 1993.

★193★
Private, 4-year undergraduate colleges and universities producing the most Ph.D.'s in the life sciences, 1981-1990

Ranking basis/background: Number of doctoral degrees granted to graduates of 914 private, 4-year U.S. undergraduate colleges and universities. Medical, law, and other professional, non-doctoral degrees are not included. **Remarks:** Original source: Office of Scientific and Engineering Personnel of the National Research Council. Report contains 50 other tables detailing the distribution of doctoral recipients by field of study over various time frames. **Number listed:** 358.

1. Oberlin College, with 136 Ph.D.'s
2. Carleton College, 116
3. Smith College, 111
4. Wellesley College, 92
5. Swarthmore College, 90
6. Pomona College, 88
7. Mount Holyoke College, 88
8. Wesleyan University, 87
9. St. Olaf College, 87
10. Barnard College, 83
11. Reed College, 81
11. Bucknell University, 81
11. Villanova University, 81
14. Colgate University, 77
15. Union College, 74
16. Muhlenberg College, 72
17. Tuskegee University, 71
18. Kalamazoo College, 70
19. Grinnell College, 66
20. Vassar College, 65
20. Wake Forest University, 65

Source: *Baccalaureate Origins of Doctorate Recipients*, 7th ed., Franklin & Marshall College, March 1993.

★194★
Top recruiters for life sciences jobs for 2000-01 bachelor's degree recipients

Ranking basis/background: Projected number of college hires from on-campus recruitment for 2000-01. **Remarks:** Numbers reflect total expected hires, not just African American projected hires. **Number listed:** 1.

1. Abbott Laboratories, with 100 projected hires

Source: "The Top 100 Employers and the Majors in Demand for the Class of 2001," *The Black Collegian*, 31: 19-35, (February 2001).

BIOLOGICAL SCIENCES–INTERNATIONAL

★195★
Canadian universities with the greatest impact in biology and biochemistry, 1993-97

Ranking basis/background: For each university, total number of citations divided by number of published articles during the same time period. **Remarks:** Original source: *National Science Indicators on Diskette, 1981-97* **Number listed:** 5.

1. University of Toronto, with 9.32 citations per paper; 2,228 total papers
2. University of Alberta, 7.69; 1,223
3. University of Calgary, 7.33; 670
4. McGill University, 7.25; 1,746
5. University of British Columbia, 7.14; 1,198

Source: "Canadian Universities: Highest Impact in Biology and Biochemistry, 1993-97," *What's Hot*, October 5, 1998.

BIOLOGY

★196★
Marine and freshwater biology journals with the greatest impact measure, 1981-98

Ranking basis/background: Citations-per-paper impact score is the total citations to a journal's published papers divided by total number of papers the journal has published over an eighteen year period. **Remarks:** Original source: *Journal Citation Reports* and *Journal Performance Indicators on Diskette*. **Number listed:** 10.

1. *Oceanography & Marine Biology*, with an impact score of 41.54
2. *Advances in Marine Biology*, 30.16
3. *Marine Biology Letters*, 23.12
4. *Marine Ecology-Progress*, 15.30
5. *Marine Biology*, 14.81
6. *Canadian Journal of Fisheries and Aquatic Sciences*, 14.58
7. *Microbial Ecology*, 13.44
8. *DANA-Journal of Fisheries and Marine Biology*, 13.06
9. *Netherlands Journal of Sea Research*, 12.95
10. *Aquatic Toxicology*, 12.76

Source: "Journals Ranked by Impact: Marine & Freshwater Biology," *What's Hot in Research* (http://www.isinet.com/hot/research) *Institute for Scientific Information*, October 11, 1999.

★197★
Marine and freshwater biology journals with the greatest impact measure, 1994-98

Ranking basis/background: Citations-per-paper impact score is the total citations to a journal's published papers divided by total number of papers the journal has published over a five year period. **Remarks:** Original source: *Journal Citation Reports* and Journal Performance Indicators on Diskette. **Number listed:** 10.
1. *Advances in Marine Biology*, with an impact score of 13.71
2. *Oceanography & Marine Biology*, 11.97
3. *Reviews in Fish Biology and Fisheries*, 7.01
4. *Netherlands Journal of Sea Research*, 6.94
5. *Marine Ecology-Progress*, 4.51
6. *Journal of the Great Lakes*, 4.23
7. *Journal of Phycology*, 4.18
8. *Aquatic Toxicology*, 4.16
9. *Canadian Journal of Fisheries and Aquatic Sciences*, 3.97
10. *Microbial Ecology*, 3.90

Source: "Journals Ranked by Impact: Marine & Freshwater Biology," *What's Hot in Research* (http://www.isinet.com/hot/research) *Institute for Scientific Information*, October 11, 1999.

★198★
Top recruiters for biology/biological science jobs for 2000-01 bachelor's degree recipients

Ranking basis/background: Projected number of college hires from on-campus recruitment for 2000-01. **Remarks:** Numbers reflect total expected hires, not just African American projected hires. **Number listed:** 10.
1. Genentech, Inc., with 86 projected hires
2. Abbott Laboratories, 80
3. Accenture, 65
4. PA Dept. Environmental Protection, 67
5. U.S. Forest Services, 24
6. Caddo Parish School Board, 20
7. Novant Health, 10
8. Wyeth-Ayerst, 4
9. Henrico County Public Schools, 2
10. Macy's West, 1

Source: "The Top 100 Employers and the Majors in Demand for the Class of 2001," *The Black Collegian*, 31: 19-35, (February 2001).

BIOLOGY, GRADUATE

★199★
Most effective ecology, evolution, and behavior research-doctorate programs as evaluated by the National Research Council

Ranking basis/background: From a survey of nearly 8,000 faculty members conducted in the spring of 1993. Respondents were asked to rate programs in their field on "effectiveness of program in educating research scholars/scientists." **Remarks:** See *Chronicle* article for more details. Scores of 3.5-5.0 indicate "extremely effective;" 2.5-3.49 "reasonably effective;" 1.5-2.49 "minimally effective;" and 0.0-1.49 "not effective." Programs also ranked by "scholarly quality of program faculty." **Number listed:** 129.
1. Duke University, with an effectiveness rating of 4.33
2. University of Chicago, 4.31
3. Cornell University, 4.24
4. Stanford University, 4.23
5. University of Washington (WA), 4.20
6. University of California, Berkeley, 4.15
7. University of Wisconsin, Madison, 4.13
8. University of California, Davis, 4.12
9. University of Michigan, 3.98
10. Princeton University, 3.96

Source: "Rankings of Research-Doctorate Programs in 41 Disciplines at 274 Institutions," *The Chronicle of Higher Education* 42: A21-A30 (September 21, 1995).

★200★
Most effective neurosciences research-doctorate programs as evaluated by the National Research Council

Ranking basis/background: From a survey of nearly 8,000 faculty members conducted in the spring of 1993. Respondents were asked to rate programs in their field on "effectiveness of program in educating research scholars/scientists." **Remarks:** See *Chronicle* article for more details. Scores of 3.5-5.0 indicate "extremely effective;" 2.5-3.49 "reasonably effective;" 1.5-2.49 "minimally effective;" and 0.0-1.49 "not effective." Programs also ranked by "scholarly quality of program faculty." **Number listed:** 102.
1. Stanford University, with an effectiveness rating of 4.56
2. University of California, San Diego, 4.48
3. University of California, San Francisco, 4.45
4. Yale University, 4.44
5. Washington University, 4.42
6. Harvard University, 4.33
6. Johns Hopkins University, 4.33
8. Columbia University, 4.29
9. Rockefeller University, 4.26
10. California Institute of Technology, 4.22

Source: "Rankings of Research-Doctorate Programs in 41 Disciplines at 274 Institutions," *The Chronicle of Higher Education* 42: A21-A30 (September 21, 1995).

★201★
Top ecology, evolution, and behavior research-doctorate programs as evaluated by the National Research Council

Ranking basis/background: From a survey of nearly 8,000 faculty members conducted in the spring of 1993. Respondents were asked to rate programs in their field on "scholarly quality of program faculty." When more than one program had the samescore, the council averaged the rank order and gave each program the same rank number (if three programs tied for the top position, each received a rank of 2). **Remarks:** See *Chronicle* article for more details. Scores of 4.01 and above indicate "distinguished;" 3.0-4.0 "strong;" 2.51-3.0 "good;" 2.0-2.5 "adequate;" 1.0-1.99 "marginal;" and 0.0-0.99 "not sufficient for doctoral education." Programs also ranked by "effectiveness of program in educating research scholars/scientists." **Number listed:** 129.
1. Stanford University, with a quality rating of 4.51
1. University of Chicago, 4.51
3. Duke University, 4.49
4. Cornell University, 4.44
5. University of California, Davis, 4.42
6. Princeton University, 4.34
7. University of Washington, 4.30
8. University of California, Berkeley, 4.29
9. University of Wisconsin, Madison, 4.18
10. State University of New York, Stony Brook, 4.12
10. University of Texas, Austin, 4.12
12. University of Michigan, 4.10
13. Washington University, 3.94
14. University of Pennsylvania, 3.90
15. University of Minnesota, 3.88

Source: "Rankings of Research-Doctorate Programs in 41 Disciplines at 274 Institutions," *The Chronicle of Higher Education* 42: A21-A30 (September 21, 1995).

★202★
Top neurosciences research-doctorate programs as evaluated by the National Research Council

Ranking basis/background: From a survey of nearly 8,000 faculty members conducted in the spring of 1993. Respondents were asked to rate programs in their field on "scholarly quality of program faculty." When more than one program had the samescore, the council averaged the rank order and gave each program the same rank number (if three programs tied for the top position, each received a rank of 2). **Remarks:** See *Chronicle* article for more details. Scores of 4.01 and above indicate "distinguished;" 3.0-4.0 "strong;" 2.51-3.0 "good;" 2.0-2.5 "adequate;" 1.0-1.99 "marginal;" and 0.0-0.99 "not sufficient for doctoral education." Programs also ranked by "effectiveness of program in educating research scholars/scientists." **Number listed:** 102.
1. University of California, San Diego, with a quality rating of 4.82
2. Yale University, 4.76
3. Harvard University, 4.73
4. University of California, San Francisco, 4.66
5. Stanford University, 4.64
6. Columbia University, 4.58
7. Johns Hopkins University, 4.47
8. Washington University, 4.43
9. University of California, Berkeley, 4.32
10. California Institute of Technology, 4.30

BIOLOGY, GRADUATE—CELLULAR/MOLECULAR

10. University of Pennsylvania, 4.30
12. University of Washington (WA), 4.28
13. Rockefeller University, 4.23
14. Massachusetts Institute of Technology, 4.21
15. University of California, Los Angeles, 3.91

Source: "Rankings of Research-Doctorate Programs in 41 Disciplines at 274 Institutions," *The Chronicle of Higher Education* 42: A21-A30 (September 21, 1995).

★203★
Top recruiters for biology/biological science jobs for 2000-01 master's degree recipients

Ranking basis/background: Projected number of college hires from on-campus recruitment for 2000-01. **Remarks:** Numbers reflect total expected hires, not just African American projected hires. **Number listed:** 5.

1. Macy's West, with 22 projected hires
2. Accenture, 5
3. Henrico County Public Schools, 3
3. U.S. Forest Services, 3
5. Wyeth-Ayerst, 1

Source: "The Top 100 Employers and the Majors in Demand for the Class of 2001," *The Black Collegian*, 31: 19-35, (February 2001).

BIOLOGY, GRADUATE–CELLULAR/MOLECULAR

★204★
Molecular biology and genetics journals with the highest impact, 1992-96

Ranking basis/background: For each journal, number of high-impact papers, total cites to high impact papers, and average cites per high impact paper. **Remarks:** Original source: *National Science Indicators on Diskette, 1981-97* **Number listed:** 8.

1. *Cell*, with 408 high-impact papers; 132,452 total cites to high-impact papers; and 324.64 average cites per high-impact paper
2. *Nature*, 175; 52,998; 302.85
3. *PNAS*, 36; 10,424; 289.56
4. *Science*, 145; 40,681; 280.56
5. *Genes & Development*, 43; 10,812; 251.44
6. *EMBO Journal*, 42; 9,803; 233.40
7. *Molecular Cellular Biology*, 20; 4,644; 232.20
8. *Nature Genetics*, 57; 11,959; 209.81

Source: "High-Impact Journals in Molecular Biology & Genetics, 1992-96," *What's Hot*, September 22, 1998.

★205★
Most effective biochemistry and molecular biology research-doctorate programs as evaluated by the National Research Council

Ranking basis/background: From a survey of nearly 8,000 faculty members conducted in the spring of 1993. Respondents were asked to rate programs in their field on "effectiveness of program in educating research scholars/scientists." **Remarks:** See *Chronicle* article for more details. Scores of 3.5-5.0 indicate "extremely effective;" 2.5-3.49 "reasonably effective;" 1.5-2.49 "minimally effective;" and 0.0-1.49 "not effective." Programs also ranked by "scholarly quality of program faculty." **Number listed:** 194.

1. University of California, San Francisco, with an effectiveness rating of 4.73
2. Massachusetts Institute of Technology, 4.68
3. University of California, Berkeley, 4.66
4. Stanford University, 4.59
5. Harvard University, 4.44
6. California Institute of Technology, 4.41
7. University of California, San Diego, 4.37
8. Yale University, 4.32
9. University of Wisconsin, Madison, 4.30
10. Johns Hopkins University, 4.26

Source: "Rankings of Research-Doctorate Programs in 41 Disciplines at 274 Institutions," *The Chronicle of Higher Education* 42: A21-A30 (September 21, 1995).

★206★
Most effective cell and developmental biology research-doctorate programs as evaluated by the National Research Council

Ranking basis/background: From a survey of nearly 8,000 faculty members conducted in the spring of 1993. Respondents were asked to rate programs in their field on "effectiveness of program in educating research scholars/scientists." **Remarks:** See *Chronicle* article for more details. Scores of 3.5-5.0 indicate "extremely effective;" 2.5-3.49 "reasonably effective;" 1.5-2.49 "minimally effective;" and 0.0-1.49 "not effective." Programs also ranked by "scholarly quality of program faculty." **Number listed:** 179.

1. California Institute of Technology, with an effectiveness rating of 4.68
2. Massachusetts Institute of Technology, 4.66
3. University of California, San Francisco, 4.57
4. Rockefeller University, 4.54
5. Princeton University, 4.45
6. Stanford University School of Medicine, 4.39
7. Harvard University, 4.33
8. Washington University, 4.24
9. University of Washington (WA), 4.23
10. Yale University, 4.22

Source: "Rankings of Research-Doctorate Programs in 41 Disciplines at 274 Institutions," *The Chronicle of Higher Education* 42: A21-A30 (September 21, 1995).

★207★
Most effective molecular and general genetics research-doctorate programs as evaluated by the National Research Council

Ranking basis/background: From a survey of nearly 8,000 faculty members conducted in the spring of 1993. Respondents were asked to rate programs in their field on "effectiveness of program in educating research scholars/scientists." **Remarks:** See *Chronicle* article for more details. Scores of 3.5-5.0 indicate "extremely effective;" 2.5-3.49 "reasonably effective;" 1.5-2.49 "minimally effective;" and 0.0-1.49 "not effective." Programs also ranked by "scholarly quality of program faculty." **Number listed:** 103.

1. University of California, San Francisco, with an effectiveness rating of 4.80
2. Massachusetts Institute of Technology, 475
3. Harvard University, 4.55
4. California Institute of Technology, 4.47
5. Stanford University, 4.44
6. University of Wisconsin, Madison, 4.40
7. Johns Hopkins University, 4.01
8. University of Chicago, 4.25
9. University of California, Berkeley, 4.18
10. University of California, San Diego, 4.17

Source: "Rankings of Research-Doctorate Programs in 41 Disciplines at 274 Institutions," *The Chronicle of Higher Education* 42: A21-A30 (September 21, 1995).

★208★
Radcliffe Institute for Advanced Study fellowship recipients in the field of molecular biology, 2000-01

Ranking basis/background: Recipient and institutional affiliation of the Radcliffe Institute for Advanced study fellowship for pursuit of advanced work across a wide range of academic disciplines, professions, and creative arts. **Number listed:** 3.

Kelly McLaughlin, Harvard Medical School
Yvonne Parsons, Harvard University
Siu The, Harvard Medical School

Source: "The Radcliffe Institute for Advanced Study," *The Chronicle of Higher Education*, 46: A59, (June 2, 2000).

★209★
Top biochemistry and molecular biology research-doctorate programs as evaluated by the National Research Council

Ranking basis/background: From a survey of nearly 8,000 faculty members conducted in the spring of 1993. Respondents were asked to rate programs in their field on "scholarly quality of program faculty." When more than one program had the samescore, the council averaged the rank order and gave each program the same rank number (if three programs tied for the top position, each received a rank of 2). **Remarks:** See *Chronicle* article for more details. Scores of 4.01 and above indicate "distinguished;" 3.0-4.0 "strong;" 2.51-3.0 "good;" 2.0-2.5 "adequate;" 1.0-1.99 "marginal;" and 0.0-0.99 "not sufficient for doctoral education." Programs also ranked by "effectiveness of program in educating research scholars/scientists." **Number listed:** 194.

1. University of California, San Francisco, with a quality rating of 4.84
2. Massachusetts Institute of Technology, 4.83
2. Stanford University, 4.83
4. University of California, Berkeley, 4.81
5. Harvard University, 4.80
6. Yale University, 4.59
7. California Institute of Technology, 4.57
8. University of Wisconsin, Madison, 4.55
9. University of California, San Diego, 4.53
10. Johns Hopkins University, 4.38
10. Columbia University, 4.38
12. University of Colorado, 4.26
13. Washington University, 4.22
14. University of California, Los Angeles, 4.20
15. Duke University, 4.18

Source: "Rankings of Research-Doctorate Programs in 41 Disciplines at 274 Institutions," *The Chronicle of Higher Education* 42: A21-A30 (September 21, 1995).

★210★
Top cell and developmental biology research-doctorate programs as evaluated by the National Research Council

Ranking basis/background: From a survey of nearly 8,000 faculty members conducted in the spring of 1993. Respondents were asked to rate programs in their field on "scholarly quality of program faculty." When more than one program had the samescore, the council averaged the rank order and gave each program the same rank number (if three programs tied for the top position, each received a rank of 2). **Remarks:** See *Chronicle* article for more details. Scores of 4.01 and above indicate "distinguished;" 3.0-4.0 "strong;" 2.51-3.0 "good;" 2.0-2.5 "adequate;" 1.0-1.99 "marginal;" and 0.0-0.99 "not sufficient for doctoral education." Programs also ranked by "effectiveness of program in educating research scholars/scientists." **Number listed:** 179.
1. Massachusetts Institute of Technology, with a quality rating of 4.86
2. Rockefeller University, 4.77
3. University of California, San Francisco, 4.76
4. California Institute of Technology, 4.73
5. Harvard University, 4.70
6. Stanford University School of Medicine, 4.55
7. University of California, San Diego, 4.50
8. University of Washington, 4.48
9. Washington University, 4.39
10. Yale University, 4.37
11. Princeton University, 4.36
11. Stanford University School of Arts and Sciences, 4.36
13. University of California, Berkeley, 4.16
14. Duke University, 4.11
15. University of Chicago, 4.10

Source: "Rankings of Research-Doctorate Programs in 41 Disciplines at 274 Institutions," *The Chronicle of Higher Education* 42: A21-A30 (September 21, 1995).

★211★
Top molecular and general genetics research-doctorate programs as evaluated by the National Research Council

Ranking basis/background: From a survey of nearly 8,000 faculty members conducted in the spring of 1993. Respondents were asked to rate programs in their field on "scholarly quality of program faculty." When more than one program had the samescore, the council averaged the rank order and gave each program the same rank number (if three programs tied for the top position, each received a rank of 2). **Remarks:** See *Chronicle* article for more details. Scores of 4.01 and above indicate "distinguished;" 3.0-4.0 "strong;" 2.51-3.0 "good;" 2.0-2.5 "adequate;" 1.0-1.99 "marginal;" and 0.0-0.99 "not sufficient for doctoral education." Programs also ranked by "effectiveness of program in educating research scholars/scientists." **Number listed:** 103.
1. Massachusetts Institute of Technology, with a quality rating of 4.88
2. University of California, San Francisco, 4.87
3. Harvard University, 4.77
4. California Institute of Technology, 4.51
5. Stanford University, 4.48
6. University of California, San Diego, 4.44
7. University of Wisconsin, Madison, 4.33
8. Yale University, 4.32
9. Johns Hopkins University, 4.26
10. University of California, Berkeley, 4.21
11. University of Chicago, 4.17
12. Columbia University, 4.14
13. University of Utah, 4.08
14. Baylor College of Medicine, 4.07
15. Duke University, 4.01

Source: "Rankings of Research-Doctorate Programs in 41 Disciplines at 274 Institutions," *The Chronicle of Higher Education* 42: A21-A30 (September 21, 1995).

★212★
U.S. universities with the greatest impact in cell and developmental biology, 1993-97

Ranking basis/background: For each university, total number of citations divided by number of published articles during the same time period. **Remarks:** Original source: *National Science Indicators on Diskette, 1981-97* **Number listed:** 5.
1. Massachusetts Institute of Technology, with 52.65 citations per paper; 452 total papers
2. Rockefeller University, 40.65; 285
3. Harvard University, 37.72; 1,679
4. Baylor College of Medicine, 35.42; 353
5. Columbia University, 34.09; 493

Source: "Cell & Developmental Biology: High-Impact U.S. Universities, 1993-97," *What's Hot*, July 20, 1998.

★213★
U.S. universities with the greatest impact in cell and developmental biology, 1994-98

Ranking basis/background: Average citations per paper from the top 100 federally funded U.S. universities that had at least 50 published papers in ISI indexed cell & developmental biology journals. Also includes total number of papers published during the five year period. **Number listed:** 5.
1. Massachusetts Institute of Technology, with 476 papers; 47.80 citations per paper
2. Rockefeller University, 284; 42.10
3. Harvard University, 1,824; 36.94
4. University of Texas, Dallas, 345; 36.13
5. Columbia University, 502; 33.77

Source: "Cell & Developmental Biology: High Impact U.S. Universities, 1994-98," *What's Hot in Research* (http://www.isinet.com/isi/hot/research) *Institute for Scientific Information*, July 24, 2000.

BIOLOGY, GRADUATE–MICROBIOLOGY

★214★
Canadian universities with the most citations per paper in the field of microbiology, 1992-96

Ranking basis/background: Citations per paper. Also includes number of papers, 1992-96. **Remarks:** Original source: ISI's *Canadian University Indicators on Diskette, 1981-97*. **Number listed:** 5.
1. McMaster University, with 9.77 citations per paper; 145 papers
2. McGill University, 6.66; 355
3. University of Alberta, 6.39; 273
4. University of Calgary, 6.33; 187
5. University of British Columbia, 6.13; 354

Source: "Canadian Universities: Highest Impact in Microbiology, 1992-96," *What's Hot*, April 27, 1998.

★215★
U.S. universities publishing the most papers in the field of microbiology, 1994-98

Ranking basis/background: Number of papers published in the field of microbiology over a five-year period, and percent of field based on each universities percentage of 76,909 papers entered in the ISI database from ISI-indexed microbiology journals. **Number listed:** 5.
1. Harvard University, with 842 papers; 1.09% of field
2. University of Wisconsin, Madison, 662; 0.86%
3. Cornell University, 535; 0.70%
4. University of Iowa, 493; 0.64%
5. Johns Hopkins University, 477; 0.62%

Source: "Microbiology: Most Prolific U.S. Universities, 1994-98," *What's Hot in Research* (http://www.isinet.com/isi/hot/research) *Institute for Scientific Information*, May 8, 2000.

★216★
U.S. universities with the greatest impact in biotechnology and applied microbiology, 1995-99

Ranking basis/background: Average citations per paper from the top 100 federally funded U.S. universities that had at least 50 published papers in ISI indexed biotechnology/applied microbiology journals. Also includes total number of papers published during the five year period. **Number listed:** 5.
1. Harvard University, with 69 papers; 10.32 citations per paper
2. Massachusetts Institute of Technology, 157; 5.26
3. University of Maryland, Baltimore, 54; 5.11
4. Rutgers University, 65; 5.05
5. University of Wisconsin, Madison, 77; 4.65

Source: "Biotechnology & Applied Microbiology: High Impact U.S. Universities, 1995-99," *What's Hot in Research* (http://www.isinet.com/isi/hot/research) *Institute for Scientific Information*.

★217★
U.S. universities with the greatest impact in microbiology, 1994-98

Ranking basis/background: Total number of microbiology papers published from each university and average number of citations per paper between 1994 and 1998. **Remarks:** Original source: University Science Indicators on Diskette, 1981-98. **Number listed:** 5.
1. New York University, with 242 astrophysics papers; 21.85 citations per paper
2. Rockefeller University, 238; 16.99
3. University of Alabama, 416; 13.56
4. Oregon Health Sciences University, 131; 13.55
5. Harvard University, 842; 12.87

Source: "Microbiology: High-Impact U.S. Universities, 1994-98," *What's Hot in Research* (http://www.isinet.com/hot/research) *Institute for Scientific Information*, December 13, 1999.

BIOMEDICAL ENGINEERING

★218★
U.S. universities with the greatest impact in microbiology, 1995-99

Ranking basis/background: Average citations per paper from the top 100 federally funded U.S. universities that had at least 50 published papers in ISI indexed microbiology journals. Also includes total number of papers published during the five year period. **Number listed:** 5.

1. Rockefeller University, with 257 papers; 20.02 citations per paper
2. New York University, 228; 19.99
3. University of Pennsylvania, 388; 14.47
4. Columbia University, 199; 14.41
5. Stanford University, 444; 13.85

Source: "Microbiology: High Impact U.S. Universities, 1995-99," *What's Hot in Research* (http://www.isinet.com/isi/hot/research) *Institute for Scientific Information*, December 11, 2000.

BIOMEDICAL ENGINEERING
See: **Engineering, Graduate–Biomedical**

BIOSTATISTICS
See: **Mathematics, Graduate–Statistics**

BLACK AMERICANS

★219★
Most important African Americans in the twentieth century

Ranking basis/background: From a JBHE readers survey of African Americans who made the greatest contributions to American society in the twentieth century. **Number listed:** 20.

1. Rev. Martin Luther King, Jr.
2. Thurgood Marshall
3. W.E.B. DuBois
4. Malcolm X
5. Rosa Parks
6. Jesse Jackson
7. George Washington Carver
8. Muhammad Ali
9. Charles Drew

Source: "JBHE Readers Select the Most Important African Americans of the Twentieth Century," *The Journal of Blacks in Higher Education, No. 25*, pp. 101-105, (Autumn 1999).

BLACK COLLEGES AND UNIVERSITIES

Related Information

★220★
Wilson, Erlene B., *The 100 Best Colleges for African American Students (revised edition)*, Penguin Group, 1998.

Remarks: Provides a listing of total number of African American students at each college, academic offerings, the African American student organizations, prominent African American alumni, the average SAT score of incoming freshmen, and health services available to students.

BLACK STUDENTS–FINANCIAL AID

★221★
Colleges offering the Thurgood Marshall Scholarship Fund

Ranking basis/background: Listing of historically black colleges and universities enrolling more than 180,000 students that offer the Thurgood Marshall Scholarship Fund. **Number listed:** 37.

Alabama A&M University
Alabama State University
Albany State College
Alcorn State University
Bowie State University
Central State University
University of Pennsylvania, Cheyney
Coppin State College
Delaware State College
Elizabeth City State University
Fayetteville State University
Florida A&M University
Fort Valley State College
Grambling State University
Jackson State University
Kentucky State University
Langston University
Lincoln University (PA)
Lincoln University (MO)
Mississippi Valley State University
Morgan State University
Norfolk State University
North Carolina A&T State University
North Carolina Central University
Prairie View A&M University
Savannah State University
South Carolina State University
Southern University
Tennessee State University
Texas Southern University
Tuskegee University
University of Arkansas, Pine Bluff
University of Maryland, Eastern Shore
Virginia State University
Winston-Salem State University
University of the Virgin Islands
University of the District of Columbia

Source: *Murray Resource Directory and Career Guide to HBCUs, Third edition.* Logical Exression in Design, 1996.

BLACKS–ENROLLMENT, COLLEGE

★222★
U.S. colleges and universities with the highest percentage of African Americans enrolled, 1997

Ranking basis/background: Total number of African Americans enrolled and percentage they comprise of total enrollment. **Remarks:** Original source: *Black Issues* analysis of IPEDS data. **Number listed:** 413.

1. Denver Conservative Baptist Seminary (CO), with 1 African American enrolled; 100% of total enrolled
1. Fisk University (TN), 700; 100%
1. Claflin College (SC), 1,005; 100%
1. Morris College (SC), 970; 100%
1. Bennett College (NC), 616; 100%
1. Tougaloo College (MS), 916; 100%
1. Benedict College (SC), 2,198; 100%
1. Clark Atlanta University (GA), 4,503; 100%
1. Barber-Scotia College (NC), 498; 100%
1. Lewis College of Business (MI), 246; 100%
1. Lane College (TN), 670; 100%
1. Miles College (AL), 1,334; 100%
13. Arkansas Baptist College (AR), 198; 99%
13. Johnson C. Smith University (NC), 1,348; 99%
13. Morehouse College (GA), 2,964; 99%
13. Talladega College (AL), 641; 99%
17. Virginia Union University (VA), 1,520; 98%
17. Voorhees College (SC), 905; 98%
17. Lawson State Community College (AL), 1,554; 98%
17. Mississippi Valley State University (MS), 2,074; 98%
17. Le Moyne-Owen College (TN), 963; 98%
17. Dillard University (LA), 1,512; 98%

Source: "Black-Serving Institutions," *Black Issues in Higher Education*, 17: 38-40, (September 28, 2000).

★223★
U.S. colleges and universities with the lowest percentage of African Americans enrolled, 1997

Ranking basis/background: Total number of African Americans enrolled and percentage they comprise of total enrollment. **Remarks:** Original source: *Black Issues* analysis of IPEDS data. **Number listed:** 413.

1. Career Point Business School (OK), with 51 African American enrolled; 25% of total enrolled
1. Devry Institute of Technology (TX), 660; 25%
1. East Central Community College (MS), 498; 25%
1. Roosevelt University (IL), 1,049; 25%
1. City University of New York, Queensborough Community College (NY), 2,588; 25%
1. Calumet College of St. Joseph (IN), 248; 25%
1. Southern Arkansas University Tech (AR), 207; 15%
1. Eti Technical College (OH), 52; 25%
1. Keiser College (FL), 584; 25%
1. New York Institute of Technology, Manhattan (NY), 430; 25%
1. University of Baltimore (MD), 487; 25%
1. Mountain View College (TX), 1,354; 25%
1. Southeastern Community College (NC), 409; 25%
1. Catholic Medical Center School of Nursing (NY), 15; 25%
1. Art Institute of Atlanta (GA), 397; 25%

Source: "Black-Serving Institutions," *Black Issues in Higher Education*, 17: 38-40, (September 28, 2000).

BOARDING SCHOOLS
See: **Schools, Elementary & Secondary Schools, Secondary**

BOOKS
See also: **Censorship Libraries**

★224★
American Library Association's most frequently challenged books of the decade

Ranking basis/background: Literature that was most challenged during the past decade according to the American Library Association. **Number listed:** 10.

1. *Scary Stories Series*
2. *Daddy's Roommate*
3. *I Know Why the Caged Bird Sings*
4. *The Chocolate War*
5. *The Adventures of Huckleberry Finn*
6. *Of Mice and Men*
7. *Forever*
8. *Bridge to Terabithia*
9. *Heather Has Two Mommies*
10. *The Catcher in the Rye*

Source: "Ban That Book," *U.S. News & World Report*, 129: 12, (September 25, 2000).

★225★
American School Board Journal's notable education books, 2000

Ranking basis/background: As chosen by the editors of *American School Board Journal*. **Number listed:** 9.

The Academic Achievement Challenge: What Really Works in the Classroom?, by Jeanne S. Chall (published by Guilford Press)
Ordinary Resurrections: Children in the Years of Hope, Jonathan Kozol (Crown)
Charter Schools in Action: Renewing Public Education, Chester E. Finn Jr., Bruno V. Manno, and Gregg Vanourek (Princeton University Press)
Millennials Rising: The Next Great Generation, Neil Howe and William Strauss (Vintage Books)
Class Dismissed: A Year in the Life of an American High School, a Glimpse into the Heart of a Nation, Meredith Maran (St. Martin's Press)
The Irreducible Needs of Children: What Every Child Must Have to Grow, Learn, and Flourish, T. Berry Brazelton, M.D. and Stanley I. Greenspan, M.D. (Perseus Books)
It Takes a City: Getting Serious about Urban School Reform, Paul T. Hill, Christine Campbell, and James Harvey (Brookings Institution Press)
When Schools Compete: A Cautionary Tale, Edward B. Fiske and Helen F. Ladd (Brookings Institutions Press)
Left Back: A Century of Failed School Reforms, Diane Ravitch (Simon & Schuster)

Source: Jones, Rebecca, "Millennium Reader," *American School Board Journal*, 188: 24-27, (January 2001).

★226★
Best selling small press releases, 2001

Ranking basis/background: Title most in demand by libraries from Quality Books nationwide, six months prior to the week ending February 10, 2001. **Number listed:** 20.

1. *Fell's Official Know-It-All Guide: Magic for Beginners*, by Walter B. Gibson (published by Frederick Fell)
2. *The Beginner's Guide to Homeschooling*, Patrick Farenga (Holt Assoc.)
3. *Exotic Paper Airplanes*, Thay Yang (Cypress House)
4. *Phonics Pathways*, Dolores G. Hiskes (Dorbooks)
5. *Attention Deficit/Hyperactivity Disorder: What Every Parent Wants To Know*, David L. Wodrich (Paul H. Brookes Pub.)
6. *Internet Basics Without Fear!*, Shaun Fawcett (Final Draft Pubns)
7. *Native American Crafts & Skills: A Fully Illustrated Guide to Wilderness Living and Survival*, David Montgomery (Lyons Press)
8. *Everyday Math Made E-Z*, Pete Reinhart (E-Z Legal Forms)
9. *Fell's Official Know-It-All Guide: Wedding Planner*, Edith Gilbert (Frederick Fell)
10. *Palm Reading for Beginners*, Richard Webster (Llwellyn)

Source: "Small Press Best Sellers," *Library Journal*, 126: 70, (March 1, 2001).

★227★
Booklist's best fiction books for library collections, 2000

Ranking basis/background: Alphabetical listing, by author, of the year's outstanding books for public-library collections. Choices are those that combine literary, intellectual, and aesthetic excellence with popular appeal. **Number listed:** 21.

The Blind Assassin, by Margaret Atwood (published by Doubleday/Nan A. Talese)
Master of the Crossroads, Madison Smartt Bell (Pantheon)
Ravelstein, Saul Bellow (Viking)
Jayber Crow: The Life Story of Jayber Crow, Barber, of the Port William Membership, as Written by Himself, Wendell Berry (Counterpoint)
A Blind Man Can See How Much I Love You, Amy Bloom (Random)
A Friend of the Earth, T.C. Boyle (Viking)
The Amazing Adventures of Kavalier and Clay, Michael Chabon (Random)
Being Dead, Jim Crace (Farrar)
The Best of Jackson Payne, Jack Fuller (Knopf)
The Beast God Forgot to Invent, Jim Harrison (Grove/Atlantic)
The Elementary Particles, Michel Houellebecq (Knopf)
English Passengers, Matthew Kneale (Doubleday/Nan A. Talese)
The Diagnosis, Alan Lightman (Pantheon)
Becoming Madame Mao, Anchee Min (Houghton)
Ghostwritten, David Mitchell (Random)
Exile, Padraic O'Conaire (Dufour Editions)
MotherKind, Jayne Anne Phillips (Knopf)
Scandalmonger, William Safire (Simon & Schuster)
In America, Susan Sontag (Farrar)
The Hill Bachelors, William Trevor (Viking)
The Golden Age, Gore Vidal (Doubleday)

Source: "Editor's Choice 2000," *Booklist*, 97: 850-868, (January 1 & 15, 2001).

★228★
Booklist's best first novels

Ranking basis/background: Alphabetical listing by author for highly recommended first novels as reviewed in *Booklist* from December 1, 1999 through November 15, 2000. **Number listed:** 10.

Aimee Bender, *An Invisible Sign of My Own* (published by Doubleday)
Liza Dalby, *The Tale of Murasaki* (Doubleday)
Helen DeWitt, *The Last Samurai* (Hyperion)
Michel Feber, *Under the Skin* (Harcourt)
Moses Isegawa, *Abyssinian Chronicles* (Knopf)
Arthur Japin, *The Two Hearts of Kwasi Boachi* (Knopf)
Jeffrey Lent, *In the Fall* (Grove/Atlantic)
David Mitchell, *Ghostwritten* (Random)
William Monahan, *Light House* (Riverhead)
Zadie Smith, *White Teeth* (Random)

Source: Smothers, Bonnie, "Top 10 First Novels," *Booklist*, 97: 615, (November 15, 2000).

★229★
Booklist's most recommended African American nonfiction

Ranking basis/background: Alphabetical listing, by author, selected from books reviewed in *Booklist* between February 15, 2000 and February 1, 2001. **Number listed:** 10.

An American Story, by Debra J. Dickerson (published by Pantheon)
Homecoming: The Story of African-American Farmers, Charlene Gilbert and Quinn Eli (Beacon)
Kind of Blue: The Making of the Miles Davis Masterpiece, Ashley Kahn (Da Capo)
W.E.B. Du Bois: The Fight for Equality and the American Century, 1919-63, David Levering Lewis (Holt/John Macrae)
Strange Fruit: Billie Holiday, Cafe Society, and an Early Call for Civil Rights, David Margolick (Running Press)
Boogie Man: The Adventures of John Lee Hooker in the American Twentieth Century, Charles Shaar Murray (St. Martin's)
The Complete Jacob Lawrence, Peter T. Nesbitt and Michelle DuBois (Univ. of Washington)
The Measure of a Man: A Spiritual Autobiography, Sidney Poitier (Harper San Francisco)
Slave Narratives (Library of America; dist. by Viking)
Black, White and Jewish: Autobiography of a Shifting Self, Rebecca Walker (Riverhead)

Source: Hooper, Brad, "Top Ten African American Nonfiction," *Booklist*, 97: 109, (February 15, 2001).

★230★
Booklist's most recommended historical novels, 2001

Ranking basis/background: As reviewed by *Booklist*. List is alphabetical by author. **Number listed:** 10.

- *Master of the Crossroads*, by Madison Smartt Bell (published by Pantheon)
- *Grant*, Max Byrd (Bantam)
- *Gemini: The Eighth Book of the House of Niccolo*, Dorothy Dunnett (Knopf)
- *Dream of the Walled City*, Lisa Huang Fleischman (Pocket)
- *Ladysmith*, Giles Foden (Knopf)
- *Flashman and the Tiger*, George MacDonald Fraser (Knopf)
- *Wild Life*, Molly Gloss (Simon & Schuster)
- *Nowhere Else of Earth*, Josephine Humphreys (Viking)
- *Honorable Company*, Allan Mallinson (Bantam)
- *The Golden Age*, Gore Vidal (Doubleday)

Source: Hooper, Brad, "Top 10 Historical Novels," *Booklist*, 97: 1452, (April 1, 2001).

★231★
Booklist's most recommended poetry books, 2001

Ranking basis/background: As reviewed by *Booklist*. List is alphabetical by author. **Number listed:** 10.

- *Some Ether*, by Nick Flynn (published by Graywolf)
- *Boss Cupid*, Thom Gunn (Farrar)
- *The Iron-Blue Vault: Selected Poems*, Attila Jozsef (Bloodaxe)
- *The House of Blue Light*, David Kirby (Louisiana State)
- *Cool, Calm & Collected Poems, 1960-2000*, Carolyn Kizer (Copper Canyon)
- *Talking Dirty to the Gods*, Yusef Komunyakaa (Farrar)
- *Ancient Acid Flashes Back*, Adrian C. Louis (University of Nevada)
- *What the Ice Gets: Shakleton's Antarctic Expedition, 1914-1916*, Melinda Mueller (Van West)
- *The New Young American Poets*, edited by Kevin Prufer (Southern Illinois University)
- *Scanning the Century: The Penguin Book of the Twentieth Century in Poetry*, edited by Peter Forbes (Penguin)

Source: Olson, Ray, "Top 10 Poetry Books," *Booklist*, 97: 1349, (March 15, 2001).

★232★
Booklist's most recommended science fiction/fantasy books

Ranking basis/background: Alphabetical list by author of fantasy book reviewed in *Booklist* from April 15, 2000 through April 1, 2001. **Number listed:** 10.

- *Daughter of the Shining Isles*, by Elizabeth Cunningham (published by Station Hill/Barrytown)
- *Under the Skin*, Michel Faber (Harcourt)
- *Ship of Destiny*, Robin Hobb (Bantam Spectra)
- *St. Patrick's Gargoyle*, Katherine Kurtz (Berkley/Ace)
- *Brightly Burning*, Mercedes Lackey (DAW)
- *Daughter of the Forest*, Juliet Marillier (Tor)
- *The Miocene Arrow*, Sean McMullen (Tor)
- *Ventus*, Karl Schuroeder (Tor)
- *Magic Terror: Seven Tales*, Peter Straub (Random)
- *The Great War: Breakthroughs*, Harry Turtledove (Del Rey)

Source: Estes, Sally, "Top 10 Fantasy Books for Youth," *Booklist*, 97: 1561, (April 15, 2001).

★233★
Canada's best fiction selections of the 20th century

Ranking basis/background: Most significant creators and works from a number of areas, selected by *Maclean's* critics and an art historian. Not listed in order of importance. **Number listed:** 10.

- *As for Me and My House*, by James Sinclair Ross
- *The Tin Flute*, Gabrielle Roy
- *The Apprenticeship of Duddy Kravitz*, Mordecai Richler
- *The Stone Angel*, Margaret Laurence
- *Fifth Business*, Robertson Davies
- *The Wars*, Timothy Findley
- *The Handmaid's Tale*, Margaret Atwood
- *The English Patient*, Michael Ondaatije
- *Selected Stories*, Alice Munro
- *The Selected Stories of Mavis Gallant*

Source: Bemrose, John, "Best of the Century," *Maclean's*, 113: 241-246, (January 1, 2000).

★234★
Canada's best nonfiction selections of the 20th century

Ranking basis/background: Most significant creators and works from a number of areas, selected by *Maclean's* critics and an art historian. Not listed in order of importance. **Number listed:** 10.

- *The Fur Trade in Canada*, by Harold Innis
- *Tales of an Empty Cabin*, Grey Owl
- *Fearful Symmetry*, Northrop Frye
- *John A. Macdonald*, Donald Creighton
- *Never Cry Wolf*, Farley Mowat
- *Understanding Media*, Marshall McLuhan
- *Lament for a Nation*, George Grant
- *The Last Spike*, Pierre Berton
- *The Canadian Establishment*, Peter C. Newman
- *Reflections of a Siamese Twin*, John Ralston Saul

Source: Bemrose, John, "Best of the Century," *Maclean's*, 113: 241-246, (January 1, 2000).

★235★
Christopher Awards winners for adult literature, 2000

Ranking basis/background: Winners of the 52nd annual Christopher Awards for literary works that "affirm the highest values of the human spirit." **Number listed:** 6.

- *Dark Midnight When I Rise*, by Andrew Ward (published by Farrar, Straus and Giroux)
- *Flags of Our Fathers*, James Bradley with Ron Powers (Bantam Books)
- *It's Not About the Bike: My Journey Back to Life*, Lance Armstrong with Sally Jenkins (Putnam)
- *Life Is So Good*, George Dawson and Richard Glaubman (Random House)
- *Ordinary Resurrections: Children in the Years of Hope*, Jonathan Kozol (Crown Publishers)
- *With Love and Prayers*, F. Washington Jarvis (David R. Godine)

Source: "The 52nd Annual Christopher Awards," *Library Journal*, 126: 111, (March 15, 2001).

★236★
Estimated book sales, 1999-2000

Ranking basis/background: Figures for total sales, in millions, and percentage of change from 1999 to 2000. **Remarks:** Original source: Book Industry Study Group Trends 2000. **Number listed:** 12.

1. Professional, with $4,974.8 million; and a 5.4% change
2. Adult Trade, $4,963.1; 3.5%
3. Elhi, $3,608.5; 5.6%
4. College, $3,382.7; 8.1%
5. Juvenile Trade, $1,896.5; 10.2%
6. Mass Market, $1,474.6; 5.1%
7. Book Clubs, $1,296.4; 3.3%
8. Religious, $1,260.7; 3.6%
9. Subscription Reference, $818.6; 3.8%
10. University Press, $431.5; 4.8%
11. Mail Order, $370.6; 10.2% decrease
12. Standardized Tests, $233.6; 6.8%

Source: Milliot, Jim, "BISG Projects 5% Gain In Book Sales in 2000," *Publishers Weekly*, 247: 9, (August 28, 2000).

★237★
Favorite African American authors

Ranking basis/background: As voted by members of the African American Literature Book Club, an independent online book-selling Web site. **Number listed:** 25.

1. Toni Morrison
2. Zora Neale Hurston
3. Maya Angelou
4. J. California Cooper
5. Alice Walker
6. Langston Hughes
7. E. Lynn Harris
8. James Baldwin
9. Terry McMillan
10. Bebe Moore Campbell

Source: "African Americans Select Their Favorite Books of the Twentieth Century," *The Journal of Blacks in Higher Education*, No. 26, pp. 122-123, (Winter 1999).

★238★
Favorite books of African Americans

Ranking basis/background: From a survey conducted by the African American Literature Book Club, an independent online book-selling Web site. **Number listed:** 10.

1. *The Color Purple*, by Alice Walker
2. *Their Eyes Were Watching God*, Zora Neale Hurston
3. *Beloved*, Toni Morrison
4. *And This Too Shall Pass*, E. Lynn Harris
5. *I Know Why the Caged Bird Sings*, Maya Angelou
6. *Some Love, Some Pain, Some Time: Stories*, J. California Cooper
7. *Dissappearing Acts*, Terry McMillan
8. *Invisible Man*, Ralph Ellison
9. *Song of Solomon*, Toni Morrison
10. *Native Son*, Richard Wright

Source: "African Americans Select Their Favorite Books of the Twentieth Century," *The Journal of Blacks in Higher Education*, No. 26, pp. 122-123, (Winter 1999).

★239★
Hardcover bestsellers by corporation, 2000

Ranking basis/background: Number of books and number of weeks on *Publishers Weekly*'s 2000 list. Also includes publisher's share of the 1530 hardcover or paperback bestseller positions during 2000. **Number listed:** 8.
1. Random House, with 69 books; and 505 weeks
2. Penguin Putnam, 39; 269
3. HarperCollins, 29; 196
3. Simon & Schuster, 29; 166
5. Time Warner, 19; 143
6. Von Holtzbrinck, 13; 57
7. Hyperion, 7; 53
8. Tyndale, 3; 19

Source: Maryles, Daisy, "Who's Topping the Charts?," *Publishers Weekly*, 249: 36-39, (January 8, 2001).

★240★
Hardcover bestsellers by publishing house, 2000

Ranking basis/background: Number of books and number of weeks on *Publishers Weekly*'s 2000 list. **Number listed:** 55.
1. Putnam, with 23 books; and 191 weeks
2. Simon & Schuster, 20; 116
3. Random House, 18; 96
4. HarperCollins, 13; 115
5. Warner, 11; 99
5. Bantam, 11; 72
7. Knopf, 10; 92
8. Delacorte, 9; 35
8. Morrow, 9; 35
10. Hyperion, 7; 53
10. Little, Brown, 7; 42
10. Viking, 7; 34
10. Dutton, 7; 29
14. Doubleday, 6; 101
14. St. Martin's, 6; 21

Source: Maryles, Daisy, "Who's Topping the Charts?," *Publishers Weekly*, 249: 36-39, (January 8, 2001).

★241★
Library Journal's best fiction audiobooks, 2000

Ranking basis/background: Alphabetical listing by author, as selected by *Library Journal*. **Number listed:** 12.
- *Darkness Peering*, by Alice Blanchard (published by Recorded Bks)
- *False Pretenses*, Catherine Coulter (Chivers Audiobks)
- *Juneteenth*, Ralph Ellison (Recorded Bks)
- *Remembering Blue*, Connie May Fowler (Audio Literature)
- *The Edge*, Dick Francis (Clipper Audio)
- *Disobedience*, Jane Hamilton (BDD Audio)
- *Archangel*, Robert Harris (Chivers Audiobks)
- *Blood and Smoke*, Stephen King (S&S Audio)
- *The Drowning People*, Richard Mason (Chivers Audiobks)
- *Walkin' the Dog*, Walter Mosley (Books on Tape)
- *Horse Heaven*, Jane Smiley (Random Audio)
- *Mortal Sins*, Penn Williamson (Time Warner Audiobks)

Source: Burns, Ann, "Best Audiobooks of 2000," *Library Journal*, 126: 142-143, (March 15, 2001).

★242★
Library Journal's best mystery titles, 2000

Ranking basis/background: Alphabetical listing, by author, from *Library Journal*'s Best Genre Fiction of 2000 list as chosen by columnist Rex Klett. **Number listed:** 5.
- *Drumsticks*, by Charlotte Carter (published by Warner)
- *The Tidal Poole*, Karen Harper (Delacorte)
- *Blue Deer Thaw*, Jamie Harrison (Hyperion)
- *The Fifth Woman*, Henning Mankell (New Press)
- *Set in Darkness*, Ian Rankin (Minotaur: St. Martin's)

Source: Bryant, Eric, et. al., "Best Books of 2000," *Library Journal*, 126: 52-56, (January 2001).

★243★
Library Journal's best nonfiction audiobooks, 2000

Ranking basis/background: Alphabetical listing by author, as selected by *Library Journal*. **Number listed:** 12.
- *A Season on the Reservation: My Sojourn with the White Mountain Apache*, by Kareem Abdul-Jabbar (published by S&S Audio)
- *Squandering Aimlessly: My Adventures in the American Marketplace*, David Brancaccio (S&S Audio)
- *In a Sunburned Country*, Bill Bryson (BDD Audio)
- *Cronkite Remembers*, Walter Cronkite (S&S Audio)
- *American Rhapsody*, Joe Eszterhas (New Millennium Audio)
- *Martin Luther King: A Concise Biography*, Harry Harmer (ISIS Audio Bks)
- *Langston Hughes Reads*, Langston Hughes (Caedmon: HarperAudio)
- *The Camino: A Journey of the Spirit*, Shirley MacLaine (S&S Audio)
- *Actual Innocence: Five Days to Execution and Other Dispatches from the Wrongly Convicted*, Barry Scheck and other (BDD Audio)
- *Me Talk Pretty One Day*, David Sedaris (Time Warner Audiobks)
- *Return to Wholeness: Embracing Body, Mind, and Spirit in the Face of Cancer*, David Simon, M.D. (Wiley Audio)
- *Sosa: An Autobiography*, Sammy Sosa with Marcos Breton (Time Warner Audiobks)

Source: Burns, Ann, "Best Audiobooks of 2000," *Library Journal*, 126: 142-143, (March 15, 2001).

★244★
Library Journal's best poetry books, 2000

Ranking basis/background: Alphabetical list by author. **Number listed:** 11.
- *Tell Me*, by Kim Addonizio (published by BOA)
- *Men in the Off Hours*, Anne Carson (Knopf)
- *Blessing the Boats: New and Selected Poems, 1988-2000*, Lucille Clifton (BOA)
- *The Ledge*, Michael Collier (Houghton)
- *Some Ether*, Nick Flynn (Graywolf)
- *Carolina Ghost Woods*, Judy Jordan (Louisiana State Univ.)
- *The Collected Poems of Stanley Kunitz*, Stanley Kunitz (Norton)
- *Ultima Thule*, David McCombs (Yale Univ.)
- *Climbing Back*, Dionisio D. Martinez (Norton)
- *Supernatural Love: Poems 1976-1992*, Gjertrud Schnackenberg (Farrar)
- *The Cradle of the Real Life*, Jean Valentine (Wesleyan Univ.)

Source: Hoffert, Barbara, "Best Poetry of 2000," *Library Journal*, 126: 102-103, (April 15, 2001).

★245★
Library Journal's best romance titles, 2000

Ranking basis/background: Alphabetical listing, by author, from *Library Journal*'s Best Genre Fiction of 2000 list as chosen by columnist Kristin Ramsdell. **Number listed:** 5.
- *The Last Good Man*, by Kathleen Eagle (published by Avon: HarperCollins)
- *First Lady*, Susan Elizabeth Phillips (Avon: HarperCollins)
- *The Burning Point*, Mary Jo Putney (Berkley)
- *No Crystal Stair*, Eva Rutland (Mira: Harlequin)
- *In the Midnight Rain*, Ruth Wind (HarperCollins)

Source: Bryant, Eric, et. al., "Best Books of 2000," *Library Journal*, 126: 52-56, (January 2001).

★246★
Library Journal's best science fiction and fantasy titles, 2000

Ranking basis/background: Alphabetical listing, by author, from *Library Journal*'s Best Genre Fiction of 2000 list as chosen by columnist Jackie Cassada. **Number listed:** 5.
- *Dark Matter*, edited by Sheree R. Thomas (published by Warner)
- *Dune: House Harkonnen*, by Brian Herbert and Kevin J. Anderson (Spectra: Bantam)
- *The Telling*, Ursula Le Guin (Harcourt)
- *Prospero's Children*, Jan Siegel (Del Rey: Ballantine)
- *Wheel of the Infinite*, Martha Wells (Avon: HarperCollins)

Source: Bryant, Eric, et. al., "Best Books of 2000," *Library Journal*, 126: 52-56, (January 2001).

★247★
Library Journal's most notable anthropology books, 2000

Ranking basis/background: As recommended by *Library Journal*'s list of 2000's Best Sci-Tech Books. **Number listed:** 1.
- *Darkness in El Dorado: How Scientists and Journalist Devastated the Amazon*, by Patrick Tierney (published by Norton)

Source: Sapp, Gregg, "Making Science Personal," *Library Journal*, 126: 46-48, (March 1, 2001).

★248★
Library Journal's most notable astronomy books, 2000

Ranking basis/background: As recommended by *Library Journal*'s list of 2000's Best Sci-Tech Books. **Number listed:** 2.

- *Einstein's Unfinished Symphony: Listening to the Sounds of Space-Time*, by Marcia Bartusiak (published by Joseph Henry Press)
- *Just Six Numbers: The Deep Forces That Shape Our Universe*, Martin Rees (Basic Bks: Perseus)

Source: Sapp, Gregg, "Making Science Personal," *Library Journal*, 126: 46-48, (March 1, 2001).

★249★
Library Journal's most notable biography books, 2000

Ranking basis/background: As recommended by *Library Journal*'s list of 2000's Best Business Books. **Number listed:** 4.

- *The Leap: A Memoir of Love and Madness in the Internet Gold Rush*, by Tom Ashbrook (published by Houghton)
- *The Millionaire Mind*, Thomas J. Stanley (Andrews McMeel)
- *Maestro: Greenspan's Fed and the American Boom*, Bob Woodward (S&S)
- *From Third World to First: The Singapore Story 1965-2000*, Le Kuan Yew (HarperCollins)

Source: Awe, Susan C., "Getting Our Dot-Com-Uppance?," *Library Journal*, 126: 42-45, (March 15, 2001).

★250★
Library Journal's most notable biology books, 2000

Ranking basis/background: As recommended by *Library Journal*'s list of 2000's Best Sci-Tech Books. **Number listed:** 2.

- *Darwin's Ghost: "The Origin of Species" Updated*, by Steve Jones (published by Random)
- *The Variety of Life: A Survey and a Celebration of All the Creatures That Have Ever Lived*, Colin Tudge (Oxford Univ.)

Source: Sapp, Gregg, "Making Science Personal," *Library Journal*, 126: 46-48, (March 1, 2001).

★251★
Library Journal's most notable books about entrepreneurship, 2000

Ranking basis/background: As recommended by *Library Journal*'s list of 2000's Best Business Books. **Number listed:** 2.

- *Start Small, Finish Big: Fifteen Key Lessons to Start-and Run-Your Own Successful Business*, by Fred DeLuca with John P. Hayes (published by Warner)
- *Entrepreneur America: Lessons from Inside Bob Ryan's High-Tech Start-Up boot Camp*, Rob Ryan (HarperBusiness:HarperCollins)

Source: Awe, Susan C., "Getting Our Dot-Com-Uppance?," *Library Journal*, 126: 42-45, (March 15, 2001).

★252★
Library Journal's most notable books about venture capital, 2000

Ranking basis/background: As recommended by *Library Journal*'s list of 2000's Best Business Books. **Number listed:** 2.

- *Done Deals: Venture Capitalists Tell Their Stories*, (published by Harvard Business Sch.)
- *eBoys: The First Inside Account of Venture Capitalists at Work*, by Randall E. Stross (Crown)

Source: Awe, Susan C., "Getting Our Dot-Com-Uppance?," *Library Journal*, 126: 42-45, (March 15, 2001).

★253★
Library Journal's most notable books on capitalism, 2000

Ranking basis/background: As recommended by *Library Journal*'s list of 2000's Best Business Books. **Number listed:** 2.

- *The Electronic B@zaar: From the Silk Road to the eRoad*, by Robin Bloor (published by Nicholas Brealey)
- *The Mystery of Capital*, Hernando de Soto (Basic Bks: Perseus)

Source: Awe, Susan C., "Getting Our Dot-Com-Uppance?," *Library Journal*, 126: 42-45, (March 15, 2001).

★254★
Library Journal's most notable books on job performance, 2000

Ranking basis/background: As recommended by *Library Journal*'s list of 2000's Best Business Books. **Number listed:** 2.

- *Play Like a Man, Win Like a Woman*, by Gail Evans (published by Broadway)
- *The Secret Handshake: Mastering the Politics of the Business Inner Circle*, Kathleen Kelley Reardon (Currency Bks)

Source: Awe, Susan C., "Getting Our Dot-Com-Uppance?," *Library Journal*, 126: 42-45, (March 15, 2001).

★255★
Library Journal's most notable computer science books, 2000

Ranking basis/background: As recommended by *Library Journal*'s list of 2000's Best Sci-Tech Books. **Number listed:** 1.

- *The Advent of the Algorithm: The Idea That Rules the World*, by David Berlinski (published by Harcourt)

Source: Sapp, Gregg, "Making Science Personal," *Library Journal*, 126: 46-48, (March 1, 2001).

★256★
Library Journal's most notable digital technology books, 2000

Ranking basis/background: As recommended by *Library Journal*'s list of 2000's Best Business Books. **Number listed:** 4.

- *Trust and Risk in Internet Commerce*, by L. Jean Camp (published by MIT)
- *The Cluetrain Manifesto*, Rick Levine and others (Perseus)
- *Immutable Laws of Internet Branding*, Al Ries and Laura Ries (HarperBusiness: HarperCollins)
- *How Digital Is Your Business?*, Adrian J. Slywotzky and David J. Morrison (Crown)

Source: Awe, Susan C., "Getting Our Dot-Com-Uppance?," *Library Journal*, 126: 42-45, (March 15, 2001).

★257★
Library Journal's most notable earth sciences books, 2000

Ranking basis/background: As recommended by *Library Journal*'s list of 2000's Best Sci-Tech Books. **Number listed:** 1.

- *Volcano Cowboys: The Rocky Evolution of a Dangerous Science*, by Dick Thompson (published by Thomas Dunne Bks: St. Martin's)

Source: Sapp, Gregg, "Making Science Personal," *Library Journal*, 126: 46-48, (March 1, 2001).

★258★
Library Journal's most notable entomology books, 2000

Ranking basis/background: As recommended by *Library Journal*'s list of 2000's Best Sci-Tech Books. **Number listed:** 1.

- *Buzzwords: A Scientist Muses on Sex, Bugs, and Rock 'n' Roll*, by May R. Berenbaum (published by Joseph Henry Pr.)

Source: Sapp, Gregg, "Making Science Personal," *Library Journal*, 126: 46-48, (March 1, 2001).

★259★
Library Journal's most notable environmental sciences books, 2000

Ranking basis/background: As recommended by *Library Journal*'s list of 2000's Best Sci-Tech Books. **Number listed:** 1.

- *Something New Under the Sun: An Environmental History of the Twentieth Century World*, by J.R. McNeill (published by Norton)

Source: Sapp, Gregg, "Making Science Personal," *Library Journal*, 126: 46-48, (March 1, 2001).

★260★
Library Journal's most notable general science books, 2000

Ranking basis/background: As recommended by *Library Journal*'s list of 2000's Best Sci-Tech Books. **Number listed:** 3.

- *The Best American Science and Nature Writing, 2000*, (published by Houghton)
- *Defenders of the Truth: The Battle for Science in the Sociobiology Debate and Beyond*, by Ullica Segerstale (Oxford Univ.)
- *Nonzero: The Logic of Human Destiny*, Robert Wright (Pantheon)

Source: Sapp, Gregg, "Making Science Personal," *Library Journal*, 126: 46-48, (March 1, 2001).

★261★
Library Journal's most notable genetics books, 2000

Ranking basis/background: As recommended by *Library Journal*'s list of 2000's Best Sci-Tech Books. **Number listed:** 1.

- *Genome: The Autobiography of a Species in 23 Chapters*, by Matt Ridley (published by HarperCollins)

Source: Sapp, Gregg, "Making Science Personal," *Library Journal*, 126: 46-48, (March 1, 2001).

★262★
Library Journal's most notable health sciences books, 2000
Ranking basis/background: As recommended by *Library Journal*'s list of 2000's Best Sci-Tech Books. **Number listed:** 3.
- *AIDS Doctors: Voices from the Epidemic*, by Ronald Bayer and Gerald Oppenheimer (published by Oxford Univ.)
- *Betrayal of Trust: The Collapse of Global Public Health*, Laurie Garrett (Hyperion)
- *The Mysteries Within: A Surgeon Reflects on Medical Myths*, Sherwin Nuland (S&S)

Source: Sapp, Gregg, "Making Science Personal," *Library Journal*, 126: 46-48, (March 1, 2001).

★263★
Library Journal's most notable history of science books, 2000
Ranking basis/background: As recommended by *Library Journal*'s list of 2000's Best Sci-Tech Books. **Number listed:** 2.
- *Atomic Fragments: A Daughter's Questions*, by Mary Palevsky (published by Univ. of California)
- *A Rum Affair: A True Story of Botanical Fraud*, Karl Sabbagh (Farrar)

Source: Sapp, Gregg, "Making Science Personal," *Library Journal*, 126: 46-48, (March 1, 2001).

★264★
Library Journal's most notable investing books, 2000
Ranking basis/background: As recommended by *Library Journal*'s list of 2000's Best Business Books. **Number listed:** 8.
- *Multiple Streams of Income*, by Robert G. Allen (published by Wiley)
- *The Power of Gold: The History of an Obsession*, Peter L. Bernstein (Wiley)
- *John Bogle on Investing*, John C. Bogle (McGraw-Hill)
- *Investment Titans*, Jonathan Burton (McGraw-Hill)
- *On Money and Markets: A Wall Street Memoir*, Henry Kaufman (McGraw-Hill)
- *When Genius Failed: The Rise and Fall of Long-Term Capital Management*, Roger Lowenstein (Random)
- *Irrational Exuberance*, Robert J. Shiller (Princeton Univ.)
- *How to Pick Stocks Like Warren Buffett*, Timothy Vick (McGraw-Hill)

Source: Awe, Susan C., "Getting Our Dot-Com-Uppance?," *Library Journal*, 126: 42-45, (March 15, 2001).

★265★
Library Journal's most notable management books, 2000
Ranking basis/background: As recommended by *Library Journal*'s list of 2000's Best Business Books. **Number listed:** 7.
- *Managing Six Sigma*, by Forrest W. Breyfogle, III (published by Wiley)
- *Global Codes of Conduct*, (Univ. of Notre Dame)
- *Leading the Revolution*, Gary Hamel (Harvard Business Sch.)
- *The Strategy-Focused Organization*, Robert S. Kaplan and David P. Norton (Harvard Business Sch.)
- *Living on the Fault Line: Managing for Shareholder Value in the Age of the Internet*, Geoffrey A. Moore (HarperBusiness: HarperCollins)
- *The Six Sigma Way*, Peter S. Pande and others (McGraw-Hill)
- *Hidden Value: How Great Companies Achieve Extraordinary Results with Ordinary People*, Jeffrey Pfeffer and Charles A. O'Reilly (Harvard Business Sch.)

Source: Awe, Susan C., "Getting Our Dot-Com-Uppance?," *Library Journal*, 126: 42-45, (March 15, 2001).

★266★
Library Journal's most notable mathematics books, 2000
Ranking basis/background: As recommended by *Library Journal*'s list of 2000's Best Sci-Tech Books. **Number listed:** 1.
- *The Math Gene: How Mathematical Thinking Evolved and Why Number Are Like Gossip*, by Keith Devlin (published by Basic Bks: Perseus)

Source: Sapp, Gregg, "Making Science Personal," *Library Journal*, 126: 46-48, (March 1, 2001).

★267★
Library Journal's most notable meteorology books, 2000
Ranking basis/background: As recommended by *Library Journal*'s list of 2000's Best Sci-Tech Books. **Number listed:** 1.
- *Tying Down the Wind: Adventures in the Worst Weather on Earth*, by Eric Pinder (published by Tarcher)

Source: Sapp, Gregg, "Making Science Personal," *Library Journal*, 126: 46-48, (March 1, 2001).

★268★
Library Journal's most notable microbiology books, 2000
Ranking basis/background: As recommended by *Library Journal*'s list of 2000's Best Sci-Tech Books. **Number listed:** 1.
- *Parasite Rex: Inside the Bizarre World of Nature's Most Dangerous Creatures*, by Carl Zimmer (published by Free Press)

Source: Sapp, Gregg, "Making Science Personal," *Library Journal*, 126: 46-48, (March 1, 2001).

★269★
Library Journal's most notable natural history books, 2000
Ranking basis/background: As recommended by *Library Journal*'s list of 2000's Best Sci-Tech Books. **Number listed:** 2.
- *Water: The Fate of Our Most Precious Resource*, by Marq de Villiers (published by Houghton)
- *The Eighth Continent: Life, Death, and Discovery in the Lost World of Madagascar*, Peter Tyson (Morrow)

Source: Sapp, Gregg, "Making Science Personal," *Library Journal*, 126: 46-48, (March 1, 2001).

★270★
Library Journal's most notable neurology books, 2000
Ranking basis/background: As recommended by *Library Journal*'s list of 2000's Best Sci-Tech Books. **Number listed:** 1.
- *Why We Hurt: The Natural History of Pain*, by Frank T. Vertosick Jr., M.D. (published by Harcourt)

Source: Sapp, Gregg, "Making Science Personal," *Library Journal*, 126: 46-48, (March 1, 2001).

★271★
Library Journal's most notable new economy books, 2000
Ranking basis/background: As recommended by *Library Journal*'s list of 2000's Best Business Books. **Number listed:** 3.
- *The Coming Internet*, by Michael J. Mandel (published by Basic Bks: Perseus)
- *Surfing the Edge of Chaos*, Richard T. Pascale and others (Crown)
- *Clicks and Mortar*, David S. Pottruck and Terry Pearce (Jossey-Bass)

Source: Awe, Susan C., "Getting Our Dot-Com-Uppance?," *Library Journal*, 126: 42-45, (March 15, 2001).

★272★
Library Journal's most notable oceanography books, 2000
Ranking basis/background: As recommended by *Library Journal*'s list of 2000's Best Sci-Tech Books. **Number listed:** 1.
- *The Eternal Darkness: A Personal History of Deep Sea Exploration*, by Robert D. Ballard (published by Princeton Univ.)

Source: Sapp, Gregg, "Making Science Personal," *Library Journal*, 126: 46-48, (March 1, 2001).

★273★
Library Journal's most notable paleontology books, 2000
Ranking basis/background: As recommended by *Library Journal*'s list of 2000's Best Sci-Tech Books. **Number listed:** 2.
- *Trilobite!: Eyewitness to Evolution*, by Richard Fortey (published by Knopf)
- *Extinct Humans*, Ian Tattersall and Jeffrey Schwartz (Westview)

Source: Sapp, Gregg, "Making Science Personal," *Library Journal*, 126: 46-48, (March 1, 2001).

★274★
Library Journal's most notable physics books, 2000
Ranking basis/background: As recommended by *Library Journal*'s list of 2000's Best Sci-Tech Books. **Number listed:** 2.
- *E=mc2: A Biography of the World's Most Famous Equation*, by David Bodanis (published by Walker)
- *Lucifer's Legacy: The Meaning of Asymmetry*, Frank Close (Oxford Univ.)

Source: Sapp, Gregg, "Making Science Personal," *Library Journal*, 126: 46-48, (March 1, 2001).

★275★
Library Journal's most notable psychology books, 2000
Ranking basis/background: As recommended by *Library Journal*'s list of 2000's Best Sci-Tech Books. **Number listed:** 1.
- *Defending the Cavewoman: And Other Tales of Clinical Neurology*, by Harold Klawans, M.D. (published by Norton)

Source: Sapp, Gregg, "Making Science Personal," *Library Journal*, 126: 46-48, (March 1, 2001).

★276★
Library Journal's most notable scientific biography books, 2000

Ranking basis/background: As recommended by *Library Journal*'s list of 2000's Best Sci-Tech Books. **Number listed:** 1.

The Monk in the Garden: The Lost and Found Genius of Gregor Mendel, the Father of Genetics, by Robin Marantz Henig (published by Houghton)

Source: Sapp, Gregg, "Making Science Personal," *Library Journal*, 126: 46-48, (March 1, 2001).

★277★
Library Journal's most notable technology books, 2000

Ranking basis/background: As recommended by *Library Journal*'s list of 2000's Best Sci-Tech Books. **Number listed:** 2.

Robo Sapiens: Evolution of a New Species, by Peter Menzel and Faith D'Aluisio (published by MIT Press)

One Good Turn: A Natural History of the Screwdriver and the Screw, Witold Rybcynski (Scribner)

Source: Sapp, Gregg, "Making Science Personal," *Library Journal*, 126: 46-48, (March 1, 2001).

★278★
Library Journal's most notable zoology books, 2000

Ranking basis/background: As recommended by *Library Journal*'s list of 2000's Best Sci-Tech Books. **Number listed:** 3.

Hope Is the Thing with Feathers: A Personal Chronicle of Vanished Birds, by Christopher Cokins (published by Tarcher)

Wild Minds: What Animals Really Think, Marc D. Hauser (Holt)

A Fish Caught in Time: The Search for the Coelacanth, Samantha Weinberg (HarperCollins)

Source: Sapp, Gregg, "Making Science Personal," *Library Journal*, 126: 46-48, (March 1, 2001).

★279★
Longest-running fiction hardcover bestsellers, 2000

Ranking basis/background: Number of weeks on *Publishers Weekly*'s 2000 list. **Number listed:** 4.
1. *The Brethren*, by John Grisham (published by Doubleday), with 30 weeks
2. *Timeline*, Michael Crichton (Knopf), 17
3. *The Lion's Game*, Nelson DeMille (Warner), 16
3. *The Bear and the Dragon*, Tom Clancy (Putnam), 16

Source: Maryles, Daisy, "Who's Topping the Charts?," *Publishers Weekly*, 249: 36-39, (January 8, 2001).

★280★
Longest-running mass market paperback bestsellers, 2000

Ranking basis/background: Number of weeks on *Publishers Weekly*'s 2000 list. **Number listed:** 7.
1. *Dr. Atkins' New Diet Revolution*, by Robert C. Atkins, M.D. (published by Avon), with 51 weeks
2. *The Testament*, John Grisham (Dell Island), 28
3. *The Cider House Rules*, John Irving (Ballantine), 20
4. *The Saving Graces*, Patricia Gaffney (HarperPaperbacks), 19
5. *The Perfect Storm*, Sebastian Junger (HarperPaperbacks), 18
6. *Angela's Ashes*, Frank McCourt (Simon & Schuster/Touchstone), 16
7. *The Carbohydrate Addict's Diet*, Dr. Richard Heller and Dr. Rachael Heller (Signet), 15

Source: Maryles, Daisy, "Who's Topping the Charts?," *Publishers Weekly*, 249: 36-39, (January 8, 2001).

★281★
Longest-running nonfiction hardcover bestsellers, 2000

Ranking basis/background: Number of weeks on *Publishers Weekly*'s 2000 list. **Number listed:** 16.
1. *Tuesdays with Morrie*, by Mitch Albom (published by Doubleday), with 51 weeks
1. *Who Moved My Cheese?*, Spencer Johnson (Putnam), 51
3. *Body for Life*, Bill Phillips and Michael D'Orso (HarperCollins), 50
4. *Relationship Rescue*, Phillip C. McGraw (Hyperion), 33
5. *Flags of Our Fathers*, James Bradley with Ron Powers (Bantam), 25
6. *It's Not About the Bike: My Journey Back to Life*, Lance Armstrong (Putnam), 23
7. *Ten Things I Wish I'd Known-Before I Went Out into the Real World*, Maria Shriver (Warner), 21
8. *The Greatest Generation*, Tom Brokaw (Random House), 20
9. *Sugar Busters!*, H. L. Steward, M. C. Bethea, S. S. Andrews and L. A. Balart (Ballantine), 19
10. *'Tis*, Frank McCourt (Scribner), 17
10. *The Rock Says*, The Rock with Joe Layden (ReganBooks), 17
10. *Eating Well for Optimum Health*, Andrew Weil, M.D. (Knopf), 17
13. *The Millionaire Mind*, Thomas J. Stanley (Andrews McMeel), 15
13. *How to Know God*, Deepak Chopra (Harmony), 15
13. *Nothing Like It in the World*, Stephen E. Ambrose (Simon & Schuster), 15
13. *Guinness World Records 2001* (Guinness Publishing), 15

Source: Maryles, Daisy, "Who's Topping the Charts?," *Publishers Weekly*, 249: 36-39, (January 8, 2001).

★282★
Longest-running trade paperback bestsellers, 2000

Ranking basis/background: Number of weeks on *Publishers Weekly*'s 2000 list. **Number listed:** 18.
1. *The Poisonwood Bible*, by Barbara Kingsolver (published by HarperPerennial), with 49 weeks
2. *The Seat of the Soul*, Gary Zukav (Simon & Schuster/Fireside), 47
3. *Rich Dad Poor Dad*, Robert T. Kiyosaki with Sharon Lechter (Warner), 33
3. *The Four Agreements*, Don Miguel Ruiz (Amber-Allen), 33
5. *The Hours*, Michael Cunningham (Picador), 32
6. *While I Was Gone*, Sue Miller (Ballantine), 30
7. *Where the Heart Is*, Billie Letts (Warner), 24
8. *A Child Called "It"*, Dave Pelzer (Health Communications), 22
8. *Girl, Interrupted*, Susanna Kaysen (Vintage), 22
10. *Life Strategies*, Phillip C. McGraw (Hyperion), 21
10. *The Girls' Guide to Hunting and Fishing*, Melissa Bank (Penguin), 21
12. *Take Time for Your Life*, Cheryl Richardson (Broadway), 20
13. *Memoirs of a Geisha*, Arthur Golden (Vintage), 18
13. *Left Behind*, Tim LaHaye and Jerry B. Jenkins (Tyndale House), 18
13. *Chicken Soup for the Teenage Soul III*, J. Canfield, M. V. Hansen and K. Kirberger (Health Communications), 18
13. *The Red Tent*, Anita Diamant (Picador), 18
17. *Plainsong*, Kent Haruf (Vintage), 16
18. *The Bluest Eye*, Toni Morrison (Plume), 15

Source: Maryles, Daisy, "Who's Topping the Charts?," *Publishers Weekly*, 249: 36-39, (January 8, 2001).

★283★
Mass market paperback bestsellers by publishing house, 2000

Ranking basis/background: Number of books and number of weeks on *Publishers Weekly*'s 2000 list. **Number listed:** 28.
1. Pocket Books, with 21 books; and 85 weeks
2. Berkley, 18; 101
3. Bantam, 14; 53
3. Jove, 14; 46
5. Dell, 12; 56
6. Avon, 11; 74
7. HarperPaperbacks, 9; 57
8. Warner, 8; 54
9. Ballantine, 7; 50
10. Signet, 6; 31

Source: Maryles, Daisy, "Who's Topping the Charts?," *Publishers Weekly*, 249: 36-39, (January 8, 2001).

★284★
Most notable fiction books, 2001

Ranking basis/background: Alphabetical list by author, compiled by the Notable Books Council, ALA Reference and User Services Association. Titles selected were published from November 1999 through October 2000 and show wide general appeal and literary merit. **Number listed:** 14.

The Blind Assassin, by Margaret Atwood (published by Doubleday/Nan)

Don't Tell Anyone, Frederick Busch (Norton)

The Amazing Adventures of Kavalier and Clay, Michael Chabon (Random)

Disgrace, J.M. Coetzee (Viking)

Being Dead, Jim Crace (Farrar)

The Last Samurai, Helen DeWitt (Hyperion/Talk Miramax)

The Delinquent Virgin, Laura Kalpakian (Graywolf)

Truth and Bright Water, Thomas King (Atlantic Monthly)

English Passengers, Matthew Kneale (Doubleday/Nan)

Living to Tell, Antonya Nelson (Scribner)

Anil's Ghost, Michael Ondaatje (Knopf)

Scar Vegas, Tom Paine (Harcourt)

White Teeth, Zadie Smith (Random)

The Quick and the Dead, Joy Williams (Knopf)
Source: ALA's 2001 "Best" Lists, *Booklist*, 97: 1362-1388, (March 15, 2001).

★285★
Most notable nonfiction books, 2001

Ranking basis/background: Alphabetical list by author, compiled by the Notable Books Council, ALA Reference and User Services Association. Titles selected were published from November 1999 through October 2000 and show wide general appeal and literary merit. **Number listed:** 8.

From Dawn to Decadence: 500 Years of Western Cultural Life, 1500 to the Present, by Jacques Barzun (published by HarperCollins)
A Heartbreaking Work of Staggering Genius, Dave Eggers (Simon & Schuster)
Barrow's Boys, Fergus Fleming (Atlantic Monthly)
The Collaborator: The Trial and Execution of Robert Brasillach, Alice Yaeger Kaplan (University of Chicago)
Genome: The Autobiography of a Species in 23 Chapters, Matt Ridley (HarperCollins)
Persian Mirrors: The Elusive Face of Iran, Elaine Sciolino (Free Press)
Bruce Chatwin, Nicholas Shakespeare (Doubleday/Nan)
In Siberia, Colin Thubron (HarperCollins)
Source: ALA's 2001 "Best" Lists, *Booklist*, 97: 1362-1388, (March 15, 2001).

★286★
Outstanding arts and literature books, 2000

Ranking basis/background: Alphabetical listing, by author, of the year's outstanding books for public-library collections. Choices are those that combine literary, intellectual, and aesthetic excellence with popular appeal. **Number listed:** 6.

Brunelleschi's Dome: How a Renaissance Genius Reinvented Architecture, by Ross King (published by Walker)
The Complete Jacob Lawrence, Peter T. Nesbitt and Michelle DuBois (University of Washington)
Letters from the Editor: The New Yorker's Harold Ross, Harold Ross (Random)
In Search of Moby Dick: The Quest for the Great White Whale, Tim Severin (Basic)
Van Gogh and Gauguin: The Search for Sacred Art, Deborah Silverman (Farrar)
Another Beauty, Adam Zagajewski (Farrar)
Source: "Editor's Choice 2000," *Booklist*, 97: 850-868, (January 1 & 15, 2001).

★287★
Outstanding audiobooks, 2000

Ranking basis/background: Alphabetical listing of the year's outstanding audiobooks for public-library collections. **Number listed:** 13.

Carnal Innocence, written by Nora Roberts; read by Tom Stechschulte (produced by Recorded Books)
Children of the River, Linda Crewe; Christina Moore (Recorded Books)
Fight Club, Chuck Palahniuk; J. Todd Adams (Highbridge)
Harry Potter and the Goblet of Fire, J.K. Rowling; Jim Dale (Listening Library)
In a Sunburned Country, Bill Bryson; read by the author (BDD)
Joey Pigza Swallowed the Key, Jack Gantos; read by the author (Listening Library)
King of the Dragons, Carol Fenner; Alan Ruck (Listening Library)
The Legend of Sleepy Hollow, Washington Irving; St. Charles Players (Monterey SoundWorks)
Lord Emsworth and Others, P.G. Wodenhouse; Nigel Lambert (Chivers)
The Picture of Dorian Gray, Oscar Wilde; Simon Callow (Trafalgar Square)
Rebecca, Daphne Du Maurier; Anna Massey (Audio Partners)
Snow Falling on Cedars, David Gusterson; Peter Marinker (Random House)
The Trolls, Polly Horvath; Julie Hagerty (Listening Library)
Source: "Editor's Choice 2000," *Booklist*, 97: 850-868, (January 1 & 15, 2001).

★288★
Outstanding biography books, 2000

Ranking basis/background: Alphabetical listing, by author, of the year's outstanding books for public-library collections. Choices are those that combine literary, intellectual, and aesthetic excellence with popular appeal. **Number listed:** 20.

Where Did It All Go Right?, by A. Alvarez (published by Morrow)
Bellow, James Atlas (Random)
Oscar Wilde: A Certain Genius, Barbara Belford (Random)
Hirohito and the Making of Modern Japan, Herbert Bix (HarperCollins)
My Mother's Ghost, Fergus Bordewich (Doubleday)
Marcel Proust, William C. Carter (Yale)
Ho Chi Minh, William J. Duiker (Hyperion)
Georgiana: Duchess of Devonshire, Amanda Foreman (Random)
Hitler, 1936-1945: Nemesis, Ian Kershaw (Norton)
The Happy Bottom Riding Club: The Life and Times of Pancho Barnes, Lauren Kessler (Random)
Marie Antoinette: The Last Queen of France, Evelyne Lever (Farrar)
W.E.B. DuBois: The Fight for Equality and the American Century, 1919-63, David Levering Lewis (Holt/John Macrae)
Lincoln: A Foreigner's Quest, Jan Morris (Simon & Schuster)
The Last Man Standing: The Tragedy and Triumph of Geronimo Pratt, Jack Olsen (Doubleday)
Dances with Luigi: A Grandson's Determined Quest to Comprehend Italy and the Italians, Paul Paolicelli (St. Martin's/Thomas Dunne)
Rimbaud, Graham Robb (Norton)
A Life in the Twentieth Century: Innocent Beginnings, 1917-1950, Arthur M. Schlesinger (Houghton)
Bruce Chatwin, Nicholas Shakespeare (Doubleday/Nan A. Talese)
Chief Buffalo Child Long Lance: The Glorious Impostor, Donald B. Smith (Red Deer)
The Circle of Hanh, Bruce Weigl (Grove)
Source: "Editor's Choice 2000," *Booklist*, 97: 850-868, (January 1 & 15, 2001).

★289★
Outstanding history books, 2000

Ranking basis/background: Alphabetical listing, by author, of the year's outstanding books for public-library collections. Choices are those that combine literary, intellectual, and aesthetic excellence with popular appeal. **Number listed:** 9.

Crucible of War: The Seven Years' War and the Faith of Empire in British North America, by Fred Anderson (published by Knopf)
The Battle for God, Karen Armstrong (Knopf)
From Dawn to Decadence: 500 Years of Western Cultural Life, 1500 to the Present, Jacques Barzun (HarperCollins)
In a Sunburned Country, Bill Bryson (Broadway)
The Great Arc: The Dramatic Tale of How India Was Mapped and Everest Was Named, John Keay (HarperCollins)
The Blood Runs like a River through My Dreams: A Memoir, Nasdijj (Houghton)
In the Heart of the Sea: The Tragedy of the Whaleship Essex, Nathaniel Philbrick (Viking)
First They Killed My Father: A Daughter of Cambodia Remembers, Loung Ung (HarperCollins)
Leap, Terry Tempest Williams (Pantheon)
Source: "Editor's Choice 2000," *Booklist*, 97: 850-868, (January 1 & 15, 2001).

★290★
Outstanding poetry books, 2000

Ranking basis/background: Alphabetical listing, by author, of the year's outstanding books for public-library collections. Choices are those that combine literary, intellectual, and aesthetic excellence with popular appeal. **Number listed:** 2.

Swarm, by Jorie Graham (published by Ecco)
Cool, Calm & Collected: Poems, 1960-2000, Carolyn Kizer (Copper Canyon)
Source: "Editor's Choice 2000," *Booklist*, 97: 850-868, (January 1 & 15, 2001).

★291★
Outstanding science books, 2000

Ranking basis/background: Alphabetical listing, by author, of the year's outstanding books for public-library collections. Choices are those that combine literary, intellectual, and aesthetic excellence with popular appeal. **Number listed:** 5.

The Advent of the Algorithm: The Idea That Rules the World, by David Berlinski (Harcourt)
Journey of the Pink Dolphins: An Amazon Quest, Sy Montgomery (Simon & Schuster)
The Mysteries Within: A Surgeon Reflects on Medical Myths, Sherwin B. Nuland (Simon & Schuster)
Genome: The Autobiography of a Species in 23 Chapters, Matt Ridley (HarperCollins)
The Variety of Life: The Meaning of Biodiversity, Colin Tudge (Oxford)
Source: "Editor's Choice 2000," *Booklist*, 97: 850-868, (January 1 & 15, 2001).

BOOKS

★292★
Outstanding social sciences books, 2000

Ranking basis/background: Alphabetical listing, by author, of the year's outstanding books for public-library collections. Choices are those that combine literary, intellectual, and aesthetic excellence with popular appeal. **Number listed:** 6.

God's Name in Vain: The Wrongs and Rights of Religion in Politics, by Stephen L. Carter (published by Basic)
I May Not Get There with You: The True Martin Luther King, Jr, Michael Eric Dyson (Free Press)
Betrayal of Trust: The Collapse of Global Public Health, Laurie Garrett (Hyperion)
Homecoming: The Story of African-American Farmers, Charlene Gilbert and Quinn Eli (Beacon)
Ordinary Resurrections: Children in the Years of Hope, Jonathan Kozol (Crown)
The Debt: What America Owes to Blacks, Randall Robinson (Dutton)

Source: "Editor's Choice 2000," *Booklist*, 97: 850-868, (January 1 & 15, 2001).

★293★
Outstanding works of fiction, 2001

Ranking basis/background: Titles published from November 1999 through October 2000 that show wide general appeal and literary merit, as selected by the Reference and User Services Association, a division of the American Library Association. **Number listed:** 14.

The Blind Assassin, by Margaret Atwood (published by Random House)
Don't Tell Anyone, Frederick Busch (Norton)
The Amazing Adventures of Kavalier and Clay, Michael Chabon (Random House)
Disgrace, J.M. Coetzee (Viking)
Being Dead, Jim Crace (Farrar Straus & Giroux)
The Last Samurai, Helen DeWitt (Hyperion)
The Delinquent Virgin, Laura Kalpakian (Graywolf)
Truth and Bright Water, Thomas King (Atlantic Monthly)
English Passengers, Matthew Kneale (Nan A. Talese)
Living to Tell, Antonya Nelson (Scribner)
Anil's Ghost, Michael Ondaatje (Knopf)
Scar Vegas, Tom Paine (Harcourt)
White Teeth, Zadie Smith (Random House)
The Quick and the Dead, Joy Williams (Knopf)

Source: "American Library Association Notable Books 2001," *Reference & User Services Quarterly*, 40: 251-252, (Spring 2001).

★294★
Outstanding works of nonfiction, 2001

Ranking basis/background: Titles published from November 1999 through October 2000 that show wide general appeal and literary merit, as selected by the Reference and User Services Association, a division of the American Library Association. **Number listed:** 8.

From Dawn to Decadence: 500 Years of Western Cultural Life, 1500 to the Present, by Jacques Barzun (published by HarperCollins)
A Heartbreaking Work of Staggering Genius, Dave Eggers (Simon & Schuster)
Barrow's Boys, Fergus Fleming (Atlantic Monthly)
The Collaborator: The Trial and Execution of Robert Brasillach, Alice Yaeger Kaplan (Univ. of Chicago)
Genome: The Autobiography of a Species in 23 Chapters, Matt Ridley (HarperCollins)
Persian Mirrors: The Elusive Face of Iran, Elaine Sciolino (Free Press)
Bruce Chatwin, Nicholas Shakespeare (Nan A. Talese)
In Siberia, Colin Thubron (HarperCollins)

Source: "American Library Association Notable Books 2001," *Reference & User Services Quarterly*, 40: 251-252, (Spring 2001).

★295★
Outstanding works of poetry, 2001

Ranking basis/background: Titles published from November 1999 through October 2000 that show wide general appeal and literary merit, as selected by the Reference and User Services Association, a division of the American Library Association. **Number listed:** 3.

Beowulf, by Seamus Heaney (published by Farrar Straus & Giroux)
Collected Poems, Stanley Kunitz (Norton)
Learning Human: Selected Poems, Les Murray (Farrar Straus & Giroux)

Source: "American Library Association Notable Books 2001," *Reference & User Services Quarterly*, 40: 251-252, (Spring 2001).

★296★
Paperback bestsellers by corporation, 2000

Ranking basis/background: Number of books and number of weeks on *Publishers Weekly*'s 2000 list. Also includes publisher's share of the 1530 hardcover or paperback bestseller positions during 2000. **Number listed:** 10.

1. Random House, with 55 books; and 377 weeks
2. Penguin Putnam Inc., 49; 266
3. Simon & Schuster, 31; 196
4. HarperCollins, 29; 216
5. Time Warner, 15; 153
6. Health Communications, 12; 63
7. Von Holtzbrinck, 9; 77
8. Silhouette, 9; 37
9. Tyndale, 4; 39
9. Hyperion, 4; 35

Source: Maryles, Daisy, "Who's Topping the Charts?," *Publishers Weekly*, 249: 36-39, (January 8, 2001).

★297★
Percentage change of libraries purchasing how-to books

Ranking basis/background: Percentage of change in libraries buying specific how-to books. **Remarks:** Original source: *Library Journal* Book Buying Survey, 2001. **Number listed:** 3.

1. Home improvement titles, 72% increase
2. Arts and crafts titles, 62% increase
3. Knitting, sewing and crocheting titles, 31% decrease

Source: Hoffert, Barbara, "Book Report 2001: The Budget Shifts," *Library Journal*, 126: 130-132, (February 15, 2001).

★298★
Percentage of libraries purchasing e-books, by population served

Ranking basis/background: Percentage of libraries buying and mean amount spent on e-books for each population served. **Remarks:** Original source: *Library Journal* Book Buying Survey, 2001. **Number listed:** 8.

Under 10,000, with 22% of libraries buying; mean amount spent of $350
10,000-24,999, 21%; $626
25,000-49,999, 33%; $833
50,000-99,999, 33%; $1,000
100,000-249,999, 25%; $3,433
250,000-499,999, 18%; $2,575
500,000-999,999, 62%; $14,971
1 million and up, 55%; $6,850

Source: Hoffert, Barbara, "Book Report 2001: The Budget Shifts," *Library Journal*, 126: 130-132, (February 15, 2001).

★299★
Projected annual revenue for e-books

Ranking basis/background: Estimated figures, in billions of dollars, for revenue from e-books. **Remarks:** Original source: Forrester Research. **Number listed:** 6.

2000, with $0.4 billion
2001, $0.8
2002, $1.7
2003, $3.6
2004, $5.4
2005, $7.8

Source: Battey, Jim, "The Evolution of E-Books," *Infoworld*, 23: 20, (April 30, 2001).

★300★
Publishers with the best industry stocks, 2000

Ranking basis/background: Stock prices and percent change from December 31, 1999 to December 29, 2000. **Number listed:** 22.

1. Scholastic, with 88.63; and a change of 42.5%
2. McGraw-Hill, 58.63; 4.9% decrease
3. Harcourt General, 57.20; 42.1%
4. Houghton Mifflin, 46.38; 9.9%
5. Reader's Digest, 39.13; 33.8%
6. Donnelley, 27.00; 8.8%
7. Barnes & Noble, 26.50; 28.5%
8. Banta Corp., 25.42; 12.7%
9. John Wiley, 21.50; 28.4%
10. Advanced Marketing Services, 17.38; 8.4% decrease

Source: Milliot, Jim, "Industry Stocks Stumbled in 2000," *Publishers Weekly*, 249: 10, (January 8, 2001).

★301★
Retail audiobook titles selling 1 million copies

Ranking basis/background: Alphabetical listing of audiobook titles with the highest sales figures according to publishers. **Number listed:** 1.

Men Are from Mars, Women Are from Venus, by John Gray (published by Harper Audio)

Source: Rosenblum, Trudi M., "Top of the Reel," *Publishers Weekly*, 247: 54-56, (June 5, 2000).

★302★
Retail audiobook titles selling 1.5 million copies

Ranking basis/background: Alphabetical listing of audiobook titles with the highest sales figures according to publishers. **Number listed:** 1.

The Seven Habits of Highly Effective People, by Stephen Covey (published by Simon & Schuster Audio)

Source: Rosenblum, Trudi M., "Top of the Reel," *Publishers Weekly*, 247: 54-56, (June 5, 2000).

★303★
Retail audiobook titles selling 300,000-400,000 copies

Ranking basis/background: Alphabetical listing of audiobook titles with the highest sales figures according to publishers. **Number listed:** 6.

The Celestine Prophecy, by James Redfield (published by Time Warner AudioBooks)
First Things First, Stephen Covey (Simon & Schuster)
More News from Lake Wobegon, Garrison Keillor (HighBridge)
Gospel Birds, Garrison Keillor (HighBridge)
Lake Wobegon Days, Garrison Keillor (HighBridge)
The Power of Positive Thinking, Dr. Norman Vincent Peale

Source: Rosenblum, Trudi M., "Top of the Reel," *Publishers Weekly*, 247: 54-56, (June 5, 2000).

★304★
Retail audiobook titles selling 400,000-500,000 copies

Ranking basis/background: Alphabetical listing of audiobook titles with the highest sales figures according to publishers. **Number listed:** 1.

Awaken the Giant Within, by Anthony Robbins (published by Simon & Schuster)

Source: Rosenblum, Trudi M., "Top of the Reel," *Publishers Weekly*, 247: 54-56, (June 5, 2000).

★305★
Retail audiobook titles selling 500,000-600,000 copies

Ranking basis/background: Alphabetical listing of audiobook titles with the highest sales figures according to publishers. **Number listed:** 1.

News from Lake Wobegon, by Garrison Keillor (published by HighBridge)

Source: Rosenblum, Trudi M., "Top of the Reel," *Publishers Weekly*, 247: 54-56, (June 5, 2000).

★306★
Subject areas with the highest library expenditures/circulation

Ranking basis/background: Percentage of libraries reporting each subject in their top five expenditures and circulation. **Remarks:** Original source: *Library Journal* Book Buying Survey, 2001. **Number listed:** 16.

Medicine/health, with 49% reporting highest expenditure; 53% reporting highest circulation
Fiction, 43%; 48%
Arts/crafts/collectibles, 41%; 39%
Biography, 40%; 48%
History, 35%; 27%
Travel, 26%; 38%
Business/personal finance, 20%; 12%
Reference, 20%; n/a
Cookbooks, 10%; 31%
Mysteries, 19%; 25%
Social science, 18%; 11%
Genre fiction, 17%; 23%
Computer books, 15%; 9%
How-to/home repair, 13%; 19%
Science/technology, 11%; 11%
Literature, 10%; 5%

Source: Hoffert, Barbara, "Book Report 2001: The Budget Shifts," *Library Journal*, 126: 130-132, (February 15, 2001).

★307★
Trade paperback bestsellers by publishing house, 2000

Ranking basis/background: Number of books and number of weeks on *Publishers Weekly*'s 2000 list. **Number listed:** 31.

1. Health Communications, with 12 books; and 63 weeks
2. Vintage, 9; 93
3. Penguin, 5; 45
4. Hyperion, 4; 35
5. Warner, 3; 64
5. Simon & Schuster/Fireside, 3; 49
5. Plume, 3; 32
5. Tyndale, 3; 25
5. Pocket, 3; 23
5. Avon, 3; 19

Source: Maryles, Daisy, "Who's Topping the Charts?," *Publishers Weekly*, 249: 36-39, (January 8, 2001).

BOOKS, CHILDREN AND YOUNG ADULT

★308★
Booklist's best art books for young people

Ranking basis/background: Alphabetical listing, by author, of the best art titles for youth as reviewed by *Booklist* from December 15,1999 through December 1, 2000. **Number listed:** 10.

Exploring World Art, by Andrea Belloli (published by Oxford) recommended for Gr. 7-up
Fireflies in the Dark: The Story of Friedl Dicker-Brandeis and the Children of Terezin, Susan Goldman Rubin (Holiday) Gr. 5-10
The Sign Painter, Alan Say (Houghton/Walter Lorraine) Gr. 5-up
In Real Life: Six Women Photographers, Leslie Sills (Holiday) Gr. 7-12
Michelangelo, Diane Stanley (HarperCollins) Gr. 5-8
The Genius of Leonardo, Guido Visconti (Barefoot) Gr. 3-6
You Can't Take a Balloon into the National Gallery, Jacqueline Preiss Weitzman (Dial) Ages 4-8
Squeaking of Art: The Mice Go to the Museum, Monica Wellington (Dutton) Ages 4-8
Gustav Klimt: Silver, Gold, and Precious Stone, Angela Wenzel (Prestel) Gr. 4-8
Oxford First Book of Art, Gillian Wolfe (Oxford) Gr. 1-4

Source: Engberg, Gillian, "Top 10 Youth Art Books," *Booklist*, 97: 8, (December 15, 2000).

★309★
Booklist's best first novels for youths

Ranking basis/background: Alphabetical listing by author for highly recommended first novels for young people as reviewed in *Booklist* from December 1, 1999 through November 15, 2000. **Number listed:** 10.

Frances Arrington, *Bluestem*, recommended for Grades 4-6 (published by Putnam/Philomel)
Adam Bagdasarian, *Forgotten Fire*, Gr. 8-12 (DK Ink/Melanie Kroupa)
Cat Bauer, *Harley, Like a Person*, Gr. 7-10 (Winslow)
J.B. Cheaney, *The Playmaker*, Gr. 7-10 (Knopf)
E.R. Frank, *Life is Funny*, Gr. 7-12 (DK Ink/Richard Jackson)
Lynn Joseph, *The Color of My Words*, Gr. 4-6 (HarperCollins/Joanna Cotler)
Tracy Mack, *Drawing Lessons from a Bear*, Gr. 4-7 (Scholastic)
Louise Rennison, *Angus, Thongs and Full-Frontal Snogging: Confessions of Georgia Nicolson*, Gr. 6-9 (HarperCollins)
Terry Trueman, *Stuck in Neutral*, Gr. 6-10 (HarperCollins)
Lori Aurelia Williams, *When Kambia Elaine Flew in from Neptune*, Gr. 7-12 (Simon & Schuster)

Source: Rochman, Hazel, "Top 10 Youth First Novels," *Booklist*, 97: 631, (November 15, 2000).

★310★
Booklist's best science books for children

Ranking basis/background: Alphabetical listing by author for highly recommended books in the field of science, technology and math for young readers, as reviewed in *Booklist* from December 1, 1999 through November 15, 2000. **Number listed:** 10.

Durga Bernhard, *Earth, Sky, Wet, Dry: A Book of Nature Opposites*, recommended for ages 4-7 (published by Orchard)
Nic Bishop, *Digging for Bird-Dinosaurs: An Expedition to Madagascar*, Gr. 4-6 (Houghton)
Franklyn M. Branley, *The International Space Station*, ages 5-8 (HarperCollins)
Stephen Budiansky, *The World According to Horses: How They Run, See, and Think*, Gr. 4-8 (Holt)
Sneed B. Collard, *The Forest in the Clouds*, Gr. 2-4 (Charlesbridge)
Doug Henderson, *Asteriod Impact*, Gr. 3-5 (Dial)
Dorothy Hinshaw Patent, *Shaping the Earth*, Gr. 4-7 (Clarion)
Laurence Pringle, *Bats! Strange and Wonderful*, Gr. 3-5 (Boyds Mills)
April Pulley Sayre, *Splish! Splash! Animal Baths*, ages 4-6 (Millbrook)
Marilyn Singer, *On the Same Day in March: A Tour of the World's Weather*, Gr. 1-3 (HarperCollins)

Source: Zvirin, Stephanie, "Top 10 Science Books for Children," *Booklist*, 97: 735, (December 1, 2000).

★311★
Booklist's most recommended black history books for youth

Ranking basis/background: Alphabetical listing, by author, selected from books reviewed in *Booklist* between February 15, 2000 and February 1, 2001. **Number listed:** 10.

- *Messenger, Messenger*, by Robert Burleigh (published by Simon & Schuster/Atheneum) recommended for ages 4-8
- *The Times They Used to Be*, Lucille Clifton (Delacorte) Gr. 4-9
- *Ida B. Wells: Mother of the Civil Rights Movement*, Dennis Brindell Fradin and Judith Bloom Fradin (Clarion) Gr. 8-12
- *Life is Funny*, E.R. Frank (DK Ink/Richard Jackson) Gr. 7-12
- *The Girl Who Spun Gold*, Virginia Hamilton (Scholastic) Ages 4-8
- *Wings*, Christopher Myers (Scholastic) Ages 4-9
- *Osceola: Memories of a Sharecropper's Daughter*, edited by Alan Govenar (Hyperion) Gr. 3-7
- *When Kambia Elaine Flew in from Neptune*, Lori Aurelia Williams (Simon & Schuster) Gr. 7-12
- *True Believer*, Virginia Euwer Wolff (Simon & Schuster/Atheneum) Gr. 7-12
- *Words with Wings: A Treasury of African-American Poetry and Art*, edited by Belinda Rochelle (HarperCollins/Amistad) Gr. 4 and up

Source: Rochman, Hazel, "Top Ten Black History Books for Youth," *Booklist*, 97: 1152, (February 15, 2001).

★312★
Booklist's most recommended fantasy books for youth

Ranking basis/background: Alphabetical list by author of fantasy book reviewed in *Booklist* from April 15, 2000 through April 1, 2001. **Number listed:** 10.

- *The Wings of Merlin*, by T.A. Barron (published by Putnam/Philomel) recommended for grades 7-10
- *Fire Bringer*, David Clement-Davis (Dutton) Gr. 7-12
- *Lord Brocktree*, Brian Jacques (Putnam/Philomel) Gr. 5.8
- *The Dark Portal*, Robin Jarvis (North-South/SeaStar) Gr. 5-8
- *Orwell's Luck*, Richard W. Jennings (Houghton/Walter Lorraine) Gr. 4-7
- *Year of the Griffin*, Diana Wynne Jones (Greenwillow) Gr. 7-10
- *Spindle's End*, Robin McKinley (Putnam) Gr. 7-12
- *Beast*, Donna Jo Napoli (Simon & Schuster/Atheneum) Gr. 7-10
- *Harry Potter and the Goblet of Fire*, J.K. Rowling (Scholastic/Arthur A. Levine) Gr. 5-8
- *The Queen of Attolia*, Megan Whalen Turner (Greenwillow) Gr. 7-12

Source: Estes, Sally, "Top 10 Fantasy Books for Youth," *Booklist*, 97: 1561, (April 15, 2001).

★313★
Booklist's most recommended geography series for young people, 2000

Ranking basis/background: Alphabetical listing by series title for outstanding geography literature that introduce young readers to new cultures, places and people, as reviewed by *Booklist*. **Number listed:** 10.

- *America the Beautiful* (published by Children's Press) recommended for Grades 4-7
- *Country Insights* (Raintree/Steck-Vaughn) Gr. 4-6
- *Cultures of the World* (Marshall Cavendish) Gr. 4-7
- *Exploring Cultures of the World* (Benchmark) Gr. 3-5
- *Families around the World* (A Family From...) (Raintree/Steck-Vaughn) Gr. 3-6
- *Hello U.S.A.* (Lerner) Gr. 3-5
- *Mapping Our World* (Benchmark) Gr. 4-6
- *Modern Nations of the World* (Lucent) Gr. 6-9
- *The Seven Continents* (Twenty-First Century) Gr. 5-8
- *World's Children (Children of ...)* (Carolrhoda) Gr. 3-5

Source: Cooper, Ilene, "Top 10 Geography Series for Youth," *Booklist*, 97: 460, (October 15, 2000).

★314★
Booklist's most recommended historical fiction for youths, 2001

Ranking basis/background: As reviewed by *Booklist* from April 1, 2000 through March 15, 2001. List is alphabetical by author. **Number listed:** 10.

- *Fever 1793*, by Laurie Halse Anderson (published by Simon & Schuster) recommended for Grades 7-10
- *Bluestem*, Frances Arrington (Putnam/Philomel) Gr. 4-6
- *Willa's New World*, Barbara Demers (Coteau: McGraw-Hill) Gr. 5-8
- *Nory Ryan's Song*, Patricia Reilly Gliff (Delacorte) Gr. 4-7
- *The Boxer*, Kathleen Karr (Farrar) Gr. 6-9
- *The Art of Keeping Cool*, Janet Taylor Lisle (Simon & Schuster) Gr. 5-8
- *A Year Down Yonder*, Richard Peck (Dial) Gr. 6-10
- *At the Sign of the Star*, Katherine Sturtevant (Farrar) Gr. 4-8
- *The Key Is Lost*, Ida Vos (HarperCollins) Gr. 5-9
- *Queen's Own Fool*, Jane Yolen and Robert J. Harris (Putnam/Philomel) Gr. 7-12

Source: Zvirin, Stephanie, "Top 10 Historical Fiction for Youth," *Booklist*, 97: 1486, (April 1, 2001).

★315★
Booklist's most recommended poetry for youths, 2001

Ranking basis/background: As reviewed by *Booklist* from March 15, 2000 through March 1, 2001. List is alphabetical by author. **Number listed:** 10.

- *Days Like This: A Collection of Small Poems*, edited by Simon James (published by Candlewick) recommended for ages 2-6
- *In Every Tiny Grain of Sand: A Child's Book of Prayers and Praise*, Reeve Lindbergh (Candlewick) Gr. 3-6
- *We, the People*, Bobbi Katz (Greenwillow) Gr. 5-8
- *Light Gathering Poems*, Liz Rosenberg (Holt) Gr. 6-12
- *My America: A Poetry Atlas of the United States*, Lee Bennett Hopkins (Simon & Schuster) Gr. 4-7
- *Salting the Ocean: 100 Poems by Young Poets*, Naomi Shihab Nye (Greenwillow) Gr. 4-12
- *Stone Bench in an Empty Park*, Paul B. Janeczko (Orchard) Gr. 5-12
- *Voices: Poetry and Art from Around the World*, Barbara Brenner (National Geographic) Gr. 6-12
- *Words with Wings: A Treasury of African-American Poetry and Art*, Belinda Rochelle (HarperCollins) Gr. 4 and up
- *You Hear Me? Poems and Writings by Teenage Boys*, Betsy Franco (Candlewick) Gr. 7-12

Source: Engberg, Gillian, "Top 10 Poetry Titles for Youth," *Booklist*, 97: 1393, (April 1, 2001).

★316★
Christopher Awards winners for youth literature, 2000

Ranking basis/background: Winners of the 52nd annual Christopher Awards for literary works that "affirm the highest values of the human spirit." **Number listed:** 5.

- *How Do Dinosaurs Say Good Night?*, by Jane Yolen (published by Blue Sky Press/Scholastic) recommended for preschool
- *The Mousery*, Charlotte Pomerantz (Gulliver Books/Harcourt) Ages 6-8
- *The Yellow Star*, Carmen Agra Deedy (Peachtree Publishers Ltd.) Ages 9-10
- *Hope Was Here*, Joan Bauer (G.P. Putnam's Sons) Ages 11-12
- *The Wanderer*, Sharon Creech (Joanna Cotler Books/HarperCollins) Young Adult

Source: "The 52nd Annual Christopher Awards," *Library Journal*, 126: 111, (March 15, 2001).

★317★
Most notable books for middle readers, 2001

Ranking basis/background: Alphabetical list by author, compiled by the Notable Children's Books Committee of the Association for Library Service to Children. Titles selected were published during 2000, include books of commendable quality in fiction, information, poetry and pictures, and have special interest and value to children through age 14. **Number listed:** 21.

- *Digging for Bird-Dinosaurs: An Expedition to Madagascar*, by Nic Bishop (published by Houghton)
- *Crazy Horse's Vision*, Joseph Bruchac (Lee & Low)
- *Satchel Paige*, Lesa Cline-Ransome (Simon & Schuster)
- *Liberty*, Lynn Curlee (Simon & Schuster)
- *Because of Winn-Dixie*, Kate DeCamillo (Candlewick)
- *Joey Pigza Loses Control*, Jack Gantos (Farrar)
- *Norman Rockwell: Storyteller with a Brush*, Beverly Gherman (Simon & Schuster/Antheneum)
- *The Amazing Life of Benjamin Franklin*, James Cross Giblin (Scholastic)

Nory Ryan's Song, Patricia Reilly Giff (Delacorte)
Frank O. Gehry: Outside In, Jan Greenberg and Sandra Jordan (DK Ink)
The Doll People, Ann M. Martin and Laura Godwin (Hyperion)
Judy Moody, Megan McDonald (Candlewick)
Wings, Christopher Myers (Scholastic)
Surviving Brick Johnson, Laurie Myers (Clarion)
Osceola: Memories of a Sharecropper's Daughter, edited by Alan Govenar (Hyperion/Jump at the Sun)
Let It Shine: Stories of Black Women Freedom Fighters, Andrea Davis Pinkney (Harcourt/Gulliver)
Freedom River, Doreen Rappaport (Hyperion/Jump at the Sun)
Only Passing Through: The Story of Sojourner Truth, Anne Rockwell (Knopf)
So You Want to Be President?, Judith St. George (Putnam/Philomel)
Space Race, Sylvia Waugh (Delacorte)
My Season with Penguins: An Antarctic Journal, Sophie Webb (Houghton)

Source: ALA's 2001 "Best" Lists, *Booklist*, 97: 1362-1388, (March 15, 2001).

★318★
Most notable books for older readers, 2001

Ranking basis/background: Alphabetical list by author, compiled by the Notable Children's Books Committee of the Association for Library Service to Children. Titles selected were published during 2000, include books of commendable quality in fiction, information, poetry and pictures, and have special interest and value to children through age 14. **Number listed:** 22.

Kit's Wilderness, by David Almond (published by Delacorte)
Sir Walter Raleigh and the Quest for El Dorado, Marc Aronson (Clarion)
Hope Was Here, Joan Bauer (Putnam)
Samir and Yonatan, Daniella Carmi (Scholastic/Arthur A. Levine)
The Wanderer, Sharon Creech (HarperCollins/Joanna Cotler)
The Longitude Prize, Joan Dash (Farrar/Frances Foster)
Ida B. Wells: Mother of the Civil Rights Movement, Dennis Brindell Fradin and Judith Bloom Fradin (Clarion)
How God Fix Jonah, Lorenz Graham (Boyds Mills)
The Color of My Words, Lynn Joseph (HarperCollins/Joanna Cotler)
Ghost Boy, Iain Lawrence (Delacorte)
Ultimate Game, Christopher Lehmann (Godine)
Freedom Like Sunlight: Praisesongs for Black Americans, Patrick J. Lewis (Creative Editions)
The Art of Keeping Cool, Janet Taylor Lisle (Simon & Schuster)
Gold Dust, Chris Lynch (HarperCollins)
Building Big, David Macaulay (Houghton/Walter Lorraine)
Blizzard! The Storm That Changed America, Jim Murphy (Scholastic)
The Wind Singer, William Nicholson (Hyperion)
A Year Down Yonder, Richard Peck (Dial)
The Amber Spyglass, Philip Pullman (Knopf)

Voices: Poetry and Art from Around the World, edited by Barbara Brenner (National Geographic)
Homeless Bird, Gloria Whelan (HarperCollins)
Pedro and Me: Friendship, Loss, and What I Learned, Judd Winick (Holt)

Source: ALA's 2001 "Best" Lists, *Booklist*, 97: 1362-1388, (March 15, 2001).

★319★
Most notable books for young readers, 2001

Ranking basis/background: Alphabetical list by author, compiled by the Notable Children's Books Committee of the Association for Library Service to Children. Titles selected were published during 2000, include books of commendable quality in fiction, information, poetry and pictures, and have special interest and value to children through age 14. **Number listed:** 20.

America's Champion Swimmer: Gertrude Ederle, by David A. Adler (published by Harcourt/Gulliver)
Night Worker, Kate Banks (Farrar/Frances Foster)
Radio Rescue, Lynne Barasch (Farrar/Frances Foster)
Uncommon Traveler: Mary Kingsley in Africa, Don Brown (Houghton)
Click, Clack, Moo: Cows That Type, Doreen Cronin (Simon & Schuster)
Days Like This: A Collection of Small Poems, edited by Simon James (Candlewick)
Olivia, Ian Falconer (Simon & Schuster)
Max, Bob Graham (Candlewick)
Iris and Walter, Elisa Haden Guest (Harcout/Gulliver)
Wemberly Worried, Kevin Henkes (Greenwillow)
Virgie Goes to School with Us Boys, Elizabeth Fitzgerald Howard (Simon & Schuster)
In Every Tiny Grain of Sand: A Child's Book of Prayers and Praise, edited by Reeve Lindbergh (Candlewick)
Seven Spools of Thread: A Kwanzaa Story, Angela Shelf Medearis (Whitman)
Kate and the Beanstalk, Mary Pope Osborne (Simon & Schuster)
Cold Little Duck, Duck, Duck, Lisa Westberg Peters (Greenwillow)
Chato and the Party Animals, Gary Soto (Putnam)
Ernest L. Thayer's Casey at the Bat: A Ballad of the Republic Sung in the Year 1888, Ernest Lawrence Thayer (Handprint)
Good Night, Good Knight, Shelley Moore Thomas (Dutton)
Off to the Sweet Shores of Africa and Other Talking Drum Rhymes, Uzo Unobagha (Chronicle)
How Do Dinosaurs Say Good Night?, Jane Yolen (Scholastic/Blue Sky)

Source: ALA's 2001 "Best" Lists, *Booklist*, 97: 1362-1388, (March 15, 2001).

★320★
Most notable children's recordings, 2001

Ranking basis/background: Alphabetical list by title, compiled by the Notable Children's Recordings committee. **Number listed:** 33.

Bud, not Buddy (produced by Listening Library)

Charlie Parker Played Be Bop! (Live Oak Media)
Daddy-Long-Legs (Recorded Books)
Dance on a Moonbeam: A Collection of Songs and Poems (Telarc)
Duke Ellington (Weston Woods)
Eleanor (Recorded Books)
The Folk Keeper (Listening Library)
Freddy the Pilot (Recorded Books)
George Washington's Mother (Weston Woods)
The Great Turkey Walk (Recorded Books)
Harry Potter and the Goblet of Fire (Listening Library)
Harry Potter and the Prisoner of Azkaban (Listening Library)
Howliday Inn (Listening Library)
I Was a Sixth Grade Alien (Listening Library)
Kit's Wilderness (Listening Library)
Lilly's Purple Plastic Purse (Live Oaks Media)
Matilda Bone (Listening Library)
Mr. Popper's Penguins (Recorded Books)
Music of the American Colonies (Enslow)
Nory Ryan's Song (Listening Library)
Ouch! (Live Oak Media)
Passage to Freedom: The Sugihara Story (Live Oak Media)
Rhythm in My Shoes (Rounder Records)
Snow (Live Oak Media)
Spider Sparrow (Listening Library)
Still the Same Me (Rounder Records)
The Subtle Knife (Listening Library)
The Trolls (Listening Library)
Water Torture, The Barking Mouse, and Other Tales of Wonder (Rounder Kids)
When Zachary Beaver Came to Town (Listening Library)
Wiley and the Hairy Man: Adapted from an American Folktale (Live Oak Media)
A Year Down Yonder (Listening Library)
Yo! Yes? (Weston Woods)

Source: ALA's 2001 "Best" Lists, *Booklist*, 97: 1362-1388, (March 15, 2001).

★321★
Most notable fiction books for reluctant young adult readers, 2001

Ranking basis/background: Alphabetical list by author, compiled by the Young Adult Library Services Association, of books published from late 1999 through 2000, that will appeal to teens who have been reluctant to read. **Number listed:** 33.

Counterfeit Son, by Elaine Marie Alphin (published by Harcourt)
Kissing Tennessee and Other Stories from the Stardust Dance, Kathi Appelt (Harcourt)
When Jeff Comes Home, Catherine Atkins (Putnam)
Demon in My View, Amelia Atwater-Rhodes (Delacorte)
Harley, Like a Person, Cat Bauer (Winslow)
Love Him Forever, Cherie Bennett (Avon)
The Edge, Ben Bo (Lerner/LernerSports)
Skullcrack, Ben Bo (Lerner/LernerSports)
The Princess Diaries, Meg Cabot (HarperCollins)
Snail Mail No More, Paula Danziger and Ann M. Martin (Scholastic)
Daughter of the Moon, Lynne Ewing (Hyperion)
Life Is Funny, E.R. Frank (DK Ink)

Meets the Eye, Christopher Golden (Pocket)
Simpson's Comics a Go-Go, Matt Groening (HarperPerennial)
Crashboomlove: A Novel in Verse, Juan Felipe Herrera (University of New Mexico)
Night of the Pompon, Sarah Jett (Pocket/Archway)
The Girls, Amy Goldman Koss (Dial)
Dancing With an Alien, Mary Logue (HarperCollins)
Love and Other Four Letter Words, Carolyn Mackler (Delacorte)
Cut, Patricia McCormick (Front Street)
145th Street: Short Stories, Walter Dean Myers (Delacorte)
Jade Green: A Ghost Story, Phyllis Reynolds Naylor (Simon & Schuster/Atheneum)
Fearless, Francine Pascal (Pocket)
Define "Normal", Julie Anne Peters (Little, Brown)
Angus, Thongs, and Full-Frontal Snogging: Confessions of Georgia Nicolson, Louise Rennison (HarperCollins)
Regeneration series, L.J. Singleton (Putnam/Berkley)
Tall Tales: Six Amazing Basketball Dreams, Charles R. Smith (Dutton)
Leslie's Journal, Allan Stratton (Annick)
Players, Joyce Sweeney (Winslow)
Treacherous Love: The Diary of an Anonymous Teenager, edited by Beatrice Sparks (Morrow/Avon)
Stuck in Neutral, Terry Trueman (HarperCollins)
Turning Seventeen series (HarperTrophy)
Playing Without the Ball, Rich Wallace (Knopf)

Source: ALA's 2001 "Best" Lists, *Booklist*, 97: 1362-1388, (March 15, 2001).

★322★

Most notable fiction books for young adults, 2001

Ranking basis/background: Alphabetical list by author, compiled by a committee of the Young Adult Library Services Association. Titles selected were published from late 1999 through 2000, span a variety of subjects and reading levels, and are found appropriate for young adults ages 12 to 18. **Number listed:** 58.

Kit's Wilderness, by David Almond (published by Delacorte)
Fever 1793, Laurie Halse Anderson (Simon & Schuster)
Kissing Tennessee and Other Stories from the Stardust Dance, Kathi Appelt (Harcourt)
Forgotten Fire, Adam Bagdasarian (DK Ink/Melanie Kroupa)
Harley, Like a Person, Cat Bauer (Winslow)
Hope Was Here, Joan Bauer (Putnam)
Shakespeare's Scribe, Gary Blackwood (Dutton)
Being with Henry, Martha Brooks (DK Ink/Melanie Kroupa)
The Princess Diaries, Meg Cabot (HarperCollins)
Aria of the Sea, Dia Calhoun (Winslow)
Girl with a Pearl Earring, Tracy Chavalier (Dutton)
Many Stones, Carolyn Coman (Front Street)
The Wanderer, Sharon Creech (HarperCollins)
Timeline, Michael Crichton (Knopf)
Tightrope, Gillian Cross (Holiday)
Dreamland, Sarah Dessen (Viking)
Night Hoops, Carl Deuker (Houghton)
Borrowed Light, Anna Feinberg (Delacorte)
Crossing Jordan, Adrian Fogelin (Peachtree)
Nory Ryan's Song, Patricia Reilly Giff (Delacorte)
Split Image, Mel Glenn (HarperCollins)
Holding Up the Earth, Dianne E. Gray (Houghton)
Plainsong, Kent Haruf (Knopf)
Pay It Forward, Catherine Ryan Hyde (Simon & Schuster)
Torn Thread, Anne Isaacs (Scholastic)
The Boxer, Kathleen Karr (Farrar)
No Condition Is Permanent, Cristina Kessler (Putnam/Philomel)
Silent to the Bone, E.L. Konigsburg (Simon & Schuster)
The Girls, Amy Goldman Koss (Dial)
Ghost Boy, Iain Lawrence (Delacorte)
Crazy, Benjamin Lebert (Knopf/Borzoi)
Dancing With an Alien, Mary Logue (HarperCollins)
Gold Dust, Chris Lynch (HarperCollins)
Daughter of the Forest, Juliet Marillier (Tor)
The Savage Damsel and the Dwarf, Gerald Morris (Houghton)
Night Flying, Rita Murphy (Delacorte)
145th Street: Short Stories, Walter Dean Myers (Delacorte)
Perfect Family, Jerrie Oughton (Houghton)
The Beet Fields: Memories of a Sixteenth Summer, Gary Paulsen (Delacorte)
A Year Down Yonder, Richard Peck (Dial)
Define "Normal", Julie Anne Peters (Little, Brown)
The Last Book in the Universe, Rodman Philbrick (Scholastic/Blue Sky)
The Likes of Me, Randall Beth Platt (Delacorte)
The Body of Christopher Creed, Carol Plum-Ucci (Harcourt)
A Dance for Three, Louise Plummer (Delacorte)
Angus, Thongs, and Full-Frontal Snogging: Confessions of Georgia Nicolson, Lousie Rennison (HarperCollins)
Esperanza Rising, Pam Munoz Ryan (Scholastic)
Send One Angel Down, Virginia Frances Schwartz (Holiday)
Stargirl, Jerry Sinelli (Knopf)
Stuck in Neutral, Terry Trueman (HarperCollins)
Playing Without the Ball, Rich Wallace (Knopf)
Meely LaBauve, Ken Wells (Random)
Homeless Bird, Gloria Whelan (HarperCollins)
Memories of Summer, Ruth White (Farrar)
When Kambia Elaine Flew in from Neptune, Lori Aurelia Williams (Simon & Schuster)
What's in a Name?, Ellen Wittlinger (Simon & Schuster)
Miracle's Boys, Jacqueline Woodson (Putnam)
Queen's Own Fool, Jane Yolen and Robert J. Harris (Putnam/Philomel)

Source: ALA's 2001 "Best" Lists, *Booklist*, 97: 1362-1388, (March 15, 2001).

★323★

Most notable nonfiction books for reluctant young adult readers, 2001

Ranking basis/background: Alphabetical list by author, compiled by the Young Adult Library Services Association, of books published from late 1999 through 2000, that will appeal to teens who have been reluctant to read. **Number listed:** 46.

Basket Counts, by Arnold Adoff (published by Simon & Schuster)
Rookie: Tamika Whitmore's First Year in the WNBA, Joan Anderson (Dutton)
Baseball's Best Shots: The Greatest Baseball Photography of All Time, (DK)
D.I.Y. Beauty, Karen W. Bressler and Susan Redstone (Penguin/Puffin/Alloy)
How to Be Gorgeous: The Ultimate Beauty Guide to Hair, Makeup and More, Elizabeth Brous (HarperCollins/Trophy)
Bobbi Brown Teenage Beauty: Everything You Need to Know to Look Pretty, Bobbi Brown and Annemarie Iverson (HarperCollins/Cliff Street)
Backstreet Boys: The Official Book, Andre Ceillag (Delacorte)
The Truly Tasteless Scratch & Sniff Book, Andrew Donkin (DK)
James Bond: The Secret World of 007, Alastair Dougall (DK)
Deal With It: A Whole New Approach to Your Body, Brain and Life as a Girl, Esther Drill and others (Pocket)
StormWatch: Force of Nature, Warren Ellis (DC Comics)
The Magic of M.C. Escher, M.C. Escher and J.L. Locher (Abrams)
Stick Figure: A Diary of My Former Self, Lori Gottlieb (Simon & Schuster)
Pop-Up Book of Phobias, Gary Greenberg (Morrow/Rob Weisbach)
Hawk: Occupation: Skateboarder, Tony Hawk and Sean Mortimer (HarperCollins)
Bicycle Stunt Riding: Catch Air!, Chris Hayhurst (Rosen)
Mountain Biking: Get on the Trail, Chris Hayhurst (Rosen)
MTV's Celebrity Deathmatch Companion, Dave Hughes and Matt Harrigan (Rizzoli/Universe)
Conquering the Beast Within: How I Fought Depression and Won...and How You Can, Too, Cati Irwin (Times)
Cool in School, Michael-Anne Johns (Scholastic)
Teen Love: On Relationships, a Book for Teenagers, Kimberly Kirberger (Health Communications)
The Boyfriend Clinic: The Final Word on Flirting, Dating, Guys and Love, Melanie Manarino (HarperCollins/Trophy)
Tom Strong, Book 1, Alan Moore (DC Comics)
Real Rules for Girls, Mindy Morgenstern (Girl Press)
JLA: Earth 2, Grant Morrison (DC Comics)
Hidden Evidence: Forty True Crime Stories and How Forensic Science Helped to Solve Them, David Owen (Firefly)
Highs! Over 150 Ways to Feel Really, Really Good...without Alcohol or Other Drugs, Alex Packer (Free Spirit)

The Pain Tree and Other Teenage Angst-Ridden Poetry, edited by Esther Pearl Watson and Mark Todd (Houghton)
The Secret Life of Teens: Young People Speak Out about Their Lives, Gayatri Patnaik and Michelle T. Shinseki (HarperSanFrancisco)
The Worst-Case Scenario Survival Handbook, Joshua Piven and David Borgenicht (Chronicle)
MTV's the Real World New Orleans: Unmasked, Alison Pollett (Pocket/MTV)
Rock and Ice Climbing: Top the Tower!, Jeremy Roberts (Rosen)
The Rock Says, The Rock and Joe Leyden (HarperCollins/Regan)
WCW: The Ultimate Guide, Bob Ryder and Dave Scherer (DK)
Total Astrology: What the Stars Say about Life and Love, Georgia Routsis Savas (HarperCollins/Trophy)
Kissing: The Complete Guide, Tamar Schreibman (Simon & Schuster/Aladdin)
The Art of Optical Illusions, Al Seckel (Carlton)
The Rose That Grew from Concrete, Tupac Shakur (Simon & Schuster)
Dreams: Explore the You That You Can't Control, Tucker Shaw (Penguin/Puffin/Alloy)
...Any Advice?, Tucker Shaw and Fiona Gibb (Penguin/Puffin/Alloy)
Katie.com: My Story, Catherine Tarbox (Dutton)
This Book Really Sucks (Planet Dexter)
SLAM, Cecily Von Ziegesar (Penguin/Puffin/Alloy)
Mummies, Bones & Body Parts, Charlotte Wilcox (Carolrhoda)
Pedro and Me: Friendship, Loss, and What I Learned, Judd Winick (Holt)
You Hear Me? Poems and Writings by Teenage Boys, edited by Betsy Franco (Candlewick)

Source: ALA's 2001 "Best" Lists, *Booklist*, 97: 1362-1388, (March 15, 2001).

★324★
Most notable nonfiction books for young adults, 2001

Ranking basis/background: Alphabetical list by author, compiled by a committee of the Young Adult Library Services Association. Titles selected were published from late 1999 through 2000, span a variety of subjects and reading levels, and are found appropriate for young adults ages 12 to 18. **Number listed:** 18.

It's Not About the Bike: My Journey Back to Life, by Lance Armstrong and Sally Jenkins (published by Putnam)
The Nazi Olympics: Berlin, 1936, Susan D. Bachrach (Little, Brown)
Kids on Strike!, Susan Campbell Bartoletti (Houghton)
My Favorite Things: 75 Works of Art from Around the World, Sister Wendy Beckett (Abrams)
Ida B. Wells: Mother of the Civil Rights Movement, Dennis Brindel Fradin and Judith Bloom Fradin (Clarion)
Give Me Liberty: The Story of the Declaration of Independence, Russell Freedman (Holiday)
Savion: My Life in Tap, Savion Glover and Bruce Weber (Morrow)
Stick Figure: A Diary of My Former Self, Lori Gottlieb (Simon & Schuster)
Geeks: How Two Lost Boys Rode the Internet out of Idaho, Jon Katz (Villard)
Spellbinder: The Life of Harry Houdini, Tom Lalicki (Holiday)
Jefferson's Children: The Story of One American Family, Shannon Lanier and Jane Feldman (Random)
Darkness over Denmark: The Danish Resistance and the Rescue of the Jews, Ellen Levine (Holiday)
Sitting Bull and His World, Albert Marrin (Dutton)
In the Line of Fire: Presidents' Lives at Stake, Judith St. George (Holiday)
Learning to Swim: A Memoir, Ann Turner (Scholastic)
First They Killed My Father: A Daughter of Cambodia Remembers, Loung Ung (HarperCollins)
Pedro and Me: Friendship, Loss, and What I Learned, Judd Winick (Holt)
You Hear Me? Poems and Writings by Teenage Boys, edited by Betsy Franco (Candlewick)

Source: ALA's 2001 "Best" Lists, *Booklist*, 97: 1362-1388, (March 15, 2001).

★325★
Outstanding audio selections for young listeners, 2000

Ranking basis/background: Alphabetical listing of the year's outstanding audio selections for public-library collections. **Number listed:** 9.

Battle of the Mad Scientists (produced by Round River Records) recommended for Ages 4-up
Early Childhood Classics: Old Favorites with a New Twist (Educational Activities) Ages 1-7
Galileo and the Stargazers (Greathall) Ages 6-12
Rhythm in My Shoes (Rounder Records) Ages 5-10
Simple Gifts (Live Oak Media) Ages 4-8
Snow (Live Oak Media) Ages 3-8
Sweet Dreams of Hope (Rounder Kids) All ages
Voices of the Shoah: Remembrances of the Holocaust (Rhino) Ages 12-adult
Yes M'am: Respect for the Elders (Diane Ferlatte) Ages 5-adult

Source: "Editor's Choice 2000," *Booklist*, 97: 850-868, (January 1 & 15, 2001).

★326★
Outstanding books for middle readers, 2000

Ranking basis/background: Alphabetical listing, by author, of the year's outstanding books for public-library collections. Choices are those that combine literary, intellectual, and aesthetic excellence with popular appeal. **Number listed:** 14.

The Wonderful Wizard of Oz: A Commemorative Pop-Up, by Frank L. Baum (published by Simon & Schuster/Little Simon) recommended for all ages
Digging for Bird-Dinosaurs: An Expedition to Madagascar, Nic Bishop (Houghton) Gr. 4-6
Satchel Paige, Lesa Cline-Ransome (Simon & Schuster) Gr. 2-4
Joey Pigza Loses Control, Jack Gantos (Farrar) Gr. 4-7
Norman Rockwell: Storyteller with a Brush, Beverly Gherman (Simon & Schuster/Atheneum) Gr. 4-7
Asteriod Impact, Douglas Henderson (Dial) Gr. 3-5
In Every Tiny Grain of Sand: A Child's Book of Prayers and Praise, edited by Reeve Lindbergh (Candlewick) Gr. 3-6
The Dark Portal, Robin Jarvis (North-South/Sea Star) Gr. 5-8
Orwell's Luck, Richard Jennings (Houghton/Walter Lorraine) Gr. 4-7
Gathering Blue, Lois Lowry (Houghton/Walter Lorraine) Gr. 5-8
Aesop's Fables, Jerry Pinkney (North-South/Sea Star) Gr. 2-4
Harry Potter and the Goblet of Fire, J.K. Rowling (Scholastic/Arthur A. Levine) Gr. 5-8
So You Want to Be President?, Judith St. George (Putnam/Philomel) Gr. 3-5
Michelangelo, Diane Stanley (HarperCollins) Gr. 5-8
At the Sign of the Star, Katherine Sturtevant (Farrar), Gr. 4-8

Source: "Editor's Choice 2000," *Booklist*, 97: 850-868, (January 1 & 15, 2001).

★327★
Outstanding books for older readers, 2000

Ranking basis/background: Alphabetical listing, by author, of the year's outstanding books for public-library collections. Choices are those that combine literary, intellectual, and aesthetic excellence with popular appeal. **Number listed:** 18.

Kit's Wilderness, by David Almond (published by Delacorte) recommended for Gr. 5-8
Forgotten Fire, Adam Bagdasarian (DK Ink/Melanie Kroupa) Gr. 8-12
Fire Bringer, David Clement-Davis (Dutton) Gr. 7-12
Many Stones, Carolyn Coman (Front Street) Gr. 7-12
The Wanderer, Sharon Creech (HarperCollins/Joanna Cotler) Gr. 6-8
Dreamland, Sarah Dessen (Viking) Gr. 8-10
Ida B. Wells: Mother of the Civil Rights Movement, Dennis Brindell Fradin and Judith Bloom Fradin (Clarion) Gr. 6-up
Life Is Funny, E.R. Frank (DK Ink) Gr. 7-12
Frank O. Gehry: Outside In, Jan Greenberg and Sandra Jordan (DK Ink) Gr. 7-12
Silent to the Bone, E.L. Konigsburg (Simon & Schuster/Atheneum) Gr. 7-10
Darkness over Denmark: The Danish Resistance and the Rescue of the Jews, Ellen Levine (Holiday) Gr. 6-12
Building Big, David Macaulay (Houghton/Walter Lorraine) Gr. 7-up
The Beet Field, Gary Paulsen (Delacorte) Gr. 9-12
A Year Down Yonder, Richard Peck (Dial) Gr. 6-10
Angus, Thongs, and Full-Frontal Snogging: Confessions of Georgia Nicolson, Louise Rennison (HarperCollins) Gr. 6-9
In Real Life: Six Women Photographers, Leslie Sills (Holiday) Gr. 7-12
Stuck in Neutral, Terry Trueman (HarperCollins) Gr. 6-10

BOOKS, CHILDREN AND YOUNG ADULT

Homeless Bird, Gloria Whelan (HarperCollins) Gr. 6-9

Source: "Editor's Choice 2000," *Booklist*, 97: 850-868, (January 1 & 15, 2001).

★328★
Outstanding books for young readers, 2000

Ranking basis/background: Alphabetical listing, by author, of the year's outstanding books for public-library collections. Choices are those that combine literary, intellectual, and aesthetic excellence with popular appeal. **Number listed:** 16.

America's Champion Swimmer: Gertrude Ederle, by David A. Adler (published by Harcourt/Gulliver) recommended for Gr. 2-4

The Night Worker, Kate Banks (Farrar) Ages 3-7

Messenger, Messenger, Robert Burleigh (Simon & Schuster/Atheneum) Ages 4-8

The Hunter: A Chinese Folktale, Mary Casanova (Simon & Schuster/Atheneum) Ages 4-8

Buttons, Brock Cole (Farrar) Ages 5-8

You Forgot Your Skirt, Amelia Bloomer!, Shana Corey (Scholastic) Ages 5-8

Olivia, Ian Falconer (Simon & Schuster/Atheneum) Ages 3-5

The Girl Who Spun Gold, Virginia Hamilton (Scholastic/Blue Sky) Ages 4-8

Hannah's Collections, Marthe Jocelyn (Dutton) Ages 3-5

Henry Hikes to Fitchburg, D.B. Johnson (Houghton) Ages 5-8

Yoshi's Feast, Kimiko Kajikawa (DK Ink) Ages 4-8

A Is for Salad, Mike Lester (Putnam/Grosset) Gr. 1-4

Wings, Christopher Myers (Scholastic) Ages 4-9

Peg and the Whale, Kenneth Oppel (Simon & Schuster) Ages 5-8

Kate and the Beanstalk, Mary Pope Osborne (Simon & Schuster/Atheneum) Ages 4-8

How Do Dinosaurs Say Good Night?, Jane Yolen (Scholastic/Blue Sky) Ages 4-6

Source: "Editor's Choice 2000," *Booklist*, 97: 850-868, (January 1 & 15, 2001).

★329★
Outstanding children's fiction books, 2000

Ranking basis/background: Alphabetical listing, by author, of the year's outstanding books for library collections. **Number listed:** 16.

David Almond, *Kit's Wilderness* (published by Delacorte)

Francesca Lia Block, *The Roses and the Beast: Fairy Tales Retold* (HarperCollins/Cotler)

Sharon Creech, *The Wanderer* (HarperCollins/Cotler)

Kate DiCamillo, *Because of Winn-Dixie* (Candlewick)

Jack Gantos, *Joey Pigza Loses Control* (FSG)

Elissa Haden Guest, *Iris and Walter* (Harcourt/Gulliver)

Diana Wynne Jones, *Year of the Griffin* (HarperCollins/Greenwillow)

E. L. Konigsburg, *Silent to the Bone* (Atheneum/Karl)

Iain Lawrence, *Ghost Boy* (Delacorte)

Julius Lester, *Pharaoh's Daughter* (Harcourt/Silver Whistle)

Ann M. Martin and Laura Godwin, *The Doll People* (Hyperion)

Megan McDonald, *Judy Moody* (Candlewick)

J. K. Rowling, *Harry Potter and the Goblet of Fire* (Scholastic/Levine)

Pam Munoz, *Esperanza Rising* (Scholastic Press)

Jerry Spinelli, *Stargirl* (Knopf)

Suzanne Fisher Staples, *Shiva's Fire* (FSG/Foster)

Source: "Best Children's Books," *Publishers Weekly*, 247: 42-45, (November 6, 2000).

★330★
Outstanding children's nonfiction books, 2000

Ranking basis/background: Alphabetical listing, by author, of the year's outstanding books for library collections. **Number listed:** 6.

Marc Aronson, *Sir Walter Raleigh and the Quest for El Dorado* (published by Clarion)

David Macaulay, *Building Big* (Houghton/Lorraine)

Mirjam Pressler, *Anne Frank: A Hidden Life* (Dutton)

Judith St. George, *So You Want to Be President?* (Philomel)

Edited by Richard B. Stolley, *LIFE: Our Century in Pictures for Young People* (Little, Brown)

Judd Winick, *Pedro and Me: Friendship, Loss, and What I Learned* (Holt)

Source: "Best Children's Books," *Publishers Weekly*, 247: 42-45, (November 6, 2000).

★331★
Outstanding children's picture books, 2000

Ranking basis/background: Alphabetical listing, by author, of the year's outstanding books for library collections. **Number listed:** 18.

Shana Corey, *You Forgot Your Skirt, Amelia Bloomer!* (published by Scholastic Press)

Sharon Creech, *Fishing in the Air* (HarperCollins/Cotler)

Doreen Cronin, *Click, Clack, Moo: Cows That Type* (Simon & Schuster)

Berlie Doherty, *Fairy Tales* (Candlewick)

Ian Falconer, *Olivia* (Atheneum/Schwartz)

Denise Fleming, *The Everything Book* (Holt)

Bob Graham, *Max* (Candlewick)

Woody Guthrie, *Bling Blang; Howdi Do* (Candlewick)

Kevin Henkes, *Wemberly Worried* (HarperCollins/Greenwillow)

D. B. Johnson, *Henry Hikes to Fitchburg* (Houghton)

Christopher Myers, *Wings* (Scholastic Press)

Jerdine Nolen, *Big Jabe* (HarperCollins)

Mary Pope Osborne, *Kate and the Beanstalk* (Atheneum/Schwartz)

Jerry Pinkney, *Aesop's Fables* (North-South/SeaStar)

Margret and H. A. Rey, *Whiteblack the Penguin Sees the World* (Houghton)

Allen Say, *The Sign Painter* (Houghton/Lorraine)

Peter Sis, *Madlenka* (FSG/Foster)

Edited by Art Spiegelman and Francoise Mouly, *Little Lit* (HarperCollins/Cotler)

Source: "Best Children's Books," *Publishers Weekly*, 247: 42-45, (November 6, 2000).

★332★
Outstanding children's religion books, 2000

Ranking basis/background: Alphabetical listing, by author, of the year's outstanding books for library collections. **Number listed:** 2.

Edited by Ann Keay Beneduce, *Joy to the World: A Family Christmas Treasury* (published by Simon & Schuster/Atheneum)

Eric A. Kimmel, *Gershon's Monster: A Story for the Jewish New Year* (Scholastic Press)

Source: "Best Children's Books," *Publishers Weekly*, 247: 42-45, (November 6, 2000).

★333★
Outstanding fiction books for young adults, 2000

Ranking basis/background: Alphabetical listing, by author, of the year's outstanding books for public-library collections. Choices are those that combine literary, intellectual, and aesthetic excellence with popular appeal. **Number listed:** 10.

Girl with a Pearl Earring, by Tracy Chevalier (published by Dutton)

Alice's Tulips, Sandra Dallas (St. Martin's)

Jim, the Boy, Tony Earley (Little, Brown)

The Keeper of Dreams, Peter Shann Ford (Simon & Schuster)

How All This Started, Pete Fromm (Picador USA)

Daughter of the Forest, Juliet Marillier (Tor)

The Floating Girl, Sujata Massey (HarperCollins)

Prospero's Children, Jan Siegel (Ballantine/Del Rey)

Diamond Dogs, Alan Watt (Little, Brown)

Sunday You Learn How to Box, Bill Wright (Scribner)

Source: "Editor's Choice 2000," *Booklist*, 97: 850-868, (January 1 & 15, 2001).

★334★
Outstanding nonfiction books for young adults, 2000

Ranking basis/background: Alphabetical listing, by author, of the year's outstanding books for public-library collections. Choices are those that combine literary, intellectual, and aesthetic excellence with popular appeal. **Number listed:** 13.

Paper Shadow: A Memoir of a Past Lost and Found, by Wayson Choy (published by Picador USA)

Counting Coup: A True Story of Basketball and Honor on the Little Big Horn, Larry Colton (Warner)

Honky, Dalton Conley (University of California)

Giant Steps: The New Generation of African American Writers, edited by Kevin Young (HarperCollins/Quill)

Geeks: How Two Lost Boys Rode the Internet out of Idaho, Jon Katz (Villard)

Las Mamis: Favorite Latino Authors Remember Their Mothers, edited by Esmeralda Santiago and Joie Davidow (Knopf)

Blackbird: A Childhood Lost, Jennifer Lauck (Pocket)
The Girls of Summer: The U.S. Women's Soccer Team and How It Changed the World, Jere Longman (HarperCollins)
The Blood Runs like a River through My Dreams: A Memoir, Nasdijj (Houghton)
The Ice Master: The Doomed 1913 Voyage of the Karluk, Jennifer Niven (Hyperion)
The Heart of the Sea: The Tragedy of the Whaleship Essex, Nathaniel Philbrick (Viking)
Real Boys' Voices, William S. Pollack and Todd Shuster (Random)
The Night My Mother Met Bruce Lee: Observations on Not Fitting In, Paisley Rekdal (Pantheon)

Source: "Editor's Choice 2000," *Booklist*, 97: 850-868, (January 1 & 15, 2001).

★335★
Publishers Weekly Off-the-Cuff Awards winner for best anthology or collection, 2000

Ranking basis/background: Taken from *Publishers Weekly* poll of children's booksellers for recommendations of their favorite (and not-so-favorite) books of the year. **Number listed:** 1.

The Serpent Slayer and Other Stories of Strong Women, retold by Katrin Tchana

Source: "The 2000 Cuffies," *Publishers Weekly*, 249: 30-31, (January 8, 2001).

★336★
Publishers Weekly Off-the-Cuff Awards winner for best audiobook, 2000

Ranking basis/background: Taken from *Publishers Weekly* poll of children's booksellers for recommendations of their favorite (and not-so-favorite) books of the year. **Number listed:** 2.

Harry Potter and the Goblet of Fire, by J.K. Rowling, read by Jim Dale
Honorable mention: *Holes*, Louis Sachar, read by Kerry Beyer

Source: "The 2000 Cuffies," *Publishers Weekly*, 249: 30-31, (January 8, 2001).

★337★
Publishers Weekly Off-the-Cuff Awards winner for best book of poetry, 2000

Ranking basis/background: Taken from *Publishers Weekly* poll of children's booksellers for recommendations of their favorite (and not-so-favorite) books of the year. **Number listed:** 2.

It's Raining Pigs & Noodles, by Jack Prelutsky
Honorable mention: *Mammalabilia*, Douglas Florian

Source: "The 2000 Cuffies," *Publishers Weekly*, 249: 30-31, (January 8, 2001).

★338★
Publishers Weekly Off-the-Cuff Awards winner for best book title, 2000

Ranking basis/background: Taken from *Publishers Weekly* poll of children's booksellers for recommendations of their favorite (and not-so-favorite) books of the year. **Number listed:** 3.

Miss Alaineus, by Debra Frasier
Honorable mention: *A Is for Salad*, Mike Lester
Honorable mention: *Click, Clack, Moo: Cows That Type*, Doreen Cronin

Source: "The 2000 Cuffies," *Publishers Weekly*, 249: 30-31, (January 8, 2001).

★339★
Publishers Weekly Off-the-Cuff Awards winner for best opening line, 2000

Ranking basis/background: Taken from *Publishers Weekly* poll of children's booksellers for recommendations of their favorite (and not-so-favorite) books of the year. **Number listed:** 1.

"My name is India Opal Buloni, and last summer my daddy, the preacher, sent me to the store for a box of macaroni-and-cheese, some white rice, and two tomatoes and I came back with a dog." from *Because of Winn-Dixie*

Source: "The 2000 Cuffies," *Publishers Weekly*, 249: 30-31, (January 8, 2001).

★340★
Publishers Weekly Off-the-Cuff Awards winner for best pop-up book, 2000

Ranking basis/background: Taken from *Publishers Weekly* poll of children's booksellers for recommendations of their favorite (and not-so-favorite) books of the year. **Number listed:** 1.

The Wonderful Wizard of Oz, illustrated by Robert Sabuda

Source: "The 2000 Cuffies," *Publishers Weekly*, 249: 30-31, (January 8, 2001).

★341★
Publishers Weekly Off-the-Cuff Awards winner for best sequel, 2000

Ranking basis/background: Taken from *Publishers Weekly* poll of children's booksellers for recommendations of their favorite (and not-so-favorite) books of the year. **Number listed:** 1.

The Amber Spyglass, by Philip Pullman

Source: "The 2000 Cuffies," *Publishers Weekly*, 249: 30-31, (January 8, 2001).

★342★
Publishers Weekly Off-the-Cuff Awards winner for best treatment of a social issue, 2000

Ranking basis/background: Taken from *Publishers Weekly* poll of children's booksellers for recommendations of their favorite (and not-so-favorite) books of the year. **Number listed:** 2.

The Christmas Gift, by Francisco Jimenez
Honorable mention: *I Love You Like Crazy Cakes*, Rose Lewis

Source: "The 2000 Cuffies," *Publishers Weekly*, 249: 30-31, (January 8, 2001).

★343★
Publishers Weekly Off-the-Cuff Awards winner for best work of nonfiction, 2000

Ranking basis/background: Taken from *Publishers Weekly* poll of children's booksellers for recommendations of their favorite (and not-so-favorite) books of the year. **Number listed:** 1.

So You Want to Be President?, by Judith St. George

Source: "The 2000 Cuffies," *Publishers Weekly*, 249: 30-31, (January 8, 2001).

★344★
Publishers Weekly Off-the-Cuff Awards winner for biggest flop, per publisher's expectations, 2000

Ranking basis/background: Taken from *Publishers Weekly* poll of children's booksellers for recommendations of their favorite (and not-so-favorite) books of the year. **Number listed:** 1.

The Giggler Treatment, by Roddy Doyle

Source: "The 2000 Cuffies," *Publishers Weekly*, 249: 30-31, (January 8, 2001).

★345★
Publishers Weekly Off-the-Cuff Awards winner for book happiest to see back in print, 2000

Ranking basis/background: Taken from *Publishers Weekly* poll of children's booksellers for recommendations of their favorite (and not-so-favorite) books of the year. **Number listed:** 5.

Angelina Ballerina books, by Katherine Holabird
Honorable mention: *Petunia*, Roger Duvoisin
Honorable mention: Lois Lenski titles
Honorable mention: *Where's Wallace?*, Hilary Knight
Honorable mention: *Mr. Willowby's Christmas Tree*, Robert Barry

Source: "The 2000 Cuffies," *Publishers Weekly*, 249: 30-31, (January 8, 2001).

★346★
Publishers Weekly Off-the-Cuff Awards winner for favorite novel of the year, 2000

Ranking basis/background: Taken from *Publishers Weekly* poll of children's booksellers for recommendations of their favorite (and not-so-favorite) books of the year. **Number listed:** 4.

Stargirl by Jerry Spinelli
Honorable mention: *Because of Winn-Dixie*, Kate DeCamillo
Honorable mention: *Esperanza Rising*, Pam Munoz Ryan
Honorable mention: *The Wanderer*, Sharon Creech

Source: "The 2000 Cuffies," *Publishers Weekly*, 249: 30-31, (January 8, 2001).

★347★
Publishers Weekly Off-the-Cuff Awards winner for favorite picture book of the year, 2000

Ranking basis/background: Taken from *Publishers Weekly* poll of children's booksellers for recommendations of their favorite (and not-so-favorite) books of the year. **Number listed:** 1.

Olivia by Ian Falconer

Source: "The 2000 Cuffies," *Publishers Weekly*, 249: 30-31, (January 8, 2001).

★348★
Publishers Weekly Off-the-Cuff Awards winner for favorite series, 2000

Ranking basis/background: Taken from *Publishers Weekly* poll of children's booksellers for recommendations of their favorite (and not-so-favorite) books of the year. **Number listed:** 2.

A Series of Unfortunate Events, by Lemony Snicket
Honorable mention: Sammy Keyes, Wendelin Van Draanen

BOOKS, CHILDREN AND YOUNG ADULT

Educational Rankings Annual • 2002

Source: "The 2000 Cuffies," *Publishers Weekly*, 249: 30-31, (January 8, 2001).

★349★
Publishers Weekly **Off-the-Cuff Awards winner for funniest novel, 2000**

Ranking basis/background: Taken from *Publishers Weekly* poll of children's booksellers for recommendations of their favorite (and not-so-favorite) books of the year. **Number listed:** 1.
  Angus, Thongs and Full-Frontal Snogging: Confessions of Georgia Nicolson, by Louise Rennison

Source: "The 2000 Cuffies," *Publishers Weekly*, 249: 30-31, (January 8, 2001).

★350★
Publishers Weekly **Off-the-Cuff Awards winner for funniest picture book, 2000**

Ranking basis/background: Taken from *Publishers Weekly* poll of children's booksellers for recommendations of their favorite (and not-so-favorite) books of the year. **Number listed:** 1.
  Click, Clack, Moo: Cows That Type

Source: "The 2000 Cuffies," *Publishers Weekly*, 249: 30-31, (January 8, 2001).

★351★
Publishers Weekly **Off-the-Cuff Awards winner for hottest selling book to go out of stock, 2000**

Ranking basis/background: Taken from *Publishers Weekly* poll of children's booksellers for recommendations of their favorite (and not-so-favorite) books of the year. **Number listed:** 4.
  Harry Potter and the Prisoner of Azkaban, by J.K. Rowling
  Honorable mention: *If You Take a Mouse to the Movies*, by Laura Joffe Numeroff
  Honorable mention: *Henry Hikes to Fitchburg*, D.B. Johnson
  Honorable mention: *The Wonderful Wizard of Oz*

Source: "The 2000 Cuffies," *Publishers Weekly*, 249: 30-31, (January 8, 2001).

★352★
Publishers Weekly **Off-the-Cuff Awards winner for most disappointing book by a favorite author (in terms of sales), 2000**

Ranking basis/background: Taken from *Publishers Weekly* poll of children's booksellers for recommendations of their favorite (and not-so-favorite) books of the year. **Number listed:** 1.
  Crickwing, by Janell Cannon

Source: "The 2000 Cuffies," *Publishers Weekly*, 249: 30-31, (January 8, 2001).

★353★
Publishers Weekly **Off-the-Cuff Awards winner for most memorable character in a lead role, 2000**

Ranking basis/background: Taken from *Publishers Weekly* poll of children's booksellers for recommendations of their favorite (and not-so-favorite) books of the year. **Number listed:** 1.
  Olivia

Source: "The 2000 Cuffies," *Publishers Weekly*, 249: 30-31, (January 8, 2001).

★354★
Publishers Weekly **Off-the-Cuff Awards winner for most objectionable book, 2000**

Ranking basis/background: Taken from *Publishers Weekly* poll of children's booksellers for recommendations of their favorite (and not-so-favorite) books of the year. **Number listed:** 2.
  But I Waaannt It!, by Dr. Laura Schlessinger
  Honorable mention: "All the badly written celebrity books-you know the ones!"

Source: "The 2000 Cuffies," *Publishers Weekly*, 249: 30-31, (January 8, 2001).

★355★
Publishers Weekly **Off-the-Cuff Awards winner for most often requested title, 2000**

Ranking basis/background: Taken from *Publishers Weekly* poll of children's booksellers for recommendations of their favorite (and not-so-favorite) books of the year. **Number listed:** 1.
  Harry Potter

Source: "The 2000 Cuffies," *Publishers Weekly*, 249: 30-31, (January 8, 2001).

★356★
Publishers Weekly **Off-the-Cuff Awards winner for most overdone subject, 2000**

Ranking basis/background: Taken from *Publishers Weekly* poll of children's booksellers for recommendations of their favorite (and not-so-favorite) books of the year. **Number listed:** 2.
  Fantasy
  Honorable mentions: divorce; variations on the Cinderella story

Source: "The 2000 Cuffies," *Publishers Weekly*, 249: 30-31, (January 8, 2001).

★357★
Publishers Weekly **Off-the-Cuff Awards winner for most promising new author, 2000**

Ranking basis/background: Taken from *Publishers Weekly* poll of children's booksellers for recommendations of their favorite (and not-so-favorite) books of the year. **Number listed:** 1.
  Kate DiCamillo

Source: "The 2000 Cuffies," *Publishers Weekly*, 249: 30-31, (January 8, 2001).

★358★
Publishers Weekly **Off-the-Cuff Awards winner for most promising new illustrator, 2000**

Ranking basis/background: Taken from *Publishers Weekly* poll of children's booksellers for recommendations of their favorite (and not-so-favorite) books of the year. **Number listed:** 2.
  Ian Falconer
  Honorable mention: D.B. Johnson

Source: "The 2000 Cuffies," *Publishers Weekly*, 249: 30-31, (January 8, 2001).

★359★
Publishers Weekly **Off-the-Cuff Awards winner for most unusual picture book, 2000**

Ranking basis/background: Taken from *Publishers Weekly* poll of children's booksellers for recommendations of their favorite (and not-so-favorite) books of the year. **Number listed:** 1.
  Little Lit, edited by Art Spiegelman and Francoise Mouly

Source: "The 2000 Cuffies," *Publishers Weekly*, 249: 30-31, (January 8, 2001).

★360★
Publishers Weekly **Off-the-Cuff Awards winners for best activity book/kit, 2000**

Ranking basis/background: Taken from *Publishers Weekly* poll of children's booksellers for recommendations of their favorite (and not-so-favorite) books of the year. **Number listed:** 2.
1. *The Way Things Work Kit*, by David Macaulay
1. *My Little Red Toolbox*, Stephen T. Johnson

Source: "The 2000 Cuffies," *Publishers Weekly*, 249: 30-31, (January 8, 2001).

★361★
Publishers Weekly **Off-the-Cuff Awards winners for best novel for older teens, 2000**

Ranking basis/background: Taken from *Publishers Weekly* poll of children's booksellers for recommendations of their favorite (and not-so-favorite) books of the year. **Number listed:** 2.
1. *Stargirl*, by Jerry Spinelli
1. *Silent to the Bone*, E.L. Konigsburg

Source: "The 2000 Cuffies," *Publishers Weekly*, 249: 30-31, (January 8, 2001).

★362★
Publishers Weekly **Off-the-Cuff Awards winners for books for adults, not for children, 2000**

Ranking basis/background: Taken from *Publishers Weekly* poll of children's booksellers for recommendations of their favorite (and not-so-favorite) books of the year. **Number listed:** 2.
1. *Made for Each Other*, by William Steig
1. *Some Things Are Scary*, Florence Parry Heide

Source: "The 2000 Cuffies," *Publishers Weekly*, 249: 30-31, (January 8, 2001).

★363★
Smithsonian's **best books for children ages 1 to 6**

Ranking basis/background: *Smithsonian*'s most recommended children's books. **Number listed:** 27.
  Baby Steps, by Peter McCarty (published by Henry Holt)
  Little Puppy, Little Lamb, Little Calf, Kim Lewis (Candlewick)
  Circus Family Dog, Andrew Clements (Clarion)
  Mr. Bear's Vacation and *Mr. Bear to the Rescue*, Debi Gliori (Orchard/Grolier)
  First Word Book, illustrated by Mandy Stanley (Kingfisher)
  Max, Bob Graham (Candlewick)
  Sophie and the New Baby, Laurence Anholt (Albert Whitman, Morton Grove)

Harry's Home, Laurence Anholt (Farrar Straus Giroux)
My First Garden, Tomek Bagacki (Farrar Straus Giroux)
Town House Mouse and Country Mouse Cottage: How We Lived One Hundred Years Ago, Nigel Brooks and Abigail Horner (Walker)
Clarence Goes Out West and Meets a Purple Horse, Jean Ekman Adams (Rising Moon)
Wombat Goes Walkabout, Michael Morpurgo (Candlewick)
The Jazz Fly, Matthew Gollub (Tortuga Press)
A Gardener's Alphabet, Mary Azarian (Houghton Mifflin)
Young Discoverers Encyclopedia of Facts and Experiments (Kingfisher)
Buttons, Brock Cole (Farrar Straus Giroux)
Yard Sale!, Mitra Modarressi (DK Ink)
Bonaparte, Marsha Wilson Chall (DK Ink)
Drawing Lessons from a Bear, David McPhail (Little, Brown)
Monk Camps Out, Emily Arnold McCully (Scholastic)
My First Oxford Book of Stories, Geraldine McCaughrean (Oxford University Press)
Madlenka, Peter Sis (Farrar Straus Giroux)
Roberto: The Insect Architect, Nina Laden (Chronicle)
Where's Wallace?, Hilary Knight (Simon & Schuster)
What's in the Tide Pool? and *What's in the Meadow?*, Anne Hunter (Houghton Mifflin)
When Night Time Comes Near, Judy Pedersen (Viking)

Source: Burke, Kathleen, "Smithsonian's Notable Books for Children, 2000," *Smithsonian*, 31: 58-72, (November 2000).

★364★
Smithsonian's best books for children ages 6 to 10

Ranking basis/background: *Smithsonian*'s most recommended children's books. **Number listed:** 22.

Basho and the Fox, by Tim Myers (published by Marshall Cavendish)
The Library of Congress: An Architectural Alphabet (Pomegranate)
Blanca's Feather, Antonio Hernandez Madrigal (Rising Moon)
Sleds on Boston Common, Louise Borden (Simon & Schuster)
Growing Seasons Elsie Lee (Putnam)
Midnight Math: Twelve Terrific Math Games, Peter Ledwon (Holiday House)
The Jumbo Book of Gardening, Karyn Morris (Kids Can Press)
Mammalabilia, Douglas Florian (Harcourt)
Trouble on Thunder Mountain, Russell Hoban (Orchard/Grolier)
Ancient Greece: Daily Life; Greek Theatre; The Original Olympics, Stewart Ross (Peter Bedrick)
The Upside Down Boy; El Nino de Cabeza, Juan Felipe Herrera (Children's Book Press)
The Second Escape of Arthur Cooper, Cynthia M. Stowe (Marshall Cavendish)
Girls Think of Everything: Stories of Ingenious Inventions by Women, Catherine Thimmesh (Houghton Mifflin)
The Year of Miss Agnes, Kirkpatrick Hill (Simon & Schuster)
The Secret Life of Fishes: From Angels to Zebras on the Coral Reef, Helen Buttfield (Abrams)
Here Comes Pontus!, Ann-Sofie Jeppson (R&S Books/Farrar Straus Giroux)
Kidtopia: 'Round the Country and Back Through Time in 60 Projects, Roberta Gould (Tricycle)
An Algonquian Year, Michael McCurdy (Houghton Mifflin)
Radio Rescue, Lynne Barasch (Farrar Straus Giroux)
When Mack Came Back, Brad Strickland (Dial/Penguin)
The Kingfisher Book of Fairy Tales, retold by Vivian French (Kingfisher)
Dogs Have the Strangest Friends & Other True Stories of Animal Feelings, Jeffrey Moussaieff Masson (Dutton)

Source: Burke, Kathleen, "Smithsonian's Notable Books for Children, 2000," *Smithsonian*, 31: 58-72, (November 2000).

★365★
Smithsonian's best books for children ages 10 and up

Ranking basis/background: *Smithsonian*'s most recommended children's books. **Number listed:** 31.

The Amber Spyglass, by Philip Pullman (published by Knopf)
Stick and Whittle, Sid Hite (Scholastic)
Let It Shine: Stories of Black Women Freedom Fighters, Andrea Davis Pinkney (Harcourt)
Miracle's Boys, Jacqueline Woodson (Putnam)
Smith and *Black Jack*, Leon Garfield (Farrar Straus Giroux)
My Season with Penguins: An Antarctic Journal, Sophie Webb (Houghton Mifflin)
Shakespeare's Scribe, Gary Blackwood (Dutton)
Dream Freedom, Sonia Levitin (Harcourt)
The Kingfisher Science Encyclopedia (Kingfisher)
Through the Burning Steppe: A Wartime Memoir, Elena Kozhina (Riverhead/Penguin Putnam)
The Book of the Lion, Michael Cadnum (Penguin/Putnam)
Because of Winn-Dixie, Kate DiCamillo (Candlewick)
Night Flying, Rita Murphy (Delacorte)
Frank O. Gehry: Outside In, Jan Greenberg and Sandra Jordan (DK Ink)
Sea Soup: Zooplankton, Mary M. Cerullo (Tilbury House)
Sunwing, Kenneth Oppel (Simon & Schuster)
The Big Six, Arthur Ransome (David R. Godine)
The Puffin Book of Nonsense Stories, Quentin Blake (Penguin/Trafalgar Square)
Bound for the North Star: True Stories of Fugitive Slaves, Dennis Brindell Fradin (Clarion)
4 Fantastic Novels, Daniel Pinkwater (Aladdin)
Esperanza Rising, Pam Munoz Ryan (Scholastic)
Cassie Loves Beethoven, Alan Arkin (Hyperion)
Digging for Bird-Dinosaurs: An Expedition to Madagascar, Nic Bishop (Houghton Mifflin)
Osceola: Memories of a Sharecropper's Daughter, Alan Govenar (Hyperion)
Torn Thread, Anne Isaacs (Scholastic)
The Mildenhall Treasure, Roald Dahl (Knopf)
Norman Rockwell: Storyteller with a Brush, Beverly Gherman (Atheneum)
LIFE: Our Century in Pictures for Young People, Richard B. Stolley (Little, Brown)
The Day the Rabbi Disappeared: Jewish Holiday Tales of Magic, Howard Schwartz (Viking)
Harry Potter and the Goblet of Fire, J.K. Rowling (Scholastic)

Source: Burke, Kathleen, "Smithsonian's Notable Books for Children, 2000," *Smithsonian*, 31: 58-72, (November 2000).

BOOKS, REFERENCE

★366★
Booklist's best science and technology books

Ranking basis/background: Alphabetical listing by author for highly recommended sci-tech titles as reviewed in *Booklist* from December 1, 1999 through November 15, 2000. **Number listed:** 10.

David Berlinski, *The Advent of the Algorithm: The Idea That Rules the World*, (published by Harcourt)
Stephen Jay Gould, *The Lying Stones of Marrakech: Penultimate Reflections in Natural History* (Crown/Harmony)
John Keay, *The Great Arc: The Dramatic Tale of How India Was Mapped and Everest Was Named* (HarperCollins)
Sy Montgomery, *Journey of the Pink Dolphins: An Amazon Quest* (Simon & Schuster)
Sherwin B. Nuland, *The Mysteries Within: A Surgeon Reflects on Medical Myths* (Simon & Schuster)
Matt Ridley, *Genome: The Autobiography of a Species in 23 Chapters* (HarperCollins)
Phil Schappert, *A World for Butterflies: Their Lives, Behavior, and Future* (Firefly)
Charles Selfe, *Zero: The Biography of a Dangerous Idea* (Viking)
Robert Sullivan, *A Whale Hunt* (Scribner)
Colin Trudge, *The Variety of Life: The Meaning of Biodiversity* (Oxford)

Source: Seaman, Donna, "Top 10 Sci-Tech Books," *Booklist*, 97: 686, (December 1, 2000).

★367★
Library Journal's best free reference websites, 2000

Ranking basis/background: Selected by *Library Journal*. **Number listed:** 15.

AltaVista Translations (babel.altavista.com/translate.dyn)
AmphibiaWeb (elib.cs.berkeley.edu/aw/index.html)
ArtStar.com (www.artstar.com)
Biography.com (www.biography.com)
The British Monarchy (www.royal.gov.uk)

BOOKS, REFERENCE

Center for Disease Control and Prevention (www.cdc.gov)
De Imperatoribus Romanis: An Online Encyclopedia of Roman Emperors (www.roman-emperors.org)
DOUGLASS: Archives of American Public Address (douglass.speech.nwu.edu)
Encyclopedia of ED Statistics (nces.ed.gov/edstats)
Federal Reserve System, Board of Governors (www.federalreserve.gov)
Latin American Network Information Center (LANIC) (www.lanic.utexas.edu)
The National Transportation Safety Board (www.ntsb.gov)
ONLINE! A Reference Guide to Using Internet Sources (www.bedfordstmartins.com/online/index.html)
PopNet (www.popnet.org)
Pulitzer Prizes (www.pulitzer.org)

Source: Etkin, Cynthia and Brian E. Coutts, "Best Reference Sources: Websites 2000," *Library Journal*, 126: 42-43, (April 15, 2001).

★368★
Library Journal's best reference books, 2000

Ranking basis/background: Selected by *Library Journal*. **Number listed:** 30.

Amphibians: The World of Frogs, Toads, Salamanders, and Newts
Barrington Atlas of the Greek and Roman World
Beaulieu Encyclopedia of the Automobile
The Biographical Dictionary of Women in Science
World Encyclopedia of Christmas
The Cambridge World History of Food
Companion to African Literatures
Encyclopedia of Biodiversity
Encyclopedia of British Columbia
Encyclopedia of Contemporary Italian Culture
Encyclopedia of Eastern Europe
Encyclopedia of German Literature
The Encyclopedia of Louisville
Encyclopedia of Psychology
Encyclopedia of Stress
Encyclopedia of the American Civil War: A Political, Social, and Military History
Encyclopedia of the American Constitution
Encyclopedia of the Korean War: A Political, Social, and Military History
Encyclopedia of the U.S. Census
Encyclopedia of Third Parties in America
Encyclopedia of World History
New Historical Atlas of Religion in America
Encyclopedia of the United States Cabinet
The Pacific-Islands: An Encyclopedia
The Encyclopedia of Ephemera
St. James Encyclopedia of Popular Culture
Biodiversity Studies: A Bibliographic Review
Sports: The Complete Visual Reference
Trade, Travel, and Exploration in the Middle Ages: An Encyclopedia
World Poets

Source: Coutts, Brian E. and John B. Richard, "Best Reference Sources 2000," *Library Journal*, 126: 40-46, (April 15, 2001).

★369★
Library Journal's best reference databases and discs, 2000

Ranking basis/background: Selected by *Library Journal*. **Number listed:** 13.

AccessScience: The Online Encyclopedia of Science and Technology (www.mcgraw-hill.com)
The Accunet/AP Photo Archive (ap.accuweather.com)
American National Biography (www.oup-usa.org)
Asian American Experience On File Online (www.factsonfile.com)
Columbia Granger's World of Poetry Online (www.grangers.org)
CQ Researcher (www.cq.com)
DISCovering Multicultural America (www.galegroup.com)
Diversity Your World (www.slinfo.com)
Grolier Multimedia Encyclopedia 2.0 (www.go.grolier.com)
History Resource Center: U.S. (www.galenet.com)
Literature in Context Online (www.gem.greenwood.com)
Routledge Encyclopedia of Philosophy Online (www.routledge-ny.com)
The Trans-Atlantic Slave Trade (CD-ROM) (www.cup.org)

Source: LaGuardia, Cheryl, "Best Reference Sources: Database & Disc 2000," *Library Journal*, 126: 44-45, (April 15, 2001).

★370★
Outstanding reference sources, 2000

Ranking basis/background: Alphabetical listing of the year's outstanding reference sources for public-library collections. **Number listed:** 29.

American Indian History and Culture: An Online Encyclopedia, (www.factsonfile.com)
American Women's History: An Online Encyclopedia (www.factsonfile.com)
Ancient Civilizations (published by Grolier)
The Biographical Dictionary of Women in Science: Pioneering Lives from Ancient Times to the Mid-20th Century (Routledge)
The Cambridge World History of Food (Cambridge)
The Chronological Encyclopedia of Discoveries in Space (Oryx)
The Columbia Granger's World of Poetry (www.grangers.org)
Encyclopedia of American Radio, 1920-1960 (McFarland)
Encyclopedia of Eastern Europe: From the Congress of Vienna to the Fall of Communism (Garland)
Encyclopedia of Major Marketing Campaigns (Gale)
Encyclopedia of Monasticism (Fitzroy Dearborn)
Encyclopedia of Psychology (Oxford)
Encyclopedia of the American Civil War: A Political, Social, and Military History (ABC-CLIO)
The Encyclopedia of the Dead Sea Scrolls (Oxford)
Encyclopedia of the Korean War: A Political, Social, and Military History (ABC-CLIO)
Encyclopedia of the Palestinians (Facts On File)
Encyclopedia of Third Parties in America (Sharpe)
Exploring Life Sciences (Marshall Cavendish)
Gay Histories and Cultures: An Encyclopedia (Garland)
Lesbian Histories and Cultures: An Encyclopedia (Garland)
Historical Encyclopedia of Atomic Energy (Greenwood)
Medieval Folklore: An Encyclopedia of Myths, Legends, Tales, Beliefs, and Customs (ABC-CLIO)
Nueva Enciclopedia Cumbre en Linea (go.grolier.com)
Oxford Companion to Fairy Tales (Oxford)
Oxford English Dictionary Online (dictionary.oed.com)
St. James Encyclopedia of Popular Culture (St. James)
Science and Its Times: Understanding the Social Significance of Scientific Discovery (Gale)
Student Resource Center (galenet.com)
World Conflicts and Confrontations (Salem)
World Poets (Scribner)

Source: "Editor's Choice 2000," *Booklist*, 97: 850-868, (January 1 & 15, 2001).

★371★
Outstanding reference sources, 2001

Ranking basis/background: High quality reference works for small to medium-sized libraries selected by the Reference and User Services Association, a division of the American Library Association. **Number listed:** 28.

Beaulieu Encyclopedia of the Automobile (published by Fitzroy-Dearborn)
The Cambridge World History of Food (Cambridge Univ.)
Contemporary American Religion (Macmillan)
Encyclopedia of Aquaculture (John Wiley)
Encyclopedia of Biodiversity (Academic Press)
Encyclopedia of Ephemera: A Guide to the Fragmentary Documents of Everyday Life for the Collector, Curator, and Historian (Routledge)
Encyclopedia of European Social History from 1350 to 2000 (Scribner)
Encyclopedia of German Literature (Fitzroy Dearborn)
Encyclopedia of Judaism (Continuum Publishing)
Encyclopedia of Lesbian and Gay Histories and Cultures (Garland)
Encyclopedia of Monasticism (Fitzroy Dearborn)
Encyclopedia of Movie Special Effects (Oryx Press)
Encyclopedia of Paleontology (Fitzroy Dearborn)
Encyclopedia of the American Civil War: A Political, Social, and Military History (ABC-CLIO)
Encyclopedia of the Palestinians (Facts On File)
Encyclopedia of Psychology (American Psychological Association)
Encyclopedia of the Scientific Revolution (Garland)
Encyclopedia of the United States Cabinet (ABC-CLIO)

Encyclopedia of Twentieth Century American Humor (Oryx Press)
Facts On File Companion to the American Short Story (Facts On File)
International Encyclopedia of Women and Sports (Macmillan Library Reference)
Ken Schultz's Fishing Encyclopedia: Worldwide Angling Guide (IDG Books)
Oxford Companion to Crime and Mystery Writing (Oxford)
Oxford Companion to Fairy Tales (Oxford)
Science and Its Times: Understanding the Social Significance of Scientific Discovery (Gale)
Scientific American Desk Reference (Wiley)
Sports: The Complete Visual Reference (Firefly Books)
Women in World History: A Biographical Encyclopedia (Gale)
Source: "Outstanding Reference Sources: The 2001 Selection of Recent Titles," *Reference & User Services Quarterly*, 40: 253-255, (Spring 2001).

★372★
Selected new editions and supplements reference books, 2000
Ranking basis/background: Part of a semiannual series begun by Constance M. Winchel and continued by Eugene Sheehy. **Number listed:** 15.
Walford's Guide to Reference Material
Directory of University Libraries in Europe
Foundation Center's Guide to Grantseeking on the Web
Oxford Companion to English Literature
Cambridge Bibliography of English Literature
A Glossary of Contemporary Literary Theory
Oxford Dictionary for Writers and Editors
Encyclopedia of American Radio: An A to Z Guide to Radio from Jack Benny to Howard Stern
American Naval History: A Guide
Encyclopedia of the American Constitution
Historical Dictionary of the 1950s
History Today Who's Who in British History
Handbook of Dates for Students of British History
Encyclopedia of the Vietnam War
Encyclopedia of Human Evolution and Prehistory
Source: McIlvaine, Eileen, "Selected Reference Books of 2000," *College and Research Libraries*, 62: 180-195, (March 2001).

★373★
Selected reference books-dictionaries, 2000
Ranking basis/background: Part of a semiannual series begun by Constance M. Winchel and continued by Eugene Sheehy. **Number listed:** 2.
Grande dizionario italiano dell'uso, by Tullio De Mauro
Il nuovo etimologico: DELI: Dizionario etimologico della lingua italiano, Manlio Cartelazzo
Source: McIlvaine, Eileen, "Selected Reference Books of 2000," *College and Research Libraries*, 62: 180-195, (March 2001).

★374★
Selected reference books in the field of archaeology, 2000
Ranking basis/background: Part of a semiannual series begun by Constance M. Winchel and continued by Eugene Sheehy. **Number listed:** 4.
Archaeological Method and Theory: An Encyclopedia
Companion Encyclopedia of Archaeology
Dictionary of Archaeology
Encyclopedia of Archaeology: The Great Archaeologists
Source: McIlvaine, Eileen, "Selected Reference Books of 2000," *College and Research Libraries*, 62: 180-195, (March 2001).

★375★
Selected reference books in the field of film, 2000
Ranking basis/background: Part of a semiannual series begun by Constance M. Winchel and continued by Eugene Sheehy. **Number listed:** 1.
BFI Companion to Eastern European and Russian Cinema
Source: McIlvaine, Eileen, "Selected Reference Books of 2000," *College and Research Libraries*, 62: 180-195, (March 2001).

★376★
Selected reference books in the field of history, 2000
Ranking basis/background: Part of a semiannual series begun by Constance M. Winchel and continued by Eugene Sheehy. **Number listed:** 5.
Barrington Atlas of the Greek and Roman World
Dictionnaire historique de la France sous l'Occupation
Encyclopedia of Contemporary Italian Culture
Encyclopedia of Eastern Europe: From the Congress of Vienna to the Fall of Communism
The Boer War: Historiography and Annotated Bibliography
Source: McIlvaine, Eileen, "Selected Reference Books of 2000," *College and Research Libraries*, 62: 180-195, (March 2001).

★377★
Selected reference books in the field of literature, 2000
Ranking basis/background: Part of a semiannual series begun by Constance M. Winchel and continued by Eugene Sheehy. **Number listed:** 5.
Encyclopedia of German Literature
English Novel, 1770-1829: A Bibliographical Survey of Prose Fiction Published in the British Isles
Index to Twentieth-Century Spanish Plays: In Collections, Anthologies, and Periodicals
Companion to African Literatures
Twentieth-Century Literary Movements Dictionary
Source: McIlvaine, Eileen, "Selected Reference Books of 2000," *College and Research Libraries*, 62: 180-195, (March 2001).

★378★
Selected reference books in the field of music, 2000
Ranking basis/background: Part of a semiannual series begun by Constance M. Winchel and continued by Eugene Sheehy. **Number listed:** 1.
Diccionario de la musica espanola e hispanoamericana
Source: McIlvaine, Eileen, "Selected Reference Books of 2000," *College and Research Libraries*, 62: 180-195, (March 2001).

★379★
Selected reference books in the field of political science, 2000
Ranking basis/background: Part of a semiannual series begun by Constance M. Winchel and continued by Eugene Sheehy. **Number listed:** 1.
Encyclopedia of Modern Separatist Movements
Source: McIlvaine, Eileen, "Selected Reference Books of 2000," *College and Research Libraries*, 62: 180-195, (March 2001).

★380★
Selected reference books in the field of religion, 2000
Ranking basis/background: Part of a semiannual series begun by Constance M. Winchel and continued by Eugene Sheehy. **Number listed:** 1.
Women in Scripture: A Dictionary of Named and Unnamed Women in the Hebrew Bible, the Apocryphal/Deuterocanonical Books and the New Testament
Source: McIlvaine, Eileen, "Selected Reference Books of 2000," *College and Research Libraries*, 62: 180-195, (March 2001).

★381★
Selected reference books in the field of science and technology, 2000
Ranking basis/background: Part of a semiannual series begun by Constance M. Winchel and continued by Eugene Sheehy. **Number listed:** 1.
American Women in Technology: An Encyclopedia
Source: McIlvaine, Eileen, "Selected Reference Books of 2000," *College and Research Libraries*, 62: 180-195, (March 2001).

BUSINESS ADMINISTRATION

★382★
Best performing companies in Standard & Poor's 500, 2001
Ranking basis/background: Composite rank calculated from eight criteria: one-year total return; three-year total return; one-year sales growth; three-year average annual sales growth; one-year profit growth; three-year average annual profit growth; net profit margins; and return on equity, with additional weight given to company sales. **Number listed:** 50.
1. Tyco International
2. Anadarko Petroleum
3. Calpine
4. Dynegy
5. Applied Materials
6. Providian Financial
7. Occidental Petroleum
8. Apache

BUSINESS ADMINISTRATION

9. Kerr-McGee
10. Oracle

Source: "The Business Week 50," *Business Week*, 3726A: 10-20, (Spring 2001).

★383★
Best small companies in the U.S.

Ranking basis/background: Top ranked small companies for profitability and business growth. **Number listed:** 200.

1. Trex
2. Albany Molecular Research
3. Inet Technologies
4. Qlogic
5. Micrel
6. Serena Software
7. Carrier Access
8. PLX Technology
9. Xeta Technologies
10. Semtech
11. Zomax
12. Pre-Paid Legal Services
13. Cognizant Technology Solutions
14. Chico's FAS
15. Sawtek
16. Advantage Learning Systems
17. Barra
18. North American Scientific
19. WebTrends
20. Richton International

Source: "200 Best Small Companies," *Forbes*, 66: 222-344, (October 30, 2000).

★384★
Best small companies worldwide

Ranking basis/background: Top ranked small companies for profitability and business growth. **Number listed:** 100.

1. Unit 4, computer hardware (Netherlands)
2. Ordina, IT services (Netherlands)
3. Fayrewood, electronics distributors (UK)
4. Computer Services, IT services (Netherlands)
5. UCC Groep, electronic equipment (Netherlands)
6. ICT Automatisering, electronic components (Netherlands)
7. Magnus Holdings, business services (Netherlands)
8. Athens Medical, hospital management (Greece)
9. Gold Zack, financial services (Germany)
10. Satyam Computer, IT services (India)

Source: "200 Best Small Companies," *Forbes*, 66: 222-344, (October 30, 2000).

★385★
Biggest information technology companies, 2000

Ranking basis/background: Figures, in millions, for current sales of the 12-month period ending Feb. 28, March 31, or April 30, as researched by Standard & Poor's Compustat, *Business Week*. **Number listed:** 10.

1. SBC Communications, with $50,269.0 million
2. Hewlett-Packard, $45,381.0
3. WorldCom, $37,976.0
4. NTT Docomo, $34,432.0
5. Dell Computer, $27,007.0
6. Ericsson, $25,331.4
7. Nortel Networks, $24,121.0
8. Microsoft, $22,916.0
9. Nokia, $21,986.2
10. Tech Data, $16,991.7

Source: "The Information Technology 100," *Business Week*, 3686: 138-154, (June 19, 2000).

★386★
Business Week's best companies in Australia

Ranking basis/background: Derived from evaluations of market value, share price and annual change, price/book value ratio, price/earnings ratio, yield, sales, profits, and return on equity. **Remarks:** Original source: Morgan Stanley Capital International Inc. **Number listed:** 15.

1. Telstra
2. News Corp.
3. National Australia Bank
4. Broken Hill Proprietary
5. Commonwealth Bank of Australia
6. Westpac Banking
7. Australia & New Zealand Banking Group
8. Cable & Wireless Optus
9. AMP Ltd.
10. Brambles Industries

Source: "The Global 100: The World's Most Valuable Companies," *Business Week*, 3689: 107-152, (July 10, 2000).

★387★
Business Week's best companies in Austria

Ranking basis/background: Derived from evaluations of market value, share price and annual change, price/book value ratio, price/earnings ratio, yield, sales, profits, and return on equity. **Remarks:** Original source: Morgan Stanley Capital International Inc. **Number listed:** 1.

1. Bank Austria

Source: "The Global 100: The World's Most Valuable Companies," *Business Week*, 3689: 107-152, (July 10, 2000).

★388★
Business Week's best companies in Belgium

Ranking basis/background: Derived from evaluations of market value, share price and annual change, price/book value ratio, price/earnings ratio, yield, sales, profits, and return on equity. **Remarks:** Original source: Morgan Stanley Capital International Inc. **Number listed:** 10.

1. Fortis
2. KBC Bancassurance Holding
3. Electrabel
4. Dexia
5. Almanij
6. Groupe Bruxelles Lambert
7. Solvay
8. Groupe UCB
9. Electrafina
10. Societe Europeenne Des Satellites

Source: "The Global 100: The World's Most Valuable Companies," *Business Week*, 3689: 107-152, (July 10, 2000).

★389★
Business Week's best companies in Britain

Ranking basis/background: Derived from evaluations of market value, share price and annual change, price/book value ratio, price/earnings ratio, yield, sales, profits, and return on equity. **Remarks:** Original source: Morgan Stanley Capital International Inc. **Number listed:** 94.

1. Vodafone Airtouch
2. BP Amoco
3. Glaxo Wellcome
4. British Telecommunications
5. HSBC Holdings
6. Shell Transport & Trading
7. Astrazeneca
8. Smithkline Beecham
9. Lloyds TSB Group
10. Cable & Wireless
11. Royal Bank of Scotland Group
12. Barclays Bank
13. British Sky Broadcasting Group
14. CGNU
15. Marconi

Source: "The Global 100: The World's Most Valuable Companies," *Business Week*, 3689: 107-152, (July 10, 2000).

★390★
Business Week's best companies in Canada

Ranking basis/background: Derived from evaluations of market value, share price and annual change, price/book value ratio, price/earnings ratio, yield, sales, profits, and return on equity. **Remarks:** Original source: Morgan Stanley Capital International Inc. **Number listed:** 32.

1. Nortel Networks
2. Seagram
3. Thomson
4. Bombardier
5. Royal Bank of Canada
6. Toronto-Dominion Bank
7. BCE (Bell Canada Enterprises)
8. Bank of Nova Scotia
9. Canadian Imperial Bank of Commerce
10. Bank of Montreal

Source: "The Global 100: The World's Most Valuable Companies," *Business Week*, 3689: 107-152, (July 10, 2000).

★391★
Business Week's best companies in Denmark

Ranking basis/background: Derived from evaluations of market value, share price and annual change, price/book value ratio, price/earnings ratio, yield, sales, profits, and return on equity. **Remarks:** Original source: Morgan Stanley Capital International Inc. **Number listed:** 5.

1. Tele Danmark
2. Novo-Nordisk
3. Dampskibsselskabet AF 1912
4. Dampskibsselskabet Svenborg
5. Den Danske Bank

Source: "The Global 100: The World's Most Valuable Companies," *Business Week*, 3689: 107-152, (July 10, 2000).

★392★
Business Week's best companies in Finland

Ranking basis/background: Derived from evaluations of market value, share price and annual change, price/book value ratio, price/earnings ratio, yield, sales, profits, and return on equity. **Remarks:** Original source: Morgan Stanley Capital International Inc. **Number listed:** 4.

1. Nokia
2. Sonera
3. Stora Enso
4. UPM-Kymmene

Source: "The Global 100: The World's Most Valuable Companies," *Business Week*, 3689: 107-152, (July 10, 2000).

★393★

Business Week's best companies in France

Ranking basis/background: Derived from evaluations of market value, share price and annual change, price/book value ratio, price/earnings ratio, yield, sales, profits, and return on equity. **Remarks:** Original source: Morgan Stanley Capital International Inc. **Number listed:** 44.
1. France Telecom
2. Totalfinaelf
3. Alcatel
4. Vivendi
5. Axa
6. STMicroelectronics
7. Aventis
8. Carrefour
9. L'Oreal
10. BNP Paribas

Source: "The Global 100: The World's Most Valuable Companies," *Business Week*, 3689: 107-152, (July 10, 2000).

★394★

Business Week's best companies in Germany

Ranking basis/background: Derived from evaluations of market value, share price and annual change, price/book value ratio, price/earnings ratio, yield, sales, profits, and return on equity. **Remarks:** Original source: Morgan Stanley Capital International Inc. **Number listed:** 35.
1. Deutsche Telekom
2. Allianz
3. Siemens
4. DaimlerChrysler
5. Munchener Rueck.
6. SAP
7. Deutsche Bank
8. Bayer
9. Hypovereinsbank
10. Veba

Source: "The Global 100: The World's Most Valuable Companies," *Business Week*, 3689: 107-152, (July 10, 2000).

★395★

Business Week's best companies in Hong Kong

Ranking basis/background: Derived from evaluations of market value, share price and annual change, price/book value ratio, price/earnings ratio, yield, sales, profits, and return on equity. **Remarks:** Original source: Morgan Stanley Capital International Inc. **Number listed:** 15.
1. Hutchison Whampoa
2. Cable & Wireless HKT
3. Pacific Century Cyberworks
4. Cheung Kong Holdings
5. Hang Seng Bank
6. Sun Hung Kai Properties
7. Citic Pacific
8. CLP Holdings
9. Swire Pacific
10. HongKong Electric Holdings

Source: "The Global 100: The World's Most Valuable Companies," *Business Week*, 3689: 107-152, (July 10, 2000).

★396★

Business Week's best companies in Ireland

Ranking basis/background: Derived from evaluations of market value, share price and annual change, price/book value ratio, price/earnings ratio, yield, sales, profits, and return on equity. **Remarks:** Original source: Morgan Stanley Capital International Inc. **Number listed:** 5.
1. Elan
2. Allied Irish Banks
3. CRH
4. Eircom
5. Bank of Ireland

Source: "The Global 100: The World's Most Valuable Companies," *Business Week*, 3689: 107-152, (July 10, 2000).

★397★

Business Week's best companies in Italy

Ranking basis/background: Derived from evaluations of market value, share price and annual change, price/book value ratio, price/earnings ratio, yield, sales, profits, and return on equity. **Remarks:** Original source: Morgan Stanley Capital International Inc. **Number listed:** 31.
1. Telecom Italia
2. TIM
3. ENEL
4. ENI
5. Assicurazioni Generali
6. Unicredito Italiano
7. Tecnost
8. Banca Intesa
9. San Paolo-IMI
10. Seat Pagine Gialle

Source: "The Global 100: The World's Most Valuable Companies," *Business Week*, 3689: 107-152, (July 10, 2000).

★398★

Business Week's best companies in Japan

Ranking basis/background: Derived from evaluations of market value, share price and annual change, price/book value ratio, price/earnings ratio, yield, sales, profits, and return on equity. **Remarks:** Original source: Morgan Stanley Capital International Inc. **Number listed:** 149.
1. NTT Docomo
2. Nippon Telegraph & Telephone
3. Toyota Motor
4. Sony
5. Seven-Eleven Japan
6. Takeda Chemical Industries
7. Bank of Tokyo-Mitsubishi
8. Fujitsu
9. Softbank
10. Matsushita Electric Industrial
11. Nomura Securities
12. Murata Manufacturing
13. Hitachi Ltd.
14. NEC
15. Sumitomo Bank
16. Canon
17. Rohm
18. Tokyo Electric Power
19. Honda Motor
20. Kyocera

Source: "The Global 100: The World's Most Valuable Companies," *Business Week*, 3689: 107-152, (July 10, 2000).

★399★

Business Week's best companies in New Zealand

Ranking basis/background: Derived from evaluations of market value, share price and annual change, price/book value ratio, price/earnings ratio, yield, sales, profits, and return on equity. **Remarks:** Original source: Morgan Stanley Capital International Inc. **Number listed:** 1.
1. Telecom Corp. of New Zealand

Source: "The Global 100: The World's Most Valuable Companies," *Business Week*, 3689: 107-152, (July 10, 2000).

★400★

Business Week's best companies in Norway

Ranking basis/background: Derived from evaluations of market value, share price and annual change, price/book value ratio, price/earnings ratio, yield, sales, profits, and return on equity. **Remarks:** Original source: Morgan Stanley Capital International Inc. **Number listed:** 1.
1. Norsk Hydro

Source: "The Global 100: The World's Most Valuable Companies," *Business Week*, 3689: 107-152, (July 10, 2000).

★401★

Business Week's best companies in Portugal

Ranking basis/background: Derived from evaluations of market value, share price and annual change, price/book value ratio, price/earnings ratio, yield, sales, profits, and return on equity. **Remarks:** Original source: Morgan Stanley Capital International Inc. **Number listed:** 3.
1. Portugal Telecom
2. Electricidade de Portugal (EDP)
3. Banco Comercial Portugues (BCP)

Source: "The Global 100: The World's Most Valuable Companies," *Business Week*, 3689: 107-152, (July 10, 2000).

★402★

Business Week's best companies in Singapore

Ranking basis/background: Derived from evaluations of market value, share price and annual change, price/book value ratio, price/earnings ratio, yield, sales, profits, and return on equity. **Remarks:** Original source: Morgan Stanley Capital International Inc. **Number listed:** 7.
1. Singapore Telecommunications
2. DBS Group Holdings
3. Chartered Semiconductor Manufacturing
4. Singapore Airlines
5. OCBC Overseas Chinese Bank
6. United Overseas Bank
7. Singapore Press Holdings

Source: "The Global 100: The World's Most Valuable Companies," *Business Week*, 3689: 107-152, (July 10, 2000).

★403★

Business Week's best companies in Spain

Ranking basis/background: Derived from evaluations of market value, share price and annual change, price/book value ratio, price/earnings ratio, yield, sales, profits, and return on equity. **Remarks:** Original source: Morgan Stanley Capital International Inc. **Number listed:** 12.
1. Telefonica

BUSINESS ADMINISTRATION

2. Banco Bilbao Vizcaya Argentaria (BBVA)
3. Banco Santander Central Hispano
4. Repsol YPF
5. Endesa
6. Terra Networks
7. Iberdrola
8. Gas Natural SDG
9. Banco Popular Espanol
10. Union Electrica Fenosa
11. Amadeus Global Travel Distribution
12. Altadis

Source: "The Global 100: The World's Most Valuable Companies," *Business Week*, 3689: 107-152, (July 10, 2000).

★404★
Business Week's best companies in Sweden

Ranking basis/background: Derived from evaluations of market value, share price and annual change, price/book value ratio, price/earnings ratio, yield, sales, profits, and return on equity. **Remarks:** Original source: Morgan Stanley Capital International Inc. **Number listed:** 18.

1. LM Ericsson
2. Skandia Forsakring
3. Hennes & Mauritz
4. Nordic Baltic Holding
5. Investor
6. Volvo
7. Svenska Handelsbanken
8. Securitas
9. Foereningssparbanken
10. Skandinaviska Enskilda Banken

Source: "The Global 100: The World's Most Valuable Companies," *Business Week*, 3689: 107-152, (July 10, 2000).

★405★
Business Week's best companies in Switzerland

Ranking basis/background: Derived from evaluations of market value, share price and annual change, price/book value ratio, price/earnings ratio, yield, sales, profits, and return on equity. **Remarks:** Original source: Morgan Stanley Capital International Inc. **Number listed:** 18.

1. Novartis
2. Roche Holding
3. Nestle
4. UBS
5. Credit Suisse Group
6. ABB
7. Swiss RE
8. Swisscom
9. Zurich Allied
10. Serono

Source: "The Global 100: The World's Most Valuable Companies," *Business Week*, 3689: 107-152, (July 10, 2000).

★406★
Business Week's best companies in terms of profits

Ranking basis/background: Profit figures, in billions of dollars. **Remarks:** Original source: Morgan Stanley Capital International Inc. **Number listed:** 10.

1. Hutchison Whampoa, with $14.25 billion
2. General Electric, $10.72
3. Citigroup, $9.99
4. Royal Dutch/Shell, $8.58
5. Exxon Mobil, $7.91
6. Bank of America, $7.88
7. Microsoft, $7.79
8. IBM, $7.71
9. Philip Morris, $7.68
10. Cheung Kong Holdings, $7.62

Source: "The Global 100: The World's Most Valuable Companies," *Business Week*, 3689: 107-152, (July 10, 2000).

★407★
Business Week's best companies in terms of return on equity

Ranking basis/background: Percentage of return on equity. **Remarks:** Original source: Morgan Stanley Capital International Inc. **Number listed:** 10.

1. General Mills, with 531.7%
2. Pacific Century Cyberworks, 377.5%
3. Campbell Soup, 308.5%
4. Quaker Oats, 183.2%
5. Imperial Chemical Industries, 174.8%
6. Reuters Group, 135.8%
7. Europolitan Holdings, 131.4%
8. US West, 114.6%
9. Shell Transport & Trading, 109.7%
10. Sara Lee, 93.5%

Source: "The Global 100: The World's Most Valuable Companies," *Business Week*, 3689: 107-152, (July 10, 2000).

★408★
Business Week's best companies in terms of sales

Ranking basis/background: Sales figures, in billions of dollars. **Remarks:** Original source: Morgan Stanley Capital International Inc. **Number listed:** 10.

1. Exxon Mobil, with $185.53 billion
2. General Motors, $173.22
3. Wal-Mart Stores, 166.81
4. Ford Motor Company, $162.56
5. DaimlerChrysler, $151.04
6. Mitsui, $129.84
7. Mitsubishi Corp., $127.05
8. Toyota Motor, $119.71
9. Itochu, $112.75
10. General Electric, $111.63

Source: "The Global 100: The World's Most Valuable Companies," *Business Week*, 3689: 107-152, (July 10, 2000).

★409★
Business Week's best companies in terms of share-price gain

Ranking basis/background: Percentage of share-price gain from 1999. **Remarks:** Original source: Morgan Stanley Capital International Inc. **Number listed:** 10.

1. SDL, with 874%
2. Brocade Communication Systems, 631%
3. BEA Systems, 609%
4. I2 Technologies, 573%
5. Applied Micro Circuits, 571%
6. PMC-Sierra, 531%
7. Broadvision, 520%
8. Integrated Device Technology, 498%
9. Veritas Software, 494%
10. Oracle, 479%

Source: "The Global 100: The World's Most Valuable Companies," *Business Week*, 3689: 107-152, (July 10, 2000).

★410★
Business Week's best companies in the Netherlands

Ranking basis/background: Derived from evaluations of market value, share price and annual change, price/book value ratio, price/earnings ratio, yield, sales, profits, and return on equity. **Remarks:** Original source: Morgan Stanley Capital International Inc. **Number listed:** 22.

1. Royal Dutch Petroleum
2. Royal Dutch Electronics
3. ING Groep
4. Aegon
5. Koninkluke KPN
6. ABN Amro Holdings
7. Unilever NV
8. Koninkluke Ahold
9. Heineken
10. ASM Lithography Holding

Source: "The Global 100: The World's Most Valuable Companies," *Business Week*, 3689: 107-152, (July 10, 2000).

★411★
Business Week's best companies in the United States

Ranking basis/background: Derived from evaluations of market value, share price and annual change, price/book value ratio, price/earnings ratio, yield, sales, profits, and return on equity. **Remarks:** Original source: Morgan Stanley Capital International Inc. **Number listed:** 484.

1. General Electric
2. Intel
3. Cisco Systems
4. Microsoft
5. Exxon Mobil
6. Wal-Mart Stores
7. Citigroup
8. Oracle
9. IBM
10. Lucent Technologies
11. American International Group
12. Merck
13. Pfizer
14. SBC Communications
15. Coca-Cola Enterprises
16. EMC
17. Johnson & Johnson
18. America Online
19. Hewlett-Packard
20. Sun Microsystems
21. Texas Instruments
22. Home Depot
23. Dell Computer
24. AT&T
25. Bristol-Myers Squibb

Source: "The Global 100: The World's Most Valuable Companies," *Business Week*, 3689: 107-152, (July 10, 2000).

★412★
Business Week's best performing companies with the greatest decline in earnings growth

Ranking basis/background: Figures, in millions of dollars, for earnings growth loss over 12-months. **Remarks:** Original source: Compustat, provided by Standard & Poor's Institutions Market Services. **Number listed:** 10.

1. Nortel Networks, with a decline of $3470.0 million
2. JDS Uniphase, $2571,7
3. Sprint PCS Group, $1868.0
4. Global Crossing, $1307.8

5. Conseco, $1130.9
6. American Home Products, $901.0
7. Barrick Gold, $766.0
8. Nextel Communications, $711.0
9. Broadcom, $693.4
10. Veritas Software, $619.8

Source: "The Business Week 50," *Business Week*, 3726A: 10-20, (Spring 2001).

★413★
Business Week's best performing companies with the highest 1-year earnings growth

Ranking basis/background: Percentage increase in earnings growth over a 1-year period. **Remarks:** Original source: Compustat, provided by Standard & Poor's Institutions Market Services. **Number listed:** 10.
1. Burlington Resources, with a 6740% increase
2. Inco, 2253%
3. Anadarko Petroleum, 1816%
4. Cabletron Systems, 1129%
5. Stryker, 1039%
6. DuPont, 957%
7. Autodesk, 851%
8. Reebok International, 632%
9. Unocal, 540%
10. Eastman Chemical Company, 531%

Source: "The Business Week 50," *Business Week*, 3726A: 10-20, (Spring 2001).

★414★
Business Week's best performing companies with the highest 1-year sales performance

Ranking basis/background: Percentage increase in sales over a 1-year period. **Remarks:** Original source: Compustat, provided by Standard & Poor's Institutions Market Services. **Number listed:** 10.
1. JDS Uniphase, with a 291% increase
2. Broadvision, 258%
3. Oneok, 222%
4. Anadarko Petroleum, 221%
5. Calpine, 178%
6. Applied Micro Circuits, 158%
7. Global Crossing, 154%
8. Enron, 151%
9. Duke Energy, 127%
10. Siebel Systems, 121%

Source: "The Business Week 50," *Business Week*, 3726A: 10-20, (Spring 2001).

★415★
Business Week's best performing companies with the highest 1-year shareholder returns

Ranking basis/background: Percentage increase in shareholder returns over a 1-year period. **Remarks:** Original source: Compustat, provided by Standard & Poor's Institutions Market Services. **Number listed:** 10.
1. Healthsouth, with a 226.6% increase
2. Reebok International, 220.0%
3. Allied Waste Industries, 187.1%
4. EOG Resources, 187.1%
5. Manor Care, 186.9%
6. Tenet Healthcare, 163.7%
7. Philip Morris, 156.0%
8. Loews, 147.6%
9. Cardinal Health, 143.1%
10. Washington Mutual, 140.0%

Source: "The Business Week 50," *Business Week*, 3726A: 10-20, (Spring 2001).

★416★
Business Week's best performing companies with the highest 3-year earnings growth

Ranking basis/background: Annual percentage increase in earnings growth over a 3-year period. **Remarks:** Original source: Compustat, provided by Standard & Poor's Institutions Market Services. **Number listed:** 10.
1. Amerada Hess, with a 444.7% increase
2. Eastman Kodak Company, 443.1%
3. Tyco International, 362.1%
4. Intuit, 307.9%
5. Dow Jones, 303.8%
6. Millipore, 247.6%
7. AOL Time Warner, 211.1%
8. ITT Industries, 200.0%
9. NCR, 192.2%
10. WorldCom, 173.4%

Source: "The Business Week 50," *Business Week*, 3726A: 10-20, (Spring 2001).

★417★
Business Week's best performing companies with the highest 3-year sales performance

Ranking basis/background: Percentage increase in sales over a 3-year period. **Remarks:** Original source: Compustat, provided by Standard & Poor's Institutions Market Services. **Number listed:** 10.
1. Broadcom, with a 204.8% increase
2. Global Crossing, 198.9%
3. JDS Uniphase, 166.3%
4. Yahoo, 153.1%
5. Broadvision, 145.9%
6. King Pharmaceuticals, 141.7%
7. Sprint PCS Group, 127.5%
8. Veritas Software, 121.2%
9. Devon Energy, 117.0%
10. Anadarko Petroleum, 112.8%

Source: "The Business Week 50," *Business Week*, 3726A: 10-20, (Spring 2001).

★418★
Business Week's best performing companies with the highest 3-year shareholder returns

Ranking basis/background: Percentage increase in shareholder returns over a 3-year period. **Remarks:** Original source: Compustat, provided by Standard & Poor's Institutions Market Services. **Number listed:** 10.
1. Calpine, with a 2142.4% increase
2. Applied Micro Circuits, 1041.2%
3. Qualcomm, 780.0%
4. Network Appliance, 706.7%
5. Veritas Software, 670.7%
6. Qlogic, 645.1%
7. Mercury Interactive, 575.9%
8. AOL Time Warner, 480.4%
9. Amgen, 442.6%
10. Scientific-Atlanta, 438.9%

Source: "The Business Week 50," *Business Week*, 3726A: 10-20, (Spring 2001).

★419★
Business Week's best performing companies with the highest net margin, 2000

Ranking basis/background: Percentage increase in net margin in 2000. **Remarks:** Original source: Compustat, provided by Standard & Poor's Institutions Market Services. **Number listed:** 10.
1. Oracle, with a 63.3% increase
2. Ambac Financial Group, 59.2%
3. MBIA, 50.0%
4. MGIC Investment, 48.8%
5. Xilinx, 43.2%
6. Linear Technology, 43.0%
7. Microsoft, 41.9%
8. Altera, 36.1%
9. Biogen, 36.0%
10. Maxim Integrated Products, 32.6%

Source: "The Business Week 50," *Business Week*, 3726A: 10-20, (Spring 2001).

★420★
Business Week's best performing companies with the highest return on equity, 2000

Ranking basis/background: Percentage increase in equity returns in 2000. **Remarks:** Original source: Compustat, provided by Standard & Poor's Institutions Market Services. **Number listed:** 10.
1. UST, with a 194.4% increase
2. Oracle, 138.0%
3. Quaker Oats, 100.5%
4. Maytag, 90.7%
5. Equifax, 74.3%
6. Ralston Purina, 67.5%
7. Colgate-Palmolive, 66.2%
8. Kellogg, 65.5%
9. Deluxe, 64.5%
10. Stilwell Financial, 60.2%

Source: "The Business Week 50," *Business Week*, 3726A: 10-20, (Spring 2001).

★421★
Business Week's best performing companies with the lowest 1-year sales performance

Ranking basis/background: Percentage decrease in sales over a 1-year period. **Remarks:** Original source: Compustat, provided by Standard & Poor's Institutions Market Services. **Number listed:** 10.
1. Qualcomm, with a 33% decrease
2. McDermott International, 29%
3. CSX, 21%
4. Cabletron Systems, 18%
5. Novell, 16%
6. Briggs & Stratton, 13%
6. Cendanta, 13%
8. Paccar, 12%
8. Navistar International, 12%
8. Parametric Technology, 12%

Source: "The Business Week 50," *Business Week*, 3726A: 10-20, (Spring 2001).

★422★
Business Week's best performing companies with the lowest 1-year shareholder returns

Ranking basis/background: Percentage decrease in shareholder returns over a 1-year period. **Remarks:** Original source: Compustat, provided by Standard & Poor's Institutions Market Services. **Number listed:** 10.
1. Broadvision, with a 91.4% decrease
2. Conexant Systems, 87.5%
3. Yahoo, 85.1%
4. Novell, 82.0%
5. JDS Uniphase, 79.7%
6. Lucent Technologies, 78.9%
7. Qlogic, 76.0%
8. Citrix Systems, 75.3%
9. Broadcom, 75.1%
10. Gateway, 75.0%

Source: "The Business Week 50," *Business Week*, 3726A: 10-20, (Spring 2001).

BUSINESS ADMINISTRATION

★423★
Business Week's best performing companies with the lowest 3-year sales performance

Ranking basis/background: Percentage decrease in sales over a 3-year period. **Remarks:** Original source: Compustat, provided by Standard & Poor's Institutions Market Services. **Number listed:** 10.
1. McDermott International, with an 18.8% decrease
2. Tektronix, 17.9%
3. Ralston Purina, 17.1%
4. Thermo Electron, 16.9%
5. Deluxe, 14.8%
6. Allegheny Technologies, 14.2%
7. Halliburton, 11.9%
8. Homestake Mining, 10.0%
9. Tricon Global Restaurants, 9.7%
10. Consolidated Stores, 9.5%

Source: "The Business Week 50," *Business Week*, 3726A: 10-20, (Spring 2001).

★424★
Business Week's best performing companies with the lowest 3-year shareholder returns

Ranking basis/background: Percentage decrease in shareholder returns over a 3-year period. **Remarks:** Original source: Compustat, provided by Standard & Poor's Institutions Market Services. **Number listed:** 10.
1. Xerox, with an 85.3% decrease
2. JC Penney, 73.1%
3. Conseco, 68.6%
4. American Greetings, 68.1%
5. Hercules, 67.6%
6. McDermott International, 66.1%
7. Cendant, 65.1%
8. Dana, 64.6%
9. Quintiles Transnational, 63.2%
10. Thomas & Betts, 62.5%

Source: "The Business Week 50," *Business Week*, 3726A: 10-20, (Spring 2001).

★425★
Business Week's best performing companies with the lowest net margin, 2000

Ranking basis/background: Percentage decrease in net margin in 2000. **Remarks:** Original source: Compustat, provided by Standard & Poor's Institutions Market Services. **Number listed:** 10.
1. JDS Uniphase, with a 97.8% decrease
2. Broadcom, 61.3%
3. Applied Micro Circuits, 59.7%
4. Barrick Gold, 57.6%
5. Veritas Software, 51.3%
6. Broadvision, 38.5%
7. Global Crossing, 34.5%
8. Sprint PCS Group, 29.5%
9. Conexant Systems, 22.4%
10. Conseco, 13.6%

Source: "The Business Week 50," *Business Week*, 3726A: 10-20, (Spring 2001).

★426★
Business Week's best performing companies with the lowest return on equity, 2000

Ranking basis/background: Percentage decrease in equity returns in 2000. **Remarks:** Original source: Compustat, provided by Standard & Poor's Institutions Market Services. **Number listed:** 10.
1. Sprint PCS Group, with a 99.5% decrease
2. Nextel Communications, 45.4%
3. Avaya, 35.5%
4. Conseco, 26.1%
5. Winn-Dixie Stores, 25.8%
6. Barrick Gold, 25.3%
7. Veritas Software, 20.8%
8. Broadvision, 15.8%
9. Conexant Systems, 15.3%
10. Nortel Networks, 14.8%

Source: "The Business Week 50," *Business Week*, 3726A: 10-20, (Spring 2001).

★427★
Business Week's top companies in terms of earning growth, 2000

Ranking basis/background: Percentage of average annual earning growth over the last three years. **Remarks:** Original source: Compustat provided by Standard & Poor's Institutional Market Services. **Number listed:** 5.
1. Bebe Stores, with 467.7%
2. Network Appliance, 446.0%
3. Comtech Telecommunications, 318.9%
4. Carrier Access, 265.5%
5. Direct Focus, 224.7%

Source: Borrus, Amy, "Hot Growth Companies," *Business Week*, 3683: 179-181, (May 29, 2000).

★428★
Business Week's top companies in terms of earnings, 2000

Ranking basis/background: Figures, in millions, for earnings over the latest four quarters. **Remarks:** Original source: Compustat provided by Standard & Poor's Institutional Market Services. **Number listed:** 5.
1. Advanced Fibre Communications, with $276.2 million in earnings
2. Citrix Systems, $129.7
3. Centex Construction Products, $108.2
4. Zebra Technologies, $72.2
5. World Wrestling Federation Entertainment, $70.0

Source: Borrus, Amy, "Hot Growth Companies," *Business Week*, 3683: 179-181, (May 29, 2000).

★429★
Business Week's top companies in terms of market value, 2000

Ranking basis/background: Figures, in millions, for market value as of May 5, 2000. **Remarks:** Original source: Compustat provided by Standard & Poor's Institutional Market Services. **Number listed:** 5.
1. Network Appliance, with $21,282 million
2. E-Tek Dynamics, $13,192
3. Network Solutions, $10,101
4. Vitesse Semiconductor, $9,583
5. Citrix Systems, $7,855

Source: Borrus, Amy, "Hot Growth Companies," *Business Week*, 3683: 179-181, (May 29, 2000).

★430★
Business Week's top companies in terms of return on capital, 2000

Ranking basis/background: Average capital return percentages for the latest three years. **Remarks:** Original source: Compustat provided by Standard & Poor's Institutional Market Services. **Number listed:** 5.
1. Somera Communications, with 82.1%
2. Direct Focus, 53.8%
3. Datalink, 51.5%
4. Plantronics, 48.2%
5. Skechers U.S.A., 42.4%

Source: Borrus, Amy, "Hot Growth Companies," *Business Week*, 3683: 179-181, (May 29, 2000).

★431★
Business Week's top companies in terms of sales, 2000

Ranking basis/background: Figures, in millions, for sales over the latest four quarters. **Remarks:** Original source: Compustat provided by Standard & Poor's Institutional Market Services. **Number listed:** 5.
1. Wackenhut Corrections, with $471.6 million in sales
2. Barr Laboratories, $470.5
3. Network Appliance, $470.1
4. Skechers U.S.A., $462.2
5. Too Inc., $542.4

Source: Borrus, Amy, "Hot Growth Companies," *Business Week*, 3683: 179-181, (May 29, 2000).

★432★
Business Week's top companies in terms of sales growth, 2000

Ranking basis/background: Percentage of average annual growth. **Remarks:** Original source: Compustat provided by Standard & Poor's Institutional Market Services. **Number listed:** 5.
1. Martha Stewart Living, with 251.4%
2. Carrier Access, 164.7%
3. Direct Focus, 146.4%
4. Jakks Pacific, 143.1%
5. Somera Communications, 128.7%

Source: Borrus, Amy, "Hot Growth Companies," *Business Week*, 3683: 179-181, (May 29, 2000).

★433★
Business Week's top companies worldwide

Ranking basis/background: Market value, in billions of dollars. **Number listed:** 100.
1. General Electric (U.S.), with a market value of $520.25 billion
2. Intel (U.S.), $416.71
3. Cisco Systems (U.S.), $395.01
4. Microsoft (U.S.), $322.82
5. Exxon Mobil (U.S.), $289.92
6. Vodafone Airtouch (Britain), $277.95
7. Wal-Mart Stores (U.S.), $256.66
8. NTT Docomo (Japan), $247.24
9. Nokia (Finland), $242.19
10. Royal Dutch/Shell (Netherlands/Britain), $213.54
11. Citigroup (U.S.), $209.86
12. BP Amoco (Britain), $207.51
13. Oracle (U.S.), $204.01
14. IBM (U.S.), $192.49
15. Nippon Telegraph & Telephone (Japan), $189.16
16. Deutsche Telekom (Germany), $187.25
17. Lucent Technologies (U.S.), $183.34
18. American International Group (U.S.), $173.50
19. Merck (U.S.), $172.87
20. Pfizer (U.S.), $171.52

Source: "The Global 100: The World's Most Valuable Companies," *Business Week*, 3689: 107-152, (July 10, 2000).

★434★
Business Week's top emerging-market companies worldwide

Ranking basis/background: Derived from evaluations of market value, share price and annual change, price/book value ratio, price/earnings ratio, yield, sales, profits, and return on equity. **Remarks:** Original source: Morgan Stanley Capital International Inc. **Number listed:** 200.
1. China Telecom (Hong Kong) (China)
2. Taiwan Semiconductor Manufacturing (Taiwan)
3. Samsung Electronics (Korea)
4. Telefonos de Mexico (Telmex) (Mexico)
5. United Microelectronics (Taiwan)
6. SK Telecom (Korea)
7. Petrobras (Brazil)
8. Korea Telecom (Korea)
9. Anglo American (South Africa)
10. Korea Electric Power (KEPCO) (Korea)
11. Turkiye Is Bankasi (Turkey)
12. Gazprom (Russia)
13. Check Point Software Technologies (Israel)
14. Cathay Life Insurance (Taiwan)
15. Hindustan Lever (India)
16. Hellenic Telecommunications Organization (Greece)
17. Asustek Computer (Taiwan)
18. Tenaga Nasional (Malaysia)
19. Telekom Malaysia (Malaysia)
20. Lukoil Holding (Russia)

Source: "The Global 100: The World's Most Valuable Companies," *Business Week*, 3689: 107-152, (July 10, 2000).

★435★
Companies that have been on *Business Week*'s top 50 list the longest

Ranking basis/background: Percentage of growth in net income from 1996 to 2000, for companies that have made *Business Week*'s top 50 list every year since its start in 1997. **Number listed:** 5.
1. Morgan Stanley Dean Witter, with 403% growth in net income
2. EMC, 291%
3. Tellabs, 290%
4. Sun Microsystems, 146%
5. Merck, 104%

Source: "The Business Week 50," *Business Week*, 3726A: 10-20, (Spring 2001).

★436★
Companies with the best two-year total returns since 1998

Ranking basis/background: Two-year return percentage calculated from stock prices as of April 28, 2000. **Remarks:** Original source: Compustat provided by Standard & Poor's Institutional Market Services. **Number listed:** 10.
1. Veritas Software, with 1222.5%
2. Powerwave Technologies, 1002.3%
3. Meade Instruments, 613.4%
4. Semtech, 471.3%
5. Advanced Digital Information, 423.9%
6. Procom Technology, 350.0%
7. Micrel, 340.8%
8. Performance Technologies, 249.4%
9. Sapient, 220.8%
10. Intest, 203.4%

Source: Byrnes, Nanette, "What Happened to the Class of '98?," *Business Week*, 3683: 198, (May 29, 2000).

★437★
Companies with the worst two-year total returns since 1998

Ranking basis/background: Two-year return percentage calculated from stock prices as of April 28, 2000. **Remarks:** Original source: Compustat provided by Standard & Poor's Institutional Market Services. **Number listed:** 10.
1. Coast Dental Services, with 91.5% decrease
2. Omni Energy Services, 98.0% decrease
3. American Coin Merchandising, 88.7% decrease
4. Retrospetiva, 88.1% decrease
5. Hagler Bailly, 85.9% decrease
6. Monarch Dental, 84.4% decrease
7. Ballantyne of Omaha, 82.0% decrease
8. Curative Health Services, 80.8% decrease
9. Shoe Pavilion, 80.0% decrease
10. Signature Eyewear, 79.1% decrease

Source: Byrnes, Nanette, "What Happened to the Class of '98?," *Business Week*, 3683: 198, (May 29, 2000).

★438★
European business moguls considered the best agenda setters

Ranking basis/background: As selected by *Business Week*. **Number listed:** 6.
  Angela Merkel, Party Leader CDU (Germany)
  Jose Bove, Activist (France)
  Patricia Hewitt, Minister of State (Britain)
  Thomas Middelhof, CEO Bertelsmann (Germany)
  Gabor Demszky, Mayor Budapest (Hungary)
  Jean-Pierre Zanoto, Magistrate (France)

Source: Rossant, John, "The Stars of Europe: Leaders at the Forefront of Change," *Business Week*, 3686: 162-163, (June 19, 2000).

★439★
European business moguls considered the best challengers

Ranking basis/background: As selected by *Business Week*. **Number listed:** 3.
  Michael O'Leary, CEO Ryanair (Ireland)
  Karl Matthaus Schmidt, Founder ConSors (Germany)
  Philippe Camus, Co-CEO EADS (France)

Source: Rossant, John, "The Stars of Europe: Leaders at the Forefront of Change," *Business Week*, 3686: 162-163, (June 19, 2000).

★440★
European business moguls considered the best dealmakers

Ranking basis/background: As selected by *Business Week*. **Number listed:** 4.
  Paul Achleitner, CFO Allianz (Germany)
  Paulo Pereira, Managing Director Morgan Stanley Dean Witter (Portugal)
  Josef Acdermann, Management Board Member Deutsche Bank (Germany)
  Carl Palmstierna, Venture Capitalist (Sweden)

Source: Rossant, John, "The Stars of Europe: Leaders at the Forefront of Change," *Business Week*, 3686: 162-163, (June 19, 2000).

★441★
European business moguls considered the best empire builders

Ranking basis/background: As selected by *Business Week*. **Number listed:** 5.
  Chris Gent, CEO Vodafone AirTouch (Britain)
  John Browne, CEO BP Amoco (Britain)
  Werner Seifert, CEO Deutsche Borse (Germany)
  John Bond, Group Chairman HSBC Holdings (Britain)
  Daniel Bernard, President Carrefour (France)

Source: Rossant, John, "The Stars of Europe: Leaders at the Forefront of Change," *Business Week*, 3686: 162-163, (June 19, 2000).

★442★
European business moguls considered the best innovators

Ranking basis/background: As selected by *Business Week*. **Number listed:** 6.
  Bruno Bonnel, CEO Infogames Entertainment (France)
  Anne Asensio, Designer General Motors (France)
  John De Mol, CEO Endemol Entertainment (Netherlands)
  Marc Lassus, Chairman Gemplus (France)
  Kari Stefansson, CEO deCode Genetics (Iceland)
  Stefan Rover, CEO Brokat Infosystems (Germany)

Source: Rossant, John, "The Stars of Europe: Leaders at the Forefront of Change," *Business Week*, 3686: 162-163, (June 19, 2000).

★443★
European business moguls considered the best turnaround artists

Ranking basis/background: As selected by *Business Week*. **Number listed:** 4.
  Marco Tronchetti Provera, CEO Pirelli (Italy)
  Alfonsa Cortina, CEO Repsol-YPF (Spain)
  Marjorie Scardino, CEO Pearson Group (Britain)
  Wendelin Wiedeking, CEO Prosche (Germany)

Source: Rossant, John, "The Stars of Europe: Leaders at the Forefront of Change," *Business Week*, 3686: 162-163, (June 19, 2000).

★444★
Fast-growing information technology companies, 2000

Ranking basis/background: Revenue growth percentages over the previous 12-month period, as researched by Standard & Poor's Compustat, *Business Week*. **Number listed:** 10.
1. Netcreations, with 615.5% revenue growth
2. Vignette, 486.0%
3. JDS Uniphase, 301.5%
4. Infospace, 265.3%
5. Viant, 252.6%
6. Art Technology Group, 235.9%
7. Veritas Software, 215.5%
8. Yahoo Japan, 210.0%
9. Voicestream Wireless, 206.2%
10. Broadvision, 167.4%

Source: "The Information Technology 100," *Business Week*, 3686: 138-154, (June 19, 2000).

BUSINESS ADMINISTRATION

★445★
Fortune's highest ranked advertising and marketing companies, 2000

Ranking basis/background: Based on a survey by Clark Martire & Bartolomeo of 10,000 executives, directors, and securities analysts rating 535 companies in 61 industries on overall management quality, products or service quality, innovativeness, value as a long-term investment, financial strength, responsibility to the community/environment, use of corporate assets, and effectiveness in business globally. **Number listed:** 4.

1. Omnicom Group, with a score of 8.54
2. Interpublic Group, 7.91
3. Young & Rubicam, 5.95
4. True North Communications, 5.72

Source: Diba, Ahmad and Lisa Munoz, "Who's Up Who's Down," *Fortune*, 143: 104-F7, (February 19, 2001).

★446★
Fortune's highest ranked aerospace companies, 2000

Ranking basis/background: Based on a survey by Clark Martire & Bartolomeo of 10,000 executives, directors, and securities analysts rating 535 companies in 61 industries on overall management quality, products or service quality, innovativeness, value as a long-term investment, financial strength, responsibility to the community/environment, use of corporate assets, and effectiveness in business globally. **Number listed:** 10.

1. United Technologies, with a score of 7.41
2. Boeing, 6.96
3. Honeywell International, 6.72
4. General Dynamics, 6.63
5. Textron, 6.52
6. Northrop Grumman, 6.36
7. Lockheed Martin, 6.00
8. B.F. Goodrich, 5.74
9. Raytheon, 5.40
10. Sequa, 5.13

Source: Diba, Ahmad and Lisa Munoz, "Who's Up Who's Down," *Fortune*, 143: 104-F7, (February 19, 2001).

★447★
Fortune's highest ranked airlines, 2000

Ranking basis/background: Based on a survey by Clark Martire & Bartolomeo of 10,000 executives, directors, and securities analysts rating 535 companies in 61 industries on overall management quality, products or service quality, innovativeness, value as a long-term investment, financial strength, responsibility to the community/environment, use of corporate assets, and effectiveness in business globally. **Number listed:** 10.

1. Southwest Airlines, with a score of 7.62
2. Continental Airlines, 7.02
3. Delta Air Lines, 6.49
4. AMR, 6.22
5. Northwest Airlines, 5.36
6. UAL, 4.69
7. Alaska Air Group, 4.31
8. Trans World Airlines, 3.38
9. America West Holdings, 3.29
10. US Airways Group, 3.22

Source: Diba, Ahmad and Lisa Munoz, "Who's Up Who's Down," *Fortune*, 143: 104-F7, (February 19, 2001).

★448★
Fortune's highest ranked apparel companies, 2000

Ranking basis/background: Based on a survey by Clark Martire & Bartolomeo of 10,000 executives, directors, and securities analysts rating 535 companies in 61 industries on overall management quality, products or service quality, innovativeness, value as a long-term investment, financial strength, responsibility to the community/environment, use of corporate assets, and effectiveness in business globally. **Number listed:** 9.

1. Nike, with a score of 7.16
2. Liz Claiborne, 7.04
3. Jones Apparel Group, 6.80
4. Polo Ralph Lauren, 6.63
5. VF, 6.08
6. Kellwood, 5.39
7. Phillips-Van Heusen, 5.35
8. Reebok International, 5.31
9. Warnaco Group, 3.13

Source: Diba, Ahmad and Lisa Munoz, "Who's Up Who's Down," *Fortune*, 143: 104-F7, (February 19, 2001).

★449★
Fortune's highest ranked automotive retailing services companies, 2000

Ranking basis/background: Based on a survey by Clark Martire & Bartolomeo of 10,000 executives, directors, and securities analysts rating 535 companies in 61 industries on overall management quality, products or service quality, innovativeness, value as a long-term investment, financial strength, responsibility to the community/environment, use of corporate assets, and effectiveness in business globally. **Number listed:** 9.

1. Avis Rent A Car, with a score of 5.86
2. Lithia Motors, 5.73
3. Group 1 Automotive, 5.66
4. Ryder System, 5.29
5. AutoNation, 5.23
6. Sonic Automotive, 5.08
7. United Auto Group, 5.06
8. Budget Group, 3.86
9. Amerco, 3.75

Source: Diba, Ahmad and Lisa Munoz, "Who's Up Who's Down," *Fortune*, 143: 104-F7, (February 19, 2001).

★450★
Fortune's highest ranked beverages companies, 2000

Ranking basis/background: Based on a survey by Clark Martire & Bartolomeo of 10,000 executives, directors, and securities analysts rating 535 companies in 61 industries on overall management quality, products or service quality, innovativeness, value as a long-term investment, financial strength, responsibility to the community/environment, use of corporate assets, and effectiveness in business globally. **Number listed:** 8.

1. PepsiCo, with a score of 8.00
2. Anheuser-Busch, 7.67
3. Adolph Coors, 7.04
4. Coca-Cola, 6.63
5. Whitman, 5.90
6. Coca-Cola Enterprises, 5.61
7. Brown-Forman, 5.58
8. Constellation Brands, 5.19

Source: Diba, Ahmad and Lisa Munoz, "Who's Up Who's Down," *Fortune*, 143: 104-F7, (February 19, 2001).

★451★
Fortune's highest ranked building materials and glass companies, 2000

Ranking basis/background: Based on a survey by Clark Martire & Bartolomeo of 10,000 executives, directors, and securities analysts rating 535 companies in 61 industries on overall management quality, products or service quality, innovativeness, value as a long-term investment, financial strength, responsibility to the community/environment, use of corporate assets, and effectiveness in business globally. **Number listed:** 8.

1. Corning, with a score of 7.77
2. Vulcan Materials, 5.13
3. USG, 4.83
4. Southdown, 4.65
5. Owens-Illinois, 4.43
6. Armstrong Holdings, 4.34
7. Johns Manville, 4.30
8. Owens Corning, 3.38

Source: Diba, Ahmad and Lisa Munoz, "Who's Up Who's Down," *Fortune*, 143: 104-F7, (February 19, 2001).

★452★
Fortune's highest ranked chemicals companies, 2000

Ranking basis/background: Based on a survey by Clark Martire & Bartolomeo of 10,000 executives, directors, and securities analysts rating 535 companies in 61 industries on overall management quality, products or service quality, innovativeness, value as a long-term investment, financial strength, responsibility to the community/environment, use of corporate assets, and effectiveness in business globally. **Number listed:** 10.

1. Du Pont, with a score of 7.43
2. Dow Chemical Co., 6.89
3. Bayer, 6.39
4. PPG Industries, 6.29
5. BASF, 6.07
6. Praxair, 5.94
7. Rohm & Haas, 5.89
8. Air Products & Chemicals, 5.75
9. Sherwin-Williams, 5.34
10. Union Carbide, 4.66

Source: Diba, Ahmad and Lisa Munoz, "Who's Up Who's Down," *Fortune*, 143: 104-F7, (February 19, 2001).

★453★
Fortune's highest ranked computer and data services companies, 2000

Ranking basis/background: Based on a survey by Clark Martire & Bartolomeo of 10,000 executives, directors, and securities analysts rating 535 companies in 61 industries on overall management quality, products or service quality, innovativeness, value as a long-term investment, financial strength, responsibility to the community/environment, use of corporate assets, and effectiveness in business globally. **Number listed:** 10.

1. America Online, with a score of 7.11
2. Automatic Data Processing, 6.86
3. First Data, 6.32
4. Computer sciences, 6.11
5. Electronic Data Systems, 6.10
6. Unisys, 5.56
7. Dun & Bradstreet, 5.52
8. Science Applications International, 5.44
9. Comdisco, 5.28
10. Micro Warehouse, 4.92

Source: Diba, Ahmad and Lisa Munoz, "Who's Up Who's Down," *Fortune*, 143: 104-F7, (February 19, 2001).

★454★
Fortune's highest ranked computer peripherals companies, 2000

Ranking basis/background: Based on a survey by Clark Martire & Bartolomeo of 10,000 executives, directors, and securities analysts rating 535 companies in 61 industries on overall management quality, products or service quality, innovativeness, value as a long-term investment, financial strength, responsibility to the community/environment, use of corporate assets, and effectiveness in business globally. **Number listed:** 8.
1. EMC, with a score of 7.76
2. Lexmark International Group, 6.36
3. Quantum, 6.15
4. Seagate Technology, 6.14
5. Maxtor, 5.92
6. Imation, 5.83
7. Storage Technology, 5.70
8. Iomega, 5.26

Source: Diba, Ahmad and Lisa Munoz, "Who's Up Who's Down," *Fortune*, 143: 104-F7, (February 19, 2001).

★455★
Fortune's highest ranked computer software companies, 2000

Ranking basis/background: Based on a survey by Clark Martire & Bartolomeo of 10,000 executives, directors, and securities analysts rating 535 companies in 61 industries on overall management quality, products or service quality, innovativeness, value as a long-term investment, financial strength, responsibility to the community/environment, use of corporate assets, and effectiveness in business globally. **Number listed:** 8.
1. Microsoft, with a score of 7.39
2. Oracle, 6.91
3. Computer Associates International, 6.46
4. PeopleSoft, 5.85
5. Novell, 5.45
6. BMC Software, 5.44
7. Electronic Arts, 5.36
8. Compuware, 4.39

Source: Diba, Ahmad and Lisa Munoz, "Who's Up Who's Down," *Fortune*, 143: 104-F7, (February 19, 2001).

★456★
Fortune's highest ranked computers and office equipment companies, 2000

Ranking basis/background: Based on a survey by Clark Martire & Bartolomeo of 10,000 executives, directors, and securities analysts rating 535 companies in 61 industries on overall management quality, products or service quality, innovativeness, value as a long-term investment, financial strength, responsibility to the community/environment, use of corporate assets, and effectiveness in business globally. **Number listed:** 10.
1. Gateway, with a score of 7.08
2. Sun Microsystems, 6.79
3. Hewlett-Packard, 6.41
4. IBM, 6.20
5. Dell Computer, 6.07
6. Compaq Computer, 5.76
7. Canon U.S.A., 4.81
8. Apple Computer, 4.60
9. NCR, 4.54
10. Xerox, 3.87

Source: Diba, Ahmad and Lisa Munoz, "Who's Up Who's Down," *Fortune*, 143: 104-F7, (February 19, 2001).

★457★
Fortune's highest ranked consumer credit companies, 2000

Ranking basis/background: Based on a survey by Clark Martire & Bartolomeo of 10,000 executives, directors, and securities analysts rating 535 companies in 61 industries on overall management quality, products or service quality, innovativeness, value as a long-term investment, financial strength, responsibility to the community/environment, use of corporate assets, and effectiveness in business globally. **Number listed:** 7.
1. American Express, with a score of 7.92
2. MBNA, 7.33
3. Capital One Financial, 7.13
4. USA Education, 6.03
5. Household International, 5.77
6. Providian Financial, 5.76
7. Associates First Capital, 5.29

Source: Diba, Ahmad and Lisa Munoz, "Who's Up Who's Down," *Fortune*, 143: 104-F7, (February 19, 2001).

★458★
Fortune's highest ranked consumer food products companies, 2000

Ranking basis/background: Based on a survey by Clark Martire & Bartolomeo of 10,000 executives, directors, and securities analysts rating 535 companies in 61 industries on overall management quality, products or service quality, innovativeness, value as a long-term investment, financial strength, responsibility to the community/environment, use of corporate assets, and effectiveness in business globally. **Number listed:** 10.
1. Nestle USA, with a score of 6.87
2. General Mills, 6.71
3. Bestfoods, 6.06
4. Nabisco Group Holdings, 5.98
5. ConAgra, 5.82
6. Sara Lee, 5.71
7. Kellogg, 5.66
8. H.J. Heinz, 5.65
9. Campbell Soup, 4.91
10. Farmland Industries, 4.20

Source: Diba, Ahmad and Lisa Munoz, "Who's Up Who's Down," *Fortune*, 143: 104-F7, (February 19, 2001).

★459★
Fortune's highest ranked electric and gas utilities companies, 2000

Ranking basis/background: Based on a survey by Clark Martire & Bartolomeo of 10,000 executives, directors, and securities analysts rating 535 companies in 61 industries on overall management quality, products or service quality, innovativeness, value as a long-term investment, financial strength, responsibility to the community/environment, use of corporate assets, and effectiveness in business globally. **Number listed:** 11.
1. Duke Energy, with a score of 7.69
2. Southern, 6.94
3. Reliant Energy, 6.55
4. UtiliCorp United, 6.36
5. TXU, 6.35
6. Entergy, 6.16
7. Edison International, 6.08
8. American Electric Power, 5.93
9. PG&E, 5.79
10. Avista, 5.29
11. Consolidated Edison, 5.21

Source: Diba, Ahmad and Lisa Munoz, "Who's Up Who's Down," *Fortune*, 143: 104-F7, (February 19, 2001).

★460★
Fortune's highest ranked electronics and electrical equipment companies, 2000

Ranking basis/background: Based on a survey by Clark Martire & Bartolomeo of 10,000 executives, directors, and securities analysts rating 535 companies in 61 industries on overall management quality, products or service quality, innovativeness, value as a long-term investment, financial strength, responsibility to the community/environment, use of corporate assets, and effectiveness in business globally. **Number listed:** 10.
1. General Electric, with a score of 7.99
2. Emerson Electric, 6.69
3. Tyco International, 6.59
4. Motorola, 6.43
5. Siemens, 6.05
6. Philips Electronics N.A., 5.96
7. Rockwell International, 5.75
8. Solectron, 5.71
9. Whirlpool, 5.60
10. Eaton, 5.54

Source: Diba, Ahmad and Lisa Munoz, "Who's Up Who's Down," *Fortune*, 143: 104-F7, (February 19, 2001).

★461★
Fortune's highest ranked engineering and construction companies, 2000

Ranking basis/background: Based on a survey by Clark Martire & Bartolomeo of 10,000 executives, directors, and securities analysts rating 535 companies in 61 industries on overall management quality, products or service quality, innovativeness, value as a long-term investment, financial strength, responsibility to the community/environment, use of corporate assets, and effectiveness in business globally. **Number listed:** 10.
1. Centex, with a score of 7.22
2. Lennar, 6.57
3. Peter Kiewit Sons', 6.57
4. Pulte, 6.55
5. Halliburton, 6.49
6. D.R. Horton, 6.05
7. Kaufman & Broad, 6.04
8. Emcor Group, 5.99
9. Fluor, 5.83
10. Foster Wheeler, 5.74

Source: Diba, Ahmad and Lisa Munoz, "Who's Up Who's Down," *Fortune*, 143: 104-F7, (February 19, 2001).

★462★
Fortune's highest ranked entertainment companies, 2000

Ranking basis/background: Based on a survey by Clark Martire & Bartolomeo of 10,000 executives, directors, and securities analysts rating 535 companies in 61 industries on overall management quality, products or service quality, innovativeness, value as a long-term investment, financial strength, responsibility to the community/environment, use of corporate assets, and effectiveness in business globally. **Number listed:** 6.
1. Viacom, with a score of 8.08
2. Time Warner, 7.12
3. Walt Disney, 6.32
4. Clear Channel Communications, 6.24
5. News America, 5.73
6. USA Networks, 5.39

Source: Diba, Ahmad and Lisa Munoz, "Who's Up Who's Down," *Fortune*, 143: 104-F7, (February 19, 2001).

BUSINESS ADMINISTRATION

★463★
Fortune's highest ranked food and drug stores, 2000

Ranking basis/background: Based on a survey by Clark Martire & Bartolomeo of 10,000 executives, directors, and securities analysts rating 535 companies in 61 industries on overall management quality, products or service quality, innovativeness, value as a long-term investment, financial strength, responsibility to the community/environment, use of corporate assets, and effectiveness in business globally. **Number listed:** 10.

1. Safeway, with a score of 7.50
2. Walgreen, 7.17
3. Publix Super Markets, 6.99
4. Kroger, 6.78
5. CVS, 6.31
6. Ahold USA, 6.27
7. Albertson's, 5.88
8. Delhaize America, 5.64
9. Winn-Dixie Stores, 4.39
10. Rite Aid, 3.96

Source: Diba, Ahmad and Lisa Munoz, "Who's Up Who's Down," *Fortune*, 143: 104-F7, (February 19, 2001).

★464★
Fortune's highest ranked food production companies, 2000

Ranking basis/background: Based on a survey by Clark Martire & Bartolomeo of 10,000 executives, directors, and securities analysts rating 535 companies in 61 industries on overall management quality, products or service quality, innovativeness, value as a long-term investment, financial strength, responsibility to the community/environment, use of corporate assets, and effectiveness in business globally. **Number listed:** 10.

1. Suiza Foods, with a score of 6.67
2. Tyson Foods, 6.37
3. Dean Foods, 6.35
4. IBP, 6.07
5. Archer Daniels Midland, 6.02
6. Seaboard, 5.33
7. Gold Kist, 5.11
8. Chiquita Brands International, 4.61
9. Agway, 4.40
10. Imperial Sugar, 4.29

Source: Diba, Ahmad and Lisa Munoz, "Who's Up Who's Down," *Fortune*, 143: 104-F7, (February 19, 2001).

★465★
Fortune's highest ranked food services companies, 2000

Ranking basis/background: Based on a survey by Clark Martire & Bartolomeo of 10,000 executives, directors, and securities analysts rating 535 companies in 61 industries on overall management quality, products or service quality, innovativeness, value as a long-term investment, financial strength, responsibility to the community/environment, use of corporate assets, and effectiveness in business globally. **Number listed:** 10.

1. Starbucks, with a score of 7.42
2. McDonald's, 7.35
3. Outback Steakhouse, 7.29
4. Brinker International, 7.08
5. Darden Restaurants, 6.98
6. Wendy's International, 6.71
7. Tricon Global Restaurants, 5.49
8. CBRL, 5.12
9. Advantica, 4.37
10. CKE Restaurants, 3.04

Source: Diba, Ahmad and Lisa Munoz, "Who's Up Who's Down," *Fortune*, 143: 104-F7, (February 19, 2001).

★466★
Fortune's highest ranked forest and paper products companies, 2000

Ranking basis/background: Based on a survey by Clark Martire & Bartolomeo of 10,000 executives, directors, and securities analysts rating 535 companies in 61 industries on overall management quality, products or service quality, innovativeness, value as a long-term investment, financial strength, responsibility to the community/environment, use of corporate assets, and effectiveness in business globally. **Number listed:** 10.

1. Kimberly-Clark, with a score of 6.83
2. Weyerhauser, 6.43
3. International Paper, 5.93
4. Mead, 5.88
5. Willamette Industries, 5.79
6. Georgia-Pacific, 5.33
7. Temple-Inland, 5.13
8. Boise Cascade, 4.74
9. Fort James, 4.58
10. Smurfit-Stone Container, 4.47

Source: Diba, Ahmad and Lisa Munoz, "Who's Up Who's Down," *Fortune*, 143: 104-F7, (February 19, 2001).

★467★
Fortune's highest ranked furniture companies, 2000

Ranking basis/background: Based on a survey by Clark Martire & Bartolomeo of 10,000 executives, directors, and securities analysts rating 535 companies in 61 industries on overall management quality, products or service quality, innovativeness, value as a long-term investment, financial strength, responsibility to the community/environment, use of corporate assets, and effectiveness in business globally. **Number listed:** 6.

1. Herman Miller, with a score of 7.97
2. Steelcase, 7.07
3. Hon Industries, 6.88
4. Leggett & Platt, 6.71
5. La-Z-Boy, 5.85
6. Furniture Brands International, 5.58

Source: Diba, Ahmad and Lisa Munoz, "Who's Up Who's Down," *Fortune*, 143: 104-F7, (February 19, 2001).

★468★
Fortune's highest ranked general merchandisers, 2000

Ranking basis/background: Based on a survey by Clark Martire & Bartolomeo of 10,000 executives, directors, and securities analysts rating 535 companies in 61 industries on overall management quality, products or service quality, innovativeness, value as a long-term investment, financial strength, responsibility to the community/environment, use of corporate assets, and effectiveness in business globally. **Number listed:** 10.

1. Wal-Mart Stores, with a score of 7.56
2. Target, 7.29
3. Nordstrom, 5.89
4. May Department Stores, 5.76
5. Federated Department Stores, 5.61
6. Sears, Roebuck, 5.31
7. Saks Corporation, 5.17
8. JC Penney, 3.84
9. Dillard's, 3.71
10. Kmart, 3.33

Source: Diba, Ahmad and Lisa Munoz, "Who's Up Who's Down," *Fortune*, 143: 104-F7, (February 19, 2001).

★469★
Fortune's highest ranked health care companies, 2000

Ranking basis/background: Based on a survey by Clark Martire & Bartolomeo of 10,000 executives, directors, and securities analysts rating 535 companies in 61 industries on overall management quality, products or service quality, innovativeness, value as a long-term investment, financial strength, responsibility to the community/environment, use of corporate assets, and effectiveness in business globally. **Number listed:** 10.

1. WellPoint Health Networks, with a score of 7.02
2. United HealthCare, 6.80
3. Cigna, 6.15
4. Tenet Healthcare, 5.43
5. HCA, 5.36
6. Anthem Insurance, 5.00
7. Health Net, 4.85
8. Humana, 4.12
9. Aetna, 3.97
10. PacifiCare Health Systems, 3.61

Source: Diba, Ahmad and Lisa Munoz, "Who's Up Who's Down," *Fortune*, 143: 104-F7, (February 19, 2001).

★470★
Fortune's highest ranked hotels, casinos and resorts, 2000

Ranking basis/background: Based on a survey by Clark Martire & Bartolomeo of 10,000 executives, directors, and securities analysts rating 535 companies in 61 industries on overall management quality, products or service quality, innovativeness, value as a long-term investment, financial strength, responsibility to the community/environment, use of corporate assets, and effectiveness in business globally. **Number listed:** 10.

1. Marriott International, with a score of 7.47
2. MGM Mirage, 6.71
3. Hilton Hotels, 6.27
4. Park Place Entertainment, 6.18
5. Harrah's Entertainment, 6.14
6. Starwood Hotels & Resorts, 6.04
7. Crestline Capital, 5.77
8. Mandalay Resort Group, 5.57
9. Wyndham International, 3.91
10. Trump Hotels & Casino Resorts, 3.33

Source: Diba, Ahmad and Lisa Munoz, "Who's Up Who's Down," *Fortune*, 143: 104-F7, (February 19, 2001).

★471★
Fortune's highest ranked industrial and farm equipment companies, 2000

Ranking basis/background: Based on a survey by Clark Martire & Bartolomeo of 10,000 executives, directors, and securities analysts rating 535 companies in 61 industries on overall management quality, products or service quality, innovativeness, value as a long-term investment, financial strength, responsibility to the community/environment, use of corporate assets, and effectiveness in business globally. **Number listed:** 10.

1. Deere, with a score of 6.87
2. Caterpillar Inc., 6.84
3. ITT Industries, 6.62
4. Ingersoll-Rand, 6.41
5. Dover, 6.40
6. Parker Hannifin, 6.16

7. Black & Decker, 6.11
8. Cummins Engine, 5.99
9. Baker Hughes, 5.87
10. American Standard, 5.76

Source: Diba, Ahmad and Lisa Munoz, "Who's Up Who's Down," *Fortune*, 143: 104-F7, (February 19, 2001).

★472★
Fortune's highest ranked life and health insurance companies, 2000

Ranking basis/background: Based on a survey by Clark Martire & Bartolomeo of 10,000 executives, directors, and securities analysts rating 535 companies in 61 industries on overall management quality, products or service quality, innovativeness, value as a long-term investment, financial strength, responsibility to the community/environment, use of corporate assets, and effectiveness in business globally. **Number listed:** 10.
1. Northwestern Mutual Life Insurance, with a score of 7.38
2. New York Life Insurance, 6.74
3. TIAA-CREF, 6.65
4. Massachusetts Mutual Life Insurance, 6.14
5. AFLAC, 6.02
6. Guardian Life of America, 5.91
7. MetLife, 5.66
8. American General, 5.58
9. Prudential Insurance of America, 5.06
10. UnumProvident, 4.67

Source: Diba, Ahmad and Lisa Munoz, "Who's Up Who's Down," *Fortune*, 143: 104-F7, (February 19, 2001).

★473★
Fortune's highest ranked mail, packaging, and freight delivery companies, 2000

Ranking basis/background: Based on a survey by Clark Martire & Bartolomeo of 10,000 executives, directors, and securities analysts rating 535 companies in 61 industries on overall management quality, products or service quality, innovativeness, value as a long-term investment, financial strength, responsibility to the community/environment, use of corporate assets, and effectiveness in business globally. **Number listed:** 6.
1. United Parcel Service of America, with a score of 8.36
2. FedEx, 7.64
3. Expeditors International of Washington, 5.43
4. Fritz, 5.10
5. Airborne Freight, 4.00
6. Pittston, 3.83

Source: Diba, Ahmad and Lisa Munoz, "Who's Up Who's Down," *Fortune*, 143: 104-F7, (February 19, 2001).

★474★
Fortune's highest ranked medical products and equipment companies, 2000

Ranking basis/background: Based on a survey by Clark Martire & Bartolomeo of 10,000 executives, directors, and securities analysts rating 535 companies in 61 industries on overall management quality, products or service quality, innovativeness, value as a long-term investment, financial strength, responsibility to the community/environment, use of corporate assets, and effectiveness in business globally. **Number listed:** 9.
1. Medtronic, with a score of 8.23
2. Guidant, 7.65
3. Baxter International, 7.30
4. Becton Dickinson, 6.08
5. Hillenbrand Industries, 5.50
6. Boston Scientific, 5.38
7. Mallinckrodt, 5.29
8. Bausch & Lomb, 5.26
9. Dade Behring, 5.11

Source: Diba, Ahmad and Lisa Munoz, "Who's Up Who's Down," *Fortune*, 143: 104-F7, (February 19, 2001).

★475★
Fortune's highest ranked metal products companies, 2000

Ranking basis/background: Based on a survey by Clark Martire & Bartolomeo of 10,000 executives, directors, and securities analysts rating 535 companies in 61 industries on overall management quality, products or service quality, innovativeness, value as a long-term investment, financial strength, responsibility to the community/environment, use of corporate assets, and effectiveness in business globally. **Number listed:** 10.
1. Fortune Brands, with a score of 7.66
2. Illinois Tool Works, 5.70
3. Danaher, 5.15
4. Newell Rubbermaid, 4.90
5. Stanley Works, 4.90
6. Ball, 4.65
7. U.S. Industries, 4.63
8. Masco, 4.61
9. General Cable, 4.23
10. Crown Cork & Seal, 4.15

Source: Diba, Ahmad and Lisa Munoz, "Who's Up Who's Down," *Fortune*, 143: 104-F7, (February 19, 2001).

★476★
Fortune's highest ranked metals companies, 2000

Ranking basis/background: Based on a survey by Clark Martire & Bartolomeo of 10,000 executives, directors, and securities analysts rating 535 companies in 61 industries on overall management quality, products or service quality, innovativeness, value as a long-term investment, financial strength, responsibility to the community/environment, use of corporate assets, and effectiveness in business globally. **Number listed:** 10.
1. Alcoa, with a score of 7.46
2. Nucor, 6.08
3. Phelps Dodge, 5.75
4. Worthington Industries, 5.52
5. AK Steel Holding, 5.21
6. Allegheny Technologies, 5.19
7. Commercial Metals, 4.62
8. Bethlehem Steel, 4.24
9. Maxxam, 4.04
10. LTV, 3.24

Source: Diba, Ahmad and Lisa Munoz, "Who's Up Who's Down," *Fortune*, 143: 104-F7, (February 19, 2001).

★477★
Fortune's highest ranked mining and crude oil companies, 2000

Ranking basis/background: Based on a survey by Clark Martire & Bartolomeo of 10,000 executives, directors, and securities analysts rating 535 companies in 61 industries on overall management quality, products or service quality, innovativeness, value as a long-term investment, financial strength, responsibility to the community/environment, use of corporate assets, and effectiveness in business globally. **Number listed:** 8.
1. Apache, with a score of 7.95
2. Unocal, 5.97
3. Burlington Resources, 5.09
4. Occidental Petroleum, 5.02
5. Newmont Mining, 4.95
6. Martin Marietta Materials, 4.92
7. Freeport-McMoran Copper & Gold, 4.63
8. Plains Resources, 4.46

Source: Diba, Ahmad and Lisa Munoz, "Who's Up Who's Down," *Fortune*, 143: 104-F7, (February 19, 2001).

★478★
Fortune's highest ranked money center banks, 2000

Ranking basis/background: Based on a survey by Clark Martire & Bartolomeo of 10,000 executives, directors, and securities analysts rating 535 companies in 61 industries on overall management quality, products or service quality, innovativeness, value as a long-term investment, financial strength, responsibility to the community/environment, use of corporate assets, and effectiveness in business globally. **Number listed:** 5.
1. Citigroup, with a score of 8.60
2. Chase Manhattan, 7.61
3. J.P. Morgan & Co., 7.05
4. Bank of New York, 6.87
5. Bank of America, 6.53

Source: Diba, Ahmad and Lisa Munoz, "Who's Up Who's Down," *Fortune*, 143: 104-F7, (February 19, 2001).

★479★
Fortune's highest ranked mortgage finance companies, 2000

Ranking basis/background: Based on a survey by Clark Martire & Bartolomeo of 10,000 executives, directors, and securities analysts rating 535 companies in 61 industries on overall management quality, products or service quality, innovativeness, value as a long-term investment, financial strength, responsibility to the community/environment, use of corporate assets, and effectiveness in business globally. **Number listed:** 10.
1. Fannie Mae, with a score of 7.17
2. Freddie Mac, 6.78
3. Golden West Financial, 6.63
4. Washington Mutual, 6.47
5. Charter One Financial, 6.14
6. Countrywide Credit Industries, 5.68
7. First American Financial, 5.31
8. Golden State Bancorp, 5.07
9. Dime Bancorp, 4.85
10. LandAmerica Financial Group, 4.60

Source: Diba, Ahmad and Lisa Munoz, "Who's Up Who's Down," *Fortune*, 143: 104-F7, (February 19, 2001).

★480★
Fortune's highest ranked motor vehicle parts companies, 2000

Ranking basis/background: Based on a survey by Clark Martire & Bartolomeo of 10,000 executives, directors, and securities analysts rating 535 companies in 61 industries on overall management quality, products or service quality, innovativeness, value as a long-term investment, financial strength, responsibility to the community/environment, use of corporate assets, and effectiveness in business globally. **Number listed:** 10.
1. Johnson Controls, with a score of 7.39
2. Delphi Automotive Systems, 7.18
3. Lear, 6.34
4. TRW, 6.10

5. Autoliv, 6.09
6. Dana, 5.95
7. Arvin Meritor, 5.60
8. Tenneco Automotive, 4.94
9. Fleetwood Enterprises, 4.92
10. Federal-Mogul, 3.21

Source: Diba, Ahmad and Lisa Munoz, "Who's Up Who's Down," *Fortune*, 143: 104-F7, (February 19, 2001).

★481★
Fortune's highest ranked motor vehicles companies, 2000

Ranking basis/background: Based on a survey by Clark Martire & Bartolomeo of 10,000 executives, directors, and securities analysts rating 535 companies in 61 industries on overall management quality, products or service quality, innovativeness, value as a long-term investment, financial strength, responsibility to the community/environment, use of corporate assets, and effectiveness in business globally. **Number listed:** 8.

1. Toyota Motor Sales USA, with a score of 7.51
2. Ford Motor Company, 7.30
3. American Honda Motor, 6.93
4. Navistar International, 5.93
5. DaimlerChrysler, 5.71
6. General Motors, 5.57
7. Paccar, 5.29
8. Oshkosh Truck, 5.06

Source: Diba, Ahmad and Lisa Munoz, "Who's Up Who's Down," *Fortune*, 143: 104-F7, (February 19, 2001).

★482★
Fortune's highest ranked network communications companies, 2000

Ranking basis/background: Based on a survey by Clark Martire & Bartolomeo of 10,000 executives, directors, and securities analysts rating 535 companies in 61 industries on overall management quality, products or service quality, innovativeness, value as a long-term investment, financial strength, responsibility to the community/environment, use of corporate assets, and effectiveness in business globally. **Number listed:** 7.

1. Cisco Systems, with a score of 8.17
2. Nortel Networks, 7.70
3. Tellabs, 6.55
4. ADC Telecommunications, 6.33
5. 3Com, 6.02
6. Lucent Technologies, 5.17
7. Cabletron Systems, 4.80

Source: Diba, Ahmad and Lisa Munoz, "Who's Up Who's Down," *Fortune*, 143: 104-F7, (February 19, 2001).

★483★
Fortune's highest ranked outsourcing services companies, 2000

Ranking basis/background: Based on a survey by Clark Martire & Bartolomeo of 10,000 executives, directors, and securities analysts rating 535 companies in 61 industries on overall management quality, products or service quality, innovativeness, value as a long-term investment, financial strength, responsibility to the community/environment, use of corporate assets, and effectiveness in business globally. **Number listed:** 10.

1. Cintas, with a score of 7.24
2. Aramark, 6.79
3. ServiceMaster, 6.72
4. Administaff, 6.68
5. Sodexho Marriott Services, 6.49
6. Wackenhut, 5.87
7. Convergys, 5.44
8. Ogden, 5.19
9. Viad, 4.99
10. Staff Leasing, 4.93

Source: Diba, Ahmad and Lisa Munoz, "Who's Up Who's Down," *Fortune*, 143: 104-F7, (February 19, 2001).

★484★
Fortune's highest ranked petroleum refining companies, 2000

Ranking basis/background: Based on a survey by Clark Martire & Bartolomeo of 10,000 executives, directors, and securities analysts rating 535 companies in 61 industries on overall management quality, products or service quality, innovativeness, value as a long-term investment, financial strength, responsibility to the community/environment, use of corporate assets, and effectiveness in business globally. **Number listed:** 10.

1. Exxon Mobil, with a score of 8.04
2. BP America, 7.95
3. Shell Oil, 7.72
4. Chevron, 7.36
5. Conoco, 6.45
6. Texaco, 6.19
7. Phillips Petroleum, 6.02
8. Tosco, 5.93
9. USX, 5.53
10. Citgo, 5.29

Source: Diba, Ahmad and Lisa Munoz, "Who's Up Who's Down," *Fortune*, 143: 104-F7, (February 19, 2001).

★485★
Fortune's highest ranked pharmaceuticals companies, 2000

Ranking basis/background: Based on a survey by Clark Martire & Bartolomeo of 10,000 executives, directors, and securities analysts rating 535 companies in 61 industries on overall management quality, products or service quality, innovativeness, value as a long-term investment, financial strength, responsibility to the community/environment, use of corporate assets, and effectiveness in business globally. **Number listed:** 10.

1. Bristol-Myers Squibb, with a score of 7.36
2. Merck, 7.21
3. Pfizer, 7.15
4. Johnson & Johnson, 6.93
5. Eli Lilly and Company, 6.87
6. Schering-Plough, 6.68
7. Pharmacia, 6.67
8. Amgen, 6.14
9. Abbott Laboratories, 5.55
10. American Home Products, 5.16

Source: Diba, Ahmad and Lisa Munoz, "Who's Up Who's Down," *Fortune*, 143: 104-F7, (February 19, 2001).

★486★
Fortune's highest ranked pipelines and energy companies, 2000

Ranking basis/background: Based on a survey by Clark Martire & Bartolomeo of 10,000 executives, directors, and securities analysts rating 535 companies in 61 industries on overall management quality, products or service quality, innovativeness, value as a long-term investment, financial strength, responsibility to the community/environment, use of corporate assets, and effectiveness in business globally. **Number listed:** 10.

1. Enron, with a score of 8.29
2. Williams, 6.86
3. El Paso Energy, 6.85
4. Dynegy, 6.75
5. Kinder Morgan, 6.63
6. MidAmerican Energy Holdings, 5.46
7. NorthWestern, 5.25
8. Western Gas Resources, 5.01
9. USEC, 4.56
10. TransMontaigne Oil, 4.46

Source: Diba, Ahmad and Lisa Munoz, "Who's Up Who's Down," *Fortune*, 143: 104-F7, (February 19, 2001).

★487★
Fortune's highest ranked printing companies, 2000

Ranking basis/background: Based on a survey by Clark Martire & Bartolomeo of 10,000 executives, directors, and securities analysts rating 535 companies in 61 industries on overall management quality, products or service quality, innovativeness, value as a long-term investment, financial strength, responsibility to the community/environment, use of corporate assets, and effectiveness in business globally. **Number listed:** 7.

1. R.R. Donnelley & Sons, with a score of 7.03
2. Banta, 5.89
3. Reynolds & Reynolds, 5.60
4. Deluxe, 5.54
5. Wallace Computer Services, 5.46
6. Standard Register, 5.33
7. Mail-Well, 4.89

Source: Diba, Ahmad and Lisa Munoz, "Who's Up Who's Down," *Fortune*, 143: 104-F7, (February 19, 2001).

★488★
Fortune's highest ranked property and casualty insurance companies, 2000

Ranking basis/background: Based on a survey by Clark Martire & Bartolomeo of 10,000 executives, directors, and securities analysts rating 535 companies in 61 industries on overall management quality, products or service quality, innovativeness, value as a long-term investment, financial strength, responsibility to the community/environment, use of corporate assets, and effectiveness in business globally. **Number listed:** 10.

1. Berkshire Hathaway, with a score of 7.61
2. USAA, 7.13
3. American International Group, 7.08
4. Hartford Financial Services Group, 6.81
5. State Farm Insurance Company, 6.66
6. Allstate, 6.46
7. Nationwide Insurance Enterprise, 5.93
8. Liberty Mutual Insurance Group, 5.92
9. St. Paul, 5.80
10. Loews, 4.94

Source: Diba, Ahmad and Lisa Munoz, "Who's Up Who's Down," *Fortune*, 143: 104-F7, (February 19, 2001).

★489★
Fortune's highest ranked publishing companies, 2000

Ranking basis/background: Based on a survey by Clark Martire & Bartolomeo of 10,000 executives, directors, and securities analysts rating 535 companies in 61 industries on overall management quality, products or service quality, innovativeness, value as a long-term investment, financial strength, responsibility to the community/environment, use of corporate assets, and effectiveness in business globally. **Number listed:** 10.

1. New York Times, with a score of 7.71

2. Tribune, 7.35
3. The Washington Post, 7.29
4. Dow Jones, 7.13
5. Gannett, 6.58
6. McGraw-Hill, 6.41
7. Knight Ridder, 6.25
8. American Greetings, 5.39
9. Primedia, 5.08
10. Reader's Digest Association, 5.05

Source: Diba, Ahmad and Lisa Munoz, "Who's Up Who's Down," *Fortune*, 143: 104-F7, (February 19, 2001).

★490★
Fortune's highest ranked railroads, 2000

Ranking basis/background: Based on a survey by Clark Martire & Bartolomeo of 10,000 executives, directors, and securities analysts rating 535 companies in 61 industries on overall management quality, products or service quality, innovativeness, value as a long-term investment, financial strength, responsibility to the community/environment, use of corporate assets, and effectiveness in business globally. **Number listed:** 5.
1. Union Pacific, with a score of 7.03
2. Burlington Northern Santa Fe, 6.32
3. Norfolk Southern, 5.79
4. CSX, 5.15
5. Kansas City So. Industries, 5.02

Source: Diba, Ahmad and Lisa Munoz, "Who's Up Who's Down," *Fortune*, 143: 104-F7, (February 19, 2001).

★491★
Fortune's highest ranked real estate companies, 2000

Ranking basis/background: Based on a survey by Clark Martire & Bartolomeo of 10,000 executives, directors, and securities analysts rating 535 companies in 61 industries on overall management quality, products or service quality, innovativeness, value as a long-term investment, financial strength, responsibility to the community/environment, use of corporate assets, and effectiveness in business globally. **Number listed:** 4.
1. Equity Office Properties, with a score of 7.92
2. Equity Residential Properties, 7.43
3. Simon Property Group, 7.22
4. Del Webb, 6.13

Source: Diba, Ahmad and Lisa Munoz, "Who's Up Who's Down," *Fortune*, 143: 104-F7, (February 19, 2001).

★492★
Fortune's highest ranked rubber and plastic products companies, 2000

Ranking basis/background: Based on a survey by Clark Martire & Bartolomeo of 10,000 executives, directors, and securities analysts rating 535 companies in 61 industries on overall management quality, products or service quality, innovativeness, value as a long-term investment, financial strength, responsibility to the community/environment, use of corporate assets, and effectiveness in business globally. **Number listed:** 10.
1. Sealed Air, with a score of 7.30
2. Goodyear Tire & Rubber, 6.92
3. Pactiv, 6.45
4. Mark IV Industries, 6.31
5. Cooper Tire & Rubber, 6.20
6. GenCorp, 5.62
7. PolyOne, 5.46
8. Carlisle, 5.45
9. Foamex International, 5.12
10. Bridgestone/Firestone, 3.31

Source: Diba, Ahmad and Lisa Munoz, "Who's Up Who's Down," *Fortune*, 143: 104-F7, (February 19, 2001).

★493★
Fortune's highest ranked scientific, photo and control equipment companies, 2000

Ranking basis/background: Based on a survey by Clark Martire & Bartolomeo of 10,000 executives, directors, and securities analysts rating 535 companies in 61 industries on overall management quality, products or service quality, innovativeness, value as a long-term investment, financial strength, responsibility to the community/environment, use of corporate assets, and effectiveness in business globally. **Number listed:** 10.
1. Applied Materials, with a score of 7.44
2. Minnesota Mining & Manufacturing, 7.11
3. Applera, 6.82
4. Teradyne, 6.48
5. Stryker, 6.04
6. Tektronix, 5.89
7. Beckman Coulter, 5.75
8. Eastman Kodak Company, 5.34
9. Thermo Electron, 5.30
10. Polaroid, 4.73

Source: Diba, Ahmad and Lisa Munoz, "Who's Up Who's Down," *Fortune*, 143: 104-F7, (February 19, 2001).

★494★
Fortune's highest ranked securities companies, 2000

Ranking basis/background: Based on a survey by Clark Martire & Bartolomeo of 10,000 executives, directors, and securities analysts rating 535 companies in 61 industries on overall management quality, products or service quality, innovativeness, value as a long-term investment, financial strength, responsibility to the community/environment, use of corporate assets, and effectiveness in business globally. **Number listed:** 10.
1. Charles Schwab, with a score of 8.07
2. Goldman Sachs, 7.81
3. Morgan Stanley Dean Witter, 7.25
4. Merrill Lynch, 7.20
5. AXA Financial, 6.55
6. A.G. Edwards, 6.00
7. Lehman Brothers Holdings, 5.94
8. Franklin Resources, 5.87
9. Paine Webber Group, 5.72
10. Bear Stearns, 5.15

Source: Diba, Ahmad and Lisa Munoz, "Who's Up Who's Down," *Fortune*, 143: 104-F7, (February 19, 2001).

★495★
Fortune's highest ranked semiconductors companies, 2000

Ranking basis/background: Based on a survey by Clark Martire & Bartolomeo of 10,000 executives, directors, and securities analysts rating 535 companies in 61 industries on overall management quality, products or service quality, innovativeness, value as a long-term investment, financial strength, responsibility to the community/environment, use of corporate assets, and effectiveness in business globally. **Number listed:** 8.
1. Texas Instruments, with a score of 7.78
2. Intel, 7.53
3. Analog Devices, 7.04
4. LSI Logic, 6.39
5. Atmel, 5.70
6. Advanced Micro Devices, 5.53
7. National Semiconductor, 5.39
8. Amkor Technology, 5.20

Source: Diba, Ahmad and Lisa Munoz, "Who's Up Who's Down," *Fortune*, 143: 104-F7, (February 19, 2001).

★496★
Fortune's highest ranked soaps and cosmetics companies, 2000

Ranking basis/background: Based on a survey by Clark Martire & Bartolomeo of 10,000 executives, directors, and securities analysts rating 535 companies in 61 industries on overall management quality, products or service quality, innovativeness, value as a long-term investment, financial strength, responsibility to the community/environment, use of corporate assets, and effectiveness in business globally. **Number listed:** 10.
1. Procter & Gamble, with a score of 7.63
2. Colgate-Palmolive, 7.62
3. Unilever U.S., 6.78
4. Gillette, 6.75
5. Estee Lauder, 6.49
6. Clorox, 6.29
7. Avon Products, 6.20
8. Alberto-Culver, 4.67
9. Revlon, 3.92
10. Dial, 3.72

Source: Diba, Ahmad and Lisa Munoz, "Who's Up Who's Down," *Fortune*, 143: 104-F7, (February 19, 2001).

★497★
Fortune's highest ranked specialty retailers, 2000

Ranking basis/background: Based on a survey by Clark Martire & Bartolomeo of 10,000 executives, directors, and securities analysts rating 535 companies in 61 industries on overall management quality, products or service quality, innovativeness, value as a long-term investment, financial strength, responsibility to the community/environment, use of corporate assets, and effectiveness in business globally. **Number listed:** 10.
1. Home Depot, with a score of 7.85
2. Limited, 6.69
3. Costco Wholesale, 6.67
4. Gap, 6.55
5. Lowe's, 6.47
6. Best Buy, 6.35
7. Staples, 6.10
8. Circuit City Group, 5.54
9. Office Depot, 5.39
10. Toys "R" Us, 4.71

Source: Diba, Ahmad and Lisa Munoz, "Who's Up Who's Down," *Fortune*, 143: 104-F7, (February 19, 2001).

★498★
Fortune's highest ranked super-regional banks, 2000

Ranking basis/background: Based on a survey by Clark Martire & Bartolomeo of 10,000 executives, directors, and securities analysts rating 535 companies in 61 industries on overall management quality, products or service quality, innovativeness, value as a long-term investment, financial strength, responsibility to the community/environment, use of corporate assets, and effectiveness in business globally. **Number listed:** 10.
1. Wells Fargo, with a score of 7.52
2. Firstar, 6.50
3. FleetBoston, 6.43
4. SunTrust Banks, 6.19

5. PNC Financial Services Group, 6.17
6. U.S. Bancorp, 5.86
7. National City, 5.73
8. Bank One, 5.32
9. First Union, 5.00
10. KeyCorp, 4.98

Source: Diba, Ahmad and Lisa Munoz, "Who's Up Who's Down," *Fortune*, 143: 104-F7, (February 19, 2001).

★499★
Fortune's highest ranked telecommunications companies, 2000

Ranking basis/background: Based on a survey by Clark Martire & Bartolomeo of 10,000 executives, directors, and securities analysts rating 535 companies in 61 industries on overall management quality, products or service quality, innovativeness, value as a long-term investment, financial strength, responsibility to the community/environment, use of corporate assets, and effectiveness in business globally. **Number listed:** 10.

1. SBC Communications, with a score of 7.36
2. BellSouth, 6.20
3. Verizon Communications, 5.94
4. Qwest Communications, 5.88
5. ALLTEL, 5.83
6. Sprint, 5.56
7. Comcast, 5.41
8. Cablevision Systems, 4.96
9. WorldCom, 4.91
10. AT&T, 4.86

Source: Diba, Ahmad and Lisa Munoz, "Who's Up Who's Down," *Fortune*, 143: 104-F7, (February 19, 2001).

★500★
Fortune's highest ranked temporary help companies, 2000

Ranking basis/background: Based on a survey by Clark Martire & Bartolomeo of 10,000 executives, directors, and securities analysts rating 535 companies in 61 industries on overall management quality, products or service quality, innovativeness, value as a long-term investment, financial strength, responsibility to the community/environment, use of corporate assets, and effectiveness in business globally. **Number listed:** 7.

1. Robert Half International, with a score of 6.92
2. Manpower, 6.36
3. Kelly Services, 5.79
4. Spherion, 5.08
5. Volt Information Sciences, 4.79
6. CDI, 4.58
7. Modis Professional Services, 4.29

Source: Diba, Ahmad and Lisa Munoz, "Who's Up Who's Down," *Fortune*, 143: 104-F7, (February 19, 2001).

★501★
Fortune's highest ranked textiles companies, 2000

Ranking basis/background: Based on a survey by Clark Martire & Bartolomeo of 10,000 executives, directors, and securities analysts rating 535 companies in 61 industries on overall management quality, products or service quality, innovativeness, value as a long-term investment, financial strength, responsibility to the community/environment, use of corporate assets, and effectiveness in business globally. **Number listed:** 8.

1. Shaw Industries, with a score of 6.68
2. Mohawk Industries, 6.42
3. Unifi, 6.30
4. Springs Industries, 6.16
5. Interface, 5.50
6. WestPoint Stevens, 5.47
7. Burlington Industries, 4.63
8. Pillowtex, 3.69

Source: Diba, Ahmad and Lisa Munoz, "Who's Up Who's Down," *Fortune*, 143: 104-F7, (February 19, 2001).

★502★
Fortune's highest ranked tobacco companies, 2000

Ranking basis/background: Based on a survey by Clark Martire & Bartolomeo of 10,000 executives, directors, and securities analysts rating 535 companies in 61 industries on overall management quality, products or service quality, innovativeness, value as a long-term investment, financial strength, responsibility to the community/environment, use of corporate assets, and effectiveness in business globally. **Number listed:** 5.

1. Philip Morris, with a score of 8.19
2. UST, 6.36
3. R.J. Reynolds Tobacco, 6.26
4. Universal, 5.85
5. Dimon, 5.47

Source: Diba, Ahmad and Lisa Munoz, "Who's Up Who's Down," *Fortune*, 143: 104-F7, (February 19, 2001).

★503★
Fortune's highest ranked trucking companies, 2000

Ranking basis/background: Based on a survey by Clark Martire & Bartolomeo of 10,000 executives, directors, and securities analysts rating 535 companies in 61 industries on overall management quality, products or service quality, innovativeness, value as a long-term investment, financial strength, responsibility to the community/environment, use of corporate assets, and effectiveness in business globally. **Number listed:** 10.

1. CNF Transportation, with a score of 6.62
2. USFreightways, 6.49
3. American Freightways, 6.43
4. Yellow, 6.32
5. Arkansas Best, 5.94
6. C.H. Robinson Worldwide, 5.92
7. Roadway Express, 5.85
8. Landstar, 5.62
9. J.B. Hunt Transport Services, 5.14
10. Consolidated Freightways, 3.81

Source: Diba, Ahmad and Lisa Munoz, "Who's Up Who's Down," *Fortune*, 143: 104-F7, (February 19, 2001).

★504★
Fortune's highest ranked waste management companies, 2000

Ranking basis/background: Based on a survey by Clark Martire & Bartolomeo of 10,000 executives, directors, and securities analysts rating 535 companies in 61 industries on overall management quality, products or service quality, innovativeness, value as a long-term investment, financial strength, responsibility to the community/environment, use of corporate assets, and effectiveness in business globally. **Number listed:** 4.

1. Waste Management, with a score of 7.35
2. Republic Services, 6.08
3. Allied Waste Industries, 5.83
4. Safety-Kleen, 3.61

Source: Diba, Ahmad and Lisa Munoz, "Who's Up Who's Down," *Fortune*, 143: 104-F7, (February 19, 2001).

★505★
Fortune's highest ranked wholesalers, 2000

Ranking basis/background: Based on a survey by Clark Martire & Bartolomeo of 10,000 executives, directors, and securities analysts rating 535 companies in 61 industries on overall management quality, products or service quality, innovativeness, value as a long-term investment, financial strength, responsibility to the community/environment, use of corporate assets, and effectiveness in business globally. **Number listed:** 10.

1. Cardinal Health, with a score of 7.55
2. Sysco, 6.64
3. Arrow Electronics, 6.33
4. Tech Data, 6.28
5. AmeriSource Health, 6.23
6. Supervalu, 5.98
7. McKesson HBOC, 5.94
8. Fleming, 5.63
9. Ingram Micro, 5.59
10. Bergen Brunswig, 5.07

Source: Diba, Ahmad and Lisa Munoz, "Who's Up Who's Down," *Fortune*, 143: 104-F7, (February 19, 2001).

★506★
Fortune's least admired companies for employee talent

Ranking basis/background: Based on a survey by Clark Martire & Bartolomeo of 10,000 executives, directors, and securities analysts who selected companies, regardless of industry, that they admire most. **Number listed:** 3.

1. Warnaco Group, with a score of 2.38
2. LTV, 2.83
3. Trans World Airlines, 2.95

Source: Diba, Ahmad and Lisa Munoz, "Who's Up Who's Down," *Fortune*, 143: 104-F7, (February 19, 2001).

★507★
Fortune's least admired companies for financial soundness

Ranking basis/background: Based on a survey by Clark Martire & Bartolomeo of 10,000 executives, directors, and securities analysts who selected companies, regardless of industry, that they admire most. **Number listed:** 3.

1. Owens Corning, with a score of 1.74
2. Federal-Mogul, 1.80
3. Trans World Airlines, 2.11

Source: Diba, Ahmad and Lisa Munoz, "Who's Up Who's Down," *Fortune*, 143: 104-F7, (February 19, 2001).

★508★
Fortune's least admired companies for innovation

Ranking basis/background: Based on a survey by Clark Martire & Bartolomeo of 10,000 executives, directors, and securities analysts who selected companies, regardless of industry, that they admire most. **Number listed:** 3.

1. JC Penney, with a score of 2.86
2. Dillard's, 3.00
3. America West Holdings, 3.15

Source: Diba, Ahmad and Lisa Munoz, "Who's Up Who's Down," *Fortune*, 143: 104-F7, (February 19, 2001).

BUSINESS ADMINISTRATION

★509★
Fortune's least admired companies for long-term investment value

Ranking basis/background: Based on a survey by Clark Martire & Bartolomeo of 10,000 executives, directors, and securities analysts who selected companies, regardless of industry, that they admire most. **Number listed:** 3.
1. Owens Corning, with a score of 1.71
2. Federal-Mogul, 2.10
3. Bridgestone/Firestone, 2.13

Source: Diba, Ahmad and Lisa Munoz, "Who's Up Who's Down," *Fortune*, 143: 104-F7, (February 19, 2001).

★510★
Fortune's least admired companies for quality of management

Ranking basis/background: Based on a survey by Clark Martire & Bartolomeo of 10,000 executives, directors, and securities analysts who selected companies, regardless of industry, that they admire most. **Number listed:** 3.
1. Warnaco Group, with a score of 2.48
2. Federal-Mogul, 2.88
3. LTV, 2.98

Source: Diba, Ahmad and Lisa Munoz, "Who's Up Who's Down," *Fortune*, 143: 104-F7, (February 19, 2001).

★511★
Fortune's least admired companies for quality of products or services

Ranking basis/background: Based on a survey by Clark Martire & Bartolomeo of 10,000 executives, directors, and securities analysts who selected companies, regardless of industry, that they admire most. **Number listed:** 3.
1. America West Holdings, with a score of 3.30
2. US Airways Group, 3.66
3. Kmart, 3.67

Source: Diba, Ahmad and Lisa Munoz, "Who's Up Who's Down," *Fortune*, 143: 104-F7, (February 19, 2001).

★512★
Fortune's least admired companies for social responsibility

Ranking basis/background: Based on a survey by Clark Martire & Bartolomeo of 10,000 executives, directors, and securities analysts who selected companies, regardless of industry, that they admire most. **Number listed:** 3.
1. Amerco, with a score of 3.11
2. Trump Hotels and Casino Resorts, 3.19
3. CKE Restaurants, 3.35

Source: Diba, Ahmad and Lisa Munoz, "Who's Up Who's Down," *Fortune*, 143: 104-F7, (February 19, 2001).

★513★
Fortune's least admired companies for use of corporate assets

Ranking basis/background: Based on a survey by Clark Martire & Bartolomeo of 10,000 executives, directors, and securities analysts who selected companies, regardless of industry, that they admire most. **Number listed:** 3.
1. Federal-Mogul, with a score of 2.55
2. Warnaco Group, 2.62
3. CKE Restaurants, 2.73

Source: Diba, Ahmad and Lisa Munoz, "Who's Up Who's Down," *Fortune*, 143: 104-F7, (February 19, 2001).

★514★
Fortune's most admired companies for employee talent

Ranking basis/background: Based on a survey by Clark Martire & Bartolomeo of 10,000 executives, directors, and securities analysts who selected companies, regardless of industry, that they admire most. **Number listed:** 3.
1. Omnicom Group, with a score of 8.76
2. Goldman Sachs, 8.70
3. Citigroup, 8.68

Source: Diba, Ahmad and Lisa Munoz, "Who's Up Who's Down," *Fortune*, 143: 104-F7, (February 19, 2001).

★515★
Fortune's most admired companies for financial soundness

Ranking basis/background: Based on a survey by Clark Martire & Bartolomeo of 10,000 executives, directors, and securities analysts who selected companies, regardless of industry, that they admire most. **Number listed:** 5.
1. Exxon Mobil, with a score of 9.30
2. Citigroup, 9.00
2. Omnicom Group, 9.00
2. United Parcel Service of America, 9.00
2. Intel, 9.00

Source: Diba, Ahmad and Lisa Munoz, "Who's Up Who's Down," *Fortune*, 143: 104-F7, (February 19, 2001).

★516★
Fortune's most admired companies for innovation

Ranking basis/background: Based on a survey by Clark Martire & Bartolomeo of 10,000 executives, directors, and securities analysts who selected companies, regardless of industry, that they admire most. **Number listed:** 3.
1. Enron, with a score of 9.28
2. Charles Schwab, 9.09
3. Citigroup, 8.52

Source: Diba, Ahmad and Lisa Munoz, "Who's Up Who's Down," *Fortune*, 143: 104-F7, (February 19, 2001).

★517★
Fortune's most admired companies for long-term investment value

Ranking basis/background: Based on a survey by Clark Martire & Bartolomeo of 10,000 executives, directors, and securities analysts who selected companies, regardless of industry, that they admire most. **Number listed:** 3.
1. Citigroup, with a score of 8.97
2. Exxon Mobil, 8.68
3. Omnicom Group, 8.62

Source: Diba, Ahmad and Lisa Munoz, "Who's Up Who's Down," *Fortune*, 143: 104-F7, (February 19, 2001).

★518★
Fortune's most admired companies for quality of management

Ranking basis/background: Based on a survey by Clark Martire & Bartolomeo of 10,000 executives, directors, and securities analysts who selected companies, regardless of industry, that they admire most. **Number listed:** 3.
1. Omnicom Group, with a score of 9.05
2. Enron, 8.97
3. Citigroup, 8.94

Source: Diba, Ahmad and Lisa Munoz, "Who's Up Who's Down," *Fortune*, 143: 104-F7, (February 19, 2001).

★519★
Fortune's most admired companies for quality of products or services

Ranking basis/background: Based on a survey by Clark Martire & Bartolomeo of 10,000 executives, directors, and securities analysts who selected companies, regardless of industry, that they admire most. **Number listed:** 3.
1. Toyota Motor Sales USA, with a score of 8.89
2. Omnicom Group, 8.86
3. New York Times, 8.73

Source: Diba, Ahmad and Lisa Munoz, "Who's Up Who's Down," *Fortune*, 143: 104-F7, (February 19, 2001).

★520★
Fortune's most admired companies for social responsibility

Ranking basis/background: Based on a survey by Clark Martire & Bartolomeo of 10,000 executives, directors, and securities analysts who selected companies, regardless of industry, that they admire most. **Number listed:** 3.
1. Du Pont, with a score of 8.19
2. McDonald's, 8.01
3. Waste Management, 8.00

Source: Diba, Ahmad and Lisa Munoz, "Who's Up Who's Down," *Fortune*, 143: 104-F7, (February 19, 2001).

★521★
Fortune's most admired companies for use of corporate assets

Ranking basis/background: Based on a survey by Clark Martire & Bartolomeo of 10,000 executives, directors, and securities analysts who selected companies, regardless of industry, that they admire most. **Number listed:** 3.
1. Citigroup, with a score of 8.71
2. Omnicom Group, 8.38
3. Exxon Mobil, 8.33

Source: Diba, Ahmad and Lisa Munoz, "Who's Up Who's Down," *Fortune*, 143: 104-F7, (February 19, 2001).

★522★
Information technology companies giving the best returns, 2000

Ranking basis/background: Percentage of shareholder returns through May 15, 2000, as researched by Standard & Poor's Compustat, *Business Week*. **Number listed:** 10.
1. BEA Systems, with 884.6%
2. Broadvision, 810.0%
3. Legend Holdings, 670.1%
4. Art Technology Group, 660.4%
5. I2 Technologies, 569.3%
6. Powerwave Technologies, 536.1%
7. Oracle, 528.6%
8. Siebel Systems, 501.1%
9. Kemet, 459.3%
10. Integrated Device Technology, 444.2%

Source: "The Information Technology 100," *Business Week*, 3686: 138-154, (June 19, 2000).

BUSINESS ADMINISTRATION

★523★
Largest private companies, 2000

Ranking basis/background: According to *Forbes* research of revenues and profits. **Number listed:** 500.

1. Cargill, Chief executive Warren Staley; type of business: international marketer and processor of agricultural and industrial commodities
2. Koch Industries, Charles Koch; oil, chemicals, minerals, energy, environmental technology, ranching
3. PricewaterhouseCoopers, James J. Schiro; accounting, auditing, tax and consulting services
4. Mars, John F. Mars; makes candy, ice cream, meals and pet food; processes rice; electronics
5. KPMG International, Stephen G. Butler; accounting, auditing, tax and construction and management
6. Publix Super Markets, Howard M. Jenkins; 631 supermarkets in Alabama, Florida, Georgia and South Carolina
7. Deloitte Touche Tomatsu, James E. Copeland Jr.; accounting, auditing, tax and consulting services
8. ContiGroup Cos, Paul J. Fribourg; processes poultry, pork and beef; mills four and feed
9. Ernst & Young, Philip A. Laskawy; accounting, auditing and tax services
10. Meijer, Hank Meijer; general merchandise and grocery stores in the Midwest
11. Andersen Consulting, Joe W. Forehand; management and consulting services
12. Fidelity Investments, Edward C. Johnson III; mutual funds, on-line discount brokerage, pension management
13. Arthur Andersen, Louis P. Salvatore; accounting, auditing, tax services
14. HE Butt Grocery, Charles C. Butt; H-E-B & H-E-B Pantry Food stores; milk plant and break bakery in Texas
15. Huntsman, Peter R. Huntsman; produces chemicals, polymers
16. Aramark, Joseph Neubauer; food and support services; uniforms; child care and educational services
17. C&S Wholesale Grocers, Richard B. Cohen; wholesales food to supermarkets, retail stores and military bases
18. JM Family Enterprises, Pat Moran; independent distributor of Toyotas; insurance, financial services
19. Marmon Group, Robert A. Pritzker; manufactures auto parts, railroad equipment and industrial products
20. Alliant Exchange, Earl L. Mason; distributes food to restaurants, hotels, hospitals and other facilities
21. Enterprise Rent-A-Car, Andrew C. Taylor; auto rental, leasing, car sales
22. Science Applications International, J. Robert Beyster; technology research and development and systems integration
23. Levi Strauss & Company, Philip Marineau; Levi's, Dockers & Slates jeans and other casual apparel
24. Premcor, William C. Rusnack; refines and markets petroleum products; convenience stores

Source: "500 Biggest Private Companies," *Forbes*, 166: 190-240, (November 27, 2000).

★524★
Leadership characteristics of dot-com CEOs

Ranking basis/background: According to a survey of more than 700 CEOs conducted by Bruson-Marsteller. **Number listed:** 5.

1. Risk-taking, with 82%
2. Creative, 81%
3. Passionate, 68%
3. Trailblazing, 68%
5. Impulsive, 62%

Source: Battey, Jim, "Survey Gauges Leadership Characteristics of CEOs," *Infoworld*, 22: 45, (12-25-00 to 1-1-01).

★525★
Leadership characteristics of Fortune 500 CEOs

Ranking basis/background: According to a survey of more than 700 CEOs conducted by Bruson-Marsteller. **Number listed:** 5.

1. Globally minded, with 79%
2. Competitive, 78%
2. Strategic, 78%
4. Good communicator, 69%
5. Trustworthy, 65%

Source: Battey, Jim, "Survey Gauges Leadership Characteristics of CEOs," *Infoworld*, 22: 45, (12-25-00 to 1-1-01).

★526★
Most influential African Americans in business

Ranking basis/background: Alphabetical listing compiled by the DuSable Museum of African American History. **Number listed:** 9.

- Robert Abbott, publisher
- Berry Gordy, recording industry
- John H. Johnson, publisher
- Robert Johnson, BET cable network founder
- Quincy Jones, recording industry
- Reginald Lewis, food industry
- Russell Simmons, recording industry
- Madame C.J. Walker, hair-care industry
- Oprah Winfrey, television/film

Source: Moffett, Nancy, "Voices of Power," *Chicago Sun-Times*, February 2, 2000, p. 39.

★527★
Most profitable information technology companies, 2000

Ranking basis/background: Return on equity percentages, determined by net income available for shareholders divided by common equity, as researched by Standard & Poor's Compustat, *Business Week*. **Number listed:** 10.

1. Netcom, with 53.8% return of equity
2. Oracle, 47.9%
3. S3, 46.1%
4. Lexmark International Group, 41.7%
5. Nokia, 39.7%
6. Xilinx, 36.7%
7. CTS, 36.5%
8. Asustek Computer, 34.0%
9. Dell Computer, 31.2%
10. Nvidia, 30.9%

Source: "The Information Technology 100," *Business Week*, 3686: 138-154, (June 19, 2000).

★528★
Software companies with the fastest growth, 2000

Ranking basis/background: Figures, in billions of dollars, for annual revenue in 2000 and percent increase since 1999. **Remarks:** Original source: Fortune **Number listed:** 10.

1. Siebel Systems, with $1.80 billion in revenue; a 127.8% increase from 1999
2. Veritas Software, $1.21; 10.34%
3. Comverse Technology, $1.23; 40.6%
4. Compuware, $2.23; 36.0%
5. BMC Software, $1.71; 31.5%
6. Adobe Systems, $1.27; 25.7%
7. PeopleSoft, $1.74; 21.7%
8. Cadence Design Systems, $1.28; 17.4%
9. Electronics Arts, $1.42; 16.4%
10. Computer Associates, $6.10; 16.2%

Source: Battey, Jim, "Fastest-Growing Software Companies," *Infoworld*, 23: 20, (April 30, 2001).

★529★
Top aerospace and defense companies in Standard & Poor's 500, 2001

Ranking basis/background: Composite rank calculated from eight criteria: one-year total return; three-year total return; one-year sales growth; three-year average annual sales growth; one-year profit growth; three-year average annual profit growth; net profit margins; and return on equity, with additional weight given to company sales. **Number listed:** 7.

1. General Dynamics, with an industry average of 40
2. United Technologies, 109
3. B.F. Goodrich, 225
4. Boeing, 249
5. Northrop Grumman, 270
6. Raytheon, 397
7. Lockheed Martin, 452

Source: "Industry Rankings of the S&P 500," *Business Week*, 3726A: 82-109, (Spring 2001).

★530★
Top automotive companies in Standard & Poor's 500, 2001

Ranking basis/background: Composite rank calculated from eight criteria: one-year total return; three-year total return; one-year sales growth; three-year average annual sales growth; one-year profit growth; three-year average annual profit growth; net profit margins; and return on equity, with additional weight given to company sales. **Number listed:** 10.

1. Ford Motor Company, with an industry average of 289
2. Cooper Tire & Rubber, 359
3. Paccar, 369
4. Eaton, 400
5. General Motors, 406
6. Delphi Automotive Systems, 408
7. Goodyear Tire & Rubber, 456
8. Dana, 458
9. Visteon, 461
10. Navistar International, 474

Source: "Industry Rankings of the S&P 500," *Business Week*, 3726A: 82-109, (Spring 2001).

BUSINESS ADMINISTRATION

★531★
Top banks in Standard & Poor's 500, 2001

Ranking basis/background: Composite rank calculated from eight criteria: one-year total return; three-year total return; one-year sales growth; three-year average annual sales growth; one-year profit growth; three-year average annual profit growth; net profit margins; and return on equity, with additional weight given to company sales. **Number listed:** 28.
1. Providian Financial, with an industry average of 6
2. Fleetboston Financial, 15
3. U.S. Bancorp, 46
4. Wells Fargo, 54
5. MBNA, 55
6. Fifth Third Bancorp, 61
7. Northern Trust, 111
8. Synovus Financial, 136
9. State Street, 137
10. SunTrust Banks, 143

Source: "Industry Rankings of the S&P 500," *Business Week*, 3726A: 82-109, (Spring 2001).

★532★
Top business schools in research performance, 1986-1998

Ranking basis/background: Determined by the number of pages a school's faculty published in the 20 top-tier business research journals over a 13 year period, from 1986 to 1998. **Number listed:** 50.
1. University of Pennsylvania
2. University of Michigan
3. Stanford University
4. New York University
5. University of Chicago
6. Columbia University
7. University of Minnesota
8. University of Texas, Austin
9. Harvard University
10. Northwestern University

Source: Trieschmann, James S., et. al., "Serving Multiple Constituencies in Business Schools: Program Versus Research Performance," *Academy of Management Journal*, 43: 1130-1141, (December 2000).

★533★
Top chemical companies in Standard & Poor's 500, 2001

Ranking basis/background: Composite rank calculated from eight criteria: one-year total return; three-year total return; one-year sales growth; three-year average annual sales growth; one-year profit growth; three-year average annual profit growth; net profit margins; and return on equity, with additional weight given to company sales. **Number listed:** 9.
1. Rohm & Haas, with an industry average of 261
2. Eastman Chemical Company, 265
3. DuPont, 281
4. Dow Chemical Co., 284
5. Great Lakes Chemical, 337
6. Praxair, 368
7. Air Products & Chemicals, 382
8. Hercules, 454
9. International Flavors & Fragrances, 455

Source: "Industry Rankings of the S&P 500," *Business Week*, 3726A: 82-109, (Spring 2001).

★534★
Top companies in terms of growth, 2000

Ranking basis/background: As researched by Standard & Poor's Compustat, *Business Week*. Ranks are calculated using three-year results in sales growth, earning growth, and return on invested capital. **Number listed:** 100.
1. Direct Focus
2. Somera Communications
3. World Wrestling Federation Entertainment
4. Albany Molecular Research
5. Skechers U.S.A.
6. Serena Software
7. Bebe Stores
8. Martha Stewart Living Omnimedia
9. U.S. Concrete
10. Neon Systems
11. PLX Technology
12. Power Integrations
13. Cunningham Graphics International
14. Finisar
15. E-Tek Dynamics
16. Netscout Systems
17. Inet Technologies
18. Cognizant Technology Solutions
19. Advanced Fibre Communications
20. Network Appliance

Source: "Hot Growth Companies," *Business Week*, 3683: 200-206, (May 29, 2000).

★535★
Top conglomerates in Standard & Poor's 500, 2001

Ranking basis/background: Composite rank calculated from eight criteria: one-year total return; three-year total return; one-year sales growth; three-year average annual sales growth; one-year profit growth; three-year average annual profit growth; net profit margins; and return on equity, with additional weight given to company sales. **Number listed:** 6.
1. General Electric, with an industry average of 79
2. Honeywell International, 228
3. Pall, 240
4. TRW, 381
5. Textron, 409
6. Allegheny Technologies, 441

Source: "Industry Rankings of the S&P 500," *Business Week*, 3726A: 82-109, (Spring 2001).

★536★
Top consumer products companies in Standard & Poor's 500, 2001

Ranking basis/background: Composite rank calculated from eight criteria: one-year total return; three-year total return; one-year sales growth; three-year average annual sales growth; one-year profit growth; three-year average annual profit growth; net profit margins; and return on equity, with additional weight given to company sales. **Number listed:** 25.
1. Bed Bath & Beyond, with an industry average of 49
2. Best Buy, 95
3. Philip Morris, 97
4. Anheuser-Busch, 154
5. Radio Shack, 157
6. Ecolab, 169
7. Colgate-Palmolive, 209
8. PepsiCo, 210
9. Adolph Coors, 252
10. UST, 272

Source: "Industry Rankings of the S&P 500," *Business Week*, 3726A: 82-109, (Spring 2001).

★537★
Top containers and packaging companies in Standard & Poor's 500, 2001

Ranking basis/background: Composite rank calculated from eight criteria: one-year total return; three-year total return; one-year sales growth; three-year average annual sales growth; one-year profit growth; three-year average annual profit growth; net profit margins; and return on equity, with additional weight given to company sales. **Number listed:** 7.
1. Westvaco, with an industry average of 285
2. Temple-Inland, 328
3. Ball, 350
4. Bemis, 352
5. Sealed Air, 379
6. Pactiv, 444
7. Potlatch, 482

Source: "Industry Rankings of the S&P 500," *Business Week*, 3726A: 82-109, (Spring 2001).

★538★
Top discount and fashion retailing companies in Standard & Poor's 500, 2001

Ranking basis/background: Composite rank calculated from eight criteria: one-year total return; three-year total return; one-year sales growth; three-year average annual sales growth; one-year profit growth; three-year average annual profit growth; net profit margins; and return on equity, with additional weight given to company sales. **Number listed:** 24.
1. Kohl's, with an industry average of 52
2. Lowe's, 117
3. Home Depot, 118
4. TJX, 121
5. Wal-Mart Stores, 125
6. Tiffany, 132
7. Target, 155
8. Gap, 175
9. Costco Wholesale, 213
10. Staples, 241

Source: "Industry Rankings of the S&P 500," *Business Week*, 3726A: 82-109, (Spring 2001).

★539★
Top electrical and electronics companies in Standard & Poor's 500, 2001

Ranking basis/background: Composite rank calculated from eight criteria: one-year total return; three-year total return; one-year sales growth; three-year average annual sales growth; one-year profit growth; three-year average annual profit growth; net profit margins; and return on equity, with additional weight given to company sales. **Number listed:** 41.
1. Micron Technology, with an industry average of 16
2. Xilinx, 17
3. Analog Devices, 23
4. Altera, 32
5. Texas Instruments, 50
6. Teradyne, 51
7. Sanmina, 60
8. Maxim Integrated Products, 62
9. Linear Technology, 63
10. Kla-Tencor, 83

Source: "Industry Rankings of the S&P 500," *Business Week*, 3726A: 82-109, (Spring 2001).

BUSINESS ADMINISTRATION

★540★
Top food companies in Standard & Poor's 500, 2001

Ranking basis/background: Composite rank calculated from eight criteria: one-year total return; three-year total return; one-year sales growth; three-year average annual sales growth; one-year profit growth; three-year average annual profit growth; net profit margins; and return on equity, with additional weight given to company sales. **Number listed:** 19.

1. Sysco, with an industry average of 80
2. Kroger, 120
3. Safeway, 141
4. Starbucks, 205
5. Quaker Oats, 223
6. Wm. Wrigley Jr., 257
7. Albertson's, 258
8. Ralston Purina, 290
9. H.J. Heinz, 292
10. General Mills, 305

Source: "Industry Rankings of the S&P 500," *Business Week*, 3726A: 82-109, (Spring 2001).

★541★
Top fuel companies in Standard & Poor's 500, 2001

Ranking basis/background: Composite rank calculated from eight criteria: one-year total return; three-year total return; one-year sales growth; three-year average annual sales growth; one-year profit growth; three-year average annual profit growth; net profit margins; and return on equity, with additional weight given to company sales. **Number listed:** 26.

1. Anadarko Petroleum, with an industry average of 2
2. Occidental Petroleum, 7
3. Apache, 8
4. Kerr-McGee, 9
5. Amerada Hess, 18
6. Phillips Petroleum, 22
7. EOG Resources, 24
8. Chevron, 35
9. Exxon Mobil, 44
10. Conoco, 59

Source: "Industry Rankings of the S&P 500," *Business Week*, 3726A: 82-109, (Spring 2001).

★542★
Top health care companies in Standard & Poor's 500, 2001

Ranking basis/background: Composite rank calculated from eight criteria: one-year total return; three-year total return; one-year sales growth; three-year average annual sales growth; one-year profit growth; three-year average annual profit growth; net profit margins; and return on equity, with additional weight given to company sales. **Number listed:** 41.

1. Forest Laboratories, with an industry average of 14
2. Cardinal Health, 25
3. Alza, 27
4. Merck, 30
5. Medtronic, 57
6. Stryker, 58
7. Biogen, 65
8. Medimmune, 68
9. Walgreen, 73
10. Pfizer, 76

Source: "Industry Rankings of the S&P 500," *Business Week*, 3726A: 82-109, (Spring 2001).

★543★
Top housing and real estate companies in Standard & Poor's 500, 2001

Ranking basis/background: Composite rank calculated from eight criteria: one-year total return; three-year total return; one-year sales growth; three-year average annual sales growth; one-year profit growth; three-year average annual profit growth; net profit margins; and return on equity, with additional weight given to company sales. **Number listed:** 7.

1. Pulte, with an industry average of 105
2. KB Home, 144
3. Centex, 203
4. Masco, 204
5. Vulcan Materials, 312
6. PPG Industries, 318
7. Sherwin-Williams, 466

Source: "Industry Rankings of the S&P 500," *Business Week*, 3726A: 82-109, (Spring 2001).

★544★
Top information technology companies, 2000

Ranking basis/background: As researched by Standard & Poor's Compustat, *Business Week*. **Number listed:** 100.

1. Nokia
2. Siebel Systems
3. Oracle
4. Nvidia
5. Taiwan Semiconductor Manufacturing
6. CDW Computer Centers
7. PC Connection
8. Legend Holdings
9. Xilinx
10. Analog Devices
11. Sun Microsystems
12. Amdocs
13. Network Appliance
14. Micron Technology
15. Yahoo Japan
16. CTS
17. Broadcom
18. Powerwave Technologies
19. S3
20. STMicroelectronics
21. China Telecom (Hong Kong)
22. Cypress Semiconductor
23. JDS Uniphase
24. Dell Computer
25. Cisco Systems

Source: "The Information Technology 100," *Business Week*, 3686: 138-154, (June 19, 2000).

★545★
Top leisure time industries in Standard & Poor's 500, 2001

Ranking basis/background: Composite rank calculated from eight criteria: one-year total return; three-year total return; one-year sales growth; three-year average annual sales growth; one-year profit growth; three-year average annual profit growth; net profit margins; and return on equity, with additional weight given to company sales. **Number listed:** 16.

1. Harley-Davidson, with an industry average of 81
2. Marriott International, 179
3. Darden Restaurants, 191
4. Starwood Hotels & Resorts, 215
5. Carnival, 239
6. McDonald's, 246
7. Eastman Kodak Company, 276
8. Wendy's International, 308
9. Viacom, 332
10. Brunswick, 342

Source: "Industry Rankings of the S&P 500," *Business Week*, 3726A: 82-109, (Spring 2001).

★546★
Top management journals

Ranking basis/background: Proportion of citations derived from the summation of all citations of a journal from the year of publication until a specified time period cut-off divided by the summation of all citations examined during the same time period. **Number listed:** 65.

1. *Journal of Applied Psychology*, with a 9.05 proportion of citations
2. *Academy of Management Journal*, 8.27
3. *Administrative Science Quarterly*, 8.03
4. *Organizational Behavior and Human Decision Processes*, 6.69
5. *Strategic Management Journal*, 6.37
5. *Academy of Management Review*, 6.37
7. *Journal of Personality and Social Psychology*, 3.43
8. *Psychological Bulletin*, 3.06
9. *Personnel Psychology*, 2.43
10. *Harvard Business Review*, 2.21
11. *Human Relations*, 2.13
12. *Industrial and Labor Relations Review*, 2.11
13. *Journal of International Business Studies*, 2.06
14. *Management Science*, 2.03
15. *American Sociological Review*, 2.01

Source: Tahai, Alireza and Michael J. Meyer, "A Revealed Preference Study of Management Journals' Direct Influences," *Strategic Management Journal*, 20: 279-296, (March 1999).

★547★
Top management journals by core impact

Ranking basis/background: Proportion of citations derived from the summation of all citations of a journal from the year of publication until a specified time period cut-off divided by the summation of all citations examined during the same time period. Core impact figures are those with limited age of citations to only citations equal to or younger than the citation mode distribution. **Number listed:** 65.

1. *Strategic Management Journal*, with a 10.64 proportion of citations
2. *Academy of Management Journal*, 9.57
3. *Journal of Applied Psychology*, 8.71
4. *Organizational Behavior and Human Decision Processes*, 7.58
5. *Academy of Management Review*, 5.55
6. *Administrative Science Quarterly*, 5.33
7. *Journal of Management*, 3.89
8. *Organization Science*, 2.91
9. *Industrial and Labor Relations Review*, 2.68
10. *Personnel Psychology*, 2.48
11. *Journal of International Business Studies*, 2.42
12. *Human Relations*, 2.17
13. *Management Science*, 2.13
14. *Long Range Planning*, 1.89
15. *Harvard Business Review*, 1.76

Source: Tahai, Alireza and Michael J. Meyer, "A Revealed Preference Study of Management Journals' Direct Influences," *Strategic Management Journal*, 20: 279-296, (March 1999).

★548★
Top manufacturing companies in Standard & Poor's 500, 2001

Ranking basis/background: Composite rank calculated from eight criteria: one-year total return; three-year total return; one-year sales growth; three-year average annual sales growth; one-year profit growth; three-year average annual profit growth; net profit margins; and return on equity, with additional weight given to company sales. **Number listed:** 25.
1. Tyco International, with an industry average of 1
2. Applied Materials, 5
3. Illinois Tool Works, 178
4. ITT Industries, 192
5. Minnesota Mining & Manufacturing, 216
6. Dover, 219
7. Johnson Controls, 230
8. Parker Hannifin, 236
9. Newell Rubbermaid, 271
10. Corning, 280

Source: "Industry Rankings of the S&P 500," *Business Week*, 3726A: 82-109, (Spring 2001).

★549★
Top metals and mining companies in Standard & Poor's 500, 2001

Ranking basis/background: Composite rank calculated from eight criteria: one-year total return; three-year total return; one-year sales growth; three-year average annual sales growth; one-year profit growth; three-year average annual profit growth; net profit margins; and return on equity, with additional weight given to company sales. **Number listed:** 13.
1. Alcoa, with an industry average of 100
2. Engelhard, 163
3. Inco, 167
4. Alcan, 255
5. Nucor, 343
6. Phelps Dodge, 426
7. Worthington Industries, 468
8. Placer Dome, 469
9. Freeport-McMoran Copper & Gold, 473
10. USX-U.S. Steel Group, 480
11. Newmont Mining, 483
12. Barrick Gold, 487
13. Homestake Mining, 491

Source: "Industry Rankings of the S&P 500," *Business Week*, 3726A: 82-109, (Spring 2001).

★550★
Top nonbank financial companies in Standard & Poor's 500, 2001

Ranking basis/background: Composite rank calculated from eight criteria: one-year total return; three-year total return; one-year sales growth; three-year average annual sales growth; one-year profit growth; three-year average annual profit growth; net profit margins; and return on equity, with additional weight given to company sales. **Number listed:** 47.
1. Lehman Brothers Holdings, with an industry average of 11
2. Capital One Financial, 21
3. Citigroup, 28
4. Marsh & McLennan, 33
5. Household International, 34
6. Washington Mutual, 39
7. Morgan Stanley Dean Witter, 42
8. Merrill Lynch, 48
9. Freddie Mac, 53
10. Stilwell Financial, 71

Source: "Industry Rankings of the S&P 500," *Business Week*, 3726A: 82-109, (Spring 2001).

★551★
Top office equipment and computers companies in Standard & Poor's 500, 2001

Ranking basis/background: Composite rank calculated from eight criteria: one-year total return; three-year total return; one-year sales growth; three-year average annual sales growth; one-year profit growth; three-year average annual profit growth; net profit margins; and return on equity, with additional weight given to company sales. **Number listed:** 45.
1. Oracle, with an industry average of 10
2. EMC, 12
3. Sun Microsystems, 29
4. Mercury Interactive, 37
5. AOL Time Warner, 38
6. Cisco Systems, 66
7. Dell Computer, 69
8. Siebel Systems, 75
9. Microsoft, 91
10. Network Appliance, 101

Source: "Industry Rankings of the S&P 500," *Business Week*, 3726A: 82-109, (Spring 2001).

★552★
Top paper and forest products companies in Standard & Poor's 500, 2001

Ranking basis/background: Composite rank calculated from eight criteria: one-year total return; three-year total return; one-year sales growth; three-year average annual sales growth; one-year profit growth; three-year average annual profit growth; net profit margins; and return on equity, with additional weight given to company sales. **Number listed:** 8.
1. Kimberly-Clark, with an industry average of 133
2. Weyerhauser, 166
3. Willamette Industries, 172
4. International Paper, 266
5. Georgia-Pacific, 282
6. Boise Cascade, 395
7. Mead, 431
8. Louisiana-Pacific, 481

Source: "Industry Rankings of the S&P 500," *Business Week*, 3726A: 82-109, (Spring 2001).

★553★
Top publishing and broadcasting companies in Standard & Poor's 500, 2001

Ranking basis/background: Composite rank calculated from eight criteria: one-year total return; three-year total return; one-year sales growth; three-year average annual sales growth; one-year profit growth; three-year average annual profit growth; net profit margins; and return on equity, with additional weight given to company sales. **Number listed:** 11.
1. Comcast, with an industry average of 41
2. Clear Channel Communications, 153
3. Univision Communications, 156
4. New York Times, 187
5. McGraw-Hill, 197
6. Gannett, 214
7. Tribune, 307
8. Dow Jones, 314
9. Knight Ridder, 345
10. Walt Disney, 422
11. Meredith, 427

Source: "Industry Rankings of the S&P 500," *Business Week*, 3726A: 82-109, (Spring 2001).

★554★
Top recruiters for business administration jobs for 2000-01 bachelor's degree recipients

Ranking basis/background: Projected number of college hires from on-campus recruitment for 2000-01. **Remarks:** Numbers reflect total expected hires, not just African American projected hires. **Number listed:** 57.
1. Footstar, with 3,000 projected hires
2. Enterprise Rent-A-Car, 2,000
3. Wells Fargo Financial, 1,300
4. EDS, 500
4. Sherwin-Williams, 500
6. Accenture, 450
7. Deloitte & Touche, 415
8. General Motors, 140
9. Office Depot, 120
9. Blockbuster Inc., 120

Source: "The Top 100 Employers and the Majors in Demand for the Class of 2001," *The Black Collegian*, 31: 19-35, (February 2001).

★555★
Top recruiters for logistics jobs for 2000-01 bachelor's degree recipients

Ranking basis/background: Projected number of college hires from on-campus recruitment for 2000-01. **Remarks:** Numbers reflect total expected hires, not just African American projected hires. **Number listed:** 3.
1. Toys "R" Us, with 15 projected hires
1. Caterpillar Inc., 15
3. Federated Department Stores, 5

Source: "The Top 100 Employers and the Majors in Demand for the Class of 2001," *The Black Collegian*, 31: 19-35, (February 2001).

★556★
Top recruiters for retail merchandising jobs for 2000-01 bachelor's degree recipients

Ranking basis/background: Projected number of college hires from on-campus recruitment for 2000-01. **Remarks:** Numbers reflect total expected hires, not just African American projected hires. **Number listed:** 6.
1. JCPenney Company, with 150 projected hires
2. Federated Department Stores, 130
3. Rich's Lazarus Goldsmiths, 70
4. May Department Stores, 20
5. Stern's, 13
6. Office Depot, 10

Source: "The Top 100 Employers and the Majors in Demand for the Class of 2001," *The Black Collegian*, 31: 19-35, (February 2001).

★557★
Top recruiters for supplier chain management jobs for 2000-01 bachelor's degree recipients

Ranking basis/background: Projected number of college hires from on-campus recruitment for 2000-01. **Remarks:** Numbers reflect total expected hires, not just African American projected hires. **Number listed:** 1.
1. General Dynamics Land Systems, with 5 projected hires

Source: "The Top 100 Employers and the Majors in Demand for the Class of 2001," *The Black Collegian*, 31: 19-35, (February 2001).

BUSINESS ADMINISTRATION

★558★
Top services industries in Standard & Poor's 500, 2001

Ranking basis/background: Composite rank calculated from eight criteria: one-year total return; three-year total return; one-year sales growth; three-year average annual sales growth; one-year profit growth; three-year average annual profit growth; net profit margins; and return on equity, with additional weight given to company sales. **Number listed:** 18.
1. Dynegy, with an industry average of 4
2. Paychex, 47
3. Omnicom Group, 70
4. Enron, 103
5. Cintas, 147
6. Robert Half International, 150
7. Convergys, 211
8. Interpublic Group, 218
9. Allied Waste Industries, 277
10. R.R. Donnelley & Sons, 291

Source: "Industry Rankings of the S&P 500," *Business Week*, 3726A: 82-109, (Spring 2001).

★559★
Top telecommunications companies in Standard & Poor's 500, 2001

Ranking basis/background: Composite rank calculated from eight criteria: one-year total return; three-year total return; one-year sales growth; three-year average annual sales growth; one-year profit growth; three-year average annual profit growth; net profit margins; and return on equity, with additional weight given to company sales. **Number listed:** 19.
1. ADC Telecommunications, with an industry average of 20
2. Verizon Communications, 26
3. SBC Communications, 36
4. Tellabs, 43
5. Scientific-Atlanta, 45
6. Comverse Technology, 67
7. ALLTEL, 72
8. BellSouth, 158
9. WorldCom, 222
10. Centurytel, 333

Source: "Industry Rankings of the S&P 500," *Business Week*, 3726A: 82-109, (Spring 2001).

★560★
Top transportation companies in Standard & Poor's 500, 2001

Ranking basis/background: Composite rank calculated from eight criteria: one-year total return; three-year total return; one-year sales growth; three-year average annual sales growth; one-year profit growth; three-year average annual profit growth; net profit margins; and return on equity, with additional weight given to company sales. **Number listed:** 10.
1. Southwest Airlines, with an industry average of 78
2. FedEx, 238
3. Union Pacific, 279
4. AMR, 320
5. Burlington Northern Santa Fe, 327
6. Delta Air Lines, 358
7. Norfolk Southern, 402
8. CSX, 410
9. Ryder System, 428
10. US Airways Group, 448

Source: "Industry Rankings of the S&P 500," *Business Week*, 3726A: 82-109, (Spring 2001).

★561★
Top utilities companies in Standard & Poor's 500, 2001

Ranking basis/background: Composite rank calculated from eight criteria: one-year total return; three-year total return; one-year sales growth; three-year average annual sales growth; one-year profit growth; three-year average annual profit growth; net profit margins; and return on equity, with additional weight given to company sales. **Number listed:** 37.
1. Calpine, with an industry average of 3
2. AES, 13
3. Duke Energy, 19
4. El Paso, 31
5. PPL, 56
6. Reliant Energy, 84
7. Oneok, 85
8. Exelon, 108
9. Xcel Energy, 113
10. Southern, 124

Source: "Industry Rankings of the S&P 500," *Business Week*, 3726A: 82-109, (Spring 2001).

★562★
U.S. cities considered to be the most affordable for IT professionals

Ranking basis/background: According to an index developed by Techies.com for measuring local salaries versus cost of living. **Number listed:** 5.
1. Austin, TX, with a rating of 105.6
2. Dallas, TX, 105.5
3. Houston, TX, 105.3
4. Twin Cities, MN, 100.1
5. Atlanta, GA, 99.7

Source: Battey, Jim, "Top Five Most Affordable Cities," *Infoworld*, 22: 45, (12-25-00 to 1-1-01).

★563★
U.S. News & World Report's undergraduate business programs with the best consulting departments, 2000-01

Ranking basis/background: Based on *U.S News* survey asking business school deans and senior faculty to rate the quality of programs they are familiar with, and name the best programs in various specialties. **Number listed:** 5.
1. University of Pennsylvania, Wharton School of Business
2. University of Michigan Business School
3. New York University, Leonard N. Stern School of Business
4. Massachusetts Institute of Technology, Alfred P. Sloan School of Management
4. University of California, Berkeley, Haas Graduate School of Business Administration

Source: "America's Best Colleges," *U.S. News & World Report*, 129: 90-132, (September 11, 2000).

★564★
U.S. News & World Report's undergraduate business programs with the best e-commerce departments, 2000-01

Ranking basis/background: Based on *U.S News* survey asking business school deans and senior faculty to rate the quality of programs they are familiar with, and name the best programs in various specialties. **Number listed:** 5.
1. Carnegie-Mellon University Graduate School of Industrial Administration
2. Massachusetts Institute of Technology, Alfred P. Sloan School of Management
3. University of Texas, Austin, McCombs School of Business
4. University of Pennsylvania, Wharton School of Business
5. University of California, Berkeley, Haas Graduate School of Business Administration

Source: "America's Best Colleges," *U.S. News & World Report*, 129: 90-132, (September 11, 2000).

★565★
U.S. News & World Report's undergraduate business programs with the best entrepreneurship departments, 2000-01

Ranking basis/background: Based on *U.S News* survey asking business school deans and senior faculty to rate the quality of programs they are familiar with, and name the best programs in various specialties. **Number listed:** 7.
1. Babson College, F.W. Olin Graduate School of Business
2. University of Pennsylvania, Wharton School of Business
2. University of Southern California, Marshall School of Business
4. Baylor University, Hankamer School of Business
5. Ball State University
5. New York University, Leonard N. Stern School of Business
5. University of Texas, Austin, McCombs School of Business

Source: "America's Best Colleges," *U.S. News & World Report*, 129: 90-132, (September 11, 2000).

★566★
U.S. News & World Report's undergraduate business programs with the best general management departments, 2000-01

Ranking basis/background: Based on *U.S News* survey asking business school deans and senior faculty to rate the quality of programs they are familiar with, and name the best programs in various specialties. **Number listed:** 5.
1. University of Pennsylvania, Wharton School of Business
2. University of Michigan Business School
3. University of California, Berkeley, Haas Graduate School of Business Administration
4. Indiana University, Kelley Graduate School of Business
5. Massachusetts Institute of Technology, Alfred P. Sloan School of Management

Source: "America's Best Colleges," *U.S. News & World Report*, 129: 90-132, (September 11, 2000).

★567★
U.S. News & World Report's undergraduate business programs with the best human resources departments, 2000-01

Ranking basis/background: Based on *U.S News* survey asking business school deans and senior faculty to rate the quality of programs they are familiar with, and name the best programs in various specialties. **Number listed:** 5.
1. University of Pennsylvania, Wharton School of Business
2. University of Michigan Business School

3. University of Illinois, Urbana-Champaign College of Commerce and Business Administration
4. Indiana University, Kelley Graduate School of Business
4. Ohio State University, Fisher School of Business

Source: "America's Best Colleges," *U.S. & World Report*, 129: 90-132, (September 11, 2000).

★568★
U.S. News & World Report's undergraduate business programs with the best management information systems departments, 2000-01

Ranking basis/background: Based on *U.S News* survey asking business school deans and senior faculty to rate the quality of programs they are familiar with, and name the best programs in various specialties. **Number listed:** 5.
1. Massachusetts Institute of Technology, Alfred P. Sloan School of Management
2. Carnegie-Mellon University Graduate School of Industrial Administration
3. University of Minnesota, Carlson School of Management
4. University of Texas, Austin, McCombs School of Business
5. University of Arizona, Eller School MBA Program

Source: "America's Best Colleges," *U.S. & World Report*, 129: 90-132, (September 11, 2000).

★569★
U.S. News & World Report's undergraduate business programs with the best production/operations departments, 2000-01

Ranking basis/background: Based on *U.S News* survey asking business school deans and senior faculty to rate the quality of programs they are familiar with, and name the best programs in various specialties. **Number listed:** 6.
1. Massachusetts Institute of Technology, Alfred P. Sloan School of Management
2. Carnegie-Mellon University Graduate School of Industrial Administration
3. Purdue University, Krannert School of Management
4. University of Michigan Business School
5. Indiana University, Kelley Graduate School of Business
5. University of Pennsylvania, Wharton School of Business

Source: "America's Best Colleges," *U.S. & World Report*, 129: 90-132, (September 11, 2000).

★570★
U.S. News & World Report's undergraduate business programs with the best real estate departments, 2000-01

Ranking basis/background: Based on *U.S News* survey asking business school deans and senior faculty to rate the quality of programs they are familiar with, and name the best programs in various specialties. **Number listed:** 5.
1. University of Pennsylvania, Wharton School of Business
2. University of California, Berkeley, Haas Graduate School of Business Administration
3. New York University, Leonard N. Stern School of Business

3. Ohio State University, Fisher School of Business
5. University of Wisconsin, Madison

Source: "America's Best Colleges," *U.S. & World Report*, 129: 90-132, (September 11, 2000).

★571★
U.S. News & World Report's undergraduate business programs with the highest academic reputation scores, 2000-01

Ranking basis/background: Based on *U.S News* survey asking business school deans and senior faculty to rate the quality of programs they are familiar with, and name the best programs in various specialties. **Number listed:** 49.
1. University of Pennsylvania, Wharton School of Business, with a score of 4.8
2. Massachusetts Institute of Technology, Alfred P. Sloan School of Management, 4.6
2. University of Michigan Business School, 4.6
4. University of California, Berkeley, Haas Graduate School of Business Administration, 4.5
5. Carnegie-Mellon University Graduate School of Industrial Administration, 4.3
5. University of North Carolina, Kenan Flagler Business School, 4.3
5. University of Texas, Austin, McCombs School of Business, 4.3
8. New York University, Leonard N. Stern School of Business, 4.2
8. University of Virginia, McIntire Graduate School of Business Administration, 4.2
10. Indiana University, Kelley Graduate School of Business, 4.1
10. University of Illinois, Urbana-Champaign College of Commerce and Business Administration, 4.1
10. University of Wisconsin, Madison

Source: "America's Best Colleges," *U.S. & World Report*, 129: 90-132, (September 11, 2000).

★572★
U.S. News & World Report's universities with the best quantitative methods departments, 1999-2000

Ranking basis/background: Based on a *U.S. News* survey asking business school deans and senior faculty to rate the quality of programs they are familiar with, and name the best programs in various specialties. **Number listed:** 5.
1. Massachusetts Institute of Technology
2. Carnegie Mellon University
3. University of Pennsylvania
4. Purdue University, West Lafayette
5. University of California, Berkeley

Source: "America's Best Colleges 2000 Annual Guide," *U.S. News & World Report*, 127: 62-105, (August 30, 1999).

★573★
U.S. News & World Report's universities with the best taxation departments, 1999-2000

Ranking basis/background: Based on a *U.S. News* survey asking business school deans and senior faculty to rate the quality of programs they are familiar with, and name the best programs in various specialties. **Number listed:** 5.
1. University of Texas, Austin
2. University of Illinois, Urbana-Champaign

3. New York University
3. University of Southern California
5. University of Florida

Source: "America's Best Colleges 2000 Annual Guide," *U.S. News & World Report*, 127: 62-105, (August 30, 1999).

★574★
U.S. universities publishing the most papers in the field of management, 1995-99

Ranking basis/background: Number of papers published in the field of management over a five-year period, and percent of field based on each universities percentage of 13,181 papers entered in the ISI database from ISI-indexed management journals. **Number listed:** 5.
1. University of Michigan, Ann Arbor, with 183 papers; 1.39% of field
2. Massachusetts Institute of Technology, 176; 1.34%
3. University of Pennsylvania, 174; 1.32%
4. Harvard University, 165; 1.25%
5. Stanford University, 140; 1.06%

Source: "Management: Most Prolific U.S. Universities, 1995-99," *What's Hot in Research* (http://www.isinet.com/isi/hot/research) Institute for Scientific Information, November 27, 2000.

★575★
U.S. universities with the greatest impact in management, 1994-98

Ranking basis/background: Average citations per paper from the top 100 federally funded U.S. universities that had at least 50 published papers in ISI indexed management journals. Also includes total number of papers published during the five year period. **Number listed:** 5.
1. Columbia University, with 118 papers; 4.69 citations per paper
2. Northwestern University, 116; 4.41
3. University of Pennsylvania, 184; 4.39
4. Stanford University, 136; 4.21
5. Massachusetts Institute of Technology, 174; 4.13

Source: "Management: High Impact U.S. Universities, 1994-98," *What's Hot in Research* (http://www.isinet.com/isi/hot/research) Institute for Scientific Information, May 15, 2000.

Related Information

★576★
Dichev, Ilia D., "How Good Are Business School Rankings?," *Journal of Business*, 72: 201-213, (April 1999).
Remarks: Investigates the predictability of future changes and the timeliness of MBA school rankings conducted by *BusinessWeek* and *U.S. News & World Report*.

BUSINESS ADMINISTRATION–ACCOUNTING

See also: **Business Administration, Graduate–Accounting**

★577★
Top accounting journals by citation proportions

Ranking basis/background: Proportion of citations. **Number listed:** 49.

BUSINESS ADMINISTRATION—FINANCE

1. *Journal of Accounting Research*, with 16.13
2. *Accounting Review*, 13.56
3. *Journal of Accounting and Economics*, 10.34
4. *Accounting Organizations and Society*, 9.23
5. *Journal of Financial Economics*, 3.65
6. *Journal of Finance*, 3.50
7. *National Tax Journal*, 3.06
8. *Auditing: A Journal of Practice & Theory*, 2.98
9. *American Economic Review*, 2.94
10. *Econometrica*, 2.58

Source: Tahai, Alireza and John T. Rigsby, "Information Processing Using Citations to Investigate Journal Influence in Accounting," *Information Processing & Management*, pp. 341-359, (March/May 1999).

★578★
Top accounting journals by half-life impact factor

Ranking basis/background: Proportion of citations. **Number listed:** 49.

1. *Accounting Review*, with 16.29
2. *Journal of Accounting Research*, 13.38
3. *Journal of Accounting and Economics*, 12.02
4. *Accounting Organizations and Society*, 11.25
5. *Auditing: A Journal of Practice & Theory*, 3.99
6. *Journal of Financial Economics*, 3.57
7. *National Tax Journal*, 3.19
8. *Journal of Finance*, 2.98
9. *Contemporary Accounting Research*, 2.52
10. *American Economic Review*, 1.82

Source: Tahai, Alireza and John T. Rigsby, "Information Processing Using Citations to Investigate Journal Influence in Accounting," *Information Processing & Management*, pp. 341-359, (March/May 1999).

★579★
Top accounting journals by mode impact factor

Ranking basis/background: Proportion of citations. **Number listed:** 49.

1. *Accounting Review*, with 18.43
2. *Journal of Accounting Research*, 13.06
3. *Journal of Accounting and Economics*, 12.26
4. *Accounting Organizations and Society*, 9.86
5. *Auditing: A Journal of Practice & Theory*, 4.57
6. *National Tax Journal*, 3.93
7. *Journal of Finance*, 3.53
7. *Contemporary Accounting Research*, 3.53
9. *Journal of Financial Economics*, 2.24
10. *Communications*, 2.16

Source: Tahai, Alireza and John T. Rigsby, "Information Processing Using Citations to Investigate Journal Influence in Accounting," *Information Processing & Management*, pp. 341-359, (March/May 1999).

★580★
Top recruiters for accounting jobs for 2000-01 bachelor's degree recipients

Ranking basis/background: Projected number of college hires from on-campus recruitment for 2000-01. **Remarks:** Numbers reflect total expected hires, not just African American projected hires. **Number listed:** 49.

1. Arthur Andersen LLP, with 1,582 projected hires
2. Deloitte & Touche, 650
3. Accenture, 130
4. EDS, 100
5. Federal Deposit Insurance Company, 60
6. Cap Gemini Ernst & Young, 50
6. Footstar, 50
7. Marriott International, 40
8. Northwestern Mutual Financial Network, 40
10. Litton Industries, 30

Source: "The Top 100 Employers and the Majors in Demand for the Class of 2001," *The Black Collegian*, 31: 19-35, (February 2001).

★581★
U.S. News & World Report's undergraduate business programs with the best accounting departments, 2000-01

Ranking basis/background: Based on *U.S News* survey asking business school deans and senior faculty to rate the quality of programs they are familiar with, and name the best programs in various specialties. **Number listed:** 5.

1. University of Illinois, Urbana-Champaign College of Commerce and Business Administration
2. University of Texas, Austin, McCombs School of Business
3. University of Michigan Business School
4. University of Pennsylvania, Wharton School of Business
4. University of Southern California, Marshall School of Business

Source: "America's Best Colleges," *U.S. News & World Report*, 129: 90-132, (September 11, 2000).

BUSINESS ADMINISTRATION–FINANCE
See also: **Business Administration, Graduate–Finance**

★582★
Top recruiters for finance/banking jobs for 2000-01 bachelor's degree recipients

Ranking basis/background: Projected number of college hires from on-campus recruitment for 2000-01. **Remarks:** Numbers reflect total expected hires, not just African American projected hires. **Number listed:** 38.

1. Wells Fargo Financial, with 300 projected hires
2. Arthur Andersen LLP, 266
3. Accenture, 150
4. EDS, 100
5. Deloitte & Touche, 80
5. May Department Stores, 80
7. Federated Department Stores, 63
8. BB&T Corporation, 55
9. Federal Deposit Insurance Company, 50
9. Footstar, 50
9. Western Southern Life, 50

Source: "The Top 100 Employers and the Majors in Demand for the Class of 2001," *The Black Collegian*, 31: 19-35, (February 2001).

BUSINESS ADMINISTRATION, GRADUATE

★583★
Academics' choices for best graduate entrepreneurship programs, 2001

Ranking basis/background: From a *U.S. News & World Report* survey of deans and directors of MBA programs. **Remarks:** Data collected by Market Facts, Inc. **Number listed:** 10.

1. Babson College, F.W. Olin Graduate School of Business
2. University of Pennsylvania, Wharton School of Business
3. Harvard University Graduate School of Business Administration
4. Stanford University Graduate School of Business
5. University of California, Los Angeles, Anderson Graduate School of Management
6. University of Southern California, Marshall School of Business
7. University of Texas, Austin, McCombs School of Business
8. Massachusetts Institute of Technology, Alfred P. Sloan School of Management
9. Northwestern University, Kellogg Graduate School of Management
10. University of California, Berkeley, Haas Graduate School of Business Administration
10. University of Michigan Business School

Source: "America's Best Graduate Schools: 2002 Annual Guide," *U.S. News & World Report*, 130: 60-97, (April 19, 2001).

★584★
Academics' choices for best graduate executive MBA programs, 2001

Ranking basis/background: From a *U.S. News & World Report* survey of deans and directors of MBA programs. **Remarks:** Data collected by Market Facts, Inc. **Number listed:** 10.

1. Northwestern University, Kellogg Graduate School of Management
2. Duke University, Fuqua School of Business
3. University of Pennsylvania, Wharton School of Business
4. University of Chicago Graduate School of Business
5. Columbia University Graduate School of Business
6. New York University, Leonard N. Stern School of Business
7. University of California, Los Angeles, Anderson Graduate School of Management
8. University of Michigan Business School
9. University of North Carolina, Kenan Flagler Business School
10. Emory University, Goizueta Graduate School of Business

Source: "America's Best Graduate Schools: 2002 Annual Guide," *U.S. News & World Report*, 130: 60-97, (April 19, 2001).

BUSINESS ADMINISTRATION, GRADUATE

★585★
Academics' choices for best graduate management information systems programs, 2001

Ranking basis/background: From a *U.S. News & World Report* survey of deans and directors of MBA programs. **Remarks:** Data collected by Market Facts, Inc. **Number listed:** 10.
1. Massachusetts Institute of Technology, Alfred P. Sloan School of Management
2. Carnegie-Mellon University Graduate School of Industrial Administration
3. University of Texas, Austin, McCombs School of Business
4. University of Arizona, Eller School MBA Program
5. Stanford University Graduate School of Business
6. University of Minnesota, Carlson School of Management
7. University of Pennsylvania, Wharton School of Business
8. New York University, Leonard N. Stern School of Business
9. University of Maryland, Smith Graduate School of Management and Technology
10. University of Michigan Business School

Source: "America's Best Graduate Schools: 2002 Annual Guide," *U.S. News & World Report*, 130: 60-97, (April 19, 2001).

★586★
Academics' choices for best graduate nonprofit organizations programs, 2001

Ranking basis/background: From a *U.S. News & World Report* survey of deans and directors of MBA programs. **Remarks:** Data collected by Market Facts, Inc. **Number listed:** 10.
1. Yale University, Ancell School of Business
2. Northwestern University, Kellogg Graduate School of Management
3. Harvard University Graduate School of Business Administration
4. Stanford University Graduate School of Business
5. University of Michigan Business School
6. University of Pennsylvania, Wharton School of Business
7. University of California, Berkeley, Haas Graduate School of Business Administration
8. Columbia University Graduate School of Business
9. Case Western Reserve University, Weatherhead School of Business
10. Cornell University, Johnson Graduate School of Business and Public Administration

Source: "America's Best Graduate Schools: 2002 Annual Guide," *U.S. News & World Report*, 130: 60-97, (April 19, 2001).

★587★
Academics' choices for best part-time MBA programs, 2000

Ranking basis/background: From a *U.S. News & World Report* survey of deans and directors of MBA programs. **Remarks:** Data collected by Market Facts Inc. **Number listed:** 10.
   New York University, Leonard N. Stern School of Business
   University of Chicago Graduate School of Business
   Northwestern University, Kellogg Graduate School of Management
   University of California, Los Angeles, Anderson Graduate School of Management
   DePaul University, Charles H. Kellstadt Graduate School of Business
   University of Michigan, Ann Arbor
   University of Southern California, Marshall Graduate School of Business
   University of California, Berkeley, Haas Graduate School of Business Administration
   Georgia State University, J. Mack Robinson College of Business
   Babson College, F.W. Olin Graduate School of Business

Source: "America's Best Graduate Schools: 2001 Annual Guide," *U.S. News & World Report*, 128: 56-94, (April 10, 2000).

★588★
Acceptance rates for *U.S. News & World Report*'s top 10 graduate business schools, 2001

Ranking basis/background: From a *U.S. News & World Report* survey of acceptance rates for 2000. **Remarks:** Data collected by Market Facts, Inc. **Number listed:** 53.
1. University of Chicago Graduate School of Business, with 25.4%
2. University of Michigan Business School, 20.8%
3. Duke University, Fuqua School of Business, 19.3%
4. Northwestern University, Kellogg Graduate School of Management, 17.7%
5. Massachusetts Institute of Technology, Alfred P. Sloan School of Management, 17.5%
6. University of Pennsylvania, Wharton School of Business, 14.4%
7. Harvard University Graduate School of Business Administration, 13.5%
7. University of California, Berkeley, Haas Graduate School of Business Administration, 13.5%
9. Columbia University Graduate School of Business, 12.5%
10. Stanford University Graduate School of Business, 8.3%

Source: "America's Best Graduate Schools: 2002 Annual Guide," *U.S. News & World Report*, 130: 60-97, (April 19, 2001).

★589★
Annual tuition at *Business Week*'s top business schools, 2000

Ranking basis/background: Annual tuition rates for the 1999-2000 academic year. As compiled by *Business Week* from a survey of graduates from the Class of 2000 and companies that actively recruit MBAs. **Number listed:** 30.
   University of Pennsylvania, Wharton School of Business, with $27,170
   Northwestern University, Kellogg Graduate School of Management, $28,677
   Harvard University Graduate School of Business Administration, $28,500
   Massachusetts Institute of Technology, Alfred P. Sloan School of Management, $29,860
   Duke University, Fuqua School of Business, $29,735
   University of Michigan Business School, $28,500
   Columbia University Graduate School of Business, $30,548
   Cornell University, Johnson Graduate School of Business and Public Administration, $27,600
   University of Virginia, Darden Graduate School of Business Administration, $24,208
   University of Chicago Graduate School of Business, $29,231

Source: "The Best B Schools," *Business Week*, 3701: 76-100, (October 2, 2000).

★590★
***Asiaweek*'s best M.B.A. programs**

Ranking basis/background: Based on a survey by *Asiaweek* of top Asian corporations and business schools. **Number listed:** 5.
1. Melbourne Business School
2. Indian Institute of Management at Ahmadabad
3. Asian Institute of Management, Philippines
4. Asian Institute of Technology, Thailand
5. NUS Business School, Singapore

Source: Watzman, Haim, "'Asiaweek' Ranks Business Schools," *The Chronicle of Higher Education*, 46: A72, (May 19, 2000).

★591★
Average GMAT scores at *U.S. News & World Report*'s top 10 graduate business schools, 2001

Ranking basis/background: From a *U.S. News & World Report* survey of average GMAT scores for 2000. **Remarks:** Data collected by Market Facts, Inc. **Number listed:** 53.
1. Stanford University Graduate School of Business, with an average GMAT score of 730
2. Harvard University Graduate School of Business Administration, 700
2. University of Pennsylvania, Wharton School of Business, 700
4. Massachusetts Institute of Technology, Alfred P. Sloan School of Management, 710
5. Columbia University Graduate School of Business, 704
6. Northwestern University, Kellogg Graduate School of Management, 695
7. University of California, Berkeley, Haas Graduate School of Business Administration, 690
7. Duke University, Fuqua School of Business, 690
9. University of Chicago Graduate School of Business, 684
10. University of Michigan Business School, 675

Source: "America's Best Graduate Schools: 2002 Annual Guide," *U.S. News & World Report*, 130: 60-97, (April 19, 2001).

★592★
Average job offers received by graduates from *Business Week*'s top business schools, 1999

Ranking basis/background: Average number of job offers received by members of the Class of 1999, as compiled by *Business Week* from data provided by the schools themselves and surveys of the most recent MBA graduates. **Number listed:** 30.
   University of Pennsylvania, Wharton School of Business, with 3.6

Northwestern University, Kellogg Graduate School of Management, 3.5
Harvard University Graduate School of Business Administration, 4.1
Massachusetts Institute of Technology, Alfred P. Sloan School of Management, 3.9
Duke University, Fuqua School of Business, 3.1
University of Michigan Business School, 3.3
Columbia University Graduate School of Business, 3.1
Cornell University, Johnson Graduate School of Business and Public Administration, 3.2
University of Virginia, Darden Graduate School of Business Administration, 3.4
University of Chicago Graduate School of Business, 3.1

Source: "The Best B Schools," *Business Week*, 3701: 76-100, (October 2, 2000).

★593★
Average undergraduate GPA at *U.S. News & World Report*'s top 10 graduate business schools, 2001

Ranking basis/background: From a *U.S. News & World Report* survey of undergraduate GPA averages for 2000. **Remarks:** Data collected by Market Facts, Inc. **Number listed:** 53.
1. Stanford University Graduate School of Business, with an average GPA of 3.60
2. University of Pennsylvania, Wharton School of Business, 3.54
3. University of California, Berkeley, Haas Graduate School of Business Administration, 3.52
4. Harvard University Graduate School of Business Administration, 3.50
4. Massachusetts Institute of Technology, Alfred P. Sloan School of Management, 3.50
6. Northwestern University, Kellogg Graduate School of Management, 3.45
6. Columbia University Graduate School of Business, 3.45
8. Duke University, Fuqua School of Business, 3.43
9. University of Chicago Graduate School of Business, 3.35
10. University of Michigan Business School, 3.32

Source: "America's Best Graduate Schools: 2002 Annual Guide," *U.S. News & World Report*, 130: 60-97, (April 19, 2001).

★594★
Business Week's institutions with the best entrepreneurship programs

Ranking basis/background: Based on *Business Week*'s survey of 273 companies. **Number listed:** 5.
1. Babson College
2. University of Pennsylvania, Wharton School of Business
3. Harvard University Graduate School of Business Administration
4. Stanford University Graduate School of Business
5. Dartmouth College, Amos Tuck School of Business Administration

Source: Enbar, Nadav, "Where Big Shots Learn to Think Like Hotshots," *Business Week*, 3651: 85, (October 18, 1999).

★595★
Business Week's top business schools, 2000

Ranking basis/background: As compiled by *Business Week* from a survey of graduates from the Class of 2000 and companies that actively recruit MBAs. **Number listed:** 30.
1. University of Pennsylvania, Wharton School of Business
2. Northwestern University, Kellogg Graduate School of Management
3. Harvard University Graduate School of Business Administration
4. Massachusetts Institute of Technology, Alfred P. Sloan School of Management
5. Duke University, Fuqua School of Business
6. University of Michigan Business School
7. Columbia University Graduate School of Business
8. Cornell University, Johnson Graduate School of Business and Public Administration
9. University of Virginia, Darden Graduate School of Business Administration
10. University of Chicago Graduate School of Business

Source: "The Best B Schools," *Business Week*, 3701: 76-100, (October 2, 2000).

★596★
Business Week's top business schools as selected by corporate recruiters, 2000

Ranking basis/background: As compiled by *Business Week* from a survey of graduates from the Class of 2000 and companies that actively recruit MBAs. **Number listed:** 30.
1. University of Pennsylvania, Wharton School of Business
2. Northwestern University, Kellogg Graduate School of Management
3. Harvard University Graduate School of Business Administration
4. University of Chicago Graduate School of Business
5. Columbia University Graduate School of Business
6. University of Michigan Business School
7. Massachusetts Institute of Technology, Alfred P. Sloan School of Management
8. Duke University, Fuqua School of Business
9. University of Virginia, Darden Graduate School of Business Administration
10. Cornell University, Johnson Graduate School of Business and Public Administration

Source: "The Best B Schools," *Business Week*, 3701: 76-100, (October 2, 2000).

★597★
Business Week's top business schools as selected by recent MBA graduates, 2000

Ranking basis/background: As compiled by *Business Week* from a survey of graduates from the Class of 2000 and companies that actively recruit MBAs. **Number listed:** 30.
1. Northwestern University, Kellogg Graduate School of Management
2. University of Virginia, Darden Graduate School of Business Administration
3. University of Pennsylvania, Wharton School of Business
4. Harvard University Graduate School of Business Administration
5. University of Michigan Business School
6. University of California, Los Angeles, Anderson Graduate School of Management
7. Massachusetts Institute of Technology, Alfred P. Sloan School of Management
8. Cornell University, Johnson Graduate School of Business and Public Administration
9. Washington University, John M. Olin School of Business
10. Duke University, Fuqua School of Business

Source: "The Best B Schools," *Business Week*, 3701: 76-100, (October 2, 2000).

★598★
Business Week's top business schools best at responding to student concerns, 2000

Ranking basis/background: As compiled by *Business Week* from data provided by the schools themselves and surveys of the most recent MBA graduates. **Number listed:** 5.
1. Washington University, John M. Olin School of Business
2. Indiana University, Kelley Graduate School of Business
3. Cornell University, Johnson Graduate School of Business and Public Administration
4. Duke University, Fuqua School of Business
5. University of North Carolina, Kenan Flagler Business School

Source: "The Best B Schools," *Business Week*, 3701: 76-100, (October 2, 2000).

★599★
Business Week's top business schools by intellectual capital, 2000

Ranking basis/background: As compiled by *Business Week* from a survey of graduates from the Class of 2000 and companies that actively recruit MBAs. **Number listed:** 30.
1. Duke University, Fuqua School of Business
2. Massachusetts Institute of Technology, Alfred P. Sloan School of Management
3. Stanford University Graduate School of Business
4. Cornell University, Johnson Graduate School of Business and Public Administration
5. Yale University, Ancell School of Business
6. Columbia University Graduate School of Business
7. University of Chicago Graduate School of Business
8. University of Pennsylvania, Wharton School of Business
9. Vanderbilt University, Owen Graduate School of Management
10. University of California, Los Angeles, Anderson Graduate School of Management

Source: "The Best B Schools," *Business Week*, 3701: 76-100, (October 2, 2000).

★600★
Business Week's top business schools for finance skills as selected by corporate recruiters, 2000

Ranking basis/background: As compiled by *Business Week* from data provided by the schools themselves and surveys of the most recent MBA graduates and selected corporate recruiters.
Number listed: 10.
1. University of Pennsylvania, Wharton School of Business
2. University of Chicago Graduate School of Business
3. Harvard University Graduate School of Business Administration
4. Columbia University Graduate School of Business
5. Northwestern University, Kellogg Graduate School of Management
6. Duke University, Fuqua School of Business
7. University of Michigan Business School
8. Massachusetts Institute of Technology, Alfred P. Sloan School of Management
9. New York University, Leonard N. Stern School of Business
10. University of Virginia, Darden Graduate School of Business Administration

Source: "The Best B Schools," *Business Week*, 3701: 76-100, (October 2, 2000).

★601★
Business Week's top business schools for general management skills as selected by corporate recruiters, 2000

Ranking basis/background: As compiled by *Business Week* from data provided by the schools themselves and surveys of the most recent MBA graduates and selected corporate recruiters.
Number listed: 10.
1. Northwestern University, Kellogg Graduate School of Management
2. Harvard University Graduate School of Business Administration
3. University of Michigan Business School
4. University of Pennsylvania, Wharton School of Business
5. University of Virginia, Darden Graduate School of Business Administration
6. Duke University, Fuqua School of Business
7. Stanford University Graduate School of Business
8. University of Chicago Graduate School of Business
9. Columbia University Graduate School of Business
10. Cornell University, Johnson Graduate School of Business and Public Administration

Source: "The Best B Schools," *Business Week*, 3701: 76-100, (October 2, 2000).

★602★
Business Week's top business schools for global scope skills as selected by corporate recruiters, 2000

Ranking basis/background: As compiled by *Business Week* from data provided by the schools themselves and surveys of the most recent MBA graduates and selected corporate recruiters.
Number listed: 10.
1. University of Pennsylvania, Wharton School of Business
2. Harvard University Graduate School of Business Administration
3. Northwestern University, Kellogg Graduate School of Management
4. University of Chicago Graduate School of Business
5. Columbia University Graduate School of Business
6. Stanford University Graduate School of Business
7. University of Michigan Business School
8. Massachusetts Institute of Technology, Alfred P. Sloan School of Management
9. Thunderbird, American Graduate School of International Management
10. Duke University, Fuqua School of Business

Source: "The Best B Schools," *Business Week*, 3701: 76-100, (October 2, 2000).

★603★
Business Week's top business schools for marketing skills as selected by corporate recruiters, 2000

Ranking basis/background: As compiled by *Business Week* from data provided by the schools themselves and surveys of the most recent MBA graduates and selected corporate recruiters.
Number listed: 10.
1. Northwestern University, Kellogg Graduate School of Management
2. University of Pennsylvania, Wharton School of Business
3. Harvard University Graduate School of Business Administration
4. Duke University, Fuqua School of Business
5. University of Michigan Business School
6. University of Virginia, Darden Graduate School of Business Administration
7. Columbia University Graduate School of Business
8. Cornell University, Johnson Graduate School of Business and Public Administration
9. University of Chicago Graduate School of Business
10. Stanford University Graduate School of Business

Source: "The Best B Schools," *Business Week*, 3701: 76-100, (October 2, 2000).

★604★
Business Week's top business schools for technology skills as selected by corporate recruiters, 2000

Ranking basis/background: As compiled by *Business Week* from data provided by the schools themselves and surveys of the most recent MBA graduates and selected corporate recruiters.
Number listed: 10.
1. Massachusetts Institute of Technology, Alfred P. Sloan School of Management
2. Carnegie-Mellon University Graduate School of Industrial Administration
3. University of Pennsylvania, Wharton School of Business
4. Northwestern University, Kellogg Graduate School of Management
5. Stanford University Graduate School of Business
6. Harvard University Graduate School of Business Administration
7. University of Chicago Graduate School of Business
8. Cornell University, Johnson Graduate School of Business and Public Administration
9. Duke University, Fuqua School of Business
10. University of Virginia, Darden Graduate School of Business Administration

Source: "The Best B Schools," *Business Week*, 3701: 76-100, (October 2, 2000).

★605★
Business Week's top business schools outside the U.S. as selected by corporate recruiters, 2000

Ranking basis/background: As compiled by *Business Week* from data provided by the schools themselves and surveys of the most recent MBA graduates and selected corporate recruiters.
Number listed: 7.
1. European Institute of Business Administration (INSEAD)
2. Insituto de Estudios Superiors de la Empresa-International Graduate School of Management
3. London Business School
4. International Institute for Management Development (IMD)
5. University of Western Ontario
6. University of Toronto
7. Rotterdam School of Management

Source: "The Best B Schools," *Business Week*, 3701: 76-100, (October 2, 2000).

★606★
Business Week's top business schools outside the U.S. as selected by recent MBA graduates, 2000

Ranking basis/background: As compiled by *Business Week* from data provided by the schools themselves and surveys of the most recent MBA graduates and selected corporate recruiters.
Number listed: 7.
1. European Institute of Business Administration (INSEAD)
2. London Business School
3. Insituto de Estudios Superiors de la Empresa-International Graduate School of Management
4. International Institute for Management Development (IMD)
5. University of Western Ontario
6. Rotterdam School of Management
7. University of Toronto

Source: "The Best B Schools," *Business Week*, 3701: 76-100, (October 2, 2000).

★607★
Business Week's top business schools outside the U.S. for intellectual capital, 2000

Ranking basis/background: As compiled by *Business Week* from data provided by the schools themselves and surveys of the most recent MBA graduates and selected corporate recruiters.
Number listed: 7.
1. London Business School
2. European Institute of Business Administration (INSEAD)
3. International Institute for Management Development (IMD)
4. University of Toronto
5. University of Western Ontario
6. Rotterdam School of Management

BUSINESS ADMINISTRATION, GRADUATE

7. Insituto de Estudios Superiors de la Empresa-International Graduate School of Management

Source: "The Best B Schools," *Business Week*, 3701: 76-100, (October 2, 2000).

★608★
Business Week's top business schools with the best placement offices, 2000

Ranking basis/background: As compiled by *Business Week* from data provided by the schools themselves and surveys of the most recent MBA graduates. **Number listed:** 5.
1. Northwestern University, Kellogg Graduate School of Management
2. University of Virginia, Darden Graduate School of Business Administration
3. University of Chicago Graduate School of Business
4. Duke University, Fuqua School of Business
5. Cornell University, Johnson Graduate School of Business and Public Administration

Source: "The Best B Schools," *Business Week*, 3701: 76-100, (October 2, 2000).

★609★
Business Week's top business schools with the best teachers, 2000

Ranking basis/background: Business schools with the best-rated teachers, as compiled by *Business Week* from a survey of graduates from the Class of 2000 and companies that actively recruit MBAs. **Number listed:** 5.
1. University of Virginia, Darden Graduate School of Business Administration
2. University of Rochester, Simon Graduate School of Management
3. Indiana University, Kelley Graduate School of Business
4. Cornell University, Johnson Graduate School of Business and Public Administration
5. Washington University, John M. Olin School of Business

Source: "The Best B Schools," *Business Week*, 3701: 76-100, (October 2, 2000).

★610★
Business Week's top business schools with the greatest decrease in MBA satisfaction, 2000

Ranking basis/background: As compiled by *Business Week* from data provided by the schools themselves and surveys of the most recent MBA graduates. **Number listed:** 5.
1. University of Chicago Graduate School of Business
2. Yale University, Ancell School of Business
3. Carnegie-Mellon University Graduate School of Industrial Administration
4. Stanford University Graduate School of Business
5. Dartmouth College, Amos Tuck School of Business Administration

Source: "The Best B Schools," *Business Week*, 3701: 76-100, (October 2, 2000).

★611★
Business Week's top business schools with the greatest rise in MBA satisfaction, 2000

Ranking basis/background: As compiled by *Business Week* from data provided by the schools themselves and surveys of the most recent MBA graduates. **Number listed:** 5.
1. University of Virginia, Darden Graduate School of Business Administration
2. Massachusetts Institute of Technology, Alfred P. Sloan School of Management
3. Harvard University Graduate School of Business Administration
4. Washington University, John M. Olin School of Business
5. University of North Carolina, Kenan Flagler Business School

Source: "The Best B Schools," *Business Week*, 3701: 76-100, (October 2, 2000).

★612★
Business Week's top business schools with the highest percentage of international students, 2000

Ranking basis/background: Percentage of international MBA students for combined years 1999-2000. As compiled by *Business Week* from a survey of graduates from the Class of 2000 and companies that actively recruit MBAs. **Number listed:** 30.
1. University of Rochester, Simon Graduate School of Management, 50%
2. Purdue University, Krannert School of Management, 41%
3. University of Pennsylvania, Wharton School of Business, 39%
4. Georgetown University, McDonough School of Business, 38%
5. Massachusetts Institute of Technology, Alfred P. Sloan School of Management, 37%
5. Carnegie-Mellon University Graduate School of Industrial Administration, 37%
7. Michigan State University, Eli Broad College of Business, 36%
8. New York University, Leonard N. Stern School of Business, 35%
8. University of Maryland, Smith Graduate School of Management and Technology, 35%
10. Washington University, John M. Olin School of Business, 33%

Source: "The Best B Schools," *Business Week*, 3701: 76-100, (October 2, 2000).

★613★
Business Week's top business schools with the highest percentage of minority enrollment, 2000

Ranking basis/background: Percentage of minority MBA students for combined years 1999-2000. As compiled by *Business Week* from a survey of graduates from the Class of 2000 and companies that actively recruit MBAs. **Number listed:** 30.
1. University of Rochester, Simon Graduate School of Management, with 17%
2. Duke University, Fuqua School of Business, 16%
3. Northwestern University, Kellogg Graduate School of Management, 14%
3. Harvard University Graduate School of Business Administration, 14%
3. University of Virginia, Darden Graduate School of Business Administration, 14%
6. Columbia University Graduate School of Business, 13%
7. University of Michigan Business School, 12%
7. Georgia Tech, DuPree College of Management, 12%
9. Massachusetts Institute of Technology, Alfred P. Sloan School of Management, 11%
9. University of North Carolina, Kenan Flagler Business School, 11%
9. University of Southern California, Marshall School of Business, 11%

Source: "The Best B Schools," *Business Week*, 3701: 76-100, (October 2, 2000).

★614★
Business Week's top business schools with the highest percentage of women enrollees, 2000

Ranking basis/background: Percentage of female MBA students for combined years 1999-2000. As compiled by *Business Week* from a survey of graduates from the Class of 2000 and companies that actively recruit MBAs. **Number listed:** 30.
1. New York University, Leonard N. Stern School of Business, with 39%
2. Duke University, Fuqua School of Business, 38%
3. Columbia University Graduate School of Business, 37%
4. Georgetown University, McDonough School of Business, 36%
5. University of Maryland, Smith Graduate School of Management and Technology, 35%
5. Stanford University Graduate School of Business, 35%
7. University of California, Berkeley, Haas Graduate School of Business Administration, 34%
8. University of Southern California, Marshall School of Business, 33%
9. Dartmouth College, Amos Tuck School of Business Administration, 32%
10. Northwestern University, Kellogg Graduate School of Management, 31%
10. Harvard University Graduate School of Business Administration, 31%
10. University of North Carolina, Kenan Flagler Business School, 31%

Source: "The Best B Schools," *Business Week*, 3701: 76-100, (October 2, 2000).

★615★
Business Week's top business schools with the lowest percentage of international students, 2000

Ranking basis/background: Percentage of international MBA students from combined years 1999-2000. As compiled by *Business Week* from a survey of graduates from the Class of 2000 and companies that actively recruit MBAs. **Number listed:** 30.
1. University of Southern California, Marshall School of Business, 23%
2. University of Virginia, Darden Graduate School of Business Administration, 25%
3. University of California, Los Angeles, Anderson Graduate School of Management, 26%
3. University of Texas, Austin, McCombs School of Business, 26%

BUSINESS ADMINISTRATION, GRADUATE

5. Duke University, Fuqua School of Business, 28%
5. Columbia University Graduate School of Business, 28%
5. Vanderbilt University, Owen Graduate School of Management, 28%
8. University of North Carolina, Kenan Flagler Business School, 29%
8. Georgia Tech, DuPree College of Management, 29%
10. Cornell University, Johnson Graduate School of Business and Public Administration, 30%

Source: "The Best B Schools," *Business Week*, 3701: 76-100, (October 2, 2000).

★616★
Business Week's top business schools with the lowest percentage of minority enrollment, 2000

Ranking basis/background: Percentage of minority MBA students for combined years 1999-2000. As compiled by *Business Week* from a survey of graduates from the Class of 2000 and companies that actively recruit MBAs. **Number listed:** 30.

1. Cornell University, Johnson Graduate School of Business and Public Administration, with 5%
1. Carnegie-Mellon University Graduate School of Industrial Administration, 5%
1. University of Texas, Austin, McCombs School of Business, 5%
1. Vanderbilt University, Owen Graduate School of Management, 5%
5. Yale University, Ancell School of Business, 6%
6. University of California, Berkeley, Haas Graduate School of Business Administration, 7%
6. University of Chicago Graduate School of Business, 7%
8. University of California, Los Angeles, Anderson Graduate School of Management, 8%
8. Georgetown University, McDonough School of Business, 8%
8. Emory University, Goizueta Graduate School of Business, 8%
8. Michigan State University, Eli Broad College of Business, 8%

Source: "The Best B Schools," *Business Week*, 3701: 76-100, (October 2, 2000).

★617★
Business Week's top business schools with the lowest percentage of women enrollees, 2000

Ranking basis/background: Percentage of female MBA students for the combines years 1999-2000. As compiled by *Business Week* from a survey of graduates from the Class of 2000 and companies that actively recruit MBAs. **Number listed:** 30.

1. Purdue University, Krannert School of Management, 21%
2. University of Chicago Graduate School of Business, 23%
3. University of Texas, Austin, McCombs School of Business, 24%
3. Indiana University, Kelley Graduate School of Business, 24%
3. University of Rochester, Simon Graduate School of Manangement, 24%
6. Washington University, John M. Olin School of Business, 25%

7. Carnegie-Mellon University Graduate School of Industrial Administration, 26%
8. Massachusetts Institute of Technology, Alfred P. Sloan School of Management, 27%
8. Cornell University, Johnson Graduate School of Business and Public Administration, 27%
8. Vanderbilt University, Owen Graduate School of Management, 27%

Source: "The Best B Schools," *Business Week*, 3701: 76-100, (October 2, 2000).

★618★
Business Week's top business schools with the most improved program as selected by corporate recruiters, 2000

Ranking basis/background: As compiled by *Business Week* from data provided by the schools themselves and surveys of the most recent MBA graduates and selected corporate recruiters. **Number listed:** 5.

1. Duke University, Fuqua School of Business
2. University of Chicago Graduate School of Business
3. Cornell University, Johnson Graduate School of Business and Public Administration
4. Northwestern University, Kellogg Graduate School of Management
5. Carnegie-Mellon University Graduate School of Industrial Administration

Source: "The Best B Schools," *Business Week*, 3701: 76-100, (October 2, 2000).

★619★
Business Week's top business schools with the most innovative curriculum as selected by corporate recruiters, 2000

Ranking basis/background: As compiled by *Business Week* from data provided by the schools themselves and surveys of the most recent MBA graduates and selected corporate recruiters. **Number listed:** 5.

1. Northwestern University, Kellogg Graduate School of Management
2. University of Pennsylvania, Wharton School of Business
3. Carnegie-Mellon University Graduate School of Industrial Administration
4. University of Virginia, Darden Graduate School of Business Administration
5. Harvard University Graduate School of Business Administration

Source: "The Best B Schools," *Business Week*, 3701: 76-100, (October 2, 2000).

★620★
Business Week's top business schools with the worst placement offices, 2000

Ranking basis/background: As compiled by *Business Week* from data provided by the schools themselves and surveys of the most recent MBA graduates. **Number listed:** 5.

1. Stanford University Graduate School of Business
2. University of Pennsylvania, Wharton School of Business
3. University of Texas, Austin, McCombs School of Business
4. University of Maryland, Smith Graduate School of Management and Technology
5. Georgetown University, McDonough School of Business

Source: "The Best B Schools," *Business Week*, 3701: 76-100, (October 2, 2000).

★621★
Business Week's top business schools worst at responding to student concerns, 2000

Ranking basis/background: As compiled by *Business Week* from data provided by the schools themselves and surveys of the most recent MBA graduates. **Number listed:** 5.

1. Stanford University Graduate School of Business
2. Harvard University Graduate School of Business Administration
3. Carnegie-Mellon University Graduate School of Industrial Administration
4. Georgia Tech, DuPree College of Management
5. University of California, Los Angeles, Anderson Graduate School of Management

Source: "The Best B Schools," *Business Week*, 3701: 76-100, (October 2, 2000).

★622★
Comparisons of investment returns for consulting MBAs

Ranking basis/background: Comparison of the fastest, slowest and average MBA investment payback as calculated from a *Business Week* survey of MBA students from 73 schools where 15 or more students responded. **Remarks:** Original source: Business Week, Jens Stephan, University of Cincinnati. **Number listed:** 3.

Fastest: University of Texas, with $120,900 total investment; 108% post-MBA salary increase; taking 3.5 years to pay back
Slowest: University of Florida, $136,900; 67%; 6.0
Average: $122,900; 95%; 4.2

Source: "The Best B Schools," *Business Week*, 3701: 76-100, (October 2, 2000).

★623★
Comparisons of investment returns for entrepreneurship MBAs

Ranking basis/background: Comparison of the fastest, slowest and average MBA investment payback as calculated from a *Business Week* survey of MBA students from 73 schools where 15 or more students responded. **Remarks:** Original source: Business Week, Jens Stephan, University of Cincinnati. **Number listed:** 3.

Fastest: Columbia University, with $156,300 total investment; 105% post-MBA salary increase; taking 4.2 years to pay back
Slowest: University of Southern California, $160,300; 39%; 8.5
Average: $135,700; 77%; 5.7

Source: "The Best B Schools," *Business Week*, 3701: 76-100, (October 2, 2000).

BUSINESS ADMINISTRATION, GRADUATE

★624★
Comparisons of investment returns for finance MBAs

Ranking basis/background: Comparison of the fastest, slowest and average MBA investment payback as calculated from a *Business Week* survey of MBA students from 73 schools where 15 or more students responded. **Remarks:** Original source: Business Week, Jens Stephan, University of Cincinnati. **Number listed:** 3.

- Fastest: University of Pittsburgh, with $80,600 total investment; 100% post-MBA salary increase; taking 3.3 years to pay back
- Slowest: University of Florida, $141,600; 56%; 6.4
- Average: $123,200; 81%; 4.6

Source: "The Best B Schools," *Business Week*, 3701: 76-100, (October 2, 2000).

★625★
Comparisons of investment returns for information technology MBAs

Ranking basis/background: Comparison of the fastest, slowest and average MBA investment payback as calculated from a *Business Week* survey of MBA students from 73 schools where 15 or more students responded. **Remarks:** Original source: Business Week, Jens Stephan, University of Cincinnati. **Number listed:** 3.

- Fastest: University of South Carolina, with $93,600 total investment; 117% post-MBA salary increase; taking 4.0 years to pay back
- Slowest: Stanford University, $197,400; 54%; 6.6
- Average: $127,100; 72%; 5.4

Source: "The Best B Schools," *Business Week*, 3701: 76-100, (October 2, 2000).

★626★
Comparisons of investment returns for marketing MBAs

Ranking basis/background: Comparison of the fastest, slowest and average MBA investment payback as calculated from a *Business Week* survey of MBA students from 73 schools where 15 or more students responded. **Remarks:** Original source: Business Week, Jens Stephan, University of Cincinnati. **Number listed:** 3.

- Fastest: Texas A&M University, with $75,200 total investment; 117% post-MBA salary increase; taking 3.4 years to pay back
- Slowest: Stanford University, $179,300; 31%; 9.3
- Average: $119,600; 82%; 4.9

Source: "The Best B Schools," *Business Week*, 3701: 76-100, (October 2, 2000).

★627★
Comparisons of investment returns for operations MBAs

Ranking basis/background: Comparison of the fastest, slowest and average MBA investment payback as calculated from a *Business Week* survey of MBA students from 73 schools where 15 or more students responded. **Remarks:** Original source: Business Week, Jens Stephan, University of Cincinnati. **Number listed:** 3.

- Fastest: Purdue University, with $104,200 total investment; 100% post-MBA salary increase; taking 3.9 years to pay back
- Slowest: Thunderbird, American Graduate School of International Management, $125,700; 75%; 5.8
- Average: $118,500; 78%; 4.9

Source: "The Best B Schools," *Business Week*, 3701: 76-100, (October 2, 2000).

★628★
European and Canadian business schools with the quickest payback on MBA investments

Ranking basis/background: Median total investment, percent salary increase, median years to payback, and median salary at graduation, as calculated from a *Business Week* survey of MBA students from 73 schools where 15 or more students responded. **Remarks:** Original source: Business Week, Jens Stephan, University of Cincinnati. **Number listed:** 3.

1. European Institute of Business Administration (INSEAD), with $101,500 median total investment; 60% post-MBA salary increase; taking 2.8 years to pay back; $90,000 median salary at graduation
2. International Institute for Management Development (IMD), $110,500; 63%; 3.0; $100,000
3. Cranfield University School of Management, $84,300; 56%; 3.4; $75,000

Source: "The Best B Schools," *Business Week*, 3701: 76-100, (October 2, 2000).

★629★
European and Canadian business schools with the slowest payback on MBA investments

Ranking basis/background: Median total investment, percent salary increase, median years to payback, and median salary at graduation, as calculated from a *Business Week* survey of MBA students from 73 schools where 15 or more students responded. **Remarks:** Original source: Business Week, Jens Stephan, University of Cincinnati. **Number listed:** 3.

1. Escuela Superior de Administracion y Direccion de Empresas (ESADE), with $92,700 median total investment; 73% post-MBA salary increase; taking 5.7 years to pay back; $50,000 median salary at graduation
1. University of Toronto, $99,000; 50%; 5.7; $57,000
3. York University, $83,000; 67%; 5.6; $41,500

Source: "The Best B Schools," *Business Week*, 3701: 76-100, (October 2, 2000).

★630★
***Financial Times* best business schools**

Ranking basis/background: Top business schools worldwide according to *Financial Times*. **Number listed:** 20.

1. Harvard University Graduate School of Business Administration
2. University of Pennsylvania, Wharton School of Business
3. Stanford University Graduate School of Business
4. Massachusetts Institute of Technology, Alfred P. Sloan School of Management
5. Columbia University Graduate School of Business
6. University of Chicago Graduate School of Business
7. Northwestern University, Kellogg Graduate School of Management
8. London Business School
9. European Institute of Business Administration (INSEAD)
10. Cornell University, Johnson Graduate School of Business and Public Administration
11. International Institute for Management Development (IMD)
12. University of California, Berkeley, Haas Graduate School of Business Administration
13. New York University, Leonard N. Stern School of Business
14. University of California, Los Angeles, Anderson Graduate School of Management
15. Dartmouth College, Amos Tuck School of Business Administration
16. University of Michigan Business School
17. Duke University, Fuqua School of Business
18. Yale University, Ancell School of Business
19. University of Western Ontario, Richard Ivey School of Business
20. University of Virginia, Darden Graduate School of Business Administration

Source: Crainer, Stuart and Des Dearlove, "The Ivory Chateau," *Across the Board*, 37: 35-40, (June 2000).

★631★
Highest post-MBA salaries for students enrolled in *Business Week*'s top business schools, 1999

Ranking basis/background: Median starting salary packages for members of the Class of 1999, as compiled by *Business Week* from data provided by the schools themselves and surveys of the most recent MBA graduates. **Number listed:** 30.

1. Stanford University Graduate School of Business, with $165,500
2. Harvard University Graduate School of Business Administration, $160,000
3. University of Pennsylvania, Wharton School of Business, $156,000
4. Dartmouth College, Amos Tuck School of Business Administration, $149,500
5. Massachusetts Institute of Technology, Alfred P. Sloan School of Management, $149,000
6. Columbia University Graduate School of Business, $142,500
7. Northwestern University, Kellogg Graduate School of Management, $142,000
8. University of Chicago Graduate School of Business, $140,000
8. New York University, Leonard N. Stern School of Business, $140,000
10. University of California, Los Angeles, Anderson Graduate School of Management, $136,500

Source: "The Best B Schools," *Business Week*, 3701: 76-100, (October 2, 2000).

★632★
Highest pre-MBA salaries for students enrolled in *Business Week*'s top business schools, 1999

Ranking basis/background: Median salaries for member of the Class of 1999 before they received their degrees, as compiled by *Business Week* from data provided by the schools themselves and surveys of the most recent MBA graduates. **Number listed:** 30.
1. Stanford University Graduate School of Business, with $65,500
2. Harvard University Graduate School of Business Administration, $65,000
3. University of Pennsylvania, Wharton School of Business, $60,000
4. Northwestern University, Kellogg Graduate School of Management, $55,000
4. Massachusetts Institute of Technology, Alfred P. Sloan School of Management, $55,000
4. University of Chicago Graduate School of Business, $55,000
4. University of California, Los Angeles, Anderson Graduate School of Management, $55,000
8. University of Michigan Business School, $50,000
8. Columbia University Graduate School of Business, $50,000
8. University of Virginia, Darden Graduate School of Business Administration, $50,000
8. Dartmouth College, Amos Tuck School of Business Administration, $50,000

Source: "The Best B Schools," *Business Week*, 3701: 76-100, (October 2, 2000).

★633★
International skills considered the most important

Ranking basis/background: Important international skills as determined by the MBA International Career Guide, 1997. **Number listed:** 10.

International awareness
Commercial thinking
Analytical skills
Interpersonal skills
Functional skills
Academic record
Leadership potential
Languages
Previous work experience
Generalist

Source: Bachhuber, Thomas, *The Best Graduate Business Schools, Third Edition*, Macmillan, 1999.

★634★
Lowest post-MBA salaries for students enrolled in *Business Week*'s top business schools, 1999

Ranking basis/background: Median starting salary packages for members of the Class of 1999, as compiled by *Business Week* from data provided by the schools themselves and surveys of the most recent MBA graduates. **Number listed:** 30.
1. Michigan State University, Eli Broad College of Business, with $93,000
2. Georgia Tech, DuPree College of Management, $95,000
3. Purdue University, Krannert School of Management, $101,500
4. University of Maryland, Smith Graduate School of Management and Technology, $105,000
4. Emory University, Goizueta Graduate School of Business, $105,000
6. University of Texas, Austin, McCombs School of Business, $107,000
7. Washington University, John M. Olin School of Business, $109,000
8. University of Rochester, Simon Graduate School of Management, $110,000
9. University of Southern California, Marshall School of Business, $112,000
10. Indiana University, Kelley Graduate School of Business, $114,000

Source: "The Best B Schools," *Business Week*, 3701: 76-100, (October 2, 2000).

★635★
Lowest pre-MBA salaries for students enrolled in *Business Week*'s top business schools, 1999

Ranking basis/background: Median salaries for member of the Class of 1999 before they received their degrees, as compiled by *Business Week* from data provided by the schools themselves and surveys of the most recent MBA graduates. **Number listed:** 30.
1. Purdue University, Krannert School of Management, with $32,000
2. Michigan State University, Eli Broad College of Business, $34,000
3. Georgia Tech, DuPree College of Management, $35,000
4. University of Maryland, Smith Graduate School of Management and Technology, $39,000
5. Indiana University, Kelley Graduate School of Business, $40,000
5. University of Rochester, Simon Graduate School of Management, $40,000
5. Vanderbilt University, Owen Graduate School of Management, $40,000
8. Washington University, John M. Olin School of Business, $40,500
9. Yale University, Ancell School of Business, $44,000
10. New York University, Leonard N. Stern School of Business, $45,000
10. Carnegie-Mellon University Graduate School of Industrial Administration, $45,000
10. University of Texas, Austin, McCombs School of Business, $45,000
10. Emory University, Goizueta Graduate School of Business, $45,000

Source: "The Best B Schools," *Business Week*, 3701: 76-100, (October 2, 2000).

★636★
Median starting salaries of graduates from *U.S. News & World Report*'s top 10 graduate business schools, 2001

Ranking basis/background: From a *U.S. News & World Report* survey of business school graduates in 2000. **Remarks:** Data collected by Market Facts, Inc. **Number listed:** 53.
1. Harvard University Graduate School of Business Administration, with a median starting salary of $117,180
2. Northwestern University, Kellogg Graduate School of Management, $112,994
3. Massachusetts Institute of Technology, Alfred P. Sloan School of Management, $112,741
4. University of Pennsylvania, Wharton School of Business, $111,747
5. Columbia University Graduate School of Business, $110,556
6. Stanford University Graduate School of Business, $108,441
7. University of Chicago Graduate School of Business, $107,895
8. Duke University, Fuqua School of Business, $106,761
9. University of Michigan Business School, $105,282
10. University of California, Berkeley, Haas Graduate School of Business Administration, $104,159

Source: "America's Best Graduate Schools: 2002 Annual Guide," *U.S. News & World Report*, 130: 60-97, (April 19, 2001).

★637★
Out-of-state tuition and fees for *U.S. News & World Report*'s top 10 graduate business schools, 2001

Ranking basis/background: From a *U.S. News & World Report* survey of graduate school tuition and fees in 2000. **Remarks:** Data collected by Market Facts, Inc. **Number listed:** 53.
1. Columbia University Graduate School of Business, with $30,548
2. Duke University, Fuqua School of Business, $28,910
3. Massachusetts Institute of Technology, Alfred P. Sloan School of Management, $29,860
4. University of Pennsylvania, Wharton School of Business, $29,250
5. University of Chicago Graduate School of Business, $29,230
6. Stanford University Graduate School of Business, $28,896
7. University of Michigan Business School, $28,686
8. Northwestern University, Kellogg Graduate School of Management, $28,677
9. Harvard University Graduate School of Business Administration, $28,500
10. University of California, Berkeley, Haas Graduate School of Business Administration, $20,702

Source: "America's Best Graduate Schools: 2002 Annual Guide," *U.S. News & World Report*, 130: 60-97, (April 19, 2001).

★638★
Percentage of applicants accepted at *Business Week*'s top business schools, 2000

Ranking basis/background: Percentage as applicants accepted for the 1999-2000 academic year. As compiled by *Business Week* from a survey of graduates from the Class of 2000 and companies that actively recruit MBAs. **Number listed:** 30.

University of Pennsylvania, Wharton School of Business, with 14%
Northwestern University, Kellogg Graduate School of Management, 18%
Harvard University Graduate School of Business Administration, 13%
Massachusetts Institute of Technology, Alfred P. Sloan School of Management, 17%
Duke University, Fuqua School of Business, 19%
University of Michigan Business School, 21%

Columbia University Graduate School of Business, 12%
Cornell University, Johnson Graduate School of Business and Public Administration, 25%
University of Virginia, Darden Graduate School of Business Administration, 19%
University of Chicago Graduate School of Business, 25%

Source: "The Best B Schools," *Business Week*, 3701: 76-100, (October 2, 2000).

★639★
Percentage of employed graduates at U.S. News & World Report's top 10 graduate business schools, 2001

Ranking basis/background: From a *U.S. News & World Report* survey based on employment upon or after graduation, median starting salaries, and ratio of on-campus recruiters to graduates. **Remarks:** Data collected by Market Facts, Inc. **Number listed:** 53.

1. Columbia University Graduate School of Business, 99.2%
2. Duke University, Fuqua School of Business, 94.4%
3. Northwestern University, Kellogg Graduate School of Management, 93.2%
3. Massachusetts Institute of Technology, Alfred P. Sloan School of Management, 93.2%
5. University of Michigan Business School, 92.3%
6. University of California, Berkeley, Haas Graduate School of Business Administration, 91.5%
7. University of Chicago Graduate School of Business, 90.4%
8. Harvard University Graduate School of Business Administration, 87.6%
9. Stanford University Graduate School of Business, with 87.5%
10. University of Pennsylvania, Wharton School of Business, 76.0%

Source: "America's Best Graduate Schools: 2002 Annual Guide," *U.S. News & World Report*, 130: 60-97, (April 19, 2001).

★640★
Percentage of graduates earning over $100,000 from Business Week's top business schools, 1999

Ranking basis/background: Percentage of Class of 1999 earning over $100,000, as compiled by *Business Week* from data provided by the schools themselves and surveys of the most recent MBA graduates. **Number listed:** 30.

University of Pennsylvania, Wharton School of Business, 89%
Northwestern University, Kellogg Graduate School of Management, 83%
Harvard University Graduate School of Business Administration, 89%
Massachusetts Institute of Technology, Alfred P. Sloan School of Management, 88%
Duke University, Fuqua School of Business, 80%
University of Michigan Business School, 81%
Columbia University Graduate School of Business, 85%
Cornell University, Johnson Graduate School of Business and Public Administration, 82%
University of Virginia, Darden Graduate School of Business Administration, 84%
University of Chicago Graduate School of Business, 86%

Source: "The Best B Schools," *Business Week*, 3701: 76-100, (October 2, 2000).

★641★
Percentage of graduates employed within 3 months of graduation from U.S. News & World Report's top 10 graduate business schools, 2001

Ranking basis/background: From a *U.S. News & World Report* survey based on employment upon or after graduation, median starting salaries, and ratio of on-campus recruiters to graduates. **Remarks:** Data collected by Market Facts, Inc. **Number listed:** 53.

1. Northwestern University, Kellogg Graduate School of Management, with 100.0%
2. Columbia University Graduate School of Business, 99.7%
3. University of Pennsylvania, Wharton School of Business, 99.3%
4. Stanford University Graduate School of Business, 98.7%
5. Harvard University Graduate School of Business Administration, 98.6%
6. University of California, Berkeley, Haas Graduate School of Business Administration, 98.5%
7. Duke University, Fuqua School of Business, 97.4%
8. University of Chicago Graduate School of Business, 95.7%
9. Massachusetts Institute of Technology, Alfred P. Sloan School of Management, 95.4%
10. University of Michigan Business School, 95.3%

Source: "America's Best Graduate Schools: 2002 Annual Guide," *U.S. News & World Report*, 130: 60-97, (April 19, 2001).

★642★
Post-MBA salaries for graduates from Business Week's top business schools outside the U.S., 2000

Ranking basis/background: Median post-MBA salary package, as compiled by *Business Week* from data provided by the schools themselves and surveys of the most recent MBA graduates and selected corporate recruiters. **Number listed:** 7.

1. London Business School, with $137,000
2. International Institute for Management Development (IMD), $126,000
3. European Institute of Business Administration (INSEAD), $124,000
4. Rotterdam School of Management, $91,000
5. Insituto de Estudios Superiors de la Empresa-International Graduate School of Management, $77,000
6. University of Western Ontario, $74,000
7. University of Toronto, $66,000

Source: "The Best B Schools," *Business Week*, 3701: 76-100, (October 2, 2000).

★643★
Pre-MBA salaries for students at Business Week's top business schools outside the U.S., 2000

Ranking basis/background: Median pre-MBA salary, as compiled by *Business Week* from data provided by the schools themselves and surveys of the most recent MBA graduates and selected corporate recruiters. **Number listed:** 7.

1. International Institute for Management Development (IMD), with $69,000
2. European Institute of Business Administration (INSEAD), $60,000
3. London Business School, $50,000
4. Rotterdam School of Management, $43,000
5. Insituto de Estudios Superiors de la Empresa-International Graduate School of Management, $40,000
6. University of Toronto, $35,500
7. University of Western Ontario, $35,000

Source: "The Best B Schools," *Business Week*, 3701: 76-100, (October 2, 2000).

★644★
Top business schools by average MBA rank, 1986-1998

Ranking basis/background: Determined by research rank in conjunction with mean MBA rank according to *U.S. News & World Report*'s top business schools over a 13 year period from 1995 to 1999. **Number listed:** 50.

1. Stanford University
2. University of Pennsylvania
3. Harvard University
4. Massachusetts Institute of Technology
5. Northwestern University
6. University of Chicago
7. University of Minnesota
8. Dartmouth University
9. Duke University
10. University of Michigan

Source: Trieschmann, James S., et. al., "Serving Multiple Constituencies in Business Schools: Program Versus Research Performance," *Academy of Management Journal*, 43: 1130-1141, (December 2000).

★645★
Top business schools for overall within-discipline research performance, 1986-1998

Ranking basis/background: Determined by the number of pages a school's faculty published in the 20 top-tier business research journals over a 13 year period, from 1986 to 1998. **Number listed:** 50.

1. University of Pennsylvania
2. University of Michigan
3. Stanford University
4. New York University
5. University of Chicago
6. Columbia University
7. University of Minnesota
8. University of Texas, Austin
9. Harvard University
10. Northwestern University

Source: Trieschmann, James S., et. al., "Serving Multiple Constituencies in Business Schools: Program Versus Research Performance," *Academy of Management Journal*, 43: 1130-1141, (December 2000).

BUSINESS ADMINISTRATION, GRADUATE

★646★

Top business schools for within-discipline research performance in management, 1986-1998

Ranking basis/background: Determined by the number of pages a school's faculty published in the 20 top-tier business research journals over a 13 year period, from 1986 to 1998. **Number listed:** 50.
1. Stanford University
2. University of Michigan
3. University of Pennsylvania
4. New York University
5. Columbia University
6. Northwestern University
7. University of Minnesota
8. Harvard University
9. University of Illinois
10. Texas A&M University, College Station

Source: Trieschmann, James S., et. al., "Serving Multiple Constituencies in Business Schools: Program Versus Research Performance," *Academy of Management Journal*, 43: 1130-1141, (December 2000).

★647★

Top business schools for within-discipline research performance in management science, 1986-1998

Ranking basis/background: Determined by the number of pages a school's faculty published in the 20 top-tier business research journals over a 13 year period, from 1986 to 1998. **Number listed:** 50.
1. Massachusetts Institute of Technology
2. Columbia University
3. University of Pennsylvania
4. Stanford University
5. University of Texas, Austin
6. Carnegie Mellon University
7. Duke University
8. University of Michigan
9. Purdue University
10. University of Washington, Seattle

Source: Trieschmann, James S., et. al., "Serving Multiple Constituencies in Business Schools: Program Versus Research Performance," *Academy of Management Journal*, 43: 1130-1141, (December 2000).

★648★

Top business schools for within-discipline research performance in production/operations management, 1986-1998

Ranking basis/background: Determined by the number of pages a school's faculty published in the 20 top-tier business research journals over a 13 year period, from 1986 to 1998. **Number listed:** 50.
1. University of Minnesota
2. Michigan State University
3. University of South Carolina
4. University of Cincinnati
5. Ohio State University
6. Texas A&M University, College Station
7. University of Indiana
8. University of North Carolina, Chapel Hill
9. University of Wisconsin, Madison
10. Arizona State University

Source: Trieschmann, James S., et. al., "Serving Multiple Constituencies in Business Schools: Program Versus Research Performance," *Academy of Management Journal*, 43: 1130-1141, (December 2000).

★649★

Top graduate business schools, 2001

Ranking basis/background: From a *U.S. News & World Report* survey based on academic reputation, student selectivity, placement success, and graduate rate. **Remarks:** Data collected by Market Facts, Inc. **Number listed:** 53.
1. Stanford University Graduate School of Business, with an overall score of 100
2. Harvard University Graduate School of Business Administration, 99
3. Northwestern University, Kellogg Graduate School of Management, 98
4. University of Pennsylvania, Wharton School of Business, 97
5. Massachusetts Institute of Technology, Alfred P. Sloan School of Management, 96
6. Columbia University Graduate School of Business, 93
7. University of California, Berkeley, Haas Graduate School of Business Administration, 91
8. Duke University, Fuqua School of Business, 90
9. University of Chicago Graduate School of Business, 89
10. University of Michigan Business School, 88

Source: "America's Best Graduate Schools: 2002 Annual Guide," *U.S. News & World Report*, 130: 60-97, (April 19, 2001).

★650★

Top graduate business schools by reputation as determined by academic personnel, 2001

Ranking basis/background: From a *U.S. News & World Report* survey based on academic reputation, student selectivity, placement success, and graduate rate. **Remarks:** Data collected by Market Facts, Inc. **Number listed:** 53.
1. Stanford University Graduate School of Business, with 4.9
1. Harvard University Graduate School of Business Administration, 4.9
3. Northwestern University, Kellogg Graduate School of Management, 4.8
3. University of Pennsylvania, Wharton School of Business, 4.8
3. Massachusetts Institute of Technology, Alfred P. Sloan School of Management, 4.8
6. University of Chicago Graduate School of Business, 4.7
7. University of California, Berkeley, Haas Graduate School of Business Administration, 4.6
8. Columbia University Graduate School of Business, 4.5
8. Duke University, Fuqua School of Business, 4.5
8. University of Michigan Business School, 4.5

Source: "America's Best Graduate Schools: 2002 Annual Guide," *U.S. News & World Report*, 130: 60-97, (April 19, 2001).

★651★

Top graduate business schools by reputation, as determined by recruiters, 2001

Ranking basis/background: From a *U.S. News & World Report* survey based on academic reputation, student selectivity, placement success, and graduate rate. **Remarks:** Data collected by Market Facts, Inc. **Number listed:** 53.
1. Harvard University Graduate School of Business Administration, with 5.0
1. Northwestern University, Kellogg Graduate School of Management, 5.0
3. University of Pennsylvania, Wharton School of Business, 4.9
4. University of Michigan Business School, 4.8
5. Stanford University Graduate School of Business, 4.6
6. Massachusetts Institute of Technology, Alfred P. Sloan School of Management, 4.4
6. University of Chicago Graduate School of Business, 4.4
8. Duke University, Fuqua School of Business, 4.3
8. University of Virginia, Darden Graduate School of Business Administration, 4.3
10. Columbia University Graduate School of Business, 4.2
10. University of California, Berkeley, Haas Graduate School of Business Administration, 4.2
10. Dartmouth College, Amos Tuck School of Business Administration, 4.2
10. New York University, Leonard N. Stern School of Business, 4.2
10. University of California, Los Angeles, Anderson Graduate School of Management, 4.2
10. Yale University, Ancell School of Business, 4.2
10. Cornell University, Johnson Graduate School of Business and Public Administration, 4.2
10. Carnegie-Mellon University Graduate School of Industrial Administration, 4.2
10. University of North Carolina, Kenan Flagler Business School, 4.2
10. University of Texas, Austin, McCombs School of Business, 4.2
10. Indiana University, Kelley Graduate School of Business, 4.2

Source: "America's Best Graduate Schools: 2002 Annual Guide," *U.S. News & World Report*, 130: 60-97, (April 19, 2001).

★652★

Top recruiters for business administration jobs for 2000-01 master's degree recipients

Ranking basis/background: Projected number of college hires from on-campus recruitment for 2000-01. **Remarks:** Numbers reflect total expected hires, not just African American projected hires. **Number listed:** 57.
1. Deloitte & Touche, with 427 projected hires
2. Accenture, 275
3. Procter & Gamble, 112
4. EDS, 100
4. Lucent Technologies, 100
6. American Management Systems, 70
7. BB&T Corporation, 55
8. General Motors, 35

9. Wachovia, 35
10. Wells Fargo Financial, 25

Source: "The Top 100 Employers and the Majors in Demand for the Class of 2001," *The Black Collegian*, 31: 19-35, (February 2001).

★653★
Top recruiters for logistics jobs for 2000-01 master's degree recipients

Ranking basis/background: Projected number of college hires from on-campus recruitment for 2000-01. **Remarks:** Numbers reflect total expected hires, not just African American projected hires. **Number listed:** 1.

1. Toys "R" Us, with 1 projected hire

Source: "The Top 100 Employers and the Majors in Demand for the Class of 2001," *The Black Collegian*, 31: 19-35, (February 2001).

★654★
U.S. business schools with the quickest payback on MBA investments

Ranking basis/background: Median total investment, percent salary increase, median years to payback, and median salary at graduation, as calculated from a *Business Week* survey of MBA students from 73 schools where 15 or more students responded. **Remarks:** Original source: Business Week, Jens Stephan, University of Cincinnati. **Number listed:** 10.

1. Brigham Young University, with $70,900 median total investment; 120% post-MBA salary increase; taking 3.5 years to pay back; $67,000 median salary at graduation
2. University of Tennessee, Knoxville, $77,200; 115%; 3.6; $65,000
3. University of Iowa, $83,400; 100%; 3.7; $70,000
4. Purdue University, $102,600; 122%; 3.8; $77,000
5. University of Pittsburgh, $82,600; 62%; 3.9; $65,000
6. Georgia Tech, $93,500; 100%; 4.0; $72,000
6. Texas A&M University, $83,000; 98%; 4.0; $68,000
8. Michigan State University, $94,200; 100%; 4.1; $71,000
8. Penn State University, $97,100; 101%; 4.1%; $73,000
8. Yale University, $148,600; 100%; 4.1; $80,000

Source: "The Best B Schools," *Business Week*, 3701: 76-100, (October 2, 2000).

★655★
U.S. business schools with the slowest payback on MBA investments

Ranking basis/background: Median total investment, percent salary increase, median years to payback, and median salary at graduation, as calculated from a *Business Week* survey of MBA students from 73 schools where 15 or more students responded. **Remarks:** Original source: Business Week, Jens Stephan, University of Cincinnati. **Number listed:** 10.

1. University of Florida, with $136,900 median total investment; 68% post-MBA salary increase; taking 6.6 years to pay back; $65,000 median salary at graduation
2. George Washington University, $125,800; 67%; 6.3; $67,000
3. University of California, Irvine, $133,400; 68%; 6.1; $75,000
4. Thunderbird, American Graduate School of International Management, $129,700; 60%; 5.8; $72,000
5. Stanford University, $179,300; 60%; 5.7; $100,000
6. Boston University, $133,200; 83%; 5.6; $80,000
7. University of Southern California, $144,600; 68%; 5.5; $80,000
7. Rutgers University, $115,400; 60%; 5.5; $66,500
9. American University, $115,200; 60%; 5.4; $67,000
9. Babson College, $132,500; 78%; 5.4; $75,000

Source: "The Best B Schools," *Business Week*, 3701: 76-100, (October 2, 2000).

Related Information

★656★

"How the Report Cards Get Graded," *Business Week*, 3701: 78-80, (October 2, 2000).

Remarks: Explains the process and calculations done to determine *Business Week*'s best MBA schools. A 37-questions survey was sent to 16,843 graduates of the Class of 2000 and 10,039 replies were received. Surveys were also sent to 419 companies that actively recruit MBAs, of those 247 responded.

★657★

"The Best B Schools," *Business Week Online* (www.businessweek.com/bschools/), October 2, 2000.

Remarks: *Business Week*'s ranking of the best MBA schools, from a 37-questions survey sent to 16,843 graduates of the Class of 2000, 10,039 replies were received. Surveys were also sent to 419 companies that actively recruit MBAs, of those 247 responded.

★658★

Colbert, Amy, Reuven R. Levary and Michael C. Shaner, "Determining the Relative Efficiency of MBA Programs Using DEA," *European Journal of Operational Research*, 125: 656-669, (September 16, 2000).

Remarks: Examines the relative efficiency of 24 top ranked U.S. MBA programs and 3 foreign MBA programs using Data envelopment analysis (DEA).

BUSINESS ADMINISTRATION, GRADUATE–ACCOUNTING

See also: **Business Administration–Accounting**

★659★
Academics' choices for best graduate accounting programs, 2001

Ranking basis/background: From a *U.S. News & World Report* survey of deans and directors of MBA programs. **Remarks:** Data collected by Market Facts, Inc. **Number listed:** 10.

1. University of Illinois, Urbana-Champaign College of Commerce and Business Administration
2. University of Pennsylvania, Wharton School of Business
3. University of Texas, Austin, McCombs School of Business
4. University of Chicago Graduate School of Business
5. University of Michigan Business School
6. Stanford University Graduate School of Business
7. New York University, Leonard N. Stern School of Business
8. University of Southern California, Marshall School of Business
9. Northwestern University, Kellogg Graduate School of Management
10. Harvard University Graduate School of Business Administration

Source: "America's Best Graduate Schools: 2002 Annual Guide," *U.S. News & World Report*, 130: 60-97, (April 19, 2001).

★660★
Top business schools for within-discipline research performance in accounting, 1986-1998

Ranking basis/background: Determined by the number of pages a school's faculty published in the 20 top-tier business research journals over a 13 year period, from 1986 to 1998. **Number listed:** 50.

1. University of Pennsylvania
2. University of Michigan
3. University of Chicago
4. Stanford University
5. University of Washington, Seattle
6. University of Rochester
7. Northwestern University
8. University of North Carolina, Chapel Hill
9. University of Iowa
10. Columbia University

Source: Trieschmann, James S., et. al., "Serving Multiple Constituencies in Business Schools: Program Versus Research Performance," *Academy of Management Journal*, 43: 1130-1141, (December 2000).

★661★
Top recruiters for accounting jobs for 2000-01 master's degree recipients

Ranking basis/background: Projected number of college hires from on-campus recruitment for 2000-01. **Remarks:** Numbers reflect total expected hires, not just African American projected hires. **Number listed:** 49.

1. Arthur Andersen LLP, with 507 projected hires
2. Deloitte & Touche, 170
3. EDS, 25
4. Federal Deposit Insurance Company, 20
4. Lucent Technologies, 20
6. Accenture, 10
6. Litton Industries, 10
8. General Motors, 5
8. Houghton Mifflin, 5
10. Novant Health, 3
10. Toys "R" Us, 3

Source: "The Top 100 Employers and the Majors in Demand for the Class of 2001," *The Black Collegian*, 31: 19-35, (February 2001).

BUSINESS ADMINISTRATION, GRADUATE–FINANCE

See also: **Business Administration–Finance**

★662★
Academics' choices for best graduate finance programs, 2001

Ranking basis/background: From a *U.S. News & World Report* survey of deans and directors of MBA programs. **Remarks:** Data collected by Market Facts, Inc. **Number listed:** 10.
1. University of Pennsylvania, Wharton School of Business
2. University of Chicago Graduate School of Business
3. New York University, Leonard N. Stern School of Business
4. Stanford University Graduate School of Business
5. Massachusetts Institute of Technology, Alfred P. Sloan School of Management
6. Columbia University Graduate School of Business
7. Northwestern University, Kellogg Graduate School of Management
8. University of California, Los Angeles, Anderson Graduate School of Management
9. Harvard University Graduate School of Business Administration
10. University of California, Berkeley, Haas Graduate School of Business Administration

Source: "America's Best Graduate Schools: 2002 Annual Guide," *U.S. News & World Report*, 130: 60-97, (April 19, 2001).

★663★
Top business schools for within-discipline research performance in finance, 1986-1998

Ranking basis/background: Determined by the number of pages a school's faculty published in the 20 top-tier business research journals over a 13 year period, from 1986 to 1998. **Number listed:** 50.
1. University of Chicago
2. University of Pennsylvania
3. New York University
4. Harvard University
5. University of Michigan
6. Ohio State University
7. University of California, Los Angeles
8. Columbia University
9. Northwestern University
10. Duke University

Source: Trieschmann, James S., et. al., "Serving Multiple Constituencies in Business Schools: Program Versus Research Performance," *Academy of Management Journal*, 43: 1130-1141, (December 2000).

★664★
Top recruiters for finance/banking jobs for 2000-01 master's degree recipients

Ranking basis/background: Projected number of college hires from on-campus recruitment for 2000-01. **Remarks:** Numbers reflect total expected hires, not just African American projected hires. **Number listed:** 38.
1. Arthur Andersen LLP, with 75 projected hires
2. BB&T Corporation, 55
3. Accenture, 50
3. Deloitte & Touche, 50
3. Federal Deposit Insurance Company, 50
6. American Airlines, 30
7. Agilent Technologies, 28
8. EDS, 25
9. Wells Fargo Financial, 10
9. Cigna, 10
9. Marriott International, 10

Source: "The Top 100 Employers and the Majors in Demand for the Class of 2001," *The Black Collegian*, 31: 19-35, (February 2001).

★665★
U.S. News & World Report's undergraduate business programs with the best finance departments, 2000-01

Ranking basis/background: Based on *U.S News* survey asking business school deans and senior faculty to rate the quality of programs they are familiar with, and name the best programs in various specialties. **Number listed:** 5.
1. University of Pennsylvania, Wharton School of Business
2. New York University, Leonard N. Stern School of Business
3. University of Michigan Business School
4. University of California, Berkeley, Haas Graduate School of Business Administration
5. Massachusetts Institute of Technology, Alfred P. Sloan School of Management

Source: "America's Best Colleges," *U.S. News & World Report*, 129: 90-132, (September 11, 2000).

BUSINESS ADMINISTRATION, GRADUATE–GENERAL MANAGEMENT

★666★
Academics' choices for best graduate general management programs, 2001

Ranking basis/background: From a *U.S. News & World Report* survey of deans and directors of MBA programs. **Remarks:** Data collected by Market Facts, Inc. **Number listed:** 10.
1. Harvard University Graduate School of Business Administration
2. Stanford University Graduate School of Business
3. Northwestern University, Kellogg Graduate School of Management
4. University of Michigan Business School
5. University of Pennsylvania, Wharton School of Business
6. University of Virginia, Darden Graduate School of Business Administration
7. Dartmouth College, Amos Tuck School of Business Administration
8. University of California, Berkeley, Haas Graduate School of Business Administration
9. Duke University, Fuqua School of Business
10. University of California, Los Angeles, Anderson Graduate School of Management

Source: "America's Best Graduate Schools: 2002 Annual Guide," *U.S. News & World Report*, 130: 60-97, (April 19, 2001).

BUSINESS ADMINISTRATION, GRADUATE–INSURANCE

See also: **Business Administration–Insurance**

★667★
Top business schools for within-discipline research performance in insurance, international business and real estate, 1986-1998

Ranking basis/background: Determined by the number of pages a school's faculty published in the 20 top-tier business research journals over a 13 year period, from 1986 to 1998. **Number listed:** 50.
1. University of Pennsylvania
2. University of South Carolina
3. University of Texas, Austin
4. University of Wisconsin, Madison
5. University of Georgia
6. University of Illinois
7. Rutgers University
8. Georgia State University
9. New York University
10. University of North Carolina, Chapel Hill

Source: Trieschmann, James S., et. al., "Serving Multiple Constituencies in Business Schools: Program Versus Research Performance," *Academy of Management Journal*, 43: 1130-1141, (December 2000).

BUSINESS ADMINISTRATION, GRADUATE–INTERNATIONAL

★668★
Academics' choices for best graduate international business programs, 2001

Ranking basis/background: From a *U.S. News & World Report* survey of deans and directors of MBA programs. **Remarks:** Data collected by Market Facts, Inc. **Number listed:** 10.
1. Thunderbird, American Graduate School of International Management
2. University of South Carolina, Darla Moore School of Business
3. University of Pennsylvania, Wharton School of Business
4. Columbia University Graduate School of Business
5. Harvard University Graduate School of Business Administration
6. New York University, Leonard N. Stern School of Business
7. University of California, Los Angeles, Anderson Graduate School of Management
8. University of Michigan Business School
9. Northwestern University, Kellogg Graduate School of Management
10. Duke University, Fuqua School of Business

Source: "America's Best Graduate Schools: 2002 Annual Guide," *U.S. News & World Report*, 130: 60-97, (April 19, 2001).

BUSINESS ADMINISTRATION, GRADUATE–MANUFACTURING

See also: **Business Administration–Manufacturing**

★669★
Top recruiters for manufacturing management jobs for 2000-01 master's degree recipients

Ranking basis/background: Projected number of college hires from on-campus recruitment for 2000-01. **Remarks:** Numbers reflect total expected hires, not just African American projected hires. **Number listed:** 3.
1. Lucent Technologies, with 50 projected hires
2. Accenture, 5
3. Wyeth-Ayerst, 2

Source: "The Top 100 Employers and the Majors in Demand for the Class of 2001," *The Black Collegian*, 31: 19-35, (February 2001).

BUSINESS ADMINISTRATION, GRADUATE–MARKETING

See also: **Business Administration–Marketing**

★670★
Academics' choices for best graduate marketing programs, 2001

Ranking basis/background: From a *U.S. News & World Report* survey of deans and directors of MBA programs. **Remarks:** Data collected by Market Facts, Inc. **Number listed:** 10.
1. Northwestern University, Kellogg Graduate School of Management
2. University of Pennsylvania, Wharton School of Business
3. Harvard University Graduate School of Business Administration
4. Duke University, Fuqua School of Business
5. University of Michigan Business School
6. Stanford University Graduate School of Business
7. Columbia University Graduate School of Business
8. University of California, Berkeley, Haas Graduate School of Business Administration
9. University of California, Los Angeles, Anderson Graduate School of Management
10. University of Chicago Graduate School of Business

Source: "America's Best Graduate Schools: 2002 Annual Guide," *U.S. News & World Report*, 130: 60-97, (April 19, 2001).

★671★
Top business schools for within-discipline research performance in marketing, 1986-1998

Ranking basis/background: Determined by the number of pages a school's faculty published in the 20 top-tier business research journals over a 13 year period, from 1986 to 1998. **Number listed:** 50.
1. University of Pennsylvania
2. University of Florida
3. University of Texas, Austin
4. University of Wisconsin, Madison
5. Columbia University
6. New York University
7. University of Arizona
8. University of Chicago
9. University of Minnesota
10. Northwestern University

Source: Trieschmann, James S., et. al., "Serving Multiple Constituencies in Business Schools: Program Versus Research Performance," *Academy of Management Journal*, 43: 1130-1141, (December 2000).

★672★
Top recruiters for marketing jobs for 2000-01 master's degree recipients

Ranking basis/background: Projected number of college hires from on-campus recruitment for 2000-01. **Remarks:** Numbers reflect total expected hires, not just African American projected hires. **Number listed:** 10.
1. Lucent Technologies, with 100 projected hires
2. Accenture, 25
3. American Airlines, 20
4. Houghton Mifflin, 10
5. Arthur Andersen LLP, 6
6. Quantum, 5
7. Wyeth-Ayerst, 4
7. Applebee's International, 4
9. Wells Fargo Financial, 3
10. SAKS Corporation, 1

Source: "The Top 100 Employers and the Majors in Demand for the Class of 2001," *The Black Collegian*, 31: 19-35, (February 2001).

BUSINESS ADMINISTRATION, GRADUATE–QUANTITATIVE ANALYSIS

★673★
Academics' choices for best graduate quantitative analysis programs, 2001

Ranking basis/background: From a *U.S. News & World Report* survey of deans and directors of MBA programs. **Remarks:** Data collected by Market Facts, Inc. **Number listed:** 10.
1. Massachusetts Institute of Technology, Alfred P. Sloan School of Management
2. Carnegie-Mellon University Graduate School of Industrial Administration
3. University of Chicago Graduate School of Business
4. Stanford University Graduate School of Business
5. University of Pennsylvania, Wharton School of Business
6. University of Michigan Business School
7. Purdue University, Krannert School of Management
8. Northwestern University, Kellogg Graduate School of Management
9. University of California, Berkeley, Haas Graduate School of Business Administration
10. Duke University, Fuqua School of Business

Source: "America's Best Graduate Schools: 2002 Annual Guide," *U.S. News & World Report*, 130: 60-97, (April 19, 2001).

BUSINESS ADMINISTRATION, GRADUATE–TECHNOLOGY MANAGEMENT

See also: **Business Administration–Technology Management**

★674★
Academics' choices for best graduate production/operations management programs, 2001

Ranking basis/background: From a *U.S. News & World Report* survey of deans and directors of MBA programs. **Remarks:** Data collected by Market Facts, Inc. **Number listed:** 10.
1. Massachusetts Institute of Technology, Alfred P. Sloan School of Management
2. Purdue University, Krannert School of Management
3. Carnegie-Mellon University Graduate School of Industrial Administration
4. Stanford University Graduate School of Business
5. University of Michigan Business School
6. Harvard University Graduate School of Business Administration
7. University of Pennsylvania, Wharton School of Business
8. Northwestern University, Kellogg Graduate School of Management
9. University of California, Los Angeles, Anderson Graduate School of Management
10. Indiana University, Kelley Graduate School of Business

Source: "America's Best Graduate Schools: 2002 Annual Guide," *U.S. News & World Report*, 130: 60-97, (April 19, 2001).

★675★
Top business schools for within-discipline research performance in management information systems, 1986-1998

Ranking basis/background: Determined by the number of pages a school's faculty published in the 20 top-tier business research journals over a 13 year period, from 1986 to 1998. **Number listed:** 50.
1. University of Minnesota
2. Massachusetts Institute of Technology
3. University of Texas, Austin
4. Georgia State University
5. Carnegie Mellon University
6. University of Georgia
7. Harvard University
8. University of Pittsburgh
9. New York University
10. University of Arizona

Source: Trieschmann, James S., et. al., "Serving Multiple Constituencies in Business Schools: Program Versus Research Performance," *Academy of Management Journal*, 43: 1130-1141, (December 2000).

★676★
Top recruiters for telecommunications jobs for 2000-01 master's degree recipients

Ranking basis/background: Projected number of college hires from on-campus recruitment for 2000-01. **Remarks:** Numbers reflect total expected hires, not just African American projected hires. **Number listed:** 1.

1. Arthur Andersen LLP, with 1 projected hire

Source: "The Top 100 Employers and the Majors in Demand for the Class of 2001," *The Black Collegian*, 31: 19-35, (February 2001).

BUSINESS ADMINISTRATION–INSURANCE
See also: **Business Administration, Graduate–Insurance**

★677★
Authors with the most published pages in impact-weighted insurance journals

Ranking basis/background: Number of pages. All totals are adjusted for coauthorship. **Number listed:** 25.
1. W. Kip Viscusi, with 289.0 pages
2. Peter C. Fishburn, 275.8
3. J. David Cummings, 269.7
4. Scott E. Harrington, 170.0
5. Richard Zeckhauser, 168.7
6. Colin F. Camerer, 157.3
7. Howard Kunreuther, 149.8
8. Richard A. Derring, 145.5
9. Greg Taylor, 136.1
10. Christian Gollier, 131.0

Source: Colquitt, Lilee, Randy E. Dumm and Sandra G. Gustavson, "Risk and Insurance Research Productivity: 1987-1996," *The Journal of Risk and Insurance*, December 1998, pp. 711-741.

★678★
Degree-granting institutions with the most published pages in *The Journal of Risk and Insurance*, 1987-1996

Ranking basis/background: Number of pages published. **Number listed:** 10.
1. University of Pennsylvania, with 787 pages
2. University of Illinois, 447
3. University of Chicago, 172
4. University of Texas, 151
5. Indiana University, 129
5. University of Georgia, 129
7. University of Wisconsin, 117
8. Ohio State University, 93
9. University of North Carolina, 90
10. Harvard University, 84

Source: Colquitt, Lilee, Randy E. Dumm and Sandra G. Gustavson, "Risk and Insurance Research Productivity: 1987-1996," *The Journal of Risk and Insurance*, December 1998, pp. 711-741.

★679★
Employing institutions with the most published pages in *The Journal of Risk and Insurance*, 1987-1996

Ranking basis/background: Number of pages published. **Number listed:** 10.
1. University of Pennsylvania, with 414 pages
2. University of Georgia, 234
3. University of South Carolina, 213
4. University of Wisconsin, 205
5. University of Texas, 163
6. Georgia State University, 161
7. University of Illinois, 135
8. Temple University, 129
9. Pennsylvania State University, 101
10. University of Minnesota, 79

Source: Colquitt, Lilee, Randy E. Dumm and Sandra G. Gustavson, "Risk and Insurance Research Productivity: 1987-1996," *The Journal of Risk and Insurance*, December 1998, pp. 711-741.

★680★
Individual authors with the most published pages in *The Journal of Risk and Insurance*, 1987-1996

Ranking basis/background: Number of pages published. **Number listed:** 10.
1. J. David Cummins, with 126 pages
2. Jack L. VanDerhei, 70
3. Mark J. Browne, 69
4. Scott E. Harrington, 68
5. Richard A. Derring, 66
6. Stephen P. D'Arcy, 65
7. Greg Taylor, 62
8. Richard Butler, 61
9. James R. Garven, 58
10. Mary A. Weiss, 57

Source: Colquitt, Lilee, Randy E. Dumm and Sandra G. Gustavson, "Risk and Insurance Research Productivity: 1987-1996," *The Journal of Risk and Insurance*, December 1998, pp. 711-741.

★681★
U.S. News & World Report's universities with the best insurance departments, 1999-2000

Ranking basis/background: Based on a *U.S. News* survey asking business school deans and senior faculty to rate the quality of programs they are familiar with, and name the best programs in various specialties. **Number listed:** 5.
1. University of Pennsylvania
2. Georgia State University
3. University of Wisconsin, Madison
4. University of Georgia
5. University of South Carolina, Columbia

Source: "America's Best Colleges 2000 Annual Guide," *U.S. News & World Report*, 127: 62-105, (August 30, 1999).

BUSINESS ADMINISTRATION–INTERNATIONAL

★682★
U.S. News & World Report's undergraduate business programs with the best international business departments, 2000-01

Ranking basis/background: Based on *U.S News* survey asking business school deans and senior faculty to rate the quality of programs they are familiar with, and name the best programs in various specialties. **Number listed:** 5.
1. University of South Carolina, Darla Moore School of Business
2. University of Pennsylvania, Wharton School of Business
3. New York University, Leonard N. Stern School of Business
4. University of Michigan Business School
5. University of Southern California, Marshall School of Business

Source: "America's Best Colleges," *U.S. News & World Report*, 129: 90-132, (September 11, 2000).

BUSINESS ADMINISTRATION–MANUFACTURING
See also: **Business Administration, Graduate–Manufacturing**

★683★
Top recruiters for manufacturing management jobs for 2000-01 bachelor's degree recipients

Ranking basis/background: Projected number of college hires from on-campus recruitment for 2000-01. **Remarks:** Numbers reflect total expected hires, not just African American projected hires. **Number listed:** 8.
1. Sherwin-Williams, with 150 projected hires
2. Accenture, 65
3. Lucent Technologies, 50
4. Wyeth-Ayerst, 15
5. Caterpillar Inc., 14
6. TOTALInternational Paper, 10
7. Litton Industries, 5
7. Abbott Laboratories, 5

Source: "The Top 100 Employers and the Majors in Demand for the Class of 2001," *The Black Collegian*, 31: 19-35, (February 2001).

BUSINESS ADMINISTRATION–MARKETING
See also: **Business Administration, Graduate–Marketing Business Periodicals**

★684★
Top recruiters for marketing jobs for 2000-01 bachelor's degree recipients

Ranking basis/background: Projected number of college hires from on-campus recruitment for 2000-01. **Remarks:** Numbers reflect total expected hires, not just African American projected hires. **Number listed:** 41.
1. Enterprise Rent-A-Car, with 2,000 projected hires
2. Sherwin-Williams, 350
3. Federated Department Stores, 161
4. Accenture, 100
4. EDS, 100
6. Macy's East, 90
7. May Department Stores, 80
7. Northwestern Mutual Financial Network, 80
9. Western Southern Life, 75
10. Office Depot, 60

Source: "The Top 100 Employers and the Majors in Demand for the Class of 2001," *The Black Collegian*, 31: 19-35, (February 2001).

★685★
U.S. News & World Report's undergraduate business programs with the best marketing departments, 2000-01

Ranking basis/background: Based on *U.S News* survey asking business school deans and senior faculty to rate the quality of programs they are familiar with, and name the best programs in various specialties. **Number listed:** 5.
1. University of Pennsylvania, Wharton School of Business
2. University of Michigan Business School

3. University of Texas, Austin, McCombs School of Business
4. University of California, Berkeley, Haas Graduate School of Business Administration
5. Indiana University, Kelley Graduate School of Business

Source: "America's Best Colleges," *U.S. News & World Report*, 129: 90-132, (September 11, 2000).

BUSINESS ADMINISTRATION–TECHNOLOGY MANAGEMENT

See also: **Business Administration, Graduate–Technology Management**

★686★
Top recruiters for telecommunications jobs for 2000-01 bachelor's degree recipients

Ranking basis/background: Projected number of college hires from on-campus recruitment for 2000-01. **Remarks:** Numbers reflect total expected hires, not just African American projected hires. **Number listed:** 1.
1. Arthur Andersen LLP, with 4 projected hires

Source: "The Top 100 Employers and the Majors in Demand for the Class of 2001," *The Black Collegian*, 31: 19-35, (February 2001).

BUSINESS PERIODICALS

See also: **Economics and Business Periodicals Real Estate Periodicals**

★687★
Authors with the most articles published in the *Journal of Business Research*, 1985 to 1999

Ranking basis/background: Number of articles published in the *Journal of Business Research* between 1985 and 1999. **Number listed:** 46.
1. William R. Darden, with 9 published articles
2. Arch G. Woodside, 8
2. William O. Bearden, 8
2. Alan J. Dubinsky, 8
5. Ronald E. Goldsmith, 7
5. Wesley J. Johnston, 7
5. O.C. Ferrell, 7
5. P. Rajan Varadarajan, 7
5. James R. Lumpkin, 7
10. Robert E. Spekman, 6
10. Barry J. Babin, 6
10. Charles M. Futrell, 6
10. Scott J. Vitell, 6

Source: Knight, Gary A., G. Tomas M. Hult and R. Edward Bashaw, "Research Productivity in the Journal of Business Research: 1985-1999," *Journal of Business Research*, 49: 303-314, (September 2000).

★688★
Business journals by citation impact, 1981-98

Ranking basis/background: Impact factor calculated by taking the number of current citations to source items published and dividing it by the number of articles published in the journal during that time period. **Number listed:** 10.
1. *Administrative Science Quarterly*, with a 36.89 impact factor
2. *Academy of Management Review*, 27.88
3. *Journal of Consumer Research*, 23.76
4. *Academy of Management Journal*, 22.27
5. *Journal of Marketing*, 22.18
6. *Journal of Marketing Research*, 17.86
7. *Strategic Management Journal*, 17.26
8. *Journal of Business*, 13.24
9. *Journal of Management*, 9.83
10. *Marketing Science*, 7.85

Source: "Journals Ranked by Impact: Business," *What's Hot in Research* (http://www.isinet.com/isi/hot/research) Institute for Scientific Information, July 17, 2000.

★689★
Business journals by citation impact, 1994-98

Ranking basis/background: Impact factor calculated by taking the number of current citations to source items published and dividing it by the number of articles published in the journal during that time period. **Number listed:** 10.
1. *Journal of Marketing*, with a 8.53 impact factor
2. *Administrative Science Quarterly*, 8.26
3. *Academy of Management Review*, 7.88
4. *Academy of Management Journal*, 6.48
5. *Journal of Consumer Research*, 5.58
6. *Strategic Management Journal*, 4.51
7. *Journal of Environmental Economics and Management*, 3.23
8. *Journal of Marketing Research*, 3.16
9. *Marketing Science*, 2.89
10. *Journal of Management*, 2.83

Source: "Journals Ranked by Impact: Business," *What's Hot in Research* (http://www.isinet.com/isi/hot/research) Institute for Scientific Information, July 17, 2000.

★690★
Business journals by citation impact, 1998

Ranking basis/background: Impact factor calculated by taking the number of current citations to source items published and dividing it by the number of articles published in the journal during that time period. **Number listed:** 10.
1. *Academy of Management Review*, with a 3.73 impact factor
2. *Administrative Science Quarterly*, 3.54
3. *Journal of Marketing*, 2.93
4. *Academy of Management Journal*, 2.45
5. *Journal of Common Market Studies*, 2.04
6. *Journal of Consumer Research*, 1.83
7. *Sloan Management Review*, 1.64
8. *Journal of Marketing Research*, 1.60
9. *California Management Review*, 1.58
10. *Marketing Science*, 1.56

Source: "Journals Ranked by Impact: Business," *What's Hot in Research* (http://www.isinet.com/isi/hot/research) Institute for Scientific Information, July 17, 2000.

★691★
Business journals receiving the most citations in five core journals, 1995-97

Ranking basis/background: Total citations received in *The Journal of World Business*, *The Journal of International Business Studies*, *Multinational Business Review*, *Management International Review*, and *International Business Review* collectively. **Number listed:** 30.
1. *Journal of International Business Studies*, with 1,184 total citations
2. *Management International Review*, 242
3. *Journal of World Business*, 219
4. *International Marketing Review*, 129
5. *International Business Review*, 49
6. *Journal of International Marketing*, 43
7. *International Studies of Management and Organization*, 39
8. *Advances in International Marketing*, 25
9. *Advances in International Comparative Management*, 16
10. *International Journal of Research in Marketing*, 13

Source: DuBois, Frank L. and David Reeb, "Ranking the International Business Journal," *Journal of International Business Studies*, 31: 689-704, (Fourth Quarter 2000).

★692★
Highest impact authors in the *Journal of Business Research*, by adjusted number of citations in 12 journals, 1985-1999

Ranking basis/background: Adjusted number of citations in 12 investigated journals. **Number listed:** 44.
1. Christian Gronroos, with 12.00 adjusted number of citations
2. William George, 10.00
3. N.C.G. Campbell, 9.00
3. John A. Czepiel, 9.00
5. Emin Babakus, 8.00
5. Gregory W. Boller, 8.00
7. Jacob Naor, 5.00
8. Lawrence B. Chonko, 3.60
9. Theresa K. Lant, 3.50
9. Barbara Loken, 3.50

Source: Knight, Gary A., G. Tomas M. Hult and R. Edward Bashaw, "Research Productivity in the Journal of Business Research: 1985-1999," *Journal of Business Research*, 49: 303-314, (September 2000).

★693★
Highest impact authors in the *Journal of Business Research*, by number of citations in 12 journals, 1985-1999

Ranking basis/background: Raw number of citations in 12 investigated journals. **Number listed:** 44.
1. Robert E. Spekman, with 19
1. Shelby D. Hunt, 19
3. Lawrence B. Chonko, 18
4. S. Tamer Cavusgil, 17
4. Charles M. Futrell, 17
6. Emin Babakus, 16
6. Gregory W. Boller, 16
6. Jeffrey K. Sager, 16
6. Mark W. Johnston, 16
6. P. Rajan Varadarajan, 16

Source: Knight, Gary A., G. Tomas M. Hult and R. Edward Bashaw, "Research Productivity in the Journal of Business Research: 1985-1999," *Journal of Business Research*, 49: 303-314, (September 2000).

★694★
Institutions, by adjusted authorship, with the most published authors in the *Journal of Business Research*, 1985 to 1999

Ranking basis/background: Number of articles and number of authors published in the *Journal of Business Research* between 1985 and 1999, and adjustment factor. **Number listed:** 50.
1. University of Lodz, Poland, with 16 articles; 29 authors; .57 adjustment factor
2. University of Colorado, Boulder, 7; 15; .47
3. University of Connecticut, 7; 15; .47
4. University of Oregon, 7; 15; .47
5. Mississippi State University, 7; 16; .44
6. University of Southern California, 17; 40; .43
7. University of Illinois, Urbana-Champaign, 9; 21; .43
8. University of North Texas, 8; 19; .42
9. Georgia Institute of Technology, 9; 22; .41
10. University of Toledo, 7; 17; .41

Source: Knight, Gary A., G. Tomas M. Hult and R. Edward Bashaw, "Research Productivity in the Journal of Business Research: 1985-1999," *Journal of Business Research*, 49: 303-314, (September 2000).

★695★
Institutions with the most published authors in the *Journal of Business Research*, 1985 to 1999

Ranking basis/background: Number of articles and number of authors published in the *Journal of Business Research* between 1985 and 1999. **Number listed:** 50.
1. Louisiana State University, with 27 articles; 78 authors
2. Texas A&M University, 20; 90
3. University of South Carolina, 19; 64
4. University of Southern California, 17; 40
5. Georgia State University, 17; 52
6. University of Memphis, 17; 62
7. University of Lodz, Poland, 16; 28
8. University of Texas, Austin, 15; 39
9. Michigan State University, 15; 47
10. Florida State University, 14; 43

Source: Knight, Gary A., G. Tomas M. Hult and R. Edward Bashaw, "Research Productivity in the Journal of Business Research: 1985-1999," *Journal of Business Research*, 49: 303-314, (September 2000).

★696★
Journals with the highest impact factor in the field of management, 1981-96

Ranking basis/background: Impact factor is calculated as a ratio between citations and recent citable items published. **Remarks:** Original source: ISI's *Journal Citations Reports* and *Journal Performance Indicators on Diskette*. **Number listed:** 10.
1. Administration Science Quarterly
2. Organ. Behavior
3. Academy of Management Review
4. Academy of Management Journal
5. Strategic Management Journal
6. *MIS Quarterly*
7. Organ. Behavior
8. Operations Research
9. Journal of Management
10. Journal of Forecasting

Source: "Journals Ranked by Impact: Management," *What's Hot*, March 30, 1998.

★697★
Most influential articles in the *Journal of Business Research*, 1985-1999

Ranking basis/background: Number of citations in 12 investigated journals. **Number listed:** 11.
1. *An Empirical Assessment of the SERVQUAL Scale*, by Emin Babakus and Gregory W. Boller (1992), with 16 citations
2. *Ethics and Marketing Management: An Empirical Examination*, Lawrence B. Chonko and Shelby D. Hunt (1985), 14
3. *The Problem-Solving Approach to Negotiations in Industrial Marketing*, John L. Graham (1986), 13
4. *Relationship Approach to Marketing in Service Contexts: The Marketing and Organizational Behavior Interface*, Christian Gronroos (1990), 12
5. *Internal Marketing and Organizational Behavior: A Partnership in Developing Customer-Conscious Employees at Every Level*, William George (1990), 10
5. *Performance and Job Satisfaction Effects on Salesperson Turnover: A Replication and Extension*, Mark W. Johnston et al (1988), 10
7. *An Interaction Approach to Organizational Buying Behavior*, N.C.G. Campbell (1985), 9
7. *Firm and Management Characteristics as Discriminators of Export Marketing Activity*, S. Tamer Cavusgil and Jacob Naor (1987), 9
7. *Service Encounters and Service Relationships: Implications for Research*, John A. Czepiel (1990), 9
10. *Influence of Firm Size on Export Planning and Performance*, Saeed Samiee and Peter G.P. Walters (1990), 8
10. *Relationship Management: Managing the Selling and the Buying Interface*, Robert E. Spekman and Wesley J. Johnston (1986), 8

Source: Knight, Gary A., G. Tomas M. Hult and R. Edward Bashaw, "Research Productivity in the Journal of Business Research: 1985-1999," *Journal of Business Research*, 49: 303-314, (September 2000).

★698★
Most influential articles in the *Journal of Business Research* from 1985 to 1989

Ranking basis/background: Number of citations in received from 1985 through 1999. **Number listed:** 6.
1. *Ethics and Marketing Management: An Empirical Examination*, Lawrence B. Chonko and Shelby D. Hunt (1985), with 14 total citations
2. *The Problem-Solving Approach to Negotiations in Industrial Marketing*, John L. Graham (1986), 13
3. *Performance and Job Satisfaction Effects on Salesperson Turnover: A Replication and Extension*, Mark W. Johnston et al (1988), 10
4. *An Interaction Approach to Organizational Buying Behavior*, N.C.G. Campbell (1985), 9
4. *Firm and Management Characteristics as Discriminators of Export Marketing Activity*, S. Tamer Cavusgil and Jacob Naor (1987), 9
6. *Relationship Management: Managing the Selling and the Buying Interface*, Robert E. Spekman and Wesley J. Johnston (1986), 8

Source: Knight, Gary A., G. Tomas M. Hult and R. Edward Bashaw, "Research Productivity in the Journal of Business Research: 1985-1999," *Journal of Business Research*, 49: 303-314, (September 2000).

★699★
Most influential articles in the *Journal of Business Research* from 1990 to 1994

Ranking basis/background: Number of citations in received from 1990 through 1999. **Number listed:** 7.
1. *An Empirical Assessment of the SERVQUAL Scale*, by Emin Babakus and Gregory W. Boller (1992), with 16 total citations
2. *Relationship Approach to Marketing in Service Contexts: The Marketing and Organizational Behavior Interface*, Christian Gronroos (1990), 12
3. *Internal Marketing and Organizational Behavior: A Partnership in Developing Customer-Conscious Employees at Every Level*, William George (1990), 10
4. *Service Encounters and Service Relationships: Implications for Research*, John A. Czepiel (1990), 9
5. *Influence of Firm Size on Export Planning and Performance*, Saeed Samiee and Peter G.P. Walters (1990), 8
6. *Antecedents to Buyer-Seller Collaboration: An Analysis from the Buyer's Perspective*, Ven Sriram, Robert Krapfel, and Robert Spekman (1992), 7
6. *Exploring the Concept of Affective Quality: Expanding the Concept of Retail Personality*, William R. Darden and Barry J. Babin (1994), 7

Source: Knight, Gary A., G. Tomas M. Hult and R. Edward Bashaw, "Research Productivity in the Journal of Business Research: 1985-1999," *Journal of Business Research*, 49: 303-314, (September 2000).

★700★
Most influential articles in the *Journal of Business Research* from 1995 to 1999

Ranking basis/background: Number of citations in received from 1995 through 1999. **Number listed:** 5.
1. *The Role of Employee Effort in Satisfaction with Service Transactions*, by Lois A. Mohr and Mary Jo Bitner (1995), with 6 total citations
2. *Moral Intensity and Ethical Decision-Making of Marketing Professionals*, Anusorn Singhapakdi, Scott J. Vitell, and Kenneth Draft (1996), 5
3. *Power, Bureaucracy, Influence and Performance: Their Relationships in Industrial Distribution Channels*, Brett A. Boyle and F. Robert Dwyer (1995), 4

BUSINESS SCHOOLS (COLLEGE)

3. *An Investigation of Relationalism across a Range of Marketing Relationships and Alliances*, Joyce A. Young, Faye W. Gilbert and Faye S. McIntyre (1996), 4
5. *The Perceived Importance of the Ethical Decision-Making of Ad Managers*, Donald P. Robin, Eric R. Reidenbach and P.J. Forrest (1996), 3

Source: Knight, Gary A., G. Tomas M. Hult and R. Edward Bashaw, "Research Productivity in the Journal of Business Research: 1985-1999," *Journal of Business Research*, 49: 303-314, (September 2000).

★701★
Most published authors, adjusted for coauthorship, in the *Journal of Business Research*, 1985 to 1999

Ranking basis/background: Number of articles, adjusted for coauthorship, published in the *Journal of Business Research* between 1985 and 1999. **Number listed:** 46.

1. Cynthia Webster, with 4 published articles; 5 total authors; .80 adjustment factor
2. Tomasz Domanski, 5; 7; .71
3. Saeed Samiee, 4; 6; .67
4. Arch G. Woodside, 8; 16; .50
5. Ronald E. Goldsmith, 7; 14; .50
6. Luis V. Dominguez, 4; 8; .50
7. Robert E. Hite, 4; 8; .50
8. Michael Y. Hu, 4; 8; .50
9. David T. Wilson, 4; 8; .50
10. Wesley J. Johnston, 7; 15; .47

Source: Knight, Gary A., G. Tomas M. Hult and R. Edward Bashaw, "Research Productivity in the Journal of Business Research: 1985-1999," *Journal of Business Research*, 49: 303-314, (September 2000).

Related Information

★702★
Inkpen, Andrew C., "A Note on Ranking the International Business Journals," *Journal of International Business Studies*, 32: 193-196, (First Quarter 2001).
Remarks: A response to the DuBois and Reeb article examining the relative quality of international business journals.

★703★
DuBois, Frank L. and David M. Reeb, "Ranking the International Business Journals: A Reply," *Journal of International Business Studies*, 32: 197-199, (First Quarter 2001).
Remarks: A counter-response to Professor Inkpen's article regarding the relative quality of international business journals.

BUSINESS SCHOOLS (COLLEGE)
See: **Business Administration Business Administration, Graduate**

CAMPUS CRIME

★704★
College stalking statistics

Ranking basis/background: Percentage of female college students stalked and length of stalking. **Remarks:** Original source: National Institute of Justice. **Number listed:** 2.
Female university students who have been stalked, 13.1%
Average length of stalkings, 60 days

Source: "The Stark Facts of College Stalking," *U.S. News & World Report*, 130: 14, (February 12, 2001).

★705★
Four-year institutions with the most drug arrests reported, 1999

Ranking basis/background: Number of drug arrests reported. Based on a survey of 6,300 college campuses. **Remarks:** Original source: U.S. Education Department. **Number listed:** 5.

1. University of California, Berkeley, with 265
2. University of Maine, 143
3. Michigan State University, 133
4. University of Washington (WA), 127
5. Indiana University, Bloomington, 126

Source: Nicklin, Julie L., "Drug and Alcohol Arrests Increased in 1999," *The Chronicle of Higher Education*, 47: A35-A37, (February 2, 2001).

★706★
Four-year institutions with the most drug referrals reported, 1999

Ranking basis/background: Number of drug referrals reported. Based on a survey of 6,300 college campuses. **Remarks:** Original source: U.S. Education Department. **Number listed:** 5.

1. Southern Illinois University, Carbondale, with 443
2. State University of New York, College at Oneonta, 305
3. University of Oregon, 275
4. University of Vermont, 238
5. Ohio State University, 234

Source: Nicklin, Julie L., "Drug and Alcohol Arrests Increased in 1999," *The Chronicle of Higher Education*, 47: A35-A37, (February 2, 2001).

★707★
Four-year institutions with the most liquor arrests reported, 1999

Ranking basis/background: Number of liquor arrests reported. Based on a survey of 6,300 college campuses. **Remarks:** Original source: U.S. Education Department. **Number listed:** 5.

1. Michigan State University, with 856
2. University of Michigan, Ann Arbor, 673
3. Western Michigan University, 623
4. University of California, Berkeley, 563
5. University of Minnesota, Twin Cities, 546

Source: Nicklin, Julie L., "Drug and Alcohol Arrests Increased in 1999," *The Chronicle of Higher Education*, 47: A35-A37, (February 2, 2001).

★708★
Four-year institutions with the most liquor referrals reported, 1999

Ranking basis/background: Number of liquor referrals reported. Based on a survey of 6,300 college campuses. **Remarks:** Original source: U.S. Education Department. **Number listed:** 5.

1. University of Southern Indiana, with 1,179
2. Bowling Green State University, 958
3. University of Vermont, 925
4. Indiana University, Bloomington, 912
5. University of Delaware, 854

Source: Nicklin, Julie L., "Drug and Alcohol Arrests Increased in 1999," *The Chronicle of Higher Education*, 47: A35-A37, (February 2, 2001).

★709★
Four-year institutions with the most weapons arrests reported, 1999

Ranking basis/background: Number of weapons arrests reported. Based on a survey of 6,300 college campuses. **Remarks:** Original source: U.S. Education Department. **Number listed:** 5.

1. Michigan State University, with 32
2. University of California, Berkeley, 26
3. University of North Carolina, Charlotte, 20
4. University of Colorado Health Sciences Center, 19
5. South Carolina State University, 16

Source: Nicklin, Julie L., "Drug and Alcohol Arrests Increased in 1999," *The Chronicle of Higher Education*, 47: A35-A37, (February 2, 2001).

★710★
Four-year institutions with the most weapons referrals reported, 1999

Ranking basis/background: Number of weapons referrals reported. Based on a survey of 6,300 college campuses. **Remarks:** Original source: U.S. Education Department. **Number listed:** 5.

1. Hampton University, with 23
2. Illinois State University, 21
3. University of Illinois, Urbana-Champaign, 19
4. University of Southern Indiana, 18
5. Howard University, 17

Source: Nicklin, Julie L., "Drug and Alcohol Arrests Increased in 1999," *The Chronicle of Higher Education*, 47: A35-A37, (February 2, 2001).

★711★
How female college students were stalked

Ranking basis/background: Percentage of female college students reporting each type of stalking. **Remarks:** Original source: National Institute of Justice. **Number listed:** 6.
By telephone, with 77.7%
Offender waiting outside/inside a building, 47.9%
Watched from afar, 44.0%
Followed, 42.0%
Received letters, 31.0%
Received E-mails, 24.7%

Source: "The Stark Facts of College Stalking," *U.S. News & World Report*, 130: 14, (February 12, 2001).

★712★
Most dangerous college campuses in the U.S.

Ranking basis/background: As assessed by APBnews.com. **Number listed:** 25.
1. Morris Brown College
2. LeMoyne-Owen College
3. Spelman College
4. Clark Atlanta University
5. Morehouse College
6. VanderCook College of Music
7. City University of New York, City College
8. Edward Waters College
9. Southern University and A&M College
10. Illinois Institute of Technology

Source: Wright, Scott W., "Campus Crimes Survey Angers HBCU Officials," *Black Issues in Higher Education*, 16: 14-16, (March 2, 2000).

★713★
Number of criminal arrests reported on U.S. college campuses, 1999

Ranking basis/background: Number of arrests reported and percentage of change in 1-year. Based on a survey of 6,300 college campuses. **Remarks:** Original source: U.S. Education Department. **Number listed:** 3.
1. Liquor-law violations, with 25,933 incidents reported; a 1-year change of 0.4%
2. Drug-law violations, 10,482; 5.8%
3. Weapons-law violations, 1,317; 1.9% decrease

Source: Nicklin, Julie L., "Drug and Alcohol Arrests Increased in 1999," *The Chronicle of Higher Education*, 47: A35-A37, (February 2, 2001).

★714★
Number of criminal incidents reported on U.S. college campuses, 1999

Ranking basis/background: Number of incidents reported and percentage of change in 1-year. Based on a survey of 6,300 college campuses. **Remarks:** Original source: U.S. Education Department. **Number listed:** 10.
1. Burglary, with 26,035 incidents reported; a 1-year change of 1.4%
2. Motor-vehicle theft, 6,201; 2.5%
3. Aggravated assault, 3,777; 2.0% decrease
4. Robbery, 1,997; 7.3%
5. Forcible sex offenses, 1,842; 4.0%
6. Arson, 1,167; n/a
7. Hate crimes, 1,067; 50.4%
8. Nonforcible sex offenses, 627; 11.0%
9. Murder and non-negligent manslaughter, 11; 54.2% decrease
10. Negligent manslaughter, 10; n/a

Source: Nicklin, Julie L., "Drug and Alcohol Arrests Increased in 1999," *The Chronicle of Higher Education*, 47: A35-A37, (February 2, 2001).

★715★
Number of criminal referrals reported on U.S. college campuses, 1999

Ranking basis/background: Number of referrals reported. Based on a survey of 6,300 college campuses. **Remarks:** Original source: U.S. Education Department. **Number listed:** 3.
1. Liquor-law violations, with 108,846
2. Drug-law violations, 18,466
3. Weapons-law violations, 1,370

Source: Nicklin, Julie L., "Drug and Alcohol Arrests Increased in 1999," *The Chronicle of Higher Education*, 47: A35-A37, (February 2, 2001).

★716★
Number of on-campus aggravated assaults reported, by type of institution, 1999

Ranking basis/background: Number of aggravated assaults reported. Based on a survey of 6,300 college campuses. **Remarks:** Original source: U.S. Education Department. **Number listed:** 3.
   Public, with 2,544
   Private, nonprofit, 1,000
   Private, for-profit, 233

Source: Nicklin, Julie L., "Drug and Alcohol Arrests Increased in 1999," *The Chronicle of Higher Education*, 47: A35-A37, (February 2, 2001).

★717★
Number of on-campus burglaries reported, by type of institution, 1999

Ranking basis/background: Number of burglaries reported. Based on a survey of 6,300 college campuses. **Remarks:** Original source: U.S. Education Department. **Number listed:** 3.
   Public, with 15,173
   Private, nonprofit, 9,772
   Private, for-profit, 1,090

Source: Nicklin, Julie L., "Drug and Alcohol Arrests Increased in 1999," *The Chronicle of Higher Education*, 47: A35-A37, (February 2, 2001).

★718★
Number of on-campus forcible sex offenses reported, by type of institution, 1999

Ranking basis/background: Number of forcible sex offenses reported. Based on a survey of 6,300 college campuses. **Remarks:** Original source: U.S. Education Department. **Number listed:** 3.
   Public, with 1,126
   Private, nonprofit, 698
   Private, for-profit, 18

Source: Nicklin, Julie L., "Drug and Alcohol Arrests Increased in 1999," *The Chronicle of Higher Education*, 47: A35-A37, (February 2, 2001).

★719★
Number of on-campus hate crimes reported, by type of offense, 1999

Ranking basis/background: Number of hate crimes reported. Based on a survey of 6,300 college campuses. **Remarks:** Original source: U.S. Education Department. **Number listed:** 7.
   Murder and non-negligent manslaughter, with 1
   Negligent manslaughter, 0
   Forcible sex offenses, 92
   Forcible rape, 33
   Simple assault, 1,677
   Aggravated assault, 232
   Arson, 32

Source: Nicklin, Julie L., "Drug and Alcohol Arrests Increased in 1999," *The Chronicle of Higher Education*, 47: A35-A37, (February 2, 2001).

★720★
Number of on-campus motor-vehicle thefts reported, by type of institution, 1999

Ranking basis/background: Number of motor-vehicle thefts reported. Based on a survey of 6,300 college campuses. **Remarks:** Original source: U.S. Education Department. **Number listed:** 3.
   Public, with 4,147
   Private, nonprofit, 1,496
   Private, for-profit, 558

Source: Nicklin, Julie L., "Drug and Alcohol Arrests Increased in 1999," *The Chronicle of Higher Education*, 47: A35-A37, (February 2, 2001).

★721★
Number of on-campus nonforcible sex offenses reported, by type of institution, 1999

Ranking basis/background: Number of nonforcible sex offenses reported. Based on a survey of 6,300 college campuses. **Remarks:** Original source: U.S. Education Department. **Number listed:** 3.
   Public, with 423
   Private, nonprofit, 189
   Private, for-profit, 15

Source: Nicklin, Julie L., "Drug and Alcohol Arrests Increased in 1999," *The Chronicle of Higher Education*, 47: A35-A37, (February 2, 2001).

★722★
Number of on-campus robberies reported, by type of institution, 1999

Ranking basis/background: Number of robberies reported. Based on a survey of 6,300 college campuses. **Remarks:** Original source: U.S. Education Department. **Number listed:** 3.
   Public, with 1,005
   Private, nonprofit, 733
   Private, for-profit, 259

Source: Nicklin, Julie L., "Drug and Alcohol Arrests Increased in 1999," *The Chronicle of Higher Education*, 47: A35-A37, (February 2, 2001).

★723★
On-campus criminal homicides, 1999

Ranking basis/background: Number of criminal homicides reported at each type of institution. **Remarks:** Original source: U.S. Department of Education Report, "The Incidence of Crime on the Campuses of the U.S. Postsecondary Education Institutions." **Number listed:** 3.
   Public, with 7
   Private, non-profit, 4
   Private, for-profit, 0

Source: Brown, Linda Meggett, "Student Deaths Shake Up College Campuses," *Black Issues in Higher Education*, 17: 22-27, (February 15, 2001).

★724★
Reported arrests from 481 U.S. college campuses with more than 5,000 students, 1998

Ranking basis/background: Total number of arrests reported and 1-year change percentages. Based on survey responses of 481 four-year institutions enrolling at least 5,000 students. **Number listed:** 3.

CAMPUS CRIME

1. Liquor-law violation, with 23,261 arrests; and a 1-year change of 24.3%
2. Drug-law violations, 8,844; 11.1%
3. Weapons-law violations, 972; 0.5%

Source: Nicklin, Julie L., "Arrests at Colleges Surge for Alcohol and Drug Violations," *The Chronicle of Higher Education*, 46: A48-A50, (June 9, 2000).

★725★
Reported incidents from 481 U.S. college campuses with more than 5,000 students, 1998

Ranking basis/background: Total number of incidents reported and 1-year change percentages. Based on survey responses of 481 four-year institutions enrolling at least 5,000 students. **Number listed:** 10.

1. Burglary, with 13,745 incidents reported; a 1-year change of 5.6% decrease
2. Motor-vehicle theft, 4,160; 2.5% decrease
3. Aggravated assault, 2,267; 2.8%
4. Forcible sex offenses, 1,240; 11.3%
5. Robbery, 1,068; 2.9% decrease
6. Arson, 539; 16.9%
7. Hate crimes, 179; 15.5%
8. Nonforcible sex offenses, 159; 27.2%
9. Murder, 20; 11.1%
10. Manslaughter, 1

Source: Nicklin, Julie L., "Arrests at Colleges Surge for Alcohol and Drug Violations," *The Chronicle of Higher Education*, 46: A48-A50, (June 9, 2000).

★726★
Total crimes reported at 4-year private institutions, 1998

Ranking basis/background: Number of crimes reported at each size institution. **Remarks:** Original source: IACLEA "1999 Campus Crime Survey." **Number listed:** 4.

Under 5,000 students, with and average of 61.9 crimes reported
5,000-15,000 students, 159.4
Over 15,000 students, 521.9
All, 137.8

Source: Brown, Linda Meggett, "Student Deaths Shake Up College Campuses," *Black Issues in Higher Education*, 17: 22-27, (February 15, 2001).

★727★
Total crimes reported at 4-year public institutions, 1998

Ranking basis/background: Number of crimes reported at each size institution. **Remarks:** Original source: IACLEA "1999 Campus Crime Survey." **Number listed:** 4.

Under 5,000 students, with and average of 45.4 crimes reported
5,000-15,000 students, 153.8
Over 15,000 students, 484
All, 287.7

Source: Brown, Linda Meggett, "Student Deaths Shake Up College Campuses," *Black Issues in Higher Education*, 17: 22-27, (February 15, 2001).

★728★
U.S. college campuses reporting murders or non-negligent manslaughters, 1999

Ranking basis/background: Number of murders or non-negligent manslaughters reported. Based on a survey of 6,300 college campuses. **Remarks:** Original source: U.S. Education Department. **Number listed:** 11.

Alabama A&M University, with 1
California State University, Sacramento, 1
Chapman University, 1
Colegio Universitario del Este, 1
Elizabeth City State University, 1
Howard University, 1
Indiana University-Purdue University, Indianapolis, 1
Kalamazoo College, 1
Southern University, 1
University of Louisiana, Lafayette, 1
Veteran Administration Medical Center School of Radiology Technology (CA), 1

Source: Nicklin, Julie L., "Drug and Alcohol Arrests Increased in 1999," *The Chronicle of Higher Education*, 47: A35-A37, (February 2, 2001).

★729★
U.S. college campuses with more than 5,000 students reporting murders or manslaughters, 1998

Ranking basis/background: Total number of murders or manslaughters reported at each campus. Based on survey responses of 481 four-year institutions enrolling at least 5,000 students. **Number listed:** 18.

1. Indiana University-Purdue University Indianapolis, with 2
1. Morgan State University, 2
3. University of Maryland, Baltimore, 1
3. California State University, Hayward, 1
3. Columbia University, 1
3. Michigan State University, 1
3. Murray State University, 1
3. Southeastern Louisiana University, 1
3. Temple University, 1
3. University of Arizona, 1
3. University of California, Davis, 1
3. University of Illinois, Urbana-Champaign, 1
3. University of Nevada, Reno, 1
3. University of New Mexico, 1
3. University of Pennsylvania, 1
3. University of Vermont, 1
3. Washington State University, 1 (manslaughter)
3. Wayne State University, 1

Source: Nicklin, Julie L., "Arrests at Colleges Surge for Alcohol and Drug Violations," *The Chronicle of Higher Education*, 46: A48-A50, (June 9, 2000).

★730★
U.S. colleges and universities reporting the most alcohol related arrests, 1998

Ranking basis/background: Total number of alcohol related arrests reported. Based on survey responses of 481 four-year institutions enrolling at least 5,000 students. **Number listed:** 5.

1. University of Wisconsin, Madison, with 792
2. Michigan State University, 655
3. University of Minnesota, Twin Cities, 606
4. Western Michigan University, 405
5. University of California, Berkeley, 382

Source: Nicklin, Julie L., "Arrests at Colleges Surge for Alcohol and Drug Violations," *The Chronicle of Higher Education*, 46: A48-A50, (June 9, 2000).

★731★
U.S. colleges and universities reporting the most drug related arrests, 1998

Ranking basis/background: Total number of drug related arrests reported. Based on survey responses of 481 four-year institutions enrolling at least 5,000 students. **Number listed:** 5.

1. University of California, Berkeley, with 280
2. Rutgers University, New Brunswick, 138
3. University of North Carolina, Greensboro, 132
4. University of Arizona, 123
5. Virginia Commonwealth University, 122

Source: Nicklin, Julie L., "Arrests at Colleges Surge for Alcohol and Drug Violations," *The Chronicle of Higher Education*, 46: A48-A50, (June 9, 2000).

★732★
U.S. colleges and universities reporting the most weapons related arrests, 1998

Ranking basis/background: Total number of weapons related arrests reported. Based on survey responses of 481 four-year institutions enrolling at least 5,000 students. **Number listed:** 5.

1. Michigan State University, with 49
2. University of California, Berkeley, 34
3. University of North Carolina, Charlotte, 26
4. University of North Carolina, Greensboro, 23
5. San Jose State University, 20

Source: Nicklin, Julie L., "Arrests at Colleges Surge for Alcohol and Drug Violations," *The Chronicle of Higher Education*, 46: A48-A50, (June 9, 2000).

★733★
U.S. colleges and universities with the largest numerical increases in alcohol arrests, 1998

Ranking basis/background: Total number of arrests and number it increased in one year. Based on survey responses of 481 four-year institutions enrolling at least 5,000 students. **Number listed:** 5.

1. University of Wisconsin, Madison, with 792 arrests in 1998; 450 more arrests than 1997
2. Washington State University, 355; 226
3. Florida State University, 320; 210
4. San Diego State University, 291; 199
5. Ball State University, 272; 177

Source: Nicklin, Julie L., "Arrests at Colleges Surge for Alcohol and Drug Violations," *The Chronicle of Higher Education*, 46: A48-A50, (June 9, 2000).

★734★
U.S. colleges and universities with the largest numerical increases in drug arrests, 1998

Ranking basis/background: Total number of arrests and number it increased in one year. Based on survey responses of 481 four-year institutions enrolling at least 5,000 students. **Number listed:** 5.

1. University of North Carolina, Greensboro, with 132 arrests in 1998; 115 more arrests than 1997
2. University of California, Berkeley, 280; 101
3. San Diego State University, 81; 66
4. Clark Atlanta University, 94; 55
5. University of California, Davis, 91; 54

Source: Nicklin, Julie L., "Arrests at Colleges Surge for Alcohol and Drug Violations," *The Chronicle of Higher Education*, 46: A48-A50, (June 9, 2000).

★735★
U.S. colleges and universities with the largest numerical increases in weapons arrests, 1998

Ranking basis/background: Total number of arrests and number it increased in one year. Based on survey responses of 481 four-year institutions enrolling at least 5,000 students. **Number listed:** 5.
1. Michigan State University, with 49 arrests in 1998; 18 more arrests than 1997
1. University of North Carolina, Greensboro, 23; 18
3. University of Wisconsin, Madison, 13; 12
4. University of Wisconsin, Oshkosh, 11; 9
4. Washington State University, 9; 9

Source: Nicklin, Julie L., "Arrests at Colleges Surge for Alcohol and Drug Violations," *The Chronicle of Higher Education*, 46: A48-A50, (June 9, 2000).

★736★
Who female college students reported stalking them

Ranking basis/background: Percentage of female college students reporting each stalker relationship. **Remarks:** Original source: National Institute of Justice. **Number listed:** 6.
  Boyfriend/ex-boyfriend, with 42.5%
  Classmate, 24.5%
  Acquaintance, 10.3%
  Friend, 5.6%
  Coworker, 5.6%
  Other, 11.5%

Source: "The Stark Facts of College Stalking," *U.S. News & World Report*, 130: 14, (February 12, 2001).

Related Information

★737★
"Fact File: Crime Data From 481 U.S. Colleges and Universities," *The Chronicle of Higher Education*, 46: A51-A57, (June 9, 2000).
  Remarks: Presents crime data as reported during the 1997-98 academic year from 481 four-year institutions with 5,000 or more students enrolled.

★738★
"The Incidence of Crime on the Campuses of U.S. Postsecondary Education Institutions," *http://www.ed.gov/offices/OPE/PPI/ReportToCongress.pdf*.
  Remarks: Education Department crime statistics of individual campuses, separated into three categories, "on campus," "noncampus," and other locations. Data was requested from 2,089 public institutions, 1,950 private, nonprofits, and 2,261 private, for-profits for the years 1997, 1998 and 1999.

CAREERS

★739★
Careers college students considered least respected, 2000

Ranking basis/background: Percentage of votes from a survey of a thousand college students and recent graduates conducted by Jobtrak.com. **Number listed:** 5.
1. Politician, with 38%
2. Salesperson, 28%
3. IRS agent, 16%
4. Lawyer, 11%
5. Journalist, 7%

Source: "Prime Numbers," *The Chronicle of Higher Education*, 47: A7, (November 24, 2000).

★740★
Careers college students considered most respected, 2000

Ranking basis/background: Percentage of votes from a survey of a thousand college students and recent graduates conducted by Jobtrak.com. **Number listed:** 5.
1. Teacher, with 40%
2. Doctor, 32%
3. Social worker, 13%
4. CEO of internet company, 8%
5. Police officer, 7%

Source: "Prime Numbers," *The Chronicle of Higher Education*, 47: A7, (November 24, 2000).

Related Information

★741★
Ashley, Martin, *Massage: A Career at Your Fingertips: The Complete Guide to Becoming a Bodywork Professional, 3rd Ed.*, Enterprise Publishing, 1999.
  Remarks: This handbook includes information on schools and license laws for the 50 states, Washington DC, and Canada. Schools offering advanced courses in massage specialties are detailed. Professional associations, suppliers, and newsletters are also listed.

CELLULAR BIOLOGY, GRADUATE
See: **Biology, Graduate–Cellular/Molecular**

CENSORSHIP

★742★
American Library Associations most frequently challenged books for the 1990s

Ranking basis/background: Most frequently challenged literature as published by the American Library Association. **Number listed:** 100.
  Scary Stories Series, by Alvin Schwartz
  Daddy's Roommate, Michael Willhoite
  I Know Why the Caged Bird Sings, Maya Angelou
  The Chocolate War, Robert Cormier
  The Adventures of Huckleberry Finn, Mark Twain
  Of Mice and Men, John Steinbeck
  Forever, Judy Blume
  Bridge to Terabithia, Katherine Paterson
  Heather Has Two Mommies, Leslea Newman
  The Catcher in the Rye, J.D. Salinger

Source: "The Good, the Bad and the Unreadable," *Chicago Tribune*, September 24, 2000, Section 2, p. 1.

★743★
Authors protested for more than one book between 1952 and 1989, according to the *Newsletter of Intellectual Freedom*

Ranking basis/background: A report based on the books listed in the *Newsletter of Intellectual Freedom* as protested/attacked/censored between 1952 and 1989. **Remarks:** Books censored the most are also listed. **Number listed:** 4.
1. J. D. Salinger, 72 times (*The Catcher in the Rye*, 71 times; *Nine Stories*, 1 time)
2. Judy Blume, 57 (*Are You There God? It's Me Margaret*, 8; *Blubber*, 4; *Deenie*, 13; *Forever*, 18; *It's Not the End of the World*, 3; *Then Again Maybe I Won't*, 11)
3. John Steinbeck, 47 (*Of Mice and Men*, 29; *Grapes of Wrath*, 16; and *In Dubious Battle*, 2)
4. Norman Klein, 14 (*Confessions of an Only Child*, 1; *Give Me One Good Reason*, 1; *It's Okay if You Don't Love Me*, 5; *Mom, The Wolfman and Me*, 2; *Naomi in the Middle*, 3, et al.)

Source: Donelson, Ken, "You Can't Have That Book in My Kid's School Library: Books under Attack in the Newsletter on Intellectual Freedom, 1952-1989," *The High School Journal* 74: 1-7 (October/November 1990).

★744★
Books censored the most between 1952 and 1989, according to the *Newsletter of Intellectual Freedom*

Ranking basis/background: A report based on the books listed in the *Newsletter of Intellectual Freedom* as protested/attacked/censored between 1952 and 1989. **Remarks:** Authors protested for more than one book are also listed. **Number listed:** 49.
1. *The Catcher in the Rye*, with 72 incidents
2. *Go Ask Alice*, 31
3. *Of Mice and Men*, 29
4. *Forever*, 18
5. *Soul on Ice*, 17
6. *The Grapes of Wrath*, 16
7. *Adventures of Huckleberry Finn*, 15
8. *Manchild in the Promised Land*, 14
8. *Flowers for Algernon*, 14
10. *Deenie*, 13

Source: Donelson, Ken, "You Can't Have That Book in My Kid's School Library: Books under Attack in the Newsletter on Intellectual Freedom, 1952-1989," *The High School Journal* 74: 1-7 (October/November 1990).

★745★
Most frequently banned books in the 1990s

Ranking basis/background: Compiled from documentation from the American Library Association's Office of Intellectual Freedom and the People for the American Way. **Number listed:** 50.
  Impressions, ed. by Jack Booth et al.

Of Mice and Men, by John Steinbeck
The Catcher in the Rye, by J. D. Salinger
The Adventures of Huckleberry Finn, by Mark Twain
The Chocolate War, by Robert Cormier
Bridge to Terabithia, by Katherine Paterson
Scary Stories to Tell in the Dark, by Alvin Schwartz
More Scary Stories to Tell in the Dark, by Alvin Schwartz
The Witches, by Roald Dahl
Daddy's Roommate, by Michael Willhoite
Curses, Hexes, and Spells, by Daviel Cohen
A Wrinkle in Time, by Madeleine L'Engle
How to Eat Fried Worms, by Thomas Rockwell
Blubber, by Judy Blume
Revolting Rhymes, by Roald Dahl
Halloween ABC, by Eve Merriam
A Day No Pigs Would Die, by Robert Peck
Heather Has Two Mommies, by Leslea Newman
Christine, by Stephen King
I Know Why the Caged Bird Sings, by Maya Angelou
Fallen Angels, by Walter Myers
The New Teenage Body Book, by Kathy McCoy and Charles Wibbelsman
Little Red Riding Hood, by Jacob and Wilhelm Grimm
The Headless Cupid, by Zilpha Snyder
Night Chills, by Dean Koontz
Lord of the Flies, by William Golding
A Separate Peace, by John Knowles
Slaughterhouse-Five, by Kurt Vonnegut
The Color Purple, by Alice Walker
James and the Giant Peach, by Roald Dahl
The Learning Tree, by Gordon Parks
The Witches of Worm, by Zilpha Snyder
My Brother Sam Is Dead, by James Lincoln Collier and Christopher Collier
The Grapes of Wrath, by John Steinbeck
Cujo, by Stephen King
The Great Gilly Hopkins, by Katherine Paterson
The Figure in the Shadows, by John Bellairs
On My Honor, by Marion Dane Bauer
In the Night Kitchen, by Maurice Sendak
Grendel, by John Champlin Gardner
I Have to Go, by Robert Munsch
Annie on My Mind, by Nancy Garden
The Adventures of Tom Sawyer, by Mark Twain
The Pigman, by Paul Zindel
My House, by Nikki Giovanni
Then Again, Maybe I Won't, by Judy Blume
The Handmaid's Tale, by Margaret Atwood
Witches, Pumpkins, and Grinning Ghosts: The Story of the Halloween Symbols, by Edna Barth
One Hundred Years of Solitude, by Gabriel Garcia Marquez
Scary Stories 3: More Tales to Chill Your Bones, by Alvin Schwartz

Source: Foerstel, Herbert N., *Banned in the U.S.A.: A Reference Guide to Book Censorship in Schools and Public Libraries*, Greenwood Press, 1994.

★746★
People for the American Way's list of most frequently challenged authors, 1982-1992

Ranking basis/background: Compiled from documentation from the American Library Association's Office of Intellectual Freedom and the People for the American Way. **Number listed:** 11.

Judy Blume
Stephen King
John Steinbeck
Robert Cormier
J. D. Salinger
Mark Twain
Roald Dahl
Alvin Schwartz
Shel Silverstein
Anonymous, *Go Ask Alice*
Katherine Paterson

Source: Foerstel, Herbert N., *Banned in the U.S.A.: A Reference Guide to Book Censorship in Schools and Public Libraries*, Greenwood Press, 1994.

★747★
People for the American Way's list of most frequently challenged books, 1982-1992

Ranking basis/background: Compiled from documentation from the American Library Association's Office of Intellectual Freedom and the People for the American Way. **Number listed:** 12.

Of Mice and Men, John Steinbeck
The Catcher in the Rye, J. D. Salinger
The Chocolate War, Robert Cormier
The Adventures of Huckleberry Finn, Mark Twain
A Light in the Attic, Shel Silverstein
Go Ask Alice, Anonymous
Blubber, Judy Blume
The Witches, Roald Dahl
Ordinary People, Judith Guest
Forever, Judy Blume
Then Again, Maybe I Won't, Judy Blume
Scary Stories Series, Alvin Schwartz

Source: Foerstel, Herbert N., *Banned in the U.S.A.: A Reference Guide to Book Censorship in Schools and Public Libraries*, Greenwood Press, 1994.

★748★
People for the American Way's list of most frequently challenged books, 1991-1992

Ranking basis/background: Compiled from documentation from the American Library Association's Office of Intellectual Freedom and the People for the American Way. **Number listed:** 11.

Of Mice and Men, John Steinbeck
More Scary Stories to Tell in the Dark, Alvin Schwartz
Scary Stories to Tell in the Dark, Alvin Schwartz
The Catcher in the Rye, J. D. Salinger
The Chocolate War, Robert Cormier
The Witches, Roald Dahl
Bridge to Terabithia, Katherine Paterson
Blubber, Judy Blume
Revolting Rhymes, Roald Dahl
A Day No Pigs Would Die, Robert Peck
A Wrinkle in Time, Madeleine L'Engle

Source: Foerstel, Herbert N., *Banned in the U.S.A.: A Reference Guide to Book Censorship in Schools and Public Libraries*, Greenwood Press, 1994.

★749★
People for the American Way's list of most frequently challenged materials, 1982-1992

Ranking basis/background: Compiled from documentation from the American Library Association's Office of Intellectual Freedom and the People for the American Way. **Number listed:** 10.

Impressions, (textbook series)
Quest, (self-esteem program)
Pumsy: In Pursuit of Excellence, (self-esteem program)
Developing Understanding of Self and Others (DUSO), (self-esteem program)
Michigan Model for Comprehensive School Health Education
Romeo and Juliet, (film)
Tactics for Thinking, (thinking skills program)
Sports Illustrated, (magazine)
Junior Great Books Series, (texts)
Finding My Way, (health textbook)

Source: Foerstel, Herbert N., *Banned in the U.S.A.: A Reference Guide to Book Censorship in Schools and Public Libraries*, Greenwood Press, 1994.

★750★
People for the American Way's list of states with the most challenges to library and school books, 1982-1992

Ranking basis/background: Compiled from documentation from the American Library Association's Office of Intellectual Freedom and the People for the American Way. **Number listed:** 11.

California
Oregon
Florida
Texas
Washington
New York
Illinois
Michigan
Colorado
Iowa
Ohio

Source: Foerstel, Herbert N., *Banned in the U.S.A.: A Reference Guide to Book Censorship in Schools and Public Libraries*, Greenwood Press, 1994.

CHEMICAL ENGINEERING
See: Engineering–Chemical Engineering, Graduate–Chemical

CHEMISTRY

★751★
American Chemical Society 2001 award winners (Group 1)

Ranking basis/background: Awards are administered by the American Chemical Society. **Number listed:** 10.

Magid A. Abou-Gharbia, winner of the Earle B. Barnes Award for Leadership in Chemical Research Management (sponsored by Dow Chemical Co.)
Paul S. Anderson, ACS Award in Industrial Chemistry (DuPont Pharmaceuticals Co.)
John N. Armor, E.V. Murphree Award in Industrial & Engineering Chemistry (ExxonMobil Research & Engineering Co. and ExxonMobil Chemical Co.)
John D. Baldeschwieler, ACS Award for Creative Invention (Corporation Associates)
Ernst Bayer, ACS Award in Chromatography (Supelco Inc.)
Alexis T. Bell, ACS Award for Creative Research in Homogeneous or Heterogeneous Catalysis (Shell Oil Foundation)
Carolyn R. Bertozzi, ACS Award in Pure Chemistry (Alpha Chi Sigma Fraternity)
Klaus Biemann, ACS Award in Analytical Chemistry (Fisher Scientific Co.)
Christina Bodurow Erwin, ACS Award for Encouraging Women into Careers in the Chemical Sciences (Camille & Henry Dreyfus Foundation)
Joan F. Brennecke, Ipatieff Prize

Source: "2001 ACS National Award Winners," *C&EN: Chemical & Engineering News,* 79: 31-37, (January 1, 2001).

★752★
American Chemical Society 2001 award winners (Group 2)

Ranking basis/background: Awards are administered by the American Chemical Society. **Number listed:** 9.

Daniel J. Brunelle, winner of the ACS Award in Applied Polymer Science
Charles T. Campbell, ACS Award in Colloid or Surface Chemistry (sponsored by Procter & Gamble Co.)
Leland C. Clark Jr., ACS Award for Creative Work in Fluorine Chemistry (Lancaster Synthesis Inc.)
F. Albert Cotton, ACS Award in Organometallic Chemistry (Dow Chemical Co. Foundation)
Omkaram Nalamasu, Francis M. Houlihan, Arturo N. Medina, Ashok T. Reddy, James M. Davidson, ACS Award for Team Innovation (ACS Corporation Associates)
John P. Fackler, ACS Award for Distinguished Service in the Advancement of Inorganic Chemistry (Strem Chemicals)
William M. Gelbart, Joel Henry Hildebrand Award in the Theoretical & Experimental Chemistry of Liquids (ExxonMobil Research & Engineering Co. and ExxonMobil Chemical Co.)
Harry B. Gray, George C. Pimentel Award in Chemical Education (Union Carbide)
Robert H. Grubbs, Herbert C. Brown Award for Creative Research in Synthetic Methods (Aldrich Chemical Co. and the Purdue Borane Research Fund)

Source: "2001 ACS National Award Winners," *C&EN: Chemical & Engineering News,* 79: 36-43, (January 8, 2001).

★753★
American Chemical Society 2001 award winners (Group 3)

Ranking basis/background: Awards are administered by the American Chemical Society. **Number listed:** 10.

Carlos G. Gutierrez, winner of the ACS Award for Encouraging Disadvantaged Students into Careers in the Chemical Sciences (sponsored by Camille & Henry Dreyfus Foundation Inc.)
Michael R. Hoffmann, ACS Award for Creative Advances in Environmental Science & Technology (Air Products & Chemicals Inc.)
Csaba Horvath, ACS Award in Separations Science & Technology (IBC Advanced Technologies Inc. and Millipore Corp.)
Eric N. Jacobsen, ACS Award for Creative Work in Synthetic Organic Chemistry (Aldrich Chemical Co.)
Martin Karplus, ACS Award for Computers in Chemical & Pharmaceutical Research
William A. Klemperer, E. Bright Wilson Award in Spectroscopy (Rohm and Haas Co.)
Yuan Chuan Lee, Claude S. Hudson Award in Carbohydrate Chemistry (National Starch & Chemical)
Tobin J. Marks, ACS Award in the Chemistry of Materials (DuPont)
Josef Michl, James Flack Norris Award in Physical Organic Chemistry (ACS Northeastern Section)
Martin T. Zanni, Nobel Laureate Signature Award for Graduate Education in Chemistry (Mallinckrodt Baker)

Source: "2001 ACS National Award Winners," *C&EN: Chemical & Engineering News,* 79: 54-60, (January 15, 2001).

★754★
American Chemical Society 2001 award winners (Group 4)

Ranking basis/background: Awards are administered by the American Chemical Society. **Number listed:** 10.

Ryoji Noyori, winner of the Roger Adams Award in Organic Chemistry (Organic Reactions Inc. and Organic Syntheses Inc.)
Iwao Ojima, E.B. Hershberg Award for Important Discoveries in Medicinally Active Substances (Schering-Plough Corp.)
Michele Parrinello, ACS Award in Theoretical Chemistry (IBM Corp.)
Robert Pasternack, ACS Award for Research at an Undergraduate Institution (Research Corp.)
David Perlman, James T. Grady-James H. Stack Award for Interpreting Chemistry for the Public
John D. Roberts, Nakanishi Prize
John Ross, Peter Debye Award in Physical Chemistry (DuPont Co.)
Peter G. Schultz, Alfred Bader Award in Bioinorganic or Bioorganic Chemistry
Helmut Schwarz, Frank H. Field & Joe L. Franklin Award for Outstanding Achievement in Mass Spectrometry (Bruker Daltonics Inc.)
Barbara Pressey Sitzman, James Bryant Conant Award in High School Chemistry Teaching (Albermarle Corp.)

Source: "2001 ACS National Award Winners," *C&EN: Chemical & Engineering News,* 79: 31-37, (January 1, 2001).

★755★
American Chemical Society 2001 award winners (Group 5)

Ranking basis/background: Awards are administered by the American Chemical Society. **Number listed:** 9.

Yoshito Kishi, winner of the Ernest Guenther Award in the Chemistry of Natural Products (sponsored by Givaudan)
Edward I. Solomon, ACS Award in Inorganic Chemistry (Aldrich Chemical Co.)
Susan S. Taylor, Francis P. Garvan-John M. Olin Medal (Olin Corp. Charitable Trust)
David A. Tirrell, ACS Award in Polymer Chemistry (ExxonMobil Chemical Co.)
Daniel F. Veber, Ralph F. Hirschmann Award in Peptide Chemistry (Merck Research Laboratories)
William B. Walters, ACS Award for Nuclear Chemistry (Gordon & Breach Publishing Group)
J.M. White, Arthur W. Adamson Award for Distinguished Service in the Advancement of Surface Chemistry (Occidental Petroleum Corp.)
Francisco Zaera, George A. Olah Award in Hydrocarbon or Petroleum Chemistry
Richard N. Zare, Charles Lathrop Parsons Award

Source: "2001 ACS National Award Winners," *C&EN: Chemical & Engineering News,* 79: 42-48, (January 29, 2001).

★756★
Bachelor's degrees awarded in chemistry, 1980 to 1997

Ranking basis/background: Number of degrees awarded by chemistry departments with ACS-approved bachelor's level programs. **Remarks:** Original source: National Center for Education Statistics. **Number listed:** 18.

1980, with 11,232
1981, 11,347
1982, 11,062
1983, 10,796
1984, 10,704
1985, 10,482
1986, 10,116
1987, 9,670
1988, 9,052
1989, 8,625
1990, 8,132
1991, 8,321
1992, 8,641
1993, 8,914
1994, 9,425
1995, 9,722
1996, 10,415
1997, 10,644

Source: Brennan, Mairin B., "Demand," *C&EN: Chemical & Engineering News,* 77: 38-46, (November 15, 1999).

CHEMISTRY

★757★
CA journal literature abstracted, by country, 2000

Ranking basis/background: Percentage of *Chemical Abstracts* journal literature abstracted. Total journal literature abstracted in 2000 was 573,469. **Remarks:** Original source: Chemical Abstracts Service. **Number listed:** 6.
1. United States, with 24%
2. Japan, 13%
3. China, 10%
4. Germany, 7%
5. United Kingdom, 5%
6. Other, 41%

Source: Raber, Linda R., "Building A Chemical Research Dynasty," *C&EN: Chemical & Engineering News*, 79: 45-46, (February 26, 2001).

★758★
CA patents abstracted, by country, 2000

Ranking basis/background: Percentage of *Chemical Abstracts* patents abstracted. Total patents abstracted in 2000 was 146,590. **Remarks:** Original source: Chemical Abstracts Service. **Number listed:** 7.
1. Japan, with 45%
2. World Intellectual Property Organization, 18%
3. United States, 8%
4. China, 7%
5. Russia, 6%
6. European Patent Organization, 5%
7. Other, 11%

Source: Raber, Linda R., "Building A Chemical Research Dynasty," *C&EN: Chemical & Engineering News*, 79: 45-46, (February 26, 2001).

★759★
Median salaries for B.S. chemists, by employment sector, 2000

Ranking basis/background: Median salary, in thousands, for full-time chemist salaries. **Remarks:** Original source: 1995 and 2000 salary and employment censuses of ACS members, 1996 through 1999 salary and employment surveys. **Number listed:** 3.
  Industry, with $54.2
  Government, $53.7
  Academia, $40.0

Source: Heylin, Michael, "Employment Outlook: Salaries & Jobs 2001," *C&EN: Chemical & Engineering News*, 78: 47-54, (November 13, 2000).

★760★
Median salaries for chemistry professors with eleven- to twelve-month contracts, by type of school

Ranking basis/background: Median base annual salary, in thousands, for both non-Ph.D. and Ph.D. schools as of March 1, 2000. **Remarks:** Original source: ACS survey. **Number listed:** 3.
  Full professor, with $95.0 thousand at non-Ph.D. schools; $106.1 thousand at Ph.D. schools
  Associate professor, $70.0; $66.2
  Assistant professor, $50.5; $56.8

Source: Heylin, Michael, "ChemCensus 2000: Salary & Employment Survey," *C&EN: Chemical & Engineering News*, 78: 46-53, (August 14, 2000).

★761★
Median salaries for chemistry professors with nine- to ten-month contracts, by type of school

Ranking basis/background: Median base annual salary, in thousands, for both non-Ph.D. and Ph.D. schools as of March 1, 2000. **Remarks:** Original source: ACS survey. **Number listed:** 3.
  Full professor, with $63.0 thousand at non-Ph.D. schools; $85.1 thousand at Ph.D. schools
  Associate professor, $48.4; $56.0
  Assistant professor, $40.0; $49.2

Source: Heylin, Michael, "ChemCensus 2000: Salary & Employment Survey," *C&EN: Chemical & Engineering News*, 78: 46-53, (August 14, 2000).

★762★
Median salaries for chemists, by degree, 2000

Ranking basis/background: Median base annual salary, in thousands, for full-time chemists as of March 1, 2000. **Remarks:** Original source: ACS survey. **Number listed:** 3.
  B.S., with $53.1 thousand
  M.S., $62.0
  Ph.D., $79.0

Source: Heylin, Michael, "ChemCensus 2000: Salary & Employment Survey," *C&EN: Chemical & Engineering News*, 78: 46-53, (August 14, 2000).

★763★
Median salaries for chemists, by degree and race/ethnicity, 2000

Ranking basis/background: Median base annual salary, in thousands, as of March 1, 2000. **Remarks:** Original source: ACS survey. **Number listed:** 3.
  B.S., with $54.0 for whites; $50.0 Asian; $47.0 African American; $48.4 Hispanic
  M.S., $63.0; $57.9; $60.0; $57.4
  Ph.D., $80.0; $76.0; $71.4; $70.0

Source: Heylin, Michael, "ChemCensus 2000: Salary & Employment Survey," *C&EN: Chemical & Engineering News*, 78: 46-53, (August 14, 2000).

★764★
Median salaries for chemists, by employment sector, 2000

Ranking basis/background: Median base annual salary, in thousands, for full-time chemists as of March 1, 2000. **Remarks:** Original source: ACS survey. **Number listed:** 3.
  Industry, with $74.5 thousand
  Government, $70.0
  Academia, $58.0

Source: Heylin, Michael, "ChemCensus 2000: Salary & Employment Survey," *C&EN: Chemical & Engineering News*, 78: 46-53, (August 14, 2000).

★765★
Median salaries for chemists, by employment sector and race/ethnicity, 2000

Ranking basis/background: Median base annual salary, in thousands, as of March 1, 2000. **Remarks:** Original source: ACS survey. **Number listed:** 3.
  Industry, with $75.0 for whites; $74.4 Asian; $62.7 African American; $64.0 Hispanic
  Government, $71.3; $67.0; $57.2; $61.0
  Academia, $58.8; $56.0; $50.0; $50.0

Source: Heylin, Michael, "ChemCensus 2000: Salary & Employment Survey," *C&EN: Chemical & Engineering News*, 78: 46-53, (August 14, 2000).

★766★
Median salaries for chemists, by gender, 2000

Ranking basis/background: Median base annual salary, in thousands, for full-time chemists as of March 1, 2000. **Remarks:** Original source: ACS survey. **Number listed:** 2.
  Men, with $74.1 thousand
  Women, $56.0

Source: Heylin, Michael, "ChemCensus 2000: Salary & Employment Survey," *C&EN: Chemical & Engineering News*, 78: 46-53, (August 14, 2000).

★767★
Median salaries for chemists, by gender and race/ethnicity, 2000

Ranking basis/background: Median base annual salary, in thousands, as of March 1, 2000. **Remarks:** Original source: ACS survey. **Number listed:** 2.
  Men, with $75.0 for whites; $75.0 Asian; $63.0 African American; $64.0 Hispanic
  Female, $55.0; $62.0; $51.0; $50.3

Source: Heylin, Michael, "ChemCensus 2000: Salary & Employment Survey," *C&EN: Chemical & Engineering News*, 78: 46-53, (August 14, 2000).

★768★
Median salaries for chemists holding a bachelor's degree, by employment sector, 2000

Ranking basis/background: Median base annual salary, in thousands, for full-time chemists as of March 1, 2000. **Remarks:** Original source: ACS survey. **Number listed:** 3.
  Industry, with $54.2 thousand
  Government, $53.7
  Academia, $40.0

Source: Heylin, Michael, "ChemCensus 2000: Salary & Employment Survey," *C&EN: Chemical & Engineering News*, 78: 46-53, (August 14, 2000).

★769★
Median salaries for chemists in the east north central region of the U.S., by degree, 2000

Ranking basis/background: Median base annual salary, in thousands, for full-time chemists as of March 1, 2000. The east north central region includes Wisconsin, Illinois, Michigan, Indiana, and Ohio. **Remarks:** Original source: ACS survey. **Number listed:** 3.
  B.S., with $52.8
  M.S., $62.0
  Ph.D., $78.0

Source: Heylin, Michael, "ChemCensus 2000: Salary & Employment Survey," *C&EN: Chemical & Engineering News*, 78: 46-53, (August 14, 2000).

★770★
Median salaries for chemists in the east south central region of the U.S., by degree, 2000

Ranking basis/background: Median base annual salary, in thousands, for full-time chemists as of March 1, 2000. The east south central region includes Kentucky, Tennessee, Alabama, and Mississippi. **Remarks:** Original source: ACS survey. **Number listed:** 3.

B.S., with $52.0
M.S., $59.6
Ph.D., $66.0
Source: Heylin, Michael, "ChemCensus 2000: Salary & Employment Survey," *C&EN: Chemical & Engineering News*, 78: 46-53, (August 14, 2000).

★771★
Median salaries for chemists in the middle Atlantic region of the U.S., by degree, 2000

Ranking basis/background: Median base annual salary, in thousands, for full-time chemists as of March 1, 2000. The middle Atlantic region includes Pennsylvania, New York, and New Jersey. **Remarks:** Original source: ACS survey. **Number listed:** 3.
  B.S., with $55.5
  M.S., $65.0
  Ph.D., $83.7
Source: Heylin, Michael, "ChemCensus 2000: Salary & Employment Survey," *C&EN: Chemical & Engineering News*, 78: 46-53, (August 14, 2000).

★772★
Median salaries for chemists in the mountain region of the U.S., by degree, 2000

Ranking basis/background: Median base annual salary, in thousands, for full-time chemists as of March 1, 2000. The mountain region includes Montana, Idaho, Colorado, Nevada, Utah, Wyoming, New Mexico, and Arizona. **Remarks:** Original source: ACS survey. **Number listed:** 3.
  B.S., with $50.1
  M.S., $54.1
  Ph.D., $75.0
Source: Heylin, Michael, "ChemCensus 2000: Salary & Employment Survey," *C&EN: Chemical & Engineering News*, 78: 46-53, (August 14, 2000).

★773★
Median salaries for chemists in the New England region of the U.S., by degree, 2000

Ranking basis/background: Median base annual salary, in thousands, for full-time chemists as of March 1, 2000. The New England region includes Maine, Delaware, Vermont, Connecticut, Rhode Island, and Massachusetts. **Remarks:** Original source: ACS survey. **Number listed:** 3.
  B.S., with $53.4
  M.S., $63.0
  Ph.D., $81.0
Source: Heylin, Michael, "ChemCensus 2000: Salary & Employment Survey," *C&EN: Chemical & Engineering News*, 78: 46-53, (August 14, 2000).

★774★
Median salaries for chemists in the Pacific region of the U.S., by degree, 2000

Ranking basis/background: Median base annual salary, in thousands, for full-time chemists as of March 1, 2000. The Pacific region includes Washington, Oregon, and California. **Remarks:** Original source: ACS survey. **Number listed:** 3.
  B.S., with $55.1
  M.S., $62.0
  Ph.D., $81.0
Source: Heylin, Michael, "ChemCensus 2000: Salary & Employment Survey," *C&EN: Chemical & Engineering News*, 78: 46-53, (August 14, 2000).

★775★
Median salaries for chemists in the south Atlantic region of the U.S., by degree, 2000

Ranking basis/background: Median base annual salary, in thousands, for full-time chemists as of March 1, 2000. The south Atlantic region includes Florida, Georgia, West Virginia, Virginia, North Carolina, South Carolina, and Maryland. **Remarks:** Original source: ACS survey. **Number listed:** 3.
  B.S., with $52.9
  M.S., $62.0
  Ph.D., $79.1
Source: Heylin, Michael, "ChemCensus 2000: Salary & Employment Survey," *C&EN: Chemical & Engineering News*, 78: 46-53, (August 14, 2000).

★776★
Median salaries for chemists in the west north central region of the U.S., by degree, 2000

Ranking basis/background: Median base annual salary, in thousands, for full-time chemists as of March 1, 2000. The west north central region includes North Dakota, South Dakota, Nebraska, Kansas, Minnesota, Iowa, and Missouri. **Remarks:** Original source: ACS survey. **Number listed:** 3.
  B.S., with $48.0
  M.S., $56.0
  Ph.D., $70.0
Source: Heylin, Michael, "ChemCensus 2000: Salary & Employment Survey," *C&EN: Chemical & Engineering News*, 78: 46-53, (August 14, 2000).

★777★
Median salaries for chemists in the west south central region of the U.S., by degree, 2000

Ranking basis/background: Median base annual salary, in thousands, for full-time chemists as of March 1, 2000. The west south central region includes Texas, Oklahoma, Arkansas, and Louisiana. **Remarks:** Original source: ACS survey. **Number listed:** 3.
  B.S., with $53.8
  M.S., $59.0
  Ph.D., $73.0
Source: Heylin, Michael, "ChemCensus 2000: Salary & Employment Survey," *C&EN: Chemical & Engineering News*, 78: 46-53, (August 14, 2000).

★778★
Median salaries for chemists with a bachelor's degree, by employment sector and race/ethnicity, 2000

Ranking basis/background: Median base annual salary, in thousands, as of March 1, 2000. **Remarks:** Original source: ACS survey. **Number listed:** 3.
  Industry, with $55.0 for whites; $50.3 Asian; $49.0 African American; $49.2 Hispanic
  Government, $54.0; $47.6; $42.9; $52.5
  Academia, $38.5; $38.5; $42.3; $35.1
Source: Heylin, Michael, "ChemCensus 2000: Salary & Employment Survey," *C&EN: Chemical & Engineering News*, 78: 46-53, (August 14, 2000).

★779★
Median salaries for M.S. chemists, by employment sector, 2000

Ranking basis/background: Median salary, in thousands, for full-time chemist salaries. **Remarks:** Original source: 1995 and 2000 salary and employment censuses of ACS members, 1996 through 1999 salary and employment surveys. **Number listed:** 3.
  Industry, with $65.5
  Government, $61.5
  Academia, $45.0
Source: Heylin, Michael, "Employment Outlook: Salaries & Jobs 2001," *C&EN: Chemical & Engineering News*, 78: 47-54, (November 13, 2000).

★780★
Median salaries for Ph.D. chemists, by employment sector, 2000

Ranking basis/background: Median salary, in thousands, for full-time chemist salaries. **Remarks:** Original source: 1995 and 2000 salary and employment censuses of ACS members, 1996 through 1999 salary and employment surveys. **Number listed:** 3.
  Industry, with $86.2
  Government, $80.0
  Academia, $60.0
Source: Heylin, Michael, "Employment Outlook: Salaries & Jobs 2001," *C&EN: Chemical & Engineering News*, 78: 47-54, (November 13, 2000).

★781★
Median salary for B.S. chemists, by field

Ranking basis/background: Median salary, in thousands, for full-time B.S. chemists salaries as of 1997. **Remarks:** Original source: National Science Foundation; Science and Engineering Indicators 2000. **Number listed:** 13.
1. Chemical engineers, with $62.0
2. All engineers, $55.0
3. Computer/math, $54.0
4. All scientists, $50.0
5. Earth sciences, $46.5
6. Physical sciences, $42.1
7. Physics/astronomy, $42.0
8. Environmental life sciences, $41.0
9. Chemistry, $41.3
10. Agriculture/food science, $37.0
11. Life-related science, $36.0
12. Biological sciences, $35.0
13. Social sciences, $25.0

Source: Heylin, Michael, "Employment Outlook: Salaries & Jobs 2001," *C&EN: Chemical & Engineering News*, 78: 47-54, (November 13, 2000).

★782★
Median salary for chemists, by employer, 2000

Ranking basis/background: Median salary, in thousands, for full-time chemist salaries. **Remarks:** Original source: 1995 and 2000 salary and employment censuses of ACS members, 1996 through 1999 salary and employment surveys. **Number listed:** 3.
  Industry, with $74.5
  Government, $58.0
  Academia, $50.0

CHEMISTRY

Source: Heylin, Michael, "Employment Outlook: Salaries & Jobs 2001," *C&EN: Chemical & Engineering News*, 78: 47-54, (November 13, 2000).

★783★
Median salary for chemists, by gender, 2000

Ranking basis/background: Median salary, in thousands, for full-time chemist salaries. **Remarks:** Original source: 1995 and 2000 salary and employment censuses of ACS members, 1996 through 1999 salary and employment surveys. **Number listed:** 2.
   Men, with $74.1
   Women, $56.0

Source: Heylin, Michael, "Employment Outlook: Salaries & Jobs 2001," *C&EN: Chemical & Engineering News*, 78: 47-54, (November 13, 2000).

★784★
Median salary for chemists, by highest degree, 2000

Ranking basis/background: Median salary, in thousands, for full-time chemist salaries. **Remarks:** Original source: 1995 and 2000 salary and employment censuses of ACS members, 1996 through 1999 salary and employment surveys. **Number listed:** 3.
   B.S., with $53.1
   M.S., $62.0
   Ph.D., $79.0

Source: Heylin, Michael, "Employment Outlook: Salaries & Jobs 2001," *C&EN: Chemical & Engineering News*, 78: 47-54, (November 13, 2000).

★785★
Median salary for M.S. chemists, by field

Ranking basis/background: Median salary, in thousands, for full-time M.S. chemists salaries as of 1997. **Remarks:** Original source: National Science Foundation; Science and Engineering Indicators 2000. **Number listed:** 13.
   1. Chemical engineers, with $70.0
   2. All engineers, $63.6
   3. Computer/math, $60.0
   4. Physics/astronomy, $58.0
   5. All scientists, $54.0
   6. Earth sciences, $53.0
   7. Environmental life sciences, $52.0
   8. Physical sciences, $51.0
   9. Chemistry, $50.0
   10. Life-related science, $42.0
   11. Biological sciences, $42.0
   12. Social sciences, $41.1
   13. Agriculture/food science, $40.0

Source: Heylin, Michael, "Employment Outlook: Salaries & Jobs 2001," *C&EN: Chemical & Engineering News*, 78: 47-54, (November 13, 2000).

★786★
Median salary for Ph.D. chemists, by field

Ranking basis/background: Median salary, in thousands, for full-time Ph.D. chemists salaries as of 1997. **Remarks:** Original source: National Science Foundation; Science and Engineering Indicators 2000. **Number listed:** 13.
   1. Physics/astronomy, with $73.0
   2. Chemical engineers, $72.1
   3. All engineers, $72.0
   4. Chemistry, $70.0
   5. Computer/math, $65.0
   5. Physical sciences, $65.0
   7. Earth sciences, $62.0
   8. All scientists, $60.0
   8. Agriculture/food science, $60.0
   10. Environmental life sciences, $59.0
   11. Life-related science, $57.5
   12. Biological sciences, $55.0
   12. Social sciences, $55.0

Source: Heylin, Michael, "Employment Outlook: Salaries & Jobs 2001," *C&EN: Chemical & Engineering News*, 78: 47-54, (November 13, 2000).

★787★
Median salary gain for chemists with bachelor's degrees, by employment sector, 2000

Ranking basis/background: Percent of median salary gain between March 1, 1999 and March 1, 2000. **Remarks:** Original source: ACS membership survey. **Number listed:** 3.
   Industry, with 5.3%
   Government, 4.9%
   Academia, 4.6%

Source: Heylin, Michael, "ChemCensus 2000: Salary & Employment Survey," *C&EN: Chemical & Engineering News*, 78: 46-53, (August 14, 2000).

★788★
Overall median salary for chemists with full-time employment, by degree, 2000

Ranking basis/background: Overall median salary, in thousands, for full-time chemists as of March 1, 2000. **Remarks:** Original source: ACS survey. **Number listed:** 3.
   B.S., with $54.2
   M.S., $65.5
   Ph.D., $86.3

Source: Heylin, Michael, "ChemCensus 2000: Salary & Employment Survey," *C&EN: Chemical & Engineering News*, 78: 46-53, (August 14, 2000).

★789★
Overall median salary for female chemists with full-time employment, by degree, 2000

Ranking basis/background: Overall median salary, in thousands, for full-time chemists as of March 1, 2000. **Remarks:** Original source: ACS survey. **Number listed:** 3.
   B.S., with $48.0
   M.S., $58.0
   Ph.D., $78.0

Source: Heylin, Michael, "ChemCensus 2000: Salary & Employment Survey," *C&EN: Chemical & Engineering News*, 78: 46-53, (August 14, 2000).

★790★
Overall median salary for full-time chemists with a bachelor's degree, by work function, 2000

Ranking basis/background: Overall median salary, in thousands, for full-time chemists as of March 1, 2000. **Remarks:** Original source: ACS survey. **Number listed:** 6.
   General management, with $72.1
   R&D management, $80.0
   Basic research, $48.7
   Applied research, $54.1
   Production, $50.0
   Marketing and sales, $67.0

Source: Heylin, Michael, "ChemCensus 2000: Salary & Employment Survey," *C&EN: Chemical & Engineering News*, 78: 46-53, (August 14, 2000).

★791★
Overall median salary for male chemists with full-time employment, by degree, 2000

Ranking basis/background: Overall median salary, in thousands, for full-time chemists as of March 1, 2000. **Remarks:** Original source: ACS survey. **Number listed:** 3.
   B.S., with $59.0
   M.S., $70.0
   Ph.D., $88.5

Source: Heylin, Michael, "ChemCensus 2000: Salary & Employment Survey," *C&EN: Chemical & Engineering News*, 78: 46-53, (August 14, 2000).

★792★
Top recruiters for chemistry jobs for 2000-01 bachelor's degree recipients

Ranking basis/background: Projected number of college hires from on-campus recruitment for 2000-01. **Remarks:** Numbers reflect total expected hires, not just African American projected hires. **Number listed:** 8.
   1. Abbott Laboratories, with 100 projected hires
   2. Accenture, 65
   3. Agilent Technologies, 20
   4. U.S. Air Force (Active Duty Hires), 10
   5. PA Dept. Environmental Protection, 5
   5. Caddo Parish School Board, 5
   7. Houghton Mifflin, 2
   7. Novant Health, 2

Source: "The Top 100 Employers and the Majors in Demand for the Class of 2001," *The Black Collegian*, 31: 19-35, (February 2001).

★793★
U.S. universities with the greatest impact in chemistry, 1994-98

Ranking basis/background: Average citations per paper from the top 100 federally funded U.S. universities that had at least 50 published papers in ISI indexed chemistry journals. Also includes total number of papers published during the five year period. **Number listed:** 5.
   1. Harvard University, with 1,111 papers; 10.12 citations per paper
   2. Caltech, 1,166; 9.81
   3. University of California, San Diego, 802; 8.53
   4. Emory University, 600; 8.46
   5. Stanford University, 1,230; 8.39

Source: "Chemistry: High Impact U.S. Universities, 1994-98," *What's Hot in Research* (http://www.isinet.com/isi/hot/research) Institute for Scientific Information, July 3, 2000.

★794★
U.S. universities with the highest concentration of papers published in the field of chemistry, 1994-98

Ranking basis/background: Number of papers published in the field of chemistry over a five-year period, and percentage they comprise of the university's total papers published. **Number listed:** 5.
   1. University of Delaware, with 1,098 papers; 26.60% of university's total papers
   2. Lehigh University, 366; 22.18%
   3. Iowa State University, 1,185; 16.97%

4. Rice University, 429; 16.74%
5. Purdue University, 1,771; 16.21%

Source: "U.S. Universities with Highest Concentrations in Chemistry, 1994-98," *What's Hot in Research* (http://www.isinet.com/isi/hot/research) Institute for Scientific Information, September 4, 2000.

★795★
Winner of the American Chemical Society's Arthur C. Cope Awards, 2001

Ranking basis/background: Recipients recognized for significant contributions in organic chemistry. **Number listed:** 11.

George A. Olah, University of Southern California
Geoffrey W. Coates, Cornell University
Michael T. Crimmins, University of North Carolina, Chapel Hill
Jean M.J. Frechet, University of California, Berkeley
Murray Goodman, University of California, San Diego
Jeffrey W. Kelly, Scripps Research Institute
John Montgomery, Wayne State University
Matthew S. Platz, Ohio State University
Nicole S. Sampson, State University of New York, Stony Brook
Richard R. Schrock, Massachusetts Institute of Technology
Victor A. Snieckus, Queen's University (ON)

Source: "2001 ACS Cope Award Winners," *C&EN: Chemical & Engineering News*, 79: 36-43, (February 5, 2001).

CHEMISTRY, GRADUATE

★796★
Median salaries for chemists holding a doctoral degree, by employment sector, 2000

Ranking basis/background: Median base annual salary, in thousands, for full-time chemists as of March 1, 2000. **Remarks:** Original source: ACS survey. **Number listed:** 3.

Industry, with $86.2 thousand
Government, $80.0
Academia, $60.0

Source: Heylin, Michael, "ChemCensus 2000: Salary & Employment Survey," *C&EN: Chemical & Engineering News*, 78: 46-53, (August 14, 2000).

★797★
Median salaries for chemists holding a master's degree, by employment sector, 2000

Ranking basis/background: Median base annual salary, in thousands, for full-time chemists as of March 1, 2000. **Remarks:** Original source: ACS survey. **Number listed:** 3.

Industry, with $65.5 thousand
Government, $61.2
Academia, $45.0

Source: Heylin, Michael, "ChemCensus 2000: Salary & Employment Survey," *C&EN: Chemical & Engineering News*, 78: 46-53, (August 14, 2000).

★798★
Median salaries for chemists with a doctoral degree, by employment sector and race/ethnicity, 2000

Ranking basis/background: Median base annual salary, in thousands, as of March 1, 2000. **Remarks:** Original source: ACS survey. **Number listed:** 3.

Industry, with $89.0 for whites; $79.0 Asian; $80.0 African American; $79.1 Hispanic
Government, $81.0; $76.7; $70.0; $76.6
Academia, $60.5; $58.0; $54.0; $51.3

Source: Heylin, Michael, "ChemCensus 2000: Salary & Employment Survey," *C&EN: Chemical & Engineering News*, 78: 46-53, (August 14, 2000).

★799★
Median salaries for chemists with a master's degree, by employment sector and race/ethnicity, 2000

Ranking basis/background: Median base annual salary, in thousands, as of March 1, 2000. **Remarks:** Original source: ACS survey. **Number listed:** 3.

Industry, with $67.7 for whites; $58.5 Asian; $65.1 African American; $60.0 Hispanic
Government, $62.0; $63.2; $55.6; $59.2
Academia, $45.0; $47.3; $42.6; $36.0

Source: Heylin, Michael, "ChemCensus 2000: Salary & Employment Survey," *C&EN: Chemical & Engineering News*, 78: 46-53, (August 14, 2000).

★800★
Median salary gain for chemists with doctoral degrees, by employment sector, 2000

Ranking basis/background: Percent of median salary gain between March 1, 1999 and March 1, 2000. **Remarks:** Original source: ACS membership survey. **Number listed:** 3.

Industry, with 5.0%
Government, 5.0%
Academia, 4.2%

Source: Heylin, Michael, "ChemCensus 2000: Salary & Employment Survey," *C&EN: Chemical & Engineering News*, 78: 46-53, (August 14, 2000).

★801★
Median salary gain for chemists with master's degrees, by employment sector, 2000

Ranking basis/background: Percent of median salary gain between March 1, 1999 and March 1, 2000. **Remarks:** Original source: ACS membership survey. **Number listed:** 3.

Industry, with 4.9%
Government, 4.9%
Academia, 4.1%

Source: Heylin, Michael, "ChemCensus 2000: Salary & Employment Survey," *C&EN: Chemical & Engineering News*, 78: 46-53, (August 14, 2000).

★802★
Most effective chemistry research-doctorate programs as evaluated by the National Research Council

Ranking basis/background: From a survey of nearly 8,000 faculty members conducted in the spring of 1993. Respondents were asked to rate programs in their field on "effectiveness of program in educating research scholars/scientists." **Remarks:** See *Chronicle* article for more details. Scores of 3.5-5.0 indicate "extremely effective;" 2.5-3.49 "reasonably effective;" 1.5-2.49 "minimally effective;" and 0.0-1.49 "not effective." Programs also ranked by "scholarly quality of program faculty." **Number listed:** 168.

1. California Institute of Technology, with an effectiveness rating of 4.75
2. University of California, Berkeley, 4.72
3. Massachusetts Institute of Technology, 4.70
4. Harvard University, 4.57
5. Stanford University, 4.57
6. Cornell University, 4.40
7. University of Illinois, Urbana-Champaign, 4.38
8. Columbia University, 4.37
9. Yale University, 4.31
10. University of Wisconsin, Madison, 4.26

Source: "Rankings of Research-Doctorate Programs in 41 Disciplines at 274 Institutions," *The Chronicle of Higher Education* 42: A21-A30 (September 21, 1995).

★803★
Overall median salary for full-time chemists with a doctoral degree, by work function, 2000

Ranking basis/background: Overall median salary, in thousands, for full-time chemists as of March 1, 2000. **Remarks:** Original source: ACS survey. **Number listed:** 6.

General management, with $110.0
R&D management, $108.8
Basic research, $86.0
Applied research, $82.0
Production, $78.0
Marketing and sales, $86.0

Source: Heylin, Michael, "ChemCensus 2000: Salary & Employment Survey," *C&EN: Chemical & Engineering News*, 78: 46-53, (August 14, 2000).

★804★
Overall median salary for full-time chemists with a master's degree, by work function, 2000

Ranking basis/background: Overall median salary, in thousands, for full-time chemists as of March 1, 2000. **Remarks:** Original source: ACS survey. **Number listed:** 6.

General management, with $86.0
R&D management, $90.0
Basic research, $62.0
Applied research, $62.9
Production, $60.0
Marketing and sales, $76.3

Source: Heylin, Michael, "ChemCensus 2000: Salary & Employment Survey," *C&EN: Chemical & Engineering News*, 78: 46-53, (August 14, 2000).

CHEMISTRY PERIODICALS

★805★
Top chemistry research-doctorate programs as evaluated by the National Research Council

Ranking basis/background: From a survey of nearly 8,000 faculty members conducted in the spring of 1993. Respondents were asked to rate programs in their field on "scholarly quality of program faculty." When more than one program had the same score, the council averaged the rank order and gave each program the same rank number (if three programs tied for the top position, each received a rank of 2). **Remarks:** See *Chronicle* article for more details. Scores of 4.01 and above indicate "distinguished;" 3.0-4.0 "strong;" 2.51-3.0 "good;" 2.0-2.5 "adequate;" 1.0-1.99 "marginal;" and 0.0-0.99 "not sufficient for doctoral education." Programs also ranked by "effectiveness of program in educating research scholars/scientists." **Number listed:** 168.
1. University of California, Berkeley, with a quality rating of 4.96
2. California Institute of Technology, 4.94
3. Harvard University, 4.87
3. Stanford University, 4.87
5. Massachusetts Institute of Technology, 4.86
6. Cornell University, 4.55
7. Columbia University, 4.54
8. University of Illinois, Urbana-Champaign, 4.48
9. University of Wisconsin, Madison, 4.46
9. University of Chicago, 4.46
9. University of California, Los Angeles, 4.46
12. Yale University, 4.38
13. University of Texas, Austin, 4.28
14. Northwestern University, 4.23
15. Texas A&M University, 4.11

Source: "Rankings of Research-Doctorate Programs in 41 Disciplines at 274 Institutions," *The Chronicle of Higher Education* 42: A21-A30 (September 21, 1995).

★806★
Top recruiters for chemistry jobs for 2000-01 master's degree recipients

Ranking basis/background: Projected number of college hires from on-campus recruitment for 2000-01. **Remarks:** Numbers reflect total expected hires, not just African American projected hires. **Number listed:** 5.
1. Lucent Technologies, 20
2. Accenture, 5
2. Agilent Technologies, 5
4. Houghton Mifflin, 2
4. Novant Health, 2

Source: "The Top 100 Employers and the Majors in Demand for the Class of 2001," *The Black Collegian*, 31: 19-35, (February 2001).

★807★
United Kingdom universities with the greatest impact in chemistry, 1993-97

Ranking basis/background: For each university, total number of citations divided by number of published articles during the same time period. **Remarks:** Original source: *National Science Indicators on Diskette, 1981-97* **Number listed:** 5.
1. University of Cambridge, with 6.06 citations per paper; 2,298 total papers
2. University of Sussex, 5.50; 738
3. University of Birmingham, 5.44; 654
4. University of Oxford, 5.16; 1,691
5. Birkbeck College, 4.66; 276

Source: "United Kingdom: High-Impact Universities in Chemistry, 1993-97," *What's Hot*, September 28, 1998.

CHEMISTRY PERIODICALS

★808★
Chemistry journals by citation impact, 1981-99

Ranking basis/background: Impact factor calculated by taking the number of current citations to source items published and dividing it by the number of articles published in the journal during that time period. **Number listed:** 10.
1. *Chemical Reviews*, with a 95.79 impact factor
2. *Accounts of Chemical Research*, 64.42
3. *Journal of the American Chemical Society*, 32.31
4. *Chemical Society Reviews*, 29.64
5. *Journal of Computational Chemistry*, 26.03
6. *Topics in Current Chemistry*, 25.87
7. *Angewandte Chemie International Edition*, 22.84
8. *Journal of the Chemical Society-Chemical Communications*, 17.05
9. *Reviews of Chemical Intermediates*, 15.90
10. *Nouveau Journal de Chemie*, 14.96

Source: "Journals Ranked by Impact: Chemistry (general)," *What's Hot in Research* (http://www.isinet.com/isi/hot/research) Institute for Scientific Information.

★809★
Chemistry journals by citation impact, 1995-99

Ranking basis/background: Impact factor calculated by taking the number of current citations to source items published and dividing it by the number of articles published in the journal during that time period. **Number listed:** 10.
1. *Chemical Reviews*, with a 40.73 impact factor
2. *Accounts of Chemical Research*, 22.47
3. *Journal of the American Chemical Society*, 11.72
4. *Journal of the Chemical Society-Chemical Communications*, 11.48
5. *Angewandte Chemie International Edition*, 10.53
6. *Chemical Society Reviews*, 9.43
7. *Reviews in Computational Chemistry*, 7.64
8. *Chemistry: A European Journal*, 6.95
9. *Chemical Research in Toxicology*, 6.57
10. *Liebigs Annalen der Chemie*, 6.50

Source: "Journals Ranked by Impact: Chemistry (general)," *What's Hot in Research* (http://www.isinet.com/isi/hot/research) Institute for Scientific Information.

★810★
Chemistry journals by citation impact, 1999

Ranking basis/background: Impact factor calculated by taking the number of current citations to source items published and dividing it by the number of articles published in the journal during that time period. **Number listed:** 10.
1. *Chemical Reviews*, with a 21.24 impact factor
2. *Accounts of Chemical Research*, 11.80
3. *Journal of Physical Chemistry*, 9.89
4. *Chemical Society Reviews*, 8.80
5. *Angewandte Chemie International Edition*, 8.00
6. *Journal of the American Chemical Society*, 5.54
7. *Chemistry: A European Journal*, 4.81
8. *Topics in Current Chemistry*, 4.15
9. *Chemical Communications*, 3.48
10. *Chemical Research in Toxicology*, 3.47

Source: "Journals Ranked by Impact: Chemistry (general)," *What's Hot in Research* (http://www.isinet.com/isi/hot/research) Institute for Scientific Information.

★811★
Inorganic and nuclear chemistry journals by citation impact, 1981-99

Ranking basis/background: Impact factor calculated by taking the number of current citations to source items published and dividing it by the number of articles published in the journal during that time period. **Number listed:** 10.
1. *Progress in Inorganic Chemistry*, with a 88.60 impact factor
2. *Advances in Organometallic Chemistry*, 76.76
3. *Progress in Solid State Chemistry*, 47.97
4. *Structure & Bonding*, 46.69
5. *Advances in Inorganic Chemistry*, 40.85
6. *Coordination Chemistry Reviews*, 22.10
7. *Inorganic Chemistry*, 16.73
8. *Organometallics*, 16.51
9. *Inorganica Chimica Acta*, 12.79
10. *Metal Ions/Biological Systems*, 12.51

Source: "Journals Ranked by Impact: Inorganic & Nuclear Chemistry," *What's Hot in Research* (http://www.isinet.com/isi/hot/research) Institute for Scientific Information, January 15, 2001.

★812★
Inorganic and nuclear chemistry journals by citation impact, 1995-99

Ranking basis/background: Impact factor calculated by taking the number of current citations to source items published and dividing it by the number of articles published in the journal during that time period. **Number listed:** 10.
1. *Progress in Inorganic Chemistry*, with a 27.07 impact factor
2. *Advances in Organometallic Chemistry*, 15.82
3. *Progress in Solid State Chemistry*, 11.20
4. *Stucture & Bonding*, 10.00
5. *Organometallics*, 6.58
6. *Metal Ions/Biological Systems*, 6.49
7. *Inorganic Chemistry*, 6.08
8. *Tetrahedron-Asymmetry*, 4.87
9. *Journal of Biology and Inorganic Chemistry*, 4.64
10. *Journal Chemical Society (London)-Dalton Transactions*, 4.56

Source: "Journals Ranked by Impact: Inorganic & Nuclear Chemistry," *What's Hot in Research* (http://www.isinet.com/isi/hot/research) Institute for Scientific Information, January 15, 2001.

★813★
Inorganic and nuclear chemistry journals by citation impact, 1999

Ranking basis/background: Impact factor calculated by taking the number of current citations to source items published and dividing it by the number of articles published in the journal during that time period. **Number listed:** 10.

1. *Advances in Organometallic Chemistry*, with a 10.10 impact factor
2. *Progress in Inorganic Chemistry*, 8.48
3. *Progress in Solid State Chemistry*, 6.29
4. *Stucture & Bonding*, 5.33
5. *Advances in Inorganic Chemistry*, 4.86
6. *Journal of Biology and Inorganic Chemistry*, 4.46
7. *Metal Ions/Biological Systems*, 3.70
8. *Organometallics*, 3.22
9. *Inorganic Chemistry*, 2.84
10. *Tetrahedron-Asymmetry*, 2.65

Source: "Journals Ranked by Impact: Inorganic & Nuclear Chemistry," *What's Hot in Research* (http://www.isinet.com/isi/hot/research) *Institute for Scientific Information*, January 15, 2001.

CIVIL ENGINEERING
See: **Engineering–Civil Engineering, Graduate–Civil**

CIVIL RIGHTS–FEDERAL AID

★814★
Proposed fiscal 2002 appropriations for civil rights

Ranking basis/background: Based on the U.S. government's proposed fiscal 2002 appropriations for civil rights. **Number listed:** 2.
   Equal Employment Opportunity Commission, with $310,406,000
   Commission on Civil Rights, $0,096,000
Source: "Bush's Fiscal 2002 Budget Plan for Higher Education and Science," *The Chronicle of Higher Education*, 47: A36-A37, (April 20, 2001).

CLASSICAL STUDIES, GRADUATE

★815★
Most effective classics research-doctorate programs as evaluated by the National Research Council

Ranking basis/background: From a survey of nearly 8,000 faculty members conducted in the spring of 1993. Respondents were asked to rate programs in their field on "effectiveness of program in educating research scholars/scientists." **Remarks:** See *Chronicle* article for more details. Scores of 3.5-5.0 indicate "extremely effective;" 2.5-3.49 "reasonably effective;" 1.5-2.49 "minimally effective;" and 0.0-1.49 "not effective." Programs also ranked by "scholarly quality of program faculty." **Number listed:** 29.
1. University of California, Berkeley, with an effectiveness rating of 4.41
2. University of Michigan, 4.26
3. Princeton University, 4.15
4. Harvard University, 3.86
5. University of North Carolina, Chapel Hill, 3.57
6. Yale University, 3.52
7. Bryn Mawr College, 3.48
8. Brown University, 3.46
9. University of Texas, Austin, 3.40
10. Cornell University, 3.38

Source: "Rankings of Research-Doctorate Programs in 41 Disciplines at 274 Institutions," *The Chronicle of Higher Education* 42: A21-A30 (September 21, 1995).

★816★
Top classics research-doctorate programs as evaluated by the National Research Council

Ranking basis/background: From a survey of nearly 8,000 faculty members conducted in the spring of 1993. Respondents were asked to rate programs in their field on "scholarly quality of program faculty." When more than one program had the samescore, the council averaged the rank order and gave each program the same rank number (if three programs tied for the top position, each received a rank of 2). **Remarks:** See *Chronicle* article for more details. Scores of 4.01 and above indicate "distinguished;" 3.0-4.0 "strong;" 2.51-3.0 "good;" 2.0-2.5 "adequate;" 1.0-1.99 "marginal;" and 0.0-0.99 "not sufficient for doctoral education." Programs also ranked by "effectiveness of program in educating research scholars/scientists." **Number listed:** 29.
1. Harvard University, with a quality rating of 4.79
2. University of California, Berkeley, 4.77
3. University of Michigan, 4.54
4. Princeton University, 4.16
5. Yale University, 4.12
6. Brown University, 4.10
7. University of Chicago, 4.00
8. University of Texas, Austin, 3.92
9. University of California, Los Angeles, 3.89
10. Columbia University, 3.86
11. University of North Carolina, Chapel Hill, 3.81
12. Cornell University, 3.73
13. University of Pennsylvania, 3.62
14. Bryn Mawr College, 3.48
15. Duke University, 3.37

Source: "Rankings of Research-Doctorate Programs in 41 Disciplines at 274 Institutions," *The Chronicle of Higher Education* 42: A21-A30 (September 21, 1995).

COLLEGE ADMINISTRATION

★817★
Characteristics of college and university presidents, 1998

Ranking basis/background: Percent of presidents in each characteristic. **Remarks:** Original source: American Council on Education. **Number listed:** 4.
   Women, with 19.3%
   Minority, 11.3%
   Currently married, 83.8%
   Had doctoral degree, 80.7%
Source: Lively, Kit, "Diversity Increases Among Presidents," *The Chronicle of Higher Education*, 47: A31, A34, (September 15, 2000).

★818★
Comparison percentages of minority presidents at private baccalaureate-granting institutions

Ranking basis/background: Percentage of minority presidents during 1998 as compared to 1986. **Remarks:** Original source: American Council on Education. **Number listed:** 2.
   1998, with 7.9%
   1986, 5.9%
Source: Lively, Kit, "Diversity Increases Among Presidents," *The Chronicle of Higher Education*, 47: A31, A34, (September 15, 2000).

★819★
Comparison percentages of minority presidents at private doctorate-granting institutions

Ranking basis/background: Percentage of minority presidents during 1998 as compared to 1986. **Remarks:** Original source: American Council on Education. **Number listed:** 2.
   1998, with 4.1%
   1986, 1.4%
Source: Lively, Kit, "Diversity Increases Among Presidents," *The Chronicle of Higher Education*, 47: A31, A34, (September 15, 2000).

★820★
Comparison percentages of minority presidents at private master's-granting institutions

Ranking basis/background: Percentage of minority presidents during 1998 as compared to 1986. **Remarks:** Original source: American Council on Education. **Number listed:** 2.
   1998, with 1.9%
   1986, 6.8%
Source: Lively, Kit, "Diversity Increases Among Presidents," *The Chronicle of Higher Education*, 47: A31, A34, (September 15, 2000).

★821★
Comparison percentages of minority presidents at private specialized institutions

Ranking basis/background: Percentage of minority presidents during 1998 as compared to 1986. **Remarks:** Original source: American Council on Education. **Number listed:** 2.
   1998, with 7.2%
   1986, 5.7%
Source: Lively, Kit, "Diversity Increases Among Presidents," *The Chronicle of Higher Education*, 47: A31, A34, (September 15, 2000).

★822★
Comparison percentages of minority presidents at private two-year institutions

Ranking basis/background: Percentage of minority presidents during 1998 as compared to 1986. **Remarks:** Original source: American Council on Education. **Number listed:** 2.
   1998, with 3.7%
   1986, 11.3%
Source: Lively, Kit, "Diversity Increases Among Presidents," *The Chronicle of Higher Education*, 47: A31, A34, (September 15, 2000).

★823★
Comparison percentages of minority presidents at public baccalaureate-granting institutions

Ranking basis/background: Percentage of minority presidents during 1998 as compared to 1986. **Remarks:** Original source: American Council on Education. **Number listed:** 2.
   1998, with 25.0%
   1986, 11.5%

COLLEGE ADMINISTRATION

Source: Lively, Kit, "Diversity Increases Among Presidents," *The Chronicle of Higher Education*, 47: A31, A34, (September 15, 2000).

★824★
Comparison percentages of minority presidents at public doctorate-granting institutions

Ranking basis/background: Percentage of minority presidents during 1998 as compared to 1986. **Remarks:** Original source: American Council on Education. **Number listed:** 2.
  1998, with 8.7%
  1986, 2.8%

Source: Lively, Kit, "Diversity Increases Among Presidents," *The Chronicle of Higher Education*, 47: A31, A34, (September 15, 2000).

★825★
Comparison percentages of minority presidents at public master's-granting institutions

Ranking basis/background: Percentage of minority presidents during 1998 as compared to 1986. **Remarks:** Original source: American Council on Education. **Number listed:** 2.
  1998, with 25.6%
  1986, 17.3%

Source: Lively, Kit, "Diversity Increases Among Presidents," *The Chronicle of Higher Education*, 47: A31, A34, (September 15, 2000).

★826★
Comparison percentages of minority presidents at public specialized institutions

Ranking basis/background: Percentage of minority presidents during 1998 as compared to 1986. **Remarks:** Original source: American Council on Education. **Number listed:** 2.
  1998, with 19.2%
  1986, 2.4%

Source: Lively, Kit, "Diversity Increases Among Presidents," *The Chronicle of Higher Education*, 47: A31, A34, (September 15, 2000).

★827★
Comparison percentages of minority presidents at public two-year institutions

Ranking basis/background: Percentage of minority presidents during 1998 as compared to 1986. **Remarks:** Original source: American Council on Education. **Number listed:** 2.
  1998, with 13.1%
  1986, 8.1%

Source: Lively, Kit, "Diversity Increases Among Presidents," *The Chronicle of Higher Education*, 47: A31, A34, (September 15, 2000).

★828★
Comparison percentages of women presidents at private baccalaureate-granting institutions

Ranking basis/background: Percentage of women presidents during 1998 as compared to 1986. **Remarks:** Original source: American Council on Education. **Number listed:** 2.
  1998, with 20.0%
  1986, 16.6%

Source: Lively, Kit, "Diversity Increases Among Presidents," *The Chronicle of Higher Education*, 47: A31, A34, (September 15, 2000).

★829★
Comparison percentages of women presidents at private doctorate-granting institutions

Ranking basis/background: Percentage of women presidents during 1998 as compared to 1986. **Remarks:** Original source: American Council on Education. **Number listed:** 2.
  1998, with 9.5%
  1986, 2.9%

Source: Lively, Kit, "Diversity Increases Among Presidents," *The Chronicle of Higher Education*, 47: A31, A34, (September 15, 2000).

★830★
Comparison percentages of women presidents at private master's-granting institutions

Ranking basis/background: Percentage of women presidents during 1998 as compared to 1986. **Remarks:** Original source: American Council on Education. **Number listed:** 2.
  1998, with 19.7%
  1986, 12.4%

Source: Lively, Kit, "Diversity Increases Among Presidents," *The Chronicle of Higher Education*, 47: A31, A34, (September 15, 2000).

★831★
Comparison percentages of women presidents at private specialized institutions

Ranking basis/background: Percentage of women presidents during 1998 as compared to 1986. **Remarks:** Original source: American Council on Education. **Number listed:** 2.
  1998, with 14.8%
  1986, 7.0%

Source: Lively, Kit, "Diversity Increases Among Presidents," *The Chronicle of Higher Education*, 47: A31, A34, (September 15, 2000).

★832★
Comparison percentages of women presidents at private two-year institutions

Ranking basis/background: Percentage of women presidents during 1998 as compared to 1986. **Remarks:** Original source: American Council on Education. **Number listed:** 2.
  1998, with 25.0%
  1986, 21.8%

Source: Lively, Kit, "Diversity Increases Among Presidents," *The Chronicle of Higher Education*, 47: A31, A34, (September 15, 2000).

★833★
Comparison percentages of women presidents at public baccalaureate-granting institutions

Ranking basis/background: Percentage of women presidents during 1998 as compared to 1986. **Remarks:** Original source: American Council on Education. **Number listed:** 2.
  1998, with 23.4%
  1986, 8.6%

Source: Lively, Kit, "Diversity Increases Among Presidents," *The Chronicle of Higher Education*, 47: A31, A34, (September 15, 2000).

★834★
Comparison percentages of women presidents at public doctorate-granting institutions

Ranking basis/background: Percentage of women presidents during 1998 as compared to 1986. **Remarks:** Original source: American Council on Education. **Number listed:** 2.
  1998, with 15.2%
  1986, 4.3%

Source: Lively, Kit, "Diversity Increases Among Presidents," *The Chronicle of Higher Education*, 47: A31, A34, (September 15, 2000).

★835★
Comparison percentages of women presidents at public master's-granting institutions

Ranking basis/background: Percentage of women presidents during 1998 as compared to 1986. **Remarks:** Original source: American Council on Education. **Number listed:** 2.
  1998, with 17.8%
  1986, 8.2%

Source: Lively, Kit, "Diversity Increases Among Presidents," *The Chronicle of Higher Education*, 47: A31, A34, (September 15, 2000).

★836★
Comparison percentages of women presidents at public specialized institutions

Ranking basis/background: Percentage of women presidents during 1998 as compared to 1986. **Remarks:** Original source: American Council on Education. **Number listed:** 2.
  1998, with 14.9%
  1986, 4.8%

Source: Lively, Kit, "Diversity Increases Among Presidents," *The Chronicle of Higher Education*, 47: A31, A34, (September 15, 2000).

★837★
Comparison percentages of women presidents at public two-year institutions

Ranking basis/background: Percentage of women presidents during 1998 as compared to 1986. **Remarks:** Original source: American Council on Education. **Number listed:** 2.
  1998, with 22.1%
  1986, 5.8%

Source: Lively, Kit, "Diversity Increases Among Presidents," *The Chronicle of Higher Education*, 47: A31, A34, (September 15, 2000).

★838★
Top challenges for college and university administrators

Ranking basis/background: Educational facilities and business issues affecting college and university administrators. **Number listed:** 10.

1. Construction and repair
2. Funding
3. Housing
4. Incorporating auxiliary services
5. Improving the learning environment
6. Maintenance and operations
7. Marketing and recruiting
8. Security and safety
9. Staff training and retention
10. Technology

Source: Kennedy, Mike, "The Top Ten Issues Impacting College Administrators," *American School & University*, 73: 24-28, (January 2001).

★839★
Top fields of study for college and university presidents, 1998

Ranking basis/background: Percent of presidents in with a background in each field of study. **Remarks:** Original source: American Council on Education. **Number listed:** 3.
- Education, with 39.9%
- Humanities, 13.5%
- Social sciences, 12.4%

Source: Lively, Kit, "Diversity Increases Among Presidents," *The Chronicle of Higher Education*, 47: A31, A34, (September 15, 2000).

Related Information

★840★
Sontz, Ann H. L., *The American College President, 1639-1989: A Critical Review and Bibliography*, Greenwood Press, 1991.
Remarks: A bibliography that includes material on colonial and 19th century academic presidents and literature written by academic administrators since the early 1960s. Contains biographical and autobiographical material on the American college president and explores educational history insofar as it contains insights that are relevant to an understanding of the academic presidency.

COLLEGE ADMINISTRATION, MINORITY

★841★
African American administrators at institutions of higher education, 1995

Ranking basis/background: Number of men and women African American administrators in 1995, percent of total administrators, and percent change from 1985 to 1995. **Remarks:** Original source: American Council on Education. **Number listed:** 2.
- Men, with 5,835 African American administrators; 7.4% of total; a 16.6% change from '85-'95
- Women, 6,822; 11.1%; 65.5%

Source: Weige, Pamela R., "As Latino Populations Grow.," *Black Issues in Higher Education*, 17: 20-25, (September 28, 2000).

★842★
Hispanic American administrators at institutions of higher education, 1995

Ranking basis/background: Number of men and women Hispanic American administrators in 1995, percent of total administrators, and percent change from 1985 to 1995. **Remarks:** Original source: American Council on Education. **Number listed:** 2.
- Men, with 1,966 Hispanic American administrators; 2.5% of total; a 26.6% change from '85-'95
- Women, 1,829; 3.0%; 115.7%

Source: Weige, Pamela R., "As Latino Populations Grow.," *Black Issues in Higher Education*, 17: 20-25, (September 28, 2000).

COLLEGE ADMISSION

★843★
Best ways to save for college

Ranking basis/background: *Parents* suggestions for best ways to start saving for a higher education. **Number listed:** 7.
1. Custodial accounts
2. Section 529 Plans
3. Prepaid college tuition plans
4. Education IRAs
5. Roth IRAs
6. Tax-deferred retirement plans
7. U.S. Government Savings Bonds

Source: Greer, Rebecca E., "7 Smart Ways to Save for College," *Parents*, 75: 165-170, (October 2000).

★844★
Comparison of acceptance rates at the top 5 liberal arts colleges in the U.S., 1990 and 2001

Ranking basis/background: Percentage of applicants accepted in 1990 and 2001. **Remarks:** Original source: Higher Education Research Institute, UCLA. **Number listed:** 5.
1. Amherst College, with 20% accepted in 1990; 19% accepted in 2001
2. Swarthmore College, 32%; 23%
3. Williams College, 28%; 24%
4. Pomona College, 36%; 29%
5. Wellesley College, 49%; 43%

Source: "Slimmer Chances for Thick Envelopes," *U.S. News & World Report*, 130: 16, (April 23, 2001).

★845★
Comparison of acceptance rates at the top 5 national universities in the U.S., 1990 and 2001

Ranking basis/background: Percentage of applicants accepted in 1990 and 2001. **Remarks:** Original source: Higher Education Research Institute, UCLA. **Number listed:** 5.
1. Harvard University, with 18% accepted in 1990; 11% accepted in 2001
2. Princeton University, 17%; 12%
3. Yale University, 20%; 14%
4. California Institute of Technology, 30%; 15%
5. Massachusetts Institute of Technology, 32%; 16%

Source: "Slimmer Chances for Thick Envelopes," *U.S. News & World Report*, 130: 16, (April 23, 2001).

COLLEGE ADMISSION–TESTS
See: **College Entrance Examinations**

COLLEGE BOOKSTORES

★846★
Contractors managing the most college bookstores, 1999

Ranking basis/background: Number of college bookstores managed. **Remarks:** Original source: National Association of College Bookstores. **Number listed:** 4.
1. Follett College Stores, with 585
2. Barnes & Noble College Bookstores, 332
3. Wallace's Bookstores, 75
4. College Bookstores of America, 74

Source: Pulley, John L., "Whose Bookstore Is It, Anyway?," *The Chronicle of Higher Education*, 46: A41-A42, (February 4, 2000).

COLLEGE CHOICE

★847★
Top college choices for Washington D.C. students

Ranking basis/background: According to the D.C. Tuition Assistance Grant Program. **Number listed:** 10.
1. Howard University
2. University of Maryland
3. Virginia State University
4. Norfolk State University
5. Montgomery College
6. Prince George's Community College
7. Morgan State University
8. Hampton University
9. Bowie State University
10. University of Maryland

Source: "Florida, Michigan, California Colleges Have Yet to Agree to D.C. Tuition Plan," *Black Issues in Higher Education*, 17: 9, (September 28, 2000).

COLLEGE ENROLLMENT
See also: **American Indians–Enrollment, College Blacks–Enrollment, College College Students Disabilities–Enrollment of Students Foreign Students–Enrollment, College Hispanic Americans–Enrollment, College Minority Groups–Enrollment, College**

★848★
College enrollment figures projected for men from 2002-2008, by status

Ranking basis/background: Based on data analysis conducted by the U.S. Department of Education. **Remarks:** Article contains projections on college enrollment, degree achievement, and high-school graduates. **Number listed:** 9.
- 2002, with 3,882,000 full-time; 2,636,000 part-time
- 2003, 3,925,000; 2,644,000
- 2004, 3,968,000; 2,660,000
- 2005, 4,010,000; 2,674,000
- 2006, 4,060,000; 2,688,000
- 2007, 4,114,000; 2,705,000
- 2008, 4,182,000; 2,724,000

COLLEGE ENROLLMENT

Source: *Projections of Education Statistics to 2008,* NCES 98-016, U.S. Department of Education, National Center for Education Statistics (June 1998).

★849★
College enrollment figures projected for the year 2002-2008, by status

Ranking basis/background: Based on data analysis conducted by the U.S. Department of Education. **Remarks:** Article contains projections on college enrollment, degree achievement, and high-school graduates. **Number listed:** 9.

   2002, with 8,696,000 full-time; 6,358,000 part-time
   2003, 8,813,000; 6,372,000
   2004, 8,946,000; 6,403,000
   2005, 9,085,000; 6,432,000
   2006, 9,243,000; 6,460,000
   2007, 9,391,000; 6,489,000
   2008, 9,562,000; 6,520,000

Source: *Projections of Education Statistics to 2008,* NCES 98-016, U.S. Department of Education, National Center for Education Statistics (June 1998).

★850★
College enrollment figures projected for the year 2002-2008, by type of institution

Ranking basis/background: Based on data analysis conducted by the U.S. Department of Education. **Remarks:** Article contains projections on college enrollment, degree achievement, and high-school graduates. **Number listed:** 9.

   2002, with 11,751,000 public; 3,303,000 private
   2003, 11,849,000; 3,335,000
   2004, 11,975,000; 3,374,000
   2005, 12,101,000; 3,415,000
   2006, 12,242,000; 3,461,000
   2007, 12,378,000; 3,502,000
   2008, 12,534,000; 3,549,000

Source: *Projections of Education Statistics to 2008,* NCES 98-016, U.S. Department of Education, National Center for Education Statistics (June 1998).

★851★
College enrollment figures projected for women from 2002-2008, by status

Ranking basis/background: Based on data analysis conducted by the U.S. Department of Education. **Remarks:** Article contains projections on college enrollment, degree achievement, and high-school graduates. **Number listed:** 9.

   2002, with 4,814,000 full-time; 3,722,000 part-time
   2003, 4,888,000; 3,728,000
   2004, 4,978,000; 3,743,000
   2005, 5,075,000; 3,758,000
   2006, 5,183,000; 3,771,000
   2007, 5,277,000; 3,784,000
   2008, 5,380,000; 3,797,000

Source: *Projections of Education Statistics to 2008,* NCES 98-016, U.S. Department of Education, National Center for Education Statistics (June 1998).

★852★
Community colleges in North America with the highest enrollment

Ranking basis/background: Number of students. **Remarks:** Original source: Statistics Canada, Universities: Enrollment and Degrees; U.S. Department of Education, Directory of Postsecondary Institutions. **Number listed:** 20.

1. Miami-Dade Community College, with 47,060 students
2. Houston Community College System, 39,541
3. Northern Virginia Community College, 37,144
4. College of Du Page (Glen Ellyn, IL), 29,888
5. Pima Community College, 27,866
6. Portland Community College, 26,540
7. City College of San Francisco, 26,019
8. Tarrant County Junior College (Ft. Worth), 25,953
9. Oakland Community College (MI), 25,913
10. Broward Community College, 25,738

Source: Savageau, David, *Places Rated Almanac,* Macmillan General Reference, 6th ed., 1999.

★853★
First-professional college enrollment figures projected for the years 2002-2008, by type of institution

Ranking basis/background: Based on data analysis conducted by the U.S. Department of Education. **Remarks:** Article contains projections on college enrollment, degree achievement, and high-school graduates. **Number listed:** 9.

   2002, with 104,000 public students; 164,000 private students
   2003, 105,000; 166,000
   2004, 106,000; 168,000
   2005, 108,000; 170,000
   2006, 109,000; 172,000
   2007, 110,000; 173,000
   2008, 111,000; 175,000

Source: *Projections of Education Statistics to 2008,* NCES 98-016, U.S. Department of Education, National Center for Education Statistics (June 1998).

★854★
Four-year college enrollment figures projected for the years 2002-2008, by type of institution

Ranking basis/background: Based on data analysis conducted by the U.S. Department of Education. **Remarks:** Article contains projections on college enrollment, degree achievement, and high-school graduates. **Number listed:** 9.

   2002, with 6,198,000 public students; 3,061,000 private students
   2003, 6,262,000; 3,092,000
   2004, 6,335,000; 3,127,000
   2005, 6,413,000; 3,165,000
   2006, 6,500,000; 3,207,000
   2007, 6,580,000; 3,246,000
   2008, 6,670,000; 3,288,000

Source: *Projections of Education Statistics to 2008,* NCES 98-016, U.S. Department of Education, National Center for Education Statistics (June 1998).

★855★
Four-year public institutions enrolling the highest number of students from the District of Columbia, 1998-99

Ranking basis/background: Four-year public institution with the most District of Columbia residents enrolled. Table also includes difference between in-state and out-of-state tuition. **Remarks:** Original source: District of Columbia Tuition Assistance Grant Program; Chronicle Reporting. **Number listed:** 12.

1. Delaware State University
2. Temple University
3. Bowie State University
4. University of Maryland, College Park
5. University of Virginia
6. Morgan State University
7. Florida A&M University
8. University of Maryland, Eastern Shore
9. University of Maryland, University College
10. University of Pittsburgh
11. University of Wisconsin, Madison
12. University of Michigan, Ann Arbor

Source: Hebel, Sara, "D.C. Students Are No Longer 'Out of State' Everywhere," *The Chronicle of Higher Education,* 46: A26-A27, A30, (July 14, 2000).

★856★
Full-time equivalent college enrollment figures projected for the years 2002-2008, by type of institution

Ranking basis/background: Full-time enrollment plus the full-time equivalent of part-time enrollment as reported by institutions. Based on data analysis conducted by the U.S. Department of Education. **Remarks:** Article contains projections on college enrollment, degree achievement, and high-school graduates. **Number listed:** 9.

   2002, with 8,285,000 public students; 2,701,000 private students
   2003, 8,375,000; 2,733,000
   2004, 8,483,000; 2,770,000
   2005, 8,593,000; 2,809,000
   2006, 8,718,000; 2,852,000
   2007, 8,836,000; 2,892,000
   2008, 8,974,000; 2,937,000

Source: *Projections of Education Statistics to 2008,* NCES 98-016, U.S. Department of Education, National Center for Education Statistics (June 1998).

★857★
Graduate college enrollment figures projected for the years 2002-2008, by type of institution

Ranking basis/background: Based on data analysis conducted by the U.S. Department of Education. **Remarks:** Article contains projections on college enrollment, degree achievement, and high-school graduates. **Number listed:** 9.

   2002, with 1,065,000 public students; 633,000 private students
   2003, 1,068,000; 635,000
   2004, 1,076,000; 639,000
   2005, 1,084,000; 644,000
   2006, 1,090,000; 648,000
   2007, 1,095,000; 651,000
   2008, 1,098,000; 653,000

Source: *Projections of Education Statistics to 2008,* NCES 98-016, U.S. Department of Education, National Center for Education Statistics (June 1998).

★858★
Percentage of enrollment at private institutions of higher education, by country, 1998

Ranking basis/background: Percentage of students enrolled for each country. **Remarks:** Original source: OECD Education Database 2000. **Number listed:** 20.

- Japan, 73.9%
- South Korea, 75.7%
- Philippines, 75.2%
- Indonesia, 70.3%
- Brazil, 59.9%
- United States, 31.1%
- Hungary, 11.8%
- Spain, 10.5%
- France, 9.0%
- Malaysia, 7.1%

Source: Cohen, David, "The Worldwide Rise of Private Colleges," *The Chronicle of Higher Education*, 47: A47-A49, (March 9, 2001).

★859★
Percentage of enrollment at public institutions of higher education, by country, 1998

Ranking basis/background: Percentage of students enrolled for each country. **Remarks:** Original source: OECD Education Database 2000. **Number listed:** 20.

1. Australia, with 100.0%
1. Canada, 100.0%
1. Czech Republic, 100.0%
4. New Zealand, 99.4%
5. Turkey, 98.3%
6. Austria, 97.4%
7. Ireland, 94.1%
8. Malaysia, 92.9%
9. France, 91.0%
10. Spain, 89.5%

Source: Cohen, David, "The Worldwide Rise of Private Colleges," *The Chronicle of Higher Education*, 47: A47-A49, (March 9, 2001).

★860★
States with the highest enrollment in private 4-year institutions of higher education

Ranking basis/background: Enrollment figures for private 4-year colleges and universities. **Remarks:** Original source: U.S. Department of Education. **Number listed:** 10.

1. New York, with 347,451
2. California, 211,950
3. Massachusetts, 192,652
4. Pennsylvania, 184,500
5. Illinois, 144,885
6. Ohio, 98,733
7. Texas, 93,240
8. Florida, 86,936
9. Missouri, 78,664
10. Michigan, 67,643

Source: "The Top Ten," *American School & University*, 73: 38-41, (January 2001).

★861★
States with the highest enrollment in public 4-year institutions of higher education

Ranking basis/background: Enrollment figures for public 4-year colleges and universities. **Remarks:** Original source: U.S. Department of Education. **Number listed:** 10.

1. California, with 443,300
2. Texas, 336,871
3. New York, 260,085
4. Ohio, 218,092
5. Michigan, 211,724
6. Pennsylvania, 203,498
7. Florida, 167,565
8. Illinois, 160,767
9. Indiana, 149,174
10. Virginia, 142,893

Source: "The Top Ten," *American School & University*, 73: 38-41, (January 2001).

★862★
Two-year college enrollment figures projected for the years 2002-2008, by type of institution

Ranking basis/background: Based on data analysis conducted by the U.S. Department of Education. **Remarks:** Article contains projections on college enrollment, degree achievement, and high-school graduates. **Number listed:** 9.

- 2002, with 5,553,000 public students; 242,000 private students
- 2003, 5,587,000; 244,000
- 2004, 5,640,000; 247,000
- 2005, 5,688,000; 250,000
- 2006, 5,742,000; 253,000
- 2007, 5,798,000; 256,000
- 2008, 5,864,000; 260,000

Source: *Projections of Education Statistics to 2008*, NCES 98-016, U.S. Department of Education, National Center for Education Statistics (June 1998).

★863★
Undergraduate college enrollment figures projected for the years 2002-2008, by type of institution

Ranking basis/background: Based on data analysis conducted by the U.S. Department of Education. **Remarks:** Article contains projections on college enrollment, degree achievement, and high-school graduates. **Number listed:** 9.

- 2002, with 10,581,000 public students; 2,505,000 private students
- 2003, 10,676,000; 2,535,000
- 2004, 10,793,000; 2,567,000
- 2005, 10,910,000; 2,601,000
- 2006, 11,044,000; 2,641,000
- 2007, 11,173,000; 2,678,000
- 2008, 11,324,000; 2,721,000

Source: *Projections of Education Statistics to 2008*, NCES 98-016, U.S. Department of Education, National Center for Education Statistics (June 1998).

★864★
U.S. catholic universities with the highest enrollment, 1999

Ranking basis/background: Total enrollment for 1999. **Remarks:** Original source: DePaul University Enrollment Management Research. **Number listed:** 11.

1. DePaul University, with 19,570
2. St. John's University, 18,478
3. Boston College, 13,853
4. Fordham University, 13,551
5. Loyola University, Chicago, 13,358
6. Georgetown University, 12,498
7. St. Louis University, 11,069
8. Marquette University, 10,780
9. University of Notre Dame, 10,654
10. University of Dayton, 10,223
11. Villanova University, 9,900
12. Seton Hall University, 9,608

Source: Allen, Linn J. and Meg McSherry Breslin, "DePaul's Gamble Paying Off," *Chicago Tribune*, December 17, 2000, Section 4, pp. 1, 4.

COLLEGE ENROLLMENT–ILLINOIS

★865★
Fall enrollment at Chicago-area city colleges, by minority percentages, 1999

Ranking basis/background: Total enrollment for 1999 and percentage of minority enrollees. Minority includes those students who identified themselves as black, Native American, Asian or Hispanic. **Remarks:** Original source: Illinois Board of Higher Education. **Number listed:** 7.

- Richard J. Daley College, out of 9,800 enrolled; 79.9% are minorities
- Kennedy King College, 6,681; 97.5%
- Malcolm X College, 8,561; 91.9%
- Olive-Harvey College, 7,778; 98.0%
- Harry S. Truman College, 14,147; 69.8%
- Harold Washington College, 8,270; 77.3%
- Wilbur Wright College, 11,560; 59.1%

Source: "Education Market Facts," *Crain's Chicago Business*, 23: F28, F30, (July 3, 2000).

★866★
Fall enrollment at Chicago-area proprietary institutions, by minority percentages, 1999

Ranking basis/background: Total enrollment for 1999 and percentage of minority enrollees. Minority includes those students who identified themselves as black, Native American, Asian or Hispanic. **Remarks:** Original source: Illinois Board of Higher Education. **Number listed:** 2.

- DeVry Institute of Technology, Chicago, out of 4,007 enrolled; 67.6% are minorities
- DeVry Institute of Technology, DuPage, 4,131; 31.5%

Source: "Education Market Facts," *Crain's Chicago Business*, 23: F28, F30, (July 3, 2000).

★867★
Fall enrollment at Chicago-area public community colleges, by minority percentages, 1999

Ranking basis/background: Total enrollment for 1999 and percentage of minority enrollees. Minority includes those students who identified themselves as black, Native American, Asian or Hispanic. **Remarks:** Original source: Illinois Board of Higher Education. **Number listed:** 13.

- DuPage Community College, out of 29,032 enrolled; 22.3% are minorities
- Elgin Community College, 9,513; 5.0%
- Harper Community College, 14,817; 27.6%
- Joliet Community College, 10,858; 15.5%
- Lake County Community College, 14,036; 27.6%
- McHenry Community College, 5,108; 4.1%
- Moraine Valley Community College, 14,414; 13.7%
- Morton Community College, 4,632; 60.6%
- Oakton Community College, 9,925; 23.8%
- Prairie State Community College, 5,188; 36.1%
- South Suburban Community College, 7,254; 51.9%
- Triton Community College, 18,697; 39.7%

COLLEGE ENTRANCE EXAMINATIONS

Waubonsee Community College, 7,276; 32.2%

Source: "Education Market Facts," *Crain's Chicago Business*, 23: F28, F30, (July 3, 2000).

★868★
Fall enrollment at Chicago-area public universities, by minority percentages, 1999

Ranking basis/background: Total enrollment for 1999 and percentage of minority enrollees. Minority includes those students who identified themselves as black, Native American, Asian or Hispanic. **Remarks:** Original source: Illinois Board of Higher Education. **Number listed:** 4.

  Chicago State University, out of 7,580 enrolled; 89.8% are minorities
  Governors State University, 6,287; 33.3%
  Northeastern Illinois University, 10,937; 46.4%
  University of Illinois, Chicago, 24,669; 42.4%

Source: "Education Market Facts," *Crain's Chicago Business*, 23: F28, F30, (July 3, 2000).

★869★
Fall enrollment at the largest Chicago-area private institutions, by minority percentages, 1999

Ranking basis/background: Total enrollment for 1999 and percentage of minority enrollees. Minority includes those students who identified themselves as black, Native American, Asian or Hispanic. **Remarks:** Original source: Illinois Board of Higher Education. **Number listed:** 11.

  Columbia College, out of 8,848 enrolled; 36.1% are minorities
  DePaul University, 19,511; 27.8%
  Illinois Institute of Technology, 6,062; 24.8%
  Lewis University, 4,084; 24.1%
  Loyola University, Chicago, 13,359; 23.7%
  National-Louis University, 6,021; 27.6%
  Northwestern University, 17,121; 23.0%
  Roosevelt University, 6,908; 36.5%
  St. Xavier University, 4,071; 22.2%
  University of Chicago, 12,337; 22.2%
  University of St. Francis, 4,321; 4.8%

Source: "Education Market Facts," *Crain's Chicago Business*, 23: F28, F30, (July 3, 2000).

COLLEGE ENTRANCE EXAMINATIONS

★870★
ACT composite scores, by gender, 2000

Ranking basis/background: Average ACT scores and 1-year change percentages. **Remarks:** Original source: ACT. **Number listed:** 2.

  Men, with an average score of 21.2; and a 1-year change of 0.1%
  Women, 20.9; 0.0%

Source: "The Nation," *The Chronicle of Higher Education*, 47: 20, (September 1, 2000).

★871★
ACT composite scores, by race/ethnicity, 2000

Ranking basis/background: Average ACT scores and 1-year change percentages. **Remarks:** Original source: ACT. **Number listed:** 6.

  Native American, with an average score of 19.0; and a 1-year change of 0.1%
  Asian American, 21.7; 0.0%
  African American, 17.0; 0.1% decrease
  Hispanic American, 18.9; 0.0%
  White, 21.8; 0.1%
  Multiracial, 21.2; 0.0%

Source: "The Nation," *The Chronicle of Higher Education*, 47: 20, (September 1, 2000).

★872★
ACT score averages, 1995 to 2000

Ranking basis/background: National composite average ACT scores. **Remarks:** Original source: ACT. **Number listed:** 6.

  1995, with 20.8
  1996, 20.9
  1997, 21.0
  1998, 21.0
  1999, 21.0
  2000, 21.0

Source: "Education Vital Signs 2000," *American School Board Journal*, 187: 31-47, (December 2000).

★873★
Decreases in Mexican American SAT verbal scores from 1990 to 2000

Ranking basis/background: Average SAT verbal score comparison from 1990 to 2000. **Remarks:** Original source: The College Board. **Number listed:** 2.

  1990, with an average score of 457
  2000, 453

Source: Hurd, Hilary, "Poor Strategies Continue to Plague Black Test-Takers," *Black Issues in Higher Education*, 17: 8, (September 28, 2000).

★874★
Illinois high schools with the highest SAT scores

Ranking basis/background: Average overall ACT score. **Remarks:** Original source: Sun-Times research. **Number listed:** 11.

1. New Trier Township High School (Winnetka), with 26.0
2. Highland Park High School (Highland Park), 25.2
3. Deerfield High School (Deerfield), 25.1
3. Naperville North High School (Naperville), 25.1
5. Lake Forest High School (Lake Forest), 25.0
6. Glenbrook North High School (Northbrook), 24.9
7. Naperville Central High School (Naperville), 24.7
8. Adlai E. Stevenson High School (Lincolnshire), 24.6
8. Barrington High School (Barrington), 24.6
8. Libertyville High School (Libertyville), 24.6
8. Whitney Young High School (Chicago), 24.6

Source: "School Report Card 2000," *Chicago Sun-Times*, November 1, 2000, pp. 1R-22R.

★875★
Increases in African American SAT math scores from 1990 to 2000

Ranking basis/background: Average SAT math score comparison from 1990 to 2000. **Remarks:** Original source: The College Board. **Number listed:** 2.

  1990, with an average score of 419
  2000, 426

Source: Hurd, Hilary, "Poor Strategies Continue to Plague Black Test-Takers," *Black Issues in Higher Education*, 17: 8, (September 28, 2000).

★876★
Increases in African American SAT verbal scores from 1990 to 2000

Ranking basis/background: Average SAT verbal score comparison from 1990 to 2000. **Remarks:** Original source: The College Board. **Number listed:** 2.

  1990, with an average score of 428
  2000, 434

Source: Hurd, Hilary, "Poor Strategies Continue to Plague Black Test-Takers," *Black Issues in Higher Education*, 17: 8, (September 28, 2000).

★877★
Increases in Asian American SAT math scores from 1990 to 2000

Ranking basis/background: Average SAT math score comparison from 1990 to 2000. **Remarks:** Original source: The College Board. **Number listed:** 2.

  1990, with an average score of 546
  2000, 565

Source: Hurd, Hilary, "Poor Strategies Continue to Plague Black Test-Takers," *Black Issues in Higher Education*, 17: 8, (September 28, 2000).

★878★
Increases in Asian American SAT verbal scores from 1990 to 2000

Ranking basis/background: Average SAT verbal score comparison from 1990 to 2000. **Remarks:** Original source: The College Board. **Number listed:** 2.

  1990, with an average score of 483
  2000, 499

Source: Hurd, Hilary, "Poor Strategies Continue to Plague Black Test-Takers," *Black Issues in Higher Education*, 17: 8, (September 28, 2000).

★879★
Increases in Hispanic American SAT math scores from 1990 to 2000

Ranking basis/background: Average SAT math score comparison from 1990 to 2000. **Remarks:** Original source: The College Board. **Number listed:** 2.

  1990, with an average score of 464
  2000, 467

Source: Hurd, Hilary, "Poor Strategies Continue to Plague Black Test-Takers," *Black Issues in Higher Education*, 17: 8, (September 28, 2000).

★880★
Increases in Hispanic American SAT verbal scores from 1990 to 2000

Ranking basis/background: Average SAT verbal score comparison from 1990 to 2000. **Remarks:** Original source: The College Board. **Number listed:** 2.

  1990, with an average score of 459
  2000, 461

Source: Hurd, Hilary, "Poor Strategies Continue to Plague Black Test-Takers," *Black Issues in Higher Education*, 17: 8, (September 28, 2000).

★881★
Increases in Mexican American SAT math scores from 1990 to 2000

Ranking basis/background: Average SAT math score comparison from 1990 to 2000. **Remarks:** Original source: The College Board. **Number listed:** 2.
   1990, with an average score of 460
   2000, 460
Source: Hurd, Hilary, "Poor Strategies Continue to Plague Black Test-Takers," *Black Issues in Higher Education*, 17: 8, (September 28, 2000).

★882★
Increases in Native American SAT math scores from 1990 to 2000

Ranking basis/background: Average SAT math score comparison from 1990 to 2000. **Remarks:** Original source: The College Board. **Number listed:** 2.
   1990, with an average score of 468
   2000, 481
Source: Hurd, Hilary, "Poor Strategies Continue to Plague Black Test-Takers," *Black Issues in Higher Education*, 17: 8, (September 28, 2000).

★883★
Increases in Native American SAT verbal scores from 1990 to 2000

Ranking basis/background: Average SAT verbal score comparison from 1990 to 2000. **Remarks:** Original source: The College Board. **Number listed:** 2.
   1990, with an average score of 466
   2000, 482
Source: Hurd, Hilary, "Poor Strategies Continue to Plague Black Test-Takers," *Black Issues in Higher Education*, 17: 8, (September 28, 2000).

★884★
Increases in Puerto Rican SAT math scores from 1990 to 2000

Ranking basis/background: Average SAT math score comparison from 1990 to 2000. **Remarks:** Original source: The College Board. **Number listed:** 2.
   1990, with an average score of 437
   2000, 451
Source: Hurd, Hilary, "Poor Strategies Continue to Plague Black Test-Takers," *Black Issues in Higher Education*, 17: 8, (September 28, 2000).

★885★
Increases in Puerto Rican SAT verbal scores from 1990 to 2000

Ranking basis/background: Average SAT verbal score comparison from 1990 to 2000. **Remarks:** Original source: The College Board. **Number listed:** 2.
   1990, with an average score of 435
   2000, 456
Source: Hurd, Hilary, "Poor Strategies Continue to Plague Black Test-Takers," *Black Issues in Higher Education*, 17: 8, (September 28, 2000).

★886★
Increases in white American SAT math scores from 1990 to 2000

Ranking basis/background: Average SAT math score comparison from 1990 to 2000. **Remarks:** Original source: The College Board. **Number listed:** 2.
   1990, with an average score of 515
   2000, 530
Source: Hurd, Hilary, "Poor Strategies Continue to Plague Black Test-Takers," *Black Issues in Higher Education*, 17: 8, (September 28, 2000).

★887★
Increases in white American SAT verbal scores from 1990 to 2000

Ranking basis/background: Average SAT verbal score comparison from 1990 to 2000. **Remarks:** Original source: The College Board. **Number listed:** 2.
   1990, with an average score of 519
   2000, 528
Source: Hurd, Hilary, "Poor Strategies Continue to Plague Black Test-Takers," *Black Issues in Higher Education*, 17: 8, (September 28, 2000).

★888★
Math SAT scores, 1989 to 1999

Ranking basis/background: Average math SAT score. **Remarks:** Original source: The College Board. **Number listed:** 11.
   1989, with 502
   1990, 501
   1991, 500
   1992, 501
   1993, 503
   1994, 504
   1995, 506
   1996, 508
   1997, 511
   1998, 512
   1999, 511
Source: Carlson, Scott, "College Board Reports Little Change in Average SAT Scores," *The Chronicle of Higher Education*, 46: A56, (September 10, 1999).

★889★
Math SAT scores for African Americans, by gender, 2000

Ranking basis/background: Average verbal SAT score for men and women. **Remarks:** Original source: The College Board. **Number listed:** 2.
   Men, with 436
   Women, 419
Source: "Disparities & Gaps in America," *Black Issues in Higher Education*, 18: 28-29, (March 1, 2001).

★890★
Math SAT scores for Asian Americans, by gender, 2000

Ranking basis/background: Average verbal SAT score for men and women. **Remarks:** Original source: The College Board. **Number listed:** 2.
   Men, with 583
   Women, 548
Source: "Disparities & Gaps in America," *Black Issues in Higher Education*, 18: 28-29, (March 1, 2001).

★891★
Math SAT scores for Hispanic Americans, by gender, 2000

Ranking basis/background: Average verbal SAT score for men and women. **Remarks:** Original source: The College Board. **Number listed:** 3.
   Mexican American, with 480 for men; 445 for women
   Puerto Rican, 471; 437
   Latin, South & Central American, 489; 451
Source: "Disparities & Gaps in America," *Black Issues in Higher Education*, 18: 28-29, (March 1, 2001).

★892★
Math SAT scores for Native Americans, by gender, 2000

Ranking basis/background: Average verbal SAT score for men and women. **Remarks:** Original source: The College Board. **Number listed:** 2.
   Men, with 498
   Women, 467
Source: "Disparities & Gaps in America," *Black Issues in Higher Education*, 18: 28-29, (March 1, 2001).

★893★
Math SAT scores for white Americans, by gender, 2000

Ranking basis/background: Average verbal SAT score for men and women. **Remarks:** Original source: The College Board. **Number listed:** 2.
   Men, with 549
   Women, 514
Source: "Disparities & Gaps in America," *Black Issues in Higher Education*, 18: 28-29, (March 1, 2001).

★894★
Mean composite ACT scores by gender, 2000

Ranking basis/background: Mean composite ACT scores. **Remarks:** Original source: ACT Inc. **Number listed:** 2.
   Men, with 21.2
   Women, 20.9
Source: *The World Almanac and Book of Facts 2001*, World Almanac Books, 2001.

★895★
Mean composite ACT scores by state, 2000

Ranking basis/background: Mean composite ACT scores. **Remarks:** Original source: ACT Inc. **Number listed:** 51.
   Alabama, with 20.2
   Alaska, 21.3
   Arizona, 21.5
   Arkansas, 20.3
   California, 21.4
   Colorado, 21.5
   Connecticut, 21.3
   Delaware, 20.6
   District of Columbia, 17.8
   Florida, 20.6
   Georgia, 19.9
   Hawaii, 21.6
   Idaho, 21.4
   Illinois, 21.5
   Indiana, 21.4
   Iowa, 22.0
   Kansas, 21.6
   Kentucky, 20.1
   Louisiana, 19.6
   Maine, 21.9
   Maryland, 20.7
   Massachusetts, 21.9
   Michigan, 21.3
   Minnesota, 22.0
   Mississippi, 18.7
   Missouri, 21.6
   Montana, 21.8
   Nebraska, 21.7
   Nevada, 21.5

COLLEGE ENTRANCE EXAMINATIONS

New Hampshire, 22.5
New Jersey, 20.7
New Mexico, 20.1
New York, 22.2
North Carolina, 19.5
North Dakota, 21.4
Ohio, 21.4
Oklahoma, 20.8
Oregon, 22.7
Pennsylvania, 21.4
Rhode Island, 21.1
South Carolina, 19.3
South Dakota, 21.5
Tennessee, 20.0
Texas, 20.3
Utah, 21.5
Vermont, 22.2
Virginia, 20.5
Washington, 22.4
West Virginia, 20.2
Wisconsin, 22.2
Wyoming, 21.6

Source: *The World Almanac and Book of Facts 2001*, World Almanac Books, 2001.

★896★
Mean English ACT scores by gender, 2000

Ranking basis/background: Mean English ACT scores. **Remarks:** Original source: ACT Inc. **Number listed:** 2.
  Men, with 20.0
  Women, 20.9

Source: *The World Almanac and Book of Facts 2001*, World Almanac Books, 2001.

★897★
Mean math ACT scores by gender, 2000

Ranking basis/background: Mean math ACT scores. **Remarks:** Original source: ACT Inc. **Number listed:** 2.
  Men, with 21.4
  Women, 20.2

Source: *The World Almanac and Book of Facts 2001*, World Almanac Books, 2001.

★898★
Mean math SAT scores by gender, 2000

Ranking basis/background: Mean math SAT scores. **Remarks:** Original source: The College Board. **Number listed:** 2.
  Men, with 533
  Women, 498

Source: *The World Almanac and Book of Facts 2001*, World Almanac Books, 2001.

★899★
Mean math SAT scores by gender for selected years

Ranking basis/background: Mean math SAT scores. **Remarks:** Original source: The College Board. **Number listed:** 4.
  1970, with 531 for men; 493 for women; 512 overall
  1980, 515; 473; 492
  1990, 521; 483; 501
  2000, 533; 498; 514

Source: "Education Vital Signs 2000," *American School Board Journal*, 187: 31-47, (December 2000).

★900★
Mean math SAT scores by state, 2000

Ranking basis/background: Mean math SAT scores. **Remarks:** Original source: The College Board. **Number listed:** 51.
  Alabama, with 555
  Alaska, 515
  Arizona, 523
  Arkansas, 554
  California, 518
  Colorado, 537
  Connecticut, 509
  Delaware, 496
  District of Columbia, 486
  Florida, 500
  Georgia, 486
  Hawaii, 519
  Idaho, 541
  Illinois, 586
  Indiana, 501
  Iowa, 600
  Kansas, 580
  Kentucky, 550
  Louisiana, 558
  Maine, 500
  Maryland, 509
  Massachusetts, 513
  Michigan, 569
  Minnesota, 594
  Mississippi, 549
  Missouri, 577
  Montana, 546
  Nebraska, 571
  Nevada, 517
  New Hampshire, 519
  New Jersey, 513
  New Mexico, 543
  New York, 506
  North Carolina, 496
  North Dakota, 609
  Ohio, 539
  Oklahoma, 560
  Oregon, 527
  Pennsylvania, 497
  Rhode Island, 500
  South Carolina, 482
  South Dakota, 588
  Tennessee, 553
  Texas, 500
  Utah, 569
  Vermont, 508
  Virginia, 500
  Washington, 528
  West Virginia, 511
  Wisconsin, 597
  Wyoming, 545

Source: *The World Almanac and Book of Facts 2001*, World Almanac Books, 2001.

★901★
Mean verbal SAT scores by gender, 2000

Ranking basis/background: Mean verbal SAT scores. **Remarks:** Original source: The College Board. **Number listed:** 2.
  Men, with 507
  Women, 504

Source: *The World Almanac and Book of Facts 2001*, World Almanac Books, 2001.

★902★
Mean verbal SAT scores by gender for selected years

Ranking basis/background: Mean verbal SAT scores. **Remarks:** Original source: The College Board. **Number listed:** 4.
  1970, with 536 for men; 538 for women; 537 overall
  1980, 506; 498; 502
  1990, 505; 496; 500
  2000, 507; 502; 505

Source: "Education Vital Signs 2000," *American School Board Journal*, 187: 31-47, (December 2000).

★903★
Mean verbal SAT scores by state, 2000

Ranking basis/background: Mean verbal SAT scores. **Remarks:** Original source: The College Board. **Number listed:** 51.
  Alabama, with 559
  Alaska, 519
  Arizona, 521
  Arkansas, 563
  California, 497
  Colorado, 534
  Connecticut, 508
  Delaware, 502
  District of Columbia, 494
  Florida, 498
  Georgia, 488
  Hawaii, 488
  Idaho, 540
  Illinois, 568
  Indiana, 498
  Iowa, 589
  Kansas, 574
  Kentucky, 548
  Louisiana, 562
  Maine, 504
  Maryland, 507
  Massachusetts, 511
  Michigan, 557
  Minnesota, 581
  Mississippi, 562
  Missouri, 572
  Montana, 543
  Nebraska, 560
  Nevada, 510
  New Hampshire, 520
  New Jersey, 498
  New Mexico, 549
  New York, 494
  North Carolina, 492
  North Dakota, 588
  Ohio, 533
  Oklahoma, 563
  Oregon, 527
  Pennsylvania, 498
  Rhode Island, 505
  South Carolina, 484
  South Dakota, 587
  Tennessee, 563
  Texas, 493
  Utah, 570
  Vermont, 513
  Virginia, 509
  Washington, 526
  West Virginia, 526
  Wisconsin, 584
  Wyoming, 545

Source: *The World Almanac and Book of Facts 2001*, World Almanac Books, 2001.

★904★
Students granted extra time to take the SAT

Ranking basis/background: Comparison numbers for students allowed extra time to take the SAT, from 1993 through 2000. **Remarks:** Original source: College Board. **Number listed:** 8.
- 1993, with 12,259
- 1994, 14,994
- 1995, 16,163
- 1996, 19,046
- 1997, 21,618
- 1998, 23,318
- 1999, 24,016
- 2000, 25,570

Source: Marcus, David L., "Extra Credit: Passing the Test of Time," *U.S. News & World Report*, 130: 50, (March 5, 2001).

★905★
Verbal SAT scores, 1989 to 1999

Ranking basis/background: Average verbal SAT score. **Remarks:** Original source: The College Board. **Number listed:** 11.
- 1989, with 504
- 1990, 500
- 1991, 499
- 1992, 500
- 1993, 500
- 1994, 499
- 1995, 504
- 1996, 505
- 1997, 505
- 1998, 505
- 1999, 505

Source: Carlson, Scott, "College Board Reports Little Change in Average SAT Scores," *The Chronicle of Higher Education*, 46: A56, (September 10, 1999).

★906★
Verbal SAT scores for African Americans, by gender, 2000

Ranking basis/background: Average verbal SAT score for men and women. **Remarks:** Original source: The College Board. **Number listed:** 2.
- Men, with 431
- Women, 436

Source: "Disparities & Gaps in America," *Black Issues in Higher Education*, 18: 28-29, (March 1, 2001).

★907★
Verbal SAT scores for Asian Americans, by gender, 2000

Ranking basis/background: Average verbal SAT score for men and women. **Remarks:** Original source: The College Board. **Number listed:** 2.
- Men, with 501
- Women, 498

Source: "Disparities & Gaps in America," *Black Issues in Higher Education*, 18: 28-29, (March 1, 2001).

★908★
Verbal SAT scores for Hispanic Americans, by gender, 2000

Ranking basis/background: Average verbal SAT score for men and women. **Remarks:** Original source: The College Board. **Number listed:** 3.
- Mexican American, 458 for men; 449 for women
- Puerto Rican, 460; 452
- Latin, South & Central American, 467; 457

Source: "Disparities & Gaps in America," *Black Issues in Higher Education*, 18: 28-29, (March 1, 2001).

★909★
Verbal SAT scores for Native Americans, by gender, 2000

Ranking basis/background: Average verbal SAT score for men and women. **Remarks:** Original source: The College Board. **Number listed:** 2.
- Men, with 482
- Women, 481

Source: "Disparities & Gaps in America," *Black Issues in Higher Education*, 18: 28-29, (March 1, 2001).

★910★
Verbal SAT scores for white Americans, by gender, 2000

Ranking basis/background: Average verbal SAT score for men and women. **Remarks:** Original source: The College Board. **Number listed:** 2.
- Men, with 529
- Women, 526

Source: "Disparities & Gaps in America," *Black Issues in Higher Education*, 18: 28-29, (March 1, 2001).

COLLEGE FACULTY

★911★
Gender breakdown of full-time faculty at comprehensive institutions in the U.S., 1998

Ranking basis/background: Percentage of men and women faculty at each type of institution. **Remarks:** Original source: U.S. Department of Education. **Number listed:** 2.
- Public, with 61.7% men; 38.3% women
- Nonprofit private, 63.3%; 36.7

Source: Wilson, Robin, "Proportion of Part-Time Faculty Members Leveled Off From 1992 to 1998, Data Show," *The Chronicle of Higher Education*, 47: A14, (May 4, 2001).

★912★
Gender breakdown of full-time faculty at doctoral institutions in the U.S., 1998

Ranking basis/background: Percentage of men and women faculty at each type of institution. **Remarks:** Original source: U.S. Department of Education. **Number listed:** 2.
- Public, with 66.7% men; 33.3% women
- Nonprofit private, 63.6%; 36.4%

Source: Wilson, Robin, "Proportion of Part-Time Faculty Members Leveled Off From 1992 to 1998, Data Show," *The Chronicle of Higher Education*, 47: A14, (May 4, 2001).

★913★
Gender breakdown of full-time faculty at liberal arts institutions in the U.S., 1998

Ranking basis/background: Percentage of men and women faculty at each type of institution. **Remarks:** Original source: U.S. Department of Education. **Number listed:** 1.
- Nonprofit private, with 62.2% men; 37.9% women

Source: Wilson, Robin, "Proportion of Part-Time Faculty Members Leveled Off From 1992 to 1998, Data Show," *The Chronicle of Higher Education*, 47: A14, (May 4, 2001).

★914★
Gender breakdown of full-time faculty at research institutions in the U.S., 1998

Ranking basis/background: Percentage of men and women faculty at each type of institution. **Remarks:** Original source: U.S. Department of Education. **Number listed:** 2.
- Public, with 70.5% men; 29.5% women
- Nonprofit private, 73.9%; 26.2

Source: Wilson, Robin, "Proportion of Part-Time Faculty Members Leveled Off From 1992 to 1998, Data Show," *The Chronicle of Higher Education*, 47: A14, (May 4, 2001).

★915★
Gender breakdown of full-time faculty at two-year institutions in the U.S., 1998

Ranking basis/background: Percentage of men and women faculty at each type of institution. **Remarks:** Original source: U.S. Department of Education. **Number listed:** 1.
- Public, with 50.1% men; 49.9% women

Source: Wilson, Robin, "Proportion of Part-Time Faculty Members Leveled Off From 1992 to 1998, Data Show," *The Chronicle of Higher Education*, 47: A14, (May 4, 2001).

★916★
Gender breakdown of part-time faculty at comprehensive institutions in the U.S., 1998

Ranking basis/background: Percentage of men and women faculty at each type of institution. **Remarks:** Original source: U.S. Department of Education. **Number listed:** 2.
- Public, with 46.5% men; 53.5% women
- Nonprofit private, 59.1%; 40.9%

Source: Wilson, Robin, "Proportion of Part-Time Faculty Members Leveled Off From 1992 to 1998, Data Show," *The Chronicle of Higher Education*, 47: A14, (May 4, 2001).

★917★
Gender breakdown of part-time faculty at doctoral institutions in the U.S., 1998

Ranking basis/background: Percentage of men and women faculty at each type of institution. **Remarks:** Original source: U.S. Department of Education. **Number listed:** 2.
- Public, with 49.6% men; 50.4% women
- Nonprofit private, 58.6%; 41.4%

Source: Wilson, Robin, "Proportion of Part-Time Faculty Members Leveled Off From 1992 to 1998, Data Show," *The Chronicle of Higher Education*, 47: A14, (May 4, 2001).

★918★
Gender breakdown of part-time faculty at liberal arts institutions in the U.S., 1998

Ranking basis/background: Percentage of men and women faculty at each type of institution. **Remarks:** Original source: U.S. Department of Education. **Number listed:** 1.
- Nonprofit private, with 44.0% men; 56.1% women

COLLEGE FACULTY, MINORITY

Source: Wilson, Robin, "Proportion of Part-Time Faculty Members Leveled Off From 1992 to 1998, Data Show," *The Chronicle of Higher Education*, 47: A14, (May 4, 2001).

★919★
Gender breakdown of part-time faculty at research institutions in the U.S., 1998

Ranking basis/background: Percentage of men and women faculty at each type of institution. **Remarks:** Original source: U.S. Department of Education. **Number listed:** 2.

    Public, with 55.2% men; 44.8%% women
    Nonprofit private, 60.3%; 39.8

Source: Wilson, Robin, "Proportion of Part-Time Faculty Members Leveled Off From 1992 to 1998, Data Show," *The Chronicle of Higher Education*, 47: A14, (May 4, 2001).

★920★
Gender breakdown of part-time faculty at two-year institutions in the U.S., 1998

Ranking basis/background: Percentage of men and women faculty at each type of institution. **Remarks:** Original source: U.S. Department of Education. **Number listed:** 1.

    Public, with 51.8% men; 48.2% women

Source: Wilson, Robin, "Proportion of Part-Time Faculty Members Leveled Off From 1992 to 1998, Data Show," *The Chronicle of Higher Education*, 47: A14, (May 4, 2001).

COLLEGE FACULTY, MINORITY

★921★
African American faculty tenure rates, 1995

Ranking basis/background: Percentage of tenure track African American faculty. **Remarks:** Original source: American Council on Education. **Number listed:** 2.

    Men, with 62%
    Women, 55%

Source: Weige, Pamela R., "As Latino Populations Grow.," *Black Issues in Higher Education*, 17: 20-25, (September 28, 2000).

★922★
Hispanic American faculty tenure rates, 1995

Ranking basis/background: Percentage of tenure track Hispanic American faculty. **Remarks:** Original source: American Council on Education. **Number listed:** 2.

    Men, with 66%
    Women, 55%

Source: Weige, Pamela R., "As Latino Populations Grow.," *Black Issues in Higher Education*, 17: 20-25, (September 28, 2000).

★923★
Institutions with the most full-time Hispanic American faculty

Ranking basis/background: Number of full-time Hispanic American faculty employed at each institution, and percentage represented of total faculty. **Remarks:** Original source: American Council on Education. **Number listed:** 100.

1. University of Miami, with 234 Hispanic American faculty; 12.7% of total faculty
2. San Francisco Community College District, 164; 10.0%
3. Miami-Dade Community College, 152; 22.5%
4. University of California, Los Angeles, 148; 4.9%
5. University of New Mexico, 131; 8.7%
6. Laredo Community College, 115; 57.8%
7. El Paso Community College, 108; 36.9%
8. Florida International University, 102; 12.3%
9. University of Washington (WA), 101; 1.9%
10. Arizona State University, 96; 6.0%
10. University of California, Davis, 96; 3.8%
12. University of Texas, Austin, 94; 4.2%
13. University of Florida, 92; 2.8%
14. University of Arizona, 90; 4.5%
15. University of Texas, Pan American, 89; 23.7%
16. University of Colorado, Boulder, 88; 4.1%
17. University of Texas, El Paso, 86; 16.6%
18. Columbia University, New York City, 85; 3.3%
18. University of Texas Health Science Center, San Antonio, 85; 9.0%
20. University of Texas, Brownsville, 83; 35.6%

Source: Weige, Pamela R., "As Latino Populations Grow.," *Black Issues in Higher Education*, 17: 20-25, (September 28, 2000).

★924★
Institutions with the most part-time Hispanic American faculty

Ranking basis/background: Number of part-time Hispanic American faculty employed at each institution, and percentage represented of total faculty. **Remarks:** Original source: American Council on Education. **Number listed:** 100.

1. Miami-Dade Community College, 713; 33.9%
2. El Paso Community College, 434; 47.6%
3. Rancho Santiago Community College District, 296; 11.7%
4. Houston Community College System, 147; 8.4%
5. Pima Community College, 140; 10.5%
6. Laredo Community College, 127; 79.4%
7. South Texas Community College, 117; 47.8%
8. Del Mar College, 109; 28.5%
9. City University of New York, Hostos Community College, 107; 37.0%
10. University of Southern California, 93; 4.0%

Source: Weige, Pamela R., "As Latino Populations Grow.," *Black Issues in Higher Education*, 17: 20-25, (September 28, 2000).

★925★
U.S. colleges and universities with the most full-time Hispanic American faculty

Ranking basis/background: Total number of Hispanic American faculty employed full-time and percentage they comprise of total faculty. **Number listed:** 103.

1. University of Miami (FL), with 234 full-time Hispanic faculty; (12.7% of total faculty)
2. San Francisco Community College District (CA), 164 (10.0%)
3. Miami-Dade Community College (FL), 152 (22.5%)
4. University of California, Los Angeles (CA), 148 (4.9%)
5. University of New Mexico (NM), 131 (8.7%)
6. Laredo Community College (TX), 115 (57.8%)
7. El Paso Community College (TX), 108 (36.9%)
8. Florida International University (FL), 102 (12.3%)
9. University of Washington (WA), 101 (1.9%)
10. Arizona State University (AZ), 96 (6.0%)
10. University of California, Davis (CA), 96 (3.8%)
12. University of Texas, Austin (TX), 94 (4.2%)
13. University of Florida (FL), 92 (2.8%)
14. University of Arizona (AZ), 90 (4.5%)
15. University of Texas, Pan American (TX), 89 (23.7%)
16. University of Colorado, Boulder (CO), 88 (4.1%)
17. University of Texas, El Paso (TX), 86 (16.6%)
18. Columbia University, New York City (NY), 85 (3.3%)
18. University of Texas Health Science Center, San Antonio (TX), 85 (9.0%)
20. University of Texas, Brownsville (TX), 83 (35.6%)

Source: "Top 100 Institutions, Full-Time Hispanic Faculty," *Black Issues in Higher Education*, 17: 24-25, (September 28, 2000).

COLLEGE GRADUATES
See also: **Degrees (Academic) Doctoral Degrees**

★926★
College graduates in the labor force, by occupational group, 1998

Ranking basis/background: Number, in thousands, of college graduates employed in each occupational group. **Number listed:** 7.

1. Professional specialty, with 14,862 thousand
2. Executive, administrative, and managerial, 9,206
3. Noncollege-level jobs, 5,864
4. Marketing and sales, 2,644
5. All other college-level jobs, 1,599
6. Technicians and related, 1,245
7. Unemployed, 679

Source: Fleetwood, Chad and Kristina Shelley, "The Outlook for College Graduates, 1998-2008: A Balancing Act," *Occupational Outlook Quarterly*, 44: 2-9, (Fall 2000).

★927★
Division I NCAA colleges with that graduated all of their African American male basketball players, 1990-91 to 1993-94

Ranking basis/background: Institutions with scholarship athletes enrolling from 1990-91 to 1993-94 and receiving a bachelor's degree within six years of entering an NCAA institution. **Number listed:** 7.

    Bucknell University
    College of the Holy Cross
    Manhattan College

Northwestern University
Providence College
Southern Utah University
Stanford University

Source: Suggs, Welch, "Graduation Rates for Athletes Hold Steady," *The Chronicle of Higher Education*, 47: A47-A49, (December 1, 2000).

★928★
Division I NCAA colleges with that graduated less than 20% of their African American male athletes, 1990-91 to 1993-94

Ranking basis/background: Institutions with scholarship athletes enrolling from 1990-91 to 1993-94 and receiving a bachelor's degree within six years of entering an NCAA institution. **Number listed:** 26.

1. University of Wisconsin, Green Bay, with 3 African American male athletes; 0% graduation rate
2. California State University, Sacramento, 14; 7%
2. Idaho State University, 28; 7%
4. Brigham Young University, 12; 8%
5. California State University, Fullerton, 22; 9%
6. University of Texas, Arlington, 20; 10%
7. Coastal Carolina University, 9; 11%
7. University of Montana, 9; 11%
7. University of Nevada, Reno, 27; 11%
7. University of Wisconsin, Milwaukee, 9; 11%
11. University of Arkansas, Little Rock, 25; 12%
12. University of Arkansas, Fayetteville, 61; 13%
12. California State University, Long Beach, 15; 13%
12. University of Texas, Pan American, 8; 13%
15. Lamar University, 20; 15%
16. University of Akron, 49; 16%
16. California State University, Fresno, 44; 16%
18. Mercer University, 6; 17%
18. Nicholls State University, 36; 17%
20. Ohio State University, 66; 18%
20. University of Louisiana, Lafayette, 57; 18%
20. Texas Southern University, 92; 18%
23. University of Nevada, Las Vegas, 53; 19%
23. San Diego State University, 47; 19%
23. Weber State University, 16; 19%
23. University of Wyoming, 31; 19%

Source: Suggs, Welch, "Graduation Rates for Athletes Hold Steady," *The Chronicle of Higher Education*, 47: A47-A49, (December 1, 2000).

★929★
Division I NCAA colleges with that graduated more than 80% of their African American male athletes, 1990-91 to 1993-94

Ranking basis/background: Institutions with scholarship athletes enrolling from 1990-91 to 1993-94 and receiving a bachelor's degree within six years of entering an NCAA institution. **Number listed:** 10.

1. Manhattan College, with 11 African American male athletes; 100% graduation rate
1. Providence College, 8; 100%
3. University of Hartford, 10; 90%
4. Stanford University, 27; 89%
5. Northwestern University, 41; 88%
6. Fairfield University, 7; 86%
6. Vanderbilt University, 58; 86%
8. Duke University, 46; 85%
9. Wofford College, 33; 82%
10. St. Francis College (PA), 5; 80%

Source: Suggs, Welch, "Graduation Rates for Athletes Hold Steady," *The Chronicle of Higher Education*, 47: A47-A49, (December 1, 2000).

★930★
Division I NCAA colleges with that graduated none of their African American male basketball players, 1990-91 to 1993-94

Ranking basis/background: Institutions with scholarship athletes enrolling from 1990-91 to 1993-94 and receiving a bachelor's degree within six years of entering an NCAA institution. **Number listed:** 47.

Ball State University
Baylor University
Brigham Young University
California State University, Long Beach
California State University, Sacramento
California State University
Eastern Kentucky University
Eastern Washington University
Georgia Institute of Technology
Georgia Southern University
Jacksonville State University
James Madison University
Louisiana State University
McNeese State University
Morehead State University (KY)
Nicholls State University
Oregon State University
Rutgers University, New Brunswick
Samford University
Southern Illinois University, Carbondale
Southern University, Baton Rouge
Southwest Missouri State University
Texas Tech University
University of Alabama, Birmingham
University of Arkansas, Fayetteville
University of Cincinnati
University of Colorado, Boulder
University of Hawaii, Manoa
University of Idaho
University of Louisville
University of Memphis
University of Michigan
University of Minnesota, Twin Cities
University of Nevada, Las Vegas
University of Nevada, Reno
University of New Orleans
University of Oklahoma
University of Texas, El Paso
University of Texas, Pan American
University of the Pacific
University of Toledo
University of Wisconsin, Green Bay
University of Wisconsin, Milwaukee
University of Wyoming
Utah State University
Virginia Commonwealth University
Western Illinois University

Source: Suggs, Welch, "Graduation Rates for Athletes Hold Steady," *The Chronicle of Higher Education*, 47: A47-A49, (December 1, 2000).

★931★
Division I NCAA colleges with the highest graduation rates for female athletes, 1990-91 to 1993-94

Ranking basis/background: Proportion of scholarship athletes enrolling from 1990-91 to 1993-94 and receiving a bachelor's degree within six years of entering an NCAA institution. **Number listed:** 20.

1. Northwestern University, with 86 female athletes; 98% graduating within six years
2. Bucknell University, 87; 97%
3. Lehigh University, 128; 96%
4. Georgetown University, 51; 94%
4. Wofford College, 33; 94%
4. University of Notre Dame, 117; 94%
7. Duke University, 69; 93%
7. Boston College, 88; 93%
7. University of Richmond, 60; 93%
7. Siena College, 29; 93%

Source: Suggs, Welch, "Graduation Rates for Athletes Hold Steady," *The Chronicle of Higher Education*, 47: A47-A49, (December 1, 2000).

★932★
Division I NCAA colleges with the highest graduation rates for female basketball players, 1990-91 to 1993-94

Ranking basis/background: Proportion of scholarship athletes enrolling from 1990-91 to 1993-94 and receiving a bachelor's degree within six years of entering an NCAA institution. **Number listed:** 11.

1. Boston College, with 100% black players; 100% white players; 100% all players
1. Lafayette College, 100%; 100%; 100%
1. Lehigh University, 0; 100%; 100%
1. Loyola University, Chicago, 0; 100%; 100%
1. St. John's University (NY), 100%; 100%; 100%
1. Santa Clara University, 100%; 100%; 100%
1. Siena College, 100%; 100%; 100%
1. Wagner College, 0; 100%; 100%
1. University of Wisconsin, Madison, 100%; 100%; 100%
1. College of Charleston, 100%; 100%; 100%
1. Wofford College, 100%; 100%; 100%

Source: Suggs, Welch, "Graduation Rates for Athletes Hold Steady," *The Chronicle of Higher Education*, 47: A47-A49, (December 1, 2000).

★933★
Division I NCAA colleges with the highest graduation rates for football players, 1990-91 to 1993-94

Ranking basis/background: Proportion of scholarship athletes enrolling from 1990-91 to 1993-94 and receiving a bachelor's degree within six years of entering an NCAA institution. **Number listed:** 10.

1. Duke University, with 87% black players; 95% white players; 91% all players
2. Northwestern University, 85%; 89%; 88%
3. University of New Hampshire, 93%; 86%; 86%
3. University of Richmond, 83%; 88%; 86%
5. Lehigh University, 88%; 81%; 83%
5. Stanford University, 88%; 82%; 83%
7. College of William and Mary, 75%; 84%; 82%

COLLEGE GRADUATES

7. University of Notre Dame, 80%; 84%; 82%
7. Wofford College, 81%; 82%; 82%
10. College of the Holy Cross, 69%; 81%; 80%

Source: Suggs, Welch, "Graduation Rates for Athletes Hold Steady," *The Chronicle of Higher Education*, 47: A47-A49, (December 1, 2000).

★934★
Division I NCAA colleges with the highest graduation rates for male athletes, 1990-91 to 1993-94

Ranking basis/background: Proportion of scholarship athletes enrolling from 1990-91 to 1993-94 and receiving a bachelor's degree within six years of entering an NCAA institution. **Number listed:** 20.

1. Northwestern University, with 166 male athletes; 90% graduating within six years
1. Duke University, 184; 90%
3. Georgetown University, 66; 88%
3. Lehigh University, 248; 88%
3. Manhattan College, 49; 88%
3. Stanford University, 162; 88%
7. Bucknell University, 223; 87%
7. University of Notre Dame, 224; 87%
9. Loyola College (MD), 49; 84%
9. La Salle University, 81; 84%

Source: Suggs, Welch, "Graduation Rates for Athletes Hold Steady," *The Chronicle of Higher Education*, 47: A47-A49, (December 1, 2000).

★935★
Division I NCAA colleges with the highest graduation rates for male basketball players, 1990-91 to 1993-94

Ranking basis/background: Proportion of scholarship athletes enrolling from 1990-91 to 1993-94 and receiving a bachelor's degree within six years of entering an NCAA institution. **Number listed:** 10.

1. Stanford University, with 100% black players; 100% white players; 100% all players
2. Manhattan College, 100%; 67%; 92%
2. Northwestern University, 100%; 83%; 92%
4. Northwestern University, 100%; 83%; 91%
4. Bucknell University, 100%; 83%; 91%
4. Southern Methodist University, 80%; 100%; 91%
7. Drexel University, 83%; 100%; 89%
8. University of San Diego, 67%; 100%; 88%
9. University of Notre Dame, 71%; 100%; 86%
9. Wofford College, 80%; 89%; 86%

Source: Suggs, Welch, "Graduation Rates for Athletes Hold Steady," *The Chronicle of Higher Education*, 47: A47-A49, (December 1, 2000).

★936★
Division I NCAA colleges with the lowest graduation rates for female athletes, 1990-91 to 1993-94

Ranking basis/background: Proportion of scholarship athletes enrolling from 1990-91 to 1993-94 and receiving a bachelor's degree within six years of entering an NCAA institution. **Number listed:** 20.

1. Chicago State University, with 30 female athletes; 27% graduating within six years
2. University of Texas, Pan American, 45; 29%
3. Mississippi Valley State University, 30; 30%
4. Florida Atlantic University, 61; 34%
5. University of Arkansas, Little Rock, 98; 35%
5. Charleston Southern University, 102; 35%
7. Weber State University, 65; 37%
8. University of Houston, 86; 40%
8. McNeese State University, 60; 40%
10. California State University, Fullerton, 66; 41%

Source: Suggs, Welch, "Graduation Rates for Athletes Hold Steady," *The Chronicle of Higher Education*, 47: A47-A49, (December 1, 2000).

★937★
Division I NCAA colleges with the lowest graduation rates for female basketball players, 1990-91 to 1993-94

Ranking basis/background: Proportion of scholarship athletes enrolling from 1990-91 to 1993-94 and receiving a bachelor's degree within six years of entering an NCAA institution. **Number listed:** 11.

1. University of Houston, with 10% black players; 0% white players; 10% all players
2. Southeastern Louisiana University, 17%; 17%; 17%
3. McNeese State University, 20%; 25%; 22%
3. University of Nevada, Reno, 50%; 0%; 22%
5. Florida Atlantic University, 0; 25%; 23%
5. University of Texas, San Antonio, 25%; 22%; 23%
7. University of Alabama, Birmingham, 11%; 38%; 24%
8. University of Missouri, Kansas City, 50%; 22%; 25%
9. Alcorn State University, 27%; 0; 27%
9. University of South Alabama, 40%; 25%; 27%
9. University of Texas, El Paso, 20%; 17%; 27%

Source: Suggs, Welch, "Graduation Rates for Athletes Hold Steady," *The Chronicle of Higher Education*, 47: A47-A49, (December 1, 2000).

★938★
Division I NCAA colleges with the lowest graduation rates for football players, 1990-91 to 1993-94

Ranking basis/background: Proportion of scholarship athletes enrolling from 1990-91 to 1993-94 and receiving a bachelor's degree within six years of entering an NCAA institution. **Number listed:** 10.

1. California State University, Fullerton, with 0% black players; 0% white players; 0% all players
2. Idaho State University, 5%; 24%; 18%
3. Boise State University, 25%; 17%; 20%
4. California State University, Long Beach, 20%; 22%; 21%
5. University of Arkansas, Fayetteville, 16%; 36%; 23%
5. University of Nevada, Reno, 11%; 32%; 23%
5. Texas Southern University, 24%; 0; 23%
8. University of Akron, 15%; 41%; 24%
9. Central Connecticut State University, 20%; 40%; 25%
9. Nicholls State University, 19%; 32%; 25%

Source: Suggs, Welch, "Graduation Rates for Athletes Hold Steady," *The Chronicle of Higher Education*, 47: A47-A49, (December 1, 2000).

★939★
Division I NCAA colleges with the lowest graduation rates for male athletes, 1990-91 to 1993-94

Ranking basis/background: Proportion of scholarship athletes enrolling from 1990-91 to 1993-94 and receiving a bachelor's degree within six years of entering an NCAA institution. **Number listed:** 20.

1. Texas Southern University, with 98 male athletes; 17% graduating within six years
2. California State University, Fullerton, 89; 20%
3. Florida Atlantic University, 84; 23%
4. University of Texas, Pan American, 83; 24%
4. Idaho State University, 117; 24%
4. Boise State University, 120; 24%
4. University of Nevada, Reno, 108; 24%
4. Oral Roberts University, 17; 24%
9. University of Arkansas, Little Rock, 168; 25%
9. University of Houston, 140; 25%
9. Nicholls State University, 121; 25%

Source: Suggs, Welch, "Graduation Rates for Athletes Hold Steady," *The Chronicle of Higher Education*, 47: A47-A49, (December 1, 2000).

★940★
Division I NCAA colleges with the lowest graduation rates for male basketball players, 1990-91 to 1993-94

Ranking basis/background: Proportion of scholarship athletes enrolling from 1990-91 to 1993-94 and receiving a bachelor's degree within six years of entering an NCAA institution. **Number listed:** 10.

1. California State University, Sacramento, with 0% black players; 0% white players; 0% all players
1. Nicholls State University, 0; 0; 0%
1. Southern University, Baton Rouge, 0; 0; 0%
1. Southwest Missouri State University, 0; 0; 0%
1. University of Idaho, 0; 0; 0%

Source: Suggs, Welch, "Graduation Rates for Athletes Hold Steady," *The Chronicle of Higher Education*, 47: A47-A49, (December 1, 2000).

★941★
Division II NCAA colleges with the 0% graduation rates for men's basketball players, 1993-94

Ranking basis/background: Institutions with none of scholarship athletes receiving their bachelor's degree within six years of entering a NCAA institution. **Remarks:** Original source: NCAA. **Number listed:** 17.

Anderson College (SC)
Bluefield State College
California State University, Bakersfield
California State University, Dominguez Hills
Cheyney University of Pennsylvania
Clayton College and State University
Colorado Christian University
Edinboro University of Pennsylvania
Livingstone College

Ohio Valley College
University of Arkansas, Monticello
University of Bridgeport
University of California, Riverside
University of Colorado, Colorado Springs
University of Hawaii, Hilo
University of West Florida
Western Oregon University

Source: Suggs, Welch, "Lack of Resources Hampers Graduation Rates in Division II," *The Chronicle of Higher Education*, 47: A49-A51, (January 5, 2001).

★942★
Division II NCAA colleges with the 0% graduation rates for women's basketball players, 1993-94

Ranking basis/background: Institutions with none of scholarship athletes receiving their bachelor's degree within six years of entering a NCAA institution. **Remarks:** Original source: NCAA. **Number listed:** 7.

Augusta State University
Lincoln Memorial University
Livingstone College
Ohio Valley College
Missouri Southern State College
University of North Alabama
University of West Alabama

Source: Suggs, Welch, "Lack of Resources Hampers Graduation Rates in Division II," *The Chronicle of Higher Education*, 47: A49-A51, (January 5, 2001).

★943★
Division II NCAA colleges with the 100% graduation rates for men's basketball players, 1993-94

Ranking basis/background: Institutions with all of scholarship athletes receiving their bachelor's degree within six years of entering a NCAA institution. **Remarks:** Original source: NCAA. **Number listed:** 12.

Adelphi University
American International College
Emporia State University
Franklin Pierce College
LeMoyne College (NY)
Merrimack College
Regis University
St. Anselm College
St. Michael's College
Shaw University
University of North Carolina, Pembroke
Wheeling Jesuit University

Source: Suggs, Welch, "Lack of Resources Hampers Graduation Rates in Division II," *The Chronicle of Higher Education*, 47: A49-A51, (January 5, 2001).

★944★
Division II NCAA colleges with the 100% graduation rates for women's basketball players, 1993-94

Ranking basis/background: Institutions with all of scholarship athletes receiving their bachelor's degree within six years of entering a NCAA institution. **Remarks:** Original source: NCAA. **Number listed:** 13.

Bentley College
College of St. Rose
Emporia State University
Franklin Pierce College
Indiana University (PA)
Merrimack College

Pace University
Queen's College
St. Michael's College
Slippery Rock University (PA)
University of Alaska, Anchorage
University of Central Oklahoma
West Liberty State College

Source: Suggs, Welch, "Lack of Resources Hampers Graduation Rates in Division II," *The Chronicle of Higher Education*, 47: A49-A51, (January 5, 2001).

★945★
Division II NCAA colleges with the highest graduation rates for all sports, 1993-94

Ranking basis/background: Proportion of scholarship athletes who received a bachelor's degree within six years of entering a NCAA institution. **Remarks:** Original source: NCAA. **Number listed:** 20.

1. St. Michael's College, with 100% male athletes; 100% female athletes
2. St. Anselm College, 100%; 92%
3. Pace University, 88%; 98%
4. Westminster College (PA), 85%; 92%
5. Merrimack College, 80%; 100%
6. Franklin Pierce College, $85%; 79%
7. Bryant College (RI), 78%; 82%
8. Bentley College, 63%; 95%
9. Stonehill College, 67%; 88%
10. Morehouse College, 78%; 0%

Source: Suggs, Welch, "Lack of Resources Hampers Graduation Rates in Division II," *The Chronicle of Higher Education*, 47: A49-A51, (January 5, 2001).

★946★
Division II NCAA colleges with the highest graduation rates for football players, 1993-94

Ranking basis/background: Percentage of scholarship athletes receiving their bachelor's degree within six years of entering a NCAA institution. **Remarks:** Original source: NCAA. **Number listed:** 11.

1. Bentley College, with 100%
2. Westminster College (PA), 84%
3. South Dakota State University, 79%
4. Morehouse College, 78%
5. Hillsdale College, 72%
6. American International College, 71%
7. Colorado School of Mines, 68%
7. Harding University, 68%
9. Truman State University, 66%
10. Livingston College, 64%
11. Lenoir-Rhyne College, 63%

Source: Suggs, Welch, "Lack of Resources Hampers Graduation Rates in Division II," *The Chronicle of Higher Education*, 47: A49-A51, (January 5, 2001).

★947★
Division II NCAA colleges with the lowest graduation rates for all sports, 1993-94

Ranking basis/background: Proportion of scholarship athletes who received a bachelor's degree within six years of entering a NCAA institution. **Remarks:** Original source: NCAA. **Number listed:** 20.

1. Ohio Valley College, with 5% male athletes; 0% female athletes
2. University of the District of Columbia, 7%; 5%
3. Clayton College and State University, 11%; 13%
4. Anderson College (SC), 12%; 19%
5. University of Arkansas, Monticello, 14%; 36%
6. Bluefield State College, 9%; 25%
7. Bowie State University, 22%; 18%
8. LeMoyne-Owen College (TN), 19%; 22%
9. Adams State College, 21%; 22%
10. University of Hawaii, Hilo, 24%; 19%

Source: Suggs, Welch, "Lack of Resources Hampers Graduation Rates in Division II," *The Chronicle of Higher Education*, 47: A49-A51, (January 5, 2001).

★948★
Division II NCAA colleges with the lowest graduation rates for football players, 1993-94

Ranking basis/background: Percentage of scholarship athletes receiving their bachelor's degree within six years of entering a NCAA institution. **Remarks:** Original source: NCAA. **Number listed:** 11.

1. West Virginia State College, with 0%
1. Western Oregon University, 0%
3. Texas A&M University, Kingsville, 10%
4. Cameron University (OK), 11%
5. Wayne State University, 13%
6. Morris Brown College, 14%
7. University of Arkansas, Monticello, 16%
8. Alderson-Broaddus College, 17%
8. Bowie State University, 17%
8. Eastern New Mexico University, 17%
8. University of Central Oklahoma, 17%

Source: Suggs, Welch, "Lack of Resources Hampers Graduation Rates in Division II," *The Chronicle of Higher Education*, 47: A49-A51, (January 5, 2001).

★949★
Employment and enrollment status of tribal college graduates

Ranking basis/background: Percentage of tribal college graduates in each employment or enrollment category. Working includes self-employment. Homemakers are included in the "neither working nor attending college" category. **Remarks:** Based on a study conducted by the Institute for Higher Education Policy, the American Indian Higher Education Consortium and the Sallie Mae Education Institute. **Number listed:** 4.

1. Working, not attending college, with 52%
2. Working, and attending college, 22%
3. Attending college, not working, 17%
4. Neither working nor attending college, 9%

Source: Wright, Scott W., "Survey Confirms Tribal College Role in Alleviating Unemployment," *Black Issues in Higher Education*, 17: 18-19, (June 22, 2000).

★950★
Graduate rates by sport for Division I NCAA colleges, 1993-94

Ranking basis/background: Percentage of black and white scholarship athletes receiving their bachelor's degree within six years of entering an NCAA institution. **Remarks:** Original source: NCAA. **Number listed:** 3.

Football, with 42% of black players; 56% of white players
Men's basketball, 34%; 56%
Women's basketball, 52%; 69%

COLLEGE GRADUATES

Source: Suggs, Welch, "Lack of Resources Hampers Graduation Rates in Division II," *The Chronicle of Higher Education,* 47: A49-A51, (January 5, 2001).

★951★
Graduate rates by sport for Division II NCAA colleges, 1993-94

Ranking basis/background: Percentage of black and white scholarship athletes receiving their bachelor's degree within six years of entering an NCAA institution. **Remarks:** Original source: NCAA. **Number listed:** 3.
- Football, with 32% of black players; 44% of white players
- Men's basketball, 38%; 58%
- Women's basketball, 51%; 60%

Source: Suggs, Welch, "Lack of Resources Hampers Graduation Rates in Division II," *The Chronicle of Higher Education,* 47: A49-A51, (January 5, 2001).

★952★
Graduate rates comparison for Division I NCAA colleges, 1993-94

Ranking basis/background: Number and proportion of all students and scholarship athletes receiving their bachelor's degree within six years of entering an NCAA institution. **Remarks:** Original source: NCAA. **Number listed:** 11.
- Number of institutions: 321
- Number of students: 523,428
- Male students, 249,609 (48% graduation rate)
- Female students, 273,819 (52%)
- Number of athletes: 14,928
- Male athletes, 8,911 (60%)
- Female athletes, 6,017 (40%)
- Black male athletes, 2,683 (30%)
- White male athletes, 5,353 (60%)
- Black female athletes, 890 (15%)
- White female athletes, 4,512 (75%)

Source: Suggs, Welch, "Lack of Resources Hampers Graduation Rates in Division II," *The Chronicle of Higher Education,* 47: A49-A51, (January 5, 2001).

★953★
Graduate rates comparison for Division II NCAA colleges, 1993-94

Ranking basis/background: Number and proportion of all students and scholarship athletes receiving their bachelor's degree within six years of entering an NCAA institution. **Remarks:** Original source: NCAA. **Number listed:** 11.
- Number of institutions: 295
- Number of students: 159,242
- Male students, 72,472 (46% graduation rate)
- Female students, 86,770 (55%)
- Number of athletes: 7,688
- Male athletes, 4,816 (66%)
- Female athletes, 2,872 (37%)
- Black male athletes, 1,045 (22%)
- White male athletes, 3,212 (67%)
- Black female athletes, 348 (12%)
- White female athletes, 2,264 (79%)

Source: Suggs, Welch, "Lack of Resources Hampers Graduation Rates in Division II," *The Chronicle of Higher Education,* 47: A49-A51, (January 5, 2001).

★954★
Graduation rates for female basketball players at Division I NCAA colleges, by race/ethnicity

Ranking basis/background: Proportion of scholarship athletes enrolling in 1993-94 and receiving a bachelor's degree within six years of entering a NCAA institution. **Number listed:** 7.
- Native American/Alaskan Native, with 60%
- Asian American/Pacific Islander, 100%
- African American, 52%
- Hispanic American, 55%
- White, 69%
- Nonresident alien, 64%
- Other, 57%

Source: Suggs, Welch, "Graduation Rates for Athletes Hold Steady," *The Chronicle of Higher Education,* 47: A47-A49, (December 1, 2000).

★955★
Graduation rates for female basketball players at Division II NCAA colleges, 1993-94

Ranking basis/background: Proportion of scholarship athletes who received a bachelor's degree within six years of entering a NCAA institution. **Remarks:** Original source: NCAA. **Number listed:** 7.
- Native American/Alaskan Native, with 14%
- Asian American, 25%
- African American, 51%
- Hispanic American, 38%
- White, 60%
- Nonresident alien, 33%
- Other, 50%

Source: Suggs, Welch, "Lack of Resources Hampers Graduation Rates in Division II," *The Chronicle of Higher Education,* 47: A49-A51, (January 5, 2001).

★956★
Graduation rates for female students and athletes at Division I NCAA colleges, by race/ethnicity

Ranking basis/background: Proportion of freshman students and scholarship athletes enrolling in 1993-94 and receiving a bachelor's degree within six years of entering a NCAA institution. **Number listed:** 7.
- Native American/Alaskan Native, with 41% for all female students; 54% for female athletes
- Asian American/Pacific Islander, 69%; 82%
- African American, 42%; 57%
- Hispanic American, 51%; 58%
- White, 61%; 71%
- Nonresident alien, 64%; 67%
- Other, 59%; 60%

Source: Suggs, Welch, "Graduation Rates for Athletes Hold Steady," *The Chronicle of Higher Education,* 47: A47-A49, (December 1, 2000).

★957★
Graduation rates for female students at Division II NCAA colleges, 1993-94

Ranking basis/background: Proportion of freshman students and scholarship athletes who received a bachelor's degree within six years of entering a NCAA institution. **Remarks:** Original source: NCAA. **Number listed:** 7.
- Native American/Alaskan Native, with 28% for all female students; 25% for female athletes
- Asian American, 56%; 41%
- African American, 39%; 45%
- Hispanic American, 46%; 46%
- White, 49%; 60%
- Nonresident alien, 45%; 55%
- Other, 42%; 50%

Source: Suggs, Welch, "Lack of Resources Hampers Graduation Rates in Division II," *The Chronicle of Higher Education,* 47: A49-A51, (January 5, 2001).

★958★
Graduation rates for football players at Division I NCAA colleges, by race/ethnicity

Ranking basis/background: Proportion of scholarship athletes enrolling in 1993-94 and receiving a bachelor's degree within six years of entering a NCAA institution. **Number listed:** 7.
- Native American/Alaskan Native, with 57%
- Asian American/Pacific Islander, 42%
- African American, 42%
- Hispanic American, 40%
- White, 55%
- Nonresident alien, 40%
- Other, 38%

Source: Suggs, Welch, "Graduation Rates for Athletes Hold Steady," *The Chronicle of Higher Education,* 47: A47-A49, (December 1, 2000).

★959★
Graduation rates for football players at Division II NCAA colleges, 1993-94

Ranking basis/background: Proportion of scholarship athletes who received a bachelor's degree within six years of entering a NCAA institution. **Remarks:** Original source: NCAA. **Number listed:** 6.
- Native American/Alaskan Native, with 71%
- Asian American, 10%
- African American, 32%
- Hispanic American, 34%
- White, 44%
- Other, 59%

Source: Suggs, Welch, "Lack of Resources Hampers Graduation Rates in Division II," *The Chronicle of Higher Education,* 47: A49-A51, (January 5, 2001).

★960★
Graduation rates for male basketball players at Division I NCAA colleges, by race/ethnicity

Ranking basis/background: Proportion of scholarship athletes enrolling in 1993-94 and receiving a bachelor's degree within six years of entering a NCAA institution. **Number listed:** 7.
- Native American/Alaskan Native, with 0%
- Asian American/Pacific Islander, 0%
- African American, 34%
- Hispanic American, 67%
- White, 56%
- Nonresident alien, 61%
- Other, 20%

Source: Suggs, Welch, "Graduation Rates for Athletes Hold Steady," *The Chronicle of Higher Education,* 47: A47-A49, (December 1, 2000).

★961★
Graduation rates for male basketball players at Division II NCAA colleges, 1993-94

Ranking basis/background: Proportion of scholarship athletes who received a bachelor's degree within six years of entering a NCAA institution. **Remarks:** Original source: NCAA. **Number listed:** 7.

- Native American/Alaskan Native, with 25%
- Asian American, 0%
- African American, 38%
- Hispanic American, 33%
- White, 58%
- Nonresident alien, 56%
- Other, 33%

Source: Suggs, Welch, "Lack of Resources Hampers Graduation Rates in Division II," *The Chronicle of Higher Education*, 47: A49-A51, (January 5, 2001).

★962★
Graduation rates for male students and athletes at Division I NCAA colleges, by race/ethnicity

Ranking basis/background: Proportion of freshman students and scholarship athletes enrolling in 1993-94 and receiving a bachelor's degree within six years of entering a NCAA institution. **Number listed:** 7.

- Native American/Alaskan Native, with 36% for all male students; 42% for male athletes
- Asian American/Pacific Islander, 63%; 47%
- African American, 32%; 41%
- Hispanic American, 44%; 44%
- White, 57%; 56%
- Nonresident alien, 59%; 61%
- Other, 55%; 46%

Source: Suggs, Welch, "Graduation Rates for Athletes Hold Steady," *The Chronicle of Higher Education*, 47: A47-A49, (December 1, 2000).

★963★
Graduation rates for male students at Division II NCAA colleges, 1993-94

Ranking basis/background: Proportion of freshman students and scholarship athletes who received a bachelor's degree within six years of entering a NCAA institution. **Remarks:** Original source: NCAA. **Number listed:** 7.

- Native American/Alaskan Native, with 24% for all male students; 54% for male athletes
- Asian American, 44%; 33%
- African American, 28%; 34%
- Hispanic American, 33%; 38%
- White, 41%; 48%
- Nonresident alien, 43%; 59%
- Other, 38%; 54%

Source: Suggs, Welch, "Lack of Resources Hampers Graduation Rates in Division II," *The Chronicle of Higher Education*, 47: A49-A51, (January 5, 2001).

★964★
Occupational fields of tribal college graduates that are currently employed

Ranking basis/background: Percentage of tribal college graduates in each occupational category. Includes those working full- or part-time or were self-employed. **Remarks:** Based on a study conducted by the Institute for Higher Education Policy, the American Indian Higher Education Consortium and the Sallie Mae Education Institute. **Number listed:** 6.

1. Construction trades, with 24%
2. Health care/nursing, 16%
3. Teacher, 13%
4. Clerk, secretary, office manager, 6%
4. Program administrator, 6%
6. Other, 35%

Source: Wright, Scott W., "Survey Confirms Tribal College Role in Alleviating Unemployment," *Black Issues in Higher Education*, 17: 18-19, (June 22, 2000).

★965★
Projected change in employment of college graduates, by occupational group, from 1998 to 2008

Ranking basis/background: Number, in thousands, for projected change in employment for college graduates in each occupational group from 1998 to 2008. **Number listed:** 6.

1. Professional specialty, with 4,390 thousand (29.5% of all graduates)
2. Executive, administrative, and managerial, 2,120 (23.0%)
3. Marketing and sales, 760 (28.8%)
4. Technicians and related, 440 (35.2%)
5. Administrative support, 300 (27.5%)
6. All other college-level jobs, 180 (35.3%)

Source: Fleetwood, Chad and Kristina Shelley, "The Outlook for College Graduates, 1998-2008: A Balancing Act," *Occupational Outlook Quarterly*, 44: 2-9, (Fall 2000).

★966★
Projected employment of college graduates, by occupational group, 2008

Ranking basis/background: Projected number, in thousands, of college graduates employed in each occupational group for 2008. **Number listed:** 6.

1. Professional specialty, with 19,250 thousand (12.1% of all graduates)
2. Executive, administrative, and managerial, 11,320 (7.1%)
3. Marketing and sales, 3,400 (2.1%)
4. Technicians and related, 1,690 (1.1%)
5. Administrative support, 1,390 (0.9%)
6. All other college-level jobs, 690 (0.4%)

Source: Fleetwood, Chad and Kristina Shelley, "The Outlook for College Graduates, 1998-2008: A Balancing Act," *Occupational Outlook Quarterly*, 44: 2-9, (Fall 2000).

COLLEGE GUIDES

Related Information

★967★
Franek, Robert, et. al., *The Best 311 Colleges*, Princeton Review Publishing, 2001 edition, 2000.

Remarks: Results from a multiple-choice survey taken at approximately 100-125 college campuses compiling the opinions of nearly 60,000 students who ranked institutions in nine categories: academics, administration, quality of life, politics, demographics, social life, extracurriculars, parties, and schools by type.

★968★
Barnes, Shirley, "ABCs of the V," *Chicago Tribune*, November 14, 1999, Section 12, pp. 1, 5.

Remarks: Article about the Harley-Davidson University, an all-inclusive facility in Milwaukee setting new standards for vocational training.

★969★
Crainer, Stuart and Des Dearlove, *Gravy Training: Inside the Business of Business Schools*, Jossey-Bass, 1999.

Remarks: An in-depth assessment of U.S. business schools by management education experts.

★970★
"New Guide Profiles Nation's Leading Colleges That Encourage Character Development-100 Colleges & Universities Named to Honor Roll," *College News*, January 2000, p. 10.

Remarks: Explains basis for *The Templeton Guide: Colleges That Encourage Character Development*. Guide profiles programs of 405 exemplary colleges in ten categories; 50 college president who are leaders in student character development; and 100 colleges and universities named on the Templeton Honor Roll for their commitment to inspiring students in leading ethical and civic-minded lives.

★971★
Fiske, Edward B., *The Fiske Guide to Colleges 2002*, Times Books, 2001.

Remarks: An annual publication consisting of individual essays on some 300 of the "best" colleges and universities. Compiled from questionnaires sent to administrators and a cross section of students. Each essay contains a set of ratings of the college or university on the basis of academic strength, social life, and overall quality of life. Includes price and geographic indices.

★972★
Fiske, Edward B. and Bruce G. Hammond, *The Fiske Guide to Getting Into the Right College*, Times Books, 2001.

Remarks: A complete guide to college admissions. Includes "One-Hour College Finder", how to fill out an application and use the Internet for speedier processing, write an application essay, and win scholarships and financial aid.

★973★
The Handbook of Historically Black Colleges & Universities: Comprehensive Profiles of Black Colleges and Universities, 3rd ed., Jireh & Associates, 1999.

Remarks: Provides an alphabetical listing of historically black U.S. colleges and universities, website contacts, glossary of terms, and applications forms.

COLLEGE LIFE

★974★
Machung, Anne, "Playing the Rankings Game," *Change*, pp. 12-16, (July/August 1998).
Remarks: Discusses the discrepancies and credibility of the *U.S. News & World Report*'s college and university rankings and the methodology in generating those rankings.

★975★
Studwell, William E. and Bruce R. Schueneman, *College Fight Songs: An Annotated Anthology*, Haworth Press, 1998.
Remarks: History of college fight songs and their composers.

★976★
Hoffman, Charlene M., *State Comparisons of Education Statistics: 1969-70 to 1996-97*, U.S. Department of Education, National Center for Education Statistics NCES 98-018, 1998.
Remarks: Statistics for demographics/enrollment, achievement and graduates, teachers and staff, and institutions and finances for all educational levels.

★977★
"Making Sense of All Those Numbers," *U.S. News & World Report*, 130: 65, (April 19, 2001).
Remarks: Provides an in-depth explanation of how *U.S. News & World Report* compiles its ranking of graduate programs.

★978★
Best Graduate Schools, U.S. News & World Report, 2001.
Remarks: Directory providing information for over 1,000 graduate programs and career outlooks for each discipline. Also includes the Campbell Interest and Skill Survey to aid in career choices.

★979★
Measuring Up 2000: The State-by-State Report Card for Higher Education, The National Center for Public Policy and Higher Education, 2000.
Remarks: Grades higher education in the U.S., by state, through a series of category and index scores including high school credentials; proficiency in math, reading and writing; college entrance and advanced placement exams; enrollment; affordability and financial aid; completion and benefits.

★980★
Greene, Howard R. and Matthew W. Greene, *Making It Into A Top College: 10 Steps to Gaining Admission to Selective Colleges and Universities*, HarperCollins, 2000.
Remarks: Explains what identifies a college or university as selective and discusses steps recommended for gaining admission.

★981★
Ehrenberg, Ronald G., *Tuition Rising: Why College Costs So Much*, Harvard University Press, 2000.
Remarks: Analyses the response to rating published in national magazines such as *U.S. News & World Report*, and discusses how they engage dysfunctional competition for students.

★982★
The Insider's Guide to the Colleges 2001, 27th edition, The Yale Daily News Publishing Company, 2000.
Remarks: Describes, explains, and interprets national rankings of colleges and academic quality. Provides further investigation of higher education through interviews of friends (and friends of friends) at 311 colleges and universities in the United States and Canada.

★983★
"Guide to Evaluating Information Technology on Campus (EDUCAUSE, 2001)," *http://www.educause.edu/consumerguide/*.
Remarks: Offers online information to aid prospective college students and their parents in evaluating technology resources used on campus. Guide is organized by four key areas: academic experience; administrative experience; social experience; and requirements, services and costs.

★984★
Guide to the Best Colleges in the U.S., Simon & Schuster, 2000.
Remarks: Comprehensive guide for selecting a college. Discusses scouting, various types of institutions, admissions processes, special considerations, and financial aid.

COLLEGE LIFE

★985★
U.S. colleges and universities least accepting of alternative lifestyles

Ranking basis/background: From a survey of nearly 60,000 students who were asked to answer 70 multiple choice question on subjects including school administration, quality of teaching, social life and campus life. The rankings from this survey are based purely on student opinion and are not to be considered objective. **Remarks:** Except for schools with less than 1,000 students enrolled, the Princeton Review heard from at least 100 students on each campus surveyed. **Number listed:** 20.
1. University of Notre Dame
2. Boston College
3. Denison University
4. Duke University
5. Grove City College
6. Wheaton College (IL)
7. Seton Hall University
8. University of Connecticut
9. Hampton University
10. Wofford College

Source: Franek, Robert, et. al., *The Best 311 Colleges, 2001 edition*, Princeton Review Publishing, 2000.

★986★
U.S. colleges and universities most accepting of alternative lifestyles

Ranking basis/background: From a survey of nearly 60,000 students who were asked to answer 70 multiple choice question on subjects including school administration, quality of teaching, social life and campus life. The rankings from this survey are based purely on student opinion and are not to be considered objective. **Remarks:** Except for schools with less than 1,000 students enrolled, the Princeton Review heard from at least 100 students on each campus surveyed. **Number listed:** 20.
1. Pitzer College
2. New York University
3. Wells College
4. Smith College
5. Mount Holyoke College
6. Connecticut College
7. Colby College
8. Sarah Lawrence College
9. Simon's Rock College of Bard
10. Reed College

Source: Franek, Robert, et. al., *The Best 311 Colleges, 2001 edition*, Princeton Review Publishing, 2000.

★987★
U.S. colleges and universities offering the best overall academic experience for undergraduates

Ranking basis/background: From a survey of nearly 60,000 students who were asked to answer 70 multiple choice question on subjects including school administration, quality of teaching, social life and campus life. The rankings from this survey are based purely on student opinion and are not to be considered objective. **Remarks:** Except for schools with less than 1,000 students enrolled, the Princeton Review heard from at least 100 students on each campus surveyed. **Number listed:** 20.
1. Princeton University
2. Swarthmore College
3. United States Air Force Academy
4. United States Coast Guard Academy
5. Williams College
6. Harvard College
7. Amherst College
8. Smith College
9. Harvey Mudd College
10. Haverford College

Source: Franek, Robert, et. al., *The Best 311 Colleges, 2001 edition*, Princeton Review Publishing, 2000.

★988★
U.S. colleges and universities that are the toughest to get into

Ranking basis/background: From a survey of nearly 60,000 students who were asked to answer 70 multiple choice question on subjects including school administration, quality of teaching, social life and campus life. The rankings from this survey are based purely on student opinion and are not to be considered objective. **Remarks:** Except for schools with less than 1,000 students enrolled, the Princeton Review heard from at least 100 students on each campus surveyed. **Number listed:** 20.
1. Princeton University
2. Harvard College
3. Cooper Union
4. United States Military Academy
5. United States Naval Academy
6. United States Air Force Academy
7. Yale University
8. Stanford University
9. Columbia University
10. Amherst College

Source: Franek, Robert, et. al., *The Best 311 Colleges, 2001 edition*, Princeton Review Publishing, 2000.

★989★
U.S. colleges and universities that devote the least course time to discussion

Ranking basis/background: From a survey of nearly 60,000 students who were asked to answer 70 multiple choice question on subjects including school administration, quality of teaching, social life and campus life. The rankings from this survey are based purely on student opinion and are not to be considered objective. **Remarks:** Except for schools with less than 1,000 students enrolled, the Princeton Review heard from at least 100 students on each campus surveyed. **Number listed:** 20.
1. University of Georgia
2. University of Wyoming
3. University of Arkansas, Fayetteville
4. University of Idaho
5. University of Toronto
6. Michigan Technological University
7. McGill University
8. City University of New York, Hunter College
9. University of Washington (WA)
10. Illinois Institute of Technology

Source: Franek, Robert, et. al., *The Best 311 Colleges, 2001 edition*, Princeton Review Publishing, 2000.

★990★
U.S. colleges and universities that devote the most course time to discussion

Ranking basis/background: From a survey of nearly 60,000 students who were asked to answer 70 multiple choice question on subjects including school administration, quality of teaching, social life and campus life. The rankings from this survey are based purely on student opinion and are not to be considered objective. **Remarks:** Except for schools with less than 1,000 students enrolled, the Princeton Review heard from at least 100 students on each campus surveyed. **Number listed:** 20.
1. Occidental College
2. Wells College
3. Georgetown University
4. Boston College
5. Sarah Lawrence College
6. Fairfield University
7. Carleton College
8. Knox College
9. Colorado College
10. Oberlin College

Source: Franek, Robert, et. al., *The Best 311 Colleges, 2001 edition*, Princeton Review Publishing, 2000.

★991★
U.S. colleges and universities where a large portion of the student body drink beer

Ranking basis/background: From a survey of nearly 60,000 students who were asked to answer 70 multiple choice question on subjects including school administration, quality of teaching, social life and campus life. The rankings from this survey are based purely on student opinion and are not to be considered objective. **Remarks:** Except for schools with less than 1,000 students enrolled, the Princeton Review heard from at least 100 students on each campus surveyed. **Number listed:** 20.
1. Union College
2. University of Texas, Austin
3. St. Bonaventure University
4. Louisiana State University, Baton Rouge
5. Florida State University
6. St. Lawrence University
7. Seton Hall University
8. Lehigh University
9. Lafayette College
10. University of Tennessee, Knoxville

Source: Franek, Robert, et. al., *The Best 311 Colleges, 2001 edition*, Princeton Review Publishing, 2000.

★992★
U.S. colleges and universities where a large portion of the student body drink hard liquor

Ranking basis/background: From a survey of nearly 60,000 students who were asked to answer 70 multiple choice question on subjects including school administration, quality of teaching, social life and campus life. The rankings from this survey are based purely on student opinion and are not to be considered objective. **Remarks:** Except for schools with less than 1,000 students enrolled, the Princeton Review heard from at least 100 students on each campus surveyed. **Number listed:** 20.
1. Bucknell University
2. Trinity College
3. Tulane University
4. Union College
5. Lehigh University
6. Louisiana State University, Baton Rouge
7. Florida State University
8. University of Wisconsin, Madison
9. St. Bonaventure University
10. University of Alabama

Source: Franek, Robert, et. al., *The Best 311 Colleges, 2001 edition*, Princeton Review Publishing, 2000.

★993★
U.S. colleges and universities where fraternities and sororities are popular

Ranking basis/background: From a survey of nearly 60,000 students who were asked to answer 70 multiple choice question on subjects including school administration, quality of teaching, social life and campus life. The rankings from this survey are based purely on student opinion and are not to be considered objective. **Remarks:** Except for schools with less than 1,000 students enrolled, the Princeton Review heard from at least 100 students on each campus surveyed. **Number listed:** 20.
1. DePauw University
2. Washington and Lee University
3. Louisiana State University, Baton Rouge
4. University of Michigan
5. University of Texas, Austin
6. Birmingham Southern College
7. Ohio University, Athens
8. University of Georgia
9. University of Alabama
10. Florida State University

Source: Franek, Robert, et. al., *The Best 311 Colleges, 2001 edition*, Princeton Review Publishing, 2000.

★994★
U.S. colleges and universities where intercollegiate sports are not popular

Ranking basis/background: From a survey of nearly 60,000 students who were asked to answer 70 multiple choice question on subjects including school administration, quality of teaching, social life and campus life. The rankings from this survey are based purely on student opinion and are not to be considered objective. **Remarks:** Except for schools with less than 1,000 students enrolled, the Princeton Review heard from at least 100 students on each campus surveyed. **Number listed:** 20.
1. Hampshire College
2. Bennington College
3. Sarah Lawrence College
4. Reed College
5. Goddard College
6. St. John's College (NM)
7. Simon's Rock College of Bard
8. Emerson College
9. Golden Gate College
10. Fordham University

Source: Franek, Robert, et. al., *The Best 311 Colleges, 2001 edition*, Princeton Review Publishing, 2000.

★995★
U.S. colleges and universities where intercollegiate sports are popular

Ranking basis/background: From a survey of nearly 60,000 students who were asked to answer 70 multiple choice question on subjects including school administration, quality of teaching, social life and campus life. The rankings from this survey are based purely on student opinion and are not to be considered objective. **Remarks:** Except for schools with less than 1,000 students enrolled, the Princeton Review heard from at least 100 students on each campus surveyed. **Number listed:** 20.
1. University of Notre Dame
2. Pennsylvania State University
3. Florida State University
4. Syracuse University
5. Michigan State University
6. University of Michigan, Ann Arbor
7. University of North Carolina, Chapel Hill
8. Villanova University
9. Colgate University
10. Wake Forest University

Source: Franek, Robert, et. al., *The Best 311 Colleges, 2001 edition*, Princeton Review Publishing, 2000.

★996★
U.S. colleges and universities where intramural sports are not popular

Ranking basis/background: From a survey of nearly 60,000 students who were asked to answer 70 multiple choice question on subjects including school administration, quality of teaching, social life and campus life. The rankings from this survey are based purely on student opinion and are not to be considered objective. **Remarks:** Except for schools with less than 1,000 students enrolled, the Princeton Review heard from at least 100 students on each campus surveyed. **Number listed:** 20.
1. Bennington College
2. Simon's Rock College of Bard
3. Evergreen State College
4. Emerson College
5. Eugene Lang College
6. Stephens College
7. Sarah Lawrence College
8. Cooper Union
9. Fordham University
10. Bryn Mawr College

Source: Franek, Robert, et. al., *The Best 311 Colleges, 2001 edition*, Princeton Review Publishing, 2000.

COLLEGE LIFE

★997★
U.S. colleges and universities where intramural sports are popular

Ranking basis/background: From a survey of nearly 60,000 students who were asked to answer 70 multiple choice question on subjects including school administration, quality of teaching, social life and campus life. The rankings from this survey are based purely on student opinion and are not to be considered objective. **Remarks:** Except for schools with less than 1,000 students enrolled, the Princeton Review heard from at least 100 students on each campus surveyed. **Number listed:** 20.
1. Wabash College
2. University of Notre Dame
3. Colgate University
4. Rice University
5. Hanover College
6. Williams College
7. Whitman College
8. University of Arizona
9. Pennsylvania State University
10. Carleton College

Source: Franek, Robert, et. al., *The Best 311 Colleges, 2001 edition*, Princeton Review Publishing, 2000.

★998★
U.S. colleges and universities where students and the local community have strained relations

Ranking basis/background: From a survey of nearly 60,000 students who were asked to answer 70 multiple choice question on subjects including school administration, quality of teaching, social life and campus life. The rankings from this survey are based purely on student opinion and are not to be considered objective. **Remarks:** Except for schools with less than 1,000 students enrolled, the Princeton Review heard from at least 100 students on each campus surveyed. **Number listed:** 20.
1. Duke University
2. College of the Atlantic
3. Babson College
4. Sarah Lawrence College
5. College of New Jersey
6. Tufts University
7. Bennington College
8. Villanova University
9. Connecticut College
10. Colorado School of Mines

Source: Franek, Robert, et. al., *The Best 311 Colleges, 2001 edition*, Princeton Review Publishing, 2000.

★999★
U.S. colleges and universities where students and the local community relate well

Ranking basis/background: From a survey of nearly 60,000 students who were asked to answer 70 multiple choice question on subjects including school administration, quality of teaching, social life and campus life. The rankings from this survey are based purely on student opinion and are not to be considered objective. **Remarks:** Except for schools with less than 1,000 students enrolled, the Princeton Review heard from at least 100 students on each campus surveyed. **Number listed:** 20.
1. Albertson College
2. Earlham College
3. Wheaton College (IL)
4. Ohio Wesleyan University
5. United States Coast Guard Academy
6. Emerson College
7. Wells College
8. St. Lawrence University
9. Seton Hall University
10. Rensselaer Polytechnic Institute

Source: Franek, Robert, et. al., *The Best 311 Colleges, 2001 edition*, Princeton Review Publishing, 2000.

★1000★
U.S. colleges and universities where students are not very politically active

Ranking basis/background: From a survey of nearly 60,000 students who were asked to answer 70 multiple choice question on subjects including school administration, quality of teaching, social life and campus life. The rankings from this survey are based purely on student opinion and are not to be considered objective. **Remarks:** Except for schools with less than 1,000 students enrolled, the Princeton Review heard from at least 100 students on each campus surveyed. **Number listed:** 20.
1. St. Bonaventure University
2. Babson College
3. Rensselaer Polytechnic Institute
4. Bennington College
5. College of New Jersey
6. Carnegie Mellon University
7. Colorado School of Mines
8. Austin College
9. University of Idaho
10. Texas Christian University

Source: Franek, Robert, et. al., *The Best 311 Colleges, 2001 edition*, Princeton Review Publishing, 2000.

★1001★
U.S. colleges and universities where students are very politically active

Ranking basis/background: From a survey of nearly 60,000 students who were asked to answer 70 multiple choice question on subjects including school administration, quality of teaching, social life and campus life. The rankings from this survey are based purely on student opinion and are not to be considered objective. **Remarks:** Except for schools with less than 1,000 students enrolled, the Princeton Review heard from at least 100 students on each campus surveyed. **Number listed:** 20.
1. Bard College
2. Lewis and Clark College
3. College of the Atlantic
4. Simon's Rock College of Bard
5. Swarthmore College
6. Vassar College
7. Evergreen State College
8. Earlham College
9. Grinnell College
10. Hampshire College

Source: Franek, Robert, et. al., *The Best 311 Colleges, 2001 edition*, Princeton Review Publishing, 2000.

★1002★
U.S. colleges and universities where students study the least

Ranking basis/background: From a survey of nearly 60,000 students who were asked to answer 70 multiple choice question on subjects including school administration, quality of teaching, social life and campus life. The rankings from this survey are based purely on student opinion and are not to be considered objective. **Remarks:** Except for schools with less than 1,000 students enrolled, the Princeton Review heard from at least 100 students on each campus surveyed. **Number listed:** 20.
1. University of Montana, Missoula
2. University of Rhode Island
3. St. Bonaventure University
4. George Mason University
5. Arizona State University
6. Seton Hall University
7. University of Georgia
8. University of Hawaii, Manoa
9. University of Alabama, Tuscaloosa
10. Providence College

Source: Franek, Robert, et. al., *The Best 311 Colleges, 2001 edition*, Princeton Review Publishing, 2000.

★1003★
U.S. colleges and universities where students study the most

Ranking basis/background: From a survey of nearly 60,000 students who were asked to answer 70 multiple choice question on subjects including school administration, quality of teaching, social life and campus life. The rankings from this survey are based purely on student opinion and are not to be considered objective. **Remarks:** Except for schools with less than 1,000 students enrolled, the Princeton Review heard from at least 100 students on each campus surveyed. **Number listed:** 20.
1. Davidson College
2. Rice University
3. Massachusetts Institute of Technology
4. California Institute of Technology
5. United States Coast Guard Academy
6. Bryn Mawr College
7. Wake Forest University
8. Carnegie Mellon University
9. Scripps College
10. Swarthmore College

Source: Franek, Robert, et. al., *The Best 311 Colleges, 2001 edition*, Princeton Review Publishing, 2000.

★1004★
U.S. colleges and universities where the general student body does not drink beer

Ranking basis/background: From a survey of nearly 60,000 students who were asked to answer 70 multiple choice question on subjects including school administration, quality of teaching, social life and campus life. The rankings from this survey are based purely on student opinion and are not to be considered objective. **Remarks:** Except for schools with less than 1,000 students enrolled, the Princeton Review heard from at least 100 students on each campus surveyed. **Number listed:** 20.
1. Wheaton College (IL)
2. Brigham Young University
3. Golden Gate University
4. College of the Ozarks
5. Wesleyan College
6. City University of New York, Queens College
7. Samford University
8. Cooper Union
9. Calvin College
10. Mount Holyoke College

Source: Franek, Robert, et. al., *The Best 311 Colleges, 2001 edition*, Princeton Review Publishing, 2000.

Educational Rankings Annual • 2002 — COLLEGE LIFE

★1005★
U.S. colleges and universities where the general student body does not drink hard liquor

Ranking basis/background: From a survey of nearly 60,000 students who were asked to answer 70 multiple choice question on subjects including school administration, quality of teaching, social life and campus life. The rankings from this survey are based purely on student opinion and are not to be considered objective. **Remarks:** Except for schools with less than 1,000 students enrolled, the Princeton Review heard from at least 100 students on each campus surveyed. **Number listed:** 20.

1. Wheaton College (IL)
2. Calvin College
3. Brigham Young University
4. Mount Holyoke College
5. Grove City College
6. Wesleyan College
7. Simon's Rock College of Bard
8. California Institute of Technology
9. Cooper Union
10. United States Coast Guard Academy

Source: Franek, Robert, et. al., *The Best 311 Colleges, 2001 edition*, Princeton Review Publishing, 2000.

★1006★
U.S. colleges and universities where the general student body does not smoke marijuana

Ranking basis/background: From a survey of nearly 60,000 students who were asked to answer 70 multiple choice question on subjects including school administration, quality of teaching, social life and campus life. The rankings from this survey are based purely on student opinion and are not to be considered objective. **Remarks:** Except for schools with less than 1,000 students enrolled, the Princeton Review heard from at least 100 students on each campus surveyed. **Number listed:** 20.

1. Grove City College
2. Wheaton College (IL)
3. College of the Ozarks
4. Brigham Young University
5. California Institute of Technology
6. Wells College
7. Golden Gate University
8. Samford University
9. Samford University
10. Centenary College of Louisiana
11. Furman University

Source: Franek, Robert, et. al., *The Best 311 Colleges, 2001 edition*, Princeton Review Publishing, 2000.

★1007★
U.S. colleges and universities where the general student body puts a strong emphasis on athletic events

Ranking basis/background: From a survey of nearly 60,000 students who were asked to answer 70 multiple choice question on subjects including school administration, quality of teaching, social life and campus life. The rankings from this survey are based purely on student opinion and are not to be considered objective. **Remarks:** Except for schools with less than 1,000 students enrolled, the Princeton Review heard from at least 100 students on each campus surveyed. **Number listed:** 20.

1. University of Notre Dame
2. Kansas State University
3. Colgate University
4. University of Arizona
5. Pennsylvania State University
6. University of Florida
7. Syracuse University
8. University of Georgia
9. University of North Carolina, Chapel Hill
10. Villanova University

Source: Franek, Robert, et. al., *The Best 311 Colleges, 2001 edition*, Princeton Review Publishing, 2000.

★1008★
U.S. colleges and universities where the general student body puts a strong emphasis on socializing

Ranking basis/background: From a survey of nearly 60,000 students who were asked to answer 70 multiple choice question on subjects including school administration, quality of teaching, social life and campus life. The rankings from this survey are based purely on student opinion and are not to be considered objective. **Remarks:** Except for schools with less than 1,000 students enrolled, the Princeton Review heard from at least 100 students on each campus surveyed. **Number listed:** 20.

1. Louisiana State University, Baton Rouge
2. University of Alabama
3. University of Texas, Austin
4. Florida State University
5. University of Colorado, Boulder
6. University of Tennessee, Knoxville
7. University of California, Santa Cruz
8. Tulane University
9. University of Wisconsin, Madison
10. Ohio University, Athens

Source: Franek, Robert, et. al., *The Best 311 Colleges, 2001 edition*, Princeton Review Publishing, 2000.

★1009★
U.S. colleges and universities where the general student body puts little emphasis on athletic events

Ranking basis/background: From a survey of nearly 60,000 students who were asked to answer 70 multiple choice question on subjects including school administration, quality of teaching, social life and campus life. The rankings from this survey are based purely on student opinion and are not to be considered objective. **Remarks:** Except for schools with less than 1,000 students enrolled, the Princeton Review heard from at least 100 students on each campus surveyed. **Number listed:** 20.

1. Connecticut College
2. Bard College
3. Hollins University
4. Simon's Rock College of Bard
5. Bennington College
6. Eugene Lang College
7. New College of the University of South Florida
8. Reed College
9. Cooper Union
10. Occidental College

Source: Franek, Robert, et. al., *The Best 311 Colleges, 2001 edition*, Princeton Review Publishing, 2000.

★1010★
U.S. colleges and universities where the general student body puts little emphasis on socializing

Ranking basis/background: From a survey of nearly 60,000 students who were asked to answer 70 multiple choice question on subjects including school administration, quality of teaching, social life and campus life. The rankings from this survey are based purely on student opinion and are not to be considered objective. **Remarks:** Except for schools with less than 1,000 students enrolled, the Princeton Review heard from at least 100 students on each campus surveyed. **Number listed:** 20.

1. Brigham Young University
2. Wheaton College (IL)
3. California Institute of Technology
4. United States Naval Academy
5. United States Coast Guard Academy
6. Samford University
7. Cooper Union
8. Wellesley College
9. Mount Holyoke College
10. Calvin College

Source: Franek, Robert, et. al., *The Best 311 Colleges, 2001 edition*, Princeton Review Publishing, 2000.

★1011★
U.S. colleges and universities where the general student body smokes marijuana

Ranking basis/background: From a survey of nearly 60,000 students who were asked to answer 70 multiple choice question on subjects including school administration, quality of teaching, social life and campus life. The rankings from this survey are based purely on student opinion and are not to be considered objective. **Remarks:** Except for schools with less than 1,000 students enrolled, the Princeton Review heard from at least 100 students on each campus surveyed. **Number listed:** 20.

1. Reed College
2. Lewis and Clark College
3. New York University
4. Lehigh University
5. Oberlin College
6. Vassar College
7. Warren Wilson College
8. Trinity College
9. New College of the University of South Florida
10. University of Colorado, Boulder

Source: Franek, Robert, et. al., *The Best 311 Colleges, 2001 edition*, Princeton Review Publishing, 2000.

★1012★
U.S. colleges and universities with a diverse student body

Ranking basis/background: From a survey of nearly 60,000 students who were asked to answer 70 multiple choice question on subjects including school administration, quality of teaching, social life and campus life. The rankings from this survey are based purely on student opinion and are not to be considered objective. **Remarks:** Except for schools with less than 1,000 students enrolled, the Princeton Review heard from at least 100 students on each campus surveyed. **Number listed:** 20.

1. Columbia University
2. Boston University
3. New York University
4. Massachusetts Institute of Technology
5. Temple University
6. Seton Hall University

COLLEGE LIFE

7. Clark University
8. Mount Holyoke College
9. University of Maryland, Baltimore
10. University of California, Berkeley

Source: Franek, Robert, et. al., *The Best 311 Colleges, 2001 edition*, Princeton Review Publishing, 2000.

★1013★
U.S. colleges and universities with a favorable surrounding town or city

Ranking basis/background: From a survey of nearly 60,000 students who were asked to answer 70 multiple choice question on subjects including school administration, quality of teaching, social life and campus life. The rankings from this survey are based purely on student opinion and are not to be considered objective. **Remarks:** Except for schools with less than 1,000 students enrolled, the Princeton Review heard from at least 100 students on each campus surveyed. **Number listed:** 20.

1. New York University
2. Boston University
3. Emerson College
4. DePauw University
5. Cooper University
6. Georgetown University
7. Emory University
8. Macalester College
9. University of Georgia
10. University of California, Berkeley

Source: Franek, Robert, et. al., *The Best 311 Colleges, 2001 edition*, Princeton Review Publishing, 2000.

★1014★
U.S. colleges and universities with a generally conservative student body

Ranking basis/background: From a survey of nearly 60,000 students who were asked to answer 70 multiple choice question on subjects including school administration, quality of teaching, social life and campus life. The rankings from this survey are based purely on student opinion and are not to be considered objective. **Remarks:** Except for schools with less than 1,000 students enrolled, the Princeton Review heard from at least 100 students on each campus surveyed. **Number listed:** 20.

1. Wheaton College (IL)
2. University of Dallas
3. Texas Christian University
4. Providence College
5. United States Coast Guard Academy
6. Sweet Briar College
7. Grove City College
8. Brigham Young University
9. Furman University
10. Villanova University

Source: Franek, Robert, et. al., *The Best 311 Colleges, 2001 edition*, Princeton Review Publishing, 2000.

★1015★
U.S. colleges and universities with a generally liberal student body

Ranking basis/background: From a survey of nearly 60,000 students who were asked to answer 70 multiple choice question on subjects including school administration, quality of teaching, social life and campus life. The rankings from this survey are based purely on student opinion and are not to be considered objective. **Remarks:** Except for schools with less than 1,000 students enrolled, the Princeton Review heard from at least 100 students on each campus surveyed. **Number listed:** 20.

1. Haverford College
2. Reed College
3. Smith College
4. Hampshire College
5. Bryn Mawr College
6. Warren Wilson College
7. Bennington College
8. Wesleyan University
9. Bard College
10. Sarah Lawrence

Source: Franek, Robert, et. al., *The Best 311 Colleges, 2001 edition*, Princeton Review Publishing, 2000.

★1016★
U.S. colleges and universities with a large student body of conservative Republicans

Ranking basis/background: From a survey of nearly 60,000 students who were asked to answer 70 multiple choice question on subjects including school administration, quality of teaching, social life and campus life. The rankings from this survey are based purely on student opinion and are not to be considered objective. **Remarks:** Except for schools with less than 1,000 students enrolled, the Princeton Review heard from at least 100 students on each campus surveyed. **Number listed:** 20.

1. Southern Methodist University
2. Wofford College
3. Rose-Hulman Institute of Technology
4. Grove City College
5. University of Dallas
6. Louisiana State University, Baton Rouge
7. Wabash College
8. Villanova University
9. Lehigh University
10. College of the Ozarks

Source: Franek, Robert, et. al., *The Best 311 Colleges, 2001 edition*, Princeton Review Publishing, 2000.

★1017★
U.S. colleges and universities with a large student body of liberal Democrats

Ranking basis/background: From a survey of nearly 60,000 students who were asked to answer 70 multiple choice question on subjects including school administration, quality of teaching, social life and campus life. The rankings from this survey are based purely on student opinion and are not to be considered objective. **Remarks:** Except for schools with less than 1,000 students enrolled, the Princeton Review heard from at least 100 students on each campus surveyed. **Number listed:** 20.

1. Lewis and Clark College
2. Reed College
3. Sarah Lawrence College
4. New College of the University of South Florida
5. College of the Atlantic
6. New York University
7. Drew University
8. Wesleyan University
9. Vassar College
10. Hampshire College

Source: Franek, Robert, et. al., *The Best 311 Colleges, 2001 edition*, Princeton Review Publishing, 2000.

★1018★
U.S. colleges and universities with a popular newspaper

Ranking basis/background: From a survey of nearly 60,000 students who were asked to answer 70 multiple choice question on subjects including school administration, quality of teaching, social life and campus life. The rankings from this survey are based purely on student opinion and are not to be considered objective. **Remarks:** Except for schools with less than 1,000 students enrolled, the Princeton Review heard from at least 100 students on each campus surveyed. **Number listed:** 20.

1. University of Pennsylvania
2. University of North Carolina, Chapel Hill
3. Wabash College
4. Tufts University
5. University of Minnesota, Twin Cities
6. Michigan State University
7. University of Florida
8. Syracuse University
9. University of Massachusetts, Amherst
10. Loyola Marymount University

Source: Franek, Robert, et. al., *The Best 311 Colleges, 2001 edition*, Princeton Review Publishing, 2000.

★1019★
U.S. colleges and universities with a popular radio station

Ranking basis/background: From a survey of nearly 60,000 students who were asked to answer 70 multiple choice question on subjects including school administration, quality of teaching, social life and campus life. The rankings from this survey are based purely on student opinion and are not to be considered objective. **Remarks:** Except for schools with less than 1,000 students enrolled, the Princeton Review heard from at least 100 students on each campus surveyed. **Number listed:** 20.

1. DePaul University
2. Emerson College
3. Brown University
4. Loyola Marymount University
5. Goddard College
6. Fordham University
7. Denison University
8. Hampton University
9. Louisiana State University, Baton Rouge
10. Bates College

Source: Franek, Robert, et. al., *The Best 311 Colleges, 2001 edition*, Princeton Review Publishing, 2000.

★1020★
U.S. colleges and universities with a popular theater group

Ranking basis/background: From a survey of nearly 60,000 students who were asked to answer 70 multiple choice question on subjects including school administration, quality of teaching, social life and campus life. The rankings from this survey are based purely on student opinion and are not to be considered objective. **Remarks:** Except for schools with less than 1,000 students enrolled, the Princeton Review heard from at least 100 students on each campus surveyed. **Number listed:** 20.

1. Emerson College
2. Ithaca College
3. Whitman College
4. Millsaps College
5. Hampshire College
6. Evergreen State College
7. Hendrix College
8. Florida A&M University

9. Brown University
10. Hamilton College

Source: Franek, Robert, et. al., *The Best 311 Colleges, 2001 edition*, Princeton Review Publishing, 2000.

★1021★
U.S. colleges and universities with a primarily non-religious student body

Ranking basis/background: From a survey of nearly 60,000 students who were asked to answer 70 multiple choice question on subjects including school administration, quality of teaching, social life and campus life. The rankings from this survey are based purely on student opinion and are not to be considered objective. **Remarks:** Except for schools with less than 1,000 students enrolled, the Princeton Review heard from at least 100 students on each campus surveyed. **Number listed:** 20.

1. Vassar College
2. Lewis and Clark College
3. Reed College
4. Macalester College
5. Wesleyan University
6. Bard College
7. Connecticut College
8. University of Vermont
9. Bates College
10. Bowdoin College

Source: Franek, Robert, et. al., *The Best 311 Colleges, 2001 edition*, Princeton Review Publishing, 2000.

★1022★
U.S. colleges and universities with a primarily religious student body

Ranking basis/background: From a survey of nearly 60,000 students who were asked to answer 70 multiple choice question on subjects including school administration, quality of teaching, social life and campus life. The rankings from this survey are based purely on student opinion and are not to be considered objective. **Remarks:** Except for schools with less than 1,000 students enrolled, the Princeton Review heard from at least 100 students on each campus surveyed. **Number listed:** 20.

1. Wheaton College (IL)
2. Brigham Young University
3. University of Dallas
4. Grove City College
5. Baylor University
6. United States Coast Guard Academy
7. Samford University
8. College of the Holy Cross
9. Morehouse College
10. Pepperdine University

Source: Franek, Robert, et. al., *The Best 311 Colleges, 2001 edition*, Princeton Review Publishing, 2000.

★1023★
U.S. colleges and universities with an unfavorable surrounding town or city

Ranking basis/background: From a survey of nearly 60,000 students who were asked to answer 70 multiple choice question on subjects including school administration, quality of teaching, social life and campus life. The rankings from this survey are based purely on student opinion and are not to be considered objective. **Remarks:** Except for schools with less than 1,000 students enrolled, the Princeton Review heard from at least 100 students on each campus surveyed. **Number listed:** 20.

1. University of Pittsburgh
2. Tufts University
3. Villanova University
4. Rensselaer Polytechnic Institute
5. University of Miami
6. Georgia Institute of Technology
7. University of Mississippi
8. University of Wyoming
9. St. Lawrence University
10. Simon's Rock College of Bard

Source: Franek, Robert, et. al., *The Best 311 Colleges, 2001 edition*, Princeton Review Publishing, 2000.

★1024★
U.S. colleges and universities with excellent instructors

Ranking basis/background: From a survey of nearly 60,000 students who were asked to answer 70 multiple choice question on subjects including school administration, quality of teaching, social life and campus life. The rankings from this survey are based purely on student opinion and are not to be considered objective. **Remarks:** Except for schools with less than 1,000 students enrolled, the Princeton Review heard from at least 100 students on each campus surveyed. **Number listed:** 20.

1. Babson College
2. Wabash College
3. Tufts University
4. Smith College
5. Villanova University
6. Colorado College
7. Austin College
8. Haverford College
9. Millsaps College
10. Pitzer College

Source: Franek, Robert, et. al., *The Best 311 Colleges, 2001 edition*, Princeton Review Publishing, 2000.

★1025★
U.S. colleges and universities with excellent library facilities

Ranking basis/background: From a survey of nearly 60,000 students who were asked to answer 70 multiple choice question on subjects including school administration, quality of teaching, social life and campus life. The rankings from this survey are based purely on student opinion and are not to be considered objective. **Remarks:** Except for schools with less than 1,000 students enrolled, the Princeton Review heard from at least 100 students on each campus surveyed. **Number listed:** 20.

1. Harvard College
2. University of Virginia
3. Knox College
4. Haverford College
5. University of Michigan, Ann Arbor
6. New York University
7. Hamilton College
8. Ohio State University, Columbus
9. Mount Holyoke College
10. Skidmore College

Source: Franek, Robert, et. al., *The Best 311 Colleges, 2001 edition*, Princeton Review Publishing, 2000.

★1026★
U.S. colleges and universities with harmonious race/class interaction

Ranking basis/background: From a survey of nearly 60,000 students who were asked to answer 70 multiple choice question on subjects including school administration, quality of teaching, social life and campus life. The rankings from this survey are based purely on student opinion and are not to be considered objective. **Remarks:** Except for schools with less than 1,000 students enrolled, the Princeton Review heard from at least 100 students on each campus surveyed. **Number listed:** 20.

1. Syracuse University
2. Babson College
3. St. Lawrence University
4. Pitzer College
5. Seton Hall University
6. Simon's Rock College of Bard
7. Bard College
8. Swarthmore College
9. Vassar College
10. Carnegie Mellon University

Source: Franek, Robert, et. al., *The Best 311 Colleges, 2001 edition*, Princeton Review Publishing, 2000.

★1027★
U.S. colleges and universities with poor instructors

Ranking basis/background: From a survey of nearly 60,000 students who were asked to answer 70 multiple choice question on subjects including school administration, quality of teaching, social life and campus life. The rankings from this survey are based purely on student opinion and are not to be considered objective. **Remarks:** Except for schools with less than 1,000 students enrolled, the Princeton Review heard from at least 100 students on each campus surveyed. **Number listed:** 20.

1. Hofstra University
2. University of Iowa
3. Georgia Institute of Technology
4. University of Pittsburgh
5. Sonoma State University
6. Miami University (OH)
7. Beloit College
8. State University of New York, Stony Brook
9. State University of New York, Buffalo
10. University of Toronto

Source: Franek, Robert, et. al., *The Best 311 Colleges, 2001 edition*, Princeton Review Publishing, 2000.

★1028★
U.S. colleges and universities with poor library facilities

Ranking basis/background: From a survey of nearly 60,000 students who were asked to answer 70 multiple choice question on subjects including school administration, quality of teaching, social life and campus life. The rankings from this survey are based purely on student opinion and are not to be considered objective. **Remarks:** Except for schools with less than 1,000 students enrolled, the Princeton Review heard from at least 100 students on each campus surveyed. **Number listed:** 20.

1. Catawba College
2. Hollins University
3. St. Lawrence University
4. Seton Hall University
5. Syracuse University
6. Hampton University
7. Hanover College

COLLEGE LIFE

8. Florida State University
9. University of North Dakota
10. Miami University (OH)

Source: Franek, Robert, et. al., *The Best 311 Colleges, 2001 edition*, Princeton Review Publishing, 2000.

★1029★
U.S. colleges and universities with strained race/class interaction

Ranking basis/background: From a survey of nearly 60,000 students who were asked to answer 70 multiple choice question on subjects including school administration, quality of teaching, social life and campus life. The rankings from this survey are based purely on student opinion and are not to be considered objective. **Remarks:** Except for schools with less than 1,000 students enrolled, the Princeton Review heard from at least 100 students on each campus surveyed. **Number listed:** 20.

1. Trinity College
2. Emory University
3. St. Bonaventure University
4. University of Pittsburgh
5. Bennington College
6. Denison University
7. Tufts University
8. Villanova University
9. Colorado School of Mines
10. University of California, Santa Barbara

Source: Franek, Robert, et. al., *The Best 311 Colleges, 2001 edition*, Princeton Review Publishing, 2000.

★1030★
U.S. colleges and universities with the best financial aid programs

Ranking basis/background: From a survey of nearly 60,000 students who were asked to answer 70 multiple choice question on subjects including school administration, quality of teaching, social life and campus life. The rankings from this survey are based purely on student opinion and are not to be considered objective. **Remarks:** Except for schools with less than 1,000 students enrolled, the Princeton Review heard from at least 100 students on each campus surveyed. **Number listed:** 20.

1. Knox College
2. Ripon College
3. Wofford College
4. Centenary College of Louisiana
5. Lake Forest College
6. Warren Wilson College
7. Agnes Scott College
8. Oglethorpe University
9. Susquehanna University
10. Ursinus College

Source: Franek, Robert, et. al., *The Best 311 Colleges, 2001 edition*, Princeton Review Publishing, 2000.

★1031★
U.S. colleges and universities with the best food service program

Ranking basis/background: From a survey of nearly 60,000 students who were asked to answer 70 multiple choice question on subjects including school administration, quality of teaching, social life and campus life. The rankings from this survey are based purely on student opinion and are not to be considered objective. **Remarks:** Except for schools with less than 1,000 students enrolled, the Princeton Review heard from at least 100 students on each campus surveyed. **Number listed:** 20.

1. College of the Atlantic
2. Wheaton College (IL)
3. Bowdoin College
4. Washington University
5. Emerson College
6. Dickinson College
7. Simon's Rock College of Bard
8. Bard College
9. Colby College
10. Albertson College

Source: Franek, Robert, et. al., *The Best 311 Colleges, 2001 edition*, Princeton Review Publishing, 2000.

★1032★
U.S. colleges and universities with the best on-campus housing facilities

Ranking basis/background: From a survey of nearly 60,000 students who were asked to answer 70 multiple choice question on subjects including school administration, quality of teaching, social life and campus life. The rankings from this survey are based purely on student opinion and are not to be considered objective. **Remarks:** Except for schools with less than 1,000 students enrolled, the Princeton Review heard from at least 100 students on each campus surveyed. **Number listed:** 20.

1. Bryn Mawr College
2. Smith College
3. Middlebury College
4. Sarah Lawrence College
5. Marlboro College
6. Swarthmore College
7. Wells College
8. Bennington College
9. Randolph-Macon Woman's College
10. Rice University

Source: Franek, Robert, et. al., *The Best 311 Colleges, 2001 edition*, Princeton Review Publishing, 2000.

★1033★
U.S. colleges and universities with the best overall administration

Ranking basis/background: From a survey of nearly 60,000 students who were asked to answer 70 multiple choice question on subjects including school administration, quality of teaching, social life and campus life. The rankings from this survey are based purely on student opinion and are not to be considered objective. **Remarks:** Except for schools with less than 1,000 students enrolled, the Princeton Review heard from at least 100 students on each campus surveyed. **Number listed:** 20.

1. United States Naval Academy
2. United States Air Force Academy
3. Williams College
4. Pomona College
5. Villanova University
6. Austin College
7. Texas Christian University
8. Harvard College
9. Haverford College
10. Millsaps College

Source: Franek, Robert, et. al., *The Best 311 Colleges, 2001 edition*, Princeton Review Publishing, 2000.

★1034★
U.S. colleges and universities with the best quality of life

Ranking basis/background: From a survey of nearly 60,000 students who were asked to answer 70 multiple choice question on subjects including school administration, quality of teaching, social life and campus life. The rankings from this survey are based purely on student opinion and are not to be considered objective. **Remarks:** Except for schools with less than 1,000 students enrolled, the Princeton Review heard from at least 100 students on each campus surveyed. **Number listed:** 20.

1. Dartmouth College
2. Davidson College
3. Agnes Scott College
4. Harvard College
5. Goddard College
6. University of Richmond
7. Claremont McKenna College
8. University of California, Santa Cruz
9. Brigham Young University
10. Rhodes College

Source: Franek, Robert, et. al., *The Best 311 Colleges, 2001 edition*, Princeton Review Publishing, 2000.

★1035★
U.S. colleges and universities with the happiest students

Ranking basis/background: From a survey of nearly 60,000 students who were asked to answer 70 multiple choice question on subjects including school administration, quality of teaching, social life and campus life. The rankings from this survey are based purely on student opinion and are not to be considered objective. **Remarks:** Except for schools with less than 1,000 students enrolled, the Princeton Review heard from at least 100 students on each campus surveyed. **Number listed:** 20.

1. St. Bonaventure University
2. College of the Atlantic
3. St. Lawrence University
4. Wabash College
5. Pomona College
6. Bard College
7. Swarthmore College
8. Bennington College
9. Tufts University
10. Pitzer College

Source: Franek, Robert, et. al., *The Best 311 Colleges, 2001 edition*, Princeton Review Publishing, 2000.

★1036★
U.S. colleges and universities with the least accessible instructors

Ranking basis/background: From a survey of nearly 60,000 students who were asked to answer 70 multiple choice question on subjects including school administration, quality of teaching, social life and campus life. The rankings from this survey are based purely on student opinion and are not to be considered objective. **Remarks:** Except for schools with less than 1,000 students enrolled, the Princeton Review heard from at least 100 students on each campus surveyed. **Number listed:** 20.

1. Arizona State University
2. Syracuse University
3. California Institute of Technology
4. University of North Dakota
5. University of Montana, Missoula
6. Sonoma State University
7. Florida State University
8. University of Missouri, Rolla

9. State University of New York, Buffalo
10. University of Maryland, Baltimore
Source: Franek, Robert, et. al., *The Best 311 Colleges, 2001 edition*, Princeton Review Publishing, 2000.

★1037★
U.S. colleges and universities with the least attractive campuses

Ranking basis/background: From a survey of nearly 60,000 students who were asked to answer 70 multiple choice question on subjects including school administration, quality of teaching, social life and campus life. The rankings from this survey are based purely on student opinion and are not to be considered objective. **Remarks:** Except for schools with less than 1,000 students enrolled, the Princeton Review heard from at least 100 students on each campus surveyed. **Number listed:** 20.
1. Drexel University
2. University of Dallas
3. State University of New York, Stony Brook
4. New Jersey Institute of Technology
5. Rochester Institute of Technology
6. Seton Hall University
7. Cooper Union
8. City University of New York, Hunter College
9. Duquesne University
10. California Institute of Technology

Source: Franek, Robert, et. al., *The Best 311 Colleges, 2001 edition*, Princeton Review Publishing, 2000.

★1038★
U.S. colleges and universities with the most accessible instructors

Ranking basis/background: From a survey of nearly 60,000 students who were asked to answer 70 multiple choice question on subjects including school administration, quality of teaching, social life and campus life. The rankings from this survey are based purely on student opinion and are not to be considered objective. **Remarks:** Except for schools with less than 1,000 students enrolled, the Princeton Review heard from at least 100 students on each campus surveyed. **Number listed:** 20.
1. United States Military Academy
2. United States Naval Academy
3. United States Coast Guard Academy
4. St. Bonaventure University
5. College of the Atlantic
6. Babson College
7. Rensselaer Polytechnic Institute
8. Tufts University
9. Villanova University
10. Colorado School of Mines

Source: Franek, Robert, et. al., *The Best 311 Colleges, 2001 edition*, Princeton Review Publishing, 2000.

★1039★
U.S. colleges and universities with the most attractive campuses

Ranking basis/background: From a survey of nearly 60,000 students who were asked to answer 70 multiple choice question on subjects including school administration, quality of teaching, social life and campus life. The rankings from this survey are based purely on student opinion and are not to be considered objective. **Remarks:** Except for schools with less than 1,000 students enrolled, the Princeton Review heard from at least 100 students on each campus surveyed. **Number listed:** 20.

1. College of the Atlantic
2. Mount Holyoke College
3. University of Richmond
4. Bryn Mawr College
5. Vassar College
6. Susquehanna University
7. Wellesley College
8. Colby College
9. Stanford University
10. University of California, Santa Barbara
11. University of California, Santa Cruz

Source: Franek, Robert, et. al., *The Best 311 Colleges, 2001 edition*, Princeton Review Publishing, 2000.

★1040★
U.S. colleges and universities with the most upper level courses taught by TAs

Ranking basis/background: From a survey of nearly 60,000 students who were asked to answer 70 multiple choice question on subjects including school administration, quality of teaching, social life and campus life. The rankings from this survey are based purely on student opinion and are not to be considered objective. **Remarks:** Except for schools with less than 1,000 students enrolled, the Princeton Review heard from at least 100 students on each campus surveyed. **Number listed:** 20.
1. University of Iowa
2. Binghamton University (SUNY)
3. State University of New York, Buffalo
4. Michigan State University
5. Arizona State University
6. Arizona State University
7. University of Pittsburgh
8. University of Hawaii, Manoa
9. University of Alabama, Tuscaloosa
10. University of Arkansas, Fayetteville
11. University of Florida

Source: Franek, Robert, et. al., *The Best 311 Colleges, 2001 edition*, Princeton Review Publishing, 2000.

★1041★
U.S. colleges and universities with the unhappiest students

Ranking basis/background: From a survey of nearly 60,000 students who were asked to answer 70 multiple choice question on subjects including school administration, quality of teaching, social life and campus life. The rankings from this survey are based purely on student opinion and are not to be considered objective. **Remarks:** Except for schools with less than 1,000 students enrolled, the Princeton Review heard from at least 100 students on each campus surveyed. **Number listed:** 20.
1. New Jersey Institute of Technology
2. State University of New York, Buffalo
3. University of California, Riverside
4. Hofstra University
5. Sonoma State University
6. University of Missouri, Rolla
7. Spelman College
8. Colorado School of Mines
9. Temple University
10. City University of New York, Queens College

Source: Franek, Robert, et. al., *The Best 311 Colleges, 2001 edition*, Princeton Review Publishing, 2000.

★1042★
U.S. colleges and universities with the worst financial aid programs

Ranking basis/background: From a survey of nearly 60,000 students who were asked to answer 70 multiple choice question on subjects including school administration, quality of teaching, social life and campus life. The rankings from this survey are based purely on student opinion and are not to be considered objective. **Remarks:** Except for schools with less than 1,000 students enrolled, the Princeton Review heard from at least 100 students on each campus surveyed. **Number listed:** 20.
1. Hampton University
2. Binghamton University (SUNY)
3. Washington State University
4. College of the Holy Cross
5. Howard University
6. University of Hawaii, Manoa
7. University of Alabama
8. State University of New York, Albany
9. Temple University
10. University of California, Santa Barbara

Source: Franek, Robert, et. al., *The Best 311 Colleges, 2001 edition*, Princeton Review Publishing, 2000.

★1043★
U.S. colleges and universities with the worst food service program

Ranking basis/background: From a survey of nearly 60,000 students who were asked to answer 70 multiple choice question on subjects including school administration, quality of teaching, social life and campus life. The rankings from this survey are based purely on student opinion and are not to be considered objective. **Remarks:** Except for schools with less than 1,000 students enrolled, the Princeton Review heard from at least 100 students on each campus surveyed. **Number listed:** 20.
1. Stevens Institute of Technology
2. Catawba College
3. Hampton University
4. Gustavus Adolphus College
5. St. Bonaventure University
6. Oglethorpe University
7. Hiram College
8. Westminster College
9. Colorado School of Mines
10. Tuskegee University

Source: Franek, Robert, et. al., *The Best 311 Colleges, 2001 edition*, Princeton Review Publishing, 2000.

★1044★
U.S. colleges and universities with the worst on-campus housing facilities

Ranking basis/background: From a survey of nearly 60,000 students who were asked to answer 70 multiple choice question on subjects including school administration, quality of teaching, social life and campus life. The rankings from this survey are based purely on student opinion and are not to be considered objective. **Remarks:** Except for schools with less than 1,000 students enrolled, the Princeton Review heard from at least 100 students on each campus surveyed. **Number listed:** 20.
1. Rutgers University, Rutgers College
2. State University of New York, Buffalo
3. State University of New York, Stony Brook
4. California Polytechnic State University, San Luis Obispo
5. University of Washington (WA)
6. University of Montana, Missoula

7. University of Georgia
8. University of Florida
9. Howard University
10. Florida A&M University

Source: Franek, Robert, et. al., *The Best 311 Colleges, 2001 edition*, Princeton Review Publishing, 2000.

★1045★
U.S. colleges and universities with the worst overall administration

Ranking basis/background: From a survey of nearly 60,000 students who were asked to answer 70 multiple choice question on subjects including school administration, quality of teaching, social life and campus life. The rankings from this survey are based purely on student opinion and are not to be considered objective. **Remarks:** Except for schools with less than 1,000 students enrolled, the Princeton Review heard from at least 100 students on each campus surveyed. **Number listed:** 20.

1. City University of New York, Hunter College
2. Hofstra University
3. Temple University
4. Howard University
5. Hampton University
6. University of Connecticut
7. University of Massachusetts, Amherst
8. Rutgers University, Rutgers College
9. Stevens Institute of Technology
10. Spelman College

Source: Franek, Robert, et. al., *The Best 311 Colleges, 2001 edition*, Princeton Review Publishing, 2000.

★1046★
U.S. colleges and universities without a diverse student body

Ranking basis/background: From a survey of nearly 60,000 students who were asked to answer 70 multiple choice question on subjects including school administration, quality of teaching, social life and campus life. The rankings from this survey are based purely on student opinion and are not to be considered objective. **Remarks:** Except for schools with less than 1,000 students enrolled, the Princeton Review heard from at least 100 students on each campus surveyed. **Number listed:** 20.

1. College of the Holy Cross
2. Boston College
3. Grove City College
4. Washington and Lee University
5. Trinity College
6. Fairfield University
7. Colgate University
8. University of Notre Dame
9. College of the Atlantic
10. Reed College

Source: Franek, Robert, et. al., *The Best 311 Colleges, 2001 edition*, Princeton Review Publishing, 2000.

COLLEGE PRESIDENTS
See: **College Administration Salaries–Colleges & Universities**

COLLEGE STUDENTS

★1047★
Activities incoming freshmen report spending six or more hours per week doing, 2000

Ranking basis/background: Survey responses of freshmen entering 2-year and 4-year institutions in the fall of 2000. Because of rounding or multiple responses, figures may total more than 100 percent. **Remarks:** Original source: "The American Freshmen: National Norms for Fall 2000," published by American Council on Education and University of California at Los Angeles Higher Education Research Institute. **Number listed:** 28.

Attended a religious service, with 82.8%
Was bored in class, 39.7%
Participated in organized demonstrations, 45.4%
Tutored another student, 53.8%
Studied with other students, 87.4%
Was a guest in a teacher's home, 27.7%
Smoked cigarettes, 10.0%
Drank beer, 48.3%
Drank wine or liquor, 53.9%
Felt overwhelmed by all I had to do, 28.1%
Felt depressed, 8.1%
Performed volunteer work, 81.0%
Played a musical instrument, 41.5%
Asked a teacher for advice after class, 23.9%
Overslept and missed class or appointment, 35.3%
Discussed politics, 16.4%
Voted in a student election, 22.8%
Socialized with someone of another racial/ethnic group, 67.6%
Came late to class, 64.5%
Attended a public recital or concert, 79.5%
Visited an art gallery or museum, 59.4%
Discussed religion, 29.8%
Communicated via e-mail, 65.6%
Used the Internet for research or homework, 67.4%
Participated in Internet chat rooms, 19.9%
Other Internet use, 52.2%
Performed community service as part of a class, 55.8%
Used a personal computer, 78.5%

Source: "Fact File: This Year's Freshmen at 4-Year Colleges: a Statistical Profile," *The Chronicle of Higher Education*, 47: A48-A49, (January 26, 2001).

★1048★
Average high school grade of incoming freshmen, 2000

Ranking basis/background: Survey responses of freshmen entering 2-year and 4-year institutions in the fall of 2000. Because of rounding or multiple responses, figures may total more than 100 percent. **Remarks:** Original source: "The American Freshmen: National Norms for Fall 2000," published by American Council on Education and University of California at Los Angeles Higher Education Research Institute. **Number listed:** 8.

A or A, with 21.2%
A-, 21.7%
B, 20.8%
B, 21.5%
B-, 8.2%
C, 4.5%
C, 2.0%
D, 0.1%

Source: "Fact File: This Year's Freshmen at 4-Year Colleges: a Statistical Profile," *The Chronicle of Higher Education*, 47: A48-A49, (January 26, 2001).

★1049★
College attended is students' first choice for incoming freshmen, 2000

Ranking basis/background: Survey responses of freshmen entering 2-year and 4-year institutions in the fall of 2000. Because of rounding or multiple responses, figures may total more than 100 percent. **Remarks:** Original source: "The American Freshmen: National Norms for Fall 2000," published by American Council on Education and University of California at Los Angeles Higher Education Research Institute. **Number listed:** 4.

First choice, with 70.6%
Second choice, 20.8%
Third choice, 5.5%
Other, 3.1%

Source: "Fact File: This Year's Freshmen at 4-Year Colleges: a Statistical Profile," *The Chronicle of Higher Education*, 47: A48-A49, (January 26, 2001).

★1050★
Expected majors for incoming freshmen, 2000

Ranking basis/background: Survey responses of freshmen entering 2-year and 4-year institutions in the fall of 2000. Because of rounding or multiple responses, figures may total more than 100 percent. **Remarks:** Original source: "The American Freshmen: National Norms for Fall 2000," published by American Council on Education and University of California at Los Angeles Higher Education Research Institute. **Number listed:** 11.

1. Business, with 16.7%
2. Arts and humanities, 12.1%
3. Professional, 11.6%
4. Education, 11.0%
5. Social sciences, 10.0%
6. Engineering, 8.7%
7. Undecided, 8.3%
8. Biological sciences, 6.6%
9. Physical sciences, 2.6%
10. Technical, 2.1%
11. Other fields, 9.9%

Source: "Fact File: This Year's Freshmen at 4-Year Colleges: a Statistical Profile," *The Chronicle of Higher Education*, 47: A48-A49, (January 26, 2001).

★1051★
High school of incoming freshmen requiring community service for graduation, 2000

Ranking basis/background: Survey responses of freshmen entering 2-year and 4-year institutions in the fall of 2000. Because of rounding or multiple responses, figures may total more than 100 percent. **Remarks:** Original source: "The American Freshmen: National Norms for Fall 2000," published by American Council on Education and University of California at Los Angeles Higher Education Research Institute. **Number listed:** 2.

Yes, with 72.7%
No, 27.3%

Source: "Fact File: This Year's Freshmen at 4-Year Colleges: a Statistical Profile," *The Chronicle of Higher Education*, 47: A48-A49, (January 26, 2001).

★1052★
Number of Advanced Placement courses taken in high school by incoming freshmen, 2000

Ranking basis/background: Survey responses of freshmen entering 2-year and 4-year institutions in the fall of 2000. Because of rounding or multiple responses, figures may total more than 100 percent. **Remarks:** Original source: "The American Freshmen: National Norms for Fall 2000," published by American Council on Education and University of California at Los Angeles Higher Education Research Institute. **Number listed:** 5.

None, with 42.6%
1 to 4, 47.0%
5 to 9, 9.1%
10 to 14, 0.9%
15 or more, 0.4%

Source: "Fact File: This Year's Freshmen at 4-Year Colleges: a Statistical Profile," *The Chronicle of Higher Education*, 47: A48-A49, (January 26, 2001).

★1053★
Number of Advanced Placement exams taken in high school by incoming freshmen, 2000

Ranking basis/background: Survey responses of freshmen entering 2-year and 4-year institutions in the fall of 2000. Because of rounding or multiple responses, figures may total more than 100 percent. **Remarks:** Original source: "The American Freshmen: National Norms for Fall 2000," published by American Council on Education and University of California at Los Angeles Higher Education Research Institute. **Number listed:** 5.

None, with 57.0%
1 to 4, 36.4%
5 to 9, 6.0%
10 to 14, 0.4%
15 or more, 0.2%

Source: "Fact File: This Year's Freshmen at 4-Year Colleges: a Statistical Profile," *The Chronicle of Higher Education*, 47: A48-A49, (January 26, 2001).

★1054★
Number of hours per week freshmen spent doing volunteer work during the last year in high school, 2000

Ranking basis/background: Survey responses of freshmen entering 2-year and 4-year institutions in the fall of 2000. Because of rounding or multiple responses, figures may total more than 100 percent. **Remarks:** Original source: "The American Freshmen: National Norms for Fall 2000," published by American Council on Education and University of California at Los Angeles Higher Education Research Institute. **Number listed:** 8.

None, with 31.0%
Less than 1, 22.2%
1 to 2, 23.5%
3 to 5, 13.5%
6 to 10, 5.4%
11 to 15, 1.9%
16 to 20, 1.0%
21 or more, 1.5%

Source: "Fact File: This Year's Freshmen at 4-Year Colleges: a Statistical Profile," *The Chronicle of Higher Education*, 47: A48-A49, (January 26, 2001).

★1055★
Number of hours per week freshmen spent studying or doing homework during the last year in high school, 2000

Ranking basis/background: Survey responses of freshmen entering 2-year and 4-year institutions in the fall of 2000. Because of rounding or multiple responses, figures may total more than 100 percent. **Remarks:** Original source: "The American Freshmen: National Norms for Fall 2000," published by American Council on Education and University of California at Los Angeles Higher Education Research Institute. **Number listed:** 8.

None, with 2.3%
Less than 1, 11.8%
1 to 2, 21.1%
3 to 5, 28.7%
6 to 10, 20.0%
11 to 15, 8.8%
16 to 20, 4.2%
21 or more, 3.0%

Source: "Fact File: This Year's Freshmen at 4-Year Colleges: a Statistical Profile," *The Chronicle of Higher Education*, 47: A48-A49, (January 26, 2001).

★1056★
Planned residence of incoming freshmen, 2000

Ranking basis/background: Survey responses of freshmen entering 2-year and 4-year institutions in the fall of 2000. Because of rounding or multiple responses, figures may total more than 100 percent. **Remarks:** Original source: "The American Freshmen: National Norms for Fall 2000," published by American Council on Education and University of California at Los Angeles Higher Education Research Institute. **Number listed:** 6.

1. Dormitory, with 75.4%
2. With family or other relatives, 17.6%
3. Other private home, apartment, or room, 4.4%
4. Other campus housing, 1.7%
5. Fraternity of sorority house, 0.5%
6. Other, 0.3%

Source: "Fact File: This Year's Freshmen at 4-Year Colleges: a Statistical Profile," *The Chronicle of Higher Education*, 47: A48-A49, (January 26, 2001).

★1057★
Political orientation of incoming freshmen, 2000

Ranking basis/background: Survey responses of freshmen entering 2-year and 4-year institutions in the fall of 2000. Because of rounding or multiple responses, figures may total more than 100 percent. **Remarks:** Original source: "The American Freshmen: National Norms for Fall 2000," published by American Council on Education and University of California at Los Angeles Higher Education Research Institute. **Number listed:** 5.

1. Middle of the road, with 51.9%
2. Liberal, 24.8%
3. Conservative, 18.9%
4. Far left, 2.9%
5. Far right, 1.4%

Source: "Fact File: This Year's Freshmen at 4-Year Colleges: a Statistical Profile," *The Chronicle of Higher Education*, 47: A48-A49, (January 26, 2001).

★1058★
Racial and ethnic background of incoming freshmen, 2000

Ranking basis/background: Survey responses of freshmen entering 2-year and 4-year institutions in the fall of 2000. Because of rounding or multiple responses, figures may total more than 100 percent. **Remarks:** Original source: "The American Freshmen: National Norms for Fall 2000," published by American Council on Education and University of California at Los Angeles Higher Education Research Institute. **Number listed:** 8.

1. White, with 76.1%
2. African American, 10.4%
3. Asian American, 7.1%
4. Hispanic American, 3.8%
5. Native American, 1.9%
6. Puerto Rican, 1.0%
7. Other Latino, 2.2%
8. Other, 3.6%

Source: "Fact File: This Year's Freshmen at 4-Year Colleges: a Statistical Profile," *The Chronicle of Higher Education*, 47: A48-A49, (January 26, 2001).

★1059★
Reasons incoming freshmen gave as "very important" in selecting a college, 2000

Ranking basis/background: Survey responses of freshmen entering 2-year and 4-year institutions in the fall of 2000. Because of rounding or multiple responses, figures may total more than 100 percent. **Remarks:** Original source: "The American Freshmen: National Norms for Fall 2000," published by American Council on Education and University of California at Los Angeles Higher Education Research Institute. **Number listed:** 23.

1. College has a very good academic reputation, 55.2%
2. College's graduates get good jobs, 50.9%
3. Wanted to go to a school about the size of the college, 35.0%
4. Offered financial assistance, 32.0%
5. College's graduates gain admission to top graduate/professional schools, 29.7%
6. College has a good reputation for its social activities, 27.9%
7. College offers special educational programs, 21.2%
8. Offered merit-based scholarship, 20.9%
9. Low tuition, 20.3%
10. Wanted to live near home, 16.9%
11. Offered need-based scholarship, 11.4%
12. Rankings in national magazines, 9.8%
13. Relatives wanted me to come here, 7.8%
14. Attracted by the religious affiliation/orientation of college, 7.3%
15. Admitted through an early-action or early-decision program, 7.1%
16. Information from a website, 6.8%
17. High-school counselor advised me, 6.1%
18. Friends are attending, 5.8%
19. Not offered aid by first choice, 5.5%
20. Offered athletic scholarship, 4.8%
21. Teacher advised me, 3.6%
22. Not accepted anywhere else, 3.2%
23. Private college counselor advised me, 2.1%

Source: "Fact File: This Year's Freshmen at 4-Year Colleges: a Statistical Profile," *The Chronicle of Higher Education*, 47: A48-A49, (January 26, 2001).

★1060★
Reasons incoming freshmen stated as "very important" in deciding to attend college, 2000

Ranking basis/background: Survey responses of freshmen entering 2-year and 4-year institutions in the fall of 2000. Because of rounding or multiple responses, figures may total more than 100 percent. **Remarks:** Original source: "The American Freshmen: National Norms for Fall 2000," published by American Council on Education and University of California at Los Angeles Higher Education Research Institute. **Number listed:** 13.

1. To learn more about things that interest me, with 76.6%
2. To get training for a specific career, 71.8%
3. To be able to get a better job, 71.6%
4. To be able to make more money, 70.0%
5. To gain a general education and appreciation of ideas, 64.5%
6. To prepare myself for graduate or professional school, 56.9%
7. To improve my reading and study skills, 41.1%
8. To make me a more cultured person, 40.5%
9. Parents wanted me to go, 35.7%
10. Wanted to get away from home, 21.4%
11. A mentor or role model encouraged me to go, 13.3%
12. Could not find a job, 4.9%
13. There was nothing better to do, 3.4%

Source: "Fact File: This Year's Freshmen at 4-Year Colleges: a Statistical Profile," *The Chronicle of Higher Education*, 47: A48-A49, (January 26, 2001).

★1061★
Religious preference of incoming freshmen, 2000

Ranking basis/background: Survey responses of freshmen entering 2-year and 4-year institutions in the fall of 2000. Because of rounding or multiple responses, figures may total more than 100 percent. **Remarks:** Original source: "The American Freshmen: National Norms for Fall 2000," published by American Council on Education and University of California at Los Angeles Higher Education Research Institute. **Number listed:** 17.

1. Roman Catholic, with 30.5%
2. None, 14.9%
3. Other Christian, 12.7%
4. Baptist, 11.6%
5. Methodist, 6.4%
6. Lutheran, 5.8%
7. Presbyterian, 4.0%
8. Jewish, 2.8%
9. Episcopal, 1.7%
10. Latter-day Saints (Mormon), 1.5%
11. United Church of Christ, 1.4%
12. Buddhist, 1.0%
13. Islamic, 0.9%
14. Eastern Orthodox, 0.7%
15. Seventh-day Adventist, 0.3%
16. Quaker, 0.2%
17. Other, 3.6%

Source: "Fact File: This Year's Freshmen at 4-Year Colleges: a Statistical Profile," *The Chronicle of Higher Education*, 47: A48-A49, (January 26, 2001).

★1062★
Sources of financial aid for incoming freshmen, 2000

Ranking basis/background: Survey responses of freshmen entering 2-year and 4-year institutions in the fall of 2000. Because of rounding or multiple responses, figures may total more than 100 percent. **Remarks:** Original source: "The American Freshmen: National Norms for Fall 2000," published by American Council on Education and University of California at Los Angeles Higher Education Research Institute. **Number listed:** 20.

1. Parents, other relatives, or friends, 82.5%
2. Savings from summer work, 49.0%
3. Other college grants, 32.5%
4. Other, savings, 32.0%
5. Stafford Loans, 26.2%
6. Part-time job on campus, 25.8%
7. Part-time job off campus, 21.9%
8. State scholarships, 21.8%
9. Pell Grants, 16.9%
10. College Work-Study, 13.2%
11. Other private grants, 11.7%
12. Other college loans, 11.4%
13. Perkins Loans, 9.5%
14. Supplemental Educational Opportunity Grants, 5.8%
15. Other government grants, 2.8%
16. Full-time job while in college, 2.7%
17. Spouse, 0.7%
18. Vocational rehabilitation funds, 0.6%
19. Other loans, 8.0%
20. Other sources, 5.2%

Source: "Fact File: This Year's Freshmen at 4-Year Colleges: a Statistical Profile," *The Chronicle of Higher Education*, 47: A48-A49, (January 26, 2001).

★1063★
Student self-ratings of above average for incoming freshmen, 2000

Ranking basis/background: Survey responses of freshmen entering 2-year and 4-year institutions in the fall of 2000. Because of rounding or multiple responses, figures may total more than 100 percent. **Remarks:** Original source: "The American Freshmen: National Norms for Fall 2000," published by American Council on Education and University of California at Los Angeles Higher Education Research Institute. **Number listed:** 20.

Academic ability, with 67.4%
Artistic ability, 29.4%
Computer skills, 33.6%
Competitiveness, 56.2%
Cooperativeness, 72.6%
Creativity, 56.9%
Drive to achieve, 70.6%
Emotional health, 53.8%
Initiative, 51.7%
Leadership ability, 60.8%
Mathematical ability, 44.3%
Physical health, 56.4%
Popularity, 40.7%
Public speaking ability, 37.4%
Self-confidence (intellectual), 60.3%
Self-confidence (social), 52.1%
Self-understanding, 57.1%
Spirituality, 44.9%
Understanding of others, 65.6%
Writing ability, 45.9%

Source: "Fact File: This Year's Freshmen at 4-Year Colleges: a Statistical Profile," *The Chronicle of Higher Education*, 47: A48-A49, (January 26, 2001).

COLLEGE STUDENTS, GRADUATE
See: **Graduate Students**

COLLEGES & UNIVERSITIES
See also: **Black Colleges and Universities**
Two-Year Colleges

★1064★
Average class size at colleges and universities in the U.S., by state

Ranking basis/background: A random sample of average class sizes at colleges and universities in the U.S. for selected states. **Remarks:** Original source: University of Phoenix. **Number listed:** 14.

Arizona, with an average class size of 14.7
California, 13.0
Colorado, 13.3
Florida, 10.6
Hawaii, 11.8
Louisiana, 14.2
Michigan, 13.2
Nevada, 14.5
New Mexico, 14.0
Oregon, 13.4
Puerto Rico, 12.0
Utah, 12.2
Washington, 14.5
On-line, 8.6

Source: Leatherman, Courtney, "U. of Phoenix Faculty Member Insists They Offer High-Quality Education," *The Chronicle of Higher Education*, October 16, 1998, pp. A14-A16.

★1065★
College freshmen's choices for exemplary undergraduate institutions

Ranking basis/background: Compiled from a survey of college students regarding size, educational mission, student characteristics, and other factors. Institutions are listed alphabetically. **Remarks:** Original source: National Survey of Student Engagement, Indiana University. **Number listed:** 3.

Columbia College (SC)
Marymount College (NY)
Medgar Evers College of the City University of New York

Source: Reisberg, Leo, "Are Students Actually Learning?," *The Chronicle of Higher Education*, 46: A67-A70, (November 17, 2000).

★1066★
First-year student's choices for exemplary special mission institutions

Ranking basis/background: Compiled from a survey of college students regarding size, educational mission, student characteristics, and other factors. Institutions are listed alphabetically. **Remarks:** Original source: National Survey of Student Engagement, Indiana University. **Number listed:** 2.

Rhode Island School of Design
Rose-Hulman Institute of Technology

Source: Reisberg, Leo, "Are Students Actually Learning?," *The Chronicle of Higher Education*, 46: A67-A70, (November 17, 2000).

★1067★
Institutions censured by the American Association of University Professors, 2001

Ranking basis/background: Listing by year of censure for institutions found with unsatisfactory conditions of academic freedom and tenure. **Number listed:** 52.

- Grove City College (first censured in 1963)
- Amarillo College (1968)
- Frank Phillips College (1969)
- Virginia Community College System (1975)
- Concordia Seminary (1975)
- Houston Baptist University (1975)
- Murray State University (1976)
- Blinn College (1976)
- Des Moines University Osteopathic Medical Center (1977)
- State University of New York (1978)
- Phillips Community College of the University of Arkansas (1978)
- Wingate University (1979)
- Olivet College (1980)
- Nichols College (1980)
- Yeshiva University (1982)
- American International College (1983)
- Illinois College of Optometry (1984)
- Metropolitan Community College (1984)
- Westminster College (UT) (1985)
- Southwestern Adventist University (1985)
- Talladega College (1986)
- Southern Nazarene University (1987)
- Pontifical Catholic University of Puerto Rico (1987)
- Husson College (1987)
- Hillsdale College (1988)
- Maryland Institute, College of Art (1988)
- Southeastern Baptist Theological Seminary (1989)
- The Catholic University of America (1990)
- New York University (1990)
- Dean College (1992)
- Baltimore City Community College (1992)
- Loma Linda University (1992)
- Clarkson College (1993)
- North Greenville College (1993)
- Savannah College of Art and Design (1993)
- University of Bridgeport (1994)
- Benedict College (1994)
- Nyack College (1995)
- Bennington College (1995)
- Alaska Pacific University (1995)
- Community College of Baltimore County, Essex (1995)
- St. Bonaventure University (1996)
- Garland County Community College (1996)
- St. Meinrad School of Theology (1997)
- Minneapolis College of Art and Design (1997)
- Brigham Young University (1998)
- University of the District of Columbia (1998)
- Lawrence Technological University (1998)
- Johnson & Wales University (1999)
- Mount Marty College (1999)
- Albertus Magnus College (2000)
- University of Central Arkansas (2000)

Source: "Censured Administrations," *Academe*, 87: 99, (March/April 2001).

★1068★
Largest degree-granting colleges and universities, by enrollment

Ranking basis/background: Enrollment figures for degree-granting colleges and universities. **Remarks:** Original source: U.S. Department of Education. **Number listed:** 10.

1. Community College of the Air Force, with 63,717
2. University of Texas, Austin, 48,857
3. Miami-Dade Community College, 48,449
4. Ohio State University, 48,278
5. University of Minnesota, Twin Cities, 45,410
6. Arizona State University, 44,255
7. Michigan State University, 42,603
8. University of Florida, 41,713
9. Texas A&M University, 41,461
10. Pennsylvania State University, 40,538

Source: "The Top Ten," *American School & University*, 73: 38-41, (January 2001).

★1069★
Proportion of U.S. institutions by Carnegie classification, 2000

Ranking basis/background: Percentage of institutions in each Carnegie class of a total 3,856 institutions. **Remarks:** Original source: Carnegie Foundation for the Advancement of Teaching. **Number listed:** 10.

1. Associate's colleges, with 42.5%
2. Specialized institutions, 19.2%
3. Master's (comprehensive) colleges and universities I, 12.7%
4. Baccalaureate colleges-general, 8.0%
5. Baccalaureate colleges-liberal arts, 5.5%
6. Doctoral/research universities-extensive, 3.8%
7. Master's (comprehensive) colleges and universities II, 3.3%
8. Doctoral/research universities-intensive, 2.9%
9. Baccalaureate/associate's colleges, 1.3%
10. Tribal colleges, 0.7%

Source: Basinger, Julianne, "A New Way of Classifying Colleges Elates Some and Perturbs Others," *The Chronicle of Higher Education*, 47: A31, A34, (August 11, 2000).

★1070★
"Report Card" for Alabama's higher education

Ranking basis/background: Each state's delivery of higher education was graded in five categories: preparation (based on high school credentials and exams); participation (based on percentage of high school students enrolling in college); Affordability (based on family income and available grants); completion (based on college follow-through); and benefits (based on contributions of college graduates). **Remarks:** Original source: The National Center for Public Policy and Higher Education. **Number listed:** 5.

- Preparation, with F
- Participation, C
- Affordability, D
- Completion, B-
- Benefits, C

Source: Selingo, Jeffrey, "Grading the States on Higher Education," *The Chronicle of Higher Education*, 47: A24-A25, (December 8, 2000).

★1071★
"Report Card" for Alaska's higher education

Ranking basis/background: Each state's delivery of higher education was graded in five categories: preparation (based on high school credentials and exams); participation (based on percentage of high school students enrolling in college); Affordability (based on family income and available grants); completion (based on college follow-through); and benefits (based on contributions of college graduates). **Remarks:** Original source: The National Center for Public Policy and Higher Education. **Number listed:** 5.

- Preparation, with A-
- Participation, D
- Affordability, C
- Completion, F
- Benefits, B

Source: Selingo, Jeffrey, "Grading the States on Higher Education," *The Chronicle of Higher Education*, 47: A24-A25, (December 8, 2000).

★1072★
"Report Card" for Arizona's higher education

Ranking basis/background: Each state's delivery of higher education was graded in five categories: preparation (based on high school credentials and exams); participation (based on percentage of high school students enrolling in college); Affordability (based on family income and available grants); completion (based on college follow-through); and benefits (based on contributions of college graduates). **Remarks:** Original source: The National Center for Public Policy and Higher Education. **Number listed:** 5.

- Preparation, with D
- Participation, D-
- Affordability, C
- Completion, D
- Benefits, D-

Source: Selingo, Jeffrey, "Grading the States on Higher Education," *The Chronicle of Higher Education*, 47: A24-A25, (December 8, 2000).

★1073★
"Report Card" for Arkansas's higher education

Ranking basis/background: Each state's delivery of higher education was graded in five categories: preparation (based on high school credentials and exams); participation (based on percentage of high school students enrolling in college); Affordability (based on family income and available grants); completion (based on college follow-through); and benefits (based on contributions of college graduates). **Remarks:** Original source: The National Center for Public Policy and Higher Education. **Number listed:** 5.

- Preparation, with D
- Participation, D-
- Affordability, C
- Completion, D
- Benefits, D-

Source: Selingo, Jeffrey, "Grading the States on Higher Education," *The Chronicle of Higher Education*, 47: A24-A25, (December 8, 2000).

COLLEGES & UNIVERSITIES

★1074★
"Report Card" for California's higher education

Ranking basis/background: Each state's delivery of higher education was graded in five categories: preparation (based on high school credentials and exams); participation (based on percentage of high school students enrolling in college); Affordability (based on family income and available grants); completion (based on college follow-through); and benefits (based on contributions of college graduates). **Remarks:** Original source: The National Center for Public Policy and Higher Education. **Number listed:** 5.

- Preparation, with C-
- Participation, B
- Affordability, A
- Completion, C
- Benefits, B

Source: Selingo, Jeffrey, "Grading the States on Higher Education," *The Chronicle of Higher Education*, 47: A24-A25, (December 8, 2000).

★1075★
"Report Card" for Colorado's higher education

Ranking basis/background: Each state's delivery of higher education was graded in five categories: preparation (based on high school credentials and exams); participation (based on percentage of high school students enrolling in college); Affordability (based on family income and available grants); completion (based on college follow-through); and benefits (based on contributions of college graduates). **Remarks:** Original source: The National Center for Public Policy and Higher Education. **Number listed:** 5.

- Preparation, with B
- Participation, B-
- Affordability, B-
- Completion, C
- Benefits, A

Source: Selingo, Jeffrey, "Grading the States on Higher Education," *The Chronicle of Higher Education*, 47: A24-A25, (December 8, 2000).

★1076★
"Report Card" for Connecticut's higher education

Ranking basis/background: Each state's delivery of higher education was graded in five categories: preparation (based on high school credentials and exams); participation (based on percentage of high school students enrolling in college); Affordability (based on family income and available grants); completion (based on college follow-through); and benefits (based on contributions of college graduates). **Remarks:** Original source: The National Center for Public Policy and Higher Education. **Number listed:** 5.

- Preparation, with A
- Participation, B
- Affordability, C
- Completion, B
- Benefits, A

Source: Selingo, Jeffrey, "Grading the States on Higher Education," *The Chronicle of Higher Education*, 47: A24-A25, (December 8, 2000).

★1077★
"Report Card" for Delaware's higher education

Ranking basis/background: Each state's delivery of higher education was graded in five categories: preparation (based on high school credentials and exams); participation (based on percentage of high school students enrolling in college); Affordability (based on family income and available grants); completion (based on college follow-through); and benefits (based on contributions of college graduates). **Remarks:** Original source: The National Center for Public Policy and Higher Education. **Number listed:** 5.

- Preparation, with C
- Participation, A
- Affordability, C-
- Completion, B
- Benefits, A

Source: Selingo, Jeffrey, "Grading the States on Higher Education," *The Chronicle of Higher Education*, 47: A24-A25, (December 8, 2000).

★1078★
"Report Card" for Florida's higher education

Ranking basis/background: Each state's delivery of higher education was graded in five categories: preparation (based on high school credentials and exams); participation (based on percentage of high school students enrolling in college); Affordability (based on family income and available grants); completion (based on college follow-through); and benefits (based on contributions of college graduates). **Remarks:** Original source: The National Center for Public Policy and Higher Education. **Number listed:** 5.

- Preparation, with C
- Participation, D
- Affordability, D
- Completion, B
- Benefits, C-

Source: Selingo, Jeffrey, "Grading the States on Higher Education," *The Chronicle of Higher Education*, 47: A24-A25, (December 8, 2000).

★1079★
"Report Card" for Georgia's higher education

Ranking basis/background: Each state's delivery of higher education was graded in five categories: preparation (based on high school credentials and exams); participation (based on percentage of high school students enrolling in college); Affordability (based on family income and available grants); completion (based on college follow-through); and benefits (based on contributions of college graduates). **Remarks:** Original source: The National Center for Public Policy and Higher Education. **Number listed:** 5.

- Preparation, with D
- Participation, F
- Affordability, D
- Completion, B-
- Benefits, C

Source: Selingo, Jeffrey, "Grading the States on Higher Education," *The Chronicle of Higher Education*, 47: A24-A25, (December 8, 2000).

★1080★
"Report Card" for Hawaii's higher education

Ranking basis/background: Each state's delivery of higher education was graded in five categories: preparation (based on high school credentials and exams); participation (based on percentage of high school students enrolling in college); Affordability (based on family income and available grants); completion (based on college follow-through); and benefits (based on contributions of college graduates). **Remarks:** Original source: The National Center for Public Policy and Higher Education. **Number listed:** 5.

- Preparation, with C
- Participation, B-
- Affordability, C-
- Completion, C
- Benefits, C

Source: Selingo, Jeffrey, "Grading the States on Higher Education," *The Chronicle of Higher Education*, 47: A24-A25, (December 8, 2000).

★1081★
"Report Card" for Idaho's higher education

Ranking basis/background: Each state's delivery of higher education was graded in five categories: preparation (based on high school credentials and exams); participation (based on percentage of high school students enrolling in college); Affordability (based on family income and available grants); completion (based on college follow-through); and benefits (based on contributions of college graduates). **Remarks:** Original source: The National Center for Public Policy and Higher Education. **Number listed:** 5.

- Preparation, with D
- Participation, D
- Affordability, B-
- Completion, C
- Benefits, C

Source: Selingo, Jeffrey, "Grading the States on Higher Education," *The Chronicle of Higher Education*, 47: A24-A25, (December 8, 2000).

★1082★
"Report Card" for Illinois's higher education

Ranking basis/background: Each state's delivery of higher education was graded in five categories: preparation (based on high school credentials and exams); participation (based on percentage of high school students enrolling in college); Affordability (based on family income and available grants); completion (based on college follow-through); and benefits (based on contributions of college graduates). **Remarks:** Original source: The National Center for Public Policy and Higher Education. **Number listed:** 5.

- Preparation, with A
- Participation, A
- Affordability, A
- Completion, C
- Benefits, B-

Source: Selingo, Jeffrey, "Grading the States on Higher Education," *The Chronicle of Higher Education*, 47: A24-A25, (December 8, 2000).

Educational Rankings Annual • 2002   COLLEGES & UNIVERSITIES

★1083★
"Report Card" for Indiana's higher education

Ranking basis/background: Each state's delivery of higher education was graded in five categories: preparation (based on high school credentials and exams); participation (based on percentage of high school students enrolling in college); Affordability (based on family income and available grants); completion (based on college follow-through); and benefits (based on contributions of college graduates). **Remarks:** Original source: The National Center for Public Policy and Higher Education. **Number listed:** 5.

    Preparation, with C-
    Participation, C-
    Affordability, C
    Completion, B-
    Benefits, C

Source: Selingo, Jeffrey, "Grading the States on Higher Education," *The Chronicle of Higher Education*, 47: A24-A25, (December 8, 2000).

★1084★
"Report Card" for Iowa's higher education

Ranking basis/background: Each state's delivery of higher education was graded in five categories: preparation (based on high school credentials and exams); participation (based on percentage of high school students enrolling in college); Affordability (based on family income and available grants); completion (based on college follow-through); and benefits (based on contributions of college graduates). **Remarks:** Original source: The National Center for Public Policy and Higher Education. **Number listed:** 5.

    Preparation, with B
    Participation, B
    Affordability, B
    Completion, A-
    Benefits, C

Source: Selingo, Jeffrey, "Grading the States on Higher Education," *The Chronicle of Higher Education*, 47: A24-A25, (December 8, 2000).

★1085★
"Report Card" for Kansas's higher education

Ranking basis/background: Each state's delivery of higher education was graded in five categories: preparation (based on high school credentials and exams); participation (based on percentage of high school students enrolling in college); Affordability (based on family income and available grants); completion (based on college follow-through); and benefits (based on contributions of college graduates). **Remarks:** Original source: The National Center for Public Policy and Higher Education. **Number listed:** 5.

    Preparation, with B
    Participation, A
    Affordability, B
    Completion, B
    Benefits, B

Source: Selingo, Jeffrey, "Grading the States on Higher Education," *The Chronicle of Higher Education*, 47: A24-A25, (December 8, 2000).

★1086★
"Report Card" for Kentucky's higher education

Ranking basis/background: Each state's delivery of higher education was graded in five categories: preparation (based on high school credentials and exams); participation (based on percentage of high school students enrolling in college); Affordability (based on family income and available grants); completion (based on college follow-through); and benefits (based on contributions of college graduates). **Remarks:** Original source: The National Center for Public Policy and Higher Education. **Number listed:** 5.

    Preparation, with C
    Participation, D
    Affordability, B
    Completion, C-
    Benefits, D

Source: Selingo, Jeffrey, "Grading the States on Higher Education," *The Chronicle of Higher Education*, 47: A24-A25, (December 8, 2000).

★1087★
"Report Card" for Louisiana's higher education

Ranking basis/background: Each state's delivery of higher education was graded in five categories: preparation (based on high school credentials and exams); participation (based on percentage of high school students enrolling in college); Affordability (based on family income and available grants); completion (based on college follow-through); and benefits (based on contributions of college graduates). **Remarks:** Original source: The National Center for Public Policy and Higher Education. **Number listed:** 5.

    Preparation, with F
    Participation, F
    Affordability, C-
    Completion, C
    Benefits, D

Source: Selingo, Jeffrey, "Grading the States on Higher Education," *The Chronicle of Higher Education*, 47: A24-A25, (December 8, 2000).

★1088★
"Report Card" for Maine's higher education

Ranking basis/background: Each state's delivery of higher education was graded in five categories: preparation (based on high school credentials and exams); participation (based on percentage of high school students enrolling in college); Affordability (based on family income and available grants); completion (based on college follow-through); and benefits (based on contributions of college graduates). **Remarks:** Original source: The National Center for Public Policy and Higher Education. **Number listed:** 5.

    Preparation, with B
    Participation, C
    Affordability, F
    Completion, B
    Benefits, C

Source: Selingo, Jeffrey, "Grading the States on Higher Education," *The Chronicle of Higher Education*, 47: A24-A25, (December 8, 2000).

★1089★
"Report Card" for Maryland's higher education

Ranking basis/background: Each state's delivery of higher education was graded in five categories: preparation (based on high school credentials and exams); participation (based on percentage of high school students enrolling in college); Affordability (based on family income and available grants); completion (based on college follow-through); and benefits (based on contributions of college graduates). **Remarks:** Original source: The National Center for Public Policy and Higher Education. **Number listed:** 5.

    Preparation, with B
    Participation, A
    Affordability, D
    Completion, B-
    Benefits, A

Source: Selingo, Jeffrey, "Grading the States on Higher Education," *The Chronicle of Higher Education*, 47: A24-A25, (December 8, 2000).

★1090★
"Report Card" for Massachusetts's higher education

Ranking basis/background: Each state's delivery of higher education was graded in five categories: preparation (based on high school credentials and exams); participation (based on percentage of high school students enrolling in college); Affordability (based on family income and available grants); completion (based on college follow-through); and benefits (based on contributions of college graduates). **Remarks:** Original source: The National Center for Public Policy and Higher Education. **Number listed:** 5.

    Preparation, with A
    Participation, A-
    Affordability, D
    Completion, A-
    Benefits, A-

Source: Selingo, Jeffrey, "Grading the States on Higher Education," *The Chronicle of Higher Education*, 47: A24-A25, (December 8, 2000).

★1091★
"Report Card" for Michigan's higher education

Ranking basis/background: Each state's delivery of higher education was graded in five categories: preparation (based on high school credentials and exams); participation (based on percentage of high school students enrolling in college); Affordability (based on family income and available grants); completion (based on college follow-through); and benefits (based on contributions of college graduates). **Remarks:** Original source: The National Center for Public Policy and Higher Education. **Number listed:** 5.

    Preparation, with B
    Participation, B
    Affordability, C
    Completion, C
    Benefits, B

Source: Selingo, Jeffrey, "Grading the States on Higher Education," *The Chronicle of Higher Education*, 47: A24-A25, (December 8, 2000).

COLLEGES & UNIVERSITIES

★1092★
"Report Card" for Minnesota's higher education

Ranking basis/background: Each state's delivery of higher education was graded in five categories: preparation (based on high school credentials and exams); participation (based on percentage of high school students enrolling in college); Affordability (based on family income and available grants); completion (based on college follow-through); and benefits (based on contributions of college graduates). **Remarks:** Original source: The National Center for Public Policy and Higher Education. **Number listed:** 5.

- Preparation, with C
- Participation, B-
- Affordability, A
- Completion, B
- Benefits, A

Source: Selingo, Jeffrey, "Grading the States on Higher Education," *The Chronicle of Higher Education*, 47: A24-A25, (December 8, 2000).

★1093★
"Report Card" for Mississippi's higher education

Ranking basis/background: Each state's delivery of higher education was graded in five categories: preparation (based on high school credentials and exams); participation (based on percentage of high school students enrolling in college); Affordability (based on family income and available grants); completion (based on college follow-through); and benefits (based on contributions of college graduates). **Remarks:** Original source: The National Center for Public Policy and Higher Education. **Number listed:** 5.

- Preparation, with D
- Participation, D-
- Affordability, C
- Completion, C
- Benefits, C

Source: Selingo, Jeffrey, "Grading the States on Higher Education," *The Chronicle of Higher Education*, 47: A24-A25, (December 8, 2000).

★1094★
"Report Card" for Missouri's higher education

Ranking basis/background: Each state's delivery of higher education was graded in five categories: preparation (based on high school credentials and exams); participation (based on percentage of high school students enrolling in college); Affordability (based on family income and available grants); completion (based on college follow-through); and benefits (based on contributions of college graduates). **Remarks:** Original source: The National Center for Public Policy and Higher Education. **Number listed:** 5.

- Preparation, with C
- Participation, C-
- Affordability, D
- Completion, B-
- Benefits, C

Source: Selingo, Jeffrey, "Grading the States on Higher Education," *The Chronicle of Higher Education*, 47: A24-A25, (December 8, 2000).

★1095★
"Report Card" for Montana's higher education

Ranking basis/background: Each state's delivery of higher education was graded in five categories: preparation (based on high school credentials and exams); participation (based on percentage of high school students enrolling in college); Affordability (based on family income and available grants); completion (based on college follow-through); and benefits (based on contributions of college graduates). **Remarks:** Original source: The National Center for Public Policy and Higher Education. **Number listed:** 5.

- Preparation, with B
- Participation, D
- Affordability, D-
- Completion, C
- Benefits, B

Source: Selingo, Jeffrey, "Grading the States on Higher Education," *The Chronicle of Higher Education*, 47: A24-A25, (December 8, 2000).

★1096★
"Report Card" for Nebraska's higher education

Ranking basis/background: Each state's delivery of higher education was graded in five categories: preparation (based on high school credentials and exams); participation (based on percentage of high school students enrolling in college); Affordability (based on family income and available grants); completion (based on college follow-through); and benefits (based on contributions of college graduates). **Remarks:** Original source: The National Center for Public Policy and Higher Education. **Number listed:** 5.

- Preparation, with A
- Participation, A
- Affordability, C
- Completion, C
- Benefits, B-

Source: Selingo, Jeffrey, "Grading the States on Higher Education," *The Chronicle of Higher Education*, 47: A24-A25, (December 8, 2000).

★1097★
"Report Card" for Nevada's higher education

Ranking basis/background: Each state's delivery of higher education was graded in five categories: preparation (based on high school credentials and exams); participation (based on percentage of high school students enrolling in college); Affordability (based on family income and available grants); completion (based on college follow-through); and benefits (based on contributions of college graduates). **Remarks:** Original source: The National Center for Public Policy and Higher Education. **Number listed:** 5.

- Preparation, with D
- Participation, D
- Affordability, B
- Completion, F
- Benefits, C-

Source: Selingo, Jeffrey, "Grading the States on Higher Education," *The Chronicle of Higher Education*, 47: A24-A25, (December 8, 2000).

★1098★
"Report Card" for New Hampshire's higher education

Ranking basis/background: Each state's delivery of higher education was graded in five categories: preparation (based on high school credentials and exams); participation (based on percentage of high school students enrolling in college); Affordability (based on family income and available grants); completion (based on college follow-through); and benefits (based on contributions of college graduates). **Remarks:** Original source: The National Center for Public Policy and Higher Education. **Number listed:** 5.

- Preparation, with B
- Participation, C
- Affordability, F
- Completion, A
- Benefits, B-

Source: Selingo, Jeffrey, "Grading the States on Higher Education," *The Chronicle of Higher Education*, 47: A24-A25, (December 8, 2000).

★1099★
"Report Card" for New Jersey's higher education

Ranking basis/background: Each state's delivery of higher education was graded in five categories: preparation (based on high school credentials and exams); participation (based on percentage of high school students enrolling in college); Affordability (based on family income and available grants); completion (based on college follow-through); and benefits (based on contributions of college graduates). **Remarks:** Original source: The National Center for Public Policy and Higher Education. **Number listed:** 5.

- Preparation, with A
- Participation, B
- Affordability, B
- Completion, B-
- Benefits, A

Source: Selingo, Jeffrey, "Grading the States on Higher Education," *The Chronicle of Higher Education*, 47: A24-A25, (December 8, 2000).

★1100★
"Report Card" for New Mexico's higher education

Ranking basis/background: Each state's delivery of higher education was graded in five categories: preparation (based on high school credentials and exams); participation (based on percentage of high school students enrolling in college); Affordability (based on family income and available grants); completion (based on college follow-through); and benefits (based on contributions of college graduates). **Remarks:** Original source: The National Center for Public Policy and Higher Education. **Number listed:** 5.

- Preparation, with D-
- Participation, B-
- Affordability, B
- Completion, D-
- Benefits, C

Source: Selingo, Jeffrey, "Grading the States on Higher Education," *The Chronicle of Higher Education*, 47: A24-A25, (December 8, 2000).

★1101★
"Report Card" for New York higher education

Ranking basis/background: Each state's delivery of higher education was graded in five categories: preparation (based on high school credentials and exams); participation (based on percentage of high school students enrolling in college); Affordability (based on family income and available grants); completion (based on college follow-through); and benefits (based on contributions of college graduates). **Remarks:** Original source: The National Center for Public Policy and Higher Education. **Number listed:** 5.

    Preparation, with B
    Participation, B-
    Affordability, D-
    Completion, A-
    Benefits, B

Source: Selingo, Jeffrey, "Grading the States on Higher Education," *The Chronicle of Higher Education*, 47: A24-A25, (December 8, 2000).

★1102★
"Report Card" for North Carolina's higher education

Ranking basis/background: Each state's delivery of higher education was graded in five categories: preparation (based on high school credentials and exams); participation (based on percentage of high school students enrolling in college); Affordability (based on family income and available grants); completion (based on college follow-through); and benefits (based on contributions of college graduates). **Remarks:** Original source: The National Center for Public Policy and Higher Education. **Number listed:** 5.

    Preparation, with B
    Participation, D
    Affordability, A
    Completion, B
    Benefits, D

Source: Selingo, Jeffrey, "Grading the States on Higher Education," *The Chronicle of Higher Education*, 47: A24-A25, (December 8, 2000).

★1103★
"Report Card" for North Dakota higher education

Ranking basis/background: Each state's delivery of higher education was graded in five categories: preparation (based on high school credentials and exams); participation (based on percentage of high school students enrolling in college); Affordability (based on family income and available grants); completion (based on college follow-through); and benefits (based on contributions of college graduates). **Remarks:** Original source: The National Center for Public Policy and Higher Education. **Number listed:** 5.

    Preparation, with B
    Participation, B
    Affordability, C
    Completion, B
    Benefits, C

Source: Selingo, Jeffrey, "Grading the States on Higher Education," *The Chronicle of Higher Education*, 47: A24-A25, (December 8, 2000).

★1104★
"Report Card" for Ohio's higher education

Ranking basis/background: Each state's delivery of higher education was graded in five categories: preparation (based on high school credentials and exams); participation (based on percentage of high school students enrolling in college); Affordability (based on family income and available grants); completion (based on college follow-through); and benefits (based on contributions of college graduates). **Remarks:** Original source: The National Center for Public Policy and Higher Education. **Number listed:** 5.

    Preparation, with C
    Participation, C-
    Affordability, D-
    Completion, B
    Benefits, C

Source: Selingo, Jeffrey, "Grading the States on Higher Education," *The Chronicle of Higher Education*, 47: A24-A25, (December 8, 2000).

★1105★
"Report Card" for Oklahoma's higher education

Ranking basis/background: Each state's delivery of higher education was graded in five categories: preparation (based on high school credentials and exams); participation (based on percentage of high school students enrolling in college); Affordability (based on family income and available grants); completion (based on college follow-through); and benefits (based on contributions of college graduates). **Remarks:** Original source: The National Center for Public Policy and Higher Education. **Number listed:** 5.

    Preparation, with D
    Participation, C
    Affordability, B-
    Completion, C-
    Benefits, C-

Source: Selingo, Jeffrey, "Grading the States on Higher Education," *The Chronicle of Higher Education*, 47: A24-A25, (December 8, 2000).

★1106★
"Report Card" for Oregon's higher education

Ranking basis/background: Each state's delivery of higher education was graded in five categories: preparation (based on high school credentials and exams); participation (based on percentage of high school students enrolling in college); Affordability (based on family income and available grants); completion (based on college follow-through); and benefits (based on contributions of college graduates). **Remarks:** Original source: The National Center for Public Policy and Higher Education. **Number listed:** 5.

    Preparation, with C-
    Participation, D
    Affordability, D-
    Completion, C
    Benefits, C

Source: Selingo, Jeffrey, "Grading the States on Higher Education," *The Chronicle of Higher Education*, 47: A24-A25, (December 8, 2000).

★1107★
"Report Card" for Pennsylvania's higher education

Ranking basis/background: Each state's delivery of higher education was graded in five categories: preparation (based on high school credentials and exams); participation (based on percentage of high school students enrolling in college); Affordability (based on family income and available grants); completion (based on college follow-through); and benefits (based on contributions of college graduates). **Remarks:** Original source: The National Center for Public Policy and Higher Education. **Number listed:** 5.

    Preparation, with C
    Participation, C
    Affordability, C
    Completion, A
    Benefits, B-

Source: Selingo, Jeffrey, "Grading the States on Higher Education," *The Chronicle of Higher Education*, 47: A24-A25, (December 8, 2000).

★1108★
"Report Card" for Rhode Island's higher education

Ranking basis/background: Each state's delivery of higher education was graded in five categories: preparation (based on high school credentials and exams); participation (based on percentage of high school students enrolling in college); Affordability (based on family income and available grants); completion (based on college follow-through); and benefits (based on contributions of college graduates). **Remarks:** Original source: The National Center for Public Policy and Higher Education. **Number listed:** 5.

    Preparation, with C
    Participation, A
    Affordability, F
    Completion, A
    Benefits, A

Source: Selingo, Jeffrey, "Grading the States on Higher Education," *The Chronicle of Higher Education*, 47: A24-A25, (December 8, 2000).

★1109★
"Report Card" for South Carolina's higher education

Ranking basis/background: Each state's delivery of higher education was graded in five categories: preparation (based on high school credentials and exams); participation (based on percentage of high school students enrolling in college); Affordability (based on family income and available grants); completion (based on college follow-through); and benefits (based on contributions of college graduates). **Remarks:** Original source: The National Center for Public Policy and Higher Education. **Number listed:** 5.

    Preparation, with C-
    Participation, D-
    Affordability, C
    Completion, B
    Benefits, B-

Source: Selingo, Jeffrey, "Grading the States on Higher Education," *The Chronicle of Higher Education*, 47: A24-A25, (December 8, 2000).

★1110★
"Report Card" for South Dakota's higher education

Ranking basis/background: Each state's delivery of higher education was graded in five categories: preparation (based on high school credentials and exams); participation (based on percentage of high school students enrolling in college); Affordability (based on family income and available grants); completion (based on college follow-through); and benefits (based on contributions of college graduates). **Remarks:** Original source: The National Center for Public Policy and Higher Education. **Number listed:** 5.

- Preparation, with C
- Participation, C
- Affordability, D
- Completion, B-
- Benefits, C-

Source: Selingo, Jeffrey, "Grading the States on Higher Education," *The Chronicle of Higher Education*, 47: A24-A25, (December 8, 2000).

★1111★
"Report Card" for Tennessee's higher education

Ranking basis/background: Each state's delivery of higher education was graded in five categories: preparation (based on high school credentials and exams); participation (based on percentage of high school students enrolling in college); Affordability (based on family income and available grants); completion (based on college follow-through); and benefits (based on contributions of college graduates). **Remarks:** Original source: The National Center for Public Policy and Higher Education. **Number listed:** 5.

- Preparation, with C-
- Participation, D-
- Affordability, C
- Completion, C
- Benefits, D

Source: Selingo, Jeffrey, "Grading the States on Higher Education," *The Chronicle of Higher Education*, 47: A24-A25, (December 8, 2000).

★1112★
"Report Card" for Texas's higher education

Ranking basis/background: Each state's delivery of higher education was graded in five categories: preparation (based on high school credentials and exams); participation (based on percentage of high school students enrolling in college); Affordability (based on family income and available grants); completion (based on college follow-through); and benefits (based on contributions of college graduates). **Remarks:** Original source: The National Center for Public Policy and Higher Education. **Number listed:** 5.

- Preparation, with C
- Participation, D
- Affordability, C
- Completion, D
- Benefits, C

Source: Selingo, Jeffrey, "Grading the States on Higher Education," *The Chronicle of Higher Education*, 47: A24-A25, (December 8, 2000).

★1113★
"Report Card" for Utah's higher education

Ranking basis/background: Each state's delivery of higher education was graded in five categories: preparation (based on high school credentials and exams); participation (based on percentage of high school students enrolling in college); Affordability (based on family income and available grants); completion (based on college follow-through); and benefits (based on contributions of college graduates). **Remarks:** Original source: The National Center for Public Policy and Higher Education. **Number listed:** 5.

- Preparation, with A
- Participation, C
- Affordability, A
- Completion, D
- Benefits, C

Source: Selingo, Jeffrey, "Grading the States on Higher Education," *The Chronicle of Higher Education*, 47: A24-A25, (December 8, 2000).

★1114★
"Report Card" for Vermont's higher education

Ranking basis/background: Each state's delivery of higher education was graded in five categories: preparation (based on high school credentials and exams); participation (based on percentage of high school students enrolling in college); Affordability (based on family income and available grants); completion (based on college follow-through); and benefits (based on contributions of college graduates). **Remarks:** Original source: The National Center for Public Policy and Higher Education. **Number listed:** 5.

- Preparation, with B-
- Participation, C-
- Affordability, D-
- Completion, A
- Benefits, B-

Source: Selingo, Jeffrey, "Grading the States on Higher Education," *The Chronicle of Higher Education*, 47: A24-A25, (December 8, 2000).

★1115★
"Report Card" for Virginia's higher education

Ranking basis/background: Each state's delivery of higher education was graded in five categories: preparation (based on high school credentials and exams); participation (based on percentage of high school students enrolling in college); Affordability (based on family income and available grants); completion (based on college follow-through); and benefits (based on contributions of college graduates). **Remarks:** Original source: The National Center for Public Policy and Higher Education. **Number listed:** 5.

- Preparation, with B
- Participation, B-
- Affordability, C
- Completion, B
- Benefits, B

Source: Selingo, Jeffrey, "Grading the States on Higher Education," *The Chronicle of Higher Education*, 47: A24-A25, (December 8, 2000).

★1116★
"Report Card" for Washington's higher education

Ranking basis/background: Each state's delivery of higher education was graded in five categories: preparation (based on high school credentials and exams); participation (based on percentage of high school students enrolling in college); Affordability (based on family income and available grants); completion (based on college follow-through); and benefits (based on contributions of college graduates). **Remarks:** Original source: The National Center for Public Policy and Higher Education. **Number listed:** 5.

- Preparation, with C
- Participation, C-
- Affordability, B-
- Completion, B-
- Benefits, B

Source: Selingo, Jeffrey, "Grading the States on Higher Education," *The Chronicle of Higher Education*, 47: A24-A25, (December 8, 2000).

★1117★
"Report Card" for West Virginia's higher education

Ranking basis/background: Each state's delivery of higher education was graded in five categories: preparation (based on high school credentials and exams); participation (based on percentage of high school students enrolling in college); Affordability (based on family income and available grants); completion (based on college follow-through); and benefits (based on contributions of college graduates). **Remarks:** Original source: The National Center for Public Policy and Higher Education. **Number listed:** 5.

- Preparation, with D
- Participation, D
- Affordability, D
- Completion, C
- Benefits, F

Source: Selingo, Jeffrey, "Grading the States on Higher Education," *The Chronicle of Higher Education*, 47: A24-A25, (December 8, 2000).

★1118★
"Report Card" for Wisconsin's higher education

Ranking basis/background: Each state's delivery of higher education was graded in five categories: preparation (based on high school credentials and exams); participation (based on percentage of high school students enrolling in college); Affordability (based on family income and available grants); completion (based on college follow-through); and benefits (based on contributions of college graduates). **Remarks:** Original source: The National Center for Public Policy and Higher Education. **Number listed:** 5.

- Preparation, with A-
- Participation, B
- Affordability, B
- Completion, B
- Benefits, B-

Source: Selingo, Jeffrey, "Grading the States on Higher Education," *The Chronicle of Higher Education*, 47: A24-A25, (December 8, 2000).

★1119★
"Report Card" for Wyoming's higher education

Ranking basis/background: Each state's delivery of higher education was graded in five categories: preparation (based on high school credentials and exams); participation (based on percentage of high school students enrolling in college); Affordability (based on family income and available grants); completion (based on college follow-through); and benefits (based on contributions of college graduates). **Remarks:** Original source: The National Center for Public Policy and Higher Education. **Number listed:** 5.
- Preparation, with C-
- Participation, B-
- Affordability, C
- Completion, B
- Benefits, C

Source: Selingo, Jeffrey, "Grading the States on Higher Education," *The Chronicle of Higher Education*, 47: A24-A25, (December 8, 2000).

★1120★
Retention rates of African American students at historically black institutions, 1997-98

Ranking basis/background: Comparison of black students and total student six-year graduation rate for student who began school in 1992-93. **Remarks:** Original source: NCCA. **Number listed:** 37.
1. Spelman College, with an 76% retention of African American students; 76% total student retention
2. Howard University, 52%; 53%
2. Hampton University, 52%; 52%
4. Elizabeth State University, 51%; 59%
5. Clark Atlanta University, 50%; 50%
6. Winston-Salem State University, 49%; 48%
7. Morehouse College, 48%; 48%
8. Florida A&M State University, 47%; 47%
9. South Carolina State University, 45%; 45%
9. North Carolina Central University, 45%; 44%

Source: Roach, Ronald, "Special Report: Minority Student Recruitment & Retention," *Black Issues in Higher Education*, 17: 36-46, (October 26, 2000).

★1121★
Retention rates of African American students at traditionally white institutions, 1997-98

Ranking basis/background: Comparison of black students and total student six-year graduation rate for student who began school in 1992-93. **Remarks:** Original source: NCCA. **Number listed:** 46.
1. University of Virginia, with an 86% retention of African American students; 92% total student retention
2. New York University, 66%; 72%
3. University of North Carolina, Chapel Hill, 64%; 80%
4. University of Michigan, Ann Arbor, 61%; 83%
4. Rutgers University, New Brunswick, 61%; 73%
4. St. John's University (NY), 61%; 66%
7. University of California, Los Angeles, 58%; 78%
8. Florida State University, 56%; 64%
9. University of Alabama, 55%; 59%
10. University of Illinois, Urbana-Champaign, 54%; 77%
10. University of Central Florida, 54%; 52%

Source: Roach, Ronald, "Special Report: Minority Student Recruitment & Retention," *Black Issues in Higher Education*, 17: 36-46, (October 26, 2000).

★1122★
U.S. News & World Report's best national universities, 2000-01

Ranking basis/background: Based on *U.S News* questionnaire sent to 1,400 four-year institutions. Scores are averaged and weighted percentages from seven attributes: academic reputation, retention, faculty resources, student selectivity, financial resources, graduation rate performance and alumni giving. **Remarks:** Comparable data was used from the U.S. Department of Education, the Council for Aid to Education, the NCAA, and Wintergreen/Orchard House publishers. **Number listed:** 51.
1. Princeton University, with an overall score of 100.0
2. Harvard University, 99.0
2. Yale University, 99.0
4. California Institute of Technology, 97.0
5. Massachusetts Institute of Technology, 96.0
6. Stanford University, 94.0
6. University of Pennsylvania, 94.0
8. Duke University, 93.0
9. Dartmouth College, 91.0
10. Columbia University, 90.0
10. Cornell University, 90.0
10. University of Chicago, 90.0

Source: "America's Best Colleges," *U.S. News & World Report*, 129: 90-132, (September 11, 2000).

★1123★
U.S. News & World Report's best public national universities, 2000-01

Ranking basis/background: Based on *U.S News* questionnaire sent to 1,400 four-year institutions. Scores are averaged and weighted percentages from seven attributes: academic reputation, retention, faculty resources, student selectivity, financial resources, graduation rate performance and alumni giving. **Remarks:** Comparable data was used from the U.S. Department of Education, the Council for Aid to Education, the NCAA, and Wintergreen/Orchard House publishers. **Number listed:** 51.
1. University of California, Berkeley
1. University of Virginia
3. University of California, Los Angeles
3. University of Michigan, Ann Arbor
3. University of North Carolina, Chapel Hill
6. College of William and Mary
7. University of California, San Diego
8. Georgia Institute of Technology
8. University of Wisconsin, Madison
10. University of California, Davis
10. University of California, Irvine
10. University of Illinois, Urbana-Champaign

Source: "America's Best Colleges," *U.S. News & World Report*, 129: 90-132, (September 11, 2000).

★1124★
U.S. News & World Report's indicators for measuring academic quality of national colleges and universities

Ranking basis/background: Weighted percentages for quality rating of national universities and liberal arts colleges. **Number listed:** 7.
- Academic reputation, with 25%
- Graduation and retention rates, 20%
- Faculty resources, 20%
- Student selectivity, 15%
- Financial resources, 10%
- Alumni giving, 5%
- Graduation rate performance, 5%

Source: Morse, Robert J. and Samuel M. Flanigan, "How We Rank the Colleges," *U.S. News & World Report*, 129: 104-105, (September 11, 2000).

★1125★
U.S. News & World Report's indicators for measuring academic quality of regional colleges and universities

Ranking basis/background: Weighted percentages for quality rating of national universities and liberal arts colleges. **Number listed:** 6.
- Academic reputation, with 25%
- Graduation and retention rates, 25%
- Faculty resources, 20%
- Student selectivity, 15%
- Financial resources, 10%
- Alumni giving, 5%

Source: Morse, Robert J. and Samuel M. Flanigan, "How We Rank the Colleges," *U.S. News & World Report*, 129: 104-105, (September 11, 2000).

★1126★
U.S. News & World Report's national universities with the best academic reputation, 2000-01

Ranking basis/background: Based on *U.S News* questionnaire sent to 1,400 four-year institutions. Scores are averaged and weighted percentages from seven attributes: academic reputation, retention, faculty resources, student selectivity, financial resources, graduation rate performance and alumni giving. **Remarks:** Comparable data was used from the U.S. Department of Education, the Council for Aid to Education, the NCAA, and Wintergreen/Orchard House publishers. **Number listed:** 51.
1. Princeton University, with a score of 4.9
1. Harvard University, 4.9
1. Yale University, 4.9
1. Massachusetts Institute of Technology, 4.9
1. Stanford University, 4.9
6. University of California, Berkeley, 4.8
7. California Institute of Technology, 4.7
7. Columbia University, 4.7
7. University of Chicago, 4.7
10. Duke University, 4.6
10. Cornell University, 4.6
10. Johns Hopkins University, 4.6

Source: "America's Best Colleges," *U.S. News & World Report*, 129: 90-132, (September 11, 2000).

★1127★
U.S. News & World Report's national universities with the best faculty resources rank, 2000-01

Ranking basis/background: Based on *U.S News* questionnaire sent to 1,400 four-year institutions. Scores are averaged and weighted percentages from seven attributes: academic reputation, retention, faculty resources, student selectivity, financial resources, graduation rate performance and alumni giving. **Remarks:** Comparable data was used from the U.S. Department of Education, the Council for Aid to Education, the NCAA, and Wintergreen/Orchard House publishers. **Number listed:** 51.
1. California Institute of Technology
2. University of Chicago
3. University of Pennsylvania
4. Rice University
5. Princeton University
6. Harvard University
7. Duke University
8. Vanderbilt University

COLLEGES & UNIVERSITIES

9. Emory University
10. Yale University

Source: "America's Best Colleges," *U.S. & World Report*, 129: 90-132, (September 11, 2000).

★1128★
U.S. News & World Report's national universities with the best freshmen retention rates, 2000-01

Ranking basis/background: Based on *U.S News* questionnaire sent to 1,400 four-year institutions. Scores are averaged and weighted percentages from seven attributes: academic reputation, retention, faculty resources, student selectivity, financial resources, graduation rate performance and alumni giving. **Remarks:** Comparable data was used from the U.S. Department of Education, the Council for Aid to Education, the NCAA, and Wintergreen/Orchard House publishers. **Number listed:** 51.

1. Princeton University, with 99%
2. Yale University, 98%
2. Stanford University, 98%
2. University of Notre Dame, 98%
5. Brown University, 97%
5. University of Virginia, 97%
5. Columbia University, 97%
5. Massachusetts Institute of Technology, 97%
5. Duke University, 97%
10. Harvard University, 96%
10. University of Pennsylvania, 96%
10. Dartmouth College, 96%
10. Cornell University, 96%
10. Georgetown University, 96%
10. University of California, Los Angeles, 96%
10. Tufts University, 96%
10. College of William and Mary, 96%

Source: "America's Best Colleges," *U.S. News & World Report*, 129: 90-132, (September 11, 2000).

★1129★
U.S. News & World Report's national universities with the best graduation and retention rank, 2000-01

Ranking basis/background: Based on *U.S News* questionnaire sent to 1,400 four-year institutions. Scores are averaged and weighted percentages from seven attributes: academic reputation, retention, faculty resources, student selectivity, financial resources, graduation rate performance and alumni giving. **Remarks:** Comparable data was used from the U.S. Department of Education, the Council for Aid to Education, the NCAA, and Wintergreen/Orchard House publishers. **Number listed:** 51.

1. Harvard University
2. Princeton University
3. Yale University
4. University of Notre Dame
5. Dartmouth College
6. Stanford University
7. Duke University
7. Brown University
9. University of Virginia
10. Massachusetts Institute of Technology
10. Northwestern University

Source: "America's Best Colleges," *U.S. News & World Report*, 129: 90-132, (September 11, 2000).

★1130★
U.S. News & World Report's national universities with the best student/faculty ratio, 2000-01

Ranking basis/background: Based on *U.S News* questionnaire sent to 1,400 four-year institutions. Scores are averaged and weighted percentages from seven attributes: academic reputation, retention, faculty resources, student selectivity, financial resources, graduation rate performance and alumni giving. **Remarks:** Comparable data was used from the U.S. Department of Education, the Council for Aid to Education, the NCAA, and Wintergreen/Orchard House publishers. **Number listed:** 51.

1. California Institute of Technology, with a student/faculty ratio of 3/1
2. University of Chicago, 4/1
3. Princeton University, 6/1
3. Emory University, 6/1
5. Yale University, 7/1
5. Massachusetts Institute of Technology, 7/1
5. University of Pennsylvania, 7/1
5. Columbia University, 7/1
9. Harvard University, 8/1
9. Stanford University, 8/1
9. Duke University, 8/1
9. Northwestern University, 8/1
9. Tufts University, 8/1

Source: "America's Best Colleges," *U.S. News & World Report*, 129: 90-132, (September 11, 2000).

★1131★
U.S. News & World Report's national universities with the highest acceptance rates, 2000-01

Ranking basis/background: Based on *U.S News* questionnaire sent to 1,400 four-year institutions. Scores are averaged and weighted percentages from seven attributes: academic reputation, retention, faculty resources, student selectivity, financial resources, graduation rate performance and alumni giving. **Remarks:** Comparable data was used from the U.S. Department of Education, the Council for Aid to Education, the NCAA, and Wintergreen/Orchard House publishers. **Number listed:** 51.

1. Yeshiva University, with 79%
2. Rensselaer Polytechnic Institute, 78%
2. Tulane University, 78%
4. University of Washington (WA), 77%
5. University of Wisconsin, Madison, 74%
6. Case Western Reserve University, 71%
6. University of Illinois, Urbana-Champaign, 71%
8. Georgia Institute of Technology, 69%
9. University of Rochester, 66%
10. University of Michigan, Ann Arbor, 64%

Source: "America's Best Colleges," *U.S. News & World Report*, 129: 90-132, (September 11, 2000).

★1132★
U.S. News & World Report's national universities with the highest alumni giving rank, 2000-01

Ranking basis/background: Based on *U.S News* questionnaire sent to 1,400 four-year institutions. Scores are averaged and weighted percentages from seven attributes: academic reputation, retention, faculty resources, student selectivity, financial resources, graduation rate performance and alumni giving. **Remarks:** Comparable data was used from the U.S. Department of Education, the Council for Aid to Education, the NCAA, and Wintergreen/Orchard House publishers. **Number listed:** 51.

1. Princeton University
2. Dartmouth College
3. Yale University
4. University of Notre Dame
5. Harvard University
6. Duke University
7. Massachusetts Institute of Technology
8. Brown University
9. California Institute of Technology
10. University of Pennsylvania

Source: "America's Best Colleges," *U.S. News & World Report*, 129: 90-132, (September 11, 2000).

★1133★
U.S. News & World Report's national universities with the highest financial resources rank, 2000-01

Ranking basis/background: Based on *U.S News* questionnaire sent to 1,400 four-year institutions. Scores are averaged and weighted percentages from seven attributes: academic reputation, retention, faculty resources, student selectivity, financial resources, graduation rate performance and alumni giving. **Remarks:** Comparable data was used from the U.S. Department of Education, the Council for Aid to Education, the NCAA, and Wintergreen/Orchard House publishers. **Number listed:** 51.

1. California Institute of Technology
2. Johns Hopkins University
3. Massachusetts Institute of Technology
4. Yale University
5. Washington University in St. Louis
6. Wake Forest University
7. University of Pennsylvania
8. Harvard University
9. Stanford University
10. Dartmouth College

Source: "America's Best Colleges," *U.S. News & World Report*, 129: 90-132, (September 11, 2000).

★1134★
U.S. News & World Report's national universities with the highest graduation rate, 1999

Ranking basis/background: Based on *U.S News* questionnaire sent to 1,400 four-year institutions. Scores are averaged and weighted percentages from seven attributes: academic reputation, retention, faculty resources, student selectivity, financial resources, graduation rate performance and alumni giving. **Remarks:** Comparable data was used from the U.S. Department of Education, the Council for Aid to Education, the NCAA, and Wintergreen/Orchard House publishers. **Number listed:** 51.

1. Harvard University, with 97%
2. Princeton University, 96%
3. University of Notre Dame, 95%
3. Dartmouth College, 94%
5. Yale University, 94%
6. Brown University, 93%
7. Duke University, 92%
7. Northwestern University, 92%
7. Yeshiva University, 92%
10. Columbia University, 91%
10. Cornell University, 91%
10. Massachusetts Institute of Technology, 91%
10. University of Virginia, 91%

Source: "America's Best Colleges," *U.S. News & World Report*, 129: 90-132, (September 11, 2000).

★1135★
U.S. News & World Report's national universities with the highest percentage of freshmen in the top 10% of their high school class, 2000-01

Ranking basis/background: Based on *U.S News* questionnaire sent to 1,400 four-year institutions. Scores are averaged and weighted percentages from seven attributes: academic reputation, retention, faculty resources, student selectivity, financial resources, graduation rate performance and alumni giving. **Remarks:** Comparable data was used from the U.S. Department of Education, the Council for Aid to Education, the NCAA, and Wintergreen/Orchard House publishers. **Number listed:** 51.

1. California Institute of Technology, with 100%
2. University of California, San Diego, 99%
3. University of California, Berkeley, 98%
4. University of California, Los Angeles, 97%
5. Yale University, 95%
5. University of California, Davis, 95%
5. University of California, Irvine, 95%
5. University of California, Santa Barbara, 95%
9. Massachusetts Institute of Technology, 94%
10. Princeton University, 92%

Source: "America's Best Colleges," *U.S. News & World Report*, 129: 90-132, (September 11, 2000).

★1136★
U.S. News & World Report's national universities with the highest percentage of full-time faculty, 2000-01

Ranking basis/background: Based on *U.S News* questionnaire sent to 1,400 four-year institutions. Scores are averaged and weighted percentages from seven attributes: academic reputation, retention, faculty resources, student selectivity, financial resources, graduation rate performance and alumni giving. **Remarks:** Comparable data was used from the U.S. Department of Education, the Council for Aid to Education, the NCAA, and Wintergreen/Orchard House publishers. **Number listed:** 51.

1. Georgia Institute of Technology, with 100%
2. Duke University, 98%
2. Cornell University, 98%
4. University of North Carolina, Chapel Hill, 97%
5. Case Western Reserve University, 97%
5. University of Texas, Austin, 97%
7. California Institute of Technology, 96%
8. University of Chicago, 95%
8. University of Virginia, 95%
8. Carnegie Mellon University, 95%
8. Pennsylvania State University, University Park, 95%

Source: "America's Best Colleges," *U.S. News & World Report*, 129: 90-132, (September 11, 2000).

★1137★
U.S. News & World Report's national universities with the highest proportion of alumni support, 2000-01

Ranking basis/background: Based on *U.S News* questionnaire sent to 1,400 four-year institutions. Scores are averaged and weighted percentages from seven attributes: academic reputation, retention, faculty resources, student selectivity, financial resources, graduation rate performance and alumni giving. **Remarks:** Comparable data was used from the U.S. Department of Education, the Council for Aid to Education, the NCAA, and Wintergreen/Orchard House publishers. **Number listed:** 51.

1. Princeton University, with 66%
2. Dartmouth College, 52%
3. Yale University, 49%
4. University of Notre Dame, 48%
5. Harvard University, 47%
6. Duke University, 45%
7. Massachusetts Institute of Technology, 43%
7. Brown University, 43%
9. California Institute of Technology, 41%
10. University of Pennsylvania, 40%

Source: "America's Best Colleges," *U.S. News & World Report*, 129: 90-132, (September 11, 2000).

★1138★
U.S. News & World Report's national universities with the highest proportion of classes with less than 20 students, 2000-01

Ranking basis/background: Based on *U.S News* questionnaire sent to 1,400 four-year institutions. Scores are averaged and weighted percentages from seven attributes: academic reputation, retention, faculty resources, student selectivity, financial resources, graduation rate performance and alumni giving. **Remarks:** Comparable data was used from the U.S. Department of Education, the Council for Aid to Education, the NCAA, and Wintergreen/Orchard House publishers. **Number listed:** 51.

1. Union Institute, with 100%
2. New School University, 89%
3. MCP Hahnemann University, 87%
4. California Institute of Technology, 78%
4. Illinois Institute of Technology, 78%
4. Yale University, 78%
7. Howard University, 76%
8. Nova Southeastern University, 74%
9. Cornell University, 73%
10. Washington University in St. Louis, 72%

Source: "America's Best Colleges," *U.S. News & World Report*, 129: 90-132, (September 11, 2000).

★1139★
U.S. News & World Report's national universities with the highest selectivity rank, 2000-01

Ranking basis/background: Based on *U.S News* questionnaire sent to 1,400 four-year institutions. Scores are averaged and weighted percentages from seven attributes: academic reputation, retention, faculty resources, student selectivity, financial resources, graduation rate performance and alumni giving. **Remarks:** Comparable data was used from the U.S. Department of Education, the Council for Aid to Education, the NCAA, and Wintergreen/Orchard House publishers. **Number listed:** 51.

1. Harvard University
2. Yale University
3. Princeton University
4. California Institute of Technology
5. Stanford University
6. Massachusetts Institute of Technology
7. Columbia University
8. Brown University
9. University of Pennsylvania
10. Dartmouth College

Source: "America's Best Colleges," *U.S. News & World Report*, 129: 90-132, (September 11, 2000).

★1140★
U.S. News & World Report's national universities with the lowest acceptance rates, 2000-01

Ranking basis/background: Based on *U.S News* questionnaire sent to 1,400 four-year institutions. Scores are averaged and weighted percentages from seven attributes: academic reputation, retention, faculty resources, student selectivity, financial resources, graduation rate performance and alumni giving. **Remarks:** Comparable data was used from the U.S. Department of Education, the Council for Aid to Education, the NCAA, and Wintergreen/Orchard House publishers. **Number listed:** 51.

1. Harvard University, with 11%
1. Princeton University, 11%
3. Columbia University, 14%
4. Stanford University, 15%
5. Yale University, 16%
6. Brown University, 17%
7. California Institute of Technology, 18%
8. Massachusetts Institute of Technology, 19%
9. Dartmouth College, 21%
10. Georgetown University, 23%

Source: "America's Best Colleges," *U.S. News & World Report*, 129: 90-132, (September 11, 2000).

★1141★
U.S. News & World Report's national universities with the lowest graduation rates, 1999

Ranking basis/background: Based on *U.S News* questionnaire sent to 1,400 four-year institutions. Scores are averaged and weighted percentages from seven attributes: academic reputation, retention, faculty resources, student selectivity, financial resources, graduation rate performance and alumni giving. **Remarks:** Comparable data was used from the U.S. Department of Education, the Council for Aid to Education, the NCAA, and Wintergreen/Orchard House publishers. **Number listed:** 51.

1. University of Texas, Austin, with 66%
2. University of California, Santa Barbara, 67%
3. Georgia Institute of Technology, 69%
4. University of Southern California, 70%
5. New York University, 72%
5. Tulane University, 72%
5. University of Washington (WA), 72%
5. Pepperdine University, 72%
9. Rensselaer Polytechnic Institute, 73%
10. University of Rochester, 74%
10. University of California, Irvine, 74%

Source: "America's Best Colleges," *U.S. News & World Report*, 129: 90-132, (September 11, 2000).

★1142★
U.S. News & World Report's national universities with the lowest proportion of classes with 50 or more students, 2000-01

Ranking basis/background: Based on *U.S News* questionnaire sent to 1,400 four-year institutions. Scores are averaged and weighted percentages from seven attributes: academic reputation, retention, faculty resources, student selectivity, financial resources, graduation rate performance and alumni giving. **Remarks:** Comparable data was used from the U.S. Department of Education, the Council for Aid to Education, the NCAA, and Wintergreen/Orchard House publishers. **Number listed:** 51.

1. Pepperdine University, with 1%
2. Wake Forest University, 2%
2. Yeshiva University, 2%

4. University of Chicago, 3%
5. Vanderbilt University, 5%
6. Lehigh University, 6%
7. University of Pennsylvania, 7%
7. Duke University, 7%
7. Emory University, 7%
7. Tufts University, 7%
7. College of William and Mary, 7%

Source: "America's Best Colleges," *U.S. News & World Report*, 129: 90-132, (September 11, 2000).

Related Information

★1143★
Tenner, Edward, "Looking Beyond the Top 20," *U.S. News & World Report*, 129: 133, (September 11, 2000).
Remarks: Commentary regarding other issues and indicators besides national publication ratings to consider when choosing an institution of higher education.

★1144★
Morse, Robert J. and Samuel M. Flanigan, "How We Rank the Colleges," *U.S. News & World Report*, 129: 104-105, (September 11, 2000).
Remarks: Provides an in-depth explanation of the indicators for rating academic reputation, retention rates, faculty resources, student selectivity, financial resources, graduation rate performance and alumni giving rate the *U.S. News* uses to measure academic quality at national and regional colleges and universities in the U.S.

★1145★
www.usnews.com.
Remarks: *U.S. News'* Online Colleges and Careers Center provides job listings, a database that rates 2000+ colleges and universities, admissions tests preparations, interactive worksheets for calculating college costs, a listing of financial aid and scholarships, options for study abroad, and an opportunity to question counselors online.

★1146★
Guide to Distance Learning Programs 2001, 5th ed., Peterson's, 2001.
Remarks: Highlights specific program information from more than 650 American and Canadian colleges and universities that offer college-level study via telecommunications media.

★1147★
The Chronicle of Higher Education.
Remarks: Table shows the Higher Education Carnegie Classification for 3,856 accredited colleges and universities in the United States, by state. Also available on-line at http://www.carnegiefoundation.org.

COLLEGES & UNIVERSITIES–CANADA

★1148★
Best Canadian universities for producing leaders of tomorrow, 2000

Ranking basis/background: Combined ranking of 47 universities from three categories. **Remarks:** Based on *Macleans* ranking on 22 performance measures of such as student body, classes, faculty, finances, library facilities, and reputation. **Number listed:** 25.
1. University of Waterloo
2. University of Toronto
3. University of Alberta
4. Queen's University
5. McGill University
6. University of British Columbia
7. University of Guelph
8. McMaster University
9. Simon Fraser University
10. Acadia University

Source: "Universities 2000: The 10th Annual Ranking," *Maclean's*, 113: 52-109, (November 20, 2000).

★1149★
Best Canadian universities overall, 2000

Ranking basis/background: Combined ranking of 47 universities from three categories. **Remarks:** Based on *Macleans* ranking on 22 performance measures of such as student body, classes, faculty, finances, library facilities, and reputation. **Number listed:** 25.
1. University of Waterloo
2. University of Toronto
3. Queen's University
4. University of Alberta
5. McGill University
6. University of British Columbia
7. McMaster University
8. University of Guelph
9. Simon Fraser University
10. Acadia University
11. University of Western
12. University of Calgary
13. Ryerson University
14. University of Montreal
15. Dalhousie University
16. Wilfrid Laurier University
17. University of Sherbrooke
18. Mount Allison University
19. University of Victoria
20. Laval University
21. York University
22. University of Saskatchewan
23. University of New Brunswick
24. St. Francis Xavier University
25. St. Mary's University (NS)

Source: "Universities 2000: The 10th Annual Ranking," *Maclean's*, 113: 52-109, (November 20, 2000).

★1150★
Best Canadian universities that are the most innovative, 2000

Ranking basis/background: Combined ranking of 47 universities from three categories. **Remarks:** Based on *Macleans* ranking on 22 performance measures of such as student body, classes, faculty, finances, library facilities, and reputation. **Number listed:** 25.
1. University of Waterloo
2. McMaster University
3. University of Toronto
4. University of Guelph
5. University of Alberta
6. Simon Fraser University
7. Queen's University
8. University of British Columbia
9. McGill University
10. Acadia University

Source: "Universities 2000: The 10th Annual Ranking," *Maclean's*, 113: 52-109, (November 20, 2000).

★1151★
Best Canadian universities with the highest quality, 2000

Ranking basis/background: Combined ranking of 47 universities from three categories. **Remarks:** Based on *Macleans* ranking on 22 performance measures of such as student body, classes, faculty, finances, library facilities, and reputation. **Number listed:** 25.
1. Queen's University
2. University of Toronto
3. McGill University
4. University of Waterloo
5. University of British Columbia
6. University of Alberta
7. McMaster University
8. Simon Fraser University
9. University of Guelph
10. University of Western

Source: "Universities 2000: The 10th Annual Ranking," *Maclean's*, 113: 52-109, (November 20, 2000).

★1152★
Canadian comprehensive universities best at producing leaders of tomorrow, 2000

Ranking basis/background: Reputational ranking of schools believed to be best at producing leaders of tomorrow. Based on *Maclean's* survey of more than 3,500 individuals including corporate CEOs, university administrators, and high school guidance counselors from across Canada who rated schools in three categories: highest quality, most innovative, and leader of tomorrow. **Number listed:** 5.
1. University of Waterloo
2. University of Guelph
3. Simon Fraser University
4. York University
5. University of New Brunswick

Source: "Universities 2000: The 10th Annual Ranking," *Maclean's*, 113: 52-109, (November 20, 2000).

★1153★
Canadian comprehensive universities by alumni support, 2000

Ranking basis/background: Percentage of alumni giving gifts to the university over the last five years. **Remarks:** Based on *Macleans* ranking on 22 performance measures of such as student body, classes, faculty, finances, library facilities, and reputation. **Number listed:** 11.
1. University of Waterloo, with 22.1%
2. University of Windsor, 16.6%
3. University of Carleton, 16.3%
4. Concordia University, 15.5%
5. Simon Fraser University, 15.1%
6. York University, 13.6%
7. University of Guelph, 13.4%
8. Memorial University, 11.5%
9. University of New Brunswick, 11.2%
10. University of Victoria, 9%

11. University of Regina, 4.5%
Source: "Universities 2000: The 10th Annual Ranking," *Maclean's*, 113: 52-109, (November 20, 2000).

★1154★
Canadian comprehensive universities by award-winning faculty members, 2000
Ranking basis/background: Number of full-time professors per 1,000 winning national awards over the past five years. **Remarks:** Based on *Macleans* ranking on 22 performance measures of such as student body, classes, faculty, finances, library facilities, and reputation. **Number listed:** 11.
1. Simon Fraser University, with 6.1
2. University of Waterloo, 5.7
3. University of Guelph, 4.5
4. York University, 4.3
5. University of Victoria, 3.3
6. Memorial University, 1.9
7. University of Carleton, 1.8
8. University of Windsor, 1.1
9. University of New Brunswick, 1
10. Concordia University, 0.8
11. University of Regina, 0.5

Source: "Universities 2000: The 10th Annual Ranking," *Maclean's*, 113: 52-109, (November 20, 2000).

★1155★
Canadian comprehensive universities by class size at the first- and second-year level, 2000
Ranking basis/background: Percentage of classes within six size ranges weighted and combined to determine overall rank. Figures for the class size having over 500 students are not shown due to the small proportion represented. **Remarks:** Based on *Macleans* ranking on 22 performance measures of such as student body, classes, faculty, finances, library facilities, and reputation. **Number listed:** 11.
1. University of Regina, with 51.41% in classes of 1-25 students; 29.74% (26-50); 12.79% (51-100); 5.52% (101-250); 0.54% (251-500)
2. Concordia University, 37.84%; 37.46%; 22.02%; 2.68%; 0.54%
3. University of New Brunswick, 38.12%; 34.53%; 21.37%; 5.13%; 0.85%
4. Memorial University, 28.99%; 46.87%; 21.71%; 1.79%; 0.64%
5. University of Victoria, 42.48%; 28.85%; 18.41%; 9.03%; 1.24%
6. Simon Fraser University, 46.17%; 19.13%; 14.54%; 16.58%; 3.57%
7. University of Guelph, 36.75%; 31.62%; 13.25%; 14.1%; 4.27%
8. University of Windsor, 31.21%; 26.97%; 22.54%; 16.38%; 2.89%
9. York University, 35.91%; 19.58%; 19.96%; 20.82%; 3.15%
10. University of Waterloo, 26.66%; 24.43%; 28.52%; 17.17%; 2.36%
11. University of Carleton, 24.74%; 24.74%; 31.02%; 16.36%; 3.14%

Source: "Universities 2000: The 10th Annual Ranking," *Maclean's*, 113: 52-109, (November 20, 2000).

★1156★
Canadian comprehensive universities by class size at the third- and forth-year level, 2000
Ranking basis/background: Percentage of classes within six size ranges weighted and combined to determine overall rank. Figures for the class size having 251-500 students and over 500 students are not shown due to the small proportion represented. **Remarks:** Based on *Macleans* ranking on 22 performance measures of such as student body, classes, faculty, finances, library facilities, and reputation. **Number listed:** 11.
1. University of Regina, with 77.15% in classes of 1-25 students; 18.78% (26-50); 4.07% (51-100); 0% (101-250)
2. Memorial University, 69.97%; 23.65%; 5.95%; 0.28%
3. Concordia University, 67.27%; 26.33%; 6.04%; 0.36%
4. University of New Brunswick, 66.19%; 25.11%; 7.99%; 0.71%
5. University of Windsor, 66.59%; 22.2%; 10.11%; 1.1%
6. Simon Fraser University, 64.67%; 22.43%; 11.06%; 1.84%
7. University of Carleton, 64.25%; 22.31%; 10.39%; 3.05%
8. York University, 62.03%; 24.95%; 10.69%; 2.26%
9. University of Guelph, 64.37%; 21.34%; 9.88%; 3.88%
10. University of Victoria, 57.6%; 30.49%; 10.94%; 0.97%
11. University of Waterloo, 61.84%; 21.99%; 11.63%; 4.11%

Source: "Universities 2000: The 10th Annual Ranking," *Maclean's*, 113: 52-109, (November 20, 2000).

★1157★
Canadian comprehensive universities by classes taught by tenured faculty, 2000
Ranking basis/background: Percentage of first-year classes taught by tenured or tenure-track faculty. **Remarks:** Based on *Macleans* ranking on 22 performance measures of such as student body, classes, faculty, finances, library facilities, and reputation. **Number listed:** 11.
1. York University, with 86.3%
2. University of Windsor, 76.2%
3. Memorial University, 67.3%
4. University of Guelph, 58.9%
5. University of New Brunswick, 54.5%
6. University of Waterloo, 50.3%
7. Simon Fraser University, 46.7%
8. University of Carleton, 44.8%
9. University of Victoria, 40.9%
10. Concordia University, 40.9%
11. University of Regina, 21%

Source: "Universities 2000: The 10th Annual Ranking," *Maclean's*, 113: 52-109, (November 20, 2000).

★1158★
Canadian comprehensive universities by faculty members with Ph.D.'s, 2000
Ranking basis/background: Percentage of full-time faculty members with Ph.D.s. **Remarks:** Based on *Macleans* ranking on 22 performance measures of such as student body, classes, faculty, finances, library facilities, and reputation. **Number listed:** 11.
1. University of Waterloo, with 96.4%
2. University of Guelph, 96.1%
3. Simon Fraser University, 94.7%
4. University of Windsor, 93.6%
4. York University, 93.6%
6. University of Victoria, 93.1%
7. Concordia University, 91%
8. University of Carleton, 89.9%
9. University of New Brunswick, 86%
10. Memorial University, 83.9%
11. University of Regina, 72.4%

Source: "Universities 2000: The 10th Annual Ranking," *Maclean's*, 113: 52-109, (November 20, 2000).

★1159★
Canadian comprehensive universities by international graduate students, 2000
Ranking basis/background: Percentage of graduate students from abroad. **Remarks:** Based on *Macleans* ranking on 22 performance measures of such as student body, classes, faculty, finances, library facilities, and reputation. **Number listed:** 11.
1. University of Windsor, with 38.5%
2. University of Regina, 26.6%
3. Memorial University, 22%
4. University of Waterloo, 21.9%
5. University of New Brunswick, 21.2%
6. University of Victoria, 20.8%
7. Simon Fraser University, 17%
8. Concordia University, 16.8%
9. University of Guelph, 14.2%
10. University of Carleton, 11.9%
11. York University, 11.6%

Source: "Universities 2000: The 10th Annual Ranking," *Maclean's*, 113: 52-109, (November 20, 2000).

★1160★
Canadian comprehensive universities by library acquisitions, 2000
Ranking basis/background: Percentage of library budget allocated to updating the university's collection. **Remarks:** Based on *Macleans* ranking on 22 performance measures of such as student body, classes, faculty, finances, library facilities, and reputation. **Number listed:** 11.
1. Simon Fraser University, with 44.19%
2. University of Waterloo, 43.55%
3. University of Windsor, 42.23%
4. University of Regina, 41.5%
5. Memorial University, 41.3%
6. University of Victoria, 38.4%
7. University of Guelph, 38.14
8. York University, 36.99%
9. Concordia University, 36.43%
10. University of Carleton, 33.56%
11. University of New Brunswick, 28.98%

Source: "Universities 2000: The 10th Annual Ranking," *Maclean's*, 113: 52-109, (November 20, 2000).

★1161★
Canadian comprehensive universities by library expenses, 2000
Ranking basis/background: Percentage of library budget allocated to maintaining library services. **Remarks:** Based on *Macleans* ranking on 22 performance measures of such as student body, classes, faculty, finances, library facilities, and reputation. **Number listed:** 11.
1. Memorial University, with 7.2%
2. University of Windsor, 6.9%
2. University of New Brunswick, 6.9%
4. University of Waterloo, 6.6%
5. University of Carleton, 6.5%

5. Simon Fraser University, 6.5%
7. University of Victoria, 6.4%
8. University of Guelph, 6.2%
9. York University, 6.0%
9. University of Regina, 6.0%
11. Concordia University 5.9%

Source: "Universities 2000: The 10th Annual Ranking," *Maclean's*, 113: 52-109, (November 20, 2000).

★1162★
Canadian comprehensive universities by library holdings per student, 2000

Ranking basis/background: Number of print volumes in all campus libraries divided by the number of full-time-equivalent students. **Remarks:** Based on *Macleans* ranking on 22 performance measures of such as student body, classes, faculty, finances, library facilities, and reputation. **Number listed:** 11.

1. University of New Brunswick, with 323
2. Memorial University, 303
3. University of Victoria, 242
4. University of Guelph, 235
5. University of Windsor, 229
6. University of Regina, 221
7. University of Carleton, 214
8. University of Waterloo, 179
9. York University, 166
10. Concordia University, 160
11. Simon Fraser University, 148

Source: "Universities 2000: The 10th Annual Ranking," *Maclean's*, 113: 52-109, (November 20, 2000).

★1163★
Canadian comprehensive universities by operating budget per student, 2000

Ranking basis/background: Figures for operating expenditures per weighted full-time-equivalent student. **Remarks:** Based on *Macleans* ranking on 22 performance measures of such as student body, classes, faculty, finances, library facilities, and reputation. **Number listed:** 11.

1. Simon Fraser University, with $8,202
2. University of Windsor, $7,856
3. Memorial University, $7,844
4. University of Victoria, $7,656
5. University of Guelph, $7,522
6. University of Regina, $7,517
7. University of Carleton, $7,246
8. University of Waterloo, $7,072
9. University of New Brunswick, $6,903
10. York University, $6,724
11. Concordia University, $6,037

Source: "Universities 2000: The 10th Annual Ranking," *Maclean's*, 113: 52-109, (November 20, 2000).

★1164★
Canadian comprehensive universities by percentage of operating budget allocated to scholarships, 2000

Ranking basis/background: Percentage of total operating expenditures allocated to scholarships and bursaries. **Remarks:** Based on *Macleans* ranking on 22 performance measures of such as student body, classes, faculty, finances, library facilities, and reputation. **Number listed:** 11.

1. University of Carleton, with 8.07%
2. York University, 7.41%
3. University of Waterloo, 6.72%
4. Memorial University, 6.05%
5. Simon Fraser University, 5.92%
6. University of Guelph, 5.88%
7. University of Victoria, 5.75%
8. University of Windsor, 5.57%
9. University of Regina, 5.01%
10. Concordia University, 4.23%
11. University of New Brunswick, 2.83%

Source: "Universities 2000: The 10th Annual Ranking," *Maclean's*, 113: 52-109, (November 20, 2000).

★1165★
Canadian comprehensive universities by percentage of operating budget allocated to student services, 2000

Ranking basis/background: Percent of total operating expenditures allocated to student services. **Remarks:** Based on *Macleans* ranking on 22 performance measures of such as student body, classes, faculty, finances, library facilities, and reputation. **Number listed:** 11.

1. York University, with 6.93%
2. University of Guelph, 6.24%
3. University of Windsor, 5.6%
4. University of Carleton, 5.34%
5. University of Regina, 4.91%
6. University of Victoria, 4.78%
7. Memorial University, 4.7%
8. Concordia University, 4.62%
9. University of New Brunswick, 4.02%
10. Simon Fraser University, 3.91%
11. University of Waterloo, 3.59%

Source: "Universities 2000: The 10th Annual Ranking," *Maclean's*, 113: 52-109, (November 20, 2000).

★1166★
Canadian comprehensive universities by social science/humanities grants per faculty member, 2000

Ranking basis/background: Average size and number of peer-adjudicated research grants from the Social Sciences and Humanities Research Council of Canada per eligible full-time faculty member; number of grants is per 100 eligible full-time faculty members. The ranking reflects a weighted average of the two. **Remarks:** Based on *Macleans* ranking on 22 performance measures of such as student body, classes, faculty, finances, library facilities, and reputation. **Number listed:** 11.

1. Simon Fraser University, with $8,265; 28.53 eligible faculty per 100
2. Concordia University, $4,891; 24.14
3. University of Victoria, $4,941; 19.79
4. York University, $4,581; 15.89
5. University of Carleton, $4,533; 15.99
6. University of Guelph, $2,986; 18.96
7. University of Waterloo, $2,928; 16.67
8. Memorial University, $1,899; 8.33
9. University of Regina, $1,515; 7.22
10. University of Windsor, $1,321; 6.11
11. University of New Brunswick, $1,183; 6.1

Source: "Universities 2000: The 10th Annual Ranking," *Maclean's*, 113: 52-109, (November 20, 2000).

★1167★
Canadian comprehensive universities by students from out of province, 2000

Ranking basis/background: Percentage of students from out of province. **Remarks:** Based on *Macleans* ranking on 22 performance measures of such as student body, classes, faculty, finances, library facilities, and reputation. **Number listed:** 11.

1. University of New Brunswick, with 18.4%
2. Concordia University, 15.1%
3. University of Carleton, 12.8%
4. University of Victoria, 10.7%
5. University of Waterloo, 8.4%
6. Simon Fraser University, 7.2%
7. Memorial University, 5.8%
8. University of Regina, 3.9%
9. University of Guelph, 2.8%
10. York University, 2%
11. University of Windsor, 1.7%

Source: "Universities 2000: The 10th Annual Ranking," *Maclean's*, 113: 52-109, (November 20, 2000).

★1168★
Canadian comprehensive universities by students winning national awards, 2000

Ranking basis/background: Number of students per 1,000 winning national awards. **Remarks:** Based on *Macleans* ranking on 22 performance measures of such as student body, classes, faculty, finances, library facilities, and reputation. **Number listed:** 11.

1. University of Waterloo, with 6.6
2. University of Guelph, 5.4
3. University of Carleton, 4.9
4. Simon Fraser University, 4.7
5. University of Victoria, 4.6
6. University of New Brunswick, 4
7. York University, 3.1
8. Concordia University, 3
9. University of Regina, 2.4
10. Memorial University, 2
11. University of Windsor, 1.5

Source: "Universities 2000: The 10th Annual Ranking," *Maclean's*, 113: 52-109, (November 20, 2000).

★1169★
Canadian comprehensive universities that are the best overall, 2000

Ranking basis/background: Reputational ranking of schools believed to be the best overall. Based on *Maclean's* survey of more than 3,500 individuals including corporate CEOs, university administrators, and high school guidance counselors from across Canada who rated schools in three categories: highest quality, most innovative, and leader of tomorrow. **Number listed:** 5.

1. University of Waterloo
2. University of Guelph
3. Simon Fraser University
4. University of Victoria
5. York University

Source: "Universities 2000: The 10th Annual Ranking," *Maclean's*, 113: 52-109, (November 20, 2000).

★1170★
Canadian comprehensive universities that are the most innovative, 2000

Ranking basis/background: Reputational ranking of schools believed to be the most innovative. Based on *Maclean's* survey of more than 3,500 individuals including corporate CEOs, university administrators, and high school guidance counselors from across Canada who rated schools in three categories: highest quality, most innovative, and leader of tomorrow. **Number listed:** 5.

1. University of Waterloo
2. University of Guelph
3. Simon Fraser Unikversity
4. University of Victoria
5. York University

★1171★
Canadian comprehensive universities with the highest quality, 2000

Ranking basis/background: Reputational ranking of schools believed to have the highest quality. Based on *Maclean's* survey of more than 3,500 individuals including corporate CEOs, university administrators, and high school guidance counselors from across Canada who rated schools in three categories: highest quality, most innovative, and leader of tomorrow. **Number listed:** 5.
1. University of Waterloo
2. Simon Fraser University
3. University of Guelph
4. University of Victoria
5. York University

Source: "Universities 2000: The 10th Annual Ranking," *Maclean's*, 113: 52-109, (November 20, 2000).

★1172★
Canadian medical/doctoral universities by alumni support, 2000

Ranking basis/background: Percentage of alumni giving gifts to the university over the last five years. **Remarks:** Based on *Macleans* ranking on 22 performance measures of such as student body, classes, faculty, finances, library facilities, and reputation. **Number listed:** 15.
1. University of Toronto, with 24.8%
2. University of Western, 24.5%
3. McGill University, 19.8%
4. Queen's University, 18.9%
5. University of Manitoba, 18.4%
6. Dalhousie University, 15.6%
7. University of Montreal, 14.6%
8. University of Sherbrooke, 14.3%
9. McMaster University, 13.7%
10. University of Alberta, 13.1%
11. University of Calgary, 13%
12. University of Ottawa, 12%
13. Laval University, 9.9%
14. University of Saskatchewan, 9.3%

Source: "Universities 2000: The 10th Annual Ranking," *Maclean's*, 113: 52-109, (November 20, 2000).

★1173★
Canadian medical/doctoral universities by award-winning faculty members, 2000

Ranking basis/background: Number of full-time professors per 1,000 winning national awards over the past five years. **Remarks:** Based on *Macleans* ranking on 22 performance measures of such as student body, classes, faculty, finances, library facilities, and reputation. **Number listed:** 15.
1. Queen's University, with 9.4
2. University of Toronto, 9.1
3. McGill University, 8.6
4. University of Montreal, 8.3
5. University of British Columbia, 8.2
6. McMaster University, 7.5
7. University of Alberta, 5.5
8. Laval University, 5.4
9. University of Manitoba, 4.9
10. University of Western, 4.1
11. University of Ottawa, 4
12. Dalhousie University, 3.8
13. University of Sherbrooke, 3.2
14. University of Calgary, 3.1
15. University of Saskatchewan, 3

Source: "Universities 2000: The 10th Annual Ranking," *Maclean's*, 113: 52-109, (November 20, 2000).

★1174★
Canadian medical/doctoral universities by class size at the first- and second-year level, 2000

Ranking basis/background: Percentage of classes within six size ranges weighted and combined to determine overall rank. Figures for the class size having over 500 students are not shown due to the small proportion represented. **Remarks:** Based on *Macleans* ranking on 22 performance measures of such as student body, classes, faculty, finances, library facilities, and reputation. **Number listed:** 15.
1. University of Sherbrooke, with 48.58% in classes of 1-25 students; 28.66% (26-50); 20.02% (51-100); 2.74% (101-250); 0% (251-500)
2. University of Western, 47.17%; 27.81%; 18.02%; 6.01%; 0.87%
3. University of British Columbia, 50.63%; 24.1%; 12.19%; 12.99%; 0.09%
4. McGill University, 51.1%; 18.7%; 16.72%; 10.45%; 2.72%
5. University of Toronto, 50.95%; 15.73%; 15.79%; 15.24%; 2.01%
6. University of Ottawa, 40.67%; 25.89%; 21.79%; 11.33%; 0.32%
7. University of Alberta, 39.49%; 28.05%; 17.4%; 13.49%; 1.56%
8. University of Saskatchewan, 34.28%; 32.19%; 22.56%; 9.89%; 1.07%
9. University of Montreal, 34.8%; 24.74%; 34.59%; 5.51%; 0.37%
10. Dalhousie University, 35.15%; 27.96%; 26.21%; 10.49%; 0%
11. Queen's University, 44.16%; 16.25%; 22.24%; 14.51%; 2.84%
12. University of Manitoba, 37.05%; 25.64%; 21.61%; 15.17%; 0.54%
13. Laval University, 33.03%; 28.04%; 26.32%; 11.8%; 0.8%
14. University of Calgary, 29.29%; 29.4%; 26.23%; 13.88%; 1.2%
15. McMaster University, 21.98%; 30.1%; 16.44%; 27.52%; 3.96%

Source: "Universities 2000: The 10th Annual Ranking," *Maclean's*, 113: 52-109, (November 20, 2000).

★1175★
Canadian medical/doctoral universities by class size at the third- and forth-year level, 2000

Ranking basis/background: Percentage of classes within six size ranges weighted and combined to determine overall rank. Figures for the class size having 251-500 students and over 500 students are not shown due to the small proportion represented. **Remarks:** Based on *Macleans* ranking on 22 performance measures of such as student body, classes, faculty, finances, library facilities, and reputation. **Number listed:** 15.
1. University of Montreal, with 83.96% in classes of 1-25 students; 9.19% (26-50); 6.11% (51-100); 0.74% (101-250)
2. McGill University, 82.4%; 9.69%; 6.17%; 1.73%
3. McMaster University, 79.81%; 11.26%; 6.36%; 2.57%
4. Queen's University, 77.76%; 14.22%; 5.51%; 2.42%
5. University of Manitoba, 75.04%; 15.69%; 8.73%; 0.53%
6. University of Calgary, 73.32%; 18.45%; 7.31%; 0.93%
7. University of British Columbia, 75.45%; 13.34%; 8.21%; 3%
8. Dalhousie University, 69.49%; 21.88%; 8.09%; 0.55%
9. University of Western, 71.65%; 16.22%; 10.87%; 1.26%
10. University of Alberta, 71.76%; 16.47%; 9.08%; 2.61%
11. University of Toronto, 68.66%; 18.96%; 10.02%; 2.1%
12. University of Saskatchewan, 64.17%; 26.29%; 8.12%; 1.42%
13. University of Ottawa, 62.74%; 23.18%; 13.11%; 0.97%
14. University of Sherbrooke, 56.56%; 32.72%; 10.72%; 0%
15. Laval University, 56.42%; 22.72%; 16.68%; 4.17%

Source: "Universities 2000: The 10th Annual Ranking," *Maclean's*, 113: 52-109, (November 20, 2000).

★1176★
Canadian medical/doctoral universities by classes taught by tenured faculty, 2000

Ranking basis/background: Percentage of first-year classes taught by tenured or tenure-track faculty. **Remarks:** Based on *Macleans* ranking on 22 performance measures of such as student body, classes, faculty, finances, library facilities, and reputation. **Number listed:** 15.
1. Laval University, with 78.3%
2. University of Western, 71.6%
3. University of Toronto, 69.8%
4. McMaster University, 64.4%
5. Dalhousie University, 63.9%
6. University of Manitoba, 62%
7. University of Ottawa, 61%
8. University of Saskatchewan, 55.3%
9. University of Montreal, 49.5%
10. University of Sherbrooke, 47.5%
11. McGill University, 46.7%
12. University of Alberta, 43.3%
13. University of British Columbia, 40.9%
14. University of Calgary, 36.9%
15. Queen's University, 28.5%

Source: "Universities 2000: The 10th Annual Ranking," *Maclean's*, 113: 52-109, (November 20, 2000).

★1177★
Canadian medical/doctoral universities by faculty members with Ph.D.'s, 2000

Ranking basis/background: Percentage of full-time faculty members with Ph.D.s. **Remarks:** Based on *Macleans* ranking on 22 performance measures of such as student body, classes, faculty, finances, library facilities, and reputation. **Number listed:** 15.
1. University of British Columbia, with 98.3%
2. University of Toronto, 97.3%
3. University of Ottawa, 96.4%
4. Queen's University, 95.5%
5. McMaster University, 95.2%
6. University of Western, 95%
7. University of Alberta, 94.2%
8. University of Calgary, 94.1%

9. McGill University, 93.9%
10. University of Manitoba, 93.8%
11. Laval University, 93.3%
12. Dalhousie University, 91.2%
13. University of Saskatchewan, 90.3%
14. University of Montreal, 90%
15. University of Sherbrooke, 86.6%

Source: "Universities 2000: The 10th Annual Ranking," *Maclean's*, 113: 52-109, (November 20, 2000).

★1178★
Canadian medical/doctoral universities by international graduate students, 2000

Ranking basis/background: Percentage of graduate students from abroad. **Remarks:** Based on *Macleans* ranking on 22 performance measures of such as student body, classes, faculty, finances, library facilities, and reputation. **Number listed:** 15.

1. University of Saskatchewan, with 24%
2. McGill University, 21.9%
3. Queen's University, 21.2%
4. Laval University, 20.8%
5. University of Alberta, 18.4%
6. University of British Columbia, 18.3%
7. University of Sherbrooke, 17.3%
8. University of Montreal, 17.1%
9. University of Ottawa, 15.7%
10. Dalhousie University, 15.1%
11. University of Calgary, 13.8%
12. University of Western, 12.3%
13. University of Toronto, 11.9%
14. University of Manitoba, 11%
15. McMaster University, 9.8%

Source: "Universities 2000: The 10th Annual Ranking," *Maclean's*, 113: 52-109, (November 20, 2000).

★1179★
Canadian medical/doctoral universities by library acquisitions, 2000

Ranking basis/background: Percentage of library budget allocated to updating the university's collection. **Remarks:** Based on *Macleans* ranking on 22 performance measures of such as student body, classes, faculty, finances, library facilities, and reputation. **Number listed:** 15.

1. Dalhousie University, with 49.34%
2. Queen's University, 47.08%
3. University of British Columbia, 47%
4. University of Sherbrooke, 46.19%
5. University of Toronto, 46.08%
6. McMaster University, 43.26
7. University of Saskatchewan, 42.7%
8. University of Alberta, 42.42%
9. University of Western, 42.36%
10. McGill University, 42.29%
11. Laval University, 38.28%
12. University of Manitoba, 37.02%
13. University of Ottawa, 35.56%
14. University of Calgary, 35.05%
15. University of Montreal, 33.31

Source: "Universities 2000: The 10th Annual Ranking," *Maclean's*, 113: 52-109, (November 20, 2000).

★1180★
Canadian medical/doctoral universities by library expenses, 2000

Ranking basis/background: Percentage of library budget allocated to maintaining library services. **Remarks:** Based on *Macleans* ranking on 22 performance measures of such as student body, classes, faculty, finances, library facilities, and reputation. **Number listed:** 15.

1. University of Toronto, with 10.2%
2. University of British Columbia, 9.2%
3. Queen's University, 7.9%
4. University of Western, 7.8%
5. University of Manitoba, 6.9%
6. University of Saskatchewan, 6.5%
7. University of Alberta, 6.4%
8. McMaster University, 6.0%
9. McGill University, 5.7%
10. Dalhousie University, 5.6%
11. University of Calgary, 5.5%
12. University of Ottawa, 5.4%
13. University of Montreal, 5.2%
14. Laval University, 5.0%
15. University of Sherbrooke, 4.0%

Source: "Universities 2000: The 10th Annual Ranking," *Maclean's*, 113: 52-109, (November 20, 2000).

★1181★
Canadian medical/doctoral universities by library holdings, 2000

Ranking basis/background: Total library holdings in millions. **Remarks:** Based on *Macleans* ranking on 22 performance measures of such as student body, classes, faculty, finances, library facilities, and reputation. **Number listed:** 15.

1. University of Toronto, with 13.974
2. University of Alberta, 9.451
3. University of British Columbia, 7.977
4. University of Western, 6.464
5. Queen's University, 5.263
6. University of Calgary, 4.763
7. University of Montreal, 4.738
8. McGill University, 4.563
9. University of Saskatchewan, 4.209
10. Laval University, 4.192
11. University of Ottawa, 3.639
12. University of Manitoba, 2.947
13. McMaster University, 2.944
14. Dalhousie University, 1.83
15. University of Sherbrooke, 1.696

Source: "Universities 2000: The 10th Annual Ranking," *Maclean's*, 113: 52-109, (November 20, 2000).

★1182★
Canadian medical/doctoral universities by library holdings per student, 2000

Ranking basis/background: Number of print volumes in all campus libraries divided by the number of full-time-equivalent students. **Remarks:** Based on *Macleans* ranking on 22 performance measures of such as student body, classes, faculty, finances, library facilities, and reputation. **Number listed:** 15.

1. University of Alberta, with 363
2. Queen's University, 327
3. University of Toronto, 304
4. University of Saskatchewan, 272
5. University of Western, 264
6. University of British Columbia, 262
7. University of Calgary, 218
8. University of Ottawa, 212
9. McGill University, 205
10. Laval University, 196
11. McMaster University, 193
12. University of Manitoba, 175
13. Dalhousie University, 167
14. University of Sherbrooke, 139
15. University of Montreal, 138

Source: "Universities 2000: The 10th Annual Ranking," *Maclean's*, 113: 52-109, (November 20, 2000).

★1183★
Canadian medical/doctoral universities by medical/science grants per faculty member, 2000

Ranking basis/background: Average size and number of peer-adjudicated research grants from the Natural Sciences and Engineering Research Council and the Medical Research Council per eligible full-time faculty member; number of grants is per 100 eligible full-time faculty members. The ranking reflects a weighted average of the two. **Remarks:** Based on *Macleans* ranking on 22 performance measures of such as student body, classes, faculty, finances, library facilities, and reputation. **Number listed:** 11.

1. University of Victoria, with $67,645; 144.51 eligible faculty per 100
2. Simon Fraser University, $56,348; 129.77
3. University of Guelph, $51,893; 126.48
4. York University, $48,152; 128.49
5. University of Waterloo, $49,341; 124.89
6. Concordia University, $33,408; 121.57
7. University of Windsor, $36,795; 108
8. University of Carleton, $41,084; 98.01
9. University of Regina, $22,972; 81.74
10. University of New Brunswick, $18,919; 68.44
11. Memorial University, $18,577; 50.45

Source: "Universities 2000: The 10th Annual Ranking," *Maclean's*, 113: 52-109, (November 20, 2000).

★1184★
Canadian medical/doctoral universities by medical/science grants per faculty member, 2000

Ranking basis/background: Average size and number of peer-adjudicated research grants from the Natural Sciences and Engineering Research Council and the Medical Research Council per eligible full-time faculty member; number of grants is per 100 eligible full-time faculty members. The ranking reflects a weighted average of the two. **Remarks:** Based on *Macleans* ranking on 22 performance measures of such as student body, classes, faculty, finances, library facilities, and reputation. **Number listed:** 15.

1. University of Alberta, with $71,274; 156.57 eligible faculty per 100
2. University of British Columbia, $74,759; 140.3
3. University of Ottawa, $70,265; 143.15
4. University of Western, $63,119; 135.76
5. University of Toronto, $67,531; 125.36
6. Queen's University, $66,108; 104.01
7. McGill University, $60,944; 108.53
8. University of Montreal, $55,184; 116.32
9. University of Calgary, $54,646; 105.17
10. Laval University $48,044; 100.7
11. McMaster University, $50,997; 91.53
12. University of Sherbrooke, $40,710; 90.91
13. University of Manitoba, $34,152; 85.09
14. Dalhousie University, $31,877; 85.82
15. University of Saskatchewan, $22,286; 57.77

Source: "Universities 2000: The 10th Annual Ranking," *Maclean's*, 113: 52-109, (November 20, 2000).

★1185★
Canadian medical/doctoral universities by operating budget per student, 2000

Ranking basis/background: Figures for operating expenditures per weighted full-time-equivalent student. **Remarks:** Based on *Macleans* ranking on 22 performance measures of such as student body, classes, faculty, finances, library facilities, and reputation. **Number listed:** 15.

1. University of Ottawa, with $10,568
2. University of Toronto, $8,557
3. University of Calgary, $8,521
4. University of Western, $8,103
5. University of Alberta, $7,926
6. Dalhousie University, $7,922
7. McGill University, $7,764
8. McMaster University, $7,636
9. University of Manitoba, $7,166
10. Queen's University, $7,001
11. Laval University, $6,858
12. University of British Columbia, $6,839
13. University of Saskatchewan, $6,739
14. University of Sherbrooke, $6,392
15. University of Montreal, $6,311

Source: "Universities 2000: The 10th Annual Ranking," *Maclean's*, 113: 52-109, (November 20, 2000).

★1186★
Canadian medical/doctoral universities by percentage of operating budget allocated to scholarships, 2000

Ranking basis/background: Percentage of total operating expenditures allocated to scholarships and bursaries. **Remarks:** Based on *Macleans* ranking on 22 performance measures of such as student body, classes, faculty, finances, library facilities, and reputation. **Number listed:** 15.

1. Queen's University, with 12.5%
2. University of Toronto, 11.09%
3. University of Alberta, 10.66%
4. University of Western, 9.94%
5. University of British Columbia, 9.82%
6. McGill University, 9.78%
7. McMaster University, 8.31%
8. University of Ottawa, 7.93%
9. University of Calgary, 7.37%
10. Dalhousie University, 7.33%
11. University of Montreal, 7.07%
12. Laval University, 5.92%
13. University of Sherbrooke, 5.22%
14. University of Saskatchewan, 4.1%
15. University of Manitoba, 4.02%

Source: "Universities 2000: The 10th Annual Ranking," *Maclean's*, 113: 52-109, (November 20, 2000).

★1187★
Canadian medical/doctoral universities by percentage of operating budget allocated to student services, 2000

Ranking basis/background: Percent of total operating expenditures allocated to student services. **Remarks:** Based on *Macleans* ranking on 22 performance measures of such as student body, classes, faculty, finances, library facilities, and reputation. **Number listed:** 15.

1. University of Toronto, with 5.59%
2. University of British Columbia, 5.57%
3. University of Alberta, 4.77%
4. Queen's University, $4.55%
5. University of Ottawa, 4.52%
5. University of Western, 4.52%
7. Dalhousie University, 4.12%
8. University of Calgary, 3.56%
9. McGill University, 3.54%
10. McMaster University, 3.37%
11. University of Saskatchewan, 3.28%
12. Laval University, 3.27%
13. University of Manitoba, 3.19%
14. University of Sherbrooke, 3.07%
15. University of Montreal, 2.6%

Source: "Universities 2000: The 10th Annual Ranking," *Maclean's*, 113: 52-109, (November 20, 2000).

★1188★
Canadian medical/doctoral universities by reputation, 2000

Ranking basis/background: Reputational ranking of schools. Based on *Maclean's* ranking of 22 performance measures of Medical/Doctoral universities such as student body, classes, faculty, finances, library facilities, and reputation. **Number listed:** 15.

1. University of Toronto
2. Queen's University
3. University of Alberta
4. McGill University
5. University of British Columbia
6. McMaster University
7. University of Western
8. University of Calgary
9. University of Montreal
10. Dalhousie University
11. University of Sherbrooke
12. Laval University
13. University of Saskatchewan
14. University of Ottawa
15. University of Manitoba

Source: "Universities 2000: The 10th Annual Ranking," *Maclean's*, 113: 52-109, (November 20, 2000).

★1189★
Canadian medical/doctoral universities by social science/humanities grants per faculty member, 2000

Ranking basis/background: Average size and number of peer-adjudicated research grants from the Social Sciences and Humanities Research Council of Canada per eligible full-time faculty member; number of grants is per 100 eligible full-time faculty members. The ranking reflects a weighted average of the two. **Remarks:** Based on *Macleans* ranking on 22 performance measures of such as student body, classes, faculty, finances, library facilities, and reputation. **Number listed:** 15.

1. University of British Columbia, with $10,001; 37.68 eligible faculty per 100
2. University of Toronto, $8,397; 41.71
3. McMaster University, $8,175; 27.84
4. University of Montreal, $6,653; 30.3
5. University of Ottawa, $8,819; 20.86
6. McGill University, $6,582; 29.14
7. Laval University, $6.723; 25.49
8. University of Alberta, $6,846; 24.83
9. Queen's University, $5,444; 27.47
10. University of Calgary, $6,705; 15.17
11. Dalhousie University, $3,909; 24.31
12. University of Western, $4,236; 21.62
13. University of Sherbrooke, $2,851; 14.53
14. University of Manitoba, $2,530; 10.43
15. University of Saskatchewan, $1,604; 6.51

Source: "Universities 2000: The 10th Annual Ranking," *Maclean's*, 113: 52-109, (November 20, 2000).

★1190★
Canadian medical/doctoral universities by students from out of province, 2000

Ranking basis/background: Percentage of students from out of province. **Remarks:** Based on *Macleans* ranking on 22 performance measures of such as student body, classes, faculty, finances, library facilities, and reputation. **Number listed:** 15.

1. Dalhousie University, with 29.7%
1. McGill University, 29.7%
3. Queen's University, 18.4%
4. University of Ottawa, 15.5%
5. University of Alberta, 12.2%
6. Laval University, 11.8%
7. University of Calgary, 9.8%
8. University of Saskatchewan, 8.8%
9. University of Western, 8%
10. University of Montreal, 7.9%
11. University of British Columbia, 7.1%
12. University of Manitoba, 6.3%
13. University of Toronto, 4%
14. University of Sherbrooke, 3%
15. McMaster University, 2.2%

Source: "Universities 2000: The 10th Annual Ranking," *Maclean's*, 113: 52-109, (November 20, 2000).

★1191★
Canadian medical/doctoral universities by students winning national awards, 2000

Ranking basis/background: Number of students per 1,000 winning national awards. **Remarks:** Based on *Macleans* ranking on 22 performance measures of such as student body, classes, faculty, finances, library facilities, and reputation. **Number listed:** 15.

1. McGill University, with 9
2. Queen's University, 8.1
3. University of British Columbia, 7.4
4. University of Toronto, 7.2
5. McMaster University, 6.8
6. Dalhousie University, 6.4
7. Laval University, 5.8
8. University of Alberta, 5.2
9. University of Montreal, 5
10. University of Manitoba, 4.5
10. University of Ottawa, 4.5
12. University of Western, 4.2
13. University of Sherbrooke, 3.7
14. University of Calgary, 3.4
15. University of Saskatchewan, 2.1

Source: "Universities 2000: The 10th Annual Ranking," *Maclean's*, 113: 52-109, (November 20, 2000).

★1192★
Canadian primarily undergraduate universities best at producing leaders of tomorrow, 2000

Ranking basis/background: Reputational ranking of schools believed to be the best at producing leaders of tomorrow. Based on *Maclean's* survey of more than 3,500 individuals including corporate CEOs, university administrators, and high school guidance counselors from across Canada who rated schools in three categories: highest quality, most innovative, and leader of tomorrow. **Number listed:** 5.

1. Acadia University

COLLEGES & UNIVERSITIES—CANADA

2. Ryerson University
3. Wilfrid Laurier University
4. Mount Allison University
5. University of Lethbridge

Source: "Universities 2000: The 10th Annual Ranking," *Maclean's*, 113: 52-109, (November 20, 2000).

★1193★
Canadian primarily undergraduate universities by alumni support, 2000

Ranking basis/background: Percentage of alumni giving gifts to the university over the last five years. **Remarks:** Based on *Macleans* ranking on 22 performance measures of such as student body, classes, faculty, finances, library facilities, and reputation. **Number listed:** 20.

1. Universite de Moncton, with 32.6%
2. University of Nipissing, 30.5%
3. Bishop's University, 30.3%
4. St. Mary's University (NS)
5. St. Francis Xavier University, 26.8%
6. Trent University, 26%
7. Brandon University, 24.7%
8. University of Winnipeg, 23.4%
9. Acadia University, 21.4%
10. St. Thomas University (NB), 20.3%
11. Wilfrid Laurier University, 20%
12. Mount Allison University, 18.4%
13. Lakehead University, 17.4%
14. University of Lethbridge, 17%
15. Mount St. Vincent University, 16.4%
16. University of Prince Edward Island, 14%
17. Brock University, 12.6%
18. University College of Cape Breton, 12%
19. Ryerson University, 11.5%
20. Laurentian University of Sudbury, 7.8%

Source: "Universities 2000: The 10th Annual Ranking," *Maclean's*, 113: 52-109, (November 20, 2000).

★1194★
Canadian primarily undergraduate universities by award-winning faculty members, 2000

Ranking basis/background: Number of full-time professors per 1,000 winning national awards over the past five years. **Remarks:** Based on *Macleans* ranking on 22 performance measures of such as student body, classes, faculty, finances, library facilities, and reputation. **Number listed:** 21.

1. Trent University, with 9.7
2. University of Lethbridge, 3.5%
3. Lakehead University, 2.5
3. University of Winnipeg, 2.5
5. University of New Brunswick, Canada, 1.7
6. Mount Allison University, 1.6
7. Acadia University, 1.1
8. Laurentian University of Sudbury, 0.6

Source: "Universities 2000: The 10th Annual Ranking," *Maclean's*, 113: 52-109, (November 20, 2000).

★1195★
Canadian primarily undergraduate universities by class size at the first and second-year level, 2000

Ranking basis/background: Percentage of classes within six size ranges weighted and combined to determine overall rank. Figures for the class size having 251-500 students and those over 500 students are not shown due to the small proportion represented. **Remarks:** Based on *Macleans* ranking on 22 performance measures of such as student body, classes, faculty, finances, library facilities, and reputation. **Number listed:** 21.

1. University College of Cape Breton, with 66.56% in classes of 1-25 students; 25.52% (26-50); 6.81% (51-100); 1.11% (101-250)
2. Trent University, 74.58%; 9.11%; 9.96%; 5.72%
3. St. Francis Xavier University, 62.63%; 24.64%; 10.88%; 1.85%
4. Bishop's University, 58.22%; 29.79%; 11.3%; 0.68%
5. Laurentian University of Sudbury, 60.28%; 26.64%; 10.05%; 3.04%
6. Universite de Moncton, 57.77%; 30.18%; 10.21%; 1.83%
7. Brandon University, 56.65%; 26.6%; 15.27%; 1.48%
8. University of Nipissing, 55.19%; 29.87%; 11.69%; 3.25%
9. Acadia University, 42.18%; 45.09%; 10.88%; 1.86%
10. Mount St. Vincent University, 41.71%; 42.65%; 14.69%; 0.95%
11. University of Prince Edward Island, 47.6%; 32.31%; 17.03%; 2.62%
12. University of Winnipeg, 39.72%; 44.8%; 14.55%; 0.92%
13. Mount Allison University, 51.63%; 23.26%; 18.14%; 6.98%
14. Lakehead University, 51.96%; 22.07%; 17.6%; 8.1%
15. St. Mary's University (NS), 40.82%; 37.66%; 18.55%; 2.97%
16. University of Lethbridge, 41.74%; 32.17%; 19.71%; 6.38%
17. University of New Brunswick, Canada, 44.3%; 26.58%; 16.46%; 12.66%
18. St. Thomas University (NB), 31.5%; 38%; 30.5%; 0%
19. Brock University, 42.7%; 29.19%; 14.32%; 11.89%
20. Wilfrid Laurier University, 44.29%; 18.91%; 28.62%; 7.5%
21. Ryerson University, 29.24%; 43.95%; 19.2%; 7.49%

Source: "Universities 2000: The 10th Annual Ranking," *Maclean's*, 113: 52-109, (November 20, 2000).

★1196★
Canadian primarily undergraduate universities by class size at the third and forth-year level, 2000

Ranking basis/background: Percentage of classes within six size ranges weighted and combined to determine overall rank. Figures for the class size having 251-500 students and over 500 students are not shown due to the small proportion represented. **Remarks:** Based on *Macleans* ranking on 22 performance measures of such as student body, classes, faculty, finances, library facilities, and reputation. **Number listed:** 21.

1. Brandon University, with 89.85% in classes of 1-25 students; 9.14% (26-50); 0.51% (51-100); 0.51% (101-250)
2. Mount Allison University, 89.14%; 10.1%; 0.76%; 0%
3. Laurentian University of Sudbury, 88.51%; 10.34%; 1.15%; 0%
4. Mount St. Vincent University, 85.52%; 14.48%; 0%; 0%
5. Bishop's University, 83.64%; 16.36%; 0%; 0%
6. University of Winnipeg, 85.46%; 13.12%; 1.42%; 0%
7. Brock University, 83.7%; 12.81%; 3.34%; 0.14%
8. Universite de Moncton, 81.32%; 17.02%; 1.65%; 0%
9. University of Nipissing, 81.94%; 15.97%; 2.08%; 0%
10. St. Mary's University (NS), 79.9%; 19.14%; 0.96%; 0%
11. University of Lethbridge, 81.42%; 15.49%; 3.1%; 0%
12. St. Francis Xavier University, 79.44%; 17.5%; 3.06%; 0%
13. Acadia University, 76.39%; 22.95%; 0%; 0.66%
14. University College of Cape Breton, 76.26%; 21.79%; 1.95%; 0%
15. Trent University, 80.11%; 13.77%; 5.93%; 0.19%
16. University of Prince Edward Island, 77.55%; 17.35%; 4.76%; 0.34%
17. Wilfrid Laurier University, 73.55%; 24.19%; 2.26%; 0%
18. University of New Brunswick, Canada, 74.47%; 19.57%; 5.53%; 0.43%
19. St. Thomas University (NB), 68.7%; 19.13%; 12.17%; 0%
20. Ryerson University, 60.12%; 31.1%; 7.61%; 1.17%
21. Lakehead University, 55.08%; 35.98%; 7.52%; 1.42%

Source: "Universities 2000: The 10th Annual Ranking," *Maclean's*, 113: 52-109, (November 20, 2000).

★1197★
Canadian primarily undergraduate universities by classes taught by tenured faculty, 2000

Ranking basis/background: Percentage of first-year classes taught by tenured or tenure-track faculty. **Remarks:** Based on *Macleans* ranking on 22 performance measures of such as student body, classes, faculty, finances, library facilities, and reputation. **Number listed:** 21.

1. University of Winnipeg, with 84.9%
2. Mount Allison University, 82.3%
3. Brandon University, 79.2%
4. St. Francis Xavier University, 70.9%
5. University College of Cape Breton, 70.6%
6. Laurentian University of Sudbury, 69.8%
7. University of Lethbridge, 66.3%
8. St. Mary's University (NS), 65.9%
9. Ryerson University, 65.3%
10. Brock University, 64.7%
11. Trent University, 63.7%
12. Universite de Moncton, 63.6%
13. University of Nipissing, 63.4%
14. Mount St. Vincent University, 60.2%
15. Bishop's University, 58.9%
16. Lakehead University, 58%
17. Acadia University, 57.9%
18. St. Thomas University (NB), 55.3%
19. University of Prince Edward Island, 54.1%

20. University of New Brunswick, Canada, 43.4%
21. Wilfrid Laurier University, 41.7%

Source: "Universities 2000: The 10th Annual Ranking," *Maclean's*, 113: 52-109, (November 20, 2000).

★1198★
Canadian primarily undergraduate universities by faculty members with Ph.D.'s, 2000

Ranking basis/background: Percentage of full-time faculty members with Ph.D.s. **Remarks:** Based on *Macleans* ranking on 22 performance measures of such as student body, classes, faculty, finances, library facilities, and reputation. **Number listed:** 21.

1. University of New Brunswick, Canada, 95.6%
2. St. Mary's University (NS), 92.4%
3. Acadia University, 92.1%
4. Brock University, 91.8%
5. Wilfrid Laurier University, 90.2%
6. St. Thomas University (NB), 89%
7. St. Francis Xavier University, 88.8%
8. Mount Allison University, 86.8%
9. Trent University, 86.3%
10. Laurentian University of Sudbury, 85.3%
11. Lakehead University, 84.3%
12. Brandon University, 82.7%
13. Mount St. Vincent University, 82.5%
14. University of Winnipeg, 82.2%
15. University of Nipissing, 78.7%
15. University of Prince Edward Island, 78.7%
17. University of Lethbridge, 76.3%
18. Bishop's University, 72.4%
19. Universite de Moncton, 66.4%
20. Ryerson University, 58.8%
21. University College of Cape Breton, 46.6%

Source: "Universities 2000: The 10th Annual Ranking," *Maclean's*, 113: 52-109, (November 20, 2000).

★1199★
Canadian primarily undergraduate universities by library acquisitions, 2000

Ranking basis/background: Percentage of library budget allocated to updating the university's collection. **Remarks:** Based on *Macleans* ranking on 22 performance measures of such as student body, classes, faculty, finances, library facilities, and reputation. **Number listed:** 21.

1. University of New Brunswick, Canada, with 63.85%
2. Mount St. Vincent University, 44.57%
3. Lakehead University, 43.97%
4. University of Prince Edward Island, 40.67%
5. St. Francis Xavier University, 38.64%
6. University of Nipissing, 38.55%
7. Mount Allison University, 37.89%
8. Ryerson University, 36.4%
9. Wilfrid Laurier University, 35.94%
10. Brock University, 35.73%
11. Laurentian University of Sudbury, 35.47%
12. Universite de Moncton, 35.44%
13. Acadia University, 35.27%
14. University of Winnipeg, 34.06%
15. Bishop's University, 33.17%
16. University of Lethbridge, 31.13%
17. St. Mary's University (NS), 29.96%
18. St. Thomas University (NB), 28.98%
19. Trent University, 28.61%
20. University College of Cape Breton, 25.76%
21. Brandon University, 24.02%

Source: "Universities 2000: The 10th Annual Ranking," *Maclean's*, 113: 52-109, (November 20, 2000).

★1200★
Canadian primarily undergraduate universities by library expenses, 2000

Ranking basis/background: Percentage of library budget allocated to maintaining library services. **Remarks:** Based on *Macleans* ranking on 22 performance measures of such as student body, classes, faculty, finances, library facilities, and reputation. **Number listed:** 21.

1. Bishop's University, with 9.4%
2. University of New Brunswick, Canada, 7.5%
3. Mount Allison University, 6.9%
4. University of Winnipeg, 6.6%
5. Trent University, 6.5%
6. Brock University, 6.4%
7. Wilfrid Laurier University, 6.2%
8. Universite de Moncton, 6.1%
8. St. Thomas University (NB), 6.1%
10. Acadia University, 5.6%
10. Lakehead University, 5.6%
12. St. Francis Xavier University, 5.5%
13. University of Lethbridge, 5.4%
14. Laurentian University of Sudbury, 5.2%
15. University of Nipissing, 5.1%
16. St. Mary's University (NS), 4.9%
17. University of Prince Edward Island, 4.6%
17. Brandon University, 4.6%
19. Mount St. Vincent University, 4.5%
20. Ryerson University, 4.1%
21. University College of Cape Breton, 4.0%

Source: "Universities 2000: The 10th Annual Ranking," *Maclean's*, 113: 52-109, (November 20, 2000).

★1201★
Canadian primarily undergraduate universities by library holdings per student, 2000

Ranking basis/background: Number of print volumes in all campus libraries divided by the number of full-time-equivalent students. **Remarks:** Based on *Macleans* ranking on 22 performance measures of such as student body, classes, faculty, finances, library facilities, and reputation. **Number listed:** 21.

1. Acadia University, with 390
2. Brandon University, 363
3. Mount Allison University, 333
4. St. Thomas University (NB), 323
5. Universite de Moncton, 300
6. University of New Brunswick, Canada, 282
7. University of Lethbridge, 238
8. St. Francis Xavier University, 238
9. Bishop's University
10. Trent University, 221
11. Laurentian University of Sudbury, 219
12. University of Nipissing, 195
13. Mount St. Vincent University, 193
14. University of Prince Edward Island, 185
15. Wilfrid Laurier University, 168
16. St. Mary's University (NS), 151
17. Lakehead University, 150
18. Brock University, 146
19. University College of Cape Breton, 142
20. University of Winnipeg, 131
21. Ryerson University, 78

Source: "Universities 2000: The 10th Annual Ranking," *Maclean's*, 113: 52-109, (November 20, 2000).

★1202★
Canadian primarily undergraduate universities by medical/science grants per faculty member, 2000

Ranking basis/background: Average size and number of peer-adjudicated research grants from the Natural Sciences and Engineering Research Council and the Medical Research Council per eligible full-time faculty member; number of grants is per 100 eligible full-time faculty members. The ranking reflects a weighted average of the two. **Remarks:** Based on *Macleans* ranking on 22 performance measures of such as student body, classes, faculty, finances, library facilities, and reputation. **Number listed:** 20.

1. Trent University, with $35,541; 93.88 eligible faculty per 100
2. University of Lethbridge, $26,832; 96.43
3. University of Winnipeg, $13,123; 88.89
4. Mount Allison University, $15,213; 64.71
5. St. Mary's University (NS), $14,422; 62
6. Brock University, $15,246; 56.41
7. St. Francis Xavier University, $14,479; 57.38
8. Wilfrid Laurier University, $14,830; 50.94
9. Lakehead University, $12,880; 53.49
10. University of New Brunswick, Canada, $11,256; 53.33
11. Laurentian University of Sudbury, $14,434; 41.18
12. Acadia University, $10,986; 49.21
13. Universite de Moncton, $8,232; 41.46
14. Ryerson University, $8,899; 37.64
15. University of Prince Edward Island, $6,212; 26.61
16. Brandon University, $4,448; 19.05
17. Mount St. Vincent University, $2,784; 18.18
18. University College of Cape Breton, $2,410; 14.29
19. University of Nipissing, $840; 9.09
20. Bishop's University, $1,263; 6.25

Source: "Universities 2000: The 10th Annual Ranking," *Maclean's*, 113: 52-109, (November 20, 2000).

★1203★
Canadian primarily undergraduate universities by operating budget per student, 2000

Ranking basis/background: Figures for operating expenditures per weighted full-time-equivalent student. **Remarks:** Based on *Macleans* ranking on 22 performance measures of such as student body, classes, faculty, finances, library facilities, and reputation. **Number listed:** 21.

1. University of Prince Edward Island, with $8,824
2. Mount Allison University, $8,068
3. University of Nipissing, $7,876
4. Trent University, $7,578
5. Lakehead University, $7,542
6. Laurentian University of Sudbury, $7,389
7. University of Lethbridge, $7,389
8. Acadia University, $6,990
9. University of New Brunswick, Canada, $6,878
10. Universite de Moncton, $6,645
11. St. Francis Xavier University, $6,638
12. Ryerson University, $6,426
13. University of Winnipeg, $6,420

14. Mount St. Vincent University, $6,095
15. Bishop's University, $6,077
16. St. Thomas University (NB), $6,021
17. St. Mary's University (NS), $5,991
18. Brandon University, $5,976
19. University College of Cape Breton, $5,423
20. Wilfrid Laurier University, $4,901
21. Brock University, $4,588

Source: "Universities 2000: The 10th Annual Ranking," *Maclean's*, 113: 52-109, (November 20, 2000).

★1204★
Canadian primarily undergraduate universities by percentage of operating budget allocated to scholarships, 2000

Ranking basis/background: Percentage of total operating expenditures allocated to scholarships and bursaries. Remarks: Based on *Macleans* ranking on 22 performance measures of such as student body, classes, faculty, finances, library facilities, and reputation. Number listed: 21.
1. Wilfrid Laurier University, with 7.23%
2. Lakehead University, 7.08%
3. Trent University, 6.91%
4. Bishop's University, 6.87%
5. Laurentian University of Sudbury, 6.85%
6. Brock University, 5.46%
7. St. Thomas University (NB), 5.1%
8. University of Nipissing, 4.68%
9. Mount Allison University, 3.91%
10. Ryerson University, 3.73%
11. St. Francis Xavier University, 3.72%
12. St. Mary's University (NS), 3.32%
13. Acadia University, 3.09%
14. Universite de Moncton, 2.78%
15. Mount St. Vincent University, 2.7%
16. University of Lethbridge, 2.5%
17. University of Winnipeg, 2.4%
18. University of Prince Edward Island, 2.02%
19. University of New Brunswick, Canada, 1.84%
20. University College of Cape Breton, 1.32%
21. Brandon University, 1.18%

Source: "Universities 2000: The 10th Annual Ranking," *Maclean's*, 113: 52-109, (November 20, 2000).

★1205★
Canadian primarily undergraduate universities by percentage of operating budget allocated to student services, 2000

Ranking basis/background: Percent of total operating expenditures allocated to student services. Remarks: Based on *Macleans* ranking on 22 performance measures of such as student body, classes, faculty, finances, library facilities, and reputation. Number listed: 21.
1. Bishop's University, with 11.76%
2. University of Lethbridge, 10.53%
3. University of Nipissing, 9.31%
4. University of Winnipeg, 9.05%
5. St. Thomas University (NB), 8.71%
6. Brock University, 6.66%
7. Wilfrid Laurier University, 6.54%
8. Lakehead University, 6.01%
9. St. Mary's University (NS), 5.7%
10. Trent University, 5.66%
11. St. Francis Xavier University, 5.6%
12. University College of Cape Breton, 5.55%
13. Acadia University, 5.53%
14. Ryerson University, 5.49%
15. Brandon University, 5.24%
16. Mount Allison University, 4.92%

17. Laurentian University of Sudbury, 4.59%
18. University of New Brunswick, Canada, 4.08%
19. Universite de Moncton, 4.06%
20. Mount St. Vincent University, 4.05%
21. University of Prince Edward Island, 2.99%

Source: "Universities 2000: The 10th Annual Ranking," *Maclean's*, 113: 52-109, (November 20, 2000).

★1206★
Canadian primarily undergraduate universities by reputation, 2000

Ranking basis/background: Reputational ranking of schools believed to be the best overall. Based on *Maclean's* survey of more than 3,500 individuals including corporate CEOs, university administrators, and high school guidance counselors from across Canada who rated schools in three categories: highest quality, most innovative, and leader of tomorrow. Number listed: 21.
1. Acadia University
2. Ryerson University
3. Wilfrid Laurier University
4. Mount Allison University
5. St. Francis Xavier University
6. St. Mary's University (NS)
7. University of Lethbridge
8. Trent University
9. Mount St. Vincent University
10. Brock University
11. University of Winnipeg
12. University of New Brunswick, Canada
13. Bishop's University
14. St. Thomas University (NB)
15. University of Prince Edward Island
16. Universite de Moncton
17. Lakehead University
18. University College of Cape Breton
19. Laurentian University of Sudbury
20. University of Nipissing
21. Brandon University

Source: "Universities 2000: The 10th Annual Ranking," *Maclean's*, 113: 52-109, (November 20, 2000).

★1207★
Canadian primarily undergraduate universities by social science/humanities grants per faculty member, 2000

Ranking basis/background: Average size and number of peer-adjudicated research grants from the Social Sciences and Humanities Research Council of Canada per eligible full-time faculty member; number of grants is per 100 eligible full-time faculty members. The ranking reflects a weighted average of the two. Remarks: Based on *Macleans* ranking on 22 performance measures of such as student body, classes, faculty, finances, library facilities, and reputation. Number listed: 21.
1. University College of Cape Breton, with $5,291; 13.56 eligible faculty per 100
2. University of New Brunswick, Canada, $2,445; 23.53
3. University of Winnipeg, $2,859; 15.91
4. Trent University, $2,484; 17.46
5. Brandon University, $4,856; 6.59
6. Wilfrid Laurier University, $2,496; 11.39
7. St. Thomas University (NB), $624; 18.06
8. St. Mary's University (NS), $2,191; 11.11
9. Acadia University, $2,305; 9.92
10. Mount Allison University, $1,449; 11.49
11. St. Francis Xavier University, $1,488; 10.26
12. Brock University, $1,810; 6.05

13. Mount St. Vincent University, $929; 9.8
14. University of Prince Edward Island, $805; 9.3
15. Universite de Moncton, $1,072; 7.21
16. Lakehead University, $729; 5
17. University of Lethbridge, $755; 3.39
18. Bishop's University, $295; 2.56
19. University of Nipissing, $0; 0

Source: "Universities 2000: The 10th Annual Ranking," *Maclean's*, 113: 52-109, (November 20, 2000).

★1208★
Canadian primarily undergraduate universities by students from out of province, 2000

Ranking basis/background: Percentage of students from out of province. Remarks: Based on *Macleans* ranking on 22 performance measures of such as student body, classes, faculty, finances, library facilities, and reputation. Number listed: 21.
1. Mount Allison University, with 60.2%
2. Bishop's University, 42.9%
3. St. Thomas University (NB), 34.6%
4. Acadia University, 32%
5. St. Francis Xavier University, 27.7%
6. University of Prince Edward Island, 19.5%
7. University of Lethbridge, 18.8%
8. St. Mary's University (NS), 15.3%
9. Mount St. Vincent University, 13.5%
10. Universite de Moncton, 9.8%
11. University College of Cape Breton, 8.6%
12. Brandon University, 7%
13. Trent University, 6.4%
14. University of New Brunswick, Canada, 5.7%
15. Lakehead University, 5%
16. Ryerson University, 3.8%
17. University of Winnipeg, 2.8%
18. Laurentian University of Sudbury, 1.8%
19. Wilfrid Laurier University, 1.7%
20. Brock University, 1.2%
21. University of Nipissing, 1.1%

Source: "Universities 2000: The 10th Annual Ranking," *Maclean's*, 113: 52-109, (November 20, 2000).

★1209★
Canadian primarily undergraduate universities by students winning national awards, 2000

Ranking basis/background: Number of students per 1,000 winning national awards. Remarks: Based on *Macleans* ranking on 22 performance measures of such as student body, classes, faculty, finances, library facilities, and reputation. Number listed: 21.
1. Mount Allison University, with 4.1
2. Acadia University, 3.9
3. St. Francis Xavier University, 3.3
4. Trent University, 2.7
5. University of Prince Edward Island, 2.5
6. University of Winnipeg, 2.1
7. Universite de Moncton, 1.9
8. Bishop's University, 1.6
9. Laurentian University of Sudbury, 1.5
10. Brock University, 1.4
10. Lakehead University, 1.4
10. University of New Brunswick, Canada, 1.4
10. St. Mary's University (NS), 1.4
14. University of Lethbridge, 1.3
14. Wilfrid Laurier University, 1.3
16. Brandon University, 1.1
17. Mount St. Vincent University, 0.7

18. Ryerson University, 0.5
19. St. Thomas University (NB), 0.3
20. University of Nipissing, 0.2
21. University College of Cape Breton, 0.1

Source: "Universities 2000: The 10th Annual Ranking," *Maclean's*, 113: 52-109, (November 20, 2000).

★1210★
Canadian primarily undergraduate universities that are the best overall, 2000

Ranking basis/background: Reputational ranking of schools believed to be the best overall. Based on *Maclean's* survey of more than 3,500 individuals including corporate CEOs, university administrators, and high school guidance counselors from across Canada who rated schools in three categories: highest quality, most innovative, and leader of tomorrow. **Number listed:** 5.

1. Acadia University
2. Ryerson University
3. Wilfrid Laurier University
4. Mount Allison University
5. St. Francis Xavier University

Source: "Universities 2000: The 10th Annual Ranking," *Maclean's*, 113: 52-109, (November 20, 2000).

★1211★
Canadian primarily undergraduate universities that are the most innovative, 2000

Ranking basis/background: Reputational ranking of schools believed to be the most innovative. Based on *Maclean's* survey of more than 3,500 individuals including corporate CEOs, university administrators, and high school guidance counselors from across Canada who rated schools in three categories: highest quality, most innovative, and leader of tomorrow. **Number listed:** 5.

1. Acadia University
2. Ryerson University
3. Wilfrid Laurier University
4. Mount Allison University
5. St. Mary's University (NS)

Source: "Universities 2000: The 10th Annual Ranking," *Maclean's*, 113: 52-109, (November 20, 2000).

★1212★
Canadian primarily undergraduate universities with the highest quality, 2000

Ranking basis/background: Reputational ranking of schools believed to have the highest quality. Based on *Maclean's* survey of more than 3,500 individuals including corporate CEOs, university administrators, and high school guidance counselors from across Canada who rated schools in three categories: highest quality, most innovative, and leader of tomorrow. **Number listed:** 5.

1. Mount Allison University
2. Acadia University
3. Wilfrid Laurier University
4. St. Francis Xavier University
5. Ryerson University

Source: "Universities 2000: The 10th Annual Ranking," *Maclean's*, 113: 52-109, (November 20, 2000).

★1213★
Canadian universities by average entering grade, 2000

Ranking basis/background: Average final year grades of freshmen students entering from high school of Quebec's CEGAP system. **Number listed:** 47.

1. Queen's University, with an average final grade of 87.7%
2. University of British Columbia, 86.5%
3. University of Guelph, 86.2%
4. University of Toronto, 85.8%
5. McGill University, 85.5%
6. Mount Allison University, 85.1%
7. Simon Fraser University, 84.7%
8. Dalhousie University, 84.5%
9. Laval University, 84%
10. University of Waterloo, 83.8%
10. University of Western, 83.8%

Source: "Universities 2000: The 10th Annual Ranking," *Maclean's*, 113: 52-109, (November 20, 2000).

★1214★
Canadian universities by graduation rate, 2000

Ranking basis/background: Percentage of full-time second-year undergraduates who completed their degree within one year of the expected graduation date. **Number listed:** 47.

1. Universite de Moncton, with 94.4%
2. St. Francis Xavier University, 93.2%
3. Queen's University, 92.6%
4. McGill University, 92.5%
5. University of Toronto, 89.9%
6. University of Montreal, 88.3%
7. University of Guelph, 87.8%
8. McMaster University, 87.2%
9. Dalhousie University, 87.1%
10. University of Ottawa, 87%

Source: "Universities 2000: The 10th Annual Ranking," *Maclean's*, 113: 52-109, (November 20, 2000).

★1215★
Canadian universities by students with 75% grade averages or higher, 2000

Ranking basis/background: Percentage of incoming students from high school of Quebec's CEGAP system with averages of 75% or higher. **Number listed:** 47.

1. Queen's University, with 99.8%
2. McGill University, 99.5%
3. University of British Columbia, 99.3%
4. University of Toronto, 98.9%
5. University of Guelph, 98.5%
6. Simon Fraser University, 98.4%
7. University of Western, 96.4%
8. University of Victoria, 91.7%
9. Dalhousie University, 89.4%
10. University of Waterloo, 88.9%

Source: "Universities 2000: The 10th Annual Ranking," *Maclean's*, 113: 52-109, (November 20, 2000).

★1216★
Canadian universities chosen as being value added, 2000

Ranking basis/background: The relationship between the caliber of incoming students and subsequent measures of student achievement to determine which universities most improve student performance. **Remarks:** Based on *Macleans* ranking on 22 performance measures of such as student body, classes, faculty, finances, library facilities, and reputation. **Number listed:** 15.

1. Trent University
2. University of Windsor
3. Lakehead University
4. Universite de Moncton
5. Brock University
6. St. Francis Xavier University
7. Laurentian University of Sudbury
8. University of Manitoba
9. University of Ottawa
10. University of Montreal
11. McMaster University
12. University of Carleton
13. McGill University
14. Concordia University
15. Brandon University

Source: "Universities 2000: The 10th Annual Ranking," *Maclean's*, 113: 52-109, (November 20, 2000).

★1217★
Canadian universities with the highest total cost, 2000

Ranking basis/background: Annual fees for tuition and compulsory ancillary fees for undergraduate arts and science programs as of September 2000. **Remarks:** Based on *Macleans* ranking on 22 performance measures of such as student body, classes, faculty, finances, library facilities, and reputation. **Number listed:** 47.

1. Acadia University, with $5,952
2. Dalhousie University (Science), $5,300
3. McGill University, $4,841
4. St. Mary's University (NS) (Science), $4,730
5. University of Waterloo, $4,708
6. University of Toronto, $4,670
7. St. Mary's University (NS) (Arts), $4,630
8. St. Francis Xavier University, $4,611
9. Mount Allison University, $4,574
10. Dalhousie University (Arts), $4,550

Source: "Universities 2000: The 10th Annual Ranking," *Maclean's*, 113: 52-109, (November 20, 2000).

★1218★
Canadian universities with the lowest total cost, 2000

Ranking basis/background: Annual fees for tuition and compulsory ancillary fees for undergraduate arts and science programs as of September 2000. **Remarks:** Based on *Macleans* ranking on 22 performance measures of such as student body, classes, faculty, finances, library facilities, and reputation. **Number listed:** 47.

1. Laval University, with $1,830
2. University of Sherbrooke, $1,910
3. University of Montreal, $2,056
4. Bishop's University, $2,095
5. Concordia University, $2,250
6. University of British Columbia, $2,466
7. Simon Fraser University, $2,517
8. University of Victoria, $2,530
9. University of New Brunswick, Canada, $2,540

10. University of Winnipeg, $2,786
Source: "Universities 2000: The 10th Annual Ranking," *Maclean's*, 113: 52-109, (November 20, 2000).

★1219★
Top Canadian comprehensive universities, 2000

Ranking basis/background: Reputational ranking of schools believed to be the best overall. Based on *Maclean's* survey of more than 3,500 individuals including corporate CEOs, university administrators, and high school guidance counselors from across Canada who rated schools in three categories: highest quality, most innovative, and leader of tomorrow. **Number listed:** 11.
1. Simon Fraser University
2. University of Guelph
3. University of Waterloo
4. University of Victoria
5. York University
6. Memorial University
7. University of Windsor
8. University of Carleton
9. Concordia University
10. University of New Brunswick
11. University of Regina

Source: "Universities 2000: The 10th Annual Ranking," *Maclean's*, 113: 52-109, (November 20, 2000).

★1220★
Top Canadian comprehensive universities by reputation, 2000

Ranking basis/background: Reputational ranking of schools believed to be the best overall. Based on *Maclean's* survey of more than 3,500 individuals including corporate CEOs, university administrators, and high school guidance counselors from across Canada who rated schools in three categories: highest quality, most innovative, and leader of tomorrow. **Number listed:** 11.
1. University of Waterloo
2. University of Guelph
3. Simon Fraser University
4. University of Victoria
5. York University
6. University of New Brunswick
7. Memorial University
8. Concordia University
9. University of Carleton
10. University of Regina
11. University of Windsor

Source: "Universities 2000: The 10th Annual Ranking," *Maclean's*, 113: 52-109, (November 20, 2000).

★1221★
Top Canadian medical/doctoral universities, 2000

Ranking basis/background: Reputational ranking of schools believed to be the best overall. Based on *Maclean's* ranking of 22 performance measures of Medical/Doctoral universities such as student body, classes, faculty, finances, library facilities, and reputation. **Number listed:** 15.
1. University of Toronto
2. University of British Columbia
3. Queen's University
4. McGill University
5. University of Western
6. University of Alberta
7. McMaster University
8. Dalhousie University
9. University of Ottawa
10. University of Montreal
11. Laval University
12. University of Calgary
13. University of Sherbrooke
14. University of Manitoba
15. University of Saskatchewan

Source: "Universities 2000: The 10th Annual Ranking," *Maclean's*, 113: 52-109, (November 20, 2000).

★1222★
Top Canadian medical/doctoral universities best at producing leaders of tomorrow, 2000

Ranking basis/background: Reputational ranking of schools believed to be the best at producing leaders of tomorrow. Based on *Maclean's* survey of more than 3,500 individuals including corporate CEOs, university administrators, and high school guidance counselors from across Canada who rated schools in three categories: highest quality, most innovative, and leader of tomorrow. **Number listed:** 5.
1. University of Toronto
2. University of Alberta
3. Queen's University
4. McGill University
5. University of British Columbia

Source: "Universities 2000: The 10th Annual Ranking," *Maclean's*, 113: 52-109, (November 20, 2000).

★1223★
Top Canadian medical/doctoral universities that are the best overall, 2000

Ranking basis/background: Reputational ranking of schools believed to be the best overall. Based on *Maclean's* survey of more than 3,500 individuals including corporate CEOs, university administrators, and high school guidance counselors from across Canada who rated schools in three categories: highest quality, most innovative, and leader of tomorrow. **Number listed:** 5.
1. University of Toronto
2. Queen's University
3. University of Alberta
4. McGill University
5. University of British Columbia

Source: "Universities 2000: The 10th Annual Ranking," *Maclean's*, 113: 52-109, (November 20, 2000).

★1224★
Top Canadian medical/doctoral universities that are the most innovative, 2000

Ranking basis/background: Reputational ranking of schools believed to be the most innovative. Based on *Maclean's* survey of more than 3,500 individuals including corporate CEOs, university administrators, and high school guidance counselors from across Canada who rated schools in three categories: highest quality, most innovative, and leader of tomorrow. **Number listed:** 5.
1. McMaster University
2. University of Toronto
3. University of Alberta
4. Queen's University
5. University of British Columbia

Source: "Universities 2000: The 10th Annual Ranking," *Maclean's*, 113: 52-109, (November 20, 2000).

★1225★
Top Canadian medical/doctoral universities with the highest quality, 2000

Ranking basis/background: Reputational ranking of schools believed to have the highest quality. Based on *Maclean's* survey of more than 3,500 individuals including corporate CEOs, university administrators, and high school guidance counselors from across Canada who rated schools in three categories: highest quality, most innovative, and leader of tomorrow. **Number listed:** 5.
1. Queen's University
2. University of Toronto
3. McGill University
4. University of British Columbia
5. University of Alberta

Source: "Universities 2000: The 10th Annual Ranking," *Maclean's*, 113: 52-109, (November 20, 2000).

★1226★
Top Canadian primarily undergraduate universities, 2000

Ranking basis/background: Reputational ranking of schools believed to be the best overall. Based on *Maclean's* survey of more than 3,500 individuals including corporate CEOs, university administrators, and high school guidance counselors from across Canada who rated schools in three categories: highest quality, most innovative, and leader of tomorrow. **Number listed:** 21.
1. Mount Allison University
2. Acadia University
3. St. Francis Xavier University
4. Trent University
5. Wilfrid Laurier University
6. Bishop's University
7. University of Winnipeg
8. University of Lethbridge
9. St. Mary's University (NS)
10. University of New Brunswick, Canada
11. Universite de Moncton
12. St. Thomas University (NB)
13. Mount St. Vincent University
14. University of Nipissing
15. Brock University
16. Brandon University
17. Laurentian University of Sudbury
18. University of Prince Edward Island
19. Ryerson University
20. University College of Cape Breton
21. Lakehead University

Source: "Universities 2000: The 10th Annual Ranking," *Maclean's*, 113: 52-109, (November 20, 2000).

Related Information

★1227★
"The Maclean's Directory," *Maclean's*, 113: 110, (November 20, 2000).
Remarks: Listing of total number of full- and part-time students enrolled at 47 Canadian universities during the 1999-2000 academic year.

★1228★
Johnston, Ann Dowsett and Mary Dwyer, "Window into the Rankings," *Maclean's*, 113: 62-64, (November 20, 2000).
Remarks: Explains the ranking criteria and methodology used in the tenth annual *Maclean's* survey of Canadian universities.

Educational Rankings Annual • 2002

★1229★

"The Maclean's Guide to Canadian Universities 2000," *Maclean Hunter*, 1999.
Remarks: Profiles 68 schools including university colleges, art colleges, and agricultural and military colleges. Provides advice on obtaining scholarships, securing loans, and investing in an RESP. Also features a financial planner, international student planner, residence report, and scholarship directory.

COLLEGES & UNIVERSITIES–ENROLLMENT

See: American Indians–Enrollment, College Blacks–Enrollment, College College Enrollment Disabilities–Enrollment of Students Foreign Students–Enrollment, College Hispanic Americans–Enrollment, College Minority Groups–Enrollment, College

COLLEGES & UNIVERSITIES–FINANCIAL SUPPORT & EXPENDITURES

See also: Research & Development Funding Research Funding

★1230★
2000 endowment values of the "wealthiest" U.S. universities

Ranking basis/background: Figures, in billions, for 2000 value and percentage for return rate. **Number listed:** 25.
1. Harvard University, with a value of $19.20 billion; and a 32.2% return rate
2. Yale University, $10.10; 41.0%
3. University of Texas System, $10.00; 16.5%
4. Stanford University, $8.57; 39.9%
5. Princeton University, $8.40; 35.5%
6. Massachusetts Institute of Technology, $6.50; n/a
7. University of California System, $5.06; 14.7%
8. Emory University, $4.90; 7.8%
9. Texas A&M University System and Foundations, $4.48; 27.2%
10. Washington University (MO), $4.30; 13.4%

Source: Pulley, John L., "No Gain, Slight Pain," *The Chronicle of Higher Education*, 47: A29-A30, (March 16, 2001).

★1231★
2000 returns on university endowments and other comparative measures

Ranking basis/background: Total return-rate percentages for the year ending June 30, 2000 based on data for 463 college and university investment pools. **Remarks:** Original source: National Association of College and University Business Officers. **Number listed:** 4.
Standard & Poor's 500 Index, with 7.2%
Russell 3000 Index, 9.6%
Lehman Brothers Aggregate Bond Index, 4.6%
Consumer Price Index, 3.7%

Source: Pulley, John L., "The Rich Got Richer in 2000, Study of Endowments Shows," *The Chronicle of Higher Education*, 47: A39-A42, (April 13, 2001).

★1232★
2000 returns on university endowments, by size

Ranking basis/background: Total return-rate percentages for the year ending June 30, 2000 based on data for 463 college and university investment pools. **Remarks:** Original source: National Association of College and University Business Officers. **Number listed:** 4.
$100-million and under, with 9.7%
Over $100-million to $500-million, 12.0%
Over $500-million to $1-billion, 18.8%
Over $1-billion, 29.2%

Source: Pulley, John L., "The Rich Got Richer in 2000, Study of Endowments Shows," *The Chronicle of Higher Education*, 47: A39-A42, (April 13, 2001).

★1233★
2000 returns on university endowments, by type of institution

Ranking basis/background: Total return-rate percentages for the year ending June 30, 2000 based on data for 463 college and university investment pools. **Remarks:** Original source: National Association of College and University Business Officers. **Number listed:** 2.
Public, with 10.6%
Private, 14.3%

Source: Pulley, John L., "The Rich Got Richer in 2000, Study of Endowments Shows," *The Chronicle of Higher Education*, 47: A39-A42, (April 13, 2001).

★1234★
2001 mid-year endowment values of the "wealthiest" U.S. universities

Ranking basis/background: Figures, in billions, for 2001 mid-year value and percentage for return rate. **Number listed:** 25.
1. University of Texas System, with a value of $10.02 billion; and a 0.6% decrease in return rate
2. Princeton University, $8.70; 4.3%
3. Stanford University, $8.57; 0.0%
4. Emory University, $5.20; 5.4%
5. University of California System, $5.01; 0.5% decrease
6. Texas A&M University System and Foundations, $4.30; 2.1%
7. Washington University (MO), $4.20; 2.7% decrease
8. University of Chicago, $3.69; 1.0% decrease
9. University of Michigan, $3.50; 0.0%
10. Cornell University, $3.43; 3.2%

Source: Pulley, John L., "No Gain, Slight Pain," *The Chronicle of Higher Education*, 47: A29-A30, (March 16, 2001).

★1235★
2002 budget request for aid to individual institutions

Ranking basis/background: Based on the U.S. government's proposed fiscal 2002 appropriations for aid to individual institutions. **Number listed:** 3.
Gallaudet University, with $89,400,000
Howard University, $232,474,000
National Technical Institute for the Deaf, $52,570,000

Source: "Bush's Fiscal 2002 Budget Plan for Higher Education and Science," *The Chronicle of Higher Education*, 47: A36-A37, (April 20, 2001).

★1236★
Average returns on university endowments and other comparative measurements from 1990-2000

Ranking basis/background: Total return-rate percentages for the years ending June 30, 1990 through 2000 based on data for 463 college and university investment pools. **Remarks:** Original source: National Association of College and University Business Officers. **Number listed:** 11.
1990, with 10.2%
1991, 7.4%
1992, 13.6%
1993, 13.7%
1994, 3.0%
1995, 15.9%
1996, 17.3%
1997, 20.7%
1998, 18.0%
1999, 11.0%
2000, 13.0%

Source: Pulley, John L., "The Rich Got Richer in 2000, Study of Endowments Shows," *The Chronicle of Higher Education*, 47: A39-A42, (April 13, 2001).

★1237★
Colleges and universities with the largest endowments, 2000

Ranking basis/background: Market value, in thousands of dollars, as of June 30, 2000. 569 institutions participated in the comparative performance study by the National Association of College and University Business Officers. **Number listed:** 569.
1. Harvard University, with $18,844,338; and a 32.2% one-year change
2. Yale University, $10,084,900; 40.1%
3. University of Texas System, $10,013,175; 23.2%
4. Stanford University, $8,649,475; 44.0%
5. Princeton University, $8,398,100; 29.8%
6. Massachusetts Institute of Technology, $6,475,506; 51.0%
7. University of California, $5,639,777; 30.7%
8. Emory University, $5,032,683; 12.4%
9. Columbia University, $4,263,972; 17.3%
10. Washington University (MO), $4,234,599; 12.6%
11. Texas A&M University System, $4,205,849; 12.3%
12. University of Chicago, $3,828,664; 38.6%
13. University of Michigan, $3,468,372; 37.3%
14. Cornell University, $3,436,926; 19.8%
15. Rice University, $3,372,458; 14.8%
16. Northwestern University, $3,368,233; 27.8%
17. University of Pennsylvania, $3,200,812; 2.5% decrease
18. University of Notre Dame, $3,089,007; 55.7%
19. Duke University, $2,663,891; 58.7%
20. Dartmouth College, $2,490,376; 45.6%

Source: Pulley, John L., "The Rich Got Richer in 2000, Study of Endowments Shows," *The Chronicle of Higher Education*, 47: A39-A42, (April 13, 2001).

COLLEGES & UNIVERSITIES—FINANCIAL SUPPORT

★1238★
Colleges and universities with the smallest endowments, 2000

Ranking basis/background: Market value, in thousands of dollars, as of June 30, 2000. 569 institutions participated in the comparative performance study by the National Association of College and University Business Officers. **Number listed:** 569.

1. Thomas College, with $968
2. Tiffin University, $2,400
3. State University of New York (all campuses except those listed separately), $5,658
4. State University of New York, Geneseo Foundation, $6,189
5. Montgomery College, $6,895
6. Central Connecticut State University, $7,051
7. Bank Street College of Education, $7,478
8. Delta College, $8,321
9. University of Wisconsin, Whitewater, $8,365
10. West Chester University of Pennsylvania, $8,598
11. Tyler Junior College Foundation, $8,668
12. City University of New York, Graduate School and University Center, $8,871
13. College Misericordia, $9,288
14. Mount Ida College, $9,794
15. Mercyhurst College, $9,941
16. University of Albany Foundation, $10,337
17. Alvernia College, $10,553
18. State University of New York, Potsdam College Foundation, $10,895
19. McKendree College, $13,933
20. Western Michigan University Foundation, $13,962

Source: Pulley, John L., "The Rich Got Richer in 2000, Study of Endowments Shows," *The Chronicle of Higher Education*, 47: A39-A42, (April 13, 2001).

★1239★
Community colleges receiving the most gifts, 1999-2000

Ranking basis/background: Figures for total amount of gifts given to each college. **Remarks:** Original source: Council for Aid to Education. **Number listed:** 20.

1. Maricopa County Community College District, with $8,311,624
2. Santa Rosa Junior College, $6,651,968
3. Santa Barbara City College, $5,620,169
4. College of Southern Idaho, $5,139,631
5. Westark College, $3,699,925
6. Somerset Community College, $3,615,779
7. State University of New York College of Technology, Alfred, $3,587,064
8. Delta College (MI), $3,150,355
9. Greenville Technical College, $3,089,718
10. Montgomery College, $2,732,123

Source: Pulley, John L., "College Fund Raising Reached Record $23.2-Billion in 1999-2000," *The Chronicle of Higher Education*, 47: A28-A30, (May 4, 2001).

★1240★
Endowment values for the wealthiest U.S. universities, 2000

Ranking basis/background: Figures, in billions, for endowment value and return rate percentages for 2000. **Remarks:** Original source: National Association of College and University Business Officers; Chronicle Reporting. **Number listed:** 25.

1. Harvard University, with a value of $19.20 billion; and a return rate of 32.2%
2. University of Texas System, $10.00; 16.5%
3. Yale University, $10.10; 41%
4. Princeton University, $8.40; 35.5%
5. Stanford University, figures not calculated yet
6. Emory University figures not calculated yet
7. University of California System, $5.06; 14.7%
8. Massachusetts Institute of Technology, figures not released yet
9. Washington University (MO), $4.30; rate of return undisclosed
10. Texas A&M University System and Foundations, $4.48; 27.2%

Source: Lively, Kit and Scott Street, "The Rich Get Richer," *The Chronicle of Higher Education*, 47: A49-A52, (October 13, 2000).

★1241★
Federal appropriations to colleges, by agency, 2000

Ranking basis/background: Percentage of funds that Congress directs federal agencies to "earmark" for projects that involve specific institutions. **Remarks:** Original source: Chronicle reporting. **Number listed:** 12.

1. Defense with 32.2%
2. Transportation, 10.2%
3. Agriculture, 9.2%
4. Education, 7.3%
5. Health and human services 6.6%
6. NASA, 6.3%
7. Justice, 5.5%
8. Housing and urban development, 5.0%
9. Commerce, 4.9%
10. EPA, 4.8%
11. Energy, 2.2%
12. Other, 5.9%

Source: Brainard, Jeffrey and Ron Southwick, "Congress Gives Colleges a Billion-Dollar Bonanza," *The Chronicle of Higher Education*, 46: A29-A31, (July 28, 2000).

★1242★
Institutions receiving the most alumni gifts, 1999-2000

Ranking basis/background: Figures for total amount of alumni gifts given to each institution. **Remarks:** Original source: Council for Aid to Education. **Number listed:** 20.

1. Yale University, with $233,715,511
2. Stanford University, $209,897,707
3. Harvard University, $188,122,681
4. Cornell University, $154,311,052
5. University of Michigan, $126,352,492
6. Massachusetts Institute of Technology, $113,172,036
7. New York University, $107,064,230
8. University of Virginia, $99,026,625
9. Johns Hopkins University, $94,006,637
10. Princeton University, $89,341,167

Source: Pulley, John L., "College Fund Raising Reached Record $23.2-Billion in 1999-2000," *The Chronicle of Higher Education*, 47: A28-A30, (May 4, 2001).

★1243★
Institutions receiving the most corporate gifts, 1999-2000

Ranking basis/background: Figures for total amount of corporate gifts given to each institution. **Remarks:** Original source: Council for Aid to Education. **Number listed:** 20.

1. Duke University, with $180,834,867
2. University of California, San Francisco, $81,705,314
3. University of Washington (WA), $73,923,141
4. Massachusetts Institute of Technology, $69,360,865
5. Ohio State University, $64,245,463
6. Stanford University, $64,047,294
7. University of Illinois, $63,828,151
8. University of Minnesota, $62,162,837
9. University of Texas, Austin, $56,724,727
10. Clemson University, $56,109,909

Source: Pulley, John L., "College Fund Raising Reached Record $23.2-Billion in 1999-2000," *The Chronicle of Higher Education*, 47: A28-A30, (May 4, 2001).

★1244★
Institutions receiving the most gifts, 1999-2000

Ranking basis/background: Figures for total amount of gifts given to each institution. **Remarks:** Original source: Council for Aid to Education. **Number listed:** 20.

1. Stanford University, with $580,473,838
2. Harvard University, $485,238,498
3. Duke University, $407,952,525
4. Yale University, $358,102,600
5. Cornell University, $308,676,394
6. John Hopkins University, $304,043,508
7. Columbia University, $292,267,910
8. University of Pennsylvania, $288,152,160
9. University of Wisconsin, Madison, $280,182,467
10. University of California, Los Angeles, $253,764,625

Source: Pulley, John L., "College Fund Raising Reached Record $23.2-Billion in 1999-2000," *The Chronicle of Higher Education*, 47: A28-A30, (May 4, 2001).

★1245★
Institutions receiving the most in federal agency appropriations to colleges, 2000

Ranking basis/background: Each year Congress directs federal agencies to "earmark" for projects that involve specific institutions. These figures show total dollar value of earmarks that Congress did not require colleges to share with any partners and also those monies they were required to share with other colleges, businesses, or government agencies. **Remarks:** Original source: Chronicle reporting. **Number listed:** 25.

1. Loma Linda University with $36,000,000 in individual funds; $0 to be shared
2. University of Missouri, Columbia, $28,573,666; $5,118,000
3. University of Hawaii, Manoa, $21,136,500; $12,738,000
4. University of Alabama, Tuscaloosa, $17,880,881; $0
5. Medical University of South Carolina, $17,312,000; $0
6. West Virginia University $17,262,333; $7,300,000
7. University of Mississippi, $15,775,000; $4,260,000

8. Dartmouth College, $15,000,000; $1,250,000
9. Wheeling Jesuit University, $14,500,000; $0
10. Louisiana State University, $13,154,000; $9,885,500

Source: Brainard, Jeffrey and Ron Southwick, "Congress Gives Colleges a Billion-Dollar Bonanza," *The Chronicle of Higher Education*, 46: A29-A31, (July 28, 2000).

★1246★
Investment percentages of university endowments, 2000

Ranking basis/background: Percentage of assets invested as of June 30, 2000. **Remarks:** Original source: National Association of College and University Business Officers. **Number listed:** 8.
1. U.S. stocks, with 50.5%
2. U.S. bonds, 21.3%
3. Non-U.S. stocks, 11.6%
4. Alternative assets, 7.4%
5. Cash, 4.1%
6. Real estate, 2.0%
7. Non-U.S. bonds, 1.2%
8. Other, 1.8%

Source: Pulley, John L., "The Rich Got Richer in 2000, Study of Endowments Shows," *The Chronicle of Higher Education*, 47: A39-A42, (April 13, 2001).

★1247★
Largest gifts to higher education, 1967-2000

Ranking basis/background: Figures, in millions of dollars, for largest amounts given to institutions by individuals and organizations. **Remarks:** Value of gifts may have increased or decreased since pledged or received. **Number listed:** 22.
1. Gates Millennium Scholars program, from the Bill and Melinda Gates foundation, $1-billion over 20 years; cash (1999)
2. Massachusetts Institute of Technology, Patrick J. and Lore Harp McGovern, estimated at $350-million over 20 years; cash; (2000)
3. Vanderbilt University, Ingram Charitable Fund, at least $300-million; stock (1998)
4. Emory University, Lettie Pate Evans, Joseph B. Whitehead, and Robert W. Woodruff Foundations, $295-million; stock (1996)
5. New York University, Sir Harold Acton, a 57-acre Italian estate, a collection of Renaissance art, and at least $25-million in cash, with a value estimated by the university of at least $250-million and perhaps as much as $500-million (1994)
6. University of Colorado System, Claudia and William T. Coleman III, $250-million over five years; stock (2001)
7. University of California, San Francisco, estate of Larry L. Hillblom, up to $240-million to establish the Larry L. Hillblom Foundation, which will support medical research at the university and benefit other charities; stock, land, and other assets (1998)
8. Franklin W. Olin College of Engineering, F.W. Olin Foundation, at least $200-million to establish the college; cash (1997)
9. Furman University, estate of John D. Hollingsworth Jr., $150-million to $200-million; real estate and other assets (2001)
10. Stanford University, James H. Clark, $150-million; nature of gift not disclosed (1999)

Source: "Major Private Gifts to Higher Education Since 1967," *The Chronicle of Higher Education*, 47: A38, (January 26, 2001).

★1248★
Largest private gifts to higher education, 1967-2000

Ranking basis/background: Figures, in millions of dollars, for largest amounts given privately to institutions by individuals and organizations. **Remarks:** Value of gifts may have increased or decreased since pledged or received. **Number listed:** 10.
1. Rensselaer Polytechnic Institute, from an anonymous donor, $360-million; nature of gift not disclosed (2001)
2. Massachusetts Institute of Technology, Patrick J. and Lore Harp McGovern, estimated at $350-million over 20 years; cash (2000)
3. Vanderbilt University, Ingram Charitable Fund, $300-million; stock (1998)
4. Emory University, Lettie Pate Evans, Joseph B. Whitehead, and Robert W. Woodruff Foundations, $295-million; stock (1996)
5. New York University, Sir Harold Acton, a 57-acre Italian estate, a collection of Renaissance art, and at least $25-million in cash, with a value estimated by the university of at least $250-million and perhaps as much as $500-million (1994)
6. University of Colorado System, Claudia and William T. Coleman III, $250-million over five years; stock (2001)
7. University of California, San Francisco, estate of Larry L. Hillblom, up to $240-million to establish the Larry L. Hillblom Foundation, which will support medical research at the university and benefit other charities; stock, land, and other assets (1998)
8. Franklin W. Olin College of Engineering, F.W. Olin Foundation, at least $200-million to establish the college; cash (1997)
9. Furman University, estate of John D. Hollingsworth Jr., $150-million to $200-million; real estate and other assets (2001)
10. Stanford University, James H. Clark, $150-million; nature of gift not disclosed (1999)

Source: Jacobson, Jennifer, "Anonymous Donor Pledges $360-Million to RPI," *The Chronicle of Higher Education*, 47: A32, (March 23, 2001).

★1249★
Lobbyist that billed the most to U.S. colleges and universities, 1999

Ranking basis/background: Approximate figures lobbyists billed to U.S. institutions in 1999. **Remarks:** Original source: Senate Office of Public Records; FEC2U.com **Number listed:** 10.
1. Cassidy & Associates, with $4,530,000
2. Van Scoyoc Associates, $2,070,000
3. Capital Associates, $1,060,000
4. Advocacy Group, $667,000
5. Jorden, Burt, Boros, Cicchetti, Berenson & Johnson, $670,000
6. Johnston and Associates, $540,000
7. Barbour, Griffith & Rogers, $380,000
8. Sagamore Associates, $320,000
9. Jefferson Government Relations, $280,000
10. Campbell-Crane & Associates, $270,000

Source: Brainard, Jeffrey, "Hired Guns Help Colleges Feed at the Pork Barrel," *The Chronicle of Higher Education*, 47: A37-A38, (October 13, 2000).

★1250★
Proposed fiscal 2002 appropriations for graduate support

Ranking basis/background: Based on the U.S. government's proposed fiscal 2002 appropriations for graduate support. **Number listed:** 3.
  Robert C. Byrd honors scholarships, with $41,001,000
  Javits Fellowships, $10,000,000
  Graduate Assistance in Areas of National Need, $31,000,000

Source: "Bush's Fiscal 2002 Budget Plan for Higher Education and Science," *The Chronicle of Higher Education*, 47: A36-A37, (April 20, 2001).

★1251★
Proposed fiscal 2002 appropriations for student assistance

Ranking basis/background: Based on the U.S. government's proposed fiscal 2002 appropriations for student assistance. **Number listed:** 6.
  Pell Grants, with $9,756,000,000
  Supplemental Grants, $691,000,000
  Federal Work-Study, $1,011,000,000
  Perkins Loans, $160,000,000
  Leveraging Educational Assistance Partnership, $55,000,000
  Federal Administration Direct Loan Program, $780,000,000

Source: "Bush's Fiscal 2002 Budget Plan for Higher Education and Science," *The Chronicle of Higher Education*, 47: A36-A37, (April 20, 2001).

★1252★
Sources of voluntary financial support for U.S. colleges and universities, 1999-2000

Ranking basis/background: Figures, in billions of dollars, and percentage of total voluntary financial support from each source. Figures do not equal 100 percent due to rounding. **Remarks:** Original source: Council for Aid to Education. **Number listed:** 6.
1. Alumni, with $6.80-billion (29%)
2. Other individuals, $5.42 (23%)
3. Foundations, $5.08 (22%)
4. Corporations, $4.15 (18%)
5. Religious organizations, $370-million (2%)
6. Other, $1.38 (6%)

Source: Pulley, John L., "College Fund Raising Reached Record $23.2-Billion in 1999-2000," *The Chronicle of Higher Education*, 47: A28-A30, (May 4, 2001).

★1253★
Spending of voluntary financial support for U.S. colleges and universities, 1999-2000

Ranking basis/background: Percentage of spending of voluntary financial support from each category. Figures do not equal 100 percent due to rounding. **Remarks:** Original source: Council for Aid to Education. **Number listed:** 6.

COLLEGES & UNIVERSITIES—FINANCIAL SUPPORT

1. Current operations (restricted), with 39.9%
2. Endowment (restricted), 34.2%
3. Property, buildings, equipment, 14.8%
4. Current operations (unrestricted), 8.7%
5. Endowment (unrestricted), 2.2%
6. Loans, 1%

Source: Pulley, John L., "College Fund Raising Reached Record $23.2-Billion in 1999-2000," *The Chronicle of Higher Education*, 47: A28-A30, (May 4, 2001).

★1254★
State appropriations for Alabama's institutions of higher education, 2000-01

Ranking basis/background: State appropriations for higher education in 2000-01, as compiled by James C. Palmer and Sandra H. Gillilan of Illinois State University. Figures are in thousands of dollars. Also includes percentage of change over one year. **Remarks:** n/c indicates figures are not comparable. **Number listed:** 17.

- University of Alabama System, with appropriations of $378,904; and a 1-year change of 6.0%
- Auburn University System, $205,735; 5.6%
- University of South Alabama, $83,514; 4.8%
- Troy State University System, $35,628; 6.3%
- Jacksonville State University, $28,989; 3.9%
- Alabama A&M University, $31,759; 5.9%
- Alabama State University, $30,092; 3.6%
- University of North Alabama, $21,591; 5.5%
- University of Montevallo, $15,255; 5.0%
- University of West Alabama, $9,467; 5.6%
- Athens State College, $8,914; 6.6%
- Community colleges, $241,221; 7.8%
- Voc-tech statewide programs, $9,384; 43.3% decrease
- Aid to private colleges and students, $12,875; 5.2%
- Marine environmental consortium, $2,788; 6.7% decrease
- Student aid, $4,704; 27.8%
- Other, $38,373; n/c

Source: "Fact File: State Appropriations for Higher Education, 2000-1," *The Chronicle of Higher Education*, 47: A35-A39, (December 15, 2000).

★1255★
State appropriations for Alaska's institutions of higher education, 2000-01

Ranking basis/background: State appropriations for higher education in 2000-01, as compiled by James C. Palmer and Sandra H. Gillilan of Illinois State University. Figures are in thousands of dollars. Also includes percentage of change over one year. **Remarks:** n/c indicates figures are not comparable. **Number listed:** 2.

- University of Alaska System, with appropriations of $189,041; and a 1-year change of 8.0%
- Other, $1,532; n/c

Source: "Fact File: State Appropriations for Higher Education, 2000-1," *The Chronicle of Higher Education*, 47: A35-A39, (December 15, 2000).

★1256★
State appropriations for Arizona's institutions of higher education, 2000-01

Ranking basis/background: State appropriations for higher education in 2000-01, as compiled by James C. Palmer and Sandra H. Gillilan of Illinois State University. Figures are in thousands of dollars. Also includes percentage of change over one year. **Remarks:** n/c indicates figures are not comparable. **Number listed:** 5.

- University of Arizona, with appropriations of $327,952; and a 1-year change of 2.6%
- Arizona State University, $324,416; 3.0%
- Northern Arizona University, $113,170; 4.4%
- Community colleges, $119,662; 3.5%
- Other, $7,421; n/c

Source: "Fact File: State Appropriations for Higher Education, 2000-1," *The Chronicle of Higher Education*, 47: A35-A39, (December 15, 2000).

★1257★
State appropriations for Arkansas's institutions of higher education, 2000-01

Ranking basis/background: State appropriations for higher education in 2000-01, as compiled by James C. Palmer and Sandra H. Gillilan of Illinois State University. Figures are in thousands of dollars. Also includes percentage of change over one year. **Remarks:** n/c indicates figures are not comparable. **Number listed:** 9.

- University of Arkansas System, with appropriations of $311,546; and a 1-year change of 2.9%
- Arkansas State University, $62,040; 1.3%
- Southern Arkansas University, $18,896; 2.0%
- University of Central Arkansas, $41,957; 2.3%
- Arkansas Tech University, $20,192; 2.5%
- Henderson State University, $16,872; 0.7%
- Community colleges, $110,279; 0.8%
- Student aid, $30,353; 1.4%
- Other, $5,992; n/c

Source: "Fact File: State Appropriations for Higher Education, 2000-1," *The Chronicle of Higher Education*, 47: A35-A39, (December 15, 2000).

★1258★
State appropriations for California's institutions of higher education, 2000-01

Ranking basis/background: State appropriations for higher education in 2000-01, as compiled by James C. Palmer and Sandra H. Gillilan of Illinois State University. Figures are in thousands of dollars. Also includes percentage of change over one year. **Remarks:** n/c indicates figures are not comparable. **Number listed:** 6.

- University of California, with appropriations of $3,205,563; and a 1-year change of 18.0%
- California State University, $2,473,014; 9.8%
- Community colleges, $2,789,424; 19.8%
- Hastings College of Law, $14,300; 0.9% decrease
- Student-aid commission, $531,463; 36.5%
- Postsecondary-education commission, $3,654; 2.2%

Source: "Fact File: State Appropriations for Higher Education, 2000-1," *The Chronicle of Higher Education*, 47: A35-A39, (December 15, 2000).

★1259★
State appropriations for Colorado's institutions of higher education, 2000-01

Ranking basis/background: State appropriations for higher education in 2000-01, as compiled by James C. Palmer and Sandra H. Gillilan of Illinois State University. Figures are in thousands of dollars. Also includes percentage of change over one year. **Remarks:** n/c indicates figures are not comparable. **Number listed:** 9.

- University of Colorado, with appropriations of $209,000; and a 1-year change of 3.7%
- State Board of Agriculture, $146,157; 2.9%
- University of Northern Colorado, $41,960; 6.4%
- Colorado School of Mines, $19,496; 4.7%
- State colleges, $73,940; 1.5%
- Community colleges, $138,406; 3.5%
- Occupational education, $29,301; 2.9%
- Student aid, $78,263; 7.2%
- Other, $6,960; n/c

Source: "Fact File: State Appropriations for Higher Education, 2000-1," *The Chronicle of Higher Education*, 47: A35-A39, (December 15, 2000).

★1260★
State appropriations for Connecticut's institutions of higher education, 2000-01

Ranking basis/background: State appropriations for higher education in 2000-01, as compiled by James C. Palmer and Sandra H. Gillilan of Illinois State University. Figures are in thousands of dollars. Also includes percentage of change over one year. **Remarks:** n/c indicates figures are not comparable. **Number listed:** 9.

- University of Connecticut, with appropriations of $252,727; and a 1-year change of 1.1%
- Central Connecticut University, $41,401; 3.6% decrease
- Southern Connecticut University, $40,686; 5.9% decrease
- Eastern Connecticut University, $23,743; 14.4%
- Western Connecticut University, $22,197; 4.1%
- State University System Central Office, $4,157; 50.5%
- Community-tech colleges, $118,998; 4.5%
- Fringe benefits, $153,694; 1.4% decrease
- Student aid and other, $52,736; 16.4%

Source: "Fact File: State Appropriations for Higher Education, 2000-1," *The Chronicle of Higher Education*, 47: A35-A39, (December 15, 2000).

★1261★
State appropriations for Delaware's institutions of higher education, 2000-01

Ranking basis/background: State appropriations for higher education in 2000-01, as compiled by James C. Palmer and Sandra H. Gillilan of Illinois State University. Figures are in thousands of dollars. Also includes percentage of change over one year. **Remarks:** n/c indicates figures are not comparable. **Number listed:** 4.

- University of Delaware, with appropriations of $101,531; and a 1-year change of 5.1%
- Delaware State College, $28,347; 5.0%
- Tech and community colleges, $50,219; 7.3%
- Other, $5,743; n/c

★1262★
State appropriations for Florida's institutions of higher education, 2000-01

Ranking basis/background: State appropriations for higher education in 2000-01, as compiled by James C. Palmer and Sandra H. Gillilan of Illinois State University. Figures are in thousands of dollars. Also includes percentage of change over one year. **Remarks:** n/c indicates figures are not comparable. **Number listed:** 14.

- University of Florida, with appropriations of $517,939; and a 1-year change of 5.8%
- University of South Florida, $268,762; 6.0%
- Florida State University, $254,835; 13.0%
- Florida International University, $147,956; 5.0%
- University of Central Florida, $157,260; 0.8% decrease
- Florida Atlantic University, $110,635; 4.9%
- Florida A&M University, $83,634; 10.9%
- University of West Florida, $47,679; 2.8%
- University of North Florida, $58,269; 2.0%
- Florida Gulf Coast University, $29,227; 0.5%
- Private colleges, $120,189; 14.9%
- Community colleges, $776,733; 2.8%
- Student aid, $157,162; 31.0%
- Other, $99,245; n/c

Source: "Fact File: State Appropriations for Higher Education, 2000-1," *The Chronicle of Higher Education*, 47: A35-A39, (December 15, 2000).

★1263★
State appropriations for Georgia's institutions of higher education, 2000-01

Ranking basis/background: State appropriations for higher education in 2000-01, as compiled by James C. Palmer and Sandra H. Gillilan of Illinois State University. Figures are in thousands of dollars. Also includes percentage of change over one year. **Remarks:** n/c indicates figures are not comparable. **Number listed:** 21.

- University of Georgia, with appropriations of $410,651; and a 1-year change of 3.5%
- Medical College of Georgia, $139,998; 14.0% decrease
- Georgia Institute of Technology, $194,806; 12.4%
- Georgia State University, $157,881; 0.2% decrease
- Georgia Southern University, $69,470; 0.4% decrease
- Valdosta State University, $43,073; 5.4% decrease
- Kennesaw State University, $50,349; 0.2% decrease
- State University of West Georgia, $38,572; 2.8%
- Georgia College and State University, $26,192; 0.4% decrease
- Columbus State University, $25,095; 3.4% decrease
- Southern Polytechnic State University, $20,031; 2.7% decrease
- Augusta State University, $22,565; 1.0% decrease
- Fort Valley State University, $21,274; 8.5%
- Armstrong Atlantic State University, $23,578; 1.9% decrease
- Savannah State University $17,367; 6.2% decrease
- Albany State University, $19,471; 2.2%
- North Georgia College and State University, $18,291; 5.2%
- Clayton College and State University, $16,831; 5.9% decrease
- Georgia Southwestern State University, $13,156; 3.4%
- Community colleges, $162,899; 1.1% decrease
- Other, $108,779; n/c

Source: "Fact File: State Appropriations for Higher Education, 2000-1," *The Chronicle of Higher Education*, 47: A35-A39, (December 15, 2000).

★1264★
State appropriations for Hawaii's institutions of higher education, 2000-01

Ranking basis/background: State appropriations for higher education in 2000-01, as compiled by James C. Palmer and Sandra H. Gillilan of Illinois State University. Figures are in thousands of dollars. Also includes percentage of change over one year. **Remarks:** n/c indicates figures are not comparable. **Number listed:** 3.

- University of Hawaii, with appropriations of $350,122; and a 1-year change of 2.1%
- Western Interstate Commission for Higher Education, $964; 0.0%
- Fringe benefits, $53,658; 16.8% decrease

Source: "Fact File: State Appropriations for Higher Education, 2000-1," *The Chronicle of Higher Education*, 47: A35-A39, (December 15, 2000).

★1265★
State appropriations for Idaho's institutions of higher education, 2000-01

Ranking basis/background: State appropriations for higher education in 2000-01, as compiled by James C. Palmer and Sandra H. Gillilan of Illinois State University. Figures are in thousands of dollars. Also includes percentage of change over one year. **Remarks:** n/c indicates figures are not comparable. **Number listed:** 8.

- University of Idaho, with appropriations of $106,353; and a 1-year change of 6.4%
- Boise State University, $66,494; 8.5%
- Idaho State University, $58,583; 7.0%
- Lewis-Clark State College, $10,141; 9.1%
- Community colleges, $15,847; 10.3%
- Vocational education, $31,254; 9.6%
- Student aid, $2,509; 0.9%
- Other, $7,029; n/c

Source: "Fact File: State Appropriations for Higher Education, 2000-1," *The Chronicle of Higher Education*, 47: A35-A39, (December 15, 2000).

★1266★
State appropriations for Illinois institutions of higher education, 2000-01

Ranking basis/background: State appropriations for higher education in 2000-01, as compiled by James C. Palmer and Sandra H. Gillilan of Illinois State University. Figures are in thousands of dollars. Also includes percentage of change over one year. **Remarks:** n/c indicates figures are not comparable. **Number listed:** 12.

- University of Illinois, with appropriations of $853,080; and a 1-year change of 5.6%
- Southern Illinois University, $256,077; 6.4%
- Northern Illinois University, $123,269; 5.3%
- Illinois State University, $97,767; 5.5%
- Western Illinois University, $67,410; 5.2%
- Eastern Illinois University, $56,536; 6.5%
- Northeastern Illinois University, $46,858; 6.6%
- Chicago State University, $44,715; 7.1%
- Governors State University, $28,829; 5.9%
- Community colleges, $388,398; 5.8%
- Student aid, $408,637; 6.0%
- Other, $327,491; n/c

Source: "Fact File: State Appropriations for Higher Education, 2000-1," *The Chronicle of Higher Education*, 47: A35-A39, (December 15, 2000).

★1267★
State appropriations for Indiana's institutions of higher education, 2000-01

Ranking basis/background: State appropriations for higher education in 2000-01, as compiled by James C. Palmer and Sandra H. Gillilan of Illinois State University. Figures are in thousands of dollars. Also includes percentage of change over one year. **Remarks:** n/c indicates figures are not comparable. **Number listed:** 9.

- Indiana University, with appropriations of $447,733; and a 1-year change of 3.4%
- Purdue University, $315,571; 3.7%
- Ball State University, $122,078; 3.2%
- Indiana State University, Terre Haute, $76,736; 2.5%
- University of Southern Indiana, $29,450; 6.2%
- Vincennes University, $29,799; 5.5%
- Ivy Tech State College, $92,972; 6.1%
- Student aid, $118,183; 14.6%
- Other, $50,675; n/c

Source: "Fact File: State Appropriations for Higher Education, 2000-1," *The Chronicle of Higher Education*, 47: A35-A39, (December 15, 2000).

★1268★
State appropriations for Iowa's institutions of higher education, 2000-01

Ranking basis/background: State appropriations for higher education in 2000-01, as compiled by James C. Palmer and Sandra H. Gillilan of Illinois State University. Figures are in thousands of dollars. Also includes percentage of change over one year. **Remarks:** n/c indicates figures are not comparable. **Number listed:** 7.

- University of Iowa, with appropriations of $281,344; and a 1-year change of 2.9%
- Iowa State University, $269,897; 3.1%
- University of Northern Iowa, $91,829; 3.8%
- Area colleges, $147,577; 4.2%
- Student aid, $9,396; 8.3%
- Private colleges, $48,830; 2.4%
- Other, $2,251; n/c

Source: "Fact File: State Appropriations for Higher Education, 2000-1," *The Chronicle of Higher Education*, 47: A35-A39, (December 15, 2000).

COLLEGES & UNIVERSITIES—FINANCIAL SUPPORT

★1269★
State appropriations for Kansas institutions of higher education, 2000-01

Ranking basis/background: State appropriations for higher education in 2000-01, as compiled by James C. Palmer and Sandra H. Gillilan of Illinois State University. Figures are in thousands of dollars. Also includes percentage of change over one year. **Remarks:** n/c indicates figures are not comparable. **Number listed:** 10.

- University of Kansas, with appropriations of $232,870; and a 1-year change of 2.7%
- Kansas State University, $160,221; 2.2%
- Wichita State University, $63,610; 3.7%
- Pittsburgh State University, $32,379; 5.0%
- Emporia State University, $29,716; 3.8%
- Fort Hays State University, $30,878; 4.8%
- Washburn University, $9,270; 13.2%
- Community colleges, $74,087; 20.0%
- Technical schools, $29,124; 1.4%
- Other, $18,158; n/c

Source: "Fact File: State Appropriations for Higher Education, 2000-1," *The Chronicle of Higher Education*, 47: A35-A39, (December 15, 2000).

★1270★
State appropriations for Kentucky's institutions of higher education, 2000-01

Ranking basis/background: State appropriations for higher education in 2000-01, as compiled by James C. Palmer and Sandra H. Gillilan of Illinois State University. Figures are in thousands of dollars. Also includes percentage of change over one year. **Remarks:** n/c indicates figures are not comparable. **Number listed:** 11.

- University of Kentucky, with appropriations of $298,388; and a 1-year change of 3.7%
- University of Louisville, $161,515; 4.4%
- Eastern Kentucky University, $64,814; 4.5%
- Western Kentucky University, $61,084; 6.9%
- Murray State University, $61,084; 6.9%
- Morehead State University, $38,538; 5.9%
- Northern Kentucky University, $35,138; 15.6%
- Kentucky State University, $20,028; 4.8%
- Community and technical college system, $172,923; 8.1%
- Student aid, $69,019; 27.2%
- Other, $33,427; n/c

Source: "Fact File: State Appropriations for Higher Education, 2000-1," *The Chronicle of Higher Education*, 47: A35-A39, (December 15, 2000).

★1271★
State appropriations for Louisiana institutions of higher education, 2000-01

Ranking basis/background: State appropriations for higher education in 2000-01, as compiled by James C. Palmer and Sandra H. Gillilan of Illinois State University. Figures are in thousands of dollars. Also includes percentage of change over one year. **Remarks:** n/c indicates figures are not comparable. **Number listed:** 14.

- Louisiana State University System, with appropriations of $403,887; and a 1-year change of 1.7%
- Southern University System, $60,049; 3.4% decrease
- Louisiana Tech, $34,405; 2.6% decrease
- University of Louisiana, Lafayette, $48,796; 2.1% decrease
- University of Louisiana, Monroe, $36,304; 1.0% decrease
- Southeastern Louisiana University, $37,643; 1.8% decrease
- McNeese State University, $21,918; 11.3% decrease
- Northwestern State University, $24,251; 8.3%
- Nicholls State University, $20,439; 0.6% decrease
- Grambling State University, $21,325; 3.1% decrease
- Community and technical college system, $124,723; 1.4%
- Louisiana University Marine Consortium, $1,809; 0.5% decrease
- Private colleges, $4,260; 0.0%
- Other, $40,255; n/c

Source: "Fact File: State Appropriations for Higher Education, 2000-1," *The Chronicle of Higher Education*, 47: A35-A39, (December 15, 2000).

★1272★
State appropriations for Maine's institutions of higher education, 2000-01

Ranking basis/background: State appropriations for higher education in 2000-01, as compiled by James C. Palmer and Sandra H. Gillilan of Illinois State University. Figures are in thousands of dollars. Also includes percentage of change over one year. **Remarks:** n/c indicates figures are not comparable. **Number listed:** 6.

- University of Maine System, with appropriations of $169,311; and a 1-year change of 7.7%
- Maine Technical College System, $36,751; 9.5%
- Maine Maritime Academy, $7,390; 3.0%
- Maine Public Broadcasting Corp., $2,329; 2.2%
- Student aid, $12,726; 1.7%
- Other, $410; n/c

Source: "Fact File: State Appropriations for Higher Education, 2000-1," *The Chronicle of Higher Education*, 47: A35-A39, (December 15, 2000).

★1273★
State appropriations for Maryland's institutions of higher education, 2000-01

Ranking basis/background: State appropriations for higher education in 2000-01, as compiled by James C. Palmer and Sandra H. Gillilan of Illinois State University. Figures are in thousands of dollars. Also includes percentage of change over one year. **Remarks:** n/c indicates figures are not comparable. **Number listed:** 7.

- University of Maryland System, with appropriations of $798,293; and a 1-year change of 10.9%
- Morgan State University, $47,912; 10.2%
- St. Mary's College (MD), $13,475; 6.4%
- Student aid, $68,386; 20.4%
- Community colleges, $162,960; 15.6%
- Private colleges, $41,615; 13.8%
- Other, $41,962; n/c

Source: "Fact File: State Appropriations for Higher Education, 2000-1," *The Chronicle of Higher Education*, 47: A35-A39, (December 15, 2000).

★1274★
State appropriations for Massachusetts's institutions of higher education, 2000-01

Ranking basis/background: State appropriations for higher education in 2000-01, as compiled by James C. Palmer and Sandra H. Gillilan of Illinois State University. Figures are in thousands of dollars. Also includes percentage of change over one year. **Remarks:** n/c indicates figures are not comparable. **Number listed:** 13.

- University of Massachusetts, with appropriations of $495,420; and a 1-year change of 6.4%
- Salem State College, $40,117; 10.2%
- Bridgewater State College, $37,300; 6.3%
- Fitchburg State College, $29,973; 11.6%
- Worcester State College, $23,063; 8.8%
- Westfield State College, $23,738; 13.0%
- Framingham State College, $23,738; 13.0%
- Massachusetts Maritime Academy, $12,742; 5.1%
- Massachusetts College of Liberal Arts, $15,501; 9.0%
- Massachusetts College of Art, $15,279; 5.5%
- Community colleges, $287,887; 17.4%
- Student aid, $112,071; 10.6%
- Other, $28,735; n/c

Source: "Fact File: State Appropriations for Higher Education, 2000-1," *The Chronicle of Higher Education*, 47: A35-A39, (December 15, 2000).

★1275★
State appropriations for Michigan's institutions of higher education, 2000-01

Ranking basis/background: State appropriations for higher education in 2000-01, as compiled by James C. Palmer and Sandra H. Gillilan of Illinois State University. Figures are in thousands of dollars. Also includes percentage of change over one year. **Remarks:** n/c indicates figures are not comparable. **Number listed:** 16.

- University of Michigan, with appropriations of $495,420; and a 1-year change of 5.9%
- Michigan State University, $388,780; 7.3%
- Wayne State University, $249,970; 5.0%
- Western Michigan University, $123,856; 6.3%
- Eastern Michigan University, $86,368; 5.5%
- Central Michigan University, $88,542; 10.0%
- Ferris State University, $54,716; 5.0%
- Michigan Technological University, $54,441; 5.0%
- Northern Michigan University, $51,259; 5.0%
- Oakland University, $51,534; 9.2%
- Grand Valley State University, $59,077; 10.0%
- Saginaw Valley State University, $26,947; 8.0%
- Lake Superior State University, $14,062; 5.0%
- Community colleges, $315,012; 6.0%
- Student aid, $257,575; 12.2%
- Other, $3,873; n/c

Source: "Fact File: State Appropriations for Higher Education, 2000-1," *The Chronicle of Higher Education*, 47: A35-A39, (December 15, 2000).

★1276★
State appropriations for Minnesota's institutions of higher education, 2000-01

Ranking basis/background: State appropriations for higher education in 2000-01, as compiled by James C. Palmer and Sandra H. Gillilan of Illinois State University. Figures are in thousands of dollars. Also includes percentage of change over one year. **Remarks:** n/c indicates figures are not comparable. **Number listed:** 5.

- University of Minnesota, with appropriations of $607,199; and a 1-year change of 3.7%
- State Colleges and Universitys System, $579,774; 5.5%
- Mayo Medical School, $1,637; 5.9%
- Student aid, $128,367; 8.9%
- Other, $32,160; n/c

Source: "Fact File: State Appropriations for Higher Education, 2000-1," *The Chronicle of Higher Education*, 47: A35-A39, (December 15, 2000).

★1277★
State appropriations for Mississippi's institutions of higher education, 2000-01

Ranking basis/background: State appropriations for higher education in 2000-01, as compiled by James C. Palmer and Sandra H. Gillilan of Illinois State University. Figures are in thousands of dollars. Also includes percentage of change over one year. **Remarks:** n/c indicates figures are not comparable. **Number listed:** 12.

- University of Mississippi, with appropriations of $239,066; and a 1-year change of 1.3%
- Mississippi State University, $157,565; 0.9%
- University of Southern Mississippi, $85,017; 0.3%
- Jackson State University, $45,589; 4.9%
- Delta State University, $22,627; 0.4%
- Alcorn State University, $28,044; 4.7%
- Mississippi University for Women, $15,012; 1.9% decrease
- Mississippi Valley State University, $16,695; 11.8%
- Community colleges, $181,607; 3.4% decrease
- Vocational education, $32,585; 0.1%
- Student aid, $34,113; 6.4%
- Other, $23,907; n/c

Source: "Fact File: State Appropriations for Higher Education, 2000-1," *The Chronicle of Higher Education*, 47: A35-A39, (December 15, 2000).

★1278★
State appropriations for Missouri's institutions of higher education, 2000-01

Ranking basis/background: State appropriations for higher education in 2000-01, as compiled by James C. Palmer and Sandra H. Gillilan of Illinois State University. Figures are in thousands of dollars. Also includes percentage of change over one year. **Remarks:** n/c indicates figures are not comparable. **Number listed:** 14.

- University of Missouri, with appropriations of $474,664; and a 1-year change of 5.3%
- Southwest Missouri State University, $87,396; 2.4%
- Central Missouri State University, $61,775; 5.0%
- Southeast Missouri State University, $50,528; 5.1%
- Truman State University, $45,422; 6.0%
- Northwest Missouri State University, $32,287; 8.9%
- Missouri Western State College, $21,981; 2.1%
- Missouri Southern State College, $21,471; 2.3%
- Lincoln University, $18,553; 8.0%
- Harris-Stowe State College, $10,673; 9.1%
- Linn State Technical College, $5,540; 14.1%
- Community colleges, $151,899; 5.4%
- Student aid, $43,315; 4.2%
- Other, $2,044; n/c

Source: "Fact File: State Appropriations for Higher Education, 2000-1," *The Chronicle of Higher Education*, 47: A35-A39, (December 15, 2000).

★1279★
State appropriations for Montana's institutions of higher education, 2000-01

Ranking basis/background: State appropriations for higher education in 2000-01, as compiled by James C. Palmer and Sandra H. Gillilan of Illinois State University. Figures are in thousands of dollars. Also includes percentage of change over one year. **Remarks:** n/c indicates figures are not comparable. **Number listed:** 5.

- University of Montana, with appropriations of $52,513; and a 1-year change of 1.8%
- Montana State University, $74,471; 2.7%
- Community colleges, $5,803; 1.8%
- Student aid, $7,670; 2.9%
- Other, $1,231; n/c

Source: "Fact File: State Appropriations for Higher Education, 2000-1," *The Chronicle of Higher Education*, 47: A35-A39, (December 15, 2000).

★1280★
State appropriations for Nebraska's institutions of higher education, 2000-01

Ranking basis/background: State appropriations for higher education in 2000-01, as compiled by James C. Palmer and Sandra H. Gillilan of Illinois State University. Figures are in thousands of dollars. Also includes percentage of change over one year. **Remarks:** n/c indicates figures are not comparable. **Number listed:** 7.

- University of Nebraska, with appropriations of $390,849; and a 1-year change of 3.7%
- Wayne State College, $13,741; 3.4%
- Chadron State College, $11,833; 3.7%
- Peru State College, $6,319; 2.0% decrease
- Tech community colleges, $95,564; 60.0%
- Student aid, $5,674; 3.9%
- Other, $2,061; n/c

Source: "Fact File: State Appropriations for Higher Education, 2000-1," *The Chronicle of Higher Education*, 47: A35-A39, (December 15, 2000).

★1281★
State appropriations for Nevada's institutions of higher education, 2000-01

Ranking basis/background: State appropriations for higher education in 2000-01, as compiled by James C. Palmer and Sandra H. Gillilan of Illinois State University. Figures are in thousands of dollars. Also includes percentage of change over one year. **Remarks:** n/c indicates figures are not comparable. **Number listed:** 3.

- University of Nevada System, with appropriations of $203,869; and a 1-year change of 2.5%
- Community colleges, $91,334; 6.0%
- Other, $21,410; n/c

Source: "Fact File: State Appropriations for Higher Education, 2000-1," *The Chronicle of Higher Education*, 47: A35-A39, (December 15, 2000).

★1282★
State appropriations for New Hampshire's institutions of higher education, 2000-01

Ranking basis/background: State appropriations for higher education in 2000-01, as compiled by James C. Palmer and Sandra H. Gillilan of Illinois State University. Figures are in thousands of dollars. Also includes percentage of change over one year. **Remarks:** n/c indicates figures are not comparable. **Number listed:** 10.

- University of New Hampshire, Durham, with appropriations of $51,859; and a 1-year change of 4.3%
- University of New Hampshire, Manchester, $1,890; 32.1%
- College of Lifelong Learning, $1,472; 4.8%
- Keene State College, $10,072; 4.8%
- Plymouth State College, $10,072; 4.8%
- New Hampshire Technical Institute, $5,570; 3.7% decrease
- Tech colleges, $13,766; 3.0% decrease
- Dartmouth Medical Grant Program, $170; 0.0%
- Student aid, $252; 16.0% decrease
- Other, $3,572; n/c

Source: "Fact File: State Appropriations for Higher Education, 2000-1," *The Chronicle of Higher Education*, 47: A35-A39, (December 15, 2000).

★1283★
State appropriations for New Jersey's institutions of higher education, 2000-01

Ranking basis/background: State appropriations for higher education in 2000-01, as compiled by James C. Palmer and Sandra H. Gillilan of Illinois State University. Figures are in thousands of dollars. Also includes percentage of change over one year. **Remarks:** n/c indicates figures are not comparable. **Number listed:** 18.

- Rutgers University, with appropriations of $332,873; and a 1-year change of 3.5%
- University of Medicine and Dentistry of New Jersey, $188,898; 3.3%
- New Jersey Institute of Technology, $51,753; 0.2%
- Montclair State College, $48,833; 9.2%
- William Paterson University of New Jersey, $40,382; 2.5%
- College of New Jersey, $37,530; 2.9%
- Kean University, $38,233; 2.8%
- New Jersey City University, $31,953; 2.3%
- Rowan University, $38,070; 2.5%
- Richard Stockton College of New Jersey, $22,888; 5.9%
- Ramapo College of New Jersey, $19,973; 1.1%
- Thomas Edison State College, $6,003; 2.5%
- Health-related programs, $2,337; 10.0%
- Community colleges, $164,400; 8.5%
- Student aid, $212,069; 6.0%
- Fringe benefits, public senior colleges, $362,838; 14.9%
- Private colleges, $25,940; 7.6%
- Other, $45,938; n/c

Source: "Fact File: State Appropriations for Higher Education, 2000-1," *The Chronicle of Higher Education*, 47: A35-A39, (December 15, 2000).

COLLEGES & UNIVERSITIES—FINANCIAL SUPPORT

★1284★
State appropriations for New Mexico's institutions of higher education, 2000-01

Ranking basis/background: State appropriations for higher education in 2000-01, as compiled by James C. Palmer and Sandra H. Gillilan of Illinois State University. Figures are in thousands of dollars. Also includes percentage of change over one year. **Remarks:** n/c indicates figures are not comparable. **Number listed:** 10.

- University of New Mexico, with appropriations of $219,056; and a 1-year change of 3.8%
- New Mexico State University, $140,522; 3.6%
- Eastern New Mexico University, $32,614; 2.9%
- New Mexico Institute of Mining and Technology, $26,306; 3.0%
- New Mexico Highlands University, $20,834; 4.1%
- Western New Mexico University, $13,530; 3.0%
- Community colleges, $45,408; 10.2%
- Voc-tech schools, $41,810; 6.9%
- Student aid, $20,484; 4.1%
- Other, $7,731; n/c

Source: "Fact File: State Appropriations for Higher Education, 2000-1," *The Chronicle of Higher Education*, 47: A35-A39, (December 15, 2000).

★1285★
State appropriations for New York's institutions of higher education, 2000-01

Ranking basis/background: State appropriations for higher education in 2000-01, as compiled by James C. Palmer and Sandra H. Gillilan of Illinois State University. Figures are in thousands of dollars. Also includes percentage of change over one year. **Remarks:** n/c indicates figures are not comparable. **Number listed:** 9.

- State University of New York College and Schools, with appropriations of $1,546,047; and a 1-year change of 11.1%
- Cornell cooperative extension, $3,863; 14.9%
- Community colleges, $452,977; 6.0%
- City University of New York, $608,376; 5.0%
- Targeted aid to private colleges, $69,250; 1.0%
- Other aid to public and private colleges, $23,450; 0.5%
- Student aid, $673,583; 3.8%
- Technology initiatives, $60,070; 18.2%
- Other, $15,020; n/c

Source: "Fact File: State Appropriations for Higher Education, 2000-1," *The Chronicle of Higher Education*, 47: A35-A39, (December 15, 2000).

★1286★
State appropriations for North Carolina's institutions of higher education, 2000-01

Ranking basis/background: State appropriations for higher education in 2000-01, as compiled by James C. Palmer and Sandra H. Gillilan of Illinois State University. Figures are in thousands of dollars. Also includes percentage of change over one year. **Remarks:** n/c indicates figures are not comparable. **Number listed:** 19.

- University of North Carolina, Chapel Hill, with appropriations of $408,884; and a 1-year change of 5.7%
- University of North Carolina Hospitals at Chapel Hill, $39,829; 7.8%
- North Carolina State University, $356,914; 4.3%
- East Carolina University, $169,038; 10.5%
- University of North Carolina, Greensboro, $94,971; 11.5%
- Appalachian State University, $87,307; 8.5%
- University of North Carolina, Charlotte, $96,923; 7.2%
- North Carolina A&T State University, $60,710; 8.0%
- Western Carolina University, $52,555; 5.5%
- University of North Carolina, Wilmington, $60,044; 7.2%
- North Carolina Central University, $44,889; 4.2%
- Fayetteville State University, $30,821; 11.5%
- Winston-Salem State University, $28,244; 8.9%
- University of North Carolina, Asheville, $25,520; 4.1%
- University of North Carolina, Pembroke, $24,227; 8.8%
- Elizabeth City State University, $21,577; 8.1%
- North Carolina School of the Arts, $16,045; 4.4%
- Community colleges, $615,498; 4.0%
- Other, $164,493; n/c

Source: "Fact File: State Appropriations for Higher Education, 2000-1," *The Chronicle of Higher Education*, 47: A35-A39, (December 15, 2000).

★1287★
State appropriations for North Dakota's institutions of higher education, 2000-01

Ranking basis/background: State appropriations for higher education in 2000-01, as compiled by James C. Palmer and Sandra H. Gillilan of Illinois State University. Figures are in thousands of dollars. Also includes percentage of change over one year. **Remarks:** n/c indicates figures are not comparable. **Number listed:** 12.

- University of North Dakota, with appropriations of $61,609; and a 1-year change of 0.4%
- North Dakota State University, $62,510; 1.5%
- Williston State College, $2,563; 0.0%
- State College of Science, $11,802; 0.0%
- Minot State University, $14,821; 0.0%
- Dickinson State University, $6,786; 0.0%
- Valley City State University, $5,597; 0.0%
- Mayville State University, $3,950; 0.0%
- Lake Region State College, $2,319; 0.0%
- Bismarck State College, $7,492; 0.0%
- Student aid, $1,230; 0.0%
- Other, $3,952; 0.0%

Source: "Fact File: State Appropriations for Higher Education, 2000-1," *The Chronicle of Higher Education*, 47: A35-A39, (December 15, 2000).

★1288★
State appropriations for Ohio's institutions of higher education, 2000-01

Ranking basis/background: State appropriations for higher education in 2000-01, as compiled by James C. Palmer and Sandra H. Gillilan of Illinois State University. Figures are in thousands of dollars. Also includes percentage of change over one year. **Remarks:** n/c indicates figures are not comparable. **Number listed:** 12.

- Ohio State University, with appropriations of $429,400; and a 1-year change of 5.6%
- University of Cincinnati, $185,012; 2.7%
- University of Akron, $97,888; 2.8%
- Ohio University, $123,840; 4.5%
- Kent State University, $97,251; 6.1%
- University of Toledo, $95,031; 5.7%
- Bowling Green State University, $85,315; 6.7%
- Wright State University, $84,961; 4.9%
- Cleveland State University, $73,284; 5.6%
- Miami University (OH), $70,584; 6.7%
- Youngstown State University, $48,688; 0.9%
- Central State University, $17,762; 1.4% decrease
- Shawnee State University, $15,596; 5.6%
- Medical College of Ohio, $37,574; 2.9%
- Northeastern Ohio University's College of Medicine, $17,468; 1.9%
- Case Western Reserve University, $4,282; 2.4%
- Community colleges, $267,904; 12.0%
- University branches, $109,293; 12.5%
- Tech colleges, $70,649; 8.6%
- Student aid, $192,325; 14.1%
- Other, $82,291; n/c

Source: "Fact File: State Appropriations for Higher Education, 2000-1," *The Chronicle of Higher Education*, 47: A35-A39, (December 15, 2000).

★1289★
State appropriations for Oklahoma's institutions of higher education, 2000-01

Ranking basis/background: State appropriations for higher education in 2000-01, as compiled by James C. Palmer and Sandra H. Gillilan of Illinois State University. Figures are in thousands of dollars. Also includes percentage of change over one year. **Remarks:** n/c indicates figures are not comparable. **Number listed:** 16.

- University of Oklahoma, with appropriations of $205,851; and a 1-year change of 6.0%
- Oklahoma State University, $208,158; 5.6%
- University of Central Oklahoma, $44,456; 5.5%
- Northeastern State University, $31,267; 5.0%
- Rogers State University, $11,367; 16.8%
- Southwestern Oklahoma State University, $21,086; 5.6%
- Cameron University, $19,278; 6.9%
- East Central University, $16,095; 4.8%
- Southeastern Oklahoma State University, $15,596; 4.6%
- Langston University, $12,895; 9.1%
- Northwestern Oklahoma State University, $8,991; 5.6%
- Oklahoma Panhandle State University, $6,367; 7.8%
- University of Science & Arts, $6,520; 4.5%
- Community colleges, $111,686; 1.0%
- Student aid, $19,512; 0.0%
- Other, $40,547; n/c

Source: "Fact File: State Appropriations for Higher Education, 2000-1," *The Chronicle of Higher Education*, 47: A35-A39, (December 15, 2000).

★1290★
State appropriations for Oregon's institutions of higher education, 2000-01

Ranking basis/background: State appropriations for higher education in 2000-01, as compiled by James C. Palmer and Sandra H. Gillilan of Illinois State University. Figures are in thousands of dollars. Also includes percentage of change over one year. **Remarks:** n/c indicates figures are not comparable. **Number listed:** 4.

- Oregon University System, with appropriations of $379,277; and a 1-year change of 0.6%
- Oregon Health Sciences University, $55,948; 0.0%
- Student aid, $16,258; 0.0%
- Community colleges, $215,753; 3.2%

Source: "Fact File: State Appropriations for Higher Education, 2000-1," *The Chronicle of Higher Education*, 47: A35-A39, (December 15, 2000).

★1291★
State appropriations for Pennsylvania's institutions of higher education, 2000-01

Ranking basis/background: State appropriations for higher education in 2000-01, as compiled by James C. Palmer and Sandra H. Gillilan of Illinois State University. Figures are in thousands of dollars. Also includes percentage of change over one year. **Remarks:** n/c indicates figures are not comparable. **Number listed:** 9.

- Pennsylvania State University, with appropriations of $331,949; and a 1-year change of 5.7%
- Temple University, $179,021; 5.7%
- University of Pittsburgh, $177,410; 5.8%
- Lincoln University, $12,942; 13.9%
- State System of Higher Education, $471,821; 6.3%
- Community colleges, $165,170; 14.8%
- Thaddeus Stevens College of Technology, $8,061; 6.6%
- State-aided private institutions, $82,876; 5.4%
- Student aid and other, $576,114; 6.6%

Source: "Fact File: State Appropriations for Higher Education, 2000-1," *The Chronicle of Higher Education*, 47: A35-A39, (December 15, 2000).

★1292★
State appropriations for Rhode Island's institutions of higher education, 2000-01

Ranking basis/background: State appropriations for higher education in 2000-01, as compiled by James C. Palmer and Sandra H. Gillilan of Illinois State University. Figures are in thousands of dollars. Also includes percentage of change over one year. **Remarks:** n/c indicates figures are not comparable. **Number listed:** 4.

- University of Rhode Island, with appropriations of $78,621; and a 1-year change of 6.9%
- Rhode Island College, $40,701; 7.7%
- Community College of Rhode Island, $37,786; 7.3%
- Other, $5,734; n/c

Source: "Fact File: State Appropriations for Higher Education, 2000-1," *The Chronicle of Higher Education*, 47: A35-A39, (December 15, 2000).

★1293★
State appropriations for South Carolina's institutions of higher education, 2000-01

Ranking basis/background: State appropriations for higher education in 2000-01, as compiled by James C. Palmer and Sandra H. Gillilan of Illinois State University. Figures are in thousands of dollars. Also includes percentage of change over one year. **Remarks:** n/c indicates figures are not comparable. **Number listed:** 14.

- University of South Carolina, with appropriations of $231,157; and a 1-year change of 9.3%
- Clemson University, $162,250; 5.7%
- Medical University of South Carolina, $145,033; 6.7%
- College of Charleston, $33,479; 8.9%
- South Carolina State University, $25,346; 8.7%
- Winthrop University, $25,404; 11.5%
- The Citadel, $17,205; 8.7%
- Francis Marion University, $16,395; 9.0%
- Coastal Carolina University, $14,783; 9.5%
- Lander University, $11,368; 9.8%
- Board of Tech & Comprehensive Education, $171,310; 9.8%
- Student aid, $1,368; 16.1%
- Grants to private-college students, $21,566; 10.1%
- Other, $3,456; n/c

Source: "Fact File: State Appropriations for Higher Education, 2000-1," *The Chronicle of Higher Education*, 47: A35-A39, (December 15, 2000).

★1294★
State appropriations for South Dakota's institutions of higher education, 2000-01

Ranking basis/background: State appropriations for higher education in 2000-01, as compiled by James C. Palmer and Sandra H. Gillilan of Illinois State University. Figures are in thousands of dollars. Also includes percentage of change over one year. **Remarks:** n/c indicates figures are not comparable. **Number listed:** 9.

- University of South Dakota, with appropriations of $35,976; and a 1-year change of 3.6%
- South Dakota State University, $46,883; 3.7%
- South Dakota School of Mines and Technology 1.5%
- Northern State University, $7,694; 1.1%
- Black Hills State University, $6,305; 0.4%
- Dakota State University, $5,623; 2.0%
- Postsecondary vocational education, $13,979; 1.5%
- Student aid, $89; 0.0%
- Other, $8,621; n/c

Source: "Fact File: State Appropriations for Higher Education, 2000-1," *The Chronicle of Higher Education*, 47: A35-A39, (December 15, 2000).

★1295★
State appropriations for Tennessee's institutions of higher education, 2000-01

Ranking basis/background: State appropriations for higher education in 2000-01, as compiled by James C. Palmer and Sandra H. Gillilan of Illinois State University. Figures are in thousands of dollars. Also includes percentage of change over one year. **Remarks:** n/c indicates figures are not comparable. **Number listed:** 11.

- University of Tennessee, with appropriations of $397,894; and a 1-year change of 6.2%
- University of Memphis, $96,992; 3.0%
- East Tennessee State University, $75,246; 3.5%
- Middle Tennessee State University, $75,326; 3.4%
- Tennessee Technological University, $39,453; 1.9%
- Tennessee State University, $33,940; 5.0% decrease
- Austin Peay State University, $27,781; 0.4% decrease
- Community colleges, $183,084; 2.7%
- Technology centers, $39,431; 7.6%
- Student aid, $32,071; 39.0%
- Other, $38,155; n/c

Source: "Fact File: State Appropriations for Higher Education, 2000-1," *The Chronicle of Higher Education*, 47: A35-A39, (December 15, 2000).

★1296★
State appropriations for Texas's institutions of higher education, 2000-01

Ranking basis/background: State appropriations for higher education in 2000-01, as compiled by James C. Palmer and Sandra H. Gillilan of Illinois State University. Figures are in thousands of dollars. Also includes percentage of change over one year. **Remarks:** n/c indicates figures are not comparable. **Number listed:** 14.

- University of Texas System, with appropriations of $1,355,483; and a 1-year change of 0.3% decrease
- Texas A&M University System, $620,742; 1.7% decrease
- University of Houston System, $180,703; 0.0%
- Texas State University System, $198,463; 3.8% decrease
- Texas Tech University System, $196,999; 1.0%
- University of North Texas System, $131,486; 2.3% decrease
- Texas State Technical College, $56,876; 6.4% decrease
- Texas Woman's University, $48,409; 0.7%
- Texas Southern University, $31,610; 4.6% decrease
- Stephen F. Austin State University, $41,694; 1.1% decrease
- Midwestern State University, $17,266; 11.6% decrease
- Community colleges, $825,708; 2.6%
- Baylor College of Medicine, $40,609; 0.0%
- Student aid and other, $283,751; 10.3% decrease

Source: "Fact File: State Appropriations for Higher Education, 2000-1," *The Chronicle of Higher Education*, 47: A35-A39, (December 15, 2000).

★1297★
State appropriations for Utah's institutions of higher education, 2000-01

Ranking basis/background: State appropriations for higher education in 2000-01, as compiled by James C. Palmer and Sandra H. Gillilan of Illinois State University. Figures are in thousands of dollars. Also includes percentage of change over one year. **Remarks:** n/c indicates figures are not comparable. **Number listed:** 6.

- University of Utah, with appropriations of $200,251; and a 1-year change of 5.9%

Utah State University, $119,459; 5.3%
Weber State University, $53,408; 6.4%
Southern Utah University, $24,594; 9.2%
Two-year colleges, $129,418; 8.5%
Other, $16,561; n/c

Source: "Fact File: State Appropriations for Higher Education, 2000-1," *The Chronicle of Higher Education*, 47: A35-A39, (December 15, 2000).

★1298★
State appropriations for Vermont's institutions of higher education, 2000-01

Ranking basis/background: State appropriations for higher education in 2000-01, as compiled by James C. Palmer and Sandra H. Gillilan of Illinois State University. Figures are in thousands of dollars. Also includes percentage of change over one year. **Remarks:** n/c indicates figures are not comparable. **Number listed:** 4.

University of Vermont, with appropriations of $32,447; and a 1-year change of 7.0%
State colleges, $19,786; 6.8%
Student aid, $14,805; 7.0%
Other, $715; n/c

Source: "Fact File: State Appropriations for Higher Education, 2000-1," *The Chronicle of Higher Education*, 47: A35-A39, (December 15, 2000).

★1299★
State appropriations for Virginia's institutions of higher education, 2000-01

Ranking basis/background: State appropriations for higher education in 2000-01, as compiled by James C. Palmer and Sandra H. Gillilan of Illinois State University. Figures are in thousands of dollars. Also includes percentage of change over one year. **Remarks:** n/c indicates figures are not comparable. **Number listed:** 19.

University of Virginia, with appropriations of $157,507; and a 1-year change of 5.9%
Virginia Commonwealth University, $174,466; 8.7%
Virginia Tech, $182,499; 5.5%
George Mason University, $109,695; 9.9%
Old Dominion University, $83,968; 3.3%
James Madison University, $64,517; 11.9%
College of William and Mary, $48,317; 9.7%
Radford University, $38,919; 7.3%
Norfolk State University, $39,166; 14.3%
Virginia State University, $25,499; 17.4%
Longwood College, $20,007; 10.4%
Mary Washington College, $18,473; 7.3%
Christopher Newport University, $22,660; 6.3%
Virginia Military Institute, $14,954; 5.3%
University of Virginia, Wise, $9,977; 12.3%
Community colleges, $310,678; 9.4%
Affiliated agencies, $80,941; 8.5%
Student aid, $78,188; 4.1%
Other, $149,345; n/c

Source: "Fact File: State Appropriations for Higher Education, 2000-1," *The Chronicle of Higher Education*, 47: A35-A39, (December 15, 2000).

★1300★
State appropriations for Washington's institutions of higher education, 2000-01

Ranking basis/background: State appropriations for higher education in 2000-01, as compiled by James C. Palmer and Sandra H. Gillilan of Illinois State University. Figures are in thousands of dollars. Also includes percentage of change over one year. **Remarks:** n/c indicates figures are not comparable. **Number listed:** 9.

University of Washington (WA), with appropriations of $341,833; and a 1-year change of 6.1%
Washington State University, $197,166; 7.6%
Western Washington University, $56,514; 6.0%
Eastern Washington University, $43,919; 5.5%
Central Washington University, $44,726; 6.3%
Evergreen State College, $24,793; 10.9%
Community and tech colleges, $490,677; 7.3%
Student aid, $120,909; 13.7%
Other, $13,374; n/c

Source: "Fact File: State Appropriations for Higher Education, 2000-1," *The Chronicle of Higher Education*, 47: A35-A39, (December 15, 2000).

★1301★
State appropriations for West Virginia's institutions of higher education, 2000-01

Ranking basis/background: State appropriations for higher education in 2000-01, as compiled by James C. Palmer and Sandra H. Gillilan of Illinois State University. Figures are in thousands of dollars. Also includes percentage of change over one year. **Remarks:** n/c indicates figures are not comparable. **Number listed:** 14.

West Virginia University, with appropriations of $207,529; and a 1-year change of 5.5%
Marshall University, $63,055; 4.8%
West Virginia School of Osteopathic Medicine, $7,545; 15.9%
Fairmont State College, $20,385; 7.8%
West Virginia State College, $13,960; 8.3%
Shepherd College, $11,716; 10.5%
West Liberty State College, $10,018; 8.2%
Concord College, $9,585; 11.5%
Glenville State College, $7,757; 5.7%
Bluefield State College, $7,468; 5.6%
West Virginia Northern Community College, $5,657; 10.1%
Southern West Virginia Community and Technical College, $7,089; 5.5%
Student aid, $16,225; 15.8%
Other, $21,339; n/c

Source: "Fact File: State Appropriations for Higher Education, 2000-1," *The Chronicle of Higher Education*, 47: A35-A39, (December 15, 2000).

★1302★
State appropriations for Wisconsin's institutions of higher education, 2000-01

Ranking basis/background: State appropriations for higher education in 2000-01, as compiled by James C. Palmer and Sandra H. Gillilan of Illinois State University. Figures are in thousands of dollars. Also includes percentage of change over one year. **Remarks:** n/c indicates figures are not comparable. **Number listed:** 4.

University of Wisconsin System, with appropriations of $954,584; and a 1-year change of 9.4%
Wisconsin Tech System, $145,072; 8.4%
Medical College of Wisconsin, $7,447; 0.0%
Higher-education aids board, $63,019; 4.0%

Source: "Fact File: State Appropriations for Higher Education, 2000-1," *The Chronicle of Higher Education*, 47: A35-A39, (December 15, 2000).

★1303★
State appropriations for Wyoming's institutions of higher education, 2000-01

Ranking basis/background: State appropriations for higher education in 2000-01, as compiled by James C. Palmer and Sandra H. Gillilan of Illinois State University. Figures are in thousands of dollars. Also includes percentage of change over one year. **Remarks:** n/c indicates figures are not comparable. **Number listed:** 3.

University of Wyoming, with appropriations of $102,850; and a 1-year change of 12.2%
Community colleges, $48,739; 5.9%
Other, $1,993; n/c

Source: "Fact File: State Appropriations for Higher Education, 2000-1," *The Chronicle of Higher Education*, 47: A35-A39, (December 15, 2000).

★1304★
States allocating the largest amount of state tax appropriations for higher education, 2000-01

Ranking basis/background: State appropriations for higher education in 2000-01, as compiled by James C. Palmer and Sandra H. Gillilan of Illinois State University. **Remarks:** Table cites appropriations for all 50 states. **Number listed:** 50.

1. California, with total state tax appropriations of $9,017,418
2. Texas, $4,029,799
3. New York, $3,452,636
4. Florida, $2,829,525
5. Illinois, $2,699,067
6. North Carolina, $2,398,489
7. Michigan, $2,231,607
8. Ohio, $2,206,398
9. Pennsylvania, $2,005,364
10. New Jersey, $1,670,911

Source: "Fact File: State Appropriations for Higher Education, 2000-1," *The Chronicle of Higher Education*, 47: A35-A39, (December 15, 2000).

★1305★
States allocating the smallest amount of state tax appropriations for higher education, 2000-01

Ranking basis/background: State appropriations for higher education in 2000-01, as compiled by James C. Palmer and Sandra H. Gillilan of Illinois State University. **Remarks:** Table cites appropriations for all 50 states. **Number listed:** 50.

1. Vermont, with total state tax appropriations of $67,753
2. New Hampshire, $98,695
3. South Dakota, $134,803
4. Montana, $141,688
5. Wyoming, $153,582
6. Rhode Island, $162,842
7. North Dakota, $184,631
8. Delaware, $185,840
9. Alaska, $190,573
10. Maine, $228,917

Educational Rankings Annual • 2002 — COLLEGES & UNIVERSITIES—FINANCIAL SUPPORT

Source: "Fact File: State Appropriations for Higher Education, 2000-1," *The Chronicle of Higher Education*, 47: A35-A39, (December 15, 2000).

★1306★
States receiving the most in federal agency appropriations to colleges, 2000

Ranking basis/background: Each year Congress directs federal agencies to "earmark" for projects that involve specific institutions. These figures show total dollar value of earmarks that Congress did not require colleges to share with any partners and also those monies they were required to share with other colleges, businesses, or government agencies. **Remarks:** Original source: Chronicle reporting. **Number listed:** 51.
1. California, with $64,124,250 in individual funds; $29,192,000 to be shared
2. Texas, $47,537,498; $67,774,317
3. Mississippi, $40,184,017; $26,289,500
4. Missouri, $39,644,166; $6,738,000
5. West Virginia, $38,862,333; $9,042,000
6. Alabama, $38,810,236; $45,500,000
7. Florida, $35,538,328; $17,024,000
8. New York, $31,327,692; $32,543,800
9. Massachusetts, $26,154,500; $23,124,000
10. Hawaii, $23,763,500; $15,488,000

Source: Brainard, Jeffrey and Ron Southwick, "Congress Gives Colleges a Billion-Dollar Bonanza," *The Chronicle of Higher Education*, 46: A29-A31, (July 28, 2000).

★1307★
States receiving the most in federal agency appropriations to colleges, from 1996 to 2000

Ranking basis/background: Each year Congress directs federal agencies to "earmark" for projects that involve specific institutions. These figures show total dollar value of earmarks that Congress did not require colleges to share with any partners and also those monies they were required to share with other colleges, businesses, or government agencies. **Remarks:** Original source: Chronicle reporting. **Number listed:** 51.
1. California, with $224,344,193 in individual funds; $146,700,000 to be shared
2. Florida, $120,184,149; $60,361,000
3. Alabama, $91,776,022; $105,250,000
4. West Virginia, $91,182,333; $37,192,000
5. Hawaii, $88,791,000; $155,297,000
6. Pennsylvania, $85,715,113; $217,593,957
7. Texas, $82,511,248; $140,696,067
8. Louisiana, $81,038,400; $102,919,500
9. New York, $79,768,388; $93,179,300
10. Mississippi, $73,803,017; $66,269,500

Source: Brainard, Jeffrey and Ron Southwick, "Congress Gives Colleges a Billion-Dollar Bonanza," *The Chronicle of Higher Education*, 46: A29-A31, (July 28, 2000).

★1308★
States with the highest percentage increase in appropriations for higher education, 2000-01

Ranking basis/background: One-year change percentages in state appropriations for higher education in 2000-01, as compiled by James C. Palmer and Sandra H. Gillilan of Illinois State University. **Remarks:** Table cites tax appropriations. **Number listed:** 51.
1. California, with an increase of 17.0%
2. Maryland, 12.5%
3. Nebraska, 10.7%
4. Massachusetts, 10.1%
5. Virginia, 10.0%
6. Wyoming 9.9%
7. Wisconsin, 8.9%
8. South Carolina, 8.3%
9. Kentucky, 8.2%
10. Alaska, 8.0%

Source: "Fact File: State Appropriations for Higher Education, 2000-1," *The Chronicle of Higher Education*, 47: A35-A39, (December 15, 2000).

★1309★
Trends in federal agency appropriations to colleges, 1989 to 2000

Ranking basis/background: Figures, in millions of dollars, that Congress directs federal agencies to "earmark" for projects that involve specific institutions. **Remarks:** Original source: Chronicle reporting. **Number listed:** 12.

1989, with $289 million
1990, $270
1991, $493
1992, $684
1993, $763
1994, $651
1995, $600
1996, $296
1997, $440
1998, $528
1999, $797
2000, $1,044

Source: Brainard, Jeffrey and Ron Southwick, "Congress Gives Colleges a Billion-Dollar Bonanza," *The Chronicle of Higher Education*, 46: A29-A31, (July 28, 2000).

★1310★
U.S. colleges and universities spending the most on independent lobbyists, 1999

Ranking basis/background: Approximate figures spent on independent lobbyists in 1999. **Remarks:** Original source: Senate Office of Public Records; FEC2U.com **Number listed:** 10.
1. Boston University, with $760,000
2. Johns Hopkins University, $460,000
3. University of Miami, $440,000
4. Northwestern University, $400,000
5. Columbia University, $360,000
5. Tulane University, $360,000
7. New York University, $280,000
7. Temple University, $280,000
7. University of Hawaii, $280,000
7. University of New Orleans, $280,000

Source: Brainard, Jeffrey, "Hired Guns Help Colleges Feed at the Pork Barrel," *The Chronicle of Higher Education*, 47: A37-A38, (October 13, 2000).

★1311★
Voluntary financial support for liberal arts institutions, 1999-2000

Ranking basis/background: Number of institutions and total amount of private donations received during 1999-2000. **Remarks:** Original source: Council for Aid to Education. **Number listed:** 3.

All liberal arts, 306 institutions; receiving $2,529,665,000 in gifts
Private, 291; $2,504,518,000
Public, 15; $25,147,000

Source: Pulley, John L., "College Fund Raising Reached Record $23.2-Billion in 1999-2000," *The Chronicle of Higher Education*, 47: A28-A30, (May 4, 2001).

★1312★
Voluntary financial support for master's institutions, 1999-2000

Ranking basis/background: Number of institutions and total amount of private donations received during 1999-2000. **Remarks:** Original source: Council for Aid to Education. **Number listed:** 3.

All master's, 292 institutions; receiving $1,718,793,000 in gifts
Private, 152; $1,067,976,000
Public, 140; $650,817,000

Source: Pulley, John L., "College Fund Raising Reached Record $23.2-Billion in 1999-2000," *The Chronicle of Higher Education*, 47: A28-A30, (May 4, 2001).

★1313★
Voluntary financial support for research institutions, 1999-2000

Ranking basis/background: Number of institutions and total amount of private donations received during 1999-2000. **Remarks:** Original source: Council for Aid to Education. **Number listed:** 3.

All research, 195 institutions; receiving $12,223,617,000 in gifts
Private, 69; $5,902,215,000
Public, 126; $6,321,403,000

Source: Pulley, John L., "College Fund Raising Reached Record $23.2-Billion in 1999-2000," *The Chronicle of Higher Education*, 47: A28-A30, (May 4, 2001).

★1314★
Voluntary financial support for specialized institutions, 1999-2000

Ranking basis/background: Number of institutions and total amount of private donations received during 1999-2000. **Remarks:** Original source: Council for Aid to Education. **Number listed:** 3.

All specialized, 61 institutions; receiving $628,092,000,000 in gifts
Private, 47; $373,083,000
Public, 14; $255,009,000

Source: Pulley, John L., "College Fund Raising Reached Record $23.2-Billion in 1999-2000," *The Chronicle of Higher Education*, 47: A28-A30, (May 4, 2001).

★1315★
Voluntary financial support for two-year institutions, 1999-2000

Ranking basis/background: Number of institutions and total amount of private donations received during 1999-2000. **Remarks:** Original source: Council for Aid to Education. **Number listed:** 3.

All two-year, 84 institutions; receiving $129,026,000 in gifts
Private, 9; $29,915,000
Public, 75; $99,111,000

Source: Pulley, John L., "College Fund Raising Reached Record $23.2-Billion in 1999-2000," *The Chronicle of Higher Education*, 47: A28-A30, (May 4, 2001).

COLLEGES & UNIVERSITIES–HONORS PROGRAMS

★1316★
Golden Key Scholar Award winners, 2000

Ranking basis/background: Alphabetical listing of Golden Key National Honor Society outstanding undergraduates in all fields of study who have reached high standards of academic achievement. **Number listed:** 11.

Victor Boutros, Baylor University, *University of Chicago Law School, JD*
Richard Burwick, Johns Hopkins University, *University of California, San Francisco, MD*
Kristina Conlin, University of Texas, San Antonio, *Northwestern University, Ph.D.*
Kathryn Gainey, California State University, Long Beach, *Harvard Law School, JD*
Zoe Greenwood, Australian National University, *The Australian National University, MS*
Jeffrey Jacobs, Utah State University, *Stanford University, Ph.D.*
Andrew Lim, University of British Columbia, *University of Toronto, MD*
My Hanh Nguyen, University of Florida, *University of Florida, MD*
Kimberly Noble, University of Wisconsin, Madison, *University of Wisconsin, Madison, MS*
Zoy Patouhas, Wayne State University, *Wayne State University, MD*
Everett Weiss, University of Southern California, *Oregon Health Sciences University MS*

Source: "Golden Key National Honor Society," *The Chronicle of Higher Education*, 47: A79, (October 13, 2000).

COLLEGES & UNIVERSITIES, LIBERAL ARTS

★1317★
College freshmen's choices for exemplary liberal arts institutions

Ranking basis/background: Compiled from a survey of college students regarding size, educational mission, student characteristics, and other factors. Institutions are listed alphabetically. **Remarks:** Original source: National Survey of Student Engagement, Indiana University. **Number listed:** 4.

Antioch College
Centre College
Denison University
Wabash College

Source: Reisberg, Leo, "Are Students Actually Learning?," *The Chronicle of Higher Education*, 46: A67-A70, (November 17, 2000).

★1318★
College senior's choices for exemplary liberal arts institutions

Ranking basis/background: Compiled from a survey of college students regarding size, educational mission, student characteristics, and other factors. Institutions are listed alphabetically. **Remarks:** Original source: National Survey of Student Engagement, Indiana University. **Number listed:** 5.

Antioch College
Centre College
Evergreen State College
Sweet Briar College
Wesleyan College (GA)

Source: Reisberg, Leo, "Are Students Actually Learning?," *The Chronicle of Higher Education*, 46: A67-A70, (November 17, 2000).

★1319★
College senior's choices for exemplary undergraduate institutions

Ranking basis/background: Compiled from a survey of college students regarding size, educational mission, student characteristics, and other factors. Institutions are listed alphabetically. **Remarks:** Original source: National Survey of Student Engagement, Indiana University. **Number listed:** 3.

Barton College
Columbia College (SC)
Covenant College

Source: Reisberg, Leo, "Are Students Actually Learning?," *The Chronicle of Higher Education*, 46: A67-A70, (November 17, 2000).

★1320★
U.S. News & World Report's best national liberal arts colleges, 2000-01

Ranking basis/background: Based on *U.S News* questionnaire sent to 1,400 four-year institutions. Scores are averaged and weighted percentages from seven attributes: academic reputation, retention, faculty resources, student selectivity, financial resources, graduation rate performance and alumni giving. **Remarks:** Comparable data was used from the U.S. Department of Education, the Council for Aid to Education, the NCAA, and Wintergreen/Orchard House publishers. **Number listed:** 51.

1. Amherst College, with an overall score of 100.0
2. Swarthmore College, 99.0
3. Williams College, 98.0
4. Wellesley College, 94.0
5. Pomona College, 93.0
6. Bowdoin College, 91.0
6. Carleton College, 91.0
6. Haverford College, 91.0
6. Middlebury College, 91.0
10. Wesleyan University, 90.0

Source: "America's Best Colleges," *U.S. News & World Report*, 129: 90-132, (September 11, 2000).

★1321★
U.S. News & World Report's national liberal arts colleges with the best faculty resources rank, 2000-01

Ranking basis/background: Based on *U.S News* questionnaire sent to 1,400 four-year institutions. Scores are averaged and weighted percentages from seven attributes: academic reputation, retention, faculty resources, student selectivity, financial resources, graduation rate performance and alumni giving. **Remarks:** Comparable data was used from the U.S. Department of Education, the Council for Aid to Education, the NCAA, and Wintergreen/Orchard House publishers. **Number listed:** 51.

1. Washington and Lee University
2. University of the South
3. Bard College
4. Willamette University
5. Pomona College
6. Grinnell College
7. Colorado College
8. Whitman College
9. Carleton College
10. Swarthmore College

Source: "America's Best Colleges," *U.S. News & World Report*, 129: 90-132, (September 11, 2000).

★1322★
U.S. News & World Report's national liberal arts colleges with the best financial resources rank, 2000-01

Ranking basis/background: Based on *U.S News* questionnaire sent to 1,400 four-year institutions. Scores are averaged and weighted percentages from seven attributes: academic reputation, retention, faculty resources, student selectivity, financial resources, graduation rate performance and alumni giving. **Remarks:** Comparable data was used from the U.S. Department of Education, the Council for Aid to Education, the NCAA, and Wintergreen/Orchard House publishers. **Number listed:** 51.

1. Wellesley College
2. Swarthmore College
3. Scripps College
4. Pomona College
5. Middlebury College
6. Mount Holyoke College
7. Williams College
8. Bowdoin College
9. Amherst College
10. Trinity College

Source: "America's Best Colleges," *U.S. News & World Report*, 129: 90-132, (September 11, 2000).

★1323★
U.S. News & World Report's national liberal arts colleges with the best freshmen retention rates, 2000-01

Ranking basis/background: Based on *U.S News* questionnaire sent to 1,400 four-year institutions. Scores are averaged and weighted percentages from seven attributes: academic reputation, retention, faculty resources, student selectivity, financial resources, graduation rate performance and alumni giving. **Remarks:** Comparable data was used from the U.S. Department of Education, the Council for Aid to Education, the NCAA, and Wintergreen/Orchard House publishers. **Number listed:** 51.

1. Pomona College, with 98%
2. Amherst College, 97%
2. Williams College, 97%
4. Swarthmore College, 96%
4. Davidson College, 96%
6. Wellesley College, 95%

6. Carleton College, 95%
6. Haverford College, 95%
6. Middlebury College, 95%
6. Wesleyan University, 95%

Source: "America's Best Colleges," *U.S. News & World Report*, 129: 90-132, (September 11, 2000).

★1324★
U.S. News & World Report's national liberal arts colleges with the best graduation and retention rank, 2000-01

Ranking basis/background: Based on *U.S News* questionnaire sent to 1,400 four-year institutions. Scores are averaged and weighted percentages from seven attributes: academic reputation, retention, faculty resources, student selectivity, financial resources, graduation rate performance and alumni giving. **Remarks:** Comparable data was used from the U.S. Department of Education, the Council for Aid to Education, the NCAA, and Wintergreen/Orchard House publishers. **Number listed:** 51.

1. Amherst College
2. Williams College
3. Swarthmore College
4. College of the Holy Cross
5. Haverford College
6. Smith College
7. Pomona College
8. Bowdoin College
9. Middlebury College
10. Carleton College

Source: "America's Best Colleges," *U.S. News & World Report*, 129: 90-132, (September 11, 2000).

★1325★
U.S. News & World Report's national liberal arts colleges with the best selectivity rank, 2000-01

Ranking basis/background: Based on *U.S News* questionnaire sent to 1,400 four-year institutions. Scores are averaged and weighted percentages from seven attributes: academic reputation, retention, faculty resources, student selectivity, financial resources, graduation rate performance and alumni giving. **Remarks:** Comparable data was used from the U.S. Department of Education, the Council for Aid to Education, the NCAA, and Wintergreen/Orchard House publishers. **Number listed:** 51.

1. Amherst College
2. Williams College
3. Swarthmore College
4. Pomona College
5. Middlebury College
6. Claremont McKenna College
7. Bowdoin College
8. Haverford College
9. Wesleyan University
10. Davidson College

Source: "America's Best Colleges," *U.S. News & World Report*, 129: 90-132, (September 11, 2000).

★1326★
U.S. News & World Report's national liberal arts colleges with the best student/faculty ratios, 2000-01

Ranking basis/background: Based on *U.S News* questionnaire sent to 1,400 four-year institutions. Scores are averaged and weighted percentages from seven attributes: academic reputation, retention, faculty resources, student selectivity, financial resources, graduation rate performance and alumni giving. **Remarks:** Comparable data was used from the U.S. Department of Education, the Council for Aid to Education, the NCAA, and Wintergreen/Orchard House publishers. **Number listed:** 51.

1. Sarah Lawrence College, with 6/1
2. Amherst College, 8/1
2. Swarthmore College, 8/1
4. Williams College, 9/1
4. Bard College, 9/1
4. Vassar College, 9/1
4. Claremont McKenna College, 9/1
4. Washington and Lee University, 9/1
4. Wesleyan University, 9/1
4. Pomona College, 9/1
4. Haverford College, 9/1
4. Wesleyan University, 9/1

Source: "America's Best Colleges," *U.S. News & World Report*, 129: 90-132, (September 11, 2000).

★1327★
U.S. News & World Report's national liberal arts colleges with the highest academic reputation scores, 2000-01

Ranking basis/background: Based on *U.S News* questionnaire sent to 1,400 four-year institutions. Scores are averaged and weighted percentages from seven attributes: academic reputation, retention, faculty resources, student selectivity, financial resources, graduation rate performance and alumni giving. **Remarks:** Comparable data was used from the U.S. Department of Education, the Council for Aid to Education, the NCAA, and Wintergreen/Orchard House publishers. **Number listed:** 51.

1. Amherst College, with a score of 4.8
1. Swarthmore College, 4.8
1. Williams College, 4.8
4. Wellesley College, 4.7
5. Carleton College, 4.5
5. Smith College, 4.5
7. Pomona College, 4.4
7. Bowdoin College, 4.4
7. Haverford College, 4.4
7. Wesleyan University, 4.4

Source: "America's Best Colleges," *U.S. News & World Report*, 129: 90-132, (September 11, 2000).

★1328★
U.S. News & World Report's national liberal arts colleges with the highest acceptance rates, 2000-01

Ranking basis/background: Based on *U.S News* questionnaire sent to 1,400 four-year institutions. Scores are averaged and weighted percentages from seven attributes: academic reputation, retention, faculty resources, student selectivity, financial resources, graduation rate performance and alumni giving. **Remarks:** Comparable data was used from the U.S. Department of Education, the Council for Aid to Education, the NCAA, and Wintergreen/Orchard House publishers. **Number listed:** 51.

1. Willamette University, with 90%
2. Centre College, 86%
3. Lawrence University, 81%
4. Rhodes College, 77%
5. University of the South, 73%
6. Scripps College, 70%
7. Denison University, 69%
8. Kenyon College, 68%
9. DePauw University, 67%
9. Beloit College, 67%

Source: "America's Best Colleges," *U.S. News & World Report*, 129: 90-132, (September 11, 2000).

★1329★
U.S. News & World Report's national liberal arts colleges with the highest alumni giving rank, 2000-01

Ranking basis/background: Based on *U.S News* questionnaire sent to 1,400 four-year institutions. Scores are averaged and weighted percentages from seven attributes: academic reputation, retention, faculty resources, student selectivity, financial resources, graduation rate performance and alumni giving. **Remarks:** Comparable data was used from the U.S. Department of Education, the Council for Aid to Education, the NCAA, and Wintergreen/Orchard House publishers. **Number listed:** 51.

1. Amherst College
2. Centre College
3. Williams College
4. Carleton College
5. Swarthmore College
6. Bowdoin College
7. Washington and Lee University
8. Scripps College
9. Davidson College
10. Bryn Mawr College

Source: "America's Best Colleges," *U.S. News & World Report*, 129: 90-132, (September 11, 2000).

★1330★
U.S. News & World Report's national liberal arts colleges with the highest graduation rates, 2000-01

Ranking basis/background: Based on *U.S News* questionnaire sent to 1,400 four-year institutions. Scores are averaged and weighted percentages from seven attributes: academic reputation, retention, faculty resources, student selectivity, financial resources, graduation rate performance and alumni giving. **Remarks:** Comparable data was used from the U.S. Department of Education, the Council for Aid to Education, the NCAA, and Wintergreen/Orchard House publishers. **Number listed:** 51.

1. Amherst College, with 96%
2. Williams College, 94%
3. College of the Holy Cross, 93%
4. Swarthmore College, 92%
5. Bowdoin College, 91%
6. Middlebury College, 90%
6. Wellesley College, 90%
8. Bucknell University, 89%
8. Carleton College, 89%
8. Colgate University, 89%
8. Davidson College, 89%
8. Pomona College, 89%

Source: "America's Best Colleges," *U.S. News & World Report*, 129: 90-132, (September 11, 2000).

★1331★
U.S. News & World Report's national liberal arts colleges with the highest percentage of alumni support, 2000-01

Ranking basis/background: Based on *U.S News* questionnaire sent to 1,400 four-year institutions. Scores are averaged and weighted percentages from seven attributes: academic reputation, retention, faculty resources, student selectivity, financial resources, graduation rate performance and alumni giving. **Remarks:** Comparable data was used from the U.S. Department of Education, the Council for Aid to Education, the NCAA, and Wintergreen/Orchard House publishers. **Number listed:** 51.

1. Amherst College, with 68%
1. Centre College, 68%
3. Williams College, 60%
4. Carleton College, 58%

5. Swarthmore College, 56%
6. Bowdoin College, 55%
7. Washington and Lee University, 54%
8. Davidson College, 53%
8. Scripps College, 53%
10. Haverford College, 52%
10. Bryn Mawr College, 52%
10. Hamilton College, 52%
10. Mount Holyoke College, 52%

Source: "America's Best Colleges," *U.S. News & World Report*, 129: 90-132, (September 11, 2000).

★1332★
U.S. News & World Report's national liberal arts colleges with the highest percentage of freshmen in the top 10% of their high school class, 2000-01

Ranking basis/background: Based on *U.S News* questionnaire sent to 1,400 four-year institutions. Scores are averaged and weighted percentages from seven attributes: academic reputation, retention, faculty resources, student selectivity, financial resources, graduation rate performance and alumni giving. **Remarks:** Comparable data was used from the U.S. Department of Education, the Council for Aid to Education, the NCAA, and Wintergreen/Orchard House publishers. **Number listed:** 51.
1. Amherst College, 88%
2. Williams College, 84%
3. Swarthmore College, 82%
4. Pomona College, 80%
5. Claremont McKenna College, 78%
6. Bowdoin College, 77%
7. Haverford College, 76%
8. Davidson College, 74%
9. Middlebury College, 72%
10. Wesleyan University, 70%

Source: "America's Best Colleges," *U.S. News & World Report*, 129: 90-132, (September 11, 2000).

★1333★
U.S. News & World Report's national liberal arts colleges with the highest percentage of full-time faculty, 2000-01

Ranking basis/background: Based on *U.S News* questionnaire sent to 1,400 four-year institutions. Scores are averaged and weighted percentages from seven attributes: academic reputation, retention, faculty resources, student selectivity, financial resources, graduation rate performance and alumni giving. **Remarks:** Comparable data was used from the U.S. Department of Education, the Council for Aid to Education, the NCAA, and Wintergreen/Orchard House publishers. **Number listed:** 51.
1. Grinnell College, with 99%
1. Denison University, 99%
1. Furman University, 99%
4. Smith College, 98%
4. Skidmore College, 98%
4. Kenyon College, 98%
7. Washington and Lee University, 97%
7. Williams College, 97%
7. Centre College, 97%
7. Colgate University, 97%
7. Bates College, 97%
7. Bucknell University, 97%
7. Connecticut College, 97%
7. Middlebury College, 97%
7. Davidson College, 97%

Source: "America's Best Colleges," *U.S. News & World Report*, 129: 90-132, (September 11, 2000).

★1334★
U.S. News & World Report's national liberal arts colleges with the highest proportion of classes having 50 or more students, 2000-01

Ranking basis/background: Based on *U.S News* questionnaire sent to 1,400 four-year institutions. Scores are averaged and weighted percentages from seven attributes: academic reputation, retention, faculty resources, student selectivity, financial resources, graduation rate performance and alumni giving. **Remarks:** Comparable data was used from the U.S. Department of Education, the Council for Aid to Education, the NCAA, and Wintergreen/Orchard House publishers. **Number listed:** 51.
1. Amherst College, with 8%
1. Barnard College, 8%
3. Bowdoin College, 7%
4. Williams College, 6%
4. Scripps College, 6%
6. Haverford College, 5%
6. Smith College, 5%
6. Trinity College, 5%
9. Wesleyan University, 4%
9. Bates College, 4%
9. Colby College, 4%
9. Oberlin College, 4%
9. Bucknell College, 4%

Source: "America's Best Colleges," *U.S. News & World Report*, 129: 90-132, (September 11, 2000).

★1335★
U.S. News & World Report's national liberal arts colleges with the highest proportion of classes with less than 20 students, 2000-01

Ranking basis/background: Based on *U.S News* questionnaire sent to 1,400 four-year institutions. Scores are averaged and weighted percentages from seven attributes: academic reputation, retention, faculty resources, student selectivity, financial resources, graduation rate performance and alumni giving. **Remarks:** Comparable data was used from the U.S. Department of Education, the Council for Aid to Education, the NCAA, and Wintergreen/Orchard House publishers. **Number listed:** 51.
1. Marlboro College, with 98%
2. Simon's Rock College of Bard, 96%
3. Sarah Lawrence College, 95%
4. Bennington College, 91%
4. Judson College, 91%
4. Sweet Briar College, 91%
7. Antioch College, 89%
8. Wells College, 86%
9. Bard College, 85%
10. Chatham College, 83%
10. Wesleyan College, 83%

Source: "America's Best Colleges," *U.S. News & World Report*, 129: 90-132, (September 11, 2000).

★1336★
U.S. News & World Report's national liberal arts colleges with the lowest acceptance rates, 2000-01

Ranking basis/background: Based on *U.S News* questionnaire sent to 1,400 four-year institutions. Scores are averaged and weighted percentages from seven attributes: academic reputation, retention, faculty resources, student selectivity, financial resources, graduation rate performance and alumni giving. **Remarks:** Comparable data was used from the U.S. Department of Education, the Council for Aid to Education, the NCAA, and Wintergreen/Orchard House publishers. **Number listed:** 51.
1. Amherst College, with 19%
2. Swarthmore College, 22%
3. Williams College, 23%
4. Middlebury College, 26%
5. Claremont McKenna College, 28%
6. Wesleyan University, 29%
7. Bowdoin College, 32%
7. Pomona College, 32%
9. Bates College, 33%
9. Colby College, 33%
9. Haverford College, 33%

Source: "America's Best Colleges," *U.S. News & World Report*, 129: 90-132, (September 11, 2000).

COLLEGES & UNIVERSITIES, LIBERAL ARTS–MIDDLE WESTERN STATES

★1337★
U.S. News & World Report's midwestern regional liberal arts colleges with students least in debt, 1999

Ranking basis/background: Based on total amount borrowed by 1999 graduates from one or more of the following sources: federal, state and local governments, financial institutions, and the colleges themselves. **Remarks:** Debt does not reflect monies borrowed by parents or others on behalf of the student. **Number listed:** 5.
1. Grand View College, with an average debt of $2,709
2. College of the Ozarks, $5,196
3. Culver-Stockton College, $8,204
4. Principia College, $8,764
5. William Tyndale College, $9,500

Source: "How Heavy is the Load?," *U.S. News & World Report*, 129: 101-102, (September 18, 2000).

★1338★
U.S. News & World Report's midwestern regional liberal arts colleges with students most in debt, 1999

Ranking basis/background: Based on total amount borrowed by 1999 graduates from one or more of the following sources: federal, state and local governments, financial institutions, and the colleges themselves. **Remarks:** Debt does not reflect monies borrowed by parents or others on behalf of the student. **Number listed:** 5.
1. Alverno College, with an average debt of $30,835
2. Barat College, $23,000
3. Mount Mary College, $22,221
4. University of Findlay, $22,000
5. Augsburg College, $20,846

Source: "How Heavy is the Load?," *U.S. News & World Report*, 129: 101-102, (September 18, 2000).

★1339★
U.S. News & World Report's midwestern regional liberal arts colleges with the best student/faculty ratios, 2000-01

Ranking basis/background: Based on *U.S News* questionnaire sent to 1,400 four-year institutions. Scores are averaged and weighted percentages from seven attributes: academic reputation, retention, faculty resources, student selectivity, financial resources, graduation rate performance and alumni giving. **Remarks:** Comparable data was used from the U.S. Department of Education, the Council for Aid to Education, the NCAA, and Wintergreen/Orchard House publishers. **Number listed:** 35.

1. Principia College, with a student/faculty ratio of 9/1
2. Stephens College, 10/1
2. Bethel College, 10/1
4. Hillsdale College, 11/1
5. St. Mary's College (IN), 12/1
5. Blufton College, 12/1
5. Marietta College, 12/1
8. Augustana College, 13/1
8. Heidelberg College, 13/1
8. Huntington College, 13/1
8. Clarke College, 13/1
8. Adrian College, 13/1
8. Loras College, 13/1
8. Ohio Northern University, 13/1
8. Millikin University, 13/1

Source: "America's Best Colleges," *U.S. News & World Report*, 129: 90-132, (September 11, 2000).

★1340★
***U.S. News & World Report*'s midwestern regional liberal arts colleges with the highest academic reputation scores, 2000-01**

Ranking basis/background: Based on *U.S News* questionnaire sent to 1,400 four-year institutions. Scores are averaged and weighted percentages from seven attributes: academic reputation, retention, faculty resources, student selectivity, financial resources, graduation rate performance and alumni giving. **Remarks:** Comparable data was used from the U.S. Department of Education, the Council for Aid to Education, the NCAA, and Wintergreen/Orchard House publishers. **Number listed:** 35.

1. St. Norbert College, with 3.8
2. St. Mary's College (IN), 3.6
2. Taylor University, 3.6
2. Millikin University, 3.6
2. Otterbein College, 3.6
6. Ohio Northern University, 3.5
6. Augustana College, 3.5
6. Augsburg College, 3.5
9. Simpson College, 3.4
9. Bethel College, 3.4

Source: "America's Best Colleges," *U.S. News & World Report*, 129: 90-132, (September 11, 2000).

★1341★
***U.S. News & World Report*'s midwestern regional liberal arts colleges with the highest acceptance rates, 2000-01**

Ranking basis/background: Based on *U.S News* questionnaire sent to 1,400 four-year institutions. Scores are averaged and weighted percentages from seven attributes: academic reputation, retention, faculty resources, student selectivity, financial resources, graduation rate performance and alumni giving. **Remarks:** Comparable data was used from the U.S. Department of Education, the Council for Aid to Education, the NCAA, and Wintergreen/Orchard House publishers. **Number listed:** 35.

1. Dordt College, with 95%
2. Ohio Northern University, 93%
3. Marietta College, 92%
3. Northwestern College, 92%
5. Mount Union College, 90%
5. St. Norbert College, 90%
5. Huntington College, 90%
5. Carroll College, 90%
9. Otterbein College, 89%
9. Doane College, 89%

Source: "America's Best Colleges," *U.S. News & World Report*, 129: 90-132, (September 11, 2000).

★1342★
***U.S. News & World Report*'s midwestern regional liberal arts colleges with the highest alumni giving rates, 2000-01**

Ranking basis/background: Based on *U.S News* questionnaire sent to 1,400 four-year institutions. Scores are averaged and weighted percentages from seven attributes: academic reputation, retention, faculty resources, student selectivity, financial resources, graduation rate performance and alumni giving. **Remarks:** Comparable data was used from the U.S. Department of Education, the Council for Aid to Education, the NCAA, and Wintergreen/Orchard House publishers. **Number listed:** 35.

1. Dordt College, with 49%
2. Heidelberg College, 41%
2. St. Mary's College (IN), 41%
4. Taylor University, 41%
5. North Park University, 38%
6. Doane College, 37%
6. Northwestern College, 37%
6. Huntington College, 37%
6. Otterbein College, 37%
10. Blufton College, 35%

Source: "America's Best Colleges," *U.S. News & World Report*, 129: 90-132, (September 11, 2000).

★1343★
***U.S. News & World Report*'s midwestern regional liberal arts colleges with the highest freshmen retention rates, 2000-01**

Ranking basis/background: Based on *U.S News* questionnaire sent to 1,400 four-year institutions. Scores are averaged and weighted percentages from seven attributes: academic reputation, retention, faculty resources, student selectivity, financial resources, graduation rate performance and alumni giving. **Remarks:** Comparable data was used from the U.S. Department of Education, the Council for Aid to Education, the NCAA, and Wintergreen/Orchard House publishers. **Number listed:** 35.

1. Hillsdale College, with 90%
2. Taylor University, 89%
3. St. Mary's College (IN), 86%
3. Principia College, 86%
3. Cedarville College, 86%
6. St. Norbert College, 83%
6. Bethel College, 83%
8. Otterbein College, 82%
8. Loras College, 82%
10. Ohio Northern University, 81%
10. Simpson College, 81%
10. Augustana College, 81%
10. Dordt College, 81%
10. Elmhurst College, 81%

Source: "America's Best Colleges," *U.S. News & World Report*, 129: 90-132, (September 11, 2000).

★1344★
***U.S. News & World Report*'s midwestern regional liberal arts colleges with the highest graduation rates, 2000-01**

Ranking basis/background: Based on *U.S News* questionnaire sent to 1,400 four-year institutions. Scores are averaged and weighted percentages from seven attributes: academic reputation, retention, faculty resources, student selectivity, financial resources, graduation rate performance and alumni giving. **Remarks:** Comparable data was used from the U.S. Department of Education, the Council for Aid to Education, the NCAA, and Wintergreen/Orchard House publishers. **Number listed:** 35.

1. St. Mary's College (IN), with 75%
2. Principia College, 74%
3. St. Norbert College, 73%
3. Taylor University, 73%
5. Bethel College, 70%
6. Otterbein College, 68%
7. Hillsdale College, 65%
7. Millikin University, 65%
9. Simpson College, 64%
9. Cedarville College, 64%

Source: "America's Best Colleges," *U.S. News & World Report*, 129: 90-132, (September 11, 2000).

★1345★
***U.S. News & World Report*'s midwestern regional liberal arts colleges with the highest percentage of freshmen in the top 25% of their high school class, 2000-01**

Ranking basis/background: Based on *U.S News* questionnaire sent to 1,400 four-year institutions. Scores are averaged and weighted percentages from seven attributes: academic reputation, retention, faculty resources, student selectivity, financial resources, graduation rate performance and alumni giving. **Remarks:** Comparable data was used from the U.S. Department of Education, the Council for Aid to Education, the NCAA, and Wintergreen/Orchard House publishers. **Number listed:** 35.

1. Hillsdale College, with 73%
2. Taylor University, 72%
3. St. Mary's College (IN), 68%
3. McKendree College, 68%
5. Cedarville College, 67%
6. Stephens College, 66%
7. Ohio Northern University, 65%
8. Mount Union College, 62%
9. Augustana College, 61%
10. St. Norbert College, 60%

Source: "America's Best Colleges," *U.S. News & World Report*, 129: 90-132, (September 11, 2000).

★1346★
***U.S. News & World Report*'s midwestern regional liberal arts colleges with the highest percentage of full-time faculty, 2000-01**

Ranking basis/background: Based on *U.S News* questionnaire sent to 1,400 four-year institutions. Scores are averaged and weighted percentages from seven attributes: academic reputation, retention, faculty resources, student selectivity, financial resources, graduation rate performance and alumni giving. **Remarks:** Comparable data was used from the U.S. Department of Education, the Council for Aid to Education, the NCAA, and Wintergreen/Orchard House publishers. **Number listed:** 35.

1. Stephens College, with 93%
2. Manchester College, 92%
2. Taylor University, 92%
4. Ohio Northern University, 91%
4. Cedarville College, 91%
6. Mount Union College, 90%
6. Buena Vista University, 90%
8. St. Norbert College, 89%
8. College of the Ozarks, 89%
8. Muskingum College, 89%

Source: "America's Best Colleges," *U.S. News & World Report*, 129: 90-132, (September 11, 2000).

★1347★
U.S. News & World Report's midwestern regional liberal arts colleges with the highest proportion of classes having 20 students or less, 2000-01

Ranking basis/background: Based on *U.S News* questionnaire sent to 1,400 four-year institutions. Scores are averaged and weighted percentages from seven attributes: academic reputation, retention, faculty resources, student selectivity, financial resources, graduation rate performance and alumni giving. **Remarks:** Comparable data was used from the U.S. Department of Education, the Council for Aid to Education, the NCAA, and Wintergreen/Orchard House publishers. **Number listed:** 35.

1. Principia College, with 93%
2. Stephens College, 89%
3. Bethel College, 83%
4. Blufton College, 81%
5. Hillsdale College, 74%
5. Alverno College, 74%
7. Clarke College, 73%
8. Loras College, 72%
9. Heidelberg College, 71%
10. Marietta College, 69%

Source: "America's Best Colleges," *U.S. News & World Report*, 129: 90-132, (September 11, 2000).

★1348★
U.S. News & World Report's midwestern regional liberal arts colleges with the lowest acceptance rates, 2000-01

Ranking basis/background: Based on *U.S News* questionnaire sent to 1,400 four-year institutions. Scores are averaged and weighted percentages from seven attributes: academic reputation, retention, faculty resources, student selectivity, financial resources, graduation rate performance and alumni giving. **Remarks:** Comparable data was used from the U.S. Department of Education, the Council for Aid to Education, the NCAA, and Wintergreen/Orchard House publishers. **Number listed:** 35.

1. College of the Ozarks, with 18%
2. Taylor University, 68%
3. Alverno College, 71%
3. McKendree College, 71%
5. Cedarville College, 74%
5. Elmhurst College, 74%
7. Millikin University, 75%
8. Augsburg College, 77%
9. Clarke College, 78%
10. Adrian College, 80%

Source: "America's Best Colleges," *U.S. News & World Report*, 129: 90-132, (September 11, 2000).

★1349★
U.S. News & World Report's top midwestern regional liberal arts colleges, 2000-01

Ranking basis/background: Based on *U.S News* questionnaire sent to 1,400 four-year institutions. Scores are averaged and weighted percentages from seven attributes: academic reputation, retention, faculty resources, student selectivity, financial resources, graduation rate performance and alumni giving. **Remarks:** Comparable data was used from the U.S. Department of Education, the Council for Aid to Education, the NCAA, and Wintergreen/Orchard House publishers. **Number listed:** 35.

1. St. Mary's College (IN), with an overall score of 100.0
2. St. Norbert College, 97.0
2. Taylor University, 97.0
4. Hillsdale College, 93.0
5. Otterbein College, 91.0
6. Principia College, 90.0
7. Ohio Northern University, 88.0
8. Simpson College, 87.0
9. Bethel College, 85.0
9. Millikin University, 85.0

Source: "America's Best Colleges," *U.S. News & World Report*, 129: 90-132, (September 11, 2000).

★1350★
U.S. News & World Report's top public midwestern regional liberal arts colleges, 2000-01

Ranking basis/background: Based on *U.S News* questionnaire sent to 1,400 four-year institutions. Scores are averaged and weighted percentages from seven attributes: academic reputation, retention, faculty resources, student selectivity, financial resources, graduation rate performance and alumni giving. **Remarks:** Comparable data was used from the U.S. Department of Education, the Council for Aid to Education, the NCAA, and Wintergreen/Orchard House publishers. **Number listed:** 4.

1. Southwest State University
2. University of Minnesota, Crookston
3. Valley City State University
4. Purdue University, North Central

Source: "America's Best Colleges," *U.S. News & World Report*, 129: 90-132, (September 11, 2000).

COLLEGES & UNIVERSITIES, LIBERAL ARTS–NORTHEASTERN STATES

★1351★
U.S. News & World Report's northern regional liberal arts colleges with students least in debt, 1999

Ranking basis/background: Based on total amount borrowed by 1999 graduates from one or more of the following sources: federal, state and local governments, financial institutions, and the colleges themselves. **Remarks:** Debt does not reflect monies borrowed by parents or others on behalf of the student. **Number listed:** 5.

1. Mount Aloysius College, with an average debt of $6,125
2. Point Park College, $7,267
3. Wesley College, $8,000
4. University of Maine, Augusta, $9,569
5. Hilbert College, $9,819

Source: "How Heavy is the Load?," *U.S. News & World Report*, 129: 101-102, (September 18, 2000).

★1352★
U.S. News & World Report's northern regional liberal arts colleges with students most in debt, 1999

Ranking basis/background: Based on total amount borrowed by 1999 graduates from one or more of the following sources: federal, state and local governments, financial institutions, and the colleges themselves. **Remarks:** Debt does not reflect monies borrowed by parents or others on behalf of the student. **Number listed:** 5.

1. Neumann College, with an average debt of $26,862
2. Keuka College, $20,525
3. Merrimack College, $20,125
4. Thiel College, $20,069
5. St. Vincent College, $19,842

Source: "How Heavy is the Load?," *U.S. News & World Report*, 129: 101-102, (September 18, 2000).

★1353★
U.S. News & World Report's northern regional liberal arts colleges with the best student/faculty ratios, 2000-01

Ranking basis/background: Based on *U.S News* questionnaire sent to 1,400 four-year institutions. Scores are averaged and weighted percentages from seven attributes: academic reputation, retention, faculty resources, student selectivity, financial resources, graduation rate performance and alumni giving. **Remarks:** Comparable data was used from the U.S. Department of Education, the Council for Aid to Education, the NCAA, and Wintergreen/Orchard House publishers. **Number listed:** 27.

1. Rosemont College, with a student/faculty ratio of 8/1
2. Marymount College, Tarrytown, 9/1
3. College of St. Elizabeth, 10/1
3. Regis College, 10/1
5. St. Vincent College, 12/1
6. Lycoming College, 13/1
6. Colby-Sawyer College, 13/1
6. Carlow College, 13/1
6. Stonehill College, 13/1
6. Elizabethtown College, 13/1
6. Lebanon Valley College, 13/1

Source: "America's Best Colleges," *U.S. News & World Report*, 129: 90-132, (September 11, 2000).

★1354★
U.S. News & World Report's northern regional liberal arts colleges with the highest academic reputation scores, 2000-01

Ranking basis/background: Based on *U.S News* questionnaire sent to 1,400 four-year institutions. Scores are averaged and weighted percentages from seven attributes: academic reputation, retention, faculty resources, student selectivity, financial resources, graduation rate performance and alumni giving. **Remarks:** Comparable data was used from the U.S. Department of Education, the Council for Aid to Education, the NCAA, and Wintergreen/Orchard House publishers. **Number listed:** 27.

1. Susquehanna University, with a score of 3.9
2. St. Anselm College, 3.7
3. Stonehill College, 3.6
4. Elizabethtown College, 3.5
5. Grove City College, 3.4
5. King's College, 3.4
7. York College of Pennsylvania, 3.3
7. Le Moyne College, 3.3
9. Messiah College, 3.2
9. Regis College, 3.2
9. Marymount Manhattan College, 3.2

Source: "America's Best Colleges," *U.S. News & World Report*, 129: 90-132, (September 11, 2000).

★1355★
U.S. News & World Report's northern regional liberal arts colleges with the highest acceptance rates, 2000-01

Ranking basis/background: Based on *U.S News* questionnaire sent to 1,400 four-year institutions. Scores are averaged and weighted percentages from seven attributes: academic reputation, retention, faculty resources, student selectivity, financial resources, graduation rate performance and alumni giving. **Remarks:** Comparable data was used from the U.S. Department of Education, the Council for Aid to Education, the NCAA, and Wintergreen/Orchard House publishers. **Number listed:** 27.
1. Regis College, with 94%
2. St. Vincent College, 88%
3. Roger Williams University, 86%
4. Marymount College, Tarrytown, 85%
5. Colby-Sawyer College, 84%
6. Rosemont College, 83%
6. College of St. Elizabeth, 83%
8. Lycoming College, 82%
9. King's College, 81%
9. Messiah College, 81%

Source: "America's Best Colleges," *U.S. News & World Report*, 129: 90-132, (September 11, 2000).

★1356★
U.S. News & World Report's northern regional liberal arts colleges with the highest alumni giving rates, 2000-01

Ranking basis/background: Based on *U.S News* questionnaire sent to 1,400 four-year institutions. Scores are averaged and weighted percentages from seven attributes: academic reputation, retention, faculty resources, student selectivity, financial resources, graduation rate performance and alumni giving. **Remarks:** Comparable data was used from the U.S. Department of Education, the Council for Aid to Education, the NCAA, and Wintergreen/Orchard House publishers. **Number listed:** 27.
1. Cedar Crest College, with 44%
2. Regis College, 37%
3. College of St. Elizabeth, 36%
4. Rosemont College, 35%
5. St. Vincent College, 34%
6. Lebanon Valley College, 33%
7. Elizabethtown College, 32%
8. St. Anselm College, 31%
9. Le Moyne College, 30%
10. Susquehanna University, 29%
10. King's College, 29%

Source: "America's Best Colleges," *U.S. News & World Report*, 129: 90-132, (September 11, 2000).

★1357★
U.S. News & World Report's northern regional liberal arts colleges with the highest freshmen retention rates, 2000-01

Ranking basis/background: Based on *U.S News* questionnaire sent to 1,400 four-year institutions. Scores are averaged and weighted percentages from seven attributes: academic reputation, retention, faculty resources, student selectivity, financial resources, graduation rate performance and alumni giving. **Remarks:** Comparable data was used from the U.S. Department of Education, the Council for Aid to Education, the NCAA, and Wintergreen/Orchard House publishers. **Number listed:** 27.
1. Grove City College, with 90%
2. Stonehill College, 89%
3. Susquehanna University, 87%
4. St. Anselm College, 86%
4. Le Moyne College, 86%
6. Messiah College, 84%
6. St. Vincent College, 84%
6. St. Joseph's College (NY), 84%
9. Elizabethtown College, 83%
10. King's College, 81%
10. Regis College, 81%
10. St. Thomas Aquinas College, 81%
10. Allentown College of St. Francis de Sales, 81%
10. Rosemont College, 81%
10. York College of Pennsylvania, 81%
10. Lycoming College, 81%

Source: "America's Best Colleges," *U.S. News & World Report*, 129: 90-132, (September 11, 2000).

★1358★
U.S. News & World Report's northern regional liberal arts colleges with the highest graduation rates, 2000-01

Ranking basis/background: Based on *U.S News* questionnaire sent to 1,400 four-year institutions. Scores are averaged and weighted percentages from seven attributes: academic reputation, retention, faculty resources, student selectivity, financial resources, graduation rate performance and alumni giving. **Remarks:** Comparable data was used from the U.S. Department of Education, the Council for Aid to Education, the NCAA, and Wintergreen/Orchard House publishers. **Number listed:** 27.
1. Stonehill College, with 77%
2. Grove City College, 76%
3. St. Anselm College, 73%
3. King's College, 73%
5. Le Moyne College, 72%
5. Messiah College, 72%
7. Susquehanna University, 70%
8. Rosemont College, 69%
9. Elizabethtown College, 68%
9. Allentown College of St. Francis de Sales, 68%

Source: "America's Best Colleges," *U.S. News & World Report*, 129: 90-132, (September 11, 2000).

★1359★
U.S. News & World Report's northern regional liberal arts colleges with the highest percentage of freshmen in the top 25% of their high school class, 2000-01

Ranking basis/background: Based on *U.S News* questionnaire sent to 1,400 four-year institutions. Scores are averaged and weighted percentages from seven attributes: academic reputation, retention, faculty resources, student selectivity, financial resources, graduation rate performance and alumni giving. **Remarks:** Comparable data was used from the U.S. Department of Education, the Council for Aid to Education, the NCAA, and Wintergreen/Orchard House publishers. **Number listed:** 27.
1. Grove City College, with 88%
2. Stonehill College, 77%
3. Marymount Manhattan College, 75%
4. Lebanon Valley College, 68%
5. Messiah College, 66%
6. York College of Pennsylvania, 65%
7. Susquehanna University, 61%
8. Elizabethtown College, 59%
9. St. Anselm College, 53%
10. Cedar Crest College, 50%

Source: "America's Best Colleges," *U.S. News & World Report*, 129: 90-132, (September 11, 2000).

★1360★
U.S. News & World Report's northern regional liberal arts colleges with the highest percentage of full-time faculty, 2000-01

Ranking basis/background: Based on *U.S News* questionnaire sent to 1,400 four-year institutions. Scores are averaged and weighted percentages from seven attributes: academic reputation, retention, faculty resources, student selectivity, financial resources, graduation rate performance and alumni giving. **Remarks:** Comparable data was used from the U.S. Department of Education, the Council for Aid to Education, the NCAA, and Wintergreen/Orchard House publishers. **Number listed:** 27.
1. Grove City College, with 90%
2. Lycoming College, 88%
3. St. Vincent College, 87%
4. St. Anselm College, 85%
4. Merrimack College, 85%
4. University of Maine, Farmington, 85%
7. Susquehanna University, 82%
7. Allentown College of St. Francis de Sales, 82%
9. Elizabethtown College, 80%
9. Mercyhurst College, 80%
9. King's College, 80%
9. Messiah College, 80%

Source: "America's Best Colleges," *U.S. News & World Report*, 129: 90-132, (September 11, 2000).

★1361★
U.S. News & World Report's northern regional liberal arts colleges with the highest proportion of classes having 20 students or less, 2000-01

Ranking basis/background: Based on *U.S News* questionnaire sent to 1,400 four-year institutions. Scores are averaged and weighted percentages from seven attributes: academic reputation, retention, faculty resources, student selectivity, financial resources, graduation rate performance and alumni giving. **Remarks:** Comparable data was used from the U.S. Department of Education, the Council for Aid to Education, the NCAA, and Wintergreen/Orchard House publishers. **Number listed:** 27.
1. Rosemont College, with 87%
1. Marymount College, Tarrytown, 87%
3. Carlow College, 79%
4. Regis College, 76%
5. Marymount Manhattan College, 72%
5. College of St. Elizabeth, 72%
7. Lebanon Valley College, 64%
8. Cedar Crest College, 62%
9. King's College, 55%
10. Elizabethtown College, 54%

Source: "America's Best Colleges," *U.S. News & World Report*, 129: 90-132, (September 11, 2000).

★1362★
U.S. News & World Report's northern regional liberal arts colleges with the lowest acceptance rates, 2000-01

Ranking basis/background: Based on *U.S News* questionnaire sent to 1,400 four-year institutions. Scores are averaged and weighted percentages from seven attributes: academic reputation, retention, faculty resources, student selectivity, financial resources, graduation rate performance and alumni giving. **Remarks:** Comparable data was used from the U.S. Department of Education, the Council for Aid to Education, the NCAA, and Wintergreen/Orchard House publishers. **Number listed:** 27.
1. Grove City College, with 44%

COLLEGES & UNIVERSITIES, LIBERAL ARTS—SOUTHERN

2. Stonehill College, 53%
3. University of Maine, Farmington, 65%
4. St. Joseph's College (NY), 66%
5. Marymount Manhattan College, 67%
6. York College of Pennsylvania, 71%
7. St. Anselm College, 72%
7. Lebanon Valley College, 72%
7. Merrimack College, 72%
10. Carlow College, 73%

Source: "America's Best Colleges," *U.S. News & World Report*, 129: 90-132, (September 11, 2000).

★1363★
U.S. News & World Report's top northern regional liberal arts colleges, 2000-01

Ranking basis/background: Based on *U.S News* questionnaire sent to 1,400 four-year institutions. Scores are averaged and weighted percentages from seven attributes: academic reputation, retention, faculty resources, student selectivity, financial resources, graduation rate performance and alumni giving. **Remarks:** Comparable data was used from the U.S. Department of Education, the Council for Aid to Education, the NCAA, and Wintergreen/Orchard House publishers. **Number listed:** 27.

1. Susquehanna University, with an overall score of 100.0
2. Stonehill College, 99.0
3. St. Anselm College, 96.0
4. Elizabethtown College, 94.0
5. Grove City College, 91.0
6. King's College, 90.0
6. Le Moyne College, 90.0
8. Messiah College, 89.0
9. Lebanon Valley College, 88.0
10. Regis College, 86.0

Source: "America's Best Colleges," *U.S. News & World Report*, 129: 90-132, (September 11, 2000).

★1364★
U.S. News & World Report's top public northern regional liberal arts colleges, 2000-01

Ranking basis/background: Based on *U.S News* questionnaire sent to 1,400 four-year institutions. Scores are averaged and weighted percentages from seven attributes: academic reputation, retention, faculty resources, student selectivity, financial resources, graduation rate performance and alumni giving. **Remarks:** Comparable data was used from the U.S. Department of Education, the Council for Aid to Education, the NCAA, and Wintergreen/Orchard House publishers. **Number listed:** 4.

1. University of Maine, Farmington
2. State University of New York, Purchase College
3. Massachusetts College of Liberal Arts
3. Ramapo College of New Jersey

Source: "America's Best Colleges," *U.S. News & World Report*, 129: 90-132, (September 11, 2000).

★1365★
U.S. News & World Report's top public western regional liberal arts colleges, 2000-01

Ranking basis/background: Based on *U.S News* questionnaire sent to 1,400 four-year institutions. Scores are averaged and weighted percentages from seven attributes: academic reputation, retention, faculty resources, student selectivity, financial resources, graduation rate performance and alumni giving. **Remarks:** Comparable data was used from the U.S. Department of Education, the Council for Aid to Education, the NCAA, and Wintergreen/Orchard House publishers. **Number listed:** 4.

1. Evergreen State College
2. Texas A&M University, Galveston
3. University of Hawaii, Hilo
4. Eastern Oregon University

Source: "America's Best Colleges," *U.S. News & World Report*, 129: 90-132, (September 11, 2000).

COLLEGES & UNIVERSITIES, LIBERAL ARTS–SOUTHERN STATES

★1366★
U.S. News & World Report's southern regional liberal arts colleges with students least in debt, 1999

Ranking basis/background: Based on total amount borrowed by 1999 graduates from one or more of the following sources: federal, state and local governments, financial institutions, and the colleges themselves. **Remarks:** Debt does not reflect monies borrowed by parents or others on behalf of the student. **Number listed:** 5.

1. Alice Lloyd College, with an average debt of $3,371
2. Fairmont State College, $6,325
3. Limestone College, $6,656
4. Bluefield State College, $7,200
5. Mount Olive College, $7,453

Source: "How Heavy is the Load?," *U.S. News & World Report*, 129: 101-102, (September 18, 2000).

★1367★
U.S. News & World Report's southern regional liberal arts colleges with students most in debt, 1999

Ranking basis/background: Based on total amount borrowed by 1999 graduates from one or more of the following sources: federal, state and local governments, financial institutions, and the colleges themselves. **Remarks:** Debt does not reflect monies borrowed by parents or others on behalf of the student. **Number listed:** 5.

1. Our Lady of Holy Cross College, with an average debt of $25,000
2. Alderson-Broaddus College, $23,250
3. Fisk University, $20,000
4. Paine College, $19,750
5. Salem-Teikyo University, $18,758

Source: "How Heavy is the Load?," *U.S. News & World Report*, 129: 101-102, (September 18, 2000).

★1368★
U.S. News & World Report's southern regional liberal arts colleges with the best student/faculty ratios, 2000-01

Ranking basis/background: Based on *U.S News* questionnaire sent to 1,400 four-year institutions. Scores are averaged and weighted percentages from seven attributes: academic reputation, retention, faculty resources, student selectivity, financial resources, graduation rate performance and alumni giving. **Remarks:** Comparable data was used from the U.S. Department of Education, the Council for Aid to Education, the NCAA, and Wintergreen/Orchard House publishers. **Number listed:** 33.

1. Lyon College, with a student/faculty ratio of 9/1
2. King College, 10/1
3. Brerea College, 11/1
3. Mary Baldwin College, 11/1
5. Berry College, 12/1
5. Union University, 12/1
5. Columbia College, 12/1
5. Coker College, 12/1
5. Thomas More College, 12/1
5. Warren Wilson College, 12/1
5. Wingate University, 12/1

Source: "America's Best Colleges," *U.S. News & World Report*, 129: 90-132, (September 11, 2000).

★1369★
U.S. News & World Report's southern regional liberal arts colleges with the highest academic reputation scores, 2000-01

Ranking basis/background: Based on *U.S News* questionnaire sent to 1,400 four-year institutions. Scores are averaged and weighted percentages from seven attributes: academic reputation, retention, faculty resources, student selectivity, financial resources, graduation rate performance and alumni giving. **Remarks:** Comparable data was used from the U.S. Department of Education, the Council for Aid to Education, the NCAA, and Wintergreen/Orchard House publishers. **Number listed:** 33.

1. Brerea College, with a score of 4.1
2. Berry College, 3.9
3. Emory and Henry College, 3.6
4. Mary Baldwin College, 3.6
5. Lyon College, 3.5
5. Roanoke College, 3.5
7. Asbury College, 3.4
7. Maryville College, 3.4
7. Carson-Newman College, 3.4
7. Mississippi University for Women, 3.4

Source: "America's Best Colleges," *U.S. News & World Report*, 129: 90-132, (September 11, 2000).

★1370★
U.S. News & World Report's southern regional liberal arts colleges with the highest acceptance rates, 2000-01

Ranking basis/background: Based on *U.S News* questionnaire sent to 1,400 four-year institutions. Scores are averaged and weighted percentages from seven attributes: academic reputation, retention, faculty resources, student selectivity, financial resources, graduation rate performance and alumni giving. **Remarks:** Comparable data was used from the U.S. Department of Education, the Council for Aid to Education, the NCAA, and Wintergreen/Orchard House publishers. **Number listed:** 33.

1. Fisk University, with 97%
2. David Lipscomb University, 93%
3. High Point University, 91%

3. Wingate University, 91%
5. Thomas More College, 90%
6. Bridgewater College, 89%
7. Carson-Newman College, 88%
8. Asbury College, 87%
9. Mary Baldwin College, 86%
10. Union University, 85%

Source: "America's Best Colleges," *U.S. News & World Report*, 129: 90-132, (September 11, 2000).

★1371★
U.S. News & World Report's southern regional liberal arts colleges with the highest alumni giving rates, 2000-01

Ranking basis/background: Based on *U.S News* questionnaire sent to 1,400 four-year institutions. Scores are averaged and weighted percentages from seven attributes: academic reputation, retention, faculty resources, student selectivity, financial resources, graduation rate performance and alumni giving. **Remarks:** Comparable data was used from the U.S. Department of Education, the Council for Aid to Education, the NCAA, and Wintergreen/Orchard House publishers. **Number listed:** 33.

1. Emory and Henry College, with 51%
2. Maryville College, 43%
3. Asbury College, 38%
4. Claflin University, 37%
5. Eastern Mennonite University, 36%
6. Columbia College, 35%
7. Mary Baldwin College, 34%
8. Roanoke College, 29%
9. Ouachita Baptist University, 28%
9. Coker College, 28%

Source: "America's Best Colleges," *U.S. News & World Report*, 129: 90-132, (September 11, 2000).

★1372★
U.S. News & World Report's southern regional liberal arts colleges with the highest freshmen retention rates, 2000-01

Ranking basis/background: Based on *U.S News* questionnaire sent to 1,400 four-year institutions. Scores are averaged and weighted percentages from seven attributes: academic reputation, retention, faculty resources, student selectivity, financial resources, graduation rate performance and alumni giving. **Remarks:** Comparable data was used from the U.S. Department of Education, the Council for Aid to Education, the NCAA, and Wintergreen/Orchard House publishers. **Number listed:** 33.

1. Fisk University, with 87%
2. Covenant College, 80%
3. John Brown University, 79%
4. Claflin University, 78%
4. Asbury College, 78%
6. Berry College, 77%
6. Bridgewater College, 77%
8. Roanoke College, 76%
8. Maryville College, 76%
8. Bryan College, 76%

Source: "America's Best Colleges," *U.S. News & World Report*, 129: 90-132, (September 11, 2000).

★1373★
U.S. News & World Report's southern regional liberal arts colleges with the highest graduation rates, 2000-01

Ranking basis/background: Based on *U.S News* questionnaire sent to 1,400 four-year institutions. Scores are averaged and weighted percentages from seven attributes: academic reputation, retention, faculty resources, student selectivity, financial resources, graduation rate performance and alumni giving. **Remarks:** Comparable data was used from the U.S. Department of Education, the Council for Aid to Education, the NCAA, and Wintergreen/Orchard House publishers. **Number listed:** 33.

1. Claflin University, with 72%
2. Emory and Henry College, 65%
3. Eastern Mennonite University, 61%
4. Roanoke College, 58%
4. Union University, 58%
6. Berry College, 56%
7. Columbia College, 55%
7. Carson-Newman College, 55%
7. Bridgewater College, 55%
10. Mary Baldwin College, 54%
10. Asbury College, 54%

Source: "America's Best Colleges," *U.S. News & World Report*, 129: 90-132, (September 11, 2000).

★1374★
U.S. News & World Report's southern regional liberal arts colleges with the highest percentage of full-time faculty, 2000-01

Ranking basis/background: Based on *U.S News* questionnaire sent to 1,400 four-year institutions. Scores are averaged and weighted percentages from seven attributes: academic reputation, retention, faculty resources, student selectivity, financial resources, graduation rate performance and alumni giving. **Remarks:** Comparable data was used from the U.S. Department of Education, the Council for Aid to Education, the NCAA, and Wintergreen/Orchard House publishers. **Number listed:** 33.

1. Bridgewater College, with 96%
2. Brerea College, 94%
3. Warren Wilson College, 93%
4. Lyon College, 91%
4. John Brown University, 91%
4. Claflin University, 91%
7. Emory and Henry College, 90%
7. Fisk University, 90%
7. Wingate University, 90%
10. University of the Ozarks, 89%
10. Covenant College, 89%

Source: "America's Best Colleges," *U.S. News & World Report*, 129: 90-132, (September 11, 2000).

★1375★
U.S. News & World Report's southern regional liberal arts colleges with the highest proportion of classes having 20 students or less, 2000-01

Ranking basis/background: Based on *U.S News* questionnaire sent to 1,400 four-year institutions. Scores are averaged and weighted percentages from seven attributes: academic reputation, retention, faculty resources, student selectivity, financial resources, graduation rate performance and alumni giving. **Remarks:** Comparable data was used from the U.S. Department of Education, the Council for Aid to Education, the NCAA, and Wintergreen/Orchard House publishers. **Number listed:** 33.

1. Coker College, with 86%
2. Bryan College, 81%
3. Thomas More College, 79%
3. King College, 79%
5. Lyon College, 74%
5. Wingate University, 74%
5. University of the Ozarks, 74%
8. Milligan College, 73%
9. High Point University, 72%
10. Louisiana College, 68%

Source: "America's Best Colleges," *U.S. News & World Report*, 129: 90-132, (September 11, 2000).

★1376★
U.S. News & World Report's southern regional liberal arts colleges with the highest proportion of freshmen in the top 25% of their high school class, 2000-01

Ranking basis/background: Based on *U.S News* questionnaire sent to 1,400 four-year institutions. Scores are averaged and weighted percentages from seven attributes: academic reputation, retention, faculty resources, student selectivity, financial resources, graduation rate performance and alumni giving. **Remarks:** Comparable data was used from the U.S. Department of Education, the Council for Aid to Education, the NCAA, and Wintergreen/Orchard House publishers. **Number listed:** 33.

1. Lyon College, with 79%
2. Berry College, 73%
3. Louisiana College, 70%
4. Mississippi University for Women, 69%
5. Bryan College, 68%
6. Brerea College, 67%
7. Maryville College, 65%
8. Union University, 64%
9. King College, 62%
10. Asbury College, 58%

Source: "America's Best Colleges," *U.S. News & World Report*, 129: 90-132, (September 11, 2000).

★1377★
U.S. News & World Report's southern regional liberal arts colleges with the lowest acceptance rates, 2000-01

Ranking basis/background: Based on *U.S News* questionnaire sent to 1,400 four-year institutions. Scores are averaged and weighted percentages from seven attributes: academic reputation, retention, faculty resources, student selectivity, financial resources, graduation rate performance and alumni giving. **Remarks:** Comparable data was used from the U.S. Department of Education, the Council for Aid to Education, the NCAA, and Wintergreen/Orchard House publishers. **Number listed:** 33.

1. Flagler College, with 31%
2. Brerea College, 34%
3. Claflin University, 56%
4. Milligan College, 69%
5. Ouachita Baptist University, 71%
6. Mississippi University for Women, 72%
7. Bryan College, 75%
8. Covenant College, 78%
9. University of the Ozarks, 79%
9. Louisiana College, 79%
9. Warren Wilson College, 79%
9. Florida Southern College, 79%

Source: "America's Best Colleges," *U.S. News & World Report*, 129: 90-132, (September 11, 2000).

COLLEGES & UNIVERSITIES, LIBERAL ARTS—STUDENT

★1378★
U.S. News & World Report's top public southern regional liberal arts colleges, 2000-01

Ranking basis/background: Based on *U.S News* questionnaire sent to 1,400 four-year institutions. Scores are averaged and weighted percentages from seven attributes: academic reputation, retention, faculty resources, student selectivity, financial resources, graduation rate performance and alumni giving. **Remarks:** Comparable data was used from the U.S. Department of Education, the Council for Aid to Education, the NCAA, and Wintergreen/Orchard House publishers. **Number listed:** 4.
1. Mississippi University for Women
2. University of Virginia, Wise
3. Christopher Newport University
3. University of South Carolina, Aiken

Source: "America's Best Colleges," *U.S. News & World Report*, 129: 90-132, (September 11, 2000).

★1379★
U.S. News & World Report's top southern regional liberal arts colleges, 2000-01

Ranking basis/background: Based on *U.S News* questionnaire sent to 1,400 four-year institutions. Scores are averaged and weighted percentages from seven attributes: academic reputation, retention, faculty resources, student selectivity, financial resources, graduation rate performance and alumni giving. **Remarks:** Comparable data was used from the U.S. Department of Education, the Council for Aid to Education, the NCAA, and Wintergreen/Orchard House publishers. **Number listed:** 33.
1. Brerea College, with an overall score of 100.0
2. Berry College, 97.0
3. Emory and Henry College, 93.0
4. Lyon College, 92.0
5. Roanoke College, 89.0
6. Mary Baldwin College, 86.0
7. Asbury College, 84.0
7. Maryville College, 84.0
9. Union University, 83.0
10. Columbia College, 82.0

Source: "America's Best Colleges," *U.S. News & World Report*, 129: 90-132, (September 11, 2000).

COLLEGES & UNIVERSITIES, LIBERAL ARTS–STUDENT COSTS

★1380★
U.S. News & World Report's best undergraduate fees among midwestern regional liberal arts colleges by discount tuition, 2000

Ranking basis/background: Based on a percentage averaged from 3 variables; ratio of quality to price, percentage of all undergraduates receiving grants meeting financial need during the 1999-2000 academic year, and average discount: percentage of a school's total costs. **Number listed:** 10.
1. Northwestern College, with a 53% average discount from total cost; and an average cost of $9,099 after receiving grants based on need
2. Simpson College, 45%; $11,853
3. Heidelberg College, 46%; $12,737
3. Manchester College, 49%; $10,818
5. Buena Vista University, 44%; $12,585
6. Muskingum College, 44%; $10,609
7. Augustana College, 41%; $11,679
7. Doane College, 36%; $11,770
9. Adrian College, 41%; $11,789
9. Mount Union College, 41%; $12,494

Source: "Great Schools at Great Prices," *U.S. News & World Report*, 129: 96, 100, (September 18, 2000).

★1381★
U.S. News & World Report's best undergraduate fees among national liberal arts colleges by discount tuition, 2000

Ranking basis/background: Based on a percentage averaged from 3 variables; ratio of quality to price, percentage of all undergraduates receiving grants meeting financial need during the 1999-2000 academic year, and average discount: percentage of a school's total costs. **Number listed:** 36.
1. Swarthmore College, with a 57% average discount from total cost; and an average cost of $14,434 after receiving grants based on need
2. Grinnell College, 51%; $12,988
3. Claremont McKenna College, 54%; $13,691
4. Wabash College, 54%; $11,249
5. University of the South, 53%; $12,140
6. Colgate University, 57%; $13,918
7. Pomona College, 52%; $16,040
8. Williams College, 52%; $16,045
9. Amherst College, 52%; $16,727
10. Knox College, 51%; $12,899

Source: "Great Schools at Great Prices," *U.S. News & World Report*, 129: 96, 100, (September 18, 2000).

★1382★
U.S. News & World Report's best undergraduate fees among northern regional liberal arts colleges by discount tuition, 2000

Ranking basis/background: Based on a percentage averaged from 3 variables; ratio of quality to price, percentage of all undergraduates receiving grants meeting financial need during the 1999-2000 academic year, and average discount: percentage of a school's total costs. **Number listed:** 10.
1. College of St. Elizabeth, with a 62% average discount from total cost; and an average cost of $8,474 after receiving grants based on need
2. Grove City College, 28%; $9,331
3. Le Moyne College, 40%; $13,650
4. Elizabethtown College, 42%; $14,339
5. St. Vincent College, 39%; $13,195
6. Susquehanna University, 41%; $15,727
7. Lebanon Valley College, 38%; $15,133
8. Cedar Crest College, 40%; $15,050
8. Rosemont College, 44%; $13,209
8. York College of Pennsylvania, 23%; $10,289

Source: "Great Schools at Great Prices," *U.S. News & World Report*, 129: 96, 100, (September 18, 2000).

★1383★
U.S. News & World Report's best undergraduate fees among southern regional liberal arts colleges by discount tuition, 2000

Ranking basis/background: Based on a percentage averaged from 3 variables; ratio of quality to price, percentage of all undergraduates receiving grants meeting financial need during the 1999-2000 academic year, and average discount: percentage of a school's total costs. **Number listed:** 10.
1. Mississippi University for Women, with a 40% average discount from total cost; and an average cost of $6,377 after receiving grants based on need
2. Ouachita Baptist University, 53%; $6,971
3. Lyon College, 52%; $8,391
4. University of the Ozarks, 55%; $7,348
5. Claflin University, 39%; $8,626
6. Emory and Henry College, 41%; $11,837
7. Berry College, 43%; $11,072
8. LaGrange College, 44%; $9,642
9. Bridgewater College, 48%; $12,010
9. Florida Southern College, 47%; $10,388
9. King College, 44%; $10,190
9. Maryville College, 44%; $13,092

Source: "Great Schools at Great Prices," *U.S. News & World Report*, 129: 96, 100, (September 18, 2000).

★1384★
U.S. News & World Report's best undergraduate fees among western regional liberal arts colleges by discount tuition, 2000

Ranking basis/background: Based on a percentage averaged from 3 variables; ratio of quality to price, percentage of all undergraduates receiving grants meeting financial need during the 1999-2000 academic year, and average discount: percentage of a school's total costs. **Number listed:** 10.
1. Texas Lutheran University, with a 36% average discount from total cost; and an average cost of $11,381 after receiving grants based on need
2. George Fox University, 38%; $14,947
3. Carroll College, 28%; $13,031
4. Pacific Union College, 36%; $13,855
5. Schreiner College, 35%; $13,402
6. McMurry University, 28%; $12,074
7. Albertson College, 23%; $17,060
7. Master's College and Seminary, 35%; $13,839
9. Oklahoma Baptist University, 14%; $13,201
10. Concordia University, 34%; $15,567

Source: "Great Schools at Great Prices," *U.S. News & World Report*, 129: 96, 100, (September 18, 2000).

★1385★
U.S. News & World Report's national liberal arts colleges with students least in debt, 1999

Ranking basis/background: Based on total amount borrowed by 1999 graduates from one or more of the following sources: federal, state and local governments, financial institutions, and the colleges themselves. **Remarks:** Debt does not reflect monies borrowed by parents or others on behalf of the student. **Number listed:** 25.

1. Christendom College, with an average debt of $8,980
2. Alma College, $9,649
3. Earlham College, $10,365
4. Hampden-Sydney College, $10,400
5. Gordon College, $10,429
6. DePauw University, $11,375
7. Hanover College, $11,735
8. Furman University, $11,750
9. Illinois College, $11,771
10. Judson College, $12,085

Source: "How Heavy is the Load?," *U.S. News & World Report*, 129: 101-102, (September 18, 2000).

★1386★
U.S. News & World Report's national liberal arts colleges with students most in debt, 1999

Ranking basis/background: Based on total amount borrowed by 1999 graduates from one or more of the following sources: federal, state and local governments, financial institutions, and the colleges themselves. **Remarks:** Debt does not reflect monies borrowed by parents or others on behalf of the student. **Number listed:** 15.

1. Wesleyan University, with an average debt of $25,342
2. Austin College, $21,550
3. Central College, $20,665
4. Pitzer College, $20,530
5. University of Puget Sound, $20,259
6. Bennington College, $19,300
7. Ohio Wesleyan University, $19,253
8. Oglethorpe University, $19,232
9. Hamline University, $18,887
10. Southwestern University, $18,879
11. Millsaps College, $18,743
12. Westmont College, $18,319
13. Scripps College, $18,278
14. Concordia College, Moorhead, $18,135

Source: "How Heavy is the Load?," *U.S. News & World Report*, 129: 101-102, (September 18, 2000).

COLLEGES & UNIVERSITIES, LIBERAL ARTS–TUITION

See: **Colleges & Universities, Liberal Arts–Student Costs**

COLLEGES & UNIVERSITIES, LIBERAL ARTS–WESTERN STATES

★1387★
Academic reputation scores for *U.S. News & World Report*'s top western regional liberal arts colleges, 2000-01

Ranking basis/background: Based on *U.S News* questionnaire sent to 1,400 four-year institutions. Scores are averaged and weighted percentages from seven attributes: academic reputation, retention, faculty resources, student selectivity, financial resources, graduation rate performance and alumni giving. **Remarks:** Comparable data was used from the U.S. Department of Education, the Council for Aid to Education, the NCAA, and Wintergreen/Orchard House publishers. **Number listed:** 17.
1. George Fox University, with a score of 3.9
2. Evergreen State College, 3.7
3. Albertson College, 3.6
3. Oklahoma Baptist University, 3.6
3. College of Sante Fe, 3.6
6. Carroll College, 3.5
6. Texas Lutheran University, 3.5
6. LeTourneau University, 3.5
6. Brigham Young University (HI), 3.5
10. Northwest Nazarene University, 3.4
10. Texas A&M University, Galveston, 3.4
10. Concordia University, 3.4
13. Oklahoma Christian University, 3.3
13. McMurry University, 3.3
15. Pacific Union College, 3.2
15. Schreiner College, 3.2
17. Master's College and Seminary, 3.1

Source: "America's Best Colleges," *U.S. News & World Report*, 129: 90-132, (September 11, 2000).

★1388★
Acceptance rates for *U.S. News & World Report*'s top western regional liberal arts colleges, 2000-01

Ranking basis/background: Based on *U.S News* questionnaire sent to 1,400 four-year institutions. Scores are averaged and weighted percentages from seven attributes: academic reputation, retention, faculty resources, student selectivity, financial resources, graduation rate performance and alumni giving. **Remarks:** Comparable data was used from the U.S. Department of Education, the Council for Aid to Education, the NCAA, and Wintergreen/Orchard House publishers. **Number listed:** 17.
1. George Fox University, with 93%
2. Carroll College, 91%
3. Oklahoma Christian University, 90%
4. Oklahoma Baptist University, 89%
5. Texas A&M University, Galveston, 89%
6. Evergreen State College, 86%
7. LeTourneau University, 85%
8. College of Sante Fe, 84%
9. Albertson College, 83%
9. Texas Lutheran University, 83%
11. Master's College and Seminary, 82%
12. Concordia University, 79%
13. Schreiner College, 72%
14. Northwest Nazarene University, 71%
15. McMurry University, 68%
16. Brigham Young University (HI), 46%
17. Pacific Union College, 44%

Source: "America's Best Colleges," *U.S. News & World Report*, 129: 90-132, (September 11, 2000).

★1389★
Alumni giving rates at *U.S. News & World Report*'s top western regional liberal arts colleges, 2000-01

Ranking basis/background: Based on *U.S News* questionnaire sent to 1,400 four-year institutions. Scores are averaged and weighted percentages from seven attributes: academic reputation, retention, faculty resources, student selectivity, financial resources, graduation rate performance and alumni giving. **Remarks:** Comparable data was used from the U.S. Department of Education, the Council for Aid to Education, the NCAA, and Wintergreen/Orchard House publishers. **Number listed:** 16.
1. Northwest Nazarene University, with 30%
2. Carroll College, 27%
3. George Fox University, 23%
4. Oklahoma Baptist University, 22%
5. Texas Lutheran University, 21%
6. Pacific Union College, 20%
7. Schreiner College, 19%
8. LeTourneau University, 16%
8. Concordia University, 16%
10. Albertson College, 15%
11. Evergreen State College, 14%
12. Oklahoma Christian University, 13%
12. McMurry University, 13%
14. College of Sante Fe, 12%
15. Master's College and Seminary, 7%
16. Brigham Young University (HI), 6%

Source: "America's Best Colleges," *U.S. News & World Report*, 129: 90-132, (September 11, 2000).

★1390★
Average freshmen retention rates for *U.S. News & World Report*'s top western regional liberal arts colleges, 2000-01

Ranking basis/background: Based on *U.S News* questionnaire sent to 1,400 four-year institutions. Scores are averaged and weighted percentages from seven attributes: academic reputation, retention, faculty resources, student selectivity, financial resources, graduation rate performance and alumni giving. **Remarks:** Comparable data was used from the U.S. Department of Education, the Council for Aid to Education, the NCAA, and Wintergreen/Orchard House publishers. **Number listed:** 17.
1. George Fox University, with 78%
1. Oklahoma Baptist University, 78%
3. Concordia University, 77%
4. Carroll College, 75%
5. Texas Lutheran University, 73%
5. Master's College and Seminary, 73%
7. Pacific Union College, 72%
7. LeTourneau University, 72%
9. Texas A&M University, Galveston, 71%
10. Albertson College, 70%
11. Northwest Nazarene University, 68%
12. Evergreen State College, 66%
13. Schreiner College, 65%
14. Oklahoma Christian University, 64%
14. McMurry University, 64%
16. College of Sante Fe, 63%
17. Brigham Young University (HI), 62%

Source: "America's Best Colleges," *U.S. News & World Report*, 129: 90-132, (September 11, 2000).

★1391★
Average graduation rates for *U.S. News & World Report*'s top western regional liberal arts colleges, 2000-01

Ranking basis/background: Based on *U.S News* questionnaire sent to 1,400 four-year institutions. Scores are averaged and weighted percentages from seven attributes: academic reputation, retention, faculty resources, student selectivity, financial resources, graduation rate performance and alumni giving. **Remarks:** Comparable data was used from the U.S. Department of Education, the Council for Aid to Education, the NCAA, and Wintergreen/Orchard House publishers. **Number listed:** 17.
1. Albertson College, with 55%
2. Concordia University, 54%
3. George Fox University, 52%
4. Evergreen State College, 50%
5. Oklahoma Baptist University, 48%
5. LeTourneau University, 48%
7. Pacific Union College, 47%
8. Texas Lutheran University, 46%
9. Northwest Nazarene University, 45%
10. Carroll College, 44%
11. Master's College and Seminary, 40%
12. McMurry University, 37%
13. Oklahoma Christian University, 36%
14. Schreiner College, 34%
15. Texas A&M University, Galveston, 29%
16. Brigham Young University (HI), 26%
16. College of Sante Fe, 26%

COLLEGES & UNIVERSITIES, LIBERAL ARTS—WESTERN

Source: "America's Best Colleges," *U.S. News & World Report*, 129: 90-132, (September 11, 2000).

★1392★
Percentage of freshmen in the top 25% of their high school class at *U.S. News & World Report*'s top western regional liberal arts colleges, 2000-01

Ranking basis/background: Based on *U.S News* questionnaire sent to 1,400 four-year institutions. Scores are averaged and weighted percentages from seven attributes: academic reputation, retention, faculty resources, student selectivity, financial resources, graduation rate performance and alumni giving. **Remarks:** Comparable data was used from the U.S. Department of Education, the Council for Aid to Education, the NCAA, and Wintergreen/Orchard House publishers. **Number listed:** 15.

1. Texas Lutheran University, with 64%
2. George Fox University, 63%
2. Pacific Union College, 63%
4. Oklahoma Baptist University, 62%
5. Albertson College, 59%
6. Master's College and Seminary, 58%
7. Northwest Nazarene University, 56%
8. Carroll College, 55%
8. Brigham Young University (HI), 55%
10. LeTourneau University, 54%
11. McMurry University, 53%
12. Texas A&M University, Galveston, 50%
13. Concordia University, 46%
14. Schreiner College, 45%
15. College of Sante Fe, 37%

Source: "America's Best Colleges," *U.S. News & World Report*, 129: 90-132, (September 11, 2000).

★1393★
Percentage of full-time faculty at *U.S. News & World Report*'s top western regional liberal arts colleges, 2000-01

Ranking basis/background: Based on *U.S News* questionnaire sent to 1,400 four-year institutions. Scores are averaged and weighted percentages from seven attributes: academic reputation, retention, faculty resources, student selectivity, financial resources, graduation rate performance and alumni giving. **Remarks:** Comparable data was used from the U.S. Department of Education, the Council for Aid to Education, the NCAA, and Wintergreen/Orchard House publishers. **Number listed:** 17.

1. Northwest Nazarene University, with 100%
2. Texas A&M University, Galveston, 98%
3. Albertson College, 95%
3. Pacific Union College, 95%
5. Oklahoma Baptist University, 85%
5. McMurry University, 85%
7. Brigham Young University (HI), 84%
8. Oklahoma Christian University, 83%
9. Schreiner College, 82%
10. Carroll College, 81%
11. George Fox University, 80%
12. Evergreen State College, 78%
13. Texas Lutheran University, 76%
14. Master's College and Seminary, 70%
15. LeTourneau University, 56%
16. College of Sante Fe, 52%
17. Concordia University, 51%

Source: "America's Best Colleges," *U.S. News & World Report*, 129: 90-132, (September 11, 2000).

★1394★
Proportion of classes having 20 students or less at *U.S. News & World Report*'s top western regional liberal arts colleges, 2000-01

Ranking basis/background: Based on *U.S News* questionnaire sent to 1,400 four-year institutions. Scores are averaged and weighted percentages from seven attributes: academic reputation, retention, faculty resources, student selectivity, financial resources, graduation rate performance and alumni giving. **Remarks:** Comparable data was used from the U.S. Department of Education, the Council for Aid to Education, the NCAA, and Wintergreen/Orchard House publishers. **Number listed:** 17.

1. College of Sante Fe, with 92%
2. Albertson College, 75%
3. Master's College and Seminary, 74%
4. Pacific Union College, 70%
4. Oklahoma Christian University, 70%
6. McMurry University, 65%
7. Schreiner College, 63%
7. Texas A&M University, Galveston, 63%
9. LeTourneau University, 61%
10. Oklahoma Baptist University, 58%
11. Carroll College, 55%
12. Texas Lutheran University, 54%
13. George Fox University, 53%
14. Evergreen State College, 52%
15. Northwest Nazarene University, 50%
16. Brigham Young University (HI), 47%
17. Concordia University, 44%

Source: "America's Best Colleges," *U.S. News & World Report*, 129: 90-132, (September 11, 2000).

★1395★
Student/faculty ratios at *U.S. News & World Report*'s top western regional liberal arts colleges, 2000-01

Ranking basis/background: Based on *U.S News* questionnaire sent to 1,400 four-year institutions. Scores are averaged and weighted percentages from seven attributes: academic reputation, retention, faculty resources, student selectivity, financial resources, graduation rate performance and alumni giving. **Remarks:** Comparable data was used from the U.S. Department of Education, the Council for Aid to Education, the NCAA, and Wintergreen/Orchard House publishers. **Number listed:** 17.

1. Carroll College, with a student/faculty ratio of 11/1
1. Texas A&M University, Galveston, 11/1
3. Albertson College, 12/1
3. Pacific Union College, 12/1
5. College of Sante Fe, 13/1
6. Oklahoma Baptist University, 14/1
6. Northwest Nazarene University, 14/1
8. Brigham Young University (HI), 15/1
9. George Fox University, 16/1
9. Texas Lutheran University, 16/1
9. Oklahoma Christian University, 16/1
9. Master's College and Seminary, 16/1
9. McMurry University, 16/1
14. Schreiner College, 17/1
14. Concordia University, 17/1
16. Evergreen State College, 20/1
16. LeTourneau University, 20/1

Source: "America's Best Colleges," *U.S. News & World Report*, 129: 90-132, (September 11, 2000).

★1396★
***U.S. News & World Report*'s top western regional liberal arts colleges, 2000-01**

Ranking basis/background: Based on *U.S News* questionnaire sent to 1,400 four-year institutions. Scores are averaged and weighted percentages from seven attributes: academic reputation, retention, faculty resources, student selectivity, financial resources, graduation rate performance and alumni giving. **Remarks:** Comparable data was used from the U.S. Department of Education, the Council for Aid to Education, the NCAA, and Wintergreen/Orchard House publishers. **Number listed:** 17.

1. Albertson College, with an overall score of 100.0
2. George Fox University, 95.0
3. Oklahoma Baptist University, 88.0
4. Evergreen State College, 86.0
5. Carroll College, 85.0
6. Texas Lutheran University, 84.0
7. Northwest Nazarene University, 83.0
7. Pacific Union College, 83.0
9. LeTourneau University, 82.0
10. Oklahoma Christian University, 79.0
11. Brigham Young University (HI), 77.0
11. College of Sante Fe, 77.0
11. Concordia University, 77.0
14. Master's College and Seminary, 76.0
14. Texas A&M University, Galveston, 76.0
16. McMurry University, 74.0
16. Schreiner College, 74.0

Source: "America's Best Colleges," *U.S. News & World Report*, 129: 90-132, (September 11, 2000).

★1397★
***U.S. News & World Report*'s western regional liberal arts colleges with students least in debt, 1999**

Ranking basis/background: Based on total amount borrowed by 1999 graduates from one or more of the following sources: federal, state and local governments, financial institutions, and the colleges themselves. **Remarks:** Debt does not reflect monies borrowed by parents or others on behalf of the student. **Number listed:** 6.

1. Oklahoma Panhandle State University, with an average debt of $4,000
2. Pacific Union College, $7,256
3. Brigham Young University, $7,536
4. University of Hawaii, Hilo, $8,500
5. Christian Heritage College, $10,000
5. Concordia University, $10,000

Source: "How Heavy is the Load?," *U.S. News & World Report*, 129: 101-102, (September 18, 2000).

★1398★
***U.S. News & World Report*'s western regional liberal arts colleges with students most in debt, 1999**

Ranking basis/background: Based on total amount borrowed by 1999 graduates from one or more of the following sources: federal, state and local governments, financial institutions, and the colleges themselves. **Remarks:** Debt does not reflect monies borrowed by parents or others on behalf of the student. **Number listed:** 5.

1. Carroll College, with an average debt of $21,364
2. University of Great Falls, $21,303
3. Rocky Mountain College, $19,328
4. Texas Lutheran University, $18,750
5. Northwest Christian College, $18,687

Source: "How Heavy is the Load?," *U.S. News & World Report*, 129: 101-102, (September 18, 2000).

COLLEGES & UNIVERSITIES–MIDDLE WESTERN STATES

★1399★
U.S. News & World Report's midwestern regional universities with students least in debt, 1999

Ranking basis/background: Based on total amount borrowed by 1999 graduates from one or more of the following sources: federal, state and local governments, financial institutions, and the colleges themselves. **Remarks:** Debt does not reflect monies borrowed by parents or others on behalf of the student. **Number listed:** 5.
1. University of St. Francis, with an average debt of $3,216
2. University of Wisconsin, Parkside, $7,725
3. University of Wisconsin, Platteville, $8,500
4. Saginaw Valley State University, $9,580
5. Minot State University, $9,665

Source: "How Heavy is the Load?," *U.S. News & World Report*, 129: 101-102, (September 18, 2000).

★1400★
U.S. News & World Report's midwestern regional universities with students most in debt, 1999

Ranking basis/background: Based on total amount borrowed by 1999 graduates from one or more of the following sources: federal, state and local governments, financial institutions, and the colleges themselves. **Remarks:** Debt does not reflect monies borrowed by parents or others on behalf of the student. **Number listed:** 5.
1. Chicago State University, with an average debt of $23,000
2. Creighton University, $20,255
3. College of St. Scholastica, $20,224
4. Franciscan University of Steubenville, $19,692
5. Baldwin-Wallace College, $19,678

Source: "How Heavy is the Load?," *U.S. News & World Report*, 129: 101-102, (September 18, 2000).

★1401★
U.S. News & World Report's midwestern regional universities with the best academic reputation scores, 2000-01

Ranking basis/background: Based on *U.S News* questionnaire sent to 1,400 four-year institutions. Scores are averaged and weighted percentages from seven attributes: academic reputation, retention, faculty resources, student selectivity, financial resources, graduation rate performance and alumni giving. **Remarks:** Comparable data was used from the U.S. Department of Education, the Council for Aid to Education, the NCAA, and Wintergreen/Orchard House publishers. **Number listed:** 34.
1. Creighton University, with a score of 4.1
2. Drake University, 4.0
3. Valparaiso University, 3.9
4. Bradley University, 3.8
4. John Carroll University, 3.8
4. University of Dayton, 3.8
4. Xavier University, 3.8
8. Butler University, 3.7
8. University of St. Thomas, 3.7
8. Truman State University, 3.7

Source: "America's Best Colleges," *U.S. News & World Report*, 129: 90-132, (September 11, 2000).

★1402★
U.S. News & World Report's midwestern regional universities with the best alumni giving rates, 2000-01

Ranking basis/background: Based on *U.S News* questionnaire sent to 1,400 four-year institutions. Scores are averaged and weighted percentages from seven attributes: academic reputation, retention, faculty resources, student selectivity, financial resources, graduation rate performance and alumni giving. **Remarks:** Comparable data was used from the U.S. Department of Education, the Council for Aid to Education, the NCAA, and Wintergreen/Orchard House publishers. **Number listed:** 34.
1. North Central College, with 40%
2. Calvin College, 35%
3. John Carroll University, 34%
4. Drury University, 33%
4. College of Mount St. Joseph, 33%
6. Rockford College, 32%
7. Bradley University, 31%
8. Carthage College, 30%
9. Valparaiso University, 27%
9. Xavier University, 27%

Source: "America's Best Colleges," *U.S. News & World Report*, 129: 90-132, (September 11, 2000).

★1403★
U.S. News & World Report's midwestern regional universities with the best student/faculty ratios, 2000-01

Ranking basis/background: Based on *U.S News* questionnaire sent to 1,400 four-year institutions. Scores are averaged and weighted percentages from seven attributes: academic reputation, retention, faculty resources, student selectivity, financial resources, graduation rate performance and alumni giving. **Remarks:** Comparable data was used from the U.S. Department of Education, the Council for Aid to Education, the NCAA, and Wintergreen/Orchard House publishers. **Number listed:** 34.
1. College of St. Catherine, with a student/faculty ratio of 8/1
2. Rockhurst University, 9/1
3. Rockford College, 10/1
4. University of St. Francis, 11/1
5. Baker University, 12/1
5. Drury University, 12/1
7. Valparaiso University, 13/1
7. Drake University, 13/1
7. John Carroll University, 13/1
7. University of Evansville, 13/1
7. Baldwin-Wallace College, 13/1
7. North Central College, 13/1
7. College of St. Scholastica, 13/1
7. Dominican University, 13/1

Source: "America's Best Colleges," *U.S. News & World Report*, 129: 90-132, (September 11, 2000).

★1404★
U.S. News & World Report's midwestern regional universities with the highest acceptance rates, 2000-01

Ranking basis/background: Based on *U.S News* questionnaire sent to 1,400 four-year institutions. Scores are averaged and weighted percentages from seven attributes: academic reputation, retention, faculty resources, student selectivity, financial resources, graduation rate performance and alumni giving. **Remarks:** Comparable data was used from the U.S. Department of Education, the Council for Aid to Education, the NCAA, and Wintergreen/Orchard House publishers. **Number listed:** 34.
1. Calvin College, with 99%
2. College of St. Scholastica, 93%
3. Creighton University, 91%
3. University of Evansville, 91%
3. Drury University, 91%
3. South Dakota State University, 91%
3. Carthage College, 91%
8. Rockhurst University, 90%
8. Drake University, 90%
10. Xavier University, 89%

Source: "America's Best Colleges," *U.S. News & World Report*, 129: 90-132, (September 11, 2000).

★1405★
U.S. News & World Report's midwestern regional universities with the highest freshmen retention rates, 2000-01

Ranking basis/background: Based on *U.S News* questionnaire sent to 1,400 four-year institutions. Scores are averaged and weighted percentages from seven attributes: academic reputation, retention, faculty resources, student selectivity, financial resources, graduation rate performance and alumni giving. **Remarks:** Comparable data was used from the U.S. Department of Education, the Council for Aid to Education, the NCAA, and Wintergreen/Orchard House publishers. **Number listed:** 34.
1. Xavier University, with 88%
1. John Carroll University, 88%
3. College of Mount St. Joseph, 87%
3. University of Dayton, 87%
3. Valparaiso University, 87%
6. Creighton University, 85%
6. Truman State University, 85%
6. University of St. Thomas, 85%
6. Calvin College, 85%
10. Baldwin-Wallace College, 84%

Source: "America's Best Colleges," *U.S. News & World Report*, 129: 90-132, (September 11, 2000).

★1406★
U.S. News & World Report's midwestern regional universities with the highest graduation rates, 2000-01

Ranking basis/background: Based on *U.S News* questionnaire sent to 1,400 four-year institutions. Scores are averaged and weighted percentages from seven attributes: academic reputation, retention, faculty resources, student selectivity, financial resources, graduation rate performance and alumni giving. **Remarks:** Comparable data was used from the U.S. Department of Education, the Council for Aid to Education, the NCAA, and Wintergreen/Orchard House publishers. **Number listed:** 34.
1. John Carroll University, with 74%
2. University of Dayton, 72%
3. Valparaiso University, 70%
4. Creighton University, 69%
5. Xavier University, 68%
6. Calvin College, 67%
7. Bradley University, 66%
7. University of St. Thomas, 66%
9. Drake University, 65%
9. College of Mount St. Joseph, 65%

Source: "America's Best Colleges," *U.S. News & World Report*, 129: 90-132, (September 11, 2000).

COLLEGES & UNIVERSITIES—NORTHERN STATES

★1407★
U.S. News & World Report's midwestern regional universities with the highest percentage of freshmen from the top 25% of their high school class, 2000-01

Ranking basis/background: Based on *U.S News* questionnaire sent to 1,400 four-year institutions. Scores are averaged and weighted percentages from seven attributes: academic reputation, retention, faculty resources, student selectivity, financial resources, graduation rate performance and alumni giving. **Remarks:** Comparable data was used from the U.S. Department of Education, the Council for Aid to Education, the NCAA, and Wintergreen/Orchard House publishers. **Number listed:** 34.

1. Truman State University, with 81%
2. Valparaiso University, 75%
3. Creighton University, 70%
4. Butler University, 69%
5. University of Evansville, 68%
6. Baldwin-Wallace College, 64%
7. Bradley University, 63%
8. Drake University, 62%
8. College of St. Scholastica, 62%
8. University of St. Thomas, 62%

Source: "America's Best Colleges," *U.S. News & World Report*, 129: 90-132, (September 11, 2000).

★1408★
U.S. News & World Report's midwestern regional universities with the highest percentage of full-time faculty, 2000-01

Ranking basis/background: Based on *U.S News* questionnaire sent to 1,400 four-year institutions. Scores are averaged and weighted percentages from seven attributes: academic reputation, retention, faculty resources, student selectivity, financial resources, graduation rate performance and alumni giving. **Remarks:** Comparable data was used from the U.S. Department of Education, the Council for Aid to Education, the NCAA, and Wintergreen/Orchard House publishers. **Number listed:** 34.

1. Rockford College, with 100%
2. South Dakota State University, 99%
3. University of Evansville, 98%
3. College of St. Scholastica, 98%
5. Truman State University, 97%
6. University of Wisconsin, Eau Claire, 94%
6. University of Wisconsin, Stevens Point, 94%
8. Calvin College, 93%
9. Valparaiso University, 91%
10. University of Northern Iowa, 90%

Source: "America's Best Colleges," *U.S. News & World Report*, 129: 90-132, (September 11, 2000).

★1409★
U.S. News & World Report's midwestern regional universities with the highest proportion of classes having 20 students or less, 2000-01

Ranking basis/background: Based on *U.S News* questionnaire sent to 1,400 four-year institutions. Scores are averaged and weighted percentages from seven attributes: academic reputation, retention, faculty resources, student selectivity, financial resources, graduation rate performance and alumni giving. **Remarks:** Comparable data was used from the U.S. Department of Education, the Council for Aid to Education, the NCAA, and Wintergreen/Orchard House publishers. **Number listed:** 34.

1. Webster University, with 84%
2. Dominican University, 79%
3. College of Mount St. Joseph, 74%
4. College of St. Catherine, 73%
5. Benedictine University, 69%
5. Carthage College, 69%
7. Concordia University, River Forest (IL), 68%
8. College of St. Scholastica, 64%
9. Drake University, 61%
9. North Central College, 61%

Source: "America's Best Colleges," *U.S. News & World Report*, 129: 90-132, (September 11, 2000).

★1410★
U.S. News & World Report's midwestern regional universities with the lowest acceptance rates, 2000-01

Ranking basis/background: Based on *U.S News* questionnaire sent to 1,400 four-year institutions. Scores are averaged and weighted percentages from seven attributes: academic reputation, retention, faculty resources, student selectivity, financial resources, graduation rate performance and alumni giving. **Remarks:** Comparable data was used from the U.S. Department of Education, the Council for Aid to Education, the NCAA, and Wintergreen/Orchard House publishers. **Number listed:** 34.

1. University of Wisconsin, Stevens Point, with 60%
2. Webster University, 62%
3. University of St. Francis, 69%
4. University of Wisconsin, La Crosse, 71%
5. Concordia University, River Forest (IL), 72%
6. University of Wisconsin, Eau Claire, 74%
7. North Central College, 76%
7. Benedictine University, 76%
7. St. Xavier University, 76%
7. Rockford College, 76%

Source: "America's Best Colleges," *U.S. News & World Report*, 129: 90-132, (September 11, 2000).

★1411★
U.S. News & World Report's top midwestern regional universities, 2000-01

Ranking basis/background: Based on *U.S News* questionnaire sent to 1,400 four-year institutions. Scores are averaged and weighted percentages from seven attributes: academic reputation, retention, faculty resources, student selectivity, financial resources, graduation rate performance and alumni giving. **Remarks:** Comparable data was used from the U.S. Department of Education, the Council for Aid to Education, the NCAA, and Wintergreen/Orchard House publishers. **Number listed:** 34.

1. Creighton University, with an overall score of 100.0
2. Valparaiso University, 97.0
3. Drake University, 95.0
4. Bradley University, 94.0
4. John Carroll University, 94.0
4. University of Dayton, 94.0
7. Xavier University, 93.0
8. Butler University, 90.0
9. University of St. Thomas, 89.0
10. Calvin College, 88.0

Source: "America's Best Colleges," *U.S. News & World Report*, 129: 90-132, (September 11, 2000).

★1412★
U.S. News & World Report's top public midwestern regional universities, 2000-01

Ranking basis/background: Based on *U.S News* questionnaire sent to 1,400 four-year institutions. Scores are averaged and weighted percentages from seven attributes: academic reputation, retention, faculty resources, student selectivity, financial resources, graduation rate performance and alumni giving. **Remarks:** Comparable data was used from the U.S. Department of Education, the Council for Aid to Education, the NCAA, and Wintergreen/Orchard House publishers. **Number listed:** 12.

1. Truman State University
2. University of Northern Iowa
3. University of Wisconsin, Eau Claire
4. South Dakota State University
4. University of Wisconsin, La Crosse
6. University of Wisconsin, Stevens Point
7. Eastern Illinois University
7. University of Wisconsin, Whitewater
7. Washburn University
10. Central Michigan University
10. University of Michigan, Dearborn
12. University of Minnesota, Duluth

Source: "America's Best Colleges," *U.S. News & World Report*, 129: 90-132, (September 11, 2000).

COLLEGES & UNIVERSITIES–NORTHERN STATES

★1413★
U.S. News & World Report's northern regional universities with students least in debt, 1999

Ranking basis/background: Based on total amount borrowed by 1999 graduates from one or more of the following sources: federal, state and local governments, financial institutions, and the colleges themselves. **Remarks:** Debt does not reflect monies borrowed by parents or others on behalf of the student. **Number listed:** 5.

1. Canisius College, with an average debt of $4,269
2. Bridgewater State College, $6,746
3. City University of New York, Bernard M. Baruch College, $6,920
4. St. Joseph College (CT), $7,541
5. Anna Maria College, $9,500

Source: "How Heavy is the Load?," *U.S. News & World Report*, 129: 101-102, (September 18, 2000).

★1414★
U.S. News & World Report's northern regional universities with students most in debt, 1999

Ranking basis/background: Based on total amount borrowed by 1999 graduates from one or more of the following sources: federal, state and local governments, financial institutions, and the colleges themselves. **Remarks:** Debt does not reflect monies borrowed by parents or others on behalf of the student. **Number listed:** 5.

1. Trinity College, with an average debt of $27,643
2. Montclair State University, $21,459
3. American International College, $20,800
4. Suffolk University, $20,384
5. Elmira College, $20,143

Source: "How Heavy is the Load?," *U.S. News & World Report*, 129: 101-102, (September 18, 2000).

★1415★
U.S. News & World Report's northern regional universities with the best academic reputation scores, 2000-01

Ranking basis/background: Based on *U.S News* questionnaire sent to 1,400 four-year institutions. Scores are averaged and weighted percentages from seven attributes: academic reputation, retention, faculty resources, student selectivity, financial resources, graduation rate performance and alumni giving. **Remarks:** Comparable data was used from the U.S. Department of Education, the Council for Aid to Education, the NCAA, and Wintergreen/Orchard House publishers. **Number listed:** 38.
1. Villanova University, with a score of 4.1
1. Rochester Institute of Technology, 4.1
3. Providence College, 3.6
3. State University of New York, College of Arts & Sciences, Geneseo, 3.6
5. Loyola College, 3.5
5. College of New Jersey, 3.5
5. Gallaudet University, 3.5
5. Ithaca College, 3.5
9. Fairfield University, 3.4
9. St. Joseph's University (PA), 3.4

Source: "America's Best Colleges," *U.S. News & World Report*, 129: 90-132, (September 11, 2000).

★1416★
U.S. News & World Report's northern regional universities with the best student/faculty ratios, 2000-01

Ranking basis/background: Based on *U.S News* questionnaire sent to 1,400 four-year institutions. Scores are averaged and weighted percentages from seven attributes: academic reputation, retention, faculty resources, student selectivity, financial resources, graduation rate performance and alumni giving. **Remarks:** Comparable data was used from the U.S. Department of Education, the Council for Aid to Education, the NCAA, and Wintergreen/Orchard House publishers. **Number listed:** 38.
1. Gallaudet University, with a student/faculty ratio of 7/1
2. St. Joseph College (CT), 10/1
2. Simmons College, 10/1
2. Hood College, 10/1
5. Ithaca College, 11/1
6. Widener University, 12/1
6. Elmira College, 12/1
6. Springfield College, 12/1
6. Nazareth College of Rochester, 12/1
6. Beaver College, 12/1
6. Alfred University, 12/1

Source: "America's Best Colleges," *U.S. News & World Report*, 129: 90-132, (September 11, 2000).

★1417★
U.S. News & World Report's northern regional universities with the highest acceptance rates, 2000-01

Ranking basis/background: Based on *U.S News* questionnaire sent to 1,400 four-year institutions. Scores are averaged and weighted percentages from seven attributes: academic reputation, retention, faculty resources, student selectivity, financial resources, graduation rate performance and alumni giving. **Remarks:** Comparable data was used from the U.S. Department of Education, the Council for Aid to Education, the NCAA, and Wintergreen/Orchard House publishers. **Number listed:** 38.
1. St. Bonaventure University, with 91%
2. Widener University, 89%
3. St. Joseph College (CT), 87%
4. Mount St. Mary's College and Seminary, 84%
5. Canisius College, 81%
5. Emerson College, 81%
5. Alfred University, 81%
8. Rider University, 80%
8. La Salle University, 80%
10. Hood College, 77%
10. Rochester Institute of Technology, 77%

Source: "America's Best Colleges," *U.S. News & World Report*, 129: 90-132, (September 11, 2000).

★1418★
U.S. News & World Report's northern regional universities with the highest alumni giving rates, 2000-01

Ranking basis/background: Based on *U.S News* questionnaire sent to 1,400 four-year institutions. Scores are averaged and weighted percentages from seven attributes: academic reputation, retention, faculty resources, student selectivity, financial resources, graduation rate performance and alumni giving. **Remarks:** Comparable data was used from the U.S. Department of Education, the Council for Aid to Education, the NCAA, and Wintergreen/Orchard House publishers. **Number listed:** 38.
1. Elmira College, with 50%
2. St. Joseph College (CT), 38%
2. Quinnipiac University, 38%
4. University of Scranton, 34%
4. St. Bonaventure University, 34%
6. Loyola College, 33%
7. Providence College, 32%
8. Springfield College, 28%
9. Fairfield University, 27%
10. Shippensburg University of Pennsylvania, 26%

Source: "America's Best Colleges," *U.S. News & World Report*, 129: 90-132, (September 11, 2000).

★1419★
U.S. News & World Report's northern regional universities with the highest average graduation rates, 2000-01

Ranking basis/background: Based on *U.S News* questionnaire sent to 1,400 four-year institutions. Scores are averaged and weighted percentages from seven attributes: academic reputation, retention, faculty resources, student selectivity, financial resources, graduation rate performance and alumni giving. **Remarks:** Comparable data was used from the U.S. Department of Education, the Council for Aid to Education, the NCAA, and Wintergreen/Orchard House publishers. **Number listed:** 38.
1. Villanova University, with 84%
2. Providence College, 82%
2. Fairfield University, 82%
4. University of Scranton, 81%
5. Loyola College, 78%
5. State University of New York, College of Arts & Sciences, Geneseo, 78%
7. College of New Jersey, 77%
7. Quinnipiac University, 77%
9. La Salle University, 72%
10. Ithaca College, 71%
10. Manhattan College, 71%
10. Wagner College, 71%
10. Assumption College, 71%
10. St. Joseph's University (PA), 71%

Source: "America's Best Colleges," *U.S. News & World Report*, 129: 90-132, (September 11, 2000).

★1420★
U.S. News & World Report's northern regional universities with the highest freshmen retention rates, 2000-01

Ranking basis/background: Based on *U.S News* questionnaire sent to 1,400 four-year institutions. Scores are averaged and weighted percentages from seven attributes: academic reputation, retention, faculty resources, student selectivity, financial resources, graduation rate performance and alumni giving. **Remarks:** Comparable data was used from the U.S. Department of Education, the Council for Aid to Education, the NCAA, and Wintergreen/Orchard House publishers. **Number listed:** 38.
1. Villanova University, with 93%
1. College of New Jersey, 93%
3. Providence College, 92%
3. Loyola College, 92%
5. State University of New York, College of Arts & Sciences, Geneseo, 91%
6. University of Scranton, 90%
6. Marist College, 90%
8. St. Joseph's University (PA), 89%
9. Fairfield University, 88%
10. Quinnipiac University, 87%

Source: "America's Best Colleges," *U.S. News & World Report*, 129: 90-132, (September 11, 2000).

★1421★
U.S. News & World Report's northern regional universities with the highest percentage of freshmen in the top 25% of their high school class, 2000-01

Ranking basis/background: Based on *U.S News* questionnaire sent to 1,400 four-year institutions. Scores are averaged and weighted percentages from seven attributes: academic reputation, retention, faculty resources, student selectivity, financial resources, graduation rate performance and alumni giving. **Remarks:** Comparable data was used from the U.S. Department of Education, the Council for Aid to Education, the NCAA, and Wintergreen/Orchard House publishers. **Number listed:** 38.
1. State University of New York, College of Arts & Sciences, Geneseo, with 92%
1. College of New Jersey, 92%
3. St. Joseph's University (PA), 89%
4. Providence College, 77%
5. Villanova University, 75%
6. Hood College, 71%
7. Nazareth College of Rochester, 69%
8. Loyola College, 68%
9. Fairfield University, 65%
10. University of Scranton, 62%

Source: "America's Best Colleges," *U.S. News & World Report*, 129: 90-132, (September 11, 2000).

★1422★
U.S. News & World Report's northern regional universities with the highest percentage of full-time faculty, 2000-01

Ranking basis/background: Based on *U.S News* questionnaire sent to 1,400 four-year institutions. Scores are averaged and weighted percentages from seven attributes: academic reputation, retention, faculty resources, student selectivity, financial resources, graduation rate performance and alumni giving. **Remarks:** Comparable data was used from the U.S. Department of Education, the Council for Aid to Education, the NCAA, and Wintergreen/Orchard House publishers. **Number listed:** 38.
1. Gallaudet University, with 100%
2. Notre Dame College, 96%
2. St. Joseph College, 96%

4. Shippensburg University of Pennsylvania, 95%
5. Alfred University, 93%
6. Providence College, 92%
6. Hood College, 92%
8. Ithaca College, 91%
9. University of Massachusetts, Dartmouth, 90%
9. Elmira College, 90%

Source: "America's Best Colleges," *U.S. News & World Report*, 129: 90-132, (September 11, 2000).

★1423★
U.S. News & World Report's northern regional universities with the highest proportion of classes with 20 students of less, 2000-01

Ranking basis/background: Based on *U.S News* questionnaire sent to 1,400 four-year institutions. Scores are averaged and weighted percentages from seven attributes: academic reputation, retention, faculty resources, student selectivity, financial resources, graduation rate performance and alumni giving. **Remarks:** Comparable data was used from the U.S. Department of Education, the Council for Aid to Education, the NCAA, and Wintergreen/Orchard House publishers. **Number listed:** 38.

1. Elmira College, with 82%
2. Notre Dame College, 76%
3. St. Joseph College (CT), 72%
4. Hood College, 71%
5. Simmons College, 69%
5. Beaver College, 69%
7. Ithaca College, 68%
8. Alfred University, 67%
9. Wagner College, 66%
10. Widener University, 61%

Source: "America's Best Colleges," *U.S. News & World Report*, 129: 90-132, (September 11, 2000).

★1424★
U.S. News & World Report's northern regional universities with the lowest acceptance rates, 2000-01

Ranking basis/background: Based on *U.S News* questionnaire sent to 1,400 four-year institutions. Scores are averaged and weighted percentages from seven attributes: academic reputation, retention, faculty resources, student selectivity, financial resources, graduation rate performance and alumni giving. **Remarks:** Comparable data was used from the U.S. Department of Education, the Council for Aid to Education, the NCAA, and Wintergreen/Orchard House publishers. **Number listed:** 38.

1. State University of New York, College of Arts & Sciences, Geneseo, with 52%
2. Rowan University, 54%
3. College of New Jersey, 55%
4. Marist College, 56%
5. Villanova University, 57%
6. Providence College, 60%
7. Fairfield University, 61%
7. St. Joseph's University (PA), 61%
9. Rutgers University, Camden, 62%
10. Beaver College, 63%

Source: "America's Best Colleges," *U.S. News & World Report*, 129: 90-132, (September 11, 2000).

★1425★
U.S. News & World Report's top northern regional universities, 2000-01

Ranking basis/background: Based on *U.S News* questionnaire sent to 1,400 four-year institutions. Scores are averaged and weighted percentages from seven attributes: academic reputation, retention, faculty resources, student selectivity, financial resources, graduation rate performance and alumni giving. **Remarks:** Comparable data was used from the U.S. Department of Education, the Council for Aid to Education, the NCAA, and Wintergreen/Orchard House publishers. **Number listed:** 38.

1. Villanova University, with an overall score of 100.0
2. Providence College, 91.0
3. Fairfield University, 89.0
4. Rochester Institute of Technology, 88.0
5. Loyola College, 87.0
6. College of New Jersey, 85.0
7. University of Scranton, 84.0
8. Ithaca College, 83.0
9. State University of New York, College of Arts & Sciences, Geneseo, 81.0
10. St. Joseph's University (PA), 80.0

Source: "America's Best Colleges," *U.S. News & World Report*, 129: 90-132, (September 11, 2000).

★1426★
U.S. News & World Report's top public northern regional universities, 2000-01

Ranking basis/background: Based on *U.S News* questionnaire sent to 1,400 four-year institutions. Scores are averaged and weighted percentages from seven attributes: academic reputation, retention, faculty resources, student selectivity, financial resources, graduation rate performance and alumni giving. **Remarks:** Comparable data was used from the U.S. Department of Education, the Council for Aid to Education, the NCAA, and Wintergreen/Orchard House publishers. **Number listed:** 12.

1. College of New Jersey
2. State University of New York, College of Arts & Sciences, Geneseo
3. Rutgers University, Camden
3. Millersville University of Pennsylvania
5. Rowan University
5. Shippensburg University of Pennsylvania
5. University of Massachusetts, Dartmouth
8. Montclair State University
8. Salisbury State University
10. Bloomsburg University of Pennsylvania
10. City University of New York, Queens College
10. Towson State University

Source: "America's Best Colleges," *U.S. News & World Report*, 129: 90-132, (September 11, 2000).

COLLEGES & UNIVERSITIES–RESEARCH
See: **Research & Development Funding Research Funding**

COLLEGES & UNIVERSITIES–REVENUE
See: **Colleges & Universities–Financial Support & Expenditures**

COLLEGES & UNIVERSITIES–SELECTION
See: **College Choice Evaluation Criteria & Methodologies**

COLLEGES & UNIVERSITIES, SMALL–STUDENT COSTS

★1427★
U.S. News & World Report's best undergraduate fees among midwestern regional universities by discount tuition, 2000

Ranking basis/background: Based on a percentage averaged from 3 variables; ratio of quality to price, percentage of all undergraduates receiving grants meeting financial need during the 1999-2000 academic year, and average discount: percentage of a school's total costs. **Number listed:** 16.

1. Drury University, with a 43% average discount from total cost; and an average cost of $8,997 after receiving grants based on need
2. South Dakota State University, 27%; $7,997
3. Bradley University, 34%; $13,836
3. Valparaiso University, 38%; $14,159
5. Calvin College, 35%; $12,910
6. College of Mount St. Joseph, 40%; $11,825
7. Drake University, 38%; $14,892
8. University of Evansville, 39%; $13,888
9. University of Dayton, 32%; $14,978
10. Butler University, 39%; $14,470
11. North Central College, 38%; $13,786
12. College of St. Scholastica, 34%; $14,246
12. St. Xavier University (IL), 38%; $13,342
14. University of St. Thomas, 32%; $15,581
15. Creighton University, 26%; $16,486
15. John Carroll University, 28%; $16,853

Source: "Great Schools at Great Prices," *U.S. News & World Report*, 129: 96, 100, (September 18, 2000).

★1428★
U.S. News & World Report's best undergraduate fees among northern regional universities by discount tuition, 2000

Ranking basis/background: Based on a percentage averaged from 3 variables; ratio of quality to price, percentage of all undergraduates receiving grants meeting financial need during the 1999-2000 academic year, and average discount: percentage of a school's total costs. **Number listed:** 15.

1. Alfred University, with a 58% average discount from total cost; and an average cost of $12,214 after receiving grants based on need
2. Hood College, 52%; $12,513
3. Rochester Institute of Technology, 36%; $16,517
4. Nazareth College of Rochester, 35%; $14,001
5. Canisius College, 41%; $13,774
6. Ithaca College, 38%; $17,480
7. College of New Jersey, 13%; $15,184
7. St. Bonaventure University, 32%; $14,701

9. St. Michael's College, 36%; $16,816
10. Simmons College, 40%; $17.974
11. St. Joseph College (CT), 36%; $15,796
12. Loyola College (MD), 35%; $17,990
13. Mount St. Mary's College and Seminary, 36%; $16,025
13. University of Scranton, 31%; $18,976
15. Elmira College, 43%; $16,804

Source: "Great Schools at Great Prices," *U.S. News & World Report*, 129: 96, 100, (September 18, 2000).

★1429★
U.S. News & World Report's best undergraduate fees among southern regional universities by discount tuition, 2000

Ranking basis/background: Based on a percentage averaged from 3 variables; ratio of quality to price, percentage of all undergraduates receiving grants meeting financial need during the 1999-2000 academic year, and average discount: percentage of a school's total costs. **Number listed:** 15.

1. Centenary College of Louisiana, with a 43% average discount from total cost; and an average cost of $10,762 after receiving grants based on need
2. University of Richmond, 39%; $15,478
3. Converse College, 46%; $11,836
4. Rollins College, 56%; $13,822
5. Stetson University, 45%; $14,165
6. Murray State University, 19%; $9,600
7. Samford University, 26%; $13,271
8. Queens College, 38%; $11,279
9. Spring Hill College, 43%; $13,367
10. Harding University, 23%; $11,334
11. East Carolina University, 21%; $9,439
12. Loyola University, New Orleans, 34%; $15,207
13. Mercer University, 34%; $15,448
14. James Madison University, 12%; $14,788
15. Appalachian State University, 14%; $13,010

Source: "Great Schools at Great Prices," *U.S. News & World Report*, 129: 96, 100, (September 18, 2000).

★1430★
U.S. News & World Report's best undergraduate fees among western regional universities by discount tuition, 2000

Ranking basis/background: Based on a percentage averaged from 3 variables; ratio of quality to price, percentage of all undergraduates receiving grants meeting financial need during the 1999-2000 academic year, and average discount: percentage of a school's total costs. **Number listed:** 16.

1. Trinity University, with a 45% average discount from total cost; and an average cost of $13,075 after receiving grants based on need
2. Loyola Marymount University, 47%; $14,581
3. St. Mary's College (CA), 51%; $13,590
4. Pacific University (OR), 41%; $13,877
5. St. Mary's University (TX), 28%; $14,210
6. University of Portland, 37%; $15,323
7. Linfield College, 34%; $16,336
7. Santa Clara University, 39%; $17,678
9. Gonzaga University, 32%; $17,224
10. Whitworth College, 34%; $16,712
11. Westminster College, 29%; $14,501

12. Oklahoma City University, 17%; $11,680
13. Pacific Lutheran University, 29%; $16,912
13. University of Redlands, 35%; $18,860
15. Abilene Christian University, 19%; $13,990
15. Chapman University, 40%; $18,322

Source: "Great Schools at Great Prices," *U.S. News & World Report*, 129: 96, 100, (September 18, 2000).

COLLEGES & UNIVERSITIES–SOUTHERN STATES

★1431★
U.S. News & World Report's southern regional universities with students least in debt, 1999

Ranking basis/background: Based on total amount borrowed by 1999 graduates from one or more of the following sources: federal, state and local governments, financial institutions, and the colleges themselves. **Remarks:** Debt does not reflect monies borrowed by parents or others on behalf of the student. **Number listed:** 5.

1. Lenoir-Rhyne College, with an average debt of $4,006
2. Gardner-Webb University, $6,770
3. University of North Carolina, Pembroke, $6,849
4. Northwestern State University of Louisiana, $7,426
5. University of South Alabama, $9,000

Source: "How Heavy is the Load?," *U.S. News & World Report*, 129: 101-102, (September 18, 2000).

★1432★
U.S. News & World Report's southern regional universities with students most in debt, 1999

Ranking basis/background: Based on total amount borrowed by 1999 graduates from one or more of the following sources: federal, state and local governments, financial institutions, and the colleges themselves. **Remarks:** Debt does not reflect monies borrowed by parents or others on behalf of the student. **Number listed:** 5.

1. Georgia Southwestern State University, with an average debt of $28,125
2. Alabama State University, $27,500
3. Hampton University, $23,000
4. Harding University, $22,420
5. Northern Kentucky University, $20,530

Source: "How Heavy is the Load?," *U.S. News & World Report*, 129: 101-102, (September 18, 2000).

★1433★
U.S. News & World Report's southern regional universities with the best academic reputation scores, 2000-01

Ranking basis/background: Based on *U.S News* questionnaire sent to 1,400 four-year institutions. Scores are averaged and weighted percentages from seven attributes: academic reputation, retention, faculty resources, student selectivity, financial resources, graduation rate performance and alumni giving. **Remarks:** Comparable data was used from the U.S. Department of Education, the Council for Aid to Education, the NCAA, and Wintergreen/Orchard House publishers. **Number listed:** 31.

1. University of Richmond, with a score of 4.3
2. James Madison University, 4.0
3. Rollins College, 3.7
3. Stetson University, 3.7
3. Samford University, 3.7
3. Mercer University, 3.7
3. Mary Washington College, 3.7
8. The Citadel, 3.6
8. Loyola University, New Orleans, 3.6
8. Appalachian State University, 3.6
8. College of Charleston, 3.6
8. University of North Carolina, Charlotte, 3.6

Source: "America's Best Colleges," *U.S. News & World Report*, 129: 90-132, (September 11, 2000).

★1434★
U.S. News & World Report's southern regional universities with the best alumni giving rates, 2000-01

Ranking basis/background: Based on *U.S News* questionnaire sent to 1,400 four-year institutions. Scores are averaged and weighted percentages from seven attributes: academic reputation, retention, faculty resources, student selectivity, financial resources, graduation rate performance and alumni giving. **Remarks:** Comparable data was used from the U.S. Department of Education, the Council for Aid to Education, the NCAA, and Wintergreen/Orchard House publishers. **Number listed:** 31.

1. University of Richmond, with 36%
2. The Citadel, 35%
2. College of Charleston, 35%
4. Spring Hill College, 32%
5. Mary Washington College, 30%
5. Bellarmine College, 30%
7. Harding University, 29%
7. Wheeling Jesuit University, 29%
9. Meredith College, 28%
10. Centenary College of Louisiana, 27%
10. Stetson University, 27%

Source: "America's Best Colleges," *U.S. News & World Report*, 129: 90-132, (September 11, 2000).

★1435★
U.S. News & World Report's southern regional universities with the best student/faculty ratios, 2000-01

Ranking basis/background: Based on *U.S News* questionnaire sent to 1,400 four-year institutions. Scores are averaged and weighted percentages from seven attributes: academic reputation, retention, faculty resources, student selectivity, financial resources, graduation rate performance and alumni giving. **Remarks:** Comparable data was used from the U.S. Department of Education, the Council for Aid to Education, the NCAA, and Wintergreen/Orchard House publishers. **Number listed:** 31.

1. Converse College, with a student/faculty ratios of 9/1
2. Belmont University, 10/1
2. Stetson University, 10/1
4. University of Richmond, 11/1
5. Rollins College, 12/1
5. Loyola University, New Orleans, 12/1
5. Queens College, 12/1
5. Wheeling Jesuit University, 12/1
5. Centenary College of Louisiana, 12/1
10. Christian Brothers University, 13/1

Source: "America's Best Colleges," *U.S. News & World Report*, 129: 90-132, (September 11, 2000).

★1436★
U.S. News & World Report's southern regional universities with the highest acceptance rates, 2000-01

Ranking basis/background: Based on *U.S News* questionnaire sent to 1,400 four-year institutions. Scores are averaged and weighted percentages from seven attributes: academic reputation, retention, faculty resources, student selectivity, financial resources, graduation rate performance and alumni giving. **Remarks:** Comparable data was used from the U.S. Department of Education, the Council for Aid to Education, the NCAA, and Wintergreen/Orchard House publishers. **Number listed:** 31.

1. Bellarmine College, with 95%
2. Mississippi College, 93%
3. Wheeling Jesuit University, 89%
3. Spring Hill College, 89%
5. Samford University, 88%
6. Loyola University, New Orleans, 86%
7. Meredith College, 85%
7. Xavier University (LA), 85%
9. Centenary College of Louisiana, 83%
10. Harding University, 82%

Source: "America's Best Colleges," *U.S. News & World Report*, 129: 90-132, (September 11, 2000).

★1437★
U.S. News & World Report's southern regional universities with the highest freshmen retention rates, 2000-01

Ranking basis/background: Based on *U.S News* questionnaire sent to 1,400 four-year institutions. Scores are averaged and weighted percentages from seven attributes: academic reputation, retention, faculty resources, student selectivity, financial resources, graduation rate performance and alumni giving. **Remarks:** Comparable data was used from the U.S. Department of Education, the Council for Aid to Education, the NCAA, and Wintergreen/Orchard House publishers. **Number listed:** 31.

1. University of Richmond, with 93%
2. James Madison University, 90%
3. Meredith College, 85%
4. Mary Washington College, 83%
4. Appalachian State University, 83%
4. Hampton College, 83%
4. Bellarmine College, 83%
4. Elon College, 83%
9. Samford University, 81%
9. Mississippi College, 81%

Source: "America's Best Colleges," *U.S. News & World Report*, 129: 90-132, (September 11, 2000).

★1438★
U.S. News & World Report's southern regional universities with the highest graduation rates, 2000-01

Ranking basis/background: Based on *U.S News* questionnaire sent to 1,400 four-year institutions. Scores are averaged and weighted percentages from seven attributes: academic reputation, retention, faculty resources, student selectivity, financial resources, graduation rate performance and alumni giving. **Remarks:** Comparable data was used from the U.S. Department of Education, the Council for Aid to Education, the NCAA, and Wintergreen/Orchard House publishers. **Number listed:** 31.

1. University of Richmond, with 83%
2. James Madison University, 81%
3. The Citadel, 74%
4. Mary Washington College, 73%
5. Meredith College, 68%
6. Appalachian State University, 63%
7. Rollins College, 62%
7. Stetson University, 62%
9. Samford University, 63%
10. Converse College, 59%

Source: "America's Best Colleges," *U.S. News & World Report*, 129: 90-132, (September 11, 2000).

★1439★
U.S. News & World Report's southern regional universities with the highest percentage of freshmen in the top 25% of their high school class, 2000-01

Ranking basis/background: Based on *U.S News* questionnaire sent to 1,400 four-year institutions. Scores are averaged and weighted percentages from seven attributes: academic reputation, retention, faculty resources, student selectivity, financial resources, graduation rate performance and alumni giving. **Remarks:** Comparable data was used from the U.S. Department of Education, the Council for Aid to Education, the NCAA, and Wintergreen/Orchard House publishers. **Number listed:** 31.

1. University of Richmond, with 91%
2. Mary Washington College, 85%
3. James Madison University, 81%
4. Converse College, 71%
5. Murray State University, 69%
5. Samford University, 69%
5. Mercer University, 69%
8. Hampton University, 68%
9. Stetson University, 65%
10. Rollins College, 64%

Source: "America's Best Colleges," *U.S. News & World Report*, 129: 90-132, (September 11, 2000).

★1440★
U.S. News & World Report's southern regional universities with the highest percentage of full-time faculty, 2000-01

Ranking basis/background: Based on *U.S News* questionnaire sent to 1,400 four-year institutions. Scores are averaged and weighted percentages from seven attributes: academic reputation, retention, faculty resources, student selectivity, financial resources, graduation rate performance and alumni giving. **Remarks:** Comparable data was used from the U.S. Department of Education, the Council for Aid to Education, the NCAA, and Wintergreen/Orchard House publishers. **Number listed:** 31.

1. Murray State University, with 98%
2. Xavier University (LA), 95%
3. Converse College, 94%
4. East Carolina University, 93%
5. The Citadel, 92%
6. Elon College, 90%
7. James Madison University, 89%
8. Appalachian State University, 88%
9. University of Richmond, 87%
9. Stetson University, 87%
9. Centenary College of Louisiana, 87%
9. Mary Washington College, 87%

Source: "America's Best Colleges," *U.S. News & World Report*, 129: 90-132, (September 11, 2000).

★1441★
U.S. News & World Report's southern regional universities with the highest proportion of classes with 20 students or less, 2000-01

Ranking basis/background: Based on *U.S News* questionnaire sent to 1,400 four-year institutions. Scores are averaged and weighted percentages from seven attributes: academic reputation, retention, faculty resources, student selectivity, financial resources, graduation rate performance and alumni giving. **Remarks:** Comparable data was used from the U.S. Department of Education, the Council for Aid to Education, the NCAA, and Wintergreen/Orchard House publishers. **Number listed:** 31.

1. Queens College, with 74%
2. Centenary College of Louisiana, 72%
2. Converse College, 72%
2. Mississippi College, 72%
5. Wheeling Jesuit University, 69%
6. Belmont University, 65%
7. Rollins College, 64%
8. Samford University, 61%
9. Stetson University, 60%
10. Mercer University, 57%

Source: "America's Best Colleges," *U.S. News & World Report*, 129: 90-132, (September 11, 2000).

★1442★
U.S. News & World Report's southern regional universities with the lowest acceptance rates, 2000-01

Ranking basis/background: Based on *U.S News* questionnaire sent to 1,400 four-year institutions. Scores are averaged and weighted percentages from seven attributes: academic reputation, retention, faculty resources, student selectivity, financial resources, graduation rate performance and alumni giving. **Remarks:** Comparable data was used from the U.S. Department of Education, the Council for Aid to Education, the NCAA, and Wintergreen/Orchard House publishers. **Number listed:** 31.

1. College of Charleston, 44%
2. University of Richmond, with 45%
3. Mary Washington College, 56%
4. University of North Carolina, Wilmington, 58%
5. Elon College, 59%
6. Hampton University, 64%
7. James Madison University, 65%
8. Appalachian State University, 66%
9. Murray State University, 70%
9. University of North Carolina, Charlotte, 70%

Source: "America's Best Colleges," *U.S. News & World Report*, 129: 90-132, (September 11, 2000).

★1443★
U.S. News & World Report's top public southern regional universities, 2000-01

Ranking basis/background: Based on *U.S News* questionnaire sent to 1,400 four-year institutions. Scores are averaged and weighted percentages from seven attributes: academic reputation, retention, faculty resources, student selectivity, financial resources, graduation rate performance and alumni giving. **Remarks:** Comparable data was used from the U.S. Department of Education, the Council for Aid to Education, the NCAA, and Wintergreen/Orchard House publishers. **Number listed:** 13.

1. James Madison University
2. Mary Washington College
3. The Citadel
4. Appalachian State University

5. College of Charleston
6. Murray State University
6. University of North Carolina, Charlotte
8. University of North Carolina, Wilmington
9. East Carolina University
9. Winthrop University
11. Longwood College
11. Radford University
11. University of North Florida

Source: "America's Best Colleges," *U.S. News & World Report*, 129: 90-132, (September 11, 2000).

★1444★
U.S. News & World Report's **top southern regional universities, 2000-01**

Ranking basis/background: Based on *U.S News* questionnaire sent to 1,400 four-year institutions. Scores are averaged and weighted percentages from seven attributes: academic reputation, retention, faculty resources, student selectivity, financial resources, graduation rate performance and alumni giving. **Remarks:** Comparable data was used from the U.S. Department of Education, the Council for Aid to Education, the NCAA, and Wintergreen/Orchard House publishers. **Number listed:** 31.
1. University of Richmond, with an overall score of 100.0
2. James Madison University, 78.0
2. Rollins College, 78.0
4. Stetson University, 77.0
5. Samford University, 74.0
6. Mary Washington College, 72.0
7. The Citadel, 71.0
7. Loyola University, New Orleans, 71.0
9. Mercer University, 69.0
10. Appalachian State University, 67.0

Source: "America's Best Colleges," *U.S. News & World Report*, 129: 90-132, (September 11, 2000).

COLLEGES & UNIVERSITIES–SPECIALITY

★1445★
U.S. tribal colleges

Ranking basis/background: Listing of tribal colleges in the U.S., alphabetical by state. **Remarks:** Original source: American Indian College Fund & American Indian Higher Education Consortium. **Number listed:** 31.
  Dine College (AZ)
  D-Q University (CA)
  Haskell Indian Nations University (KS)
  Bay Mills Community College (MI)
  Fond du Lac Tribal and Community College (MN)
  Leech Lake Tribal College (MN)
  White Earth Tribal College (MN)
  Blackfeet Community College (MT)
  Dull Knife Memorial College (MT)
  Fort Belknap College (MT)
  Fort Peck Community College (MT)
  Little Big Horn College (MT)
  Salish Kootenai College (MT)
  Stone Child College (MT)
  Little Priest Tribal College (NE)
  Nebraska Indian Community College (NE)
  Crowpoint Institute of Technology (NM)
  Institute of American Indian Arts (NM)
  Southwestern Indian Polytechnic Institute (NM)
  Fort Berthold Community College (ND)
  Cankdeska Cikana Community College (ND)
  Sitting Bull College (ND)
  Turtle Mountain Community College (ND)
  United Tribes Technical College (ND)
  Si Tanka College (SD)
  Oglala Lakota College (SD)
  Sinte Gleska University (SD)
  Sisseton-Wahpeton Community College (SD)
  Northwest Indian College (WA)
  College of the Menominee Nations (WI)
  Lac Courte Oreilles Ojibwa Community College (WI)

Source: Wright, Scott W., "Survey Confirms Tribal College Role in Alleviating Unemployment," *Black Issues in Higher Education*, 17: 18-19, (June 22, 2000).

COLLEGES & UNIVERSITIES–STATE AID
See: **Colleges & Universities–Financial Support & Expenditures**

COLLEGES & UNIVERSITIES–STUDENT COSTS
See also: **Colleges & Universities, Liberal Arts–Student Costs Colleges & Universities, Small–Student Costs**

★1446★
Average expenditures for commuters attending 2-year private colleges in the U.S., 2000

Ranking basis/background: Breakdown of charges incurred by the average undergraduate enrolled full-time. Total average costs is $12,219. Room in not included for commuter students. **Remarks:** Original source: The College Board. **Number listed:** 5.
  Tuition and fees, with $7,458
  Books and supplies, $661
  Room and board, $2,032
  Transportation, $980
  Other, $1,088

Source: Brownstein, Andrew, "Tuition Rises Faster Than Inflation, and Faster Than in Previous Year," *The Chronicle of Higher Education* (http://www.chronicle.com/free/v47/i09/09a05001.htm#avcosts), 47: 1-3, (October 27, 2000).

★1447★
Average expenditures for commuters attending 2-year public colleges in the U.S., 2000

Ranking basis/background: Breakdown of charges incurred by the average undergraduate enrolled full-time. Total average costs is $7,024. Room is not included for commuter students. **Remarks:** Original source: The College Board. **Number listed:** 5.
  Tuition and fees, with $1,705
  Books and supplies, $663
  Room and board, $2,426
  Transportation, $1,035
  Other, $1,195

Source: Brownstein, Andrew, "Tuition Rises Faster Than Inflation, and Faster Than in Previous Year," *The Chronicle of Higher Education* (http://www.chronicle.com/free/v47/i09/09a05001.htm#avcosts), 47: 1-3, (October 27, 2000).

★1448★
Average expenditures for commuters attending 4-year private colleges in the U.S., 2000

Ranking basis/background: Breakdown of charges incurred by the average undergraduate enrolled full-time. Total average costs is $21,704. Room is not included for commuter students. **Remarks:** Original source: The College Board. **Number listed:** 5.
  Tuition and fees, with $16,332
  Books and supplies, $730
  Room and board, $2,495
  Transportation, $926
  Other, $1,221

Source: Brownstein, Andrew, "Tuition Rises Faster Than Inflation, and Faster Than in Previous Year," *The Chronicle of Higher Education* (http://www.chronicle.com/free/v47/i09/09a05001.htm#avcosts), 47: 1-3, (October 27, 2000).

★1449★
Average expenditures for commuters attending 4-year public colleges in the U.S., 2000

Ranking basis/background: Breakdown of charges incurred by the average undergraduate enrolled full-time. Total average costs is $9,229. Room not included for commuter students. **Remarks:** Original source: The College Board. **Number listed:** 5.
  Tuition and fees, with $3,510
  Books and supplies, $704
  Room and board, $2,444
  Transportation, $1,014
  Other, $1,557

Source: Brownstein, Andrew, "Tuition Rises Faster Than Inflation, and Faster Than in Previous Year," *The Chronicle of Higher Education* (http://www.chronicle.com/free/v47/i09/09a05001.htm#avcosts), 47: 1-3, (October 27, 2000).

★1450★
Average expenditures for residents attending 2-year private colleges in the U.S., 2000

Ranking basis/background: Breakdown of charges incurred by the average undergraduate enrolled full-time. Total average costs is $14,679. **Remarks:** Original source: The College Board. **Number listed:** 5.
  Tuition and fees, with $7,458
  Books and supplies, $661
  Room and board, $4,736
  Transportation, $679
  Other, $1,145

Source: Brownstein, Andrew, "Tuition Rises Faster Than Inflation, and Faster Than in Previous Year," *The Chronicle of Higher Education* (http://www.chronicle.com/free/v47/i09/09a05001.htm#avcosts), 47: 1-3, (October 27, 2000).

COLLEGES & UNIVERSITIES—STUDENT COSTS

★1451★
Average expenditures for residents attending 2-year public colleges in the U.S., 2000

Ranking basis/background: Breakdown of charges incurred by the average undergraduate enrolled full-time. **Remarks:** Original source: The College Board. **Number listed:** 2.

- Tuition and fees, with $1,705
- Books and supplies, $663

Source: Brownstein, Andrew, "Tuition Rises Faster Than Inflation, and Faster Than in Previous Year," *The Chronicle of Higher Education* (http://www.chronicle.com/free/v47/i09/09a05001.htm#avcosts), 47: 1-3, (October 27, 2000).

★1452★
Average expenditures for residents attending 4-year private colleges in the U.S., 2000

Ranking basis/background: Breakdown of charges incurred by the average undergraduate enrolled full-time. Total average costs is $24,946. **Remarks:** Original source: The College Board. **Number listed:** 5.

- Tuition and fees, with $16,332
- Books and supplies, $730
- Room and board, $6,209
- Transportation, $573
- Other, $1,102

Source: Brownstein, Andrew, "Tuition Rises Faster Than Inflation, and Faster Than in Previous Year," *The Chronicle of Higher Education* (http://www.chronicle.com/free/v47/i09/09a05001.htm#avcosts), 47: 1-3, (October 27, 2000).

★1453★
Average expenditures for residents attending 4-year public colleges in the U.S., 2000

Ranking basis/background: Breakdown of charges incurred by the average undergraduate enrolled full-time. Total average costs is $11,338. **Remarks:** Original source: The College Board. **Number listed:** 5.

- Tuition and fees, with $3,510
- Books and supplies, $704
- Room and board, $4,960
- Transportation, $643
- Other, $1,521

Source: Brownstein, Andrew, "Tuition Rises Faster Than Inflation, and Faster Than in Previous Year," *The Chronicle of Higher Education* (http://www.chronicle.com/free/v47/i09/09a05001.htm#avcosts), 47: 1-3, (October 27, 2000).

★1454★
Average expenditures for undergraduates at 4-year private colleges in the U.S., 1990-91 through 2000-01

Ranking basis/background: Average tuition and fees at 4-year private colleges for undergraduate students enrolled full-time. **Remarks:** Original source: The College Board. **Number listed:** 11.

- 1990-91, with $9,391
- 1991-92, $10,017
- 1992-93, $10,498
- 1993-94, $11,025
- 1994-95, $11,709
- 1995-96, $12,432
- 1996-97, $12,823
- 1997-98, $13,664
- 1998-99, $14,709
- 1999-00, $15,380
- 2000-01, $16,332

Source: Brownstein, Andrew, "Tuition Rises Faster Than Inflation, and Faster Than in Previous Year," *The Chronicle of Higher Education* (http://www.chronicle.com/free/v47/i09/09a05001.htm#avcosts), 47: 1-3, (October 27, 2000).

★1455★
Average expenses at private 2-year colleges, 2000-01

Ranking basis/background: Costs for resident and commuter students at 2-year private colleges for 2000-01. Room costs not included for commuter students. Figures are weighted by enrollment to reflect the charges incurred by the average undergraduate enrolled at each type of institution. **Remarks:** Original source: The College Board. **Number listed:** 6.

- Tuition and fees, $7,458 (resident); $7,458 (commuter)
- Books and supplies, $661; $661
- Room and board, $4,736; $2,032
- Transportation, $679; $980
- Other, $1,145; $1,088
- Total, $14,679; $12,219

Source: Brownstein, Andrew, "Tuition Rises Faster Than Inflation, and Faster Than in Previous Year," *The Chronicle of Higher Education*, 47: A50-A52, (October 27, 2000).

★1456★
Average expenses at private 4-year colleges, 2000-01

Ranking basis/background: Costs for resident and commuter students at 4-year private colleges for 2000-01. Room costs not included for commuter students. Figures are weighted by enrollment to reflect the charges incurred by the average undergraduate enrolled at each type of institution. **Remarks:** Original source: The College Board. **Number listed:** 6.

- Tuition and fees, $16,332 (resident); $16,332 (commuter)
- Books and supplies, $730; $730
- Room and board, $6,209; $2,495
- Transportation, $573; $926
- Other, $1,102; $1,221
- Total, $24,946; $21,704

Source: Brownstein, Andrew, "Tuition Rises Faster Than Inflation, and Faster Than in Previous Year," *The Chronicle of Higher Education*, 47: A50-A52, (October 27, 2000).

★1457★
Average expenses at public 2-year colleges, 2000-01

Ranking basis/background: Costs for resident and commuter students at 2-year public colleges for 2000-01. Room costs not included for commuter students. Figures are weighted by enrollment to reflect the charges incurred by the average undergraduate enrolled at each type of institution. **Remarks:** Original source: The College Board. **Number listed:** 6.

- Tuition and fees, $1,705 (resident); $1,705 (commuter)
- Books and supplies, $663; $663
- Room and board, n/a; $2,426
- Transportation, n/a; $1,035
- Other, n/a; $1,195
- Total, $2,368; $7,024

Source: Brownstein, Andrew, "Tuition Rises Faster Than Inflation, and Faster Than in Previous Year," *The Chronicle of Higher Education*, 47: A50-A52, (October 27, 2000).

★1458★
Average expenses at public 4-year colleges, 2000-01

Ranking basis/background: Costs for resident and commuter students at 4-year public colleges for 2000-01. Room costs not included for commuter students. Figures are weighted by enrollment to reflect the charges incurred by the average undergraduate enrolled at each type of institution. **Remarks:** Original source: The College Board. **Number listed:** 6.

- Tuition and fees, $3,510 (resident); $3,510 (commuter)
- Books and supplies, $704; $704
- Room and board, $4,960; $2,444
- Transportation, $643; $1,014
- Other, $1,521; $1,557
- Total, $11,338; $9,229

Source: Brownstein, Andrew, "Tuition Rises Faster Than Inflation, and Faster Than in Previous Year," *The Chronicle of Higher Education*, 47: A50-A52, (October 27, 2000).

★1459★
Fiske Guide's best buys for private colleges and universities, 2001

Ranking basis/background: According to *Fiske Guide*'s questionnaire asking administrators and a cross section of students, to rate college or university on the basis of academic strength, social life, and overall quality of life. **Number listed:** 21.

1. Baylor University
2. Birmingham Southern College
3. Brigham Young University
4. California Institute of Technology
5. Calvin College
6. Centre College
7. Cooper Union
8. Deep Springs College
9. Grinnell College
10. Hendrix College
11. Hope College
12. Millsaps College
13. Morehouse College
14. Presbyterian College
15. Randolph-Macon Woman's College
16. Rice University
17. St. John's University and College of St. Benedict
18. University of the South, Sewanee
19. Spelman College
20. Trinity University
21. Washington and Lee University

Source: Fiske, Edward B., *The Fiske Guide to Colleges 2001 - 17th ed.*, Three Rivers Press, 2000.

★1460★
Fiske Guide's best buys for public colleges and universities, 2001

Ranking basis/background: According to *Fiske Guide*'s questionnaire asking administrators and a cross section of students, to rate college or university on the basis of academic strength, social life, and overall quality of life. **Number listed:** 19.

1. University of British Columbia, Canada
2. University of California, Los Angeles
3. University of California, Riverside
4. University of California, San Diego
5. University of Colorado, Boulder
6. Evergreen State College
7. Georgia Institute of Technology
8. University of Iowa
9. University of Kansas
10. Mary Washington College
11. McGill University

12. Miami University (OH)
13. New College of the University of South Florida
14. University of North Carolina, Asheville
15. University of North Carolina, Chapel Hill
16. University of Oregon
17. University of Texas, Austin
18. University of Toronto
19. University of Wisconsin, Madison

Source: Fiske, Edward B., *The Fiske Guide to Colleges 2001 - 17th ed.*, Three Rivers Press, 2000.

★1461★

Highest undergraduate tuition and fees at private nonprofit, 4-year or above colleges and universities

Ranking basis/background: These figures for in-state tuition and fees at over 3,000 colleges and universities were collected by the College Board in the Annual Survey of Colleges, 2000-01. Figures represent charges to first-time, full-time undergraduates based on a nine-month academic year of 30 semester hours or 45 quarter hours. **Remarks:** A separate table for each state, the District of Columbia, and Puerto Rico is included. Listing also shows added out-of-state tuition and 1999-2000 tuition and fees. **Number listed:** 1094.

1. Sarah Lawrence College, with tuition and fees of $26,668
2. Brown University, $26,374
3. Brandeis University, $26,241
4. Wesleyan University, $26,180
5. Hampshire College, $26,125
6. Amherst College, $26,080
6. Kenyon College, $26,080
8. Massachusetts Institute of Technology, $26,050
9. Bowdoin College, $25,890
10. Dartmouth College, $25,763
11. Colgate University, $25,740
12. Tufts University, $25,714
13. Duke University, $25,630
14. University of Chicago, $25,489
15. Tulane University, $25,480
16. Skidmore College, $25,465
17. Trinity College, $25,440
18. Johns Hopkins University, $25,430
18. Princeton University, $25,430
20. Bard College, $25,380
21. Mount Holyoke College, $25,360
22. Oberlin College, $25,355
23. Pitzer College, $25,238
24. Yale University, $25,220
25. Swarthmore College, $25,200

Source: "Tuition and Fees 2000-01: Private Nonprofit, 4-Year or Above," *The Chronicle of Higher Education* (http://chronicle.com/stats/tuition/tuition-results.php3), 47:, (October 27, 2000).

★1462★

Highest undergraduate tuition and fees at public 2-year colleges and universities

Ranking basis/background: These figures for in-state tuition and fees at over 3,000 colleges and universities were collected by the College Board in the Annual Survey of Colleges, 2000-01. Figures represent charges to first-time, full-time undergraduates based on a nine-month academic year of 30 semester hours or 45 quarter hours. **Remarks:** A separate table for each state, the District of Columbia, and Puerto Rico is included. Listing also shows added out-of-state tuition and 1999-2000 tuition and fees. **Number listed:** 853.

1. Georgia Military College, with tuition and fees of $10,790
2. Thaddeus Stevens State School of Technology, $4,820
3. Texas Southmost College, $4,796
4. New Hampshire Technical Institute, $4,070
5. State University of New York College of Technology, Canton, $3,925
6. State University of New York, College of A&T, Morrisville, $3,805
6. State University of New York College of Technology, Delhi, $3,805
8. Community College of Vermont, $3,730
9. Ohio State University A&T Institute, $3,408
10. University of Cincinnati, Raymond Walters College, $3,396
11. University of Akron, Wayne College, $3,273
12. Bowling Green State University, Firelands College, $3,186
13. Sisseton-Wahpeton Community College, $3,160
14. Montana State University, College of Technology, Billings, $3,052
15. Kent State University, Ashtabula, $3,004
15. Kent State University, East Liverpool, $3,004
15. Kent State University, Salem, $3,004
15. Kent State University, Stark, $3,004
15. Kent State University, Trumbull, $3,004
15. Kent State University, Tuscarawas, $3,004
21. Quincy College, $2,970
22. University of Cincinnati, Clermont College, $2,943
23. Cayuga County Community College, $2,878
24. Corning Community College, $2,874
25. Jamestown Community College, $2,850

Source: "Tuition and Fees 2000-01: Public, 2-Year," *The Chronicle of Higher Education* (http://chronicle.com/stats/tuition/tuition-results.php3), 47:, (October 27, 2000).

★1463★

Highest undergraduate tuition and fees at public, 4-year or above colleges and universities

Ranking basis/background: These figures for in-state tuition and fees at over 3,000 colleges and universities were collected by the College Board in the Annual Survey of Colleges, 2000-01. Figures represent charges to first-time, full-time undergraduates based on a nine-month academic year of 30 semester hours or 45 quarter hours. **Remarks:** A separate table for each state, the District of Columbia, and Puerto Rico is included. Listing also shows added out-of-state tuition and 1999-2000 tuition and fees. **Number listed:** 552.

1. New York State College of Ceramics, Alfred University, with tuition and fees of $9,976
2. Franklin Institute of Boston, $9,700
3. University of Vermont, $8,268
4. Pennsylvania College of Technology, $7,422
5. University of New Hampshire, $7,395
6. St. Mary's College (MD), $7,360
7. University of Pittsburgh, $7,002
8. Temple University, $6,948
9. Penn State University, Behrend College, $6,852
10. Penn State University, Harrisburg, $6,832
11. Penn State University, University Park, $6,756
12. Penn State University, Altoona, $6,742
12. Penn State University, Berks, $6,742
14. New Jersey Institute of Technology, $6,730
15. Penn State University, Abington, $6,722
16. Penn State University, Beaver, $6,646
16. Penn State University, Hazleton, $6,646
16. Penn State University, Lehigh Valley, $6,646
16. Penn State University, Wilkes-Barre, $6,464
20. Penn State University, Delaware County, $6,636
20. Penn State University, Mont Alto, $6,636
20. Penn State University, New Kensington, $6,636
20. Penn State University, Shenango, $6,636
24. Penn State University, Dubois, $6,626
24. Penn State University, Fayette, $6,626
24. Penn State University, McKeesport, $6,626
24. Penn State University, Capital College, $6,626
24. Penn State University, Worthington Scranton, $6,626
24. Penn State University, York, $6,626

Source: "Tuition and Fees 2000-01: Public, 4-Year or Above," *The Chronicle of Higher Education* (http://chronicle.com/stats/tuition/tuition-results.php3), 47:, (October 27, 2000).

★1464★

Lowest undergraduate tuition and fees at private nonprofit, 4-year or above colleges and universities

Ranking basis/background: These figures for in-state tuition and fees at over 3,000 colleges and universities were collected by the College Board in the Annual Survey of Colleges, 2000-01. Figures represent charges to first-time, full-time undergraduates based on a nine-month academic year of 30 semester hours or 45 quarter hours. **Remarks:** A separate table for each state, the District of Columbia, and Puerto Rico is included. Listing also shows added out-of-state tuition and 1999-2000 tuition and fees. **Number listed:** 1094.

1. Berea College, with tuition and fees of $199
2. Baptist Missionary Association Theological Seminary, $2,190
3. Arkansas Baptist College, $2,230
4. Institute for Christian Studies, $2,250
5. Salish Kootenai College, $2,355
6. Brigham Young University, $2,830
7. University of Rio Grande, $2,916
8. Brigham Young University (HI), $2,988
9. American Baptist College of ABT Seminary, $3,090
10. Baptist Bible College, $3,164
11. Medcenter One College of Nursing, $3,186
12. Mirrer Yeshiva Central Institute, $3,300
13. Universidad Metropolitana, $3,324
14. Wesley College, $3,400
15. Yeshiva Beth Yehuda-Yeshiva Gedolah of Greater Detroit, $3,500
15. Beth Hatalmud Rabbinical College, $3,500
17. Southeastern Baptist College, $3,520
18. Yeshiva of Nitra, $3,600
18. Rabbinical College Bobover Yeshiva B'nei Zion, $3,600
20. Arlington Baptist College, $3,650
21. University of Puerto Rico, San German, $3,700
21. University of Puerto Rico, Ponce, $3,700
21. University of Puerto Rico, Metropolitan, $3,700
21. University of Puerto Rico, Bayamon, $3,700

COLLEGES & UNIVERSITIES—STUDENT COSTS

21. University of Puerto Rico, Barranquitas, $3,700
21. University of Puerto Rico, Arecibo, $3,700
21. University of Puerto Rico, Aguadilla, $3,700

Source: "Tuition and Fees 2000-01: Private Nonprofit, 4-Year or Above," *The Chronicle of Higher Education* (http://chronicle.com/stats/tuition/tuition-results.php3), 47:, (October 27, 2000).

★1465★
Lowest undergraduate tuition and fees at public 2-year colleges and universities

Ranking basis/background: These figures for in-state tuition and fees at over 3,000 colleges and universities were collected by the College Board in the Annual Survey of Colleges, 2000-01. Figures represent charges to first-time, full-time undergraduates based on a nine-month academic year of 30 semester hours or 45 quarter hours. **Remarks:** A separate table for each state, the District of Columbia, and Puerto Rico is included. Listing also shows added out-of-state tuition and 1999-2000 tuition and fees. **Number listed:** 853.

1. Lake Tahoe Community College, with tuition and fees of $324
2. Vista Community College, $330
2. San Joaquin Delta College, $330
2. Sacramento City College, $330
2. Pasadena City College, $330
2. Palo Verde College, $330
2. Merritt College, $330
2. Imperial Valley College, $330
2. Diablo Valley College, $330
2. Contra Costa College, $330
2. Compton Community College, $330
2. Chabot College, $330
2. Cerro Coso Community College, $330
2. College of Marin Kentfield, $330
2. Barstow College, $330
2. Antelope Valley College, $330
2. American River College, $330
18. Napa Valley College, $332
18. Los Medanos College, $332
20. Laney College, $334
20. College of Alameda, $334
22. Hartnell College, $338
23. Victor Valley College, $340
24. West Hills Community College, $341
25. Yuba College, $342

Source: "Tuition and Fees 2000-01: Public, 2-Year," *The Chronicle of Higher Education* (http://chronicle.com/stats/tuition/tuition-results.php3), 47:, (October 27, 2000).

★1466★
Lowest undergraduate tuition and fees at public, 4-year or above colleges and universities

Ranking basis/background: These figures for in-state tuition and fees at over 3,000 colleges and universities were collected by the College Board in the Annual Survey of Colleges, 2000-01. Figures represent charges to first-time, full-time undergraduates based on a nine-month academic year of 30 semester hours or 45 quarter hours. **Remarks:** A separate table for each state, the District of Columbia, and Puerto Rico is included. Listing also shows added out-of-state tuition and 1999-2000 tuition and fees. **Number listed:** 552.

1. University of Puerto Rico, Mayaguez, with tuition and fees of $1,010
2. University of Puerto Rico, Cayey University, $1,020
3. University of Puerto Rico, Rio Piedras, $1,120
4. University of Puerto Rico, Humacao University, $1,125
5. University of Texas Medical Branch, Galveston, $1,200
6. Conservatory of Music of Puerto Rico, $1,420
7. West Virginia University, Parkersburg, $1,437
8. Macon State College, $1,438
9. University of Hawaii, Hilo, $1,466
10. Fayetteville State University, $1,542
11. California State University, Sacramento, $1,650
12. University of Texas, Brownsville, $1,676
13. California State University, Stanislaus, $1,678
14. Utah Valley State College, $1,682
15. Elizabeth City State University, $1,686
16. California State University, San Marcos, $1,706
17. California State University, Hayward, $1,728
18. California State University, Los Angeles, $1,732
19. California State University, Dominguez Hills, $1,738
20. California State University, Long Beach, $1,744
21. California State University, Fresno, $1,746
22. California State University, San Bernardino, $1,749
23. San Diego State University, $1,776
24. California State Polytechnic University, Pomona, $1,778
25. Winston-Salem State University, $1,805

Source: "Tuition and Fees 2000-01: Public, 4-Year or Above," *The Chronicle of Higher Education* (http://chronicle.com/stats/tuition/tuition-results.php3), 47:, (October 27, 2000).

★1467★
Private 4-year institutions with the highest tuition, 2000-01

Ranking basis/background: Figures for tuition and fees charged to first-time, full-time undergraduates enrolled for a nine-month academic year of 30 semester hours or 45 quarter hours. Excluded are private, for-profit colleges, institutions in Puerto Rico, and those classified as theological seminaries or specialized faith-based institutions. **Remarks:** Original source: Chronicle analysis of College Board statistics. **Number listed:** 10.

1. Columbia University School of General Studies, with $29,057
2. Sarah Lawrence College, $26,668
3. Brown University, $26,374
4. Brandeis University, $26,241
5. Wesleyan University, $26,180
6. Hampshire College, $26,125
7. Hamilton College, $26,100
8. Amherst College, $26,090
9. Kenyon College, $26,080
10. Massachusetts Institute of Technology, $26,050

Source: Brownstein, Andrew, "Tuition Rises Faster Than Inflation, and Faster Than in Previous Year," *The Chronicle of Higher Education*, 47: A50-A52, (October 27, 2000).

★1468★
Private 4-year institutions with the lowest tuition, 2000-01

Ranking basis/background: Figures for tuition and fees charged to first-time, full-time undergraduates enrolled for a nine-month academic year of 30 semester hours or 45 quarter hours. Excluded are private, for-profit colleges, institutions in Puerto Rico, and those classified as theological seminaries or specialized faith-based institutions. **Remarks:** Original source: Chronicle analysis of College Board statistics. **Number listed:** 10.

1. Berea College, with $199
2. Arkansas Baptist College, $2,230
3. Brigham Young University, $2,830
4. University of Rio Grande, $2,916
5. Brigham Young University (HI), $2,988
6. Medcenter One College of Nursing, $3,186
7. Philander Smith College, $3,842
8. Bellevue University, $4,030
9. Sojourner-Douglass College, $4,470
10. College of the Southwest, $4,715

Source: Brownstein, Andrew, "Tuition Rises Faster Than Inflation, and Faster Than in Previous Year," *The Chronicle of Higher Education*, 47: A50-A52, (October 27, 2000).

★1469★
Projected college costs at public and private institutions, 2002-2015

Ranking basis/background: Projected total costs including tuition, fees, books, and room and board for four years. Hypothetical rate of increase is 6% per year. **Number listed:** 16.

2002, with $58,946 for public college; $125,421 for private college
2003, $62,483; $132,946
2004, $66,232; $140,923
2005, $70,206; $149,378
2006, $74,418; $158,341
2007, $78,883; $167,841
2008, $83,616; $177,912
2009, $88,633; $188,587
2010, $93,951; $199,902
2011, $99,588; $211,896
2012, $105,564; $224,610
2013, $111,897; $238,086
2014, $118,611; $252,371
2015, $125,728; $267,514

Source: "How Will You Meet the Rising Cost of College?," *Guide to Your Personal Finances*, IIAACREEF, 1998.

★1470★
Projected monthly savings needed to meet college costs at public and private institutions, 2002-2015

Ranking basis/background: Projected monthly saving needed to cover total costs including tuition, fees, books, and room and board for four years. Assumes an 8% annual return on investments up to the fourth year of college. Monthly saving figures are based upon a saving starting date of September 1997. **Number listed:** 16.

Student to begin college in 2002, with $499 monthly savings needed for public college; and $1,062 for private college
2003, $451; $959
2004, $412; $876
2005, $380; $809
2006, $353; $752
2007, $331; $703
2008, $311; $662
2009, $294; $626
2010, $279; $594

2011, $266; $566
2012, $254; $540
2013, $243; $518
2014, $234; $497
2015, $225; $478

Source: "How Will You Meet the Rising Cost of College?," *Guide to Your Personal Finances*, IIAACREEF, 1998.

★1471★
Public 4-year institutions with the highest tuition, 2000-01

Ranking basis/background: Figures for tuition and fees charged to first-time, full-time undergraduates enrolled for a nine-month academic year of 30 semester hours or 45 quarter hours. Excluded are private, for-profit colleges, institutions in Puerto Rico, and those classified as theological seminaries or specialized faith-based institutions. **Remarks:** Original source: Chronicle analysis of College Board statistics. **Number listed:** 10.

1. New York State College of Ceramics, Alfred University, with $9,976
2. University of Vermont, $8,268
3. Pennsylvania College of Technology, $7,422
4. University of New Hampshire, $7,395
5. St. Mary's College (MD), $7,360
6. University of Pittsburgh, $7,002
7. Temple University, $6,948
8. Penn State University, Erie, $6,852
9. Penn State University, Harrisburg, $6,832
10. Penn State University, University Park, $6,756

Source: Brownstein, Andrew, "Tuition Rises Faster Than Inflation, and Faster Than in Previous Year," *The Chronicle of Higher Education*, 47: A50-A52, (October 27, 2000).

★1472★
Public 4-year institutions with the lowest tuition, 2000-01

Ranking basis/background: Figures for tuition and fees charged to first-time, full-time undergraduates enrolled for a nine-month academic year of 30 semester hours or 45 quarter hours. Excluded are private, for-profit colleges, institutions in Puerto Rico, and those classified as theological seminaries or specialized faith-based institutions. **Remarks:** Original source: Chronicle analysis of College Board statistics. **Number listed:** 10.

1. University of Texas Medical Branch, Galveston, with $1,200
2. West Virginia University, Parkersburg, $1,437
3. Macon State College, $1,438
4. University of Hawaii, Hilo, $1,466
5. Fayetteville State University, $1,542
6. California State University, Sacramento, $1,650
7. University of Texas, Brownsville, $1,676
8. California State University, Stanislaus, $1,678
9. Utah Valley State College, $1,682
10. Elizabeth City State University, $1,686

Source: Brownstein, Andrew, "Tuition Rises Faster Than Inflation, and Faster Than in Previous Year," *The Chronicle of Higher Education*, 47: A50-A52, (October 27, 2000).

★1473★
Tuition and fees for undergraduates at public 4-year institutions, 1990-91 to 2000-01

Ranking basis/background: Average costs of tuition and fees for undergraduates at 4-year public institutions from 1999-91 through 2000-01. **Remarks:** Original source: The College Board. **Number listed:** 11.

1990-91, with and average cost of $9,391
1991-92, $10,017
1992-93, $10,498
1993-94, $11,025
1994-95, $11,709
1995-96, $12,432
1996-97, $12,823
1997-98, $13,664
1998-99, $14,709
1999-2000, $15,380
2000-01, $16,332

Source: Brownstein, Andrew, "Tuition Rises Faster Than Inflation, and Faster Than in Previous Year," *The Chronicle of Higher Education*, 47: A50-A52, (October 27, 2000).

★1474★
U.S. News & World Report's best undergraduate fees among national universities by discount tuition, 2000

Ranking basis/background: Based on a percentage averaged from 3 variables; ratio of quality to price, percentage of all undergraduates receiving grants meeting financial need during the 1999-2000 academic year, and average discount: percentage of a school's total costs. **Number listed:** 49.

1. California Institute of Technology, with a 53% average discount from total cost; and an average cost of $14,090 after receiving grants based on need
2. Harvard University, 53%; $16,379
3. Rice University, 45%; $13,083
4. Stanford University, 54%; $15,437
5. Princeton University, 52%; $16,380
6. Dartmouth College, 52%; $16,520
7. University of Rochester, 51%; $15,634
8. Massachusetts Institute of Technology, 47%; $18,373
9. Yale University, 48%; $18,071
10. Case Western Reserve University, 45%; $15,093

Source: "Great Schools at Great Prices," *U.S. News & World Report*, 129: 96, 100, (September 18, 2000).

★1475★
U.S. News & World Report's national universities with students least in debt, 1999

Ranking basis/background: Based on total amount borrowed by 1999 graduates from one or more of the following sources: federal, state and local governments, financial institutions, and the colleges themselves. **Remarks:** Debt does not reflect monies borrowed by parents or others on behalf of the student. **Number listed:** 25.

1. Indiana State University, with an average debt of $4,129
2. Florida International University, $4,750
3. Illinois State University, $9,283
4. University of North Carolina, Greensboro, $10,026
5. Yeshiva University, $10,807
6. New Jersey Institute of Technology, $11,000
7. Rice University, $11,393
8. Ball State University, $11,400
9. University of Washington (WA), $11,445
10. Southern Illinois University, Carbondale, $11,475

Source: "How Heavy is the Load?," *U.S. News & World Report*, 129: 101-102, (September 18, 2000).

★1476★
U.S. News & World Report's national universities with students most in debt, 1999

Ranking basis/background: Based on total amount borrowed by 1999 graduates from one or more of the following sources: federal, state and local governments, financial institutions, and the colleges themselves. **Remarks:** Debt does not reflect monies borrowed by parents or others on behalf of the student. **Number listed:** 15.

1. New School University, with an average debt of $27,125
2. Union Institute, $26,300
3. Florida Institute of Technology, $24,265
4. Andrews University, $24,163
5. Pepperdine University, $24,117
6. University of San Diego, $23,100
7. Massachusetts Institute of Technology, $22,529
8. Virginia Commonwealth University, $22,379
9. Brown University, $22,240
10. University of San Francisco, $22,238
11. University of Missouri, Kansas City, $22,127
12. University of Pennsylvania, $21,600
13. University of Vermont, $21,500
14. University of Tulsa, $21,376
15. Cleveland State University, $21,106

Source: "How Heavy is the Load?," *U.S. News & World Report*, 129: 101-102, (September 18, 2000).

Related Information

★1477★
"Trends in College Pricing 2000," *http://www.collegeboard.org*.
Remarks: Pricing data from the Annual Survey of Colleges for the 2000-2001 academic year. Includes average fixed charges for undergraduates (tuition, fees, room and board); average non-fixed budget components (books and supplies, transportation, and other expenses); and sample student budgets for each type of institution on grant, loan, and work-study funds.

★1478★
"Trends in Student Aid 2000," *http://www.collegeboard.org*.
Remarks: Presents annual data on the amount of financial assistance (grants, loans, and work-study-federal, state, and institutional) available to help students pay for postsecondary education including tuition, fees, living costs, transportation, books, and supplies.

COLLEGES & UNIVERSITIES–STUDENT COSTS–ALABAMA

★1479★
Highest undergraduate tuition and fees at colleges and universities in Alabama

Ranking basis/background: These figures for in-state tuition and fees at over 3,000 colleges and universities were collected by the College Board in the Annual Survey of Colleges, 2000-01. Figures represent charges to first-time, full-time undergraduates based on a nine-month academic year of 30 semester hours or 45 quarter hours. **Remarks:** A separate table for each state, the District of Columbia, and Puerto Rico is included. Listing also shows added out-of-state tuition and 1999-2000 tuition and fees. **Number listed:** 65.

1. Birmingham Southern College, with tuition and fees of $16,264
2. Spring Hill College, $16,254
3. Huntington College, $11,910
4. Samford University, $10,738
5. Tuskegee University, $10,006
6. Southern Christian University, $9,375
7. Marion Military Institute, $9,200
8. Oakwood College, $9,058
9. University of Mobile, $8,280
10. Faulkner College, $7,800

Source: "Tuition and Fees 2000-01," *The Chronicle of Higher Education (http://chronicle.com/stats/tuition/tuition-results.php3)*, 47:, (October 27, 2000).

★1480★
Lowest undergraduate tuition and fees at colleges and universities in Alabama

Ranking basis/background: These figures for in-state tuition and fees at over 3,000 colleges and universities were collected by the College Board in the Annual Survey of Colleges, 2000-01. Figures represent charges to first-time, full-time undergraduates based on a nine-month academic year of 30 semester hours or 45 quarter hours. **Remarks:** A separate table for each state, the District of Columbia, and Puerto Rico is included. Listing also shows added out-of-state tuition and 1999-2000 tuition and fees. **Number listed:** 65.

1. Wallace State Community College, with tuition and fees of $1,260
2. Northeast Alabama Community College, $1,410
3. Snead State Community College, $1,470
4. Shelton State Community College, $1,560
4. J. F. Drake State Technical College, $1,560
4. Douglas MacArthur State Technical College, $1,560
7. Bessemer State Technical College, $1,584
8. Wallace Community College, $1,620
8. Trenholm State Technical College, $1,620
8. Reid State Technical College, $1,620
8. John M. Patterson State Technical College, $1,620
8. George C. Wallace State Community College, $1,620

Source: "Tuition and Fees 2000-01," *The Chronicle of Higher Education (http://chronicle.com/stats/tuition/tuition-results.php3)*, 47:, (October 27, 2000).

COLLEGES & UNIVERSITIES–STUDENT COSTS–ALASKA

★1481★
Undergraduate tuition and fees at colleges and universities in Alaska

Ranking basis/background: These figures for in-state tuition and fees at over 3,000 colleges and universities were collected by the College Board in the Annual Survey of Colleges, 2000-01. Figures represent charges to first-time, full-time undergraduates based on a nine-month academic year of 30 semester hours or 45 quarter hours. **Remarks:** A separate table for each state, the District of Columbia, and Puerto Rico is included. Listing also shows added out-of-state tuition and 1999-2000 tuition and fees. **Number listed:** 7.

1. Alaska Pacific University, with tuition and fees of $10,480
2. Sheldon Jackson College, $7,620
3. Alaska Bible College, $4,750
4. University of Alaska, Fairbanks, $3,420
5. University of Alaska, Anchorage, $2,769
6. University of Alaska, Southeast, $2,626
7. Prince William Sound Community College, $2,088

Source: "Tuition and Fees 2000-01," *The Chronicle of Higher Education (http://chronicle.com/stats/tuition/tuition-results.php3)*, 47:, (October 27, 2000).

COLLEGES & UNIVERSITIES–STUDENT COSTS–ARIZONA

★1482★
Highest undergraduate tuition and fees at colleges and universities in Arizona

Ranking basis/background: These figures for in-state tuition and fees at over 3,000 colleges and universities were collected by the College Board in the Annual Survey of Colleges, 2000-01. Figures represent charges to first-time, full-time undergraduates based on a nine-month academic year of 30 semester hours or 45 quarter hours. **Remarks:** A separate table for each state, the District of Columbia, and Puerto Rico is included. Listing also shows added out-of-state tuition and 1999-2000 tuition and fees. **Number listed:** 29.

1. Al Collins Graphic Design School, with tuition and fees of $18,600
2. Embry-Riddle Aeronautical University, $14,820
3. Prescott College, $13,264
4. Grand Canyon University, $9,660
5. DeVry Institute of Technology, Phoenix, $8,390
6. Southwestern College, $8,310
7. University of Phoenix, $7,200
7. Western International University, $7,200
9. American Indian College of the Assemblies of God, $4,330
10. University of Arizona, $2,348

Source: "Tuition and Fees 2000-01," *The Chronicle of Higher Education (http://chronicle.com/stats/tuition/tuition-results.php3)*, 47:, (October 27, 2000).

★1483★
Lowest undergraduate tuition and fees at colleges and universities in Arizona

Ranking basis/background: These figures for in-state tuition and fees at over 3,000 colleges and universities were collected by the College Board in the Annual Survey of Colleges, 2000-01. Figures represent charges to first-time, full-time undergraduates based on a nine-month academic year of 30 semester hours or 45 quarter hours. **Remarks:** A separate table for each state, the District of Columbia, and Puerto Rico is included. Listing also shows added out-of-state tuition and 1999-2000 tuition and fees. **Number listed:** 29.

1. Dine College, with tuition and fees of $660
2. Mohave Community College, $720
3. Eastern Arizona College, $748
4. Northland Pioneer College, $750
5. Central Arizona College, $910
6. Cochise College, $960
6. Arizona Western College, $960
8. Pima Community College, $1,060
9. Yavapai College, $1,240
9. South Mountain Community College, $1,240
9. Scottsdale Community College, $1,240
9. Rio Salado College, $1,240
9. Phoenix College, $1,240
9. Paradise Valley Community College, $1,240
9. Mesa Community College, $1,240
9. Glendale Community College, $1,240
9. Gateway Community College, $1,240

Source: "Tuition and Fees 2000-01," *The Chronicle of Higher Education (http://chronicle.com/stats/tuition/tuition-results.php3)*, 47:, (October 27, 2000).

COLLEGES & UNIVERSITIES–STUDENT COSTS–ARKANSAS

★1484★
Highest undergraduate tuition and fees at colleges and universities in Arkansas

Ranking basis/background: These figures for in-state tuition and fees at over 3,000 colleges and universities were collected by the College Board in the Annual Survey of Colleges, 2000-01. Figures represent charges to first-time, full-time undergraduates based on a nine-month academic year of 30 semester hours or 45 quarter hours. **Remarks:** A separate table for each state, the District of Columbia, and Puerto Rico is included. Listing also shows added out-of-state tuition and 1999-2000 tuition and fees. **Number listed:** 32.

1. Hendrix College, with tuition and fees of $12,920
2. John Brown University, $11,492
3. Lyon College, $10,955
4. Ouachita Baptist University, $10,000
5. University of the Ozarks, $9,106
6. Harding University, $8,525
7. Williams Baptist College, $6,270
8. Central Baptist College, $6,088
9. University of Arkansas, $3,872
10. Philander Smith College, $3,842

Source: "Tuition and Fees 2000-01," *The Chronicle of Higher Education (http://chronicle.com/stats/tuition/tuition-results.php3)*, 47:, (October 27, 2000).

★1485★

Lowest undergraduate tuition and fees at colleges and universities in Arkansas

Ranking basis/background: These figures for in-state tuition and fees at over 3,000 colleges and universities were collected by the College Board in the Annual Survey of Colleges, 2000-01. Figures represent charges to first-time, full-time undergraduates based on a nine-month academic year of 30 semester hours or 45 quarter hours. **Remarks:** A separate table for each state, the District of Columbia, and Puerto Rico is included. Listing also shows added out-of-state tuition and 1999-2000 tuition and fees. **Number listed:** 32.

1. Rich Mountain Community College, with tuition and fees of $888
2. Mississippi County Community College, $980
2. Garland County Community College, $980
4. North Arkansas College, $1,008
5. East Arkansas Community College, $1,050
6. Westark College, $1,260
7. Northwest Arkansas Community College, $1,290
7. Arkansas State University, Beebe Branch, $1,290
9. Arkansas State University, Mountain Home, $1,330
10. University of Arkansas, Phillips Community College, $1,356

Source: "Tuition and Fees 2000-01," *The Chronicle of Higher Education (http://chronicle.com/stats/tuition/tuition-results.php3),* 47:, (October 27, 2000).

COLLEGES & UNIVERSITIES–STUDENT COSTS–CALIFORNIA

★1486★

Highest undergraduate tuition and fees at colleges and universities in California

Ranking basis/background: These figures for in-state tuition and fees at over 3,000 colleges and universities were collected by the College Board in the Annual Survey of Colleges, 2000-01. Figures represent charges to first-time, full-time undergraduates based on a nine-month academic year of 30 semester hours or 45 quarter hours. **Remarks:** A separate table for each state, the District of Columbia, and Puerto Rico is included. Listing also shows added out-of-state tuition and 1999-2000 tuition and fees. **Number listed:** 235.

1. Pitzer College, with tuition and fees of $25,238
2. Stanford University, $24,441
3. University of Southern California, $24,229
4. Pomona College, $24,170
5. Pepperdine University, $24,050
6. Occidental College, $24,030
7. Harvey Mudd College, $23,187
8. Scripps College, $22,600
9. Claremont McKenna College, $22,580
10. Chapman University, $21,049

Source: "Tuition and Fees 2000-01," *The Chronicle of Higher Education (http://chronicle.com/stats/tuition/tuition-results.php3),* 47:, (October 27, 2000).

★1487★

Lowest undergraduate tuition and fees at colleges and universities in California

Ranking basis/background: These figures for in-state tuition and fees at over 3,000 colleges and universities were collected by the College Board in the Annual Survey of Colleges, 2000-01. Figures represent charges to first-time, full-time undergraduates based on a nine-month academic year of 30 semester hours or 45 quarter hours. **Remarks:** A separate table for each state, the District of Columbia, and Puerto Rico is included. Listing also shows added out-of-state tuition and 1999-2000 tuition and fees. **Number listed:** 235.

1. Lake Tahoe Community College, with tuition and fees of $324
2. Vista Community College, $330
2. San Joaquin Delta College, $330
2. Sacramento City College, $330
2. Pasadena City College, $330
2. Palo Verde College, $330
2. Merritt College, $330
2. Imperial Valley College, $330
2. Contra Costa College, $330
2. Diablo Valley College, $330
2. Chabot College, $330
2. Cerro Coso Community College, $330
2. Barstow College, $330
2. American River College, $330

Source: "Tuition and Fees 2000-01," *The Chronicle of Higher Education (http://chronicle.com/stats/tuition/tuition-results.php3),* 47:, (October 27, 2000).

COLLEGES & UNIVERSITIES–STUDENT COSTS–COLORADO

★1488★

Highest undergraduate tuition and fees at colleges and universities in Colorado

Ranking basis/background: These figures for in-state tuition and fees at over 3,000 colleges and universities were collected by the College Board in the Annual Survey of Colleges, 2000-01. Figures represent charges to first-time, full-time undergraduates based on a nine-month academic year of 30 semester hours or 45 quarter hours. **Remarks:** A separate table for each state, the District of Columbia, and Puerto Rico is included. Listing also shows added out-of-state tuition and 1999-2000 tuition and fees. **Number listed:** 46.

1. Colorado College, with tuition and fees of $22,800
2. University of Denver, $20,556
3. Regis University, $17,570
4. Art Institute of Colorado, $15,000
5. Naropa University, $14,090
6. Colorado Christian University, $11,400
7. Rocky Mountain College of Art & Design, $10,752
8. Technical Trades Institute, $10,200
9. Westwood College of Aviation Technology, $8,900
10. National American University, Denver, $8,600

Source: "Tuition and Fees 2000-01," *The Chronicle of Higher Education (http://chronicle.com/stats/tuition/tuition-results.php3),* 47:, (October 27, 2000).

★1489★

Lowest undergraduate tuition and fees at colleges and universities in Colorado

Ranking basis/background: These figures for in-state tuition and fees at over 3,000 colleges and universities were collected by the College Board in the Annual Survey of Colleges, 2000-01. Figures represent charges to first-time, full-time undergraduates based on a nine-month academic year of 30 semester hours or 45 quarter hours. **Remarks:** A separate table for each state, the District of Columbia, and Puerto Rico is included. Listing also shows added out-of-state tuition and 1999-2000 tuition and fees. **Number listed:** 46.

1. Colorado Mountain College, Timberline Campus, with tuition and fees of $1,380
1. Colorado Mountain College, Spring Valley Campus, $1,380
1. Colorado Mountain College, Alpine Campus, $1,380
4. Aims Community College, $1,530
5. Community College of Aurora, $1,830
6. Pikes Peak Community College, $1,854
7. Arapahoe Community College, $1,861
8. Morgan Community College, $1,884
9. Colorado Northwestern Community College, $1,894
10. Otero Junior College, $1,902

Source: "Tuition and Fees 2000-01," *The Chronicle of Higher Education (http://chronicle.com/stats/tuition/tuition-results.php3),* 47:, (October 27, 2000).

COLLEGES & UNIVERSITIES–STUDENT COSTS–CONNECTICUT

★1490★

Highest undergraduate tuition and fees at colleges and universities in Connecticut

Ranking basis/background: These figures for in-state tuition and fees at over 3,000 colleges and universities were collected by the College Board in the Annual Survey of Colleges, 2000-01. Figures represent charges to first-time, full-time undergraduates based on a nine-month academic year of 30 semester hours or 45 quarter hours. **Remarks:** A separate table for each state, the District of Columbia, and Puerto Rico is included. Listing also shows added out-of-state tuition and 1999-2000 tuition and fees. **Number listed:** 34.

1. Wesleyan University, with tuition and fees of $26,180
2. Trinity College, $25,440
3. Yale University, $25,220
4. Gibbs College, $24,192
5. Fairfield University, $21,435
6. University of Hartford, $19,696
7. Quinnipiac University, $17,780
8. St. Joseph College, $17,430
9. Sacred Heart University, $15,589
10. University of New Haven, $15,520

Source: "Tuition and Fees 2000-01," *The Chronicle of Higher Education (http://chronicle.com/stats/tuition/tuition-results.php3),* 47:, (October 27, 2000).

COLLEGES & UNIVERSITIES—STUDENT COSTS–DELAWARE

★1491★
Lowest undergraduate tuition and fees at colleges and universities in Connecticut

Ranking basis/background: These figures for in-state tuition and fees at over 3,000 colleges and universities were collected by the College Board in the Annual Survey of Colleges, 2000-01. Figures represent charges to first-time, full-time undergraduates based on a nine-month academic year of 30 semester hours or 45 quarter hours. **Remarks:** A separate table for each state, the District of Columbia, and Puerto Rico is included. Listing also shows added out-of-state tuition and 1999-2000 tuition and fees. **Number listed:** 34.

1. Charter Oak State College, with tuition and fees of $517
2. Tunxis Community College, $1,886
2. Three Rivers Community-Technical College, $1,886
2. Quinebaug Valley Community College, $1,886
2. Norwalk Community-Technical College, $1,886
2. Northwestern Connecticut Community-Technical College, $1,886
2. Naugatuck Valley Community-Technical College, $1,886
2. Middlesex Community-Technical College, $1,886
2. Manchester Community-Technical College, $1,886
2. Housatonic Community-Technical College, $1,886
2. Gateway Community College, $1,886
2. Capital Community College, $1,886
2. Asnuntuck Community-Technical College, $1,886

Source: "Tuition and Fees 2000-01," *The Chronicle of Higher Education* (http://chronicle.com/stats/tuition/tuition-results.php3), 47:, (October 27, 2000).

COLLEGES & UNIVERSITIES–STUDENT COSTS–DELAWARE

★1492★
Undergraduate tuition and fees at colleges and universities in Delaware

Ranking basis/background: These figures for in-state tuition and fees at over 3,000 colleges and universities were collected by the College Board in the Annual Survey of Colleges, 2000-01. Figures represent charges to first-time, full-time undergraduates based on a nine-month academic year of 30 semester hours or 45 quarter hours. **Remarks:** A separate table for each state, the District of Columbia, and Puerto Rico is included. Listing also shows added out-of-state tuition and 1999-2000 tuition and fees. **Number listed:** 9.

1. Wesley College, with tuition and fees of $11,919
2. Goldey-Beacom College, $8,280
3. Wilmington College, $6,290
4. University of Delaware, $5,004
5. Delaware State University, $3,470
6. Delaware Technical and Community College, Owens Campus, $1,616
6. Delaware Technical and Community College, Stanton/Wilmington Campus, $1,616
6. Delaware Technical and Community College, Terry Campus, $1,616

Source: "Tuition and Fees 2000-01," *The Chronicle of Higher Education* (http://chronicle.com/stats/tuition/tuition-results.php3), 47:, (October 27, 2000).

COLLEGES & UNIVERSITIES–STUDENT COSTS–DISTRICT OF COLUMBIA

★1493★
Undergraduate tuition and fees at colleges and universities in the District of Columbia

Ranking basis/background: These figures for in-state tuition and fees at over 3,000 colleges and universities were collected by the College Board in the Annual Survey of Colleges, 2000-01. Figures represent charges to first-time, full-time undergraduates based on a nine-month academic year of 30 semester hours or 45 quarter hours. **Remarks:** A separate table for each state, the District of Columbia, and Puerto Rico is included. Listing also shows added out-of-state tuition and 1999-2000 tuition and fees. **Number listed:** 10.

1. George Washington University, with tuition and fees of $25,040
2. Georgetown University, $24,168
3. American University, $21,399
4. Catholic University of America, $19,930
5. Corcoran College of Art and Design, $15,550
6. Trinity College, $14,440
7. Howard University, $9,745
8. Southeastern University, $9,300
9. Gallaudet University, $7,660
10. University of the District of Columbia, $2,070

Source: "Tuition and Fees 2000-01," *The Chronicle of Higher Education* (http://chronicle.com/stats/tuition/tuition-results.php3), 47:, (October 27, 2000).

COLLEGES & UNIVERSITIES–STUDENT COSTS–FLORIDA

★1494★
Highest undergraduate tuition and fees at colleges and universities in Florida

Ranking basis/background: These figures for in-state tuition and fees at over 3,000 colleges and universities were collected by the College Board in the Annual Survey of Colleges, 2000-01. Figures represent charges to first-time, full-time undergraduates based on a nine-month academic year of 30 semester hours or 45 quarter hours. **Remarks:** A separate table for each state, the District of Columbia, and Puerto Rico is included. Listing also shows added out-of-state tuition and 1999-2000 tuition and fees. **Number listed:** 81.

1. Rollins College, with tuition and fees of $22,868
2. University of Miami, $22,526
3. Lynn University, $19,250
4. Eckerd College, $18,785
5. Florida Institute of Technology, $18,450
6. Stetson University, $18,385
7. Barry University, $16,815
8. University of Tampa, $16,032
9. Ringling School of Art and Design, $15,670
10. Jacksonville University, $15,510

Source: "Tuition and Fees 2000-01," *The Chronicle of Higher Education* (http://chronicle.com/stats/tuition/tuition-results.php3), 47:, (October 27, 2000).

★1495★
Lowest undergraduate tuition and fees at colleges and universities in Florida

Ranking basis/background: These figures for in-state tuition and fees at over 3,000 colleges and universities were collected by the College Board in the Annual Survey of Colleges, 2000-01. Figures represent charges to first-time, full-time undergraduates based on a nine-month academic year of 30 semester hours or 45 quarter hours. **Remarks:** A separate table for each state, the District of Columbia, and Puerto Rico is included. Listing also shows added out-of-state tuition and 1999-2000 tuition and fees. **Number listed:** 81.

1. Okaloosa-Walton Community College, with tuition and fees of $1,256
2. Lake City Community College, $1,294
3. Broward Community College, $1,403
4. North Florida Community College, $1,411
5. St. Johns River Community College, $1,419
6. Brevard Community College, $1,425
7. Tallahassee Community College, $1,440
7. Palm Beach Community College, $1,440
7. Indian River Community College, $1,440
7. Chipola Junior College, $1,440

Source: "Tuition and Fees 2000-01," *The Chronicle of Higher Education* (http://chronicle.com/stats/tuition/tuition-results.php3), 47:, (October 27, 2000).

COLLEGES & UNIVERSITIES–STUDENT COSTS–GEORGIA

★1496★
Highest undergraduate tuition and fees at colleges and universities in Georgia

Ranking basis/background: These figures for in-state tuition and fees at over 3,000 colleges and universities were collected by the College Board in the Annual Survey of Colleges, 2000-01. Figures represent charges to first-time, full-time undergraduates based on a nine-month academic year of 30 semester hours or 45 quarter hours. **Remarks:** A separate table for each state, the District of Columbia, and Puerto Rico is included. Listing also shows added out-of-state tuition and 1999-2000 tuition and fees. **Number listed:** 78.

1. Emory University, with tuition and fees of $24,532
2. Oglethorpe University, $18,485
3. Oxford College of Emory University, $17,840
4. Mercer University, $17,028
5. Agnes Scott College, $16,745
6. Savannah College of Art and Design, $16,700
7. Wesleyan College, $16,300
8. Covenant College, $15,960
9. Atlanta College of Art, $14,095
10. Art Institute of Atlanta, $13,868

Source: "Tuition and Fees 2000-01," *The Chronicle of Higher Education (http://chronicle.com/stats/tuition/tuition-results.php3)*, 47:, (October 27, 2000).

★1497★
Lowest undergraduate tuition and fees at colleges and universities in Georgia

Ranking basis/background: These figures for in-state tuition and fees at over 3,000 colleges and universities were collected by the College Board in the Annual Survey of Colleges, 2000-01. Figures represent charges to first-time, full-time undergraduates based on a nine-month academic year of 30 semester hours or 45 quarter hours. **Remarks:** A separate table for each state, the District of Columbia, and Puerto Rico is included. Listing also shows added out-of-state tuition and 1999-2000 tuition and fees. **Number listed:** 78.
1. Athens Area Technical Institute, with tuition and fees of $933
2. Chattahoochee Technical Institute, $978
3. Columbus Technical Institute, $1,008
4. Gwinnett Technical Institute, $1,107
5. DeKalb Technical Institute, $1,206
6. Savannah Technical Institute, $1,268
7. East Georgia College, $1,376
8. Dalton State College, $1,394
9. Bainbridge College, $1,404
10. Gainesville College, $1,408

Source: "Tuition and Fees 2000-01," *The Chronicle of Higher Education (http://chronicle.com/stats/tuition/tuition-results.php3)*, 47:, (October 27, 2000).

COLLEGES & UNIVERSITIES–STUDENT COSTS–HAWAII

★1498★
Undergraduate tuition and fees at colleges and universities in Hawaii

Ranking basis/background: These figures for in-state tuition and fees at over 3,000 colleges and universities were collected by the College Board in the Annual Survey of Colleges, 2000-01. Figures represent charges to first-time, full-time undergraduates based on a nine-month academic year of 30 semester hours or 45 quarter hours. **Remarks:** A separate table for each state, the District of Columbia, and Puerto Rico is included. Listing also shows added out-of-state tuition and 1999-2000 tuition and fees. **Number listed:** 15.
1. TransPacific Hawaii College, with tuition and fees of $15,021
2. Chaminade University, Honolulu, $12,240
3. Hawaii Pacific University, $8,920
4. Heald Business College, Honolulu, $7,560
5. University of Hawaii, Manoa, $3,157
6. Brigham Young University (HI), $2,988
7. University of Hawaii, West Oahu, $1,906
8. University of Hawaii, Hilo, $1,466
9. University of Hawaii, Kapiolani Community College, $1,092
10. University of Hawaii, Hawaii Community College, $1,082
11. University of Hawaii, Leeward Community College, 1,057
12. University of Hawaii, Honolulu Community College, $1,052
12. University of Hawaii, Windward Community College, $1,052
14. University of Hawaii, Maui Community College, $1,050
15. University of Hawaii, Kauai Community College, $1,042

Source: "Tuition and Fees 2000-01," *The Chronicle of Higher Education (http://chronicle.com/stats/tuition/tuition-results.php3)*, 47:, (October 27, 2000).

COLLEGES & UNIVERSITIES–STUDENT COSTS–IDAHO

★1499★
Undergraduate tuition and fees at colleges and universities in Idaho

Ranking basis/background: These figures for in-state tuition and fees at over 3,000 colleges and universities were collected by the College Board in the Annual Survey of Colleges, 2000-01. Figures represent charges to first-time, full-time undergraduates based on a nine-month academic year of 30 semester hours or 45 quarter hours. **Remarks:** A separate table for each state, the District of Columbia, and Puerto Rico is included. Listing also shows added out-of-state tuition and 1999-2000 tuition and fees. **Number listed:** 11.
1. Albertson College, with tuition and fees of $16,600
2. Northwest Nazarene University, $13,500
3. Boise Bible College, $4,880
4. Idaho State University, $2,578
5. University of Idaho, $2,476
6. Boise State University, $2,451
7. Lewis-Clark State College, $2,360
8. Ricks College, $2,250
9. College of Southern Idaho, $1,330
10. North Idaho College, $1,296
11. Eastern Idaho Technical College, $1,248

Source: "Tuition and Fees 2000-01," *The Chronicle of Higher Education (http://chronicle.com/stats/tuition/tuition-results.php3)*, 47:, (October 27, 2000).

COLLEGES & UNIVERSITIES–STUDENT COSTS–ILLINOIS

★1500★
Highest undergraduate tuition and fees at colleges and universities in Illinois

Ranking basis/background: These figures for in-state tuition and fees at over 3,000 colleges and universities were collected by the College Board in the Annual Survey of Colleges, 2000-01. Figures represent charges to first-time, full-time undergraduates based on a nine-month academic year of 30 semester hours or 45 quarter hours. **Remarks:** A separate table for each state, the District of Columbia, and Puerto Rico is included. Listing also shows added out-of-state tuition and 1999-2000 tuition and fees. **Number listed:** 130.
1. University of Chicago, with tuition and fees of $25,489
2. Northwestern University, $24,648
3. Lake Forest College, $21,190
4. Knox College, $21,174
5. Illinois Wesleyan University, $20,410
6. School of the Art Institute of Chicago, $20,220
7. Loyola University, Chicago, $18,726
8. Illinois Institute of Technology, $18,100
9. Augustana College, $17,913
10. North Park University, $16,910

Source: "Tuition and Fees 2000-01," *The Chronicle of Higher Education (http://chronicle.com/stats/tuition/tuition-results.php3)*, 47:, (October 27, 2000).

★1501★
Lowest undergraduate tuition and fees at colleges and universities in Illinois

Ranking basis/background: These figures for in-state tuition and fees at over 3,000 colleges and universities were collected by the College Board in the Annual Survey of Colleges, 2000-01. Figures represent charges to first-time, full-time undergraduates based on a nine-month academic year of 30 semester hours or 45 quarter hours. **Remarks:** A separate table for each state, the District of Columbia, and Puerto Rico is included. Listing also shows added out-of-state tuition and 1999-2000 tuition and fees. **Number listed:** 130.
1. Southeastern Illinois College, with tuition and fees of $1,170
2. Shawnee Community College, $1,200
3. Rend Lake College, $1,260
3. Kaskaskia College, $1,260
3. Kankakee Community College, $1,260
3. Wabash Valley College, $1,260
3. Olney Central College, $1,260
3. Lincoln Trail College, $1,260
3. Frontier Community College, $1,260
10. Danville Area Community College, $1,320

Source: "Tuition and Fees 2000-01," *The Chronicle of Higher Education (http://chronicle.com/stats/tuition/tuition-results.php3)*, 47:, (October 27, 2000).

COLLEGES & UNIVERSITIES–STUDENT COSTS–INDIANA

★1502★
Highest undergraduate tuition and fees at colleges and universities in Indiana

Ranking basis/background: These figures for in-state tuition and fees at over 3,000 colleges and universities were collected by the College Board in the Annual Survey of Colleges, 2000-01. Figures represent charges to first-time, full-time undergraduates based on a nine-month academic year of 30 semester hours or 45 quarter hours. **Remarks:** A separate table for each state, the District of Columbia, and Puerto Rico is included. Listing also shows added out-of-state tuition and 1999-2000 tuition and fees. **Number listed:** 63.
1. University of Notre Dame, with tuition and fees of $23,357
2. Earlham College, $21,070
3. Rose-Hulman Institute of Technology, $20,904
4. DePauw University, $20,550
5. St. Mary's College (IN), $18,300
6. Wabash College, $18,294
7. Butler University, $18,230
8. Valparaiso University, $17,636
9. University of Evansville, $16,404
10. Taylor University, $15,820

COLLEGES & UNIVERSITIES—STUDENT COSTS–IOWA

Source: "Tuition and Fees 2000-01," *The Chronicle of Higher Education* (http://chronicle.com/stats/tuition/tuition-results.php3), 47:, (October 27, 2000).

★1503★
Lowest undergraduate tuition and fees at colleges and universities in Indiana

Ranking basis/background: These figures for in-state tuition and fees at over 3,000 colleges and universities were collected by the College Board in the Annual Survey of Colleges, 2000-01. Figures represent charges to first-time, full-time undergraduates based on a nine-month academic year of 30 semester hours or 45 quarter hours. **Remarks:** A separate table for each state, the District of Columbia, and Puerto Rico is included. Listing also shows added out-of-state tuition and 1999-2000 tuition and fees. **Number listed:** 63.
1. Ivy Tech. State College, Whitewater, with tuition and fees of $1,986
1. Ivy Tech State College, Wabash Valley, $1,986
1. Ivy Tech State College, Southwest, $1,986
1. Ivy Tech State College, Southeast, $1,986
1. Ivy Tech State College, Southcentral, $1,986
1. Ivy Tech State College, Northwest, $1,986
1. Ivy Tech State College, Northeast, $1,986
1. Ivy Tech State College, Northcentral, $1,986
1. Ivy Tech State College, Lafayette, $1,986
1. Ivy Tech State College, Kokomo, $1,986
1. Ivy Tech State College, Eastcentral, $1,986
1. Ivy Tech State College, Columbus, $1,986
1. Ivy Tech State College, Central Indiana, $1,986

Source: "Tuition and Fees 2000-01," *The Chronicle of Higher Education* (http://chronicle.com/stats/tuition/tuition-results.php3), 47:, (October 27, 2000).

COLLEGES & UNIVERSITIES–STUDENT COSTS–IOWA

★1504★
Highest undergraduate tuition and fees at colleges and universities in Iowa

Ranking basis/background: These figures for in-state tuition and fees at over 3,000 colleges and universities were collected by the College Board in the Annual Survey of Colleges, 2000-01. Figures represent charges to first-time, full-time undergraduates based on a nine-month academic year of 30 semester hours or 45 quarter hours. **Remarks:** A separate table for each state, the District of Columbia, and Puerto Rico is included. Listing also shows added out-of-state tuition and 1999-2000 tuition and fees. **Number listed:** 57.
1. Grinnell College, with tuition and fees of $20,500
2. Cornell College, $19,570
3. Coe College, $18,415
4. Luther College, $18,080
5. Buena Vista University, $17,176
6. Drake University, $17,090
7. Wartburg College, $15,765
8. Maharishi University of Management, $15,630
9. Loras College, $15,329
10. Simpson College, $15,150

Source: "Tuition and Fees 2000-01," *The Chronicle of Higher Education* (http://chronicle.com/stats/tuition/tuition-results.php3), 47:, (October 27, 2000).

★1505★
Lowest undergraduate tuition and fees at colleges and universities in Iowa

Ranking basis/background: These figures for in-state tuition and fees at over 3,000 colleges and universities were collected by the College Board in the Annual Survey of Colleges, 2000-01. Figures represent charges to first-time, full-time undergraduates based on a nine-month academic year of 30 semester hours or 45 quarter hours. **Remarks:** A separate table for each state, the District of Columbia, and Puerto Rico is included. Listing also shows added out-of-state tuition and 1999-2000 tuition and fees. **Number listed:** 57.
1. Indian Hills Community College, with tuition and fees of $1,860
2. Northwest Iowa Community College, $1,905
3. Scott Community College, $1,950
3. Muscatine Community College, $1,950
3. Kirkwood Community College, $1,950
3. Clinton Community College, $1,950
7. Southeastern Community College, South Campus, $1,980
8. Southeastern Community College, North Campus, $2,000
9. Iowa Central Community College, $2,078
10. Des Moines Area Community College, $2,082

Source: "Tuition and Fees 2000-01," *The Chronicle of Higher Education* (http://chronicle.com/stats/tuition/tuition-results.php3), 47:, (October 27, 2000).

COLLEGES & UNIVERSITIES–STUDENT COSTS–KANSAS

★1506★
Highest undergraduate tuition and fees at colleges and universities in Kansas

Ranking basis/background: These figures for in-state tuition and fees at over 3,000 colleges and universities were collected by the College Board in the Annual Survey of Colleges, 2000-01. Figures represent charges to first-time, full-time undergraduates based on a nine-month academic year of 30 semester hours or 45 quarter hours. **Remarks:** A separate table for each state, the District of Columbia, and Puerto Rico is included. Listing also shows added out-of-state tuition and 1999-2000 tuition and fees. **Number listed:** 47.
1. Benedictine College, with tuition and fees of $12,700
2. Tabor College, $12,410
3. Baker University, $12,380
4. Bethany College, $12,304
5. Southwestern College, $12,260
6. St. Mary College (KS), $12,070
7. Bethel College, $11,800
7. Kansas Wesleyan University, $11,800
9. Sterling College, $11,782
10. Hesston College, $11,700
10. McPherson College, $11,700

★1507★
Lowest undergraduate tuition and fees at colleges and universities in Kansas

Ranking basis/background: These figures for in-state tuition and fees at over 3,000 colleges and universities were collected by the College Board in the Annual Survey of Colleges, 2000-01. Figures represent charges to first-time, full-time undergraduates based on a nine-month academic year of 30 semester hours or 45 quarter hours. **Remarks:** A separate table for each state, the District of Columbia, and Puerto Rico is included. Listing also shows added out-of-state tuition and 1999-2000 tuition and fees. **Number listed:** 47.
1. Independence Community College, with tuition and fees of $1,245
2. Allen County Community College, $1,260
3. Kansas City Kansas Community College, $1,290
4. Seward County Community College, $1,320
4. Garden City Community College, $1,320
6. Neosho County Community College, $1,350
6. Labette Community College, $1,350
6. Fort Scott Community College, $1,350
6. Cowley County Community College, $1,350
6. Colby Community College, $1,350
6. Coffeyville Community College, $1,350

Source: "Tuition and Fees 2000-01," *The Chronicle of Higher Education* (http://chronicle.com/stats/tuition/tuition-results.php3), 47:, (October 27, 2000).

COLLEGES & UNIVERSITIES–STUDENT COSTS–KENTUCKY

★1508★
Highest undergraduate tuition and fees at colleges and universities in Kentucky

Ranking basis/background: These figures for in-state tuition and fees at over 3,000 colleges and universities were collected by the College Board in the Annual Survey of Colleges, 2000-01. Figures represent charges to first-time, full-time undergraduates based on a nine-month academic year of 30 semester hours or 45 quarter hours. **Remarks:** A separate table for each state, the District of Columbia, and Puerto Rico is included. Listing also shows added out-of-state tuition and 1999-2000 tuition and fees. **Number listed:** 50.
1. Centre College, with tuition and fees of $16,900
2. Transylvania University, $15,270
3. Asbury College, $14,056
4. Bellarmine College, $13,760
5. Thomas More College, $12,580
6. Georgetown College, $12,380
7. Spalding University, $11,496
8. Union College, $11,120
9. Kentucky Wesleyan College, $10,420
10. Louisville Technical Institute, $10,250

★1509★
Lowest undergraduate tuition and fees at colleges and universities in Kentucky

Ranking basis/background: These figures for in-state tuition and fees at over 3,000 colleges and universities were collected by the College Board in the Annual Survey of Colleges, 2000-01. Figures represent charges to first-time, full-time undergraduates based on a nine-month academic year of 30 semester hours or 45 quarter hours. **Remarks:** A separate table for each state, the District of Columbia, and Puerto Rico is included. Listing also shows added out-of-state tuition and 1999-2000 tuition and fees. **Number listed:** 50.

1. Berea College, with tuition and fees of $199
2. Southeast Community College, $1,230
2. Somerset Community College, $1,230
2. Prestonsburg Community College, $1,230
2. Paducah Community College, $1,230
2. Owensboro Community College, $1,230
2. Maysville Community College, $1,230
2. Madisonville Community College, $1,230
2. Jefferson Community College, $1,230
2. Hopkinsville Community College, $1,230
2. Henderson Community College, $1,230
2. Hazard Community College, $1,230
2. Elizabethtown Community College, $1,230
2. Ashland Community College, $1,230

Source: "Tuition and Fees 2000-01," *The Chronicle of Higher Education (http://chronicle.com/stats/tuition/tuition-results.php3)*, 47:, (October 27, 2000).

COLLEGES & UNIVERSITIES–STUDENT COSTS–LOUISIANA

★1510★
Highest undergraduate tuition and fees at colleges and universities in Louisiana

Ranking basis/background: These figures for in-state tuition and fees at over 3,000 colleges and universities were collected by the College Board in the Annual Survey of Colleges, 2000-01. Figures represent charges to first-time, full-time undergraduates based on a nine-month academic year of 30 semester hours or 45 quarter hours. **Remarks:** A separate table for each state, the District of Columbia, and Puerto Rico is included. Listing also shows added out-of-state tuition and 1999-2000 tuition and fees. **Number listed:** 30.

1. Tulane University, with tuition and fees of $25,480
2. Remington College-Education American, Inc., $15,550
3. Loyola University, New Orleans, $15,481
4. Centenary College of Louisiana, $14,600
5. Xavier University (LA), $9,700
6. Dillard University, $9,200
7. St. Joseph Seminary College, $7,775
8. Louisiana College, $7,150
9. Our Lady of Holy Cross College, $6,240
10. Grantham College of Engineering, $5,200

Source: "Tuition and Fees 2000-01," *The Chronicle of Higher Education (http://chronicle.com/stats/tuition/tuition-results.php3)*, 47:, (October 27, 2000).

★1511★
Lowest undergraduate tuition and fees at colleges and universities in Louisiana

Ranking basis/background: These figures for in-state tuition and fees at over 3,000 colleges and universities were collected by the College Board in the Annual Survey of Colleges, 2000-01. Figures represent charges to first-time, full-time undergraduates based on a nine-month academic year of 30 semester hours or 45 quarter hours. **Remarks:** A separate table for each state, the District of Columbia, and Puerto Rico is included. Listing also shows added out-of-state tuition and 1999-2000 tuition and fees. **Number listed:** 30.

1. Southern University, with tuition and fees of $1,260
2. Bossier Parish Community College, $1,360
3. Louisiana State University, Alexandria, $1,397
4. Louisiana State University, Eunice, $1,414
5. Nunez Community College, $1,450
6. Delgado Community College, $1,506
7. Southern University, New Orleans, $2,169
8. Southern University and A&M College, $2,286
9. University of Louisiana, Lafayette, $2,289
10. Louisiana State University, Shreveport, $2,300

Source: "Tuition and Fees 2000-01," *The Chronicle of Higher Education (http://chronicle.com/stats/tuition/tuition-results.php3)*, 47:, (October 27, 2000).

COLLEGES & UNIVERSITIES–STUDENT COSTS–MAINE

★1512★
Highest undergraduate tuition and fees at colleges and universities in Maine

Ranking basis/background: These figures for in-state tuition and fees at over 3,000 colleges and universities were collected by the College Board in the Annual Survey of Colleges, 2000-01. Figures represent charges to first-time, full-time undergraduates based on a nine-month academic year of 30 semester hours or 45 quarter hours. **Remarks:** A separate table for each state, the District of Columbia, and Puerto Rico is included. Listing also shows added out-of-state tuition and 1999-2000 tuition and fees. **Number listed:** 25.

1. Bowdoin College, with tuition and fees of $25,890
2. College of the Atlantic, $20,361
3. Maine College of Art, $17,558
4. University of New England, $16,325
5. St. Joseph's College, $14,415
6. Unity College, $12,795
7. Thomas College, $12,780
8. Husson College, $9,580
9. Central Maine Medical Center School of Nursing, $5,931
10. Andover College, $5,400

Source: "Tuition and Fees 2000-01," *The Chronicle of Higher Education (http://chronicle.com/stats/tuition/tuition-results.php3)*, 47:, (October 27, 2000).

★1513★
Lowest undergraduate tuition and fees at colleges and universities in Maine

Ranking basis/background: These figures for in-state tuition and fees at over 3,000 colleges and universities were collected by the College Board in the Annual Survey of Colleges, 2000-01. Figures represent charges to first-time, full-time undergraduates based on a nine-month academic year of 30 semester hours or 45 quarter hours. **Remarks:** A separate table for each state, the District of Columbia, and Puerto Rico is included. Listing also shows added out-of-state tuition and 1999-2000 tuition and fees. **Number listed:** 25.

1. Washington County Technical College, with tuition and fees of $2,085
2. Southern Maine Technical College, $2,155
3. Northern Maine Technical College, $2,190
4. Central Maine Technical College, $2,220
5. Kennebec Valley Technical College, $2,250
6. Eastern Maine Technical College, $2,380
7. Beal College, $2,825
8. University of Maine, Fort Kent, $3,434
9. University of Maine, Presque Isle, $3,520
10. University of Maine, Augusta, $3,525

Source: "Tuition and Fees 2000-01," *The Chronicle of Higher Education (http://chronicle.com/stats/tuition/tuition-results.php3)*, 47:, (October 27, 2000).

COLLEGES & UNIVERSITIES–STUDENT COSTS–MARYLAND

★1514★
Highest undergraduate tuition and fees at colleges and universities in Maryland

Ranking basis/background: These figures for in-state tuition and fees at over 3,000 colleges and universities were collected by the College Board in the Annual Survey of Colleges, 2000-01. Figures represent charges to first-time, full-time undergraduates based on a nine-month academic year of 30 semester hours or 45 quarter hours. **Remarks:** A separate table for each state, the District of Columbia, and Puerto Rico is included. Listing also shows added out-of-state tuition and 1999-2000 tuition and fees. **Number listed:** 54.

1. Johns Hopkins University, with tuition and fees of $25,430
2. St. John's College, $24,770
3. Johns Hopkins University, Peabody Conservatory of Music, $23,475
4. Loyola College (MD), $21,750
5. Goucher College, $21,300
5. Washington College, $21,300
7. Maryland Institute, College of Art, $20,080
8. Western Maryland College, $19,600
9. Hood College, $18,620
10. Mount St. Mary's College and Seminary, $17,400

Source: "Tuition and Fees 2000-01," *The Chronicle of Higher Education (http://chronicle.com/stats/tuition/tuition-results.php3)*, 47:, (October 27, 2000).

COLLEGES & UNIVERSITIES—STUDENT COSTS

★1515★
Lowest undergraduate tuition and fees at colleges and universities in Maryland
Ranking basis/background: These figures for in-state tuition and fees at over 3,000 colleges and universities were collected by the College Board in the Annual Survey of Colleges, 2000-01. Figures represent charges to first-time, full-time undergraduates based on a nine-month academic year of 30 semester hours or 45 quarter hours. **Remarks:** A separate table for each state, the District of Columbia, and Puerto Rico is included. Listing also shows added out-of-state tuition and 1999-2000 tuition and fees. **Number listed:** 54.
1. Wor-Wic Community College, with tuition and fees of $1,764
2. Anne Arundel Community College, $1,900
3. Harford Community College, $1,944
4. Cecil Community College, $1,975
5. Baltimore City Community College, $1,980
6. Community College of Baltimore County, Catonsville, $2,115
7. Community College of Baltimore County, Essex, $2,116
7. Community College of Baltimore County, Dundalk, $2,116
9. Carroll Community College, $2,160
10. Hagerstown Community College, $2,280
10. Chesapeake College, $2,280

Source: "Tuition and Fees 2000-01," *The Chronicle of Higher Education (http://chronicle.com/stats/tuition/tuition-results.php3)*, 47:, (October 27, 2000).

★1517★
Lowest undergraduate tuition and fees at colleges and universities in Massachusetts
Ranking basis/background: These figures for in-state tuition and fees at over 3,000 colleges and universities were collected by the College Board in the Annual Survey of Colleges, 2000-01. Figures represent charges to first-time, full-time undergraduates based on a nine-month academic year of 30 semester hours or 45 quarter hours. **Remarks:** A separate table for each state, the District of Columbia, and Puerto Rico is included. Listing also shows added out-of-state tuition and 1999-2000 tuition and fees. **Number listed:** 95.
1. Holyoke Community College, with tuition and fees of $1,756
2. Quinsigamond Community College, $1,890
2. Massachusetts Bay Community College, $1,890
4. Bunker Hill Community College, $1,950
5. Mount Wachusett Community College, $1,992
6. Massasoit Community College, $2,040
7. Bristol Community College, $2,070
8. Northern Essex Community College, $2,190
8. North Shore Community College, $2,190
10. Springfield Technical Community College, $2,198

Source: "Tuition and Fees 2000-01," *The Chronicle of Higher Education (http://chronicle.com/stats/tuition/tuition-results.php3)*, 47:, (October 27, 2000).

★1519★
Lowest undergraduate tuition and fees at colleges and universities in Michigan
Ranking basis/background: These figures for in-state tuition and fees at over 3,000 colleges and universities were collected by the College Board in the Annual Survey of Colleges, 2000-01. Figures represent charges to first-time, full-time undergraduates based on a nine-month academic year of 30 semester hours or 45 quarter hours. **Remarks:** A separate table for each state, the District of Columbia, and Puerto Rico is included. Listing also shows added out-of-state tuition and 1999-2000 tuition and fees. **Number listed:** 89.
1. Kalamazoo Valley Community College, with tuition and fees of $1,341
2. Muskegon Community College, $1,500
3. Lansing Community College, $1,525
4. Oakland Community College, $1,531
5. Gogebic Community College, $1,540
6. Monroe County Community College, $1,544
7. North Central Michigan College, $1,550
8. Lake Michigan College, $1,575
9. Kellogg Community College, $1,635
10. Glen Oaks Community College, $1,650

Source: "Tuition and Fees 2000-01," *The Chronicle of Higher Education (http://chronicle.com/stats/tuition/tuition-results.php3)*, 47:, (October 27, 2000).

COLLEGES & UNIVERSITIES–STUDENT COSTS–MASSACHUSETTS

★1516★
Highest undergraduate tuition and fees at colleges and universities in Massachusetts
Ranking basis/background: These figures for in-state tuition and fees at over 3,000 colleges and universities were collected by the College Board in the Annual Survey of Colleges, 2000-01. Figures represent charges to first-time, full-time undergraduates based on a nine-month academic year of 30 semester hours or 45 quarter hours. **Remarks:** A separate table for each state, the District of Columbia, and Puerto Rico is included. Listing also shows added out-of-state tuition and 1999-2000 tuition and fees. **Number listed:** 95.
1. Brandeis University, with tuition and fees of $26,241
2. Hampshire College, $26,125
3. Amherst College, $26,080
4. Massachusetts Institute of Technology, $26,050
5. Tufts University, $25,714
6. Mount Holyoke College, $25,360
7. Harvard College, $25,128
8. Boston University, $25,044
9. Simon's Rock College of Bard, $24,850
10. Williams College, $24,790

Source: "Tuition and Fees 2000-01," *The Chronicle of Higher Education (http://chronicle.com/stats/tuition/tuition-results.php3)*, 47:, (October 27, 2000).

COLLEGES & UNIVERSITIES–STUDENT COSTS–MICHIGAN

★1518★
Highest undergraduate tuition and fees at colleges and universities in Michigan
Ranking basis/background: These figures for in-state tuition and fees at over 3,000 colleges and universities were collected by the College Board in the Annual Survey of Colleges, 2000-01. Figures represent charges to first-time, full-time undergraduates based on a nine-month academic year of 30 semester hours or 45 quarter hours. **Remarks:** A separate table for each state, the District of Columbia, and Puerto Rico is included. Listing also shows added out-of-state tuition and 1999-2000 tuition and fees. **Number listed:** 89.
1. Kalamazoo College, with tuition and fees of $19,834
2. Albion College, $18,912
3. Hope College, $16,714
4. Center for Creative Studies College of Art and Design, $16,526
5. Kettering University, $16,096
6. Alma College, $15,878
7. University of Detroit Mercy, $15,000
8. Adrian College, $14,250
9. Calvin College, $14,040
10. Aquinas College, $14,034

Source: "Tuition and Fees 2000-01," *The Chronicle of Higher Education (http://chronicle.com/stats/tuition/tuition-results.php3)*, 47:, (October 27, 2000).

COLLEGES & UNIVERSITIES–STUDENT COSTS–MINNESOTA

★1520★
Highest undergraduate tuition and fees at colleges and universities in Minnesota
Ranking basis/background: These figures for in-state tuition and fees at over 3,000 colleges and universities were collected by the College Board in the Annual Survey of Colleges, 2000-01. Figures represent charges to first-time, full-time undergraduates based on a nine-month academic year of 30 semester hours or 45 quarter hours. **Remarks:** A separate table for each state, the District of Columbia, and Puerto Rico is included. Listing also shows added out-of-state tuition and 1999-2000 tuition and fees. **Number listed:** 74.
1. Carleton College, with tuition and fees of $24,390
2. Macalester College, $21,614
3. St. Olaf College, $19,400
4. Minneapolis College of Art and Design, $19,360
5. Gustavus Adolphus College, $18,270
6. University of St. Thomas, $17,313
7. College of St. Benedict, $17,241
7. St. John's University, $17,241
9. College of St. Catherine, $16,442
10. Hamline University, $16,425

Source: "Tuition and Fees 2000-01," *The Chronicle of Higher Education (http://chronicle.com/stats/tuition/tuition-results.php3)*, 47:, (October 27, 2000).

★1521★
Lowest undergraduate tuition and fees at colleges and universities in Minnesota

Ranking basis/background: These figures for in-state tuition and fees at over 3,000 colleges and universities were collected by the College Board in the Annual Survey of Colleges, 2000-01. Figures represent charges to first-time, full-time undergraduates based on a nine-month academic year of 30 semester hours or 45 quarter hours. **Remarks:** A separate table for each state, the District of Columbia, and Puerto Rico is included. Listing also shows added out-of-state tuition and 1999-2000 tuition and fees. **Number listed:** 74.

1. Northwest Technical College, with tuition and fees of $2,257
2. St. Cloud Technical College, $2,325
3. St. Paul Technical College, $2,329
4. Hennepin Technical College, $2,336
5. Minnesota West Community and Technical College, $2,356
6. Alexandria Technical College, $2,381
7. Riverland Community College Agricultural Technical and Community College, $2,387
8. Pine Technical College, $2,400
9. South Central Technical College, $2,408
10. Hibbing Community College Agricultural Technical and Community College, $2,453

Source: "Tuition and Fees 2000-01," *The Chronicle of Higher Education* (http://chronicle.com/stats/tuition/tuition-results.php3), 47:, (October 27, 2000).

COLLEGES & UNIVERSITIES–STUDENT COSTS–MISSISSIPPI

★1522★
Highest undergraduate tuition and fees at colleges and universities in Mississippi

Ranking basis/background: These figures for in-state tuition and fees at over 3,000 colleges and universities were collected by the College Board in the Annual Survey of Colleges, 2000-01. Figures represent charges to first-time, full-time undergraduates based on a nine-month academic year of 30 semester hours or 45 quarter hours. **Remarks:** A separate table for each state, the District of Columbia, and Puerto Rico is included. Listing also shows added out-of-state tuition and 1999-2000 tuition and fees. **Number listed:** 38.

1. Millsaps College, with tuition and fees of $15,814
2. Belhaven College, $10,860
3. Mississippi College, $9,614
4. Tougaloo College, $7,070
5. William Carey College, $6,780
6. Blue Mountain College, $5,630
7. Rust College, $5,400
8. Wood College, $5,230
9. Magnolia Bible College, $4,540
10. Mary Holmes College, $4,100

Source: "Tuition and Fees 2000-01," *The Chronicle of Higher Education* (http://chronicle.com/stats/tuition/tuition-results.php3), 47:, (October 27, 2000).

★1523★
Lowest undergraduate tuition and fees at colleges and universities in Mississippi

Ranking basis/background: These figures for in-state tuition and fees at over 3,000 colleges and universities were collected by the College Board in the Annual Survey of Colleges, 2000-01. Figures represent charges to first-time, full-time undergraduates based on a nine-month academic year of 30 semester hours or 45 quarter hours. **Remarks:** A separate table for each state, the District of Columbia, and Puerto Rico is included. Listing also shows added out-of-state tuition and 1999-2000 tuition and fees. **Number listed:** 38.

1. Jones County Junior College, with tuition and fees of $908
2. Southwest Mississippi Community College, $950
3. Mississippi Gulf Coast Community College, Perkinston, $972
3. Mississippi Gulf Coast Community College, Jefferson Davis Campus, $972
3. Mississippi Gulf Coast Community College, Jackson County Campus, $972
6. Northwest Mississippi Community College, $1,000
6. Itawamba Community College, $1,000
6. East Central Community College, $1,000
9. Mississippi Delta Community College, $1,020
10. East Mississippi Community College, $1,040

Source: "Tuition and Fees 2000-01," *The Chronicle of Higher Education* (http://chronicle.com/stats/tuition/tuition-results.php3), 47:, (October 27, 2000).

COLLEGES & UNIVERSITIES–STUDENT COSTS–MISSOURI

★1524★
Highest undergraduate tuition and fees at colleges and universities in Missouri

Ranking basis/background: These figures for in-state tuition and fees at over 3,000 colleges and universities were collected by the College Board in the Annual Survey of Colleges, 2000-01. Figures represent charges to first-time, full-time undergraduates based on a nine-month academic year of 30 semester hours or 45 quarter hours. **Remarks:** A separate table for each state, the District of Columbia, and Puerto Rico is included. Listing also shows added out-of-state tuition and 1999-2000 tuition and fees. **Number listed:** 74.

1. Washington University, with tuition and fees of 24,745
2. St. Louis University, $18,438
3. Kansas City Art Institute, $18,218
4. Stephens College, $15,770
5. Westminster College, $14,300
6. Research College of Nursing, $14,100
7. Rockhurst University, $13,840
8. William Jewell College, $13,800
9. William Woods University, $13,350
10. St. Louis College of Pharmacy, $13,120

Source: "Tuition and Fees 2000-01," *The Chronicle of Higher Education* (http://chronicle.com/stats/tuition/tuition-results.php3), 47:, (October 27, 2000).

★1525★
Lowest undergraduate tuition and fees at colleges and universities in Missouri

Ranking basis/background: These figures for in-state tuition and fees at over 3,000 colleges and universities were collected by the College Board in the Annual Survey of Colleges, 2000-01. Figures represent charges to first-time, full-time undergraduates based on a nine-month academic year of 30 semester hours or 45 quarter hours. **Remarks:** A separate table for each state, the District of Columbia, and Puerto Rico is included. Listing also shows added out-of-state tuition and 1999-2000 tuition and fees. **Number listed:** 74.

1. St. Louis Community College, Meramec, with tuition and fees of $1,260
1. St. Louis Community College, Forest Park, $1,260
1. St. Louis Community College, Florissant Valley, $1,260
1. Mineral Area College, $1,260
5. Moberly Area Community College, $1,368
6. Jefferson College, $1,410
7. State Fair Community College, $1,470
8. St. Charles County Community College, $1,500
8. Crowder College, $1,500
10. Penn Valley Community College, $1,590
10. North Central Missouri College, $1,590
10. Maple Woods Community College, $1,590
10. Longview Community College, $1,590

Source: "Tuition and Fees 2000-01," *The Chronicle of Higher Education* (http://chronicle.com/stats/tuition/tuition-results.php3), 47:, (October 27, 2000).

COLLEGES & UNIVERSITIES–STUDENT COSTS–MONTANA

★1526★
Highest undergraduate tuition and fees at colleges and universities in Montana

Ranking basis/background: These figures for in-state tuition and fees at over 3,000 colleges and universities were collected by the College Board in the Annual Survey of Colleges, 2000-01. Figures represent charges to first-time, full-time undergraduates based on a nine-month academic year of 30 semester hours or 45 quarter hours. **Remarks:** A separate table for each state, the District of Columbia, and Puerto Rico is included. Listing also shows added out-of-state tuition and 1999-2000 tuition and fees. **Number listed:** 23.

1. Rocky Mountain College, with tuition and fees of $12,243
2. Carroll College, $12,238
3. University of Great Falls, $10,260
4. Montana State University, Bozeman, $3,079
5. Montana State University, Billings, $3,052
5. Montana State University, Billings College of Technology, $3,052
7. Montana Tech, $3,006
8. Montana State University, Northern, $2,692
9. Western Montana College, $2,603
10. University of Montana, Missoula, $2,600

Source: "Tuition and Fees 2000-01," *The Chronicle of Higher Education* (http://chronicle.com/stats/tuition/tuition-results.php3), 47:, (October 27, 2000).

★1527★
Lowest undergraduate tuition and fees at colleges and universities in Montana

Ranking basis/background: These figures for in-state tuition and fees at over 3,000 colleges and universities were collected by the College Board in the Annual Survey of Colleges, 2000-01. Figures represent charges to first-time, full-time undergraduates based on a nine-month academic year of 30 semester hours or 45 quarter hours. **Remarks:** A separate table for each state, the District of Columbia, and Puerto Rico is included. Listing also shows added out-of-state tuition and 1999-2000 tuition and fees. **Number listed:** 23.

1. Fort Peck Community College, with tuition and fees of $1,540
2. Dawson Community College, $1,596
3. Flathead Valley Community College, $1,750
4. Miles Community College, $1,890
5. Blackfeet Community College, $1,941
6. Stone Child College, $1,950
7. Montana State University College of Technology, Great Falls, $2,085
8. Dull Knife Memorial College, $2,100
9. Montana Tech of the University of Montana, $2,220
10. Helena College of Technology, $2,260

Source: "Tuition and Fees 2000-01," *The Chronicle of Higher Education (http://chronicle. com/stats/tuition/tuition-results.php3)*, 47:, (October 27, 2000).

COLLEGES & UNIVERSITIES–STUDENT COSTS–NEBRASKA

★1528★
Highest undergraduate tuition and fees at colleges and universities in Nebraska

Ranking basis/background: These figures for in-state tuition and fees at over 3,000 colleges and universities were collected by the College Board in the Annual Survey of Colleges, 2000-01. Figures represent charges to first-time, full-time undergraduates based on a nine-month academic year of 30 semester hours or 45 quarter hours. **Remarks:** A separate table for each state, the District of Columbia, and Puerto Rico is included. Listing also shows added out-of-state tuition and 1999-2000 tuition and fees. **Number listed:** 33.

1. Creighton University, with tuition and fees of $14,910
2. Midland Lutheran College, $13,940
3. Nebraska Wesleyan University, $13,704
4. College of St. Mary (NE), $13,350
5. Dana College, $13,300
6. Hastings College, $12,916
7. Doane College, $12,820
8. Concordia University, $12,470
9. Union College, $10,940
10. Nebraska Methodist College of Nursing and Allied Health, $9,090

Source: "Tuition and Fees 2000-01," *The Chronicle of Higher Education (http://chronicle. com/stats/tuition/tuition-results.php3)*, 47:, (October 27, 2000).

★1529★
Lowest undergraduate tuition and fees at colleges and universities in Nebraska

Ranking basis/background: These figures for in-state tuition and fees at over 3,000 colleges and universities were collected by the College Board in the Annual Survey of Colleges, 2000-01. Figures represent charges to first-time, full-time undergraduates based on a nine-month academic year of 30 semester hours or 45 quarter hours. **Remarks:** A separate table for each state, the District of Columbia, and Puerto Rico is included. Listing also shows added out-of-state tuition and 1999-2000 tuition and fees. **Number listed:** 33.

1. Metropolitan Community College, with tuition and fees of $1,350
2. Mid Plains Community College Area, $1,408
3. Western Nebraska Community College, $1,440
4. Northeast Community College, $1,478
5. Central Community College, $1,560
6. Nebraska College of Technical Agriculture, $1,946
7. Southeast Community College, Milford Campus, $1,950
7. Southeast Community College, Lincoln Campus, $1,950
9. Southeast Community College, Beatrice Campus, $1,998
10. Peru State College, $2,355

Source: "Tuition and Fees 2000-01," *The Chronicle of Higher Education (http://chronicle. com/stats/tuition/tuition-results.php3)*, 47:, (October 27, 2000).

COLLEGES & UNIVERSITIES–STUDENT COSTS–NEVADA

★1530★
Undergraduate tuition and fees at colleges and universities in Nevada

Ranking basis/background: These figures for in-state tuition and fees at over 3,000 colleges and universities were collected by the College Board in the Annual Survey of Colleges, 2000-01. Figures represent charges to first-time, full-time undergraduates based on a nine-month academic year of 30 semester hours or 45 quarter hours. **Remarks:** A separate table for each state, the District of Columbia, and Puerto Rico is included. Listing also shows added out-of-state tuition and 1999-2000 tuition and fees. **Number listed:** 8.

1. Sierra Nevada College, with tuition and fees of $11,500
2. Las Vegas College, $9,360
3. University of Nevada, Reno, $2,454
4. University of Nevada, Las Vegas, $2,386
5. Truckee Meadows Community College, $1,395
5. Western Nevada Community College, $1,395
7. Community College of Southern Nevada, $1,275
7. Great Basin College, $1,275

Source: "Tuition and Fees 2000-01," *The Chronicle of Higher Education (http://chronicle. com/stats/tuition/tuition-results.php3)*, 47:, (October 27, 2000).

COLLEGES & UNIVERSITIES–STUDENT COSTS–NEW HAMPSHIRE

★1531★
Highest undergraduate tuition and fees at colleges and universities in New Hampshire

Ranking basis/background: These figures for in-state tuition and fees at over 3,000 colleges and universities were collected by the College Board in the Annual Survey of Colleges, 2000-01. Figures represent charges to first-time, full-time undergraduates based on a nine-month academic year of 30 semester hours or 45 quarter hours. **Remarks:** A separate table for each state, the District of Columbia, and Puerto Rico is included. Listing also shows added out-of-state tuition and 1999-2000 tuition and fees. **Number listed:** 25.

1. Dartmouth College, with tuition and fees of $25,763
2. Colby-Sawyer College, $19,218
3. Franklin Pierce College, $18,985
4. St. Anselm College, $18,850
5. New England College, $18,382
6. Daniel Webster College, $16,770
7. New Hampshire College, $15,848
8. Rivier College, $15,835
9. Notre Dame College, $15,782
10. McIntosh College, $13,100

Source: "Tuition and Fees 2000-01," *The Chronicle of Higher Education (http://chronicle. com/stats/tuition/tuition-results.php3)*, 47:, (October 27, 2000).

★1532★
Lowest undergraduate tuition and fees at colleges and universities in New Hampshire

Ranking basis/background: These figures for in-state tuition and fees at over 3,000 colleges and universities were collected by the College Board in the Annual Survey of Colleges, 2000-01. Figures represent charges to first-time, full-time undergraduates based on a nine-month academic year of 30 semester hours or 45 quarter hours. **Remarks:** A separate table for each state, the District of Columbia, and Puerto Rico is included. Listing also shows added out-of-state tuition and 1999-2000 tuition and fees. **Number listed:** 25.

1. New Hampshire Community Technical College, Laconia, with tuition and fees of $3,800
1. New Hampshire Community Technical College, Berline, $3,800
3. New Hampshire Community Technical College, Nashua, $3,830
3. New Hampshire Community Technical College, Manchester, $3,830
3. New Hampshire Community Technical College, Claremont, $3,830
6. New Hampshire Community Technical College, Stratham, $3,860
7. New Hampshire Technical Institute, $4,070
8. University of New Hampshire, Manchester, $4,930
9. College for Lifelong Learning, $5,170
10. Plymouth State College, $5,254

Source: "Tuition and Fees 2000-01," *The Chronicle of Higher Education (http://chronicle. com/stats/tuition/tuition-results.php3)*, 47:, (October 27, 2000).

COLLEGES & UNIVERSITIES–STUDENT COSTS–NEW JERSEY

★1533★
Highest undergraduate tuition and fees at colleges and universities in New Jersey

Ranking basis/background: These figures for in-state tuition and fees at over 3,000 colleges and universities were collected by the College Board in the Annual Survey of Colleges, 2000-01. Figures represent charges to first-time, full-time undergraduates based on a nine-month academic year of 30 semester hours or 45 quarter hours. **Remarks:** A separate table for each state, the District of Columbia, and Puerto Rico is included. Listing also shows added out-of-state tuition and 1999-2000 tuition and fees. **Number listed:** 65.

1. Princeton University, with tuition and fees of $25,430
2. Drew University, $24,018
3. Stevens Institute of Technology, $22,439
4. Seton Hall University, $18,290
5. Westminster Choir College of Rider University, $17,760
6. Rider University, $17,650
7. Fairleigh Dickinson University, $16,856
8. Monmouth University, $16,326
9. St. Peter's College, $15,606
10. Centenary College, $15,120

Source: "Tuition and Fees 2000-01," *The Chronicle of Higher Education (http://chronicle.com/stats/tuition/tuition-results.php3),* 47:, (October 27, 2000).

★1534★
Lowest undergraduate tuition and fees at colleges and universities in New Jersey

Ranking basis/background: These figures for in-state tuition and fees at over 3,000 colleges and universities were collected by the College Board in the Annual Survey of Colleges, 2000-01. Figures represent charges to first-time, full-time undergraduates based on a nine-month academic year of 30 semester hours or 45 quarter hours. **Remarks:** A separate table for each state, the District of Columbia, and Puerto Rico is included. Listing also shows added out-of-state tuition and 1999-2000 tuition and fees. **Number listed:** 65.

1. Burlington County College, with tuition and fees of $1,800
2. Camden County College, $1,838
3. Atlantic Cape Community College, $1,961
4. Ocean County College, $2,130
5. Warren County Community College, $2,144
6. Passaic County Community College, $2,190
7. Gloucester County College, $2,280
8. Raritan Valley Community College, $2,290
9. Salem Community College, $2,305
10. County College of Morris, $2,310

Source: "Tuition and Fees 2000-01," *The Chronicle of Higher Education (http://chronicle.com/stats/tuition/tuition-results.php3),* 47:, (October 27, 2000).

COLLEGES & UNIVERSITIES–STUDENT COSTS–NEW MEXICO

★1535★
Highest undergraduate tuition and fees at colleges and universities in New Mexico

Ranking basis/background: These figures for in-state tuition and fees at over 3,000 colleges and universities were collected by the College Board in the Annual Survey of Colleges, 2000-01. Figures represent charges to first-time, full-time undergraduates based on a nine-month academic year of 30 semester hours or 45 quarter hours. **Remarks:** A separate table for each state, the District of Columbia, and Puerto Rico is included. Listing also shows added out-of-state tuition and 1999-2000 tuition and fees. **Number listed:** 21.

1. St. John's College, with tuition and fees of $24,770
2. College of Santa Fe, $16,110
3. College of the Southwest, $4,715
4. University of New Mexico, $2,795
5. New Mexico State University, $2,790
6. New Mexico Institute of Mining and Technology, $2,499
7. Institute of American Indian Arts, $2,440
8. New Mexico Military Institute, $2,126
9. New Mexico Highlands University, $2,073
10. Eastern New Mexico University, $1,944

Source: "Tuition and Fees 2000-01," *The Chronicle of Higher Education (http://chronicle.com/stats/tuition/tuition-results.php3),* 47:, (October 27, 2000).

★1536★
Lowest undergraduate tuition and fees at colleges and universities in New Mexico

Ranking basis/background: These figures for in-state tuition and fees at over 3,000 colleges and universities were collected by the College Board in the Annual Survey of Colleges, 2000-01. Figures represent charges to first-time, full-time undergraduates based on a nine-month academic year of 30 semester hours or 45 quarter hours. **Remarks:** A separate table for each state, the District of Columbia, and Puerto Rico is included. Listing also shows added out-of-state tuition and 1999-2000 tuition and fees. **Number listed:** 21.

1. San Juan College, with tuition and fees of $360
2. New Mexico Junior College, $362
3. Clovis Community College, $548
4. Santa Fe Community College, $750
5. Eastern New Mexico University, Roswell, $765
6. Northern New Mexico Community College, $771
7. New Mexico State University, Carlsbad, $840
8. Dona Ana Branch Community College, $840
9. New Mexico State University, Alamogordo, $1,050
10. Albuquerque Technical Vocational Institute, $1,255

Source: "Tuition and Fees 2000-01," *The Chronicle of Higher Education (http://chronicle.com/stats/tuition/tuition-results.php3),* 47:, (October 27, 2000).

COLLEGES & UNIVERSITIES–STUDENT COSTS–NEW YORK

★1537★
Highest undergraduate tuition and fees at colleges and universities in New York

Ranking basis/background: These figures for in-state tuition and fees at over 3,000 colleges and universities were collected by the College Board in the Annual Survey of Colleges, 2000-01. Figures represent charges to first-time, full-time undergraduates based on a nine-month academic year of 30 semester hours or 45 quarter hours. **Remarks:** A separate table for each state, the District of Columbia, and Puerto Rico is included. Listing also shows added out-of-state tuition and 1999-2000 tuition and fees. **Number listed:** 226.

1. Sarah Lawrence College, with tuition and fees of $26,668
2. Hamilton College, $26,100
3. Columbia University, Columbia College, $25,922
3. Columbia University Foundation School of Engineering and Applied Science, $25,922
5. Colgate University, $25,740
6. Skidmore College, $25,465
7. Bard College, $25,380
8. Hobart and William Smith College, $25,192
9. Union College, $24,963
10. Columbia University School of General Studies, $24,944

Source: "Tuition and Fees 2000-01," *The Chronicle of Higher Education (http://chronicle.com/stats/tuition/tuition-results.php3),* 47:, (October 27, 2000).

★1538★
Lowest undergraduate tuition and fees at colleges and universities in New York

Ranking basis/background: These figures for in-state tuition and fees at over 3,000 colleges and universities were collected by the College Board in the Annual Survey of Colleges, 2000-01. Figures represent charges to first-time, full-time undergraduates based on a nine-month academic year of 30 semester hours or 45 quarter hours. **Remarks:** A separate table for each state, the District of Columbia, and Puerto Rico is included. Listing also shows added out-of-state tuition and 1999-2000 tuition and fees. **Number listed:** 226.

1. Nassau Community College, with tuition and fees of $2,320
2. Orange County Community College, $2,375
3. Dutchess Community College, $2,420
4. Columbia-Greene Community College, $2,454
5. Schenectady County Community College, $2,455
6. Andirondack Community College, $2,476
7. Clinton Community College, $2,492
8. Finger Lakes Community College, $2,520
9. Herkimer County Community College, $2,530
10. Rockland Community College, $2,545

Source: "Tuition and Fees 2000-01," *The Chronicle of Higher Education (http://chronicle.com/stats/tuition/tuition-results.php3),* 47:, (October 27, 2000).

COLLEGES & UNIVERSITIES–STUDENT COSTS–NORTH CAROLINA

★1539★

Highest undergraduate tuition and fees at colleges and universities in North Carolina

Ranking basis/background: These figures for in-state tuition and fees at over 3,000 colleges and universities were collected by the College Board in the Annual Survey of Colleges, 2000-01. Figures represent charges to first-time, full-time undergraduates based on a nine-month academic year of 30 semester hours or 45 quarter hours. **Remarks:** A separate table for each state, the District of Columbia, and Puerto Rico is included. Listing also shows added out-of-state tuition and 1999-2000 tuition and fees. **Number listed:** 115.

1. Duke University, with tuition and fees of $25,630
2. Davidson College, $23,094
3. Wake Forest University, $22,410
4. Guilford College, $16,970
5. St. Andrews Presbyterian College, $14,440
6. Warren Wilson College, $14,375
7. Salem College, $13,945
8. Elon College, $13,781
9. Catawba College, $13,670
10. Methodist College, $13,404

Source: "Tuition and Fees 2000-01," *The Chronicle of Higher Education* (http://chronicle.com/stats/tuition/tuition-results.php3), 47:, (October 27, 2000).

★1540★

Lowest undergraduate tuition and fees at colleges and universities in North Carolina

Ranking basis/background: These figures for in-state tuition and fees at over 3,000 colleges and universities were collected by the College Board in the Annual Survey of Colleges, 2000-01. Figures represent charges to first-time, full-time undergraduates based on a nine-month academic year of 30 semester hours or 45 quarter hours. **Remarks:** A separate table for each state, the District of Columbia, and Puerto Rico is included. Listing also shows added out-of-state tuition and 1999-2000 tuition and fees. **Number listed:** 115.

1. Forsyth Technical Community College, with tuition and fees of $825
2. Pamlico Community College, $840
2. Alamance Community College, $840
4. Wake Technical Community College, $841
5. McDowell Technical Community College, $843
5. Beaufort County Community College, $843
7. Fayetteville Technical Community College, $844
8. Haywood Community College, $845
9. Wilson Technical Community College, $846
9. Tri-County Community College, $846

Source: "Tuition and Fees 2000-01," *The Chronicle of Higher Education* (http://chronicle.com/stats/tuition/tuition-results.php3), 47:, (October 27, 2000).

COLLEGES & UNIVERSITIES–STUDENT COSTS–NORTH DAKOTA

★1541★

Highest undergraduate tuition and fees at colleges and universities in North Dakota

Ranking basis/background: These figures for in-state tuition and fees at over 3,000 colleges and universities were collected by the College Board in the Annual Survey of Colleges, 2000-01. Figures represent charges to first-time, full-time undergraduates based on a nine-month academic year of 30 semester hours or 45 quarter hours. **Remarks:** A separate table for each state, the District of Columbia, and Puerto Rico is included. Listing also shows added out-of-state tuition and 1999-2000 tuition and fees. **Number listed:** 19.

1. University of Mary, with tuition and fees of $8,800
2. Jamestown College, $7,550
3. Trinity Bible College, $6,520
4. Medcenter One College of Nursing, $3,186
5. Mayville State University, $3,182
6. Valley City State University, $3,173
7. University of North Dakota, $3,088
8. North Dakota State University, $3,010
9. Fort Berthold Community College, $2,540
9. Sitting Bull College, $2,540
9. United Tribes Technical College, $2,540

Source: "Tuition and Fees 2000-01," *The Chronicle of Higher Education* (http://chronicle.com/stats/tuition/tuition-results.php3), 47:, (October 27, 2000).

★1542★

Lowest undergraduate tuition and fees at colleges and universities in North Dakota

Ranking basis/background: These figures for in-state tuition and fees at over 3,000 colleges and universities were collected by the College Board in the Annual Survey of Colleges, 2000-01. Figures represent charges to first-time, full-time undergraduates based on a nine-month academic year of 30 semester hours or 45 quarter hours. **Remarks:** A separate table for each state, the District of Columbia, and Puerto Rico is included. Listing also shows added out-of-state tuition and 1999-2000 tuition and fees. **Number listed:** 19.

1. North Dakota State College of Science, with tuition and fees of $1,850
2. Williston State College, $1,916
3. Minot State University, Bottineau, $1,958
4. Bismarck State College, $1,970
5. Little Hoop Community College, $1,985
6. Lake Region State College, $2,078
7. Dickinson State University, $2,378
8. Minot State University, $2,425

Source: "Tuition and Fees 2000-01," *The Chronicle of Higher Education* (http://chronicle.com/stats/tuition/tuition-results.php3), 47:, (October 27, 2000).

COLLEGES & UNIVERSITIES–STUDENT COSTS–OHIO

★1543★

Highest undergraduate tuition and fees at colleges and universities in Ohio

Ranking basis/background: These figures for in-state tuition and fees at over 3,000 colleges and universities were collected by the College Board in the Annual Survey of Colleges, 2000-01. Figures represent charges to first-time, full-time undergraduates based on a nine-month academic year of 30 semester hours or 45 quarter hours. **Remarks:** A separate table for each state, the District of Columbia, and Puerto Rico is included. Listing also shows added out-of-state tuition and 1999-2000 tuition and fees. **Number listed:** 138.

1. Kenyon College, with tuition and fees of $26,080
2. Oberlin College, $25,355
3. Denison University, $22,210
4. Ohio Wesleyan University, $21,880
5. Wittenberg University, $21,640
6. College of Wooster, $21,520
7. Ohio Northern University, $21,435
8. Case Western Reserve University, $20,260
9. Antioch College, $20,242
10. Cleveland Institute of Music, $19,395

Source: "Tuition and Fees 2000-01," *The Chronicle of Higher Education* (http://chronicle.com/stats/tuition/tuition-results.php3), 47:, (October 27, 2000).

★1544★

Lowest undergraduate tuition and fees at colleges and universities in Ohio

Ranking basis/background: These figures for in-state tuition and fees at over 3,000 colleges and universities were collected by the College Board in the Annual Survey of Colleges, 2000-01. Figures represent charges to first-time, full-time undergraduates based on a nine-month academic year of 30 semester hours or 45 quarter hours. **Remarks:** A separate table for each state, the District of Columbia, and Puerto Rico is included. Listing also shows added out-of-state tuition and 1999-2000 tuition and fees. **Number listed:** 138.

1. Cuyahoga Community College, Western, with tuition and fees of $1,740
1. Cuyahoga Community College, Metropolitan, $1,740
1. Cuyahoga Community College, Eastern, $1,740
4. Owens Community College, Toledo, $1,800
4. Owens Community College, Findlay, $1,800
6. Lakeland Community College, $1,917
7. Terra Community College, $1,944
8. Jefferson Community College, $1,965
9. Central Ohio Technical College, $2,052
10. Columbus State Community College, $2,121

Source: "Tuition and Fees 2000-01," *The Chronicle of Higher Education* (http://chronicle.com/stats/tuition/tuition-results.php3), 47:, (October 27, 2000).

COLLEGES & UNIVERSITIES–STUDENT COSTS–OKLAHOMA

★1545★
Highest undergraduate tuition and fees at colleges and universities in Oklahoma

Ranking basis/background: These figures for in-state tuition and fees at over 3,000 colleges and universities were collected by the College Board in the Annual Survey of Colleges, 2000-01. Figures represent charges to first-time, full-time undergraduates based on a nine-month academic year of 30 semester hours or 45 quarter hours. **Remarks:** A separate table for each state, the District of Columbia, and Puerto Rico is included. Listing also shows added out-of-state tuition and 1999-2000 tuition and fees. **Number listed:** 38.

1. University of Tulsa, with tuition and fees of $13,810
2. Oral Roberts University, $11,650
3. Oklahoma Christian University of Science and Arts, $10,440
4. Oklahoma City University, $10,045
5. Southern Nazarene University, $9,868
6. Bartlesville Wesleyan College, $9,700
7. Oklahoma Baptist University, $9,440
8. St. Gregory's University, $9,084
9. National Education Center Spartan School of Aeronautics, $8,500
10. Mid-America Bible College, $6,244

Source: "Tuition and Fees 2000-01," *The Chronicle of Higher Education* (http://chronicle.com/stats/tuition/tuition-results.php3), 47:, (October 27, 2000).

★1546★
Lowest undergraduate tuition and fees at colleges and universities in Oklahoma

Ranking basis/background: These figures for in-state tuition and fees at over 3,000 colleges and universities were collected by the College Board in the Annual Survey of Colleges, 2000-01. Figures represent charges to first-time, full-time undergraduates based on a nine-month academic year of 30 semester hours or 45 quarter hours. **Remarks:** A separate table for each state, the District of Columbia, and Puerto Rico is included. Listing also shows added out-of-state tuition and 1999-2000 tuition and fees. **Number listed:** 38.

1. Northern Oklahoma College, with tuition and fees of $1,265
2. Connors State College, $1,334
3. Carl Albert State College, $1,349
4. Western Oklahoma State College, $1,350
5. Northeastern Oklahoma A&M College, $1,365
6. Oklahoma City Community College, $1,368
7. Rose State College, $1,421
8. Murray State College, $1,427
9. Redlands Community College, $1,448
10. Seminole State College, $1,461

Source: "Tuition and Fees 2000-01," *The Chronicle of Higher Education* (http://chronicle.com/stats/tuition/tuition-results.php3), 47:, (October 27, 2000).

COLLEGES & UNIVERSITIES–STUDENT COSTS–OREGON

★1547★
Highest undergraduate tuition and fees at colleges and universities in Oregon

Ranking basis/background: These figures for in-state tuition and fees at over 3,000 colleges and universities were collected by the College Board in the Annual Survey of Colleges, 2000-01. Figures represent charges to first-time, full-time undergraduates based on a nine-month academic year of 30 semester hours or 45 quarter hours. **Remarks:** A separate table for each state, the District of Columbia, and Puerto Rico is included. Listing also shows added out-of-state tuition and 1999-2000 tuition and fees. **Number listed:** 37.

1. Reed College, with tuition and fees of $25,020
2. Williamette University, $22,422
3. Lewis and Clark College, $22,072
4. Linfield College, $18,600
5. University of Portland, $18,060
6. Pacific University (OR), $17,800
7. George Fox University, $17,610
8. Concordia University, $15,500
9. Warner Pacific College, $14,755
10. Northwest Christian College, $13,905

Source: "Tuition and Fees 2000-01," *The Chronicle of Higher Education* (http://chronicle.com/stats/tuition/tuition-results.php3), 47:, (October 27, 2000).

★1548★
Lowest undergraduate tuition and fees at colleges and universities in Oregon

Ranking basis/background: These figures for in-state tuition and fees at over 3,000 colleges and universities were collected by the College Board in the Annual Survey of Colleges, 2000-01. Figures represent charges to first-time, full-time undergraduates based on a nine-month academic year of 30 semester hours or 45 quarter hours. **Remarks:** A separate table for each state, the District of Columbia, and Puerto Rico is included. Listing also shows added out-of-state tuition and 1999-2000 tuition and fees. **Number listed:** 37.

1. Clatsop Community College, with tuition and fees of $1,476
2. Lane Community College, $1,695
3. Chemeketa Community College, $1,710
4. Linn-Benton Community College, $1,711
5. Umpqua Community College, $1,755
6. Mount Hood Community College, $1,778
7. Southwestern Oregon Community College, $1,824
8. Blue Mountain Community College, $1,824
9. Clackamas Community College, $1,845
10. Portland Community College, $1,913

Source: "Tuition and Fees 2000-01," *The Chronicle of Higher Education* (http://chronicle.com/stats/tuition/tuition-results.php3), 47:, (October 27, 2000).

COLLEGES & UNIVERSITIES–STUDENT COSTS–PENNSYLVANIA

★1549★
Highest undergraduate tuition and fees at colleges and universities in Pennsylvania

Ranking basis/background: These figures for in-state tuition and fees at over 3,000 colleges and universities were collected by the College Board in the Annual Survey of Colleges, 2000-01. Figures represent charges to first-time, full-time undergraduates based on a nine-month academic year of 30 semester hours or 45 quarter hours. **Remarks:** A separate table for each state, the District of Columbia, and Puerto Rico is included. Listing also shows added out-of-state tuition and 1999-2000 tuition and fees. **Number listed:** 177.

1. Swarthmore College, with tuition and fees of $25,200
2. University of Pennsylvania, $25,170
3. Haverford College, $24,940
4. Gettysburg College, $24,875
5. Franklin and Marshall College, $24,816
6. Carnegie Mellon University, $24,792
7. Dickinson College, $24,475
8. Lehigh University, $24,000
9. Bryn Mawr College, $23,940
10. Lafayette College, $23,846

Source: "Tuition and Fees 2000-01," *The Chronicle of Higher Education* (http://chronicle.com/stats/tuition/tuition-results.php3), 47:, (October 27, 2000).

★1550★
Lowest undergraduate tuition and fees at colleges and universities in Pennsylvania

Ranking basis/background: These figures for in-state tuition and fees at over 3,000 colleges and universities were collected by the College Board in the Annual Survey of Colleges, 2000-01. Figures represent charges to first-time, full-time undergraduates based on a nine-month academic year of 30 semester hours or 45 quarter hours. **Remarks:** A separate table for each state, the District of Columbia, and Puerto Rico is included. Listing also shows added out-of-state tuition and 1999-2000 tuition and fees. **Number listed:** 177.

1. Westmoreland County Community College, with tuition and fees of $1,560
2. Community College of Allegheny County, $1,781
3. Butler County Community College, $1,800
4. Delaware County Community College, $1,890
5. Luzerne County Community College, $1,980
6. Berean Institute, $2,100
7. Reading Area Community College, $2,160
8. Harrisburg Area Community College, $2,175
9. Community College of Beaver County, $2,310
10. Lehigh Carbon Community College, $2,325

Source: "Tuition and Fees 2000-01," *The Chronicle of Higher Education* (http://chronicle.com/stats/tuition/tuition-results.php3), 47:, (October 27, 2000).

COLLEGES & UNIVERSITIES–STUDENT COSTS–PUERTO RICO

★1551★
Highest undergraduate tuition and fees at colleges and universities in Puerto Rico

Ranking basis/background: These figures for in-state tuition and fees at over 3,000 colleges and universities were collected by the College Board in the Annual Survey of Colleges, 2000-01. Figures represent charges to first-time, full-time undergraduates based on a nine-month academic year of 30 semester hours or 45 quarter hours. **Remarks:** A separate table for each state, the District of Columbia, and Puerto Rico is included. Listing also shows added out-of-state tuition and 1999-2000 tuition and fees. **Number listed:** 38.
1. ICPR Junior College, with tuition and fees of $4,875
2. Caribbean University, $4,600
3. University of Sacred Heart (PR), $4,440
4. Universidad Politecnica de Puerta Rico, $4,150
5. Turabo University $4,110
6. Colegio Universitario del Este, $4,100
7. Columbia College, $3,960
8. Atlantic College, $3,830
9. Pontifical Catholic University, Puerto Rico, $3,726
10. University of Puerto Rico, Aguadilla, $3,700
10. University of Puerto Rico, Arecibo, $3,700
10. University of Puerto Rico, Barranquitas, $3,700
10. University of Puerto Rico, Bayamon, $3,700
10. University of Puerto Rico, Fajardo, $3,700
10. University of Puerto Rico, Guayama, $3,700
10. University of Puerto Rico, Metropolitan, $3,700
10. University of Puerto Rico, Ponce, $3,700
10. University of Puerto Rico, San German, $3,700

Source: "Tuition and Fees 2000-01," *The Chronicle of Higher Education (http://chronicle.com/stats/tuition/tuition-results.php3),* 47:, (October 27, 2000).

★1552★
Lowest undergraduate tuition and fees at colleges and universities in Puerto Rico

Ranking basis/background: These figures for in-state tuition and fees at over 3,000 colleges and universities were collected by the College Board in the Annual Survey of Colleges, 2000-01. Figures represent charges to first-time, full-time undergraduates based on a nine-month academic year of 30 semester hours or 45 quarter hours. **Remarks:** A separate table for each state, the District of Columbia, and Puerto Rico is included. Listing also shows added out-of-state tuition and 1999-2000 tuition and fees. **Number listed:** 38.
1. University of Puerto Rico, Bayamon, with tuition and fees of $970
2. University of Puerto Rico, Utuado, $972
2. University of Puerto Rico, Carolina Regional College, $972
4. University of Puerto Rico, Aguadilla, $975
5. University of Puerto Rico, Ponce, $976
6. University of Puerto Rico, Mayaguez, $1,010
7. University of Puerto Rico Medical Sciences Campus, $1,011
8. University of Puerto Rico, Cayey University, $1,020
9. University of Puerto Rico, Rio Piedras, $1,120
10. University of Puerto Rico, Humacao University, $1,125
10. University of Puerto Rico, Arecibo, $1,125

Source: "Tuition and Fees 2000-01," *The Chronicle of Higher Education (http://chronicle.com/stats/tuition/tuition-results.php3),* 47:, (October 27, 2000).

COLLEGES & UNIVERSITIES–STUDENT COSTS–RHODE ISLAND

★1553★
Undergraduate tuition and fees at colleges and universities in Rhode Island

Ranking basis/background: These figures for in-state tuition and fees at over 3,000 colleges and universities were collected by the College Board in the Annual Survey of Colleges, 2000-01. Figures represent charges to first-time, full-time undergraduates based on a nine-month academic year of 30 semester hours or 45 quarter hours. **Remarks:** A separate table for each state, the District of Columbia, and Puerto Rico is included. Listing also shows added out-of-state tuition and 1999-2000 tuition and fees. **Number listed:** 10.
1. Brown University, with tuition and fees of $26,374
2. Rhode Island School of Design, $21,860
3. Providence College, $18,935
4. Roger Williams University, $18,130
5. Salve Regina University, $17,550
6. Bryant College, $17,330
7. New England Institute of Technology, $11,870
8. University of Rhode Island, $5,154
9. Rhode Island College, $3,371
10. Community College of Rhode Island, $1,806

Source: "Tuition and Fees 2000-01," *The Chronicle of Higher Education (http://chronicle.com/stats/tuition/tuition-results.php3),* 47:, (October 27, 2000).

COLLEGES & UNIVERSITIES–STUDENT COSTS–SOUTH CAROLINA

★1554★
Highest undergraduate tuition and fees at colleges and universities in South Carolina

Ranking basis/background: These figures for in-state tuition and fees at over 3,000 colleges and universities were collected by the College Board in the Annual Survey of Colleges, 2000-01. Figures represent charges to first-time, full-time undergraduates based on a nine-month academic year of 30 semester hours or 45 quarter hours. **Remarks:** A separate table for each state, the District of Columbia, and Puerto Rico is included. Listing also shows added out-of-state tuition and 1999-2000 tuition and fees. **Number listed:** 54.
1. Furman University, with tuition and fees of $19,156
2. Wofford College, $17,730
3. Presbyterian College, $17,342
4. Converse College, $15,840
5. Erskine College, $15,712
6. Coker College, $15,397
7. Columbia College, $15,060
8. Newberry College, $14,632
9. Southern Wesleyan University, $12,104
10. Charleston Southern University, $11,346

Source: "Tuition and Fees 2000-01," *The Chronicle of Higher Education (http://chronicle.com/stats/tuition/tuition-results.php3),* 47:, (October 27, 2000).

★1555★
Lowest undergraduate tuition and fees at colleges and universities in South Carolina

Ranking basis/background: These figures for in-state tuition and fees at over 3,000 colleges and universities were collected by the College Board in the Annual Survey of Colleges, 2000-01. Figures represent charges to first-time, full-time undergraduates based on a nine-month academic year of 30 semester hours or 45 quarter hours. **Remarks:** A separate table for each state, the District of Columbia, and Puerto Rico is included. Listing also shows added out-of-state tuition and 1999-2000 tuition and fees. **Number listed:** 54.
1. Williamsburg Technical College, with tuition and fees of $1,080
1. Denmark Technical College, $1,080
3. Chesterfield-Marlboro Technical College, $1,200
3. Central Carolina Technical College, $1,200
5. Tri-County Technical College, $1,215
6. York Technical College, $1,236
7. Technical College of the Lowcountry, $1,250
8. Trident Technical College, $1,300
8. Aiken Technical College, $1,300
10. Orangeburg-Calhoun Technical College, $1,311

Source: "Tuition and Fees 2000-01," *The Chronicle of Higher Education (http://chronicle.com/stats/tuition/tuition-results.php3),* 47:, (October 27, 2000).

COLLEGES & UNIVERSITIES–STUDENT COSTS–SOUTH DAKOTA

★1556★
Highest undergraduate tuition and fees at colleges and universities in South Dakota

Ranking basis/background: These figures for in-state tuition and fees at over 3,000 colleges and universities were collected by the College Board in the Annual Survey of Colleges, 2000-01. Figures represent charges to first-time, full-time undergraduates based on a nine-month academic year of 30 semester hours or 45 quarter hours. **Remarks:** A separate table for each state, the District of Columbia, and Puerto Rico is included. Listing also shows added out-of-state tuition and 1999-2000 tuition and fees. **Number listed:** 21.
1. Augustana College, with tuition and fees of $14,754
2. University of Sioux Falls, $12,100
3. Mount Marty College, $10,634
4. Dakota Wesleyan University, $10,611
5. National American University, Rapid City, $9,675
6. Huron University, $9,450
7. Presentation College, $8,068
8. Kilian Community College, $4,740
9. Dakota State University, $3,578
10. University of South Dakota, $3,448

Source: "Tuition and Fees 2000-01," *The Chronicle of Higher Education* (http://chronicle.com/stats/tuition/tuition-results.php3), 47:, (October 27, 2000).

★1557★
Lowest undergraduate tuition and fees at colleges and universities in South Dakota

Ranking basis/background: These figures for in-state tuition and fees at over 3,000 colleges and universities were collected by the College Board in the Annual Survey of Colleges, 2000-01. Figures represent charges to first-time, full-time undergraduates based on a nine-month academic year of 30 semester hours or 45 quarter hours. **Remarks:** A separate table for each state, the District of Columbia, and Puerto Rico is included. Listing also shows added out-of-state tuition and 1999-2000 tuition and fees. **Number listed:** 21.
1. Sinte Gleska University, with tuition and fees of $2,130
2. Southeast Technical Institute, $2,550
3. Oglala Lakota College, $2,660
4. Western Dakota Technical Institute, $2,800
5. Lake Area Technical Institute, $2,880
6. Mitchell Technical Institute, $2,895
7. Sisseton-Wahpeton Community College, $3,160
8. Northern State University, $3,312
9. South Dakota State University, $3,365
10. South Dakota School of Mines and Technology, $3,391

Source: "Tuition and Fees 2000-01," *The Chronicle of Higher Education* (http://chronicle.com/stats/tuition/tuition-results.php3), 47:, (October 27, 2000).

COLLEGES & UNIVERSITIES–STUDENT COSTS–TENNESSEE

★1558★
Highest undergraduate tuition and fees at colleges and universities in Tennessee

Ranking basis/background: These figures for in-state tuition and fees at over 3,000 colleges and universities were collected by the College Board in the Annual Survey of Colleges, 2000-01. Figures represent charges to first-time, full-time undergraduates based on a nine-month academic year of 30 semester hours or 45 quarter hours. **Remarks:** A separate table for each state, the District of Columbia, and Puerto Rico is included. Listing also shows added out-of-state tuition and 1999-2000 tuition and fees. **Number listed:** 62.
1. Vanderbilt University, with tuition and fees of $24,700
2. University of the South, $20,130
3. Rhodes College, $19,503
4. Maryville College, $16,649
5. Christian Brothers University, $13,790
6. King College, $12,700
7. Memphis College of Art, $12,690
8. Tusculum College, $12,500
9. Milligan College, $12,300
10. Belmont University, $12,240

Source: "Tuition and Fees 2000-01," *The Chronicle of Higher Education* (http://chronicle.com/stats/tuition/tuition-results.php3), 47:, (October 27, 2000).

★1559★
Lowest undergraduate tuition and fees at colleges and universities in Tennessee

Ranking basis/background: These figures for in-state tuition and fees at over 3,000 colleges and universities were collected by the College Board in the Annual Survey of Colleges, 2000-01. Figures represent charges to first-time, full-time undergraduates based on a nine-month academic year of 30 semester hours or 45 quarter hours. **Remarks:** A separate table for each state, the District of Columbia, and Puerto Rico is included. Listing also shows added out-of-state tuition and 1999-2000 tuition and fees. **Number listed:** 62.
1. Nashville State Technical Institute, with tuition and fees of $1,424
2. Walters State Community College, $1,433
3. Volunteer State Community College, $1,435
3. Dyersburg State Community College, $1,435
3. Cleveland State Community College, $1,435
6. Roane State Community College, $1,439
7. Columbia State Community College, $1,440
8. Motlow State Community College, $1,441
9. Shelby State Community College, $1,445
9. Jackson State Community College, $1,445

Source: "Tuition and Fees 2000-01," *The Chronicle of Higher Education* (http://chronicle.com/stats/tuition/tuition-results.php3), 47:, (October 27, 2000).

COLLEGES & UNIVERSITIES–STUDENT COSTS–TEXAS

★1560★
Highest undergraduate tuition and fees at colleges and universities in Texas

Ranking basis/background: These figures for in-state tuition and fees at over 3,000 colleges and universities were collected by the College Board in the Annual Survey of Colleges, 2000-01. Figures represent charges to first-time, full-time undergraduates based on a nine-month academic year of 30 semester hours or 45 quarter hours. **Remarks:** A separate table for each state, the District of Columbia, and Puerto Rico is included. Listing also shows added out-of-state tuition and 1999-2000 tuition and fees. **Number listed:** 153.
1. Southwest School of Electronics, with tuition and fees of $21,800
2. Southern Methodist University, $19,620
3. Rice University, $16,445
4. Hallmark Institute of Technology, $15,996
5. Trinity University, $15,804
6. Southwestern University, $15,750
7. Austin College, $15,427
8. University of Dallas, $15,188
9. St. Mary's University (TX), $13,757
10. Texas Christian University, $13,125

Source: "Tuition and Fees 2000-01," *The Chronicle of Higher Education* (http://chronicle.com/stats/tuition/tuition-results.php3), 47:, (October 27, 2000).

★1561★
Lowest undergraduate tuition and fees at colleges and universities in Texas

Ranking basis/background: These figures for in-state tuition and fees at over 3,000 colleges and universities were collected by the College Board in the Annual Survey of Colleges, 2000-01. Figures represent charges to first-time, full-time undergraduates based on a nine-month academic year of 30 semester hours or 45 quarter hours. **Remarks:** A separate table for each state, the District of Columbia, and Puerto Rico is included. Listing also shows added out-of-state tuition and 1999-2000 tuition and fees. **Number listed:** 153.
1. College of the Mainland, with tuition and fees of $535
2. Amarillo College, $558
3. Trinity Valley Community College, $570
4. Angelina College, $612
5. San Jacinto College, North, $644
5. San Jacinto College, Central, $644
7. Brazosport College, $680
8. Richland College, $700
8. North Lake College, $700
8. Mountain View College, $700
8. El Centro College, $700
8. Eastfield College, $700
8. Cedar Valley College, $700
8. Brookhaven College, $700

Source: "Tuition and Fees 2000-01," *The Chronicle of Higher Education* (http://chronicle.com/stats/tuition/tuition-results.php3), 47:, (October 27, 2000).

COLLEGES & UNIVERSITIES–STUDENT COSTS–UTAH

★1562★
Undergraduate tuition and fees at colleges and universities in Utah

Ranking basis/background: These figures for in-state tuition and fees at over 3,000 colleges and universities were collected by the College Board in the Annual Survey of Colleges, 2000-01. Figures represent charges to first-time, full-time undergraduates based on a nine-month academic year of 30 semester hours or 45 quarter hours. **Remarks:** A separate table for each state, the District of Columbia, and Puerto Rico is included. Listing also shows added out-of-state tuition and 1999-2000 tuition and fees. **Number listed:** 14.

1. Stevens-Henager College of Business, with tuition and fees of $17,775
2. Westminster College, $13,730
3. Mountain West College, $9,765
4. University of Utah, $2,897
5. Brigham Young University, $2,830
6. Utah State University, $2,403
7. LDS Business College, $2,160
8. Weber State University, $2,118
9. Southern Utah University, $2,066
10. Dixie State College, $1,792
11. Utah Valley State College, $1,682
12. Salt Lake Community College, $1,636
13. College of Eastern Utah, $1,466
14. Snow College, $1,312

Source: "Tuition and Fees 2000-01," *The Chronicle of Higher Education* (http://chronicle.com/stats/tuition/tuition-results.php3), 47:, (October 27, 2000).

COLLEGES & UNIVERSITIES–STUDENT COSTS–VERMONT

★1563★
Undergraduate tuition and fees at colleges and universities in Vermont

Ranking basis/background: These figures for in-state tuition and fees at over 3,000 colleges and universities were collected by the College Board in the Annual Survey of Colleges, 2000-01. Figures represent charges to first-time, full-time undergraduates based on a nine-month academic year of 30 semester hours or 45 quarter hours. **Remarks:** A separate table for each state, the District of Columbia, and Puerto Rico is included. Listing also shows added out-of-state tuition and 1999-2000 tuition and fees. **Number listed:** 20.

1. Landmark College, with tuition and fees of $30,700
2. Bennington College, $23,600
3. Goddard College, $20,038
4. Marlboro College, $19,660
5. New England Culinary Institute, $19,035
6. St. Michael's College, $18,782
7. Green Mountain College, $17,600
8. Norwich University, $15,450
9. Trinity College (VT), $14,568
10. Sterling College, $13,630
11. College of St. Joseph (VT), $11,700
12. Champlain College, $11,005
13. Southern Vermont College, $10,990
14. Burlington College, $9,750
15. University of Vermont, $8,268
16. Vermont Technical College, $5,830
17. Johnson State College, $5,294
18. Castleton State College, $5,030
19. Lyndon State College, $5,028
20. Community College of Vermont, $3,730

Source: "Tuition and Fees 2000-01," *The Chronicle of Higher Education* (http://chronicle.com/stats/tuition/tuition-results.php3), 47:, (October 27, 2000).

COLLEGES & UNIVERSITIES–STUDENT COSTS–VIRGINIA

★1564★
Highest undergraduate tuition and fees at colleges and universities in Virginia

Ranking basis/background: These figures for in-state tuition and fees at over 3,000 colleges and universities were collected by the College Board in the Annual Survey of Colleges, 2000-01. Figures represent charges to first-time, full-time undergraduates based on a nine-month academic year of 30 semester hours or 45 quarter hours. **Remarks:** A separate table for each state, the District of Columbia, and Puerto Rico is included. Listing also shows added out-of-state tuition and 1999-2000 tuition and fees. **Number listed:** 68.

1. University of Richmond, with tuition and fees of $20,140
2. Lynchburg College, $18,105
3. Randolph-Macon College, $18,100
4. Washington and Lee University, $17,965
5. Roanoke College, $17,960
6. Randolph-Macon Woman's College, $17,480
7. Sweet Briar College, $17,324
8. Hollins University, $17,210
9. Hampden-Sydney College, $17,189
10. Shenandoah University, $16,300

Source: "Tuition and Fees 2000-01," *The Chronicle of Higher Education* (http://chronicle.com/stats/tuition/tuition-results.php3), 47:, (October 27, 2000).

★1565★
Lowest undergraduate tuition and fees at colleges and universities in Virginia

Ranking basis/background: These figures for in-state tuition and fees at over 3,000 colleges and universities were collected by the College Board in the Annual Survey of Colleges, 2000-01. Figures represent charges to first-time, full-time undergraduates based on a nine-month academic year of 30 semester hours or 45 quarter hours. **Remarks:** A separate table for each state, the District of Columbia, and Puerto Rico is included. Listing also shows added out-of-state tuition and 1999-2000 tuition and fees. **Number listed:** 68.

1. Danville Community College, with tuition and fees of $1,114
2. Paul D. Camp Community College, $1,159
3. John Tyler Community College, $1,164
4. Virginia Western Community College, $1,167
5. Patrick Henry Community College, $1,169
6. Wytheville Community College, $1,174
7. Central Virginia Community College, $1,179
8. Piedmont Virginia Community College, $1,181
9. Virginia Highlands Community College, $1,182
9. Dabney S. Lancaster Community College, $1,182

Source: "Tuition and Fees 2000-01," *The Chronicle of Higher Education* (http://chronicle.com/stats/tuition/tuition-results.php3), 47:, (October 27, 2000).

COLLEGES & UNIVERSITIES–STUDENT COSTS–WASHINGTON

★1566★
Highest undergraduate tuition and fees at colleges and universities in Washington

Ranking basis/background: These figures for in-state tuition and fees at over 3,000 colleges and universities were collected by the College Board in the Annual Survey of Colleges, 2000-01. Figures represent charges to first-time, full-time undergraduates based on a nine-month academic year of 30 semester hours or 45 quarter hours. **Remarks:** A separate table for each state, the District of Columbia, and Puerto Rico is included. Listing also shows added out-of-state tuition and 1999-2000 tuition and fees. **Number listed:** 56.

1. Whitman College, with tuition and fees of $21,742
2. University of Puget Sound, $21,425
3. Gonzaga University, $17,610
4. Seattle University, $17,010
5. Whitworth College, $16,928
6. Pacific Lutheran University, $16,800
7. Seattle Pacific University, $15,381
8. Cornish College of the Arts, $15,100
9. St. Martin's College, $14,930
10. Walla Walla College, $14,568

Source: "Tuition and Fees 2000-01," *The Chronicle of Higher Education* (http://chronicle.com/stats/tuition/tuition-results.php3), 47:, (October 27, 2000).

★1567★
Lowest undergraduate tuition and fees at colleges and universities in Washington

Ranking basis/background: These figures for in-state tuition and fees at over 3,000 colleges and universities were collected by the College Board in the Annual Survey of Colleges, 2000-01. Figures represent charges to first-time, full-time undergraduates based on a nine-month academic year of 30 semester hours or 45 quarter hours. **Remarks:** A separate table for each state, the District of Columbia, and Puerto Rico is included. Listing also shows added out-of-state tuition and 1999-2000 tuition and fees. **Number listed:** 56.

1. Lake Washington Technical College, with tuition and fees of $1,263
2. Everett Community College, $1,634
3. Spokane Falls Community College, $1,637
4. Big Bend Community College, $1,641
5. Olympic College, $1,671
6. Whatcom Community College, $1,680
7. Skagit Valley College, $1,686
8. Yakima Valley Community College, $1,716
9. Highline Community College, $1,716
10. Wenatchee Valley College, $1,737
10. Spokane Community College, $1,737

COLLEGES & UNIVERSITIES–STUDENT COSTS–WEST VIRGINIA

★1568★
Highest undergraduate tuition and fees at colleges and universities in West Virginia

Ranking basis/background: These figures for in-state tuition and fees at over 3,000 colleges and universities were collected by the College Board in the Annual Survey of Colleges, 2000-01. Figures represent charges to first-time, full-time undergraduates based on a nine-month academic year of 30 semester hours or 45 quarter hours. **Remarks:** A separate table for each state, the District of Columbia, and Puerto Rico is included. Listing also shows added out-of-state tuition and 1999-2000 tuition and fees. **Number listed:** 28.
1. Bethany College, with tuition and fees of $19,695
2. West Virginia Wesleyan College, $18,050
3. Corinthian Schools National Institute of Technology, $16,300
4. Wheeling Jesuit University, $16,230
5. Alderson-Broaddus College, $13,890
6. University of Charleston, $13,200
7. Salem-Teikyo University, $13,040
8. Davis and Elkins College, $12,824
9. Mountain State College, $9,515
10. Ohio Valley College, $8,316

Source: "Tuition and Fees 2000-01," *The Chronicle of Higher Education* (http://chronicle.com/stats/tuition/tuition-results.php3), 47:, (October 27, 2000).

★1569★
Lowest undergraduate tuition and fees at colleges and universities in West Virginia

Ranking basis/background: These figures for in-state tuition and fees at over 3,000 colleges and universities were collected by the College Board in the Annual Survey of Colleges, 2000-01. Figures represent charges to first-time, full-time undergraduates based on a nine-month academic year of 30 semester hours or 45 quarter hours. **Remarks:** A separate table for each state, the District of Columbia, and Puerto Rico is included. Listing also shows added out-of-state tuition and 1999-2000 tuition and fees. **Number listed:** 28.
1. West Virginia University, Parkersburg, with tuition and fees of $1,437
2. Southern West Virginia Community and Technical College, $1,440
3. West Virginia Northern Community College, $1,632
4. Potomac State College, $2,192
5. Bluefield State College, $2,288
6. Fairmont State College, $2,316
7. Glenville State College, $2,376
8. West Liberty State College, $2,420
9. West Virginia State College, $2,464
10. Shepherd College, $2,508

Source: "Tuition and Fees 2000-01," *The Chronicle of Higher Education* (http://chronicle.com/stats/tuition/tuition-results.php3), 47:, (October 27, 2000).

COLLEGES & UNIVERSITIES–STUDENT COSTS–WISCONSIN

★1570★
Highest undergraduate tuition and fees at colleges and universities in Wisconsin

Ranking basis/background: These figures for in-state tuition and fees at over 3,000 colleges and universities were collected by the College Board in the Annual Survey of Colleges, 2000-01. Figures represent charges to first-time, full-time undergraduates based on a nine-month academic year of 30 semester hours or 45 quarter hours. **Remarks:** A separate table for each state, the District of Columbia, and Puerto Rico is included. Listing also shows added out-of-state tuition and 1999-2000 tuition and fees. **Number listed:** 68.
1. Lawrence University, with tuition and fees of $21,855
2. Beloit College, $21,550
3. Milwaukee School of Engineering, $20,985
4. Ripon College, $18,240
5. Carthage College, $17,350
5. Milwaukee Institute of Art & Design, $17,350
7. Marquette University, $17,336
8. St. Norbert College, $16,770
9. Carroll College, $15,580
9. Columbia College of Nursing, $15,580

Source: "Tuition and Fees 2000-01," *The Chronicle of Higher Education* (http://chronicle.com/stats/tuition/tuition-results.php3), 47:, (October 27, 2000).

★1571★
Lowest undergraduate tuition and fees at colleges and universities in Wisconsin

Ranking basis/background: These figures for in-state tuition and fees at over 3,000 colleges and universities were collected by the College Board in the Annual Survey of Colleges, 2000-01. Figures represent charges to first-time, full-time undergraduates based on a nine-month academic year of 30 semester hours or 45 quarter hours. **Remarks:** A separate table for each state, the District of Columbia, and Puerto Rico is included. Listing also shows added out-of-state tuition and 1999-2000 tuition and fees. **Number listed:** 68.
1. Southwest Wisconsin Technical College, with tuition and fees of $1,890
1. Gateway Technical College, $1,890
3. Nicolet Area Technical College, $1,898
4. Northeast Wisconsin Technical College, $1,905
4. Blackhawk Technical College, $1,905
6. Lakeshore Technical College, $1,926
7. Moraine Park Technical College, $1,935
8. Mid-State Technical College, $1,937
9. Wisconsin Indianhead Technical College, $1,941
10. Chippewa Valley Technical College, $1,946

Source: "Tuition and Fees 2000-01," *The Chronicle of Higher Education* (http://chronicle.com/stats/tuition/tuition-results.php3), 47:, (October 27, 2000).

COLLEGES & UNIVERSITIES–STUDENT COSTS–WYOMING

★1572★
Undergraduate tuition and fees at colleges and universities in Wyoming

Ranking basis/background: These figures for in-state tuition and fees at over 3,000 colleges and universities were collected by the College Board in the Annual Survey of Colleges, 2000-01. Figures represent charges to first-time, full-time undergraduates based on a nine-month academic year of 30 semester hours or 45 quarter hours. **Remarks:** A separate table for each state, the District of Columbia, and Puerto Rico is included. Listing also shows added out-of-state tuition and 1999-2000 tuition and fees. **Number listed:** 9.
1. Wyoming Technical Institute, with tuition and fees of $16,750
2. University of Wyoming, $2,575
3. Northwest College, $1,610
4. Eastern Wyoming College, $1,608
5. Central Wyoming College, $1,524
6. Laramie County Community College, $1,428
7. Sheridan College, $1,416
8. Western Wyoming Community College, $1,344
9. Casper College, $1,248

Source: "Tuition and Fees 2000-01," *The Chronicle of Higher Education* (http://chronicle.com/stats/tuition/tuition-results.php3), 47:, (October 27, 2000).

COLLEGES & UNIVERSITIES–TUITION

See: **Colleges & Universities–Student Costs**

COLLEGES & UNIVERSITIES–WESTERN STATES

★1573★
***U.S. News & World Report*'s top public western regional universities, 2000-01**

Ranking basis/background: Based on *U.S News* questionnaire sent to 1,400 four-year institutions. Scores are averaged and weighted percentages from seven attributes: academic reputation, retention, faculty resources, student selectivity, financial resources, graduation rate performance and alumni giving. **Remarks:** Comparable data was used from the U.S. Department of Education, the Council for Aid to Education, the NCAA, and Wintergreen/Orchard House publishers. **Number listed:** 13.
1. California Polytechnic State University, San Luis Obispo
2. Western Washington University
3. California State Polytechnic University, Pomona
3. Montana Tech of the University of Montana
5. California State University, Chico
6. Humboldt State University
6. Sonoma State University
8. University of Nevada, Las Vegas
9. San Jose State University

9. University of Colorado, Colorado Springs
11. California State University, Fresno
11. California State University, Sacramento
11. Weber State University

Source: "America's Best Colleges," *U.S. News & World Report*, 129: 90-132, (September 11, 2000).

★1574★
U.S. News & World Report's top western regional universities, 2000-01

Ranking basis/background: Based on *U.S News* questionnaire sent to 1,400 four-year institutions. Scores are averaged and weighted percentages from seven attributes: academic reputation, retention, faculty resources, student selectivity, financial resources, graduation rate performance and alumni giving. **Remarks:** Comparable data was used from the U.S. Department of Education, the Council for Aid to Education, the NCAA, and Wintergreen/Orchard House publishers. **Number listed:** 28.
1. Trinity University, with an overall score of 100.0
2. Santa Clara University, 90.0
3. Loyola Marymount University, 83.0
4. Gonzaga University, 80.0
5. California Polytechnic State University, San Luis Obispo, 77.0
6. Linfield College, 76.0
6. University of Portland, 76.0
6. University of Redlands, 76.0
9. Pacific Lutheran University, 74.0
9. St. Mary's College (CA), 74.0
9. Whitworth College, 74.0

Source: "America's Best Colleges," *U.S. News & World Report*, 129: 90-132, (September 11, 2000).

★1575★
U.S. News & World Report's western regional universities with students least in debt, 1999

Ranking basis/background: Based on total amount borrowed by 1999 graduates from one or more of the following sources: federal, state and local governments, financial institutions, and the colleges themselves. **Remarks:** Debt does not reflect monies borrowed by parents or others on behalf of the student. **Number listed:** 5.
1. Northeastern State University, with an average debt of $5,500
2. University of Texas, El Paso, $6,242
3. California State University, Long Beach, $6,400
4. Dallas Baptist University, $6,540
5. Southwestern Oklahoma State University, $7,500

Source: "How Heavy is the Load?," *U.S. News & World Report*, 129: 101-102, (September 18, 2000).

★1576★
U.S. News & World Report's western regional universities with students most in debt, 1999

Ranking basis/background: Based on total amount borrowed by 1999 graduates from one or more of the following sources: federal, state and local governments, financial institutions, and the colleges themselves. **Remarks:** Debt does not reflect monies borrowed by parents or others on behalf of the student. **Number listed:** 5.
1. Mount St. Mary's College and Seminary, with an average debt of $35,000
2. Oral Roberts University, $25,223
3. Abilene Christian University, $23,405
4. St. Edward's University, $22,733
5. University of Redlands, $20,673

Source: "How Heavy is the Load?," *U.S. News & World Report*, 129: 101-102, (September 18, 2000).

★1577★
U.S. News & World Report's western regional universities with the best academic reputation scores, 2000-01

Ranking basis/background: Based on *U.S News* questionnaire sent to 1,400 four-year institutions. Scores are averaged and weighted percentages from seven attributes: academic reputation, retention, faculty resources, student selectivity, financial resources, graduation rate performance and alumni giving. **Remarks:** Comparable data was used from the U.S. Department of Education, the Council for Aid to Education, the NCAA, and Wintergreen/Orchard House publishers. **Number listed:** 28.
1. Trinity University, with a score of 4.3
2. Santa Clara University, 3.9
2. California Polytechnic State University, San Luis Obispo, 3.9
4. Loyola Marymount University, 3.7
4. Gonzaga University, 3.7
6. University of Portland, 3.5
6. California State Polytechnic University, Pomona, 3.5
8. Whitworth College, 3.4
8. Seattle University, 3.4
10. Linfield College, 3.3
10. University of Redlands, 3.3
10. Pacific Lutheran University, 3.3
10. St. Mary's College (CA), 3.3

Source: "America's Best Colleges," *U.S. News & World Report*, 129: 90-132, (September 11, 2000).

★1578★
U.S. News & World Report's western regional universities with the best student/faculty ratios, 2000-01

Ranking basis/background: Based on *U.S News* questionnaire sent to 1,400 four-year institutions. Scores are averaged and weighted percentages from seven attributes: academic reputation, retention, faculty resources, student selectivity, financial resources, graduation rate performance and alumni giving. **Remarks:** Comparable data was used from the U.S. Department of Education, the Council for Aid to Education, the NCAA, and Wintergreen/Orchard House publishers. **Number listed:** 28.
1. Marylhurst University, with a student/faculty ratio of 7/1
2. Pacific University (OR), 10/1
3. Trinity University, 11/1
4. Chapman University, 12/1
4. Gonzaga University, 12/1
6. St. Mary's University (TX), 13/1
6. Santa Clara University, 13/1
6. Loyola Marymount University, 13/1
6. Linfield College, 13/1
6. University of Portland, 13/1
6. St. Mary's College (CA), 13/1

Source: "America's Best Colleges," *U.S. News & World Report*, 129: 90-132, (September 11, 2000).

★1579★
U.S. News & World Report's western regional universities with the highest acceptance rates, 2000-01

Ranking basis/background: Based on *U.S News* questionnaire sent to 1,400 four-year institutions. Scores are averaged and weighted percentages from seven attributes: academic reputation, retention, faculty resources, student selectivity, financial resources, graduation rate performance and alumni giving. **Remarks:** Comparable data was used from the U.S. Department of Education, the Council for Aid to Education, the NCAA, and Wintergreen/Orchard House publishers. **Number listed:** 28.
1. Montana Tech of the University of Montana, with 95%
2. Seattle Pacific University, 93%
3. Linfield College, 92%
4. University of Portland, 89%
5. Gonzaga University, 87%
5. Marylhurst University, 87%
5. Whitworth College, 87%
8. Westminster College, 86%
8. St. Mary's University (TX), 86%
8. Pacific University (OR), 86%

Source: "America's Best Colleges," *U.S. News & World Report*, 129: 90-132, (September 11, 2000).

★1580★
U.S. News & World Report's western regional universities with the highest alumni giving rates, 2000-01

Ranking basis/background: Based on *U.S News* questionnaire sent to 1,400 four-year institutions. Scores are averaged and weighted percentages from seven attributes: academic reputation, retention, faculty resources, student selectivity, financial resources, graduation rate performance and alumni giving. **Remarks:** Comparable data was used from the U.S. Department of Education, the Council for Aid to Education, the NCAA, and Wintergreen/Orchard House publishers. **Number listed:** 28.
1. Santa Clara University, with 29%
2. Linfield College, 28%
2. Marylhurst University, 28%
4. University of Redlands, 26%
4. Pacific University (OR), 26%
6. University of Portland, 25%
6. Whitworth College, 25%
8. Gonzaga University, 23%
8. St. Mary's University (TX), 23%
8. Montana Tech of the University of Montana, 23%

Source: "America's Best Colleges," *U.S. News & World Report*, 129: 90-132, (September 11, 2000).

★1581★
U.S. News & World Report's western regional universities with the highest freshmen retention rates, 2000-01

Ranking basis/background: Based on *U.S News* questionnaire sent to 1,400 four-year institutions. Scores are averaged and weighted percentages from seven attributes: academic reputation, retention, faculty resources, student selectivity, financial resources, graduation rate performance and alumni giving. **Remarks:** Comparable data was used from the U.S. Department of Education, the Council for Aid to Education, the NCAA, and Wintergreen/Orchard House publishers. **Number listed:** 28.
1. Santa Clara University, with 91%
2. Gonzaga University, 88%
3. California Polytechnic State University, San Luis Obispo, 87%

4. Trinity University, 86%
4. Loyola Marymount University, 86%
6. Mount St. Mary's College and Seminary, 84%
7. St. Mary's College (CA), 83%
7. Whitworth College, 83%
7. Regis University, 83%
10. Pacific Lutheran University, 82%
10. Chapman University, 82%
10. St. Mary's University (TX), 82%

Source: "America's Best Colleges," *U.S. News & World Report*, 129: 90-132, (September 11, 2000).

★1582★
U.S. News & World Report's western regional universities with the highest graduation rates, 2000-01

Ranking basis/background: Based on *U.S News* questionnaire sent to 1,400 four-year institutions. Scores are averaged and weighted percentages from seven attributes: academic reputation, retention, faculty resources, student selectivity, financial resources, graduation rate performance and alumni giving. **Remarks:** Comparable data was used from the U.S. Department of Education, the Council for Aid to Education, the NCAA, and Wintergreen/Orchard House publishers. **Number listed:** 28.

1. Santa Clara University, with 80%
2. Trinity University, 76%
3. Loyola Marymount University, 73%
4. St. Mary's College (CA), 67%
5. Linfield College, 65%
5. Pacific Lutheran University, 65%
7. Western Washington University, 63%
8. Gonzaga University, 62%
8. University of Portland, 62%
10. Mount St. Mary's College and Seminary, 61%

Source: "America's Best Colleges," *U.S. News & World Report*, 129: 90-132, (September 11, 2000).

★1583★
U.S. News & World Report's western regional universities with the highest percentage of freshmen in the top 25% of their high school class, 2000-01

Ranking basis/background: Based on *U.S News* questionnaire sent to 1,400 four-year institutions. Scores are averaged and weighted percentages from seven attributes: academic reputation, retention, faculty resources, student selectivity, financial resources, graduation rate performance and alumni giving. **Remarks:** Comparable data was used from the U.S. Department of Education, the Council for Aid to Education, the NCAA, and Wintergreen/Orchard House publishers. **Number listed:** 28.

1. Trinity University, with 82%
2. Seattle Pacific University, 79%
3. Whitworth College, 78%
4. Marylhurst University, 77%
5. California Polytechnic State University, San Luis Obispo, 73%
6. Santa Clara University, 71%
6. Pacific Lutheran University, 71%
6. Pacific University (OR), 71%
9. University of Redlands, 69%
10. University of Portland, 67%

Source: "America's Best Colleges," *U.S. News & World Report*, 129: 90-132, (September 11, 2000).

★1584★
U.S. News & World Report's western regional universities with the highest percentage of full-time faculty, 2000-01

Ranking basis/background: Based on *U.S News* questionnaire sent to 1,400 four-year institutions. Scores are averaged and weighted percentages from seven attributes: academic reputation, retention, faculty resources, student selectivity, financial resources, graduation rate performance and alumni giving. **Remarks:** Comparable data was used from the U.S. Department of Education, the Council for Aid to Education, the NCAA, and Wintergreen/Orchard House publishers. **Number listed:** 28.

1. Gonzaga University, with 97%
2. Whitworth College, 95%
3. Linfield College, 93%
4. Trinity University, 92%
5. Montana Tech of the University of Montana, 91%
6. Pacific Lutheran University, 89%
6. Western Washington University, 89%
8. Abilene Christian University, 86%
9. Santa Clara University, 85%
9. St. Mary's University, San Antonio, 85%
9. Seattle University, 85%
9. University of Portland, 85%

Source: "America's Best Colleges," *U.S. News & World Report*, 129: 90-132, (September 11, 2000).

★1585★
U.S. News & World Report's western regional universities with the highest proportion of classes with 20 students or less, 2000-01

Ranking basis/background: Based on *U.S News* questionnaire sent to 1,400 four-year institutions. Scores are averaged and weighted percentages from seven attributes: academic reputation, retention, faculty resources, student selectivity, financial resources, graduation rate performance and alumni giving. **Remarks:** Comparable data was used from the U.S. Department of Education, the Council for Aid to Education, the NCAA, and Wintergreen/Orchard House publishers. **Number listed:** 28.

1. Marylhurst University, with 95%
2. Regis University, 89%
3. Westminster College, 75%
4. University of Redlands, 74%
5. Oklahoma City University, 69%
6. Pacific University (OR), 65%
6. Notre Dame College, 65%
8. Linfield College, 64%
8. Whitworth College, 64%
10. Montana Tech of the University of Montana, 63%

Source: "America's Best Colleges," *U.S. News & World Report*, 129: 90-132, (September 11, 2000).

★1586★
U.S. News & World Report's western regional universities with the lowest acceptance rates, 2000-01

Ranking basis/background: Based on *U.S News* questionnaire sent to 1,400 four-year institutions. Scores are averaged and weighted percentages from seven attributes: academic reputation, retention, faculty resources, student selectivity, financial resources, graduation rate performance and alumni giving. **Remarks:** Comparable data was used from the U.S. Department of Education, the Council for Aid to Education, the NCAA, and Wintergreen/Orchard House publishers. **Number listed:** 28.

1. California Polytechnic State University, San Luis Obispo, with 42%
2. Chapman University, 60%
3. Loyola Marymount University, 62%
4. Oklahoma City University, 63%
5. Santa Clara University, 70%
6. California State Polytechnic University, Pomona, 71%
7. Mount St. Mary's College and Seminary, 74%
8. Trinity University, 76%
9. California Lutheran University, 77%
10. Abilene Christian University, 79%

Source: "America's Best Colleges," *U.S. News & World Report*, 129: 90-132, (September 11, 2000).

COLLEGES, JUNIOR
See: **Two-Year Colleges**

COMMUNICATION
See: **Data Communications–North America Mass Media Speech Communication**

COMMUNITY COLLEGES
See: **Two-Year Colleges**

COMPARATIVE LITERATURE, GRADUATE

★1587★
Most effective comparative literature research-doctorate programs as evaluated by the National Research Council

Ranking basis/background: From a survey of nearly 8,000 faculty members conducted in the spring of 1993. Respondents were asked to rate programs in their field on "effectiveness of program in educating research scholars/scientists." **Remarks:** See *Chronicle* article for more details. Scores of 3.5-5.0 indicate "extremely effective;" 2.5-3.49 "reasonably effective;" 1.5-2.49 "minimally effective;" and 0.0-1.49 "not effective." Programs also ranked by "scholarly quality of program faculty." **Number listed:** 44.

1. Yale University, with an effectiveness rating of 4.30
2. Johns Hopkins University, 4.12
3. Princeton University, 3.96
4. University of California, Berkeley, 3.83
5. Columbia University, 3.82
6. Harvard University, 3.81
7. Duke University, 3.80
8. Cornell University, 3.78
9. Stanford University, 3.75
10. University of California, Berkeley, 3.83

Source: "Rankings of Research-Doctorate Programs in 41 Disciplines at 274 Institutions," *The Chronicle of Higher Education* 42: A21-A30 (September 21, 1995).

★1588★
Top comparative literature research-doctorate programs as evaluated by the National Research Council

Ranking basis/background: From a survey of nearly 8,000 faculty members conducted in the spring of 1993. Respondents were asked to rate programs in their field on "scholarly quality of program faculty." When more than one program had the samescore, the council averaged the rank order and gave each program the same rank number (if three programs tied for the top position, each received a rank of 2). **Remarks:** See *Chronicle* article for more details. Scores of 4.01 and above indicate "distinguished;" 3.0-4.0 "strong;" 2.51-3.0 "good;" 2.0-2.5 "adequate;" 1.0-1.99 "marginal;" and 0.0-0.99 "not sufficient for doctoral education." Programs also ranked by "effectiveness of program in educating research scholars/scientists." **Number listed:** 44.

1. Yale University, with a quality rating of 4.70
2. Duke University, 4.51
3. Columbia University, 4.44
4. Harvard University, 4.37
5. Princeton University, 4.32
6. Cornell University, 4.31
7. Johns Hopkins University, 4.18
8. University of California, Irvine, 4.06
9. Stanford University, 4.05
10. University of California, Berkeley, 4.00
11. University of Pennsylvania, 3.99
12. University of Chicago, 3.56
13. New York University, 3.49
14. University of Washington (WA), 3.37
15. University of Michigan, 3.23

Source: "Rankings of Research-Doctorate Programs in 41 Disciplines at 274 Institutions," *The Chronicle of Higher Education* 42: A21-A30 (September 21, 1995).

COMPETENCY TESTS FOR STUDENTS
See: **Achievement Tests–Schools, Elementary & Secondary College Entrance Examinations**

COMPUTER ENGINEERING
See: **Engineering–Computer Engineering, Graduate–Computer**

COMPUTER SCIENCE
See also: **Data Communications–North America**

★1589★
Canadian universities producing the most-cited papers in the field of computer science, 1992-96

Ranking basis/background: Citations per paper. Also includes total number of papers published, 1992-96. **Remarks:** Original source: ISI's *Canadian University Indicators on Diskette, 1981-96.* **Number listed:** 6.

1. Simon Fraser University, with 1.84 citations per paper; 88 total papers
2. University of British Columbia, 1.42; 112
3. University of Waterloo, 1.26; 218
4. Queen's University, 1.24; 96
4. University of Toronto, 1.24; 207
6. University of Alberta, 1.22; 82

Source: "Canadian Universities: Highest Impact in Computer Science, 1992-96," *What's Hot,* February 2, 1998.

★1590★
Top recruiters for computer science jobs for 2000-01 bachelor's degree recipients

Ranking basis/background: Projected number of college hires from on-campus recruitment for 2000-01. **Remarks:** Numbers reflect total expected hires, not just African American projected hires. **Number listed:** 44.

1. EDS, with 1,000 projected hires
2. Lucent Technologies, 300
2. Cap Gemini Ernst & Young, 300
4. American Management Systems, 220
5. Alcatel, 125
6. Accenture, 100
6. Telcordia Technologies, 100
6. Deloitte & Touche, 100
6. Unisys, 100
6. State Farm Insurance Company, 100

Source: "The Top 100 Employers and the Majors in Demand for the Class of 2001," *The Black Collegian,* 31: 19-35, (February 2001).

★1591★
U.S. universities publishing the most papers in the field of computer science, 1994-98

Ranking basis/background: Number of papers published in the field of computer science over a five-year period, and percent of field based on each universities percentage of 39,205 papers entered in the ISI database from ISI-indexed computer science journals. **Number listed:** 5.

1. Massachusetts Institute of Technology, with 492 papers; 1.25% of field
2. University of Maryland, College Park, 404; 1.03%
3. Stanford University, 378; 0.96%
4. University of Illinois, Urbana-Champaign, 344; 0.88%
5. Carnegie Mellon University, 321; 0.82%

Source: "Computer Science: Most Prolific U.S. Universities, 1994-98," *What's Hot in Research* (http://www.isinet.com/isi/hot/research) *Institute for Scientific Information,* July 10, 2000.

★1592★
U.S. universities with the greatest impact in computer science, 1994-98

Ranking basis/background: Total number of computer science papers published from each university and average number of citations per paper between 1994 and 1998. **Remarks:** Original source: University Science Indicators on Diskette, 1981-98. **Number listed:** 5.

1. University of California, Berkeley, with 307 computer science papers; 2.61 citations per paper
2. University of Illinois, Urbana-Champaign, 344; 2.51
3. Princeton University, 213; 2.50
4. Stanford University, 378; 2.39
5. Massachusetts Institute of Technology, 492; 2.36

Source: "Computer Science: High-Impact U.S. Universities, 1994-98," *What's Hot in Research* (http://www.isinet.com/hot/research) *Institute for Scientific Information,* October 11, 1999.

★1593★
U.S. universities with the greatest impact in computer science, 1995-99

Ranking basis/background: Average citations per paper from the top 100 federally funded U.S. universities that had at least 50 published papers in ISI indexed computer science journals. Also includes total number of papers published during the five year period. **Number listed:** 5.

1. Princeton University, with 195 papers; 3.65 citations per paper
2. University of California, Berkeley, 346; 3.02
3. University of Illinois, Urbana-Champaign, 348; 2.82
4. University of Virginia, 106; 2.65
5. Columbia University, 150; 2.56

Source: "Computer Science: High Impact U.S. Universities, 1995-99," *What's Hot in Research* (http://www.isinet.com/isi/hot/research) *Institute for Scientific Information,* September 11, 2000.

COMPUTER SCIENCE, GRADUATE
See also: **Engineering, Graduate–Computer**

★1594★
Most effective computer science research-doctorate programs as evaluated by the National Research Council

Ranking basis/background: From a survey of nearly 8,000 faculty members conducted in the spring of 1993. Respondents were asked to rate programs in their field on "effectiveness of program in educating research scholars/scientists." **Remarks:** See *Chronicle* article for more details. Scores of 3.5-5.0 indicate "extremely effective;" 2.5-3.49 "reasonably effective;" 1.5-2.49 "minimally effective;" and 0.0-1.49 "not effective." Programs also ranked by "scholarly quality of program faculty." **Number listed:** 108.

1. Massachusetts Institute of Technology, with an effectiveness rating of 4.62
2. Stanford University, 4.60
3. University of California, Berkeley, 4.58
4. Cornell University, 4.47
5. Carnegie Mellon University, 4.38
6. University of Washington (WA), 4.05
7. California Institute of Technology, 3.97
8. University of Illinois, Urbana-Champaign, 3.93
9. University of Wisconsin, Madison, 3.87
10. Princeton University, 3.84

Source: "Rankings of Research-Doctorate Programs in 41 Disciplines at 274 Institutions," *The Chronicle of Higher Education* 42: A21-A30 (September 21, 1995).

COMPUTER SOFTWARE

★1595★
Private, 4-year undergraduate colleges and universities producing the most Ph.D.'s in the computer sciences, 1920-1990

Ranking basis/background: Number of doctoral degrees granted to graduates of 914 private, 4-year U.S. undergraduate colleges and universities. Medical, law, and other professional, non-doctoral degrees are not included. **Remarks:** Original source: Office of Scientific and Engineering Personnel of the National Research Council. Report contains 50 other tables detailing the distribution of doctoral recipients by field of study over various time frames. **Number listed:** 222.
1. Oberlin College, with 13 Ph.D.'s
2. Reed College, 12
3. Polytechnic University, 9
3. Swarthmore College, 9
3. Wesleyan University, 9
3. Stevens Institute of Technology, 9
7. Carleton College, 8
7. Manhattan College, 8
9. Williams College, 7
10. Union College, 6
10. Bucknell University, 6
10. Harvey Mudd College, 6
10. University of Dayton, 6
10. Santa Clara University, 6
10. Moravian College, 6
16. St. Olaf College, 5
16. Clarkson University, 5
16. Amherst College, 5
16. Pomona College, 5
16. Furman University, 5
16. Occidental College, 5
16. Antioch College, 5
16. Cooper Union, 5
16. North Park College & Theological Seminary, 5

Source: *Baccalaureate Origins of Doctorate Recipients, 7th ed.,* Franklin & Marshall College, March 1993.

★1596★
Private, 4-year undergraduate colleges and universities producing the most Ph.D.'s in the computer sciences, 1981-1990

Ranking basis/background: Number of doctoral degrees granted to graduates of 914 private, 4-year U.S. undergraduate colleges and universities. Medical, law, and other professional, non-doctoral degrees are not included. **Remarks:** Original source: Office of Scientific and Engineering Personnel of the National Research Council. Report contains 50 other tables detailing the distribution of doctoral recipients by field of study over various time frames. **Number listed:** 201.
1. Oberlin College, with 13 Ph.D.'s
2. Wesleyan University, 9
3. Carleton College, 8
3. Reed College, 8
3. Swarthmore College, 8
6. Williams College, 7
6. Polytechnic University, 7
6. Stevens Institute of Technology, 7
9. Union College, 6
9. Moravian College, 6
11. Bucknell University, 5
11. Clarkson University, 5
11. Pomona College, 5
11. Manhattan College, 5
11. University of Dayton, 5
11. Amherst College, 5
11. North Park College & Theological Seminary, 5
11. Harvey Mudd College, 5

Source: *Baccalaureate Origins of Doctorate Recipients, 7th ed.,* Franklin & Marshall College, March 1993.

★1597★
Top computer science research-doctorate programs as evaluated by the National Research Council

Ranking basis/background: From a survey of nearly 8,000 faculty members conducted in the spring of 1993. Respondents were asked to rate programs in their field on "scholarly quality of program faculty." When more than one program had the samescore, the council averaged the rank order and gave each program the same rank number (if three programs tied for the top position, each received a rank of 2). **Remarks:** See *Chronicle* article for more details. Scores of 4.01 and above indicate "distinguished;" 3.0-4.0 "strong;" 2.51-3.0 "good;" 2.0-2.5 "adequate;" 1.0-1.99 "marginal;" and 0.0-0.99 "not sufficient for doctoral education." Programs also ranked by "effectiveness of program in educating research scholars/scientists." **Number listed:** 108.
1. Stanford University, with a quality rating of 4.97
2. Massachusetts Institute of Technology, 4.91
3. University of California, Berkeley, 4.88
4. Carnegie Mellon University, 4.76
5. Cornell University, 4.64
6. Princeton University, 4.31
7. University of Texas, Austin, 4.18
8. University of Illinois, Urbana-Champaign, 4.09
9. University of Washington (WA), 4.04
10. University of Wisconsin, Madison, 4.00
11. Harvard University, 3.94
12. California Institute of Technology, 3.93
13. Brown University, 3.86
14. University of California, Los Angeles, 3.73
14. Yale University, 3.73

Source: "Rankings of Research-Doctorate Programs in 41 Disciplines at 274 Institutions," *The Chronicle of Higher Education* 42: A21-A30 (September 21, 1995).

★1598★
Top recruiters for computer science jobs for 2000-01 master's degree recipients

Ranking basis/background: Projected number of college hires from on-campus recruitment for 2000-01. **Remarks:** Numbers reflect total expected hires, not just African American projected hires. **Number listed:** 44.
1. Lucent Technologies, with 300 projected hires
2. EDS, 100
3. Accenture, 50
4. Tellabs, 40
5. Telcordia Technologies, 20
5. Federal Deposit Insurance Company, 20
7. Agilent Technologies, 15
8. Procter & Gamble, 10
8. Litton Industries, 10
8. ALLTEL, 10
8. Qualcomm, 10

Source: "The Top 100 Employers and the Majors in Demand for the Class of 2001," *The Black Collegian,* 31: 19-35, (February 2001).

COMPUTER SOFTWARE

★1599★
Top selling home education software, 2000

Ranking basis/background: Based on average U.S. sales from January to June 2000. **Remarks:** Original source: PC Data, Reston, VA. **Number listed:** 10.
1. Jumpstart Phonics
2. Pokemon Studio Blue
3. Winnie The Pooh Preschool
4. Jumpstart First Grade
5. Winnie The Pooh Kindergarten
6. Winnie The Pooh Toddler
7. Mavis Beacon Teaches Typing 10.0
8. Jumpstart Second Grade
9. Jumpstart Preschool
10. Pokemon Studio Red

Source: *The World Almanac and Book of Facts 2001,* World Almanac Books, 2001.

★1600★
Top selling personal productivity software, 2000

Ranking basis/background: Based on average U.S. sales from January to June 2000. **Remarks:** Original source: PC Data, Reston, VA. **Number listed:** 10.
1. Microsoft Expedia Streets
2. Print Shop Deluxe
3. Microsoft Greetings
4. Microsoft Home Publishing Suite
5. Microsoft Home Publishing
6. Microsoft Works Suite
7. Printmaster Gold
8. Microsoft Picture It
9. Printmaster Silver
10. Easy CD Creator Deluxe 4.0

Source: *The World Almanac and Book of Facts 2001,* World Almanac Books, 2001.

★1601★
Top selling reference software, 2000

Ranking basis/background: Based on average U.S. sales from January to June 2000. **Remarks:** Original source: PC Data, Reston, VA. **Number listed:** 5.
1. Microsoft Encarta Encyclopedia
2. American Heritage Talking Dictionary Classic
3. Microsoft Encarta Encyclopedia Deluxe
4. Microsoft Encarta Reference Suite
5. Webster's Gold Encyclopedia 2000

Source: *The World Almanac and Book of Facts 2001,* World Almanac Books, 2001.

★1602★
Top selling software in all categories, 2000

Ranking basis/background: Based on average U.S. sales from January to June 2000. **Remarks:** Original source: PC Data, Reston, VA. **Number listed:** 20.
1. Turbo Tax Deluxe
2. Turbo Tax
3. The Sims
4. Norton Antivirus 2000 6.0
5. Who Wants To Be A Millionaire
6. Taxcut 1000 Federal Filling Edition Deluxe
7. Taxcut 1999 Federal Filling Edition
8. MS Windows 98 2nd Edition Upgrade

COMPUTER USES AT HOME

9. Turbo Tax Multi State
10. MP Roller Coaster Tycoon

Source: *The World Almanac and Book of Facts 2001*, World Almanac Books, 2001.

COMPUTER USES AT HOME

★1603★
Countries with the most computers, 2000

Ranking basis/background: Projected figures, in millions, for total number of computers in 2000. **Remarks:** Original source: Computer Industry Almanac Inc. **Number listed:** 15.

1. United States, with 160.50 million computers
2. Japan, 46.80
3. Germany, 29.80
4. United Kingdom, 26.00
5. France, 21.80
6. Italy, 17.50
7. Canada, 15.30
8. China, 13.30
9. South Korea, 10.60
10. Australia, 10.20

Source: Brunner, editor, Borgna, *The Time Almanac 2000*, Information Please, 1999.

★1604★
Countries with the most computers per capita, 2000

Ranking basis/background: Projected figures for number of computers per every 1,000 people. **Remarks:** Original source: Computer Industry Almanac Inc. **Number listed:** 16.

1. United States, with 580.0
2. Australia, 525.7
3. Norway, 515.4
4. Canada, 511.9
5. Denmark, 510.2
6. Sweden, 508.9
7. Finland, 505.0
8. New Zealand, 499.2
9. Netherlands, 450.3
10. United Kingdom, 441.1

Source: Brunner, editor, Borgna, *The Time Almanac 2000*, Information Please, 1999.

★1605★
Percentage of computer usage in U.S. households, by income

Ranking basis/background: Percentage of computer usage by annual family income. **Remarks:** Original source: U.S. Census Bureau. **Number listed:** 4.

$5,000-$9,999, with 11.0%
$20,000-$24,999, 23.5%
$35,000-$49,999, 46.9%
Over $75,000, 76.8%

Source: "Disparities & Gaps in America," *Black Issues in Higher Education*, 18: 28-29, (March 1, 2001).

COMPUTER USES IN EDUCATION
See also: **Distance Education**

★1606★
Percentage of instructional classrooms with Internet access

Ranking basis/background: Percentage of classrooms with internet access for selected years. **Remarks:** Original source: U.S. Department of Education. **Number listed:** 4.

1994, with 3%
1996, 14%
1998, 51%
1999, 63%

Source: "Education Vital Signs 2000," *American School Board Journal*, 187: 31-47, (December 2000).

★1607★
U.S. public schools with computers, 2000

Ranking basis/background: Number of schools and percentage of total schools that have computers, by elementary, middle/jr. high, senior high, K-12, and special ed/adult ed. **Remarks:** Original source: Quality Education Data, Inc., Denver, CO. **Number listed:** 5.

Elementary, with 43,968 schools with computers (82.5% of all schools)
Middle/jr. high, 12,848 (87.3%)
Senior high, 14,548 (81.6%)
K-12, 1,721 (72.2%)
Special ed./Adult ed., 994 (42.0%)

Source: *The World Almanac and Book of Facts 2001*, World Almanac Books, 2001.

★1608★
U.S. public schools with Internet access, 2000

Ranking basis/background: Number of schools and percentage of total schools that have Internet access, by elementary, middle/jr. high, senior high, K-12, and special ed/adult ed. **Remarks:** Original source: Quality Education Data, Inc., Denver, CO. **Number listed:** 5.

Elementary, with 35,994 schools with computers (67.5% of all schools)
Middle/jr. high, 12,210 (82.9%)
Senior high, 13,857 (77.8%)
K-12, 1,573 (66.0%)
Special ed./Adult ed., 584 (24.7%)

Source: *The World Almanac and Book of Facts 2001*, World Almanac Books, 2001.

★1609★
U.S. public schools with LANs, 2000

Ranking basis/background: Number of schools and percentage of total schools that have LANs (Local area networks), by elementary, middle/jr. high, senior high, K-12, and special ed/adult ed. **Remarks:** Original source: Quality Education Data, Inc., Denver, CO. **Number listed:** 5.

Elementary, with 22,398 schools with computers (42.0% of all schools)
Middle/jr. high, 8,184 (55.6%)
Senior high, 10,982 (61.6%)
K-12, 1,309 (54.9%)
Special ed./Adult ed., 345 (14.6%)

Source: *The World Almanac and Book of Facts 2001*, World Almanac Books, 2001.

CONSUMER RESEARCH
See: **Business Administration, Graduate–Marketing Business Administration–Marketing**

COOKING INSTRUCTION

Related Information

★1610★
The Guide to Cooking Schools, 13th ed., ShawGuides, 2001.

Remarks: A detailed guide to 1100 school and travel programs in restaurants, cookware shops, private homes, vocational schools and colleges both for nonprofessionals and those seeking a career in this field. Geographic and subject indexes are included. Includes apprenticeships and wine instruction. Online at http://cookingcareer.shawguides.com/

CRIMINAL JUSTICE
See also: **Law Enforcement**

★1611★
Criminology and penology journals with the greatest impact measure, 1981-98

Ranking basis/background: Citations-per-paper impact score is the total citations to a journal's published papers divided by total number of papers the journal has published over an eighteen year period. **Remarks:** Original source: *Journal Citation Reports* and Journal Performance Indicators on Diskette. **Number listed:** 10.

1. *Criminology*, with an impact score of 12.69
2. *Journal of Research in Crime and Delinquency*, 7.68
3. *Crime & Justice*, 6.68
4. *Crime & Delinquency*, 5.14
5. *Criminal Justice and Behavior*, 4.88
6. *Journal of Interpersonal Violence*, 4.46
7. *Journal of Criminal Law and Criminology*, 4.46
8. *British Journal of Criminology*, 3.56
9. *Journal of Police Science & Administration*, 3.03
10. *American Criminal Law Review*, 2.27

Source: "Journals Ranked by Impact: Criminology & Penology," *What's Hot in Research* (http://www.isinet.com/hot/research) Institute for Scientific Information, February 14, 2000.

★1612★
Criminology and penology journals with the greatest impact measure, 1994-98

Ranking basis/background: Citations-per-paper impact score is the total citations to a journal's published papers divided by total number of papers the journal has published over a five year period. **Remarks:** Original source: *Journal Citation Reports* and Journal Performance Indicators on Diskette. **Number listed:** 10.

1. *Criminology*, with an impact score of 3.92
2. *Journal of Research in Crime and Delinquency*, 2.78

3. *Journal of Criminal Law and Criminology*, 2.11
4. *Criminal Justice and Behavior*, 2.05
5. *Journal of Interpersonal Violence*, 1.94
6. *Journal of Quantitative Criminology*, 1.88
7. *British Journal of Criminology*, 1.35
8. *Crime & Delinquency*, 1.31
9. *Canadian Journal of Criminology*, 0.90
10. *American Criminal Law Review*, 0.86

Source: "Journals Ranked by Impact: Criminology & Penology," *What's Hot in Research* (http://www.isinet.com/hot/research) *Institute for Scientific Information*, February 14, 2000.

★1613★
Most cited authors in the journal *Australian and New Zealand Journals of Criminology*, 1990 to 1995

Ranking basis/background: Total number of citations. **Number listed:** 5.
1. John Braithwaite, with 25 citations
2. Brent Fisse, 11
3. R.V. Ericson, 10
4. D.B. Moore, 8
4. L.W. Sherman, 8

Source: Cohn, Ellen G. and David P. Farrington, "Changes in the Most-Cited Scholars in Twenty Criminology and Criminal Justice Journals Between 1990 and 1995," *Journal of Criminal Justice*, 27: 345-359, (July/August 1999).

★1614★
Most cited authors in the journal *British Journal of Criminology*, 1990 to 1995

Ranking basis/background: Total number of citations. **Number listed:** 4.
1. K. Pease, with 20 citations
2. David P. Farrington, 14
3. J. Young, 12
4. P.M. Mayhew, 11

Source: Cohn, Ellen G. and David P. Farrington, "Changes in the Most-Cited Scholars in Twenty Criminology and Criminal Justice Journals Between 1990 and 1995," *Journal of Criminal Justice*, 27: 345-359, (July/August 1999).

★1615★
Most cited authors in the journal *Canadian Journal of Criminology*, 1990 to 1995

Ranking basis/background: Total number of citations. **Number listed:** 6.
1. M.A. Straus, with 28 citations
2. M.D. Smith, 13
3. R.E. Dobash, 12
3. Russell P. Dobash, 12
5. R.J. Gelles, 9
5. E.A. Stanko, 9

Source: Cohn, Ellen G. and David P. Farrington, "Changes in the Most-Cited Scholars in Twenty Criminology and Criminal Justice Journals Between 1990 and 1995," *Journal of Criminal Justice*, 27: 345-359, (July/August 1999).

★1616★
Most cited authors in the journal *Crime and Delinquency*, 1990 to 1995

Ranking basis/background: Total number of citations. **Number listed:** 5.
1. L.W. Sherman, with 19 citations
2. R.A. Berk, 10
2. R.E. Dobash, 10
2. Russell P. Dobash, 10
2. K.J. Ferraro, 10

Source: Cohn, Ellen G. and David P. Farrington, "Changes in the Most-Cited Scholars in Twenty Criminology and Criminal Justice Journals Between 1990 and 1995," *Journal of Criminal Justice*, 27: 345-359, (July/August 1999).

★1617★
Most cited authors in the journal *Crime and Justice*, 1990 to 1995

Ranking basis/background: Total number of citations. **Number listed:** 5.
1. K. Pease, with 46 citations
2. David P. Farrington, 31
3. R.V.G. Clarke, 28
4. L.W. Sherman, 26
5. P.M. Mayhew, 24

Source: Cohn, Ellen G. and David P. Farrington, "Changes in the Most-Cited Scholars in Twenty Criminology and Criminal Justice Journals Between 1990 and 1995," *Journal of Criminal Justice*, 27: 345-359, (July/August 1999).

★1618★
Most cited authors in the journal *Crime, Law, and Social Change*, 1990 to 1995

Ranking basis/background: Total number of citations. **Number listed:** 4.
1. E. Fromm, with 8 citations
2. P. Arlacchi, 6
2. L.I. Shelley, 6
4. T. Goldstein, 5

Source: Cohn, Ellen G. and David P. Farrington, "Changes in the Most-Cited Scholars in Twenty Criminology and Criminal Justice Journals Between 1990 and 1995," *Journal of Criminal Justice*, 27: 345-359, (July/August 1999).

★1619★
Most cited authors in the journal *Criminal Justice and Behavior*, 1990 to 1995

Ranking basis/background: Total number of citations. **Number listed:** 5.
1. R. Rogers, with 12 citations
2. G.L. Wells, 10
3. B.L. Cutler, 8
3. R.D. Hare, 8
3. H.C. Quay, 8

Source: Cohn, Ellen G. and David P. Farrington, "Changes in the Most-Cited Scholars in Twenty Criminology and Criminal Justice Journals Between 1990 and 1995," *Journal of Criminal Justice*, 27: 345-359, (July/August 1999).

★1620★
Most cited authors in the journal *Criminal Justice Review*, 1990 to 1995

Ranking basis/background: Total number of citations. **Number listed:** 7.
1. W.A. Geller, with 8 citations
1. L.W. Sherman, 8
3. J.J. Fyfe, 7
3. A.J. Reiss, 7
5. D.H. Bayley, 5
5. H. Tooch, 5
5. R.G. Worden, 5

Source: Cohn, Ellen G. and David P. Farrington, "Changes in the Most-Cited Scholars in Twenty Criminology and Criminal Justice Journals Between 1990 and 1995," *Journal of Criminal Justice*, 27: 345-359, (July/August 1999).

★1621★
Most cited authors in the journal *Criminologie*, 1990 to 1995

Ranking basis/background: Total number of citations. **Number listed:** 4.
1. P. Landreville, with 8 citations
2. P. Fitzpatrick, 6
3. J.I. Desroches, 5
3. P. Robert, 5

Source: Cohn, Ellen G. and David P. Farrington, "Changes in the Most-Cited Scholars in Twenty Criminology and Criminal Justice Journals Between 1990 and 1995," *Journal of Criminal Justice*, 27: 345-359, (July/August 1999).

★1622★
Most cited authors in the journal *Criminology*, 1990 to 1995

Ranking basis/background: Total number of citations. **Number listed:** 5.
1. Travis Hirschi, with 22 citations
2. John L. Hagan, 16
3. Michael R. Gottfredson, 14
3. H.G. Grasmick, 14
3. Robert J. Sampson, 14

Source: Cohn, Ellen G. and David P. Farrington, "Changes in the Most-Cited Scholars in Twenty Criminology and Criminal Justice Journals Between 1990 and 1995," *Journal of Criminal Justice*, 27: 345-359, (July/August 1999).

★1623★
Most cited authors in the journal *Federal Probation*, 1990 to 1995

Ranking basis/background: Total number of citations. **Number listed:** 5.
1. P. Gendreau, with 18 citations
2. D.A. Andrews, 13
3. Francis T. Cullen, 12
4. J. Bonta, 8
4. J. Petersilia, 8

Source: Cohn, Ellen G. and David P. Farrington, "Changes in the Most-Cited Scholars in Twenty Criminology and Criminal Justice Journals Between 1990 and 1995," *Journal of Criminal Justice*, 27: 345-359, (July/August 1999).

★1624★
Most cited authors in the journal *International Journal of Comparative and Applied Criminal Justice*, 1990 to 1995

Ranking basis/background: Total number of citations. **Number listed:** 6.
1. R.J. Sampson, with 13 citations
2. J.S.T. Quah, 12
3. B.A.K. Rider, 9
4. F.T. Cullen, 5
4. J. Eisenstein, 5
4. S. Quah, 5

Source: Cohn, Ellen G. and David P. Farrington, "Changes in the Most-Cited Scholars in Twenty Criminology and Criminal Justice Journals Between 1990 and 1995," *Journal of Criminal Justice*, 27: 345-359, (July/August 1999).

★1625★
Most cited authors in the journal *International Journal of Offender Therapy and Comparative Criminology*, 1990 to 1995

Ranking basis/background: Total number of citations. **Number listed:** 2.
1. J.V. Becker, with 14 citations

2. S.W. Henggeler, 7

Source: Cohn, Ellen G. and David P. Farrington, "Changes in the Most-Cited Scholars in Twenty Criminology and Criminal Justice Journals Between 1990 and 1995," *Journal of Criminal Justice*, 27: 345-359, (July/August 1999).

★1626★
Most cited authors in the journal *Journal of Criminal Justice*, 1990 to 1995

Ranking basis/background: Total number of citations. **Number listed:** 5.
1. J. Habermas, with 14 citations
2. Travis Hirschi, 13
3. Michael R. Gottfredson, 10
4. C.R. Tittle, 9
5. R.V. Del Carmen, 8

Source: Cohn, Ellen G. and David P. Farrington, "Changes in the Most-Cited Scholars in Twenty Criminology and Criminal Justice Journals Between 1990 and 1995," *Journal of Criminal Justice*, 27: 345-359, (July/August 1999).

★1627★
Most cited authors in the journal *Journal of Interpersonal Violence*, 1990 to 1995

Ranking basis/background: Total number of citations. **Number listed:** 7.
1. D. Finkelhor, with 30 citations
2. M.A. Straus, 15
3. D.E.H. Russell, 12
4. A. Browne, 11
4. M.P. Koss, 11
4. M. Runtz, 11
4. D.A. Wolfe, 11

Source: Cohn, Ellen G. and David P. Farrington, "Changes in the Most-Cited Scholars in Twenty Criminology and Criminal Justice Journals Between 1990 and 1995," *Journal of Criminal Justice*, 27: 345-359, (July/August 1999).

★1628★
Most cited authors in the journal *Journal of Quantitative Criminology*, 1990 to 1995

Ranking basis/background: Total number of citations. **Number listed:** 5.
1. Alfred Blumstein, with 18 citations
2. David P. Farrington, 14
2. Travis Hirschi, 14
4. Jacqueline Cohen, 13
5. R.J. Sampson, 12

Source: Cohn, Ellen G. and David P. Farrington, "Changes in the Most-Cited Scholars in Twenty Criminology and Criminal Justice Journals Between 1990 and 1995," *Journal of Criminal Justice*, 27: 345-359, (July/August 1999).

★1629★
Most cited authors in the journal *Journal of Research in Crime and Delinquency*, 1990 to 1995

Ranking basis/background: Total number of citations. **Number listed:** 5.
1. Delbert S. Elliott, with 19 citations
2. Travis Hirschi, 16
3. David P. Farrington, 13
3. David Huizinga, 13
5. L.W. Sherman, 12

Source: Cohn, Ellen G. and David P. Farrington, "Changes in the Most-Cited Scholars in Twenty Criminology and Criminal Justice Journals Between 1990 and 1995," *Journal of Criminal Justice*, 27: 345-359, (July/August 1999).

★1630★
Most cited authors in the journal *Justice Quarterly*, 1990 to 1995

Ranking basis/background: Total number of citations. **Number listed:** 5.
1. L.W. Sherman, with 24 citations
2. John L. Hagan, 17
3. Meda Chesney-Lind, 13
4. Travis Hirschi, 11
4. D. Weisburd, 11

Source: Cohn, Ellen G. and David P. Farrington, "Changes in the Most-Cited Scholars in Twenty Criminology and Criminal Justice Journals Between 1990 and 1995," *Journal of Criminal Justice*, 27: 345-359, (July/August 1999).

★1631★
Most cited authors in the journal *Social Justice*, 1990 to 1995

Ranking basis/background: Total number of citations. **Number listed:** 6.
1. I. Wallerstein, with 10 citations
2. J. Asker, 9
3. Michael Foucault, 7
3. M. Maurer, 7
5. S. Amin, 6
5. J. Young, 6

Source: Cohn, Ellen G. and David P. Farrington, "Changes in the Most-Cited Scholars in Twenty Criminology and Criminal Justice Journals Between 1990 and 1995," *Journal of Criminal Justice*, 27: 345-359, (July/August 1999).

★1632★
Most cited authors in the journal *Violence and Victims*, 1990 to 1995

Ranking basis/background: Total number of citations. **Number listed:** 5.
1. M.A. Straus, with 56 citations
2. R.J. Gelles, 21
3. K.D. O'Leary, 20
4. M.P. Koss, 16
5. L.E. Walker, 15

Source: Cohn, Ellen G. and David P. Farrington, "Changes in the Most-Cited Scholars in Twenty Criminology and Criminal Justice Journals Between 1990 and 1995," *Journal of Criminal Justice*, 27: 345-359, (July/August 1999).

★1633★
Most cited authors in three criminal justice journals

Ranking basis/background: Most cited authors in *Justice Quarterly*, *Journal of Criminal Justice*, and *Criminal Justice and Behavior* combined, by number of citations. **Remarks:** Articles reviewed for the study include comments, rejoinders, research notes, and unpublished reports and conference papers (if cited), but exclude editorials, letters, obituaries, book reviews, and book review articles. All cited authors were counted, not just first authors. **Number listed:** 30.
1. Francis T. Cullen, with 120 citations
2. John L. Hagan, 99
3. Travis Hirschi, 98
4. L.W. Sherman, 93
5. James Q. Wilson, 92
6. Michael R. Gottfredson, 87
7. J. Petersilia, 85
8. Lawrence E. Cohen, 79
9. Marvin E. Wolfgang, 71
10. Alfred Blumstein, 68

Source: Cohn, Ellen G. and David P. Farrington, "Changes in the Most-Cited Scholars in Major American Criminology and Criminal Justice Journals 1986-1990 and 1991-1995," *Journal of Criminal Justice*, 26: 99-116, (March/April 1998).

★1634★
Most cited authors in three criminology journals

Ranking basis/background: Most cited authors in *Criminology*, *Journal of Quantitative Criminology*, and *Journal of Research in Criminal Delinquency* combined, by number of citations. **Remarks:** Articles reviewed for the study include comments, rejoinders, research notes, and unpublished reports and conference papers (if cited), but exclude editorials, letters, obituaries, book reviews, and book review articles. All cited authors were counted, not just first authors. **Number listed:** 30.
1. Travis Hirschi, with 150 citations
2. David P. Farrington, 143
3. Michael R. Gottfredson, 142
4. Delbert S. Elliott, 140
5. Robert J. Sampson, 134
6. David Huizinga, 131
7. Alfred Blumstein, 130
8. Lawrence E. Cohen, 118
9. Jacqueline Cohen, 116
10. Marvin E. Wolfgang, 108

Source: Cohn, Ellen G. and David P. Farrington, "Changes in the Most-Cited Scholars in Major American Criminology and Criminal Justice Journals 1986-1990 and 1991-1995," *Journal of Criminal Justice*, 26: 99-116, (March/April 1998).

★1635★
Most cited scholars in academic literature dealing with corrections

Ranking basis/background: Incidence of citations, which is the number of times scholars and/or works were cited in 209 articles and/or research notes. **Number listed:** 50.
1. Francis T. Cullen, with 182 incidence of citations
2. J. Petersilia, 126
3. Timothy J. Flanagan, 105
4. Bruce G. Link, 98
5. Nancy Travis Wolfe, 93
6. Hans Toch, 91
7. John J. Dilulio, Jr., 88
8. John T. Whitehead, 85
9. Todd R. Clear, 78
10. Jacqueline Cohen, 77

Source: Wright, Richard A. and J. Mitchell Miller, "The Most-Cited Scholars and Works in Corrections," *The Prison Journal*, 79: 5-22, (March 1, 1999).

★1636★
Most-cited scholars in *Australian and New Zealand Journal of Criminology*

Ranking basis/background: Total citations between 1991 and 1995. **Number listed:** 49.
1. John Braithwaite, with 58 citations
2. John Walker, 26
3. Paul R. Wilson, 25
4. Pat O'Malley, 24
5. Peter Grabosky, 23
6. David Biles, 22
6. Jock Young, 22
8. Stanley Cohen, 21

9. Chris Cunneen, 19
9. Brent Fisse, 19

Source: Cohn, Ellen G. and David P. Farrington, "Changes in the Most-Cited Scholars in Major International Journals between 1986-90 and 1991-95," *British Journal of Criminology*, 38: 156-170, (Winter 1998).

★1637★
Most-cited scholars in *British Journal of Criminology*

Ranking basis/background: Total citations between 1991 and 1995. **Number listed:** 49.
1. Patricia M. Mayhew, with 45 citations
2. J. Michael Hough, 41
3. Ken Pease, 40
3. Jock Young, 40
5. Ronald V.G. Clarke, 35
5. David P. Farrington, 35
7. Alfred Blumstein, 26
7. Anthony E. Bottoms, 26
7. Travis Hirschi, 26
10. John Braithwaite, 25

Source: Cohn, Ellen G. and David P. Farrington, "Changes in the Most-Cited Scholars in Major International Journals between 1986-90 and 1991-95," *British Journal of Criminology*, 38: 156-170, (Winter 1998).

★1638★
Most-cited scholars in *Canadian Journal of Criminology*

Ranking basis/background: Total citations between 1991 and 1995. **Number listed:** 49.
1. M.A. Straus, with 33 citations
2. Anthony N. Doob, 29
2. Peter G. Jaffe, 29
4. Alan W. Leschied, 23
4. Alan E. Markwart, 23
6. Raymond R. Carrado, 21
7. Nicholas Bala, 20
8. Travis Hirschi, 19
9. Wesley G. Skogan, 16
10. Don A. Andrews, 15

Source: Cohn, Ellen G. and David P. Farrington, "Changes in the Most-Cited Scholars in Major International Journals between 1986-90 and 1991-95," *British Journal of Criminology*, 38: 156-170, (Winter 1998).

★1639★
Most-cited scholars in *Criminology*

Ranking basis/background: Total citations between 1991 and 1995. **Number listed:** 49.
1. Travis Hirschi, with 153 citations
2. Michael R. Gottfredson, 10
3. David P. Farrington, 98
4. Delbert S. Elliott, 83
5. Alfred Blumstein, 77
6. Jacqueline Cohen, 66
7. Robert J. Sampson, 65
8. C.R. Tittle, 63
9. David Huizinga, 56
9. Raymond Paternoster, 56

Source: Cohn, Ellen G. and David P. Farrington, "Changes in the Most-Cited Scholars in Major International Journals between 1986-90 and 1991-95," *British Journal of Criminology*, 38: 156-170, (Winter 1998).

★1640★
Most cited scholars in critical criminology

Ranking basis/background: Total number of citations analyzed from three journals and 18 books in the area of criminology. **Number listed:** 50.
1. Jock Young, with 724 citations
2. Richard Quinney, 371
3. Brian D. MacLean, 209
4. John Lea, 206
5. Michael Foucault, 179
6. Ian Taylor, 173
7. William J. Chambliss, 158
7. Trevor Jones, 158
9. Stanley Cohen, 139
10. Roger Matthews, 135

Source: Wright, Richard A. and David O. Friedrichs, "The Most-Cited Scholars and Works in Critical Criminology," *Journal of Criminal Justice Education: JCJE*, 9: 211-231, (Fall 1999).

★1641★
Most-cited scholars in critical criminology publications

Ranking basis/background: Number of citations in 412 criminology publications examined between 1991 and 1995. Scholars had to be cited at least 30 times in a minimum of five publications. **Number listed:** 50.
1. Jock Young, with 724 citations
2. Richard Quinney, 371
3. Brian D. MacLean, 209
4. John Lea, 206
5. Michael Foucault, 179
6. Ian Taylor, 173
7. William J. Chambliss, 159
8. Trevor Jones, 158
9. Stanley Cohen, 139
10. Roger Matthews, 135

Source: Wright, Richard A. and David O. Friedrichs, "The Most-Cited Scholars and Works in Critical Criminology," *Journal of Criminal Justice Education*, 9: 211-231, (Fall 1998).

★1642★
Most-cited scholars in women and crime publications

Ranking basis/background: Incidence and prevalence of citations in 174 separate women and crime publications from 1990 to 1996. **Number listed:** 50.
1. Meda Chesney-Lind, with 261 incidence of citations/42 prevalence of citations
2. Carol Smart, 142/34
3. Kathleen Daly, 137/37
4. Lynn E. Zimmer, 125/18
5. Rebecca Emerson Dobash, 111/20
5. Russell P. Dobash, 111/20
7. Nicole Hahn Rafter, 110/29
8. Susan Ehrlich Martin, 109/28
9. Allison Morris, 102/18
10. Estelle B. Freedman, 96/14

Source: Wright, Richard A. and Cindy Sheridan, "The Most-Cited Scholars and Works in Women and Crime Publications," *Women & Criminal Justice*, 8: 41-60, (1997).

★1643★
Most cited works in academic literature dealing with corrections

Ranking basis/background: Incidence of citations, which is the number of times works were cited in 209 articles and/or research notes. **Number listed:** 25.

1. Hammett, Harrold, Gross, & Epstein, (1994) *1992 Update: HIV/AIDS in Correctional Facilities*, with 55 incidence of citations
2. Dilulio, (1987) *Governing Prisons: A Comparative Study of Correctional Management*, 48
3. Maguire, Pastore, & Flanagan (1995) *Sourcebook of Criminal Justice Statistics-1994*, 39
4. Whitehead & Lindquist (1989) "Determinants of Correctional Officers Professional Orientation," 35
5. Cullen, Link, Wolfe, & Frank (1985), "The Social Dimensions of Correctional Officer Stress," 33

Source: Wright, Richard A. and J. Mitchell Miller, "The Most-Cited Scholars and Works in Corrections," *The Prison Journal*, 79: 5-22, (March 1, 1999).

★1644★
Most cited works in critical criminology

Ranking basis/background: Total number of citations and number of publications citing the work, analyzed from three journals and 18 books in the area of criminology. **Number listed:** 25.
1. Michael Foucault (1977), *Discipline and Punish: Birth of the Prison*, with 101 citations; and 31 publications citing the work
2. Trevor Jones, Brian D. MacLean, and Jock Young (1986), *The Islington Crime Survey: Crime, Victimization, and Policing in Inner-City London*, 97; 33
3. John Lea and Jock Young (1984), *What Is to Be Done about Law and Order*, 94; 35
4. Richard Quinney (1980), *Class, State, and Crime*, 79; 28
5. Ian Taylor, Paul Walton, and Jock Young (1973), *The New Criminology: For a Social Theory of Deviance*, 78; 46

Source: Wright, Richard A. and David O. Friedrichs, "The Most-Cited Scholars and Works in Critical Criminology," *Journal of Criminal Justice Education: JCJE*, 9: 211-231, (Fall 1999).

★1645★
Most-cited works in critical criminology publications

Ranking basis/background: Number of citations in 412 criminology publications examined between 1991 and 1995. Works had to be cited at least 30 times in a minimum of five publications. **Number listed:** 25.
1. *Punish: Birth of the Prison* (1977), by Michael Foucault, with 101 citations/in 31 publications
2. *The Islington Crime Survey: Crime Victimization, and Policing in Inner-City London* (1986), Trevor Jones, Brian D. MacLean, and Jock Young, 97/33
3. *What Is to Be Done About Law and Order?* (1984), John Lea and Jock Young, 94/35
4. *Class, State, and Crime* (1980), Richard Quinney, 79/28
5. *The New Criminology: For a Social Theory of Deviance* (1973), Ian Taylor, Paul Walton, and Jock Young, 78/46
6. *Losing the Fight against Crime* (1986), Richard Kinsey, John Lea, and Jock Young, 71/27

CRITICAL JUSTICE

7. *Richer and the Poor Get Prison: Ideology, Crime, and Criminal Justice* (1995), Jeffrey Reiman, 67/21
8. *Order, Law, and Crime: An Introduction to Criminology* (1985), Raymond J. Michalowski, 67/15
9. *Capitalism, Patriarchy, and Crime: Toward a Socialist Feminist Criminology* (1986), James W. Messerchmidt, 59/21
10. *Critique of Legal Order: Crime Control in Capitalist Society* (1974), Richard Quinney, 57/13

Source: Wright, Richard A. and David O. Friedrichs, "The Most-Cited Scholars and Works in Critical Criminology," *Journal of Criminal Justice Education*, 9: 211-231, (Fall 1998).

★1646★
Most-cited works in women and crime publications

Ranking basis/background: Incidence and prevalence of citations in 174 separate women and crime publications from 1990 to 1996. **Number listed:** 29.

1. *Women Guarding Men* (1986), by Lynn E. Zimmer, with 94 incidence of citations/15 prevalence of citations
2. *Partial Justice: Women, Prisons, and Social Control* (1990), Nicole Hahn Rafter, 67/14
3. *Women, Crime and Criminal Justice* (1987), Allison Morris, 67/11
4. *Women, Crime and Criminology: A Feminist Critque* (1976), Carol Smart, 59/21
5. *Their Sisters' Keepers: Women's Prison Reform in America, 1830-1930* (1981), Estelle B. Freedman, 55/10
6. "Feminism and Criminology" (1988), Kathleen Daly and Meda Chesney-Lind, 54/25
7. *Breaking and Entering: Policewomen on Patrol* (1980), Susan Ehrlich Martin, 54/16
8. *Women in the Criminal Justice System* (1994), Clarice Feinman, 51/19
9. *In a Different Voice: Psychological Theory and Women's Development* (1982), Carol Gilligan, 45/18
10. *When Battered Women Kill* (1987), Angela Browne, 45/16

Source: Wright, Richard A. and Cindy Sheridan, "The Most-Cited Scholars and Works in Women and Crime Publications," *Women & Criminal Justice*, 8: 41-60, (1997).

★1647★
Top recruiters for criminal justice jobs for 2000-01 bachelor's degree recipients

Ranking basis/background: Projected number of college hires from on-campus recruitment for 2000-01. **Remarks:** Numbers reflect total expected hires, not just African American projected hires. **Number listed:** 5.

1. Eckerd Youth Alternatives, Inc., with 50 projected hires
2. U.S. Air Force (Active Duty Hires), 40
3. Wells Fargo Financial, 10
4. Caddo Parish School Board, 5
5. U.S. Air Force (Civilian Hires), 4

Source: "The Top 100 Employers and the Majors in Demand for the Class of 2001," *The Black Collegian*, 31: 19-35, (February 2001).

★1648★
Universities with the most-cited scholars in *Criminal Justice and Behavior*

Ranking basis/background: Number of faculty at each university and mean number of citations between 1991 and 1995. **Number listed:** 20.

1. University of Cincinnati (with 11 criminal justice faculty), 2.36 citation average
2. University of Maryland (12), 2.25
3. State University of New York, Albany (13), 2.23
4. Pennsylvania State University (13), 1.00
5. Temple University (15), .80
6. University of Nebraska, Omaha (13), .69
7. Michigan State University (19), .68
8. Rutgers University, Newark (13), .62
9. University of Delaware (15), .53
10. Sam Houston State University (28), .50

Source: Cohn, Ellen G. and David P. Farrington, "Assessing the Quality of American Doctoral Program Faculty in Criminology and Criminal Justice, 1991-1995," *Journal of Criminal Justice Education: JCJE*, 9: 187-210, (Fall 1998).

★1649★
Universities with the most-cited scholars in *Criminology*

Ranking basis/background: Number of faculty at each university and mean number of citations between 1991 and 1995. **Number listed:** 20.

1. University of Maryland (with 12 criminal justice faculty), 12.58 citation average
2. Rutgers University, Newark (13), 6.69
3. State University of New York, Albany (13), 5.46
4. University of Cincinnati (11), 4.18
5. University of California, Irvine (9), 3.56
6. Northeastern University (12), 4.08
7. University of Missouri, St. Louis (8), 3.00
8. Pennsylvania State University (13), 3.46
9. Florida State University (17), 3.88
10. Temple University (15), 2.60

Source: Cohn, Ellen G. and David P. Farrington, "Assessing the Quality of American Doctoral Program Faculty in Criminology and Criminal Justice, 1991-1995," *Journal of Criminal Justice Education: JCJE*, 9: 187-210, (Fall 1998).

★1650★
Universities with the most-cited scholars in *Journal of Quantitative Criminology*

Ranking basis/background: Number of faculty at each university and mean number of citations between 1991 and 1995. **Number listed:** 20.

1. University of Maryland (with 12 criminal justice faculty), 7.75 citation average
2. State University of New York, Albany (13), 3.46
3. University of Missouri, St. Louis (8), 2.25
4. Pennsylvania State University (13), 2.23
5. University of California, Irvine (9), 2.11
6. Northeastern University (12), 2.00
7. University of Cincinnati (11), 1.73
8. Temple University (15), 1.47
9. University of Nebraska, Omaha (13), 1.38
10. Rutgers University, Newark (13), 1.23

Source: Cohn, Ellen G. and David P. Farrington, "Assessing the Quality of American Doctoral Program Faculty in Criminology and Criminal Justice, 1991-1995," *Journal of Criminal Justice Education: JCJE*, 9: 187-210, (Fall 1998).

★1651★
Universities with the most-cited scholars in *Journal of Research in Crime and Delinquency*

Ranking basis/background: Number of faculty at each university and mean number of citations between 1991 and 1995. **Number listed:** 20.

1. University of Maryland (with 12 criminal justice faculty), 9.92 citation average
2. Rutgers University, Newark (13), 5.62
3. University of Cincinnati (11), 3.18
4. State University of New York, Albany (13), 3.00
5. University of California, Irvine (9), 2.89
6. University of Missouri, St. Louis (8), 2.88
7. Florida State University (17), 2.35
8. Northeastern University (12), 2.25
9. Temple University (15), 2.07
10. Pennsylvania State University (13), 1.62

Source: Cohn, Ellen G. and David P. Farrington, "Assessing the Quality of American Doctoral Program Faculty in Criminology and Criminal Justice, 1991-1995," *Journal of Criminal Justice Education: JCJE*, 9: 187-210, (Fall 1998).

★1652★
Universities with the most-cited scholars in *Justice Quarterly*

Ranking basis/background: Number of faculty at each university and mean number of citations between 1991 and 1995. **Number listed:** 20.

1. University of Maryland (with 12 criminal justice faculty), 11.17 citation average
2. University of Cincinnati (11), 6.91
3. Rutgers University, Newark (13), 6.00
4. State University of New York, Albany (13), 4.85
5. University of California, Irvine (9), 4.56
6. Temple University (15), 3.80
7. Pennsylvania State University (13), 3.77
8. University of Nebraska, Omaha (13), 3.46
9. Arizona State University (16), 3.06
10. University of Missouri, St. Louis (8), 2.63

Source: Cohn, Ellen G. and David P. Farrington, "Assessing the Quality of American Doctoral Program Faculty in Criminology and Criminal Justice, 1991-1995," *Journal of Criminal Justice Education: JCJE*, 9: 187-210, (Fall 1998).

Related Information

★1653★
Cohn, Ellen G. and David P. Farrington, "Assessing the Quality of American Doctoral Program Faculty in Criminology and Criminal Justice, 1991-1995," *Journal of Criminal Justice Education: JCJE*, 9: 187-210, (Fall 1998).

Remarks: A study of the quality of American doctoral program faculty in the field of criminology and criminal justice. Article assesses 299 faculty in 20 American doctoral programs by counting the number of citations of their work is six major American criminology and criminal justice journals published between 1991 and 1995.

CRYSTALLOGRAPHY

★1654★
Crystallography journals by citation impact, 1981-98

Ranking basis/background: Impact factor calculated by taking the number of current citations to source items published and dividing it by the number of articles published in the journal during that time period. **Number listed:** 10.
1. *Acta Crystallography A*, with a 19.88 impact factor
2. *Journal of Applied Crystallography*, 15.57
3. *Journal of Molecular Graphics/Models*, 12.12
4. *Acta Crystallography B*, 11.32
5. *Journal Inclusion Phenomena and Molecular Recognition*, 9.33
6. *Molecular Crystallography and Liquid Crystals*, 8.53
7. *Journal of Crystallography and Molecular Structures*, 8.52
8. *Journal of Crystal Growth*, 8.14
9. *Liquid Crystals*, 7.55
10. *Crystallography Lattice Defects*, 6.68

Source: "Journals Ranked by Impact: Crystallography," *What's Hot in Research (http://www.isinet.com/isi/hot/research) Institute for Scientific Information*, June 19, 2000.

★1655★
Crystallography journals by citation impact, 1994-98

Ranking basis/background: Impact factor calculated by taking the number of current citations to source items published and dividing it by the number of articles published in the journal during that time period. **Number listed:** 10.
1. *Acta Crystallography A*, with a 5.06 impact factor
2. *Acta Crystallography D*, 4.84
3. *Journal of Molecular Graphics/Models*, 4.28
4. *Acta Crystallography B*, 3.41
5. *Journal of Applied Crystallography*, 3.00
6. *Liquid Crystals*, 2.87
7. *Journal of Crystal Growth*, 2.47
8. *Polyhedron*, 2.41
9. *Journal Inclusion Phenomena and Molecular Recognition*, 2.29
10. *Journal of Crystallographic and Spectroscopal Research*, 1.70

Source: "Journals Ranked by Impact: Crystallography," *What's Hot in Research (http://www.isinet.com/isi/hot/research) Institute for Scientific Information*, June 19, 2000.

★1656★
Crystallography journals by citation impact, 1998

Ranking basis/background: Impact factor calculated by taking the number of current citations to source items published and dividing it by the number of articles published in the journal during that time period. **Number listed:** 10.
1. *Journal of Molecular Graphics/Models*, with a 4.94 impact factor
2. *Acta Crystallography D*, 2.24
3. *Acta Crystallography A*, 2.15
4. *Acta Crystallography B*, 1.61
5. *Journal of Applied Crystallography*, 1.57
6. *Liquid Crystals*, 1.44
7. *Polyhedron*, 1.36
8. *Journal of Crystal Growth*, 1.31
9. *Crystal Research and Technology*, 0.80
10. *Journal Inclusion Phenomena and Molecular Recognition*, 0.69

Source: "Journals Ranked by Impact: Crystallography," *What's Hot in Research (http://www.isinet.com/isi/hot/research) Institute for Scientific Information*, June 19, 2000.

DATA COMMUNICATIONS–NORTH AMERICA
See also: **Computer Science**

★1657★
U.S. universities with the greatest impact in communication, 1995-99

Ranking basis/background: Average citations per paper from the top 100 federally funded U.S. universities that had at least 50 published papers in ISI indexed communication journals. Also includes total number of papers published during the five year period. **Number listed:** 5.
1. University of Michigan, with 63 papers; 2.27 citations per paper
2. University of Wisconsin, Madison, 141; 1.87
3. Northwestern University, 58; 1.83
4. Purdue University, 57; 1.74
5. University of Georgia, 106; 1.51

Source: "Communication: High Impact U.S. Universities, 1995-99," *What's Hot in Research (http://www.isinet.com/isi/hot/research) Institute for Scientific Information*, January 15, 2001.

DEFAULT RATE ON STUDENT LOANS
See: **Loan Repayment**

DEGREES (ACADEMIC)
See also: **Doctoral Degrees Degrees (Academic)–Minority Groups**

★1658★
Associate degree figures projected for men for the years 2002-2008

Ranking basis/background: Based on data analysis conducted by the U.S. Department of Education. **Remarks:** Article contains projections on college enrollment, degree achievement, and high-school graduates. **Number listed:** 9.
  2002, with 211,000 degrees
  2003, 212,000
  2004, 213,000
  2005, 213,000
  2006, 214,000
  2007, 215,000
  2008, 216,000

Source: *Projections of Education Statistics to 2008*, NCES 98-016, U.S. Department of Education, National Center for Education Statistics (June 1998).

★1659★
Associate degree figures projected for the years 2002-2007, by gender

Ranking basis/background: Based on data analysis conducted by the U.S. Department of Education. **Remarks:** Original source: U.S. Department of Education, National Center for Education Statistics, *Earned Degrees Conferred; Projection of Education Statistics to 2007*; Higher Education General Information Survey, Degrees and Other Formal Awards Conferred surveys; and Integrated Postsecondary Education Data System, Completions surveys. **Number listed:** 7.
  2001-02, with 545,000 total; 211,000 to men; and 333,000 to women
  2002-03, 556,000; 213,000; 343,000
  2003-04, 566,000; 214,000; 352,000
  2004-05, 572,000; 215,000; 357,000
  2005-06, 579,000; 216,000; 363,000
  2006-07, 587,000; 217,000; 369,000

Source: Snyder, Thomas D., *Digest of Education Statistics, 1997*, National Center for Education Statistics, 1997.

★1660★
Associate degree figures projected for women for the years 2002-2008

Ranking basis/background: Based on data analysis conducted by the U.S. Department of Education. **Remarks:** Article contains projections on college enrollment, degree achievement, and high-school graduates. **Number listed:** 9.
  2002, with 339,000 degrees
  2003, 343,000
  2004, 346,000
  2005, 347,000
  2006, 351,000
  2007, 357,000
  2008, 363,000

Source: *Projections of Education Statistics to 2008*, NCES 98-016, U.S. Department of Education, National Center for Education Statistics (June 1998).

★1661★
Bachelor's degree figures projected for men for the years 2002-2008

Ranking basis/background: Based on data analysis conducted by the U.S. Department of Education. **Remarks:** Article contains projections on college enrollment, degree achievement, and high-school graduates. **Number listed:** 9.
  2002, with 510,000 degrees
  2003, 515,000
  2004, 519,000
  2005, 520,000
  2006, 524,000
  2007, 527,000
  2008, 530,000

Source: *Projections of Education Statistics to 2008*, NCES 98-016, U.S. Department of Education, National Center for Education Statistics (June 1998).

DEGREES (ACADEMIC)—MINORITY GROUPS

★1662★
Bachelor's degree figures projected for the years 2002-2007, by gender

Ranking basis/background: Based on data analysis conducted by the U.S. Department of Education. **Remarks:** Original source: U.S. Department of Education, National Center for Education Statistics, *Earned Degrees Conferred; Projection of Education Statistics to 2007*; Higher Education General Information Survey, Degrees and Other Formal Awards Conferred surveys; and Integrated Postsecondary Education Data System, Completions surveys. **Number listed:** 7.

    2001-02, with 1,169,000 total; 508,000 to men; and 660,000 to women
    2002-03, 1,191,000; 516,000; 675,000
    2003-04, 1,216,000; 522,000; 694,000
    2004-05, 1,237,000; 524,000; 713,000
    2005-06, 1,253,000; 529,000; 724,000
    2006-07, 1,268,000; 532,000; 735,000

Source: Snyder, Thomas D., *Digest of Education Statistics, 1997*, National Center for Education Statistics, 1997.

★1663★
Bachelor's degree figures projected for women for the years 2002-2008

Ranking basis/background: Based on data analysis conducted by the U.S. Department of Education. **Remarks:** Article contains projections on college enrollment, degree achievement, and high-school graduates. **Number listed:** 9.

    2002, with 685,000 degrees
    2003, 699,000
    2004, 708,000
    2005, 716,000
    2006, 719,000
    2007, 729,000
    2008, 739,000

Source: *Projections of Education Statistics to 2008*, NCES 98-016, U.S. Department of Education, National Center for Education Statistics (June 1998).

★1664★
Bachelor's degree recipients by socioeconomic status

Ranking basis/background: Percentage of 1989 beginning postsecondary students receiving a bachelor's degree or higher by 1994. **Remarks:** Original source: U.S. Department of Education. **Number listed:** 3.

1. Highest quartile, with 41.1%
2. Middle quartiles, 18.7%
3. Lowest quartile, 6.1%

Source: Burd, Stephen, "Lack of Need-Based Financial Aid Still Impedes Access to College for Low-Income Students, Report Finds," *The Chronicle of Higher Education*, 47: A26, (March 2, 2001).

★1665★
Doctoral degree figures projected for the years 2002-2007, by gender

Ranking basis/background: Based on data analysis conducted by the U.S. Department of Education. **Remarks:** Original source: U.S. Department of Education, National Center for Education Statistics, *Earned Degrees Conferred; Projection of Education Statistics to 2007*; Higher Education General Information Survey, Degrees and Other Formal Awards Conferred surveys; and Integrated Postsecondary Education Data System, Completions surveys. **Number listed:** 7.

    2001-02, with 46,000 total; 26,300 to men; and 19,700 to women
    2002-03, 46,400; 26,200; 20,200
    2003-04, 46,800; 26,100; 20,700
    2004-05, 47,200; 26,000; 21,200
    2005-06, 47,500; 25,900; 21,600
    2006-07, 47,900; 25,800; 22,100

Source: Snyder, Thomas D., *Digest of Education Statistics, 1997*, National Center for Education Statistics, 1997.

★1666★
Master's degree figures projected for men for the years 2002-2008

Ranking basis/background: Based on data analysis conducted by the U.S. Department of Education. **Remarks:** Article contains projections on college enrollment, degree achievement, and high-school graduates. **Number listed:** 9.

    2002, with 191,000 degrees
    2003, 193,000
    2004, 195,000
    2005, 197,000
    2006, 199,000
    2007, 201,000
    2008, 203,000

Source: *Projections of Education Statistics to 2008*, NCES 98-016, U.S. Department of Education, National Center for Education Statistics (June 1998).

★1667★
Master's degree figures projected for the years 2002-2007, by gender

Ranking basis/background: Based on data analysis conducted by the U.S. Department of Education. **Remarks:** Original source: U.S. Department of Education, National Center for Education Statistics, *Earned Degrees Conferred; Projection of Education Statistics to 2007*; Higher Education General Information Survey, Degrees and Other Formal Awards Conferred surveys; and Integrated Postsecondary Education Data System, Completions surveys. **Number listed:** 7.

    2002-03, with 434,000 total; 206,000 to men; and 228,000 to women
    2003-04, 438,000; 208,000; 230,000
    2004-05, 442,000; 210,000; 232,000
    2005-06, 446,000; 212,000; 234,000
    2006-07, 450,000; 214,000; 236,000

Source: Snyder, Thomas D., *Digest of Education Statistics, 1997*, National Center for Education Statistics, 1997.

★1668★
Master's degree figures projected for women for the years 2002-2008

Ranking basis/background: Based on data analysis conducted by the U.S. Department of Education. **Remarks:** Article contains projections on college enrollment, degree achievement, and high-school graduates. **Number listed:** 9.

    2002, with 231,000 degrees
    2003, 233,000
    2004, 235,000
    2005, 237,000
    2006, 239,000
    2007, 241,000
    2008, 243,000

Source: *Projections of Education Statistics to 2008*, NCES 98-016, U.S. Department of Education, National Center for Education Statistics (June 1998).

DEGREES (ACADEMIC)–MINORITY GROUPS

★1669★
Bachelor's degree recipients by race/ethnicity

Ranking basis/background: Percentage of 1989 beginning postsecondary students receiving a bachelor's degree or higher by 1994. **Remarks:** Original source: U.S. Department of Education. **Number listed:** 3.

1. White, non-Hispanic, with 27.3%
2. Hispanic American, 17.8%
3. Black, non-Hispanic, 16.9%

Source: Burd, Stephen, "Lack of Need-Based Financial Aid Still Impedes Access to College for Low-Income Students, Report Finds," *The Chronicle of Higher Education*, 47: A26, (March 2, 2001).

★1670★
Historically black colleges and universities awarding the most master's degrees to African Americans

Ranking basis/background: Total master's degrees conferred to African American students at historically black colleges and universities, in all disciplines combined, during the 1997-98 academic year. **Remarks:** Original source: *Black Issues* analysis of U.S. Department of Education reports of data submitted by institutions. **Number listed:** 25.

1. Howard University (DC)
2. Clark Atlanta University (GA)
3. Bowie State University (MD)
4. Prairie View A&M University (TX)
5. Jackson State University (MS)
6. Southern University and A&M College (LA)
7. Florida A&M State University (FL)
8. South Carolina State University (SC)
9. North Carolina A&T State University (NC)
10. Alabama A&M University (AL)
11. Tennessee State University (TN)
11. Norfolk State University (VA)
13. North Carolina Central University (NC)
14. Fort Valley State University (GA)
15. Alabama State University (AL)
16. Grambling State University (LA)
17. Lincoln University (PA)
17. Virginia State University (VA)
19. Alcorn State University (MS)
20. Choppin State College (MD)

Source: "Top 100 Degree Producers," *Black Issues in Higher Education*, 17: 48-89, (July 7, 2000).

★1671★
Master's degrees conferred to African Americans by historically black colleges and universities, 1997-98

Ranking basis/background: Total number of degrees awarded to African Americans at historically black institutions compared to all other institutions, plus the average annual percentage of change. **Remarks:** Original source: *Black Issues* analysis of U.S. Department of Education reports of data submitted by institutions. **Number listed:** 3.

    Historically black institutions, with 4,364 degrees awarded; and a 9.7% average annual change
    All other institutions, 24,140; 8.4%
    Total, 28,504; 8.6%

Source: Borden, Victor M.H., "The Top 100: Interpreting the Data," *Black Issues in Higher Education*, 17: 46-47, (July 6, 2000).

★1672★
Top bachelor's degree disciplines for African Americans, 1997-98

Ranking basis/background: From a list of each ethnic group's Top 10 disciplines in number of bachelor's degrees conferred in 1997-98. **Number listed:** 15.
1. Business management and administrative services
2. Social sciences and history
3. Education
4. Health professional and related sciences
5. Psychology
6. Biological sciences/life sciences
7. Communications
8. Liberal arts, general studies, humanities
9. Protective services
10. Public administration and services
11. English language, literature, and letters
12. Visual and performing arts
13. Engineering
14. Computer and information science
15. Multi-cultural/interdisciplinary studies

Source: Collison, Michele N-K, "Degree-Producer Analysis Offers Good and Bad News," *Black Issues in Higher Education*, 17: 45-47, (June 22, 2000).

★1673★
Top bachelor's degree disciplines for Asian Americans, 1997-98

Ranking basis/background: From a list of each ethnic group's Top 10 disciplines in number of bachelor's degrees conferred in 1997-98. **Number listed:** 15.
1. Business management and administrative services
2. Biological sciences/life sciences
3. Social sciences and history
4. Engineering
5. Health professional and related sciences
6. Psychology
7. Computer and information science
8. Visual and performing arts
9. English language, literature, and letters
10. Education
11. Multi-cultural/interdisciplinary studies
12. Communications
13. Liberal arts, general studies, humanities
14. Public administration and services
15. Protective services

Source: Collison, Michele N-K, "Degree-Producer Analysis Offers Good and Bad News," *Black Issues in Higher Education*, 17: 45-47, (June 22, 2000).

★1674★
Top bachelor's degree disciplines for Hispanic Americans, 1997-98

Ranking basis/background: From a list of each ethnic group's Top 10 disciplines in number of bachelor's degrees conferred in 1997-98. **Number listed:** 15.
1. Business management and administrative services
2. Social sciences and history
3. Education
4. Psychology
5. Health professional and related sciences
6. Biological sciences/life sciences
7. Liberal arts, general studies, humanities
8. Engineering
9. Communications
10. Multi-cultural/interdisciplinary studies
11. Protective services
12. English language, literature, and letters
13. Visual and performing arts
14. Public administration and services
15. Computer and information science

Source: Collison, Michele N-K, "Degree-Producer Analysis Offers Good and Bad News," *Black Issues in Higher Education*, 17: 45-47, (June 22, 2000).

★1675★
Top bachelor's degree disciplines for Native Americans, 1997-98

Ranking basis/background: From a list of each ethnic group's Top 10 disciplines in number of bachelor's degrees conferred in 1997-98. **Number listed:** 15.
1. Business management and administrative services
2. Education
3. Social sciences and history
4. Health professional and related sciences
5. Psychology
6. Biological sciences/life sciences
7. Liberal arts, general studies, humanities
8. Visual and performing arts
9. English language, literature, and letters
10. Communications
11. Engineering
12. Public administration and services
13. Protective services
14. Multi-cultural/interdisciplinary studies
15. Computer and information science

Source: Collison, Michele N-K, "Degree-Producer Analysis Offers Good and Bad News," *Black Issues in Higher Education*, 17: 45-47, (June 22, 2000).

★1676★
Top bachelor's degree disciplines for non-minorities, 1997-98

Ranking basis/background: From a list of each ethnic group's Top 10 disciplines in number of bachelor's degrees conferred in 1997-98. **Number listed:** 15.
1. Business management and administrative services
2. Social sciences and history
3. Education
4. Health professional and related sciences
5. Psychology
6. Biological sciences/life sciences
7. Engineering
8. Visual and performing arts
9. English language, literature, and letters
10. Communications
11. Liberal arts, general studies, humanities
12. Computer and information science
13. Multi-cultural/interdisciplinary studies
14. Protective services
15. Public administration and services

Source: Collison, Michele N-K, "Degree-Producer Analysis Offers Good and Bad News," *Black Issues in Higher Education*, 17: 45-47, (June 22, 2000).

★1677★
Top colleges in terms of total associate degrees awarded to minorities, 1997-98

Ranking basis/background: A ranking of total associate degrees in all disciplines combined conferred to minority men and women plus the overall total for 1997-98. **Remarks:** Original source: U.S. Department of Education reports of data submitted by institutions. **Number listed:** 99.
1. Miami-Dade Community College, with 1,653 degrees awarded to minority men; 2,526 awarded to minority women; and 4,179 awarded overall
2. City University of New York, Borough of Manhattan Community College, 419; 1,216; 1,635
3. City University of New York, John Jay College of Criminal Justice, 878; 202; 1,080
4. City University of New York, Laguardia Community College, 268; 754; 1,022
5. City University of New York, New York City Technical College, 390; 520; 910
6. Central Texas College, 504; 340; 844
7. Valencia Community College, 312; 512; 824
8. City University of New York, Bronx Community College, 204; 614; 818
9. Broward Community College, 266; 549; 815
10. Monroe College, 179; 606; 785

Source: "9th Annual Top 100 Degree Producers," *Black Issues in Higher Education*, 17: 50-78, (June 22, 2000).

★1678★
Top colleges in terms of total baccalaureate degrees awarded to minorities, 1997-98

Ranking basis/background: A ranking of total baccalaureate degrees in all disciplines combined conferred to minority men and women plus the overall total for 1997-98. **Remarks:** Original source: U.S. Department of Education reports of data submitted by institutions. **Number listed:** 100.
1. University of California, Los Angeles, with 1,451 degrees awarded to minority men; 1,785 awarded to minority women; and 3,236 awarded overall
2. University of California, Berkeley, 1,448; 1,564; 3,012
3. Florida International University, 1,012; 1,640; 2,652
4. University of Texas, Austin, 1,025; 1,175; 2,200
5. University of Hawaii, Manoa, 846; 1,138; 1,984
6. San Jose State University, 862; 1,084; 1,946
7. University of California, Irvine, 843; 1,087; 1,930
8. University of California, Davis, 827; 1,055; 1,882
9. California State University, Fullerton, 703; 1,106; 1,809
10. San Diego State University, 745; 983; 1,728

Source: "9th Annual Top 100 Degree Producers," *Black Issues in Higher Education*, 17: 50-78, (June 22, 2000).

★1679★
Total baccalaureate biology/life sciences degrees awarded to African Americans from U.S. colleges and universities, 1997-98

Ranking basis/background: A ranking of total baccalaureate biology/life sciences degrees conferred to African Americans in 1997-98. **Remarks:** Original source: U.S. Department of Education reports of data submitted by institutions. **Number listed:** 54.
1. Xavier University (LA), with 165 degrees awarded

2. Howard University, 103
2. Hampton University, 103
4. Jackson State University, 98
5. University of Maryland, College Park, 67
6. Clark Atlanta University, 66
7. Prairie View A&M University, 64
8. Morehouse College, 57
9. Grambling State University, 55
9. Tennessee State University, 55

Source: "9th Annual Top 100 Degree Producers," *Black Issues in Higher Education*, 17: 50-78, (June 22, 2000).

★1680★
Total baccalaureate biology/life sciences degrees awarded to Asian Americans from U.S. colleges and universities, 1997-98

Ranking basis/background: A ranking of total baccalaureate biology/life sciences degrees conferred to Asian Americans in 1997-98. **Remarks:** Original source: U.S. Department of Education reports of data submitted by institutions. **Number listed:** 50.
1. University of California, Los Angeles, with 501 degrees awarded
2. University of California, Berkeley, 427
3. University of California, Irvine, 420
4. University of California, Davis, 402
5. University of California, San Diego, 320
6. University of Texas, Austin, 178
7. Rutgers University, New Brunswick, 173
8. University of California, Riverside, 165
9. University of Washington (WA), 162
10. University of Illinois, Urbana-Champaign, 134

Source: "9th Annual Top 100 Degree Producers," *Black Issues in Higher Education*, 17: 50-78, (June 22, 2000).

★1681★
Total baccalaureate biology/life sciences degrees awarded to Hispanic Americans from U.S. colleges and universities, 1997-98

Ranking basis/background: A ranking of total baccalaureate biology/life sciences degrees conferred to Hispanic Americans in 1997-98. **Remarks:** Original source: U.S. Department of Education reports of data submitted by institutions. **Number listed:** 52.
1. University of Texas, San Antonio, with 89 degrees awarded
2. University of California, San Diego, 73
2. University of Texas, Austin, 73
4. University of Arizona, 70
5. Florida International University, 68
6. University of California, Davis, 63
6. University of New Mexico, 63
8. University of California, Los Angeles, 61
9. University of California, Irvine, 59
10. University of Texas, El Paso, 46

Source: "9th Annual Top 100 Degree Producers," *Black Issues in Higher Education*, 17: 50-78, (June 22, 2000).

★1682★
Total baccalaureate biology/life sciences degrees awarded to Native Americans from U.S. colleges and universities, 1997-98

Ranking basis/background: A ranking of total baccalaureate biology/life sciences degrees conferred to Native Americans in 1997-98. **Remarks:** Original source: U.S. Department of Education reports of data submitted by institutions. **Number listed:** 36.
1. University of North Carolina, Pembroke, with 17 degrees awarded
2. Northeastern State University, 16
3. University of Oklahoma, Norman, 12
4. Oklahoma State University, 11
5. University of New Mexico, 9
6. University of California, Davis, 8
6. Southeastern Oklahoma State University, 8
6. University of Washington (WA), 8
9. University of Arizona, 6
9. Washington State University, 6

Source: "9th Annual Top 100 Degree Producers," *Black Issues in Higher Education*, 17: 50-78, (June 22, 2000).

★1683★
Total baccalaureate business management and administrative services degrees awarded to African Americans from U.S. colleges and universities, 1997-98

Ranking basis/background: A ranking of total baccalaureate business management and administrative services degrees conferred to African Americans in 1997-98. **Remarks:** Original source: U.S. Department of Education reports of data submitted by institutions. **Number listed:** 50.
1. City University of New York, Bernard M. Baruch College, with 238 degrees awarded
2. St. Leo College, 220
3. North Carolina A&T State University, 200
4. Georgia State University, 189
5. Howard University, 183
6. Hampton University, 175
7. Park College, 170
8. Grambling State University, 164
9. Morehouse College, 149
10. Florida A&M University, 147

Source: "9th Annual Top 100 Degree Producers," *Black Issues in Higher Education*, 17: 50-78, (June 22, 2000).

★1684★
Total baccalaureate business management and administrative services degrees awarded to Asian Americans from U.S. colleges and universities, 1997-98

Ranking basis/background: A ranking of total baccalaureate business management and administrative services degrees conferred to Asian Americans in 1997-98. **Remarks:** Original source: U.S. Department of Education reports of data submitted by institutions. **Number listed:** 50.
1. California State University, Fullerton, with 538 degrees awarded
2. San Francisco State University, 466
3. University of Hawaii, Manoa, 463
4. San Jose State University, 405
5. California State Polytechnic University, Pomona, 369
6. City University of New York, Bernard M. Baruch College, 320
7. California State University, Hayward, 294
8. University of Southern California, 287
9. California State University, Los Angeles, 272
10. California State University, Northridge, 217

Source: "9th Annual Top 100 Degree Producers," *Black Issues in Higher Education*, 17: 50-78, (June 22, 2000).

★1685★
Total baccalaureate business management and administrative services degrees awarded to Hispanic Americans from U.S. colleges and universities, 1997-98

Ranking basis/background: A ranking of total baccalaureate business management and administrative services degrees conferred to Hispanic Americans in 1997-98. **Remarks:** Original source: U.S. Department of Education reports of data submitted by institutions. **Number listed:** 50.
1. Florida International University, with 511 degrees awarded
2. University of Texas, El Paso, 242
3. University of Texas, San Antonio, 192
4. University of Texas, Pan American, 191
5. City University of New York, Bernard M. Baruch College, 179
6. San Diego State University, 159
7. California State Polytechnic University, Pomona, 149
8. California State University, Fullerton, 146
9. University of Houston, University Park, 143
10. University of Southern California, 125

Source: "9th Annual Top 100 Degree Producers," *Black Issues in Higher Education*, 17: 50-78, (June 22, 2000).

★1686★
Total baccalaureate business management and administrative services degrees awarded to Native Americans from U.S. colleges and universities, 1997-98

Ranking basis/background: A ranking of total baccalaureate business management and administrative services degrees conferred to Native Americans in 1997-98. **Remarks:** Original source: U.S. Department of Education reports of data submitted by institutions. **Number listed:** 60.
1. Northeastern State University, with 46 degrees awarded
2. University of Oklahoma, Norman, 33
3. Oklahoma State University, 26
4. Southeastern Oklahoma State University, 22
5. East Central University, 17
6. University of New Mexico, 16
7. Arizona State University, 14
7. University of North Carolina, Pembroke, 14
9. Northern Arizona University, 12
9. University of Washington (WA), 12

Source: "9th Annual Top 100 Degree Producers," *Black Issues in Higher Education*, 17: 50-78, (June 22, 2000).

★1687★
Total baccalaureate communications degrees awarded to African Americans from U.S. colleges and universities, 1997-98

Ranking basis/background: A ranking of total baccalaureate communications degrees conferred to African Americans in 1997-98. **Remarks:** Original source: U.S. Department of Education reports of data submitted by institutions. **Number listed:** 53.
1. Howard University, with 176 degrees awarded
2. Clark Atlanta University, 95
3. Hampton University, 81
4. Temple University, 73
5. University of North Carolina, Chapel Hill, 68
6. Norfolk State University, 63
7. Grambling State University, 53
8. Florida A&M State University, 49
9. Morgan State University, 45
10. University of Florida, 43

Source: "9th Annual Top 100 Degree Producers," *Black Issues in Higher Education*, 17: 50-78, (June 22, 2000).

★1688★
Total baccalaureate communications degrees awarded to Asian Americans from U.S. colleges and universities, 1997-98

Ranking basis/background: A ranking of total baccalaureate communications degrees conferred to Asian Americans in 1997-98. **Remarks:** Original source: U.S. Department of Education reports of data submitted by institutions. **Number listed:** 53.
1. University of Hawaii, Manoa, with 105 degrees awarded
2. California State University, Fullerton, 58
3. University of Texas, Austin, 48
4. San Jose State University, 35
5. University of California, Santa Barbara, 34
6. University of Washington (WA), 33
7. University of California, Berkeley, 32
8. University of California, San Diego, 31
9. University of Southern California, 24
10. Boston University, 23

Source: "9th Annual Top 100 Degree Producers," *Black Issues in Higher Education*, 17: 50-78, (June 22, 2000).

★1689★
Total baccalaureate communications degrees awarded to Hispanic Americans from U.S. colleges and universities, 1997-98

Ranking basis/background: A ranking of total baccalaureate communications degrees conferred to Hispanic Americans in 1997-98. **Remarks:** Original source: U.S. Department of Education reports of data submitted by institutions. **Number listed:** 51.
1. University of Texas, Austin, with 108 degrees awarded
2. California State University, Fullerton, 86
3. Florida International University, 75
4. Arizona State University, 53
5. University of Florida, 51
6. University of Texas, El Paso, 48
7. California State University, Northridge, 38
7. Rutgers University, New Brunswick, 38
9. University of Miami, 37
10. University of North Texas, 28

Source: "9th Annual Top 100 Degree Producers," *Black Issues in Higher Education*, 17: 50-78, (June 22, 2000).

★1690★
Total baccalaureate communications degrees awarded to Native Americans from U.S. colleges and universities, 1997-98

Ranking basis/background: A ranking of total baccalaureate communications degrees conferred to Native Americans in 1997-98. **Remarks:** Original source: U.S. Department of Education reports of data submitted by institutions. **Number listed:** 23.
1. University of Oklahoma, Norman, with 8 degrees awarded
2. Arizona State University, 6
2. California State University, Sacramento, 6
4. California State University, Fullerton, 5
4. Northeastern State University, 5
4. Southeastern Oklahoma State University, 5
4. University of Texas, Austin, 5
8. California State University, Chico, 4
8. University of North Carolina, Chapel Hill, 4
8. Oklahoma State University, 4
8. Purdue University, 4

Source: "9th Annual Top 100 Degree Producers," *Black Issues in Higher Education*, 17: 50-78, (June 22, 2000).

★1691★
Total baccalaureate computer and information science degrees awarded to African Americans from U.S. colleges and universities, 1997-98

Ranking basis/background: A ranking of total baccalaureate computer and information science degrees conferred to African Americans in 1997-98. **Remarks:** Original source: U.S. Department of Education reports of data submitted by institutions. **Number listed:** 50.
1. Grambling State University, with 74 degrees awarded
2. Florida A&M University, 72
3. DeVry Institute of Technology, Decatur, 69
4. City University of New York, Bernard M. Baruch College, 49
5. University of Maryland, Baltimore, 44
6. Strayer College, Alexandria, 41
7. North Carolina A&T State University, 40
8. Alabama State University, 39
9. Morgan State University, 35
10. Georgia State University, 34

Source: "9th Annual Top 100 Degree Producers," *Black Issues in Higher Education*, 17: 50-78, (June 22, 2000).

★1692★
Total baccalaureate computer and information science degrees awarded to Asian Americans from U.S. colleges and universities, 1997-98

Ranking basis/background: A ranking of total baccalaureate computer and information science degrees conferred to Asian Americans in 1997-98. **Remarks:** Original source: U.S. Department of Education reports of data submitted by institutions. **Number listed:** 51.
1. University of California, Irvine, with 90 degrees awarded
2. California State University, Los Angeles, 83
3. City University of New York, Bernard M. Baruch College, 76
4. San Jose State University, 69
5. University of Maryland, College Park, 66
6. New York University, 55
7. George Mason University, 54
8. University of Texas, Dallas, 49
9. University of California, Berkeley, 47
10. University of California, Davis, 45

Source: "9th Annual Top 100 Degree Producers," *Black Issues in Higher Education*, 17: 50-78, (June 22, 2000).

★1693★
Total baccalaureate computer and information science degrees awarded to Hispanic Americans from U.S. colleges and universities, 1997-98

Ranking basis/background: A ranking of total baccalaureate computer and information science degrees conferred to Hispanic Americans in 1997-98. **Remarks:** Original source: U.S. Department of Education reports of data submitted by institutions. **Number listed:** 53.
1. Florida International University, with 86 degrees awarded
2. City University of New York, Lehman College, 54
3. City University of New York, Bernard M. Baruch College, 41
4. DeVry Institute of Technology, Pomona, 20
4. DeVry Institute of Technology, Chicago, 20
6. University of Texas, Austin, 16
7. Fordham University, 15
7. Our Lady of the Lake University, San Antonio, 15
9. California State University, Los Angeles, 13
9. Metropolitan State College, Devner, 13
9. University of Texas, Pan American, 13

Source: "9th Annual Top 100 Degree Producers," *Black Issues in Higher Education*, 17: 50-78, (June 22, 2000).

★1694★
Total baccalaureate computer and information science degrees awarded to Native Americans from U.S. colleges and universities, 1997-98

Ranking basis/background: A ranking of total baccalaureate computer and information science degrees conferred to Native Americans in 1997-98. **Remarks:** Original source: U.S. Department of Education reports of data submitted by institutions. **Number listed:** 5.
1. Northern Arizona University, with 5 degrees awarded
2. Southeastern Oklahoma State University, 4
3. Fort Lewis College, 3
3. Hawaii Pacific University, 3
3. University of Texas, Austin, 3

Source: "9th Annual Top 100 Degree Producers," *Black Issues in Higher Education*, 17: 50-78, (June 22, 2000).

DEGREES (ACADEMIC)—MINORITY GROUPS

★1695★
Total baccalaureate degrees awarded to African Americans, by Carnegie classification, 1997-98

Ranking basis/background: A ranking of total baccalaureate degrees conferred to minorities at accredited postsecondary institutions within the 50 states and the District of Columbia for 1997-98.
Number listed: 13.

    Research I, with 15,025 degrees awarded
    Research II, 4,464
    Doctoral I, 6,616
    Doctoral II, 6,085
    Master's I, 37,820
    Master's II, 2,996
    Bachelor's I, 2,729
    Bachelor's II, 14,872
    Associates, 300
    Specialized, 3,496
    Tribal, 19
    Unclassified, 1,102
    Historically black colleges and universities, 25,586

Source: Collison, Michele N-K, "Degree-Producer Analysis Offers Good and Bad News," *Black Issues in Higher Education*, 17: 45-47, (June 22, 2000).

★1696★
Total baccalaureate degrees awarded to African Americans, by type of institution, 1997-98

Ranking basis/background: A ranking of total baccalaureate degrees conferred to minorities at accredited postsecondary institutions within the 50 states and the District of Columbia for 1997-98.
Number listed: 3.

    Public, with 61,986 degrees awarded
    Private, non-profit, 31,953
    Proprietary, 1,585

Source: Collison, Michele N-K, "Degree-Producer Analysis Offers Good and Bad News," *Black Issues in Higher Education*, 17: 45-47, (June 22, 2000).

★1697★
Total baccalaureate degrees awarded to African Americans from historically black colleges, 1997-98

Ranking basis/background: A ranking of total baccalaureate degrees in all disciplines combined conferred to African Americans in 1997-98.
Remarks: Original source: U.S. Department of Education reports of data submitted by institutions.
Number listed: 42.

1. Florida A&M University, with 1,201 degrees awarded
2. Howard University, 1,183
3. Southern University and A&M College, 1,015
4. North Carolina A&T State University, 951
5. Grambling State University, 834
6. Hampton University, 797
7. Norfolk State University, 718
8. Morgan State University, 652
9. North Carolina Central University, 648
10. Jackson State University, 600

Source: "9th Annual Top 100 Degree Producers," *Black Issues in Higher Education*, 17: 50-78, (June 22, 2000).

★1698★
Total baccalaureate degrees awarded to African Americans from traditionally white institutions, 1997-98

Ranking basis/background: A ranking of total baccalaureate degrees in all disciplines combined conferred to African Americans in 1997-98.
Remarks: Original source: U.S. Department of Education reports of data submitted by institutions.
Number listed: 50.

1. Chicago State University, with 747 degrees awarded
2. Temple University, 683
3. Georgia State University, 650
4. College of New Rochelle, 589
5. City University of New York, York College, 558
6. University of Maryland, University College, 531
7. University of Maryland, College Park, 529
8. Florida International University, 522
9. Southern Illinois University, Carbondale, 520
10. City University of New York, City College, 498

Source: "9th Annual Top 100 Degree Producers," *Black Issues in Higher Education*, 17: 50-78, (June 22, 2000).

★1699★
Total baccalaureate degrees awarded to African Americans from U.S. colleges and universities, 1997-98

Ranking basis/background: A ranking of total baccalaureate degrees in all disciplines combined conferred to African Americans in 1997-98.
Remarks: Original source: U.S. Department of Education reports of data submitted by institutions.
Number listed: 50.

1. Florida A&M University, with 1,201 degrees awarded
2. Howard University, 1,183
3. Southern University and A&M College, 1,015
4. North Carolina A&T State University, 951
5. Grambling State University, 834
6. Hampton University, 797
7. Chicago State University, 747
8. Norfolk State University, 718
9. Temple University, 683
10. Morgan State University, 652

Source: "9th Annual Top 100 Degree Producers," *Black Issues in Higher Education*, 17: 50-78, (June 22, 2000).

★1700★
Total baccalaureate degrees awarded to Asian Americans, by Carnegie classification, 1997-98

Ranking basis/background: A ranking of total baccalaureate degrees conferred to minorities at accredited postsecondary institutions within the 50 states and the District of Columbia for 1997-98.
Number listed: 13.

    Research I, with 31,027 degrees awarded
    Research II, 4,195
    Doctoral I, 3,463
    Doctoral II, 4,285
    Master's I, 17,846
    Master's II, 698
    Bachelor's I, 2,520
    Bachelor's II, 2,510
    Associates, 90
    Specialized, 2,192
    Tribal, 0
    Unclassified, 661

Source: Collison, Michele N-K, "Degree-Producer Analysis Offers Good and Bad News," *Black Issues in Higher Education*, 17: 45-47, (June 22, 2000).

★1701★
Total baccalaureate degrees awarded to Asian Americans, by type of institution, 1997-98

Ranking basis/background: A ranking of total baccalaureate degrees conferred to minorities at accredited postsecondary institutions within the 50 states and the District of Columbia for 1997-98.
Number listed: 3.

    Public, with 48,773 degrees awarded
    Private, non-profit, 19,926
    Proprietary, 788

Source: Collison, Michele N-K, "Degree-Producer Analysis Offers Good and Bad News," *Black Issues in Higher Education*, 17: 45-47, (June 22, 2000).

★1702★
Total baccalaureate degrees awarded to Asian Americans from U.S. colleges and universities, 1997-98

Ranking basis/background: A ranking of total baccalaureate degrees in all disciplines combined conferred to Asian Americans in 1997-98.
Remarks: Original source: U.S. Department of Education reports of data submitted by institutions.
Number listed: 50.

1. University of California, Los Angeles, with 2,131
2. University of California, Berkeley, 2,071
3. University of Hawaii, Manoa, 1,948
4. University of California, Irvine, 1,473
5. University of California, Davis, 1,306
6. San Jose State University, 1,296
7. University of Washington (WA), 1,221
8. San Francisco State University, 1,102
9. University of California, San Diego, 1,029
10. California State Polytechnic University, Pomona, 943
10. California State University, Fullerton, 943

Source: "9th Annual Top 100 Degree Producers," *Black Issues in Higher Education*, 17: 50-78, (June 22, 2000).

★1703★
Total baccalaureate degrees awarded to Hispanic Americans, by Carnegie classification, 1997-98

Ranking basis/background: A ranking of total baccalaureate degrees conferred to minorities at accredited postsecondary institutions within the 50 states and the District of Columbia for 1997-98.
Number listed: 12.

    Research I, with 14,331 degrees awarded
    Research II, 2,999
    Doctoral I, 2,779
    Doctoral II, 5,526
    Master's I, 21,896
    Master's II, 704
    Bachelor's I, 877
    Bachelor's II, 2,964
    Associates, 76
    Specialized, 1,766
    Tribal, 0
    Unclassified, 708

Source: Collison, Michele N-K, "Degree-Producer Analysis Offers Good and Bad News," *Black Issues in Higher Education*, 17: 45-47, (June 22, 2000).

★1704★
Total baccalaureate degrees awarded to Hispanic Americans, by type of institution, 1997-98

Ranking basis/background: A ranking of total baccalaureate degrees conferred to minorities at accredited postsecondary institutions within the 50 states and the District of Columbia for 1997-98. **Number listed:** 3.
- Public, with 40,650 degrees awarded
- Private, non-profit, 13,002
- Proprietary, 974

Source: Collison, Michele N-K, "Degree-Producer Analysis Offers Good and Bad News," *Black Issues in Higher Education*, 17: 45-47, (June 22, 2000).

★1705★
Total baccalaureate degrees awarded to Hispanic Americans from U.S. colleges and universities, 1997-98

Ranking basis/background: A ranking of total baccalaureate degrees in all disciplines combined conferred to Hispanic Americans in 1997-98. **Remarks:** Original source: U.S. Department of Education reports of data submitted by institutions. **Number listed:** 50.
1. Florida International University, with 1,968 degrees awarded
2. University of Texas, Pan American, 1,108
3. University of Texas, El Paso, 1,063
4. University of Texas, Austin, 1,042
5. University of Texas, San Antonio, 864
6. San Diego State University, 856
7. California State University, Los Angeles, 825
8. University of California, Los Angeles, 784
9. California State University, Fullerton, 726
10. University of New Mexico, 704

Source: "9th Annual Top 100 Degree Producers," *Black Issues in Higher Education*, 17: 50-78, (June 22, 2000).

★1706★
Total baccalaureate degrees awarded to minorities, by Carnegie classification, 1997-98

Ranking basis/background: A ranking of total baccalaureate degrees conferred to minorities at accredited postsecondary institutions within the 50 states and the District of Columbia for 1997-98. **Number listed:** 12.
- Research I, with 61,884 degrees awarded
- Research II, 12,365
- Doctoral I, 13,325
- Doctoral II, 16,448
- Master's I, 80,514
- Master's II, 4,584
- Bachelor's I, 6,293
- Bachelor's II, 21,150
- Associates, 484
- Specialized, 7,662
- Tribal, 67
- Unclassified, 2,555

Source: Collison, Michele N-K, "Degree-Producer Analysis Offers Good and Bad News," *Black Issues in Higher Education*, 17: 45-47, (June 22, 2000).

★1707★
Total baccalaureate degrees awarded to minorities, by type of institution, 1997-98

Ranking basis/background: A ranking of total baccalaureate degrees conferred to minorities at accredited postsecondary institutions within the 50 states and the District of Columbia for 1997-98. **Number listed:** 3.
- Public, with 157,369
- Private, non-profit, 66,527
- Proprietary, 3,454

Source: Collison, Michele N-K, "Degree-Producer Analysis Offers Good and Bad News," *Black Issues in Higher Education*, 17: 45-47, (June 22, 2000).

★1708★
Total baccalaureate degrees awarded to Native Americans, by Carnegie classification, 1997-98

Ranking basis/background: A ranking of total baccalaureate degrees conferred to minorities at accredited postsecondary institutions within the 50 states and the District of Columbia for 1997-98. **Number listed:** 12.
- Research I, with 1,501 degrees awarded
- Research II, 707
- Doctoral I, 467
- Doctoral II, 552
- Master's I, 2,952
- Master's II, 180
- Bachelor's I, 167
- Bachelor's II, 804
- Associates, 18
- Specialized, 208
- Tribal, 48
- Unclassified, 84

Source: Collison, Michele N-K, "Degree-Producer Analysis Offers Good and Bad News," *Black Issues in Higher Education*, 17: 45-47, (June 22, 2000).

★1709★
Total baccalaureate degrees awarded to Native Americans, by type of institution, 1997-98

Ranking basis/background: A ranking of total baccalaureate degrees conferred to minorities at accredited postsecondary institutions within the 50 states and the District of Columbia for 1997-98. **Number listed:** 3.
- Public, with 5,960 degrees awarded
- Private, non-profit, 1,646
- Proprietary, 88

Source: Collison, Michele N-K, "Degree-Producer Analysis Offers Good and Bad News," *Black Issues in Higher Education*, 17: 45-47, (June 22, 2000).

★1710★
Total baccalaureate degrees awarded to Native Americans from U.S. colleges and universities, 1997-98

Ranking basis/background: A ranking of total baccalaureate degrees in all disciplines combined conferred to Native Americans in 1997-98. **Remarks:** Original source: U.S. Department of Education reports of data submitted by institutions. **Number listed:** 50.
1. Northeastern State University, with 276 degrees awarded
2. Southeastern Oklahoma State University, 175
3. Oklahoma State University, 145
4. University of Oklahoma, Norman, 140
5. University of New Mexico, 131
6. Northern Arizona University, 130
7. University of North Carolina, Pembroke, 113
8. East Central University, 100
9. Arizona State University, 92
10. Fort Lewis College, 91

Source: "9th Annual Top 100 Degree Producers," *Black Issues in Higher Education*, 17: 50-78, (June 22, 2000).

★1711★
Total baccalaureate education degrees awarded to African Americans from U.S. colleges and universities, 1997-98

Ranking basis/background: A ranking of total baccalaureate education degrees conferred to African Americans in 1997-98. **Remarks:** Original source: U.S. Department of Education reports of data submitted by institutions. **Number listed:** 52.
1. Florida A&M State University, with 232 degrees awarded
2. Alabama State University, 178
3. Southern Illinois University, Carbondale, 157
4. Southern University, New Orleans, 123
5. Alabama A&M University, 117
6. Temple University, 115
7. Southern University and A&M College, 109
8. Chicago State University, 90
9. North Carolina A&T State University, 88
10. Nova Southeastern University, 79

Source: "9th Annual Top 100 Degree Producers," *Black Issues in Higher Education*, 17: 50-78, (June 22, 2000).

★1712★
Total baccalaureate education degrees awarded to Asian Americans from U.S. colleges and universities, 1997-98

Ranking basis/background: A ranking of total baccalaureate education degrees conferred to Asian Americans in 1997-98. **Remarks:** Original source: U.S. Department of Education reports of data submitted by institutions. **Number listed:** 56.
1. University of Hawaii, Manoa, with 163 degrees awarded
2. San Francisco State University, 53
3. California State University, Los Angeles, 47
4. California State University, Fullerton, 45
5. California State University, Sacramento, 35
6. San Diego State University, 31
6. San Jose State University, 31
8. California State University, Northridge, 28
9. California State University, Long Beach, 24
10. University of California, Berkeley, 22
10. University of California, Davis, 22
10. Southern Illinois University, Carbondale, 22
10. Rutgers University, New Brunswick, 22

Source: "9th Annual Top 100 Degree Producers," *Black Issues in Higher Education*, 17: 50-78, (June 22, 2000).

★1713★
Total baccalaureate education degrees awarded to Hispanic Americans from U.S. colleges and universities, 1997-98

Ranking basis/background: A ranking of total baccalaureate education degrees conferred to Hispanic Americans in 1997-98. **Remarks:** Original source: U.S. Department of Education reports of data submitted by institutions. **Number listed:** 52.
1. Florida International University, with 265 degrees awarded
2. California State University, Los Angeles, 174
3. University of Arizona, 126
3. University of New Mexico, 126
5. Nova Southeastern University, 124
6. New Mexico State University, 95
7. City University of New York, City College, 93
8. California State University, Fullerton, 91
9. Arizona State University, 78
10. Barry University, 72

Source: "9th Annual Top 100 Degree Producers," *Black Issues in Higher Education*, 17: 50-78, (June 22, 2000).

★1714★
Total baccalaureate education degrees awarded to Native Americans from U.S. colleges and universities, 1997-98

Ranking basis/background: A ranking of total baccalaureate education degrees conferred to Native Americans in 1997-98. **Remarks:** Original source: U.S. Department of Education reports of data submitted by institutions. **Number listed:** 50.
1. Northeastern State University, with 110 degrees awarded
2. Southeastern Oklahoma State University, 71
3. Northern Arizona University, 52
4. University of New Mexico, 29
5. University of Central Oklahoma, 27
6. East Central University, 23
7. Oklahoma State University, 20
8. University of North Carolina, Pembroke, 19
9. Prescott College, 18
10. University of Alaska, Fairbanks, 16

Source: "9th Annual Top 100 Degree Producers," *Black Issues in Higher Education*, 17: 50-78, (June 22, 2000).

★1715★
Total baccalaureate engineering degrees awarded to minorities from U.S. colleges and universities, 1997-98

Ranking basis/background: A ranking of total baccalaureate engineering degrees conferred to minorities in 1997-98. **Remarks:** Original source: U.S. Department of Education reports of data submitted by institutions. **Number listed:** 103.
1. North Carolina A&T State University, with 226 degrees awarded
2. Georgia Institute of Technology, 192
3. Florida International University, 173
4. Texas A&M University, 160
5. FAMU/FSU College of Engineering, 142
6. University of Florida, 121
7. University of Texas, Austin, 111
8. University of Texas, El Paso, 105
9. City University of New York, City College, 103
9. Prairie View A&M University, 103

Source: "9th Annual Top 100 Degree Producers," *Black Issues in Higher Education*, 17: 50-78, (June 22, 2000).

★1716★
Total baccalaureate English language, literature, and letters degrees awarded to African Americans from U.S. colleges and universities, 1997-98

Ranking basis/background: A ranking of total baccalaureate English language, literature, and letters degrees conferred to African Americans in 1997-98. **Remarks:** Original source: U.S. Department of Education reports of data submitted by institutions. **Number listed:** 58.
1. University of Illinois, Urbana-Champaign, with 59 degrees awarded
2. Hampton University, 54
3. Spelman College, 48
4. University of Maryland, College Park, 47
4. Jackson State University, 47
6. Howard University, 36
6. Morehouse College, 36
6. State University of New York, Albany, 6
9. University of South Carolina, Columbia, 35
9. University of Virginia, 35
9. Virginia State University, 35

Source: "9th Annual Top 100 Degree Producers," *Black Issues in Higher Education*, 17: 50-78, (June 22, 2000).

★1717★
Total baccalaureate English language, literature, and letters degrees awarded to Asian Americans from U.S. colleges and universities, 1997-98

Ranking basis/background: A ranking of total baccalaureate English language, literature, and letters degrees conferred to Asian Americans in 1997-98. **Remarks:** Original source: U.S. Department of Education reports of data submitted by institutions. **Number listed:** 52.
1. University of California, Los Angeles, with 92 degrees awarded
2. University of California, Berkeley, 85
3. University of Hawaii, Manoa, 77
4. University of Washington (WA), 55
5. University of California, Davis, 38
5. University of California, Irvine, 38
7. Rutgers University, New Brunswick, 36
8. California State University, Long Beach, 30
9. University of Illinois, Urbana-Champaign, 26
9. University of Michigan, Ann Arbor, 26
9. State University of New York, Albany, 26
9. George Mason University, 26

Source: "9th Annual Top 100 Degree Producers," *Black Issues in Higher Education*, 17: 50-78, (June 22, 2000).

★1718★
Total baccalaureate English language, literature, and letters degrees awarded to Hispanic Americans from U.S. colleges and universities, 1997-98

Ranking basis/background: A ranking of total baccalaureate English language, literature, and letters degrees conferred to Hispanic Americans in 1997-98. **Remarks:** Original source: U.S. Department of Education reports of data submitted by institutions. **Number listed:** 55.
1. University of California, Los Angeles, with 64 degrees awarded
2. University of Texas, Austin, 62
3. University of California, Berkeley, 61
4. California State University, Long Beach, 52
5. University of Texas, Pan American, 48
6. Florida International University, 41
6. University of Texas, El Paso, 41
8. California State University, Northridge, 37
8. San Diego State University, 37
10. City University of New York, Hunter College, 36

Source: "9th Annual Top 100 Degree Producers," *Black Issues in Higher Education*, 17: 50-78, (June 22, 2000).

★1719★
Total baccalaureate English language, literature, and letters degrees awarded to Native Americans from U.S. colleges and universities, 1997-98

Ranking basis/background: A ranking of total baccalaureate English language, literature, and letters degrees conferred to Native Americans in 1997-98. **Remarks:** Original source: U.S. Department of Education reports of data submitted by institutions. **Number listed:** 26.
1. University of California, Los Angeles, with 8 degrees awarded
2. University of California, Berkeley, 6
2. University of New Mexico, 6
2. East Central University, 6
2. University of Oklahoma, Norman, 6
6. University of California, Berkeley, 5
6. University of Michigan, Ann Arbor, 5
6. Northeastern State University, 5
9. California State University, Long Beach, 4
9. San Diego State University, 4
9. Fort Lewis College, 4
9. Eastern Michigan University, 4
9. University of North Carolina, Pembroke, 4
9. Old Dominion University, 4
9. University of Washington (WA), 4

Source: "9th Annual Top 100 Degree Producers," *Black Issues in Higher Education*, 17: 50-78, (June 22, 2000).

★1720★
Total baccalaureate ethnic/cultural studies degrees awarded to African Americans from U.S. colleges and universities, 1997-98

Ranking basis/background: A ranking of total baccalaureate ethnic/cultural studies degrees conferred to African Americans for 1997-98. **Remarks:** Original source: U.S. Department of Education reports of data self reported by institutions. **Number listed:** 50.
1. University of California, Berkeley, with 27 degrees awarded
2. State University of New York, College at Old Westbury, 21
3. California State University, Long Beach, 19
3. Wesleyan University, 19
3. Rutgers University, New Brunswick, 19
6. Ohio State University, 17
7. University of California, Santa Barbara, 15
8. California State University, Northridge, 14
8. City University of New York, Hunter College, 14
8. State University of New York, Albany, 14

Source: Hamilton, Kendra, "African American Studies," *Black Issues in Higher Education*, 17: 28-31, (May 25, 2000).

★1721★
Total baccalaureate health professions and related sciences degrees awarded to African Americans from U.S. colleges and universities, 1997-98

Ranking basis/background: A ranking of total baccalaureate health professions and related sciences degrees conferred to African Americans in 1997-98. **Remarks:** Original source: U.S. Department of Education reports of data submitted by institutions. **Number listed:** 50.
1. Howard University, with 200 degrees awarded
2. Southern University and A&M College, 187
3. Florida A&M State University, 173
4. Florida International University, 127
5. St. Joseph's College (NY), 106
6. Texas Southern University, 103
7. Dillard University, 102
8. Southern Illinois University, Carbondale, 96
8. City University of New York, Lehman College, 96
10. State University of New York, Health Science Center, Brooklyn, 92

Source: "9th Annual Top 100 Degree Producers," *Black Issues in Higher Education*, 17: 50-78, (June 22, 2000).

★1722★
Total baccalaureate health professions and related sciences degrees awarded to Asian Americans from U.S. colleges and universities, 1997-98

Ranking basis/background: A ranking of total baccalaureate health professions and related sciences degrees conferred to Asian Americans in 1997-98. **Remarks:** Original source: U.S. Department of Education reports of data submitted by institutions. **Number listed:** 50.
1. San Jose State University, with 152 degrees awarded
2. Long Island University, Brooklyn, 114
3. University of Hawaii, Manoa, 86
4. University of Southern California, 77
4. Temple University, 77
6. Loma Linda University, 71
7. California State University, Long Beach, 70
7. Rutgers University, New Brunswick, 70
9. San Francisco State University, 69
10. St. John's University (NY), 63

Source: "9th Annual Top 100 Degree Producers," *Black Issues in Higher Education*, 17: 50-78, (June 22, 2000).

★1723★
Total baccalaureate health professions and related sciences degrees awarded to Hispanic Americans from U.S. colleges and universities, 1997-98

Ranking basis/background: A ranking of total baccalaureate health professions and related sciences degrees conferred to Hispanic Americans in 1997-98. **Remarks:** Original source: U.S. Department of Education reports of data submitted by institutions. **Number listed:** 50.
1. Florida International University, with 129 degrees awarded
2. University of Texas, El Paso, 91
3. University of Texas, Pan American, 87
4. City University of New York, Lehman College, 80
5. University of New Mexico, 75
6. University of Texas Health Science Center, San Antonio, 71
7. University of Miami, 66
8. University of Central Florida, 60
9. University of Texas, Austin, 57
10. University of Texas Medical Branch, Galveston, 55

Source: "9th Annual Top 100 Degree Producers," *Black Issues in Higher Education*, 17: 50-78, (June 22, 2000).

★1724★
Total baccalaureate health professions and related sciences degrees awarded to Native Americans from U.S. colleges and universities, 1997-98

Ranking basis/background: A ranking of total baccalaureate health professions and related sciences degrees conferred to Native Americans in 1997-98. **Remarks:** Original source: U.S. Department of Education reports of data submitted by institutions. **Number listed:** 60.
1. University of Oklahoma Health Sciences Center, with 24 degrees awarded
2. Northeast Louisiana University, 17
3. University of New Mexico, 15
3. University of North Dakota, 15
5. Northeastern State University, 14
6. St. Xavier University, 13
7. Old Dominion University, 10
8. California State University, Fresno, 8
8. Southwestern Oklahoma State University, 8
10. East Central University, 7
10. University of Washington (WA), 7

Source: "9th Annual Top 100 Degree Producers," *Black Issues in Higher Education*, 17: 50-78, (June 22, 2000).

★1725★
Total baccalaureate law and legal studies degrees awarded to African Americans from U.S. colleges and universities, 1997-98

Ranking basis/background: A ranking of total baccalaureate law and legal studies degrees conferred to African Americans in 1997-98. **Remarks:** Original source: U.S. Department of Education reports of data submitted by institutions. **Number listed:** 29.
1. University of the District of Columbia, with 27 degrees awarded
2. University of Central Florida, 13
3. University of Detroit Mercy, 10
4. University of West Los Angeles, 9
5. Mississippi University for Women, 8
6. University of California, Santa Barbara, 7
6. Amherst College, 7
6. University of Massachusetts, Amherst, 7
9. Morris Brown College, 6
9. Valdosta State University, 6

Source: "9th Annual Top 100 Degree Producers," *Black Issues in Higher Education*, 17: 50-78, (June 22, 2000).

★1726★
Total baccalaureate law and legal studies degrees awarded to Asian Americans from U.S. colleges and universities, 1997-98

Ranking basis/background: A ranking of total baccalaureate law and legal studies degrees conferred to Asian Americans in 1997-98. **Remarks:** Original source: U.S. Department of Education reports of data submitted by institutions. **Number listed:** 5.
1. University of California, Santa Barbara, with 25 degrees awarded
2. University of California, Berkeley, 21
3. Chapman University, 5
4. University of West Florida, 3
5. University of Massachusetts, Amherst, 2

Source: "9th Annual Top 100 Degree Producers," *Black Issues in Higher Education*, 17: 50-78, (June 22, 2000).

★1727★
Total baccalaureate law and legal studies degrees awarded to Hispanic Americans from U.S. colleges and universities, 1997-98

Ranking basis/background: A ranking of total baccalaureate law and legal studies degrees conferred to Hispanic Americans in 1997-98. **Remarks:** Original source: U.S. Department of Education reports of data submitted by institutions. **Number listed:** 9.
1. University of California, Santa Barbara, with 26 degrees awarded
2. University of Central Florida, 18
3. Barry University, 10
4. University of California, Berkeley, 6
5. Chapman University, 4
5. University of Houston, Clear Lake, 4
7. University of Massachusetts, Amherst, 3
7. Stephen F. Austin State University, 3
7. Texas Weslyan University, 3

Source: "9th Annual Top 100 Degree Producers," *Black Issues in Higher Education*, 17: 50-78, (June 22, 2000).

★1728★
Total baccalaureate law and legal studies degrees awarded to Native Americans from U.S. colleges and universities, 1997-98

Ranking basis/background: A ranking of total baccalaureate law and legal studies degrees conferred to Native Americans in 1997-98. **Remarks:** Original source: U.S. Department of Education reports of data submitted by institutions. **Number listed:** 2.
1. University of California, Santa Barbara, with 4 degrees awarded
2. East Central University, 3

Source: "9th Annual Top 100 Degree Producers," *Black Issues in Higher Education*, 17: 50-78, (June 22, 2000).

★1729★
Total baccalaureate mathematics degrees awarded to African Americans from U.S. colleges and universities, 1997-98

Ranking basis/background: A ranking of total baccalaureate mathematics degrees conferred to African Americans in 1997-98. **Remarks:** Original source: U.S. Department of Education reports of data submitted by institutions. **Number listed:** 58.

1. City University of New York, York College, with 56 degrees awarded
2. Clark Atlanta University, 23
3. Spelman College, 22
4. Morehouse College, 21
4. Southern University and A&M College, 21
4. South Carolina State University, 21
7. Florida A&M State University, 19
8. Georgia State University, 14
9. Jackson State University, 13
9. Texas A&M University, 13

Source: "9th Annual Top 100 Degree Producers," *Black Issues in Higher Education*, 17: 50-78, (June 22, 2000).

★1730★
Total baccalaureate mathematics degrees awarded to Asian Americans from U.S. colleges and universities, 1997-98

Ranking basis/background: A ranking of total baccalaureate mathematics degrees conferred to Asian Americans in 1997-98. **Remarks:** Original source: U.S. Department of Education reports of data submitted by institutions. **Number listed:** 56.
1. University of California, Los Angeles, with 50 degrees awarded
2. State University of New York, Stony Brook, 34
3. University of California, Berkeley, 20
4. New York University, 19
4. University of Washington (WA), 19
6. University of California, Irvine, 18
6. Texas A&M University, 18
8. Rutgers University, New Brunswick, 17
9. University of California, Davis, 14
10. University of California, Santa Barbara, 13

Source: "9th Annual Top 100 Degree Producers," *Black Issues in Higher Education*, 17: 50-78, (June 22, 2000).

★1731★
Total baccalaureate mathematics degrees awarded to Hispanic Americans from U.S. colleges and universities, 1997-98

Ranking basis/background: A ranking of total baccalaureate mathematics degrees conferred to Hispanic Americans in 1997-98. **Remarks:** Original source: U.S. Department of Education reports of data submitted by institutions. **Number listed:** 52.
1. University of California, Los Angeles, with 21 degrees awarded
1. Texas A&M University, 21
3. University of Texas, Austin, 19
4. University of Texas, Pan American, 18
4. University of Texas, San Antonio, 18
6. Texas A&M International University, 13
7. San Diego State University, 12
7. Jersey City State College, 12
9. University of Houston, University Park, 9
10. City University of New York, York College, 8
10. State University of New York, Stony Brook, 8

Source: "9th Annual Top 100 Degree Producers," *Black Issues in Higher Education*, 17: 50-78, (June 22, 2000).

★1732★
Total baccalaureate mathematics degrees awarded to Native Americans from U.S. colleges and universities, 1997-98

Ranking basis/background: A ranking of total baccalaureate mathematics degrees conferred to Native Americans in 1997-98. **Remarks:** Original source: U.S. Department of Education reports of data submitted by institutions. **Number listed:** 1.
1. University of North Carolina, Pembroke, with 6 degrees awarded

Source: "9th Annual Top 100 Degree Producers," *Black Issues in Higher Education*, 17: 50-78, (June 22, 2000).

★1733★
Total baccalaureate physical sciences degrees awarded to African Americans from U.S. colleges and universities, 1997-98

Ranking basis/background: A ranking of total baccalaureate physical sciences degrees conferred to African Americans in 1997-98. **Remarks:** Original source: U.S. Department of Education reports of data submitted by institutions. **Number listed:** 52.
1. Xavier University (LA), with 55 degrees awarded
2. Southern University and A&M College, 23
3. Howard University, 21
4. Lincoln University, 20
5. Spelman College, 17
5. Jackson State University, 17
7. Morgan State University, 16
7. Benedict College, 16
9. United States Naval Academy, 15
9. Alcorn State University, 15

Source: "9th Annual Top 100 Degree Producers," *Black Issues in Higher Education*, 17: 50-78, (June 22, 2000).

★1734★
Total baccalaureate physical sciences degrees awarded to Asian Americans from U.S. colleges and universities, 1997-98

Ranking basis/background: A ranking of total baccalaureate physical sciences degrees conferred to Asian Americans in 1997-98. **Remarks:** Original source: U.S. Department of Education reports of data submitted by institutions. **Number listed:** 52.
1. University of California, Irvine, with 67 degrees awarded
2. University of California, Berkeley, 42
2. University of California, Los Angeles, 42
4. University of California, San Diego, 37
5. Massachusetts Institute of Technology, 31
6. San Jose State University, 29
6. Harvard University, 29
8. University of Hawaii, Manoa, 27
9. University of North Carolina, Chapel Hill, 26
10. Cornell University, 25

Source: "9th Annual Top 100 Degree Producers," *Black Issues in Higher Education*, 17: 50-78, (June 22, 2000).

★1735★
Total baccalaureate physical sciences degrees awarded to Hispanic Americans from U.S. colleges and universities, 1997-98

Ranking basis/background: A ranking of total baccalaureate physical sciences degrees conferred to Hispanic Americans in 1997-98. **Remarks:** Original source: U.S. Department of Education reports of data submitted by institutions. **Number listed:** 41.
1. Florida International University, with 19 degrees awarded
2. University of California, Irvine, 11
2. University of Texas, El Paso, 11
4. Texas A&M University, 9
5. University of Arizona, 8
5. California State Polytechnic University, Pomona, 8
5. University of Texas, Austin, 8
8. University of California, Davis, 7
8. University of Miami, 7
8. United States Naval Academy, 7

Source: "9th Annual Top 100 Degree Producers," *Black Issues in Higher Education*, 17: 50-78, (June 22, 2000).

★1736★
Total baccalaureate physical sciences degrees awarded to Native Americans from U.S. colleges and universities, 1997-98

Ranking basis/background: A ranking of total baccalaureate physical sciences degrees conferred to Native Americans in 1997-98. **Remarks:** Original source: U.S. Department of Education reports of data submitted by institutions. **Number listed:** 5.
1. University of North Carolina, with 7 degrees awarded
2. Southeastern Oklahoma State University, 6
3. Southwestern Oklahoma State University, 4
4. University of New Mexico, 3
4. University of Oklahoma, Norman, 3

Source: "9th Annual Top 100 Degree Producers," *Black Issues in Higher Education*, 17: 50-78, (June 22, 2000).

★1737★
Total baccalaureate psychology degrees awarded to African Americans from U.S. colleges and universities, 1997-98

Ranking basis/background: A ranking of total baccalaureate psychology degrees conferred to African Americans in 1997-98. **Remarks:** Original source: U.S. Department of Education reports of data submitted by institutions. **Number listed:** 52.
1. City University of New York, York College, with 107 degrees awarded
2. Howard University, 84
3. Hampton University, 83
4. Spelman College, 82
5. Florida A&M University, 76
6. City University of New York, John Jay College of Criminal Justice, 71
7. Chicago State University, 70
8. Clark Atlanta University, 61
8. Morehouse College, 61
10. Grambling State University, 58

Source: "9th Annual Top 100 Degree Producers," *Black Issues in Higher Education*, 17: 50-78, (June 22, 2000).

★1738★
Total baccalaureate psychology degrees awarded to Asian Americans from U.S. colleges and universities, 1997-98

Ranking basis/background: A ranking of total baccalaureate psychology degrees conferred to Asian Americans in 1997-98. **Remarks:** Original source: U.S. Department of Education reports of data submitted by institutions. **Number listed:** 52.
1. University of California, Los Angeles, with 215 degrees awarded
2. University of California, Davis, 162
3. University of California, Irvine, 141
4. University of Hawaii, Manoa, 116
5. University of California, San Diego, 112
6. University of California, Berkeley, 109
7. Rutgers University, New Brunswick, 78
8. University of Washington (WA), 68
9. University of Illinois, Urbana-Champaign, 67
10. University of Michigan, Ann Arbor, 64

Source: "9th Annual Top 100 Degree Producers," *Black Issues in Higher Education*, 17: 50-78, (June 22, 2000).

★1739★
Total baccalaureate psychology degrees awarded to Hispanic Americans from U.S. colleges and universities, 1997-98

Ranking basis/background: A ranking of total baccalaureate psychology degrees conferred to Hispanic Americans in 1997-98. **Remarks:** Original source: U.S. Department of Education reports of data submitted by institutions. **Number listed:** 51.
1. Florida International University, with 202 degrees awarded
2. San Diego State University, 106
3. City University of New York, Hunter College, 89
4. University of California, Los Angeles, 86
5. University of Texas, Austin, 77
6. California State University, Northridge, 74
7. City University of New York, Lehman College, 73
8. University of California, Davis, 71
9. California State University, Long Beach, 67
9. California State University, Los Angeles, 67

Source: "9th Annual Top 100 Degree Producers," *Black Issues in Higher Education*, 17: 50-78, (June 22, 2000).

★1740★
Total baccalaureate psychology degrees awarded to Native Americans from U.S. colleges and universities, 1997-98

Ranking basis/background: A ranking of total baccalaureate psychology degrees conferred to Native Americans in 1997-98. **Remarks:** Original source: U.S. Department of Education reports of data submitted by institutions. **Number listed:** 50.
1. Northeastern State University, with 20 degrees awarded
2. University of Washington (WA), 12
3. University of Oklahoma, Norman, 11
4. University of California, San Diego, 7
4. Southeastern Oklahoma State University, 7
6. Northern Arizona University, 6
6. California State University, Fullerton, 6
6. University of New Mexico, 6
6. University of North Dakota, 6
6. Oklahoma State University, 6

Source: "9th Annual Top 100 Degree Producers," *Black Issues in Higher Education*, 17: 50-78, (June 22, 2000).

★1741★
Total baccalaureate social sciences and history degrees awarded to African Americans from U.S. colleges and universities, 1997-98

Ranking basis/background: A ranking of total baccalaureate social sciences and history degrees conferred to African Americans in 1997-98. **Remarks:** Original source: U.S. Department of Education reports of data submitted by institutions. **Number listed:** 51.
1. University of Maryland, College Park, with 133 degrees awarded
1. North Carolina Central University, 133
3. University of California, Los Angeles, 120
4. Spelman College, 118
5. Howard University, 117
6. Southern University and A&M College, 111
7. St. Leo College, 109
7. Norfolk State University, 109
9. City University of New York, Hunter College, 90
10. Morehouse College, 89
10. Virginia State University, 89

Source: "9th Annual Top 100 Degree Producers," *Black Issues in Higher Education*, 17: 50-78, (June 22, 2000).

★1742★
Total baccalaureate social sciences and history degrees awarded to Asian Americans from U.S. colleges and universities, 1997-98

Ranking basis/background: A ranking of total baccalaureate social sciences and history degrees conferred to Asian Americans in 1997-98. **Remarks:** Original source: U.S. Department of Education reports of data submitted by institutions. **Number listed:** 53.
1. University of California, Los Angeles, with 544 degrees awarded
2. University of California, Berkeley, 374
3. University of California, Irvine, 362
4. University of Washington (WA), 227
5. University of Hawaii, Manoa, 199
6. University of California, San Diego, 197
7. Rutgers University, New Brunswick, 125
8. University of California, Davis, 124
9. University of Chicago, 117
10. New York University, 107

Source: "9th Annual Top 100 Degree Producers," *Black Issues in Higher Education*, 17: 50-78, (June 22, 2000).

★1743★
Total baccalaureate social sciences and history degrees awarded to Hispanic Americans from U.S. colleges and universities, 1997-98

Ranking basis/background: A ranking of total baccalaureate social sciences and history degrees conferred to Hispanic Americans in 1997-98. **Remarks:** Original source: U.S. Department of Education reports of data submitted by institutions. **Number listed:** 52.
1. University of California, Los Angeles, with 313 degrees awarded
2. University of California, Berkeley, 195
3. Florida International University, 173
4. University of Texas, Austin, 162
5. University of California, Santa Barbara, 144
6. San Diego State University, 106
7. California State University, Northridge, 97
8. California State University, Fresno, 92
9. City University of New York, Hunter College, 91
10. University of California, Santa Cruz, 89

Source: "9th Annual Top 100 Degree Producers," *Black Issues in Higher Education*, 17: 50-78, (June 22, 2000).

★1744★
Total baccalaureate social sciences and history degrees awarded to Native Americans from U.S. colleges and universities, 1997-98

Ranking basis/background: A ranking of total baccalaureate social sciences and history degrees conferred to Native Americans in 1997-98. **Remarks:** Original source: U.S. Department of Education reports of data submitted by institutions. **Number listed:** 60.
1. University of California, Los Angeles, with 27 degrees awarded
2. University of North Carolina, Pembroke, 16
3. University of California, Santa Barbara, 15
3. University of Washington (WA), 15
5. Arizona State University, 14
5. University of New Mexico, 14
7. University of Arizona, 13
8. California State University, Sacramento, 12
8. University of California, Berkeley, 12
8. Fort Lewis College, 12
8. Oglala Lakota College, 12
8. Western Washington University, 12

Source: "9th Annual Top 100 Degree Producers," *Black Issues in Higher Education*, 17: 50-78, (June 22, 2000).

★1745★
Total ethnic/cultural studies doctoral degrees awarded to African Americans from U.S. colleges and universities, 1997-98

Ranking basis/background: A ranking of total ethnic/cultural studies doctoral degrees conferred to African Americans for 1997-98. **Remarks:** Original source: U.S. Department of Education reports of data self reported by institutions. **Number listed:** 1.
1. Temple University, with 9 degrees awarded

Source: Hamilton, Kendra, "African American Studies," *Black Issues in Higher Education*, 17: 28-31, (May 25, 2000).

★1746★
Total ethnic/cultural studies doctoral degrees awarded to minorities from U.S. colleges and universities, 1997-98

Ranking basis/background: A ranking of total ethnic/cultural studies doctoral degrees conferred to minorities for 1997-98. **Remarks:** Original source: U.S. Department of Education reports of data self reported by institutions. **Number listed:** 2.
1. Temple University, with 9 degrees awarded
2. University of California, Berkeley, 6

Source: Hamilton, Kendra, "African American Studies," *Black Issues in Higher Education*, 17: 28-31, (May 25, 2000).

DEGREES (ACADEMIC)—MINORITY GROUPS

★1747★
Total ethnic/cultural studies master's degrees awarded to African Americans from U.S. colleges and universities, 1997-98

Ranking basis/background: A ranking of total ethnic/cultural studies master's degrees conferred to African Americans for 1997-98. **Remarks:** Original source: U.S. Department of Education reports of data self reported by institutions. **Number listed:** 8.

1. Ohio State University, with 15 degrees awarded
2. Northeastern Illinois University, 14
3. Temple University, 12
4. University of Iowa, 7
5. University of California, Los Angeles, 5
5. Yale University, 5
7. Georgetown University, 4
7. Clark Atlanta University, 4

Source: Hamilton, Kendra, "African American Studies," *Black Issues in Higher Education*, 17: 28-31, (May 25, 2000).

★1748★
Total ethnic/cultural studies master's degrees awarded to minorities from U.S. colleges and universities, 1997-98

Ranking basis/background: A ranking of total ethnic/cultural studies master's degrees conferred to minorities for 1997-98. **Remarks:** Original source: U.S. Department of Education reports of data self reported by institutions. **Number listed:** 34.

1. University of California, Los Angeles, with 18 degrees awarded
2. Ohio State University, 15
3. Northeastern Illinois University, 14
4. University of Arizona, 12
4. University of California, Berkeley, 12
4. Temple University, 12
7. University of New Mexico, 11
8. University of Hawaii, Manoa, 10
8. Stanford University, 10
10. University of Pennsylvania, 9

Source: Hamilton, Kendra, "African American Studies," *Black Issues in Higher Education*, 17: 28-31, (May 25, 2000).

★1749★
Total master's degrees awarded to African Americans, by type of institutions, 1997-98

Ranking basis/background: Total number of master's degrees conferred to African American students in 1997-98 by carnegie classification. **Remarks:** Original source: *Black Issues* analysis of U.S. Department of Education data. **Number listed:** 15.

Public, with 16,321
Private, nonprofit, 11,639
Proprietary, 544
Research I, 6,059
Research II, 1,527
Doctorate I, 3,103
Doctorate II, 1,883
Master's I, 12,660
Master's II, 649
Bachelor's I, 142
Bachelor's II, 455
Associate's, 2
Specialized, 1,533
Tribal, 491
Unclassified, 4,364

Source: St. John, Eric, "More Doctorates in the House," *Black Issues in Higher Education*, 17: 38-44, (July 6, 2000).

★1750★
Total master's degrees awarded to Asian Americans, by type of institutions, 1997-98

Ranking basis/background: Total number of master's degrees conferred to Asian American students in 1997-98 by carnegie classification. **Remarks:** Original source: *Black Issues* analysis of U.S. Department of Education data. **Number listed:** 15.

Public, with 9,907
Private, nonprofit, 9,489
Proprietary, 453
Research I, 7,936
Research II, 874
Doctorate I, 1,527
Doctorate II, 1,829
Master's I, 5,065
Master's II, 181
Bachelor's I, 129
Bachelor's II, 219
Associate's, 5
Specialized, 1,619
Tribal, 0
Unclassified, 465

Source: St. John, Eric, "More Doctorates in the House," *Black Issues in Higher Education*, 17: 38-44, (July 6, 2000).

★1751★
Total master's degrees awarded to Hispanic Americans, by type of institutions, 1997-98

Ranking basis/background: Total number of master's degrees conferred to Hispanic American students in 1997-98 by carnegie classification. **Remarks:** Original source: *Black Issues* analysis of U.S. Department of Education data. **Number listed:** 15.

Public, with 7,112
Private, nonprofit, 4,828
Proprietary, 255
Research I, 3,347
Research II, 546
Doctorate I, 1,284
Doctorate II, 1,307
Master's I, 4,646
Master's II, 164
Bachelor's I, 50
Bachelor's II, 95
Associate's, 0
Specialized, 566
Tribal, 0
Unclassified, 190

Source: St. John, Eric, "More Doctorates in the House," *Black Issues in Higher Education*, 17: 38-44, (July 6, 2000).

★1752★
Total master's degrees awarded to minorities, by type of institutions, 1997-98

Ranking basis/background: Total number of master's degrees conferred to minority students in 1997-98 by carnegie classification. **Remarks:** Original source: *Black Issues* analysis of U.S. Department of Education data. **Number listed:** 15.

Public, with 34,600
Private, nonprofit, 26,615
Proprietary, 1,280
Research I, 17,867
Research II, 3,112
Doctorate I, 6,102
Doctorate II, 5,158
Master's I, 23,025
Master's II, 1,037
Bachelor's I, 347
Bachelor's II, 841
Associate's, 8
Specialized, 3,822
Tribal, 2
Unclassified, 1,174

Source: St. John, Eric, "More Doctorates in the House," *Black Issues in Higher Education*, 17: 38-44, (July 6, 2000).

★1753★
Total master's degrees awarded to Native Americans, by type of institutions, 1997-98

Ranking basis/background: Total number of master's degrees conferred to Native American students in 1997-98 by carnegie classification. **Remarks:** Original source: *Black Issues* analysis of U.S. Department of Education data. **Number listed:** 15.

Public, with 1,260
Private, nonprofit, 659
Proprietary, 28
Research I, 525
Research II, 165
Doctorate I, 188
Doctorate II, 139
Master's I, 654
Master's II, 43
Bachelor's I, 26
Bachelor's II, 72
Associate's, 1
Specialized, 104
Tribal, 2
Unclassified, 28

Source: St. John, Eric, "More Doctorates in the House," *Black Issues in Higher Education*, 17: 38-44, (July 6, 2000).

★1754★
Total of all degrees conferred to African Americans by historically black colleges and universities, 1997-98

Ranking basis/background: Total number of all degrees awarded to African Americans at historically black institutions compared to all other institutions, plus the average annual percentage of change. **Remarks:** Original source: *Black Issues* analysis of U.S. Department of Education reports of data submitted by institutions. **Number listed:** 3.

Historically black institutions, with 32,366 degrees awarded; and a 4.0% average annual change
All other institutions, 151,256; 5.6%
Total, 183,622; 5.3%

Source: Borden, Victor M.H., "The Top 100: Interpreting the Data," *Black Issues in Higher Education*, 17: 46-47, (July 6, 2000).

★1755★
Traditionally white institutions awarding the most master's degrees to African Americans

Ranking basis/background: Total master's degrees conferred to African American students at traditionally white institutions of higher education, in all disciplines combined, during the 1997-98 academic year. **Remarks:** Original source: *Black Issues* analysis of U.S. Department of Education reports of data submitted by institutions. **Number listed:** 50.
1. Webster University (MO)
2. Central Michigan University (MI)
3. Cambridge College (MA)
4. New York University (NY)
5. Wayne State University (MI)
6. Nova Southeastern University (FL)
7. National-Louis University (IL)
8. Long Island University, Brooklyn (NY)
9. Chicago State University (IL)
10. City University of New York, Brooklyn College (NY)
11. City University of New York, City College (NY)
12. University of Michigan, Ann Arbor (MI)
12. Temple University (PA)
12. University of South Carolina, Columbia (SC)
15. University of Maryland, College Park (MD)
16. Georgia State University (GA)
17. Columbia University (NY)
18. Marygrove College (MI)
19. Florida International University (FL)
19. Johns Hopkins University (MD)

Source: "Top 100 Degree Producers," *Black Issues in Higher Education*, 17: 48-89, (July 7, 2000).

★1756★
U.S. colleges and universities awarding the most biological and life sciences master's degrees to African Americans

Ranking basis/background: Total master's degrees conferred to African American students in the field of biological and life sciences during the 1997-98 academic year. **Remarks:** Original source: *Black Issues* analysis of U.S. Department of Education reports of data submitted by institutions. **Number listed:** 18.
1. Howard University (DC)
2. Alcorn State University (MS)
2. Tennessee State University (TN)
4. Jackson State University (MD)
4. Hampton University (VA)
6. Virginia State University (VA)
7. Johns Hopkins University (MD)
7. Long Island University, Brooklyn (NY)
9. Barry University (FL)
9. New York University (NY)
11. Georgia Southern University (GA)
11. University of Illinois, Urbana-Champaign (IL)
11. Louisiana State University Medical Center (LA)
11. New York Medical College (NY)
11. North Carolina Central University (NC)
11. North Carolina State University (NC)
11. Brown University (RI)
11. Texas Southern University (TX)

Source: "Top 100 Degree Producers," *Black Issues in Higher Education*, 17: 48-89, (July 7, 2000).

★1757★
U.S. colleges and universities awarding the most biological and life sciences master's degrees to Asian Americans

Ranking basis/background: Total master's degrees conferred to Asian American students in the field of biological and life sciences during the 1997-98 academic year. **Remarks:** Original source: *Black Issues* analysis of U.S. Department of Education reports of data submitted by institutions. **Number listed:** 60.
1. Finch University of Health Science, Chicago (IL)
2. Georgetown University (DC)
3. University of Hawaii, Manoa (HI)
4. University of California, Los Angeles (CA)
5. Wayne State University (MI)
5. New York University (NY)
7. Barry University (FL)
7. University of Illinois, Urbana-Champaign (IL)
9. Washington University (MO)
10. University of Michigan, Ann Arbor (MI)
10. Columbia University, New York City (NY)
12. Stanford University (CA)
13. University of California, Riverside (CA)
13. Northwestern University (IL)
15. University of California, San Diego (CA)
15. Johns Hopkins University (MD)
15. Rutgers University, New Brunswick (NJ)
15. Thomas Jefferson University (PA)
19. George Washington University (DC)
19. University of Texas, San Antonio (TX)

Source: "Top 100 Degree Producers," *Black Issues in Higher Education*, 17: 48-89, (July 7, 2000).

★1758★
U.S. colleges and universities awarding the most biological and life sciences master's degrees to Hispanic Americans

Ranking basis/background: Total master's degrees conferred to Hispanic American students in the field of biological and life sciences during the 1997-98 academic year. **Remarks:** Original source: *Black Issues* analysis of U.S. Department of Education reports of data submitted by institutions. **Number listed:** 8.
1. University of Texas, San Antonio (TX)
2. Barry University (FL)
2. University of the Incarnate Word
4. New Mexico State University (NM)
4. Cornell University (NY)
6. University of Miami (FL)
6. University of Illinois, Urbana-Champaign (IL)
6. University of Missouri, St. Louis (MO)

Source: "Top 100 Degree Producers," *Black Issues in Higher Education*, 17: 48-89, (July 7, 2000).

★1759★
U.S. colleges and universities awarding the most business management and administrative services master's degrees to African Americans

Ranking basis/background: Total master's degrees conferred to African American students in the field of business management and administrative services during the 1997-98 academic year. **Remarks:** Original source: *Black Issues* analysis of U.S. Department of Education reports of data submitted by institutions. **Number listed:** 51.
1. Webster University (MO)
2. Central Michigan University (MI)
3. University of Maryland, University College (MD)
4. Lincoln University (PA)
5. Nova Southeastern University (FL)
6. Clark Atlanta University (GA)
7. National-Louis University (IL)
8. Keller Graduate School of Management, Inc.(GA)
9. Bowie State University (MD)
10. Johns Hopkins University (MD)
11. Florida Institute of Technology (FL)
12. Georgia State University (GA)
12. Northwestern University (IL)
14. Keller Graduate School of Management, Inc. (IL)
15. Roosevelt University (IL)
16. Averett College (VA)
17. Mercer University (GA)
18. Wilmington College, New Castle (DE)
19. University of Michigan, Ann Arbor (MI)
20. University of Phoenix (AZ)

Source: "Top 100 Degree Producers," *Black Issues in Higher Education*, 17: 48-89, (July 7, 2000).

★1760★
U.S. colleges and universities awarding the most business management and administrative services master's degrees to Asian Americans

Ranking basis/background: Total master's degrees conferred to Asian American students in the field of business management and administrative services during the 1997-98 academic year. **Remarks:** Original source: *Black Issues* analysis of U.S. Department of Education reports of data submitted by institutions. **Number listed:** 50.
1. University of Southern California (CA)
2. Golden Gate University, San Francisco (CA)
3. University of Chicago (IL)
4. Northwestern University (IL)
5. California State University, Hayward (CA)
6. New York University (NY)
7. University of California, Los Angeles (CA)
7. Santa Clara University (CA)
9. Harvard University (MA)
10. Pepperdine University (CA)
11. City University of New York, Bernard M. Baruch College (NY)
12. University of Hawaii, Manoa (HI)
13. Southeastern University (DC)
13. University of Maryland, University College (MD)
15. DePaul University (IL)
16. Webster University (MO)
17. University of California, Berkeley (CA)
18. San Francisco State University (CA)
18. Baker College Center for Graduate Studies (MI)
20. Rutgers University, Newark (NJ)

Source: "Top 100 Degree Producers," *Black Issues in Higher Education*, 17: 48-89, (July 7, 2000).

DEGREES (ACADEMIC)—MINORITY GROUPS

★1761★
U.S. colleges and universities awarding the most business management and administrative services master's degrees to Hispanic Americans

Ranking basis/background: Total master's degrees conferred to Hispanic American students in the field of business management and administrative services during the 1997-98 academic year. **Remarks:** Original source: *Black Issues* analysis of U.S. Department of Education reports of data submitted by institutions. **Number listed:** 50.

1. Florida International University (FL)
2. Webster University (MO)
3. University of Miami (FL)
4. Nova Southeastern University (FL)
5. University of Texas, Austin (TX)
6. University of Phoenix (AZ)
7. Pepperdine University (CA)
8. Texas A&M International University (TX)
9. University of Southern California (CA)
10. Our Lady of the Lake University, San Antonio (TX)
11. New York University, (NY)
12. National University (CA)
12. San Diego State University (CA)
14. Central Michigan University (MI)
15. Golden Gate University, San Francisco (CA)
16. St. Thomas University (FL)
16. Arthur D. Little School of Management (MA)
18. University of California, Los Angeles, (CA)
18. University of Maryland, University College (MD)
18. University of Michigan, Ann Arbor (MI)
18. Stevens Institute of Technology (NJ)

Source: "Top 100 Degree Producers," *Black Issues in Higher Education*, 17: 48-89, (July 7, 2000).

★1762★
U.S. colleges and universities awarding the most business management and administrative services master's degrees to Native Americans

Ranking basis/background: Total master's degrees conferred to Native American students in the field of business management and administrative services during the 1997-98 academic year. **Remarks:** Original source: *Black Issues* analysis of U.S. Department of Education reports of data submitted by institutions. **Number listed:** 32.

1. Central Michigan University (MI)
2. University of Phoenix (AZ)
2. University of Southern California (CA)
2. Webster University (MO)
2. East Central University (OK)
2. Oklahoma City University (OK)
7. Arizona State University (AZ)
7. University of Illinois, Urbana-Champaign (IL)
7. Northwestern University (IL)
10. Florida Institute of Technology (FL)
10. Boston University (MA)
10. University of Findlay (OH)
10. Northeastern State University (OK)
10. Southeastern Oklahoma State University (OK)
10. University of Dallas (TX)

Source: "Top 100 Degree Producers," *Black Issues in Higher Education*, 17: 48-89, (July 7, 2000).

★1763★
U.S. colleges and universities awarding the most communications master's degrees to African Americans

Ranking basis/background: Total master's degrees conferred to African American students in the field of communications during the 1997-98 academic year. **Remarks:** Original source: *Black Issues* analysis of U.S. Department of Education reports of data submitted by institutions. **Number listed:** 49.

1. Howard University (DC)
2. American University (DC)
3. Northwestern University (IL)
4. Bowie State University (MD)
5. Governors State University (IL)
6. New York University (NY)
7. Syracuse University (NY)
8. Columbia University, New York City (NY)
9. Southern University and A&M College (LA)
9. Michigan State University (MI)
11. University of Maryland, College Park (MD)
11. Temple University (PA)
13. University of Southern Mississippi (MS)
13. University of Missouri, Columbia (MO)
15. Seton Hall University (NJ)
16. Norfolk State University (VA)
17. Boston University (MA)
17. Wayne State University (MI)
17. Webster University (MO)
17. Rowan University (NJ)
17. City University of New York, Brooklyn College (NY)
17. New School for Social Research (NY)
17. Virginia Commonwealth University (VA)

Source: "Top 100 Degree Producers," *Black Issues in Higher Education*, 17: 48-89, (July 7, 2000).

★1764★
U.S. colleges and universities awarding the most communications master's degrees to Asian Americans

Ranking basis/background: Total master's degrees conferred to Asian American students in the field of communications during the 1997-98 academic year. **Remarks:** Original source: *Black Issues* analysis of U.S. Department of Education reports of data submitted by institutions. **Number listed:** 21.

1. Columbia University, New York City (NY)
2. University of Southern California (CA)
3. Northwestern University (IL)
4. Fort Hays State University (KS)
4. New York University (NY)
6. University of Hawaii, Manoa (HI)
6. Boston University (MA)
8. University of California, Berkeley, (CA)
8. Syracuse University (NY)
10. Ithaca College (NY)
10. Pace University (NY)
10. University of Pittsburgh (PA)
13. Michigan State University (MI)
14. San Diego State University (CA)
14. San Francisco State University (CA)
16. San Jose State University (CA)
16. University of Denver (CO)
16. Wheaton College (IL)
16. University of Missouri, Columbia (MO)

16. Wake Forest University (NC)
16. Stanford University (CA)

Source: "Top 100 Degree Producers," *Black Issues in Higher Education*, 17: 48-89, (July 7, 2000).

★1765★
U.S. colleges and universities awarding the most communications master's degrees to Hispanic Americans

Ranking basis/background: Total master's degrees conferred to Hispanic American students in the field of communications during the 1997-98 academic year. **Remarks:** Original source: *Black Issues* analysis of U.S. Department of Education reports of data submitted by institutions. **Number listed:** 18.

1. Florida International University (FL)
2. New York University (NY)
3. Syracuse University (NY)
4. Northwestern University (IL)
4. University of Texas, El Paso (TX)
6. University of California, Berkeley, (CA)
6. University of Denver (CO)
6. American University (DC)
6. St. Mary's University (TX)
10. Columbia University, New York City (NY)
11. University of Florida, (FL)
11. University of Miami (FL)
13. Loyola Marymount University (CA)
13. San Francisco State University (CA)
13. Florida State University (FL)
13. College of New Rochelle (NY)
13. New School for Social Research (NY)
13. University of Texas, Austin (TX)

Source: "Top 100 Degree Producers," *Black Issues in Higher Education*, 17: 48-89, (July 7, 2000).

★1766★
U.S. colleges and universities awarding the most computer and information sciences master's degrees to African Americans

Ranking basis/background: Total master's degrees conferred to African American students in the field of computer and information sciences during the 1997-98 academic year. **Remarks:** Original source: *Black Issues* analysis of U.S. Department of Education reports of data submitted by institutions. **Number listed:** 47.

1. Bowie State University (MD)
2. Clark Atlanta University (GA)
3. American University (DC)
4. North Carolina A&T State University (NC)
5. Colorado Technical University (CO)
5. Syracuse University (NY)
5. Pace University, White Plains (NY)
8. Johns Hopkins University (MD)
9. Alabama A&M University (AL)
9. Troy State University, Montgomery (AL)
9. Strayer College, Alexandria (VA)
12. Golden Gate University, San Francisco (CA)
12. University of Denver (CO)
12. University of St. Thomas (MN)
15. George Washington University (DC)
15. Hawaii Pacific University (HI)
15. Illinois Institute of Technology (IL)
15. Southern University and A&M College (LA)
15. City University of New York, Bernard M. Baruch College (NY)
15. City University of New York, Brooklyn College (NY)

15. Pace University (NY)
15. North Carolina Central University (NC)
15. Drexel University (PA)
Source: "Top 100 Degree Producers," *Black Issues in Higher Education*, 17: 48-89, (July 7, 2000).

★1767★
U.S. colleges and universities awarding the most computer and information sciences master's degrees to Asian Americans

Ranking basis/background: Total master's degrees conferred to Asian American students in the field of computer and information sciences during the 1997-98 academic year. **Remarks:** Original source: *Black Issues* analysis of U.S. Department of Education reports of data submitted by institutions. **Number listed:** 50.
1. Wayne State University (MI)
2. Southeastern University (DC)
3. University of Texas, Dallas (TX)
4. University of Southwestern Louisiana (LA)
5. New Jersey Institute of Technology (NJ)
6. George Mason University (VA)
7. Illinois Institute of Technology (IL)
8. Villanova University (PA)
9. Stanford University (CA)
10. City University of New York, City College (NY)
11. St. Joseph's University (PA)
12. Johns Hopkins University (MD)
13. DePaul University (IL)
13. City University of New York, Bernard M. Baruch College (NY)
15. Golden Gate University, San Francisco (CA)
15. Hawaii Pacific University (HI)
17. University of Southern California (CA)
18. California State University, Long Beach (CA)
18. Georgia State University (GA)
20. New York University (NY)
Source: "Top 100 Degree Producers," *Black Issues in Higher Education*, 17: 48-89, (July 7, 2000).

★1768★
U.S. colleges and universities awarding the most computer and information sciences master's degrees to Hispanic Americans

Ranking basis/background: Total master's degrees conferred to Hispanic American students in the field of computer and information sciences during the 1997-98 academic year. **Remarks:** Original source: *Black Issues* analysis of U.S. Department of Education reports of data submitted by institutions. **Number listed:** 15.
1. Pace University (NY)
2. University of Phoenix, Albuquerque (NM)
3. St. Mary's University (TX)
4. American University (DC)
5. New Jersey Institute of Technology (NJ)
5. Stevens Institute of Technology (NJ)
5. George Mason University (VA)
5. Pace University, White Plains (NY)
9. Regis University (CO)
9. Illinois Institute of Technology (IL)
9. New York University (NY)
9. University of Pittsburgh (PA)
9. Temple University (PA)
9. Southern Methodist University (TX)
9. Strayer College, Alexandria (VA)
Source: "Top 100 Degree Producers," *Black Issues in Higher Education*, 17: 48-89, (July 7, 2000).

★1769★
U.S. colleges and universities awarding the most education master's degrees to African Americans

Ranking basis/background: Total master's degrees conferred to African American students in the field of education during the 1997-98 academic year. **Remarks:** Original source: *Black Issues* analysis of U.S. Department of Education reports of data submitted by institutions. **Number listed:** 50.
1. Cambridge College (MA)
2. Prairie View A&M University (TX)
3. National-Louis University (IL)
4. Nova Southeastern University (FL)
5. Marygrove College (MI)
6. Chicago State University (IL)
7. City University of New York, City College (NY)
8. City University of New York, Brooklyn College (NY)
9. Florida A&M University (FL)
10. Clark Atlanta University (GA)
11. Wayne State University (MI)
12. Long Island University, Brooklyn (NY)
13. Fort Valley State University (GA)
14. Jackson State University (MS)
15. Alabama A&M University (AL)
16. University of South Carolina, Columbia (SC)
17. Bowie State University (MD)
18. Old Dominion University (VA)
19. Norfolk State University (VA)
20. Cheyney University of Pennsylvania (PA)
Source: "Top 100 Degree Producers," *Black Issues in Higher Education*, 17: 48-89, (July 7, 2000).

★1770★
U.S. colleges and universities awarding the most education master's degrees to Asian Americans

Ranking basis/background: Total master's degrees conferred to Asian American students in the field of education during the 1997-98 academic year. **Remarks:** Original source: *Black Issues* analysis of U.S. Department of Education reports of data submitted by institutions. **Number listed:** 57.
1. University of Hawaii, Manoa (HI)
2. Teachers College, Columbia University (NY)
3. California State University, Los Angeles (CA)
4. National University (CA)
4. Harvard University (MA)
6. University of California, Los Angeles (CA)
7. Madonna University (MI)
8. San Francisco State University (CA)
8. City University of New York, City College (NY)
10. San Diego State University (CA)
11. New York University (NY)
12. California State University, Dominguez Hills (CA)
13. University of California, Berkeley (CA)
14. California State University, Long Beach (CA)
14. California State University, Northridge (CA)
14. San Jose State University (CA)
14. Lesley College (MA)
14. City University of New York, Hunter College (NY)
14. George Mason University (VA)
14. Stanford University (CA)
Source: "Top 100 Degree Producers," *Black Issues in Higher Education*, 17: 48-89, (July 7, 2000).

★1771★
U.S. colleges and universities awarding the most education master's degrees to Hispanic Americans

Ranking basis/background: Total master's degrees conferred to Hispanic American students in the field of education during the 1997-98 academic year. **Remarks:** Original source: *Black Issues* analysis of U.S. Department of Education reports of data submitted by institutions. **Number listed:** 52.
1. City University of New York, City College (NY)
2. Northern Arizona University (AZ)
3. Florida International University (FL)
4. Nova Southeastern University (FL)
5. California State University, Los Angeles (CA)
6. University of Texas (TX)
7. University of New Mexico (NM)
7. Texas A&M University, Corpus Christi (TX)
9. National University (CA)
10. San Diego State University (CA)
11. Azusa Pacific University (CA)
12. City University of New York, Lehman College (NY)
13. Sul Ross State University (TX)
13. University of Texas, El Paso (TX)
15. City University of New York, Hunter College (NY)
16. Texas A&M University, Kingsville (TX)
17. National-Louis University (IL)
18. Barry University (FL)
19. California State University, Dominguez Hills (CA)
20. New Mexico State University (NM)
Source: "Top 100 Degree Producers," *Black Issues in Higher Education*, 17: 48-89, (July 7, 2000).

★1772★
U.S. colleges and universities awarding the most education master's degrees to Native Americans

Ranking basis/background: Total master's degrees conferred to Native American students in the field of education during the 1997-98 academic year. **Remarks:** Original source: *Black Issues* analysis of U.S. Department of Education reports of data submitted by institutions. **Number listed:** 55.
1. Northern Arizona University (AZ)
2. Doane College (NE)
3. Northeastern State University (OK)
4. University of New Mexico (NM)
5. Harvard University (MA)
6. Lesley College (MA)
7. Western New Mexico University (NM)
7. Southeastern Oklahoma State University (OK)
7. City University (WA)
7. Gonzaga University (WA)
11. East Central University (OK)
12. University of Central Oklahoma (OK)
12. Heritage College (WA)
14. University of Northern Colorado (CO)
14. University of Oklahoma, Norman (OK)
16. San Diego State University (CA)

17. National University (CA)
17. Michigan State University (MI)
17. Old Dominion University (VA)
17. University of Puget Sound (WA)

Source: "Top 100 Degree Producers," *Black Issues in Higher Education,* 17: 48-89, (July 7, 2000).

★1773★
U.S. colleges and universities awarding the most English language/literature/letters master's degrees to African Americans

Ranking basis/background: Total master's degrees conferred to African American students in the field of English language/literature/letters during the 1997-98 academic year. **Remarks:** Original source: *Black Issues* analysis of U.S. Department of Education reports of data submitted by institutions. **Number listed:** 38.

1. New York University (NY)
2. Chicago State University (IL)
3. Northern Illinois University (IL)
3. Old Dominion University (VA)
5. Jacksonville State University (AL)
5. Howard University (DC)
5. Jackson State University (MS)
5. City University of New York, City College (NY)
9. Columbia University, New York City (NY)
9. Long Island University, Brooklyn (NY)
11. Southern Polytechnic State University (GA)
11. Southern Illinois University, Edwardsville (IL)
11. Iowa State University (IA)
11. Morgan State University (MD)
11. Teachers College, Columbia University (NY)
11. North Carolina State University (NC)
11. Pennsylvania State University, University Park (PA)
11. University of Pittsburgh (PA)
11. Brown University (RI)
11. Winthrop University (SC)

Source: "Top 100 Degree Producers," *Black Issues in Higher Education,* 17: 48-89, (July 7, 2000).

★1774★
U.S. colleges and universities awarding the most English language/literature/letters master's degrees to Asian Americans

Ranking basis/background: Total master's degrees conferred to Asian American students in the field of English language/literature/letters during the 1997-98 academic year. **Remarks:** Original source: *Black Issues* analysis of U.S. Department of Education reports of data submitted by institutions. **Number listed:** 25.

1. San Francisco State University (CA)
2. University of Hawaii, Manoa (HI)
3. University of California, Los Angeles (CA)
4. University of Michigan, Ann Arbor (MI)
5. Columbia University, New York City (NY)
6. School of the Art Institute of Chicago (IL)
7. New York University (NY)
8. Stanford University (CA)
9. University of California, Berkeley (CA)
10. San Diego State University (CA)
11. University of Illinois, Chicago (IL)
12. Mankato State University (MN)
13. California State University, Fullerton, (CA)
14. California State University, Hayward (CA)
15. California State University, Los Angeles (CA)
16. University of California, Irvine (CA)
17. University of California, San Diego (CA)
18. University of California, Santa Cruz (CA)
19. Mills College (CA)
20. University of Iowa (IA)

Source: "Top 100 Degree Producers," *Black Issues in Higher Education,* 17: 48-89, (July 7, 2000).

★1775★
U.S. colleges and universities awarding the most English language/literature/letters master's degrees to Hispanic Americans

Ranking basis/background: Total master's degrees conferred to Hispanic American students in the field of English language/literature/letters during the 1997-98 academic year. **Remarks:** Original source: *Black Issues* analysis of U.S. Department of Education reports of data submitted by institutions. **Number listed:** 20.

1. University of Texas, El Paso (TX)
2. San Diego State University (CA)
3. San Francisco State University (CA)
3. City University of New York, Queens College (NY)
3. New York University (NY)
6. Arizona State University (AZ)
6. Texas A&M International University (TX)
8. California State University, Dominguez Hills (CA)
8. California State University, Los Angeles (CA)
8. University of Colorado, Boulder (CO)
8. Colorado State University (CO)
8. University of Texas, Austin (TX)
13. California State University, Sacramento (CA)
13. University of California, Los Angeles (CA)
13. University of Miami (FL)
13. University of Iowa (IA)
13. University of New Mexico (NM)
13. Our Lady of the Lake University, San Antonio (TX)
13. University of Texas, Pan American (TX)
13. Southern Methodist University (TX)

Source: "Top 100 Degree Producers," *Black Issues in Higher Education,* 17: 48-89, (July 7, 2000).

★1776★
U.S. colleges and universities awarding the most English language/literature/letters master's degrees to Native Americans

Ranking basis/background: Total master's degrees conferred to Native American students in the field of English language/literature/letters during the 1997-98 academic year. **Remarks:** Original source: *Black Issues* analysis of U.S. Department of Education reports of data submitted by institutions. **Number listed:** 1.

1. Oklahoma State University (OK)

Source: "Top 100 Degree Producers," *Black Issues in Higher Education,* 17: 48-89, (July 7, 2000).

★1777★
U.S. colleges and universities awarding the most health professions and related sciences master's degrees to African Americans

Ranking basis/background: Total master's degrees conferred to African American students in the field of health professions and related sciences during the 1997-98 academic year. **Remarks:** Original source: *Black Issues* analysis of U.S. Department of Education reports of data submitted by institutions. **Number listed:** 51.

1. Central Michigan University (MI)
2. South Carolina State University (SC)
3. Emory University (GA)
4. Florida International University (FL)
5. Columbia University, New York City (NY)
5. City University of New York, Hunter College (NY)
7. University of Alabama, Birmingham (AL)
8. Governors State University (IL)
9. Long Island University, Brooklyn (NY)
10. Barry University (FL)
11. University of North Carolina, Chapel Hill (NC)
12. Southern University and A&M College (LA)
12. Tulane University (LA)
14. George Washington University (DC)
14. Johns Hopkins University (MD)
14. New York University (NY)
14. University of Phoenix (MI)
18. University of South Carolina, Columbia (SC)
19. University of Pittsburgh (PA)
20. University of Michigan, Ann Arbor (MI)
20. Webster University (MO)

Source: "Top 100 Degree Producers," *Black Issues in Higher Education,* 17: 48-89, (July 7, 2000).

★1778★
U.S. colleges and universities awarding the most health professions and related sciences master's degrees to Asian Americans

Ranking basis/background: Total master's degrees conferred to Asian American students in the field of health professions and related sciences during the 1997-98 academic year. **Remarks:** Original source: *Black Issues* analysis of U.S. Department of Education reports of data submitted by institutions. **Number listed:** 56.

1. South Baylo University (CA)
2. University of California, Los Angeles (CA)
3. Johns Hopkins University (MD)
4. Loma Linda University (CA)
5. University of Hawaii, Manoa (HI)
6. Boston University (MA)
7. University of Southern California (CA)
8. Emory University (GA)
9. University of Michigan, Ann Arbor (MI)
10. University of California, Berkeley (CA)
10. Columbia University, New York City (NY)
12. Yale University (CT)
13. Harvard University (MA)
13. University of Texas Health Science Center (TX)
15. University of California, San Francisco (CA)
15. New York University (NY)
17. California State University, Long Beach (CA)
17. George Washington University (DC)
19. University of Washington (WA)

20. San Diego State University (CA)

Source: "Top 100 Degree Producers," *Black Issues in Higher Education*, 17: 48-89, (July 7, 2000).

★1779★
U.S. colleges and universities awarding the most health professions and related sciences master's degrees to Hispanic Americans

Ranking basis/background: Total master's degrees conferred to Hispanic American students in the field of health professions and related sciences during the 1997-98 academic year. **Remarks:** Original source: *Black Issues* analysis of U.S. Department of Education reports of data submitted by institutions. **Number listed:** 56.

1. Nova Southeastern University (FL)
2. San Diego State University (CA)
3. University of South Florida (FL)
4. University of California, Los Angeles (CA)
4. Loma Linda University (CA)
4. University of Miami (FL)
4. University of Texas Health Science Center (TX)
8. Florida International University (FL)
8. New York University (NY)
10. Tulane University (LA)
11. New Mexico Highlands University (NM)
12. Texas Woman's University (TX)
13. Barry University (FL)
13. University of Texas, El Paso (TX)
15. Columbia University, New York City (NY)
16. Johns Hopkins University (MD)
17. University of California, San Francisco (CA)
17. University of Nebraska Medical Center (NE)
19. University of Illinois, Chicago (IL)
19. Texas A&M University, Corpus Christi (TX)

Source: "Top 100 Degree Producers," *Black Issues in Higher Education*, 17: 48-89, (July 7, 2000).

★1780★
U.S. colleges and universities awarding the most health professions and related sciences master's degrees to Native Americans

Ranking basis/background: Total master's degrees conferred to Native American students in the field of health professions and related sciences during the 1997-98 academic year. **Remarks:** Original source: *Black Issues* analysis of U.S. Department of Education reports of data submitted by institutions. **Number listed:** 14.

1. University of Oklahoma Health Sciences Center (OK)
2. University of Washington (WA)
3. University of Arizona (AZ)
3. University of Nebraska Medical Center (NE)
3. New Mexico Highlands University (NM)
6. University of California, Los Angeles (CA)
6. Howard University (DC)
6. University of Minnesota, Twin Cities (MN)
6. Temple University (PA)
10. University of California, Berkeley (CA)
10. University of Hawaii, Manoa (HI)
10. Boston University (MA)
10. University of Tulsa (OK)
10. Texas Woman's University (TX)

Source: "Top 100 Degree Producers," *Black Issues in Higher Education*, 17: 48-89, (July 7, 2000).

★1781★
U.S. colleges and universities awarding the most law and legal studies master's degrees to African Americans

Ranking basis/background: Total master's degrees conferred to African American students in the field of law and legal studies during the 1997-98 academic year. **Remarks:** Original source: *Black Issues* analysis of U.S. Department of Education reports of data submitted by institutions. **Number listed:** 13.

1. University of Baltimore (MD)
2. Georgetown University (DC)
3. Temple University (PA)
4. George Washington University (DC)
4. Howard University (DC)
6. Webster University (MO)
7. Loyola University, Chicago (IL)
7. New York University (NY)
9. University of Florida (FL)
9. Boston University (MA)
9. Case Western Reserve University (OH)
9. Marymount University (VA)
9. Widener University (DE)

Source: "Top 100 Degree Producers," *Black Issues in Higher Education*, 17: 48-89, (July 7, 2000).

★1782★
U.S. colleges and universities awarding the most law and legal studies master's degrees to Asian Americans

Ranking basis/background: Total master's degrees conferred to Asian American students in the field of law and legal studies during the 1997-98 academic year. **Remarks:** Original source: *Black Issues* analysis of U.S. Department of Education reports of data submitted by institutions. **Number listed:** 10.

1. New York University (NY)
2. Georgetown University (DC)
3. University of the Pacific (CA)
4. Golden Gate University, San Francisco (CA)
5. University of San Diego (CA)
5. George Washington University (DC)
5. Dickinson School of Law (IL)
8. Loyola University, Chicago, (IL)
8. Touro College (NY)
8. Southern Methodist University (TX)

Source: "Top 100 Degree Producers," *Black Issues in Higher Education*, 17: 48-89, (July 7, 2000).

★1783★
U.S. colleges and universities awarding the most law and legal studies master's degrees to Hispanic Americans

Ranking basis/background: Total master's degrees conferred to Hispanic American students in the field of law and legal studies during the 1997-98 academic year. **Remarks:** Original source: *Black Issues* analysis of U.S. Department of Education reports of data submitted by institutions. **Number listed:** 8.

1. Georgetown University (DC)
2. University of Miami (FL)
3. New York University (NY)
4. University of San Diego (CA)
4. Tulane University (LA)
6. John Marshall Law School (IL)
7. University of the Pacific (CA)
7. American University (DC)

Source: "Top 100 Degree Producers," *Black Issues in Higher Education*, 17: 48-89, (July 7, 2000).

★1784★
U.S. colleges and universities awarding the most law and legal studies master's degrees to Native Americans

Ranking basis/background: Total master's degrees conferred to Native American students in the field of law and legal studies during the 1997-98 academic year. **Remarks:** Original source: *Black Issues* analysis of U.S. Department of Education reports of data submitted by institutions. **Number listed:** 1.

1. Georgetown University (DC)

Source: "Top 100 Degree Producers," *Black Issues in Higher Education*, 17: 48-89, (July 7, 2000).

★1785★
U.S. colleges and universities awarding the most master's degrees to African Americans

Ranking basis/background: Total master's degrees conferred to African American students in all disciplines combined during the 1997-98 academic year. **Remarks:** Original source: *Black Issues* analysis of U.S. Department of Education reports of data submitted by institutions. **Number listed:** 50.

1. Webster University (MO)
2. Central Michigan University (MI)
3. Howard University (DC)
4. Clark Atlanta University (GA)
5. Cambridge College (MA)
6. New York University (NY)
7. Wayne State University (MI)
8. Bowie State University (MD)
9. Nova Southeastern University (FL)
10. Prairie View A&M University (TX)
11. National-Louis University (IL)
12. Jackson State University (MS)
13. Long Island University, Brooklyn (NY)
14. Chicago State University (IL)
14. Southern University and A&M College (LA)
16. Florida A&M University (FL)
17. City University of New York, Brooklyn College (NY)
18. City University of New York, City College (NY)
19. University of Michigan, Ann Arbor (MI)
19. Temple University (PA)

Source: "Top 100 Degree Producers," *Black Issues in Higher Education*, 17: 48-89, (July 7, 2000).

★1786★
U.S. colleges and universities awarding the most master's degrees to Asian Americans

Ranking basis/background: Total master's degrees conferred to Asian American students in all disciplines combined during the 1997-98 academic year. **Remarks:** Original source: *Black Issues* analysis of U.S. Department of Education reports of data submitted by institutions. **Number listed:** 50.

1. University of Hawaii, Manoa (HI)
2. University of Southern California (CA)
3. South Baylo University (CA)
4. University of California, Los Angeles (CA)
5. Wayne State University (MI)

6. Stanford University (CA)
7. New York University (NY)
8. University of California, Berkeley (CA)
9. Columbia University, New York City (NY)
10. Harvard University (MA)
11. University of Michigan, Ann Arbor (MI)
12. San Jose State University (CA)
13. San Francisco State University (CA)
14. Northwestern University (IL)
15. George Washington University (DC)
15. Johns Hopkins University (MD)
17. San Diego State University (CA)
18. Boston University (MS)
19. Golden Gate University, San Francisco (CA)
20. Santa Clara University (CA)

Source: "Top 100 Degree Producers," *Black Issues in Higher Education*, 17: 48-89, (July 7, 2000).

★1787★
U.S. colleges and universities awarding the most master's degrees to Hispanic Americans

Ranking basis/background: Total master's degrees conferred to Hispanic American students in all disciplines combined during the 1997-98 academic year. Remarks: Original source: *Black Issues* analysis of U.S. Department of Education reports of data submitted by institutions. Number listed: 50.
1. Florida International University (FL)
2. Nova Southeastern University (FL)
3. San Diego State University (CA)
4. New York University (NY)
5. University of Texas, Austin (TX)
6. University of Miami (FL)
7. City University of New York, City College (NY)
8. Webster University (MO)
9. Northern Arizona University (AZ)
10. California State University, Los Angeles (CA)
11. National University (CA)
11. University of Texas, El Paso (TX)
13. University of New Mexico (NM)
14. University of Texas, Pan American (TX)
15. University of Southern California (CA)
16. University of California, Los Angeles (CA)
16. City University of New York, Hunter College (NY)
18. Texas A&M University, Corpus Christi (TX)
19. Barry University (FL)
20. Arizona State University (AZ)

Source: "Top 100 Degree Producers," *Black Issues in Higher Education*, 17: 48-89, (July 7, 2000).

★1788★
U.S. colleges and universities awarding the most master's degrees to minorities

Ranking basis/background: Total master's degrees conferred to minority students in all disciplines combined during the 1997-98 academic year. Remarks: Original source: *Black Issues* analysis of U.S. Department of Education reports of data submitted by institutions. Number listed: 100.
1. Webster University (MO)
2. New York University (NY)
3. University of Southern California (CA)
4. Wayne State University (MI)
5. Florida International University (FL)
6. University of California, Los Angeles, (CA)
7. University of Hawaii (HI)
8. Nova Southeastern University (FL)
9. Central Michigan University (MI)
10. Columbia University, New York City (NY)
11. University of Michigan, Ann Arbor (MI)
12. Harvard University (MA)
13. City University of New York, City College (NY)
14. San Diego State University (CA)
15. Stanford University (CA)
16. National University (CA)
17. University of California, Berkeley (CA)
18. South Baylo University (CA)
19. University of Texas, Austin, (TX)
20. George Washington University (DC)

Source: "Top 100 Degree Producers," *Black Issues in Higher Education*, 17: 48-89, (July 7, 2000).

★1789★
U.S. colleges and universities awarding the most master's degrees to Native Americans

Ranking basis/background: Total master's degrees conferred to Native American students in all disciplines combined during the 1997-98 academic year. Remarks: Original source: *Black Issues* analysis of U.S. Department of Education reports of data submitted by institutions. Number listed: 57.
1. Northern Arizona University (AZ)
2. University of Oklahoma, Norman (OK)
3. Doane College (NE)
4. Northeastern State University (OK)
5. University of Washington (WA)
6. Arizona State University (AZ)
7. University of New Mexico (NM)
7. Oklahoma State University (OK)
9. University of Arizona (AZ)
9. Webster University (MO)
9. Southeastern Oklahoma State University (OK)
12. Harvard University (MA)
13. University of California, Berkeley (CA)
13. University of Oklahoma Health Sciences Center (OK)
15. East Central University (OK)
16. University of Kansas (KS)
16. Central Michigan University (MI)
16. University of Utah (UT)
19. Lesley College (MS)
19. Oklahoma City University (OK)
19. City University (WA)

Source: "Top 100 Degree Producers," *Black Issues in Higher Education*, 17: 48-89, (July 7, 2000).

★1790★
U.S. colleges and universities awarding the most mathematics master's degrees to African Americans

Ranking basis/background: Total master's degrees conferred to African American students in the field of mathematics during the 1997-98 academic year. Remarks: Original source: *Black Issues* analysis of U.S. Department of Education reports of data submitted by institutions. Number listed: 14.
1. Clark Atlanta University (GA)
2. North Carolina A&T State University (NC)
2. North Carolina State University (NC)
4. Southern University and A&M College (LA)
5. Chicago State University (IL)
5. Tennessee State University (TN)
7. Auburn University (AL)
7. Fayetteville State University (NC)
7. Virginia State University (VA)
10. University of Arkansas, Little Rock (AK)
10. University of Central Florida (FL)
10. Johns Hopkins University (MD)
10. University of Maryland, College Park (MD)
10. St. John's University (NY)

Source: "Top 100 Degree Producers," *Black Issues in Higher Education*, 17: 48-89, (July 7, 2000).

★1791★
U.S. colleges and universities awarding the most mathematics master's degrees to Asian Americans

Ranking basis/background: Total master's degrees conferred to Asian American students in the field of mathematics during the 1997-98 academic year. Remarks: Original source: *Black Issues* analysis of U.S. Department of Education reports of data submitted by institutions. Number listed: 27.
1. Eastern Michigan University (MI)
2. University of California, Los Angeles (CA)
3. San Diego State University (CA)
4. Columbia University (NY)
5. California State University, Hayward (CA)
5. Stanford University (CA)
7. University of California, Berkeley (CA)
7. Claremont Graduate University (CA)
7. University of Chicago (IL)
7. University of Southwestern Louisiana (LA)
7. Southern Methodist University (TX)

Source: "Top 100 Degree Producers," *Black Issues in Higher Education*, 17: 48-89, (July 7, 2000).

★1792★
U.S. colleges and universities awarding the most mathematics master's degrees to Hispanic Americans

Ranking basis/background: Total master's degrees conferred to Hispanic American students in the field of mathematics during the 1997-98 academic year. Remarks: Original source: *Black Issues* analysis of U.S. Department of Education reports of data submitted by institutions. Number listed: 5.
1. California State University, Los Angeles (CA)
1. Claremont Graduate University (CA)
1. San Diego State University (CA)
1. State University of New York, Stony Brook (NY)
1. Angelo State University (TX)

Source: "Top 100 Degree Producers," *Black Issues in Higher Education*, 17: 48-89, (July 7, 2000).

★1793★
U.S. colleges and universities awarding the most physical sciences master's degrees to African Americans

Ranking basis/background: Total master's degrees conferred to African American students in the field of physical sciences during the 1997-98 academic year. Remarks: Original source: *Black Issues* analysis of U.S. Department of Education reports of data submitted by institutions. Number listed: 14.
1. Clark Atlanta University (GA)
2. Johns Hopkins University (MD)
2. University of South Carolina, Columbia (SC)

4. Howard University (DC)
   5. Georgia Institute of Technology (GA)
   6. Alabama A&M University (AL)
   6. Washington University (MO)
   6. Fisk University (TN)
   6. Hampton University (VA)
   10. Delaware State University (DE)
   10. George Washington University (DC)
   10. Florida A&M State University (FL)
   10. Georgia State University (GA)
   10. University of North Carolina, Chapel Hill (NC)

Source: "Top 100 Degree Producers," *Black Issues in Higher Education*, 17: 48-89, (July 7, 2000).

★1794★
U.S. colleges and universities awarding the most physical sciences master's degrees to Asian Americans

Ranking basis/background: Total master's degrees conferred to Asian American students in the field of physical sciences during the 1997-98 academic year. **Remarks:** Original source: *Black Issues* analysis of U.S. Department of Education reports of data submitted by institutions. **Number listed:** 33.

   1. University of California, San Diego (CA)
   2. University of Hawaii, Manoa (HI)
   3. University of Illinois, Chicago (IL)
   4. University of California, Berkeley (CA)
   4. University of California, Davis (CA)
   4. University of California, Santa Barbara (CA)
   4. San Jose State University (CA)
   4. George Washington University (DC)
   4. Stanford University (CA)
   10. California State University, Los Angeles (CA)
   10. San Diego State University (CA)
   10. Florida Atlantic University (FL)
   10. University of Illinois, Urbana-Champaign (IL)
   10. Johns Hopkins University (MD)
   10. University of Michigan, Ann Arbor (MI)
   10. Wayne State University (MI)
   10. Rutgers University, New Brunswick (NJ)
   10. Long Island University, Brooklyn (NY)
   10. State University of New York, Stony Brook (NY)
   10. Villanova University (PA)
   10. University of Washington (WA)

Source: "Top 100 Degree Producers," *Black Issues in Higher Education*, 17: 48-89, (July 7, 2000).

★1795★
U.S. colleges and universities awarding the most physical sciences master's degrees to Hispanic Americans

Ranking basis/background: Total master's degrees conferred to Hispanic American students in the field of physical sciences during the 1997-98 academic year. **Remarks:** Original source: *Black Issues* analysis of U.S. Department of Education reports of data submitted by institutions. **Number listed:** 4.

   1. George Washington University (DC)
   1. Florida International University (FL)
   3. San Diego State University (CA)
   3. Florida Atlantic University (FL)

Source: "Top 100 Degree Producers," *Black Issues in Higher Education*, 17: 48-89, (July 7, 2000).

★1796★
U.S. colleges and universities awarding the most physical sciences master's degrees to Native Americans

Ranking basis/background: Total master's degrees conferred to Native American students in the field of physical sciences during the 1997-98 academic year. **Remarks:** Original source: *Black Issues* analysis of U.S. Department of Education reports of data submitted by institutions. **Number listed:** 1.

   1. Northern Arizona University (AZ)

Source: "Top 100 Degree Producers," *Black Issues in Higher Education*, 17: 48-89, (July 7, 2000).

★1797★
U.S. colleges and universities awarding the most psychology master's degrees to African Americans

Ranking basis/background: Total master's degrees conferred to African American students in the field of psychology during the 1997-98 academic year. **Remarks:** Original source: *Black Issues* analysis of U.S. Department of Education reports of data submitted by institutions. **Number listed:** 60.

   1. Webster University (MO)
   2. Bowie State University (MD)
   3. National University (CA)
   4. California State University, Dominguez Hills (CA)
   5. Teachers College, Columbia University (NY)
   6. Amber University (TX)
   7. Troy State University (AL)
   8. Governors State University (IL)
   9. Southern University and A&M College (LA)
   10. Pepperdine University (CA)
   10. Johns Hopkins University (MD)
   10. Long Island University, Brooklyn (NY)
   13. Troy State University, Montgomery (AL)
   13. Towson State University (MD)
   15. Martin University (IN)
   16. University of Baltimore (MD)
   16. City University of New York, John Jay College of Criminal Justice (NY)
   18. Alabama A&M University (AL)
   18. University of Detroit Mercy (MI)
   18. Cameron University (OK)
   18. Marymount University (VA)

Source: "Top 100 Degree Producers," *Black Issues in Higher Education*, 17: 48-89, (July 7, 2000).

★1798★
U.S. colleges and universities awarding the most psychology master's degrees to Asian Americans

Ranking basis/background: Total master's degrees conferred to Asian American students in the field of psychology during the 1997-98 academic year. **Remarks:** Original source: *Black Issues* analysis of U.S. Department of Education reports of data submitted by institutions. **Number listed:** 35.

   1. Teachers College, Columbia University (NY)
   2. Pepperdine University (CA)
   3. Chaminade University, Honolulu (HI)
   4. National University (CA)
   5. Webster University (MO)
   6. John F. Kennedy University (CA)
   7. California School of Professional Psychology (CA)
   7. California State University, Dominguez Hills (CA)
   7. Boston College (MA)
   10. Azusa Pacific University (CA)
   10. University of Hawaii, Manoa (HI)
   10. Long Island University, Brooklyn (NY)
   10. New York University (NY)
   14. California State University, Long Beach (CA)
   14. University of California, Los Angeles (CA)
   14. Golden Gate University, San Francisco (CA)
   14. Notre Dame College (CA)
   14. Boston University (MA)
   14. St. John's University (NY)
   14. Lewis and Clark College (OR)
   14. City University (WA)
   14. Stanford University (CA)

Source: "Top 100 Degree Producers," *Black Issues in Higher Education*, 17: 48-89, (July 7, 2000).

★1799★
U.S. colleges and universities awarding the most psychology master's degrees to Hispanic Americans

Ranking basis/background: Total master's degrees conferred to Hispanic American students in the field of psychology during the 1997-98 academic year. **Remarks:** Original source: *Black Issues* analysis of U.S. Department of Education reports of data submitted by institutions. **Number listed:** 55.

   1. Webster University (MO)
   2. Caribbean Center for Advanced Studies (FL)
   3. National University (CA)
   4. Pepperdine University (CA)
   5. Nova Southeastern University (FL)
   6. Long Island University, Brooklyn (NY)
   7. St. Thomas University (FL)
   8. Texas A&M University, Kingsville (TX)
   9. University of Miami (FL)
   10. City University of New York, John Jay College of Criminal Justice (NY)
   11. City University of New York, City College (NY)
   11. St. Mary's University (TX)
   13. Barry University (FL)
   14. California School of Professional Psychology (CA)
   14. California State University, Los Angeles (CA)
   14. Adams State College (CO)
   14. Teachers College, Columbia University (NY)
   18. California State University, Fullerton (CA)
   18. Governors State University (IL)
   18. Fairleigh Dickinson University (NJ)
   18. Texas A&M International University (TX)
   18. Antioch University, Los Angeles (CA)

Source: "Top 100 Degree Producers," *Black Issues in Higher Education*, 17: 48-89, (July 7, 2000).

DEGREES (ACADEMIC)—MINORITY GROUPS

★1800★
U.S. colleges and universities awarding the most psychology master's degrees to Native Americans

Ranking basis/background: Total master's degrees conferred to Native American students in the field of psychology during the 1997-98 academic year. **Remarks:** Original source: *Black Issues* analysis of U.S. Department of Education reports of data submitted by institutions. **Number listed:** 7.
1. Webster University (MO)
2. Southeastern Oklahoma State University (OK)
3. Lewis and Clark College (OR)
4. Pepperdine University (CA)
4. San Francisco State University (CA)
4. City University of New York, John Jay College of Criminal Justice (NY)
4. Utah State University (UT)

Source: "Top 100 Degree Producers," *Black Issues in Higher Education*, 17: 48-89, (July 7, 2000).

★1801★
U.S. colleges and universities awarding the most social sciences and history master's degrees to African Americans

Ranking basis/background: Total master's degrees conferred to African American students in the field of social sciences and history during the 1997-98 academic year. **Remarks:** Original source: *Black Issues* analysis of U.S. Department of Education reports of data submitted by institutions. **Number listed:** 49.
1. University of Oklahoma, Norman (OK)
2. Florida A&M University (FL)
3. City University of New York, Brooklyn College (NY)
4. New School for Social Research (NY)
5. American University (DC)
5. Prairie View A&M University (TX)
5. Jackson State University (MS)
8. Howard University (DC)
9. University of Chicago (IL)
10. Columbia University, New York City (NY)
10. University of Memphis (TN)
12. Columbus State University (GA)
12. Southern University and A&M College (LA)
12. City University of New York, City College (NY)
15. City University of New York, Queens College (NY)
15. St. John's University (NY)
15. Ohio University (OH)
15. Stanford University (CA)
19. Florida State University (FL)
19. University of Michigan, Ann Arbor (MI)

Source: "Top 100 Degree Producers," *Black Issues in Higher Education*, 17: 48-89, (July 7, 2000).

★1802★
U.S. colleges and universities awarding the most social sciences and history master's degrees to Asian Americans

Ranking basis/background: Total master's degrees conferred to Asian American students in the field of social sciences and history during the 1997-98 academic year. **Remarks:** Original source: *Black Issues* analysis of U.S. Department of Education reports of data submitted by institutions. **Number listed:** 60.
1. Columbia University, New York City (NY)
2. University of California, Berkeley (CA)
2. University of Hawaii, Manoa (HI)
4. George Washington University (DC)
4. Stanford University (CA)
6. University of California, San Diego (CA)
7. Johns Hopkins University (MD)
8. University of California, Los Angeles (CA)
8. George Mason University (VA)
10. University of Southern California (CA)
11. Tufts University (MA)
12. American University (DC)
13. Yale University (CT)
13. University of Chicago (IL)
13. Boston University (MA)
13. University of Oklahoma, Norman (OK)
17. University of California, Irvine (CA)
18. New School for Social Research (NY)
18. New York University (NY)
20. San Francisco State University (CA)

Source: "Top 100 Degree Producers," *Black Issues in Higher Education*, 17: 48-89, (July 7, 2000).

★1803★
U.S. colleges and universities awarding the most social sciences and history master's degrees to Hispanic Americans

Ranking basis/background: Total master's degrees conferred to Hispanic American students in the field of social sciences and history during the 1997-98 academic year. **Remarks:** Original source: *Black Issues* analysis of U.S. Department of Education reports of data submitted by institutions. **Number listed:** 51.
1. University of Oklahoma, Norman (OK)
1. St. Mary's University (TX)
3. American University (DC)
4. Columbia University, New York City (NY)
5. George Mason University (VA)
6. Tufts University (MA)
6. Trinity University (TX)
8. University of California, Berkeley (CA)
8. University of California, San Diego (CA)
8. New School for Social Research (NY)
11. University of California, Santa Barbara (CA)
11. Texas A&M International University (TX)
13. Florida International University (FL)
13. George Washington University (DC)
13. Johns Hopkins University (MD)
13. Stanford University (CA)
17. Claremont Graduate University (CA)
17. Georgetown University (DC)
17. New York University (NY)
17. University of Houston, University Park (TX)

Source: "Top 100 Degree Producers," *Black Issues in Higher Education*, 17: 48-89, (July 7, 2000).

★1804★
U.S. colleges and universities awarding the most social sciences and history master's degrees to Native Americans

Ranking basis/background: Total master's degrees conferred to Native American students in the field of social sciences and history during the 1997-98 academic year. **Remarks:** Original source: *Black Issues* analysis of U.S. Department of Education reports of data submitted by institutions. **Number listed:** 2.
1. University of Oklahoma, Norman (OK)
2. Bellevue University (NE)

Source: "Top 100 Degree Producers," *Black Issues in Higher Education*, 17: 48-89, (July 7, 2000).

★1805★
U.S. institutions awarding the most associate degrees to African Americans in agribusiness and production, 1998

Ranking basis/background: Institutions conferring the most associate degrees in agribusiness and production to African American students during the 1996-97 academic year. **Number listed:** 4.
1. Ohio State University A&T Institute (OH)
2. Trenholm State Technical College (AL)
3. Mississippi Delta Community College (MS)
3. Virginia Tech (VA)

Source: "Top 100 Agriculture Degree Producers, 1998," *Black Issues in Higher Education*, 17: 27-29, (June 8, 2000).

★1806★
U.S. institutions awarding the most associate degrees to African Americans in ethnic/cultural studies, 1997-98

Ranking basis/background: Institutions awarding the most ethnic/cultural associate degrees to African American students in 1997-98. **Remarks:** Original source: *Black Issues* analysis of U.S. Department of Education data. **Number listed:** 2.
1. San Diego City College (CA)
1. San Diego Mesa College (CA)

Source: Hamilton, Kendra, "A New Spectrum," *Black Issues in Higher Education*, 17: 24-27, (May 25, 2000).

★1807★
U.S. institutions awarding the most associate degrees to Hispanic Americans in agricultural sciences, 1998

Ranking basis/background: Institutions conferring the most associate degrees in agricultural sciences to Hispanic American students during the 1996-97 academic year. **Number listed:** 2.
1. Texas State Technical College, Harlingen (TX)
2. Santa Fe Community College, Gainesville (FL)

Source: "Top 100 Agriculture Degree Producers, 1998," *Black Issues in Higher Education*, 17: 27-29, (June 8, 2000).

★1808★
U.S. institutions awarding the most associate degrees to minorities in agribusiness and production, 1998

Ranking basis/background: Institutions conferring the most associate degrees in agribusiness and production to minority students during the 1996-97 academic year. **Number listed:** 10.
1. Ohio University A&T Institute (OH)
2. Trenholm State Technical College (AL)
3. Bakersfield College (CA)
4. Butte College (CA)
4. Moorpark College (CA)
4. Kirkwood Community College (IA)
4. University of Massachusetts, Amherst (MA)
4. Mississippi Delta Community College (MS)
4. Rogers University, Claremore (OK)
4. Virginia Tech (VA)

Source: "Top 100 Agriculture Degree Producers, 1998," *Black Issues in Higher Education*, 17: 27-29, (June 8, 2000).

★1809★
U.S. institutions awarding the most associate degrees to minorities in agricultural sciences, 1998

Ranking basis/background: Institutions conferring the most associate degrees in agricultural sciences to minority students during the 1996-97 academic year. **Number listed:** 6.
1. Eastern Oklahoma State College (OK)
2. Texas State Technical College, Harlingen (TX)
3. State University of New York, College of A&T, Cobleskill (NY)
3. State University of New York, College of A&T, Morrisville (NY)
5. Santa Fe Community College, Gainesville (FL)
5. Connors State College (OK)

Source: "Top 100 Agriculture Degree Producers, 1998," *Black Issues in Higher Education*, 17: 27-29, (June 8, 2000).

★1810★
U.S. institutions awarding the most associate degrees to minorities in ethnic/cultural studies, 1997-98

Ranking basis/background: Institutions awarding the most ethnic/cultural associate degrees to minority students in 1997-98. **Remarks:** Original source: *Black Issues* analysis of U.S. Department of Education data. **Number listed:** 5.
1. Dine College (AZ)
2. Oglala Lakota College (SD)
3. San Diego Mesa College (CA)
4. San Diego City College (CA)
4. Bay Mills Community College (MI)

Source: Hamilton, Kendra, "A New Spectrum," *Black Issues in Higher Education*, 17: 24-27, (May 25, 2000).

★1811★
U.S. institutions awarding the most associate degrees to Native Americans in agribusiness and production, 1998

Ranking basis/background: Institutions conferring the most associate degrees in agribusiness and production to Native American students during the 1996-97 academic year. **Number listed:** 1.
1. Rogers University, Claremore (OK)

Source: "Top 100 Agriculture Degree Producers, 1998," *Black Issues in Higher Education*, 17: 27-29, (June 8, 2000).

★1812★
U.S. institutions awarding the most associate degrees to Native Americans in agricultural sciences, 1998

Ranking basis/background: Institutions conferring the most associate degrees in agricultural sciences to Native American students during the 1996-97 academic year. **Number listed:** 1.
1. Eastern Oklahoma State College (OK)

Source: "Top 100 Agriculture Degree Producers, 1998," *Black Issues in Higher Education*, 17: 27-29, (June 8, 2000).

★1813★
U.S. institutions awarding the most baccalaureate degrees to African Americans in agribusiness and production, 1998

Ranking basis/background: Institutions conferring the most baccalaureate degrees in agribusiness and production to African American students during the 1996-97 academic year. **Number listed:** 20.
1. Alcorn State University (MS)
2. Florida A&M State University (FL)
3. Michigan State University (MI)
4. Southern University and A&M College (LA)
5. Ohio State University (OH)
6. Cornell University (NY)
7. Fort Valley State University (GA)
8. University of Florida (FL)
9. Delaware State University (DE)
10. University of Maryland, College Park (MD)
10. University of Maryland, Eastern Shore (MD)
10. South Carolina State University (SC)

Source: "Top 100 Agriculture Degree Producers, 1998," *Black Issues in Higher Education*, 17: 27-29, (June 8, 2000).

★1814★
U.S. institutions awarding the most baccalaureate degrees to African Americans in agricultural sciences, 1998

Ranking basis/background: Institutions conferring the most baccalaureate degrees in agricultural sciences to African American students during the 1996-97 academic year. **Number listed:** 29.
1. Alabama A&M University (AL)
2. Tuskegee University (AL)
3. University of Arkansas, Pine Bluff (AR)
4. Tennessee State University (TN)
5. Alcorn State University (MS)
5. North Carolina A&T State University (NC)
5. Prairie View A&M University (TX)
8. Southern University and A&M College (LA)
9. Florida A&M State University (FL)
10. University of Florida (FL)

Source: "Top 100 Agriculture Degree Producers, 1998," *Black Issues in Higher Education*, 17: 27-29, (June 8, 2000).

★1815★
U.S. institutions awarding the most baccalaureate degrees to Asian Americans in agribusiness and production, 1998

Ranking basis/background: Institutions conferring the most baccalaureate degrees in agribusiness and production to Asian American students during the 1996-97 academic year. **Number listed:** 7.
1. University of California, Davis (CA)
2. Cornell University (NY)
3. California Polytechnic State University (CA)
4. Michigan State University (MI)
5. University of Florida (FL)
6. Oregon State University (OR)
7. California State University, Chico (CA)

Source: "Top 100 Agriculture Degree Producers, 1998," *Black Issues in Higher Education*, 17: 27-29, (June 8, 2000).

★1816★
U.S. institutions awarding the most baccalaureate degrees to Asian Americans in agricultural sciences, 1998

Ranking basis/background: Institutions conferring the most baccalaureate degrees in agricultural sciences to Asian American students during the 1996-97 academic year. **Number listed:** 21.
1. University of California, Davis (CA)
2. University of Florida (FL)
3. Cornell University (NY)
4. California State University, Fresno (CA)
4. University of Hawaii, Hilo (HI)
4. University of Minnesota, Twin Cities (MN)
7. California State Polytechnic University (CA)
7. University of Illinois, Urbana-Champaign (IL)
9. California Polytechnic State University (CA)
10. University of Hawaii, Manoa (HI)

Source: "Top 100 Agriculture Degree Producers, 1998," *Black Issues in Higher Education*, 17: 27-29, (June 8, 2000).

★1817★
U.S. institutions awarding the most baccalaureate degrees to Hispanic Americans in agribusiness and production, 1998

Ranking basis/background: Institutions conferring the most baccalaureate degrees in agribusiness and production to Hispanic American students during the 1996-97 academic year. **Number listed:** 8.
1. California Polytechnic State University (CA)
2. Texas A&M University (TX)
3. University of California, Davis (CA)
4. California State University, Fresno (CA)
4. Cornell University (NY)
6. University of Florida (FL)
6. Texas A&M University, Kingsville (TX)
6. Arizona State University, East (AZ)

Source: "Top 100 Agriculture Degree Producers, 1998," *Black Issues in Higher Education*, 17: 27-29, (June 8, 2000).

★1818★
U.S. institutions awarding the most baccalaureate degrees to Hispanic Americans in agricultural sciences, 1998

Ranking basis/background: Institutions conferring the most baccalaureate degrees in agricultural sciences to Hispanic American students during the 1996-97 academic year. **Number listed:** 17.
1. University of Florida (FL)
2. Texas A&M University (TX)
3. California Polytechnic State University (CA)
4. California State Polytechnic University (CA)
5. University of California, Davis (CA)
6. University of Arizona (AZ)
6. Iowa State University (IA)
6. Louisiana State University and A&M College (LA)
6. New Mexico State University (NM)
10. Colorado State University (CO)

Source: "Top 100 Agriculture Degree Producers, 1998," *Black Issues in Higher Education*, 17: 27-29, (June 8, 2000).

DEGREES (ACADEMIC)—MINORITY GROUPS

★1819★
U.S. institutions awarding the most baccalaureate degrees to minorities in agribusiness and production, 1998

Ranking basis/background: Institutions conferring the most baccalaureate degrees in agribusiness and production to minority students during the 1996-97 academic year. **Number listed:** 34.
1. University of California, Davis (CA)
2. Cornell University (NY)
3. Alcorn State University (MS)
4. California Polytechnic State University (CA)
5. Michigan State University (MI)
6. Texas A&M University (TX)
7. Florida A&M State University (TX)
8. University of Florida (FL)
9. Southern University and A&M College (FL)
10. Ohio State University (OH)

Source: "Top 100 Agriculture Degree Producers, 1998," *Black Issues in Higher Education*, 17: 27-29, (June 8, 2000).

★1820★
U.S. institutions awarding the most baccalaureate degrees to minorities in agricultural sciences, 1998

Ranking basis/background: Institutions conferring the most baccalaureate degrees in agricultural sciences to minority students during the 1996-97 academic year. **Number listed:** 55.
1. University of Florida (FL)
2. University of California, Davis (CA)
3. Texas A&M University (TX)
4. California Polytechnic State University (CA)
5. Alabama A&M University (AL)
5. California State Polytechnic University (CA)
7. Tuskegee University (AL)
8. University of Arkansas, Pine Bluff (AR)
8. Colorado State University (CO)
10. New Mexico State University (NM)

Source: "Top 100 Agriculture Degree Producers, 1998," *Black Issues in Higher Education*, 17: 27-29, (June 8, 2000).

★1821★
U.S. institutions awarding the most baccalaureate degrees to minorities in ethnic/cultural studies, 1997-98

Ranking basis/background: Institutions awarding the most ethnic/cultural baccalaureate degrees to minority students in 1997-98. **Remarks:** Original source: *Black Issues* analysis of U.S. Department of Education data. **Number listed:** 50.
1. University of California, Berkeley (CA)
2. University of California, Santa Barbara (CA)
3. University of Hawaii, Manoa (HI)
4. University of Washington (WA)
5. University of California, Los Angeles (CA)
6. Rutgers University, New Brunswick (NJ)
7. University of California, Santa Cruz (CA)
8. Wesleyan University (CT)
9. University of California, San Diego (CA)
10. California State University, Northridge (CA)

Source: Hamilton, Kendra, "A New Spectrum," *Black Issues in Higher Education*, 17: 24-27, (May 25, 2000).

★1822★
U.S. institutions awarding the most baccalaureate degrees to Native Americans in agribusiness and production, 1998

Ranking basis/background: Institutions conferring the most baccalaureate degrees in agribusiness and production to Native American students during the 1996-97 academic year. **Number listed:** 3.
1. California Polytechnic State University (CA)
1. Oklahoma State University (OK)
3. Colorado State University (CO)

Source: "Top 100 Agriculture Degree Producers, 1998," *Black Issues in Higher Education*, 17: 27-29, (June 8, 2000).

★1823★
U.S. institutions awarding the most baccalaureate degrees to Native Americans in agricultural sciences, 1998

Ranking basis/background: Institutions conferring the most baccalaureate degrees in agricultural sciences to Native American students during the 1996-97 academic year. **Number listed:** 5.
1. Oklahoma State University (OK)
2. New Mexico State University (NM)
3. Colorado State University (CO)
4. California Polytechnic State University (CA)
4. South Dakota State University (SD)

Source: "Top 100 Agriculture Degree Producers, 1998," *Black Issues in Higher Education*, 17: 27-29, (June 8, 2000).

★1824★
U.S. institutions awarding the most master's degrees to African Americans in agribusiness and production, 1998

Ranking basis/background: Institutions conferring the most master's degrees in agribusiness and production to African American students during the 1996-97 academic year. **Number listed:** 5.
1. South Carolina State University (SC)
2. Alabama A&M University (AL)
2. Prairie View A&M University (TX)
4. University of Illinois, Urbana-Champaign (IL)
4. North Carolina A&T State University (NC)

Source: "Top 100 Agriculture Degree Producers, 1998," *Black Issues in Higher Education*, 17: 27-29, (June 8, 2000).

★1825★
U.S. institutions awarding the most master's degrees to African Americans in agricultural sciences, 1998

Ranking basis/background: Institutions conferring the most master's degrees in agricultural sciences to African American students during the 1996-97 academic year. **Number listed:** 7.
1. Alcorn State University (MS)
2. North Carolina A&T State University (NC)
3. Alabama A&M University (AL)
4. Prairie View A&M University (TX)
5. Tennessee State University (TN)
6. University of Illinois, Urbana-Champaign (IL)
6. Cornell University (NY)

Source: "Top 100 Agriculture Degree Producers, 1998," *Black Issues in Higher Education*, 17: 27-29, (June 8, 2000).

★1826★
U.S. institutions awarding the most master's degrees to Asian Americans in agribusiness and production, 1998

Ranking basis/background: Institutions conferring the most master's degrees in agribusiness and production to Asian American students during the 1996-97 academic year. **Number listed:** 1.
1. University of California, Davis (CA)

Source: "Top 100 Agriculture Degree Producers, 1998," *Black Issues in Higher Education*, 17: 27-29, (June 8, 2000).

★1827★
U.S. institutions awarding the most master's degrees to Asian Americans in agricultural sciences, 1998

Ranking basis/background: Institutions conferring the most master's degrees in agricultural sciences to Asian American students during the 1996-97 academic year. **Number listed:** 2.
1. University of Hawaii, Manoa (HI)
2. Rutgers University, New Brunswick (NJ)

Source: "Top 100 Agriculture Degree Producers, 1998," *Black Issues in Higher Education*, 17: 27-29, (June 8, 2000).

★1828★
U.S. institutions awarding the most master's degrees to Hispanic Americans in agricultural sciences, 1998

Ranking basis/background: Institutions conferring the most master's degrees in agricultural sciences to Hispanic American students during the 1996-97 academic year. **Number listed:** 1.
Texas A&M University (TX)

Source: "Top 100 Agriculture Degree Producers, 1998," *Black Issues in Higher Education*, 17: 27-29, (June 8, 2000).

★1829★
U.S. institutions awarding the most master's degrees to minorities in agribusiness and production, 1998

Ranking basis/background: Institutions conferring the most master's degrees in agribusiness and production to minority students during the 1996-97 academic year. **Number listed:** 8.
1. South Carolina State University (SC)
2. University of California, Davis (CA)
3. Alabama A&M University (AL)
3. University of Illinois, Urbana-Champaign (IL)
3. Prairie View A&M University (TX)
6. Michigan State University (MI)
6. Cornell University (NY)
6. North Carolina A&T State University (NC)

Source: "Top 100 Agriculture Degree Producers, 1998," *Black Issues in Higher Education*, 17: 27-29, (June 8, 2000).

★1830★
U.S. institutions awarding the most master's degrees to minorities in agricultural sciences, 1998

Ranking basis/background: Institutions conferring the most master's degrees in agricultural sciences to minority students during the 1996-97 academic year. **Number listed:** 15.
1. Alcorn State University (MS)
2. North Carolina A&T State University (NC)
3. University of Hawaii, Manoa (HI)
4. Alabama A&M University (AL)

5. University of Illinois, Urbana-Champaign (IL)
5. Tennessee State University (TN)
5. Prairie View A&M University (TX)
8. Rutgers University, New Brunswick (NJ)
8. Oklahoma State University (OK)
8. Texas A&M University (TX)

Source: "Top 100 Agriculture Degree Producers, 1998," *Black Issues in Higher Education*, 17: 27-29, (June 8, 2000).

★1831★
U.S. institutions awarding the most master's degrees to Native Americans in agricultural sciences, 1998

Ranking basis/background: Institutions conferring the most master's degrees in agricultural sciences to Native American students during the 1996-97 academic year. **Number listed:** 1.

1. Oklahoma State University (OK)

Source: "Top 100 Agriculture Degree Producers, 1998," *Black Issues in Higher Education*, 17: 27-29, (June 8, 2000).

Related Information

★1832★
Borden, Victor M.H., "The Top 100: Interpreting the Data," *Black Issues in Higher Education*, 17: 46-47, (July 6, 2000).
> **Remarks:** Explains the collection criteria for number of degrees and other formal awards conferred in academic, vocational and continuing professional education programs to students with minority status. The 100 institutions listed combine all minority groups and disciplines by degree level.

★1833★
Borden, Dr. Victor M.H., "The Top 100: Interpreting the Data," *Black Issues in Higher Education*, 17: 48-49, (June 22, 2000).
> **Remarks:** Explains the methodology and data sources for *Black Issues in Higher Education*'s ranking of the top 100 institutions awarding baccalaureate degrees to minority students across all disciplines and in specific disciplines during the 1997-98 academic year.

DEGREES (PROFESSIONAL)

★1834★
First professional degrees conferred to African Americans by historically black colleges and universities, 1997-98

Ranking basis/background: Total number of degrees awarded to African Americans at historically black institutions compared to all other institutions, plus the average annual percentage of change. **Remarks:** Original source: *Black Issues* analysis of U.S. Department of Education reports of data submitted by institutions. **Number listed:** 3.

Historically black institutions, with 910 degrees awarded; and a 7.7% average annual change
All other institutions, 4,384; 4.9%
Total, 5,294; 5.4%

Source: Borden, Victor M.H., "The Top 100: Interpreting the Data," *Black Issues in Higher Education*, 17: 46-47, (July 6, 2000).

★1835★
Historically black colleges and universities awarding the most first professional degrees to African Americans

Ranking basis/background: Total first professional degrees conferred to African American students at historically black colleges and universities in all disciplines combined during the 1997-98 academic year. **Remarks:** Original source: *Black Issues* analysis of U.S. Department of Education reports of data submitted by institutions. **Number listed:** 10.

1. Howard University (DC)
2. Meharry Medical College (TN)
3. Xavier University (LA)
4. Texas Southern University (TX)
5. Southern University and A&M College (LA)
6. Interdenominational Theological Center (GA)
7. North Carolina Central University (NC)
8. Florida A&M State University (FL)
9. Tuskegee University (AL)
10. Morehouse School of Medicine (GA)

Source: "Top 100 Degree Producers," *Black Issues in Higher Education*, 17: 48-89, (July 7, 2000).

★1836★
Top recruiters for jobs requiring a graduate professional degree (attorney-JD)

Ranking basis/background: Projected number of college hires from on-campus recruitment for 2000-01. **Remarks:** Numbers reflect total expected hires, not just African American projected hires. **Number listed:** 1.

1. Procter & Gamble, with 10 projected hires

Source: "The Top 100 Employers and the Majors in Demand for the Class of 2001," *The Black Collegian*, 31: 19-35, (February 2001).

★1837★
Total first professional degrees awarded to African Americans, by type of institutions, 1997-98

Ranking basis/background: Total number of first professional degrees conferred to African American students in 1997-98 by carnegie classification. **Remarks:** Original source: *Black Issues* analysis of U.S. Department of Education data. **Number listed:** 15.

Public, with 2,122
Private, nonprofit, 3,162
Proprietary, 10
Research I, 1,991
Research II, 271
Doctorate I, 409
Doctorate II, 387
Master's I, 757
Master's II, 27
Bachelor's I, 53
Bachelor's II, 62
Associate's, 0
Specialized, 1,285
Tribal, 0
Unclassified, 52

Source: St. John, Eric, "More Doctorates in the House," *Black Issues in Higher Education*, 17: 38-44, (July 6, 2000).

★1838★
Total first professional degrees awarded to Asian Americans, by type of institutions, 1997-98

Ranking basis/background: Total number of first professional degrees conferred to Asian American students in 1997-98 by carnegie classification. **Remarks:** Original source: *Black Issues* analysis of U.S. Department of Education data. **Number listed:** 15.

Public, with 2,993
Private, nonprofit, 4,494
Proprietary, 32
Research I, 3,251
Research II, 339
Doctorate I, 394
Doctorate II, 612
Master's I, 475
Master's II, 21
Bachelor's I, 68
Bachelor's II, 49
Associate's, 0
Specialized, 2,275
Tribal, 0
Unclassified, 35

Source: St. John, Eric, "More Doctorates in the House," *Black Issues in Higher Education*, 17: 38-44, (July 6, 2000).

★1839★
Total first professional degrees awarded to Hispanic Americans, by type of institutions, 1997-98

Ranking basis/background: Total number of first professional degrees conferred to Hispanic American students in 1997-98 by carnegie classification. **Remarks:** Original source: *Black Issues* analysis of U.S. Department of Education data. **Number listed:** 15.

Public, with 1,369
Private, nonprofit, 1,793
Proprietary, 34
Research I, 1,251
Research II, 197
Doctorate I, 308
Doctorate II, 224
Master's I, 319
Master's II, 18
Bachelor's I, 45
Bachelor's II, 10
Associate's, 0
Specialized, 784
Tribal, 0
Unclassified, 40

Source: St. John, Eric, "More Doctorates in the House," *Black Issues in Higher Education*, 17: 38-44, (July 6, 2000).

★1840★
Total first professional degrees awarded to minorities, by type of institutions, 1997-98

Ranking basis/background: Total number of first professional degrees conferred to minority students in 1997-98 by carnegie classification. **Remarks:** Original source: *Black Issues* analysis of U.S. Department of Education data. **Number listed:** 15.

Public, with 6,765
Private, nonprofit, 9,711
Proprietary, 77
Research I, 6,691
Research II, 851
Doctorate I, 1,149
Doctorate II, 1,278

DEGREES (PROFESSIONAL)

Master's I, 1,622
Master's II, 68
Bachelor's I, 177
Bachelor's II, 121
Associate's, 0
Specialized, 4,465
Tribal, 0
Unclassified, 131

Source: St. John, Eric, "More Doctorates in the House," *Black Issues in Higher Education*, 17: 38-44, (July 6, 2000).

★1841★
Total first professional degrees awarded to Native Americans, by type of institutions, 1997-98

Ranking basis/background: Total number of first professional degrees conferred to Native American students in 1997-98 by carnegie classification. **Remarks:** Original source: *Black Issues* analysis of U.S. Department of Education data. **Number listed:** 15.

Public, with 281
Private, nonprofit, 262
Proprietary, 1
Research I, 198
Research II, 44
Doctorate I, 38
Doctorate II, 55
Master's I, 71
Master's II, 2
Bachelor's I, 11
Bachelor's II, 0
Associate's, 0
Specialized, 121
Tribal, 0
Unclassified, 4

Source: St. John, Eric, "More Doctorates in the House," *Black Issues in Higher Education*, 17: 38-44, (July 6, 2000).

★1842★
Traditionally white institutions awarding the most first professional degrees to African Americans

Ranking basis/background: Total first professional degrees conferred to African American students at traditionally white institutions in all disciplines combined during the 1997-98 academic year. **Remarks:** Original source: *Black Issues* analysis of U.S. Department of Education reports of data submitted by institutions. **Number listed:** 48.

1. University of Maryland, Baltimore (MD)
2. Georgetown University (DC)
3. Harvard University (MA)
4. University of Florida (FL)
5. George Washington University (DC)
6. Temple University (PA)
7. University of Virginia (VA)
8. University of Miami (FL)
9. University of Baltimore (MD)
10. University of Michigan, Ann Arbor (MI)
11. University of North Carolina, Chapel Hill (NC)
11. Ohio State University (OH)
13. Columbia University (NY)
14. Emory University (GA)
15. University of Southern California (CA)
15. Nova Southeastern University (FL)
15. University of Illinois, Chicago (IL)
15. University of Wisconsin, Madison (WI)
19. Wayne State University (MI)
19. Fordham University (NY)

Source: "Top 100 Degree Producers," *Black Issues in Higher Education*, 17: 48-89, (July 7, 2000).

★1843★
U.S. colleges and universities awarding the most first professional degrees to African Americans

Ranking basis/background: Total first professional degrees conferred to African American students in all disciplines combined during the 1997-98 academic year. **Remarks:** Original source: *Black Issues* analysis of U.S. Department of Education reports of data submitted by institutions. **Number listed:** 54.

1. Howard University (DC)
2. Meharry Medical College (TN)
3. Xavier University (LA)
4. Texas Southern University (TX)
5. University of Maryland, Baltimore (MD)
6. Georgetown University (DC)
7. Harvard University (MA)
8. University of Florida (FL)
9. George Washington University (DC)
10. Temple University (PA)
11. Southern University and A&M College (LA)
12. Interdenominational Theological Center (GA)
13. University of Virginia (VA)
14. University of Miami (FL)
15. University of Baltimore (MD)
16. University of Michigan, Ann Arbor (MI)
17. North Carolina Central University (NC)
18. Florida A&M University (FL)
19. University of North Carolina, Chapel Hill (NC)
19. Ohio State University (OH)

Source: "Top 100 Degree Producers," *Black Issues in Higher Education*, 17: 48-89, (July 7, 2000).

★1844★
U.S. colleges and universities awarding the most first professional degrees to Asian Americans

Ranking basis/background: Total first professional degrees conferred to Asian American students in all disciplines combined during the 1997-98 academic year. **Remarks:** Original source: *Black Issues* analysis of U.S. Department of Education reports of data submitted by institutions. **Number listed:** 52.

1. University of Southern California (CA)
2. University of the Pacific (CA)
3. New York University (NY)
4. University of Illinois, Chicago (IL)
5. University of California, San Francisco (CA)
6. Harvard University (MA)
7. University of Medicine and Dentistry of New Jersey (NJ)
8. University of California, Los Angeles (CA)
9. Northwestern University (IL)
10. University of Hawaii, Manoa (HI)
11. Loyola Marymount University (CA)
12. Temple University (PA)
13. University of Maryland, Baltimore (MD)
14. Boston University (MA)
15. Tufts University (MA)
16. University of Michigan, Ann Arbor (MI)
17. Loma Linda University (CA)
18. University of Pennsylvania (PA)
19. Columbia University, New York City (NY)
20. Ohio State University (OH)

Source: "Top 100 Degree Producers," *Black Issues in Higher Education*, 17: 48-89, (July 7, 2000).

★1845★
U.S. colleges and universities awarding the most first professional degrees to Hispanic Americans

Ranking basis/background: Total first professional degrees conferred to Hispanic American students in all disciplines combined during the 1997-98 academic year. **Remarks:** Original source: *Black Issues* analysis of U.S. Department of Education reports of data submitted by institutions. **Number listed:** 52.

1. University of Miami (FL)
2. Nova Southeastern University (FL)
3. University of Texas, Austin (TX)
4. University of Southern California (CA)
5. Loyola Marymount University (CA)
6. University of California, Los Angeles (CA)
7. George Washington University (DC)
8. University of Texas Health Science Center, Houston (TX)
9. University of Florida (FL)
9. University of New Mexico (NM)
11. University of California, Berkeley (CA)
11. University of Illinois, Chicago (IL)
11. Texas Southern University (TX)
14. Georgetown University (DC)
14. New York University (NY)
16. University of Texas Medical Branch, Galveston (TX)
17. Temple University (PA)
18. University of Medicine and Dentistry of New Jersey (NJ)
19. Stanford University (CA)
20. University of California, Davis, (CA)
20. University of the Pacific (CA)
20. St. John's University (NY)
20. University of Texas Health Science Center, San Antonio (TX)
20. University of Wisconsin, Madison (WI)
20. Harvard University (MA)

Source: "Top 100 Degree Producers," *Black Issues in Higher Education*, 17: 48-89, (July 7, 2000).

★1846★
U.S. colleges and universities awarding the most first professional degrees to Native Americans

Ranking basis/background: Total first professional degrees conferred to Native American students in all disciplines combined during the 1997-98 academic year. **Remarks:** Original source: *Black Issues* analysis of U.S. Department of Education reports of data submitted by institutions. **Number listed:** 67.

1. University of Minnesota, Twin Cities (MN)
2. University of Oklahoma Health Sciences Center (OK)
3. University of New Mexico (NM)
4. University of Tulsa (OK)
5. College of Osteopathic Medicine (OK)
5. Oklahoma City University (OK)
5. Seattle University (WA)
5. University of Washington (WA)
9. University of North Carolina, Chapel Hill (NC)
9. University of Wisconsin, Madison (WI)
11. University of the Pacific (CA)
11. Georgetown University (DC)
13. University of Colorado, Boulder (CO)
14. University of Arizona (AZ)

14. University of California, San Francisco (CA)
14. Life University (GA)
14. Tulane University (LA)
14. University of North Dakota (ND)
14. University of Oklahoma, Norman (OK)
14. University of Houston, University Park (TX)
14. Texas Tech University (TX)

Source: "Top 100 Degree Producers," *Black Issues in Higher Education*, 17: 48-89, (July 7, 2000).

★1847★
U.S. colleges and universities awarding the most health professions and related sciences first professional degrees to African Americans

Ranking basis/background: Total first professional degrees conferred to African American students in the field of health professions and related sciences during the 1997-98 academic year. **Remarks:** Original source: *Black Issues* analysis of U.S. Department of Education reports of data submitted by institutions. **Number listed:** 58.

1. Meharry Medical College (TN)
2. Howard University (DC)
3. Xavier University (LA)
4. Florida A&M State University (FL)
4. University of Maryland, Baltimore (MD)
6. University of Illinois, Chicago (IL)
7. University of Medicine and Dentistry of New Jersey (NJ)
7. Temple University (PA)
9. Tuskegee University (AL)
10. Morehouse School of Medicine (GA)
11. Life University (GA)
12. Louisiana State University Medical Center (LA)
12. Wayne State University (MI)
12. Ohio State University (OH)
12. Allegheny University of the Health Sciences (PA)
12. University of Tennessee, Memphis (TN)
17. Harvard University (MA)
17. Medical University of South Carolina (SC)
19. Virginia Commonwealth University (VA)
20. Georgetown University (DC)
20. University of Michigan, Ann Arbor (MI)
20. University of North Carolina, Chapel Hill (NC)
20. University of Cincinnati (OH)
20. University of Virginia (VA)

Source: "Top 100 Degree Producers," *Black Issues in Higher Education*, 17: 48-89, (July 7, 2000).

★1848★
U.S. colleges and universities awarding the most health professions and related sciences first professional degrees to Asian Americans

Ranking basis/background: Total first professional degrees conferred to Asian American students in the field of health professions and related sciences during the 1997-98 academic year. **Remarks:** Original source: *Black Issues* analysis of U.S. Department of Education reports of data submitted by institutions. **Number listed:** 51.

1. University of Southern California (CA)
2. University of the Pacific (CA)
3. University of Illinois, Chicago (IL)
4. University of California, San Francisco (CA)
5. New York University (NY)
6. University of Medicine and Dentistry of New Jersey (NJ)
7. Northwestern University (IL)
8. Tufts University (MA)
9. Loma Linda University (CA)
10. Los Angeles College of Chiropractic (CA)
10. State University of New York, Health Science Center, Brooklyn (NY)
12. Ohio State University (OH)
12. University of Texas Health Science Center, San Antonio (TX)
14. New York Medical College (NY)
14. Temple University (PA)
16. University of Maryland, Baltimore (MD)
16. Harvard University (MA)
18. Columbia University, New York City (NY)
18. University of Pennsylvania (PA)
20. University of Michigan, Ann Arbor (MI)

Source: "Top 100 Degree Producers," *Black Issues in Higher Education*, 17: 48-89, (July 7, 2000).

★1849★
U.S. colleges and universities awarding the most health professions and related sciences first professional degrees to Hispanic Americans

Ranking basis/background: Total first professional degrees conferred to Hispanic American students in the field of health professions and related sciences during the 1997-98 academic year. **Remarks:** Original source: *Black Issues* analysis of U.S. Department of Education reports of data submitted by institutions. **Number listed:** 56.

1. University of Texas Health Science Center, Houston (TX)
2. University of Illinois, Chicago (IL)
3. University of Texas Medical Branch, Galveston (TX)
4. Nova Southeastern University (FL)
5. University of Medicine and Dentistry of New Jersey (NJ)
6. University of Texas Health Science Center, San Antonio (TX)
7. University of California, Los Angeles (CA)
7. Life University (GA)
9. University of Southern California (CA)
10. University of California, San Francisco (CA)
11. University of Texas Southwest Medical Center (TX)
12. University of Florida (FL)
13. Tufts University (MA)
14. New York University (NY)
15. New York Institute of Technology, Old Westbury (NY)
16. Temple University (PA)
17. Michigan State University (MI)
18. Los Angeles College of Chiropractic (CA)
18. University of Colorado Health Sciences Center (CO)
20. Texas Tech University Health Sciences Center (TX)

Source: "Top 100 Degree Producers," *Black Issues in Higher Education*, 17: 48-89, (July 7, 2000).

★1850★
U.S. colleges and universities awarding the most health professions and related sciences first professional degrees to minorities

Ranking basis/background: Total first professional degrees conferred to minority students in the field of health professions and related sciences during the 1997-98 academic year. **Remarks:** Original source: *Black Issues* analysis of U.S. Department of Education reports of data submitted by institutions. **Number listed:** 51.

1. University of Southern California (CA)
2. University of Illinois, Chicago (IL)
3. University of California, San Francisco (CA)
4. University of Medicine and Dentistry of New Jersey (NJ)
5. University of the Pacific (CA)
6. New York University (NY)
7. Howard University (DC)
8. Meharry Medical College (TN)
9. Temple University (PA)
10. University of Maryland, Baltimore (MD)
11. Xavier University (LA)
12. Tufts University (MA)
13. University of Texas Health Science Center, San Antonio (TX)
14. Ohio State University (OH)
14. University of Texas Health Science Center, Houston (TX)
16. Northwestern University (IL)
17. Nova Southeastern University (FL)
18. Harvard University (MA)
19. University of Michigan, Ann Arbor (MI)
19. State University of New York Health Science Center, Brooklyn (NY)

Source: "Top 100 Degree Producers," *Black Issues in Higher Education*, 17: 48-89, (July 7, 2000).

★1851★
U.S. colleges and universities awarding the most health professions and related sciences first professional degrees to Native Americans

Ranking basis/background: Total first professional degrees conferred to Native American students in the field of health professions and related sciences during the 1997-98 academic year. **Remarks:** Original source: *Black Issues* analysis of U.S. Department of Education reports of data submitted by institutions. **Number listed:** 26.

1. University of Oklahoma Health Sciences Center (OK)
2. University of Minnesota, Twin Cities (MN)
3. College of Osteopathic Medicine of Oklahoma (OK)
4. University of California, San Francisco (CA)
4. Life University (GA)
4. University of Wisconsin, Madison (WI)
7. University of Arizona (AZ)
7. University of North Dakota (ND)
7. Oklahoma State University (OK)
10. Indiana University-Purdue University (IN)
10. University of North Carolina, Chapel Hill (NC)
10. University of North Texas Health Science Center, Fort Worth (TX)
13. University of Alabama, Birmingham (AL)
13. Life Chiropractic College, West (CA)
13. University of Southern California (CA)
13. Colorado State University (CO)
13. University of South Florida (FL)

DEMOGRAPHY

13. Palmer College of Chiropractic (IA)
13. Tulane University (LA)
13. Tufts University (MA)
13. Michigan State University (MI)
13. Wayne State University (MI)
13. University of New Mexico (NM)
13. University of Texas Medical Branch, Galveston (TX)
13. University of Washington (WA)
13. Marquette University (WI)

Source: "Top 100 Degree Producers," *Black Issues in Higher Education*, 17: 48-89, (July 7, 2000).

★1852★
U.S. colleges and universities awarding the most law and legal studies first professional degrees to African Americans

Ranking basis/background: Total first professional degrees conferred to African American students in the field of law and legal studies during the 1997-98 academic year. **Remarks:** Original source: *Black Issues* analysis of U.S. Department of Education reports of data submitted by institutions. **Number listed:** 53.

1. Howard University (DC)
2. Texas Southern University (TX)
3. Southern University and A&M College (LA)
4. George Washington University (DC)
5. Georgetown University (DC)
5. University of Florida (FL)
7. Harvard University (MA)
8. University of Baltimore (MD)
9. University of Maryland, Baltimore (MD)
9. North Carolina Central University (NC)
11. University of Miami (FL)
12. Fordham University (NY)
13. Temple University (PA)
13. University of Virginia (VA)
15. Columbia University, New York City (NY)
15. University of Texas, Austin (TX)
17. Tulane University (LA)
17. Georgia State University (GA)
17. New York Law School (NY)
17. Touro College (NY)
17. University of Wisconsin, Madison (WI)

Source: "Top 100 Degree Producers," *Black Issues in Higher Education*, 17: 48-89, (July 7, 2000).

★1853★
U.S. colleges and universities awarding the most law and legal studies first professional degrees to Asian Americans

Ranking basis/background: Total first professional degrees conferred to Asian American students in the field of law and legal studies during the 1997-98 academic year. **Remarks:** Original source: *Black Issues* analysis of U.S. Department of Education reports of data submitted by institutions. **Number listed:** 52.

1. Loyola Marymount University (CA)
2. University of California, Los Angeles (CA)
3. University of California, Hastings (CA)
3. Santa Clara University (CA)
3. Harvard University (MA)
6. New York University (NY)
7. Georgetown University (DC)
8. University of Hawaii, Manoa (HI)
9. Southwestern University School of Law (CA)
10. American University (DC)
11. University of the Pacific (CA)

11. George Washington University (DC)
13. University of San Francisco (CA)
14. Brooklyn Law School (NY)
15. University of California, Berkeley (CA)
16. University of California, Davis (CA)
17. University of San Diego (CA)
18. Illinois Institute of Technology (IL)
19. Boston University (MA)
20. Fordham University (NY)

Source: "Top 100 Degree Producers," *Black Issues in Higher Education*, 17: 48-89, (July 7, 2000).

★1854★
U.S. colleges and universities awarding the most law and legal studies first professional degrees to Hispanic Americans

Ranking basis/background: Total first professional degrees conferred to Hispanic American students in the field of law and legal studies during the 1997-98 academic year. **Remarks:** Original source: *Black Issues* analysis of U.S. Department of Education reports of data submitted by institutions. **Number listed:** 53.

1. University of Texas, Austin (TX)
2. University of Miami (FL)
3. Loyola Marymount University (CA)
4. George Washington University (DC)
5. Texas Southern University (TX)
6. Nova Southeastern University (FL)
7. University of California, Berkeley (CA)
7. Georgetown University (DC)
9. St. John's University (NY)
10. University of Southern California (CA)
11. Southwestern University School of Law (CA)
11. University of New Mexico (NM)
13. Fordham University (NY)
14. University of the Pacific (CA)
14. Rutgers University, Newark (NJ)
14. St. Mary's University (TX)
14. Stanford University (CA)
18. St. Thomas University (FL)
19. University of Florida (FL)
19. University of Pennsylvania (PA)
19. South Texas College of Law (TX)

Source: "Top 100 Degree Producers," *Black Issues in Higher Education*, 17: 48-89, (July 7, 2000).

★1855★
U.S. colleges and universities awarding the most law and legal studies first professional degrees to Native Americans

Ranking basis/background: Total first professional degrees conferred to Native American students in the field of law and legal studies during the 1997-98 academic year. **Remarks:** Original source: *Black Issues* analysis of U.S. Department of Education reports of data submitted by institutions. **Number listed:** 44.

1. University of New Mexico (NM)
1. University of Tulsa (OK)
3. Oklahoma City University (OK)
3. Seattle University (WA)
5. University of the Pacific (CA)
6. University of Colorado, Boulder (CO)
6. Georgetown University (DC)
6. University of Washington (WA)
9. University of Oklahoma, Norman (OK)
10. Texas Tech University (TX)
11. American University (DC)
11. Boston University (MA)
11. Hamline University (MN)

11. University of North Carolina, Chapel Hill (NC)
11. University of Houston, University Park (TX)
11. Gonzaga University (WA)

Source: "Top 100 Degree Producers," *Black Issues in Higher Education*, 17: 48-89, (July 7, 2000).

DEMOGRAPHY

★1856★
Demography journals with the highest average citations after 5 years

Ranking basis/background: Average number of citations per article after five years. **Number listed:** 16.

1. *Family Planning Perspectives*, with 13.98
2. *Population and Development Review*, 7.21
3. *Population Bulletin*, 8.50
4. *Demography*, 7.84
5. *Studies in Family Planning*, 5.55
6. *Population Studies*, 4.81
7. *International Migration Review*, 2.06
8. *Journal of Population Economics*, 1.85
9. *Journal of Biosocial Science*, 1.41
10. *Social Biology*, 1.29

Source: Van Dalen, Hendrik P. and Kene Henkens, "How Influential Are Demography Journals," *Population and Development Review*, 25: 229-251, (June 1999).

★1857★
Most cited demography journals, 1991-95

Ranking basis/background: Total number of citations received annually. **Number listed:** 16.

1. *Demography*, with 1,049.0 citations received
2. *Family Planning Perspectives*, 975.2
3. *Population and Development Review*, 698.8
4. *Population Studies*, 592.2
5. *Studies in Family Planning*, 549.0
6. *Journal of Biosocial Science*, 336.2
7. *International Migration Review*, 314.6
8. *Social Biology*, 233.4
9. *Population*, 204.8
10. *Population Bulletin*, 115.0

Source: Van Dalen, Hendrik P. and Kene Henkens, "How Influential Are Demography Journals," *Population and Development Review*, 25: 229-251, (June 1999).

★1858★
"Outside" journals most frequently citing *Demography*, 1991-95

Ranking basis/background: Total number of citations. **Number listed:** 3.

1. *Journal of Marriage and the Family*, with 311 cites
2. *Social Forces*, 139
3. *American Sociological Review*, 119

Source: Van Dalen, Hendrik P. and Kene Henkens, "How Influential Are Demography Journals," *Population and Development Review*, 25: 229-251, (June 1999).

★1859★
"Outside" journals most frequently citing *Family Planning Perspectives*, 1991-95

Ranking basis/background: Total number of citations. Number listed: 3.
1. *Journal of Adolescent Health*, with 227 cites
2. *American Journal of Public Health*, 209
3. *Adolescence*, 167

Source: Van Dalen, Hendrik P. and Kene Henkens, "How Influential Are Demography Journals," *Population and Development Review*, 25: 229-251, (June 1999).

★1860★
"Outside" journals most frequently citing *Population and Development Review*, 1991-95

Ranking basis/background: Total number of citations. Number listed: 3.
1. *Social Science and Medicine*, with 187 cites
2. *Annual Review of Sociology*, 100
3. *Economic and Political Weekly*, 51

Source: Van Dalen, Hendrik P. and Kene Henkens, "How Influential Are Demography Journals," *Population and Development Review*, 25: 229-251, (June 1999).

★1861★
"Outside" journals most frequently citing *Population Studies*, 1991-95

Ranking basis/background: Total number of citations. Number listed: 3.
1. *Social Science and Medicine*, with 137 cites
2. *Journal of Family History*, 62
2. *Social History of Medicine*, 62

Source: Van Dalen, Hendrik P. and Kene Henkens, "How Influential Are Demography Journals," *Population and Development Review*, 25: 229-251, (June 1999).

★1862★
"Outside" journals most frequently citing *Studies in Family Planning*, 1991-95

Ranking basis/background: Total number of citations. Number listed: 3.
1. *Contraception*, with 174 cites
2. *Social Science and Medicine*, 171
3. *International Journal of Gynecology and Obstetrics*, 89

Source: Van Dalen, Hendrik P. and Kene Henkens, "How Influential Are Demography Journals," *Population and Development Review*, 25: 229-251, (June 1999).

★1863★
Top demography journals by average impact factor, 1991-95

Ranking basis/background: Average impact factor for the years 1991 to 1995. Number listed: 16.
1. *Demography*, with 1.63
2. *Population Bulletin*, 1.37
3. *Family Planning Perspectives*, 1.32
4. *Population and Development Review*, 1.29
5. *Studies in Family Planning*, 1.12
5. *Population Studies*, 1.12
7. *Journal of Biosocial Science*, 0.39
7. *International Migration Review*, 0.39

9. *Population Research and Policy Review*, 0.38
10. *Population and Environment*, 0.32

Source: Van Dalen, Hendrik P. and Kene Henkens, "How Influential Are Demography Journals," *Population and Development Review*, 25: 229-251, (June 1999).

DENTISTRY

★1864★
Endodontic articles with the most citations, 1974 through 1999

Ranking basis/background: Total number of citations received between January 1974 and January 1999. Number listed: 11.
1. *The effects of surgical exposures of dental pulps in germ-free and conventional laboratory rats*, by S. Kakehashi, H.R. Stanley, R.J. Fitzgerald, with 156 citations
2. *Radiographic and direct observations of experimental lesions in bone 1*, I.B. Bender, S. Seltzer, 118
3. *Cleaning and shaping the root canal*, H. Schilder, 111
4. *The hydrodynamics of the dentine; its possible relationship to dentinal pain*, M. Brannstrom, A. Astrom, 107
4. *Filling root canals in three dimensions*, H. Schilder, 107
6. *Bacteriologic studies of necrotic dental pulps*, G. Sundqvist, 103
7. *The "balanced force" concept for instrumentation of curved canals*, J.B. Roane, C.L. Sabala, M.G. Duncanson Jr., 90
8. *Microscopic investigation of root apexes*, Y. Kuttler, 67
9. *Reaction of rat connective tissue to polyethylene tube implants. Parts I and II*, C.D. Torneck, 62
10. *Endodontic success-who's reading the radiograph?*, M. Goldman, A.H. Pearson, N. Darzenta, 59
11. *Wound healing in the tissues of the periodontium following periradicular surgery. 1. The incisional wound and 2. The dissectional wound*, J.W. Harrison, K.A. Jurosky, 16

Source: Johnson, Bradford R., "The Essential Endodontic Literature: A Survey of Postgraduate Program Directors," *Journal of Endodontics*, 26: 447-449, (August 2000).

★1865★
U.S. universities publishing the most papers in the field of dentistry/oral surgery and medicine, 1995-99

Ranking basis/background: Number of papers published in the field of dentistry/oral surgery and medicine over a five-year period, and percent of field based on each universities percentage of 16,899 papers entered in the ISI database from ISI-indexed dentistry journals. Number listed: 6.
1. University of Texas, Austin, with 321 papers; 1.90% of field
2. University of Texas, San Antonio, 318; 1.88%
3. University of North Carolina, Chapel Hill, 271; 1.60%
4. University of Michigan, 266; 1.57%

4. University of Iowa, 265; 1.57%
6. University of Washington (WA), 246; 1.46%

Source: "Dentistry/Oral Surgery & Medicine: Most Prolific U.S. Universities, 1995-99," *What's Hot in Research* (http://www.isinet.com/isi/hot/research) Institute for Scientific Information.

★1866★
U.S. universities with the greatest impact in dentistry/oral surgery, 1994-98

Ranking basis/background: Total number of dentistry/oral surgery papers published from each university and average number of citations per paper between 1994 and 1998. Remarks: Original source: University Science Indicators on Diskette, 1981-98. Number listed: 5.
1. State University of New York, Buffalo, with 120 dentistry/oral surgery papers; 5.47 citations per paper
2. University of Minnesota, 109; 3.64
3. University of North Carolina, Chapel Hill, 257; 3.41
4. University of Southern California, 103; 3.40
5. University of Alabama, 106; 3.05

Source: "Dentistry/Oral Surgery & Medicine: High-Impact U.S. Universities, 1994-98," *What's Hot in Research* (http://www.isinet.com/hot/research) Institute for Scientific Information, June 28, 1999.

★1867★
U.S. universities with the greatest impact in dentistry/oral surgery and medicine, 1995-99

Ranking basis/background: Average citations per paper from the top 100 federally funded U.S. universities that had at least 50 published papers in ISI indexed dentistry/oral surgery & medicine journals. Also includes total number of papers published during the five year period. Number listed: 5.
1. State University of New York, Buffalo, with 123 papers; 4.43 citations per paper
2. University of Southern California, 110; 4.02
3. University of North Carolina, Chapel Hill, 271; 3.18
4. University of Texas, Houston, 194; 3.03
5. University of Washington (WA), 246; 3.02

Source: "Dentistry/Oral Surgery & Medicine: High Impact U.S. Universities, 1995-99," *What's Hot in Research* (http://www.isinet.com/isi/hot/research) Institute for Scientific Information, September 18, 2000.

★1868★
U.S. universities with the highest concentration of dentistry papers published, 1994-98

Ranking basis/background: Total number of dentistry papers published from each university and percentage they comprise of university's total papers between 1994 and 1998. Remarks: Original source: University Science Indicators on Diskette, 1981-98. Number listed: 5.
1. University of Texas, San Antonio, with 280 dentistry papers; 5.80% of university's total papers
2. University of Iowa, 261; 2.48%
3. University of North Carolina, Chapel Hill, 257; 2.12%
4. University of Texas, Houston, 190; 1.99%

5. University of Connecticut, 129; 1.92%
Source: "U.S. Universities with Highest Concentrations in Dentistry, 1994-98," *What's Hot in Research (http://www.isinet.com/hot/research) Institute for Scientific Information*, October 18, 1999.

DERMATOLOGY

★1869★
Leading categories of dermatologic disease covered by top articles in the field, 1945-1990

Ranking basis/background: Number of articles published pertaining to each category, 1945-1990. **Remarks:** Other tables included cover the most-cited journals, most-cited articles, and most published authors. Original source: Institute for Scientific Information/*Science Citation Index*. **Number listed:** 12.

1. Neoplasia, with 23 articles
2. Dermatitis, 19
3. Psoriasis, 16
4. Connective tissue disease, 10
5. Drug reaction, 9
6. Bullous dermatoses, 8
7. Congenital dermatologic disease, 6
8. Infectious dermatologic disease, 4
8. Systemic dermatologic disease manifestations, 4
10. Acne, 3
10. Keratinocyte biology, 3
10. Langerhan's cell, 3

Source: Dubin, Daniel, Arthur W. Hafner, and Kenneth A. Arndt, "Citation Classics in Clinical Dermatologic Journals," *Archives of Dermatology* 129: 1121-1129 (September 1993).

★1870★
Most cited authors in dermatology journals, 1981 to 1996

Ranking basis/background: Total number of citations for papers appearing in dermatology journals, irrespective of authorship placement, from 1981 through 1996 according to the Institute of Scientific Information database. **Number listed:** 25.

1. J.J. Voorhees, with 4,706 citations
2. B.J. Nickoloff, 3,481
3. H.I. Miabach, 2,915
4. K. Wolff, 2,791
5. J. Thivolet, 2,688
6. P.M. Elias, 2,656
7. R.K. Winkelmann, 2,463
8. S.I. Katz, 2,264
9. G. Stingl, 2,172
10. D.M. MacDonald, 2,033

Source: Stern, Robert S. and Kenneth A. Arndt, "Top Cited Authors in Dermatology," *Archives of Dermatology*, 135: 299-302, (March 2000).

★1871★
Most cited first authors in dermatology journals, 1981 to 1996

Ranking basis/background: Total number of citations for papers appearing in dermatology journals, with first author placement, from 1981 through 1996 according to the Institute of Scientific Information database. **Number listed:** 25.

1. J.D. Fine, with 813 citations
2. W.R. Gammon, 766
3. K. Kragballe, 731
4. D.N. Sauder, 719
5. B.J. Nickoloff, 707
6. C.E.M. Griffiths, 634
7. S.T. Boyce, 572
8. N.S. Penneys, 517
9. W. Aberer, 509
10. R. Willemze, 498

Source: Stern, Robert S. and Kenneth A. Arndt, "Top Cited Authors in Dermatology," *Archives of Dermatology*, 135: 299-302, (March 2000).

★1872★
Most frequently cited clinical dermatology articles, 1945-1990

Ranking basis/background: Number of citations per article, 1945-1990. Articles are from the 10 most frequently cited dermatologic journals. To be ranked, an article must have been cited at least 100 times, 1945-1990. **Remarks:** Original source: Institute for Scientific Information/*Science Citation Index*. **Number listed:** 129.

1. A. W. McKenzie and R. B. Stoughton, "Method for comparing percutaneous absorption of steroids," *Archives of Dermatology* 86:608-610, 1962, with 360 citations
2. D. L. Tuffanelli and R. K. Winklemann, "Systemic scleroderma: a clinical study of 727 cases," *Archives of Dermatology* 84:359-371, 1961, 358
3. E. J. Van Scott and T. M. Ekel, "Kinetics of hyperplasia in psoriasis," *Archives of Dermatology* 88:373-381, 1963, 246
4. L. Juhlin, S. G. O. Johansson, and H. Bennich, et al., "Immunoglobulin E in dermatoses: levels in atopic dermatitis and urticaria," *Archives of Dermatology* 100:12-16, 1969, 240
5. W. H. Clark, Jr., R. R. Reimer, and M. Greene, et al., "Origin of familial malignant melanomas from heritable melanocytic lesions: 'the B-K mole syndrome,'" *Archives of Dermatology* 114:732-738, 1978, 237
6. A. Lyell, "Toxic epidermal necrolysis: an eruption resembling scalding of the skin," *British Journal of Dermatology* 68:355-361, 1956, 235
6. K. Wolff, T. B. Fitzpatrick, and J. A. Parrish, et al., "Photochemotherapy for psoriasis with orally administered methoxsalen," *Archives of Dermatology* 112:943-950, 1976, 235
8. R. B. Stoughton and W. Fritsch, "Influence of dimethylsulfoxide (DMSO) on human percutaneous absorption," *Archives of Dermatology* 90:512-517, 1964, 213
9. M. A. Lutzner, J. W. Hobbs, and P. Horvath, "Ultrastructure of abnormal cells in Sezary syndrome, mycosis fungoides, and parasoriasis en plaque," *Archives of Dermatology* 103:375-386, 1971, 207
10. P. M. Elias and M. L. Williams, "Retinoids, cancer, and the skin," *Archives of Dermatology* 117:160-180, 1981, 202

Source: Dubin, Daniel, Arthur W. Hafner, and Kenneth A. Arndt, "Citation Classics in Clinical Dermatologic Journals," *Archives of Dermatology* 129: 1121-1129 (September 1993).

★1873★
Number of citations and papers for original articles appearing in dermatology journals, 1981 to 1996

Ranking basis/background: Total number of citations and papers, for original articles only, appearing in dermatology journals from 1981 through 1996 according to the Institute of Scientific Information database. **Number listed:** 25.

1. *Journal of Investigative Dermatology*, with 70,547 citations; 3,821 papers
2. *Journal of American Academy of Dermatology*, 39,566; 3,644
3. *British Journal of Dermatology*, 33,579; 3,294
4. *Archives of Dermatology*, 28,286; 2,467
5. *Contact Dermatitis*, 11,047; 1,479
6. *Archives of Dermatology Research*, 8,999; 1,328
7. *Acta Dermato-Venereologica*, 8,655; 1,390
8. *Dermatologic Clinics*, 7,599; 1,264
9. *Dermatologic Surgery*, 7,040; 1,695
10. *American Journal of Dermatopathology*, 6,734; 1,208

Source: Stern, Robert S. and Kenneth A. Arndt, "Top Cited Authors in Dermatology," *Archives of Dermatology*, 135: 299-302, (March 2000).

★1874★
Number of citations and papers in dermatology journals, 1981 to 1996

Ranking basis/background: Total number of citations and papers appearing in dermatology journals from 1981 through 1996 according to the Institute of Scientific Information database. **Number listed:** 25.

1. *Journal of Investigative Dermatology*, with 93,789 citations; 18,712 papers
2. *Journal of American Academy of Dermatology*, 60,481; 8,309
3. *British Journal of Dermatology*, 42,339; 6,444
4. *Archives of Dermatology*, 42,134; 5,597
5. *Contact Dermatitis*, 18,478; 3,926
6. *Acta Dermato-Venereologica*, 13,623; 2,877
7. *Archives of Dermatology Research*, 11,653; 2,110
8. *International Journal of Dermatology*, 9,937; 3,614
9. *Dermatologic Clinics*, 9,193; 1,989
10. *Dermatologic Surgery*, 8,574; 2,987

Source: Stern, Robert S. and Kenneth A. Arndt, "Top Cited Authors in Dermatology," *Archives of Dermatology*, 135: 299-302, (March 2000).

★1875★
U.S. universities with the greatest impact in dermatology, 1994-98

Ranking basis/background: Total number of dermatology papers published from each university and average number of citations per paper between 1994 and 1998. **Remarks:** Original source: University Science Indicators on Diskette, 1981-98. **Number listed:** 5.

1. University of Michigan, with 156 dermatology papers; 6.97 citations per paper
2. University of Washington (WA), 82; 6.73
3. Yale University, 103; 6.23
4. Case Western Reserve University, 100; 5.58
5. Emory University, 51; 5.35

Source: "Dermatology: High-Impact U.S. Universities, 1994-98," *What's Hot in Research* (http://www.isinet.com/hot/research) *Institute for Scientific Information*, January 17, 2000.

★1876★
U.S. universities with the greatest impact in dermatology, 1995-99

Ranking basis/background: Average citations per paper from the top 100 federally funded U.S. universities that had at least 50 published papers in ISI indexed dermatology journals. Also includes total number of papers published during the five year period. **Number listed:** 5.

1. University of Michigan, with 133 papers; 6.50 citations per paper
2. University of Washington (WA), 85; 6.33
3. University of California, Los Angeles, 87; 5.91
4. Harvard University, 293; 5.89
5. State University of New York, Stony Brook, 78; 5.86

Source: "Dermatology: High Impact U.S. Universities, 1995-99," *What's Hot in Research* (http://www.isinet.com/isi/hot/research) *Institute for Scientific Information*.

DIPLOMA MILLS
See: **Degrees (Academic)**

DISABILITIES–ENROLLMENT OF STUDENTS

★1877★
Disabled students served in U.S. public school programs, 1998-99

Ranking basis/background: Number, in thousands, of children from 6 to 21 years old served in educational programs annually. **Remarks:** Original source: Office of Special Education and Rehabilitative Services, U.S. Department of Education. **Number listed:** 13.

All disabilities, with 5,541 thousand
Learning disabilities, 2,817
Speech impairments, 1,075
Mental retardation, 611
Emotional disturbance, 463
Multiple disabilities, 108
Hearing impairments, 71
Orthopedic impairments, 69
Other health impairments, 221
Visual impairments, 26
Autism, 54
Deaf-blindness, 2
Traumatic brain injury, 13

Source: *The World Almanac and Book of Facts 2001*, World Almanac Books, 2001.

DISABILITIES–FEDERAL AID

★1878★
2002 budget request for education of the handicapped

Ranking basis/background: Based on the U.S. government's proposed fiscal 2002 appropriations for education for the handicapped. **Number listed:** 5.

National Institute on Disability and Rehabilitation Research, with $110,000,000
Research and innovation, $70,000,000
Technical assistance, $53,481,000
Professional development, $81,952,000
Technology development, $31,710,000

Source: "Bush's Fiscal 2002 Budget Plan for Higher Education and Science," *The Chronicle of Higher Education*, 47: A36-A37, (April 20, 2001).

DISABILITIES, LEARNING
See: **Learning Disabilities**

DISADVANTAGED–FEDERAL AID

★1879★
Proposed fiscal 2002 appropriations for aid to the disadvantaged

Ranking basis/background: Based on the U.S. government's proposed fiscal 2002 appropriations for aid to the disadvantaged. **Number listed:** 4.

TRIO programs for disadvantaged students, with $780,000,000
Gaining Early Awareness and Readiness for Undergraduate Programs (GEAR UP), $227,000,000
Minority Institutions Science and Engineering Improvement, $8,500,000
College-aid migrant programs, $10,000,000

Source: "Bush's Fiscal 2002 Budget Plan for Higher Education and Science," *The Chronicle of Higher Education*, 47: A36-A37, (April 20, 2001).

DISTANCE EDUCATION
See also: **Computer Uses in Education**

Related Information

★1880★
The Best Distance Learning Graduate Schools: Earning Your Degree Without Leaving Home, Princeton Review Publishing, 1999.
Remarks: Provides information on U.S. colleges and universities that offer programs via telecommunications media.

★1881★
Peterson's MBA Distance Learning Programs, Peterson's, 2000.
Remarks: Provides information on U.S. colleges and universities, that offer MBA programs via telecommunications media.

DOCTORAL DEGREES
See also: **Degrees (Academic)**

★1882★
Age grouping of doctorate recipients, by broad field, 1999

Ranking basis/background: Based on the 1998-99 Survey of Earned Doctorates (SED) conducted by the National Research Council's Office of Scientific and Engineering Personnel (OSEP). The doctorates are reported by academic year and include research and applied research doctorates in all fields. **Remarks:** The *Summary Report* is the 33rd in an annual series of reports that began in 1967. **Number listed:** 7.

Physical sciences, with 88 (21-25 yrs); 3,074 (26-30 yrs); 1,761 (31-35 yrs); 654 (36-40 yrs); 265 (41-45 yrs); 143 (over 45)
Engineering, 68; 2,211; 1,649; 739; 216; 132
Life sciences, 36; 3,140; 2,470; 1,079; 579; 512
Social sciences, 27; 2,216; 2,026; 988; 610; 747
Humanities, 7; 1,084; 1,751; 1,035; 589; 738
Education, 8; 436; 963; 976; 1,145; 2,762
Professional/other fields, 7; 305; 594; 435; 327; 455

Source: Sanderson, A., et. al., *Doctorate Recipients from United States Universities: Summary Report 1999*, Chicago: National Opinion Research Center, 2000.

★1883★
Age grouping of doctorate recipients, by citizenship, 1999

Ranking basis/background: Based on the 1998-99 Survey of Earned Doctorates (SED) conducted by the National Research Council's Office of Scientific and Engineering Personnel (OSEP). The doctorates are reported by academic year and include research and applied research doctorates in all fields. **Remarks:** The *Summary Report* is the 33rd in an annual series of reports that began in 1967. **Number listed:** 4.

U.S. citizen, with 137 (21-25 yrs); 8,858 (26-30 yrs); 6,697 (31-35 yrs); 3,854 (36-40 yrs); 2,900 (41-45 yrs); 4,936 (over 45)
Permanent Visa, 11; 492; 885; 510; 233; 147
Temporary Visa, 86; 3,034; 3,557; 1,476; 545; 250
Unknown, 7; 82; 75; 66; 53; 156

Source: Sanderson, A., et. al., *Doctorate Recipients from United States Universities: Summary Report 1999*, Chicago: National Opinion Research Center, 2000.

★1884★
Age grouping of doctorate recipients, by gender, 1999

Ranking basis/background: Based on the 1998-99 Survey of Earned Doctorates (SED) conducted by the National Research Council's Office of Scientific and Engineering Personnel (OSEP). The doctorates are reported by academic year and include research and applied research doctorates in all fields. **Remarks:** The *Summary Report* is the 33rd in an annual series of reports that began in 1967. **Number listed:** 2.

DOCTORAL DEGREES

Men, with 166 (21-25 yrs); 7,559 (26-30 yrs); 7,026 (31-35 yrs); 3,579 (36-40 yrs); 1,955 (41-45 yrs); 2,092 (over 45)
Women, 75; 4,905; 4,187; 2,327; 1,776; 3,397

Source: Sanderson, A., et. al., *Doctorate Recipients from United States Universities: Summary Report 1999*, Chicago: National Opinion Research Center, 2000.

★1885★
Age grouping of doctorate recipients, by race/ethnicity, 1999

Ranking basis/background: Based on the 1998-99 Survey of Earned Doctorates (SED) conducted by the National Research Council's Office of Scientific and Engineering Personnel (OSEP). The doctorates are reported by academic year and include research and applied research doctorates in all fields.
Remarks: The *Summary Report* is the 33rd in an annual series of reports that began in 1967.
Number listed: 5.

Asian American/Pacific Islander, with 15 (21-25 yrs); 619 (26-30 yrs); 347 (31-35 yrs); 160 (36-40 yrs); 73 (41-45 yrs); 90 (over 45)
African American, 8; 341; 308; 234; 220; 468
Hispanic American, 2; 312; 277; 179; 144; 183
Native American/Alaskan Native, 0; 36; 49; 36; 34; 61
White, 108; 7,444; 5,628; 3,192; 2,385; 4,062

Source: Sanderson, A., et. al., *Doctorate Recipients from United States Universities: Summary Report 1999*, Chicago: National Opinion Research Center, 2000.

★1886★
Agricultural sciences doctorates awarded at U.S. colleges and universities, by subfield, 1999

Ranking basis/background: Based on the 1998-99 Survey of Earned Doctorates (SED) conducted by the National Research Council's Office of Scientific and Engineering Personnel (OSEP). The doctorates are reported by academic year and include research and applied research doctorates in all fields.
Remarks: The *Summary Report* is the 33rd in an annual series of reports that began in 1967.
Number listed: 26.

Agricultural economics, with 149
Agricultural business and management, 2
Animal breeding and genetics, 21
Animal nutrition, 46
Dairy science, 12
Poultry science, 8
Fisheries science and management, 38
Animal sciences, other, 71
Agronomy and crop science, 106
Plant breeding and genetics, 44
Plant pathology, 66
Plant sciences, other, 38
Food engineering, 7
Soil chemistry/microbiology, 29
Soil sciences, other, 67
Horticulture science, 66
Forest biology, 14
Forest engineering, 1
Forest management, 17
Wood science and pulp/paper technology, 21
Conservation/renewable national resources, 25
Forestry and related sciences, other, 49
Wildlife/range management, 44
Agricultural sciences, general, 8
Agricultural sciences, other, 30

Source: Sanderson, A., et. al., *Doctorate Recipients from United States Universities: Summary Report 1999*, Chicago: National Opinion Research Center, 2000.

★1887★
Biological sciences doctorates awarded at U.S. colleges and universities, by subfield, 1999

Ranking basis/background: Based on the 1998-99 Survey of Earned Doctorates (SED) conducted by the National Research Council's Office of Scientific and Engineering Personnel (OSEP). The doctorates are reported by academic year and include research and applied research doctorates in all fields.
Remarks: The *Summary Report* is the 33rd in an annual series of reports that began in 1967.
Number listed: 30.

Biochemistry, with 763
Biomedical sciences, 177
Biophysics, 173
Biotechnology research, 19
Bacteriology, 13
Plant genetics, 31
Plant pathology, 36
Plant physiology, 54
Botany, other, 68
Anatomy, 33
Biometrics and biostatistics, 76
Cell biology, 285
Ecology, 272
Developmental biology/embryology, 108
Endocrinology, 19
Entomology, 113
Biological immunology, 223
Molecular biology, 719
Microbiology, 382
Neuroscience, 437
Nutritional sciences, 104
Parasitology, 13
Toxicology, 115
Human and animal genetics, 217
Human and animal pathology, 120
Human and animal pharmacology, 243
Human and animal physiology, 243
Zoology, other, 126
Biological sciences, general, 182
Biological sciences, other, 225

Source: Sanderson, A., et. al., *Doctorate Recipients from United States Universities: Summary Report 1999*, Chicago: National Opinion Research Center, 2000.

★1888★
Business and management doctorates awarded at U.S. colleges and universities, by subfield, 1999

Ranking basis/background: Based on the 1998-99 Survey of Earned Doctorates (SED) conducted by the National Research Council's Office of Scientific and Engineering Personnel (OSEP). The doctorates are reported by academic year and include research and applied research doctorates in all fields.
Remarks: The *Summary Report* is the 33rd in an annual series of reports that began in 1967.
Number listed: 11.

Accounting, with 153
Banking/financial support services, 75
Business administration and management, 311
Business/managerial economics, 42
International business, 34
Management information systems/business data processing, 83
Marketing management, 127
Operations research, 52
Organizational behavior, 100
Business management/administrative services, general, 50
Business management/administrative services, other, 77

Source: Sanderson, A., et. al., *Doctorate Recipients from United States Universities: Summary Report 1999*, Chicago: National Opinion Research Center, 2000.

★1889★
Chemistry doctorates awarded at U.S. colleges and universities, by subfield, 1999

Ranking basis/background: Based on the 1998-99 Survey of Earned Doctorates (SED) conducted by the National Research Council's Office of Scientific and Engineering Personnel (OSEP). The doctorates are reported by academic year and include research and applied research doctorates in all fields.
Remarks: The *Summary Report* is the 33rd in an annual series of reports that began in 1967.
Number listed: 10.

Analytical, with 333
Inorganic, 279
Nuclear, 10
Organic, 564
Medicinal/pharmaceutical, 132
Physical, 310
Polymer, 95
Theoretical, 56
Chemistry, general, 196
Chemistry, other, 159

Source: Sanderson, A., et. al., *Doctorate Recipients from United States Universities: Summary Report 1999*, Chicago: National Opinion Research Center, 2000.

★1890★
Citizenship of doctoral recipients in all fields at U.S. colleges and universities, 1999

Ranking basis/background: Based on the 1998-99 Survey of Earned Doctorates (SED) conducted by the National Research Council's Office of Scientific and Engineering Personnel (OSEP). The doctorates are reported by academic year and include research and applied research doctorates in all fields.
Remarks: The *Summary Report* is the 33rd in an annual series of reports that began in 1967.
Number listed: 4.

U.S. Citizens, with 27,622 doctorates awarded
Non-U.S. (Permanent Visa), 2,300
Non-U.S. (Temporary Visa), 9,068
Unknown, 2,150

Source: Sanderson, A., et. al., *Doctorate Recipients from United States Universities: Summary Report 1999*, Chicago: National Opinion Research Center, 2000.

★1891★
Citizenship of doctoral recipients in education at U.S. colleges and universities, 1999

Ranking basis/background: Based on the 1998-99 Survey of Earned Doctorates (SED) conducted by the National Research Council's Office of Scientific and Engineering Personnel (OSEP). The doctorates are reported by academic year and include research and applied research doctorates in all fields.
Remarks: The *Summary Report* is the 33rd in an annual series of reports that began in 1967.
Number listed: 4.
- U.S. Citizens, with 5,429 doctorates awarded
- Non-U.S. (Permanent Visa), 180
- Non-U.S. (Temporary Visa), 519
- Unknown, 429

Source: Sanderson, A., et. al., *Doctorate Recipients from United States Universities: Summary Report 1999*, Chicago: National Opinion Research Center, 2000.

★1892★
Citizenship of doctoral recipients in engineering at U.S. colleges and universities, 1999

Ranking basis/background: Based on the 1998-99 Survey of Earned Doctorates (SED) conducted by the National Research Council's Office of Scientific and Engineering Personnel (OSEP). The doctorates are reported by academic year and include research and applied research doctorates in all fields.
Remarks: The *Summary Report* is the 33rd in an annual series of reports that began in 1967.
Number listed: 4.
- U.S. Citizens, with 2,474 doctorates awarded
- Non-U.S. (Permanent Visa), 399
- Non-U.S. (Temporary Visa), 2,193
- Unknown, 271

Source: Sanderson, A., et. al., *Doctorate Recipients from United States Universities: Summary Report 1999*, Chicago: National Opinion Research Center, 2000.

★1893★
Citizenship of doctoral recipients in humanities at U.S. colleges and universities, 1999

Ranking basis/background: Based on the 1998-99 Survey of Earned Doctorates (SED) conducted by the National Research Council's Office of Scientific and Engineering Personnel (OSEP). The doctorates are reported by academic year and include research and applied research doctorates in all fields.
Remarks: The *Summary Report* is the 33rd in an annual series of reports that began in 1967.
Number listed: 4.
- U.S. Citizens, with 4,267 doctorates awarded
- Non-U.S. (Permanent Visa), 309
- Non-U.S. (Temporary Visa), 640
- Unknown, 252

Source: Sanderson, A., et. al., *Doctorate Recipients from United States Universities: Summary Report 1999*, Chicago: National Opinion Research Center, 2000.

★1894★
Citizenship of doctoral recipients in life sciences at U.S. colleges and universities, 1999

Ranking basis/background: Based on the 1998-99 Survey of Earned Doctorates (SED) conducted by the National Research Council's Office of Scientific and Engineering Personnel (OSEP). The doctorates are reported by academic year and include research and applied research doctorates in all fields.
Remarks: The *Summary Report* is the 33rd in an annual series of reports that began in 1967.
Number listed: 4.
- U.S. Citizens, with 5,121 doctorates awarded
- Non-U.S. (Permanent Visa), 605
- Non-U.S. (Temporary Visa), 2,109
- Unknown, 291

Source: Sanderson, A., et. al., *Doctorate Recipients from United States Universities: Summary Report 1999*, Chicago: National Opinion Research Center, 2000.

★1895★
Citizenship of doctoral recipients in physical sciences, mathematics, and computer sciences at U.S. colleges and universities, 1999

Ranking basis/background: Based on the 1998-99 Survey of Earned Doctorates (SED) conducted by the National Research Council's Office of Scientific and Engineering Personnel (OSEP). The doctorates are reported by academic year and include research and applied research doctorates in all fields.
Remarks: The *Summary Report* is the 33rd in an annual series of reports that began in 1967.
Number listed: 4.
- U.S. Citizens, with 3,443 doctorates awarded
- Non-U.S. (Permanent Visa), 429
- Non-U.S. (Temporary Visa), 2,146
- Unknown, 306

Source: Sanderson, A., et. al., *Doctorate Recipients from United States Universities: Summary Report 1999*, Chicago: National Opinion Research Center, 2000.

★1896★
Citizenship of doctoral recipients in professional/other fields, at U.S. colleges and universities, 1999

Ranking basis/background: Based on the 1998-99 Survey of Earned Doctorates (SED) conducted by the National Research Council's Office of Scientific and Engineering Personnel (OSEP). The doctorates are reported by academic year and include research and applied research doctorates in all fields.
Remarks: The *Summary Report* is the 33rd in an annual series of reports that began in 1967.
Number listed: 4.
- U.S. Citizens, with 1,536 doctorates awarded
- Non-U.S. (Permanent Visa), 120
- Non-U.S. (Temporary Visa), 492
- Unknown, 144

Source: Sanderson, A., et. al., *Doctorate Recipients from United States Universities: Summary Report 1999*, Chicago: National Opinion Research Center, 2000.

★1897★
Citizenship of doctoral recipients in social sciences at U.S. colleges and universities, 1999

Ranking basis/background: Based on the 1998-99 Survey of Earned Doctorates (SED) conducted by the National Research Council's Office of Scientific and Engineering Personnel (OSEP). The doctorates are reported by academic year and include research and applied research doctorates in all fields.
Remarks: The *Summary Report* is the 33rd in an annual series of reports that began in 1967.
Number listed: 4.
- U.S. Citizens, with 5,352 doctorates awarded
- Non-U.S. (Permanent Visa), 258
- Non-U.S. (Temporary Visa), 969
- Unknown, 457

Source: Sanderson, A., et. al., *Doctorate Recipients from United States Universities: Summary Report 1999*, Chicago: National Opinion Research Center, 2000.

★1898★
Communications doctorates awarded at U.S. colleges and universities, by subfield, 1999

Ranking basis/background: Based on the 1998-99 Survey of Earned Doctorates (SED) conducted by the National Research Council's Office of Scientific and Engineering Personnel (OSEP). The doctorates are reported by academic year and include research and applied research doctorates in all fields.
Remarks: The *Summary Report* is the 33rd in an annual series of reports that began in 1967.
Number listed: 5.
- Communications research, with 50
- Mass communications, 153
- Communications theory, 47
- Communications, general, 69
- Communications, other, 60

Source: Sanderson, A., et. al., *Doctorate Recipients from United States Universities: Summary Report 1999*, Chicago: National Opinion Research Center, 2000.

★1899★
Comparative data of women receiving doctorate degrees in selected fields in 1950 and 1998

Ranking basis/background: Number of degrees awarded to women in each field in 1950 and 1998.
Number listed: 11.
- Physics Ph.D.s, with 6 in 1950; and 201 in 1998
- Math Ph.D.s, 11; 297
- Chemistry Ph.D.s, 37; 695
- Engineering Ph.D.s, 1; 769
- Physical sciences Ph.D.s, 58; 1,600
- Social sciences Ph.D.s, 122; 3,838
- Life sciences Ph.D.s, 113; 3,876
- Education Doctorates, 160; 4,120
- Doctorates in all fields, 613; 17,856
- M.D.s, 346; 6,450
- Law degrees, 288; 17,531

Source: Ivie, Rachel and Katie Stowe, "Women in Physics, 2000," *AIP: American Institute of Physics Report*, June 2000, pp. 1-16.

DOCTORAL DEGREES

★1900★
Computer science doctorates awarded at U.S. colleges and universities, by subfield, 1999

Ranking basis/background: Based on the 1998-99 Survey of Earned Doctorates (SED) conducted by the National Research Council's Office of Scientific and Engineering Personnel (OSEP). The doctorates are reported by academic year and include research and applied research doctorates in all fields. **Remarks:** The *Summary Report* is the 33rd in an annual series of reports that began in 1967. **Number listed:** 2.

Computer science, with 735
Information sciences and systems, 115

Source: Sanderson, A., et. al., *Doctorate Recipients from United States Universities: Summary Report 1999*, Chicago: National Opinion Research Center, 2000.

★1901★
Countries of origin for non-U.S. citizens awarded doctorates at U.S. colleges and universities, 1999

Ranking basis/background: Based on the 1998-99 Survey of Earned Doctorates (SED) conducted by the National Research Council's Office of Scientific and Engineering Personnel (OSEP). The doctorates are reported by academic year and include research and applied research doctorates in all fields. **Remarks:** The *Summary Report* is the 33rd in an annual series of reports that began in 1967. **Number listed:** 30.

1. People's Republic of China, with 2,400 U.S. doctorates awarded
2. India, 1,077
3. Korea, 1,017
4. Republic of China (Taiwan), 981
5. Canada, 473
6. Germany, 266
7. Japan, 238
8. Russia, 231
9. Turkey, 224
10. United Kingdom, 215
11. Brazil, 205
12. Mexico, 191
13. Thailand, 181
14. Greece, 117
15. France, 110
16. Iran, 103
17. Italy, 102
18. Romania, 101
19. Spain, 100
20. Jordan, 84
21. Venezuela, 80
22. Australia, 75
23. Egypt, 73
24. Saudi Arabia, 71
25. Yugoslavia, 67
25. Hong Kong, 67
25. Pakistan, 67
28. Indonesia, 64
28. Argentina, 64
30. Malaysia, 63

Source: Sanderson, A., et. al., *Doctorate Recipients from United States Universities: Summary Report 1999*, Chicago: National Opinion Research Center, 2000.

★1902★
Doctoral degree distribution by broad field, 1999

Ranking basis/background: Percentage of doctoral degrees awarded in each field. **Remarks:** Original source: NSF, NIH, USED, NEH, USDA, NASA. **Number listed:** 7.

1. Life sciences, 19.8%
2. Social sciences, 17.1%
3. Education, 15.9%
4. Physical science/math, 15.4%
5. Humanities, 13.3%
6. Engineering, 13.0%
7. Professional/other fields, 5.6%

Source: Sanderson, A., et. al., *Doctorate Recipients from United States Universities: Summary Report 1999*, Chicago: National Opinion Research Center, 2000.

★1903★
Doctoral degree figures projected for men for the years 2002-2008

Ranking basis/background: Based on data analysis conducted by the U.S. Department of Education. **Remarks:** Article contains projections on college enrollment, degree achievement, and high-school graduates. **Number listed:** 9.

2002, with 27,200 degrees
2003, 27,100
2004, 27,000
2005, 26,900
2006, 26,800
2007, 26,700
2008, 26,600

Source: *Projections of Education Statistics to 2008*, NCES 98-016, U.S. Department of Education, National Center for Education Statistics (June 1998).

★1904★
Doctoral degree figures projected for women for the years 2002-2008

Ranking basis/background: Based on data analysis conducted by the U.S. Department of Education. **Remarks:** Article contains projections on college enrollment, degree achievement, and high-school graduates. **Number listed:** 9.

2002, with 20,000 degrees
2003, 20,500
2004, 20,900
2005, 21,400
2006, 21,900
2007, 22,400
2008, 22,900

Source: *Projections of Education Statistics to 2008*, NCES 98-016, U.S. Department of Education, National Center for Education Statistics (June 1998).

★1905★
Doctoral degrees conferred to African Americans by historically black colleges and universities, 1997-98

Ranking basis/background: Total number of degrees awarded to African Americans at historically black institutions compared to all other institutions, plus the average annual percentage of change. **Remarks:** Original source: *Black Issues* analysis of U.S. Department of Education reports of data submitted by institutions. **Number listed:** 3.

Historically black institutions, with 260 degrees awarded; and a 15.2% average annual change
All other institutions, 1,735; 7.8%
Total, 1,995; 8.6%

Source: Borden, Victor M.H., "The Top 100: Interpreting the Data," *Black Issues in Higher Education*, 17: 46-47, (July 6, 2000).

★1906★
Doctorate-granting-institutions awarding the most non-U.S. citizen doctoral degrees, 1999

Ranking basis/background: Based on the 1998-99 Survey of Earned Doctorates (SED) conducted by the National Research Council's Office of Scientific and Engineering Personnel (OSEP). The doctorates are reported by academic year and include research and applied research doctorates in all fields. **Remarks:** The *Summary Report* is the 33rd in an annual series of reports that began in 1967. **Number listed:** 20.

1. University of Illinois, Urbana-Champaign, with 243 non-U.S. citizen doctorates awarded
2. Ohio State University, 237
3. University of Texas, Austin, 230
4. Purdue University, 221
5. University of Wisconsin, Madison, 212
6. University of Minnesota, Twin Cities, 204
7. Texas A&M University, 199
8. University of Michigan, Ann Arbor, 192
9. Cornell University, Endowed Colleges, 188
10. Pennsylvania State University, 182

Source: Sanderson, A., et. al., *Doctorate Recipients from United States Universities: Summary Report 1999*, Chicago: National Opinion Research Center, 2000.

★1907★
Doctorate-granting-institutions with the highest percentage of non-U.S. citizen doctoral degrees awarded, 1999

Ranking basis/background: Based on the 1998-99 Survey of Earned Doctorates (SED) conducted by the National Research Council's Office of Scientific and Engineering Personnel (OSEP). The doctorates are reported by academic year and include research and applied research doctorates in all fields. **Remarks:** The *Summary Report* is the 33rd in an annual series of reports that began in 1967. **Number listed:** 20.

1. New Jersey Institute of Technology, with 79.5% of doctoral degrees awarded to non-U.S. citizens
2. Stevens Institute of Technology, 72.2%
3. Clarkson University, 68.4%
4. Rockefeller University, 61.1%
5. Illinois Institute of Technology, 60.9%
6. Polytechnic University, 60.7%
7. Michigan Technological University, 58.3%
8. University of Missouri, Rolla, 56.8%
9. Rutgers University, Newark, 54.3%
10. University of Massachusetts, Lowell, 50.0%

Source: Sanderson, A., et. al., *Doctorate Recipients from United States Universities: Summary Report 1999*, Chicago: National Opinion Research Center, 2000.

★1908★
Doctorates awarded by U.S. colleges and universities per institution, 1961 to 1999

Ranking basis/background: Based on the 1998-99 Survey of Earned Doctorates (SED) conducted by the National Research Council's Office of Scientific and Engineering Personnel (OSEP). The doctorates are reported by academic year and include research and applied research doctorates in all fields. **Remarks:** The *Summary Report* is the 33rd in an annual series of reports that began in 1967. **Number listed:** 36.

    1961, with 10,413 doctorates awarded; at 174 institutions; 60 doctorates awarded per institution
    1962, 11,500; 175; 66
    1963, 12,728; 186; 68
    1964, 14,325; 196; 73
    1965, 16,340; 206; 79
    1966, 17,949; 216; 83
    1967, 20,403; 220; 93
    1968, 22,937; 230; 100
    1969, 25,743; 232; 111
    1970, 29,498; 242; 122
    1971, 31,867; 264; 121
    1972, 33,041; 271; 122
    1973, 33,755; 290; 116
    1974, 33,047; 297; 111
    1975, 32,952; 297; 111
    1976, 32,946; 299; 110
    1977, 31,716; 309; 103
    1978, 30,875; 316; 98
    1979, 31,239; 316; 99
    1980, 31,020; 325; 95
    1981, 31,356; 328; 96
    1982, 31,111; 333; 93
    1983, 31,281; 337; 93
    1984, 31,337; 336; 93
    1985, 31,297; 342; 92
    1986, 31,902; 345; 92
    1987, 32,370; 353; 92
    1988, 33,500; 355; 94
    1989, 34,327; 360; 95
    1990, 36,067; 358; 101
    1991, 37,534; 367; 102
    1992, 38,890; 370; 105
    1993, 39,801; 375; 106
    1994, 41,034; 377; 109
    1995, 41,743; 384; 109
    1996, 42,415; 392; 108
    1997, 42,555; 382; 111
    1998, 42,683; 387; 110
    1999, 41,140; 392; 105

Source: Sanderson, A., et. al., *Doctorate Recipients from United States Universities: Summary Report 1999*, Chicago: National Opinion Research Center, 2000.

★1909★
Earth, atmosphere, and marine science doctorates awarded at U.S. colleges and universities, by subfield, 1999

Ranking basis/background: Based on the 1998-99 Survey of Earned Doctorates (SED) conducted by the National Research Council's Office of Scientific and Engineering Personnel (OSEP). The doctorates are reported by academic year and include research and applied research doctorates in all fields. **Remarks:** The *Summary Report* is the 33rd in an annual series of reports that began in 1967. **Number listed:** 19.

    Atmospheric physics and chemistry, with 43
    Atmospheric dynamics, 16
    Meteorology, 22
    Atmospheric science/meteorology, general, 33
    Atmospheric science/meteorology, other, 10
    Geology, 158
    Geochemistry, 55
    Geophysics and seismology, 100
    Paleontology, 15
    Mineralogy, petrology, 14
    Stratigraphy, sedimentation, 17
    Geomorphology and glacial geology, 18
    Geological and related science, general, 9
    Geological and related science, other, 35
    Environmental science, 100
    Hydrology and water resources, 32
    Oceanography, 100
    Marine sciences, 30
    Misc. physical sciences, other, 17

Source: Sanderson, A., et. al., *Doctorate Recipients from United States Universities: Summary Report 1999*, Chicago: National Opinion Research Center, 2000.

★1910★
Education accumulated debt of doctorate recipients, 1999

Ranking basis/background: Number of graduates and percentages for each level of debt. Based on the 1998-99 Survey of Earned Doctorates (SED) conducted by the National Research Council's Office of Scientific and Engineering Personnel (OSEP). The doctorates are reported by academic year and include research and applied research doctorates in all fields. **Remarks:** The *Summary Report* is the 33rd in an annual series of reports that began in 1967. **Number listed:** 8.

    $5,000 or less, with 3,561 (9.6%)
    $5,001-$10,000, 2,946 (7.9%)
    $10,001-$15,000, 2,401 (6.5%)
    $15,001-$20,000, 1,945 (5.2%)
    $20,001-$25,000, 1,534 (4.1%)
    $25,001-$30,000, 1,309 (3.5%)
    $30,001 or more, 4,946 (13.3%)
    No debt, 18,545 (49.9%)

Source: Sanderson, A., et. al., *Doctorate Recipients from United States Universities: Summary Report 1999*, Chicago: National Opinion Research Center, 2000.

★1911★
Education accumulated debt of doctorate recipients, by citizenship, 1999

Ranking basis/background: Number of graduates and percentages for each level of debt. Based on the 1998-99 Survey of Earned Doctorates (SED) conducted by the National Research Council's Office of Scientific and Engineering Personnel (OSEP). The doctorates are reported by academic year and include research and applied research doctorates in all fields. **Remarks:** The *Summary Report* is the 33rd in an annual series of reports that began in 1967. **Number listed:** 8.

    $5,000 or less, with 2,504 (9.4%) U.S. citizens; 212 (9.7%) Permanent Visa; 837 (10.0%) Temporary Visa
    $5,001-$10,000, 2,292 (8.6%); 147 (6.7%); 503 (6.0%)
    $10,001-$15,000, 1,988 (7.5%); 103 (4.7%); 306 (3.6%)
    $15,001-$20,000, 1,663 (6.3%); 80 (3.7%); 198 (2.4%)
    $20,001-$25,000, 1,325 (5.0%); 63 (2.9%); 144 (1.7%)
    $25,001-$30,000, 1,143 (4.3%); 48 (2.2%); 116 (1.4%)
    $30,001 or more, 4,160 (15.7%); 175 (8.0%); 606 (7.2%)
    No debt, 11,457 (43.2%); 1,360 (62.2%); 5,694 (67.8%)

Source: Sanderson, A., et. al., *Doctorate Recipients from United States Universities: Summary Report 1999*, Chicago: National Opinion Research Center, 2000.

★1912★
Education accumulated debt of doctorate recipients, by gender, 1999

Ranking basis/background: Number of graduates and percentages for each level of debt. Based on the 1998-99 Survey of Earned Doctorates (SED) conducted by the National Research Council's Office of Scientific and Engineering Personnel (OSEP). The doctorates are reported by academic year and include research and applied research doctorates in all fields. **Remarks:** The *Summary Report* is the 33rd in an annual series of reports that began in 1967. **Number listed:** 8.

    $5,000 or less, with 2,128 (10.0%) men; 1,433 (9.1%) women
    $5,001-$10,000, 1,688 (7.9%); 1,258 (7.9%)
    $10,001-$15,000, 1,366 (6.4%); 1,036 (6.5%)
    $15,001-$20,000, 1,113 (5.2%); 832 (5.3%)
    $20,001-$25,000, 853 (4.0%); 681 (4.3%)
    $25,001-$30,000, 726 (3.4%); 583 (3.7%)
    $30,001 or more, 2,590 (12.1%); 2,356 (14.9%)
    No debt, 10,889 (51.9%); 7,653 (48.3%)

Source: Sanderson, A., et. al., *Doctorate Recipients from United States Universities: Summary Report 1999*, Chicago: National Opinion Research Center, 2000.

★1913★
Education accumulated debt of doctorate recipients, by race/ethnicity, 1999

Ranking basis/background: Number of graduates and percentages for each level of debt. Based on the 1998-99 Survey of Earned Doctorates (SED) conducted by the National Research Council's Office of Scientific and Engineering Personnel (OSEP). The doctorates are reported by academic year and include research and applied research doctorates in all fields. **Remarks:** The *Summary Report* is the 33rd in an annual series of reports that began in 1967. **Number listed:** 8.

    $5,000 or less, with 116 (9.2%) Asian American/Pacific Islander; 168 (11.1%) African American; 112 (11.0%) Hispanic American; 21 (10.4%) Native American/Alaskan Native; and 2,046 (9.2%) White
    $5,001-$10,000, 125 (9.9%); 117 (7.7%); 82 (8.0%); 17 (8.4%); 1,913 (8.6%)
    $10,001-$15,000, 110 (8.7%); 111 (7.3%); 81 (7.9%); 13 (6.4%); 1,638 (7.4%)
    $15,001-$20,000, 65 (5.1%); 108 (7.1%); 72 (7.1%); 10 (5.0%); 1,394 (6.3%)
    $20,001-$25,000, 57 (4.5%); 109 (7.2%); 55 (5.4%); 13 (6.4%); 1,079 (4.9%)
    $25,001-$30,000, 46 (3.6%); 88 (5.8%); 52 (5.1%); 12 (5.9%); 931 (4.2%)
    $30,001 or more, 152 (12.0%); 401 (26.5%); 208 (20.4%); 48 (23.8%); 3,301 (14.9%)
    No debt, 594 (47.0%); 412 (27.2%); 359 (35.2%); 68 (33.7%); 9,867 (44.5%)

DOCTORAL DEGREES

Source: Sanderson, A., et. al., *Doctorate Recipients from United States Universities: Summary Report 1999*, Chicago: National Opinion Research Center, 2000.

★1914★
Education accumulated debt of education doctorate recipients, 1999

Ranking basis/background: Number of graduates and percentages for each level of debt. Based on the 1998-99 Survey of Earned Doctorates (SED) conducted by the National Research Council's Office of Scientific and Engineering Personnel (OSEP). The doctorates are reported by academic year and include research and applied research doctorates in all fields. **Remarks:** The *Summary Report* is the 33rd in an annual series of reports that began in 1967. **Number listed: 8.**

$5,000 or less, with 533 (9.1%)
$5,001-$10,000, 400 (6.9%)
$10,001-$15,000, 317 (5.4%)
$15,001-$20,000, 267 (4.6%)
$20,001-$25,000, 233 (4.0%)
$25,001-$30,000, 189 (3.2%)
$30,001 or more, 799 (13.7%)
No debt, 3,095 (53.1%)

Source: Sanderson, A., et. al., *Doctorate Recipients from United States Universities: Summary Report 1999*, Chicago: National Opinion Research Center, 2000.

★1915★
Education accumulated debt of engineering doctorate recipients, 1999

Ranking basis/background: Number of graduates and percentages for each level of debt. Based on the 1998-99 Survey of Earned Doctorates (SED) conducted by the National Research Council's Office of Scientific and Engineering Personnel (OSEP). The doctorates are reported by academic year and include research and applied research doctorates in all fields. **Remarks:** The *Summary Report* is the 33rd in an annual series of reports that began in 1967. **Number listed: 8.**

$5,000 or less, with 497 (10.3%)
$5,001-$10,000, 332 (6.9%)
$10,001-$15,000, 267 (5.5%)
$15,001-$20,000, 173 (3.6%)
$20,001-$25,000, 146 (3.0%)
$25,001-$30,000, 91 (1.9%)
$30,001 or more, 381 (7.9%)
No debt, 2,958 (61.1%)

Source: Sanderson, A., et. al., *Doctorate Recipients from United States Universities: Summary Report 1999*, Chicago: National Opinion Research Center, 2000.

★1916★
Education accumulated debt of humanities doctorate recipients, 1999

Ranking basis/background: Number of graduates and percentages for each level of debt. Based on the 1998-99 Survey of Earned Doctorates (SED) conducted by the National Research Council's Office of Scientific and Engineering Personnel (OSEP). The doctorates are reported by academic year and include research and applied research doctorates in all fields. **Remarks:** The *Summary Report* is the 33rd in an annual series of reports that began in 1967. **Number listed: 8.**

$5,000 or less, with 462 (9.3%)
$5,001-$10,000, 462 (9.3%)
$10,001-$15,000, 385 (7.7%)
$15,001-$20,000, 332 (6.7%)
$20,001-$25,000, 278 (5.6%)
$25,001-$30,000, 238 (4.8%)
$30,001 or more, 774 (15.5%)
No debt, 2,059 (41.3%)

Source: Sanderson, A., et. al., *Doctorate Recipients from United States Universities: Summary Report 1999*, Chicago: National Opinion Research Center, 2000.

★1917★
Education accumulated debt of life sciences doctorate recipients, 1999

Ranking basis/background: Number of graduates and percentages for each level of debt. Based on the 1998-99 Survey of Earned Doctorates (SED) conducted by the National Research Council's Office of Scientific and Engineering Personnel (OSEP). The doctorates are reported by academic year and include research and applied research doctorates in all fields. **Remarks:** The *Summary Report* is the 33rd in an annual series of reports that began in 1967. **Number listed: 8.**

$5,000 or less, with 801 (10.6%)
$5,001-$10,000, 637 (8.5%)
$10,001-$15,000, 532 (7.1%)
$15,001-$20,000, 392 (5.2%)
$20,001-$25,000, 280 (3.7%)
$25,001-$30,000, 230 (3.1%)
$30,001 or more, 767 (10.2%)
No debt, 3,885 (51.6%)

Source: Sanderson, A., et. al., *Doctorate Recipients from United States Universities: Summary Report 1999*, Chicago: National Opinion Research Center, 2000.

★1918★
Education accumulated debt of physical sciences, mathematics, and computer sciences doctorate recipients, 1999

Ranking basis/background: Number of graduates and percentages for each level of debt. Based on the 1998-99 Survey of Earned Doctorates (SED) conducted by the National Research Council's Office of Scientific and Engineering Personnel (OSEP). The doctorates are reported by academic year and include research and applied research doctorates in all fields. **Remarks:** The *Summary Report* is the 33rd in an annual series of reports that began in 1967. **Number listed: 8.**

$5,000 or less, with 626 (10.8%)
$5,001-$10,000, 482 (8.4%)
$10,001-$15,000, 367 (6.4%)
$15,001-$20,000, 232 (4.0%)
$20,001-$25,000, 171 (3.0%)
$25,001-$30,000, 140 (2.4%)
$30,001 or more, 357 (6.2%)
No debt, 3,395 (58.8%)

Source: Sanderson, A., et. al., *Doctorate Recipients from United States Universities: Summary Report 1999*, Chicago: National Opinion Research Center, 2000.

★1919★
Education accumulated debt of professional/other doctorate recipients, 1999

Ranking basis/background: Number of graduates and percentages for each level of debt. Based on the 1998-99 Survey of Earned Doctorates (SED) conducted by the National Research Council's Office of Scientific and Engineering Personnel (OSEP). The doctorates are reported by academic year and include research and applied research doctorates in all fields. **Remarks:** The *Summary Report* is the 33rd in an annual series of reports that began in 1967. **Number listed: 8.**

$5,000 or less, with 158 (7.9%)
$5,001-$10,000, 162 (8.1%)
$10,001-$15,000, 102 (5.1%)
$15,001-$20,000, 119 (5.9%)
$20,001-$25,000, 83 (4.1%)
$25,001-$30,000, 83 (4.1%)
$30,001 or more, 353 (17.6%)
No debt, 943 (47.1%)

Source: Sanderson, A., et. al., *Doctorate Recipients from United States Universities: Summary Report 1999*, Chicago: National Opinion Research Center, 2000.

★1920★
Education accumulated debt of social sciences doctorate recipients, 1999

Ranking basis/background: Number of graduates and percentages for each level of debt. Based on the 1998-99 Survey of Earned Doctorates (SED) conducted by the National Research Council's Office of Scientific and Engineering Personnel (OSEP). The doctorates are reported by academic year and include research and applied research doctorates in all fields. **Remarks:** The *Summary Report* is the 33rd in an annual series of reports that began in 1967. **Number listed: 8.**

$5,000 or less, with 484 (7.8%)
$5,001-$10,000, 471 (7.6%)
$10,001-$15,000, 432 (6.9%)
$15,001-$20,000, 430 (6.9%)
$20,001-$25,000, 343 (5.5%)
$25,001-$30,000, 338 (5.4%)
$30,001 or more, 1,515 (24.3%)
No debt, 2,210 (35.5%)

Source: Sanderson, A., et. al., *Doctorate Recipients from United States Universities: Summary Report 1999*, Chicago: National Opinion Research Center, 2000.

★1921★
Education doctorates awarded at U.S. colleges and universities, by subfield, 1999

Ranking basis/background: Based on the 1998-99 Survey of Earned Doctorates (SED) conducted by the National Research Council's Office of Scientific and Engineering Personnel (OSEP). The doctorates are reported by academic year and include research and applied research doctorates in all fields. **Remarks:** The *Summary Report* is the 33rd in an annual series of reports that began in 1967. **Number listed: 16.**

Curriculum and instruction, with 996
Educational administration and supervision, 897
Educational leadership, 1,150
Educational/instructional media design, 123
Educational statistics/research methods, 57
Educational assessment, testing and measures, 39
Educational psychology, 298
School psychology, 109
Social/philosophical foundations of education, 125
Special education, 263
Counseling education/counseling and guidance, 261
Higher education/evaluation and research, 464
Pre-elementary/early childhood, 49
Elementary education, 59
Secondary education, 31
Adult and continuing education, 153

Source: Sanderson, A., et. al., *Doctorate Recipients from United States Universities: Summary Report 1999*, Chicago: National Opinion Research Center, 2000.

★1922★
Education doctorates awarded to U.S. citizens/permanent residents at U.S. colleges and universities, by race/ethnicity and subfield, 1999

Ranking basis/background: Based on the 1998-99 Survey of Earned Doctorates (SED) conducted by the National Research Council's Office of Scientific and Engineering Personnel (OSEP). The doctorates are reported by academic year and include research and applied research doctorates in all fields.
Remarks: The *Summary Report* is the 33rd in an annual series of reports that began in 1967.
Number listed: 3.
  Teacher education, with 5 to Asian Americans; 30 to African Americans; 8 to Hispanic Americans; 2 to Native Americans; and 195 to Whites
  Teaching fields, 14; 52; 26; 9; 590
  Other education, 84; 539; 218; 49; 3,539
Source: Sanderson, A., et. al., *Doctorate Recipients from United States Universities: Summary Report 1999*, Chicago: National Opinion Research Center, 2000.

★1923★
Engineering doctorates awarded at U.S. colleges and universities, by subfield, 1999

Ranking basis/background: Based on the 1998-99 Survey of Earned Doctorates (SED) conducted by the National Research Council's Office of Scientific and Engineering Personnel (OSEP). The doctorates are reported by academic year and include research and applied research doctorates in all fields.
Remarks: The *Summary Report* is the 33rd in an annual series of reports that began in 1967.
Number listed: 26.
  Aerospace, aeronautic., astronautic., with 207
  Agricultural, 59
  Bioengineering and biomedical, 245
  Ceramic sciences, 33
  Chemical, 580
  Civil, 507
  Communications, 38
  Computer, 206
  Electrical, electronics, 1,233
  Engineering, mechanics, 68
  Engineering physics, 28
  Engineering science, 51
  Environmental health engineering, 78
  Industrial/manufacturing, 209
  Materials science, 394
  Mechanical, 785
  Metallurgical, 43
  Mining and mineral, 18
  Nuclear, 77
  Ocean, 16
  Operations research, 67
  Petroleum, 45
  Polymer/plastics, 53
  Systems, 42
  Engineering, general, 39
  Engineering, other, 216
Source: Sanderson, A., et. al., *Doctorate Recipients from United States Universities: Summary Report 1999*, Chicago: National Opinion Research Center, 2000.

★1924★
First-professional degree figures projected for men for the years 2002-2008

Ranking basis/background: Based on data analysis conducted by the U.S. Department of Education. **Remarks:** Article contains projections on college enrollment, degree achievement, and high-school graduates. **Number listed:** 9.
  2002, with 40,500 degrees
  2003, 40,100
  2004, 39,800
  2005, 39,900
  2006, 40,100
  2007, 40,500
  2008, 40,800
Source: *Projections of Education Statistics to 2008*, NCES 98-016, U.S. Department of Education, National Center for Education Statistics (June 1998).

★1925★
First-professional degree figures projected for women for the years 2002-2008

Ranking basis/background: Based on data analysis conducted by the U.S. Department of Education. **Remarks:** Article contains projections on college enrollment, degree achievement, and high-school graduates. **Number listed:** 9.
  2002, with 31,800 degrees
  2003, 31,800
  2004, 32,000
  2005, 32,400
  2006, 33,000
  2007, 33,600
  2008, 34,200
Source: *Projections of Education Statistics to 2008*, NCES 98-016, U.S. Department of Education, National Center for Education Statistics (June 1998).

★1926★
Gender breakdown of agricultural sciences doctorate recipients, by subfield, 1999

Ranking basis/background: Number of men and women doctorate recipients for each subfield. Based on the 1998-99 Survey of Earned Doctorates (SED) conducted by the National Research Council's Office of Scientific and Engineering Personnel (OSEP). The doctorates are reported by academic year and include research and applied research doctorates in all fields. **Remarks:** The *Summary Report* is the 33rd in an annual series of reports that began in 1967. **Number listed:** 26.
  Agricultural economics, with 110 men; 39 women
  Agricultural business and management, 2; 0
  Animal breeding and genetics, 14; 7
  Animal nutrition, 34; 12
  Dairy science, 7; 5
  Poultry science, 4; 2
  Fisheries science and management, 31; 7
  Animal sciences, other, 48; 23
  Agronomy and crop science, 90; 16
  Plant breeding and genetics, 31; 13
  Plant pathology, 39; 27
  Plant sciences, other, 26; 12
  Food engineering, 5; 2
  Soil chemistry/microbiology, 21; 8
  Soil sciences, other, 55; 11
  Horticulture science, 50; 16
  Forest biology, 10; 4
  Forest engineering, 1; 0
  Forest management, 14; 3
  Wood science and pulp/paper technology, 15; 6
  Conservation/renewable national resources, 16; 9
  Forestry and related sciences, other, 32; 16
  Wildlife/range management, 36; 8
  Agricultural sciences, general, 8; 0
  Agricultural sciences, other, 24; 6
Source: Sanderson, A., et. al., *Doctorate Recipients from United States Universities: Summary Report 1999*, Chicago: National Opinion Research Center, 2000.

★1927★
Gender breakdown of biological sciences doctorate recipients, by subfield, 1999

Ranking basis/background: Number of men and women doctorate recipients for each subfield. Based on the 1998-99 Survey of Earned Doctorates (SED) conducted by the National Research Council's Office of Scientific and Engineering Personnel (OSEP). The doctorates are reported by academic year and include research and applied research doctorates in all fields. **Remarks:** The *Summary Report* is the 33rd in an annual series of reports that began in 1967. **Number listed:** 30.
  Biochemistry, with 451 men; 310 women
  Biomedical sciences, 101; 72
  Biophysics, 124; 49
  Biotechnology research, 17; 2
  Bacteriology, 7; 6
  Plant genetics, 22; 9
  Plant pathology, 24; 12
  Plant physiology, 31; 23
  Botany, other, 42; 26
  Anatomy, 17; 16
  Biometrics and biostatistics, 39; 36
  Cell biology, 148; 136
  Ecology, 150; 121
  Developmental biology/embryology, 54; 54
  Endocrinology, 10; 9
  Entomology, 77; 36
  Biological immunology, 123; 100
  Molecular biology, 419; 299
  Microbiology, 218; 163
  Neuroscience, 253; 183
  Nutritional sciences, 34; 69
  Parasitology, 7; 6
  Toxicology, 62; 53
  Human and animal genetics, 110; 106
  Human and animal pathology, 65; 54
  Human and animal pharmacology, 134; 108
  Human and animal physiology, 134; 108
  Zoology, other, 79; 47
  Biological sciences, general, 104; 75
  Biological sciences, other, 118; 107
Source: Sanderson, A., et. al., *Doctorate Recipients from United States Universities: Summary Report 1999*, Chicago: National Opinion Research Center, 2000.

DOCTORAL DEGREES

★1928★
Gender breakdown of business and management doctorate recipients, by subfield, 1999

Ranking basis/background: Number of men and women doctorate recipients for each subfield. Based on the 1998-99 Survey of Earned Doctorates (SED) conducted by the National Research Council's Office of Scientific and Engineering Personnel (OSEP). The doctorates are reported by academic year and include research and applied research doctorates in all fields. **Remarks:** The *Summary Report* is the 33rd in an annual series of reports that began in 1967. **Number listed:** 11.

Accounting, with 92 men; 60 women
Banking/financial support services, 62; 13
Business administration and management, 228; 80
Business/managerial economics, 32; 10
International business, 26; 8
Management information systems/business data processing, 59; 24
Marketing management, 89; 38
Operations research, 45; 7
Organizational behavior, 42; 58
Business management/administrative services, general, 31; 17
Business management/administrative services, other, 50; 27

Source: Sanderson, A., et. al., *Doctorate Recipients from United States Universities: Summary Report 1999*, Chicago: National Opinion Research Center, 2000.

★1929★
Gender breakdown of chemistry doctorate recipients, by subfield, 1999

Ranking basis/background: Number of men and women doctorate recipients for each subfield. Based on the 1998-99 Survey of Earned Doctorates (SED) conducted by the National Research Council's Office of Scientific and Engineering Personnel (OSEP). The doctorates are reported by academic year and include research and applied research doctorates in all fields. **Remarks:** The *Summary Report* is the 33rd in an annual series of reports that began in 1967. **Number listed:** 10.

Analytical, with 225 men; 108 women
Inorganic, 189; 90
Nuclear, 9; 1
Organic, 399; 163
Medicinal/pharmaceutical, 81; 51
Physical, 235; 75
Polymer, 64; 31
Theoretical, 47; 9
Chemistry, general, 139; 52
Chemistry, other, 106; 53

Source: Sanderson, A., et. al., *Doctorate Recipients from United States Universities: Summary Report 1999*, Chicago: National Opinion Research Center, 2000.

★1930★
Gender breakdown of communications doctorate recipients, by subfield, 1999

Ranking basis/background: Number of men and women doctorate recipients for each subfield. Based on the 1998-99 Survey of Earned Doctorates (SED) conducted by the National Research Council's Office of Scientific and Engineering Personnel (OSEP). The doctorates are reported by academic year and include research and applied research doctorates in all fields. **Remarks:** The *Summary Report* is the 33rd in an annual series of reports that began in 1967. **Number listed:** 5.

Communications research, with 28 men; 22 women
Mass communications, 78; 74
Communications theory, 20; 27
Communications, general, 28; 41
Communications, other, 27; 33

Source: Sanderson, A., et. al., *Doctorate Recipients from United States Universities: Summary Report 1999*, Chicago: National Opinion Research Center, 2000.

★1931★
Gender breakdown of computer science doctorate recipients, by subfield, 1999

Ranking basis/background: Number of men and women doctorate recipients for each subfield. Based on the 1998-99 Survey of Earned Doctorates (SED) conducted by the National Research Council's Office of Scientific and Engineering Personnel (OSEP). The doctorates are reported by academic year and include research and applied research doctorates in all fields. **Remarks:** The *Summary Report* is the 33rd in an annual series of reports that began in 1967. **Number listed:** 2.

Computer science, with 609 men; 119 women
Information sciences and systems, 78; 37

Source: Sanderson, A., et. al., *Doctorate Recipients from United States Universities: Summary Report 1999*, Chicago: National Opinion Research Center, 2000.

★1932★
Gender breakdown of earth, atmosphere, and marine science doctorate recipients, by subfield, 1999

Ranking basis/background: Number of men and women doctorate recipients for each subfield. Based on the 1998-99 Survey of Earned Doctorates (SED) conducted by the National Research Council's Office of Scientific and Engineering Personnel (OSEP). The doctorates are reported by academic year and include research and applied research doctorates in all fields. **Remarks:** The *Summary Report* is the 33rd in an annual series of reports that began in 1967. **Number listed:** 19.

Atmospheric physics and chemistry, with 32 men; 11 women
Atmospheric dynamics, 12; 4
Meteorology, 21; 1
Atmospheric science/meteorology, general, 29; 3
Atmospheric science/meteorology, other, 7; 3
Geology, 117; 41
Geochemistry, 34; 21
Geophysics and seismology, 84; 15
Paleontology, 11; 4
Mineralogy, petrology, 11; 3
Stratigraphy, sedimentation, 14; 3
Geomorphology and glacial geology, 9; 9
Geological and related science, general, 7; 1
Geological and related science, other, 25; 10
Environmental science, 68; 31
Hydrology and water resources, 27; 5
Oceanography, 64; 36
Marine sciences, 21; 9
Misc. physical sciences, other, 11; 6

Source: Sanderson, A., et. al., *Doctorate Recipients from United States Universities: Summary Report 1999*, Chicago: National Opinion Research Center, 2000.

★1933★
Gender breakdown of education doctorate recipients, by subfield, 1999

Ranking basis/background: Number of men and women doctorate recipients for each subfield. Based on the 1998-99 Survey of Earned Doctorates (SED) conducted by the National Research Council's Office of Scientific and Engineering Personnel (OSEP). The doctorates are reported by academic year and include research and applied research doctorates in all fields. **Remarks:** The *Summary Report* is the 33rd in an annual series of reports that began in 1967. **Number listed:** 16.

Curriculum and instruction, with 280 men; 712 women
Educational administration and supervision, 361; 536
Educational leadership, 456; 693
Educational/instructional media design, 69; 54
Educational statistics/research methods, 23; 33
Educational assessment, testing and measures, 20; 19
Educational psychology, 80; 218
School psychology, 19; 90
Social/philosophical foundations of education, 60; 65
Special education, 58; 204
Counseling education/counseling and guidance, 97; 164
Higher education/evaluation and research, 182; 281
Pre-elementary/early childhood, 4; 45
Elementary education, 12; 47
Secondary education, 12; 19
Adult and continuing education, 62; 90

Source: Sanderson, A., et. al., *Doctorate Recipients from United States Universities: Summary Report 1999*, Chicago: National Opinion Research Center, 2000.

★1934★
Gender breakdown of engineering doctorate recipients, by subfield, 1999

Ranking basis/background: Number of men and women doctorate recipients for each subfield. Based on the 1998-99 Survey of Earned Doctorates (SED) conducted by the National Research Council's Office of Scientific and Engineering Personnel (OSEP). The doctorates are reported by academic year and include research and applied research doctorates in all fields. **Remarks:** The *Summary Report* is the 33rd in an annual series of reports that began in 1967. **Number listed:** 26.

Aerospace, aeronautic., astronautic., with 189 men; 17 women
Agricultural, 47; 12
Bioengineering and biomedical, 181; 63
Ceramic sciences, 24; 9
Chemical, 477; 102
Civil, 430; 76
Communications, 32; 6
Computer, 171; 33
Electrical, electronics, 1,105; 117
Engineering, mechanics, 56; 11
Engineering physics, 24; 4
Engineering science, 46; 4
Environmental health engineering, 65; 13
Industrial/manufacturing, 166; 43
Materials science, 316; 75
Mechanical, 693; 84
Metallurgical, 37; 4
Mining and mineral, 16; 2
Nuclear, 69; 8

Ocean, 15; 1
Operations research, 51; 16
Petroleum, 40; 5
Polymer/plastics, 36; 17
Systems, 34; 7
Engineering, general, 32; 4
Engineering, other, 151; 58

Source: Sanderson, A., et. al., *Doctorate Recipients from United States Universities: Summary Report 1999*, Chicago: National Opinion Research Center, 2000.

★1935★
Gender breakdown of health sciences doctorate recipients, by subfield, 1999

Ranking basis/background: Number of men and women doctorate recipients for each subfield. Based on the 1998-99 Survey of Earned Doctorates (SED) conducted by the National Research Council's Office of Scientific and Engineering Personnel (OSEP). The doctorates are reported by academic year and include research and applied research doctorates in all fields. **Remarks:** The *Summary Report* is the 33rd in an annual series of reports that began in 1967. **Number listed:** 12.

Speech-language pathology and audiology, with 31 men; 55 women
Environmental health, 39; 28
Health systems/services administration, 22; 38
Public health, 57; 112
Epidemiology, 67; 112
Exercise physiology/science, kinesiology, 70; 34
Nursing, 15; 340
Pharmacy, 82; 55
Rehabilitation/therapeutic services, 6; 20
Veterinary medicine, 27; 22
Health sciences, general, 13; 19
Health sciences, other, 70; 66

Source: Sanderson, A., et. al., *Doctorate Recipients from United States Universities: Summary Report 1999*, Chicago: National Opinion Research Center, 2000.

★1936★
Gender breakdown of humanities doctorate recipients, by subfield, 1999

Ranking basis/background: Number of men and women doctorate recipients for each subfield. Based on the 1998-99 Survey of Earned Doctorates (SED) conducted by the National Research Council's Office of Scientific and Engineering Personnel (OSEP). The doctorates are reported by academic year and include research and applied research doctorates in all fields. **Remarks:** The *Summary Report* is the 33rd in an annual series of reports that began in 1967. **Number listed:** 19.

History, American, with 253 men; 165 women
History, Asian, 45; 23
History, European, 144; 91
History/philosophy of science and technology, 31; 18
History, general, 50; 26
History, other, 88; 77
Classics, 46; 31
Comparative literature, 67; 98
Linguistics, 99; 147
Speech and rhetorical studies, 65; 85
Letters, general, 6; 13
Letters, other, 30; 53
American studies, 40; 56
Archeology, 14; 12
Art history/criticism/conservation, 56; 132
Music, 426; 323
Philosophy, 290; 96
Religion, 255; 82
Drama/theater arts, 50; 49

Source: Sanderson, A., et. al., *Doctorate Recipients from United States Universities: Summary Report 1999*, Chicago: National Opinion Research Center, 2000.

★1937★
Gender breakdown of language and literature doctorate recipients, by subfield, 1999

Ranking basis/background: Number of men and women doctorate recipients for each subfield. Based on the 1998-99 Survey of Earned Doctorates (SED) conducted by the National Research Council's Office of Scientific and Engineering Personnel (OSEP). The doctorates are reported by academic year and include research and applied research doctorates in all fields. **Remarks:** The *Summary Report* is the 33rd in an annual series of reports that began in 1967. **Number listed:** 15.

American, with 147 men; 225 women
English, 271; 379
French, 44; 105
German, 32; 58
Italian, 7; 13
Spanish, 81; 120
Russian, 9; 17
Slavic, 10; 7
Chinese, 10; 17
Japanese, 6; 4
Hebrew, 2; 2
Arabic, 7; 5
Other language and literature, 35; 36

Source: Sanderson, A., et. al., *Doctorate Recipients from United States Universities: Summary Report 1999*, Chicago: National Opinion Research Center, 2000.

★1938★
Gender breakdown of mathematics doctorate recipients, by subfield, 1999

Ranking basis/background: Number of men and women doctorate recipients for each subfield. Based on the 1998-99 Survey of Earned Doctorates (SED) conducted by the National Research Council's Office of Scientific and Engineering Personnel (OSEP). The doctorates are reported by academic year and include research and applied research doctorates in all fields. **Remarks:** The *Summary Report* is the 33rd in an annual series of reports that began in 1967. **Number listed:** 12.

Applied mathematics, with 193 men; 59 women
Algebra, 58; 25
Analysis and functional analysis, 68; 19
Geometry, 49; 16
Logic, 18; 5
Number theory, 38; 12
Mathematical statistics, 128; 46
Topology, 50; 15
Computing theory and practice, 11; 3
Operations research, 12; 9
Mathematics, general, 93; 22
Mathematics, other, 87; 46

Source: Sanderson, A., et. al., *Doctorate Recipients from United States Universities: Summary Report 1999*, Chicago: National Opinion Research Center, 2000.

★1939★
Gender breakdown of physics and astronomy doctorate recipients, by subfield, 1999

Ranking basis/background: Number of men and women doctorate recipients for each subfield. Based on the 1998-99 Survey of Earned Doctorates (SED) conducted by the National Research Council's Office of Scientific and Engineering Personnel (OSEP). The doctorates are reported by academic year and include research and applied research doctorates in all fields. **Remarks:** The *Summary Report* is the 33rd in an annual series of reports that began in 1967. **Number listed:** 13.

Astronomy, with 43 men; 17 women
Astrophysics, 85; 15
Acoustics, 15; 1
Chemical and atomic/molecular, 85; 14
Elementary particles, 152; 17
Fluids, 19; 2
Nuclear, 67; 9
Optics, 84; 12
Plasma and high-temperature, 47; 2
Polymer, 21; 7
Solid state and low-temperature, 266; 42
Physics, general, 177; 23
Physics, other, 170; 31

Source: Sanderson, A., et. al., *Doctorate Recipients from United States Universities: Summary Report 1999*, Chicago: National Opinion Research Center, 2000.

★1940★
Gender breakdown of professional doctorate recipients, by subfield, 1999

Ranking basis/background: Number of men and women doctorate recipients for each subfield. Based on the 1998-99 Survey of Earned Doctorates (SED) conducted by the National Research Council's Office of Scientific and Engineering Personnel (OSEP). The doctorates are reported by academic year and include research and applied research doctorates in all fields. **Remarks:** The *Summary Report* is the 33rd in an annual series of reports that began in 1967. **Number listed:** 10.

Architectural environmental design, with 45 men; 20 women
Home economics, 6; 17
Law, 26; 10
Library science, 10; 29
Parks/recreation/leisure/fitness, 17; 12
Public administration, 71; 48
Social work, 58; 171
Theology/religious education, 130; 38
Professional fields, general, 2; 7
Professional fields, other, 31; 32

Source: Sanderson, A., et. al., *Doctorate Recipients from United States Universities: Summary Report 1999*, Chicago: National Opinion Research Center, 2000.

★1941★
Gender breakdown of psychology doctorate recipients, by subfield, 1999

Ranking basis/background: Number of men and women doctorate recipients for each subfield. Based on the 1998-99 Survey of Earned Doctorates (SED) conducted by the National Research Council's Office of Scientific and Engineering Personnel (OSEP). The doctorates are reported by academic year and include research and applied research doctorates in all fields. **Remarks:** The *Summary Report* is the 33rd in an annual series of reports that began in 1967. **Number listed:** 18.

Clinical, with 408 men; 1,040 women

Cognitive and psycholinguistics, 73; 70
Comparative, 4; 7
Counseling, 165; 296
Developmental and child, 44; 149
Human/individual and family counseling, 23; 107
Experimental, 20; 45
Educational, 20; 45
Family and marriage counseling, 17; 38
Industrial and organizational, 59; 99
Personality, 5; 11
Physiological/psychobiology, 37; 50
Psychometrics, 13; 2
Quantitative, 7; 7
School, 32; 88
Social, 60; 114
Psychology, general, 97; 125
Psychology, other, 73; 135

Source: Sanderson, A., et. al., *Doctorate Recipients from United States Universities: Summary Report 1999*, Chicago: National Opinion Research Center, 2000.

★1942★
Gender breakdown of social sciences doctorate recipients, by subfield, 1999

Ranking basis/background: Number of men and women doctorate recipients for each subfield. Based on the 1998-99 Survey of Earned Doctorates (SED) conducted by the National Research Council's Office of Scientific and Engineering Personnel (OSEP). The doctorates are reported by academic year and include research and applied research doctorates in all fields. **Remarks:** The *Summary Report* is the 33rd in an annual series of reports that began in 1967. **Number listed:** 15.

Anthropology, with 200 men; 261 women
Area studies, 8; 3
Criminology, 31; 20
Demography/population studies, 10; 17
Economics, 661; 247
Econometrics, 10; 5
Geography, 95; 49
International relations/affairs, 81; 38
Political science and government, 435; 215
Public policy analysis, 68; 55
Sociology, 218; 324
Statistics, 49; 21
Urban affairs/studies, 40; 17
Social sciences, general, 11; 14
Social sciences, other, 67; 86

Source: Sanderson, A., et. al., *Doctorate Recipients from United States Universities: Summary Report 1999*, Chicago: National Opinion Research Center, 2000.

★1943★
Gender breakdown of teaching fields doctorate recipients, by subfield, 1999

Ranking basis/background: Number of men and women doctorate recipients for each subfield. Based on the 1998-99 Survey of Earned Doctorates (SED) conducted by the National Research Council's Office of Scientific and Engineering Personnel (OSEP). The doctorates are reported by academic year and include research and applied research doctorates in all fields. **Remarks:** The *Summary Report* is the 33rd in an annual series of reports that began in 1967. **Number listed:** 20.

Agricultural education, with 24 men; 14 women
Art education, 16; 31
Business education, 14; 30
English education, 13; 51
Foreign language education, 17; 45
Health education, 18; 40
Home economics education, 2; 8
Technical/industrial arts education, 15; 6
Mathematics education, 38; 62
Music education, 37; 41
Nursing education, 3; 19
Physical education and coaching, 63; 51
Reading education, 9; 59
Science education, 30; 28
Social science education, 7; 2
Technical education, 21; 6
Trade and industrial education, 11; 3
Teacher education/special academics and vocations, 21; 33
Education, general, 57; 137
Education, other, 133; 260

Source: Sanderson, A., et. al., *Doctorate Recipients from United States Universities: Summary Report 1999*, Chicago: National Opinion Research Center, 2000.

★1944★
Health sciences doctorates awarded at U.S. colleges and universities, by subfield, 1999

Ranking basis/background: Based on the 1998-99 Survey of Earned Doctorates (SED) conducted by the National Research Council's Office of Scientific and Engineering Personnel (OSEP). The doctorates are reported by academic year and include research and applied research doctorates in all fields. **Remarks:** The *Summary Report* is the 33rd in an annual series of reports that began in 1967. **Number listed:** 12.

Speech-language pathology and audiology, with 86
Environmental health, 69
Health systems/services administration, 62
Public health, 171
Epidemiology, 180
Exercise physiology/science, kinesiology, 104
Nursing, 358
Pharmacy, 137
Rehabilitation/therapeutic services, 26
Veterinary medicine, 49
Health sciences, general, 32
Health sciences, other, 136

Source: Sanderson, A., et. al., *Doctorate Recipients from United States Universities: Summary Report 1999*, Chicago: National Opinion Research Center, 2000.

★1945★
Historically black colleges and universities awarding the most doctorate degrees to African Americans

Ranking basis/background: Total doctoral degrees conferred to African American students in all disciplines combined during the 1997-98 academic year. **Remarks:** Original source: *Black Issues* analysis of U.S. Department of Education reports of data submitted by institutions. **Number listed:** 9.

1. Howard University (DC)
2. Virginia Union University (VA)
3. Clark Atlanta University (GA)
4. Jackson State University (MS)
5. Meharry Medical College (TN)
6. South Carolina State University (SC)
7. Texas Southern University (TX)
8. Tennessee State University (TN)
9. Interdenominational Theological Center (GA)

Source: "Top 100 Degree Producers," *Black Issues in Higher Education*, 17: 48-89, (July 7, 2000).

★1946★
Humanities doctorates awarded at U.S. colleges and universities, by subfield, 1999

Ranking basis/background: Based on the 1998-99 Survey of Earned Doctorates (SED) conducted by the National Research Council's Office of Scientific and Engineering Personnel (OSEP). The doctorates are reported by academic year and include research and applied research doctorates in all fields. **Remarks:** The *Summary Report* is the 33rd in an annual series of reports that began in 1967. **Number listed:** 19.

History, American, with 418
History, Asian, 68
History, European, 235
History/philosophy of science and technology, 49
History, general, 76
History, other, 165
Classics, 77
Comparative literature, 166
Linguistics, 250
Speech and rhetorical studies, 150
Letters, general, 19
Letters, other, 83
American studies, 98
Archeology, 26
Art history/criticism/conservation, 189
Music, 769
Philosophy, 387
Religion, 337
Drama/theater arts, 99

Source: Sanderson, A., et. al., *Doctorate Recipients from United States Universities: Summary Report 1999*, Chicago: National Opinion Research Center, 2000.

★1947★
Humanities doctorates awarded to U.S. citizens/permanent residents at U.S. colleges and universities, by race/ethnicity and subfield, 1999

Ranking basis/background: Based on the 1998-99 Survey of Earned Doctorates (SED) conducted by the National Research Council's Office of Scientific and Engineering Personnel (OSEP). The doctorates are reported by academic year and include research and applied research doctorates in all fields. **Remarks:** The *Summary Report* is the 33rd in an annual series of reports that began in 1967. **Number listed:** 4.

History, with 27 to Asian Americans; 28 to African Americans; 23 to Hispanic Americans; 4 to Native Americans; and 743 to Whites
American and English language and literature, 19; 37; 33; 2; 783
Foreign language and literature, 17; 16; 53; 3; 307
Other humanities, 63; 91; 61; 16; 1,862

Source: Sanderson, A., et. al., *Doctorate Recipients from United States Universities: Summary Report 1999*, Chicago: National Opinion Research Center, 2000.

★1948★
Institutions awarding the most doctorate degrees to African Americans, 1997-98

Ranking basis/background: Total doctorate degrees awarded to men and women, in all disciplines combined, during the 1997-98 academic year. **Remarks:** Original source: U.S. Department of Education reports of data submitted by institutions, ranking are based on the third review of 1997-98 preliminary data. **Number listed:** 52.

1. Nova Southern University, with 12 doctorate to men; 65 doctorates to women; 77 doctorates total
2. Howard University, 25; 39; 64
3. Virginia Union University, 48; 15; 63
4. United Theological Seminary, 34; 16; 50
5. Clark Atlanta University, 13; 28; 41
6. Virginia Polytechnic Institute and State University, 3; 30; 33
7. Harvard University, 12; 20; 32
8. Florida State University, 17; 14; 31
9. Union Institute, 11; 19; 30
10. Columbia University, Teachers College, 11; 18; 29

Source: Lum, Lydia, "Will Historic Inequities Ever Be Remedied?," *Black Issues in Higher Education*, 18: 32-29, (March 29, 2001).

★1949★
Language and literature doctorates awarded at U.S. colleges and universities, by subfield, 1999

Ranking basis/background: Based on the 1998-99 Survey of Earned Doctorates (SED) conducted by the National Research Council's Office of Scientific and Engineering Personnel (OSEP). The doctorates are reported by academic year and include research and applied research doctorates in all fields. **Remarks:** The *Summary Report* is the 33rd in an annual series of reports that began in 1967. **Number listed:** 15.

American, with 372
English, 652
French, 149
German, 90
Italian, 20
Spanish, 201
Russian, 26
Slavic, 17
Chinese, 27
Japanese, 10
Hebrew, 4
Arabic, 12
Other language and literature, 72

Source: Sanderson, A., et. al., *Doctorate Recipients from United States Universities: Summary Report 1999*, Chicago: National Opinion Research Center, 2000.

★1950★
Life sciences doctorates awarded to U.S. citizens/permanent residents at U.S. colleges and universities, by race/ethnicity and subfield, 1999

Ranking basis/background: Based on the 1998-99 Survey of Earned Doctorates (SED) conducted by the National Research Council's Office of Scientific and Engineering Personnel (OSEP). The doctorates are reported by academic year and include research and applied research doctorates in all fields. **Remarks:** The *Summary Report* is the 33rd in an annual series of reports that began in 1967. **Number listed:** 3.

Biological sciences, with 297 to Asian Americans; 109 to African Americans; 145 to Hispanic Americans; 20 to Native Americans; and 3,028 to Whites
Health sciences, 43; 51; 39; 6; 815
Agricultural sciences, 21; 18; 11; 2; 442

Source: Sanderson, A., et. al., *Doctorate Recipients from United States Universities: Summary Report 1999*, Chicago: National Opinion Research Center, 2000.

★1951★
Mathematics doctorates awarded at U.S. colleges and universities, by subfield, 1999

Ranking basis/background: Based on the 1998-99 Survey of Earned Doctorates (SED) conducted by the National Research Council's Office of Scientific and Engineering Personnel (OSEP). The doctorates are reported by academic year and include research and applied research doctorates in all fields. **Remarks:** The *Summary Report* is the 33rd in an annual series of reports that began in 1967. **Number listed:** 12.

Applied mathematics, with 252
Algebra, 84
Analysis and functional analysis, 87
Geometry, 65
Logic, 23
Number theory, 50
Mathematical statistics, 174
Topology, 65
Computing theory and practice, 14
Operations research, 21
Mathematics, general, 117
Mathematics, other, 133

Source: Sanderson, A., et. al., *Doctorate Recipients from United States Universities: Summary Report 1999*, Chicago: National Opinion Research Center, 2000.

★1952★
Median age at conferral of doctoral degree from U.S. universities, by discipline, 1999

Ranking basis/background: Median age at doctorate conferral for each field of study. **Remarks:** Original source: "Survey of Earned Doctorates." **Number listed:** 9.

All fields, with a median age of 33.8
Arts and humanities, 35.1
Business, 36.1
Education, 44.3
Engineering, 31.4
Life sciences, 32.1
Physical sciences, 30.7
Social sciences, 33.2
Professional fields, 39.1

Source: Leatherman, Courtney, "The Number of New Ph.D.'s Drops For the First Time Since 1985," *The Chronicle of Higher Education*, 47: A10-A11, (February 9, 2001).

★1953★
Median age of doctorate recipients in all fields, 1999

Ranking basis/background: Age distribution percentages of Ph.D. recipients for all fields of study. Data collected is from an annual Survey of Earned Doctorates and a census of research doctoral recipients earning their degree between July 1, 1998 and June 30, 1999. **Remarks:** Original source: NSF, NIH, USED, NEH, USDA, NASA. **Number listed:** 4.

21-30 years, with 32.5%
31-40 years, 43.8%
41 years & older, 23.6%

Source: Sanderson, A., et. al., *Doctorate Recipients from United States Universities: Summary Report 1999*, Chicago: National Opinion Research Center, 2000.

★1954★
Median age of doctorate recipients in education, 1999

Ranking basis/background: Age distribution percentages of Ph.D. recipients in education. Data collected is from an annual Survey of Earned Doctorates and a census of research doctoral recipients earning their degree between July 1, 1998 and June 30, 1999. **Remarks:** Original source: NSF, NIH, USED, NEH, USDA, NASA. **Number listed:** 4.

21-30 years, with 7.1%
31-40 years, 30.8%
41 years & older, 62.1%

Source: Sanderson, A., et. al., *Doctorate Recipients from United States Universities: Summary Report 1999*, Chicago: National Opinion Research Center, 2000.

★1955★
Median age of doctorate recipients in engineering, 1999

Ranking basis/background: Age distribution percentages of Ph.D. recipients in engineering. Data collected is from an annual Survey of Earned Doctorates and a census of research doctoral recipients earning their degree between July 1, 1998 and June 30, 1999. **Remarks:** Original source: NSF, NIH, USED, NEH, USDA, NASA. **Number listed:** 4.

21-30 years, with 45.4%
31-40 years, 47.6%
41 years & older, 6.9%

Source: Sanderson, A., et. al., *Doctorate Recipients from United States Universities: Summary Report 1999*, Chicago: National Opinion Research Center, 2000.

★1956★
Median age of doctorate recipients in humanities, 1999

Ranking basis/background: Age distribution percentages of Ph.D. recipients in humanities. Data collected is from an annual Survey of Earned Doctorates and a census of research doctoral recipients earning their degree between July 1, 1998 and June 30, 1999. **Remarks:** Original source: NSF, NIH, USED, NEH, USDA, NASA. **Number listed:** 4.

21-30 years, with 21.0%
31-40 years, 53.5%
41 years & older, 25.5%

Source: Sanderson, A., et. al., *Doctorate Recipients from United States Universities: Summary Report 1999*, Chicago: National Opinion Research Center, 2000.

★1957★
Median age of doctorate recipients in life sciences, 1999

Ranking basis/background: Age distribution percentages of Ph.D. recipients in life sciences. Data collected is from an annual Survey of Earned Doctorates and a census of research doctoral recipients earning their degree between July 1, 1998 and June 30, 1999. **Remarks:** Original source: NSF, NIH, USED, NEH, USDA, NASA. **Number listed:** 4.

DOCTORAL DEGREES

21-30 years, with 40.6%
31-40 years, 45.4%
41 years & older, 14.0%

Source: Sanderson, A., et. al., *Doctorate Recipients from United States Universities: Summary Report 1999*, Chicago: National Opinion Research Center, 2000.

★1958★
Median age of doctorate recipients in physical sciences, 1999

Ranking basis/background: Age distribution percentages of Ph.D. recipients in physical sciences. Data collected is from an annual Survey of Earned Doctorates and a census of research doctoral recipients earning their degree between July 1, 1998 and June 30, 1999. **Remarks:** Original source: NSF, NIH, USED, NEH, USDA, NASA. **Number listed:** 4.

21-30 years, with 52.8%
31-40 years, 40.4%
41 years & older, 6.8%

Source: Sanderson, A., et. al., *Doctorate Recipients from United States Universities: Summary Report 1999*, Chicago: National Opinion Research Center, 2000.

★1959★
Median age of doctorate recipients in professional and other fields, 1999

Ranking basis/background: Age distribution percentages of Ph.D. recipients in professional and other fields. Data collected is from an annual Survey of Earned Doctorates and a census of research doctoral recipients earning their degree between July 1, 1998 and June 30, 1999. **Remarks:** Original source: NSF, NIH, USED, NEH, USDA, NASA. **Number listed:** 4.

21-30 years, with 14.7%
31-40 years, 48.5%
41 years & older, 36.8%

Source: Sanderson, A., et. al., *Doctorate Recipients from United States Universities: Summary Report 1999*, Chicago: National Opinion Research Center, 2000.

★1960★
Median age of doctorate recipients in social sciences, 1999

Ranking basis/background: Age distribution percentages of Ph.D. recipients in social sciences. Data collected is from an annual Survey of Earned Doctorates and a census of research doctoral recipients earning their degree between July 1, 1998 and June 30, 1999. **Remarks:** Original source: NSF, NIH, USED, NEH, USDA, NASA. **Number listed:** 4.

21-30 years, with 33.9%
31-40 years, 45.6%
41 years & older, 20.5%

Source: Sanderson, A., et. al., *Doctorate Recipients from United States Universities: Summary Report 1999*, Chicago: National Opinion Research Center, 2000.

★1961★
Number and percentage of doctorate recipients in all fields, at U.S. colleges and universities, by gender, 1999

Ranking basis/background: Based on the 1998-99 Survey of Earned Doctorates (SED) conducted by the National Research Council's Office of Scientific and Engineering Personnel (OSEP). The doctorates are reported by academic year and include research and applied research doctorates in all fields. **Remarks:** The *Summary Report* is the 33rd in an annual series of reports that began in 1967. **Number listed:** 2.

Men, with 23,460; 57.0%
Women, 17,493; 42.5%

Source: Sanderson, A., et. al., *Doctorate Recipients from United States Universities: Summary Report 1999*, Chicago: National Opinion Research Center, 2000.

★1962★
Number and percentage of education doctorate recipients, at U.S. colleges and universities, by gender, 1999

Ranking basis/background: Based on the 1998-99 Survey of Earned Doctorates (SED) conducted by the National Research Council's Office of Scientific and Engineering Personnel (OSEP). The doctorates are reported by academic year and include research and applied research doctorates in all fields. **Remarks:** The *Summary Report* is the 33rd in an annual series of reports that began in 1967. **Number listed:** 2.

Men, with 2,344; 35.8%
Women, 4,196; 64.2%

Source: Sanderson, A., et. al., *Doctorate Recipients from United States Universities: Summary Report 1999*, Chicago: National Opinion Research Center, 2000.

★1963★
Number and percentage of engineering doctorate recipients, at U.S. colleges and universities, by gender, 1999

Ranking basis/background: Based on the 1998-99 Survey of Earned Doctorates (SED) conducted by the National Research Council's Office of Scientific and Engineering Personnel (OSEP). The doctorates are reported by academic year and include research and applied research doctorates in all fields. **Remarks:** The *Summary Report* is the 33rd in an annual series of reports that began in 1967. **Number listed:** 2.

Men, with 4,503; 85.1%
Women, 791; 14.9%

Source: Sanderson, A., et. al., *Doctorate Recipients from United States Universities: Summary Report 1999*, Chicago: National Opinion Research Center, 2000.

★1964★
Number and percentage of humanities doctorate recipients, at U.S. colleges and universities, by gender, 1999

Ranking basis/background: Based on the 1998-99 Survey of Earned Doctorates (SED) conducted by the National Research Council's Office of Scientific and Engineering Personnel (OSEP). The doctorates are reported by academic year and include research and applied research doctorates in all fields. **Remarks:** The *Summary Report* is the 33rd in an annual series of reports that began in 1967. **Number listed:** 2.

Men, with 2,777; 35.8%
Women, 2,658; 48.9%

Source: Sanderson, A., et. al., *Doctorate Recipients from United States Universities: Summary Report 1999*, Chicago: National Opinion Research Center, 2000.

★1965★
Number and percentage of life sciences doctorate recipients, at U.S. colleges and universities, by gender, 1999

Ranking basis/background: Based on the 1998-99 Survey of Earned Doctorates (SED) conducted by the National Research Council's Office of Scientific and Engineering Personnel (OSEP). The doctorates are reported by academic year and include research and applied research doctorates in all fields. **Remarks:** The *Summary Report* is the 33rd in an annual series of reports that began in 1967. **Number listed:** 2.

Men, with 4,473; 55.3%
Women, 3,620; 44.7%

Source: Sanderson, A., et. al., *Doctorate Recipients from United States Universities: Summary Report 1999*, Chicago: National Opinion Research Center, 2000.

★1966★
Number and percentage of physical sciences doctorate recipients, at U.S. colleges and universities, by gender, 1999

Ranking basis/background: Based on the 1998-99 Survey of Earned Doctorates (SED) conducted by the National Research Council's Office of Scientific and Engineering Personnel (OSEP). The doctorates are reported by academic year and include research and applied research doctorates in all fields. **Remarks:** The *Summary Report* is the 33rd in an annual series of reports that began in 1967. **Number listed:** 2.

Men, with 4,821; 76.6%
Women, 1,474; 23.4%

Source: Sanderson, A., et. al., *Doctorate Recipients from United States Universities: Summary Report 1999*, Chicago: National Opinion Research Center, 2000.

★1967★
Number and percentage of professional/other doctorate recipients, at U.S. colleges and universities, by gender, 1999

Ranking basis/background: Based on the 1998-99 Survey of Earned Doctorates (SED) conducted by the National Research Council's Office of Scientific and Engineering Personnel (OSEP). The doctorates are reported by academic year and include research and applied research doctorates in all fields. **Remarks:** The *Summary Report* is the 33rd in an annual series of reports that began in 1967. **Number listed:** 2.

Men, with 1,348; 59.0%
Women, 935; 41.0%

Source: Sanderson, A., et. al., *Doctorate Recipients from United States Universities: Summary Report 1999*, Chicago: National Opinion Research Center, 2000.

DOCTORAL DEGREES

★1968★
Number and percentage of social sciences doctorate recipients, at U.S. colleges and universities, by gender, 1999

Ranking basis/background: Based on the 1998-99 Survey of Earned Doctorates (SED) conducted by the National Research Council's Office of Scientific and Engineering Personnel (OSEP). The doctorates are reported by aeademic year and include research and applied research doctorates in all fields.
Remarks: The *Summary Report* is the 33rd in an annual series of reports that began in 1967.
Number listed: 2.
- Men, with 3,194; 45.5%
- Women, 3,819; 54.5%

Source: Sanderson, A., et. al., *Doctorate Recipients from United States Universities: Summary Report 1999*, Chicago: National Opinion Research Center, 2000.

★1969★
Number of doctorate recipients at U.S. colleges and universities, by field, 1999

Ranking basis/background: Based on the 1998-99 Survey of Earned Doctorates (SED) conducted by the National Research Council's Office of Scientific and Engineering Personnel (OSEP). The doctorates are reported by academic year and include research and applied research doctorates in all fields.
Remarks: The *Summary Report* is the 33rd in an annual series of reports that began in 1967.
Number listed: 7.
- Physical sciences, with 6,324 doctorate recipients
- Engineering, 5,337
- Life sciences, 8,126
- Social sciences, 7,036
- Humanities, 5,468
- Education, 6,557
- Professional/other, 2,292

Source: Sanderson, A., et. al., *Doctorate Recipients from United States Universities: Summary Report 1999*, Chicago: National Opinion Research Center, 2000.

★1970★
Number of doctorates awarded by U.S. colleges and universities and percentage of annual change for each year, 1957 to 1999

Ranking basis/background: Based on the 1998-99 Survey of Earned Doctorates (SED) conducted by the National Research Council's Office of Scientific and Engineering Personnel (OSEP). The doctorates are reported by academic year and include research and applied research doctorates in all fields.
Remarks: The *Summary Report* is the 33rd in an annual series of reports that began in 1967.
Number listed: 41.
- 1957, with 8,611 doctorates; 1.1% change
- 1958, 8,773; 1.9%
- 1959, 9,213; 5.0%
- 1960, 9,733; 5.6%
- 1961, 10,413; 7.0%
- 1962, 11,500; 10.4%
- 1963, 12,728; 10.7%
- 1964, 14,325; 12.5%
- 1965, 16,340; 14.1%
- 1966, 17,949; 9.8%
- 1967, 20,403; 13.7%
- 1968, 22,937; 12.4%
- 1969, 25,743; 12.2%
- 1970, 29,498; 14.6%
- 1971, 31,867; 8.0%
- 1972, 33,041; 3.7%
- 1973, 33,755; 2.2%
- 1974, 33,047; 2.1% decrease
- 1975, 32,952; 0.3% decrease
- 1976, 32,946; 0.0%
- 1977, 31,716; 3.7% decrease
- 1978, 30,875; 2.7% decrease
- 1979, 31,239; 1.2%
- 1980, 31,020; 0.7% decrease
- 1981, 31,356; 1.1%
- 1982, 31,111; 0.8% decrease
- 1983, 31,281; 0.5%
- 1984, 31,337; 0.2%
- 1985, 31,297; 0.1% decrease
- 1986, 31,902; 1.9%
- 1987, 32,370; 1.5%
- 1988, 33,500; 3.5%
- 1989, 34,327; 2.5%
- 1990, 36,067; 5.1%
- 1991, 37,534; 4.1%
- 1992, 38,890; 3.6%
- 1993, 39,801; 2.3%
- 1994, 41,034; 3.1%
- 1995, 41,743; 1.7%
- 1996, 42,414; 1.7%
- 1997, 42,555; 0.3%
- 1998, 42,683; 0.3%
- 1999, 41,140; 3.6% decrease

Source: Sanderson, A., et. al., *Doctorate Recipients from United States Universities: Summary Report 1999*, Chicago: National Opinion Research Center, 2000.

★1971★
Number of education doctorate recipients at U.S. colleges and universities, by field, 1999

Ranking basis/background: Based on the 1998-99 Survey of Earned Doctorates (SED) conducted by the National Research Council's Office of Scientific and Engineering Personnel (OSEP). The doctorates are reported by academic year and include research and applied research doctorates in all fields.
Remarks: The *Summary Report* is the 33rd in an annual series of reports that began in 1967.
Number listed: 3.
- Teacher education, with 292 doctorate recipients
- Teaching fields, 891
- Other education, 5,374

Source: Sanderson, A., et. al., *Doctorate Recipients from United States Universities: Summary Report 1999*, Chicago: National Opinion Research Center, 2000.

★1972★
Number of engineering doctorate recipients at U.S. colleges and universities, by field, 1999

Ranking basis/background: Based on the 1998-99 Survey of Earned Doctorates (SED) conducted by the National Research Council's Office of Scientific and Engineering Personnel (OSEP). The doctorates are reported by academic year and include research and applied research doctorates in all fields.
Remarks: The *Summary Report* is the 33rd in an annual series of reports that began in 1967.
Number listed: 1.
- Engineering, with 5,337 doctorate recipients

Source: Sanderson, A., et. al., *Doctorate Recipients from United States Universities: Summary Report 1999*, Chicago: National Opinion Research Center, 2000.

★1973★
Number of humanities doctorate recipients at U.S. colleges and universities, by field, 1999

Ranking basis/background: Based on the 1998-99 Survey of Earned Doctorates (SED) conducted by the National Research Council's Office of Scientific and Engineering Personnel (OSEP). The doctorates are reported by academic year and include research and applied research doctorates in all fields.
Remarks: The *Summary Report* is the 33rd in an annual series of reports that began in 1967.
Number listed: 4.
- History, with 1,011 doctorate recipients
- English language and literature, 1,024
- Foreign language and literature, 628
- Other humanities, 2,805

Source: Sanderson, A., et. al., *Doctorate Recipients from United States Universities: Summary Report 1999*, Chicago: National Opinion Research Center, 2000.

★1974★
Number of life sciences doctorate recipients at U.S. colleges and universities, by field, 1999

Ranking basis/background: Based on the 1998-99 Survey of Earned Doctorates (SED) conducted by the National Research Council's Office of Scientific and Engineering Personnel (OSEP). The doctorates are reported by academic year and include research and applied research doctorates in all fields.
Remarks: The *Summary Report* is the 33rd in an annual series of reports that began in 1967.
Number listed: 3.
- Biological sciences, with 5,600 doctorate recipients
- Health sciences, 1,410
- Agricultural sciences, 1,116

Source: Sanderson, A., et. al., *Doctorate Recipients from United States Universities: Summary Report 1999*, Chicago: National Opinion Research Center, 2000.

★1975★
Number of physical sciences doctorate recipients at U.S. colleges and universities, by field, 1999

Ranking basis/background: Based on the 1998-99 Survey of Earned Doctorates (SED) conducted by the National Research Council's Office of Scientific and Engineering Personnel (OSEP). The doctorates are reported by academic year and include research and applied research doctorates in all fields.
Remarks: The *Summary Report* is the 33rd in an annual series of reports that began in 1967.
Number listed: 5.
- Physics and astronomy, with 1,431 doctorate recipients
- Chemistry, 2,134
- Earth, atmosphere, and marine science, 824
- Mathematics, 1,085
- Computer sciences, 850

Source: Sanderson, A., et. al., *Doctorate Recipients from United States Universities: Summary Report 1999*, Chicago: National Opinion Research Center, 2000.

DOCTORAL DEGREES

★1976★
Number of professional/other doctorate recipients at U.S. colleges and universities, by field, 1999

Ranking basis/background: Based on the 1998-99 Survey of Earned Doctorates (SED) conducted by the National Research Council's Office of Scientific and Engineering Personnel (OSEP). The doctorates are reported by academic year and include research and applied research doctorates in all fields.
Remarks: The *Summary Report* is the 33rd in an annual series of reports that began in 1967.
Number listed: 4.
- Business and management, with 1,104 doctorate recipients
- Communications, 379
- Other professional fields, 781
- Other fields, 28

Source: Sanderson, A., et. al., *Doctorate Recipients from United States Universities: Summary Report 1999*, Chicago: National Opinion Research Center, 2000.

★1977★
Number of social sciences doctorate recipients at U.S. colleges and universities, by field, 1999

Ranking basis/background: Based on the 1998-99 Survey of Earned Doctorates (SED) conducted by the National Research Council's Office of Scientific and Engineering Personnel (OSEP). The doctorates are reported by academic year and include research and applied research doctorates in all fields.
Remarks: The *Summary Report* is the 33rd in an annual series of reports that began in 1967.
Number listed: 6.
- Psychology, with 3,667 doctorate recipients
- Anthropology, 461
- Economics, 927
- Political science and international relations, 773
- Sociology, 543
- Other social sciences, 665

Source: Sanderson, A., et. al., *Doctorate Recipients from United States Universities: Summary Report 1999*, Chicago: National Opinion Research Center, 2000.

★1978★
Number of U.S. citizen/permanent resident doctorate recipients in all fields at U.S. colleges and universities, by race/ethnicity, 1999

Ranking basis/background: Based on the 1998-99 Survey of Earned Doctorates (SED) conducted by the National Research Council's Office of Scientific and Engineering Personnel (OSEP). The doctorates are reported by academic year and include research and applied research doctorates in all fields.
Remarks: The *Summary Report* is the 33rd in an annual series of reports that began in 1967.
Number listed: 5.
- Asian American, with 1,324
- African American, 1,596
- Hispanic American, 1,109
- Native American, 219
- White, 22,929

Source: Sanderson, A., et. al., *Doctorate Recipients from United States Universities: Summary Report 1999*, Chicago: National Opinion Research Center, 2000.

★1979★
Number of U.S. citizen/permanent resident doctorate recipients in education at U.S. colleges and universities, by race/ethnicity, 1999

Ranking basis/background: Based on the 1998-99 Survey of Earned Doctorates (SED) conducted by the National Research Council's Office of Scientific and Engineering Personnel (OSEP). The doctorates are reported by academic year and include research and applied research doctorates in all fields.
Remarks: The *Summary Report* is the 33rd in an annual series of reports that began in 1967.
Number listed: 5.
- Asian American, with 103
- African American, 621
- Hispanic American, 252
- Native American, 60
- White, 4,324

Source: Sanderson, A., et. al., *Doctorate Recipients from United States Universities: Summary Report 1999*, Chicago: National Opinion Research Center, 2000.

★1980★
Number of U.S. citizen/permanent resident doctorate recipients in engineering at U.S. colleges and universities, by race/ethnicity, 1999

Ranking basis/background: Based on the 1998-99 Survey of Earned Doctorates (SED) conducted by the National Research Council's Office of Scientific and Engineering Personnel (OSEP). The doctorates are reported by academic year and include research and applied research doctorates in all fields.
Remarks: The *Summary Report* is the 33rd in an annual series of reports that began in 1967.
Number listed: 5.
- Asian American, with 266
- African American, 84
- Hispanic American, 71
- Native American, 12
- White, 1,982

Source: Sanderson, A., et. al., *Doctorate Recipients from United States Universities: Summary Report 1999*, Chicago: National Opinion Research Center, 2000.

★1981★
Number of U.S. citizen/permanent resident doctorate recipients in humanities at U.S. colleges and universities, by race/ethnicity, 1999

Ranking basis/background: Based on the 1998-99 Survey of Earned Doctorates (SED) conducted by the National Research Council's Office of Scientific and Engineering Personnel (OSEP). The doctorates are reported by academic year and include research and applied research doctorates in all fields.
Remarks: The *Summary Report* is the 33rd in an annual series of reports that began in 1967.
Number listed: 5.
- Asian American, with 126
- African American, 172
- Hispanic American, 170
- Native American, 25
- White, 3,695

Source: Sanderson, A., et. al., *Doctorate Recipients from United States Universities: Summary Report 1999*, Chicago: National Opinion Research Center, 2000.

★1982★
Number of U.S. citizen/permanent resident doctorate recipients in life sciences at U.S. colleges and universities, by race/ethnicity, 1999

Ranking basis/background: Based on the 1998-99 Survey of Earned Doctorates (SED) conducted by the National Research Council's Office of Scientific and Engineering Personnel (OSEP). The doctorates are reported by academic year and include research and applied research doctorates in all fields.
Remarks: The *Summary Report* is the 33rd in an annual series of reports that began in 1967.
Number listed: 5.
- Asian American, with 361
- African American, 178
- Hispanic American, 195
- Native American, 28
- White, 4,285

Source: Sanderson, A., et. al., *Doctorate Recipients from United States Universities: Summary Report 1999*, Chicago: National Opinion Research Center, 2000.

★1983★
Number of U.S. citizen/permanent resident doctorate recipients in physical sciences, mathematics, and computer sciences at U.S. colleges and universities, by race/ethnicity, 1999

Ranking basis/background: Based on the 1998-99 Survey of Earned Doctorates (SED) conducted by the National Research Council's Office of Scientific and Engineering Personnel (OSEP). The doctorates are reported by academic year and include research and applied research doctorates in all fields.
Remarks: The *Summary Report* is the 33rd in an annual series of reports that began in 1967.
Number listed: 5.
- Asian American, with 216
- African American, 91
- Hispanic American, 93
- Native American, 18
- White, 2,953

Source: Sanderson, A., et. al., *Doctorate Recipients from United States Universities: Summary Report 1999*, Chicago: National Opinion Research Center, 2000.

★1984★
Number of U.S. citizen/permanent resident doctorate recipients in professional/other fields at U.S. colleges and universities, by race/ethnicity, 1999

Ranking basis/background: Based on the 1998-99 Survey of Earned Doctorates (SED) conducted by the National Research Council's Office of Scientific and Engineering Personnel (OSEP). The doctorates are reported by academic year and include research and applied research doctorates in all fields.
Remarks: The *Summary Report* is the 33rd in an annual series of reports that began in 1967.
Number listed: 5.
- Asian American, with 64
- African American, 139
- Hispanic American, 50
- Native American, 16
- White, 1,249

Source: Sanderson, A., et. al., *Doctorate Recipients from United States Universities: Summary Report 1999*, Chicago: National Opinion Research Center, 2000.

★1985★

Number of U.S. citizen/permanent resident doctorate recipients in social sciences at U.S. colleges and universities, by race/ethnicity, 1999

Ranking basis/background: Based on the 1998-99 Survey of Earned Doctorates (SED) conducted by the National Research Council's Office of Scientific and Engineering Personnel (OSEP). The doctorates are reported by academic year and include research and applied research doctorates in all fields.
Remarks: The *Summary Report* is the 33rd in an annual series of reports that began in 1967.
Number listed: 5.

Asian American, with 188
African American, 311
Hispanic American, 278
Native American, 60
White, 4,441

Source: Sanderson, A., et. al., *Doctorate Recipients from United States Universities: Summary Report 1999*, Chicago: National Opinion Research Center, 2000.

★1986★

Percentage of all doctorate recipients awarded to women from 1921-1996

Ranking basis/background: Based on the 1995-96 Survey of Earned Doctorates (SED) conducted by the National Research Council's Office of Scientific and Engineering Personnel (OSEP). The doctorates are reported by academic year and include research and applied research doctorates in all fields.
Remarks: The *Summary Report* is the 30th in an annual series of reports that began in 1967.
Number listed: 75.

1921, with 16.2%
1922, 14.4%
1923, 14.8%
1924, 15.0%
1925, 16.7%
1926, 13.9%
1927, 15.1%
1928, 14.5%
1929, 16.7%
1930, 15.1%
1931, 15.4%
1932, 16.0%
1933, 14.1%
1934, 13.0%
1935, 14.6%
1936, 15.2%
1937, 14.6%
1938, 15.2%
1939, 14.4%
1940, 13.1%
1941, 11.6%
1942, 12.4%
1943, 15.2%
1944, 17.1%
1945, 20.3%
1946, 19.2%
1947, 14.0%
1948, 12.1%
1949, 10.0%
1950, 9.5%
1951, 9.3%
1952, 9.5%
1953, 9.4%
1954, 9.1%
1955, 9.9%
1956, 9.5%
1957, 11.6%
1958, 11.3%
1959, 10.6%
1960, 10.7%
1961, 10.8%
1962, 10.7%
1963, 10.9%
1964, 10.9%
1965, 10.8%
1966, 11.6%
1967, 12.0%
1968, 12.8%
1969, 13.2%
1970, 13.5%
1971, 14.4%
1972, 16.0%
1973, 18.0%
1974, 19.5%
1975, 21.9%
1976, 23.3%
1977, 24.8%
1978, 27.0%
1979, 28.6%
1980, 30.3%
1981, 31.5%
1982, 32.4%
1983, 33.7%
1984, 34.1%
1985, 34.3%
1986, 35.4%
1987, 35.3%
1988, 35.3%
1989, 36.5%
1990, 36.3%
1991, 37.0%
1992, 37.1%
1993, 38.0%
1994, 38.6%
1995, 39.3%
1996, 40.0%

Source: Henderson, P.H., J.E. Clarke and C. Woods, *Summary Report 1996: Doctorate Recipients from United States Universities*, National Academy Press, 1998.

★1987★

Percentage of doctoral degree recipients at U.S. universities, by race/ethnicity, 1999

Ranking basis/background: Percentage of doctorates granted to each ethnic group in 1999. Total doctorates awarded to minorities is 27,622, the includes U.S. citizens only. **Remarks:** Original source: "Survey of Earned Doctorates." **Number listed:** 6.

1. White, with 83.0%
2. African American, 5.8%
3. Asian American, 4.8%
4. Hispanic American, 4.0%
5. Native American, 0.8%
6. Race unknown, 1.6%

Source: Leatherman, Courtney, "The Number of New Ph.D.'s Drops For the First Time Since 1985," *The Chronicle of Higher Education*, 47: A10-A11, (February 9, 2001).

★1988★

Percentage of female doctorate recipients at U.S. colleges and universities, by subfield, 1999

Ranking basis/background: Based on the 1998-99 Survey of Earned Doctorates (SED) conducted by the National Research Council's Office of Scientific and Engineering Personnel (OSEP). The doctorates are reported by academic year and include research and applied research doctorates in all fields.
Remarks: The *Summary Report* is the 33rd in an annual series of reports that began in 1967.
Number listed: 25.

Mathematics, with 1,085 doctorate recipients; 25.5% female; and a 26.3% change in number of doctorates from 1989 to 1999
Computer science, 850; 18.4%; 38.9%
Physics and astronomy, 1,431; 13.4%; 12.3%
Chemistry, 2,134; 29.7%; 8.3%
Earth, atmosphere, and marine science, 824; 26.2%; 11.4%
Biochemistry, 763; 40.6%; 14.1%
Cell biology, 285; 47.7%; 114.3%
Ecology, 272; 44.5%; 68.9%
Molecular biology, 719; 41.6%; 74.1%
Microbiology, 382; 42.7%; 12.4%
Neuroscience, 437; 41.9%; 141.4%
Health sciences, 1,410; 63.9%; 44.8%
Agricultural sciences, 1,116; 28.6%; 10.9% decrease
Psychology, 3,667; 66.7%; 14.3%
Anthropology, 461; 56.6%; 41.8%
Economics, 912; 27.1%; 4.6%
Political science and government, 653; 32.9%; 51.9%
Sociology, 543; 59.7%; 24.5%
History, 1,011; 39.6%; 87.9%
Linguistics, 250; 58.8%; 33.0%
Art history, 189; 69.8%; 30.3%
Music, 769; 42.0%; 47.6%
Philosophy, 387; 24.8%; 43.3%
Language and literature, 1,652; 59.8%; 43.4%
Business and management, 1,104; 31.0%; 4.9%

Source: Sanderson, A., et. al., *Doctorate Recipients from United States Universities: Summary Report 1999*, Chicago: National Opinion Research Center, 2000.

★1989★

Percentage of female doctorate recipients, by broad field, 1999

Ranking basis/background: Distribution percentages of female Ph.D. recipients for each field of study. **Remarks:** Original source: NSF, NIH, USED, NEH, USDA, NASA. **Number listed:** 8.

1. Education, 64%
2. Social sciences, 55%
3. Humanities, 49%
4. Life sciences, 45%
5. Physical sciences, 23%
6. Engineering, 15%
7. Professional/other, 41%
8. All fields, 43%

Source: Sanderson, A., et. al., *Doctorate Recipients from United States Universities: Summary Report 1999*, Chicago: National Opinion Research Center, 2000.

★1990★

Percentage of minority doctorate recipients in the U.S., 1999

Ranking basis/background: Distribution percentages of minority Ph.D. recipients. **Remarks:** Original source: NSF, NIH, USED, NEH, USDA, NASA. **Number listed:** 4.

1. African American, with 5.9%
2. Asian American, 4.9%
3. Hispanic American, 4.1%
4. Native American, 0.8%

Source: Sanderson, A., et. al., *Doctorate Recipients from United States Universities: Summary Report 1999*, Chicago: National Opinion Research Center, 2000.

DOCTORAL DEGREES

★1991★
Percentage of minority doctorate recipients in the U.S., by broad field, 1999

Ranking basis/background: Distribution percentages of minority Ph.D. recipients in each field. **Remarks:** Original source: NSF, NIH, USED, NEH, USDA, NASA. **Number listed:** 8.
1. Education, with 19.3%
2. Engineering, 17.9%
3. Social sciences, 15.9%
4. Life sciences, 15.1%
5. Physical sciences, 12.4%
6. Humanities, 11.8%
7. Professional/other, 17.7%
8. All fields, 15.6%

Source: Sanderson, A., et. al., *Doctorate Recipients from United States Universities: Summary Report 1999*, Chicago: National Opinion Research Center, 2000.

★1992★
Percentage of minority doctorate recipients in the U.S., by gender, 1999

Ranking basis/background: Distribution percentages of male and female minority Ph.D. recipients. **Remarks:** Original source: NSF, NIH, USED, NEH, USDA, NASA. **Number listed:** 4.
- African American, with 37.8% male; 62.2% female
- Asian American, 58.3%; 41.7%%
- Hispanic American, 43.8%; 56.2%
- Native American, 44.7%; 55.3%

Source: Sanderson, A., et. al., *Doctorate Recipients from United States Universities: Summary Report 1999*, Chicago: National Opinion Research Center, 2000.

★1993★
Physical sciences, mathematics, and computer sciences doctorates awarded to U.S. citizens/permanent residents at U.S. colleges and universities, by race/ethnicity and subfield, 1999

Ranking basis/background: Based on the 1998-99 Survey of Earned Doctorates (SED) conducted by the National Research Council's Office of Scientific and Engineering Personnel (OSEP). The doctorates are reported by academic year and include research and applied research doctorates in all fields. **Remarks:** The *Summary Report* is the 33rd in an annual series of reports that began in 1967. **Number listed:** 5.
- Physics and astronomy, with 36 to Asian Americans; 8 to African Americans; 13 to Hispanic Americans; 5 to Native Americans; and 680 to Whites
- Chemistry, 92; 46; 38; 5; 1,052
- Earth, atmosphere, and marine science, 15; 11; 18; 6; 418
- Mathematics, 31; 10; 12; 1; 474
- Computer sciences, 42; 16; 12; 1; 329

Source: Sanderson, A., et. al., *Doctorate Recipients from United States Universities: Summary Report 1999*, Chicago: National Opinion Research Center, 2000.

★1994★
Physics and astronomy doctorates awarded at U.S. colleges and universities, by subfield, 1999

Ranking basis/background: Based on the 1998-99 Survey of Earned Doctorates (SED) conducted by the National Research Council's Office of Scientific and Engineering Personnel (OSEP). The doctorates are reported by academic year and include research and applied research doctorates in all fields. **Remarks:** The *Summary Report* is the 33rd in an annual series of reports that began in 1967. **Number listed:** 13.
- Astronomy, with 60
- Astrophysics, 100
- Acoustics, 16
- Chemical and atomic/molecular, 99
- Elementary particles, 169
- Fluids, 23
- Nuclear, 76
- Optics, 97
- Plasma and high-temperature, 49
- Polymer, 28
- Solid state and low-temperature, 308
- Physics, general, 205
- Physics, other, 201

Source: Sanderson, A., et. al., *Doctorate Recipients from United States Universities: Summary Report 1999*, Chicago: National Opinion Research Center, 2000.

★1995★
Primary source of financial support for doctorate recipients in all fields, 1999

Ranking basis/background: Percentages of Ph.D. recipients receiving financial support from each source. Data collected is from an annual Survey of Earned Doctorates and a census of research doctoral recipients earning their degree between July 1, 1998 and June 30, 1999. **Remarks:** Original source: NSF, NIH, USED, NEH, USDA, NASA. **Number listed:** 5.
- Teaching, with 17.4%
- Research, 25.2%
- Fellowship, 18.3%
- Own, 32.6%
- Other, 6.5%

Source: Sanderson, A., et. al., *Doctorate Recipients from United States Universities: Summary Report 1999*, Chicago: National Opinion Research Center, 2000.

★1996★
Primary source of financial support for doctorate recipients in education, 1999

Ranking basis/background: Percentages of Ph.D. recipients receiving financial support from each source. Data collected is from an annual Survey of Earned Doctorates and a census of research doctoral recipients earning their degree between July 1, 1998 and June 30, 1999. **Remarks:** Original source: NSF, NIH, USED, NEH, USDA, NASA. **Number listed:** 5.
- Teaching, with 7.1%
- Research, 6.5%
- Fellowship, 7.3%
- Own, 69.2%
- Other, 10.0%

Source: Sanderson, A., et. al., *Doctorate Recipients from United States Universities: Summary Report 1999*, Chicago: National Opinion Research Center, 2000.

★1997★
Primary source of financial support for doctorate recipients in engineering, 1999

Ranking basis/background: Percentages of Ph.D. recipients receiving financial support from each source. Data collected is from an annual Survey of Earned Doctorates and a census of research doctoral recipients earning their degree between July 1, 1998 and June 30, 1999. **Remarks:** Original source: NSF, NIH, USED, NEH, USDA, NASA. **Number listed:** 5.
- Teaching, with 8.8%
- Research, 51.9%
- Fellowship, 15.7%
- Own, 12.6%
- Other, 11.0%

Source: Sanderson, A., et. al., *Doctorate Recipients from United States Universities: Summary Report 1999*, Chicago: National Opinion Research Center, 2000.

★1998★
Primary source of financial support for doctorate recipients in humanities, 1999

Ranking basis/background: Percentages of Ph.D. recipients receiving financial support from each source. Data collected is from an annual Survey of Earned Doctorates and a census of research doctoral recipients earning their degree between July 1, 1998 and June 30, 1999. **Remarks:** Original source: NSF, NIH, USED, NEH, USDA, NASA. **Number listed:** 5.
- Teaching, with 32.8%
- Research, 1.2%
- Fellowship, 23.5%
- Own, 39.4%
- Other, 3.0%

Source: Sanderson, A., et. al., *Doctorate Recipients from United States Universities: Summary Report 1999*, Chicago: National Opinion Research Center, 2000.

★1999★
Primary source of financial support for doctorate recipients in life sciences, 1999

Ranking basis/background: Percentages of Ph.D. recipients receiving financial support from each source. Data collected is from an annual Survey of Earned Doctorates and a census of research doctoral recipients earning their degree between July 1, 1998 and June 30, 1999. **Remarks:** Original source: NSF, NIH, USED, NEH, USDA, NASA. **Number listed:** 5.
- Teaching, with 10.6%
- Research, 38.0%
- Fellowship, 28.0%
- Own, 17.4%
- Other, 6.0%

Source: Sanderson, A., et. al., *Doctorate Recipients from United States Universities: Summary Report 1999*, Chicago: National Opinion Research Center, 2000.

★2000★
Primary source of financial support for doctorate recipients in physical sciences, 1999

Ranking basis/background: Percentages of Ph.D. recipients receiving financial support from each source. Data collected is from an annual Survey of Earned Doctorates and a census of research doctoral recipients earning their degree between July 1, 1998 and June 30, 1999. **Remarks:** Original source: NSF, NIH, USED, NEH, USDA, NASA. **Number listed:** 5.

Teaching, with 27.7%
Research, 43.0%
Fellowship, 14.9%
Own, 9.7%
Other, 4.7%

Source: Sanderson, A., et. al., *Doctorate Recipients from United States Universities: Summary Report 1999*, Chicago: National Opinion Research Center, 2000.

★2001★
Primary source of financial support for doctorate recipients in professional and other fields, 1999

Ranking basis/background: Percentages of Ph.D. recipients receiving financial support from each source. Data collected is from an annual Survey of Earned Doctorates and a census of research doctoral recipients earning their degree between July 1, 1998 and June 30, 1999. **Remarks:** Original source: NSF, NIH, USED, NEH, USDA, NASA. **Number listed:** 5.

Teaching, with 20.2%
Research, 10.5%
Fellowship, 14.0%
Own, 46.5%
Other, 8.9%

Source: Sanderson, A., et. al., *Doctorate Recipients from United States Universities: Summary Report 1999*, Chicago: National Opinion Research Center, 2000.

★2002★
Primary source of financial support for doctorate recipients in social sciences, 1999

Ranking basis/background: Percentages of Ph.D. recipients receiving financial support from each source. Data collected is from an annual Survey of Earned Doctorates and a census of research doctoral recipients earning their degree between July 1, 1998 and June 30, 1999. **Remarks:** Original source: NSF, NIH, USED, NEH, USDA, NASA. **Number listed:** 5.

Teaching, with 19.2%
Research, 13.8%
Fellowship, 19.0%
Own, 43.8%
Other, 4.3%

Source: Sanderson, A., et. al., *Doctorate Recipients from United States Universities: Summary Report 1999*, Chicago: National Opinion Research Center, 2000.

★2003★
Primary sources of financial support for doctorate recipients, by citizenship, 1999

Ranking basis/background: Percentage of doctorate recipients receiving support from each category by citizenship. Based on the 1998-99 Survey of Earned Doctorates (SED) conducted by the National Research Council's Office of Scientific and Engineering Personnel (OSEP). The doctorates are reported by academic year and include research and applied research doctorates in all fields. **Remarks:** The *Summary Report* is the 33rd in an annual series of reports that began in 1967. **Number listed:** 7.

Teaching assistantships, with 16.0% U.S. citizens; 21.3% non-U.S. (Permanent Visa); and 20.7% non-U.S. (Temporary Visa)
Research assistantships/traineeships, 19.6%; 33.7%; 40.6%
Fellowships/dissertation grants, 18.8%; 17.2%; 17.0%
Own resources, 40.6%; 22.1%; 10.2%
Foreign government, 0.2%; 3.2%; 10.3%
Employer, 4.1%; 2.3%; 1.1%
Other, 0.7%; 0.3%; 0.1%

Source: Sanderson, A., et. al., *Doctorate Recipients from United States Universities: Summary Report 1999*, Chicago: National Opinion Research Center, 2000.

★2004★
Primary sources of financial support for doctorate recipients, by gender, 1999

Ranking basis/background: Percentage of men and women doctorate recipients receiving support from each category. Based on the 1998-99 Survey of Earned Doctorates (SED) conducted by the National Research Council's Office of Scientific and Engineering Personnel (OSEP). The doctorates are reported by academic year and include research and applied research doctorates in all fields. **Remarks:** The *Summary Report* is the 33rd in an annual series of reports that began in 1967. **Number listed:** 7.

Teaching assistantships, with 18.1% men; and 16.5% women
Research assistantships/traineeships, 30.2%; 18.4%
Fellowships/dissertation grants, 17.9%; 18.8%
Own resources, 26.1%; 41.2%
Foreign government, 3.5%; 1.6%
Employer, 3.6%; 3.0%
Other, 0.6%; 0.5%

Source: Sanderson, A., et. al., *Doctorate Recipients from United States Universities: Summary Report 1999*, Chicago: National Opinion Research Center, 2000.

★2005★
Primary sources of financial support for doctorate recipients, by race/ethnicity, 1999

Ranking basis/background: Percentage of doctorate recipients receiving support from each category by race/ethnicity. Based on the 1998-99 Survey of Earned Doctorates (SED) conducted by the National Research Council's Office of Scientific and Engineering Personnel (OSEP). The doctorates are reported by academic year and include research and applied research doctorates in all fields. **Remarks:** The *Summary Report* is the 33rd in an annual series of reports that began in 1967. **Number listed:** 7.

Teaching assistantships, with 14.0% Asian American/Pacific Islander; 7.5% African American; 12.3% Hispanic American; 9.6% Native American/Alaskan Native; and 17.0% White
Research assistantships/traineeships, 31.8%; 7.9%; 12.4%; 16.2%; 20.1%
Fellowships/dissertation grants, 27.1%; 29.9%; 30.1%; 24.7%; 16.9%
Own resources, 22.7%; 48.6%; 40.7%; 44.4%; 41.0%
Foreign government, 1.1%; 0.3%; 0.6%; 1.5%; 0.1%
Employer, 2.7%; 4.8%; 3.9%; 2.5%; 4.2%
Other, 0.6%; 1.0%; 0.1%; 1.0%; 0.7%

Source: Sanderson, A., et. al., *Doctorate Recipients from United States Universities: Summary Report 1999*, Chicago: National Opinion Research Center, 2000.

★2006★
Primary sources of financial support for education doctorate recipients, by citizenship, 1999

Ranking basis/background: Percentage of doctorate recipients receiving support from each category by citizenship. Based on the 1998-99 Survey of Earned Doctorates (SED) conducted by the National Research Council's Office of Scientific and Engineering Personnel (OSEP). The doctorates are reported by academic year and include research and applied research doctorates in all fields. **Remarks:** The *Summary Report* is the 33rd in an annual series of reports that began in 1967. **Number listed:** 7.

Teaching assistantships, with 6.2% U.S. citizens; 12.7% non-U.S. (Permanent Visa); and 15.5% non-U.S. (Temporary Visa)
Research assistantships/traineeships, 5.3%; 12.0%; 18.1%
Fellowships/dissertation grants, 6.5%; 11.4%; 15.7%
Own resources, 72.7%; 55.1%; 33.1%
Foreign government, 0.1%; 3.8%; 14.8%
Employer, 8.2%; 4.4%; 2.9%
Other, 1.1%; 0.6%; 0.0%

Source: Sanderson, A., et. al., *Doctorate Recipients from United States Universities: Summary Report 1999*, Chicago: National Opinion Research Center, 2000.

★2007★
Primary sources of financial support for education doctorate recipients, by gender, 1999

Ranking basis/background: Percentage of men and women doctorate recipients receiving support from each category. Based on the 1998-99 Survey of Earned Doctorates (SED) conducted by the National Research Council's Office of Scientific and Engineering Personnel (OSEP). The doctorates are reported by academic year and include research and applied research doctorates in all fields. **Remarks:** The *Summary Report* is the 33rd in an annual series of reports that began in 1967. **Number listed:** 7.

Teaching assistantships, with 7.4% men; and 6.9% women
Research assistantships/traineeships, 7.1%; 6.2%
Fellowships/dissertation grants, 6.9%; 7.5%
Own resources, 66.3%; 70.8%
Foreign government, 2.0%; 1.0%
Employer, 8.9%; 7.0%
Other, 1.4%; 0.7%

Source: Sanderson, A., et. al., *Doctorate Recipients from United States Universities: Summary Report 1999*, Chicago: National Opinion Research Center, 2000.

DOCTORAL DEGREES

★2008★
Primary sources of financial support for education doctorate recipients, by race/ethnicity, 1999

Ranking basis/background: Percentage of doctorate recipients receiving support from each category by race/ethnicity. Based on the 1998-99 Survey of Earned Doctorates (SED) conducted by the National Research Council's Office of Scientific and Engineering Personnel (OSEP). The doctorates are reported by academic year and include research and applied research doctorates in all fields.
Remarks: The *Summary Report* is the 33rd in an annual series of reports that began in 1967.
Number listed: 7.

- Teaching assistantships, with 3.2% Asian American/Pacific Islander; 3.5% African American; 3.5% Hispanic American; 3.8% Native American/Alaskan Native; and 6.7% White
- Research assistantships/traineeships, 14.0%; 3.5%; 4.8%; 11.3%; 5.3%
- Fellowships/dissertation grants, 19.4%; 11.9%; 15.0%; 15.1%; 4.8%
- Own resources, 57.0%; 72.1%; 69.2%; 64.2%; 73.5%
- Foreign government, 2.2%; 0.3%; 0.0%; 0.0%; 0.1%
- Employer, 4.3%; 7.3%; 7.5%; 3.8%; 8.6%
- Other, 0.0%; 1.4%; 0.0%; 1.9%; 1.1%

Source: Sanderson, A., et. al., *Doctorate Recipients from United States Universities: Summary Report 1999*, Chicago: National Opinion Research Center, 2000.

★2009★
Primary sources of financial support for engineering doctorate recipients, by citizenship, 1999

Ranking basis/background: Percentage of doctorate recipients receiving support from each category by citizenship. Based on the 1998-99 Survey of Earned Doctorates (SED) conducted by the National Research Council's Office of Scientific and Engineering Personnel (OSEP). The doctorates are reported by academic year and include research and applied research doctorates in all fields.
Remarks: The *Summary Report* is the 33rd in an annual series of reports that began in 1967.
Number listed: 7.

- Teaching assistantships, with 7.1% U.S. citizens; 11.0% non-U.S. (Permanent Visa); and 10.6% non-U.S. (Temporary Visa)
- Research assistantships/traineeships, 44.1%; 55.5%; 60.2%
- Fellowships/dissertation grants, 22.6%; 9.9%; 8.7%
- Own resources, 16.9%; 13.4%; 7.5%
- Foreign government, 0.2%; 5.8%; 11.2%
- Employer, 8.3%; 4.5%; 1.8%
- Other, 0.8%; 0.0%; 0.1%

Source: Sanderson, A., et. al., *Doctorate Recipients from United States Universities: Summary Report 1999*, Chicago: National Opinion Research Center, 2000.

★2010★
Primary sources of financial support for engineering doctorate recipients, by gender, 1999

Ranking basis/background: Percentage of men and women doctorate recipients receiving support from each category. Based on the 1998-99 Survey of Earned Doctorates (SED) conducted by the National Research Council's Office of Scientific and Engineering Personnel (OSEP). The doctorates are reported by academic year and include research and applied research doctorates in all fields.
Remarks: The *Summary Report* is the 33rd in an annual series of reports that began in 1967.
Number listed: 7.

- Teaching assistantships, with 8.9% men; and 8.2% women
- Research assistantships/traineeships, 51.9%; 51.8%
- Fellowships/dissertation grants, 14.2%; 24.6%
- Own resources, 13.2%; 9.2%
- Foreign government, 5.8%; 3.1%
- Employer, 5.5%; 3.2%
- Other, 0.5%; 0.0%

Source: Sanderson, A., et. al., *Doctorate Recipients from United States Universities: Summary Report 1999*, Chicago: National Opinion Research Center, 2000.

★2011★
Primary sources of financial support for engineering doctorate recipients, by race/ethnicity, 1999

Ranking basis/background: Percentage of doctorate recipients receiving support from each category by race/ethnicity. Based on the 1998-99 Survey of Earned Doctorates (SED) conducted by the National Research Council's Office of Scientific and Engineering Personnel (OSEP). The doctorates are reported by academic year and include research and applied research doctorates in all fields.
Remarks: The *Summary Report* is the 33rd in an annual series of reports that began in 1967.
Number listed: 7.

- Teaching assistantships, with 9.5% Asian American/Pacific Islander; 5.0% African American; 7.7% Hispanic American; 0.0% Native American/Alaskan Native; and 6.9% White
- Research assistantships/traineeships, 53.6%; 18.8%; 29.2%; 25.0%; 44.7%
- Fellowships/dissertation grants, 19.0%; 56.3%; 36.9%; 25.0%; 21.0%
- Own resources, 11.5%; 15.0%; 20.0%; 25.0%; 17.7%
- Foreign government, 0.8%; 0.0%; 0.0%; 8.3%; 0.1%
- Employer, 5.2%; 5.0%; 6.2%; 16.7%; 8.8%
- Other, 0.4%; 0.0%; 0.0%; 0.0%; 0.7%

Source: Sanderson, A., et. al., *Doctorate Recipients from United States Universities: Summary Report 1999*, Chicago: National Opinion Research Center, 2000.

★2012★
Primary sources of financial support for humanities doctorate recipients, by citizenship, 1999

Ranking basis/background: Percentage of doctorate recipients receiving support from each category by citizenship. Based on the 1998-99 Survey of Earned Doctorates (SED) conducted by the National Research Council's Office of Scientific and Engineering Personnel (OSEP). The doctorates are reported by academic year and include research and applied research doctorates in all fields.
Remarks: The *Summary Report* is the 33rd in an annual series of reports that began in 1967.
Number listed: 7.

- Teaching assistantships, with 31.7% U.S. citizens; 38.5% non-U.S. (Permanent Visa); and 37.5% non-U.S. (Temporary Visa)
- Research assistantships/traineeships, 1.2%; 0.7%; 2.0%
- Fellowships/dissertation grants, 22.6%; 21.7%; 30.9%
- Own resources, 42.5%; 33.2%; 21.1%
- Foreign government, 0.2%; 4.2%; 7.4%
- Employer, 1.4%; 1.7%; 0.5%
- Other, 0.4%; 0.0%; 0.5%

Source: Sanderson, A., et. al., *Doctorate Recipients from United States Universities: Summary Report 1999*, Chicago: National Opinion Research Center, 2000.

★2013★
Primary sources of financial support for humanities doctorate recipients, by gender, 1999

Ranking basis/background: Percentage of men and women doctorate recipients receiving support from each category. Based on the 1998-99 Survey of Earned Doctorates (SED) conducted by the National Research Council's Office of Scientific and Engineering Personnel (OSEP). The doctorates are reported by academic year and include research and applied research doctorates in all fields.
Remarks: The *Summary Report* is the 33rd in an annual series of reports that began in 1967.
Number listed: 7.

- Teaching assistantships, with 30.5% men; and 35.2% women
- Research assistantships/traineeships, 1.3%; 1.2%
- Fellowships/dissertation grants, 24.2%; 22.8%
- Own resources, 40.2%; 38.6%
- Foreign government, 1.7%; 0.9%
- Employer, 1.6%; 1.0%
- Other, 0.6%; 0.2%

Source: Sanderson, A., et. al., *Doctorate Recipients from United States Universities: Summary Report 1999*, Chicago: National Opinion Research Center, 2000.

★2014★
Primary sources of financial support for humanities doctorate recipients, by race/ethnicity, 1999

Ranking basis/background: Percentage of doctorate recipients receiving support from each category by race/ethnicity. Based on the 1998-99 Survey of Earned Doctorates (SED) conducted by the National Research Council's Office of Scientific and Engineering Personnel (OSEP). The doctorates are reported by academic year and include research and applied research doctorates in all fields.
Remarks: The *Summary Report* is the 33rd in an annual series of reports that began in 1967.
Number listed: 7.
- Teaching assistantships, with 28.6% Asian American/Pacific Islander; 13.2% African American; 31.8% Hispanic American; 40.9% Native American/Alaskan Native; and 32.7% White
- Research assistantships/traineeships, 1.7%; 1.3%; 0.6%; 0.0%; 1.2%
- Fellowships/dissertation grants, 29.4%; 46.5%; 23.6%; 27.3%; 21.2%
- Own resources, 37.0%; 33.3%; 40.8%; 31.8%; 43.0%
- Foreign government, 3.4%; 0.6%; 0.6%; 0.0%; 0.1%
- Employer, 0.0%; 3.1%; 2.5%; 0.0%; 1.4%
- Other, 0.0%; 1.9%; 0.0%; 0.0%; 0.4%

Source: Sanderson, A., et. al., *Doctorate Recipients from United States Universities: Summary Report 1999*, Chicago: National Opinion Research Center, 2000.

★2015★
Primary sources of financial support for life sciences doctorate recipients, by citizenship, 1999

Ranking basis/background: Percentage of doctorate recipients receiving support from each category by citizenship. Based on the 1998-99 Survey of Earned Doctorates (SED) conducted by the National Research Council's Office of Scientific and Engineering Personnel (OSEP). The doctorates are reported by academic year and include research and applied research doctorates in all fields.
Remarks: The *Summary Report* is the 33rd in an annual series of reports that began in 1967.
Number listed: 7.
- Teaching assistantships, with 10.2% U.S. citizens; 12.4% non-U.S. (Permanent Visa); and 11.1% non-U.S. (Temporary Visa)
- Research assistantships/traineeships, 32.8%; 46.2%; 48.4%
- Fellowships/dissertation grants, 30.7%; 24.4%; 22.7%
- Own resources, 22.2%; 13.9%; 5.9%
- Foreign government, 0.3%; 1.0%; 10.8%
- Employer, 3.0%; 1.2%; 0.8%
- Other, 0.6%; 0.9%; 0.2%

Source: Sanderson, A., et. al., *Doctorate Recipients from United States Universities: Summary Report 1999*, Chicago: National Opinion Research Center, 2000.

★2016★
Primary sources of financial support for life sciences doctorate recipients, by gender, 1999

Ranking basis/background: Percentage of men and women doctorate recipients receiving support from each category. Based on the 1998-99 Survey of Earned Doctorates (SED) conducted by the National Research Council's Office of Scientific and Engineering Personnel (OSEP). The doctorates are reported by academic year and include research and applied research doctorates in all fields.
Remarks: The *Summary Report* is the 33rd in an annual series of reports that began in 1967.
Number listed: 7.
- Teaching assistantships, with 11.8% men; and 9.1% women
- Research assistantships/traineeships, 40.2%; 35.2%
- Fellowships/dissertation grants, 26.8%; 29.5%
- Own resources, 14.7%; 20.7%
- Foreign government, 3.7%; 2.4%
- Employer, 2.2%; 2.5%
- Other, 0.6%; 0.5%

Source: Sanderson, A., et. al., *Doctorate Recipients from United States Universities: Summary Report 1999*, Chicago: National Opinion Research Center, 2000.

★2017★
Primary sources of financial support for life sciences doctorate recipients, by race/ethnicity, 1999

Ranking basis/background: Percentage of doctorate recipients receiving support from each category by race/ethnicity. Based on the 1998-99 Survey of Earned Doctorates (SED) conducted by the National Research Council's Office of Scientific and Engineering Personnel (OSEP). The doctorates are reported by academic year and include research and applied research doctorates in all fields.
Remarks: The *Summary Report* is the 33rd in an annual series of reports that began in 1967.
Number listed: 7.
- Teaching assistantships, with 5.8% Asian American/Pacific Islander; 7.8% African American; 7.7% Hispanic American; 0.0% Native American/Alaskan Native; and 6.9% White
- Research assistantships/traineeships, 34.5%; 16.8%; 23.0%; 32.1%; 34.1%
- Fellowships/dissertation grants, 44.1%; 47.9%; 48.1%; 35.7%; 27.9%
- Own resources, 11.6%; 23.4%; 17.5%; 28.6%; 23.2%
- Foreign government, 1.2%; 0.0%; 1.1%; 3.6%; 0.2%
- Employer, 1.4%; 2.4%; 2.2%; 0.0%; 3.3%
- Other, 1.4%; 1.8%; 0.5%; 0.0%; 0.5%

Source: Sanderson, A., et. al., *Doctorate Recipients from United States Universities: Summary Report 1999*, Chicago: National Opinion Research Center, 2000.

★2018★
Primary sources of financial support for physical sciences, mathematics, and computer sciences doctorate recipients, by citizenship, 1999

Ranking basis/background: Percentage of doctorate recipients receiving support from each category by citizenship. Based on the 1998-99 Survey of Earned Doctorates (SED) conducted by the National Research Council's Office of Scientific and Engineering Personnel (OSEP). The doctorates are reported by academic year and include research and applied research doctorates in all fields.
Remarks: The *Summary Report* is the 33rd in an annual series of reports that began in 1967.
Number listed: 7.
- Teaching assistantships, with 24.4% U.S. citizens; 33.3% non-U.S. (Permanent Visa); and 32.1% non-U.S. (Temporary Visa)
- Research assistantships/traineeships, 40.5%; 43.8%; 46.8%
- Fellowships/dissertation grants, 18.0%; 11.0%; 10.6%
- Own resources, 13.8%; 8.3%; 3.3%
- Foreign government, 0.1%; 1.5%; 6.6%
- Employer, 3.0%; 2.4%; 0.4%
- Other, 0.2%; 0.0%; 0.1%

Source: Sanderson, A., et. al., *Doctorate Recipients from United States Universities: Summary Report 1999*, Chicago: National Opinion Research Center, 2000.

★2019★
Primary sources of financial support for physical sciences, mathematics, and computer sciences doctorate recipients, by gender, 1999

Ranking basis/background: Percentage of men and women doctorate recipients receiving support from each category. Based on the 1998-99 Survey of Earned Doctorates (SED) conducted by the National Research Council's Office of Scientific and Engineering Personnel (OSEP). The doctorates are reported by academic year and include research and applied research doctorates in all fields.
Remarks: The *Summary Report* is the 33rd in an annual series of reports that began in 1967.
Number listed: 7.
- Teaching assistantships, with 27.9% men; and 27.1% women
- Research assistantships/traineeships, 44.3%; 38.7%
- Fellowships/dissertation grants, 13.5%; 19.4%
- Own resources, 9.1%; 11.4%
- Foreign government, 2.7%; 2.0%
- Employer, 2.2%; 1.4%
- Other, 0.2%; 0.0%

Source: Sanderson, A., et. al., *Doctorate Recipients from United States Universities: Summary Report 1999*, Chicago: National Opinion Research Center, 2000.

DOCTORAL DEGREES   Educational Rankings Annual • 2002

★2020★
Primary sources of financial support for physical sciences, mathematics, and computer sciences doctorate recipients, by race/ethnicity, 1999

Ranking basis/background: Percentage of doctorate recipients receiving support from each category by race/ethnicity. Based on the 1998-99 Survey of Earned Doctorates (SED) conducted by the National Research Council's Office of Scientific and Engineering Personnel (OSEP). The doctorates are reported by academic year and include research and applied research doctorates in all fields.
Remarks: The *Summary Report* is the 33rd in an annual series of reports that began in 1967.
Number listed: 7.
- Teaching assistantships, with 22.8% Asian American/Pacific Islander; 12.9% African American; 16.7% Hispanic American; 21.4% Native American/Alaskan Native; and 25.2% White
- Research assistantships/traineeships, 47.6%; 25.9%; 24.4%; 57.1%; 40.8%
- Fellowships/dissertation grants, 18.0%; 41.2%; 38.9%; 7.1%; 16.7%
- Own resources, 6.8%; 15.3%; 14.4%; 14.3%; 14.1%
- Foreign government, 0.5%; 0.0%; 1.1%; 0.0%; 0.1%
- Employer, 4.4%; 4.7%; 4.4%; 0.0%; 2.8%
- Other, 0.0%; 0.0%; 0.0%; 0.0%; 0.3%

Source: Sanderson, A., et. al., *Doctorate Recipients from United States Universities: Summary Report 1999*, Chicago: National Opinion Research Center, 2000.

★2021★
Primary sources of financial support for professional/other doctorate recipients, by citizenship, 1999

Ranking basis/background: Percentage of doctorate recipients receiving support from each category by citizenship. Based on the 1998-99 Survey of Earned Doctorates (SED) conducted by the National Research Council's Office of Scientific and Engineering Personnel (OSEP). The doctorates are reported by academic year and include research and applied research doctorates in all fields.
Remarks: The *Summary Report* is the 33rd in an annual series of reports that began in 1967.
Number listed: 7.
- Teaching assistantships, with 18.0% U.S. citizens; 24.1% non-U.S. (Permanent Visa); and 26.8% non-U.S. (Temporary Visa)
- Research assistantships/traineeships, 9.0%; 13.0%; 14.6%
- Fellowships/dissertation grants, 11.2%; 14.8%; 22.8%
- Own resources, 54.6%; 38.9%; 21.4%
- Foreign government, 0.2%; 6.5%; 12.2%
- Employer, 6.0%; 1.9%; 1.9%
- Other, 1.0%; 0.9%; 0.2%

Source: Sanderson, A., et. al., *Doctorate Recipients from United States Universities: Summary Report 1999*, Chicago: National Opinion Research Center, 2000.

★2022★
Primary sources of financial support for professional/other doctorate recipients, by gender, 1999

Ranking basis/background: Percentage of men and women doctorate recipients receiving support from each category. Based on the 1998-99 Survey of Earned Doctorates (SED) conducted by the National Research Council's Office of Scientific and Engineering Personnel (OSEP). The doctorates are reported by academic year and include research and applied research doctorates in all fields.
Remarks: The *Summary Report* is the 33rd in an annual series of reports that began in 1967.
Number listed: 7.
- Teaching assistantships, with 20.1% men; and 20.3% women
- Research assistantships/traineeships, 11.0%; 9.7%
- Fellowships/dissertation grants, 15.5%; 11.8%
- Own resources, 43.0%; 51.7%
- Foreign government, 3.9%; 2.0%
- Employer, 5.6%; 3.8%
- Other, 0.9%; 0.7%

Source: Sanderson, A., et. al., *Doctorate Recipients from United States Universities: Summary Report 1999*, Chicago: National Opinion Research Center, 2000.

★2023★
Primary sources of financial support for professional/other doctorate recipients, by race/ethnicity, 1999

Ranking basis/background: Percentage of doctorate recipients receiving support from each category by race/ethnicity. Based on the 1998-99 Survey of Earned Doctorates (SED) conducted by the National Research Council's Office of Scientific and Engineering Personnel (OSEP). The doctorates are reported by academic year and include research and applied research doctorates in all fields.
Remarks: The *Summary Report* is the 33rd in an annual series of reports that began in 1967.
Number listed: 7.
- Teaching assistantships, with 23.3% Asian American/Pacific Islander; 11.7% African American; 4.1% Hispanic American; 0.0% Native American/Alaskan Native; and 19.3% White
- Research assistantships/traineeships, 13.3%; 3.9%; 8.2%; 6.3%; 9.4%
- Fellowships/dissertation grants, 18.3%; 28.1%; 32.7%; 25.0%; 7.8%
- Own resources, 41.7%; 52.3%; 49.0%; 62.5%; 55.6%
- Foreign government, 0.0%; 0.8%; 0.0%; 0.0%; 0.2%
- Employer, 1.7%; 3.1%; 6.1%; 6.3%; 6.6%
- Other, 1.7%; 0.0%; 0.0%; 0.0%; 1.2%

Source: Sanderson, A., et. al., *Doctorate Recipients from United States Universities: Summary Report 1999*, Chicago: National Opinion Research Center, 2000.

★2024★
Primary sources of financial support for social sciences doctorate recipients, by citizenship, 1999

Ranking basis/background: Percentage of doctorate recipients receiving support from each category by citizenship. Based on the 1998-99 Survey of Earned Doctorates (SED) conducted by the National Research Council's Office of Scientific and Engineering Personnel (OSEP). The doctorates are reported by academic year and include research and applied research doctorates in all fields.
Remarks: The *Summary Report* is the 33rd in an annual series of reports that began in 1967.
Number listed: 7.
- Teaching assistantships, with 17.3% U.S. citizens; 22.9% non-U.S. (Permanent Visa); and 28.9% non-U.S. (Temporary Visa)
- Research assistantships/traineeships, 13.8%; 14.6%; 13.3%
- Fellowships/dissertation grants, 17.5%; 22.1%; 26.4%
- Own resources, 49.0%; 36.3%; 15.8%
- Foreign government, 0.2%; 3.8%; 14.5%
- Employer, 1.5%; 0.4%; 1.1%
- Other, 0.6%; 0.0%; 0.0%

Source: Sanderson, A., et. al., *Doctorate Recipients from United States Universities: Summary Report 1999*, Chicago: National Opinion Research Center, 2000.

★2025★
Primary sources of financial support for social sciences doctorate recipients, by gender, 1999

Ranking basis/background: Percentage of men and women doctorate recipients receiving support from each category. Based on the 1998-99 Survey of Earned Doctorates (SED) conducted by the National Research Council's Office of Scientific and Engineering Personnel (OSEP). The doctorates are reported by academic year and include research and applied research doctorates in all fields.
Remarks: The *Summary Report* is the 33rd in an annual series of reports that began in 1967.
Number listed: 7.
- Teaching assistantships, with 21.0% men; and 17.6% women
- Research assistantships/traineeships, 13.4%; 14.1%
- Fellowships/dissertation grants, 20.6%; 17.7%
- Own resources, 39.1%; 47.7%
- Foreign government, 3.6%; 1.3%
- Employer, 1.9%; 0.9%
- Other, 0.4%; 0.6%

Source: Sanderson, A., et. al., *Doctorate Recipients from United States Universities: Summary Report 1999*, Chicago: National Opinion Research Center, 2000.

★2026★
Primary sources of financial support for social sciences doctorate recipients, by race/ethnicity, 1999

Ranking basis/background: Percentage of doctorate recipients receiving support from each category by race/ethnicity. Based on the 1998-99 Survey of Earned Doctorates (SED) conducted by the National Research Council's Office of Scientific and Engineering Personnel (OSEP). The doctorates are reported by academic year and include research and applied research doctorates in all fields. **Remarks:** The *Summary Report* is the 33rd in an annual series of reports that began in 1967. **Number listed:** 7.

- Teaching assistantships, with 18.5% Asian American/Pacific Islander; 9.2% African American; 12.5% Hispanic American; 9.4% Native American/Alaskan Native; and 18.1% White
- Research assistantships/traineeships, 12.9%; 8.8%; 10.8%; 9.4%; 14.5%
- Fellowships/dissertation grants, 21.9%; 36.1%; 29.3%; 32.1%; 15.3%
- Own resources, 44.9%; 42.5%; 45.3%; 45.3%; 49.9%
- Foreign government, 0.6%; 0.0%; 0.9%; 1.9%; 0.1%
- Employer, 1.1%; 3.1%; 1.3%; 0.0%; 1.4%
- Other, 0.0%; 0.3%; 0.0%; 1.9%; 0.7%

Source: Sanderson, A., et. al., *Doctorate Recipients from United States Universities: Summary Report 1999*, Chicago: National Opinion Research Center, 2000.

★2027★
Private, 4-year undergraduate colleges and universities producing the most Ph.D.s in all fields of study, 1920-1990

Ranking basis/background: Number of doctoral degrees granted to graduates of 914 private, 4-year U.S. undergraduate colleges and universities. Medical, law, and other professional, non-doctoral degrees are not included. **Remarks:** Original source: Office of Scientific and Engineering Personnel of the National Research Council. Report contains 50 other tables detailing the distribution of doctoral recipients by field of study over various time frames. **Number listed:** 360.

1. Oberlin College, with 3,900 Ph.D.'s
2. Swarthmore College, 2,174
3. Barnard College, 1,935
4. Wellesley College, 1,811
5. Amherst College, 1,719
6. Pomona College, 1,703
7. Carleton College, 1,697
8. Smith College, 1,652
9. Wesleyan University, 1,616
10. Reed College, 1,531
11. Wheaton College, 1,489
12. DePauw University, 1,455
13. Vassar College, 1,403
14. College of Wooster, 1,401
15. Mount Holyoke College, 1,345
16. Williams College, 1,339
17. St. Olaf College, 1,338
18. Bucknell University, 1,292
19. Antioch College, 1,248
20. Polytechnic University, 1,238

Source: *Baccalaureate Origins of Doctorate Recipients*, 7th ed., Franklin & Marshall College, March 1993.

★2028★
Private, 4-year undergraduate colleges and universities producing the most Ph.D.'s in all fields of study, 1981-1990

Ranking basis/background: Number of doctoral degrees granted to graduates of 914 private, 4-year U.S. undergraduate colleges and universities. Medical, law, and other professional, non-doctoral degrees are not included. **Remarks:** Original source: Office of Scientific and Engineering Personnel of the National Research Council. Report contains 50 other tables detailing the distribution of doctoral recipients by field of study over various time frames. **Number listed:** 358.

1. Oberlin College, with 946 Ph.D.'s
2. Wellesley College, 572
3. Barnard College, 569
4. Smith College, 562
5. Carleton College, 537
6. Swarthmore College, 532
7. Wesleyan University, 472
8. Vassar College, 444
9. Wheaton College, 441
9. Mount Holyoke College, 441
11. Pomona College, 438
12. Bucknell University, 428
13. Reed College, 400
14. St. Olaf College, 398
15. Wake Forest University, 356
16. University of Dayton, 339
16. Williams College, 339
18. Clark University, 336
19. Amherst College, 333
20. Villanova University, 326

Source: *Baccalaureate Origins of Doctorate Recipients*, 7th ed., Franklin & Marshall College, March 1993.

★2029★
Private, 4-year undergraduate colleges and universities producing the most Ph.D.'s in all fields of study, 1990

Ranking basis/background: Number of doctoral degrees granted to graduates of 914 private, 4-year U.S. undergraduate colleges and universities. Medical, law, and other professional, non-doctoral degrees are not included. **Remarks:** Original source: Office of Scientific and Engineering Personnel of the National Research Council. Report contains 50 other tables detailing the distribution of doctoral recipients by field of study over various time frames. **Number listed:** 328.

1. Oberlin College, with 90 Ph.D.'s
2. Carleton College, 65
3. Reed College, 60
4. Wellesley College, 58
5. Smith College, 55
6. Swarthmore College, 53
6. Wesleyan University, 53
8. Vassar College, 49
9. St. Olaf College, 46
9. Pomona College, 46
11. Wheaton College, 42
11. Bucknell University, 42
13. Barnard College, 41
13. Mount Holyoke College, 41
15. College of Wooster, 39
16. Colgate University, 36
16. Connecticut College, 36
18. Bryn Mawr College, 35
19. Macalester College, 34
19. Colorado College, 34
19. Grinnell College, 34

Source: *Baccalaureate Origins of Doctorate Recipients*, 7th ed., Franklin & Marshall College, March 1993.

★2030★
Private, 4-year undergraduate colleges and universities producing the most Ph.D.'s in nonscience fields, 1920-1990

Ranking basis/background: Number of doctoral degrees granted to graduates of 914 private, 4-year U.S. undergraduate colleges and universities. Medical, law, and other professional, non-doctoral degrees are not included. **Remarks:** Original source: Office of Scientific and Engineering Personnel of the National Research Council. Report contains 50 other tables detailing the distribution of doctoral recipients by field of study over various time frames. **Number listed:** 359.

1. Oberlin College, with 1,647 Ph.D.'s
2. Wellesley College, 917
3. Barnard College, 908
4. Wheaton College, 898
5. Smith College, 873
6. Amherst College, 735
7. Swarthmore College, 661
8. Wesleyan University, 659
9. Vassar College, 658
10. St. Olaf College, 585
11. College of Wooster, 584
12. Calvin College, 573
13. DePauw University, 571
14. Bryn Mawr College, 565
15. Wake Forest University, 564
16. Mount Holyoke College, 559
17. Duquesne University, 557
18. Pomona College, 552
19. Ohio Wesleyan University, 550
20. Carleton College, 546

Source: *Baccalaureate Origins of Doctorate Recipients*, 7th ed., Franklin & Marshall College, March 1993.

★2031★
Private, 4-year undergraduate colleges and universities producing the most Ph.D.'s in nonscience fields, 1981-1990

Ranking basis/background: Number of doctoral degrees granted to graduates of 914 private, 4-year U.S. undergraduate colleges and universities. Medical, law, and other professional, non-doctoral degrees are not included. **Remarks:** Original source: Office of Scientific and Engineering Personnel of the National Research Council. Report contains 50 other tables detailing the distribution of doctoral recipients by field of study over various time frames. **Number listed:** 349.

1. Oberlin College, with 429 Ph.D.'s
2. Wellesley College, 266
3. Smith College, 264
4. Wheaton College, 262
5. Barnard College, 255
6. Duquesne University, 198
7. Vassar College, 196
8. Mount Holyoke College, 186
9. Wesleyan University, 169
10. Calvin College, 165
11. Swarthmore College, 160
12. Wake Forest University, 157
13. St. Olaf College, 156
14. Bryn Mawr College, 147
15. College of Wooster, 142
16. Mississippi College, 134
17. Carleton College, 133
17. Drake University, 133
19. Pomona College, 130

DOCTORAL DEGREES

20. Villanova University, 129

Source: *Baccalaureate Origins of Doctorate Recipients, 7th ed.*, Franklin & Marshall College, March 1993.

★2032★
Private, 4-year undergraduate colleges and universities producing the most Ph.D.'s in nonscience fields, 1990

Ranking basis/background: Number of doctoral degrees granted to graduates of 914 private, 4-year U.S. undergraduate colleges and universities. Medical, law, and other professional, non-doctoral degrees are not included. **Remarks:** Original source: Office of Scientific and Engineering Personnel of the National Research Council. Report contains 50 other tables detailing the distribution of doctoral recipients by field of study over various time frames. **Number listed:** 286.

1. Oberlin College, with 36 Ph.D.s
2. Wellesley College, 28
3. Smith College, 25
4. Wesleyan University, 23
5. Wheaton College, 22
6. Mississippi College, 21
7. Vassar College, 20
7. College of Wooster, 20
9. Pomona College, 17
10. Bucknell University, 16
10. Connecticut College, 16
10. Wake Forest University, 16
10. Villanova University, 16
14. St. Olaf College, 15
14. Barnard College, 15
14. Hampton University, 15
17. Bryn Mawr College, 14
17. Colorado College, 14
17. Duquesne University, 14
17. Spelman College, 14

Source: *Baccalaureate Origins of Doctorate Recipients, 7th ed.*, Franklin & Marshall College, March 1993.

★2033★
Professional doctorates awarded at U.S. colleges and universities, by subfield, 1999

Ranking basis/background: Based on the 1998-99 Survey of Earned Doctorates (SED) conducted by the National Research Council's Office of Scientific and Engineering Personnel (OSEP). The doctorates are reported by academic year and include research and applied research doctorates in all fields. **Remarks:** The *Summary Report* is the 33rd in an annual series of reports that began in 1967. **Number listed:** 10.

Architectural environmental design, with 65
Home economics, 23
Law, 37
Library science, 39
Parks/recreation/leisure/fitness, 29
Public administration, 119
Social work, 229
Theology/religious education, 168
Professional fields, general, 9
Professional fields, other, 63

Source: Sanderson, A., et. al., *Doctorate Recipients from United States Universities: Summary Report 1999*, Chicago: National Opinion Research Center, 2000.

★2034★
Professional/other doctorates awarded to U.S. citizens/permanent residents at U.S. colleges and universities, by race/ethnicity and subfield, 1999

Ranking basis/background: Based on the 1998-99 Survey of Earned Doctorates (SED) conducted by the National Research Council's Office of Scientific and Engineering Personnel (OSEP). The doctorates are reported by academic year and include research and applied research doctorates in all fields. **Remarks:** The *Summary Report* is the 33rd in an annual series of reports that began in 1967. **Number listed:** 3.

Business and management, with 32 to Asian Americans; 54 to African Americans; 13 to Hispanic Americans; 5 to Native Americans; and 585 to Whites
Other professional fields, 32; 84; 36; 11; 660
Other fields, 0; 1; 1; 0; 4

Source: Sanderson, A., et. al., *Doctorate Recipients from United States Universities: Summary Report 1999*, Chicago: National Opinion Research Center, 2000.

★2035★
Profile of median number of years from baccalaureate to doctorate award for all fields, 1999

Ranking basis/background: Based on the 1998-99 Survey of Earned Doctorates (SED) conducted by the National Research Council's Office of Scientific and Engineering Personnel (OSEP). The doctorates are reported by academic year and include research and applied research doctorates in all fields. **Remarks:** The *Summary Report* is the 33rd in an annual series of reports that began in 1967. **Number listed:** 3.

Sex: Men, with 10.0 years elapsed time from baccalaureate (7.3 years registered time from baccalaureate); and Women with 11.3 years elapsed time from baccalaureate (7.6 years registered time from baccalaureate)
Citizenship: U.S. citizen, 10.7 (7.5); Non-U.S.-Permanent Visa, 11.4 (8.0); Non-U.S.-Temporary Visa, 9.8 (7.0)
Race/ethnicity: Asian American, 8.5 (7.0); African American, 13.7 (7.9); Hispanic American, 11.2 (7.9); Native American, 13.0 (8.2); White, 10.6 (7.5)

Source: Sanderson, A., et. al., *Doctorate Recipients from United States Universities: Summary Report 1999*, Chicago: National Opinion Research Center, 2000.

★2036★
Profile of median number of years from baccalaureate to education doctorate, 1999

Ranking basis/background: Based on the 1998-99 Survey of Earned Doctorates (SED) conducted by the National Research Council's Office of Scientific and Engineering Personnel (OSEP). The doctorates are reported by academic year and include research and applied research doctorates in all fields. **Remarks:** The *Summary Report* is the 33rd in an annual series of reports that began in 1967. **Number listed:** 3.

Sex: Men, with 18.3 years elapsed time from baccalaureate (8.1 years registered time from baccalaureate); and Women with 20.5 years elapsed time from baccalaureate (8.2 years registered time from baccalaureate)
Citizenship: U.S. citizen, 20.9 (8.4); Non-U.S.-Permanent Visa, 15.0 (8.0); Non-U.S.-Temporary Visa, 13.0 (6.9)
Race/ethnicity: Asian American, 15.0 (7.6); African American, 21.6 (8.0); Hispanic American, 18.8 (9.0); Native American, 20.5 (9.0); White, 21.0 (8.4)

Source: Sanderson, A., et. al., *Doctorate Recipients from United States Universities: Summary Report 1999*, Chicago: National Opinion Research Center, 2000.

★2037★
Profile of median number of years from baccalaureate to engineering doctorate, 1999

Ranking basis/background: Based on the 1998-99 Survey of Earned Doctorates (SED) conducted by the National Research Council's Office of Scientific and Engineering Personnel (OSEP). The doctorates are reported by academic year and include research and applied research doctorates in all fields. **Remarks:** The *Summary Report* is the 33rd in an annual series of reports that began in 1967. **Number listed:** 3.

Sex: Men, with 8.9 years elapsed time from baccalaureate (6.7 years registered time from baccalaureate); and Women with 8.0 years elapsed time from baccalaureate (6.3 years registered time from baccalaureate)
Citizenship: U.S. citizen, 8.0 (6.5); Non-U.S.-Permanent Visa, 10.6 (7.5); Non-U.S.-Temporary Visa, 9.1 (6.6)
Race/ethnicity: Asian American, 7.6 (6.7); African American, 9.3 (7.0); Hispanic American, 7.9 (6.7); Native American, 10.7 (8.9); White, 8.0 (6.5)

Source: Sanderson, A., et. al., *Doctorate Recipients from United States Universities: Summary Report 1999*, Chicago: National Opinion Research Center, 2000.

★2038★
Profile of median number of years from baccalaureate to humanities doctorate, 1999

Ranking basis/background: Based on the 1998-99 Survey of Earned Doctorates (SED) conducted by the National Research Council's Office of Scientific and Engineering Personnel (OSEP). The doctorates are reported by academic year and include research and applied research doctorates in all fields. **Remarks:** The *Summary Report* is the 33rd in an annual series of reports that began in 1967. **Number listed:** 3.

Sex: Men, with 11.8 years elapsed time from baccalaureate (8.9 years registered time from baccalaureate); and Women with 11.6 years elapsed time from baccalaureate (8.9 years registered time from baccalaureate)
Citizenship: U.S. citizen, 11.8 (9.0); Non-U.S.-Permanent Visa, 12.2 (9.4); Non-U.S.-Temporary Visa, 11.0 (8.1)
Race/ethnicity: Asian American, 11.0 (9.0); African American, 12.2 (8.9); Hispanic American, 11.7 (8.5); Native American, 14.9 (10.0); White, 11.7 (9.0)

★2039★
Profile of median number of years from baccalaureate to life sciences doctorate, 1999

Ranking basis/background: Based on the 1998-99 Survey of Earned Doctorates (SED) conducted by the National Research Council's Office of Scientific and Engineering Personnel (OSEP). The doctorates are reported by academic year and include research and applied research doctorates in all fields.
Remarks: The *Summary Report* is the 33rd in an annual series of reports that began in 1967.
Number listed: 3.
- Sex: Men, with 9.0 years elapsed time from baccalaureate (7.0 years registered time from baccalaureate); and Women with 9.0 years elapsed time from baccalaureate (7.0 years registered time from baccalaureate)
- Citizenship: U.S. citizen, 8.5 (7.0); Non-U.S.-Permanent Visa, 11.0 (7.8); Non-U.S.-Temporary Visa, 9.9 (7.0)
- Race/ethnicity: Asian American, 7.9 (6.6); African American, 10.0 (7.6); Hispanic American, 8.9 (7.3); Native American, 10.0 (8.0); White, 8.5 (6.9)

Source: Sanderson, A., et. al., *Doctorate Recipients from United States Universities: Summary Report 1999*, Chicago: National Opinion Research Center, 2000.

★2040★
Profile of median number of years from baccalaureate to physical sciences doctorate, 1999

Ranking basis/background: Based on the 1998-99 Survey of Earned Doctorates (SED) conducted by the National Research Council's Office of Scientific and Engineering Personnel (OSEP). The doctorates are reported by academic year and include research and applied research doctorates in all fields.
Remarks: The *Summary Report* is the 33rd in an annual series of reports that began in 1967.
Number listed: 3.
- Sex: Men, with 8.0 years elapsed time from baccalaureate (6.8 years registered time from baccalaureate); and Women with 7.9 years elapsed time from baccalaureate (6.6 years registered time from baccalaureate)
- Citizenship: U.S. citizen, 7.2 (6.6); Non-U.S.-Permanent Visa, 10.1 (7.5); Non-U.S.-Temporary Visa, 8.9 (7.0)
- Race/ethnicity: Asian American, 7.6 (7.0); African American, 7.9 (6.8); Hispanic American, 8.0 (7.3); Native American, 9.6 (6.8); White, 7.0 (6.5)

Source: Sanderson, A., et. al., *Doctorate Recipients from United States Universities: Summary Report 1999*, Chicago: National Opinion Research Center, 2000.

★2041★
Profile of median number of years from baccalaureate to professional/other doctorate, 1999

Ranking basis/background: Based on the 1998-99 Survey of Earned Doctorates (SED) conducted by the National Research Council's Office of Scientific and Engineering Personnel (OSEP). The doctorates are reported by academic year and include research and applied research doctorates in all fields.
Remarks: The *Summary Report* is the 33rd in an annual series of reports that began in 1967.
Number listed: 3.
- Sex: Men, with 13.6 years elapsed time from baccalaureate (8.0 years registered time from baccalaureate); and Women with 14.8 years elapsed time from baccalaureate (8.0 years registered time from baccalaureate)
- Citizenship: U.S. citizen, 15.4 (8.1); Non-U.S.-Permanent Visa, 13.0 (8.8); Non-U.S.-Temporary Visa, 11.0 (7.5)
- Race/ethnicity: Asian American, 12.8 (8.0); African American, 16.0 (7.6); Hispanic American, 14.5 (8.1); Native American, 19.3 (8.9); White, 15.5 (8.2)

Source: Sanderson, A., et. al., *Doctorate Recipients from United States Universities: Summary Report 1999*, Chicago: National Opinion Research Center, 2000.

★2042★
Profile of median number of years from baccalaureate to social sciences doctorate, 1999

Ranking basis/background: Based on the 1998-99 Survey of Earned Doctorates (SED) conducted by the National Research Council's Office of Scientific and Engineering Personnel (OSEP). The doctorates are reported by academic year and include research and applied research doctorates in all fields.
Remarks: The *Summary Report* is the 33rd in an annual series of reports that began in 1967.
Number listed: 3.
- Sex: Men, with 10.0 years elapsed time from baccalaureate (7.6 years registered time from baccalaureate); and Women with 9.8 years elapsed time from baccalaureate (7.5 years registered time from baccalaureate)
- Citizenship: U.S. citizen, 9.7 (7.5); Non-U.S.-Permanent Visa, 11.8 (8.2); Non-U.S.-Temporary Visa, 10.0 (7.5)
- Race/ethnicity: Asian American, 9.0 (7.2); African American, 9.9 (7.4); Hispanic American, 9.7 (7.6); Native American, 10.0 (8.0); White, 9.7 (7.5)

Source: Sanderson, A., et. al., *Doctorate Recipients from United States Universities: Summary Report 1999*, Chicago: National Opinion Research Center, 2000.

★2043★
Psychology doctorates awarded at U.S. colleges and universities, by subfield, 1999

Ranking basis/background: Based on the 1998-99 Survey of Earned Doctorates (SED) conducted by the National Research Council's Office of Scientific and Engineering Personnel (OSEP). The doctorates are reported by academic year and include research and applied research doctorates in all fields.
Remarks: The *Summary Report* is the 33rd in an annual series of reports that began in 1967.
Number listed: 18.
- Clinical, with 1,449
- Cognitive and psycholinguistics, 143
- Comparative, 11
- Counseling, 461
- Developmental and child, 193
- Human/individual and family counseling, 130
- Experimental, 66
- Educational, 66
- Family and marriage counseling, 55
- Industrial and organizational, 158
- Personality, 16
- Physiological/psychobiology, 87
- Psychometrics, 15
- Quantitative, 14
- School, 120
- Social, 175
- Psychology, general, 229
- Psychology, other, 208

Source: Sanderson, A., et. al., *Doctorate Recipients from United States Universities: Summary Report 1999*, Chicago: National Opinion Research Center, 2000.

★2044★
Social sciences doctorates awarded at U.S. colleges and universities, by subfield, 1999

Ranking basis/background: Based on the 1998-99 Survey of Earned Doctorates (SED) conducted by the National Research Council's Office of Scientific and Engineering Personnel (OSEP). The doctorates are reported by academic year and include research and applied research doctorates in all fields.
Remarks: The *Summary Report* is the 33rd in an annual series of reports that began in 1967.
Number listed: 15.
- Anthropology, with 461
- Area studies, 11
- Criminology, 51
- Demography/population studies, 28
- Economics, 912
- Econometrics, 15
- Geography, 144
- International relations/affairs, 120
- Political science and government, 653
- Public policy analysis, 124
- Sociology, 543
- Statistics, 72
- Urban affairs/studies, 57
- Social sciences, general, 25
- Social sciences, other, 153

Source: Sanderson, A., et. al., *Doctorate Recipients from United States Universities: Summary Report 1999*, Chicago: National Opinion Research Center, 2000.

★2045★
Social sciences doctorates awarded to U.S. citizens/permanent residents at U.S. colleges and universities, by race/ethnicity and subfield, 1999

Ranking basis/background: Based on the 1998-99 Survey of Earned Doctorates (SED) conducted by the National Research Council's Office of Scientific and Engineering Personnel (OSEP). The doctorates are reported by academic year and include research and applied research doctorates in all fields.
Remarks: The *Summary Report* is the 33rd in an annual series of reports that began in 1967.
Number listed: 5.
- Psychology, with 107 to Asian Americans; 169 to African Americans; 192 to Hispanic Americans; 36 to Native Americans; and 2,632 to Whites

DOCTORAL DEGREES

Economics, 19; 21; 17; 1; 334
Anthropology and sociology, 26; 55; 33; 12; 624
Political science and international relations, 17; 32; 21; 6; 479
Other social sciences, 19; 34; 15; 5; 372

Source: Sanderson, A., et. al., *Doctorate Recipients from United States Universities: Summary Report 1999*, Chicago: National Opinion Research Center, 2000.

★2046★
Teaching fields doctorates awarded at U.S. colleges and universities, by subfield, 1999

Ranking basis/background: Based on the 1998-99 Survey of Earned Doctorates (SED) conducted by the National Research Council's Office of Scientific and Engineering Personnel (OSEP). The doctorates are reported by academic year and include research and applied research doctorates in all fields. **Remarks:** The *Summary Report* is the 33rd in an annual series of reports that began in 1967. **Number listed:** 20.

Agricultural education, with 38
Art education, 47
Business education, 45
English education, 64
Foreign language education, 62
Health education, 58
Home economics education, 10
Technical/industrial arts education, 21
Mathematics education, 101
Music education, 79
Nursing education, 22
Physical education and coaching, 114
Reading education, 68
Science education, 58
Social science education, 9
Technical education, 27
Trade and industrial education, 14
Teacher education/special academics and vocations, 54
Education, general, 199
Education, other, 393

Source: Sanderson, A., et. al., *Doctorate Recipients from United States Universities: Summary Report 1999*, Chicago: National Opinion Research Center, 2000.

★2047★
Top doctorate granting institutions, 1999

Ranking basis/background: Based on the 1998-99 Survey of Earned Doctorates (SED) conducted by the National Research Council's Office of Scientific and Engineering Personnel (OSEP). The doctorates are reported by academic year and include research and applied research doctorates in all fields. **Remarks:** The *Summary Report* is the 33rd in an annual series of reports that began in 1967. **Number listed:** 50.

1. University of Texas, Austin, with 752 doctorates granted
2. University of California, Berkeley, 717
3. University of Wisconsin, Madison, 685
4. University of Minnesota, Twin Cities, 656
5. University of Michigan, Ann Arbor, 655
6. University of Illinois, Urbana-Champaign, 643
7. University of California, Los Angeles, 588
8. Pennsylvania State University, 580
9. Nova Southeastern University, 573
10. Harvard University, 564

Source: Sanderson, A., et. al., *Doctorate Recipients from United States Universities: Summary Report 1999*, Chicago: National Opinion Research Center, 2000.

★2048★
Top doctorate granting states, 1999

Ranking basis/background: Number of doctoral degrees awarded in each state. **Remarks:** Original source: NSF, NIH, USED, NEH, USDA, NASA. **Number listed:** 18.

1. California, with 4,724
2. New York, 3,511
3. Texas, 2,697
4. Illinois, 2,201
5. Massachusetts, 2,132
6. Pennsylvania, 2,115
7. Florida, 1,944
8. Ohio, 1,638

Source: Sanderson, A., et. al., *Doctorate Recipients from United States Universities: Summary Report 1999*, Chicago: National Opinion Research Center, 2000.

★2049★
Total doctoral degrees awarded to African Americans, by type of institutions, 1997-98

Ranking basis/background: Total number of doctoral degrees conferred to African American students in 1997-98 by carnegie classification. **Remarks:** Original source: *Black Issues* analysis of U.S. Department of Education data. **Number listed:** 15.

Public, with 1,083
Private, nonprofit, 887
Proprietary, 25
Research I, 929
Research II, 177
Doctorate I, 392
Doctorate II, 94
Master's I, 107
Master's II, 0
Bachelor's I, 12
Bachelor's II, 64
Associate's, 0
Specialized, 205
Tribal, 0
Unclassified, 15

Source: St. John, Eric, "More Doctorates in the House," *Black Issues in Higher Education*, 17: 38-44, (July 6, 2000).

★2050★
Total doctoral degrees awarded to Asian Americans, by type of institutions, 1997-98

Ranking basis/background: Total number of doctoral degrees conferred to Asian American students in 1997-98 by carnegie classification. **Remarks:** Original source: *Black Issues* analysis of U.S. Department of Education data. **Number listed:** 15.

Public, with 1,461
Private, nonprofit, 754
Proprietary, 6
Research I, 1,538
Research II, 150
Doctorate I, 168
Doctorate II, 94
Master's I, 37
Master's II, 0
Bachelor's I, 13
Bachelor's II, 2
Associate's, 0
Specialized, 211
Tribal, 0
Unclassified, 8

Source: St. John, Eric, "More Doctorates in the House," *Black Issues in Higher Education*, 17: 38-44, (July 6, 2000).

★2051★
Total doctoral degrees awarded to Hispanic Americans, by type of institutions, 1997-98

Ranking basis/background: Total number of doctoral degrees conferred to Hispanic American students in 1997-98 by carnegie classification. **Remarks:** Original source: *Black Issues* analysis of U.S. Department of Education data. **Number listed:** 15.

Public, with 446
Private, nonprofit, 221
Proprietary, 10
Research I, 416
Research II, 51
Doctorate I, 60
Doctorate II, 43
Master's I, 39
Master's II, 0
Bachelor's I, 0
Bachelor's II, 0
Associate's, 0
Specialized, 65
Tribal, 0
Unclassified, 3

Source: St. John, Eric, "More Doctorates in the House," *Black Issues in Higher Education*, 17: 38-44, (July 6, 2000).

★2052★
Total doctoral degrees awarded to minorities, by type of institutions, 1997-98

Ranking basis/background: Total number of doctoral degrees conferred to minority students in 1997-98 by carnegie classification. **Remarks:** Original source: *Black Issues* analysis of U.S. Department of Education data. **Number listed:** 15.

Public, with 3,096
Private, nonprofit, 1,919
Proprietary, 58
Research I, 2,966
Research II, 415
Doctorate I, 639
Doctorate II, 242
Master's I, 187
Master's II, 0
Bachelor's I, 25
Bachelor's II, 66
Associate's, 0
Specialized, 491
Tribal, 0
Unclassified, 42

Source: St. John, Eric, "More Doctorates in the House," *Black Issues in Higher Education*, 17: 38-44, (July 6, 2000).

★2053★
Total doctoral degrees awarded to Native Americans, by type of institutions, 1997-98

Ranking basis/background: Total number of doctoral degrees conferred to Native American students in 1997-98 by carnegie classification. **Remarks:** Original source: *Black Issues* analysis of U.S. Department of Education data. **Number listed:** 15.

Public, with 106

Private, nonprofit, 57
Proprietary, 17
Research I, 83
Research II, 37
Doctorate I, 19
Doctorate II, 11
Master's I, 4
Master's II, 0
Bachelor's I, 0
Bachelor's II, 0
Associate's, 0
Specialized, 10
Tribal, 0
Unclassified, 16

Source: St. John, Eric, "More Doctorates in the House," *Black Issues in Higher Education*, 17: 38-44, (July 6, 2000).

★2054★
Total doctorate recipients by state, 1999

Ranking basis/background: Based on the 1998-99 Survey of Earned Doctorates (SED) conducted by the National Research Council's Office of Scientific and Engineering Personnel (OSEP). The doctorates are reported by academic year and include research and applied research doctorates in all fields.
Remarks: The *Summary Report* is the 33rd in an annual series of reports that began in 1967.
Number listed: 52.

1. California, with 4,747
2. New York, 3,511
3. Texas, 2,697
4. Illinois, 2,201
5. Massachusetts, 2,132
6. Pennsylvania, 2,115
7. Florida, 1,944
8. Ohio, 1,638
9. Michigan, 1,428
10. North Carolina, 1,105
11. Indiana, 1,057
12. Virginia, 1,026
13. Maryland, 1,006
14. Georgia, 935
15. Wisconsin, 873
16. New Jersey, 822
17. Minnesota, 774
18. Colorado, 754
19. Arizona, 729
20. Washington, 706
21. Tennessee, 667
22. Missouri, 666
23. Iowa, 583
24. Connecticut, 574
25. Louisiana, 557
26. District of Columbia, 524
27. Alabama, 494
28. Kansas, 433
29. South Carolina, 416
30. Oregon, 386
31. Oklahoma, 383
32. Mississippi, 365
33. Utah, 365
34. Kentucky, 317
35. Nebraska, 291
36. New Mexico, 276
37. Rhode Island, 237
38. Delaware, 166
39. Hawaii, 160
40. Puerto Rico, 141
41. West Virginia, 140
42. Arkansas, 121
43. New Hampshire, 97
44. Nevada, 85
45. Montana, 83
46. Idaho, 80
47. South Dakota, 77
48. North Dakota, 68
49. Wyoming, 64
50. Vermont, 53
51. Maine, 37
52. Alaska, 27

Source: Sanderson, A., et. al., *Doctorate Recipients from United States Universities: Summary Report 1999*, Chicago: National Opinion Research Center, 2000.

★2055★
Total number of doctorates awarded to African American men and women at U.S. colleges and universities for selected years between 1979 through 1999

Ranking basis/background: Based on the 1998-99 Survey of Earned Doctorates (SED) conducted by the National Research Council's Office of Scientific and Engineering Personnel (OSEP). The doctorates are reported by academic year and include research and applied research doctorates in all fields.
Remarks: The *Summary Report* is the 33rd in an annual series of reports that began in 1967.
Number listed: 13.

1979, with 1,443
1984, 1,496
1989, 1,247
1990, 1,354
1991, 1,466
1992, 1,434
1993, 1,615
1994, 1,683
1995, 1,823
1996, 1,836
1997, 1,774
1998, 1,914
1999, 2,071

Source: Sanderson, A., et. al., *Doctorate Recipients from United States Universities: Summary Report 1999*, Chicago: National Opinion Research Center, 2000.

★2056★
Total number of doctorates awarded to African American men at U.S. colleges and universities for selected years between 1979 through 1999

Ranking basis/background: Based on the 1998-99 Survey of Earned Doctorates (SED) conducted by the National Research Council's Office of Scientific and Engineering Personnel (OSEP). The doctorates are reported by academic year and include research and applied research doctorates in all fields.
Remarks: The *Summary Report* is the 33rd in an annual series of reports that began in 1967.
Number listed: 13.

1979, with 898
1984, 904
1989, 685
1990, 733
1991, 788
1992, 771
1993, 840
1994, 889
1995, 881
1996, 933
1997, 863
1998, 824
1999, 919

Source: Sanderson, A., et. al., *Doctorate Recipients from United States Universities: Summary Report 1999*, Chicago: National Opinion Research Center, 2000.

★2057★
Total number of doctorates awarded to African American women at U.S. colleges and universities for selected years between 1979 through 1999

Ranking basis/background: Based on the 1998-99 Survey of Earned Doctorates (SED) conducted by the National Research Council's Office of Scientific and Engineering Personnel (OSEP). The doctorates are reported by academic year and include research and applied research doctorates in all fields.
Remarks: The *Summary Report* is the 33rd in an annual series of reports that began in 1967.
Number listed: 13.

1979, with 545
1984, 592
1989, 562
1990, 621
1991, 678
1992, 663
1993, 773
1994, 792
1995, 942
1996, 903
1997, 911
1998, 1,088
1999, 1,152

Source: Sanderson, A., et. al., *Doctorate Recipients from United States Universities: Summary Report 1999*, Chicago: National Opinion Research Center, 2000.

★2058★
Total number of doctorates awarded to Asian American/Pacific Islander men and women at U.S. colleges and universities for selected years between 1979 through 1999

Ranking basis/background: Based on the 1998-99 Survey of Earned Doctorates (SED) conducted by the National Research Council's Office of Scientific and Engineering Personnel (OSEP). The doctorates are reported by academic year and include research and applied research doctorates in all fields.
Remarks: The *Summary Report* is the 33rd in an annual series of reports that began in 1967.
Number listed: 13.

1979, with 2,602
1984, 3,403
1989, 5,195
1990, 6,293
1991, 7,528
1992, 8,291
1993, 8,674
1994, 9,369
1995, 9,709
1996, 9,830
1997, 9,011
1998, 8,592
1999, 8,032

Source: Sanderson, A., et. al., *Doctorate Recipients from United States Universities: Summary Report 1999*, Chicago: National Opinion Research Center, 2000.

DOCTORAL DEGREES

★2059★
Total number of doctorates awarded to Asian American/Pacific Islander men at U.S. colleges and universities for selected years between 1979 through 1999

Ranking basis/background: Based on the 1998-99 Survey of Earned Doctorates (SED) conducted by the National Research Council's Office of Scientific and Engineering Personnel (OSEP). The doctorates are reported by academic year and include research and applied research doctorates in all fields.
Remarks: The *Summary Report* is the 33rd in an annual series of reports that began in 1967.
Number listed: 13.

    1979, with 2,158
    1984, 2,789
    1989, 4,166
    1990, 5,030
    1991, 5,872
    1992, 6,418
    1993, 6,605
    1994, 7,061
    1995, 7,103
    1996, 7,209
    1997, 6,423
    1998, 6,040
    1999, 5,543

Source: Sanderson, A., et. al., *Doctorate Recipients from United States Universities: Summary Report 1999*, Chicago: National Opinion Research Center, 2000.

★2060★
Total number of doctorates awarded to Asian American/Pacific Islander women at U.S. colleges and universities for selected years between 1979 through 1999

Ranking basis/background: Based on the 1998-99 Survey of Earned Doctorates (SED) conducted by the National Research Council's Office of Scientific and Engineering Personnel (OSEP). The doctorates are reported by academic year and include research and applied research doctorates in all fields.
Remarks: The *Summary Report* is the 33rd in an annual series of reports that began in 1967.
Number listed: 13.

    1979, with 444
    1984, 614
    1989, 1,029
    1990, 1,262
    1991, 1,648
    1992, 1,862
    1993, 2,055
    1994, 2,298
    1995, 2,599
    1996, 2,616
    1997, 2,581
    1998, 2,536
    1999, 2,488

Source: Sanderson, A., et. al., *Doctorate Recipients from United States Universities: Summary Report 1999*, Chicago: National Opinion Research Center, 2000.

★2061★
Total number of doctorates awarded to Hispanic American men and women at U.S. colleges and universities for selected years between 1979 through 1999

Ranking basis/background: Based on the 1998-99 Survey of Earned Doctorates (SED) conducted by the National Research Council's Office of Scientific and Engineering Personnel (OSEP). The doctorates are reported by academic year and include research and applied research doctorates in all fields.
Remarks: The *Summary Report* is the 33rd in an annual series of reports that began in 1967.
Number listed: 13.

    1979, with 908
    1984, 916
    1989, 1,063
    1990, 1,228
    1991, 1,320
    1992, 1,402
    1993, 1,431
    1994, 1,534
    1995, 1,534
    1996, 1,621
    1997, 1,685
    1998, 1,869
    1999, 1,842

Source: Sanderson, A., et. al., *Doctorate Recipients from United States Universities: Summary Report 1999*, Chicago: National Opinion Research Center, 2000.

★2062★
Total number of doctorates awarded to Hispanic American men at U.S. colleges and universities for selected years between 1979 through 1999

Ranking basis/background: Based on the 1998-99 Survey of Earned Doctorates (SED) conducted by the National Research Council's Office of Scientific and Engineering Personnel (OSEP). The doctorates are reported by academic year and include research and applied research doctorates in all fields.
Remarks: The *Summary Report* is the 33rd in an annual series of reports that began in 1967.
Number listed: 13.

    1979, with 681
    1984, 620
    1989, 662
    1990, 760
    1991, 807
    1992, 860
    1993, 874
    1994, 866
    1995, 909
    1996, 927
    1997, 978
    1998, 1,055
    1999, 968

Source: Sanderson, A., et. al., *Doctorate Recipients from United States Universities: Summary Report 1999*, Chicago: National Opinion Research Center, 2000.

★2063★
Total number of doctorates awarded to Hispanic American women at U.S. colleges and universities for selected years between 1979 through 1999

Ranking basis/background: Based on the 1998-99 Survey of Earned Doctorates (SED) conducted by the National Research Council's Office of Scientific and Engineering Personnel (OSEP). The doctorates are reported by academic year and include research and applied research doctorates in all fields.
Remarks: The *Summary Report* is the 33rd in an annual series of reports that began in 1967.
Number listed: 13.

    1979, with 227
    1984, 296
    1989, 401
    1990, 468
    1991, 513
    1992, 542
    1993, 556
    1994, 668
    1995, 625
    1996, 694
    1997, 707
    1998, 812
    1999, 874

Source: Sanderson, A., et. al., *Doctorate Recipients from United States Universities: Summary Report 1999*, Chicago: National Opinion Research Center, 2000.

★2064★
Total number of doctorates awarded to men and women at U.S. colleges and universities for selected years between 1979 through 1999

Ranking basis/background: Total includes men, women, and individuals who did not report sex. Based on the 1998-99 Survey of Earned Doctorates (SED) conducted by the National Research Council's Office of Scientific and Engineering Personnel (OSEP). The doctorates are reported by academic year and include research and applied research doctorates in all fields. **Remarks:** The *Summary Report* is the 33rd in an annual series of reports that began in 1967. **Number listed:** 13.

    1979, with 31,239
    1984, 31,337
    1989, 34,327
    1990, 36,067
    1991, 37,534
    1992, 38,890
    1993, 39,801
    1994, 41,034
    1995, 41,743
    1996, 42,414
    1997, 42,555
    1998, 42,683
    1999, 41,140

Source: Sanderson, A., et. al., *Doctorate Recipients from United States Universities: Summary Report 1999*, Chicago: National Opinion Research Center, 2000.

★2065★
Total number of doctorates awarded to men and women with unreported race/ethnicity at U.S. colleges and universities for selected years between 1979 through 1999

Ranking basis/background: Based on the 1998-99 Survey of Earned Doctorates (SED) conducted by the National Research Council's Office of Scientific and Engineering Personnel (OSEP). The doctorates are reported by academic year and include research and applied research doctorates in all fields.
Remarks: The *Summary Report* is the 33rd in an annual series of reports that began in 1967.
Number listed: 13.

    1979, with 2,520
    1984, 2,029
    1989, 3,365
    1990, 2,184
    1991, 1,751
    1992, 1,690
    1993, 1,510
    1994, 1,194
    1995, 1,415
    1996, 1,756
    1997, 3,674
    1998, 3,290
    1999, 2,526

Source: Sanderson, A., et. al., *Doctorate Recipients from United States Universities: Summary Report 1999*, Chicago: National Opinion Research Center, 2000.

★2066★
Total number of doctorates awarded to men at U.S. colleges and universities for selected years between 1979 through 1999

Ranking basis/background: Based on the 1998-99 Survey of Earned Doctorates (SED) conducted by the National Research Council's Office of Scientific and Engineering Personnel (OSEP). The doctorates are reported by academic year and include research and applied research doctorates in all fields.
Remarks: The *Summary Report* is the 33rd in an annual series of reports that began in 1967.
Number listed: 13.

    1979, with 22,302
    1984, 20,638
    1989, 21,814
    1990, 22,960
    1991, 23,525
    1992, 24,235
    1993, 24,384
    1994, 25,059
    1995, 25,159
    1996, 25,274
    1997, 24,944
    1998, 24,659
    1999, 23,460

Source: Sanderson, A., et. al., *Doctorate Recipients from United States Universities: Summary Report 1999*, Chicago: National Opinion Research Center, 2000.

★2067★
Total number of doctorates awarded to men with unreported race/ethnicity at U.S. colleges and universities for selected years between 1979 through 1999

Ranking basis/background: Based on the 1998-99 Survey of Earned Doctorates (SED) conducted by the National Research Council's Office of Scientific and Engineering Personnel (OSEP). The doctorates are reported by academic year and include research and applied research doctorates in all fields.
Remarks: The *Summary Report* is the 33rd in an annual series of reports that began in 1967.
Number listed: 13.

    1979, with 1,846
    1984, 1,488
    1989, 2,403
    1990, 1,618
    1991, 1,169
    1992, 1,067
    1993, 850
    1994, 735
    1995, 862
    1996, 1,026
    1997, 1,946
    1998, 1,924
    1999, 1,409

Source: Sanderson, A., et. al., *Doctorate Recipients from United States Universities: Summary Report 1999*, Chicago: National Opinion Research Center, 2000.

★2068★
Total number of doctorates awarded to minority men and women at U.S. colleges and universities for selected years between 1979 through 1999

Ranking basis/background: Based on the 1998-99 Survey of Earned Doctorates (SED) conducted by the National Research Council's Office of Scientific and Engineering Personnel (OSEP). The doctorates are reported by academic year and include research and applied research doctorates in all fields.
Remarks: The *Summary Report* is the 33rd in an annual series of reports that began in 1967.
Number listed: 13.

    1979, with 28,719
    1984, 29,308
    1989, 30,962
    1990, 33,883
    1991, 35,783
    1992, 37,200
    1993, 38,291
    1994, 39,840
    1995, 40,328
    1996, 40,658
    1997, 38,881
    1998, 39,393
    1999, 38,614

Source: Sanderson, A., et. al., *Doctorate Recipients from United States Universities: Summary Report 1999*, Chicago: National Opinion Research Center, 2000.

★2069★
Total number of doctorates awarded to minority men at U.S. colleges and universities for selected years between 1979 through 1999

Ranking basis/background: Based on the 1998-99 Survey of Earned Doctorates (SED) conducted by the National Research Council's Office of Scientific and Engineering Personnel (OSEP). The doctorates are reported by academic year and include research and applied research doctorates in all fields.
Remarks: The *Summary Report* is the 33rd in an annual series of reports that began in 1967.
Number listed: 13.

    1979, with 20,456
    1984, 19,150
    1989, 19,411
    1990, 21,342
    1991, 22,356
    1992, 23,168
    1993, 23,534
    1994, 24,324
    1995, 24,297
    1996, 24,248
    1997, 22,998
    1998, 22,735
    1999, 22,051

Source: Sanderson, A., et. al., *Doctorate Recipients from United States Universities: Summary Report 1999*, Chicago: National Opinion Research Center, 2000.

★2070★
Total number of doctorates awarded to minority women at U.S. colleges and universities for selected years between 1979 through 1999

Ranking basis/background: Based on the 1998-99 Survey of Earned Doctorates (SED) conducted by the National Research Council's Office of Scientific and Engineering Personnel (OSEP). The doctorates are reported by academic year and include research and applied research doctorates in all fields.
Remarks: The *Summary Report* is the 33rd in an annual series of reports that began in 1967.
Number listed: 13.

    1979, with 8,263
    1984, 10,158
    1989, 11,551
    1990, 12,540
    1991, 13,417
    1992, 14,019
    1993, 14,738
    1994, 15,501
    1995, 16,023
    1996, 16,405
    1997, 15,870
    1998, 16,663
    1999, 16,562

Source: Sanderson, A., et. al., *Doctorate Recipients from United States Universities: Summary Report 1999*, Chicago: National Opinion Research Center, 2000.

DOCTORAL DEGREES

★2071★
Total number of doctorates awarded to Native American/Alaskan Native men and women at U.S. colleges and universities for selected years between 1979 through 1999

Ranking basis/background: Based on the 1998-99 Survey of Earned Doctorates (SED) conducted by the National Research Council's Office of Scientific and Engineering Personnel (OSEP). The doctorates are reported by academic year and include research and applied research doctorates in all fields.
Remarks: The *Summary Report* is the 33rd in an annual series of reports that began in 1967.
Number listed: 13.
  1979, with 84
  1984, 74
  1989, 94
  1990, 98
  1991, 132
  1992, 152
  1993, 121
  1994, 146
  1995, 148
  1996, 190
  1997, 166
  1998, 190
  1999, 219

Source: Sanderson, A., et. al., *Doctorate Recipients from United States Universities: Summary Report 1999*, Chicago: National Opinion Research Center, 2000.

★2072★
Total number of doctorates awarded to Native American/Alaskan Native men at U.S. colleges and universities for selected years between 1979 through 1999

Ranking basis/background: Based on the 1998-99 Survey of Earned Doctorates (SED) conducted by the National Research Council's Office of Scientific and Engineering Personnel (OSEP). The doctorates are reported by academic year and include research and applied research doctorates in all fields.
Remarks: The *Summary Report* is the 33rd in an annual series of reports that began in 1967.
Number listed: 13.
  1979, with 59
  1984, 54
  1989, 49
  1990, 52
  1991, 74
  1992, 82
  1993, 61
  1994, 74
  1995, 80
  1996, 104
  1997, 78
  1998, 104
  1999, 98

Source: Sanderson, A., et. al., *Doctorate Recipients from United States Universities: Summary Report 1999*, Chicago: National Opinion Research Center, 2000.

★2073★
Total number of doctorates awarded to Native American/Alaskan Native women at U.S. colleges and universities for selected years between 1979 through 1999

Ranking basis/background: Based on the 1998-99 Survey of Earned Doctorates (SED) conducted by the National Research Council's Office of Scientific and Engineering Personnel (OSEP). The doctorates are reported by academic year and include research and applied research doctorates in all fields.
Remarks: The *Summary Report* is the 33rd in an annual series of reports that began in 1967.
Number listed: 13.
  1979, with 25
  1984, 20
  1989, 45
  1990, 46
  1991, 58
  1992, 70
  1993, 60
  1994, 72
  1995, 68
  1996, 86
  1997, 88
  1998, 86
  1999, 121

Source: Sanderson, A., et. al., *Doctorate Recipients from United States Universities: Summary Report 1999*, Chicago: National Opinion Research Center, 2000.

★2074★
Total number of doctorates awarded to white men and women at U.S. colleges and universities for selected years between 1979 through 1999

Ranking basis/background: Based on the 1998-99 Survey of Earned Doctorates (SED) conducted by the National Research Council's Office of Scientific and Engineering Personnel (OSEP). The doctorates are reported by academic year and include research and applied research doctorates in all fields.
Remarks: The *Summary Report* is the 33rd in an annual series of reports that began in 1967.
Number listed: 13.
  1979, with 23,682
  1984, 23,419
  1989, 23,363
  1990, 24,910
  1991, 25,337
  1992, 25,921
  1993, 26,450
  1994, 27,108
  1995, 27,114
  1996, 27,181
  1997, 26,245
  1998, 26,828
  1999, 26,450

Source: Sanderson, A., et. al., *Doctorate Recipients from United States Universities: Summary Report 1999*, Chicago: National Opinion Research Center, 2000.

★2075★
Total number of doctorates awarded to white men at U.S. colleges and universities for selected years between 1979 through 1999

Ranking basis/background: Based on the 1998-99 Survey of Earned Doctorates (SED) conducted by the National Research Council's Office of Scientific and Engineering Personnel (OSEP). The doctorates are reported by academic year and include research and applied research doctorates in all fields.
Remarks: The *Summary Report* is the 33rd in an annual series of reports that began in 1967.
Number listed: 13.
  1979, with 16,660
  1984, 14,783
  1989, 13,849
  1990, 14,767
  1991, 14,815
  1992, 15,037
  1993, 15,154
  1994, 15,434
  1995, 15,324
  1996, 15,075
  1997, 14,656
  1998, 14,712
  1999, 14,523

Source: Sanderson, A., et. al., *Doctorate Recipients from United States Universities: Summary Report 1999*, Chicago: National Opinion Research Center, 2000.

★2076★
Total number of doctorates awarded to white women at U.S. colleges and universities for selected years between 1979 through 1999

Ranking basis/background: Based on the 1998-99 Survey of Earned Doctorates (SED) conducted by the National Research Council's Office of Scientific and Engineering Personnel (OSEP). The doctorates are reported by academic year and include research and applied research doctorates in all fields.
Remarks: The *Summary Report* is the 33rd in an annual series of reports that began in 1967.
Number listed: 13.
  1979, with 7,022
  1984, 8,636
  1989, 9,514
  1990, 10,143
  1991, 10,520
  1992, 10,882
  1993, 11,294
  1994, 11,671
  1995, 11,789
  1996, 12,106
  1997, 11,583
  1998, 12,111
  1999, 11,927

Source: Sanderson, A., et. al., *Doctorate Recipients from United States Universities: Summary Report 1999*, Chicago: National Opinion Research Center, 2000.

★2077★
Total number of doctorates awarded to women at U.S. colleges and universities for selected years between 1979 through 1999

Ranking basis/background: Based on the 1998-99 Survey of Earned Doctorates (SED) conducted by the National Research Council's Office of Scientific and Engineering Personnel (OSEP). The doctorates are reported by academic year and include research and applied research doctorates in all fields.
Remarks: The *Summary Report* is the 33rd in an annual series of reports that began in 1967.
Number listed: 13.
    1979, with 8,937
    1984, 10,669
    1989, 12,513
    1990, 13,106
    1991, 13,873
    1992, 14,436
    1993, 15,122
    1994, 15,820
    1995, 16,414
    1996, 16,944
    1997, 17,251
    1998, 17,858
    1999, 17,493
Source: Sanderson, A., et. al., *Doctorate Recipients from United States Universities: Summary Report 1999*, Chicago: National Opinion Research Center, 2000.

★2078★
Total number of doctorates awarded to women with unreported race/ethnicity at U.S. colleges and universities for selected years between 1979 through 1999

Ranking basis/background: Based on the 1998-99 Survey of Earned Doctorates (SED) conducted by the National Research Council's Office of Scientific and Engineering Personnel (OSEP). The doctorates are reported by academic year and include research and applied research doctorates in all fields.
Remarks: The *Summary Report* is the 33rd in an annual series of reports that began in 1967.
Number listed: 13.
    1979, with 674
    1984, 541
    1989, 962
    1990, 566
    1991, 456
    1992, 417
    1993, 384
    1994, 319
    1995, 391
    1996, 539
    1997, 1,381
    1998, 1,225
    1999, 931
Source: Sanderson, A., et. al., *Doctorate Recipients from United States Universities: Summary Report 1999*, Chicago: National Opinion Research Center, 2000.

★2079★
Traditionally white institutions awarding the most doctorate degrees to African Americans

Ranking basis/background: Total doctoral degrees conferred to African American students in all disciplines combined during the 1997-98 academic year. **Remarks:** Original source: *Black Issues* analysis of U.S. Department of Education reports of data submitted by institutions. **Number listed:** 52.

1. Nova Southeastern University (FL)
2. United Theological Seminary, Dayton (OH)
3. Virginia Polytechnic Institute and State University (VA)
4. Harvard University (MA)
5. Florida State University (FL)
6. Union Institute, Cincinnati (OH)
7. Teachers College, Columbia University (NY)
8. Temple University (PA)
9. University of Michigan, Ann Arbor (MI)
9. Michigan State University (MI)
9. Ohio State University (OH)

Source: "Top 100 Degree Producers," *Black Issues in Higher Education*, 17: 48-89, (July 7, 2000).

★2080★
Trends in doctoral degrees granted at U.S. universities, by gender, 1987 through 1999

Ranking basis/background: Number, in thousands, of doctorates granted to men and women for each year. **Remarks:** Original source: "Survey of Earned Doctorates." **Number listed:** 13.
    1987, with 11.4 thousand doctorates awarded to women; 20.9 thousand awarded to men
    1988, 11.8; 21.7
    1989, 12.5; 21.8
    1990, 13.1; 23.0
    1991, 13.9; 23.5
    1992, 14.4; 24.2
    1993, 15.1; 24.4
    1994, 15.8; 25.1
    1995, 16.4; 25.2
    1996, 16.9; 25.3
    1997, 17.3; 24.9
    1998, 17.9; 24.7
    1999, 17.5; 23.5
Source: Leatherman, Courtney, "The Number of New Ph.D.'s Drops For the First Time Since 1985," *The Chronicle of Higher Education*, 47: A10-A11, (February 9, 2001).

★2081★
Trends in doctorates awarded to African American women

Ranking basis/background: Percentage of doctorates awarded to African American women for selected years. **Number listed:** 9.
    1977, with 38.7%
    1991, 58.7%
    1992, 59.4%
    1993, 60.2%
    1994, 62.7%
    1995, 62.5%
    1996, 59.3%
    1997, 60.5%
    1998, 64.6%
Source: "Vital Signs," *The Journal of Blacks in Higher Education*, No. 26, pp. 79-85, (Winter 1999).

★2082★
U.S. colleges and universities awarding the most biological and life sciences doctorate degrees to African Americans

Ranking basis/background: Total doctoral degrees conferred to African American students in the field of biological and life sciences during the 1997-98 academic year. **Remarks:** Original source: *Black Issues* analysis of U.S. Department of Education reports of data submitted by institutions. **Number listed:** 6.

1. Meharry Medical College (TN)
2. Howard University (DC)
3. Johns Hopkins University (MD)
4. Medical College of Georgia (GA)
4. Harvard University (MA)
4. Ohio State University (OH)

Source: "Top 100 Degree Producers," *Black Issues in Higher Education*, 17: 48-89, (July 7, 2000).

★2083★
U.S. colleges and universities awarding the most biological and life sciences doctorate degrees to Asian Americans

Ranking basis/background: Total doctoral degrees conferred to Asian American students in the field of biological and life sciences during the 1997-98 academic year. **Remarks:** Original source: *Black Issues* analysis of U.S. Department of Education reports of data submitted by institutions. **Number listed:** 51.

1. University of California, Los Angeles (CA)
1. University of Hawaii, Manoa (HI)
3. University of Texas Southwest Medical Center (TX)
4. University of California, Berkeley (CA)
4. Louisiana State University Medical Center (LA)
4. Columbia University, New York City (NY)
7. City University of New York, Graduate School and University Center (NY)
8. Washington University (MO)
9. University of Chicago (IL)
10. University of Alabama, Birmingham (AL)
10. University of California, Davis (CA)
10. University of Southern California (CA)
10. University of Minnesota, Twin Cities (MN)
10. University of Medicine and Dentistry of New Jersey (NJ)
10. State University of New York, Stony Brook (NY)
10. University of North Carolina, Chapel Hill (NC)
10. Baylor College of Medicine (TX)
10. University of Texas, Austin (TX)
10. Virginia Commonwealth University (VA)

Source: "Top 100 Degree Producers," *Black Issues in Higher Education*, 17: 48-89, (July 7, 2000).

★2084★
U.S. colleges and universities awarding the most biological and life sciences doctorate degrees to Hispanic Americans

Ranking basis/background: Total doctoral degrees conferred to Hispanic American students in the field of biological and life sciences during the 1997-98 academic year. **Remarks:** Original source: *Black Issues* analysis of U.S. Department of Education reports of data submitted by institutions. **Number listed:** 6.

1. University of California, Davis (CA)
2. Stanford University (CA)
3. University of California, Berkeley (CA)
4. University of Connecticut (CT)
4. State University of New York, Stony Brook (NY)
4. Baylor College of Medicine (TX)

Source: "Top 100 Degree Producers," *Black Issues in Higher Education*, 17: 48-89, (July 7, 2000).

DOCTORAL DEGREES

★2085★
U.S. colleges and universities awarding the most business management and administrative services doctorate degrees to African Americans

Ranking basis/background: Total doctoral degrees conferred to African American students in the field of business management and administrative services during the 1997-98 academic year. **Remarks:** Original source: *Black Issues* analysis of U.S. Department of Education reports of data submitted by institutions. **Number listed:** 2.
1. Walden University (MN)
1. Florida State University (FL)

Source: "Top 100 Degree Producers," *Black Issues in Higher Education*, 17: 48-89, (July 7, 2000).

★2086★
U.S. colleges and universities awarding the most business management and administrative services doctorate degrees to Asian Americans

Ranking basis/background: Total doctoral degrees conferred to Asian American students in the field of business management and administrative services during the 1997-98 academic year. **Remarks:** Original source: *Black Issues* analysis of U.S. Department of Education reports of data submitted by institutions. **Number listed:** 3.
1. Temple University (PA)
2. University of Texas, Arlington (TX)
3. New York University (NY)

Source: "Top 100 Degree Producers," *Black Issues in Higher Education*, 17: 48-89, (July 7, 2000).

★2087★
U.S. colleges and universities awarding the most business management and administrative services doctorate degrees to Hispanic Americans

Ranking basis/background: Total doctoral degrees conferred to Hispanic American students in the field of business management and administrative services during the 1997-98 academic year. **Remarks:** Original source: *Black Issues* analysis of U.S. Department of Education reports of data submitted by institutions. **Number listed:** 1.
1. University of Phoenix (AZ)

Source: "Top 100 Degree Producers," *Black Issues in Higher Education*, 17: 48-89, (July 7, 2000).

★2088★
U.S. colleges and universities awarding the most communications doctorate degrees to African Americans

Ranking basis/background: Total doctoral degrees conferred to African American students in the field of communications during the 1997-98 academic year. **Remarks:** Original source: *Black Issues* analysis of U.S. Department of Education reports of data submitted by institutions. **Number listed:** 2.
1. Howard University (DC)
2. Wayne State University (MI)

Source: "Top 100 Degree Producers," *Black Issues in Higher Education*, 17: 48-89, (July 7, 2000).

★2089★
U.S. colleges and universities awarding the most computer and information sciences doctorate degrees to African Americans

Ranking basis/background: Total doctoral degrees conferred to African American students in the field of computer and information sciences during the 1997-98 academic year. **Remarks:** Original source: *Black Issues* analysis of U.S. Department of Education reports of data submitted by institutions. **Number listed:** 1.
1. Nova Southeastern University (FL)

Source: "Top 100 Degree Producers," *Black Issues in Higher Education*, 17: 48-89, (July 7, 2000).

★2090★
U.S. colleges and universities awarding the most computer and information sciences doctorate degrees to Asian Americans

Ranking basis/background: Total doctoral degrees conferred to Asian American students in the field of computer and information sciences during the 1997-98 academic year. **Remarks:** Original source: *Black Issues* analysis of U.S. Department of Education reports of data submitted by institutions. **Number listed:** 5.
1. University of Illinois, Urbana-Champaign (IL)
2. University of California, Berkeley (CA)
3. Illinois Institute of Technology (IL)
3. Wayne State University (MI)
3. Stanford University (CA)

Source: "Top 100 Degree Producers," *Black Issues in Higher Education*, 17: 48-89, (July 7, 2000).

★2091★
U.S. colleges and universities awarding the most doctoral degrees to African Americans from 1995 to 1999

Ranking basis/background: Based on the 1998-99 Survey of Earned Doctorates (SED) conducted by the National Research Council's Office of Scientific and Engineering Personnel (OSEP). The doctorates are reported by academic year and include research and applied research doctorates in all fields. **Remarks:** The *Summary Report* is the 33rd in an annual series of reports that began in 1967. **Number listed:** 20.
1. University of Texas, Austin, with 189 doctorates awarded
2. University of Puerto Rico, Rio Piedras, 162
3. University of California, Berkeley, 152
4. Carlos Albizu University, San Juan, 143
5. University of California, Los Angeles, 118
6. Texas A&M University, 105
7. Arizona State University, 84
7. Harvard University, 84
9. University of Michigan, Ann Arbor, 79
9. Stanford University, 79

Source: Sanderson, A., et. al., *Doctorate Recipients from United States Universities: Summary Report 1999*, Chicago: National Opinion Research Center, 2000.

★2092★
U.S. colleges and universities awarding the most doctoral degrees to American Indians and Alaskan Natives from 1995 to 1999

Ranking basis/background: Based on the 1998-99 Survey of Earned Doctorates (SED) conducted by the National Research Council's Office of Scientific and Engineering Personnel (OSEP). The doctorates are reported by academic year and include research and applied research doctorates in all fields. **Remarks:** The *Summary Report* is the 33rd in an annual series of reports that began in 1967. **Number listed:** 20.
1. Oklahoma State University, with 29 doctorates awarded
2. University of Oklahoma, 26
3. University of California, Los Angeles, 18
3. Pennsylvania State University, 18
3. University of Washington (WA), 18
6. University of Arkansas, Fayetteville, 17
7. University of Michigan, Ann Arbor, 15
7. Stanford University, 15
9. University of Arizona, 14
10. University of Minnesota, Twin Cities, 13
10. North Carolina State University, Raleigh, 13
10. University of Texas, Austin, 13

Source: Sanderson, A., et. al., *Doctorate Recipients from United States Universities: Summary Report 1999*, Chicago: National Opinion Research Center, 2000.

★2093★
U.S. colleges and universities awarding the most doctoral degrees to Asian Americans and Pacific Islanders from 1995 to 1999

Ranking basis/background: Based on the 1998-99 Survey of Earned Doctorates (SED) conducted by the National Research Council's Office of Scientific and Engineering Personnel (OSEP). The doctorates are reported by academic year and include research and applied research doctorates in all fields. **Remarks:** The *Summary Report* is the 33rd in an annual series of reports that began in 1967. **Number listed:** 20.
1. University of California, Berkeley, with 317 doctorates awarded
2. University of California, Los Angeles, 285
3. Stanford University, 203
4. Massachusetts Institute of Technology, 145
5. Harvard University, 141
6. University of Michigan, Ann Arbor, 132
7. University of Illinois, Urbana-Champaign, 123
8. University of California, Davis, 120
9. Columbia University, New York City, 117
10. University of Southern California, 111

Source: Sanderson, A., et. al., *Doctorate Recipients from United States Universities: Summary Report 1999*, Chicago: National Opinion Research Center, 2000.

★2094★
U.S. colleges and universities awarding the most doctoral degrees to Hispanic Americans from 1995 to 1999

Ranking basis/background: Based on the 1998-99 Survey of Earned Doctorates (SED) conducted by the National Research Council's Office of Scientific and Engineering Personnel (OSEP). The doctorates are reported by academic year and include research and applied research doctorates in all fields. **Remarks:** The *Summary Report* is the 33rd in an annual series of reports that began in 1967. **Number listed:** 20.

1. Nova Southeastern University, with 290 doctorates awarded
2. Howard University, 239
3. University of Michigan, Ann Arbor, 143
4. Ohio State University, 131
5. University of Maryland, College Park, 122
6. Virginia Polytechnic Institute and State University, 122
7. Wayne State University, 114
8. Teachers College, Columbia University, 101
9. Florida State University, 100
10. Temple University, 96

Source: Sanderson, A., et. al., *Doctorate Recipients from United States Universities: Summary Report 1999*, Chicago: National Opinion Research Center, 2000.

★2095★
U.S. colleges and universities awarding the most doctorate degrees to African Americans

Ranking basis/background: Total doctoral degrees conferred to African American students in all disciplines combined during the 1997-98 academic year. **Remarks:** Original source: *Black Issues* analysis of U.S. Department of Education reports of data submitted by institutions. **Number listed:** 52.

1. Nova Southeastern University (FL)
2. Howard University (DC)
3. Virginia Union University (VA)
4. United Theological Seminary, Dayton (OH)
5. Clark Atlanta University (GA)
6. Virginia Polytechnic Institute and State University (VA)
7. Harvard University (MA)
8. Florida State University (FL)
9. Union Institute, Cincinnati (OH)
10. Teachers College, Columbia University (NY)
10. Temple University (PA)
12. University of Michigan, Ann Arbor (MI)
12. Michigan State University (MI)
12. Ohio State University (OH)
15. Jackson State University (MS)
16. North Carolina State University (NC)
16. Pennsylvania State University, University Park (PA)
18. University of California, Los Angeles (CA)
18. George Washington University (DC)
18. University of Cincinnati (OH)

Source: "Top 100 Degree Producers," *Black Issues in Higher Education*, 17: 48-89, (July 7, 2000).

★2096★
U.S. colleges and universities awarding the most doctorate degrees to Asian Americans

Ranking basis/background: Total doctoral degrees conferred to Asian American students in all disciplines combined during the 1997-98 academic year. **Remarks:** Original source: *Black Issues* analysis of U.S. Department of Education reports of data submitted by institutions. **Number listed:** 53.

1. University of California, Berkeley (CA)
2. University of California, Los Angeles (CA)
3. University of Hawaii, Manoa (HI)
4. University of Southern California (CA)
5. University of Illinois, Urbana-Champaign (IL)
6. Wayne University (MI)
7. University of Texas, Austin (TX)
8. University of Michigan, Ann Arbor (MI)
8. Stanford University (CA)
10. University of Washington (WA)
11. Columbia University, New York City (NY)
12. New York University (NY)
13. McCormick Theological Seminary (IL)
13. Rutgers University, New Brunswick (NJ)
15. University of California, San Diego (CA)
16. University of Maryland, College Park (MD)
16. Harvard University (MA)
16. Texas A&M University (TX)
16. Purdue University (IN)
20. State University of New York, Stony Brook (NY)

Source: "Top 100 Degree Producers," *Black Issues in Higher Education*, 17: 48-89, (July 7, 2000).

★2097★
U.S. colleges and universities awarding the most doctorate degrees to Hispanic Americans

Ranking basis/background: Total doctoral degrees conferred to Hispanic American students in all disciplines combined during the 1997-98 academic year. **Remarks:** Original source: *Black Issues* analysis of U.S. Department of Education reports of data submitted by institutions. **Number listed:** 60.

1. University of Texas, Austin (TX)
2. University of California, Los Angeles (CA)
3. University of California, Berkeley (CA)
4. Arizona State University (AZ)
5. University of Southern California (CA)
5. University of Michigan, Ann Arbor (MI)
7. University of New Mexico (NM)
8. Caribbean Center for Advanced Studies (FL)
9. Texas A&M University, Kingsville (TX)
9. Nova Southeastern University (FL)
11. University of Houston (TX)
12. University of California, Santa Barbara (CA)
12. New York University (NY)
14. University of California, Davis (CA)
14. University of Miami (FL)
14. Texas A&M University (TX)
14. University of Wisconsin, Madison (WI)
14. Stanford University (CA)
19. California School of Professional Psychology (CA)
19. San Diego State University (CA)
19. McCormick Theological Seminary (IL)
19. Union Institute, Cincinnati (OH)

Source: "Top 100 Degree Producers," *Black Issues in Higher Education*, 17: 48-89, (July 7, 2000).

★2098★
U.S. colleges and universities awarding the most doctorate degrees to minorities

Ranking basis/background: Total doctoral degrees conferred to minority students in all disciplines combined during the 1997-98 academic year. **Remarks:** Original source: *Black Issues* analysis of U.S. Department of Education reports of data submitted by institutions. **Number listed:** 110.

1. University of California, Los Angeles (CA)
2. University of California, Berkeley (CA)
3. Nova Southeastern University (FL)
4. University of Southern California (CA)
4. University of Texas, Austin (TX)
6. University of Hawaii, Manoa (HI)
7. University of Michigan, Ann Arbor (MI)
8. Harvard University (MA)
9. University of Illinois, Urbana-Champaign (IL)
10. Howard University (DC)
11. Virginia Union University (VA)
12. Stanford University (CA)
13. Wayne State University (MI)
14. Ohio State University (OH)
14. Temple University (PA)
16. Michigan State University (MI)
16. New York University (NY)
16. United Theological Seminary, Dayton (OH)
19. Pennsylvania State University, University Park (PA)
20. Rutgers University, New Brunswick (NJ)

Source: "Top 100 Degree Producers," *Black Issues in Higher Education*, 17: 48-89, (July 7, 2000).

★2099★
U.S. colleges and universities awarding the most doctorate degrees to Native Americans

Ranking basis/background: Total doctoral degrees conferred to Native American students in all disciplines combined during the 1997-98 academic year. **Remarks:** Original source: *Black Issues* analysis of U.S. Department of Education reports of data submitted by institutions. **Number listed:** 14.

1. Minnesota School of Professional Psychology (MN)
2. Harvard University (MA)
3. Pennsylvania State University, University Park (PA)
4. George Washington University (DC)
4. Michigan State University (MI)
4. Oklahoma State University (OK)
4. University of Oregon (OR)
4. Stanford University (CA)
9. University of Arkansas, Fayetteville (AR)
9. University of California, Los Angeles (CA)
9. University of Georgia (GA)
9. University of Illinois, Urbana-Champaign (IL)
9. University of Minnesota (MN)
9. University of North Dakota (NC)

Source: "Top 100 Degree Producers," *Black Issues in Higher Education*, 17: 48-89, (July 7, 2000).

DOCTORAL DEGREES

★2100★
U.S. colleges and universities awarding the most doctorates in all fields, 1999

Ranking basis/background: Based on the 1998-99 Survey of Earned Doctorates (SED) conducted by the National Research Council's Office of Scientific and Engineering Personnel (OSEP). The doctorates are reported by academic year and include research and applied research doctorates in all fields.
Remarks: The *Summary Report* is the 33rd in an annual series of reports that began in 1967.
Number listed: 20.
1. University of Texas, Austin, with 752 doctorates awarded
2. University of California, Berkeley, 717
3. University of Wisconsin, Madison, 685
4. University of Minnesota, Twin Cities, 656
5. University of Michigan, Ann Arbor, 655
6. University of Illinois, Urbana-Champaign, 643
7. University of California, Los Angeles, 588
8. Pennsylvania State University, 580
9. Nova Southeastern University, 573
10. Harvard University, 564

Source: Sanderson, A., et. al., *Doctorate Recipients from United States Universities: Summary Report 1999*, Chicago: National Opinion Research Center, 2000.

★2101★
U.S. colleges and universities awarding the most doctorates in education, 1999

Ranking basis/background: Based on the 1998-99 Survey of Earned Doctorates (SED) conducted by the National Research Council's Office of Scientific and Engineering Personnel (OSEP). The doctorates are reported by academic year and include research and applied research doctorates in all fields.
Remarks: The *Summary Report* is the 33rd in an annual series of reports that began in 1967.
Number listed: 20.
1. Nova Southeastern University, with 428 doctorates awarded
2. Teachers College, Columbia University, 182
3. Loyola University, Chicago, 119
4. University of Texas, Austin, 116
5. Pennsylvania State University, 113
6. Ohio State University, 101
7. Virginia Polytechnic Institute and State University, 99
8. University of Minnesota, Twin Cities, 97
9. University of Georgia, 85
10. Oklahoma State University, 84

Source: Sanderson, A., et. al., *Doctorate Recipients from United States Universities: Summary Report 1999*, Chicago: National Opinion Research Center, 2000.

★2102★
U.S. colleges and universities awarding the most doctorates in engineering, 1999

Ranking basis/background: Based on the 1998-99 Survey of Earned Doctorates (SED) conducted by the National Research Council's Office of Scientific and Engineering Personnel (OSEP). The doctorates are reported by academic year and include research and applied research doctorates in all fields.
Remarks: The *Summary Report* is the 33rd in an annual series of reports that began in 1967.
Number listed: 20.
1. Massachusetts Institute of Technology, with 194 doctorates awarded
2. Stanford University, 168
3. Georgia Institute of Technology, 162
3. University of Texas, Austin, 162
5. University of California, Berkeley, 149
6. University of Michigan, Ann Arbor, 145
7. Pennsylvania State University, 142
8. Purdue University, 136
9. University of Illinois, Urbana-Champaign, 130
10. North Carolina State University, Raleigh, 112

Source: Sanderson, A., et. al., *Doctorate Recipients from United States Universities: Summary Report 1999*, Chicago: National Opinion Research Center, 2000.

★2103★
U.S. colleges and universities awarding the most doctorates in humanities, 1999

Ranking basis/background: Based on the 1998-99 Survey of Earned Doctorates (SED) conducted by the National Research Council's Office of Scientific and Engineering Personnel (OSEP). The doctorates are reported by academic year and include research and applied research doctorates in all fields.
Remarks: The *Summary Report* is the 33rd in an annual series of reports that began in 1967.
Number listed: 20.
1. Harvard University, with 146 doctorates awarded
2. New York University, 143
3. University of Chicago, 133
4. Yale University, 128
5. Indiana University, Bloomington, 124
6. University of California, Los Angeles, 120
7. University of Michigan, Ann Arbor, 118
8. University of California, Berkeley, 115
9. Columbia University, New York City, 114
10. University of Texas, Austin, 113

Source: Sanderson, A., et. al., *Doctorate Recipients from United States Universities: Summary Report 1999*, Chicago: National Opinion Research Center, 2000.

★2104★
U.S. colleges and universities awarding the most doctorates in life sciences, 1999

Ranking basis/background: Based on the 1998-99 Survey of Earned Doctorates (SED) conducted by the National Research Council's Office of Scientific and Engineering Personnel (OSEP). The doctorates are reported by academic year and include research and applied research doctorates in all fields.
Remarks: The *Summary Report* is the 33rd in an annual series of reports that began in 1967.
Number listed: 20.
1. University of Wisconsin, Madison, with 178 doctorates awarded
2. Johns Hopkins University, 175
2. University of Minnesota, Twin Cities, 175
4. Cornell University, Endowed Colleges, 159
5. Harvard University, 156
6. University of Washington (WA), 143
7. University of California, Davis, 141
8. University of Florida, 139
9. University of California, Berkeley, 128
10. Ohio State University, 127

Source: Sanderson, A., et. al., *Doctorate Recipients from United States Universities: Summary Report 1999*, Chicago: National Opinion Research Center, 2000.

★2105★
U.S. colleges and universities awarding the most doctorates in physical sciences, mathematics, and computer sciences, 1999

Ranking basis/background: Based on the 1998-99 Survey of Earned Doctorates (SED) conducted by the National Research Council's Office of Scientific and Engineering Personnel (OSEP). The doctorates are reported by academic year and include research and applied research doctorates in all fields.
Remarks: The *Summary Report* is the 33rd in an annual series of reports that began in 1967.
Number listed: 20.
1. University of California, Berkeley, with 172 doctorates awarded
2. Massachusetts Institute of Technology, 156
3. University of Wisconsin, Madison, 124
4. University of Texas, Austin, 121
5. University of Illinois, Urbana-Champaign, 118
6. Stanford University, 116
7. University of Michigan, Ann Arbor, 115
8. University of Maryland, College Park, 106
9. University of Washington (WA), 103
10. Texas A&M University, 102

Source: Sanderson, A., et. al., *Doctorate Recipients from United States Universities: Summary Report 1999*, Chicago: National Opinion Research Center, 2000.

★2106★
U.S. colleges and universities awarding the most doctorates in professional and other fields, 1999

Ranking basis/background: Based on the 1998-99 Survey of Earned Doctorates (SED) conducted by the National Research Council's Office of Scientific and Engineering Personnel (OSEP). The doctorates are reported by academic year and include research and applied research doctorates in all fields.
Remarks: The *Summary Report* is the 33rd in an annual series of reports that began in 1967.
Number listed: 20.
1. University of Texas, Austin, with 51 doctorates awarded
2. Nova Southeastern University, 47
3. Virginia Polytechnic Institute and State University, 39
4. University of Southern California, 38
4. New York University, 38
4. Pennsylvania State University, 38
7. Indiana University, Bloomington, 35
7. Ohio State University, 35
7. University of Pennsylvania, 35
10. Michigan State University, 34
10. University of Minnesota, Twin Cities, 34

Source: Sanderson, A., et. al., *Doctorate Recipients from United States Universities: Summary Report 1999*, Chicago: National Opinion Research Center, 2000.

★2107★
U.S. colleges and universities awarding the most doctorates in social sciences, 1999

Ranking basis/background: Based on the 1998-99 Survey of Earned Doctorates (SED) conducted by the National Research Council's Office of Scientific and Engineering Personnel (OSEP). The doctorates are reported by academic year and include research and applied research doctorates in all fields.
Remarks: The *Summary Report* is the 33rd in an annual series of reports that began in 1967.
Number listed: 20.

1. University of Texas, Austin, with 113 doctorates awarded
2. Harvard University, 111
2. University of Michigan, Ann Arbor, 111
4. University of Chicago, 110
5. University of Wisconsin, Madison, 106
6. University of California, Berkeley, 102
7. University of Maryland, College Park, 100
8. University of California, Los Angeles, 99
9. Columbia University, New York City, 96
10. University of Illinois, Urbana-Champaign, 91

Source: Sanderson, A., et. al., *Doctorate Recipients from United States Universities: Summary Report 1999*, Chicago: National Opinion Research Center, 2000.

★2108★
U.S. colleges and universities awarding the most education doctorate degrees to African Americans

Ranking basis/background: Total doctoral degrees conferred to African American students in the field of education during the 1997-98 academic year. **Remarks:** Original source: *Black Issues* analysis of U.S. Department of Education reports of data submitted by institutions. **Number listed:** 48.
1. Nova Southeastern University (FL)
2. Clark Atlanta University (GA)
3. Virginia Polytechnic Institute and State University (VA)
4. Teachers College, Columbia University (NY)
5. George Washington University (DC)
6. University of Illinois, Urbana-Champaign (IL)
6. Jackson State University (MS)
6. University of Southern Mississippi (MS)
6. Ohio State University (OH)
6. South Carolina State University (SC)

Source: "Top 100 Degree Producers," *Black Issues in Higher Education*, 17: 48-89, (July 7, 2000).

★2109★
U.S. colleges and universities awarding the most education doctorate degrees to Asian Americans

Ranking basis/background: Total doctoral degrees conferred to Asian American students in the field of education during the 1997-98 academic year. **Remarks:** Original source: *Black Issues* analysis of U.S. Department of Education reports of data submitted by institutions. **Number listed:** 16.
1. University of California, Los Angeles (CA)
1. University of San Francisco (CA)
1. University of Southern California (CA)
4. Northern Illinois University (IL)
4. New York University (NY)
4. Teachers College, Columbia University (NY)
4. University of Texas, Austin (TX)
8. University of Arizona (AZ)
8. Nova Southeastern University (FL)
8. Indiana University, Bloomington (IN)
8. Wayne University (MI)
8. Pennsylvania State University, University Park (PA)
8. University of Pittsburgh (PA)
8. Texas A&M University, Commerce (TX)
8. Seattle University (WA)
8. University of Washington (WA)

Source: "Top 100 Degree Producers," *Black Issues in Higher Education*, 17: 48-89, (July 7, 2000).

★2110★
U.S. colleges and universities awarding the most education doctorate degrees to Hispanic Americans

Ranking basis/background: Total doctoral degrees conferred to Hispanic American students in the field of education during the 1997-98 academic year. **Remarks:** Original source: *Black Issues* analysis of U.S. Department of Education reports of data submitted by institutions. **Number listed:** 24.
1. University of Texas, Austin (TX)
2. Texas A&M University, Kingsville (TX)
3. Arizona State University (AZ)
4. University of Southern California (CA)
5. University of California, Los Angeles (CA)
6. University of New Mexico (NM)
7. University of Wisconsin, Madison (WI)
8. University of California, Santa Barbara (CA)
8. University of LaVerne (CA)
8. San Diego State University (CA)
8. University of Houston, University Park (TX)

Source: "Top 100 Degree Producers," *Black Issues in Higher Education*, 17: 48-89, (July 7, 2000).

★2111★
U.S. colleges and universities awarding the most education doctorate degrees to Native Americans

Ranking basis/background: Total doctoral degrees conferred to Native American students in the field of education during the 1997-98 academic year. **Remarks:** Original source: *Black Issues* analysis of U.S. Department of Education reports of data submitted by institutions. **Number listed:** 1.
1. Pennsylvania State University, University Park (PA)

Source: "Top 100 Degree Producers," *Black Issues in Higher Education*, 17: 48-89, (July 7, 2000).

★2112★
U.S. colleges and universities awarding the most English language/literature/ letters doctorate degrees to African Americans

Ranking basis/background: Total doctoral degrees conferred to African American students in the field of English language/literature/letter during the 1997-98 academic year. **Remarks:** Original source: *Black Issues* analysis of U.S. Department of Education reports of data submitted by institutions. **Number listed:** 4.
1. University of California, Berkeley (CA)
1. Columbia University, New York City (NY)
1. Indiana University (PA)
1. University of Pennsylvania (PA)

Source: "Top 100 Degree Producers," *Black Issues in Higher Education*, 17: 48-89, (July 7, 2000).

★2113★
U.S. colleges and universities awarding the most English language/literature/ letters doctorate degrees to Asian Americans

Ranking basis/background: Total doctoral degrees conferred to Asian American students in the field of English language/literature/letter during the 1997-98 academic year. **Remarks:** Original source: *Black Issues* analysis of U.S. Department of Education reports of data submitted by institutions. **Number listed:** 3.
1. Indiana University (PA)
2. University of California, Berkeley (CA)
3. Columbia University, New York City (NY)

Source: "Top 100 Degree Producers," *Black Issues in Higher Education*, 17: 48-89, (July 7, 2000).

★2114★
U.S. colleges and universities awarding the most health professions and related sciences doctorate degrees to African Americans

Ranking basis/background: Total doctoral degrees conferred to African American students in the field of health professions and related sciences during the 1997-98 academic year. **Remarks:** Original source: *Black Issues* analysis of U.S. Department of Education reports of data submitted by institutions. **Number listed:** 7.
1. Howard University (DC)
2. University of Alabama, Birmingham (AL)
2. Johns Hopkins University (MD)
4. Harvard University (MD)
4. University of Massachusetts, Amherst (MA)
4. University of Oklahoma Health Sciences Center (OK)
4. University of Pittsburgh (PA)

Source: "Top 100 Degree Producers," *Black Issues in Higher Education*, 17: 48-89, (July 7, 2000).

★2115★
U.S. colleges and universities awarding the most health professions and related sciences doctorate degrees to Asian Americans

Ranking basis/background: Total doctoral degrees conferred to Asian American students in the field of health professions and related sciences during the 1997-98 academic year. **Remarks:** Original source: *Black Issues* analysis of U.S. Department of Education reports of data submitted by institutions. **Number listed:** 21.
1. University of Southern California (CA)
2. Wayne State University (MI)
3. Johns Hopkins University (MD)
3. Harvard University (MA)
5. University of California, Los Angeles (CA)
6. University of Washington (WA)
7. University of California, Berkeley (CA)
8. University of California, San Diego (CA)
9. University of Texas Health Science Center, Houston (TX)
10. University of California, San Francisco (CA)
10. University of Florida (FL)
10. Rush University (IL)
10. University of Oklahoma Health Sciences Center (OK)
10. University of Pittsburgh (PA)
10. University of Wisconsin (WI)

DOCTORAL DEGREES

Source: "Top 100 Degree Producers," *Black Issues in Higher Education*, 17: 48-89, (July 7, 2000).

★2116★
U.S. colleges and universities awarding the most health professions and related sciences doctorate degrees to Hispanic Americans

Ranking basis/background: Total doctoral degrees conferred to Hispanic American students in the field of health professions and related sciences during the 1997-98 academic year. **Remarks:** Original source: *Black Issues* analysis of U.S. Department of Education reports of data submitted by institutions. **Number listed:** 21.
1. University of Southern California (CA)
2. Wayne State University (MI)
3. Johns Hopkins University (MD)
3. Harvard University (MA)
5. University of California, Los Angeles (CA)
6. University of Washington (WA)
7. University of California, Berkeley (CA)
8. University of California, San Diego (CA)
9. University of Texas Health Science Center, Houston (TX)
10. University of California, San Francisco (CA)
10. University of Florida (FL)
10. Rush University (IL)
10. University of Oklahoma Health Sciences Center (OK)
10. University of Pittsburgh (PA)
10. University of Wisconsin, Madison (WI)

Source: "Top 100 Degree Producers," *Black Issues in Higher Education*, 17: 48-89, (July 7, 2000).

★2117★
U.S. colleges and universities awarding the most mathematics doctorate degrees to Asian Americans

Ranking basis/background: Total doctoral degrees conferred to Asian American students in the field of mathematics during the 1997-98 academic year. **Remarks:** Original source: *Black Issues* analysis of U.S. Department of Education reports of data submitted by institutions. **Number listed:** 4.
1. University of California, Los Angeles (CA)
1. University of California, Riverside (CA)
1. University of Southwestern Louisiana (LA)
1. Rutgers University, New Brunswick (NJ)

Source: "Top 100 Degree Producers," *Black Issues in Higher Education*, 17: 48-89, (July 7, 2000).

★2118★
U.S. colleges and universities awarding the most physical sciences doctorate degrees to African Americans

Ranking basis/background: Total doctoral degrees conferred to African American students in the field of physical sciences during the 1997-98 academic year. **Remarks:** Original source: *Black Issues* analysis of U.S. Department of Education reports of data submitted by institutions. **Number listed:** 6.
1. Howard University (DC)
1. University of Michigan, Ann Arbor (MI)
3. Alabama A&M University (AL)
3. University of Florida (FL)
3. Massachusetts Institute of Technology (MA)

3. University of North Carolina, Chapel Hill (NC)

Source: "Top 100 Degree Producers," *Black Issues in Higher Education*, 17: 48-89, (July 7, 2000).

★2119★
U.S. colleges and universities awarding the most physical sciences doctorate degrees to Asian Americans

Ranking basis/background: Total doctoral degrees conferred to Asian American students in the field of physical sciences during the 1997-98 academic year. **Remarks:** Original source: *Black Issues* analysis of U.S. Department of Education reports of data submitted by institutions. **Number listed:** 30.
1. University of California, Los Angeles (CA)
2. University of Hawaii, Manoa (HI)
3. California Institute of Technology (CA)
3. University of California, Berkeley (CA)
5. University of Chicago (IL)
6. University of California, San Diego (CA)
6. University of California, Santa Barbara (CA)
6. University of Illinois, Urbana-Champaign (IL)
6. University of Washington (WA)
6. Stanford University (CA)

Source: "Top 100 Degree Producers," *Black Issues in Higher Education*, 17: 48-89, (July 7, 2000).

★2120★
U.S. colleges and universities awarding the most psychology doctorate degrees to African Americans

Ranking basis/background: Total doctoral degrees conferred to African American students in the field of psychology during the 1997-98 academic year. **Remarks:** Original source: *Black Issues* analysis of U.S. Department of Education reports of data submitted by institutions. **Number listed:** 20.
1. Howard University (DC)
2. Wright State University (OH)
3. California School of Professional Psychology, Alameda (CA)
4. California School of Professional Psychology, Los Angeles (CA)
4. Temple University (PA)
6. California School of Professional Psychology, Fresno (CA)
6. University of Georgia (GA)
8. U.S. International University (CA)
8. Adler School of Professional Psychology (IL)
8. University of Detroit Mercy (MI)
8. Union Institute, Cincinnati (OH)

Source: "Top 100 Degree Producers," *Black Issues in Higher Education*, 17: 48-89, (July 7, 2000).

★2121★
U.S. colleges and universities awarding the most psychology doctorate degrees to Asian Americans

Ranking basis/background: Total doctoral degrees conferred to Asian American students in the field of psychology during the 1997-98 academic year. **Remarks:** Original source: *Black Issues* analysis of U.S. Department of Education reports of data submitted by institutions. **Number listed:** 9.
1. California School of Professional Psychology, Alameda (CA)
2. Colorado State University (CO)
2. New York University (NY)
4. California School of Professional Psychology, Los Angeles (CA)
4. California School of Professional Psychology, San Diego (CA)
4. University of California, Los Angeles (CA)
4. Illinois School of Professional Psychology (IL)
4. Southern Illinois University, Carbondale (IL)
4. Teachers College, Columbia University (NY)

Source: "Top 100 Degree Producers," *Black Issues in Higher Education*, 17: 48-89, (July 7, 2000).

★2122★
U.S. colleges and universities awarding the most psychology doctorate degrees to Hispanic Americans

Ranking basis/background: Total doctoral degrees conferred to Hispanic American students in the field of psychology during the 1997-98 academic year. **Remarks:** Original source: *Black Issues* analysis of U.S. Department of Education reports of data submitted by institutions. **Number listed:** 14.
1. Caribbean Center for Advanced Studies (FL)
2. California School of Professional Psychology, Los Angeles (CA)
3. Nova Southeastern University (FL)
4. California School of Professional Psychology, San Diego (CA)
4. San Diego State University (CA)
4. Florida International University (FL)
4. Boston University (MA)
4. University of Massachusetts, Amherst (MA)
4. University of Michigan, Ann Arbor (MI)
4. City University of New York, Graduate School and University Center (NY)
11. California School of Professional Psychology, Alameda (CA)
11. University of Miami (FL)
11. Illinois School of Professional Psychology (IL)
11. Rutgers University, New Brunswick (NJ)

Source: "Top 100 Degree Producers," *Black Issues in Higher Education*, 17: 48-89, (July 7, 2000).

★2123★
U.S. colleges and universities awarding the most psychology doctorate degrees to Native Americans

Ranking basis/background: Total doctoral degrees conferred to Native American students in the field of psychology during the 1997-98 academic year. **Remarks:** Original source: *Black Issues* analysis of U.S. Department of Education reports of data submitted by institutions. **Number listed:** 1.
1. Minnesota School of Professional Psychology (MN)

Source: "Top 100 Degree Producers," *Black Issues in Higher Education*, 17: 48-89, (July 7, 2000).

★2124★
U.S. colleges and universities awarding the most social sciences and history doctorate degrees to African Americans

Ranking basis/background: Total doctoral degrees conferred to African American students in the field of social sciences and history during the 1997-98 academic year. **Remarks:** Original source: *Black Issues* analysis of U.S. Department of Education reports of data submitted by institutions. **Number listed:** 21.
1. Harvard University (MA)
2. Clark Atlanta University (GA)
3. Howard University (DC)
3. Old Dominion University (VA)
5. The Fielding Institute (CA)
6. University of Chicago (IL)
7. University of California, Los Angeles (CA)
7. American University (DC)
7. Michigan State University (MI)
7. Wayne State University (MI)
7. City University of New York, Graduate School and University Center (NY)

Source: "Top 100 Degree Producers," *Black Issues in Higher Education*, 17: 48-89, (July 7, 2000).

★2125★
U.S. colleges and universities awarding the most social sciences and history doctorate degrees to Asian Americans

Ranking basis/background: Total doctoral degrees conferred to Asian American students in the field of social sciences and history during the 1997-98 academic year. **Remarks:** Original source: *Black Issues* analysis of U.S. Department of Education reports of data submitted by institutions. **Number listed:** 15.
1. University of Hawaii, Manoa (HI)
2. University of California, Berkeley (CA)
3. University of California, Los Angeles (CA)
4. University of Southern California (CA)
5. Columbia University, New York City (NY)
5. New York University (NY)
7. Yale University (CT)
8. Duke University (NC)
9. Texas A&M University (TX)
10. University of California, Riverside (CA)
10. University of Chicago (IL)
10. Northwestern University (IL)
10. Harvard University (MA)
10. State University of New York, Stony Brook (NY)
10. Stanford University (CA)

Source: "Top 100 Degree Producers," *Black Issues in Higher Education*, 17: 48-89, (July 7, 2000).

★2126★
U.S. colleges and universities awarding the most social sciences and history doctorate degrees to Hispanic Americans

Ranking basis/background: Total doctoral degrees conferred to Hispanic American students in the field of social sciences and history during the 1997-98 academic year. **Remarks:** Original source: *Black Issues* analysis of U.S. Department of Education reports of data submitted by institutions. **Number listed:** 4.
1. University of California, Berkeley (CA)
2. University of California, Los Angeles (CA)
3. Harvard University (MA)
3. University of Michigan, Ann Arbor (MI)

Source: "Top 100 Degree Producers," *Black Issues in Higher Education*, 17: 48-89, (July 7, 2000).

★2127★
U.S. colleges and universities awarding the most social sciences and history doctorate degrees to Native Americans

Ranking basis/background: Total doctoral degrees conferred to Native American students in the field of social sciences and history during the 1997-98 academic year. **Remarks:** Original source: *Black Issues* analysis of U.S. Department of Education reports of data submitted by institutions. **Number listed:** 1.
1. Harvard University (MA)

Source: "Top 100 Degree Producers," *Black Issues in Higher Education*, 17: 48-89, (July 7, 2000).

★2128★
U.S. institutions awarding the most doctoral degrees to Asian Americans in agribusiness and production, 1998

Ranking basis/background: Institutions conferring the most doctoral degrees in agribusiness and production to Asian American students during the 1996-97 academic year. **Number listed:** 1.
1. University of Hawaii, Manoa (HI)

Source: "Top 100 Agriculture Degree Producers, 1998," *Black Issues in Higher Education*, 17: 27-29, (June 8, 2000).

★2129★
U.S. institutions awarding the most doctoral degrees to Asian Americans in agricultural sciences, 1998

Ranking basis/background: Institutions conferring the most doctoral degrees in agricultural sciences to Asian American students during the 1996-97 academic year. **Number listed:** 1.
1. University of Hawaii, Manoa (HI)

Source: "Top 100 Agriculture Degree Producers, 1998," *Black Issues in Higher Education*, 17: 27-29, (June 8, 2000).

★2130★
U.S. institutions awarding the most doctoral degrees to minorities in agribusiness and production, 1998

Ranking basis/background: Institutions conferring the most doctoral degrees in agribusiness and production to minority students during the 1996-97 academic year. **Number listed:** 1.
1. University of Hawaii, Manoa (HI)

Source: "Top 100 Agriculture Degree Producers, 1998," *Black Issues in Higher Education*, 17: 27-29, (June 8, 2000).

★2131★
U.S. institutions awarding the most doctoral degrees to minorities in agricultural sciences, 1998

Ranking basis/background: Institutions conferring the most doctoral degrees in agricultural sciences to minority students during the 1996-97 academic year. **Number listed:** 5.
1. University of Hawaii, Manoa (HI)
1. Michigan State University (MI)
1. Texas A&M University (TX)
4. Alabama A&M University (AL)
4. University of Florida (FL)

Source: "Top 100 Agriculture Degree Producers, 1998," *Black Issues in Higher Education*, 17: 27-29, (June 8, 2000).

★2132★
U.S. institutions awarding the most doctorate degrees, 1999

Ranking basis/background: Number of doctorates awarded in all disciplines from each institutions in 1999. **Remarks:** Original source: "Survey of Earned Doctorates." **Number listed:** 50.
1. University of Texas, Austin, with 752
2. University of California, Berkeley, 717
3. University of Wisconsin, Madison, 685
4. University of Minnesota, Twin Cities, 656
5. University of Michigan, Ann Arbor, 655
6. University of Illinois, Urbana-Champaign, 643
7. University of California, Los Angeles, 588
8. Pennsylvania State University, 580
9. Nova Southeastern University, 573
10. Harvard University, 564

Source: Leatherman, Courtney, "The Number of New Ph.D.'s Drops For the First Time Since 1985," *The Chronicle of Higher Education*, 47: A10-A11, (February 9, 2001).

Related Information

★2133★
Sanderson, A., et. al., "Doctorate Recipients from United States Universities: Summary Report 1999," http://www.nsf.gov/sbe/srs/sengdr/start.htm.

Remarks: Data collected in the Survey of Earned Doctorates including trends in doctorate recipients, postgraduate plans, employment and location, and interstate migration patterns of doctorate recipients.

DOCTORAL STUDENTS
See: **Graduate Students**

DROPOUTS

★2134★
College dropout rates for selected countries

Ranking basis/background: Percentage of college dropouts **Remarks:** Original source: O.E.C.D. **Number listed:** 3.
1. Italy, with 65% (highest)
2. United States, 37%
3. Japan, 11% (lowest)

Source: Wheeler, David L., "Falling Behind: U.S. Trails 3 European Nations in Rate of College Graduation," *The Chronicle of Higher Education*, 46: A63, (May 26, 2000).

★2135★
High school dropouts in the U.S., by race and gender, 1999

Ranking basis/background: Total number of dropouts and percent of total. 1999 total dropouts is 524,000. **Remarks:** Original source: U.S. Department of Labor. **Number listed:** 5.
   Men, with 243,000 dropouts; 46.4% of total
   Women, 282,000; 53.8%

DRUG EDUCATION

White, 377,000; 71.9%
African American, 118,000; 22.5%
Hispanic American, 119,000; 22.7%
Source: "Disparities & Gaps in America," *Black Issues in Higher Education*, 18: 28-29, (March 1, 2001).

DRUG EDUCATION
See: **Substance Abuse and Education**

EARLY ADMISSION, COLLEGE
See: **College Admission**

EARLY PARENTHOOD
See: **Teen Pregnancy**

EARTH SCIENCE

★2136★
Ecology journals by citation impact, 1981-99

Ranking basis/background: Impact factor calculated by taking the number of current citations to source items published and dividing it by the number of articles published in the journal during that time period. **Number listed:** 10.
1. *Annual Reviews of Ecological Systems*, with a 79.98 impact factor
2. *Advances in Ecological Research*, 69.62
3. *Ecological Monographs*, 58.03
4. *Advances in Microbial Ecology*, 47.15
5. *Ecology*, 30.20
6. *American Naturalist*, 29.63
7. *Evolution*, 28.09
8. *ZBL Bakter./Mikrobiology*, 23.11
9. *Journal of Animal Ecology*, 21.66
10. *Trends in Ecology/Evolution*, 19.72

Source: "Journals Ranked by Impact: Ecology," *What's Hot in Research* (http://www.isinet.com/isi/hot/research) Institute for Scientific Information.

★2137★
Ecology journals by citation impact, 1995-99

Ranking basis/background: Impact factor calculated by taking the number of current citations to source items published and dividing it by the number of articles published in the journal during that time period. **Number listed:** 10.
1. *Advances in Ecological Research*, with a 34.20 impact factor
2. *Trends in Ecology/Evolution*, 13.72
3. *Annual Reviews of Ecological Systems*, 12.81
4. *Ecological Monographs*, 10.49
5. *Advances in Microbial Ecology*, 8.20
6. *Evolution*, 8.05
7. *Ecologist*, 7.57
8. *American Naturalist*, 7.16
9. *Journal of Ecology*, 6.05
10. *Journal of Animal Ecology*, 6.39

Source: "Journals Ranked by Impact: Ecology," *What's Hot in Research* (http://www.isinet.com/isi/hot/research) Institute for Scientific Information.

★2138★
Ecology journals by citation impact, 1999

Ranking basis/background: Impact factor calculated by taking the number of current citations to source items published and dividing it by the number of articles published in the journal during that time period. **Number listed:** 10.
1. *Advances in Ecological Research*, with a 9.60 impact factor
2. *Trends in Ecology/Evolution*, 7.62
3. *Annual Review of Ecological Systems*, 5.69
4. *Ecological Monographs*, 4.45
5. *Wildlife Monographs*, 4.44
6. *American Naturalist*, 3.93
7. *Evolution*, 3.73
8. *Ecology*, 3.57
9. *Molecular Ecology*, 3.44
10. *Journal of Evolutionary Biology*, 3.26

Source: "Journals Ranked by Impact: Ecology," *What's Hot in Research* (http://www.isinet.com/isi/hot/research) Institute for Scientific Information.

★2139★
Oceanography journals by citation impact, 1981-99

Ranking basis/background: Impact factor calculated by taking the number of current citations to source items published and dividing it by the number of articles published in the journal during that time period. **Number listed:** 10.
1. *Oceanography & Marine Biology*, with a 47.86 impact factor
2. *Journal of Geophysical Research-Oceans and Atmospheres*, 33.49
3. *Deep-Sea Research Part A*, 25.77
4. *Limnology & Oceanography*, 25.13
5. *Journal of Marine Research*, 21.67
6. *Estuarine and Coastal Marine Science*, 19.93
7. *Progress in Oceanography*, 18.65
8. *Journal of Geophysical Research-Space Physics*, 16.79
9. *Journal of Geophysical Research-Atmosphere*, 16.19
10. *Journal of Physical Oceanography*, 15.93

Source: "Journals Ranked by Impact: Oceanography," *What's Hot in Research* (http://www.isinet.com/isi/hot/research) Institute for Scientific Information, October 23, 2000.

★2140★
Oceanography journals by citation impact, 1995-99

Ranking basis/background: Impact factor calculated by taking the number of current citations to source items published and dividing it by the number of articles published in the journal during that time period. **Number listed:** 10.
1. *Oceanography & Marine Biology*, with a 12.33 impact factor
2. *Deep Sea Research, Part II*, 7.77
3. *Paleoceanography*, 7.44
4. *Netherlands Journal of Sea Research*, 6.56
5. *Limnology & Oceanography*, 6.50
6. *Journal of Geophysical Research-Atmosphere*, 6.43
7. *Journal of Geophysical Research-Solid*, 6.05
8. *Journal of Geophysical Research-Oceans*, 5.39
9. *Marine Chemistry*, 5.13
10. *Deep-Sea Research, Part I*, 4.90

Source: "Journals Ranked by Impact: Oceanography," *What's Hot in Research* (http://www.isinet.com/isi/hot/research) Institute for Scientific Information, October 23, 2000.

★2141★
Oceanography journals by citation impact, 1999

Ranking basis/background: Impact factor calculated by taking the number of current citations to source items published and dividing it by the number of articles published in the journal during that time period. **Number listed:** 10.
1. *Paleoceanography*, with a 3.97 impact factor
2. *Limnology & Oceanography*, 3.02
3. *Journal of Physical Oceanography*, 2.33
4. *Marine Chemistry*, 2.29
5. *Journal of Marine Research*, 1.97
6. *Deep-Sea Research, Part I*, 1.94
7. *Fisheries Oceanography*, 1.48
8. *Estuarine and Coastal Shelf Science*, 1.47
9. *Atmosphere-Ocean*, 1.42
10. *Progress in Oceanography*, 1.29

Source: "Journals Ranked by Impact: Oceanography," *What's Hot in Research* (http://www.isinet.com/isi/hot/research) Institute for Scientific Information, October 23, 2000.

★2142★
Top recruiters for meteorology jobs for 2000-01 bachelor's degree recipients

Ranking basis/background: Projected number of college hires from on-campus recruitment for 2000-01. **Remarks:** Numbers reflect total expected hires, not just African American projected hires. **Number listed:** 1.
1. U.S. Air Force Randolph AFB, with 40 projected hires

Source: "The Top 100 Employers and the Majors in Demand for the Class of 2001," *The Black Collegian*, 31: 19-35, (February 2001).

★2143★
Top United Kingdom universities by citation impact in the field of geosciences, 1991-95

Ranking basis/background: Average citations per paper published from a list of over 100 U.K. universities between 1991 and 1995. **Remarks:** Source: ISI's *United Kingdom Universities Indicators on Diskette, 1981-95*. **Number listed:** 3.
1. Open University, with 5.21 citations per paper
2. University of Oxford, 4.83
3. University of East Anglia, 4.74

Source: "Citation Records Reveal Top U.K. Universities in 21 Fields," *The Scientist*, 11: 12, (March 3, 1997).

★2144★
Top United Kingdom universities by citation impact in the field of plant and animal sciences, 1991-95

Ranking basis/background: Average citations per paper published from a list of over 100 U.K. universities between 1991 and 1995. **Remarks:** Source: ISI's *United Kingdom Universities Indicators on Diskette, 1981-95*. **Number listed:** 3.
1. University of Leicester, with 6.76 citations per paper
2. University of East Anglia, 5.68
3. University of Lancaster, 4.49

Source: "Citation Records Reveal Top U.K. Universities in 21 Fields," *The Scientist*, 11: 12, (March 3, 1997).

★2145★
Top United Kingdom universities by total citations in the field of agricultural sciences, 1991-95

Ranking basis/background: Total citations by field from a list of over 100 U.K. universities between 1991 and 1995. **Remarks:** Source: ISI's *United Kingdom Universities Indicators on Diskette, 1981-95*. **Number listed:** 3.
1. University of Reading, with 847 total citations
2. University of East Anglia, 617
3. University of Aberdeen, 588

Source: "Citation Records Reveal Top U.K. Universities in 21 Fields," *The Scientist*, March 3, 1997, p. 12.

★2146★
Top United Kingdom universities by total citations in the field of ecology/ environmental, 1991-95

Ranking basis/background: Total citations by field from a list of over 100 U.K. universities between 1991 and 1995. **Remarks:** Source: ISI's *United Kingdom Universities Indicators on Diskette, 1981-95*. **Number listed:** 3.
1. University of Oxford, with 1,314 total citations
2. Imperial College, 1,299
3. University of Lancaster, 864

Source: "Citation Records Reveal Top U.K. Universities in 21 Fields," *The Scientist*, March 3, 1997, p. 12.

★2147★
Top United Kingdom universities by total citations in the field of geosciences, 1991-95

Ranking basis/background: Total citations by field from a list of over 100 U.K. universities between 1991 and 1995. **Remarks:** Source: ISI's *United Kingdom Universities Indicators on Diskette, 1981-95*. **Number listed:** 3.
1. University of Cambridge, with 2,993 total citations
2. University of Oxford, 2,292
3. University of Edinburgh, 1,558

Source: "Citation Records Reveal Top U.K. Universities in 21 Fields," *The Scientist*, March 3, 1997, p. 12.

★2148★
Top United Kingdom universities by total citations in the field of plant and animal sciences, 1991-95

Ranking basis/background: Total citations by field from a list of over 100 U.K. universities between 1991 and 1995. **Remarks:** Source: ISI's *United Kingdom Universities Indicators on Diskette, 1981-95*. **Number listed:** 3.
1. University of East Anglia, with 3,570 total citations
2. University of Oxford, 2,212
3. University of Bristol, 2,209

Source: "Citation Records Reveal Top U.K. Universities in 21 Fields," *The Scientist*, March 3, 1997, p. 12.

★2149★
U.S. universities with the greatest impact in geosciences, 1994-98

Ranking basis/background: Average citations per paper from the top 100 federally funded U.S. universities that had at least 50 published papers in ISI indexed geosciences journals. Also includes total number of papers published during the five year period. **Number listed:** 5.
1. Georgia Institute of Technology, with 231 papers; 8.90 citations per paper
2. Harvard University, 435; 8.71
3. University of New Hampshire, 299; 8.56
4. University of California, Irvine, 221; 8.40
5. Columbia University, 766; 8.01

Source: "Geosciences: High Impact U.S. Universities, 1994-98," *What's Hot in Research* (http://www.isinet.com/isi/hot/research) Institute for Scientific Information, August 14, 2000.

EARTH SCIENCE, GRADUATE

★2150★
Most effective geosciences research-doctorate programs as evaluated by the National Research Council

Ranking basis/background: From a survey of nearly 8,000 faculty members conducted in the spring of 1993. Respondents were asked to rate programs in their field on "effectiveness of program in educating research scholars/scientists." **Remarks:** See *Chronicle* article for more details. Scores of 3.5-5.0 indicate "extremely effective;" 2.5-3.49 "reasonably effective;" 1.5-2.49 "minimally effective;" and 0.0-1.49 "not effective." Programs also ranked by "scholarly quality of program faculty." **Number listed:** 100.
1. California Institute of Technology, with an effectiveness rating of 4.63
2. Massachusetts Institute of Technology, 4.52
3. Columbia University, 4.14
4. University of California, Berkeley, 4.09
5. University of California, San Diego, 4.06
5. Stanford University, 4.06
7. University of Chicago, 4.03
8. Stanford University Program in Geophysics, 3.96
8. Brown University, 3.96
10. Johns Hopkins University, 3.94

Source: "Rankings of Research-Doctorate Programs in 41 Disciplines at 274 Institutions," *The Chronicle of Higher Education* 42: A21-A30 (September 21, 1995).

★2151★
Private, 4-year undergraduate colleges and universities producing the most Ph.D.'s in the earth sciences, 1981-1990

Ranking basis/background: Number of doctoral degrees granted to graduates of 914 private, 4-year U.S. undergraduate colleges and universities. Medical, law, and other professional, non-doctoral degrees are not included. **Remarks:** Original source: Office of Scientific and Engineering Personnel of the National Research Council. Report contains 50 other tables detailing the distribution of doctoral recipients by field of study over various time frames. **Number listed:** 238.
1. Carleton College, with 37 Ph.D.'s
2. Pomona College, 30
3. Franklin and Marshall College, 29
3. Colgate University, 29
5. Middlebury College, 27
6. Oberlin College, 22
7. Amherst College, 20
8. Colorado College, 18
9. Wesleyan University, 15
9. Williams College, 15
9. Earlham College, 15
12. Harvey Mudd College, 14
12. Swarthmore College, 14
12. Bucknell University, 14
15. Wellesley College, 13
15. Occidental College, 13
15. Dickinson College, 13
15. Beloit College, 13
15. Long Island University, Southhampton College, 13

Source: *Baccalaureate Origins of Doctorate Recipients, 7th ed.*, Franklin & Marshall College, March 1993.

★2152★
Top geosciences research-doctorate programs as evaluated by the National Research Council

Ranking basis/background: From a survey of nearly 8,000 faculty members conducted in the spring of 1993. Respondents were asked to rate programs in their field on "scholarly quality of program faculty." When more than one program had the samescore, the council averaged the rank order and gave each program the same rank number (if three programs tied for the top position, each received a rank of 2). **Remarks:** See *Chronicle* article for more details. Scores of 4.01 and above indicate "distinguished;" 3.0-4.0 "strong;" 2.51-3.0 "good;" 2.0-2.5 "adequate;" 1.0-1.99 "marginal;" and 0.0-0.99 "not sufficient for doctoral education." Programs also ranked by "effectiveness of program in educating research scholars/scientists." **Number listed:** 100.
1. California Institute of Technology, with a quality rating of 4.87
2. Massachusetts Institute of Technology, 4.67
3. University of California, Berkeley, 4.45
4. Columbia University, 4.38
5. Stanford University Program in Geophysics, 4.33
6. University of California, San Diego, 4.23
7. University of Chicago, 4.22
8. Harvard University, 4.20
9. Stanford University, 4.15
9. Cornell University, 4.15
11. University of California, Los Angeles, 4.11
11. Pennsylvania State University, 4.11
11. Brown University, 4.11
14. Princeton University, 4.01
15. University of Texas, Austin, 3.96
15. Stanford University Program in Applied Earth Sciences, 3.96

Source: "Rankings of Research-Doctorate Programs in 41 Disciplines at 274 Institutions," *The Chronicle of Higher Education* 42: A21-A30 (September 21, 1995).

ECONOMETRICS

★2153★
Top oceanography research-doctorate programs as evaluated by the National Research Council

Ranking basis/background: From a survey of nearly 8,000 faculty members conducted in the spring of 1993. Respondents were asked to rate programs in their field on "scholarly quality of program faculty." When more than one program had the samescore, the council averaged the rank order and gave each program the same rank number (if three programs tied for the top position, each received a rank of 2). **Remarks:** See *Chronicle* article for more details. Scores of 4.01 and above indicate "distinguished;" 3.0-4.0 "strong;" 2.51-3.0 "good;" 2.0-2.5 "adequate;" 1.0-1.99 "marginal;" and 0.0-0.99 "not sufficient for doctoral education." Programs also ranked by "effectiveness of program in educating research scholars/scientists." **Number listed:** 26.

1. University of California, San Diego, with a quality rating of 4.69
2. Massachusetts Institute of Technology, 4.62
3. University of Washington (WA), 4.31
4. Columbia University, 4.30
5. Oregon State University, 3.88
6. University of Rhode Island, 3.68
7. University of Hawaii, Manoa, 3.50
8. State University of New York, Stony Brook, 3.49
9. Florida State University, 3.48
10. University of Maryland, College Park, 3.42
11. University of Miami, 3.29
12. Texas A&M University, 3.26
13. University of North Carolina, Chapel Hill, 3.22
13. Duke University, 3.22
15. University of South Florida, 3.07

Source: "Rankings of Research-Doctorate Programs in 41 Disciplines at 274 Institutions," *The Chronicle of Higher Education* 42: A21-A30 (September 21, 1995).

★2154★
United Kingdom universities with the greatest impact in geosciences, 1993-97

Ranking basis/background: For each university, total number of citations divided by number of published articles during the same time period. **Remarks:** Original source: *National Science Indicators on Diskette, 1981-97* **Number listed:** 5.

1. University of Cambridge, with 5.28 citations per paper; 868 total papers
2. University of East Anglia, 5.25; 279
3. Open University, 5.17; 235
4. Queens University of Belfast, 5.02; 112
5. University of Bristol, 4.80; 397

Source: "United Kingdom: High-Impact Universities in Geosciences, 1993-97," *What's Hot*, October 19, 1998.

★2155★
U.S. universities with the greatest impact in geosciences, 1993-97

Ranking basis/background: For each university, total number of citations divided by number of published articles during the same time period. **Remarks:** Original source: *National Science Indicators on Diskette, 1981-97* **Number listed:** 5.

1. University of California, Irvine, with 9.48 citations per paper; 188 total papers
2. Georgia Institute of Technology, 9.39; 204
3. University of New Hampshire, 9.02; 239
4. Columbia University, 8.92; 773
5. Harvard University, 8.88; 465

Source: "Geosciences: High-Impact U.S. Universities, 1993-97," *What's Hot*, September 16, 1998.

ECONOMETRICS
See: **Economics**

ECONOMICS

★2156★
Authors most frequently contributing to the *American Economic Review* from 1911-1990

Ranking basis/background: Data includes all articles and notes appearing in *American Economic Review* from 1911-1990. Excluded are comments, replies, abstracts, and book reviews. **Remarks:** Total number of entries published in *American Economic Review* from 1911-1990 is 3,644. These articles were written by 2,946 different authors who were employed by at least 398 different academic institutions. **Number listed:** 100.

1. R. G. Blakey, with 18 articles
2. William Baumol, 17
3. Paul Samuelson, 15
3. Joseph Stiglitz, 15
5. Frank Fetter, 11
5. Irving Fisher, 11
5. George J. Stigler, 11
8. G. C. Blakey, 10
8. James M. Buchanan, 10
8. J. Maurice Clark, 10
8. Franco Modigliani, 10
8. Vernon Smith, 10

Source: Heck, Jean Louis, "Eight Decades of Contributing Authors and Institutions to the *American Economic Review*: A Historical Summary," *Journal of Economic Education* 24: 163-170 (Spring 1993).

★2157★
Authors most frequently contributing to the *American Economic Review* from 1951-1990

Ranking basis/background: Data includes all articles and notes appearing in *American Economic Review* from 1951-1990. Excluded are comments, replies, abstracts and book reviews. **Remarks:** Also cites authors frequently contributing from 1911-1990 and the institutions most frequently contributing to *American Economic Review*. **Number listed:** 105.

1. William Baumol, with 17 articles
2. Joseph Stiglitz, 15
3. Franco Modigliani, 10
3. Vernon Smith, 10
5. James M. Buchanan, 9
5. Martin S. Feldstein, 9
5. Jerome Stein, 9
8. Robert Eisner, 8
8. Eugene Fama, 8
8. Elhanan Helpman, 8
8. David Leuhan, 8
8. Paul Samuelson, 8

Source: Heck, Jean Louis, "Eight Decades of Contributing Authors and Institutions to the *American Economic Review*: A Historical Summary," *Journal of Economic Education* 24: 163-170 (Spring 1993).

★2158★
Economics departments by number of citations by top economists, 1971-92

Ranking basis/background: Total number of citations by top economists, based on a citation analysis of 250 economists at U.S. universities during the period 1971-92. **Number listed:** 15.

1. Harvard University, with 57,155 citations
2. University of Chicago, 33,348
3. Stanford University, 27,425
4. Massachusetts Institute of Technology, 27,054
5. Princeton University, 16,571
6. University of California, Berkeley, 15,837
7. Columbia University, 15,648
8. Yale University, 14,862
9. University of California, Los Angeles, 13,946
10. University of Maryland, 10,685
11. University of Pennsylvania, 9,828
12. University of Wisconsin, 9,023
13. University of Minnesota, 6,512
14. University of Michigan, 6,441
15. Northwestern University, 6,301

Source: Medoff, Marshall, "A Citation-Based Analysis of Economists and Economics Programs," *The American Economist*, pp. 46-59, (Spring 1996).

★2159★
Economics departments by number of citations per top economist, 1971-92

Ranking basis/background: Number of citations per top economist, based on a citation analysis of 250 economists at U.S. universities during the period 1971-92. **Number listed:** 15.

1. University of Chicago, with 2,382.00 citations per top economist
2. Harvard University, 1,970.86
3. Massachusetts Institute of Technology, 1,932.43
4. University of Maryland, 1,780.83
5. Columbia University, 1,564.80
6. University of California, Berkeley, 1,439.73
7. University of Minnesota, 1,302.40
8. Princeton University, 1,274.69
9. University of California, Los Angeles, 1,267.82
10. Northwestern University, 1,260.20
11. Stanford University, 1,246.59
12. University of Pennsylvania, 1,228.50
13. Yale University, 1,143.23
14. University of Wisconsin, 1,127.88
15. University of Michigan, 1,073.50

Source: Medoff, Marshall, "A Citation-Based Analysis of Economists and Economics Programs," *The American Economist*, pp. 46-59, (Spring 1996).

★2160★
Economics departments by number of top economists, 1971-92

Ranking basis/background: Total number of top economists, based on a citation analysis of 250 economists at U.S. universities during the period 1971-92. **Number listed:** 15.

1. Harvard University, with 29 top economists
2. Stanford University, 22
3. University of Chicago, 14
3. Massachusetts Institute of Technology, 14
5. Princeton University, 13
5. Yale University, 13
7. University of California, Berkeley, 11
7. University of California, Los Angeles, 11
9. Columbia University, 10
10. University of Pennsylvania, 8

10. University of Wisconsin, 8
12. University of Maryland, 6
12. University of Michigan, 6
14. University of Minnesota, 5
14. Northwestern University, 5

Source: Medoff, Marshall, "A Citation-Based Analysis of Economists and Economics Programs," *The American Economist*, pp. 46-59, (Spring 1996).

★2161★
Economics journals with the greatest impact measure, 1981-98

Ranking basis/background: Citations-per-paper impact score is the total citations to a journal's published papers divided by total number of papers the journal has published over an eighteen year period. **Remarks:** Original source: *Journal Citation Reports* and Journal Performance Indicators on Diskette. **Number listed:** 10.

1. *Journal of Economic Literature*, with an impact score of 34.63
2. *Econometrica*, 34.17
3. *Journal of Financial Economics*, 43.27
4. *Journal of Political Economics*, 28.83
5. *Bell Journal of Economics*, 26.95
6. *Quarterly Journal of Economics*, 17.31
7. *Journal of Monetary Economics*, 16.59
8. *American Economic Review*, 15.66
9. *Journal of Law and Economics*, 14.99
10. *Review of Economic Studies*, 14.72

Source: "Journals Ranked by Impact: Economics," *What's Hot in Research* (http://www.isinet.com/hot/research) Institute for Scientific Information, June 28, 1999.

★2162★
Economics journals with the greatest impact measure, 1994-98

Ranking basis/background: Citations-per-paper impact score is the total citations to a journal's published papers divided by total number of papers the journal has published over a five year period. **Remarks:** Original source: *Journal Citation Reports* and Journal Performance Indicators on Diskette. **Number listed:** 10.

1. *Journal of Economic Literature*, with an impact score of 8.89
2. *Quarterly Journal of Economics*, 6.26
3. *Journal of Economic Perspectives*, 5.71
4. *Journal of Political Economics*, 5.55
5. *Econometrica*, 4.75
6. *Journal of Financial Economics*, 4.01
7. *American Economic Review*, 3.81
8. *Journal of Monetary Economics*, 3.58
9. *Review of Economic Studies*, 3.53
10. *Journal of Health Economics*, 3.23

Source: "Journals Ranked by Impact: Economics," *What's Hot in Research* (http://www.isinet.com/hot/research) Institute for Scientific Information, June 28, 1999.

★2163★
Economics journals with the greatest impact measure, 1997

Ranking basis/background: Ratio of citations and recent citable items published. **Remarks:** Original source: *Journal Citation Reports* and Journal Performance Indicators on Diskette. **Number listed:** 10.

1. *The Economist*, with a ratio of 9.17
2. *Journal of Economic Literature*, 5.82
3. *Quarterly Journal of Economics*, 3.07
4. *Journal of Political Economics*, 2.85
5. *Journal of Economic Perspectives*, 2.77
6. *Journal of Financial Economics*, 2.51
7. *Brookings Papers in Economics*, 2.07
8. *Economy and Society*, 1.98
9. *Journal of Health Economics*, 1.73
10. *Econometrica*, 1.71

Source: "Journals Ranked by Impact: Economics," *What's Hot in Research* (http://www.isinet.com/hot/research) Institute for Scientific Information, June 28, 1999.

★2164★
Elite liberal arts colleges ranked by per capita quality adjusted scholarship articles in the field of economics, 1975-94

Ranking basis/background: Listed in rank order based on an index calculated to measure per capita research productivity. **Number listed:** 40.

1. Barnard College
2. Bates College
3. Wesleyan University
4. Swarthmore College
5. Pomona College
6. Bowdoin College
7. Claremont McKenna College
8. Grinnell College
9. Colby College
10. Amherst College

Source: Bodenhorn, Howard, "Teachers and Scholars Too: Economic Scholarship at Elite Liberal Arts Colleges," *Journal of Economic Education*, pp. 323-336, (Fall 1997).

★2165★
Elite liberal arts colleges ranked by quality adjusted scholarship articles in the field of economics, 1975-94

Ranking basis/background: Listed in rank order based on an index calculated to measure research productivity. **Number listed:** 40.

1. Wesleyan University
2. Barnard College
3. Claremont McKenna College
4. Swarthmore College
5. Williams College
6. Bowdoin College
7. Bates College
8. Pomona College
9. Smith College
10. Grinnell College

Source: Bodenhorn, Howard, "Teachers and Scholars Too: Economic Scholarship at Elite Liberal Arts Colleges," *Journal of Economic Education*, pp. 323-336, (Fall 1997).

★2166★
Individuals producing the most economic education research articles, 1963-1990

Ranking basis/background: Total number of pages of economic education research articles, from 1963-1990. **Remarks:** Original source: *REED* database. Data is also ranked by number of adjusted pages, raw pages, and raw articles. **Number listed:** 20.

1. William B. Walstad, with 14.87 articles
2. J. J. Siegfried, 14.30
3. John C. Soper, 14.03
4. William E. Becker, 13.50
5. Marilyn Kourilsky, 12.50
6. Philip Saunders, 10.50
7. W. Lee Hansen, 8.17
8. Allen C. Kelley, 7.83
9. Michael W. Watts, 7.70
10. Keith G. Lumsden, 7.58

Source: Marlin, W. James, Jr. and Garey C. Durden, "An Analysis of Contributions and Contributors in Economic Education Research," *Journal of Economic Education* 24: 171-186 (Spring 1993).

★2167★
Institutions generating the most economic education research text, 1963-1990

Ranking basis/background: Total number of pages of economic education research text from 1963-1990, by page count. The top ten schools are predominantly schools where there are several prolific economic education research writers. **Remarks:** Original source: *REED* database. Data is also ranked by number of adjusted articles. **Number listed:** 20.

1. University of Nebraska, with 293.80 pages
2. Vanderbilt University, 240.17
3. Indiana University, 231.96
4. University of California, Los Angeles, 153.67
5. John Carroll University, 153.30
6. Purdue University, 132.80
7. Stanford University, 129.40
8. University of Minnesota, 128.67
9. University of Georgia, 126.64
10. Duke University, 110.80
11. London University, 107.00
12. University of Wisconsin, 102.36
13. University of Illinois, 100.50
14. JCEE, 100.10
15. University of Chicago, 97.00
16. Clemson University, 89.67
17. Louisiana State University, 75.2
18. Illinois State University, 74.04
19. University of Colorado, 70.66
20. Heriot-Watt, 60.70

Source: Marlin, W. James, Jr. and Garey C. Durden, "An Analysis of Contributions and Contributors in Economic Education Research," *Journal of Economic Education* 24: 171-186 (Spring 1993).

★2168★
Institutions most frequently contributing to the *American Economic Review* from 1911-1990

Ranking basis/background: Total number of adjusted articles contributed to *American Economic Review* by the faculty of these academic institutions from 1911-1990. Excluded are comments, replies, abstracts, and book reviews. **Remarks:** Fractional credit is given to institutions of co-authored articles. **Number listed:** 94.

1. Harvard University, with 140.17 articles
2. Princeton University, 124.58
3. University of California, Berkeley, 107.00
4. University of Chicago, 101.87
5. Massachusetts Institute of Technology, 100.37
6. Yale University, 92.50
7. Columbia College, 87.33
8. University of Pennsylvania, 82.00
9. Stanford University, 81.83
10. University of Wisconsin, 77.37

Source: Heck, Jean Louis, "Eight Decades of Contributing Authors and Institutions to the *American Economic Review*: A Historical Summary," *Journal of Economic Education* 24: 163-170 (Spring 1993).

ECONOMICS

★2169★
Institutions most frequently contributing to the *American Economic Review* from 1951-1990

Ranking basis/background: Data identifies academic institutions whose faculty have contributed most frequently to *American Economic Review* from 1951-1990. Included are all articles and notes; excluded are comments, replies, abstracts, and book reviews. **Remarks:** Fractional credit is given to institutions of co-authored articles. **Number listed:** 98.

1. Massachusetts Institute of Technology, with 83.17 articles
2. University of Chicago, 81.67
3. Princeton University, 81.58
4. University of California, Berkeley, 77.00
5. Harvard University, 73.17
6. Stanford University, 65.83
7. University of Pennsylvania, 64.00
8. University of California, Los Angeles, 59.59
9. Yale University, 55.50
10. University of Wisconsin, 53.37

Source: Heck, Jean Louis, "Eight Decades of Contributing Authors and Institutions to the *American Economic Review*: A Historical Summary," *Journal of Economic Education* 24: 163-170 (Spring 1993).

★2170★
Journals publishing the most articles on economic education research from 1963-1990

Ranking basis/background: Total number of articles on economic education in these journals between 1963-1990. **Remarks:** Original source: REED database. Table also breaks down the data for years 1963-1979 and 1980-1990. **Number listed:** 23.

1. *Journal of Economic Education*, with 491 articles
2. *American Economic Review (Proceedings)*, 73
3. *Economics*, 36
4. *Theory and Research in Social Education*, 17
5. *Social Education*, 16
6. *Economic Inquiry/Western Economic Journal*, 14
6. *Southern Economic Journal*, 14
8. *American Economic Review*, 13
9. *Theory into Practice*, 10
10. *Social Science Computer Review*, 9

Source: Marlin, W. James, Jr. and Garey C. Durden, "An Analysis of Contributions and Contributors in Economic Education Research," *Journal of Economic Education* 24: 171-186 (Spring 1993).

★2171★
Radcliffe Institute for Advanced Study fellowship recipient in the field of economic and social development, 2000-01

Ranking basis/background: Recipient and institutional affiliation of the Radcliffe Institute for Advanced study fellowship for pursuit of advanced work across a wide range of academic disciplines, professions, and creative arts. **Number listed:** 1.

Sarah Kuhn, University of Massachusetts, Lowell

Source: "The Radcliffe Institute for Advanced Study," *The Chronicle of Higher Education*, 46: A59, (June 2, 2000).

★2172★
Radcliffe Institute for Advanced Study fellowship recipients in the field of economics, 2000-01

Ranking basis/background: Recipient and institutional affiliation of the Radcliffe Institute for Advanced study fellowship for pursuit of advanced work across a wide range of academic disciplines, professions, and creative arts. **Number listed:** 2.

Marilyn Carr, United Nations
Nancy Goldstein, University of Southern Maine

Source: "The Radcliffe Institute for Advanced Study," *The Chronicle of Higher Education*, 46: A59, (June 2, 2000).

★2173★
Top assistant professor economists at elite liberal arts colleges, 1975-94

Ranking basis/background: Listed in rank order based on an index calculated to measure research productivity. **Number listed:** 15.

1. R. Grossman, affiliated with Wesleyan University
2. D. Barbezat, Colby College
3. D. Zimmerman, Williams College
4. P. Mehrling, Barnard College
5. H. Bodenhorn, Lafayette College
6. C. Conrad, Barnard College
7. C. Campbell, Colgate University
8. D. Mann, Williams College
9. E. Gamber, Lafayette College
10. J. Jacobsen, Wesleyan University

Source: Bodenhorn, Howard, "Teachers and Scholars Too: Economic Scholarship at Elite Liberal Arts Colleges," *Journal of Economic Education*, pp. 323-336, (Fall 1997).

★2174★
Top associate professor economists at elite liberal arts colleges, 1975-94

Ranking basis/background: Listed in rank order based on an index calculated to measure research productivity. **Number listed:** 15.

1. M. Jones, affiliated with Bowdoin College
2. J. Mullahy, Trinity College
3. M. Montgomery, Grinnell College
4. D. Haas-Wilson, Smith College
5. B. Bateman, Grinnell College
6. J. Caskey, Swarthmore College
7. E. Brown, Pomona College
8. R. Connelly, Bowdoin College
9. S. Golub, Swarthmore College
10. R. Burdekin, Claremont McKenna College

Source: Bodenhorn, Howard, "Teachers and Scholars Too: Economic Scholarship at Elite Liberal Arts Colleges," *Journal of Economic Education*, pp. 323-336, (Fall 1997).

★2175★
Top full professor economists at elite liberal arts colleges, 1975-94

Ranking basis/background: Listed in rank order based on an index calculated to measure research productivity. **Number listed:** 15.

1. D. Foley, affiliated with Barnard College
2. F. Pryor, Swarthmore College
3. M. Lovell, Wesleyan University
4. John H. Mutti, Grinnell College
5. M. Murray, Bates College
6. G. Woglom, Amherst College
7. G. Smith, Pomona College
8. D. Aschauer, Bates College
9. D. Jones, Hamilton College
10. T. Willett, Claremont McKenna College

Source: Bodenhorn, Howard, "Teachers and Scholars Too: Economic Scholarship at Elite Liberal Arts Colleges," *Journal of Economic Education*, pp. 323-336, (Fall 1997).

★2176★
U.S. academic economists by mean number of citations, 1971-92

Ranking basis/background: Mean number of citations among economists at U.S. universities, excluding self-citations, based on a review of the 1971-92 *Social Sciences Citation Index*. Nobel Prize winners and economists over seventy years old as of 1992 were not included. **Number listed:** 250.

1. E.F. Fama, University of Chicago, with 268.25 mean citations
2. Martin S. Feldstein, Harvard University, 226.20
3. Robert J. Barro, Harvard University, 215.08
4. O.E. Williamson, University of California, Berkeley, 197.03
5. Robert E. Lucas, University of Chicago, 187.78
6. J.J. Heckman, University of Chicago, 163.90
7. R.W. Dornbusch, Massachusetts Institute of Technology, 155.09
8. A.K. Sen, Harvard University, 154.45
9. M.C. Jensen, Harvard University, 151.45
10. T.J. Sargent, University of Minnesota, 148.91
11. M.E. Porter, Harvard University, 144.15
12. R.B. Freeman, Harvard University, 143.04
13. M. Olson, University of Maryland, 139.86
14. Joseph Stiglitz, Stanford University, 135.23
15. S.J. Grossman, University of Pennsylvania, 132.23
16. H. Theil, University of Florida, 131.19
17. F.M. Scherer, Harvard University, 131.00
18. J.N. Bhagwati, Columbia University, 122.60
19. C.W.J. Granger, University of California, San Diego, 96.06
20. R.E. Hall, Stanford University, 106.60

Source: Medoff, Marshall, "A Citation-Based Analysis of Economists and Economics Programs," *The American Economist*, pp. 46-59, (Spring 1996).

★2177★
U.S. academic economists by total citations, 1971-92

Ranking basis/background: Total number of citations among economists at U.S. universities, excluding self-citations, based on a review of the 1971-92 *Social Sciences Citation Index*. Nobel Prize winners and economists over seventy years old as of 1992 were not included. **Number listed:** 250.

1. E.F. Fama, University of Chicago, with 7,511 citations
2. O.E. Williamson, University of California, Berkeley, 5,714
3. Martin S. Feldstein, Harvard University, 5,655
4. H. Theil, University of Florida, 5,379
5. Robert E. Lucas, University of Chicago, 5,241
6. A.K. Sen, Harvard University, 5,097

7. Robert J. Barro, Harvard University, 4,947
8. M. Olson, University of Maryland, 4,056
9. F.M. Scherer, Harvard University, 3,799
10. M.C. Jensen, Harvard University, 3,635
11. T.J. Sargent, University of Minnesota, 3,574
12. Joseph Stiglitz, Stanford University, 3,516
13. J.J. Heckman, University of Chicago, 3,442
14. R.B. Freeman, Harvard University, 3,433
15. R.W. Dornbusch, Massachusetts Institute of Technology, 3,257
16. C.W.J. Granger, University of California, San Diego, 3,170
17. Z. Griliches, Harvard University, 3,162
18. J.N. Bhagwati, Columbia University, 3,065
19. S. Bowles, University of Massachusetts, 2,866
20. A. Zellner, University of Chicago, 2,808

Source: Medoff, Marshall, "A Citation-Based Analysis of Economists and Economics Programs," *The American Economist*, pp. 46-59, (Spring 1996).

★2178★
U.S. universities publishing the most papers in the field of economics and business, 1995-99

Ranking basis/background: Number of papers published in the field of economics and business over a five-year period, and percent of field based on each universities percentage of 47,333 papers entered in the ISI database from ISI-indexed economics and business journals. **Number listed:** 5.

1. Harvard University, with 990 papers; 2.09% of field
2. University of Pennsylvania, 731; 1.54
3. Stanford University, 617; 1.30
4. Massachusetts Institute of Technology, 599; 1.27%
5. University of California, Berkeley, 577; 1.22%

Source: "Economics & Business: Most Prolific U.S. Universities, 1995-99," *What's Hot in Research* (http://www.isinet.com/isi/hot/research) *Institute for Scientific Information*, November 6, 2000.

★2179★
U.S. universities with the greatest impact in economics, 1995-99

Ranking basis/background: Average citations per paper from the top 100 federally funded U.S. universities that had at least 50 published papers in ISI indexed economics journals. Also includes total number of papers published during the five year period. **Number listed:** 5.

1. University of Chicago, with 475 papers; 4.22 citations per paper
2. Princeton University, 262; 4.21
3. Harvard University, 825; 3.86
4. Massachusetts Institute of Technology, 423; 3.64
5. University of Pennsylvania, 557; 3.29

Source: "Economics: High Impact U.S. Universities, 1995-99," *What's Hot in Research* (http://www.isinet.com/isi/hot/research) *Institute for Scientific Information*.

ECONOMICS AND BUSINESS PERIODICALS
See also: **Real Estate Periodicals**

★2180★
Alternative general economics journals, by non-uniform weighting of subdisciplinary impacts, including self-citations

Ranking basis/background: According to *Applied Economics* research of journals by subdiscipline. **Number listed:** 10.

1. *Econometrica*, with 100.0
2. *American Economic Review*, 85.70
3. *Journal of Political Economics*, 74.09
4. *Journal of Economic Theory*, 39.18
5. *Journal of Finance*, 36.49
6. *Journal of Financial Economics*, 36.18
7. *Review of Economic Studies*, 35.90
8. *Quarterly Journal of Economics*, 28.44
9. *Rand Journal of Economics*, 20.94
10. *Journal of Monetary Economics*, 18.13

Source: Barrett, Christopher B., Aliakbar Olia and Dee Van Bailey, "Subdiscipline-Specific Journal Rankings: Whither Applied Economics?," *Applied Economics*, 32: 239-252, (February 10, 2000).

★2181★
Alternative general economics journals, by uniform weighting of subdisciplinary impacts, including self-citations

Ranking basis/background: According to *Applied Economics* research of journals by subdiscipline. **Number listed:** 10.

1. *American Economic Review*, with 100.0
2. *Journal of Political Economics*, 76.68
3. *Econometrica*, 69.95
4. *Journal of Financial Economics*, 30.00
5. *Journal of Economic Theory*, 29.56
6. *Quarterly Journal of Economics*, 29.01
7. *Review of Economic Studies*, 26.60
8. *Rand Journal of Economics*, 26.57
9. *Public Choice*, 25.88
10. *Journal of Finance*, 25.73

Source: Barrett, Christopher B., Aliakbar Olia and Dee Van Bailey, "Subdiscipline-Specific Journal Rankings: Whither Applied Economics?," *Applied Economics*, 32: 239-252, (February 10, 2000).

★2182★
Economics journals by citation impact, 1981-98

Ranking basis/background: Impact factor calculated by taking the number of current citations to source items published and dividing it by the number of articles published in the journal during that time period. **Number listed:** 10.

1. *Journal of Economic Literature*, with a 37.68 impact factor
2. *Econometrica*, 36.42
3. *Journal of Political Economics*, 31.00
4. *Journal of Financial Economics*, 29.73
5. *Bell Journal of Economics*, 28.96
6. *Quarterly Journal of Economics*, 19.51
7. *Journal of Monetary Economics*, 17.38
8. *American Economic Review*, 16.81
9. *Review of Economic Studies*, 15.76
10. *Journal of Law and Economics*, 15.11

Source: "Journals Ranked by Impact: Economics," *What's Hot in Research* (http://www.isinet.com/isi/hot/research) *Institute for Scientific Information*, July 31, 2000.

★2183★
Economics journals by citation impact, 1995-98

Ranking basis/background: Impact factor calculated by taking the number of current citations to source items published and dividing it by the number of articles published in the journal during that time period. **Number listed:** 10.

1. *Journal of Economic Literature*, with a 11.04 impact factor
2. *Quarterly Journal of Economics*, 6.83
3. *Journal of Political Economics*, 6.01
4. *Journal of Economic Perspectives*, 5.53
5. *Journal of Financial Economics*, 4.41
6. *Econometrica*, 4.36
7. *American Economic Review*, 3.97
8. *World Bank Economic Review*, 3.57
9. *Journal of Health Economics*, 3.51
10. *Journal of Environmental Economics and Management*, 3.28

Source: "Journals Ranked by Impact: Economics," *What's Hot in Research* (http://www.isinet.com/isi/hot/research) *Institute for Scientific Information*, July 31, 2000.

★2184★
Economics journals by citation impact, 1998

Ranking basis/background: Impact factor calculated by taking the number of current citations to source items published and dividing it by the number of articles published in the journal during that time period. **Number listed:** 10.

1. *The Economist*, with a 10.49 impact factor
2. *Journal of Economic Literature*, 6.41
3. *Quarterly Journal of Economics*, 3.54
4. *Journal of Economic Perspectives*, 3.09
5. *Journal of Political Economics*, 2.61
6. *Health Economics*, 2.16
7. *Journal of Health Economics*, 2.13
8. *Economic Geography*, 2.08
9. *Econometrica*, 2.07
10. *American Economic Review*, 1.98

Source: "Journals Ranked by Impact: Economics," *What's Hot in Research* (http://www.isinet.com/isi/hot/research) *Institute for Scientific Information*, July 31, 2000.

★2185★
Most cited economists

Ranking basis/background: Total number of citations in principles of economics texts. **Number listed:** 16.

1. John Maynard Keynes, with 78 citations
2. Adam Smith, 76
3. Milton Friedman, 45
4. David Ricardo, 37
5. Karl Marx, 34
6. Thomas Malthus, 30
7. Alfred Marshall, 20
8. Joseph Schumpeter, 20
9. Arthur Okun, 19
10. George J. Stigler, 16
11. Ronald H. Coase, 14
12. John K. Galbraith, 12
12. Simon Kuznets, 12
12. Robert E. Lucas, 12
15. Gary Becker, 11
15. Martin S. Feldstein, 11

Source: Hoaas, David J. and Lauren J. Madigan, "A Citation Analysis of Economists in Principles of Economics Textbooks," *Social Science Journal*, 36: 525-532, (1999).

ECONOMICS AND BUSINESS PERIODICALS

★2186★
Top ranked AACSB publications

Ranking basis/background: From a nationwide survey of American Assembly of Collegiate Schools of Business institutions and non-AACSB institutions rating 80 publications for value in reviews of research performance. **Number listed:** 80.

1. *MIS Quarterly*
2. *Management Science*
3. *Communications of the Association of Computing Machinery*
4. *Information Systems Research*
5. *Decision Sciences*
6. *Harvard Business Review*
7. *Journal of Management Information Systems*
8. *Sloan Management Review*
9. *IEEE transactions on various subjects*
10. *Journal of the ACM*

Source: Whitman, Michael E., Anthony R. Hendrickson and Anthony M. Townsend, "Research Commentary. Academic Rewards for Teaching, Research, and Service: Data and Discourse," *Information Systems Research*, 10: 99-109, (June 1999).

★2187★
Top ranked agricultural and natural resource economics journals

Ranking basis/background: According to *Applied Economics* research of journals by subdiscipline. **Number listed:** 10.

1. *American Journal of Agricultural Economics*
2. *Econometrica*
3. *American Economic Review*
4. *Journal of Political Economics*
5. *Review of Economics and Statistics*
6. *Journal of Econometrics*
7. *Review of Economic Studies*
8. *Journal of Agricultural and Resource Economics*
9. *International Economic Review*
10. *Land Economics*

Source: Barrett, Christopher B., Aliakbar Olia and Dee Van Bailey, "Subdiscipline-Specific Journal Rankings: Whither Applied Economics?," *Applied Economics*, 32: 239-252, (February 10, 2000).

★2188★
Top ranked business administration and business economics journals

Ranking basis/background: According to *Applied Economics* research of journals by subdiscipline. **Number listed:** 10.

1. *Journal of Accounting and Economics*
2. *Journal of Financial Economics*
3. *Journal of Accounting Research*
4. *Journal of Finance*
5. *Accounting Review*
6. *Journal of Business*
7. *American Economic Review*
8. *Journal of Political Economics*
9. *Econometrica*
10. *Rand Journal of Economics*

Source: Barrett, Christopher B., Aliakbar Olia and Dee Van Bailey, "Subdiscipline-Specific Journal Rankings: Whither Applied Economics?," *Applied Economics*, 32: 239-252, (February 10, 2000).

★2189★
Top ranked economic development, technological change, and growth journals

Ranking basis/background: According to *Applied Economics* research of journals by subdiscipline. **Number listed:** 10.

1. *World Development*
2. *American Economic Review*
3. *Journal of Development Economics*
4. *Economic Development and Cultural Change*
5. *Journal of Political Economics*
6. *Economic Journal*
7. *Review of Economics and Statistics*
8. *Econometrica*
9. *Journal of Development Studies*
10. *Quarterly Journal of Economics*

Source: Barrett, Christopher B., Aliakbar Olia and Dee Van Bailey, "Subdiscipline-Specific Journal Rankings: Whither Applied Economics?," *Applied Economics*, 32: 239-252, (February 10, 2000).

★2190★
Top ranked economic history journals

Ranking basis/background: According to *Applied Economics* research of journals by subdiscipline. **Number listed:** 10.

1. *Journal of Economic History*
2. *Economic History Review*
3. *Explorations in Economic History*
4. *American Economic Review*
5. *Business History Review*
6. *Journal of Political Economics*
7. *Agricultural History Review*
8. *Economic Journal*
9. *Past Present*
10. *Social History*

Source: Barrett, Christopher B., Aliakbar Olia and Dee Van Bailey, "Subdiscipline-Specific Journal Rankings: Whither Applied Economics?," *Applied Economics*, 32: 239-252, (February 10, 2000).

★2191★
Top ranked economic systems journals

Ranking basis/background: According to *Applied Economics* research of journals by subdiscipline. **Number listed:** 10.

1. *Journal of Comparative Economics*
2. *American Economic Review*
3. *Econometrica*
4. *Review of Economic Studies*
5. *Economic Journal*
6. *Journal of Political Economics*
7. *Quarterly Journal of Economics*
8. *Rand Journal of Economics*
9. *Review of Economics and Statistics*
10. *Economica*

Source: Barrett, Christopher B., Aliakbar Olia and Dee Van Bailey, "Subdiscipline-Specific Journal Rankings: Whither Applied Economics?," *Applied Economics*, 32: 239-252, (February 10, 2000).

★2192★
Top ranked financial economics journals

Ranking basis/background: According to *Applied Economics* research of journals by subdiscipline. **Number listed:** 10.

1. *Journal of Financial Economics*
2. *Journal of Finance*
3. *Journal of Futures Markets*
4. *Journal of Business*
5. *Journal of Political Economics*
6. *Econometrica*
7. *American Economic Review*
8. *Journal of Financial and Quantitative Analysis*
9. *Rand Journal of Economics*
10. *Journal of Economic Theory*

Source: Barrett, Christopher B., Aliakbar Olia and Dee Van Bailey, "Subdiscipline-Specific Journal Rankings: Whither Applied Economics?," *Applied Economics*, 32: 239-252, (February 10, 2000).

★2193★
Top ranked health, education, and welfare journals

Ranking basis/background: According to *Applied Economics* research of journals by subdiscipline. **Number listed:** 10.

1. *Journal of Economic Education*
2. *American Economic Review*
3. *Journal of Political Economics*
4. *Journal of Economic Literature*
5. *Journal of Human Resources*
6. *Review of Economics and Statistics*
7. *Econometrica*
8. *Industrial and Labor Relations Review*
9. *Review of Economic Studies*
10. *Economic Inquiry*

Source: Barrett, Christopher B., Aliakbar Olia and Dee Van Bailey, "Subdiscipline-Specific Journal Rankings: Whither Applied Economics?," *Applied Economics*, 32: 239-252, (February 10, 2000).

★2194★
Top ranked industrial organization journals

Ranking basis/background: According to *Applied Economics* research of journals by subdiscipline. **Number listed:** 10.

1. *Rand Journal of Economics*
2. *American Economic Review*
3. *Journal of Law and Economics*
4. *Journal of Political Economics*
5. *Econometrica*
6. *Quarterly Journal of Economics*
7. *Review of Economic Studies*
8. *Journal of Economic Theory*
9. *Journal of Financial Economics*
10. *Review of Economics and Statistics*

Source: Barrett, Christopher B., Aliakbar Olia and Dee Van Bailey, "Subdiscipline-Specific Journal Rankings: Whither Applied Economics?," *Applied Economics*, 32: 239-252, (February 10, 2000).

★2195★
Top ranked international economics journals

Ranking basis/background: According to *Applied Economics* research of journals by subdiscipline. **Number listed:** 10.

1. *Journal of International Economics*
2. *Journal of Political Economics*
3. *American Economic Review*
4. *Quarterly Journal of Economics*
5. *Econometrica*
6. *Economic Journal*
7. *Journal of Monetary Economics*
8. *Review of Economic Studies*
9. *Canadian Journal of Economics*
10. *International Economic Review*

Source: Barrett, Christopher B., Aliakbar Olia and Dee Van Bailey, "Subdiscipline-Specific Journal Rankings: Whither Applied Economics?," *Applied Economics*, 32: 239-252, (February 10, 2000).

★2196★
Top ranked labor and demographic economics journals

Ranking basis/background: According to *Applied Economics* research of journals by subdiscipline. **Number listed:** 10.
1. *Industrial and Labor Relations Review*
2. *Monthly Labor Review*
3. *American Economic Review*
4. *Journal of Political Economics*
5. *Industrial Relations*
6. *Journal of Human Resources*
7. *Review of Economics and Statistics*
8. *Journal of Labor Research*
9. *Econometrica*
10. *Quarterly Journal of Economics*

Source: Barrett, Christopher B., Aliakbar Olia and Dee Van Bailey, "Subdiscipline-Specific Journal Rankings: Whither Applied Economics?," *Applied Economics*, 32: 239-252, (February 10, 2000).

★2197★
Top ranked law and economics journals

Ranking basis/background: According to *Applied Economics* research of journals by subdiscipline. **Number listed:** 10.
1. *Public Choice*
2. *American Economic Review*
3. *Journal of Political Economics*
4. *Journal of Law and Economics*
5. *American Political Science Review*
6. *Econometrica*
7. *Journal of Public Economics*
8. *National Tax Journal*
9. *Rand Journal of Economics*
10. *Quarterly Journal of Economics*

Source: Barrett, Christopher B., Aliakbar Olia and Dee Van Bailey, "Subdiscipline-Specific Journal Rankings: Whither Applied Economics?," *Applied Economics*, 32: 239-252, (February 10, 2000).

★2198★
Top ranked mathematical and quantitative methods journals

Ranking basis/background: According to *Applied Economics* research of journals by subdiscipline. **Number listed:** 10.
1. *Econometrica*
2. *Journal of Economic Theory*
3. *Review of Economic Studies*
4. *Journal of Econometrics*
5. *American Economic Review*
6. *Journal of Political Economics*
7. *Journal of American Statistical Assn.*
8. *International Economic Review*
9. *Annals of Mathematical Statistics*
10. *Annals of Statistics*

Source: Barrett, Christopher B., Aliakbar Olia and Dee Van Bailey, "Subdiscipline-Specific Journal Rankings: Whither Applied Economics?," *Applied Economics*, 32: 239-252, (February 10, 2000).

★2199★
Top ranked microeconomics and monetary economics journals

Ranking basis/background: According to *Applied Economics* research of journals by subdiscipline. **Number listed:** 10.
1. *Journal of Political Economics*
2. *Journal of Monetary Economics*
3. *American Economic Review*
4. *Econometrica*
5. *Journal of Money, Credit & Banking*
6. *Journal of Finance*
7. *Quarterly Journal of Economics*
8. *Brookings Papers on Economic Activity*
9. *Journal of Economic Theory*
10. *Carnegie-Rochester Conference Series on Public Policy*

Source: Barrett, Christopher B., Aliakbar Olia and Dee Van Bailey, "Subdiscipline-Specific Journal Rankings: Whither Applied Economics?," *Applied Economics*, 32: 239-252, (February 10, 2000).

★2200★
Top ranked microeconomics journals

Ranking basis/background: According to *Applied Economics* research of journals by subdiscipline. **Number listed:** 10.
1. *Journal of Economic Theory*
2. *Econometrica*
3. *Review of Economic Studies*
4. *Journal of Political Economics*
5. *American Economic Review*
6. *Journal of Mathematical Economics*
7. *Quarterly Journal of Economics*
8. *Rand Journal of Economics*
9. *International Economic Review*
10. *International Journal of Game Theory*

Source: Barrett, Christopher B., Aliakbar Olia and Dee Van Bailey, "Subdiscipline-Specific Journal Rankings: Whither Applied Economics?," *Applied Economics*, 32: 239-252, (February 10, 2000).

★2201★
Top ranked public economics journals

Ranking basis/background: According to *Applied Economics* research of journals by subdiscipline. **Number listed:** 10.
1. *Public Choice*
2. *American Economic Review*
3. *Journal of Public Economics*
4. *Journal of Political Economics*
5. *Econometrica*
6. *Journal of Law of Economics*
7. *American Political Science Review*
8. *Quarterly Journal of Economics*
9. *National Tax Journal*
10. *Review of Economic Studies*

Source: Barrett, Christopher B., Aliakbar Olia and Dee Van Bailey, "Subdiscipline-Specific Journal Rankings: Whither Applied Economics?," *Applied Economics*, 32: 239-252, (February 10, 2000).

★2202★
Top ranked urban, rural and regional economics journals

Ranking basis/background: According to *Applied Economics* research of journals by subdiscipline. **Number listed:** 10.
1. *Journal of Urban Economics*
2. *American Economic Review*
3. *Journal of Regional Science*
4. *Journal of Political Economics*
5. *Review of Economics and Statistics*
6. *Econometrica*
7. *Urban Studies*
8. *Journal of Public Economics*
9. *Regional Science and Urban Economics*
10. *Land Economics*

Source: Barrett, Christopher B., Aliakbar Olia and Dee Van Bailey, "Subdiscipline-Specific Journal Rankings: Whither Applied Economics?," *Applied Economics*, 32: 239-252, (February 10, 2000).

★2203★
United Kingdom universities contributing the most papers in the field of economics and business, 1993-97

Ranking basis/background: Total number of papers from 1993 to 1997 and average number of citations per paper. **Remarks:** Original source: United Kingdom University Indicators of Diskette, 1981-97. **Number listed:** 5.
1. University College London, with 173 papers; and an average of 2.23 citations per paper
2. University of Oxford, 327; 2.13
3. University of Sussex, 103; 1.92
4. Birkbeck College, 101; 1.82
5. London University, 963; 1.80

Source: "United Kingdom: High-Impact Universities in Economics & Business, 1993-97," *What's Hot in Research,* http://www.isinet.com/whatshot/whatshot.html, Institute for Scientific Information, (February 16, 1999).

ECONOMICS, GRADUATE

★2204★
Economics Ph.D. programs by number of citations of top economist graduates, 1971-92

Ranking basis/background: Total number of citations of top economist graduates, based on a citation analysis of 250 economists at U.S. universities during the period 1971-92. **Number listed:** 15.
1. Harvard University, with 77,324 citations
2. Massachusetts Institute of Technology, 60,030
3. University of Chicago, 55,860
4. Yale University, 16,362
5. University of California, Berkeley, 12,160
6. Carnegie Mellon University, 11,088
7. Princeton University, 11,063
8. Northwestern University, 9,801
9. Stanford University, 9,435
10. University of Minnesota, 7,605
11. Johns Hopkins University, 7,391
12. Columbia University, 7,058
13. University of Wisconsin, 6,649
14. University of Michigan, 5,278
15. University of Pennsylvania, 4,883

Source: Medoff, Marshall, "A Citation-Based Analysis of Economists and Economics Programs," *The American Economist,* pp. 46-59, (Spring 1996).

★2205★
Economics Ph.D. programs by number of citations per top economist graduate, 1971-92

Ranking basis/background: Number of citations per top economist graduate, based on a citation analysis of 250 economists at U.S. universities during the period 1971-92. **Number listed:** 15.
1. University of Chicago, with 1,801.93 citations per top economist graduate
2. Northwestern University, 1,633.50
3. Harvard University, 1,546.48
4. Columbia University, 1,411.60
5. Carnegie Mellon University, 1,386.00
6. University of Wisconsin, 1,329.80
7. University of Michigan, 1,319.50
8. Massachusetts Institute of Technology, 1,305.00

ECONOMICS, GRADUATE

9. University of Minnesota, 1,267.50
10. Johns Hopkins University, 1,231.83
11. Princeton University, 1,229.22
12. University of Pennsylvania, 1,220.75
13. University of California, Berkeley, 1,105.45
14. Yale University, 1,090.80
15. Stanford University, 1,048.33

Source: Medoff, Marshall, "A Citation-Based Analysis of Economists and Economics Programs," *The American Economist*, pp. 46-59, (Spring 1996).

★2206★
Economics Ph.D. programs by number of top economist graduates, 1971-92

Ranking basis/background: Total number of top economist graduates, based on a citation analysis of 250 economists at U.S. universities during the period 1971-92. **Number listed:** 15.

1. Harvard University, with 50 top economist graduates
2. Massachusetts Institute of Technology, 46
3. University of Chicago, 31
4. Yale University, 15
5. University of California, Berkeley, 11
6. Princeton University, 9
6. Stanford University, 9
8. Carnegie Mellon University, 8
9. Northwestern University, 6
9. University of Minnesota, 6
9. Johns Hopkins University, 6
12. Columbia University, 5
12. University of Wisconsin, 5
14. University of Michigan, 4
14. University of Pennsylvania, 4

Source: Medoff, Marshall, "A Citation-Based Analysis of Economists and Economics Programs," *The American Economist*, pp. 46-59, (Spring 1996).

★2207★
Most effective economics research-doctorate programs as evaluated by the National Research Council

Ranking basis/background: From a survey of nearly 8,000 faculty members conducted in the spring of 1993. Respondents were asked to rate programs in their field on "effectiveness of program in educating research scholars/scientists." **Remarks:** See *Chronicle* article for more details. Scores of 3.5-5.0 indicate "extremely effective;" 2.5-3.49 "reasonably effective;" 1.5-2.49 "minimally effective;" and 0.0-1.49 "not effective." Programs also ranked by "scholarly quality of program faculty." **Number listed:** 107.

1. Massachusetts Institute of Technology, with an effectiveness rating of 4.71
2. Princeton University, 4.69
3. University of Chicago, 4.63
4. Stanford University, 4.58
5. Harvard University, 4.33
6. University of Minnesota, 4.08
7. University of California, Berkeley, 4.05
8. Northwestern University, 4.04
9. Yale University, 4.01
10. University of Rochester, 3.96

Source: "Rankings of Research-Doctorate Programs in 41 Disciplines at 274 Institutions," *The Chronicle of Higher Education* 42: A21-A30 (September 21, 1995).

★2208★
Origin of doctorate for dissertation chairs in economics

Ranking basis/background: Number of dissertations chaired at doctoral origin of economics faculty. **Number listed:** 30.

1. Harvard University, with 70.9 dissertations chaired
2. Massachusetts Institute of Technology, 70.4
3. University of Chicago, 51.7
4. Stanford University, 37.9
5. Princeton University, 30.7
6. Northwestern University, 28.5
7. University of California, Berkeley, 28.4
8. Yale University, 25.9
9. University of Minnesota, 17.8
10. Columbia University, 15.5

Source: Pieper, Paul J. and Rachel A. Willis, "The Doctoral Origins of Economics Faculty and the Education of New Economics Doctorates," *Journal of Economic Education*, pp. 80-88, (Winter 1999).

★2209★
Origin of doctorate for economics faculty at Ph.D.-granting institutions

Ranking basis/background: Doctoral school of economics faculty. **Number listed:** 75.

1. Harvard University
2. Massachusetts Institute of Technology
3. University of Chicago
4. University of California, Berkeley
5. Stanford University
6. Yale University
7. University of Wisconsin
8. University of Minnesota
9. Princeton University
10. Columbia University
11. University of Pennsylvania
12. Northwestern University
13. University of Michigan
14. Cornell University
15. University of Rochester

Source: Pieper, Paul J. and Rachel A. Willis, "The Doctoral Origins of Economics Faculty and the Education of New Economics Doctorates," *Journal of Economic Education*, pp. 80-88, (Winter 1999).

★2210★
Origin of doctorate for economics faculty at Ph.D.-granting institutions, by Ph.D. equivalents produced

Ranking basis/background: Number of Ph.D. equivalents produced at doctoral origin of economics faculty. **Number listed:** 69.

1. Harvard University, with 82.6 Ph.D. equivalents produced
2. Massachusetts Institute of Technology, 75.0
3. University of Chicago, 52.1
4. University of California, Berkeley, 45.2
5. Stanford University, 42.3
6. Yale University, 39.3
7. University of Wisconsin, 33.4
8. University of Minnesota, 29.3
9. Princeton University, 28.0
10. Columbia University, 27.8
11. Northwestern University, 24.4
12. University of Pennsylvania, 22.1
13. University of Michigan, 20.2
14. University of Rochester, 16.5
15. Cornell University, 13.6

Source: Pieper, Paul J. and Rachel A. Willis, "The Doctoral Origins of Economics Faculty and the Education of New Economics Doctorates," *Journal of Economic Education*, pp. 80-88, (Winter 1999).

★2211★
Private, 4-year undergraduate colleges and universities producing the most Ph.D.'s in economics, 1920-1990

Ranking basis/background: Number of doctoral degrees granted to graduates of 914 private, 4-year U.S. undergraduate colleges and universities. Medical, law, and other professional, non-doctoral degrees are not included. **Remarks:** Original source: Office of Scientific and Engineering Personnel of the National Research Council. Report contains 50 other tables detailing the distribution of doctoral recipients by field of study over various time frames. **Number listed:** 311.

1. Oberlin College, with 172 Ph.D.'s
2. Swarthmore College, 161
3. Amherst College, 113
4. Williams College, 101
5. Wesleyan University, 76
6. Wellesley College, 74
7. Carleton College, 72
8. Grinnell College, 70
9. Pomona College, 68
10. Reed College, 62
11. Ohio Wesleyan University, 59
12. Haverford College, 51
13. Smith College, 48
14. College of Wooster, 45
15. Berea College, 41
15. University of Richmond, 41
17. Santa Clara University, 39
17. Occidental College, 39
17. Colorado College, 39
17. Barnard College, 39
17. Vassar College, 39

Source: *Baccalaureate Origins of Doctorate Recipients 7th ed.*, Franklin & Marshall College, March 1993.

★2212★
Private, 4-year undergraduate colleges and universities producing the most Ph.D.'s in economics, 1981-1990

Ranking basis/background: Number of doctoral degrees granted to graduates of 914 private 4-year U.S. undergraduate colleges and universities. Medical, law, and other professional, non-doctoral degrees are not included. **Remarks:** Original source: Office of Scientific and Engineering Personnel of the National Research Council. Report contains 50 other tables detailing the distribution of doctoral recipients by field of study over various time frames. **Number listed:** 325.

1. Swarthmore College, with 47 Ph.D.'s
2. Oberlin College, 38
3. Williams College, 28
4. Wesleyan University, 27
5. Pomona College, 22
5. Wellesley College, 22
7. Amherst College, 18
7. Carleton College, 18
9. Bucknell University, 17
9. Grinnell College, 17
11. Reed College, 15
12. Smith College, 14
13. Haverford College, 13
13. La Salle University, 13
13. Vassar College, 13
16. Kalamazoo College, 12
16. Bowdoin College, 12

Source: *Baccalaureate Origins of Doctorate Recipients, 7th ed.*, Franklin & Marshall College, March 1993.

★2213★
Top economics research-doctorate programs as evaluated by the National Research Council

Ranking basis/background: From a survey of nearly 8,000 faculty members conducted in the spring of 1993. Respondents were asked to rate programs in their field on "scholarly quality of program faculty." When more than one program had the samescore, the council averaged the rank order and gave each program the same rank number (if three programs tied for the top position, each received a rank of 2). **Remarks:** See *Chronicle* article for more details. Scores of 4.01 and above indicate "distinguished;" 3.0-4.0 "strong;" 2.51-3.0 "good;" 2.0-2.5 "adequate;" 1.0-1.99 "marginal;" and 0.0-0.99 "not sufficient for doctoral education." Programs also ranked by "effectiveness of program in educating research scholars/scientists." **Number listed:** 107.
1. University of Chicago, with a quality rating of 4.95
1. Harvard University, 4.95
3. Massachusetts Institute of Technology, 4.93
4. Stanford University, 4.92
5. Princeton University, 4.84
6. Yale University, 4.70
7. University of California, Berkeley, 4.55
8. University of Pennsylvania, 4.43
9. Northwestern University, 4.39
10. University of Minnesota, 4.22
11. University of California, Los Angeles, 4.12
12. Columbia University, 4.07
13. University of Michigan, 4.03
14. University of Rochester, 4.01
15. University of Wisconsin, Madison, 3.93

Source: "Rankings of Research-Doctorate Programs in 41 Disciplines at 274 Institutions," *The Chronicle of Higher Education* 42: A21-A30 (September 21, 1995).

★2214★
Undergraduate institutions with the most graduates who received Ph.D.s in economics, 1920-1984

Ranking basis/background: Based on responses to questionnaires sent to nine liberal arts colleges (Amherst, Haverford, Middlebury, Oberlin, Smith, Swarthmore, Wellesley, Wesleyan, and Williams), each a large supplier of entering Ph.D. students, asking about their economics curricula, students, and faculty. Number of graduates for 1975-1984 also included. **Number listed:** 17.
1. Oberlin College, with 150
2. Swarthmore College, 127
3. Amherst College, 104
4. Williams College, 82
5. Wesleyan University, 65
6. Carleton College, 61
6. Grinnell College, 61
6. Wellesley College, 61
9. Ohio Wesleyan University, 58
10. Pomona College, 56

Source: Kasper, Hirschel, et al., "The Education of Economists: From Undergraduate to Graduate Study," *Journal of Economic Literature* 29: 1088-1109 (September 1991).

ECONOMICS, GRADUATE–CANADA

★2215★
Canadian universities publishing the most papers in the fields of economics and business, 1992-96

Ranking basis/background: For each university, total number of papers published. **Remarks:** Original source: ISI's *Canadian University Indicators on Diskette, 1981-97*. **Number listed:** 5.
1. University of Montreal, with 265 papers
2. University of Western Ontario, 187
3. Queen's University, 163
4. McMaster University, 161
5. Simon Fraser University, 112

Source: "Canadian Universities: Highest Impact in Economics and Business, 1992-96," *Institute for Scientific Information: What's Hot*, March 9, 1998.

ECONOMICS–REAL ESTATE
See: **Real Estate**

EDUCATION
See also: **Higher Education School Districts & School Systems Schools, Elementary & Secondary Teacher Education**

★2216★
Most influential African Americans in education

Ranking basis/background: Alphabetical listing compiled by the DuSable Museum of African American History. **Number listed:** 6.
  Mary McLeod Bethune, educator
  John Hope Franklin, historian
  Henry Louis Gates Jr., scholar-author
  Benjamin Mays, educator
  Booker T. Washington, educator
  Cornel West, scholar-author

Source: Moffett, Nancy, "Voices of Power," *Chicago Sun-Times*, February 2, 2000, p. 39.

★2217★
Pivotal events in education during the 20th century

Ranking basis/background: Education events as compiled by Ben Brodinsky from *EdPress News*. **Number listed:** 10.
1. G.I. Bill of Rights
2. Desegregation
3. Education of All Handicapped Act
4. Federal support
5. Innovative thoughts
6. Standardized testing
7. Reading instruction
8. Computers in the classroom
9. Teacher organizations
10. Public high schools

Source: Brodinsky, Ben, "Top 10 Education Events of the 20th Century," *The Education Digest*, April 1999, pp. 4-7.

★2218★
Radcliffe Institute for Advanced Study fellowship recipient in the field of education, 2000-01

Ranking basis/background: Recipient and institutional affiliation of the Radcliffe Institute for Advanced study fellowship for pursuit of advanced work across a wide range of academic disciplines, professions, and creative arts. **Number listed:** 1.
  Annie Rogers, Harvard University

Source: "The Radcliffe Institute for Advanced Study," *The Chronicle of Higher Education*, 46: A59, (June 2, 2000).

★2219★
U.S. universities publishing the most papers in the field of education, 1994-98

Ranking basis/background: Number of papers published in the field of education over a five-year period, and percent of field based on each universities percentage of 12,828 papers entered in the ISI database from ISI-indexed education journals. **Number listed:** 5.
1. University of Wisconsin, Madison, with 215 papers; 1.68% of field
2. University of Georgia, 196; 1.53%
3. University of Michigan, Ann Arbor, 166; 1.29%
4. Indiana University, 153; 1.19%
5. University of California, Los Angeles, 146; 1.14%

Source: "Education: Most Prolific U.S. Universities, 1994-98," *What's Hot in Research* (http://www.isinet.com/isi/hot/research) *Institute for Scientific Information*, June 12, 2000.

★2220★
U.S. universities with the greatest impact in education, 1993-97

Ranking basis/background: For each university, total number of citations divided by number of published articles during the same time period. **Remarks:** Original source: *National Science Indicators on Diskette, 1981-97* **Number listed:** 6.
1. University of Michigan, with 2.51 citations per paper; 186 total papers
2. Michigan State University, 2.48; 124
3. Stanford University, 2.22; 142
4. University of Maryland, College Park, 1.78; 140
4. University of Illinois, Urbana-Champaign, 1.78; 147
6. Purdue University, 1.75; 136

Source: "Education: High-Impact U.S. Universities, 1993-97," *What's Hot*, October 26, 1998.

★2221★
U.S. universities with the greatest impact in education, 1994-98

Ranking basis/background: Total number of education papers published from each university and average number of citations per paper between 1994 and 1998. **Remarks:** Original source: University Science Indicators on Diskette, 1981-98. **Number listed:** 5.
1. Stanford University, with 126 education papers; 2.25 citations per paper
2. University of Michigan, 166; 2.14
3. Michigan State University, 113; 2.11
4. Vanderbilt University, 100; 2.03
5. University of California, Los Angeles, 146; 1.99

EDUCATION—FINANCIAL SUPPORT

Source: "Education: High-Impact U.S. Universities, 1994-98," *What's Hot in Research* (http://www.isinet.com/hot/research) Institute for Scientific Information, February 7, 2000.

★2222★
U.S. universities with the greatest impact in education, 1995-99

Ranking basis/background: Average citations per paper from the top 100 federally funded U.S. universities that had at least 50 published papers in ISI indexed education journals. Also includes total number of papers published during the five year period. **Number listed:** 5.
1. University of Pittsburgh, with 88 papers; 2.68 citations per paper
2. Vanderbilt University, 105; 2.44
3. University of Illinois, Chicago, 91; 2.07
4. Purdue University, 130; 2.05
5. University of Wisconsin, Madison, 210; 1.96

Source: "Education: High Impact U.S. Universities, 1995-99," *What's Hot in Research* (http://www.isinet.com/isi/hot/research) Institute for Scientific Information.

★2223★
U.S. universities with the highest concentration of education papers published, 1994-98

Ranking basis/background: Total number of education papers published from each university and percentage they comprise of university's total papers between 1994 and 1998. **Remarks:** Original source: University Science Indicators on Diskette, 1981-98. **Number listed:** 5.
1. Lehigh University, with 48 education papers; 2.82% of university's total papers
2. University of Georgia, 196; 2.41%
3. University of Oregon, 54; 1.85%
4. Utah State University, 36; 1.65%
5. University of New Hampshire, 29; 1.60%

Source: "U.S. Universities with Highest Concentrations in Education, 1994-98," *What's Hot in Research* (http://www.isinet.com/hot/research) Institute for Scientific Information, September 27, 1999.

Related Information

★2224★
Berres, Michael S., et. al., *Creating Tomorrow's Schools Today: Stories of Inclusion, Change, and Renewal*, Teachers College Press, 1996.
Remarks: Provides case studies of three stories of educational change: Seattle's Lawton Elementary School; a partnership between the University of Oregon and South Valley Elementary School; and Souhegan High School in New Hampshire.

★2225★
Digest of Education Statistics, National Center for Education Statistics, Annual.
Remarks: Gives statistics and other data related to education in the United States for elementary and secondary schools as well as for institutions of higher education. A core statistical source.

★2226★
Pellegrino, James W., Lee R. Jones and Karen J. Mitchel, editors, *Grading the Nation's Report Card: Evaluating NAEP and Transforming the Assessment of Educational Progress*, National Academy Press, 1999.
Remarks: Examines school system factors that influence student achievement and recommends strategies for improving NAEP's effectiveness.

EDUCATION–FINANCIAL SUPPORT
See also: **Colleges & Universities–Financial Support & Expenditures Expenditures per Pupil Schools, Elementary & Secondary–Revenue**

★2227★
2002 budget request for adult and vocational education

Ranking basis/background: Based on the U.S. government's proposed fiscal 2002 appropriations for adult and vocational programs. **Number listed:** 4.
- Adult education with $556,060,000
- Vocational education: State grants, $1,100,000,000
- Vocational education: Tech-Prep education, $106,000,000
- Tribally controlled vocational education, $5,600,000

Source: "Bush's Fiscal 2002 Budget Plan for Higher Education and Science," *The Chronicle of Higher Education*, 47: A36-A37, (April 20, 2001).

★2228★
2002 budget request for education research and statistics

Ranking basis/background: Based on the U.S. government's proposed fiscal 2002 appropriations for education research and statistics. **Number listed:** 2.
- Education research, with $188,067,000
- Education statistics, $85,000,000

Source: "Bush's Fiscal 2002 Budget Plan for Higher Education and Science," *The Chronicle of Higher Education*, 47: A36-A37, (April 20, 2001).

★2229★
2002 budget request for miscellaneous education programs

Ranking basis/background: Based on the U.S. government's proposed fiscal 2002 appropriations for miscellaneous education programs. **Number listed:** 10.
- State grants for improving teacher quality, with $2,600,000,000
- Teacher training in technology, $0
- Teacher Quality Enhancement Grants, $54,000,000
- Reading and literacy grants, $0
- Office for Civil Rights, $79,934,000
- Inspector General, $38,720,000
- Fund for the Improvement of Postsecondary Education, $51,200,000
- Fees for Advanced Placement Tests, $22,000,000
- Women's education equity, $0
- Learning Anytime Anywhere Partnerships, $0

Source: "Bush's Fiscal 2002 Budget Plan for Higher Education and Science," *The Chronicle of Higher Education*, 47: A36-A37, (April 20, 2001).

★2230★
Fiscal 2002 requested budget as compared with Fiscal 2001 budget for other agencies

Ranking basis/background: Based on the U.S. government's proposed fiscal 2002 budget request as compared with the fiscal 2001 budget. **Number listed:** 9.
- National Institutes of Health, with 13.4%
- National Science Foundation: research, 0.5% decrease
- Agriculture Department: cooperative extension, 4.4% decrease
- Agriculture Department: cooperative research, 19.4%
- Energy Department: high-energy and nuclear physics, 0.9%
- Energy Department: basic energy sciences, 1.3%
- National Endowment for the Humanities, 0.2%
- National Endowment for the Arts, 0.2%
- AmeriCorps, 2.8%

Source: "Bush's Fiscal 2002 Budget Plan for Higher Education and Science," *The Chronicle of Higher Education*, 47: A36-A37, (April 20, 2001).

★2231★
Fiscal 2002 requested budget as compared with Fiscal 2001 budget for the Education Department

Ranking basis/background: Based on the U.S. government's proposed fiscal 2002 budget requested in the Department of Education as compared with the fiscal 2001 budget. **Number listed:** 17.
- Pell Grants, with 11.4%
- Supplemental Grants, 0.0%
- Work-Study, 0.0%
- Perkins Loans, 0.0%
- Leveraging Educational Assistance Partnership, 0.0%
- Federal Administration Direct Loan Program, 1.3%
- Aid to historically black colleges, 6.5%
- Aid to Hispanic-serving institutions, 5.8%
- Tech-prep education, 0.0%
- TRIO programs for disadvantaged students, 6.8%
- Education research, 1.3%
- Education statistics, 6.3%
- Office for Civil Rights, 5.4%
- Fund for the Improvement of Postsecondary Education, 65.1% decrease
- Learning Anytime Anywhere Partnerships, 100.0% decrease
- GEAR UP, 23.1% decrease
- Teacher Quality Enhancement Grants, 44.9%

Source: "Bush's Fiscal 2002 Budget Plan for Higher Education and Science," *The Chronicle of Higher Education*, 47: A36-A37, (April 20, 2001).

★2232★
Proposed fiscal 2002 appropriations for institutional assistance

Ranking basis/background: Based on the U.S. government's proposed fiscal 2002 appropriations for institutional assistance. **Number listed:** 7.
- Aid to historically black colleges, with $245,000,000

Institutional support, $73,000,000
Hispanic-serving institutions, $72,500,000
Tribal colleges, $15,000,000
College-housing and academic-facilities loans, $762,000,000
Interest-subsidy grants, $5,000,000
International education, $78,022,000

Source: "Bush's Fiscal 2002 Budget Plan for Higher Education and Science," *The Chronicle of Higher Education*, 47: A36-A37, (April 20, 2001).

★2233★
State tax expenditures, 1999-2000

Ranking basis/background: Percentage of state tax dollars spent on each area. **Remarks:** Original source: National Association of State Budget Officers. **Number listed:** 7.
1. Elementary and secondary education, with 35.5%
2. Medicaid, 14.6%
3. Higher education, 13.0%
4. Corrections, 6.9%
5. Public assistance, 2.5%
6. Transportation, 0.7%
7. Other, 26.8%

Source: Schmidt, Peter, "State Budgets Indicate Lean Times for Public Colleges," *The Chronicle of Higher Education*, 47: A21-A22, (February 2, 2001).

EDUCATION–INTERNATIONAL

★2234★
Japan's ten great educators

Ranking basis/background: Educators are those who were individualists and strived to counteract the tendency of Japanese education to produce uniformity. All helped to correct and enrich Japanese education. **Number listed:** 10.

Fukuzawa Yukichi
Mori Arinori
Naruse Jinzo
Uchimura Kanzo
Nitobe Inazo
Tsuda Ume
Sawayanagi Masataro
Shimonaka Yasaburo
Nambara Shigeru
Munakata Seiya

Source: Duke, Benjamin C., *Ten Great Educators of Modern Japan*, University of Tokyo Press, 1989.

EDUCATION PERIODICALS

★2235★
Education and educational research journals by citation impact, 1981-99

Ranking basis/background: Impact factor calculated by taking the number of current citations to source items published and dividing it by the number of articles published in the journal during that time period. **Number listed:** 10.
1. *Reviews in Educational Research*, with a 27.88 impact factor
2. *Reading Research Quarterly*, 17.93
3. *American Educational Research Journal*, 14.37
4. *Sociology of Education*, 12.88
5. *Harvard Education Review*, 12.03
6. *Reviews of Research in Education*, 10.45
7. *Journal of Educational Statistics*, 8.01
8. *Journal of Reading Behavior*, 7.11
9. *ECTJ-Education, Communication, Technology Journal*, 7.02
10. *Resource for Teaching of English*, 6.73

Source: "Journals Ranked by Impact: Education & Educational Research," *What's Hot in Research* (http://www.isinet.com/isi/hot/research) Institute for Scientific Information, October 9, 2000.

★2236★
Education and educational research journals by citation impact, 1995-99

Ranking basis/background: Impact factor calculated by taking the number of current citations to source items published and dividing it by the number of articles published in the journal during that time period. **Number listed:** 10.
1. *Reviews in Educational Research*, with a 6.86 impact factor
2. *American Educational Research Journal*, 5.81
3. *Reviews of Research in Education*, 4.15
4. *Reading Research Quarterly*, 4.14
5. *Journal of Learning Sciences*, 3.53
6. *Sociology of Education*, 3.04
7. *Journal of Reading Behavior*, 2.84
8. *AIDS Education & Prevention*, 2.82
9. *Harvard Education Review*, 2.29
10. *Journal of Research and Science Teaching*, 2.20

Source: "Journals Ranked by Impact: Education & Educational Research," *What's Hot in Research* (http://www.isinet.com/isi/hot/research) Institute for Scientific Information, October 9, 2000.

★2237★
Education and educational research journals by citation impact, 1999

Ranking basis/background: Impact factor calculated by taking the number of current citations to source items published and dividing it by the number of articles published in the journal during that time period. **Number listed:** 10.
1. *Reviews in Educational Research*, with a 3.03 impact factor
2. *Reviews of Research in Education*, 2.50
3. *Reading Research Quarterly*, 1.95
4. *Journal of Learning Sciences*, 1.82
5. *American Educational Research Journal*, 1.50
6. *Harvard Education Review*, 1.26
7. *Journal of American College Health*, 1.16
8. *AIDS Education & Prevention*, 1.06
9. *Journal of Research and Science Teaching*, 1.01
10. *Science Education*, 0.99

Source: "Journals Ranked by Impact: Education & Educational Research," *What's Hot in Research* (http://www.isinet.com/isi/hot/research) Institute for Scientific Information, October 9, 2000.

★2238★
Education and educational research journals with the greatest impact measure

Ranking basis/background: Ratio of citations and recent citable items published. **Remarks:** Original source: *National Science Indicators on Diskette, 1981-97* **Number listed:** 10.
1. *Educational Research*, with a ratio of 4.33
2. *Reviews in Educational Research*, 3.88
3. *Review of Research in Education*, 2.00
4. *American Educational Research Journal*, 1.95
5. *Sociology of Education*, 1.57
6. *AIDS Education & Prevention*, 1.13
7. *Journal of Higher Education*, 1.09
8. *Journal of Educational Statistics*, 1.00
8. *American Journal of Education*, 1.00
10. *Harvard Education Review*, 0.98

Source: "Journals Ranked by Impact: Education & Educational Research," *What's Hot*, July 6, 1998.

EDUCATION, SCHOOLS OF
See: **Teacher Education**

EDUCATIONAL FINANCE
See: **Colleges & Universities–Financial Support & Expenditures Education–Financial Support Expenditures per Pupil Schools, Elementary & Secondary–Revenue**

ELECTRICAL ENGINEERING
See: **Engineering-Electrical/Electronic Engineering, Graduate–Electrical/Electronic**

EMPIRICAL SCIENCES
See: **Physical Sciences, Graduate**

EMPLOYMENT

★2239★
Annual leave days for employees in selected countries

Ranking basis/background: Typical number of annual leave days allowed employees in each country. **Number listed:** 10.
1. Austria, with 30 days
1. Germany, 30
1. Brazil, 30
4. Sweden, 25
5. United Kingdom, 23
6. Belgium, 20
6. Ireland, 20
8. Japan, 16
9. United States, 15
10. Canada, 10

Source: Reilly, Shannon and Adrienne Lewis, "Annual Leave Varies Around the World," *USA Today*, March 21, 2001, Section B, p. 1B.

★2240★
Best jobs, by career field, 2000

Ranking basis/background: Top jobs in each career field as compiled by *U.S. News & World Report*. **Number listed:** 20.

Agriculture: Plant geneticists
Architecture: Virtual-reality architects

EMPLOYMENT

Communications: Hispanic marketing specialist
Construction: Steel house framer
Cuisine: Supermarkets chefs
Education: Educational consultants
Engineering: Robotics engineers
Fashion: High-tech clothing designer
Finance: Quantitative analysts
Human resources: Talent wizards
Information tech: Chief experience officer
Law: Law practice technologists
Manufacturing: Enterprise Application Integration evangelist
Medicine: Web doctor
Personal Services: Executive coach
Politics: Internet Political Strategists
Privacy: Chief privacy officer
Recreation: Youth soccer coach
Technology: Nanotechnologist
Travel: Adventure travel gurus

Source: Benjamin, Matthew, et. al., "Flip-of-the-Coin Jobs," *U.S. News & World Report*, 128: 72-84, (November 6, 2000).

★2241★
"Blue-collar" jobs considered the least physically demanding

Ranking basis/background: Physical demand rank based on analysis of various aspects of physicality involved in each occupation. **Number listed:** 29.
1. Bus driver, with 142
2. Office machine repairer, 146
3. Guard, 147
4. Electrical equipment repairer, 153
5. Correction officer, 155
6. Precision assembler, 157
7. Automobile assembler, 158
8. Forklift operator, 163
9. Appliance repairer, 166
9. Vending machine repairer, 166
9. Communications equipment mechanic, 166

Source: *Jobs Rated Almanac: The Best and Worst Jobs-250 in All-Ranked by More Than a Dozen Vital Factors Including Salary, Stress, Benefits and More, 5th ed.*, St. Martin's Griffin, 2000.

★2242★
Countries with the highest percentage of workers satisfied with their job

Ranking basis/background: Based on a study conducted by Vancouver-based public opinion firm Ipsos-Reid which polled 9,300 working-age adults in 39 countries. **Number listed:** 5.
1. Denmark, with 61%
2. India, 55%
3. Norway, 54%
4. United States, 50%
5. Ireland, 49%

Source: Boyle, Matthew, "Nothing is Rotten in Denmark," *Fortune*, 143: 242, (February 19, 2001).

★2243★
Countries with the lowest percentage of workers satisfied with their job

Ranking basis/background: Based on a study conducted by Vancouver-based public opinion firm Ipsos-Reid which polled 9,300 working-age adults in 39 countries. **Number listed:** 5.
1. Hungary, with 9%
2. Ukraine, 10%
2. Czech Republic, 10%
4. China, 11%
4. Estonia, 11%

Source: Boyle, Matthew, "Nothing is Rotten in Denmark," *Fortune*, 143: 242, (February 19, 2001).

★2244★
Jobs considered the loneliest

Ranking basis/background: Alphabetical list of jobs that are confining and offer little or no personal interaction. **Number listed:** 20.
- Author (books)
- Automobile assembler
- Automobile painter
- Computer operator
- Computer programmer
- Cook/chef
- Dental laboratory technician
- Dishwasher
- Disk jockey
- Dressmaker
- Drill-press operator
- Guard
- Machine tool operator
- Machinist
- Medical laboratory technician
- Photographic process worker
- Precision assembler
- Shoe maker/repairer
- Software engineer
- Tool-and-die maker

Source: *Jobs Rated Almanac: The Best and Worst Jobs-250 in All-Ranked by More Than a Dozen Vital Factors Including Salary, Stress, Benefits and More, 5th ed.*, St. Martin's Griffin, 2000.

★2245★
Jobs considered the most competitive

Ranking basis/background: Alphabetical list with stress rank, based on 23 different job factors expected to evoke stress. Higher points were given if a particular demand was a major part of the job, lower points for a small part of the job, and no points if the demand was not required normally. **Number listed:** 21.
- Actor, with 213
- Advertising account executive, 235
- Astronaut, 244
- Attorney, 220
- Automobile salesperson, 203
- Baseball player (Major League), 194
- Basketball coach (NCAA), 236
- Basketball player (NBA), 202
- Choreographer, 198
- Congressperson/Senator, 232
- Corporate executive (senior), 248
- Dancer, 219
- Disk jockey, 140
- Fashion model, 204
- Football player (NFL), 242
- Jockey, 237
- Mayor, 238
- Newscaster, 193
- Photojournalist, 233
- President (U.S.), 250
- Race car driver (Indy Class), 247

Source: *Jobs Rated Almanac: The Best and Worst Jobs-250 in All-Ranked by More Than a Dozen Vital Factors Including Salary, Stress, Benefits and More, 5th ed.*, St. Martin's Griffin, 2000.

★2246★
Jobs that are potentially the highest paying

Ranking basis/background: Jobs with incomes in the 90th percentile of the earnings scale in the highest paying jobs. **Number listed:** 30.
1. Basketball player (NBA), with $7,755,000
2. Race car driver (Indy Class), $5,740,000
3. Football player (NFL), $5,156,000
4. Baseball player (Major League), $4,878,000
5. Symphony conductor, $746,000
6. Jockey, $454,000
7. Surgeon, $427,000
8. President (U.S.), $400,000
9. Corporate executive (senior), $320,000
10. Computer consultant, $269,000

Source: *Jobs Rated Almanac: The Best and Worst Jobs-250 in All-Ranked by More Than a Dozen Vital Factors Including Salary, Stress, Benefits and More, 5th ed.*, St. Martin's Griffin, 2000.

★2247★
Jobs with the best environment scores

Ranking basis/background: Environment scores are based on the physical and emotional components of each job. Points were given for each adverse working condition typically encountered, thus the greater the points the worse the rank. **Number listed:** 250.
1. Statistician, with a score of 89.52
2. Mathematician, 89.72
3. Computer systems analyst, 90.78
4. Hospital administrator, 93.14
5. Historian, 136.41
6. Software engineer, 150.00
7. Typist/work processor, 160.64
8. Medical records technician, 165.20
9. Industrial designer, 177.00
10. Actuary, 179.44

Source: *Jobs Rated Almanac: The Best and Worst Jobs-250 in All-Ranked by More Than a Dozen Vital Factors Including Salary, Stress, Benefits and More, 5th ed.*, St. Martin's Griffin, 2000.

★2248★
Jobs with the best income scores

Ranking basis/background: Income scores are computed by adding the estimated mid-level income and the Growth Potential and are rounded to the nearest $1,000. **Number listed:** 250.
1. Basketball player (NBA), with $2,587,264
2. Baseball player (Major League), $1,668,257
3. Football player (NFL), $1,120,478
4. Race car driver (Indy Class), $489,844
5. President (U.S.), $400,000
6. Surgeon, $241,256
7. Corporate executive (senior), $182,442
8. Congressperson/Senator, $157,027
9. Baseball umpire (Major League), $145,149
10. Judge (Federal), $141,015

Source: *Jobs Rated Almanac: The Best and Worst Jobs-250 in All-Ranked by More Than a Dozen Vital Factors Including Salary, Stress, Benefits and More, 5th ed.*, St. Martin's Griffin, 2000.

★2249★
Jobs with the best outlook scores

Ranking basis/background: Point system is based on four factors: unemployment rates in recent years based on an index of one to five (one being very low; five very high); expected employment growth through the year 2005, as forecast by the Department of Labor; potential salary growth; and potential for promotion. **Number listed:** 250.
1. Financial planner, with a score of 533
2. Hospital administrator, 529
3. Website manager, 525
4. Physician assistant, 513
5. Advertising account executive, 503
6. Physician (general practice), 488
7. Computer consultant, 487
8. Meteorologist, 486
9. Veterinarian, 482
10. Highway patrol officer, 473

Educational Rankings Annual • 2002

EMPLOYMENT

Source: *Jobs Rated Almanac: The Best and Worst Jobs-250 in All-Ranked by More Than a Dozen Vital Factors Including Salary, Stress, Benefits and More*, 5th ed., St. Martin's Griffin, 2000.

★2250★
Jobs with the best physical demands scores

Ranking basis/background: Based on data used by the Department of Labor, one point was given for each physical component of the job, such as, lifting, pulling, pushing, standing, walking, stooping, kneeling, crawling, climbing, crouching, or reaching. Points were also given for hazards faced, exposure to weather, the need for stamina, and the work environment. **Number listed:** 250.
1. Statistician, with a score of 3.95
2. Actuary, 3.97
2. Mathematician, 3.97
4. Executive search consultant, 4.00
4. Website manager, 4.00
6. Market research analyst, 4.09
6. Economist, 4.09
8. Accountant, 4.23
9. Advertising account executive, 4.62
10. Bank officer, 4.76

Source: *Jobs Rated Almanac: The Best and Worst Jobs-250 in All-Ranked by More Than a Dozen Vital Factors Including Salary, Stress, Benefits and More*, 5th ed., St. Martin's Griffin, 2000.

★2251★
Jobs with the best security scores

Ranking basis/background: Scores based on three factors: anticipated employment growth or decline up to 2005; recent unemployment rates; and physical hazards which could impair one's ability to work, such as life-threatening job situations. **Number listed:** 250.
1. Web developer, with a score of 158
2. Website manager, 150
3. Computer consultant, 149
4. Software engineer, negative 43
5. Computer systems analyst, negative 56
6. Audiologist, negative 61
7. Biologist, negative 65
8. Attorney, negative 83
8. Mayor, negative 83
10. Agency director (nonprofit), negative 84

Source: *Jobs Rated Almanac: The Best and Worst Jobs-250 in All-Ranked by More Than a Dozen Vital Factors Including Salary, Stress, Benefits and More*, 5th ed., St. Martin's Griffin, 2000.

★2252★
Jobs with the best stress scores

Ranking basis/background: A range of points was assigned for 23 different job factors expected to evoke stress. Higher points were given if a particular demand was a major part of the job, lower points for a small part of the job, and no points if the demand was not required normally. **Number listed:** 250.
1. Medical records technician, with a score of 15.48
2. Janitor, 16.32
3. Forklift operator, 18.18
4. Musical instrument repairer, 18.77
5. Florist, 18.80
6. Actuary, 20.18
7. Appliance repairer, 21.12
8. Medical secretary, 21.14
9. Librarian, 21.40
10. Bookkeeper, 21.46

Source: *Jobs Rated Almanac: The Best and Worst Jobs-250 in All-Ranked by More Than a Dozen Vital Factors Including Salary, Stress, Benefits and More*, 5th ed., St. Martin's Griffin, 2000.

★2253★
Jobs with the greatest potential income for beginners

Ranking basis/background: Potential percentage increases relative to starting and top-level pay. **Number listed:** 31.
1. Race car driver (Indy Class), with 1,584%
2. Football player (NFL), 2,478%
3. Basketball player (NBA), 2,264%
4. Baseball player (Major League), 2,257%
5. Fashion model, 1,836%
6. Symphony conductor, 1,720%
7. Jockey, 1,521%
8. Airplane pilot, 1,231%
9. Dancer, 980%
10. Author (books), 967%

Source: *Jobs Rated Almanac: The Best and Worst Jobs-250 in All-Ranked by More Than a Dozen Vital Factors Including Salary, Stress, Benefits and More*, 5th ed., St. Martin's Griffin, 2000.

★2254★
Jobs with the highest employment growth

Ranking basis/background: Percentage of job opening through the year 2005, according to the Bureau of Labor Statistics and various industry sources. **Number listed:** 24.
1. Website manager, with 200%
2. Web developer, 108%
3. Software engineer, 107%
4. Computer consultant, 99%
5. Computer systems analyst, 94%
6. Paralegal assistant, 62%
7. Physician assistant, 48%
8. Medical records technician, 44%
9. Respiratory therapist, 43%
10. Stockbroker, 41%
10. Dental hygienist, 41%

Source: *Jobs Rated Almanac: The Best and Worst Jobs-250 in All-Ranked by More Than a Dozen Vital Factors Including Salary, Stress, Benefits and More*, 5th ed., St. Martin's Griffin, 2000.

★2255★
Jobs with the highest starting salaries

Ranking basis/background: Average starting salary. **Number listed:** 24.
1. President (U.S.), with $400,000
2. Basketball player (NBA), $328,000
3. Baseball player (Major League), $207,000
4. Football player (NFL), $200,000
5. Congressperson/Senator, $143,000
6. Judge (Federal), $130,000
7. Surgeon, $120,000
8. Baseball umpire (Major League), $83,000
9. Psychiatrist, $64,000
9. Dentist, $64,000

Source: *Jobs Rated Almanac: The Best and Worst Jobs-250 in All-Ranked by More Than a Dozen Vital Factors Including Salary, Stress, Benefits and More*, 5th ed., St. Martin's Griffin, 2000.

★2256★
Jobs with the highest unemployment

Ranking basis/background: Alphabetical list with security rank, which is based on anticipated employment growth or decline up to 2005, recent unemployment rates, and physical hazards. **Number listed:** 27.

Bricklayer, with a security rank of 248
Carpenter, 230
Carpet installer, 234
Compositor/typesetter, 216
Construction machinery operator, 220
Construction worker (laborer), 232
Cowboy, 236
Diary farmer, 239
Dishwasher, 227
Drill-press operator, 241
Drywall applicator/finisher, 249
Electrician, 225
Farmer, 239
Fisherman, 247
Forklift operator, 230
Garbage collector, 250
Glazier, 234
Ironworker, 228
Janitor, 222
Lumberjack, 237
Maid, 222
Plumber, 233
Railroad conductor, 238
Roofer, 222
Roustabout, 242
Sheet metal worker, 221
Stevedore, 225

Source: *Jobs Rated Almanac: The Best and Worst Jobs-250 in All-Ranked by More Than a Dozen Vital Factors Including Salary, Stress, Benefits and More*, 5th ed., St. Martin's Griffin, 2000.

★2257★
Jobs with the longest work weeks

Ranking basis/background: Jobs requiring the most hours of work per week but generally are among the highest paying. **Number listed:** 28.
1. President (U.S.), with 65.00 hours weekly
2. Firefighter, 55.00
2. Corporate executive (senior), 55.00
2. Psychiatrist, 55.00
2. Osteopath, 55.00
2. Physician (general practice), 55.00
2. Rabbi, 55.00
2. Surgeon, 55.00
9. Farmer, 52.50
9. Dairy farmer, 52.50
9. Catholic priest, 52.50
9. Protestant minister, 52.50

Source: *Jobs Rated Almanac: The Best and Worst Jobs-250 in All-Ranked by More Than a Dozen Vital Factors Including Salary, Stress, Benefits and More*, 5th ed., St. Martin's Griffin, 2000.

★2258★
Jobs with the lowest unemployment

Ranking basis/background: Alphabetical list with security rank, which is based on anticipated employment growth or decline up to 2005, recent unemployment rates, and physical hazards. **Number listed:** 31.

Agency director (nonprofit), with a security rank of 10
Agricultural scientist, 30
Airplane pilot, 12
Archeologist, 32
Astronomer, 14
Attorney, 8
Audiologist, 6
Biologist, 7
Chemist, 44
Congressperson/Senator, 15
Conservationist, 34
Dietician, 30
Geologist, 42
Judge (Federal), 13

EMPLOYMENT

Mayor, 8
Meteorologist, 43
Occupational therapist, 21
Oceanographer, 39
Optometrist, 49
Pharmacist, 52
Physical therapist, 21
Physician (general practice), 27
Physician assistant, 17
Physiologist, 36
Podiatrist, 30
President (U.S.), 15
Psychiatrist, 33
Respiratory therapist, 18
Speech pathologist, 20
Surgeon, 28
Zoologist, 37

Source: *Jobs Rated Almanac: The Best and Worst Jobs-250 in All-Ranked by More Than a Dozen Vital Factors Including Salary, Stress, Benefits and More, 5th ed.*, St. Martin's Griffin, 2000.

★2259★
Jobs with the most stringent quotas

Ranking basis/background: Cumulative points scored in three categories: deadlines, quotas and time sensitive-levels. **Number listed:** 33.

1. Corporate executive (senior), with 17.00
2. Stenographer/court reporter, 14.00
2. Compositor/typesetter, 14.00
2. Air traffic controller, 14.00
2. President (U.S.), 14.00
6. Stevedore, 13.00
6. Stockbroker, 13.00
8. Typist/work processor, 12.00
8. Insurance underwriter, 12.00
8. Purchasing agent, 12.00
8. Secretary, 12.00
8. Motion picture editor, 12.00
8. Technical writer, 12.00
8. Social worker, 12.00
8. Teacher, 12.00
8. Author (books), 12.00
8. Nurse (registered), 12.00
8. Reporter (newspaper), 12.00
8. Photojournalist, 12.00
8. Real estate agent, 12.00
8. Public relations executive, 12.00

Source: *Jobs Rated Almanac: The Best and Worst Jobs-250 in All-Ranked by More Than a Dozen Vital Factors Including Salary, Stress, Benefits and More, 5th ed.*, St. Martin's Griffin, 2000.

★2260★
Jobs with the worst environment scores

Ranking basis/background: Environment scores are based on the physical and emotional components of each job. Points were given for each adverse working condition typically encountered, thus the greater the points the worse the rank. **Number listed:** 250.

1. President (U.S.), with a score of 3,630.00
2. Firefighter, 3,314.03
3. Race car driver (Indy Class), 2,522.25
4. Football player (NFL), 2,401.85
5. Taxi driver, 2,317.21
6. Astronaut, 2,270.84
7. Jockey, 2,079.75
8. Surgeon, 1,962.00
9. Police officer, 1,877.85
10. Lumberjack, 1,817.53

Source: *Jobs Rated Almanac: The Best and Worst Jobs-250 in All-Ranked by More Than a Dozen Vital Factors Including Salary, Stress, Benefits and More, 5th ed.*, St. Martin's Griffin, 2000.

★2261★
Jobs with the worst income scores

Ranking basis/background: Income scores are computed by adding the estimated mid-level income and the Growth Potential and are rounded to the nearest $1,000. **Number listed:** 250.

1. Waiter/waitress, with $14,042
2. Dishwasher, $14,058
3. Bartender, $15,067
4. Dressmaker, $16,069
5. Cashier, $16,070
6. Child care worker, $16,075
7. Maid, $16,083
8. Catholic priest, $16,175
9. Actor, $16,608
10. Nurse's aide, $18,092

Source: *Jobs Rated Almanac: The Best and Worst Jobs-250 in All-Ranked by More Than a Dozen Vital Factors Including Salary, Stress, Benefits and More, 5th ed.*, St. Martin's Griffin, 2000.

★2262★
Jobs with the worst outlook scores

Ranking basis/background: Point system is based on four factors: unemployment rates in recent years based on an index of one to five (one being very low; five very high); expected employment growth through the year 2005, as forecast by the Department of Labor; potential salary growth; and potential for promotion. **Number listed:** 250.

1. Dressmaker, with a score of negative 99
2. Shoe maker/repairer, negative 98
3. Drill-press operator, negative 73
4. Lumberjack, negative 70
5. Railroad conductor, negative 66
6. Fisherman, negative 59
7. Computer operator, negative 58
8. Jeweler, negative 56
9. Musical instrument repairers, negative 50
9. Cowboy, negative 50

Source: *Jobs Rated Almanac: The Best and Worst Jobs-250 in All-Ranked by More Than a Dozen Vital Factors Including Salary, Stress, Benefits and More, 5th ed.*, St. Martin's Griffin, 2000.

★2263★
Jobs with the worst physical demands scores

Ranking basis/background: Based on data used by the Department of Labor, one point was given for each physical component of the job, such as, lifting, pulling, pushing, standing, walking, stooping, kneeling, crawling, climbing, crouching, or reaching. Points were also given for hazards faced, exposure to weather, the need for stamina, and the work environment. **Number listed:** 250.

1. Football player (NFL), with a score of 43.73
2. Firefighter, 43.23
3. Cowboy, 41.00
4. Lumberjack, 38.87
5. Basketball player (NBA), 38.00
6. Baseball player (Major League), 37.00
7. Roustabout, 36.89
8. Ironworker, 36.85
9. Garbage collector, 36.55
10. Construction worker (laborer), 36.41

Source: *Jobs Rated Almanac: The Best and Worst Jobs-250 in All-Ranked by More Than a Dozen Vital Factors Including Salary, Stress, Benefits and More, 5th ed.*, St. Martin's Griffin, 2000.

★2264★
Jobs with the worst security scores

Ranking basis/background: Scores based on three factors: anticipated employment growth or decline up to 2005; recent unemployment rates; and physical hazards which could impair one's ability to work, such as life-threatening job situations. **Number listed:** 250.

1. Garbage collector, with a score of negative 446
2. Drywall applicator/finisher, negative 442
3. Bricklayer, negative 438
4. Fisherman, negative 423
5. Football player (NFL), negative 422
5. Basketball player (NBA), negative 422
5. Baseball player (Major League), negative 422
5. Baseball umpire (Major League), negative 422
9. Roustabout, negative 421
10. Drill-press operator, negative 419

Source: *Jobs Rated Almanac: The Best and Worst Jobs-250 in All-Ranked by More Than a Dozen Vital Factors Including Salary, Stress, Benefits and More, 5th ed.*, St. Martin's Griffin, 2000.

★2265★
Jobs with the worst stress scores

Ranking basis/background: A range of points was assigned for 23 different job factors expected to evoke stress. Higher points were given if a particular demand was a major part of the job, lower points for a small part of the job, and no points if the demand was not required normally. **Number listed:** 250.

1. President (U.S.), with a score of 176.55
2. Firefighter, 110.93
3. Corporate executive (senior), 108.62
4. Race car driver (Indy Class), 101.77
5. Taxi driver, 100.49
6. Surgeon, 99.46
7. Astronaut, 99.34
8. Police officer, 93.89
9. Football player (NFL), 92.79
10. Air traffic controller, 83.13

Source: *Jobs Rated Almanac: The Best and Worst Jobs-250 in All-Ranked by More Than a Dozen Vital Factors Including Salary, Stress, Benefits and More, 5th ed.*, St. Martin's Griffin, 2000.

★2266★
Least desirable jobs

Ranking basis/background: Rankings based on cumulative scores in six core job factors: environment, income, outlook, physical demands, security and stress. **Number listed:** 250.

1. Fisherman
2. Roustabout
3. Lumberjack
4. Cowboy
5. Ironworker
6. Garbage collector
7. Construction worker (laborer)
8. Taxi driver
9. Stevedore
10. Welder

Source: *Jobs Rated Almanac: The Best and Worst Jobs-250 in All-Ranked by More Than a Dozen Vital Factors Including Salary, Stress, Benefits and More, 5th ed.*, St. Martin's Griffin, 2000.

Educational Rankings Annual • 2002 — EMPLOYMENT

★2267★
Most desirable jobs
Ranking basis/background: Rankings based on cumulative scores in six core job factors: environment, income, outlook, physical demands, security and stress. **Number listed:** 250.
1. Financial planner
2. Website manager
3. Computer systems analyst
4. Actuary
5. Computer programmer
6. Software engineering
7. Meteorologist
8. Biologist
9. Astronomer
10. Paralegal assistant

Source: *Jobs Rated Almanac: The Best and Worst Jobs-250 in All-Ranked by More Than a Dozen Vital Factors Including Salary, Stress, Benefits and More, 5th ed.*, St. Martin's Griffin, 2000.

★2268★
Most desirable jobs in agriculture
Ranking basis/background: Rankings based on cumulative scores in six core job factors: environment, income, outlook, physical demands, security and stress. **Number listed:** 6.
1. Agricultural scientist
2. Farmer
3. Seaman
4. Dairy farmer
5. Cowboy
6. Fisherman

Source: *Jobs Rated Almanac: The Best and Worst Jobs-250 in All-Ranked by More Than a Dozen Vital Factors Including Salary, Stress, Benefits and More, 5th ed.*, St. Martin's Griffin, 2000.

★2269★
Most desirable jobs in athletics
Ranking basis/background: Rankings based on cumulative scores in six core job factors: environment, income, outlook, physical demands, security and stress. **Number listed:** 8.
1. Basketball coach (NCAA)
2. Sports instructor
3. Baseball player (Major League)
4. Basketball player (NBA)
5. Race car driver (Indy Class)
6. Football player (NFL)
7. Baseball umpire (Major League)
8. Jockey

Source: *Jobs Rated Almanac: The Best and Worst Jobs-250 in All-Ranked by More Than a Dozen Vital Factors Including Salary, Stress, Benefits and More, 5th ed.*, St. Martin's Griffin, 2000.

★2270★
Most desirable jobs in business/finance
Ranking basis/background: Rankings based on cumulative scores in six core job factors: environment, income, outlook, physical demands, security and stress. **Number listed:** 28.
1. Financial planner
2. Paralegal assistant
3. Bank officer
4. Accountant
5. Economist
6. Insurance underwriter
7. Purchasing agent
8. Executive search consultant
9. Market research analyst
10. Bookkeeper

Source: *Jobs Rated Almanac: The Best and Worst Jobs-250 in All-Ranked by More Than a Dozen Vital Factors Including Salary, Stress, Benefits and More, 5th ed.*, St. Martin's Griffin, 2000.

★2271★
Most desirable jobs in communications
Ranking basis/background: Rankings based on cumulative scores in six core job factors: environment, income, outlook, physical demands, security and stress. **Number listed:** 14.
1. Technical writer
2. Editor
3. Broadcast technician
4. Advertising account executive
5. Artist (commercial)
6. Public relations executive
7. Newswriter (radio/TV)
8. Newscaster
9. Author (books)
10. Advertising salesperson
11. Photographer
12. Reporter (newspaper)
13. Disk jockey
14. Photojournalist

Source: *Jobs Rated Almanac: The Best and Worst Jobs-250 in All-Ranked by More Than a Dozen Vital Factors Including Salary, Stress, Benefits and More, 5th ed.*, St. Martin's Griffin, 2000.

★2272★
Most desirable jobs in construction trades
Ranking basis/background: Rankings based on cumulative scores in six core job factors: environment, income, outlook, physical demands, security and stress. **Number listed:** 14.
1. Surveyor
2. Construction foreman
3. Carpet installer
4. Construction machinery operator
5. Plasterer
6. Painter
7. Drywall applicator/finisher
8. Glazier
9. Bricklayer
10. Sheet metal worker
11. Carpenter
12. Roofer
13. Construction worker (laborer)
14. Ironworker

Source: *Jobs Rated Almanac: The Best and Worst Jobs-250 in All-Ranked by More Than a Dozen Vital Factors Including Salary, Stress, Benefits and More, 5th ed.*, St. Martin's Griffin, 2000.

★2273★
Most desirable jobs in healthcare/medicine
Ranking basis/background: Rankings based on cumulative scores in six core job factors: environment, income, outlook, physical demands, security and stress. **Number listed:** 32.
1. Hospital administrator
2. Dietician
3. Audiologist
4. Dental hygienist
5. Physiologist
6. Occupational therapist
7. Speech pathologist
8. Medical technologist
9. Medical records technician
10. Chiropractor

Source: *Jobs Rated Almanac: The Best and Worst Jobs-250 in All-Ranked by More Than a Dozen Vital Factors Including Salary, Stress, Benefits and More, 5th ed.*, St. Martin's Griffin, 2000.

★2274★
Most desirable jobs in math/science
Ranking basis/background: Rankings based on cumulative scores in six core job factors: environment, income, outlook, physical demands, security and stress. **Number listed:** 12.
1. Actuary
2. Meteorologist
3. Biologist
4. Astronomer
5. Statistician
6. Mathematician
7. Physicist
8. Geologist
9. Industrial engineer
10. Chemist
11. Zoologist
12. Oceanographer

Source: *Jobs Rated Almanac: The Best and Worst Jobs-250 in All-Ranked by More Than a Dozen Vital Factors Including Salary, Stress, Benefits and More, 5th ed.*, St. Martin's Griffin, 2000.

★2275★
Most desirable jobs in personal services
Ranking basis/background: Rankings based on cumulative scores in six core job factors: environment, income, outlook, physical demands, security and stress. **Number listed:** 7.
1. Barber
2. Undertaker
3. Cosmetologist
4. Child care worker
5. Chauffeur
6. Maid
7. Taxi driver

Source: *Jobs Rated Almanac: The Best and Worst Jobs-250 in All-Ranked by More Than a Dozen Vital Factors Including Salary, Stress, Benefits and More, 5th ed.*, St. Martin's Griffin, 2000.

★2276★
Most desirable jobs in production/manufacturing
Ranking basis/background: Rankings based on cumulative scores in six core job factors: environment, income, outlook, physical demands, security and stress. **Number listed:** 29.
1. Industrial designer
2. Aerospace engineer
3. Electrical engineer
4. Petroleum engineer
5. Nuclear engineer
6. Civil engineer
7. Mechanical engineer
8. Engineering technician
9. Lithographer/photoengraver
10. Photographic process worker

Source: *Jobs Rated Almanac: The Best and Worst Jobs-250 in All-Ranked by More Than a Dozen Vital Factors Including Salary, Stress, Benefits and More, 5th ed.*, St. Martin's Griffin, 2000.

★2277★
Most desirable jobs in the arts
Ranking basis/background: Rankings based on cumulative scores in six core job factors: environment, income, outlook, physical demands, security and stress. **Number listed:** 15.
1. Motion picture editor

EMPLOYMENT OPPORTUNITIES

2. Architectural drafter
3. Antique dealer
4. Set designer
5. Architect
6. Museum curator
7. Artist (fine art)
8. Fashion designer
9. Symphony conductor
10. Fashion model
11. Musician
12. Actor
13. Singer
14. Choreographer
15. Dancer

Source: *Jobs Rated Almanac: The Best and Worst Jobs-250 in All-Ranked by More Than a Dozen Vital Factors Including Salary, Stress, Benefits and More,* 5th ed., St. Martin's Griffin, 2000.

★2278★
Most desirable jobs in travel/food service

Ranking basis/background: Rankings based on cumulative scores in six core job factors: environment, income, outlook, physical demands, security and stress. **Number listed:** 11.

1. Hotel manager
2. Airplane pilot
3. Flight attendant
4. Ticket agent
5. Travel agent
6. Cook/chef
7. Waiter/waitress
8. Railroad conductor
9. Bartender
10. Truck driver
11. Dishwasher

Source: *Jobs Rated Almanac: The Best and Worst Jobs-250 in All-Ranked by More Than a Dozen Vital Factors Including Salary, Stress, Benefits and More,* 5th ed., St. Martin's Griffin, 2000.

★2279★
Most desirable public sector jobs

Ranking basis/background: Rankings based on cumulative scores in six core job factors: environment, income, outlook, physical demands, security and stress. **Number listed:** 32.

1. Judge (Federal)
2. Parole officer
3. Postal inspector
4. School principal
5. Urban/regional planner
6. Conservationist
7. College professor
8. Military (commissioned officer)
9. Librarian
10. Social worker

Source: *Jobs Rated Almanac: The Best and Worst Jobs-250 in All-Ranked by More Than a Dozen Vital Factors Including Salary, Stress, Benefits and More,* 5th ed., St. Martin's Griffin, 2000.

★2280★
Most desirable social sciences jobs

Ranking basis/background: Rankings based on cumulative scores in six core job factors: environment, income, outlook, physical demands, security and stress. **Number listed:** 8.

1. Historian
2. Archeologist
3. Sociologist
4. Philosopher
5. Political scientist
6. Anthropologist
7. Home economist
8. Recreation worker

Source: *Jobs Rated Almanac: The Best and Worst Jobs-250 in All-Ranked by More Than a Dozen Vital Factors Including Salary, Stress, Benefits and More,* 5th ed., St. Martin's Griffin, 2000.

★2281★
Most desirable technical/repair jobs

Ranking basis/background: Rankings based on cumulative scores in six core job factors: environment, income, outlook, physical demands, security and stress. **Number listed:** 25.

1. Website manager
2. Computer systems analyst
3. Computer programmer
4. Software engineer
5. Web developer
6. Musical instrument repairer
7. Electrical technician
8. Computer consultant
9. Computer service technician
10. Office machine repairer

Source: *Jobs Rated Almanac: The Best and Worst Jobs-250 in All-Ranked by More Than a Dozen Vital Factors Including Salary, Stress, Benefits and More,* 5th ed., St. Martin's Griffin, 2000.

★2282★
Most inquired issues regarding new employment

Ranking basis/background: Percent of applicants inquiring about each issue, after salary and bonuses. **Remarks:** Original source: Robert Half International. **Number listed:** 6.

1. Benefits, with 36%
2. Corporate culture, 34%
3. Equity opportunities/stock options, 11%
4. Job security/career opportunities, 7%
5. Other, 4%
6. Don't know/no answer, 1%

Source: Haralson, Darryl and Gary Visgaitis, "More About This Job," *USA Today*, October 12, 2000, Section B, p. 1B.

★2283★
Qualifications of job candidates that employers/recruiters find most important

Ranking basis/background: Percentage of employers/recruiters stating each qualification as very important/important. **Number listed:** 9.

1. Communication skills, with 82%
2. Teamwork, 79%
3. Leadership skills, 69%
4. Computer/technical aptitudes, 67%
5. GPA, 65%
6. Resume, 52%
7. Internship/Co-op, 51%
8. Appearance, 41%
9. Extracurricular activities, 38%

Source: "The Top 100 Employers and the Majors in Demand for the Class of 2001," *The Black Collegian*, 31: 19-35, (February 2001).

★2284★
U.S. cities with the highest number of high-tech employees, 1998

Ranking basis/background: Total number of high-tech employees in 1998 and percent of change since 1993. **Remarks:** Original source: AEA. **Number listed:** 10.

1. San Jose, CA, with 252,900 high-tech employees; 36.2% change
2. Boston, 234,800; 10.2%

Educational Rankings Annual • 2002

3. Chicago, 180,400; 26.9%
4. Washington, 177,700; 35.3%
5. Dallas, 176,600; 54.2%
6. Los Angeles, 160,500; 6.6%
7. Atlanta, 117,300; 48.9%
8. New York, 115,900; 28.2%
9. Minneapolis/St. Paul, 98,400; 25.7%
10. Orange County, CA, 93,600; 28.4%

Source: "High-tech Cities," *Infoworld*, 22: 16, (December 18, 2000).

★2285★
"White-collar" jobs considered the most physically demanding

Ranking basis/background: Physical demand rank based on analysis of various aspects of physicality involved in each occupation. **Number listed:** 23.

1. Veterinarian, with 197
2. Conservationist, 187
3. Surgeon, 185
4. Osteopath, 186
5. Musician, 183
5. Photojournalist, 183
7. Basketball coach (NCAA), 182
8. Physical therapist, 180
9. Undertaker, 178
10. Occupational safety/health inspector, 173

Source: *Jobs Rated Almanac: The Best and Worst Jobs-250 in All-Ranked by More Than a Dozen Vital Factors Including Salary, Stress, Benefits and More,* 5th ed., St. Martin's Griffin, 2000.

Related Information

★2286★

Jobs Rated Almanac: The Best and Worst Jobs-250 in All-Ranked by More Than a Dozen Vital Factors Including Salary, Stress, Benefits and More, 5th ed., St. Martin's Griffin, 2000.
   Remarks: Provides rankings of 250 occupations based on six core job criteria: Environment, Income, Outlook, Physical Demands, Security and Stress

---

EMPLOYMENT OPPORTUNITIES

★2287★
Employment change projections by major industry division from 1998 to 2008

Ranking basis/background: Projected change in jobs, by total (in thousands) and percentage, for each major industry division between 1998 and 2008. **Number listed:** 16.

   Nonfarm wage and salary, with 19,640 thousand (16%)
   Goods producing, 347 (1%)
   Mining, 115 less (19% decrease)
   Construction, 550 (9%)
   Manufacturing, 89 less (0%)
   Durable, 107 (1%)
   Nondurable, 196 less (3% decrease)
   Service producing, 19,293 (19%)
   Transportation, communications, and utilities, 941 (14%)
   Wholesale trade, 499 (7%)
   Retail trade, 3,067 (14%)
   Finance, insurance, and real estate, 960 (13%)
   Services, 11,957 (33%)
   Government, 1,869 (9%)

Federal government, 136 less (5% decrease)
State and local government, 2,005 (12%)
Source: "Futurework," *Occupational Outlook Quarterly,* 44: 31-36, (Summer 2000).

★2288★
Employment change projections by major occupational group from 1998 to 2008

Ranking basis/background: Projected change in number employed, in thousands, for each major occupational group between 1998 and 2008. Also includes percent distribution. **Number listed:** 9.
- Executive, administrative, and managerial, with 2,426 (16%)
- Professional specialty, 5,343 (27%)
- Technicians and related support, 1,098 (22%)
- Marketing and sales, 2,287 (15%)
- Administrative support, including clerical, 2,198 (9%)
- Service, 3,853 (17%)
- Agriculture, forestry, fishing, and related, 71 (2%)
- Precision production, craft, and repair, 1,252 (8%)
- Operators, fabricators, and laborers, 1,753 (9%)

Source: "Futurework," *Occupational Outlook Quarterly,* 44: 31-36, (Summer 2000).

★2289★
Employment distribution projections by education and training category for 2008

Ranking basis/background: Projected percentage of employment for each educational and training category in 2008. **Number listed:** 11.
1. Short-term on-the-job training, with 39.0%
2. Moderate-term on-the-job training, 13.7%
3. Bachelor's degree, 13.4%
4. Long-term on-the-job training, 9.1%
5. Work experience in a related occupation, 7.8%
6. Work experience plus bachelor's or higher degree, 7.0%
7. Associate degree, 4.0%
8. Postsecondary vocational training, 3.2%
9. First professional degree, 1.4%
10. Doctoral degree, 0.8%
11. Master's degree, 0.7%

Source: "Futurework," *Occupational Outlook Quarterly,* 44: 31-36, (Summer 2000).

★2290★
Employment projections by major industry division for 2008

Ranking basis/background: Projected number of jobs, in thousands, for each major industry division in 2008. **Number listed:** 16.
- Nonfarm wage and salary, with 144,526 thousand
- Goods producing, 25,694
- Mining, 475
- Construction, 6,535
- Manufacturing, 18,684
- Durable, 11,277
- Nondurable, 7,406
- Service producing, 118,832
- Transportation, communications, and utilities, 7,541
- Wholesale trade, 7,330
- Retail trade, 25,363
- Finance, insurance, and real estate, 8,367
- Services, 48,543
- Government, 21,668
- Federal government, 2,550
- State and local government, 19,138

Source: "Futurework," *Occupational Outlook Quarterly,* 44: 31-36, (Summer 2000).

★2291★
Employment projections by major occupational group for 2008

Ranking basis/background: Projected number employed, in thousands, for each major occupational group in 2008. Also includes percent distribution. **Number listed:** 9.
- Executive, administrative, and managerial, with 17,196 thousand (11%)
- Professional specialty, 25,145 (16%)
- Technicians and related support, 6,048 (4%)
- Marketing and sales, 17,627 (11%)
- Administrative support, including clerical, 26,659 (17%)
- Service, 26,401 (16%)
- Agriculture, forestry, fishing, and related, 4,506 (3%)
- Precision production, craft, and repair, 16,871 (11%)
- Operators, fabricators, and laborers, 20,341 (13%)

Source: "Futurework," *Occupational Outlook Quarterly,* 44: 31-36, (Summer 2000).

★2292★
Projections for the fastest growing occupations requiring a bachelor's degree or more from 1998 to 2008

Ranking basis/background: Projected percent change for each occupation between 1998 and 2008. **Number listed:** 21.
1. Computer engineers, with a change of 108%
2. Computer systems analysts, 94%
3. Database administrators, 77%
4. Physician assistants, 48%
5. Residential counselors, 46%
6. Engineering, natural science, and computer systems managers, 43%
7. Securities, commodities, and financial services sales agents, 41%
8. Speech-language pathologists and audiologists, 38%
9. Social workers, 36%
10. Biological scientists, 35%

Source: "OOChart," *Occupational Outlook Quarterly,* 44: 36, (Fall 2000).

EMPLOYMENT OUTLOOK

★2293★
Employment change by class of worker, 2008

Ranking basis/background: Percentage projected employment change for each worker class, between 1998 and 2008. **Number listed:** 2.
- Self-employed and unpaid family workers, with a 6% change
- Wage and salary workers, 15%

Source: "Occupational Employment," *Occupational Outlook Quarterly,* 43: 8-24, (Winter 1999).

★2294★
Employment growth percentages for selected industries, 1998-2000

Ranking basis/background: Percentage projections for nonfarm wage and salary employment growth, for selected industries between 1998 and 2008. **Number listed:** 20.
1. Computer and data processing services, with 117% employment growth
2. Home health care services, 80%
3. Residential care facilities, 57%
4. Security and commodity exchanges and services, 55%
4. Nonstore retailers, including mail order, 55%
6. Local and suburban transportation, 45%
6. Management and public relations, 45%
8. Personnel supply services, 43%
9. Museums and botanical and zoological gardens, 42%
10. Offices of physicians, 41%
11. Research and testing services, 40%
12. Freight transportation arrangement, 39%
13. Security and commodity brokers, 35%
14. Federal and business credit institutions, 34%
14. Water supply and sanitary services, 34%
16. Personal credit institutions, 33%
17. Individual, family, and other social services, 32%
17. Child day care services, 32%
17. Credit reporting and collection, 32%
17. School bus operation, 32%

Source: "Industry Employment," *Occupational Outlook Quarterly,* 43: 25-30, (Winter 1999).

★2295★
Employment in college-level jobs, by occupational group, 2006

Ranking basis/background: Number of jobs projected for 2006. **Number listed:** 7.
1. Executive, administrative, and managerial, with 10,210
2. Professional specialty, 17,930
3. Technicians and related support, 1,600
4. Marketing and sales, 3,250
5. Administrative support, 1,420
6. All other college-level jobs, 530
7. Noncollege-level jobs, 116,000

Source: Mittelhauser, Mark, "The Outlook for College Graduates, 1996-2006: Prepare Yourself," *Occupational Outlook Quarterly,* pp. 2-9, (Summer 1998).

★2296★
Employment outlook for the year 2005 for major occupations

Ranking basis/background: Total number employed in each field. Percentage increase over 1990 is shown in parentheses. The U.S. Department of Labor projects employment for the year 2005 on the assumption of "moderate" economic growth. Major and selected occupations are listed. **Number listed:** 9.
1. Administrative support, clerical, with 24,835,000 (13% increase over 1990)
2. Service, 24,806,000 (29%)
3. Professional specialty, 20,907,000 (32%)
4. Operators, fabricators, laborers, 17,961,000 (4%)
5. Marketing, sales, 17,489,000 (24%)
6. Precision production, craft, repair, 15,909,000 (13%)
7. Executive, administrative, and managerial, 15,866,000 (27%)

EMPLOYMENT OUTLOOK

8. Technician, 5,754,000 (37%)
9. Agriculture, forestry, and fishing, 3,665,000 (5%)

Source: "Trends and Indicators," *The Chronicle of Higher Education* 38: A14 (July 22, 1992).

★2297★
Employment outlook for the year 2005 for selected occupations

Ranking basis/background: Total number employed in each field. Percentage increase over 1990 is shown in parentheses. The U.S. Department of Labor projects employment outlooks for the year 2005 on the assumption of "moderate" economic growth. Major and selected occupations are listed. **Number listed:** 7.

1. Secondary teachers, with 1,717,000 (34% increase over 1990)
2. Elementary teachers, 1,675,000 (23%)
3. Teacher aides, 1,086,000 (34%)
4. College teachers, 846,000 (19%)
5. Pre-school, kindergarten teachers, 598,000 (41%)
6. Special education teachers, 467,000 (41%)
7. Education administrators, 434,000 (25%)

Source: "Trends & Indicators," *The Chronicle of Higher Education* 38: A14 (July 22, 1992).

★2298★
Employment outlook in college-level jobs, 2005

Ranking basis/background: Projected employment, in thousands for the year 2005. Also includes the percent change for 1994-2005. **Number listed:** 9.

- Executive, administrative, and managerial, with 9,202 thousand; 22.1% change
- Professional specialty, 17,214; 32.0%
- Technicians, 1,547; 38.4%
- Sales representatives and supervisors, 3,162; 33.4%
- Administrative support occupations, 1,417; 36.3%
- All other college-level jobs, 535; 16.1%
- All college-level jobs, 33,077; 29.4%
- Noncollege-level jobs, 111,631; 10.0%
- Total, 144,708; 13.9%

Source: Shelley, Kristina J., "1994-2005: Lots of College-Level Jobs-But Not For All Graduates," *Occupational Outlook Quarterly*, 40: 2-9, (Summer 1996).

★2299★
Employment projections by class of worker, 2008

Ranking basis/background: Number, in millions, of projected employment for each worker class, for 1998 and 2008. **Number listed:** 2.

- Self-employed and unpaid family workers, with 12.3 million in 1998; 128.2 million in 2008
- Wage and salary workers, 13.1; 147.7

Source: "Occupational Employment," *Occupational Outlook Quarterly*, 43: 8-24, (Winter 1999).

★2300★
Ethnic breakdown of executives and managers in Silicon Valley firms, 1997

Ranking basis/background: Percentage of managers from each race, according to the U.S. Equal Employment Opportunity Commission, in all industries combined. **Number listed:** 5.

1. White managers, 88%
2. African American managers, 6%
3. Hispanic American managers, 4%
4. Asian American managers, 3%
4. Native American managers, 3%

Source: "Technology: Bits & Bytes," *Black Issues in Higher Education*, 18: 40-41, (March 15, 2001).

★2301★
Fastest growing jobs, 1996-2006

Ranking basis/background: Percent increase from 1996 to 2006. **Number listed:** 10.

1. Database manager, with an 118% increase
2. Computer engineer, 109%
3. Systems analyst, 103%
4. Personal/home aide, 85%
5. Physical-therapy assistant, 79%
6. Home health aide, 76%
7. Medical assistant, 74%
7. Desktop publisher, 74%
9. Physical therapist, 71%
10. Occupational therapist, 69%

Source: McGinn, Daniel and John McCormick, "Your Next Job," *Newsweek*, February 1, 1999, pp. 42-45.

★2302★
Fastest growing occupations, 1998-2008

Ranking basis/background: Percentage of projected employment growth for each occupation, between 1998 and 2008. **Number listed:** 20.

1. Computer engineers, with a 108% growth
2. Computer support specialists, 102%
3. Computer systems analysts, 94%
4. Database administrators, 77%
5. Desktop publishing specialists, 73%
6. Paralegals and legal assistants, 62%
7. Personal care and home health aides, 58%
7. Medical assistants, 58%
9. Social and human service assistants, 53%
10. Physician assistants, 48%
11. Data processing equipment repairers, 47%
12. Residential counselors, 46%
13. Electronic semiconductor processors, 45%
14. Health information technicians, 44%
14. Physical therapy assistants and aides, 44%
16. Engineering, science, and computer systems managers, 43%
16. Respiratory therapists, 43%
18. Dental assistants, 42%
18. Surgical technologists, 42%
20. Securities and financial services sales agents, 41%

Source: "Occupational Employment," *Occupational Outlook Quarterly*, 43: 8-24, (Winter 1999).

★2303★
Highest projected employment growth by industry, 1996-2006

Ranking basis/background: Percentage of increase in industry employment. **Remarks:** Original source: Bureau of Labor Statistics. **Number listed:** 10.

1. Computer services, with an increase of 108%
2. Health services, 68%
3. Public relations, management, 60%
3. Transportation services, 60%
5. Residential care, 59%
6. Personnel supply services, 53%
7. Water and sanitation, 51%
8. Misc. social services, 50%
9. Health practitioners, 47%
10. Amusement and recreation, 41%

Source: "Employment Projections," *Chicago Tribune*, December 13, 1998, Section 6, p. 1.

★2304★
Industries in Illinois with the highest projected worker increase through 2006

Ranking basis/background: Projected number of workers needed in each industry. **Number listed:** 10.

1. Professional and technical, with 269,355 workers needed
2. Services (excluding health), 141,924
3. Marketing and sales, 104,421
4. Business administration and management, 87,515
5. Administrative support, 51,892
6. Health services, 39,805
7. Transportation, material handling, 35,666
8. Construction and extracting, 24,373
9. Production and manufacturing, 18,671
10. Agriculture, 8,040

Source: Roeder, David, "What New Year Holds for Chicago's Economy," *Chicago Sun-Times*, January 5, 2000, pp. 6-7.

★2305★
Industries with the highest percentage of projected employment growth from 1998 through 2008

Ranking basis/background: Change percentages, number of jobs, in thousands, for 1998 and projected numbers for 2008 in each industry. **Remarks:** Original source: Bureau of Labor Statistics. **Number listed:** 10.

1. Computer and data processing, with 1,599 jobs in 1998; 3,472 jobs in 2008; and a 117% change
2. Health services, 1,209; 2,018; 67%
3. Residential care, 747; 1,171; 57%
4. Management and public relations, 1,034; 1,500; 45%
5. Personnel supply services, 3,230; 4,623; 43%
5. Equipment rental and leasing, 258; 369; 43%
7. Museums, 93; 131; 42%
8. Research and testing services, 614; 861; 40%
8. Transportation services, 236; 329; 40%
8. Security and commodity brokers, 645; 900; 40%

Source: "Career Ideas," *Chicago Tribune*, January 2, 2000, Section 17, p. 15.

★2306★
Industries with the highest projected growth rate, 1994-2005

Ranking basis/background: Percentage change in employment, 1994-2005. **Remarks:** Original source: Bureau of Labor Statistics. **Number listed:** 9.

1. Health services, with an 84.1% increase
2. Residential care, 82.7%
3. Computer and data processing services, 69.5%
4. Individual and miscellaneous Social services, 68.8%
5. Miscellaneous Business services, 68.4%
6. Child day care services, 59.4%
7. Personnel supply services, 58.1%
8. Services to buildings, 58.0%
9. Miscellaneous Equipment rental and leasing, 50.8%

Source: Scheetz, L. Patrick and Rebecca Gratz, "Careers for the New Millennium," *The Black Collegian*, October 1996, pp. 32-33, 131-133.

★2307★
Industry employment for selected years
Ranking basis/background: Number, in millions, of nonfarm wage and salary employment, by industry sector, for 1998 and 2008 projections. **Number listed:** 2.

    Service producing, with 100.5 million in 1998; and a projected 119.6 million in 2008
    Goods producing, 25.3; 25.7

Source: "Industry Employment," *Occupational Outlook Quarterly*, 43: 25-30, (Winter 1999).

★2308★
Monster.com's most searched job listings
Ranking basis/background: Job listings that get searched for the most on Monster.com. **Number listed:** 10.

1. Project manager (entry level)
2. Sports agents mentorship
3. Marketing and sales manager
4. Event planner
5. Technical consultant
6. Sales/medical
7. Project manager
8. Human resources assistant
9. Production supervisor
10. Plant manager

Source: "What's Hot in Jobs," *Chicago Tribune*, July 16, 2000, Section 17, p. 17.

★2309★
Number employed by education/training category, 1998-2008
Ranking basis/background: Number, in millions, of people employed, for each education/training category between 1998 and 2008. **Number listed:** 11.

    First professional degree, with 2 million
    Doctoral degree, 1
    Master's degree, 1
    Work experience plus bachelor's or higher degree, 10
    Bachelor's degree, 17
    Associate degree, 5
    Postsecondary vocational training, 5
    Work experience in a related occupation, 11
    Long-term on-the-job training, 13
    Moderate-term on-the-job training, 21
    Short-term on-the-job training, 55

Source: "Occupational Employment," *Occupational Outlook Quarterly*, 43: 8-24, (Winter 1999).

★2310★
Occupations with the highest decline in employment, 1998-2008
Ranking basis/background: Number, in thousands, of projected employment loss for each occupation, between 1998 and 2008. **Number listed:** 20.

1. Farmers, with 173 jobs eliminated
2. Sewing machine operators, garment, 112
3. Child-care workers, private household, 97
4. Typists/word processors, 93
5. Bookkeeping, accounting, and auditing clerks, 81
6. Cleaners and servants, private household, 71
7. Farm workers, 57
8. Computer operators, except peripheral equipment, 54
9. Textile draw-out and winding machine operators, 50
10. Bank tellers, 31
11. Switchboard operators, 30
12. Inspectors, testers, and graders, precision, 22
12. Machine tool cutting operators, 22
14. Butchers and meatcutters, 15
15. Payroll and timekeeping clerks, 11
16. Peripheral computer equipment operators, 10
16. Woodworking machine operators, 10
18. Offset lithographic press operators, 9
18. Fisherman, 9
18. Procurement clerks, 9

Source: "Occupational Employment," *Occupational Outlook Quarterly*, 43: 8-24, (Winter 1999).

★2311★
Occupations with the highest number of self-employed workers, 1998
Ranking basis/background: Number, in thousands, of self-employed workers in each occupation in 1998. **Number listed:** 20.

1. Farmers, with 1,301
2. Marketing and sales worker supervisors, 875
3. Child-care workers, except private household, 494
4. Carpenters, 343
5. Hairstylists and cosmetologists, 275
6. Truck drivers, except driver/salesworkers, 266
7. Lawyers, 244
8. Blue-collar worker supervisors, 230
9. Bookkeeping, accounting, and auditing clerks, 209
10. Food service and lodging managers, 208
10. Painters and paperhangers, 208
12. Sales agents, real estate, 204
13. Management analysts, 184
14. Laborers, landscaping and groundskeeping, 182
15. Artists and commercial artists, 177
16. Automotive mechanics, 175
17. Retail salespersons, 161
18. Janitors and cleaners, 152
19. Property and real estate managers, 150
20. Designers, except interior designers, 148

Source: "Occupational Employment," *Occupational Outlook Quarterly*, 43: 8-24, (Winter 1999).

★2312★
Occupations with the largest projected employment growth, 1998-2008
Ranking basis/background: Number, in thousands, of projected employment growth for selected occupations, between 1998 and 2008. **Number listed:** 20.

1. Computer systems analysts, with 577 new jobs
2. Retail salespersons, 563
3. Cashiers, 556
4. General managers and top executives, 551
5. Truck drivers, except driver/salesworkers, 493
6. Office clerks, general, 463
7. Registered nurses, 451
8. Computer support specialists, 439
9. Personal care and home health aides, 433
10. Teacher assistants, 375
11. Janitors and cleaners, 365
12. Nursing aides and attendants, 325
13. Computer engineers, 323
14. Teachers, secondary school, 322
15. Office and administrative support supervisors and managers, 313
16. Receptionists and information clerks, 305
17. Waiters and waitresses, 303
18. Guards, 294
19. Marketing and sales worker supervisors, 263
20. Food counter and related workers, 247

Source: "Occupational Employment," *Occupational Outlook Quarterly*, 43: 8-24, (Winter 1999).

★2313★
Percentage of projected employment growth by education/training, 1998-2008
Ranking basis/background: Percentage of employment growth for each education/training category between 1998 and 2008. **Number listed:** 11.

    First professional degree, with 16%
    Doctoral degree, 23%
    Master's degree, 19%
    Work experience plus bachelor's or higher degree, 18%
    Bachelor's degree, 24%
    Associate degree, 31%
    Postsecondary vocational training, 14%
    Work experience in a related occupation, 12%
    Long-term on-the-job training, 9%
    Moderate-term on-the-job training, 7%
    Short-term on-the-job training, 14%

Source: "Occupational Employment," *Occupational Outlook Quarterly*, 43: 8-24, (Winter 1999).

★2314★
Percentages for projected employment growth by occupational group, 1998-2008
Ranking basis/background: Percentage of new employment anticipated for each occupational group in between 1998 to 2008. **Number listed:** 9.

1. Professional specialty, with a 27% growth
2. Technicians and related support, 22%
3. Service, 17%
4. Executive, administrative, and managerial, 16%
5. Marketing and sales, 15%
6. Administrative support, including clerical, 9%
6. Operators, fabricators, and laborers, 9%
8. Precision production, craft, and repair, 8%
9. Agriculture, forestry, fishing, and related, 2%

Source: "Occupational Employment," *Occupational Outlook Quarterly*, 43: 8-24, (Winter 1999).

★2315★
Projected employment growth by education/training, 1998-2008
Ranking basis/background: Number, in thousands, of projected employment change for each education/training category between 1998 and 2008. **Number listed:** 11.

    First professional degree, with 308 new jobs
    Doctoral degree, 232
    Master's degree, 174

EMPLOYMENT OUTLOOK

Work experience plus bachelor's or higher degree, 1,680
Bachelor's degree, 4,217
Associate degree, 1,537
Postsecondary vocational training, 643
Work experience in a related occupation, 1,316
Long-term on-the-job training, 1,168
Moderate-term on-the-job training, 1,430
Short-term on-the-job training, 7,576

Source: "Occupational Employment," *Occupational Outlook Quarterly*, 43: 8-24, (Winter 1999).

★2316★
Projected employment growth by occupational group, 1998-2008

Ranking basis/background: Number, in thousands, of new employment anticipated in each occupational group in between 1998 to 2008. **Number listed:** 9.

1. Professional specialty, with 5,343 new jobs
2. Service, 3,853
3. Executive, administrative, and managerial, 2,426
4. Marketing and sales, 2,287
5. Administrative support, including clerical, 2,198
6. Operators, fabricators, and laborers, 1,753
7. Precision production, craft, and repair, 1,252
8. Technicians and related support, 1,098
9. Agriculture, forestry, fishing, and related, 71

Source: "Occupational Employment," *Occupational Outlook Quarterly*, 43: 8-24, (Winter 1999).

★2317★
Projected employment growth for selected occupations that require a bachelor's degree or more, 1998-2008

Ranking basis/background: Number, in thousands, of projected employment growth for selected occupations that usually require a bachelor's degree or work experience plus a bachelor's or higher degree, between 1998 and 2008. **Number listed:** 20.

1. Computer systems analysts, with 577 new jobs
2. General managers and top executives, 551
3. Computer engineers, 323
4. Teachers, secondary school, 322
5. Social workers, 218
6. Teachers, elementary school, 205
7. Computer programmers, 191
8. Engineering, natural science, and computer systems managers, 142
9. Teachers, special education, 137
10. Securities and financial services sales agents, 124
11. Accountants and auditors, 122
12. Advertising, marketing, and public relations managers, 112
13. Management analysts, 98
14. Financial managers, 97
15. Electrical engineers, 93
16. Teachers, preschool, 92
17. Designers, except interior designers, 91
18. Residential counselors, 88
19. Writers and editors, 83
20. Artists and commercial artists, 79

Source: "Occupational Employment," *Occupational Outlook Quarterly*, 43: 8-24, (Winter 1999).

★2318★
Projected employment growth for selected occupations that require advanced education, 1998-2008

Ranking basis/background: Number, in thousands, of projected employment growth for selected occupations that usually require a master's, doctoral, or first professional degree, between 1998 and 2008. **Number listed:** 20.

1. College and university faculty, with 195 new jobs
2. Physicians, 122
3. Lawyers, 117
4. Counselors, 46
5. Physical therapists, 41
6. Speech-language pathologists and audiologists, 40
7. Biological scientists, 28
8. Clergy, 20
9. Psychologists, 19
10. Veterinarians, 14
10. Pharmacists, 14
12. Chiropractors, 11
13. Medical scientists, 8
14. Librarians, 7
14. Operations research analysts, 7
16. Urban/regional planners, 6
17. Dentists, 5
18. Optometrists, 4
19. Archivists, curators, and conservators, 3
20. Podiatrists, 1

Source: "Occupational Employment," *Occupational Outlook Quarterly*, 43: 8-24, (Winter 1999).

★2319★
Projected employment growth for selected occupations that require an associate degree or less, 1998-2008

Ranking basis/background: Number, in thousands, of projected employment growth for selected occupations that usually require an associate degree or postsecondary vocational training, between 1998 and 2008. **Number listed:** 20.

Registered nurses, with 451 new jobs
Computer support specialists, 439
Licensed practical nurses, 136
Automotive mechanics and service technicians, 132
Paralegals and legal assistants, 84
Hairstylists and cosmetologists, 62
Dental hygienists, 58
Electrical and electronic technicians and technologists, 56
Emergency medical technicians, 47
Health information technicians, 41
Data processing equipment repairers, 37
Legal secretaries, 37
Respiratory therapists, 37
Physical therapy assistants and aides, 36
Radiologic technologists and technicians, 32
Medical secretaries, 26
Sales agents, real estate, 26
Travel agents, 25
Surgical technologists, 23
Drafters, 18

Source: "Occupational Employment," *Occupational Outlook Quarterly*, 43: 8-24, (Winter 1999).

★2320★
Projected employment growth for selected occupations that require long-term on-the-job training, 1998-2008

Ranking basis/background: Number, in thousands, of projected employment growth for selected occupations that usually require related work experience or long-term on-the-job training, between 1998 and 2008. **Number listed:** 20.

1. Office and administrative support supervisors and managers, with 313 new jobs
2. Marketing and sales worker supervisors, 263
3. Blue-collar worker supervisors, 196
4. Corrections officers, 148
5. Cooks, restaurants, 146
6. Police patrol officers, 141
7. Food service and lodging managers, 97
8. Maintenance repairers, general utility, 95
9. Carpenters, 74
10. Electricians, 68
11. Telephone/cable TV installers and repairers, 55
12. Heating, air conditioning, and refrigeration mechanics, 48
13. Teachers and instructors, vocational education, 46
14. Musicians, singers, and related workers, 41
15. Actors, directors, and producers, 38
16. Insurance adjusters, examiners, and investigators, 37
17. Automotive body and related repairers, 36
18. Instructors, adults (nonvocational) education, 35
19. Sheriffs and deputy sheriffs, 31
19. Welders and cutters, 31

Source: "Occupational Employment," *Occupational Outlook Quarterly*, 43: 8-24, (Winter 1999).

★2321★
Projected employment growth for selected occupations that require shortor moderate-term on-the-job training, 1998-2008

Ranking basis/background: Number, in thousands, of projected employment growth for selected occupations that usually require short- or moderate-term on-the-job training, between 1998 and 2008. **Number listed:** 20.

1. Retail salesperson, with 563 new jobs
2. Cashiers, 556
3. Truck drivers, except driver/salesworkers, 493
4. Office clerks, general, 463
5. Personal care and home health aides, 433
6. Teacher assistants, 375
7. Janitors and cleaners, 365
8. Nursing aides and attendants, 325
9. Receptionists and information clerks, 305
10. Waiters and waitresses, 303
11. Guards, 294
12. Food counter and related workers, 247
13. Child-care workers, except private household, 236
14. Laborers, landscaping and groundskeeping, 234
15. Hand packers and packagers, 213
16. Adjustment clerks, 163
17. Medical assistants, 146
18. Social and human service assistants, 141
19. Stock clerks and order fillers, 131
19. Food preparation workers, 131

Source: "Occupational Employment," *Occupational Outlook Quarterly*, 43: 8-24, (Winter 1999).

★2322★
Projected employment growth in the U.S., by level of education, from 1996 to 2006

Ranking basis/background: Percentage of projected growth for each educational attainment level. **Number listed:** 12.
1. Bachelor's degree, with a 25.4% growth
2. Associate's degree, 22.2%
3. Doctoral degree, 19.0%
4. First professional degree, 18.0%
5. Work experience plus bachelor's or higher degree, 17.8%
6. Master's degree, 15.0%
7. Total, all occupations, 14.0%
8. Short-term on-the-job training, 13.3%
9. Work experience in a related occupation, 12.2%
10. Long-term on-the-job training, 9.1%
11. Moderate-term on-the-job training, 8.7%
12. Post-secondary vocational training, 7.4%

Source: "Education Rules in Job Growth," *Chicago Tribune*, January 2, 2000, Section 17, p. 30.

★2323★
Top bachelor's and master's degree majors in demand for employment, 2001

Ranking basis/background: Projected number of college hires from on-campus recruitment of all degree recipients for 2000-01. **Remarks:** Numbers reflect total expected hires, not just African American projected hires. **Number listed:** 46.
1. Business administration and management, with 11,447
2. Multidisciplinary major, 10,462
3. Education, 6,044
4. Accounting, 5,042
5. Liberal arts, 4,446
6. Computer science, 4,006
7. Marketing, 3,965
8. Information technology (MIS), 3,915
9. Electrical/electrical engineering, 2,319
10. Finance/banking, 2,113

Source: "The Top 100 Employers and the Majors in Demand for the Class of 2001," *The Black Collegian*, 31: 19-35, (February 2001).

★2324★
Top bachelor's degree majors in demand for employment, 2001

Ranking basis/background: Projected number of college hires from on-campus recruitment of all degree recipients for 2000-01. **Remarks:** Numbers reflect total expected hires, not just African American projected hires. **Number listed:** 46.
1. Multidisciplinary major, with 10,017
2. Business administration and management, 10,015
3. Liberal arts, 4,311
4. Accounting, 3,990
5. Marketing, 3,771
6. Information technology (MIS), 3,405
7. Computer science, 3,401
8. Education, 3,346
9. Electrical/electrical engineering, 1,751
10. Finance/banking, 1,743

Source: "The Top 100 Employers and the Majors in Demand for the Class of 2001," *The Black Collegian*, 31: 19-35, (February 2001).

★2325★
Top employers of college graduates, 2001

Ranking basis/background: Projected number of college hires from on-campus recruitment of all degree recipients for 2000-01. **Remarks:** Numbers reflect total expected hires, not just African American projected hires. **Number listed:** 100.
1. Enterprise Rent-A-Car, with 6,000 projected hires
2. Ford Motor Company, 5,000
3. Footstar, 4,944
4. EDS, 4,350
5. Accenture, 4,003
6. Lucent Technologies, 3,245
7. Immigration and Naturalization Service, 3,000
8. Arthur Andersen LLP, 2,999
9. Fairfax County Public Schools, 2,035
10. Deloitte & Touche LLP, 1,938

Source: "The Top 100 Employers and the Majors in Demand for the Class of 2001," *The Black Collegian*, 31: 19-35, (February 2001).

★2326★
Top master's degree majors in demand for employment, 2001

Ranking basis/background: Projected number of college hires from on-campus recruitment of all degree recipients for 2000-01. **Remarks:** Numbers reflect total expected hires, not just African American projected hires. **Number listed:** 46.
1. Education, with 2,698
2. Business administration and management, 1,432
3. Accounting, 1,052
4. Computer science, 605
5. Electrical/electrical engineering, 568
6. Information technology (MIS), 510
7. Multidisciplinary major, 445
8. Finance/banking, 370
9. Computer engineering, 293
10. Math/actuarial science, 198

Source: "The Top 100 Employers and the Majors in Demand for the Class of 2001," *The Black Collegian*, 31: 19-35, (February 2001).

★2327★
Top recruiters for multidisciplinary majors jobs for 2000-01 bachelor's degree recipients

Ranking basis/background: Projected number of college hires from on-campus recruitment for 2000-01. **Remarks:** Numbers reflect total expected hires, not just African American projected hires. **Number listed:** 8.
1. Ford Motor Company, with 5,000 projected hires
2. Immigration and Naturalization Service, 3,000
3. U.S. Marine Corps, 1,320
4. NASA Headquarters, 300
5. U.S. Air Force (Active Duty Hires), 272
6. Kroger, 75
7. May Department Stores, 40
8. Bechtel National, 10

Source: "The Top 100 Employers and the Majors in Demand for the Class of 2001," *The Black Collegian*, 31: 19-35, (February 2001).

★2328★
Top recruiters for multidisciplinary majors jobs for 2000-01 master's degree recipients

Ranking basis/background: Projected number of college hires from on-campus recruitment for 2000-01. **Remarks:** Numbers reflect total expected hires, not just African American projected hires. **Number listed:** 3.
1. U.S. Marine Corps, 330
2. Deloitte & Touche, 100
3. Kroger, 15

Source: "The Top 100 Employers and the Majors in Demand for the Class of 2001," *The Black Collegian*, 31: 19-35, (February 2001).

Related Information

★2329★
Recruiting Trends 2000-2001.
Remarks: The Collegiate Employment Research Institute at Michigan State University's results of an annual survey of 320 employers regarding job growth and the current job market. Online at http://www.csp.msu.edu/ceri/pubs/rectrends9899.htm

EMPLOYMENT POTENTIAL

★2330★
Job openings for high-tech workers

Ranking basis/background: Total number of job openings projected in the next 12 months for each type of job and projected number of positions that will not be filled. Based on a survey of 700 firms. **Remarks:** Original source: Information Technology Association of America. **Number listed:** 9.
1. Tech support, with 616,055 openings; 327,835 that won't be filled
2. Database development, 271,487; 147,489
3. Programming/software engineering, 213,890; 109,948
4. Network design, 165,585; 79,374
5. Web development, 161,301; 90,137
6. Technical writing, 63,753; 31,167
7. Enterprise analysis, 46,337; 22,077
8. Digital media, 31,110; 13,969
9. Other, 38,980; 21,332

Source: "Help Wanted-Badly," *U.S. News & World Report*, 129: 12, (September 25, 2000).

★2331★
U.S. school districts with the highest number of vacancies for K-12 teachers

Ranking basis/background: Number of K-12 teacher vacancies in each district. **Number listed:** 10.
1. New York City, with 12,000
2. Los Angeles, 4,000
3. Miami-Dade, 3,200
4. Chicago, 3,000
5. Clark County, NV, 1,600
6. Houston, 1,000
7. Baltimore, 900
8. Philadelphia, 800
9. Newark, NJ, 600
10. Boston, 500

Source: Lord, Mary, "Good Teachers, the Newest Imports," *U.S. News & World Report*, 130: 54, (April 9, 2001).

ENDOWMENT, COLLEGE

See: **Colleges & Universities–Financial Support & Expenditures**

ENGINEERING

★2332★
Top institutions in systems and software engineering publications

Ranking basis/background: A ranking of institutions with the most published works in the field of systems and software engineering. **Number listed:** 15.
1. Carnegie Mellon/SEI
2. University of Maryland
3. Bell Labs, Lucent
4. National Chiao Tung University
5. National University of Singapore
6. Iowa State University
7. University of York (U.K.)
8. University of Illinois
9. Ohio State University
10. University of Texas

Source: Glass, Robert L., "An Assessment of Systems and Software Engineering Scholars and Institutions (1993-1997)," *Journal of Systems & Software*, 43: 59-64, (October 1999).

★2333★
Top published scholars in the field of systems and software engineering

Ranking basis/background: A ranking of scholars with the most published works in the field of systems and software engineering. **Number listed:** 16.
1. Johnny S.K. Wong (Iowa State)
2. Richard Lai (La Trobe)
3. Elaine J. Weyuker (AT&T Labs)
4. Victor R. Basili (Maryland)
5. Robert L. Glass (Computing Trends)
6. Shari Lawrence Pfleeger (Systems/Software)
7. Jen-Yen Chen (National Chiao Tung)
8. Kassem Saleh, (Kuwiat)
9. Alfonso Fuggetta (Politecnico di Milano)
10. Norman Fenton (City University London)

Source: Glass, Robert L., "An Assessment of Systems and Software Engineering Scholars and Institutions (1993-1997)," *Journal of Systems & Software*, 43: 59-64, (October 1999).

★2334★
Top recruiters for engineering jobs for 2000-01 bachelor's degree recipients

Ranking basis/background: Projected number of college hires from on-campus recruitment for 2000-01. **Remarks:** Numbers reflect total expected hires, not just African American projected hires. **Number listed:** 1.
1. Corning, with 8 projected hires

Source: "The Top 100 Employers and the Majors in Demand for the Class of 2001," *The Black Collegian*, 31: 19-35, (February 2001).

★2335★
Top recruiters for multidisciplinary engineers jobs for 2000-01 bachelor's degree recipients

Ranking basis/background: Projected number of college hires from on-campus recruitment for 2000-01. **Remarks:** Numbers reflect total expected hires, not just African American projected hires. **Number listed:** 3.
1. Schlumberger, with 400 projected hires
2. NASA Headquarters, 300
3. PA Department of Transportation, 105

Source: "The Top 100 Employers and the Majors in Demand for the Class of 2001," *The Black Collegian*, 31: 19-35, (February 2001).

★2336★
Top recruiters for systems engineer jobs for 2000-01 bachelor's degree recipients

Ranking basis/background: Projected number of college hires from on-campus recruitment for 2000-01. **Remarks:** Numbers reflect total expected hires, not just African American projected hires. **Number listed:** 12.
1. EDS, with 1,000 projected hires
2. Lucent Technologies, 100
3. Accenture, 50
4. Footstar, 25
5. Unisys, 20
6. Arthur Andersen LLP, 15
7. CNF Inc., 10
7. American Management Systems, 10
7. State Farm Insurance Company, 10
10. Corning, 6
11. Agilent Technologies, 5
11. Bechtel National, 5

Source: "The Top 100 Employers and the Majors in Demand for the Class of 2001," *The Black Collegian*, 31: 19-35, (February 2001).

★2337★
U.S. News & World Report's undergraduate engineering programs with the highest academic reputation scores, 2000-01

Ranking basis/background: Based on *U.S News* survey asking engineering school deans and senior faculty to rate the quality of programs they are familiar with, and name the best programs in various specialties. **Number listed:** 50.
1. Rose-Hulman Institute of Technology, with a score of 4.4
2. Harvey Mudd College, 4.3
3. Cooper Union, 4.0
4. Bucknell University, 3.7
4. Rochester Institute of Technology, 3.7
4. United States Air Force Academy, 3.7
4. United States Military Academy, 3.7
4. United States Naval Academy, 3.7
9. California Polytechnic State University, San Luis Obispo, 3.6
10. Swarthmore College, 3.5

Source: "America's Best Colleges," *U.S. News & World Report*, 129: 90-132, (September 11, 2000).

★2338★
U.S. universities contributing the most papers in the field of AI, robotics, and auto control, 1993-97

Ranking basis/background: Total number of papers and average number of citations per paper. **Remarks:** Original source: University Science Indicators of Diskette, 1981-97. **Number listed:** 5.
1. University of California, Berkeley, with 174 papers; and an average 3.87 citations per paper
2. Caltech, 173; 3.44
3. University of Texas, Austin, 106; 3.06
4. University of Illinois, Urbana-Champaign, 171; 2.78
5. University of Southern California, 158; 2.64

Source: "AI, Robotics, & Auto Control: High-Impact U.S. Universities, 1993-97," *What's Hot in Research*, http://www.isinet.com/whatshot/whatshot.html, Institute for Scientific Information, (February 22, 1999).

ENGINEERING–AERONAUTICAL

See also: **Engineering, Graduate–Aeronautical**

★2339★
Top recruiters for aeronautical engineering jobs for 2000-01 bachelor's degree recipients

Ranking basis/background: Projected number of college hires from on-campus recruitment for 2000-01. **Remarks:** Numbers reflect total expected hires, not just African American projected hires. **Number listed:** 3.
1. U.S. Air Force (Active Duty Hires), with 42 projected hires
2. U.S. Air Force (Civilian Hires), 10
3. Accenture, 5

Source: "The Top 100 Employers and the Majors in Demand for the Class of 2001," *The Black Collegian*, 31: 19-35, (February 2001).

ENGINEERING–AEROSPACE

See also: **Engineering, Graduate–Aerospace**

★2340★
Top recruiters for aerospace engineering jobs for 2000-01 bachelor's degree recipients

Ranking basis/background: Projected number of college hires from on-campus recruitment for 2000-01. **Remarks:** Numbers reflect total expected hires, not just African American projected hires. **Number listed:** 4.
1. Litton Industries, with 25 projected hires
2. U.S. Air Force (Active Duty Hires), 20
3. Rockwell Collins, 9
4. Accenture, 5

Source: "The Top 100 Employers and the Majors in Demand for the Class of 2001," *The Black Collegian*, 31: 19-35, (February 2001).

★2341★
U.S. News & World Report's undergraduate engineering programs with the best aerospace departments, 2000-01

Ranking basis/background: Based on *U.S News* survey asking engineering school deans and senior faculty to rate the quality of programs they are familiar with, and name the best programs in various specialties. **Number listed:** 6.
1. Embry-Riddle Aeronautical University

2. United States Air Force Academy
3. United States Naval Academy
4. California State Polytechnic University, Pomona
4. California Polytechnic State University, San Luis Obispo
4. St. Louis University

Source: "America's Best Colleges," *U.S. News & World Report*, 129: 90-132, (September 11, 2000).

ENGINEERING–CHEMICAL
See also: **Engineering, Graduate–Chemical**

★2342★
Bachelor's degrees awarded in chemical engineering, 1980 to 1997

Ranking basis/background: Number of degrees awarded each year. **Remarks:** Original source: National Center for Education Statistics. **Number listed:** 18.
   1980, with 6,320
   1981, 6,527
   1982, 6,740
   1983, 7,185
   1984, 7,475
   1985, 7,146
   1986, 5,877
   1987, 4,991
   1988, 3,917
   1989, 3,663
   1990, 3,430
   1991, 3,444
   1992, 3,754
   1993, 4,459
   1994, 5,163
   1995, 5,901
   1996, 6,319
   1997, 6,564

Source: Brennan, Mairin B., "Demand," *C&EN: Chemical & Engineering News*, 77: 38-46, (November 15, 1999).

★2343★
Top recruiters for chemical engineering jobs for 2000-01 bachelor's degree recipients

Ranking basis/background: Projected number of college hires from on-campus recruitment for 2000-01. **Remarks:** Numbers reflect total expected hires, not just African American projected hires. **Number listed:** 15.
1. Procter & Gamble, with 150 projected hires
2. Abbott Laboratories, 40
3. Accenture, 30
4. Eastman Chemical Company, 23
5. International Paper, 20
6. Agilent Technologies, 19
7. PA Dept. Environmental Protection, 18
8. Corning, 16
9. Bechtel National, 15
10. U.S. Air Force (Active Duty Hires), 10
11. Caterpillar Inc., 8
12. Texaco, 7
13. Westinghouse, 6
14. Honda of America Manufacturing Inc., 5
15. Life Scan, 3

Source: "The Top 100 Employers and the Majors in Demand for the Class of 2001," *The Black Collegian*, 31: 19-35, (February 2001).

★2344★
***U.S. News & World Report*'s undergraduate engineering programs with the best chemical departments, 2000-01**

Ranking basis/background: Based on *U.S News* survey asking engineering school deans and senior faculty to rate the quality of programs they are familiar with, and name the best programs in various specialties. **Number listed:** 5.
1. Rose-Hulman Institute of Technology
2. Bucknell University
2. Cooper Union
2. Manhattan College
2. University of Minnesota, Duluth

Source: "America's Best Colleges," *U.S. News & World Report*, 129: 90-132, (September 11, 2000).

★2345★
U.S. universities with the highest concentration of papers published in the field of chemical engineering, 1994-98

Ranking basis/background: Number of papers published in the field of chemical engineering over a five-year period, and percentage they comprise of the university's total papers published. **Number listed:** 5.
1. Lehigh University, with 104 papers; 6.11% of university's total papers
2. University of Delaware, 168; 3.92%
3. Carnegie Mellon University, 151; 3.52%
4. Georgia Institute of Technology, 129; 2.73%
5. West Virginia University, 71; 2.35%

Source: "Chemical Engineering: High Concentration U.S. Universities, 1994-98," *What's Hot in Research (http://www.isinet.com/isi/hot/research) Institute for Scientific Information*, August 21, 2000.

ENGINEERING–CIVIL
See also: **Engineering, Graduate–Civil**

★2346★
Top recruiters for civil engineering jobs for 2000-01 bachelor's degree recipients

Ranking basis/background: Projected number of college hires from on-campus recruitment for 2000-01. **Remarks:** Numbers reflect total expected hires, not just African American projected hires. **Number listed:** 11.
1. Illinois Department of Transportation, with 113 projected hires
2. PA Department of Transportation, 100
3. Gannett Fleming, Inc., 30
3. Accenture, 30
5. Dewberry & Davis LLC, 20
6. Ingalls Shipbuilding, 15
6. Bechtel National, 15
8. U.S. Forest Services, 11
9. International Paper, 10
9. Newport News Shipbuilding, 10
11. U.S. Air Force (Civilian Hires), 8

Source: "The Top 100 Employers and the Majors in Demand for the Class of 2001," *The Black Collegian*, 31: 19-35, (February 2001).

★2347★
***U.S. News & World Report*'s undergraduate engineering programs with the best civil departments, 2000-01**

Ranking basis/background: Based on *U.S News* survey asking engineering school deans and senior faculty to rate the quality of programs they are familiar with, and name the best programs in various specialties. **Number listed:** 7.
1. Rose-Hulman Institute of Technology
2. United States Military Academy
3. Cooper Union
4. United States Air Force Academy
5. Bucknell University
5. California Polytechnic State University, San Luis Obispo
5. Harvey Mudd College

Source: "America's Best Colleges," *U.S. News & World Report*, 129: 90-132, (September 11, 2000).

★2348★
U.S. universities publishing the most papers in the field of civil engineering, 1994-98

Ranking basis/background: Total number of papers published from each university. **Remarks:** Original source: University Science Indicators on Diskette, 1981-97. **Number listed:** 5.
1. University of California, Berkeley, with 326 papers
2. Massachusetts Institute of Technology, 207
3. University of Arizona, 190
4. University of Texas, Austin, 182
5. Purdue University, 176

Source: "Civil Engineering: Most Prolific U.S. Universities, 1994-98," *What's Hot in Research (http://www.isinet.com/hot/research) Institute for Scientific Information*, September 20, 1999.

★2349★
U.S. universities publishing the most papers in the field of civil engineering, 1995-99

Ranking basis/background: Number of papers published in the field of civil engineering over a five-year period, and percent of field based on each universities percentage of 19,910 papers entered in the ISI database from ISI-indexed civil engineering journals. **Number listed:** 5.
1. University of California, Berkeley, with 325 papers; 1.63% of field
2. Massachusetts Institute of Technology, 194; 0.97%
3. Texas A&M University, 186; 0.93%
4. University of Arizona, 182; 0.91%
5. University of Texas, Austin, 177; 0.89

Source: "Civil Engineering: Most Prolific U.S. Universities, 1995-99," *What's Hot in Research (http://www.isinet.com/isi/hot/research) Institute for Scientific Information*.

★2350★
U.S. universities with the greatest impact in civil engineering, 1995-99

Ranking basis/background: Average citations per paper from the top 100 federally funded U.S. universities that had at least 50 published papers in ISI indexed civil engineering journals. Also includes total number of papers published during the five year period. **Number listed:** 5.
1. University of Arizona, with 182 papers; 3.41 citations per paper
2. University of Colorado, 153; 2.87
3. Princeton University, 68; 2.82

ENGINEERING—COMPUTER

4. Stanford University, 124; 2.67
5. Utah State University, 85; 2.51

Source: "Civil Engineering: High Impact U.S. Universities, 1995-99," *What's Hot in Research* (http://www.isinet.com/isi/hot/research) *Institute for Scientific Information*, October 16, 2000.

★2351★
U.S. universities with the highest concentration of civil engineering papers published, 1994-98

Ranking basis/background: Total number of civil engineering papers published from each university and percentage they comprise of university's total papers between 1994 and 1998. **Remarks:** Original source: University Science Indicators on Diskette, 1981-98. **Number listed:** 5.

1. Utah State University, with 89 civil engineering papers; 4.09% of university's total papers
2. Colorado State University, 132; 2.60%
3. Georgia Institute of Technology, 122; 2.59%
4. Virginia Polytechnic Institute and State University, 118; 1.98%
5. University of Delaware, 79; 1.84%

Source: "U.S. Universities with Highest Concentrations in Civil Engineering, 1994-98," *What's Hot in Research* (http://www.isinet.com/hot/research) *Institute for Scientific Information*, December 6, 1999.

ENGINEERING–COMPUTER
See also: **Engineering, Graduate–Computer**

★2352★
Top recruiters for computer engineering jobs for 2000-01 bachelor's degree recipients

Ranking basis/background: Projected number of college hires from on-campus recruitment for 2000-01. **Remarks:** Numbers reflect total expected hires, not just African American projected hires. **Number listed:** 26.

1. Lucent Technologies, with 200 projected hires
2. Deloitte & Touche, 130
3. Alcatel, 125
4. Accenture, 60
5. Unisys, 50
6. Litton Industries, 40
6. U.S. Air Force (Active Duty Hires), 40
8. Tellabs, 35
9. CNF Inc., 25
9. General Dynamics Land Systems, 25

Source: "The Top 100 Employers and the Majors in Demand for the Class of 2001," *The Black Collegian*, 31: 19-35, (February 2001).

★2353★
U.S. News & World Report's undergraduate engineering programs with the best computer departments, 2000-01

Ranking basis/background: Based on *U.S News* survey asking engineering school deans and senior faculty to rate the quality of programs they are familiar with, and name the best programs in various specialties. **Number listed:** 5.

1. California Polytechnic State University, San Luis Obispo
1. Rose-Hulman Institute of Technology
3. Rochester Institute of Technology
4. Cooper Union
4. Milwaukee School of Engineering

Source: "America's Best Colleges," *U.S. News & World Report*, 129: 90-132, (September 11, 2000).

ENGINEERING–ELECTRICAL/ELECTRONIC
See also: **Engineering, Graduate–Electrical/Electronic**

★2354★
Top recruiters for electrical/electronic engineering jobs for 2000-01 bachelor's degree recipients

Ranking basis/background: Projected number of college hires from on-campus recruitment for 2000-01. **Remarks:** Numbers reflect total expected hires, not just African American projected hires. **Number listed:** 36.

1. Lucent Technologies, with 300 projected hires
2. Accenture, 160
3. Alcatel, 125
4. General Motors, 115
5. Agilent Technologies, 100
5. Cap Gemini Ernst & Young, 100
7. U.S. Air Force (Active Duty Hires), 81
8. Exelon, 80
9. Rockwell Collins, 77
10. Telcordia Technologies, 75

Source: "The Top 100 Employers and the Majors in Demand for the Class of 2001," *The Black Collegian*, 31: 19-35, (February 2001).

★2355★
U.S. News & World Report's undergraduate engineering programs with the best electrical departments, 2000-01

Ranking basis/background: Based on *U.S News* survey asking engineering school deans and senior faculty to rate the quality of programs they are familiar with, and name the best programs in various specialties. **Number listed:** 6.

1. Rose-Hulman Institute of Technology
2. Harvey Mudd College
3. California Polytechnic State University, San Luis Obispo
4. Cooper Union
5. Rochester Institute of Technology
5. United States Air Force Academy

Source: "America's Best Colleges," *U.S. News & World Report*, 129: 90-132, (September 11, 2000).

★2356★
U.S. universities with the greatest impact in electrical and electronic engineering, 1994-99

Ranking basis/background: Average citations per paper from the top 100 federally funded U.S. universities that had at least 50 published papers in ISI indexed electrical and electronic engineering journals. Also includes total number of papers published during the five year period. **Number listed:** 5.

1. University of California, San Francisco, with 285 papers; 3.38 citations per paper
2. University of California, Santa Barbara, 273; 3.30
3. Stanford University, 392; 3.25
4. Massachusetts Institute of Technology, 504; 3.22
5. University of Illinois, Urbana-Champaign, 473; 3.14

Source: "Electrical & Electronic Engineering: High Impact U.S. Universities, 1994-98," *What's Hot in Research* (http://www.isinet.com/isi/hot/research) *Institute for Scientific Information*, July 17, 2000.

ENGINEERING–ENVIRONMENTAL
See also: **Engineering, Graduate–Environmental**

★2357★
Top recruiters for environmental engineering jobs for 2000-01 bachelor's degree recipients

Ranking basis/background: Projected number of college hires from on-campus recruitment for 2000-01. **Remarks:** Numbers reflect total expected hires, not just African American projected hires. **Number listed:** 9.

1. U.S. Air Force (Active Duty Hires), with 39 projected hires
2. PA Dept. Environmental Protection, 18
3. International Paper, 14
4. General Motors, 5
4. Abbott Laboratories, 5
4. Bechtel National, 5
4. Marathon Oil, 5
8. Gannett Fleming, Inc., 4
9. Dewberry & Davis LLC, 2

Source: "The Top 100 Employers and the Majors in Demand for the Class of 2001," *The Black Collegian*, 31: 19-35, (February 2001).

ENGINEERING, GRADUATE

★2358★
Acceptance rates for U.S. News & World Report's top 10 graduate engineering schools, 2001

Ranking basis/background: From a *U.S. News & World Report* survey of acceptance rates for 2000. **Remarks:** Data collected by Market Facts, Inc. **Number listed:** 50.

1. Stanford University, with 39.0%
2. University of Michigan, Ann Arbor, 38.2%
3. University of Texas, Austin, 31.5%
4. Massachusetts Institute of Technology, 29.5%
5. Cornell University, 28.4%
6. University of California, Berkeley, 23.8%
7. Georgia Institute of Technology, 22.1%
8. University of Illinois, Urbana-Champaign, 19.7%
9. Carnegie Mellon University, 16.4%
10. California Institute of Technology, 10.1%

Source: "America's Best Graduate Schools: 2002 Annual Guide," *U.S. News & World Report*, 130: 60-97, (April 19, 2001).

ENGINEERING, GRADUATE

★2359★
Average analytic GRE scores for *U.S. News & World Report*'s top 10 graduate engineering schools, 2001

Ranking basis/background: From a *U.S. News & World Report* survey of average GRE scores for 2000. **Remarks:** Data collected by Market Facts, Inc. **Number listed:** 50.
1. California Institute of Technology, with 783
2. Carnegie Mellon University, 718
3. Massachusetts Institute of Technology, 716
4. University of Illinois, Urbana-Champaign, 707
5. Stanford University, 703
5. University of Michigan, Ann Arbor, 703
7. Cornell University, 700
8. University of California, Berkeley, 696
9. Georgia Institute of Technology, 693
10. University of Texas, Austin, 679

Source: "America's Best Graduate Schools: 2002 Annual Guide," *U.S. News & World Report*, 130: 60-97, (April 19, 2001).

★2360★
Average quantitative GRE scores for *U.S. News & World Report*'s top 10 graduate engineering schools, 2001

Ranking basis/background: From a *U.S. News & World Report* survey of average GRE scores for 2000. **Remarks:** Data collected by Market Facts, Inc. **Number listed:** 50.
1. California Institute of Technology, with 773
2. Carnegie Mellon University, 770
3. Stanford University, 769
4. Cornell University, 768
5. Massachusetts Institute of Technology, 767
6. University of Michigan, Ann Arbor, 765
6. University of Illinois, Urbana-Champaign, 765
8. University of California, Berkeley, 760
9. University of Texas, Austin, 756
10. Georgia Institute of Technology, 754

Source: "America's Best Graduate Schools: 2002 Annual Guide," *U.S. News & World Report*, 130: 60-97, (April 19, 2001).

★2361★
Doctoral student-faculty ratios at *U.S. News & World Report*'s top 10 graduate engineering schools, 2001

Ranking basis/background: From a *U.S. News & World Report* survey of number of doctoral students per faculty member in 2000. **Remarks:** Data collected by Market Facts, Inc. **Number listed:** 50.
1. University of Texas, Austin, with 3.0 doctoral students per faculty member
2. Georgia Institute of Technology, 3.1
2. University of Illinois, Urbana-Champaign, 3.1
4. University of Michigan, Ann Arbor, 3.3
5. Massachusetts Institute of Technology, 3.4
6. Carnegie Mellon University, 3.5
7. Cornell University, 3.7
8. California Institute of Technology, 4.7
9. University of California, Berkeley, 4.9
10. Stanford University, 5.0

Source: "America's Best Graduate Schools: 2002 Annual Guide," *U.S. News & World Report*, 130: 60-97, (April 19, 2001).

★2362★
Faculty membership in National Academy of Engineering at *U.S. News & World Report*'s top 10 graduate engineering schools, 2001

Ranking basis/background: From a *U.S. News & World Report* survey of percentage of faculty with membership in the National Academy of Engineering in 2000. **Remarks:** Data collected by Market Facts, Inc. **Number listed:** 50.
1. University of California, Berkeley, with 19.5%
2. California Institute of Technology, 17.2%
3. Stanford University, 17.1%
4. University of Texas, Austin, 12.8%
5. Massachusetts Institute of Technology, with 12.3%
6. Carnegie Mellon University, 9.2%
7. Cornell University, 6.7%
8. Georgia Institute of Technology, 4.4%
9. University of Illinois, Urbana-Champaign, 3.8%
10. University of Michigan, Ann Arbor, 3.7%

Source: "America's Best Graduate Schools: 2002 Annual Guide," *U.S. News & World Report*, 130: 60-97, (April 19, 2001).

★2363★
Ph.D.s granted at *U.S. News & World Report*'s top 10 graduate engineering schools, 2001

Ranking basis/background: From a *U.S. News & World Report* survey of Ph.D.s granted during the 1999-2000. **Remarks:** Data collected by Market Facts, Inc. **Number listed:** 50.
1. Massachusetts Institute of Technology, with 229
2. Stanford University, 203
3. University of Michigan, Ann Arbor, 202
4. University of Illinois, Urbana-Champaign, 195
5. University of California, Berkeley, 174
5. Georgia Institute of Technology, 174
7. Carnegie Mellon University, 171
8. University of Texas, Austin, 132
9. Cornell University, 104
10. California Institute of Technology, 48

Source: "America's Best Graduate Schools: 2002 Annual Guide," *U.S. News & World Report*, 130: 60-97, (April 19, 2001).

★2364★
Research expenditures per faculty member at *U.S. News & World Report*'s top 10 graduate engineering schools, 2001

Ranking basis/background: From a *U.S. News & World Report* survey of total research expenditures, in thousands of dollars, per faculty member in 2000. **Remarks:** Data collected by Market Facts, Inc. **Number listed:** 50.
1. University of Michigan, Ann Arbor, with $595.6 thousand
2. Cornell University, $568.9
3. Carnegie Mellon University, $551.5
4. Stanford University, $548.3
5. Massachusetts Institute of Technology, $532.9
6. California Institute of Technology, $498.4
7. University of Texas, Austin, $467.0
8. University of California, Berkeley, $462.4
9. Georgia Institute of Technology, $399.4
10. University of Illinois, Urbana-Champaign, $360.4

Source: "America's Best Graduate Schools: 2002 Annual Guide," *U.S. News & World Report*, 130: 60-97, (April 19, 2001).

★2365★
Research funding allocated to *U.S. News & World Report*'s top 10 graduate engineering schools, 2001

Ranking basis/background: From a *U.S. News & World Report* survey of total research funding, in millions of dollars, given for 2000. **Remarks:** Data collected by Market Facts, Inc. **Number listed:** 50.
1. Massachusetts Institute of Technology, with $178.0 million
2. Georgia Institute of Technology, $172.5
3. University of Illinois, Urbana-Champaign, $135.9
4. University of Michigan, Ann Arbor, $134.0
5. University of California, Berkeley, $101.3
6. University of Texas, Austin, $91.1
7. Carnegie Mellon University, $91.0
8. Stanford University, $90.5
9. Cornell University, $82.5
10. California Institute of Technology, $43.4

Source: "America's Best Graduate Schools: 2002 Annual Guide," *U.S. News & World Report*, 130: 60-97, (April 19, 2001).

★2366★
Top graduate engineering schools, 2001

Ranking basis/background: From a *U.S. News & World Report* survey based on academic reputation, reputation by practicing engineers, student selectivity, research activity, and faculty resources. **Remarks:** Data collected by Market Facts, Inc. **Number listed:** 50.
1. Massachusetts Institute of Technology, with an overall score of 100
2. Stanford University, 91
3. University of California, Berkeley, 88
4. University of Michigan, Ann Arbor, 86
5. Georgia Institute of Technology, 85
6. University of Illinois, Urbana-Champaign, 83
7. California Institute of Technology, 82
8. Carnegie Mellon University, 80
9. Cornell University, 78
10. University of Texas, Austin, 77

Source: "America's Best Graduate Schools: 2002 Annual Guide," *U.S. News & World Report*, 130: 60-97, (April 19, 2001).

★2367★
Top graduate engineering schools by reputation, as determined by academic personnel, 2001

Ranking basis/background: From a *U.S. News & World Report* survey of engineering school deans and deans of academic affairs. **Remarks:** Data collected by Market Facts, Inc. **Number listed:** 50.
1. Massachusetts Institute of Technology, with a reputation score of 5.0
2. Stanford University, 4.9
2. University of California, Berkeley, 4.9
4. California Institute of Technology, 4.8
5. University of Illinois, Urbana-Champaign, 4.7
6. University of Michigan, Ann Arbor, 4.6
7. Georgia Institute of Technology, 4.5
8. Carnegie Mellon University, 4.4
8. Cornell University, 4.4
10. University of Texas, Austin, 4.2
10. Purdue University, West Lafayette, 4.2
10. Princeton University, 4.2

ENGINEERING, GRADUATE—AERONAUTICAL

Source: "America's Best Graduate Schools: 2002 Annual Guide," *U.S. News & World Report*, 130: 60-97, (April 19, 2001).

★2368★

Top graduate engineering schools by reputation, as determined by engineers and recruiters, 2001

Ranking basis/background: From a *U.S. News & World Report* survey of National Academy of Engineering members' and corporate recruiters' rankings of the top 25 engineering schools. **Remarks:** Data collected by Market Facts, Inc. **Number listed:** 50.
1. Massachusetts Institute of Technology, with a reputational score of 5.0
2. Georgia Institute of Technology, 4.7
3. University of Michigan, Ann Arbor, 4.5
3. Purdue University, West Lafayette, 4.5
5. Stanford University, 4.4
5. University of California, Berkeley, 4.4
5. University of Illinois, Urbana-Champaign, 4.4
8. California Institute of Technology, 4.3
8. Carnegie Mellon University, 4.3
8. Cornell University, 4.3
8. University of Texas, Austin, 4.3
8. Penn State University, University Park, 4.3
8. University of Wisconsin, Madison, 4.3

Source: "America's Best Graduate Schools: 2002 Annual Guide," *U.S. News & World Report*, 130: 60-97, (April 19, 2001).

★2369★

Top recruiters for engineering jobs for 2000-01 master's degree recipients

Ranking basis/background: Projected number of college hires from on-campus recruitment for 2000-01. **Remarks:** Numbers reflect total expected hires, not just African American projected hires. **Number listed:** 1.
1. Corning, with 19 projected hires

Source: "The Top 100 Employers and the Majors in Demand for the Class of 2001," *The Black Collegian*, 31: 19-35, (February 2001).

★2370★

Top recruiters for multidisciplinary engineers jobs for 2000-01 master's degree recipients

Ranking basis/background: Projected number of college hires from on-campus recruitment for 2000-01. **Remarks:** Numbers reflect total expected hires, not just African American projected hires. **Number listed:** 1.
1. Schlumberger, with 100 projected hires

Source: "The Top 100 Employers and the Majors in Demand for the Class of 2001," *The Black Collegian*, 31: 19-35, (February 2001).

★2371★

Top recruiters for systems engineer jobs for 2000-01 master's degree recipients

Ranking basis/background: Projected number of college hires from on-campus recruitment for 2000-01. **Remarks:** Numbers reflect total expected hires, not just African American projected hires. **Number listed:** 6.
1. EDS, with 100 projected hires
1. Lucent Technologies, 100
3. Accenture, 12
4. Corning, 4
5. CNF Inc., 2
6. Arthur Andersen LLP, 1

Source: "The Top 100 Employers and the Majors in Demand for the Class of 2001," *The Black Collegian*, 31: 19-35, (February 2001).

★2372★

U.S. News & World Report's graduate engineering programs with the highest academic reputation scores, 2000-01

Ranking basis/background: Based on *U.S News* survey asking engineering school deans and senior faculty to rate the quality of programs they are familiar with, and name the best programs in various specialties. **Number listed:** 85.
1. Massachusetts Institute of Technology, with a score of 4.9
2. Stanford University, 4.7
2. University of California, Berkeley, 4.7
4. California Institute of Technology, 4.6
5. University of Illinois, Urbana-Champaign, 4.5
5. University of Michigan, Ann Arbor, 4.5
7. Cornell University, 4.4
7. Georgia Institute of Technology, 4.4
9. Carnegie Mellon University, 4.3
9. Purdue University, West Lafayette, 4.3
9. University of Texas, Austin, 4.3

Source: "America's Best Colleges," *U.S. News & World Report*, 129: 90-132, (September 11, 2000).

ENGINEERING, GRADUATE–AERONAUTICAL
See also: **Engineering–Aeronautical**

★2373★

Top recruiters for aeronautical engineering jobs for 2000-01 master's degree recipients

Ranking basis/background: Projected number of college hires from on-campus recruitment for 2000-01. **Remarks:** Numbers reflect total expected hires, not just African American projected hires. **Number listed:** 2.
1. U.S. Air Force (Active Duty Hires), with 2 projected hires
2. Accenture, 1

Source: "The Top 100 Employers and the Majors in Demand for the Class of 2001," *The Black Collegian*, 31: 19-35, (February 2001).

ENGINEERING, GRADUATE–AEROSPACE
See also: **Engineering–Aerospace**

★2374★

Academics' choices for best graduate aerospace/aeronautical/astronautical engineering programs, 2001

Ranking basis/background: From a *U.S. News & World Report* survey of engineering school deans. **Remarks:** Data collected by Market Facts, Inc. **Number listed:** 10.
1. Massachusetts Institute of Technology
2. Stanford University
3. Georgia Institute of Technology
4. University of Michigan, Ann Arbor
5. California Institute of Technology
6. Purdue University, West Lafayette
7. University of Texas, Austin
8. University of Illinois, Urbana-Champaign
9. Princeton University
10. Cornell University

Source: "America's Best Graduate Schools: 2002 Annual Guide," *U.S. News & World Report*, 130: 60-97, (April 19, 2001).

★2375★

Most effective aerospace engineering research-doctorate programs as evaluated by the National Research Council

Ranking basis/background: From a survey of nearly 8,000 faculty members conducted in the spring of 1993. Respondents were asked to rate programs in their field on "effectiveness of program in educating research scholars/scientists." **Remarks:** See *Chronicle* article for more details. Scores of 3.5-5.0 indicate "extremely effective;" 2.5-3.49 "reasonably effective;" 1.5-2.49 "minimally effective;" and 0.0-1.49 "not effective." Programs also ranked by "scholarly quality of program faculty." **Number listed:** 33.
1. California Institute of Technology, with an effectiveness rating of 4.43
2. Massachusetts Institute of Technology, 4.31
3. Stanford University, 4.26
4. Princeton University, 4.03
5. University of Michigan, 3.80
6. Cornell University, 3.75
7. University of Texas, Austin, 3.64
8. Georgia Institute of Technology, 3.49
9. Purdue University, 3.46
10. University of California, Los Angeles, 3.44

Source: "Rankings of Research-Doctorate Programs in 41 Disciplines at 274 Institutions," *The Chronicle of Higher Education* 42: A21-A30 (September 21, 1995).

★2376★

Top aerospace engineering research-doctorate programs as evaluated by the National Research Council

Ranking basis/background: From a survey of nearly 8,000 faculty members conducted in the spring of 1993. Respondents were asked to rate programs in their field on "scholarly quality of program faculty." When more than one program had the samescore, the council averaged the rank order and gave each program the same rank number (if three programs tied for the top position, each received a rank of 2). **Remarks:** See *Chronicle* article for more details. Scores of 4.01 and above indicate "distinguished;" 3.0-4.0 "strong;" 2.51-3.0 "good;" 2.0-2.5 "adequate;" 1.0-1.99 "marginal;" and 0.0-0.99 "not sufficient for doctoral education." Programs also ranked by "effectiveness of program in educating research scholars/scientists." **Number listed:** 33.
1. California Institute of Technology, with a quality rating of 4.61
2. Massachusetts Institute of Technology, 4.54
3. Stanford University, 4.50
4. Princeton University, 4.30
5. University of Michigan, 4.05
6. Cornell University, 3.93
7. Purdue University, 3.71
8. University of Texas, Austin, 3.67
9. Georgia Institute of Technology, 3.66
10. University of California, San Diego, 3.62
10. University of California, Los Angeles, 3.62
12. University of Minnesota, 3.40
13. University of Colorado, 3.35
14. University of Illinois, Urbana-Champaign, 3.34

15. Virginia Polytechnic Institute and State University, 3.24
Source: "Rankings of Research-Doctorate Programs in 41 Disciplines at 274 Institutions," *The Chronicle of Higher Education* 42: A21-A30 (September 21, 1995).

★2377★
Top recruiters for aerospace engineering jobs for 2000-01 master's degree recipients

Ranking basis/background: Projected number of college hires from on-campus recruitment for 2000-01. **Remarks:** Numbers reflect total expected hires, not just African American projected hires. **Number listed:** 2.
1. Litton Industries, with 10 projected hires
2. Accenture, 1

Source: "The Top 100 Employers and the Majors in Demand for the Class of 2001," *The Black Collegian*, 31: 19-35, (February 2001).

★2378★
***U.S. News & World Report*'s graduate engineering programs with the best aerospace departments, 2000-01**

Ranking basis/background: Based on *U.S News* survey asking engineering school deans and senior faculty to rate the quality of programs they are familiar with, and name the best programs in various specialties. **Number listed:** 5.
1. Massachusetts Institute of Technology
2. Georgia Institute of Technology
3. University of Michigan, Ann Arbor
4. Stanford University
5. Purdue University, West Lafayette

Source: "America's Best Colleges," *U.S. News & World Report*, 129: 90-132, (September 11, 2000).

ENGINEERING, GRADUATE–AGRICULTURAL

★2379★
Academics' choices for best graduate agricultural engineering programs, 2001

Ranking basis/background: From a *U.S. News & World Report* survey of engineering school deans. **Remarks:** Data collected by Market Facts, Inc. **Number listed:** 10.
1. Texas A&M University, College Station
2. Purdue University, West Lafayette
3. University of Illinois, Urbana-Champaign
4. University of California, Davis
5. Cornell University
6. University of Nebraska, Lincoln
7. North Carolina State University
8. Penn State University, University Park
9. Iowa State University
10. University of Florida

Source: "America's Best Graduate Schools: 2002 Annual Guide," *U.S. News & World Report*, 130: 60-97, (April 19, 2001).

ENGINEERING, GRADUATE–BIOCHEMICAL

★2380★
***U.S. News & World Report*'s undergraduate engineering programs with the best industrial manufacturing departments, 2000-01**

Ranking basis/background: Based on *U.S News* survey asking engineering school deans and senior faculty to rate the quality of programs they are familiar with, and name the best programs in various specialties. **Number listed:** 5.
1. Kettering University
2. Bradley University
2. California Polytechnic State University, San Luis Obispo
2. Rochester Institute of Technology
2. University of Wisconsin, Platteville

Source: "America's Best Colleges," *U.S. News & World Report*, 129: 90-132, (September 11, 2000).

ENGINEERING, GRADUATE–BIOMEDICAL

★2381★
Academics' choices for best graduate bioengineering/biomedical engineering programs, 2001

Ranking basis/background: From a *U.S. News & World Report* survey of engineering school deans. **Remarks:** Data collected by Market Facts, Inc. **Number listed:** 10.
1. Johns Hopkins University
2. Duke University
3. University of California, San Diego
4. Massachusetts Institute of Technology
5. Case Western Reserve University
6. Georgia Institute of Technology
7. University of Washington (WA)
8. University of Pennsylvania
9. University of Michigan, Ann Arbor
10. University of California, Berkeley

Source: "America's Best Graduate Schools: 2002 Annual Guide," *U.S. News & World Report*, 130: 60-97, (April 19, 2001).

★2382★
Most-cited biomedical scientists, 1990-97

Ranking basis/background: For each scientist/affiliation, total citations and number of papers. **Remarks:** Original source: *National Science Indicators on Diskette, 1981-97* **Number listed:** 5.
1. Bert Vogelstein (Howard Hughes Medical Institute Johns Hopkins University), with 27,901 total citations; 190 papers
2. Salvador Moncada (University College London), 20,354; 342
3. Solomon H. Snyder (Johns Hopkins University), 19,793; 251
4. Joseph Schlessinger (New York University Medical Center), 18,315; 228
5. Pierre Chambon (Institute of Genetics/Molecular Cellular Biology), 15,035; 328

Source: "Superstars of Biomedicine, 1990-97," *What's Hot*, June 29, 1998.

★2383★
Most effective biomedical engineering research-doctorate programs as evaluated by the National Research Council

Ranking basis/background: From a survey of nearly 8,000 faculty members conducted in the spring of 1993. Respondents were asked to rate programs in their field on "effectiveness of program in educating research scholars/scientists." **Remarks:** See *Chronicle* article for more details. Scores of 3.5-5.0 indicate "extremely effective;" 2.5-3.49 "reasonably effective;" 1.5-2.49 "minimally effective;" and 0.0-1.49 "not effective." Programs also ranked by "scholarly quality of program faculty." **Number listed:** 38.
1. University of California, San Diego, with an effectiveness rating of 4.17
2. Massachusetts Institute of Technology, 4.17
3. Johns Hopkins University, 409
4. Rice University, 3.95
5. University of California, San Francisco, 3.89
6. University of Washington (WA), 3.85
7. University of California, Berkeley, 3.84
8. Stanford University, 3.83
9. University of Pennsylvania, 3.82
10. University of Utah, 3.69

Source: "Rankings of Research-Doctorate Programs in 41 Disciplines at 274 Institutions," *The Chronicle of Higher Education* 42: A21-A30 (September 21, 1995).

★2384★
Top biomedical engineering research-doctorate programs as evaluated by the National Research Council

Ranking basis/background: From a survey of nearly 8,000 faculty members conducted in the spring of 1993. Respondents were asked to rate programs in their field on "scholarly quality of program faculty." When more than one program had the samescore, the council averaged the rank order and gave each program the same rank number (if three programs tied for the top position, each received a rank of 2). **Remarks:** See *Chronicle* article for more details. Scores of 4.01 and above indicate "distinguished;" 3.0-4.0 "strong;" 2.51-3.0 "good;" 2.0-2.5 "adequate;" 1.0-1.99 "marginal;" and 0.0-0.99 "not sufficient for doctoral education." Programs also ranked by "effectiveness of program in educating research scholars/scientists." **Number listed:** 38.
1. Massachusetts Institute of Technology, with a quality rating of 4.62
2. University of California, San Diego, 4.45
3. University of Washington (WA), 4.35
4. Duke University, 4.33
5. University of Pennsylvania, 4.28
6. Johns Hopkins University, 4.25
7. University of California, San Francisco, 4.19
8. University of California, Berkeley, 4.08
9. University of Utah, 3.97
10. Rice University, 3.94
11. University of Michigan, 3.91
12. Stanford University, 3.86
13. Case Western Reserve University, 3.84
14. Northwestern University, 3.82
15. University of Rochester, 3.67

Source: "Rankings of Research-Doctorate Programs in 41 Disciplines at 274 Institutions," *The Chronicle of Higher Education* 42: A21-A30 (September 21, 1995).

ENGINEERING, GRADUATE—CHEMICAL

★2385★
U.S. News & World Report's graduate engineering programs with the best biomedical departments, 2000-01

Ranking basis/background: Based on *U.S News* survey asking engineering school deans and senior faculty to rate the quality of programs they are familiar with, and name the best programs in various specialties. **Number listed:** 5.
1. Johns Hopkins University
2. Duke University
3. University of California, San Diego
4. Case Western Reserve University
5. Massachusetts Institute of Technology

Source: "America's Best Colleges," *U.S. News & World Report*, 129: 90-132, (September 11, 2000).

ENGINEERING, GRADUATE–CHEMICAL
See also: **Engineering–Chemical**

★2386★
Academics' choices for best graduate chemical engineering programs, 2001

Ranking basis/background: From a *U.S. News & World Report* survey of engineering school deans. **Remarks:** Data collected by Market Facts, Inc. **Number listed:** 10.
1. Massachusetts Institute of Technology
2. University of California, Berkeley
3. University of Minnesota, Twin Cities
4. California Institute of Technology
5. Stanford University
6. University of Texas, Austin
7. University of Wisconsin, Madison
8. University of Delaware
9. Princeton University
10. University of Illinois, Urbana-Champaign

Source: "America's Best Graduate Schools: 2002 Annual Guide," *U.S. News & World Report*, 130: 60-97, (April 19, 2001).

★2387★
Doctoral degrees awarded in chemical engineering, 1980 to 1997

Ranking basis/background: Number of degrees awarded each year. **Remarks:** Original source: National Center for Education Statistics. **Number listed:** 18.
1980, with 284
1981, 300
1982, 311
1983, 319
1984, 330
1985, 418
1986, 446
1987, 497
1988, 579
1989, 602
1990, 562
1991, 611
1992, 590
1993, 595
1994, 604
1995, 571
1996, 670
1997, 650

Source: Brennan, Mairin B., "Demand," *C&EN: Chemical & Engineering News*, 77: 38-46, (November 15, 1999).

★2388★
Master's degrees awarded in chemical engineering, 1980 to 1997

Ranking basis/background: Number of degrees awarded each year. **Remarks:** Original source: National Center for Education Statistics. **Number listed:** 18.
1980, with 1,270
1981, 1,267
1982, 1,285
1983, 1,368
1984, 1,514
1985, 1,544
1986, 1,361
1987, 1,184
1988, 1,088
1989, 1,093
1990, 1,035
1991, 903
1992, 956
1993, 990
1994, 1,032
1995, 1,085
1996, 1,176
1997, 1,131

Source: Brennan, Mairin B., "Demand," *C&EN: Chemical & Engineering News*, 77: 38-46, (November 15, 1999).

★2389★
Most effective chemical engineering research-doctorate programs as evaluated by the National Research Council

Ranking basis/background: From a survey of nearly 8,000 faculty members conducted in the spring of 1993. Respondents were asked to rate programs in their field on "effectiveness of program in educating research scholars/scientists." **Remarks:** See *Chronicle* article for more details. Scores of 3.5-5.0 indicate "extremely effective;" 2.5-3.49 "reasonably effective;" 1.5-2.49 "minimally effective;" and 0.0-1.49 "not effective." Programs also ranked by "scholarly quality of program faculty." **Number listed:** 93.
1. University of Minnesota, with an effectiveness rating of 4.57
2. Massachusetts Institute of Technology, 4.43
2. University of California, Berkeley, 4.43
4. University of Wisconsin, Madison, 4.37
5. Stanford University, 4.31
6. University of Illinois, Urbana-Champaign, 4.28
7. California Institute of Technology, 4.24
8. University of Delaware, 4.21
9. Princeton University, 4.02
10. University of Pennsylvania, 3.81
10. Cornell University, 3.81

Source: "Rankings of Research-Doctorate Programs in 41 Disciplines at 274 Institutions," *The Chronicle of Higher Education* 42: A21-A30 (September 21, 1995).

★2390★
Top chemical engineering research-doctorate programs as evaluated by the National Research Council

Ranking basis/background: From a survey of nearly 8,000 faculty members conducted in the spring of 1993. Respondents were asked to rate programs in their field on "scholarly quality of program faculty." When more than one program had the same score, the council averaged the rank order and gave each program the same rank number (if three programs tied for the top position, each received a rank of 2). **Remarks:** See *Chronicle* article for more details. Scores of 4.01 and above indicate "distinguished;" 3.0-4.0 "strong;" 2.51-3.0 "good;" 2.0-2.5 "adequate;" 1.0-1.99 "marginal;" and 0.0-0.99 "not sufficient for doctoral education." Programs also ranked by "effectiveness of program in educating research scholars/scientists." **Number listed:** 93.
1. University of Minnesota, with a quality rating of 4.86
2. Massachusetts Institute of Technology, 4.73
3. University of California, Berkeley, 4.63
4. University of Wisconsin, Madison, 4.62
5. University of Illinois, Urbana-Champaign, 4.42
6. California Institute of Technology, 4.41
7. Stanford University, 4.35
8. University of Delaware, 4.34
9. Princeton University, 4.14
10. University of Texas, Austin, 4.08
11. University of Pennsylvania, 3.97
12. Carnegie Mellon University, 3.87
13. Cornell University, 3.86
14. University of California, Santa Barbara, 3.75
15. Northwestern University, 3.75

Source: "Rankings of Research-Doctorate Programs in 41 Disciplines at 274 Institutions," *The Chronicle of Higher Education* 42: A21-A30 (September 21, 1995).

★2391★
Top recruiters for chemical engineering jobs for 2000-01 master's degree recipients

Ranking basis/background: Projected number of college hires from on-campus recruitment for 2000-01. **Remarks:** Numbers reflect total expected hires, not just African American projected hires. **Number listed:** 5.
1. Lucent Technologies, with 30 projected hires
2. Procter & Gamble, 20
3. Accenture, 8
4. Corning, 3
4. Life Scan, 3

Source: "The Top 100 Employers and the Majors in Demand for the Class of 2001," *The Black Collegian*, 31: 19-35, (February 2001).

★2392★
U.S. News & World Report's graduate engineering programs with the best chemical departments, 2000-01

Ranking basis/background: Based on *U.S News* survey asking engineering school deans and senior faculty to rate the quality of programs they are familiar with, and name the best programs in various specialties. **Number listed:** 5.
1. Massachusetts Institute of Technology
2. University of California, Berkeley
3. University of Minnesota, Twin Cities

4. University of Delaware
4. University of Wisconsin, Madison
Source: "America's Best Colleges," *U.S. News & World Report*, 129: 90-132, (September 11, 2000).

★2393★
U.S. universities with the greatest impact in chemical engineering, 1994-98

Ranking basis/background: Total number of chemical engineering papers published from each university and average number of citations per paper between 1994 and 1998. **Remarks:** Original source: University Science Indicators on Diskette, 1981-98. **Number listed:** 5.
1. Northwestern University, with 113 chemical engineering papers; 6.49 citations per paper
2. University of Pittsburgh, 126; 5.40
3. University of Wisconsin, Madison, 137; 4.73
4. University of Delaware, 168; 4.64
5. Lehigh University, 104; 4.36

Source: "Chemical Engineering: High-Impact U.S. Universities, 1994-98," *What's Hot in Research* (http://www.isinet.com/hot/research) Institute for Scientific Information, April 10, 2000.

ENGINEERING, GRADUATE–CIVIL
See also: **Engineering–Civil**

★2394★
Academics' choices for best graduate civil engineering programs, 2001

Ranking basis/background: From a *U.S. News & World Report* survey of engineering school deans. **Remarks:** Data collected by Market Facts, Inc. **Number listed:** 10.
1. University of California, Berkeley
1. University of Illinois, Urbana-Champaign
3. University of Texas, Austin
4. Massachusetts Institute of Technology
5. Purdue University, West Lafayette
6. Georgia Institute of Technology
6. Stanford University
8. University of Michigan, Ann Arbor
9. Cornell University
10. California Institute of Technology
10. Texas A&M University, College Station

Source: "America's Best Graduate Schools: 2002 Annual Guide," *U.S. News & World Report*, 130: 60-97, (April 19, 2001).

★2395★
Most effective civil engineering research-doctorate programs as evaluated by the National Research Council

Ranking basis/background: From a survey of nearly 8,000 faculty members conducted in the spring of 1993. Respondents were asked to rate programs in their field on "effectiveness of program in educating research scholars/scientists." **Remarks:** See *Chronicle* article for more details. Scores of 3.5-5.0 indicate "extremely effective;" 2.5-3.49 "reasonably effective;" 1.5-2.49 "minimally effective;" and 0.0-1.49 "not effective." Programs also ranked by "scholarly quality of program faculty." **Number listed:** 86.
1. Massachusetts Institute of Technology, with an effectiveness rating of 4.47
2. California Institute of Technology, 4.42
3. Stanford University, 4.29
4. University of Texas, Austin, 4.27
5. University of Illinois, Urbana-Champaign, 4.23
6. University of California, Berkeley, 4.22
7. Cornell University, 4.08
8. Princeton University, 3.89
9. University of Michigan, 3.82
10. Carnegie Mellon University, 3.79

Source: "Rankings of Research-Doctorate Programs in 41 Disciplines at 274 Institutions," *The Chronicle of Higher Education* 42: A21-A30 (September 21, 1995).

★2396★
Top civil engineering research-doctorate programs as evaluated by the National Research Council

Ranking basis/background: From a survey of nearly 8,000 faculty members conducted in the spring of 1993. Respondents were asked to rate programs in their field on "scholarly quality of program faculty." When more than one program had the samescore, the council averaged the rank order and gave each program the same rank number (if three programs tied for the top position, each received a rank of 2). **Remarks:** See *Chronicle* article for more details. Scores of 4.01 and above indicate "distinguished;" 3.0-4.0 "strong;" 2.51-3.0 "good;" 2.0-2.5 "adequate;" 1.0-1.99 "marginal;" and 0.0-0.99 "not sufficient for doctoral education." Programs also ranked by "effectiveness of program in educating research scholars/scientists." **Number listed:** 86.
1. Massachusetts Institute of Technology, with a quality rating of 4.61
2. University of California, Berkeley, 4.56
3. Stanford University, 4.44
4. University of Texas, Austin, 4.42
5. University of Illinois, Urbana-Champaign, 4.41
6. Cornell University, 4.30
7. California Institute of Technology, 4.27
8. Princeton University, 3.99
9. Northwestern University, 3.96
10. University of Michigan, 3.90
11. Purdue University, 3.89
12. Carnegie Mellon University, 3.85
13. University of Minnesota, 3.76
14. University of Washington (WA), 3.67
15. University of North Carolina, Chapel Hill, 3.58

Source: "Rankings of Research-Doctorate Programs in 41 Disciplines at 274 Institutions," *The Chronicle of Higher Education* 42: A21-A30 (September 21, 1995).

★2397★
Top recruiters for civil engineering jobs for 2000-01 master's degree recipients

Ranking basis/background: Projected number of college hires from on-campus recruitment for 2000-01. **Remarks:** Numbers reflect total expected hires, not just African American projected hires. **Number listed:** 4.
1. Gannett Fleming, Inc., with 10 projected hires
2. Accenture, 8
3. Dewberry & Davis LLC, 5
3. Ingalls Shipbuilding, 5

Source: "The Top 100 Employers and the Majors in Demand for the Class of 2001," *The Black Collegian*, 31: 19-35, (February 2001).

★2398★
U.S. News & World Report's graduate engineering programs with the best civil departments, 2000-01

Ranking basis/background: Based on *U.S News* survey asking engineering school deans and senior faculty to rate the quality of programs they are familiar with, and name the best programs in various specialties. **Number listed:** 5.
1. University of California, Berkeley
2. University of Illinois, Urbana-Champaign
3. Massachusetts Institute of Technology
4. Georgia Institute of Technology
5. University of Texas, Austin

Source: "America's Best Colleges," *U.S. News & World Report*, 129: 90-132, (September 11, 2000).

ENGINEERING, GRADUATE–COMPUTER
See also: **Engineering–Computer**

★2399★
Academics' choices for best graduate computer engineering programs, 2001

Ranking basis/background: From a *U.S. News & World Report* survey of engineering school deans. **Remarks:** Data collected by Market Facts, Inc. **Number listed:** 10.
1. Carnegie Mellon University
2. Massachusetts Institute of Technology
3. Stanford University
4. University of California, Berkeley
5. University of Illinois, Urbana-Champaign
6. University of Texas, Austin
7. University of Washington (WA)
8. University of Michigan, Ann Arbor
9. Princeton University
10. Cornell University

Source: "America's Best Graduate Schools: 2002 Annual Guide," *U.S. News & World Report*, 130: 60-97, (April 19, 2001).

★2400★
Top recruiters for computer engineering jobs for 2000-01 master's degree recipients

Ranking basis/background: Projected number of college hires from on-campus recruitment for 2000-01. **Remarks:** Numbers reflect total expected hires, not just African American projected hires. **Number listed:** 10.
1. Lucent Technologies, with 200 projected hires
2. Litton Industries, 30
3. Deloitte & Touche, 20
4. Accenture, 15
5. Federal Deposit Insurance Company, 10
6. ALLTEL, 5
7. Automated Analysis Corporation, 4
8. CNF Inc., 2
9. Arthur Andersen LLP, 1
9. Novant Health, 1

Source: "The Top 100 Employers and the Majors in Demand for the Class of 2001," *The Black Collegian*, 31: 19-35, (February 2001).

★2401★
U.S. News & World Report's graduate engineering programs with the best computer departments, 2000-01

Ranking basis/background: Based on *U.S News* survey asking engineering school deans and senior faculty to rate the quality of programs they are familiar with, and name the best programs in various specialties. **Number listed:** 5.
1. Massachusetts Institute of Technology
2. Stanford University
2. University of California, Berkeley
4. University of Illinois, Urbana-Champaign
5. Carnegie Mellon University

Source: "America's Best Colleges," *U.S. News & World Report*, 129: 90-132, (September 11, 2000).

★2402★
U.S. universities with the highest concentrations in artificial intelligence, 1992-96

Ranking basis/background: For each university, percentage of total number of papers that are artificial intelligence papers and total artificial intelligence papers published during a five-year period. **Remarks:** Original source: *National Science Indicators on Diskette, 1981-97* **Number listed:** 5.
1. Massachusetts Institute of Technology, with 1.26% of university's total papers; 234 artificial intelligence papers
2. University of Michigan, 1.22%; 227
3. Carnegie Mellon University, 1.20%; 222
4. University of Maryland, College Park, 1.09%; 203
5. Purdue University, 1.06; 196

Source: "Artificial Intelligence: Most Prolific U.S. Universities, 1992-96," *What's Hot*, June 29, 1998.

ENGINEERING, GRADUATE–ELECTRICAL/ELECTRONIC

See also: **Engineering–Electrical/Electronic**

★2403★
Academics' choices for best graduate electrical/electronic/communications engineering programs, 2001

Ranking basis/background: From a *U.S. News & World Report* survey of engineering school deans. **Remarks:** Data collected by Market Facts, Inc. **Number listed:** 10.
1. Massachusetts Institute of Technology
2. Stanford University
3. University of Illinois, Urbana-Champaign
4. University of California, Berkeley
5. University of Michigan, Ann Arbor
6. California Institute of Technology
7. Georgia Institute of Technology
8. Cornell University
9. Purdue University, West Lafayette
10. Carnegie Mellon University

Source: "America's Best Graduate Schools: 2002 Annual Guide," *U.S. News & World Report*, 130: 60-97, (April 19, 2001).

★2404★
Most effective electrical engineering research-doctorate programs as evaluated by the National Research Council

Ranking basis/background: From a survey of nearly 8,000 faculty members conducted in the spring of 1993. Respondents were asked to rate programs in their field on "effectiveness of program in educating research scholars/scientists." **Remarks:** See *Chronicle* article for more details. Scores of 3.5-5.0 indicate "extremely effective;" 2.5-3.49 "reasonably effective;" 1.5-2.49 "minimally effective;" and 0.0-1.49 "not effective." Programs also ranked by "scholarly quality of program faculty." **Number listed:** 126.
1. Stanford University, with an effectiveness rating of 4.68
2. Massachusetts Institute of Technology, 4.61
3. University of Illinois, Urbana-Champaign, 4.57
4. University of California, Berkeley, 4.46
5. California Institute of Technology, 4.34
6. University of Michigan, 4.17
7. Cornell University, 4.08
8. Carnegie Mellon University, 4.05
9. Princeton University, 4.00
10. Purdue University, 3.94

Source: "Rankings of Research-Doctorate Programs in 41 Disciplines at 274 Institutions," *The Chronicle of Higher Education* 42: A21-A30 (September 21, 1995).

★2405★
Top electrical engineering research-doctorate programs as evaluated by the National Research Council

Ranking basis/background: From a survey of nearly 8,000 faculty members conducted in the spring of 1993. Respondents were asked to rate programs in their field on "scholarly quality of program faculty." When more than one program had the samescore, the council averaged the rank order and gave each program the same rank number (if three programs tied for the top position, each received a rank of 2). **Remarks:** See *Chronicle* article for more details. Scores of 4.01 and above indicate "distinguished;" 3.0-4.0 "strong;" 2.51-3.0 "good;" 2.0-2.5 "adequate;" 1.0-1.99 "marginal;" and 0.0-0.99 "not sufficient for doctoral education." Programs also ranked by "effectiveness of program in educating research scholars/scientists." **Number listed:** 126.
1. Stanford University, with a quality rating of 4.83
2. Massachusetts Institute of Technology, 4.79
3. University of Illinois, Urbana-Champaign, 4.70
4. University of California, Berkeley, 4.69
5. California Institute of Technology, 4.46
6. University of Michigan, 4.38
7. Cornell University, 4.35
8. Purdue University, 4.02
9. Princeton University, 4.01
10. University of Southern California, 4.00
10. University of California, Los Angeles, 4.00
12. Carnegie Mellon University, 3.94
13. Georgia Institute of Technology, 3.93
14. University of Texas, Austin, 3.88
15. Columbia University, 3.79

Source: "Rankings of Research-Doctorate Programs in 41 Disciplines at 274 Institutions," *The Chronicle of Higher Education* 42: A21-A30 (September 21, 1995).

★2406★
Top recruiters for electrical/electronic engineering jobs for 2000-01 master's degree recipients

Ranking basis/background: Projected number of college hires from on-campus recruitment for 2000-01. **Remarks:** Numbers reflect total expected hires, not just African American projected hires. **Number listed:** 36.
1. Lucent Technologies, with 300 projected hires
2. Accenture, 65
3. Agilent Technologies, 48
4. Tellabs, 40
5. Qualcomm, 25
6. Corning, 21
7. General Motors, 20
7. Telcordia Technologies, 20
9. Automated Analysis Corporation, 10
10. Procter & Gamble, 5
10. Ingalls Shipbuilding, 5
10. ALLTEL, 5

Source: "The Top 100 Employers and the Majors in Demand for the Class of 2001," *The Black Collegian*, 31: 19-35, (February 2001).

★2407★
U.S. News & World Report's graduate engineering programs with the best electrical departments, 2000-01

Ranking basis/background: Based on *U.S News* survey asking engineering school deans and senior faculty to rate the quality of programs they are familiar with, and name the best programs in various specialties. **Number listed:** 5.
1. Massachusetts Institute of Technology
2. University of California, Berkeley
3. Stanford University
3. University of Illinois, Urbana-Champaign
5. University of Michigan, Ann Arbor

Source: "America's Best Colleges," *U.S. News & World Report*, 129: 90-132, (September 11, 2000).

ENGINEERING, GRADUATE–ENVIRONMENTAL

See also: **Engineering–Environmental**

★2408★
Academics' choices for best graduate environmental/environmental health engineering programs, 2001

Ranking basis/background: From a *U.S. News & World Report* survey of engineering school deans. **Remarks:** Data collected by Market Facts, Inc. **Number listed:** 10.
1. Stanford University
2. University of Michigan, Ann Arbor
3. University of Illinois, Urbana-Champaign
4. University of California, Berkeley
5. University of Texas, Austin
6. Johns Hopkins University
7. Massachusetts Institute of Technology
8. California Institute of Technology
9. Georgia Institute of Technology
10. University of North Carolina, Chapel Hill

Source: "America's Best Graduate Schools: 2002 Annual Guide," *U.S. News & World Report*, 130: 60-97, (April 19, 2001).

★2409★
Top recruiters for environmental engineering jobs for 2000-01 master's degree recipients

Ranking basis/background: Projected number of college hires from on-campus recruitment for 2000-01. **Remarks:** Numbers reflect total expected hires, not just African American projected hires. **Number listed:** 3.
1. Dewberry & Davis LLC, with 3 projected hires
2. Gannett Fleming, Inc., 2
3. International Paper, 1

Source: "The Top 100 Employers and the Majors in Demand for the Class of 2001," *The Black Collegian*, 31: 19-35, (February 2001).

★2410★
U.S. News & World Report's graduate engineering programs with the best environmental departments, 2000-01

Ranking basis/background: Based on *U.S News* survey asking engineering school deans and senior faculty to rate the quality of programs they are familiar with, and name the best programs in various specialties. **Number listed:** 5.
1. University of Illinois, Urbana-Champaign
2. Stanford University
3. Massachusetts Institute of Technology
3. University of California, Berkeley
3. University of Michigan, Ann Arbor

Source: "America's Best Colleges," *U.S. News & World Report*, 129: 90-132, (September 11, 2000).

ENGINEERING, GRADUATE–INDUSTRIAL
See also: **Engineering–Industrial**

★2411★
Academics' choices for best graduate industrial/manufacturing engineering programs, 2001

Ranking basis/background: From a *U.S. News & World Report* survey of engineering school deans. **Remarks:** Data collected by Market Facts, Inc. **Number listed:** 10.
1. Georgia Institute of Technology
2. University of Michigan, Ann Arbor
3. Purdue University, West Lafayette
4. Penn State University, University Park
5. University of California, Berkeley
6. Texas A&M University, College Station
7. Stanford University
8. Northwestern University
9. Virginia Tech
10. University of Wisconsin, Madison

Source: "America's Best Graduate Schools: 2002 Annual Guide," *U.S. News & World Report*, 130: 60-97, (April 19, 2001).

★2412★
Most effective industrial engineering research-doctorate programs as evaluated by the National Research Council

Ranking basis/background: From a survey of nearly 8,000 faculty members conducted in the spring of 1993. Respondents were asked to rate programs in their field on "effectiveness of program in educating research scholars/scientists." **Remarks:** See *Chronicle* article for more details. Scores of 3.5-5.0 indicate "extremely effective;" 2.5-3.49 "reasonably effective;" 1.5-2.49 "minimally effective;" and 0.0-1.49 "not effective." Programs also ranked by "scholarly quality of program faculty." **Number listed:** 37.
1. University of California, Berkeley, with an effectiveness rating of 4.31
2. Georgia Institute of Technology, 4.30
3. University of Michigan, 4.19
4. Purdue University, 4.07
5. Virginia Polytechnic Institute and State University, 3.68
6. Northwestern University, 3.62
7. Stanford University, 3.60
8. Pennsylvania State University, 3.52
9. University of Wisconsin, Madison, 3.48
10. Texas A&M University, 3.44

Source: "Rankings of Research-Doctorate Programs in 41 Disciplines at 274 Institutions," *The Chronicle of Higher Education* 42: A21-A30 (September 21, 1995).

★2413★
Top industrial engineering research-doctorate programs as evaluated by the National Research Council

Ranking basis/background: From a survey of nearly 8,000 faculty members conducted in the spring of 1993. Respondents were asked to rate programs in their field on "scholarly quality of program faculty." When more than one program had the same score, the council averaged the rank order and gave each program the same rank number (if three programs tied for the top position, each received a rank of 2). **Remarks:** See *Chronicle* article for more details. Scores of 4.01 and above indicate "distinguished;" 3.0-4.0 "strong;" 2.51-3.0 "good;" 2.0-2.5 "adequate;" 1.0-1.99 "marginal;" and 0.0-0.99 "not sufficient for doctoral education." Programs also ranked by "effectiveness of program in educating research scholars/scientists." **Number listed:** 37.
1. Georgia Institute of Technology, with a quality rating of 4.71
2. University of California, Berkeley, 4.44
3. Purdue University, 4.43
4. University of Michigan, 4.36
5. Texas A&M University, 3.81
6. Northwestern University, 3.73
7. Stanford University, 3.68
8. Virginia Polytechnic Institute and State University, 3.66
9. Pennsylvania State University, 3.50
10. University of Wisconsin, Madison, 3.48
11. North Carolina State University, 3.46
12. Ohio State University, 3.24
13. University of Illinois, Urbana-Champaign, 3.13
14. Rensselaer Polytechnic Institute, 3.12
15. Lehigh University, 3.03

Source: "Rankings of Research-Doctorate Programs in 41 Disciplines at 274 Institutions," *The Chronicle of Higher Education* 42: A21-A30 (September 21, 1995).

★2414★
Top recruiters for industrial engineering jobs for 2000-01 master's degree recipients

Ranking basis/background: Projected number of college hires from on-campus recruitment for 2000-01. **Remarks:** Numbers reflect total expected hires, not just African American projected hires. **Number listed:** 2.
1. Corning, with 7 projected hires
2. Cigna, 6

Source: "The Top 100 Employers and the Majors in Demand for the Class of 2001," *The Black Collegian*, 31: 19-35, (February 2001).

★2415★
U.S. News & World Report's graduate engineering programs with the best industrial manufacturing departments, 2000-01

Ranking basis/background: Based on *U.S News* survey asking engineering school deans and senior faculty to rate the quality of programs they are familiar with, and name the best programs in various specialties. **Number listed:** 5.
1. Purdue University, West Lafayette
2. Georgia Institute of Technology
3. University of Michigan, Ann Arbor
4. University of California, Berkeley
5. Texas A&M University, College Station

Source: "America's Best Colleges," *U.S. News & World Report*, 129: 90-132, (September 11, 2000).

ENGINEERING, GRADUATE–MARINE
See also: **Engineering–Marine**

★2416★
Top recruiters for marine engineering jobs for 2000-01 master's degree recipients

Ranking basis/background: Projected number of college hires from on-campus recruitment for 2000-01. **Remarks:** Numbers reflect total expected hires, not just African American projected hires. **Number listed:** 1.
1. Ingalls Shipbuilding, with 5 projected hires

Source: "The Top 100 Employers and the Majors in Demand for the Class of 2001," *The Black Collegian*, 31: 19-35, (February 2001).

ENGINEERING, GRADUATE–MATERIALS/METALLURGICAL
See also: **Engineering–Materials/Metallurgical**

★2417★
Academics' choices for best graduate materials engineering programs, 2001

Ranking basis/background: From a *U.S. News & World Report* survey of engineering school deans. **Remarks:** Data collected by Market Facts, Inc. **Number listed:** 10.
1. Massachusetts Institute of Technology
2. Northwestern University
3. Stanford University
4. University of Illinois, Urbana-Champaign

ENGINEERING, GRADUATE—MECHANICAL

5. University of California, Berkeley
6. University of Michigan, Ann Arbor
7. University of California, Santa Barbara
8. Cornell University
9. Penn State University, University Park
10. University of Florida

Source: "America's Best Graduate Schools: 2002 Annual Guide," *U.S. News & World Report*, 130: 60-97, (April 19, 2001).

★2418★
Most effective materials science research-doctorate programs as evaluated by the National Research Council

Ranking basis/background: From a survey of nearly 8,000 faculty members conducted in the spring of 1993. Respondents were asked to rate programs in their field on "effectiveness of program in educating research scholars/scientists." **Remarks:** See *Chronicle* article for more details. Scores of 3.5-5.0 indicate "extremely effective;" 2.5-3.49 "reasonably effective;" 1.5-2.49 "minimally effective;" and 0.0-1.49 "not effective." Programs also ranked by "scholarly quality of program faculty." **Number listed:** 65.

1. Massachusetts Institute of Technology, with an effectiveness rating of 4.22
2. University of Massachusetts, Amherst, 4.21
3. Cornell University, 4.10
4. Northwestern University, 4.08
5. University of California, Berkeley, 4.08
6. Stanford University, 4.00
7. University of Illinois, Urbana-Champaign, 3.93
8. Pennsylvania State University, 3.83
9. Carnegie Mellon University, 3.72
10. Rensselaer Polytechnic Institute, 3.65

Source: "Rankings of Research-Doctorate Programs in 41 Disciplines at 274 Institutions," *The Chronicle of Higher Education* 42: A21-A30 (September 21, 1995).

★2419★
Top materials science research-doctorate programs as evaluated by the National Research Council

Ranking basis/background: From a survey of nearly 8,000 faculty members conducted in the spring of 1993. Respondents were asked to rate programs in their field on "scholarly quality of program faculty." When more than one program had the samescore, the council averaged the rank order and gave each program the same rank number (if three programs tied for the top position, each received a rank of 2). **Remarks:** See *Chronicle* article for more details. Scores of 4.01 and above indicate "distinguished;" 3.0-4.0 "strong;" 2.51-3.0 "good;" 2.0-2.5 "adequate;" 1.0-1.99 "marginal;" and 0.0-0.99 "not sufficient for doctoral education." Programs also ranked by "effectiveness of program in educating research scholars/scientists." **Number listed:** 65.

1. Massachusetts Institute of Technology, with a quality rating of 4.61
2. Northwestern University, 4.47
3. Cornell University, 4.35
4. University of California, Berkeley, 4.33
5. University of Illinois, Urbana-Champaign, 4.29
6. Stanford University, 4.24
7. University of Massachusetts, Amherst, 4.20
8. University of California, Santa Barbara, 4.18
9. Pennsylvania State University, 3.97
10. University of Pennsylvania, 3.79
11. Carnegie Mellon University, 3.75
11. California Institute of Technology, 3.75
13. Rensselaer Polytechnic Institute, 3.68
14. University of Wisconsin, Madison, 3.66
14. University of Michigan, 3.66

Source: "Rankings of Research-Doctorate Programs in 41 Disciplines at 274 Institutions," *The Chronicle of Higher Education* 42: A21-A30 (September 21, 1995).

★2420★
Top recruiters for metallurgical/mining engineering jobs for 2000-01 master's degree recipients

Ranking basis/background: Projected number of college hires from on-campus recruitment for 2000-01. **Remarks:** Numbers reflect total expected hires, not just African American projected hires. **Number listed:** 1.

1. Automated Analysis Corporation, with 3 projected hires

Source: "The Top 100 Employers and the Majors in Demand for the Class of 2001," *The Black Collegian*, 31: 19-35, (February 2001).

★2421★
U.S. News & World Report's graduate engineering programs with the best materials departments, 2000-01

Ranking basis/background: Based on *U.S News* survey asking engineering school deans and senior faculty to rate the quality of programs they are familiar with, and name the best programs in various specialties. **Number listed:** 6.

1. University of Illinois, Urbana-Champaign
2. Massachusetts Institute of Technology
3. Northwestern University
4. University of Michigan, Ann Arbor
5. Pennsylvania State University, University Park
5. Stanford University

Source: "America's Best Colleges," *U.S. News & World Report*, 129: 90-132, (September 11, 2000).

ENGINEERING, GRADUATE–MECHANICAL
See also: **Engineering–Mechanical**

★2422★
Academics' choices for best graduate mechanical engineering programs, 2001

Ranking basis/background: From a *U.S. News & World Report* survey of engineering school deans. **Remarks:** Data collected by Market Facts, Inc. **Number listed:** 10.

1. Massachusetts Institute of Technology
2. Stanford University
3. University of California, Berkeley
4. University of Illinois, Urbana-Champaign
5. University of Michigan, Ann Arbor
6. Georgia Institute of Technology
7. Purdue University, West Lafayette
8. California Institute of Technology
9. Cornell University
10. University of Minnesota, Twin Cities
10. University of Texas, Austin

Source: "America's Best Graduate Schools: 2002 Annual Guide," *U.S. News & World Report*, 130: 60-97, (April 19, 2001).

★2423★
Most effective mechanical engineering research-doctorate programs as evaluated by the National Research Council

Ranking basis/background: From a survey of nearly 8,000 faculty members conducted in the spring of 1993. Respondents were asked to rate programs in their field on "effectiveness of program in educating research scholars/scientists." **Remarks:** See *Chronicle* article for more details. Scores of 3.5-5.0 indicate "extremely effective;" 2.5-3.49 "reasonably effective;" 1.5-2.49 "minimally effective;" and 0.0-1.49 "not effective." Programs also ranked by "scholarly quality of program faculty." **Number listed:** 110.

1. Stanford University, with an effectiveness rating of 4.50
1. University of California, Berkeley, 4.50
3. Massachusetts Institute of Technology, 4.45
4. California Institute of Technology, 4.30
5. Princeton University, 4.09
6. University of Illinois, Urbana-Champaign, 4.02
7. Purdue University, 4.01
8. University of Michigan, 4.00
9. Cornell University, 3.99
10. Northwestern University, 3.87

Source: "Rankings of Research-Doctorate Programs in 41 Disciplines at 274 Institutions," *The Chronicle of Higher Education* 42: A21-A30 (September 21, 1995).

★2424★
Top recruiters for mechanical engineering jobs for 2000-01 master's degree recipients

Ranking basis/background: Projected number of college hires from on-campus recruitment for 2000-01. **Remarks:** Numbers reflect total expected hires, not just African American projected hires. **Number listed:** 6.

1. General Motors, with 50 projected hires
2. Automated Analysis Corporation, 20
3. Accenture, 15
4. Corning, 13
5. Procter & Gamble, 10
6. Ingalls Shipbuilding, 5

Source: "The Top 100 Employers and the Majors in Demand for the Class of 2001," *The Black Collegian*, 31: 19-35, (February 2001).

★2425★
U.S. News & World Report's graduate engineering programs with the best mechanical departments, 2000-01

Ranking basis/background: Based on *U.S News* survey asking engineering school deans and senior faculty to rate the quality of programs they are familiar with, and name the best programs in various specialties. **Number listed:** 5.

1. Massachusetts Institute of Technology
2. University of California, Berkeley
3. Stanford University
4. University of Michigan, Ann Arbor
5. University of Illinois, Urbana-Champaign

Source: "America's Best Colleges," *U.S. News & World Report*, 129: 90-132, (September 11, 2000).

ENGINEERING, GRADUATE–NUCLEAR
See also: **Engineering–Nuclear**

★2426★
Academics' choices for best graduate nuclear engineering schools, 2000

Ranking basis/background: From a *U.S. News & World Report* survey of engineering school deans. **Remarks:** Data collected by Market Facts Inc. **Number listed:** 10.
1. Massachusetts Institute of Technology
2. University of Illinois, Urbana-Champaign
3. University of Michigan, Ann Arbor
4. University of California, Berkeley
5. University of Wisconsin, Madison
6. Penn State University, University Park
7. North Carolina State University
8. Purdue University, West Lafayette
9. Texas A&M University, College Station
10. University of Florida

Source: "America's Best Graduate Schools: 2001 Annual Guide," *U.S. News & World Report*, 128: 56-94, (April 10, 2000).

★2427★
Top recruiters for nuclear engineering jobs for 2000-01 master's degree recipients

Ranking basis/background: Projected number of college hires from on-campus recruitment for 2000-01. **Remarks:** Numbers reflect total expected hires, not just African American projected hires. **Number listed:** 1.
1. Accenture, with 3 projected hires

Source: "The Top 100 Employers and the Majors in Demand for the Class of 2001," *The Black Collegian*, 31: 19-35, (February 2001).

★2428★
***U.S. News & World Report*'s graduate engineering programs with the best nuclear departments, 2000-01**

Ranking basis/background: Based on *U.S News* survey asking engineering school deans and senior faculty to rate the quality of programs they are familiar with, and name the best programs in various specialties. **Number listed:** 5.
1. University of Michigan, Ann Arbor
2. Massachusetts Institute of Technology
3. University of California, Berkeley
4. University of Wisconsin, Madison
5. Pennsylvania State University, University Park

Source: "America's Best Colleges," *U.S. News & World Report*, 129: 90-132, (September 11, 2000).

ENGINEERING, GRADUATE–PETROLEUM
See also: **Engineering–Petroleum**

★2429★
Academics' choices for best graduate petroleum engineering schools, 2000

Ranking basis/background: From a *U.S. News & World Report* survey of engineering school deans. **Remarks:** Data collected by Market Facts Inc. **Number listed:** 10.
1. Texas A&M University, College Station
2. University of Texas, Austin
3. Stanford University
4. Colorado School of Mines
4. University of Oklahoma
6. Louisiana State University, Baton Rouge
7. University of Tulsa
8. Texas Tech University
9. Penn State University, University Park
10. New Mexico Institute of Mining and Technology

Source: "America's Best Graduate Schools: 2001 Annual Guide," *U.S. News & World Report*, 128: 56-94, (April 10, 2000).

★2430★
Top recruiters for petroleum engineering jobs for 2000-01 master's degree recipients

Ranking basis/background: Projected number of college hires from on-campus recruitment for 2000-01. **Remarks:** Numbers reflect total expected hires, not just African American projected hires. **Number listed:** 1.
1. Accenture, with 2 projected hires

Source: "The Top 100 Employers and the Majors in Demand for the Class of 2001," *The Black Collegian*, 31: 19-35, (February 2001).

★2431★
***U.S. News & World Report*'s graduate engineering programs with the best petroleum departments, 2000-01**

Ranking basis/background: Based on *U.S News* survey asking engineering school deans and senior faculty to rate the quality of programs they are familiar with, and name the best programs in various specialties. **Number listed:** 5.
1. Texas A&M University, College Station
2. University of Texas, Austin
3. Colorado School of Mines
4. University of Oklahoma
4. University of Tulsa

Source: "America's Best Colleges," *U.S. News & World Report*, 129: 90-132, (September 11, 2000).

ENGINEERING–INDUSTRIAL
See also: **Engineering, Graduate–Industrial**

★2432★
Top recruiters for industrial engineering jobs for 2000-01 bachelor's degree recipients

Ranking basis/background: Projected number of college hires from on-campus recruitment for 2000-01. **Remarks:** Numbers reflect total expected hires, not just African American projected hires. **Number listed:** 7.
1. Graybar Electric, Inc., with 200 projected hires
2. Honda of America Manufacturing, Inc., 27
3. Parker Hannifin, 20
4. Cap Gemini Ernst & Young, 20
5. Bechtel National, 10
6. Agilent Technologies, 6
7. Corning, 3

Source: "The Top 100 Employers and the Majors in Demand for the Class of 2001," *The Black Collegian*, 31: 19-35, (February 2001).

ENGINEERING–MARINE
See also: **Engineering, Graduate–Marine**

★2433★
Top recruiters for marine engineering jobs for 2000-01 bachelor's degree recipients

Ranking basis/background: Projected number of college hires from on-campus recruitment for 2000-01. **Remarks:** Numbers reflect total expected hires, not just African American projected hires. **Number listed:** 1.
1. Ingalls Shipbuilding, with 20 projected hires

Source: "The Top 100 Employers and the Majors in Demand for the Class of 2001," *The Black Collegian*, 31: 19-35, (February 2001).

ENGINEERING–MATERIALS/METALLURGICAL
See also: **Engineering, Graduate–Materials/Metallurgical**

★2434★
Top recruiters for metallurgical/mining engineering jobs for 2000-01 bachelor's degree recipients

Ranking basis/background: Projected number of college hires from on-campus recruitment for 2000-01. **Remarks:** Numbers reflect total expected hires, not just African American projected hires. **Number listed:** 4.
1. U.S. Air Force (Active Duty Hires), with 10 projected hires
2. General Motors, 5
2. Caterpillar Inc., 5
4. Automated Analysis Corporation, 3

Source: "The Top 100 Employers and the Majors in Demand for the Class of 2001," *The Black Collegian*, 31: 19-35, (February 2001).

★2435★
U.S. universities with the greatest impact in metallurgy, 1995-99

Ranking basis/background: Average citations per paper from the top 100 federally funded U.S. universities that had at least 50 published papers in ISI indexed metallurgy journals. Also includes total number of papers published during the five year period. **Number listed:** 5.
1. University of Southern California, with 52 papers; 10.17 citations per paper
2. University of California, Santa Barbara, 73; 6.59
3. University of California, San Francisco, 75; 6.45
4. University of Michigan, 87; 3.14
5. University of California, Irvine, 63; 3.06

Source: "Metallurgy: High Impact U.S. Universities, 1995-99," *What's Hot in Research* (http://www.isinet.com/isi/hot/research) *Institute for Scientific Information*, January 8, 2001.

ENGINEERING—MECHANICAL

★2436★
U.S. universities with the highest concentration of metallurgy papers published, 1994-98

Ranking basis/background: Total number of metallurgy papers published from each university and percentage they comprise of university's total papers between 1994 and 1998. **Remarks:** Original source: University Science Indicators on Diskette, 1981-98. **Number listed:** 5.
1. Lehigh University, with 59 metallurgy papers; 3.46% of university's total papers
2. Carnegie Mellon University, 103; 2.40%
3. Washington State University, 63; 1.27%
4. University of Virginia, 113; 1.24%
5. Massachusetts Institute of Technology, 169; 1.17%

Source: "U.S. Universities with Highest Concentrations in Metallurgy, 1994-98," *What's Hot in Research* (http://www.isinet.com/hot/research) Institute for Scientific Information, August 23, 1999.

ENGINEERING–MECHANICAL
See also: **Engineering, Graduate–Mechanical**

★2437★
Top recruiters for mechanical engineering jobs for 2000-01 bachelor's degree recipients

Ranking basis/background: Projected number of college hires from on-campus recruitment for 2000-01. **Remarks:** Numbers reflect total expected hires, not just African American projected hires. **Number listed:** 24.
1. General Motors, with 300 projected hires
2. Caterpillar Inc., 236
3. Procter & Gamble, 65
4. Accenture, 60
5. U.S. Air Force (Active Duty Hires), 40
5. Parker Hannifin, 40
5. Westinghouse, 40
8. Newport News Shipbuilding, 30
9. Abbott Laboratories, 25
9. International Paper, 25
9. Honda of America Manufacturing, Inc., 25

Source: "The Top 100 Employers and the Majors in Demand for the Class of 2001," *The Black Collegian*, 31: 19-35, (February 2001).

★2438★
U.S. News & World Report's undergraduate engineering programs with the best mechanical departments, 2000-01

Ranking basis/background: Based on *U.S News* survey asking engineering school deans and senior faculty to rate the quality of programs they are familiar with, and name the best programs in various specialties. **Number listed:** 6.
1. Rose-Hulman Institute of Technology
2. Cooper Union
3. Harvey Mudd College
4. Bucknell University
5. California Polytechnic State University, San Luis Obispo
5. United States Military Academy

Source: "America's Best Colleges," *U.S. News & World Report*, 129: 90-132, (September 11, 2000).

★2439★
U.S. universities with the greatest impact in mechanical engineering, 1994-98

Ranking basis/background: Average citations per paper from the top 100 federally funded U.S. universities that had at least 50 published papers in ISI indexed mechanical engineering journals. Also includes total number of papers published during the five year period. **Number listed:** 5.
1. Brown University, with 110 papers; 4.68 citations per paper
2. Stanford University, 300; 4.18
3. University of California, Santa Barbara, 102; 3.77
4. University of California, San Francisco, 106; 3.66
5. Caltech, 257; 2.68

Source: "Mechanical Engineering: High Impact U.S. Universities, 1994-98," *What's Hot in Research* (http://www.isinet.com/isi/hot/research) Institute for Scientific Information, June 19, 2000.

ENGINEERING–NUCLEAR
See also: **Engineering, Graduate–Nuclear**

★2440★
Top recruiters for nuclear engineering jobs for 2000-01 bachelor's degree recipients

Ranking basis/background: Projected number of college hires from on-campus recruitment for 2000-01. **Remarks:** Numbers reflect total expected hires, not just African American projected hires. **Number listed:** 5.
1. Newport News Shipbuilding, with 50 projected hires
2. Accenture, 10
2. U.S. Air Force (Active Duty Hires), 10
4. Westinghouse, 8
5. Bechtel National, 5

Source: "The Top 100 Employers and the Majors in Demand for the Class of 2001," *The Black Collegian*, 31: 19-35, (February 2001).

ENGINEERING–PETROLEUM
See also: **Engineering, Graduate–Petroleum**

★2441★
Top recruiters for petroleum engineering jobs for 2000-01 bachelor's degree recipients

Ranking basis/background: Projected number of college hires from on-campus recruitment for 2000-01. **Remarks:** Numbers reflect total expected hires, not just African American projected hires. **Number listed:** 2.
1. Accenture, with 10 projected hires
1. Marathon Oil, 10

Source: "The Top 100 Employers and the Majors in Demand for the Class of 2001," *The Black Collegian*, 31: 19-35, (February 2001).

ENGLISH ACT OR SAT SCORES
See: **College Entrance Examinations**

ENGLISH LANGUAGE AND LITERATURE
See also: **Theatre Arts**

★2442★
Radcliffe Institute for Advanced Study fellowship recipient in the field of American literature, 2000-01

Ranking basis/background: Recipient and institutional affiliation of the Radcliffe Institute for Advanced study fellowship for pursuit of advanced work across a wide range of academic disciplines, professions, and creative arts. **Number listed:** 1.
  Francesca Sawaya, Portland State University

Source: "The Radcliffe Institute for Advanced Study," *The Chronicle of Higher Education*, 46: A59, (June 2, 2000).

★2443★
Radcliffe Institute for Advanced Study fellowship recipient in the field of English literature, 2000-01

Ranking basis/background: Recipient and institutional affiliation of the Radcliffe Institute for Advanced study fellowship for pursuit of advanced work across a wide range of academic disciplines, professions, and creative arts. **Number listed:** 1.
  Janis Caldwell, Wake Forest University

Source: "The Radcliffe Institute for Advanced Study," *The Chronicle of Higher Education*, 46: A59, (June 2, 2000).

★2444★
Radcliffe Institute for Advanced Study fellowship recipient in the field of poetry, 2000-01

Ranking basis/background: Recipient and institutional affiliation of the Radcliffe Institute for Advanced study fellowship for pursuit of advanced work across a wide range of academic disciplines, professions, and creative arts. **Number listed:** 1.
  Natasha Trethewey, Auburn University

Source: "The Radcliffe Institute for Advanced Study," *The Chronicle of Higher Education*, 46: A59, (June 2, 2000).

★2445★
Top essayists from 1946-1996

Ranking basis/background: Number of reprints. **Remarks:** Original source: "College English" Vol. 61, No.4. **Number listed:** 10.
1. George Orwell, with 357
2. E.B. White, 268
3. Joan Didion, 219
4. Lewis Thomas, 204
5. Henry David Thoreau, 180
6. Virginia Woolf, 177
7. Jonathan Swift, 173
8. Rev. Martin Luther King, Jr., 165
9. James Thurber, 158
10. Mark Twain, 143

Source: Heller, Scott, "Essays That Live On: A Scholar Examines an Overlooked Canon," *The Chronicle of Higher Education*, April 2, 1999, pp. A20-A21.

★2446★

Top recruiters for language/literature jobs for 2000-01 bachelor's degree recipients

Ranking basis/background: Projected number of college hires from on-campus recruitment for 2000-01. **Remarks:** Numbers reflect total expected hires, not just African American projected hires. **Number listed:** 7.
1. Footstar, with 500 projected hires
2. Houghton Mifflin, 50
2. Accenture, 50
4. Eckerd Youth Alternatives, Inc., 10
5. Henrico County Public Schools, 6
6. Countrywide Home Loans, 5
6. Caddo Parish School Board, 5

Source: "The Top 100 Employers and the Majors in Demand for the Class of 2001," *The Black Collegian*, 31: 19-35, (February 2001).

★2447★

U.S. universities publishing the most papers in the field of literature, 1994-98

Ranking basis/background: Number of papers published in the field of literature over a five-year period, and percent of field based on each universities percentage of 20,094 papers entered in the ISI database from ISI-indexed literature journals. **Number listed:** 7.
1. Indiana University, with 188 papers; 0.94% of field
2. Pennsylvania State University, 184; 0.92%
3. City University of New York, 172; 0.86%
4. University of Michigan, Ann Arbor, 155; 0.77%
4. University of California, Berkeley, 154; 0.77%
6. University of California, Los Angeles, 153; 0.76%
6. Columbia University, 152; 0.76%

Source: "Literature: Most Prolific U.S. Universities, 1994-98," *What's Hot in Research* (http://www.isinet.com/isi/hot/research) Institute for Scientific Information, May 22, 2000.

ENGLISH LANGUAGE AND LITERATURE, GRADUATE

★2448★

Most effective English language and literature research-doctorate programs as evaluated by the National Research Council

Ranking basis/background: From a survey of nearly 8,000 faculty members conducted in the spring of 1993. Respondents were asked to rate programs in their field on "effectiveness of program in educating research scholars/scientists." **Remarks:** See *Chronicle* article for more details. Scores of 3.5-5.0 indicate "extremely effective;" 2.5-3.49 "reasonably effective;" 1.5-2.49 "minimally effective;" and 0.0-1.49 "not effective." Programs also ranked by "scholarly quality of program faculty." **Number listed:** 127.
1. University of California, Berkeley, with an effectiveness rating of 4.53
2. Yale University, 4.43
2. Cornell University, 4.43
4. Stanford University, 4.30
5. University of Virginia, 4.27
6. University of Pennsylvania, 4.24

7. University of Chicago, 4.20
8. Harvard University, 4.14
9. Johns Hopkins University, 3.99
10. Duke University, 3.98

Source: "Rankings of Research-Doctorate Programs in 41 Disciplines at 274 Institutions," *The Chronicle of Higher Education* 42: A21-A30 (September 21, 1995).

★2449★

Private, 4-year undergraduate colleges and universities producing the most Ph.D.'s in English, 1920-1990

Ranking basis/background: Number of doctoral degrees granted to graduates of 914 private, 4-year U.S. undergraduate colleges and universities. Medical, law, and other professional, non-doctoral degrees are not included. **Remarks:** Original source: Office of Scientific and Engineering Personnel of the National Research Council. Report contains 50 other tables detailing the distribution of doctoral recipients by field of study over various time frames. **Number listed:** 355.
1. Oberlin College, with 222 Ph.D.'s
2. Amherst College, 196
3. Wellesley College, 178
4. Smith College, 159
5. Barnard College, 153
6. Swarthmore College, 129
6. Wesleyan University, 129
8. Williams College, 123
9. Mount Holyoke College, 112
10. Vassar College, 109
11. Carleton College, 106
12. Bryn Mawr College, 105
13. Hamilton College, 97
14. College of the Holy Cross, 96
15. Middlebury College, 87
16. Wheaton College, 84
17. Kenyon College, 81
18. University of the South, 80
19. Colgate University, 78
19. Haverford College, 78

Source: *Baccalaureate Origins of Doctorate Recipients, 7th ed.*, Franklin & Marshall College, March 1993.

★2450★

Private, 4-year undergraduate colleges and universities producing the most Ph.D.'s in English, 1981-1990

Ranking basis/background: Number of doctoral degrees granted to graduates of 914 private, 4-year U.S. undergraduate colleges and universities. Medical, law, and other professional, non-doctoral degrees are not included. **Remarks:** Original source: Office of Scientific and Engineering Personnel of the National Research Council. Report contains 50 other tables detailing the distribution of doctoral recipients by field of study over various time frames. **Number listed:** 277.
1. Oberlin College, with 46 Ph.D.'s
2. Wellesley College, 42
3. Smith College, 36
4. Barnard College, 27
5. Wheaton College, 26
6. Amherst College, 24
7. Bryn Mawr College, 23
7. Kenyon College, 23
9. Calvin College, 22
10. Vassar College, 21
11. Swarthmore College, 20
12. Middlebury College, 19
13. Carleton College, 18
13. Pomona College, 18

13. Bucknell University, 18
13. Colgate University, 18
17. Mount Holyoke College, 17
17. Reed College, 17
19. Duquesne University, 16
19. Wesleyan University, 16
19. Wake Forest University, 16
19. Williams College, 16

Source: *Baccalaureate Origins of Doctorate Recipients, 7th ed.*, Franklin & Marshall College, March 1993.

★2451★

Top English language and literature research-doctorate programs as evaluated by the National Research Council

Ranking basis/background: From a survey of nearly 8,000 faculty members conducted in the spring of 1993. Respondents were asked to rate programs in their field on "scholarly quality of program faculty." When more than one program had the samescore, the council averaged the rank order and gave each program the same rank number (if three programs tied for the top position, each received a rank of 2). **Remarks:** See *Chronicle* article for more details. Scores of 4.01 and above indicate "distinguished;" 3.0-4.0 "strong;" 2.51-3.0 "good;" 2.0-2.5 "adequate;" 1.0-1.99 "marginal;" and 0.0-0.99 "not sufficient for doctoral education." Programs also ranked by "effectiveness of program in educating research scholars/scientists." **Number listed:** 127.
1. Yale University, with a quality rating of 4.77
1. University of California, Berkeley, 4.77
1. Harvard University, 4.77
4. University of Virginia, 4.58
5. Duke University, 4.55
5. Stanford University, 4.55
7. Cornell University, 4.49
8. University of Pennsylvania, 4.47
9. Columbia University, 4.47
10. University of Chicago, 4.41
11. Johns Hopkins University, 4.33
12. University of California, Los Angeles, 4.10
13. Princeton University, 4.05
14. Brown University, 3.99
15. University of California, Irvine, 3.95

Source: "Rankings of Research-Doctorate Programs in 41 Disciplines at 274 Institutions," *The Chronicle of Higher Education* 42: A21-A30 (September 21, 1995).

★2452★

Top recruiters for language/literature jobs for 2000-01 master's degree recipients

Ranking basis/background: Projected number of college hires from on-campus recruitment for 2000-01. **Remarks:** Numbers reflect total expected hires, not just African American projected hires. **Number listed:** 3.
1. Houghton Mifflin, with 10 projected hires
1. Accenture, 10
3. Henrico County Public Schools, 7

Source: "The Top 100 Employers and the Majors in Demand for the Class of 2001," *The Black Collegian*, 31: 19-35, (February 2001).

ENROLLMENT, COLLEGE

See: American Indians–Enrollment, College Blacks–Enrollment, College College Enrollment Disabilities–Enrollment of Students Foreign Students–Enrollment, College Hispanic Americans–Enrollment, College Minority Groups–Enrollment, College

ENROLLMENT, SCHOOL

See: Disabilities–Enrollment of Students School Enrollment

ENTOMOLOGY

★2453★
Entomology journals by citation impact, 1981-98

Ranking basis/background: Impact factor calculated by taking the number of current citations to source items published and dividing it by the number of articles published in the journal during that time period. **Number listed:** 10.
1. *Annual Review of Entomology*, with a 38.94 impact factor
2. *Advances in Insect Physiology*, 31.09
3. *Insect Biochemistry*, 15.60
4. *Pesticide Biochemistry and Physiology*, 11.54
5. *Journal of Insect Physiology*, 11.21
6. *Ecological Entomology*, 10.26
7. *Physiological Entomology*, 9.48
8. *Archives of Insect Biochemistry*, 8.31
9. *Bulletin of Entology Research*, 6.86
10. *Entomologia Experiments and Applications*, 6.35

Source: "Journals Ranked by Impact: Entomology," *What's Hot in Research (http://www.isinet.com/isi/hot/research) Institute for Scientific Information*, May 8, 2000.

★2454★
Entomology journals by citation impact, 1994-98

Ranking basis/background: Impact factor calculated by taking the number of current citations to source items published and dividing it by the number of articles published in the journal during that time period. **Number listed:** 10.
1. *Advances in Insect Physiology*, with a 14.17 impact factor
2. *Annual Review of Entomology*, 11.28
3. *Insect Molecular Biology*, 5.57
4. *Insect Biochemistry and Molecular Biology*, 4.70
5. *Journal of Insect Physiology*, 3.41
6. *Archives of Insect Biochemistry*, 2.84
7. *Ecological Entomology*, 2.79
8. *Pesticide Biochemistry and Physiology*, 2.68
9. *Physiological Entomology*, 2.43
10. *Biological Control*, 2.27

Source: "Journals Ranked by Impact: Entomology," *What's Hot in Research (http://www.isinet.com/isi/hot/research) Institute for Scientific Information*, May 8, 2000.

★2455★
Entomology journals by citation impact, 1998

Ranking basis/background: Impact factor calculated by taking the number of current citations to source items published and dividing it by the number of articles published in the journal during that time period. **Number listed:** 10.
1. *Annual Review of Entomology*, with a 5.36 impact factor
2. *Advances in Insect Physiology*, 4.50
3. *Insect Molecular Biology*, 2.08
4. *Insect Biochemistry and Molecular Biology*, 1.93
5. *Ecological Entomology*, 1.53
6. *Archives of Insect Biochemistry*, 1.36
7. *Journal of Insect Physiology*, 1.32
8. *Pesticide Science*, 1.13
9. *Biological Control*, 1.11
10. *Journal of Medical Entomology*, 1.07

Source: "Journals Ranked by Impact: Entomology," *What's Hot in Research (http://www.isinet.com/isi/hot/research) Institute for Scientific Information*, May 8, 2000.

ENVIRONMENTAL EDUCATION

★2456★
Highest impact economics journals in energy from 1974 to 1979

Ranking basis/background: Number of citations and average citations per article as research by the *Journal of Environmental Economics and Management*. **Number listed:** 5.
1. *Review of Economics and Statistics*, with 540 citations; and average of 60 citations per article
2. *Journal of Political Economics*, 167; 56
3. *Bell Journal of Economics*, 692; 41
4. *American Economic Review*, 397; 25
5. *Southern Economic Journal*, 147; 16

Source: Kolstad, Charles D., "Energy and Depletable Resources: Economics and Policy, 1973-1998," *Journal of Environmental Economics and Management*, 39: 282-305, (May 2000).

★2457★
Highest impact economics journals in energy from 1980 to 1989

Ranking basis/background: Number of citations and average citations per article as research by the *Journal of Environmental Economics and Management*. **Number listed:** 5.
1. *Econometrica*, with 540 citations; an average of 60 citations per article
2. *Journal of Political Economics*, 212; 35
3. *American Economic Review*, 335; 26
4. *Journal of Law and Economics*, 91; 18
5. *International Economic Review*, 70; 14

Source: Kolstad, Charles D., "Energy and Depletable Resources: Economics and Policy, 1973-1998," *Journal of Environmental Economics and Management*, 39: 282-305, (May 2000).

★2458★
Highest impact economics journals in energy from 1990 to 1998

Ranking basis/background: Number of citations and average citations per article as research by the *Journal of Environmental Economics and Management*. **Number listed:** 5.
1. *Economic Journal*, with 304 citations; an average of 18 citations per article
2. *Journal of Political Economics*, 45; 15
3. *American Economic Review*, 252; 13
4. *Review of Economic Studies*, 18; 9
5. *Journal of Finance*, 41; 8

Source: Kolstad, Charles D., "Energy and Depletable Resources: Economics and Policy, 1973-1998," *Journal of Environmental Economics and Management*, 39: 282-305, (May 2000).

★2459★
Highest impact economics journals in exhaustible resources from 1974 to 1979

Ranking basis/background: Number of citations and average citations per article during the five-year period as research by the *Journal of Environmental Economics and Management*. **Number listed:** 5.
1. *Journal of Political Economics*, with 269 citations; an average of 67 citations per article
2. *Review of Economics and Statistics*, 123; 62
3. *American Economic Review*, 362; 45
4. *Bell Journal of Economics*, 119; 40
5. *Review of Economic Studies*, 439; 32

Source: Kolstad, Charles D., "Energy and Depletable Resources: Economics and Policy, 1973-1998," *Journal of Environmental Economics and Management*, 39: 282-305, (May 2000).

★2460★
Highest impact economics journals in exhaustible resources from 1980 to 1989

Ranking basis/background: Number of citations and average citations per article as research by the *Journal of Environmental Economics and Management*. **Number listed:** 5.
1. *Journal of Business*, with 118 citations; an average of 58 citations per article
2. *Journal of Political Economics*, 212; 30
3. *Scandinavian Journal of Economics*, 97; 16
4. *Econometrica*, 102; 11
5. *Journal of Environmental Economics and Management*, 318; 8

Source: Kolstad, Charles D., "Energy and Depletable Resources: Economics and Policy, 1973-1998," *Journal of Environmental Economics and Management*, 39: 282-305, (May 2000).

★2461★
Highest impact economics journals in exhaustible resources from 1990 to 1998

Ranking basis/background: Number of citations and average citations per article as research by the *Journal of Environmental Economics and Management*. **Number listed:** 6.
1. *American Economic Review*, with 32 citations; an average of 16 citations per article
2. *Review of Economics and Statistics*, 26; 13
3. *Journal of Public Economics*, 75; 11
4. *Scandinavian Journal of Economics*, 50; 6
5. *Journal of Development Economics*, 20; 5
6. *Review of Economic Studies*, 10; 5

Source: Kolstad, Charles D., "Energy and Depletable Resources: Economics and Policy, 1973-1998," *Journal of Environmental Economics and Management*, 39: 282-305, (May 2000).

★2462★
Journal of Environmental Economics and Management's best articles in depletable resources and energy

Ranking basis/background: Total number of citations. **Number listed:** 10.

1. *Trends in Natural Resource Commodity Prices-An Analysis of the Time Domain*, by Slade (1982), with 65 citations
2. *Optimal Use of Non-Renewable Resources-Theory of Extraction*, Schulze (1974), 42
3. *Control Theory Applied to Natural and Environmental Resources-Exposition*, Smith (1977), 41
4. *Concepts and Measures of Natural Resource Scarcity with a Summary of Recent Trends*, Hall and Hall (1984), 36
5. *Taxation of Non-Replenishable Natural Resources*, Burness (1976), 35
6. *Mineral Depletion with Cost as the Extraction Limit...*, Stollery (1983), 30
7. *Optimal Pricing, Use, and Exploration of Uncertain Natural ChangResource Stocks*, Arrow and Chang (1982), 28
8. *Measuring Natural Resource Scarcity-Theory and Practice*, Smith (1978), 24
9. *Natural Resource Scarcity-Empirical Evidence and Public Policy*, Johnson et al. (1980), 22
10. *Model of Mining and Exploring for Exhaustible Resources*, Peterson (1978), 21

Source: Kolstad, Charles D., "Energy and Depletable Resources: Economics and Policy, 1973-1998," *Journal of Environmental Economics and Management*, 39: 282-305, (May 2000).

★2463★
Top cited energy papers from 1974 to 1978

Ranking basis/background: Number of citations during the five-year period as research by the *Journal of Environmental Economics and Management*. **Number listed:** 3.

1. *Technology, Prices and the Derived Demand for Energy*, by Berndt and Wood, with 350 citations
2. *U.S. Energy Policy and Economic Growth, 1975-2000*, Hudson and Jorgenson, 232
3. *Intercountry Translog Model of Energy Substitution Responses*, Griffin and Gregory, 130

Source: Kolstad, Charles D., "Energy and Depletable Resources: Economics and Policy, 1973-1998," *Journal of Environmental Economics and Management*, 39: 282-305, (May 2000).

★2464★
Top cited energy papers from 1979 to 1983

Ranking basis/background: Number of citations during the five-year period as research by the *Journal of Environmental Economics and Management*. **Number listed:** 3.

1. *Engineering and Econometric Interpretation of Energy-Capital Complementarity*, by Berndt and Wood, with 152 citations
2. *Individual Discount Rates and the Purchase and Utilization of Energy-Using Durables*, Hausman, 149
3. *Oil and the Macroeconomy Since World War II*, J.D. Hamilton, 123

Source: Kolstad, Charles D., "Energy and Depletable Resources: Economics and Policy, 1973-1998," *Journal of Environmental Economics and Management*, 39: 282-305, (May 2000).

★2465★
Top cited energy papers from 1984 to 1988

Ranking basis/background: Number of citations during the five-year period as research by the *Journal of Environmental Economics and Management*. **Number listed:** 3.

1. *Contract Duration and Relationship-Specific Investments-Empirical Evidence from Coal Markets*, by Joskow, with 85 citations
2. *Exports, Policy Choices, and Economic Growth in Developing Countries after 1973 Oil Shock*, Balassa, 62
3. *Testing for the Effects of Oil-Price Rises Using Vector Autoregression*, Burbidge and Harrison, 43

Source: Kolstad, Charles D., "Energy and Depletable Resources: Economics and Policy, 1973-1998," *Journal of Environmental Economics and Management*, 39: 282-305, (May 2000).

★2466★
Top cited energy papers from 1989 to 1993

Ranking basis/background: Number of citations during the five-year period as research by the *Journal of Environmental Economics and Management*. **Number listed:** 3.

1. *The Great Crash, the Oil Price Shock, and The Unit-Root Hypothesis*, by Perron, with 435 citations
2. *To Slow or Not to Slow-The Economics of the Greenhouse Effect*, Nordhaus, 167
3. *Some Economics of Global Warming*, Schelling, 50

Source: Kolstad, Charles D., "Energy and Depletable Resources: Economics and Policy, 1973-1998," *Journal of Environmental Economics and Management*, 39: 282-305, (May 2000).

★2467★
Top cited energy papers from 1994 to 1998

Ranking basis/background: Number of citations during the five-year period as research by the *Journal of Environmental Economics and Management*. **Number listed:** 3.

1. *The Impact of Global Warming on Agriculture-A Ricardian Analysis*, by Mendelsohn et al., with 35 citations
2. *Access Pricing and Competition*, Laffont and Tirole, 23
3. *A Regional Dynamic General-Equilibrium Model of Alternative Climate Change Strategies*, Nordhaus and Yang, 22

Source: Kolstad, Charles D., "Energy and Depletable Resources: Economics and Policy, 1973-1998," *Journal of Environmental Economics and Management*, 39: 282-305, (May 2000).

★2468★
Top cited nonrenewable resource papers from 1974 to 1978

Ranking basis/background: Number of citations during the five-year period as research by the *Journal of Environmental Economics and Management*. **Number listed:** 3.

1. *Economics of Resources or Resources of Economics*, by Solow, with 175 citations
2. *Common Property as a Concept in Natural Resources Policy*, Ciriacy-Wantrup and Bishop, 111
3. *Intergenerational Equity and Exhaustible Resources*, Solow, 107

Source: Kolstad, Charles D., "Energy and Depletable Resources: Economics and Policy, 1973-1998," *Journal of Environmental Economics and Management*, 39: 282-305, (May 2000).

★2469★
Top cited nonrenewable resource papers from 1979 to 1983

Ranking basis/background: Number of citations during the five-year period as research by the *Journal of Environmental Economics and Management*. **Number listed:** 3.

1. *Uncertainty and Exhaustible Resource Markets*, by Pindyck, with 74 citations
2. *Common Property Externalities-Isolation, Assurance, and Resource Depletion in a Traditional Grazing Context*, Runge, 72
3. *Trends in Natural Resource Commodity Prices-An Analysis of the Time Domain*, Slade, 65

Source: Kolstad, Charles D., "Energy and Depletable Resources: Economics and Policy, 1973-1998," *Journal of Environmental Economics and Management*, 39: 282-305, (May 2000).

★2470★
Top cited nonrenewable resource papers from 1984 to 1988

Ranking basis/background: Number of citations during the five-year period as research by the *Journal of Environmental Economics and Management*. **Number listed:** 3.

1. *Evaluating Natural Resource Investment*, by Brennan and Schwartz, with 116 citations
2. *On the Intergenerational Allocation of Natural Resources*, Solow, 72
3. *Oligopoly Extraction of a Common Property Natural Resource-The Importance of the Period of Commitment in Dynamic Games*, Reinganum and Stokey, 54

Source: Kolstad, Charles D., "Energy and Depletable Resources: Economics and Policy, 1973-1998," *Journal of Environmental Economics and Management*, 39: 282-305, (May 2000).

★2471★
Top cited nonrenewable resource papers from 1989 to 1993

Ranking basis/background: Number of citations during the five-year period as research by the *Journal of Environmental Economics and Management*. **Number listed:** 3.

1. *Natural Resources, National Accounting, and Economic Depreciation*, by Hartwick, with 47 citations
2. *Mineral Depletion, with Special Reference to Petroleum*, Adelman, 26
3. *The Evolution of Policy Responses to Stratospheric Ozone Depletion*, Morrisette, 21

Source: Kolstad, Charles D., "Energy and Depletable Resources: Economics and Policy, 1973-1998," *Journal of Environmental Economics and Management*, 39: 282-305, (May 2000).

ENVIRONMENTAL ENGINEERING

★2472★
Top cited nonrenewable resource papers from 1994 to 1998

Ranking basis/background: Number of citations during the five-year period as research by the *Journal of Environmental Economics and Management*. **Number listed:** 3.
1. *Net National Product as an Indicator of Sustainability*, by Asheim, with 24 citations
2. *Economics and Sustainability-Balancing Trade-Offs and Imperatives*, Toman, 16
3. *The Environment as a Factor of Production-The Effects of Economic Growth and Trade Liberalization*, Lopez, 8

Source: Kolstad, Charles D., "Energy and Depletable Resources: Economics and Policy, 1973-1998," *Journal of Environmental Economics and Management*, 39: 282-305, (May 2000).

★2473★
U.S. universities publishing the most papers in the field of ecology/environmental sciences, 1994-98

Ranking basis/background: Total number of papers published from each university. **Remarks:** Original source: University Science Indicators on Diskette, 1981-97. **Number listed:** 6.
1. University of California, Davis, with 809 papers
2. University of California, Berkeley, 649
3. University of Minnesota, 574
4. University of Florida, 570
5. Cornell University, 567
6. Colorado State University, 561

Source: "Ecology/Environmental Sciences: Most Prolific U.S. Universities, 1994-98," *What's Hot in Research* (http://www.isinet.com/hot/research) Institute for Scientific Information, December 20, 1999.

★2474★
U.S. universities with the greatest impact in ecology/environmental sciences, 1994-98

Ranking basis/background: Average citations per paper from the top 100 federally funded U.S. universities that had at least 50 published papers in ISI indexed ecology/environmental sciences journals. Also includes total number of papers published during the five year period. **Number listed:** 5.
1. Caltech, with 128 papers; 6.38 citations per paper
2. Carnegie Mellon University, 104; 6.08
3. Stanford University, 354; 5.95
4. University of New Hampshire, 141; 5.86
5. University of California, Santa Barbara, 164; 5.81

Source: "Ecology/Environmental Sciences: High Impact U.S. Universities, 1994-98," *What's Hot in Research* (http://www.isinet.com/isi/hot/research) Institute for Scientific Information, August 28, 2000.

ENVIRONMENTAL ENGINEERING
See: **Engineering–Environmental Engineering, Graduate–Environmental**

EVALUATION CRITERIA & METHODOLOGIES

Related Information

★2475★
Webster, David S., "Advantages and Disadvantages of Methods of Assessing Quality," *Change* 13: 20-24 (October 1981).
Remarks: Webster, the "godfather" of academic rankings research discusses the types of ranking methodologies being employed to evaluate the quality of departments and institutions.

EVALUATION CRITERIA & METHODOLOGIES—BIBLIOGRAPHIES

Related Information

★2476★
Hattendorf, Lynn C., "College and University Rankings: Part 5– An Annotated Bibliography of Analysis, Criticism, and Evaluation," *RQ* 29: 402-420 (Spring 1990).
Remarks: Presents an annotated bibliography of 63 books and articles providing information about college and university rankings.

★2477★
Hattendorf, Lynn C., "College and University Rankings: Part 4–An Annotated Bibliography of Analysis, Criticism, and Evaluation," *RQ* 28: 340-367 (Spring 1989).
Remarks: Presents an annotated bibliography of 77 books and articles in the field of academic quality, rankings, and research published from 1986 through 1988.

★2478★
Hattendorf, Lynn C., "College and University Rankings: Part 2–An Annotated Bibliography of Analysis, Criticism, and Evaluation," *RQ* 26: 315-322 (Spring 1987).
Remarks: This annotated bibliography of 29 articles and books on academic rankings updates an article in *RQ* 25: 332-347 (Spring 1986).

★2479★
Hattendorf, Lynn C., "College and University Rankings: Part 3–An Annotated Bibliography of Analysis, Criticism, and Evaluation," *RQ* 27: 337-357 (Spring 1988).
Remarks: Provides an annotated bibliography of 56 books and articles published in 1986 and 1987 with information about college and university rankings.

★2480★
Hattendorf, Lynn C., "College and University Rankings: An Annotated Bibliography of Analysis, Criticism, and Evaluation," *RQ* 25: 332-347 (Spring 1986).
Remarks: Presents a comprehensive, annotated bibliography of 83 books and articles that provide general information on ratings and rankings since 1981.

EVALUATION CRITERIA & METHODOLOGIES–INSTITUTIONS
See also: **College Choice Colleges & Universities**

Related Information

★2481★
Webster, David S., "Ranking Academic Quality: The Undergraduate Story," *Change* 18: 34-41 (November/December 1986).
Remarks: Provides an historical overview of fifteen undergraduate ranking studies done since 1950.

★2482★
Webster, David S., *Academic Quality Rankings of American Colleges and Universities*, Charles C. Thomas Publisher, 1986.
Remarks: The first and only book to present a history of the entire field of educational rankings research.

★2483★
Haworth, Jennifer Grant and Clifton F. Conrad, *Emblems of Quality in Higher Education: Developing and Sustaining High-Quality Programs*, Allyn & Bacon, 1997.
Remarks: Presents five views of determining program quality in higher education: faculty view, resources view, student quality-and-effort view, curriculum requirements view, and a multidimensional/multilevel view.

EVALUATION CRITERIA & METHODOLOGIES–PEERS

★2484★
Compilers of major multi-disciplinary peer assessment rankings

Ranking basis/background: Peer ranking listing of at least 15 academic and/or professional fields. Listing is chronological by year published. **Remarks:** Article also includes National Academy of Sciences rankings of the best academic programs. **Number listed:** 9.
- Hughes (1925), with 20 fields rated
- Hughes (1935), 35
- Keniston (1959), 24
- Cartter (1966), 29
- Roose & Anderson (1970), 36
- Margulies & Blau (1973), 17
- Blau & Margulies (1974-1975), 18
- Ladd & Lipset (1979), 19
- National Academy of Sciences (1982), 32

Source: Webster, David S., "Institutional Effectiveness Using Scholarly Peer Assessments as Major Criteria," *The Review of Higher Education* 9: 67-82 (1985)., January 1, 1990.

EVALUATION CRITERIA & METHODOLOGIES–PROGRAMS (ACADEMIC)

Related Information

★2485★
Magner, Denise K., "Ratings War," *The Chronicle of Higher Education* 42: A19-A20 (October 27, 1995).
Remarks: Article examines reaction to the National Research Council's 1995 report "Research-Doctorate Programs in the United States: Continuity and Change," which ranked 3,634 programs at 274 institutions.

EVALUATION OF PERIODICALS
See: **Periodicals**

EXPENDITURES PER PUPIL

★2486★
Trends in per-pupil spending at elementary and secondary schools in the U.S.

Ranking basis/background: Figures for annual per-pupil spending for selected years. **Remarks:** Original source: National Center for Education Statistics. 2001 figure is a projection. **Number listed:** 4.
1986, with $3,479
1991, $4,902
1996, $5,689
2001, $7,489
Source: Laird, Bob, "Per-Pupil Spending is Climbing," *USA Today*, February 5, 2001, Section A, p. 1A.

FACULTY
See: **College Faculty Teachers, Elementary and Secondary**

FACULTY-STUDENT RATIO
See: **Schools, Elementary & Secondary–Teacher-Student Ratio**

FEDERAL AID

★2487★
Proposed fiscal 2002 appropriations for miscellaneous federal aid

Ranking basis/background: Based on the U.S. government's proposed fiscal 2002 appropriations for miscellaneous federal aid. **Number listed:** 5.
Corporation for Public Broadcasting, with $370,000,000
Digital Transition Fund, $20,000,000
AmeriCorps, $236,980,000
U.S. Department of State educational and cultural exchanges, $242,000,000
District of Columbia Resident Tuition Support, $17,000,000
Source: "Bush's Fiscal 2002 Budget Plan for Higher Education and Science," *The Chronicle of Higher Education*, 47: A36-A37, (April 20, 2001).

FEDERAL AID TO EDUCATION
See: **Colleges & Universities–Financial Support & Expenditures Education–Financial Support Expenditures per Pupil Schools, Elementary & Secondary–Revenue Student Financial Aid**

FEDERAL AID TO THE DISADVANTAGED
See: **Disadvantaged–Federal Aid**

FEDERAL AID TO THE HANDICAPPED
See: **Disabilities–Federal Aid**

FEDERAL GRANTS IN RESEARCH
See: **Research Funding Research & Development Funding Scientific & Technological Research & Development Funding Scientific & Technological Research Funding**

FEDERAL STUDENT GRANTS
See: **Student Financial Aid**

FILM
See: **Motion Pictures**

FILM STUDIES
See: **Mass Media**

FINANCE
See: **Business Administration–Finance Business Administration, Graduate–Finance**

FINANCIAL AID TO STUDENTS
See: **Student Financial Aid**

FOOTBALL
See: **Athletics**

FOREIGN COUNTRIES

★2488★
Countries with the highest spending per student on higher education, 1997

Ranking basis/background: Total expenditures per student on higher education for each country. **Remarks:** Original source: O.E.C.D. **Number listed:** 32.
1. Paraguay, with $19,271
2. United States, $17,466
3. Switzerland, $16,376
4. Canada, $14,809
5. Sweden, $12,981
6. Argentina, $11,552
7. Australia, $11,240
8. Brazil, $10,791
9. Japan, $10,157
10. Norway, $10,108
Source: Wheeler, David L., "Falling Behind: U.S. Trails 3 European Nations in Rate of College Graduation," *The Chronicle of Higher Education*, 46: A63, (May 26, 2000).

★2489★
Countries with the lowest spending per student on higher education, 1997

Ranking basis/background: Total expenditures per student on higher education for each country. **Remarks:** Original source: O.E.C.D. **Number listed:** 32.
1. Philippines, with $2,170
2. Uruguay, $2,394
3. Turkey, $2,397
4. Greece, $3,990
5. Poland, $4,395
6. Mexico, $4,519
7. Spain, $5,166
8. Czech Republic, $5,351
9. Hungary, $5,430
10. Italy, $5,972
Source: Wheeler, David L., "Falling Behind: U.S. Trails 3 European Nations in Rate of College Graduation," *The Chronicle of Higher Education*, 46: A63, (May 26, 2000).

★2490★
Eastern European countries with the highest citation impact, 1999

Ranking basis/background: Number of cites per paper from 1993 to 1997. **Number listed:** 10.
1. Hungary, with 2.64 cites per paper
2. Estonia, 2.29
3. Lithuania, 2.27
4. Slovenia, 2.19
5. Poland, 2.11
6. Latvia, 1.59
7. Czech Republic, 1.57
8. Bulgaria, 1.52
9. Romania, 1.30
10. Slovak Republic, 1.17
Source: Koening, Robert, "Eastern Europe's Research Gamble," *Science*, January 1, 1999, pp. 22-24.

FOREIGN LANGUAGE PROGRAMS

FOREIGN LANGUAGE PROGRAMS
See: **Language Programs**

FOREIGN STUDENTS–ENROLLMENT, COLLEGE

★2491★
Academic levels profile of foreign students enrolled in U.S. institutions of higher education, 1998-99

Ranking basis/background: Academic level, by percentage. **Number listed:** 5.
1. Undergraduate, with 46%
2. Graduate, 42%
3. Practical training, 5%
4. Intensive English training, 4%
5. Non-degree, 3%

Source: "Open Doors, 2000," *Institute of International Education*, 2000.

★2492★
Bachelor's institutions with the highest enrollment of foreign students, 1998-99

Ranking basis/background: Total number of foreign students enrolled at institution and proportion of foreign students to total enrollment. **Number listed:** 10.
1. University of Dallas, with 500 foreign students enrolled (16.2% of total enrollment)
2. Mount Holyoke College, 278 (14.6%)
3. Penn State, Commonwealth College, 240 (1.7%)
4. Wesleyan University, 225 (7.0%)
5. Ohio Wesleyan University, 215 (11.7%)
6. Macalester College, 203 (11.4%)
7. Oberlin College, 201 (6.9%)
8. Eckerd College, 196 (12.8%)
9. Smith College, 180 (7.2%)
10. Teikyo Loretto Height University, 177 (96.7%)

Source: "Open Doors, 2000," *Institute of International Education*, 2000.

★2493★
Community colleges with the highest enrollment of foreign students, 1998-99

Ranking basis/background: Total number of foreign students enrolled at institution and proportion of foreign students to total enrollment. **Number listed:** 10.
1. Northern Virginia Community College, with 2,984 foreign students enrolled (8.0% of total enrollment)
2. Montgomery College, Rockville, 2,748 (13.2%)
3. Santa Monica College, 2,702 (10.4%)
4. Houston Community College System, 2,466 (4.8%)
5. Miami-Dade Community College, 1,401 (2.3%)
6. City College of San Francisco, 1,325 (1.5%)
7. City University of New York, Borough of Manhattan Community College, 1,222 (7.6%)
8. Orange Coast College, 1,118 (4.9%)
9. Moraine Valley Community College, 1,114 (7.7%)
10. Pasadena City College, 1,067 (4.6%)

Source: "Open Doors, 2000," *Institute of International Education*, 2000.

★2494★
Doctoral institutions with the highest enrollment of foreign students, 1998-99

Ranking basis/background: Total number of foreign students enrolled at institution and proportion of foreign students to total enrollment. **Number listed:** 10.
1. University of North Texas, with 1,736 foreign students enrolled (6.6% of total enrollment)
2. American University, 1,711 (15.6%)
3. New School University, 1,648 (21.4%)
4. Drexel University, 1,605 (13.8%)
5. Illinois Institute of Technology, 1,541 (25.4%)
6. Western Michigan University, 1,502 (5.5%)
7. University of Texas, Arlington, 1,453 (7.8%)
8. University of Texas, Dallas, 1,350 (14.2%)
9. University of Toledo, 1,313 (6.3%)
10. Georgia State University, 1,160 (4.9%)

Source: "Open Doors, 2000," *Institute of International Education*, 2000.

★2495★
Fields of study profile of foreign students enrolled in U.S. institutions of higher education, 1998-99

Ranking basis/background: Discipline of study, by percentage. **Number listed:** 12.
1. Business, with 20%
2. Engineering, 15%
3. Math and computer science, 11%
4. Social sciences, 8%
5. Physical and life sciences, 7%
6. Fine or applied arts, 6%
6. Liberal arts and general studies, 6%
8. Health professions, 4%
8. Intensive English language, 4%
10. Humanities, 3%
10. Education, 3%
12. Other, 13%

Source: "Open Doors, 2000," *Institute of International Education*, 2000.

★2496★
Foreign countries with the highest enrollment of foreign students, 1999-2000

Ranking basis/background: Total number of students from each country enrolled at U.S. institutions of higher education. Table includes only countries sending more than 3,000 students to academic institutions in the U.S. **Number listed:** 65.
1. China, 54,466
2. Japan, 46,872
3. India, 42,337
4. Republic of Korea, 41,191
5. Taiwan, 29,234
6. Canada, 23,544
7. Indonesia, 11,300
8. Thailand, 10,983
9. Mexico, 10,607
10. Turkey, 10,100

Source: "Open Doors, 2000," *Institute of International Education*, 2000.

★2497★
Gender profile of foreign students enrolled in U.S. institutions of higher education, 1998-99

Ranking basis/background: Gender breakdown, by percentage. **Number listed:** 2.
Men, with 58%
Women, 43%

Source: "Open Doors, 2000," *Institute of International Education*, 2000.

★2498★
Institution profile of foreign students enrolled in U.S. institutions of higher education, 1998-99

Ranking basis/background: Type of institution, by percentage. **Number listed:** 6.
Research, with 40%
Doctoral, 13%
Master's, 19%
Bachelor's, 5%
Two-year, 17%
Other, 6%

Source: "Open Doors, 2000," *Institute of International Education*, 2000.

★2499★
Master's institutions with the highest enrollment of foreign students, 1998-99

Ranking basis/background: Total number of foreign students enrolled at institution and proportion of foreign students to total enrollment. **Number listed:** 10.
1. City University of New York, Bernard M. Baruch College, with 2,899 foreign students enrolled (19.4% of total enrollment)
2. Hawaii Pacific University, 2,255 (28.0%)
3. San Francisco State University, 2,146 (7.8%)
4. University of Texas, El Paso, 1,649 (11.2%)
5. California State University, Long Beach, 1,587 (5.3%)
6. University of Central Oklahoma, 1,534 (10.7%)
7. City University of New York, City College, 1,436 (11.8%)
8. University of Bridgeport, 1,400 (52.1%)
9. San Jose State University, 1,324 (5.0%)
10. California State University, Fullerton, 1,237 (4.8%)

Source: "Open Doors, 2000," *Institute of International Education*, 2000.

★2500★
Percentage of students enrolled in institutions of higher education that were not citizens of the country where they studied, 1998

Ranking basis/background: Percentage of students enrolled in institutions of higher education for each country, that were not citizens of the country where they studied. **Remarks:** Original source: O.E.C.D. **Number listed:** 23.
1. Switzerland, with 15.9%
2. Australia, 12.6%
3. Austria, 11.5%
4. Britain, 10.8%
5. Germany, 8.2%
6. France, 7.3%
7. Denmark, 6.0%
8. Ireland, 4.8%
9. Sweden, 4.5%

10. Canada, 3.8%

Source: Wheeler, David L., "Falling Behind: U.S. Trails 3 European Nations in Rate of College Graduation," *The Chronicle of Higher Education*, 46: A63, (May 26, 2000).

★2501★
Professional or specialized institutions with the highest enrollment of foreign students, 1998-99

Ranking basis/background: Total number of foreign students enrolled at institution and proportion of foreign students to total enrollment. **Number listed:** 10.
1. Academy of Art College, with 1,595 foreign students enrolled (29.4% of total enrollment)
2. Johnson & Wales University, 1,119 (9.1%)
3. Berklee College of Music, 1,058 (35.1%)
4. Fashion Institute of Technology, 1,016 (14.1%)
5. Pratt Institute, 950 (22.9%)
6. Thunderbird, American Graduate School of International Management, 775 (51.9%)
7. New Hampshire College, 730 (13.0%)
8. Bentley College, 640 (11.1%)
9. Babson College, 565 (16.5%)
10. Southern Polytechnic State University, 542 (14.9%)

Source: "Open Doors, 2000," *Institute of International Education*, 2000.

★2502★
Region of origin of foreign students enrolled in U.S. institutions of higher education, 1998-99

Ranking basis/background: Percentage of students from each region of origin. Total foreign students enrolled in U.S. institutions in 1998-99 is 514,723. **Number listed:** 7.
1. Asia, with 54.4%
2. Europe, 15.2%
3. Latin America, 12.1%
4. Middle East, 6.8%
5. Africa, 5.9%
6. North America, 4.7%
7. Oceania, 0.9%

Source: "Open Doors, 2000," *Institute of International Education*, 2000.

★2503★
Research institutions with the highest enrollment of foreign students, 1998-99

Ranking basis/background: Total number of foreign students enrolled at institution and proportion of foreign students to total enrollment. **Number listed:** 20.
1. New York University, with 4,890 foreign students enrolled (13.2% of total enrollment)
2. University of Southern California, 4,564 (15.8%)
3. Columbia University, 4,532 (21.1%)
4. University of Wisconsin, Madison, 4,154 (10.1%)
5. Purdue University, 4,133 (11.2%)
6. Boston University, 4,126 (14.5%)
7. University of Michigan, Ann Arbor, 4,101 (10.8%)
8. University of Texas, Austin, 3,992 (8.2%)
9. Ohio State University, 3,880 (8.1%)
10. University of Illinois, Urbana-Champaign, 3,454 (9.4%)

Source: "Open Doors, 2000," *Institute of International Education*, 2000.

★2504★
Total enrollment of foreign students at U.S. institutions for selected years

Ranking basis/background: Number of foreign students enrolled at U.S. institutions of higher education. **Number listed:** 21.
1. 1954-55, with 34,232
2. 1959-60, 48,486
3. 1964-65, 82,045
4. 1969-70, 134,959
5. 1974-75, 154,580
6. 1979-80, 286,343
7. 1984-85, 342,113
8. 1985-86, 343,777
9. 1986-87, 349,609
10. 1987-88, 356,187
11. 1988-89, 366,354
12. 1989-90, 386,851
13. 1990-91, 407,529
14. 1991-92, 419,585
15. 1992-93, 438,618
16. 1993-94, 449,749
17. 1994-95, 452,653
18. 1995-96, 453,787
19. 1996-97, 457,984
20. 1997-98, 481,280
21. 1998-99, 490,933

Source: *Open Doors, 1998-99: Report on International Educational Exchange* (http://www.opendoorsweb.org/), Institute of International Education, 1999.

★2505★
U.S. counties with the highest international enrollment, 1999-2000

Ranking basis/background: Number of international students enrolled at institutions within each county. **Number listed:** 4.
1. Los Angeles County, with 22,859
2. Manhattan, 22,606
3. Cook County, IL, 12,322
4. Middlesex County, MA, 8,456

Source: "Open Doors, 2000," *Institute of International Education*, 2000.

FOREIGN STUDY

★2506★
Academic levels profile of U.S. students studying abroad, 1998-99

Ranking basis/background: Academic level, by percentage. **Number listed:** 10.
Freshman, with 3%
Sophomore, 13%
Junior, 40%
Senior, 19%
Associate, 2%
Bachelor's, unspecified, 13%
Master's, 5%
Graduate, unspecified, 3%
Doctoral, 1%
Other, 1%

Source: "Open Doors, 2000," *Institute of International Education*, 2000.

★2507★
Fields of study profile of U.S. students studying abroad, 1998-99

Ranking basis/background: Discipline of study, by percentage. **Number listed:** 13.
1. Social sciences, with 20%
2. Business, 18%
3. Humanities, 15%
4. Foreign languages, 8%
4. Fine or applied arts, 8%
6. Physical sciences, 7%
7. Education, 4%
7. Health sciences, 4%
9. Engineering, 3%
10. Math and computer science, 2%
11. Agriculture, 1%
12. Undeclared, 4%
13. Other, 6%

Source: "Open Doors, 2000," *Institute of International Education*, 2000.

★2508★
Gender profile of U.S. students studying abroad, 1998-99

Ranking basis/background: Gender breakdown by percentage. **Number listed:** 2.
Men, with 35%
Women, 65%

Source: "Open Doors, 2000," *Institute of International Education*, 2000.

★2509★
Race/ethnicity profile of U.S. students studying abroad, 1998-99

Ranking basis/background: Race/ethnicity breakdown by percentage. **Number listed:** 6.
White, with 85%
Hispanic American, 5%
Asian American, 4%
African American, 3%
Native American, 1%
Multiracial, 1%

Source: "Open Doors, 2000," *Institute of International Education*, 2000.

★2510★
Top countries of study for U.S. students studying abroad, 1998-99

Ranking basis/background: Number of U.S. students studying at each destination and 1-year percentage changes. Total number of students studying abroad for 1998-99 is 129,770. **Number listed:** 30.
1. Britain, with 27,720 U.S. students; and a 7.0% 1-year change
2. Spain, 12,292; 18.3%
3. Italy, 11,281; 11.2%
4. France, 10,479; 7.2%
5. Mexico, 7,363; 2.8% decrease
6. Multiple countries, 6,702; 22.8%
7. Australia, 5,368; 23.3%
8. Germany, 4,534; 9.4%
9. Costa Rica, 3,449; 16.0%
10. Israel, 3,302; 66.1%

Source: "Open Doors, 2000," *Institute of International Education*, 2000.

★2511★
U.S. bachelor's institutions with the largest number of students studying abroad, 1998-99

Ranking basis/background: Number of U.S. students studying abroad during the 1998-99 academic year. **Number listed:** 20.
1. St. Olaf College, with 632
2. Colgate University, 470
3. DePauw University, 440
4. Colorado College, 439
5. Trinity College (CT), 426

FOUNDATIONS (INSTITUTIONS)

6. College of St. Benedict/St. John (MN), 418
7. Gustavus Adolphus College, 408
8. Bates College, 378
9. Messiah College, 369
10. Colby College, 364

Source: "Open Doors, 2000," *Institute of International Education*, 2000.

★2512★
U.S. doctoral institutions with the largest number of students studying abroad, 1998-99

Ranking basis/background: Number of U.S. students studying abroad during the 1998-99 academic year. **Number listed:** 20.

1. Miami University (OH), with 1,110
2. Dartmouth College, 700
3. George Mason University, 671
4. Boston College, 626
5. Pepperdine University, 621
6. American University, 495
7. Baylor University, 470
8. Florida International University, 453
9. University of New Hampshire, 438
10. Ball State University, 432

Source: "Open Doors, 2000," *Institute of International Education*, 2000.

★2513★
U.S. master's institutions with the largest number of students studying abroad, 1998-99

Ranking basis/background: Number of U.S. students studying abroad during the 1998-99 academic year. **Number listed:** 20.

1. University of St. Thomas (MN), with 673
2. James Madison University, 568
3. California Polytechnic State University, San Luis Obispo, 525
4. Elon College, 499
5. Santa Clara University, 472
6. Calvin College, 442
7. Appalachian State University, 441
8. University of Northern Iowa, 406
9. Villanova University, 381
10. Pacific Lutheran University

Source: "Open Doors, 2000," *Institute of International Education*, 2000.

★2514★
U.S. research institutions with the largest number of students studying abroad, 1998-99

Ranking basis/background: Number of U.S. students studying abroad during the 1998-99 academic year. **Number listed:** 20.

1. Brigham Young University, with 1,862
2. Michigan State University, 1,565
3. University of Texas, Austin, 1,452
4. University of Pennsylvania, 1,349
5. New York University, 1,304
6. University of Wisconsin, Madison, 1,204
7. University of North Carolina, Chapel Hill, 1,061
8. University of Arizona, 1,040
9. University of Colorado, Boulder, 1,019
10. University of Illinois, Urbana-Champaign, 1,005

Source: "Open Doors, 2000," *Institute of International Education*, 2000.

★2515★
World regions hosting U.S. students studying abroad, 1998-99

Ranking basis/background: Percentage of U.S. students studying in each world region. Total number of students studying abroad for 1998-99 is 129,770. **Number listed:** 8.

1. Europe, with 62.7%
2. Latin America, 15.0%
3. Asia, 6.0%
4. Multiple regions, 5.2%
5. Oceania, 4.9%
6. Middle East, 2.8%
6. Africa, 2.8%
8. North America, 0.7%

Source: "Open Doors, 2000," *Institute of International Education*, 2000.

FOUNDATIONS (INSTITUTIONS)
See: **Philanthropic Foundations**

FRENCH LANGUAGE AND LITERATURE, GRADUATE

★2516★
Top French language and literature research-doctorate programs as evaluated by the National Research Council

Ranking basis/background: From a survey of nearly 8,000 faculty members conducted in the spring of 1993. Respondents were asked to rate programs in their field on "scholarly quality of program faculty." When more than one program had the samescore, the council averaged the rank order and gave each program the same rank number (if three programs tied for the top position, each received a rank of 2). **Remarks:** See *Chronicle* article for more details. Scores of 4.01 and above indicate "distinguished;" 3.0-4.0 "strong;" 2.51-3.0 "good;" 2.0-2.5 "adequate;" 1.0-1.99 "marginal;" and 0.0-0.99 "not sufficient for doctoral education." Programs also ranked by "effectiveness of program in educating research scholars/scientists." **Number listed:** 45.

1. Yale University, 4.68
2. Princeton University, 4.55
3. Duke University, 4.43
4. Columbia University, 4.40
5. University of Pennsylvania, 4.37
6. Stanford University, 4.20
7. University of California, Berkeley, 4.19
8. Cornell University, 4.08
9. University of Michigan, 3.97
10. University of California, Irvine, 3.78
11. University of Wisconsin, Madison, 3.74
12. New York University, 3.66
13. University of Virginia, 3.60
14. City University of New York, Graduate School and University Center, 3.48
15. Emory University, 3.38

Source: "Rankings of Research-Doctorate Programs in 41 Disciplines at 274 Institutions," *The Chronicle of Higher Education* 42: A21-A30 (September 21, 1995).

FRESHMEN, COLLEGE
See: **College Students**

FUNDRAISING, COLLEGE
See: **Colleges & Universities–Financial Support & Expenditures**

GEOGRAPHY

★2517★
Radcliffe Institute for Advanced Study fellowship recipient in the field of geography, 2000-01

Ranking basis/background: Recipient and institutional affiliation of the Radcliffe Institute for Advanced study fellowship for pursuit of advanced work across a wide range of academic disciplines, professions, and creative arts. **Number listed:** 1.

Susanne Freidberg, Dartmouth College

Source: "The Radcliffe Institute for Advanced Study," *The Chronicle of Higher Education*, 46: A59, (June 2, 2000).

GEOGRAPHY, GRADUATE

★2518★
Faculty's scholarly reputation in the Ph.D.-granting departments of geography, 1925-1982

Ranking basis/background: Ranking from the National Academy of Sciences study is also given, as well as the ranking for the total number of articles published in 1978-80 and the ratings of the department's reputation in the eyes of other academic geographers. **Remarks:** Article also lists the ratings of Hughes, Keniston, Thomson, Cartter, Roose-Anderson, Beaumont, Sopher-Duncan, and Morrill. Also cited in *Journal of Geography* 164-169 (September/October 1981). **Number listed:** 15.

1. University of Minnesota, with 71 points
2. Pennsylvania State University, 68
3. University of Chicago, 67
4. University of California, Berkeley, 66
4. University of Wisconsin, Madison, 66
6. University of California, Los Angeles, 64
7. Ohio State University, 63
8. Clark University, 62
9. Johns Hopkins University, 59
9. Syracuse University, 59
9. University of Washington (WA), 59
12. University of Illinois, 58
13. University of Iowa, 57
14. University of Kansas, 56
15. University of Georgia, 55
15. Louisiana State University, 55
15. State University of New York, Buffalo, 55

Source: Webster, David, "The Highest Ranked American Ph.D.-Granting Geography Departments: 1925-1982," *Directions* 25: 125-143 (Fall 1983).

★2519★
Most effective geography research-doctorate programs as evaluated by the National Research Council

Ranking basis/background: From a survey of nearly 8,000 faculty members conducted in the spring of 1993. Respondents were asked to rate programs in their field on "effectiveness of program in educating research scholars/scientists." **Remarks:** See *Chronicle* article for more details. Scores of 3.5-5.0 indicate "extremely effective;" 2.5-3.49 "reasonably effective;" 1.5-2.49 "minimally effective;" and 0.0-1.49 "not effective." Programs also ranked by "scholarly quality of program faculty." **Number listed:** 36.

1. Pennsylvania State University, 4.18
2. University of Wisconsin, Madison, 4.14
3. University of Minnesota, 3.95
3. University of California, Santa Barbara, 3.95
3. Ohio State University, 3.95
6. Syracuse University, 3.78
7. University of California, Berkeley, 3.73
8. Clark University, 3.63
9. University of Colorado, 3.61
10. University of Washington (WA), 3.55

Source: "Rankings of Research-Doctorate Programs in 41 Disciplines at 274 Institutions," *The Chronicle of Higher Education* 42: A21-A30 (September 21, 1995).

★2520★
Top geography research-doctorate programs as evaluated by the National Research Council

Ranking basis/background: From a survey of nearly 8,000 faculty members conducted in the spring of 1993. Respondents were asked to rate programs in their field on "scholarly quality of program faculty." When more than one program had the samescore, the council averaged the rank order and gave each program the same rank number (if three programs tied for the top position, each received a rank of 2). **Remarks:** See *Chronicle* article for more details. Scores of 4.01 and above indicate "distinguished;" 3.0-4.0 "strong;" 2.51-3.0 "good;" 2.0-2.5 "adequate;" 1.0-1.99 "marginal;" and 0.0-0.99 "not sufficient for doctoral education." Programs also ranked by "effectiveness of program in educating research scholars/scientists." **Number listed:** 36.

1. Pennsylvania State University, with a quality rating of 4.59
2. University of Wisconsin, Madison, 4.40
3. University of Minnesota, 4.22
4. University of California, Santa Barbara, 4.16
5. Ohio State University, 4.07
6. University of California, Berkeley, 3.99
6. Syracuse University, 3.99
8. University of California, Los Angeles, 3.95
9. Clark University, 3.82
10. University of Washington (WA), 3.66
11. State University of New York, Buffalo, 3.63
12. University of Colorado, 3.57
13. Rutgers University, New Brunswick, 3.39
14. University of Texas, Austin, 3.38
15. Arizona State University, 3.35

Source: "Rankings of Research-Doctorate Programs in 41 Disciplines at 274 Institutions," *The Chronicle of Higher Education* 42: A21-A30 (September 21, 1995).

★2521★
Top Ph.D.-granting departments of geography from 1925-1982

Ranking basis/background: Ranking from the National Academy of Sciences study. The ranking for the total number of articles published in 1978-80, the rating of the faculty's scholarly reputation, and the rating of the department's reputation in the eyes of other academic geographers are also given. **Remarks:** Article also lists the ratings of Hughes, Keniston, Thomson, Cartter, Roose-Anderson, Beaumont, Sopher-Duncan, and Morrill. Also cited in *Journal of Geography* 164-169 (September/October 1981). **Number listed:** 10.

1. University of Wisconsin, with 78.5 points
2. University of Chicago, 71
3. University of California, Berkeley, 56
4. University of Washington, Seattle, 43
5. University of Michigan, 39.5
6. University of Minnesota, 38.5
7. University of California, Los Angeles, 28.5
8. Northwestern University, 25
9. Clark University, 22
10. Syracuse University, 21.5

Source: Webster, David, "The Highest Ranked American Ph.D.-Granting Geography Departments: 1925-1982," *Directions* 25: 125-143 (Fall 1983).

GEOLOGY
See also: **Earth Science**

★2522★
Top recruiters for geology/geophysics jobs for 2000-01 bachelor's degree recipients

Ranking basis/background: Projected number of college hires from on-campus recruitment for 2000-01. **Remarks:** Numbers reflect total expected hires, not just African American projected hires. **Number listed:** 5.

1. Accenture, with 40 projected hires
2. Dewberry & Davis LLC, 25
3. U.S. Air Force (Active Duty Hires), 20
4. Marathon Oil, 10
5. PA Dept. Environmental Protection, 6

Source: "The Top 100 Employers and the Majors in Demand for the Class of 2001," *The Black Collegian*, 31: 19-35, (February 2001).

★2523★
Top recruiters for jobs requiring a graduate professional degree (Ph.D.)

Ranking basis/background: Projected number of college hires from on-campus recruitment for 2000-01. **Remarks:** Numbers reflect total expected hires, not just African American projected hires. **Number listed:** 1.

1. Procter & Gamble, with 40 projected hires

Source: "The Top 100 Employers and the Majors in Demand for the Class of 2001," *The Black Collegian*, 31: 19-35, (February 2001).

GEOLOGY, GRADUATE
See also: **Earth Science, Graduate**

★2524★
Top recruiters for geology/geophysics jobs for 2000-01 master's degree recipients

Ranking basis/background: Projected number of college hires from on-campus recruitment for 2000-01. **Remarks:** Numbers reflect total expected hires, not just African American projected hires. **Number listed:** 2.

1. Accenture, with 3 projected hires
2. Texaco, 6

Source: "The Top 100 Employers and the Majors in Demand for the Class of 2001," *The Black Collegian*, 31: 19-35, (February 2001).

GEOLOGY PERIODICALS

★2525★
Geology journals with the greatest impact measure, 1981-98

Ranking basis/background: Citations-per-paper impact score is the total citations to a journal's published papers divided by total number of papers the journal has published over an eighteen year period. **Remarks:** Original source: *Journal Citation Reports* and Journal Performance Indicators on Diskette. **Number listed:** 10.

1. *Isotope Geoscience*, with an impact score of 18.83
2. *Economic Geology*, 16.54
3. *Journal of Metamorphic Geology*, 15.65
4. *Journal of Geology*, 15.16
5. *Journal of Sedimentary Petrology*, 14.97
6. *Geology*, 14.51
7. *Journal of the Geological Society of Australia*, 12.67
8. *Sedimentology*, 12.18
9. *Quarternary Science Review*, 9.54
10. *Journal of the International Association of Mathematical Geology*, 6.60

Source: "Journals Ranked by Impact: Geology," *What's Hot in Research* (http://www.isinet.com/hot/research) Institute for Scientific Information, July 12, 1999.

★2526★
Geology journals with the greatest impact measure, 1994-98

Ranking basis/background: Citations-per-paper impact score is the total citations to a journal's published papers divided by total number of papers the journal has published over a five year period. **Remarks:** Original source: *Journal Citation Reports* and Journal Performance Indicators on Diskette. **Number listed:** 10.

1. *Journal of Sedimentology Research*, with an impact score of 5.01
2. *Geology*, 4.60
3. *Journal of Sedimentology Research Part A*, 4.33
4. *Journal of Metamorphic Geology*, 4.22
5. *Quarternary Science Review*, 4.04
6. *Journal of Geology*, 3.80
7. *Journal of Sedimentary Petrology*, 3.24
8. *Sedimentology*, 3.08
9. *Palaios*, 2.65
10. *Ore Geology Reviews*, 2.30

Source: "Journals Ranked by Impact: Geology," *What's Hot in Research* (http://www.isinet.com/hot/research) Institute for Scientific Information, July 12, 1999.

GEOPHYSICS PERIODICALS
See: **Physics Periodicals**

GEOSCIENCE
See: **Earth Science, Graduate**

GERMAN LANGUAGE AND LITERATURE, GRADUATE

★2527★
Most effective German language and literature research-doctorate programs as evaluated by the National Research Council

Ranking basis/background: From a survey of nearly 8,000 faculty members conducted in the spring of 1993. Respondents were asked to rate programs in their field on "effectiveness of program in educating research scholars/scientists." **Remarks:** See *Chronicle* article for more details. Scores of 3.5-5.0 indicate "extremely effective;" 2.5-3.49 "reasonably effective;" 1.5-2.49 "minimally effective;" and 0.0-1.49 "not effective." Programs also ranked by "scholarly quality of program faculty." **Number listed:** 32.

1. Princeton University, with an effectiveness rating of 3.91
2. University of California, Berkeley, 3.88
3. Harvard University, 3.78
4. Cornell University, 3.73
5. Yale University, 3.68
6. University of Wisconsin, Madison, 3.65
7. Stanford University, 3.61
8. Washington University, 3.55
9. University of Virginia, 3.54
10. University of Minnesota, 3.48

Source: "Rankings of Research-Doctorate Programs in 41 Disciplines at 274 Institutions," *The Chronicle of Higher Education* 42: A21-A30 (September 21, 1995).

★2528★
Top German language and literature research-doctorate programs as evaluated by the National Research Council

Ranking basis/background: From a survey of nearly 8,000 faculty members conducted in the spring of 1993. Respondents were asked to rate programs in their field on "scholarly quality of program faculty." When more than one program had the samescore, the council averaged the rank order and gave each program the same rank number (if three programs tied for the top position, each received a rank of 2). **Remarks:** See *Chronicle* article for more details. Scores of 4.01 and above indicate "distinguished;" 3.0-4.0 "strong;" 2.51-3.0 "good;" 2.0-2.5 "adequate;" 1.0-1.99 "marginal;" and 0.0-0.99 "not sufficient for doctoral education." Programs also ranked by "effectiveness of program in educating research scholars/scientists." **Number listed:** 32.

1. University of California, Berkeley, with a quality rating of 4.32
2. Princeton University, 4.22
3. Cornell University, 4.19
4. Harvard University, 4.01
5. Yale University, 3.95
6. Stanford University, 3.83
7. Washington University, 3.81
8. University of Virginia, 3.77
9. Johns Hopkins University, 3.75
10. University of Wisconsin, Madison, 3.74
11. University of Minnesota, 3.68
12. University of Washington (WA), 3.60
13. University of Texas, Austin, 3.40
14. Indiana University, 3.28
14. University of California, Irvine, 3.28

Source: "Rankings of Research-Doctorate Programs in 41 Disciplines at 274 Institutions," *The Chronicle of Higher Education* 42: A21-A30 (September 21, 1995).

GMAT

★2529★
Average GMAT scores for *U.S. News & World Report*'s top 10 graduate business schools, 2000

Ranking basis/background: From a *U.S. News & World Report* survey of GMAT scores for 1999. **Remarks:** Data collected by Market Facts Inc. **Number listed:** 50.

Harvard University, with an average GMAT score of 690
Stanford University, 725
University of Pennsylvania, Wharton School of Business, 691
Massachusetts Institute of Technology, Alfred P. Sloan School of Management, 700
Northwestern University, Kellogg Graduate School of Management, 690
Columbia University Graduate School of Business, 700
University of Chicago Graduate School of Business, 690
Duke University, Fuqua School of Business, 677
University of Michigan, Ann Arbor, 675
University of California, Berkeley, Haas Graduate School of Business Administration, 682

Source: "America's Best Graduate Schools: 2001 Annual Guide," *U.S. News & World Report*, 128: 56-94, (April 10, 2000).

GRADUATE DEGREES
See: **Degrees (Academic) Doctoral Degrees**

GRADUATE EDUCATION (GENERAL)

Related Information

★2530★
Research-Doctorate Programs in the United States: Continuity and Change, National Research Council, 1995.

Remarks: Study examines the reputation, quality, and effectiveness of 3,634 doctoral programs at 274 universities. It updates and expands the National Research Council's 1982 assessment of graduate education in the U.S.

GRADUATE SCHOOLS
See: **Colleges & Universities**

GRADUATE STUDENTS
See also: **Graduate Education (General)**

★2531★
College senior's choices for exemplary doctoral-extensive universities

Ranking basis/background: Compiled from a survey of college students regarding size, educational mission, student characteristics, and other factors. Institutions are listed alphabetically. **Remarks:** Original source: National Survey of Student Engagement, Indiana University. **Number listed:** 4.

Brigham Young University
Loyola University, Chicago
University of Michigan, Ann Arbor
University of Virginia

Source: Reisberg, Leo, "Are Students Actually Learning?," *The Chronicle of Higher Education*, 46: A67-A70, (November 17, 2000).

★2532★
College senior's choices for exemplary doctoral-intensive universities

Ranking basis/background: Compiled from a survey of college students regarding size, educational mission, student characteristics, and other factors. Institutions are listed alphabetically. **Remarks:** Original source: National Survey of Student Engagement, Indiana University. **Number listed:** 3.

Miami University (OH)
Pepperdine University
State University of New York College of Environmental Science and Forestry

Source: Reisberg, Leo, "Are Students Actually Learning?," *The Chronicle of Higher Education*, 46: A67-A70, (November 17, 2000).

★2533★
College senior's choices for exemplary master's institutions

Ranking basis/background: Compiled from a survey of college students regarding size, educational mission, student characteristics, and other factors. Institutions are listed alphabetically. **Remarks:** Original source: National Survey of Student Engagement, Indiana University. **Number listed:** 4.

College of St. Catherine (MN)
Regis College (MA)
St. Michael's College
University of Richmond

Source: Reisberg, Leo, "Are Students Actually Learning?," *The Chronicle of Higher Education*, 46: A67-A70, (November 17, 2000).

★2534★
First-year student's choices for exemplary doctoral-extensive universities
Ranking basis/background: Compiled from a survey of college students regarding size, educational mission, student characteristics, and other factors. Institutions are listed alphabetically.
Remarks: Original source: National Survey of Student Engagement, Indiana University. **Number listed:** 4.

American University
Indiana University, Bloomington
Rice University
University of Michigan, Ann Arbor

Source: Reisberg, Leo, "Are Students Actually Learning?," *The Chronicle of Higher Education*, 46: A67-A70, (November 17, 2000).

★2535★
First-year student's choices for exemplary doctoral-intensive universities
Ranking basis/background: Compiled from a survey of college students regarding size, educational mission, student characteristics, and other factors. Institutions are listed alphabetically.
Remarks: Original source: National Survey of Student Engagement, Indiana University. **Number listed:** 3.

Pepperdine University
Polytechnic University (NY)
Seton Hall University

Source: Reisberg, Leo, "Are Students Actually Learning?," *The Chronicle of Higher Education*, 46: A67-A70, (November 17, 2000).

★2536★
First-year student's choices for exemplary master's institutions
Ranking basis/background: Compiled from a survey of college students regarding size, educational mission, student characteristics, and other factors. Institutions are listed alphabetically.
Remarks: Original source: National Survey of Student Engagement, Indiana University. **Number listed:** 4.

College of Notre Dame (MD)
Loyola College (MD)
Regis College (MA)
University of Richmond

Source: Reisberg, Leo, "Are Students Actually Learning?," *The Chronicle of Higher Education*, 46: A67-A70, (November 17, 2000).

GRADUATES, COLLEGE
See: **College Graduates Degrees (Academic) Doctoral Degrees Salaries–College Graduates**

GRADUATES, HIGH-SCHOOL
See: **Schools, Secondary–Graduates**

GRADUATION RATES–COLLEGE
See: **College Graduates**

GRANTS, FEDERAL
See: **Research Funding Research & Development Funding Scientific & Technological Research & Development Funding Scientific & Technological Research Funding Student Financial Aid**

GRAPHIC ARTS
See: **Art**

HANDICAPPED
See: **Disabilities–Enrollment of Students Disabilities–Federal Aid**

HEALTH

★2537★
Health policy and services journals by citation impact, 1981-99
Ranking basis/background: Impact factor calculated by taking the number of current citations to source items published and dividing it by the number of articles published in the journal during that time period. **Number listed:** 10.

1. *Milbank Members Fund Quarterly*, with a 21.01 impact factor
2. *Medical Care*, 17.50
3. *Milbank Quarterly*, 13.72
4. *Journal of Health Economics*, 10.79
5. *Inquiry-Journal of Health Care*, 9.51
6. *Health Services Research*, 8.93
7. *Health Affairs*, 6.74
8. *Journal of Health Politics and Policy*, 5.98
9. *International Journal of Health Services*, 5.37
10. *Community Mental Health Journal*, 5.20

Source: "Journals Ranked by Impact: Health Policy & Services," *What's Hot in Research* (http://www.isinet.com/isi/hot/research) *Institute for Scientific Information*, January 1, 2001.

★2538★
Health policy and services journals by citation impact, 1995-99
Ranking basis/background: Impact factor calculated by taking the number of current citations to source items published and dividing it by the number of articles published in the journal during that time period. **Number listed:** 10.

1. *Milbank Quarterly*, with a 6.30 impact factor
2. *Health Affairs*, 5.04
3. *Psychology, Public Policy, and Law*, 4.69
4. *Medical Care*, 4.59
5. *Future of Children*, 4.07
6. *Health Care Financial Review*, 3.73
7. *Inquiry-Journal of Health Care*, 3.57
8. *Journal of Health Economics*, 3.51
9. *Journal of Mental Health Administration*, 3.35
10. *Health Services Research*, 3.25

Source: "Journals Ranked by Impact: Health Policy & Services," *What's Hot in Research* (http://www.isinet.com/isi/hot/research) *Institute for Scientific Information*, January 1, 2001.

★2539★
Health policy and services journals by citation impact, 1999
Ranking basis/background: Impact factor calculated by taking the number of current citations to source items published and dividing it by the number of articles published in the journal during that time period. **Number listed:** 10.

1. *Health Affairs*, with a 5.08 impact factor
2. *Milbank Quarterly*, 3.43
3. *Health Economics*, 2.40
4. *Journal of Health Economics*, 2.37
5. *Medical Care*, 2.08
6. *Journal of Health Politics and Policy*, 2.06
7. *Psychiatric Services*, 1.75
8. *Health Services Research*, 1.73
9. *The Joint Commission Journal on Quality Improvement*, 1.54
10. *Psychology, Public Policy, and Law*, 1.41

Source: "Journals Ranked by Impact: Health Policy & Services," *What's Hot in Research* (http://www.isinet.com/isi/hot/research) *Institute for Scientific Information*, January 1, 2001.

★2540★
Top recruiters for allied health/biomedical science jobs for 2000-01 bachelor's degree recipients
Ranking basis/background: Projected number of college hires from on-campus recruitment for 2000-01. **Remarks:** Numbers reflect total expected hires, not just African American projected hires. **Number listed:** 2.

1. U.S. Air Force (Active Duty Hires), with 314 projected hires
2. Wyeth-Ayerst, 4

Source: "The Top 100 Employers and the Majors in Demand for the Class of 2001," *The Black Collegian*, 31: 19-35, (February 2001).

★2541★
Top recruiters for health jobs for 2000-01 bachelor's degree recipients
Ranking basis/background: Projected number of college hires from on-campus recruitment for 2000-01. **Remarks:** Numbers reflect total expected hires, not just African American projected hires. **Number listed:** 8.

1. JCPenney Company, with 75 projected hires
2. Accenture, 50
3. Cap Gemini Ernst & Young, 20
4. Applebee's International, 8
5. Wyeth-Ayerst, 6
6. Novant Health, 5
6. Sherwin-Williams, 5
8. Arthur Andersen LLP, 1

Source: "The Top 100 Employers and the Majors in Demand for the Class of 2001," *The Black Collegian*, 31: 19-35, (February 2001).

HEALTH–FEDERAL AID

★2542★
National Institutes of Health growth trends, 1997 to 2002

Ranking basis/background: Figures, in billions, from the U.S. government's fiscal appropriations for the National Institutes for Health programs. **Number listed:** 6.
- 1997, with $12.7 billion
- 1998, $13.6
- 1999, $15.6
- 2000, $17.9
- 2001, $20.5
- 2002, $23.2 (proposed)

Source: Brainard, Jeffrey and Ron Southwick, "NIH Soars, Other Science Agencies Struggle in President's First Budget Plan," *The Chronicle of Higher Education*, 47: A35, A38-A39, (April 20, 2001).

★2543★
Proposed fiscal 2002 appropriations for health professions

Ranking basis/background: Based on the U.S. government's proposed fiscal 2002 appropriations for health professions. **Number listed:** 3.
- Training programs for minority and disadvantaged students, with $45,807,000
- Graduate medical education at children's hospitals, $200,000,000
- Training for other health professions, $93,946,000

Source: "Bush's Fiscal 2002 Budget Plan for Higher Education and Science," *The Chronicle of Higher Education*, 47: A36-A37, (April 20, 2001).

HEALTH, GRADUATE

★2544★
Top recruiters for allied health/biomedical science jobs for 2000-01 master's degree recipients

Ranking basis/background: Projected number of college hires from on-campus recruitment for 2000-01. **Remarks:** Numbers reflect total expected hires, not just African American projected hires. **Number listed:** 3.
1. U.S. Air Force (Active Duty Hires), with 42 projected hires
2. Novant Health, 20
3. Wyeth-Ayerst, 2

Source: "The Top 100 Employers and the Majors in Demand for the Class of 2001," *The Black Collegian*, 31: 19-35, (February 2001).

★2545★
Top recruiters for health jobs for 2000-01 master's degree recipients

Ranking basis/background: Projected number of college hires from on-campus recruitment for 2000-01. **Remarks:** Numbers reflect total expected hires, not just African American projected hires. **Number listed:** 5.
- U.S. Air Force (Active Duty Hires), with 53 projected hires
- Arthur Andersen LLP, 12
- Accenture, 10
- Wyeth-Ayerst, 10
- Novant Health, 2

Source: "The Top 100 Employers and the Majors in Demand for the Class of 2001," *The Black Collegian*, 31: 19-35, (February 2001).

HIGH SCHOOL DROPOUTS
See: **Dropouts**

HIGH SCHOOLS
See: **Schools, Secondary**

HIGHER EDUCATION

★2546★
New trends in higher education

Ranking basis/background: List of trends to watch for in higher education. **Number listed:** 10.
- Impact of technology
- Cross-disciplinary training
- Global impact
- A demographic shift
- Continuing education
- Institutional involvement in community
- Creating creative learning methods
- Cost and accountability
- Diversity dilemma
- New leadership

Source: Hamilton, Kendra, "The New Academic Year," *Black Issues in Higher Education*, 17: 24-27, (September 14, 2000).

HIGHER EDUCATION–FINANCIAL SUPPORT
See: **Colleges & Universities–Financial Support & Expenditures**

HIGHER EDUCATION INSTITUTIONS
See: **Black Colleges and Universities Colleges & Universities Two-Year Colleges**

HISPANIC AMERICANS–ENROLLMENT, COLLEGE

★2547★
Hispanic American enrollment at Hispanic-serving institutions of higher education, by state, 1997

Ranking basis/background: Percentage of Hispanic American students enrolled at Hispanic-serving institutions in each state. **Remarks:** Original source: Hispanic Association of Colleges and Universities. **Number listed:** 13.
1. California, with 30.8%
2. Puerto Rico, 23.4%
3. Texas, 18.8%
4. Florida, 8.1%
5. New York, 5.5%
6. New Mexico, 4.8%
7. Arizona, 2.7%
8. Illinois, 3.6%
9. Colorado, 0.8%
9. New Jersey, 0.8%
11. Washington, 0.4%
12. Kansas, 0.3%
13. Oregon, 0.01%

Source: Dervarics, Charles, "Hispanic-Serving Institutions Make Impressive Strides," *Black Issues in Higher Education*, 17: 32-35, (September 28, 2000).

★2548★
Hispanic American enrollment in higher education, 1997

Ranking basis/background: Number, in thousands, of Hispanic Americans enrolled at each type of institution, and percentage change since 1988. **Remarks:** Original source: American Council on Education. **Number listed:** 3.
- All institutions, with 1,218 thousand enrolled; a 79.2% change since 1988
- Four-year institutions, 530; 79.0%
- Two-year institutions, 89; 79.4%

Source: Weige, Pamela R., "As Latino Populations Grow.," *Black Issues in Higher Education*, 17: 20-25, (September 28, 2000).

HISTORY

★2549★
Radcliffe Institute for Advanced Study fellowship recipients in the field of history, 2000-01

Ranking basis/background: Recipient and institutional affiliation of the Radcliffe Institute for Advanced study fellowship for pursuit of advanced work across a wide range of academic disciplines, professions, and creative arts. **Number listed:** 8.
- Kathy Davis, Utrecht University
- Virginia Drachman, Tufts University
- Glenda Gilmore, Yale University
- Ellen More, University of Texas
- Lisa Herschbach, Rutgers University
- Kenda Mutongi, Williams College
- Helen Horowitz, Smith College
- Regina Kunzel, Williams College

Source: "The Radcliffe Institute for Advanced Study," *The Chronicle of Higher Education*, 46: A59, (June 2, 2000).

★2550★
Top recruiters for history jobs for 2000-01 bachelor's degree recipients

Ranking basis/background: Projected number of college hires from on-campus recruitment for 2000-01. **Remarks:** Numbers reflect total expected hires, not just African American projected hires. **Number listed:** 4.
1. Houghton Mifflin, with 10 projected hires
1. Wells Fargo Financial, 10
1. Eckerd Youth Alternatives, Inc., 10
4. Henrico County Public Schools, 3

Source: "The Top 100 Employers and the Majors in Demand for the Class of 2001," *The Black Collegian*, 31: 19-35, (February 2001).

★2551★
U.S. universities contributing the most papers in the field of history, 1993-97

Ranking basis/background: Average citations per paper. Also includes total number of papers from 1993 to 1997. **Remarks:** Original source: University Science Indicators of Diskette, 1981-97. **Number listed:** 5.
1. Harvard University, with 147 papers; 0.95 citations per paper
2. University of California, Berkeley, 123; 0.79
3. University of California, Los Angeles, 119; 0.77
4. University of Michigan, 117; 0.75
5. City University of New York, 106; 0.68

Source: "History: Most Prolific U.S. Universities, 1993-97," *What's Hot in Research,* http://www.isinet.com/whatshot/whatshot.html, Institute for Scientific Information (March 29, 1999).

HISTORY, GRADUATE

★2552★
Private, 4-year undergraduate colleges and universities producing the most Ph.D.'s in history, 1920-1990

Ranking basis/background: Number of doctoral degrees granted to graduates of 914 private, 4-year U.S. undergraduate colleges and universities. Medical, law, and other professional, non-doctoral degrees are not included. **Remarks:** Original source: Office of Scientific and Engineering Personnel of the National Research Council. Report contains 50 other tables detailing the distribution of doctoral recipients by field of study over various time frames. **Number listed:** 338.
1. Oberlin College, with 195 Ph.D.'s
2. Amherst College, 161
3. Swarthmore College, 141
4. Smith College, 134
5. Wesleyan University, 124
6. Wellesley College, 116
7. Barnard College, 113
8. College of Wooster, 107
9. Vassar College, 100
10. Williams College, 97
11. Carleton College, 92
12. Mount Holyoke College, 82
12. Pomona College, 82
12. Wheaton College, 82
15. DePauw University, 78
16. Davidson College, 75
16. Grinnell College, 75
18. Reed College, 73
19. College of the Holy Cross, 72
20. Bryn Mawr College, 71

Source: *Baccalaureate Origins of Doctorate Recipients, 7th ed.,* Franklin & Marshall College, March 1993.

★2553★
Private, 4-year undergraduate colleges and universities producing the most Ph.D.'s in history, 1981-1990

Ranking basis/background: Number of doctoral degrees granted to graduates of 914 private, 4-year U.S. undergraduate colleges and universities. Medical, law, and other professional, non-doctoral degrees are not included. **Remarks:** Original source: Office of Scientific and Engineering Personnel of the National Research Council. Report contains 50 other tables detailing the distribution of doctoral recipients by field of study over various time frames. **Number listed:** 292.
1. Oberlin College, with 37 Ph.D.s
2. Wellesley College, 36
3. Smith College, 27
3. Wesleyan University, 27
5. Barnard College, 26
6. Swarthmore College, 24
7. Amherst College, 21
8. Mount Holyoke College, 20
8. Vassar College, 20
10. Reed College, 18
11. Carleton College, 17
11. College of Wooster, 17
13. Bryn Mawr College, 15
13. Pomona College, 15
15. Grinnell College, 14
16. Calvin College, 13
17. Wheaton College, 12
17. Wake Forest University, 12
17. Williams College, 12
17. College of the Holy Cross, 12
17. Colorado College, 12

Source: *Baccalaureate Origins of Doctorate Recipients, 7th ed.,* Franklikn & Marshall College, March 1993.

★2554★
Top history research-doctorate programs as evaluated by the National Research Council

Ranking basis/background: From a survey of nearly 8,000 faculty members conducted in the spring of 1993. Respondents were asked to rate programs in their field on "scholarly quality of program faculty." When more than one program had the samescore, the council averaged the rank order and gave each program the same rank number (if three programs tied for the top position, each received a rank of 2). **Remarks:** See *Chronicle* article for more details. Scores of 4.01 and above indicate "distinguished;" 3.0-4.0 "strong;" 2.51-3.0 "good;" 2.0-2.5 "adequate;" 1.0-1.99 "marginal;" and 0.0-0.99 "not sufficient for doctoral education." Programs also ranked by "effectiveness of program in educating research scholars/scientists." **Number listed:** 111.
1. Yale University, with a quality rating of 4.89
2. University of California, Berkeley, 4.79
3. Princeton University, 4.75
4. Harvard University, 4.71
5. Columbia University, 4.63
6. University of California, Los Angeles, 4.59
7. Stanford University, 4.56
8. University of Chicago, 4.49
9. Johns Hopkins University, 4.42
10. University of Wisconsin, Madison, 4.37
11. University of Michigan, 4.30
12. University of Pennsylvania, 4.24
13. Cornell University, 4.22
14. Brown University, 3.96
15. Duke University, 3.93

Source: "Rankings of Research-Doctorate Programs in 41 Disciplines at 274 Institutions," *The Chronicle of Higher Education* 42: A21-A30 (September 21, 1995).

★2555★
Top recruiters for history jobs for 2000-01 master's degree recipients

Ranking basis/background: Projected number of college hires from on-campus recruitment for 2000-01. **Remarks:** Numbers reflect total expected hires, not just African American projected hires. **Number listed:** 1.
1. Henrico County Public Schools, with 8 projected hires

Source: "The Top 100 Employers and the Majors in Demand for the Class of 2001," *The Black Collegian,* 31: 19-35, (February 2001).

HOME SCHOOLING

Related Information

★2556★
Deckard, Steve, *Home Schooling Laws and Resource Guide for All Fifty States, annual.,* Vision Publishing.
Remarks: Describes state laws on educating a child at home. Entries list application process, curriculum, teacher requirements, record-keeping, and testing requirements. Name, address, and phone number for each state contact is also given.

HOMEWORK

★2557★
Time students spend doing homework daily, by age group

Ranking basis/background: Percentage of time spent on homework each day, by age group. **Remarks:** Original source: National Center for Education Statistics. **Number listed:** 4.
None, with 26% 9-year olds; 24% 13-year olds; 26% 17-year olds
Less than 1 hour, 52%; 37%; 26%
1-2 hours, 12%; 26%; 23%
More than 2 hours, 5%; 8%; 12%

Source: Simmons, Keith, "Not Much Homework Getting Done," *USA Today,* May 4, 2001, Section A, p. 1A.

HOTEL AND RESTAURANT MANAGEMENT

★2558★
Top recruiters for hospitality/hotel/restaurant management jobs for 2000-01 bachelor's degree recipients

Ranking basis/background: Projected number of college hires from on-campus recruitment for 2000-01. **Remarks:** Numbers reflect total expected hires, not just African American projected hires. **Number listed:** 6.
1. Marriott International, with 550 projected hires

HUMAN RESOURCES

2. Hyatt Hotels & Resorts, 350
3. Applebee's International, 60
4. Sherwin-Williams, 40
5. Federated Department Stores, 14
6. Macy's East, 10

Source: "The Top 100 Employers and the Majors in Demand for the Class of 2001," *The Black Collegian*, 31: 19-35, (February 2001).

HUMAN RESOURCES

★2559★
Top recruiters for human resources jobs for 2000-01 bachelor's degree recipients

Ranking basis/background: Projected number of college hires from on-campus recruitment for 2000-01. **Remarks:** Numbers reflect total expected hires, not just African American projected hires. **Number listed:** 3.

1. Footstar, with 20 projected hires
2. Caterpillar Inc., 6
3. International Paper, 3

Source: "The Top 100 Employers and the Majors in Demand for the Class of 2001," *The Black Collegian*, 31: 19-35, (February 2001).

HUMAN RESOURCES, GRADUATE

★2560★
Top recruiters for human resources jobs for 2000-01 master's degree recipients

Ranking basis/background: Projected number of college hires from on-campus recruitment for 2000-01. **Remarks:** Numbers reflect total expected hires, not just African American projected hires. **Number listed:** 2.

1. Footstar, with 5 projected hires
2. International Paper, 3

Source: "The Top 100 Employers and the Majors in Demand for the Class of 2001," *The Black Collegian*, 31: 19-35, (February 2001).

INCOME

See also: **Salaries–College Graduates**
Salaries–Colleges & Universities
Salaries–Schools, Elementary & Secondary

★2561★
Counties with the highest per capita income

Ranking basis/background: Per capita income for each U.S. county. **Remarks:** Original source: Woods & Poole Economics; includes earned and unearned income. **Number listed:** 20.

1. Manhattan, NY, with $69,157
2. Marin, CA, $54,608
3. Pitkin, CO, $54,076
4. Fairfield, CT, $53,474
5. Somerset, NJ, $51,605
6. Alexandria, VA, $50,752
7. Westchester, NY, $50,402
8. Morris, NJ, $49,640
9. Bergen, NJ, $48,137
10. Arlington, VA, $47,252
11. Montgomery, MD, $46,911
12. Teton, WY, $45,758
13. San Francisco, CA, $45,694
14. Montgomery, PA, $45,553
15. Fairfax, VA, $45,493
16. Lake, IL, $45,218
17. Nassau, NY, $45,176
18. Oakland, MI, $44,767
19. Nantucket, MA, $44,534
20. San Mateo, CA, $43,884

Source: Whitman, David, "When East Beats West," *U.S. News & World Report*, 128: 28, (May 8, 2000).

INDUSTRIAL ORGANIZATION
See: **Economics**

INFORMATION SCIENCE
See: **Library Science**

INFORMATION SYSTEMS

★2562★
Book publishers with the most citations (Class 1)

Ranking basis/background: Number of citations, from a sample of 123 citing journal articles and 82 proceeding articles. Citing articles refer to 6,901 publications, namely 3,128 journal articles, 1,532 proceeding articles, 1,577 books, and 664 other publications. **Number listed:** 3.

1. Springer-Verlag, with 169
2. Wiley, 143
3. Addison-Wesley, 131

Source: Kleijnen, Jack P.C. and William Van Groenendaal, "Measuring the Quality of Publications: New Methodology and Case Study," *Information Processing and Management*, 36: 551-570, (July 2000).

★2563★
Book publishers with the most citations (Class 2)

Ranking basis/background: Number of citations, from a sample of 123 citing journal articles and 82 proceeding articles. Citing articles refer to 6,901 publications, namely 3,128 journal articles, 1,532 proceeding articles, 1,577 books, and 664 other publications. **Number listed:** 3.

1. Prentice Hall, with 101
2. MIT Press, 83
3. Cambridge University Press, 76

Source: Kleijnen, Jack P.C. and William Van Groenendaal, "Measuring the Quality of Publications: New Methodology and Case Study," *Information Processing and Management*, 36: 551-570, (July 2000).

★2564★
Book publishers with the most citations (Class 3)

Ranking basis/background: Number of citations, from a sample of 123 citing journal articles and 82 proceeding articles. Citing articles refer to 6,901 publications, namely 3,128 journal articles, 1,532 proceeding articles, 1,577 books, and 664 other publications. **Number listed:** 6.

1. Morgan Kaufmann Publishers, with 57
2. Sage Publications, 56
3. Academic Press, 55
4. McGraw-Hill, 51
5. Elsevier, 39
6. Lawrence Erlbaum Associates, 37

Source: Kleijnen, Jack P.C. and William Van Groenendaal, "Measuring the Quality of Publications: New Methodology and Case Study," *Information Processing and Management*, 36: 551-570, (July 2000).

★2565★
Book publishers with the most citations (Class 4)

Ranking basis/background: Number of citations, from a sample of 123 citing journal articles and 82 proceeding articles. Citing articles refer to 6,901 publications, namely 3,128 journal articles, 1,532 proceeding articles, 1,577 books, and 664 other publications. **Number listed:** 9.

1. Oxford University Press, with 34
2. North-Holland, 31
3. Macmillan, 31
3. Free Press, 31
5. Kluwer, 29
6. Jossey-Bass, 27
7. Benjamin-Cummings, 25
8. JAI Press, 24
9. Houghton Mifflin, 21

Source: Kleijnen, Jack P.C. and William Van Groenendaal, "Measuring the Quality of Publications: New Methodology and Case Study," *Information Processing and Management*, 36: 551-570, (July 2000).

★2566★
Book publishers with the most citations (Class 5)

Ranking basis/background: Number of citations, from a sample of 123 citing journal articles and 82 proceeding articles. Citing articles refer to 6,901 publications, namely 3,128 journal articles, 1,532 proceeding articles, 1,577 books, and 664 other publications. **Number listed:** 21.

1. University of Chicago Press, with 20
2. University of California Press, 19
2. Harvard Business School Press, 19
4. Heinemann, 18
4. Blackwell, Basil, 18
6. Harvard University Press, 17
6. Routledge, 17
8. Freeman, 16
9. Harper and Row, 15
10. Pitman, 14

Source: Kleijnen, Jack P.C. and William Van Groenendaal, "Measuring the Quality of Publications: New Methodology and Case Study," *Information Processing and Management*, 36: 551-570, (July 2000).

★2567★
Journals and proceedings with the most citations (Class 1)

Ranking basis/background: Number of citations, from a sample of 123 citing journal articles and 82 proceeding articles. Citing articles refer to 6,901 publications, namely 3,128 journal articles, 1,532 proceeding articles, 1,577 books, and 664 other publications. **Number listed:** 5.

1. *MIS Quarterly*, with 135
2. *Management Science*, 132
3. *Communications of the Association of Computing Machinery*, 123

4. *Proceedings of the International Conference on Very Large Databases (VLDB)*, 87
4. *Proceedings of the ACM Conference on Management of Data (SIGMOD)*, 87

Source: Kleijnen, Jack P.C. and William Van Groenendaal, "Measuring the Quality of Publications: New Methodology and Case Study," *Information Processing and Management*, 36: 551-570, (July 2000).

★2568★
Journals and proceedings with the most citations (Class 2)

Ranking basis/background: Number of citations, from a sample of 123 citing journal articles and 82 proceeding articles. Citing articles refer to 6,901 publications, namely 3,128 journal articles, 1,532 proceeding articles, 1,577 books, and 664 other publications. **Number listed:** 31.

1. *Administrative Science Quarterly*, with 63
2. *Artificial Intelligence*, 55
3. *Journal of Management Information Systems*, 47
3. *Journal of Personality and Social Psychology*, 47
5. *Harvard Business Review*, 45
6. *European Journal of Operational Research*, 44
6. *Journal of Accounting Research*, 44
6. *Proceedings of the National Conference on Artificial Intelligence (AAAI)*, 44
9. *Academy of Management Review*, 43
10. *Journal of the ACM*, 42
10. *IEEE Transactions on Software Engineering*, 42
10. *Econometrica*, 42

Source: Kleijnen, Jack P.C. and William Van Groenendaal, "Measuring the Quality of Publications: New Methodology and Case Study," *Information Processing and Management*, 36: 551-570, (July 2000).

★2569★
Journals and proceedings with the most citations (Class 3)

Ranking basis/background: Number of citations, from a sample of 123 citing journal articles and 82 proceeding articles. Citing articles refer to 6,901 publications, namely 3,128 journal articles, 1,532 proceeding articles, 1,577 books, and 664 other publications. **Number listed:** 51.

1. *ACM Computing Surveys*, with 34
1. *Proceedings of the International Joint Conference on Artificial Intelligence (IJCAI)*, 34
3. *Psychological Review*, 32
4. *IEEE Transactions on Knowledge and Data Engineering*, 31
4. *Information and Management*, 31
6. *ACM SIGMOD Record*, 30
6. *IEEE Transactions on Systems, Man and Cybernetics*, 30
6. *Proceedings of the ACM Symposium on the Theory of Computing (STOC)*, 30
6. *Proceedings of the IEEE International Conference on Data Engineering (ICDE)*, 30
10. *Proceedings of the International Conference on Information Systems (ICIS)*, 29
10. *Proceedings of the International Conference on Logic Programming (ICLP)*, 29

Source: Kleijnen, Jack P.C. and William Van Groenendaal, "Measuring the Quality of Publications: New Methodology and Case Study," *Information Processing and Management*, 36: 551-570, (July 2000).

★2570★
Journals and proceedings with the most citations (Class 4)

Ranking basis/background: Number of citations, from a sample of 123 citing journal articles and 82 proceeding articles. Citing articles refer to 6,901 publications, namely 3,128 journal articles, 1,532 proceeding articles, 1,577 books, and 664 other publications. **Number listed:** 123.

1. *Interfaces*, with 17
2. *ACM Transactions on Office Information Systems*, 16
2. *Journal of Management*, 16
2. *Proceedings of the IEEE Symposium on Foundations of Computer Science (FOCS)*, 16
2. *Proceedings of the IEEE*, 16
6. *Information Processing and Management*, 15
6. *International Journal of Production Research*, 15
6. *Proceedings of the International Conference on Machine Learning (ICML)*, 15
9. *Annual Review of Psychology*, 14
9. *Personnel Psychology*, 14
9. *Journal of Marketing*, 14
9. *Neural Computation*, 14
9. *Proceedings of the International Symposium on Computer Architecture*, 14
9. *Proceedings of the IEEE International Computer Conference (COMPCON)*, 14
9. *Proceedings of the International Conference on Principles of Knowledge*, 14
9. *Representation and Reasoning*, 14
9. *Proceedings of the IEEE Real-Time Systems Symposium*, 14

Source: Kleijnen, Jack P.C. and William Van Groenendaal, "Measuring the Quality of Publications: New Methodology and Case Study," *Information Processing and Management*, 36: 551-570, (July 2000).

★2571★
Publishers, journals and proceedings with the lowest citations (Class 6)

Ranking basis/background: Number of citations, from a sample of 123 citing journal articles and 82 proceeding articles. Citing articles refer to 6,901 publications, namely 3,128 journal articles, 1,532 proceeding articles, 1,577 books, and 664 other publications. **Number listed:** 50.

1. Simon & Schuster, with 10
1. World Scientific Publishing, 10
3. Norton, 9
3. Computer Science Press, 9
5. Greenwood Press, 8
5. Gorcum, Van, 8
5. Taylor & Francis, 8
8. University of Michigan, 7
8. Clarendon Press, 7
8. Pergamon Press, 7

Source: Kleijnen, Jack P.C. and William Van Groenendaal, "Measuring the Quality of Publications: New Methodology and Case Study," *Information Processing and Management*, 36: 551-570, (July 2000).

INSTITUTIONAL EVALUATION
See: Evaluation Criteria & Methodologies–Institutions

INSURANCE
See: Business Administration, Graduate–Insurance Business Administration–Insurance

INTERNATIONAL BUSINESS
See: Business Administration

INTERNATIONAL ECONOMICS
See: Economics

INTERNATIONAL RELATIONS
See: Political Science

INTERNET

★2572★
American cities with the highest percentage of people with Internet access

Ranking basis/background: Percentage of people with Internet access in each designated market area. **Number listed:** 20.

1. San Francisco/Oakland/San Jose, with 61.0%
2. San Diego, 58.0%
3. Washington, DC, 56.1%
4. Seattle/Tacoma, 55.9%
5. Portland, OR, 54.0%
6. Boston, 51.7%
7. Dallas/Fort Worth, 47.6%
8. Denver, 47.3%
9. Atlanta, 46.1%
10. Los Angeles, 43.9%

Source: "Wired Cities," *American Demographics*, 22: 64, (June 2000).

★2573★
America's most wired cities, 2001

Ranking basis/background: From research of home and business Internet use, the prevalence of online companies, number of networked computers in a given area, and the quantity and quality of city-related content available online. **Number listed:** 50.

1. San Jose, CA
2. San Francisco, CA
3. Austin-San Marcos, TX
4. Washington, DC
5. Orange County, CA
6. Las Vegas, NV
7. Oxnard-Ventura, CA
8. Raleigh-Durham-Chapel Hill, NC
9. Seattle, WA
10. Middlesex-Somerset-Hunterdon, NJ

INTERNET

Source: "America's 50 Most Wired Cities," *Yahoo! Internet Life*, 7: 102-103, (April 2001).

★2574★
America's most wired cities with the highest domain density, 2001

Ranking basis/background: Number of commercial domain names registered divided by the total number of firms. From research of home and business Internet use, the prevalence of online companies, number of networked computers in a given area, and the quantity and quality of city-related content available online. **Number listed:** 50.

1. San Jose, CA, 10.0
2. San Francisco, CA, 9.3
3. Oakland, CA, 5.9
3. Los Angeles-Long Beach, CA, 5.9
5. Washington, DC, 5.5
6. Las Vegas, NV, 5.2
6. San Diego, CA, 5.2
8. Austin-San Marcos, TX, 5.0
9. Orange County, CA, 4.7
10. Phoenix-Mesa, AZ, 4.3

Source: "America's 50 Most Wired Cities," *Yahoo! Internet Life*, 7: 102-103, (April 2001).

★2575★
America's most wired towns, 2001

Ranking basis/background: From research of home and business Internet use, the prevalence of online companies, number of networked computers in a given area, and the quantity and quality of city-related content available online. **Number listed:** 6.

1. Abingdon, VA
2. Ashland, OR
3. Glasgow, MT
4. Tomball, TX
5. Windham, NH
6. Murray, KY

Source: Knopper, Steve, "The Most Wired Towns," *Yahoo! Internet Life*, 7: 104-105, (April 2001).

★2576★
Cities with the highest online spending per Internet user

Ranking basis/background: From research of home and business Internet use, the prevalence of online companies, number of networked computers in a given area, and the quantity and quality of city-related content available online. **Remarks:** Original source: Forrester Research. **Number listed:** 10.

1. San Jose, CA, with $297
2. San Francisco, CA, $211
3. Middlesex-Somerset-Hunterdon, NJ, $194
4. Austin-San Marcos, TX, $189
5. Newark, NJ, $185
6. Oakland, CA, $181
7. Boston, MA, $180
7. Washington, DC, $180
7. Orange County, CA, $180
10. Dallas, TX, $179

Source: "America's 50 Most Wired Cities," *Yahoo! Internet Life*, 7: 102-103, (April 2001).

★2577★
Cities with the highest percentage of adults using the Internet at home

Ranking basis/background: From research of home and business Internet use, the prevalence of online companies, number of networked computers in a given area, and the quantity and quality of city-related content available online. **Remarks:** Original source: Forrester Research, using data from the U.S. Census Bureau and Bureau of Labor Statistics, *Current Population Survey*. **Number listed:** 10.

1. Austin-San Marcos, TX, with 69.7%
2. San Jose, CA, 67.6%
3. Raleigh-Durham-Chapel Hill, NC, 67.0%
4. Washington, DC, 64.9%
5. San Francisco, CA, 62.5%
6. Middlesex-Somerset-Hunterdon, NJ, 60.7%
7. Orange County, CA, 59.1%
8. Newark, NJ, 58.5%
9. Dallas, TX, 58.4%
10. Atlanta, GA, 58.2%

Source: "America's 50 Most Wired Cities," *Yahoo! Internet Life*, 7: 102-103, (April 2001).

★2578★
Cities with the highest percentage of broadband use and interest

Ranking basis/background: From research of home and business Internet use, the prevalence of online companies, number of networked computers in a given area, and the quantity and quality of city-related content available online. **Remarks:** Original source: Forrester Research. **Number listed:** 10.

1. Oxnard-Ventura, CA, with 62.7%
2. Bakersfield, CA, 61.0%
3. Stockton-Lodi, CA, 56.7%
4. Raleigh-Durham-Chapel Hill, NC, 54.9%
5. San Jose, CA, 54.5%
6. Las Vegas, NV, 53.7%
7. Salt Lake City-Ogden, UT, 52.7%
8. Oklahoma City, OK, 52.3%
9. Fort Worth-Arlington, TX, 52.2%
10. Sacramento, CA, 51.7%

Source: "America's 50 Most Wired Cities," *Yahoo! Internet Life*, 7: 102-103, (April 2001).

★2579★
Cities with the most domains per 1,000 firms

Ranking basis/background: From research of home and business Internet use, the prevalence of online companies, number of networked computers in a given area, and the quantity and quality of city-related content available online. **Remarks:** Original source: Matthew Zook. **Number listed:** 10.

1. San Jose, CA, with 3,486.8
2. San Francisco, CA, 3,239.8
3. Los Angeles-Long Beach, CA, 2,074.5
4. Oakland, CA, 2,044.1
5. Washington, DC, 1,934.0
6. Orange County, CA, 1,922.8
7. New York, NY, 1,845.5
8. Oxnard-Ventura, CA, 1,826.9
9. San Diego, CA, 1,809.4
10. Austin-San Marcos, TX, 1,733.1

Source: "America's 50 Most Wired Cities," *Yahoo! Internet Life*, 7: 102-103, (April 2001).

★2580★
Cities with the most Yahoo! listings per million residents

Ranking basis/background: From research of home and business Internet use, the prevalence of online companies, number of networked computers in a given area, and the quantity and quality of city-related content available online. **Remarks:** Original source: Forrester Research, using data from the U.S. Census Bureau and Bureau of Labor Statistics, *Current Population Survey*. **Number listed:** 10.

1. Las Vegas, NV, with 180.7
2. Harrisburg-Lebanon-Carlisle, PA, 124.2
3. Greenville-Spartanburg-Anderson, SC, 109.2
4. Austin, TX, 102.4
5. Orlando, FL, 98.8
6. Salt Lake City-Ogden, UT, 97.0
7. Boston, MA, 85.6
8. Albany-Schenectady-Troy, NY, 84.6
9. Minneapolis/St. Paul, MN, 78.7
10. Phoenix, AZ, 78.7

Source: "America's 50 Most Wired Cities," *Yahoo! Internet Life*, 7: 102-103, (April 2001).

★2581★
Comparison data of internet use, by income for 1998 and 2000

Ranking basis/background: Percentage of users for each income level in December 1998 and August 2000. **Remarks:** Original source: NTIA and ESA, U.S. Department of Commerce, Using U.S. Bureau of the Census current population survey. **Number listed:** 6.

Under $15,000, with 13.7% in Dec. 98; 18.9% in Aug. 2000
$15,000 to $24,999, 18.4%; 25.5%
$25,000-$34,999, 25.3%; 35.7%
$35,000-$49,999, 34.7%; 46.5%
$50,000-$74,999, 45.5%; 57.7%
$75,000 and above, 58.9%; 70.1%

Source: "Technology: Bits & Bytes," *Black Issues in Higher Education*, 18: 40-41, (March 15, 2001).

★2582★
Comparison data of internet use, by race/ethnicity for 1998 and 2000

Ranking basis/background: Percentage of users for each race, in December 1998 and August 2000. **Remarks:** Original source: NTIA and ESA, U.S. Department of Commerce, Using U.S. Bureau of the Census current population survey. **Number listed:** 5.

White, with 37.6% in Dec. 98; 50.3% in Aug. 2000
Asian American/Pacific Islander, 35.8%; 49.4%
African American, 19%; 29.3%
Hispanic American, 16.6%; 23.7%
Total, 32.7%; 44.4%

Source: "Technology: Bits & Bytes," *Black Issues in Higher Education*, 18: 40-41, (March 15, 2001).

★2583★
Countries with the most Internet users

Ranking basis/background: Population of country; number, in millions, of Internet users; and percentage of net user penetration. **Remarks:** Original source: Morgan Stanley Dean Witter. **Number listed:** 10.

1. United States, with a population of 276 million; 91.0 million Internet users; 33.0% Net user penetration
2. Japan, 127; 29.0; 22.8%
3. Germany, 83; 18.9; 22.8%

4. United Kingdom, 60; 18.8; 31.3%
5. South Korea, 46; 14.0; 30.4%
6. France, 59; 10.7; 18.1%
7. China, 1.3 billion; 10.0; 0.8%
8. Canada, 31; 9.7; 31.3%
9. Australia, 19; 7.4; 38.9%
10. Italy, 58; 6.6; 11.4%

Source: Battey, Jim, "Internet Countries," *Infoworld*, 23: 16, (March 12, 2001).

★2584★
Internet use by age, 1998

Ranking basis/background: Percentage of people using the Internet in each age group. **Number listed:** 8.

   Age 3-17, with 30%
   Age 18-24, 44%
   Age 25-34, 42%
   Age 35-44, 40%
   Age 45-54, 39%
   Age 55-64, 25%
   Age 65-74, 10%
   Age 75 and over, 4%

Source: Schau, Terry, "Internet Use: Here, There, and Everywhere," *Occupational Outlook Quarterly*, 44: 40-47, (Winter 2000).

★2585★
Internet use by educational level, 1998

Ranking basis/background: Percentage of people using the Internet in each educational level. **Number listed:** 7.

   Professional degree, with 67%
   Master's degree, 66%
   Bachelor's degree, 59%
   Associate degree, 43%
   Some college, no degree, 42%
   High school diploma or equivalent, 21%
   Less than high school diploma, 7%

Source: Schau, Terry, "Internet Use: Here, There, and Everywhere," *Occupational Outlook Quarterly*, 44: 40-47, (Winter 2000).

★2586★
Internet use by industry, 1998

Ranking basis/background: Percentage of people using the Internet in each industry. **Number listed:** 7.

1. Public administration, with 32%
2. Finance, insurance, and real estate, 30%
3. Services, 23%
4. Transportation, communications, and utilities, 19%
5. Manufacturing, construction, and mining, 16%
6. Wholesale and retail trade, 9%
7. Agriculture, forestry, and fishing, 3%

Source: Schau, Terry, "Internet Use: Here, There, and Everywhere," *Occupational Outlook Quarterly*, 44: 40-47, (Winter 2000).

★2587★
Internet use by major occupational group, 1998

Ranking basis/background: Percentage of people using the Internet in each occupational group. **Number listed:** 8.

1. Managerial and professional specialty, with 37%
2. Technicians and related support, 29%
3. Administrative support, 19%
4. Sales, 16%
5. Precision production, craft, and repair, 8%
6. Service, 4%
7. Operators, fabricators, and laborers, 3%
8. Farming, forestry, and fishing, 1%

Source: Schau, Terry, "Internet Use: Here, There, and Everywhere," *Occupational Outlook Quarterly*, 44: 40-47, (Winter 2000).

★2588★
Internet use, by race/ethnicity and gender breakdown, 2000

Ranking basis/background: Percentage of users for each race and gender. **Remarks:** Original source: NTIA and ESA, U.S. Department of Commerce, Using U.S. Bureau of the Census current population survey. **Number listed:** 5.

   White, with 50.7% male; 49.9% female
   Asian American/Pacific Islander, 52.7%; 46.1%
   African American, 27.9%; 30.6%
   Hispanic American, 22.7%; 24.7%
   Total, 44.6%; 44.2%

Source: "Technology: Bits & Bytes," *Black Issues in Higher Education*, 18: 40-41, (March 15, 2001).

★2589★
Internet use for 12- to 23-year olds, 1998

Ranking basis/background: Percentage of people using the Internet in each age group. **Number listed:** 6.

   Age 12-13, with 44%
   Age 14-15, 51%
   Age 16-17, 52%
   Age 18-19, 48%
   Age 20-21, 43%
   Age 22-23, 42%

Source: Schau, Terry, "Internet Use: Here, There, and Everywhere," *Occupational Outlook Quarterly*, 44: 40-47, (Winter 2000).

★2590★
Internet users by income group

Ranking basis/background: Number, in millions, of Internet users in each income group for February 2000 and February 2001, according to Nielsen//Netratings. **Number listed:** 6.

   $0-$25,000, with 4.3 million in February 2000; 6.3 million in February 2001
   $25,001-$50,000, 18.8; 26.4
   $50,001-$75,000, 21.4; 30.4
   $75,001-$100,000, 12.3; 16.2
   $100,001-$150,000, 7.8; 10.4
   More than $150,000, 3.8; 4.8

Source: Battey, Jim, "Low-Wage Surfers are Web's Fastest-Growing Group," *Infoworld*, 23: 18, (March 26, 2001).

★2591★
Medical Library Association's top health related web sites

Ranking basis/background: Medical Library Association's recommendations for best consumer health sites. **Number listed:** 10.
1. AMA Health Insight (*www.ama-assn.org/consumer.html*)
2. Centers for Disease Control and Prevention (*www.cdc.gov*)
3. Healthfinder (*www.healthfinder.org/default.htm*)
4. Health Web (*www.healthweb.org*)
5. HIV InSite (*http://hivinsite.ucsf.edu*)
6. Mayo Clinic Health Oasis (*www.mayohealth.org*)
7. MEDLINEplus (*www.nlm.nih.gov/medlineplus*)
8. National Women's Health Information Center (*www.4women.gov*)
9. NOAH: New York Online Access to Health (*www.noah.cuny.edu*)
10. Oncolink (*www.oncolink.upenn.edu*)

Source: Ritter, Jim, "Medical Librarians List Top Web Sites," *Chicago Sun-Times*, October 23, 2000, p. 19.

★2592★
Most frequently referenced web sites

Ranking basis/background: Based on research by OCLC Office of Research. **Number listed:** 50.
1. http://www.microsoft.com
2. http://www.netscape.com
3. http://www.geocities.com (geocities.yahoo.com/home/)
4. http://members.aol.com
5. http://www.yahoo.com
6. http://www.adobe.com
7. http://www.amazon.com
8. http://www.altavista.com
9. http://member.tripod.com (www.tripod.lycos.com/)
10. http://www.macromedia.com

Source: Bennett, Rick, "OCLC Web Characterization Project Names Top 50 Site References on the Web," *OCLC Newsletter*, 249: 32, (January/February 2001).

★2593★
Most notable children's web sites, 2001

Ranking basis/background: Alphabetical list by title, compiled by the Notable Children's Web Sites committee. **Number listed:** 11.

   Between the Lions (http://www.pbs.org/wgbh/lions)
   California's Untold Stories Gold Rush (http://www.museumca.org/goldrush)
   Discovery School's Puzzlemaker (http://puzzlemaker.school.discovery.com)
   Good Night Mr. Snoozleberg (http://sarbakan.com/snooz)
   Harry Potter (http://www.scholastic.com/harrypotter/home.asp)
   Library of Congress Presents America's Story from America's Library (http://www.americaslibrary.gov)
   Narnia (http://www.narnia.com)
   Ology (http://ology.amnh.org)
   Online Adventures of Captain Underpants (http://www.scholastic.com/captainunderpants.home.htm)
   Robotics: Sensing-Thinking-Acting (http://www.thetech.org/robotics/)
   Zillions-Consumer Reports Online for Kids (http://www.zillions.org)

Source: ALA's 2001 "Best" Lists, *Booklist*, 97: 1362-1388, (March 15, 2001).

★2594★
Most visited websites, 2000

Ranking basis/background: Number of unique visitors in August 2000. **Remarks:** Original source: Media Metrix, Inc. **Number listed:** 20.
1. http://www.yahoo.com, with 49,300
2. http://www.msn.com, 41,643
3. http://www.aol.com, 35,155
4. http://www.microsoft.com, 30,080
5. http://www.lycos.com, 27,612
6. http://www.passport.com, 24,102
7. http://www.hotmail.com, 22,262
8. http://www.go.com, 21,094
9. http://www.netscape.com, 18,355
10. http://www.excite.com, 15,654

INTERNET

Source: *The World Almanac and Book of Facts 2001*, World Almanac Books, 2001.

★2595★
Most wired colleges, 2000

Ranking basis/background: Based on Yahoo's evaluation of access and infrastructure, administrative aspects, general on-line resources, and support technology. **Remarks:** Original source: ZDNET: College Guide: America's Most Wired Colleges, 2000. **Number listed:** 20.

1. Williams College
2. Colgate University
3. Bates College
4. Occidental College
5. Oberlin College
6. Sweet Briar College
7. Albion College
8. Illinois Wesleyan University
9. Smith College
10. Trinity College

Source: "Technology: Bits & Bytes," *Black Issues in Higher Education*, 18: 40-41, (March 15, 2001).

★2596★
Most wired countries, 2001

Ranking basis/background: Determined by ability to access and absorb information technology. Four criteria categories are: computer, information, internet, and social infrastructures. **Remarks:** Original source: IDC. **Number listed:** 6.

1. Sweden
2. Norway
3. Finland
4. United States
5. Denmark
6. Britain

Source: "The Big Picture: How the U.S. Rates in the Wired World," *Business Week*, 3724: 10, (March 19, 2001).

★2597★
Most wired historically black colleges and universities, 2000

Ranking basis/background: Based on Yahoo's evaluation of access and infrastructure, administrative aspects, general on-line resources, and support technology. **Remarks:** Original source: ZDNET: College Guide: America's Most Wired Colleges, 2000. **Number listed:** 3.

1. Tennessee State University
2. Hampton University
3. Morehouse College

Source: "Technology: Bits & Bytes," *Black Issues in Higher Education*, 18: 40-41, (March 15, 2001).

★2598★
Most wired universities, 2000

Ranking basis/background: Based on Yahoo's evaluation of access and infrastructure, administrative aspects, general on-line resources, and support technology. **Remarks:** Original source: ZDNET: College Guide: America's Most Wired Colleges, 2000. **Number listed:** 20.

1. Carnegie Mellon University
2. University of Delaware
3. New Jersey Institute of Technology
4. Indiana University, Bloomington
5. Dartmouth University
6. Massachusetts Institute of Technology
7. Rensselaer Polytechnic Institute
8. University of Virginia
9. Washington State University
10. University of California, Los Angeles

Source: "Technology: Bits & Bytes," *Black Issues in Higher Education*, 18: 40-41, (March 15, 2001).

★2599★
Percentage of internet usage for selected countries

Ranking basis/background: Percentage of internet users per country. **Remarks:** Original source: American Express, www.americanexpress.com. **Number listed:** 10.

1. Sweden, with 74%
2. United States, 66%
3. Brazil, 62%
4. Canada, 60%
4. Australia, 60%
6. Hong Kong, 46%
7. Argentina, 35%
8. United Kingdom, 35%
9. Japan, 27%
10. Italy, 24%

Source: "The World Connected," *Chicago Sun-Times*, November 7, 2000, p. 47.

★2600★
Percentage of internet usage in U.S. households, by race/ethnicity

Ranking basis/background: Percentage of households using the internet in each area type. **Remarks:** Original source: National Telecommunications and Information Administration, 1999. **Number listed:** 4.

White, non Hispanic, with 30% in the U.S.; 24% in Rural areas; 32% in Urban areas; 32% in Central City areas
Black, non Hispanic, 11%; 7%; 12%; 10%
Other, non Hispanic, 33%; 17%; 35%; 32%
Hispanic, 13%; 10%; 13%; 10%

Source: "Disparities & Gaps in America," *Black Issues in Higher Education*, 18: 28-29, (March 1, 2001).

★2601★
Percentage of people using the internet, by educational level

Ranking basis/background: Based on a survey of 2,096 households by the UCLA Center for Communication Policy in Spring 2000. **Remarks:** Original source: *The UCLA Internet Report: Surveying the Digital Future.* **Number listed:** 5.

Less than a high school education, 31%
High school graduates, 53%
Some college education, 70%
College graduates, 86%
Advanced degrees, 86%

Source: Joseph, Lori and Marcy E. Mullins, "Who's Using the Internet?," *USA Today*, February 12, 2001, Section A, p. 1A.

★2602★
Top career-related Web sites

Ranking basis/background: Number, in millions, of page views in January, as determined by Alexa Research. **Number listed:** 10.

1. Monster.com (www.monster.com), with 614.9 million page views
2. HotJobs.com (www.hotjobs.com), 178.3
3. Headhunter.net (www.headhunter.net), 157.3
4. Craigslist (www.craigslist.org), 98.9
5. Dice.com (www.dice.com), 71.5
6. JobsOnline (www.jobsonline.com), 56.6
7. FlipDog.com (www.flipdog.com), 55.6
8. CareerBuilder (www.careerbuilder.com), 26.6
9. Vault.com (www.vault.com), 19.9
10. Net-Temps (www.net-temps.com), 18.9

Source: Battey, Jim, "The Top Ten List: Career-Related Web Sites," *Infoworld*, 23: 16, (March 5, 2001).

★2603★
Top E-commerce web sites

Ranking basis/background: According to Alexa Research. **Number listed:** 10.

1. eBay
2. Amazon.com
3. Travelocity
4. Expedia
5. Dell.com
6. Cdnow
7. eToys
8. Buy.com
9. Barnesandnoble.com
10. JCPenney.com

Source: Battey, Jim, "E-commerce Sites," *Infoworld*, 23: 16, (February 26, 2001).

★2604★
Top E-recruiting providers, 2000

Ranking basis/background: Annual revenue, in millions, and percent change from 1999 revenue as determined by IDC. **Number listed:** 10.

1. Monster.com, with $349.2 million in revenue; a 223.3% change since 1999
2. Futurestep, $82.0; 274.4%
3. HotJobs.com, $74.7; 378.8%
4. Headhunter.net, $49.2; 429.0%
5. Dice.com, $48.5; 205.0%
6. StepStone, $48.1; 272.9%
7. BrassRing, $40.0; 100.0%
8. CareerBuilder, $39.0; 161.7%
9. JobPilot, $30.8; 187.9%
10. Jobline International, $22.7; 224.3%

Source: Battey, Jim, "The Top Ten List: E-Recruiting Providers," *Infoworld*, 23: 18, (March 26, 2001).

★2605★
Top sites for educators

Ranking basis/background: Web sites chosen for their comprehensiveness, creativity, and relevance for educators interested in technology. **Number listed:** 40.

1. EdWeb (http://edweb.cnidr.org:90/)
2. New Media Centers (http://www.csulb.edu/gc/nmc/index.html)
3. Texas Center for Educational Technology (http://www.tcet.unt.edu/)
4. On the Horizon (http://sunsite.unc.edu/horizon/index.hrml)
5. Internet Resources for Technology Education (http://ed1.eng.ohio-state.edu/guide/resources.html)
6. Virtual Classroom (http://www.enmu.edu/virtual/virt.hrml)
7. The Technology Coordinator's Web Site (http://www.wwu.edu/~kenr/TCsite/home.html)
8. The Virtual Library for Information Technology (http://tecfa.unige.ch/info-edu-comp.html)
9. Campus Computing Survey (http://www.campuscomputing.net)
10. The Annenberg/CPB Project Learner Online Home Page for Educators (http://www.learner.org)

Source: "Syllabus Web: Top 40 Education Web Sites," *Syllabus Web (http://www.syllabus.com/syllabustop40/top40.cfm).*

★2606★
U.S. cities with the most wired households, 2001

Ranking basis/background: Percentage of households with Internet access from a personal computer. **Remarks:** Original source: Nielsen/Netratings. **Number listed:** 10.

1. Portland, OR, with 69.7%
2. Seattle, WA, 69.6%
3. San Francisco, 69.1%
4. Boston, 68.4%
5. San Diego, 66.2%
6. Washington, 65.2%
7. Denver, 63.2%
8. Orlando, FL, 61.4%
9. Hartford/New Haven, CT, 61.3%
10. Kansas City, MO, 61.2%

Source: Battey, Jim, "Most-Wired Cities," *Infoworld*, 23: 16, (April 23, 2001).

★2607★
U.S. market areas with the highest percentage of adults having internet access

Ranking basis/background: Percentage of adults with internet access in selected U.S. cities. **Number listed:** 20.

1. Denver, with 74%
1. Seattle/Tacoma, 74%
3. San Francisco/Oakland/San Jose, 73%
4. Atlanta, 71%
5. Phoenix, 70%
6. Dallas/Fort Worth, 69%
7. Minneapolis/St. Paul, 68%
7. Sacramento/Stockton/Modesto, CA, 68%
9. Houston, 67%
9. Los Angeles, 67%
11. Boston, 66%
12. Philadelphia, 65%
13. Miami/Fort Lauderdale, FL, 64%
13. New York, 64%
15. Chicago, 63%
15. Tampa/St. Petersburg/Sarasota, FL, 63%
17. Washington, DC, 62%
17. Cleveland, 62%
17. Detroit, 62%
20. Pittsburgh, 55%

Source: "Telecommunications," *Crain's Chicago Business*, 23: F16, (July 3, 2000).

★2608★
Web pages with the highest access percentages

Ranking basis/background: How Web pages are accessed by percentage. **Remarks:** Original source: Websnapshot.com. **Number listed:** 4.

1. Internal links, with 42%
2. Bookmarks/typed-in URLs, 28%
3. Other web sites, 23%
4. Search engines, 7%

Source: Battey, Jim, "Where's All That Traffic Coming From?," *Infoworld*, 23: 16, (February 26, 2001).

★2609★
Web sites where internet users spend the most time

Ranking basis/background: Average time spent per person as determined by Nielsen//NetRatings. **Number listed:** 9.

1. eBay, with 1 hr., 39 min. average time spent at site
2. Yahoo, 1 hr, 31 min.
3. AOL Time Warner, 53 min., 30 sec.
4. Excite@Home, 32 min., 35 sec.
5. Walt Disney, 29 min., 11 sec.
6. Uproar, 18 min., 51 sec.
7. AltaVista, 17 min., 58 sec.
8. Viacom, 17 min., 13 sec.
9. Google, 17 min., 7 sec.

Source: Battey, Jim, "eBay Rates as the Web's Stickiest Site," *Infoworld*, 23: 16, (February 26, 2001).

INTERNSHIPS

★2610★
Most selective internships in the U.S., 2001

Ranking basis/background: Alphabetical list, selected by Mark Oldman and Samer Hamadeh, *The Best 106 Internships* (Random House/Princeton Review). **Number listed:** 129.

Abbott Laboratories
The Academy for Advanced and Strategic Studies
Academy of Television Arts & Sciences
Actors Theatre of Louisville
Advocates for Children of New York
Aigner Associates
American Bar Association
American Civil Liberties Union
American Committee on Africa/The Africa Fund
American Forests
Anchorage Daily News
Anheuser-Busch
Aperture Foundation
Apple Computer
Assistant Directors Training Program
Association of Trial Lawyers of America
Bernstein-Rein
Betsey Johnson
Black Enterprise
The Blade
Boeing
Bozell Public Relations
Brooklyn Museum
Brown Miller Communications
Bucks County Courier Times
California State Senate
The Callaghan Group
Callaway Advanced Technology
Center for Coastal Studies
Chicago Bulls
The Citizens Network for Foreign Affairs
The Conservative Caucus
Council on Hemispheric Affairs
Creamer Dickson Basford
Crown Capital
Dallas Cowboys
Davis Hays & Co.
Design Tech International
DuPont
Dykeman Associates
Edelman Public Relations Worldwide
Federal Bureau of Investigation
Federal Reserve Bank of New York
Forbes
The Ford Foundation
Forty Acres and a Mule Filmworks
Gensler
GTE
Hallmark Cards
Hill and Holiday Advertising, Inc.
Hoffman-La Roche
Insurance Services Office
International Creative Management
The International Foundation for Education & Self-Help
The Jim Henson Company
John Wiley & Sons
KCSA Public Relations
Lake Charles American Press
Late Show with David Letterman
The Library of Congress
Lincoln Center for the Performing Arts
Lucasfilm/LucasDigital
Maine State Music Theater
Makovsky & Company
Manhattan Theater Club
Merck
Merrill Lynch
Miller Brewing Company
The Milwaukee Journal Sentinel
Miss Porter's School
Mother Jones
The Nation
The National Audubon Society
National Center for Fair and Open Testing
National Collegiate Athletic Association
National Endowment for the Humanities
National Football League
National Journal
National Review
National Wildlife Federation
National Women's Health Network
The New Republic
The Newshour with Jim Lehrer
Newsweek
New York Times
Nightline
NIKE
Northwestern Mutual Financial Network
NOW Legal Defense and Education Fund
Octel Communications
Oklahoma Redhawks Baseball Club
Open City Films
Oscar Meyer Wienermobile
Ove Arup & Partners
The Paris Review
Pella
Pittsburgh Post-Gazette
Playhouse on the Square
PMK Public Relations
Pro-Found Software
Quaker United National Office
Raychem
Reebok
Renew America
Rolling Stone
Rosenbluth International
Ruder-Finn
San Diego Zoo
San Francisco Chronicle
San Francisco 49ers
Savvy Management
Science News
The Seattle Times
Student Works Painting
Supreme Court of the United States
Symantec Corporation
Tellabs
Tyco Toys
United Talent Agency
Varsity Student Painters
The Wall Street Journal
Wall Street Music
Washington Office on Latin America
The Washington Post
Wells Fargo Bank
WGN-Chicago
The Widmeyer Baker Group
The Wilson Quarterly

INTERPERSONAL COMMUNICATION

Xerox
Source: *The Princeton Review: The Internship Bible*, Random House, 2001.

★2611★
Top internships in the U.S. with the highest compensation, 2001

Ranking basis/background: Alphabetical list, selected by Mark Oldman and Samer Hamadeh, *The Best 106 Internships* (Random House/Princeton Review). **Number listed:** 71.

    Abbott Laboratories
    Aetna Life Inc.
    The Boston Globe
    BP
    Chevron
    Citibank
    Deloitte & Touche
    Dow Chemical Co.
    DuPont
    Eastman Kodak Company
    Exxon
    The Ford Foundation
    Ford Motor Company
    Frito-Lay
    General Mills
    GMC Truck
    GTE
    Hallmark Cards
    Hewitt Associates
    Hewlett-Packard
    Inroads
    Intel
    J.P. Morgan & Co.
    Kraft Foods, Inc.
    Lawrence Livermore National Laboratory
    Lincoln Center for the Performing Arts
    Mattel Toys
    Merck
    Microsoft
    Miller Brewing Company
    Morrison & Foerster
    Nabisco
    National Consortium for Graduate Degrees for Minorities in Engineering and Science
    National Security Agency
    New York Times
    Newsday/New York Newsday
    Newsweek
    Octel Communications
    Office of Job Corps
    Oldsmobile
    Oscar Meyer Wienermobile
    Peace Corps
    Peggy Guggenheim Collection
    Pella
    Pfizer
    The Philadelphia Inquirer
    Pro-Found Software
    Rand
    Raychem
    Reebok
    Renew America
    St. Paul's School
    San Francisco Chronicle
    Schulumberger
    SGI
    The Southwestern Company
    Sponsors for Educational Opportunity
    State Teachers Retirement System of Ohio
    Student Works Painting
    Symantec Corporation
    Tellabs
    Texas Instruments
    Union Carbide
    United States Senate Youth Program
    Varsity Student Painters
    The Wall Street Journal
    The Washington Post
    Weyerhauser
    Writers Guild of American, West
    Xerox
    Xerox Palo Alto Research Center

Source: *The Princeton Review: The Internship Bible*, Random House, 2001.

★2612★
Top internships in the U.S., 2001

Ranking basis/background: As selected by Mark Oldman and Samer Hamadeh, *The Best 106 Internships* (Random House/Princeton Review). **Number listed:** 10.

    Academy of Television Arts & Sciences
    The Coro Foundation
    CNN
    Hewlett-Packard
    Inroads
    Northwestern Mutual Life Insurance
    Procter & Gamble
    Summerbridge International
    Supreme Court of the United States
    The Washington Post

Source: *The Princeton Review: The Internship Bible*, Random House, 2001.

INTERPERSONAL COMMUNICATION
See: **Speech Communication**

JOURNALISM
See: **Mass Media–Journalism**

JUNIOR COLLEGES
See: **Two-Year Colleges**

LABOR ECONOMICS
See: **Economics**

LANGUAGE PROGRAMS

★2613★
Radcliffe Institute for Advanced Study fellowship recipient in the field of Asian literature, 2000-01

Ranking basis/background: Recipient and institutional affiliation of the Radcliffe Institute for Advanced study fellowship for pursuit of advanced work across a wide range of academic disciplines, professions, and creative arts. **Number listed:** 1.

    Cathy Silber, Williams College

Source: "The Radcliffe Institute for Advanced Study," *The Chronicle of Higher Education*, 46: A59, (June 2, 2000).

★2614★
Top recruiters for foreign language jobs for 2000-01 bachelor's degree recipients

Ranking basis/background: Projected number of college hires from on-campus recruitment for 2000-01. **Remarks:** Numbers reflect total expected hires, not just African American projected hires. **Number listed:** 5.

1. Accenture, with 40 projected hires
2. U.S. Air Force (Active Duty Hires), 25
3. Houghton Mifflin, 10
4. Henrico County Public Schools, 10
5. Federated Department Stores, 6

Source: "The Top 100 Employers and the Majors in Demand for the Class of 2001," *The Black Collegian*, 31: 19-35, (February 2001).

LANGUAGE PROGRAMS, GRADUATE
See also: **English Language and Literature French Language and Literature, Graduate German Language and Literature, Graduate Spanish Language and Literature, Graduate**

★2615★
Top recruiters for foreign language jobs for 2000-01 master's degree recipients

Ranking basis/background: Projected number of college hires from on-campus recruitment for 2000-01. **Remarks:** Numbers reflect total expected hires, not just African American projected hires. **Number listed:** 2.

1. Accenture, with 10 projected hires
2. Houghton Mifflin, 2

Source: "The Top 100 Employers and the Majors in Demand for the Class of 2001," *The Black Collegian*, 31: 19-35, (February 2001).

Related Information

★2616★
Benseler, David P. and Suzanne S. Moore, "Doctoral Degrees Granted in Foreign Languages in the United States: 1999," *Modern Language Journal*, 84: 406-422, (Autumn 2000).
    Remarks: Presents an annual survey of doctoral degrees granted in foreign languages, literatures, cultures, and linguistics and in foreign language education in the U.S. Each dissertation, completed during the 1999 calendar year, includes author, title, and director, as well as the type of doctoral degree granted (DML, EdD, PhD).

LAW

★2617★
Law journals by citation impact, 1981-96

Ranking basis/background: For each journal, total number of citations divided by number of published articles during the same time period. **Remarks:** Original source: ISI's *Journal Citation Reports* and *Journal Performance Indicators on Diskette*. **Number listed:** 10.

1. *Harvard Law Review*, with 17.17 citations per paper
2. *Stanford Law Review*, 14.30

3. *Journal of Legal Studies*, 13.45
4. *Yale Law Journal*, 13.31
5. *Journal of Law and Economics*, 13.26
6. *University of Chicago Law Review*, 9.78
7. *Columbia Law Review*, 9.43
8. *Michigan Law Review*, 8.99
9. *Virginia Law Review*, 8.74
10. *Pennsylvania Law Review*, 8.64

Source: "Journals Ranked by Impact: Law," *Institute for Scientific Information: What's Hot,* February 2, 1998.

★2618★
Law journals with the greatest impact measure, 1981-98

Ranking basis/background: Citations-per-paper impact score is the total citations to a journal's published papers divided by total number of papers the journal has published over an eighteen year period. **Remarks:** Original source: *Journal Citation Reports* and Journal Performance Indicators on Diskette. **Number listed:** 10.

1. *Harvard Law Review*, with an impact score of 18.80
2. *Stanford Law Review*, 15.66
3. *Yale Law Journal*, 15.33
4. *Journal of Law and Economics*, 14.99
5. *Journal of Legal Studies*, 14.61
6. *University of Chicago Law Review*, 11.31
7. *Columbia Law Review*, 11.28
8. *Michigan Law Review*, 10.92
9. *University of Pennsylvania Law Review*, 10.38
10. *Virginia Law Review*, 10.23

Source: "Journals Ranked by Impact: Law," *What's Hot in Research* (http://www.isinet.com/hot/research) *Institute for Scientific Information,* September 20, 1999.

★2619★
Most frequently-cited law reviews and legal periodicals, 1924-1986: a compilation

Ranking basis/background: Based on a compilation of rankings determined in six other similar studies described in this article. Those rankings, in turn, are based on number of citations. **Number listed:** 50.

1. *Harvard Law Review*
2. *Yale Law Review*
3. *Columbia Law Review*
4. *Pennsylvania Law Review*
5. *Michigan Law Review*
6. *University of Chicago Law Review*
7. *Virginia Law Review*
8. *Business Lawyer*
9. *New York University Law Review*
10. *California Law Review*

Source: Finet, Scott, "The Most Frequently Cited Law Reviews and Legal Periodicals," *Legal Reference Services Quarterly* 9: 227-240 (No. 3, 1989).

★2620★
Most frequently-cited law reviews and legal periodicals, according to *Shepard's Law Review Citations*, 1957-1986

Ranking basis/background: Ranked by the estimated number of citations appearing in *SLRC*, derived by calculating the average number of citations per page and multiplying that number by the number of pages of citations for each title. **Number listed:** 50.

1. *Harvard Law Review*
2. *Yale Law Review*

3. *Columbia Law Review*
4. *Pennsylvania Law Review*
5. *Michigan Law Review*
6. *California Law Review*
7. *ABA Journal*
8. *Virginia Law Review*
9. *University of Chicago Law Review*
10. *New York University Law Review*

Source: Finet, Scott, "The Most Frequently Cited Law Reviews and Legal Periodicals," *Legal Reference Services Quarterly* 9: 227-240 (No. 3, 1989).

★2621★
Radcliffe Institute for Advanced Study fellowship recipient in the field of law, 2000-01

Ranking basis/background: Recipient and institutional affiliation of the Radcliffe Institute for Advanced study fellowship for pursuit of advanced work across a wide range of academic disciplines, professions, and creative arts. **Number listed:** 1.

Vicki Schultz, Yale Law School

Source: "The Radcliffe Institute for Advanced Study," *The Chronicle of Higher Education*, 46: A59, (June 2, 2000).

★2622★
Radcliffe Institute for Advanced Study fellowship recipients in the field of public policy, 2000-01

Ranking basis/background: Recipient and institutional affiliation of the Radcliffe Institute for Advanced study fellowship for pursuit of advanced work across a wide range of academic disciplines, professions, and creative arts. **Number listed:** 2.

Lisa Dodson, Harvard University
Jane Fountain, Harvard University

Source: "The Radcliffe Institute for Advanced Study," *The Chronicle of Higher Education*, 46: A59, (June 2, 2000).

★2623★
U.S. universities publishing the most papers in the field of law, 1994-98

Ranking basis/background: Total number of papers published from each university. **Remarks:** Original source: University Science Indicators on Diskette, 1981-97. **Number listed:** 5.

1. Harvard University, with 285 papers
2. University of Chicago, 260
3. Georgetown University, 239
4. Yale University, 197
5. University of Virginia, 185

Source: "Law: Most Prolific U.S. Universities, 1994-98," *What's Hot in Research* (http://www.isinet.com/hot/research) *Institute for Scientific Information,* November 15, 1999.

LAW ENFORCEMENT
See also: **Criminal Justice**

★2624★
Most-cited scholars in police studies articles/research notes

Ranking basis/background: Incidence of citations and prevalence of citations for each author, from an examination of 370 police studies articles/research notes from 1991 to 1995. **Number listed:** 60.

1. Lawrence W. Sherman, with incidence of citations 331/prevalence of citations 83

2. David H. Bayley, 217/76
3. Herman Goldstein, 202/76
4. James Q. Wilson, 149/69
5. Jerome H. Skolnick, 143/79
6. George L. Kelling, 130/58
7. Peter K. Manning, 122/47
8. Robert J. Trojanowicz, 120/41
9. Geoffrey P. Alpert, 114/32
10. Samuel Walker, 113/47

Source: Wright, Richard A. and J. Mitchell Miller, "The Most-Cited Scholars and Works in Police Studies," *Policing: An International Journal of Police Strategies & Management,* 21: 240-254, (1998).

★2625★
Most-cited works in police studies articles/research notes

Ranking basis/background: Incidence of citations and prevalence of citations for each article, from an examination of 370 police studies articles/research notes from 1991 to 1995. **Number listed:** 36.

1. *Problem-Oriented Policing*, by Herman Goldstein (first published in 1990), with incidence of citations 97/prevalence of citations 41
2. *Justice Without Trial: Law Enforcement in a Democratic Society*, Jerome H. Skolnick (1975), 57/36
3. *Varieties of Police Behavior: The Management of Law and Order in Eight Communities*, James Q. Wilson (1968), 56/39
4. *Police: Streetcorner Politicians*, William Ker Muir, Jr. (1977), 50/18
5. *Community Policing: A Contemporary Perspective*, Robert Trojanowicz and Bonnie Bucqueroux (1990), 49/27
6. "Broken windows: the police and neighborhood safety", James Q. Wilson and Gerge L. Kelling (1982), 46/21
7. *Sourcebook of Criminal Justice Statistics, 1994*, Kathleen Maguire and Ann L. Pastore editors (1995)
8. *Policing a Free Society*, Herman Goldstein (1977), 42/26
9. *The Politics of the Police*, Robert Reiner (1992), 41/27
10. *The New Blue Line: Police Innovation in Six American Cities*, Jerome H. Skolnick and David H. Bayley (1986), 41/27

Source: Wright, Richard A. and J. Mitchell Miller, "The Most-Cited Scholars and Works in Police Studies," *Policing: An International Journal of Police Strategies & Management,* 21: 240-254, (1998).

LAW SCHOOLS

★2626★
Academics' choices for best clinical law programs, 2001

Ranking basis/background: From a *U.S. News & World Report* survey of academic specialists, senior faculty, and law school deans. **Remarks:** Data collected by Market Facts, Inc. **Number listed:** 10.

1. Georgetown University
2. New York University
3. American University
4. City University of New York, Queens College
5. University of Maryland
6. Yale University

LAW SCHOOLS

7. University of New Mexico
8. Northwestern University
9. University of Michigan, Ann Arbor
10. Rutgers State University, Newark

Source: "America's Best Graduate Schools: 2002 Annual Guide," *U.S. News & World Report*, 130: 60-97, (April 19, 2001).

★2627★
Academics' choices for best dispute resolution programs, 2001

Ranking basis/background: From a *U.S. News & World Report* survey of academic specialists, senior faculty, and law school deans. **Remarks:** Data collected by Market Facts, Inc. **Number listed:** 10.

1. University of Missouri, Columbia
2. Pepperdine University
3. Harvard University
4. Ohio State University
5. Hamline University
6. Willamette University
7. Cardozo-Yeshiva University
8. Georgetown University
9. University of Texas, Austin
10. Stanford University

Source: "America's Best Graduate Schools: 2002 Annual Guide," *U.S. News & World Report*, 130: 60-97, (April 19, 2001).

★2628★
Academics' choices for best environmental law programs, 2001

Ranking basis/background: From a *U.S. News & World Report* survey of academic specialists, senior faculty, and law school deans. **Remarks:** Data collected by Market Facts, Inc. **Number listed:** 10.

1. Vermont Law School
2. Lewis and Clark College
3. Pace University
4. University of Colorado, Boulder
5. University of Maryland
6. Tulane University
7. University of California, Berkeley
8. Georgetown University
9. George Washington University
10. Stanford University

Source: "America's Best Graduate Schools: 2002 Annual Guide," *U.S. News & World Report*, 130: 60-97, (April 19, 2001).

★2629★
Academics' choices for best health law programs, 2001

Ranking basis/background: From a *U.S. News & World Report* survey of academic specialists, senior faculty, and law school deans. **Remarks:** Data collected by Market Facts, Inc. **Number listed:** 10.

1. University of Houston
2. St. Louis University
3. Loyola University, Chicago
4. University of Maryland
5. Seton Hall University
6. Case Western Reserve University
7. Indiana University, Indianapolis
8. Widener University
9. Boston University
10. DePaul University

Source: "America's Best Graduate Schools: 2002 Annual Guide," *U.S. News & World Report*, 130: 60-97, (April 19, 2001).

★2630★
Academics' choices for best intellectual property law programs, 2001

Ranking basis/background: From a *U.S. News & World Report* survey of academic specialists, senior faculty, and law school deans. **Remarks:** Data collected by Market Facts, Inc. **Number listed:** 10.

1. University of California, Berkeley
2. George Washington University
3. Franklin Pierce Law Center
4. University of Houston
5. Cardozo-Yeshiva University
6. New York University
7. Stanford University
8. Santa Clara University
9. Boston University
10. DePaul University

Source: "America's Best Graduate Schools: 2002 Annual Guide," *U.S. News & World Report*, 130: 60-97, (April 19, 2001).

★2631★
Academics' choices for best international law programs, 2001

Ranking basis/background: From a *U.S. News & World Report* survey of academic specialists, senior faculty, and law school deans. **Remarks:** Data collected by Market Facts, Inc. **Number listed:** 10.

1. New York University
2. Georgetown University
3. Harvard University
4. Columbia University
5. Yale University
6. University of California, Berkeley
7. University of Michigan, Ann Arbor
8. University of Virginia
9. American University
10. George Washington University

Source: "America's Best Graduate Schools: 2002 Annual Guide," *U.S. News & World Report*, 130: 60-97, (April 19, 2001).

★2632★
Academics' choices for best tax law programs, 2001

Ranking basis/background: From a *U.S. News & World Report* survey of academic specialists, senior faculty, and law school deans. **Remarks:** Data collected by Market Facts, Inc. **Number listed:** 11.

1. New York University
2. University of Florida
3. Georgetown University
4. Harvard University
5. University of Texas, Austin
6. Stanford University
7. University of Miami
8. Yale University
9. Boston University
9. University of Chicago
9. University of Virginia

Source: "America's Best Graduate Schools: 2002 Annual Guide," *U.S. News & World Report*, 130: 60-97, (April 19, 2001).

★2633★
Academics' choices for best trial advocacy programs, 2001

Ranking basis/background: From a *U.S. News & World Report* survey of academic specialists, senior faculty, and law school deans. **Remarks:** Data collected by Market Facts, Inc. **Number listed:** 12.

1. Temple University
2. Stetson University
3. Northwestern University
4. Georgetown University
5. South Texas College of Law
5. University of Notre Dame
7. New York University
8. Loyola Law School
9. Emory University
9. John Marshall Law School
9. University of Texas, Austin
9. William Mitchell College of Law

Source: "America's Best Graduate Schools: 2002 Annual Guide," *U.S. News & World Report*, 130: 60-97, (April 19, 2001).

★2634★
Acceptance rates at *U.S. News & World Report*'s top 10 law schools, 2001

Ranking basis/background: From a *U.S. News & World Report* survey of the acceptance rates for 2000 applicants. **Remarks:** Data collected by Market Facts, Inc. **Number listed:** 54.

1. University of Michigan, Ann Arbor, with 35.3%
2. University of Virginia, 28.9%
3. University of Pennsylvania, 27.6%
4. Duke University, 24.8%
5. University of Chicago, 23.1%
6. New York University, 22.2%
7. Columbia University, 17.4%
8. University of California, Berkeley, 16.5%
9. Harvard University, 16.0%
10. Stanford University, 11.3%
11. Yale University, 8.4%

Source: "America's Best Graduate Schools: 2002 Annual Guide," *U.S. News & World Report*, 130: 60-97, (April 19, 2001).

★2635★
Graduate employment after graduation percentage for *U.S. News & World Report*'s top 10 law schools, 2001

Ranking basis/background: From a *U.S. News & World Report* survey of the percentage of 2000 class employed upon graduation or within six months after graduation, ratio of last year's on-campus recruiters to number of 2000 graduates, and median starting salary for 2000 graduates. **Remarks:** Data collected by Market Facts, Inc. **Number listed:** 54.

1. Columbia University, with 100%
1. New York University, 100%
1. University of Chicago, 100%
1. University of Virginia, 100%
1. Duke University, 100%
1. University of Pennsylvania, 100%
7. University of Michigan, Ann Arbor, 99%
7. Yale University, 99%
7. Stanford University, 99%
10. University of California, Berkeley, 98%

Source: "America's Best Graduate Schools: 2002 Annual Guide," *U.S. News & World Report*, 130: 60-97, (April 19, 2001).

★2636★
Graduate employment percentage for *U.S. News & World Report*'s top 10 law schools, 2001

Ranking basis/background: From a *U.S. News & World Report* survey of the percentage of 2000 class employed upon graduation or within six months after graduation, ratio of last year's on-campus recruiters to number of 2000 graduates, and median starting salary for 2000 graduates. **Remarks:** Data collected by Market Facts, Inc. **Number listed:** 54.

1. Yale University, with 99%

1. Stanford University, 99%
1. University of Virginia, 99%
1. University of Pennsylvania, 99%
5. University of Chicago, 98%
6. Harvard University, 97%
6. Columbia University, 97%
8. New York University, 96%
8. Duke University, 96%
10. University of Michigan, Ann Arbor, 93%
10. University of California, Berkeley, 93%

Source: "America's Best Graduate Schools: 2002 Annual Guide," *U.S. News & World Report*, 130: 60-97, (April 19, 2001).

★2637★
Jurisdiction's overall bar passage rate for *U.S. News & World Report*'s top 10 law schools, 2001

Ranking basis/background: From a *U.S. News & World Report* survey of the jurisdiction's overall bar passage rate for 2000. **Remarks:** Data collected by Market Facts, Inc. **Number listed:** 54.

Yale University, with 73%
Stanford University, 61%
Harvard University, 73%
Columbia University, 73%
New York University, 73%
University of Chicago, 82%
University of Michigan, Ann Arbor, 73%
University of Virginia, 73%
University of California, Berkeley, 61%
Duke University, 73%
University of Pennsylvania, 73%

Source: "America's Best Graduate Schools: 2002 Annual Guide," *U.S. News & World Report*, 130: 60-97, (April 19, 2001).

★2638★
Law schools with the best administrative law faculty, 1999-2000

Ranking basis/background: Alphabetical list of law schools with outstanding faculty in a specific area as compiled by consultation with experts in various fields and anthologies of leading articles in each field. **Number listed:** 7.

Columbia University
George Washington University
New York University
Northwestern University
University of Chicago
University of Virginia
Yale University

Source: Leiter, Brian, "New Educational Quality Ranking of U.S. Law Schools for 1999-2000," *http://www.dia.utexas.edu/depts/philosophy/faculty/leiter/LGOURMET.HTM*, November 1999.

★2639★
Law schools with the best bankruptcy faculty, 1999-2000

Ranking basis/background: Alphabetical list of law schools with outstanding faculty in a specific area as compiled by consultation with experts in various fields and anthologies of leading articles in each field. **Number listed:** 6.

Harvard University
New York University
University of Chicago
University of Texas, Austin
Vanderbilt University
Yale University

Source: Leiter, Brian, "New Educational Quality Ranking of U.S. Law Schools for 1999-2000," *http://www.dia.utexas.edu/depts/philosophy/faculty/leiter/LGOURMET.HTM*, November 1999.

★2640★
Law schools with the best civil procedure faculty, 1999-2000

Ranking basis/background: Alphabetical list of law schools with outstanding faculty in a specific area as compiled by consultation with experts in various fields and anthologies of leading articles in each field. **Number listed:** 6.

Duke University
Harvard University
University of California, Hastings
University of Pennsylvania
University of Texas, Austin
Yale University

Source: Leiter, Brian, "New Educational Quality Ranking of U.S. Law Schools for 1999-2000," *http://www.dia.utexas.edu/depts/philosophy/faculty/leiter/LGOURMET.HTM*, November 1999.

★2641★
Law schools with the best commercial law faculty, 1999-2000

Ranking basis/background: Alphabetical list of law schools with outstanding faculty in a specific area as compiled by consultation with experts in various fields and anthologies of leading articles in each field. **Number listed:** 7.

Harvard University
New York University
Stanford University
University of Chicago
University of Michigan
University of Virginia
Yale University

Source: Leiter, Brian, "New Educational Quality Ranking of U.S. Law Schools for 1999-2000," *http://www.dia.utexas.edu/depts/philosophy/faculty/leiter/LGOURMET.HTM*, November 1999.

★2642★
Law schools with the best comparative law faculty, 1999-2000

Ranking basis/background: Alphabetical list of law schools with outstanding faculty in a specific area as compiled by consultation with experts in various fields and anthologies of leading articles in each field. **Number listed:** 6.

Columbia University
Harvard University
University of Michigan
University of Pennsylvania
University of Texas, Austin
Yale University

Source: Leiter, Brian, "New Educational Quality Ranking of U.S. Law Schools for 1999-2000," *http://www.dia.utexas.edu/depts/philosophy/faculty/leiter/LGOURMET.HTM*, November 1999.

★2643★
Law schools with the best constitutional law (freedom of religion) faculty, 1999-2000

Ranking basis/background: Alphabetical list of law schools with outstanding faculty in a specific area as compiled by consultation with experts in various fields and anthologies of leading articles in each field. **Number listed:** 7.

Case Western Reserve University
Columbia University
George Washington University
New York University
University of California, Berkeley
University of Texas, Austin
University of Utah

Source: Leiter, Brian, "New Educational Quality Ranking of U.S. Law Schools for 1999-2000," *http://www.dia.utexas.edu/depts/philosophy/faculty/leiter/LGOURMET.HTM*, November 1999.

★2644★
Law schools with the best constitutional law (freedom of speech) faculty, 1999-2000

Ranking basis/background: Alphabetical list of law schools with outstanding faculty in a specific area as compiled by consultation with experts in various fields and anthologies of leading articles in each field. **Number listed:** 8.

Columbia University
Cornell University
University of California, Berkeley
University of Chicago
University of Pennsylvania
University of Texas, Austin
University of Virginia
Yale University

Source: Leiter, Brian, "New Educational Quality Ranking of U.S. Law Schools for 1999-2000," *http://www.dia.utexas.edu/depts/philosophy/faculty/leiter/LGOURMET.HTM*, November 1999.

★2645★
Law schools with the best constitutional law (general) faculty, 1999-2000

Ranking basis/background: Alphabetical list of law schools with outstanding faculty in a specific area as compiled by consultation with experts in various fields and anthologies of leading articles in each field. **Number listed:** 9.

Columbia University
Duke University
Georgetown University
Harvard University
Stanford University
University of Chicago
University of Miami
University of Texas, Austin
Yale University

Source: Leiter, Brian, "New Educational Quality Ranking of U.S. Law Schools for 1999-2000," *http://www.dia.utexas.edu/depts/philosophy/faculty/leiter/LGOURMET.HTM*, November 1999.

★2646★
Law schools with the best corporate law and securities regulation faculty, 1999-2000

Ranking basis/background: Alphabetical list of law schools with outstanding faculty in a specific area as compiled by consultation with experts in various fields and anthologies of leading articles in each field. **Number listed:** 6.

Columbia University
Harvard University
New York University
Stanford University
University of Chicago
Yale University

Source: Leiter, Brian, "New Educational Quality Ranking of U.S. Law Schools for 1999-2000," *http://www.dia.utexas.edu/depts/philosophy/faculty/leiter/LGOURMET.HTM*, November 1999.

LAW SCHOOLS

★2647★
Law schools with the best criminal law (substantive) faculty, 1999-2000

Ranking basis/background: Alphabetical list of law schools with outstanding faculty in a specific area as compiled by consultation with experts in various fields and anthologies of leading articles in each field. **Number listed:** 6.
- Columbia University
- Northwestern University
- University of California, Berkeley
- University of California, Los Angeles
- University of Chicago
- University of Pennsylvania

Source: Leiter, Brian, "New Educational Quality Ranking of U.S. Law Schools for 1999-2000," *http://www.dia.utexas.edu/depts/philosophy/faculty/leiter/LGOURMET.HTM*, November 1999.

★2648★
Law schools with the best criminal procedure faculty, 1999-2000

Ranking basis/background: Alphabetical list of law schools with outstanding faculty in a specific area as compiled by consultation with experts in various fields and anthologies of leading articles in each field. **Number listed:** 5.
- Harvard University
- University of Chicago
- University of Florida
- University of Michigan
- Yale University

Source: Leiter, Brian, "New Educational Quality Ranking of U.S. Law Schools for 1999-2000," *http://www.dia.utexas.edu/depts/philosophy/faculty/leiter/LGOURMET.HTM*, November 1999.

★2649★
Law schools with the best critical race theory faculty, 1999-2000

Ranking basis/background: Alphabetical list of law schools with outstanding faculty in a specific area as compiled by consultation with experts in various fields and anthologies of leading articles in each field. **Number listed:** 6.
- Columbia University
- Duke University
- Georgetown University
- New York University
- University of California, Berkeley
- University of Colorado

Source: Leiter, Brian, "New Educational Quality Ranking of U.S. Law Schools for 1999-2000," *http://www.dia.utexas.edu/depts/philosophy/faculty/leiter/LGOURMET.HTM*, November 1999.

★2650★
Law schools with the best environmental law faculty, 1999-2000

Ranking basis/background: Alphabetical list of law schools with outstanding faculty in a specific area as compiled by consultation with experts in various fields and anthologies of leading articles in each field. **Number listed:** 7.
- Chicago-Kent College of Law, Illinois Institute of Technology
- Georgetown University
- New York University
- University of California, Berkeley
- University of Texas, Austin
- University of Washington, Seattle
- Yale University

Source: Leiter, Brian, "New Educational Quality Ranking of U.S. Law Schools for 1999-2000," *http://www.dia.utexas.edu/depts/philosophy/faculty/leiter/LGOURMET.HTM*, November 1999.

★2651★
Law schools with the best feminist legal theory faculty, 1999-2000

Ranking basis/background: Alphabetical list of law schools with outstanding faculty in a specific area as compiled by consultation with experts in various fields and anthologies of leading articles in each field. **Number listed:** 8.
- Cornell University
- Duke University
- Georgetown University
- Harvard University
- Stanford University
- University of California, Los Angeles
- University of Chicago
- University of Michigan

Source: Leiter, Brian, "New Educational Quality Ranking of U.S. Law Schools for 1999-2000," *http://www.dia.utexas.edu/depts/philosophy/faculty/leiter/LGOURMET.HTM*, November 1999.

★2652★
Law schools with the best health law (excluding medical ethics) faculty, 1999-2000

Ranking basis/background: Alphabetical list of law schools with outstanding faculty in a specific area as compiled by consultation with experts in various fields and anthologies of leading articles in each field. **Number listed:** 5.
- Duke University
- Georgetown University
- Ohio State University
- University of Houston
- University of Maryland

Source: Leiter, Brian, "New Educational Quality Ranking of U.S. Law Schools for 1999-2000," *http://www.dia.utexas.edu/depts/philosophy/faculty/leiter/LGOURMET.HTM*, November 1999.

★2653★
Law schools with the best intellectual property faculty, 1999-2000

Ranking basis/background: Alphabetical list of law schools with outstanding faculty in a specific area as compiled by consultation with experts in various fields and anthologies of leading articles in each field. **Number listed:** 6.
- Boston University
- Columbia University
- New York University
- Stanford University
- University of California, Berkeley
- University of Texas, Austin

Source: Leiter, Brian, "New Educational Quality Ranking of U.S. Law Schools for 1999-2000," *http://www.dia.utexas.edu/depts/philosophy/faculty/leiter/LGOURMET.HTM*, November 1999.

★2654★
Law schools with the best international law faculty, 1999-2000

Ranking basis/background: Alphabetical list of law schools with outstanding faculty in a specific area as compiled by consultation with experts in various fields and anthologies of leading articles in each field. **Number listed:** 5.
- Columbia University
- Georgetown University
- Harvard University
- New York University
- Yale University

Source: Leiter, Brian, "New Educational Quality Ranking of U.S. Law Schools for 1999-2000," *http://www.dia.utexas.edu/depts/philosophy/faculty/leiter/LGOURMET.HTM*, November 1999.

★2655★
Law schools with the best jurisprudence faculty, 1999-2000

Ranking basis/background: Alphabetical list of law schools with outstanding faculty in a specific area as compiled by consultation with experts in various fields and anthologies of leading articles in each field. **Number listed:** 8.
- Yeshiva University, Cardozo Law School
- Columbia University
- New York University
- University of California, Los Angeles
- University of Michigan
- University of Pennsylvania
- University of Texas, Austin
- Yale University

Source: Leiter, Brian, "New Educational Quality Ranking of U.S. Law Schools for 1999-2000," *http://www.dia.utexas.edu/depts/philosophy/faculty/leiter/LGOURMET.HTM*, November 1999.

★2656★
Law schools with the best labor law faculty, 1999-2000

Ranking basis/background: Alphabetical list of law schools with outstanding faculty in a specific area as compiled by consultation with experts in various fields and anthologies of leading articles in each field. **Number listed:** 8.
- Columbia University
- Cornell University
- Harvard University
- Northeastern University
- Ohio State University
- University of Illinois
- University of Pennsylvania
- University of Texas, Austin

Source: Leiter, Brian, "New Educational Quality Ranking of U.S. Law Schools for 1999-2000," *http://www.dia.utexas.edu/depts/philosophy/faculty/leiter/LGOURMET.HTM*, November 1999.

★2657★
Law schools with the best law and economics faculty, 1999-2000

Ranking basis/background: Alphabetical list of law schools with outstanding faculty in a specific area as compiled by consultation with experts in various fields and anthologies of leading articles in each field. **Number listed:** 7.
- Columbia University
- Harvard University
- New York University
- Stanford University
- University of California, Berkeley
- University of Chicago
- Yale University

Source: Leiter, Brian, "New Educational Quality Ranking of U.S. Law Schools for 1999-2000," *http://www.dia.utexas.edu/depts/philosophy/faculty/leiter/LGOURMET.HTM*, November 1999.

★2658★
Law schools with the best law and religion (excluding First Amendment issues) faculty, 1999-2000

Ranking basis/background: Alphabetical list of law schools with outstanding faculty in a specific area as compiled by consultation with experts in various fields and anthologies of leading articles in each field. **Number listed:** 6.

- Duke University
- Emory University
- University of Georgia
- University of Notre Dame
- Wake Forest University
- Yale University

Source: Leiter, Brian, "New Educational Quality Ranking of U.S. Law Schools for 1999-2000," http://www.dia.utexas.edu/depts/philosophy/faculty/leiter/LGOURMET.HTM, November 1999.

★2659★
Law schools with the best law and social science plus psychology and sociology faculty, 1999-2000

Ranking basis/background: Alphabetical list of law schools with outstanding faculty in a specific area as compiled by consultation with experts in various fields and anthologies of leading articles in each field. **Number listed:** 7.

- Northwestern University
- University of California, Berkeley
- University of California, Los Angeles
- University of Michigan
- University of Pennsylvania
- University of Virginia
- University of Wisconsin, Madison

Source: Leiter, Brian, "New Educational Quality Ranking of U.S. Law Schools for 1999-2000," http://www.dia.utexas.edu/depts/philosophy/faculty/leiter/LGOURMET.HTM, November 1999.

★2660★
Law schools with the best legal ethics, professional responsibility, and legal profession faculty, 1999-2000

Ranking basis/background: Alphabetical list of law schools with outstanding faculty in a specific area as compiled by consultation with experts in various fields and anthologies of leading articles in each field. **Number listed:** 7.

- Boston University
- Georgetown University
- Stanford University
- University of Pennsylvania
- University of Texas, Austin
- University of Wisconsin, Madison
- Yale University

Source: Leiter, Brian, "New Educational Quality Ranking of U.S. Law Schools for 1999-2000," http://www.dia.utexas.edu/depts/philosophy/faculty/leiter/LGOURMET.HTM, November 1999.

★2661★
Law schools with the best legal history faculty, 1999-2000

Ranking basis/background: Alphabetical list of law schools with outstanding faculty in a specific area as compiled by consultation with experts in various fields and anthologies of leading articles in each field. **Number listed:** 7.

- Harvard University
- New York University
- Stanford University
- University of Michigan
- University of Texas, Austin
- University of Virginia
- Yale University

Source: Leiter, Brian, "New Educational Quality Ranking of U.S. Law Schools for 1999-2000," http://www.dia.utexas.edu/depts/philosophy/faculty/leiter/LGOURMET.HTM, November 1999.

★2662★
Law schools with the best moral and political theory (Anglo-American traditions) faculty, 1999-2000

Ranking basis/background: Alphabetical list of law schools with outstanding faculty in a specific area as compiled by consultation with experts in various fields and anthologies of leading articles in each field. **Number listed:** 6.

- Boston University
- Columbia University
- New York University
- University of California, Berkeley
- University of Michigan
- Yale University

Source: Leiter, Brian, "New Educational Quality Ranking of U.S. Law Schools for 1999-2000," http://www.dia.utexas.edu/depts/philosophy/faculty/leiter/LGOURMET.HTM, November 1999.

★2663★
Law schools with the best moral and political theory (Continental traditions) faculty, 1999-2000

Ranking basis/background: Alphabetical list of law schools with outstanding faculty in a specific area as compiled by consultation with experts in various fields and anthologies of leading articles in each field. **Number listed:** 4.

- Yeshiva University, Cardozo Law School
- University of Chicago
- University of Texas, Austin
- Yale University

Source: Leiter, Brian, "New Educational Quality Ranking of U.S. Law Schools for 1999-2000," http://www.dia.utexas.edu/depts/philosophy/faculty/leiter/LGOURMET.HTM, November 1999.

★2664★
Law schools with the best tax faculty, 1999-2000

Ranking basis/background: Alphabetical list of law schools with outstanding faculty in a specific area as compiled by consultation with experts in various fields and anthologies of leading articles in each field. **Number listed:** 6.

- Harvard University
- New York University
- Stanford University
- University of Chicago
- University of Texas, Austin
- Yale University

Source: Leiter, Brian, "New Educational Quality Ranking of U.S. Law Schools for 1999-2000," http://www.dia.utexas.edu/depts/philosophy/faculty/leiter/LGOURMET.HTM, November 1999.

★2665★
Law schools with the best Torts (including products liability) faculty, 1999-2000

Ranking basis/background: Alphabetical list of law schools with outstanding faculty in a specific area as compiled by consultation with experts in various fields and anthologies of leading articles in each field. **Number listed:** 6.

- Cornell University
- University of California, Los Angeles
- University of Chicago
- University of Texas, Austin
- University of Virginia
- Yale University

Source: Leiter, Brian, "New Educational Quality Ranking of U.S. Law Schools for 1999-2000," http://www.dia.utexas.edu/depts/philosophy/faculty/leiter/LGOURMET.HTM, November 1999.

★2666★
Law schools with the highest quality, 1999-2000

Ranking basis/background: Educational Quality Ranking is based on the schools performance in three categories: faculty quality (scholarly productivity, scholarly impact of faculty work, and reputation); student quality (data from the American Bar Association on student in the 75th and 25th percentile of the entering class); and teaching quality. Also includes resident costs. **Number listed:** 50.

1. University of Chicago
2. Yale University
3. Harvard University
4. Stanford University
5. Columbia University
5. New York University
7. University of Michigan
8. University of California, Berkeley
8. University of Virginia
10. Cornell University
11. University of Pennsylvania
11. University of Texas, Austin
13. Georgetown University
13. Northwestern University
15. Duke University
15. University of California, Los Angeles

Source: Leiter, Brian, "New Educational Quality Ranking of U.S. Law Schools for 1999-2000," http://www.dia.utexas.edu/depts/philosophy/faculty/leiter/LGOURMET.HTM, November 1999.

★2667★
School's bar passage rate in jurisdiction at *U.S. News & World Report*'s top 10 law schools, 2001

Ranking basis/background: From a *U.S. News & World Report* survey of the school's bar passage rate in jurisdiction for 2000. **Remarks:** Data collected by Market Facts, Inc. **Number listed:** 54.

- Yale University, with 95.1% overall bar passage rate; in the NY jurisdiction
- Stanford University, 92.8%; CA
- Harvard University, 95.9%; NY
- Columbia University, 92.4%; NY
- New York University, 93.8%; NY
- University of Chicago, 93.7%; IL
- University of Michigan, Ann Arbor, 89.7%; NY
- University of Virginia, 96.1%; VA
- University of California, Berkeley, 86.3%; CA
- Duke University, 92.3%; NY
- University of Pennsylvania, 86.5%; NY

Source: "America's Best Graduate Schools: 2002 Annual Guide," *U.S. News & World Report*, 130: 60-97, (April 19, 2001).

★2668★
States with the most law schools

Ranking basis/background: Number of law schools. **Number listed:** 10.

1. California, with 19 law schools

LAW SCHOOLS—STUDENTS

2. New York, 15
3. Illinois, 9
3. Ohio, 9
3. Texas, 9
6. Massachusetts, 7
6. Pennsylvania, 7
8. Florida, 6
8. District of Columbia, 6
8. Virginia, 6

Source: Baker, Mark, *The Insider's Book of Law School Lists*, Simon & Schuster, 1997.

★2669★
Student-faculty ratios at *U.S. News & World Report*'s top 10 law schools, 2001

Ranking basis/background: From a *U.S. News & World Report* survey of number of students per faculty member in 2000. **Remarks:** Data collected by Market Facts, Inc. **Number listed:** 54.

1. Yale University, with 10.8 students per faculty member
2. University of Chicago, 11.0
3. New York University, 12.5
4. Columbia University, 12.9
5. Stanford University, 13.4
6. University of Virginia, 14.2
7. University of Michigan, Ann Arbor, 14.7
8. University of Pennsylvania, 14.8
9. University of California, Berkeley, 15.9
10. Duke University, 16.0
11. Harvard University, 19.7

Source: "America's Best Graduate Schools: 2002 Annual Guide," *U.S. News & World Report*, 130: 60-97, (April 19, 2001).

★2670★
Top law schools, 2001

Ranking basis/background: From a *U.S. News & World Report* survey based on academic reputation, student selectivity, faculty resources, and placement success. **Remarks:** Data collected by Market Facts, Inc. **Number listed:** 54.

1. Yale University, with an overall score of 100
2. Stanford University, 96
3. Harvard University, 92
4. Columbia University, 90
5. New York University, 88
6. University of Chicago, 86
7. University of Michigan, Ann Arbor, 84
7. University of Virginia, 84
9. University of California, Berkeley, 83
10. Duke University, 82
10. University of Pennsylvania, 82

Source: "America's Best Graduate Schools: 2002 Annual Guide," *U.S. News & World Report*, 130: 60-97, (April 19, 2001).

★2671★
Top law schools by reputation, as determined by academic personnel, 2001

Ranking basis/background: From a *U.S. News & World Report* survey of law school deans and senior faculty. **Remarks:** Data collected by Market Facts, Inc. **Number listed:** 54.

1. Yale University, with a score of 4.9
1. Stanford University, 4.9
1. Harvard University, 4.9
4. Columbia University, 4.8
5. University of Chicago, 4.8
6. University of Michigan, Ann Arbor, 4.7
6. University of California, Berkeley, 4.7
8. New York University, 4.6
9. University of Virginia, 4.5
9. University of Pennsylvania, 4.5

Source: "America's Best Graduate Schools: 2002 Annual Guide," *U.S. News & World Report*, 130: 60-97, (April 19, 2001).

★2672★
Top law schools by reputation, as determined by lawyers and judges, 2001

Ranking basis/background: From a *U.S. News & World Report* survey of lawyers, hiring partners, and senior judges. **Remarks:** Data collected by Market Facts, Inc. **Number listed:** 54.

1. Yale University, with a score of 4.9
1. Stanford University, 4.9
1. Harvard University, 4.9
4. Columbia University, 4.8
5. University of Chicago, 4.8
6. University of Michigan, Ann Arbor, 4.7
7. New York University, 4.6
7. University of Virginia, 4.6
7. University of California, Berkeley, 4.6
10. Duke University, 4.5
10. University of Pennsylvania, 4.5

Source: "America's Best Graduate Schools: 2002 Annual Guide," *U.S. News & World Report*, 130: 60-97, (April 19, 2001).

LAW SCHOOLS–STUDENTS

★2673★
Top law school student bodies, 1999-2000

Ranking basis/background: Educational Quality Ranking is based on the schools performance in three categories: faculty quality (scholarly productivity, scholarly impact of faculty work, and reputation); student quality (data from the American Bar Association on student in the 75th and 25th percentile of the entering class); and teaching quality. Also includes total student body size. **Number listed:** 50.

1. Yale University
2. Harvard University
3. University of Chicago
4. New York University
5. Stanford University
6. Columbia University
7. University of Virginia
8. University of California, Berkeley
9. University of Pennsylvania
10. Georgetown University
10. University of Michigan

Source: Leiter, Brian, "New Educational Quality Ranking of U.S. Law Schools for 1999-2000," http://www.dia.utexas.edu/depts/philosophy/faculty/leiter/LGOURMET.HTM, November 1999.

LEARNING DISABILITIES

Related Information

★2674★

Kravets, Marybeth and Imy F. Wax, *The K&W Guide to Colleges for Students with Learning Disabilities or Attention Deficit Disorders*, 2000 edition, Random House, 1999.

Remarks: Provides in-depth information about services and programs available at colleges and universities for students with learning disabilities. Includes general profiles of the schools, policies and procedures regarding course waivers or substitutions, information about special admission procedures, the applications process, and specific courses and programs.

LECTURERS, COLLEGE
See: **College Faculty Salaries–Colleges & Universities**

LIBERAL ARTS

★2675★
Top recruiters for liberal arts jobs for 2000-01 bachelor's degree recipients

Ranking basis/background: Projected number of college hires from on-campus recruitment for 2000-01. **Remarks:** Numbers reflect total expected hires, not just African American projected hires. **Number listed:** 35.

1. Enterprise Rent-A-Car, with 2,000 projected hires
2. Footstar, 500
3. GAP Inc., 250
4. Accenture, 200
5. Lucent Technologies, 100
5. Wells Fargo Financial, 100
5. EDS, 100
5. Sherwin-Williams, 100
5. Houghton Mifflin, 100
10. Federated Department Stores, 91

Source: "The Top 100 Employers and the Majors in Demand for the Class of 2001," *The Black Collegian*, 31: 19-35, (February 2001).

LIBERAL-ARTS COLLEGES
See: **Colleges & Universities, Liberal Arts**

LIBERAL ARTS, GRADUATE

★2676★
Top recruiters for liberal arts jobs for 2000-01 master's degree recipients

Ranking basis/background: Projected number of college hires from on-campus recruitment for 2000-01. **Remarks:** Numbers reflect total expected hires, not just African American projected hires. **Number listed:** 4.

1. Lucent Technologies, with 100 projected hires
2. Accenture, 20
3. Federal Deposit Insurance Company, 10
4. Deloitte & Touche, 5

Source: "The Top 100 Employers and the Majors in Demand for the Class of 2001," *The Black Collegian*, 31: 19-35, (February 2001).

LIBRARIES

★2677★
Illinois institutions with the highest article output

Ranking basis/background: Number of articles produced. Based on a study of 281 entries identified 210 articles written by 166 different Illinois academic librarians from 1995 through January 1999. **Number listed:** 8.
1. University of Illinois, Urbana-Champaign, with 43.45
2. University of Illinois, Chicago, 42.86
3. Southern Illinois University, 21.50
4. Northern Illinois University, 14.83
5. Illinois State University, 13.66
6. Western Illinois University, 13.40
7. Northwestern University, 5.83
8. Loyola University, 5.00

Source: Joswick, Kathleen E., "Article Publication Patterns of Academic Librarians: An Illinois Case Study," *College & Research Libraries*, 60: 340-349, (July 1999).

★2678★
Institutions with the most productive libraries, 1993-1997

Ranking basis/background: Number of authors and articles, from an examination of 32 articles with 3,624 peer-reviewed articles published from 1993 to 1997. **Number listed:** 20.
1. Pennsylvania State University, with 35 authors; 46 articles
2. Cornell University, 32; 32
3. University of Illinois, Urbana-Champaign, 31; 40
4. University of Minnesota, 31; 28
5. University of Illinois, Chicago, 30; 38
6. Iowa State University, 29; 35
7. Ohio State University, 27; 41
8. Rutgers University, 27; 27
9. Texas A&M University, 26; 25
10. University of Florida, 22; 19

Source: Weller, Ann C., Julie M. Hurd and Stephen E. Wiberley, Jr., "Publication Patterns of U.S. Academic Librarians from 1993 to 1997," *College & Research Libraries*, 60: 352-363, (July 1999).

★2679★
Languages of requested materials from OCLC ILL, 1999

Ranking basis/background: Language requests made, other than English, during 1999 through the OCLC Interlibrary Loan service. **Number listed:** 24.
1. French, with 113,856
2. German, 106,803
3. Spanish, 100,356
4. Italian, 36,787
5. Russian, 26,484
6. Unknown, 25,471
7. Japanese, 24,705
8. Chinese, 16,858
9. Multilingual, 14,881
10. Portuguese, 9,908

Source: "Top 25 Languages of Materials Requested on the OCLC ILL Service during 1999," *OCLC Newsletter*, No. 244, p. 17, (March/April 2000).

★2680★
North America's first ten public libraries

Ranking basis/background: First ten public libraries that opened in North America according to the National Library of Canada. **Number listed:** 10.
1. Quebec City Library (opened in 1779)
2. Montreal Public Library (1796)
3. Niagara Library (1800)
4. Halifax Library (1806)
5. St. Andres Social Library (1815)
6. Fredericton Social Library (1816)
7. Newport Library (1820)
8. Halifax Public Library (1824)
9. Peterboro Public Library (1833)
10. New Orleans Public Library (1843)

Source: "Emporium," *Maclean's*, January 11, 1999, p. 16.

★2681★
State library associations with most full-time staff

Ranking basis/background: Total full-time equivalents. **Remarks:** Original source: State Library Association Executive Directors. **Number listed:** 10.
1. Texas, with 12
2. Ohio, 10
3. Michigan, 5
4. California, 4
4. New York, 4
6. Pennsylvania, 3
7. Illinois, 2.5
8. New Jersey, 2
9. Louisiana, 1.25
10. Iowa, .75

Source: "The State of State Library Associations," *The Illinois Library Association Reporter*, 18: 11-13, (October 2000).

★2682★
State library associations with the highest annual revenue

Ranking basis/background: Annual revenue for 2000. **Remarks:** Original source: State Library Association Executive Directors. **Number listed:** 12.
1. Texas, with $2,100,000
2. Ohio, $1,500,000
3. Illinois, $900,000
4. California, $638,000
5. New York, $500,000
6. Michigan, $450,000
7. New Jersey, $303,438
8. Pennsylvania, $280,000
9. Florida, $260,000
10. Iowa, $154,000
11. Kentucky, $120,000
12. Louisiana, $100,000

Source: "The State of State Library Associations," *The Illinois Library Association Reporter*, 18: 11-13, (October 2000).

★2683★
State library associations with the highest conference attendance

Ranking basis/background: Total paid attendance to conferences. **Remarks:** Original source: State Library Association Executive Directors. **Number listed:** 10.
1. Texas, with 6,000
2. New York, 1,450
3. Illinois, 1,250
4. Ohio, 1,100
5. Michigan, 1,000
6. Florida, 900
7. Kentucky, 800
8. New Jersey, 700
9. Louisiana, 650
10. Pennsylvania, 600

Source: "The State of State Library Associations," *The Illinois Library Association Reporter*, 18: 11-13, (October 2000).

★2684★
State library associations with the highest unrestricted net assets

Ranking basis/background: Unrestricted net assets for 2000. **Remarks:** Original source: State Library Association Executive Directors. **Number listed:** 11.
1. Texas, with $2,500,000
2. California, $533,000
3. Ohio, $250,000
4. Illinois, $175,702
5. New York, $148,132
6. Louisiana, $101,000
7. New Jersey, $98,381
8. Florida, $90,000
9. Iowa, $70,000
10. Michigan, $60,000
11. Pennsylvania, $36,000

Source: "The State of State Library Associations," *The Illinois Library Association Reporter*, 18: 11-13, (October 2000).

★2685★
State library associations with the largest membership

Ranking basis/background: Total membership. **Remarks:** Original source: State Library Association Executive Directors. **Number listed:** 12.
1. Texas, with 7,311
2. Ohio, 5,525
3. Illinois, 3,011
4. New York, 3,000
5. Michigan, 2,280
6. California, 2,094
7. Kentucky, 1,800
8. Pennsylvania, 1,603
9. New Jersey, 1,520
10. Iowa, 1,415
11. Florida, 1,405
12. Louisiana, 1,400

Source: "The State of State Library Associations," *The Illinois Library Association Reporter*, 18: 11-13, (October 2000).

LIBRARIES, LAW

★2686★
Law library web sites, by luminosity

Ranking basis/background: Total luminosity, or number of external links, to the law library web site. **Number listed:** 156.
1. Washburn University, with 8,769 external links
2. Emory University, 4,426
3. Georgetown University, 4,179
4. University of Texas, 3,060
5. Regent University, 2,521
6. University of Chicago, 2,517
7. Cornell University, 1,956
8. University of Southern California, 1,910
9. University of Notre Dame, 1,852

LIBRARIES, PUBLIC

10. University of Nebraska, 1,522

Source: Vreeland, Robert C., "Law Libraries in Hyperspace: A Citation Analysis of World Wide Web Sites," *Law Library Journal*, 92: 9-25, (Winter).

★2687★
Law library web sites, by visibility

Ranking basis/background: Alta Vista search engine indexes to the law library web site. **Number listed:** 156.

1. Washburn University, with 6,237
2. Emory University, 3,718
3. Georgetown University, 1,978
4. University of Southern California, 1,514
5. University of Texas, Austin, 811
6. University of Pennsylvania, 507
7. Gonzaga University, 381
8. Cornell University, 372
8. Harvard University, 372
10. Pace University, 356

Source: Vreeland, Robert C., "Law Libraries in Hyperspace: A Citation Analysis of World Wide Web Sites," *Law Library Journal*, 92: 9-25, (Winter).

★2688★
Law library web sites with the most visible external hostnames

Ranking basis/background: Visibility of external hostnames. **Number listed:** 200.

1. http://www.law.cornell.edu, with 1,316
2. http://www.access.gpo.gov, 904
3. http://193.135.156.15, 701
4. http://www.findlaw.com, 651
5. http://law.house.gov, 618
6. http://www.abanet.org, 542
7. http://www.law.emory.edu, 534
8. http://lawlib.wuacc.edu, 517
9. http://www.house.gov, 504
10. http://www.yahoo.com, 422

Source: Vreeland, Robert C., "Law Libraries in Hyperspace: A Citation Analysis of World Wide Web Sites," *Law Library Journal*, 92: 9-25, (Winter).

★2689★
Law library web sites with the most visible external URLs

Ranking basis/background: Number of URLs linked. **Number listed:** 80.

1. http://thomas.loc.gov, with 93
2. http://www.findlaw.com, 89
3. http://law.house.gov, 78
4. http://www.un.org, 72
5. http://www.law.cornell.edu, 68
6. http://www.yahoo.com, 64
7. http://www.abanet.org, 63
8. http://www.access.gpo.gov/su_docs/aces/aces140.html, 61
9. http://www.senate.gov, 59
10. http://www.law.cornell.edu/uscode, 58

Source: Vreeland, Robert C., "Law Libraries in Hyperspace: A Citation Analysis of World Wide Web Sites," *Law Library Journal*, 92: 9-25, (Winter).

LIBRARIES, PUBLIC

★2690★
Average Hennen's American Public Library Ratings, by state

Ranking basis/background: Average HAPLR index ratings. **Number listed:** 50.

1. Ohio, with an average rating of 657
2. Indiana, 607
3. Massachusetts, 599
4. Washington, 592
5. Minnesota, 591
6. Utah, 576
7. Wisconsin, 576
8. Kansas, 566
9. New York, 560
10. Connecticut, 553

Source: Hennen, Thomas J., "Great American Public Libraries: HAPLR Ratings, 2000," *American Libraries*, 31: 50-54, (November 2000).

★2691★
Highest Hennen's American Public Library Ratings for libraries serving a population of 999 and under

Ranking basis/background: HAPLR index ratings. **Number listed:** 10.

1. Lynnville Public Library (Lynnville, IA), with an index rating of 913
2. Brownsville Public Library (Brownsville, WI), 883
3. Clayville Library Association (Clayville, NY), 882
4. Poland Public Library (Poland, NY), 880
5. Raquette Lake Free Library (Raquette Lake), 867
6. Easton Library (Greenwich, NY), 852
7. Falls City Public Library (Falls City, TX), 846
8. Wide-Awake Club Library (Fillmore, NY), 845
9. Mill Pond Public Library (Kingston, WI), 843
10. Ellisburg Free Library (Ellisburg, NY), 842

Source: Hennen, Thomas J., "Great American Public Libraries: HAPLR Ratings, 2000," *American Libraries*, 31: 50-54, (November 2000).

★2692★
Highest Hennen's American Public Library Ratings for libraries serving a population of 1,000 to 2,499

Ranking basis/background: HAPLR index ratings. **Number listed:** 10.

1. Hazel L. Meyer Memorial Library (De Smet, SD), with an index rating of 888
2. Moose Lake Public Library (Moose Lake, MN), 884
3. Jones Memorial Library (Orleans, VT), 868
4. Perham Area Public Library (Perham, MN), 865
5. Mary Cotton Public Library (Sabetha, KS), 864
6. Union Public Library (Union, IA), 864
7. Fairfax Community Library (Fairfax, VT), 860
8. Seneca Free Library (Seneca, KS), 857
9. Odon Winkelpleck Memorial Library (Odon, IN), 854
10. Runals Memorial Library (Edgerton, MN), 852

Source: Hennen, Thomas J., "Great American Public Libraries: HAPLR Ratings, 2000," *American Libraries*, 31: 50-54, (November 2000).

★2693★
Highest Hennen's American Public Library Ratings for libraries serving a population of 2,500 to 4,999

Ranking basis/background: HAPLR index ratings. **Number listed:** 10.

1. Hagerstown-Jefferson Township Public Library (Hagerstown, IN), with an index rating of 936
2. Falconer Public Library (Falconer, NY), 899
3. GAR Memorial Library (West Newbury, MA), 892
4. North Liberty Community Library (North Liberty, IA), 887
5. Tracy Memorial Library (New London, NH), 880
6. Vineyard Haven Public Library (Vineyard Haven, MA), 877
7. Lee Public Library (Lee, NH), 868
8. East Syracuse Free Library (East Syracuse, NY), 867
9. Hamilton Public Library (Hamilton, NY), 864
10. Central City Public Library (Central City, NE), 861

Source: Hennen, Thomas J., "Great American Public Libraries: HAPLR Ratings, 2000," *American Libraries*, 31: 50-54, (November 2000).

★2694★
Highest Hennen's American Public Library Ratings for libraries serving a population of 5,000 to 9,999

Ranking basis/background: HAPLR index ratings. **Number listed:** 10.

1. Morris Public Library (Morris, MN), with an index rating of 904
2. Bridgeport Public Library (Bridgeport, WV), 898
3. Westfield Public Library (Westfield, IN), 882
4. Manlius Library (Manlius, NY), 879
5. Fayetteville Free Library (Fayetteville, NY), 877
6. Bernardsville Public Library (Bernardsville, NJ), 876
7. Mukwonago Community Library (Mukwonago, WI), 871
8. Redwood Falls Public Library (Redwood Falls, MN), 865
9. Williamson Free Public Library (Williamson, NY), 865
10. Cresco Public Library (Cresco, IA), 855

Source: Hennen, Thomas J., "Great American Public Libraries: HAPLR Ratings, 2000," *American Libraries*, 31: 50-54, (November 2000).

★2695★
Highest Hennen's American Public Library Ratings for libraries serving a population of 10,000 to 24,999

Ranking basis/background: HAPLR index ratings. **Number listed:** 10.

1. Hays Public Library (Hays, KS), with an index rating of 902
2. Brown Deer Public Library (Brown Deer, WI), 883
3. Wickliffe Public Library (Wickliffe, OH), 879

4. Peters Township Public Library (McMurray, PA), 869
5. Staunton Public Library (Staunton, VA), 867
6. Fergus Falls Public Library (Fergus Falls, MN), 863
7. Delphos Public Library (Delphos, OH), 859
8. Darien Library (Darien, CT), 854
9. Twinsburg Public Library (Twinsburg, OH), 853
10. George F. Johnson Memorial Library (Endicott, NY), 852

Source: Hennen, Thomas J., "Great American Public Libraries: HAPLR Ratings, 2000," *American Libraries*, 31: 50-54, (November 2000).

★2696★
Highest Hennen's American Public Library Ratings for libraries serving a population of 25,000 to 49,999

Ranking basis/background: HAPLR index ratings. **Number listed:** 10.
1. Washington-Centerville Public Library (Centerville, OH), with an index rating of 918
2. Carmel Clay Public Library (Carmel, IN), 884
3. James Prendergast Library Association (Jamestown, NY), 878
4. Elmhurst Public Library (Elmhurst, IL), 851
5. Urbana Free Library (Urbana, IL), 850
6. Wright Memorial Public Library (Oakwood, OH), 849
7. Cook Memorial Public Library District (Libertyville, IL), 848
8. Cary Memorial Library (Lexington, MA), 847
9. Concord Pike Library (Wilmington, DE), 846
10. Downers Grove Public Library (Downers Grove, IL), 842

Source: Hennen, Thomas J., "Great American Public Libraries: HAPLR Ratings, 2000," *American Libraries*, 31: 50-54, (November 2000).

★2697★
Highest Hennen's American Public Library Ratings for libraries serving a population of 50,000 to 99,999

Ranking basis/background: HAPLR index ratings. **Number listed:** 10.
1. Lower Merion Library System (Ardmore, PA), with an index rating of 884
2. Newtown Free Library (Newton, MA), 882
3. Newport Beach Public Library (Newport Beach, CA), 873
4. Palatine Public Library District (Palatine, IL), 865
5. Westerville Public Library (Westerville, OH), 851
6. Wheaton Public Library (Wheaton, IL), 846
7. Cleveland Heights-University Heights Public Library (Cleveland Hts., OH), 842
8. Findlay-Hancock County Public Library (Findlay, OH), 841
9. Ames Public Library (Ames, IA), 838
10. Carlsbad City Library (Carlsbad, CA), 830

Source: Hennen, Thomas J., "Great American Public Libraries: HAPLR Ratings, 2000," *American Libraries*, 31: 50-54, (November 2000).

★2698★
Highest Hennen's American Public Library Ratings for libraries serving a population of 100,000 to 249,999

Ranking basis/background: HAPLR index ratings. **Number listed:** 10.
1. Naperville Public Libraries (Naperville, IL), with an index rating of 887
2. St. Charles City-County Library District (St. Peters, MO), 880
3. Porter County Public Library System (Valparaiso, IN), 839
4. Tippecanoe County Public Library (Lafayette, IN), 832
5. St. Joseph County Public Library (South Bend, IN), 831
6. Schaumburg Township District Library (Schaumburg, IL), 830
7. Loudoun County Public Library (Leesburg, VA), 822
8. Santa Clara City Library (Santa Clara, CA), 820
9. Middletown Public Library (Middletown, OH), 818
10. Beaverton City Library (Beaverton, OR), 815

Source: Hennen, Thomas J., "Great American Public Libraries: HAPLR Ratings, 2000," *American Libraries*, 31: 50-54, (November 2000).

★2699★
Highest Hennen's American Public Library Ratings for libraries serving a population of 250,000 to 499,999

Ranking basis/background: HAPLR index ratings. **Number listed:** 10.
1. Santa Clara County Free Library (San Jose, CA), with an index rating of 859
2. Johnson County Library (Shawnee Mission, KS), 857
3. Prince William Public Library System (Prince William, VA), 824
4. Richland County Public Library (Columbia, SC), 791
5. Anne Arundel County Public Library (Annapolis, MD), 785
6. Dayton & Montgomery County Public Library (Dayton, OH), 782
7. Toledo-Lucas County Public Library (Toledo, OH), 760
8. Allen County Public Library (Fort Wayne, IN), 753
9. Sarasota County Library System (Sarasota, FL), 749
10. Dakota County Library (Eagan, MN), 745

Source: Hennen, Thomas J., "Great American Public Libraries: HAPLR Ratings, 2000," *American Libraries*, 31: 50-54, (November 2000).

★2700★
Highest Hennen's American Public Library Ratings for libraries serving a population of over 500,000

Ranking basis/background: HAPLR index ratings. **Number listed:** 10.
1. Denver Public Library (Denver, CO), with an index rating of 890
2. Columbus Metropolitan Library (Columbus, OH), 831
3. Indianapolis-Marion County Public Library (Indianapolis, IN), 788
4. Hennepin County Library (Minnetonka, MN), 787
5. St. Louis County Library (St. Louis, MO), 738
6. Fairfax County Public Library (Fairfax, VA), 714
7. Gwinnett County Public Library System (Lawrenceville, GA), 685
8. Mid-Continent Consolidated Library District (Independence, MO), 684
9. Multnomah County Library (Portland, OR), 680
10. Public Library of Charlotte & Mecklenburg Co. (Charlotte, NC), 676

Source: Hennen, Thomas J., "Great American Public Libraries: HAPLR Ratings, 2000," *American Libraries*, 31: 50-54, (November 2000).

★2701★
Public library average materials budget, by population served, 2001

Ranking basis/background: Average materials budget. **Remarks:** Original source: *Library Journal* Budget Report 2001. **Number listed:** 7.
Fewer than 10,000, with $35,000
10,000-24,999, $85,000
25,000-49,999, $135,000
50,000-99,999, $221,000
100,000-499,999, $860,000
500,000-999,999, $3,697,000
1 million or more, $5,193,000

Source: St. Lifer, Evan, "The Library as Anchor," *Library Journal*, 126: 59-61, (January 2001).

★2702★
Public library average net maintenance costs, by population served, 2000

Ranking basis/background: Average net maintenance costs. **Remarks:** Original source: *Library Journal* Budget Report 2001. **Number listed:** 7.
Fewer than 10,000, with $4,500
10,000-24,999, $13,900
25,000-49,999, $14,000
50,000-99,999, $37,100
100,000-499,999, $108,700
500,000-999,999, $593,100
1 million or more, $722,000

Source: St. Lifer, Evan, "The Library as Anchor," *Library Journal*, 126: 59-61, (January 2001).

★2703★
Public library average operating budget, by population served, 2001

Ranking basis/background: Average operating budget. **Remarks:** Original source: *Library Journal* Budget Report 2001. **Number listed:** 7.
Fewer than 10,000, with $193,000
10,000-24,999, $558,000
25,000-49,999, $968,000
50,000-99,999, $1,503,000
100,000-499,999, $5,664,000
500,000-999,999, $23,957,000
1 million or more, $39,820,000

Source: St. Lifer, Evan, "The Library as Anchor," *Library Journal*, 126: 59-61, (January 2001).

★2704★
Public library average salary budget, by population served, 2001

Ranking basis/background: Average salary budget. **Remarks:** Original source: *Library Journal* Budget Report 2001. **Number listed:** 7.
Fewer than 10,000, with $119,000
10,000-24,999, $320,000
25,000-49,999, $630,000

50,000-99,999, $774,000
100,000-499,999, $3,666,000
500,000-999,999, $12,628,000
1 million or more, $23,117,000
Source: St. Lifer, Evan, "The Library as Anchor," *Library Journal*, 126: 59-61, (January 2001).

LIBRARIES, RESEARCH–NORTH AMERICA

★2705★
Average operating expenditures for university research libraries in the U.S. and Canada, 1998-99

Ranking basis/background: Percentage breakdown of the $2.07-billion total for operating expenditures in U.S. and Canada libraries, 1998-99. Figures do not equal 100 percent due to rounding.
Remarks: Original source: Association of Research Libraries. **Number listed:** 4.
1. Salaries, with 47%
2. Library materials, 38%
3. Contract binding, 1%
4. Other, 14%

Source: "Holdings of University Research Libraries in U.S. and Canada, 1998-99," *The Chronicle of Higher Education* (http://www.chronicle.com/weekly/v46/i37/stats/4637libraries.htm), 46:, (May 19, 2000).

★2706★
Top university research libraries in the U.S. and Canada, 1998-99

Ranking basis/background: Based on an index developed by the Association of Research Libraries to measure the relative size of university libraries. Takes into account the number of volumes held, number of volumes added during the previous year, number of current serials, total expenditures, and staff size. **Remarks:** Number of volumes in library is included as an indication of relative size.
Number listed: 111.
1. Harvard University, with 14,190,704 volumes in library
2. Yale University, 10,294,792
3. Stanford University, 7,151,546
4. University of Toronto, 8,668,036
5. University of California, Berkeley, 8,946,754
6. University of California, Los Angeles, 7,401,780
7. University of Michigan, 7,195,097
8. University of Illinois, Urbana-Champaign, 9,302,203
9. Columbia University, 7,144,703
10. Cornell University, 6,448,496
11. University of Texas, 7,783,847
12. University of Washington (WA), 5,937,690
13. Pennsylvania State University, 4,391,055
14. University of Minnesota, 5,747,805
15. Indiana University, 6,177,219
16. University of Wisconsin, 5,962,889
17. Princeton University, 5,751,978
18. University of North Carolina, 5,024,221
19. University of Pennsylvania, 4,791,947
20. University of Chicago, 6,419,386

Source: "Holdings of University Research Libraries in U.S. and Canada, 1998-99," *The Chronicle of Higher Education* (http://www.chronicle.com/weekly/v46/i37/stats/4637libraries.htm), 46:, (May 19, 2000).

★2707★
University research libraries in the U.S. and Canada with the largest decreases in total expenditures from 1993-94 to 1998-99

Ranking basis/background: Percentage of decrease in expenditures from 1992-93 to 1997-98.
Remarks: Original source: Association of Research Libraries. **Number listed:** 11.
1. Laval University, with a 25.0% decrease
2. University of Waterloo, 12.8%
3. University of Western Ontario, 9.7%
4. McMaster University, 8.5%
5. University of Guelph, 8.5%
6. York University (Ontario), 6.7%
7. University of Hawaii, 6.1%
8. McGill University, 5.0%
9. University of Alberta, 3.7%
10. University of Miami, 2.1%
11. University of British Columbia, 1.0%

Source: "Holdings of University Research Libraries in U.S. and Canada, 1998-99," *The Chronicle of Higher Education* (http://www.chronicle.com/weekly/v46/i37/stats/4637libraries.htm), 46:, (May 19, 2000).

★2708★
University research libraries in the U.S. and Canada with the largest increases in total expenditures from 1993-94 to 1998-99

Ranking basis/background: Percentage of increase in expenditures from 1992-93 to 1997-98.
Remarks: Original source: Association of Research Libraries. **Number listed:** 15.
1. University of Notre Dame, with a 67.9% increase
2. Howard University, 65.9%
3. North Carolina State University, 63.8%
4. University of Utah, 62.8%
5. University of South Carolina, 60.3%
6. University of Kentucky, 59.1%
7. Texas A&M University, 52.6%
8. University of Connecticut, 49.2%
9. Pennsylvania State University, 48.4%
10. Stanford University, 48.1%
11. University of Pennsylvania, 44.0%
12. University of Virginia, 43.6%
13. Washington University (MO), 43.4%
14. Georgia Institute of Technology, 41.3%
15. University of Georgia, 41.1%

Source: "Holdings of University Research Libraries in U.S. and Canada, 1998-99," *The Chronicle of Higher Education* (http://www.chronicle.com/weekly/v46/i37/stats/4637libraries.htm), 46:, (May 19, 2000).

LIBRARY SCIENCE

★2709★
Comparison of library and information science programs composite rankings with *U.S. News & World Report* survey

Ranking basis/background: Composite rank, points, and *U.S. News* survey ranking. **Number listed:** 15.
University of Indiana, with 59.5 points (ranked 6 in *U.S. News*)
University of Illinois, 54.5 (1)
University of North Carolina, 52.5 (1)
Rutgers University, 50.5 (6)
University of California, Los Angeles, 45.5 (10)
University of California, Berkeley, 39.0 (Not rated)
University of Michigan, 36.0 (3)
Simmons University, 33.5 (12)
University of Maryland, 33.0 (14)
University of Tennessee, 30.0 (20)

Source: Budd, John M., "Scholarly Productivity of U.S. LIS Faculty: An Update," *Library Quarterly*, 70: 230-245, (April 2000).

★2710★
Library and information science faculty with the most citations to journal articles, 1993-1998

Ranking basis/background: Total number of citations to journal articles published between 1993 and 1998. **Number listed:** 25.
1. Hal Varian, with 673 citations
2. Nicholas Belkin, 440
3. Tefko Saracevic, 425
4. Gary Marchionini, 366
5. Blaise Cronin, 350
6. Marcia J. Bates, 338
7. Christine Borgman, 336
8. Charles McClure, 316
9. Peter Hernon, 276
10. Carol Kuhlthau, 253

Source: Budd, John M., "Scholarly Productivity of U.S. LIS Faculty: An Update," *Library Quarterly*, 70: 230-245, (April 2000).

★2711★
Library and information science faculty with the most journal articles, 1993-1998

Ranking basis/background: Total number of journal articles published between 1993 and 1998. **Number listed:** 20.
1. Carol Tenopir, with 43 articles
2. Peter Jacso, 32
3. Blaise Cronin, 26
4. Martha E. Williams, 23
5. Amanda Spink, 22
6. Peter Hernon, 20
6. Charles McClure, 20
8. A.J. Anderson, 19
9. John M. Budd, 15
9. Alexandra Dimitroff, 15
11. Bryce Allen, 13
11. Marcia J. Bates, 13
11. Robert Losee, 13
11. Dietmar Wolfram, 13
15. Paul Kantor, 12
15. Tefko Saracevic, 12
17. Linda C. Smith, 11
17. Hal Varian, 11
19. MaryEllen Sievert, 10
19. Darlene Weingand, 10

Source: Budd, John M., "Scholarly Productivity of U.S. LIS Faculty: An Update," *Library Quarterly*, 70: 230-245, (April 2000).

★2712★
Library and information science programs with the most citations to journal articles, 1993-1998

Ranking basis/background: Total number of citations to journal articles published between 1993 and 1998. **Number listed:** 15.
Rutgers University, with 1,321 citations to journal articles
University of California, Berkeley, 1,214
University of Indiana, 1,121
University of California, Los Angeles, 937

University of Michigan, 695
University of North Carolina, 674
University of Illinois, 620
Syracuse University, 559
Simmons University, 553
University of Maryland, 546
Drexel University, 496
University of North Texas, 453
University of Pittsburgh, 430
University of Washington (WA), 347
University of Tennessee, 266

Source: Budd, John M., "Scholarly Productivity of U.S. LIS Faculty: An Update," *Library Quarterly*, 70: 230-245, (April 2000).

★2713★
Library and information science programs with the most journal articles, 1993-1998

Ranking basis/background: Total number of journal articles published between 1993 and 1998. **Number listed:** 15.
1. University of Illinois, with 68 publications
1. University of Indiana, 68
3. University of Tennessee, 57
4. University of North Carolina, 56
5. University of Hawaii, 52
5. University of Wisconsin, Milwaukee, 52
7. Simmons University, 49
8. Rutgers University, 48
8. University of California, Los Angeles, 48
10. University of Missouri, 41
10. University of Pittsburgh, 41
12. University of North Texas, 35
13. Syracuse University, 35
14. University of Maryland, 33
15. University of California, Berkeley, 30

Source: Budd, John M., "Scholarly Productivity of U.S. LIS Faculty: An Update," *Library Quarterly*, 70: 230-245, (April 2000).

★2714★
Library and information science programs with the most journal articles per capita, 1993-1998

Ranking basis/background: Total number of per capita publications between 1993 and 1998. **Number listed:** 15.
1. University of Hawaii, with 8.67 publications
2. University of Tennessee, 6.00
3. University of Missouri, 5.86
4. University of Wisconsin, Milwaukee, 5.47
5. University of Indiana, 4.00
6. University of Illinois, 3.95
7. University of California, Berkeley, 3.90
8. University of California, Los Angeles, 3.84
9. University of North Carolina, 3.57
10. Simmons University, 3.55
11. University of Arizona, 3.40
12. Rutgers University, 2.79
13. University of Maryland, 2.60
14. University of Michigan, 2.32
15. University of North Texas, 2.29

Source: Budd, John M., "Scholarly Productivity of U.S. LIS Faculty: An Update," *Library Quarterly*, 70: 230-245, (April 2000).

★2715★
Library and information science programs with the most per capita citations to journal articles, 1993-1998

Ranking basis/background: Total number of per capita citations to journal articles published between 1993 and 1998. **Number listed:** 15.

1. University of California, Berkeley, with 157.66 per capita citations
2. Rutgers University, 76.80
3. University of California, Los Angeles, 74.96
4. University of Indiana, 65.94
5. University of Michigan, 55.90
6. University of Maryland, 42.99
7. University of North Carolina, 42.93
8. Simmons University, 40.07
9. University of Washington (WA), 39.43
10. University of Illinois, 36.05
11. University of Missouri, 35.71
12. Drexel University, 30.62
13. University of North Texas, 29.61
14. University of Tennessee, 28.95
15. University of Hawaii, 28.17

Source: Budd, John M., "Scholarly Productivity of U.S. LIS Faculty: An Update," *Library Quarterly*, 70: 230-245, (April 2000).

★2716★
Top recruiters for library science jobs for 2000-01 bachelor's degree recipients

Ranking basis/background: Projected number of college hires from on-campus recruitment for 2000-01. **Remarks:** Numbers reflect total expected hires, not just African American projected hires. **Number listed:** 1.
1. Accenture, with 25 projected hires

Source: "The Top 100 Employers and the Majors in Demand for the Class of 2001," *The Black Collegian*, 31: 19-35, (February 2001).

★2717★
Top recruiters for library science jobs for 2000-01 master's degree recipients

Ranking basis/background: Projected number of college hires from on-campus recruitment for 2000-01. **Remarks:** Numbers reflect total expected hires, not just African American projected hires. **Number listed:** 2.
1. Lucent Technologies, with 10 projected hires
2. Accenture, 5

Source: "The Top 100 Employers and the Majors in Demand for the Class of 2001," *The Black Collegian*, 31: 19-35, (February 2001).

★2718★
U.S. universities publishing the most papers in the field of library and information science, 1995-99

Ranking basis/background: Number of papers published in the field of library and information science over a five-year period, and percent of field based on each universities percentage of 9,077 papers entered in the ISI database from ISI-indexed library & information science journals. **Number listed:** 5.
1. Indiana University, with 160 papers; 1.76% of field
2. University of Illinois, Urbana-Champaign, 151; 1.66
3. Rutgers University, 96; 1.06%
4. University of North Carolina, Chapel Hill, 95; 1.05%
5. Pennsylvania State University, 93; 1.02%

Source: "Library & Information Science: Most Prolific U.S. Universities, 1995-99," *What's Hot in Research* (http://www.isinet.com/isi/hot/research) *Institute for Scientific Information*, December 18, 2000.

★2719★
U.S. universities with the greatest impact in library and information science, 1994-98

Ranking basis/background: Total number of library and information science papers published from each university and average number of citations per paper between 1994 and 1998. **Remarks:** Original source: University Science Indicators on Diskette, 1981-98. **Number listed:** 5.
1. Columbia University, with 50 library and information science papers; 6.30 citations per paper
2. University of Pittsburgh, 66; 2.88
3. Stanford University, 60; 2.45
4. Harvard University, 60; 1.90
5. University of North Carolina, Chapel Hill, 84; 1.89

Source: "Library & Information Science: High-Impact U.S. Universities, 1994-98," *What's Hot in Research* (http://www.isinet.com/hot/research) *Institute for Scientific Information*, April 3, 2000.

★2720★
Universities contributing the greatest number of papers to the field of library and information science

Ranking basis/background: Universities with the most papers in the field of library science between 1993 and 1997. Based on each university's percentage of the 9,309 papers in the ISI database. **Remarks:** Original source: University Science Indicators on Diskette, 1981-97. **Number listed:** 5.
1. Indiana University, with 146 papers (1.57% of field)
2. University of Illinois, Urbana-Champaign, 126 (1.35%)
3. Rutgers University, 119 (1.28%)
4. University of Michigan, 104 (1.12%)
5. University of North Carolina, Chapel Hill, 96 (1.03%)

Source: "Library & Information Science: Most Prolific U.S. Universities, 1993-97," *What's Hot in Research*, http://www.isinet.com/whatshot/whatshot.html, Institute for Scientific Information (April 26, 1999).

Related Information

★2721★
Bair, Jeffrey H. and Janice C. Barrons, "The Academic Elite in Library Science: Linkages Among Top-Ranked Graduate Programs," *College & Research Libraries*, May 1997, pp. 233-235.
  Remarks: Presents a 1996 *U.S. News & World Report* ranking of leading library science graduate programs and discusses the extent to which graduates of the top-ranked schools become employed by other schools within the top-ranked group.

★2722★
Gregory, Vicki L. and Sonia Ramirez Wohlmuth, "Better Pay, More Jobs," *Library Journal*, 125: 30-36, (October 15, 2000).
  Remarks: Reports and tables the status of library science graduates including salary and placement data.

LIBRARY SCIENCE PERIODICALS

★2723★
Authors that most frequently cite *Libri* publications from 1972 to 1999

Ranking basis/background: Number of citations. **Number listed:** 30.
1. D. Schmidmaier, with 11 citations
2. M.P. Satija, 9
2. W.A. Wiegand, 9
4. C.C. Aguolu, 7
4. D. Anderson, 7
6. B. Cronin, 6
6. E. Garfield, 6
6. S.J. Haider, 6
6. M.B. Line, 6
6. A. Schubert, 6

Source: Wormell, Irene, "Libri's Golden Jubilee in a Bibliometric Mirror," *Libri*, 50: 75-94, (June 2000).

★2724★
Information and library science journals by citation impact, 1981-99

Ranking basis/background: Impact factor calculated by taking the number of current citations to source items published and dividing it by the number of articles published in the journal during that time period. **Number listed:** 10.
1. *ACM Transactions on Office Information Systems*, with a 17.45 impact factor
2. *MIS Quarterly*, 15.28
3. *Information Technology R&D Applications*, 8.52
4. *Annual Review of Information Sciences*, 8.08
5. *Knowledge Acquisition*, 7.29
6. *Journal of Documentation*, 7.05
7. *Journal of American Society of Information Sciences*, 6.89
8. *International Journal of Geographical Information Systems*, 5.63
9. *Information Processing and Management*, 5.11
10. *Social Science Information Studies*, 4.50

Source: "Journals Ranked by Impact: Information & Library Science," *What's Hot in Research (http://www.isinet.com/isi/hot/research) Institute for Scientific Information*, September 25, 2000.

★2725★
Information and library science journals by citation impact, 1995-99

Ranking basis/background: Impact factor calculated by taking the number of current citations to source items published and dividing it by the number of articles published in the journal during that time period. **Number listed:** 10.
1. *Knowledge Acquisition*, with a 5.40 impact factor
2. *MIS Quarterly*, 3.65
3. *International Journal of Geographical Information Systems*, 3.42
4. *Journal of American Medical Informatics Association*, 3.34
5. *Information Systems Research*, 2.74
6. *Annual Review of Information Sciences*, 2.63
7. *Scientist*, 2.62
8. *Journal of Documentation*, 2.48
9. *Journal of American Society of Information Sciences*, 2.31
10. *Library Quarterly*, 1.95

Source: "Journals Ranked by Impact: Information & Library Science," *What's Hot in Research (http://www.isinet.com/isi/hot/research) Institute for Scientific Information*, September 25, 2000.

★2726★
Information and library science journals by citation impact, 1999

Ranking basis/background: Impact factor calculated by taking the number of current citations to source items published and dividing it by the number of articles published in the journal during that time period. **Number listed:** 10.
1. *Library and Information Science Research*, with a 3.17 impact factor
2. *Journal of American Medical Informatics Association*, 2.36
3. *Journal of Documentation*, 1.60
4. *Annual Review of Information Sciences*, 1.44
5. *Journal of American Society of Information Sciences*, 1.33
6. *MIS Quarterly*, 1.17
7. *Library Quarterly*, 1.08
8. *College and Research Libraries*, 1.06
9. *International Journal of Geographical Information Systems*, 0.94
10. *Scientometrics*, 0.93

Source: "Journals Ranked by Impact: Information & Library Science," *What's Hot in Research (http://www.isinet.com/isi/hot/research) Institute for Scientific Information*, September 25, 2000.

★2727★
Information and library science journals with the greatest impact measure, 1981-98

Ranking basis/background: Citations-per-paper impact score is the total citations to a journal's published papers divided by total number of papers the journal has published over an eighteen year period. **Remarks:** Original source: *Journal Citation Reports* and *Journal Performance Indicators on Diskette*. **Number listed:** 10.
1. *ACM Transactions on Office Information Systems*, with an impact score of 16.45
2. *MIS Quarterly*, 14.35
3. *IEEE Transcripts on Information Theory*, 9.13
4. *Information Technology R&D Applications*, 8.37
5. *Annual Review of Information Sciences*, 7.50
6. *Journal of Chemical Information and Computer Sciences*, 7.28
7. *Transaction on Information Systems*, 7.20
8. *Journal of Documentation*, 6.91
9. *Journal of American Society of Information Sciences*, 6.79
10. *Knowledge Acquisition*, 6.03

Source: "Journals Ranked by Impact: Information & Library Science," *What's Hot in Research (http://www.isinet.com/hot/research) Institute for Scientific Information*, August 2, 1999.

★2728★
Journal of the American Society for Information Science's best papers, by citations per year

Ranking basis/background: Ranked by number of citations received per year. **Number listed:** 5.
1. *A Study of Information Seeking and Retrieving, Parts I-III*, (May 1988)
2. *Variations in Relevance Assessments and the Measurements of Retrieval Effectiveness* (January 1996)
3. *Information Search Tactics*, (July 1979)
4. *Searchers' Selection of Search Keys* (August 1991)
5. *Information-Seeking Strategies of Novices Using a Full-Text Encyclopedia* (January 1989)

Source: Brooks, Terrence A., "How Good Are the Best Papers of JASIS?," *Journal of the American Society for Information Science*, 51: 485-486, (March 15, 2000).

★2729★
Journal of the American Society for Information Science's best papers, by total citations

Ranking basis/background: Ranked by total number of citations received. **Number listed:** 5.
1. *A Study of Information Seeking and Retrieving, Parts I-III* (May 1988)
2. *Information Search Tactics* (July 1979)
3. *On Selecting a Measure of Retrieval Effectiveness* (March-April 1973)
4. *An Experimental Comparison of the Effectiveness of Computers and Humans as Search Intermediaries* (November 1983)
5. *A Case-Based Model of Searching Behavior* (July 1984)

Source: Brooks, Terrence A., "How Good Are the Best Papers of JASIS?," *Journal of the American Society for Information Science*, 51: 485-486, (March 15, 2000).

★2730★
Most frequently cited *Libri* articles

Ranking basis/background: Publications most frequently included in the list of references of other publications published in all kinds of journals by number of citations received. **Number listed:** 23.
1. *Weeking the Collection: A Review of Research on Identifying Obsolete Stock*, by Carol A. Seymour (1972), with 27 citations
2. *The Subject Specialist in National and University Libraries with Special Reference to Book Selection*, J. Periam Danton (1967), 23
3. *PRECIS in a Multilingual Context*, Derek Austin (1967), 20
3. *Authorship Characteristics in Five International Library Journals*, Paschalis Raptis (1992), 20
5. *Subject Specialization in Three British University Libraries*, Peter Woodhead (1974), 18
5. *Bibliometrics: Its Theoretical Foundations, Methods and Applications*, S.M. Lawani (1981), 18
7. *Determining the Optimal Number of Volumes for a Library's Core Collection*, Richard W. Trueswell (1966), 16
8. *Portrait in Paradox: Commitment and Ambivalence in American Librarianship, 1876-1976*, Michael H. Harris (1976), 13
8. *Information and Information Science in Context*, Peter Ingwersen (1992), 13
10. *The Subject Specialist on the Academic Library Staff*, Ann Coppin (1974), 9

Source: Wormell, Irene, "Libri's Golden Jubilee in a Bibliometric Mirror," *Libri*, 50: 75-94, (June 2000).

LIFE SCIENCES
See: **Biological Sciences**

LINGUISTICS

★2731★
Language and linguistics journals with the greatest impact measure, 1981-98

Ranking basis/background: Citations-per-paper impact score is the total citations to a journal's published papers divided by total number of papers the journal has published over a five year period. **Remarks:** Original source: *Journal Citation Reports* and Journal Performance Indicators on Diskette. **Number listed:** 10.
1. *Journal of Verbal Learning and Behavior*, with an impact score of 46.17
2. *Journal of Memory and Language*, 21.11
3. *Brain and Language*, 13.78
4. *Linguistic Inquiry*, 13.48
5. *Journal of Speech and Hearing Disorders*, 12.82
6. *Language*, 11.20
7. *Journal of Speech and Hearing Research*, 10.28
8. *Journal of Child Language*, 9.32
9. *Applied Psycholinguistics*, 8.01
10. *Natural Language & Linguistics Theory*, 7.47

Source: "Journals Ranked by Impact: Language & Linguistics," *What's Hot in Research* (http://www.isinet.com/hot/research) Institute for Scientific Information, August 23, 1999.

LINGUISTICS, GRADUATE

★2732★
Most effective linguistics research-doctorate programs as evaluated by the National Research Council

Ranking basis/background: From a survey of nearly 8,000 faculty members conducted in the spring of 1993. Respondents were asked to rate programs in their field on "effectiveness of program in educating research scholars/scientists." **Remarks:** See *Chronicle* article for more details. Scores of 3.5-5.0 indicate "extremely effective;" 2.5-3.49 "reasonably effective;" 1.5-2.49 "minimally effective;" and 0.0-1.49 "not effective." Programs also ranked by "scholarly quality of program faculty." **Number listed:** 41.
1. University of Massachusetts, Amherst, with an effectiveness rating of 4.44
2. Massachusetts Institute of Technology, 4.39
3. University of California, Los Angeles, 4.17
4. Stanford University, 4.01
5. Cornell University, 3.89
6. University of California, Santa Cruz, 3.80
7. University of Arizona, 3.51
8. University of Connecticut, 3.51
9. University of Pennsylvania, 3.68
10. University of Chicago, 3.64

Source: "Rankings of Research-Doctorate Programs in 41 Disciplines at 274 Institutions," *The Chronicle of Higher Education* 42: A21-A30 (September 21, 1995).

★2733★
Top linguistics research-doctorate programs as evaluated by the National Research Council

Ranking basis/background: From a survey of nearly 8,000 faculty members conducted in the spring of 1993. Respondents were asked to rate programs in their field on "scholarly quality of program faculty." When more than one program had the samescore, the council averaged the rank order and gave each program the same rank number (if three programs tied for the top position, each received a rank of 2). **Remarks:** See *Chronicle* article for more details. Scores of 4.01 and above indicate "distinguished;" 3.0-4.0 "strong;" 2.51-3.0 "good;" 2.0-2.5 "adequate;" 1.0-1.99 "marginal;" and 0.0-0.99 "not sufficient for doctoral education." Programs also ranked by "effectiveness of program in educating research scholars/scientists." **Number listed:** 41.
1. Massachusetts Institute of Technology, with a quality rating of 4.79
2. Stanford University, 4.59
3. University of California, Los Angeles, 4.56
4. University of Massachusetts, Amherst, 4.44
5. University of Pennsylvania, 4.16
6. University of Chicago, 3.97
6. University of California, Berkeley, 3.97
8. Ohio State University, 3.80
9. Cornell University, 3.78
10. University of California, Santa Cruz, 3.66
11. University of Texas, Austin, 3.61
12. University of Southern California, 3.58
12. University of Arizona, 3.58
14. University of California, San Diego, 3.43
15. City University of New York, Graduate School and University Center, 3.41

Source: "Rankings of Research-Doctorate Programs in 41 Disciplines at 274 Institutions," *The Chronicle of Higher Education* 42: A21-A30 (September 21, 1995).

LITERACY

★2734★
U.S. universities with the highest concentration of papers published in the field of literary studies, 1994-98

Ranking basis/background: Number of papers published in the field of literary studies over a five-year period, and percentage they comprise of the university's total papers published. **Number listed:** 5.
1. City University of New York, with 172 papers; 2.42% of university's total papers
2. Brandeis University, 35; 2.01%
3. University of New Hampshire, 33; 1.82%
4. Loyola University, 55; 1.65%
5. University of California, Riverside, 63; 1.59%

Source: "Literary Studies: High-Concentration U.S. Universities, 1994-98," *What's Hot in Research* (http://www.isinet.com/isi/hot/research) Institute for Scientific Information, June 26, 2000.

LITERARY CRITICISM

★2735★
U.S. universities with the highest concentrations in literary criticism, 1992-96

Ranking basis/background: Percent literature papers represent of university's total papers. Also includes number of literature papers, 1992-96. **Remarks:** Original source: ISI's *University Science Indicators on Diskette, 1981-97*. **Number listed:** 5.
1. City University of New York, with 2.80%; 212 literature papers
2. University of New Hampshire, 2.37%; 40
3. University of California, Riverside, 1.86%; 70
4. University of Oregon, 1.82%; 51
5. Indiana University, 1.75%; 195

Source: "U.S. Universities with Highest Concentrations in Literary Criticism, 1992-96," *What's Hot*, April 13, 1998.

LOAN REPAYMENT

★2736★
Historically black colleges and universities with high student loan default rates, 1998

Ranking basis/background: Default rates, by percentage. **Remarks:** Original source: U.S. Department of Education. **Number listed:** 4.
1. Texas College, with 38.2%
2. Southwestern Christian College, 34.6%
3. Barber-Scotia College, 33.9%
4. Livingston College, 33.5%

Source: "HBCUs Making Major Progress in Curbing Loan Defaults," *Black Issues in Higher Education*, 17: 8-9, (November 9, 2000).

★2737★
Historically black colleges and universities with major improvements in student loan default rates, 1998

Ranking basis/background: Default rates, by percentage. **Remarks:** Original source: U.S. Department of Education. **Number listed:** 8.
1. Paul Quinn College, with 23.6%
2. Miles College, 21.8%
3. Allen University, 21.5%
4. Huston-Tillotson College, 20.3%
5. Central State University, 16.5%
6. Mary Holmes College, 17.7%
7. Lane College, 17.0%
8. Texas Southern University, 15.7%

Source: "HBCUs Making Major Progress in Curbing Loan Defaults," *Black Issues in Higher Education*, 17: 8-9, (November 9, 2000).

MACROECONOMICS
See: **Economics**

MANAGEMENT COURSES (CREDIT)
See: **Business Administration**

MANAGEMENT INFORMATION SYSTEMS

★2738★
Top recruiters for information technology (MIS) jobs for 2000-01 bachelor's degree recipients

Ranking basis/background: Projected number of college hires from on-campus recruitment for 2000-01. **Remarks:** Numbers reflect total expected hires, not just African American projected hires. **Number listed:** 45.
1. EDS, with 1,000 projected hires
2. Accenture, 650
3. Deloitte & Touche, 225
4. Footstar, 220
5. Arthur Andersen LLP, 205
6. Lucent Technologies, 150
7. Cap Gemini Ernst & Young, 100
8. American Management Systems, 85
9. Principal Financial Group, 60
10. Houghton Mifflin, 50
10. Caterpillar Inc., 50

Source: "The Top 100 Employers and the Majors in Demand for the Class of 2001," *The Black Collegian*, 31: 19-35, (February 2001).

★2739★
Top recruiters for information technology (MIS) jobs for 2000-01 master's degree recipients

Ranking basis/background: Projected number of college hires from on-campus recruitment for 2000-01. **Remarks:** Numbers reflect total expected hires, not just African American projected hires. **Number listed:** 45.
1. Lucent Technologies, with 150 projected hires
2. EDS, 100
3. Accenture, 50
4. Deloitte & Touche, 38
5. Agilent Technologies, 35
6. Footstar, 30
7. Arthur Andersen LLP, 31
8. Houghton Mifflin, 30
9. Tellabs, 15
10. ALLTEL, 10

Source: "The Top 100 Employers and the Majors in Demand for the Class of 2001," *The Black Collegian*, 31: 19-35, (February 2001).

MANAGEMENT SCIENCE
See: **Business Administration**

MARKETING
See: **Business Administration, Graduate–Marketing Business Administration–Marketing**

MASS MEDIA

★2740★
Areas of specialization in journalism and mass communications programs with the highest enrollment, 1999

Ranking basis/background: Number of student enrolled. Figures are based on the annual enrollment survey conducted by the University of Georgia, in the Henry W. Grady College of Journalism and Mass Communication. **Number listed:** 20.
1. Public relations, with 3,337 students enrolled
2. Advertising, 2,820
3. Broadcast news, 2,287
4. News editorial, 2,140
5. RTV/telecommunications, 1,973
6. Journalism, 1,385
7. Public relations/advertising combined, 1,004
8. Mass communications, 788
9. Speech, 547
10. Organizational communication, 531

Source: Becker, Lee B., et. al., "Undergrad Enrollments Level Off, Graduate Education Declines," *Journalism & Mass Communication Educator*, 55: 68-80, (Autumn).

★2741★
Bachelor's degrees granted in journalism and mass communications programs, by gender, 1999

Ranking basis/background: Number of degrees granted. Figures are based on the annual enrollment survey conducted by the University of Georgia, in the Henry W. Grady College of Journalism and Mass Communication. **Number listed:** 2.
1. Women, with 13,131
2. Men, 7,500

Source: Becker, Lee B., et. al., "Undergrad Enrollments Level Off, Graduate Education Declines," *Journalism & Mass Communication Educator*, 55: 68-80, (Autumn).

★2742★
Bachelor's degrees granted in journalism and mass communications programs, by race/ethnicity, 1999

Ranking basis/background: Number of degrees granted. Figures are based on the annual enrollment survey conducted by the University of Georgia, in the Henry W. Grady College of Journalism and Mass Communication. **Number listed:** 7.
   African American, with 1,360 degrees granted
   Hispanic American, 793
   Asian American, 393
   Native American, 178
   White, 10,083
   Other, 150
   Foreign, 280

Source: Becker, Lee B., et. al., "Undergrad Enrollments Level Off, Graduate Education Declines," *Journalism & Mass Communication Educator*, 55: 68-80, (Autumn).

★2743★
Bachelor's enrollment in journalism and mass communications programs, by gender, 1999

Ranking basis/background: Number of students enrolled. Figures are based on the annual enrollment survey conducted by the University of Georgia, in the Henry W. Grady College of Journalism and Mass Communication. **Number listed:** 2.
1. Women, with 54,118
2. Men, 33,735

Source: Becker, Lee B., et. al., "Undergrad Enrollments Level Off, Graduate Education Declines," *Journalism & Mass Communication Educator*, 55: 68-80, (Autumn).

★2744★
Bachelor's enrollments in journalism and mass communications programs, by race/ethnicity, 1999

Ranking basis/background: Number of students enrolled. Figures are based on the annual enrollment survey conducted by the University of Georgia, in the Henry W. Grady College of Journalism and Mass Communication. **Number listed:** 7.
   African American, with 8,239 students enrolled
   Hispanic American, 5,070
   Asian American, 1,673
   Native American, 533
   White, 49,329
   Other, 1,084
   Foreign, 1,133

Source: Becker, Lee B., et. al., "Undergrad Enrollments Level Off, Graduate Education Declines," *Journalism & Mass Communication Educator*, 55: 68-80, (Autumn).

★2745★
Degrees granted in the ten largest undergraduate journalism and mass communications programs, 1999

Ranking basis/background: Number of degrees granted during the 1998-99 academic year. Figures are based on the annual enrollment survey conducted by the University of Georgia, in the Henry W. Grady College of Journalism and Mass Communication. **Number listed:** 10.
1. University of Florida, with 668 degrees granted
2. Boston University, 582
3. Pennsylvania State University, 572
4. California State University, Fullerton, 555
5. Ohio State University, 410
6. University of Central Florida, 407
7. Middle Tennessee State University, 383
8. Syracuse University, 381
9. Ithaca College, 364
10. University of Georgia, 349

Source: Becker, Lee B., et. al., "Undergrad Enrollments Level Off, Graduate Education Declines," *Journalism & Mass Communication Educator*, 55: 68-80, (Autumn).

★2746★
Enrollment of students in the ten largest undergraduate journalism and mass communications programs, 1999

Ranking basis/background: Number of students enrolled in Autumn of 1999. Figures are based on the annual enrollment survey conducted by the University of Georgia, in the Henry W. Grady College of Journalism and Mass Communication. **Number listed:** 10.

1. Pennsylvania State University, with 2,919 undergraduate enrolled
2. Middle Tennessee State University, 2,794
3. University of Florida, 2,695
4. California State University, Fullerton, 2,040
5. Boston University, 1,914
6. University of Sacred Heart (PR), 1,773
7. Ball State University, 1,727
8. Syracuse University, 1,660
9. University of Alabama, 1,453
10. Towson State University, 1,352

Source: Becker, Lee B., et. al., "Undergrad Enrollments Level Off, Graduate Education Declines," *Journalism & Mass Communication Educator*, 55: 68-80, (Autumn).

★2747★
Highest ranked active communication studies researchers

Ranking basis/background: Most prolific researchers in communications studies. **Number listed:** 100.
1. J. McCroskey, University of West Virginia
2. M. Beatty, University of Missouri, St. Louis
3. J. Burgoon, University of Arizona
4. D. Infante, Kent State University
5. V. Richmond, University of West Virginia
6. B. Greenberg, Michigan State University
7. M. Burgoon, University of Arizona
8. J. Ayres, Washington State University
9. S. Becker, University of Iowa
10. L. Rosenfeld, University of North Carolina

Source: Hickson III, Mark, Don W. Stacks and Jean Bodon, "The Status of Research Productivity in Communication, 1915-1995," *Communication Monographs*, 66: 178-197, (June 1999).

★2748★
Highest ranked inactive communication studies researchers

Ranking basis/background: Most prolific researchers in communications studies. **Number listed:** 26.
1. G. Miller, Michigan State University
2. L. Crocker, Denison University
3. L. Barker, Auburn University
4. W. Braden, Louisiana State University
5. T. Clevenger, Florida State University
6. G. Phillips, Penn State University
7. R. Oliver, Penn State University
8. W. Thompson, University of Houston
9. P. Gillespie, University of Maryland
10. J. Black, Ohio State University

Source: Hickson III, Mark, Don W. Stacks and Jean Bodon, "The Status of Research Productivity in Communication, 1915-1995," *Communication Monographs*, 66: 178-197, (June 1999).

★2749★
Institutions with the most prolific communication studies researchers

Ranking basis/background: Number of cites per top 100 faculty. **Number listed:** 25.
1. West Virginia University, with 206
2. Kent State University, 145
3. University of Texas, 133
4. University of Georgia, 111
5. University of Arizona, 102
6. Purdue University, 95
6. University of Wisconsin, 95
8. California State University, Long Beach, 78
9. Michigan State University, 71
10. University of California, Davis, 70
10. University of California, Santa Barbara, 70
10. University of Indiana, 70

Source: Hickson III, Mark, Don W. Stacks and Jean Bodon, "The Status of Research Productivity in Communication, 1915-1995," *Communication Monographs*, 66: 178-197, (June 1999).

★2750★
Magazines with the largest circulation

Ranking basis/background: Total average paid circulation during the 6 months ending December 31, 1999. **Remarks:** Original source: Audit Bureau of Circulations, Schaumburg, IL. **Number listed:** 100.
1. *Reader's Digest*, with a circulation of 12,556,410
2. *TV Guide*, 11,116,180
3. *National Geographic Magazine*, 8,514,274
4. *Better Homes and Gardens*, 7,611,023
5. *Family Circle*, 5,002,875
6. *Good Housekeeping*, 4,549,975
7. *Ladies' Home Journal*, 4,525,455
8. *Woman's Day*, 4,280,909
9. *McCall's*, 4,208,988
10. *Time*, 4,122,699

Source: *The World Almanac and Book of Facts 2001*, World Almanac Books, 2001.

★2751★
Radcliffe Institute for Advanced Study fellowship recipient in the field of film making, 2000-01

Ranking basis/background: Recipient and institutional affiliation of the Radcliffe Institute for Advanced study fellowship for pursuit of advanced work across a wide range of academic disciplines, professions, and creative arts. **Number listed:** 1.
  Charlene Gilbert, State University of New York, Buffalo

Source: "The Radcliffe Institute for Advanced Study," *The Chronicle of Higher Education*, 46: A59, (June 2, 2000).

★2752★
Sources of new faculty members in journalism and mass communications programs, 1999-2000

Ranking basis/background: Percentage of new faculty hired from each area, estimated for 1999-2000. **Number listed:** 5.
  Hired from industry or from other universities, with 73.8%
  Hired from doctoral program with Ph.D., 49.6%
  Hired from doctoral program ABD, 33.6%
  Hired directly from graduate school, 26.2%
  Hired from master's program, 16.8%

Source: Becker, Lee B., et. al., "Undergrad Enrollments Level Off, Graduate Education Declines," *Journalism & Mass Communication Educator*, 55: 68-80, (Autumn).

★2753★
Total degrees granted in journalism and mass communications programs, 1998-99

Ranking basis/background: Total degrees granted as reported by schools. Also includes the number of schools reporting at each level. Figures are based on the annual enrollment survey conducted by the University of Georgia, in the Henry W. Grady College of Journalism and Mass Communication. **Number listed:** 3.
  Undergraduate, with 408 schools reporting; 31,778 degrees granted
  Master's, 431; 2,776
  Doctoral, 451; 177

Source: Becker, Lee B., et. al., "Undergrad Enrollments Level Off, Graduate Education Declines," *Journalism & Mass Communication Educator*, 55: 68-80, (Autumn).

★2754★
Undergraduate enrollment in journalism and mass communications programs by grade level, 1999

Ranking basis/background: Actual enrollment count reported by schools. Also includes the number of schools reporting at each level. Figures are based on the annual enrollment survey conducted by the University of Georgia, in the Henry W. Grady College of Journalism and Mass Communication. **Number listed:** 4.
  Freshmen, with 276 schools reporting; 22,180 student enrolled
  Sophomores, 279; 21,466
  Juniors, 281; 29,178
  Seniors, 281; 30,570

Source: Becker, Lee B., et. al., "Undergrad Enrollments Level Off, Graduate Education Declines," *Journalism & Mass Communication Educator*, 55: 68-80, (Autumn).

★2755★
U.S. universities publishing the most papers in the field of communication, 1994-98

Ranking basis/background: Total number of papers published from each university. **Remarks:** Original source: University Science Indicators on Diskette, 1981-97. **Number listed:** 6.
1. University of Wisconsin, Madison, with 119 papers
2. Indiana University, 75
2. Michigan State University, 75
4. University of Texas, Austin, 69
5. University of Minnesota, 68
6. University of Georgia, 64

Source: "Communication: Prolific U.S. Universities, 1994-98," *What's Hot in Research (http://www.isinet.com/hot/research) Institute for Scientific Information*, February 14, 2000.

MASS MEDIA, GRADUATE

★2756★
Degrees granted in the ten largest doctoral journalism and mass communications programs, 1999

Ranking basis/background: Number of degrees granted during the 1998-99 academic year. Figures are based on the annual enrollment survey conducted by the University of Georgia, in the Henry W. Grady College of Journalism and Mass Communication. **Number listed:** 12.
1. Ohio State University, with 14 doctorates granted
2. University of Alabama, 10
2. University of Wisconsin, Madison, 10
2. University of Utah, 10
2. Howard University, 10
6. University of Colorado, 8
6. University of Florida, 8
6. University of Georgia, 8
9. University of Tennessee, 7
9. Indiana University, 7
9. University of North Carolina, 7

9. University of Texas, Austin, 7

Source: Becker, Lee B., et. al., "Undergrad Enrollments Level Off, Graduate Education Declines," *Journalism & Mass Communication Educator,* 55: 68-80, (Autumn).

★2757★
Degrees granted in the ten largest master's journalism and mass communications programs, 1999

Ranking basis/background: Number of degrees granted during the 1998-99 academic year. Figures are based on the annual enrollment survey conducted by the University of Georgia, in the Henry W. Grady College of Journalism and Mass Communication. **Number listed:** 10.

1. Columbia University, with 255 degrees granted
2. Boston University, 158
3. Syracuse University, 132
4. Ball State University, 131
5. Virginia Commonwealth University, 112
6. Northwestern University, 100
7. Roosevelt University, 82
8. University of Colorado, 46
9. University of Florida, 43
9. University of Missouri, 43

Source: Becker, Lee B., et. al., "Undergrad Enrollments Level Off, Graduate Education Declines," *Journalism & Mass Communication Educator,* 55: 68-80, (Autumn).

★2758★
Doctoral degrees granted in journalism and mass communications programs, by gender, 1999

Ranking basis/background: Number of degrees granted. Figures are based on the annual enrollment survey conducted by the University of Georgia, in the Henry W. Grady College of Journalism and Mass Communication. **Number listed:** 2.

1. Women, 83
2. Men, 85

Source: Becker, Lee B., et. al., "Undergrad Enrollments Level Off, Graduate Education Declines," *Journalism & Mass Communication Educator,* 55: 68-80, (Autumn).

★2759★
Doctoral degrees granted in journalism and mass communications programs, by race/ethnicity, 1999

Ranking basis/background: Number of degrees granted. Figures are based on the annual enrollment survey conducted by the University of Georgia, in the Henry W. Grady College of Journalism and Mass Communication. **Number listed:** 7.

African American, with 16 doctorates granted
Hispanic American, 3
Asian American, 5
Native American, 2
White, 90
Other, 3
Foreign, 30

Source: Becker, Lee B., et. al., "Undergrad Enrollments Level Off, Graduate Education Declines," *Journalism & Mass Communication Educator,* 55: 68-80, (Autumn).

★2760★
Doctoral enrollment in journalism and mass communications programs, by gender, 1999

Ranking basis/background: Number of students enrolled. Figures are based on the annual enrollment survey conducted by the University of Georgia, in the Henry W. Grady College of Journalism and Mass Communication. **Number listed:** 2.

1. Women, with 525
2. Men, 411

Source: Becker, Lee B., et. al., "Undergrad Enrollments Level Off, Graduate Education Declines," *Journalism & Mass Communication Educator,* 55: 68-80, (Autumn).

★2761★
Doctoral enrollments in journalism and mass communications programs, by race/ethnicity, 1999

Ranking basis/background: Number of students enrolled. Figures are based on the annual enrollment survey conducted by the University of Georgia, in the Henry W. Grady College of Journalism and Mass Communication. **Number listed:** 7.

African American, with 46 students enrolled
Hispanic American, 12
Asian American, 54
Native American, 6
White, 449
Other, 18
Foreign, 175

Source: Becker, Lee B., et. al., "Undergrad Enrollments Level Off, Graduate Education Declines," *Journalism & Mass Communication Educator,* 55: 68-80, (Autumn).

★2762★
Enrollment of students in the ten largest doctoral journalism and mass communications programs, 1999

Ranking basis/background: Number of students enrolled in Autumn of 1999. Figures are based on the annual enrollment survey conducted by the University of Georgia, in the Henry W. Grady College of Journalism and Mass Communication. **Number listed:** 11.

1. Howard University, with 78 doctoral students enrolled
2. University of Utah, 67
3. University of North Carolina, 60
4. University of Wisconsin, Madison, 56
5. University of Florida, 50
5. University of Southern Mississippi, 50
7. Purdue University, 45
8. University of Minnesota, 43
8. Pennsylvania State University, 43
10. University of Iowa, 42
10. Southern Illinois University, 42

Source: Becker, Lee B., et. al., "Undergrad Enrollments Level Off, Graduate Education Declines," *Journalism & Mass Communication Educator,* 55: 68-80, (Autumn).

★2763★
Enrollment of students in the ten largest master's journalism and mass communications programs, 1999

Ranking basis/background: Number of students enrolled in Autumn of 1999. Figures are based on the annual enrollment survey conducted by the University of Georgia, in the Henry W. Grady College of Journalism and Mass Communication. **Number listed:** 10.

1. Boston University, with 371 master's student enrolled
2. American University, 329
3. Columbia University, 299
4. Northwestern University, 268
5. Syracuse University, 248
6. Roosevelt University, 242
7. Ball State University, 224
8. New York University, 200
9. University of Missouri, 175
10. University of Florida, 156

Source: Becker, Lee B., et. al., "Undergrad Enrollments Level Off, Graduate Education Declines," *Journalism & Mass Communication Educator,* 55: 68-80, (Autumn).

★2764★
Graduate enrollment in journalism and mass communications programs by degree level, 1999

Ranking basis/background: Actual enrollment count reported by schools. Also includes the number of schools reporting at each level. Figures are based on the annual enrollment survey conducted by the University of Georgia, in the Henry W. Grady College of Journalism and Mass Communication. **Number listed:** 2.

Master's, with 446 schools reporting; 10,041 students enrolled
Doctoral, 451; 1,121

Source: Becker, Lee B., et. al., "Undergrad Enrollments Level Off, Graduate Education Declines," *Journalism & Mass Communication Educator,* 55: 68-80, (Autumn).

★2765★
Master's degrees granted in journalism and mass communications programs, by gender, 1999

Ranking basis/background: Number of degrees granted. Figures are based on the annual enrollment survey conducted by the University of Georgia, in the Henry W. Grady College of Journalism and Mass Communication. **Number listed:** 2.

1. Women, 1,283
2. Men, 749

Source: Becker, Lee B., et. al., "Undergrad Enrollments Level Off, Graduate Education Declines," *Journalism & Mass Communication Educator,* 55: 68-80, (Autumn).

★2766★
Master's degrees granted in journalism and mass communications programs, by race/ethnicity, 1999

Ranking basis/background: Number of degrees granted. Figures are based on the annual enrollment survey conducted by the University of Georgia, in the Henry W. Grady College of Journalism and Mass Communication. **Number listed:** 7.

African American, with 133 degrees granted
Hispanic American, 59
Asian American, 90

Native American, 11
White, 1,091
Other, 57
Foreign, 272

Source: Becker, Lee B., et. al., "Undergrad Enrollments Level Off, Graduate Education Declines," *Journalism & Mass Communication Educator*, 55: 68-80, (Autumn).

★2767★
Master's enrollment in journalism and mass communications programs, by gender, 1999

Ranking basis/background: Number of students enrolled. Figures are based on the annual enrollment survey conducted by the University of Georgia, in the Henry W. Grady College of Journalism and Mass Communication. **Number listed:** 2.

1. Women, with 3,439
2. Men, 1,987

Source: Becker, Lee B., et. al., "Undergrad Enrollments Level Off, Graduate Education Declines," *Journalism & Mass Communication Educator*, 55: 68-80, (Autumn).

★2768★
Master's enrollments in journalism and mass communications programs, by race/ethnicity, 1999

Ranking basis/background: Number of students enrolled. Figures are based on the annual enrollment survey conducted by the University of Georgia, in the Henry W. Grady College of Journalism and Mass Communication. **Number listed:** 7.

African American, with 399 students enrolled
Hispanic American, 259
Asian American, 167
Native American, 13
White, 2,977
Other, 109
Foreign, 708

Source: Becker, Lee B., et. al., "Undergrad Enrollments Level Off, Graduate Education Declines," *Journalism & Mass Communication Educator*, 55: 68-80, (Autumn).

MASS MEDIA–JOURNALISM

★2769★
Best U.S. works of journalism in the 20th century

Ranking basis/background: Selected by the New York University Journalism faculty and 17 other panelists. **Number listed:** 100.

1. John Hersey, "Hiroshima," entire issue of *The New Yorker* (1946)
2. Rachel Carson, "Silent Spring," book (1962)
3. Bob Woodward and Carl Bernstein, Watergate investigations for the *Washington Post* (1972-73)
4. Edward R. Murrow, "This is London..." radio reports for CBS on the German bombing of London (1940)
5. Ida Tarbell, "The History of the Standard Oil Company," investigation in *McClure*'s magazine (1902-1904)
6. Lincoln Steffens, "The Shame of the Cities," investigation in *McClure*'s magazine (1902-1904)
7. John Reed, "Ten Days That Shook the World," book (1919)
8. H.L. Mencken, coverage of the Scopes "monkey" trial in the *Baltimore Sun* (1925)
9. Ernie Pyle, reports from Europe and the Pacific during World War II for the Scripps-Howard newspapers (1940-45)
10. Edward R. Murrow and Fred Friendly, See It Now CBS television documentary taking on Senator Joseph McCarthy (1954)
11. Edward R. Murrow, David Lowe and Fred Friendly, CBS Reports television documentary "Harvest of Shame" (1960)
12. Seymour Hersh, investigation of massacre committed by American soldiers at My Lai in Vietnam for Dispatch News Services (1969)
13. New York Times, publication of the Pentagon Papers (1971)
14. James Agee and Walker Evans, "Let Us Now Praise Famous Men," book (1941)
15. W.E.B. DuBois, "The Souls of Black Folk," collected articles (1903)
16. I.F. Stone, I.F. Stone's Weekly (1953-67)
17. Henry Hampton, "Eyes on the Prize," documentary (1987)
18. Tom Wolfe, "The Electric Kool-Aid Acid Test," book (1968)
19. Norman Mailer, "The Armies of the Night," book (1968)
20. Hannah Arendt, "Eichmann in Jerusalem: A Report on the Banality of Evil," collected articles (1963)
21. William Shirer, "Berlin Dairy: The Journal of a Foreign Correspondent, 1939-1941," book (1941)
22. Truman Capote, "In Cold Blood: A True Account of a Multiple Murder and Its Consequences," book (1965)
23. Joan Didion, "Slouching Towards Bethlehem," collected articles (1968)
24. Tom Wolfe, "The Kandy-Kolored Tangerine-Flake Streamline Baby," collected articles (1965)
25. Michael Herr, "Dispatches," book (1977)

Source: "The Top 100 Works of Journalism in the United States in the 20th Century," http://www.nyu.edu/gsas/dept/journal/Dept-news/News-stories/990301-topjourn.htm.

★2770★
Top editorial cartoonists used in teaching journalism history

Ranking basis/background: Subjective list of cartoonists considered to have made an outstanding contribution to American journalism. **Number listed:** 10.

Thomas Nast (1840-1902)
Joseph Keppler (1838-94)
Clifford Berryman (1869-1949)
Rollin Kirby (1875-1952)
J. Norwood "Ding" Darling (1876-1962)
Daniel R. Fitzpatrick (1881-1969)
Edmund Duffy (1899-1962)
Herbert (Herblock) Block (1909-)
Bill Mauldin (1921-)
Pat Oliphant (1935-)

Source: Harrison, S.L., "Cartoons as a Teaching Tool in Journalism History," *Journalism & Mass Communication Educator*, pp. 95-101, (Spring 1998).

MATERIALS/METALLURGICAL ENGINEERING
See: **Engineering, Graduate–Materials/Metallurgical Engineering–Materials/Metallurgical**

MATHEMATICAL ACT OR SAT SCORES
See: **College Entrance Examinations**

MATHEMATICS

★2771★
Top recruiters for math/actuarial science jobs for 2000-01 bachelor's degree recipients

Ranking basis/background: Projected number of college hires from on-campus recruitment for 2000-01. **Remarks:** Numbers reflect total expected hires, not just African American projected hires. **Number listed:** 13.

1. Deloitte & Touche, with 95 projected hires
2. Accenture, 65
3. Lucent Technologies, 50
4. American Management Systems, 45
5. U.S. Air Force (Active Duty Hires), 20
6. State Farm Insurance Company, 18
7. Cigna, 15
8. Principal Financial Group, 10
8. Houghton Mifflin, 10
8. Federal Deposit Insurance Company, 10
8. Caddo Parish School Board, 10
12. Arthur Andersen LLP, 9
13. Henrico County Public Schools, 8

Source: "The Top 100 Employers and the Majors in Demand for the Class of 2001," *The Black Collegian*, 31: 19-35, (February 2001).

★2772★
U.S. universities with the greatest impact in mathematics, 1995-99

Ranking basis/background: Average citations per paper from the top 100 federally funded U.S. universities that had at least 50 published papers in ISI indexed mathematics journals. Also includes total number of papers published during the five year period. **Number listed:** 5.

1. Harvard University, with 357 papers; 3.73 citations per paper
2. Stanford University, 398; 3.59
3. University of Minnesota, 461; 2.87
4. New York University, 338; 2.68
5. Cornell University, 419; 2.47

Source: "Mathematics: High Impact U.S. Universities, 1995-99," *What's Hot in Research* (http://www.isinet.com/isi/hot/research) *Institute for Scientific Information*, October 2, 2000.

MATHEMATICS ACHIEVEMENT

★2773★
Eighth grade mathematics achievement scores from selected countries, 1999

Ranking basis/background: Average achievement score received for each country from results of the Third International Mathematics and Science Study. International average score is 487. **Number listed:** 28.

1. Singapore, with 604
2. South Korea, 587
3. Taiwan, 585
4. Japan, 579
5. Netherlands, 540
6. Hungary, 532
7. Canada, 531
8. Russia, 526
9. Australia, 525
10. Finland, 520
10. Czech Republic, 520
12. Bulgaria, 511
13. United States, 502
14. England, 496
15. New Zealand, 491
16. Lithuania, 482
17. Italy, 479
18. Romania, 472
19. Thailand, 467
20. Israel, 466
21. Tunisia, 448
22. Turkey, 429
23. Jordan, 428
24. Iran, 422
25. Indonesia, 403
26. Chile, 392
27. Philippines, 345
28. South Africa, 275

Source: Holden, Constance, "Asia Stays on Top, U.S. in Middle in New Global Rankings," *Science*, 290: 6, (December 8, 2000).

MATHEMATICS, GRADUATE

★2774★
Australian universities with the greatest impact in mathematics, 1993-97

Ranking basis/background: For each university, total number of citations divided by number of published articles during the same time period. **Remarks:** Original source: *National Science Indicators on Diskette, 1981-97* **Number listed:** 5.

1. University of Melbourne, with 24.16 citations per paper; 213 total papers
2. University of Queensland, 13.86; 112
3. Monash University, 11.42; 96
4. Institute of Advanced Studies, 8.12; 269
5. La Trobe University, 7.72; 87

Source: "Australia: High-Impact Universities in Mathematics, 1993-97," *What's Hot*, November 9, 1998.

★2775★
Most effective mathematics research-doctorate programs as evaluated by the National Research Council

Ranking basis/background: From a survey of nearly 8,000 faculty members conducted in the spring of 1993. Respondents were asked to rate programs in their field on "effectiveness of program in educating research scholars/scientists." **Remarks:** See *Chronicle* article for more details. Scores of 3.5-5.0 indicate "extremely effective;" 2.5-3.49 "reasonably effective;" 1.5-2.49 "minimally effective;" and 0.0-1.49 "not effective." Programs also ranked by "scholarly quality of program faculty." **Number listed:** 139.

1. Princeton University, with an effectiveness rating of 4.37
2. University of Chicago, 4.64
3. Harvard University, 4.58
4. Massachusetts Institute of Technology, 4.57
5. Stanford University, 4.41
6. University of California, Berkeley, 4.37
7. New York University, 4.26
8. Yale University, 4.11
9. Brown University Program in Applied Mathematics, 4.06
10. Cornell University, 3.96

Source: "Rankings of Research-Doctorate Programs in 41 Disciplines at 274 Institutions," *The Chronicle of Higher Education* 42: A21-A30 (September 21, 1995).

★2776★
Private, 4-year undergraduate colleges and universities producing the most Ph.D.'s in mathematics, 1920-1990

Ranking basis/background: Number of doctoral degrees granted to graduates of 914 private 4-year U.S. undergraduate colleges and universities. Medical, law, and other professional, non-doctoral degrees are not included. **Remarks:** Original source: Office of Scientific and Engineering Personnel of the National Research Council. Report contains 50 other tables detailing the distribution of doctoral recipients by field of study over various time frames. **Number listed:** 313.

1. Oberlin College, with 134 Ph.D.'s
2. Reed College, 125
3. Swarthmore College, 116
4. Polytechnic University, 86
4. Pomona College, 86
6. Harvey Mudd College, 71
7. Carleton College, 68
7. University of Dayton, 68
9. Haverford College, 54
10. Bucknell University, 50
10. Amherst College, 50
12. Wesleyan University, 49
13. College of the Holy Cross, 48
14. Cooper Union, 46
15. Stevens Institute of Technology, 45
16. Knox College, 44
16. Davidson College, 44
18. Manhattan College, 43
18. Union College, 43
20. St. Olaf College, 42

Source: *Baccalaureate Origins of Doctorate Recipients, 7th ed.*, Franklin & Marshall College, March 1993.

★2777★
Private, 4-year undergraduate colleges and universities producing the most Ph.D.'s in mathematics, 1981-1990

Ranking basis/background: Number of doctoral degrees granted to graduates of 914 private, 4-year U.S. undergraduate colleges and universities. Medical, law, and other professional, non-doctoral degrees are not included. **Remarks:** Original source: Office of Scientific and Engineering Personnel of the National Research Council. Report contains 50 other tables detailing the distribution of doctoral recipients by field of study over various time frames. **Number listed:** 335.

1. Harvey Mudd College, with 29 Ph.D.'s
2. Reed College, 24
3. Oberlin College, 23
4. Pomona College, 23
5. St. Olaf College, 19
6. Carleton College, 18
7. Santa Clara University, 14
8. Wesleyan University, 13
9. Knox College, 12
10. Swarthmore College, 11
10. Bucknell University, 11
12. Williams College, 10
12. Stevens Institute of Technology, 10
12. Kalamazoo College, 10
15. Polytechnic University, 9
15. Wheaton College, 9
15. Haverford College, 9
15. Vassar College, 9
15. Middlebury College, 9

Source: *Baccalaureate Origins of Doctorate Recipients, 7th ed.*, Franklin & Marshall College, March 1993.

★2778★
Top mathematics research-doctorate programs as evaluated by the National Research Council

Ranking basis/background: From a survey of nearly 8,000 faculty members conducted in the spring of 1993. Respondents were asked to rate programs in their field on "scholarly quality of program faculty." When more than one program had the samescore, the council averaged the rank order and gave each program the same rank number (if three programs tied for the top position, each received a rank of 2). **Remarks:** See *Chronicle* article for more details. Scores of 4.01 and above indicate "distinguished;" 3.0-4.0 "strong;" 2.51-3.0 "good;" 2.0-2.5 "adequate;" 1.0-1.99 "marginal;" and 0.0-0.99 "not sufficient for doctoral education." Programs also ranked by "effectiveness of program in educating research scholars/scientists." **Number listed:** 139.

1. University of California, Berkeley, with a quality rating of 4.94
1. Princeton University, 4.94
3. Massachusetts Institute of Technology, 4.92
4. Harvard University, 4.90
5. University of Chicago, 4.69
6. Stanford University, 4.68
7. Yale University, 4.55
8. New York University, 4.49
9. University of Michigan, 4.23
9. Columbia University, 4.23
11. California Institute of Technology, 4.19
12. University of California, Los Angeles, 4.14
13. University of Wisconsin, Madison, 4.10
14. University of Minnesota, 4.08
15. Cornell University, 4.05

★2779★
Top recruiters for math/actuarial science jobs for 2000-01 master's degree recipients

Ranking basis/background: Projected number of college hires from on-campus recruitment for 2000-01. **Remarks:** Numbers reflect total expected hires, not just African American projected hires. **Number listed:** 4.
1. Lucent Technologies, with 150 projected hires
2. Deloitte & Touche, 35
3. Henrico County Public Schools, 7
4. Accenture, 5

Source: "The Top 100 Employers and the Majors in Demand for the Class of 2001," *The Black Collegian*, 31: 19-35, (February 2001).

MATHEMATICS, GRADUATE–STATISTICS

★2780★
Most effective statistics and biostatistics research-doctorate programs as evaluated by the National Research Council

Ranking basis/background: From a survey of nearly 8,000 faculty members conducted in the spring of 1993. Respondents were asked to rate programs in their field on "effectiveness of program in educating research scholars/scientists." **Remarks:** See *Chronicle* article for more details. Scores of 3.5-5.0 indicate "extremely effective;" 2.5-3.49 "reasonably effective;" 1.5-2.49 "minimally effective;" and 0.0-1.49 "not effective." Programs also ranked by "scholarly quality of program faculty." **Number listed:** 65.
1. Stanford University, with an effectiveness rating of 4.44
2. University of California, Berkeley, 4.33
3. University of Chicago, 4.09
4. University of Washington Program in Biostatistics, 408
5. University of Wisconsin, Madison, 4.07
6. Cornell University, 4.06
7. University of California, Berkeley, 4.01
8. Iowa State University, 3.99
9. University of Washington Program in Statistics, 3.85
10. Carnegie Mellon University, 3.84

Source: "Rankings of Research-Doctorate Programs in 41 Disciplines at 274 Institutions," *The Chronicle of Higher Education* 42: A21-A30 (September 21, 1995).

★2781★
Top recruiters for statistics jobs for 2000-01 master's degree recipients

Ranking basis/background: Projected number of college hires from on-campus recruitment for 2000-01. **Remarks:** Numbers reflect total expected hires, not just African American projected hires. **Number listed:** 3.
1. Accenture, with 10 projected hires
2. Lucent Technologies, 50
3. Houghton Mifflin, 10

Source: "The Top 100 Employers and the Majors in Demand for the Class of 2001," *The Black Collegian*, 31: 19-35, (February 2001).

★2782★
Top statistics and biostatistics research-doctorate programs as evaluated by the National Research Council

Ranking basis/background: From a survey of nearly 8,000 faculty members conducted in the spring of 1993. Respondents were asked to rate programs in their field on "scholarly quality of program faculty." When more than one program had the samescore, the council averaged the rank order and gave each program the same rank number (if three programs tied for the top position, each received a rank of 2). **Remarks:** See *Chronicle* article for more details. Scores of 4.01 and above indicate "distinguished;" 3.0-4.0 "strong;" 2.51-3.0 "good;" 2.0-2.5 "adequate;" 1.0-1.99 "marginal;" and 0.0-0.99 "not sufficient for doctoral education." Programs also ranked by "effectiveness of program in educating research scholars/scientists." **Number listed:** 65.
1. Stanford University, with a quality rating of 4.76
1. University of California, Berkeley Program in Statistics, 4.76
3. University of California, Berkeley Program in Biostatistics, 4.43
4. Cornell University, 4.37
5. University of Chicago, 4.34
6. University of Washington Program in Biostatistics, 4.21
7. Harvard University, 4.17
8. University of Wisconsin, Madison, 4.06
9. University of Washington Program in Statistics, 4.01
10. Purdue University, 4.00
11. University of North Carolina, Chapel Hill Program in Statistics, 3.98
12. University of California, Los Angeles, 3.93
13. University of Minnesota Program in Statistics, 3.91
14. Iowa State University, 3.89
15. Texas A&M University, 3.78

Source: "Rankings of Research-Doctorate Programs in 41 Disciplines at 274 Institutions," *The Chronicle of Higher Education* 42: A21-A30 (September 21, 1995).

MATHEMATICS PERIODICALS

★2783★
Mathematics journals by impact factor

Ranking basis/background: Ratio of current citations to source items published and number of articles published over the previous two years. **Remarks:** Original source: *Journal Citation Reports* and Journal Performances Indicators on Diskette. **Number listed:** 10.
1. *Annals of Mathematics*, with 2.07
2. *Journal of the American Mathematical Society*, 1.40
3. *Inventiones Mathematical*, 1.13
4. *Bulletin of the American Mathematical Society*, 1.10
5. *Acta Mathematica*, 1.03
6. *Memoirs of the American Mathematical Society*, 1.02
7. *Journal des Mathematiques Pures et Appliquees*, 1.00
8. *Journal of Differential Geometry*, 0.93
9. *Annales Scientifiques de L'Ecole Normale Superieure*, 0.92
10. *Communications on Pure and Applied Mathematics*, 0.91

Source: "Journals Ranked by Impact: Mathematics," *What's Hot in Research,* http://www.isinet.com/whatshot/whatshot.html, Institute for Scientific Information (March 29, 1999).

★2784★
Mathematics journals by impact factor, 1981 to 1997

Ranking basis/background: Current citations to a journal's published papers divided by total papers published over an 18-year period. **Remarks:** Original source: *Journal Citation Reports* and Journal Performances Indicators on Diskette. **Number listed:** 10.
1. *Annals of Mathematics*, with 16.48
2. *Communications on Pure and Applied Mathematics*, 13.66
3. *Acta Mathematica*, 13.31
4. *Journal of Differential Geometry*, 10.96
5. *Inventiones Mathematical*, 10.79
6. *Bulletin of the American Mathematical Society*, 9.67
7. *Annales Scientifiques de L'Ecole Normale Superieure*, 8.19
8. *Advances in Mathematics*, 7.80
9. *Proceedings of the London Mathematical Society*, 6.47
10. *Topology*, 6.33

Source: "Journals Ranked by Impact: Mathematics," *What's Hot in Research,* http://www.isinet.com/whatshot/whatshot.html, Institute for Scientific Information (March 29, 1999).

★2785★
Mathematics journals by impact factor, 1993 to 1997

Ranking basis/background: Current citations to a journal's published papers divided by total papers published over the past five years. **Remarks:** Original source: *Journal Citation Reports* and Journal Performances Indicators on Diskette. **Number listed:** 10.
1. *Bulletin of the American Mathematical Society*, with 3.84
2. *Annals of Mathematics*, 3.24
3. *Acta Mathematica*, 3.24
4. *Communications on Pure and Applied Mathematics*, 2.70
5. *Inventiones Mathematical,* 2.27
6. *Annals of Mathematics Studies*, 1.99
7. *Journal of Differential Geometry*, 1.93
8. *Annales Scientifiques de L'Ecole Normale Superieure*, 1.88
9. *Journal of Functional Analysis*, 1.74
10. *Duke Mathematical Journal*, 1.68

Source: "Journals Ranked by Impact: Mathematics," *What's Hot in Research,* http://www.isinet.com/whatshot/whatshot.html, Institute for Scientific Information (March 29, 1999).

MATHEMATICS–STATISTICS

★2786★
Top recruiters for statistics jobs for 2000-01 bachelor's degree recipients

Ranking basis/background: Projected number of college hires from on-campus recruitment for 2000-01. **Remarks:** Numbers reflect total expected hires, not just African American projected hires. **Number listed:** 5.
1. Accenture, with 130 projected hires
2. Lucent Technologies, 25
2. Houghton Mifflin, 25
4. U.S. Air Force (Active Duty Hires), 10
5. Federal Deposit Insurance Company, 5

Source: "The Top 100 Employers and the Majors in Demand for the Class of 2001," *The Black Collegian*, 31: 19-35, (February 2001).

MEASUREMENT
See: **Evaluation Criteria & Methodologies**

MECHANICAL ENGINEERING
See: **Engineering, Graduate–Mechanical Engineering–Mechanical**

MEDICAL CENTERS

★2787★
Top cancer hospitals in the U.S., 2000

Ranking basis/background: U.S. News index based on reputation among specialists, cancer mortality rate, Council of Teaching Hospitals member, technology score, discharge planning, and hospital wide ration of full-time R.N.s to beds. **Number listed:** 50.
1. University of Texas, M.D. Anderson Cancer Center (Houston), with an overall index score of 100.0
2. Memorial Sloan-Kettering Cancer Center (New York), 98.9
3. Johns Hopkins Hospital (Baltimore), 64.6
4. Mayo Clinic (Rochester, MN), 57.6
5. Duke University Medical Center (Durham, NC), 38.8
6. University of Chicago Hospitals (Chicago), 36.2
7. Massachusetts General Hospital (Boston), 36.1
8. UCLA Medical Center (Los Angeles), 36.0
9. Roswell Park Cancer Institute (Buffalo), 34.8
10. Clarian Health Partners (Indianapolis), 34.3

Source: "America's Best Hospitals, 2000," *U.S. News & World Report*, 129: 50-107, (July 17, 2000).

★2788★
Top cardiology and heart surgery hospitals in the U.S., 2000

Ranking basis/background: U.S. News index based on reputation among specialists, cardiology mortality rate, Council of Teaching Hospitals member, technology score, discharge planning, hospital wide ration of full-time R.N.s to beds, and trauma center. **Number listed:** 50.
1. Cleveland Clinic (Cleveland), with an overall index score of 100.0
2. Mayo Clinic (Rochester, MN), 89.7
3. Massachusetts General Hospital (Boston), 60.3
4. Johns Hopkins Hospital (Baltimore), 54.8
5. Duke University Medical Center (Durham, NC), 54.4
6. Brigham and Women's Hospital (Boston), 50.8
7. Texas Heart Institute-St. Luke's Episcopal Hospital (Houston), 47.4
8. Stanford University Hospital (Stanford, CA), 43.6
9. Emory University Hospital (Atlanta), 39.5
10. Barnes-Jewish Hospital (St. Louis), 34.6

Source: "America's Best Hospitals, 2000," *U.S. News & World Report*, 129: 50-107, (July 17, 2000).

★2789★
Top endocrinology hospitals in the U.S., 2000

Ranking basis/background: U.S. News index based on reputation among specialists, endocrinology mortality rate, Council of Teaching Hospitals member, technology score, discharge planning, hospital wide ration of full-time R.N.s to beds, and trauma center. **Number listed:** 50.
1. Mayo Clinic (Rochester, MN), with an overall index score of 100.0
2. Massachusetts General Hospital (Boston), 86.1
3. Johns Hopkins Hospital (Baltimore), 54.9
4. Brigham and Women's Hospital (Boston), 50.0
5. University of California, San Francisco Medical Center (San Francisco), 49.2
6. University of Virginia Health Sciences Center (Charlottesville), 45.7
7. Barnes-Jewish Hospital (St. Louis), 43.6
8. University of Chicago Hospitals (Chicago), 43.3
9. Cleveland Clinic (Cleveland), 41.1
10. University of Michigan Medical Center (Ann Arbor), 38.9

Source: "America's Best Hospitals, 2000," *U.S. News & World Report*, 129: 50-107, (July 17, 2000).

★2790★
Top gastroenterology hospitals in the U.S., 2000

Ranking basis/background: U.S. News index based on reputation among specialists, gastroenterology mortality rate, Council of Teaching Hospitals member, technology score, discharge planning, hospital wide ration of full-time R.N.s to beds, and trauma center. **Number listed:** 50.
1. Mayo Clinic (Rochester, MN), with an overall index score of 100.0
2. Cleveland Clinic (Cleveland), 66.8
3. Johns Hopkins Hospital (Baltimore), 66.1
4. Massachusetts General Hospital (Boston), 62.2
5. Mount Sinai Medical Center (New York), 51.1
6. UCLA Medical Center (Los Angeles), 45.0
7. University of Chicago Hospitals (Chicago), 40.1
8. Duke University Medical Center (Durham, NC), 35.8
9. University of California, San Francisco Medical Center (San Francisco), 35.0
10. University of Pittsburgh Medical Center (Pittsburgh), 31.0

Source: "America's Best Hospitals, 2000," *U.S. News & World Report*, 129: 50-107, (July 17, 2000).

★2791★
Top geriatrics hospitals in the U.S., 2000

Ranking basis/background: U.S. News index based on reputation among specialists, hospitalwide mortality rate, Council of Teaching Hospitals member, technology score, discharge planning, hospital wide ration of full-time R.N.s to beds, and number of geriatric outpatient and community services offered. **Number listed:** 50.
1. UCLA Medical Center (Los Angeles), with an overall index score of 100.0
2. Johns Hopkins Hospital (Baltimore), 82.5
3. Mount Sinai Medical Center (New York), 75.9
4. Duke University Medical Center (Durham, NC), 62.3
5. Massachusetts General Hospital (Boston), 61.7
6. Mayo Clinic (Rochester, MN), 45.4
7. St. Louis University Hospital (St. Louis), 45.4
8. University of Michigan Medical Center (Ann Arbor), 41.7
9. Cleveland Clinic (Cleveland), 39.9
10. Yale-New Haven Hospital (New Haven, CT), 37.7

Source: "America's Best Hospitals, 2000," *U.S. News & World Report*, 129: 50-107, (July 17, 2000).

★2792★
Top gynecology hospitals in the U.S., 2000

Ranking basis/background: U.S. News index based on reputation among specialists, hospitalwide mortality rate, Council of Teaching Hospitals member, technology score, discharge planning, hospital wide ration of full-time R.N.s to beds, trauma center, and number of gynecology services. **Number listed:** 50.
1. Johns Hopkins Hospital (Baltimore), with an overall index score of 100.0
2. Mayo Clinic (Rochester, MN), 76.9
3. Brigham and Women's Hospital (Boston), 69.3
4. UCLA Medical Center (Los Angeles), 58.0
5. New York Presbyterian Hospital (New York), 55.8
6. University of Texas, M.D. Anderson Cancer Center (Houston), 55.0
7. Massachusetts General Hospital (Boston), 54.2
8. Duke University Medical Center (Durham, NC), 53.2
9. Parkland Memorial Hospitals (Dallas), 52.8
10. Memorial Sloan-Kettering Cancer Center (New York), 44.9

Source: "America's Best Hospitals, 2000," *U.S. News & World Report*, 129: 50-107, (July 17, 2000).

★2793★
Top hospitals in the U.S., 2000

Ranking basis/background: These hospitals ranked high in a least six of 17 specialties in the *U.S. News* ranking. A high ranking means at least two standard deviations above the mean, a statistical measure. Two points were awarded for ranking at least three standard deviations above the mean, 1 point for ranking between two and three standard deviations above the mean. **Number listed:** 15.
1. Johns Hopkins Hospital, with 31 points earned in 16 specialties
2. Mayo Clinic, 27; 14
3. Massachusetts General Hospital, 25; 13
4. Cleveland Clinic, 23; 12
5. UCLA Medical Center, 21; 13
6. Duke University Medical Center, 21; 12
7. Barnes-Jewish Hospital, 16; 10
8. Brigham and Women's Hospital, 16; 10
9. Stanford University Hospital, 16; 10
10. University of California, San Francisco Medical Center, 12; 7
11. Hospital of the University of Pennsylvania, 11; 8
12. University of Michigan Medical Center, 11; 8
13. University of Chicago Hospitals, 10; 8
14. University of Washington Medical Center, 10; 6
15. University of Pittsburgh Medical Center, 7; 6

Source: "America's Best Hospitals, 2000," *U.S. News & World Report*, 129: 50-107, (July 17, 2000).

★2794★
Top nephrology hospitals in the U.S., 2000

Ranking basis/background: *U.S. News* index based on reputation among specialists, nephrology mortality rate, Council of Teaching Hospitals member, technology score, discharge planning, hospital wide ration of full-time R.N.s to beds, and trauma center. **Number listed:** 50.
1. Brigham and Women's Hospital (Boston), with an overall index score of 100.00
2. Massachusetts General Hospital (Boston), 92.7
3. Cleveland Clinic (Cleveland), 82.3
4. University Hospital (Denver), 76.6
5. Mayo Clinic (Rochester, MN), 75.7
6. Barnes-Jewish Hospital (St. Louis), 72.1
7. Duke University Medical Center (Durham, NC), 70.8
8. New York Presbyterian Hospital (New York), 67.8
9. Vanderbilt University Hospital and Clinic (Nashville), 67.3
10. Johns Hopkins Hospital (Baltimore), 64.1

Source: "America's Best Hospitals, 2000," *U.S. News & World Report*, 129: 50-107, (July 17, 2000).

★2795★
Top neurology and neurosurgery hospitals in the U.S., 2000

Ranking basis/background: *U.S. News* index based on reputation among specialists, neurology mortality rate, Council of Teaching Hospitals member, technology score, discharge planning, hospital wide ration of full-time R.N.s to beds, and trauma center. **Number listed:** 50.
1. Mayo Clinic (Rochester, MN), with an overall index score of 100.0
2. Massachusetts General Hospital (Boston), 87.3
3. Johns Hopkins Hospital (Baltimore), 78.3
4. New York Presbyterian Hospital (New York), 69.7
5. University of California, San Francisco Medical Center (San Francisco), 56.1
6. Cleveland Clinic (Cleveland), 49.5
7. Hospital of the University of Pennsylvania (Philadelphia), 38.5
8. UCLA Medical Center (Los Angeles), 37.9
9. Barnes-Jewish Hospital (St. Louis), 37.3
10. Brigham and Women's Hospital (Boston), 35.0

Source: "America's Best Hospitals, 2000," *U.S. News & World Report*, 129: 50-107, (July 17, 2000).

★2796★
Top ophthalmology hospitals in the U.S., 2000

Ranking basis/background: Reputational scores from physician surveys conducted over the past three years. Hospitals on the list had to be recommended by at least 3 percent of the 150 board-certified specialists polled in each specialty. **Number listed:** 18.
1. Johns Hopkins Hospital (Wilmer Eye Institute), with a reputational score of 71.7%
2. University of Miami (Bascom Palmer Eye Institute), 67.5%
3. Wills Eye Hospital, 59.2%
4. Massachusetts Eye and Ear Infirmary, 43.8%
5. UCLA Medical Center (Jules Stein Eye Institute), 28.2%
6. University of Iowa Hospitals and Clinics, 17.4%
7. USC Medical Center (Doheny Eye Institute), 10.4%
8. Emory University Hospital, 9.3%
9. New York Eye and Ear Infirmary, 8.1%
10. Duke University Medical Center, 7.5%
11. Barnes-Jewish Hospital, 6.5%
12. University of California, San Francisco Medical Center, 6.4%
13. Mayo Clinic, 5.4%
14. Manhattan Eye, Ear and Throat Hospital, 4.6%
15. Methodist Hospital (Cullen Eye Institute), 4.5%
16. University of Wisconsin Hospital and Clinics, 4.4%
17. Cleveland Clinic, 4.2%
18. University of Illinois Hospital and Clinics, 3.4%

Source: "America's Best Hospitals, 2000," *U.S. News & World Report*, 129: 50-107, (July 17, 2000).

★2797★
Top orthopedics hospitals in the U.S., 2000

Ranking basis/background: *U.S. News* index based on reputation among specialists, orthopedic mortality rate, Council of Teaching Hospitals member, technology score, discharge planning, hospital wide ration of full-time R.N.s to beds, and trauma center. **Number listed:** 50.
1. Mayo Clinic (Rochester, MN), with an overall index score of 100.0
2. Hospital for Special Surgery (New York), 90.3
3. Massachusetts General Hospital (Boston), 66.6
4. Johns Hopkins Hospital (Baltimore), 50.1
5. Cleveland Clinic (Cleveland), 45.8
6. Duke University Medical Center (Durham, NC), 44.1
7. Harborview Medical Center (Seattle), 37.0
8. University of Washington Medical Center (Seattle), 36.5
9. University of Iowa Hospitals and Clinics (Iowa City), 35.5
10. UCLA Medical Center (Los Angeles), 34.0

Source: "America's Best Hospitals, 2000," *U.S. News & World Report*, 129: 50-107, (July 17, 2000).

★2798★
Top ortolaryngology hospitals in the U.S., 2000

Ranking basis/background: *U.S. News* index based on reputation among specialists, hospitalwide mortality rate, Council of Teaching Hospitals member, technology score, discharge planning, hospital wide ration of full-time R.N.s to beds, and trauma center. **Number listed:** 50.
1. Johns Hopkins Hospital (Baltimore), with an overall index score of 100.0
2. University of Iowa Hospitals and Clinics (Iowa City), 83.3
3. Massachusetts Eye and Ear Infirmary (Boston), 77.6
4. University of Pittsburgh Medical Center (Pittsburgh), 63.1
5. Mayo Clinic (Rochester, MN), 62.5
6. UCLA Medical Center (Los Angeles), 61.5
7. University of Michigan Medical Center (Ann Arbor), 58.0
8. Barnes-Jewish Hospital (St. Louis), 46.7
9. Hospital of the University of Pennsylvania (Philadelphia), 46.6
10. Cleveland Clinic (Cleveland), 46.1

Source: "America's Best Hospitals, 2000," *U.S. News & World Report*, 129: 50-107, (July 17, 2000).

★2799★
Top pediatrics hospitals in the U.S., 2000

Ranking basis/background: Reputational scores from physician surveys conducted over the past three years. Hospitals on the list had to be recommended by at least 3 percent of the 150 board-certified specialists polled in each specialty. **Number listed:** 22.
1. Children's Hospital, Boston, with a reputational score of 47.8%
2. Children's Hospital of Philadelphia, 40.8%
3. Johns Hopkins Hospital, 28.3%
4. Children's Hospital, Denver, 12.8%
5. Children's Hospital, Los Angeles, 12.4%
6. University Hospitals of Cleveland (Rainbow Babies & Children's Hospital), 12.0%
7. Children's Hospital of Pittsburgh, 11.2%
8. Texas Children's Hospital, Houston, 10.6%
9. New York Presbyterian Hospital (Babies & Children's Hospital), 9.3%
10. Children's Memorial Hospital, Chicago, 9.0%

Source: "America's Best Hospitals, 2000," *U.S. News & World Report*, 129: 50-107, (July 17, 2000).

MEDICAL PERIODICALS

★2800★
Top psychiatric hospitals in the U.S., 2000

Ranking basis/background: Reputational scores from physician surveys conducted over the past three years. Hospitals on the list had to be recommended by at least 3 percent of the 150 board-certified specialists polled in each specialty. **Number listed:** 19.

1. Massachusetts General Hospital, Boston, with a reputational score of 27.5%
2. New York Presbyterian Hospital, 22.4%
3. McLean Hospital, 21.5%
4. C.F. Menninger Memorial Hospital, 19.4%
5. Johns Hopkins Hospital, 15.9%
6. UCLA Neuropsychiatric Hospital, 14.9%
7. Yale-New Haven Hospital, 9.7%
8. Mayo Clinic, 8.0%
9. Duke University Medical Center, 7.0%
10. University of Pittsburgh Medical Center, 5.2%

Source: "America's Best Hospitals, 2000," *U.S. News & World Report*, 129: 50-107, (July 17, 2000).

★2801★
Top rehabilitation hospitals in the U.S., 2000

Ranking basis/background: Reputational scores from physician surveys conducted over the past three years. Hospitals on the list had to be recommended by at least 3 percent of the 150 board-certified specialists polled in each specialty. **Number listed:** 19.

1. Rehabilitation Institute of Chicago, with a reputational score of 63.8%
2. University of Washington Medical Center, 35.0%
3. The Institute for Rehabilitation and Research, 34.7%
4. Kessler Institute for Rehabilitation, 28.5%
5. Mayo Clinic, 20.9%
6. Craig Hospital, 19.6%
7. New York University Medical Center (Rusk Institute), 13.3%
8. Ohio State University Medical Center, 12.6%
9. University of Michigan Medical Center, 12.3%
10. Thomas Jefferson University Hospital, 10.0%

Source: "America's Best Hospitals, 2000," *U.S. News & World Report*, 129: 50-107, (July 17, 2000).

★2802★
Top rheumatology hospitals in the U.S., 2000

Ranking basis/background: *U.S. News* index based on reputation among specialists, hospitalwide mortality rate, Council of Teaching Hospitals member, technology score, discharge planning, and hospital wide ration of full-time R.N.s to beds. **Number listed:** 50.

1. Mayo Clinic (Rochester, MN), with an overall index score of 100.0
2. Johns Hopkins Hospital (Baltimore), 79.5
3. Hospital for Special Surgery (New York), 78.1
4. Brigham and Women's Hospital (Boston), 68.8
5. University of Alabama Hospital at Birmingham (Birmingham), 57.9
6. Cleveland Clinic (Cleveland), 55.8
7. Massachusetts General Hospital (Boston), 55.2
8. UCLA Medical Center (Los Angeles), 54.4
9. Stanford University Hospital (Stanford, CA), 43.2
10. Duke University Medical Center (Durham, NC), 42.0

Source: "America's Best Hospitals, 2000," *U.S. News & World Report*, 129: 50-107, (July 17, 2000).

★2803★
Top urology hospitals in the U.S., 2000

Ranking basis/background: *U.S. News* index based on reputation among specialists, urology mortality rate, Council of Teaching Hospitals member, technology score, discharge planning, hospital wide ration of full-time R.N.s to beds, and trauma center. **Number listed:** 50.

1. Johns Hopkins Hospital (Baltimore), with an overall index score of 100.0
2. Cleveland Clinic (Cleveland), 65.2
3. Mayo Clinic (Rochester, MN), 65.2
4. UCLA Medical Center (Los Angeles), 53.2
5. New York Presbyterian Hospital (New York), 45.9
6. Duke University Medical Center (Durham, NC), 45.0
7. Stanford University Hospital (Stanford, CA), 41.2
8. Massachusetts General Hospital (Boston), 39.3
9. Memorial Sloan-Kettering Cancer Center (New York), 39.1
10. Barnes-Jewish Hospital (St. Louis), 37.9

Source: "America's Best Hospitals, 2000," *U.S. News & World Report*, 129: 50-107, (July 17, 2000).

Related Information

★2804★

Comarow, Avery, "How We Selected the Best Hospitals," *U.S. News & World Report*, 129: 75, (July 19, 2000). **Remarks:** An in-depth description of "America's Best Hospitals" ranking basis for reputational scores, purpose of mortality calculations, definition of terms, eligibility for ranking, and additional data considered in scoring 6,247 medical centers.

MEDICAL PERIODICALS

★2805★
Geriatrics and gerontology journals with the greatest impact measure, 1981-98

Ranking basis/background: Citations-per-paper impact score is the total citations to a journal's published papers divided by total number of papers the journal has published over an eighteen year period. **Remarks:** Original source: *Journal Citation Reports* and Journal Performance Indicators on Diskette. **Number listed:** 10.

1. *Journal of Gerontology*, with an impact score of 21.03
2. *Neurobiology of Aging*, 16.74
3. *Psychology and Aging*, 14.11
4. *Journal of the American Geriatric Society*, 13.88
5. *Gerontologist*, 10.47
6. *Mechanisms of Ageing and Development*, 9.89
7. *Age and Aging*, 8.29
8. *Maturitas*, 8.21
9. *Experiments in Aging Research*, 7.99
10. *Experimental Gerontology*, 7.92

Source: "Journals Ranked by Impact: Geriatrics & Gerontology," *What's Hot in Research* (http://www.isinet.com/hot/research) *Institute for Scientific Information*, March 27, 2000.

★2806★
Geriatrics and gerontology journals with the greatest impact measure, 1994-98

Ranking basis/background: Citations-per-paper impact score is the total citations to a journal's published papers divided by total number of papers the journal has published over a five year period. **Remarks:** Original source: *Journal Citation Reports* and Journal Performance Indicators on Diskette. **Number listed:** 10.

1. *Journal of Gerontology*, with an impact score of 12.74
2. *Neurobiology of Aging*, 5.69
3. *Journal of the American Geriatric Society*, 5.24
4. *Psychology and Aging*, 4.72
5. *Gerontologist*, 3.51
6. *Journals of Gerontology, Series B: Psychological Sciences & Social Sciences*, 3.29
7. *Experimental Gerontology*, 3.24
8. *Age and Aging*, 2.87
9. *Maturitas*, 2.85
10. *Journal of Geriatric Psychology and Neurology*, 2.84

Source: "Journals Ranked by Impact: Geriatrics & Gerontology," *What's Hot in Research* (http://www.isinet.com/hot/research) *Institute for Scientific Information*, March 27, 2000.

★2807★
Geriatrics and gerontology journals with the greatest impact measure, 1998

Ranking basis/background: Ratio of citations and recent citable items published. **Remarks:** Original source: *Journal Citation Reports* and Journal Performance Indicators on Diskette. **Number listed:** 10.

1. *Neurobiology of Aging*, with a ratio of 3.52
2. *Age*, 3.23
3. *Journal of the American Geriatric Society*, 2.79
4. *Experimental Gerontology*, 1.64
5. *Drugs and Aging*, 1.60
6. *Mechanisms of Ageing and Development*, 1.58
7. *Gerontology*, 1.50
8. *Maturitas*, 1.49
9. *Age and Aging*, 1.43
10. *Journals of Gerontology, Series B: Psychological Sciences & Social Sciences*, 1.22

Source: "Journals Ranked by Impact: Geriatrics & Gerontology," *What's Hot in Research* (http://www.isinet.com/hot/research) *Institute for Scientific Information*, March 27, 2000.

★2808★
Hematology journals with the greatest impact measure, 1981-98

Ranking basis/background: Citations-per-paper impact score is the total citations to a journal's published papers divided by total number of papers the journal has published over an eighteen year period. **Remarks:** Original source: *Journal Citation Reports* and *Journal Performance Indicators on Diskette.* **Number listed:** 10.
1. *Circulation Research*, with an impact score of 45.55
2. *Circulation*, 38.85
3. *Blood*, 36.97
4. *Journal of Cerebral Blood Flow*, 32.04
5. *Clinics in Haematology*, 29.25
6. *Seminars in Hematology*, 21.25
7. *Thrombosis and Haemostasis*, 16.46
8. *CRC Critical Reviews in Oncology and Hematology*, 16.00
9. *British Journal of Haematology*, 15.88
10. *Journal of Leukocyte Biology*, 15.47

Source: "Journals Ranked by Impact: Hematology," *What's Hot in Research* (http://www.isinet.com/hot/research) *Institute for Scientific Information*, April 24, 2000.

★2809★
Hematology journals with the greatest impact measure, 1994-98

Ranking basis/background: Citations-per-paper impact score is the total citations to a journal's published papers divided by total number of papers the journal has published over a five year period. **Remarks:** Original source: *Journal Citation Reports* and *Journal Performance Indicators on Diskette.* **Number listed:** 10.
1. *Circulation Research*, with an impact score of 16.44
2. *Blood*, 15.72
3. *Circulation*, 15.22
4. *Journal of Cerebral Blood Flow*, 10.94
5. *Journal of Leukocyte Biology*, 9.06
6. *Experimental Hematology*, 7.65
7. *Blood Cells*, 7.03
8. *Thrombosis and Haemostasis*, 6.95
9. *Arteriosclerosis, Thrombosis and Vascular Biology*, 6.64
10. *Journal of Inflammation*, 6.33

Source: "Journals Ranked by Impact: Hematology," *What's Hot in Research* (http://www.isinet.com/hot/research) *Institute for Scientific Information*, April 24, 2000.

★2810★
Immunology journals with the greatest impact measure, 1981-98

Ranking basis/background: Citations-per-paper impact score is the total citations to a journal's published papers divided by total number of papers the journal has published over an eighteen year period. **Remarks:** Original source: *Journal Citation Reports* and *Journal Performance Indicators on Diskette.* **Number listed:** 10.
1. *Annual Review of Immunology*, with an impact score of 201.31
2. *Advances in Immunology*, 116.40
3. *Journal of Experimental Medicine*, 72.70
4. *Immunology Today*, 56.43
5. *Immunological Reviews*, 53.91
6. *Journal of Immunology*, 39.81
7. *Immunity*, 37.22
8. *CRC Critical Reviews in Immunology*, 31.48
9. *Reviews of Infectious Diseases*, 28.39
10. *European Journal of Immunology*, 26.93

Source: "Journals Ranked by Impact: Immunology," *What's Hot in Research* (http://www.isinet.com/hot/research) *Institute for Scientific Information*, April 10, 2000.

★2811★
Immunology journals with the greatest impact measure, 1994-98

Ranking basis/background: Citations-per-paper impact score is the total citations to a journal's published papers divided by total number of papers the journal has published over a five year period. **Remarks:** Original source: *Journal Citation Reports* and *Journal Performance Indicators on Diskette.* **Number listed:** 10.
1. *Annual Review of Immunology*, with an impact score of 97.52
2. *Advances in Immunology*, 50.33
3. *Immunity*, 37.22
4. *Immunology Today*, 33.78
5. *Journal of Experimental Medicine*, 31.52
6. *Current Opinion in Immunology*, 20.17
7. *Journal of Immunology*, 13.42
8. *Immunological Reviews*, 12.94
9. *European Journal of Immunology*, 11.98
10. *Journal of Leukocyte Biology*, 9.06

Source: "Journals Ranked by Impact: Immunology," *What's Hot in Research* (http://www.isinet.com/hot/research) *Institute for Scientific Information*, April 10, 2000.

★2812★
Neurosciences journals with the greatest impact measure, 1981-98

Ranking basis/background: Citations-per-paper impact score is the total citations to a journal's published papers divided by total number of papers the journal has published over an eighteen year period. **Remarks:** Original source: *Journal Citation Reports* and *Journal Performance Indicators on Diskette.* **Number listed:** 10.
1. *Annual Review of Neuroscience*, with an impact score of 145.82
2. *Neuron*, 70.24
3. *Brain Research Review*, 66.27
4. *Trends in Neuroscience*, 59.48
5. *Journal of Neuroscience*, 41.11
6. *Annals of Neurology*, 40.09
7. *Cerebrovascular and Brain Metabolism Reviews*, 39.43
8. *Progress in Neurobiology*, 39.02
9. *Brain*, 33.63
10. *Journal of Cerebral Blood Flow and Metabolism*, 32.04

Source: "Journals Ranked by Impact: Neurosciences," *What's Hot in Research* (http://www.isinet.com/hot/research) *Institute for Scientific Information*, November 22, 1999.

★2813★
Neurosciences journals with the greatest impact measure, 1994-98

Ranking basis/background: Citations-per-paper impact score is the total citations to a journal's published papers divided by total number of papers the journal has published over a five year period. **Remarks:** Original source: *Journal Citation Reports* and *Journal Performance Indicators on Diskette.* **Number listed:** 10.
1. *Annual Review of Neuroscience*, with an impact score of 65.12
2. *Neuron*, 35.68
3. *Trends in Neuroscience*, 33.30
4. *Cerebrovascular and Brain Metabolism Reviews*, 21.44
5. *Annals of Neurology*, 16.36
6. *Journal of Neuroscience*, 15.74
7. *Current Opinion in Neurobiology*, 15.73
8. *Frontal Neuroendocrinology*, 14.40
9. *Progress in Neurobiology*, 12.07
10. *Brain*, 11.67

Source: "Journals Ranked by Impact: Neurosciences," *What's Hot in Research* (http://www.isinet.com/hot/research) *Institute for Scientific Information*, November 22, 1999.

★2814★
Surgery journals with the greatest impact measure, 1981-98

Ranking basis/background: Citations-per-paper impact score is the total citations to a journal's published papers divided by total number of papers the journal has published over an eighteen year period. **Remarks:** Original source: *Journal Citation Reports* and *Journal Performance Indicators on Diskette.* **Number listed:** 10.
1. *Annals of Surgery*, with an impact score of 30.86
2. *American Journal of Surgical Pathology*, 22.69
3. *Journal of Neurosurgery*, 22.29
4. *Journal of Thoracic and Cardiovascular Surgery*, 17.70
5. *Transplantation*, 17.08
6. *Archives of Surgery*, 17.03
7. *Surgery*, 16.99
8. *Journal of Neurology Neurosurgery and Psychiatry*, 16.09
9. *Journal of Vascular Surgery*, 14.09
10. *American Journal of Surgery*, 13.88

Source: "Journals Ranked by Impact: Surgery," *What's Hot in Research* (http://www.isinet.com/hot/research) *Institute for Scientific Information*, November 15, 1999.

★2815★
Surgery journals with the greatest impact measure, 1994-98

Ranking basis/background: Citations-per-paper impact score is the total citations to a journal's published papers divided by total number of papers the journal has published over a five year period. **Remarks:** Original source: *Journal Citation Reports* and *Journal Performance Indicators on Diskette.* **Number listed:** 10.
1. *Annals of Surgery*, with an impact score of 10.89
2. *Transplantation*, 7.04
3. *American Journal of Surgical Pathology*, 7.02
4. *Journal of Neurosurgery*, 6.31
5. *Journal of Thoracic and Cardiovascular Surgery*, 6.05
6. *Journal of Vascular Surgery*, 5.88
7. *Archives of Surgery*, 5.23
8. *British Journal of Surgery*, 5.14
9. *Journal of Neurology Neurosurgery and Psychiatry*, 4.97
10. *American Journal of Surgery*, 4.59

Source: "Journals Ranked by Impact: Surgery," *What's Hot in Research* (http://www.isinet.com/hot/research) *Institute for Scientific Information*, November 15, 1999.

MEDICAL SCHOOLS

★2816★
Urology and nephrology journals with the greatest impact measure, 1981-98

Ranking basis/background: Citations-per-paper impact score is the total citations to a journal's published papers divided by total number of papers the journal has published over an eighteen year period. **Remarks:** Original source: *Journal Citation Reports* and Journal Performance Indicators on Diskette. **Number listed:** 10.

1. *Kidney International*, with an impact score of 21.45
2. *Journal of Urology*, 12.82
3. *Investigative Urology*, 12.49
4. *Prostate*, 11.89
5. *Clinical Nephrology*, 11.35
6. *American Journal of Kidney Diseases*, 10.49
7. *Urologic Clinics of North America*, 10.36
8. *Journal of the American Society of Nephrology*, 9.60
9. *Renal Physiology & Biochemistry*, 9.53
10. *Nephron*, 9.10

Source: "Journals Ranked by Impact: Urology & Nephrology," *What's Hot in Research (http://www.isinet.com/hot/research) Institute for Scientific Information*, November 1, 1999.

★2817★
Urology and nephrology journals with the greatest impact measure, 1994-98

Ranking basis/background: Citations-per-paper impact score is the total citations to a journal's published papers divided by total number of papers the journal has published over a five year period. **Remarks:** Original source: *Journal Citation Reports* and Journal Performance Indicators on Diskette. **Number listed:** 10.

1. *Kidney International*, with an impact score of 7.96
2. *Journal of the American Society of Nephrology*, 5.85
3. *American Journal of Kidney Diseases*, 5.50
4. *Journal of Urology*, 4.62
5. *Urology*, 4.31
6. *Prostate*, 4.05
7. *Urologic Clinics of North America*, 3.86
8. *Seminars in Nephrology*, 3.64
9. *Genitourinary Medicine*, 3.44
10. *Renal Physiology & Biochemistry*, 3.38

Source: "Journals Ranked by Impact: Urology & Nephrology," *What's Hot in Research (http://www.isinet.com/hot/research) Institute for Scientific Information*, November 1, 1999.

MEDICAL SCHOOLS

★2818★
Academics' choices for best AIDS programs, 2001

Ranking basis/background: From a *U.S. News & World Report* survey of medical school deans and senior faculty. **Remarks:** Data collected by Market Facts, Inc. **Number listed:** 10.

1. University of California, San Francisco
2. Harvard University
3. Johns Hopkins University
4. University of Alabama, Birmingham
5. University of California, Los Angeles
6. University of Washington (WA)
7. New York University
8. Columbia University College of Physicians and Surgeons
9. Stanford University
10. University of Miami

Source: "America's Best Graduate Schools: 2002 Annual Guide," *U.S. News & World Report*, 130: 60-97, (April 19, 2001).

★2819★
Academics' choices for best drug and alcohol abuse programs, 2001

Ranking basis/background: From a *U.S. News & World Report* survey of medical school deans and senior faculty. **Remarks:** Data collected by Market Facts, Inc. **Number listed:** 11.

1. Yale University
2. Harvard University
3. Johns Hopkins University
4. Columbia University College of Physicians and Surgeons
4. University of California, San Francisco
6. Brown University
6. University of California, Los Angeles
8. New York University
8. University of Pennsylvania
10. University of California, San Diego
10. Washington University (MO)

Source: "America's Best Graduate Schools: 2002 Annual Guide," *U.S. News & World Report*, 130: 60-97, (April 19, 2001).

★2820★
Academics' choices for best family medicine programs, 2001

Ranking basis/background: From a *U.S. News & World Report* survey of medical school deans and senior faculty. **Remarks:** Data collected by Market Facts, Inc. **Number listed:** 11.

1. University of Washington (WA)
2. University of Missouri, Columbia
3. University of North Carolina, Chapel Hill
4. Oregon Health Sciences University
4. University of Iowa
6. University of New Mexico
7. University of Colorado Health Sciences Center
8. University of Michigan, Ann Arbor
9. Case Western Reserve University
9. Michigan State University
9. University of Minnesota, Twin Cities

Source: "America's Best Graduate Schools: 2002 Annual Guide," *U.S. News & World Report*, 130: 60-97, (April 19, 2001).

★2821★
Academics' choices for best geriatrics programs, 2001

Ranking basis/background: From a *U.S. News & World Report* survey of medical school deans and senior faculty. **Remarks:** Data collected by Market Facts, Inc. **Number listed:** 10.

1. Harvard University
2. Johns Hopkins University
3. Mount Sinai School of Medicine
4. Duke University
5. University of California, Los Angeles
6. University of Washington (WA)
7. University of Michigan, Ann Arbor
8. Wake Forest University
9. Yale University
10. University of Pennsylvania

Source: "America's Best Graduate Schools: 2002 Annual Guide," *U.S. News & World Report*, 130: 60-97, (April 19, 2001).

★2822★
Academics' choices for best internal medicine programs, 2001

Ranking basis/background: From a *U.S. News & World Report* survey of medical school deans and senior faculty. **Remarks:** Data collected by Market Facts, Inc. **Number listed:** 10.

1. Harvard University
2. Johns Hopkins University
3. University of California, San Francisco
4. Duke University
5. Washington University (MO)
6. University of Pennsylvania
7. University of Michigan, Ann Arbor
8. University of Washington (WA)
9. Yale University
10. Stanford University

Source: "America's Best Graduate Schools: 2002 Annual Guide," *U.S. News & World Report*, 130: 60-97, (April 19, 2001).

★2823★
Academics' choices for best pediatrics programs, 2001

Ranking basis/background: From a *U.S. News & World Report* survey of medical school deans and senior faculty. **Remarks:** Data collected by Market Facts, Inc. **Number listed:** 10.

1. Johns Hopkins University
2. Harvard University
3. University of Pennsylvania
4. University of Washington (WA)
5. University of California, San Francisco
6. University of Cincinnati
7. Washington University (MO)
8. Yale University
9. Duke University
10. Stanford University

Source: "America's Best Graduate Schools: 2002 Annual Guide," *U.S. News & World Report*, 130: 60-97, (April 19, 2001).

★2824★
Academics' choices for best rural medicine programs, 2001

Ranking basis/background: From a *U.S. News & World Report* survey of medical school deans and senior faculty. **Remarks:** Data collected by Market Facts, Inc. **Number listed:** 12.

1. University of Washington (WA)
2. University of New Mexico
3. University of Iowa
4. East Tennessee State University
4. University of North Dakota
6. Michigan State University
6. University of Minnesota, Duluth
8. East Carolina University
8. Oregon Health Sciences University
8. University of North Carolina, Chapel Hill
8. University of South Dakota

Source: "America's Best Graduate Schools: 2002 Annual Guide," *U.S. News & World Report*, 130: 60-97, (April 19, 2001).

★2825★
Academics' choices for best women's health medical programs, 2001

Ranking basis/background: From a *U.S. News & World Report* survey of medical school deans and senior faculty. **Remarks:** Data collected by Market Facts, Inc. **Number listed:** 11.

1. Harvard University
2. University of California, San Francisco
3. Johns Hopkins University

3. University of Pennsylvania
5. University of Washington (WA)
6. Duke University
7. Yale University
8. Northwestern University
9. Columbia University College of Physicians and Surgeons
10. University of California, Los Angeles
10. Washington University (MO)

Source: "America's Best Graduate Schools: 2002 Annual Guide," *U.S. News & World Report*, 130: 60-97, (April 19, 2001).

★2826★
Acceptance rates for *U.S. News & World Report*'s top 10 primary-care medical schools, 2001

Ranking basis/background: From a *U.S. News & World Report* survey of medical school acceptance rates in 2000. **Remarks:** Data collected by Market Facts, Inc. **Number listed:** 54.
1. University of Massachusetts, Worcester, 22.2%
2. University of Iowa, 10.7%
3. University of Minnesota, Duluth, 10.3%
4. University of New Mexico, 10.1%
5. University of Colorado Health Sciences Center, 8.9%
6. University of Washington (WA), with 7.3%
7. University of North Carolina, Chapel Hill, 7.0%
8. Oregon Health Sciences University, 6.4%
9. Michigan State University, 6.3%
10. University of California, San Francisco, 5.0%

Source: "America's Best Graduate Schools: 2002 Annual Guide," *U.S. News & World Report*, 130: 60-97, (April 19, 2001).

★2827★
Acceptance rates for *U.S. News & World Report*'s top 10 research-oriented medical schools, 2001

Ranking basis/background: From a *U.S. News & World Report* survey of medical school acceptance rates in 2000. **Remarks:** Data collected by Market Facts, Inc. **Number listed:** 51.
1. Washington University (MO), with 9.9%
2. Columbia University College of Physicians and Surgeons, 9.8%
3. University of Michigan, Ann Arbor, 7.3%
4. Yale University, 6.0%
5. University of Pennsylvania, 5.2%
6. Harvard University, 5.1%
7. Johns Hopkins University, 5.0%
7. University of California, San Francisco, 5.0%
9. Duke University, 4.5%
10. Stanford University, 3.3%

Source: "America's Best Graduate Schools: 2002 Annual Guide," *U.S. News & World Report*, 130: 60-97, (April 19, 2001).

★2828★
Acceptance rates of all applicants to U.S. medical schools, by age, 1999-2000

Ranking basis/background: Acceptance rates for the 1999-2000 entering class, by age groups. **Remarks:** Original source: AAMC Data Warehouse: Applicant Matriculant File (11/15/99). **Number listed:** 7.
  20 and under, 2.4% of applicants in the age bracket were accepted (620 total applicants in the age bracket; accounting of 1.6% of all applicants)
  21-23, 62.6% (20,770; 53.9%)
  24-27, 24.7% (11,336; 29.4%)
  28-31, 6.7% (3,448; 8.9%)
  32-34, 1.7% (1,007; 2.6%)
  35-37, 1% (585; 1.5%)
  38 and over, 1% (763; 2%)

Source: Coleman, Editor, Cari L., *Medical School Admission Requirements, 2001-2002, United States and Canada*, Association of American Medical Colleges, 2000.

★2829★
Acceptance rates of all female applicants to U.S. medical schools, by age, 1999-2000

Ranking basis/background: Acceptance rates for the 1999-2000 entering class, by age groups. **Remarks:** Original source: AAMC Data Warehouse: Applicant Matriculant File (11/15/99). **Number listed:** 7.
  20 and under, 2.7% of applicants in the age bracket were accepted (325 total applicants in the age bracket; accounting of 1.9% of all applicants)
  21-23, 65.1% (9,994; 57.3%)
  24-27, 22.2% (4,627; 26.5%)
  28-31, 6.4% (1,426; 8.2%)
  32-34, 1.5% (423; 2.4%)
  35-37, 1% (249; 1.4%)
  38 and over, 1.2% (389; 2.2%)

Source: Coleman, Editor, Cari L., *Medical School Admission Requirements, 2001-2002, United States and Canada*, Association of American Medical Colleges, 2000.

★2830★
Acceptance rates of all male applicants to U.S. medical schools, by age, 1999-2000

Ranking basis/background: Acceptance rates for the 1999-2000 entering class, by age groups. **Remarks:** Original source: AAMC Data Warehouse: Applicant Matriculant File (11/15/99). **Number listed:** 7.
  20 and under, 2.1% of applicants in the age bracket were accepted (295 total applicants in the age bracket; accounting of 1.4% of all applicants)
  21-23, 60.4% (10,776; 51.1%)
  24-27, 26.8% (6,709; 31.8%)
  28-31, 7% (2,022; 9.6%)
  32-34, 1.9% (584; 2.8%)
  35-37, 1% (336; 1.6%)
  38 and over, 0.8% (374; 1.8%)

Source: Coleman, Editor, Cari L., *Medical School Admission Requirements, 2001-2002, United States and Canada*, Association of American Medical Colleges, 2000.

★2831★
Application and acceptance rates of African American applicants to first-year classes in U.S. medical schools, 1995-96 through 1999-2000

Ranking basis/background: Shows number of minority applicants, percentage of all applicants, number accepted, and percentage of all applicants accepted for each class. **Remarks:** Original source: AAMC Data Warehouse: Applicant Matriculant File (11/15/99). **Number listed:** 5.
  1995-96, with 3,487 African American applicants (7.5% of all applicants); and 1,365 accepted (39.1% of African American applicants accepted)
  1996-97, 3,524 (7.5%); 1,266 (35.9%)
  1997-98, 3,168 (7.4%); 1,202 (37.9%)
  1998-99, 3,151 (7.7%); 1,269 (40.3%)
  1999-00, 2,940 (7.6%); 1,199 (40.8%)

Source: Coleman, Editor, Cari L., *Medical School Admission Requirements, 2001-2002, United States and Canada*, Association of American Medical Colleges, 2000.

★2832★
Application and acceptance rates of mainland Puerto Rican applicants to first-year classes in U.S. medical schools, 1995-96 through 1999-2000

Ranking basis/background: Shows number of minority applicants, percentage of all applicants, number accepted, and percentage of all applicants accepted for each class. **Remarks:** Original source: AAMC Data Warehouse: Applicant Matriculant File (11/15/99). **Number listed:** 5.
  1995-96, with 267 mainland Puerto Rican applicants (0.6% of all applicants); and 116 accepted (43.4% of mainland Puerto Rican applicants accepted)
  1996-97, 272 (0.6%); 146 (53.7%)
  1997-98, 214 (0.5%); 116 (54.2%)
  1998-99, 220 (0.5%); 111 (50.5%)
  1999-00, 217 (0.6%); 119 (54.8%)

Source: Coleman, Editor, Cari L., *Medical School Admission Requirements, 2001-2002, United States and Canada*, Association of American Medical Colleges, 2000.

★2833★
Application and acceptance rates of Mexican American/Chicano applicants to first-year classes in U.S. medical schools, 1995-96 through 1999-2000

Ranking basis/background: Shows number of minority applicants, percentage of all applicants, number accepted, and percentage of all applicants accepted for each class. **Remarks:** Original source: AAMC Data Warehouse: Applicant Matriculant File (11/15/99). **Number listed:** 5.
  1995-96, with 933 Mexican American/Chicano applicants (2.0% of all applicants); and 504 accepted (54.0% of Mexican American/Chicano applicants accepted)
  1996-97, 975 (2.1%); 470 (48.2%)
  1997-98, 838 (1.9%); 418 (49.9%)
  1998-99, 822 (2.0%); 435 (52.9%)
  1999-00, 777 (2.0%); 415 (53.4%)

Source: Coleman, Editor, Cari L., *Medical School Admission Requirements, 2001-2002, United States and Canada*, Association of American Medical Colleges, 2000.

★2834★
Application and acceptance rates of Native American applicants to first-year classes in U.S. medical schools, 1995-96 through 1999-2000

Ranking basis/background: Shows number of minority applicants, percentage of all applicants, number accepted, and percentage of all applicants accepted for each class. **Remarks:** Original source: AAMC Data Warehouse: Applicant Matriculant File (11/15/99). **Number listed:** 5.

1995-96, with 358 Native American applicants (0.8% of all applicants); and 152 accepted (42.7% of Native American applicants accepted)
1996-97, 383 (0.8%); 154 (40.2%)
1997-98, 330 (0.8%); 137 (41.5%)
1998-99, 294 (0.7%); 155 (52.7%)
1999-00, 247 (0.6%); 117 (47.4%)

Source: Coleman, Editor, Cari L., *Medical School Admission Requirements, 2001-2002, United States and Canada*, Association of American Medical Colleges, 2000.

★2835★
Average MCAT scores at *U.S. News & World Report*'s top 10 primary-care medical schools, 2001

Ranking basis/background: From a *U.S. News & World Report* survey of average MCAT scores for 2000. **Remarks:** Data collected by Market Facts, Inc. **Number listed:** 54.

1. University of California, San Francisco, with 11.4
2. University of Massachusetts, Worcester, 10.6
3. University of Washington (WA), 10.4
4. University of North Carolina, Chapel Hill, 10.3
5. University of Iowa, 10.2
6. Oregon Health Sciences University, 10.0
6. University of Colorado Health Sciences Center, 10.0
8. University of New Mexico, 9.6
9. University of Minnesota, Duluth, 9.4
10. Michigan State University, 9.2

Source: "America's Best Graduate Schools: 2002 Annual Guide," *U.S. News & World Report*, 130: 60-97, (April 19, 2001).

★2836★
Average MCAT scores at *U.S. News & World Report*'s top 10 research-oriented medical schools, 2001

Ranking basis/background: From a *U.S. News & World Report* survey of average MCAT scores for 2000. **Remarks:** Data collected by Market Facts, Inc. **Number listed:** 51.

1. Washington University (MO), with 12.0
2. University of Pennsylvania, 11.7
2. Columbia University College of Physicians and Surgeons, 11.7
4. Duke University, 11.6
5. University of California, San Francisco, 11.4
6. Johns Hopkins University, 11.2
7. Harvard University, 11.1
7. Yale University, 11.1
7. Stanford University, 11.1
7. University of Michigan, Ann Arbor, 11.1

Source: "America's Best Graduate Schools: 2002 Annual Guide," *U.S. News & World Report*, 130: 60-97, (April 19, 2001).

★2837★
Average undergraduate GPA at *U.S. News & World Report*'s top 10 primary-care medical schools, 2001

Ranking basis/background: From a *U.S. News & World Report* survey of average undergraduate GPAs for 2000. **Remarks:** Data collected by Market Facts, Inc. **Number listed:** 54.

1. University of Iowa, with 3.72
2. University of California, San Francisco, 3.71
3. University of Washington (WA), 3.65
4. Oregon Health Sciences University, 3.61
5. University of Minnesota, Duluth, 3.60
6. University of New Mexico, 3.49
7. University of Massachusetts, Worcester, 3.58
7. University of Colorado Health Sciences Center, 3.58
9. University of North Carolina, Chapel Hill, 3.57
10. Michigan State University, 3.50

Source: "America's Best Graduate Schools: 2002 Annual Guide," *U.S. News & World Report*, 130: 60-97, (April 19, 2001).

★2838★
Average undergraduate GPA at *U.S. News & World Report*'s top 10 research-oriented medical schools, 2001

Ranking basis/background: From a *U.S. News & World Report* survey of undergraduate GPAs for 2000. **Remarks:** Data collected by Market Facts, Inc. **Number listed:** 51.

1. Washington University (MO), with 3.81
2. Harvard University, 3.80
2. Johns Hopkins University, 3.80
2. University of Pennsylvania, 3.80
5. Duke University, 3.77
6. Columbia University College of Physicians and Surgeons, 3.75
7. University of California, San Francisco, 3.71
8. Stanford University, 3.70
9. Yale University, 3.69
10. University of Michigan, Ann Arbor, 3.60

Source: "America's Best Graduate Schools: 2002 Annual Guide," *U.S. News & World Report*, 130: 60-97, (April 19, 2001).

★2839★
Comparative data for female applicants to U.S. medical schools, 1995-96 through 1999-2000

Ranking basis/background: Shows number of applicants, number of accepted, and percentage of women accepted in each class. **Remarks:** Original source: AAMC Data Warehouse: Applicant Matriculant File (11/15/99). **Number listed:** 5.

1995-96, with 19,779 female applicants (7,437 or 37.6% accepted)
1996-97, 20,031 (7,439; 37.1%)
1997-98, 18,273 (7,485; 41.0%)
1998-99, 17,787 (7,686; 43.2%)
1999-00, 17,433 (7,980; 45.8%)

Source: Coleman, Editor, Cari L., *Medical School Admission Requirements, 2001-2002, United States and Canada*, Association of American Medical Colleges, 2000.

★2840★
Comparative data for male applicants to U.S. medical schools, 1995-96 through 1999-2000

Ranking basis/background: Shows number of applicants, number of accepted, and percentage of men accepted in each class. **Remarks:** Original source: AAMC Data Warehouse: Applicant Matriculant File (11/15/99). **Number listed:** 5.

1995-96, with 26,812 male applicants (9,920 or 37.0% accepted)
1996-97, 26,937 (9,946; 36.9%)
1997-98, 24,747 (9,828; 39.7%)
1998-99, 23,216 (9,693; 41.8%)
1999-00, 21,096 (9,465; 44.9%)

Source: Coleman, Editor, Cari L., *Medical School Admission Requirements, 2001-2002, United States and Canada*, Association of American Medical Colleges, 2000.

★2841★
Faculty-student ratios at *U.S. News & World Report*'s top 10 primary-care medical schools, 2001

Ranking basis/background: From a *U.S. News & World Report* survey of number of students per faculty member in 2000. **Remarks:** Data collected by Market Facts, Inc. **Number listed:** 54.

1. University of Minnesota, Duluth, with 0.4 students per faculty member
2. Michigan State University, 0.8
3. University of Iowa, 1.0
4. University of North Carolina, Chapel Hill, 1.5
5. University of Massachusetts, Worcester, 1.6
6. University of Colorado Health Sciences Center, 1.7
7. University of New Mexico, 1.9
8. University of Washington (WA), 2.1
9. University of California, San Francisco, 2.3
10. Oregon Health Sciences University, 2.4

Source: "America's Best Graduate Schools: 2002 Annual Guide," *U.S. News & World Report*, 130: 60-97, (April 19, 2001).

★2842★
Faculty-student ratios at *U.S. News & World Report*'s top 10 research-oriented medical schools, 2001

Ranking basis/background: From a *U.S. News & World Report* survey of number of students per faculty member in 2000. **Remarks:** Data collected by Market Facts, Inc. **Number listed:** 51.

1. Stanford University, with 1.4 students per faculty member
2. University of Michigan, Ann Arbor, 2.3
2. University of California, San Francisco, 2.3
4. Washington University (MO), 2.4
5. Yale University, 2.8
6. University of Pennsylvania, 3.2
7. Columbia University College of Physicians and Surgeons, 3.7
8. Johns Hopkins University, 3.8
8. Duke University, 3.8
10. Harvard University, 7.5

Source: "America's Best Graduate Schools: 2002 Annual Guide," *U.S. News & World Report*, 130: 60-97, (April 19, 2001).

★2843★
First-year new women entrants to U.S. medical schools, 1995-96 through 1999-2000

Ranking basis/background: Shows number of women applicants, number of total applicants, and percentage that women comprise of the total for each class. First-year entrants are students entering medical school for the first time. **Remarks:** Original source: AAMC Data Warehouse: Applicant Matriculant File (11/15/99). **Number listed:** 5.

1995-96, with 6,941 new women entrants (42.7% of 16,253 total first-year new entrants)
1996-97, 6,918 (42.7%; 16,201)
1997-98, 6,995 (43.3%; 16,165)
1998-99, 7,162 (44.3%; 16,170)
1999-00, 7,412 (45.7%; 16,221)

Source: Coleman, Editor, Cari L., *Medical School Admission Requirements, 2001-2002, United States and Canada*, Association of American Medical Colleges, 2000.

★2844★
Graduate origin of first-year medical school residencies, 1999

Ranking basis/background: Percent of first-year medical residents from each graduate origin, based on a total of 22,320 first-year residencies. **Remarks:** Original source: American Medical Association. **Number listed:** 3.
1. Graduates of medical schools in the U.S., with 72%
2. Graduates of foreign medical schools, 25%
3. Graduates of osteopathic schools, 3%

Source: Mangan, Katherine S., "Should Medical Schools Admit More Applicants?," *The Chronicle of Higher Education*, 46: A42, (August 4, 2000).

★2845★
NIH research grants for *U.S. News & World Report*'s top 10 research-oriented medical schools, 2001

Ranking basis/background: Figures, in million of dollars, for NIH research grants received in 2000. From a *U.S. News & World Report* survey. **Remarks:** Data collected by Market Facts, Inc. **Number listed:** 51.
1. Harvard University, with $676.8 million
2. University of Pennsylvania, $328.5
3. Johns Hopkins University, $314.8
4. Washington University (MO), $251.3
5. University of California, San Francisco, $243.0
6. Columbia University College of Physicians and Surgeons, $237.6
7. Yale University, $216.9
8. University of Michigan, Ann Arbor, $200.4
9. Stanford University, $187.0
10. Duke University, $164.7

Source: "America's Best Graduate Schools: 2002 Annual Guide," *U.S. News & World Report*, 130: 60-97, (April 19, 2001).

★2846★
Out-of-state tuition and fees at *U.S. News & World Report*'s top 10 primary-care medical schools, 2001

Ranking basis/background: From a *U.S. News & World Report* survey of out-of-state tuition and fees in 2000. **Remarks:** Data collected by Market Facts, Inc. **Number listed:** 54.
1. University of Colorado Health Sciences Center, with $58,621
2. Michigan State University, $36,007
3. University of Minnesota, Duluth, $35,824
4. Oregon Health Sciences University, $34,165
5. University of Iowa, $28,575
6. University of North Carolina, Chapel Hill, $25,045
7. University of New Mexico, $24,859
8. University of Washington (WA), $24,484
9. University of California, San Francisco, $20,448
10. University of Massachusetts, Worcester, n/a

Source: "America's Best Graduate Schools: 2002 Annual Guide," *U.S. News & World Report*, 130: 60-97, (April 19, 2001).

★2847★
Out-of-state tuition and fees for *U.S. News & World Report*'s top 10 research-oriented medical schools, 2001

Ranking basis/background: From a *U.S. News & World Report* survey of out-of-state tuition and fees for 2000. **Remarks:** Data collected by Market Facts, Inc. **Number listed:** 51.
1. Washington University (MO), with $32,960
2. Columbia University College of Physicians and Surgeons, $32,757
3. University of Pennsylvania, $32,432
4. Duke University, $31,012
5. Stanford University, $30,439
6. Yale University, $30,075
7. Harvard University, $29,736
8. Johns Hopkins University, $29,136
9. University of Michigan, Ann Arbor, $28,814
10. University of California, San Francisco, $20,448

Source: "America's Best Graduate Schools: 2002 Annual Guide," *U.S. News & World Report*, 130: 60-97, (April 19, 2001).

★2848★
Percentage of graduates entering *U.S. News & World Report*'s top 10 primary-care medical schools, 2001

Ranking basis/background: From a *U.S. News & World Report* survey of graduates entering primary-care medical schools from 1998-2000. **Remarks:** Data collected by Market Facts, Inc. **Number listed:** 54.
1. University of Minnesota, Duluth, with 73.3%
2. University of Massachusetts, Worcester, 63.6%
3. University of New Mexico, 62.7%
4. Michigan State University, 61.4%
5. Oregon Health Sciences University, 59.0%
6. University of Iowa, 55.2%
7. University of California, San Francisco, 52.0%
8. University of Washington (WA), with 51.4%
9. University of Colorado Health Sciences Center, 51.3%
10. University of North Carolina, Chapel Hill, 46.6%

Source: "America's Best Graduate Schools: 2002 Annual Guide," *U.S. News & World Report*, 130: 60-97, (April 19, 2001).

★2849★
States with the most medical schools

Ranking basis/background: Number of medical schools. **Number listed:** 11.
1. New York, with 13 medical schools
2. California, 10
3. Pennsylvania, 8
3. Texas, 8
5. Illinois, 7
6. Ohio, 6
6. Missouri, 6
8. Georgia, 4
8. Florida, 4
8. Massachusetts, 4
8. North Carolina, 4

Source: Baker, Mark, *The Insider's Book of Medical School Lists*, Simon & Schuster, 1997.

★2850★
Subjects required by the most U.S. medical schools for the 2000-01 entering class

Ranking basis/background: Figures based on data provided by 125 medical schools. Fall 1999. **Remarks:** Florida, Northwestern, Southern Illinois, Weill, SUNY Syracuse, Northeastern Ohio, University of Pennsylvania, Medical University of South Carolina, Texas Tech, and University of Washington did not indicate specific course requirements and are not included in tabulations. **Number listed:** 11.
1. Physics, with 110 schools
1. Inorganic (general) chemistry, 110
1. Organic chemistry, 110
4. Biology, 67
5. English, 57
6. Biology or zoology, 50
7. Calculus, 21
8. College mathematics, 19
9. Humanities, 16
10. Social sciences, 15
11. Behavioral sciences, 13

Source: Coleman, Editor, Cari L., *Medical School Admission Requirements, 2001-2002, United States and Canada*, Association of American Medical Colleges, 2000.

★2851★
Top biological science majors for accepted applicants to U.S. medical schools, 1999-2000

Ranking basis/background: Percentage of biological sciences majors accepted for the 1999-2000 entering class. **Remarks:** Original source: AAMC Data Warehouse: Applicant Matriculant File (11/15/99). **Number listed:** 5.
- Biology, with 43.1% (6,137 accepted; out of 14,249 applicants)
- Microbiology, 41.4% (431; 1,041)
- Physiology, 38.0% (212; 558)
- Science (other biology), 48.1% (510; 1,061)
- Zoology, 44.5% (327; 735)

Source: Coleman, Editor, Cari L., *Medical School Admission Requirements, 2001-2002, United States and Canada*, Association of American Medical Colleges, 2000.

★2852★
Top health professions majors for accepted applicants to U.S. medical schools, 1999-2000

Ranking basis/background: Percentage of health profession majors accepted for the 1999-2000 entering class. **Remarks:** Original source: AAMC Data Warehouse: Applicant Matriculant File (11/15/99). **Number listed:** 3.
- Medical technology, with 18.2% (31 accepted; out of 170 applicants)
- Nursing, 27.0% (72; 267)
- Pharmacy, 24.9% (48; 193)

Source: Coleman, Editor, Cari L., *Medical School Admission Requirements, 2001-2002, United States and Canada*, Association of American Medical Colleges, 2000.

MEDICAL SCHOOLS

★2853★
Top mixed discipline majors for accepted applicants to U.S. medical schools, 1999-2000

Ranking basis/background: Percentage of mixed discipline majors accepted for the 1999-2000 entering class. **Remarks:** Original source: AAMC Data Warehouse: Applicant Matriculant File (11/15/99). **Number listed:** 5.

- Double major science, with 49.8% (433 accepted; out of 869 applicants)
- Double major science/nonscience, 56.1% (834; 1,487)
- Interdisciplinary studies, 58.8% (130; 221)
- Premedical, 36.2% (204; 563)
- Preprofessional, 47.5% (66; 139)

Source: Coleman, Editor, Cari L., *Medical School Admission Requirements, 2001-2002, United States and Canada*, Association of American Medical Colleges, 2000.

★2854★
Top nonscience majors for accepted applicants to U.S. medical schools, 1999-2000

Ranking basis/background: Percentage of nonscience majors accepted for the 1999-2000 entering class. **Remarks:** Original source: AAMC Data Warehouse: Applicant Matriculant File (11/15/99). **Number listed:** 10.

- Anthropology, with 55.3% (182 accepted; out of 329 applicants)
- Economics, 56.8% (193; 340)
- English, 52.7% (244; 463)
- Foreign Language, 50.9% (142; 279)
- History, 58.9% (244; 414)
- Philosophy, 51.6% (95; 184)
- Political science, 51.6% (131; 254)
- Psychobiology, 55.3% (168; 304)
- Psychology, 42.7% (769; 1,802)
- Sociology, 43.6% (85; 195)

Source: Coleman, Editor, Cari L., *Medical School Admission Requirements, 2001-2002, United States and Canada*, Association of American Medical Colleges, 2000.

★2855★
Top physical science majors for accepted applicants to U.S. medical schools, 1999-2000

Ranking basis/background: Percentage of physical sciences majors accepted for the 1999-2000 entering class. **Remarks:** Original source: AAMC Data Warehouse: Applicant Matriculant File (11/15/99). **Number listed:** 10.

- Biochemistry, with 49.1% (1,172 accepted; out of 2,389 applicants)
- Biomedical engineering, 57.6% (212; 368)
- Chemical engineering, 53.9% (173; 321)
- Chemistry, 48.3% (1,020; 2,110)
- Chemistry and biology, 40.8% (128; 314)
- Electrical engineering, 46.8% (81; 173)
- Mathematics, 44.0% (99; 225)
- Natural sciences, 44.6% (91; 204)
- Physics, 46.8% (88; 188)
- Science (general), 39.8% (70; 176)

Source: Coleman, Editor, Cari L., *Medical School Admission Requirements, 2001-2002, United States and Canada*, Association of American Medical Colleges, 2000.

★2856★
Top primary-care medical schools, 2001

Ranking basis/background: From a *U.S. News & World Report* survey of primary-care medical schools based on academic reputation, reputation by intern-residency program directors, student selectivity, and faculty resources. **Remarks:** Data collected by Market Facts, Inc. **Number listed:** 54.

1. University of Washington (WA), with an overall score of 100.0
2. Oregon Health Sciences University, 87.0
3. University of New Mexico, 82.0
4. University of California, San Francisco, 77.0
4. University of Massachusetts, Worcester, 77.0
6. Michigan State University, 76.0
6. University of North Carolina, Chapel Hill, 76.0
8. University of Colorado Health Sciences Center, 73.0
8. University of Iowa, 73.0
8. University of Minnesota, Duluth, 73.0

Source: "America's Best Graduate Schools: 2002 Annual Guide," *U.S. News & World Report*, 130: 60-97, (April 19, 2001).

★2857★
Top primary-care medical schools by reputation, as determined by academic personnel, 2001

Ranking basis/background: From a *U.S. News & World Report* survey of primary-care medical schools based on academic reputation, reputation by intern-residency program directors, student selectivity, and faculty resources. **Remarks:** Data collected by Market Facts, Inc. **Number listed:** 54.

1. University of Washington (WA), with a score of 4.2
2. University of New Mexico, 3.7
2. University of North Carolina, Chapel Hill, 3.7
4. Oregon Health Sciences University, 3.6
5. Michigan State University, 3.5
6. University of California, San Francisco, 3.4
6. University of Colorado Health Sciences Center, 3.4
6. University of Wisconsin, Madison, 3.4
9. University of Iowa, 3.3
9. East Carolina University, 3.3

Source: "America's Best Graduate Schools: 2002 Annual Guide," *U.S. News & World Report*, 130: 60-97, (April 19, 2001).

★2858★
Top primary-care medical schools by student selectivity rank, 2001

Ranking basis/background: From a *U.S. News & World Report* survey of primary-care medical schools based on academic reputation, reputation by intern-residency program directors, student selectivity, and faculty resources. **Remarks:** Data collected by Market Facts, Inc. **Number listed:** 54.

1. Washington University (MO)
2. University of Pennsylvania
3. Duke University
5. Mayo Medical School
6. Johns Hopkins University
7. Harvard University
8. University of California, San Francisco
9. Baylor College of Medicine
12. Cornell University

Source: "America's Best Graduate Schools: 2002 Annual Guide," *U.S. News & World Report*, 130: 60-97, (April 19, 2001).

★2859★
Top research-oriented medical schools, 2001

Ranking basis/background: From a *U.S. News & World Report* survey based on academic reputation, reputation by intern-residency program directors, student selectivity, faculty resources, and research activity. **Remarks:** Data collected by Market Facts, Inc. **Number listed:** 51.

1. Harvard University, with an overall score of 100
2. Johns Hopkins University, 94
3. Duke University, 90
4. University of Pennsylvania, 89
4. Washington University (MO), 89
6. Columbia University College of Physicians and Surgeons, 87
7. University of California, San Francisco, 85
8. Yale University, 82
9. Stanford University, 81
9. University of Michigan, Ann Arbor, 81

Source: "America's Best Graduate Schools: 2002 Annual Guide," *U.S. News & World Report*, 130: 60-97, (April 19, 2001).

★2860★
Top research-oriented medical schools by reputation, as determined by academic personnel, 2001

Ranking basis/background: From a *U.S. News & World Report* survey based on academic reputation, reputation by intern-residency program directors, student selectivity, faculty resources, and research activity. **Remarks:** Data collected by Market Facts, Inc. **Number listed:** 51.

1. Harvard University, with a score of 4.9
1. Johns Hopkins University, 4.9
3. Duke University, 4.7
3. University of California, San Francisco, 4.7
5. Washington University (MO), 4.6
5. Stanford University, 4.6
7. University of Michigan, Ann Arbor, 4.5
7. University of Pennsylvania, 4.5
7. University of Washington (WA), 4.5
10. Columbia University College of Physicians and Surgeons, 4.3
10. Yale University, 4.3

Source: "America's Best Graduate Schools: 2002 Annual Guide," *U.S. News & World Report*, 130: 60-97, (April 19, 2001).

★2861★
Top research-oriented medical schools by reputation, as determined by intern/residency directors, 2001

Ranking basis/background: From a *U.S. News & World Report* survey based on academic reputation, reputation by intern-residency program directors, student selectivity, faculty resources, and research activity. **Remarks:** Data collected by Market Facts, Inc. **Number listed:** 51.

1. Harvard University, with a score of 5.0
1. Johns Hopkins University, 5.0
3. Duke University, 4.9
4. Columbia University College of Physicians and Surgeons, 4.4
4. University of Michigan, Ann Arbor, 4.4
6. University of Pennsylvania, 4.3
6. Washington University (MO), 4.3
6. Yale University, 4.3
6. Stanford University, 4.3
10. University of California, San Francisco, 4.2

MEDICINE

Source: "America's Best Graduate Schools: 2002 Annual Guide," *U.S. News & World Report*, 130: 60-97, (April 19, 2001).

★2862★
Top research-oriented medical schools by student selectivity, 2001

Ranking basis/background: From a *U.S. News & World Report* survey based on academic reputation, reputation by intern-residency program directors, student selectivity, faculty resources, and research activity. **Remarks:** Data collected by Market Facts, Inc. **Number listed:** 51.
1. Washington University (MO)
2. University of Pennsylvania
3. Duke University
4. Columbia University College of Physicians and Surgeons
5. Mayo Medical School
6. Johns Hopkins University
7. Harvard University
8. University of California, San Francisco
9. Baylor College of Medicine
10. Stanford University

Source: "America's Best Graduate Schools: 2002 Annual Guide," *U.S. News & World Report*, 130: 60-97, (April 19, 2001).

★2863★
U.S. medical school enrollment of U.S. citizens by racial/ethnic category, 1999-2000

Ranking basis/background: Total enrollment of 16,221 medical students identified by racial/ethnic category. There were additionally 155 foreign students and 385 unidentified students. **Remarks:** Original source: AAMC Data Warehouse: Applicant Matriculant File (11/15/99). **Number listed:** 6.
- White, with 10,276 enrolled (63.3% of total)
- African American, 1,122 (6.9%)
- Mexican American/Chicano, 389 (2.4%)
- Asian American/Pacific Islander, 3,255 (19.9%)
- Native American, 109 (0.7%)
- Puerto Rican, 199 (1.2%)

Source: Coleman, Editor, Cari L., *Medical School Admission Requirements, 2001-2002, United States and Canada*, Association of American Medical Colleges, 2000.

MEDICAL SCHOOLS–ENROLLMENT

★2864★
African American enrollment in first-year classes in U.S. medical schools, 1990-91 through 1999-2000

Ranking basis/background: Shows number of African Americans enrolled and percentage they comprise of total enrollment. First-year class enrollment figures include new entrants and those students repeating, reentering, or continuing the initial year. **Remarks:** Original source: AAMC Data Warehouse: Applicant Matriculant File (11/15/99). **Number listed:** 10.
- 1990-91, with 1,046 enrolled (6.5% of total first-year enrollment)
- 1991-92, 1,063 (6.6%)
- 1992-93, 1,196 (7.3%)
- 1993-94, 1,275 (7.8%)
- 1994-95, 1,309 (8.0%)
- 1995-96, 1,289 (7.9%)
- 1996-97, 1,190 (7.3%)
- 1997-98, 1,134 (7.0%)
- 1998-99, 1,201 (7.4%)
- 1999-00, 1,122 (6.9%)

Source: Coleman, Editor, Cari L., *Medical School Admission Requirements, 2001-2002, United States and Canada*, Association of American Medical Colleges, 2000.

★2865★
Mainland Puerto Rican enrollment in first-year classes in U.S. medical schools, 1990-91 through 1999-2000

Ranking basis/background: Shows number of mainland Puerto Ricans enrolled and percentage they comprise of total enrollment. First-year class enrollment figures include new entrants and those students repeating, reentering, or continuing the initial year. **Remarks:** Original source: AAMC Data Warehouse: Applicant Matriculant File (11/15/99). **Number listed:** 10.
- 1990-91, with 99 enrolled (0.6% of total first-year enrollment)
- 1991-92, 110 (0.7%)
- 1992-93, 108 (0.7%)
- 1993-94, 96 (0.6%)
- 1994-95, 129 (0.8%)
- 1995-96, 109 (0.7%)
- 1996-97, 141 (0.9%)
- 1997-98, 108 (0.7%)
- 1998-99, 106 (0.7%)
- 1999-00, 112 (0.7%)

Source: Coleman, Editor, Cari L., *Medical School Admission Requirements, 2001-2002, United States and Canada*, Association of American Medical Colleges, 2000.

★2866★
Mexican American/Chicano enrollment in first-year classes in U.S. medical schools, 1990-91 through 1999-2000

Ranking basis/background: Shows number of Mexican American/Chicanos enrolled and percentage they comprise of total enrollment. First-year class enrollment figures include new entrants and those students repeating, reentering, or continuing the initial year. **Remarks:** Original source: AAMC Data Warehouse: Applicant Matriculant File (11/15/99). **Number listed:** 10.
- 1990-91, with 272 enrolled (1.7% of total first-year enrollment)
- 1991-92, 313 (1.9%)
- 1992-93, 409 (2.5%)
- 1993-94, 382 (2.3%)
- 1994-95, 458 (2.8%)
- 1995-96, 480 (3.0%)
- 1996-97, 453 (2.8%)
- 1997-98, 397 (2.5%)
- 1998-99, 418 (2.6%)
- 1999-00, 389 (2.4%)

Source: Coleman, Editor, Cari L., *Medical School Admission Requirements, 2001-2002, United States and Canada*, Association of American Medical Colleges, 2000.

★2867★
Native American enrollment in first-year classes in U.S. medical schools, 1990-91 through 1999-2000

Ranking basis/background: Shows number of Native Americans enrolled and percentage they comprise of total enrollment. First-year class enrollment figures include new entrants and those students repeating, reentering, or continuing the initial year. **Remarks:** Original source: AAMC Data Warehouse: Applicant Matriculant File (11/15/99). **Number listed:** 10.
- 1990-91, with 68 enrolled (0.4% of total first-year enrollment)
- 1991-92, 94 (0.6%)
- 1992-93, 118 (0.7%)
- 1993-94, 129 (0.8%)
- 1994-95, 128 (0.8%)
- 1995-96, 145 (0.9%)
- 1996-97, 142 (0.9%)
- 1997-98, 123 (0.8%)
- 1998-99, 147 (0.9%)
- 1999-00, 109 (0.7%)

Source: Coleman, Editor, Cari L., *Medical School Admission Requirements, 2001-2002, United States and Canada*, Association of American Medical Colleges, 2000.

MEDICINE

★2868★
Authors with the greatest impact measure in cardiovascular research, 1993-98

Ranking basis/background: Number of high-impact papers and citations. **Remarks:** Original source: ISI High-Impact Papers, 1993-98. **Number listed:** 6.
1. Eric J. Topol, Cleveland Clinic Foundation, with 17 high-impact papers; 2,157 citations
2. Robert M. Califf, Duke University, 14; 1,483
3. Charles H. Hennekens, Harvard University, 11; 2,277
4. Valentin Fuster, Mt. Sinai Medical Center, 11; 1,120
5. Meir J. Stampfer, Harvard University, 10; 2,502
6. Michael R. Bristow, University of Colorado Health Sciences Center, 10; 1,416

Source: "Cardiovascular Research: High-Impact Authors, 1993-98," *What's Hot in Research* (http://www.isinet.com/hot/research) *Institute for Scientific Information*, September 6, 1999.

★2869★
Cities with the highest productivity of paper in the discipline of cardiovascular systems, 1994-96

Ranking basis/background: Cities with the highest number of papers. Total papers from 1994 to 1996 in the discipline of cardiovascular systems is 17,724. **Number listed:** 10.
- London
- Amsterdam-Hague-Rotterdam-Utrecht
- Paris
- Milan
- Edinburgh-Glasgow
- Munich

Berlin
Dortmund-Dusseldorf-Cologne
Copenhagen-Lund
Rome

Source: Matthiessen, Christian Wichmann and Annette Winkel Schwarz, "Scientific Centres in Europe: An Analysis of Research Strength and Pattern of Specialization Based on Bibliometric Indicators," *Urban Studies*, 36: 453-477, (March 1999).

★2870★
Cities with the highest productivity of paper in the discipline of hematology, 1994-96

Ranking basis/background: Cities with the highest number of papers. Total papers from 1994 to 1996 in the discipline of hematology is 17,128. **Number listed:** 10.

London
Amsterdam-Hague-Rotterdam-Utrecht
Paris
Milan
Rome
Berlin
Vienna
Mannheim-Heidelberg
Munich

Source: Matthiessen, Christian Wichmann and Annette Winkel Schwarz, "Scientific Centres in Europe: An Analysis of Research Strength and Pattern of Specialization Based on Bibliometric Indicators," *Urban Studies*, 36: 453-477, (March 1999).

★2871★
Cities with the highest productivity of paper in the discipline of immunology, 1994-96

Ranking basis/background: Cities with the highest number of papers. Total papers from 1994 to 1996 in the discipline of immunology is 19,003. **Number listed:** 10.

London
Paris
Amsterdam-Hague-Rotterdam-Utrecht
Copenhagen-Lund
Stockholm-Uppsala
Basel-Mulhouse-Freiburg
Milan
Rome
Oxford-Reading
Brussels-Antwerp

Source: Matthiessen, Christian Wichmann and Annette Winkel Schwarz, "Scientific Centres in Europe: An Analysis of Research Strength and Pattern of Specialization Based on Bibliometric Indicators," *Urban Studies*, 36: 453-477, (March 1999).

★2872★
Cities with the highest productivity of paper in the discipline of medicine (general and internal), 1994-96

Ranking basis/background: Cities with the highest number of papers. Total papers from 1994 to 1996 in the discipline of medicine (general and internal) is 27,981. **Number listed:** 10.

London
Paris
Edinburgh-Glasgow
Manchester-Liverpool
Amsterdam-Hague-Rotterdam-Utrecht
Oxford-Reading
Barcelona

Sheffield-Leeds
Madrid
Copenhagen-Lund

Source: Matthiessen, Christian Wichmann and Annette Winkel Schwarz, "Scientific Centres in Europe: An Analysis of Research Strength and Pattern of Specialization Based on Bibliometric Indicators," *Urban Studies*, 36: 453-477, (March 1999).

★2873★
Clinical medicine subfields with the highest impact measure, 1981-1997

Ranking basis/background: Average cites per paper published and cited in ISI indexed journals of clinical medicine between 1981 and 1997. **Remarks:** Original source: National Science Indicators Database, 1981-97. **Number listed:** 22.

1. Oncology, with 17.79
2. Endocrinology, metabolism and nutrition, 17.01
3. Hematology, 14.83
4. Clinical psychology and psychiatry, 13.49
5. Cardiology, 11.48
6. Neurology, 11.43
7. Clinical immunology and infectious diseases, 11.19
8. Gastroenterology and hepatology, 11.07
9. Rheumatology, 10.59
10. General and internal medicine, 10.32

Source: "Top Docs: Medicine's Most Cited, 1981-98," *Science Watch*, 10: 1-2, (May/June 1999).

★2874★
Most-cited researchers in cardiology, 1981-1998

Ranking basis/background: Total citations from papers published and cited in ISI indexed journals of clinical medicine from 1981 to June 1998. **Remarks:** Original source: National Science Indicators Database, 1981-June 1998. **Number listed:** 10.

1. Eugene Braunwald, Harvard University, with 19,451 citations
2. William B. Kannel, Boston University, 15,727
3. Eric J. Topol, Cleveland Clinic Foundation, 14,917
4. John H. Laragh, Cornell Medical Center, 13,539
5. Valentin Fuster, Mt. Sinai Medical Center, 13,376
6. Patrick W. Senuys, Erasmus University, 12,529
7. Robert M. Califf, Duke University, 12,373
8. David R. Holmes, Mayo Clinic, 12,268
9. Peter J. Barnes, Imperial College, 11,768
10. Stephen E. Epstein, National Heart Lung Blood Institute, 11,103

Source: "Top Docs: Medicine's Most Cited, 1981-98," *Science Watch*, 10: 1-2, (May/June 1999).

★2875★
Most-cited researchers in clinical medicine, 1981-1998

Ranking basis/background: Total citations from papers published and cited in ISI indexed journals of clinical medicine from 1981 to June 1998. **Remarks:** Original source: National Science Indicators Database, 1981-June 1998. **Number listed:** 20.

1. Thomas E. Starzi, from University of Pittsburgh (in the field of transplantation), with 26,456 citations
2. Steven A. Rosenberg, National Cancer Institute (Oncology), 22,734
3. Meir J. Stampfer, Harvard University (Epidemiology), 20,225
4. E. Donnall Thomas, F. Hutchinson Cancer Center (Transplantation), 19,781
5. Charles H. Hennekens, Harvard University (Epidemiology), 19,645
6. Eugene Braunwald, Harvard University (Cardiology), 19,451
7. Walter C. Willett, Harvard University (Epidemiology), 19,281
8. Robert C. Gallo, Institute of Human Viruses, University of Maryland (Virology/HIV), 18,659
9. Anthony S. Fauci, National Institute of Allergy Infection Disorders (Virology/HIV), 18,114
10. Rainer Storb, F. Hutchinson Cancer Center (Oncology), 17,560

Source: "Top Docs: Medicine's Most Cited, 1981-98," *Science Watch*, 10: 1-2, (May/June 1999).

★2876★
Most-cited researchers in epidemiology, 1981-1998

Ranking basis/background: Total citations from papers published and cited in ISI indexed journals of clinical medicine from 1981 to June 1998. **Remarks:** Original source: National Science Indicators Database, 1981-June 1998. **Number listed:** 10.

1. Meir J. Stampfer, Harvard University, with 20,225 citations
2. Charles H. Hennekens, Harvard University, 19,645
3. Walter C. Willett, Harvard University, 19,281
4. Frank E. Speizer, Harvard University, 15,480
5. Graham A. Colditz, Harvard University, 14,296
6. Bernard Rosner, Harvard University, 13,931
7. L. Joseph Melton, Mayo Clinic, 10,186
8. Joseph F. Fraumeni, National Cancer Institute, 10,090
9. William P. Castelli, Harvard University, 9,608
10. Richard Peto, University of Oxford, 9,406

Source: "Top Docs: Medicine's Most Cited, 1981-98," *Science Watch*, 10: 1-2, (May/June 1999).

★2877★
Most-cited researchers in oncology, 1981-1998

Ranking basis/background: Total citations from papers published and cited in ISI indexed journals of clinical medicine from 1981 to June 1998. **Remarks:** Original source: National Science Indicators Database, 1981-June 1998. **Number listed:** 10.

1. Steven A. Rosenberg, National Cancer Institute, with 22,734 citations
2. Rainer Storb, F. Hutchinson Cancer Center, 17,560
3. C. Dean Buckner, Response Oncology, Inc., 13,984
4. Frederick R. Appelbaum, F. Hutchinson Cancer Center, 12,262
5. David Y. Mason, University of Oxford/J. Radcliffe Hospital, 12,233
6. Robert P. Gale, Salick Health Care Inc., 12,232

7. Jerome E. Groopman, Harvard University, 12,123
8. Daniel Catovsky, Institute of Cancer Research, 11,045
9. Elaine S. Jaffe, National Cancer Institute, 10,688
10. Michael T. Lotze, University of Pittsburgh, 10,413

Source: "Top Docs: Medicine's Most Cited, 1981-98," *Science Watch*, 10: 1-2, (May/June 1999).

★2878★
Most-cited researchers in surgery/transplantation, 1981-1998

Ranking basis/background: Total citations from papers published and cited in ISI indexed journals of clinical medicine from 1981 to June 1998. **Remarks:** Original source: National Science Indicators Database, 1981-June 1998. **Number listed:** 10.

1. Thomas E. Starzi, University of Pittsburgh, with 26,456 citations
2. E. Donnall Thomas, F. Hutchinson Cancer Center, 19,781
3. Shunzabora Iwatsuki, University of Pittsburgh, 10,496
4. Satoru Todo, University of Pittsburgh, 10,415
5. David Van Thiel, Loyola University Medical Center, 10,020
6. Richard L. Simmons, University of Pittsburgh, 9,369
7. H. Joachim Deeg, University of Washington, 9,149
8. John S. Najarlan, University of Minnesota, 9,078
9. David E.R. Sutherland, University of Minnesota, 9,049
10. Byers W. Shaw, University of Nebraska, 7,253

Source: "Top Docs: Medicine's Most Cited, 1981-98," *Science Watch*, 10: 1-2, (May/June 1999).

★2879★
Most influential African Americans in medicine and science

Ranking basis/background: Alphabetical listing compiled by the DuSable Museum of African American History. **Number listed:** 6.

Ben Carson, brain surgeon
George Washington Carver, scientist-inventor
Charles Drew, scientist
Clara Hale, AIDS hospice founder
Mae Jemison, astronaut
Daniel Hale Williams, surgeon

Source: Moffett, Nancy, "Voices of Power," *Chicago Sun-Times*, February 2, 2000, p. 39.

★2880★
Radcliffe Institute for Advanced Study fellowship recipients in the field of biomedicine, 2000-01

Ranking basis/background: Recipient and institutional affiliation of the Radcliffe Institute for Advanced study fellowship for pursuit of advanced work across a wide range of academic disciplines, professions, and creative arts. **Number listed:** 2.

Joanna Gilbert, Harvard Medical School
Hiromi Gunshin, Children's Hospital, Boston

Source: "The Radcliffe Institute for Advanced Study," *The Chronicle of Higher Education*, 46: A59, (June 2, 2000).

★2881★
Top recruiters for medical technology jobs for 2000-01 bachelor's degree recipients

Ranking basis/background: Projected number of college hires from on-campus recruitment for 2000-01. **Remarks:** Numbers reflect total expected hires, not just African American projected hires. **Number listed:** 3.

1. Abbott Laboratories, with 40 projected hires
2. U.S. Air Force (Active Duty Hires), 5
2. Novant Health, 5

Source: "The Top 100 Employers and the Majors in Demand for the Class of 2001," *The Black Collegian*, 31: 19-35, (February 2001).

MERIT SCHOLARSHIPS
See: **Student Financial Aid**

METALLURGICAL ENGINEERING
See: **Engineering, Graduate–Materials/Metallurgical Engineering–Materials/Metallurgical**

MICROBIOLOGY
See: **Biology, Graduate–Microbiology**

MICROECONOMICS
See: **Economics**

MILITARY SCHOOLS

★2882★
Most influential African Americans in the military

Ranking basis/background: Alphabetical listing compiled by the DuSable Museum of African American History. **Number listed:** 3.

Benjamin Davis, Army general, Tuskegee Airman
Daniel "Chappie" James, Army general, Tuskegee Airman
Colin Powell, chairman, U.S. Joint Chiefs of Staff

Source: Moffett, Nancy, "Voices of Power," *Chicago Sun-Times*, February 2, 2000, p. 39.

MINORITY GROUPS–ENROLLMENT, COLLEGE

★2883★
State grades for affordability of higher education for minority students, 2000

Ranking basis/background: Grades received, by state, for how affordable higher education is in the state. **Remarks:** Original source: The National Center for Public Policy and Higher Education. **Number listed:** 50.

Alabama, with D
Alaska, C
Arizona, C-
Arkansas, C
California, A
Colorado, B-
Connecticut, C
Delaware, C-
Florida, D
Georgia, D
Hawaii, C-
Idaho, B-
Illinois, A
Indiana, C
Iowa, B
Kansas, B
Kentucky, B
Louisiana, C-
Maine, F
Maryland, D
Massachusetts, D
Michigan, C
Minnesota, A
Mississippi, C
Missouri, D
Montana, D-
Nebraska, C
Nevada, B
New Hampshire, F
New Jersey, B
New Mexico, B
New York, D-
North Carolina, A
North Dakota, C
Ohio, D-
Oklahoma, B-
Oregon, D-
Pennsylvania, C
Rhode Island, F
South Carolina, C
South Dakota, D
Tennessee, C
Texas, C
Utah, A
Vermont, D-
Virginia, C
Washington, B-
West Virginia, D
Wisconsin, B
Wyoming, C

Source: Hurd, Hilary, "State Policies Greatly Impact Minority Access to Higher Education," *Black Issues in Higher Education*, 17: 18-19, (December 21, 2000).

★2884★
State grades for benefits state receives for educating its minority students, 2000

Ranking basis/background: Grades received, by state, for what economic and civic benefits each state receives from education its residents. **Remarks:** Original source: The National Center for Public Policy and Higher Education. **Number listed:** 50.

MINORITY GROUPS—ENROLLMENT, COLLEGE

Alabama, with C
Alaska, B
Arizona, B-
Arkansas, D-
California, B
Colorado, A
Connecticut, A
Delaware, A
Florida, C-
Georgia, C
Hawaii, C
Idaho, C
Illinois, B-
Indiana, B
Iowa, C
Kansas, B
Kentucky, D
Louisiana, D
Maine, C
Maryland, A
Massachusetts, A-
Michigan, B
Minnesota, A
Mississippi, C
Missouri, C
Montana, B
Nebraska, B-
Nevada, C-
New Hampshire, B-
New Jersey, A
New Mexico, C
New York, B
North Carolina, D
North Dakota, C
Ohio, C
Oklahoma, C-
Oregon, C
Pennsylvania, B-
Rhode Island, A
South Carolina, B-
South Dakota, C-
Tennessee, D
Texas, C
Utah, B-
Vermont, B-
Virginia, B
Washington, B
West Virginia, F
Wisconsin, B-
Wyoming, C

Source: Hurd, Hilary, "State Policies Greatly Impact Minority Access to Higher Education," *Black Issues in Higher Education*, 17: 18-19, (December 21, 2000).

★2885★
State grades for completion of higher education by minority students, 2000

Ranking basis/background: Grades received, by state, according to how many minorities that enroll in higher education complete their academic or vocational programs. **Remarks:** Original source: The National Center for Public Policy and Higher Education. **Number listed:** 50.

Alabama, with B-
Alaska, F
Arizona, C-
Arkansas, D
California, C
Colorado, C
Connecticut, B
Delaware, B
Florida, B
Georgia, B-
Hawaii, C
Idaho, C

Illinois, C
Indiana, B-
Iowa, A-
Kansas, B
Kentucky, C-
Louisiana, C
Maine, C
Maryland, B-
Massachusetts, A-
Michigan, C
Minnesota, B
Mississippi, C
Missouri, B-
Montana, B
Nebraska, C
Nevada, F
New Hampshire, A
New Jersey, B-
New Mexico, D-
New York, A-
North Carolina, B
North Dakota, B
Ohio, B
Oklahoma, C-
Oregon, C
Pennsylvania, A
Rhode Island, A
South Carolina, B
South Dakota, B-
Tennessee, C
Texas, D
Utah, D
Vermont, A
Virginia, B
Washington, B-
West Virginia, C
Wisconsin, B
Wyoming, B

Source: Hurd, Hilary, "State Policies Greatly Impact Minority Access to Higher Education," *Black Issues in Higher Education*, 17: 18-19, (December 21, 2000).

★2886★
State grades for participation of minority students in higher education, 2000

Ranking basis/background: Grades received, by state, for state residents enrolling in college-level programs. **Remarks:** Original source: The National Center for Public Policy and Higher Education. **Number listed:** 50.

Alabama, with C
Alaska, D
Arizona, C
Arkansas, D-
California, B
Colorado, B-
Connecticut, B
Delaware, A
Florida, D
Georgia, F
Hawaii, B-
Idaho, D
Illinois, A
Indiana, C-
Iowa, B
Kansas, A
Kentucky, D
Louisiana, F
Maine, C
Maryland, A
Massachusetts, A-
Michigan, B
Minnesota, B-
Mississippi, D-

Missouri, C-
Montana, D
Nebraska, A
Nevada, D
New Hampshire, C
New Jersey, B
New Mexico, B-
New York, B-
North Carolina, D
North Dakota, B
Ohio, C-
Oklahoma, C
Oregon, D
Pennsylvania, C
Rhode Island, A
South Carolina, D-
South Dakota, C
Tennessee, D-
Texas, D
Utah, C
Vermont, C-
Virginia, B-
Washington, C-
West Virginia, D
Wisconsin, B
Wyoming, B-

Source: Hurd, Hilary, "State Policies Greatly Impact Minority Access to Higher Education," *Black Issues in Higher Education*, 17: 18-19, (December 21, 2000).

★2887★
State grades for preparing minority students for higher education, 2000

Ranking basis/background: Grades received, by state, for how well students are prepared to take advantage of higher education. **Remarks:** Original source: The National Center for Public Policy and Higher Education. **Number listed:** 50.

Alabama, with F
Alaska, A-
Arizona, D
Arkansas, D
California, C-
Colorado, B
Connecticut, A
Delaware, C
Florida, C
Georgia, D
Hawaii, C
Idaho, D
Illinois, A
Indiana, C-
Iowa, B
Kansas, B
Kentucky, C
Louisiana, F
Maine, B
Maryland, B
Massachusetts, A
Michigan, B
Minnesota, C
Mississippi, D
Missouri, C
Montana, B
Nebraska, A-
Nevada, D
New Hampshire, B
New Jersey, A
New Mexico, D-
New York, B
North Carolina, B
North Dakota, B
Ohio, C
Oklahoma, D
Oregon, C-

Pennsylvania, C
Rhode Island, C
South Carolina, C
South Dakota, C
Tennessee, C-
Texas, C
Utah, A
Vermont, B-
Virginia, B
Washington, C
West Virginia, D
Wisconsin, A-
Wyoming, C-

Source: Hurd, Hilary, "State Policies Greatly Impact Minority Access to Higher Education," *Black Issues in Higher Education*, 17: 18-19, (December 21, 2000).

★2888★
Trends in college enrollment rates of 18- to 24-year olds, by race/ethnicity

Ranking basis/background: Percentage of 18- to 24-year olds enrolled for selected years. **Remarks:** Original source: Digest of Education Statistics, 1998. **Number listed:** 10.
 1980, with 25% whites; 19% African Americans; 16% Hispanic Americans
 1982, 27%; 20%; 17%
 1984, 28%; 20%; 18%
 1986, 29%; 22%; 18%
 1988, 31%; 21%; 17%
 1990, 33%; 25%; 16%
 1992, 37%; 25%; 21%
 1994, 38%; 28%; 19%
 1996, 40%; 27%; 20%
 1997, 41%; 30%; 22%

Source: Dervarics, Charles, "Hispanic-Serving Institutions Make Impressive Strides," *Black Issues in Higher Education*, 17: 32-35, (September 28, 2000).

MOLECULAR BIOLOGY
See: **Biology, Graduate–Cellular/Molecular**

MOTION PICTURES

★2889★
Most notable children's videos, 2001

Ranking basis/background: Alphabetical list by title, compiled by the Notable Children's Videos committee. **Number listed:** 14.
 Antarctic Antics: A Book of Penguin Poems (produced by Weston Woods)
 Black Cat (Spoken Arts)
 Bully Dance (Bullfrog)
 Cuckoo, Mr. Edgar! (National Film Board of Canada)
 Duke Ellington, (Weston Woods)
 George and Martha (Sony Wonder)
 Korea: Yu Sings Pansori (New Dimension Media)
 Mary Cassatt: American Impressionist (Devine Entertainment)
 Peter Pan (New Video Group)
 The Scrambled States of America (Weston Woods)
 Strega Nona (Weston Woods)
 Tiny's Hat (Spoken Arts)
 Winslow Homer: An American Original (Devine Entertainment)
 Yo! Yes? (Weston Woods)

Source: ALA's 2001 "Best" Lists, *Booklist*, 97: 1362-1388, (March 15, 2001).

★2890★
Most notable DVDs and videos for young adults, 2001

Ranking basis/background: Alphabetical list by title, compiled by the Young Adult Library Services Association, recognizes features for technical merit, content, and use with and interest to youth ages 12 to 18. **Number listed:** 10.
 Daring to Resist: Three Women Face the Holocaust (produced by Women Make Movies)
 DUI: Dead in 5 Seconds (Goldhil Home Media)
 Everest: The Death Zone (WGBH)
 George Lucas in Love (MediaTrip.com)
 Invisible Revolution: A Youth Subculture of Hate (Filmakers Library)
 Killing Us Softly III: Advertising's Image of Women (California Newsreel)
 The Mirror Lied (Filmakers Library)
 Slender Existence (Filmakers Library)
 The Truth About Violence (AIMS Multimedia)

Source: ALA's 2001 "Best" Lists, *Booklist*, 97: 1362-1388, (March 15, 2001).

★2891★
Most notable videos for adults, 2001

Ranking basis/background: Alphabetical list by title, compiled by the American Library Association Video Round Table, are best videos released over the past two years. **Number listed:** 15.
 42 Up (produced by First Run/Icarus)
 American Movie: The Making of Northwestern (Home video sources)
 Ayn Rand: A Sense of Life (Strand Home Video)
 The Brandon Teena Story (New Video)
 Cinema Verite: Defining the Moment (National Film Board of Canada)
 Coming to Light: Edward S. Curtis and the North American Indians (Bullfrog)
 Jeni LeGon: Living in a Great Big Way (Cinema Guild)
 The Legacy: Murder and Media Politics and Prison (Films for the Humanities & Sciences)
 On Our Own Terms: Moyers on Death and Dying in America (Films for the Humanities & Science)
 One Day Longer: Story of the Frontier Strike (Transit Media)
 Rabbit in the Moon (Transit Media)
 Sing Faster: The Stagehand's Ring Cycle (Direct Cinema)
 Stranger with a Camera (California Newsreel)
 Walking with Dinosaurs (Home video sources)
 Well-Founded Fear (Epidavros Project)

Source: ALA's 2001 "Best" Lists, *Booklist*, 97: 1362-1388, (March 15, 2001).

★2892★
Outstanding videos for library collections, 2000

Ranking basis/background: Alphabetical listing of the year's outstanding videos for public-library collections. **Number listed:** 20.
 Almost Elvis: Elvis Impersonators and Their Quest for the Crown (produced by Blue Suede Films) recommended for Gr. 9-up
 America's Crayfish: Crawling in Troubled Waters (Earthwave) Gr. 9-up
 Building Big (WGBH Boston) Gr. 7-up
 Cuckoo, Mr. Edgar! (National Film Board of Canada) Gr. 1-5
 Daring to Resist: Three Women Face the Holocaust (Women Make Movies) Gr. 7-up
 Duke Ellington: The Piano Prince and His Orchestra (Weston Woods) Gr. 1-5
 Free a Man to Fight: Women Soldiers of WWII (Two Girls from Back East Productions) Gr. 9-up
 The Island of the Skog (Weston Woods) Ages 4-7
 Long Night's Journey into Day (California Newsreel) Gr. 9-up
 Ludovic: The Snow Gift (National Film Board of Canada) Ages 4-8
 The Man That Corrupted Hadleyburg (Globalstage) Gr. 6-up
 New York (PBS) Gr. 7-up
 Not for Ourselves Alone: The Story of Elizabeth Cady Stanton and Susan B. Anthony (PBS) Gr. 7-up
 On Our Own Terms: Moyers on Death and Dying in America (Films for the Humanities & Sciences) Gr. 10-up
 Silent Sentinels (Bullfrog) Gr. 6-up
 Sing, Dance 'n Sign! (Kimbo Educational) Ages 3-9
 Stranger with a Camera (California Newsreel) Gr. 9-up
 That's a Family! (Women's Educational Media) Gr. 1-6
 White Hotel (Sub Rosa Studios) Adult
 Winslow Homer: An American Original (Devine Entertainment) Gr. 3-up

Source: "Editor's Choice 2000," *Booklist*, 97: 850-868, (January 1 & 15, 2001).

MUSIC
See also: **Opera**

★2893★
Radcliffe Institute for Advanced Study fellowship recipient in the field of music composition, 2000-01

Ranking basis/background: Recipient and institutional affiliation of the Radcliffe Institute for Advanced study fellowship for pursuit of advanced work across a wide range of academic disciplines, professions, and creative arts. **Number listed:** 1.
 Barbara White, Princeton University

Source: "The Radcliffe Institute for Advanced Study," *The Chronicle of Higher Education*, 46: A59, (June 2, 2000).

★2894★
Top recruiters for music jobs for 2000-01 bachelor's degree recipients

Ranking basis/background: Projected number of college hires from on-campus recruitment for 2000-01. **Remarks:** Numbers reflect total expected hires, not just African American projected hires. **Number listed:** 1.
1. Caddo Parish School Board, with 5 projected hires

MUSIC, GRADUATE

Source: "The Top 100 Employers and the Majors in Demand for the Class of 2001," *The Black Collegian*, 31: 19-35, (February 2001).

MUSIC, GRADUATE

★2895★
Most effective music research-doctorate programs as evaluated by the National Research Council

Ranking basis/background: From a survey of nearly 8,000 faculty members conducted in the spring of 1993. Respondents were asked to rate programs in their field on "effectiveness of program in educating research scholars/scientists." **Remarks:** See *Chronicle* article for more details. Scores of 3.5-5.0 indicate "extremely effective;" 2.5-3.49 "reasonably effective;" 1.5-2.49 "minimally effective;" and 0.0-1.49 "not effective." Programs also ranked by "scholarly quality of program faculty." **Number listed:** 65.

1. University of Chicago, with an effectiveness rating of 4.26
2. Harvard University, 4.26
3. Princeton University, 4.18
4. University of California, Berkeley, 4.11
4. Yale University, 4.11
6. University of Rochester, 4.03
6. University of Michigan, 4.03
8. Cornell University, 3.90
9. City University of New York, Graduate School and University Center, 3.79
10. Brandeis University, 3.73

Source: "Rankings of Research-Doctorate Programs in 41 Disciplines at 274 Institutions," *The Chronicle of Higher Education* 42: A21-A30 (September 21, 1995).

★2896★
Top music research-doctorate programs as evaluated by the National Research Council

Ranking basis/background: From a survey of nearly 8,000 faculty members conducted in the spring of 1993. Respondents were asked to rate programs in their field on "scholarly quality of program faculty." When more than one program had the samescore, the council averaged the rank order and gave each program the same rank number (if three programs tied for the top position, each received a rank of 2). **Remarks:** See *Chronicle* article for more details. Scores of 4.01 and above indicate "distinguished;" 3.0-4.0 "strong;" 2.51-3.0 "good;" 2.0-2.5 "adequate;" 1.0-1.99 "marginal;" and 0.0-0.99 "not sufficient for doctoral education." Programs also ranked by "effectiveness of program in educating research scholars/scientists." **Number listed:** 65.

1. Harvard University, with a quality rating of 4.59
2. University of Chicago, 4.53
3. University of California, Berkeley, 4.51
4. City University of New York, Graduate School and University Center, 4.41
5. Yale University, 4.40
6. Princeton University, 4.39
7. University of Pennsylvania, 4.35
8. University of Rochester, 4.24
9. University of Michigan, 4.16
10. University of Illinois, Urbana-Champaign, 4.11
11. Columbia University, 4.05
11. Cornell University, 4.05
13. Brandeis University, 3.85
14. State University of New York, Stony Brook, 3.80
15. Stanford University, 3.79

Source: "Rankings of Research-Doctorate Programs in 41 Disciplines at 274 Institutions," *The Chronicle of Higher Education* 42: A21-A30 (September 21, 1995).

NATURAL SCIENCE ACT SCORES
See: **College Entrance Examinations**

NEWSPAPERS

★2897★
Most memorable news stories of the 20th century

Ranking basis/background: In order of importance as determined by a survey of journalists and historians. **Number listed:** 100.

1. United States drops atomic bombs on Hiroshima, Nagasaki: Japan surrenders to end World War II (1945)
2. American astronaut Neil Armstrong becomes the first human to walk on the moon (1969)
3. Japan bombs Pearl Harbor: United States enters World War II (1941)
4. Wilbur and Orville Wright fly the first powered airplane (1903)
5. Women win the vote (1920)
6. President John F. Kennedy assassinated in Dallas (1963)
7. Horrors of Nazi Holocaust, concentration camps exposed (1945)
8. World War I begins in Europe (1914)
9. *Brown v. Board of Education* ends "separate but equal" school segregation (1954)
10. U.S. stock market crashes: The Great Depression sets in (1929)
11. Alexander Fleming discovers the first antibiotic, penicillin (1928)
12. Structure of DNA discovered (1953)
13. Soviet Union dissolves, Mikhail Gorbachev resigns: Boris Yeltsin takes over (1991)
14. President Richard M. Nixon resigns after Watergate scandal (1974)
15. Germany invades Poland: World War II begins in Europe (1939)
16. Russian Revolution ends: Communists take over (1917)
17. Henry Ford organizes the first major U.S. assembly line to produce Model T cars (1913)
18. Soviets launch Sputnik, first space satellite: space race begins (1957)
19. Albert Einstein presents special theory of relativity: general relativity theory to follow (1905)
20. FDA approves birth-control pill (1960)

Source: *The World Almanac and Book of Facts 2000*, World Almanac Books, 1999.

NUCLEAR ENGINEERING
See: **Engineering, Graduate–Nuclear**

NURSING

★2898★
Top recruiters for nursing jobs for 2000-01 bachelor's degree recipients

Ranking basis/background: Projected number of college hires from on-campus recruitment for 2000-01. **Remarks:** Numbers reflect total expected hires, not just African American projected hires. **Number listed:** 2.

1. Novant Health, with 100 projected hires
2. U.S. Air Force (Active Duty Hires), 58

Source: "The Top 100 Employers and the Majors in Demand for the Class of 2001," *The Black Collegian*, 31: 19-35, (February 2001).

Related Information

★2899★
Official Guide to Undergraduate Nursing Schools, Jones and Bartlett, 2000.
Remarks: Provides up-to-date information about 2-year, 3-year, and 4-year nursing schools based on annual surveys of the National League for Nursing. Includes profiles of all undergraduate nursing schools; information on special programs, distance learning, and part-time studies; practice pre-entrance exam; scholarship advice; and future employment trends. Comes with a companion CD-ROM.

★2900★
Official Guide to Undergraduate and Graduate Nursing Schools, Jones and Bartlett, 2000.
Remarks: Provides up-to-date information about 2-year, 3-year, 4-year, and graduate nursing schools based on annual surveys of the National League for Nursing. Includes profiles of all nursing schools; information on special programs, distance learning, and part-time studies; practice pre-entrance exam; scholarship advice; and future employment trends. Comes with a companion CD-ROM.

NURSING–GRADUATE

Related Information

★2901★
Official Guide to Graduate Nursing Schools, Jones and Bartlett, 2000.
Remarks: Provides up-to-date information about graduate nursing schools based on annual surveys of the National League for Nursing. Includes profiles of all graduate nursing schools; information on special programs, distance learning, and part-time studies; scholarship advice; and future employment trends. Comes with a companion CD-ROM.

NUTRITION

★2902★
Food science and technology journals by citation impact, 1991-99

Ranking basis/background: Impact factor calculated by taking the number of current citations to source items published and dividing it by the number of articles published in the journal during that time period. **Number listed:** 10.

1. *CRC-Critical Review of Food Sciences*, with a 29.63 impact factor
2. *Food/Cosmetics Toxicology*, 19.78
3. *Critical Review of Food Sciences*, 14.16
4. *Food Microstructure*, 11.82
5. *Netherlands Milk/Dairy Journal*, 11.67
6. *Journal of Dairy Research*, 10.96
7. *Journal of Cereal Science*, 10.83
8. *Journal of Dairy Science*, 10.71
9. *Chemical Senses*, 10.29
10. *Starke*, 9.57

Source: "Journals Ranked by Impact: Food Science & Technology," *What's Hot in Research* (http://www.isinet.com/isi/hot/research) Institute for Scientific Information, August 28, 2000.

★2903★
Food science and technology journals by citation impact, 1995-99

Ranking basis/background: Impact factor calculated by taking the number of current citations to source items published and dividing it by the number of articles published in the journal during that time period. **Number listed:** 10.

1. *Critical Review of Food Sciences*, with a 6.38 impact factor
2. *Trends in Food Science and Technology*, 4.75
3. *Netherlands Milk/Dairy Journal*, 4.07
4. *Chemical Senses*, 3.50
5. *Zeit. fur Lebensmittel*, 3.40
6. *Biotechnology Progress*, 3.30
7. *Journal of Cereal Science*, 3.14
8. *Journal of Dairy Research*, 3.11
9. *International Journal of Food Microbiology*, 3.05
10. *Journal of Agriculture and Food Chemistry*, 2.95

Source: "Journals Ranked by Impact: Food Science & Technology," *What's Hot in Research* (http://www.isinet.com/isi/hot/research) Institute for Scientific Information, August 28, 2000.

★2904★
Food science and technology journals by citation impact, 1999

Ranking basis/background: Impact factor calculated by taking the number of current citations to source items published and dividing it by the number of articles published in the journal during that time period. **Number listed:** 10.

1. *Critical Review of Food Sciences*, with a 3.40 impact factor
2. *Chemical Senses*, 2.16
3. *Trends in Food Science and Technology*, 2.09
4. *Biotechnology Progress*, 1.81
5. *Journal of Dairy Science*, 1.67
6. *International Journal of Food Microbiology*, 1.67
7. *Lait*, 1.66
8. *Journal of Cereal Science*, 1.49
9. *Journal of Agriculture and Food Chemistry*, 1.45
10. *Journal of Food Protection*, 1.41

Source: "Journals Ranked by Impact: Food Science & Technology," *What's Hot in Research* (http://www.isinet.com/isi/hot/research) Institute for Scientific Information, August 28, 2000.

OCEANOGRAPHY
See: **Earth Science**

OPERA
See also: **Music**

★2905★
Most frequently produced operas in North America, 1999-2000

Ranking basis/background: Number of productions in North America during the 1999-2000 season. **Remarks:** Original source: *OPERA America*. **Number listed:** 5.

1. *Madame Butterfly*, by Puccini, with 23 productions
2. *The Barber of Seville*, Rossini, 22
3. *Tosca*, Puccini, 19
4. *La Boheme*, Puccini, 18
5. *Don Giovanni*, Mozart, 15

Source: Umminger, April and Genevieve Lynn, "Most Frequently Produced Operas," *USA Today*, February 3, 2000, Section D, p. 1D.

OPTICS

★2906★
Optics journals by citation impact, 1981-99

Ranking basis/background: Impact factor calculated by taking the number of current citations to source items published and dividing it by the number of articles published in the journal during that time period. **Number listed:** 10.

1. *Journal of the Optical Society of America*, with a 18.64 impact factor
2. *Physical Review A*, 14.88
3. *Journal of the Optical Society of America B*, 13.20
4. *Optics Letters*, 13.07
5. *Progress in Optics*, 12.16
6. *Journal of Physics B*, 11.12
7. *Advances in Atomic Molecular Optics*, 10.95
8. *Journal of the Optical Society of America A-Optics Image Science and Vision*, 10.45
9. *Optica Acta*, 8.63
10. *Journal of Lightwave Technology*, 8.34

Source: "Journals Ranked by Impact: Optics," *What's Hot in Research* (http://www.isinet.com/isi/hot/research) Institute for Scientific Information, December 18, 2000.

★2907★
Optics journals by citation impact, 1995-99

Ranking basis/background: Impact factor calculated by taking the number of current citations to source items published and dividing it by the number of articles published in the journal during that time period. **Number listed:** 10.

1. *Advances in Atomic Molecular Optics*, with a 11.41 impact factor
2. *Progress in Optics*, 7.71
3. *Optics Letters*, 6.02
4. *Physical Review A*, 5.52
5. *Journal of the Optical Society of America B*, 4.29
6. *IEEE Journal of Selected Topics in Quantum Electronics*, 4.15
7. *Journal of the Optical Society of America A-Optics Image Science and Vision*, 3.76
8. *Journal of Physics B-Atomic Molecular Optics*, 3.68
9. *IEEE Photonics Technology*, 3.62
10. *Journal of Lightwave Technology*, 3.28

Source: "Journals Ranked by Impact: Optics," *What's Hot in Research* (http://www.isinet.com/isi/hot/research) Institute for Scientific Information, December 18, 2000.

★2908★
Optics journals by citation impact, 1999

Ranking basis/background: Impact factor calculated by taking the number of current citations to source items published and dividing it by the number of articles published in the journal during that time period. **Number listed:** 10.

1. *Advances in Atomic Molecular Optics*, with a 6.67 impact factor
2. *Progress in Optics*, 4.25
3. *Optics Letters*, 3.54
4. *Journal of Physics B-Atomic Molecular Optics*, 2.64
5. *Physical Review A*, 2.64
6. *IEEE Journal of Selected Topics in Quantum Electronics*, 2.51
7. *IEEE Photonics Technology*, 2.14
8. *Journal of the Optical Society of America B*, 2.03
9. *Journal of Lightwave Technology*, 1.99
10. *Journal of the Optical Society of America A-Optics Image Science and Vision*, 1.86

Source: "Journals Ranked by Impact: Optics," *What's Hot in Research* (http://www.isinet.com/isi/hot/research) Institute for Scientific Information, December 18, 2000.

★2909★
Optics journals with the greatest impact measure, 1981-98

Ranking basis/background: Citations-per-paper impact score is the total citations to a journal's published papers divided by total number of papers the journal has published over an eighteen year period. **Remarks:** Original source: *Journal Citation Reports* and Journal Performance Indicators on Diskette. **Number listed:** 10.

1. *Journal of the Optical Society of America*, with an impact score of 17.62
2. *Journal of the Optical Society of America B*, 12.34
3. *Optics Letters*, 12.06
4. *Journal of Physics B*, 10.79
5. *Progress in Optics*, 10.15
6. *Journal of the Optical Society of America A-Optics Image Science and Vision*, 9.50
7. *Advances in Atomic Molecular Optics*, 8.50

8. *Optica Acta*, 8.25
9. *Journal of Lightwave Technology*, 7.85
10. *Applied Optics*, 7.27

Source: "Journals Ranked by Impact: Optics," *What's Hot in Research* (http://www.isinet.com/hot/research) Institute for Scientific Information, January 17, 2000.

★2910★
Optics journals with the greatest impact measure, 1994-98

Ranking basis/background: Citations-per-paper impact score is the total citations to a journal's published papers divided by total number of papers the journal has published over a five year period. **Remarks:** Original source: *Journal Citation Reports* and Journal Performance Indicators on Diskette. **Number listed:** 10.
1. *Advances in Atomic Molecular Optics*, with an impact score of 8.24
2. *Optics Letters*, 5.36
3. *IEE Proceedings-Optoelectronics*, 3.95
4. *Journal of the Optical Society of America A-Optics Image Science and Vision*, 3.88
5. *Journal of the Optical Society of America B*, 3.80
6. *Journal of Physics B*, 3.69
7. *Progress in Optics*, 3.66
8. *IEEE Photonics Technology*, 3.39
9. *Applied Physics B: Lasers and Optics*, 2.87
10. *Journal of Lightwave Technology*, 2.80

Source: "Journals Ranked by Impact: Optics," *What's Hot in Research* (http://www.isinet.com/hot/research) Institute for Scientific Information, January 17, 2000.

★2911★
U.S. universities with the greatest impact in optics and acoustics, 1994-98

Ranking basis/background: Total number of optics and acoustics papers published from each university and average number of citations per paper between 1994 and 1998. **Remarks:** Original source: University Science Indicators on Diskette, 1981-98. **Number listed:** 5.
1. Stanford University, with 260 optics and acoustics papers; 4.76 citations per paper
2. Caltech, 219; 4.33
3. University of California, San Diego, 209; 4.24
4. Massachusetts Institute of Technology, 405; 4.23
5. University of Michigan, 274; 3.87

Source: "Optics & Acoustics: High-Impact U.S. Universities, 1994-98," *What's Hot in Research* (http://www.isinet.com/hot/research) Institute for Scientific Information, April 24, 2000.

★2912★
U.S. universities with the greatest impact in optics and acoustics, 1995-99

Ranking basis/background: Average citations per paper from the top 100 federally funded U.S. universities that had at least 50 published papers in ISI indexed optics and acoustics journals. Also includes total number of papers published during the five year period. **Number listed:** 5.
1. Princeton University, with 104 papers; 7.25 citations per paper
2. Stanford University, 232; 6.16
3. Cornell University, 101; 5.78
4. Harvard University, 106; 5.28
5. University of Pennsylvania, 101; 4.68

Source: "Optics & Acoustics: High Impact U.S. Universities, 1995-99," *What's Hot in Research* (http://www.isinet.com/isi/hot/research) Institute for Scientific Information.

ORAL INTERPRETATION
See: **Speech Communication**

ORGANIZATIONS

★2913★
Institutions in the Worker Rights Consortium

Ranking basis/background: Alphabetical list. **Number listed:** 44.
Albion College
Bard College
Boston College
Brown University
College of the Holy Cross
Columbia University
Cornell University
DePaul University
Earlham College
Georgetown University
Haverford College
Indiana University, Bloomington
Loyola University, Chicago
Loyola University, New Orleans
Macalester College
Miami University (OH)
Middlebury College
New York University
Northern Illinois University
Oberlin College
St. Cloud State University
St. Mary's College
San Francisco State University
Smith College
Transylvania University
University of California, Berkeley
University of California, Davis
University of California, Irvine
University of California, Los Angeles
University of California, Merced
University of California, Riverside
University of California, San Diego
University of California, San Francisco
University of California, Santa Barbara
University of California, Santa Cruz
University of Illinois, Urbana-Champaign
University of Iowa
University of Michigan, Ann Arbor
University of Minnesota, Twin Cities
University of North Carolina, Chapel Hill
University of Oregon
University of Wisconsin, Madison
University of Wisconsin, Stevens Point
Western Michigan University

Source: Van Der Werf, Martin, "The Worker Rights Consortium Makes Strides Toward Legitimacy," *The Chronicle of Higher Education*, 46: A41-A42, (April 21, 2000).

ORGANIZATIONAL COMMUNICATION
See: **Speech Communication**

ORGANIZATIONAL THEORY AND BEHAVIOR
See: **Business Administration**

PEER EVALUATION
See: **Evaluation Criteria & Methodologies–Peers**

PERIODICALS

★2914★
African periodical prices, 2001

Ranking basis/background: Average price per title. **Remarks:** Based on EBSCO's database of 260,000 serial title listings. Only prepriced titles were included. **Number listed:** 1.
Africa, with $90.89

Source: Born, Kathleen and Lee Van Orsdel, "Searching for Serials Utopia," *Library Journal*, 126: 53-58, (April 15, 2001).

★2915★
Arts and humanities periodical prices, 2001

Ranking basis/background: Average price per title. **Remarks:** Based on EBSCO's database of 260,000 serial title listings. Only prepriced titles were included. **Number listed:** 2.
U.S., with $146.78
Non-U.S., $253.68

Source: Born, Kathleen and Lee Van Orsdel, "Searching for Serials Utopia," *Library Journal*, 126: 53-58, (April 15, 2001).

★2916★
Asian periodical prices by country, 2001

Ranking basis/background: Average price per title. **Remarks:** Based on EBSCO's database of 260,000 serial title listings. Only prepriced titles were included. **Number listed:** 2.
1. Japan, with $290.40
2. Other, $464.83

Source: Born, Kathleen and Lee Van Orsdel, "Searching for Serials Utopia," *Library Journal*, 126: 53-58, (April 15, 2001).

★2917★
Australia and New Zealand periodical prices, 2001

Ranking basis/background: Average price per title. **Remarks:** Based on EBSCO's database of 260,000 serial title listings. Only prepriced titles were included. **Number listed:** 1.
Australia and New Zealand, with $328.38

Source: Born, Kathleen and Lee Van Orsdel, "Searching for Serials Utopia," *Library Journal*, 126: 53-58, (April 15, 2001).

★2918★
Average costs for Academic Search titles by subject, 2001

Ranking basis/background: Average costs per title for college and medium-sized university libraries, alphabetical by subject. **Remarks:** Based on EBSCO's database of 260,000 serial title listings. Only prepriced titles were included. **Number listed:** 31.

Agriculture, with an average cost per title of $79.14
Anthropology, $126.96
Art and architecture, $168.48
Astronomy, $115.98
Biology, $416.03
Botany, $185.00
Business and economics, $176.02
Chemistry, $1,777.00
Education, $244.60
Engineering, $320.22
Food science, $130.37
General science, $237.68
General works, $67.20
Geography, $149.31
Health sciences, $282.81
History, $122.98
Language and literature, $108.66
Law, $116.49
Library and information science, $105.13
Math and computer science, $282.45
Military and Naval science, $105.42
Music, $83.00
Philosophy and religion, $88.00
Physics, $1,850.38
Political science, $208.26
Psychology, $272.32
Recreation, $60.61
Sociology, $234.03
Technology, $113.16
Zoology, $16.00

Source: Born, Kathleen and Lee Van Orsdel, "Searching for Serials Utopia," *Library Journal*, 126: 53-58, (April 15, 2001).

★2919★
Average costs of Magazine Article Summaries titles, 2001

Ranking basis/background: Average costs per title of those most often subscribed to by school and public libraries. **Remarks:** Based on EBSCO's database of 260,000 serial title listings. Only prepriced titles were included. **Number listed:** 2.

U.S. subscriptions, with $66.97
Non-U.S., $411.85

Source: Born, Kathleen and Lee Van Orsdel, "Searching for Serials Utopia," *Library Journal*, 126: 53-58, (April 15, 2001).

★2920★
Best-selling youth magazines

Ranking basis/background: Circulation figures for best-selling youth magazines. **Remarks:** Original source: Paid circulation analysis filed with the Audit Bureau of Circulations. **Number listed:** 10.

1. *Boy's Life*, with a circulation of 1,252,920
2. *Contact Kids*, 310,690
3. *Kid City Magazine*, 261,806
4. *Beckett Baseball Card Monthly*, 209,768
5. *Bop*, 136,915
6. *Super Teen*, 127,308
7. *16 Magazine*, 123,149
8. *Teen Beat*, 122,512
9. *Beckett Football Card Monthly*, 108,374
10. *Beckett Basketball Card Monthly*, 98,690

Source: "Bestsellers," *U.S. News & World Report*, 128: 62, (May 15, 2000).

★2921★
European periodical prices by country, 2001

Ranking basis/background: Average price per title. **Remarks:** Based on EBSCO's database of 260,000 serial title listings. Only prepriced titles were included. **Number listed:** 8.

1. Netherlands, with $1,755.34
2. Ireland, $1,514.90
3. Germany, $853.30
4. United Kingdom, $848.44
5. Switzerland, $649.82
6. France, $269.62
7. Italy, $120.85
8. Other, $363.62

Source: Born, Kathleen and Lee Van Orsdel, "Searching for Serials Utopia," *Library Journal*, 126: 53-58, (April 15, 2001).

★2922★
Institute for Scientific Information periodical prices by country, 2001

Ranking basis/background: Average price per title. **Remarks:** Based on EBSCO's database of 260,000 serial title listings. Only prepriced titles were included. **Number listed:** 28.

1. Netherlands, with 497 titles; with an average price per title of $1,755.34
2. Ireland, 45; $1,154.90
3. Singapore, 11; $1,280.18
4. Austria, 26; $994.37
5. England, 1,338; $857.51
6. Germany, 355; $853.30
7. Switzerland, 95; $649.82
8. United States, 2,550; $473.57
9. New Zealand, 27; $456.05
10. Denmark, 56; $387.75
11. Russia, 29; $356.24
12. Japan, 76; $290.40
13. Scotland, 15; $289.53
14. Australia, 61; $271.87
15. Israel, 13; $270.00
16. France, 153; $269.62
17. Sweden, 17; $199.01
18. Hungary, 9; $183.00
19. Spain, 11; $182.23
20. Czech Republic, 8; $166.53
21. Norway, 13; $153.64
22. Canada, 122; $141.55
23. Italy, 64; $120.85
24. Belgium, 16; $103.75
25. Taiwan, 7; $90.86
26. India, 9; $87.11
27. Mexico, 9; $71.89
28. South Africa, 12; $71.45

Source: Born, Kathleen and Lee Van Orsdel, "Searching for Serials Utopia," *Library Journal*, 126: 53-58, (April 15, 2001).

★2923★
***Library Journal*'s notable new magazines, 1999**

Ranking basis/background: Alphabetical listing by magazine title. **Number listed:** 10.

Bride Again
Code
eBay Magazine
Garden Escape
Hero: The Magazine for the Rest of Us
In Touch
National Geographic Adventure
Talk
Tin House
Wicked

Source: Colford, Michael, "Best New Magazines of 1999," *Library Journal*, 125: 50-51, (May 1, 2000).

★2924★
North American periodical prices by country, 2001

Ranking basis/background: Average price per title. **Remarks:** Based on EBSCO's database of 260,000 serial title listings. Only prepriced titles were included. **Number listed:** 3.

1. United States, with $473.57
2. Canada, $85.60
3. Other, $85.60

Source: Born, Kathleen and Lee Van Orsdel, "Searching for Serials Utopia," *Library Journal*, 126: 53-58, (April 15, 2001).

★2925★
Periodical prices by LC subject, 2001

Ranking basis/background: Average price per title, alphabetical by LC subject. **Remarks:** Based on EBSCO's database of 260,000 serial title listings. Only prepriced titles were included. **Number listed:** 31.

Agriculture, with an average price per title of $529.22
Anthropology, $256.68
Art and architecture, $109.53
Astronomy, $1,083.91
Biology, $1,064.33
Botany, $790.28
Business and economics, $500.94
Chemistry, $1,918.09
Education, $249.81
Engineering, $1,142.84
Food science, $731.26
General science, $830.55
General works, $89.50
Geography, $682.29
Geology, $914.51
Health sciences, $728.14
History, $120.05
Language and literature, $101.34
Law, $159.91
Library and information science, $259.69
Math and computer science, $1,018.57
Military and Naval science, $329.00
Music, $79.94
Philosophy and religion, $136.48
Physics, $2,011.13
Political science, $254.19
Psychology, $326.00
Recreation, $127.20
Sociology, $297.18
Technology, $1,013.34
Zoology, $866.03

Source: Born, Kathleen and Lee Van Orsdel, "Searching for Serials Utopia," *Library Journal*, 126: 53-58, (April 15, 2001).

★2926★
Periodical prices by scientific discipline, 2001

Ranking basis/background: Average price per title. **Remarks:** Based on EBSCO's database of 260,000 serial title listings. Only prepriced titles were included. **Number listed:** 14.

1. Physics, with an average price per title of $2,011.13
2. Chemistry, $1,918.09
3. Engineering, $1,142.84
4. Astronomy, $1,083.91

PETROLEUM ENGINEERING

5. Biology, $1,064.33
6. Math and computer science, $1,018.57
7. Technology, $1,013.34
8. Geology, $914.51
9. Zoology, $866.03
10. General science, $830.55
11. Botany, $790.28
12. Food science, $731.26
13. Health sciences, $728.14
14. Geography, $682.29

Source: Born, Kathleen and Lee Van Orsdel, "Searching for Serials Utopia," *Library Journal*, 126: 53-58, (April 15, 2001).

★2927★
Projected costs of all arts and humanities periodical titles, 2001

Ranking basis/background: Projected total cost in 2002. **Remarks:** Based on EBSCO's database of 260,000 serial title listings. Only prepriced titles were included. **Number listed:** 2.
U.S. subscriptions, with $123,579
Non-U.S., $220,232

Source: Born, Kathleen and Lee Van Orsdel, "Searching for Serials Utopia," *Library Journal*, 126: 53-58, (April 15, 2001).

★2928★
Projected costs of all science periodical titles, 2001

Ranking basis/background: Projected total cost in 2002. **Remarks:** Based on EBSCO's database of 260,000 serial title listings. Only prepriced titles were included. **Number listed:** 2.
U.S. subscriptions, with $1,044,250
Non-U.S., $2,324,724

Source: Born, Kathleen and Lee Van Orsdel, "Searching for Serials Utopia," *Library Journal*, 126: 53-58, (April 15, 2001).

★2929★
Projected costs of all social science periodical titles, 2001

Ranking basis/background: Projected total cost in 2002. **Remarks:** Based on EBSCO's database of 260,000 serial title listings. Only prepriced titles were included. **Number listed:** 2.
U.S. subscriptions, with $524,131
Non-U.S., $1,046,758

Source: Born, Kathleen and Lee Van Orsdel, "Searching for Serials Utopia," *Library Journal*, 126: 53-58, (April 15, 2001).

★2930★
Projected total costs for Academic Search titles, 2001

Ranking basis/background: Number of titles, total cost in 2001, and projected total cost in 2002. **Remarks:** Based on EBSCO's database of 260,000 serial title listings. Only prepriced titles were included. **Number listed:** 2.
U.S. subscriptions, with 711 titles; a total cost of $104,809 in 2001; a projected costs of $115,814 in 2002
Non-U.S., $230; $87,108; $97,561

Source: Born, Kathleen and Lee Van Orsdel, "Searching for Serials Utopia," *Library Journal*, 126: 53-58, (April 15, 2001).

★2931★
Science periodical prices, 2001

Ranking basis/background: Average price per title. **Remarks:** Based on EBSCO's database of 260,000 serial title listings. Only prepriced titles were included. **Number listed:** 2.
U.S., with $799.76
Non-U.S., $1,211.06

Source: Born, Kathleen and Lee Van Orsdel, "Searching for Serials Utopia," *Library Journal*, 126: 53-58, (April 15, 2001).

★2932★
Social science periodical prices, 2001

Ranking basis/background: Average price per title. **Remarks:** Based on EBSCO's database of 260,000 serial title listings. Only prepriced titles were included. **Number listed:** 2.
U.S., with $357.44
Non-U.S., $735.93

Source: Born, Kathleen and Lee Van Orsdel, "Searching for Serials Utopia," *Library Journal*, 126: 53-58, (April 15, 2001).

★2933★
South American periodical prices, 2001

Ranking basis/background: Average price per title. **Remarks:** Based on EBSCO's database of 260,000 serial title listings. Only prepriced titles were included. **Number listed:** 1.
South America, with $76.85

Source: Born, Kathleen and Lee Van Orsdel, "Searching for Serials Utopia," *Library Journal*, 126: 53-58, (April 15, 2001).

PETROLEUM ENGINEERING
See: **Engineering, Graduate–Petroleum Engineering–Petroleum**

PHARMACY

★2934★
Top recruiters for pharmacology/pharmaceutical jobs for 2000-01 bachelor's degree recipients

Ranking basis/background: Projected number of college hires from on-campus recruitment for 2000-01. **Remarks:** Numbers reflect total expected hires, not just African American projected hires. **Number listed:** 2.
1. Abbott Laboratories, with 80 projected hires
2. Novant Health, 10

Source: "The Top 100 Employers and the Majors in Demand for the Class of 2001," *The Black Collegian*, 31: 19-35, (February 2001).

★2935★
Trends in pharmacy school applications, 1994 through 2000

Ranking basis/background: Number, in thousands, of pharmacy school applications filed each year. **Remarks:** Original source: American Association of Colleges of Pharmacy. **Number listed:** 7.
1994, with 34.2 thousand
1995, 32.7
1996, 33.9
1997, 29.1
1998, 25.0
1999, 23.7
2000, 24.1

Source: Mangan, Katherine S., "Pharmacy Schools Struggle to Fill Their Classes," *The Chronicle of Higher Education*, 47: A43-A44, (March 2, 2001).

★2936★
U.S. universities with the greatest impact in pharmacology, 1994-98

Ranking basis/background: Average citations per paper from the top 100 federally funded U.S. universities that had at least 50 published papers in ISI indexed pharmacology journals. Also includes total number of paper published during the five year period. **Number listed:** 5.
1. Vanderbilt University, with 297 papers; 11.51 citations per paper
2. University of Chicago, 137; 10.01
3. University of California, Los Angeles, 220; 9.88
4. Duke University, 242; 9.86
5. Oregon Health Sciences University, 119; 9.84

Source: "Pharmacology: High Impact U.S. Universities, 1994-98," *What's Hot in Research* (http://www.isinet.com/isi/hot/research) *Institute for Scientific Information*, June 5, 2000.

★2937★
U.S. universities with the highest concentration of papers published in the field of pharmacology, 1995-99

Ranking basis/background: Number of papers published in the field of pharmacology over a five-year period, and percentage they comprise of the university's total papers published. **Number listed:** 5.
1. Virginia Commonwealth University, with 274 papers; 6.12% of university's total papers
2. University of Kansas, 302; 5.66%
3. University of North Carolina, Chapel Hill, 543; 4.50%
4. West Virginia University, 118; 4.04%
5. University of Illinois, Chicago, 319; 4.00%

Source: "U.S. Universities with Highest Concentrations in Pharmacology, 1995-99," *What's Hot in Research* (http://www.isinet.com/isi/hot/research) *Institute for Scientific Information*, January 1, 2001.

PHARMACY, GRADUATE

★2938★
Most effective pharmacology research-doctorate programs as evaluated by the National Research Council

Ranking basis/background: From a survey of nearly 8,000 faculty members conducted in the spring of 1993. Respondents were asked to rate programs in their field on "effectiveness of program in educating research scholars/scientists." **Remarks:** See *Chronicle* article for more details. Scores of 3.5-5.0 indicate "extremely effective;" 2.5-3.49 "reasonably effective;" 1.5-2.49 "minimally effective;" and 0.0-1.49 "not effective." Programs also ranked by "scholarly quality of program faculty." **Number listed:** 127.
1. Yale University, with an effectiveness rating of 4.32

2. Johns Hopkins University, 4.22
3. Vanderbilt University, 4.15
4. University of North Carolina, Chapel Hill interdisciplinary with the Schools of Medicine, Pharmacology, and Public Health, 4.14
5. University of Texas Southwest Medical Center, 4.04
6. Duke University, 4.03
7. University of Pennsylvania, 4.02
8. University of Washington (WA), 4.01
9. Harvard University, 4.00
10. University of North Carolina, Chapel Hill School of Arts and Sciences, 3.99

Source: "Rankings of Research-Doctorate Programs in 41 Disciplines at 274 Institutions," *The Chronicle of Higher Education* 42: A21-A30 (September 21, 1995).

★2939★
Top pharmacology research-doctorate programs as evaluated by the National Research Council

Ranking basis/background: From a survey of nearly 8,000 faculty members conducted in the spring of 1993. Respondents were asked to rate programs in their field on "scholarly quality of program faculty." When more than one program had the same score, the council averaged the rank order and gave each program the same rank number (if three programs tied for the top position, each received a rank of 2). **Remarks:** See *Chronicle* article for more details. Scores of 4.01 and above indicate "distinguished;" 3.0-4.0 "strong;" 2.51-3.0 "good;" 2.0-2.5 "adequate;" 1.0-1.99 "marginal;" and 0.0-0.99 "not sufficient for doctoral education." Programs also ranked by "effectiveness of program in educating research scholars/scientists." **Number listed:** 127.
1. Yale University, with a quality rating of 4.45
2. University of Texas Southwest Medical Center, 4.39
3. University of California, San Diego, 4.36
4. Johns Hopkins University, 4.21
5. Duke University, 4.18
6. Vanderbilt University, 4.17
7. Harvard University, 4.14
8. University of North Carolina, Chapel Hill School of Arts and Sciences, 4.03
9. University of Washington (WA), 4.02
9. University of Pennsylvania, 4.02
11. Massachusetts Institute of Technology, 3.90
12. University of Wisconsin, Madison, 3.89
13. University of Michigan Medical Center, 3.85
14. New York University, 3.84
15. Emory University, 3.83

Source: "Rankings of Research-Doctorate Programs in 41 Disciplines at 274 Institutions," *The Chronicle of Higher Education* 42: A21-A30 (September 21, 1995).

★2940★
Top recruiters for pharmacology/pharmaceutical jobs for 2000-01 master's degree recipients

Ranking basis/background: Projected number of college hires from on-campus recruitment for 2000-01. **Remarks:** Numbers reflect total expected hires, not just African American projected hires. **Number listed:** 2.
1. Novant Health, with 20 projected hires
2. U.S. Air Force (Active Duty Hires), 12

Source: "The Top 100 Employers and the Majors in Demand for the Class of 2001," *The Black Collegian*, 31: 19-35, (February 2001).

PH.D.
See: **Doctoral Degrees**

PHILANTHROPIC FOUNDATIONS

★2941★
Corporations making the most contributions to African American communities, 1995

Ranking basis/background: Figures, in millions, for grants awarded to African American communities. A total of 3,518 grants were awarded, totaling $61,496,128. **Remarks:** Original source: National Committee for Responsive Philanthropy. **Number listed:** 4.
1. Coca-Cola Enterprises, with $2.71 million
2. Exxon, $2.69
2. Ford Motor Company, $2.69
4. General Motors, $2.55

Source: Collison, Michele N-K, "The Changing Face of Philanthropy," *Black Issues in Higher Education*, 17: 18-23, (May 25, 2000).

★2942★
National Society of Fund-Raising Executives, by race/ethnicity

Ranking basis/background: Percentage of representative in each racial category. **Remarks:** Original source: National Society of Fund-Raising Executives. **Number listed:** 5.
1. White, with 96.2%
2. African American, 1.9%
3. Hispanic American, 1.1%
4. Asian American, .4%
4. Native American, .4%

Source: Collison, Michele N-K, "The Changing Face of Philanthropy," *Black Issues in Higher Education*, 17: 18-23, (May 25, 2000).

★2943★
Organizations with the most charitable contributions raised, 1999

Ranking basis/background: Amount raised, in millions, of charitable giving by individuals, corporations, and foundation. **Remarks:** Original source: The Chronicle of Philanthropy. **Number listed:** 10.
1. Salvation Army, with $1,400 million raised
2. YMCA of the USA, $693
3. American Red Cross, $678
4. American Cancer Society, $620
5. Fidelity Investments Charitable Gift Fund, $573
6. Lutheran Services in America, $559
7. United Jewish Communities, $524
8. America's Second Harvest, $472
9. Habitat for Humanity International, $467
10. Harvard University, $452

Source: "A Giving Spree," *U.S. News & World Report*, 129: 12, (December 11, 2000).

★2944★
Top recipients of corporate contributions to African American communities, 1995

Ranking basis/background: Figures, in millions, for grants awarded to African American communities. A total of 3,518 grants were awarded, totaling $61,496,128. **Remarks:** Original source: National Committee for Responsive Philanthropy. **Number listed:** 4.
1. The College Fund/UNCF, with $8.78 million
2. Urban League, $2.63
3. NAACP, $1.14
4. Howard University, $.88

Source: Collison, Michele N-K, "The Changing Face of Philanthropy," *Black Issues in Higher Education*, 17: 18-23, (May 25, 2000).

PHILOSOPHY, GRADUATE

★2945★
Most effective philosophy research-doctorate programs as evaluated by the National Research Council

Ranking basis/background: From a survey of nearly 8,000 faculty members conducted in the spring of 1993. Respondents were asked to rate programs in their field on "effectiveness of program in educating research scholars/scientists." **Remarks:** See *Chronicle* article for more details. Scores of 3.5-5.0 indicate "extremely effective;" 2.5-3.49 "reasonably effective;" 1.5-2.49 "minimally effective;" and 0.0-1.49 "not effective." Programs also ranked by "scholarly quality of program faculty." **Number listed:** 72.
1. Princeton University, with an effectiveness rating of 4.56
2. University of Pittsburgh, 4.43
3. University of Pittsburgh, Program in History and Philosophy of Science, 4.26
4. Cornell University, 4.14
5. Stanford University, 4.02
6. University of California, Los Angeles, 4.01
7. Massachusetts Institute of Technology, 3.91
8. University of Michigan, 3.88
9. Harvard University, 3.77
10. University of Arizona, 3.74

Source: "Rankings of Research-Doctorate Programs in 41 Disciplines at 274 Institutions," *The Chronicle of Higher Education* 42: A21-A30 (September 21, 1995).

★2946★
Radcliffe Institute for Advanced Study fellowship recipients in the field of philosophy, 2000-01

Ranking basis/background: Recipient and institutional affiliation of the Radcliffe Institute for Advanced study fellowship for pursuit of advanced work across a wide range of academic disciplines, professions, and creative arts. **Number listed:** 2.
  Angelica Nuzzo, DePaul University
  Daryl Tress, Fordham University

Source: "The Radcliffe Institute for Advanced Study," *The Chronicle of Higher Education*, 46: A59, (June 2, 2000).

PHYSICAL SCIENCES, GRADUATE

★2947★
Top philosophy research-doctorate programs as evaluated by the National Research Council

Ranking basis/background: From a survey of nearly 8,000 faculty members conducted in the spring of 1993. Respondents were asked to rate programs in their field on "scholarly quality of program faculty." When more than one program had the same score, the council averaged the rank order and gave each program the same rank number (if three programs tied for the top position, each received a rank of 2). **Remarks:** See *Chronicle* article for more details. Scores of 4.01 and above indicate "distinguished;" 3.0-4.0 "strong;" 2.51-3.0 "good;" 2.0-2.5 "adequate;" 1.0-1.99 "marginal;" and 0.0-0.99 "not sufficient for doctoral education." Programs also ranked by "effectiveness of program in educating research scholars/scientists." **Number listed:** 72.

1. Princeton University, with a quality rating of 4.93
2. University of Pittsburgh, 4.73
3. Harvard University, 4.69
4. University of California, Berkeley, 4.66
5. University of Pittsburgh, Program in History and Philosophy of Science, 4.47
6. University of California, Los Angeles, 4.42
7. Stanford University, 4.20
8. University of Michigan, 4.15
9. Cornell University, 4.11
10. Massachusetts Institute of Technology, 4.01
11. University of Arizona, 3.99
12. University of Chicago, 3.88
13. Rutgers University, New Brunswick, 3.82
13. Brown University, 3.82
15. University of California, San Diego, 3.79

Source: "Rankings of Research-Doctorate Programs in 41 Disciplines at 274 Institutions," *The Chronicle of Higher Education* 42: A21-A30 (September 21, 1995).

★2948★
U.S. universities publishing the most papers in the field of philosophy, 1995-99

Ranking basis/background: Number of papers published in the field of philosophy over a five-year period, and percent of field based on each universities percentage of 10,777 papers entered in the ISI database from ISI-indexed philosophy journals. **Number listed:** 5.

1. University of Wisconsin, Madison, with 105 papers; 0.97% of field
2. University of Pittsburgh, 94; 0.87%
3. Harvard University, 86; 0.80%
4. Princeton University, 85; 0.79%
5. City University of New York, 79; 0.73%

Source: "Philosophy: Most Prolific U.S. Universities, 1995-99," *What's Hot in Research* (http://www.isinet.com/isi/hot/research) *Institute for Scientific Information*, September 25, 2000.

PHYSICAL SCIENCES, GRADUATE
See also: **Chemistry, Graduate Earth Science, Graduate Engineering, Graduate Physics, Graduate**

★2949★
Private, 4-year undergraduate colleges and universities producing the most Ph.D.'s in physics and astronomy, 1920-1990

Ranking basis/background: Number of doctoral degrees granted to graduates of 914 private, 4-year U.S. undergraduate colleges and universities. Medical, law, and other professional, non-doctoral degrees are not included. **Remarks:** Original source: Office of Scientific and Engineering Personnel of the National Research Council. Report contains 50 other tables detailing the distribution of doctoral recipients by field of study over various time frames. **Number listed:** 335.

1. Oberlin College, with 205 Ph.D.'s
2. Polytechnic University, 197
3. Swarthmore College, 177
4. Reed College, 158
5. Carleton College, 149
6. Union College, 134
7. Stevens Institute of Technology, 132
8. Pomona College, 123
9. Worcester Polytechnic Institute, 119
10. Harvey Mudd College, 118
11. Amherst College, 116
12. Cooper Union, 112
13. Wesleyan University, 104
14. Manhattan College, 103
15. Williams College, 100
16. St. Olaf College, 85
16. Haverford College, 85
18. St. Joseph's University, 75
19. Villanova University, 68

Source: *Baccalaureate Origins of Doctorate Recipients*, 7th ed., Franklin & Marshall College, March 1993.

PHYSICS

★2950★
African American physics faculty, by type of institution, 2000

Ranking basis/background: Number of African American physics faculty at each type of institution in 2000. **Remarks:** Original source: 2000 AWF Survey. **Number listed:** 3.

Ph.D., with 38
Master's, 41
Bachelor's, 62

Source: Ivie, Rachel, Katie Stowe and Roman Czujko, "2000 Physics Academic Workforce Report," *AIP: American Institute of Physics Report*, March 2001.

★2951★
Current positions of new physics faculty at bachelor's-granting institutions in 2000

Ranking basis/background: Percentage of new physics faculty at each employment level. **Remarks:** Original source: 2000 AWF Survey. **Number listed:** 6.

Full professor, with 2%
Associate professor, 5%
Assistant professor, 63%
Research professor, 1%
Instructor/adjunct, 23%
Visiting professor, 6%

Source: Ivie, Rachel, Katie Stowe and Roman Czujko, "2000 Physics Academic Workforce Report," *AIP: American Institute of Physics Report*, March 2001.

★2952★
Current positions of new physics faculty at master's-granting institutions in 2000

Ranking basis/background: Percentage of new physics faculty at each employment level. **Remarks:** Original source: 2000 AWF Survey. **Number listed:** 6.

Full professor, with 1%
Associate professor, 5%
Assistant professor, 52%
Research professor, 1%
Instructor/adjunct, 39%
Visiting professor, 2%

Source: Ivie, Rachel, Katie Stowe and Roman Czujko, "2000 Physics Academic Workforce Report," *AIP: American Institute of Physics Report*, March 2001.

★2953★
Current positions of new physics faculty at Ph.D.-granting institutions in 2000

Ranking basis/background: Percentage of new physics faculty at each employment level. **Remarks:** Original source: 2000 AWF Survey. **Number listed:** 6.

Full professor, with 13%
Associate professor, 9%
Assistant professor, 50%
Research professor, 6%
Instructor/adjunct, 15%
Visiting professor, 7%

Source: Ivie, Rachel, Katie Stowe and Roman Czujko, "2000 Physics Academic Workforce Report," *AIP: American Institute of Physics Report*, March 2001.

★2954★
Distribution of physics faculty at bachelor's-granting institutions, 2000

Ranking basis/background: Number of departments and median number of physics faculty in 2000. **Remarks:** Original source: 2000 AWF Survey. **Number listed:** 2.

Number of departments: 513
Median number of faculty: 4

Source: Ivie, Rachel, Katie Stowe and Roman Czujko, "2000 Physics Academic Workforce Report," *AIP: American Institute of Physics Report*, March 2001.

★2955★
Distribution of physics faculty at master's-granting institutions, 2000

Ranking basis/background: Number of departments and median number of physics faculty in 2000. **Remarks:** Original source: 2000 AWF Survey. **Number listed:** 2.

Number of departments: 67
Median number of faculty: 10

Source: Ivie, Rachel, Katie Stowe and Roman Czujko, "2000 Physics Academic Workforce Report," *AIP: American Institute of Physics Report*, March 2001.

PHYSICS

★2956★
Distribution of physics faculty at Ph.D.-granting institutions, 2000

Ranking basis/background: Number of departments and median number of physics faculty in 2000. **Remarks:** Original source: 2000 AWF Survey. **Number listed:** 2.
- Number of departments: 186
- Median number of faculty: 22

Source: Ivie, Rachel, Katie Stowe and Roman Czujko, "2000 Physics Academic Workforce Report," *AIP: American Institute of Physics Report*, March 2001.

★2957★
Full-time equivalent physics faculty, by type of institution, 2000

Ranking basis/background: Total number of full-time equivalent physics faculty and mean number of faculty in 2000. **Remarks:** Original source: 2000 AWF Survey. **Number listed:** 4.
- Ph.D., with 5,000 full-time equivalent physics faculty; mean number of faculty, 27
- Master's, 775; 11
- Bachelor's, 2,600; 5
- Total, 8,375; 11

Source: Ivie, Rachel, Katie Stowe and Roman Czujko, "2000 Physics Academic Workforce Report," *AIP: American Institute of Physics Report*, March 2001.

★2958★
Hispanic American physics faculty, by type of institution, 2000

Ranking basis/background: Number of Hispanic American physics faculty at each type of institution in 2000. **Remarks:** Original source: 2000 AWF Survey. **Number listed:** 3.
- Ph.D., with 81
- Master's, 32
- Bachelor's, 42

Source: Ivie, Rachel, Katie Stowe and Roman Czujko, "2000 Physics Academic Workforce Report," *AIP: American Institute of Physics Report*, March 2001.

★2959★
Institutions with the most female physics bachelor's recipients, 1994-1998

Ranking basis/background: Alphabetical list of institutions graduating at least five physics majors, with at least two female recipients. Women's colleges excluded. **Number listed:** 20.
- Baylor University
- Belmont University
- Catholic University of America
- Dickinson College
- Dillard University
- Drew University
- Fisk University
- Fordham University
- Gordon College
- Grambling State University
- Hiram College
- Jackson State University
- Lincoln University (PA)
- Mary Washington College
- Southern University (LA)
- Tougaloo College
- University of Denver
- University of Michigan, Dearborn
- University of Minnesota, Morris
- Xavier University (LA)

Source: "Prime Numbers," *The Chronicle of Higher Education*, 47: A9, (January 12, 2001).

★2960★
Often-cited papers appearing in the *American Journal of Physics*, 1945-1990

Ranking basis/background: AJP papers published between 1945-1990 with 100 or more citations in ISI's *Science Citation Index*. **Number listed:** 13.
1. J. Kraitchman, "Determination of Molecular Structure from Microwave Spectroscopic Data", 21(1), 17-24 (1953), with 677 citations
2. Michael E. Fisher, "Magnetism in One-Dimensional Systems–The Heisenberg Model for Infinite Spin", 32(5), 343-46 (1964), 445
3. N. Bloembergen, "The Stimulated Raman Effect", 35(11), 989-1023 (1967), 204
4. O.M.P. Bilaniuk, V.K. Deshpande, and E.C.G. Sudarshan, "'Meta' Relativity", 30(10),718-23 (1962), 195
5. Eugene P. Wigner, "The Problem of Measurement", 31(1), 6-15 (1963), 175
6. G.K. Horton, "Ideal Rare-Gas Crystals", 36(2), 93-119 (1968), 150
7. W. Martienssen and E. Spiller, "Coherence and Fluctuations in Light Beams", 32(12), 919-26 (1964), 119
8. N.R. Werthamer, "Theory of Quantum Crystals", 37(8), 763-82 (1969), 115
9. H.F. Stimson, "Heat Units and Temperature Scales for Calorimetry", 23(9), 614-22 (1955), 112
10. Abraham Goldberg and Harry M. Schey, "Computer-Generated Motion Pictures of One-Dimensional Quantum-Mechanical Transmission and Reflection Phenomena", 35(3), 177-186 (1967), 107
11. J.A. Brinkman, "Production of Atomic Displacements by High-Energy Particles", 24(4), 246-67 (1956), 106
12. Rodney Loudon, "One-Dimensional Hydrogen Atom", 27(9), 649-55 (1959), 106
13. Arnold G. Meister and Forrest F. Cleveland, "Application of Group Theory to the Calculation of Vibrational Frequencies of Polyatomic Molecules", 14(1), 13-27 (1946), 103

Source: "Science Citation Index Leaders," *American Journal of Physics* 61: 103-106 (February 1993).

★2961★
Physics degrees awarded at bachelors-granting institutions, by degree, 1998-99

Ranking basis/background: Number of physics degrees awarded at each level. **Number listed:** 1.
- Bachelors, with 1,683

Source: Nicholson, Starr and Patrick J. Mulvey, "Roster of Physics Departments with Enrollment and Degree Data, 1999," *AIP: American Institute of Physics Report*, August 2000.

★2962★
Physics departments at bachelor's-granting institutions recruiting new faculty members for 2001

Ranking basis/background: Number and percent of department recruiting tenured or tenure-track faculty and number and percent of department recruiting visiting faculty. **Remarks:** Original source: 2000 AWF Survey. **Number listed:** 4.
- Percent of department recruiting tenured or tenure-track faculty: 28%
- Number of tenured or tenure track recruitments, 173
- Percent of departments recruiting visiting faculty, 19%
- Number of visiting recruitments, 118

Source: Ivie, Rachel, Katie Stowe and Roman Czujko, "2000 Physics Academic Workforce Report," *AIP: American Institute of Physics Report*, March 2001.

★2963★
Physics departments at master's-granting institutions recruiting new faculty members for 2001

Ranking basis/background: Number and percent of department recruiting tenured or tenure-track faculty and number and percent of department recruiting visiting faculty. **Remarks:** Original source: 2000 AWF Survey. **Number listed:** 4.
- Percent of department recruiting tenured or tenure-track faculty: 52%
- Number of tenured or tenure track recruitments, 54
- Percent of departments recruiting visiting faculty, 8%
- Number of visiting recruitments, 9

Source: Ivie, Rachel, Katie Stowe and Roman Czujko, "2000 Physics Academic Workforce Report," *AIP: American Institute of Physics Report*, March 2001.

★2964★
Physics departments at Ph.D.-granting institutions recruiting new faculty members for 2001

Ranking basis/background: Number and percent of department recruiting tenured or tenure-track faculty and number and percent of department recruiting visiting faculty. **Remarks:** Original source: 2000 AWF Survey. **Number listed:** 4.
- Percent of department recruiting tenured or tenure-track faculty: 74%
- Number of tenured or tenure track recruitments, 282
- Percent of departments recruiting visiting faculty, 17%
- Number of visiting recruitments, 60

Source: Ivie, Rachel, Katie Stowe and Roman Czujko, "2000 Physics Academic Workforce Report," *AIP: American Institute of Physics Report*, March 2001.

★2965★
Physics faculty, by race/ethnicity, 2000

Ranking basis/background: Percentage of physics faculty from each ethnic group in 2000. **Remarks:** Original source: 2000 AWF Survey. **Number listed:** 5.
- African American, with 1.8%
- Asian American, 9.9%
- Hispanic American, 2.0%
- White, 84.2%
- Other, 2.0%

Source: Ivie, Rachel, Katie Stowe and Roman Czujko, "2000 Physics Academic Workforce Report," *AIP: American Institute of Physics Report*, March 2001.

PHYSICS

★2966★
Physics faculty hired at bachelor's-granting institutions in 2000

Ranking basis/background: Total faculty, total tenured and tenure-track faculty, percentage of departments hiring any faculty and hiring tenured and tenured-track faculty. All figures are estimated. **Remarks:** Original source: 2000 AWF Survey. **Number listed:** 4.
- All faculty, with 304
- Tenured and tenure-track, 335
- Departments hiring any faculty, 54%
- Department hiring tenured and tenure-track, 35%

Source: Ivie, Rachel, Katie Stowe and Roman Czujko, "2000 Physics Academic Workforce Report," *AIP: American Institute of Physics Report*, March 2001.

★2967★
Physics faculty hired at master's-granting institutions in 2000

Ranking basis/background: Total faculty, total tenured and tenure-track faculty, percentage of departments hiring any faculty and hiring tenured and tenured-track faculty. All figures are estimated. **Remarks:** Original source: 2000 AWF Survey. **Number listed:** 4.
- All faculty, with 69
- Tenured and tenure-track, 28
- Departments hiring any faculty, 62%
- Department hiring tenured and tenure-track, 41%

Source: Ivie, Rachel, Katie Stowe and Roman Czujko, "2000 Physics Academic Workforce Report," *AIP: American Institute of Physics Report*, March 2001.

★2968★
Physics faculty hired at Ph.D.-granting institutions in 2000

Ranking basis/background: Total faculty, total tenured and tenure-track faculty, percentage of departments hiring any faculty and hiring tenured and tenured-track faculty. All figures are estimated. **Remarks:** Original source: 2000 AWF Survey. **Number listed:** 4.
- All faculty, with 285
- Tenured and tenure-track, 191
- Departments hiring any faculty, 76%
- Department hiring tenured and tenure-track, 65%

Source: Ivie, Rachel, Katie Stowe and Roman Czujko, "2000 Physics Academic Workforce Report," *AIP: American Institute of Physics Report*, March 2001.

★2969★
Radcliffe Institute for Advanced Study fellowship recipient in the field of geophysics, 2000-01

Ranking basis/background: Recipient and institutional affiliation of the Radcliffe Institute for Advanced study fellowship for pursuit of advanced work across a wide range of academic disciplines, professions, and creative arts. **Number listed:** 1.
- Svetlana Panasyuk, Harvard University

Source: "The Radcliffe Institute for Advanced Study," *The Chronicle of Higher Education*, 46: A59, (June 2, 2000).

★2970★
Radcliffe Institute for Advanced Study fellowship recipient in the field of physics, 2000-01

Ranking basis/background: Recipient and institutional affiliation of the Radcliffe Institute for Advanced study fellowship for pursuit of advanced work across a wide range of academic disciplines, professions, and creative arts. **Number listed:** 1.
- Elizabeth Simmons, Boston University

Source: "The Radcliffe Institute for Advanced Study," *The Chronicle of Higher Education*, 46: A59, (June 2, 2000).

★2971★
Retirement rates of physics faculty at bachelor's-granting institutions during 1999 and 2000

Ranking basis/background: Estimated number of retirements per year, estimated percentage of departments with retirements per year, and estimated annual retirement rate. **Remarks:** Original source: 2000 AWF Survey. **Number listed:** 3.
- Retirements per year, with 85
- Departments with retirements per year, 13%
- Annual retirement rate, 3.9

Source: Ivie, Rachel, Katie Stowe and Roman Czujko, "2000 Physics Academic Workforce Report," *AIP: American Institute of Physics Report*, March 2001.

★2972★
Retirement rates of physics faculty at master's-granting institutions during 1999 and 2000

Ranking basis/background: Estimated number of retirements per year, estimated percentage of departments with retirements per year, and estimated annual retirement rate. **Remarks:** Original source: 2000 AWF Survey. **Number listed:** 3.
- Retirements per year, with 25
- Departments with retirements per year, 23%
- Annual retirement rate, 3.8

Source: Ivie, Rachel, Katie Stowe and Roman Czujko, "2000 Physics Academic Workforce Report," *AIP: American Institute of Physics Report*, March 2001.

★2973★
Retirement rates of physics faculty at Ph.D.-granting institutions during 1999 and 2000

Ranking basis/background: Estimated number of retirements per year, estimated percentage of departments with retirements per year, and estimated annual retirement rate. **Remarks:** Original source: 2000 AWF Survey. **Number listed:** 3.
- Retirements per year, with 127
- Departments with retirements per year, 32%
- Annual retirement rate, 2.9

Source: Ivie, Rachel, Katie Stowe and Roman Czujko, "2000 Physics Academic Workforce Report," *AIP: American Institute of Physics Report*, March 2001.

★2974★
Top recruiters for physics jobs for 2000-01 bachelor's degree recipients

Ranking basis/background: Projected number of college hires from on-campus recruitment for 2000-01. **Remarks:** Numbers reflect total expected hires, not just African American projected hires. **Number listed:** 4.
1. Accenture, with 65 projected hires
2. U.S. Air Force (Active Duty Hires), 10
3. Agilent Technologies, 6
4. Corning, 5

Source: "The Top 100 Employers and the Majors in Demand for the Class of 2001," *The Black Collegian*, 31: 19-35, (February 2001).

★2975★
Undergraduate physics majors enrolled at all institutional types, 1999-2000

Ranking basis/background: Number of physics majors for each year of study. **Number listed:** 2.
- Juniors, with 5,227
- Seniors, 5,913

Source: Nicholson, Starr and Patrick J. Mulvey, "Roster of Physics Departments with Enrollment and Degree Data, 1999," *AIP: American Institute of Physics Report*, August 2000.

★2976★
Undergraduate physics majors enrolled at bachelor's-granting institutions, 1999-2000

Ranking basis/background: Number of physics majors for each year of study. **Number listed:** 2.
- Juniors, with 2,348
- Seniors, 2,271

Source: Nicholson, Starr and Patrick J. Mulvey, "Roster of Physics Departments with Enrollment and Degree Data, 1999," *AIP: American Institute of Physics Report*, August 2000.

★2977★
U.S. institutions with more than 40% female bachelor's graduates in their physics departments, 1994-98

Ranking basis/background: Alphabetical list of institutions with physics departments having over 40% women among bachelor's graduates. **Number listed:** 20.
- Baylor University
- Belmont University
- Catholic University
- University of Denver
- Dickinson College
- Dillard University
- Drew University
- Fisk University
- Fordham University
- Gordon College
- Grambling State University
- Hiram College
- Jackson State University
- Lincoln University (PA)
- Mary Washington College
- University of Michigan, Dearborn
- University of Minnesota, Morris
- Southern University
- Tougaloo College
- Xavier University (LA)

Source: Ivie, Rachel and Katie Stowe, "Women in Physics, 2000," *AIP: American Institute of Physics Report*, June 2000, pp. 1-16.

PHYSICS, GRADUATE

★2978★
U.S. universities publishing the most papers in the field of astrophysics, 1995-99

Ranking basis/background: Number of papers published in the field of astrophysics over a five-year period, and percent of field based on each universities percentage of 41,064 papers entered in the ISI database from ISI-indexed astrophysics journals. **Number listed:** 5.
1. Caltech, with 2,113 papers; 5.15% of field
2. University of California, Berkeley, 1,309; 3.19%
3. University of Arizona, 1,058; 2.58%
4. Johns Hopkins University, 914; 2.23%
5. University of Maryland, College Park, 753; 1.83%

Source: "Astrophysics: Most Prolific U.S. Universities, 1995-99," *What's Hot in Research* (http://www.isinet.com/isi/hot/research) *Institute for Scientific Information*, October 23, 2000.

★2979★
U.S. universities with the greatest impact in astrophysics, 1994-98

Ranking basis/background: Total number of astrophysics papers published from each university and average number of citations per paper between 1994 and 1998. **Remarks:** Original source: University Science Indicators on Diskette, 1981-98. **Number listed:** 5.
1. University of California, Santa Cruz, with 547 astrophysics papers; 13.45 citations per paper
2. Princeton University, 462; 12.35
3. Arizona State University, 308; 10.84
4. University of Michigan, 475; 10.81
5. University of Wisconsin, Madison, 433; 10.21

Source: "Astrophysics: High-Impact U.S. Universities, 1994-98," *What's Hot in Research* (http://www.isinet.com/hot/research) *Institute for Scientific Information*, August 30, 1999.

★2980★
U.S. universities with the greatest impact in physics, 1994-98

Ranking basis/background: Average citations per paper from the top 100 federally funded U.S. universities that had at least 50 published papers in ISI indexed physics journals. Also includes total number of paper published during the five year period. **Number listed:** 5.
1. University of California, Santa Cruz, with 513 papers; 11.12 citations per paper
2. Rice University, 504; 9.86
3. University of California, Santa Barbara, 2,590; 9.19
4. University of California, San Francisco, 2,634; 9.10
5. Rutgers University, 1,471; 9.08

Source: "Physics: High Impact U.S. Universities, 1994-98," *What's Hot in Research* (http://www.isinet.com/isi/hot/research) *Institute for Scientific Information*, July 31, 2000.

★2981★
Women faculty in Ph.D. physics departments at U.S. institutions, 1998

Ranking basis/background: Alphabetical list of institutions with four or more women faculty in their Ph.D. physics departments. **Number listed:** 17.

University of California, Davis
University of California, Santa Barbara
California Institute of Technology
Columbia University (Department of Applied Physics and Applied Mathematics)
Florida State University
University of Iowa
John Hopkins University
University of Kansas
University of Massachusetts, Amherst
Massachusetts Institute of Technology
Michigan State University
Northwestern University
University of Notre Dame
Oregon State University
University of Pennsylvania
Rutgers University
Washington State University

Source: Ivie, Rachel and Katie Stowe, "Women in Physics, 2000," *AIP: American Institute of Physics Report*, June 2000, pp. 1-16.

★2982★
Women's colleges granting physics bachelor's degrees, 2000

Ranking basis/background: Alphabetical list of women's institutions granting bachelor's in physics degrees. **Number listed:** 16.

Agnes Scott College
Barnard College
Bryn Mawr College
Chatham College
Georgian Court College
Hollins University
Mary Baldwin College
Mount Holyoke College
College of Notre Dame (MD)
Randolph-Macon Woman's College
College of St. Catherine
Scripps College
Smith College
Spelman College
Sweet Briar College
Wellesley College

Source: Ivie, Rachel and Katie Stowe, "Women in Physics, 2000," *AIP: American Institute of Physics Report*, June 2000, pp. 1-16.

★2983★
Women's physics faculty, by academic rank, 1998

Ranking basis/background: Percentage of women physics faculty for each academic ranking. **Remarks:** Original source: Blake, *1993-94 Academic Workforce Report*, AIP, and Ivie & Stowe, *1997-98 Academic Workforce Report*, AIP. **Number listed:** 4.

Full professor, with 3%
Associate professor, 10%
Assistant professor, 17%
Other ranks, 13%

Source: Ivie, Rachel and Katie Stowe, "Women in Physics, 2000," *AIP: American Institute of Physics Report*, June 2000, pp. 1-16.

★2984★
Women's physics faculty, by type of department, 1998

Ranking basis/background: Percentage of women physics faculty for each department type. **Remarks:** Original source: Blake, *1993-94 Academic Workforce Report*, AIP, and Ivie & Stowe, *1997-98 Academic Workforce Report*, AIP. **Number listed:** 3.

Ph.D.-granting, with 6%
Master's-granting, 9%
Bachelor's-granting, 11%

Source: Ivie, Rachel and Katie Stowe, "Women in Physics, 2000," *AIP: American Institute of Physics Report*, June 2000, pp. 1-16.

PHYSICS, GRADUATE

★2985★
Citizenship of first-year physics and astronomy graduate students enrolled at master's-granting institutions, 1997-98

Ranking basis/background: Percentage of first-year physics and astronomy graduate students by citizenship. **Number listed:** 2.
U.S., with 65%
Foreign, 35%

Source: Mulvey, Patrick J. and Casey Langer, "1998 Graduate Student Report: First-Year Students," *AIP: American Institute of Physics Report*, November 2000.

★2986★
Citizenship of first-year physics and astronomy graduate students enrolled at Ph.D.-granting institutions, 1997-98

Ranking basis/background: Percentage of first-year physics and astronomy graduate students by citizenship. **Number listed:** 2.
U.S., with 48%
Foreign, 52%

Source: Mulvey, Patrick J. and Casey Langer, "1998 Graduate Student Report: First-Year Students," *AIP: American Institute of Physics Report*, November 2000.

★2987★
First-year physics and astronomy graduate students from Asia, 1997-98

Ranking basis/background: Percentage of first-year physics graduate students from each Asian country. **Remarks:** During the 1997-98 academic year 1,183 foreign citizens were enrolled as first-year students in U.S. physics and astronomy graduate programs. **Number listed:** 7.
1. People's Republic of China, with 27%
2. India, 7%
3. South Korea, 4%
4. Taiwan, 2%
5. Japan, 1%
5. Pakistan, 1%
7. Other Asia, 3%

Source: Mulvey, Patrick J. and Casey Langer, "1998 Graduate Student Report: First-Year Students," *AIP: American Institute of Physics Report*, November 2000.

★2988★
First-year physics and astronomy graduate students from Europe, 1997-98

Ranking basis/background: Percentage of first-year physics graduate students from Europe. **Remarks:** During the 1997-98 academic year 1,183 foreign citizens were enrolled as first-year students in U.S. physics and astronomy graduate programs. **Number listed:** 2.
1. Eastern and Central Europe, with 22%
2. Western Europe, 18%

PHYSICS, GRADUATE

Source: Mulvey, Patrick J. and Casey Langer, "1998 Graduate Student Report: First-Year Students," *AIP: American Institute of Physics Report*, November 2000.

★2989★
First-year physics and astronomy graduate students from selected countries, 1997-98

Ranking basis/background: Percentage of first-year physics graduate students from each country. Remarks: During the 1997-98 academic year 1,183 foreign citizens were enrolled as first-year students in U.S. physics and astronomy graduate programs. Number listed: 3.
1. Middle East, with 5%
2. Africa, 3%
3. Australia, New Zealand, 1%

Source: Mulvey, Patrick J. and Casey Langer, "1998 Graduate Student Report: First-Year Students," *AIP: American Institute of Physics Report*, November 2000.

★2990★
First-year physics and astronomy graduate students from the Americas, 1997-98

Ranking basis/background: Percentage of first-year physics graduate students from the Americas. Remarks: During the 1997-98 academic year 1,183 foreign citizens were enrolled as first-year students in U.S. physics and astronomy graduate programs. Number listed: 2.
1. Mexico, South and Central America, with 4%
2. Canada, 2%

Source: Mulvey, Patrick J. and Casey Langer, "1998 Graduate Student Report: First-Year Students," *AIP: American Institute of Physics Report*, November 2000.

★2991★
First-year physics graduate students, by citizenship, 1997-98

Ranking basis/background: Percentage of U.S. and foreign first-year physics graduate students. Number listed: 2.
U.S., with 50%
Foreign, 50%

Source: Mulvey, Patrick J. and Casey Langer, "1998 Graduate Student Report: First-Year Students," *AIP: American Institute of Physics Report*, November 2000.

★2992★
First-year physics graduate students, by gender, 1997-98

Ranking basis/background: Percentage of male and female first-year physics graduate students. Number listed: 2.
Men, with 80%
Women, 20%

Source: Mulvey, Patrick J. and Casey Langer, "1998 Graduate Student Report: First-Year Students," *AIP: American Institute of Physics Report*, November 2000.

★2993★
Foreign citizens enrolled as first-year physics graduate students, by age, 1997-98

Ranking basis/background: Percentage of foreign first-year physics graduate students from in each age group. Number listed: 3.
23 or younger, with 11%
24-25, 34%
26 or older, 55%

Source: Mulvey, Patrick J. and Casey Langer, "1998 Graduate Student Report: First-Year Students," *AIP: American Institute of Physics Report*, November 2000.

★2994★
Foreign graduate physics students enrollment, 1999-2000

Ranking basis/background: Number of first-year physics graduate students at each type of institution. Number listed: 2.
Ph.D.-granting, with 5,053
Master's-granting, 191

Source: Nicholson, Starr and Patrick J. Mulvey, "Roster of Physics Departments with Enrollment and Degree Data, 1999," *AIP: American Institute of Physics Report*, August 2000.

★2995★
Gender breakdown of first-year physics and astronomy graduate students enrolled at master's-granting institutions, 1997-98

Ranking basis/background: Percentage of male and female first-year physics and astronomy graduate students. Number listed: 2.
Men, with 76%
Women, 24%

Source: Mulvey, Patrick J. and Casey Langer, "1998 Graduate Student Report: First-Year Students," *AIP: American Institute of Physics Report*, November 2000.

★2996★
Gender breakdown of first-year physics and astronomy graduate students enrolled at Ph.D.-granting institutions, 1997-98

Ranking basis/background: Percentage of male and female first-year physics and astronomy graduate students. Number listed: 2.
Men, with 81%
Women, 19%

Source: Mulvey, Patrick J. and Casey Langer, "1998 Graduate Student Report: First-Year Students," *AIP: American Institute of Physics Report*, November 2000.

★2997★
Graduate physics students enrolled at master's-granting institutions, 1999-2000

Ranking basis/background: Number of first-year physics graduate students. Number listed: 1.
First-year, with 206

Source: Nicholson, Starr and Patrick J. Mulvey, "Roster of Physics Departments with Enrollment and Degree Data, 1999," *AIP: American Institute of Physics Report*, August 2000.

★2998★
Graduate physics students enrolled at Ph.D.-granting institutions, 1999-2000

Ranking basis/background: Number of first-year physics graduate students. Number listed: 1.
First-year, with 2,304

Source: Nicholson, Starr and Patrick J. Mulvey, "Roster of Physics Departments with Enrollment and Degree Data, 1999," *AIP: American Institute of Physics Report*, August 2000.

★2999★
Graduate physics students enrollment, 1999-2000

Ranking basis/background: Number of first-year physics graduate students. Number listed: 1.
First-year, with 2,510

Source: Nicholson, Starr and Patrick J. Mulvey, "Roster of Physics Departments with Enrollment and Degree Data, 1999," *AIP: American Institute of Physics Report*, August 2000.

★3000★
Highest degree desired of first-year physics and astronomy graduate students enrolled at master's-granting institutions, 1997-98

Ranking basis/background: Percentage of first-year physics and astronomy graduate students planning to obtain each type of degree. Number listed: 2.
Ph.D., with 53%
Master's, 47%

Source: Mulvey, Patrick J. and Casey Langer, "1998 Graduate Student Report: First-Year Students," *AIP: American Institute of Physics Report*, November 2000.

★3001★
Highest degree desired of first-year physics and astronomy graduate students enrolled at Ph.D.-granting institutions, 1997-98

Ranking basis/background: Percentage of first-year physics and astronomy graduate students planning to obtain each degree. Number listed: 2.
Ph.D., with 93%
Master's, 7%

Source: Mulvey, Patrick J. and Casey Langer, "1998 Graduate Student Report: First-Year Students," *AIP: American Institute of Physics Report*, November 2000.

★3002★
Major influences for first-year physics or astronomy graduate students from foreign countries in choosing their academic specialty, 1997-98

Ranking basis/background: Percentage of first-year physics or astronomy graduate students stating each influence as their "Top 3" in importance and "most important" in selecting their academic specialty. Number listed: 8.
Interest in the subject matter, with 96% putting it in their Top 3; 76% stating it most important
College professor, 39%; 5%
Career prospects, 37%; 2%
High school teacher, 46%; 7%
Fellow students, 30%; 1%
Parents, 31%; 6%
Expected salary & benefits, 10%; 1%
Other, 11%; 2%

Source: Mulvey, Patrick J. and Casey Langer, "1998 Graduate Student Report: First-Year Students," *AIP: American Institute of Physics Report*, November 2000.

★3003★
Major influences for first-year physics or astronomy graduate students from the U.S. in choosing their academic specialty, 1997-98

Ranking basis/background: Percentage of first-year physics or astronomy graduate students stating each influence as their "Top 3" in importance and "most important" in selecting their academic specialty. **Number listed:** 8.
- Interest in the subject matter, with 96% putting it in their Top 3; 78% stating it most important
- College professor, 56%; 7%
- Career prospects, 47%; 3%
- High school teacher, 33%; 5%
- Fellow students, 21%; 2%
- Parents, 19%; 1%
- Expected salary & benefits, 12%; 0%
- Other, 16%; 4%

Source: Mulvey, Patrick J. and Casey Langer, "1998 Graduate Student Report: First-Year Students," *AIP: American Institute of Physics Report*, November 2000.

★3004★
Major subfields of first-year physics and astronomy graduate students who are foreign citizens planning to receive a Ph.D., 1997-98

Ranking basis/background: Percentage of foreign citizen first-year physics and astronomy graduate students in each subfield. **Number listed:** 9.
1. Condensed matter, with 25%
2. Undecided, 24%
3. Particles and fields, 13%
4. Astronomy/astrophysics, 8%
5. Nuclear, 5%
6. Optics/photonics, 4%
7. Atomic and molecular, 3%
7. Materials science, 3%
9. Biophysics, 2%

Source: Mulvey, Patrick J. and Casey Langer, "1998 Graduate Student Report: First-Year Students," *AIP: American Institute of Physics Report*, November 2000.

★3005★
Major subfields of first-year physics and astronomy graduate students who are U.S. citizens planning to receive a Ph.D., 1997-98

Ranking basis/background: Percentage of U.S. citizen first-year physics and astronomy graduate students in each subfield. **Number listed:** 9.
1. Undecided, with 22%
2. Astronomy/astrophysics, 18%
3. Particles and fields, 13%
4. Condensed matter, 12%
5. Atomic and molecular, 6%
6. Nuclear, 4%
6. Optics/photonics, 4%
6. Biophysics, 4%
9. Materials science, 3%

Source: Mulvey, Patrick J. and Casey Langer, "1998 Graduate Student Report: First-Year Students," *AIP: American Institute of Physics Report*, November 2000.

★3006★
Most effective astrophysics and astronomy research-doctorate programs as evaluated by the National Research Council

Ranking basis/background: From a survey of nearly 8,000 faculty members conducted in the spring of 1993. Respondents were asked to rate programs in their field on "effectiveness of program in educating research scholars/scientists." **Remarks:** See *Chronicle* article for more details. Scores of 3.5-5.0 indicate "extremely effective;" 2.5-3.49 "reasonably effective;" 1.5-2.49 "minimally effective;" and 0.0-1.49 "not effective." Programs also ranked by "scholarly quality of program faculty." **Number listed:** 33.
1. California Institute of Technology, with an effectiveness rating of 4.75
2. University of California, Berkeley, 4.53
3. Princeton University, 4.38
4. University of California, Santa Cruz, 4.14
5. Cornell University, 3.97
6. Harvard University, 3.92
7. University of Chicago, 3.85
8. University of Arizona, 3.69
9. Massachusetts Institute of Technology, 3.68
10. University of Wisconsin, Madison, 3.47

Source: "Rankings of Research-Doctorate Programs in 41 Disciplines at 274 Institutions," *The Chronicle of Higher Education* 42: A21-A30 (September 21, 1995).

★3007★
Most effective physics research-doctorate programs as evaluated by the National Research Council

Ranking basis/background: From a survey of nearly 8,000 faculty members conducted in the spring of 1993. Respondents were asked to rate programs in their field on "effectiveness of program in educating research scholars/scientists." **Remarks:** See *Chronicle* article for more details. Scores of 3.5-5.0 indicate "extremely effective;" 2.5-3.49 "reasonably effective;" 1.5-2.49 "minimally effective;" and 0.0-1.49 "not effective." Programs also ranked by "scholarly quality of program faculty." **Number listed:** 147.
1. Harvard University, 4.71
2. Princeton University, 4.69
3. Massachusetts Institute of Technology, 4.64
4. California Institute of Technology, 4.61
5. University of Chicago, 4.55
6. Cornell University, 4.54
7. University of California, Berkeley, 4.49
8. University of Illinois, Urbana-Champaign, 4.39
9. Stanford University, 4.35
10. Yale University, 4.03

Source: "Rankings of Research-Doctorate Programs in 41 Disciplines at 274 Institutions," *The Chronicle of Higher Education* 42: A21-A30 (September 21, 1995).

★3008★
Physics degrees awarded at master's-granting institutions, by degree, 1998-99

Ranking basis/background: Number of physics degrees awarded at each level. **Number listed:** 2.
- Bachelors, with 275
- Masters, 184

Source: Nicholson, Starr and Patrick J. Mulvey, "Roster of Physics Departments with Enrollment and Degree Data, 1999," *AIP: American Institute of Physics Report*, August 2000.

★3009★
Physics degrees awarded at Ph.D.-granting institutions, by degree, 1998-99

Ranking basis/background: Number of physics degrees awarded at each level. **Number listed:** 4.
- Bachelors, with 1,688
- Masters, 487
- Masters enroute, 627
- Ph.D., 1,262

Source: Nicholson, Starr and Patrick J. Mulvey, "Roster of Physics Departments with Enrollment and Degree Data, 1999," *AIP: American Institute of Physics Report*, August 2000.

★3010★
Physics degrees granted, by type of degree, 1998-99

Ranking basis/background: Number of physics degrees awarded at each level. **Number listed:** 4.
- Bachelors, with 3,646
- Masters, 671
- Masters enroute, 627
- Ph.D., 1,262

Source: Nicholson, Starr and Patrick J. Mulvey, "Roster of Physics Departments with Enrollment and Degree Data, 1999," *AIP: American Institute of Physics Report*, August 2000.

★3011★
Physics departments by highest degree program offered, 1999-2000

Ranking basis/background: Number of departments offering degree. **Number listed:** 3.
- Ph.D.-granting, with 184 departments
- Master's-granting, 70
- Bachelor's-granting, 508

Source: Nicholson, Starr and Patrick J. Mulvey, "Roster of Physics Departments with Enrollment and Degree Data, 1999," *AIP: American Institute of Physics Report*, August 2000.

★3012★
Study status of first-year physics and astronomy graduate students enrolled at master's-granting institutions, 1997-98

Ranking basis/background: Percentage of first-year physics and astronomy graduate students in each study status. **Number listed:** 2.
- Full-time, with 82%
- Part-time, 18%

Source: Mulvey, Patrick J. and Casey Langer, "1998 Graduate Student Report: First-Year Students," *AIP: American Institute of Physics Report*, November 2000.

★3013★
Study status of first-year physics and astronomy graduate students enrolled at Ph.D.-granting institutions, 1997-98

Ranking basis/background: Percentage of first-year physics and astronomy graduate students in each study status. **Number listed:** 2.
- Full-time, with 99%
- Part-time, 1%

Source: Mulvey, Patrick J. and Casey Langer, "1998 Graduate Student Report: First-Year Students," *AIP: American Institute of Physics Report*, November 2000.

★3014★
Top astrophysics and astronomy research-doctorate programs as evaluated by the National Research Council

Ranking basis/background: From a survey of nearly 8,000 faculty members conducted in the spring of 1993. Respondents were asked to rate programs in their field on "scholarly quality of program faculty." When more than one program had the samescore, the council averaged the rank order and gave each program the same rank number (if three programs tied for the top position, each received a rank of 2). **Remarks:** See *Chronicle* article for more details. Scores of 4.01 and above indicate "distinguished;" 3.0-4.0 "strong;" 2.51-3.0 "good;" 2.0-2.5 "adequate;" 1.0-1.99 "marginal;" and 0.0-0.99 "not sufficient for doctoral education." Programs also ranked by "effectiveness of program in educating research scholars/scientists." **Number listed:** 33.
1. California Institute of Technology, with a quality rating of 4.91
2. Princeton University, 4.79
3. University of California, Berkeley, 4.65
4. Harvard University, 4.49
5. University of Chicago, 4.36
6. University of California, Santa Cruz, 4.31
7. University of Arizona, 4.10
8. Massachusetts Institute of Technology, 4.00
9. Cornell University, 3.98
10. University of Texas, Austin, 3.65
11. University of Hawaii, Manoa, 3.60
12. University of Colorado, 3.54
13. University of Illinois, Urbana-Champaign, 3.53
14. University of Wisconsin, Madison, 3.46
15. Yale University, 3.31

Source: "Rankings of Research-Doctorate Programs in 41 Disciplines at 274 Institutions," *The Chronicle of Higher Education* 42: A21-A30 (September 21, 1995).

★3015★
Top physics research-doctorate programs as evaluated by the National Research Council

Ranking basis/background: From a survey of nearly 8,000 faculty members conducted in the spring of 1993. Respondents were asked to rate programs in their field on "scholarly quality of program faculty." When more than one program had the samescore, the council averaged the rank order and gave each program the same rank number (if three programs tied for the top position, each received a rank of 2). **Remarks:** See *Chronicle* article for more details. Scores of 4.01 and above indicate "distinguished;" 3.0-4.0 "strong;" 2.51-3.0 "good;" 2.0-2.5 "adequate;" 1.0-1.99 "marginal;" and 0.0-0.99 "not sufficient for doctoral education." Programs also ranked by "effectiveness of program in educating research scholars/scientists." **Number listed:** 147.
1. Harvard University, with a quality rating of 4.91
2. Princeton University, 4.89
3. Massachusetts Institute of Technology, 4.87
3. University of California, Berkeley, 4.87
5. California Institute of Technology, 4.81
6. Cornell University, 4.75
7. University of Chicago, 4.69
8. University of Illinois, Urbana-Champaign, 4.66
9. Stanford University, 4.53
10. University of California, Santa Barbara, 4.43
11. University of Texas, Austin, 4.33
12. Columbia University, 4.25
13. Yale University, 4.21
14. University of Washington (WA), 4.20
15. University of California, Los Angeles, 4.18

Source: "Rankings of Research-Doctorate Programs in 41 Disciplines at 274 Institutions," *The Chronicle of Higher Education* 42: A21-A30 (September 21, 1995).

★3016★
Top recruiters for physics jobs for 2000-01 master's degree recipients

Ranking basis/background: Projected number of college hires from on-campus recruitment for 2000-01. **Remarks:** Numbers reflect total expected hires, not just African American projected hires. **Number listed:** 3.
1. Lucent Technologies, with 200 projected hires
2. Corning, 6
3. Accenture, 5

Source: "The Top 100 Employers and the Majors in Demand for the Class of 2001," *The Black Collegian*, 31: 19-35, (February 2001).

★3017★
Undergraduate physics majors enrolled at master's-granting institutions, 1999-2000

Ranking basis/background: Number of physics majors for each year of study. **Number listed:** 2.
  Juniors, with 465
  Seniors, 589

Source: Nicholson, Starr and Patrick J. Mulvey, "Roster of Physics Departments with Enrollment and Degree Data, 1999," *AIP: American Institute of Physics Report*, August 2000.

★3018★
Undergraduate physics majors enrolled at Ph.D.-granting institutions, 1999-2000

Ranking basis/background: Number of physics majors for each year of study. **Number listed:** 2.
  Juniors, with 2,414
  Seniors, 3,053

Source: Nicholson, Starr and Patrick J. Mulvey, "Roster of Physics Departments with Enrollment and Degree Data, 1999," *AIP: American Institute of Physics Report*, August 2000.

★3019★
U.S. citizens enrolled as first-year physics graduate students, by age, 1997-98

Ranking basis/background: Percentage of first-year physics graduate students from the U.S. in each age group. **Number listed:** 3.
  23 or younger, with 48%
  24-25, 23%
  26 or older, 29%

Source: Mulvey, Patrick J. and Casey Langer, "1998 Graduate Student Report: First-Year Students," *AIP: American Institute of Physics Report*, November 2000.

PHYSICS PERIODICALS

★3020★
Physics journals with the greatest impact measure, 1981-98

Ranking basis/background: Citations-per-paper impact score is the total citations to a journal's published papers divided by total number of papers the journal has published over an eighteen year period. **Remarks:** Original source: *Journal Citation Reports* and Journal Performance Indicators on Diskette. **Number listed:** 10.
1. *Review of Modern Physics*, with an impact score of 132.07
2. *Physics Reports*, 46.53
3. *Reports on Progress in Physics*, 44.90
4. *Physical Review Letters*, 33.14
5. *Journal de Physique Letters*, 24.78
6. *NMR-Basic Principles and Progress*, 24.17
7. *Annals of Physics*, 18.00
8. *Physics Letters B*, 15.74
9. *Physica D*, 14.39
10. *Physical Review A*, 14.17

Source: "Journals Ranked by Impact: Physics," *What's Hot in Research* (http://www.isinet.com/hot/research) Institute for Scientific Information, September 6, 1999.

PHYSIOLOGY, GRADUATE

★3021★
Most effective physiology research-doctorate programs as evaluated by the National Research Council

Ranking basis/background: From a survey of nearly 8,000 faculty members conducted in the spring of 1993. Respondents were asked to rate programs in their field on "effectiveness of program in educating research scholars/scientists." **Remarks:** See *Chronicle* article for more details. Scores of 3.5-5.0 indicate "extremely effective;" 2.5-3.49 "reasonably effective;" 1.5-2.49 "minimally effective;" and 0.0-1.49 "not effective." Programs also ranked by "scholarly quality of program faculty." **Number listed:** 140.
1. Yale University, with an effectiveness rating of 4.38
2. University of California, San Diego, 4.47
3. Stanford University, 4.17
4. University of Washington (WA), 4.10
5. University of California, Los Angeles, 4.02
6. University of California, San Francisco, 4.00
7. University of Pennsylvania, 3.95
8. University of Illinois, Urbana-Champaign, 3.92
9. University of Chicago, 3.86
10. Baylor College of Medicine, 3.84

Source: "Rankings of Research-Doctorate Programs in 41 Disciplines at 274 Institutions," *The Chronicle of Higher Education* 42: A21-A30 (September 21, 1995).

★3022★
Top physiology research-doctorate programs as evaluated by the National Research Council

Ranking basis/background: From a survey of nearly 8,000 faculty members conducted in the spring of 1993. Respondents were asked to rate programs in their field on "scholarly quality of program faculty." When more than one program had the samescore, the council averaged the rank order and gave each program the same rank number (if three programs tied for the top position, each received a rank of 2). **Remarks:** See *Chronicle* article for more details. Scores of 4.01 and above indicate "distinguished;" 3.0-4.0 "strong;" 2.51-3.0 "good;" 2.0-2.5 "adequate;" 1.0-1.99 "marginal;" and 0.0-0.99 "not sufficient for doctoral education." Programs also ranked by "effectiveness of program in educating research scholars/scientists." **Number listed:** 140.
1. Yale University, with a quality rating of 4.48
2. University of California, San Diego, 4.47
3. University of Pennsylvania, 4.27
4. University of California, Los Angeles, 4.23
5. University of California, San Francisco, 4.21
5. Baylor College of Medicine, 4.21
7. University of Washington (WA), 4.20
7. Stanford University, 4.20
9. University of Virginia, 4.19
9. Columbia University, 4.19
11. University of Chicago, 4.00
12. University of Iowa, 3.99
13. California Institute of Technology, 3.98
14. New York University, 3.91
15. University of Michigan, 3.89
15. Vanderbilt University, 3.89

Source: "Rankings of Research-Doctorate Programs in 41 Disciplines at 274 Institutions," *The Chronicle of Higher Education* 42: A21-A30 (September 21, 1995).

PLAYWRIGHTING
See: **Theatre Arts**

POLITICAL CANDIDATES

★3023★
Members of Congress receiving the largest contributions from the Sallie Mae Inc. Political Action Committee

Ranking basis/background: Total contribution made to each Congress member during the 2000 election cycle. **Remarks:** Original source: Federal Election Commission. **Number listed:** 10.
1. Rep. Thomas M. Davis III (VA), Republican, with $10,000
1. Sen. James M. Jeffords (VT), Republican, $10,000
3. Rep. Howard P. (Buck) McKeon (CA), Republican, $8,000
3. Sen. Edward M. Kennedy (MA) Democrat, $8,000
5. Rep. Thomas E. Petri (WI) Republican, $7,500
5. Sen. Charles S. Robb (VA) Democrat, $7,500
7. Rep. James P. Moran (VA) Democrat, $6,000
7. Rep. Dale E. Kildee (MI) Democrat, $6,000
7. Rep. David E. Bonior (MI) Democrat, $6,000
10. Rep. Paul E. Kanjorski (PA) Democrat, $5,500

Source: Burd, Stephen, "Should Borrowers Fear a Student-Loan Behemoth?," *The Chronicle of Higher Education*, 46: A24-A26, (August 11, 2000).

POLITICAL SCIENCE

★3024★
Authorship in the American Political Science Association in the field of electoral behavior, 1995-97

Ranking basis/background: Number of books and authors published in the field, plus percentage of male and female authors. **Number listed:** 4.
Books, with 10
Authors, 182
Male authors, 89%
Female authors, 11%

Source: Mathews, Lanethea A. and Kristi Andersen, "A Gender Gap in Publishing? Women's Representation in Edited Political Science Books," *PS: Political Science & Politics*, 34: 143-147, (March 2001).

★3025★
Authorship in the American Political Science Association in the field of environmental policy, 1995-97

Ranking basis/background: Number of books and authors published in the field, plus percentage of male and female authors. **Number listed:** 4.
Books, with 10
Authors, 152
Male authors, 84%
Female authors, 16%

Source: Mathews, Lanethea A. and Kristi Andersen, "A Gender Gap in Publishing? Women's Representation in Edited Political Science Books," *PS: Political Science & Politics*, 34: 143-147, (March 2001).

★3026★
Authorship in the American Political Science Association in the field of international politics, 1995-97

Ranking basis/background: Number of books and authors published in the field, plus percentage of male and female authors. **Number listed:** 4.
Books, with 22
Authors, 310
Male authors, 86%
Female authors, 14%

Source: Mathews, Lanethea A. and Kristi Andersen, "A Gender Gap in Publishing? Women's Representation in Edited Political Science Books," *PS: Political Science & Politics*, 34: 143-147, (March 2001).

★3027★
Authorship in the American Political Science Association in the field of Latin American politics, 1995-97

Ranking basis/background: Number of books and authors published in the field, plus percentage of male and female authors. **Number listed:** 4.
Books, with 6
Authors, 91
Male authors, 59%
Female authors, 41%

Source: Mathews, Lanethea A. and Kristi Andersen, "A Gender Gap in Publishing? Women's Representation in Edited Political Science Books," *PS: Political Science & Politics*, 34: 143-147, (March 2001).

★3028★
Authorship in the American Political Science Association in the field of political philosophy and theory, 1995-97

Ranking basis/background: Number of books and authors published in the field, plus percentage of male and female authors. **Number listed:** 4.
Books, with 30
Authors, 307
Male authors, 70%
Female authors, 30%

Source: Mathews, Lanethea A. and Kristi Andersen, "A Gender Gap in Publishing? Women's Representation in Edited Political Science Books," *PS: Political Science & Politics*, 34: 143-147, (March 2001).

★3029★
Female representation in the American Political Science Association in the field of electoral behavior, 1995-97

Ranking basis/background: Percentage of female members and authors. **Number listed:** 2.
Female members, with 19%
Female authors, 11%

Source: Mathews, Lanethea A. and Kristi Andersen, "A Gender Gap in Publishing? Women's Representation in Edited Political Science Books," *PS: Political Science & Politics*, 34: 143-147, (March 2001).

★3030★
Female representation in the American Political Science Association in the field of environmental policy, 1995-97

Ranking basis/background: Percentage of female members and authors. **Number listed:** 2.
Female members, with 23.3%
Female authors, 16%

Source: Mathews, Lanethea A. and Kristi Andersen, "A Gender Gap in Publishing? Women's Representation in Edited Political Science Books," *PS: Political Science & Politics*, 34: 143-147, (March 2001).

★3031★
Female representation in the American Political Science Association in the field of international politics, 1995-97

Ranking basis/background: Percentage of female members and authors. **Number listed:** 2.
Female members, with 22.6%
Female authors, 14%

Source: Mathews, Lanethea A. and Kristi Andersen, "A Gender Gap in Publishing? Women's Representation in Edited Political Science Books," *PS: Political Science & Politics*, 34: 143-147, (March 2001).

★3032★
Female representation in the American Political Science Association in the field of Latin American politics, 1995-97

Ranking basis/background: Percentage of female members and authors. **Number listed:** 2.
- Female members, with 26.4%
- Female authors, 41%

Source: Mathews, Lanethea A. and Kristi Andersen, "A Gender Gap in Publishing? Women's Representation in Edited Political Science Books," *PS: Political Science & Politics*, 34: 143-147, (March 2001).

★3033★
Female representation in the American Political Science Association in the field of political philosophy and theory, 1995-97

Ranking basis/background: Percentage of female members and authors. **Number listed:** 2.
- Female members, with 21.6%
- Female authors, 30%

Source: Mathews, Lanethea A. and Kristi Andersen, "A Gender Gap in Publishing? Women's Representation in Edited Political Science Books," *PS: Political Science & Politics*, 34: 143-147, (March 2001).

★3034★
Membership in the American Political Science Association in the field of electoral behavior, by gender, 1995-97

Ranking basis/background: Total members in the field, plus number of percentage of male and female members. **Number listed:** 3.
- Total members, with 168
- Male members, 136 (81%)
- Female members, 32 (19%)

Source: Mathews, Lanethea A. and Kristi Andersen, "A Gender Gap in Publishing? Women's Representation in Edited Political Science Books," *PS: Political Science & Politics*, 34: 143-147, (March 2001).

★3035★
Membership in the American Political Science Association in the field of environmental policy, by gender, 1995-97

Ranking basis/background: Total members in the field, plus number of percentage of male and female members. **Number listed:** 3.
- Total members, with 477
- Male members, 366 (77%)
- Female members, 111 (23%)

Source: Mathews, Lanethea A. and Kristi Andersen, "A Gender Gap in Publishing? Women's Representation in Edited Political Science Books," *PS: Political Science & Politics*, 34: 143-147, (March 2001).

★3036★
Membership in the American Political Science Association in the field of international politics, by gender, 1995-97

Ranking basis/background: Total members in the field, plus number of percentage of male and female members. **Number listed:** 3.
- Total members, with 3,587
- Male members, 2,776 (77%)
- Female members, 811 (23%)

Source: Mathews, Lanethea A. and Kristi Andersen, "A Gender Gap in Publishing? Women's Representation in Edited Political Science Books," *PS: Political Science & Politics*, 34: 143-147, (March 2001).

★3037★
Membership in the American Political Science Association in the field of Latin American politics, by gender, 1995-97

Ranking basis/background: Total members in the field, plus number of percentage of male and female members. **Number listed:** 3.
- Total members, with 538
- Male members, 396 (74%)
- Female members, 142 (26%)

Source: Mathews, Lanethea A. and Kristi Andersen, "A Gender Gap in Publishing? Women's Representation in Edited Political Science Books," *PS: Political Science & Politics*, 34: 143-147, (March 2001).

★3038★
Membership in the American Political Science Association in the field of political philosophy and theory, by gender, 1995-97

Ranking basis/background: Total members in the field, plus number of percentage of male and female members. **Number listed:** 3.
- Total members, with 2,177
- Male members, 1,707 (78%)
- Female members, 470 (22%)

Source: Mathews, Lanethea A. and Kristi Andersen, "A Gender Gap in Publishing? Women's Representation in Edited Political Science Books," *PS: Political Science & Politics*, 34: 143-147, (March 2001).

★3039★
Most frequently downloaded *American Political Science Review* articles

Ranking basis/background: Total number of viewings and printings from January 1997 until June 1999. **Remarks:** Original source: JSTOR (www.jstor.org) **Number listed:** 25.
1. Graham T. Allison (1969) "Conceptual Models and the Cuban Missile Crisis," with 1,055 viewings; and 713 printings
2. Stephen Anolabehere, et al. (1994) "Does Attack Advertising Demobilize the Electorate?", 530; 297
3. Sidney Verba, et al. (1993) "Citizen Activity: Who Participates? What Do They Say?", 476; 319
4. James G. March, Johan P. Olsen (1984) "The New Institutionalism: Organizational Factors in Political Life," 395; 400
5. Roger M. Smith (1993) "Beyond Tocqueville, Myrdal, and Hartz: The Multiple Traditions in America," 525; 249
6. Larry M. Bartels (1993) "Messages Received: The Political Impact of Media Exposure," 462; 278
7. Benjamin I. Page, et al. (1987) "What Moves Public Opinion?" 478; 260
8. Ross E. Burkhart, et al. (1994) "Comparative Democracy: The Economic Development Thesis," 508; 206
9. Benjamin I. Page, et al. (1983) "Effects of Public Opinion on Policy," 471;207
10. G. Bingham Powell, Jr. (1986) "American Voter Turnout in Comparative Perspective" 392; 262

Source: "At the Click of a Mouse: APSR's Most Downloaded Articles," *PS: Political Science & Politics*, 32: 654, (September 1999).

★3040★
Most influential African Americans in politics and civil rights

Ranking basis/background: Alphabetical listing compiled by the DuSable Museum of African American History. **Number listed:** 22.
- Daisy Bates, The Little Rock 9
- Shirley Chisholm, congresswoman
- Johnnie L. Cochran, Jr., attorney
- Angela Davis, Black Panther Party
- W.E.B. DuBois, author-educator
- Medgar Evers, civil rights
- Fannie Lou Hamer, civil rights
- Dorothy Height, National Council of Negro Women
- Leon Higginbotham, Jr., NAACP
- Rev. Jesse L. Jackson, Sr., civil rights
- Barbara Jordan, congresswoman
- Rev. Martin Luther King, Jr., civil rights
- John Lewis, congressman
- Thurgood Marshall, Supreme Court justice
- Huey Newton, Black Panther Party
- Rosa Parks, civil rights
- Adam Clayton Powell, congressman-minister
- A. Philip Randolph, union activist
- Harold Washington, mayor of Chicago, congressman
- Walter White, NAACP founder
- Roy Wilkins, president NAACP
- Malcolm X, black activist

Source: Moffett, Nancy, "Voices of Power," *Chicago Sun-Times*, February 2, 2000, p. 39.

★3041★
Radcliffe Institute for Advanced Study fellowship recipient in the field of political science, 2000-01

Ranking basis/background: Recipient and institutional affiliation of the Radcliffe Institute for Advanced study fellowship for pursuit of advanced work across a wide range of academic disciplines, professions, and creative arts. **Number listed:** 1.
- Cynthia Enloe, Clark University

Source: "The Radcliffe Institute for Advanced Study," *The Chronicle of Higher Education*, 46: A59, (June 2, 2000).

Related Information

★3042★
Wilson, Robin, "In Political Science: Interpreting the Rankings Shuffle," *The Chronicle of Higher Education* 42: A31 (September 22, 1995).
Remarks: Article provides results of a survey of 207 political scientists asked to assess 98 Ph.D. programs in their discipline.

POLITICAL SCIENCE, GRADUATE

★3043★
Most effective political science research-doctorate programs as evaluated by the National Research Council

Ranking basis/background: From a survey of nearly 8,000 faculty members conducted in the spring of 1993. Respondents were asked to rate programs in their field on "effectiveness of program in educating research scholars/scientists." **Remarks:** See *Chronicle* article for more details. Scores of 3.5-5.0 indicate "extremely effective;" 2.5-3.49 "reasonably effective;" 1.5-2.49 "minimally effective;" and 0.0-1.49 "not effective." Programs also ranked by "scholarly quality of program faculty." **Number listed:** 98.
1. University of Michigan, with an effectiveness rating of 4.60
2. Yale University, 4.24
3. Harvard University, 4.17
4. University of California, Berkeley, 4.13
5. Stanford University, 4.02
6. University of Rochester, 4.00
7. University of Minnesota, 3.92
8. Princeton University, 3.91
9. University of Wisconsin, Madison, 3.86
10. University of Chicago, 3.83

Source: "Rankings of Research-Doctorate Programs in 41 Disciplines at 274 Institutions," *The Chronicle of Higher Education* 42: A21-A30 (September 21, 1995).

★3044★
Private, 4-year undergraduate colleges and universities producing the most Ph.D.'s in political science and international relations, 1920-1990

Ranking basis/background: Number of doctoral degrees granted to graduates of 914 private, 4-year U.S. undergraduate colleges and universities. Medical, law, and other professional, non-doctoral degrees are not included. **Remarks:** Original source: Office of Scientific and Engineering Personnel of the National Research Council. Report contains 50 other tables detailing the distribution of doctoral recipients by field of study over various time frames. **Number listed:** 334.
1. Oberlin College, with 185 Ph.D.'s
2. Swarthmore College, 106
3. Williams College, 71
4. Pomona College, 70
5. Amherst College, 64
5. Smith College, 64
5. Barnard College, 64
8. Wellesley College, 63
9. Reed College, 58
10. Wesleyan University, 57
10. Occidental College, 57
12. Macalester College, 52
13. Carleton College, 50
14. Ohio Wesleyan University, 49
14. Haverford College, 49
16. Antioch College, 46
17. DePauw University, 45
18. Bowdoin College, 44
19. Grinnell College, 43
20. Colgate University, 42

Source: *Baccalaureate Origins of Doctorate Recipients*, 7th ed., Franklin & Marshall College, March 1993.

★3045★
Private, 4-year undergraduate colleges and universities producing the most Ph.D.'s in political science and international relations, 1981-1990

Ranking basis/background: Number of doctoral degrees granted to graduates of 914 private, 4-year U.S. undergraduate colleges and universities. Medical, law, and other professional, non-doctoral degrees are not included. **Remarks:** Original source: Office of Scientific and Engineering Personnel of the National Research Council. Report contains 50 other tables detailing the distribution of doctoral recipients by field of study over various time frames. **Number listed:** 339.
1. Oberlin College, with 24 Ph.D.'s
2. Pomona College, 18
3. Swarthmore College, 17
3. Smith College, 17
5. Wellesley College, 15
6. Macalester College, 14
6. Antioch College, 14
8. Barnard College, 13
9. Williams College, 12
10. Carleton College, 11
10. Franklin and Marshall College, 11
10. Clark University, 11
13. Wesleyan University, 10
13. Amherst College, 10
13. Wake Forest University, 10
13. Colorado College, 10
13. Mount Holyoke College, 10
18. Haverford College, 9
18. Bowdoin College, 9
18. Occidental College, 9
18. St. Mary's University (TX), 9

Source: *Baccalaureate Origins of Doctorate Recipients*, 7th ed., Franklin & Marshall College, March 1993.

★3046★
Top political science research-doctorate programs as evaluated by the National Research Council

Ranking basis/background: From a survey of nearly 8,000 faculty members conducted in the spring of 1993. Respondents were asked to rate programs in their field on "scholarly quality of program faculty." When more than one program had the samescore, the council averaged the rank order and gave each program the same rank number (if three programs tied for the top position, each received a rank of 2). **Remarks:** See *Chronicle* article for more details. Scores of 4.01 and above indicate "distinguished;" 3.0-4.0 "strong;" 2.51-3.0 "good;" 2.0-2.5 "adequate;" 1.0-1.99 "marginal;" and 0.0-0.99 "not sufficient for doctoral education." Programs also ranked by "effectiveness of program in educating research scholars/scientists." **Number listed:** 98.
1. Harvard University, with a quality rating of 4.88
2. University of California, Berkeley, 4.66
3. Yale University, 4.60
3. University of Michigan, 4.60
5. Stanford University, 4.50
6. University of Chicago, 4.41
7. Princeton University, 4.39
8. University of California, Los Angeles, 4.25
9. University of California, San Diego, 4.13
10. University of Wisconsin, Madison, 4.09
11. University of Rochester, 4.01
12. Massachusetts Institute of Technology, 3.96
13. University of Minnesota, 3.95
14. Duke University, 3.94
15. Cornell University, 3.85

Source: "Rankings of Research-Doctorate Programs in 41 Disciplines at 274 Institutions," *The Chronicle of Higher Education* 42: A21-A30 (September 21, 1995).

POLITICAL SCIENCE PERIODICALS

★3047★
Authors most frequently published in *American Political Science Review*, 1974-94

Ranking basis/background: Total articles published. **Remarks:** Source: University of Iowa *APSR* Author Data Set. **Number listed:** 10.
1. Paul R. Abramson, with 10 articles
1. Arthur H. Miller, 10
1. Edward N. Muller, 10
4. Peter C. Ordeshook, 9
4. Kenneth A. Shepsle, 9
6. Bruce Bueno de Mesquita, 8
6. Robert S. Erikson, 8
6. John A. Ferejohn, 8
6. Richard G. Niemi, 8
6. Charles W. Ostrom, 8

Source: Miller, Arthur H., Charles Tien and Andrew A. Peebler, "The *American Political Science Review* Hall of Fame: Assessments and Implications for an Evolving Discipline," *PS: Political Science & Politics*, March 1996, pp. 73-83.

★3048★
Authors with the most citations among authors published in *American Political Science Review*, 1974-94

Ranking basis/background: Total citations. **Remarks:** Source: University of Iowa *APSR* Author Data Set. **Number listed:** 50.
1. R. Brown, with 14,423 citations
2. N. H. Nie, 14,269
3. W. J. Dixon, 9,693
4. M. Olson, 8,903
5. J. G. March, 8,487
6. E. Jones, 6,542
7. S. P. Huntington, 5,884
8. A. Wildavsky, 5,568
9. G. Tullock, 5,505
10. C. E. Lindblom, 5,450

Source: Miller, Arthur H., Charles Tien and Andrew A. Peebler, "The *American Political Science Review* Hall of Fame: Assessments and Implications for an Evolving Discipline," *PS: Political Science & Politics*, March 1996, pp. 73-83.

★3049★
Political science journals with the greatest impact measure, 1981-98

Ranking basis/background: Citations-per-paper impact score is the total citations to a journal's published papers divided by total number of papers the journal has published over an eighteen year period. **Remarks:** Original source: *Journal Citation Reports* and Journal Performance Indicators on Diskette. **Number listed:** 10.
1. *American Political Science Review*, with an impact score of 17.38
2. *American Journal of Political Science*, 11.25
3. *Public Opinion Quarterly*, 9.33
4. *Journal of Conflict Resolution*, 9.11

5. *Journal of Politics*, 6.61
6. *Politics & Society*, 5.55
7. *British Journal of Political Science*, 5.48
8. *Legislative Studies Quarterly*, 5.22
9. *Comparative Political Studies*, 4.76
10. *American Politics Quarterly*, 3.98

Source: "Journals Ranked by Impact: Political Science," *What's Hot in Research (http://www.isinet.com/hot/research) Institute for Scientific Information*, December 13, 1999.

★3050★
Political science journals with the greatest impact measure, 1994-98

Ranking basis/background: Citations-per-paper impact score is the total citations to a journal's published papers divided by total number of papers the journal has published over a five year period. **Remarks:** Original source: *Journal Citation Reports* and Journal Performance Indicators on Diskette. **Number listed:** 10.
1. *American Political Science Review*, with an impact score of 5.03
2. *American Journal of Political Science*, 2.82
3. *Journal of Conflict Resolution*, 2.70
4. *British Journal of Political Science*, 2.22
5. *Comparative Political Studies*, 2.20
6. *Public Opinion Quarterly*, 2.03
7. *Political Geography*, 1.91
8. *New Left Review*, 1.81
9. *Political Research Quarterly*, 1.79
10. *Journal of Politics*, 1.73

Source: "Journals Ranked by Impact: Political Science," *What's Hot in Research (http://www.isinet.com/hot/research) Institute for Scientific Information*, December 13, 1999.

★3051★
Political science journals with the greatest percentage of articles by multiple authors, 1974-94

Ranking basis/background: Percentage of articles with more than one author. **Remarks:** Source: University of Iowa *APSR* Article Data Set and tables of contents for other journals. **Number listed:** 6.
1. *Journal of Politics*, with 57%
2. *American Sociological Review*, 44%
3. *American Political Science Review*, 41%
4. *American Journal of Political Science*, 40%
5. *Comparative Political Studies*, 28%
6. *World Politics*, 14%

Source: Miller, Arthur H., Charles Tien and Andrew A. Peebler, "The *American Political Science Review* Hall of Fame: Assessments and Implications for an Evolving Discipline," *PS: Political Science & Politics*, March 1996, pp. 73-83.

PREPARATORY SCHOOLS
See: **Schools, Secondary**

PRIVATE SCHOOLS
See: **Schools, Elementary & Secondary Schools, Secondary**

PROFESSIONAL ASSOCIATIONS

★3052★
Scholarly societies with the highest membership, 1999

Ranking basis/background: Total number of members, number of foreign members and proportion percentages. **Number listed:** 7.
1. American Association for the Advancement of Science, with 138,000 members; and 24,000 foreign members (a proportion of 17.4%)
2. American Physical Society, 41,786; 9,100 (21.8%)
3. American Mathematical Society, 27,537; 10,389 (37.7%)
4. Modern Language Association of America, 30,692; 3,221 (10.5%)
5. Organization of American Historians, 8,080; 465 (5.8%)
6. American Academy of Religion, 9,960; 1,248 (12.5%)
7. American Psychological Association, 148,867; 3,711 (2.5%)

Source: McMurtrie, Beth, "America's Scholarly Societies Raise Their Flags Abroad," *The Chronicle of Higher Education*, 46: A53-A54, (January 28, 2000).

PSYCHIATRY

★3053★
Institutions with the highest impact in psychiatry research, 1990-98

Ranking basis/background: Average citations per high-impact paper, compiled from the 200 most-cited papers published each year in ISI indexed psychiatry journals between 1990 and 1998. **Number listed:** 5.
1. Max Planck Institute of Psychiatry, with an average of 113.7 citations per paper
2. Karolinska Institute, 106.0
3. University of Michigan, 99.4
4. Medical Research Council (UK), 95.7
5. Virginia Commonwealth University, 88.4

Source: "High-Impact Research in Psychiatry, 1990-98," *What's Hot in Research (http://www.isinet.com/isi/hot/research) Institute for Scientific Information*, June 12, 2000.

★3054★
Psychiatry journals by citation impact, 1981-98

Ranking basis/background: Impact factor calculated by taking the number of current citations to source items published and dividing it by the number of articles published in the journal during that time period. **Number listed:** 10.
1. *Archives of General Psychiatry*, with a 79.43 impact factor
2. *American Journal of Psychiatry*, 31.41
3. *Schizophrenia Bulletin*, 28.90
4. *Psychosomatic Medicine*, 23.88
5. *Psychological Medicine*, 21.95
6. *British Journal of Psychiatry*, 21.49
7. *Journal of Clinical Psychopharmacy*, 19.52
8. *Psychopharmacology*, 19.20
9. *Journal of the American Academy of Child and Adolescent Psychiatry*, 18.10
10. *Journal of Clinical Psychiatry*, 17.57

Source: "Journals Ranked by Impact: Psychiatry," *What's Hot in Research (http://www.isinet.com/isi/hot/research) Institute for Scientific Information*, August 14, 2000.

★3055★
Psychiatry journals by citation impact, 1995-98

Ranking basis/background: Impact factor calculated by taking the number of current citations to source items published and dividing it by the number of articles published in the journal during that time period. **Number listed:** 10.
1. *Archives of General Psychiatry*, with a 19.80 impact factor
2. *American Journal of Psychiatry*, 11.35
3. *Schizophrenia Bulletin*, 9.31
4. *Journal of Clinical Psychopharmacy*, 8.74
5. *Dementia*, 8.61
6. *Neuropsychopharmacology*, 7.58
7. *British Journal of Psychiatry*, 7.51
8. *Journal of the American Academy of Child And Adolescent Psychiatry*, 7.12
9. *Molecular Psychiatry*, 7.05
10. *Journal of Clinical Psychiatry*, 6.92

Source: "Journals Ranked by Impact: Psychiatry," *What's Hot in Research (http://www.isinet.com/isi/hot/research) Institute for Scientific Information*, August 14, 2000.

★3056★
Psychiatry journals by citation impact, 1998

Ranking basis/background: Impact factor calculated by taking the number of current citations to source items published and dividing it by the number of articles published in the journal during that time period. **Number listed:** 10.
1. *Archives of General Psychiatry*, with a 9.40 impact factor
2. *American Journal of Psychiatry*, 5.94
3. *Schizophrenia Bulletin*, 4.46
4. *Journal of Clinical Psychiatry*, 4.07
5. *Journal of the American Academy of Child and Adolescent Psychiatry*, 3.73
6. *British Journal of Psychiatry*, 3.50
7. *Psychological Medicine*, 3.12
8. *Psychosomatic Medicine*, 3.05
9. *Psychopharmacology Bulletin*, 2.59
10. *Journal of Child Psychology, Psychiatry and Allied Disciplines*, 2.55

Source: "Journals Ranked by Impact: Psychiatry," *What's Hot in Research (http://www.isinet.com/isi/hot/research) Institute for Scientific Information*, August 14, 2000.

★3057★
Psychiatry journals by impact factor, 1981 to 1998

Ranking basis/background: Current citations to a journal's published papers divided by total papers published over an 18-year period. **Remarks:** Original source: *Journal Citation Reports* and Journal Performances Indicators on Diskette. **Number listed:** 10.
1. *Archives of General Psychiatry*, with 75.30
2. *American Journal of Psychiatry*, 29.59
3. *Schizophrenia Bulletin*, 26.36
4. *Psychosomatic Medicine*, 22.94
5. *Psychological Medicine*, 20.56
6. *British Journal of Psychiatry*, 19.95
7. *Journal of Clinical Psychopharmacology*, 18.48
8. *Psychopharmacology*, 18.40
9. *Journal of Clinical Psychiatry*, 16.95

10. *Journal of the American Academy of Child and Adolescent Psychiatry*, 16.75

Source: "Journals Ranked by Impact: Psychiatry," *What's Hot in Research,* http://www.isinet.com/whatshot/whatshot.html, Institute for Scientific Information (April 12, 1999).

★3058★
Psychiatry journals by impact factor, 1994 to 1998

Ranking basis/background: Current citations to a journal's published papers divided by total papers published over the past five years. **Remarks:** Original source: *Journal Citation Reports* and *Journal Performances Indicators on Diskette*. **Number listed:** 10.
1. *Archives of General Psychiatry*, with 21.70
2. *American Journal of Psychiatry*, 11.13
3. *Schizophrenia Bulletin*, 8.32
4. *Journal of Clinical Psychopharmacology*, 8.29
5. *Journal of Clinical Psychiatry*, 7.82
6. *Dementia*, 7.18
7. *British Journal of Psychiatry*, 7.12
8. *Journal of the American Academy of Child and Adolescent Psychiatry*, 6.68
9. *Neuropsychopharmacology*, 6.59
10. *Psychopharmacology*, 6.24

Source: "Journals Ranked by Impact: Psychiatry," *What's Hot in Research,* http://www.isinet.com/whatshot/whatshot.html, Institute for Scientific Information (April 12, 1999).

★3059★
U.S. institutions with the most citations in psychiatry research, 1990-98

Ranking basis/background: Number of citations to high-impact papers, compiled from the 200 most-cited papers published each year in ISI indexed psychiatry journals between 1990 and 1998. **Number listed:** 5.
1. Harvard University, with 9,738 citations to high-impact papers
2. National Institute of Mental Health, 9,436
3. Yale University, 7,888
4. Columbia University, 7,683
5. New York State Psychiatric Institute, 6,358

Source: "High-Impact Research in Psychiatry, 1990-98," *What's Hot in Research (http://www.isinet.com/isi/hot/research) Institute for Scientific Information,* June 12, 2000.

★3060★
U.S. universities with the greatest impact in psychiatry, 1995-99

Ranking basis/background: Average citations per paper from the top 100 federally funded U.S. universities that had at least 50 published papers in ISI indexed psychiatry journals. Also includes total number of paper published during the five year period. **Number listed:** 5.
1. Emory University, with 142 papers; 8.49 citations per paper
2. University of Michigan, 193; 8.24
3. Case Western Reserve University, 169; 8.22
4. Washington University, 164; 7.70
5. University of Cincinnati, 101; 7.68

Source: "Psychiatry: High Impact U.S. Universities, 1995-99," *What's Hot in Research (http://www.isinet.com/isi/hot/research) Institute for Scientific Information,* November 13, 2000.

★3061★
U.S. universities with the highest concentration of papers published in the field of psychiatry, 1994-98

Ranking basis/background: Number of papers published in the field of psychiatry over a five-year period, and percentage they comprise of the university's total papers published. **Number listed:** 5.
1. Yale University, with 551 papers; 3.74% of university's total papers
2. Columbia University, 554; 3.64%
3. University of Pittsburgh, 489; 3.61%
4. Virginia Commonwealth University, 160; 3.52%
5. Brown University, 199; 3.34%

Source: "Psychiatry: High-Concentration U.S. Universities, 1994-98," *What's Hot in Research (http://www.isinet.com/isi/hot/research) Institute for Scientific Information,* May 1, 2000.

PSYCHOLOGY

★3062★
Radcliffe Institute for Advanced Study fellowship recipients in the field of psychology, 2000-01

Ranking basis/background: Recipient and institutional affiliation of the Radcliffe Institute for Advanced study fellowship for pursuit of advanced work across a wide range of academic disciplines, professions, and creative arts. **Number listed:** 3.
   Deborah Belle, Boston University
   Brian Little, Carleton University
   Joseph Trimble, Western Washington University

Source: "The Radcliffe Institute for Advanced Study," *The Chronicle of Higher Education,* 46: A59, (June 2, 2000).

★3063★
Top recruiters for psychology jobs for 2000-01 bachelor's degree recipients

Ranking basis/background: Projected number of college hires from on-campus recruitment for 2000-01. **Remarks:** Numbers reflect total expected hires, not just African American projected hires. **Number listed:** 12.
1. Accenture, with 165 projected hires
2. Federated Department Stores, 33
3. Eckerd Youth Alternatives, Inc., 25
4. Macy's East, 20
5. Houghton Mifflin, 10
5. Toys "R" Us, 10
7. Footstar, 10
8. U.S. Air Force (Civilian Hires), 6
9. Caddo Parish School Board, 5
9. Arthur Andersen LLP, 5
9. Countrywide Home Loans, 5
9. Macy's West, 5

Source: "The Top 100 Employers and the Majors in Demand for the Class of 2001," *The Black Collegian,* 31: 19-35, (February 2001).

★3064★
U.S. universities with the greatest impact in psychology, 1995-99

Ranking basis/background: Average citations per paper from the top 100 federally funded U.S. universities that had at least 50 published papers in ISI indexed psychology journals. Also includes total number of paper published during the five year period. **Number listed:** 5.
1. Carnegie Mellon University, with 276 papers; 5.84 citations per paper
2. University of Rochester, 259; 5.50
3. Massachusetts Institute of Technology, 117; 5.17
4. Yale University, 581; 4.95
5. University of Pittsburgh, 579; 4.85

Source: "Psychology: High Impact U.S. Universities, 1995-99," *What's Hot in Research (http://www.isinet.com/isi/hot/research) Institute for Scientific Information,* January 29, 2001.

PSYCHOLOGY, GRADUATE

★3065★
Most effective psychology research-doctorate programs as evaluated by the National Research Council

Ranking basis/background: From a survey of nearly 8,000 faculty members conducted in the spring of 1993. Respondents were asked to rate programs in their field on "effectiveness of program in educating research scholars/scientists." **Remarks:** See *Chronicle* article for more details. Scores of 3.5-5.0 indicate "extremely effective;" 2.5-3.49 "reasonably effective;" 1.5-2.49 "minimally effective;" and 0.0-1.49 "not effective." Programs also ranked by "scholarly quality of program faculty." **Number listed:** 185.
1. Stanford University, with an effectiveness rating of 4.64
2. University of Michigan, 4.40
3. University of Illinois, Urbana-Champaign, 4.36
4. University of Minnesota, 4.33
5. Yale University, 4.31
6. University of Pennsylvania, 4.18
7. Carnegie Mellon University, 4.13
8. University of California, San Diego, 4.12
9. Princeton University, 4.10
10. Harvard University, 4.09

Source: "Rankings of Research-Doctorate Programs in 41 Disciplines at 274 Institutions," *The Chronicle of Higher Education* 42: A21-A30 (September 21, 1995).

★3066★
Private, 4-year undergraduate colleges and universities producing the most Ph.D.'s in psychology, 1920-1990

Ranking basis/background: Number of doctoral degrees granted to graduates of 914 private, 4-year U.S. undergraduate colleges and universities. Medical, law, and other professional, non-doctoral degrees are not included. **Remarks:** Original source: Office of Scientific and Engineering Personnel of the National Research Council. Report contains 50 other tables detailing the distribution of doctoral recipients by field of study over various time frames. **Number listed:** 345.
1. Oberlin College, with 421 Ph.D.'s
2. Barnard College, 361
3. Swarthmore College, 259

4. Antioch College, 249
4. Wellesley College, 249
6. Clark University, 244
7. Vassar College, 230
8. Smith College, 215
9. Wesleyan University, 194
10. DePauw University, 186
11. Bucknell University, 184
12. Mount Holyoke College, 173
13. Pomona College, 166
14. Roosevelt University, 164
15. Occidental College, 163
16. Denison University, 162
17. Reed College, 154
18. Franklin and Marshall College, 152
19. Wheaton College, 139
20. Union College, 133

Source: *Baccalaureate Origins of Doctorate Recipients, 7th ed.,* Franklin & Marshall College, March 1993.

★3067★
Private, 4-year undergraduate colleges and universities producing the most Ph.D.'s in psychology, 1981-1990

Ranking basis/background: Number of doctoral degrees granted to graduates of 914 private, 4-year U.S. undergraduate colleges and universities. Medical, law, and other professional, non-doctoral degrees are not included. **Remarks:** Original source: Office of Scientific and Engineering Personnel of the National Research Council. Report contains 50 other tables detailing the distribution of doctoral recipients by field of study over various time frames. **Number listed:** 342.

1. Barnard College, with 128 Ph.D.'s
2. Oberlin College, 126
3. Clark University, 116
4. Wellesley College, 99
5. Vassar College, 95
6. Smith College, 90
7. Mount Holyoke College, 77
8. Swarthmore College, 75
9. Wesleyan University, 63
9. Wheaton College, 63
11. Antioch College, 60
12. Pomona College, 57
13. Williams College, 56
13. Bucknell University, 56
15. Union College, 52
15. Sarah Lawrence College, 52
17. Franklin and Marshall College, 50
17. Wake Forest University, 50
19. Denison University, 48

Source: *Baccalaureate Origins of Doctorate Recipients, 7th ed.,* Franklin & Marshall College, March 1993.

★3068★
Top psychology research-doctorate programs as evaluated by the National Research Council

Ranking basis/background: From a survey of nearly 8,000 faculty members conducted in the spring of 1993. Respondents were asked to rate programs in their field on "scholarly quality of program faculty." When more than one program had the samescore, the council averaged the rank order and gave each program the same rank number (if three programs tied for the top position, each received a rank of 2). **Remarks:** See *Chronicle* article for more details. Scores of 4.01 and above indicate "distinguished;" 3.0-4.0 "strong;" 2.51-3.0 "good;" 2.0-2.5 "adequate;" 1.0-1.99 "marginal;" and 0.0-0.99 "not sufficient for doctoral education." Programs also ranked by "effectiveness of program in educating research scholars/scientists." **Number listed:** 185.

1. Stanford University, with a quality rating of 4.82
2. University of Michigan, 4.63
3. Yale University, 4.62
4. University of California, Los Angeles, 4.61
5. University of Illinois, Urbana-Champaign, 4.58
6. Harvard University, 4.48
7. University of Minnesota, 4.46
8. University of Pennsylvania, 4.35
9. University of California, Berkeley, 4.33
10. University of California, San Diego, 4.32
11. Carnegie Mellon University, 4.29
12. University of Washington (WA), 4.24
13. Princeton University, 4.22
14. Cornell University, 4.15
15. University of Wisconsin, Madison, 4.09

Source: "Rankings of Research-Doctorate Programs in 41 Disciplines at 274 Institutions," *The Chronicle of Higher Education* 42: A21-A30 (September 21, 1995).

★3069★
Top recruiters for psychology jobs for 2000-01 master's degree recipients

Ranking basis/background: Projected number of college hires from on-campus recruitment for 2000-01. **Remarks:** Numbers reflect total expected hires, not just African American projected hires. **Number listed:** 2.

1. Accenture, with 30 projected hires
2. Houghton Mifflin, 2

Source: "The Top 100 Employers and the Majors in Demand for the Class of 2001," *The Black Collegian,* 31: 19-35, (February 2001).

PSYCHOLOGY PERIODICALS

★3070★
Most cited sources in experimental analyses of human behavior between 1990 and 1999

Ranking basis/background: Total number of citations received in four journals, *Journal of the Experimental Analysis of Behavior, The Psychological Record, The Analysis of Verbal Behavior,* and *Experimental Analysis of Behavior,* between 1990 and 1999. Self citation were excluded. **Number listed:** 98.

1. M. Sidman & W. Tailby (1982), Conditional discrimination vs. matching-to-sample: An expansion of the testing paradigm, *Journal of the Experimental Analysis of Human Behavior,* with 73 citations
2. B.F. Skinner (1957), *The Analysis of Verbal Behavior,* 54
3. E. Wulfert & S.C Hayes (1988), Transfer of a conditional ordering response through conditional equivalence classes, *Journal of the Experimental Analysis of Behavior,* 47
4. J.M. Devany, S.C. Hayes & R.O. Nelson (1986), Equivalence class formation in language-able and language-disabled children, *Journal of Experimental Analysis of Behavior,* 45
5. M. Sidman (1971), Reading and auditory-visual equivalencies, *Journal of Speech and Hearing Research,* 39
6. M. Sidman (1990), Equivalence relations: Where do they come from? *Behavior Analysis in Theory and Practice: Contributions and Controversies,* 38
7. K.M. Bush, M. Sidman & J. de Rose (1989), Contextual control of emergent equivalence relations, *Journal of the Experimental Analysis of Behavior,* 36
8. M. Sidman (1986), Functional analysis of emergent verbal classes, *Analysis and Integration of Behavioral Units,* 34
9. R.R. Saunders, K.J. Saunders, K.C. Kirby & J.E. Spradlin (1988), The merger of equivalence classes by unreinforced conditional section of comparison stimuli, *Journal of the Experimental Analysis of Behavior,* 33
10. A. Baron & M. Galizio (1983), Instructional control of human operant behavior, *The Psychological Record,* 32
10. M. Sidman, B. Kirk, & M. Willson-Morris (1985), Six-member stimulus classes generated by conditional-discrimination procedures, *Journal of the Experimental Analysis of Behavior,* 32

Source: Critchfield, T.S., et. al., "Sources Cited Most Frequently in the Experimental Analysis of Human Behavior," *The Behavior Analyst,* 23: 255-266, (Fall 2000).

★3071★
Most frequently cited contribution articles in psychology journals from 1986 to 1996

Ranking basis/background: Total number of citations. **Number listed:** 10.

1. Gelso *Research in Counseling: Methodological and Professional Issues* (1980), with 100 citations
2. Gelso & Carter *The Relationship in Counseling and Psychotherapy: Components, Consequences, and Theoretical Antecedents* (1985), 90
2. Loganbill, Hardy, & Delworth *Supervision: A Conceptual Model* (1982), 90
4. Astin *The Meaning of Work in Women's Lives: A Sociopsychological Model of Career Choice and Work Behavior* (1984), 80
5. Hoshmand *Alternate Research Paradigms: A Review and Teaching Proposal* (1989), 61

6. Kitchener *Intuition, Critical Evaluation and Ethical Principles: The Foundation for Ethical Decisions in Counseling Psychology* (1984), 58
7. Heppner & Krauskopf *An Information-Procession Approach to Personal Problem Solving* (1987), 46
8. Schlossberg *A Model for Analyzing Human Adaptation to Transition* (1987), 43
9. Katz *The Sociopolitical Nature of Counseling* (1985), 42
10. Mahoney *Recent Developments in Cognitive Approaches to Counseling and Psychotherapy* (1988), 41

Source: Flores, Lisa Y., et. al., "Trend Analyses of Major Contribution in the Counseling Psychologist Cited from 1986 to 1996: Impact and Implication," *Counseling Psychologist*, 27: 73-95, (January 1999).

PUBLIC ADDRESS
See: **Speech Communication**

PUBLIC AFFAIRS
See: **Political Science**

PUBLIC SCHOOLS
See: **Schools, Elementary & Secondary Schools, Secondary**

PUBLISHING

★3072★
Highest revenues of publicly held book publishers, 1999

Ranking basis/background: Revenue figures in millions for the 1999 fiscal year. **Number listed:** 16.
1. Harcourt, with $2,142.6 in revenue
2. McGraw-Hill, $1,734.9
3. Reader's Digest, $1,561.8
4. Scholastic, $1,402.5
5. HarperCollins, $1,031.0
6. Houghton Mifflin, $920.1
7. Simon & Schuster, $610.7
8. John Wiley, $594.8
9. Tribune Ed., $339.6
10. Thomas Nelson, $261.8
11. IDG Books, $179.8
12. Golden Books, $165.8
13. Millbrook, $18.8
14. EDC, $16.8

Source: Milliot, Jim, "Publishers' Profits Had Solid Gains in 1999," *Publishers Weekly*, 247: 11, (September 4, 2000).

★3073★
Small publishers with the highest sales growth between 1997 and 1999

Ranking basis/background: Sales growth percentages between 1997 and 1999. Also includes number of titles published in 1999 and number of employees in 1999. **Number listed:** 11.

1. Gallopade International (Peachtree City, PA), with 600% sales growth; 500 titles; and 30 employees
2. Seven Stories Press (New York, NY), 440%; 25; 7
3. 300Incredible.com (Marietta, GA), 380%; 8; 5
4. Overlook Press (New York, NY), 133%; 77; 16
5. Lyons Press (New York, NY), 97%; 190; 22
6. Avalon Publishing (New York, NY), 93%; 105; 10
7. Arcadia Publishing (Charleston, SC), 45%; 350; 40
8. Charlesbridge Publishing (Watertown, MA), 39%; 34; 18
9. Brookes Publishing (Baltimore, MD), 36%; 32; 42
10. Gibbs, Smith Publisher (Layton, UT), 33%; 44; 35
11. Hay House (Carlsbad, CA), 27%; 60; 40

Source: Milliot, Jim, "Small Publishers On a Growing Spree," *Publishers Weekly*, 247: 38-40, (November 20, 2000).

★3074★
Top children's book publishers, 1999

Ranking basis/background: Estimated net sales figures, in millions, for the 1999 fiscal year. **Number listed:** 15.
1. Scholastic, with $230.0
2. Random House, $192.7
3. HarperCollins, $178.5
4. Penguin Putnam, $160.0
5. Golden Books, $132.6
6. Simon & Schuster, $126.0
7. DK Publishing, $101.5
8. Disney Juvenile Pub., $85.0
9. Landoll's, $70.0
10. Houghton Mifflin, $32.6
11. Harcourt, $30.0
12. Little, Brown, $28.5
13. Holtzbrinck, $23.0
14. Candlewick, $21.9
15. Tommy Nelson, $21.0

Source: Milliot, Jim and Diane Roback, "Scholastic Catapults To Top Slot Among Children's Publishers," *Publishers Weekly*, 247: 33-34, (October 16, 2000).

QUALITY RATINGS
See: **Evaluation Criteria & Methodologies**

REAL ESTATE

★3075★
Best big cities to live in

Ranking basis/background: Places most recommended for retirees, as selected by a team from *Modern Maturity*. **Number listed:** 10.
1. Boston, MA
2. San Francisco, CA
3. Sarasota, FL
4. Raleigh-Durham-Chapel Hill, NC
5. San Diego, CA
6. Seattle, WA
7. New York, NY
8. Chicago, IL
9. San Antonio, TX
10. Minneapolis/St. Paul, MN

Source: "The 50 Most Alive Places to Live," *Modern Maturity*, 43R: 52-82, (May/June 2000).

★3076★
Best college towns to live in

Ranking basis/background: Places most recommended for retirees, as selected by a team from *Modern Maturity*. **Number listed:** 10.
1. Austin, TX
2. Charlottesville, VA
3. Columbia, MO
4. Madison, WI
5. Princeton, NJ
6. Iowa City, IA
7. Bloomington, IN
8. Las Cruces, NM
9. State College, PA
10. Ann Arbor, MI

Source: "The 50 Most Alive Places to Live," *Modern Maturity*, 43R: 52-82, (May/June 2000).

★3077★
Best "green & clean" places to live

Ranking basis/background: Places most recommended for retirees, as selected by a team from *Modern Maturity*. **Number listed:** 10.
1. Boulder, CO
2. Bend, OR
3. Annapolis, MD
4. Bellingham, WA
5. Coeur d'Alene, ID
6. Portland, OR/Vancouver, WA
7. Flagstaff, AZ
8. Tucson, AZ
9. Burlington, VT
10. Boise, ID

Source: "The 50 Most Alive Places to Live," *Modern Maturity*, 43R: 52-82, (May/June 2000).

★3078★
Best place to live in the midwest U.S.

Ranking basis/background: As chosen by *Money* magazine for it's economical vibrancy, and success in managing growth and providing a high quality of life. **Number listed:** 1.

Chicago, IL
Population: 7,743,400
Median home price: $170,200
Public school spending per pupil: $5,996
Student/teacher ratio: 17.6
Average commute time: 28 minutes
Future job growth rate: 11%
Top neighborhoods: Andersonville, Hyde Park, Lakeview, Wicker Park
Hot spot: The Goodman Theatre, with its new $65 million state-of-the-art theater complex in the North Loop area

Source: Pachetti, Nick and Alan Mirabella, "The Best Places to Live," *Money*, 29: 148-159, (December 2000).

★3079★
Best place to live in the northeastern U.S.

Ranking basis/background: As chosen by *Money* magazine for it's economical vibrancy, and success in managing growth and providing a high quality of life. **Number listed:** 1.

Providence, RI
Population: 1,128,100
Median home price: $128,900
Public school spending per pupil: $6,754
Student/teacher ratio: 14

Average commute time: 19.5 minutes
Future job growth rate: 5.7%
Top neighborhoods: Armory, East Side, Downtown, Elmwood
Hot spot: Providence Oyster Bar, seafood spot in the popular Federal Hill district
Source: Pachetti, Nick and Alan Mirabella, "The Best Places to Live," *Money*, 29: 148-159, (December 2000).

★3080★
Best place to live in the southern U.S.
Ranking basis/background: As chosen by *Money* magazine for it's economical vibrancy, and success in managing growth and providing a high quality of life. **Number listed:** 1.
Raleigh-Durham-Chapel Hill, NC
Population: 1,031,600
Median home price: $164,600
Public school spending per pupil: $4,869
Student/teacher ratio: 14.2
Average commute time: 20 minutes
Future job growth rate: 24.8%
Top neighborhoods: Downtown (Raleigh), Trinity Park, West Village (both Durham)
Hot spot: Brightleaf 905 eatery, located in a renovated tobacco warehouse (Durham)
Source: Pachetti, Nick and Alan Mirabella, "The Best Places to Live," *Money*, 29: 148-159, (December 2000).

★3081★
Best place to live in the U.S.
Ranking basis/background: As chosen by *Money* magazine for it's economical vibrancy, and success in managing growth and providing a high quality of life. **Number listed:** 1.
Portland, OR
Population: 1,765,400
Median home price: $165,700
Public school spending per pupil: $5,270
Student/teacher ratio: 20.1
Average commute time: 20.7 minutes
Future job growth rate: 26%
Top neighborhoods: Irvington, Multnomah Village, Pearl District, Sellwood
Hot spot: Brazen Bean bar for its great happy hour and $3 martinis
Source: Pachetti, Nick and Alan Mirabella, "The Best Places to Live," *Money*, 29: 148-159, (December 2000).

★3082★
Best place to live in the western U.S.
Ranking basis/background: As chosen by *Money* magazine for it's economical vibrancy, and success in managing growth and providing a high quality of life. **Number listed:** 1.
Salt Lake City, UT
Population: 1,221,000
Median home price: $138,700
Public school spending per pupil: $3,659
Student/teacher ratio: 21.2
Average commute time: 19.5 minutes
Future job growth rate: 28.5%
Top neighborhoods: East Bench, Gilmour Park
Hot spot: Brewvies movie theater and restaurant, where you can dine while watching flicks
Source: Pachetti, Nick and Alan Mirabella, "The Best Places to Live," *Money*, 29: 148-159, (December 2000).

★3083★
Best "quirky" places to live
Ranking basis/background: Places most recommended for retirees, as selected by a team from *Modern Maturity*. **Number listed:** 10.
1. Sonoma County, CA
2. Key West, FL
3. Reno, NV
4. Hot Springs, AZ
5. Wilmington, NC
6. Santa Cruz, CA
7. Branson, MO
8. Seaside, FL
9. Bisbee, AZ
10. Sioux Falls, SD

Source: "The 50 Most Alive Places to Live," *Modern Maturity*, 43R: 52-82, (May/June 2000).

★3084★
Best small city in the U.S.
Ranking basis/background: As chosen by *Money* magazine for it's economical vibrancy, and success in managing growth and providing a high quality of life. **Number listed:** 1.
Sarasota, FL
Population: 530,900
Median home price: $126,100
Public school spending per pupil: $5,491
Student/teacher ratio: 18
Average commute time: 18.4 minutes
Future job growth rate: 30.6%
Top neighborhoods: Burns Court, Lakewood Ranch
Hot spot: Fred's restaurant, downtown
Source: Pachetti, Nick and Alan Mirabella, "The Best Places to Live," *Money*, 29: 148-159, (December 2000).

★3085★
Best small towns to live in
Ranking basis/background: Places most recommended for retirees, as selected by a team from *Modern Maturity*. **Number listed:** 10.
1. Asheville, NC
2. Ashland, OR
3. Silver City, NM
4. Chestertown, MD
5. Fort Collins, CO
6. Biloxi/Gulfport, MS
7. Oxford, MS
8. Texas Hill Country
9. Prescott, AZ
10. Naperville, IL

Source: "The 50 Most Alive Places to Live," *Modern Maturity*, 43R: 52-82, (May/June 2000).

★3086★
Most polite cities in the U.S.
Ranking basis/background: American cities considering the best mannered, according to etiquette expert Marjabelle Young Stewart. **Number listed:** 10.
1. Charleston, SC
2. Davenport, Bettendorf, IA-Moline, Rock Island, IL
3. Milwaukee, WI
4. Las Vegas, NV
5. Mobile, AL
6. Seattle, WA
7. Savannah, GA
8. San Francisco, CA
9. Chicago, IL
10. Omaha, NE-Council Bluffs, IA

Source: Baca, Kim, "Charleston, S.C., No. 1 in Courtesy," *Chicago Sun-Times*, November 25, 2000, p. 18.

★3087★
U.S. cities with the highest home prices
Ranking basis/background: As determined by *Money* magazine. **Number listed:** 5.
San Francisco, CA, with an average price of $372,700
San Jose, CA, $327,800
Honolulu, HI, $296,500
Santa Rosa, CA, $294,400
Stamford, CT, $290,300
Source: Pachetti, Nick and Alan Mirabella, "The Best Places to Live," *Money*, 29: 148-159, (December 2000).

★3088★
U.S. cities with the lowest rate of violent crime
Ranking basis/background: As determined by *Money* magazine. **Number listed:** 5.
1. Nashua, NH
2. Appleton, WI
3. Owensboro, KY
4. State College, PA
5. Portsmouth, NH

Source: Pachetti, Nick and Alan Mirabella, "The Best Places to Live," *Money*, 29: 148-159, (December 2000).

★3089★
U.S. cities with the most single people
Ranking basis/background: As determined by *Money* magazine. **Number listed:** 5.
Bryant/College Station, TX
Gainesville, FL
Bloomington, IN
Lawrence, KS
New York City
Source: Pachetti, Nick and Alan Mirabella, "The Best Places to Live," *Money*, 29: 148-159, (December 2000).

REAL ESTATE PERIODICALS

★3090★
Highly cited real estate journals, 1990 to 1995
Ranking basis/background: Based on total number of citations in base journals from 1990 to 1995. **Number listed:** 19.
1. *Real Estate Economics*, with 714 total citations
2. *Journal of Finance*, 557
3. *Journal of Urban Economics*, 388
4. *Journal of Financial Economics*, 362
5. *American Economic Review*, 286
6. *Journal of Political Economics*, 183
7. *Land Economics*, 182
8. *Econometrika*, 178
9. *Journal of Real Estate Finance & Economics*, 174
10. *Appraisal Journal*, 167

Source: Redman, Arnold L., Herman Manakyan and John R. Tanner, "A Normalized Citation Analysis of Real Estate Journals," *Real Estate Economics*, 27: 169-182, (Spring 1999).

RELIGION, GRADUATE

★3091★
Most influential African Americans in religion

Ranking basis/background: Alphabetical listing compiled by the DuSable Museum of African American History. **Number listed:** 7.
- Willie Taplin Barrow, civil rights
- Rev. Johnnie Colemon, Christ Universal Temple
- Thomas A. Dorsey, gospel music composer
- Louis Farrakhan, Nation of Islam
- Mahalia Jackson, gospel music artist
- Elijah Muhammad, Black Muslim leader
- Samuel Proctor, minister
- Howard Thurman, theologian
- Albertina Walker, gospel music artist

Source: Moffett, Nancy, "Voices of Power," *Chicago Sun-Times*, February 2, 2000, p. 39.

★3092★
Radcliffe Institute for Advanced Study fellowship recipients in the field of religion, 2000-01

Ranking basis/background: Recipient and institutional affiliation of the Radcliffe Institute for Advanced study fellowship for pursuit of advanced work across a wide range of academic disciplines, professions, and creative arts. **Number listed:** 3.
- Denise Buell, Williams College
- Kimerer LaMothe, Harvard University
- Kathleen Sands, University of Massachusetts, Boston

Source: "The Radcliffe Institute for Advanced Study," *The Chronicle of Higher Education*, 46: A59, (June 2, 2000).

★3093★
Top religion research-doctorate programs as evaluated by the National Research Council

Ranking basis/background: From a survey of nearly 8,000 faculty members conducted in the spring of 1993. Respondents were asked to rate programs in their field on "scholarly quality of program faculty." When more than one program had the same score, the council averaged the rank order and gave each program the same rank number (if three programs tied for the top position, each received a rank of 2). **Remarks:** See *Chronicle* article for more details. Scores of 4.01 and above indicate "distinguished;" 3.0-4.0 "strong;" 2.51-3.0 "good;" 2.0-2.5 "adequate;" 1.0-1.99 "marginal;" and 0.0-0.99 "not sufficient for doctoral education." Programs also ranked by "effectiveness of program in educating research scholars/scientists." **Number listed:** 38.
1. University of Chicago, with a quality rate of 4.76
2. Harvard University, 4.73
3. Princeton University, 4.33
4. Duke University, 4.25
5. Emory University, 4.05
6. University of Virginia, 3.96
7. Vanderbilt University, 3.85
8. Princeton Theological Seminary, 3.84
9. University of California, Santa Barbara, 3.82
10. Jewish Theological Seminary, 3.74
10. University of Pennsylvania, 3.74
12. University of Notre Dame, 3.73
13. Hebrew Union College, 3.71
14. Columbia University, 3.57
15. Brown University, 3.55

Source: "Rankings of Research-Doctorate Programs in 41 Disciplines at 274 Institutions," *The Chronicle of Higher Education* 42: A21-A30 (September 21, 1995).

★3094★
U.S. universities with the highest concentrations in religion and theology, 1992-96

Ranking basis/background: For each university, percentage of total number of papers that are religion and theology papers and total religion and theology papers published during a five-year period. **Remarks:** Original source: *National Science Indicators on Diskette, 1981-97* **Number listed:** 5.
1. University of Chicago, with 0.90% of university's total papers; 67 religion and theology papers
2. Princeton University, 0.85; 63
3. Duke University, 0.82; 61
4. Harvard University, 0.73; 54
5. Emory University, 0.71; 53
5. Indiana University, 0.71; 53

Source: "Religion & Theology: Most Prolific U.S. Universities, 1992-96," *What's Hot*, May 18, 1998.

RESEARCH & DEVELOPMENT

★3095★
Highest licensing royalties income for universities or research facilities, 1999

Ranking basis/background: Adjusted royalties received, in dollars. Excludes income on shared patents collected by an institution and later dispersed to others. **Remarks:** Original source: Association of University Technology Managers, Data from all 139 respondents is available at *The Chronicle*'s web site. **Number listed:** 46.
1. Columbia University, with $89,159,556 in licensing income
2. University of California System, $74,133,000
3. Florida State University, $57,313,014
4. Yale University, $40,695,606
5. Washington Research Foundation, University of Washington, $27,878,900
6. Stanford University, $27,699,355
7. Michigan State University, $23,711,867
8. University of Florida, $21,649,577
9. Wisconsin Alumni Research Foundation, University of Wisconsin, Madison, $18,011,400
10. Massachusetts Institute of Technology, $16,131,334

Source: Blumenstyk, Goldie, "Universities Collected $641-Million in Royalties on Inventions in 1999," *The Chronicle of Higher Education*, 47: A49, (November 24, 2000).

★3096★
Mean age of first and best contribution of scientists and inventors, by discipline

Ranking basis/background: Ages from which 1,884 scientists and inventors made key discoveries in their field according to a survey of historical and biographical reference books. "Best contribution" is one mentioned most often in reference books. **Remarks:** Original source: Dean K. Simonton, University of California, Davis. **Number listed:** 9.

Mathematics, with a mean age of 27.3 for first contributions; a mean age of 38.8 for best contribution
Astronomy, 30.5; 40.6
Physics, 29.7; 38.2
Chemistry, 30.5; 38.0
Biology, 29.4; 40.5
Medicine, 32.3; 42.1
Technology, 31.6; 39.7
Earth sciences, 30.9; 42.5
Other, 33.4; 41.6

Source: Guterman, Lila, "Are Mathematicians Past Their Prime at 35?," *The Chronicle of Higher Education*, 47: A18-A20, (December 1, 2000).

★3097★
Most patents issued to universities or research facilities, 1999

Ranking basis/background: Patents received. **Remarks:** Original source: Association of University Technology Managers, Data from all 139 respondents is available at *The Chronicle*'s web site (autm.net). **Number listed:** 46.
1. University of California System, with 281 patents issued
2. Massachusetts Institute of Technology, 154
3. Johns Hopkins University, 111
4. Stanford University, 90
5. University of Pennsylvania, 82
6. Wisconsin Alumni Research Foundation, University of Wisconsin, Madison, 79
7. Columbia University, 77
8. Harvard University, 72
9. Cornell Research Foundation, 70
10. Michigan State University, 63

Source: Blumenstyk, Goldie, "Universities Collected $641-Million in Royalties on Inventions in 1999," *The Chronicle of Higher Education*, 47: A49, (November 24, 2000).

★3098★
U.S. colleges and universities spending the most on chemical engineering research and development, 1998

Ranking basis/background: Figures, in thousands of dollars, for 1998 chemical engineering R&D spending; percentage of federal funds in 1998; annual percent change since 1997. **Remarks:** Original source: National Science Foundation, 2000 Survey of Scientific and Engineering Expenditures at Universities and Colleges: Fiscal Year 1998; WebCASPAR Database System. **Number listed:** 25.
1. North Carolina State University, with $13,306 in chemical engineering R&D spending; 34.9% of federal funds; and a 76.3% change from 1997
2. University of Minnesota, $11,132; 78.0%; 3.7% decrease
3. Texas A&M University, $9,899; 15.2%; 15.6%
4. Massachusetts Institute of Technology, $8,614; 48.6%; 24.2%
5. New Mexico State University, $8,263; 88.8%; 17.8% decrease
6. Stanford University, $7,376; 93.0%; 15.7%
7. Case Western Reserve University, $7,292; 56.4%; 4.5% decrease
8. University of Wisconsin, Madison, $6,732; 57.2%; 8.1% decrease
9. University of Delaware, $6,357; 50.8%; 16.5% decrease
10. University of Texas, Austin, $6,229; 51.6%; 59.1% decrease

RESEARCH & DEVELOPMENT

Source: "Academic R&D Spending: Growth Continued in '98," *C&EN: Chemical & Engineering News*, 78: 55-62, (October 30, 2000).

★3099★
U.S. colleges and universities spending the most on chemical research and development, 1998

Ranking basis/background: Figures, in thousands of dollars, for 1998 chemical R&D spending; percentage of federal funds in 1998; annual percent change since 1997. **Remarks:** Original source: National Science Foundation, 2000 Survey of Scientific and Engineering Expenditures at Universities and Colleges: Fiscal Year 1998; WebCASPAR Database System. **Number listed:** 50.

1. University of California, Berkeley, with $20,638 in chemical R&D spending; 70% of federal funds; and a 9.5% change from 1997
2. Johns Hopkins University, $18,541; 99%; 100.1%
3. California Institute of Technology, $17,760; 99%; 0.9%
4. Pennsylvania State University, $16,075; 55%; 24.8%
5. University of Illinois, Urbana-Champaign, $13,760; 58%; 1.1%
6. University of Colorado, $12,948; 81%; 17.4%
7. Purdue University, $12,548; 65%; 2.4%
8. Stanford University, $12,306; 87%; 0.9%
9. Cornell University, $12,031; 72%; 5.7%
10. University of Wisconsin, Madison, $12,011; 64%; 5.0%

Source: "Academic R&D Spending: Growth Continued in '98," *C&EN: Chemical & Engineering News*, 78: 55-62, (October 30, 2000).

★3100★
U.S. colleges and universities spending the most on chemical research equipment, 1998

Ranking basis/background: Figures, in thousands of dollars, for 1998 spending on chemical research equipment; percentage of federal funds in 1998; annual percent change since 1997. **Remarks:** Original source: National Science Foundation, 2000 Survey of Scientific and Engineering Expenditures at Universities and Colleges: Fiscal Year 1998; WebCASPAR Database System. **Number listed:** 25.

1. Pennsylvania State University, with $2,730; 47.7% of federal funds; and an 89.2% change from 1997
2. Ohio State University, $2,563; 14.4%; 386.3%
3. Case Western Reserve University, $2,302; 82.3%; 144.4%
4. Stanford University, $2,124; 97.6%; 86.3%
5. University of Pennsylvania, $1,974; 99.5%; 74.7%
6. University of Colorado, $1,665; 98.8%; 115.4%
7. California Institute of Technology, $1,621; 98.7%; 48.6%
8. University of California, Berkeley, $1,590; 80.4%; 34.6%
9. Purdue University, $1,546; 86.4%; 29.5%
10. University of Chicago, $1,527; 86.6%; 18.2% decrease

Source: "Academic R&D Spending: Growth Continued in '98," *C&EN: Chemical & Engineering News*, 78: 55-62, (October 30, 2000).

★3101★
U.S. colleges and universities with the most federal support for chemical engineering research and development, 1998

Ranking basis/background: Figures, in thousands of dollars, for 1998 federal support of chemical engineering R&D, and annual percent change since 1997. **Remarks:** Original source: National Science Foundation, 2000 Survey of Scientific and Engineering Expenditures at Universities and Colleges: Fiscal Year 1998; WebCASPAR Database System. **Number listed:** 25.

1. University of Minnesota, with $8,684 in federal support; 5.3% decrease since 1997
2. New Mexico State University, $7,334; 18.8% decrease
3. Stanford University, $6,858; 19.4%
4. Johns Hopkins University, $4,809; 6.1%
5. North Carolina State University, $4,642; 58.2%
6. Massachusetts Institute of Technology, $4,187; 1.5%
7. Case Western Reserve University, $4,116; 16.7% decrease
8. University of Wisconsin, Madison, $3,853; 12.2% decrease
9. University of Delaware, $3,227; 9.7% decrease
10. University of Texas, Austin, $3,214; 140.5%

Source: "Academic R&D Spending: Growth Continued in '98," *C&EN: Chemical & Engineering News*, 78: 55-62, (October 30, 2000).

★3102★
U.S. colleges and universities with the most federal support for chemical research and development, 1998

Ranking basis/background: Figures, in thousands of dollars, for 1998 federal support for chemical R&D and annual percent change since 1997. **Remarks:** Original source: National Science Foundation, 2000 Survey of Scientific and Engineering Expenditures at Universities and Colleges: Fiscal Year 1998; WebCASPAR Database System. **Number listed:** 50.

1. Johns Hopkins University, with $18,280 in federal support; a 103.5% change from 1997
2. California Institute of Technology, $17,629; 16.0%
3. University of California, Berkeley, $14,447; 8.7% decrease
4. University of Pennsylvania, $11,283; 8.3%
5. Stanford University, $10,658; 2.0%
6. Harvard University, $10,639; 30.9%
7. University of Colorado, $10,446; 19.2%
8. University of California, Los Angeles, $9,530; 0.5%
9. Massachusetts Institute of Technology, $9,201; 4.3%
10. Pennsylvania State University, $8,852; 2.6%

Source: "Academic R&D Spending: Growth Continued in '98," *C&EN: Chemical & Engineering News*, 78: 55-62, (October 30, 2000).

★3103★
U.S. colleges and universities with the most federal support for chemical research equipment, 1998

Ranking basis/background: Figures, in thousands of dollars, for 1998 federal support for chemical research equipment and annual percent change since 1997. **Remarks:** Original source: National Science Foundation, 2000 Survey of Scientific and Engineering Expenditures at Universities and Colleges: Fiscal Year 1998; WebCASPAR Database System. **Number listed:** 25.

1. Stanford University, with $2,073 in federal support; an 85.9% change from 1997
2. University of Pennsylvania, $1,964; 80.7%
3. Case Western Reserve University, $1,895; 243.9%
4. University of Colorado, $1,645; 118.5%
5. California Institute of Technology, $1,600; 64.9%
6. Purdue University, $1,336; 87.4%
7. University of Chicago, $1,323; 22.7% decrease
8. Pennsylvania State University, $1,302; 33.0%
9. University of California, Berkeley, $1,279; 26.5%
10. Massachusetts Institute of Technology, $1,272; 60.4%

Source: "Academic R&D Spending: Growth Continued in '98," *C&EN: Chemical & Engineering News*, 78: 55-62, (October 30, 2000).

★3104★
U.S. universities spending the most on research and development, 1998

Ranking basis/background: Figures, in millions of dollars, for total R&D spending in 1998. **Remarks:** Original source: National Science Foundation, 2000, "Academic Research and Development Expenditures: Fiscal Year 1998." **Number listed:** 30.

1. Johns Hopkins University, with $872.2 million
2. University of Michigan, $504.5
3. University of California, Los Angeles, $459.2
4. University of Wisconsin, Madison, $455.8
5. University of Washington (WA), $439.5
6. University of California, Berkeley, $441.1
7. University of California, San Diego, $429.1
8. Massachusetts Institute of Technology, $424.1
9. Stanford University, $422.6
10. Texas A&M University, $403.4

Source: "Academic R&D Spending: Growth Continued in '98," *C&EN: Chemical & Engineering News*, 78: 55-62, (October 30, 2000).

RESEARCH & DEVELOPMENT FUNDING

See also: **Scientific & Technological Research Funding**

★3105★
Institutions receiving the most federal research and development expenditures, 1999

Ranking basis/background: Federal R&D expenditures, in dollars. Table also includes expenditures for 1998. **Remarks:** Original source: National Science Foundation. **Number listed:** 100.

1. Johns Hopkins University, with $770,580,000
2. University of Washington (WA), $368,112,000
3. Stanford University, $353,947,000
4. University of Michigan, $334,226,000
5. Massachusetts Institute of Technology, $308,921,000
6. University of California, San Diego, $292,007,000
7. University of Pennsylvania, $279,013,000
8. Harvard University, $266,019,000
9. University of California, Los Angeles, $251,999,000
10. University of Wisconsin, Madison, $249,961,000
11. University of Colorado, $244,686,000
12. Columbia University, $240,158,000
13. Cornell University, $234,792,000
14. University of California, San Francisco, $233,181,000
15. Washington University (MO), $218,598,000
16. Yale University, $213,404,000
17. University of Minnesota, $207,761,000
18. University of Southern California, $199,619,000
19. Pennsylvania State University, 199,105,000
20. California Institute of Technology, $195,303,000

Source: "Top Institutions in Federal Research-and-Development Expenditures, 1998 and 1999," *The Chronicle of Higher Education*, 47: A26, (March 16, 2001).

★3106★
Proposed fiscal 2002 appropriations for Department of Agriculture research

Ranking basis/background: Based on the U.S. government's proposed fiscal 2002 appropriations for Department of Agriculture Research. **Number listed:** 7.

- Cooperative research, with $407,000,000
- Formula and competitive grants Hatch Act support, $180,000,000
- Payments to black colleges, $61,000,000
- National Research Initiative competitive grants, $106,000,000
- Initiative for Future Agriculture and Food Systems, $120,000,000
- Cooperative extension, $413,000,000
- Agricultural Research Service, $969,000,000

Source: "Bush's Fiscal 2002 Budget Plan for Higher Education and Science," *The Chronicle of Higher Education*, 47: A36-A37, (April 20, 2001).

★3107★
Proposed fiscal 2002 appropriations for Department of Commerce research

Ranking basis/background: Based on the U.S. government's proposed fiscal 2002 appropriations for Department of Commerce research. **Number listed:** 10.

- National Institute of Standards and Technology, with $487,447,000
- National Oceanic and Atmospheric Administration, $3,053,600,000
- National Telecommunications and Information Administration Information Infrastructure Grants, $15,503,000
- Department of Energy: Basic energy sciences, $1,004,705,000
- Department of Energy: High-energy and nuclear physics, $1,081,610,000
- Environmental Protection Agency Science and technology, $640,538,000
- National Aeronautics and Space Administration: Space science, $2,453,000,000
- National Aeronautics and Space Administration: Space station, $2,087,400,000
- National Aeronautics and Space Administration: Earth science, $1,278,000,000
- National Aeronautics and Space Administration: Biological and physical research, $291,300,000

Source: "Bush's Fiscal 2002 Budget Plan for Higher Education and Science," *The Chronicle of Higher Education*, 47: A36-A37, (April 20, 2001).

★3108★
Proposed fiscal 2002 appropriations for National Institutes of Health scientific research

Ranking basis/background: Based on the U.S. government's proposed fiscal 2002 appropriations for scientific research for the National Institutes of Health, totaling $23,218,630,000. **Number listed:** 21.

- Cancer Institute, with $4,177,203,000
- Heart, Lung, and Blood Institute, $2,567,429,000
- Institute of General Medical Sciences, $1,720,206,000
- Institute of Diabetes and Digestive and Kidney Diseases, $1,457,915,000
- Institute of Neurological Disorders and Stroke, $1,316,448,000
- Institute of Allergy and Infectious Diseases, $2,355,325,000
- Institute of Mental Health, $1,238,305,000
- Institute of Child Health and Human Development, $1,096,650,000
- Institute on Aging, $879,961,000
- Institute on Drug Abuse, $907,369,000
- Eye Institute, $571,126,000
- Institute of Environmental Health Sciences, $561,750,000
- Institute of Arthritis and Musculoskeletal and Skin Diseases, $443,565,000
- Human Genome Research Institute, $426,739,000
- Institute on Alcohol Abuse and Alcoholism, $381,966,000
- Institute on Deafness and Other Communication Disorders, $336,757,000
- Institute of Dental and Craniofacial Research, $341,898,000
- Institute of Nursing Research, $117,686,000
- Center for Research Resources, $974,038,000
- Library of Medicine, $275,725,000
- International Center, $56,449,000

Source: "Bush's Fiscal 2002 Budget Plan for Higher Education and Science," *The Chronicle of Higher Education*, 47: A36-A37, (April 20, 2001).

★3109★
Proposed fiscal 2002 appropriations for the National Science Foundation

Ranking basis/background: Based on the U.S. government's proposed fiscal 2002 appropriations for the National Science Foundation, totaling $4,472,490,000. **Number listed:** 10.

- National Science Foundation Research, with $3,326,980,000
- Science and engineering education, $872,410,000
- Major research equipment, $96,300,000
- Mathematical and physical sciences, $863,580,000
- Geosciences, $558,540,000
- Computer science, $470,360,000
- Engineering, $431,050,000
- Biological science, $483,110,000
- Polar programs, $276,570,000
- Social, behavioral, and economic science, $163,160,000

Source: "Bush's Fiscal 2002 Budget Plan for Higher Education and Science," *The Chronicle of Higher Education*, 47: A36-A37, (April 20, 2001).

RESEARCH FUNDING

See also: **Research & Development Funding Scientific & Technological Research & Development Funding Scientific & Technological Research Funding**

★3110★
Energy Department research funding, 2001

Ranking basis/background: Figures, in millions of dollars, and percentage of funding being allocated to each area of research. **Remarks:** Original source: Department of Energy. **Number listed:** 6.

1. Basic energy sciences, with $991.7-million (33.5%)
2. High-energy physics, $712.0-million (24.0%)
3. Biological and environmental research, $482.5-million (16.3%)
4. Nuclear physics, $360.5-million (12.2%)
5. Fusion energy sciences, $248.5-million (8.4%)
6. Advanced scientific-computing research, $165.7-million (5.6%)

Source: Southwick, Ron, "Researchers Worry About Direction and Budgets of the Energy Department," *The Chronicle of Higher Education*, 47: A20-A21, (March 23, 2001).

★3111★
Institutions receiving the largest Energy Department research grants, 2000

Ranking basis/background: Figures, in millions of dollars, of funding being allocated to each institution. **Remarks:** Original source: Department of Energy. **Number listed:** 10.

1. University of California System, with $55-million
2. University of Wisconsin System, $23
3. University of Washington (WA), $14
3. University of Illinois System, $14
5. Massachusetts Institute of Technology, $12
5. University of Michigan, $12
7. University of Minnesota System, $10
7. California Institute of Technology, $10
9. Yale University, $9
9. University of Maryland System, $9

Source: Southwick, Ron, "Researchers Worry About Direction and Budgets of the Energy Department," *The Chronicle of Higher Education*, 47: A20-A21, (March 23, 2001).

★3112★
National Science Foundation grant applications

Ranking basis/background: Total number of grant applications, in thousands, submitted to the National Science Foundation from 1995 to 1999. **Remarks:** Original source: National Science Foundation. **Number listed:** 5.

1995, with 30.7
1996, 30.2
1997, 30.2
1998, 28.3
1999, 28.5

Source: Southwick, Ron, "NSF Officials Worry as Number of New Grant Applicants Falls," *The Chronicle of Higher Education*, 46: A30, (June 9, 2000).

★3113★
National Science Foundation grants awarded to first-time applicants

Ranking basis/background: Total number of grant applications, in thousands, submitted to the National Science Foundation by first-time applicants and total grants awarded to first-time applicants from 1995 to 1999. **Remarks:** Original source: National Science Foundation. **Number listed:** 5.

1995, with 14.2 thousands first-time applicants; 3.4 thousand awarded
1996, 13.6; 3.0
1997, 13.3; 3.3
1998, 12.2; 3.0
1999, 11.8; 2.7

Source: Southwick, Ron, "NSF Officials Worry as Number of New Grant Applicants Falls," *The Chronicle of Higher Education*, 46: A30, (June 9, 2000).

★3114★
National Science Foundation grants awarded to minority researchers

Ranking basis/background: Total number of grant applications submitted to the National Science Foundation by minority researchers and total number of grants awarded to minorities from 1995 to 1999. NSF regards minorities as black, Hispanic, Native American, Native Alaskan, and Pacific Islanders. **Remarks:** Original source: National Science Foundation. **Number listed:** 5.

1995, with 1,521 minority applicants; 422 grants awarded
1996, 1,527; 472
1997, 1,452; 459
1998, 1,377; 408
1999, 1,418; 430

Source: Southwick, Ron, "NSF Officials Worry as Number of New Grant Applicants Falls," *The Chronicle of Higher Education*, 46: A30, (June 9, 2000).

RESEARCH UNIVERSITIES–SALARIES
See: **Salaries–Colleges & Universities**

RETAILING
See: **Business Administration, Graduate–Marketing Business Administration–Marketing**

RHETORIC
See: **Speech Communication**

SALARIES

★3115★
Average annual salaries for individuals obtaining a bachelor's degree, by race/ethnicity

Ranking basis/background: Average annual income. **Remarks:** Original source: U.S. Census Bureau. **Number listed:** 3.

White, with $41,439
African American, $32,062
Hispanic American, $33,465

Source: "Disparities & Gaps in America," *Black Issues in Higher Education*, 18: 28-29, (March 1, 2001).

★3116★
Average annual salaries for individuals obtaining a high school degree, by race/ethnicity

Ranking basis/background: Average annual income. **Remarks:** Original source: U.S. Census Bureau. **Number listed:** 3.

White, with $23,618
African American, $18,980
Hispanic American, $19,558

Source: "Disparities & Gaps in America," *Black Issues in Higher Education*, 18: 28-29, (March 1, 2001).

★3117★
Average annual salaries for individuals obtaining a master's degree, by race/ethnicity

Ranking basis/background: Average annual income. **Remarks:** Original source: U.S. Census Bureau. **Number listed:** 3.

White, with $52,475
African American, $40,610
Hispanic American, $46,556

Source: "Disparities & Gaps in America," *Black Issues in Higher Education*, 18: 28-29, (March 1, 2001).

★3118★
Average annual salaries for individuals without a high school degree, by race/ethnicity

Ranking basis/background: Average annual income. **Remarks:** Original source: U.S. Census Bureau. **Number listed:** 3.

White, with $16,596
African American, $13,185
Hispanic American, $15,069

Source: "Disparities & Gaps in America," *Black Issues in Higher Education*, 18: 28-29, (March 1, 2001).

★3119★
Average salaries for occupations requiring on-the-job training

Ranking basis/background: Median annual earnings in 1998. **Number listed:** 10.

1. Elevator installers and repairers, with an annual salary of $47,860
2. Electrical powerline installers and repairers, $42,600
3. Insurance adjusters, examiners, and investigators, $38,290
4. Flight attendants, $37,800
5. Police patrol officers, $37,710
6. Tool and die makers, $37,250
7. Electricians, $35,310
8. Operating engineers, $35,260
9. Bricklayers, blockmasons, and stonemasons, $35,190
10. Postal mail carriers, $34,840

Source: "High-Paying Jobs Requiring On-the-Job Training," *Occupational Outlook Quarterly*, 44: 50, (Winter 2000).

★3120★
Countries with the highest leader's salary

Ranking basis/background: Annual salary of the country's chief executive. **Number listed:** 9.

1. Singapore, with $520,380
2. Hong Kong, $417,684
3. Japan, $406,632
4. United States, $400,000
5. Taiwan, $323,412
6. Great Britain, $163,939
7. Australia, $136,380
8. Canada, $104,694
9. South Korea, $91,896

Source: "Kale to the Chief," *U.S. News & World Report*, 128: 16, (November 13, 2000).

★3121★
Countries with the lowest leader's salary

Ranking basis/background: Annual salary of the country's chief executive. **Number listed:** 9.

1. Estonia, with $1,451
2. China, $3,192
3. Nepal, $3,600
4. India, $7,020
5. Nigeria, $12,820
6. Philippines, $14,688
7. Kenya, $15,960
8. Thailand, $20,328
9. Indonesia, $24,396

Source: "Kale to the Chief," *U.S. News & World Report*, 128: 16, (November 13, 2000).

★3122★
Median annual earnings for computer technology jobs, 1998

Ranking basis/background: Median annual salary. **Remarks:** Original source: Bureau of Labor Statistics. **Number listed:** 5.

1. Computer engineers, with $61,910
2. Computer systems analysts, $52,180
3. Database administrators, $47,980
4. Computer support specialists, $37,120
5. All other computer scientists, $46,670

Source: "Technology: Bits & Bytes," *Black Issues in Higher Education*, 18: 40-41, (March 15, 2001).

★3123★
States with the highest per capita income

Ranking basis/background: Average per capita income by state. **Remarks:** Original source: Bureau of Economic Analysis. **Number listed:** 51.
1. Connecticut, with $40,640
2. Massachusetts, $37,992
3. Washington, DC, $37,383
4. New Jersey, $36,983
5. New York, $34,547
6. Maryland, $33,872
7. New Hampshire, $33,332
8. Colorado, $32,949
9. California, $32,275
10. Illinois, $32,259
11. Minnesota, $32,101

Source: "Salary Too Small? Try Moving to Connecticut," *U.S. News & World Report*, 130: 12, (May 7, 2001).

★3124★
States with the largest growth in income

Ranking basis/background: Percentage of growth in income. **Remarks:** Original source: Bureau of Economic Analysis. **Number listed:** 5.
1. Colorado, with 10.8%
2. California, 10.5%
3. Massachusetts, 9.9%
4. New Hampshire, 9.5%
5. Idaho, 9.3%

Source: "Salary Too Small? Try Moving to Connecticut," *U.S. News & World Report*, 130: 12, (May 7, 2001).

SALARIES–COLLEGE GRADUATES

★3125★
Average annual salaries for full-time, year-round workers, by educational level, 1998

Ranking basis/background: Median annual earnings of full-time, year-round employees in 1998. **Number listed:** 5.
- High school diploma, with $25,062
- Bachelor's degree, $40,387
- Master's degree, $48,772
- Doctoral degree, $60,729
- First-professional degree, $71,258

Source: Crosby, Olivia, "Degrees to Dollars: Earning of College Graduates in 1998," *Occupational Outlook Quarterly*, 44: 30-38, (Winter 2000).

★3126★
Average annual salaries of college graduates, by age, 1998

Ranking basis/background: Median annual earnings in 1998. **Number listed:** 6.
- Age 25-20, with $32,622
- Age 30-39, $42,199
- Age 40-49, $47,836
- Age 50-59, $51,207
- Age 60-64, $51,859
- Age 65 and over, $50,599

Source: Crosby, Olivia, "Degrees to Dollars: Earning of College Graduates in 1998," *Occupational Outlook Quarterly*, 44: 30-38, (Winter 2000).

★3127★
Average salaries for individuals with a bachelor's degree, by race/ethnicity

Ranking basis/background: Average annual salary. **Remarks:** Original source: U.S. Census Bureau. **Number listed:** 3.
- White, with $41,439
- African American, $32,062
- Hispanic American, $33,465

Source: Borden, Dr. Victor M.H., "The Top 100: Interpreting the Data," *Black Issues in Higher Education*, 17: 48-49, (June 22, 2000).

★3128★
Average salaries for individuals with a master's degree, by race/ethnicity

Ranking basis/background: Average annual salary. **Remarks:** Original source: U.S. Census Bureau. **Number listed:** 3.
- White, with $52,475
- African American, $40,610
- Hispanic American, $46,556

Source: Borden, Dr. Victor M.H., "The Top 100: Interpreting the Data," *Black Issues in Higher Education*, 17: 48-49, (June 22, 2000).

★3129★
Average starting salaries for college graduates, by field, 2000

Ranking basis/background: Average starting salaries from July 2000 and percentage increase since July 1999. **Remarks:** Original source: National Association of Colleges and Employers *Salary Survey*. **Number listed:** 13.
1. Computer engineering, with an average starting salary of $49,505; and a change of 9.6%
2. Computer science, $48,740; 9.9%
3. Electrical engineering, $48,492; 7.5%
4. Mechanical engineering, $45,617; 5.4%
5. Industrial engineering, $45,612; 5.9%
6. Information systems, $43,402; 10.6%
7. Political science, $37,748; 11.8%
8. Economics or finance, $37,502; 7.5%
9. Accounting, $36,919; 7.1%
10. Marketing management, $33,141; 5.1%
11. History, $31,359; 9.5%
12. English language and literature, $29,845; 10.5%
13. Psychology, $28,674; 8.9%

Source: "Higher Salaries for Recent Grads," *Occupational Outlook Quarterly*, 44: 27, (Fall 2000).

★3130★
Expected starting salaries of 2000-01 bachelor's degree recipients, by general major

Ranking basis/background: Expected starting salary range. **Number listed:** 8.
- Humanities/social science, with $28,300-$32,700
- Sciences, $41,700-$43,700
- Business, $35,600-$39,100
- Engineering, $41,700-$44,400
- Computer sciences, $42,750-$46,900
- Communication/telecommunication, $30,300-$31,400
- Allied health, $31,300-$33,000
- All reported salaries, $37,300-$41,200

Source: Gardner, Philip, "In a Slowing Economy, Job Opportunities Still Abound for 2001 Graduates," *The Black Collegian*, 31: 36-43, (February 2001).

★3131★
Expected starting salaries of 2000-01 bachelor's degree recipients, by specific major

Ranking basis/background: Expected starting salary range. **Number listed:** 21.
- Construction, with $31,300-$33,800
- Psychology, $28,400-$30,000
- Social work, $28,800-$32,200
- Accounting, $33,700-$37,200
- Business administration, $30,900-$34,300
- Economics, $32,100-$37,100
- Finance, $33,600-$38,200
- Hospitality, $28,800-$34,200
- Human resources, $36,200-$41,300
- Logistics/supply chain management, $32,700-$37,700
- Marketing, $29,700-$34,700
- Civil engineering, $40,400-$42,400
- Chemical engineering, $46,800-$48,600
- Computer engineering, $45,400-$50,300
- Electrical engineering, $44,400-$48,300
- Engineering technology, $41,500-$44,100
- Industrial engineering, $39,900-$43,400
- Mechanical engineering, $44,100-$47,800
- Computer science, $43,700-$48,300
- Information sciences (MIS), $42,400-$46,500
- Programming, $46,800-$49,600

Source: Gardner, Philip, "In a Slowing Economy, Job Opportunities Still Abound for 2001 Graduates," *The Black Collegian*, 31: 36-43, (February 2001).

★3132★
Occupations with the highest average annual salaries for college graduates, 1998

Ranking basis/background: Median annual earnings in 1998. **Number listed:** 10.
1. Physician, with $109,935
2. Dentist, $101,319
3. Lawyer, $81,068
4. Marketing, advertising, and public relations manager, $71,557
5. Pharmacist, $62,140
6. Electrical and electronic engineer, $61,852
7. Mechanical engineer, $61,594
8. Computer systems analyst, $60,565
9. Financial manager, $57,648
10. Civil engineer, $56,532

Source: Crosby, Olivia, "Degrees to Dollars: Earning of College Graduates in 1998," *Occupational Outlook Quarterly*, 44: 30-38, (Winter 2000).

SALARIES–COLLEGES & UNIVERSITIES

★3133★
Largest benefit packages awarded to presidents at institutions of higher education, 1998-99

Ranking basis/background: Figures include total benefits received. **Number listed:** 8.

SALARIES—COLLEGES & UNIVERSITIES

1. Harry C. Payne, Williams College, with benefits totaling $645,672
2. Thomas K. Hearn Jr., Wake Forest University, $244,102
3. Hunter R. Rawlings III, Cornell University, $220,760
4. William R. Brody, John Hopkins University, $200,282
5. Torsten N. Wiesel, Rockefeller University, $189,402
6. John B. Duff, Columbia College (IL), $174,814
7. Richard C. Levin, Yale University, $134,437
8. Peggy A. Stock, Westminster College (UT), $123,257

Source: Nicklin, Julie L., "Colleges are Evasive About Presidents' Benefits Packages," *The Chronicle of Higher Education*, 47: A28, (November 24, 2000).

★3134★
Median salaries of academic personnel at all institutions, 2000-01

Ranking basis/background: Figures are based on the reports of 1,466 public and private institutions and "are meant to provide a broad overview of salaries in higher education." **Remarks:** Original source: College and University Professional Association for Human Resources. **Number listed:** 55.

- Chief academic officer, with $104,193
- Associate chief academic officer, $83,950
- Chief health-professions officer, $122,179
- Director, library services, $63,228
- Acquisitions librarian, $43,080
- Chief technical-services librarian, $45,554
- Chief public-services librarian, $46,396
- Director, institutional research, $61,315
- Associate director, institutional research, $52,060
- Director, education media-services center, $50,224
- Director, learning-resources center, $46,275
- Director, international education, $65,000
- Director, international-studies education, $54,150
- Director, academic computing, $66,873
- Associate director, academic computing, $60,263
- Chief research officer, $139,460
- Chief technology-transfer officer, $108,989
- Senior technology-licensing officer, $71,809
- Director, sponsored research and programs, $70,000
- Dean, architecture, $120,000
- Dean, agriculture, $125,923
- Dean, arts and letters, $85,245
- Dean, arts and sciences, $94,666
- Dean, business, $101,082
- Dean, communications, $81,138
- Dean, continuing education, $80,351
- Dean, cooperative extension, $95,873
- Dean, dentistry, $176,158
- Dean, education, $96,906
- Dean, engineering, $146,938
- Dean, external degree programs, $74,360
- Dean, fine arts, $94,515
- Dean, graduate programs, $96,919
- Dean, health-related programs, $85,700
- Dean, home economics, $124,663
- Dean, humanities, $73,000
- Dean, instruction, $67,274
- Dean, law, $180,150
- Dean, library and information sciences, $97,888
- Dean, mathematics, $69,449
- Dean, medicine, $272,200
- Dean, music, $97,457
- Dean, nursing, $86,717
- Dean, occupational or vocational education, $71,278
- Dean, pharmacy, $143,066
- Dean, public health, $167,127
- Dean, sciences, $85,000
- Dean, social sciences, $72,877
- Dean, social work, $112,531
- Dean, special programs, $69,180
- Dean, undergraduate programs, $90,135
- Dean, veterinary medicine, $162,373
- Dean, honors program, $84,259
- Director, continuing education, $58,744
- Director, distance learning, $58,000

Source: "Fact File: Median Salaries of College Administrators by Type of Institution, 2000-1," *The Chronicle of Higher Education*, 47: A32, (March 16, 2001).

★3135★
Median salaries of academic personnel at baccalaureate institutions, 2000-01

Ranking basis/background: Figures are based on the reports of 1,466 public and private institutions and "are meant to provide a broad overview of salaries in higher education." **Remarks:** Original source: College and University Professional Association for Human Resources. **Number listed:** 55.

- Chief academic officer, with $96,989
- Associate chief academic officer, $68,000
- Chief health-professions officer, $82,239
- Director, library services, $53,586
- Acquisitions librarian, $38,805
- Chief technical-services librarian, $38,970
- Chief public-services librarian, $39,985
- Director, institutional research, $52,900
- Associate director, institutional research, $37,145
- Director, education media-services center, $40,500
- Director, learning-resources center, $37,967
- Director, international education, $50,700
- Director, international-studies education, $46,850
- Director, academic computing, $56,914
- Associate director, academic computing, $46,530
- Chief research officer, n/a
- Chief technology-transfer officer, n/a
- Senior technology-licensing officer, n/a
- Director, sponsored research and programs, $54,459
- Dean, architecture, n/a
- Dean, agriculture, n/a
- Dean, arts and letters, $75,000
- Dean, arts and sciences, $71,306
- Dean, business, $67,473
- Dean, communications, $48,051
- Dean, continuing education, $64,200
- Dean, cooperative extension, n/a
- Dean, dentistry, n/a
- Dean, education, $63,444
- Dean, engineering, $100,296
- Dean, external degree programs, $46,749
- Dean, fine arts, $60,510
- Dean, graduate programs, $69,704
- Dean, health-related programs, $68,220
- Dean, home economics, n/a
- Dean, humanities, $66,930
- Dean, instruction, n/a
- Dean, law, $163,500
- Dean, library and information sciences, $56,666
- Dean, mathematics, $69,000
- Dean, medicine, n/a
- Dean, music, $51,568
- Dean, nursing, $65,988
- Dean, occupational or vocational education, n/a
- Dean, pharmacy, n/a
- Dean, public health, n/a
- Dean, sciences, $69,282
- Dean, social sciences, $70,040
- Dean, social work, $60,000
- Dean, special programs, $59,000
- Dean, undergraduate programs, $72,500
- Dean, veterinary medicine, n/a
- Dean, honors program, $60,458
- Director, continuing education, $48,930
- Director, distance learning, $50,401

Source: "Fact File: Median Salaries of College Administrators by Type of Institution, 2000-1," *The Chronicle of Higher Education*, 47: A32, (March 16, 2001).

★3136★
Median salaries of academic personnel at comprehensive institutions, 2000-01

Ranking basis/background: Figures are based on the reports of 1,466 public and private institutions and "are meant to provide a broad overview of salaries in higher education." **Remarks:** Original source: College and University Professional Association for Human Resources. **Number listed:** 55.

- Chief academic officer, with $115,380
- Associate chief academic officer, $87,827
- Chief health-professions officer, $123,408
- Director, library services, $70,301
- Acquisitions librarian, $41,917
- Chief technical-services librarian, $45,800
- Chief public-services librarian, $45,855
- Director, institutional research, $60,083
- Associate director, institutional research, $45,355
- Director, education media-services center, $51,144
- Director, learning-resources center, $45,564
- Director, international education, $61,764
- Director, international-studies education, $53,000
- Director, academic computing, $64,335
- Associate director, academic computing, $55,000
- Chief research officer, $99,750
- Chief technology-transfer officer, $88,667
- Senior technology-licensing officer, n/a
- Director, sponsored research and programs, $62,590
- Dean, architecture, $97,500
- Dean, agriculture, $98,176
- Dean, arts and letters, $93,500
- Dean, arts and sciences, $93,936
- Dean, business, $104,500
- Dean, communications, $78,006
- Dean, continuing education, $84,864
- Dean, cooperative extension, $87,239
- Dean, dentistry, n/a
- Dean, education, $90,043
- Dean, engineering, $120,154
- Dean, external degree programs, $80,700
- Dean, fine arts, $96,716
- Dean, graduate programs, $87,502
- Dean, health-related programs, $97,859
- Dean, home economics, $85,584
- Dean, humanities, $74,819
- Dean, instruction, n/a

Dean, law, $165,000
Dean, library and information sciences, $91,000
Dean, mathematics, $75,015
Dean, medicine, $139,169
Dean, music, $77,720
Dean, nursing, $85,290
Dean, occupational or vocational education, $96,690
Dean, pharmacy, $133,300
Dean, public health, n/a
Dean, sciences, $92,386
Dean, social sciences, $89,775
Dean, social work, $79,313
Dean, special programs, $73,587
Dean, undergraduate programs, $87,918
Dean, veterinary medicine, n/a
Dean, honors program, $69,000
Director, continuing education, $60,434
Director, distance learning, $57,845

Source: "Fact File: Median Salaries of College Administrators by Type of Institution, 2000-1," *The Chronicle of Higher Education*, 47: A32, (March 16, 2001).

★3137★
Median salaries of academic personnel at doctoral institutions, 2000-01

Ranking basis/background: Figures are based on the reports of 1,466 public and private institutions and "are meant to provide a broad overview of salaries in higher education." **Remarks:** Original source: College and University Professional Association for Human Resources. **Number listed:** 55.

Chief academic officer, with $174,713
Associate chief academic officer, $123,737
Chief health-professions officer, $325,000
Director, library services, $111,999
Acquisitions librarian, $54,804
Chief technical-services librarian, $70,410
Chief public-services librarian, $74,390
Director, institutional research, $77,532
Associate director, institutional research, $59,275
Director, education media-services center, $68,974
Director, learning-resources center, $65,742
Director, international education, $83,750
Director, international-studies education, $69,981
Director, academic computing, $91,915
Associate director, academic computing, $79,940
Chief research officer, $149,557
Chief technology-transfer officer, $110,470
Senior technology-licensing officer, $75,677
Director, sponsored research and programs, $82,120
Dean, architecture, $140,000
Dean, agriculture, $151,520
Dean, arts and letters, $127,327
Dean, arts and sciences, $141,814
Dean, business, $165,925
Dean, communications, $132,823
Dean, continuing education, $113,920
Dean, cooperative extension, $127,380
Dean, dentistry, $192,086
Dean, education, $127,000
Dean, engineering, $165,898
Dean, external degree programs, $110,377
Dean, fine arts, $119,952
Dean, graduate programs, $116,776
Dean, health-related programs, $128,004
Dean, home economics, $129,549
Dean, humanities, $142,100

Dean, instruction, n/a
Dean, law, $188,317
Dean, library and information sciences, $124,189
Dean, mathematics, $112,999
Dean, medicine, $286,550
Dean, music, $120,945
Dean, nursing, $132,334
Dean, occupational or vocational education, $108,369
Dean, pharmacy, $148,843
Dean, public health, $171,400
Dean, sciences, $138,516
Dean, social sciences, $138,000
Dean, social work, $131,040
Dean, special programs, n/a
Dean, undergraduate programs, $111,500
Dean, veterinary medicine, $163,350
Dean, honors program, $99,882
Director, continuing education, $83,323
Director, distance learning, $68,051

Source: "Fact File: Median Salaries of College Administrators by Type of Institution, 2000-1," *The Chronicle of Higher Education*, 47: A32, (March 16, 2001).

★3138★
Median salaries of academic personnel at two-year institutions, 2000-01

Ranking basis/background: Figures are based on the reports of 1,466 public and private institutions and "are meant to provide a broad overview of salaries in higher education." **Remarks:** Original source: College and University Professional Association for Human Resources. **Number listed:** 55.

Chief academic officer, with $84,814
Associate chief academic officer, $67,943
Chief health-professions officer, $67,725
Director, library services, $53,455
Acquisitions librarian, $38,604
Chief technical-services librarian, $41,299
Chief public-services librarian, $40,998
Director, institutional research, $55,000
Associate director, institutional research, $49,767
Director, education media-services center, $47,094
Director, learning-resources center, $52,599
Director, international education, $60,338
Director, international-studies education, $57,289
Director, academic computing, $57,454
Associate director, academic computing, $51,730
Chief research officer, $75,024
Chief technology-transfer officer, n/a
Senior technology-licensing officer, n/a
Director, sponsored research and programs, $60,000
Dean, architecture, 65,444
Dean, agriculture, $65,942
Dean, arts and letters, $64,775
Dean, arts and sciences, $65,363
Dean, business, $66,064
Dean, communications, $64,135
Dean, continuing education, $67,500
Dean, cooperative extension, $62,913
Dean, dentistry, n/a
Dean, education, $60,883
Dean, engineering, $63,774
Dean, external degree programs, $70,297
Dean, fine arts, $73,659
Dean, graduate programs, n/a
Dean, health-related programs, $67,346
Dean, home economics, n/a

Dean, humanities, $66,074
Dean, instruction, $68,387
Dean, law, n/a
Dean, library and information sciences, $65,954
Dean, mathematics, $67,124
Dean, medicine, n/a
Dean, music, n/a
Dean, nursing, $65,000
Dean, occupational or vocational education, $66,635
Dean, pharmacy, n/a
Dean, public health, n/a
Dean, sciences, $65,696
Dean, social sciences, $65,146
Dean, social work, n/a
Dean, special programs, $69,672
Dean, undergraduate programs, $70,205
Dean, veterinary medicine, $50,863
Dean, honors program, n/a
Director, continuing education, $57,680
Director, distance learning, $53,000

Source: "Fact File: Median Salaries of College Administrators by Type of Institution, 2000-1," *The Chronicle of Higher Education*, 47: A32, (March 16, 2001).

★3139★
Median salaries of administrative personnel at all institutions, 2000-01

Ranking basis/background: Figures are based on the reports of 1,466 public and private institutions and "are meant to provide a broad overview of salaries in higher education." **Remarks:** Original source: College and University Professional Association for Human Resources. **Number listed:** 53.

Chief business officer, with $101,000
Chief administration officer, $100,240
Chief financial officer, $86,900
Chief investment officer, $95,750
Director, environmental health and safety, $62,718
Director, telecommunications/networking, $62,920
Chief planning officer, $86,453
Chief budgeting officer, $73,477
Associate budget director, $62,400
Chief planning and budget officer, $98,856
General counsel, $105,563
Chief personnel/human resources officer, $68,345
Associate director, personnel/human resources, $54,376
Manager, benefits, $45,508
Manager, training and development, $51,259
Manager, employee relations, $55,175
Manager, labor relations, $72,982
Manager, employment, $46,301
Manager, wage and salary, $54,282
Manager, personnel information systems, $55,182
Director, affirmative action and equal employment, $70,100
Associate director, affirmative action and equal employment, $55,147
Director, personnel and affirmative action, $60,000
Chief information-systems officer, $81,330
Associate director, information systems, $68,600
Data-base administrator, $56,643
System analyst, highest level, $52,326
Director, administrative computing, $67,500

Associate director, administrative computing, $57,372
Chief physical-plant officer, $69,361
Associate director, physical plant, $55,000
Manager, landscape and grounds, $41,200
Manager, building maintenance trades, $46,734
Manager, technical trades, $48,000
Manager, custodial services, $39,084
Manager, power plant, $53,280
Comptroller, $67,707
Manager, payroll, $42,433
Director, accounting, $55,676
Bursar, $50,038
Associate bursar, $40,000
Director, purchasing, $54,081
Associate director, purchasing, $47,037
Director, bookstore, $40,807
Associate director, bookstore, $34,044
Director, internal audit, $67,859
Director, auxiliary services, $68,000
Director, campus security, $51,500
Director, risk management and insurance, $64,284
Administrator, hospital medical center, $231,750
Public-relations director, hospital medical center, $94,839
Personnel director, hospital medical center, $92,500

Source: "Fact File: Median Salaries of College Administrators by Type of Institution, 2000-1," *The Chronicle of Higher Education*, 47: A32, (March 16, 2001).

★3140★
Median salaries of administrative personnel at baccalaureate institutions, 2000-01

Ranking basis/background: Figures are based on the reports of 1,466 public and private institutions and "are meant to provide a broad overview of salaries in higher education." **Remarks:** Original source: College and University Professional Association for Human Resources. **Number listed:** 53.

Chief business officer, with $94,800
Chief administration officer, $89,353
Chief financial officer, $72,445
Chief investment officer, $87,813
Director, environmental health and safety, $47,858
Director, telecommunications/networking, $49,000
Chief planning officer, $70,313
Chief budgeting officer, $62,422
Associate budget director, $56,700
Chief planning and budget officer, $69,880
General counsel, $86,483
Chief personnel/human resources officer, $52,445
Associate director, personnel/human resources, $48,400
Manager, benefits, $35,942
Manager, training and development, $41,700
Manager, employee relations, $40,205
Manager, labor relations, n/a
Manager, employment, $41,756
Manager, wage and salary, $41,070
Manager, personnel information systems, $44,100
Director, affirmative action and equal employment, $63,272
Associate director, affirmative action and equal employment, n/a
Director, personnel and affirmative action, $52,700
Chief information-systems officer, $71,029
Associate director, information systems, $49,347
Data-base administrator, $46,000
System analyst, highest level, $46,479
Director, administrative computing, $57,200
Associate director, administrative computing, $47,268
Chief physical-plant officer, $60,056
Associate director, physical plant, $46,800
Manager, landscape and grounds, $35,823
Manager, building maintenance trades, $42,231
Manager, technical trades, $43,890
Manager, custodial services, $34,446
Manager, power plant, $49,920
Comptroller, $60,250
Manager, payroll, $33,823
Director, accounting, $44,824
Bursar, $39,309
Associate bursar, $30,306
Director, purchasing, $46,371
Associate director, purchasing, $38,950
Director, bookstore, $34,827
Associate director, bookstore, $29,656
Director, internal audit, $61,000
Director, auxiliary services, $65,000
Director, campus security, $41,280
Director, risk management and insurance, $55,625
Administrator, hospital medical center, n/a
Public-relations director, hospital medical center, n/a
Personnel director, hospital medical center, n/a

Source: "Fact File: Median Salaries of College Administrators by Type of Institution, 2000-1," *The Chronicle of Higher Education*, 47: A32, (March 16, 2001).

★3141★
Median salaries of administrative personnel at comprehensive institutions, 2000-01

Ranking basis/background: Figures are based on the reports of 1,466 public and private institutions and "are meant to provide a broad overview of salaries in higher education." **Remarks:** Original source: College and University Professional Association for Human Resources. **Number listed:** 53.

Chief business officer, with $110,002
Chief administration officer, $95,937
Chief financial officer, $90,504
Chief investment officer, $62,857
Director, environmental health and safety, $53,531
Director, telecommunications/networking, $59,173
Chief planning officer, $86,078
Chief budgeting officer, $68,911
Associate budget director, $54,059
Chief planning and budget officer, $72,225
General counsel, $87,466
Chief personnel/human resources officer, $67,003
Associate director, personnel/human resources, $51,466
Manager, benefits, $41,330
Manager, training and development, $44,592
Manager, employee relations, $49,663
Manager, labor relations, $64,652
Manager, employment, $41,849
Manager, wage and salary, $46,076
Manager, personnel information systems, $47,019
Director, affirmative action and equal employment, $64,916
Associate director, affirmative action and equal employment, $56,532
Director, personnel and affirmative action, $56,562
Chief information-systems officer, $83,600
Associate director, information systems, $65,514
Data-base administrator, $56,000
System analyst, highest level, $52,296
Director, administrative computing, $67,306
Associate director, administrative computing, $56,551
Chief physical-plant officer, $72,243
Associate director, physical plant, $53,820
Manager, landscape and grounds, $40,132
Manager, building maintenance trades, $44,000
Manager, technical trades, $47,240
Manager, custodial services, $37,829
Manager, power plant, $47,773
Comptroller, $67,300
Manager, payroll, $39,630
Director, accounting, $56,038
Bursar, $47,696
Associate bursar, $36,333
Director, purchasing, $51,400
Associate director, purchasing, $40,635
Director, bookstore, $42,834
Associate director, bookstore, $34,193
Director, internal audit, $56,650
Director, auxiliary services, $66,312
Director, campus security, $52,070
Director, risk management and insurance, $53,123
Administrator, hospital medical center, n/a
Public-relations director, hospital medical center, n/a
Personnel director, hospital medical center, $59,173

Source: "Fact File: Median Salaries of College Administrators by Type of Institution, 2000-1," *The Chronicle of Higher Education*, 47: A32, (March 16, 2001).

★3142★
Median salaries of administrative personnel at doctoral institutions, 2000-01

Ranking basis/background: Figures are based on the reports of 1,466 public and private institutions and "are meant to provide a broad overview of salaries in higher education." **Remarks:** Original source: College and University Professional Association for Human Resources. **Number listed:** 53.

Chief business officer, with $153,700
Chief administration officer, $145,800
Chief financial officer, $132,200
Chief investment officer, $128,256
Director, environmental health and safety, $78,072
Director, telecommunications/networking, $82,436
Chief planning officer, $105,373
Chief budgeting officer, $90,802
Associate budget director, $68,580
Chief planning and budget officer, $110,125
General counsel, $130,000
Chief personnel/human resources officer, $98,867

Associate director, personnel/human resources, $67,748
Manager, benefits, $58,325
Manager, training and development, $55,000
Manager, employee relations, $55,550
Manager, labor relations, $72,800
Manager, employment, $55,000
Manager, wage and salary, $59,217
Manager, personnel information systems, $63,045
Director, affirmative action and equal employment, $81,775
Associate director, affirmative action and equal employment, $56,220
Director, personnel and affirmative action, $82,500
Chief information-systems officer, $125,845
Associate director, information systems, $92,450
Data-base administrator, $68,175
System analyst, highest level, $59,757
Director, administrative computing, $95,000
Associate director, administrative computing, $83,496
Chief physical-plant officer, $101,875
Associate director, physical plant, $77,419
Manager, landscape and grounds, $52,043
Manager, building maintenance trades, $58,443
Manager, technical trades, $56,640
Manager, custodial services, $53,004
Manager, power plant, $59,500
Comptroller, $98,200
Manager, payroll, $55,500
Director, accounting, $72,300
Bursar, $67,586
Associate bursar, $47,539
Director, purchasing, $74,985
Associate director, purchasing, $53,895
Director, bookstore, $66,963
Associate director, bookstore, $49,958
Director, internal audit, $78,210
Director, auxiliary services, $89,600
Director, campus security, $78,454
Director, risk management and insurance, $69,505
Administrator, hospital medical center, $279,384
Public-relations director, hospital medical center, $101,573
Personnel director, hospital medical center, $102,297

Source: "Fact File: Median Salaries of College Administrators by Type of Institution, 2000-1," *The Chronicle of Higher Education*, 47: A32, (March 16, 2001).

★3143★
Median salaries of administrative personnel at two-year institutions, 2000-01

Ranking basis/background: Figures are based on the reports of 1,466 public and private institutions and "are meant to provide a broad overview of salaries in higher education." **Remarks:** Original source: College and University Professional Association for Human Resources. **Number listed:** 53.

Chief business officer, with $79,709
Chief administration officer, $81,854
Chief financial officer, $68,000
Chief investment officer, n/a
Director, environmental health and safety, $49,767
Director, telecommunications/networking, $58,520
Chief planning officer, $68,658
Chief budgeting officer, $61,094
Associate budget director, $53,465
Chief planning and budget officer, $71,204
General counsel, $100,000
Chief personnel/human resources officer, $58,904
Associate director, personnel/human resources, $47,376
Manager, benefits, $41,996
Manager, training and development, $55,196
Manager, employee relations, $44,803
Manager, labor relations, $69,030
Manager, employment, $44,367
Manager, wage and salary, $43,589
Manager, personnel information systems, $53,211
Director, affirmative action and equal employment, $65,000
Associate director, affirmative action and equal employment, n/a
Director, personnel and affirmative action, $57,901
Chief information-systems officer, $67,514
Associate director, information systems, $64,894
Data-base administrator, $55,846
System analyst, highest level, $49,248
Director, administrative computing, $58,794
Associate director, administrative computing, $48,400
Chief physical-plant officer, $58,569
Associate director, physical plant, $47,547
Manager, landscape and grounds, $33,170
Manager, building maintenance trades, $42,964
Manager, technical trades, $46,369
Manager, custodial services, $34,878
Manager, power plant, $46,897
Comptroller, $58,889
Manager, payroll, $39,996
Director, accounting, $49,428
Bursar, $45,017
Associate bursar, $36,279
Director, purchasing, $48,071
Associate director, purchasing, $41,130
Director, bookstore, $36,668
Associate director, bookstore, $30,568
Director, internal audit, $52,700
Director, auxiliary services, $52,295
Director, campus security, $43,127
Director, risk management and insurance, $43,568
Administrator, hospital medical center, n/a
Public-relations director, hospital medical center, n/a
Personnel director, hospital medical center, n/a

Source: "Fact File: Median Salaries of College Administrators by Type of Institution, 2000-1," *The Chronicle of Higher Education*, 47: A32, (March 16, 2001).

★3144★
Median salaries of executive personnel at all institutions, 2000-01

Ranking basis/background: Figures are based on the reports of 1,466 public and private institutions and "are meant to provide a broad overview of salaries in higher education." **Remarks:** Original source: College and University Professional Association for Human Resources. **Number listed:** 5.

Chief executive of a system, with $206,195
Assistant to chief executive of a system, $88,076
Chief executive of a single institution, $147,920
Assistant to president of a single institution, $67,325
Executive vice president, $110,584

Source: "Fact File: Median Salaries of College Administrators by Type of Institution, 2000-1," *The Chronicle of Higher Education*, 47: A32, (March 16, 2001).

★3145★
Median salaries of executive personnel at baccalaureate institutions, 2000-01

Ranking basis/background: Figures are based on the reports of 1,466 public and private institutions and "are meant to provide a broad overview of salaries in higher education." **Remarks:** Original source: College and University Professional Association for Human Resources. **Number listed:** 3.

Chief executive of a single institution, $146,280
Assistant to president of a single institution, $54,375
Executive vice president, $94,041

Source: "Fact File: Median Salaries of College Administrators by Type of Institution, 2000-1," *The Chronicle of Higher Education*, 47: A32, (March 16, 2001).

★3146★
Median salaries of executive personnel at comprehensive institutions, 2000-01

Ranking basis/background: Figures are based on the reports of 1,466 public and private institutions and "are meant to provide a broad overview of salaries in higher education." **Remarks:** Original source: College and University Professional Association for Human Resources. **Number listed:** 3.

Chief executive of a single institution, $156,229
Assistant to president of a single institution, $69,763
Executive vice president, $114,600

Source: "Fact File: Median Salaries of College Administrators by Type of Institution, 2000-1," *The Chronicle of Higher Education*, 47: A32, (March 16, 2001).

★3147★
Median salaries of executive personnel at doctoral institutions, 2000-01

Ranking basis/background: Figures are based on the reports of 1,466 public and private institutions and "are meant to provide a broad overview of salaries in higher education." **Remarks:** Original source: College and University Professional Association for Human Resources. **Number listed:** 5.

Chief executive of a system, with $255,000
Assistant to chief executive of a system, $88,483
Chief executive of a single institution, $225,454
Assistant to president of a single institution, $90,420
Executive vice president, $192,250

SALARIES—COLLEGES & UNIVERSITIES

Source: "Fact File: Median Salaries of College Administrators by Type of Institution, 2000-1," *The Chronicle of Higher Education*, 47: A32, (March 16, 2001).

★3148★
Median salaries of executive personnel at two-year institutions, 2000-01

Ranking basis/background: Figures are based on the reports of 1,466 public and private institutions and "are meant to provide a broad overview of salaries in higher education." **Remarks:** Original source: College and University Professional Association for Human Resources. **Number listed:** 3.

- Chief executive of a single institution, $115,268
- Assistant to president of a single institution, $52,047
- Executive vice president, $98,696

Source: "Fact File: Median Salaries of College Administrators by Type of Institution, 2000-1," *The Chronicle of Higher Education*, 47: A32, (March 16, 2001).

★3149★
Median salaries of external affairs personnel at all institutions, 2000-01

Ranking basis/background: Figures are based on the reports of 1,466 public and private institutions and "are meant to provide a broad overview of salaries in higher education." **Remarks:** Original source: College and University Professional Association for Human Resources. **Number listed:** 17.

- Chief development officer, with $93,000
- Director, annual giving, $46,800
- Director, corporate and foundation relations, $58,830
- Director, planned giving, $64,000
- Chief public-relations officer, $61,706
- Director, governmental relations, $90,000
- Chief development and public-relations officer, $99,240
- Director, alumni affairs, $50,000
- Director, development and alumni affairs, $62,100
- Director, major gifts, $63,180
- Director, church relations, $45,501
- Director, community services, $49,288
- Director, publications, $50,000
- Associate director, publications, $40,142
- Manager, printing services, $41,090
- Director, information office, $49,430
- Director, news bureau, $44,074

Source: "Fact File: Median Salaries of College Administrators by Type of Institution, 2000-1," *The Chronicle of Higher Education*, 47: A32, (March 16, 2001).

★3150★
Median salaries of external affairs personnel at baccalaureate institutions, 2000-01

Ranking basis/background: Figures are based on the reports of 1,466 public and private institutions and "are meant to provide a broad overview of salaries in higher education." **Remarks:** Original source: College and University Professional Association for Human Resources. **Number listed:** 17.

- Chief development officer, with $88,000
- Director, annual giving, $42,500
- Director, corporate and foundation relations, $51,250
- Director, planned giving, $58,328
- Chief public-relations officer, $51,000
- Director, governmental relations, $49,400
- Chief development and public-relations officer, $75,580
- Director, alumni affairs, $43,151
- Director, development and alumni affairs, $54,636
- Director, major gifts, $62,586
- Director, church relations, $42,855
- Director, community services, $37,440
- Director, publications, $43,691
- Associate director, publications, $35,320
- Manager, printing services, $30,892
- Director, information office, $40,000
- Director, news bureau, $37,295

Source: "Fact File: Median Salaries of College Administrators by Type of Institution, 2000-1," *The Chronicle of Higher Education*, 47: A32, (March 16, 2001).

★3151★
Median salaries of external affairs personnel at comprehensive institutions, 2000-01

Ranking basis/background: Figures are based on the reports of 1,466 public and private institutions and "are meant to provide a broad overview of salaries in higher education." **Remarks:** Original source: College and University Professional Association for Human Resources. **Number listed:** 17.

- Chief development officer, with $98,000
- Director, annual giving, $45,262
- Director, corporate and foundation relations, $56,000
- Director, planned giving, $59,000
- Chief public-relations officer, $61,529
- Director, governmental relations, $79,283
- Chief development and public-relations officer, $105,924
- Director, alumni affairs, $49,895
- Director, development and alumni affairs, $66,560
- Director, major gifts, $55,075
- Director, church relations, $53,740
- Director, community services, $41,412
- Director, publications, $48,444
- Associate director, publications, $35,627
- Manager, printing services, $39,394
- Director, information office, $49,017
- Director, news bureau, $42,000

Source: "Fact File: Median Salaries of College Administrators by Type of Institution, 2000-1," *The Chronicle of Higher Education*, 47: A32, (March 16, 2001).

★3152★
Median salaries of external affairs personnel at doctoral institutions, 2000-01

Ranking basis/background: Figures are based on the reports of 1,466 public and private institutions and "are meant to provide a broad overview of salaries in higher education." **Remarks:** Original source: College and University Professional Association for Human Resources. **Number listed:** 17.

- Chief development officer, with $140,000
- Director, annual giving, $62,087
- Director, corporate and foundation relations, $74,500
- Director, planned giving, $81,700
- Chief public-relations officer, $101,200
- Director, governmental relations, $102,040
- Chief development and public-relations officer, $139,941
- Director, alumni affairs, $76,431
- Director, development and alumni affairs, $109,125
- Director, major gifts, $76,100
- Director, church relations, n/a
- Director, community services, $71,984
- Director, publications, $61,991
- Associate director, publications, $46,668
- Manager, printing services, $56,792
- Director, information office, $69,039
- Director, news bureau, $61,282

Source: "Fact File: Median Salaries of College Administrators by Type of Institution, 2000-1," *The Chronicle of Higher Education*, 47: A32, (March 16, 2001).

★3153★
Median salaries of external affairs personnel at two-year institutions, 2000-01

Ranking basis/background: Figures are based on the reports of 1,466 public and private institutions and "are meant to provide a broad overview of salaries in higher education." **Remarks:** Original source: College and University Professional Association for Human Resources. **Number listed:** 17.

- Chief development officer, with $65,602
- Director, annual giving, $44,039
- Director, corporate and foundation relations, $59,740
- Director, planned giving, $47,094
- Chief public-relations officer, $53,283
- Director, governmental relations, $76,253
- Chief development and public-relations officer, $67,700
- Director, alumni affairs, $43,127
- Director, development and alumni affairs, $50,348
- Director, major gifts, $50,713
- Director, church relations, n/a
- Director, community services, $53,316
- Director, publications, $50,462
- Associate director, publications, $40,827
- Manager, printing services, $36,189
- Director, information office, $45,979
- Director, news bureau, $33,252

Source: "Fact File: Median Salaries of College Administrators by Type of Institution, 2000-1," *The Chronicle of Higher Education*, 47: A32, (March 16, 2001).

★3154★
Median salaries of student services personnel at all institutions, 2000-01

Ranking basis/background: Figures are based on the reports of 1,466 public and private institutions and "are meant to provide a broad overview of salaries in higher education." **Remarks:** Original source: College and University Professional Association for Human Resources. **Number listed:** 38.

- Chief student-affairs officer, with $85,000
- Associate chief student-affairs officer, $64,293
- Dean, students, $67,000
- Chief admissions officer, $62,500
- Associate director, admissions, $42,454
- Director, academic advising, $47,924
- Director, admissions and registrar, $58,241
- Registrar, $53,103
- Associate registrar, $41,430
- Assistant registrar, $33,250

Director, admissions and financial aid, $68,881
Director, student financial aid, $54,390
Associate director, student financial aid, $36,690
Director, food services, $57,728
Associate director, food services, $47,193
Director, student housing, $48,000
Associate director, student housing, $41,787
Housing officer, administrative operations, $42,500
Housing officer, residence life, $33,882
Director, student union and student activities, $51,343
Director, foreign students, $43,977
Director, student union, $55,587
Associate director, student union, $44,000
Director, student activities, $39,292
Director, career development and placement, $48,404
Director, student counseling, $55,102
Associate director, student counseling, $45,933
Director, student health services, physician, $107,525
Director, student health services, nurse, $44,353
Director, campus ministries, $45,000
Director, athletics, $70,000
Director, men's athletics, $55,944
Director, women's athletics, $53,910
Director, sports information, $35,351
Director, campus recreation, $44,125
Chief, enrollment management, $79,975
Director, minority affairs, $46,756
Director, conferences, $43,910

Source: "Fact File: Median Salaries of College Administrators by Type of Institution, 2000-1," *The Chronicle of Higher Education*, 47: A32, (March 16, 2001).

★3155★
Median salaries of student services personnel at baccalaureate institutions, 2000-01

Ranking basis/background: Figures are based on the reports of 1,466 public and private institutions and "are meant to provide a broad overview of salaries in higher education." **Remarks:** Original source: College and University Professional Association for Human Resources. **Number listed:** 38.

Chief student-affairs officer, with $76,084
Associate chief student-affairs officer, $50,022
Dean, students, $52,540
Chief admissions officer, $60,000
Associate director, admissions, $38,000
Director, academic advising, $42,305
Director, admissions and registrar, $48,477
Registrar, $47,380
Associate registrar, $34,500
Assistant registrar, $28,800
Director, admissions and financial aid, $83,028
Director, student financial aid, $48,400
Associate director, student financial aid, $34,600
Director, food services, $59,000
Associate director, food services, $43,600
Director, student housing, $39,000
Associate director, student housing, $30,286
Housing officer, administrative operations, $30,600

Housing officer, residence life, $27,264
Director, student union and student activities, $41,896
Director, foreign students, $37,500
Director, student union, $40,600
Associate director, student union, $30,608
Director, student activities, $32,100
Director, career development and placement, $42,000
Director, student counseling, $48,274
Associate director, student counseling, $38,299
Director, student health services, physician, $80,750
Director, student health services, nurse, $37,111
Director, campus ministries, $43,680
Director, athletics, $58,968
Director, men's athletics, $55,384
Director, women's athletics, $41,704
Director, sports information, $30,000
Director, campus recreation, $35,800
Chief, enrollment management, $75,000
Director, minority affairs, $40,000
Director, conferences, $38,410

Source: "Fact File: Median Salaries of College Administrators by Type of Institution, 2000-1," *The Chronicle of Higher Education*, 47: A32, (March 16, 2001).

★3156★
Median salaries of student services personnel at comprehensive institutions, 2000-01

Ranking basis/background: Figures are based on the reports of 1,466 public and private institutions and "are meant to provide a broad overview of salaries in higher education." **Remarks:** Original source: College and University Professional Association for Human Resources. **Number listed:** 38.

Chief student-affairs officer, with $93,202
Associate chief student-affairs officer, $67,568
Dean, students, $64,060
Chief admissions officer, $62,400
Associate director, admissions, $42,434
Director, academic advising, $47,940
Director, admissions and registrar, $66,048
Registrar, $55,942
Associate registrar, $40,499
Assistant registrar, $32,945
Director, admissions and financial aid, $64,500
Director, student financial aid, $57,000
Associate director, student financial aid, $40,950
Director, food services, $55,848
Associate director, food services, $45,178
Director, student housing, $48,045
Associate director, student housing, $39,593
Housing officer, administrative operations, $40,234
Housing officer, residence life, $33,200
Director, student union and student activities, $51,379
Director, foreign students, $40,000
Director, student union, $50,867
Associate director, student union, $41,187
Director, student activities, $39,089
Director, career development and placement, $48,340
Director, student counseling, $53,112
Associate director, student counseling, $42,950

Director, student health services, physician, $95,143
Director, student health services, nurse, $45,006
Director, campus ministries, $41,596
Director, athletics, $73,109
Director, men's athletics, $61,885
Director, women's athletics, $53,842
Director, sports information, $35,013
Director, campus recreation, $41,900
Chief, enrollment management, $83,000
Director, minority affairs, $46,248
Director, conferences, $42,267

Source: "Fact File: Median Salaries of College Administrators by Type of Institution, 2000-1," *The Chronicle of Higher Education*, 47: A32, (March 16, 2001).

★3157★
Median salaries of student services personnel at doctoral institutions, 2000-01

Ranking basis/background: Figures are based on the reports of 1,466 public and private institutions and "are meant to provide a broad overview of salaries in higher education." **Remarks:** Original source: College and University Professional Association for Human Resources. **Number listed:** 38.

Chief student-affairs officer, with $131,120
Associate chief student-affairs officer, $92,500
Dean, students, $83,238
Chief admissions officer, $81,159
Associate director, admissions, $53,185
Director, academic advising, $58,738
Director, admissions and registrar, $92,592
Registrar, $75,574
Associate registrar, $53,725
Assistant registrar, $41,456
Director, admissions and financial aid, $85,235
Director, student financial aid, $76,683
Associate director, student financial aid, $52,150
Director, food services, $78,712
Associate director, food services, $56,104
Director, student housing, $71,678
Associate director, student housing, $55,297
Housing officer, administrative operations, $48,977
Housing officer, residence life, $49,690
Director, student union and student activities, $64,645
Director, foreign students, $54,575
Director, student union, $65,214
Associate director, student union, $49,275
Director, student activities, $51,795
Director, career development and placement, $65,719
Director, student counseling, $72,372
Associate director, student counseling, $56,460
Director, student health services, physician, $120,859
Director, student health services, nurse, $59,451
Director, campus ministries, $65,975
Director, athletics, $125,566
Director, men's athletics, $61,034
Director, women's athletics, $69,058
Director, sports information, $47,234
Director, campus recreation, $59,724
Chief, enrollment management, $105,400
Director, minority affairs, $60,000

SALARIES—COLLEGES & UNIVERSITIES

Director, conferences, $57,783

Source: "Fact File: Median Salaries of College Administrators by Type of Institution, 2000-1," *The Chronicle of Higher Education*, 47: A32, (March 16, 2001).

★3158★
Median salaries of student services personnel at two-year institutions, 2000-01

Ranking basis/background: Figures are based on the reports of 1,466 public and private institutions and "are meant to provide a broad overview of salaries in higher education." **Remarks:** Original source: College and University Professional Association for Human Resources. **Number listed:** 38.

Chief student-affairs officer, with $72,986
Associate chief student-affairs officer, $57,211
Dean, students, $65,963
Chief admissions officer, $52,073
Associate director, admissions, $41,431
Director, academic advising, $45,420
Director, admissions and registrar, $55,470
Registrar, $46,520
Associate registrar, $39,729
Assistant registrar, $34,000
Director, admissions and financial aid, $53,526
Director, student financial aid, $50,000
Associate director, student financial aid, $37,551
Director, food services, $39,972
Associate director, food services, $29,000
Director, student housing, $36,650
Associate director, student housing, $25,630
Housing officer, administrative operations, n/a
Housing officer, residence life, $30,942
Director, student union and student activities, $41,547
Director, foreign students, $38,358
Director, student union, n/a
Associate director, student union, n/a
Director, student activities, $45,000
Director, career development and placement, $43,548
Director, student counseling, $53,303
Associate director, student counseling, $42,485
Director, student health services, physician, n/a
Director, student health services, nurse, $40,206
Director, campus ministries, $35,280
Director, athletics, $54,444
Director, men's athletics, $43,233
Director, women's athletics, $32,040
Director, sports information, $40,372
Director, campus recreation, $34,374
Chief, enrollment management, $61,002
Director, minority affairs, $47,094
Director, conferences, $48,531

Source: "Fact File: Median Salaries of College Administrators by Type of Institution, 2000-1," *The Chronicle of Higher Education*, 47: A32, (March 16, 2001).

★3159★
Presidents with the highest pay at Baccalaureate I colleges, 1998-99

Ranking basis/background: Figures include salary and benefits. **Number listed:** 10.

1. Harry C. Payne, Williams College, with $878,222
2. Russell K. Osgood, Grinnell College, $381,188
3. James H. Daughdrill Jr., Rhodes College, $367,372
4. A. Lee Fritschler, Dickinson College, $358,273
5. Ruth Simmons, Smith College, $354,489
6. Frances D. Fergusson, Vassar College, $319,224
7. Roy B. Shilling Jr., Southwestern University (TX), $316,621
8. Esther L. Barazzone, Chatham College, $308,440
9. Tom Gerety, Amherst College, $299,803
10. Claire Gaudiani, Connecticut College, $299,387

Source: Nicklin, Julie L., "74 Private-College Presidents Earned More Than $300,000 in 1998-99," *The Chronicle of Higher Education*, 47: A26-A28, (November 24, 2000).

★3160★
Presidents with the highest pay at Doctoral I and II universities, 1998-99

Ranking basis/background: Figures include salary and benefits. **Number listed:** 10.

1. Thomas K. Hearn Jr., Wake Forest University, with $451,102
2. John E. Murray Jr., Duquesne University, $442,645
3. James M. Shuart, Hofstra University, $442,220
4. Constantine N. Papadakis, Drexel University, $435,738
5. Jonathan F. Fanton, New School University, $378,000
6. James E. Wright, Dartmouth College, $363,532
7. Harold J. Raveche, Steven Institute of Technology, $362,458
8. R. Gerald Turner, Southern Methodist University, $359,744
9. Benjamin Lakner, American University, $348,132
10. Michael R. Ferrari, Texas Christian University, $335,567

Source: Nicklin, Julie L., "74 Private-College Presidents Earned More Than $300,000 in 1998-99," *The Chronicle of Higher Education*, 47: A26-A28, (November 24, 2000).

★3161★
Presidents with the highest pay at Master's I and II colleges and universities, 1998-99

Ranking basis/background: Figures include salary and benefits. **Number listed:** 10.

1. Victor P. Meskill, Downing College, with $451,779
2. Jerry C. Lee, National University (CA), $403,750
3. John B. Duff, Columbia College (IL), $400,896
4. Rebecca Stafford, Monmouth University (NJ), $390,816
5. William E. Cooper, University of Richmond, $382,932
6. Anthony J. Cemera, Sacred Heart University (CT), $376,832
7. Audrey K. Doberstein, Wilmington College (DE), $373,022
8. John L. Lahey, Quinnipiac University, $370,000
9. David J. Steinberg, Long Island University, $366,100
10. John R. Brazil, Bradley University, $357,081

Source: Nicklin, Julie L., "74 Private-College Presidents Earned More Than $300,000 in 1998-99," *The Chronicle of Higher Education*, 47: A26-A28, (November 24, 2000).

★3162★
Presidents with the highest pay at Research I and II universities, 1998-99

Ranking basis/background: Figures include salary and benefits. **Number listed:** 10.

1. Judith Rodin, University of Pennsylvania, with $655,557
2. L. Jay Oliva, New York University, $649,633
3. William R. Brody, Johns Hopkins University, $645,710
4. Joe B. Wyatt, Vanderbilt University, $532,461
5. Richard C. Levin, Yale University, $525,687
6. George Rupp, Columbia University, $500,204
7. Malcolm Gillis, Rice University, $497,691
8. Stephen J. Trachtenberg, George Washington University, $473,233
9. Harold T. Shapiro, Princeton University, $456,170
10. Edward T. Foote II, University of Miami, $442,519

Source: Nicklin, Julie L., "74 Private-College Presidents Earned More Than $300,000 in 1998-99," *The Chronicle of Higher Education*, 47: A26-A28, (November 24, 2000).

★3163★
Top pay and benefits for the chief executive and top paid employees at Abilene Christian University

Ranking basis/background: Annual pay and benefits for the chief executives and top paid officers, as reported on Internal Revenue Service Form 990 by private colleges and universities in the U.S. for the 1998-99 academic year. **Number listed:** 6.

Royce L. Money, president, with $161,498 annual pay; $51,349 in benefits
Dwayne VanRheenen, provost, $131,398; $11,964
Jack W. Rich, executive VP, $123,247; $17,803
Dan Garrett, vice chancellor, $98,686; $9,890
John Tyson, VP, development, $79,318; $17,269
Jack Griggs, dean, college of business administration, $93,852; $0

Source: "Pay and Benefits of Leaders at 479 Private Colleges and Universities: a Survey," *The Chronicle of Higher Education*, 47: A29-A48, (November 24, 2000).

★3164★
Top pay and benefits for the chief executive and top paid employees at Adelphi University

Ranking basis/background: Annual pay and benefits for the chief executives and top paid officers, as reported on Internal Revenue Service Form 990 by private colleges and universities in the U.S. for the 1998-99 academic year. **Number listed:** 7.

Matthew Goldstein, president, with $251,923 annual pay; $27,246 in benefits
Steven Isenberg, interim president, $21,808; $0
Catherine Hennessy, VP, finance; treasurer, $190,000; $15,200
Timothy Burton, associate treasurer, $145,000; $17,300
Armstrong Starkey, provost, $142,369; $16,273
Angelo B. Proto, chief operating officer; VP, enrollment management and student affairs, $133,692; $15,381
Carl Rheins, special assistant to the president, $132,500; $12,369

Source: "Pay and Benefits of Leaders at 479 Private Colleges and Universities: a Survey," *The Chronicle of Higher Education*, 47: A29-A48, (November 24, 2000).

★3165★
Top pay and benefits for the chief executive and top paid employees at Agnes Scott College

Ranking basis/background: Annual pay and benefits for the chief executives and top paid officers, as reported on Internal Revenue Service Form 990 by private colleges and universities in the U.S. for the 1998-99 academic year. **Number listed:** 6.

Mary Brown Bullock, president, with $175,000 annual pay; $27,915 in benefits
William E. Gailey, VP, finance and business, $136,240; $23,777
Gue Hudson, dean of students; VP, student life and community relations; $110,880; $20,824
Sarah R. Blanshei, dean of the college, $105,000; $16,524
Elsa Pena, director, facilities, $81,868; $17,359
Sandra T. Bowden, professor, biology, $79,219; $16,181

Source: "Pay and Benefits of Leaders at 479 Private Colleges and Universities: a Survey," *The Chronicle of Higher Education*, 47: A29-A48, (November 24, 2000).

★3166★
Top pay and benefits for the chief executive and top paid employees at Alaska Pacific University

Ranking basis/background: Annual pay and benefits for the chief executives and top paid officers, as reported on Internal Revenue Service Form 990 by private colleges and universities in the U.S. for the 1998-99 academic year. **Number listed:** 5.

Douglas McKay North, president, with $105,629 annual pay; $5,435 in benefits
Liz Hartshorn, business manager, $76,095; $3,805
Charles Fahl, academic dean, $73,587; $3,740
Steven D. Berkshire, associate professor, management; associate dean, adult programs, $69,514; $3,400
Jeffrey Ickes, professor, psychology, $64,828; $7,936

Source: "Pay and Benefits of Leaders at 479 Private Colleges and Universities: a Survey," *The Chronicle of Higher Education*, 47: A29-A48, (November 24, 2000).

★3167★
Top pay and benefits for the chief executive and top paid employees at Albion College

Ranking basis/background: Annual pay and benefits for the chief executives and top paid officers, as reported on Internal Revenue Service Form 990 by private colleges and universities in the U.S. for the 1998-99 academic year. **Number listed:** 6.

Peter T. Mitchell, president, with $171,154 annual pay; $61,607 in benefits
Ben E. Hancock Jr., VP, institutional advancement, $122,838; $32,483
Dale R. Dopp, VP, finance and management, $102,920; $35,096
Robert Johnson, VP, enrollment, $108,610; $26,686
Jeffrey C. Carrier, VP, academic affairs, $94,000; $22,796
Sally J. Walker, VP, student affairs, $78,564; $23,526

Source: "Pay and Benefits of Leaders at 479 Private Colleges and Universities: a Survey," *The Chronicle of Higher Education*, 47: A29-A48, (November 24, 2000).

★3168★
Top pay and benefits for the chief executive and top paid employees at Albright College

Ranking basis/background: Annual pay and benefits for the chief executives and top paid officers, as reported on Internal Revenue Service Form 990 by private colleges and universities in the U.S. for the 1998-99 academic year. **Number listed:** 6.

Ellen S. Hurwitz, president, with $137,464 annual pay; $38,289 in benefits
Paul Gazzerro Jr., executive VP, administration and finance, $152,067; $19,193
Donald Kirkwood, VP, advancement, $99,492; $25,420
Daniel Falabella, chair; professor, computer science, $105,553; $8,104
Ronald G. Green, executive VP, academic affairs, $92,430; $12,217
Jerry Lee, professor, psychology, $78,498; $23,053

Source: "Pay and Benefits of Leaders at 479 Private Colleges and Universities: a Survey," *The Chronicle of Higher Education*, 47: A29-A48, (November 24, 2000).

★3169★
Top pay and benefits for the chief executive and top paid employees at Alfred University

Ranking basis/background: Annual pay and benefits for the chief executives and top paid officers, as reported on Internal Revenue Service Form 990 by private colleges and universities in the U.S. for the 1998-99 academic year. **Number listed:** 6.

Edward G. Coll Jr., president, with $158,221 annual pay; $75,121 in benefits
W. Richard Ott, provost, $129,966; $28,150
Michael E. Hyde, VP, university relations, $123,307; $29,901
Janice M. Stroh, VP, business and finance, $114,372; $33,219
Alan H. Goldstein, professor and chair, biology, $92,847; $29,125
Susan R. Strong, associate provost; VP, enrollment management, $85,448; $30,877

Source: "Pay and Benefits of Leaders at 479 Private Colleges and Universities: a Survey," *The Chronicle of Higher Education*, 47: A29-A48, (November 24, 2000).

★3170★
Top pay and benefits for the chief executive and top paid employees at Allegheny College

Ranking basis/background: Annual pay and benefits for the chief executives and top paid officers, as reported on Internal Revenue Service Form 990 by private colleges and universities in the U.S. for the 1998-99 academic year. **Number listed:** 6.

Richard J. Cook, president, with $170,000 annual pay; $20,530 in benefits
Bruce J. Smith, dean of the college, $106,636; $14,739
John C. Reynders, VP, administrative services; treasurer, $103,000; $14,394
John O. McCandless, VP, development, $100,000; $6,261
David Anderson, professor, psychology, $89,260; $8,436
Earl W. Adams, professor, economics, $88,644; $8,410

Source: "Pay and Benefits of Leaders at 479 Private Colleges and Universities: a Survey," *The Chronicle of Higher Education*, 47: A29-A48, (November 24, 2000).

★3171★
Top pay and benefits for the chief executive and top paid employees at Alma College

Ranking basis/background: Annual pay and benefits for the chief executives and top paid officers, as reported on Internal Revenue Service Form 990 by private colleges and universities in the U.S. for the 1998-99 academic year. **Number listed:** 6.

Alan J. Stone, president, with $175,900 annual pay; $18,042 in benefits
Leslie Ellen Brown, VP, academic affairs; provost, $104,000; $12,164
Jerry L. Scoby, VP, finance, $87,500; $10,541
Alan Hill, VP, enrollment, $82,712; $9,791
Carol Hyble, VP, development, $80,000; $10,612
Joseph D. Walser, professor, religious studies, $78,794; $10,550

Source: "Pay and Benefits of Leaders at 479 Private Colleges and Universities: a Survey," *The Chronicle of Higher Education*, 47: A29-A48, (November 24, 2000).

★3172★
Top pay and benefits for the chief executive and top paid employees at Amber University

Ranking basis/background: Annual pay and benefits for the chief executives and top paid officers, as reported on Internal Revenue Service Form 990 by private colleges and universities in the U.S. for the 1998-99 academic year. **Number listed:** 6.

Rev. Douglas W. Warner, president, with $185,000 annual pay; $25,518 in benefits
Algia G. Allen, VP, academic services, $101,400; $23,429
Melinda H. Reagan, VP, administrative services, $96,900; $19,503
Jo Lynn Loyd, VP, student services, $81,500; $14,276
Margaret Pinder, professor, human behavior, $62,300; $15,629
Ken Johnson, professor, counseling, $64,000; $12,368

Source: "Pay and Benefits of Leaders at 479 Private Colleges and Universities: a Survey," *The Chronicle of Higher Education*, 47: A29-A48, (November 24, 2000).

★3173★
Top pay and benefits for the chief executive and top paid employees at American International College

Ranking basis/background: Annual pay and benefits for the chief executives and top paid officers, as reported on Internal Revenue Service Form 990 by private colleges and universities in the U.S. for the 1998-99 academic year. **Number listed:** 6.

Harry J. Courniotes, president, with $187,100 annual pay; $36,613 in benefits
Carol A. Jobe, provost, $85,200; $3,673
Richard F. Bedard, VP, administration; comptroller, $68,000; $7,071
Ira A. Smolowitz, dean, school of business research, $67,690; $6,003
Elizabeth Ayres, dean, continuing education and graduate studies, $66,700; $5,953
Richard Sprinthall, chair, PhD program and psychology; professor, psychology, $63,200; $7,723

Source: "Pay and Benefits of Leaders at 479 Private Colleges and Universities: a Survey," *The Chronicle of Higher Education*, 47: A29-A48, (November 24, 2000).

★3174★
Top pay and benefits for the chief executive and top paid employees at American University

Ranking basis/background: Annual pay and benefits for the chief executives and top paid officers, as reported on Internal Revenue Service Form 990 by private colleges and universities in the U.S. for the 1998-99 academic year. **Number listed:** 6.

Benjamin Ladner, president, with $320,008 annual pay; $28,124 in benefits
Roderick French, chancellor, American University of Sharjah, United Arab Emirates, $224,445; $23,901
Cornelius Kerwin, provost, $207,834; $36,275
Donald L. Myers, VP, finance; treasurer, $214,355; $25,759
Claudio Grossman, dean and professor, law, $193,933; $25,427
Myron Roomkin, dean and professor, business, $162,500; $28,311

Source: "Pay and Benefits of Leaders at 479 Private Colleges and Universities: a Survey," *The Chronicle of Higher Education*, 47: A29-A48, (November 24, 2000).

★3175★
Top pay and benefits for the chief executive and top paid employees at Amherst College

Ranking basis/background: Annual pay and benefits for the chief executives and top paid officers, as reported on Internal Revenue Service Form 990 by private colleges and universities in the U.S. for the 1998-99 academic year. **Number listed:** 6.

Tom Gerety, president, with $224,000 annual pay; $75,803 in benefits
Lisa R. Raskin, dean of the faculty, $160,000; $26,861
Werner L. Gundersheimer, director, Folger Shakespeare Library, $151,840; $27,123
Sharon G. Siegel, treasurer, $150,000; $28,885
Michael Kiefer, chief advancement officer, $145,000; $27,979
Richard Goldsby, professor, biology, $127,113; $24,603

Source: "Pay and Benefits of Leaders at 479 Private Colleges and Universities: a Survey," *The Chronicle of Higher Education*, 47: A29-A48, (November 24, 2000).

★3176★
Top pay and benefits for the chief executive and top paid employees at Andrews University

Ranking basis/background: Annual pay and benefits for the chief executives and top paid officers, as reported on Internal Revenue Service Form 990 by private colleges and universities in the U.S. for the 1998-99 academic year. **Number listed:** 6.

Niels-Erik A. Andreasen, president, with $52,051 annual pay; $18,895 in benefits
Duane McBride, department chair; professor, behavioral science, $79,119; $30,065
Judith Anderson, professor, education, $67,787; $25,759
Karen Graham, dean, education, $67,485; $25,644
Charles W. Habenicht, department chair and professor, physical therapy, $64,581; $24,541
John C. Banks, professor, physical therapy, $64,375; $24,462

Source: "Pay and Benefits of Leaders at 479 Private Colleges and Universities: a Survey," *The Chronicle of Higher Education*, 47: A29-A48, (November 24, 2000).

★3177★
Top pay and benefits for the chief executive and top paid employees at Anna Maria College

Ranking basis/background: Annual pay and benefits for the chief executives and top paid officers, as reported on Internal Revenue Service Form 990 by private colleges and universities in the U.S. for the 1998-99 academic year. **Number listed:** 6.

Bernard S. Parker, president, with $87,582 annual pay; $27,545 in benefits
Cynthia M. Patterson, dean; VP, academic affairs, $70,000; $3,500
William J. Mulford, chief financial officer, $67,500; $3,375
John E. Price, chief technical officer, $67,500; $3,375
Linda L. Dodge, director, institutional advancement, $62,000; $3,100
Paul M. Chenevert, director, physical plant and security, $53,884; $2,692

Source: "Pay and Benefits of Leaders at 479 Private Colleges and Universities: a Survey," *The Chronicle of Higher Education*, 47: A29-A48, (November 24, 2000).

★3178★
Top pay and benefits for the chief executive and top paid employees at Antioch University

Ranking basis/background: Annual pay and benefits for the chief executives and top paid officers, as reported on Internal Revenue Service Form 990 by private colleges and universities in the U.S. for the 1998-99 academic year. **Number listed:** 7.

James W. Hall, chancellor, with $160,000 annual pay; $32,257 in benefits
Robert Devine, president, Antioch College, $119,368; $17,810
Alan E. Guskin, distinguished university professor emeritus, $150,106; $14,753
James Craiglow, president, Antioch New England, $110,000; $19,024
Glenn Watts, vice chancellor; chief financial officer, $110,000; $16,341
Dale Johnston, president emeritus, $105,575; $20,340
Mark Schulman, president, Antioch Southern California, $107,667; $15,182

Source: "Pay and Benefits of Leaders at 479 Private Colleges and Universities: a Survey," *The Chronicle of Higher Education*, 47: A29-A48, (November 24, 2000).

★3179★
Top pay and benefits for the chief executive and top paid employees at Aquinas College in Michigan

Ranking basis/background: Annual pay and benefits for the chief executives and top paid officers, as reported on Internal Revenue Service Form 990 by private colleges and universities in the U.S. for the 1998-99 academic year. **Number listed:** 6.

Harry J. Knopke, president, with $145,013 annual pay; $6,125 in benefits
Gary Konow, provost, $87,878; $8,511
James Garofalo, dean, school of education, $78,738; $7,615
Maribeth Wardrop, VP, development, $77,117; $7,574
William G. Shefferly, VP, operations and finance, $81,050; $3,438
Michael Keller, VP, planning, $72,146; $7,093

Source: "Pay and Benefits of Leaders at 479 Private Colleges and Universities: a Survey," *The Chronicle of Higher Education*, 47: A29-A48, (November 24, 2000).

★3180★
Top pay and benefits for the chief executive and top paid employees at Ashland University

Ranking basis/background: Annual pay and benefits for the chief executives and top paid officers, as reported on Internal Revenue Service Form 990 by private colleges and universities in the U.S. for the 1998-99 academic year. **Number listed:** 6.

G. William Benz, president, with $211,548 annual pay; $17,401 in benefits
James A. Barnes, VP, business affairs, $118,677; $11,303
Mary Ellen Drushal, provost, $116,860; $11,149
William Etling, VP, development, $114,219; $10,921
Frederick Finks, president, Ashland Theological Seminary, $108,750; $10,281
Peter W. Schramm, executive director, Ashbrook Center; professor, political science, $100,200; $9,840

Source: "Pay and Benefits of Leaders at 479 Private Colleges and Universities: a Survey," *The Chronicle of Higher Education*, 47: A29-A48, (November 24, 2000).

★3181★
Top pay and benefits for the chief executive and top paid employees at Assumption College

Ranking basis/background: Annual pay and benefits for the chief executives and top paid officers, as reported on Internal Revenue Service Form 990 by private colleges and universities in the U.S. for the 1998-99 academic year. **Number listed:** 6.

Thomas Plough, president, with $91,525 annual pay; $10,049 in benefits
Joseph H. Hagan, president emeritus, $201,077; $18,242
Francis P. Gurley, executive VP; treasurer, $148,741; $18,560
Charles L. Flynn Jr., interim provost of the college; dean of the college, $123,529; $14,058
Richard Oehling, professor, history, $77,236; $12,449
J. Richard Christiansen, VP, student activities, $77,737; $10,176

Source: "Pay and Benefits of Leaders at 479 Private Colleges and Universities: a Survey," *The Chronicle of Higher Education*, 47: A29-A48, (November 24, 2000).

★3182★
Top pay and benefits for the chief executive and top paid employees at Augustana College in Illinois

Ranking basis/background: Annual pay and benefits for the chief executives and top paid officers, as reported on Internal Revenue Service Form 990 by private colleges and universities in the U.S. for the 1998-99 academic year. **Number listed:** 6.

Thomas Tredway, president, with $186,000 annual pay; $26,325 in benefits
Paul D. Pearson, chief business and financial officer, $106,438; $19,677
Albert J. DeSimone, VP, development, $103,954; $19,441
John W. Hullett, dean, enrollment, $103,333; $19,282
Richard T. Jurasek, dean of the college, $90,958; $16,873
Evelyn S. Campbell, dean, student services, $83,588; $16,453

Source: "Pay and Benefits of Leaders at 479 Private Colleges and Universities: a Survey," *The Chronicle of Higher Education*, 47: A29-A48, (November 24, 2000).

★3183★
Top pay and benefits for the chief executive and top paid employees at Aurora University

Ranking basis/background: Annual pay and benefits for the chief executives and top paid officers, as reported on Internal Revenue Service Form 990 by private colleges and universities in the U.S. for the 1998-99 academic year. **Number listed:** 6.

Thomas H. Zarle, president, with $195,542 annual pay; $8,080 in benefits
Mark Wasicko, VP, academic affairs; provost, $117,867; $7,347
Richard C. Kleckner, VP, advancement, $113,667; $7,552
Joseph McKane, treasurer; VP, finance and administration, $108,667; $7,135
Sandy Alcorn, dean, George Williams College and school of social work, $80,751; $5,141
Rita Yerkes, associate dean, physical education and recreation administration, $79,768; $4,714

Source: "Pay and Benefits of Leaders at 479 Private Colleges and Universities: a Survey," *The Chronicle of Higher Education*, 47: A29-A48, (November 24, 2000).

★3184★
Top pay and benefits for the chief executive and top paid employees at Austin College

Ranking basis/background: Annual pay and benefits for the chief executives and top paid officers, as reported on Internal Revenue Service Form 990 by private colleges and universities in the U.S. for the 1998-99 academic year. **Number listed:** 6.

Oscar C. Page, president, with $180,000 annual pay; $0 in benefits
Jim Lewis, VP, institutional advancement, $112,289; $0
George Rowland, VP, business affairs, $108,000; $0
David Jordan, VP, academic affairs, $106,536; $0
Nan Massingill, VP, institutional enrollment, $85,000; $0
Karen Nelson, assistant dean, academic affairs, $75,695; $6,056

Source: "Pay and Benefits of Leaders at 479 Private Colleges and Universities: a Survey," *The Chronicle of Higher Education*, 47: A29-A48, (November 24, 2000).

★3185★
Top pay and benefits for the chief executive and top paid employees at Averett College

Ranking basis/background: Annual pay and benefits for the chief executives and top paid officers, as reported on Internal Revenue Service Form 990 by private colleges and universities in the U.S. for the 1998-99 academic year. **Number listed:** 6.

Frank Campbell, president, with $137,259 annual pay; $15,186 in benefits
Charles D. Terry, VP, administration and finance, $86,668; $7,201
Brian Satterlee, dean, graduate studies, $73,320; $11,110
John Termini, director, graduate and professional studies, Virginia Beach region, $77,465; $3,792
Gary L. Sherman, VP, enrollment management, $71,276; $3,863
Norman P. Fenton, director, southern Virginia region, $70,050; $4,763

Source: "Pay and Benefits of Leaders at 479 Private Colleges and Universities: a Survey," *The Chronicle of Higher Education*, 47: A29-A48, (November 24, 2000).

★3186★
Top pay and benefits for the chief executive and top paid employees at Avila College

Ranking basis/background: Annual pay and benefits for the chief executives and top paid officers, as reported on Internal Revenue Service Form 990 by private colleges and universities in the U.S. for the 1998-99 academic year. **Number listed:** 5.

Larry Kramer, president, with $131,180 annual pay; $8,576 in benefits
James T. Barry, VP, advancement, $72,150; $7,784
Esther Mills, associate dean, $64,111; $5,248
Richard Woodall, chair; professor, business economics, $63,664; $5,447
Norman Gerhart, VP, fiscal affairs, $62,500; $5,400

Source: "Pay and Benefits of Leaders at 479 Private Colleges and Universities: a Survey," *The Chronicle of Higher Education*, 47: A29-A48, (November 24, 2000).

★3187★
Top pay and benefits for the chief executive and top paid employees at Azusa Pacific University

Ranking basis/background: Annual pay and benefits for the chief executives and top paid officers, as reported on Internal Revenue Service Form 990 by private colleges and universities in the U.S. for the 1998-99 academic year. **Number listed:** 6.

Richard Felix, president, with $157,537 annual pay; $37,400 in benefits
Fred Garlett, director, Center for Accelerated Degree Programs, $113,392; $11,806
Jon Wallace, executive VP; chief operating officer, $110,215; $13,736
Clifford Hamlow, VP, university services, $107,000; $13,400
Patricia Anderson, provost, $106,015; $13,400
Hank Bode, VP, legal affairs and special projects, $100,765; $12,980

Source: "Pay and Benefits of Leaders at 479 Private Colleges and Universities: a Survey," *The Chronicle of Higher Education*, 47: A29-A48, (November 24, 2000).

★3188★
Top pay and benefits for the chief executive and top paid employees at Baker University

Ranking basis/background: Annual pay and benefits for the chief executives and top paid officers, as reported on Internal Revenue Service Form 990 by private colleges and universities in the U.S. for the 1998-99 academic year. **Number listed:** 5.

Daniel M. Lambert, president, with $139,313 annual pay; $12,033 in benefits
Russell W. Pieken, internal development and design consultant for secondary-education programming, $132,207; $0
Donald B. Clardy, executive VP; dean, School of Professional and Graduate Studies, $79,606; $16,456
Robert A. Layton, VP, financial services, $88,050; $6,919
Stuart B. Dorsey, VP; dean, college of arts and sciences, $79,550; $6,390

Source: "Pay and Benefits of Leaders at 479 Private Colleges and Universities: a Survey," *The Chronicle of Higher Education*, 47: A29-A48, (November 24, 2000).

★3189★
Top pay and benefits for the chief executive and top paid employees at Baldwin-Wallace College

Ranking basis/background: Annual pay and benefits for the chief executives and top paid officers, as reported on Internal Revenue Service Form 990 by private colleges and universities in the U.S. for the 1998-99 academic year. **Number listed:** 6.

Neal Malicky, president, with $170,272 annual pay; $27,043 in benefits
Mark H. Collier, VP, academic affairs, $126,667; $15,066
Keith Mathews, VP, finance, $112,958; $13,681
Richard Fletcher, VP, advancement, $107,671; $14,582
Roger Grugle, associate professor, business, $105,011; $10,601
Richard Little, professor, mathematics and computer science, $105,259; $7,186

Source: "Pay and Benefits of Leaders at 479 Private Colleges and Universities: a Survey," *The Chronicle of Higher Education*, 47: A29-A48, (November 24, 2000).

★3190★
Top pay and benefits for the chief executive and top paid employees at Bard College

Ranking basis/background: Annual pay and benefits for the chief executives and top paid officers, as reported on Internal Revenue Service Form 990 by private colleges and universities in the U.S. for the 1998-99 academic year. **Number listed:** 6.

Leon Botstein, president, with $205,104 annual pay; $24,190 in benefits
Dimitri Papadimitriou, executive director, Jerome Levy Economics Institute, $188,166; $97,950
David Levy, director of forecasting, Jerome Levy Economics Institute, $170,000; $20,816
John Ashbery, professor, languages and literature, $127,182; $16,377
Joel Perlmann, research professor, history, $126,027; $13,321
Stuart Levine, dean of the college; professor, psychology, $119,925; $15,639

Source: "Pay and Benefits of Leaders at 479 Private Colleges and Universities: a Survey," *The Chronicle of Higher Education*, 47: A29-A48, (November 24, 2000).

★3191★
Top pay and benefits for the chief executive and top paid employees at Barnard College

Ranking basis/background: Annual pay and benefits for the chief executives and top paid officers, as reported on Internal Revenue Service Form 990 by private colleges and universities in the U.S. for the 1998-99 academic year. **Number listed:** 6.

Judith R. Shapiro, president, with $235,000 annual pay; $37,054 in benefits
Rae Silver, professor, psychology, $171,114; $35,180
Barry Kaufman, VP, finance and administration, $153,500; $34,237
Carol Herring, VP, development and alumni affairs, $153,000; $34,662
Elizabeth S. Boylan, provost; dean of the faculty, $142,000; $37,052
Demetrios Caraley, professor, political science, $136,590; $31,795

Source: "Pay and Benefits of Leaders at 479 Private Colleges and Universities: a Survey," *The Chronicle of Higher Education*, 47: A29-A48, (November 24, 2000).

★3192★
Top pay and benefits for the chief executive and top paid employees at Barry University

Ranking basis/background: Annual pay and benefits for the chief executives and top paid officers, as reported on Internal Revenue Service Form 990 by private colleges and universities in the U.S. for the 1998-99 academic year. **Number listed:** 6.

Sister Jeanne O'Laughlin, O.P., president, with $162,225 annual pay; $12,978 in benefits
John P. Nelson, associate professor; associate dean, graduate medical sciences, $143,529; $8,400
Thomas Merrill, professor, graduate medical sciences, $135,423; $6,275
Charles Southerland, professor, graduate medical sciences, $135,238; $5,712
Chester Evans, associate VP, professor; dean, graduate medical sciences, $129,000; $10,320
J. Patrick Lee, provost; senior VP, academic affairs, $121,025; $9,682

Source: "Pay and Benefits of Leaders at 479 Private Colleges and Universities: a Survey," *The Chronicle of Higher Education*, 47: A29-A48, (November 24, 2000).

★3193★
Top pay and benefits for the chief executive and top paid employees at Bates College

Ranking basis/background: Annual pay and benefits for the chief executives and top paid officers, as reported on Internal Revenue Service Form 990 by private colleges and universities in the U.S. for the 1998-99 academic year. **Number listed:** 6.

Donald W. Harward, president, with $231,750 annual pay; $28,187 in benefits
Victoria Devlin, VP, development and alumni, $160,000; $26,429
Bernard R. Carpenter, treasurer emeritus, $135,000; $24,233
Peter C. Fackler, treasurer, $125,000; $21,060
Michael P. Murray, professor, economics, $116,030; $23,724
Carl Straub, professor, religion and environmental studies, $116,030; $21,871

Source: "Pay and Benefits of Leaders at 479 Private Colleges and Universities: a Survey," *The Chronicle of Higher Education*, 47: A29-A48, (November 24, 2000).

★3194★
Top pay and benefits for the chief executive and top paid employees at Baylor University

Ranking basis/background: Annual pay and benefits for the chief executives and top paid officers, as reported on Internal Revenue Service Form 990 by private colleges and universities in the U.S. for the 1998-99 academic year. **Number listed:** 7.

Robert B. Sloan Jr., president, with $275,459 annual pay; $21,580 in benefits
Herbert H. Reynolds, chancellor, $200,004; $29,054
Donald D. Schmeltekopt, provost; VP, academic affairs, $169,000; $29,117
David M. Guinn, professor, law, $161,623; $26,653
Bradley J.B. Toben, dean, law, $156,383; $27,080
Richard D. Scott, VP, university development, $150,150; $27,200
William D. Underwood, professor, law, $142,109; $25,547

Source: "Pay and Benefits of Leaders at 479 Private Colleges and Universities: a Survey," *The Chronicle of Higher Education*, 47: A29-A48, (November 24, 2000).

★3195★
Top pay and benefits for the chief executive and top paid employees at Beaver College

Ranking basis/background: Annual pay and benefits for the chief executives and top paid officers, as reported on Internal Revenue Service Form 990 by private colleges and universities in the U.S. for the 1998-99 academic year. **Number listed:** 6.

Bette E. Landman, president, with $140,519 annual pay; $15,500 in benefits
David C. Larsen, VP; director, international programs, $139,681; $15,400
Frank C. Vogel, VP, institutional advancement, $111,894; $12,300
Richard Speller, VP, finance; treasurer, $110,324; $12,100
William Biggs, professor; chair, health administration; professor business and economics, $106,765; $11,750
Michael Berger, VP, academic affairs; dean of the college, $97,367; $10,700

Source: "Pay and Benefits of Leaders at 479 Private Colleges and Universities: a Survey," *The Chronicle of Higher Education*, 47: A29-A48, (November 24, 2000).

★3196★
Top pay and benefits for the chief executive and top paid employees at Bellarmine University

Ranking basis/background: Annual pay and benefits for the chief executives and top paid officers, as reported on Internal Revenue Service Form 990 by private colleges and universities in the U.S. for the 1998-99 academic year. **Number listed:** 6.

- Joseph J. McGowan Jr., president, with $179,000 annual pay; $52,692 in benefits
- Vincent M. Maniaci, VP, institutional advancement, $130,000; $21,558
- John A. Oppelt, provost, $108,000; $20,595
- Edward T.L. Popper, dean, business, $104,500; $16,755
- Fred W. Rhodes, dean of students; VP, student affairs, $98,700; $19,476
- Robert L. Zimlich, VP, business affairs, $90,000; $18,474

Source: "Pay and Benefits of Leaders at 479 Private Colleges and Universities: a Survey," *The Chronicle of Higher Education*, 47: A29-A48, (November 24, 2000).

★3197★
Top pay and benefits for the chief executive and top paid employees at Bellevue University

Ranking basis/background: Annual pay and benefits for the chief executives and top paid officers, as reported on Internal Revenue Service Form 990 by private colleges and universities in the U.S. for the 1998-99 academic year. **Number listed:** 6.

- John Muller, president, with $216,000 annual pay; $13,189 in benefits
- Patricia Morocco, president, Bellevue University Foundation, $200,965; $13,012
- Jon Kayne, VP, academic affairs, $109,629; $9,733
- Ed Rauchut, associate professor, professional studies, $105,838; $5,812
- Harold Carpenter, dean, international programs, $94,046; $8,606
- Douglas Frost, dean, college of business, $92,922; $5,867

Source: "Pay and Benefits of Leaders at 479 Private Colleges and Universities: a Survey," *The Chronicle of Higher Education*, 47: A29-A48, (November 24, 2000).

★3198★
Top pay and benefits for the chief executive and top paid employees at Belmont University

Ranking basis/background: Annual pay and benefits for the chief executives and top paid officers, as reported on Internal Revenue Service Form 990 by private colleges and universities in the U.S. for the 1998-99 academic year. **Number listed:** 6.

- William T. Troutt, president, with $200,000 annual pay; $0 in benefits
- James M. Clapper, dean, college of business administration, $106,500; $0
- Jerry L. Warren, provost, $96,639; $0
- Susan Hillenmeyer, VP, administration, $88,625; $0
- Steven T. Lasley, VP finance, $86,552; $0
- Gipsie Ranney, professor, school of business, $85,698; $0

Source: "Pay and Benefits of Leaders at 479 Private Colleges and Universities: a Survey," *The Chronicle of Higher Education*, 47: A29-A48, (November 24, 2000).

★3199★
Top pay and benefits for the chief executive and top paid employees at Beloit College

Ranking basis/background: Annual pay and benefits for the chief executives and top paid officers, as reported on Internal Revenue Service Form 990 by private colleges and universities in the U.S. for the 1998-99 academic year. **Number listed:** 6.

- Victor E. Ferrall Jr., president, with $184,700 annual pay; $0 in benefits
- Bruce Wyatt, VP, external affairs, $106,812; $0
- Brock Spencer, professor, chemistry, $84,161; $16,926
- Dave Burrows, VP, academic affairs, $100,395; $0
- John Nicholas, VP, administration, $99,050; $0
- John Jungck, professor, biology, $81,906; $16,835

Source: "Pay and Benefits of Leaders at 479 Private Colleges and Universities: a Survey," *The Chronicle of Higher Education*, 47: A29-A48, (November 24, 2000).

★3200★
Top pay and benefits for the chief executive and top paid employees at Benedictine University

Ranking basis/background: Annual pay and benefits for the chief executives and top paid officers, as reported on Internal Revenue Service Form 990 by private colleges and universities in the U.S. for the 1998-99 academic year. **Number listed:** 6.

- William J. Carroll, president, with $133,738 annual pay; $6,687 in benefits
- Robert Head, VP, finance and administration, $106,900; $5,345
- Sam Ross, VP, institutional advancement, $102,000; $5,100
- Bruce Buchowicz, professor, graduate studies, $97,449; $4,872
- Richard MacLean, executive director, international programs, $94,600; $3,300
- Phyllis Little, special assistant to the president, $92,820; $4,641

Source: "Pay and Benefits of Leaders at 479 Private Colleges and Universities: a Survey," *The Chronicle of Higher Education*, 47: A29-A48, (November 24, 2000).

★3201★
Top pay and benefits for the chief executive and top paid employees at Bennington College

Ranking basis/background: Annual pay and benefits for the chief executives and top paid officers, as reported on Internal Revenue Service Form 990 by private colleges and universities in the U.S. for the 1998-99 academic year. **Number listed:** 6.

- Elizabeth Coleman, president, with $176,789 annual pay; $14,734 in benefits
- Lawrence W. Lee, treasurer, $102,000; $7,162
- Mary Runyon, director, 21st Century Fund, $89,301; $6,013
- William Reichblum, dean of the college, $81,600; $7,753
- Robert Waldman, director, information services, $73,542; $7,310
- David Rees, director, development, $76,500; $3,737

Source: "Pay and Benefits of Leaders at 479 Private Colleges and Universities: a Survey," *The Chronicle of Higher Education*, 47: A29-A48, (November 24, 2000).

★3202★
Top pay and benefits for the chief executive and top paid employees at Bethany College in West Virginia

Ranking basis/background: Annual pay and benefits for the chief executives and top paid officers, as reported on Internal Revenue Service Form 990 by private colleges and universities in the U.S. for the 1998-99 academic year. **Number listed:** 3.

- D. Duane Cummins, president, with $102,275 annual pay; $27,614 in benefits
- Joseph M. Kurey, VP, finance; treasurer, $73,950; $129,666
- Pamela Balch, VP, academic affairs; dean of the faculty, $90,000; $24,300

Source: "Pay and Benefits of Leaders at 479 Private Colleges and Universities: a Survey," *The Chronicle of Higher Education*, 47: A29-A48, (November 24, 2000).

★3203★
Top pay and benefits for the chief executive and top paid employees at Biola University

Ranking basis/background: Annual pay and benefits for the chief executives and top paid officers, as reported on Internal Revenue Service Form 990 by private colleges and universities in the U.S. for the 1998-99 academic year. **Number listed:** 6.

- Clyde Cook, president, with $168,500 annual pay; $18,341 in benefits
- Sherwood Lingenfelter, provost, $106,056; $7,967
- Wesley Wilmer, VP, advancement, $101,244; $7,641
- Carl W. Schreiber, VP, financial affairs and information systems; treasurer, $94,649; $7,366
- James Moreland, professor, philosophy, $94,533; $6,143
- John M. Reynolds, professor, philosophy, $95,190; $5,199

Source: "Pay and Benefits of Leaders at 479 Private Colleges and Universities: a Survey," *The Chronicle of Higher Education*, 47: A29-A48, (November 24, 2000).

★3204★
Top pay and benefits for the chief executive and top paid employees at Birmingham-Southern College

Ranking basis/background: Annual pay and benefits for the chief executives and top paid officers, as reported on Internal Revenue Service Form 990 by private colleges and universities in the U.S. for the 1998-99 academic year. **Number listed:** 6.

Neal R. Berte, president, with $183,516 annual pay; $105,203 in benefits
Henry Irvin Penfield, VP, academic affairs; provost, $121,172; $21,677
E. Byron Chew, dean, graduate programs; professor, business management, $118,343; $21,425
Edward S. LaMonte, VP, administration; dean, adult studies; professor, political science, $104,933; $19,211
A. Duane Reboul, head coach, men's basketball, $107,930; $13,823
Johnny A. Johnson, VP, business and finance, $100,744; $16,955

Source: "Pay and Benefits of Leaders at 479 Private Colleges and Universities: a Survey," *The Chronicle of Higher Education*, 47: A29-A48, (November 24, 2000).

★3205★
Top pay and benefits for the chief executive and top paid employees at Boston College

Ranking basis/background: Annual pay and benefits for the chief executives and top paid officers, as reported on Internal Revenue Service Form 990 by private colleges and universities in the U.S. for the 1998-99 academic year. **Remarks:** The institution paid $4-million to the Society of Jesus, which included compensation to Reverend Leahy and other Jesuit officers. **Number listed:** 7.

Rev. William P. Leahy, S.J., president, with $0 annual pay; $0 in benefits
J. Donald Monan, S.J., chancellor, $0; $0
Francis B. Campanella, executive VP, $281,643; $23,803
Peter C. McKenzie, VP, finance; treasurer, $251,844; $23,200
David R. Burgess, VP, academics; dean, faculties, $247,206; $6,078
Daniel R. Coquillette, professor, law, $225,050; $23,200
Eugene B. DiFilippo Jr., director, athletics, $213,275; $20,603

Source: "Pay and Benefits of Leaders at 479 Private Colleges and Universities: a Survey," *The Chronicle of Higher Education*, 47: A29-A48, (November 24, 2000).

★3206★
Top pay and benefits for the chief executive and top paid employees at Boston University

Ranking basis/background: Annual pay and benefits for the chief executives and top paid officers, as reported on Internal Revenue Service Form 990 by private colleges and universities in the U.S. for the 1998-99 academic year. **Remarks:** Chancellor Silber's pay includes a $250,000 loan that was forgiven. **Number listed:** 7.

Jon Westling, president, with $385,000 annual pay; $49,257 in benefits
John R. Silber, chancellor, $650,000; $164,956
James M. Becker, professor and chair, surgery, $651,661; $26,651
Timothy E. Foster, assistant professor, orthopedic surgery, $574,301; $15,961
Joseph Lascalzo, professor and chair, medicine, $454,605; $23,471
Joseph Mercurio, executive VP, $365,000; $83,238
Gary S. Rogers, professor dematologic surgery; director, dermatology, $427,773; $18,837

Source: "Pay and Benefits of Leaders at 479 Private Colleges and Universities: a Survey," *The Chronicle of Higher Education*, 47: A29-A48, (November 24, 2000).

★3207★
Top pay and benefits for the chief executive and top paid employees at Bowdoin College

Ranking basis/background: Annual pay and benefits for the chief executives and top paid officers, as reported on Internal Revenue Service Form 990 by private colleges and universities in the U.S. for the 1998-99 academic year. **Number listed:** 6.

Robert H. Edwards, president, with $242,428 annual pay; $40,121 in benefits
William A. Torrey, VP, planning and development, $140,000; $33,262
Kent John Chabotar, VP, finance and administration; treasurer, $135,000, $32,262
Charles R. Beitz, dean, academic affairs; professor, government, $128,750; $31,012
Richard E. Steele, dean, admissions, $122,000; $29,659
John L. Howland, professor, biology, $108,000; $26,857

Source: "Pay and Benefits of Leaders at 479 Private Colleges and Universities: a Survey," *The Chronicle of Higher Education*, 47: A29-A48, (November 24, 2000).

★3208★
Top pay and benefits for the chief executive and top paid employees at Bradley University

Ranking basis/background: Annual pay and benefits for the chief executives and top paid officers, as reported on Internal Revenue Service Form 990 by private colleges and universities in the U.S. for the 1998-99 academic year. **Number listed:** 6.

John R. Brazil, president, with $300,122 annual pay; $56,959 in benefits
Jim Molinari, head coach, men's basketball, $158,870; $47,166
D. Paul Mehta, professor, mechanical engineering, $159,354; $20,116
Gary M. Anna, VP; business affairs; treasurer, $143,578; $34,046
Stan Liberty, VP, academic affairs; provost, $141,370; $21,292
Robert Weinstein, president, Illinois Manufacturing Extension Center, $133,925; $21,464

Source: "Pay and Benefits of Leaders at 479 Private Colleges and Universities: a Survey," *The Chronicle of Higher Education*, 47: A29-A48, (November 24, 2000).

★3209★
Top pay and benefits for the chief executive and top paid employees at Brandeis University

Ranking basis/background: Annual pay and benefits for the chief executives and top paid officers, as reported on Internal Revenue Service Form 990 by private colleges and universities in the U.S. for the 1998-99 academic year. **Number listed:** 6.

Jehuda Reinharz, president, with $296,890 annual pay; $21,671 in benefits
Peter B. French, executive VP; chief operating officer, $234,465; $22,160
Irving R. Epstein, senior VP, academic affairs; provost, $210,817; $17,830
Nancy Winship, senior VP, development and alumni relations, $196,258; $14,630
James R. Lackner, director, Graybiel Laboratory; professor, physiology, $174,169; $19,018
Greg Petsko, professor, biochemistry and molecular pharmacodynamics; director, Rosenstiel Basic Medical Sciences Research Center, $158,445; $17,484

Source: "Pay and Benefits of Leaders at 479 Private Colleges and Universities: a Survey," *The Chronicle of Higher Education*, 47: A29-A48, (November 24, 2000).

★3210★
Top pay and benefits for the chief executive and top paid employees at Brenau University

Ranking basis/background: Annual pay and benefits for the chief executives and top paid officers, as reported on Internal Revenue Service Form 990 by private colleges and universities in the U.S. for the 1998-99 academic year. **Number listed:** 6.

John S. Burd, president, with $128,280 annual pay; $57,768 in benefits
Helen C. Ray, VP, academic affairs, $91,074; $14,186
David L. Gines, VP, institutional advancement, $84,986; $12,949
Frank Booth, dean, Brenau Academy, $74,023; $11,822
L. Dick Childers, VP, business and finance, $73,278; $12,512
Larry Andrews, VP, administration services, $73,054; $12,244

Source: "Pay and Benefits of Leaders at 479 Private Colleges and Universities: a Survey," *The Chronicle of Higher Education*, 47: A29-A48, (November 24, 2000).

★3211★
Top pay and benefits for the chief executive and top paid employees at Brown University

Ranking basis/background: Annual pay and benefits for the chief executives and top paid officers, as reported on Internal Revenue Service Form 990 by private colleges and universities in the U.S. for the 1998-99 academic year. **Number listed:** 6.

E. Gordon Gee, president, with $305,290 annual pay; $30,526 in benefits
Kirby Isaac Bland, chair; professor, surgery, $390,234; $19,912
Edward Wing, professor, medical science, $350,000; $30,230
Martin B. Keller, department chair; professor, psychiatry and human behavior, $298,775; $19,773
H. Denman Scott, professor, community health and medicine; associate dean, medicine, $250,000; $23,820
Vartan Gregorian, president emeritus, $241,576; $5,318

Source: "Pay and Benefits of Leaders at 479 Private Colleges and Universities: a Survey," *The Chronicle of Higher Education*, 47: A29-A48, (November 24, 2000).

★3212★
Top pay and benefits for the chief executive and top paid employees at Bryn Mawr College

Ranking basis/background: Annual pay and benefits for the chief executives and top paid officers, as reported on Internal Revenue Service Form 990 by private colleges and universities in the U.S. for the 1998-99 academic year. **Number listed:** 6.

- Nancy Vickers, president, with $191,694 annual pay; $26,995 in benefits
- Jerry Berenson, treasurer; CFO, $133,194; $21,588
- Robert J. Dostal, provost; professor, philosophy, $131,500; $21,271
- Frank Mallory, professor, chemistry, $118,377; $20,303
- Judith Porter, professor, sociology, $113,498; $19,655
- Rhonda Hughes, professor, mathematics, $110,418; $19,172

Source: "Pay and Benefits of Leaders at 479 Private Colleges and Universities: a Survey," *The Chronicle of Higher Education*, 47: A29-A48, (November 24, 2000).

★3213★
Top pay and benefits for the chief executive and top paid employees at Bucknell University

Ranking basis/background: Annual pay and benefits for the chief executives and top paid officers, as reported on Internal Revenue Service Form 990 by private colleges and universities in the U.S. for the 1998-99 academic year. **Number listed:** 6.

- William D. Adams, president, with $174,406 annual pay; $32,265 in benefits
- Margaret Plympton, VP, finance, $145,000; $26,825
- Richard Johnson, VP, university relations, $132,150; $24,450
- Gary Sojka, professor, biology, $125,298; $23,180
- Daniel Little, VP, academic affairs, $124,935; $23,115
- Barry Maxwell, VP, finance and administration, $117,492; $21,735

Source: "Pay and Benefits of Leaders at 479 Private Colleges and Universities: a Survey," *The Chronicle of Higher Education*, 47: A29-A48, (November 24, 2000).

★3214★
Top pay and benefits for the chief executive and top paid employees at Butler University

Ranking basis/background: Annual pay and benefits for the chief executives and top paid officers, as reported on Internal Revenue Service Form 990 by private colleges and universities in the U.S. for the 1998-99 academic year. **Number listed:** 6.

- Geoffrey Bannister, president, with $232,464 annual pay; $27,997 in benefits
- Barry S. Collier, head coach, men's basketball, $135,600; $14,381
- Thomas R. Snider, VP, enrollment management, $131,250; $17,598
- Richard D. Skooglund, VP, university advancement, $126,300; $15,973
- Bruce E. Arick, VP, finance and administration; treasurer, $118,850; $15,303
- Steve Kaplan, dean, liberal arts and sciences, $120,000; $14,139

Source: "Pay and Benefits of Leaders at 479 Private Colleges and Universities: a Survey," *The Chronicle of Higher Education*, 47: A29-A48, (November 24, 2000).

★3215★
Top pay and benefits for the chief executive and top paid employees at Cabrini College

Ranking basis/background: Annual pay and benefits for the chief executives and top paid officers, as reported on Internal Revenue Service Form 990 by private colleges and universities in the U.S. for the 1998-99 academic year. **Number listed:** 6.

- Antoinette Iadarola, president, with $107,288 annual pay; $13,205 in benefits
- Stephen J. Lightcap, VP, finance and administration, $87,634; $11,477
- Albert C. Mollica, VP, institutional advancement, $77,138; $10,689
- William Kuhns, associate professor, education; director, student-teaching program, $77,805; $8,694
- Joseph J. Romano, professor, philosophy; coordinator of honors program, $74,870; $9,737
- James Hedtke, associate professor, history, $75,835; $7,887

Source: "Pay and Benefits of Leaders at 479 Private Colleges and Universities: a Survey," *The Chronicle of Higher Education*, 47: A29-A48, (November 24, 2000).

★3216★
Top pay and benefits for the chief executive and top paid employees at California Lutheran University

Ranking basis/background: Annual pay and benefits for the chief executives and top paid officers, as reported on Internal Revenue Service Form 990 by private colleges and universities in the U.S. for the 1998-99 academic year. **Number listed:** 6.

- Luther Luedtke, president, with $156,633 annual pay; $16,208 in benefits
- George Engdahl, VP, university advancement, $124,676; $13,611
- Carl Swanson, professor, music, $122,920; $2,079
- Robert Shoup, professor, physical education, $115,420; $0
- Pam Jolicoeur, VP, academic affairs; provost, $102,884; $11,052
- Dennis Gillette, VP, administrative services, $99,350; $10,665

Source: "Pay and Benefits of Leaders at 479 Private Colleges and Universities: a Survey," *The Chronicle of Higher Education*, 47: A29-A48, (November 24, 2000).

★3217★
Top pay and benefits for the chief executive and top paid employees at Calvin College

Ranking basis/background: Annual pay and benefits for the chief executives and top paid officers, as reported on Internal Revenue Service Form 990 by private colleges and universities in the U.S. for the 1998-99 academic year. **Number listed:** 6.

- Gaylen J. Byker, president, with $144,833 annual pay; $24,206 in benefits
- Joel A. Carpenter, provost, $96,745; $16,647
- James Kraai, VP, administration and finance, $91,000; $17,658
- David DeHeer, professor, biology, $92,818; $11,674
- Cornelius Plantinga Jr., dean, chapel, $85,246; $13,058
- Henry E. DeVries II, VP, information services, $73,500; $14,080

Source: "Pay and Benefits of Leaders at 479 Private Colleges and Universities: a Survey," *The Chronicle of Higher Education*, 47: A29-A48, (November 24, 2000).

★3218★
Top pay and benefits for the chief executive and top paid employees at Campbell University

Ranking basis/background: Annual pay and benefits for the chief executives and top paid officers, as reported on Internal Revenue Service Form 990 by private colleges and universities in the U.S. for the 1998-99 academic year. **Number listed:** 6.

- Norman A. Wiggins, president, with $309,000 annual pay; $12,210 in benefits
- Willis P. Whichard, dean, law, $150,000; $14,760
- Ronald Maddox, dean and professor, pharmacy, $143,325; $14,226
- Patrick Hetrick, dean and professor, law, $111,800; $11,800
- Richard Lord, professor, law, $111,500; $11,680
- James B. McLaughlin, associate dean and professor, law, $111,500; $11,680

Source: "Pay and Benefits of Leaders at 479 Private Colleges and Universities: a Survey," *The Chronicle of Higher Education*, 47: A29-A48, (November 24, 2000).

★3219★
Top pay and benefits for the chief executive and top paid employees at Canisius College

Ranking basis/background: Annual pay and benefits for the chief executives and top paid officers, as reported on Internal Revenue Service Form 990 by private colleges and universities in the U.S. for the 1998-99 academic year. **Number listed:** 6.

- Rev. Vincent M. Cooke, S.J., president, with $131,960 annual pay; $13,866 in benefits
- Richard Shick, dean business, $114,584; $33,491
- Herbert J. Nelson, VP, academic affairs, $118,000; $16,273
- Laurence W. Franz, VP, finance and business; treasurer, $116,163; $17,941

SALARIES—COLLEGES & UNIVERSITIES

Edward Gress, professor, accounting, $112,765; $13,898
J. Patrick Greenwald, executive director, campaigns for Canisius

Source: "Pay and Benefits of Leaders at 479 Private Colleges and Universities: a Survey," *The Chronicle of Higher Education*, 47: A29-A48, (November 24, 2000).

★3220★
Top pay and benefits for the chief executive and top paid employees at Capital University

Ranking basis/background: Annual pay and benefits for the chief executives and top paid officers, as reported on Internal Revenue Service Form 990 by private colleges and universities in the U.S. for the 1998-99 academic year. **Number listed:** 6.

Ronald Volpe, interim president, with $142,117 annual pay; $16,105 in benefits
Steven Bahls, dean, law, $146,250; $17,957
Josiah Blackmore, professor, law, $144,328; $17,092
Brian Freeman, associate dean, law, $135,238; $14,179
Daniel Turack, professor, law, $129,750; $14,870
Stanton Darling, professor, law, $122,563; $13,460

Source: "Pay and Benefits of Leaders at 479 Private Colleges and Universities: a Survey," *The Chronicle of Higher Education*, 47: A29-A48, (November 24, 2000).

★3221★
Top pay and benefits for the chief executive and top paid employees at Cardinal Stritch University

Ranking basis/background: Annual pay and benefits for the chief executives and top paid officers, as reported on Internal Revenue Service Form 990 by private colleges and universities in the U.S. for the 1998-99 academic year. **Number listed:** 6.

Sister Mary Lea Schneider, O.S.F., president, with $112,250 annual pay; $13,379 in benefits
Robert L. Anderson, VP, operations and facilities, $96,400; $18,291
Laramie Jung, VP, university advancement, $80,340; $30,497
Marna E. Boyle, VP, academic affairs; dean of the faculty, $91,050; $18,826
Robert Abene, VP, student development; dean of students, $77,650; $13,200
Anthea Bojar, dean, education, $76,530; $13,010

Source: "Pay and Benefits of Leaders at 479 Private Colleges and Universities: a Survey," *The Chronicle of Higher Education*, 47: A29-A48, (November 24, 2000).

★3222★
Top pay and benefits for the chief executive and top paid employees at Carleton College

Ranking basis/background: Annual pay and benefits for the chief executives and top paid officers, as reported on Internal Revenue Service Form 990 by private colleges and universities in the U.S. for the 1998-99 academic year. **Number listed:** 6.

Stephen R. Lewis Jr., president, with $192,500 annual pay; $35,988 in benefits
Carol N. Campbell, VP; treasurer, $136,250; $26,153
Elizabeth McKinsey, dean of the college, $118,250; $25,675
Mark E. Kronholm, VP, external relations, $112,375; $25,166
Stephen Kelly, acting dean, budget and planning; professor, music, $104,083; $23,572
Clifford E. Clark Jr., professor, history and American studies; director, summer academic programs, $102,972; $20,147

Source: "Pay and Benefits of Leaders at 479 Private Colleges and Universities: a Survey," *The Chronicle of Higher Education*, 47: A29-A48, (November 24, 2000).

★3223★
Top pay and benefits for the chief executive and top paid employees at Carnegie Mellon University

Ranking basis/background: Annual pay and benefits for the chief executives and top paid officers, as reported on Internal Revenue Service Form 990 by private colleges and universities in the U.S. for the 1998-99 academic year. **Number listed:** 6.

Jared L. Cohon, president, with $334,615 annual pay; $20,760 in benefits
Chester S. Spatt, professor, economics and finance, $247,741; $31,346
Douglas Dunn, professor and dean, graduate school of industrial administration, $229,427; $48,051
Paul Christiano, provost, $232,618; $30,220
Raj Reddy, professor and dean, computer science, $231,292; $29,603
Allan Meltzer, professor, political economy, $222,702; $25,150

Source: "Pay and Benefits of Leaders at 479 Private Colleges and Universities: a Survey," *The Chronicle of Higher Education*, 47: A29-A48, (November 24, 2000).

★3224★
Top pay and benefits for the chief executive and top paid employees at Carthage College

Ranking basis/background: Annual pay and benefits for the chief executives and top paid officers, as reported on Internal Revenue Service Form 990 by private colleges and universities in the U.S. for the 1998-99 academic year. **Number listed:** 6.

F. Gregory Campbell, president, with $169,978 annual pay; $21,908 in benefits
Robert Dittus, VP, business and finance, $104,266; $13,398
Kent Henning, VP, college relations, $101,407; $13,145
Brenda Poggendorf, VP, enrollment, $101,407; $13,145
Kurt Piepenburg, dean of the college, $100,889; $13,145
Irene Kraemer, dean, school of professional studies, $89,354; $11,684

Source: "Pay and Benefits of Leaders at 479 Private Colleges and Universities: a Survey," *The Chronicle of Higher Education*, 47: A29-A48, (November 24, 2000).

★3225★
Top pay and benefits for the chief executive and top paid employees at Case Western Reserve University

Ranking basis/background: Annual pay and benefits for the chief executives and top paid officers, as reported on Internal Revenue Service Form 990 by private colleges and universities in the U.S. for the 1998-99 academic year. **Number listed:** 6.

Agnar Pytte, president, with $340,000 annual pay; $31,570 in benefits
Jeffrey Blumer, professor, pediatrics, $301,000; $30,859
Jerry M. Shuck, chair and professor, surgery, $291,527; $32,599
Ellis D. Avner, chair and professor, pediatrics, $290,000; $30,534
Dennis Landis, chair and professor, neurology, $273,182; $30,994
Nathan A. Berger, VP; dean, medical affairs, $270,000; $31,407

Source: "Pay and Benefits of Leaders at 479 Private Colleges and Universities: a Survey," *The Chronicle of Higher Education*, 47: A29-A48, (November 24, 2000).

★3226★
Top pay and benefits for the chief executive and top paid employees at Central College in Iowa

Ranking basis/background: Annual pay and benefits for the chief executives and top paid officers, as reported on Internal Revenue Service Form 990 by private colleges and universities in the U.S. for the 1998-99 academic year. **Number listed:** 6.

David Roe, president, with $135,000 annual pay; $14,565 in benefits
Thomas Iverson, provost; senior VP, $90,000; $17,904
James Hamlin, VP, college advancement, $78,011; $15,886
Barbara Bowzer, VP, business and finance, $74,160; $9,710
Donald Meyer, professor, mathematics, $62,348; $13,163
John Olsen, VP, admissions and student enrollment services, $60,750; $11,893

Source: "Pay and Benefits of Leaders at 479 Private Colleges and Universities: a Survey," *The Chronicle of Higher Education*, 47: A29-A48, (November 24, 2000).

★3227★
Top pay and benefits for the chief executive and top paid employees at Centre College

Ranking basis/background: Annual pay and benefits for the chief executives and top paid officers, as reported on Internal Revenue Service Form 990 by private colleges and universities in the U.S. for the 1998-99 academic year. **Number listed:** 7.

John Roush, president, with $181,500 annual pay; $19,028 in benefits
John Ward, VP, academic affairs; dean of the college; professor, English, $107,800; $13,188
Richard L. Bauer, VP, finance; treasurer, $97,533; $12,074
Richard Trollinger, VP, college relations, $97,533; $12,074

Milton Reigelman, professor, English; director, international program, $91,132; $9,942
Walter Gooch, VP, administrative services, $86,250; $10,851
Carey Thompson, dean, admissions, $82,600; $9,503

Source: "Pay and Benefits of Leaders at 479 Private Colleges and Universities: a Survey," *The Chronicle of Higher Education*, 47: A29-A48, (November 24, 2000).

★3228★
Top pay and benefits for the chief executive and top paid employees at Chapman University

Ranking basis/background: Annual pay and benefits for the chief executives and top paid officers, as reported on Internal Revenue Service Form 990 by private colleges and universities in the U.S. for the 1998-99 academic year. **Number listed:** 6.

James L. Doti, president, with $174,290 annual pay; $69,756 in benefits
Gary Brahm, executive VP, finance and administration, $179,000; $57,871
Parham Williams, VP; dean, law school, $178,795; $19,801
Leonard Nelson III, associate dean, student and academic affairs, $142,980; $15,999
Harry Hamilton, senior VP; provost, $138,250; $14,846
Richard McDowell, dean, school of business and economics, $137,704; $13,978

Source: "Pay and Benefits of Leaders at 479 Private Colleges and Universities: a Survey," *The Chronicle of Higher Education*, 47: A29-A48, (November 24, 2000).

★3229★
Top pay and benefits for the chief executive and top paid employees at Charleston Southern University

Ranking basis/background: Annual pay and benefits for the chief executives and top paid officers, as reported on Internal Revenue Service Form 990 by private colleges and universities in the U.S. for the 1998-99 academic year. **Number listed:** 6.

Jairy C. Hunter Jr., president, with $157,070 annual pay; $30,823 in benefits
A. Kennerley Bonnette, VP, academic affairs; provost, $101,837; $8,056
Lester McTier Anderson, professor, business administration, $75,957; $6,643
Robert N. Stevens, VP, enrollment management, $75,900; $6,454
Kenton C. Brasher, VP, business affairs, $76,744; $4,488
Albert E. Parish Jr., director, MBA program, $66,898; $5,707

Source: "Pay and Benefits of Leaders at 479 Private Colleges and Universities: a Survey," *The Chronicle of Higher Education*, 47: A29-A48, (November 24, 2000).

★3230★
Top pay and benefits for the chief executive and top paid employees at Chatham College

Ranking basis/background: Annual pay and benefits for the chief executives and top paid officers, as reported on Internal Revenue Service Form 990 by private colleges and universities in the U.S. for the 1998-99 academic year. **Number listed:** 6.

Esther L. Barazzone, president, with $292,440 annual pay; $16,000 in benefits
Susan A. Bemis, assistant dean, health sciences; director, physical therapy, $116,706; $11,435
G. Timothy Bowman, VP, finance and administration, $108,481; $11,002
Anne C. Steele, VP, academic affairs; dean of the faculty, $107,933; $10,850
Mary Kay Poppenberg, VP, institutional advancement, $96,553; $9,800
Linda G. Allison, program and medical director, physician-assistant studies, $92,762; $9,313

Source: "Pay and Benefits of Leaders at 479 Private Colleges and Universities: a Survey," *The Chronicle of Higher Education*, 47: A29-A48, (November 24, 2000).

★3231★
Top pay and benefits for the chief executive and top paid employees at Chestnut Hill College

Ranking basis/background: Annual pay and benefits for the chief executives and top paid officers, as reported on Internal Revenue Service Form 990 by private colleges and universities in the U.S. for the 1998-99 academic year. **Number listed:** 6.

Sister Carol Jean Vale, S.S.J., president, with $0 annual pay; $0 in benefits
William Walker, VP, academic affairs, $79,900; $8,693
Elizabeth Kroger, VP, financial affairs, $72,000; $8,100
Lorraine Aurely, VP, institutional advancement, $62,903; $7,717
Kathleen Anderson, dean, accelerated divisions; VP, enrollment management, $60,103; $7,507
Scott Wells Browning, associate professor, psychology, $60,215; $7,141

Source: "Pay and Benefits of Leaders at 479 Private Colleges and Universities: a Survey," *The Chronicle of Higher Education*, 47: A29-A48, (November 24, 2000).

★3232★
Top pay and benefits for the chief executive and top paid employees at Christendom College

Ranking basis/background: Annual pay and benefits for the chief executives and top paid officers, as reported on Internal Revenue Service Form 990 by private colleges and universities in the U.S. for the 1998-99 academic year. **Number listed:** 4.

Timothy O'Donnell, president, with $113,854 annual pay; $3,117 in benefits
Mark McShurley, executive VP, $52,791; $1,443
Robert Rice, VP, academic affairs, $47,065; $1,298
John Ciskanik, VP, development, $46,566; $1,226

Source: "Pay and Benefits of Leaders at 479 Private Colleges and Universities: a Survey," *The Chronicle of Higher Education*, 47: A29-A48, (November 24, 2000).

★3233★
Top pay and benefits for the chief executive and top paid employees at Christian Brothers University

Ranking basis/background: Annual pay and benefits for the chief executives and top paid officers, as reported on Internal Revenue Service Form 990 by private colleges and universities in the U.S. for the 1998-99 academic year. **Number listed:** 6.

Bro. Michael J. McGinniss, F.S.C., president, with $0 annual pay; $0 in benefits
Nicholas W. Scully, VP, institutional advancement and student affairs, $92,268; $5,536
Ray S. House, dean, school of business, $83,304; $4,998
R. Craig Blackman, VP, information systems, $77,292; $4,638
Mark Smith, VP, academic affairs, $75,180; $4,511
Ray Brown, dean, engineering, $66,096; $3,966

Source: "Pay and Benefits of Leaders at 479 Private Colleges and Universities: a Survey," *The Chronicle of Higher Education*, 47: A29-A48, (November 24, 2000).

★3234★
Top pay and benefits for the chief executive and top paid employees at City University in Washington

Ranking basis/background: Annual pay and benefits for the chief executives and top paid officers, as reported on Internal Revenue Service Form 990 by private colleges and universities in the U.S. for the 1998-99 academic year. **Number listed:** 6.

Vi Tasler, acting president, with $41,923 annual pay; $0 in benefits
Earl Sedlik, director, business programs, $62,625; $0
Robert Dolan, dean, faculty development, $55,887; $4,117
Chris Rigos, dean, graduate business programs, $55,383; $2,920
Jodey Lingg, senior faculty, accounting and finance, $56,005; $1,594
Karen Dowdell, dean, undergraduate school of business, $54,955; $2,523

Source: "Pay and Benefits of Leaders at 479 Private Colleges and Universities: a Survey," *The Chronicle of Higher Education*, 47: A29-A48, (November 24, 2000).

★3235★
Top pay and benefits for the chief executive and top paid employees at Claremont Graduate University

Ranking basis/background: Annual pay and benefits for the chief executives and top paid officers, as reported on Internal Revenue Service Form 990 by private colleges and universities in the U.S. for the 1998-99 academic year. **Number listed:** 6.

Steadman Upham, president, with $175,000 annual pay; $33,956 in benefits

John Maguire, president emeritus; senior fellow, $171,921; $25,534
John Dorger, executive VP, Claremont University Center, $157,500; $25,516
Jacek Kugler, professor, politics and policy, $144,979; $22,654
Ann Weaver-Hart, provost, $137,500; $28,593
David Drew, dean; professor, education, $134,733; $24,732

Source: "Pay and Benefits of Leaders at 479 Private Colleges and Universities: a Survey," *The Chronicle of Higher Education*, 47: A29-A48, (November 24, 2000).

★3236★
Top pay and benefits for the chief executive and top paid employees at Claremont McKenna College

Ranking basis/background: Annual pay and benefits for the chief executives and top paid officers, as reported on Internal Revenue Service Form 990 by private colleges and universities in the U.S. for the 1998-99 academic year. **Number listed:** 6.

Jack L. Stark, president, with $267,279 annual pay; $30,574 in benefits
Jon C. Keates, VP, development, $141,500; $26,746
Anthony Fucaloro, VP; dean of the faculty, $139,500; $26,962
Ralph Rossum, research professor, political science, $139,125; $26,980
Frederick M. Weis, VP; treasurer, $137,300; $25,881
Chae-Jin Lee, director, Keck Center for International and Strategic Studies; professor, Pacific-basin studies, $133,000; $24,362

Source: "Pay and Benefits of Leaders at 479 Private Colleges and Universities: a Survey," *The Chronicle of Higher Education*, 47: A29-A48, (November 24, 2000).

★3237★
Top pay and benefits for the chief executive and top paid employees at Clark Atlanta University

Ranking basis/background: Annual pay and benefits for the chief executives and top paid officers, as reported on Internal Revenue Service Form 990 by private colleges and universities in the U.S. for the 1998-99 academic year. **Number listed:** 6.

Thomas W. Cole Jr., president, with $140,000 annual pay; $7,000 in benefits
Charles Teamer, VP, administration and finance, $159,400; $7,250
Ronald Mickens, professor, physics, $123,198; $6,159
Kofi Bota, VP, research and sponsored programs, $122,000; $6,100
Winfred Harris, VP, academic affairs; provost, $120,000; $6,000
Helena Mitchell, professor, distance learning, $118,750; $6,008

Source: "Pay and Benefits of Leaders at 479 Private Colleges and Universities: a Survey," *The Chronicle of Higher Education*, 47: A29-A48, (November 24, 2000).

★3238★
Top pay and benefits for the chief executive and top paid employees at Clark University

Ranking basis/background: Annual pay and benefits for the chief executives and top paid officers, as reported on Internal Revenue Service Form 990 by private colleges and universities in the U.S. for the 1998-99 academic year. **Number listed:** 6.

Richard P. Traina, president, with $146,800 annual pay; $46,811 in benefits
James E. Collins, VP; treasurer, $135,000; $14,618
Frederick Greenaway, provost, $122,341; $14,932
Harold M. Wingood, dean, admissions, $119,550; $16,549
Daeg S. Brenner, professor, chemistry, $118,500; $16,252
Roger E. Kasperson, professor, geography, $116,012; $16,025

Source: "Pay and Benefits of Leaders at 479 Private Colleges and Universities: a Survey," *The Chronicle of Higher Education*, 47: A29-A48, (November 24, 2000).

★3239★
Top pay and benefits for the chief executive and top paid employees at Clarkson University

Ranking basis/background: Annual pay and benefits for the chief executives and top paid officers, as reported on Internal Revenue Service Form 990 by private colleges and universities in the U.S. for the 1998-99 academic year. **Number listed:** 6.

Dennis G. Brown, president, with $170,000 annual pay; $82,725 in benefits
Anthony G. Collins, VP, academic affairs; dean, engineering, $142,500; $26,358
Janos H. Fendler, professor, chemistry, $138,250; $25,920
Stig Friberg, professor, chemistry, $137,334; $24,361
Philip K. Hopke, chair, professor, chemistry, $129,260; $22,801
Michael E. Cooper, VP, institutional advancement, $122,500; $25,224

Source: "Pay and Benefits of Leaders at 479 Private Colleges and Universities: a Survey," *The Chronicle of Higher Education*, 47: A29-A48, (November 24, 2000).

★3240★
Top pay and benefits for the chief executive and top paid employees at Coe College

Ranking basis/background: Annual pay and benefits for the chief executives and top paid officers, as reported on Internal Revenue Service Form 990 by private colleges and universities in the U.S. for the 1998-99 academic year. **Number listed:** 6.

James Phifer, president, with $153,000 annual pay; $15,233 in benefits
Richard Meisterling, VP, advancement, $105,545; $8,593
Richard Rheinschmidt, controller, $96,095; $10,170
Barron Bremner, director, athletics; assistant to the president, $92,483; $9,892

Laura Skandera Trombley, VP, academic affairs; dean of the faculty, $91,960; $9,852
Louis Stark, VP, student affairs; dean of students, $85,000; $9,317

Source: "Pay and Benefits of Leaders at 479 Private Colleges and Universities: a Survey," *The Chronicle of Higher Education*, 47: A29-A48, (November 24, 2000).

★3241★
Top pay and benefits for the chief executive and top paid employees at Colby College

Ranking basis/background: Annual pay and benefits for the chief executives and top paid officers, as reported on Internal Revenue Service Form 990 by private colleges and universities in the U.S. for the 1998-99 academic year. **Number listed:** 6.

William R. Cotter, president, with $222,000 annual pay; $57,415 in benefits
Robert L. McArthur, professor, philosophy, $155,353; $26,480
Peyton R. Helm, VP, development and alumni relations, $150,000; $23,166
W. Arnold Yasinski, administrative VP, $142,000; $22,241
Douglas Archibald, professor, English, $138,696; $23,338
Edward H. Yeterian, VP, academic affairs; dean of the faculty, $136,000; $23,235

Source: "Pay and Benefits of Leaders at 479 Private Colleges and Universities: a Survey," *The Chronicle of Higher Education*, 47: A29-A48, (November 24, 2000).

★3242★
Top pay and benefits for the chief executive and top paid employees at Colgate University

Ranking basis/background: Annual pay and benefits for the chief executives and top paid officers, as reported on Internal Revenue Service Form 990 by private colleges and universities in the U.S. for the 1998-99 academic year. **Number listed:** 6.

Neil R. Grabois, president, with $240,500 annual pay; $37,609 in benefits
Elizabeth Eismeier, VP, finance; treasurer, $128,500; $27,114
Jane L. Pinchin, provost; dean of the faculty, $123,800; $29,398
Robert L. Tyburski, VP, university relations, $119,700; $25,647
Merrill L. Miller, director, student health services, $118,700; $25,534
Charles E. McClennen, associate dean of the faculty; professor, geology, $116,200; $27,901

Source: "Pay and Benefits of Leaders at 479 Private Colleges and Universities: a Survey," *The Chronicle of Higher Education*, 47: A29-A48, (November 24, 2000).

★3243★
Top pay and benefits for the chief executive and top paid employees at College Misericordia

Ranking basis/background: Annual pay and benefits for the chief executives and top paid officers, as reported on Internal Revenue Service Form 990 by private colleges and universities in the U.S. for the 1998-99 academic year. **Number listed:** 6.

- Michael MacDowell, president, with $117,173 annual pay; $23,722 in benefits
- David Payne, chair, humanities; associate professor, literature, language, and communication, $74,963; $45,627
- Helen J. Speziali, chair, health sciences; professor, nursing, $77,327; $12,384
- Catherine Wilkinson, chair and professor, health sciences, $76,579; $11,157
- John Risboskin, VP, finance and administration, $78,179; $8,900
- Margo Holm, professor, occupational therapy, $68,456; $16,143

Source: "Pay and Benefits of Leaders at 479 Private Colleges and Universities: a Survey," *The Chronicle of Higher Education*, 47: A29-A48, (November 24, 2000).

★3244★
Top pay and benefits for the chief executive and top paid employees at College of Mount St. Joseph

Ranking basis/background: Annual pay and benefits for the chief executives and top paid officers, as reported on Internal Revenue Service Form 990 by private colleges and universities in the U.S. for the 1998-99 academic year. **Remarks:** Sister Thrailkill's pay is donated to the Ursulines of the Roman Union, Ursuline Provincialate. **Number listed:** 6.

- Sister Francis Marie Thrailkill, O.S.U., president, with $122,010 annual pay; $13,112 in benefits
- Susan C. Wajert, assistant professor, management of health-care services, $75,976; $29,487
- Gene Kritsky, chair, health sciences, $81,522; $15,476
- Mark Pavlovich, VP, institutional advancement, $78,860; $13,835
- Joseph J. Ahern, chair, business administration, $71,949; $16,294
- Anne Marie Wagner, executive director, business and finance, $70,965; $12,215

Source: "Pay and Benefits of Leaders at 479 Private Colleges and Universities: a Survey," *The Chronicle of Higher Education*, 47: A29-A48, (November 24, 2000).

★3245★
Top pay and benefits for the chief executive and top paid employees at College of Saint Benedict

Ranking basis/background: Annual pay and benefits for the chief executives and top paid officers, as reported on Internal Revenue Service Form 990 by private colleges and universities in the U.S. for the 1998-99 academic year. **Number listed:** 6.

- Mary E. Lyons, president, with $180,769 annual pay; $25,631 in benefits
- Clark Hendley, provost, $112,200; $19,882
- Sister Miriam Ardolf, O.S.B., VP, finance and administrative services, $101,653; $19,127
- Charles J. Villette, dean; rector, Benedictine University College, the Bahamas, $95,645; $15,310
- Gilbert Hayes, executive director, institutional marketing and communications, $89,606; $18,634
- Kathleen Allen, VP, student development, $89,720; $15,713

Source: "Pay and Benefits of Leaders at 479 Private Colleges and Universities: a Survey," *The Chronicle of Higher Education*, 47: A29-A48, (November 24, 2000).

★3246★
Top pay and benefits for the chief executive and top paid employees at College of the Atlantic

Ranking basis/background: Annual pay and benefits for the chief executives and top paid officers, as reported on Internal Revenue Service Form 990 by private colleges and universities in the U.S. for the 1998-99 academic year. **Number listed:** 6.

- Steven K. Katona, president, with $111,183 annual pay; $5,559 in benefits
- Richard Borden, dean, academics, $67,801; $3,390
- Fran Day, director, development, $67,218; $3,361
- William Carpenter, professor, literature, $61,359; $3,068
- JoAnne Carpenter, professor, art, $58,998; $2,950
- Clair Bradstreet, comptroller, $58,101; $2,950

Source: "Pay and Benefits of Leaders at 479 Private Colleges and Universities: a Survey," *The Chronicle of Higher Education*, 47: A29-A48, (November 24, 2000).

★3247★
Top pay and benefits for the chief executive and top paid employees at College of the Holy Cross

Ranking basis/background: Annual pay and benefits for the chief executives and top paid officers, as reported on Internal Revenue Service Form 990 by private colleges and universities in the U.S. for the 1998-99 academic year. **Number listed:** 6.

- Frank Vellaccio, acting president, with $196,960 annual pay; $20,201 in benefits
- Diane Bell, professor, $308,114; $10,639
- William R. Durgin, VP; treasurer, $197,067; $20,218
- Stephen King, director, information-technology services, $126,700; $42,733
- Paul Sheff, VP, development and alumni relations, $133,900; $30,378
- Gerard Zimmermann, director, physical plant, $131,500; $17,422

Source: "Pay and Benefits of Leaders at 479 Private Colleges and Universities: a Survey," *The Chronicle of Higher Education*, 47: A29-A48, (November 24, 2000).

★3248★
Top pay and benefits for the chief executive and top paid employees at Colorado Christian University

Ranking basis/background: Annual pay and benefits for the chief executives and top paid officers, as reported on Internal Revenue Service Form 990 by private colleges and universities in the U.S. for the 1998-99 academic year. **Number listed:** 6.

- Larry Donnithorne, president, with $126,250 annual pay; $6,312 in benefits
- John White, VP, finance, $99,775; $7,152
- Gary Ewen, executive director, information-systems group, $93,153; $8,264
- Sidney Buzzel, VP, academic affairs, $89,480; $8,630
- Sandra Kay Baylock, VP, support operations, $85,870; $9,583
- Thomas Varney, dean and professor, counseling and spiritual theology, $82,500; $7,732

Source: "Pay and Benefits of Leaders at 479 Private Colleges and Universities: a Survey," *The Chronicle of Higher Education*, 47: A29-A48, (November 24, 2000).

★3249★
Top pay and benefits for the chief executive and top paid employees at Colorado College

Ranking basis/background: Annual pay and benefits for the chief executives and top paid officers, as reported on Internal Revenue Service Form 990 by private colleges and universities in the U.S. for the 1998-99 academic year. **Number listed:** 6.

- Kathryn Mohrman, president, with $185,000 annual pay; $22,809 in benefits
- Janice Legoza, VP, business and finance, $131,200; $21,537
- Don Wilson, VP, alumni development and college relations, $130,000; $22,521
- Timothy Fuller, dean of the college, $127,500; $23,289
- Donald J. Lucia, head coach, hockey, $107,683; $19,236
- Robert D. Loevy, professor, political science, $98,538; $18,268

Source: "Pay and Benefits of Leaders at 479 Private Colleges and Universities: a Survey," *The Chronicle of Higher Education*, 47: A29-A48, (November 24, 2000).

★3250★
Top pay and benefits for the chief executive and top paid employees at Columbia College in Illinois

Ranking basis/background: Annual pay and benefits for the chief executives and top paid officers, as reported on Internal Revenue Service Form 990 by private colleges and universities in the U.S. for the 1998-99 academic year. **Number listed:** 6.

- John B. Duff, president, with $226,082 annual pay; $174,814 in benefits
- Zafra Lerman, head, Institute for Science Education and Science Communication, $181,553; $46,767
- Albert C. Gall, executive VP; provost, $149,067; $43,230

Samuel A. Floyd, director, Center for Black Music Research, $153,767; $38,189
R. Michael DeSalle, VP, finance, $138,266; $40,097
Philip J. Klukoff, associate VP, continuing education, $141,782; $32,298

Source: "Pay and Benefits of Leaders at 479 Private Colleges and Universities: a Survey," *The Chronicle of Higher Education*, 47: A29-A48, (November 24, 2000).

★3251★
Top pay and benefits for the chief executive and top paid employees at Columbia University

Ranking basis/background: Annual pay and benefits for the chief executives and top paid officers, as reported on Internal Revenue Service Form 990 by private colleges and universities in the U.S. for the 1998-99 academic year. **Number listed:** 6.

George Rupp, president, with $472,750 annual pay; $27,454 in benefits
Eric Allen Rose, professor; chair, surgery, $1,875,000; $25,440
Craig Richey Smith, professor, surgery, $1,010,000; $27,488
Mehmet C. Oz, associate professor, surgery, $898,333; $25,878
Jan Modest Quaegebeaur, professor, surgery, $900,000; $23,645
Lanny G. Close, professor, otolaryngology, $884,585; $24,198

Source: "Pay and Benefits of Leaders at 479 Private Colleges and Universities: a Survey," *The Chronicle of Higher Education*, 47: A29-A48, (November 24, 2000).

★3252★
Top pay and benefits for the chief executive and top paid employees at Concordia College-Moorhead

Ranking basis/background: Annual pay and benefits for the chief executives and top paid officers, as reported on Internal Revenue Service Form 990 by private colleges and universities in the U.S. for the 1998-99 academic year. **Number listed:** 2.

Paul J. Dovre, president, with $140,667 annual pay; $21,146 in benefits
Clyde E. Allen Jr., VP, business affairs; treasurer, $106,667; $16,543

Source: "Pay and Benefits of Leaders at 479 Private Colleges and Universities: a Survey," *The Chronicle of Higher Education*, 47: A29-A48, (November 24, 2000).

★3253★
Top pay and benefits for the chief executive and top paid employees at Concordia University in Illinois

Ranking basis/background: Annual pay and benefits for the chief executives and top paid officers, as reported on Internal Revenue Service Form 990 by private colleges and universities in the U.S. for the 1998-99 academic year. **Number listed:** 6.

George C. Heider, president, with $79,857 annual pay; $6,930 in benefits
Alan Zacharias, senior VP, university advancement, $114,275; $5,400
Dianne Dinkel, VP, administration, $73,630; $3,465
Myrna S. Marseille, director, deferred giving, $65,333; $3,012
Norman E. Young, provost, $29,508; $6,024
Robert Hayes, VP, student services, $25,173; $3,201

Source: "Pay and Benefits of Leaders at 479 Private Colleges and Universities: a Survey," *The Chronicle of Higher Education*, 47: A29-A48, (November 24, 2000).

★3254★
Top pay and benefits for the chief executive and top paid employees at Connecticut College

Ranking basis/background: Annual pay and benefits for the chief executives and top paid officers, as reported on Internal Revenue Service Form 990 by private colleges and universities in the U.S. for the 1998-99 academic year. **Number listed:** 6.

Claire Gaudiani, president, with $264,221 annual pay; $35,166 in benefits
Frank V. Church, professor, music, $56,683; $284,867
Brian Rogers, librarian, $64,363; $168,981
Lynn Alan Brooks, VP, finance, $144,360; $44,467
Claire Matthews, VP, development, $134,560; $27,686
David K. Lewis, provost, $126,360; $24,918

Source: "Pay and Benefits of Leaders at 479 Private Colleges and Universities: a Survey," *The Chronicle of Higher Education*, 47: A29-A48, (November 24, 2000).

★3255★
Top pay and benefits for the chief executive and top paid employees at Converse College

Ranking basis/background: Annual pay and benefits for the chief executives and top paid officers, as reported on Internal Revenue Service Form 990 by private colleges and universities in the U.S. for the 1998-99 academic year. **Number listed:** 6.

Charles Glassick, president, with $66,000 annual pay; $0 in benefits
Thomas McDaniel, provost, $99,819; $9,082
Anita P. Davis, professor, education, $100,661; $6,256
John Hegman, VP, finance and administration, $88,022; $8,802
Scott Rawles, VP, institutional advancement, $84,719; $8,052
Joe P. Dunn, professor and chair, history and politics; director, summer programs, $81,183; $7,918

Source: "Pay and Benefits of Leaders at 479 Private Colleges and Universities: a Survey," *The Chronicle of Higher Education*, 47: A29-A48, (November 24, 2000).

★3256★
Top pay and benefits for the chief executive and top paid employees at Cornell College in Iowa

Ranking basis/background: Annual pay and benefits for the chief executives and top paid officers, as reported on Internal Revenue Service Form 990 by private colleges and universities in the U.S. for the 1998-99 academic year. **Number listed:** 6.

Leslie H. Garner Jr., president, with $150,000 annual pay; $14,800 in benefits
Terry G. Gibson, VP, alumni and college advancement, $119,325; $12,193
Glenn W. Dodd, VP, business affairs, $114,986; $11,824
Dennis D. Moore, VP, academic affairs; dean of the college, $95,460; $10,164
Joan M. Claar, VP; dean of students, $83,799; $9,173
Harlan D. Graber, professor, physics, $73,969; $8,337

Source: "Pay and Benefits of Leaders at 479 Private Colleges and Universities: a Survey," *The Chronicle of Higher Education*, 47: A29-A48, (November 24, 2000).

★3257★
Top pay and benefits for the chief executive and top paid employees at Cornell University

Ranking basis/background: Annual pay and benefits for the chief executives and top paid officers, as reported on Internal Revenue Service Form 990 by private colleges and universities in the U.S. for the 1998-99 academic year. **Number listed:** 6.

Hunter R. Rawlings III, president, with $204,670 annual pay; $220,760 in benefits
Zev Rosenwaks, professor, reproductive medicine in obstetrics and gynecology, $1,831,721; $49,888
O. Wayne Isom, chair, cardiothoracic surgery, $1,520,858; $29,396
Karl H. Krieger, professor, cardiothoracic surgery, $1,253,150; $12,401
Samuel J. Lang, associate professor, clinical cardiothoracic surgery in pediatrics, $893,710; $12,087
Owen Davis, associate professor, obstetrics and gynecology, $805,513; $12,033

Source: "Pay and Benefits of Leaders at 479 Private Colleges and Universities: a Survey," *The Chronicle of Higher Education*, 47: A29-A48, (November 24, 2000).

★3258★
Top pay and benefits for the chief executive and top paid employees at Cornerstone University

Ranking basis/background: Annual pay and benefits for the chief executives and top paid officers, as reported on Internal Revenue Service Form 990 by private colleges and universities in the U.S. for the 1998-99 academic year. **Number listed:** 6.

Rex M. Rogers, president, with $114,974 annual pay; $17,050 in benefits
John R. Lillis, executive VP; provost, $74,286; $13,141
Robert Nienhuis, VP, seminary, $71,400; $12,081
Jack P. Powell, associate provost, $70,000; $12,026
Robert Mol, VP, business, $66,931; $11,898
Lee Geysbeek, VP, broadcasting, $52,216; $10,675

Source: "Pay and Benefits of Leaders at 479 Private Colleges and Universities: a Survey," *The Chronicle of Higher Education*, 47: A29-A48, (November 24, 2000).

★3259★
Top pay and benefits for the chief executive and top paid employees at Creighton University

Ranking basis/background: Annual pay and benefits for the chief executives and top paid officers, as reported on Internal Revenue Service Form 990 by private colleges and universities in the U.S. for the 1998-99 academic year. **Remarks:** Reverend Morrison's pay is donated to the Wisconsin Province of the Society of Jesus. **Number listed:** 6.

- Rev. Michael G. Morrison, S.J., president, with $0 annual pay; $0 in benefits
- Jeffrey T. Sugimoto, associate professor, cardio surgery, $442,343; $23,838
- Michael H. McGuire, professor, surgery, $417,358; $27,977
- Joel N. Bleicher, associate professor, plastic surgery, $396,804; $26,055
- Tammy K. Ramos, assistant professor, surgery, $379,141; $28,311
- Robert J. Fitzgibbons Jr., professor, general surgery, $360,031; $22,530

Source: "Pay and Benefits of Leaders at 479 Private Colleges and Universities: a Survey," *The Chronicle of Higher Education*, 47: A29-A48, (November 24, 2000).

★3260★
Top pay and benefits for the chief executive and top paid employees at Cumberland College

Ranking basis/background: Annual pay and benefits for the chief executives and top paid officers, as reported on Internal Revenue Service Form 990 by private colleges and universities in the U.S. for the 1998-99 academic year. **Number listed:** 5.

- James H. Taylor, president, with $96,255 annual pay; $4,457 in benefits
- Joseph E. Early, VP, academic affairs, $70,009; $6,504
- George G. Ramey, VP, business affairs, $69,546; $6,488
- Sue Wake, VP, institutional advancement, $61,812; $6,080
- Reinhold Henkelmann, director, Life Science Museum, $55,000; $3,300

Source: "Pay and Benefits of Leaders at 479 Private Colleges and Universities: a Survey," *The Chronicle of Higher Education*, 47: A29-A48, (November 24, 2000).

★3261★
Top pay and benefits for the chief executive and top paid employees at Curry College

Ranking basis/background: Annual pay and benefits for the chief executives and top paid officers, as reported on Internal Revenue Service Form 990 by private colleges and universities in the U.S. for the 1998-99 academic year. **Number listed:** 6.

- Kenneth K. Quigley Jr., president, with $177,192 annual pay; $0 in benefits
- Gerard F. Linskey, VP, finance, $96,389; $0
- Bruce D. Steinberg, chair, behavioral sciences and education, $86,946; $0
- Dennis M. Thibeault, director, information services, $86,242; $0
- James Salvucci, professor, management, $85,689; $0
- Peter C. Hainer, director, experiential education, career development and placement, $84,406; $0

Source: "Pay and Benefits of Leaders at 479 Private Colleges and Universities: a Survey," *The Chronicle of Higher Education*, 47: A29-A48, (November 24, 2000).

★3262★
Top pay and benefits for the chief executive and top paid employees at Dallas Baptist University

Ranking basis/background: Annual pay and benefits for the chief executives and top paid officers, as reported on Internal Revenue Service Form 990 by private colleges and universities in the U.S. for the 1998-99 academic year. **Number listed:** 6.

- Gary R. Cook, president, with $150,870 annual pay; $8,671 in benefits
- Harold E. Norris, senior VP, financial affairs, $119,272; $10,000
- Andrew C. Schaffer, assistant professor, finance and business, $84,242; $10,202
- Gail G. Linam, academic dean; VP, undergraduate affairs, $82,905; $10,004
- Larry H. Linamen, provost; VP, graduate affairs, $88,482; $4,424
- David H. Arnott, assistant professor, management, $79,476; $10,000

Source: "Pay and Benefits of Leaders at 479 Private Colleges and Universities: a Survey," *The Chronicle of Higher Education*, 47: A29-A48, (November 24, 2000).

★3263★
Top pay and benefits for the chief executive and top paid employees at Dartmouth College

Ranking basis/background: Annual pay and benefits for the chief executives and top paid officers, as reported on Internal Revenue Service Form 990 by private colleges and universities in the U.S. for the 1998-99 academic year. **Number listed:** 6.

- James E. Wright, president, with $306,630 annual pay; $56,852 in benefits
- James O. Freedman, president emeritus, $834,928; $85,981
- John C. Baldwin, VP, health affairs; dean, medical school, $425,000; $76,292
- Andrew G. Wallace, dean, emeritus, medical school; VP emeritus, health affairs, $308,700; $55,248
- Richard W. Dow, chief surgical services, Veterans Administration Hospital, $296,018; $53,091
- Vijay Govindarajan, professor, international business, $252,984; $28,192

Source: "Pay and Benefits of Leaders at 479 Private Colleges and Universities: a Survey," *The Chronicle of Higher Education*, 47: A29-A48, (November 24, 2000).

★3264★
Top pay and benefits for the chief executive and top paid employees at Davidson College

Ranking basis/background: Annual pay and benefits for the chief executives and top paid officers, as reported on Internal Revenue Service Form 990 by private colleges and universities in the U.S. for the 1998-99 academic year. **Number listed:** 6.

- Robert F. Vagt, president, with $236,731 annual pay; $27,584 in benefits
- John W. Kuykendall, president emeritus; professor, religion, $150,629; $23,920
- James W. May Jr., VP, college relations, $120,879; $46,747
- Robert C. Norfleet, VP, business and finance, $136,369; $22,205
- Clark G. Ross, VP, academic affairs; dean of the faculty, $123,291; $21,006
- Julio J. Ramirez, professor, psychology, $119,798; $18,773

Source: "Pay and Benefits of Leaders at 479 Private Colleges and Universities: a Survey," *The Chronicle of Higher Education*, 47: A29-A48, (November 24, 2000).

★3265★
Top pay and benefits for the chief executive and top paid employees at Denison University

Ranking basis/background: Annual pay and benefits for the chief executives and top paid officers, as reported on Internal Revenue Service Form 990 by private colleges and universities in the U.S. for the 1998-99 academic year. **Number listed:** 7.

- Michele Tolela Myers, president, with $119,875 annual pay; $17,739 in benefits
- Dale T. Knobel, president, $96,000; $15,674
- Mary Jane McDonald, VP, university resources and public affairs, $130,050; $22,273
- Charles J. Morris, provost, $114,975; $27,780
- Samuel J. Thios, VP, student affairs; dean of students, $108,118; $28,215
- Seth H. Patton, VP, finance and management, $113,112; $18,759
- Ronald Winters, professor, physics and astronomy, $103,558; $26,313

Source: "Pay and Benefits of Leaders at 479 Private Colleges and Universities: a Survey," *The Chronicle of Higher Education*, 47: A29-A48, (November 24, 2000).

★3266★
Top pay and benefits for the chief executive and top paid employees at DePaul University

Ranking basis/background: Annual pay and benefits for the chief executives and top paid officers, as reported on Internal Revenue Service Form 990 by private colleges and universities in the U.S. for the 1998-99 academic year. **Remarks:** The institutions paid $841,817 to the Congregation of the Mission-Vincentian Fathers of DePaul University on behalf of the president and other members of the order. **Number listed:** 7.

- Rev. John P. Minogue, C.M., president, with $0 annual pay; $0 in benefits
- Rev. John T. Richardson, C.M., chancellor, $0; $0
- Joseph P. Kennedy, head coach, men's basketball, $219,213; $48,290
- Richard J. Meister, executive VP, academic affairs, $214,860; $32,146
- Helmut P. Epp, dean, school of computer science, telecommunication and information systems, $215,923; $25,486
- Kenneth A. McHugh, executive VP; VP, business and finance, $209,044; $29,941

M. Cherif Bassiouni, professor, law, $198,637; $30,329

Source: "Pay and Benefits of Leaders at 479 Private Colleges and Universities: a Survey," *The Chronicle of Higher Education*, 47: A29-A48, (November 24, 2000).

★3267★
Top pay and benefits for the chief executive and top paid employees at DePauw University

Ranking basis/background: Annual pay and benefits for the chief executives and top paid officers, as reported on Internal Revenue Service Form 990 by private colleges and universities in the U.S. for the 1998-99 academic year. **Number listed:** 6.

- Robert G. Bottoms, president, with $180,772 annual pay; $75,483 in benefits
- Thomas E. Dixon, VP, finance and administration, $127,975; $32,553
- James Lincoln, VP, student services, $146,645; $11,841
- Paul W. Hartman, VP, development and alumni relations, $123,792; $29,841
- Madeleine R. Eagon, VP, admissions and financial aid, $99,268; $24,999
- Stephen K. Gauly, executive director, development, $87,894; $34,099

Source: "Pay and Benefits of Leaders at 479 Private Colleges and Universities: a Survey," *The Chronicle of Higher Education*, 47: A29-A48, (November 24, 2000).

★3268★
Top pay and benefits for the chief executive and top paid employees at Dickinson College

Ranking basis/background: Annual pay and benefits for the chief executives and top paid officers, as reported on Internal Revenue Service Form 990 by private colleges and universities in the U.S. for the 1998-99 academic year. **Number listed:** 7.

- A. Lee Fritschler, president, with $310,541 annual pay; $47,732 in benefits
- Robert E. Freelen, VP, external affairs, $137,920; $24,826
- Neil Weissman, dean, academic affairs, $120,750; $21,735
- Betsy K. Emerick, dean, education services, $96,075; $17,294
- Priscilla W. Laws, professor, physics, $95,847; $17,252
- Annette S. Parker, $89,600; $16,128
- Nickolas Stamos, VP, campus operations, $89,600; $16,128

Source: "Pay and Benefits of Leaders at 479 Private Colleges and Universities: a Survey," *The Chronicle of Higher Education*, 47: A29-A48, (November 24, 2000).

★3269★
Top pay and benefits for the chief executive and top paid employees at Dominican University in Illinois

Ranking basis/background: Annual pay and benefits for the chief executives and top paid officers, as reported on Internal Revenue Service Form 990 by private colleges and universities in the U.S. for the 1998-99 academic year. **Number listed:** 6.

- Donna M. Carroll, president, with $121,275 annual pay; $27,494 in benefits
- Norman E. Carroll, VP, academic affairs, $103,786; $20,601
- Maryalyce Burke, dean, business, $92,629; $19,592
- Hugh McElwain, dean, arts and sciences, $92,476; $19,578
- Amy McCormack, VP, business affairs, $96,062; $12,215
- Prudence Dalrymple, dean, life sciences, $88,253; $19,196

Source: "Pay and Benefits of Leaders at 479 Private Colleges and Universities: a Survey," *The Chronicle of Higher Education*, 47: A29-A48, (November 24, 2000).

★3270★
Top pay and benefits for the chief executive and top paid employees at Dominican University of California

Ranking basis/background: Annual pay and benefits for the chief executives and top paid officers, as reported on Internal Revenue Service Form 990 by private colleges and universities in the U.S. for the 1998-99 academic year. **Number listed:** 6.

- Joseph R. Fink, president, with $278,119 annual pay; $43,601 in benefits
- Jeffrey V. Bialik, executive VP, $148,344; $13,701
- Vern Ummel, VP, institutional advancement, $109,194; $15,086
- Denise M. Lucy, VP, academic affairs, $111,514; $9,048
- Charles R. Billings, professor, psychology, $97,149; $8,255
- Sherry Volk, dean, arts and sciences, $94,171; $8,091

Source: "Pay and Benefits of Leaders at 479 Private Colleges and Universities: a Survey," *The Chronicle of Higher Education*, 47: A29-A48, (November 24, 2000).

★3271★
Top pay and benefits for the chief executive and top paid employees at Dowling College

Ranking basis/background: Annual pay and benefits for the chief executives and top paid officers, as reported on Internal Revenue Service Form 990 by private colleges and universities in the U.S. for the 1998-99 academic year. **Number listed:** 6.

- Victor P. Meskill, president, with $385,700 annual pay; $66,079 in benefits
- Barbara Ellen Black, treasurer, $227,970; $24,620
- Joseph Monahan, associate professor, finance, $213,412; $17,588
- Russell T. Lauper, chief of staff, $189,394; $29,081
- Clifford R. Bragdon, VP, advanced technologies, $178,542; $21,440
- Albert E. Donor, provost, $160,313; $27,441

Source: "Pay and Benefits of Leaders at 479 Private Colleges and Universities: a Survey," *The Chronicle of Higher Education*, 47: A29-A48, (November 24, 2000).

★3272★
Top pay and benefits for the chief executive and top paid employees at Drake University

Ranking basis/background: Annual pay and benefits for the chief executives and top paid officers, as reported on Internal Revenue Service Form 990 by private colleges and universities in the U.S. for the 1998-99 academic year. **Number listed:** 8.

- Robert D. Ray, president, with $256,106 annual pay; $314 in benefits
- Michael R. Ferrari, president, $38,554; $4,156
- David E. Maxwell, president, $7,500; $0
- Peter Goplerud, dean, law, $173,000; $17,577
- R. Barbara Gitenstein, provost, $145,026; $11,320
- Victoria F. Payseur, VP, business and finance, $140,000; $13,669
- Patrick Heaston, director and professor, accounting, $128,268; $10,791
- James Romig, director, Drake curriculum, $125,191; $11,929

Source: "Pay and Benefits of Leaders at 479 Private Colleges and Universities: a Survey," *The Chronicle of Higher Education*, 47: A29-A48, (November 24, 2000).

★3273★
Top pay and benefits for the chief executive and top paid employees at Drew University

Ranking basis/background: Annual pay and benefits for the chief executives and top paid officers, as reported on Internal Revenue Service Form 990 by private colleges and universities in the U.S. for the 1998-99 academic year. **Number listed:** 6.

- Thomas H. Kean, president, with $137,520 annual pay; $14,247 in benefits
- Leonard V. Sweet, VP; dean, theological school, $170,639; $17,627
- Margaret E. L. Howard, VP, administration and university relations, $151,226; $12,826
- Paolo Cucchi, VP; dean, college of liberal arts, $141,474; $17,654
- Joseph Angeletti, VP, development and alumni affairs, $138,173; $19,059
- Michael B. McKitish, VP, finance and business affairs, $138,173; $13,278

Source: "Pay and Benefits of Leaders at 479 Private Colleges and Universities: a Survey," *The Chronicle of Higher Education*, 47: A29-A48, (November 24, 2000).

★3274★
Top pay and benefits for the chief executive and top paid employees at Drexel University

Ranking basis/background: Annual pay and benefits for the chief executives and top paid officers, as reported on Internal Revenue Service Form 990 by private colleges and universities in the U.S. for the 1998-99 academic year. **Number listed:** 6.

- Constantine N. Papadakis, president, with $390,000 annual pay; $45,738 in benefits
- Ahmet Aktan, professor, infrastructure, $234,154; $35,592

Richard A. Astro, provost; senior VP, academic affairs, $215,087; $28,527
Anthony T. Caneris, senior VP, student life and administrative services, $197,627; $29,115
Frank J. Bachich, senior VP, finance; treasurer, $194,747; $27,708
Barbara S. Spiro, senior VP, institutional affairs, $190,577; $30,611

Source: "Pay and Benefits of Leaders at 479 Private Colleges and Universities: a Survey," *The Chronicle of Higher Education*, 47: A29-A48, (November 24, 2000).

★3275★
Top pay and benefits for the chief executive and top paid employees at Drury University

Ranking basis/background: Annual pay and benefits for the chief executives and top paid officers, as reported on Internal Revenue Service Form 990 by private colleges and universities in the U.S. for the 1998-99 academic year. **Number listed:** 6.

John E. Moore Jr., president, with $135,358 annual pay; $6,700 in benefits
Rabindra Roy, chair, chemistry, $102,963; $3,845
Stephen H. Good, VP, academic affairs, $92,456; $4,495
Thomas Zimmerer, director, Breech School; professor, business administration, $90,583; $5,400
Paul J. Nowak, professor, business administration, $83,376; $10,006
Judy Martin, VP, development and alumni relations, $84,558; $4,992

Source: "Pay and Benefits of Leaders at 479 Private Colleges and Universities: a Survey," *The Chronicle of Higher Education*, 47: A29-A48, (November 24, 2000).

★3276★
Top pay and benefits for the chief executive and top paid employees at Duke University

Ranking basis/background: Annual pay and benefits for the chief executives and top paid officers, as reported on Internal Revenue Service Form 990 by private colleges and universities in the U.S. for the 1998-99 academic year. **Number listed:** 6.

Nannerl O. Keohane, president, with $350,000 annual pay; $27,889 in benefits
Mike Kryzewski, head coach, men's basketball, $521,500; $30,387
Ralph Snyderman, chancellor, health affairs; dean, school of medicine; professor, medicine and immunology, $400,300; $28,622
Eugene J. McDonald, executive VP, asset management, $377,700; $28,292
Alvis Swinney, vice chancellor, $270,000; $24,514
Tallman Trask III, executive VP, $265,000; $27,338

Source: "Pay and Benefits of Leaders at 479 Private Colleges and Universities: a Survey," *The Chronicle of Higher Education*, 47: A29-A48, (November 24, 2000).

★3277★
Top pay and benefits for the chief executive and top paid employees at Duquesne University

Ranking basis/background: Annual pay and benefits for the chief executives and top paid officers, as reported on Internal Revenue Service Form 990 by private colleges and universities in the U.S. for the 1998-99 academic year. **Number listed:** 5.

John E. Murray Jr., president, with $398,380 annual pay; $44,265 in benefits
Isadore R. Lenglet, executive VP, management and business, $199,810; $28,649
Michael P. Weber, provost; VP, academics, $194,911; $29,074
Nicholas P. Cafardi, dean, law, $151,357; $24,897
Thomas J. Murrin, dean, business, $148,361; $20,318

Source: "Pay and Benefits of Leaders at 479 Private Colleges and Universities: a Survey," *The Chronicle of Higher Education*, 47: A29-A48, (November 24, 2000).

★3278★
Top pay and benefits for the chief executive and top paid employees at D'Youville College

Ranking basis/background: Annual pay and benefits for the chief executives and top paid officers, as reported on Internal Revenue Service Form 990 by private colleges and universities in the U.S. for the 1998-99 academic year. **Remarks:** Sister Roche's pay is donated to the Grey Nuns of the Sacred Heart. **Number listed:** 6.

Sister Denise A. Roche, president, with $116,025 annual pay; $6,962 in benefits
James P. Klyczek, dean, school of health and human sciences, $102,542; $6,153
Donald Keller, VP, operations, $86,512; $3,906
Michael R. Cipolla, VP, finance; treasurer, $84,278; $5,057
Robert A. DiSibio, dean, arts and sciences, $80,441; $3,818
Robert P. Murphy, VP, student affairs, $73,087; $4,385

Source: "Pay and Benefits of Leaders at 479 Private Colleges and Universities: a Survey," *The Chronicle of Higher Education*, 47: A29-A48, (November 24, 2000).

★3279★
Top pay and benefits for the chief executive and top paid employees at Earlham College

Ranking basis/background: Annual pay and benefits for the chief executives and top paid officers, as reported on Internal Revenue Service Form 990 by private colleges and universities in the U.S. for the 1998-99 academic year. **Number listed:** 6.

Douglas Bennett, president, with $164,042 annual pay; $0 in benefits
Leonard Clark, provost; academic dean; professor, philosophy, $116,660; $11,664
Richard K. Smith, VP, financial affairs, $111,700; $11,172
James P. Thompson, VP, institutional advancement and alumni development, $106,050; $10,608
Paul A. Lacey, professor, English, $89,900; $9,000
Jeffrey Rickey, dean, admissions and financial aid, $91,300; $0

Source: "Pay and Benefits of Leaders at 479 Private Colleges and Universities: a Survey," *The Chronicle of Higher Education*, 47: A29-A48, (November 24, 2000).

★3280★
Top pay and benefits for the chief executive and top paid employees at Eastern College in Pennsylvania

Ranking basis/background: Annual pay and benefits for the chief executives and top paid officers, as reported on Internal Revenue Service Form 990 by private colleges and universities in the U.S. for the 1998-99 academic year. **Number listed:** 5.

David Black, president, with $150,150 annual pay; $25,483 in benefits
Harold C. Howard, provost, $95,658; $11,800
John A. Schauss, chief operating officer, $89,612; $12,467
Alvin Jepson, VP, board and college relations, $86,725; $11,470
Allen Guelzo, dean, Templeton Honors College and Eastern College, $82,550; $6,947

Source: "Pay and Benefits of Leaders at 479 Private Colleges and Universities: a Survey," *The Chronicle of Higher Education*, 47: A29-A48, (November 24, 2000).

★3281★
Top pay and benefits for the chief executive and top paid employees at Eastern Nazarene College

Ranking basis/background: Annual pay and benefits for the chief executives and top paid officers, as reported on Internal Revenue Service Form 990 by private colleges and universities in the U.S. for the 1998-99 academic year. **Number listed:** 6.

Kent R. Hill, president, with $104,744 annual pay; $13,811 in benefits
Kenneth E. Gorton, VP, financial affairs, $83,647; $6,574
Al Socci, associate dean, adult and continuing education, $75,006; $11,580
David Kale, VP, academic affairs, $74,388; $11,534
Norene Fiacco, associate professor, English, $68,373; $7,538
Wayne Dunlop, associate dean, academics, $63,373; $10,708

Source: "Pay and Benefits of Leaders at 479 Private Colleges and Universities: a Survey," *The Chronicle of Higher Education*, 47: A29-A48, (November 24, 2000).

★3282★
Top pay and benefits for the chief executive and top paid employees at Eckerd College

Ranking basis/background: Annual pay and benefits for the chief executives and top paid officers, as reported on Internal Revenue Service Form 990 by private colleges and universities in the U.S. for the 1998-99 academic year. **Number listed:** 6.

Peter H. Armacost, president, with $150,740 annual pay; $18,780 in benefits

Peter K. Hammerschmidt, professor, economics, $139,400; $9,810
Salvatore Capobianco, professor, psychology, $121,100; $8,750
J. Webster Hull, VP, finance; treasurer, $112,350; $14,940
Lloyd W. Chapin, VP; dean of the faculty, $104,500; $14,155
Richard T. Haskins, VP, development, $101,500; $13,855

Source: "Pay and Benefits of Leaders at 479 Private Colleges and Universities: a Survey," *The Chronicle of Higher Education*, 47: A29-A48, (November 24, 2000).

★3283★
Top pay and benefits for the chief executive and top paid employees at Edgewood College

Ranking basis/background: Annual pay and benefits for the chief executives and top paid officers, as reported on Internal Revenue Service Form 990 by private colleges and universities in the U.S. for the 1998-99 academic year. **Number listed:** 6.

James A. Ebben, president, with $146,088 annual pay; $8,881 in benefits
Virginia H. Wirtz, professor; chair, nursing, $76,050; $8,767
Joseph E. Schmiedicke, professor; chair, education; director, summer session, $76,868; $6,182
Daniel Klotzbach, chief financial officer, $67,950; $8,726
Albert J. Rouse, business manager, $67,500; $8,755
Judith Wimmer, dean, academics, $69,000; $6,217

Source: "Pay and Benefits of Leaders at 479 Private Colleges and Universities: a Survey," *The Chronicle of Higher Education*, 47: A29-A48, (November 24, 2000).

★3284★
Top pay and benefits for the chief executive and top paid employees at Elmira College

Ranking basis/background: Annual pay and benefits for the chief executives and top paid officers, as reported on Internal Revenue Service Form 990 by private colleges and universities in the U.S. for the 1998-99 academic year. **Number listed:** 6.

Thomas K. Meier, president, with $134,196 annual pay; $17,392 in benefits
Bryan D. Reddick, academic VP; dean of the faculty; $100,000; $13,792
Roger G. Penland, VP, development and alumni affairs, $93,833; $13,121
Thomas K. Rutan, VP, public relations; assistant to the president, $90,600; $12,977
Jerry B. Gapp, financial VP; treasurer, $90,000; $12,903
Gerald T. Dees, VP and dean, student life, $90,000; $12,702

Source: "Pay and Benefits of Leaders at 479 Private Colleges and Universities: a Survey," *The Chronicle of Higher Education*, 47: A29-A48, (November 24, 2000).

★3285★
Top pay and benefits for the chief executive and top paid employees at Elon College

Ranking basis/background: Annual pay and benefits for the chief executives and top paid officers, as reported on Internal Revenue Service Form 990 by private colleges and universities in the U.S. for the 1998-99 academic year. **Number listed:** 6.

J. Fred Young, president, with $234,951 annual pay; $32,800 in benefits
Gerald L. Francis, provost, $138,233; $12,760
Elizabeth A. Rogers, assistant dean, physical therapy, $120,600; $13,764
Gerald O. Whittington, VP, business, finance, and technology, $119,655; $13,316
John C. Burbridge, dean, business, $114,400; $13,212
Julianne Maher, VP, academic affairs, $105,700; $10,480

Source: "Pay and Benefits of Leaders at 479 Private Colleges and Universities: a Survey," *The Chronicle of Higher Education*, 47: A29-A48, (November 24, 2000).

★3286★
Top pay and benefits for the chief executive and top paid employees at Embry-Riddle Aeronautical University

Ranking basis/background: Annual pay and benefits for the chief executives and top paid officers, as reported on Internal Revenue Service Form 990 by private colleges and universities in the U.S. for the 1998-99 academic year. **Number listed:** 7.

George Ebbs, president, with $128,173 annual pay; $32,223 in benefits
Steven M. Sliwa, president, $69,173; $17,390
Ira D. Jacobson, executive VP, academics, $140,538; $35,331
Robert A. Jost, VP, business and finance, $120,462; $30,284
Jeffrey H. Ledewitz, executive VP, student life, $117,450; $29,526
Paul McDuffee, VP, university relations, $110,423; $27,760
Iraj Hirmanpour, professor, computing and mathematics, $126,686; $7,465

Source: "Pay and Benefits of Leaders at 479 Private Colleges and Universities: a Survey," *The Chronicle of Higher Education*, 47: A29-A48, (November 24, 2000).

★3287★
Top pay and benefits for the chief executive and top paid employees at Emerson College

Ranking basis/background: Annual pay and benefits for the chief executives and top paid officers, as reported on Internal Revenue Service Form 990 by private colleges and universities in the U.S. for the 1998-99 academic year. **Number listed:** 6.

Jacqueline Liebergott, president, with $177,252 annual pay; $22,499 in benefits
Robert Silverman, VP, administration, $158,590; $22,184
Murray Schwartz, VP, academic affairs, $154,219; $11,606
Dorothy Aram, chair, communication disorders, $132,385; $17,258
Suzanne Swope, VP, enrollment, $130,334; $15,553
Joseph Cofield, VP, institutional advancement, $120,315; $9,672

Source: "Pay and Benefits of Leaders at 479 Private Colleges and Universities: a Survey," *The Chronicle of Higher Education*, 47: A29-A48, (November 24, 2000).

★3288★
Top pay and benefits for the chief executive and top paid employees at Emmanuel College in Massachusetts

Ranking basis/background: Annual pay and benefits for the chief executives and top paid officers, as reported on Internal Revenue Service Form 990 by private colleges and universities in the U.S. for the 1998-99 academic year. **Number listed:** 6.

Sister Janet Eisner, S.N.D., president, with $0 annual pay; $2,809 in benefits
Jacquelyn Armitage, VP, enrollment management, $97,375; $11,281
Kieran McTague, VP, development and alumnae relations, $100,783; $7,145
Rosemary Tobin, professor, education, $101,544; $6,022
Louise Cash, professor, music and speech communication and theater arts, $82,216; $9,969
Audrey Ashton-Savage, associate dean, CAS management programs, $84,198; $6,219

Source: "Pay and Benefits of Leaders at 479 Private Colleges and Universities: a Survey," *The Chronicle of Higher Education*, 47: A29-A48, (November 24, 2000).

★3289★
Top pay and benefits for the chief executive and top paid employees at Emory University

Ranking basis/background: Annual pay and benefits for the chief executives and top paid officers, as reported on Internal Revenue Service Form 990 by private colleges and universities in the U.S. for the 1998-99 academic year. **Number listed:** 6.

William M. Chace, president, with $372,584 annual pay; $20,704 in benefits
Michael M.E. Johns, executive VP, health affairs; director, Robert Woodruff Health Sciences Center, $677,038; $20,704
Douglas E. Mattox, professor and chair, otolaryngology, $433,333; $20,704
John A. Rock, professor and chair, gynecology and obstetrics, $386,973; $30,704
Charles B. Nemeroff, professor and chair, psychiatry, school of medicine, $352,229; $20,704
John D. Henry Sr., CEO, Emory Hospitals, $339,098; $20,704

Source: "Pay and Benefits of Leaders at 479 Private Colleges and Universities: a Survey," *The Chronicle of Higher Education*, 47: A29-A48, (November 24, 2000).

★3290★
Top pay and benefits for the chief executive and top paid employees at Erskine College

Ranking basis/background: Annual pay and benefits for the chief executives and top paid officers, as reported on Internal Revenue Service Form 990 by private colleges and universities in the U.S. for the 1998-99 academic year. **Number listed:** 7.

- John L. Carson, president, with $90,000 annual pay; $6,750 in benefits
- James W. Strobel, former president, $30,640; $2,298
- Jim Gettys, VP; dean of the college, $73,933; $5,545
- R. J. Gore, VP and dean, Erskine Theological Seminary, $65,000; $4,875
- Steve Sniteman, VP, enrollment management and technology, $60,000; $4,500
- Lee Logan, VP, development, $58,000; $4,350
- Loyd Melton, professor, New Testament; associate dean, postgraduate studies, $58,000; $4,350

Source: "Pay and Benefits of Leaders at 479 Private Colleges and Universities: a Survey," *The Chronicle of Higher Education*, 47: A29-A48, (November 24, 2000).

★3291★
Top pay and benefits for the chief executive and top paid employees at Fairfield University

Ranking basis/background: Annual pay and benefits for the chief executives and top paid officers, as reported on Internal Revenue Service Form 990 by private colleges and universities in the U.S. for the 1998-99 academic year. **Remarks:** Reverend Kelley's pay is donated to the Fairfield Jesuit Community. **Number listed:** 6.

- Rev. Aloysius P. Kelley, S.J., president, with $155,250 annual pay; $29,924 in benefits
- L. William Miles, VP, administration, $154,003; $28,247
- George E. Diffley, VP, university advancement, $140,301; $26,521
- Walter Ryba Jr. dean, business, $138,601; $26,201
- Robert E. Wall academic VP, $133,302; $25,735
- William J. Lucas VP, finance; treasurer, $132,301; $25,634

Source: "Pay and Benefits of Leaders at 479 Private Colleges and Universities: a Survey," *The Chronicle of Higher Education*, 47: A29-A48, (November 24, 2000).

★3292★
Top pay and benefits for the chief executive and top paid employees at Fairleigh Dickinson University

Ranking basis/background: Annual pay and benefits for the chief executives and top paid officers, as reported on Internal Revenue Service Form 990 by private colleges and universities in the U.S. for the 1998-99 academic year. **Number listed:** 6.

- Francis J. Mertz, president, with $235,000 annual pay; $26,077 in benefits
- Sheldon Drucker, VP, finance; treasurer, $156,684; $20,012
- Carl Viola, executive VP, $149,688; $23,458
- Charles R. Dees Jr., senior VP, institutional advancement, $142,188; $18,718
- Paul Lerman, dean, college of business administration, $125,895; $16,925
- Peter Falley, provost, $119,336; $21,004

Source: "Pay and Benefits of Leaders at 479 Private Colleges and Universities: a Survey," *The Chronicle of Higher Education*, 47: A29-A48, (November 24, 2000).

★3293★
Top pay and benefits for the chief executive and top paid employees at Florida Institute of Technology

Ranking basis/background: Annual pay and benefits for the chief executives and top paid officers, as reported on Internal Revenue Service Form 990 by private colleges and universities in the U.S. for the 1998-99 academic year. **Number listed:** 6.

- Lynn Edward Weaver, president, with $210,000 annual pay; $11,941 in benefits
- Joshua Rokach, director, school of science and liberal arts; professor, chemistry, $155,333; $12,090
- Robert L. Sullivan, VP, research and graduate programs, $148,000; $9,236
- R.L. Bartrem, VP, financial affairs, $135,000; $8,705
- A.T. Hollingsworth, dean, school of business, $124,000; $6,406
- A.R. Revay, VP, academic affairs, $109,000; $8,564

Source: "Pay and Benefits of Leaders at 479 Private Colleges and Universities: a Survey," *The Chronicle of Higher Education*, 47: A29-A48, (November 24, 2000).

★3294★
Top pay and benefits for the chief executive and top paid employees at Fontbonne College

Ranking basis/background: Annual pay and benefits for the chief executives and top paid officers, as reported on Internal Revenue Service Form 990 by private colleges and universities in the U.S. for the 1998-99 academic year. **Number listed:** 6.

- Dennis C. Golden, president, with $141,000 annual pay; $9,924 in benefits
- Cheryl Turner, VP, finance and administration; treasurer, $83,150; $5,821
- Timothy Willard, VP, institutional advancement, $83,150; $5,821
- Gary Zack, VP, enrollment management, $83,150; $5,821
- Susan Dunton, VP, academic affairs, $73,000; $5,110
- David Imler, director, information technology, $61,123; $7,168

Source: "Pay and Benefits of Leaders at 479 Private Colleges and Universities: a Survey," *The Chronicle of Higher Education*, 47: A29-A48, (November 24, 2000).

★3295★
Top pay and benefits for the chief executive and top paid employees at Fordham University

Ranking basis/background: Annual pay and benefits for the chief executives and top paid officers, as reported on Internal Revenue Service Form 990 by private colleges and universities in the U.S. for the 1998-99 academic year. **Remarks:** Reverend O'Hare's pay is donated to the Jesuits of Fordham, Inc. **Number listed:** 6.

- Rev. Joseph A. O'Hara, S.J., president, with $0 annual pay; $0 in benefits
- John Feerick, dean, law school, $245,000; $36,261
- Michael Martin, associate dean; professor, law, $199,800; $35,262
- Joseph M. Perillo, professor, law, $197,800; $33,136
- Constantine Katsoris, professor, law, $184,800; $34,766
- Daniel Capra, professor, law, $184,300; $34,920

Source: "Pay and Benefits of Leaders at 479 Private Colleges and Universities: a Survey," *The Chronicle of Higher Education*, 47: A29-A48, (November 24, 2000).

★3296★
Top pay and benefits for the chief executive and top paid employees at Franklin and Marshall College

Ranking basis/background: Annual pay and benefits for the chief executives and top paid officers, as reported on Internal Revenue Service Form 990 by private colleges and universities in the U.S. for the 1998-99 academic year. **Number listed:** 6.

- Richard Kneedler, president, with $197,500 annual pay; $24,000 in benefits
- Alice Drum, VP; dean, educational services, $152,000; $48,630
- Thomas J. Kingston, VP, finance; treasurer, $152,000; $40,701
- P. Bruce Pipes, VP, academic affairs; dean of the college, $152,000; $39,501
- Cathleen Voelker, VP, college advancement, $130,000; $32,363
- James R. Wetzel, senior assistant to the president; director, planned giving and special projects, $128,704; $20,583

Source: "Pay and Benefits of Leaders at 479 Private Colleges and Universities: a Survey," *The Chronicle of Higher Education*, 47: A29-A48, (November 24, 2000).

★3297★
Top pay and benefits for the chief executive and top paid employees at Franklin College of Indiana

Ranking basis/background: Annual pay and benefits for the chief executives and top paid officers, as reported on Internal Revenue Service Form 990 by private colleges and universities in the U.S. for the 1998-99 academic year. **Number listed:** 7.

- Paul Marion, president, with $147,000 annual pay; $27,650 in benefits
- William Bryan Martin, chancellor, $140,300; $26,639
- Richard Swindle, VP, development and public affairs, $91,550; $19,250
- Larry Griffith, VP, business and finance, $86,730; $18,171

Allen Berger, VP, academic affairs; interim dean of the college, $83,250; $17,894
Richard M. Park, professor, mathematical sciences, $75,612; $11,378
B. Stephen Richards, dean, enrollment, $63,930; $14,992

Source: "Pay and Benefits of Leaders at 479 Private Colleges and Universities: a Survey," *The Chronicle of Higher Education*, 47: A29-A48, (November 24, 2000).

★3298★
Top pay and benefits for the chief executive and top paid employees at Fresno Pacific University

Ranking basis/background: Annual pay and benefits for the chief executives and top paid officers, as reported on Internal Revenue Service Form 990 by private colleges and universities in the U.S. for the 1998-99 academic year. **Number listed:** 5.

Allen Carden, president, with $89,610 annual pay; $0 in benefits
Mark Deffenbacher, director, planned giving; director, Fresno Pacific Foundation, $73,924; $0
Howard J. Loewen, provost, $70,000; $0
Ruth Heinrichs, VP, business affairs, $64,000; $0
Stephen Varvis, dean of the college, $63,860; $0

Source: "Pay and Benefits of Leaders at 479 Private Colleges and Universities: a Survey," *The Chronicle of Higher Education*, 47: A29-A48, (November 24, 2000).

★3299★
Top pay and benefits for the chief executive and top paid employees at Friends University

Ranking basis/background: Annual pay and benefits for the chief executives and top paid officers, as reported on Internal Revenue Service Form 990 by private colleges and universities in the U.S. for the 1998-99 academic year. **Number listed:** 6.

Phillip K. Green, president, with $167,408 annual pay; $39,501 in benefits
Al Saber, professor, information technology, $114,199; $7,468
G. Robert Dove, VP, academic affairs, $93,583; $9,187
Hervey W. Wright III, VP, university advancement, $88,384; $13,661
Randall C. Doerksen, VP, administration and finance, $91,303; $9,403
Sheryl C. Wilson, VP, student affairs, $91,303; $8,223

Source: "Pay and Benefits of Leaders at 479 Private Colleges and Universities: a Survey," *The Chronicle of Higher Education*, 47: A29-A48, (November 24, 2000).

★3300★
Top pay and benefits for the chief executive and top paid employees at Furman University

Ranking basis/background: Annual pay and benefits for the chief executives and top paid officers, as reported on Internal Revenue Service Form 990 by private colleges and universities in the U.S. for the 1998-99 academic year. **Number listed:** 6.

David E. Shi, president, with $180,000 annual pay; $32,911 in benefits

Lon B. Knight Jr., professor, chemistry, $135,923; $24,957
Kenneth C. Abernethy, professor, computer science, $135,907; $20,679
Archie V. Huff, VP, academic affairs, $118,542; $27,887
Donald J. Lineback, VP, development, $113,661; $26,971
Charles A. Arrington, professor, chemistry, $115,425; $24,539

Source: "Pay and Benefits of Leaders at 479 Private Colleges and Universities: a Survey," *The Chronicle of Higher Education*, 47: A29-A48, (November 24, 2000).

★3301★
Top pay and benefits for the chief executive and top paid employees at Gallaudet University

Ranking basis/background: Annual pay and benefits for the chief executives and top paid officers, as reported on Internal Revenue Service Form 990 by private colleges and universities in the U.S. for the 1998-99 academic year. **Number listed:** 6.

I. King Jordan, president, with $305,821 annual pay; $35,802 in benefits
Paul Kelly, VP, administration and finance, $189,814; $24,074
Roslyn Rosen, VP, academic affairs, $148,381; $17,589
Jane Fernandes, VP, national pre-college program, $127,430; $27,260
William A. Moses, professor, art, $125,905; $17,613
Carol J. LaSasso, professor, education, $124,873; $17,508

Source: "Pay and Benefits of Leaders at 479 Private Colleges and Universities: a Survey," *The Chronicle of Higher Education*, 47: A29-A48, (November 24, 2000).

★3302★
Top pay and benefits for the chief executive and top paid employees at Gannon University

Ranking basis/background: Annual pay and benefits for the chief executives and top paid officers, as reported on Internal Revenue Service Form 990 by private colleges and universities in the U.S. for the 1998-99 academic year. **Number listed:** 6.

Msgr. David A. Rubino, president, with $42,846 annual pay; $2,613 in benefits
Michael Ferralli, assistant professor, physics, $166,581; $7,827
Hamid Torab, professor, mechanical engineering, $120,045; $9,103
Thomas S. Ostrowski, provost; VP, academic affairs, $115,208; $13,141
Mahesh C. Aggarwal, professor, mechanical engineering, $118,214; $9,085
Stephen A. Schillo, VP, finance and administration, $103,069; $15,416

Source: "Pay and Benefits of Leaders at 479 Private Colleges and Universities: a Survey," *The Chronicle of Higher Education*, 47: A29-A48, (November 24, 2000).

★3303★
Top pay and benefits for the chief executive and top paid employees at Gardner-Webb University

Ranking basis/background: Annual pay and benefits for the chief executives and top paid officers, as reported on Internal Revenue Service Form 990 by private colleges and universities in the U.S. for the 1998-99 academic year. **Number listed:** 6.

M. Christopher White, president, with $179,505 annual pay; $2,408 in benefits
Ralph Dixon, VP, enrollment management, $95,370; $10,115
A. Frank Bonner, senior VP; provost, $85,000; $9,386
Drew Van Horn, VP, university relations, $84,000; $8,807
Donnie Clary, VP, business and finance; assistant treasurer, $84,000; $8,687
Bruce Moore, VP, student development, $65,000; $18,099

Source: "Pay and Benefits of Leaders at 479 Private Colleges and Universities: a Survey," *The Chronicle of Higher Education*, 47: A29-A48, (November 24, 2000).

★3304★
Top pay and benefits for the chief executive and top paid employees at George Washington University

Ranking basis/background: Annual pay and benefits for the chief executives and top paid officers, as reported on Internal Revenue Service Form 990 by private colleges and universities in the U.S. for the 1998-99 academic year. **Number listed:** 6.

Stephen J. Trachtenberg, president, with $421,035 annual pay; $52,198 in benefits
Lalaigam N. Sekhar, clinical professor, neurological surgery, $476,783; $19,078
Thomas Penders, head coach, men's basketball, $431,100; $9,587
Andrew Foster, associate professor, surgery, $385,990; $16,330
Samuel Potolicchio, professor, neurology, $338,329; $15,915
John F. Williams, VP, health affairs, $320,948; $16,328

Source: "Pay and Benefits of Leaders at 479 Private Colleges and Universities: a Survey," *The Chronicle of Higher Education*, 47: A29-A48, (November 24, 2000).

★3305★
Top pay and benefits for the chief executive and top paid employees at Georgetown College in Kentucky

Ranking basis/background: Annual pay and benefits for the chief executives and top paid officers, as reported on Internal Revenue Service Form 990 by private colleges and universities in the U.S. for the 1998-99 academic year. **Number listed:** 5.

William H. Crouch Jr., president, with $165,230 annual pay; $0 in benefits
Charles N. Boehms, senior VP; dean, academics, $93,175; $0
Robert H. Osborne Jr., head coach, men's basketball, $83,376; $0
Ernie W. Stamper, VP, advancement, $78,795; $0

Sally B. Schott, president's liaison, $73,060

Source: "Pay and Benefits of Leaders at 479 Private Colleges and Universities: a Survey," *The Chronicle of Higher Education*, 47: A29-A48, (November 24, 2000).

★3306★
Top pay and benefits for the chief executive and top paid employees at Georgetown University

Ranking basis/background: Annual pay and benefits for the chief executives and top paid officers, as reported on Internal Revenue Service Form 990 by private colleges and universities in the U.S. for the 1998-99 academic year. **Remarks:** Reverend O'Donovan's pay is donated to the Society of Jesus. **Number listed:** 6.

- Reverend Leo J. O'Donovan, S.J., president, with $400,000 annual pay; $0 in benefits
- James L. Cox, professor and chief, cardiovascular surgery, $1,200,000; $21,332
- William C. Laureman, associate professor and chief, orthopedics, $848,764; $24,472
- Sam W. Wiesel, executive VP, health sciences; executive dean, medicine, $658,524; $24,466
- John R. Thompson, head coach emeritus, men's basketball, $610,040; $24,529
- Scott L. Spear, professor and chief, plastic and reconstructive surgery, $609,781; $24,529

Source: "Pay and Benefits of Leaders at 479 Private Colleges and Universities: a Survey," *The Chronicle of Higher Education*, 47: A29-A48, (November 24, 2000).

★3307★
Top pay and benefits for the chief executive and top paid employees at Georgian Court College

Ranking basis/background: Annual pay and benefits for the chief executives and top paid officers, as reported on Internal Revenue Service Form 990 by private colleges and universities in the U.S. for the 1998-99 academic year. **Number listed:** 6.

- Sister Barbara Williams, R.S.M., president, with $0 annual pay; $0 in benefits
- Mary Lee Batesko, professor and chair, education, $76,850; $4,995
- Linda James, professor, psychology, $75,830; $4,929
- Patricia Clyne-Lindberg, VP, college advancement, $75,029; $4,877
- Rita Carney, VP, planning, $70,456; $4,580
- Frank Decaro, professor, business administration, $67,223; $4,369

Source: "Pay and Benefits of Leaders at 479 Private Colleges and Universities: a Survey," *The Chronicle of Higher Education*, 47: A29-A48, (November 24, 2000).

★3308★
Top pay and benefits for the chief executive and top paid employees at Gettysburg College

Ranking basis/background: Annual pay and benefits for the chief executives and top paid officers, as reported on Internal Revenue Service Form 990 by private colleges and universities in the U.S. for the 1998-99 academic year. **Number listed:** 6.

- Gordon A. Haaland, president, with $209,053 annual pay; $40,262 in benefits
- Jennie L. Mingolelli, VP, finance and administration, $148,481; $22,079
- Daniel DeNicola, provost, $140,481; $21,650
- Lex O. McMillan, VP, college relations, $132,979; $23,614
- Julie L. Ramsey, dean of the college, $111,967; $19,277
- Gabor Bolitt, professor, history, $103,384; $25,107

Source: "Pay and Benefits of Leaders at 479 Private Colleges and Universities: a Survey," *The Chronicle of Higher Education*, 47: A29-A48, (November 24, 2000).

★3309★
Top pay and benefits for the chief executive and top paid employees at Goddard College

Ranking basis/background: Annual pay and benefits for the chief executives and top paid officers, as reported on Internal Revenue Service Form 990 by private colleges and universities in the U.S. for the 1998-99 academic year. **Number listed:** 3.

- Barbara Mossberg, president, with $106,901 annual pay; $18,220 in benefits
- Terry Keeney, dean, academic affairs, $58,294; $5,830
- Daniel Gribbin, dean, administration, $53,669; $5,598

Source: "Pay and Benefits of Leaders at 479 Private Colleges and Universities: a Survey," *The Chronicle of Higher Education*, 47: A29-A48, (November 24, 2000).

★3310★
Top pay and benefits for the chief executive and top paid employees at Golden Gate University

Ranking basis/background: Annual pay and benefits for the chief executives and top paid officers, as reported on Internal Revenue Service Form 990 by private colleges and universities in the U.S. for the 1998-99 academic year. **Number listed:** 7.

- Phillip Friedman, president, with $202,500 annual pay; $17,219 in benefits
- Thomas M. Stauffer, former president, $217,000; $13,609
- Sharon Meyer, former VP, operations; assistant treasurer, $281,500; $20,992
- Anthony J. Pagano, dean, law, $184,895; $13,193
- John Sylvester, associate dean; professor, law, $150,100; $13,840
- Marci Kelly, associate dean; director, LLM tax program, school of law, $143,150; $11,858
- Mort Cohen, professor, law, $135,000; $11,082

Source: "Pay and Benefits of Leaders at 479 Private Colleges and Universities: a Survey," *The Chronicle of Higher Education*, 47: A29-A48, (November 24, 2000).

★3311★
Top pay and benefits for the chief executive and top paid employees at Gonzaga University

Ranking basis/background: Annual pay and benefits for the chief executives and top paid officers, as reported on Internal Revenue Service Form 990 by private colleges and universities in the U.S. for the 1998-99 academic year. **Number listed:** 6.

- Robert Spitzer, S.J., president, with $125,000 annual pay; $10,000 in benefits
- Gary Randall, professor emeritus, law, $131,245; $7,547
- Harry H. Sladich, acting president; VP, administration and planning, $109,916; $6,320
- Raymond A. Birgenheier, professor, engineering, $108,762; $6,254
- Charles J. Murphy, VP, finance, $108,730; $6,252
- Leonard Doohan, dean, graduate school; professor, religious studies, $104,945; $6,034

Source: "Pay and Benefits of Leaders at 479 Private Colleges and Universities: a Survey," *The Chronicle of Higher Education*, 47: A29-A48, (November 24, 2000).

★3312★
Top pay and benefits for the chief executive and top paid employees at Gordon College in Massachusetts

Ranking basis/background: Annual pay and benefits for the chief executives and top paid officers, as reported on Internal Revenue Service Form 990 by private colleges and universities in the U.S. for the 1998-99 academic year. **Number listed:** 6.

- R. Judson Carlberg, president, with $147,839 annual pay; $27,138 in benefits
- Craig Hammon, executive VP, $103,181; $21,964
- Mark Sargent, provost, $90,888; $21,037
- Timothy Stebbings, VP, finance, $86,052; $20,087
- Stephen MacLeod, dean, college planning, $74,002; $18,363
- Thomas Askew, professor, history; associate director, East/West Institute, $74,757; $14,529

Source: "Pay and Benefits of Leaders at 479 Private Colleges and Universities: a Survey," *The Chronicle of Higher Education*, 47: A29-A48, (November 24, 2000).

★3313★
Top pay and benefits for the chief executive and top paid employees at Goshen College

Ranking basis/background: Annual pay and benefits for the chief executives and top paid officers, as reported on Internal Revenue Service Form 990 by private colleges and universities in the U.S. for the 1998-99 academic year. **Number listed:** 1.

SALARIES—COLLEGES & UNIVERSITIES

Shirley H. Showalter, president, with $76,218 annual pay; $12,321 in benefits
Source: "Pay and Benefits of Leaders at 479 Private Colleges and Universities: a Survey," *The Chronicle of Higher Education*, 47: A29-A48, (November 24, 2000).

★3314★
Top pay and benefits for the chief executive and top paid employees at Goucher College

Ranking basis/background: Annual pay and benefits for the chief executives and top paid officers, as reported on Internal Revenue Service Form 990 by private colleges and universities in the U.S. for the 1998-99 academic year. **Number listed:** 6.

- Judy Jolley Mohraz, president, with $177,500 annual pay; $44,375 in benefits
- Lucie Lapovsky, VP, finance, $115,000; $28,750
- Robert S. Welch, VP; dean, academics, $110,000; $27,500
- Mark W. Jones, VP, development and alumni affairs, $107,500; $26,875
- Barbara Fritze, VP, enrollment management, $100,000; $25,000
- David Horn, professor, chemistry, $91,087; $22,772

Source: "Pay and Benefits of Leaders at 479 Private Colleges and Universities: a Survey," *The Chronicle of Higher Education*, 47: A29-A48, (November 24, 2000).

★3315★
Top pay and benefits for the chief executive and top paid employees at Grinnell College

Ranking basis/background: Annual pay and benefits for the chief executives and top paid officers, as reported on Internal Revenue Service Form 990 by private colleges and universities in the U.S. for the 1998-99 academic year. **Number listed:** 6.

- Russell K. Osgood, president, with $350,000 annual pay; $31,188 in benefits
- Pamela A. Ferguson, former president; professor, mathematics and computer science, $266,182; $47,625
- Charles L. Duke, former interim president; former VP, academic affairs; former dean of the college; professor, physics, $175,000; $38,168
- David S. Clay, VP, business; treasurer, $165,000; $33,361
- James E. Swartz, professor, chemistry; VP, academic affairs; dean of the college, $128,000; $23,070
- John H. Mutti, professor, international economics, $121,175; $22,228

Source: "Pay and Benefits of Leaders at 479 Private Colleges and Universities: a Survey," *The Chronicle of Higher Education*, 47: A29-A48, (November 24, 2000).

★3316★
Top pay and benefits for the chief executive and top paid employees at Guilford College

Ranking basis/background: Annual pay and benefits for the chief executives and top paid officers, as reported on Internal Revenue Service Form 990 by private colleges and universities in the U.S. for the 1998-99 academic year. **Number listed:** 6.

- Donald W. McNemar, president, with $172,252 annual pay; $42,002 in benefits
- Charles Patterson, VP, advancement, $152,500; $38,500
- Arthur L. Gillis, VP; chief financial officer, $141,500; $36,300
- Bobby Wayne Clark, VP, public affairs, $130,000; $30,000
- Martha H. Cooley, VP; dean, academics, $116,500; $34,000
- Alton E. Newell, dean, admissions, $77,000; $19,250

Source: "Pay and Benefits of Leaders at 479 Private Colleges and Universities: a Survey," *The Chronicle of Higher Education*, 47: A29-A48, (November 24, 2000).

★3317★
Top pay and benefits for the chief executive and top paid employees at Gustavus Adolphus College

Ranking basis/background: Annual pay and benefits for the chief executives and top paid officers, as reported on Internal Revenue Service Form 990 by private colleges and universities in the U.S. for the 1998-99 academic year. **Number listed:** 6.

- Axel Steuer, president, with $142,100 annual pay; $20,329 in benefits
- Elizabeth Baer, VP, academic affairs; dean of the faculty, $105,700; $16,394
- Kenneth Westphal, VP, finance; treasurer, $98,500; $15,718
- Richard L. Torgerson, VP, development, $97,500; $16,304
- Dennis Johnson, VP, college relations, $85,500; $15,221
- Owen Sammelson, VP, administration, $77,900; $14,535

Source: "Pay and Benefits of Leaders at 479 Private Colleges and Universities: a Survey," *The Chronicle of Higher Education*, 47: A29-A48, (November 24, 2000).

★3318★
Top pay and benefits for the chief executive and top paid employees at Gwynedd-Mercy College

Ranking basis/background: Annual pay and benefits for the chief executives and top paid officers, as reported on Internal Revenue Service Form 990 by private colleges and universities in the U.S. for the 1998-99 academic year. **Number listed:** 6.

- Sister Linda M. Bevilacqua, O.P., president, with $0 annual pay; $0 in benefits
- Dorothy A. Prisco, VP, academic affairs, $76,800; $6,905
- Jules Tasca, professor, English, $70,824; $6,487
- Walter J. Griffin, VP, finance, $67,200; $6,338

Educational Rankings Annual • 2002

- JoAnne Trotter, dean, business and computer science, $66,670; $6,825
- Joseph F. Coleman, executive director, lifelong learning, $67,610; $4,856

Source: "Pay and Benefits of Leaders at 479 Private Colleges and Universities: a Survey," *The Chronicle of Higher Education*, 47: A29-A48, (November 24, 2000).

★3319★
Top pay and benefits for the chief executive and top paid employees at Hamilton College

Ranking basis/background: Annual pay and benefits for the chief executives and top paid officers, as reported on Internal Revenue Service Form 990 by private colleges and universities in the U.S. for the 1998-99 academic year. **Number listed:** 7.

- Eugene M. Tobin, president, with $230,000 annual pay; $37,436 in benefits
- Daniel J. O'Leary, VP, administration and finance, $161,200; $28,542
- Derek Jones, professor, economics, $134,078; $45,240
- Richard C. Tantillo, VP, communications and development, $140,500; $25,813
- Thomas E. Murphy, professor, physical education; director, athletics, $119,240; $45,891
- Richard M. Fuller, dean, admissions and financial aid, $125,000; $23,553
- Bobby Fong, dean of the faculty, $125,000; $23,553

Source: "Pay and Benefits of Leaders at 479 Private Colleges and Universities: a Survey," *The Chronicle of Higher Education*, 47: A29-A48, (November 24, 2000).

★3320★
Top pay and benefits for the chief executive and top paid employees at Hamline University

Ranking basis/background: Annual pay and benefits for the chief executives and top paid officers, as reported on Internal Revenue Service Form 990 by private colleges and universities in the U.S. for the 1998-99 academic year. **Number listed:** 6.

- Larry Osnes, president, with $180,733 annual pay; $36,944 in benefits
- Orwin L. Carter, VP, finance and administration, $148,589; $13,837
- Edwin Butterfoss, dean, law, $131,058; $16,562
- Daniel Loritz, VP, university relations, $129,913; $13,843
- Larry Bakken, professor, law, $125,811; $16,360
- Peter Thompson, professor, law, $115,264; $16,444

Source: "Pay and Benefits of Leaders at 479 Private Colleges and Universities: a Survey," *The Chronicle of Higher Education*, 47: A29-A48, (November 24, 2000).

★3321★
Top pay and benefits for the chief executive and top paid employees at Hampden-Sydney College

Ranking basis/background: Annual pay and benefits for the chief executives and top paid officers, as reported on Internal Revenue Service Form 990 by private colleges and universities in the U.S. for the 1998-99 academic year. **Number listed:** 6.

- Samuel V. Wilson, president, with $165,986 annual pay; $16,250 in benefits
- C. Norman Krueger, VP, business affairs; treasurer, $111,320; $11,110
- Lewis H. Drew, dean of students, $100,171; $9,982
- Anita Garland, dean, admissions, $93,420; $9,333
- Lawrence H. Martin, dean of the faculty, $90,900; $9,068
- C. Beeler Brush, VP, institutional advancement, $90,320; $9,018

Source: "Pay and Benefits of Leaders at 479 Private Colleges and Universities: a Survey," *The Chronicle of Higher Education,* 47: A29-A48, (November 24, 2000).

★3322★
Top pay and benefits for the chief executive and top paid employees at Hampshire College

Ranking basis/background: Annual pay and benefits for the chief executives and top paid officers, as reported on Internal Revenue Service Form 990 by private colleges and universities in the U.S. for the 1998-99 academic year. **Number listed:** 6.

- Gregory S. Prince Jr., president, with $128,109 annual pay; $21,012 in benefits
- Ali Mirsepassi, assistant dean of the faculty for multicultural education, $96,039; $16,471
- Peter C. Correa, treasurer, $96,655; $13,201
- Penina M. Glazer, professor, history, $92,847; $15,923
- Aaron Berman, dean of the faculty, $81,200; $15,703
- Steve Weisler, professor, linguistics, $80,928; $13,879

Source: "Pay and Benefits of Leaders at 479 Private Colleges and Universities: a Survey," *The Chronicle of Higher Education,* 47: A29-A48, (November 24, 2000).

★3323★
Top pay and benefits for the chief executive and top paid employees at Hampton University

Ranking basis/background: Annual pay and benefits for the chief executives and top paid officers, as reported on Internal Revenue Service Form 990 by private colleges and universities in the U.S. for the 1998-99 academic year. **Number listed:** 6.

- William R. Harvey, president, with $199,344 annual pay; $36,879 in benefits
- M. Patrick McCormick, professor, physics, $155,755; $28,815
- James Russell, professor, physics, $143,967; $26,634
- Calvin Lowe, VP, research, $111,436; $20,616
- Leon L. Scott, VP, business affairs; treasurer, $111,286; $20,588
- Donald Lyons, professor, physics, $110,811; $20,500

Source: "Pay and Benefits of Leaders at 479 Private Colleges and Universities: a Survey," *The Chronicle of Higher Education,* 47: A29-A48, (November 24, 2000).

★3324★
Top pay and benefits for the chief executive and top paid employees at Hanover College

Ranking basis/background: Annual pay and benefits for the chief executives and top paid officers, as reported on Internal Revenue Service Form 990 by private colleges and universities in the U.S. for the 1998-99 academic year. **Number listed:** 6.

- Russell Nichols, president, with $157,250 annual pay; $19,986 in benefits
- Jane Jakoubek, VP; dean, academic affairs, $95,633; $13,561
- Kris Kindelsperger, VP, development, $88,667; $13,259
- Paul Blume, professor, economics and business administration, $86,705; $12,632
- Frank Williams, VP, business affairs, $85,667; $11,821
- Tom Evans, professor, theater, $84,267; $12,798

Source: "Pay and Benefits of Leaders at 479 Private Colleges and Universities: a Survey," *The Chronicle of Higher Education,* 47: A29-A48, (November 24, 2000).

★3325★
Top pay and benefits for the chief executive and top paid employees at Hardin-Simmons University

Ranking basis/background: Annual pay and benefits for the chief executives and top paid officers, as reported on Internal Revenue Service Form 990 by private colleges and universities in the U.S. for the 1998-99 academic year. **Number listed:** 6.

- Lanny Hall, president, with $146,000 annual pay; $15,245 in benefits
- Craig Turner, executive VP, academic affairs, $93,000; $11,615
- Harold Preston, senior VP, finance and management, $91,500; $11,512
- William Gould, head, physical therapy; director, graduate studies, $89,400; $11,368
- Wayne Roy, VP, advancement, $88,500; $11,307
- Michael Whitehorn, VP, student development, $76,000; $10,450

Source: "Pay and Benefits of Leaders at 479 Private Colleges and Universities: a Survey," *The Chronicle of Higher Education,* 47: A29-A48, (November 24, 2000).

★3326★
Top pay and benefits for the chief executive and top paid employees at Hartwick College

Ranking basis/background: Annual pay and benefits for the chief executives and top paid officers, as reported on Internal Revenue Service Form 990 by private colleges and universities in the U.S. for the 1998-99 academic year. **Number listed:** 6.

- Richard A. Detweiler, president, with $164,528 annual pay; $25,103 in benefits
- John M. Pontius Jr., VP, finance, $108,187; $19,964
- Susan Gotsch, VP, academic affairs; dean of the faculty, $99,779; $18,087
- Steven T. Zvengrowski, professor, music; director, summer music festival, $86,447; $16,663
- James C. Link, VP, institutional advancement, $85,290; $15,970
- David J. Bachner, dean, global studies, $82,531; $16,974

Source: "Pay and Benefits of Leaders at 479 Private Colleges and Universities: a Survey," *The Chronicle of Higher Education,* 47: A29-A48, (November 24, 2000).

★3327★
Top pay and benefits for the chief executive and top paid employees at Harvard University

Ranking basis/background: Annual pay and benefits for the chief executives and top paid officers, as reported on Internal Revenue Service Form 990 by private colleges and universities in the U.S. for the 1998-99 academic year. **Number listed:** 6.

- Neil L. Rudenstine, president, with $315,000 annual pay; $27,599 in benefits
- Joseph B. Martin, dean, faculty of medicine; professor, neurobiology and clinical neuroscience, $340,000; $22,357
- Kim B. Clark, professor and dean, business, $278,000; $26,801
- Harvey V. Fineberg, provost, $253,000; $23,292
- Nancy S. Zeckhauser, VP, administration, $247,000; $23,309
- Alvin E. Roth, professor, economics, $252,222; $4,806

Source: "Pay and Benefits of Leaders at 479 Private Colleges and Universities: a Survey," *The Chronicle of Higher Education,* 47: A29-A48, (November 24, 2000).

★3328★
Top pay and benefits for the chief executive and top paid employees at Hastings College

Ranking basis/background: Annual pay and benefits for the chief executives and top paid officers, as reported on Internal Revenue Service Form 990 by private colleges and universities in the U.S. for the 1998-99 academic year. **Number listed:** 6.

- Richard E. Hoover, president, with $137,592 annual pay; $18,275 in benefits
- Roger Doerr, president, Hastings College Foundation, $112,000; $11,077

SALARIES—COLLEGES & UNIVERSITIES

Phillip Dudley, VP of the college, $95,550; $7,908
Dennis Krienert, treasurer, $95,550; $7,908
Dwayne Strasheim, dean, academics, $70,750; $6,492
Kenneth Rhodus, dean of students, $63,000; $6,032

Source: "Pay and Benefits of Leaders at 479 Private Colleges and Universities: a Survey," *The Chronicle of Higher Education*, 47: A29-A48, (November 24, 2000).

★3329★
Top pay and benefits for the chief executive and top paid employees at Haverford College

Ranking basis/background: Annual pay and benefits for the chief executives and top paid officers, as reported on Internal Revenue Service Form 990 by private colleges and universities in the U.S. for the 1998-99 academic year. **Number listed:** 6.

Thomas Tritton, president, with $187,500 annual pay; $38,260 in benefits
G. Richard Wynn, VP, finance and administration, $158,600; $33,336
G. Holger Hansen, VP, institutional advancement, $124,900; $30,283
Jerry P. Gollub, professor, physics, $117,450; $23,991
Bruce Partridge, professor, astronomy, $112,800; $28,416
Elaine Hansen, provost, $112,400; $27,400

Source: "Pay and Benefits of Leaders at 479 Private Colleges and Universities: a Survey," *The Chronicle of Higher Education*, 47: A29-A48, (November 24, 2000).

★3330★
Top pay and benefits for the chief executive and top paid employees at Hawaii Pacific University

Ranking basis/background: Annual pay and benefits for the chief executives and top paid officers, as reported on Internal Revenue Service Form 990 by private colleges and universities in the U.S. for the 1998-99 academic year. **Number listed:** 5.

Chatt G. Wright, president, with $211,667 annual pay; $17,600 in benefits
L. Jim Hochberg, senior VP, $362,081; $0
Donald S. Gedeon, VP, finance and operations, $152,056; $16,726
Anthony Sellitto, athletics director; head basketball coach, $117,320; $12,905
David Lohman, director, institutional advancement, $111,748; $12,292

Source: "Pay and Benefits of Leaders at 479 Private Colleges and Universities: a Survey," *The Chronicle of Higher Education*, 47: A29-A48, (November 24, 2000).

★3331★
Top pay and benefits for the chief executive and top paid employees at Hendrix College

Ranking basis/background: Annual pay and benefits for the chief executives and top paid officers, as reported on Internal Revenue Service Form 990 by private colleges and universities in the U.S. for the 1998-99 academic year. **Number listed:** 6.

Ann H. Die, president, with $165,500 annual pay; $24,804 in benefits
Timothy J. Hill, VP, business and finance, $107,500; $11,394
John Churchill, VP, academic affairs; dean of the college, $101,700; $17,148
Rev. Rock Jones, VP, enrollment; dean, admissions and financial aid; chaplain of the college, $105,038; $11,186
J. Timothy Cloyd, VP, development and college relations, $99,311; $10,788
Harold Robertson, professor, education, $81,782; $14,947

Source: "Pay and Benefits of Leaders at 479 Private Colleges and Universities: a Survey," *The Chronicle of Higher Education*, 47: A29-A48, (November 24, 2000).

★3332★
Top pay and benefits for the chief executive and top paid employees at Heritage College

Ranking basis/background: Annual pay and benefits for the chief executives and top paid officers, as reported on Internal Revenue Service Form 990 by private colleges and universities in the U.S. for the 1998-99 academic year. **Number listed:** 6.

Kathleen A. Ross, S.N.J.M., president, with $95,000 annual pay; $6,074 in benefits
Richard Wueste, VP, administration; chief operations officer, $88,000; $7,851
Sneh Veena, VP, academics, $77,000; $7,228
Robert Plumb, assistant dean, graduate program development, $75,000; $7,100
Margaret Marik, assistant VP, development, $75,000; $7,100
Patricia Whitfield, assistant professor, education and psychology, $59,512; $6,436

Source: "Pay and Benefits of Leaders at 479 Private Colleges and Universities: a Survey," *The Chronicle of Higher Education*, 47: A29-A48, (November 24, 2000).

★3333★
Top pay and benefits for the chief executive and top paid employees at Hiram College

Ranking basis/background: Annual pay and benefits for the chief executives and top paid officers, as reported on Internal Revenue Service Form 990 by private colleges and universities in the U.S. for the 1998-99 academic year. **Number listed:** 6.

G. Benjamin Oliver, president, with $154,120 annual pay; $45,146 in benefits
Sylvia Yankey, VP, development, $103,500; $15,787
Richard W. Powers, VP, business and finance, $101,000; $15,888
Michael Grajek, VP; dean of the college, $93,700; $16,760
Monty Curtis, VP, admissions and college relations, $84,200; $13,707
Edward Smerek, professor; chair, mathematics, $78,605; $14,523

Source: "Pay and Benefits of Leaders at 479 Private Colleges and Universities: a Survey," *The Chronicle of Higher Education*, 47: A29-A48, (November 24, 2000).

★3334★
Top pay and benefits for the chief executive and top paid employees at Hobart and William Smith Colleges

Ranking basis/background: Annual pay and benefits for the chief executives and top paid officers, as reported on Internal Revenue Service Form 990 by private colleges and universities in the U.S. for the 1998-99 academic year. **Number listed:** 6.

Richard H. Hersh, president, with $167,623 annual pay; $21,964 in benefits
Carol George, professor, history, $140,375; $6,863
Sheila K. Bennett, provost; dean of the faculty, $120,243; $14,275
Loren Loomis Hubbell, VP, finance, $115,201; $13,758
Sharon P. Best, VP, development and gift planning, $98,655; $12,060
Debra K. DeMeis, dean, William Smith College, $83,805; $10,536

Source: "Pay and Benefits of Leaders at 479 Private Colleges and Universities: a Survey," *The Chronicle of Higher Education*, 47: A29-A48, (November 24, 2000).

★3335★
Top pay and benefits for the chief executive and top paid employees at Hofstra University

Ranking basis/background: Annual pay and benefits for the chief executives and top paid officers, as reported on Internal Revenue Service Form 990 by private colleges and universities in the U.S. for the 1998-99 academic year. **Number listed:** 6.

James M. Shuart, president, with $407,527 annual pay; $34,693 in benefits
Stuart Rabinowitz, dean, law school, $276,934; $43,366
Lawrence Kessler, professor, law, $199,015; $39,093
M. Patricia Adamski, vice dean, law school; professor, law, $188,148; $39,774
Malachy Mahon, professor, law, $185,037; $38,355
Bernard Jacob, professor, law, $178,149; $36,971

Source: "Pay and Benefits of Leaders at 479 Private Colleges and Universities: a Survey," *The Chronicle of Higher Education*, 47: A29-A48, (November 24, 2000).

★3336★
Top pay and benefits for the chief executive and top paid employees at Hollins University

Ranking basis/background: Annual pay and benefits for the chief executives and top paid officers, as reported on Internal Revenue Service Form 990 by private colleges and universities in the U.S. for the 1998-99 academic year. **Number listed:** 6.

Janet Rasmussen, president, with $122,500 annual pay; $14,655 in benefits
L. Wayne Market, VP, academic affairs, $97,500; $12,274
Charles W. Crist, VP, business and finance, $98,900; $8,429
Cynthia Woolbright, VP, development and external relations, $90,000; $11,634

C. Renee Romano, VP, student affairs, $81,000; $11,115
Thomas L. Edwards, associate VP, academic affairs; professor, economics, $81,900; $9,140

Source: "Pay and Benefits of Leaders at 479 Private Colleges and Universities: a Survey," *The Chronicle of Higher Education*, 47: A29-A48, (November 24, 2000).

★3337★
Top pay and benefits for the chief executive and top paid employees at Holy Names College

Ranking basis/background: Annual pay and benefits for the chief executives and top paid officers, as reported on Internal Revenue Service Form 990 by private colleges and universities in the U.S. for the 1998-99 academic year. **Number listed:** 7.

Rosemarie Nassif, S.N.D., president, with $25,000 annual pay; $1,250 in benefits
Robert D. Hite, VP, finance, $78,000; $3,900
David Fike, VP, academic affairs, $72,500; $3,625
Charles Beauchamp, chair, nursing, $63,000; $3,150
Gary Yee, chair, education, $60,000; $3,000
Bill Sadler, professor, sociology and business, $57,916; $2,896
Sheila Gibson, professor, philosophy; chair, arts and humanities, $57,916; $2,896

Source: "Pay and Benefits of Leaders at 479 Private Colleges and Universities: a Survey," *The Chronicle of Higher Education*, 47: A29-A48, (November 24, 2000).

★3338★
Top pay and benefits for the chief executive and top paid employees at Hood College

Ranking basis/background: Annual pay and benefits for the chief executives and top paid officers, as reported on Internal Revenue Service Form 990 by private colleges and universities in the U.S. for the 1998-99 academic year. **Number listed:** 6.

Shirley D. Peterson, president, with $150,000 annual pay; $37,500 in benefits
Bruce E. Bigelow, VP, development and college relations, $89,080; $22,270
Cornelius R. Fay III, chief technology officer, $87,500; $21,875
Thomas M. Berger, VP, finance and administration; chief financial officer; treasurer, $87,500; $21,875
Tom Samet, VP, academic affairs; dean of the faculty, $84,248; $21,062
Robert Brill, associate VP, external relations; campaign director, $83,000; $20,750

Source: "Pay and Benefits of Leaders at 479 Private Colleges and Universities: a Survey," *The Chronicle of Higher Education*, 47: A29-A48, (November 24, 2000).

★3339★
Top pay and benefits for the chief executive and top paid employees at Hope College

Ranking basis/background: Annual pay and benefits for the chief executives and top paid officers, as reported on Internal Revenue Service Form 990 by private colleges and universities in the U.S. for the 1998-99 academic year. **Number listed:** 7.

John H. Jacobson, president, with $164,892 annual pay; $33,048 in benefits
William K. Anderson, VP, finance, $118,154; $18,184
Robert DeYoung, VP, college advancement, $108,638; $26,544
Jacob E. Nyenhuis, provost; $108,654; $26,528
James R. Bekkering, VP, admissions, $94,976; $25,557
Greg J. Maybury, director, operations and technology, $90,773; $16,006
Ben J. Patterson, dean, chapel, $91,587; $15,172

Source: "Pay and Benefits of Leaders at 479 Private Colleges and Universities: a Survey," *The Chronicle of Higher Education*, 47: A29-A48, (November 24, 2000).

★3340★
Top pay and benefits for the chief executive and top paid employees at Hope International University

Ranking basis/background: Annual pay and benefits for the chief executives and top paid officers, as reported on Internal Revenue Service Form 990 by private colleges and universities in the U.S. for the 1998-99 academic year. **Number listed:** 6.

E. LeRoy Lawson, president, with $10,609 annual pay; $2,862 in benefits
Leroy M. Fulton, VP, administration, $70,951; $2,347
Eugene Sonnenberg, dean, graduate studies, $70,349; $2,106
Edgar J. Elliston, VP, academic affairs; provost; $68,809; $2,584
James Woest, associate professor, management, $60,509; $126
Knofel Staton, professor, biblical studies, $58,411; $1,750

Source: "Pay and Benefits of Leaders at 479 Private Colleges and Universities: a Survey," *The Chronicle of Higher Education*, 47: A29-A48, (November 24, 2000).

★3341★
Top pay and benefits for the chief executive and top paid employees at Houghton College

Ranking basis/background: Annual pay and benefits for the chief executives and top paid officers, as reported on Internal Revenue Service Form 990 by private colleges and universities in the U.S. for the 1998-99 academic year. **Number listed:** 6.

Daniel R. Chamberlain, president, with $108,494 annual pay; $10,708 in benefits
Jeffrey B. Spear, VP, finance; treasurer, $67,404; $8,357
Carl Schultz, professor, Old Testament, $67,866; $7,624
John F. VanWicklin, professor, psychology, $59,577; $7,476
Paul D. Young, professor, psychology, $58,528; $7,412
Michael D. Lastoria, director, counseling services, $58,155; $7,509

Source: "Pay and Benefits of Leaders at 479 Private Colleges and Universities: a Survey," *The Chronicle of Higher Education*, 47: A29-A48, (November 24, 2000).

★3342★
Top pay and benefits for the chief executive and top paid employees at Houston Baptist University

Ranking basis/background: Annual pay and benefits for the chief executives and top paid officers, as reported on Internal Revenue Service Form 990 by private colleges and universities in the U.S. for the 1998-99 academic year. **Number listed:** 6.

E. D. Hodo, president, with $137,500 annual pay; $9,499 in benefits
R. Bruce Garrison, professor, business and economics, $128,800; $12,880
Don Looser, VP, academic affairs, $94,000; $18,826
Cindy Garbs, VP, advancement, $84,333; $22,587
Richard D. Parker, VP, financial affairs, $86,200; $2,873
Don R. Byrnes, VP, enrollment management, $73,650; $13,394

Source: "Pay and Benefits of Leaders at 479 Private Colleges and Universities: a Survey," *The Chronicle of Higher Education*, 47: A29-A48, (November 24, 2000).

★3343★
Top pay and benefits for the chief executive and top paid employees at Howard University

Ranking basis/background: Annual pay and benefits for the chief executives and top paid officers, as reported on Internal Revenue Service Form 990 by private colleges and universities in the U.S. for the 1998-99 academic year. **Number listed:** 6.

H. Patrick Swygert, president, with $298,252 annual pay; $22,545 in benefits
Sarah J. Tyce, general sales manager, WHUR radio, $388,823; $17,625
Millard J. Watkins III, general manager, WHUR radio and WHUT television station, $317,353; $9,807
Melville Wyche, professor and chair, anesthesiology, $249,837; $24,490
Alfred Goldson, professor and chair, radiation oncology, $240,779; $23,997
Floyd Malveaux, VP, health affairs; dean, college of medicine, $235,476; $20,288

Source: "Pay and Benefits of Leaders at 479 Private Colleges and Universities: a Survey," *The Chronicle of Higher Education*, 47: A29-A48, (November 24, 2000).

SALARIES—COLLEGES & UNIVERSITIES

★3344★
Top pay and benefits for the chief executive and top paid employees at Huntingdon College

Ranking basis/background: Annual pay and benefits for the chief executives and top paid officers, as reported on Internal Revenue Service Form 990 by private colleges and universities in the U.S. for the 1998-99 academic year. **Number listed:** 6.

- Wanda Bigham, president, with $115,960 annual pay; $17,394 in benefits
- William F. Pollard, dean of the college; VP, academic affairs, $81,900; $12,514
- Jay A. Dorman, VP, business and finance, $79,530; $7,953
- Terrel W. Haines, VP; executive assistant to the president for national advancement, $66,161; $6,616
- Suellen Ofe, VP, enrollment management, $61,329; $6,133
- Gracie Hanchrow, VP, development and college relations, $59,500; $5,950

Source: "Pay and Benefits of Leaders at 479 Private Colleges and Universities: a Survey," *The Chronicle of Higher Education*, 47: A29-A48, (November 24, 2000).

★3345★
Top pay and benefits for the chief executive and top paid employees at Illinois College

Ranking basis/background: Annual pay and benefits for the chief executives and top paid officers, as reported on Internal Revenue Service Form 990 by private colleges and universities in the U.S. for the 1998-99 academic year. **Number listed:** 6.

- Richard A. Pfau, president, with $140,200 annual pay; $9,802 in benefits
- Robert J. Lane, VP, development, $97,109; $5,875
- Frederick F. Ohles, VP, academic affairs; dean of the college, $89,000; $5,450
- Meryle G. Rinker, VP, business affairs, $84,500; $5,068
- Carole Ann Ryan, associate VP, academic affairs; professor, French, $81,000; $4,770
- William M. Cross, professor, sociology, $71,212; $3,953

Source: "Pay and Benefits of Leaders at 479 Private Colleges and Universities: a Survey," *The Chronicle of Higher Education*, 47: A29-A48, (November 24, 2000).

★3346★
Top pay and benefits for the chief executive and top paid employees at Illinois Institute of Technology

Ranking basis/background: Annual pay and benefits for the chief executives and top paid officers, as reported on Internal Revenue Service Form 990 by private colleges and universities in the U.S. for the 1998-99 academic year. **Number listed:** 6.

- L.M. Collens, president, with $229,516 annual pay; $13,500 in benefits
- H.H. Perritt, VP, downtown campus; dean, Chicago Kent College of Law, $248,310; $13,500
- S. L. Cooper, VP; chief academic officer, $177,315; $13,500
- T.S. Garrow, VP, institutional advancement, $175,300; $13,500
- Darsh T. Wasan, VP, international affairs, $173,531; $13,500
- Lori Andrews, professor, law, $174,175; $11,616

Source: "Pay and Benefits of Leaders at 479 Private Colleges and Universities: a Survey," *The Chronicle of Higher Education*, 47: A29-A48, (November 24, 2000).

★3347★
Top pay and benefits for the chief executive and top paid employees at Illinois Wesleyan University

Ranking basis/background: Annual pay and benefits for the chief executives and top paid officers, as reported on Internal Revenue Service Form 990 by private colleges and universities in the U.S. for the 1998-99 academic year. **Number listed:** 5.

- Minor Myers Jr., president, with $208,500 annual pay; $35,939 in benefits
- Kenneth C. Browning, VP, business and finance, $119,890; $22,180
- James Ruoti, dean, admissions, $111,815; $23,221
- Janet McNew, provost, $112,370; $22,468
- Richard Whitlock, VP, university advancement, $109,000; $22,843

Source: "Pay and Benefits of Leaders at 479 Private Colleges and Universities: a Survey," *The Chronicle of Higher Education*, 47: A29-A48, (November 24, 2000).

★3348★
Top pay and benefits for the chief executive and top paid employees at Immaculata College

Ranking basis/background: Annual pay and benefits for the chief executives and top paid officers, as reported on Internal Revenue Service Form 990 by private colleges and universities in the U.S. for the 1998-99 academic year. **Number listed:** 6.

- Sister Marie Roseanne Bonfini, I.H.M., president, with $0 annual pay; $0 in benefits
- Kevin Manning, VP, development, $96,110; $10,528
- Thomas P. Ford, VP, finance, $89,550; $7,259
- Kenneth Rasp, dean, enrollment, $74,325; $6,321
- James Mooney, professor, English, $69,246; $9,273
- Jed Yalof, professor, psychology, $64,550; $8,591

Source: "Pay and Benefits of Leaders at 479 Private Colleges and Universities: a Survey," *The Chronicle of Higher Education*, 47: A29-A48, (November 24, 2000).

★3349★
Top pay and benefits for the chief executive and top paid employees at Indiana Wesleyan University

Ranking basis/background: Annual pay and benefits for the chief executives and top paid officers, as reported on Internal Revenue Service Form 990 by private colleges and universities in the U.S. for the 1998-99 academic year. **Number listed:** 5.

- James Barnes, president, with $109,072 annual pay; $18,938 in benefits
- Terry Munday, VP, advancement, $83,841; $10,853
- Todd Voss, VP, student development, $83,407; $4,539
- Glenn Martin, chair, social sciences, $68,948; $12,870
- David J. Wright, VP, adult and professional studies, $78,815; $2,711

Source: "Pay and Benefits of Leaders at 479 Private Colleges and Universities: a Survey," *The Chronicle of Higher Education*, 47: A29-A48, (November 24, 2000).

★3350★
Top pay and benefits for the chief executive and top paid employees at Iona College

Ranking basis/background: Annual pay and benefits for the chief executives and top paid officers, as reported on Internal Revenue Service Form 990 by private colleges and universities in the U.S. for the 1998-99 academic year. **Number listed:** 6.

- Bro. James A. Liguori, C.F.C., president, with $200,000 annual pay; $13,329 in benefits
- Nicholas J. Beutell, dean, business, $153,796; $21,446
- Judson Shaver, provost; VP, academic affairs, $152,271; $21,906
- Warren Rosenberg, dean, arts and sciences, $139,309; $25,908
- Ronald R. Yager, professor, information and decision technology management and accounting, $136,821; $19,908
- John M. Braunstein, vice provost, enrollment management, $129,420; $20,256

Source: "Pay and Benefits of Leaders at 479 Private Colleges and Universities: a Survey," *The Chronicle of Higher Education*, 47: A29-A48, (November 24, 2000).

★3351★
Top pay and benefits for the chief executive and top paid employees at Ithaca College

Ranking basis/background: Annual pay and benefits for the chief executives and top paid officers, as reported on Internal Revenue Service Form 990 by private colleges and universities in the U.S. for the 1998-99 academic year. **Number listed:** 6.

- Peggy R. Williams, president, with $183,750 annual pay; $16,377 in benefits
- Thomas R. Salm, VP, business and administrative affairs, $134,100; $14,280
- Carl Sgrecci, VP; treasurer, $125,250; $12,652
- Mary Lee Seibert, acting provost, $116,774; $16,386
- John Oblak, VP, student affairs and campus life, $116,450; $11,944
- Bonnie Gordon, former VP, institutional advancement, $113,615; $12,626

Source: "Pay and Benefits of Leaders at 479 Private Colleges and Universities: a Survey," *The Chronicle of Higher Education*, 47: A29-A48, (November 24, 2000).

★3352★
Top pay and benefits for the chief executive and top paid employees at Jacksonville University

Ranking basis/background: Annual pay and benefits for the chief executives and top paid officers, as reported on Internal Revenue Service Form 990 by private colleges and universities in the U.S. for the 1998-99 academic year. **Number listed:** 6.

- Paul S. Tipton, president, with $150,000 annual pay; $31,875 in benefits
- Terry W. Mullins, dean, business, $115,000; $5,750
- Eugene J. McAllister, VP, financial affairs, $110,000; $5,500
- Matthew G. Flanigan, VP, university relations, $100,000; $5,000
- Jesse Robertson, VP, academic affairs, $97,500; $4,875
- James Brady, professor, economics, $90,079; $4,504

Source: "Pay and Benefits of Leaders at 479 Private Colleges and Universities: a Survey," *The Chronicle of Higher Education*, 47: A29-A48, (November 24, 2000).

★3353★
Top pay and benefits for the chief executive and top paid employees at John Carroll University

Ranking basis/background: Annual pay and benefits for the chief executives and top paid officers, as reported on Internal Revenue Service Form 990 by private colleges and universities in the U.S. for the 1998-99 academic year. **Number listed:** 6.

- Rev. Edward Glynn, S.J., president, with $135,000 annual pay; $8,100 in benefits
- Raj Aggarwal, professor, economics and finance, $160,566; $9,634
- Frederick Travis, VP, academics; provost, $124,060; $7,444
- Paul Kantz, VP, development, $122,096; $7,326
- Richard Fleischman, professor, accountancy, $120,693; $7,242
- Frank Navratil, professor, economics and finance; dean, business, $120,525; $7,232

Source: "Pay and Benefits of Leaders at 479 Private Colleges and Universities: a Survey," *The Chronicle of Higher Education*, 47: A29-A48, (November 24, 2000).

★3354★
Top pay and benefits for the chief executive and top paid employees at John F. Kennedy University

Ranking basis/background: Annual pay and benefits for the chief executives and top paid officers, as reported on Internal Revenue Service Form 990 by private colleges and universities in the U.S. for the 1998-99 academic year. **Number listed:** 6.

- Charles E. Glasser, president, with $146,874 annual pay; $1,800 in benefits
- Ron Dollinger, VP, university advancement, $102,602; $1,800
- Cynthia A. Walters, VP, student services and administration, $92,128; $1,800
- Josefina Baltodano, VP, university advancement, $90,861; $1,800
- Ronald Levinson, dean, graduate school of professional psychology, $90,263; $1,800
- H. Keith McConnell, associate dean, graduate school of professional psychology, $83,863; $1,800

Source: "Pay and Benefits of Leaders at 479 Private Colleges and Universities: a Survey," *The Chronicle of Higher Education*, 47: A29-A48, (November 24, 2000).

★3355★
Top pay and benefits for the chief executive and top paid employees at Johns Hopkins University

Ranking basis/background: Annual pay and benefits for the chief executives and top paid officers, as reported on Internal Revenue Service Form 990 by private colleges and universities in the U.S. for the 1998-99 academic year. **Number listed:** 6.

- William R. Brody, president, with $445,428 annual pay; $200,282 in benefits
- Walter Jackson Stark, professor, ophthalmology, $673,706; $65,389
- John L. Cameron, professor and chair, surgery, $568,203; $66,945
- Morton F. Goldberg, professor and director, ophthalmology, $582,399; $68,378
- Gary Smith, director, applied physics, $679,645; $39,746
- Elias A. Zerhouni, executive vice dean, school of medicine, $530,196; $78,837

Source: "Pay and Benefits of Leaders at 479 Private Colleges and Universities: a Survey," *The Chronicle of Higher Education*, 47: A29-A48, (November 24, 2000).

★3356★
Top pay and benefits for the chief executive and top paid employees at Judson College in Alabama

Ranking basis/background: Annual pay and benefits for the chief executives and top paid officers, as reported on Internal Revenue Service Form 990 by private colleges and universities in the U.S. for the 1998-99 academic year. **Number listed:** 5.

- David E. Potts, president, with $101,010 annual pay; $14,028 in benefits
- J. Tom Helton, VP; chief financial officer, $57,033; $5,251
- Judith Roberts, VP, academics, $52,489; $4,963
- Mark Tew, VP, institutional research; director, adult studies, $51,009; $4,861
- Jack Fowler, chair, social-science division, $49,000; $4,250

Source: "Pay and Benefits of Leaders at 479 Private Colleges and Universities: a Survey," *The Chronicle of Higher Education*, 47: A29-A48, (November 24, 2000).

★3357★
Top pay and benefits for the chief executive and top paid employees at Juniata College

Ranking basis/background: Annual pay and benefits for the chief executives and top paid officers, as reported on Internal Revenue Service Form 990 by private colleges and universities in the U.S. for the 1998-99 academic year. **Number listed:** 6.

- Thomas R. Kepple Jr., president, with $140,000 annual pay; $0 in benefits
- Robert W. Neff, former president, $148,600; $0
- William R. Alexander, VP, finance and operations, $94,500; $0
- James Lakso, provost; VP, student development; professor, economics and business administration, $92,000; $0
- David Hawsey, associate VP, college advancement and marketing, $77,250; $0
- Dale L. Wampler, professor, computer science, $71,075; $0

Source: "Pay and Benefits of Leaders at 479 Private Colleges and Universities: a Survey," *The Chronicle of Higher Education*, 47: A29-A48, (November 24, 2000).

★3358★
Top pay and benefits for the chief executive and top paid employees at Kalamazoo College

Ranking basis/background: Annual pay and benefits for the chief executives and top paid officers, as reported on Internal Revenue Service Form 990 by private colleges and universities in the U.S. for the 1998-99 academic year. **Number listed:** 6.

- James F. Jones Jr., president, with $171,582 annual pay; $62,787 in benefits
- Thomas M. Ponto, VP, business and finance, $103,906; $33,107
- Gregory S. Mahler, provost, $94,208; $26,293
- Bernard S. Palchick, VP, college advancement, $86,506; $25,251
- Thomas Breznau, executive director, L. Lee Stryker Center, $79,182; $25,544
- Joellen Silberman, dean, enrollment, $78,295; $25,389

Source: "Pay and Benefits of Leaders at 479 Private Colleges and Universities: a Survey," *The Chronicle of Higher Education*, 47: A29-A48, (November 24, 2000).

★3359★
Top pay and benefits for the chief executive and top paid employees at Kenyon College

Ranking basis/background: Annual pay and benefits for the chief executives and top paid officers, as reported on Internal Revenue Service Form 990 by private colleges and universities in the U.S. for the 1998-99 academic year. **Number listed:** 6.

- Robert A. Oden, president, with $231,720 annual pay; $26,026 in benefits
- Douglas Givens, VP, development, $127,941; $20,937
- Katherine H. Will, provost, $122,250; $16,928
- Joseph G. Nelson, VP, finance, $118,237; $20,217
- Harry Clor, professor, political science, $104,468; $17,348
- Tracy W. Schermer, college physician; director, health and counseling center, $100,733; $18,299

Source: "Pay and Benefits of Leaders at 479 Private Colleges and Universities: a Survey," *The Chronicle of Higher Education*, 47: A29-A48, (November 24, 2000).

SALARIES—COLLEGES & UNIVERSITIES

★3360★
Top pay and benefits for the chief executive and top paid employees at Knox College

Ranking basis/background: Annual pay and benefits for the chief executives and top paid officers, as reported on Internal Revenue Service Form 990 by private colleges and universities in the U.S. for the 1998-99 academic year. **Number listed:** 6.

- Richard S. Millman, president, with $87,500 annual pay; $7,298 in benefits
- Lawrence B. Breitborde, VP, academic affairs; dean of the college, $98,704; $7,064
- Pamela F. Faria, VP, administrative services, $95,607; $6,301
- Janet C. Hunter, VP, enrollment and institutional planning, $93,062; $6,486
- John R. Mohr, VP, development and alumni affairs, $89,231; $5,503
- Stephen Bailey, associate dean of the college, $89,231; $5,451

Source: "Pay and Benefits of Leaders at 479 Private Colleges and Universities: a Survey," *The Chronicle of Higher Education*, 47: A29-A48, (November 24, 2000).

★3361★
Top pay and benefits for the chief executive and top paid employees at Lafayette College

Ranking basis/background: Annual pay and benefits for the chief executives and top paid officers, as reported on Internal Revenue Service Form 990 by private colleges and universities in the U.S. for the 1998-99 academic year. **Number listed:** 6.

- Arthur J. Rothkopf, president, with $190,000 annual pay; $0 in benefits
- Gary A. Evans, VP, college relations and development, $164,000; $28,865
- Frederick J. Quivey, VP, business affairs; treasurer, $150,000; $27,694
- June Schlueter, provost, $137,000; $26,025
- Jean-Pierro Cap, professor emeritus, foreign languages and literatures, $140,150; $20,602
- Leslie F. Muhlfelder, VP, human resources; general counsel, $128,000; $24,986

Source: "Pay and Benefits of Leaders at 479 Private Colleges and Universities: a Survey," *The Chronicle of Higher Education*, 47: A29-A48, (November 24, 2000).

★3362★
Top pay and benefits for the chief executive and top paid employees at Lake Erie College

Ranking basis/background: Annual pay and benefits for the chief executives and top paid officers, as reported on Internal Revenue Service Form 990 by private colleges and universities in the U.S. for the 1998-99 academic year. **Number listed:** 6.

- Harold F. Laydon, president, with $127,500 annual pay; $34,062 in benefits
- Carol Ramsay, associate dean, teacher education, $94,861; $12,390
- Dario Muzina, VP, institutional advancement, $76,173; $14,999
- James J. White, VP, administration, $75,000; $14,965
- Mary Ann Naso, VP; dean, college services, $70,000; $14,527
- Maria de la Camara, associate dean, arts and sciences, $65,207; $13,658

Source: "Pay and Benefits of Leaders at 479 Private Colleges and Universities: a Survey," *The Chronicle of Higher Education*, 47: A29-A48, (November 24, 2000).

★3363★
Top pay and benefits for the chief executive and top paid employees at Lake Forest College

Ranking basis/background: Annual pay and benefits for the chief executives and top paid officers, as reported on Internal Revenue Service Form 990 by private colleges and universities in the U.S. for the 1998-99 academic year. **Number listed:** 6.

- David Spadafora, president, with $140,000 annual pay; $24,902 in benefits
- Steven P. Galovich, provost; dean of the faculty; professor, mathematics, $98,000; $19,631
- Fred Van Sickle, VP, alumni development, $95,000; $19,562
- Leslie T. Chapman, VP, business; treasurer, $92,000; $18,468
- George L. Speros, associate provost, associate dean of the faculty, $91,000; $17,682
- Elizabeth Fischer, dean of the college, $88,000; $17,308

Source: "Pay and Benefits of Leaders at 479 Private Colleges and Universities: a Survey," *The Chronicle of Higher Education*, 47: A29-A48, (November 24, 2000).

★3364★
Top pay and benefits for the chief executive and top paid employees at LaRoche College

Ranking basis/background: Annual pay and benefits for the chief executives and top paid officers, as reported on Internal Revenue Service Form 990 by private colleges and universities in the U.S. for the 1998-99 academic year. **Number listed:** 6.

- Msgr. William A. Kerr, president, with $102,731 annual pay; $9,146 in benefits
- Paul F. Stabile, executive director, development, $99,350; $8,431
- Sister Carolyn Winschel, executive VP, $99,166; $7,990
- Regina A. Borum, VP, academic affairs, $97,219; $5,360
- Arthur T. Shuker Jr., treasurer, $93,529; $8,070
- Dan S. Soller, VP, student life, $89,342; $7,589

Source: "Pay and Benefits of Leaders at 479 Private Colleges and Universities: a Survey," *The Chronicle of Higher Education*, 47: A29-A48, (November 24, 2000).

★3365★
Top pay and benefits for the chief executive and top paid employees at LaSalle University

Ranking basis/background: Annual pay and benefits for the chief executives and top paid officers, as reported on Internal Revenue Service Form 990 by private colleges and universities in the U.S. for the 1998-99 academic year. **Number listed:** 6.

- Nicholas A. Giordano, president, with $186,293 annual pay; $22,128 in benefits
- David C. Fleming, VP, business affairs; treasurer, $155,633; $25,204
- Richard A. Nigro, provost, $154,702; $25,109
- Thomas M. Brennan, director, athletics, $133,774; $22,974
- Scott E. Stickel, professor, accounting, $122,169; $21,793
- Madjid Tavana, associate professor, management, $119,248; $21,495

Source: "Pay and Benefits of Leaders at 479 Private Colleges and Universities: a Survey," *The Chronicle of Higher Education*, 47: A29-A48, (November 24, 2000).

★3366★
Top pay and benefits for the chief executive and top paid employees at LaSierra University

Ranking basis/background: Annual pay and benefits for the chief executives and top paid officers, as reported on Internal Revenue Service Form 990 by private colleges and universities in the U.S. for the 1998-99 academic year. **Number listed:** 6.

- Lawrence T. Geraty, president, with $60,839 annual pay; $4,411 in benefits
- Alejo Pizarro, VP, finance, $67,835; $4,918
- Charles Thomas Smith, associate VP, enrollment services, $56,843; $4,121
- Adeny Schmidt, VP, academic administration, $55,835; $4,048
- Lennard Jorgensen, VP, enrollment management, $55,835; $4,048
- Gregory Gerard, VP, advancement and university relations, $55,835; $4,048

Source: "Pay and Benefits of Leaders at 479 Private Colleges and Universities: a Survey," *The Chronicle of Higher Education*, 47: A29-A48, (November 24, 2000).

★3367★
Top pay and benefits for the chief executive and top paid employees at Lawrence University

Ranking basis/background: Annual pay and benefits for the chief executives and top paid officers, as reported on Internal Revenue Service Form 990 by private colleges and universities in the U.S. for the 1998-99 academic year. **Number listed:** 6.

- Richard Warch, president, with $190,800 annual pay; $16,618 in benefits
- William F. Hodgkiss, VP, business affairs and administration, $117,000; $12,901
- Gregory A. Volk, VP, development and external affairs, $114,000; $12,675
- Steven T. Syverson, dean, admissions and financial aid, $94,000; $11,183

Bertrand Goldgar, professor, English, $88,000; $9,049
Robert K. Dodson, dean, conservatory of music, $87,750; $8,245

Source: "Pay and Benefits of Leaders at 479 Private Colleges and Universities: a Survey," *The Chronicle of Higher Education*, 47: A29-A48, (November 24, 2000).

★3368★
Top pay and benefits for the chief executive and top paid employees at Lehigh University

Ranking basis/background: Annual pay and benefits for the chief executives and top paid officers, as reported on Internal Revenue Service Form 990 by private colleges and universities in the U.S. for the 1998-99 academic year. **Number listed:** 6.

Gregory Farrington, president, with $267,823 annual pay; $40,369 in benefits
William Hittinger, interim president, $44,564; $6,986
Nelson G. Markley, VP, academic affairs; provost, $194,870; $33,637
Emory Zimmers, professor, industrial and manufacturing systems engineering, $188,894; $29,341
John Fisher, professor, civil and environmental engineering; director, ATLSS Center, $188,823; $28,229
Roger N. Nagel, director, Intelligent Systems Laboratory; professor, manufacturing systems engineering, $181,090; $33,130
Rhonda I. Gross, VP, finance and administration, $184,310; $27,309

Source: "Pay and Benefits of Leaders at 479 Private Colleges and Universities: a Survey," *The Chronicle of Higher Education*, 47: A29-A48, (November 24, 2000).

★3369★
Top pay and benefits for the chief executive and top paid employees at Lenoir-Rhyne College

Ranking basis/background: Annual pay and benefits for the chief executives and top paid officers, as reported on Internal Revenue Service Form 990 by private colleges and universities in the U.S. for the 1998-99 academic year. **Number listed:** 6.

Ryan A. LaHurd, president, with $127,481 annual pay; $20,212 in benefits
Robert R. Warren, VP, advancement, $80,012; $15,367
Robert L. Spuller, VP; dean, academic affairs; $78,355; $15,416
G. E. Duhlstine, VP, finance and administration, $69,940; $14,409
H. Lowell Ashman, professor, political science, $66,237; $13,603
Jerald R. Gober, professor, business, $62,650; $13,169

Source: "Pay and Benefits of Leaders at 479 Private Colleges and Universities: a Survey," *The Chronicle of Higher Education*, 47: A29-A48, (November 24, 2000).

★3370★
Top pay and benefits for the chief executive and top paid employees at Lesley College

Ranking basis/background: Annual pay and benefits for the chief executives and top paid officers, as reported on Internal Revenue Service Form 990 by private colleges and universities in the U.S. for the 1998-99 academic year. **Number listed:** 6.

Margaret A. McKenna, president, with $213,210 annual pay; $37,133 in benefits
Alan Fein, VP, administration and finance, $149,978; $15,719
Carol Streit, dean, school of undergraduate studies; manager, capital campaign, $121,728; $7,339
William Dandridge, dean, education, $108,986; $7,711
Paul Karoff, VP, public affairs, $104,000; $11,046
Susan Moulton, VP, new ventures, $103,509; $11,426

Source: "Pay and Benefits of Leaders at 479 Private Colleges and Universities: a Survey," *The Chronicle of Higher Education*, 47: A29-A48, (November 24, 2000).

★3371★
Top pay and benefits for the chief executive and top paid employees at Lewis and Clark College in Oregon

Ranking basis/background: Annual pay and benefits for the chief executives and top paid officers, as reported on Internal Revenue Service Form 990 by private colleges and universities in the U.S. for the 1998-99 academic year. **Number listed:** 6.

Michael Mooney, president, with $260,500 annual pay; $30,189 in benefits
James L. Huffman, dean, law, $155,000; $21,867
Jane Atkinson, dean of the college, $134,000; $17,411
Wayne D. Pederson, VP, business and finance; treasurer, $132,875; $18,073
Scott Staff, VP, college relations, $128,750; $19,885
Stephen Kanter, professor, law, $129,500; $18,068

Source: "Pay and Benefits of Leaders at 479 Private Colleges and Universities: a Survey," *The Chronicle of Higher Education*, 47: A29-A48, (November 24, 2000).

★3372★
Top pay and benefits for the chief executive and top paid employees at Lewis University

Ranking basis/background: Annual pay and benefits for the chief executives and top paid officers, as reported on Internal Revenue Service Form 990 by private colleges and universities in the U.S. for the 1998-99 academic year. **Remarks:** Brother Gaffney's compensation is paid to Christian Brothers of the Midwest, Inc. **Number listed:** 6.

Bro. James Gaffney, F.S.C., president, with $130,000 annual pay; $8,450 in benefits
Wayne J. Draudt, VP, business and finance, $103,255; $6,712
Lawrence Hill, professor, economics, $91,848; $5,970
Henry W. Smorynski, VP, academic affairs, $89,865; $5,841
Sue Barrett, professor, nursing, $89,783; $5,836
Robert DeRose, associate VP, business and finance, $88,836; $5,774

Source: "Pay and Benefits of Leaders at 479 Private Colleges and Universities: a Survey," *The Chronicle of Higher Education*, 47: A29-A48, (November 24, 2000).

★3373★
Top pay and benefits for the chief executive and top paid employees at Liberty University

Ranking basis/background: Annual pay and benefits for the chief executives and top paid officers, as reported on Internal Revenue Service Form 990 by private colleges and universities in the U.S. for the 1998-99 academic year. **Number listed:** 7.

John M. Borek Jr., president, with $207,500 annual pay; $17,318 in benefits
Jerry Falwell, chancellor, $267,088; $16,922
A. Pierre Guillermin, president emeritus, $122,490; $6,125
Mel Hankinson, coach, basketball, $89,223; $10,693
David Lewis Young, VP, administration and finance, $80,617; $10,294
Boyd C. Rist, VP, academic affairs, $74,823; $11,784
Ellen Black, VP, planning, research, and assessment, $73,857; $11,683

Source: "Pay and Benefits of Leaders at 479 Private Colleges and Universities: a Survey," *The Chronicle of Higher Education*, 47: A29-A48, (November 24, 2000).

★3374★
Top pay and benefits for the chief executive and top paid employees at Lincoln Memorial University

Ranking basis/background: Annual pay and benefits for the chief executives and top paid officers, as reported on Internal Revenue Service Form 990 by private colleges and universities in the U.S. for the 1998-99 academic year. **Number listed:** 6.

Jerry Bishop, president, with $90,000 annual pay; $0 in benefits
D. D. Thompson, senior VP, finance; treasurer, $61,600; $0
John C. Irvine, VP; dean of the faculty, $54,676; $0
Phyliss B. Noah, dean, education, $54,356; $0
Cynthia Whitt, senior VP, alumni and development, $54,000; $0
James McCune, VP, administration, $54,000; $0

Source: "Pay and Benefits of Leaders at 479 Private Colleges and Universities: a Survey," *The Chronicle of Higher Education*, 47: A29-A48, (November 24, 2000).

SALARIES—COLLEGES & UNIVERSITIES

★3375★
Top pay and benefits for the chief executive and top paid employees at Lindenwood University

Ranking basis/background: Annual pay and benefits for the chief executives and top paid officers, as reported on Internal Revenue Service Form 990 by private colleges and universities in the U.S. for the 1998-99 academic year. **Number listed:** 6.

- Dennis C. Spellmann, president, with $335,000 annual pay; $8,000 in benefits
- James D. Evans, dean of the faculty; professor, psychology, $77,583; $3,879
- David R. Williams, dean of the college; professor, social science, $75,083; $3,754
- Dominic Soda, professor, mathematics, $74,042; $3,702
- Nancy Matheny, dean, management, $70,417; $3,521
- David Kandel, controller; chief financial officer, $69,667; $3,483

Source: "Pay and Benefits of Leaders at 479 Private Colleges and Universities: a Survey," *The Chronicle of Higher Education*, 47: A29-A48, (November 24, 2000).

★3376★
Top pay and benefits for the chief executive and top paid employees at Linfield College

Ranking basis/background: Annual pay and benefits for the chief executives and top paid officers, as reported on Internal Revenue Service Form 990 by private colleges and universities in the U.S. for the 1998-99 academic year. **Number listed:** 6.

- Vivian A. Bull, president, with $144,999 annual pay; $65,218 in benefits
- Carl B. Vance, VP, finance and administration, $111,948; $25,504
- Marvin Henberg, VP, academic affairs, $95,523; $22,301
- Lee N. Howard, VP, college relations, $89,202; $21,302
- John Reed, VP, enrollment, $82,364; $22,416
- David Groff, associate VP, academic affairs, $71,900; $21,088

Source: "Pay and Benefits of Leaders at 479 Private Colleges and Universities: a Survey," *The Chronicle of Higher Education*, 47: A29-A48, (November 24, 2000).

★3377★
Top pay and benefits for the chief executive and top paid employees at Loma Linda University

Ranking basis/background: Annual pay and benefits for the chief executives and top paid officers, as reported on Internal Revenue Service Form 990 by private colleges and universities in the U.S. for the 1998-99 academic year. **Number listed:** 6.

- B. Lyn Behrens, president, with $117,391 annual pay; $7,674 in benefits
- J. David Moorhead, president; CEO, medical center, $302,400; $8,587
- Terrence A. Hansen, executive VP; chief operating officer, medical center, $273,000; $8,587
- Teresa M. Day, senior VP; CFO, medical center, $262,500; $8,587
- Michael Jackson, senior VP, medical center, $212,720; $8,587
- Eileen Zorn, senior VP, medical center, $183,750; $8,587

Source: "Pay and Benefits of Leaders at 479 Private Colleges and Universities: a Survey," *The Chronicle of Higher Education*, 47: A29-A48, (November 24, 2000).

★3378★
Top pay and benefits for the chief executive and top paid employees at Long Island University

Ranking basis/background: Annual pay and benefits for the chief executives and top paid officers, as reported on Internal Revenue Service Form 990 by private colleges and universities in the U.S. for the 1998-99 academic year. **Number listed:** 6.

- David J. Steinberg, president, with $335,493 annual pay; $30,607 in benefits
- Mary M. Lai, VP, finance; treasurer, $212,968; $25,782
- Gale Stevens Haynes, provost, Brooklyn Campus, $181,000; $23,716
- Michael Arons, VP, academic affairs, $168,143; $25,693
- George Sutton, university attorney, $147,500; $32,357
- Joseph Shenker, provost, C.W. Post Campus, $145,000; $24,735

Source: "Pay and Benefits of Leaders at 479 Private Colleges and Universities: a Survey," *The Chronicle of Higher Education*, 47: A29-A48, (November 24, 2000).

★3379★
Top pay and benefits for the chief executive and top paid employees at Loyola College in Maryland

Ranking basis/background: Annual pay and benefits for the chief executives and top paid officers, as reported on Internal Revenue Service Form 990 by private colleges and universities in the U.S. for the 1998-99 academic year. **Number listed:** 6.

- Rev. Harold Ridley, S.J., president, with $250,939 annual pay; $2,723 in benefits
- Thomas E. Scheye, academic VP, provost, $179,600; $21,618
- John A. Palmucci, VP, administration and finance, $178,700; $20,586
- Peter Lorenzi, dean, business and management, $155,819; $21,437
- Robert D. Shelton, director, International Research Institute; professor, electrical engineering, $157,084; $13,384
- Charles R. Margenthaler, professor emeritus, operations management, $161,720; $0

Source: "Pay and Benefits of Leaders at 479 Private Colleges and Universities: a Survey," *The Chronicle of Higher Education*, 47: A29-A48, (November 24, 2000).

★3380★
Top pay and benefits for the chief executive and top paid employees at Loyola Marymount University

Ranking basis/background: Annual pay and benefits for the chief executives and top paid officers, as reported on Internal Revenue Service Form 990 by private colleges and universities in the U.S. for the 1998-99 academic year. **Remarks:** Reverend O'Malley's compensation is paid directly to the Jesuit Community. **Number listed:** 6.

- Rev. Thomas P. O'Malley, S.J., president, with $0 annual pay; $0 in benefits
- Gerald T. McLaughlin, dean, law, $218,690; $14,670
- Georgene M. Vairo, professor, law, $180,499; $14,557
- Roger Findley, professor, law, $180,237; $14,505
- Lawrence B. Solum, professor, law, $167,562; $13,350
- John R. Oester, VP, business and finance, $158,293; $13,675

Source: "Pay and Benefits of Leaders at 479 Private Colleges and Universities: a Survey," *The Chronicle of Higher Education*, 47: A29-A48, (November 24, 2000).

★3381★
Top pay and benefits for the chief executive and top paid employees at Loyola University New Orleans

Ranking basis/background: Annual pay and benefits for the chief executives and top paid officers, as reported on Internal Revenue Service Form 990 by private colleges and universities in the U.S. for the 1998-99 academic year. **Number listed:** 6.

- Rev. Bernard P. Knoth, S.J., president, with $160,000 annual pay; $0 in benefits
- John Makdisi, dean, law, $163,000; $32,600
- David C. Danahar, VP, academic affairs; provost, $159,120; $31,824
- James Klebba, associate dean, law, $149,713; $29,943
- Joseph Mansfield, VP, institutional advancement, $142,475; $28,495
- Bernard Vetter, professor, law, $125,359; $25,072

Source: "Pay and Benefits of Leaders at 479 Private Colleges and Universities: a Survey," *The Chronicle of Higher Education*, 47: A29-A48, (November 24, 2000).

★3382★
Top pay and benefits for the chief executive and top paid employees at Loyola University of Chicago

Ranking basis/background: Annual pay and benefits for the chief executives and top paid officers, as reported on Internal Revenue Service Form 990 by private colleges and universities in the U.S. for the 1998-99 academic year. **Remarks:** Reverend Piderit's pay is donated to the Society of Jesus. **Number listed:** 6.

- Rev. John Piderit, S.J., president, with $0 annual pay; $0 in benefits
- Marion Brocks, chair, medicine, $314,885; $50,602
- Robert C. Morris, associate professor, trauma surgery, $299,000; $48,049

John R. Canning, professor, surgery, $282,700; $45,430
Daniel H. Winship, dean, school of medicine, $265,414; $42,652
Ralph P. Leischner, senior associate director, educational affairs and medical school, $255,955; $41,132

Source: "Pay and Benefits of Leaders at 479 Private Colleges and Universities: a Survey," *The Chronicle of Higher Education*, 47: A29-A48, (November 24, 2000).

★3383★
Top pay and benefits for the chief executive and top paid employees at Luther College

Ranking basis/background: Annual pay and benefits for the chief executives and top paid officers, as reported on Internal Revenue Service Form 990 by private colleges and universities in the U.S. for the 1998-99 academic year. **Number listed:** 7.

Jeffrey D. Baker, president, with $200,009 annual pay; $25,771 in benefits
Richard E. Hemp, interim president, $29,615; $3,157
David J. Roslien, VP, college advancement, $109,529; $15,745
David R. Anderson, VP, academic affairs; dean of the college, $93,409; $13,972
David L. Sallee, VP, enrollment, $87,649; $13,537
Anne C. Highum, VP; dean, student life, $85,491; $13,147
Diane L. Tacke, VP, finance and administration, $88,332; $9,898

Source: "Pay and Benefits of Leaders at 479 Private Colleges and Universities: a Survey," *The Chronicle of Higher Education*, 47: A29-A48, (November 24, 2000).

★3384★
Top pay and benefits for the chief executive and top paid employees at Lynchburg College

Ranking basis/background: Annual pay and benefits for the chief executives and top paid officers, as reported on Internal Revenue Service Form 990 by private colleges and universities in the U.S. for the 1998-99 academic year. **Number listed:** 6.

Charles O. Warren, president, with $169,418 annual pay; $19,912 in benefits
Mitchell Wesolowski, VP, business and finance, $111,375; $11,485
Jacqueline W. Asbury, dean of the college, $109,565; $12,611
Stewart W. Husted, dean; professor, business and economics, $86,359; $11,526
David G. Behrs, VP, enrollment management, $85,500; $8,374
Eugene G. Frantz, VP, development and external affairs, $75,479; $11,245

Source: "Pay and Benefits of Leaders at 479 Private Colleges and Universities: a Survey," *The Chronicle of Higher Education*, 47: A29-A48, (November 24, 2000).

★3385★
Top pay and benefits for the chief executive and top paid employees at Macalester College

Ranking basis/background: Annual pay and benefits for the chief executives and top paid officers, as reported on Internal Revenue Service Form 990 by private colleges and universities in the U.S. for the 1998-99 academic year. **Number listed:** 6.

Michael S. McPherson, president, with $206,624 annual pay; $33,603 in benefits
Richard A. Ammons, VP, college advancement, $121,965; $25,937
David A. Lanegran, professor, geography, $121,468; $25,485
Craig H. Aase, VP, administration; treasurer, $117,362; $23,222
A. Wayne Roberts, provost, $114,679; $24,739
Sung Kyu Kim, professor, physics and astronomy, $113,500; $20,045

Source: "Pay and Benefits of Leaders at 479 Private Colleges and Universities: a Survey," *The Chronicle of Higher Education*, 47: A29-A48, (November 24, 2000).

★3386★
Top pay and benefits for the chief executive and top paid employees at Madonna University

Ranking basis/background: Annual pay and benefits for the chief executives and top paid officers, as reported on Internal Revenue Service Form 990 by private colleges and universities in the U.S. for the 1998-99 academic year. **Remarks:** Sister Mary Francilene's compensation is paid directly to the Felician Sisters of Livonia. **Number listed:** 6.

Sister Mary Francilene, C.S.S.F., president, with $94,000 annual pay; $0 in benefits
Charlotte Neuhauser, professor, management, marketing, and economics, $89,899; $8,452
Ernest Nolan, VP, academic administration, $84,927; $9,658
Leonard Wilhelm, VP, business, finance, and operations, $80,517; $12,454
Stewart Arends, professor and dean, business, $85,140; $7,333
Lynn Kelly, professor, computer and quantitative systems, $81,456; $8,321

Source: "Pay and Benefits of Leaders at 479 Private Colleges and Universities: a Survey," *The Chronicle of Higher Education*, 47: A29-A48, (November 24, 2000).

★3387★
Top pay and benefits for the chief executive and top paid employees at Manhattan College

Ranking basis/background: Annual pay and benefits for the chief executives and top paid officers, as reported on Internal Revenue Service Form 990 by private colleges and universities in the U.S. for the 1998-99 academic year. **Remarks:** Brother Scanlan's pay is donated to the Christian Brothers Community at Manhattan College. **Number listed:** 6.

Bro. Thomas J. Scanlan, F.S.C., president, with $119,021 annual pay; $39,622 in benefits
Laurence M. Lerner, executive vice chairman; senior VP, college development; senior VP, capital campaign, $119,789; $39,878
E. Joseph Lee, VP, student services, $113,855; $37,902
Weldon Jackson, provost, $113,568; $37,807
Joseph Dillon, VP, advancement, $104,000; $34,622
Robert A. Mahan, VP, facilities management, $100,475; $33,448

Source: "Pay and Benefits of Leaders at 479 Private Colleges and Universities: a Survey," *The Chronicle of Higher Education*, 47: A29-A48, (November 24, 2000).

★3388★
Top pay and benefits for the chief executive and top paid employees at Manhattanville College

Ranking basis/background: Annual pay and benefits for the chief executives and top paid officers, as reported on Internal Revenue Service Form 990 by private colleges and universities in the U.S. for the 1998-99 academic year. **Number listed:** 6.

Richard A. Berman, president, with $155,288 annual pay; $23,304 in benefits
Sebastian Persico, VP, finance and administration, $133,535; $22,971
Mary Corrarino, VP, student affairs; general counsel, $124,172; $18,982
Luis A. Losada, provost; dean of the faculty, $110,423; $15,666
Anthony J. LaMagra, professor, music, $95,929; $18,642
Sylvia Blake, dean, education, $91,222; $19,578

Source: "Pay and Benefits of Leaders at 479 Private Colleges and Universities: a Survey," *The Chronicle of Higher Education*, 47: A29-A48, (November 24, 2000).

★3389★
Top pay and benefits for the chief executive and top paid employees at Marian College of Fond Du Lac

Ranking basis/background: Annual pay and benefits for the chief executives and top paid officers, as reported on Internal Revenue Service Form 990 by private colleges and universities in the U.S. for the 1998-99 academic year. **Number listed:** 6.

Richard I. Ridenour, president, with $130,000 annual pay; $0 in benefits
Gary Boelhower, interim VP, academic affairs, $78,952; $10,961
Kathleen Mailer, VP, academic affairs; dean of the faculty, $79,750; $8,165
Bruce Prall, professor, mathematics and sciences, MNS division, $76,351; $10,766
Janet Hanson, VP, business and finance, $74,000; $5,550
Elizabeth Pareto, division chair, nursing studies, $68,200; $10,155

Source: "Pay and Benefits of Leaders at 479 Private Colleges and Universities: a Survey," *The Chronicle of Higher Education*, 47: A29-A48, (November 24, 2000).

SALARIES—COLLEGES & UNIVERSITIES

Educational Rankings Annual • 2002

★3390★
Top pay and benefits for the chief executive and top paid employees at Marist College

Ranking basis/background: Annual pay and benefits for the chief executives and top paid officers, as reported on Internal Revenue Service Form 990 by private colleges and universities in the U.S. for the 1998-99 academic year. **Number listed:** 6.

- Dennis J. Murray, president, with $284,200 annual pay; $29,446 in benefits
- Roy Merolli, executive VP, $131,080; $14,207
- Artin Arslanian, academic VP, dean of the faculty, $130,431; $11,442
- Anthony Campilii, chief financial officer; VP, business affairs, $109,002; $17,534
- Gerard A. Cox, VP; dean, student affairs, $101,696; $20,004
- Thomas Daly, director, physical plant, $100,475; $14,554

Source: "Pay and Benefits of Leaders at 479 Private Colleges and Universities: a Survey," *The Chronicle of Higher Education*, 47: A29-A48, (November 24, 2000).

★3391★
Top pay and benefits for the chief executive and top paid employees at Marlboro College

Ranking basis/background: Annual pay and benefits for the chief executives and top paid officers, as reported on Internal Revenue Service Form 990 by private colleges and universities in the U.S. for the 1998-99 academic year. **Number listed:** 3.

- Paul J. LeBlanc, president, with $100,000 annual pay; $5,000 in benefits
- Arthur Scott, VP, finance, $73,750; $0
- William Wootton, director, institutional advancement, $61,532; $3,077

Source: "Pay and Benefits of Leaders at 479 Private Colleges and Universities: a Survey," *The Chronicle of Higher Education*, 47: A29-A48, (November 24, 2000).

★3392★
Top pay and benefits for the chief executive and top paid employees at Marquette University

Ranking basis/background: Annual pay and benefits for the chief executives and top paid officers, as reported on Internal Revenue Service Form 990 by private colleges and universities in the U.S. for the 1998-99 academic year. **Remarks:** Reverend Wild's pay is donated to the Marquette Jesuit Association. **Number listed:** 6.

- Rev. Robert A. Wild, S.J., president, with $0 annual pay; $0 in benefits
- Jerry A. Viscione, executive VP, $209,167; $31,936
- Howard B. Eisenberg, dean, law, $178,750; $27,080
- Kenneth H. Smits, VP, administration, $178,541; $27,120
- David Buckholdt, VP, academic affairs, $160,000; $35,657
- James P. Lyddy, VP, university advancement, $158,875; $26,605

Source: "Pay and Benefits of Leaders at 479 Private Colleges and Universities: a Survey," *The Chronicle of Higher Education*, 47: A29-A48, (November 24, 2000).

★3393★
Top pay and benefits for the chief executive and top paid employees at Marycrest International University

Ranking basis/background: Annual pay and benefits for the chief executives and top paid officers, as reported on Internal Revenue Service Form 990 by private colleges and universities in the U.S. for the 1998-99 academic year. **Number listed:** 6.

- Laurence M. Conner, president, with $132,473 annual pay; $17,993 in benefits
- Alan Garfield, associate professor; chair, communication graphics and computer science, $74,687; $8,134
- Judy Stark, assistant VP, business and finance, $54,469; $17,686
- Michelle Schiffgens, chair and professor, education, $52,754; $6,153
- Delores Hilden, chair and professor, nursing, $50,310; $5,972
- J. Thomas Jacobs, professor, communication graphics and computer science, $51,169; $4,646

Source: "Pay and Benefits of Leaders at 479 Private Colleges and Universities: a Survey," *The Chronicle of Higher Education*, 47: A29-A48, (November 24, 2000).

★3394★
Top pay and benefits for the chief executive and top paid employees at Marylhurst University

Ranking basis/background: Annual pay and benefits for the chief executives and top paid officers, as reported on Internal Revenue Service Form 990 by private colleges and universities in the U.S. for the 1998-99 academic year. **Number listed:** 5.

- Nancy Wilgenbusch, president, with $134,836 annual pay; $13,484 in benefits
- Joan Neice, VP, institutional advancement, $74,550; $7,455
- Denis G. Lawrence, VP, academics, $68,630; $6,863
- Michael Lammers, VP, finance, $62,406; $6,241
- Janet Williams, VP, human resources, $57,200; $5,720

Source: "Pay and Benefits of Leaders at 479 Private Colleges and Universities: a Survey," *The Chronicle of Higher Education*, 47: A29-A48, (November 24, 2000).

★3395★
Top pay and benefits for the chief executive and top paid employees at Marymount University

Ranking basis/background: Annual pay and benefits for the chief executives and top paid officers, as reported on Internal Revenue Service Form 990 by private colleges and universities in the U.S. for the 1998-99 academic year. **Remarks:** Sister Eymard Gallagher and Sister Michelle Murphy's pay is donated to the Religious Order of the Sacred Heart of Mary. **Number listed:** 6.

- Sister Eymard Gallagher, R.S.H.M., president, with $155,400 annual pay; $11,655 in benefits
- Linda McMahon, VP, student services, $123,218; $9,241
- Robert Sigethy, dean, business administration, $112,462; $8,435
- Sister Michelle Murphy, R.S.H.M., VP, financial affairs; treasurer, $108,921; $8,169
- Lawrence Padberg, VP, academic affairs, $105,425; $7,907
- Wayne A. Lesko, dean, education and human services, $103,330; $7,750

Source: "Pay and Benefits of Leaders at 479 Private Colleges and Universities: a Survey," *The Chronicle of Higher Education*, 47: A29-A48, (November 24, 2000).

★3396★
Top pay and benefits for the chief executive and top paid employees at Marywood University

Ranking basis/background: Annual pay and benefits for the chief executives and top paid officers, as reported on Internal Revenue Service Form 990 by private colleges and universities in the U.S. for the 1998-99 academic year. **Number listed:** 6.

- Sister Mary Reap, I.H.M., president, with $15,048 annual pay; $5,184 in benefits
- Clayton N. Pheasant, VP, university advancement, $92,583; $7,536
- Michael D. Shaler, director, Military Family Institute, $99,725; $0
- Alan Levine, deputy director, research; professor, nutrition and dietetics, $88,626; $9,601
- Steven D. Karcher, VP, business affairs, $82,858; $10,897
- Raymond P. Heath, VP, student life, $84,921; $6,961

Source: "Pay and Benefits of Leaders at 479 Private Colleges and Universities: a Survey," *The Chronicle of Higher Education*, 47: A29-A48, (November 24, 2000).

★3397★
Top pay and benefits for the chief executive and top paid employees at Massachusetts Institute of Technology

Ranking basis/background: Annual pay and benefits for the chief executives and top paid officers, as reported on Internal Revenue Service Form 990 by private colleges and universities in the U.S. for the 1998-99 academic year. **Number listed:** 6.

- Charles M. Vest, president, with $355,500 annual pay; $63,387 in benefits
- Alan S. Bufferd, treasurer, $429,860; $28,744
- R. Bruce Journey, publisher and CEO, Technology Review, Alumni Magazine of MIT, $329,601; $22,747
- Edward B. Roberts, professor, management of technology, school of management, $300,312; $23,497
- Robert A. Brown, provost, $278,509; $25,162
- Jeremy C. Stein, associate professor, management, $269,484; $25,926

Source: "Pay and Benefits of Leaders at 479 Private Colleges and Universities: a Survey," *The Chronicle of Higher Education*, 47: A29-A48, (November 24, 2000).

★3398★
Top pay and benefits for the chief executive and top paid employees at Mercer University

Ranking basis/background: Annual pay and benefits for the chief executives and top paid officers, as reported on Internal Revenue Service Form 990 by private colleges and universities in the U.S. for the 1998-99 academic year. **Number listed:** 6.

- R. Kirby Godsey, president, with $261,450 annual pay; $26,369 in benefits
- W. Douglas Skelton, senior VP, health affairs; dean, medicine, $282,572; $15,515
- Paul H. D'Amato, associate professor, internal medicine, $248,680; $11,179
- William H. Nelson, professor, psychiatry and behavioral sciences, $230,471; $28,263
- Oscar S. Spivey, professor, pediatrics, $203,573; $14,060
- John T. Mitchell, VP, public and government affairs, $180,250; $27,538

Source: "Pay and Benefits of Leaders at 479 Private Colleges and Universities: a Survey," *The Chronicle of Higher Education*, 47: A29-A48, (November 24, 2000).

★3399★
Top pay and benefits for the chief executive and top paid employees at Meredith College

Ranking basis/background: Annual pay and benefits for the chief executives and top paid officers, as reported on Internal Revenue Service Form 990 by private colleges and universities in the U.S. for the 1998-99 academic year. **Number listed:** 6.

- John E. Weems, president, with $224,506 annual pay; $16,329 in benefits
- Charles E. Taylor Jr., VP, business and finance, $99,962; $8,409
- LaRose F. Spooner, VP, administrative affairs, $87,397; $7,540
- Nancy Jean Jackson, VP, student development, $84,450; $6,523
- Murphy M. Osborne Jr., VP, institutional advancement, $75,986; $6,985
- Ruth Ann Balla, manager, technology services, $74,491; $5,526

Source: "Pay and Benefits of Leaders at 479 Private Colleges and Universities: a Survey," *The Chronicle of Higher Education*, 47: A29-A48, (November 24, 2000).

★3400★
Top pay and benefits for the chief executive and top paid employees at Midamerica Nazarene University

Ranking basis/background: Annual pay and benefits for the chief executives and top paid officers, as reported on Internal Revenue Service Form 990 by private colleges and universities in the U.S. for the 1998-99 academic year. **Number listed:** 6.

- Richard L. Spindle, president, with $89,422 annual pay; $22,993 in benefits
- Franklin M. Moore, VP; dean, academic affairs, $83,837; $12,949
- John W. Stephens, VP, finance, $79,265; $15,650
- Robert K. Drummond, VP, campus life, $77,258; $14,334
- Phylis J. Deisher, assistant professor, nursing, $75,438; $13,787
- Douglas D. Henning, dean, graduate and adult studies, $71,381; $14,306

Source: "Pay and Benefits of Leaders at 479 Private Colleges and Universities: a Survey," *The Chronicle of Higher Education*, 47: A29-A48, (November 24, 2000).

★3401★
Top pay and benefits for the chief executive and top paid employees at Middlebury College

Ranking basis/background: Annual pay and benefits for the chief executives and top paid officers, as reported on Internal Revenue Service Form 990 by private colleges and universities in the U.S. for the 1998-99 academic year. **Number listed:** 6.

- John M. McCardell Jr., president, with $209,400 annual pay; $28,752 in benefits
- Bruce Peterson, professor, mathematics, $129,650; $20,882
- David W. Ginevan, executive VP, facilities planning, $198,362; $35,608
- William F. Melton II, VP, external affairs, $161,316; $26,376
- Ronald D. Liebowitz, VP; provost, $152,000; $22,374
- Edward Knox, professor, French, $124,177; $21,051

Source: "Pay and Benefits of Leaders at 479 Private Colleges and Universities: a Survey," *The Chronicle of Higher Education*, 47: A29-A48, (November 24, 2000).

★3402★
Top pay and benefits for the chief executive and top paid employees at Mills College

Ranking basis/background: Annual pay and benefits for the chief executives and top paid officers, as reported on Internal Revenue Service Form 990 by private colleges and universities in the U.S. for the 1998-99 academic year. **Number listed:** 6.

- Janet L. Holmgren, president, with $207,223 annual pay; $26,852 in benefits
- Mary Ann Kinkead, provost; dean of the faculty, $147,399; $17,550
- Sally Randel, VP, institutional advancement, $129,000; $15,288
- Peter Michell, VP, finance and administration; treasurer, $125,000; $15,626
- Edna Mitchell, professor, education; director, Women's Leadership Institute, $115,709; $14,099
- Elizabeth Burwell, assistant VP, business affairs, $101,360; $13,018

Source: "Pay and Benefits of Leaders at 479 Private Colleges and Universities: a Survey," *The Chronicle of Higher Education*, 47: A29-A48, (November 24, 2000).

★3403★
Top pay and benefits for the chief executive and top paid employees at Millsaps College

Ranking basis/background: Annual pay and benefits for the chief executives and top paid officers, as reported on Internal Revenue Service Form 990 by private colleges and universities in the U.S. for the 1998-99 academic year. **Number listed:** 6.

- George M. Harmon, president, with $211,138 annual pay; $29,800 in benefits
- Gary L. Fretwell, VP, enrollment and student affairs, $113,750; $11,375
- John Pilgrim, VP, business affairs, $124,850; $0
- Jesse D. Beeler, assistant professor, accounting, $108,410; $10,841
- Richard A. Smith, VP; dean of the college, $117,700; $0
- Walter Neely, professor, finance, $96,790; $7,933

Source: "Pay and Benefits of Leaders at 479 Private Colleges and Universities: a Survey," *The Chronicle of Higher Education*, 47: A29-A48, (November 24, 2000).

★3404★
Top pay and benefits for the chief executive and top paid employees at Mississippi College

Ranking basis/background: Annual pay and benefits for the chief executives and top paid officers, as reported on Internal Revenue Service Form 990 by private colleges and universities in the U.S. for the 1998-99 academic year. **Number listed:** 6.

- Howell W. Todd, president, with $175,000 annual pay; $10,394 in benefits
- Sidney L. Moller, interim dean, law; professor, law, $141,790; $4,940
- Shirley Jones, professor, law, $123,444; $4,387
- William H. Page, professor, law, $106,333; $4,093
- Scott F. Norberg, professor, law, $100,711; $3,563
- J. Larry Lee, professor, law, $94,333; $3,617

Source: "Pay and Benefits of Leaders at 479 Private Colleges and Universities: a Survey," *The Chronicle of Higher Education*, 47: A29-A48, (November 24, 2000).

★3405★
Top pay and benefits for the chief executive and top paid employees at Monmouth College in Illinois

Ranking basis/background: Annual pay and benefits for the chief executives and top paid officers, as reported on Internal Revenue Service Form 990 by private colleges and universities in the U.S. for the 1998-99 academic year. **Number listed:** 6.

- Richard F. Giese, president, with $157,000 annual pay; $12,852 in benefits
- George F. Arnold, VP, academic affairs, $86,320; $7,904
- Richard Valentine, VP, external relations, $85,540; $7,850
- Donald Gladfelter, VP, finance and business, $83,200; $7,686

SALARIES—COLLEGES & UNIVERSITIES

Jacquelyn Condon, VP, student life, $72,800; $6,958
Terry L. Glasgow, director, athletics, $72,078; $6,557

Source: "Pay and Benefits of Leaders at 479 Private Colleges and Universities: a Survey," *The Chronicle of Higher Education*, 47: A29-A48, (November 24, 2000).

★3406★
Top pay and benefits for the chief executive and top paid employees at Monmouth University in New Jersey

Ranking basis/background: Annual pay and benefits for the chief executives and top paid officers, as reported on Internal Revenue Service Form 990 by private colleges and universities in the U.S. for the 1998-99 academic year. **Number listed:** 6.

Rebecca Stafford, president, with $379,898 annual pay; $10,918 in benefits
Thomas S. Pearson, provost; senior VP, academic affairs, $140,060; $9,783
William G. Craig, VP, finance, $137,903; $9,632
Dennis C. Macro, VP, institutional advancement, $123,558; $8,583
Patricia Swannack, VP, administrative services, $120,500; $8,431
Grey Dimenna, VP; general counsel, $119,500; $8,349

Source: "Pay and Benefits of Leaders at 479 Private Colleges and Universities: a Survey," *The Chronicle of Higher Education*, 47: A29-A48, (November 24, 2000).

★3407★
Top pay and benefits for the chief executive and top paid employees at Moravian College

Ranking basis/background: Annual pay and benefits for the chief executives and top paid officers, as reported on Internal Revenue Service Form 990 by private colleges and universities in the U.S. for the 1998-99 academic year. **Number listed:** 6.

Ervin Rokke, president, with $140,000 annual pay; $16,738 in benefits
Susanne I. Shaw, VP, institutional advancement, $90,600; $11,498
John R. Dilendik Jr., professor, education, $81,512; $8,513
Rudy Ackerman, professor, arts, $75,111; $8,871
Richard Dull, director, athletics, $73,163; $9,645
Winfred A. Kohls, professor, history, $73,722; $9,018

Source: "Pay and Benefits of Leaders at 479 Private Colleges and Universities: a Survey," *The Chronicle of Higher Education*, 47: A29-A48, (November 24, 2000).

★3408★
Top pay and benefits for the chief executive and top paid employees at Morehouse College

Ranking basis/background: Annual pay and benefits for the chief executives and top paid officers, as reported on Internal Revenue Service Form 990 by private colleges and universities in the U.S. for the 1998-99 academic year. **Number listed:** 6.

Walter E. Massey, president, with $215,250 annual pay; $27,983 in benefits
John Hopps, senior VP for academic affairs; provost, $166,040; $9,962
Jim Fletcher, VP, finance, $135,850; $8,151
Julius Coles, director, international affairs, $118,131; $7,088
Laron Clark, VP, institutional advancement, $112,500; $6,750
Walter Fluker, executive director, leadership center, $110,750; $6,645

Source: "Pay and Benefits of Leaders at 479 Private Colleges and Universities: a Survey," *The Chronicle of Higher Education*, 47: A29-A48, (November 24, 2000).

★3409★
Top pay and benefits for the chief executive and top paid employees at Mount Holyoke College

Ranking basis/background: Annual pay and benefits for the chief executives and top paid officers, as reported on Internal Revenue Service Form 990 by private colleges and universities in the U.S. for the 1998-99 academic year. **Number listed:** 6.

Joanne Creighton, president, with $217,085 annual pay; $28,272 in benefits
John Erwin, professor emeritus, French, $256,852; $5,507
Donald O'Shea, dean of the faculty, $143,124; $25,736
Wayne Gass, dean, administration, $135,346; $25,838
Peter Berek, professor, English, $141,926; $17,939
Mary Jo Maydew, treasurer, $135,346; $21,912

Source: "Pay and Benefits of Leaders at 479 Private Colleges and Universities: a Survey," *The Chronicle of Higher Education*, 47: A29-A48, (November 24, 2000).

★3410★
Top pay and benefits for the chief executive and top paid employees at Mount Saint Mary College in New York

Ranking basis/background: Annual pay and benefits for the chief executives and top paid officers, as reported on Internal Revenue Service Form 990 by private colleges and universities in the U.S. for the 1998-99 academic year. **Number listed:** 6.

Sister Ann Sakac, president, with $83,601 annual pay; $8,778 in benefits
Sister Agnes Boyle, VP, academic affairs, $80,579; $8,461
Roy M. Huckabee, professor, business, $77,472; $7,176
Richard M. Dickerman, VP, finance, $74,989; $7,874
James F. Cotter, professor, English, $74,098; $7,754
Ernest R. Mills II, VP, development, $73,323; $7,699

Source: "Pay and Benefits of Leaders at 479 Private Colleges and Universities: a Survey," *The Chronicle of Higher Education*, 47: A29-A48, (November 24, 2000).

★3411★
Top pay and benefits for the chief executive and top paid employees at Mount Saint Mary's College in California

Ranking basis/background: Annual pay and benefits for the chief executives and top paid officers, as reported on Internal Revenue Service Form 990 by private colleges and universities in the U.S. for the 1998-99 academic year. **Number listed:** 6.

Sister Karen Kennelly, C.S.J., president, with $103,774 annual pay; $16,787 in benefits
Jacqueline P. Doud, VP, academics; dean of the faculty; provost, $102,289; $5,294
MaryAnn Bonino, director, Da Camera Society, $89,388; $8,669
Pamela Hillman, VP, institutional advancement, $92,256; $4,793
Lawrence Smith, associate VP, information support services, $87,251; $8,562
Sister Annette Bower, professor, biological sciences, $81,361; $13,952

Source: "Pay and Benefits of Leaders at 479 Private Colleges and Universities: a Survey," *The Chronicle of Higher Education*, 47: A29-A48, (November 24, 2000).

★3412★
Top pay and benefits for the chief executive and top paid employees at Mount Saint Mary's College in Maryland

Ranking basis/background: Annual pay and benefits for the chief executives and top paid officers, as reported on Internal Revenue Service Form 990 by private colleges and universities in the U.S. for the 1998-99 academic year. **Remarks:** Sister Paula Marie Buley's pay donated to religious congregation. **Number listed:** 6.

George Houston, president, with $144,200 annual pay; $11,536 in benefits
Carol Hinds, VP; provost, $92,000; $7,360
Sister Paula Marie Buley, I.H.M., VP; treasurer, $87,000; $6,960
Frank S. DeLuca, VP, institutional advancement, $80,000; $6,400
John W. Campbell, professor, education, $70,600; $5,648
James Phelan, head coach, men's basketball, $66,548; $5,323

Source: "Pay and Benefits of Leaders at 479 Private Colleges and Universities: a Survey," *The Chronicle of Higher Education*, 47: A29-A48, (November 24, 2000).

★3413★
Top pay and benefits for the chief executive and top paid employees at Muhlenberg College

Ranking basis/background: Annual pay and benefits for the chief executives and top paid officers, as reported on Internal Revenue Service Form 990 by private colleges and universities in the U.S. for the 1998-99 academic year. **Number listed:** 6.

Arthur R. Taylor, president, with $184,060 annual pay; $26,047 in benefits
Ann Neitzel, VP, development, $102,280; $16,387
James Steffy, VP, administration, $101,980; $15,957

Alton Slane, professor, political science, $96,979; $8,132

George Heitmann, professor; dean, international programs; chair, accounting and business, $93,381; $9,848

Curtis Dretsch, dean of the faculty, $90,000; $12,228

Source: "Pay and Benefits of Leaders at 479 Private Colleges and Universities: a Survey," *The Chronicle of Higher Education*, 47: A29-A48, (November 24, 2000).

★3414★
Top pay and benefits for the chief executive and top paid employees at National-Louis University in Illinois

Ranking basis/background: Annual pay and benefits for the chief executives and top paid officers, as reported on Internal Revenue Service Form 990 by private colleges and universities in the U.S. for the 1998-99 academic year. **Number listed:** 7.

Curtis L. McCray, president, with $212,133 annual pay; $24,080 in benefits

Orley R. Herron, former president, $137,750; $137,750

Edward Risinger, senior VP; interim president, $152,138; $14,973

Kerry Kopera, VP, financial services, $114,583; $10,583

Thomas Kennedy, VP, human resources, $110,515; $6,408

Dave McCulloch, VP, university services, $105,638; $11,214

David Freitas, associate dean, National College of Education, $105,653; $10,643

Source: "Pay and Benefits of Leaders at 479 Private Colleges and Universities: a Survey," *The Chronicle of Higher Education*, 47: A29-A48, (November 24, 2000).

★3415★
Top pay and benefits for the chief executive and top paid employees at National University in California

Ranking basis/background: Annual pay and benefits for the chief executives and top paid officers, as reported on Internal Revenue Service Form 990 by private colleges and universities in the U.S. for the 1998-99 academic year. **Number listed:** 6.

Jerry C. Lee, president, with $335,000 annual pay; $68,750 in benefits

Jerry Alston, VP, academic affairs, $135,000; $8,327

Kevin Casey, VP, administration and business, $128,500; $9,043

Patricia Potter, VP, marketing and educational services, $120,000; $8,400

Ellen Curtis-Pierce, dean, education, $110,000; $6,417

Shahram Azordegan, dean, business and technology, $101,000; $6,822

Source: "Pay and Benefits of Leaders at 479 Private Colleges and Universities: a Survey," *The Chronicle of Higher Education*, 47: A29-A48, (November 24, 2000).

★3416★
Top pay and benefits for the chief executive and top paid employees at Nazareth College of Rochester

Ranking basis/background: Annual pay and benefits for the chief executives and top paid officers, as reported on Internal Revenue Service Form 990 by private colleges and universities in the U.S. for the 1998-99 academic year. **Number listed:** 7.

Rose Marie Beston, president, with $333,760 annual pay; $1,594 in benefits

Robert A. Miller, president, $139,069; $13,414

Stephen C. LaSalle, VP, finance, $122,483; $17,357

Dennis Silva, VP, academic affairs, $111,171; $16,206

Paul Buntich, VP, student affairs, $85,164; $12,203

Mary T. Bush, secretary of the college; assistant to the VP, academic affairs, $81,145; $10,770

Richard Matzek, director, library, $77,625; $12,393

Source: "Pay and Benefits of Leaders at 479 Private Colleges and Universities: a Survey," *The Chronicle of Higher Education*, 47: A29-A48, (November 24, 2000).

★3417★
Top pay and benefits for the chief executive and top paid employees at Nebraska Wesleyan University

Ranking basis/background: Annual pay and benefits for the chief executives and top paid officers, as reported on Internal Revenue Service Form 990 by private colleges and universities in the U.S. for the 1998-99 academic year. **Number listed:** 7.

Jeanie Watson, president, with $142,901 annual pay; $17,390 in benefits

John White Jr., chancellor, $8,333; $166,660

Norval Kneten, VP, academic affairs, $95,000; $8,739

Sara Boatman, VP, student affairs, $78,500; $7,685

Kenneth Keith, professor and chair, psychology, $72,832; $6,018

W. Leonard Staudinger, professor, chemistry, $71,841; $6,710

Richard Vogt, professor, computer science, $61,685; $6,456

Source: "Pay and Benefits of Leaders at 479 Private Colleges and Universities: a Survey," *The Chronicle of Higher Education*, 47: A29-A48, (November 24, 2000).

★3418★
Top pay and benefits for the chief executive and top paid employees at New School University

Ranking basis/background: Annual pay and benefits for the chief executives and top paid officers, as reported on Internal Revenue Service Form 990 by private colleges and universities in the U.S. for the 1998-99 academic year. **Number listed:** 6.

Jonathan F. Fanton, president, with $362,000 annual pay; $16,000 in benefits

Richard Gorman, senior VP, external affairs, $193,274; $16,000

Judith Walzer, professor, literature, $190,000; $16,000

James Murtha, executive VP, $175,000; $16,000

Elizabeth Dickey, acting provost, $172,000; $16,000

Frank Moore, VP, information technology, $156,000; $15,600

Source: "Pay and Benefits of Leaders at 479 Private Colleges and Universities: a Survey," *The Chronicle of Higher Education*, 47: A29-A48, (November 24, 2000).

★3419★
Top pay and benefits for the chief executive and top paid employees at New York University

Ranking basis/background: Annual pay and benefits for the chief executives and top paid officers, as reported on Internal Revenue Service Form 990 by private colleges and universities in the U.S. for the 1998-99 academic year. **Number listed:** 6.

L. Jay Oliva, president, with $626,000 annual pay; $23,633 in benefits

James A. Grifo, professor, obstetrics and gynecology, $2,151,044; $22,514

Nicole Noyes, assistant professor, obstetrics and gynecology, $1,620,016; $20,935

Alan Berkeley, professor, clinical obstetrics and gynecology, $1,524,917; $22,514

Frederick Licciardi, assistant professor, obstetrics and gynecology, $1,311,440; $20,935

Robert M. Glickman, dean, school of medicine, $769,458; $27,179

Source: "Pay and Benefits of Leaders at 479 Private Colleges and Universities: a Survey," *The Chronicle of Higher Education*, 47: A29-A48, (November 24, 2000).

★3420★
Top pay and benefits for the chief executive and top paid employees at Niagara University

Ranking basis/background: Annual pay and benefits for the chief executives and top paid officers, as reported on Internal Revenue Service Form 990 by private colleges and universities in the U.S. for the 1998-99 academic year. **Remarks:** Reverend Golden's pay is donated to the Congregation of the Mission. **Number listed:** 6.

Rev. Paul L. Golden, C.M., president, with $0 annual pay; $0 in benefits

Keith Miller, dean, college of business, $100,064; $18,722

Dolores Bower, dean, college of nursing, $98,767; $19,855

Susan E. Mason, VP, academic affairs, $100,683; $14,600

Richard S. Hopkins, VP, university advancement, $88,838; $18,888

John Stranges, university professor, $85,685; $15,987

Source: "Pay and Benefits of Leaders at 479 Private Colleges and Universities: a Survey," *The Chronicle of Higher Education*, 47: A29-A48, (November 24, 2000).

SALARIES—COLLEGES & UNIVERSITIES

★3421★
Top pay and benefits for the chief executive and top paid employees at North Central College in Illinois

Ranking basis/background: Annual pay and benefits for the chief executives and top paid officers, as reported on Internal Revenue Service Form 990 by private colleges and universities in the U.S. for the 1998-99 academic year. **Number listed:** 6.

- Harold R. Wilde, president, with $200,897 annual pay; $25,539 in benefits
- R. Devadoss Pandian, VP, academic affairs; dean of the faculty, $119,688; $18,121
- Rick E. Spencer, VP, institutional advancement, $118,150; $18,046
- Paul H. Loscheider, VP, business affairs, $113,750; $17,323
- Michael Joseph, VP, enrollment management and student affairs, $108,250; $14,677
- Richard Wilders, professor, mathematics; assistant VP, institutional research and assessment, $85,232; $14,582

Source: "Pay and Benefits of Leaders at 479 Private Colleges and Universities: a Survey," *The Chronicle of Higher Education*, 47: A29-A48, (November 24, 2000).

★3422★
Top pay and benefits for the chief executive and top paid employees at Northeastern University

Ranking basis/background: Annual pay and benefits for the chief executives and top paid officers, as reported on Internal Revenue Service Form 990 by private colleges and universities in the U.S. for the 1998-99 academic year. **Number listed:** 6.

- Richard M. Freeland, president, with $305,807 annual pay; $25,143 in benefits
- Laurence F. Mucciolo, senior VP, administration and finance, $238,144; $24,427
- John Adams, professor and chair economics, $230,750; $28,496
- Judith Brown, professor, law, $248,388; $5,421
- David Hall, provost, $218,500; $22,709
- Ira R. Weiss, dean, college of business administration, $195,553; $23,247

Source: "Pay and Benefits of Leaders at 479 Private Colleges and Universities: a Survey," *The Chronicle of Higher Education*, 47: A29-A48, (November 24, 2000).

★3423★
Top pay and benefits for the chief executive and top paid employees at Northwestern University

Ranking basis/background: Annual pay and benefits for the chief executives and top paid officers, as reported on Internal Revenue Service Form 990 by private colleges and universities in the U.S. for the 1998-99 academic year. **Number listed:** 6.

- Henry S. Bienen, president, with $359,653 annual pay; $47,995 in benefits
- Dipak C. Jain, professor, marketing management, $505,635; $20,018
- Artur Raviv, professor, finance, $472,522; $20,946
- Eugene S. Sunshine, senior VP, business and finance, $457,403; $20,352
- David L. Wagner, VP; chief investment officer, $440,977; $20,946
- Gary L. Barnett, head coach, men's football, $402,270; $20,282

Source: "Pay and Benefits of Leaders at 479 Private Colleges and Universities: a Survey," *The Chronicle of Higher Education*, 47: A29-A48, (November 24, 2000).

★3424★
Top pay and benefits for the chief executive and top paid employees at Norwich University in Vermont

Ranking basis/background: Annual pay and benefits for the chief executives and top paid officers, as reported on Internal Revenue Service Form 990 by private colleges and universities in the U.S. for the 1998-99 academic year. **Number listed:** 6.

- Richard W. Schneider, president, with $160,000 annual pay; $9,693 in benefits
- Hubert D. Maultsby, provost, $100,000; $4,875
- Richard S. Hansen, senior VP, $94,425; $6,138
- Jackson Kytle, VP, dean, Vermont College, $79,856; $5,191
- David Magida, chief administrative officer, $75,672; $4,919
- Frank E. Griffis Jr., dean, admissions, $72,692; $4,725

Source: "Pay and Benefits of Leaders at 479 Private Colleges and Universities: a Survey," *The Chronicle of Higher Education*, 47: A29-A48, (November 24, 2000).

★3425★
Top pay and benefits for the chief executive and top paid employees at Notre Dame College in New Hampshire

Ranking basis/background: Annual pay and benefits for the chief executives and top paid officers, as reported on Internal Revenue Service Form 990 by private colleges and universities in the U.S. for the 1998-99 academic year. **Number listed:** 5.

- Sister Carol J. J. Descoteaux, C.S.C., president, with $79,400 annual pay; $3,013 in benefits
- Gregory Landroche, executive VP; CFO, $100,000; $12,255
- Jane Walter, dean, sciences, $90,413; $7,564
- Alicia Finn, VP, student development, $64,065; $6,089
- Carolyn Hill, VP, academic affairs, $62,200; $3,533

Source: "Pay and Benefits of Leaders at 479 Private Colleges and Universities: a Survey," *The Chronicle of Higher Education*, 47: A29-A48, (November 24, 2000).

★3426★
Top pay and benefits for the chief executive and top paid employees at Nova Southeastern University

Ranking basis/background: Annual pay and benefits for the chief executives and top paid officers, as reported on Internal Revenue Service Form 990 by private colleges and universities in the U.S. for the 1998-99 academic year. **Number listed:** 6.

- Ray Ferrero Jr., president, with $276,000 annual pay; $10,287 in benefits
- Randolph Pohlman, dean, business and entrepreneurship, $288,914; $12,086
- Terry Morton, chancellor, health-professions division, $263,752; $14,777
- Joseph Harbaugh, dean and professor, law, $221,845; $10,000
- Ronald Levant, dean, Center for Psychological Studies, $183,264; $11,986
- Anthony Silvagni, dean, medicine, $189,309; $5,035

Source: "Pay and Benefits of Leaders at 479 Private Colleges and Universities: a Survey," *The Chronicle of Higher Education*, 47: A29-A48, (November 24, 2000).

★3427★
Top pay and benefits for the chief executive and top paid employees at Oberlin College

Ranking basis/background: Annual pay and benefits for the chief executives and top paid officers, as reported on Internal Revenue Service Form 990 by private colleges and universities in the U.S. for the 1998-99 academic year. **Number listed:** 6.

- Nancy S. Dye, president, with $210,468 annual pay; $53,022 in benefits
- Andrew B. Evans, VP, finance, $146,836; $39,274
- Richard Miller, professor, singing, $131,358; $45,124
- John C. Hays, associate VP, development, $138,721; $37,447
- M. Kay Thomson, VP, development, $130,375; $39,067
- Clayton R. Koppes, dean, arts and sciences, $127,398; $39,235

Source: "Pay and Benefits of Leaders at 479 Private Colleges and Universities: a Survey," *The Chronicle of Higher Education*, 47: A29-A48, (November 24, 2000).

★3428★
Top pay and benefits for the chief executive and top paid employees at Occidental College

Ranking basis/background: Annual pay and benefits for the chief executives and top paid officers, as reported on Internal Revenue Service Form 990 by private colleges and universities in the U.S. for the 1998-99 academic year. **Number listed:** 6.

- John B. Slaughter, president, with $192,355 annual pay; $17,513 in benefits
- William D. Tingley, VP; dean, admissions and financial aid, $155,000; $14,057
- Phillip Osbourne Bethea, VP, institutional advancement, $139,000; $13,753
- Harold W. Hewitt, VP, administration and finance, $135,000; $16,233
- David Axeen, VP; dean of the faculty, $130,000; $15,789
- Hazel Scott, VP, student services; dean of students, $127,500; $12,884

Source: "Pay and Benefits of Leaders at 479 Private Colleges and Universities: a Survey," *The Chronicle of Higher Education*, 47: A29-A48, (November 24, 2000).

SALARIES—COLLEGES & UNIVERSITIES

★3429★
Top pay and benefits for the chief executive and top paid employees at Oglethorpe University

Ranking basis/background: Annual pay and benefits for the chief executives and top paid officers, as reported on Internal Revenue Service Form 990 by private colleges and universities in the U.S. for the 1998-99 academic year. **Number listed:** 7.

- Larry D. Large, president, with $44,600 annual pay; $2,735 in benefits
- Donald S. Stanton, former president, $170,350; $13,071
- John B. Knott III, executive VP, $120,000; $11,076
- Robert Buccino, VP, advancement, $102,600; $9,790
- Nancy Kerr, provost, $102,600; $9,790
- William O. Shropshire, professor, economics, $94,600; $9,178
- G. Malcolm Amerson, professor, biology, $84,000; $8,348

Source: "Pay and Benefits of Leaders at 479 Private Colleges and Universities: a Survey," *The Chronicle of Higher Education*, 47: A29-A48, (November 24, 2000).

★3430★
Top pay and benefits for the chief executive and top paid employees at Ohio Wesleyan University

Ranking basis/background: Annual pay and benefits for the chief executives and top paid officers, as reported on Internal Revenue Service Form 990 by private colleges and universities in the U.S. for the 1998-99 academic year. **Number listed:** 6.

- Thomas B. Courtice, president, with $185,000 annual pay; $52,551 in benefits
- William C. Louthan, provost, $132,000; $19,270
- George J. Elsbeck, VP, business affairs, $113,550; $17,331
- Audry K. Carter, VP, university relations, $102,000; $16,117
- Alvin I. Sher, program director, Great Lakes College Association New York Arts Program, $99,812; $13,831
- Margaret Drugovich, VP, admission and financial aid, $92,742; $15,114

Source: "Pay and Benefits of Leaders at 479 Private Colleges and Universities: a Survey," *The Chronicle of Higher Education*, 47: A29-A48, (November 24, 2000).

★3431★
Top pay and benefits for the chief executive and top paid employees at Oklahoma City University

Ranking basis/background: Annual pay and benefits for the chief executives and top paid officers, as reported on Internal Revenue Service Form 990 by private colleges and universities in the U.S. for the 1998-99 academic year. **Number listed:** 8.

- Stephen Jennings, president, with $188,641 annual pay; $20,817 in benefits
- David Cawthon, interim president, $4,891; $770
- Jerald Walker, chancellor, $185,822; $62,395
- Lawrence Hellman, dean, law, $150,000; $19,498
- Nancy Kenderdine, associate dean and professor, law, $110,762; $14,272
- Karlie Harmon, professor, mass communications, $113,984; $10,800
- Dennis Arrow, professor, law, $108,970; $14,232
- Daniel Morgan, professor, law, $102,784; $15,780

Source: "Pay and Benefits of Leaders at 479 Private Colleges and Universities: a Survey," *The Chronicle of Higher Education*, 47: A29-A48, (November 24, 2000).

★3432★
Top pay and benefits for the chief executive and top paid employees at Olivet Nazarene University

Ranking basis/background: Annual pay and benefits for the chief executives and top paid officers, as reported on Internal Revenue Service Form 990 by private colleges and universities in the U.S. for the 1998-99 academic year. **Number listed:** 6.

- John C. Bowling, president, with $101,283 annual pay; $13,471 in benefits
- Douglas Perry, VP, finance, $78,386; $11,243
- Gary W. Streit, VP, academic affairs, $78,382; $11,242
- Richard Colling, professor, biology; chair, biological sciences department, $64,511; $8,279
- Norma Wood, chair, nursing, $62,881; $8,766
- Dianne Schaafsma, director, financial services, $62,310; $9,293

Source: "Pay and Benefits of Leaders at 479 Private Colleges and Universities: a Survey," *The Chronicle of Higher Education*, 47: A29-A48, (November 24, 2000).

★3433★
Top pay and benefits for the chief executive and top paid employees at Oral Roberts University

Ranking basis/background: Annual pay and benefits for the chief executives and top paid officers, as reported on Internal Revenue Service Form 990 by private colleges and universities in the U.S. for the 1998-99 academic year. **Number listed:** 7.

- Richard L. Roberts, president, with $97,500 annual pay; $0 in benefits
- G. Oral Roberts, chancellor, $72,500; $0
- Ralph Fagin, VP, academic affairs, $104,500; $0
- David J. Ellsworth, VP, operations and finance, $104,500; $0
- David M. Bernard, VP, information and communication systems, $104,500; $0
- Jeff Ogle, VP, student services, $104,500; $0
- Walter Richardson, general manager, television, $90,150; $0

Source: "Pay and Benefits of Leaders at 479 Private Colleges and Universities: a Survey," *The Chronicle of Higher Education*, 47: A29-A48, (November 24, 2000).

★3434★
Top pay and benefits for the chief executive and top paid employees at Our Lady of the Lake University

Ranking basis/background: Annual pay and benefits for the chief executives and top paid officers, as reported on Internal Revenue Service Form 990 by private colleges and universities in the U.S. for the 1998-99 academic year. **Number listed:** 6.

- Sally Mahoney, president, with $166,917 annual pay; $9,819 in benefits
- Robert E. Gibbons, executive VP, $102,500; $7,212
- Howard Benoist, VP and dean, academic affairs, $96,443; $7,294
- Allen R. Klaus, VP, finance and facilities, $93,589; $9,586
- Robert Carignan, professor, business administration; dean, business, $94,341; $4,394
- Jasper Arnold, associate professor, business administration, $89,023; $8,735

Source: "Pay and Benefits of Leaders at 479 Private Colleges and Universities: a Survey," *The Chronicle of Higher Education*, 47: A29-A48, (November 24, 2000).

★3435★
Top pay and benefits for the chief executive and top paid employees at Pace University

Ranking basis/background: Annual pay and benefits for the chief executives and top paid officers, as reported on Internal Revenue Service Form 990 by private colleges and universities in the U.S. for the 1998-99 academic year. **Number listed:** 6.

- Patricia O'Donnell Ewers, president, with $255,880 annual pay; $50,984 in benefits
- Arthur L. Centonze, dean, Lubin School of Business, $184,077; $53,684
- John R. Nolon, professor, law, $194,911; $26,089
- Leonard C. Sippel, executive VP, finance and administration, $160,470; $46,097
- Michael B. Mushlin, professor, law, $168,252; $31,419
- Marilyn Jaffe-Ruiz, VP, academic affairs, $165,000; $29,827

Source: "Pay and Benefits of Leaders at 479 Private Colleges and Universities: a Survey," *The Chronicle of Higher Education*, 47: A29-A48, (November 24, 2000).

★3436★
Top pay and benefits for the chief executive and top paid employees at Pacific Lutheran University

Ranking basis/background: Annual pay and benefits for the chief executives and top paid officers, as reported on Internal Revenue Service Form 990 by private colleges and universities in the U.S. for the 1998-99 academic year. **Number listed:** 7.

- Loren J. Anderson, president, with $179,490 annual pay; $17,885 in benefits
- Charles R. Upshaw, VP, finance, $105,770; $11,392
- Erving S. Severtson, VP; dean, student life, $97,881; $17,373

David Aubrey, VP, development and university relations, $88,000; $18,654
Donald R. Bell, dean, business, $97,750; $8,126
Paul T. Menzel, provost, $81,947; $10,330
Laura J. Polcyn, VP, admissions and enrollment, $69,300; $8,324

Source: "Pay and Benefits of Leaders at 479 Private Colleges and Universities: a Survey," *The Chronicle of Higher Education*, 47: A29-A48, (November 24, 2000).

★3437★
Top pay and benefits for the chief executive and top paid employees at Pacific University in Oregon

Ranking basis/background: Annual pay and benefits for the chief executives and top paid officers, as reported on Internal Revenue Service Form 990 by private colleges and universities in the U.S. for the 1998-99 academic year. **Number listed:** 6.

Faith Gabelnick, president, with $161,480 annual pay; $43,732 in benefits
Leland Carr, dean, optometry, $132,600; $9,285
Murry Sidlin, professor, conducting, $115,000; $5,823
William Willey, VP, finance, $105,029; $6,726
Timothy O'Malley, VP, university relations, $100,000; $8,396
Michel Hersen, dean and professor, psychology, $92,971; $8,112

Source: "Pay and Benefits of Leaders at 479 Private Colleges and Universities: a Survey," *The Chronicle of Higher Education*, 47: A29-A48, (November 24, 2000).

★3438★
Top pay and benefits for the chief executive and top paid employees at Park University

Ranking basis/background: Annual pay and benefits for the chief executives and top paid officers, as reported on Internal Revenue Service Form 990 by private colleges and universities in the U.S. for the 1998-99 academic year. **Number listed:** 6.

Donald J. Breckon, president, with $127,829 annual pay; $79,519 in benefits
Paul H. Gault, VP, business and finance, $87,662; $7,511
Paul A. Rounds, executive VP, administration, $87,076; $7,482
Demetri Karakitsos, associate professor, $77,090; $11,713
Z. Clara Brennan, VP, academic affairs, $79,596; $7,828
Terry Snapp, VP, institutional advancement, $74,211; $5,461

Source: "Pay and Benefits of Leaders at 479 Private Colleges and Universities: a Survey," *The Chronicle of Higher Education*, 47: A29-A48, (November 24, 2000).

★3439★
Top pay and benefits for the chief executive and top paid employees at Pfeiffer University

Ranking basis/background: Annual pay and benefits for the chief executives and top paid officers, as reported on Internal Revenue Service Form 990 by private colleges and universities in the U.S. for the 1998-99 academic year. **Number listed:** 6.

Charles M. Ambrose, president, with $120,350 annual pay; $6,018 in benefits
Thomas C. Leitzel, dean, school of graduate studies, $82,750; $4,138
Ronald Hunady, professor, business, $82,667; $4,133
Joel Vickers, professor; director, MBA/MHA program, $77,617; $3,881
Mike M. Riemann, provost; dean, academics, $77,250; $3,863
David Olive, VP, institutional advancement, $74,000; $3,700

Source: "Pay and Benefits of Leaders at 479 Private Colleges and Universities: a Survey," *The Chronicle of Higher Education*, 47: A29-A48, (November 24, 2000).

★3440★
Top pay and benefits for the chief executive and top paid employees at Philadelphia University

Ranking basis/background: Annual pay and benefits for the chief executives and top paid officers, as reported on Internal Revenue Service Form 990 by private colleges and universities in the U.S. for the 1998-99 academic year. **Number listed:** 6.

James P. Gallagher, president, with $180,000 annual pay; $26,200 in benefits
David Brookstein, dean, school of textiles and materials technology, $108,994; $9,270
Randall D. Gentzler, VP, business and finance; treasurer, $108,212; $9,739
Christopher Pastore, associate professor, textiles, materials engineering, and textile engineering; coordinator, textile technology program, $109,746; $6,365
Frank Glazer, VP, institutional advancement, $106,090; $9,548
Carol Fixman, VP, academic affairs, $105,000; $9,450

Source: "Pay and Benefits of Leaders at 479 Private Colleges and Universities: a Survey," *The Chronicle of Higher Education*, 47: A29-A48, (November 24, 2000).

★3441★
Top pay and benefits for the chief executive and top paid employees at Pitzer College

Ranking basis/background: Annual pay and benefits for the chief executives and top paid officers, as reported on Internal Revenue Service Form 990 by private colleges and universities in the U.S. for the 1998-99 academic year. **Number listed:** 6.

Marilyn Chapin Massey, president, with $178,104 annual pay; $31,576 in benefits
Vicke Selk, VP, administration; treasurer, $136,690; $27,508
Alice Holzman, VP, college advancement, $128,125; $24,670
Susan Seymour, VP; dean of the faculty, $120,387; $25,270
Arnaldo Rodriguez, VP, admissions and financial aid, $113,260; $23,792
Leah Light, professor, psychology, $109,611; $21,123

Source: "Pay and Benefits of Leaders at 479 Private Colleges and Universities: a Survey," *The Chronicle of Higher Education*, 47: A29-A48, (November 24, 2000).

★3442★
Top pay and benefits for the chief executive and top paid employees at Point Loma Nazarene University

Ranking basis/background: Annual pay and benefits for the chief executives and top paid officers, as reported on Internal Revenue Service Form 990 by private colleges and universities in the U.S. for the 1998-99 academic year. **Number listed:** 5.

Bob Brower, president, with $139,680 annual pay; $24,356 in benefits
Arthur L. Shingler, VP, financial affairs, $99,380; $20,432
Alton P. Allen, VP, academic affairs; provost, $101,358; $17,343
Richard Alderson, VP, university advancement, $96,786; $12,170
Barry Ryan, VP, university relations, $89,105; $19,645

Source: "Pay and Benefits of Leaders at 479 Private Colleges and Universities: a Survey," *The Chronicle of Higher Education*, 47: A29-A48, (November 24, 2000).

★3443★
Top pay and benefits for the chief executive and top paid employees at Polytechnic University

Ranking basis/background: Annual pay and benefits for the chief executives and top paid officers, as reported on Internal Revenue Service Form 990 by private colleges and universities in the U.S. for the 1998-99 academic year. **Number listed:** 7.

David Chang, president, with $260,000 annual pay; $16,000 in benefits
George Bugliarello, chancellor, $175,000; $16,000
Mel Horwitch, professor, management; director, Institute of Technology and Enterprise, $167,170; $14,140
Gregory D. Smith, VP, finance and administration, $167,000; $12,710
William McShane, VP; dean, engineering and applied science, $153,769; $14,438
Alan Myerson, professor, chemical engineering and chemistry, $140,069; $14,578
Ivan Frisch, executive VP; provost, $138,549; $13,828

Source: "Pay and Benefits of Leaders at 479 Private Colleges and Universities: a Survey," *The Chronicle of Higher Education*, 47: A29-A48, (November 24, 2000).

★3444★
Top pay and benefits for the chief executive and top paid employees at Pomona College

Ranking basis/background: Annual pay and benefits for the chief executives and top paid officers, as reported on Internal Revenue Service Form 990 by private colleges and universities in the U.S. for the 1998-99 academic year. **Number listed:** 6.

- Peter W. Stanley, president, with $204,266 annual pay; $36,063 in benefits
- Carlene Miller, VP; treasurer, $146,340; $30,022
- Hans C. Palmer, VP; dean of the college, $145,000; $28,914
- Gary Dicovitsky, VP, development; secretary, $142,698; $29,429
- Richard A. Fass, VP, planning, $134,340; $26,549
- Deborah M. Burke, chair, psychology, $135,428; $24,165

Source: "Pay and Benefits of Leaders at 479 Private Colleges and Universities: a Survey," *The Chronicle of Higher Education*, 47: A29-A48, (November 24, 2000).

★3445★
Top pay and benefits for the chief executive and top paid employees at Presbyterian College

Ranking basis/background: Annual pay and benefits for the chief executives and top paid officers, as reported on Internal Revenue Service Form 990 by private colleges and universities in the U.S. for the 1998-99 academic year. **Number listed:** 6.

- John V. Griffith, president, with $160,000 annual pay; $7,467 in benefits
- J. David Gillespie, VP, academic affairs; dean of the faculty, $97,500; $7,225
- George Dupuy, professor, economics, $85,015; $6,056
- George E. Zubrod, VP, finance, $80,266; $6,467
- Ann B. Stidham, professor, psychology, $80,945; $4,956
- Foard H. Tarbert, professor, business, $80,401; $5,323

Source: "Pay and Benefits of Leaders at 479 Private Colleges and Universities: a Survey," *The Chronicle of Higher Education*, 47: A29-A48, (November 24, 2000).

★3446★
Top pay and benefits for the chief executive and top paid employees at Princeton University

Ranking basis/background: Annual pay and benefits for the chief executives and top paid officers, as reported on Internal Revenue Service Form 990 by private colleges and universities in the U.S. for the 1998-99 academic year. **Number listed:** 6.

- Harold T. Shapiro, president, with $413,000 annual pay; $43,170 in benefits
- Andrew K. Golden, president, Princeton University Investment Company, $318,488; $42,285
- Jeremiah P. Ostriker, provost, $297,164; $40,359
- Yacine Ait-Sahalia, professor, economics, $273,167; $44,985
- Daniel Kahneman, professor, psychology and public affairs, $260,324; $38,474
- Michael Rothschild, dean, school of public and international affairs; professor, public affairs and economics, $253,769; $38,563

Source: "Pay and Benefits of Leaders at 479 Private Colleges and Universities: a Survey," *The Chronicle of Higher Education*, 47: A29-A48, (November 24, 2000).

★3447★
Top pay and benefits for the chief executive and top paid employees at Providence College

Ranking basis/background: Annual pay and benefits for the chief executives and top paid officers, as reported on Internal Revenue Service Form 990 by private colleges and universities in the U.S. for the 1998-99 academic year. **Number listed:** 6.

- Rev. Philip A. Smith, O.P., president, with $0 annual pay; $0 in benefits
- Timothy J. Welsh, coach, men's basketball, $179,148; $11,197
- Thomas Canavan, VP, academic administration, $138,550; $19,601
- Edward J. Caron, VP, college relations and planning, $130,589; $20,113
- Michael V. Frazier, VP, business and finance, $125,396; $14,367
- Joseph P. Brum, VP, development, $117,325; $17,748

Source: "Pay and Benefits of Leaders at 479 Private Colleges and Universities: a Survey," *The Chronicle of Higher Education*, 47: A29-A48, (November 24, 2000).

★3448★
Top pay and benefits for the chief executive and top paid employees at Queens College in North Carolina

Ranking basis/background: Annual pay and benefits for the chief executives and top paid officers, as reported on Internal Revenue Service Form 990 by private colleges and universities in the U.S. for the 1998-99 academic year. **Number listed:** 6.

- Billy O. Wireman, president, with $180,500 annual pay; $23,646 in benefits
- Richard Rankin, VP, institutional advancement, $78,690; $9,400
- Laurie Guy, VP, administration and finance, $77,692; $8,443
- S. Cathy Anderson, provost, $77,541; $8,094
- Robert L. Finley, professor, business administration, $75,297; $7,089
- Glenn Loomer, director, computer services, $73,950; $8,216

Source: "Pay and Benefits of Leaders at 479 Private Colleges and Universities: a Survey," *The Chronicle of Higher Education*, 47: A29-A48, (November 24, 2000).

★3449★
Top pay and benefits for the chief executive and top paid employees at Quinnipiac University

Ranking basis/background: Annual pay and benefits for the chief executives and top paid officers, as reported on Internal Revenue Service Form 990 by private colleges and universities in the U.S. for the 1998-99 academic year. **Number listed:** 5.

- John L. Lahey, president, with $330,000 annual pay; $40,000 in benefits
- Patrick J. Healy, VP, finance and administration, $215,000; $36,000
- Neil H. Cogan, dean, law, $205,000; $33,000
- John B. Bennett, provost; VP, academic affairs, $190,000; $32,000
- Martin B. Margulies, professor, law, $129,500; $29,000

Source: "Pay and Benefits of Leaders at 479 Private Colleges and Universities: a Survey," *The Chronicle of Higher Education*, 47: A29-A48, (November 24, 2000).

★3450★
Top pay and benefits for the chief executive and top paid employees at Radcliffe College

Ranking basis/background: Annual pay and benefits for the chief executives and top paid officers, as reported on Internal Revenue Service Form 990 by private colleges and universities in the U.S. for the 1998-99 academic year. **Number listed:** 6.

- Linda Wilson, president, with $166,500 annual pay; $22,146 in benefits
- Bonnie Clendenning, VP, college relations, $143,276; $14,252
- Joanna Brode, director, development, $99,072; $14,569
- Tamar March, dean, educational programs, $93,759; $11,313
- Paula Rayman, director, public-policy institute, $92,776; $8,611
- Mary Maples Dunn, dean, Radcliffe Institute for Advanced Study, $87,842; $10,715

Source: "Pay and Benefits of Leaders at 479 Private Colleges and Universities: a Survey," *The Chronicle of Higher Education*, 47: A29-A48, (November 24, 2000).

★3451★
Top pay and benefits for the chief executive and top paid employees at Randolph-Macon College

Ranking basis/background: Annual pay and benefits for the chief executives and top paid officers, as reported on Internal Revenue Service Form 990 by private colleges and universities in the U.S. for the 1998-99 academic year. **Number listed:** 7.

- Roger H. Martin, president, with $151,500 annual pay; $17,712 in benefits
- John A. Ahladas treasurer, $94,096; $12,351
- Edward G. Moore, VP, development, $94,096; $12,351
- Howard E. Davis, professor, political science, $94,642; $11,714
- John C. Conkright, dean, admissions and financial aid, $94,096; $9,413

M. Thomas Inge, professor, humanities, $92,215; $10,497
Ira Andrews, dean of students, $86,254; $10,875

Source: "Pay and Benefits of Leaders at 479 Private Colleges and Universities: a Survey," *The Chronicle of Higher Education*, 47: A29-A48, (November 24, 2000).

★3452★
Top pay and benefits for the chief executive and top paid employees at Randolph-Macon Woman's College

Ranking basis/background: Annual pay and benefits for the chief executives and top paid officers, as reported on Internal Revenue Service Form 990 by private colleges and universities in the U.S. for the 1998-99 academic year. **Number listed:** 6.

Kathleen G. Bowman, president, with $158,000 annual pay; $15,800 in benefits
James C. Kughn Jr., VP, development and public relations, $112,283; $11,228
William A. Burns, treasurer, $98,269; $9,827
Anita Solow, VP and dean, academic affairs, $97,500; $9,750
Connie Gores, VP, enrollment, $90,177; $9,018
Donnie Morgan, dean of students, $69,680; $6,968

Source: "Pay and Benefits of Leaders at 479 Private Colleges and Universities: a Survey," *The Chronicle of Higher Education*, 47: A29-A48, (November 24, 2000).

★3453★
Top pay and benefits for the chief executive and top paid employees at Reed College

Ranking basis/background: Annual pay and benefits for the chief executives and top paid officers, as reported on Internal Revenue Service Form 990 by private colleges and universities in the U.S. for the 1998-99 academic year. **Number listed:** 7.

Steven S. Koblik, president, with $176,637 annual pay; $39,567 in benefits
Edwin O. McFarlane, VP; treasurer, $120,000; $26,880
Peter Steinberger, dean of the faculty, $110,512; $24,755
Larry D. Large, executive VP, $106,740; $23,910
Raymond Kierstead, professor, history, $87,055; $27,422
Joseph Roberts, mathematics, $87,055; $27,422
Hugh Porter, VP, development, $92,048; $20,619

Source: "Pay and Benefits of Leaders at 479 Private Colleges and Universities: a Survey," *The Chronicle of Higher Education*, 47: A29-A48, (November 24, 2000).

★3454★
Top pay and benefits for the chief executive and top paid employees at Regis University in Colorado

Ranking basis/background: Annual pay and benefits for the chief executives and top paid officers, as reported on Internal Revenue Service Form 990 by private colleges and universities in the U.S. for the 1998-99 academic year. **Remarks:** Reverend Sheeran's pay is donated to the Society of Jesus. **Number listed:** 6.

Rev. Michael J. Sheeran, S.J., president, with $143,173 annual pay; $29,317 in benefits
Allan L. Service, VP, academic affairs, $112,772; $19,216
James R. Schoemer, treasurer; VP, administration and finance, $107,963; $18,552
John Alexander, VP, development, $103,240; $17,902
Thomas E. Reynolds, VP, student life, $91,495; $16,838
Tom Kennedy, VP, new ventures, $89,995; $16,632

Source: "Pay and Benefits of Leaders at 479 Private Colleges and Universities: a Survey," *The Chronicle of Higher Education*, 47: A29-A48, (November 24, 2000).

★3455★
Top pay and benefits for the chief executive and top paid employees at Rensselaer Polytechnic Institute

Ranking basis/background: Annual pay and benefits for the chief executives and top paid officers, as reported on Internal Revenue Service Form 990 by private colleges and universities in the U.S. for the 1998-99 academic year. **Number listed:** 6.

Cornelius Barton, president, with $0 annual pay; $3,685 in benefits
Daniel Berg, professor, decision sciences and engineering systems, $306,701; $151,176
Martin Glicksman, professor, materials science and engineering, $186,302; $69,283
Shyam Muraka, professor, materials sciences and engineering, $196,102; $59,223
Jack Wilson, acting provost, $185,000; $68,890
Richard Lahey, dean, school of engineering, $184,000; $68,588

Source: "Pay and Benefits of Leaders at 479 Private Colleges and Universities: a Survey," *The Chronicle of Higher Education*, 47: A29-A48, (November 24, 2000).

★3456★
Top pay and benefits for the chief executive and top paid employees at Rhodes College

Ranking basis/background: Annual pay and benefits for the chief executives and top paid officers, as reported on Internal Revenue Service Form 990 by private colleges and universities in the U.S. for the 1998-99 academic year. **Number listed:** 7.

James H. Daughdrill Jr., president, with $275,670 annual pay; $91,702 in benefits
David L. Harlow, chancellor; chief operating officer, $197,562; $32,474
James Allen Boone, dean, administrative services, $160,000; $28,760
Arthur L. Criscillis, dean, development, $150,000; $27,185
John Planchon, associate dean, academic affairs; dean, special studies, $150,000; $27,179
David James Wottle, dean, admissions and financial aid, $140,000; $25,613
Melody Richey, dean of students, $115,000; $21,680

Source: "Pay and Benefits of Leaders at 479 Private Colleges and Universities: a Survey," *The Chronicle of Higher Education*, 47: A29-A48, (November 24, 2000).

★3457★
Top pay and benefits for the chief executive and top paid employees at Rice University

Ranking basis/background: Annual pay and benefits for the chief executives and top paid officers, as reported on Internal Revenue Service Form 990 by private colleges and universities in the U.S. for the 1998-99 academic year. **Number listed:** 6.

Malcolm Gillis, president, with $399,719 annual pay; $97,972 in benefits
Kenneth W. Hatfield, head coach, football, $289,719; $78,939
Richard E. Smalley, professor, chemistry and physics, $334,621; $26,604
Dean W. Currie, VP, finance and administration, $314,719; $32,664
David H. Auston, provost, $315,919; $29,220
Kenneth W. Kennedy, Jr., professor, computer science and mathematics, $312,255; $25,585

Source: "Pay and Benefits of Leaders at 479 Private Colleges and Universities: a Survey," *The Chronicle of Higher Education*, 47: A29-A48, (November 24, 2000).

★3458★
Top pay and benefits for the chief executive and top paid employees at Rider University

Ranking basis/background: Annual pay and benefits for the chief executives and top paid officers, as reported on Internal Revenue Service Form 990 by private colleges and universities in the U.S. for the 1998-99 academic year. **Number listed:** 6.

J. Barton Luedeke, president, with $164,152 annual pay; $29,303 in benefits
Phyllis M. Frakt, VP, academic affairs; provost, $129,916; $19,620
Christina Petruska, VP, institutional planning, $114,704; $27,208
Julie Karns, VP, finance, $121,935; $18,457
Michael Epstein, professor, psychology, $114,502; $20,884
Mark E. Sandberg, dean, business administration, $119,145; $13,752

Source: "Pay and Benefits of Leaders at 479 Private Colleges and Universities: a Survey," *The Chronicle of Higher Education*, 47: A29-A48, (November 24, 2000).

SALARIES—COLLEGES & UNIVERSITIES

★3459★
Top pay and benefits for the chief executive and top paid employees at Ripon College

Ranking basis/background: Annual pay and benefits for the chief executives and top paid officers, as reported on Internal Revenue Service Form 990 by private colleges and universities in the U.S. for the 1998-99 academic year. **Number listed:** 6.

- Paul B. Ranslow, president, with $155,000 annual pay; $23,306 in benefits
- David B. Seligman, VP; dean of the faculty, $97,541; $17,572
- Mary M. deRegnier, VP, finance, $92,700; $17,089
- Scott J. Goplin, VP; dean, admissions and financial aid, $92,700; $17,089
- David K. Williams, VP, development, $92,700; $17,089
- Robert H. Young, VP; dean of students, $75,190; $15,342

Source: "Pay and Benefits of Leaders at 479 Private Colleges and Universities: a Survey," *The Chronicle of Higher Education*, 47: A29-A48, (November 24, 2000).

★3460★
Top pay and benefits for the chief executive and top paid employees at Rivier College

Ranking basis/background: Annual pay and benefits for the chief executives and top paid officers, as reported on Internal Revenue Service Form 990 by private colleges and universities in the U.S. for the 1998-99 academic year. **Remarks:** Sister Lucille Thibodeau's pay is contributed to religious order. **Number listed:** 6.

- Sister Lucille Thibodeau, P.M., president, with $0 annual pay; $0 in benefits
- Joseph A. Fagan, VP, finance and administration, $96,410; $15,235
- Charles L. Mitsakos, chair; professor, education, $89,847; $13,535
- Lynn Jansky, VP, student development, $78,000; $13,195
- Kenneth Binder, VP, institutional advancement, $78,000; $11,912
- Steven Trainor, professor, education; dean, school of arts and sciences, $75,281; $13,736

Source: "Pay and Benefits of Leaders at 479 Private Colleges and Universities: a Survey," *The Chronicle of Higher Education*, 47: A29-A48, (November 24, 2000).

★3461★
Top pay and benefits for the chief executive and top paid employees at Rochester Institute of Technology

Ranking basis/background: Annual pay and benefits for the chief executives and top paid officers, as reported on Internal Revenue Service Form 990 by private colleges and universities in the U.S. for the 1998-99 academic year. **Number listed:** 6.

- Albert J. Simone, president, with $269,711 annual pay; $26,110 in benefits
- Stanley D. McKenzie, provost; VP, academic affairs, $180,097; $19,057
- Nathan Robfogel, VP, university relations, $172,518; $20,789
- Robert R. Davila, VP, National Technical Institute for the Deaf, $174,375; $17,483
- William M. Dempsey, president and dean, American College of Management, $152,573; $35,744
- Ian Gatley, director, Chester F. Carlson Center for Imaging Science, $162,000; $19,795

Source: "Pay and Benefits of Leaders at 479 Private Colleges and Universities: a Survey," *The Chronicle of Higher Education*, 47: A29-A48, (November 24, 2000).

★3462★
Top pay and benefits for the chief executive and top paid employees at Rockefeller University

Ranking basis/background: Annual pay and benefits for the chief executives and top paid officers, as reported on Internal Revenue Service Form 990 by private colleges and universities in the U.S. for the 1998-99 academic year. **Number listed:** 7.

- Torsten N. Wiesel, former president, with $189,583 annual pay; $189,402 in benefits
- Arnold Levine, president, $270,833; $82,949
- Frederick M. Bohen, executive VP, $300,000; $155,453
- Carol B. Eniger, VP, investment management, $240,000; $116,107
- James E. Darnell, professor, molecular-cell biology, $261,000; $65,345
- Robert G. Roeder, professor, biochemistry and molecular biology, $252,500; $45,765
- Paul Greengard, professor and head, laboratory of molecular and cellular neuroscience, $218,500; $40,521

Source: "Pay and Benefits of Leaders at 479 Private Colleges and Universities: a Survey," *The Chronicle of Higher Education*, 47: A29-A48, (November 24, 2000).

★3463★
Top pay and benefits for the chief executive and top paid employees at Rockford College in Illinois

Ranking basis/background: Annual pay and benefits for the chief executives and top paid officers, as reported on Internal Revenue Service Form 990 by private colleges and universities in the U.S. for the 1998-99 academic year. **Number listed:** 6.

- William A. Shields, president, with $174,250 annual pay; $17,112 in benefits
- John A. Gallagher, VP, institutional advancement, $96,074; $11,406
- Noe A. Marinelli, VP, finance and administration, $93,465; $11,449
- William T. O'Hare, academic VP, $88,452; $8,844
- Gerald Caton, professor, mathematics and computer science; department chair, mathematics, $67,385; $8,086
- Chris Moderson, VP, enrollment management, $68,084; $6,808

Source: "Pay and Benefits of Leaders at 479 Private Colleges and Universities: a Survey," *The Chronicle of Higher Education*, 47: A29-A48, (November 24, 2000).

★3464★
Top pay and benefits for the chief executive and top paid employees at Rockhurst University

Ranking basis/background: Annual pay and benefits for the chief executives and top paid officers, as reported on Internal Revenue Service Form 990 by private colleges and universities in the U.S. for the 1998-99 academic year. **Number listed:** 5.

- W. Earl Walker, dean, school of management, with $94,904 annual pay; $5,694 in benefits
- Anthony Tocco, professor, accounting, management school, $93,411; $5,695
- Thomas L. Lyon Jr., professor, finance, management school, $91,980; $5,850
- Robin Harris, VP, institutional advancement, $86,692; $5,362
- Roger McCoy, VP, finance, $84,134; $5,113

Source: "Pay and Benefits of Leaders at 479 Private Colleges and Universities: a Survey," *The Chronicle of Higher Education*, 47: A29-A48, (November 24, 2000).

★3465★
Top pay and benefits for the chief executive and top paid employees at Rollins College

Ranking basis/background: Annual pay and benefits for the chief executives and top paid officers, as reported on Internal Revenue Service Form 990 by private colleges and universities in the U.S. for the 1998-99 academic year. **Number listed:** 6.

- Rita Bornstein, president, with $200,092 annual pay; $52,649 in benefits
- Edward A. Moses, dean, business; professor, finance, $158,528; $17,444
- George Herbst, VP, finance; treasurer, $136,084; $16,855
- Charles Edmondson, VP, academic affairs, $124,583; $16,064
- Charles Brandon, professor, accounting, $128,825; $10,352
- Ronnie Clayton, associate professor, finance, $123,520; $11,380

Source: "Pay and Benefits of Leaders at 479 Private Colleges and Universities: a Survey," *The Chronicle of Higher Education*, 47: A29-A48, (November 24, 2000).

★3466★
Top pay and benefits for the chief executive and top paid employees at Roosevelt University

Ranking basis/background: Annual pay and benefits for the chief executives and top paid officers, as reported on Internal Revenue Service Form 990 by private colleges and universities in the U.S. for the 1998-99 academic year. **Number listed:** 6.

- Theodore L. Gross, president, with $250,156 annual pay; $25,906 in benefits
- Stuart I. Fagan, provost; VP, academic affairs, $149,783; $21,545
- John E. Allerson, VP, business and finance, $141,360; $23,586
- Richard Krieg, executive director, Institute for Metropolitan Affairs, $141,140; $5,844

James S. Cicarelli, dean, Walter E. Meller College of Business Administration, $119,348; $20,119
Ronald Champagne, VP, development, $115,873; $17,475

Source: "Pay and Benefits of Leaders at 479 Private Colleges and Universities: a Survey," *The Chronicle of Higher Education*, 47: A29-A48, (November 24, 2000).

★3467★
Top pay and benefits for the chief executive and top paid employees at Sacred Heart University in Connecticut

Ranking basis/background: Annual pay and benefits for the chief executives and top paid officers, as reported on Internal Revenue Service Form 990 by private colleges and universities in the U.S. for the 1998-99 academic year. **Number listed:** 6.

Anthony J. Cernera, president, with $361,752 annual pay; $15,080 in benefits
Paul K. Madonna, VP, finance and administration, $168,066; $10,040
James M. Barquinero, VP, enrollment planning and student affairs, $159,435; $9,800
Thomas Forget, acting VP, academic affairs, $133,107; $8,297
Luke P. Doyle, VP, institutional advancement, $120,942; $8,800
Benoit Boyer, dean, business, $111,500; $8,240

Source: "Pay and Benefits of Leaders at 479 Private Colleges and Universities: a Survey," *The Chronicle of Higher Education*, 47: A29-A48, (November 24, 2000).

★3468★
Top pay and benefits for the chief executive and top paid employees at St. Ambrose University

Ranking basis/background: Annual pay and benefits for the chief executives and top paid officers, as reported on Internal Revenue Service Form 990 by private colleges and universities in the U.S. for the 1998-99 academic year. **Number listed:** 6.

Edward Rogalski, president, with $135,000 annual pay; $118,511 in benefits
John Collis, dean, business, $109,584; $11,014
Edward Henkhaus, VP, finance, $79,711; $22,189
Daniel S. Bozik, dean, human services, $86,379; $10,816
Steven R. Goebel, VP, university relations, $82,043; $11,298
Donald J. Moeller, provost, $81,728; $11,274

Source: "Pay and Benefits of Leaders at 479 Private Colleges and Universities: a Survey," *The Chronicle of Higher Education*, 47: A29-A48, (November 24, 2000).

★3469★
Top pay and benefits for the chief executive and top paid employees at St. Andrews Presbyterian College

Ranking basis/background: Annual pay and benefits for the chief executives and top paid officers, as reported on Internal Revenue Service Form 990 by private colleges and universities in the U.S. for the 1998-99 academic year. **Number listed:** 5.

Warren L. Board, president, with $92,700 annual pay; $7,787 in benefits
Paul Baldasare, VP, institutional advancement, $65,000; $3,900
William H. Gearhart, VP, administration and finance, $65,000; $3,900
Marcia K. Nance, dean of students, $65,000; $3,900
Lawrence E. Schulz, VP, academic affairs; dean of the college; professor, politics, $53,560; $3,214

Source: "Pay and Benefits of Leaders at 479 Private Colleges and Universities: a Survey," *The Chronicle of Higher Education*, 47: A29-A48, (November 24, 2000).

★3470★
Top pay and benefits for the chief executive and top paid employees at Saint Bonaventure University

Ranking basis/background: Annual pay and benefits for the chief executives and top paid officers, as reported on Internal Revenue Service Form 990 by private colleges and universities in the U.S. for the 1998-99 academic year. **Number listed:** 7.

Robert J. Wickenheiser, president, with $125,000 annual pay; $17,981 in benefits
Dean Bruno, VP, university advancement, $102,500; $14,188
James Baron, head coach, men's basketball, $100,654; $14,060
Carol Anne Pierson, dean, education, $94,750; $13,346
Leibert Coppola, dean, school of journalism and mass communication, $94,750; $13,346
David Diles, director, athletics, $91,579; $13,023
Michael Fischer, dean, business, $89,231; $12,916

Source: "Pay and Benefits of Leaders at 479 Private Colleges and Universities: a Survey," *The Chronicle of Higher Education*, 47: A29-A48, (November 24, 2000).

★3471★
Top pay and benefits for the chief executive and top paid employees at St. Edward's University

Ranking basis/background: Annual pay and benefits for the chief executives and top paid officers, as reported on Internal Revenue Service Form 990 by private colleges and universities in the U.S. for the 1998-99 academic year. **Number listed:** 6.

Robert N. Funk, interim president, with $125,000 annual pay; $11,658 in benefits
David A. Dickson Jr., VP, financial affairs, $98,000; $13,860
Sister Donna M. Jurick, S.N.D., executive VP; academic dean, $100,000; $7,767
John G. Houghton, VP, professional and graduate studies, $80,000; $12,486
Richard H. Kinsey, assistant to the president, $75,815; $11,457
Joseph E. Pluta, professor, business and administration, $73,343; $11,903

Source: "Pay and Benefits of Leaders at 479 Private Colleges and Universities: a Survey," *The Chronicle of Higher Education*, 47: A29-A48, (November 24, 2000).

★3472★
Top pay and benefits for the chief executive and top paid employees at Saint John Fisher College in New York

Ranking basis/background: Annual pay and benefits for the chief executives and top paid officers, as reported on Internal Revenue Service Form 990 by private colleges and universities in the U.S. for the 1998-99 academic year. **Number listed:** 6.

Katherine E. Keough, president, with $129,808 annual pay; $22,756 in benefits
J. David Arnold, provost; dean of the college, $112,981; $11,857
Gerard J. Rooney, dean and VP, enrollment management, $106,927; $17,280
W. James Whelan, VP, financial affairs, $108,173; $10,912
Kathleen Powers, dean, school of adult graduate education, $88,664; $15,623
H. Wendall Howard, professor, English, $89,367; $10,617

Source: "Pay and Benefits of Leaders at 479 Private Colleges and Universities: a Survey," *The Chronicle of Higher Education*, 47: A29-A48, (November 24, 2000).

★3473★
Top pay and benefits for the chief executive and top paid employees at St. John's College in Maryland and New Mexico

Ranking basis/background: Annual pay and benefits for the chief executives and top paid officers, as reported on Internal Revenue Service Form 990 by private colleges and universities in the U.S. for the 1998-99 academic year. **Number listed:** 8.

Christopher B. Nelson, president, Annapolis, with $136,765 annual pay; $0 in benefits
John Agresto, president, Santa Fe, $122,852; $0
Fred H. Billups Jr., treasurer, Annapolis, $109,177; $0
Jeffrey Bishop, VP, advancement, Annapolis, $109,177; $0
Harvey Flaumenhaft, dean, Annapolis, $93,245; $12,588
Anthony J. Carey, dean, Santa Fe, $91,246; $10,761
Bryan Valentine, treasurer, Santa Fe, $99,220; $0
Robert Glick, VP, Santa Fe, $96,675; $0

Source: "Pay and Benefits of Leaders at 479 Private Colleges and Universities: a Survey," *The Chronicle of Higher Education*, 47: A29-A48, (November 24, 2000).

★3474★

Top pay and benefits for the chief executive and top paid employees at St. John's University in New York

Ranking basis/background: Annual pay and benefits for the chief executives and top paid officers, as reported on Internal Revenue Service Form 990 by private colleges and universities in the U.S. for the 1998-99 academic year. **Remarks:** Reverend Harrington's pay is donated to the Congregation of the Mission. **Number listed:** 6.

- Rev. Donald J. Harrington, C.M., president, with $0 annual pay; $0 in benefits
- Michael Jarvis, head coach, men's football, $705,000; $155,093
- Fran Fraschilla, former head coach, men's basketball, $400,024; $9,513
- Patrick Rohan, professor, law; dean emeritus, $254,182; $39,047
- Rudolph Hasi, dean, school of law, $254,182; $35,555
- Robert J. Crimmins, executive VP, $231,720; $40,129

Source: "Pay and Benefits of Leaders at 479 Private Colleges and Universities: a Survey," *The Chronicle of Higher Education*, 47: A29-A48, (November 24, 2000).

★3475★

Top pay and benefits for the chief executive and top paid employees at Saint Joseph College in Connecticut

Ranking basis/background: Annual pay and benefits for the chief executives and top paid officers, as reported on Internal Revenue Service Form 990 by private colleges and universities in the U.S. for the 1998-99 academic year. **Number listed:** 6.

- Winifred E. Coleman, president, with $148,500 annual pay; $18,527 in benefits
- Sister Maureen Reardon, R.S.M., executive VP; chief operations officer, $103,000; $12,450
- David Theall, VP, finance; treasurer, $100,785; $10,780
- Diane Goncalves, director, Gengras Center, $95,800; $14,280
- Harold McKone, professor, chemistry, $84,433; $11,027
- Mary Alice Wolf, professor, gerontology, $74,420; $14,799

Source: "Pay and Benefits of Leaders at 479 Private Colleges and Universities: a Survey," *The Chronicle of Higher Education*, 47: A29-A48, (November 24, 2000).

★3476★

Top pay and benefits for the chief executive and top paid employees at Saint Joseph's University

Ranking basis/background: Annual pay and benefits for the chief executives and top paid officers, as reported on Internal Revenue Service Form 990 by private colleges and universities in the U.S. for the 1998-99 academic year. **Number listed:** 6.

- Rev. Nicholas S. Rashford, S.J., president, with $0 annual pay; $0 in benefits
- Timothy W. Joyce, VP, finance, $176,000; $23,060
- Daniel J. Curran Jr., provost, $161,000; $22,389
- Richard Kochersperger, director, Center for Food Marketing, $163,427; $0
- Maureen Cullen, VP, development, $120,000; $17,574
- Linda Dunphy, VP, student services, $118,000; $16,796

Source: "Pay and Benefits of Leaders at 479 Private Colleges and Universities: a Survey," *The Chronicle of Higher Education*, 47: A29-A48, (November 24, 2000).

★3477★

Top pay and benefits for the chief executive and top paid employees at St. Lawrence University

Ranking basis/background: Annual pay and benefits for the chief executives and top paid officers, as reported on Internal Revenue Service Form 990 by private colleges and universities in the U.S. for the 1998-99 academic year. **Number listed:** 6.

- Daniel F. Sullivan, president, with $197,954 annual pay; $21,260 in benefits
- Linda R. Pettit, VP, university advancement, $120,225; $17,128
- Thomas B. Coburn, dean, academic affairs; VP, university, $114,640; $14,953
- Terry Cowdrey, dean, admissions, $112,417; $15,225
- David Richardson, professor; chair, economics, $108,954; $15,456
- Kathryn Mullaney, VP, finance, $106,090; $15,705

Source: "Pay and Benefits of Leaders at 479 Private Colleges and Universities: a Survey," *The Chronicle of Higher Education*, 47: A29-A48, (November 24, 2000).

★3478★

Top pay and benefits for the chief executive and top paid employees at St. Louis University

Ranking basis/background: Annual pay and benefits for the chief executives and top paid officers, as reported on Internal Revenue Service Form 990 by private colleges and universities in the U.S. for the 1998-99 academic year. **Remarks:** Reverend Biondi's pay is donated to the Jesuit community. **Number listed:** 6.

- Rev. Lawrence Biondi, S.J., president, with $0 annual pay; $0 in benefits
- Richard D. Bucholz, professor, surgery, division of neurosurgery, $445,653; $18,069
- Robert E. Burdge, professor and chair, orthopedic surgery, $439,081; $18,535
- Alan L. Williams, professor and chair, radiology, $401,179; $18,600
- James Regan Thomas, professor and chair, head and neck surgery, $397,911; $18,557
- Lawrence R. McBride, professor, cardiothoracic surgery, $355,739; $18,545

Source: "Pay and Benefits of Leaders at 479 Private Colleges and Universities: a Survey," *The Chronicle of Higher Education*, 47: A29-A48, (November 24, 2000).

★3479★

Top pay and benefits for the chief executive and top paid employees at Saint Martin's College in Washington

Ranking basis/background: Annual pay and benefits for the chief executives and top paid officers, as reported on Internal Revenue Service Form 990 by private colleges and universities in the U.S. for the 1998-99 academic year. **Number listed:** 6.

- David R. Spangler, president, with $105,000 annual pay; $16,584 in benefits
- Jacqueline Johnson, VP, academics, $75,000; $16,330
- Mary Sigmen, VP, finance, $73,000; $12,510
- Gary Mulhall, director, institutional advancement, $67,511; $13,365
- Leslie G. Bailey, professor, English, $60,280; $6,801
- Tony de Sam Lazaro, professor, mechanical engineering, $59,386; $6,008

Source: "Pay and Benefits of Leaders at 479 Private Colleges and Universities: a Survey," *The Chronicle of Higher Education*, 47: A29-A48, (November 24, 2000).

★3480★

Top pay and benefits for the chief executive and top paid employees at Saint Mary's College of California

Ranking basis/background: Annual pay and benefits for the chief executives and top paid officers, as reported on Internal Revenue Service Form 990 by private colleges and universities in the U.S. for the 1998-99 academic year. **Remarks:** Brother Franz's pay is donated to the Order of the Brothers of the Christian Schools. **Number listed:** 6.

- Bro. Craig Franz, president, with $0 annual pay; $0 in benefits
- William Hynes, VP, academic affairs, $125,468; $13,857
- Michael Ferrigno, VP, advancement, $120,865; $15,314
- Fannie Preston, dean, education, $123,864; $11,213
- William McLeod, VP, student affairs; gifts officer, $119,928; $14,351
- Lionel Chan, VP, financial office, $119,600; $13,546

Source: "Pay and Benefits of Leaders at 479 Private Colleges and Universities: a Survey," *The Chronicle of Higher Education*, 47: A29-A48, (November 24, 2000).

★3481★

Top pay and benefits for the chief executive and top paid employees at Saint Mary's University in Texas

Ranking basis/background: Annual pay and benefits for the chief executives and top paid officers, as reported on Internal Revenue Service Form 990 by private colleges and universities in the U.S. for the 1998-99 academic year. **Number listed:** 6.

- Rev. John Moder, S.M., president, with $108,406 annual pay; $7,588 in benefits
- Barbara Bader Aldave, dean, school of law; professor, law, $194,088; $10,500
- Robert William Piatt, dean, school of law, $175,000; $11,200

Charles E. Cantu, professor, law, $139,733; $8,470

Aloysius A. Leopold, professor, law, $135,000; $9,450

David A. Schlueter, professor, law, $123,300; $7,419

Source: "Pay and Benefits of Leaders at 479 Private Colleges and Universities: a Survey," *The Chronicle of Higher Education*, 47: A29-A48, (November 24, 2000).

★3482★
Top pay and benefits for the chief executive and top paid employees at Saint Mary's University of Minnesota

Ranking basis/background: Annual pay and benefits for the chief executives and top paid officers, as reported on Internal Revenue Service Form 990 by private colleges and universities in the U.S. for the 1998-99 academic year. **Number listed:** 6.

Bro. Louis DeThomasis, F.S.C., president, with $135,003 annual pay; $13,361 in benefits

Thomas J. Burchill, executive director, Hendrickson Institute, $114,346; $15,620

Merri Moody, director, nursing, $82,465; $13,155

Daniel Maloney, VP; chief operating officer, Twin Cities campus, $80,089; $12,950

Donald Olson, director, athletics, $76,670; $12,530

David Roffers, director, graduate education program, $73,737; $12,247

Source: "Pay and Benefits of Leaders at 479 Private Colleges and Universities: a Survey," *The Chronicle of Higher Education*, 47: A29-A48, (November 24, 2000).

★3483★
Top pay and benefits for the chief executive and top paid employees at Saint Michael's College

Ranking basis/background: Annual pay and benefits for the chief executives and top paid officers, as reported on Internal Revenue Service Form 990 by private colleges and universities in the U.S. for the 1998-99 academic year. **Number listed:** 6.

Marc A. Vander Heyden, president, with $147,000 annual pay; $29,209 in benefits

Jerry E. Flanagan, VP, admission and enrollment planning, $92,675; $39,391

Janet A. Sheeran, provost; VP, academic affairs, $110,000; $21,366

Mark Birger Benson, associate professor, business administration and accounting, $80,780; $50,058

John Gutman, former VP, administration, $111,945; $17,045

Barbara M. Wessel, VP, institutional advancement, $103,466; $22,575

Source: "Pay and Benefits of Leaders at 479 Private Colleges and Universities: a Survey," *The Chronicle of Higher Education*, 47: A29-A48, (November 24, 2000).

★3484★
Top pay and benefits for the chief executive and top paid employees at St. Olaf College

Ranking basis/background: Annual pay and benefits for the chief executives and top paid officers, as reported on Internal Revenue Service Form 990 by private colleges and universities in the U.S. for the 1998-99 academic year. **Number listed:** 6.

Mark U. Edwards, president, with $174,417 annual pay; $26,924 in benefits

Jim Pence, senior VP, dean of the college, $114,446; $20,550

Gordon Soenksen, VP, advancement, $110,000; $19,981

Alan Norton, VP; treasurer, $106,379; $19,518

Wesley Pearson, professor, chemistry, $85,809; $15,997

Mary Skorheim, VP, dean of students, $83,691; $16,615

Source: "Pay and Benefits of Leaders at 479 Private Colleges and Universities: a Survey," *The Chronicle of Higher Education*, 47: A29-A48, (November 24, 2000).

★3485★
Top pay and benefits for the chief executive and top paid employees at Saint Peter's College

Ranking basis/background: Annual pay and benefits for the chief executives and top paid officers, as reported on Internal Revenue Service Form 990 by private colleges and universities in the U.S. for the 1998-99 academic year. **Remarks:** Reverend Loughran's pay is donated to the Jesuits of Saint Peter's College, Inc. **Number listed:** 6.

Rev. James N. Loughran, S.J., president, with $0 annual pay; $0 in benefits

Katherine Restaino, dean, undergraduate evening and summer sessions, $140,093; $0

George Martin, VP, academic affairs, $129,912; $0

Peter Alexander, dean, academics, $125,345; $0

Frank J. Barletta, VP, finance and administrative services, $123,964; $0

Edward W. Reuter, VP, student affairs, $118,541; $0

Source: "Pay and Benefits of Leaders at 479 Private Colleges and Universities: a Survey," *The Chronicle of Higher Education*, 47: A29-A48, (November 24, 2000).

★3486★
Top pay and benefits for the chief executive and top paid employees at Saint Thomas University in Florida

Ranking basis/background: Annual pay and benefits for the chief executives and top paid officers, as reported on Internal Revenue Service Form 990 by private colleges and universities in the U.S. for the 1998-99 academic year. **Number listed:** 6.

Rev. Msgr. Franklyn M. Casale, president, with $89,600 annual pay; $20,608 in benefits

Daniel Morrissey, dean, law, $131,063; $31,455

Jay Silver, associate dean, law, $125,749; $30,180

Alfred Light, professor, law, $114,874; $27,570

Mark Wolff, professor, law, $110,100; $26,424

Norman Blair, VP, administrative affairs, $107,000; $25,680

Source: "Pay and Benefits of Leaders at 479 Private Colleges and Universities: a Survey," *The Chronicle of Higher Education*, 47: A29-A48, (November 24, 2000).

★3487★
Top pay and benefits for the chief executive and top paid employees at Saint Xavier University

Ranking basis/background: Annual pay and benefits for the chief executives and top paid officers, as reported on Internal Revenue Service Form 990 by private colleges and universities in the U.S. for the 1998-99 academic year. **Number listed:** 6.

Richard Yanikoski, president, with $134,400 annual pay; $9,408 in benefits

George Matthews, VP, academic affairs, $102,400; $8,192

Susan Piros, VP, business and finance, $92,500; $7,400

Robert Cummings, VP, university advancement, $89,200; $6,244

John Eber, dean, school of management, $88,000; $7,040

Lawrence Frank, dean, school of arts and sciences, $87,300; $6,984

Source: "Pay and Benefits of Leaders at 479 Private Colleges and Universities: a Survey," *The Chronicle of Higher Education*, 47: A29-A48, (November 24, 2000).

★3488★
Top pay and benefits for the chief executive and top paid employees at Salem College

Ranking basis/background: Annual pay and benefits for the chief executives and top paid officers, as reported on Internal Revenue Service Form 990 by private colleges and universities in the U.S. for the 1998-99 academic year. **Number listed:** 6.

Julianne Still Thrift, president, with $150,000 annual pay; $14,365 in benefits

D. Wayne Burkette, VP, Salem Academy and College; headmaster, Salem Academy, $83,200; $8,758

Eileen Wilson-Oyelaran, VP, Salem Academy and College; dean of the college, $80,600; $8,556

Gary Ljungquist, professor, modern languages, $69,028; $6,022

Susan Bourner, director, institutional advancement, $64,272; $7,284

Cynthia Joy Pendleton, dean of students, $63,696; $7,239

Source: "Pay and Benefits of Leaders at 479 Private Colleges and Universities: a Survey," *The Chronicle of Higher Education*, 47: A29-A48, (November 24, 2000).

★3489★
Top pay and benefits for the chief executive and top paid employees at Salve Regina University

Ranking basis/background: Annual pay and benefits for the chief executives and top paid officers, as reported on Internal Revenue Service Form 990 by private colleges and universities in the U.S. for the 1998-99 academic year. **Number listed:** 6.

- Sister M. Therese Antone, R.S.M., president, with $0 annual pay; $16,230 in benefits
- Eileen Donnelly, former professor, nursing, $124,355; $16,525
- William B. Hall, VP, business and financial affairs, $107,977; $15,274
- Dominic Varisco, executive VP, $104,231; $11,326
- Thomas Flanagan, VP, administrative services, $82,023; $12,586
- Michael Semenza, VP, development and institutional advancement, $81,231; $10,224

Source: "Pay and Benefits of Leaders at 479 Private Colleges and Universities: a Survey," *The Chronicle of Higher Education*, 47: A29-A48, (November 24, 2000).

★3490★
Top pay and benefits for the chief executive and top paid employees at Samford University

Ranking basis/background: Annual pay and benefits for the chief executives and top paid officers, as reported on Internal Revenue Service Form 990 by private colleges and universities in the U.S. for the 1998-99 academic year. **Number listed:** 6.

- Thomas E. Corts, president, with $243,433 annual pay; $95,323 in benefits
- Charles D. Cole, professor, law, $168,289; $35,729
- Howard P. Walthall, professor, law, $155,924; $34,361
- James S. Netherton, provost, $152,801; $29,788
- Barry A. Currier, dean, law, $161,340; $19,126
- Thomas B. Bishop, professor, law, $150,227; $29,890

Source: "Pay and Benefits of Leaders at 479 Private Colleges and Universities: a Survey," *The Chronicle of Higher Education*, 47: A29-A48, (November 24, 2000).

★3491★
Top pay and benefits for the chief executive and top paid employees at Santa Clara University in California

Ranking basis/background: Annual pay and benefits for the chief executives and top paid officers, as reported on Internal Revenue Service Form 990 by private colleges and universities in the U.S. for the 1998-99 academic year. **Number listed:** 6.

- Rev. Paul L. Locatelli, S.J., president, with $0 annual pay; $0 in benefits
- James Sepe, associate professor, accounting, $194,268; $19,373
- Mark A. Player, dean, law, $182,271; $24,050
- Albert Bruno, professor, marketing, $180,694; $19,914
- Richard J. Davey, coach, men's basketball, $176,007; $20,529
- George Alexander, professor, law, $169,500; $22,033

Source: "Pay and Benefits of Leaders at 479 Private Colleges and Universities: a Survey," *The Chronicle of Higher Education*, 47: A29-A48, (November 24, 2000).

★3492★
Top pay and benefits for the chief executive and top paid employees at Sarah Lawrence College

Ranking basis/background: Annual pay and benefits for the chief executives and top paid officers, as reported on Internal Revenue Service Form 990 by private colleges and universities in the U.S. for the 1998-99 academic year. **Number listed:** 6.

- Michele Tolela Myers, president, with $187,668 annual pay; $22,827 in benefits
- Alice Stone Ilchman, president emeritus, $170,000; $23,896
- Dennis Cross, VP, finance and planning, $133,501; $21,697
- Shirley Kaplan, director, theater program, $120,578; $12,172
- Barbara Kaplan, dean of the college, $108,326; $13,818
- Barbara Allar, director, capital campaign, $100,168; $18,363

Source: "Pay and Benefits of Leaders at 479 Private Colleges and Universities: a Survey," *The Chronicle of Higher Education*, 47: A29-A48, (November 24, 2000).

★3493★
Top pay and benefits for the chief executive and top paid employees at Scripps College

Ranking basis/background: Annual pay and benefits for the chief executives and top paid officers, as reported on Internal Revenue Service Form 990 by private colleges and universities in the U.S. for the 1998-99 academic year. **Number listed:** 6.

- Nancy Y. Bekavac, president, with $195,825 annual pay; $30,379 in benefits
- Michael Lamkin, VP; dean of the faculty, $139,600; $30,322
- James H. Manifold, VP, business affairs; treasurer, $130,400; $25,145
- Linda Davis-Taylor, VP, development, $114,512; $20,576
- Alan Hartley, professor, psychology, $105,503; $20,394
- David Lloyd, professor, humanities, $96,609; $26,962

Source: "Pay and Benefits of Leaders at 479 Private Colleges and Universities: a Survey," *The Chronicle of Higher Education*, 47: A29-A48, (November 24, 2000).

★3494★
Top pay and benefits for the chief executive and top paid employees at Seattle Pacific University

Ranking basis/background: Annual pay and benefits for the chief executives and top paid officers, as reported on Internal Revenue Service Form 990 by private colleges and universities in the U.S. for the 1998-99 academic year. **Number listed:** 6.

- Philip Eaton, president, with $160,874 annual pay; $47,635 in benefits
- Donald Mortenson, VP, business and planning, $118,500; $35,088
- Bruce Murphy, provost, $98,514; $29,170
- Robert McIntosh, VP, university advancement, $98,000; $29,018
- Marjorie Johnson, VP, university relations; assistant to the president, $97,800; $28,959
- Thomas Trzyna, associate provost, $86,121; $25,500

Source: "Pay and Benefits of Leaders at 479 Private Colleges and Universities: a Survey," *The Chronicle of Higher Education*, 47: A29-A48, (November 24, 2000).

★3495★
Top pay and benefits for the chief executive and top paid employees at Seattle University

Ranking basis/background: Annual pay and benefits for the chief executives and top paid officers, as reported on Internal Revenue Service Form 990 by private colleges and universities in the U.S. for the 1998-99 academic year. **Number listed:** 6.

- Rev. Steven Sundborg, S.J., president, with $0 annual pay; $0 in benefits
- James Bond, dean, law, $172,226; $17,223
- Denis Ransmeier, VP, finance and administration, $147,475; $14,748
- John Eshelman, provost, $149,946; $9,070
- David Engdahl, professor, law, $125,546; $12,555
- Linda Hanson, VP, university relations, $122,078; $11,708

Source: "Pay and Benefits of Leaders at 479 Private Colleges and Universities: a Survey," *The Chronicle of Higher Education*, 47: A29-A48, (November 24, 2000).

★3496★
Top pay and benefits for the chief executive and top paid employees at Seton Hall University

Ranking basis/background: Annual pay and benefits for the chief executives and top paid officers, as reported on Internal Revenue Service Form 990 by private colleges and universities in the U.S. for the 1998-99 academic year. **Remarks:** The institution made a donation to the Dominican order on Very Rev. Peterson's behalf. **Number listed:** 7.

- Msgr. Robert Sheeran, S.T.D., president, with $19,180 annual pay; $8,684 in benefits
- Very Rev. Thomas R. Peterson, O.P., chancellor, $0; $16,773
- George Blaney, former coach, men's basketball, $199,668; $179,362
- H. Tommy Amaker, coach, men's basketball, $260,301; $10,660
- John A. Paterson, dean, graduate medical education, $245,435; $9,404
- Mark W. Rocha, VP; assistant to the president; provost, $203,617; $16,758
- Ronald J. Riccio, dean, law school, $187,703; $16,479

Source: "Pay and Benefits of Leaders at 479 Private Colleges and Universities: a Survey," *The Chronicle of Higher Education*, 47: A29-A48, (November 24, 2000).

SALARIES—COLLEGES & UNIVERSITIES

★3497★
Top pay and benefits for the chief executive and top paid employees at Shenandoah University

Ranking basis/background: Annual pay and benefits for the chief executives and top paid officers, as reported on Internal Revenue Service Form 990 by private colleges and universities in the U.S. for the 1998-99 academic year. **Number listed:** 6.

- James A. Davis, president, with $182,500 annual pay; $14,600 in benefits
- Alan McKay, dean, pharmacy, $120,238; $9,619
- Jerry Van Voorhis, VP, development, $110,334; $8,827
- Joel R. Stegall, VP, academic programs, $105,333; $8,427
- Richard C. Shickle, VP, administration and finance, $103,333; $8,267
- Daniel Pavsek, dean, business, $93,318; $7,465

Source: "Pay and Benefits of Leaders at 479 Private Colleges and Universities: a Survey," *The Chronicle of Higher Education*, 47: A29-A48, (November 24, 2000).

★3498★
Top pay and benefits for the chief executive and top paid employees at Siena College

Ranking basis/background: Annual pay and benefits for the chief executives and top paid officers, as reported on Internal Revenue Service Form 990 by private colleges and universities in the U.S. for the 1998-99 academic year. **Number listed:** 6.

- Rev. Kevin E. Mackin, O.F.M., president, with $0 annual pay; $0 in benefits
- Paul H. Hewitt, basketball coach, $125,449; $2,347
- Anthony G. Pondillo, VP, finance and administration, $105,410; $9,845
- Gregory Stahl, VP, institutional advancement, $104,799; $4,997
- James Nolan, dean, business, $91,757; $13,376
- David B. Smith, assistant VP, institutional advancement, $86,781; $12,304

Source: "Pay and Benefits of Leaders at 479 Private Colleges and Universities: a Survey," *The Chronicle of Higher Education*, 47: A29-A48, (November 24, 2000).

★3499★
Top pay and benefits for the chief executive and top paid employees at Simmons College

Ranking basis/background: Annual pay and benefits for the chief executives and top paid officers, as reported on Internal Revenue Service Form 990 by private colleges and universities in the U.S. for the 1998-99 academic year. **Number listed:** 7.

- Daniel S. Cheever Jr., president, with $164,000 annual pay; $14,760 in benefits
- Patricia O'Brien, dean, graduate school of management, $143,500; $12,915
- Kristina Schaefer, VP, advancement, $141,000; $12,690
- Lisa Mayer, dean, enrollment services, $140,454; $12,640
- Anne Jardim, professor and co-dean, graduate school of management, $140,172; $12,615
- Margaret Hennig, professor and co-dean, graduate school of management, $140,172; $12,615
- Lisa Chapnick, senior VP, administration and planning, $138,500; $4,260

Source: "Pay and Benefits of Leaders at 479 Private Colleges and Universities: a Survey," *The Chronicle of Higher Education*, 47: A29-A48, (November 24, 2000).

★3500★
Top pay and benefits for the chief executive and top paid employees at Skidmore College

Ranking basis/background: Annual pay and benefits for the chief executives and top paid officers, as reported on Internal Revenue Service Form 990 by private colleges and universities in the U.S. for the 1998-99 academic year. **Number listed:** 6.

- David Porter, president, with $199,975 annual pay; $30,971 in benefits
- Phyllis Roth, interim president; dean of the faculty, $149,439; $29,462
- Karl Broekhuizen, VP, business affairs; treasurer, $149,074; $25,676
- Christine Hoek, VP, development and alumni affairs, $131,505; $25,520
- Regis Brodie, professor, studio art; director, Summer SIX art program, $118,810; $19,581
- Robert DeSieno, professor, computer science; assistant dean of the faculty, $106,250; $21,215

Source: "Pay and Benefits of Leaders at 479 Private Colleges and Universities: a Survey," *The Chronicle of Higher Education*, 47: A29-A48, (November 24, 2000).

★3501★
Top pay and benefits for the chief executive and top paid employees at Smith College

Ranking basis/background: Annual pay and benefits for the chief executives and top paid officers, as reported on Internal Revenue Service Form 990 by private colleges and universities in the U.S. for the 1998-99 academic year. **Number listed:** 6.

- Ruth Simmons, president, with $279,650 annual pay; $74,839 in benefits
- John Connolly, provost; dean of the faculty, $156,589; $30,285
- Elliot M. Offner, professor, humanities and art, $134,415; $45,199
- Ruth Constantine, chief financial officer; treasurer, $140,000; $30,279
- Lester Little, professor, history, $143,060; $21,303
- Joseph O'Rourke, professor, computer science, $125,773; $29,688

Source: "Pay and Benefits of Leaders at 479 Private Colleges and Universities: a Survey," *The Chronicle of Higher Education*, 47: A29-A48, (November 24, 2000).

★3502★
Top pay and benefits for the chief executive and top paid employees at Southern Methodist University

Ranking basis/background: Annual pay and benefits for the chief executives and top paid officers, as reported on Internal Revenue Service Form 990 by private colleges and universities in the U.S. for the 1998-99 academic year. **Number listed:** 6.

- R. Gerald Turner, president, with $307,299 annual pay; $52,445 in benefits
- Michael Cavan, head coach, football, $300,173; $45,805
- Michael D. Dement, head coach, basketball, $298,878; $31,671
- Albert Niemi Jr., dean, business school, $284,498; $29,876
- W. James Copeland Jr., director, athletics, $264,286; $30,265
- Ross C. Murfin, VP, academic affairs; provost, $216,922; $29,973

Source: "Pay and Benefits of Leaders at 479 Private Colleges and Universities: a Survey," *The Chronicle of Higher Education*, 47: A29-A48, (November 24, 2000).

★3503★
Top pay and benefits for the chief executive and top paid employees at Southern Nazarene University

Ranking basis/background: Annual pay and benefits for the chief executives and top paid officers, as reported on Internal Revenue Service Form 990 by private colleges and universities in the U.S. for the 1998-99 academic year. **Number listed:** 5.

- Loren Gresham, president, with $100,016 annual pay; $7,463 in benefits
- Don W. Dunnington, VP, academic affairs, $64,849; $4,351
- Wayne Murrow, dean, continuing and adult studies, $62,343; $3,890
- David Alexander, VP, university advancement, $60,127; $4,089
- Hal Cauthron, department chair, religion and philosophy, $60,401; $3,012

Source: "Pay and Benefits of Leaders at 479 Private Colleges and Universities: a Survey," *The Chronicle of Higher Education*, 47: A29-A48, (November 24, 2000).

★3504★
Top pay and benefits for the chief executive and top paid employees at Southwest Baptist University

Ranking basis/background: Annual pay and benefits for the chief executives and top paid officers, as reported on Internal Revenue Service Form 990 by private colleges and universities in the U.S. for the 1998-99 academic year. **Number listed:** 6.

- C. Pat Taylor, president, with $96,751 annual pay; $17,459 in benefits
- Dorothy E. Hash, director, physical therapy, $87,296; $11,087
- Deona M. Lilly, professor, physical therapy, $81,839; $10,507
- Bill F. Little, VP, external programs; director, international studies, $67,774; $10,968
- Bob R. Derryberry, chair, communications, $64,789; $10,653

Gary C. Hunt, professor, physical therapy, $65,473; $8,769

Source: "Pay and Benefits of Leaders at 479 Private Colleges and Universities: a Survey," *The Chronicle of Higher Education*, 47: A29-A48, (November 24, 2000).

★3505★
Top pay and benefits for the chief executive and top paid employees at Southwestern University in Texas

Ranking basis/background: Annual pay and benefits for the chief executives and top paid officers, as reported on Internal Revenue Service Form 990 by private colleges and universities in the U.S. for the 1998-99 academic year. **Number listed:** 5.

- Roy B. Shilling Jr., president, with $297,589 annual pay; $19,032 in benefits
- Rick Eason, VP, development, $139,700; $16,490
- Richard L. Anderson, VP, fiscal affairs, $136,067; $18,521
- William B. Jones, executive VP, $131,267; $15,470
- Vincent Villa, professor, biology, $112,763; $21,920

Source: "Pay and Benefits of Leaders at 479 Private Colleges and Universities: a Survey," *The Chronicle of Higher Education*, 47: A29-A48, (November 24, 2000).

★3506★
Top pay and benefits for the chief executive and top paid employees at Spalding University

Ranking basis/background: Annual pay and benefits for the chief executives and top paid officers, as reported on Internal Revenue Service Form 990 by private colleges and universities in the U.S. for the 1998-99 academic year. **Number listed:** 6.

- Thomas R. Oates, president, with $147,785 annual pay; $26,200 in benefits
- Lewis Randy Strickland, professor and director, occupational therapy, $84,465; $14,915
- M. Janice Murphy, provost; dean, graduate studies, $81,900; $14,500
- Jeffrey Ashley, VP, university advancement, $75,000; $13,463
- Mary Angela Shaughnessy, professor, education; legal counsel, $74,082; $13,237
- Wayne Milligan, VP, finance, $73,000; $14,115

Source: "Pay and Benefits of Leaders at 479 Private Colleges and Universities: a Survey," *The Chronicle of Higher Education*, 47: A29-A48, (November 24, 2000).

★3507★
Top pay and benefits for the chief executive and top paid employees at Spelman College

Ranking basis/background: Annual pay and benefits for the chief executives and top paid officers, as reported on Internal Revenue Service Form 990 by private colleges and universities in the U.S. for the 1998-99 academic year. **Number listed:** 6.

- Audrey F. Manley, president, with $189,036 annual pay; $10,194 in benefits
- Robert D. Flanigan Jr., treasurer; VP, business and financial affairs, $138,650; $13,738
- Etta Z. Falconer, interim provost; professor, mathematics, $125,080; $11,392
- Pamela Gunter-Smith, professor, physiology; chair, biology, $101,034; $8,030
- Sylvia Bozeman, professor and director, scientific applications for mathematics, $98,073; $8,016
- Beverly Guy-Sheftall, professor, English; director, women's resource and research center, $94,451; $8,459

Source: "Pay and Benefits of Leaders at 479 Private Colleges and Universities: a Survey," *The Chronicle of Higher Education*, 47: A29-A48, (November 24, 2000).

★3508★
Top pay and benefits for the chief executive and top paid employees at Spring Hill College

Ranking basis/background: Annual pay and benefits for the chief executives and top paid officers, as reported on Internal Revenue Service Form 990 by private colleges and universities in the U.S. for the 1998-99 academic year. **Remarks:** Reverend Lucey's pay is donated to the Jesuit Community. **Number listed:** 6.

- Rev. Gregory F. Lucey, S.J., president, with $0 annual pay; $0 in benefits
- Noreen Carrocci, VP, academic affairs, $96,462; $0
- Thomas Hickey, VP, finance; treasurer, $91,450; $0
- Elizabeth A. Stafford, VP, development and college relations, $90,000; $0
- Steve Pochard, dean, enrollment management, $70,297; $0
- Charles Kargleder, chair, languages and literature, $63,153; $0

Source: "Pay and Benefits of Leaders at 479 Private Colleges and Universities: a Survey," *The Chronicle of Higher Education*, 47: A29-A48, (November 24, 2000).

★3509★
Top pay and benefits for the chief executive and top paid employees at Springfield College in Massachusetts

Ranking basis/background: Annual pay and benefits for the chief executives and top paid officers, as reported on Internal Revenue Service Form 990 by private colleges and universities in the U.S. for the 1998-99 academic year. **Number listed:** 8.

- Randolph W. Bromery, president, with $157,505 annual pay; $18,965 in benefits
- Robert N. Aebersold, president, $69,270; $6,234
- Richard B. Flynn, president, $42,498; $4,699
- William D. McGarry, VP, administration and finance, $123,504; $15,073
- Edward Bilik, director, athletics; professor, physical education, $121,207; $13,481
- William J. Sullivan, director, graduate studies, $118,557; $15,223
- Corinne P. Kowpak, dean of students; VP, student affairs, $108,185; $12,235
- Thomas J. Ruscio Jr., professor, rehabilitation; department chair, rehabilitation services, $103,709; $14,154

Source: "Pay and Benefits of Leaders at 479 Private Colleges and Universities: a Survey," *The Chronicle of Higher Education*, 47: A29-A48, (November 24, 2000).

★3510★
Top pay and benefits for the chief executive and top paid employees at Stanford University

Ranking basis/background: Annual pay and benefits for the chief executives and top paid officers, as reported on Internal Revenue Service Form 990 by private colleges and universities in the U.S. for the 1998-99 academic year. **Number listed:** 6.

- Gerhard Casper, president, with $398,500 annual pay; $32,278 in benefits
- Edward Manche, professor, ophthalmology, $992,761; $40,895
- Amin A. Milki, professor, obstetrics and gynecology, $783,949; $37,867
- Laurance R. Hoagland, Jr., CEO, Stanford Management Company, $783,949; $37,016
- Curtis Feeny, executive VP, management, $704,000; $36,708
- Gary Steinberg, professor, neurosurgery, $657,005; $36,027

Source: "Pay and Benefits of Leaders at 479 Private Colleges and Universities: a Survey," *The Chronicle of Higher Education*, 47: A29-A48, (November 24, 2000).

★3511★
Top pay and benefits for the chief executive and top paid employees at Stetson University

Ranking basis/background: Annual pay and benefits for the chief executives and top paid officers, as reported on Internal Revenue Service Form 990 by private colleges and universities in the U.S. for the 1998-99 academic year. **Number listed:** 6.

- H. Douglas Lee, president, with $215,209 annual pay; $21,626 in benefits
- Lizabeth A. Moody, VP; dean, law, $193,796; $23,835
- Michael I. Swygert, professor, law, $152,364; $12,960
- Bradford Stone, professor, law, $152,725; $12,283
- W. Gary Vause, dean, law, $148,643; $14,464
- Thomas Marks Jr., professor, law, $144,345; $12,280

Source: "Pay and Benefits of Leaders at 479 Private Colleges and Universities: a Survey," *The Chronicle of Higher Education*, 47: A29-A48, (November 24, 2000).

★3512★
Top pay and benefits for the chief executive and top paid employees at Stevens Institute of Technology

Ranking basis/background: Annual pay and benefits for the chief executives and top paid officers, as reported on Internal Revenue Service Form 990 by private colleges and universities in the U.S. for the 1998-99 academic year. **Number listed:** 6.

SALARIES—COLLEGES & UNIVERSITIES

Harold J. Raveche, president, with $340,681 annual pay; $21,777 in benefits
Jerry Luftman, associate professor, management; professor and director, Master of Science, $276,250; $9,621
Donald N. Merino, professor, management and engineering management, $234,302
Patrick Flanagan, dean, applied sciences, $174,838; $13,260
Erich E. Kunhardt, professor, physics and engineering, $169,964; $15,531
Dilhan Kalyon, professor and director, Highly Filled Materials Institute, $151,703; $16,397

Source: "Pay and Benefits of Leaders at 479 Private Colleges and Universities: a Survey," *The Chronicle of Higher Education*, 47: A29-A48, (November 24, 2000).

★3513★
Top pay and benefits for the chief executive and top paid employees at Suffolk University

Ranking basis/background: Annual pay and benefits for the chief executives and top paid officers, as reported on Internal Revenue Service Form 990 by private colleges and universities in the U.S. for the 1998-99 academic year. **Number listed:** 7.

David J. Sargent, president, with $267,350 annual pay; $43,072 in benefits
William Corbett, acting dean, law, $177,739; $27,982
Francis X. Flannery, VP; treasurer, $168,276; $25,804
John E. Fenton Jr., dean, law, $167,687; $23,789
Marguerite J. Dennis, VP, development and enrollment, $163,383; $22,234
Michael R. Ronayne, dean, liberal arts and sciences, $153,701; $28,472
John F. Brennan, dean, school of management, $153,701; $28,472

Source: "Pay and Benefits of Leaders at 479 Private Colleges and Universities: a Survey," *The Chronicle of Higher Education*, 47: A29-A48, (November 24, 2000).

★3514★
Top pay and benefits for the chief executive and top paid employees at Swarthmore College

Ranking basis/background: Annual pay and benefits for the chief executives and top paid officers, as reported on Internal Revenue Service Form 990 by private colleges and universities in the U.S. for the 1998-99 academic year. **Number listed:** 6.

Alfred H. Bloom, president, with $238,736 annual pay; $17,708 in benefits
Jennie Keith, provost, $177,525; $16,684
Paul J. Aslanian, VP, finance and planning, $155,007; $18,763
Robert F. Pasternack, professor, chemistry, $131,083; $13,941
Lawrence M. Schall, associate VP, facilities and services, $125,000; $14,598
Steven I. Piker, professor, anthropology, $125,658; $11,811

Source: "Pay and Benefits of Leaders at 479 Private Colleges and Universities: a Survey," *The Chronicle of Higher Education*, 47: A29-A48, (November 24, 2000).

★3515★
Top pay and benefits for the chief executive and top paid employees at Sweet Briar College

Ranking basis/background: Annual pay and benefits for the chief executives and top paid officers, as reported on Internal Revenue Service Form 990 by private colleges and universities in the U.S. for the 1998-99 academic year. **Number listed:** 6.

Elisabeth Muhlenfeld, president, with $159,542 annual pay; $23,647 in benefits
George Lenz, dean of the college, $101,928; $10,118
Mary Lou Merkt, VP, finance and administration, $92,755; $9,276
Reuben Miller, professor, economics, $78,767; $7,875
Paul Cronin, professor, riding, $75,556; $7,296
Emile Langlois, resident director, junior year in France, $74,166; $7,380

Source: "Pay and Benefits of Leaders at 479 Private Colleges and Universities: a Survey," *The Chronicle of Higher Education*, 47: A29-A48, (November 24, 2000).

★3516★
Top pay and benefits for the chief executive and top paid employees at Syracuse University

Ranking basis/background: Annual pay and benefits for the chief executives and top paid officers, as reported on Internal Revenue Service Form 990 by private colleges and universities in the U.S. for the 1998-99 academic year. **Number listed:** 6.

Kenneth A. Shaw, president, with $242,285 annual pay; $42,207 in benefits
Paul L. Pasqualoni, head coach football, $228,014; $103,739
James A. Boeheim Jr., head coach, men's basketball, $191,770; $72,739
Geoffrey Fox, professor, electrical engineering, computer science, and physics; director, Northeast Parallel Architecture Center, $207,671; $22,710
Gershon Vincow, vice chancellor, academic affairs, $197,837; $25,770
Louis G. Marcoccia, senior VP, business, finance, and administrative services, $180,871; $25,223

Source: "Pay and Benefits of Leaders at 479 Private Colleges and Universities: a Survey," *The Chronicle of Higher Education*, 47: A29-A48, (November 24, 2000).

★3517★
Top pay and benefits for the chief executive and top paid employees at Teachers College, Columbia University

Ranking basis/background: Annual pay and benefits for the chief executives and top paid officers, as reported on Internal Revenue Service Form 990 by private colleges and universities in the U.S. for the 1998-99 academic year. **Number listed:** 6.

Arthur Levine, president, with $200,000 annual pay; $40,467 in benefits
Fred A. Schnur, VP, finance and administration, $177,920; $35,488
Karen Zumwalt, dean of the college, $168,460; $33,355
Jeanne Brooks-Gunn, professor, child and parent development and education, $159,378; $31,307
Joseph Brosnan, VP, development and external affairs, $149,935; $29,177
Herbert Ginsburg, professor, psychology and education, $146,765; $28,462

Source: "Pay and Benefits of Leaders at 479 Private Colleges and Universities: a Survey," *The Chronicle of Higher Education*, 47: A29-A48, (November 24, 2000).

★3518★
Top pay and benefits for the chief executive and top paid employees at Texas Christian University

Ranking basis/background: Annual pay and benefits for the chief executives and top paid officers, as reported on Internal Revenue Service Form 990 by private colleges and universities in the U.S. for the 1998-99 academic year. **Number listed:** 6.

Michael R. Ferrari, chancellor, with $317,167 annual pay; $18,400 in benefits
Dennis W. Franchione, coach, men's football, $638,875; $58,400
Billy D. Tubbs, coach, men's basketball, $345,404; $18,400
Eric C. Hyman, director, athletics, $257,667; $48,400
James A. McGowan, vice chancellor, finance and business, $195,479; $18,400
William H. Koehler, vice chancellor, academic affairs, $193,825; $18,400

Source: "Pay and Benefits of Leaders at 479 Private Colleges and Universities: a Survey," *The Chronicle of Higher Education*, 47: A29-A48, (November 24, 2000).

★3519★
Top pay and benefits for the chief executive and top paid employees at Texas Wesleyan University

Ranking basis/background: Annual pay and benefits for the chief executives and top paid officers, as reported on Internal Revenue Service Form 990 by private colleges and universities in the U.S. for the 1998-99 academic year. **Number listed:** 6.

Jake B. Schrum, president, with $160,059 annual pay; $9,267 in benefits
Frank K. Walwer, dean, law, $163,345; $12,783
Wylie H. Davis, professor, law, $138,074; $11,046
Frank W. Elliot, professor, law, $135,000; $10,988
Denny O. Ingram, professor, law, $122,000; $9,760
James P. George, professor, law, $121,584; $8,272

Source: "Pay and Benefits of Leaders at 479 Private Colleges and Universities: a Survey," *The Chronicle of Higher Education*, 47: A29-A48, (November 24, 2000).

★3520★
Top pay and benefits for the chief executive and top paid employees at the Allegheny University of the Health Sciences

Ranking basis/background: Annual pay and benefits for the chief executives and top paid officers, as reported on Internal Revenue Service Form 990 by private colleges and universities in the U.S. for the 1998-99 academic year. **Remarks:** In November 1998 the institution filed for bankruptcy and Drexel University took over operations under the name MCP Hahnemann University. Employee titles were unavailable. **Number listed:** 6.

- Anthony Sanzo, president, with $286,317 annual pay; $0 in benefits
- Joseph Maroon, $1,002,288; $2,272
- James McMaste, $601,778; $1,772
- Norman Wolmark, $517,906; $37,906
- Mark Roh, $457,119; $35,956
- Michael Strong, $453,333; $0

Source: "Pay and Benefits of Leaders at 479 Private Colleges and Universities: a Survey," *The Chronicle of Higher Education*, 47: A29-A48, (November 24, 2000).

★3521★
Top pay and benefits for the chief executive and top paid employees at the California Institute of Technology

Ranking basis/background: Annual pay and benefits for the chief executives and top paid officers, as reported on Internal Revenue Service Form 990 by private colleges and universities in the U.S. for the 1998-99 academic year. **Number listed:** 6.

- David Baltimore, president, with $375,000 annual pay; $36,780 in benefits
- Edward C. Stone, VP and director, Jet Propulsion Laboratory; professor, physics, $280,000; $37,756
- Paul C. Jennings, acting VP, business and finance, $247,000; $37,621
- Steven E. Koonin, VP, provost; professor, theoretical physics, $242,500; $32,490
- Harry M. Yohalem, general counsel, $215,508; $38,544
- Jerry E. Nunnally, VP, institute relations, $195,000; $31,364

Source: "Pay and Benefits of Leaders at 479 Private Colleges and Universities: a Survey," *The Chronicle of Higher Education*, 47: A29-A48, (November 24, 2000).

★3522★
Top pay and benefits for the chief executive and top paid employees at the Catholic University of America

Ranking basis/background: Annual pay and benefits for the chief executives and top paid officers, as reported on Internal Revenue Service Form 990 by private colleges and universities in the U.S. for the 1998-99 academic year. **Number listed:** 6.

- Rev. David M. O'Connell, president, with $163,955 annual pay; $20,119 in benefits
- Ralph H. Beaudoin, VP, finance; treasurer, $185,790; $28,586
- Bernard Dobranski, dean, school of law, $174,199; $26,711
- John J. Convey Jr., provost; professor, education, $156,650; $26,122
- Yun Chow Wang, professor, mechanical engineering, $154,611; $24,422
- Ralph J. Rohner, professor, law, $156,244; $22,317

Source: "Pay and Benefits of Leaders at 479 Private Colleges and Universities: a Survey," *The Chronicle of Higher Education*, 47: A29-A48, (November 24, 2000).

★3523★
Top pay and benefits for the chief executive and top paid employees at the Centenary College of Louisiana

Ranking basis/background: Annual pay and benefits for the chief executives and top paid officers, as reported on Internal Revenue Service Form 990 by private colleges and universities in the U.S. for the 1998-99 academic year. **Number listed:** 6.

- Kenneth L. Schwab, president, with $181,375 annual pay; $0 in benefits
- Thomas Phizacklea, VP, finance and administration, $103,196; $0
- Robert Bareikis, provost, $99,990; $0
- Eugene Gregory, VP, development, $93,920; $0
- Barrie Richardson, dean, Frost School of Business, $89,719; $0
- Earle Labor, professor, English, $76,924; $0

Source: "Pay and Benefits of Leaders at 479 Private Colleges and Universities: a Survey," *The Chronicle of Higher Education*, 47: A29-A48, (November 24, 2000).

★3524★
Top pay and benefits for the chief executive and top paid employees at the Chaminade University of Honolulu

Ranking basis/background: Annual pay and benefits for the chief executives and top paid officers, as reported on Internal Revenue Service Form 990 by private colleges and universities in the U.S. for the 1998-99 academic year. **Number listed:** 6.

- Mary C. Wesselkamper, president, with $101,399 annual pay; $5,070 in benefits
- Ronald W. Rex, VP, finance and operations, $93,298; $4,665
- James Fagin, professor, criminal justice, $85,708; $4,300
- Robert Santee, professor, counseling and psychology, $82,591; $4,200
- Bryan Man, professor, sociology, $80,016; $4,000
- Caryn Callahan, professor, business, $78,988; $4,000

Source: "Pay and Benefits of Leaders at 479 Private Colleges and Universities: a Survey," *The Chronicle of Higher Education*, 47: A29-A48, (November 24, 2000).

★3525★
Top pay and benefits for the chief executive and top paid employees at the College of New Rochelle

Ranking basis/background: Annual pay and benefits for the chief executives and top paid officers, as reported on Internal Revenue Service Form 990 by private colleges and universities in the U.S. for the 1998-99 academic year. **Number listed:** 6.

- Stephen J. Sweeny, president, with $187,200 annual pay; $16,000 in benefits
- Walter McCarthy, VP, financial affairs, $180,377; $16,000
- Joan E. Bailey, senior VP, academic affairs, $130,000; $16,000
- Bessie W. Blake, dean, School of New Resources, $124,339; $12,434
- Joan Bristol, VP, student services, $112,658; $11,266
- Connie N. Vance, dean, school of nursing, $111,006; $11,101

Source: "Pay and Benefits of Leaders at 479 Private Colleges and Universities: a Survey," *The Chronicle of Higher Education*, 47: A29-A48, (November 24, 2000).

★3526★
Top pay and benefits for the chief executive and top paid employees at the College of Notre Dame in California

Ranking basis/background: Annual pay and benefits for the chief executives and top paid officers, as reported on Internal Revenue Service Form 990 by private colleges and universities in the U.S. for the 1998-99 academic year. **Number listed:** 6.

- Margaret A. Huber, president, with $153,083 annual pay; $32,147 in benefits
- Anthony Macias, VP, development, $133,771; $28,092
- Lucille Sansing, VP, academic affairs, $111,477; $23,410
- Carol Probstfeld, VP, academic affairs, $109,065; $22,904
- Janifer Stackhouse, dean, arts and sciences, $100,997; $21,209
- Elaine Cohen, graduate dean, $90,914; $19,092

Source: "Pay and Benefits of Leaders at 479 Private Colleges and Universities: a Survey," *The Chronicle of Higher Education*, 47: A29-A48, (November 24, 2000).

★3527★
Top pay and benefits for the chief executive and top paid employees at the College of Notre Dame in Maryland

Ranking basis/background: Annual pay and benefits for the chief executives and top paid officers, as reported on Internal Revenue Service Form 990 by private colleges and universities in the U.S. for the 1998-99 academic year. **Number listed:** 6.

- Mary Pat Seurkamp, president, with $151,186 annual pay; $13,729 in benefits
- Patricia Bosse, VP, institutional advancement, $85,025; $8,870
- Leonard Bowman, VP, academic affairs, $78,752; $8,472
- Richard L. Staisloff, VP, financial affairs, $76,407; $9,869
- Joseph Caruso, director, facility management, $69,165; $9,457
- Warren Szelistowski, director, information systems, $63,839; $9,111

Source: "Pay and Benefits of Leaders at 479 Private Colleges and Universities: a Survey," *The Chronicle of Higher Education*, 47: A29-A48, (November 24, 2000).

SALARIES—COLLEGES & UNIVERSITIES

★3528★
Top pay and benefits for the chief executive and top paid employees at the College of St. Catherine

Ranking basis/background: Annual pay and benefits for the chief executives and top paid officers, as reported on Internal Revenue Service Form 990 by private colleges and universities in the U.S. for the 1998-99 academic year. **Remarks:** Ms. Lee's pay is donated to the Sister Servants of the Immaculate Heart of Mary. **Number listed:** 7.
- Andrea J. Lee, I.H.M., president, with $0 annual pay; $7,560 in benefits
- Mary E. Broderick, former president, $111,800; $32,566
- William S. Halloran, VP, business and finance; treasurer, $144,977; $33,160
- Randi S.N. Yoder, VP, institutional advancement, $94,004; $7,520
- Calvin N. Ryan-Mosley, director, admissions, $97,100; $0
- Colleen Hegranes, VP, student affairs, $94,209; $0
- Kenneth G. Baltes, director, computer services, $82,931; $6,634

Source: "Pay and Benefits of Leaders at 479 Private Colleges and Universities: a Survey," *The Chronicle of Higher Education*, 47: A29-A48, (November 24, 2000).

★3529★
Top pay and benefits for the chief executive and top paid employees at the College of St. Rose

Ranking basis/background: Annual pay and benefits for the chief executives and top paid officers, as reported on Internal Revenue Service Form 990 by private colleges and universities in the U.S. for the 1998-99 academic year. **Number listed:** 6.
- R. Mark Sullivan, president, with $146,934 annual pay; $20,761 in benefits
- William Lowe, VP, academic affairs, $101,014; $15,379
- Kathleen Sinel, VP, finance and administration, $95,000; $13,682
- Jeanne Kobuszewski, VP, institutional advancement, $85,000; $10,711
- Charles E. Greene Jr., associate VP, administration, $77,000; $13,669
- Andrew Harnichar, director, administrative information systems, $75,900; $13,210

Source: "Pay and Benefits of Leaders at 479 Private Colleges and Universities: a Survey," *The Chronicle of Higher Education*, 47: A29-A48, (November 24, 2000).

★3530★
Top pay and benefits for the chief executive and top paid employees at the College of St. Scholastica

Ranking basis/background: Annual pay and benefits for the chief executives and top paid officers, as reported on Internal Revenue Service Form 990 by private colleges and universities in the U.S. for the 1998-99 academic year. **Number listed:** 6.
- Larry Goodwin, president, with $106,500 annual pay; $13,037 in benefits
- Chandra Mehrotra, dean, graduate studies, $90,503; $10,024
- Cecelia Taylor, VP, academic affairs, $81,200; $11,499
- Gerald Cizadlo, professor, biology, $85,402; $7,032
- Richard Davis, VP, institutional advancement, $77,429; $10,410
- Tommy Boone, professor, exercise physiology, $77,638; $9,834

Source: "Pay and Benefits of Leaders at 479 Private Colleges and Universities: a Survey," *The Chronicle of Higher Education*, 47: A29-A48, (November 24, 2000).

★3531★
Top pay and benefits for the chief executive and top paid employees at the College of Wooster

Ranking basis/background: Annual pay and benefits for the chief executives and top paid officers, as reported on Internal Revenue Service Form 990 by private colleges and universities in the U.S. for the 1998-99 academic year. **Number listed:** 6.
- R. Stanton Hales, president, with $161,333 annual pay; $22,694 in benefits
- Sara L. Patton, VP, development, $115,833; $16,893
- William H. Snoddy, VP, business and finance, $115,833; $16,893
- Barbara Hetrick, VP, academic affairs, $117,833; $2,974
- W. A. Hayden Schilling, special assistant to the president; professor, English and history; head coach, men's tennis, $98,941; $14,214
- Steve L. Moore, director, basketball camps; head men's basketball coach, $94,673; $13,849

Source: "Pay and Benefits of Leaders at 479 Private Colleges and Universities: a Survey," *The Chronicle of Higher Education*, 47: A29-A48, (November 24, 2000).

★3532★
Top pay and benefits for the chief executive and top paid employees at the Franciscan University of Steubenville

Ranking basis/background: Annual pay and benefits for the chief executives and top paid officers, as reported on Internal Revenue Service Form 990 by private colleges and universities in the U.S. for the 1998-99 academic year. **Remarks:** Reverend Scanlan's and Reverend Bourque's pay is donated to the Franciscan Friars. **Number listed:** 6.
- Rev. Michael Scanlan, T.O.R., president, with $98,400 annual pay; $23,209 in benefits
- Michael Healy, dean of the faculty, $83,520; $24,479
- David Skiviat, VP, finance and management services, $77,214; $23,778
- Rev. Thomas Bourque, T.O.R., executive VP
- Nicholas Healy Jr., VP, university relations, $70,070; $21,835
- Randall Cirner, dean of students, $63,400; $20,255

Source: "Pay and Benefits of Leaders at 479 Private Colleges and Universities: a Survey," *The Chronicle of Higher Education*, 47: A29-A48, (November 24, 2000).

★3533★
Top pay and benefits for the chief executive and top paid employees at the Maharishi University of Management

Ranking basis/background: Annual pay and benefits for the chief executives and top paid officers, as reported on Internal Revenue Service Form 990 by private colleges and universities in the U.S. for the 1998-99 academic year. **Number listed:** 6.
- Bevan Morris, president, with $18,000 annual pay; $0 in benefits
- John Hagelin, director, Institute of Science, Technology, and Public Policy, $113,004; $0
- Robert Schneider, dean, College of Maharishi Vedic Medicine; professor, Maharishi Vedic Medicine and physiology; director, Center of Health and Aging Studies, $62,054; $0
- Keith Wallace, executive VP, $17,400; $0
- Carolyn King, associate professor, social psychology, $15,140; $0
- Michael Spivak, treasurer, $7,200; $0

Source: "Pay and Benefits of Leaders at 479 Private Colleges and Universities: a Survey," *The Chronicle of Higher Education*, 47: A29-A48, (November 24, 2000).

★3534★
Top pay and benefits for the chief executive and top paid employees at the Maryville University of Saint Louis

Ranking basis/background: Annual pay and benefits for the chief executives and top paid officers, as reported on Internal Revenue Service Form 990 by private colleges and universities in the U.S. for the 1998-99 academic year. **Number listed:** 6.
- Keith Lovin, president, with $156,283 annual pay; $10,000 in benefits
- Larry Hays, assistant treasurer, $113,091; $7,916
- Mark Bates, VP, institutional advancement, $103,569; $7,250
- Edgar O. Rasch, special assistant to the president; VP, planning, information, and institutional research, $102,627; $7,184
- Patricia Thro, VP, academic and student affairs, $101,000; $7,070
- Charlie Barnes, controller, $99,600, $6,972

Source: "Pay and Benefits of Leaders at 479 Private Colleges and Universities: a Survey," *The Chronicle of Higher Education*, 47: A29-A48, (November 24, 2000).

★3535★
Top pay and benefits for the chief executive and top paid employees at the New York Institute of Technology

Ranking basis/background: Annual pay and benefits for the chief executives and top paid officers, as reported on Internal Revenue Service Form 990 by private colleges and universities in the U.S. for the 1998-99 academic year. **Number listed:** 6.
- Matthew Schure, president, with $282,601 annual pay; $8,000 in benefits
- Stanley Schiowitz, dean, college of osteopathic medicine, $294,208; $8,000
- Edward Guiliano, VP, academic affairs, $181,878; $8,588
- James Gillespie, special assistant to the president, $181,788; $8,657

Maryse Prezeau, VP, student affairs, $177,462; $8,249
Arnold Nagler, senior associate dean, preclinical medical education, $158,875; $15,090

Source: "Pay and Benefits of Leaders at 479 Private Colleges and Universities: a Survey," *The Chronicle of Higher Education*, 47: A29-A48, (November 24, 2000).

★3536★
Top pay and benefits for the chief executive and top paid employees at the Sage Colleges in New York

Ranking basis/background: Annual pay and benefits for the chief executives and top paid officers, as reported on Internal Revenue Service Form 990 by private colleges and universities in the U.S. for the 1998-99 academic year. **Number listed:** 6.

Jeanne H. Neff, president, with $143,000 annual pay; $16,882 in benefits
David W. Marcell, VP, external relations, $100,683; $10,537
D'Ann Campbell, VP, academic affairs, $92,700; $11,633
William E. Beckman, VP, finance and administration, $90,125; $11,503
Sally Lawrence, dean, junior college and evening college, $82,462; $10,589
Stephen L. Schechter, professor, global and social sciences, $78,749; $5,980

Source: "Pay and Benefits of Leaders at 479 Private Colleges and Universities: a Survey," *The Chronicle of Higher Education*, 47: A29-A48, (November 24, 2000).

★3537★
Top pay and benefits for the chief executive and top paid employees at the University of Chicago

Ranking basis/background: Annual pay and benefits for the chief executives and top paid officers, as reported on Internal Revenue Service Form 990 by private colleges and universities in the U.S. for the 1998-99 academic year. **Number listed:** 6.

Hugo Sonnenschein, president, with $397,433 annual pay; $12,000 in benefits
Glenn D. Steele, Jr., VP, medical affairs, Pritzker School of Medicine; dean of biological sciences, $707,688; $12,000
Valluvan Jeevanandam, associate professor and chief, department of surgery; chief vascular surgery, $529,546; $12,000
Daniel P. Mass, professor, clinical and orthopedic surgery, $522,509; $12,000
Anthony A. Kossiakoff, professor, chair, and co-director, institute of biophysical dynamics in the department of biochemistry and molecular biology, $509,000; $12,000
Bruce Gewertz, professor and chair, surgery, $505,647; $12,000

Source: "Pay and Benefits of Leaders at 479 Private Colleges and Universities: a Survey," *The Chronicle of Higher Education*, 47: A29-A48, (November 24, 2000).

★3538★
Top pay and benefits for the chief executive and top paid employees at the University of Dallas

Ranking basis/background: Annual pay and benefits for the chief executives and top paid officers, as reported on Internal Revenue Service Form 990 by private colleges and universities in the U.S. for the 1998-99 academic year. **Number listed:** 6.

Msgr. Milam J. Joseph, president, with $139,387 annual pay; $12,018 in benefits
Robert M. Galecke, VP, finance and administration, $133,325; $9,333
David Gordon, professor, graduate school of management, $122,174; $6,151
Paula Ann Hughes, dean, graduate school of management, $116,605; $7,360
Robert G. Lynch, associate professor, graduate school of management, $110,988; $6,021
Glen E. Thurow, provost, $108,739; $7,415

Source: "Pay and Benefits of Leaders at 479 Private Colleges and Universities: a Survey," *The Chronicle of Higher Education*, 47: A29-A48, (November 24, 2000).

★3539★
Top pay and benefits for the chief executive and top paid employees at the University of Dayton

Ranking basis/background: Annual pay and benefits for the chief executives and top paid officers, as reported on Internal Revenue Service Form 990 by private colleges and universities in the U.S. for the 1998-99 academic year. **Remarks:** Brother Fitz's compensation is paid to the Society of Mary. **Number listed:** 6.

Bro. Raymond L. Fitz, S.M., president, with $188,000 annual pay; $14,400 in benefits
Oliver G. Purnell Jr., head coach, men's basketball, $345,333; $6,226
James A. Snide, professor, chemical and materials engineering, $202,674; $8,431
Frances E. Evans, VP, advancement, $174,533; $10,184
Gordon A. Sargent, VP, graduate studies; dean, graduate school; director, research institute, $171,839; $12,654
Richard P. Perna, professor, law, $163,477; $11,216

Source: "Pay and Benefits of Leaders at 479 Private Colleges and Universities: a Survey," *The Chronicle of Higher Education*, 47: A29-A48, (November 24, 2000).

★3540★
Top pay and benefits for the chief executive and top paid employees at the University of Denver

Ranking basis/background: Annual pay and benefits for the chief executives and top paid officers, as reported on Internal Revenue Service Form 990 by private colleges and universities in the U.S. for the 1998-99 academic year. **Number listed:** 6.

Daniel Ritchie, chancellor, with $0 annual pay; $0 in benefits
Mark A. Vogel, director, graduate tax program, college of law, $338,996; $11,834

Neil J. Newton, dean, law, $182,700; $15,717
Robert P. McGowan, professor and chair, management department of business administration, $176,036; $14,768
Dennis Lynch, dean emeritus, college of law, $174,380; $12,810
James R. Griesemer, dean, business, $155,152; $12,838

Source: "Pay and Benefits of Leaders at 479 Private Colleges and Universities: a Survey," *The Chronicle of Higher Education*, 47: A29-A48, (November 24, 2000).

★3541★
Top pay and benefits for the chief executive and top paid employees at the University of Detroit Mercy

Ranking basis/background: Annual pay and benefits for the chief executives and top paid officers, as reported on Internal Revenue Service Form 990 by private colleges and universities in the U.S. for the 1998-99 academic year. **Number listed:** 6.

Sister Maureen A. Fay, O.P., president, with $170,000 annual pay; $18,403 in benefits
Bruce Graham, dean, school of dentistry, $171,105; $25,664
Stephen Mazurak, dean, school of law, $175,000; $14,000
Leo Hanifin, dean, college of engineering and sciences, $144,942; $23,401
Perry Watson, head coach, men's basketball, $133,866; $17,856
Gary Giamartino, dean, college of business administration, $129,330; $15,262

Source: "Pay and Benefits of Leaders at 479 Private Colleges and Universities: a Survey," *The Chronicle of Higher Education*, 47: A29-A48, (November 24, 2000).

★3542★
Top pay and benefits for the chief executive and top paid employees at the University of Dubuque

Ranking basis/background: Annual pay and benefits for the chief executives and top paid officers, as reported on Internal Revenue Service Form 990 by private colleges and universities in the U.S. for the 1998-99 academic year. **Number listed:** 8.

Rev. Jeffrey Bullock, president, with $115,000 annual pay; $31,050 in benefits
John Agria, former president, $11,086; $15,794
Walter Peterson, chancellor, $40,800; $3,121
Paul Kessler, VP, academic affairs; provost, $87,800; $14,203
Ron Heath, VP, advancement, $84,530; $14,030
Tracy A. Wagner, VP, finance and auxiliary services, $85,000; $11,028
Bradley Longfield, VP; dean, seminary, $72,150; $17,384
Dale Zschoche, associate VP, advancement; director, seminary development, $57,950; $11,214

Source: "Pay and Benefits of Leaders at 479 Private Colleges and Universities: a Survey," *The Chronicle of Higher Education*, 47: A29-A48, (November 24, 2000).

SALARIES—COLLEGES & UNIVERSITIES

★3543★
Top pay and benefits for the chief executive and top paid employees at the University of Evansville

Ranking basis/background: Annual pay and benefits for the chief executives and top paid officers, as reported on Internal Revenue Service Form 990 by private colleges and universities in the U.S. for the 1998-99 academic year. **Number listed:** 6.

- James S. Vinson, president, with $196,075 annual pay; $29,087 in benefits
- James S. Crews, coach, men's basketball, $154,728; $26,864
- Robert E. Gallman, VP, fiscal affairs, $114,000; $22,044
- Robin Cooper, coach, football, $109,350; $24,938
- Stephen Greiner, VP, academic affairs, $106,020; $19,732
- Philip M. Gerhart, dean, college of engineering and computer science, $101,556; $21,976

Source: "Pay and Benefits of Leaders at 479 Private Colleges and Universities: a Survey," *The Chronicle of Higher Education*, 47: A29-A48, (November 24, 2000).

★3544★
Top pay and benefits for the chief executive and top paid employees at the University of Hartford

Ranking basis/background: Annual pay and benefits for the chief executives and top paid officers, as reported on Internal Revenue Service Form 990 by private colleges and universities in the U.S. for the 1998-99 academic year. **Number listed:** 6.

- Walter Harrison, president, with $210,000 annual pay; $17,550 in benefits
- Elizabeth Klein, provost, $139,400; $12,546
- W. Stephen Jeffrey, VP, development, $136,581; $12,292
- Beverly Maksin, VP, finance and administration, $128,750; $11,588
- Stuart Schar, dean, Hartford Art School, $125,838; $11,325
- Edward Gray, dean, Hillger and Hartford College of Women, $112,016; $10,081

Source: "Pay and Benefits of Leaders at 479 Private Colleges and Universities: a Survey," *The Chronicle of Higher Education*, 47: A29-A48, (November 24, 2000).

★3545★
Top pay and benefits for the chief executive and top paid employees at the University of Indianapolis

Ranking basis/background: Annual pay and benefits for the chief executives and top paid officers, as reported on Internal Revenue Service Form 990 by private colleges and universities in the U.S. for the 1998-99 academic year. **Number listed:** 6.

- Jerry Israel, president, with $172,500 annual pay; $15,315 in benefits
- Lynn R. Youngblood, senior VP; provost, $128,700; $22,079
- Kendall L. Hottell, VP, business and finance; treasurer, $119,200; $15,487
- Gerald L. Speth, director, graduate school of business, $102,136; $8,486
- Michael Ferin, VP, institutional advancement, $96,000; $12,431
- G. Benjamin Lantz Jr., president emeritus, $88,645; $12,472

Source: "Pay and Benefits of Leaders at 479 Private Colleges and Universities: a Survey," *The Chronicle of Higher Education*, 47: A29-A48, (November 24, 2000).

★3546★
Top pay and benefits for the chief executive and top paid employees at the University of Judaism

Ranking basis/background: Annual pay and benefits for the chief executives and top paid officers, as reported on Internal Revenue Service Form 990 by private colleges and universities in the U.S. for the 1998-99 academic year. **Number listed:** 6.

- Rabbi Robert Wexler, president, with $159,962 annual pay; $14,645 in benefits
- Daniel Rothblatt, VP, development, $120,600; $17,746
- Mark Bookman, VP, administration and business affairs, $107,103; $16,470
- Daniel Gordis, VP, community outreach and public affairs; dean, rabbinic studies, $107,103; $10,416
- Hanan Alexander, VP, academic affairs, $106,581; $10,374
- Ronald Wolfson, VP; director, Whizin Center, $96,049; $15,246

Source: "Pay and Benefits of Leaders at 479 Private Colleges and Universities: a Survey," *The Chronicle of Higher Education*, 47: A29-A48, (November 24, 2000).

★3547★
Top pay and benefits for the chief executive and top paid employees at the University of La Verne

Ranking basis/background: Annual pay and benefits for the chief executives and top paid officers, as reported on Internal Revenue Service Form 990 by private colleges and universities in the U.S. for the 1998-99 academic year. **Number listed:** 6.

- Stephen C. Morgan, president, with $171,793 annual pay; $16,776 in benefits
- Philip Hawkey, executive VP, $151,026; $15,504
- Thomas McGuire, professor, education, $145,529; $0
- William Cook, VP, academic affairs; professor, English, $116,671; $10,500
- David Kung, professor, business administration, $123,260; $0
- Margaret Redman, associate professor, English, $122,302; $0

Source: "Pay and Benefits of Leaders at 479 Private Colleges and Universities: a Survey," *The Chronicle of Higher Education*, 47: A29-A48, (November 24, 2000).

★3548★
Top pay and benefits for the chief executive and top paid employees at the University of Mary

Ranking basis/background: Annual pay and benefits for the chief executives and top paid officers, as reported on Internal Revenue Service Form 990 by private colleges and universities in the U.S. for the 1998-99 academic year. **Number listed:** 6.

- Sister Thomas Welder, president, with $95,170 annual pay; $0 in benefits
- Harold Miller, former president, $110,550; $0
- Thomas Johnson, VP, academic affairs, $82,980; $0
- Kathy Perrin, chair, occupational therapy, $77,200; $0
- Neal Kalberer, VP, public affairs, $75,220; $0
- Jerry Fischer, VP, financial affairs, $75,060; $0

Source: "Pay and Benefits of Leaders at 479 Private Colleges and Universities: a Survey," *The Chronicle of Higher Education*, 47: A29-A48, (November 24, 2000).

★3549★
Top pay and benefits for the chief executive and top paid employees at the University of Mary Hardin-Baylor

Ranking basis/background: Annual pay and benefits for the chief executives and top paid officers, as reported on Internal Revenue Service Form 990 by private colleges and universities in the U.S. for the 1998-99 academic year. **Number listed:** 6.

- Jerry G. Bawcom, president, with $133,794 annual pay; $16,659 in benefits
- Kenneth W. Johnson, VP, administrative and academic affairs, $93,050; $12,464
- Edward E. Martin, VP, business and finance, $83,830; $11,514
- Curtis Beaird, VP, external affairs, $76,679; $10,778
- Michael P. West, director, health-service management, $70,376; $10,129
- Lee E. Baldwin, dean, business, $70,166; $10,107

Source: "Pay and Benefits of Leaders at 479 Private Colleges and Universities: a Survey," *The Chronicle of Higher Education*, 47: A29-A48, (November 24, 2000).

★3550★
Top pay and benefits for the chief executive and top paid employees at the University of Miami

Ranking basis/background: Annual pay and benefits for the chief executives and top paid officers, as reported on Internal Revenue Service Form 990 by private colleges and universities in the U.S. for the 1998-99 academic year. **Number listed:** 6.

- Edward T. Foote II, president, with $374,680 annual pay; $67,839 in benefits
- Barth A. Green, professor and chair, neurological surgery, $812,013; $112,677
- Roberto C. Heros, professor and co-chair, neurological surgery, $626,784; $82,191
- Mark S. Soloway, professor and chair, neurology, $547,288; $78,616

Mark D. Brown, professor and chair, orthopedics and rehabilitation services, $524,423; $78,586

William E. Smiddy, associate professor ophthalmology, $470,108; $79,709

Source: "Pay and Benefits of Leaders at 479 Private Colleges and Universities: a Survey," *The Chronicle of Higher Education*, 47: A29-A48, (November 24, 2000).

★3551★
Top pay and benefits for the chief executive and top paid employees at the University of Mobile

Ranking basis/background: Annual pay and benefits for the chief executives and top paid officers, as reported on Internal Revenue Service Form 990 by private colleges and universities in the U.S. for the 1998-99 academic year. **Number listed:** 6.

- Mark Foley, president, with $150,000 annual pay; $9,513 in benefits
- Geneva R. Johnson, dean, physical therapy, $132,613; $17,283
- Audrey Eubanks, VP, academic affairs, $77,250; $13,323
- Carol Ann Lewando, assistant professor, physical therapy, $77,250; $10,960
- Herman Shoemaker, VP, student development, $68,000; $12,027
- Steve Lee, VP, business affairs, $65,000; $12,330

Source: "Pay and Benefits of Leaders at 479 Private Colleges and Universities: a Survey," *The Chronicle of Higher Education*, 47: A29-A48, (November 24, 2000).

★3552★
Top pay and benefits for the chief executive and top paid employees at the University of New England

Ranking basis/background: Annual pay and benefits for the chief executives and top paid officers, as reported on Internal Revenue Service Form 990 by private colleges and universities in the U.S. for the 1998-99 academic year. **Number listed:** 6.

- Sandra Featherman, president, with $182,300 annual pay; $10,027 in benefits
- John W. Thompson, staff physician, $233,625; $7,009
- Stephen Shannon, dean, osteopathic medicine, $162,399; $8,932
- Bruce P. Bates, associate dean, clinical affairs, $140,745; $7,741
- Boyd Buser, associate professor and chair, osteopathic and manipulative medicine, $135,265; $7,440
- George J. Pasquaraello, staff physician, $128,865; $7,088

Source: "Pay and Benefits of Leaders at 479 Private Colleges and Universities: a Survey," *The Chronicle of Higher Education*, 47: A29-A48, (November 24, 2000).

★3553★
Top pay and benefits for the chief executive and top paid employees at the University of New Haven

Ranking basis/background: Annual pay and benefits for the chief executives and top paid officers, as reported on Internal Revenue Service Form 990 by private colleges and universities in the U.S. for the 1998-99 academic year. **Number listed:** 6.

- Lawrence J. DeNardis, president, with $159,499 annual pay; $18,247 in benefits
- James W. Uebelacker, VP, academic affairs; provost, $101,681; $14,354
- William M. Leete Jr., VP, student affairs and athletics, $96,065; $13,151
- Duncan P. Gifford, VP, finance, $93,778; $11,548
- Thomas A. Johnson, dean, public safety and professional studies, $96,640; $7,619
- M. Jerry Kenig, dean, engineering, $86,891; $12,649

Source: "Pay and Benefits of Leaders at 479 Private Colleges and Universities: a Survey," *The Chronicle of Higher Education*, 47: A29-A48, (November 24, 2000).

★3554★
Top pay and benefits for the chief executive and top paid employees at the University of Notre Dame

Ranking basis/background: Annual pay and benefits for the chief executives and top paid officers, as reported on Internal Revenue Service Form 990 by private colleges and universities in the U.S. for the 1998-99 academic year. **Number listed:** 6.

- Rev. Edward A. Malloy, C.S.C., president, with $265,000 annual pay; $18,238 in benefits
- Nathan O. Hatch, provost, $241,500; $30,656
- Scott C. Malpass, associate VP, finance; chief investment officer, $237,083; $28,944
- Rev. E. William Beauchamp, C.S.C, executive VP, $235,000; $18,238
- Frank J. Castellino, dean, college of science, $220,080; $30,405
- Frank Incropera, dean, engineering, $202,157; $35,325

Source: "Pay and Benefits of Leaders at 479 Private Colleges and Universities: a Survey," *The Chronicle of Higher Education*, 47: A29-A48, (November 24, 2000).

★3555★
Top pay and benefits for the chief executive and top paid employees at the University of Pennsylvania

Ranking basis/background: Annual pay and benefits for the chief executives and top paid officers, as reported on Internal Revenue Service Form 990 by private colleges and universities in the U.S. for the 1998-99 academic year. **Number listed:** 6.

- Judith Rodin, president, with $603,165 annual pay; $52,392 in benefits
- John P. Wynne Jr., chief financial officer, health systems, $845,502; $1,989,529
- William N. Kelley, CEO, health systems and medical center; dean, medicine, $1,357,128; $18,505
- Thomas L. Spray, professor, surgery; division chief, cardiac surgery, $1,150,000; $13,951
- Paul J. Marcotte, assistant professor, neurosurgery, $900,803; $7,997
- Leslie Sutton, professor, surgery; chief, neurosurgery, $816,552; $15,795

Source: "Pay and Benefits of Leaders at 479 Private Colleges and Universities: a Survey," *The Chronicle of Higher Education*, 47: A29-A48, (November 24, 2000).

★3556★
Top pay and benefits for the chief executive and top paid employees at the University of Portland

Ranking basis/background: Annual pay and benefits for the chief executives and top paid officers, as reported on Internal Revenue Service Form 990 by private colleges and universities in the U.S. for the 1998-99 academic year. **Remarks:** Reverend Tyson's compensation is paid to the Congregation of the Holy Cross. **Number listed:** 6.

- Rev. David T. Tyson, C.S.C., president, with $142,140 annual pay; $24,091 in benefits
- Zia Yamayee, dean, engineering, $116,442; $20,497
- Ronald P. Hill, dean, business, $118,417; $18,405
- Anthony J. DiSpigno, VP, university relations, $105,535; $20,598
- John Goveia, professor, business, $100,475; $18,895
- Howard Feldman, professor, business, $99,814; $17,529

Source: "Pay and Benefits of Leaders at 479 Private Colleges and Universities: a Survey," *The Chronicle of Higher Education*, 47: A29-A48, (November 24, 2000).

★3557★
Top pay and benefits for the chief executive and top paid employees at the University of Puget Sound

Ranking basis/background: Annual pay and benefits for the chief executives and top paid officers, as reported on Internal Revenue Service Form 990 by private colleges and universities in the U.S. for the 1998-99 academic year. **Number listed:** 6.

- Susan Resneck Pierce, president, with $228,400 annual pay; $65,097 in benefits
- Michael Oman, VP, university relations, $147,999; $21,022
- Michael Rothman, VP, finance and administration, $145,500; $20,718
- Terry A. Cooney, academic VP, dean of the university, professor, history, $124,232; $18,042
- George H. Mills, VP, enrollment, $99,314; $14,901
- Mott T. Green, professor, honors program, $96,895; $14,519

Source: "Pay and Benefits of Leaders at 479 Private Colleges and Universities: a Survey," *The Chronicle of Higher Education*, 47: A29-A48, (November 24, 2000).

SALARIES—COLLEGES & UNIVERSITIES

★3558★
Top pay and benefits for the chief executive and top paid employees at the University of Redlands

Ranking basis/background: Annual pay and benefits for the chief executives and top paid officers, as reported on Internal Revenue Service Form 990 by private colleges and universities in the U.S. for the 1998-99 academic year. **Number listed:** 6.

- James R. Appleton, president, with $217,909 annual pay; $14,400 in benefits
- Phillip L. Doolittle, VP, finance and administration, $132,832; $11,955
- Ronald J. Stephany, VP, university relations, $109,960; $9,896
- Philip A. Glotzbach, VP, academic affairs, $107,000; $9,630
- Yasuyuki Owada, director, Johnston Center, $96,144; $8,653
- David B. Bragg, professor, mathematics and computer science, $94,749; $8,527

Source: "Pay and Benefits of Leaders at 479 Private Colleges and Universities: a Survey," *The Chronicle of Higher Education*, 47: A29-A48, (November 24, 2000).

★3559★
Top pay and benefits for the chief executive and top paid employees at the University of Richmond

Ranking basis/background: Annual pay and benefits for the chief executives and top paid officers, as reported on Internal Revenue Service Form 990 by private colleges and universities in the U.S. for the 1998-99 academic year. **Number listed:** 6.

- William E. Cooper, president, with $336,165 annual pay; $46,767 in benefits
- Richard L. Morrill, chancellor, $256,500; $43,715
- John Beilein, head coach, men's basketball, $164,823; $85,658
- Edward M. Fouhy, director, Pew Center on the States, $192,470; $39,100
- Joe B. Hoyle, associate professor, accounting, $199,186; $24,762
- Zeddie P. Bowen, VP; provost, $166,848; $32,386

Source: "Pay and Benefits of Leaders at 479 Private Colleges and Universities: a Survey," *The Chronicle of Higher Education*, 47: A29-A48, (November 24, 2000).

★3560★
Top pay and benefits for the chief executive and top paid employees at the University of Rochester

Ranking basis/background: Annual pay and benefits for the chief executives and top paid officers, as reported on Internal Revenue Service Form 990 by private colleges and universities in the U.S. for the 1998-99 academic year. **Number listed:** 6.

- Thomas H. Jackson, president, with $329,300 annual pay; $18,610 in benefits
- Richard M. Green, professor, surgery, $863,275; $18,610
- John U. Coniglio, associate professor, surgery, $630,000; $18,610
- Webster H. Pilcher, associate professor, neurosurgery, $574,561; $18,610
- Joseph M. Serletti, associate professor, surgery, $570,000; $18,610
- Robert J. Maciumas, professor, neurosurgery, $481,780; $2,690

Source: "Pay and Benefits of Leaders at 479 Private Colleges and Universities: a Survey," *The Chronicle of Higher Education*, 47: A29-A48, (November 24, 2000).

★3561★
Top pay and benefits for the chief executive and top paid employees at the University of Saint Francis in Illinois

Ranking basis/background: Annual pay and benefits for the chief executives and top paid officers, as reported on Internal Revenue Service Form 990 by private colleges and universities in the U.S. for the 1998-99 academic year. **Number listed:** 6.

- James Doppke, president, with $140,000 annual pay; $18,100 in benefits
- Michael J. Brown, VP, business affairs; treasurer, $92,180; $17,011
- Thomas Brodnicki, VP, university advancement, $94,760; $12,543
- Martin Larrey, VP, academic affairs, $95,000; $8,457
- F. William Kelley Jr., dean, college of graduate studies, $89,780; $8,134
- Lyle Hicks, dean, business and professional studies, $81,500; $11,714

Source: "Pay and Benefits of Leaders at 479 Private Colleges and Universities: a Survey," *The Chronicle of Higher Education*, 47: A29-A48, (November 24, 2000).

★3562★
Top pay and benefits for the chief executive and top paid employees at the University of Saint Francis in Indiana

Ranking basis/background: Annual pay and benefits for the chief executives and top paid officers, as reported on Internal Revenue Service Form 990 by private colleges and universities in the U.S. for the 1998-99 academic year. **Number listed:** 5.

- Sister Mary Elise Kriss, O.S.F., president, with $75,643 annual pay; $0 in benefits
- Jiya Jain, chair, business administration, $68,048; $4,083
- John J. Kessen, VP, finance, $60,044; $4,803
- Marcia Sauter, chair, nursing, $60,332; $3,017
- Richard Groves, VP, institutional advancement, $56,244; $2,812

Source: "Pay and Benefits of Leaders at 479 Private Colleges and Universities: a Survey," *The Chronicle of Higher Education*, 47: A29-A48, (November 24, 2000).

★3563★
Top pay and benefits for the chief executive and top paid employees at the University of St. Thomas in Minnesota

Ranking basis/background: Annual pay and benefits for the chief executives and top paid officers, as reported on Internal Revenue Service Form 990 by private colleges and universities in the U.S. for the 1998-99 academic year. **Number listed:** 6.

- Rev. Dennis Dease, president, with $28,540 annual pay; $26,531 in benefits
- Charles Keffer, provost, $181,606; $10,538
- Peter B. Vaill, chair, management education, $163,349; $18,954
- L. Thomas Kelly, editor, Catholic Digest, $146,538; $19,829
- Quentin J. Hietpas, senior VP, external affairs, $116,618; $48,077
- Kenneth Goodpaster, chair, business ethics, $142,407; $17,838

Source: "Pay and Benefits of Leaders at 479 Private Colleges and Universities: a Survey," *The Chronicle of Higher Education*, 47: A29-A48, (November 24, 2000).

★3564★
Top pay and benefits for the chief executive and top paid employees at the University of Saint Thomas in Texas

Ranking basis/background: Annual pay and benefits for the chief executives and top paid officers, as reported on Internal Revenue Service Form 990 by private colleges and universities in the U.S. for the 1998-99 academic year. **Number listed:** 5.

- Rev. Michael Miller, president, with $130,000 annual pay; $10,084 in benefits
- Jim Booth, VP, finance, $125,500; $12,446
- Yhi-Min Ho, dean, Cameron School of Business, $114,000; $10,259
- Lee J. Williams, VP, academic affairs, $112,000; $11,636
- Hassan Shirvani, professor, economics and finance, $96,878; $9,136

Source: "Pay and Benefits of Leaders at 479 Private Colleges and Universities: a Survey," *The Chronicle of Higher Education*, 47: A29-A48, (November 24, 2000).

★3565★
Top pay and benefits for the chief executive and top paid employees at the University of San Diego

Ranking basis/background: Annual pay and benefits for the chief executives and top paid officers, as reported on Internal Revenue Service Form 990 by private colleges and universities in the U.S. for the 1998-99 academic year. **Number listed:** 6.

- Alice B. Hayes, president, with $191,835 annual pay; $23,630 in benefits
- Francis M. Lazarus, VP; provost, $177,977; $22,675
- John G. McNamara, VP, university relation, $147,500; $18,925
- Thomas Burke Jr., VP, student affairs; dean of students, $137,667; $24,504
- Paul E. Bissonnette, VP, finance and administration, $129,167; $25,601
- Grant Morris, professor, law, $130,917; $21,840

Source: "Pay and Benefits of Leaders at 479 Private Colleges and Universities: a Survey," *The Chronicle of Higher Education*, 47: A29-A48, (November 24, 2000).

★3566★
Top pay and benefits for the chief executive and top paid employees at the University of San Francisco

Ranking basis/background: Annual pay and benefits for the chief executives and top paid officers, as reported on Internal Revenue Service Form 990 by private colleges and universities in the U.S. for the 1998-99 academic year. **Number listed:** 6.

- Rev. J. Schlogel, S.J., president, with $0 annual pay; $0 in benefits
- H.J. Foldberg, dean, law, $197,298; $39,262
- Stanley Nel, dean, arts and sciences, $178,495; $35,877
- James Wiser, VP, academic affairs, $174,720; $35,119
- Willard H. Nutting, VP, business and finance, $168,972; $34,132
- Gary G. Williams, dean, business, $153,375; $32,976

Source: "Pay and Benefits of Leaders at 479 Private Colleges and Universities: a Survey," *The Chronicle of Higher Education*, 47: A29-A48, (November 24, 2000).

★3567★
Top pay and benefits for the chief executive and top paid employees at the University of Scranton

Ranking basis/background: Annual pay and benefits for the chief executives and top paid officers, as reported on Internal Revenue Service Form 990 by private colleges and universities in the U.S. for the 1998-99 academic year. **Number listed:** 6.

- Rev. Joseph McShane, S.J., president, with $0 annual pay; $6,474 in benefits
- Richard H. Passon, academic VP; provost, $125,660; $27,674
- David E. Christiansen, VP, finance; treasurer, $125,660; $25,530
- Ronald Johnson, dean, Kani School of Management, $112,640; $23,178
- Robert J. Sylvester, VP, institutional advancement, $98,513; $24,201
- Joseph H. Dreisbach, dean; professor, college of arts and sciences, $98,255; $24,151

Source: "Pay and Benefits of Leaders at 479 Private Colleges and Universities: a Survey," *The Chronicle of Higher Education*, 47: A29-A48, (November 24, 2000).

★3568★
Top pay and benefits for the chief executive and top paid employees at the University of Southern California

Ranking basis/background: Annual pay and benefits for the chief executives and top paid officers, as reported on Internal Revenue Service Form 990 by private colleges and universities in the U.S. for the 1998-99 academic year. **Number listed:** 6.

- Steven B. Sample, president, with $434,579 annual pay; $42,912 in benefits
- Stephen J. Ryan Jr., senior VP, $549,000; $65,368
- Paul R. Hackett, head coach, football, $400,000; $46,578
- Charlie Henry Bibby, head coach, basketball, $376,688; $50,482
- Dale Clinton Garell, professor and chair, clinical medicine and pediatrics, $325,400; $40,054
- Brian E. Henderson, professor, neurology and preventive medicine, $320,000; $39,911

Source: "Pay and Benefits of Leaders at 479 Private Colleges and Universities: a Survey," *The Chronicle of Higher Education*, 47: A29-A48, (November 24, 2000).

★3569★
Top pay and benefits for the chief executive and top paid employees at the University of Tampa

Ranking basis/background: Annual pay and benefits for the chief executives and top paid officers, as reported on Internal Revenue Service Form 990 by private colleges and universities in the U.S. for the 1998-99 academic year. **Number listed:** 6.

- Ronald L. Vaughn, president, with $170,000 annual pay; $38,026 in benefits
- Alfred Page, dean, business, $136,850; $11,178
- Barbara Strickler, VP, enrollment and admissions, $115,700; $9,731
- Robert E. Forschner Jr., VP, administration and finance, $109,188; $12,985
- Daniel T. Gura, VP, development and university relations, $110,112; $9,558
- Robert A. Clark, professor, finance; director, MBA program, $92,543; $8,292

Source: "Pay and Benefits of Leaders at 479 Private Colleges and Universities: a Survey," *The Chronicle of Higher Education*, 47: A29-A48, (November 24, 2000).

★3570★
Top pay and benefits for the chief executive and top paid employees at the University of the Incarnate Word

Ranking basis/background: Annual pay and benefits for the chief executives and top paid officers, as reported on Internal Revenue Service Form 990 by private colleges and universities in the U.S. for the 1998-99 academic year. **Number listed:** 6.

- Louis J. Agnese Jr., president, with $194,000 annual pay; $12,250 in benefits
- Eduardo S. Paderon, VP, academic affairs, $104,300; $7,161
- David M. Jurenovich, VP, planning and marketing, $103,050; $7,073
- Douglas B. Endsley, VP, finance, $96,000; $6,580
- Thomas K. Plofchan, VP, institutional advancement, $96,000; $6,580
- Donald R. Traylor, dean, graduate studies, $80,538; $5,638

Source: "Pay and Benefits of Leaders at 479 Private Colleges and Universities: a Survey," *The Chronicle of Higher Education*, 47: A29-A48, (November 24, 2000).

★3571★
Top pay and benefits for the chief executive and top paid employees at the University of the Pacific

Ranking basis/background: Annual pay and benefits for the chief executives and top paid officers, as reported on Internal Revenue Service Form 990 by private colleges and universities in the U.S. for the 1998-99 academic year. **Number listed:** 6.

- Donald V. DeRosa, president, with $195,472 annual pay; $40,500 in benefits
- Arthur Dugoni, dean, dental school, $209,750; $12,000
- Gerald Caplan, dean, law, $186,250; $12,000
- Robert Boyd, professor, dentistry, $172,864; $12,000
- Joshua Dressler, professor, law, $166,134; $12,000
- Robert Christofferson, executive associate dean of the college, $164,000; $12,000

Source: "Pay and Benefits of Leaders at 479 Private Colleges and Universities: a Survey," *The Chronicle of Higher Education*, 47: A29-A48, (November 24, 2000).

★3572★
Top pay and benefits for the chief executive and top paid employees at the University of the South

Ranking basis/background: Annual pay and benefits for the chief executives and top paid officers, as reported on Internal Revenue Service Form 990 by private colleges and universities in the U.S. for the 1998-99 academic year. **Number listed:** 6.

- Samuel Williamson, president; vice chancellor, with $205,500 annual pay; $43,139 in benefits
- Arthur M. Schaefer, professor, economics, $117,800; $26,362
- Laurence Alvarez, associate provost; professor, mathematics, $112,000; $27,133
- David Simpson, VP, business and community relations, $115,180; $22,348
- Frederick Croom, provost; professor, mathematics, $111,000; $25,176
- Tommy G. Watson, university librarian, $103,250; $25,608

Source: "Pay and Benefits of Leaders at 479 Private Colleges and Universities: a Survey," *The Chronicle of Higher Education*, 47: A29-A48, (November 24, 2000).

★3573★
Top pay and benefits for the chief executive and top paid employees at the University of Tulsa

Ranking basis/background: Annual pay and benefits for the chief executives and top paid officers, as reported on Internal Revenue Service Form 990 by private colleges and universities in the U.S. for the 1998-99 academic year. **Number listed:** 6.

- Robert W. Lawless, president, with $260,000 annual pay; $54,944 in benefits
- Bill E. Self, head coach, men's basketball, $275,122; $75,113
- Robert H. Donaldson, professor, political science, $229,162; $18,193

SALARIES—COLLEGES & UNIVERSITIES

James R. Brill, professor, $151,949; $20,559
James D. Rader, dean, law, $143,356; $20,343
Roger N. Blais, provost, $140,488; $18,511

Source: "Pay and Benefits of Leaders at 479 Private Colleges and Universities: a Survey," *The Chronicle of Higher Education*, 47: A29-A48, (November 24, 2000).

★3574★
Top pay and benefits for the chief executive and top paid employees at Thomas Aquinas College in California

Ranking basis/background: Annual pay and benefits for the chief executives and top paid officers, as reported on Internal Revenue Service Form 990 by private colleges and universities in the U.S. for the 1998-99 academic year. **Number listed:** 6.

Thomas E. Dillon, president, with $68,786 annual pay; $11,571 in benefits
Thomas J. Kaiser, tutor, $81,624; $10,708
Thomas J. Susanka Jr., director, admissions, $80,160; $11,052
Kevin D. Kolbeck, tutor, $76,691; $10,504
Richard D. Ferrier, tutor, $74,807; $10,807
Marcus R. Berquist, tutor, $70,258; $11,317

Source: "Pay and Benefits of Leaders at 479 Private Colleges and Universities: a Survey," *The Chronicle of Higher Education*, 47: A29-A48, (November 24, 2000).

★3575★
Top pay and benefits for the chief executive and top paid employees at Transylvania University

Ranking basis/background: Annual pay and benefits for the chief executives and top paid officers, as reported on Internal Revenue Service Form 990 by private colleges and universities in the U.S. for the 1998-99 academic year. **Number listed:** 6.

Charles L. Shearer, president, with $150,000 annual pay; $15,000 in benefits
James G. Mosely, VP, academics; dean of the college; professor, religion, $109,600; $10,960
James E. Miller, professor, mathematics and computer science, $101,900; $9,690
J. Barton Meyer, VP, development, $94,300; $9,430
Jerry Ray, chief financial officer, $90,200; $9,020
Michael Vetter, dean of students, $79,000; $7,900

Source: "Pay and Benefits of Leaders at 479 Private Colleges and Universities: a Survey," *The Chronicle of Higher Education*, 47: A29-A48, (November 24, 2000).

★3576★
Top pay and benefits for the chief executive and top paid employees at Trevecca Nazarene University

Ranking basis/background: Annual pay and benefits for the chief executives and top paid officers, as reported on Internal Revenue Service Form 990 by private colleges and universities in the U.S. for the 1998-99 academic year. **Number listed:** 6.

Millard Reed, president, with $113,000 annual pay; $16,145 in benefits
Stephen M. Pusey, VP, academic affairs, $77,178; $12,536
Mark William Myers, VP, financial services, $74,887; $14,046
Stephen Harris, dean, student development, $69,374; $13,420
Jan Forman, dean, enrollment management, $67,813; $13,629
Harold McCue, VP, university advancement, $67,813; $10,452

Source: "Pay and Benefits of Leaders at 479 Private Colleges and Universities: a Survey," *The Chronicle of Higher Education*, 47: A29-A48, (November 24, 2000).

★3577★
Top pay and benefits for the chief executive and top paid employees at Trinity College in Connecticut

Ranking basis/background: Annual pay and benefits for the chief executives and top paid officers, as reported on Internal Revenue Service Form 990 by private colleges and universities in the U.S. for the 1998-99 academic year. **Number listed:** 6.

Evan S. Dobelle, president, with $210,000 annual pay; $30,236 in benefits
Joseph Bronzino, professor, applied science, $165,509; $24,497
Robert A. Pedemonti, VP; treasurer, $155,000; $28,430
Raymond W. Baker, dean of the faculty, $144,500; $27,404
Linda S. Campanella, senior VP, operations and planning, $139,000; $27,522
Brodie Remington, VP, development and alumni programs, $139,000; $26,974

Source: "Pay and Benefits of Leaders at 479 Private Colleges and Universities: a Survey," *The Chronicle of Higher Education*, 47: A29-A48, (November 24, 2000).

★3578★
Top pay and benefits for the chief executive and top paid employees at Trinity College in Washington D.C.

Ranking basis/background: Annual pay and benefits for the chief executives and top paid officers, as reported on Internal Revenue Service Form 990 by private colleges and universities in the U.S. for the 1998-99 academic year. **Number listed:** 6.

Patricia A. McGuire, president, with $114,480 annual pay; $14,972 in benefits
Patricia Weitzel-O'Neill, VP, academic affairs, $98,333; $11,648
Sandra Oyewole, professor; dean of the faculty, $86,283; $14,216
Joseph W. Smolskis, VP; treasurer, $85,121; $11,308
Camille Hazeur, dean, student services, $79,170; $7,526
Loretta Shpunt, professor, English, $73,583; $8,881

Source: "Pay and Benefits of Leaders at 479 Private Colleges and Universities: a Survey," *The Chronicle of Higher Education*, 47: A29-A48, (November 24, 2000).

★3579★
Top pay and benefits for the chief executive and top paid employees at Trinity University in Texas

Ranking basis/background: Annual pay and benefits for the chief executives and top paid officers, as reported on Internal Revenue Service Form 990 by private colleges and universities in the U.S. for the 1998-99 academic year. **Number listed:** 6.

Ronald Calgaard, president, with $250,000 annual pay; $33,000 in benefits
Edward C. Roy, VP, academic affairs, $154,500; $29,825
William Stone, professor, biology, $158,100; $24,417
Philip L. Cooley, professor, business administration, $157,000; $23,385
Robert E. Jensen, professor, business administration, $147,000; $22,241
William Breit, professor, economics, $143,300; $21,817

Source: "Pay and Benefits of Leaders at 479 Private Colleges and Universities: a Survey," *The Chronicle of Higher Education*, 47: A29-A48, (November 24, 2000).

★3580★
Top pay and benefits for the chief executive and top paid employees at Tufts University

Ranking basis/background: Annual pay and benefits for the chief executives and top paid officers, as reported on Internal Revenue Service Form 990 by private colleges and universities in the U.S. for the 1998-99 academic year. **Number listed:** 6.

John DiBiaggio, president, with $309,350 annual pay; $41,126 in benefits
John Harrington, dean, medical school, $290,512; $26,182
Maria Papageorge, associate professor, oral surgery, $260,383; $22,141
Steven Manos, executive VP, $239,529; $42,562
Naushirwan R. Mehta, associate professor, periodontology, $251,205; $22,060
Thomas Murnane, senior VP, $232,390; $36,713

Source: "Pay and Benefits of Leaders at 479 Private Colleges and Universities: a Survey," *The Chronicle of Higher Education*, 47: A29-A48, (November 24, 2000).

★3581★
Top pay and benefits for the chief executive and top paid employees at Tulane University

Ranking basis/background: Annual pay and benefits for the chief executives and top paid officers, as reported on Internal Revenue Service Form 990 by private colleges and universities in the U.S. for the 1998-99 academic year. **Number listed:** 6.

Scott S. Cowen, president, with $328,490 annual pay; $2,899 in benefits
Vassyl A. Lonchyna, professor, surgery and cardiotherapy, $713,031; $3,130
Thomas S. Whitecloud, III, professor and chair, orthopedics, $654,436; $18,899
James C. Butler, associate professor, orthopedics, $533,646; $14,089
Mark J. Hontas, assistant professor, orthopedics, $530,105; $12,257

Delmar R. Caldwell, professor and chair, ophthalmology, $468,200; $18,899

Source: "Pay and Benefits of Leaders at 479 Private Colleges and Universities: a Survey," *The Chronicle of Higher Education*, 47: A29-A48, (November 24, 2000).

★3582★
Top pay and benefits for the chief executive and top paid employees at Tusculum College

Ranking basis/background: Annual pay and benefits for the chief executives and top paid officers, as reported on Internal Revenue Service Form 990 by private colleges and universities in the U.S. for the 1998-99 academic year. **Number listed:** 5.

Robert E. Knott, president, with $125,652 annual pay; $8,006 in benefits
John E. Mays, senior VP, external relations, $108,942; $8,602
James F. Reid, VP, residential college, $87,125; $7,559
Suzanne Hine, VP, graduate and professional studies, $71,775; $3,589
Mark A. Stokes, VP, student and auxiliary services, $67,482; $6,294

Source: "Pay and Benefits of Leaders at 479 Private Colleges and Universities: a Survey," *The Chronicle of Higher Education*, 47: A29-A48, (November 24, 2000).

★3583★
Top pay and benefits for the chief executive and top paid employees at Tuskegee University

Ranking basis/background: Annual pay and benefits for the chief executives and top paid officers, as reported on Internal Revenue Service Form 990 by private colleges and universities in the U.S. for the 1998-99 academic year. **Number listed:** 6.

Benjamin F. Payton, president, with $155,268 annual pay; $48,435 in benefits
Michael B. Hill, senior VP, university advancement, $115,468; 5,720
Billy R. Owens, VP, business and finance, $108,501; $5,330
William L. Lester, provost, $103,495; $5,142
Tsegaye Habtermariam, director and associate dean, biomedical informatics medical systems program; professor, pathobiology, $103,828; $4,490
Shalk Jeelani, assistant VP, sponsored programs and research, $102,128; $5,106

Source: "Pay and Benefits of Leaders at 479 Private Colleges and Universities: a Survey," *The Chronicle of Higher Education*, 47: A29-A48, (November 24, 2000).

★3584★
Top pay and benefits for the chief executive and top paid employees at Union College in Kentucky

Ranking basis/background: Annual pay and benefits for the chief executives and top paid officers, as reported on Internal Revenue Service Form 990 by private colleges and universities in the U.S. for the 1998-99 academic year. **Number listed:** 6.

David C. Joyce, president, with $104,000 annual pay; $11,190 in benefits
Vernon Miles, VP, academic affairs, $58,500; $5,623
William Bernhardt, dean, graduate academic affairs, $57,692; $5,517
Jodie Barnes, VP, advancement, $57,500; $5,550
Edward H. Black, VP, planning and human resources, $52,000; $7,129
Lawrence Inkster, director, athletics; professor, health and physical education, $51,545; $7,088

Source: "Pay and Benefits of Leaders at 479 Private Colleges and Universities: a Survey," *The Chronicle of Higher Education*, 47: A29-A48, (November 24, 2000).

★3585★
Top pay and benefits for the chief executive and top paid employees at Union College in New York

Ranking basis/background: Annual pay and benefits for the chief executives and top paid officers, as reported on Internal Revenue Service Form 990 by private colleges and universities in the U.S. for the 1998-99 academic year. **Number listed:** 6.

Roger H. Hull, president, with $230,000 annual pay; $27,956 in benefits
Diane Blake, VP, finance and administration, $115,000; $13,840
Dan Lundquist, VP, admissions, $110,000; $13,589
Frank E. Wicks, associate professor, mechanical engineering, $107,920; $12,618
Donald Arnold, professor, Graduate Management Institute, $102,119; $16,437
Linda Cool, VP, academic affairs; dean of the faculty, $101,764; $14,533

Source: "Pay and Benefits of Leaders at 479 Private Colleges and Universities: a Survey," *The Chronicle of Higher Education*, 47: A29-A48, (November 24, 2000).

★3586★
Top pay and benefits for the chief executive and top paid employees at Union Institute

Ranking basis/background: Annual pay and benefits for the chief executives and top paid officers, as reported on Internal Revenue Service Form 990 by private colleges and universities in the U.S. for the 1998-99 academic year. **Number listed:** 7.

Robert T. Conley, president, with $177,301 annual pay; $59,678 in benefits
Meaven Cadwallader, acting president, $81,909; $27,223
Mark Rosenman, VP, office of social responsibility, $116,196; $34,572
Susan J. Wood, VP, finance and administration, $112,476; $38,282
Peter Hellister, VP, institutional advancement, $106,830; $34,251
Dick Genardi, dean, psychology, $97,314; $33,491
Alvin Hall, dean, school of interdisciplinary arts and sciences, $89,826; $29,078

Source: "Pay and Benefits of Leaders at 479 Private Colleges and Universities: a Survey," *The Chronicle of Higher Education*, 47: A29-A48, (November 24, 2000).

★3587★
Top pay and benefits for the chief executive and top paid employees at United States International University

Ranking basis/background: Annual pay and benefits for the chief executives and top paid officers, as reported on Internal Revenue Service Form 990 by private colleges and universities in the U.S. for the 1998-99 academic year. **Number listed:** 6.

Garry D. Hays, president, with $153,606 annual pay; $17,064 in benefits
N. John Schaedler, VP, finance and administration; treasurer, $115,755; $11,059
Joseph M. Marron, VP, student services and enrollment management, $97,003; $9,699
Ramona Kunard, dean, college of arts and sciences, $89,366; $9,182
Mink Stavenga, dean, college of business administration, $87,096; $8,981
Clark Hampton, controller, $84,749; $2,500

Source: "Pay and Benefits of Leaders at 479 Private Colleges and Universities: a Survey," *The Chronicle of Higher Education*, 47: A29-A48, (November 24, 2000).

★3588★
Top pay and benefits for the chief executive and top paid employees at University of Bridgeport

Ranking basis/background: Annual pay and benefits for the chief executives and top paid officers, as reported on Internal Revenue Service Form 990 by private colleges and universities in the U.S. for the 1998-99 academic year. **Number listed:** 6.

Richard L. Rubenstein, president, with $169,125 annual pay; $22,210 in benefits
Michael J. Grant, provost, $130,000; $17,777
Stoyan Ganev, VP, international affairs; director, New England Center for International and Regional Studies; professor, international studies, $125,859; $13,236
Tarek M. Sobh, professor, computer science and engineering, $120,101; $13,461
Ausif Mahmood, assistant professor, computer science and engineering, $114,284; $13,380
Francis A. Zolli, dean, college of chiropractics, $109,730; $14,784

Source: "Pay and Benefits of Leaders at 479 Private Colleges and Universities: a Survey," *The Chronicle of Higher Education*, 47: A29-A48, (November 24, 2000).

★3589★
Top pay and benefits for the chief executive and top paid employees at University of Central Texas

Ranking basis/background: Annual pay and benefits for the chief executives and top paid officers, as reported on Internal Revenue Service Form 990 by private colleges and universities in the U.S. for the 1998-99 academic year. **Number listed:** 5.

Pauline S. Moseley, president, with $99,300 annual pay; $9,351 in benefits

Jerome Hill, professor, computer science, $64,000; $6,880

B. J. Lyon, professor, human resource management, $55,746; $6,302

J. T. Reynolds, dean, university services, $53,960; $6,177

R. Alford, associate professor, $51,870; $6,031

Source: "Pay and Benefits of Leaders at 479 Private Colleges and Universities: a Survey," *The Chronicle of Higher Education*, 47: A29-A48, (November 24, 2000).

★3590★
Top pay and benefits for the chief executive and top paid employees at University of Charleston

Ranking basis/background: Annual pay and benefits for the chief executives and top paid officers, as reported on Internal Revenue Service Form 990 by private colleges and universities in the U.S. for the 1998-99 academic year. **Number listed:** 6.

Edwin H. Welch, president, with $162,300 annual pay; $9,738 in benefits

Robert L. Frey, VP, academic life, $75,225; $4,513

Jayson Gee, head coach, men's basketball; associate athletics director, $73,348; $4,400

Fred D. Boothe, VP, advancement, $68,000; $4,080

Jerry Forster, VP, administration and finance, $66,000; $3,960

Sandra S. Bowles, dean, health sciences, $64,091; $3,845

Source: "Pay and Benefits of Leaders at 479 Private Colleges and Universities: a Survey," *The Chronicle of Higher Education*, 47: A29-A48, (November 24, 2000).

★3591★
Top pay and benefits for the chief executive and top paid employees at Ursinus College

Ranking basis/background: Annual pay and benefits for the chief executives and top paid officers, as reported on Internal Revenue Service Form 990 by private colleges and universities in the U.S. for the 1998-99 academic year. **Number listed:** 6.

John Strassburger, president, with $152,650 annual pay; $16,228 in benefits

Judith Levy, VP, academic affairs, professor, chemistry, $118,000; $13,603

John King, director, computing services, $97,000; $13,772

Hudson B. Scattergood, VP, college relations, $98,250; $12,100

Richard DiFeliciantonio, VP, enrollment, $96,000; $13,696

William E. Akin, director of athletics, $93,267; $11,777

Source: "Pay and Benefits of Leaders at 479 Private Colleges and Universities: a Survey," *The Chronicle of Higher Education*, 47: A29-A48, (November 24, 2000).

★3592★
Top pay and benefits for the chief executive and top paid employees at Valparaiso University

Ranking basis/background: Annual pay and benefits for the chief executives and top paid officers, as reported on Internal Revenue Service Form 990 by private colleges and universities in the U.S. for the 1998-99 academic year. **Number listed:** 6.

Alan F. Harre, president, with $150,000 annual pay; $16,048 in benefits

Homer W. Drew, men's basketball coach, $175,610; $19,375

Jay Conison, interim dean, law, $150,000; $11,250

Roy A. Austensen, provost, $130,000; $9,750

William M. Moore, dean, business administration, $108,804; $8,160

David E. Vandercoy, professor, law, $108,430; $8,132

Source: "Pay and Benefits of Leaders at 479 Private Colleges and Universities: a Survey," *The Chronicle of Higher Education*, 47: A29-A48, (November 24, 2000).

★3593★
Top pay and benefits for the chief executive and top paid employees at Vanderbilt University

Ranking basis/background: Annual pay and benefits for the chief executives and top paid officers, as reported on Internal Revenue Service Form 990 by private colleges and universities in the U.S. for the 1998-99 academic year. **Number listed:** 6.

Joe B. Wyatt, chancellor, with $462,000 annual pay; $70,461 in benefits

Davis Drinkwater Jr., professor and chair, cardiac and thoracic surgery, $1,148,550; $26,783

Harry R. Jacobson, vice chancellor, health affairs, $677,000; $27,917

Joseph A. Smith, professor and chair, urologic surgery, $658,951; $27,083

Bruce R. Shack, associate professor and chair, plastic surgery, $598,525; $27,083

Ming X. Wang, assistant professor, eye center, $591,125; $23,957

Source: "Pay and Benefits of Leaders at 479 Private Colleges and Universities: a Survey," *The Chronicle of Higher Education*, 47: A29-A48, (November 24, 2000).

★3594★
Top pay and benefits for the chief executive and top paid employees at Vassar College

Ranking basis/background: Annual pay and benefits for the chief executives and top paid officers, as reported on Internal Revenue Service Form 990 by private colleges and universities in the U.S. for the 1998-99 academic year. **Number listed:** 6.

Frances D. Fergusson, president, with $282,500 annual pay; $36,724 in benefits

Anthony C. Stellato, VP; treasurer; chief financial officer, $171,800; $34,602

Norman Fainstein, dean of the faculty, $135,050; $29,337

Colton Johnson, dean of the college, $119,025; $26,454

Robert Pounder, assistant to the president, $108,700; $24,275

Alexander Thompson, professor, economics, $106,509; $21,275

Source: "Pay and Benefits of Leaders at 479 Private Colleges and Universities: a Survey," *The Chronicle of Higher Education*, 47: A29-A48, (November 24, 2000).

★3595★
Top pay and benefits for the chief executive and top paid employees at Villanova University

Ranking basis/background: Annual pay and benefits for the chief executives and top paid officers, as reported on Internal Revenue Service Form 990 by private colleges and universities in the U.S. for the 1998-99 academic year. **Remarks:** Reverend Dobbin's compensation is paid to the Order of St. Augustine. **Number listed:** 6.

Rev. Edmund J. Dobbin, O.S.A., president, with $198,650 annual pay; $21,973 in benefits

Stephen Lappas, head coach, men's basketball, $463,347; $29,735

Mark Sargent, dean; professor, law, $200,000; $27,145

Steven P. Frankino, professor, law, $190,000; $28,238

John F. Murphy, professor, law, $182,785; $26,212

Arnold B. Cohen, professor, law, $178,645; $26,887

Source: "Pay and Benefits of Leaders at 479 Private Colleges and Universities: a Survey," *The Chronicle of Higher Education*, 47: A29-A48, (November 24, 2000).

★3596★
Top pay and benefits for the chief executive and top paid employees at Virginia Wesleyan College

Ranking basis/background: Annual pay and benefits for the chief executives and top paid officers, as reported on Internal Revenue Service Form 990 by private colleges and universities in the U.S. for the 1998-99 academic year. **Number listed:** 6.

William T. Greer Jr., president, with $136,000 annual pay; $19,051 in benefits

James R. Bergdoll, VP, college relations, $110,552; $10,447

Stephen S. Mansfield, VP, academic affairs, $98,018; $15,281

David E. Buckingham, VP, student affairs, $89,467; $14,545

William T. Joseph, VP, business affairs, $87,995; $13,425

Rene Perez-Lopez, VP, information systems, $77,635; $13,277

Source: "Pay and Benefits of Leaders at 479 Private Colleges and Universities: a Survey," *The Chronicle of Higher Education*, 47: A29-A48, (November 24, 2000).

★3597★
Top pay and benefits for the chief executive and top paid employees at Viterbo University

Ranking basis/background: Annual pay and benefits for the chief executives and top paid officers, as reported on Internal Revenue Service Form 990 by private colleges and universities in the U.S. for the 1998-99 academic year. **Number listed:** 6.

- William J. Medland, president, with $126,000 annual pay; $11,844 in benefits
- Christine Valenti, director, off-campus graduate programs, $81,887; $7,528
- Thomas Thibodeau, assistant professor, religious studies, $85,037; $2,077
- John Havertape, VP, academics, $75,664; $9,082
- Susan Batell, dean, education, $75,504; $7,908
- John Schroeder, director, graduate programs, $70,071; $2,619

Source: "Pay and Benefits of Leaders at 479 Private Colleges and Universities: a Survey," *The Chronicle of Higher Education*, 47: A29-A48, (November 24, 2000).

★3598★
Top pay and benefits for the chief executive and top paid employees at Wabash College

Ranking basis/background: Annual pay and benefits for the chief executives and top paid officers, as reported on Internal Revenue Service Form 990 by private colleges and universities in the U.S. for the 1998-99 academic year. **Number listed:** 6.

- Andrew T. Ford, president, with $175,000 annual pay; $21,898 in benefits
- Raymond B. Williams, professor, religion and philosophy, $120,486; $17,284
- Paul P. Pribbenow, dean, college advancement, $116,803; $16,946
- P. Donald Herring, dean of the college, $109,834; $16,320
- Deana S. McCormick, treasurer, $92,000; $14,475
- Paul McKinney, professor, chemistry, $87,400; $13,987

Source: "Pay and Benefits of Leaders at 479 Private Colleges and Universities: a Survey," *The Chronicle of Higher Education*, 47: A29-A48, (November 24, 2000).

★3599★
Top pay and benefits for the chief executive and top paid employees at Wagner College

Ranking basis/background: Annual pay and benefits for the chief executives and top paid officers, as reported on Internal Revenue Service Form 990 by private colleges and universities in the U.S. for the 1998-99 academic year. **Number listed:** 6.

- Norman R. Smith, president, with $181,000 annual pay; $24,739 in benefits
- Richard Guarasci, provost, $120,000; $10,800
- Frank Kamenar, VP, administration and finance, $115,000; $10,350
- Ivana Pelnar-Zaiko, VP, development, $107,000; $9,630
- Walter L. Hameline, director, athletics, $92,000; $9,200
- Geoffrey Coward, professor, education, $78,331; $6,400

Source: "Pay and Benefits of Leaders at 479 Private Colleges and Universities: a Survey," *The Chronicle of Higher Education*, 47: A29-A48, (November 24, 2000).

★3600★
Top pay and benefits for the chief executive and top paid employees at Wake Forest University

Ranking basis/background: Annual pay and benefits for the chief executives and top paid officers, as reported on Internal Revenue Service Form 990 by private colleges and universities in the U.S. for the 1998-99 academic year. **Number listed:** 6.

- Thomas K. Hearn Jr., president, with $207,000 annual pay; $244,102 in benefits
- John A. Wilson, assistant professor, neurosurgical science, $600,503; $33,769
- Charles L. Branch Jr., associate professor, surgical sciences, neurosurgery, $600,503; $33,745
- David L. Kelly Jr., professor, surgical sciences; department chair, neurosurgery, $600,503; $33,255
- Steven S. Glazier, assistant professor, neurosurgical science, $600,503; $32,988
- Berry Leshin, assistant professor, dermatological science, $557,392; $33,479

Source: "Pay and Benefits of Leaders at 479 Private Colleges and Universities: a Survey," *The Chronicle of Higher Education*, 47: A29-A48, (November 24, 2000).

★3601★
Top pay and benefits for the chief executive and top paid employees at Walla Walla College

Ranking basis/background: Annual pay and benefits for the chief executives and top paid officers, as reported on Internal Revenue Service Form 990 by private colleges and universities in the U.S. for the 1998-99 academic year. **Number listed:** 6.

- W. G. Nelson, president, with $39,074 annual pay; $15,630 in benefits
- John Brunt, VP, academic administration, $38,833; $15,533
- Manford Simcock, VP, financial administration, $38,833; $15,533
- Karen Johnson, VP, college advancement, $38,833; $15,533
- Nelson Thomas, VP, student administration, $38,833; $15,533
- Victor Brown, VP, admissions, $31,929; $12,772

Source: "Pay and Benefits of Leaders at 479 Private Colleges and Universities: a Survey," *The Chronicle of Higher Education*, 47: A29-A48, (November 24, 2000).

★3602★
Top pay and benefits for the chief executive and top paid employees at Walsh University

Ranking basis/background: Annual pay and benefits for the chief executives and top paid officers, as reported on Internal Revenue Service Form 990 by private colleges and universities in the U.S. for the 1998-99 academic year. **Number listed:** 6.

- Kenneth N. Hamilton Jr., president, with $104,544 annual pay; $8,046 in benefits
- David Dunham, VP, development, $79,363; $5,533
- John Wray, treasurer, $78,000; $5,460
- James Foster, secretary, $70,795; $4,950
- Brett Freshour, dean, enrollment, $70,250; $2,928
- Janis Daly, professor, physical therapy, $66,640; $4,665

Source: "Pay and Benefits of Leaders at 479 Private Colleges and Universities: a Survey," *The Chronicle of Higher Education*, 47: A29-A48, (November 24, 2000).

★3603★
Top pay and benefits for the chief executive and top paid employees at Wartburg College

Ranking basis/background: Annual pay and benefits for the chief executives and top paid officers, as reported on Internal Revenue Service Form 990 by private colleges and universities in the U.S. for the 1998-99 academic year. **Number listed:** 7.

- John R. Ohle, president, with $137,500 annual pay; $13,971 in benefits
- Robert L. Vogel, president, $45,597; $2,164
- Michael Book, VP, administration and finance, $87,832; $10,615
- Alexander F. Smith, VP, student life; dean of students, $82,796; $10,267
- Alvin B. Koeneman, VP, development, $73,980; $9,656
- Fredric A. Waldstein, professor, political science, $71,948; $9,471
- Donald Juhl, director, food service, $66,363; $9,153

Source: "Pay and Benefits of Leaders at 479 Private Colleges and Universities: a Survey," *The Chronicle of Higher Education*, 47: A29-A48, (November 24, 2000).

★3604★
Top pay and benefits for the chief executive and top paid employees at Washington and Jefferson College

Ranking basis/background: Annual pay and benefits for the chief executives and top paid officers, as reported on Internal Revenue Service Form 990 by private colleges and universities in the U.S. for the 1998-99 academic year. **Number listed:** 6.

- Brian Mitchell, president, with $160,000 annual pay; $21,661 in benefits
- John L. Luckhardt, chair, physical education and athletics; head football coach, $105,170; $36,198
- G. Andrew Rembert, VP, academic affairs; dean of the college, $120,000; $17,503
- Duane L. Lantz, VP, business and finance, $116,000; $16,134

Harold G. Moss, VP, development, $100,544; $12,122

Dennis G. Trelka, professor, biology, $83,950; $28,106

Source: "Pay and Benefits of Leaders at 479 Private Colleges and Universities: a Survey," *The Chronicle of Higher Education*, 47: A29-A48, (November 24, 2000).

★3605★
Top pay and benefits for the chief executive and top paid employees at Washington and Lee University

Ranking basis/background: Annual pay and benefits for the chief executives and top paid officers, as reported on Internal Revenue Service Form 990 by private colleges and universities in the U.S. for the 1998-99 academic year. **Number listed:** 6.

John Elrod, president, with $193,437 annual pay; $26,151 in benefits

Barry Sullivan, dean; professor, law, $199,981; $27,322

Doug Rendleman, professor, law, $165,000; $24,988

Frederic Kirgis, professor, law, $158,662; $23,777

Andrew McThenia, professor, law, $155,610; $24,767

Larry Peppers, professor and dean, Williams School of Economics, $152,416; $24,775

Source: "Pay and Benefits of Leaders at 479 Private Colleges and Universities: a Survey," *The Chronicle of Higher Education*, 47: A29-A48, (November 24, 2000).

★3606★
Top pay and benefits for the chief executive and top paid employees at Washington College

Ranking basis/background: Annual pay and benefits for the chief executives and top paid officers, as reported on Internal Revenue Service Form 990 by private colleges and universities in the U.S. for the 1998-99 academic year. **Number listed:** 6.

John S. Toll, president, with $150,728 annual pay; $18,428 in benefits

H. Louis Stettler III, senior VP, finance and management, $114,100; $15,714

Robert Smith, VP, development, $94,550; $15,290

Joachim Scholz, dean; provost, $92,600; $15,613

Kevin Coveney, VP, admissions, $74,800; $13,878

Frank Creegan, professor, chemistry, $68,196; $12,939

Source: "Pay and Benefits of Leaders at 479 Private Colleges and Universities: a Survey," *The Chronicle of Higher Education*, 47: A29-A48, (November 24, 2000).

★3607★
Top pay and benefits for the chief executive and top paid employees at Washington University in Missouri

Ranking basis/background: Annual pay and benefits for the chief executives and top paid officers, as reported on Internal Revenue Service Form 990 by private colleges and universities in the U.S. for the 1998-99 academic year. **Number listed:** 6.

Mark S. Wrighton, chancellor, with $398,700 annual pay; $13,600 in benefits

Joel D. Cooper, professor, cardiac surgery, $767,100; $18,400

Timothy J. Eberlein, professor, surgery and pathology, $751,000; $0

Robert L. Tychsen, professor, ophthalmology and visual sciences in pediatrics, $702,484; $13,600

Jay S. Pepose, professor, ophthalmology and visual sciences, $700,350

Ralph G. Dacey Jr., professor and chair, neurological surgery, $678,468; $13,600

Source: "Pay and Benefits of Leaders at 479 Private Colleges and Universities: a Survey," *The Chronicle of Higher Education*, 47: A29-A48, (November 24, 2000).

★3608★
Top pay and benefits for the chief executive and top paid employees at Webster University

Ranking basis/background: Annual pay and benefits for the chief executives and top paid officers, as reported on Internal Revenue Service Form 990 by private colleges and universities in the U.S. for the 1998-99 academic year. **Number listed:** 7.

Richard S. Meyers, president, with $280,000 annual pay; $15,596 in benefits

Neil J. George, executive VP; VP, academic affairs, $135,000; $11,875

David Garafola, VP, finance and administration, $124,000; $10,450

Fred H. Stopsky, professor, multidisciplinary studies, $119,599; $10,206

William S. Huddleston Berry, chair; professor, behavioral and social sciences, college of arts and sciences, $118,971; $8,699

Russ Viehmann, VP, development, $110,000; $9,500

Karen Luebbert, VP; executive assistant to the president, $110,000; $9,500

Source: "Pay and Benefits of Leaders at 479 Private Colleges and Universities: a Survey," *The Chronicle of Higher Education*, 47: A29-A48, (November 24, 2000).

★3609★
Top pay and benefits for the chief executive and top paid employees at Wellesley College

Ranking basis/background: Annual pay and benefits for the chief executives and top paid officers, as reported on Internal Revenue Service Form 990 by private colleges and universities in the U.S. for the 1998-99 academic year. **Number listed:** 6.

Diana Chapman Walsh, president, with $224,059 annual pay; $18,371 in benefits

William S. Reed, VP, finance and administration, $187,739; $18,371

David Blinder, VP, resources and public affairs, $187,601; $18,371

Nancy H. Kolodny, dean of the college, $182,423; $16,506

James O'Gorman, professor, art history, $146,383; $15,637

Mary Lefkowitz, professor, classical studies, $143,799; $15,323

Source: "Pay and Benefits of Leaders at 479 Private Colleges and Universities: a Survey," *The Chronicle of Higher Education*, 47: A29-A48, (November 24, 2000).

★3610★
Top pay and benefits for the chief executive and top paid employees at Wells College

Ranking basis/background: Annual pay and benefits for the chief executives and top paid officers, as reported on Internal Revenue Service Form 990 by private colleges and universities in the U.S. for the 1998-99 academic year. **Number listed:** 6.

Lisa Marsh Ryerson, president, with $115,000 annual pay; $19,349 in benefits

Ellen Hall, dean of the college, $80,213; $15,374

Arthur Bellinzoni, professor, religion; director, planned and leadership giving, $71,532; $12,763

Diane L. Hutchinson, VP; treasurer, $69,630; $12,475

Aurelio Torres, professor, psychology, $61,246; $12,500

Crawford Thoburn, professor, music, $59,707; $12,267

Source: "Pay and Benefits of Leaders at 479 Private Colleges and Universities: a Survey," *The Chronicle of Higher Education*, 47: A29-A48, (November 24, 2000).

★3611★
Top pay and benefits for the chief executive and top paid employees at Wesleyan College in Georgia

Ranking basis/background: Annual pay and benefits for the chief executives and top paid officers, as reported on Internal Revenue Service Form 990 by private colleges and universities in the U.S. for the 1998-99 academic year. **Number listed:** 6.

Nora K. Bell, president, with $140,000 annual pay; $14,000 in benefits

Jonathan Stroud, dean, admissions, $96,000; $0

B. David Rowe, VP, institutional advancement, $85,000; $8,500

Delmas Crisp, professor, English, $75,500; $7,550

Priscilla Danheiser, dean, academics, $75,000; $7,500

Jeanette Shackelford, chair, music department, $70,579; $7,057

Source: "Pay and Benefits of Leaders at 479 Private Colleges and Universities: a Survey," *The Chronicle of Higher Education*, 47: A29-A48, (November 24, 2000).

★3612★
Top pay and benefits for the chief executive and top paid employees at Wesleyan University in Connecticut

Ranking basis/background: Annual pay and benefits for the chief executives and top paid officers, as reported on Internal Revenue Service Form 990 by private colleges and universities in the U.S. for the 1998-99 academic year. **Number listed:** 6.

Douglas J. Bennet, president, with $220,000 annual pay; $42,661 in benefits

Robert B. Taylor, VP, treasurer, $183,700; $41,563

David Beveridge, dean, natural sciences, mathematics, and academic affairs; professor, chemistry, $190,898; $33,855

Jeanine D. Basinger, professor, film studies, $143,746; $30,334

Richard W. Boyd, VP, academic affairs; provost, $140,300; $29,752

Michael Lovell, professor, economics, $135,640; $28,133

Source: "Pay and Benefits of Leaders at 479 Private Colleges and Universities: a Survey," *The Chronicle of Higher Education*, 47: A29-A48, (November 24, 2000).

★3613★
Top pay and benefits for the chief executive and top paid employees at West Virginia Wesleyan College

Ranking basis/background: Annual pay and benefits for the chief executives and top paid officers, as reported on Internal Revenue Service Form 990 by private colleges and universities in the U.S. for the 1998-99 academic year. **Number listed:** 6.

William R. Haden, president, with $147,472 annual pay; $26,831 in benefits

G. Michael Goins, VP, finance, $96,425; $19,844

Richard G. Weeks Jr., VP, academic affairs, $91,667; $20,339

Joanne C. Soliday, VP, external relations, $91,350; $17,957

J. Brooks Jones, director, gift planning, $75,000; $16,746

Joseph E. Wiest, professor, physics and engineering, $74,631; $15,070

Source: "Pay and Benefits of Leaders at 479 Private Colleges and Universities: a Survey," *The Chronicle of Higher Education*, 47: A29-A48, (November 24, 2000).

★3614★
Top pay and benefits for the chief executive and top paid employees at Western Maryland College

Ranking basis/background: Annual pay and benefits for the chief executives and top paid officers, as reported on Internal Revenue Service Form 990 by private colleges and universities in the U.S. for the 1998-99 academic year. **Number listed:** 6.

Robert H. Chambers, president, with $216,000 annual pay; $57,243 in benefits

Joan Develin Coley, provost; dean of academic affairs, $119,000; $35,714

Richard Kief, VP, institutional advancement, $119,421; $21,637

Ethan Seidel, VP, administration and finance, $117,000; $18,268

Philip R. Sayre, dean, student affairs, $92,000; $15,733

Francis Fennell, professor, education, $87,868; $18,151

Source: "Pay and Benefits of Leaders at 479 Private Colleges and Universities: a Survey," *The Chronicle of Higher Education*, 47: A29-A48, (November 24, 2000).

★3615★
Top pay and benefits for the chief executive and top paid employees at Western New England College

Ranking basis/background: Annual pay and benefits for the chief executives and top paid officers, as reported on Internal Revenue Service Form 990 by private colleges and universities in the U.S. for the 1998-99 academic year. **Number listed:** 6.

Anthony S. Caprio, president, with $190,000 annual pay; $26,020 in benefits

Donald Dunn, dean, law, $152,000; $22,315

Robert Lusardi, associate dean; professor, law, $124,454; $19,668

Jerry A. Hirsch, VP, academic affairs, $125,000; $18,258

Howard Kalodner, professor, law, $121,803; $19,188

Judith Brissette, VP, administration and planning, $116,905; $15,030

Source: "Pay and Benefits of Leaders at 479 Private Colleges and Universities: a Survey," *The Chronicle of Higher Education*, 47: A29-A48, (November 24, 2000).

★3616★
Top pay and benefits for the chief executive and top paid employees at Westminster College in Missouri

Ranking basis/background: Annual pay and benefits for the chief executives and top paid officers, as reported on Internal Revenue Service Form 990 by private colleges and universities in the U.S. for the 1998-99 academic year. **Number listed:** 7.

James F. Traer, president, with $122,000 annual pay; $9,455 in benefits

Ken Rueter, VP, business and finance, $68,000; $5,270

John Schultz, professor, chemistry, $56,635; $4,389

Douglas Fickess, professor, biology, $56,575; $4,385

Dan Diedriech, assistant VP, college relations, $56,230; $4,358

David Humphrey, dean, student life, $56,230; $4,358

Warrington Williams, professor, biology, $55,560; $4,306

Source: "Pay and Benefits of Leaders at 479 Private Colleges and Universities: a Survey," *The Chronicle of Higher Education*, 47: A29-A48, (November 24, 2000).

★3617★
Top pay and benefits for the chief executive and top paid employees at Westminster College in Pennsylvania

Ranking basis/background: Annual pay and benefits for the chief executives and top paid officers, as reported on Internal Revenue Service Form 990 by private colleges and universities in the U.S. for the 1998-99 academic year. **Number listed:** 7.

R. Thomas Williamson Jr., president, with $186,000 annual pay; $11,478 in benefits

Oscar E. Remick, president emeritus, $739,190; $4,686

William J. Birkhead, VP, finance and management services, $98,428; $7,242

John Deegan Jr., VP, academic affairs; dean of the college; professor, political science, $92,033; $6,768

Gail L. Miller, chair, economics and business administration; professor, business, $78,091; $4,896

Clarence Harms, professor, biology, $77,052; $4,800

Neal A. Edman, dean, student affairs, $69,980; $5,148

Source: "Pay and Benefits of Leaders at 479 Private Colleges and Universities: a Survey," *The Chronicle of Higher Education*, 47: A29-A48, (November 24, 2000).

★3618★
Top pay and benefits for the chief executive and top paid employees at Westminster College in Utah

Ranking basis/background: Annual pay and benefits for the chief executives and top paid officers, as reported on Internal Revenue Service Form 990 by private colleges and universities in the U.S. for the 1998-99 academic year. **Number listed:** 6.

Peggy A. Stock, president, with $196,069 annual pay; $123,257 in benefits

Stephen R. Morgan, executive VP; treasurer, $108,080; $15,317

Janet A. Glaeser, VP, institutional advancement, $100,000; $14,592

Stephen R. Baar, dean of the faculty; VP, academic affairs, $93,600; $13,125

Philip J. Alletto, VP, student development and enrollment management, $87,696; $12,662

James E. Seidelman, dean, school of business, $83,340; $11,151

Source: "Pay and Benefits of Leaders at 479 Private Colleges and Universities: a Survey," *The Chronicle of Higher Education*, 47: A29-A48, (November 24, 2000).

★3619★
Top pay and benefits for the chief executive and top paid employees at Westmont College

Ranking basis/background: Annual pay and benefits for the chief executives and top paid officers, as reported on Internal Revenue Service Form 990 by private colleges and universities in the U.S. for the 1998-99 academic year. **Number listed:** 6.

David K. Winter, president, with $149,176 annual pay; $10,442 in benefits

Edward Birch, executive VP, $111,345; $7,794

Stan Gaede, provost, $110,535; $7,737

Ronald Cronk, VP, finance and administration, $93,938; $6,576

Steve Baker, VP, development, $90,419; $6,329

David Morley, director, admissions, $85,678; $5,997

Source: "Pay and Benefits of Leaders at 479 Private Colleges and Universities: a Survey," *The Chronicle of Higher Education*, 47: A29-A48, (November 24, 2000).

SALARIES—COLLEGES & UNIVERSITIES

★3620★
Top pay and benefits for the chief executive and top paid employees at Wheaton College in Illinois

Ranking basis/background: Annual pay and benefits for the chief executives and top paid officers, as reported on Internal Revenue Service Form 990 by private colleges and universities in the U.S. for the 1998-99 academic year. **Number listed:** 6.

- A. Duane Litfin, president, with $152,565 annual pay; $14,790 in benefits
- David E. Johnston, senior VP; treasurer, $128,665; $12,354
- Stanton L. Jones, provost; dean, graduate school, $118,052; $12,966
- R. Mark Dillon, VP, advancement, $105,875; $12,200
- Ward A. Kriegbaum, interim dean, natural and social sciences, $89,781; $11,187
- Samuel A. Shellhamer, VP, student development, $89,169; $7,509

Source: "Pay and Benefits of Leaders at 479 Private Colleges and Universities: a Survey," *The Chronicle of Higher Education*, 47: A29-A48, (November 24, 2000).

★3621★
Top pay and benefits for the chief executive and top paid employees at Wheaton College in Massachusetts

Ranking basis/background: Annual pay and benefits for the chief executives and top paid officers, as reported on Internal Revenue Service Form 990 by private colleges and universities in the U.S. for the 1998-99 academic year. **Number listed:** 6.

- Dale Rogers Marshall, president, with $175,000 annual pay; $17,131 in benefits
- Edwin J. Merck, VP, finance and operations, $140,233; $19,892
- Catherine Conover, VP, college advancement, $125,000; $16,430
- Gail Berson, dean, admissions, $120,000; $17,557
- Sue Alexander, dean of students, $110,000; $14,699
- Gordon Weil, professor, economics, $105,000; $9,498

Source: "Pay and Benefits of Leaders at 479 Private Colleges and Universities: a Survey," *The Chronicle of Higher Education*, 47: A29-A48, (November 24, 2000).

★3622★
Top pay and benefits for the chief executive and top paid employees at Wheeling Jesuit University

Ranking basis/background: Annual pay and benefits for the chief executives and top paid officers, as reported on Internal Revenue Service Form 990 by private colleges and universities in the U.S. for the 1998-99 academic year. **Remarks:** Reverend Acker's compensation is donated to the Society of Jesus. **Number listed:** 8.

- Rev. Thomas S. Acker, S.J., president, with $0 annual pay; $0 in benefits
- Joseph Allen, president, National Technology Transfer Center, $123,600; $7,416
- Carole T. Coleman, executive VP; chief financial officer, $120,000; $7,200
- Sylvester Scott, VP, market and technology assessment, $120,000; $7,200
- Terry Bradford, VP, commercialization, $102,308; $6,138
- Arsev Eraslan, chief scientist, National Technology Transfer Center, $100,373; $6,022
- A. Ozer Arnas, visiting professor, $95,000; $5,700
- Nitin Naik, president, Center for Educational Technologies, $95,000; $5,700

Source: "Pay and Benefits of Leaders at 479 Private Colleges and Universities: a Survey," *The Chronicle of Higher Education*, 47: A29-A48, (November 24, 2000).

★3623★
Top pay and benefits for the chief executive and top paid employees at Whitman College

Ranking basis/background: Annual pay and benefits for the chief executives and top paid officers, as reported on Internal Revenue Service Form 990 by private colleges and universities in the U.S. for the 1998-99 academic year. **Number listed:** 7.

- Thomas E. Cronin, president, with $180,000 annual pay; $48,000 in benefits
- Stephen Becker, VP, development, $103,726; $10,373
- Patrick Keef, dean of the faculty, $98,000; $9,800
- Charles E. Cleveland, dean of students, $90,000; $9,000
- Peter Harvey, treasurer; CEO, $90,000; $9,000
- Keiko Pitter, chief technology officer, $87,000; $8,700
- John Desmond, professor, English, $86,000; $8,600

Source: "Pay and Benefits of Leaders at 479 Private Colleges and Universities: a Survey," *The Chronicle of Higher Education*, 47: A29-A48, (November 24, 2000).

★3624★
Top pay and benefits for the chief executive and top paid employees at Whittier College

Ranking basis/background: Annual pay and benefits for the chief executives and top paid officers, as reported on Internal Revenue Service Form 990 by private colleges and universities in the U.S. for the 1998-99 academic year. **Number listed:** 6.

- James L. Ash, president, with $188,700 annual pay; $19,386 in benefits
- John Fitzrandolph, dean, law; VP, legal education, $200,479; $17,780
- Jo Ann Hankin, VP, finance, $153,000; $14,077
- William Patton, professor, law, $152,654; $10,911
- Howard Foss, professor, law, $143,808; $11,261
- Warren Cohen, professor, law, $137,247; $14,544

Source: "Pay and Benefits of Leaders at 479 Private Colleges and Universities: a Survey," *The Chronicle of Higher Education*, 47: A29-A48, (November 24, 2000).

★3625★
Top pay and benefits for the chief executive and top paid employees at Whitworth College

Ranking basis/background: Annual pay and benefits for the chief executives and top paid officers, as reported on Internal Revenue Service Form 990 by private colleges and universities in the U.S. for the 1998-99 academic year. **Number listed:** 6.

- William P. Robinson, president, with $128,294 annual pay; $41,412 in benefits
- Tammy A. Reid, VP, academic affairs, dean of the faculty, $92,970; $9,536
- Thomas A. Johnson, VP, business affairs, $92,970; $9,362
- Kristine A. Burns, VP, institutional advancement, $82,633; $8,750
- Kathy H. Storm, VP, student life, $75,030; $8,108
- Gordon Jackson, associate dean, academic affairs, $71,481; $7,788

Source: "Pay and Benefits of Leaders at 479 Private Colleges and Universities: a Survey," *The Chronicle of Higher Education*, 47: A29-A48, (November 24, 2000).

★3626★
Top pay and benefits for the chief executive and top paid employees at Widener University

Ranking basis/background: Annual pay and benefits for the chief executives and top paid officers, as reported on Internal Revenue Service Form 990 by private colleges and universities in the U.S. for the 1998-99 academic year. **Number listed:** 6.

- Robert J. Bruce, president, with $252,500 annual pay; $30,300 in benefits
- Barry R. Furrow, dean of the faculty, school of law, $151,554; $15,155
- W. David Eckard III, VP, administration and finance, $143,000; $14,300
- Lawrence P. Buck, VP, academics; provost, $130,000; $13,000
- Peter Caputo, VP, development, $125,000; $12,500
- Loren Prescott, dean of the faculty and administration, law school's Harrisburg campus, $122,325; $12,233

Source: "Pay and Benefits of Leaders at 479 Private Colleges and Universities: a Survey," *The Chronicle of Higher Education*, 47: A29-A48, (November 24, 2000).

★3627★
Top pay and benefits for the chief executive and top paid employees at Wilkes University

Ranking basis/background: Annual pay and benefits for the chief executives and top paid officers, as reported on Internal Revenue Service Form 990 by private colleges and universities in the U.S. for the 1998-99 academic year. **Number listed:** 6.

- Christopher N. Breiseth, president, with $117,906 annual pay; $10,953 in benefits
- Bernard W. Graham, dean, Nesbitt School of Pharmacy, $97,602; $9,532
- Paul A. O'Hop, VP, business affairs and auxiliary enterprises, $96,357; $8,920

Joseph T. Bellucci, director, regional computer resource center; director, graduate teacher education, $92,984; $8,859

Umid Nejib, professor, electrical and computer engineering, $91,918; $8,719

J. Michael Lennon, VP, academic affairs, $90,998; $9,070

Source: "Pay and Benefits of Leaders at 479 Private Colleges and Universities: a Survey," *The Chronicle of Higher Education*, 47: A29-A48, (November 24, 2000).

★3628★
Top pay and benefits for the chief executive and top paid employees at Willamette University

Ranking basis/background: Annual pay and benefits for the chief executives and top paid officers, as reported on Internal Revenue Service Form 990 by private colleges and universities in the U.S. for the 1998-99 academic year. **Number listed:** 6.

M. Lee Pelton, president, with $180,000 annual pay; $37,495 in benefits

Robert Ackerman, dean, law, $152,400; $26,235

Bryan Johnston, dean, Atkinson Graduate School of Management, $120,000; $24,395

Larry Cress, dean, college of liberal arts, $115,300; $22,913

Brian Hardin, treasurer, $113,000; $22,559

Robert Misner, professor, law, $102,025; $21,271

Source: "Pay and Benefits of Leaders at 479 Private Colleges and Universities: a Survey," *The Chronicle of Higher Education*, 47: A29-A48, (November 24, 2000).

★3629★
Top pay and benefits for the chief executive and top paid employees at William Carey College

Ranking basis/background: Annual pay and benefits for the chief executives and top paid officers, as reported on Internal Revenue Service Form 990 by private colleges and universities in the U.S. for the 1998-99 academic year. **Number listed:** 6.

Larry W. Kennedy, president, with $116,793 annual pay; $9,304 in benefits

William M. Hetrick, dean, education, $83,500; $4,812

Van Oliphant, executive VP; provost, $67,415; $4,699

Mary Ware, dean, nursing, $67,586; $4,469

Bennie Crockett Jr., VP, institutional effectiveness and planning, $64,020; $7,822

B. J. Martin, dean, arts, humanities, and sciences; chair and professor, biology, $66,451; $4,953

Source: "Pay and Benefits of Leaders at 479 Private Colleges and Universities: a Survey," *The Chronicle of Higher Education*, 47: A29-A48, (November 24, 2000).

★3630★
Top pay and benefits for the chief executive and top paid employees at William Jewell College

Ranking basis/background: Annual pay and benefits for the chief executives and top paid officers, as reported on Internal Revenue Service Form 990 by private colleges and universities in the U.S. for the 1998-99 academic year. **Number listed:** 6.

W. Christian Sizemore, president, with $145,590 annual pay; $49,748 in benefits

Thad A. Henry, VP, advancement, $93,000; $17,794

Nina Pollard, provost; VP, academic affairs, $89,000; $15,323

Sandra M. Hader, VP, administrative services, $87,000; $15,510

Gerald B. Williams, professor and chair, business administration and economics, $81,410; $15,454

Ray Jones, executive director, college relations, $78,000; $9,949

Source: "Pay and Benefits of Leaders at 479 Private Colleges and Universities: a Survey," *The Chronicle of Higher Education*, 47: A29-A48, (November 24, 2000).

★3631★
Top pay and benefits for the chief executive and top paid employees at Williams College

Ranking basis/background: Annual pay and benefits for the chief executives and top paid officers, as reported on Internal Revenue Service Form 990 by private colleges and universities in the U.S. for the 1998-99 academic year. **Number listed:** 6.

Harry C. Payne, president, with $232,550 annual pay; $645,672 in benefits

Stuart Crampton, provost, $154,108; $29,586

George R. Goethals II, professor, psychology, $151,939; $25,342

Stephen R. Birrell, VP, alumni relations and development, $142,000; $29,590

Gordon C. Winston, professor, political economy, $142,889; $21,881

Jean-Bernard Bucky, professor, theater, $123,900; $25,474

Source: "Pay and Benefits of Leaders at 479 Private Colleges and Universities: a Survey," *The Chronicle of Higher Education*, 47: A29-A48, (November 24, 2000).

★3632★
Top pay and benefits for the chief executive and top paid employees at Wilmington College in Delaware

Ranking basis/background: Annual pay and benefits for the chief executives and top paid officers, as reported on Internal Revenue Service Form 990 by private colleges and universities in the U.S. for the 1998-99 academic year. **Number listed:** 5.

Audrey K. Doberstein, president, with $360,000 annual pay; $13,022 in benefits

Jack P. Varsalona, executive VP: provost, $257,500; $14,912

Heather A. O'Connell, VP, enrollment management, $104,470; $19,846

James L. Spartz, VP and dean, academic affairs, $115,228; $5,075

Michael E. Lee, director, admissions and financial aid, $107,470; $4,926

Source: "Pay and Benefits of Leaders at 479 Private Colleges and Universities: a Survey," *The Chronicle of Higher Education*, 47: A29-A48, (November 24, 2000).

★3633★
Top pay and benefits for the chief executive and top paid employees at Wittenberg University

Ranking basis/background: Annual pay and benefits for the chief executives and top paid officers, as reported on Internal Revenue Service Form 990 by private colleges and universities in the U.S. for the 1998-99 academic year. **Number listed:** 6.

Baird Tipson, president, with $145,916 annual pay; $23,193 in benefits

Sammye Greer, provost, $117,447; $14,474

Peter Gus Geil, VP, business and finance, $115,701; $12,425

Charles A. Dominick, VP, institutional relations and advancement, $109,421; $16,276

Richard Veler, general secretary, $105,122; $15,812

Kenneth G. Benne, dean, admissions, $83,229; $15,910

Source: "Pay and Benefits of Leaders at 479 Private Colleges and Universities: a Survey," *The Chronicle of Higher Education*, 47: A29-A48, (November 24, 2000).

★3634★
Top pay and benefits for the chief executive and top paid employees at Wofford College

Ranking basis/background: Annual pay and benefits for the chief executives and top paid officers, as reported on Internal Revenue Service Form 990 by private colleges and universities in the U.S. for the 1998-99 academic year. **Number listed:** 6.

Joab M. Lesesne Jr., president, with $150,000 annual pay; $65,363 in benefits

Dan Maultsby, senior VP and dean, academics, $127,000; $26,255

Daniel B. Morrison, senior VP, campus support programs, $110,500; $23,189

Larry T. McGehee, VP, enrollment planning, marketing, and institutional-research evaluating, $105,500; $22,260

Benjamin Dunlap, professor, humanities, $92,500; $19,844

Charlotte P. Tinsley, treasurer; chief financial officer, $90,600; $19,492

Source: "Pay and Benefits of Leaders at 479 Private Colleges and Universities: a Survey," *The Chronicle of Higher Education*, 47: A29-A48, (November 24, 2000).

★3635★
Top pay and benefits for the chief executive and top paid employees at Woodbury University

Ranking basis/background: Annual pay and benefits for the chief executives and top paid officers, as reported on Internal Revenue Service Form 990 by private colleges and universities in the U.S. for the 1998-99 academic year. **Number listed:** 6.

Kenneth R. Nielsen, president, with $171,600 annual pay; $32,421 in benefits

Louis Naidorf, dean, school of architecture and design, $95,191; $6,350

Geraldine Forbes, assistant dean, architecture, San Diego campus, $85,149; $7,866

Richard King, dean, business and management, $85,023; $7,858

Zelda Gilbert, VP, academic affairs, $82,483; $9,468

Leo O'Hara, dean, evening and weekend college, $79,500; $9,275

Source: "Pay and Benefits of Leaders at 479 Private Colleges and Universities: a Survey," *The Chronicle of Higher Education*, 47: A29-A48, (November 24, 2000).

★3636★
Top pay and benefits for the chief executive and top paid employees at Worcester Polytechnic Institute

Ranking basis/background: Annual pay and benefits for the chief executives and top paid officers, as reported on Internal Revenue Service Form 990 by private colleges and universities in the U.S. for the 1998-99 academic year. **Number listed:** 6.

Edward A. Parrish, president, with $223,000 annual pay; $21,395 in benefits

John F. Carney III, provost, $165,500; $21,395

Diran Apelian, professor, mechanical engineering; director, metal institute, $164,975; $18,369

Stephen J. Hebert, VP, administration, $138,000; $18,970

John L. Hely, VP, university relations, $126,900; $17,754

Homer Walker, department head and professor, mathematical science, $126,894; $17,754

Source: "Pay and Benefits of Leaders at 479 Private Colleges and Universities: a Survey," *The Chronicle of Higher Education*, 47: A29-A48, (November 24, 2000).

★3637★
Top pay and benefits for the chief executive and top paid employees at Xavier University in Ohio

Ranking basis/background: Annual pay and benefits for the chief executives and top paid officers, as reported on Internal Revenue Service Form 990 by private colleges and universities in the U.S. for the 1998-99 academic year. **Remarks:** Reverend Hoff's compensation is paid directly to the Jesuit order. **Number listed:** 6.

Rev. James E. Hoff, S.J., president, with $187,000 annual pay; $30,121 in benefits

J. Richard Hirte, VP, financial administration, $158,000; $28,429

George E. Prosser, head coach, men's basketball, $147,500; $26,439

James E. Bundschuh, VP, academic affairs, $140,000; $23,889

John F. Kucia, VP, administration, $123,000; $24,255

Phillip D. Jones, executive director, the Cintas Center, $121,000; $22,323

Source: "Pay and Benefits of Leaders at 479 Private Colleges and Universities: a Survey," *The Chronicle of Higher Education*, 47: A29-A48, (November 24, 2000).

★3638★
Top pay and benefits for the chief executive and top paid employees at Xavier University of Louisiana

Ranking basis/background: Annual pay and benefits for the chief executives and top paid officers, as reported on Internal Revenue Service Form 990 by private colleges and universities in the U.S. for the 1998-99 academic year. **Number listed:** 6.

Norman C. Francis, president, with $145,000 annual pay; $10,873 in benefits

Marcellus Grace, dean; professor, college of pharmacy, $117,023; $8,131

Deidre D. Labat, VP, academic affairs, $105,000; $7,642

Vimal Kishore, chair, basic pharmaceutical sciences, $103,647; $7,599

George Baker, director, engineering program, $98,455; $7,019

Robert L. Thomas, associate dean, pharmacy, $94,250; $6,980

Source: "Pay and Benefits of Leaders at 479 Private Colleges and Universities: a Survey," *The Chronicle of Higher Education*, 47: A29-A48, (November 24, 2000).

★3639★
Top pay and benefits for the chief executive and top paid employees at Yale University

Ranking basis/background: Annual pay and benefits for the chief executives and top paid officers, as reported on Internal Revenue Service Form 990 by private colleges and universities in the U.S. for the 1998-99 academic year. **Number listed:** 6.

Richard C. Levin, president, with $391,250 annual pay; $134,437 in benefits

David F. Swensen, chief investment officer, $688,974; $23,292

John A. Elefteriades, clinical professor and section chief, cardiothoracic surgery, $656,647; $26,202

Gary S. Kopf, clinical professor, cardiothoracic surgery, $620,363; $23,219

Michael W. Cleman, clinical professor, internal medicine and cardiology, $500,834; $24,369

Henry S. Cabin, clinical professor, internal medicine and cardiology, $491,750; $23,083

Source: "Pay and Benefits of Leaders at 479 Private Colleges and Universities: a Survey," *The Chronicle of Higher Education*, 47: A29-A48, (November 24, 2000).

★3640★
Top pay and benefits for the chief executive and top paid employees at Yeshiva University

Ranking basis/background: Annual pay and benefits for the chief executives and top paid officers, as reported on Internal Revenue Service Form 990 by private colleges and universities in the U.S. for the 1998-99 academic year. **Number listed:** 6.

Norman Lamm, president, with $225,500 annual pay; $8,531 in benefits

Irwin R. Merkatz, professor and chair, obstetrics and gynecology and women's health, $391,131; $10,000

James Scheuer, professor and chair, medicine, $386,003; $10,000

I. David Goldman, professor, medicine and molecular pharmacology, $347,256; $10,000

Michael B. Prystowsky, professor and chair, pathology, $336,450; $10,000

Dominick Purpura, dean, school of medicine, $325,000; $10,000

Source: "Pay and Benefits of Leaders at 479 Private Colleges and Universities: a Survey," *The Chronicle of Higher Education*, 47: A29-A48, (November 24, 2000).

★3641★
Top pay and benefits for the chief executive and top paid employees Saint Francis College in Pennsylvania

Ranking basis/background: Annual pay and benefits for the chief executives and top paid officers, as reported on Internal Revenue Service Form 990 by private colleges and universities in the U.S. for the 1998-99 academic year. **Number listed:** 6.

Rev. Christian Oravec, T.O.R., president, with $130,291 annual pay; $11,656 in benefits

Albert Simon, chair, physician-assistant department, $94,288; $9,204

Randy Frye, chair, business, $94,094; $9,194

Kathleen Owens, VP, academic affairs, $91,899; $9,012

William Duryea, director, master-of-medical-science program, $84,103; $8,405

Raymond Ponchione, director, development, $82,907; $8,337

Source: "Pay and Benefits of Leaders at 479 Private Colleges and Universities: a Survey," *The Chronicle of Higher Education*, 47: A29-A48, (November 24, 2000).

Related Information

★3642★
"Pay and Benefits of Leaders at 479 Private Colleges and Universities: a Survey," *The Chronicle of Higher Education*, 47: A29-A48, (November 24, 2000).

Remarks: Provides pay and benefits for presidents and executives at 479 private colleges and universities for the 1997-98 and 1998-99 fiscal years. Information was compiled from the Internal Revenue Service Form 990, filed annually by each institution.

SALARIES–COLLEGES & UNIVERSITIES, FACULTY

★3643★
Average compensation for assistant professors at institutions in the East North Central states, 2000-01

Ranking basis/background: Compensation is total annual salary plus major fringe benefits, based on the responses of 1,433 institutions providing data to the annual salary survey of the American Association of University Professors. **Remarks:** The East North Central region includes Illinois, Indiana, Michigan, Ohio and Wisconsin. **Number listed:** 4.

- Doctoral institutions, with an average annual salary of $65,400
- Comprehensive institutions, $56,797
- Baccalaureate institutions, $51,527
- Two-year institutions, $50,529

Source: "Uncertain Times: The Annual Report on the Economic Status of the Profession," *Academe*, 87: 25-98, (March/April 2001).

★3644★
Average compensation for assistant professors at institutions in the East South Central states, 2000-01

Ranking basis/background: Compensation is total annual salary plus major fringe benefits, based on the responses of 1,433 institutions providing data to the annual salary survey of the American Association of University Professors. **Remarks:** The East South Central region includes Alabama, Kentucky, Mississippi and Tennessee. **Number listed:** 4.

- Doctoral institutions, with an average annual salary of $58,590
- Comprehensive institutions, $52,942
- Baccalaureate institutions, $46,983
- Two-year institutions, $43,805

Source: "Uncertain Times: The Annual Report on the Economic Status of the Profession," *Academe*, 87: 25-98, (March/April 2001).

★3645★
Average compensation for assistant professors at institutions in the Middle Atlantic states, 2000-01

Ranking basis/background: Compensation is total annual salary plus major fringe benefits, based on the responses of 1,433 institutions providing data to the annual salary survey of the American Association of University Professors. **Remarks:** The Middle Atlantic region includes New Jersey, New York and Pennsylvania. **Number listed:** 4.

- Doctoral institutions, with an average annual salary of $72,448
- Comprehensive institutions, $61,045
- Baccalaureate institutions, $56,048
- Two-year institutions, $57,957

Source: "Uncertain Times: The Annual Report on the Economic Status of the Profession," *Academe*, 87: 25-98, (March/April 2001).

★3646★
Average compensation for assistant professors at institutions in the Mountain states, 2000-01

Ranking basis/background: Compensation is total annual salary plus major fringe benefits, based on the responses of 1,433 institutions providing data to the annual salary survey of the American Association of University Professors. **Remarks:** The Mountain region includes Arizona, Colorado, Idaho, Montana, Nevada, New Mexico, Utah and Wyoming. **Number listed:** 4.

- Doctoral institutions, with an average annual salary of $59,702
- Comprehensive institutions, $56,898
- Baccalaureate institutions, $47,536
- Two-year institutions, $47,272

Source: "Uncertain Times: The Annual Report on the Economic Status of the Profession," *Academe*, 87: 25-98, (March/April 2001).

★3647★
Average compensation for assistant professors at institutions in the New England states, 2000-01

Ranking basis/background: Compensation is total annual salary plus major fringe benefits, based on the responses of 1,433 institutions providing data to the annual salary survey of the American Association of University Professors. **Remarks:** The New England region includes Connecticut, Maine, Massachusetts, New Hampshire, Vermont and Rhode Island. **Number listed:** 4.

- Doctoral institutions, with an average annual salary of $72,200
- Comprehensive institutions, $60,642
- Baccalaureate institutions, $59,649
- Two-year institutions, $45,599

Source: "Uncertain Times: The Annual Report on the Economic Status of the Profession," *Academe*, 87: 25-98, (March/April 2001).

★3648★
Average compensation for assistant professors at institutions in the Pacific states, 2000-01

Ranking basis/background: Compensation is total annual salary plus major fringe benefits, based on the responses of 1,433 institutions providing data to the annual salary survey of the American Association of University Professors. **Remarks:** The Pacific region includes Alaska, California, Hawaii, Oregon and Washington. **Number listed:** 4.

- Doctoral institutions, with an average annual salary of $68,956
- Comprehensive institutions, $59,610
- Baccalaureate institutions, $54,611
- Two-year institutions, $53,110

Source: "Uncertain Times: The Annual Report on the Economic Status of the Profession," *Academe*, 87: 25-98, (March/April 2001).

★3649★
Average compensation for assistant professors at institutions in the South Atlantic states, 2000-01

Ranking basis/background: Compensation is total annual salary plus major fringe benefits, based on the responses of 1,433 institutions providing data to the annual salary survey of the American Association of University Professors. **Remarks:** The South Atlantic region includes Delaware, District of Columbia, Florida, Georgia, Maryland, North Carolina, South Carolina, Virginia and West Virginia. **Number listed:** 4.

- Doctoral institutions, with an average annual salary of $65,731
- Comprehensive institutions, $56,070
- Baccalaureate institutions, $50,572
- Two-year institutions, $52,119

Source: "Uncertain Times: The Annual Report on the Economic Status of the Profession," *Academe*, 87: 25-98, (March/April 2001).

★3650★
Average compensation for assistant professors at institutions in the West North Central states, 2000-01

Ranking basis/background: Compensation is total annual salary plus major fringe benefits, based on the responses of 1,433 institutions providing data to the annual salary survey of the American Association of University Professors. **Remarks:** The West North Central region includes Iowa, Kansas, Minnesota, Missouri, Nebraska, North Dakota and South Dakota. **Number listed:** 4.

- Doctoral institutions, with an average annual salary of $62,824
- Comprehensive institutions, $54,376
- Baccalaureate institutions, $50,299
- Two-year institutions, $48,837

Source: "Uncertain Times: The Annual Report on the Economic Status of the Profession," *Academe*, 87: 25-98, (March/April 2001).

★3651★
Average compensation for assistant professors at institutions in the West South Central states, 2000-01

Ranking basis/background: Compensation is total annual salary plus major fringe benefits, based on the responses of 1,433 institutions providing data to the annual salary survey of the American Association of University Professors. **Remarks:** The West South Central region includes Arkansas, Louisiana, Oklahoma, and Texas. **Number listed:** 4.

- Doctoral institutions, with an average annual salary of $63,726
- Comprehensive institutions, $51,847
- Baccalaureate institutions, $49,403
- Two-year institutions, $55,010

Source: "Uncertain Times: The Annual Report on the Economic Status of the Profession," *Academe*, 87: 25-98, (March/April 2001).

★3652★
Average compensation for associate professors at institutions in the East North Central states, 2000-01

Ranking basis/background: Compensation is total annual salary plus major fringe benefits, based on the responses of 1,433 institutions providing data to the annual salary survey of the American Association of University Professors. **Remarks:** The East North Central region includes Illinois, Indiana, Michigan, Ohio and Wisconsin. **Number listed:** 4.

- Doctoral institutions, with an average annual salary of $78,401
- Comprehensive institutions, $68,799
- Baccalaureate institutions, $61,882
- Two-year institutions, $60,646

Source: "Uncertain Times: The Annual Report on the Economic Status of the Profession," *Academe*, 87: 25-98, (March/April 2001).

★3653★
Average compensation for associate professors at institutions in the East South Central states, 2000-01

Ranking basis/background: Compensation is total annual salary plus major fringe benefits, based on the responses of 1,433 institutions providing data to the annual salary survey of the American Association of University Professors. **Remarks:** The East South Central region includes Alabama, Kentucky, Mississippi and Tennessee. **Number listed:** 4.

- Doctoral institutions, with an average annual salary of $70,660
- Comprehensive institutions, $62,587
- Baccalaureate institutions, $55,047
- Two-year institutions, $51,380

Source: "Uncertain Times: The Annual Report on the Economic Status of the Profession," *Academe*, 87: 25-98, (March/April 2001).

★3654★
Average compensation for associate professors at institutions in the Middle Atlantic states, 2000-01

Ranking basis/background: Compensation is total annual salary plus major fringe benefits, based on the responses of 1,433 institutions providing data to the annual salary survey of the American Association of University Professors. **Remarks:** The Middle Atlantic region includes New Jersey, New York and Pennsylvania. **Number listed:** 4.

- Doctoral institutions, with an average annual salary of $88,393
- Comprehensive institutions, $76,269
- Baccalaureate institutions, $70,547
- Two-year institutions, $67,078

Source: "Uncertain Times: The Annual Report on the Economic Status of the Profession," *Academe*, 87: 25-98, (March/April 2001).

★3655★
Average compensation for associate professors at institutions in the Mountain states, 2000-01

Ranking basis/background: Compensation is total annual salary plus major fringe benefits, based on the responses of 1,433 institutions providing data to the annual salary survey of the American Association of University Professors. **Remarks:** The Mountain region includes Arizona, Colorado, Idaho, Montana, Nevada, New Mexico, Utah and Wyoming. **Number listed:** 4.

- Doctoral institutions, with an average annual salary of $69,907
- Comprehensive institutions, $67,662
- Baccalaureate institutions, $55,081
- Two-year institutions, $52,248

Source: "Uncertain Times: The Annual Report on the Economic Status of the Profession," *Academe*, 87: 25-98, (March/April 2001).

★3656★
Average compensation for associate professors at institutions in the New England states, 2000-01

Ranking basis/background: Compensation is total annual salary plus major fringe benefits, based on the responses of 1,433 institutions providing data to the annual salary survey of the American Association of University Professors. **Remarks:** The New England region includes Connecticut, Maine, Massachusetts, New Hampshire, Vermont and Rhode Island. **Number listed:** 4.

- Doctoral institutions, with an average annual salary of $85,771
- Comprehensive institutions, $73,941
- Baccalaureate institutions, $73,187
- Two-year institutions, $50,213

Source: "Uncertain Times: The Annual Report on the Economic Status of the Profession," *Academe*, 87: 25-98, (March/April 2001).

★3657★
Average compensation for associate professors at institutions in the Pacific states, 2000-01

Ranking basis/background: Compensation is total annual salary plus major fringe benefits, based on the responses of 1,433 institutions providing data to the annual salary survey of the American Association of University Professors. **Remarks:** The Pacific region includes Alaska, California, Hawaii, Oregon and Washington. **Number listed:** 4.

- Doctoral institutions, with an average annual salary of $79,202
- Comprehensive institutions, $73,050
- Baccalaureate institutions, $64,929
- Two-year institutions, $58,356

Source: "Uncertain Times: The Annual Report on the Economic Status of the Profession," *Academe*, 87: 25-98, (March/April 2001).

★3658★
Average compensation for associate professors at institutions in the South Atlantic states, 2000-01

Ranking basis/background: Compensation is total annual salary plus major fringe benefits, based on the responses of 1,433 institutions providing data to the annual salary survey of the American Association of University Professors. **Remarks:** The South Atlantic region includes Delaware, District of Columbia, Florida, Georgia, Maryland, North Carolina, South Carolina, Virginia and West Virginia. **Number listed:** 4.

- Doctoral institutions, with an average annual salary of $79,193
- Comprehensive institutions, $68,171
- Baccalaureate institutions, $61,463
- Two-year institutions, $60,102

Source: "Uncertain Times: The Annual Report on the Economic Status of the Profession," *Academe*, 87: 25-98, (March/April 2001).

★3659★
Average compensation for associate professors at institutions in the West North Central states, 2000-01

Ranking basis/background: Compensation is total annual salary plus major fringe benefits, based on the responses of 1,433 institutions providing data to the annual salary survey of the American Association of University Professors. **Remarks:** The West North Central region includes Iowa, Kansas, Minnesota, Missouri, Nebraska, North Dakota and South Dakota. **Number listed:** 4.

- Doctoral institutions, with an average annual salary of $73,823
- Comprehensive institutions, $65,770
- Baccalaureate institutions, $59,342
- Two-year institutions, $53,060

Source: "Uncertain Times: The Annual Report on the Economic Status of the Profession," *Academe*, 87: 25-98, (March/April 2001).

★3660★
Average compensation for associate professors at institutions in the West South Central states, 2000-01

Ranking basis/background: Compensation is total annual salary plus major fringe benefits, based on the responses of 1,433 institutions providing data to the annual salary survey of the American Association of University Professors. **Remarks:** The West South Central region includes Arkansas, Louisiana, Oklahoma, and Texas. **Number listed:** 4.

- Doctoral institutions, with an average annual salary of $69,890
- Comprehensive institutions, $62,049
- Baccalaureate institutions, $58,263
- Two-year institutions, $58,723

Source: "Uncertain Times: The Annual Report on the Economic Status of the Profession," *Academe*, 87: 25-98, (March/April 2001).

★3661★
Average compensation for instructors at institutions in the East North Central states, 2000-01

Ranking basis/background: Compensation is total annual salary plus major fringe benefits, based on the responses of 1,433 institutions providing data to the annual salary survey of the American Association of University Professors. **Remarks:** The East North Central region includes Illinois, Indiana, Michigan, Ohio and Wisconsin. **Number listed:** 4.

- Doctoral institutions, with an average annual salary of $54,011
- Comprehensive institutions, $42,643
- Baccalaureate institutions, $42,782
- Two-year institutions, $42,914

Source: "Uncertain Times: The Annual Report on the Economic Status of the Profession," *Academe*, 87: 25-98, (March/April 2001).

★3662★
Average compensation for instructors at institutions in the East South Central states, 2000-01

Ranking basis/background: Compensation is total annual salary plus major fringe benefits, based on the responses of 1,433 institutions providing data to the annual salary survey of the American Association of University Professors. **Remarks:** The East South Central region includes Alabama, Kentucky, Mississippi and Tennessee. **Number listed:** 4.
  Doctoral institutions, with an average annual salary of $40,761
  Comprehensive institutions, $42,804
  Baccalaureate institutions, $39,890
  Two-year institutions, $39,369
Source: "Uncertain Times: The Annual Report on the Economic Status of the Profession," *Academe*, 87: 25-98, (March/April 2001).

★3663★
Average compensation for instructors at institutions in the Middle Atlantic states, 2000-01

Ranking basis/background: Compensation is total annual salary plus major fringe benefits, based on the responses of 1,433 institutions providing data to the annual salary survey of the American Association of University Professors. **Remarks:** The Middle Atlantic region includes New Jersey, New York and Pennsylvania. **Number listed:** 4.
  Doctoral institutions, with an average annual salary of $49,636
  Comprehensive institutions, $48,567
  Baccalaureate institutions, $46,751
  Two-year institutions, $49,084
Source: "Uncertain Times: The Annual Report on the Economic Status of the Profession," *Academe*, 87: 25-98, (March/April 2001).

★3664★
Average compensation for instructors at institutions in the Mountain states, 2000-01

Ranking basis/background: Compensation is total annual salary plus major fringe benefits, based on the responses of 1,433 institutions providing data to the annual salary survey of the American Association of University Professors. **Remarks:** The Mountain region includes Arizona, Colorado, Idaho, Montana, Nevada, New Mexico, Utah and Wyoming. **Number listed:** 4.
  Doctoral institutions, with an average annual salary of $46,169
  Comprehensive institutions, $45,742
  Baccalaureate institutions, $41,356
  Two-year institutions, $44,390
Source: "Uncertain Times: The Annual Report on the Economic Status of the Profession," *Academe*, 87: 25-98, (March/April 2001).

★3665★
Average compensation for instructors at institutions in the New England states, 2000-01

Ranking basis/background: Compensation is total annual salary plus major fringe benefits, based on the responses of 1,433 institutions providing data to the annual salary survey of the American Association of University Professors. **Remarks:** The New England region includes Connecticut, Maine, Massachusetts, New Hampshire, Vermont and Rhode Island. **Number listed:** 4.
  Doctoral institutions, with an average annual salary of $62,243
  Comprehensive institutions, $50,979
  Baccalaureate institutions, $49,240
  Two-year institutions, $43,166
Source: "Uncertain Times: The Annual Report on the Economic Status of the Profession," *Academe*, 87: 25-98, (March/April 2001).

★3666★
Average compensation for instructors at institutions in the Pacific states, 2000-01

Ranking basis/background: Compensation is total annual salary plus major fringe benefits, based on the responses of 1,433 institutions providing data to the annual salary survey of the American Association of University Professors. **Remarks:** The Pacific region includes Alaska, California, Hawaii, Oregon and Washington. **Number listed:** 4.
  Doctoral institutions, with an average annual salary of $49,020
  Comprehensive institutions, $47,149
  Baccalaureate institutions, $48,600
  Two-year institutions, $46,004
Source: "Uncertain Times: The Annual Report on the Economic Status of the Profession," *Academe*, 87: 25-98, (March/April 2001).

★3667★
Average compensation for instructors at institutions in the South Atlantic states, 2000-01

Ranking basis/background: Compensation is total annual salary plus major fringe benefits, based on the responses of 1,433 institutions providing data to the annual salary survey of the American Association of University Professors. **Remarks:** The South Atlantic region includes Delaware, District of Columbia, Florida, Georgia, Maryland, North Carolina, South Carolina, Virginia and West Virginia. **Number listed:** 4.
  Doctoral institutions, with an average annual salary of $47,987
  Comprehensive institutions, $45,070
  Baccalaureate institutions, $41,793
  Two-year institutions, $44,870
Source: "Uncertain Times: The Annual Report on the Economic Status of the Profession," *Academe*, 87: 25-98, (March/April 2001).

★3668★
Average compensation for instructors at institutions in the West North Central states, 2000-01

Ranking basis/background: Compensation is total annual salary plus major fringe benefits, based on the responses of 1,433 institutions providing data to the annual salary survey of the American Association of University Professors. **Remarks:** The West North Central region includes Iowa, Kansas, Minnesota, Missouri, Nebraska, North Dakota and South Dakota. **Number listed:** 4.
  Doctoral institutions, with an average annual salary of $46,377
  Comprehensive institutions, $43,625
  Baccalaureate institutions, $42,603
  Two-year institutions, $42,893
Source: "Uncertain Times: The Annual Report on the Economic Status of the Profession," *Academe*, 87: 25-98, (March/April 2001).

★3669★
Average compensation for instructors at institutions in the West South Central states, 2000-01

Ranking basis/background: Compensation is total annual salary plus major fringe benefits, based on the responses of 1,433 institutions providing data to the annual salary survey of the American Association of University Professors. **Remarks:** The West South Central region includes Arkansas, Louisiana, Oklahoma, and Texas. **Number listed:** 4.
  Doctoral institutions, with an average annual salary of $42,463
  Comprehensive institutions, $40,017
  Baccalaureate institutions, $40,228
  Two-year institutions, $47,272
Source: "Uncertain Times: The Annual Report on the Economic Status of the Profession," *Academe*, 87: 25-98, (March/April 2001).

★3670★
Average compensation for lecturers at institutions in the East North Central states, 2000-01

Ranking basis/background: Compensation is total annual salary plus major fringe benefits, based on the responses of 1,433 institutions providing data to the annual salary survey of the American Association of University Professors. **Remarks:** The East North Central region includes Illinois, Indiana, Michigan, Ohio and Wisconsin. **Number listed:** 4.
  Doctoral institutions, with an average annual salary of $42,652
  Comprehensive institutions, $45,734
  Baccalaureate institutions, $41,418
  Two-year institutions, $51,867
Source: "Uncertain Times: The Annual Report on the Economic Status of the Profession," *Academe*, 87: 25-98, (March/April 2001).

★3671★
Average compensation for lecturers at institutions in the East South Central states, 2000-01

Ranking basis/background: Compensation is total annual salary plus major fringe benefits, based on the responses of 1,433 institutions providing data to the annual salary survey of the American Association of University Professors. **Remarks:** The East South Central region includes Alabama, Kentucky, Mississippi and Tennessee. **Number listed:** 4.
  Doctoral institutions, with an average annual salary of $43,310
  Comprehensive institutions, $36,232
  Baccalaureate institutions, $37,090
  Two-year institutions, $34,667
Source: "Uncertain Times: The Annual Report on the Economic Status of the Profession," *Academe*, 87: 25-98, (March/April 2001).

★3672★
Average compensation for lecturers at institutions in the Middle Atlantic states, 2000-01

Ranking basis/background: Compensation is total annual salary plus major fringe benefits, based on the responses of 1,433 institutions providing data to the annual salary survey of the American Association of University Professors. **Remarks:** The Middle Atlantic region includes New Jersey, New York and Pennsylvania. **Number listed:** 4.

Doctoral institutions, with an average annual salary of $58,281
Comprehensive institutions, $49,126
Baccalaureate institutions, $51,280
Two-year institutions, $46,037

Source: "Uncertain Times: The Annual Report on the Economic Status of the Profession," *Academe*, 87: 25-98, (March/April 2001).

★3673★
Average compensation for lecturers at institutions in the Mountain states, 2000-01

Ranking basis/background: Compensation is total annual salary plus major fringe benefits, based on the responses of 1,433 institutions providing data to the annual salary survey of the American Association of University Professors. **Remarks:** The Mountain region includes Arizona, Colorado, Idaho, Montana, Nevada, New Mexico, Utah and Wyoming. **Number listed:** 4.

Doctoral institutions, with an average annual salary of $48,355
Comprehensive institutions, $50,140
Baccalaureate institutions, $39,378
Two-year institutions, $42,403

Source: "Uncertain Times: The Annual Report on the Economic Status of the Profession," *Academe*, 87: 25-98, (March/April 2001).

★3674★
Average compensation for lecturers at institutions in the New England states, 2000-01

Ranking basis/background: Compensation is total annual salary plus major fringe benefits, based on the responses of 1,433 institutions providing data to the annual salary survey of the American Association of University Professors. **Remarks:** The New England region includes Connecticut, Maine, Massachusetts, New Hampshire, Vermont and Rhode Island. **Number listed:** 3.

Doctoral institutions, with an average annual salary of $59,805
Comprehensive institutions, $53,251
Baccalaureate institutions, $59,122

Source: "Uncertain Times: The Annual Report on the Economic Status of the Profession," *Academe*, 87: 25-98, (March/April 2001).

★3675★
Average compensation for lecturers at institutions in the Pacific states, 2000-01

Ranking basis/background: Compensation is total annual salary plus major fringe benefits, based on the responses of 1,433 institutions providing data to the annual salary survey of the American Association of University Professors. **Remarks:** The Pacific region includes Alaska, California, Hawaii, Oregon and Washington. **Number listed:** 3.

Doctoral institutions, with an average annual salary of $59,547
Comprehensive institutions, $47,821
Baccalaureate institutions, $52,818

Source: "Uncertain Times: The Annual Report on the Economic Status of the Profession," *Academe*, 87: 25-98, (March/April 2001).

★3676★
Average compensation for lecturers at institutions in the South Atlantic states, 2000-01

Ranking basis/background: Compensation is total annual salary plus major fringe benefits, based on the responses of 1,433 institutions providing data to the annual salary survey of the American Association of University Professors. **Remarks:** The South Atlantic region includes Delaware, District of Columbia, Florida, Georgia, Maryland, North Carolina, South Carolina, Virginia and West Virginia. **Number listed:** 4.

Doctoral institutions, with an average annual salary of $49,586
Comprehensive institutions, $43,664
Baccalaureate institutions, $45,767
Two-year institutions, $44,944

Source: "Uncertain Times: The Annual Report on the Economic Status of the Profession," *Academe*, 87: 25-98, (March/April 2001).

★3677★
Average compensation for lecturers at institutions in the West North Central states, 2000-01

Ranking basis/background: Compensation is total annual salary plus major fringe benefits, based on the responses of 1,433 institutions providing data to the annual salary survey of the American Association of University Professors. **Remarks:** The West North Central region includes Iowa, Kansas, Minnesota, Missouri, Nebraska, North Dakota and South Dakota. **Number listed:** 4.

Doctoral institutions, with an average annual salary of $43,688
Comprehensive institutions, $38,086
Baccalaureate institutions, $43,596
Two-year institutions, $36,101

Source: "Uncertain Times: The Annual Report on the Economic Status of the Profession," *Academe*, 87: 25-98, (March/April 2001).

★3678★
Average compensation for lecturers at institutions in the West South Central states, 2000-01

Ranking basis/background: Compensation is total annual salary plus major fringe benefits, based on the responses of 1,433 institutions providing data to the annual salary survey of the American Association of University Professors. **Remarks:** The West South Central region includes Arkansas, Louisiana, Oklahoma, and Texas. **Number listed:** 4.

Doctoral institutions, with an average annual salary of $45,798
Comprehensive institutions, $42,791
Baccalaureate institutions, $38,618
Two-year institutions, $38,922

Source: "Uncertain Times: The Annual Report on the Economic Status of the Profession," *Academe*, 87: 25-98, (March/April 2001).

★3679★
Average compensation for professors at institutions in the East North Central states, 2000-01

Ranking basis/background: Compensation is total annual salary plus major fringe benefits, based on the responses of 1,433 institutions providing data to the annual salary survey of the American Association of University Professors. **Remarks:** The East North Central region includes Illinois, Indiana, Michigan, Ohio and Wisconsin. **Number listed:** 4.

Doctoral institutions, with an average annual salary of $108,987
Comprehensive institutions, $83,614
Baccalaureate institutions, $77,007
Two-year institutions, $72,382

Source: "Uncertain Times: The Annual Report on the Economic Status of the Profession," *Academe*, 87: 25-98, (March/April 2001).

★3680★
Average compensation for professors at institutions in the East South Central states, 2000-01

Ranking basis/background: Compensation is total annual salary plus major fringe benefits, based on the responses of 1,433 institutions providing data to the annual salary survey of the American Association of University Professors. **Remarks:** The East South Central region includes Alabama, Kentucky, Mississippi and Tennessee. **Number listed:** 4.

Doctoral institutions, with an average annual salary of $95,838
Comprehensive institutions, $78,173
Baccalaureate institutions, $67,815
Two-year institutions, $62,170

Source: "Uncertain Times: The Annual Report on the Economic Status of the Profession," *Academe*, 87: 25-98, (March/April 2001).

★3681★
Average compensation for professors at institutions in the Middle Atlantic states, 2000-01

Ranking basis/background: Compensation is total annual salary plus major fringe benefits, based on the responses of 1,433 institutions providing data to the annual salary survey of the American Association of University Professors. **Remarks:** The Middle Atlantic region includes New Jersey, New York and Pennsylvania. **Number listed:** 4.

Doctoral institutions, with an average annual salary of $127,154
Comprehensive institutions, $94,797
Baccalaureate institutions, $91,059
Two-year institutions, $82,018

Source: "Uncertain Times: The Annual Report on the Economic Status of the Profession," *Academe*, 87: 25-98, (March/April 2001).

★3682★
Average compensation for professors at institutions in the Mountain states, 2000-01

Ranking basis/background: Compensation is total annual salary plus major fringe benefits, based on the responses of 1,433 institutions providing data to the annual salary survey of the American Association of University Professors. **Remarks:** The Mountain region includes Arizona, Colorado, Idaho, Montana, Nevada, New Mexico, Utah and Wyoming. **Number listed:** 4.

Doctoral institutions, with an average annual salary of $93,526
Comprehensive institutions, $83,726
Baccalaureate institutions, $69,750
Two-year institutions, $55,746

Source: "Uncertain Times: The Annual Report on the Economic Status of the Profession," *Academe*, 87: 25-98, (March/April 2001).

★3683★
Average compensation for professors at institutions in the New England states, 2000-01

Ranking basis/background: Compensation is total annual salary plus major fringe benefits, based on the responses of 1,433 institutions providing data to the annual salary survey of the American Association of University Professors. **Remarks:** The New England region includes Connecticut, Maine, Massachusetts, New Hampshire, Vermont and Rhode Island. **Number listed:** 4.

Doctoral institutions, with an average annual salary of $124,554
Comprehensive institutions, $94,716
Baccalaureate institutions, $101,694
Two-year institutions, $61,178

Source: "Uncertain Times: The Annual Report on the Economic Status of the Profession," *Academe*, 87: 25-98, (March/April 2001).

★3684★
Average compensation for professors at institutions in the Pacific states, 2000-01

Ranking basis/background: Compensation is total annual salary plus major fringe benefits, based on the responses of 1,433 institutions providing data to the annual salary survey of the American Association of University Professors. **Remarks:** The Pacific region includes Alaska, California, Hawaii, Oregon and Washington. **Number listed:** 4.

Doctoral institutions, with an average annual salary of $111,646
Comprehensive institutions, $91,427
Baccalaureate institutions, $86,698
Two-year institutions, $65,347

Source: "Uncertain Times: The Annual Report on the Economic Status of the Profession," *Academe*, 87: 25-98, (March/April 2001).

★3685★
Average compensation for professors at institutions in the South Atlantic states, 2000-01

Ranking basis/background: Compensation is total annual salary plus major fringe benefits, based on the responses of 1,433 institutions providing data to the annual salary survey of the American Association of University Professors. **Remarks:** The South Atlantic region includes Delaware, District of Columbia, Florida, Georgia, Maryland, North Carolina, South Carolina, Virginia and West Virginia. **Number listed:** 4.

Doctoral institutions, with an average annual salary of $109,546
Comprehensive institutions, $84,390
Baccalaureate institutions, $76,379
Two-year institutions, $73,590

Source: "Uncertain Times: The Annual Report on the Economic Status of the Profession," *Academe*, 87: 25-98, (March/April 2001).

★3686★
Average compensation for professors at institutions in the West North Central states, 2000-01

Ranking basis/background: Compensation is total annual salary plus major fringe benefits, based on the responses of 1,433 institutions providing data to the annual salary survey of the American Association of University Professors. **Remarks:** The West North Central region includes Iowa, Kansas, Minnesota, Missouri, Nebraska, North Dakota and South Dakota. **Number listed:** 4.

Doctoral institutions, with an average annual salary of $103,956
Comprehensive institutions, $79,401
Baccalaureate institutions, $75,028
Two-year institutions, $66,241

Source: "Uncertain Times: The Annual Report on the Economic Status of the Profession," *Academe*, 87: 25-98, (March/April 2001).

★3687★
Average compensation for professors at institutions in the West South Central states, 2000-01

Ranking basis/background: Compensation is total annual salary plus major fringe benefits, based on the responses of 1,433 institutions providing data to the annual salary survey of the American Association of University Professors. **Remarks:** The West South Central region includes Arkansas, Louisiana, Oklahoma, and Texas. **Number listed:** 4.

Doctoral institutions, with an average annual salary of $99,164
Comprehensive institutions, $76,128
Baccalaureate institutions, $68,235
Two-year institutions, $67,123

Source: "Uncertain Times: The Annual Report on the Economic Status of the Profession," *Academe*, 87: 25-98, (March/April 2001).

★3688★
Average faculty salaries for institutions of higher education in Alabama, 2000-01

Ranking basis/background: Average salaries for instructional staff employed full-time for a nine-month work year. **Remarks:** Original source: American Association of University Professors. **Number listed:** 17.

Alabama A&M University, with $63.2 for professors; $53.3 for associate professors; $42.1 for assistant professors; and $33.4 for instructors
Auburn University, $76.6; $56.4; $48.1; $29.7
Auburn University, Montgomery, $65.8; $51.2; $44.1; $34.8
Birmingham-Southern College, $67.9; $52.9; $44.0; n/a
Huntingdon College, $45.8; $42.0; $37.4; n/a
Jacksonville State University, $59.4; $49.1; $42.4; $37.9
Samford University, $71.6; $51.6; $43.3; $32.8
Spring Hill College, $51.8; $43.2; $36.7; $33.2
Troy State University, $55.0; $46.0; $40.0; $28.9
Troy State University, Montgomery, $59.5; $44.7; $43.6; n/a
University of Alabama, Tuscaloosa, $77.9; $57.2; $47.3; $30.6
University of Alabama, Birmingham, $78.4; $55.2; $47.9; $33.7
University of Alabama, Huntsville, $76.6; $53.9; $48.6; $41.2
University of Montevallo, $57.2; $47.3; $37.1; $33.7
University of North Alabama, $57.8; $50.8; $44.0; $39.4
University of South Alabama, $72.0; $55.3; $47.5; $35.4
University of West Alabama, $51.5; $43.9; $38.1; n/a

Source: "Faculty Salaries at More Than 1,400 Institutions," *The Chronicle of Higher Education*, 47: A20-A23, (April 20, 2001).

★3689★
Average faculty salaries for institutions of higher education in Alaska, 2000-01

Ranking basis/background: Average salaries for instructional staff employed full-time for a nine-month work year. **Remarks:** Original source: American Association of University Professors. **Number listed:** 3.

University of Alaska, Anchorage, with $67.2 for professors; $53.0 for associate professors; $45.2 for assistant professors; and $37.4 for instructors
University of Alaska, Fairbanks, $70.5; $54.8; $45.5; $39.2
University of Alaska, Southeast, $66.7; $51.9; $41.4; $31.4

Source: "Faculty Salaries at More Than 1,400 Institutions," *The Chronicle of Higher Education*, 47: A20-A23, (April 20, 2001).

★3690★
Average faculty salaries for institutions of higher education in Arizona, 2000-01

Ranking basis/background: Average salaries for instructional staff employed full-time for a nine-month work year. **Remarks:** Original source: American Association of University Professors. **Number listed:** 6.

Arizona State University, with $85.0 for professors; $60.9 for associate professors; $52.3 for assistant professors; and $37.5 for instructors
Arizona State University, East, $79.7; $64.5; $57.4; n/a
Arizona State University, West, $83.8; $61.6; $47.5; n/a
Grand Canyon University, $42.5; $36.2; $32.0; $23.9
Northern Arizona University, $67.5; $53.2; $41.7; $29.3
University of Arizona, $84.9; $60.0; $52.0; n/a

Source: "Faculty Salaries at More Than 1,400 Institutions," *The Chronicle of Higher Education*, 47: A20-A23, (April 20, 2001).

★3691★
Average faculty salaries for institutions of higher education in Arkansas, 2000-01

Ranking basis/background: Average salaries for instructional staff employed full-time for a nine-month work year. **Remarks:** Original source: American Association of University Professors. **Number listed:** 13.

Arkansas State University, with $63.4 for professors; $53.6 for associate professors; $41.8 for assistant professors; and $32.4 for instructors

SALARIES—COLLEGES & UNIVERSITIES, FACULTY

Arkansas Tech University, $54.9; $47.8; $38.4; $28.4
Henderson State University, $54.3; $48.5; $40.0; $34.1
Hendrix College, $61.6; $51.4; $42.4; n/a
John Brown University, $52.2; $45.4; $39.7; $31.3
Lyon College, $55.6; $44.8; $38.5; n/a
Ouachita Baptist University, $56.6; $46.0; $41.0; $34.7
Southern Arkansas University, $58.3; $47.4; $39.5; $32.4
University of Arkansas, $76.3; $57.1; $50.4; $37.4
University of Arkansas, Pine Bluff, $52.3; $46.3; $40.2; $32.1
University of Central Arkansas, $60.3; $53.4; $44.2; $35.4
University of the Ozarks, $57.7; $48.1; $37.2; $26.5
Williams Baptist College, $38.4; n/a; $31.5; n/a

Source: "Faculty Salaries at More Than 1,400 Institutions," *The Chronicle of Higher Education*, 47: A20-A23, (April 20, 2001).

★3692★
Average faculty salaries for institutions of higher education in California, 2000-01

Ranking basis/background: Average salaries for instructional staff employed full-time for a nine-month work year. **Remarks:** Original source: American Association of University Professors. **Number listed:** 69.

Azusa Pacific University, with $60.2 for professors; $52.4 for associate professors; $42.5 for assistant professors; and $36.4 for instructors
Biola University, $59.4; $49.8; $41.0; n/a
California Institute of Technology, $122.2; $85.9; $73.4; n/a
California Lutheran University, $60.3; $49.2; $42.8; n/a
California Maritime Academy, $76.9; n/a; $50.0; $43.8
California Polytechnic State University, San Luis Obispo, $75.9; $62.1; $49.9; $37.9
California State Polytechnic University, Pomona, $77.3; $61.3; $49.1; $39.8
California State University, Bakersfield, $75.5; $59.6; $48.3; $35.9
California State University, Chico, $75.5; $60.2; $46.6; $37.9
California State University, Dominguez Hills, $75.4; $59.1; $47.6; $39.5
California State University, Fresno, $75.6; $61.2; $46.4; $38.0
California State University, Fullerton, $77.0; $60.8; $47.8; $37.5
California State University, Hayward, $76.6; $63.0; $50.6; $39.9
California State University, Long Beach, $75.7; $60.6; $49.3; $38.6
California State University, Los Angeles, $75.8; $; 60.7; $49.7; $36.0
California State University, Monterey Bay, $77.4; $61.2; $50.1; $37.0
California State University, Northridge, $75.6; $61.5; $48.6; $39.0
California State University, Sacramento, $75.2; $58.8; $47.7; $38.8
California State University, San Bernardino, $74.8; $60.0; $48.9; $37.0
California State University, San Marcos, $76.1; $59.7; $50.8; $36.7
California State University, Stanislaus, $74.3; $56.2; $47.9; $39.3
Humboldt State University, $74.4; $58.5; $49.2; $40.4
San Diego State University, $76.5; $61.4; $50.1; $38.4
San Francisco State University, $76.2; $63.5; $51.5; $34.6
San Jose State University, $75.7; $63.4; $50.8; $36.1
Sonoma State University, $74.7; $60.6; $47.4; n/a
Chapman University, $77.8; $64.3; $51.8; n/a
Claremont Graduate University, $94.6; $70.3; $54.7; n/a
Notre Dame College, $63.8; $48.8; $43.0; n/a
Concordia University, $52.6; $40.8; $37.3; n/a
Dominican College of San Rafael, $69.6; $51.3; $44.1; n/a
Fuller Theological Seminary, $68.3; $52.6; n/a; n/a
Harvey Mudd College, $94.2; $70.6; $60.9; n/a
La Sierra University, $50.2; $41.5; $35.0; n/a
Los Angeles College of Chiropractic, $53.5; $44.8; $36.7; n/a
Loyola Marymount University, $92.8; $64.1; $47.4; n/a
Menlo College, $65.9; n/a; $52.6; n/a
Mount St. Mary's College and Seminary, $76.4; $54.8; $49.7; $46.7
National University, $68.7; $52.3; $45.2; $39.9
Occidental College, $83.3; $58.8; $47.9; $44.3
Pacific School of Religion, n/a; $56.0; n/a; n/a
Pacific Union College, $49.1; $42.5; $37.6; $30.8
Pepperdine University, $89.1; $74.7; $62.4; n/a
Pitzer College, $77.3; $53.4; $47.9; n/a
Point Loma Nazarene College, $63.0; $51.0; $42.9; n/a
Pomona College, $93.6; $66.1; $50.5; n/a
St. Mary's College (CA), $70.5; $53.7; $n/a; n/a
Santa Clara University, $103.9; $75.0; $64.2; n/a
Scripps College, $85.5; $64.3; $48.3; n/a
Stanford University, $126.7; $88.1; $69.1; n/a
US International University, $60.3; $43.4; $38.5; n/a
University of California, Berkeley, $113.6; $73.2; $62.5; n/a
University of California, Davis, $95.4; $66.4; $56.4; n/a
University of California, Irvine, $100.5; $69.1; $60.3; n/a
University of California, Los Angeles, $112.7; $72.4; $63.0; n/a
University of California, Riverside, $97.4; $66.3; $60.5; n/a
University of California, San Diego, $104.3; $67.0; $58.2; n/a
University of California, San Francisco, $87.2; $61.6; $50.6; n/a
University of California, Santa Barbara, $102.2; $65.8; $55.6; n/a
University of California, Santa Cruz, $95.4; $65.0; $54.5; n/a
University of LaVerne, $65.5; $49.0; $43.0; n/a
University of the Pacific, $79.1; $57.5; $49.5; $55.4
University of Redlands, $69.6; $54.2; $41.9; n/a
University of Southern California, $104.2; $71.7; $62.8; $47.9
Vanguard University of Southern California, $56.4; $49.3; $42.5; n/a
Westmont College, $60.8; $49.2; $41.2; n/a
Whittier College, $85.9; $54.5; $41.7; n/a
Woodbury University, $64.6; $51.1; $45.8; n/a

Source: "Faculty Salaries at More Than 1,400 Institutions," *The Chronicle of Higher Education*, 47: A20-A23, (April 20, 2001).

★3693★
Average faculty salaries for institutions of higher education in Colorado, 2000-01

Ranking basis/background: Average salaries for instructional staff employed full-time for a nine-month work year. **Remarks:** Original source: American Association of University Professors. **Number listed:** 16.

Colorado College, with $81.2 for professors; $58.0 for associate professors; $45.4 for assistant professors; and $41.3 for instructors
Colorado School of Mines, $93.9; $65.6; $56.0; $34.8
Colorado State University, $78.9; $59.3; $50.4; n/a
Fort Lewis College, $56.1; $47.0; $34.2; $32.2
University of Southern Colorado, $55.8; $46.6; $42.4; $27.5
Community College of Denver, $48.5; $39.8; $35.4; n/a
Iliff School of Theology, $76.9; n/a; n/a; n/a
Regis University, $60.7; $52.8; $41.5; n/a
Adams State College, $54.4; $44.9; $36.9; $33.0
Mesa State College, $54.5; $44.6; $38.2; n/a
Western State College of Colorado, $53.9; $44.3; $39.9; n/a
University of Colorado, Boulder, $85.7; $62.4; $52.0; $39.8
University of Colorado, Colorado Springs, $73.4; $56.2; $48.7; $31.2
University of Colorado, Denver, $77.6; $57.4; $49.0; $35.0
University of Denver, $79.1; $61.3; $49.1; n/a
University of Northern Colorado, $64.4; $49.2; $43.8; $30.2

Source: "Faculty Salaries at More Than 1,400 Institutions," *The Chronicle of Higher Education*, 47: A20-A23, (April 20, 2001).

★3694★
Average faculty salaries for institutions of higher education in Connecticut, 2000-01

Ranking basis/background: Average salaries for instructional staff employed full-time for a nine-month work year. **Remarks:** Original source: American Association of University Professors. **Number listed:** 15.

Albertus Magnus College, with $52.1 for professors; $47.4 for associate professors; $39.8 for assistant professors; and n/a for instructors
Connecticut College, $83.0; $61.5; $47.1; n/a
Central Connecticut State University, $79.3; $59.5; $47.6; $42.9
Eastern Connecticut State University, $76.0; $59.3; $43.3; $38.4
Southern Connecticut State University, $77.1; $63.7; $48.0; n/a
Western Connecticut State University, $79.0; $61.1; $49.8; n/a
Fairfield University, $83.2; $66.4; $55.7; $42.1
Quinnipiac College, $88.2; $64.6; $53.9; n/a
Sacred Heart University, $73.9; $58.3; $47.1; $42.8
St. Joseph College, $67.1; $55.8; $41.6; n/a
Trinity College, $96.1; $67.5; $49.0; n/a
University of Connecticut, $98.0; $71.8; $56.5; $49.4
University of Hartford, $66.0; $51.7; $45.5; $34.5
University of New Haven, $65.1; $55.5; $44.7; n/a
Yale University, $124.1; $69.4; $58.0; $47.8

Source: "Faculty Salaries at More Than 1,400 Institutions," *The Chronicle of Higher Education*, 47: A20-A23, (April 20, 2001).

★3695★
Average faculty salaries for institutions of higher education in Delaware, 2000-01

Ranking basis/background: Average salaries for instructional staff employed full-time for a nine-month work year. Remarks: Original source: American Association of University Professors. Number listed: 4.

Delaware State University, with $69.8 for professors; $57.0 for associate professors; $46.5 for assistant professors; and $39.2 for instructors
University of Delaware, $95.7; $67.1; $53.5; $41.7
Wesley College, $53.1; $43.5; $37.2; n/a
Wilmington College, n/a; $47.1; $41.4; n/a

Source: "Faculty Salaries at More Than 1,400 Institutions," *The Chronicle of Higher Education*, 47: A20-A23, (April 20, 2001).

★3696★
Average faculty salaries for institutions of higher education in Florida, 2000-01

Ranking basis/background: Average salaries for instructional staff employed full-time for a nine-month work year. Remarks: Original source: American Association of University Professors. Number listed: 22.

Barry University, with $64.9 for professors; $52.2 for associate professors; $45.5 for assistant professors; and $34.7 for instructors
Bethune-Cookman College, $52.4; $48.2; $41.6; $33.3
Brevard Community College, $50.5; $44.0; $41.8; $37.8
Eckerd College, $62.7; $50.3; $42.4; n/a
Embry-Riddle Aeronautical University, $63.0; $49.6; $44.3; n/a
Florida Southern College, $57.6; $47.9; $41.0; n/a
Jacksonville University, $56.7; $47.9; $40.6; n/a
Miami-Dade Community College, $62.6; $49.6; $41.7; $35.5
Nova Southeastern University, $76.8; $54.6; $49.4; $40.2
Palm Beach Atlantic College, $51.4; $44.6; $38.7; $33.6
Rollins College, $70.0; $53.6; $38.1; n/a
St. Leo University, $51.8; $44.6; $38.8; n/a
Florida Atlantic University, $74.4; $56.9; $46.1; $36.1
Florida Gulf Coast University, $71.5; $55.4; $45.7; $35.3
Florida State University, $76.4; $55.2; $49.1; $26.7
University of Central Florida, $79.1; $60.1; $48.6; $31.6
University of Florida, $82.0; $61.4; $53.7; $56.7
University of South Florida, $72.4; $55.0; $43.9; $35.0
University of West Florida, $65.1; $53.1; $42.2; $36.6
Stetson University, $76.2; $52.7; $43.2; $36.9
University of Miami, $90.8; $60.4; $54.1; $39.7
University of Tampa, $60.7; n/a; $45.9; $34.2

Source: "Faculty Salaries at More Than 1,400 Institutions," *The Chronicle of Higher Education*, 47: A20-A23, (April 20, 2001).

★3697★
Average faculty salaries for institutions of higher education in Georgia, 2000-01

Ranking basis/background: Average salaries for instructional staff employed full-time for a nine-month work year. Remarks: Original source: American Association of University Professors. Number listed: 34.

Agnes Scott College, with $66.9 for professors; $54.0 for associate professors; $44.8 for assistant professors; and n/a for instructors
Armstrong Atlantic State University, $63.9; $50.4; $42.6; $32.9
Atlanta Metropolitan College, $57.6; $49.4; $41.8; n/a
Augusta State University, $66.6; $52.7; $41.5; $30.7
Berry College, $70.7; $55.2; $42.4; n/a
Brenau University, $54.0; $46.6; $39.2; n/a
Brunswick College, $56.6; $44.0; $42.8; $37.8
Columbia Theological Seminary, $62.1; $47.1; n/a; n/a
Columbus State University, $64.2; $52.3; $39.2; $30.9
Covenant College, $54.2; $46.9; $37.6; n/a
Dalton State College, $56.9; $51.3; $43.8; $35.5
Emory University, $111.8; $70.9; $59.9; n/a
Floyd College, $52.6; $43.6; $37.9; n/a
Georgia College and State University, $61.1; $50.7; $44.1; $35.4
Georgia Institute of Technology, $104.1; $73.0; $62.3; n/a
Georgia Perimeter College, $58.5; $48.2; $40.6; $34.3
Georgia Southern University, $68.2; $54.7; $43.7; $32.7
Georgia State University, $101.5; $65.0; $53.7; $33.3
Institute of Paper Science & Technology, $104.9; $73.7; n/a; n/a
Kennesaw State University, $70.4; $57.8; $44.6; $36.1
La Grange College, $55.4; $45.7; $42.5; n/a
Macon State College, $60.9; $52.1; $43.6; $35.4
Mercer University, $74.4; $54.2; $43.7; $34.4
Morehouse College, $67.5; $52.6; $43.4; $33.2
North Georgia College and State University, $64.3; $53.0; $41.8; $33.4
Oglethorpe University, $65.0; $50.6; $41.7; n/a
Piedmont College, $51.5; $49.7; $40.7; n/a
Reinhardt College, $49.2; $45.3; $37.5; $30.3
Shorter College, $47.3; $40.9; $33.4; n/a
Southern Polytechnic State University, $64.0; $55.6; $48.0; $40.9
Truett-McConnell College, $37.3; $36.6; $33.3; $30.9
University of Georgia, $85.0; $60.5; $52.2; $39.5
Valdosta State University, $63.6; $52.4; $44.6; $34.9

Source: "Faculty Salaries at More Than 1,400 Institutions," *The Chronicle of Higher Education*, 47: A20-A23, (April 20, 2001).

★3698★
Average faculty salaries for institutions of higher education in Hawaii, 2000-01

Ranking basis/background: Average salaries for instructional staff employed full-time for a nine-month work year. Remarks: Original source: American Association of University Professors. Number listed: 10.

University of Hawaii, Manoa, with $77.3 for professors; $57.9 for associate professors; $49.0 for assistant professors; and $38.8 for instructors
University of Hawaii, Hilo, $62.0; $51.0; $43.4; $32.2
University of Hawaii, West Oahu, $55.3; $49.4; n/a; n/a
Hawaii Community College, $55.5; $48.4; $43.4; $38.5
Honolulu Community College, $56.3; $48.9; $47.2; $38.5
Kapiolani Community College, $59.0; $50.9; $44.8; $37.8
Kauai Community College, $56.4; $50.4; $45.7; $39.9
Leeward Community College, $56.9; $48.7; $42.5; $37.6
Maui Community College, $58.6; $50.3; $45.9; $38.6
Windward Community College, $54.8; $48.5; $45.4; n/a

Source: "Faculty Salaries at More Than 1,400 Institutions," *The Chronicle of Higher Education*, 47: A20-A23, (April 20, 2001).

SALARIES—COLLEGES & UNIVERSITIES, FACULTY

★3699★
Average faculty salaries for institutions of higher education in Idaho, 2000-01

Ranking basis/background: Average salaries for instructional staff employed full-time for a nine-month work year. **Remarks:** Original source: American Association of University Professors. **Number listed:** 3.

- Albertson College, with $55.6 for professors; $44.8 for associate professors; $37.5 for assistant professors; and n/a for instructors
- Boise State University, $60.2; $50.9; $44.1; n/a
- University of Idaho, $66.7; $52.5; $45.6; $35.7

Source: "Faculty Salaries at More Than 1,400 Institutions," *The Chronicle of Higher Education*, 47: A20-A23, (April 20, 2001).

★3700★
Average faculty salaries for institutions of higher education in Illinois, 2000-01

Ranking basis/background: Average salaries for instructional staff employed full-time for a nine-month work year. **Remarks:** Original source: American Association of University Professors. **Number listed:** 48.

- Augustana College, with $63.8 for professors; $53.5 for associate professors; $42.1 for assistant professors; and $40.4 for instructors
- Black Hawk College, $62.5; $54.0; $42.9; $34.7
- Bradley University, $70.2; $56.4; $45.9; $34.3
- DePaul University, $91.1; $66.8; $53.0; $48.1
- Dominican University, $58.7; $48.0; $46.5; n/a
- Eastern Illinois University, $59.8; $51.5; $39.9; $27.8
- Elmhurst College, $65.9; $52.0; $46.7; $39.5
- Eureka College, $49.0; $40.8; $35.6; n/a
- Greenville College, $44.6; $40.1; $33.8; n/a
- Illinois Central College, $54.2; $45.5; $37.7; $32.7
- Illinois College, $60.7; $50.2; $38.7; n/a
- Illinois Institute of Technology, $88.8; $65.9; $58.2; $42.5
- Illinois State University, $68.8; $53.9; $46.2; n/a
- Illinois Wesleyan University, $71.9; $56.5; $43.4; $37.4
- John A. Logan College, $59.6; $51.3; $45.9; $43.1
- Joliet Junior College, $66.4; $45.0; $39.2; n/a
- Judson College, $52.9; $49.8; $32.8; n/a
- Knox College, $62.1; $48.2; $40.2; $38.3
- Judson College, $52.9; $49.8; $32.8; n/a
- Knox College, $62.1; $48.2; $40.2; $38.3
- Lake Forest College, $72.0; $56.5; $44.2; $37.2
- Lincoln Christian College and Seminary, $46.4; $40.1; $38.6; n/a
- Loyola University, Chicago, $84.6; $60.4; $51.2; n/a
- McCormick Theological Seminary, $57.5; $50.4; $45.1; n/a
- McKendree College, $54.3; $48.7; $41.3; $35.4
- Millikin University, $56.8; $49.5; $39.3; $35.3
- Monmouth College, $57.0; $48.3; $39.5; n/a
- Moraine Valley Community College, $69.9; $58.8; $40.3; $32.8
- National-Louis University, $62.0; $47.9; $40.9; $34.6
- North Central College, $60.4; $52.2; $43.7; n/a
- Northeastern Illinois University, $69.7; $56.0; $48.3; n/a
- Northern Illinois University, $74.7; $55.5; $47.5; $28.7
- Northwestern University, $116.2; $78.5; $65.8; n/a
- Olivet Nazarene University, $48.6; $41.3; $31.6; n/a
- Principia College, $56.6; $48.0; $43.4; $35.8
- Quincy University, $48.6; $42.3; $36.5; n/a
- Rockford College, $53.6; $43.0; $34.8; n/a
- Roosevelt University, $71.5; $55.5; $47.7; n/a
- St. Xavier University, $64.4; $54.4; $43.5; n/a
- Southern Illinois University, Carbondale, $69.9; $52.8; $43.8; $30.8
- Southern Illinois University, Edwardsville, $68.7; $57.8; $46.8; $33.3
- Southwestern Illinois College, $66.3; $46.6; $38.8; n/a
- Trinity International University, $59.3; $51.0; $38.9; n/a
- University of Chicago, $124.8; $79.5; $67.1; $45.2
- University of Illinois, Chicago, $90.2; $64.7; $55.4; $42.5
- University of Illinois, Springfield, $66.9; $56.2; $43.4; n/a
- University of Illinois, Urbana-Champaign, $95.6; $66.3; $56.8; n/a
- University of St. Francis, $56.6; $50.2; $44.2; n/a
- Western Illinois University, $65.7; $52.7; $42.7; $31.1
- Wheaton College, $66.4; $55.4; $45.5; n/a

Source: "Faculty Salaries at More Than 1,400 Institutions," *The Chronicle of Higher Education*, 47: A20-A23, (April 20, 2001).

★3701★
Average faculty salaries for institutions of higher education in Indiana, 2000-01

Ranking basis/background: Average salaries for instructional staff employed full-time for a nine-month work year. **Remarks:** Original source: American Association of University Professors. **Number listed:** 36.

- Anderson University, with $48.1 for professors; $41.4 for associate professors; $38.6 for assistant professors; and $30.4 for instructors
- Ball State University, $68.9; $54.3; $41.7; $31.0
- Bethel College, $47.5; $41.7; $38.5; n/a
- Butler University, $67.3; $55.8; $44.7; $38.9
- Calumet College of St. Joseph, $43.4; n/a; $35.5; n/a
- DePauw University, $69.8; $56.4; $45.2; n/a
- Earlham College, $61.3; $48.2; $40.2; n/a
- Goshen College, $50.5; $41.9; $36.1; n/a
- Grace College, $43.7; $36.4; n/a; n/a
- Hanover College, $66.4; $51.1; $41.4; $39.7
- Huntington College, $54.2; $46.1; $38.8; n/a
- Indiana State University, $64.1; $50.7; $41.8; $39.7
- Indiana University, Bloomington, $88.2; $61.1; $49.8; n/a
- Indiana University, East, $57.7; $47.1; $38.0; n/a
- Indiana University, Kokomo, $61.8; $52.3; $43.7; n/a
- Indiana University, Northwest, $62.5; $56.4; $41.9; n/a
- Indiana University-Purdue University, Fort Wayne, $63.3; $50.9; $43.9; $32.0
- Indiana University-Purdue University, Indianapolis, $78.8; $59.3; $50.1; $37.7
- Indiana University, South Bend, $67.7; $51.8; $41.4; n/a
- Indiana University, Southeast, $64.4; $54.7; $45.8; n/a
- Ivy Tech State College, $43.0; $38.4; $34.3; $31.8
- Manchester College, $47.2; $42.2; $36.1; n/a
- Purdue University, $87.4; $60.6; $53.0; $30.3
- Purdue University, Calumet, $66.9; $51.4; $41.1; $28.9
- Purdue University, North Central, $69.5; $48.6; $40.5; n/a
- Rose-Hulman Institute of Technology, $81.6; $64.2; $57.0; n/a
- St. Joseph's College (IN), $44.0; $36.7; $35.6; n/a
- St. Mary-of-the-Woods College, $45.1; $37.5; $33.5; n/a
- St. Mary's College (IN), $62.8; $51.0; $42.7; n/a
- Taylor University, Upland, $49.6; $41.4; $36.5; $29.9
- Taylor University, Fort Wayne, n/a; $37.6; n/a; n/a
- University of Evansville, $67.3; $53.6; $42.4; $40.2
- University of Indianapolis, $61.5; $52.3; $43.2; $35.6
- University of Notre Dame, $106.0; $70.8; $59.0; $61.7
- University of Southern Indiana, $64.7; $52.5; $44.6; $35.5
- Vincennes University, $52.6; $45.7; $41.3; $32.9
- Wabash, $74.7; $57.9; $45.1; n/a

Source: "Faculty Salaries at More Than 1,400 Institutions," *The Chronicle of Higher Education*, 47: A20-A23, (April 20, 2001).

★3702★
Average faculty salaries for institutions of higher education in Iowa, 2000-01

Ranking basis/background: Average salaries for instructional staff employed full-time for a nine-month work year. **Remarks:** Original source: American Association of University Professors. **Number listed:** 26.

- Iowa State University, with $85.2 for professors; $63.1 for associate professors; $52.7 for assistant professors; and $40.5 for instructors
- University of Iowa, $94.3; $62.5; $54.6; n/a
- University of Northern Iowa, $72.1; $55.5; $45.8; $38.8

Briar Cliff College, $42.3; $36.7; $33.3; n/a
Buena Vista University, $67.4; $53.2; $40.9; $38.6
Central College, $54.4; $45.9; $39.2; $33.3
Coe College, $60.8; $45.5; $41.6; n/a
Cornell University, $61.0; $47.8; $40.2; n/a
Dordt College, $53.5; $43.5; $40.9; $34.6
Drake University, $70.1; $50.8; $44.7; $41.3
Faith Baptist Bible College and Seminary, $36.1; $30.3; n/a; n/a
Graceland University, $53.0; $42.4; $36.5; n/a
Grinnell College, $89.2; $63.4; $47.3; $43.6
Kirkwood Community College, $46.6; $40.0; $34.6; $33.1
Loras College, $50.6; $43.1; $38.0; n/a
Luther College, $60.3; $49.7; $40.4; $35.1
Morningside College, $45.4; $40.1; $37.3; $31.3
Mount Mercy College, $49.1; $42.3; $38.2; n/a
Northwestern College, $51.7; $44.8; $38.1; n/a
Palmer College of Chiropractic, $49.3; $46.8; $38.2; $34.7
St. Ambrose University, $53.9; $42.9; $41.0; n/a
Simpson College, $60.0; $45.2; $38.8; $37.4
Upper Iowa University, n/a; $41.8; $37.1; n/a
Waldorf College, n/a; $38.5; $33.2; n/a
Wartburg College, $56.0; $44.6; $41.4; n/a
Warburg Theological Seminary, $46.6; $40.6; n/a; n/a

Source: "Faculty Salaries at More Than 1,400 Institutions," *The Chronicle of Higher Education*, 47: A20-A23, (April 20, 2001).

★3703★
Average faculty salaries for institutions of higher education in Kansas, 2000-01

Ranking basis/background: Average salaries for instructional staff employed full-time for a nine-month work year. **Remarks:** Original source: American Association of University Professors. **Number listed:** 20.

Baker University, with $49.8 for professors; $41.8 for associate professors; $36.2 for assistant professors; and n/a for instructors
Bethany College, $35.9; $31.0; $28.8; n/a
Bethel College, $37.4; $30.4; $34.0; n/a
Emporia State University, $57.6; $49.4; $42.1; $31.7
Fort Hays State University, $57.8; $48.7; $41.1; $35.0
Friends University, $50.2; $43.0; $43.1; n/a
Johnson County Community College, $56.3; $47.2; $42.9; n/a
Kansas City Kansas Community College, $58.1; $47.0; $42.6; $35.8
Kansas State University, $70.7; $55.3; $48.8; $36.1
Kansas Wesleyan University, $37.6; $34.5; $31.3; n/a
McPherson College, $35.8; $33.0; $28.9; n/a
University of Ottawa, $44.5; $38.4; $34.8; n/a
Pittsburg State University, $60.6; $51.5; $42.1; $34.7
St. Mary College (KS), $43.6; $37.0; $32.9; $29.4
Southwestern College, $45.3; $38.3; $33.0; n/a
Sterling College, $39.7; n/a; $31.1; n/a
Tabor College, $35.4; $29.9; $26.4; $23.5
University of Kansas, $79.6; $56.1; $48.8; n/a
Washburn University, $71.2; $54.8; $40.5; $36.7
Wichita State University, $71.6; $55.3; $47.7; $36.5

Source: "Faculty Salaries at More Than 1,400 Institutions," *The Chronicle of Higher Education*, 47: A20-A23, (April 20, 2001).

★3704★
Average faculty salaries for institutions of higher education in Kentucky, 2000-01

Ranking basis/background: Average salaries for instructional staff employed full-time for a nine-month work year. **Remarks:** Original source: American Association of University Professors. **Number listed:** 21.

Ashbury College, with $49.4 for professors; $42.3 for associate professors; $34.9 for assistant professors; and n/a for instructors
Ashbury Theological Seminary, $62.9; n/a; $43.8; n/a
Berea College, $63.4; $50.0; $42.7; n/a
Centre College, $66.5; $52.4; $42.3; n/a
Eastern Kentucky University, $66.2; $54.1; $43.3; $34.8
Georgetown College, $55.6; $43.6; $38.0; $32.1
Kentucky Christian College, $38.8; n/a; $33.5; n/a
Kentucky State University, $57.2; $49.9; $42.0; $33.3
Kentucky Wesleyan College, $43.2; $37.8; $32.1; n/a
Lexington Community College, $52.1; $42.6; $36.5; $32.2
Lindsey Wilson College, $53.5; $40.1; $35.2; $30.8
Midway College, n/a; n/a; $34.6; n/a
Morehead State University, $59.8; $46.2; $40.9; $28.1
Murray State University, $63.5; $52.3; $43.3; n/a
Northern Kentucky University, $64.6; $49.9; $42.4; n/a
Pikeville College, $55.6; $39.7; $34.2; $34.0
Transylvania University, $64.5; $54.5; $40.9; n/a
University of Kentucky, $79.6; $58.5; $49.4; n/a
University of Louisville, $77.6; $58.3; $45.9; 34.6
Western Kentucky University, $66.6; $51.3; $43.4; $33.7

Source: "Faculty Salaries at More Than 1,400 Institutions," *The Chronicle of Higher Education*, 47: A20-A23, (April 20, 2001).

★3705★
Average faculty salaries for institutions of higher education in Louisiana, 2000-01

Ranking basis/background: Average salaries for instructional staff employed full-time for a nine-month work year. **Remarks:** Original source: American Association of University Professors. **Number listed:** 17.

Centenary College of Louisiana, with $56.7 for professors; $45.9 for associate ofessors; $38.4 for assistant professors; and n/a for instructors
Louisiana College, $47.0; $41.7; $37.0; n/a
Louisiana State University and A&M College, $72.5; $53.1; $46.5; $31.7
Louisiana State University, Shreveport, $53.8; $44.1; n/a; $32.6
Loyola University, New Orleans, $72.7; $55.8; $44.1; n/a
Southern University, Baton Rouge, $60.4; $48.4; $40.2; $30.4
Tulane University, $94.5; $66.1; $58.7; $42.0
Grambling State University, $55.0; $45.7; $39.6; $30.6
Louisiana Tech, $61.4; $51.9; $44.2; $27.7
McNeese State University, $54.6; $44.6; $37.0; $32.3
Nicholls State University, $56.6; $45.7; $39.0; $20.6
Northwestern State University, $55.7; $45.5; $36.9; $27.1
Southeastern Louisiana University, $59.8; $49.2; $41.8; $32.1
University of Louisiana, Lafayette, $70.8; $53.6; $43.5; $32.9
University of Louisiana, Monroe, $54.5; $46.2; $38.7; $28.2
Elaine Nunez Community College, n/a; n/a; $35.0; $26.6
Xavier University (LA), $64.0; $49.6; $41.6; $31.8

Source: "Faculty Salaries at More Than 1,400 Institutions," *The Chronicle of Higher Education*, 47: A20-A23, (April 20, 2001).

★3706★
Average faculty salaries for institutions of higher education in Maine, 2000-01

Ranking basis/background: Average salaries for instructional staff employed full-time for a nine-month work year. **Remarks:** Original source: American Association of University Professors. **Number listed:** 15.

Andover College, with n/a for professors; n/a for associate professors; $30.4 for assistant professors; and $28.8 for instructors
Bates College, $83.2; $61.3; $46.8; n/a
Bowdoin College, $92.1; $66.4; $52.7; $46.1
Colby College, $93.0; $64.0; $49.6; n/a
Husson College, $48.7; $46.0; $41.8; $28.0
St. Joseph's College (ME), n/a; $45.4; $37.4; n/a
Thomas College, $33.8; $30.1; $27.6; n/a
University of Maine, $66.2; $55.3; $47.7; $37.6
University of Maine, Augusta, $52.8; $43.9; $36.0; n/a
University of Maine, Farmington, $52.8; $44.1; $34.8; $37.8
University of Maine, Fort Kent, $50.3; $43.3; $35.8; n/a

SALARIES—COLLEGES & UNIVERSITIES, FACULTY

University of Maine, Manchias, $45.8; $44.3; $33.9; n/a
University of Maine, Presque Isle, $48.6; $44.2; $36.9; n/a
University of Southern Maine, $68.4; $53.9; $42.2; n/a
University of New England, $57.3; $46.9; $39.7; $31.4

Source: "Faculty Salaries at More Than 1,400 Institutions," *The Chronicle of Higher Education*, 47: A20-A23, (April 20, 2001).

★3707★
Average faculty salaries for institutions of higher education in Maryland, 2000-01

Ranking basis/background: Average salaries for instructional staff employed full-time for a nine-month work year. **Remarks:** Original source: American Association of University Professors. **Number listed:** 25.

Cecil Community College, with $58.5 for professors; $50.4 for associate professors; $41.0 for assistant professors; and n/a for instructors
Chesapeake College, $56.6; $47.8; $43.4; n/a
College of Notre Dame (MD), $53.7; $45.2; $36.3; n/a
Columbia Union College, $42.1; $40.1; $37.8; $33.3
Goucher College, $76.6; $57.2; $43.0; n/a
Hagerstown College, $54.3; $43.1; $36.7; n/a
Harford Community College, $62.5; $57.7; $49.4; $38.7
Hood College, $58.6; $47.9; $38.5; n/a
Howard Community College, $62.5; $50.9; $44.3; $35.9
Loyola College (MD), $77.6; $61.1; $47.1; $36.2
Montegomery College, $62.9; $52.3; $44.0; $37.7
Morgan State University, $78.6; $62.0; $54.1; $43.4
Mount St. Mary's College and Seminary, $57.5; $44.7; $36.7; n/a
Prince George's Community College, $61.8; $46.6; $39.1; n/a
St. Mary's College (MD), $74.7; $55.4; $41.9; n/a
United States Naval Academy, $85.9; $67.1; $55.3; n/a
University of Maryland, College Park, $98.1; $69.2; $64.2; $46.1
University of Maryland, Baltimore, $86.2; $61.1; $52.3; $37.8
University of Maryland, Eastern Shore, $67.7; $61.1; $49.9; $42.4
Bowie State University, $70.8; $56.6; $49.3; $40.1
Frostburg State University, $67.3; $56.6; $47.2; $40.5
Salisbury State University, $68.7; $53.9; $48.3; $43.4
Towson State University, $67.2; $55.8; $45.2; $45.9
Washington College, $64.4; $53.0; $44.8; n/a
Western Maryland College, $65.8; $54.3; $43.3; n/a

Source: "Faculty Salaries at More Than 1,400 Institutions," *The Chronicle of Higher Education*, 47: A20-A23, (April 20, 2001).

★3708★
Average faculty salaries for institutions of higher education in Massachusetts, 2000-01

Ranking basis/background: Average salaries for instructional staff employed full-time for a nine-month work year. **Remarks:** Original source: American Association of University Professors. **Number listed:** 50.

Amherst College, with $97.8 for professors; $65.9 for associate professors; $55.3 for assistant professors; and n/a for instructors
Andover Newton Theological School, n/a; $47.4; n/a; n/a
Babson College, $116.6; $81.7; $76.0; n/a
Bentley College, $92.8; $77.3; $64.9; $50.5
Berklee College of Music, $57.5; $50.5; $45.0; n/a
Boston College, $108.2; $72.6; $57.7; $47.6
Brandeis University, $84.4; $62.0; $52.5; n/a
Clark University, $77.9; $59.2; $51.9; n/a
College of the Holy Cross, $84.2; $62.6; $48.4; n/a
Elms College, $48.3; $39.4; $33.1; n/a
Curry College, $59.3; $47.2; $39.8; n/a
Emerson College, $87.2; $67.4; $49.7; n/a
Endicott College, $51.1; $47.9; $42.7; n/a
Gordon College, $59.4; $49.8; $43.6; n/a
Hampshire College, $68.2; $55.9; $43.8; n/a
Harvard University, $135.2; $79.2; $71.6; $56.9
University of Massachusetts, Amherst, $88.4; $68.7; $54.3; n/a
University of Massachusetts, Boston, $81.9; $67.4; $54.1; n/a
University of Massachusetts, Dartmouth, $76.5; $64.5; $53.5; n/a
University of Massachusetts, Lowell, $84.8; $69.9; $56.0; n/a
Bridgewater State College, $56.6; $49.1; $40.6; $37.0
Westfield State College, $56.3; $49.6; $38.2; n/a
Bunker Hill Community College, $45.7; $39.0; $40.3; $42.2
Cape Cod Community College, $49.4; $39.8; $38.6; n/a
Holyoke Community College, $44.7; $35.8; $36.4; $36.0
Massasoit Community College, $47.7; $37.1; $32.1; $32.8
Mount Wachusett Community College, $47.0; $35.0; $37.5; $35.8
Northern Essex Community College, $47.6; $41.2; $38.7; $36.4
Springfield Technical Community College, $50.1; $42.8; $41.2; $38.7
Massachusetts Institute of Technology, $117.0; $78.7; $72.1; $38.4
Merrimack College, $61.9; $50.7; $45.3; n/a
Mount Holyoke College, $89.8; $65.3; $52.4; n/a
New England College of Optometry, $71.9; $57.8; $45.2; n/a
New England School of Law, $105.1; n/a; n/a; n/a
Northeastern University, $88.1; $64.4; $58.3; n/a
Pine Manor College, $50.4; $38.8; $33.2; n/a
Regis College, $58.6; $49.0; $39.2; n/a
Simmons College, $73.7; $58.2; $48.4; $44.2
Smith College, $94.8; $66.4; $52.9; n/a
Springfield College, $66.7; $51.4; $41.5; $30.9
Stonehill College, $62.8; $51.5; $40.6; n/a
Suffolk University, $91.6; 63.7; $51.6; $40.5
Tufts University, $92.6; $68.4; $52.0; $47.6
Wellesley College, $100.8; $70.7; $57.1; n/a
Western New England College, $84.1; $57.9; $56.6; $40.6
Wheaton College, $84.0; $58.1; $49.3; $41.8
Wheelock College, $70.1; $55.6; $45.5; n/a
Williams College, $98.5; $69.2; $55.6; n/a
Worcester Polytechnic Institute, $88.4; $66.3; $61.9; $46.0

Source: "Faculty Salaries at More Than 1,400 Institutions," *The Chronicle of Higher Education*, 47: A20-A23, (April 20, 2001).

★3709★
Average faculty salaries for institutions of higher education in Michigan, 2000-01

Ranking basis/background: Average salaries for instructional staff employed full-time for a nine-month work year. **Remarks:** Original source: American Association of University Professors. **Number listed:** 29.

Adrian College, with $54.4 for professors; $46.4 for associate professors; $39.6 for assistant professors; and n/a for instructors
Albion College, $62.5; $50.7; $41.4; $35.1
Alma College, $66.4; $53.1; $44.1; n/a
Aquinas College, $47.3; $40.2; $33.9; n/a
Calvin College, $56.4; $48.6; $42.4; n/a
Central Michigan University, $71.5; $55.9; $46.2; $35.7
Cleary College, n/a; $41.4; n/a; n/a
Cornerstone University, $43.7; $39.6; $32.6; n/a
Ferris State University, $61.9; $54.0; $46.6; $41.8
Finlandia University, n/a; $36.9; n/a; n/a
Grand Valley State University, $73.5; $58.9; $47.0; $41.8
Hope College, $62.5; $49.1; $41.1; n/a
Kalamazoo College, $64.9; $50.3; $43.0; n/a
Lake Superior State University, $62.6; $50.7; $43.9; n/a
Madonna University, $59.1; $49.4; $43.0; $37.1
Michigan State University, $85.2; $63.9; $51.2; $33.8
Michigan Technological University, $81.2; $60.7; $53.9; $35.1
North Central Michigan College, $56.1; n/a; n/a; $47.9
Northern Michigan University, $67.3; $54.1; $42.3; $36.9
Oakland University, $76.8; $60.9; $52.2; $43.5
Olivet College, $45.7; $41.4; $37.5; n/a
Sacred Heart Major Seminary, n/a; n/a; $40.9; n/a
Siena Heights University, $54.3; $44.0; $38.8; n/a
Spring Arbor College, $43.4; $33.9; $32.1; $30.6

University of Michigan, Ann Arbor, $105.2; $73.3; $59.7; $54.2
University of Michigan, Dearborn, $74.2; $59.4; $51.3; n/a
University of Michigan, Flint, $69.0; $55.8; $45.7; n/a
Wayne State University, $87.2; $67.0; $52.5; $45.7
Western Michigan University, $77.5; $60.3; $49.3; $36.6

Source: "Faculty Salaries at More Than 1,400 Institutions," *The Chronicle of Higher Education*, 47: A20-A23, (April 20, 2001).

★3710★
Average faculty salaries for institutions of higher education in Minnesota, 2000-01

Ranking basis/background: Average salaries for instructional staff employed full-time for a nine-month work year. **Remarks:** Original source: American Association of University Professors. **Number listed:** 26.

Augsburg College, with $55.0 for professors; $45.5 for associate professors; $39.2 for assistant professors; and $31.8 for instructors
Bethel College, $53.9; $46.4; $39.8; $37.6
Carleton College, $82.2; $60.9; $50.6; n/a
College of St. Benedict, $57.9; $49.9; $42.0; $36.1
College of St. Scholastica, $48.7; $43.1; $39.6; $34.8
Concordia College, Moorhead, $60.8; $50.9; $41.0; $35.9
Gustavus Adolphus College, $64.3; $52.4; $43.7; $39.3
Hamline University, $70.0; $51.7; $38.9; $40.8
Macalester College, $82.9; $62.1; $48.3; $39.5
Minneapolis College of Art and Design, $55.4; $45.5; n/a; n/a
Bemidji State University, $60.6; $48.6; $43.5; $34.4
Metropolitan State University, $64.3; $53.5; $45.3; n/a
Minnesota State University, Mankato, $66.3; $57.3; $46.6; $34.4
Minnesota State University, Moorhead, $61.4; $35.1; $43.4; $31.3
St. Cloud State University, $63.9; $53.1; $46.5; $21.8
Southwest State University, $63.5; $53.2; $46.0; $35.9
Winona State University, $64.8; $52.0; $43.3; $32.6
Northwestern College, $48.3; $42.0; $38.8; n/a
St. John's University, $62.2; $48.9; $40.7; $37.0
St. Mary's University (MN), $54.7; $46.3; $38.1; $30.1
St. Olaf College, $65.5; $53.5; $42.4; $41.1
University of Minnesota, Crookston, n/a; $46.6; $44.2; n/a
University of Minnesota, Duluth, $73.6; $58.5; $47.6; $34.4
University of Minnesota, Morris, $66.7; $53.3; $38.7; $36.6
University of Minnesota, Twin Cities, $93.6; $66.1; $55.4; $47.1
University of St. Thomas, $70.1; $55.2; $44.9; $41.3

Source: "Faculty Salaries at More Than 1,400 Institutions," *The Chronicle of Higher Education*, 47: A20-A23, (April 20, 2001).

★3711★
Average faculty salaries for institutions of higher education in Mississippi, 2000-01

Ranking basis/background: Average salaries for instructional staff employed full-time for a nine-month work year. **Remarks:** Original source: American Association of University Professors. **Number listed:** 8.

Alcorn State University, with $57.0 for professors; $49.6 for associate professors; $44.4 for assistant professors; and $31.6 for instructors
Delta State University, $52.0; $45.5; $40.7; $36.1
Jackson State University, $56.9; $52.8; $42.7; $33.9
Millsaps College, $64.3; $48.3; $42.2; n/a
Mississippi State University, $73.8; $56.0; $47.4; $33.4
Mississippi University for Women, $52.5; $45.0; $39.0; $37.6
University of Mississippi, $72.9; $57.2; $45.0; $26.2
University of Southern Mississippi, $68.7; $52.3; $42.7; $36.7

Source: "Faculty Salaries at More Than 1,400 Institutions," *The Chronicle of Higher Education*, 47: A20-A23, (April 20, 2001).

★3712★
Average faculty salaries for institutions of higher education in Missouri, 2000-01

Ranking basis/background: Average salaries for instructional staff employed full-time for a nine-month work year. **Remarks:** Original source: American Association of University Professors. **Number listed:** 31.

Avila College, with $48.6 for professors; $43.0 for associate professors; $37.6 for assistant professors; and n/a for instructors
Central Missouri State University, $61.9; $52.2; $42.8; $32.0
College of the Ozarks, $52.0; $47.0; $40.2; n/a
Columbia College, $47.8; $41.5; $39.0; $35.2
Cottey College, $52.3; $41.7; n/a; n/a
Covenant Theological Seminary, $49.0; $44.3; n/a; n/a
Culver-Stockton College, $45.2; $42.0; $36.6; n/a
Drury College, $60.5; $48.4; $40.7; $38.2
Harris-Stowe State College, $55.7; $49.1; $40.7; $38.2
Kansas City Art Institute, $51.0; $44.2; $36.1; $28.4
Lincoln University, $56.7; $44.4; $36.1; $28.4
Maryville University, St. Louis, $57.0; $47.3; $41.1; n/a
Missouri Baptist College, n/a; $37.3; $37.3; $33.2
Missouri Southern State College, $59.4; $47.6; $39.4; $35.5
Missouri Western State College, $57.4; $47.4; $40.1; n/a
Northwest Missouri State University, $65.0; $51.5; $42.6; $33.8
Rockhurst University, $65.1; $52.0; $40.1; n/a
St. Charles County Community College, $52.4; $45.8; $38.5; n/a
St. Louis College of Pharmacy, $69.2; $57.2; $49.5; $22.5
St. Louis University, $84.9; $59.8; $48.7; $41.0
Southeast Missouri State University, $63.9; $52.2; $42.1; $35.7
Southwest Missouri State University, $65.1; $52.1; $43.6; $40.2
Truman State University, $64.4; $52.5; $40.2; $33.6
University of Missouri, Columbia, $84.4; $61.9; $50.8
University of Missouri, Kansas City, $83.4; $58.7; $47.0; $44.8
University of Missouri, Rolla, $87.5; $65.2; $54.0; $36.9
University of Missouri, St. Louis, $78.1; $57.8; $48.0; n/a
Washington University (MO), $106.4; $67.0; $64.7; n/a
Webster University, $66.3; $49.5; $41.0; n/a
Westminster College, $51.2; $44.0; $38.4; n/a
William Jewell College, $57.8; $45.9; $40.3; n/a

Source: "Faculty Salaries at More Than 1,400 Institutions," *The Chronicle of Higher Education*, 47: A20-A23, (April 20, 2001).

★3713★
Average faculty salaries for institutions of higher education in Montana, 2000-01

Ranking basis/background: Average salaries for instructional staff employed full-time for a nine-month work year. **Remarks:** Original source: American Association of University Professors. **Number listed:** 6.

Carroll College, with $45.1 for professors; $40.1 for associate professors; $32.0 for assistant professors; and n/a for instructors
Montana State University, Bozeman, $64.8; $51.1; $43.8; $30.2
Montana State University, Billings, $54.3; $43.9; $39.4; n/a
University of Montana, $64.5; $49.1; $43.3; $38.5
Montana Tech, $56.4; $46.8; $41.7; $36.1
Western Montana College, $49.0; $40.4; $36.7; $30.9

Source: "Faculty Salaries at More Than 1,400 Institutions," *The Chronicle of Higher Education*, 47: A20-A23, (April 20, 2001).

★3714★
Average faculty salaries for institutions of higher education in Nebraska, 2000-01

Ranking basis/background: Average salaries for instructional staff employed full-time for a nine-month work year. **Remarks:** Original source: American Association of University Professors. **Number listed:** 13.

Concordia University, with $35.4 for professors; $33.6 for associate professors; $30.1 for assistant professors; and n/a for instructors
Creighton UNIVERSITY, $84.1; $57.7; $45.1; $36.3
Doane College, $55.8; $47.7; $39.1; 30.6

SALARIES—COLLEGES & UNIVERSITIES, FACULTY

Grace University, n/a; $36.5; $29.2; n/a
Hastings College, $53.7; $42.4; $38.5; $35.6
Midland Lutheran College, $49.6; $41.3; $37.2; $30.9
Chadron State College, $57.2; $44.3; $37.5; $31.1
Peru State College, $55.1; $38.9; $35.9; $33.1
Wayne State College, $51.8; $44.8; $37.5; $27.6
Nebraska Wesleyan University, $58.9; $47.0; $39.2; n/a
University of Nebraska, Kearney, $60.5; $51.6; $41.3; $42.2
University of Nebraska, Lincoln, $81.5; $58.4; $49.7; n/a
University of Nebraska, Omaha, $64.8; $57.0; $45.4; $33.3

Source: "Faculty Salaries at More Than 1,400 Institutions," *The Chronicle of Higher Education*, 47: A20-A23, (April 20, 2001).

★3715★
Average faculty salaries for institutions of higher education in Nevada, 2000-01

Ranking basis/background: Average salaries for instructional staff employed full-time for a nine-month work year. **Remarks:** Original source: American Association of University Professors. **Number listed:** 3.

University of Nevada, Las Vegas, with $83.3 for professors; $62.7 for associate professors; $48.9 for assistant professors; and n/a for instructors
University of Nevada, Reno, $85.7; $62.6; $50.1; $39.3
Great Basin College, $50.1; n/a; n/a; $39.8

Source: "Faculty Salaries at More Than 1,400 Institutions," *The Chronicle of Higher Education*, 47: A20-A23, (April 20, 2001).

★3716★
Average faculty salaries for institutions of higher education in New Hampshire, 2000-01

Ranking basis/background: Average salaries for instructional staff employed full-time for a nine-month work year. **Remarks:** Original source: American Association of University Professors. **Number listed:** 14.

Dartmouth College, with $101.5 for professors; $72.7 for associate professors; $60.3 for assistant professors; and $42.4 for instructors
Franklin Pierce Law Center, $86.6; n/a; n/a; n/a
New England College, $44.6; $36.3; $28.4; n/a
New Hampshire College, $70.9; $53.6; $44.9; n/a
New Hampshire Community Tech College Berlin/Laconia, $43.3; $37.5; $33.4; $31.2
New Hampshire Community Tech College Manchester/Stratham, $42.2; $36.4; $32.3; n/a
New Hampshire Community Tech College Nashua/Claremont, $43.6; $36.9; $33.2; n/a
New Hampshire Technical Institute, $42.8; $36.3; n/a; n/a
Notre Dame College, n/a; $36.2; $33.2; $35.2
Rivier College, $50.6; $45.5; $41.3; $38.2

St. Anselm College, $60.5; $47.3; $41.4; $35.2
University of New Hampshire, $80.1; $60.4; $46.9; n/a
Keene State College, $62.8; $50.2; $41.1; $36.4
Plymouth State College, $63.1; $49.5; $41.9; n/a

Source: "Faculty Salaries at More Than 1,400 Institutions," *The Chronicle of Higher Education*, 47: A20-A23, (April 20, 2001).

★3717★
Average faculty salaries for institutions of higher education in New Jersey, 2000-01

Ranking basis/background: Average salaries for instructional staff employed full-time for a nine-month work year. **Remarks:** Original source: American Association of University Professors. **Number listed:** 21.

Bloomfield College, with $63.7 for professors; $52.4 for associate professors; $44.2 for assistant professors; and n/a for instructors
Caldwell College, $60.3; $45.8; $37.3; n/a
College of New Jersey, $81.4; $65.2; $51.1; n/a
College of St. Elizabeth, $55.7; $48.8; $41.5; n/a
Cumberland County College, n/a; $59.6; $41.0; n/a
Drew University, $75.5; $54.0; $42.5; n/a
Felician College, n/a; $46.5; $42.7; $39.2
Georgian Court College, $59.4; $49.2; $42.2; n/a
Gloucester County College, $80.4; $74.9; $69.4; $54.2
Monmouth University, $82.6; $66.5; $49.3; $32.4
Montclair State University, $81.0; $65.1; $51.1; $32.4
Passaic County Community College, $85.1; $66.1; $47.4; $35.4
Princeton University, $125.7; $80.2; $62.6; $56.4
Ramapo College, $81.1; $64.2; $50.3; n/a
Rider University, $76.8; $68.4; $51.4; n/a
Rutgers University, Camden, $103.9; $76.2; $56.2; $37.1
Rutgers University, New Brunswick, $102.4; $72.8; $55.3; $35.3
Rutgers University, Newark, $110.1; $79.9; $61.7; $43.4
St. Peter's College, $63.5; $53.3; $42.0; $37.3
Salem Community College, n/a; n/a; $45.4; $37.3
William Paterson University, $80.6; $64.3; $50.4; $41.9

Source: "Faculty Salaries at More Than 1,400 Institutions," *The Chronicle of Higher Education*, 47: A20-A23, (April 20, 2001).

★3718★
Average faculty salaries for institutions of higher education in New Mexico, 2000-01

Ranking basis/background: Average salaries for instructional staff employed full-time for a nine-month work year. **Remarks:** Original source: American Association of University Professors. **Number listed:** 11.

College of Sante Fe, with $54.4 for professors; $46.9 for associate professors; $37.8 for assistant professors; and n/a for instructors
Eastern New Mexico University, $55.7; $44.8; $38.9; $34.4
New Mexico State University, $63.5; $50.5; $43.7; $28.8
New Mexico State University, Alamogordo, n/a; $38.6; $35.0; $30.5
New Mexico State University, Carlsbad, n/a; $39.3; n/a; $32.5
New Mexico State University, Dona Ana, $42.0; $36.1; $34.1; $30.5
New Mexico State University, Grants, n/a; n/a; n/a; $34.7
University of New Mexico, $73.5; $54.3; $47.4; n/a
University of New Mexico, Gallup, n/a; n/a; $39.4; n/a
University of New Mexico, Valencia, n/a; $42.6; n/a; n/a
Western New Mexico University, $50.9; $37.4; $33.9; n/a

Source: "Faculty Salaries at More Than 1,400 Institutions," *The Chronicle of Higher Education*, 47: A20-A23, (April 20, 2001).

★3719★
Average faculty salaries for institutions of higher education in New York, 2000-01

Ranking basis/background: Average salaries for instructional staff employed full-time for a nine-month work year. **Remarks:** Original source: American Association of University Professors. **Number listed:** 124.

Adelphi University, with $76.5 for professors; $63.7 for associate professors; $54.3 for assistant professors; and n/a for instructors
Albany College of Pharmacy, $75.7; $57.4; $51.4; $38.0
Albany Law School, $110.6; $79.9; n/a; n/a
Alfred University, $65.7; $48.5; $41.4; n/a
Bard College, $86.2; $61.4; $48.1; n/a
Canisius College, $64.6; $58.1; $44.1; n/a
Cazenovia College, $52.1; $41.6; $37.1; n/a
Clarkson University, $82.3; $62.6; $54.2; $47.4
Colgate University, $95.4; $70.4; $52.8; n/a
College of Aeronautics, $55.9; $51.6; $42.8; $39.4
College of New Rochelle, $74.2; $56.6; $47.0; n/a
College of St. Rose, $61.1; $49.8; $40.5; $35.6
Columbia University, $120.2; $76.0; $60.0; $81.6
Columbia University, Barnard College, $95.7; $62.8; $51.7; n/a
Cooper Union, $68.3; $62.5; n/a; n/a
Cornell University, Endowed Colleges, $103.0; $75.8; $66.4; n/a
Daemen College, $53.2; $45.3; $39.3; n/a
Dominican College, Blauvelt, $56.7; $48.4; $44.7; $37.1
Elmira College, $60.7; $44.5; $38.4; n/a
Fordham University, $97.2; $72.1; $54.9; $43.4
Hamilton College, $84.3; $63.6; $48.6; n/a
Hartwick College, $63.9; $51.0; $41.6; n/a
Hilbert College, $45.2; $40.4; $35.8; n/a

Hobart and William Smith College, $72.8; $56.1; $41.3; $35.0
Hofstra University, $97.2; $67.8; $52.8; $43.9
Houghton College, $51.5; $45.8; $37.3; n/a
Iona College, $74.6; $57.4; $46.3; n/a
Ithaca College, $69.9; $55.7; $42.2; $37.3
Keuka College, $48.6; $42.7; $38.0; n/a
Le Moyne College, $72.1; $59.1; $43.3; n/a
Long Island University, $83.6; $63.8; $56.1; $49.7
Manhattan College, $75.2; $61.6; $50.1; $39.3
Marist College, $69.4; $57.9; $45.7; n/a
Marymount College, $50.2; $48.4; $40.9; n/a
Marymount Manhattan College, $61.0; $48.8; $38.5; n/a
Medaille College, $61.8; $47.6; $41.2; n/a
Mercy College, $68.0; $64.9; $50.4; $46.7
Molloy College, $69.7; $50.0; $43.5; n/a
Mount St. Mary College, $62.0; $50.5; $42.0; n/a
Nazareth College of Rochester, $62.1; $52.5; $42.6; n/a
New York Institute of Technology, $84.5; $66.3; $56.1; n/a
New York University, $120.8; $76.0; $66.7; $35.8
Niagara University, $64.0; $53.6; $44.4; $39.2
Pace University, $96.1; $73.1; $58.3; n/a
Polytechnic University, $86.6; $64.0; $59.9; $37.0
Pratt Institute, $50.9; $45.2; $38.4; n/a
Rensselaer Polytechnic Institute, $93.4; $65.7; $57.9; n/a
Rochester Institute of Technology, $82.3; $64.1; $52.6; $45.4
Rockefeller University, $138.1; $85.2; $56.4; $38.5
St. Bonaventure University, $55.1; $45.6; $42.5; n/a
St. Francis College, $71.4; n/a; $42.1; $32.1
St. John Fisher College, $59.8; $52.4; $43.7; n/a
St. John's University (NY), $101.1; $67.9; $55.7; n/a
St. Joseph's College, $71.6; $55.2; $45.8; $34.7
St. Lawrence University, $75.3; $55.2; $42.6; n/a
St. Thomas Aquinas College, $67.7; $52.8; $45.4; n/a
Sarah Lawrence College, $80.5; $63.2; $48.7; n/a
Siena College, $63.2; $53.5; $45.1; $34.8
Skidmore College, $80.1; $61.2; $47.5; n/a
State University of New York, Albany, $88.5; $63.4; $52.2; n/a
State University of New York, Binghamton, $85.5; $63.6; $52.4; $41.7
State University of New York, Buffalo, $94.5; $67.4; $54.5; n/a
State University of New York, Farmingdale, $75.6; $57.4; $47.8; $40.3
State University of New York, New Paltz, $69.8; $54.7; $44.7; n/a
State University of New York, Stony Brook, $93.8; $67.3; $55.6; n/a
State University of New York, College at Brockport, $73.9; $62.2; $46.8; $41.9
State University of New York, College at Buffalo, $63.5; $52.9; $46.4; n/a
State University of New York, College at Cortland, $62.8; $49.6; $40.6; n/a
State University of New York, College at Fredonia, $65.0; $50.7; $40.5; $31.5
State University of New York, College at Geneseo, $63.8; $51.8; $43.4; $36.3
State University of New York, College at Old Westbury, $72.5; $54.8; $42.6; $38.1
State University of New York, College at Oneonta, $65.0; $51.9; $43.4; n/a
State University of New York, College at Oswego, $62.9; $53.3; $42.7; n/a
State University of New York, College at Plattsburgh, $62.5; $51.8; $41.6; n/a
State University of New York, College at Potsdam, $63.4; $47.1; $39.9; $31.0
State University of New York, College at Purchase, $67.4; $55.1; $42.5; n/a
State University of New York, College of A&T, Cobleskill, $53.8; $45.9; $40.4; $33.6
State University of New York, College of A&T, Morrisville, $55.7; $47.0; $41.0; 34.7
State University of New York, College of Environmental Science and Forestry, $73.3; $56.2; $49.7; n/a
State University of New York, College of Optometry, $83.2; $69.5; $51.8; $22.4
State University of New York College of Technology, Alfred, $57.9; $46.3; $40.4; $33.6
State University of New York College of Technology, Canton, $54.0; $48.0; $43.1; $37.2
State University of New York College of Technology, Delhi, $55.0; $46.1; $40.8; $35.1
State University of New York College of Technology, Utica-Rome, $66.4; $58.2; $51.8; n/a
Empire State College, $63.9; $53.3; $44.1; n/a
Maritime College, $57.7; $53.1; $41.8; n/a
New York State College of Ceramics, Alfred University, $68.9; $60.8; $45.8; n/a
Cornell University Statutory Colleges, $85.5; $65.9; $54.7; $36.4
Fashion Institute of Technology, $86.1; $70.3; $58.0; $42.4
Adirondack Community College, $56.9; $42.1; $39.6; n/a
Broome Community College, $60.9; $54.4; $40.8; n/a
Cayuga County Community College, $60.1; n/a; $43.8; $38.8
Clinton Community College, $47.0; $41.0; $32.6; n/a
Columbia-Greene Community College, $47.6; $48.5; $35.9; $34.3
Corning Community College, $58.7; $42.7; $35.1; $31.1
Dutchess Community College, $62.1; $51.5; $42.1; $33.4
Finger Lakes Community College, $64.5; $52.0; $39.7; $33.5
Fulton-Montgomery Community College, $68.1; $58.4; $44.9; $34.3
Genesee Community College, $58.2; $46.7; $40.9; $32.1
Herkimer County Community College, $46.7; $42.6; $37.0; n/a
Hudson Valley Community College, $67.5; $55.4; $42.8; $34.7
Jamestown Community College, $53.5; $45.6; $39.4; $34.5
Jefferson Community College, $65.3; $50.3; $43.4; $36.6
Mohawk Valley Community College, $56.0; $43.3; $37.1; $29.7
Monroe Community College, $69.9; $55.3; $43.7; $34.4
Nassau Community College, $84.4; $66.4; $56.7; $46.8
Niagara County Community College, $69.8; $59.7; $50.5; $37.9
North Country Community College, n/a; n/a; $38.6; $31.1
Onondaga Community College, $60.1; $51.3; $43.7; $39.1
Orange County Community College, $60.4; $48.9; $39.8; $33.3
Schenectady County Community College, $50.5; $39.3; $33.7; n/a
Suffolk County Community College, Ammerman, $80.7; $58.5; $52.1; $44.3
Suffolk County Community College, Eastern, $77.3; $59.6; $52.8; $44.9
Suffolk County Community College, Western, $77.4; $60.9; $53.4; $44.5
Sullivan County Community College, $52.0; $42.8; $37.1; $32.8
Tompkins-Cortland Community College, $57.2; $41.6; n/a; n/a
Ulster County Community College, $60.8; $50.2; $41.8; $36.2
Westchester Community College, $87.2; $76.3; $62.7; n/a
Syracuse University, $78.6; $61.0; $49.0; $45.1
Union College, $83.7; $64.1; $49.6; n/a
University of Rochester, $94.3; $68.6; $64.2; n/a
Vassar College, $92.0; $65.0; $49.6; $43.3
Wagner College, $66.0; $52.5; $44.2; n/a
Wells College, $58.8; $47.5; $38.2; n/a

Source: "Faculty Salaries at More Than 1,400 Institutions," *The Chronicle of Higher Education*, 47: A20-A23, (April 20, 2001).

★3720★
Average faculty salaries for institutions of higher education in North Carolina, 2000-01

Ranking basis/background: Average salaries for instructional staff employed full-time for a nine-month work year. **Remarks:** Original source: American Association of University Professors. **Number listed:** 45.

Barber-Scotia College, with $38.8 for professors; n/a for associate professors; $31.1 for assistant professors; and n/a for instructors
Barton College, $46.2; $39.4; $33.5; n/a
Belmont Abbey College, $46.6; $42.6; $32.7; n/a
Brevard College, $52.0; $37.8; $31.1; $25.3
Catawba College, $51.0; $45.5; $38.0; $30.6
Chowan College, $46.3; $40.5; $36.9; $32.5
Davidson College, $80.1; $57.5; $45.8; n/a
Duke University, $113.6; $75.7; $62.5; n/a
Elon College, $62.8; $50.8; $44.3; $34.2
Gardner-Webb University, $48.8; $44.2; $40.9; $33.0
Greensboro College, $52.7; $46.9; $37.9; n/a

SALARIES—COLLEGES & UNIVERSITIES, FACULTY

Guilford College, $50.1; $46.9; $37.9; $36.3
High Point University, $64.1; $51.1; $44.1; $36.6
Lees-McRae College, $36.8; $35.2; $32.9; $29.8
Lenoir-Rhyne College, $42.9; $43.9; $36.1; $27.2
Mars Hill College, $45.1; $38.8; $35.0; $27.6
Meredith College, $60.0; $47.2; $40.6; n/a
Methodist College, $45.1; $40.8; $34.1; n/a
Montreat College, n/a; $42.0; $36.5; n/a
Richmond Community College, $55.8; n/a; $42.4; $36.9
Sandhills Community College, $46.7; $37.8; n/a; $35.3
North Carolina Wesleyan College, $44.2; $38.1; $35.2; n/a
Pfeiffer University, $43.3; $35.6; $32.0; n/a
Queens College, $54.6; $46.7; $34.7; n/a
St. Andrews Presbyterian College, $39.9; $34.2; $32.1; n/a
Salem College, $47.6; $42.8; $36.0; n/a
Shaw University, n/a; $44.3; $36.6; $32.0
Appalachian State University, $67.1; $55.9; $45.1; $40.9
East Carolina University, $73.2; $57.6; $48.9; $42.4
Elizabeth City State University, $59.9; $47.1; $42.5; n/a
Fayetteville State University, $67.4; $56.3; $49.5; n/a
North Carolina A&T State University, $69.4; $59.1; $50.9; $36.7
North Carolina Central University, $75.9; $58.3; $49.0; n/a
North Carolina State University, $91.5; $66.5; $56.8; $49.4
University of North Carolina, Asheville, $67.3; $51.6; $40.9; n/a
University of North Carolina, Chapel Hill, $100.9; $71.4; $58.4; $60.5
University of North Carolina, Charlotte, $78.5; $59.0; $50.0; n/a
University of North Carolina, Greensboro, $78.8; $56.9; $46.6; $49.7
University of North Carolina, Pembroke, $72.6; $55.3; $45.8; n/a
University of North Carolina, Wilmington, $69.9; $54.7; $48.0; n/a
Western Carolina University, $67.1; $54.7; $45.8; n/a
Winston-Salem State University, $65.3; $56.4; $47.7; $38.8
Wake Forest University, $95.3; $69.0; $51.2; $36.3
Warren Wilson College, $49.4; $41.1; $35.6; $35.4
Wingate University, $43.1; $39.7; $36.4; $31.5

Source: "Faculty Salaries at More Than 1,400 Institutions," *The Chronicle of Higher Education*, 47: A20-A23, (April 20, 2001).

★3721★
Average faculty salaries for institutions of higher education in North Dakota, 2000-01

Ranking basis/background: Average salaries for instructional staff employed full-time for a nine-month work year. **Remarks:** Original source: American Association of University Professors. **Number listed:** 9.

Jamestown College, with $45.3 for professors; $38.1 for associate professors; $36.2 for assistant professors; and $29.4 for instructors
University of North Dakota, $57.1; $48.6; $42.3; $39.0
Dickinson State University, $46.8; $42.4; $36.6; n/a
Mayville State University, $44.6; $38.4; $34.1; $29.1
Minot State University, $50.5; $45.5; $39.6; $33.7
North Dakota State University, $60.3; $50.7; $44.8; n/a
Valley City State University, $48.0; $41.1; $35.5; $31.2
Bismarck State College, n/a; $40.2; $36.6; $31.3
North Dakota State College of Science, n/a; $38.8; $32.7; $31.9
Williston State College, n/a; n/a; n/a; $34.7

Source: "Faculty Salaries at More Than 1,400 Institutions," *The Chronicle of Higher Education*, 47: A20-A23, (April 20, 2001).

★3722★
Average faculty salaries for institutions of higher education in Ohio, 2000-01

Ranking basis/background: Average salaries for instructional staff employed full-time for a nine-month work year. **Remarks:** Original source: American Association of University Professors. **Number listed:** 75.

Antioch University, with $53.8 for professors; $44.1 for associate professors; $36.5 for assistant professors; and n/a for instructors
Antioch University, McGregor, $35.3; $37.6; n/a; n/a
Baldwin-Wallace College, $61.8; $49.8; $41.0; n/a
Blufton College, $51.4; $41.3; $36.8; n/a
Bowling Green State University, $74.2; $58.2; $46.1; $32.9
Bowling Green State University, Firelands College, n/a; $55.6; $47.6; n/a
Capital University, $69.5; $44.6; $37.4; $27.5
Case Western Reserve University, $92.9; $67.2; $56.8; $45.3
Cedarville University, $55.5; $47.2; $39.0; n/a
Central State University, $54.9; $48.3; $42.2; n/a
Cleveland State University, $72.5; $56.9; $45.2; $35.9
College of Mount St. Joseph, $56.5; $47.4; $40.3; $33.1
College of Wooster, $65.3; $51.2; $41.9; n/a
Defiance College, $43.8; $41.1; $37.2; n/a
Denison University, $72.8; $52.3; $43.7; n/a
Franciscan University of Steubenville, $52.0; $43.6; $37.6; $30.0
Heidelberg College, $54.7; $44.1; $38.7; $31.2
Hiram College, $59.7; $45.2; $37.6; n/a
John Carroll University, $73.5; $56.2; $46.9; $36.2
Kent State University, $83.1; $61.4; $48.0; n/a
Kent State University, Ashtabula, n/a; n/a; $52.3; n/a
Kent State University, East Liverpool, n/a; n/a; $43.0; n/a
Kent State University, Geauga, n/a; n/a; $45.0; n/a
Kent State University, Salem, n/a; $56.0; $49.7; n/a
Kent State University, Stark, n/a; $59.8; $48.3; n/a
Kent State University, Trumbull, n/a; $60.9; $47.1; $45.4
Kent State University, Tuscarawas, n/a; $60.9; $41.4; n/a
Kenyon College, $72.4; $52.6; $42.7; n/a
Lorain County Community College, $63.8; $58.0; $48.1; $39.2
Malone College, $51.6; $43.8; $38.1; n/a
Marietta College, $57.8; $45.6; $38.4; n/a
Methodist Theological School Ohio, $57.0; n/a; n/a; n/a
Miami University, Oxford, $82.4; $60.0; $45.9; $32.2
Miami University, Hamilton, n/a; $61.3; $40.9; $30.6
Miami University, Middletown, $74.5; $56.1; $44.3; $30.9
Mount Union College, $61.2; $47.7; $40.7; $35.0
Muskingum College, $57.5; $45.3; $37.7; n/a
North Central State College, $42.7; $39.4; $37.7; $35.4
Notre Dame College, $42.4; $38.1; $31.8; n/a
Oberlin College, $82.3; $63.7; $51.7; n/a
Ohio Dominican College, $57.1; $48.4; $40.0; $33.2
Ohio Northern University, $66.6; $54.0; $46.4; $35.2
Ohio State University, $92.2; $63.8; $54.4; $57.0
Ohio State University A&T Institute, n/a; $54.4; $43.1; n/a
Ohio State University, Lima, n/a; $55.2; $40.8; n/a
Ohio State University, Mansfield, n/a; $53.8; $44.2; n/a
Ohio State University, Marion, $70.6; $51.6; $41.4; n/a
Ohio State University, Newark, $70.3; $53.9; $42.8; n/a
Ohio University, $79.0; $58.8; $48.0; n/a
Ohio University, Chillicothe, n/a; $51.0; $41.4; n/a
Ohio University, Eastern, n/a; n/a; $45.2; n/a
Ohio University, Lancaster, n/a; $53.5; $42.3; n/a
Ohio University, Zanesville, n/a; $53.9; $42.6; n/a
Ohio Wesleyan University, $61.0; $44.4; $41.0; n/a
Otterbein College, $58.9; $47.6; $42.0; n/a
Shawnee State University, $59.3; $50.3; $41.9; $32.0
Sinclair Community College, $60.2; $46.2; $38.4; $34.8
Southern State Community College, n/a; $48.4; $42.4; $33.7
Terra State Community College, $52.2; $46.5; $42.1; n/a
Tiffin University, $61.3; $46.5; $44.8; n/a
University of Akron, $73.1; $55.9; $47.6; $39.9
University of Akron, Wayne College, n/a; $54.0; $40.4; n/a
University of Cincinnati, $80.5; $60.1; $48.2; $37.9

Clermont College, $57.6; $45.2; $34.1; n/a
Raymond Waters College, $61.5; $49.1; $36.9; n/a
University of Dayton, $75.3; $57.8; $46.5; n/a
University of Findlay, $53.6; $47.9; $39.7; $30.8
University of Rio Grande, $53.0; $45.5; $40.1; n/a
Urbana University, $39.5; $33.9; $29.2; $26.5
Ursuline College, n/a; $41.4; $36.1; $31.8
Walsh University, $49.9; $41.7; $38.3; n/a
Wilmington College, $48.9; $42.0; $37.3; n/a
Wittenberg University, $62.9; $48.8; $39.8; $37.3
Wright State University, $77.6; $57.6; $47.4; $32.9
Wright State University, Lake, n/a; $52.5; n/a; n/a
Xavier University, $69.5; $56.9; $45.5; $38.6
Youngstown State University, $69.1; $52.9; $44.0; $33.3

Source: "Faculty Salaries at More Than 1,400 Institutions," *The Chronicle of Higher Education,* 47: A20-A23, (April 20, 2001).

★3723★
Average faculty salaries for institutions of higher education in Oklahoma, 2000-01

Ranking basis/background: Average salaries for instructional staff employed full-time for a nine-month work year. **Remarks:** Original source: American Association of University Professors.
Number listed: 15.
Cameron University, with $54.6 for professors; $46.0 for associate professors; $41.0 for assistant professors; and $29.8 for instructors
East Central University, $53.2; $45.3; $39.7; $34.7
Northeastern State University, $57.5; $50.2; $43.1; $37.4
Oklahoma Baptist University, $45.5; $39.9; $34.9; $26.6
Oklahoma Christian University, $53.6; $44.2; $38.0; n/a
Oklahoma City University, $60.3; $49.1; $36.4; $34.9
Oklahoma State University, $73.1; $55.7; $48.0; $37.4
Oklahoma State University, Oklahoma City, $50.8; $40.5; $35.8; $30.2
Oklahoma State University, Tech, n/a; n/a; n/a; $34.6
Oral Roberts University, $51.6; $41.8; $34.8; $29.5
Southeastern Oklahoma State University, $56.6; $47.9; $41.8; $34.4
Southwestern Oklahoma State University, Weatherford, $56.9; $49.2; $39.5; $32.9
Southwestern Oklahoma State University, Syre, n/a; n/a; n/a; $32.7
University of Central Oklahoma, $59.0; $52.2; $46.2; $38.7
University of Oklahoma, $81.3; $55.3; $44.8; $28.2
University of Science and Arts of Oklahoma, $48.0; $39.4; $36.2; $33.0
University of Tulsa, $80.7; $58.3; $48.8; $31.8

Source: "Faculty Salaries at More Than 1,400 Institutions," *The Chronicle of Higher Education,* 47: A20-A23, (April 20, 2001).

★3724★
Average faculty salaries for institutions of higher education in Oregon, 2000-01

Ranking basis/background: Average salaries for instructional staff employed full-time for a nine-month work year. **Remarks:** Original source: American Association of University Professors.
Number listed: 14.
George Fox University, with $54.1 for professors; $46.5 for associate professors; $40.6 for assistant professors; and n/a for instructors
Linfield College, $58.8; $44.3; $37.4; n/a
Multnomah Bible College and Biblical Seminary, $43.1; n/a; $38.0; $32.2
Eastern Oregon University, $51.9; $41.0; $35.4; n/a
Oregon Institute of Technology, $56.7; $49.3; $43.9; $35.8
Oregon State University, $75.9; $59.9; $48.7; $34.7
Portland State University, $68.5; $52.4; $45.7; $34.0
Southern Oregon University, $55.7; $47.6; $38.7; $33.3
University of Oregon, $75.6; $55.4; $47.0; $36.1
Western Oregon University, $51.6; $43.0; $35.4; $28.0
Pacific University (OR), $62.4; $49.0; $40.6; $26.1
Reed College, $76.6; $57.4; $48.3; n/a
Warner Pacific College, $44.4; $37.1; $31.5; n/a
Western Baptist College, $43.7; $37.1; $32.3; n/a

Source: "Faculty Salaries at More Than 1,400 Institutions," *The Chronicle of Higher Education,* 47: A20-A23, (April 20, 2001).

★3725★
Average faculty salaries for institutions of higher education in Pennsylvania, 2000-01

Ranking basis/background: Average salaries for instructional staff employed full-time for a nine-month work year. **Remarks:** Original source: American Association of University Professors.
Number listed: 95.
Albright College, with $56.6 for professors; $48.4 for associate professors; $39.9 for assistant professors; and $27.0 for instructors
Allegheny College, $66.1; $52.1; $40.5; n/a
American College, $75.9; $75.9; n/a; n/a
Arcadia University, $73.0; $58.2; $47.6; $43.6
Bryn Mawr College, $89.6; $64.4; $50.6; $35.1
Bucknell University, $84.5; $63.9; $51.7; n/a
Butler County Community College, $52.5; $44.8; $36.7; $33.2
Cabrini College, $57.5; $48.2; $38.4; n/a
Carlow College, n/a; $63.2; $39.4; $31.7
Carnegie Mellon University, $105.0; $73.5; $68.1; n/a
Cedar Crest College, $59.6; $48.8; $40.5; $31.8
Chatham College, $61.1; $51.2; $42.5; n/a
Chestnut Hill College, $49.3; $40.9; $35.7; $32.2
College Misericordia, $58.4; $48.4; $32.4; n/a
Community College of Allegheny County, $52.8; $45.2; $44.0; n/a
Community College of Beaver County, $53.5; $50.3; n/a; n/a
Delaware Valley College, $64.3; $53.2; $41.9; n/a
DeSales University, n/a; $50.7; $44.2; $37.4
Dickinson College, $72.2; $55.8; $43.3; $39.5
Drexel University, $89.1; $67.6; $64.3; $39.2
Duquesne University, $74.7; $57.0; $48.9; $39.5
Eastern Baptist Theological Seminary, $50.2; n/a; n/a; n/a
Eastern College, $69.8; $52.6; $40.5; n/a
Elizabethtown College, $67.0; $54.2; $44.6; n/a
Franklin and Marshall College, $85.1; $59.8; $48.7; n/a
Gannon University, $56.2; $42.9; $36.6; $27.8
Geneva College, $50.7; $44.9; $38.2; n/a
Gettysburg College, $78.1; $58.1; $46.5; $41.6
Gwynedd-Mercy College, $60.0; $48.4; $40.5; $35.0
Harcum College, n/a; $39.6; $33.6; $31.4
Harrisburg Area Community College, $63.8; $45.8; $40.4; $32.2
Haverford College, $86.1; $64.0; $51.1; n/a
Holy Family College, $60.1; $45.8; $41.6; n/a
Immaculate College, n/a; $45.4; $35.0; $34.5
Juniata College, $62.8; $47.7; $40.9; n/a
King's College, $59.8; $49.7; $32.4; $41.9
La Roche College, $61.4; $52.3; $40.3; n/a
La Salle University, $71.2; $57.3; $46.9; n/a
Lafayette College, $84.5; $66.2; $50.2; n/a
Lancaster Bible College, $41.0; n/a; $32.3; n/a
Lebanon Valley College, $59.7; $47.2; $41.9; n/a
Lehigh Carbon Community College, $60.8; $48.9; $44.6; $36.8
Lehigh University, $91.2; $65.6; $56.3; n/a
Lincoln University, $59.7; $45.5; $36.5; $33.4
Luzerne County Community College, $63.2; $45.6; $38.9; $38.5
Lycoming College, $60.6; $52.5; $44.5; $35.2
Marywood University, $61.3; $49.9; $41.4; n/a
Mercyhurst College, $57.9; $47.4; $39.0; $30.4
Messiah College, $58.8; $50.3; $41.9; $36.7
Moravian College, $64.0; $51.0; $42.7; n/a
Muhlenberg College, $67.1; $52.5; $43.0; n/a
Neumann College, $48.0; $45.7; $38.6; n/a
Northampton County Area Community College, $61.8; $52.8; $42.6; $35.7
Pennsylvania State University, University Park, $93.8; $63.4; $52.7; $35.9
Philadelphia College of Bible, $45.5; $42.1; $37.2; n/a

Philadelphia University, $64.7; $54.5; $44.4; n/a
Pittsburgh Theological Seminary, $69.2; $59.3; n/a; n/a
St. Joseph's University (PA), $79.3; $62.6; $50.9; n/a
St. Vincent College, $59.2; $49.6; $40.0; n/a
Seton Hill College, $52.8; $44.3; $38.5; n/a
Bloomsburg University, $79.4; $64.6; $49.5; n/a
California University, $81.4; $64.1; $52.8; $37.0
Cheyney University, $81.3; $64.9; $50.6; $39.4
Clarion University, $80.6; $64.5; $48.9; $35.9
Edinboro University, $79.4; $62.6; $51.3; $38.2
Indiana University (PA), $80.2; $63.8; $50.1; $36.5
Kutztown University, $80.6; $65.1; $46.9; $37.2
Lock Haven University, $79.2; $62.8; $47.9; $37.4
Mansfield University, $79.1; $63.9; $49.9; $36.9
Millersville University, $80.3; $63.8; $49.6; n/a
Shippensburg University, $80.7; $63.8; $49.6; n/a
West Chester University, $80.2; $65.0; $51.4; $46.2
Susquehanna University, $64.7; $53.1; $42.5; n/a
Swarthmore College, $98.7; $69.1; $53.3; n/a
Temple University, $95.4; $69.3; $50.0; $43.7
Thiel College, $49.5; $39.6; $34.9; n/a
University of the Arts, $57.8; $45.0; $26.8; n/a
University of Pennsylvania, $120.3; $83.5; $73.1; n/a
University of Pittsburgh, $90.0; $63.6; $53.1; $39.4
University of Pittsburgh, Bradford, $59.2; $49.4; $39.8; $34.6
University of Pittsburgh, Greensburg, $57.2; $48.8; $39.2; $34.1
University of Pittsburgh, Johnstown, $61.0; $50.1; $39.6; $34.8
University of Pittsburgh, Titusville, n/a; $41.6; $35.7; n/a
University of the Sciences in Philadelphia, $69.9; $56.0; $48.5; $38.0
University of Scranton, $70.0; $62.5; $48.4; n/a
Ursinus College, $66.5; $57.8; $46.1; n/a
Valley Forge Christian College, n/a; n/a; $36.5; n/a
Villanova University, $94.2; $64.8; $53.7; $40.2
Washington and Jefferson College, $67.0; $50.9; $40.3; $39.3
Waynesburg College, $52.2; $39.9; $38.0; $32.0
Westminster College, $59.8; $46.6; $39.2; $33.9
Westmoreland County Community College, $62.7; $48.8; $40.1; n/a
Widener University, $76.9; $63.5; $44.9; $47.1
Wilkes University, $61.9; $51.5; $42.5; n/a
York College of Pennyslvania, $74.4; $59.1; $50.7; n/a

Source: "Faculty Salaries at More Than 1,400 Institutions," *The Chronicle of Higher Education*, 47: A20-A23, (April 20, 2001).

★3726★
Average faculty salaries for institutions of higher education in Puerto Rico, 2000-01

Ranking basis/background: Average salaries for instructional staff employed full-time for a nine-month work year. **Remarks:** Original source: American Association of University Professors. **Number listed:** 3.

Pontifical Catholic University, with $40.5 for professors; $29.8 for associate professors; $28.4 for assistant professors; and $21.6 for instructors
University of Puerto Rico, Humacao University, $51.7; $42.0; $36.4; $30.3
University of Puerto Rico, Ponce, $47.6; $40.1; $34.5; $29.9

Source: "Faculty Salaries at More Than 1,400 Institutions," *The Chronicle of Higher Education*, 47: A20-A23, (April 20, 2001).

★3727★
Average faculty salaries for institutions of higher education in Rhode Island, 2000-01

Ranking basis/background: Average salaries for instructional staff employed full-time for a nine-month work year. **Remarks:** Original source: American Association of University Professors. **Number listed:** 8.

Brown University, with $96.6 for professors; $64.8 for associate professors; $55.5 for assistant professors; and n/a for instructors
Bryant College, $88.3; $75.5; $58.1; n/a
Community College of Rhode Island, $56.2; $41.2; $36.8; n/a
Providence College, $78.6; $65.0; $51.5; $39.5
Rhode Island College, $60.4; $52.5; $45.3; n/a
Rhode Island School of Design, $75.3; $57.3; $46.6; n/a
Salve Regina University, $61.8; $51.8; $41.8; $37.4
University of Rhode Island, $78.8; $59.5; $48.1; n/a

Source: "Faculty Salaries at More Than 1,400 Institutions," *The Chronicle of Higher Education*, 47: A20-A23, (April 20, 2001).

★3728★
Average faculty salaries for institutions of higher education in South Carolina, 2000-01

Ranking basis/background: Average salaries for instructional staff employed full-time for a nine-month work year. **Remarks:** Original source: American Association of University Professors. **Number listed:** 23.

Charleston Southern University, with $52.5 for professors; $44.5 for associate professors; $38.9 for assistant professors; and $33.1 for instructors
The Citadel, $65.3; $52.7; $44.5; n/a
Clemson University, $77.0; $58.5; $47.8; $30.4
Coastal Carolina University, $60.4; $49.8; $42.7; $32.8
College of Charleston, $63.8; $52.2; $41.9; $35.5
Converse College, $56.9; $44.8; $38.8; n/a
Erskine College, $52.8; $46.0; $37.1; n/a
Francis Marion University, $58.0; $50.4; $41.1; $34.2
Furman University, $68.9; $51.4; $43.0; n/a
Lander University, $57.2; $46.2; $40.4; $33.9
Limestone College, n/a; $35.1; $30.2; n/a
Lutheran Theological Southern Seminary, $42.4; n/a; n/a; n/a
Presbyterian College, $57.7; $46.3; $38.1; n/a
Southern Wesleyan University, $38.3; $34.0; $28.5; n/a
University of South Carolina, Columbia, $82.9; $60.6; $50.3; $37.6
University of South Carolina, Aiken, $61.4; $48.5; $44.0; $35.5
University of South Carolina, Beaufort, $52.6; $42.0; $38.2; n/a
University of South Carolina, Lancaster, $57.4; $50.0; n/a; n/a
University of South Carolina, Salkehatchie, $54.4; n/a; $35.3; n/a
University of South Carolina, Spartanburg, $58.8; $48.1; $41.2; $33.9
University of South Carolina, Sumter, $56.1; $47.4; $38.8; n/a
Winthrop University, $56.6; $47.9; $41.5; $30.9
Wofford College, $63.2; $50.8; $40.6; n/a

Source: "Faculty Salaries at More Than 1,400 Institutions," *The Chronicle of Higher Education*, 47: A20-A23, (April 20, 2001).

★3729★
Average faculty salaries for institutions of higher education in South Dakota, 2000-01

Ranking basis/background: Average salaries for instructional staff employed full-time for a nine-month work year. **Remarks:** Original source: American Association of University Professors. **Number listed:** 9.

Augustana College, with $54.5 for professors; $44.8 for associate professors; $37.5 for assistant professors; and n/a for instructors
Dakota Wesleyan University, $41.6; $36.7; $28.2; n/a
Presentation College, n/a; n/a; $31.6; $25.2
University of South Dakota, $63.4; $45.1; $40.9; $30.3
Black Hills State University, $52.5; $45.4; $39.6; $34.6
Dakota State University, n/a; $47.9; $47.9; $32.7
South Dakota School of Mines and Technology, $67.8; $52.7; $45.2; n/a
South Dakota State University, $58.5; $48.9; $42.9; $37.4
University of Sioux Falls, $46.4; $41.5; $35.7; n/a

Source: "Faculty Salaries at More Than 1,400 Institutions," *The Chronicle of Higher Education*, 47: A20-A23, (April 20, 2001).

★3730★
Average faculty salaries for institutions of higher education in Tennessee, 2000-01

Ranking basis/background: Average salaries for instructional staff employed full-time for a nine-month work year. **Remarks:** Original source: American Association of University Professors. **Number listed:** 43.

Belmont University, with $56.8 for professors; $48.6 for associate professors; $46.1 for assistant professors; and $33.6 for instructors
Bethel College, $35.5; $34.9; $33.4; n/a
Carson-Newman College, $49.1; $42.3; $37.4; $30.1
Crichton College, $44.9; n/a; $36.8; n/a
Fisk University, $52.3; $40.4; $35.5; n/a
Freed-Hardeman University, $51.0; $47.8; $37.7; $32.0
Lambuth University, $38.5; $34.6; $33.8; $32.9
Lane College, n/a; $28.4; $31.2; $30.2
Lee University, $45.2; $39.8; $37.0; $31.3
LeMoyne-Owen College, $44.3; $37.7; $31.7; $30.6
Lincoln Memorial University, $36.4; $34.6; $35.0; $28.1
Lipscomb University, $55.1; $45.1; $38.1; $29.9
Maryville College, $57.6; $45.9; $36.9; $32.2
Milligan College, $45.7; $39.6; $35.9; n/a
Rhodes College, $79.5; $54.9; $44.5; $42.4
Southern Adventist University, $33.4; $32.2; $31.1; n/a
Austin Peay State University, $58.6; $43.5; $38.0; $30.1
East Tennessee State University, $61.2; $49.6; $41.8; $32.5
Middle Tennessee State University, $64.8; $48.3; $42.5; $29.6
Tennessee Tech University, $62.9; $49.1; $41.3; $30.7
University of Memphis, $71.4; $52.5; $45.1; $31.3
Chattanooga State Tech Community College, $51.8; $41.3; $36.3; $28.0
Cleveland State Community College, $51.1; $41.3; $36.0; $31.1
Dyersburg State Community College, $49.3; $41.3; n/a; $31.6
Motlow State Community College, $52.2; $43.4; $35.5; $31.8
Nashville State Technical Institute, $43.5; $40.6; $33.3; $32.4
Northeast State Tech Community College, n/a; $38.0; $33.1; $30.3
Pellissippi State Tech Community College, $50.6; $43.3; $37.0; $33.1
Roane State Community College, $48.7; $42.1; $34.7; $34.4
Southwest Tennessee Community College, $49.8; $40.0; $33.8; $31.5
Volunteer State Community College, $49.5; $39.4; $32.8; $30.5
Walters State Community College, $53.2; $42.5; $32.7; $26.0
Tennessee Wesleyan College, $37.2; $31.6; $29.1; $29.6
Trevecca Nazarene University, $47.1; $43.1; $35.4; n/a
Tusculum College, $43.6; $37.5; $34.0; n/a
Union University, $53.0; $45.6; $40.8; $36.7
University of the South, $73.7; $53.1; $43.9; $42.9
University of Tennessee, Knoxville, $79.6; $60.1; $47.3; $34.2
University of Tennessee Institute of Agriculture, $72.3; $59.3; $49.1; n/a
University of Tennessee, Memphis, $74.8; $56.3; $51.4; $42.0
University of Tennessee, Chattanooga, $61.3; $48.9; $43.5; $31.8
University of Tennessee, Martin, $58.0; $46.7; $41.6; $35.8
Vanderbilt University, $103.2; $66.5; $54.4; n/a

Source: "Faculty Salaries at More Than 1,400 Institutions," *The Chronicle of Higher Education*, 47: A20-A23, (April 20, 2001).

★3731★
Average faculty salaries for institutions of higher education in Texas, 2000-01

Ranking basis/background: Average salaries for instructional staff employed full-time for a nine-month work year. **Remarks:** Original source: American Association of University Professors. **Number listed:** 60.

Abilene Christian University, with $57.7 for professors; $39.1 for associate professors; $41.0 for assistant professors; and $32.9 for instructors
Alamo Community College, Palto Alto, n/a; $48.9; $43.8; $39.8
Alamo Community College, St. Philip's, $56.7; $51.5; $46.1; $38.4
Alamo Community College, San Antonio, $57.3; $51.4; $45.3; $39.4
Amber University, $54.5; n/a; n/a; n/a
Austin College, $66.4; $53.2; $42.7; n/a
Austin Community College, $63.1; $41.7; $38.3; n/a
Baylor University, $79.3; $60.5; $47.5; n/a
College of the Mainland, $50.1; $44.3; $41.7; n/a
Del Mar College, $53.6; $46.1; $40.2; $34.5
East Texas Baptist University, $43.8; $37.4; $36.5; $31.1
Hardin-Simmons University, $52.4; $50.2; $39.1; $34.0
Houston Baptist University, $49.6; $41.7; $38.6; n/a
LeTourneau University, %51.5; $45.4; $40.7; $38.1
Lubbock Christian University, $46.3; $39.6; $34.1; $30.6
McMurry University, $50.4; $44.1; $36.8; $31.2
Midwestern State University, $60.7; $52.3; $45.5; $33.9
Odessa College, $48.1; $40.2; $38.3; $34.6
Our Lady of the Lake University, San Antonio, $59.6; $49.9; $40.4; $33.6
Rice University, $108.9; $69.4; $65.7; $47.2
St. Edward's University, $58.5; $49.3; $41.6; n/a
St. Mary's University (TX), $79.1; $52.7; $42.3; $23.8
Schreiner College, $44.8; n/a; $31.1; n/a
Southern Methodist University, $95.7; $62.3; $59.2; n/a
Southwestern University, $77.6; $57.5; $44.8; n/a
Stephen F. Austin State University, $57.7; $47.5; $40.3; $35.6
Tarrant County College District, $54.0; $52.0; $50.2; $41.1
Prairie View A&M University, $56.6; $48.2; $42.5; n/a
Tarleton State University, $58.3; $49.0; $42.2; $34.9
Texas A&M International University, $71.3; $54.0; $45.5; $35.2
Texas A&M University, College Station, $85.0; $61.1; n/a; n/a
Texas A&M University, Commerce, $62.6; $50.4; $43.0; $37.4
Texas A&M University, Corpus Christi, $60.7; $52.2; $44.4; n/a
Texas A&M University, Kingsville, $54.1; $46.7; $40.8; n/a
West Texas A&M University, $55.8; $48.2; $41.7; $35.0
Texas Christian University, $84.4; $61.5; $54.8; $45.5
Texas Lutheran University, $54.5; $43.9; $37.6; n/a
Texas Tech University, $82.3; $57.7; $46.2; $31.6
Lamar State College, n/a; n/a; $35.5; $31.1
Sam Houston State University, $64.8; $50.8; $44.8; $32.3
Southwest Texas State University, $65.5; $52.7; $41.3; $29.9
Sul Ross State University, $59.3; $47.6; $38.1; n/a
Texas Wesleyan University, $69.3; $62.8; $38.1; n/a
Texas Woman's University, $60.9; $48.3; $41.7; $36.0
Trinity University, $86.6; $57.6; $45.7; n/a
University of Houston, University Park, $83.9; $57.9; $51.8; $48.6
University of Houston, Clear Lake, $71.9; $58.6; $44.4; n/a
University of Houston, Downtown, $61.6; $49.4; $42.8; $36.3
University of Houston, Victoria, $65.5; $57.2; $46.6; n/a
University of the Incarnate Word, $53.9; $46.9; $42.2; $35.3
University of North Texas, $73.2; $56.1; $46.4; n/a
University of St. Thomas, $67.4; $55.7; $46.1; $33.8
University of Texas, Arlington, $77.2; $56.3; $49.3; n/a
University of Texas, Austin, $94.1; $60.8; $57.3; $40.0
University of Texas, Brownsville, $56.4; $49.9; $45.5; $40.2
University of Texas, Dallas, $86.0; $63.4; $66.0; n/a
University of Texas, El Paso, $86.0; $63.4; $66.9; n/a
University of Texas, Pan American, $67.5; $56.3; $49.8; n/a
University of Texas, Tyler, $61.7; $50.7; $46.3; n/a
University of Texas, Permian Basin, $58.3; $46.0; $42.5; n/a

Source: "Faculty Salaries at More Than 1,400 Institutions," *The Chronicle of Higher Education*, 47: A20-A23, (April 20, 2001).

SALARIES—COLLEGES & UNIVERSITIES, FACULTY

★3732★
Average faculty salaries for institutions of higher education in the District of Columbia, 2000-01

Ranking basis/background: Average salaries for instructional staff employed full-time for a nine-month work year. **Remarks:** Original source: American Association of University Professors. **Number listed:** 7.

- American University, with $97.3 for professors; $67.0 for associate professors; $52.4 for assistant professors; and $35.3 for instructors
- Catholic University of America, $74.4; $54.7; $46.6; n/a
- Gallaudet University, $86.6; $61.3; $51.0; $38.1
- George Washington University, $98.3; $72.2; $56.9; $45.3
- Georgetown University, $107.4; $68.0; $53.4; $54.8
- Howard University, $78.5; $59.3; $49.5; $42.8
- Trinity College, $56.9; $45.5; $38.0; n/a

Source: "Faculty Salaries at More Than 1,400 Institutions," *The Chronicle of Higher Education*, 47: A20-A23, (April 20, 2001).

★3733★
Average faculty salaries for institutions of higher education in Utah, 2000-01

Ranking basis/background: Average salaries for instructional staff employed full-time for a nine-month work year. **Remarks:** Original source: American Association of University Professors. **Number listed:** 5.

- University of Utah, with $81.2 for professors; $55.2 for associate professors; $49.4 for assistant professors; and $39.6 for instructors
- Utah State University, $67.5; $53.2; $44.4; $37.3
- Weber State University, $59.0; $47.8; $40.2; $36.4
- Salt Lake Community College, $45.3; $41.1; $38.1; $34.7
- Westminster College, $53.1; $47.3; $43.2; $35.9

Source: "Faculty Salaries at More Than 1,400 Institutions," *The Chronicle of Higher Education*, 47: A20-A23, (April 20, 2001).

★3734★
Average faculty salaries for institutions of higher education in Vermont, 2000-01

Ranking basis/background: Average salaries for instructional staff employed full-time for a nine-month work year. **Remarks:** Original source: American Association of University Professors. **Number listed:** 8.

- Champlain College, with $47.8 for professors; $45.0 for associate professors; $37.8 for assistant professors; and n/a for instructors
- Landmark College, n/a; $35.7; $26.6; $23.4
- Middlebury College, $91.8; $63.9; $50.9; $46.9
- University of Vermont, $72.5; $55.3; $45.3; n/a
- Castleton State College, $50.7; $41.4; $34.3; n/a
- Johnson State College, $52.0; $42.1; $33.2; n/a
- Lyndon State College, $51.6; $42.2; $32.7; n/a
- Vermont Technical College, $48.8; $39.1; $32.6; n/a

Source: "Faculty Salaries at More Than 1,400 Institutions," *The Chronicle of Higher Education*, 47: A20-A23, (April 20, 2001).

★3735★
Average faculty salaries for institutions of higher education in Virginia, 2000-01

Ranking basis/background: Average salaries for instructional staff employed full-time for a nine-month work year. **Remarks:** Original source: American Association of University Professors. **Number listed:** 40.

- Averett College, with $45.6 for professors; $39.7 for associate professors; $37.5 for assistant professors; and $35.3 for instructors
- Bridgewater College, $52.7; $47.9; $40.1; $31.1
- Christopher Newport University, $74.9; $59.8; $48.2; $39.4
- College of William and Mary, $98.3; $66.5; $54.0; $37.0
- Eastern Mennonite University, $48.4; $40.2; $35.2; $30.5
- Emory and Henry College, $61.2; $46.7; $36.7; n/a
- George Mason University, $99.5; $69.1; $51.2; $43.4
- Hampden-Sydney College, $65.2; $53.2; $41.1; n/a
- Hollins University, $62.4; $48.3; $41.8; n/a
- James Madison University, $72.2; $59.7; $46.5; $39.4
- Liberty University, $46.6; $39.5; $33.6; $26.6
- Longwood College, $65.9; $53.5; $42.9; n/a
- Lynchburg College, $56.4; $50.9; $43.5; n/a
- Mary Baldwin College, $57.2; $47.3; $39.7; n/a
- Mary Washington College, $68.4; $53.2; $41.3; n/a
- Marymount University, $62.7; $51.4; $43.0; n/a
- Old Dominion University, $84.9; $60.3; $50.3; $41.7
- Radford University, $61.5; $49.9; $39.7; $34.2
- Randolph-Macon College, $62.2; $45.6; $39.4; n/a
- Randolph-Macon Woman's College, $61.6; $50.5; $41.1; n/a
- Richard Bland College, $56.6; $50.2; $40.2; n/a
- Roanoke College, $59.7; $49.3; $38.7; n/a
- St. Paul's College, $37.9; n/a; $33.1; $28.1
- Shenandoah University, $61.7; $51.5; $45.0; $38.4
- Sweet Briar College, $60.2; $50.7; $41.5; n/a
- Union Theological Seminary (VA), $74.4; n/a; n/a; n/a
- University of Richmond, $93.4; $64.9; $53.1; n/a
- University of Virginia, $106.2; $71.4; $56.6; $45.9
- University of Virginia, College at Wise, $68.2; $57.8; $46.9; n/a
- Virginia Commonwealth University, $87.5; $68.4; $53.7; $35.5
- Germanna Community College, $52.7; $46.4; $39.1; $38.4
- Lord Fairfax Community College, n/a; $45.6; $41.6; $35.9
- Thomas Nelson Community College, $55.8; $47.3; $42.5; $35.6
- Virginia Intermont College, $40.1; $36.6; $32.0; n/a
- Virginia Military Institute, $70.3; n/a; $42.2; n/a
- Virginia Tech, $88.9; $64.1; $54.2; $33.9
- Virginia State University, $67.4; $59.2; $47.4; $38.3
- Virginia Union University, $57.6; $46.0; $34.8; $30.3
- Virginia Wesleyan College, $57.6; $46.1; $37.1; n/a
- Washington and Lee University, $85.3; $55.8; $50.8; n/a

Source: "Faculty Salaries at More Than 1,400 Institutions," *The Chronicle of Higher Education*, 47: A20-A23, (April 20, 2001).

★3736★
Average faculty salaries for institutions of higher education in Washington, 2000-01

Ranking basis/background: Average salaries for instructional staff employed full-time for a nine-month work year. **Remarks:** Original source: American Association of University Professors. **Number listed:** 17.

- Central Washington University, with $58.8 for professors; $49.3 for associate professors; $42.1 for assistant professors; and $34.8 for instructors
- Eastern Washington University, $59.1; $49.7; $43.9; n/a
- Northwest College, $48.9; $41.0; $37.8; n/a
- Pacific Lutheran University, $59.9; $50.9; $42.1; n/a
- Peninsula College, $45.6; $44.1; $38.7; $33.3
- St. Martin's College, $44.6; $39.6; $34.5; n/a
- Seattle Pacific University, $60.4; $49.9; $43.1; $33.9
- Seattle University, $81.1; $60.2; $48.0; $43.2
- University of Puget Sound, $77.5; $58.1; $48.0; $46.3
- University of Washington, Seattle, $85.5; $62.6; $53.6; $36.9
- University of Washington, Bothell, $73.0; $62.1; $59.4; n/a
- University of Washington, Tacoma, $73.9; $58.6; $55.0; n/a
- Walla Walla College, $40.8; $38.7; $37.1; $32.3
- Washington State University, $74.5; $57.5; $50.6; $35.6
- Western Washington University, $63.6; $51.8; $43.9; $37.3
- Whitman College, $77.4; $58.4; $46.4; n/a
- Whitworth College, $58.6; $46.8; $39.3; $33.1

Source: "Faculty Salaries at More Than 1,400 Institutions," *The Chronicle of Higher Education*, 47: A20-A23, (April 20, 2001).

★3737★
Average faculty salaries for institutions of higher education in West Virginia, 2000-01

Ranking basis/background: Average salaries for instructional staff employed full-time for a nine-month work year. **Remarks:** Original source: American Association of University Professors. **Number listed:** 15.

- Bethany College, with $52.9 for professors; $41.6 for associate professors; $32.4 for assistant professors; and n/a for instructors
- Davis and Elkins College, $42.4; $40.0; $33.7; n/a
- Ohio Valley College, $38.6; $38.8; n/a; n/a
- Salem-Teikyo University, n/a; $36.7; $30.3; n/a
- Bluefield State College, $57.2; $45.6; $40.2; $33.5
- Concord College, $56.5; $51.0; $43.2; $34.4
- Fairmont State College, $54.5; $46.6; $40.0; $36.8
- Glenville State College, $61.3; $49.3; $39.2; n/a
- West Liberty State College, $55.6; $45.5; $35.4; $31.0
- Southern West Virginia Community and Technical College, $51.9; $43.0; $37.4; $30.7
- University System of West Virginia Institute of Tech, n/a; $43.4; $34.5; $29.1
- Marshall University, $58.6; $48.9; $38.1; $30.0
- West Virginia University, $72.4; $55.3; $44.3; $35.7
- West Virginia Wesleyan College, $52.1; $44.0; $37.2; n/a
- Wheeling Jesuit University, $48.5; $45.4; $40.7; $37.3

Source: "Faculty Salaries at More Than 1,400 Institutions," *The Chronicle of Higher Education*, 47: A20-A23, (April 20, 2001).

★3738★
Average faculty salaries for institutions of higher education in Wisconsin, 2000-01

Ranking basis/background: Average salaries for instructional staff employed full-time for a nine-month work year. **Remarks:** Original source: American Association of University Professors. **Number listed:** 30.

- Alverno College, with $50.6 for professors; $39.6 for associate professors; $33.4 for assistant professors; and n/a for instructors
- Beloit College, $67.0; $51.7; $42.8; n/a
- Cardinal Stritch University, $53.0; $47.6; $37.4; $31.5
- Carroll College, $55.0; $50.3; $41.5; $32.4
- Carthage College, $59.0; $49.9; $40.7; n/a
- Concordia University, $52.6; $48.9; $55.4; $37.2
- Edgewood College, $51.6; $43.4; $37.5; $33.5
- Lakeland College, $53.0; $45.6; $39.6; n/a
- Lawrence University, $69.4; $54.4; $44.2; n/a
- Marian College of Fond du Lac, $54.9; $43.1; $36.3; $31.3
- Marquette University, $77.5; $60.6; $51.3; n/a
- Milwaukee School of Engineering, $61.2; $51.9; $51.3; n/a
- Mount Mary College, $48.1; $40.8; $34.0; n/a
- Northland College, $51.0; $41.4; $34.8; n/a
- Ripon College, $54.4; $44.5; $35.8; n/a
- Silver Lake College, n/a; $39.1; $33.2; n/a
- University of Wisconsin, Madison, $90.4; $68.0; $59.8; $44.6
- University of Wisconsin, Eau Claire, $61.9; $51.5; $43.9; n/a
- University of Wisconsin, Green Bay, $60.3; $51.1; $43.7; n/a
- University of Wisconsin, La Crosse, $65.9; $53.7; $46.3; n/a
- University of Wisconsin, Milwaukee, $78.1; $60.5; $52.0; $36.9
- University of Wisconsin, Oshkosh, $65.4; $53.3; $46.9; n/a
- University of Wisconsin, Parkside, $66.4; $55.7; $43.6; n/a
- University of Wisconsin, Platteville, $65.2; $50.5; $45.6; n/a
- University of Wisconsin, River Falls, $60.1; $49.0; $46.3; n/a
- University of Wisconsin, Stevens Point, $63.8; $51.2; $42.8; $36.6
- University of Wisconsin, Stout, $62.7; $50.9; $44.7; n/a
- University of Wisconsin, Superior, $59.8; $50.4; $43.2; n/a
- University of Wisconsin, Whitewater, $67.4; $53.5; $45.9; n/a
- Viterbo College, $51.3; $43.5; $37.8; $33.1

Source: "Faculty Salaries at More Than 1,400 Institutions," *The Chronicle of Higher Education*, 47: A20-A23, (April 20, 2001).

★3739★
Average faculty salaries for institutions of higher education in Wyoming, 2000-01

Ranking basis/background: Average salaries for instructional staff employed full-time for a nine-month work year. **Remarks:** Original source: American Association of University Professors. **Number listed:** 3.

- Central Wyoming University, with $40.0 for professors; n/a for associate professors; $31.3 for assistant professors; and $28.0 for instructors
- Northwest College, $43.2; $39.1; $34.9; $28.7
- University of Wyoming, $67.4; $51.6; $48.0; $43.3

Source: "Faculty Salaries at More Than 1,400 Institutions," *The Chronicle of Higher Education*, 47: A20-A23, (April 20, 2001).

★3740★
Average faculty salaries for institutions of higher education without academic ranks in Alabama, 2000-01

Ranking basis/background: Average salaries for instructional staff employed full-time for a nine-month work year. **Remarks:** Original source: American Association of University Professors. **Number listed:** 8.

- Chattahoochee Valley Community College, with $43.4
- Enterprise State Junior College, $43.3
- J.F. Drake State Tech College, $58.0
- Jefferson State College, $42.5
- John M Patterson State Tech College, $45.3
- Lurleen B Wallace Junior College, $42.8
- Northwest Shoals Community College, $43.5
- Southern Union State Community College, $41.7

Source: "Faculty Salaries at More Than 1,400 Institutions," *The Chronicle of Higher Education*, 47: A20-A23, (April 20, 2001).

★3741★
Average faculty salaries for institutions of higher education without academic ranks in Arizona, 2000-01

Ranking basis/background: Average salaries for instructional staff employed full-time for a nine-month work year. **Remarks:** Original source: American Association of University Professors. **Number listed:** 5.

- Arizona Western College, with $39.2
- Central Arizona College, $49.4
- Cochise College, $42.1
- Maricopa County Community College, $63.4
- Yavapai College, $42.8

Source: "Faculty Salaries at More Than 1,400 Institutions," *The Chronicle of Higher Education*, 47: A20-A23, (April 20, 2001).

★3742★
Average faculty salaries for institutions of higher education without academic ranks in Arkansas, 2000-01

Ranking basis/background: Average salaries for instructional staff employed full-time for a nine-month work year. **Remarks:** Original source: American Association of University Professors. **Number listed:** 1.

- North Arkansas College, with $41.6

Source: "Faculty Salaries at More Than 1,400 Institutions," *The Chronicle of Higher Education*, 47: A20-A23, (April 20, 2001).

★3743★
Average faculty salaries for institutions of higher education without academic ranks in California, 2000-01

Ranking basis/background: Average salaries for instructional staff employed full-time for a nine-month work year. **Remarks:** Original source: American Association of University Professors. **Number listed:** 6.

- California Institute of the Arts, with $52.4
- College of the Redwoods, $55.8
- Cuesta College, $60.7
- Palo Verde College, $58.2
- Peralta Community College, $60.7
- Ventura County Community College $60.7

Source: "Faculty Salaries at More Than 1,400 Institutions," *The Chronicle of Higher Education*, 47: A20-A23, (April 20, 2001).

★3744★
Average faculty salaries for institutions of higher education without academic ranks in Colorado, 2000-01

Ranking basis/background: Average salaries for instructional staff employed full-time for a nine-month work year. **Remarks:** Original source: American Association of University Professors. **Number listed:** 3.

- Morgan Community College, with $35.9
- Pikes Peak Community College, $41.4

Red Rocks Community College, $39.7
Source: "Faculty Salaries at More Than 1,400 Institutions," *The Chronicle of Higher Education*, 47: A20-A23, (April 20, 2001).

★3745★
Average faculty salaries for institutions of higher education without academic ranks in Florida, 2000-01

Ranking basis/background: Average salaries for instructional staff employed full-time for a nine-month work year. **Remarks:** Original source: American Association of University Professors. **Number listed:** 3.
    Okaloosa-Walton Community College, with $42.8
    South Florida Community College, $39.9
    Valencia Community College, $50.8
Source: "Faculty Salaries at More Than 1,400 Institutions," *The Chronicle of Higher Education*, 47: A20-A23, (April 20, 2001).

★3746★
Average faculty salaries for institutions of higher education without academic ranks in Idaho, 2000-01

Ranking basis/background: Average salaries for instructional staff employed full-time for a nine-month work year. **Remarks:** Original source: American Association of University Professors. **Number listed:** 1.
    Northwest Nazarene University, with $41.6
Source: "Faculty Salaries at More Than 1,400 Institutions," *The Chronicle of Higher Education*, 47: A20-A23, (April 20, 2001).

★3747★
Average faculty salaries for institutions of higher education without academic ranks in Illinois, 2000-01

Ranking basis/background: Average salaries for instructional staff employed full-time for a nine-month work year. **Remarks:** Original source: American Association of University Professors. **Number listed:** 7.
    Carl Sandburg College, with $40.8
    Columbia College, $51.9
    Governors State University, $53.7
    Highland Community College, $53.9
    Lincoln College, $37.4
    McHenry County College, $52.3
    Springfield College, $28.9
Source: "Faculty Salaries at More Than 1,400 Institutions," *The Chronicle of Higher Education*, 47: A20-A23, (April 20, 2001).

★3748★
Average faculty salaries for institutions of higher education without academic ranks in Iowa, 2000-01

Ranking basis/background: Average salaries for instructional staff employed full-time for a nine-month work year. **Remarks:** Original source: American Association of University Professors. **Number listed:** 3.
    Indian Hills Community College, with $40.5
    North Iowa Area Community College, $41.2
    Southeastern Community College, $49.3
Source: "Faculty Salaries at More Than 1,400 Institutions," *The Chronicle of Higher Education*, 47: A20-A23, (April 20, 2001).

★3749★
Average faculty salaries for institutions of higher education without academic ranks in Maine, 2000-01

Ranking basis/background: Average salaries for instructional staff employed full-time for a nine-month work year. **Remarks:** Original source: American Association of University Professors. **Number listed:** 3.
    Central Maine Technical College, with $40.9
    Northern Maine Technical College, $42.1
    Southern Maine Technical College, $36.6
Source: "Faculty Salaries at More Than 1,400 Institutions," *The Chronicle of Higher Education*, 47: A20-A23, (April 20, 2001).

★3750★
Average faculty salaries for institutions of higher education without academic ranks in Maryland, 2000-01

Ranking basis/background: Average salaries for instructional staff employed full-time for a nine-month work year. **Remarks:** Original source: American Association of University Professors. **Number listed:** 1.
    University of Maryland, University College, with $49.7
Source: "Faculty Salaries at More Than 1,400 Institutions," *The Chronicle of Higher Education*, 47: A20-A23, (April 20, 2001).

★3751★
Average faculty salaries for institutions of higher education without academic ranks in Massachusetts, 2000-01

Ranking basis/background: Average salaries for instructional staff employed full-time for a nine-month work year. **Remarks:** Original source: American Association of University Professors. **Number listed:** 1.
    Simon's Rock College of Bard, with $53.5
Source: "Faculty Salaries at More Than 1,400 Institutions," *The Chronicle of Higher Education*, 47: A20-A23, (April 20, 2001).

★3752★
Average faculty salaries for institutions of higher education without academic ranks in Michigan, 2000-01

Ranking basis/background: Average salaries for instructional staff employed full-time for a nine-month work year. **Remarks:** Original source: American Association of University Professors. **Number listed:** 3.
    Kirkland Community College, with $51.8
    Schoolcraft College, $65.6
    Wayne County Community College, $56.1
Source: "Faculty Salaries at More Than 1,400 Institutions," *The Chronicle of Higher Education*, 47: A20-A23, (April 20, 2001).

★3753★
Average faculty salaries for institutions of higher education without academic ranks in Minnesota, 2000-01

Ranking basis/background: Average salaries for instructional staff employed full-time for a nine-month work year. **Remarks:** Original source: American Association of University Professors. **Number listed:** 27.
    Alexandria Technical College, with $48.4
    Anoka-Hennepin Tech College, $52.0
    Anoka-Ramsey Community College, $56.6
    Central Lakes College, $49.0
    Century College, $52.2
    Dakota County Tech College, $50.2
    Fergus Falls Community College, $51.5
    Fond du Lac Tribal and Community College, $50.4
    Hennepin Technical College, $48.4
    Hibbing Community College Tech and Community College, $49.8
    Inver Hills Community College, $55.6
    Lake Superior College, $49.2
    Minneapolis Community and Technical College, $54.9
    Minnesota State College Southeast Tech, $49.9
    Minnesota West Community and Technical College, $47.6
    Normandale Community College, $54.9
    North Hennepin Community College, $57.7
    Northland Community and Technical College, $45.5
    Northwest Technical College, $42.2
    Pine Technical College, $43.8
    Rainy River Community College, $54.3
    Ridgewater College, $48.1
    Riverland Community College, $48.2
    Rochester Community and Technical College, $52.7
    St. Cloud Technical College, $48.8
    St. Paul Technical College, $50.2
    South Central Technical College, $48.9
Source: "Faculty Salaries at More Than 1,400 Institutions," *The Chronicle of Higher Education*, 47: A20-A23, (April 20, 2001).

★3754★
Average faculty salaries for institutions of higher education without academic ranks in Mississippi, 2000-01

Ranking basis/background: Average salaries for instructional staff employed full-time for a nine-month work year. **Remarks:** Original source: American Association of University Professors. **Number listed:** 2.
    Copiah-Lincoln Community College, with $42.1
    Hinds Community College, $40.3
Source: "Faculty Salaries at More Than 1,400 Institutions," *The Chronicle of Higher Education*, 47: A20-A23, (April 20, 2001).

★3755★
Average faculty salaries for institutions of higher education without academic ranks in Missouri, 2000-01

Ranking basis/background: Average salaries for instructional staff employed full-time for a nine-month work year. **Remarks:** Original source: American Association of University Professors. **Number listed:** 4.
    Longview Community College, with $44.5
    Maple Woods Community College, $47.6
    Penn Valley Community College, $44.5
    State Fair Community College, $39.4
Source: "Faculty Salaries at More Than 1,400 Institutions," *The Chronicle of Higher Education*, 47: A20-A23, (April 20, 2001).

★3756★
Average faculty salaries for institutions of higher education without academic ranks in Montana, 2000-01

Ranking basis/background: Average salaries for instructional staff employed full-time for a nine-month work year. **Remarks:** Original source: American Association of University Professors. **Number listed:** 1.
- Dawson Community College, with $34.9

Source: "Faculty Salaries at More Than 1,400 Institutions," *The Chronicle of Higher Education*, 47: A20-A23, (April 20, 2001).

★3757★
Average faculty salaries for institutions of higher education without academic ranks in Nebraska, 2000-01

Ranking basis/background: Average salaries for instructional staff employed full-time for a nine-month work year. **Remarks:** Original source: American Association of University Professors. **Number listed:** 3.
- Central Community College, with $35.9
- Northeast Community College, $36.5
- Western Nebraska Community College, $31.8

Source: "Faculty Salaries at More Than 1,400 Institutions," *The Chronicle of Higher Education*, 47: A20-A23, (April 20, 2001).

★3758★
Average faculty salaries for institutions of higher education without academic ranks in New Jersey, 2000-01

Ranking basis/background: Average salaries for instructional staff employed full-time for a nine-month work year. **Remarks:** Original source: American Association of University Professors. **Number listed:** 1.
- Berkeley College of Business, with $36.4

Source: "Faculty Salaries at More Than 1,400 Institutions," *The Chronicle of Higher Education*, 47: A20-A23, (April 20, 2001).

★3759★
Average faculty salaries for institutions of higher education without academic ranks in New Mexico, 2000-01

Ranking basis/background: Average salaries for instructional staff employed full-time for a nine-month work year. **Remarks:** Original source: American Association of University Professors. **Number listed:** 2.
- Clovis Community College, with $36.8
- New Mexico Junior College, $38.5

Source: "Faculty Salaries at More Than 1,400 Institutions," *The Chronicle of Higher Education*, 47: A20-A23, (April 20, 2001).

★3760★
Average faculty salaries for institutions of higher education without academic ranks in New York, 2000-01

Ranking basis/background: Average salaries for instructional staff employed full-time for a nine-month work year. **Remarks:** Original source: American Association of University Professors. **Number listed:** 1.
- Berkeley College, with $35.4

Source: "Faculty Salaries at More Than 1,400 Institutions," *The Chronicle of Higher Education*, 47: A20-A23, (April 20, 2001).

★3761★
Average faculty salaries for institutions of higher education without academic ranks in North Carolina, 2000-01

Ranking basis/background: Average salaries for instructional staff employed full-time for a nine-month work year. **Remarks:** Original source: American Association of University Professors. **Number listed:** 42.
- Asheville-Buncombe Tech Community College, with $39.0
- Beaufort County Community College, $35.5
- Bladen Community College, $41.8
- Blue Ridge Community College, $37.1
- Brunswick Community College, $33.6
- Caldwell Community College and Technical Institute, $36.0
- Cape Fear Community College, $42.5
- Catawba Valley Community College, $38.2
- Central Carolina Community College, $38.4
- Central Piedmont Community College, $38.8
- College of the Albemarle, $33.6
- Craven Community College, $37.7
- Durham Tech Community College, $40.6
- Edgecombe Community College, $35.9
- Fayetteville Technical Community College, $39.5
- Gaston College, $46.3
- Halifax Community College, $37.3
- Haywood Community College, $40.2
- Johnston Community College, $37.5
- Lenoir Community College, $35.1
- Martin Community College, $34.3
- McDowell Technical Community College, $31.5
- Mitchell Community College, $38.5
- Montgomery Community College, $36.9
- Nash Community College, $37.2
- Pamlico Community College, $35.3
- Piedmont Community College, $35.0
- Pitt Community College, $40.0
- Randolph Community College, $38.6
- Roanoke-Chowan Community College, $35.7
- Robeson Community College, $37.5
- Rockingham Community College, $39.0
- Sampson Community College, $38.6
- Southwestern Community College, $38.1
- Stanley Community College, $35.4
- Surry Community College, $39.6
- Tri-County Community College, $32.7
- Vance-Granville Community College, $36.7
- Wake Technical Community College, $35.1
- Wayne Community College, $40.8
- Western Piedmont Community College, $44.3
- Wilson Technical Community College, $38.1

Source: "Faculty Salaries at More Than 1,400 Institutions," *The Chronicle of Higher Education*, 47: A20-A23, (April 20, 2001).

★3762★
Average faculty salaries for institutions of higher education without academic ranks in North Dakota, 2000-01

Ranking basis/background: Average salaries for instructional staff employed full-time for a nine-month work year. **Remarks:** Original source: American Association of University Professors. **Number listed:** 1.
- Sitting Bull College, with $30.0

Source: "Faculty Salaries at More Than 1,400 Institutions," *The Chronicle of Higher Education*, 47: A20-A23, (April 20, 2001).

★3763★
Average faculty salaries for institutions of higher education without academic ranks in Oklahoma, 2000-01

Ranking basis/background: Average salaries for instructional staff employed full-time for a nine-month work year. **Remarks:** Original source: American Association of University Professors. **Number listed:** 5.
- Eastern Oklahoma State College, with $38.5
- Oklahoma City Community College, $43.4
- Redlands Community College, $31.9
- Rose State College, $41.0
- Seminole State College, $35.8

Source: "Faculty Salaries at More Than 1,400 Institutions," *The Chronicle of Higher Education*, 47: A20-A23, (April 20, 2001).

★3764★
Average faculty salaries for institutions of higher education without academic ranks in Oregon, 2000-01

Ranking basis/background: Average salaries for instructional staff employed full-time for a nine-month work year. **Remarks:** Original source: American Association of University Professors. **Number listed:** 3.
- Clackamas Community College, with $49.4
- Lane Community College, $45.1
- Linn-Benton Community College, $43.8

Source: "Faculty Salaries at More Than 1,400 Institutions," *The Chronicle of Higher Education*, 47: A20-A23, (April 20, 2001).

★3765★
Average faculty salaries for institutions of higher education without academic ranks in South Carolina, 2000-01

Ranking basis/background: Average salaries for instructional staff employed full-time for a nine-month work year. **Remarks:** Original source: American Association of University Professors. **Number listed:** 3.
- Florence-Darlington Tech College, with $39.3
- Midlands Tech College, $39.6
- Technical College of the Lowcountry, $38.6

Source: "Faculty Salaries at More Than 1,400 Institutions," *The Chronicle of Higher Education*, 47: A20-A23, (April 20, 2001).

★3766★
Average faculty salaries for institutions of higher education without academic ranks in Texas, 2000-01

Ranking basis/background: Average salaries for instructional staff employed full-time for a nine-month work year. **Remarks:** Original source: American Association of University Professors. **Number listed:** 16.
- Alvin Community College, with $40.1
- Bee County College, $36.7
- Brookhaven College, $49.7
- Cedar Valley College, $50.7
- Eastfield College, $56.0
- El Centro College, $50.3
- Mountain View College, $55.4
- North Lake College, $51.6

Richland College, $55.6
Houston Community College System, $44.0
Laredo Community College, $44.5
Midland College, $40.2
North Central Texas, $36.7
Southwest Texas Junior College, $39.4
Tyler Junior College, $39.6
Vernon Regional Junior College, $34.0

Source: "Faculty Salaries at More Than 1,400 Institutions," *The Chronicle of Higher Education*, 47: A20-A23, (April 20, 2001).

★3767★
Average faculty salaries for institutions of higher education without academic ranks in the District of Columbia, 2000-01

Ranking basis/background: Average salaries for instructional staff employed full-time for a nine-month work year. **Remarks:** Original source: American Association of University Professors. **Number listed:** 1.

Strayer University, with $39.8

Source: "Faculty Salaries at More Than 1,400 Institutions," *The Chronicle of Higher Education*, 47: A20-A23, (April 20, 2001).

★3768★
Average faculty salaries for institutions of higher education without academic ranks in Washington, 2000-01

Ranking basis/background: Average salaries for instructional staff employed full-time for a nine-month work year. **Remarks:** Original source: American Association of University Professors. **Number listed:** 7.

Centralia College, with $43.9
City University, $32.7
Tacoma Community College, $39.1
Spokane Community College, $45.7
Spokane Falls Community College, $43.8
Wenatchee Valley College, $29.4
Whatcom Community College, $38.6

Source: "Faculty Salaries at More Than 1,400 Institutions," *The Chronicle of Higher Education*, 47: A20-A23, (April 20, 2001).

★3769★
Average faculty salaries for institutions of higher education without academic ranks in Wyoming, 2000-01

Ranking basis/background: Average salaries for instructional staff employed full-time for a nine-month work year. **Remarks:** Original source: American Association of University Professors. **Number listed:** 3.

Casper College, with $37.1
Eastern Wyoming College, $32.1
Laramie County Community College, $36.3

Source: "Faculty Salaries at More Than 1,400 Institutions," *The Chronicle of Higher Education*, 47: A20-A23, (April 20, 2001).

★3770★
Average salaries for accounting faculty at 4-year institutions, 1999-2000

Ranking basis/background: Average salary for faculty at public and private 4-year institutions. From a survey of professors in 80 disciplines at 363 public colleges and 501 private institutions, excluding medical professors. **Remarks:** Original source: College and University Personnel Association. **Number listed:** 2.

Private, with $67,549
Public, $70,634

Source: Magner, Denise K., "Law Professors are Academe's Best-Paid Faculty Members, Survey Finds," *The Chronicle of Higher Education*, 46: A20, (May 12, 2000).

★3771★
Average salaries for administrative and secretarial services faculty at 4-year institutions, 1999-2000

Ranking basis/background: Average salary for faculty at public and private 4-year institutions. From a survey of professors in 80 disciplines at 363 public colleges and 501 private institutions, excluding medical professors. **Remarks:** Original source: College and University Personnel Association. **Number listed:** 2.

Private, with $38,850
Public, $52,372

Source: Magner, Denise K., "Law Professors are Academe's Best-Paid Faculty Members, Survey Finds," *The Chronicle of Higher Education*, 46: A20, (May 12, 2000).

★3772★
Average salaries for agricultural business and production faculty at 4-year institutions, 1999-2000

Ranking basis/background: Average salary for faculty at public and private 4-year institutions. From a survey of professors in 80 disciplines at 363 public colleges and 501 private institutions, excluding medical professors. **Remarks:** Original source: College and University Personnel Association. **Number listed:** 2.

Private, with $45,195
Public, $64,644

Source: Magner, Denise K., "Law Professors are Academe's Best-Paid Faculty Members, Survey Finds," *The Chronicle of Higher Education*, 46: A20, (May 12, 2000).

★3773★
Average salaries for anthropology faculty at 4-year institutions, 1999-2000

Ranking basis/background: Average salary for faculty at public and private 4-year institutions. From a survey of professors in 80 disciplines at 363 public colleges and 501 private institutions, excluding medical professors. **Remarks:** Original source: College and University Personnel Association. **Number listed:** 2.

Private, with $60,085
Public, $56,391

Source: Magner, Denise K., "Law Professors are Academe's Best-Paid Faculty Members, Survey Finds," *The Chronicle of Higher Education*, 46: A20, (May 12, 2000).

★3774★
Average salaries for architecture and related programs faculty at 4-year institutions, 1999-2000

Ranking basis/background: Average salary for faculty at public and private 4-year institutions. From a survey of professors in 80 disciplines at 363 public colleges and 501 private institutions, excluding medical professors. **Remarks:** Original source: College and University Personnel Association. **Number listed:** 2.

Private, with $59,059
Public, $59,357

Source: Magner, Denise K., "Law Professors are Academe's Best-Paid Faculty Members, Survey Finds," *The Chronicle of Higher Education*, 46: A20, (May 12, 2000).

★3775★
Average salaries for area, ethnic, and cultural studies faculty at 4-year institutions, 1999-2000

Ranking basis/background: Average salary for faculty at public and private 4-year institutions. From a survey of professors in 80 disciplines at 363 public colleges and 501 private institutions, excluding medical professors. **Remarks:** Original source: College and University Personnel Association. **Number listed:** 2.

Private, with $56,257
Public, $59,697

Source: Magner, Denise K., "Law Professors are Academe's Best-Paid Faculty Members, Survey Finds," *The Chronicle of Higher Education*, 46: A20, (May 12, 2000).

★3776★
Average salaries for assistant professors at institutions in the East North Central states, 2000-01

Ranking basis/background: Based on the responses of 1,433 institutions providing data to the annual salary survey of the American Association of University Professors. **Remarks:** The East North Central region includes Illinois, Indiana, Michigan, Ohio, and Wisconsin. **Number listed:** 4.

Doctoral institutions, with an average annual salary of $51,600
Comprehensive institutions, $44,740
Baccalaureate institutions, $40,918
Two-year institutions, $39,507

Source: "Uncertain Times: The Annual Report on the Economic Status of the Profession," *Academe*, 87: 25-98, (March/April 2001).

★3777★
Average salaries for assistant professors at institutions in the East South Central states, 2000-01

Ranking basis/background: Based on the responses of 1,433 institutions providing data to the annual salary survey of the American Association of University Professors. **Remarks:** The East South Central region includes Alabama, Kentucky, Mississippi and Tennessee. **Number listed:** 4.

Doctoral institutions, with an average annual salary of $47,365
Comprehensive institutions, $42,663
Baccalaureate institutions, $38,354
Two-year institutions, $34,854

Source: "Uncertain Times: The Annual Report on the Economic Status of the Profession," *Academe*, 87: 25-98, (March/April 2001).

★3778★
Average salaries for assistant professors at institutions in the Middle Atlantic states, 2000-01

Ranking basis/background: Based on the responses of 1,433 institutions providing data to the annual salary survey of the American Association of University Professors. **Remarks:** The Middle Atlantic region includes New Jersey, New York, and Pennsylvania. **Number listed:** 4.

Doctoral institutions, with an average annual salary of $56,974
Comprehensive institutions, $47,690

Baccalaureate institutions, $44,307
Two-year institutions, $45,307
Source: "Uncertain Times: The Annual Report on the Economic Status of the Profession," *Academe*, 87: 25-98, (March/April 2001).

★3779★
Average salaries for assistant professors at institutions in the Mountain states, 2000-01

Ranking basis/background: Based on the responses of 1,433 institutions providing data to the annual salary survey of the American Association of University Professors. **Remarks:** The Mountain region includes Arizona, Colorado, Idaho, Montana, Nevada, New Mexico, Utah and Wyoming. **Number listed:** 4.

Doctoral institutions, with an average annual salary of $48,102
Comprehensive institutions, $45,331
Baccalaureate institutions, $38,345
Two-year institutions, $36,440

Source: "Uncertain Times: The Annual Report on the Economic Status of the Profession," *Academe*, 87: 25-98, (March/April 2001).

★3780★
Average salaries for assistant professors at institutions in the New England states, 2000-01

Ranking basis/background: Based on the responses of 1,433 institutions providing data to the annual salary survey of the American Association of University Professors. **Remarks:** The New England region includes Connecticut, Maine, Massachusetts, New Hampshire, Vermont, and Rhode Island. **Number listed:** 4.

Doctoral institutions, with an average annual salary of $57,506
Comprehensive institutions, $47,533
Baccalaureate institutions, $47,250
Two-year institutions, $34,415

Source: "Uncertain Times: The Annual Report on the Economic Status of the Profession," *Academe*, 87: 25-98, (March/April 2001).

★3781★
Average salaries for assistant professors at institutions in the Pacific states, 2000-01

Ranking basis/background: Based on the responses of 1,433 institutions providing data to the annual salary survey of the American Association of University Professors. **Remarks:** The Pacific region includes Alaska, California, Hawaii, Oregon, and Washington. **Number listed:** 4.

Doctoral institutions, with an average annual salary of $54,799
Comprehensive institutions, $48,077
Baccalaureate institutions, $43,439
Two-year institutions, $44,331

Source: "Uncertain Times: The Annual Report on the Economic Status of the Profession," *Academe*, 87: 25-98, (March/April 2001).

★3782★
Average salaries for assistant professors at institutions in the South Atlantic states, 2000-01

Ranking basis/background: Based on the responses of 1,433 institutions providing data to the annual salary survey of the American Association of University Professors. **Remarks:** The South Atlantic region includes Delaware, District of Columbia, Florida, Georgia, Maryland, North Carolina, South Carolina, Virginia, and West Virginia. **Number listed:** 4.

Doctoral institutions, with an average annual salary of $53,037
Comprehensive institutions, $44,902
Baccalaureate institutions, $40,714
Two-year institutions, $41,044

Source: "Uncertain Times: The Annual Report on the Economic Status of the Profession," *Academe*, 87: 25-98, (March/April 2001).

★3783★
Average salaries for assistant professors at institutions in the West North Central states, 2000-01

Ranking basis/background: Based on the responses of 1,433 institutions providing data to the annual salary survey of the American Association of University Professors. **Remarks:** The West North Central region includes Iowa, Kansas, Minnesota, Missouri, Nebraska, North Dakota and South Dakota. **Number listed:** 4.

Doctoral institutions, with an average annual salary of $50,923
Comprehensive institutions, $43,364
Baccalaureate institutions, $40,021
Two-year institutions, $38,230

Source: "Uncertain Times: The Annual Report on the Economic Status of the Profession," *Academe*, 87: 25-98, (March/April 2001).

★3784★
Average salaries for assistant professors at institutions in the West South Central states, 2000-01

Ranking basis/background: Based on the responses of 1,433 institutions providing data to the annual salary survey of the American Association of University Professors. **Remarks:** The West South Central region includes Arkansas, Louisiana, Oklahoma and Texas. **Number listed:** 4.

Doctoral institutions, with an average annual salary of $52,599
Comprehensive institutions, $42,313
Baccalaureate institutions, $39,880
Two-year institutions, $44,946

Source: "Uncertain Times: The Annual Report on the Economic Status of the Profession," *Academe*, 87: 25-98, (March/April 2001).

★3785★
Average salaries for assistant professors at private institutions in preclinical department of medical schools, 2000-01

Ranking basis/background: Salaries are on a 12-month basis and are rounded to the nearest $100. Data was reported for all faculty (M.D., other doctoral, and nondoctoral). **Remarks:** Original source: Association of American Medical Colleges. **Number listed:** 8.

Anatomy, with an average salary of $58,700
Biochemistry, $59,700
Genetics, $70,800
Microbiology, $60,800
Molecular/cellular biology, $61,600
Pharmacology, $59,700
Physiology, $57,500
Other basic sciences, $64,400

Source: "Uncertain Times: The Annual Report on the Economic Status of the Profession," *Academe*, 87: 25-98, (March/April 2001).

★3786★
Average salaries for assistant professors at public and private institutions in preclinical department of medical schools, 2000-01

Ranking basis/background: Salaries are on a 12-month basis and are rounded to the nearest $100. Data was reported for all faculty (M.D., other doctoral, and nondoctoral). **Remarks:** Original source: Association of American Medical Colleges. **Number listed:** 8.

Anatomy, with an average salary of $58,500
Biochemistry, $59,500
Genetics, $67,800
Microbiology, $60,600
Molecular/cellular biology, $62,100
Pharmacology, $60,600
Physiology, $59,300
Other basic sciences, $64,200

Source: "Uncertain Times: The Annual Report on the Economic Status of the Profession," *Academe*, 87: 25-98, (March/April 2001).

★3787★
Average salaries for assistant professors at public institutions in preclinical department of medical schools, 2000-01

Ranking basis/background: Salaries are on a 12-month basis and are rounded to the nearest $100. Data was reported for all faculty (M.D., other doctoral, and nondoctoral). **Remarks:** Original source: Association of American Medical Colleges. **Number listed:** 8.

Anatomy, with an average salary of $58,400
Biochemistry, $59,300
Genetics, $64,300
Microbiology, $60,400
Molecular/cellular biology, $62,600
Pharmacology, $61,200
Physiology, $60,600
Other basic sciences, $63,900

Source: "Uncertain Times: The Annual Report on the Economic Status of the Profession," *Academe*, 87: 25-98, (March/April 2001).

★3788★
Average salaries for assistant professors in church-related institutions, 2000-01

Ranking basis/background: Based on the responses of 1,433 institutions providing data to the annual salary survey of the American Association of University Professors. **Remarks:** Table also includes percentage increases in salary for continuing faculty by category, affiliation, and academic rank. **Number listed:** 4.

Doctoral institutions, with an average annual salary of $53,599
Comprehensive institutions, $44,460
Baccalaureate institutions, $39,257
Two-year institutions, $35,005

Source: "Uncertain Times: The Annual Report on the Economic Status of the Profession," *Academe*, 87: 25-98, (March/April 2001).

SALARIES—COLLEGES & UNIVERSITIES, FACULTY

★3789★
Average salaries for assistant professors in private-independent institutions, 2000-01

Ranking basis/background: Based on the responses of 1,433 institutions providing data to the annual salary survey of the American Association of University Professors. **Remarks:** Table also includes percentage increases in salary for continuing faculty by category, affiliation, and academic rank. **Number listed:** 4.

- Doctoral institutions, with an average annual salary of $60,853
- Comprehensive institutions, $47,045
- Baccalaureate institutions, $44,774
- Two-year institutions, $32,368

Source: "Uncertain Times: The Annual Report on the Economic Status of the Profession," *Academe*, 87: 25-98, (March/April 2001).

★3790★
Average salaries for assistant professors in public institutions, 2000-01

Ranking basis/background: Based on the responses of 1,433 institutions providing data to the annual salary survey of the American Association of University Professors. **Remarks:** Table also includes percentage increases in salary for continuing faculty by category, affiliation, and academic rank. **Number listed:** 4.

- Doctoral institutions, with an average annual salary of $50,635
- Comprehensive institutions, $45,147
- Baccalaureate institutions, $42,311
- Two-year institutions, $41,575

Source: "Uncertain Times: The Annual Report on the Economic Status of the Profession," *Academe*, 87: 25-98, (March/April 2001).

★3791★
Average salaries for associate professors at institutions in the East North Central states, 2000-01

Ranking basis/background: Based on the responses of 1,433 institutions providing data to the annual salary survey of the American Association of University Professors. **Remarks:** The East North Central region includes Illinois, Indiana, Michigan, Ohio, and Wisconsin. **Number listed:** 4.

- Doctoral institutions, with an average annual salary of $62,039
- Comprehensive institutions, $54,000
- Baccalaureate institutions, $48,390
- Two-year institutions, $48,008

Source: "Uncertain Times: The Annual Report on the Economic Status of the Profession," *Academe*, 87: 25-98, (March/April 2001).

★3792★
Average salaries for associate professors at institutions in the East South Central states, 2000-01

Ranking basis/background: Based on the responses of 1,433 institutions providing data to the annual salary survey of the American Association of University Professors. **Remarks:** The East South Central region includes Alabama, Kentucky, Mississippi and Tennessee. **Number listed:** 4.

- Doctoral institutions, with an average annual salary of $57,296
- Comprehensive institutions, $50,169
- Baccalaureate institutions, $44,503
- Two-year institutions, $41,290

Source: "Uncertain Times: The Annual Report on the Economic Status of the Profession," *Academe*, 87: 25-98, (March/April 2001).

★3793★
Average salaries for associate professors at institutions in the Middle Atlantic states, 2000-01

Ranking basis/background: Based on the responses of 1,433 institutions providing data to the annual salary survey of the American Association of University Professors. **Remarks:** The Middle Atlantic region includes New Jersey, New York, and Pennsylvania. **Number listed:** 4.

- Doctoral institutions, with an average annual salary of $69,100
- Comprehensive institutions, $59,846
- Baccalaureate institutions, $55,530
- Two-year institutions, $52,769

Source: "Uncertain Times: The Annual Report on the Economic Status of the Profession," *Academe*, 87: 25-98, (March/April 2001).

★3794★
Average salaries for associate professors at institutions in the Mountain states, 2000-01

Ranking basis/background: Based on the responses of 1,433 institutions providing data to the annual salary survey of the American Association of University Professors. **Remarks:** The Mountain region includes Arizona, Colorado, Idaho, Montana, Nevada, New Mexico, Utah and Wyoming. **Number listed:** 4.

- Doctoral institutions, with an average annual salary of $56,542
- Comprehensive institutions, $54,475
- Baccalaureate institutions, $45,863
- Two-year institutions, $39,866

Source: "Uncertain Times: The Annual Report on the Economic Status of the Profession," *Academe*, 87: 25-98, (March/April 2001).

★3795★
Average salaries for associate professors at institutions in the New England states, 2000-01

Ranking basis/background: Based on the responses of 1,433 institutions providing data to the annual salary survey of the American Association of University Professors. **Remarks:** The New England region includes Connecticut, Maine, Massachusetts, New Hampshire, Vermont, and Rhode Island. **Number listed:** 4.

- Doctoral institutions, with an average annual salary of $67,536
- Comprehensive institutions, $58,010
- Baccalaureate institutions, $57,302
- Two-year institutions, $38,842

Source: "Uncertain Times: The Annual Report on the Economic Status of the Profession," *Academe*, 87: 25-98, (March/April 2001).

★3796★
Average salaries for associate professors at institutions in the Pacific states, 2000-01

Ranking basis/background: Based on the responses of 1,433 institutions providing data to the annual salary survey of the American Association of University Professors. **Remarks:** The Pacific region includes Alaska, California, Hawaii, Oregon, and Washington. **Number listed:** 4.

- Doctoral institutions, with an average annual salary of $62,976
- Comprehensive institutions, $58,709
- Baccalaureate institutions, $51,227
- Two-year institutions, $48,970

Source: "Uncertain Times: The Annual Report on the Economic Status of the Profession," *Academe*, 87: 25-98, (March/April 2001).

★3797★
Average salaries for associate professors at institutions in the South Atlantic states, 2000-01

Ranking basis/background: Based on the responses of 1,433 institutions providing data to the annual salary survey of the American Association of University Professors. **Remarks:** The South Atlantic region includes Delaware, District of Columbia, Florida, Georgia, Maryland, North Carolina, South Carolina, Virginia, and West Virginia. **Number listed:** 4.

- Doctoral institutions, with an average annual salary of $64,004
- Comprehensive institutions, $55,077
- Baccalaureate institutions, $49,386
- Two-year institutions, $48,052

Source: "Uncertain Times: The Annual Report on the Economic Status of the Profession," *Academe*, 87: 25-98, (March/April 2001).

★3798★
Average salaries for associate professors at institutions in the West North Central states, 2000-01

Ranking basis/background: Based on the responses of 1,433 institutions providing data to the annual salary survey of the American Association of University Professors. **Remarks:** The West North Central region includes Iowa, Kansas, Minnesota, Missouri, Nebraska, North Dakota and South Dakota. **Number listed:** 4.

- Doctoral institutions, with an average annual salary of $59,730
- Comprehensive institutions, $52,701
- Baccalaureate institutions, $46,880
- Two-year institutions, $42,828

Source: "Uncertain Times: The Annual Report on the Economic Status of the Profession," *Academe*, 87: 25-98, (March/April 2001).

★3799★
Average salaries for associate professors at institutions in the West South Central states, 2000-01

Ranking basis/background: Based on the responses of 1,433 institutions providing data to the annual salary survey of the American Association of University Professors. **Remarks:** The West South Central region includes Arkansas, Louisiana, Oklahoma and Texas. **Number listed:** 4.

- Doctoral institutions, with an average annual salary of $58,464
- Comprehensive institutions, $50,839
- Baccalaureate institutions, $46,886
- Two-year institutions, $48,376

Source: "Uncertain Times: The Annual Report on the Economic Status of the Profession," *Academe*, 87: 25-98, (March/April 2001).

★3800★
Average salaries for associate professors at private institutions in preclinical department of medical schools, 2000-01

Ranking basis/background: Salaries are on a 12-month basis and are rounded to the nearest $100. Data was reported for all faculty (M.D., other doctoral, and nondoctoral). **Remarks:** Original source: Association of American Medical Colleges. **Number listed:** 8.
- Anatomy, with an average salary of $77,200
- Biochemistry, $75,200
- Genetics, $89,800
- Microbiology, $77,900
- Molecular/cellular biology, $84,800
- Pharmacology, $76,200
- Physiology, $77,100
- Other basic sciences, $87,800

Source: "Uncertain Times: The Annual Report on the Economic Status of the Profession," *Academe*, 87: 25-98, (March/April 2001).

★3801★
Average salaries for associate professors at public and private institutions in preclinical department of medical schools, 2000-01

Ranking basis/background: Salaries are on a 12-month basis and are rounded to the nearest $100. Data was reported for all faculty (M.D., other doctoral, and nondoctoral). **Remarks:** Original source: Association of American Medical Colleges. **Number listed:** 8.
- Anatomy, with an average salary of $75,600
- Biochemistry, $74,200
- Genetics, $85,100
- Microbiology, $76,000
- Molecular/cellular biology, $82,200
- Pharmacology, $76,400
- Physiology, $76,200
- Other basic sciences, $83,800

Source: "Uncertain Times: The Annual Report on the Economic Status of the Profession," *Academe*, 87: 25-98, (March/April 2001).

★3802★
Average salaries for associate professors at public institutions in preclinical department of medical schools, 2000-01

Ranking basis/background: Salaries are on a 12-month basis and are rounded to the nearest $100. Data was reported for all faculty (M.D., other doctoral, and nondoctoral). **Remarks:** Original source: Association of American Medical Colleges. **Number listed:** 8.
- Anatomy, with an average salary of $75,000
- Biochemistry, $73,700
- Genetics, $82,300
- Microbiology, $74,800
- Molecular/cellular biology, $78,200
- Pharmacology, $76,500
- Physiology, $75,600
- Other basic sciences, $76,100

Source: "Uncertain Times: The Annual Report on the Economic Status of the Profession," *Academe*, 87: 25-98, (March/April 2001).

★3803★
Average salaries for associate professors in church-related institutions, 2000-01

Ranking basis/background: Based on the responses of 1,433 institutions providing data to the annual salary survey of the American Association of University Professors. **Remarks:** Table also includes percentage increases in salary for continuing faculty by category, affiliation, and academic rank. **Number listed:** 4.
- Doctoral institutions, with an average annual salary of $65,221
- Comprehensive institutions, $54,638
- Baccalaureate institutions, $46,598
- Two-year institutions, $38,737

Source: "Uncertain Times: The Annual Report on the Economic Status of the Profession," *Academe*, 87: 25-98, (March/April 2001).

★3804★
Average salaries for associate professors in private-independent institutions, 2000-01

Ranking basis/background: Based on the responses of 1,433 institutions providing data to the annual salary survey of the American Association of University Professors. **Remarks:** Table also includes percentage increases in salary for continuing faculty by category, affiliation, and academic rank. **Number listed:** 4.
- Doctoral institutions, with an average annual salary of $70,314
- Comprehensive institutions, $57,832
- Baccalaureate institutions, $54,933
- Two-year institutions, $45,052

Source: "Uncertain Times: The Annual Report on the Economic Status of the Profession," *Academe*, 87: 25-98, (March/April 2001).

★3805★
Average salaries for associate professors in public institutions, 2000-01

Ranking basis/background: Based on the responses of 1,433 institutions providing data to the annual salary survey of the American Association of University Professors. **Remarks:** Table also includes percentage increases in salary for continuing faculty by category, affiliation, and academic rank. **Number listed:** 4.
- Doctoral institutions, with an average annual salary of $60,571
- Comprehensive institutions, $54,886
- Baccalaureate institutions, $50,811
- Two-year institutions, $47,323

Source: "Uncertain Times: The Annual Report on the Economic Status of the Profession," *Academe*, 87: 25-98, (March/April 2001).

★3806★
Average salaries for bioengineering and biomedical engineering faculty at 4-year institutions, 1999-2000

Ranking basis/background: Average salary for faculty at public and private 4-year institutions. From a survey of professors in 80 disciplines at 363 public colleges and 501 private institutions, excluding medical professors. **Remarks:** Original source: College and University Personnel Association. **Number listed:** 2.
- Private, with $77,089
- Public, $69,118

Source: Magner, Denise K., "Law Professors are Academe's Best-Paid Faculty Members, Survey Finds," *The Chronicle of Higher Education*, 46: A20, (May 12, 2000).

★3807★
Average salaries for botany faculty at 4-year institutions, 1999-2000

Ranking basis/background: Average salary for faculty at public and private 4-year institutions. From a survey of professors in 80 disciplines at 363 public colleges and 501 private institutions, excluding medical professors. **Remarks:** Original source: College and University Personnel Association. **Number listed:** 2.
- Private, with $48,168
- Public, $57,931

Source: Magner, Denise K., "Law Professors are Academe's Best-Paid Faculty Members, Survey Finds," *The Chronicle of Higher Education*, 46: A20, (May 12, 2000).

★3808★
Average salaries for business administration and management faculty at 4-year institutions, 1999-2000

Ranking basis/background: Average salary for faculty at public and private 4-year institutions. From a survey of professors in 80 disciplines at 363 public colleges and 501 private institutions, excluding medical professors. **Remarks:** Original source: College and University Personnel Association. **Number listed:** 2.
- Private, with $65,054
- Public, $66,464

Source: Magner, Denise K., "Law Professors are Academe's Best-Paid Faculty Members, Survey Finds," *The Chronicle of Higher Education*, 46: A20, (May 12, 2000).

★3809★
Average salaries for business and managerial economics faculty at 4-year institutions, 1999-2000

Ranking basis/background: Average salary for faculty at public and private 4-year institutions. From a survey of professors in 80 disciplines at 363 public colleges and 501 private institutions, excluding medical professors. **Remarks:** Original source: College and University Personnel Association. **Number listed:** 2.
- Private, with $63,826
- Public, $65,029

Source: Magner, Denise K., "Law Professors are Academe's Best-Paid Faculty Members, Survey Finds," *The Chronicle of Higher Education*, 46: A20, (May 12, 2000).

★3810★
Average salaries for business management and administrative services faculty at 4-year institutions, 1999-2000

Ranking basis/background: Average salary for faculty at public and private 4-year institutions. From a survey of professors in 80 disciplines at 363 public colleges and 501 private institutions, excluding medical professors. **Remarks:** Original source: College and University Personnel Association. **Number listed:** 2.
- Private, with $65,077
- Public, $77,628

SALARIES—COLLEGES & UNIVERSITIES, FACULTY

Source: Magner, Denise K., "Law Professors are Academe's Best-Paid Faculty Members, Survey Finds," *The Chronicle of Higher Education*, 46: A20, (May 12, 2000).

★3811★
Average salaries for cell and molecular biology faculty at 4-year institutions, 1999-2000

Ranking basis/background: Average salary for faculty at public and private 4-year institutions. From a survey of professors in 80 disciplines at 363 public colleges and 501 private institutions, excluding medical professors. **Remarks:** Original source: College and University Personnel Association. **Number listed:** 2.
  Private, with $59,876
  Public, $61,379
Source: Magner, Denise K., "Law Professors are Academe's Best-Paid Faculty Members, Survey Finds," *The Chronicle of Higher Education*, 46: A20, (May 12, 2000).

★3812★
Average salaries for chemical engineering faculty at 4-year institutions, 1999-2000

Ranking basis/background: Average salary for faculty at public and private 4-year institutions. From a survey of professors in 80 disciplines at 363 public colleges and 501 private institutions, excluding medical professors. **Remarks:** Original source: College and University Personnel Association. **Number listed:** 2.
  Private, with $80,931
  Public, $77,474
Source: Magner, Denise K., "Law Professors are Academe's Best-Paid Faculty Members, Survey Finds," *The Chronicle of Higher Education*, 46: A20, (May 12, 2000).

★3813★
Average salaries for chemistry faculty at 4-year institutions, 1999-2000

Ranking basis/background: Average salary for faculty at public and private 4-year institutions. From a survey of professors in 80 disciplines at 363 public colleges and 501 private institutions, excluding medical professors. **Remarks:** Original source: College and University Personnel Association. **Number listed:** 2.
  Private, with $55,556
  Public, $58,977
Source: Magner, Denise K., "Law Professors are Academe's Best-Paid Faculty Members, Survey Finds," *The Chronicle of Higher Education*, 46: A20, (May 12, 2000).

★3814★
Average salaries for civil engineering faculty at 4-year institutions, 1999-2000

Ranking basis/background: Average salary for faculty at public and private 4-year institutions. From a survey of professors in 80 disciplines at 363 public colleges and 501 private institutions, excluding medical professors. **Remarks:** Original source: College and University Personnel Association. **Number listed:** 2.
  Private, with $71,230
  Public, $70,705
Source: Magner, Denise K., "Law Professors are Academe's Best-Paid Faculty Members, Survey Finds," *The Chronicle of Higher Education*, 46: A20, (May 12, 2000).

★3815★
Average salaries for classical and ancient Near Eastern languages and literatures faculty at 4-year institutions, 1999-2000

Ranking basis/background: Average salary for faculty at public and private 4-year institutions. From a survey of professors in 80 disciplines at 363 public colleges and 501 private institutions, excluding medical professors. **Remarks:** Original source: College and University Personnel Association. **Number listed:** 2.
  Private, with $56,368
  Public, $58,360
Source: Magner, Denise K., "Law Professors are Academe's Best-Paid Faculty Members, Survey Finds," *The Chronicle of Higher Education*, 46: A20, (May 12, 2000).

★3816★
Average salaries for clinical psychology faculty at 4-year institutions, 1999-2000

Ranking basis/background: Average salary for faculty at public and private 4-year institutions. From a survey of professors in 80 disciplines at 363 public colleges and 501 private institutions, excluding medical professors. **Remarks:** Original source: College and University Personnel Association. **Number listed:** 2.
  Private, with $54,961
  Public, $55,174
Source: Magner, Denise K., "Law Professors are Academe's Best-Paid Faculty Members, Survey Finds," *The Chronicle of Higher Education*, 46: A20, (May 12, 2000).

★3817★
Average salaries for communications faculty at 4-year institutions, 1999-2000

Ranking basis/background: Average salary for faculty at public and private 4-year institutions. From a survey of professors in 80 disciplines at 363 public colleges and 501 private institutions, excluding medical professors. **Remarks:** Original source: College and University Personnel Association. **Number listed:** 2.
  Private, with $47,588
  Public, $50,148
Source: Magner, Denise K., "Law Professors are Academe's Best-Paid Faculty Members, Survey Finds," *The Chronicle of Higher Education*, 46: A20, (May 12, 2000).

★3818★
Average salaries for communications technologies faculty at 4-year institutions, 1999-2000

Ranking basis/background: Average salary for faculty at public and private 4-year institutions. From a survey of professors in 80 disciplines at 363 public colleges and 501 private institutions, excluding medical professors. **Remarks:** Original source: College and University Personnel Association. **Number listed:** 2.
  Private, with $49,331
  Public, $53,184
Source: Magner, Denise K., "Law Professors are Academe's Best-Paid Faculty Members, Survey Finds," *The Chronicle of Higher Education*, 46: A20, (May 12, 2000).

★3819★
Average salaries for computer and information sciences faculty at 4-year institutions, 1999-2000

Ranking basis/background: Average salary for faculty at public and private 4-year institutions. From a survey of professors in 80 disciplines at 363 public colleges and 501 private institutions, excluding medical professors. **Remarks:** Original source: College and University Personnel Association. **Number listed:** 2.
  Private, with $58,260
  Public, $66,240
Source: Magner, Denise K., "Law Professors are Academe's Best-Paid Faculty Members, Survey Finds," *The Chronicle of Higher Education*, 46: A20, (May 12, 2000).

★3820★
Average salaries for counselor education faculty at 4-year institutions, 1999-2000

Ranking basis/background: Average salary for faculty at public and private 4-year institutions. From a survey of professors in 80 disciplines at 363 public colleges and 501 private institutions, excluding medical professors. **Remarks:** Original source: College and University Personnel Association. **Number listed:** 2.
  Private, with $54,045
  Public, $52,681
Source: Magner, Denise K., "Law Professors are Academe's Best-Paid Faculty Members, Survey Finds," *The Chronicle of Higher Education*, 46: A20, (May 12, 2000).

★3821★
Average salaries for criminal justice and corrections faculty at 4-year institutions, 1999-2000

Ranking basis/background: Average salary for faculty at public and private 4-year institutions. From a survey of professors in 80 disciplines at 363 public colleges and 501 private institutions, excluding medical professors. **Remarks:** Original source: College and University Personnel Association. **Number listed:** 2.
  Private, with $43,434
  Public, $51,159
Source: Magner, Denise K., "Law Professors are Academe's Best-Paid Faculty Members, Survey Finds," *The Chronicle of Higher Education*, 46: A20, (May 12, 2000).

★3822★
Average salaries for curriculum and instruction faculty at 4-year institutions, 1999-2000

Ranking basis/background: Average salary for faculty at public and private 4-year institutions. From a survey of professors in 80 disciplines at 363 public colleges and 501 private institutions, excluding medical professors. **Remarks:** Original source: College and University Personnel Association. **Number listed:** 2.
  Private, with $52,735
  Public, $50,535
Source: Magner, Denise K., "Law Professors are Academe's Best-Paid Faculty Members, Survey Finds," *The Chronicle of Higher Education*, 46: A20, (May 12, 2000).

SALARIES—COLLEGES & UNIVERSITIES, FACULTY

★3823★
Average salaries for dentistry faculty at 4-year institutions, 1999-2000

Ranking basis/background: Average salary for faculty at public and private 4-year institutions. From a survey of professors in 80 disciplines at 363 public colleges and 501 private institutions, excluding medical professors. **Remarks:** Original source: College and University Personnel Association. **Number listed:** 2.
  Private, with $66,139
  Public, $71,671
Source: Magner, Denise K., "Law Professors are Academe's Best-Paid Faculty Members, Survey Finds," *The Chronicle of Higher Education*, 46: A20, (May 12, 2000).

★3824★
Average salaries for drama and theater arts faculty at 4-year institutions, 1999-2000

Ranking basis/background: Average salary for faculty at public and private 4-year institutions. From a survey of professors in 80 disciplines at 363 public colleges and 501 private institutions, excluding medical professors. **Remarks:** Original source: College and University Personnel Association. **Number listed:** 2.
  Private, with $48,134
  Public, $49,218
Source: Magner, Denise K., "Law Professors are Academe's Best-Paid Faculty Members, Survey Finds," *The Chronicle of Higher Education*, 46: A20, (May 12, 2000).

★3825★
Average salaries for economics faculty at 4-year institutions, 1999-2000

Ranking basis/background: Average salary for faculty at public and private 4-year institutions. From a survey of professors in 80 disciplines at 363 public colleges and 501 private institutions, excluding medical professors. **Remarks:** Original source: College and University Personnel Association. **Number listed:** 2.
  Private, with $67,255
  Public, $66,682
Source: Magner, Denise K., "Law Professors are Academe's Best-Paid Faculty Members, Survey Finds," *The Chronicle of Higher Education*, 46: A20, (May 12, 2000).

★3826★
Average salaries for education administration and supervision faculty at 4-year institutions, 1999-2000

Ranking basis/background: Average salary for faculty at public and private 4-year institutions. From a survey of professors in 80 disciplines at 363 public colleges and 501 private institutions, excluding medical professors. **Remarks:** Original source: College and University Personnel Association. **Number listed:** 2.
  Private, with $55,249
  Public, $56,221
Source: Magner, Denise K., "Law Professors are Academe's Best-Paid Faculty Members, Survey Finds," *The Chronicle of Higher Education*, 46: A20, (May 12, 2000).

★3827★
Average salaries for education faculty at 4-year institutions, 1999-2000

Ranking basis/background: Average salary for faculty at public and private 4-year institutions. From a survey of professors in 80 disciplines at 363 public colleges and 501 private institutions, excluding medical professors. **Remarks:** Original source: College and University Personnel Association. **Number listed:** 2.
  Private, with $49,137
  Public, $54,369
Source: Magner, Denise K., "Law Professors are Academe's Best-Paid Faculty Members, Survey Finds," *The Chronicle of Higher Education*, 46: A20, (May 12, 2000).

★3828★
Average salaries for electrical, electronics, and communications engineering faculty at 4-year institutions, 1999-2000

Ranking basis/background: Average salary for faculty at public and private 4-year institutions. From a survey of professors in 80 disciplines at 363 public colleges and 501 private institutions, excluding medical professors. **Remarks:** Original source: College and University Personnel Association. **Number listed:** 2.
  Private, with $76,683
  Public, $73,795
Source: Magner, Denise K., "Law Professors are Academe's Best-Paid Faculty Members, Survey Finds," *The Chronicle of Higher Education*, 46: A20, (May 12, 2000).

★3829★
Average salaries for engineering-related technology faculty at 4-year institutions, 1999-2000

Ranking basis/background: Average salary for faculty at public and private 4-year institutions. From a survey of professors in 80 disciplines at 363 public colleges and 501 private institutions, excluding medical professors. **Remarks:** Original source: College and University Personnel Association. **Number listed:** 2.
  Private, with $46,978
  Public, $53,195
Source: Magner, Denise K., "Law Professors are Academe's Best-Paid Faculty Members, Survey Finds," *The Chronicle of Higher Education*, 46: A20, (May 12, 2000).

★3830★
Average salaries for English composition faculty at 4-year institutions, 1999-2000

Ranking basis/background: Average salary for faculty at public and private 4-year institutions. From a survey of professors in 80 disciplines at 363 public colleges and 501 private institutions, excluding medical professors. **Remarks:** Original source: College and University Personnel Association. **Number listed:** 2.
  Private, with $40,991
  Public, $41,840
Source: Magner, Denise K., "Law Professors are Academe's Best-Paid Faculty Members, Survey Finds," *The Chronicle of Higher Education*, 46: A20, (May 12, 2000).

★3831★
Average salaries for English language and literature faculty at 4-year institutions, 1999-2000

Ranking basis/background: Average salary for faculty at public and private 4-year institutions. From a survey of professors in 80 disciplines at 363 public colleges and 501 private institutions, excluding medical professors. **Remarks:** Original source: College and University Personnel Association. **Number listed:** 2.
  Private, with $50,931
  Public, $51,960
Source: Magner, Denise K., "Law Professors are Academe's Best-Paid Faculty Members, Survey Finds," *The Chronicle of Higher Education*, 46: A20, (May 12, 2000).

★3832★
Average salaries for enterprise management and operation faculty at 4-year institutions, 1999-2000

Ranking basis/background: Average salary for faculty at public and private 4-year institutions. From a survey of professors in 80 disciplines at 363 public colleges and 501 private institutions, excluding medical professors. **Remarks:** Original source: College and University Personnel Association. **Number listed:** 2.
  Private, with $77,737
  Public, $68,049
Source: Magner, Denise K., "Law Professors are Academe's Best-Paid Faculty Members, Survey Finds," *The Chronicle of Higher Education*, 46: A20, (May 12, 2000).

★3833★
Average salaries for environmental and environmental health engineering faculty at 4-year institutions, 1999-2000

Ranking basis/background: Average salary for faculty at public and private 4-year institutions. From a survey of professors in 80 disciplines at 363 public colleges and 501 private institutions, excluding medical professors. **Remarks:** Original source: College and University Personnel Association. **Number listed:** 2.
  Private, with $57,809
  Public, $56,005
Source: Magner, Denise K., "Law Professors are Academe's Best-Paid Faculty Members, Survey Finds," *The Chronicle of Higher Education*, 46: A20, (May 12, 2000).

★3834★
Average salaries for female assistant professors in church-related institutions, 2000-01

Ranking basis/background: Based on the responses of 1,433 institutions providing data to the annual salary survey of the American Association of University Professors. **Remarks:** Table also includes percentage increases in salary for continuing faculty by category, affiliation, and academic rank. **Number listed:** 4.
  Doctoral institutions, with an average annual salary of $51,255
  Comprehensive institutions, $43,053
  Baccalaureate institutions, $38,996
  Two-year institutions, $34,585
Source: "Uncertain Times: The Annual Report on the Economic Status of the Profession," *Academe*, 87: 25-98, (March/April 2001).

SALARIES—COLLEGES & UNIVERSITIES, FACULTY

★3835★
Average salaries for female assistant professors in private-independent institutions, 2000-01

Ranking basis/background: Based on the responses of 1,433 institutions providing data to the annual salary survey of the American Association of University Professors. **Remarks:** Table also includes percentage increases in salary for continuing faculty by category, affiliation, and academic rank. **Number listed:** 4.

- Doctoral institutions, with an average annual salary of $56,901
- Comprehensive institutions, $45,935
- Baccalaureate institutions, $44,227
- Two-year institutions, $30,716

Source: "Uncertain Times: The Annual Report on the Economic Status of the Profession," *Academe*, 87: 25-98, (March/April 2001).

★3836★
Average salaries for female assistant professors in public institutions, 2000-01

Ranking basis/background: Based on the responses of 1,433 institutions providing data to the annual salary survey of the American Association of University Professors. **Remarks:** Table also includes percentage increases in salary for continuing faculty by category, affiliation, and academic rank. **Number listed:** 4.

- Doctoral institutions, with an average annual salary of $48,106
- Comprehensive institutions, $44,222
- Baccalaureate institutions, $41,306
- Two-year institutions, $40,736

Source: "Uncertain Times: The Annual Report on the Economic Status of the Profession," *Academe*, 87: 25-98, (March/April 2001).

★3837★
Average salaries for female associate professors in church-related institutions, 2000-01

Ranking basis/background: Based on the responses of 1,433 institutions providing data to the annual salary survey of the American Association of University Professors. **Remarks:** Table also includes percentage increases in salary for continuing faculty by category, affiliation, and academic rank. **Number listed:** 4.

- Doctoral institutions, with an average annual salary of $61,972
- Comprehensive institutions, $51,979
- Baccalaureate institutions, $45,686
- Two-year institutions, $39,378

Source: "Uncertain Times: The Annual Report on the Economic Status of the Profession," *Academe*, 87: 25-98, (March/April 2001).

★3838★
Average salaries for female associate professors in private-independent institutions, 2000-01

Ranking basis/background: Based on the responses of 1,433 institutions providing data to the annual salary survey of the American Association of University Professors. **Remarks:** Table also includes percentage increases in salary for continuing faculty by category, affiliation, and academic rank. **Number listed:** 4.

- Doctoral institutions, with an average annual salary of $66,851
- Comprehensive institutions, $55,990
- Baccalaureate institutions, $53,722
- Two-year institutions, $41,337

Source: "Uncertain Times: The Annual Report on the Economic Status of the Profession," *Academe*, 87: 25-98, (March/April 2001).

★3839★
Average salaries for female associate professors in public institutions, 2000-01

Ranking basis/background: Based on the responses of 1,433 institutions providing data to the annual salary survey of the American Association of University Professors. **Remarks:** Table also includes percentage increases in salary for continuing faculty by category, affiliation, and academic rank. **Number listed:** 4.

- Doctoral institutions, with an average annual salary of $57,796
- Comprehensive institutions, $53,338
- Baccalaureate institutions, $48,943
- Two-year institutions, $45,748

Source: "Uncertain Times: The Annual Report on the Economic Status of the Profession," *Academe*, 87: 25-98, (March/April 2001).

★3840★
Average salaries for female instructors in church-related institutions, 2000-01

Ranking basis/background: Based on the responses of 1,433 institutions providing data to the annual salary survey of the American Association of University Professors. **Remarks:** Table also includes percentage increases in salary for continuing faculty by category, affiliation, and academic rank. **Number listed:** 4.

- Doctoral institutions, with an average annual salary of $44,745
- Comprehensive institutions, $34,317
- Baccalaureate institutions, $33,248
- Two-year institutions, $30,158

Source: "Uncertain Times: The Annual Report on the Economic Status of the Profession," *Academe*, 87: 25-98, (March/April 2001).

★3841★
Average salaries for female instructors in private-independent institutions, 2000-01

Ranking basis/background: Based on the responses of 1,433 institutions providing data to the annual salary survey of the American Association of University Professors. **Remarks:** Table also includes percentage increases in salary for continuing faculty by category, affiliation, and academic rank. **Number listed:** 4.

- Doctoral institutions, with an average annual salary of $40,882
- Comprehensive institutions, $37,439
- Baccalaureate institutions, $36,201
- Two-year institutions, $26,745

Source: "Uncertain Times: The Annual Report on the Economic Status of the Profession," *Academe*, 87: 25-98, (March/April 2001).

★3842★
Average salaries for female instructors in public institutions, 2000-01

Ranking basis/background: Based on the responses of 1,433 institutions providing data to the annual salary survey of the American Association of University Professors. **Remarks:** Table also includes percentage increases in salary for continuing faculty by category, affiliation, and academic rank. **Number listed:** 4.

- Doctoral institutions, with an average annual salary of $34,688
- Comprehensive institutions, $34,091
- Baccalaureate institutions, $33,724
- Two-year institutions, $35,299

Source: "Uncertain Times: The Annual Report on the Economic Status of the Profession," *Academe*, 87: 25-98, (March/April 2001).

★3843★
Average salaries for female lecturers in church-related institutions, 2000-01

Ranking basis/background: Based on the responses of 1,433 institutions providing data to the annual salary survey of the American Association of University Professors. **Remarks:** Table also includes percentage increases in salary for continuing faculty by category, affiliation, and academic rank. **Number listed:** 3.

- Doctoral institutions, with an average annual salary of $38,354
- Comprehensive institutions, $36,799
- Baccalaureate institutions, $33,333

Source: "Uncertain Times: The Annual Report on the Economic Status of the Profession," *Academe*, 87: 25-98, (March/April 2001).

★3844★
Average salaries for female lecturers in private-independent institutions, 2000-01

Ranking basis/background: Based on the responses of 1,433 institutions providing data to the annual salary survey of the American Association of University Professors. **Remarks:** Table also includes percentage increases in salary for continuing faculty by category, affiliation, and academic rank. **Number listed:** 4.

- Doctoral institutions, with an average annual salary of $42,824
- Comprehensive institutions, $37,235
- Baccalaureate institutions, $42,750
- Two-year institutions, $30,100

Source: "Uncertain Times: The Annual Report on the Economic Status of the Profession," *Academe*, 87: 25-98, (March/April 2001).

★3845★
Average salaries for female lecturers in public institutions, 2000-01

Ranking basis/background: Based on the responses of 1,433 institutions providing data to the annual salary survey of the American Association of University Professors. **Remarks:** Table also includes percentage increases in salary for continuing faculty by category, affiliation, and academic rank. **Number listed:** 4.

- Doctoral institutions, with an average annual salary of $38,004
- Comprehensive institutions, $34,451
- Baccalaureate institutions, $34,043
- Two-year institutions, $34,650

Source: "Uncertain Times: The Annual Report on the Economic Status of the Profession," *Academe*, 87: 25-98, (March/April 2001).

★3846★
Average salaries for female professors in church-related institutions, 2000-01

Ranking basis/background: Based on the responses of 1,433 institutions providing data to the annual salary survey of the American Association of University Professors. **Remarks:** Table also includes percentage increases in salary for continuing faculty by category, affiliation, and academic rank. **Number listed:** 4.

- Doctoral institutions, with an average annual salary of $89,176
- Comprehensive institutions, $65,112
- Baccalaureate institutions, $54,616
- Two-year institutions, $39,356

Source: "Uncertain Times: The Annual Report on the Economic Status of the Profession," *Academe*, 87: 25-98, (March/April 2001).

★3847★
Average salaries for female professors in private-independent institutions, 2000-01

Ranking basis/background: Based on the responses of 1,433 institutions providing data to the annual salary survey of the American Association of University Professors. **Remarks:** Table also includes percentage increases in salary for continuing faculty by category, affiliation, and academic rank. **Number listed:** 4.

- Doctoral institutions, with an average annual salary of $98,905
- Comprehensive institutions, $71,976
- Baccalaureate institutions, $70,986
- Two-year institutions, $47,609

Source: "Uncertain Times: The Annual Report on the Economic Status of the Profession," *Academe*, 87: 25-98, (March/April 2001).

★3848★
Average salaries for female professors in public institutions, 2000-01

Ranking basis/background: Based on the responses of 1,433 institutions providing data to the annual salary survey of the American Association of University Professors. **Remarks:** Table also includes percentage increases in salary for continuing faculty by category, affiliation, and academic rank. **Number listed:** 4.

- Doctoral institutions, with an average annual salary of $77,379
- Comprehensive institutions, $66,795
- Baccalaureate institutions, $59,425
- Two-year institutions, $55,268

Source: "Uncertain Times: The Annual Report on the Economic Status of the Profession," *Academe*, 87: 25-98, (March/April 2001).

★3849★
Average salaries for financial management and services faculty at 4-year institutions, 1999-2000

Ranking basis/background: Average salary for faculty at public and private 4-year institutions. From a survey of professors in 80 disciplines at 363 public colleges and 501 private institutions, excluding medical professors. **Remarks:** Original source: College and University Personnel Association. **Number listed:** 2.

- Private, with $84,762
- Public, $77,229

Source: Magner, Denise K., "Law Professors are Academe's Best-Paid Faculty Members, Survey Finds," *The Chronicle of Higher Education*, 46: A20, (May 12, 2000).

★3850★
Average salaries for fine arts and art studies faculty at 4-year institutions, 1999-2000

Ranking basis/background: Average salary for faculty at public and private 4-year institutions. From a survey of professors in 80 disciplines at 363 public colleges and 501 private institutions, excluding medical professors. **Remarks:** Original source: College and University Personnel Association. **Number listed:** 2.

- Private, with $48,619
- Public, $51,249

Source: Magner, Denise K., "Law Professors are Academe's Best-Paid Faculty Members, Survey Finds," *The Chronicle of Higher Education*, 46: A20, (May 12, 2000).

★3851★
Average salaries for foreign languages and literatures faculty at 4-year institutions, 1999-2000

Ranking basis/background: Average salary for faculty at public and private 4-year institutions. From a survey of professors in 80 disciplines at 363 public colleges and 501 private institutions, excluding medical professors. **Remarks:** Original source: College and University Personnel Association. **Number listed:** 2.

- Private, with $49,323
- Public, $50,984

Source: Magner, Denise K., "Law Professors are Academe's Best-Paid Faculty Members, Survey Finds," *The Chronicle of Higher Education*, 46: A20, (May 12, 2000).

★3852★
Average salaries for full professors at private research institutions for selected years

Ranking basis/background: Average salaries for full professors. **Remarks:** Original source: F. King Alexander; Chronicle analysis of American Association of University Professors Salary Data. **Number listed:** 5.

- 1980, with $72,900
- 1985, $82,500
- 1990, $93,700
- 1995, $98,200
- 2001, $110,700

Source: Smallwood, Scott, "The Price Professors Pay for Teaching at Public Universities," *The Chronicle of Higher Education*, 47: A18, A23-A24, (April 20, 2001).

★3853★
Average salaries for full professors at public research institutions for selected years

Ranking basis/background: Average salaries for full professors. **Remarks:** Original source: F. King Alexander; Chronicle analysis of American Association of University Professors Salary Data. **Number listed:** 5.

- 1980, with $71,500
- 1985, $70,000
- 1990, $78,400
- 1995, $77,200
- 2001, $88,600

Source: Smallwood, Scott, "The Price Professors Pay for Teaching at Public Universities," *The Chronicle of Higher Education*, 47: A18, A23-A24, (April 20, 2001).

★3854★
Average salaries for full-time instructors at private institutions in preclinical department of medical schools, 2000-01

Ranking basis/background: Salaries are on a 12-month basis and are rounded to the nearest $100. Data was reported for all faculty (M.D., other doctoral, and nondoctoral). **Remarks:** Original source: Association of American Medical Colleges. **Number listed:** 8.

- Anatomy, with an average salary of $35,100
- Biochemistry, $36,900
- Genetics, $44,100
- Microbiology, $41,900
- Molecular/cellular biology, $44,300
- Pharmacology, $36,400
- Physiology, $41,900
- Other basic sciences, $43,300

Source: "Uncertain Times: The Annual Report on the Economic Status of the Profession," *Academe*, 87: 25-98, (March/April 2001).

★3855★
Average salaries for full-time instructors at public and private institutions in preclinical department of medical schools, 2000-01

Ranking basis/background: Salaries are on a 12-month basis and are rounded to the nearest $100. Data was reported for all faculty (M.D., other doctoral, and nondoctoral). **Remarks:** Original source: Association of American Medical Colleges. **Number listed:** 8.

- Anatomy, with an average salary of $42,500
- Biochemistry, $38,300
- Genetics, $45,000
- Microbiology, $46,000
- Molecular/cellular biology, $43,000
- Pharmacology, $39,500
- Physiology, $41,900
- Other basic sciences, $43,600

Source: "Uncertain Times: The Annual Report on the Economic Status of the Profession," *Academe*, 87: 25-98, (March/April 2001).

★3856★
Average salaries for full-time instructors at public institutions in preclinical department of medical schools, 2000-01

Ranking basis/background: Salaries are on a 12-month basis and are rounded to the nearest $100. Data was reported for all faculty (M.D., other doctoral, and nondoctoral). **Remarks:** Original source: Association of American Medical Colleges. **Number listed:** 8.

- Anatomy, with an average salary of $49,300
- Biochemistry, $40,300
- Genetics, $49,200
- Microbiology, $49,500
- Molecular/cellular biology, $41,700
- Pharmacology, $41,700
- Physiology, $41,800
- Other basic sciences, $43,400

Source: "Uncertain Times: The Annual Report on the Economic Status of the Profession," *Academe*, 87: 25-98, (March/April 2001).

SALARIES—COLLEGES & UNIVERSITIES, FACULTY

★3857★
Average salaries for general biology faculty at 4-year institutions, 1999-2000

Ranking basis/background: Average salary for faculty at public and private 4-year institutions. From a survey of professors in 80 disciplines at 363 public colleges and 501 private institutions, excluding medical professors. **Remarks:** Original source: College and University Personnel Association. **Number listed:** 2.
   Private, with $53,155
   Public, $58,396
Source: Magner, Denise K., "Law Professors are Academe's Best-Paid Faculty Members, Survey Finds," *The Chronicle of Higher Education*, 46: A20, (May 12, 2000).

★3858★
Average salaries for general engineering faculty at 4-year institutions, 1999-2000

Ranking basis/background: Average salary for faculty at public and private 4-year institutions. From a survey of professors in 80 disciplines at 363 public colleges and 501 private institutions, excluding medical professors. **Remarks:** Original source: College and University Personnel Association. **Number listed:** 2.
   Private, with $76,060
   Public, $78,024
Source: Magner, Denise K., "Law Professors are Academe's Best-Paid Faculty Members, Survey Finds," *The Chronicle of Higher Education*, 46: A20, (May 12, 2000).

★3859★
Average salaries for general teacher education faculty at 4-year institutions, 1999-2000

Ranking basis/background: Average salary for faculty at public and private 4-year institutions. From a survey of professors in 80 disciplines at 363 public colleges and 501 private institutions, excluding medical professors. **Remarks:** Original source: College and University Personnel Association. **Number listed:** 2.
   Private, with $44,348
   Public, $50,802
Source: Magner, Denise K., "Law Professors are Academe's Best-Paid Faculty Members, Survey Finds," *The Chronicle of Higher Education*, 46: A20, (May 12, 2000).

★3860★
Average salaries for geography faculty at 4-year institutions, 1999-2000

Ranking basis/background: Average salary for faculty at public and private 4-year institutions. From a survey of professors in 80 disciplines at 363 public colleges and 501 private institutions, excluding medical professors. **Remarks:** Original source: College and University Personnel Association. **Number listed:** 2.
   Private, with $55,561
   Public, $54,327
Source: Magner, Denise K., "Law Professors are Academe's Best-Paid Faculty Members, Survey Finds," *The Chronicle of Higher Education*, 46: A20, (May 12, 2000).

★3861★
Average salaries for geological and related sciences faculty at 4-year institutions, 1999-2000

Ranking basis/background: Average salary for faculty at public and private 4-year institutions. From a survey of professors in 80 disciplines at 363 public colleges and 501 private institutions, excluding medical professors. **Remarks:** Original source: College and University Personnel Association. **Number listed:** 2.
   Private, with $64,132
   Public, $58,800
Source: Magner, Denise K., "Law Professors are Academe's Best-Paid Faculty Members, Survey Finds," *The Chronicle of Higher Education*, 46: A20, (May 12, 2000).

★3862★
Average salaries for health and medical administrative services faculty at 4-year institutions, 1999-2000

Ranking basis/background: Average salary for faculty at public and private 4-year institutions. From a survey of professors in 80 disciplines at 363 public colleges and 501 private institutions, excluding medical professors. **Remarks:** Original source: College and University Personnel Association. **Number listed:** 2.
   Private, with $47,035
   Public, $59,671
Source: Magner, Denise K., "Law Professors are Academe's Best-Paid Faculty Members, Survey Finds," *The Chronicle of Higher Education*, 46: A20, (May 12, 2000).

★3863★
Average salaries for health and physical education faculty at 4-year institutions, 1999-2000

Ranking basis/background: Average salary for faculty at public and private 4-year institutions. From a survey of professors in 80 disciplines at 363 public colleges and 501 private institutions, excluding medical professors. **Remarks:** Original source: College and University Personnel Association. **Number listed:** 2.
   Private, with $44,310
   Public, $48,713
Source: Magner, Denise K., "Law Professors are Academe's Best-Paid Faculty Members, Survey Finds," *The Chronicle of Higher Education*, 46: A20, (May 12, 2000).

★3864★
Average salaries for history faculty at 4-year institutions, 1999-2000

Ranking basis/background: Average salary for faculty at public and private 4-year institutions. From a survey of professors in 80 disciplines at 363 public colleges and 501 private institutions, excluding medical professors. **Remarks:** Original source: College and University Personnel Association. **Number listed:** 2.
   Private, with $54,363
   Public, $54,937
Source: Magner, Denise K., "Law Professors are Academe's Best-Paid Faculty Members, Survey Finds," *The Chronicle of Higher Education*, 46: A20, (May 12, 2000).

★3865★
Average salaries for home economics faculty at 4-year institutions, 1999-2000

Ranking basis/background: Average salary for faculty at public and private 4-year institutions. From a survey of professors in 80 disciplines at 363 public colleges and 501 private institutions, excluding medical professors. **Remarks:** Original source: College and University Personnel Association. **Number listed:** 2.
   Private, with $46,117
   Public, $53,316
Source: Magner, Denise K., "Law Professors are Academe's Best-Paid Faculty Members, Survey Finds," *The Chronicle of Higher Education*, 46: A20, (May 12, 2000).

★3866★
Average salaries for human-resources management faculty at 4-year institutions, 1999-2000

Ranking basis/background: Average salary for faculty at public and private 4-year institutions. From a survey of professors in 80 disciplines at 363 public colleges and 501 private institutions, excluding medical professors. **Remarks:** Original source: College and University Personnel Association. **Number listed:** 2.
   Private, with $63,661
   Public, $68,472
Source: Magner, Denise K., "Law Professors are Academe's Best-Paid Faculty Members, Survey Finds," *The Chronicle of Higher Education*, 46: A20, (May 12, 2000).

★3867★
Average salaries for information sciences and systems faculty at 4-year institutions, 1999-2000

Ranking basis/background: Average salary for faculty at public and private 4-year institutions. From a survey of professors in 80 disciplines at 363 public colleges and 501 private institutions, excluding medical professors. **Remarks:** Original source: College and University Personnel Association. **Number listed:** 2.
   Private, with $65,724
   Public, $67,611
Source: Magner, Denise K., "Law Professors are Academe's Best-Paid Faculty Members, Survey Finds," *The Chronicle of Higher Education*, 46: A20, (May 12, 2000).

★3868★
Average salaries for instructors at institutions in the East North Central states, 2000-01

Ranking basis/background: Based on the responses of 1,433 institutions providing data to the annual salary survey of the American Association of University Professors. **Remarks:** The East North Central region includes Illinois, Indiana, Michigan, Ohio, and Wisconsin. **Number listed:** 4.
   Doctoral institutions, with an average annual salary of $34,887
   Comprehensive institutions, $33,781
   Baccalaureate institutions, $34,382
   Two-year institutions, $34,335
Source: "Uncertain Times: The Annual Report on the Economic Status of the Profession," *Academe*, 87: 25-98, (March/April 2001).

★3869★
Average salaries for instructors at institutions in the East South Central states, 2000-01

Ranking basis/background: Based on the responses of 1,433 institutions providing data to the annual salary survey of the American Association of University Professors. **Remarks:** The East South Central region includes Alabama, Kentucky, Mississippi and Tennessee. **Number listed:** 4.
- Doctoral institutions, with an average annual salary of $32,552
- Comprehensive institutions, $33,389
- Baccalaureate institutions, $32,752
- Two-year institutions, $31,204

Source: "Uncertain Times: The Annual Report on the Economic Status of the Profession," *Academe*, 87: 25-98, (March/April 2001).

★3870★
Average salaries for instructors at institutions in the Middle Atlantic states, 2000-01

Ranking basis/background: Based on the responses of 1,433 institutions providing data to the annual salary survey of the American Association of University Professors. **Remarks:** The Middle Atlantic region includes New Jersey, New York, and Pennsylvania. **Number listed:** 4.
- Doctoral institutions, with an average annual salary of $39,169
- Comprehensive institutions, $38,267
- Baccalaureate institutions, $37,009
- Two-year institutions, $37,705

Source: "Uncertain Times: The Annual Report on the Economic Status of the Profession," *Academe*, 87: 25-98, (March/April 2001).

★3871★
Average salaries for instructors at institutions in the Mountain states, 2000-01

Ranking basis/background: Based on the responses of 1,433 institutions providing data to the annual salary survey of the American Association of University Professors. **Remarks:** The Mountain region includes Arizona, Colorado, Idaho, Montana, Nevada, New Mexico, Utah and Wyoming. **Number listed:** 4.
- Doctoral institutions, with an average annual salary of $36,112
- Comprehensive institutions, $34,272
- Baccalaureate institutions, $33,874
- Two-year institutions, $33,371

Source: "Uncertain Times: The Annual Report on the Economic Status of the Profession," *Academe*, 87: 25-98, (March/April 2001).

★3872★
Average salaries for instructors at institutions in the New England states, 2000-01

Ranking basis/background: Based on the responses of 1,433 institutions providing data to the annual salary survey of the American Association of University Professors. **Remarks:** The New England region includes Connecticut, Maine, Massachusetts, New Hampshire, Vermont, and Rhode Island. **Number listed:** 4.
- Doctoral institutions, with an average annual salary of $45,604
- Comprehensive institutions, $40,757
- Baccalaureate institutions, $39,996
- Two-year institutions, $33,367

Source: "Uncertain Times: The Annual Report on the Economic Status of the Profession," *Academe*, 87: 25-98, (March/April 2001).

★3873★
Average salaries for instructors at institutions in the Pacific states, 2000-01

Ranking basis/background: Based on the responses of 1,433 institutions providing data to the annual salary survey of the American Association of University Professors. **Remarks:** The Pacific region includes Alaska, California, Hawaii, Oregon, and Washington. **Number listed:** 4.
- Doctoral institutions, with an average annual salary of $36,847
- Comprehensive institutions, $37,509
- Baccalaureate institutions, $38,700
- Two-year institutions, $37,771

Source: "Uncertain Times: The Annual Report on the Economic Status of the Profession," *Academe*, 87: 25-98, (March/April 2001).

★3874★
Average salaries for instructors at institutions in the South Atlantic states, 2000-01

Ranking basis/background: Based on the responses of 1,433 institutions providing data to the annual salary survey of the American Association of University Professors. **Remarks:** The South Atlantic region includes Delaware, District of Columbia, Florida, Georgia, Maryland, North Carolina, South Carolina, Virginia, and West Virginia. **Number listed:** 4.
- Doctoral institutions, with an average annual salary of $37,940
- Comprehensive institutions, $35,716
- Baccalaureate institutions, $34,009
- Two-year institutions, $35,441

Source: "Uncertain Times: The Annual Report on the Economic Status of the Profession," *Academe*, 87: 25-98, (March/April 2001).

★3875★
Average salaries for instructors at institutions in the West North Central states, 2000-01

Ranking basis/background: Based on the responses of 1,433 institutions providing data to the annual salary survey of the American Association of University Professors. **Remarks:** The West North Central region includes Iowa, Kansas, Minnesota, Missouri, Nebraska, North Dakota and South Dakota. **Number listed:** 4.
- Doctoral institutions, with an average annual salary of $37,530
- Comprehensive institutions, $33,965
- Baccalaureate institutions, $34,054
- Two-year institutions, $32,895

Source: "Uncertain Times: The Annual Report on the Economic Status of the Profession," *Academe*, 87: 25-98, (March/April 2001).

★3876★
Average salaries for instructors at institutions in the West South Central states, 2000-01

Ranking basis/background: Based on the responses of 1,433 institutions providing data to the annual salary survey of the American Association of University Professors. **Remarks:** The West South Central region includes Arkansas, Louisiana, Oklahoma and Texas. **Number listed:** 4.
- Doctoral institutions, with an average annual salary of $34,571
- Comprehensive institutions, $32,438
- Baccalaureate institutions, $32,338
- Two-year institutions, $36,718

Source: "Uncertain Times: The Annual Report on the Economic Status of the Profession," *Academe*, 87: 25-98, (March/April 2001).

★3877★
Average salaries for instructors in church-related institutions, 2000-01

Ranking basis/background: Based on the responses of 1,433 institutions providing data to the annual salary survey of the American Association of University Professors. **Remarks:** Table also includes percentage increases in salary for continuing faculty by category, affiliation, and academic rank. **Number listed:** 4.
- Doctoral institutions, with an average annual salary of $45,603
- Comprehensive institutions, $34,804
- Baccalaureate institutions, $33,600
- Two-year institutions, $31,046

Source: "Uncertain Times: The Annual Report on the Economic Status of the Profession," *Academe*, 87: 25-98, (March/April 2001).

★3878★
Average salaries for instructors in private-independent institutions, 2000-01

Ranking basis/background: Based on the responses of 1,433 institutions providing data to the annual salary survey of the American Association of University Professors. **Remarks:** Table also includes percentage increases in salary for continuing faculty by category, affiliation, and academic rank. **Number listed:** 4.
- Doctoral institutions, with an average annual salary of $42,516
- Comprehensive institutions, $38,140
- Baccalaureate institutions, $36,855
- Two-year institutions, $27,967

Source: "Uncertain Times: The Annual Report on the Economic Status of the Profession," *Academe*, 87: 25-98, (March/April 2001).

★3879★
Average salaries for instructors in public institutions, 2000-01

Ranking basis/background: Based on the responses of 1,433 institutions providing data to the annual salary survey of the American Association of University Professors. **Remarks:** Table also includes percentage increases in salary for continuing faculty by category, affiliation, and academic rank. **Number listed:** 4.
- Doctoral institutions, with an average annual salary of $35,210
- Comprehensive institutions, $34,404
- Baccalaureate institutions, $34,428
- Two-year institutions, $35,573

Source: "Uncertain Times: The Annual Report on the Economic Status of the Profession," *Academe*, 87: 25-98, (March/April 2001).

★3880★
Average salaries for law faculty at 4-year institutions, 1999-2000

Ranking basis/background: Average salary for faculty at public and private 4-year institutions. From a survey of professors in 80 disciplines at 363 public colleges and 501 private institutions, excluding medical professors. **Remarks:** Original source: College and University Personnel Association. **Number listed:** 2.
  Private, with $102,513
  Public, $95,829
Source: Magner, Denise K., "Law Professors are Academe's Best-Paid Faculty Members, Survey Finds," *The Chronicle of Higher Education*, 46: A20, (May 12, 2000).

★3881★
Average salaries for lecturers at institutions in the East North Central states, 2000-01

Ranking basis/background: Based on the responses of 1,433 institutions providing data to the annual salary survey of the American Association of University Professors. **Remarks:** The East North Central region includes Illinois, Indiana, Michigan, Ohio, and Wisconsin. **Number listed:** 4.
  Doctoral institutions, with an average annual salary of $41,548
  Comprehensive institutions, $35,290
  Baccalaureate institutions, $33,398
  Two-year institutions, $39,879
Source: "Uncertain Times: The Annual Report on the Economic Status of the Profession," *Academe*, 87: 25-98, (March/April 2001).

★3882★
Average salaries for lecturers at institutions in the East South Central states, 2000-01

Ranking basis/background: Based on the responses of 1,433 institutions providing data to the annual salary survey of the American Association of University Professors. **Remarks:** The East South Central region includes Alabama, Kentucky, Mississippi and Tennessee. **Number listed:** 4.
  Doctoral institutions, with an average annual salary of $35,494
  Comprehensive institutions, $28,722
  Baccalaureate institutions, $29,966
  Two-year institutions, $28,625
Source: "Uncertain Times: The Annual Report on the Economic Status of the Profession," *Academe*, 87: 25-98, (March/April 2001).

★3883★
Average salaries for lecturers at institutions in the Middle Atlantic states, 2000-01

Ranking basis/background: Based on the responses of 1,433 institutions providing data to the annual salary survey of the American Association of University Professors. **Remarks:** The Middle Atlantic region includes New Jersey, New York, and Pennsylvania. **Number listed:** 4.
  Doctoral institutions, with an average annual salary of $44,624
  Comprehensive institutions, $38,768
  Baccalaureate institutions, $40,033
  Two-year institutions, $36,261
Source: "Uncertain Times: The Annual Report on the Economic Status of the Profession," *Academe*, 87: 25-98, (March/April 2001).

★3884★
Average salaries for lecturers at institutions in the Mountain states, 2000-01

Ranking basis/background: Based on the responses of 1,433 institutions providing data to the annual salary survey of the American Association of University Professors. **Remarks:** The Mountain region includes Arizona, Colorado, Idaho, Montana, Nevada, New Mexico, Utah and Wyoming. **Number listed:** 4.
  Doctoral institutions, with an average annual salary of $39,254
  Comprehensive institutions, $40,531
  Baccalaureate institutions, $31,531
  Two-year institutions, $34,736
Source: "Uncertain Times: The Annual Report on the Economic Status of the Profession," *Academe*, 87: 25-98, (March/April 2001).

★3885★
Average salaries for lecturers at institutions in the New England states, 2000-01

Ranking basis/background: Based on the responses of 1,433 institutions providing data to the annual salary survey of the American Association of University Professors. **Remarks:** The New England region includes Connecticut, Maine, Massachusetts, New Hampshire, Vermont, and Rhode Island. **Number listed:** 3.
  Doctoral institutions, with an average annual salary of $47,674
  Comprehensive institutions, $42,519
  Baccalaureate institutions, $47,165
Source: "Uncertain Times: The Annual Report on the Economic Status of the Profession," *Academe*, 87: 25-98, (March/April 2001).

★3886★
Average salaries for lecturers at institutions in the Pacific states, 2000-01

Ranking basis/background: Based on the responses of 1,433 institutions providing data to the annual salary survey of the American Association of University Professors. **Remarks:** The Pacific region includes Alaska, California, Hawaii, Oregon, and Washington. **Number listed:** 3.
  Doctoral institutions, with an average annual salary of $46,282
  Comprehensive institutions, $37,788
  Baccalaureate institutions, $42,400
Source: "Uncertain Times: The Annual Report on the Economic Status of the Profession," *Academe*, 87: 25-98, (March/April 2001).

★3887★
Average salaries for lecturers at institutions in the South Atlantic states, 2000-01

Ranking basis/background: Based on the responses of 1,433 institutions providing data to the annual salary survey of the American Association of University Professors. **Remarks:** The South Atlantic region includes Delaware, District of Columbia, Florida, Georgia, Maryland, North Carolina, South Carolina, Virginia, and West Virginia. **Number listed:** 4.
  Doctoral institutions, with an average annual salary of $39,549
  Comprehensive institutions, $36,249
  Baccalaureate institutions, $37,137
  Two-year institutions, $36,028
Source: "Uncertain Times: The Annual Report on the Economic Status of the Profession," *Academe*, 87: 25-98, (March/April 2001).

★3888★
Average salaries for lecturers at institutions in the West North Central states, 2000-01

Ranking basis/background: Based on the responses of 1,433 institutions providing data to the annual salary survey of the American Association of University Professors. **Remarks:** The West North Central region includes Iowa, Kansas, Minnesota, Missouri, Nebraska, North Dakota and South Dakota. **Number listed:** 4.
  Doctoral institutions, with an average annual salary of $34,744
  Comprehensive institutions, $30,244
  Baccalaureate institutions, $33,853
  Two-year institutions, $28,004
Source: "Uncertain Times: The Annual Report on the Economic Status of the Profession," *Academe*, 87: 25-98, (March/April 2001).

★3889★
Average salaries for lecturers at institutions in the West South Central states, 2000-01

Ranking basis/background: Based on the responses of 1,433 institutions providing data to the annual salary survey of the American Association of University Professors. **Remarks:** The West South Central region includes Arkansas, Louisiana, Oklahoma and Texas. **Number listed:** 4.
  Doctoral institutions, with an average annual salary of $38,285
  Comprehensive institutions, $34,777
  Baccalaureate institutions, $32,041
  Two-year institutions, $33,605
Source: "Uncertain Times: The Annual Report on the Economic Status of the Profession," *Academe*, 87: 25-98, (March/April 2001).

★3890★
Average salaries for lecturers in church-related institutions, 2000-01

Ranking basis/background: Based on the responses of 1,433 institutions providing data to the annual salary survey of the American Association of University Professors. **Remarks:** Table also includes percentage increases in salary for continuing faculty by category, affiliation, and academic rank. **Number listed:** 3.
  Doctoral institutions, with an average annual salary of $41,430
  Comprehensive institutions, $38,841
  Baccalaureate institutions, $33,769
Source: "Uncertain Times: The Annual Report on the Economic Status of the Profession," *Academe*, 87: 25-98, (March/April 2001).

★3891★
Average salaries for lecturers in private-independent institutions, 2000-01

Ranking basis/background: Based on the responses of 1,433 institutions providing data to the annual salary survey of the American Association of University Professors. **Remarks:** Table also includes percentage increases in salary for continuing faculty by category, affiliation, and academic rank. **Number listed:** 4.
  Doctoral institutions, with an average annual salary of $45,703
  Comprehensive institutions, $38,851

Baccalaureate institutions, $44,442
Two-year institutions, $30,100
Source: "Uncertain Times: The Annual Report on the Economic Status of the Profession," *Academe*, 87: 25-98, (March/April 2001).

★3892★
Average salaries for lecturers in public institutions, 2000-01

Ranking basis/background: Based on the responses of 1,433 institutions providing data to the annual salary survey of the American Association of University Professors. **Remarks:** Table also includes percentage increases in salary for continuing faculty by category, affiliation, and academic rank. **Number listed:** 4.

Doctoral institutions, with an average annual salary of $39,928
Comprehensive institutions, $35,188
Baccalaureate institutions, $35,635
Two-year institutions, $35,595

Source: "Uncertain Times: The Annual Report on the Economic Status of the Profession," *Academe*, 87: 25-98, (March/April 2001).

★3893★
Average salaries for library science faculty at 4-year institutions, 1999-2000

Ranking basis/background: Average salary for faculty at public and private 4-year institutions. From a survey of professors in 80 disciplines at 363 public colleges and 501 private institutions, excluding medical professors. **Remarks:** Original source: College and University Personnel Association. **Number listed:** 2.

Private, with $43,401
Public, $54,121

Source: Magner, Denise K., "Law Professors are Academe's Best-Paid Faculty Members, Survey Finds," *The Chronicle of Higher Education*, 46: A20, (May 12, 2000).

★3894★
Average salaries for male assistant professors in church-related institutions, 2000-01

Ranking basis/background: Based on the responses of 1,433 institutions providing data to the annual salary survey of the American Association of University Professors. **Remarks:** Table also includes percentage increases in salary for continuing faculty by category, affiliation, and academic rank. **Number listed:** 4.

Doctoral institutions, with an average annual salary of $55,510
Comprehensive institutions, $45,916
Baccalaureate institutions, $39,503
Two-year institutions, $35,465

Source: "Uncertain Times: The Annual Report on the Economic Status of the Profession," *Academe*, 87: 25-98, (March/April 2001).

★3895★
Average salaries for male assistant professors in private-independent institutions, 2000-01

Ranking basis/background: Based on the responses of 1,433 institutions providing data to the annual salary survey of the American Association of University Professors. **Remarks:** Table also includes percentage increases in salary for continuing faculty by category, affiliation, and academic rank. **Number listed:** 4.

Doctoral institutions, with an average annual salary of $63,228
Comprehensive institutions, $48,172
Baccalaureate institutions, $45,319
Two-year institutions, $34,459

Source: "Uncertain Times: The Annual Report on the Economic Status of the Profession," *Academe*, 87: 25-98, (March/April 2001).

★3896★
Average salaries for male assistant professors in public institutions, 2000-01

Ranking basis/background: Based on the responses of 1,433 institutions providing data to the annual salary survey of the American Association of University Professors. **Remarks:** Table also includes percentage increases in salary for continuing faculty by category, affiliation, and academic rank. **Number listed:** 4.

Doctoral institutions, with an average annual salary of $52,611
Comprehensive institutions, $45,986
Baccalaureate institutions, $43,154
Two-year institutions, $42,462

Source: "Uncertain Times: The Annual Report on the Economic Status of the Profession," *Academe*, 87: 25-98, (March/April 2001).

★3897★
Average salaries for male associate professors in church-related institutions, 2000-01

Ranking basis/background: Based on the responses of 1,433 institutions providing data to the annual salary survey of the American Association of University Professors. **Remarks:** Table also includes percentage increases in salary for continuing faculty by category, affiliation, and academic rank. **Number listed:** 4.

Doctoral institutions, with an average annual salary of $66,905
Comprehensive institutions, $56,202
Baccalaureate institutions, $47,218
Two-year institutions, $38,329

Source: "Uncertain Times: The Annual Report on the Economic Status of the Profession," *Academe*, 87: 25-98, (March/April 2001).

★3898★
Average salaries for male associate professors in private-independent institutions, 2000-01

Ranking basis/background: Based on the responses of 1,433 institutions providing data to the annual salary survey of the American Association of University Professors. **Remarks:** Table also includes percentage increases in salary for continuing faculty by category, affiliation, and academic rank. **Number listed:** 4.

Doctoral institutions, with an average annual salary of $71,940
Comprehensive institutions, $58,933
Baccalaureate institutions, $55,822
Two-year institutions, $48,384

Source: "Uncertain Times: The Annual Report on the Economic Status of the Profession," *Academe*, 87: 25-98, (March/April 2001).

★3899★
Average salaries for male associate professors in public institutions, 2000-01

Ranking basis/background: Based on the responses of 1,433 institutions providing data to the annual salary survey of the American Association of University Professors. **Remarks:** Table also includes percentage increases in salary for continuing faculty by category, affiliation, and academic rank. **Number listed:** 4.

Doctoral institutions, with an average annual salary of $61,912
Comprehensive institutions, $55,812
Baccalaureate institutions, $51,937
Two-year institutions, $48,826

Source: "Uncertain Times: The Annual Report on the Economic Status of the Profession," *Academe*, 87: 25-98, (March/April 2001).

★3900★
Average salaries for male instructors in church-related institutions, 2000-01

Ranking basis/background: Based on the responses of 1,433 institutions providing data to the annual salary survey of the American Association of University Professors. **Remarks:** Table also includes percentage increases in salary for continuing faculty by category, affiliation, and academic rank. **Number listed:** 4.

Doctoral institutions, with an average annual salary of $46,671
Comprehensive institutions, $35,579
Baccalaureate institutions, $34,073
Two-year institutions, $32,081

Source: "Uncertain Times: The Annual Report on the Economic Status of the Profession," *Academe*, 87: 25-98, (March/April 2001).

★3901★
Average salaries for male instructors in private-independent institutions, 2000-01

Ranking basis/background: Based on the responses of 1,433 institutions providing data to the annual salary survey of the American Association of University Professors. **Remarks:** Table also includes percentage increases in salary for continuing faculty by category, affiliation, and academic rank. **Number listed:** 4.

Doctoral institutions, with an average annual salary of $44,040
Comprehensive institutions, $39,277
Baccalaureate institutions, $37,626
Two-year institutions, $30,283

Source: "Uncertain Times: The Annual Report on the Economic Status of the Profession," *Academe*, 87: 25-98, (March/April 2001).

★3902★
Average salaries for male instructors in public institutions, 2000-01

Ranking basis/background: Based on the responses of 1,433 institutions providing data to the annual salary survey of the American Association of University Professors. **Remarks:** Table also includes percentage increases in salary for continuing faculty by category, affiliation, and academic rank. **Number listed:** 4.

Doctoral institutions, with an average annual salary of $36,008
Comprehensive institutions, $34,889
Baccalaureate institutions, $35,478
Two-year institutions, $35,877

SALARIES—COLLEGES & UNIVERSITIES, FACULTY

Source: "Uncertain Times: The Annual Report on the Economic Status of the Profession," *Academe*, 87: 25-98, (March/April 2001).

★3903★
Average salaries for male lecturers in church-related institutions, 2000-01

Ranking basis/background: Based on the responses of 1,433 institutions providing data to the annual salary survey of the American Association of University Professors. **Remarks:** Table also includes percentage increases in salary for continuing faculty by category, affiliation, and academic rank. **Number listed:** 3.

Doctoral institutions, with an average annual salary of $46,518
Comprehensive institutions, $41,374
Baccalaureate institutions, $34,311

Source: "Uncertain Times: The Annual Report on the Economic Status of the Profession," *Academe*, 87: 25-98, (March/April 2001).

★3904★
Average salaries for male lecturers in private-independent institutions, 2000-01

Ranking basis/background: Based on the responses of 1,433 institutions providing data to the annual salary survey of the American Association of University Professors. **Remarks:** Table also includes percentage increases in salary for continuing faculty by category, affiliation, and academic rank. **Number listed:** 3.

Doctoral institutions, with an average annual salary of $48,850
Comprehensive institutions, $40,771
Baccalaureate institutions, $47,026

Source: "Uncertain Times: The Annual Report on the Economic Status of the Profession," *Academe*, 87: 25-98, (March/April 2001).

★3905★
Average salaries for male lecturers in public institutions, 2000-01

Ranking basis/background: Based on the responses of 1,433 institutions providing data to the annual salary survey of the American Association of University Professors. **Remarks:** Table also includes percentage increases in salary for continuing faculty by category, affiliation, and academic rank. **Number listed:** 4.

Doctoral institutions, with an average annual salary of $42,140
Comprehensive institutions, $36,235
Baccalaureate institutions, $36,819
Two-year institutions, $36,501

Source: "Uncertain Times: The Annual Report on the Economic Status of the Profession," *Academe*, 87: 25-98, (March/April 2001).

★3906★
Average salaries for male professors in church-related institutions, 2000-01

Ranking basis/background: Based on the responses of 1,433 institutions providing data to the annual salary survey of the American Association of University Professors. **Remarks:** Table also includes percentage increases in salary for continuing faculty by category, affiliation, and academic rank. **Number listed:** 4.

Doctoral institutions, with an average annual salary of $96,905
Comprehensive institutions, $72,251
Baccalaureate institutions, $57,747
Two-year institutions, $42,578

Source: "Uncertain Times: The Annual Report on the Economic Status of the Profession," *Academe*, 87: 25-98, (March/April 2001).

★3907★
Average salaries for male professors in private-independent institutions, 2000-01

Ranking basis/background: Based on the responses of 1,433 institutions providing data to the annual salary survey of the American Association of University Professors. **Remarks:** Table also includes percentage increases in salary for continuing faculty by category, affiliation, and academic rank. **Number listed:** 4.

Doctoral institutions, with an average annual salary of $109,303
Comprehensive institutions, $76,066
Baccalaureate institutions, $75,072
Two-year institutions, $57,041

Source: "Uncertain Times: The Annual Report on the Economic Status of the Profession," *Academe*, 87: 25-98, (March/April 2001).

★3908★
Average salaries for male professors in public institutions, 2000-01

Ranking basis/background: Based on the responses of 1,433 institutions providing data to the annual salary survey of the American Association of University Professors. **Remarks:** Table also includes percentage increases in salary for continuing faculty by category, affiliation, and academic rank. **Number listed:** 4.

Doctoral institutions, with an average annual salary of $85,259
Comprehensive institutions, $69,454
Baccalaureate institutions, $62,915
Two-year institutions, $59,743

Source: "Uncertain Times: The Annual Report on the Economic Status of the Profession," *Academe*, 87: 25-98, (March/April 2001).

★3909★
Average salaries for marketing management and research faculty at 4-year institutions, 1999-2000

Ranking basis/background: Average salary for faculty at public and private 4-year institutions. From a survey of professors in 80 disciplines at 363 public colleges and 501 private institutions, excluding medical professors. **Remarks:** Original source: College and University Personnel Association. **Number listed:** 2.

Private, with $72,034
Public, $69,864

Source: Magner, Denise K., "Law Professors are Academe's Best-Paid Faculty Members, Survey Finds," *The Chronicle of Higher Education*, 46: A20, (May 12, 2000).

★3910★
Average salaries for mathematics faculty at 4-year institutions, 1999-2000

Ranking basis/background: Average salary for faculty at public and private 4-year institutions. From a survey of professors in 80 disciplines at 363 public colleges and 501 private institutions, excluding medical professors. **Remarks:** Original source: College and University Personnel Association. **Number listed:** 2.

Private, with $54,087
Public, $57,871

Source: Magner, Denise K., "Law Professors are Academe's Best-Paid Faculty Members, Survey Finds," *The Chronicle of Higher Education*, 46: A20, (May 12, 2000).

★3911★
Average salaries for mechanical engineering faculty at 4-year institutions, 1999-2000

Ranking basis/background: Average salary for faculty at public and private 4-year institutions. From a survey of professors in 80 disciplines at 363 public colleges and 501 private institutions, excluding medical professors. **Remarks:** Original source: College and University Personnel Association. **Number listed:** 2.

Private, with $74,644
Public, $71,468

Source: Magner, Denise K., "Law Professors are Academe's Best-Paid Faculty Members, Survey Finds," *The Chronicle of Higher Education*, 46: A20, (May 12, 2000).

★3912★
Average salaries for multi-interdisciplinary studies faculty at 4-year institutions, 1999-2000

Ranking basis/background: Average salary for faculty at public and private 4-year institutions. From a survey of professors in 80 disciplines at 363 public colleges and 501 private institutions, excluding medical professors. **Remarks:** Original source: College and University Personnel Association. **Number listed:** 2.

Private, with $51,632
Public, $58,484

Source: Magner, Denise K., "Law Professors are Academe's Best-Paid Faculty Members, Survey Finds," *The Chronicle of Higher Education*, 46: A20, (May 12, 2000).

★3913★
Average salaries for music faculty at 4-year institutions, 1999-2000

Ranking basis/background: Average salary for faculty at public and private 4-year institutions. From a survey of professors in 80 disciplines at 363 public colleges and 501 private institutions, excluding medical professors. **Remarks:** Original source: College and University Personnel Association. **Number listed:** 2.

Private, with $48,291
Public, $49,823

Source: Magner, Denise K., "Law Professors are Academe's Best-Paid Faculty Members, Survey Finds," *The Chronicle of Higher Education*, 46: A20, (May 12, 2000).

★3914★
Average salaries for nursing faculty at 4-year institutions, 1999-2000

Ranking basis/background: Average salary for faculty at public and private 4-year institutions. From a survey of professors in 80 disciplines at 363 public colleges and 501 private institutions, excluding medical professors. **Remarks:** Original source: College and University Personnel Association. **Number listed:** 2.

Private, with $45,164
Public, $48,987

Source: Magner, Denise K., "Law Professors are Academe's Best-Paid Faculty Members, Survey Finds," *The Chronicle of Higher Education*, 46: A20, (May 12, 2000).

SALARIES—COLLEGES & UNIVERSITIES, FACULTY

★3915★
Average salaries for occupational therapy faculty at 4-year institutions, 1999-2000

Ranking basis/background: Average salary for faculty at public and private 4-year institutions. From a survey of professors in 80 disciplines at 363 public colleges and 501 private institutions, excluding medical professors. **Remarks:** Original source: College and University Personnel Association. **Number listed:** 2.
- Private, with $46,099
- Public, $51,145

Source: Magner, Denise K., "Law Professors are Academe's Best-Paid Faculty Members, Survey Finds," *The Chronicle of Higher Education*, 46: A20, (May 12, 2000).

★3916★
Average salaries for parks, recreation, and leisure studies faculty at 4-year institutions, 1999-2000

Ranking basis/background: Average salary for faculty at public and private 4-year institutions. From a survey of professors in 80 disciplines at 363 public colleges and 501 private institutions, excluding medical professors. **Remarks:** Original source: College and University Personnel Association. **Number listed:** 2.
- Private, with $48,276
- Public, $52,532

Source: Magner, Denise K., "Law Professors are Academe's Best-Paid Faculty Members, Survey Finds," *The Chronicle of Higher Education*, 46: A20, (May 12, 2000).

★3917★
Average salaries for philosophy and religion faculty at 4-year institutions, 1999-2000

Ranking basis/background: Average salary for faculty at public and private 4-year institutions. From a survey of professors in 80 disciplines at 363 public colleges and 501 private institutions, excluding medical professors. **Remarks:** Original source: College and University Personnel Association. **Number listed:** 2.
- Private, with $49,997
- Public, $56,925

Source: Magner, Denise K., "Law Professors are Academe's Best-Paid Faculty Members, Survey Finds," *The Chronicle of Higher Education*, 46: A20, (May 12, 2000).

★3918★
Average salaries for philosophy faculty at 4-year institutions, 1999-2000

Ranking basis/background: Average salary for faculty at public and private 4-year institutions. From a survey of professors in 80 disciplines at 363 public colleges and 501 private institutions, excluding medical professors. **Remarks:** Original source: College and University Personnel Association. **Number listed:** 2.
- Private, with $54,856
- Public, $55,105

Source: Magner, Denise K., "Law Professors are Academe's Best-Paid Faculty Members, Survey Finds," *The Chronicle of Higher Education*, 46: A20, (May 12, 2000).

★3919★
Average salaries for physical sciences faculty at 4-year institutions, 1999-2000

Ranking basis/background: Average salary for faculty at public and private 4-year institutions. From a survey of professors in 80 disciplines at 363 public colleges and 501 private institutions, excluding medical professors. **Remarks:** Original source: College and University Personnel Association. **Number listed:** 2.
- Private, with $52,348
- Public, $77,225

Source: Magner, Denise K., "Law Professors are Academe's Best-Paid Faculty Members, Survey Finds," *The Chronicle of Higher Education*, 46: A20, (May 12, 2000).

★3920★
Average salaries for physical therapy faculty at 4-year institutions, 1999-2000

Ranking basis/background: Average salary for faculty at public and private 4-year institutions. From a survey of professors in 80 disciplines at 363 public colleges and 501 private institutions, excluding medical professors. **Remarks:** Original source: College and University Personnel Association. **Number listed:** 2.
- Private, with $53,329
- Public, $55,710

Source: Magner, Denise K., "Law Professors are Academe's Best-Paid Faculty Members, Survey Finds," *The Chronicle of Higher Education*, 46: A20, (May 12, 2000).

★3921★
Average salaries for physics faculty at 4-year institutions, 1999-2000

Ranking basis/background: Average salary for faculty at public and private 4-year institutions. From a survey of professors in 80 disciplines at 363 public colleges and 501 private institutions, excluding medical professors. **Remarks:** Original source: College and University Personnel Association. **Number listed:** 2.
- Private, with $63,516
- Public, $63,537

Source: Magner, Denise K., "Law Professors are Academe's Best-Paid Faculty Members, Survey Finds," *The Chronicle of Higher Education*, 46: A20, (May 12, 2000).

★3922★
Average salaries for political science and government faculty at 4-year institutions, 1999-2000

Ranking basis/background: Average salary for faculty at public and private 4-year institutions. From a survey of professors in 80 disciplines at 363 public colleges and 501 private institutions, excluding medical professors. **Remarks:** Original source: College and University Personnel Association. **Number listed:** 2.
- Private, with $57,645
- Public, $56,027

Source: Magner, Denise K., "Law Professors are Academe's Best-Paid Faculty Members, Survey Finds," *The Chronicle of Higher Education*, 46: A20, (May 12, 2000).

★3923★
Average salaries for professors at institutions in the East North Central states, 2000-01

Ranking basis/background: Based on the responses of 1,433 institutions providing data to the annual salary survey of the American Association of University Professors. **Remarks:** The East North Central region includes Illinois, Indiana, Michigan, Ohio, and Wisconsin. **Number listed:** 4.
- Doctoral institutions, with an average annual salary of $88,179
- Comprehensive institutions, $66,688
- Baccalaureate institutions, $60,160
- Two-year institutions, $58,941

Source: "Uncertain Times: The Annual Report on the Economic Status of the Profession," *Academe*, 87: 25-98, (March/April 2001).

★3924★
Average salaries for professors at institutions in the East South Central states, 2000-01

Ranking basis/background: Based on the responses of 1,433 institutions providing data to the annual salary survey of the American Association of University Professors. **Remarks:** The East South Central region includes Alabama, Kentucky, Mississippi and Tennessee. **Number listed:** 4.
- Doctoral institutions, with an average annual salary of $78,595
- Comprehensive institutions, $63,027
- Baccalaureate institutions, $54,499
- Two-year institutions, $50,270

Source: "Uncertain Times: The Annual Report on the Economic Status of the Profession," *Academe*, 87: 25-98, (March/April 2001).

★3925★
Average salaries for professors at institutions in the Middle Atlantic states, 2000-01

Ranking basis/background: Based on the responses of 1,433 institutions providing data to the annual salary survey of the American Association of University Professors. **Remarks:** The Middle Atlantic region includes New Jersey, New York, and Pennsylvania. **Number listed:** 4.
- Doctoral institutions, with an average annual salary of $100,953
- Comprehensive institutions, $75,397
- Baccalaureate institutions, $71,686
- Two-year institutions, $65,260

Source: "Uncertain Times: The Annual Report on the Economic Status of the Profession," *Academe*, 87: 25-98, (March/April 2001).

★3926★
Average salaries for professors at institutions in the Mountain states, 2000-01

Ranking basis/background: Based on the responses of 1,433 institutions providing data to the annual salary survey of the American Association of University Professors. **Remarks:** The Mountain region includes Arizona, Colorado, Idaho, Montana, Nevada, New Mexico, Utah and Wyoming. **Number listed:** 4.
- Doctoral institutions, with an average annual salary of $77,346
- Comprehensive institutions, $68,445
- Baccalaureate institutions, $57,681
- Two-year institutions, $44,306

SALARIES—COLLEGES & UNIVERSITIES, FACULTY

Source: "Uncertain Times: The Annual Report on the Economic Status of the Profession," *Academe*, 87: 25-98, (March/April 2001).

★3927★
Average salaries for professors at institutions in the New England states, 2000-01

Ranking basis/background: Based on the responses of 1,433 institutions providing data to the annual salary survey of the American Association of University Professors. **Remarks:** The New England region includes Connecticut, Maine, Massachusetts, New Hampshire, Vermont, and Rhode Island. **Number listed:** 4.

Doctoral institutions, with an average annual salary of $100,907
Comprehensive institutions, $75,115
Baccalaureate institutions, $79,862
Two-year institutions, $47,909

Source: "Uncertain Times: The Annual Report on the Economic Status of the Profession," *Academe*, 87: 25-98, (March/April 2001).

★3928★
Average salaries for professors at institutions in the Pacific states, 2000-01

Ranking basis/background: Based on the responses of 1,433 institutions providing data to the annual salary survey of the American Association of University Professors. **Remarks:** The Pacific region includes Alaska, California, Hawaii, Oregon, and Washington. **Number listed:** 4.

Doctoral institutions, with an average annual salary of $92,759
Comprehensive institutions, $74,850
Baccalaureate institutions, $69,671
Two-year institutions, $55,284

Source: "Uncertain Times: The Annual Report on the Economic Status of the Profession," *Academe*, 87: 25-98, (March/April 2001).

★3929★
Average salaries for professors at institutions in the South Atlantic states, 2000-01

Ranking basis/background: Based on the responses of 1,433 institutions providing data to the annual salary survey of the American Association of University Professors. **Remarks:** The South Atlantic region includes Delaware, District of Columbia, Florida, Georgia, Maryland, North Carolina, South Carolina, Virginia, and West Virginia. **Number listed:** 4.

Doctoral institutions, with an average annual salary of $90,679
Comprehensive institutions, $68,660
Baccalaureate institutions, $61,545
Two-year institutions, $59,449

Source: "Uncertain Times: The Annual Report on the Economic Status of the Profession," *Academe*, 87: 25-98, (March/April 2001).

★3930★
Average salaries for professors at institutions in the West North Central states, 2000-01

Ranking basis/background: Based on the responses of 1,433 institutions providing data to the annual salary survey of the American Association of University Professors. **Remarks:** The West North Central region includes Iowa, Kansas, Minnesota, Missouri, Nebraska, North Dakota and South Dakota. **Number listed:** 4.

Doctoral institutions, with an average annual salary of $85,410
Comprehensive institutions, $64,260
Baccalaureate institutions, $59,446
Two-year institutions, $52,973

Source: "Uncertain Times: The Annual Report on the Economic Status of the Profession," *Academe*, 87: 25-98, (March/April 2001).

★3931★
Average salaries for professors at institutions in the West South Central states, 2000-01

Ranking basis/background: Based on the responses of 1,433 institutions providing data to the annual salary survey of the American Association of University Professors. **Remarks:** The West South Central region includes Arkansas, Louisiana, Oklahoma and Texas. **Number listed:** 4.

Doctoral institutions, with an average annual salary of $83,536
Comprehensive institutions, $62,150
Baccalaureate institutions, $54,943
Two-year institutions, $54,449

Source: "Uncertain Times: The Annual Report on the Economic Status of the Profession," *Academe*, 87: 25-98, (March/April 2001).

★3932★
Average salaries for professors at private institutions in preclinical department of medical schools, 2000-01

Ranking basis/background: Salaries are on a 12-month basis and are rounded to the nearest $100. Data was reported for all faculty (M.D., other doctoral, and nondoctoral). **Remarks:** Original source: Association of American Medical Colleges. **Number listed:** 8.

Anatomy, with an average salary of $106,400
Biochemistry, $115,400
Genetics, $131,600
Microbiology, $116,100
Molecular/cellular biology, $131,700
Pharmacology, $116,400
Physiology, $113,700
Other basic sciences, $126,500

Source: "Uncertain Times: The Annual Report on the Economic Status of the Profession," *Academe*, 87: 25-98, (March/April 2001).

★3933★
Average salaries for professors at public and private institutions in preclinical department of medical schools, 2000-01

Ranking basis/background: Salaries are on a 12-month basis and are rounded to the nearest $100. Data was reported for all faculty (M.D., other doctoral, and nondoctoral). **Remarks:** Original source: Association of American Medical Colleges. **Number listed:** 8.

Anatomy, with an average salary of $104,100
Biochemistry, $114,300
Genetics, $120,100
Microbiology, $111,500
Molecular/cellular biology, $124,600
Pharmacology, $110,800
Physiology, $108,900
Other basic sciences, $119,400

Source: "Uncertain Times: The Annual Report on the Economic Status of the Profession," *Academe*, 87: 25-98, (March/April 2001).

★3934★
Average salaries for professors at public institutions in preclinical department of medical schools, 2000-01

Ranking basis/background: Salaries are on a 12-month basis and are rounded to the nearest $100. Data was reported for all faculty (M.D., other doctoral, and nondoctoral). **Remarks:** Original source: Association of American Medical Colleges. **Number listed:** 8.

Anatomy, with an average salary of $103,000
Biochemistry, $113,600
Genetics, $109,500
Microbiology, $108,900
Molecular/cellular biology, $115,100
Pharmacology, $107,900
Physiology, $106,900
Other basic sciences, $106,500

Source: "Uncertain Times: The Annual Report on the Economic Status of the Profession," *Academe*, 87: 25-98, (March/April 2001).

★3935★
Average salaries for professors in church-related institutions, 2000-01

Ranking basis/background: Based on the responses of 1,433 institutions providing data to the annual salary survey of the American Association of University Professors. **Remarks:** Table also includes percentage increases in salary for continuing faculty by category, affiliation, and academic rank. **Number listed:** 4.

Doctoral institutions, with an average annual salary of $95,550
Comprehensive institutions, $70,523
Baccalaureate institutions, $57,012
Two-year institutions, $41,815

Source: "Uncertain Times: The Annual Report on the Economic Status of the Profession," *Academe*, 87: 25-98, (March/April 2001).

★3936★
Average salaries for professors in private-independent institutions, 2000-01

Ranking basis/background: Based on the responses of 1,433 institutions providing data to the annual salary survey of the American Association of University Professors. **Remarks:** Table also includes percentage increases in salary for continuing faculty by category, affiliation, and academic rank. **Number listed:** 4.

Doctoral institutions, with an average annual salary of $107,633
Comprehensive institutions, $75,143
Baccalaureate institutions, $74,031
Two-year institutions, $54,628

Source: "Uncertain Times: The Annual Report on the Economic Status of the Profession," *Academe*, 87: 25-98, (March/April 2001).

★3937★
Average salaries for professors in public institutions, 2000-01

Ranking basis/background: Based on the responses of 1,433 institutions providing data to the annual salary survey of the American Association of University Professors. **Remarks:** Table also includes percentage increases in salary for continuing faculty by category, affiliation, and academic rank. **Number listed:** 4.

Doctoral institutions, with an average annual salary of $84,007
Comprehensive institutions, $68,828

Baccalaureate institutions, $62,059
Two-year institutions, $57,932
Source: "Uncertain Times: The Annual Report on the Economic Status of the Profession," *Academe*, 87: 25-98, (March/April 2001).

★3938★
Average salaries for psychology faculty at 4-year institutions, 1999-2000

Ranking basis/background: Average salary for faculty at public and private 4-year institutions. From a survey of professors in 80 disciplines at 363 public colleges and 501 private institutions, excluding medical professors. **Remarks:** Original source: College and University Personnel Association. **Number listed:** 2.
  Private, with $53,188
  Public, $58,157
Source: Magner, Denise K., "Law Professors are Academe's Best-Paid Faculty Members, Survey Finds," *The Chronicle of Higher Education*, 46: A20, (May 12, 2000).

★3939★
Average salaries for public administration faculty at 4-year institutions, 1999-2000

Ranking basis/background: Average salary for faculty at public and private 4-year institutions. From a survey of professors in 80 disciplines at 363 public colleges and 501 private institutions, excluding medical professors. **Remarks:** Original source: College and University Personnel Association. **Number listed:** 2.
  Private, with $64,572
  Public, $59,825
Source: Magner, Denise K., "Law Professors are Academe's Best-Paid Faculty Members, Survey Finds," *The Chronicle of Higher Education*, 46: A20, (May 12, 2000).

★3940★
Average salaries for public health faculty at 4-year institutions, 1999-2000

Ranking basis/background: Average salary for faculty at public and private 4-year institutions. From a survey of professors in 80 disciplines at 363 public colleges and 501 private institutions, excluding medical professors. **Remarks:** Original source: College and University Personnel Association. **Number listed:** 2.
  Private, with $84,018
  Public, $62,460
Source: Magner, Denise K., "Law Professors are Academe's Best-Paid Faculty Members, Survey Finds," *The Chronicle of Higher Education*, 46: A20, (May 12, 2000).

★3941★
Average salaries for reading teacher education faculty at 4-year institutions, 1999-2000

Ranking basis/background: Average salary for faculty at public and private 4-year institutions. From a survey of professors in 80 disciplines at 363 public colleges and 501 private institutions, excluding medical professors. **Remarks:** Original source: College and University Personnel Association. **Number listed:** 2.
  Private, with $47,184
  Public, $51,878
Source: Magner, Denise K., "Law Professors are Academe's Best-Paid Faculty Members, Survey Finds," *The Chronicle of Higher Education*, 46: A20, (May 12, 2000).

★3942★
Average salaries for religion and religious studies faculty at 4-year institutions, 1999-2000

Ranking basis/background: Average salary for faculty at public and private 4-year institutions. From a survey of professors in 80 disciplines at 363 public colleges and 501 private institutions, excluding medical professors. **Remarks:** Original source: College and University Personnel Association. **Number listed:** 2.
  Private, with $53,318
  Public, $57,878
Source: Magner, Denise K., "Law Professors are Academe's Best-Paid Faculty Members, Survey Finds," *The Chronicle of Higher Education*, 46: A20, (May 12, 2000).

★3943★
Average salaries for romance languages and literatures faculty at 4-year institutions, 1999-2000

Ranking basis/background: Average salary for faculty at public and private 4-year institutions. From a survey of professors in 80 disciplines at 363 public colleges and 501 private institutions, excluding medical professors. **Remarks:** Original source: College and University Personnel Association. **Number listed:** 2.
  Private, with $51,776
  Public, $51,205
Source: Magner, Denise K., "Law Professors are Academe's Best-Paid Faculty Members, Survey Finds," *The Chronicle of Higher Education*, 46: A20, (May 12, 2000).

★3944★
Average salaries for social sciences faculty at 4-year institutions, 1999-2000

Ranking basis/background: Average salary for faculty at public and private 4-year institutions. From a survey of professors in 80 disciplines at 363 public colleges and 501 private institutions, excluding medical professors. **Remarks:** Original source: College and University Personnel Association. **Number listed:** 2.
  Private, with $56,137
  Public, $72,571
Source: Magner, Denise K., "Law Professors are Academe's Best-Paid Faculty Members, Survey Finds," *The Chronicle of Higher Education*, 46: A20, (May 12, 2000).

★3945★
Average salaries for social work faculty at 4-year institutions, 1999-2000

Ranking basis/background: Average salary for faculty at public and private 4-year institutions. From a survey of professors in 80 disciplines at 363 public colleges and 501 private institutions, excluding medical professors. **Remarks:** Original source: College and University Personnel Association. **Number listed:** 2.
  Private, with $50,421
  Public, $52,648
Source: Magner, Denise K., "Law Professors are Academe's Best-Paid Faculty Members, Survey Finds," *The Chronicle of Higher Education*, 46: A20, (May 12, 2000).

★3946★
Average salaries for sociology faculty at 4-year institutions, 1999-2000

Ranking basis/background: Average salary for faculty at public and private 4-year institutions. From a survey of professors in 80 disciplines at 363 public colleges and 501 private institutions, excluding medical professors. **Remarks:** Original source: College and University Personnel Association. **Number listed:** 2.
  Private, with $53,242
  Public, $54,471
Source: Magner, Denise K., "Law Professors are Academe's Best-Paid Faculty Members, Survey Finds," *The Chronicle of Higher Education*, 46: A20, (May 12, 2000).

★3947★
Average salaries for special education faculty at 4-year institutions, 1999-2000

Ranking basis/background: Average salary for faculty at public and private 4-year institutions. From a survey of professors in 80 disciplines at 363 public colleges and 501 private institutions, excluding medical professors. **Remarks:** Original source: College and University Personnel Association. **Number listed:** 2.
  Private, with $47,619
  Public, $52,978
Source: Magner, Denise K., "Law Professors are Academe's Best-Paid Faculty Members, Survey Finds," *The Chronicle of Higher Education*, 46: A20, (May 12, 2000).

★3948★
Average salaries for speech and rhetorical studies faculty at 4-year institutions, 1999-2000

Ranking basis/background: Average salary for faculty at public and private 4-year institutions. From a survey of professors in 80 disciplines at 363 public colleges and 501 private institutions, excluding medical professors. **Remarks:** Original source: College and University Personnel Association. **Number listed:** 2.
  Private, with $45,351
  Public, $48,746
Source: Magner, Denise K., "Law Professors are Academe's Best-Paid Faculty Members, Survey Finds," *The Chronicle of Higher Education*, 46: A20, (May 12, 2000).

★3949★
Average salaries for speech pathology and audiology faculty at 4-year institutions, 1999-2000

Ranking basis/background: Average salary for faculty at public and private 4-year institutions. From a survey of professors in 80 disciplines at 363 public colleges and 501 private institutions, excluding medical professors. **Remarks:** Original source: College and University Personnel Association. **Number listed:** 2.
  Private, with $51,401
  Public, $51,756
Source: Magner, Denise K., "Law Professors are Academe's Best-Paid Faculty Members, Survey Finds," *The Chronicle of Higher Education*, 46: A20, (May 12, 2000).

SALARIES—COLLEGES & UNIVERSITIES, FACULTY

★3950★
Average salaries for teacher education, specific academic and vocational programs faculty at 4-year institutions, 1999-2000

Ranking basis/background: Average salary for faculty at public and private 4-year institutions. From a survey of professors in 80 disciplines at 363 public colleges and 501 private institutions, excluding medical professors. **Remarks:** Original source: College and University Personnel Association. **Number listed:** 2.
    Private, with $46,480
    Public, $49,893

Source: Magner, Denise K., "Law Professors are Academe's Best-Paid Faculty Members, Survey Finds," *The Chronicle of Higher Education*, 46: A20, (May 12, 2000).

★3951★
Average salaries for technology and industrial-arts teacher education faculty at 4-year institutions, 1999-2000

Ranking basis/background: Average salary for faculty at public and private 4-year institutions. From a survey of professors in 80 disciplines at 363 public colleges and 501 private institutions, excluding medical professors. **Remarks:** Original source: College and University Personnel Association. **Number listed:** 2.
    Private, with $0
    Public, $53,237

Source: Magner, Denise K., "Law Professors are Academe's Best-Paid Faculty Members, Survey Finds," *The Chronicle of Higher Education*, 46: A20, (May 12, 2000).

★3952★
Average salaries for theological studies and religious vocations faculty at 4-year institutions, 1999-2000

Ranking basis/background: Average salary for faculty at public and private 4-year institutions. From a survey of professors in 80 disciplines at 363 public colleges and 501 private institutions, excluding medical professors. **Remarks:** Original source: College and University Personnel Association. **Number listed:** 2.
    Private, with $47,169
    Public, $0

Source: Magner, Denise K., "Law Professors are Academe's Best-Paid Faculty Members, Survey Finds," *The Chronicle of Higher Education*, 46: A20, (May 12, 2000).

★3953★
Average salaries for visual and performing arts faculty at 4-year institutions, 1999-2000

Ranking basis/background: Average salary for faculty at public and private 4-year institutions. From a survey of professors in 80 disciplines at 363 public colleges and 501 private institutions, excluding medical professors. **Remarks:** Original source: College and University Personnel Association. **Number listed:** 2.
    Private, with $46,642
    Public, $56,392

Source: Magner, Denise K., "Law Professors are Academe's Best-Paid Faculty Members, Survey Finds," *The Chronicle of Higher Education*, 46: A20, (May 12, 2000).

★3954★
Average salaries for zoology faculty at 4-year institutions, 1999-2000

Ranking basis/background: Average salary for faculty at public and private 4-year institutions. From a survey of professors in 80 disciplines at 363 public colleges and 501 private institutions, excluding medical professors. **Remarks:** Original source: College and University Personnel Association. **Number listed:** 2.
    Private, with $46,638
    Public, $62,791

Source: Magner, Denise K., "Law Professors are Academe's Best-Paid Faculty Members, Survey Finds," *The Chronicle of Higher Education*, 46: A20, (May 12, 2000).

★3955★
Average salary increase percentages for continuing faculty members at U.S. institutions of higher education, 1971-72 through 2000-01

Ranking basis/background: Annual percentage increases in salaries for all faculty ranks. **Number listed:** 22.
    1971-72 to 1973-74, with 11.6%
    1973-74 to 1975-76, 15.6%
    1975-76 to 1977-78, 13.0%
    1977-78 to 1979-80, 16.1%
    1979-80 to 1981-82, 20.9%
    1981-82 to 1983-84, 14.1%
    1983-84 to 1985-86, 14.9%
    1985-86 to 1986-87, 6.6%
    1986-87 to 1987-88, 6.5%
    1987-88 to 1988-89, 6.8%
    1988-89 to 1989-90, 7.3%
    1989-90 to 1990-91, 6.6%
    1990-91 to 1991-92, 4.3%
    1991-92 to 1992-93, 3.6%
    1992-93 to 1993-94, 4.2%
    1993-94 to 1994-95, 4.6%
    1994-95 to 1995-96, 4.0%
    1995-96 to 1996-97, 3.5%
    1996-97 to 1997-98, 4.3%
    1997-98 to 1998-99, 4.8%
    1998-99 to 1999-00, 4.8%
    1999-00 to 2000-01, 5.3%

Source: "Uncertain Times: The Annual Report on the Economic Status of the Profession," *Academe*, 87: 25-98, (March/April 2001).

★3956★
Average salary increase percentages for continuing faculty members at U.S. institutions of higher education, 1989-90 through 1999-2000

Ranking basis/background: Annual percentage increases in salaries both with and without inflation adjustments for continuing faculty members. Inflation adjustments are based on the December-to-December change in the Consumer Price Index. **Remarks:** Original source: American Association of University Professors. **Number listed:** 11.
    1989-90, with 7.3% not adjusted for inflation; 2.7% adjusted for inflation
    1990-91, 6.6%; 0.5%
    1991-92, 4.3%; 1.2%
    1992-93, 3.6%; 0.7%
    1993-94, 4.2%; 1.5%
    1994-95, 4.6%; 1.9%
    1995-96, 4.0%; 1.5%
    1996-97, 3.5%; 0.2%
    1997-98, 4.3%; 2.6%
    1998-99, 4.8%; 3.2%
    1999-2000, 4.8%; 2.1%

Source: Magner, Denise K., "Faculty Salaries Increased 3.7% in 1999-2000," *The Chronicle of Higher Education*, 46: A20-A21, (April 14, 2000).

★3957★
Average salary increase percentages for faculty members at U.S. institutions of higher education, 1971-72 through 2000-01

Ranking basis/background: Annual percentage increases in salaries for all faculty ranks. **Number listed:** 22.
    1971-72 to 1973-74, with 9.4%
    1973-74 to 1975-76, 12.1%
    1975-76 to 1977-78, 10.2%
    1977-78 to 1979-80, 13.3%
    1979-80 to 1981-82, 18.5%
    1981-82 to 1983-84, 11.4%
    1983-84 to 1985-86, 13.1%
    1985-86 to 1986-87, 5.9%
    1986-87 to 1987-88, 4.9%
    1987-88 to 1988-89, 5.8%
    1988-89 to 1989-90, 5.8%
    1989-90 to 1990-91, 6.1%
    1990-91 to 1991-92, 3.5%
    1991-92 to 1992-93, 2.5%
    1992-93 to 1993-94, 3.0%
    1993-94 to 1994-95, 3.4%
    1994-95 to 1995-96, 2.9%
    1995-96 to 1996-97, 3.0%
    1996-97 to 1997-98, 3.3%
    1997-98 to 1998-99, 3.6%
    1998-99 to 1999-00, 3.7%
    1999-00 to 2000-01, 3.5%

Source: "Uncertain Times: The Annual Report on the Economic Status of the Profession," *Academe*, 87: 25-98, (March/April 2001).

★3958★
Average salary increase percentages for faculty members at U.S. institutions of higher education, 1989-90 through 1999-2000

Ranking basis/background: Annual percentage increases in salaries both with and without inflation adjustments for all faculty members. Inflation adjustments are based on the December-to-December change in the Consumer Price Index. **Remarks:** Original source: American Association of University Professors. **Number listed:** 11.
    1989-90, with 6.1% not adjusted for inflation; 1.5% adjusted for inflation
    1990-91, 5.4%; 0.7% decrease
    1991-92, 3.5%; 0.4%
    1992-93, 2.5%; 0.4% decrease
    1993-94, 3.0%; 0.3%
    1994-95, 3.4%; 0.7%
    1995-96, 2.9%; 0.4%
    1996-97, 3.0%; 0.3% decrease
    1997-98, 3.3%; 1.6%
    1998-99, 3.6%; 2.0%
    1999-2000, 3.7%; 1.0%

Source: Magner, Denise K., "Faculty Salaries Increased 3.7% in 1999-2000," *The Chronicle of Higher Education*, 46: A20-A21, (April 14, 2000).

★3959★
Institutional costs of major fringe benefits for faculty at church-related institutions, 2000-01

Ranking basis/background: Average costs of benefits in dollars and as a percentage of salary, based on the responses of 1,433 institutions providing data to the annual salary survey of the American Association of University Professors. Average total for church-related institutions is $13,297 or 25.0% of salary. **Number listed:** 10.
- Retirement, with an average cost of $4,262; representing 8.0% of salary
- Medical Insurance, $3,154; 5.9%
- Disability, $201; 0.4%
- Tuition, $991; 1.9%
- Dental Insurance, $113; 0.2%
- Social Security, $3,774; 7.1%
- Unemployment, $122; 0.2%
- Group Life, $167; 0.3%
- Worker's Compensation, $262; 0.5%
- Benefits in Kind, $250; 0.5%

Source: "Uncertain Times: The Annual Report on the Economic Status of the Profession," *Academe*, 87: 25-98, (March/April 2001).

★3960★
Institutional costs of major fringe benefits for faculty at private-independent institutions, 2000-01

Ranking basis/background: Average costs of benefits in dollars and as a percentage of salary, based on the responses of 1,433 institutions providing data to the annual salary survey of the American Association of University Professors. Average total for private institutions is $17,521 or 25.1% of salary. **Number listed:** 10.
- Retirement, with an average cost of $6,278; representing 9.0% of salary
- Medical Insurance, $3,925; 5.6%
- Disability, $209; 0.3%
- Tuition, $1,240; 1.8%
- Dental Insurance, $171; 0.2%
- Social Security, $4,694; 6.7%
- Unemployment, $142; 0.2%
- Group Life, $210; 0.3%
- Worker's Compensation, $378; 0.5%
- Benefits in Kind, $273; 0.4%

Source: "Uncertain Times: The Annual Report on the Economic Status of the Profession," *Academe*, 87: 25-98, (March/April 2001).

★3961★
Institutional costs of major fringe benefits for faculty at public institutions, 2000-01

Ranking basis/background: Average costs of benefits in dollars and as a percentage of salary, based on the responses of 1,433 institutions providing data to the annual salary survey of the American Association of University Professors. Average total for public institutions is $13,965 or 23.8% of salary. **Number listed:** 10.
- Retirement, with an average cost of $5,475; representing 9.3% of salary
- Medical Insurance, $3,855; 6.6%
- Disability, $150; 0.3%
- Tuition, $113; 0.2%
- Dental Insurance, $181; 0.3%
- Social Security, $3,563; 6.1%
- Unemployment, $102; 0.2%
- Group Life, $135; 0.2%
- Worker's Compensation, $268; 0.5%
- Benefits in Kind, $121; 0.2%

Source: "Uncertain Times: The Annual Report on the Economic Status of the Profession," *Academe*, 87: 25-98, (March/April 2001).

★3962★
Percentage change in salary levels for assistant professors in church-related institutions, 1999-2000 to 2000-01

Ranking basis/background: Based on the responses of 1,433 institutions providing data to the annual salary survey of the American Association of University Professors. **Remarks:** Table also includes percentage increases in salary for continuing faculty by category, affiliation, and academic rank. **Number listed:** 4.
- Doctoral institutions, with a percentage increase in salary levels of 3.3%
- Comprehensive institutions, 4.1%
- Baccalaureate institutions, 3.9%
- Two-year institutions, 4.6%

Source: "Uncertain Times: The Annual Report on the Economic Status of the Profession," *Academe*, 87: 25-98, (March/April 2001).

★3963★
Percentage change in salary levels for assistant professors in private-independent institutions, 1999-2000 to 2000-01

Ranking basis/background: Based on the responses of 1,433 institutions providing data to the annual salary survey of the American Association of University Professors. **Remarks:** Table also includes percentage increases in salary for continuing faculty by category, affiliation, and academic rank. **Number listed:** 4.
- Doctoral institutions, with a percentage increase in salary levels of 5.1%
- Comprehensive institutions, 3.7%
- Baccalaureate institutions, 3.9%
- Two-year institutions, 1.5%

Source: "Uncertain Times: The Annual Report on the Economic Status of the Profession," *Academe*, 87: 25-98, (March/April 2001).

★3964★
Percentage change in salary levels for assistant professors in public institutions, 1999-2000 to 2000-01

Ranking basis/background: Based on the responses of 1,433 institutions providing data to the annual salary survey of the American Association of University Professors. **Remarks:** Table also includes percentage increases in salary for continuing faculty by category, affiliation, and academic rank. **Number listed:** 4.
- Doctoral institutions, with a percentage increase in salary levels of 5.1%
- Comprehensive institutions, 3.9%
- Baccalaureate institutions, 3.6%
- Two-year institutions, 2.5%

Source: "Uncertain Times: The Annual Report on the Economic Status of the Profession," *Academe*, 87: 25-98, (March/April 2001).

★3965★
Percentage change in salary levels for associate professors in church-related institutions, 1999-2000 to 2000-01

Ranking basis/background: Based on the responses of 1,433 institutions providing data to the annual salary survey of the American Association of University Professors. **Remarks:** Table also includes percentage increases in salary for continuing faculty by category, affiliation, and academic rank. **Number listed:** 4.
- Doctoral institutions, with a percentage increase in salary levels of 3.5%
- Comprehensive institutions, 3.3%
- Baccalaureate institutions, 3.7%
- Two-year institutions, 2.5%

Source: "Uncertain Times: The Annual Report on the Economic Status of the Profession," *Academe*, 87: 25-98, (March/April 2001).

★3966★
Percentage change in salary levels for associate professors in private-independent institutions, 1999-2000 to 2000-01

Ranking basis/background: Based on the responses of 1,433 institutions providing data to the annual salary survey of the American Association of University Professors. **Remarks:** Table also includes percentage increases in salary for continuing faculty by category, affiliation, and academic rank. **Number listed:** 4.
- Doctoral institutions, with a percentage increase in salary levels of 4.7%
- Comprehensive institutions, 3.0%
- Baccalaureate institutions, 4.2%
- Two-year institutions, 3.5%

Source: "Uncertain Times: The Annual Report on the Economic Status of the Profession," *Academe*, 87: 25-98, (March/April 2001).

★3967★
Percentage change in salary levels for associate professors in public institutions, 1999-2000 to 2000-01

Ranking basis/background: Based on the responses of 1,433 institutions providing data to the annual salary survey of the American Association of University Professors. **Remarks:** Table also includes percentage increases in salary for continuing faculty by category, affiliation, and academic rank. **Number listed:** 4.
- Doctoral institutions, with a percentage increase in salary levels of 4.5%
- Comprehensive institutions, 3.8%
- Baccalaureate institutions, 3.9%
- Two-year institutions, 2.6%

Source: "Uncertain Times: The Annual Report on the Economic Status of the Profession," *Academe*, 87: 25-98, (March/April 2001).

★3968★
Percentage change in salary levels for instructors in church-related institutions, 1999-2000 to 2000-01

Ranking basis/background: Based on the responses of 1,433 institutions providing data to the annual salary survey of the American Association of University Professors. **Remarks:** Table also includes percentage increases in salary for continuing faculty by category, affiliation, and academic rank. **Number listed:** 4.
- Doctoral institutions, with a percentage increase in salary levels of 3.3%

SALARIES—COLLEGES & UNIVERSITIES, FACULTY

Comprehensive institutions, 1.2% decrease
Baccalaureate institutions, 4.3%
Two-year institutions, 4.4%

Source: "Uncertain Times: The Annual Report on the Economic Status of the Profession," *Academe*, 87: 25-98, (March/April 2001).

★3969★
Percentage change in salary levels for instructors in private-independent institutions, 1999-2000 to 2000-01

Ranking basis/background: Based on the responses of 1,433 institutions providing data to the annual salary survey of the American Association of University Professors. **Remarks:** Table also includes percentage increases in salary for continuing faculty by category, affiliation, and academic rank. **Number listed:** 4.

Doctoral institutions, with a percentage increase in salary levels of 1.2%
Comprehensive institutions, 5.3%
Baccalaureate institutions, 2.3%
Two-year institutions, 10.6%

Source: "Uncertain Times: The Annual Report on the Economic Status of the Profession," *Academe*, 87: 25-98, (March/April 2001).

★3970★
Percentage change in salary levels for instructors in public institutions, 1999-2000 to 2000-01

Ranking basis/background: Based on the responses of 1,433 institutions providing data to the annual salary survey of the American Association of University Professors. **Remarks:** Table also includes percentage increases in salary for continuing faculty by category, affiliation, and academic rank. **Number listed:** 4.

Doctoral institutions, with a percentage increase in salary levels of 4.5%
Comprehensive institutions, 3.9%
Baccalaureate institutions, 4.8%
Two-year institutions, 2.2%

Source: "Uncertain Times: The Annual Report on the Economic Status of the Profession," *Academe*, 87: 25-98, (March/April 2001).

★3971★
Percentage change in salary levels for professors in church-related institutions, 1999-2000 to 2000-01

Ranking basis/background: Based on the responses of 1,433 institutions providing data to the annual salary survey of the American Association of University Professors. **Remarks:** Table also includes percentage increases in salary for continuing faculty by category, affiliation, and academic rank. **Number listed:** 4.

Doctoral institutions, with a percentage increase in salary levels of 4.5%
Comprehensive institutions, 3.7%
Baccalaureate institutions, 3.4%
Two-year institutions, 1.6%

Source: "Uncertain Times: The Annual Report on the Economic Status of the Profession," *Academe*, 87: 25-98, (March/April 2001).

★3972★
Percentage change in salary levels for professors in private-independent institutions, 1999-2000 to 2000-01

Ranking basis/background: Based on the responses of 1,433 institutions providing data to the annual salary survey of the American Association of University Professors. **Remarks:** Table also includes percentage increases in salary for continuing faculty by category, affiliation, and academic rank. **Number listed:** 4.

Doctoral institutions, with a percentage increase in salary levels of 4.7%
Comprehensive institutions, 4.0%
Baccalaureate institutions, 4.1%
Two-year institutions, 3.2%

Source: "Uncertain Times: The Annual Report on the Economic Status of the Profession," *Academe*, 87: 25-98, (March/April 2001).

★3973★
Percentage change in salary levels for professors in public institutions, 1999-2000 to 2000-01

Ranking basis/background: Based on the responses of 1,433 institutions providing data to the annual salary survey of the American Association of University Professors. **Remarks:** Table also includes percentage increases in salary for continuing faculty by category, affiliation, and academic rank. **Number listed:** 4.

Doctoral institutions, with a percentage increase in salary levels of 4.8%
Comprehensive institutions, 3.8%
Baccalaureate institutions, 4.1%
Two-year institutions, 3.7%

Source: "Uncertain Times: The Annual Report on the Economic Status of the Profession," *Academe*, 87: 25-98, (March/April 2001).

★3974★
Private institutions of higher education that pay the highest salaries to female professors, 2000-01

Ranking basis/background: Average annual salaries for female professors. **Number listed:** 10.

1. Rockefeller University, with $141,000
2. Harvard University, $125,400
3. Stanford University, $122,200
4. Princeton University, $121,500
5. Yale University, $115,000
6. University of Chicago, $114,200
7. University of Pennsylvania, $113,500
8. Babson College, $113,200
9. Columbia University, $111,600
10. New York University, $110,400

Source: "Uncertain Times: The Annual Report on the Economic Status of the Profession," *Academe*, 87: 25-98, (March/April 2001).

★3975★
Public institutions of higher education that pay the highest salaries to female professors, 2000-01

Ranking basis/background: Average annual salaries for female professors. **Number listed:** 10.

1. Rutgers University, Newark, with $104,100
2. University of California, Berkeley, $103,600
3. University of California, Los Angeles, $102,800
4. College of William and Mary, $99,700
5. University of Michigan, Ann Arbor, $99,000
6. University of Virginia, $98,400
7. Georgia Institute of Technology, $98,000
8. Georgia State University, $96,800
9. Rutgers University, New Brunswick, $96,300
10. University of North Carolina, Chapel Hill, $95,300

Source: "Uncertain Times: The Annual Report on the Economic Status of the Profession," *Academe*, 87: 25-98, (March/April 2001).

★3976★
U.S. community colleges with the highest paid full professors, 2001

Ranking basis/background: Average annual salary figures, in thousand, for full professors. **Remarks:** Original source: American Association of University Professors Salary Data. **Number listed:** 15.

1. Westchester Community College, with $87.2
2. Fashion Institute of Technology, $86.1
3. Passaic County Community College, $85.1
4. Nassau Community College, $84.4
5. Suffolk County Community College, Ammerman, $80.7
6. Gloucester County College, $80.4
7. Suffolk County Community College, Western, $77.4
8. Suffolk County Community College, Eastern, $77.3
9. American College (PA), $75.9
10. Miami University, Middletown, $74.5
11. Moraine Valley Community College, $69.9
11. Monroe Community College, $69.9
13. Niagara County Community College, $69.8
14. Purdue University, North Central, $69.5
15. Pennsylvania State University, $68.2

Source: Smallwood, Scott, "The Price Professors Pay for Teaching at Public Universities," *The Chronicle of Higher Education*, 47: A18, A23-A24, (April 20, 2001).

★3977★
U.S. institutions with the highest paid assistant professors, 2001

Ranking basis/background: Average annual salary figures, in thousand, for assistant professors. **Remarks:** Original source: American Association of University Professors Salary Data. **Number listed:** 15.

1. Babson College, with $76.0
2. California Institute of Technology, $73.4
3. University of Pennsylvania, $73.1
4. Massachusetts Institute of Technology, $72.1
5. Harvard University, $71.6
6. Gloucester County College, $69.4
7. Stanford University, $69.1
8. Carnegie Mellon University, $68.1
9. University of Chicago, $67.1
10. University of Texas, Dallas, $66.9
11. New York University, $66.7
12. Cornell University, Endowed Colleges, $66.4
13. Northwestern University, $65.8
14. Rice University, $65.7
15. Bentley College, $64.9

Source: Smallwood, Scott, "The Price Professors Pay for Teaching at Public Universities," *The Chronicle of Higher Education*, 47: A18, A23-A24, (April 20, 2001).

★3978★

U.S. institutions with the highest paid full professors, 2001

Ranking basis/background: Average annual salary figures, in thousand, for full professors earning more than $100,000 per year. **Remarks:** Original source: American Association of University Professors Salary Data. **Number listed:** 44.

1. Rockefeller University, with $138.1
2. Harvard University, $135.2
3. Stanford University, $126.7
4. Princeton University, $125.7
5. University of Chicago, $124.8
6. Yale University, $124.1
7. California Institute of Technology, $122.2
8. New York University, $120.8
9. University of Pennsylvania, $120.3
10. Columbia University, $120.2

Source: Smallwood, Scott, "The Price Professors Pay for Teaching at Public Universities," *The Chronicle of Higher Education*, 47: A18, A23-A24, (April 20, 2001).

★3979★

U.S. institutions with the lowest paid full professors, 2001

Ranking basis/background: Average annual salary figures, in thousand, for full professors. **Remarks:** Original source: American Association of University Professors Salary Data. **Number listed:** 15.

1. Southern Adventist University, with $33.4
2. Thomas College, $33.8
3. Antioch University, McGregor, $35.3
4. Tabor College, $35.4
5. Concordia University (NE), $35.4
6. Bethel College (TN), $35.5
7. McPherson College, $35.8
8. Bethany College (KS), $35.9
9. Faith Baptist Bible College and Theological Seminary, $36.1
10. Lincoln Memorial University, $36.4
11. Lees-McRae College, $36.8
12. Tennessee Wesleyan College, $37.2
13. Truett-McConnell College, $37.3
14. Bethel College (KS), $37.4
15. Kansas Wesleyan University, $37.6

Source: Smallwood, Scott, "The Price Professors Pay for Teaching at Public Universities," *The Chronicle of Higher Education*, 47: A18, A23-A24, (April 20, 2001).

★3980★

U.S. liberal arts colleges with the highest paid full professors, 2001

Ranking basis/background: Average annual salary figures, in thousand, for full professors. **Remarks:** Original source: American Association of University Professors Salary Data. **Number listed:** 15.

1. Wellesley College, with $100.8
2. Swarthmore College, $98.7
3. Williams College, $98.5
4. Amherst College, $97.8
5. Trinity College (CT), $96.1
6. Claremont McKenna College, $95.7
7. Barnard College, $95.7
8. Colgate University, $95.4
9. Harvey Mudd College, $94.2
10. Pomona College, $93.6
11. Colby College, $93.0
12. Bowdoin College, $92.1
13. Vassar College, $92.0
14. Middlebury College, $91.8
15. Mount Holyoke College, $89.8

Source: Smallwood, Scott, "The Price Professors Pay for Teaching at Public Universities," *The Chronicle of Higher Education*, 47: A18, A23-A24, (April 20, 2001).

Related Information

★3981★

"Faculty Salaries at More Than 1,400 Institutions," *The Chronicle of Higher Education*, 47: A20-A23, (April 20, 2001).

Remarks: Provides average faculty salaries at more than 1,400 colleges and universities for the 2000-01 academic year. Information was compiled by the American Association of University Professors.

SALARIES–HIGH SCHOOL GRADUATES

★3982★

Average salaries for individuals with a high school degree, by race/ethnicity

Ranking basis/background: Average annual salary. **Remarks:** Original source: U.S. Census Bureau. **Number listed:** 3.

White, with $23,618
African American, $18,980
Hispanic American, $19,558

Source: Borden, Dr. Victor M.H., "The Top 100: Interpreting the Data," *Black Issues in Higher Education*, 17: 48-49, (June 22, 2000).

★3983★

Average salaries for individuals without a high school degree, by race/ethnicity

Ranking basis/background: Average annual salary. **Remarks:** Original source: U.S. Census Bureau. **Number listed:** 3.

White, with $16,596
African American, $13,185
Hispanic American, $15,069

Source: Borden, Dr. Victor M.H., "The Top 100: Interpreting the Data," *Black Issues in Higher Education*, 17: 48-49, (June 22, 2000).

SALARIES–SCHOOLS, ELEMENTARY & SECONDARY

★3984★

Illinois elementary school districts with the highest teacher salaries, 1999

Ranking basis/background: Average annual salary in 1999. **Remarks:** Original source: 1999 School Report Card/Illinois Board of Education. **Number listed:** 13.

1. Salt Creek School, District 48, with an average annual teacher salary of $56,774
2. Schaumburg Community, District 54, $56,352
3. Lombard, District 44, $53,437
4. Evanston Community, District 65, $53,292
5. Northbrook School, District 28, $51,082
6. Rosemont, District 78, $48,361
7. Gurnee, District 56, $44,365
8. South Holland, District 151, $40,666
9. Western Springs, District 101, $40,656
10. Oak Lawn-Hometown, District 123, $38,700
11. Cary Community, District 26, $38,287
12. Bellwood, District 88, $37,928
13. Mundelein, District 75, $35,893

Source: Kelly, Maura, "Behind the Pay Curve," *Chicago Tribune*, July 16, 2000, Section 17, p. 3.

★3985★

Illinois high school districts with the highest teacher salaries, 1999

Ranking basis/background: Average annual salary in 1999. **Remarks:** Original source: 1999 School Report Card/Illinois Board of Education. **Number listed:** 9.

1. Palatine Township 211, with an average annual teacher salary of $76,473
2. Arlington Heights Township 214, $73,848
3. New Trier Township 203, $71,984
4. Thornton Township 205, $68,047
5. Homewood-Flossmoor Community 233, $67,537
6. Adlai E. Stevenson 125, $63,789
7. Oak Park and River Forest District 200, $63,215
8. Crystal Lake Community 155, $62,112
9. Proviso Township 209, $59,611

Source: Kelly, Maura, "Behind the Pay Curve," *Chicago Tribune*, July 16, 2000, Section 17, p. 3.

★3986★

Illinois school districts with the highest paid superintendents, 1999-2000

Ranking basis/background: Annual salary in 1999-2000. **Remarks:** Original source: Illinois State Board of Education. **Number listed:** 7.

1. Villa Park High School, District 88, with $253,876
2. Palatine High School, District 211, $226,116
3. Palatine Consolidated, District 15, $222,789
4. Illinois State Superintendent, Glenn "Max" McGee, $208,791
5. Proviso High School, District 209 (Maywood), $196,515
6. Carpentersville Unit, District 300, $195,731
7. City of Chicago School District 299 Cook, $150,000

Source: Rossi, Rosalind, "Vallas Given $30,000 Raise," *Chicago Sun-Times*, March 29, 2001, pp. 1-2.

★3987★

Salaries for full-time public school teachers in Chicago, 1998-99

Ranking basis/background: Average salary including extra duty pay, board-paid retirement, flexible benefit plan and other compensation treated as earnings by the Teachers Retirement System for the 1998-99 academic year. Also includes percentage of change from previous year, and total number of teachers. **Remarks:** Original source: Illinois State Board of Education. **Number listed:** 3.

Average salary, $49,163
Change from previous year, 3.9%
Total number of teachers, 23,639

Source: "Education Market Facts," *Crain's Chicago Business*, 23: F28, F30, (July 3, 2000).

★3988★
Salaries for full-time public school teachers in the state of Illinois, 1998-99

Ranking basis/background: Average salary including extra duty pay, board-paid retirement, flexible benefit plan and other compensation treated as earnings by the Teachers Retirement System for the 1998-99 academic year. Also includes percentage of change from previous year, and total number of teachers. **Remarks:** Original source: Illinois State Board of Education. **Number listed:** 3.

Average salary, $45,286
Change from previous year, 3.6%
Total number of teachers, 121,179

Source: "Education Market Facts," *Crain's Chicago Business*, 23: F28, F30, (July 3, 2000).

★3989★
Salaries for full-time public school teachers outside of Chicago, 1998-99

Ranking basis/background: Average salary including extra duty pay, board-paid retirement, flexible benefit plan and other compensation treated as earnings by the Teachers Retirement System for the 1998-99 academic year. Also includes percentage of change from previous year, and total number of teachers. **Remarks:** Original source: Illinois State Board of Education. **Number listed:** 3.

Average salary, $44,346
Change from previous year, 3.6%
Total number of teachers, 97,540

Source: "Education Market Facts," *Crain's Chicago Business*, 23: F28, F30, (July 3, 2000).

★3990★
Superintendents' salaries at the largest U.S. schools districts, 1999-2000

Ranking basis/background: Enrollment figures for the 1998-99 school year and average annual salary. **Remarks:** Original source: U.S. Department of Education. **Number listed:** 5.
1. New York City, with an enrollment of 1,000,000; average supt. salary of $245,000, with an option for annual increases
2. Los Angeles, 696,000; $250,000, with an option for annual pay hikes as well as annual performance bonuses of up to $100,000
3. Chicago, 431,000; $180,000
4. Dade County, FL, 353,000; $251,690
5. Broward County, FL, 231,000; $175,000, with an option for annual performance bonuses of 7 to 25 percent ($11,000 last year)

Source: Rossi, Rosalind, "Vallas Given $30,000 Raise," *Chicago Sun-Times*, March 29, 2001, pp. 1-2.

SAT
See: **College Entrance Examinations**

SCHOLARSHIPS
See: **Student Financial Aid**

SCHOOL ADMINISTRATION

★3991★
Top challenges for school administrators

Ranking basis/background: Facilities and business issues affecting elementary and secondary school administrators. **Number listed:** 10.
1. Charter schools
2. Construction and repair of facilities
3. Enrollment boom
4. Funding
5. Improving the learning environment
6. Security and safety
7. Maintenance and operations
8. Staff training and retention
9. Technology
10. Unfunded mandates

Source: Kennedy, Mike, "The Top Ten Issues Impacting School Administrators," *American School & University*, 73: 18-22, (January 2001).

SCHOOL DISTRICTS & SCHOOL SYSTEMS

★3992★
Educational program activities expenditures, 2000

Ranking basis/background: Figures, in billions, for federal expenditures allocated to education-program activities during the fiscal 2000 year. **Remarks:** Original source: Federal Support for Education Fiscal Years 1980-2000, National Center for Education Statistics. **Number listed:** 10.
1. Child nutrition, with $9.4 billion
2. Education for the disadvantaged, $8.4
3. Special education, $5.4
4. Head start, $5.3
5. Training programs, $3.5
6. School-improvement programs, $2.7
7. Vocational and adult education, $1.5
8. Education reforms–Goals 2000, $1.1
9. Impact aid, $1.0
10. Job Corps, $1.0

Source: "The Top Ten," *American School & University*, 73: 38-41, (January 2001).

★3993★
States expelling the highest ratio of students for violating the Gun-Free Schools Act, 1998-99

Ranking basis/background: Ratio of students per 1,000 expelled for Gun-Free Schools Act violations. **Remarks:** Original source: U.S. Department of Education. **Number listed:** 10.
1. Alabama, with 0.233
2. Missouri, 0.187
3. District of Columbia, 0.181
4. Alaska, 0.177
5. Tennessee, 0.168
6. Nevada, 0.167
7. Georgia, 0.148
8. Arkansas, 0.146
9. New Mexico, 0.143
10. Colorado, 0.134

Source: "The Top Ten," *American School & University*, 73: 38-41, (January 2001).

★3994★
States expelling the most students for violating the Gun-Free Schools Act, 1998-99

Ranking basis/background: Number of students expelled for Gun-Free Schools Act violations. **Remarks:** Original source: U.S. Department of Education. **Number listed:** 10.
1. Texas, with 294
2. California, 290
3. Georgia, 208
4. New York, 206
5. Alabama, 174
6. Missouri, 171
7. Tennessee, 152
8. Pennsylvania, 145
9. North Carolina, 141
10. Virginia/Washington, 115

Source: "The Top Ten," *American School & University*, 73: 38-41, (January 2001).

★3995★
States with the highest number of high school graduates, 1999-2000

Ranking basis/background: Total number of high school graduates from the 1999-2000 academic year and estimated percentage of change from 1999-2000 to 2004-2005. **Remarks:** Original source: U.S. Department of Education, National Center for Education Statistics, Common Core of Data surveys and State Public High School Graduates Model. **Number listed:** 50.
1. California, with 299,870 graduates; and a 6.7% increase by 2004-05
2. Texas, 200,910; 4.6%
3. New York, 146,060; 3.4%
4. Illinois, 130,910; 14.6%
5. Ohio, 116,210; 3.2% decrease
6. Pennsylvania, 115,810; 4.9%
7. Florida, 110,290; 10.3%
8. Michigan, 90,950; 3.6%
9. New Jersey, 72,930; 5.0%
10. North Carolina, 66,350; 13.4%

Source: "Education Market Facts," *Crain's Chicago Business*, 23: F28, F30, (July 3, 2000).

★3996★
States with the highest per-pupil expenditures

Ranking basis/background: Total per-pupil expenditures. **Remarks:** Original source: U.S. Department of Education. **Number listed:** 10.
1. New Jersey, with $9,643
2. Connecticut, $8,904
3. New York, $8,852
4. District of Columbia, $8,393
5. Alaska, $8,271
6. Rhode Island, $7,928
7. Massachusetts, $7,778
8. Delaware, $7,420
9. Pennsylvania, $7,209
10. Wisconsin, $7,123

Source: "The Top Ten," *American School & University*, 73: 38-41, (January 2001).

SCHOOL DISTRICTS & SCHOOL SYSTEMS–CHICAGO METROPOLITAN AREA

★3997★
States with the lowest number of high school graduates, 1999-2000

Ranking basis/background: Total number of high school graduates from the 1999-2000 academic year and estimated percentage of change from 1999-2000 to 2004-2005. **Remarks:** Original source: U.S. Department of Education, National Center for Education Statistics, Common Core of Data surveys and State Public High School Graduates Model. **Number listed:** 50.
1. District of Columbia, with 2,660 graduates; and a 13.9% decrease by 2004-05
2. Delaware, 6,500; 2.2% increase
3. Wyoming, 6,780; 12.8% decrease
4. Vermont, 6,960; 0.3% decrease
5. Alaska, 6,980; 2.0% increase
6. Rhode Island, 8,540; 5.5% increase
7. North Dakota, 9,010; 8.3% decrease
8. South Dakota, 10,080; 6.7% decrease
9. Hawaii, 10,670; 3.2% increase
10. Montana, 11,310; 4.4% decrease

Source: "Education Market Facts," *Crain's Chicago Business*, 23: F28, F30, (July 3, 2000).

★3998★
States with the lowest per-pupil expenditures

Ranking basis/background: Total per-pupil expenditures. **Remarks:** Original source: U.S. Department of Education. **Number listed:** 10.
1. Utah, with $3,969
2. Mississippi, $4,288
3. Arizona, $4,595
4. South Dakota, $4,669
5. Arkansas, $4,708
6. Idaho, $4,721
7. Alabama, $4,849
8. Tennessee, $4,937
9. New Mexico, $5,005
10. Oklahoma, $5,003

Source: "The Top Ten," *American School & University*, 73: 38-41, (January 2001).

★3999★
States with the most public school districts

Ranking basis/background: Total public school districts. **Remarks:** Original source: U.S. Department of Education. **Number listed:** 10.
1. Texas, with 1,042
2. California, 988
3. Illinois, 936
4. New York, 705
5. Michigan, 687
6. Ohio, 625
7. Nebraska, 596
8. New Jersey, 581
9. Oklahoma, 547
10. Missouri, 523

Source: "The Top Ten," *American School & University*, 73: 38-41, (January 2001).

SCHOOL DISTRICTS & SCHOOL SYSTEMS–CHICAGO METROPOLITAN AREA

★4000★
Acceptance rates at Chicago college prep magnet schools, 2000-01

Ranking basis/background: Number of applicants plus number and percentage enrolled from those applying as freshmen to college prep magnet schools that require a minimum test score to apply. **Remarks:** Original source: Chicago Board of Education. **Number listed:** 7.
1. Northside College Prep, with 3,500 applicants; 229 enrolled; 6.54% of applicants accepted
2. Jones College Prep, 2,817; 284; 10.08%
3. Lindblom College Prep, 641; 76; 11.86%
4. Whitney Young, 3,783; 629; 16.63%
5. Payton College Prep, 2,280; 381; 16.71%
6. Southside College Prep, 1,250; 209; 16.72%
7. Lane Technical, 4,321; 1,118; 25.87%

Source: Rossi, Rosalind, "Rules Change Could Boost College Prep Competition," *Chicago Sun-Times*, December 18, 2000, p. 6.

★4001★
Admissions to college prep schools in Chicago that are the toughest to get into, 2001

Ranking basis/background: Number of applicants, number and percentage accepted, and percentage of each racial group accepted, according to the Chicago Board of Education. **Number listed:** 8.
1. Northside College Prep, with 4,658 applicants; 237 (or 5%) accepted; 40% white; 6% black; 32% Asian; 20% Hispanic
2. Jones Academic College Prep, 4,397; 150 (3%); 25%; 37%; 9%; 28%
3. Walter Payton College Prep, 5,758; 219 (4%); 35%; 35%; 5%; 23%
4. Whitney Young Magnet, 6,708; 528 (8%); 17%; 41%; 16%; 25%
5. Lane Technical, 5,543; 1,304 (24%); 30%; 15%; 12%; 42%
6. Gwendolyn Brooks (Southside) College Prep, 2,105; 244 (12%); 2%; 83%;
7. Lindblom College Prep, 1,187; 140 (12%); 2%; 95%; 1%; 1%
8. Dr. Martin Luther King Jr. College Prep, 564; 52 (9%); 0%; 92%; 0%; 6%

Source: Rossi, Rosalind, "City's Toughest Prep Schools," *Chicago Sun-Times*, April 2, 2001, pp. 1-2.

★4002★
Chicago elementary magnet schools with the highest acceptance rates, 2000-01

Ranking basis/background: Number of applicants plus number and percentage enrolled from those applying at the entry level grade in elementary magnet schools that accept students citywide. **Remarks:** Original source: Chicago Board of Education. **Number listed:** 32.
1. Ericson Scholastic, with 180 applicants; 114 enrolled; 63.3% of applicants accepted
2. Galileo Scholastic, 98; 57; 58.2%
3. Saucedo Scholastic, 282; 126; 44.7%
4. Keller Gifted, 98; 29; 29.6%
5. Gunsaulus Scholastic, 244; 71; 29.1%
6. Inter-American, 238; 68; 28.6%
7. Lenart Gifted, 123; 31; 25.2%
8. Beasley Elementary, 478; 116; 24.3%
9. Sabin Bicultural, 263; 58; 22.1%
10. O.A. Thorp Scholastic, 372; 78; 20.9%

Source: Rossi, Rosalind, "Magnet? Take A Number," *Chicago Sun-Times*, December 18, 2000, p. 6.

★4003★
Chicago elementary magnet schools with the lowest acceptance rates, 2000-01

Ranking basis/background: Number of applicants plus number and percentage enrolled from those applying at the entry level grade in elementary magnet schools that accept students citywide. **Remarks:** Original source: Chicago Board of Education. **Number listed:** 32.
1. Decatur Classical, with 603 applicants; 26 enrolled; 4.3% of applicants accepted
2. McDade Classical, 589; 29; 4.9%
3. Black Elementary, 468; 27; 5.8%
4. Poe Classical, 435; 27; 6.2%
5. Franklin Fine Arts, 463; 29; 6.3%
5. Murray Language, 461; 29; 6.3%
7. Edison Gifted Elementary School, 453; 30; 6.6%
8. Vanderpoel Humanities, 386; 30; 7.8%
9. LaSalle Language, 773; 66; 8.5%
10. Turner Drew Language, 290; 28; 9.7%

Source: Rossi, Rosalind, "Magnet? Take A Number," *Chicago Sun-Times*, December 18, 2000, p. 6.

★4004★
Chicago neighborhood schools with the highest ISAT scores in reading and math

Ranking basis/background: Percentile of percentage of students statewide scoring the same as or worse than the average student. Only schools that tested at least two grades (3rd, 5th or 8th) were included. **Remarks:** Original source: Sun-Times research. **Number listed:** 10.
1. Edgebrook Elementary School, with a percentile of 80.8
2. Bell Elementary School, 79.7
3. Oriole Park Elementary School, 76.1
4. Lincoln Elementary School, 72.9
5. Recovering the Gifted Child, 64.8
6. George Washington Elementary School, 64.4
7. Earhart Opt for Knowledge, 63.7
8. Solomon Elementary School, 63.3
9. Beaubien Elementary School, 62.6
10. Norwood Park Elementary School, 60.6

Source: "School Report Card 2000," *Chicago Sun-Times*, November 1, 2000, pp. 1R-22R.

★4005★
College prep schools in Chicago that are the toughest to get into

Ranking basis/background: According to the Chicago Board of Education. **Number listed:** 8.
1. Northside College Prep
2. Jones Academic College Prep
3. Walter Payton College Prep
4. Whitney Young Magnet
5. Lane Technical
6. Gwendolyn Brooks (Southside) College Prep
7. Lindblom College Prep
8. Dr. Martin Luther King Jr. College Prep

SCHOOL DISTRICTS & SCHOOL SYSTEMS—ENROLLMENT

Source: Rossi, Rosalind, "City's Toughest Prep Schools," *Chicago Sun-Times*, April 2, 2001, pp. 1-2.

★4006★
Illinois elementary schools chosen to be "demonstration sites" for struggling schools

Ranking basis/background: Percentage of low income students enrolled and percentage of students reading at or above national norms on the Iowa Tests of Basic Skills. **Remarks:** Original source: Chicago Board of Education. **Number listed:** 26.

- Budlong Elementary School, with 90% low income students; 48% reading at or above national Iowa norms
- Oriole Park Elementary School, 44%; 89%
- Stockton Elementary School, 93%; 47%
- Norwood Park Elementary School, 25%; 73%
- Hayt Elementary School, 89%; 45%
- Burley Elementary School, 84%; 53%
- Chase Elementary School, 96%; 32%
- Lincoln Elementary School, 23%; 84%
- H.C. Andersen Elementary School, 94%; 42%
- Kellman Elementary School, 85%; 58%
- Orozco Elementary School, 98%; 44%
- Walsh Elementary School, 94%; 41%
- Haines Elementary School, 97%; 55%
- Saucedo Elementary School, 95%; 47%
- Beethoven Elementary School, 98%; 46%
- Healy Elementary School, 82%; 63%
- Seward Elementary School, 96%; 37%
- Carson Elementary School, 97%; 42%
- Carnegie Elementary School, 99%; 44%
- Ray Elementary School, 31%; 71%
- Dixon Elementary School, 71%; 57%
- Ninos Heros Elementary School, 94%; 41%
- Marsh Elementary School, 90%; 57%
- Pirie Elementary School, 87%; 60%
- Sutherland Elementary School, 12%; 76%
- Cullen Elementary School, 92%; 41%

Source: Rossi, Rosalind, "Schools to Teach Each Other," *Chicago Sun-Times*, April 17, 2001, p. 6.

SCHOOL DISTRICTS & SCHOOL SYSTEMS–ENROLLMENT
See: **School Enrollment**

SCHOOL DISTRICTS & SCHOOL SYSTEMS–ILLINOIS

★4007★
Illinois school districts spending the least for elementary school education 1997-98

Ranking basis/background: Operating expenditures per pupil in the six-county region. **Remarks:** Original source: Illinois Board of Higher Education. **Number listed:** 5.

1. Channahon School, District 17, with $4,043.95
2. Elwood Community Consolidated School, District 203, $4,038.92
3. New Lenox School, District 122, $3,918.04
4. Lockport Township School, District 91, $3,827.98
5. Will County School, District 92, $3,774.51

Source: "Education Market Facts," *Crain's Chicago Business*, 23: F28, F30, (July 3, 2000).

★4008★
Illinois school districts spending the least for high school education 1997-98

Ranking basis/background: Operating expenditures per pupil in the six-county region. **Remarks:** Original source: Illinois Board of Higher Education. **Number listed:** 5.

1. Grayslake High School, District 127, with $7,790.84
2. Lockport Township High School, District 205, $7,761.95
3. Lincoln-Way Community High School, District 210, $6,970.46
4. McHenry Community High School, District 156, $6,261.06
5. Marengo Community High School, District 154, $5,699.37

Source: "Education Market Facts," *Crain's Chicago Business*, 23: F28, F30, (July 3, 2000).

★4009★
Illinois school districts spending the most for elementary school education 1997-98

Ranking basis/background: Operating expenditures per pupil in the six-county region. **Remarks:** Original source: Illinois Board of Higher Education. **Number listed:** 5.

1. Rondout Elementary School, District 72, with $14,718.36
2. Butler Elementary School, District 53, $12,069.82
3. Bannockburn School, District 106, $11,158.37
4. Northbrook School, District 27, $10,826.72
5. Avoca Public School, District 37, $10,743.28

Source: "Education Market Facts," *Crain's Chicago Business*, 23: F28, F30, (July 3, 2000).

★4010★
Illinois school districts spending the most for high school education 1997-98

Ranking basis/background: Operating expenditures per pupil in the six-county region. **Remarks:** Original source: Illinois Board of Higher Education. **Number listed:** 5.

1. Township High School, District 113, with $15,482.92
2. Lake Forest Community High School, District 115, $15,199.60
3. Evanston Township High School, District 202, $14,366.51
4. New Trier High School, District 203, $13,527.65
5. Oak Park and River Forest District 200, $13,024.60

Source: "Education Market Facts," *Crain's Chicago Business*, 23: F28, F30, (July 3, 2000).

★4011★
Illinois school districts spending the most per pupil for instruction

Ranking basis/background: Spending per pupil for school districts in the six-county area. **Remarks:** Original source: Sun-Times research. **Number listed:** 10.

1. Rondout School, District 72, with $9,023
2. Butler Elementary School, District 53, $7,340
3. Kenilworth School, District 38, $6,900
4. Northbrook School, District 28, $6,846
5. Bannockburn School, District 106, 6,775
6. Salt Creek School, District 48, $6,588
7. Lincolnwood School, District 74, $6,465
8. Niles Elementary School, District 71, $6,333
9. Rhodes School, District 84-5, $6,241
10. La Grange School, District 105 (South), $6,130

Source: "School Report Card 2000," *Chicago Sun-Times*, November 1, 2000, pp. 1R-22R.

★4012★
Illinois school districts with the most average years of teacher experience

Ranking basis/background: Average years of teacher experience for school districts in the six-county area. **Remarks:** Original source: Sun-Times research. **Number listed:** 11.

1. Oak Lawn High School, District 218, with 22.70 years
2. Ford Heights, District 169, 19.60
3. Rich Township, District 227, 19.40
4. Valley View, District 365, 19.20
5. Thornton Township High School, District 205, 18.90
6. Lyons Township High School, District 204, 18.50
6. Union Ridge School District 86, 18.50
8. Atwood Heights, District 125, 18.40
9. Palatine High School, District 211, 18.40
10. Homewood-Flossmoor High School, District 233, 18.30
10. Arlington Heights High School, District 214, 18.30

Source: "School Report Card 2000," *Chicago Sun-Times*, November 1, 2000, pp. 1R-22R.

Related Information

★4013★
"School Report Card 2000," *Chicago Sun-Times*, November 1, 2000, pp. 1R-22R.

Remarks: Lists Chicago area schools statistics including percentage of students from low income families, 1997 tax rate on residential property per $100 of assessed valuation contributed to district, percentage of 10th graders who meet/exceed state standards on reading, math and science ISAT and IGAP test, percentage of students graduating, average ACT scores and percentage of students testing.

SCHOOL ENROLLMENT
See also: **Disabilities–Enrollment of Students**

★4014★
Elementary and secondary school enrollment projections for the years 2002-2008, by control of institution

Ranking basis/background: Number, in thousands, of projected enrollment for the years 2002-2008. **Remarks:** Original source: U.S. Department of Education, National Center for Education Statistics. Reports from various common core of Data surveys of Public and Private Elementary and Secondary Schools from 1983 through 1993. **Number listed:** 12.

2002, with 53,987 (K-12); 38,795 (K-8); 15,192 (9-12)
2003, 54,153; 38,795; 15,358
2004, 54,308; 38,606; 15,702
2005, 54,426; 38,376; 16,050
2006, 54,457; 38,181; 16,276
2007, 54,425; 38,073; 16,352
2008, 54,268; 38,034; 16,234

Source: *Projections of Education Statistics to 2008,* NCES 98-016, U.S. Department of Education, National Center for Education Statistics (June 1998).

★4015★
Elementary and secondary school enrollment projections for the years 2002-2008, by organizational level

Ranking basis/background: Number, in thousands, of projected enrollment for the years 2002-2008. **Remarks:** Original source: U.S. Department of Education, National Center for Education Statistics. Reports from various common core of Data surveys of Public and Private Elementary and Secondary Schools from 1983 through 1993. **Number listed:** 12.
2002, with 53,987 (K-12); 35,495 (Elementary); 18,492 (Secondary)
2003, 54,153; 35,408; 18,745
2004, 54,308; 35,215; 19,094
2005, 54,426; 35,025; 19,401
2006, 54,457; 34,877; 19,579
2007, 54,425; 34,797; 19,628
2008, 54,268; 34,775; 19,492

Source: *Projections of Education Statistics to 2008,* NCES 98-016, U.S. Department of Education, National Center for Education Statistics (June 1998).

★4016★
Largest public school districts in the U.S.

Ranking basis/background: Enrollment in public school districts. **Number listed:** 10.
1. New York City, with 1,093,071
2. Los Angeles, 722,727
3. Chicago, 431,750
4. Dade County, FL, 360,202
5. Broward County, FL, 249,923
6. Clark County, NV, 231,125
7. Houston, 210,000
8. Philadelphia, 208,170
9. Hawaii, 182,328
10. Detroit, 166,300

Source: "The Top Ten," *American School & University,* 73: 38-41, (January 2001).

★4017★
Midwest region enrollment projections for grades 9-12 in public elementary and secondary schools for the years 2002-2008

Ranking basis/background: Number, in thousands, of projected enrollment for grades 9-12 in public elementary and secondary schools for the Midwestern region of the U.S., which includes Illinois, Indiana, Iowa, Kansas, Michigan, Minnesota, Missouri, Nebraska, North Dakota, Ohio, South Dakota, and Wisconsin. **Remarks:** Original source: U.S. Department of Education, National Center for Education Statistics, Common Core of Data surveys. **Number listed:** 9.
2002, with 3,187
2003, 3,180
2004, 3,204
2005, 3,221
2006, 3,234
2007, 3,220
2008, 3,176

Source: *Projections of Education Statistics to 2008,* NCES 98-016, U.S. Department of Education, National Center for Education Statistics (June 1998).

★4018★
Midwest region enrollment projections for grades K-8 in public elementary and secondary schools for the years 2002-2008

Ranking basis/background: Number, in thousands, of projected enrollment for grades K-8 in public elementary and secondary schools for the Midwest region of the U.S., which includes Illinois, Indiana, Iowa, Kansas, Michigan, Minnesota, Missouri, Nebraska, North Dakota, Ohio, South Dakota, and Wisconsin. **Remarks:** Original source: U.S. Department of Education, National Center for Education Statistics, Common Core of Data surveys. **Number listed:** 9.
2002, with 7,429
2003, 7,392
2004, 7,328
2005, 7,271
2006, 7,224
2007, 7,191
2008, 7,168

Source: *Projections of Education Statistics to 2008,* NCES 98-016, U.S. Department of Education, National Center for Education Statistics (June 1998).

★4019★
Midwest region enrollment projections for grades K-12 in public elementary and secondary schools for the years 2002-2008

Ranking basis/background: Number, in thousands, of projected enrollment for grades K-12 in public elementary and secondary schools for the Midwest region of the U.S., which includes Illinois, Indiana, Iowa, Kansas, Michigan, Minnesota, Missouri, Nebraska, North Dakota, Ohio, South Dakota, and Wisconsin. **Remarks:** Original source: U.S. Department of Education, National Center for Education Statistics, Common Core of Data surveys. **Number listed:** 9.
2002, with 10,617
2003, 10,572
2004, 10,532
2005, 10,492
2006, 10,457
2007, 10,411
2008, 10,344

Source: *Projections of Education Statistics to 2008,* NCES 98-016, U.S. Department of Education, National Center for Education Statistics (June 1998).

★4020★
Northeast region enrollment projections for grades 9-12 in public elementary and secondary schools for the years 2002-2008

Ranking basis/background: Number, in thousands, of projected enrollment for grades 9-12 in public elementary and secondary schools for the northeast region of the U.S., which includes Connecticut, Maine, Massachusetts, New Hampshire, New Jersey, New York, Pennsylvania, Rhode Island, and Vermont. **Remarks:** Original source: U.S. Department of Education, National Center for Education Statistics, Common Core of Data surveys. **Number listed:** 9.
2002, with 2,486
2003, 2,515
2004, 2,562
2005, 2,597
2006, 2,616
2007, 2,605
2008, 2,565

Source: *Projections of Education Statistics to 2008,* NCES 98-016, U.S. Department of Education, National Center for Education Statistics (June 1998).

★4021★
Northeast region enrollment projections for grades K-8 in public elementary and secondary schools for the years 2002-2008

Ranking basis/background: Number, in thousands, of projected enrollment for grades K-8 in public elementary and secondary schools for the northeast region of the U.S., which includes Connecticut, Maine, Massachusetts, New Hampshire, New Jersey, New York, Pennsylvania, Rhode Island, Vermont. **Remarks:** Original source: U.S. Department of Education, National Center for Education Statistics, Common Core of Data surveys. **Number listed:** 9.
2002, with 5,819
2003, 5,781
2004, 5,717
2005, 5,655
2006, 5,600
2007, 5,562
2008, 5,535

Source: *Projections of Education Statistics to 2008,* NCES 98-016, U.S. Department of Education, National Center for Education Statistics (June 1998).

★4022★
Northeast region enrollment projections for grades K-12 in public elementary and secondary schools for the years 2002-2008

Ranking basis/background: Number, in thousands, of projected enrollment for grades K-12 in public elementary and secondary schools for the northeast region of the U.S., which includes Connecticut, Maine, Massachusetts, New Hampshire, New Jersey, New York, Pennsylvania, Rhode Island, and Vermont. **Remarks:** Original source: U.S. Department of Education, National Center for Education Statistics, Common Core of Data surveys. **Number listed:** 9.
2002, with 8,305
2003, 8,296
2004, 8,279
2005, 8,252
2006, 8,216

SCHOOL ENROLLMENT

2007, 8,168
2008, 8,100
Source: *Projections of Education Statistics to 2008,* NCES 98-016, U.S. Department of Education, National Center for Education Statistics (June 1998).

★4023★
Private elementary and secondary school enrollment projections for the years 2002-2008, by control of institution

Ranking basis/background: Number, in thousands, of projected enrollment for the years 2002-2008. **Remarks:** Original source: U.S. Department of Education, National Center for Education Statistics. Reports from various common core of Data surveys of Public and Private Elementary and Secondary Schools from 1983 through 1993. **Number listed:** 12.
    2002, with 6,063 (K-12); 4,671 (K-8); 1,392 (9-12)
    2003, 6,078; 4,671; 1,407
    2004, 6,087; 4,648; 1,439
    2005, 6,091; 4,620; 1,471
    2006, 6,088; 4,597; 1,491
    2007, 6,082; 4,584; 1,498
    2008, 6,067; 4,579; 1,488
Source: *Projections of Education Statistics to 2008,* NCES 98-016, U.S. Department of Education, National Center for Education Statistics (June 1998).

★4024★
Private elementary and secondary school enrollment projections for the years 2002-2008, by organizational level

Ranking basis/background: Number, in thousands, of projected enrollment for the years 2002-2008. **Remarks:** Original source: U.S. Department of Education, National Center for Education Statistics. Reports from various common core of Data surveys of Public and Private Elementary and Secondary Schools from 1983 through 1993. **Number listed:** 12.
    2002, with 6,063 (K-12); 4,671 (Elementary); 1,392 (Secondary)
    2003, 6,078; 4,671; 1,407
    2004, 6,087; 4,648; 1,439
    2005, 6,091; 4,620; 1,471
    2006, 6,088; 4,597; 1,491
    2007, 6,082; 4,584; 1,498
    2008, 6,067; 4,579; 1,488
Source: *Projections of Education Statistics to 2008,* NCES 98-016, U.S. Department of Education, National Center for Education Statistics (June 1998).

★4025★
Projected enrollment for U.S. public and private schools, 2009-10

Ranking basis/background: Projected enrollment figures, in thousands, for 2009-10. **Remarks:** Original source: National Center for Education Statistics, U.S. Department of Education. **Number listed:** 2.
    Public, with 47,109 thousand
    Private, 5,947
Source: *The World Almanac and Book of Facts 2001,* World Almanac Books, 2001.

★4026★
Public and private school enrollment in the U.S.

Ranking basis/background: Number, in millions, of students in kindergarten through 12th grade enrolled in public and private schools. **Remarks:** Original source: Department of Education. **Number listed:** 2.
1. Public, with 47.5 million
2. Private, 6 million

Source: Wasson, Hilary and Bob Laird, "1 in 9 Children are in Private Schools," *USA Today,* June 1, 2000, Section A, p. 1A.

★4027★
Public elementary and secondary school enrollment projections for the years 2002-2008, by control of institution

Ranking basis/background: Number, in thousands, of projected enrollment for the years 2002-2008. **Remarks:** Original source: U.S. Department of Education, National Center for Education Statistics. Reports from various common core of Data surveys of Public and Private Elementary and Secondary Schools from 1983 through 1993. **Number listed:** 12.
    2002, with 47,924 (K-12); 34,124 (K-8); 13,800 (9-12)
    2003, 48,075; 34,124; 13,951
    2004, 48,221; 33,958; 14,263
    2005, 48,335; 33,756; 14,579
    2006, 48,368; 33,584; 14785
    2007, 48,342; 33,489; 14,854
    2008, 48,201; 33,455; 14,746
Source: *Projections of Education Statistics to 2008,* NCES 98-016, U.S. Department of Education, National Center for Education Statistics (June 1998).

★4028★
Public elementary and secondary school enrollment projections for the years 2002-2008, by organizational level

Ranking basis/background: Number, in thousands, of projected enrollment for the years 2002-2008. **Remarks:** Original source: U.S. Department of Education, National Center for Education Statistics. Reports from various common core of Data surveys of Public and Private Elementary and Secondary Schools from 1983 through 1993. **Number listed:** 12.
    2002, with 47,924 (K-12); 30,824 (Elementary); 17,100 (Secondary)
    2003, 48,075; 30,737; 17,338
    2004, 48,221; 30,566; 17,655
    2005, 48,335; 30,405; 17,930
    2006, 48,368; 30,281; 18,088
    2007, 48,342; 30,213; 18,130
    2008, 48,201; 30,196; 18,005
Source: *Projections of Education Statistics to 2008,* NCES 98-016, U.S. Department of Education, National Center for Education Statistics (June 1998).

★4029★
Southern region enrollment projections for grades 9-12 in public elementary and secondary schools for the years 2002-2008

Ranking basis/background: Number, in thousands, of projected enrollment for grades 9-12 in public elementary and secondary schools for the southern region of the U.S., which includes Alabama, Arkansas, Delaware, District of Columbia, Florida, Georgia, Kentucky, Louisiana, Maryland, Mississippi, North Carolina, Oklahoma, South Carolina, Tennessee, Texas, Virginia, and West Virginia. **Remarks:** Original source: U.S. Department of Education, National Center for Education Statistics, Common Core of Data surveys. **Number listed:** 9.
    2002, with 4,812
    2003, 4,875
    2004, 4,993
    2005, 5,110
    2006, 5,188
    2007, 5,223
    2008, 5,199
Source: *Projections of Education Statistics to 2008,* NCES 98-016, U.S. Department of Education, National Center for Education Statistics (June 1998).

★4030★
Southern region enrollment projections for grades K-8 in public elementary and secondary schools for the years 2002-2008

Ranking basis/background: Number, in thousands, of projected enrollment for grades K-8 in public elementary and secondary schools for the southern region of the U.S., which includes Alabama, Arkansas, Delaware, District of Columbia, Florida, Georgia, Kentucky, Louisiana, Maryland, Mississippi, North Carolina, Oklahoma, South Carolina, Tennessee, Texas, Virginia, and West Virginia. **Remarks:** Original source: U.S. Department of Education, National Center for Education Statistics, Common Core of Data surveys. **Number listed:** 9.
    2002, with 12,582
    2003, 12,594
    2004, 12,541
    2005, 12,468
    2006, 12,396
    2007, 12,340
    2008, 12,302
Source: *Projections of Education Statistics to 2008,* NCES 98-016, U.S. Department of Education, National Center for Education Statistics (June 1998).

★4031★
Southern region enrollment projections for grades K-12 in public elementary and secondary schools for the years 2002-2008

Ranking basis/background: Number, in thousands, of projected enrollment for grades K-12 in public elementary and secondary schools for the southern region of the U.S., which includes Alabama, Arkansas, Delaware, District of Columbia, Florida, Georgia, Kentucky, Louisiana, Maryland, Mississippi, North Carolina, Oklahoma, South Carolina, Tennessee, Texas, Virginia, and West Virginia. **Remarks:** Original source: U.S. Department of Education, National Center for Education Statistics, Common Core of Data surveys. **Number listed:** 9.

2002, with 17,394
2003, 17,468
2004, 17,534
2005, 17,578
2006, 17,583
2007, 17,563
2008, 17,501

Source: *Projections of Education Statistics to 2008,* NCES 98-016, U.S. Department of Education, National Center for Education Statistics (June 1998).

★4032★
States with the highest average enrollment in public elementary schools

Ranking basis/background: Average public elementary school enrollment. **Remarks:** Original source: Digest of Education Statistics, 1999. **Number listed:** 10.

1. Florida, with 797
2. Georgia, 664
3. California, 631
4. Hawaii, 627
5. Nevada, 620
6. New York, 616
7. Delaware, 596
8. Maryland, 566
9. Arizona, 553
10. Texas, 552

Source: "The Top Ten," *American School & University,* 73: 38-41, (January 2001).

★4033★
States with the highest average enrollment in public secondary schools

Ranking basis/background: Average public secondary school enrollment. **Remarks:** Original source: Digest of Education Statistics, 1999. **Number listed:** 10.

1. Florida, with 1,662
2. Hawaii, 1,389
3. California, 1,387
4. Maryland, 1,220
5. Georgia, 1,196
6. Virginia, 1,082
7. Nevada, 1,052
8. Utah, 1,048
9. Delaware, 1,002
10. New York, 986

Source: "The Top Ten," *American School & University,* 73: 38-41, (January 2001).

★4034★
States with the highest K-12 public school enrollment

Ranking basis/background: Total state enrollment for K-12 public schools. **Remarks:** Original source: U.S. Department of Education. **Number listed:** 10.

1. California, with 5,924,964
2. Texas, 3,945,367
3. New York, 2,877,143
4. Florida, 2,337,633
5. Illinois, 2,011,530
6. Ohio, 1,842,559
7. Pennsylvania, 1,816,414
8. Michigan, 1,720,266
9. Georgia, 1,401,291
10. New Jersey, 1,268,996

Source: "The Top Ten," *American School & University,* 73: 38-41, (January 2001).

★4035★
States with the highest projected K-12 public school enrollment for 2010

Ranking basis/background: Projected enrollment figures for 2010. **Remarks:** Original source: "Projection of Education Statistics to 2010," National Center for Education Statistics. **Number listed:** 10.

1. California, with 6,305,000
2. Texas, 4,243,000
3. New York, 2,742,000
4. Florida, 2,348,000
5. Illinois, 2,050,000
6. Ohio, 1,731,000
7. Pennsylvania, 1,718,000
8. Michigan, 1,604,000
9. Georgia, 1,518,000
10. North Carolina, 1,275,000

Source: "The Top Ten," *American School & University,* 73: 38-41, (January 2001).

★4036★
Western region enrollment projections for grades 9-12 in public elementary and secondary schools for the years 2002-2008

Ranking basis/background: Number, in thousands, of projected enrollment for grades 9-12 in public elementary and secondary schools for the western region of the U.S., which includes Alaska, Arizona, California, Colorado, Hawaii, Idaho, Montana, Nevada, New Mexico, Oregon, Utah, Washington, and Wyoming. **Remarks:** Original source: U.S. Department of Education, National Center for Education Statistics, Common Core of Data surveys. **Number listed:** 9.

2002, with 3,314
2003, 3,381
2004, 3,504
2005, 3,650
2006, 3,748
2007, 3,805
2008, 3,807

Source: *Projections of Education Statistics to 2008,* NCES 98-016, U.S. Department of Education, National Center for Education Statistics (June 1998).

★4037★
Western region enrollment projections for grades K-8 in public elementary and secondary schools for the years 2002-2008

Ranking basis/background: Number, in thousands, of projected enrollment for grades K-8 in public elementary and secondary schools for the western region of the U.S., which includes Alaska, Arizona, California, Colorado, Hawaii, Idaho, Montana, Nevada, New Mexico, Oregon, Utah, Washington, and Wyoming. **Remarks:** Original source: U.S. Department of Education, National Center for Education Statistics, Common Core of Data surveys. **Number listed:** 9.

2002, with 8,294
2003, 8,357
2004, 8,372
2005, 8,362
2006, 8,364
2007, 8,395
2008, 8,450

Source: *Projections of Education Statistics to 2008,* NCES 98-016, U.S. Department of Education, National Center for Education Statistics (June 1998).

★4038★
Western region enrollment projections for grades K-12 in public elementary and secondary schools for the years 2002-2008

Ranking basis/background: Number, in thousands, of projected enrollment for grades K-12 in public elementary and secondary schools for the western region of the U.S., which includes Alaska, Arizona, California, Colorado, Hawaii, Idaho, Montana, Nevada, New Mexico, Oregon, Utah, Washington, and Wyoming. **Remarks:** Original source: U.S. Department of Education, National Center for Education Statistics, Common Core of Data surveys. **Number listed:** 9.

2002, with 11,608
2003, 11,739
2004, 11,876
2005, 12,012
2006, 12,112
2007, 12,201
2008, 12,257

Source: *Projections of Education Statistics to 2008,* NCES 98-016, U.S. Department of Education, National Center for Education Statistics (June 1998).

SCHOOL FACILITIES

★4039★
Elementary and secondary school facility design and planning solutions

Ranking basis/background: Better ways to build schools in an effort to help the way students learn. **Number listed:** 10.

1. Alternative school sites
2. Ecologically friendly
3. Flexible spaces
4. Outdoor spaces
5. Schools as communities
6. Smaller schools
7. Security
8. Technology
9. Welcoming the greater community
10. Universal design

Source: Kennedy, Mike, "The Top Ten Facility Design and Planning Solutions," *American School & University,* 73: 30-38, (January 2001).

★4040★
States with the highest funding needs for school-building modernization

Ranking basis/background: Figures, in billions, needed for school-building modernization. **Remarks:** Original source: National Education Association, "Modernizing Our Schools: What Will It Cost?" **Number listed:** 10.

1. New York, with $47.6 billion
2. Ohio, $23.0
3. California, $22.0
4. New Jersey, $20.7
5. Texas, $9.5
6. Illinois, $9.2
7. Massachusetts, $8.9
8. Pennsylvania, $8.5
9. Utah, $8.5
10. Michigan, $8.0

Source: "The Top Ten," *American School & University,* 73: 38-41, (January 2001).

SCHOOL SYSTEMS

★4041★
States with the highest funding needs for school-technology modernization

Ranking basis/background: Figures, in billions, needed for school-technology modernization. **Remarks:** Original source: National Education Association, "Modernizing Our Schools: What Will It Cost?" **Number listed:** 10.
1. California, with $10.9 billion
2. Texas, $4.2
3. New York, $3.0
4. Florida, $2.2
5. Illinois, $2.1
6. Ohio, $2.0
7. Michigan, $1.9
8. Pennsylvania, $1.9
9. Georgia, $1.5
10. New Jersey, $1.3

Source: "The Top Ten," *American School & University*, 73: 38-41, (January 2001).

SCHOOL SYSTEMS
See: **School Districts & School Systems**

SCHOOLS, ELEMENTARY & SECONDARY
See also: **Schools, Secondary**

★4042★
Ideas for improving U.S. schools

Ranking basis/background: Education reform theories. **Number listed:** 7.
1. Pay teachers for performance
2. Make schools smaller
3. Hold educators accountable
4. Offer more variety
5. Provide adequate funding
6. Increase time in school
7. Use technology effectively

Source: Symonds, William C., "How to Fix America's Schools," *Business Week*, 3724: 66-72, (March 19, 2001).

★4043★
Low alternative projections for average daily attendance at public elementary and secondary schools for the years 2002-2008

Ranking basis/background: Number, in thousands, for average daily attendance at public elementary and secondary schools for the years 2002-2008. **Remarks:** Original source: U.S. Department of Education, National Center for Education Statistics, *Statistics of State School Systems*; Common core of Data survey; Early Estimates survey; and National Education Association, annual *Estimates of School Statistics*. **Number listed:** 12.
  2002, with 44,213 in attendance
  2003, 44,422
  2004, 44,562
  2005, 44,697
  2006, 44,803
  2007, 44,834
  2008, 44,810

Source: *Projections of Education Statistics to 2008*, NCES 98-016, U.S. Department of Education, National Center for Education Statistics (June 1998).

★4044★
Middle alternative projections for average daily attendance at public elementary and secondary schools for the years 2002-2008

Ranking basis/background: Number, in thousands, for average daily attendance at public elementary and secondary schools for the years 2002-2008. **Remarks:** Original source: U.S. Department of Education, National Center for Education Statistics, *Statistics of State School Systems*; Common core of Data survey; Early Estimates survey; and National Education Association, annual *Estimates of School Statistics*. **Number listed:** 12.
  2002, with 44,213 in attendance
  2003, 44,422
  2004, 44,562
  2005, 44,697
  2006, 44,803
  2007, 44,834
  2008, 44,810

Source: *Projections of Education Statistics to 2008*, NCES 98-016, U.S. Department of Education, National Center for Education Statistics (June 1998).

★4045★
Opinion poll on prayer in school

Ranking basis/background: Percentage of pollees stating each view, from an Alloy Poll survey of 1,440 adults. **Number listed:** 3.
1. Say it should be voluntary, with 62%
2. Say it should be mandatory, 22%
3. Say it should be banned, 16%

Source: Joseph, Lori and Suzy Parker, "Views Vary on Prayer in School," *USA Today*, February 27, 2001, Section A, p. 1A.

★4046★
Projected public school retention rates for 2003 and 2008, by grade

Ranking basis/background: Projected retention rates. **Remarks:** Original source: U.S. Department of Education, National Center for Education Statistics, Common Core of Data surveys. **Number listed:** 11.
  Grade 1 to 2, with 97.1 (2003); 97.1 (2008)
  2 to 3, 100.2; 100.2
  3 to 4, 99.9; 99.9
  4 to 5, 100.3; 100.3
  5 to 6, 100.9; 100.9
  6 to 7, 101.6; 101.6
  7 to 8, 98.5; 98.5
  8 to 9, 111.5; 111.5
  9 to 10, 90.4; 90.4
  10 to 11, 90.5; 90.5
  11 to 12, 90.8; 90.8

Source: *Projections of Education Statistics to 2008*, NCES 98-016, U.S. Department of Education, National Center for Education Statistics (June 1998).

★4047★
Sex education topics taught in public secondary schools

Ranking basis/background: Percentage of parents wanting topic to be taught; and percentage of students claiming topic is taught. From a survey of 1,501 public school secondary students and their parents. **Remarks:** Original source: Kaiser Family Foundation "Sex Education in America: A View from Inside the Nation's Classrooms." **Number listed:** 6.
  What to do if raped, with 97% of parents wanting topic taught; 59% of students saying it's taught
  How to talk with parents, 97%; 62%
  How to get tested for disease, 92%; 69%
  How to use condoms, 85%; 68%
  Abortion, 79%; 61%
  Sexual orientation, 76%; 41%

Source: "Birds Do It. Do Teachers Teach It?," *U.S. News & World Report*, 129: 12, (October 9, 2000).

★4048★
States with the most charter schools

Ranking basis/background: Total charter schools in each state. **Remarks:** Original source: The Center for Education Reform. **Number listed:** 10.
1. Arizona, with 408
2. California, 261
3. Michigan, 181
4. Texas, 178
5. Florida, 151
6. North Carolina, 95
6. Wisconsin, 95
8. Ohio, 85
9. Colorado, 76
10. Minnesota, 75

Source: "The Top Ten," *American School & University*, 73: 38-41, (January 2001).

★4049★
States with the most K-12 public schools

Ranking basis/background: Total K-12 public schools. **Remarks:** Original source: U.S. Department of Education. **Number listed:** 10.
1. California, with 8,334
2. Texas, 7,228
3. Illinois, 4,251
4. New York, 4,224
5. Ohio, 3,732
6. Michigan, 3,656
7. Pennsylvania, 3,139
8. Florida, 3,044
9. New Jersey, 2,317
10. Missouri, 2,221

Source: "The Top Ten," *American School & University*, 73: 38-41, (January 2001).

★4050★
Students participating in gifted and talented programs, by race ethnicity, 1997

Ranking basis/background: Percentage of total K-12 population and percentage of gifted and talented program population for each ethnic group. **Remarks:** Original source: U.S. Department of Education. **Number listed:** 5.
  White, with 64% of total K-12 population; 77% of GATE program population
  African American, 17%; 7%
  Hispanic American, 14%; 9%
  Asian American, 3%; 7%

Native American, 1%; 1%
Source: "Education Vital Signs 2000," *American School Board Journal*, 187: 31-47, (December 2000).

★4051★
Subjects students most want to see on classroom TV

Ranking basis/background: Percentage of students, ages 6-11, wanting to see each subject on classroom TV. **Remarks:** Original source: Opinion Research Corporation for DirecTV. **Number listed:** 4.
1. Science/nature, with 42%
2. Math, 31%
3. History, 16%
4. Social studies, 11%

Source: Hall, Cindy and Frank Pompa, "TV Goes to School," *USA Today*, March 27, 2001, Section D, p. 5D.

★4052★
Tough issues students face at school

Ranking basis/background: From a survey of 823 adolescents conducted in December and January asking kids 12 to 15 what are the biggest problems they face at school. **Remarks:** Original source: Nickelodeon/Kaiser Family Foundation/Children Now. **Number listed:** 7.
1. Teasing and bullying, with 68%
2. Discrimination, 63%
3. Violence, 62%
4. Alcohol or drugs, 58%
5. Pressure to have sex, 49%
6. HIV/AIDS, 36%
7. Racism, 35%

Source: "Bully-Whipped," *U.S. News & World Report*, 130: 12, (March 19, 2000).

★4053★
U.S. students being bullied

Ranking basis/background: From a survey of 15,686 students grades 6 to 10 enrolled in U.S. schools. **Remarks:** Original source: National Institute of Child Health and Human Development. **Number listed:** 8.
- Students bullied during the current school term, with 16%
- Sixth graders who have been bullied weekly, 13.3%
- Tenth graders who have been bullied weekly, 4.8%
- Of students bullied, those picked on because of their looks or speech, 61.6%
- Of students bullied, those picked on because of religion or race, 25.8%
- Of students bullied, those who were the subject of rumors, 59.5%
- Of students bullied, those who were hit, slapped, or pushed, 55.6%
- Of students bullied, those who were the subject of sexual comments or gestures, 52%

Source: "Raging Bullies," *U.S. News & World Report*, 130: 12, (May 7, 2001).

Related Information

★4054★
QED's School Guides, Quality Education Data, annual.
Remarks: Gives detailed information state by state on U.S. schools, both public and private. The *Summary of School Market Management Statistics*, arranged in seven regional volumes, provides a statistical overview of the individual volumes of *QED's School Guide,*.

★4055★
Sargent, Porter, *The Handbook of Private Schools: An Annual Descriptive Survey of Independent Education*, annual.
Remarks: Contains descriptive information to aid the user in identifying private schools by types of curriculum.

★4056★
Nathan, Joe, *Charter Schools: Creating Hope and Opportunity for American Education*, Jossey-Bass Publishers, 1996.
Remarks: Provides a history of the charter school movement. Includes examples of existing charter schools, including City Academy (St. Paul, MN), O'Farrell Community School (San Diego, CA), Minnesota New Country School (LeSueur, MN), Academy Charter School (Castle Rock, CO), Hickman Charter School (San Joaquin, CA), New Visions School (Minneapolis, MN), and PS1 (Denver, CO).

★4057★
Gender Gaps: Where Schools Fail Our Children, American Association of University Women Educational Foundation, 1998.
Remarks: Examines the progress and identifies new issues in gender equity in the schools.

SCHOOLS, ELEMENTARY & SECONDARY–ENROLLMENT
See: **School Enrollment**

SCHOOLS, ELEMENTARY & SECONDARY–FINANCIAL SUPPORT
See: **Schools, Elementary & Secondary–Revenue**

SCHOOLS, ELEMENTARY & SECONDARY–INTERNATIONAL

★4058★
Canadian provinces by teaching days per year

Ranking basis/background: Annual number of teaching days. The average for Canada is 195. **Number listed:** 10.
1. Alberta, with 200 days
1. Manitoba, 200
1. Quebec, 200
4. Saskatchewan, 197
5. Prince Edward Island, 196
6. New Brunswick, 195
6. Nova Scotia, 195
8. British Columbia, 194
9. Ontario, 188
10. Newfoundland, 185

Source: Jenish, D'arcy, "Going to the Wall," *Maclean's*, November 10, 1997, pp. 18-20.

Related Information

★4059★
Haynes, Richard M. and Donald M. Chalker, "World Class Schools," *The American School Board Journal*, May 1997, pp. 20-26.
Remarks: Reviews the findings of a 35-variable study on the educational systems of Canada, France, Germany, Great Britain, Israel, Japan, New Zealand, South Korea, Taiwan, and the United States.

SCHOOLS, ELEMENTARY & SECONDARY–REVENUE
See also: **Expenditures per Pupil**

★4060★
Countries spending the highest percentage of gross domestic product on education

Ranking basis/background: Percentage of gross domestic product spent on education. **Remarks:** Original source: U.S. Department of Education. **Number listed:** 10.
1. Sweden, with 6.8%
2. Norway, 6.6%
3. New Zealand, 6.1%
4. France, 5.8%
4. Portugal, 5.8%
6. Canada, 5.4%
6. Switzerland, 5.4%
8. United States, 5.2%
9. Belgium, 4.8%
10. Spain, 4.7%

Source: "School Yardsticks," *U.S. News & World Report*, 130: 14, (February 12, 2001).

SCHOOLS, ELEMENTARY & SECONDARY–STUDENTS

Related Information

★4061★
Halstead, Kent, *Three R's: Race Retention Rates by States,* Research Associates of Washington, biennial.
Remarks: Surveys public education systems by high school graduation rates, college admissions, and college graduates, by ethnicity and race.

SCHOOLS, ELEMENTARY & SECONDARY–TEACHER-STUDENT RATIO

★4062★
High alternative projections for student-teacher ratios at elementary and secondary schools for the years 2002-2008

Ranking basis/background: Student-teacher ratios at elementary and secondary schools for the years 2002-2008. **Remarks:** Original source: U.S. Department of Education, National Center for Education Statistics. Reports from various common core of Data surveys of Public and Private Elementary and Secondary Schools from 1983 through 1993. **Number listed:** 12.

    2002, with 18.2 (Elementary); 14.2 (Secondary)
    2003, 18.1; 14.2
    2004, 17.9; 14.3
    2005, 17.8; 14.3
    2006, 17.7; 14.3
    2007, 17.6; 14.3
    2008, 17.5; 14.1

Source: *Projections of Education Statistics to 2008*, NCES 98-016, U.S. Department of Education, National Center for Education Statistics (June 1998).

★4063★
High alternative projections for student-teacher ratios at private elementary and secondary schools for the years 2002-2008

Ranking basis/background: Student-teacher ratios at private elementary and secondary schools for the years 2002-2008. **Remarks:** Original source: U.S. Department of Education, National Center for Education Statistics. Reports from various common core of Data surveys of Public and Private Elementary and Secondary Schools from 1983 through 1993. **Number listed:** 12.

    2002, with 16.2 (Elementary); 11.3 (Secondary)
    2003, 16.1; 11.2
    2004, 15.9; 11.3
    2005, 15.8; 11.4
    2006, 15.7; 11.5
    2007, 15.6; 11.4
    2008, 15.5; 11.3

Source: *Projections of Education Statistics to 2008*, NCES 98-016, U.S. Department of Education, National Center for Education Statistics (June 1998).

★4064★
High alternative projections for student-teacher ratios at public elementary and secondary schools for the years 2002-2008

Ranking basis/background: Student-teacher ratios at public elementary and secondary schools for the years 2002-2008. **Remarks:** Original source: U.S. Department of Education, National Center for Education Statistics. Reports from various common core of Data surveys of Public and Private Elementary and Secondary Schools from 1983 through 1993. **Number listed:** 12.

    2002, with 18.6 (Elementary); 14.6 (Secondary)
    2003, 18.4; 14.5
    2004, 18.3; 14.6
    2005, 18.1; 14.6
    2006, 18.0; 14.6
    2007, 17.9; 14.6
    2008, 17.8; 14.4

Source: *Projections of Education Statistics to 2008*, NCES 98-016, U.S. Department of Education, National Center for Education Statistics (June 1998).

★4065★
Low alternative projections for student-teacher ratios at elementary and secondary schools for the years 2002-2008

Ranking basis/background: Student-teacher ratios at elementary and secondary schools for the years 2002-2008. **Remarks:** Original source: U.S. Department of Education, National Center for Education Statistics. Reports from various common core of Data surveys of Public and Private Elementary and Secondary Schools from 1983 through 1993. **Number listed:** 12.

    2002, with 17.8 (Elementary); 14.0 (Secondary)
    2003, 17.6; 13.9
    2004, 17.4; 13.9
    2005, 17.1; 13.9
    2006, 17.0; 13.8
    2007, 16.8; 13.7
    2008, 16.6; 13.6

Source: *Projections of Education Statistics to 2008*, NCES 98-016, U.S. Department of Education, National Center for Education Statistics (June 1998).

★4066★
Low alternative projections for student-teacher ratios at private elementary and secondary schools for the years 2002-2008

Ranking basis/background: Student-teacher ratios at private elementary and secondary schools for the years 2002-2008. **Remarks:** Original source: U.S. Department of Education, National Center for Education Statistics. Reports from various common core of Data surveys of Public and Private Elementary and Secondary Schools from 1983 through 1993. **Number listed:** 12.

    2002, with 15.8 (Elementary); 11.1 (Secondary)
    2003, 15.6; 11.0
    2004, 15.4; 11.0
    2005, 15.2; 11.1
    2006, 15.1; 11.1
    2007, 14.9; 11.0
    2008, 14.8; 10.9

Source: *Projections of Education Statistics to 2008*, NCES 98-016, U.S. Department of Education, National Center for Education Statistics (June 1998).

★4067★
Low alternative projections for student-teacher ratios at public elementary and secondary schools for the years 2002-2008

Ranking basis/background: Student-teacher ratios at public elementary and secondary schools for the years 2002-2008. **Remarks:** Original source: U.S. Department of Education, National Center for Education Statistics. Reports from various common core of Data surveys of Public and Private Elementary and Secondary Schools from 1983 through 1993. **Number listed:** 12.

    2002, with 18.2 (Elementary); 14.3 (Secondary)
    2003, 17.9; 14.2
    2004, 17.7; 14.2
    2005, 17.5; 14.2
    2006, 17.3; 14.1
    2007, 17.1; 14.0
    2008, 17.0; 13.8

Source: *Projections of Education Statistics to 2008*, NCES 98-016, U.S. Department of Education, National Center for Education Statistics (June 1998).

★4068★
Middle alternative projections for student-teacher ratios at elementary and secondary schools for the years 2002-2008

Ranking basis/background: Student-teacher ratios at elementary and secondary schools for the years 2002-2008. **Remarks:** Original source: U.S. Department of Education, National Center for Education Statistics. Reports from various common core of Data surveys of Public and Private Elementary and Secondary Schools from 1983 through 1993. **Number listed:** 12.

    2002, with 18.0 (Elementary); 14.1 (Secondary)
    2003, 17.8; 14.0
    2004, 17.6; 14.0
    2005, 17.4; 14.0
    2006, 17.3; 14.0
    2007, 17.1; 13.9
    2008, 17.0; 13.8

Source: *Projections of Education Statistics to 2008*, NCES 98-016, U.S. Department of Education, National Center for Education Statistics (June 1998).

★4069★
Middle alternative projections for student-teacher ratios at private elementary and secondary schools for the years 2002-2008

Ranking basis/background: Student-teacher ratios at private elementary and secondary schools for the years 2002-2008. **Remarks:** Original source: U.S. Department of Education, National Center for Education Statistics. Reports from various common core of Data surveys of Public and Private Elementary and Secondary Schools from 1983 through 1993. **Number listed:** 12.

    2002, with 15.9 (Elementary); 11.2 (Secondary)
    2003, 15.8; 11.1
    2004, 15.6; 11.1
    2005, 15.5; 11.2
    2006, 15.3; 11.2
    2007, 15.2; 11.2
    2008, 15.1; 11.1

Source: *Projections of Education Statistics to 2008*, NCES 98-016, U.S. Department of Education, National Center for Education Statistics (June 1998).

SCHOOLS, SECONDARY

★4070★
Middle alternative projections for student-teacher ratios at public elementary and secondary schools for the years 2002-2008

Ranking basis/background: Student-teacher ratios at public elementary and secondary schools for the years 2002-2008. **Remarks:** Original source: U.S. Department of Education, National Center for Education Statistics. Reports from various common core of Data surveys of Public and Private Elementary and Secondary Schools from 1983 through 1993. **Number listed:** 12.

  2002, with 18.4 (Elementary); 14.4 (Secondary)
  2003, 18.2; 14.3
  2004, 17.9; 14.3
  2005, 17.7; 14.3
  2006, 17.6; 14.3
  2007, 17.5; 14.2
  2008, 17.3; 14.1

Source: *Projections of Education Statistics to 2008*, NCES 98-016, U.S. Department of Education, National Center for Education Statistics (June 1998).

★4071★
States with the largest average class size

Ranking basis/background: Average number of students per class. **Remarks:** Original source: U.S. Department of Education. **Number listed:** 5.

1. California, with 30.1 students per class
2. Maryland, 28.7
2. Utah, 28.7
4. Washington, 28.6
5. Florida, 27.7

Source: Toch, Thomas and Betsy Streisand, "Does Class Size Matter?," *U.S. News & World Report*, October 13, 1997, pp. 22-29.

★4072★
States with the smallest average class size

Ranking basis/background: Average number of students per class. **Remarks:** Original source: U.S. Department of Education. **Number listed:** 5.

1. Vermont, with 20.4 students per class
2. South Dakota, 20.7
3. Kansas, 21.0
4. Montana, 21.5
5. Arkansas, 21.6

Source: Toch, Thomas and Betsy Streisand, "Does Class Size Matter?," *U.S. News & World Report*, October 13, 1997, pp. 22-29.

SCHOOLS, ELEMENTARY & SECONDARY–TEACHERS

See: **Teachers, Elementary and Secondary Salaries–Schools, Elementary & Secondary**

SCHOOLS, ELEMENTARY & SECONDARY–TESTS

See: **Achievement Tests–Schools, Elementary & Secondary Advanced Placement Tests**

SCHOOLS, PRIVATE

See: **Schools, Elementary & Secondary Schools, Secondary**

SCHOOLS, SECONDARY

★4073★
Outstanding Catholic high schools in Metro Boston

Ranking basis/background: According to success ratios measuring number of Advanced Placement tests taken divided by number of seniors, percentage of students taking college-admissions tests, percentage of students passing the math and reading sections of the Massachusetts Educational Assessment Program, and average colleges admissions test scores. **Number listed:** 3.

  Boston College
  Malden Catholic High School
  Xaverian Brothers High School

Source: "Outstanding High Schools," *U.S. News & World Report*, January 18, 1999, pp. 46-82.

★4074★
Outstanding Catholic high schools in Metro Chicago

Ranking basis/background: According to success ratios measuring number of Advanced Placement tests taken divided by number of seniors, percentage of students taking college-admissions tests, percentage of students passing the math and reading sections of the Illinois Goal Assessment Program, and average colleges admissions test scores. **Number listed:** 6.

  Archbishop Quigley Preparatory Seminary
  Benet Academy
  Fenwick High School
  Marian Catholic High School
  Resurrection High School
  St. Rita of Cascia High School

Source: "Outstanding High Schools," *U.S. News & World Report*, January 18, 1999, pp. 46-82.

★4075★
Outstanding Catholic high schools in Metro Detroit

Ranking basis/background: According to success ratios measuring number of Advanced Placement tests taken divided by number of seniors, percentage of students taking college-admissions tests, percentage of students passing the math and reading sections of Michigan's High School Proficiency Test, and average colleges admissions test scores. **Number listed:** 4.

  Catholic Central High School
  De La Salle Collegiate High School
  Immaculate Conception Ukrainian Catholic High School
  Ladywood High School

Source: "Outstanding High Schools," *U.S. News & World Report*, January 18, 1999, pp. 46-82.

★4076★
Outstanding Catholic high schools in Metro New York

Ranking basis/background: According to success ratios measuring number of Advanced Placement tests taken divided by number of seniors, percentage of students taking college-admissions tests, percentage of students passing the Regents Comprehensive English and Math III exams, and average colleges admissions test scores. **Number listed:** 6.

  Auinas High School
  Archbishop Molloy High School
  Monsignor Farrell High School
  Notre Dame School
  St. Francis Preparatory School
  St. Saviour High School

Source: "Outstanding High Schools," *U.S. News & World Report*, January 18, 1999, pp. 46-82.

★4077★
Outstanding independent high schools in Metro Chicago

Ranking basis/background: According to success ratios measuring number of Advanced Placement tests taken divided by number of seniors, percentage of students taking college-admissions tests, percentage of students passing the math and reading sections of the Illinois Goal Assessment Program, and average colleges admissions test scores. **Number listed:** 3.

  Hanna Sacks Bais Yaakov High School
  Northridge Preparatory High School
  Timothy Christian High School

Source: "Outstanding High Schools," *U.S. News & World Report*, January 18, 1999, pp. 46-82.

★4078★
Outstanding secondary schools in Akron, Ohio

Ranking basis/background: Determined by each state's superintendent of instruction and the Council for American Private Education from evaluations of curricula and academic achievement, buildings and classrooms, classes and assemblies, cafeteria lunches, and interviews with students, parents, teachers, and administrators. **Number listed:** 3.

  Archbishop Hoban High School (Akron)
  Aurora High School (Aurora)
  Revere High School (Richfield)

Source: Savageau, David, *Places Rated Almanac*, Macmillan General Reference, 6th ed., 1999.

★4079★
Outstanding secondary schools in Albany-Schenectady-Troy, New York

Ranking basis/background: Determined by each state's superintendent of instruction and the Council for American Private Education from evaluations of curricula and academic achievement, buildings and classrooms, classes and assemblies, cafeteria lunches, and interviews with students, parents, teachers, and administrators. **Number listed:** 5.

  Academy of the Holy Names (Albany)
  Bouton High School (Voorheesville)
  La Salle Institute (Troy)
  O'Brien Academy (Albany)
  Shaker Junior High School (Latham)

Source: Savageau, David, *Places Rated Almanac*, Macmillan General Reference, 6th ed., 1999.

SCHOOLS, SECONDARY

★4080★
Outstanding secondary schools in Albuquerque, New Mexico

Ranking basis/background: Determined by each state's superintendent of instruction and the Council for American Private Education from evaluations of curricula and academic achievement, buildings and classrooms, classes and assemblies, cafeteria lunches, and interviews with students, parents, teachers, and administrators. **Number listed:** 6.

- Cleveland Middle School (Albuquerque)
- Lyndon Johnson Middle School (Albuquerque)
- McKinley Middle School (Albuquerque)
- Roosevelt Middle School (Tijeras)
- Taylor Middle School (Albuquerque)
- Van Buren Middle School (Albuquerque)

Source: Savageau, David, *Places Rated Almanac*, Macmillan General Reference, 6th ed., 1999.

★4081★
Outstanding secondary schools in Allentown-Bethlehem-Easton, Pennsylvania

Ranking basis/background: Determined by each state's superintendent of instruction and the Council for American Private Education from evaluations of curricula and academic achievement, buildings and classrooms, classes and assemblies, cafeteria lunches, and interviews with students, parents, teachers, and administrators. **Number listed:** 3.

- Central Catholic High School (Allentown)
- Feaser Middle School (Middletown)
- Southern Lehigh Middle School (Center Valley)

Source: Savageau, David, *Places Rated Almanac*, Macmillan General Reference, 6th ed., 1999.

★4082★
Outstanding secondary schools in Amarillo, Texas

Ranking basis/background: Determined by each state's superintendent of instruction and the Council for American Private Education from evaluations of curricula and academic achievement, buildings and classrooms, classes and assemblies, cafeteria lunches, and interviews with students, parents, teachers, and administrators. **Number listed:** 1.

- Crockett Middle School (Amarillo)

Source: Savageau, David, *Places Rated Almanac*, Macmillan General Reference, 6th ed., 1999.

★4083★
Outstanding secondary schools in Anchorage, Alaska

Ranking basis/background: Determined by each state's superintendent of instruction and the Council for American Private Education from evaluations of curricula and academic achievement, buildings and classrooms, classes and assemblies, cafeteria lunches, and interviews with students, parents, teachers, and administrators. **Number listed:** 2.

- East Anchorage High School
- West Anchorage High School

Source: Savageau, David, *Places Rated Almanac*, Macmillan General Reference, 6th ed., 1999.

★4084★
Outstanding secondary schools in Ann Arbor, Michigan

Ranking basis/background: Determined by each state's superintendent of instruction and the Council for American Private Education from evaluations of curricula and academic achievement, buildings and classrooms, classes and assemblies, cafeteria lunches, and interviews with students, parents, teachers, and administrators. **Number listed:** 2.

- Hartland High School (Hartland)
- Pinckney Middle School (Pinckney)

Source: Savageau, David, *Places Rated Almanac*, Macmillan General Reference, 6th ed., 1999.

★4085★
Outstanding secondary schools in Appleton-Oshkosh-Neenah, Wisconsin

Ranking basis/background: Determined by each state's superintendent of instruction and the Council for American Private Education from evaluations of curricula and academic achievement, buildings and classrooms, classes and assemblies, cafeteria lunches, and interviews with students, parents, teachers, and administrators. **Number listed:** 2.

- Hortonville Middle School (Hortonville)
- Seymour Middle School (Seymour)

Source: Savageau, David, *Places Rated Almanac*, Macmillan General Reference, 6th ed., 1999.

★4086★
Outstanding secondary schools in Athens, Georgia

Ranking basis/background: Determined by each state's superintendent of instruction and the Council for American Private Education from evaluations of curricula and academic achievement, buildings and classrooms, classes and assemblies, cafeteria lunches, and interviews with students, parents, teachers, and administrators. **Number listed:** 1.

- Cedar Shoals High School

Source: Savageau, David, *Places Rated Almanac*, Macmillan General Reference, 6th ed., 1999.

★4087★
Outstanding secondary schools in Atlanta, Georgia

Ranking basis/background: Determined by each state's superintendent of instruction and the Council for American Private Education from evaluations of curricula and academic achievement, buildings and classrooms, classes and assemblies, cafeteria lunches, and interviews with students, parents, teachers, and administrators. **Number listed:** 18.

- Banneker High School (College Park)
- Chamblee High School (Chamblee)
- Duluth High School (Duluth)
- Edwards Middle School (Conyers)
- Flat Rock Middle School (Tyrone)
- Lost Mountain Middle School (Kennesaw)
- McCleskey Middle School (Marietta)
- Mundy's Mill Middle School (Jonesboro)
- Otwell Middle School (Cumming)
- Pinckneyville Middle School (Norcross)
- Ralph Bunche Middle School (Atlanta)
- Roswell High School (Roswell)
- St. John Neumann High School (Lilburn)
- St. John the Evangelist High School (Hapeville)
- Samuel Inman Middle School (Atlanta)
- South Cobb High School (Austell)
- Sprayberry High School (Marietta)
- Trickum Middle School (Lilburn)

Source: Savageau, David, *Places Rated Almanac*, Macmillan General Reference, 6th ed., 1999.

★4088★
Outstanding secondary schools in Atlantic-Cape May, New Jersey

Ranking basis/background: Determined by each state's superintendent of instruction and the Council for American Private Education from evaluations of curricula and academic achievement, buildings and classrooms, classes and assemblies, cafeteria lunches, and interviews with students, parents, teachers, and administrators. **Number listed:** 3.

- Mainland Regional High School (Linwood)
- Our Lady Star of the Sea School (Cape May)
- Teitelman Middle School (Cape May)

Source: Savageau, David, *Places Rated Almanac*, Macmillan General Reference, 6th ed., 1999.

★4089★
Outstanding secondary schools in Augusta-Aiken, Georgia-South Carolina

Ranking basis/background: Determined by each state's superintendent of instruction and the Council for American Private Education from evaluations of curricula and academic achievement, buildings and classrooms, classes and assemblies, cafeteria lunches, and interviews with students, parents, teachers, and administrators. **Number listed:** 1.

- Thomson High School (Thomson)

Source: Savageau, David, *Places Rated Almanac*, Macmillan General Reference, 6th ed., 1999.

★4090★
Outstanding secondary schools in Austin-San Marcos, Texas

Ranking basis/background: Determined by each state's superintendent of instruction and the Council for American Private Education from evaluations of curricula and academic achievement, buildings and classrooms, classes and assemblies, cafeteria lunches, and interviews with students, parents, teachers, and administrators. **Number listed:** 9.

- Canyon Vista Middle School (Austin)
- Chisholm Trail Middle School (Round Rock)
- Georgetown High School (Georgetown)
- Grisham Middle School (Austin)
- Hill Country Middle School (Austin)
- James Bowie High School (Austin)
- Lanier High School (Austin)
- West Ridge Middle School (Austin)
- Westwood High School (Austin)

Source: Savageau, David, *Places Rated Almanac*, Macmillan General Reference, 6th ed., 1999.

★4091★
Outstanding secondary schools in Bakersfield, California

Ranking basis/background: Determined by each state's superintendent of instruction and the Council for American Private Education from evaluations of curricula and academic achievement, buildings and classrooms, classes and assemblies, cafeteria lunches, and interviews with students, parents, teachers, and administrators. **Number listed:** 2.

- Fruitvale High School
- Highland High School

Source: Savageau, David, *Places Rated Almanac*, Macmillan General Reference, 6th ed., 1999.

Educational Rankings Annual • 2002 SCHOOLS, SECONDARY

★4092★
Outstanding secondary schools in Baltimore, Maryland

Ranking basis/background: Determined by each state's superintendent of instruction and the Council for American Private Education from evaluations of curricula and academic achievement, buildings and classrooms, classes and assemblies, cafeteria lunches, and interviews with students, parents, teachers, and administrators. **Number listed:** 9.
  Archbishop Spalding High School (Severn)
  Atholton High School (Columbia)
  Baltimore School for the Arts (Baltimore)
  Dumbarton Middle School (Baltimore)
  Havre de Grace High School (Havre de Grace)
  Howard High School (Ellicott City)
  John Carroll High School (Bel Air)
  Kennedy Drieger Middle School (Baltimore)
  North Harford Middle School (Pylesville)
Source: Savageau, David, *Places Rated Almanac*, Macmillan General Reference, 6th ed., 1999.

★4093★
Outstanding secondary schools in Baton Rouge, Louisiana

Ranking basis/background: Determined by each state's superintendent of instruction and the Council for American Private Education from evaluations of curricula and academic achievement, buildings and classrooms, classes and assemblies, cafeteria lunches, and interviews with students, parents, teachers, and administrators. **Number listed:** 3.
  Catholic High School
  Episcopal High School
  St. Joseph's Academy
Source: Savageau, David, *Places Rated Almanac*, Macmillan General Reference, 6th ed., 1999.

★4094★
Outstanding secondary schools in Beaumont-Port Arthur, Texas

Ranking basis/background: Determined by each state's superintendent of instruction and the Council for American Private Education from evaluations of curricula and academic achievement, buildings and classrooms, classes and assemblies, cafeteria lunches, and interviews with students, parents, teachers, and administrators. **Number listed:** 1.
  Monsignor Kelly High School (Beaumont)
Source: Savageau, David, *Places Rated Almanac*, Macmillan General Reference, 6th ed., 1999.

★4095★
Outstanding secondary schools in Benton Harbor, Michigan

Ranking basis/background: Determined by each state's superintendent of instruction and the Council for American Private Education from evaluations of curricula and academic achievement, buildings and classrooms, classes and assemblies, cafeteria lunches, and interviews with students, parents, teachers, and administrators. **Number listed:** 1.
  McCord Renaissance Center
Source: Savageau, David, *Places Rated Almanac*, Macmillan General Reference, 6th ed., 1999.

★4096★
Outstanding secondary schools in Bergen-Passaic, New Jersey

Ranking basis/background: Determined by each state's superintendent of instruction and the Council for American Private Education from evaluations of curricula and academic achievement, buildings and classrooms, classes and assemblies, cafeteria lunches, and interviews with students, parents, teachers, and administrators. **Number listed:** 6.
  Benjamin Franklin Middle School (Ridgewood)
  Fair Lawn High School (Fair Lawn)
  Immaculate Heart Academy (Washington)
  Northern Valley Regional High School (Old Tappan)
  Queen of Peace High School (North Arlington)
  River Dell Regional High School (Oradell)
Source: Savageau, David, *Places Rated Almanac*, Macmillan General Reference, 6th ed., 1999.

★4097★
Outstanding secondary schools in Binghamton, New York

Ranking basis/background: Determined by each state's superintendent of instruction and the Council for American Private Education from evaluations of curricula and academic achievement, buildings and classrooms, classes and assemblies, cafeteria lunches, and interviews with students, parents, teachers, and administrators. **Number listed:** 1.
  East Middle School
Source: Savageau, David, *Places Rated Almanac*, Macmillan General Reference, 6th ed., 1999.

★4098★
Outstanding secondary schools in Birmingham, Alabama

Ranking basis/background: Determined by each state's superintendent of instruction and the Council for American Private Education from evaluations of curricula and academic achievement, buildings and classrooms, classes and assemblies, cafeteria lunches, and interviews with students, parents, teachers, and administrators. **Number listed:** 6.
  Grantswood Community School (Irondale)
  Hewitt-Trussville High School (Trussville)
  Homewood Middle School (Homewood)
  Louis Pizitz Middle School (Birmingham)
  Mountain Brook High School (Mountain Brook)
  Vestavia Hills High School (Vestavia Hills)
Source: Savageau, David, *Places Rated Almanac*, Macmillan General Reference, 6th ed., 1999.

★4099★
Outstanding secondary schools in Bismarck, North Dakota

Ranking basis/background: Determined by each state's superintendent of instruction and the Council for American Private Education from evaluations of curricula and academic achievement, buildings and classrooms, classes and assemblies, cafeteria lunches, and interviews with students, parents, teachers, and administrators. **Number listed:** 1.
  Century High School
Source: Savageau, David, *Places Rated Almanac*, Macmillan General Reference, 6th ed., 1999.

★4100★
Outstanding secondary schools in Boston, Massachusetts-New Hampshire

Ranking basis/background: Determined by each state's superintendent of instruction and the Council for American Private Education from evaluations of curricula and academic achievement, buildings and classrooms, classes and assemblies, cafeteria lunches, and interviews with students, parents, teachers, and administrators. **Number listed:** 8.
  Broad Meadows Middle School (Quincy)
  Clarke Middle School (Lexington)
  Coyle and Cassidy High School (Tauton)
  Fay School (Southborough)
  Mansfield High School (Mansfield)
  Marblehead Middle School (Marblehead)
  Simonds Middle School (Burlington)
  Timilty Middle School (Roxbury)
Source: Savageau, David, *Places Rated Almanac*, Macmillan General Reference, 6th ed., 1999.

★4101★
Outstanding secondary schools in Bridgeport, Connecticut

Ranking basis/background: Determined by each state's superintendent of instruction and the Council for American Private Education from evaluations of curricula and academic achievement, buildings and classrooms, classes and assemblies, cafeteria lunches, and interviews with students, parents, teachers, and administrators. **Number listed:** 1.
  Stratfield School (Fairfield)
Source: Savageau, David, *Places Rated Almanac*, Macmillan General Reference, 6th ed., 1999.

★4102★
Outstanding secondary schools in Buffalo-Niagara Falls, New York

Ranking basis/background: Determined by each state's superintendent of instruction and the Council for American Private Education from evaluations of curricula and academic achievement, buildings and classrooms, classes and assemblies, cafeteria lunches, and interviews with students, parents, teachers, and administrators. **Number listed:** 2.
  Ben Franklin Middle School (Kenmore)
  Kenmore East High School (Tonawanda)
Source: Savageau, David, *Places Rated Almanac*, Macmillan General Reference, 6th ed., 1999.

★4103★
Outstanding secondary schools in Canton-Massillon, Ohio

Ranking basis/background: Determined by each state's superintendent of instruction and the Council for American Private Education from evaluations of curricula and academic achievement, buildings and classrooms, classes and assemblies, cafeteria lunches, and interviews with students, parents, teachers, and administrators. **Number listed:** 1.
  Canton Country Day School (Canton)
Source: Savageau, David, *Places Rated Almanac*, Macmillan General Reference, 6th ed., 1999.

★4104★
Outstanding secondary schools in Cedar Rapids, Iowa

Ranking basis/background: Determined by each state's superintendent of instruction and the Council for American Private Education from evaluations of curricula and academic achievement, buildings and classrooms, classes and assemblies, cafeteria lunches, and interviews with students, parents, teachers, and administrators. **Number listed:** 3.

SCHOOLS, SECONDARY

Harding Middle School
Metro High School
Washington High School
Source: Savageau, David, *Places Rated Almanac*, Macmillan General Reference, 6th ed., 1999.

★4105★
Outstanding secondary schools in Champaign-Urbana, Illinois

Ranking basis/background: Determined by each state's superintendent of instruction and the Council for American Private Education from evaluations of curricula and academic achievement, buildings and classrooms, classes and assemblies, cafeteria lunches, and interviews with students, parents, teachers, and administrators. **Number listed:** 1.

Champaign Central High School

Source: Savageau, David, *Places Rated Almanac*, Macmillan General Reference, 6th ed., 1999.

★4106★
Outstanding secondary schools in Charleston-North Charleston, South Carolina

Ranking basis/background: Determined by each state's superintendent of instruction and the Council for American Private Education from evaluations of curricula and academic achievement, buildings and classrooms, classes and assemblies, cafeteria lunches, and interviews with students, parents, teachers, and administrators. **Number listed:** 1.

Williams Middle School

Source: Savageau, David, *Places Rated Almanac*, Macmillan General Reference, 6th ed., 1999.

★4107★
Outstanding secondary schools in Charleston, West Virginia

Ranking basis/background: Determined by each state's superintendent of instruction and the Council for American Private Education from evaluations of curricula and academic achievement, buildings and classrooms, classes and assemblies, cafeteria lunches, and interviews with students, parents, teachers, and administrators. **Number listed:** 4.

Capital High School (Charleston)
DuPont Junior High School (Belle)
Jackson Middle School (Cross Lanes)
Winfield High School (Winfield)

Source: Savageau, David, *Places Rated Almanac*, Macmillan General Reference, 6th ed., 1999.

★4108★
Outstanding secondary schools in Charlotte-Gastonia-Rock Hill, North Carolina-South Carolina

Ranking basis/background: Determined by each state's superintendent of instruction and the Council for American Private Education from evaluations of curricula and academic achievement, buildings and classrooms, classes and assemblies, cafeteria lunches, and interviews with students, parents, teachers, and administrators. **Number listed:** 5.

Charlotte Latin School (Charlotte)
Piedmont Middle School (Monroe)
Piedmont Open Middle School (Charlotte)
Providence Senior High School (Charlotte)
West Rowan High School (Mount Ulla)

Source: Savageau, David, *Places Rated Almanac*, Macmillan General Reference, 6th ed., 1999.

★4109★
Outstanding secondary schools in Chattanooga, Tennessee-Georgia

Ranking basis/background: Determined by each state's superintendent of instruction and the Council for American Private Education from evaluations of curricula and academic achievement, buildings and classrooms, classes and assemblies, cafeteria lunches, and interviews with students, parents, teachers, and administrators. **Number listed:** 3.

Fort Oglethorpe High School (Fort Oglethorpe)
Girls Prep (Chattanooga)
Red Bank High School (Chattanooga)

Source: Savageau, David, *Places Rated Almanac*, Macmillan General Reference, 6th ed., 1999.

★4110★
Outstanding secondary schools in Chicago, Illinois

Ranking basis/background: Determined by each state's superintendent of instruction and the Council for American Private Education from evaluations of curricula and academic achievement, buildings and classrooms, classes and assemblies, cafeteria lunches, and interviews with students, parents, teachers, and administrators. **Number listed:** 44.

Adlai E. Stevenson High School (Lincolnshire)
Adlai E. Stevenson High School (Prairie View)
Barrington High School (Barrington)
Carmel High School (Mundelein)
Community High School (West Chicago)
Conant High School (Hoffman Estates)
Crete-Monee Middle School (Crete)
Deer Path Junior High School (Lake Forest)
Deerfield High School (Deerfield)
Elk Grove High School (Elk Grove Village)
Flossmoor High School (Flossmoor)
Frankfort Junior High School (Frankfort)
Grayslake Middle School (Grayslake)
Highland Middle School (Libertyville)
Immaculate Heart of Mary High School (Westchester)
James Hart Middle School (Homewood)
Lake Bluff Junior High School (Lake Bluff)
Lake Forest Country Day School (Lake Forest)
Libertyville High School (Libertyville)
Madonna High School (Chicago)
Maine Township High School West (Des Plains)
Margaret Mead Junior High School (Elk Grove Village)
Marian Catholic High School (Chicago Heights)
Mother McAuley High School (Chicago)
Mundelein High School (Mundelein)
New Trier Township High School (Winnetka)
Niles North High School (Skokie)
Niles West High School (Skokie)
Northbrook Junior High School (Northbrook)
Northwood Middle School (Woodstock)
Our Lady of the Wayside School (Arlington Heights)
Palatine High School (Palatine)
Plum Grove Junior High School (Rolling Meadows)
Prospect High School (Mount Prospect)
Regina Dominican High School (Wilmette)
Rolling Meadows High School (Rolling Meadows)
St. Charles High School (St. Charles)
St. Damian School (Oak Forest)
St. Luke School (River Forest)
Schaumburg High School (Schaumburg)
Stagg High School (Palos Hills)
Trinity Lutheran School (Roselle)
Walter R. Sundling Junior High School (Palatine)
Wilmette Junior High School (Wilmette)

Source: Savageau, David, *Places Rated Almanac*, Macmillan General Reference, 6th ed., 1999.

★4111★
Outstanding secondary schools in Chico-Paradise, California

Ranking basis/background: Determined by each state's superintendent of instruction and the Council for American Private Education from evaluations of curricula and academic achievement, buildings and classrooms, classes and assemblies, cafeteria lunches, and interviews with students, parents, teachers, and administrators. **Number listed:** 1.

Chico High School

Source: Savageau, David, *Places Rated Almanac*, Macmillan General Reference, 6th ed., 1999.

★4112★
Outstanding secondary schools in Cincinnati, Ohio-Kentucky-Indiana

Ranking basis/background: Determined by each state's superintendent of instruction and the Council for American Private Education from evaluations of curricula and academic achievement, buildings and classrooms, classes and assemblies, cafeteria lunches, and interviews with students, parents, teachers, and administrators. **Number listed:** 13.

Anderson High School (Cincinnati)
Blessed Sacrament School (Fort Mitchell)
Madeira High School (Cincinnati)
Mason H (Mason)
Notre Dame Academy (Park Hills)
Princeton High School (Cincinnati)
Princeton Junior High School (Cincinnati)
Reading Central Community School (Reading)
St. James White Oak School (Cincinnati)
St. Mary School (Cincinnati)
Sellman Middle School (Cincinnati)
William Henry Harrison High School (Harrison)

Source: Savageau, David, *Places Rated Almanac*, Macmillan General Reference, 6th ed., 1999.

★4113★
Outstanding secondary schools in Clarkesville-Hoplinsville, Tennessee-Kentucky

Ranking basis/background: Determined by each state's superintendent of instruction and the Council for American Private Education from evaluations of curricula and academic achievement, buildings and classrooms, classes and assemblies, cafeteria lunches, and interviews with students, parents, teachers, and administrators. **Number listed:** 2.

Fort Campbell High School (Fort Campbell North)
Mahaffey Middle School (Fort Campbell North)

Source: Savageau, David, *Places Rated Almanac*, Macmillan General Reference, 6th ed., 1999.

Educational Rankings Annual • 2002   SCHOOLS, SECONDARY

★4114★
Outstanding secondary schools in Cleveland-Lorain-Elyria, Ohio

Ranking basis/background: Determined by each state's superintendent of instruction and the Council for American Private Education from evaluations of curricula and academic achievement, buildings and classrooms, classes and assemblies, cafeteria lunches, and interviews with students, parents, teachers, and administrators. **Number listed:** 22.

- Beachwood Middle School (Beachwood)
- Beaumont Catholic High School (Cleveland Heights)
- Elyria Catholic High School (Elyria)
- Gesu Catholic School (University Heights)
- Kenston High School (Bainbridge)
- Kirtland Middle School (Kirtland)
- Mentor Shore Junior High School (Mentor)
- Metro Catholic Parish School (Cleveland)
- Olmsted Falls High School (Olmsted Falls)
- Orange High School (Pepper Pike)
- Perry High School (Perry)
- Regina High School (South Euclid)
- Rocky River High School (Rocky River)
- Rocky River Middle School (Rocky River)
- St. Edward High School (Lakewood)
- St. John Bosco School (Parma Heights)
- St. Joseph Academy (Cleveland)
- St. Martin of Tours School (Maple Heights)
- St. Thomas More School (Brooklyn)
- Solon High School (Solon)
- Whitney Young Middle School (Cleveland)
- Willoughby South High School (Willoughby)

Source: Savageau, David, *Places Rated Almanac*, Macmillan General Reference, 6th ed., 1999.

★4115★
Outstanding secondary schools in Colorado Springs, Colorado

Ranking basis/background: Determined by each state's superintendent of instruction and the Council for American Private Education from evaluations of curricula and academic achievement, buildings and classrooms, classes and assemblies, cafeteria lunches, and interviews with students, parents, teachers, and administrators. **Number listed:** 1.

- Rampart High School

Source: Savageau, David, *Places Rated Almanac*, Macmillan General Reference, 6th ed., 1999.

★4116★
Outstanding secondary schools in Columbia, Missouri

Ranking basis/background: Determined by each state's superintendent of instruction and the Council for American Private Education from evaluations of curricula and academic achievement, buildings and classrooms, classes and assemblies, cafeteria lunches, and interviews with students, parents, teachers, and administrators. **Number listed:** 2.

- Hickman High School
- Jefferson Junior High School

Source: Savageau, David, *Places Rated Almanac*, Macmillan General Reference, 6th ed., 1999.

★4117★
Outstanding secondary schools in Columbia, South Carolina

Ranking basis/background: Determined by each state's superintendent of instruction and the Council for American Private Education from evaluations of curricula and academic achievement, buildings and classrooms, classes and assemblies, cafeteria lunches, and interviews with students, parents, teachers, and administrators. **Number listed:** 11.

- Chapin High School (Chapin)
- Chapin Middle School (Chapin)
- Dent Middle School (Columbia)
- Dutch Fork High School (Irmo)
- Heathwood Hall Episcopal School (Columbia)
- Irmo High School (Columbia)
- Irmo Middle School (Columbia)
- Lexington Middle School (Lexington)
- Richland Northeast High School (Columbia)
- Spring Valley High School (Columbia)
- Summit Parkway Middle School (Columbia)

Source: Savageau, David, *Places Rated Almanac*, Macmillan General Reference, 6th ed., 1999.

★4118★
Outstanding secondary schools in Columbus, Ohio

Ranking basis/background: Determined by each state's superintendent of instruction and the Council for American Private Education from evaluations of curricula and academic achievement, buildings and classrooms, classes and assemblies, cafeteria lunches, and interviews with students, parents, teachers, and administrators. **Number listed:** 8.

- Columbus School for Girls (Columbus)
- Granville High School (Granville)
- Immaculate Conception School (Columbus)
- Kilbourne High School (Worthington)
- Our Lady of Perpetual Help School (Grove City)
- St. Andrew School (Columbus)
- St. Francis DeSales High School (Columbus)
- St. Joseph Montessori School (Columbus)

Source: Savageau, David, *Places Rated Almanac*, Macmillan General Reference, 6th ed., 1999.

★4119★
Outstanding secondary schools in Corpus Christi, Texas

Ranking basis/background: Determined by each state's superintendent of instruction and the Council for American Private Education from evaluations of curricula and academic achievement, buildings and classrooms, classes and assemblies, cafeteria lunches, and interviews with students, parents, teachers, and administrators. **Number listed:** 1.

- St. James Episcopal School

Source: Savageau, David, *Places Rated Almanac*, Macmillan General Reference, 6th ed., 1999.

★4120★
Outstanding secondary schools in Dallas, Texas

Ranking basis/background: Determined by each state's superintendent of instruction and the Council for American Private Education from evaluations of curricula and academic achievement, buildings and classrooms, classes and assemblies, cafeteria lunches, and interviews with students, parents, teachers, and administrators. **Number listed:** 28.

- Anna Middle School (Anna)
- Armstrong Middle School (Plano)
- Bishop Lynch High School (Dallas)
- Blalack Junior High School (Carrollton)
- BT Washington Performing Arts High School (Dallas)
- Carpenter Middle School (Plano)
- Christ the King Catholic School (Dallas)
- Clark High School (Plano)
- Coppell Middle School (Dallas)
- Forest Meadow Junior High School (Dallas)
- Good Shepherd Episcopal School (Dallas)
- Jesuit Prep (Dallas)
- Lyles Middle School (Garland)
- Marcus High School (Flower Mound)
- McCulloch Middle School (Dallas)
- Milliken Middle School (Lewisville)
- Newman Smith High School (Carrollton)
- Parkhill Junior High School (Dallas)
- Plano East Senior High School (Plano)
- Plano High School (Plano)
- Renner Middle School (Plano)
- Richardson Junior High School (Richardson)
- St. Mark the Evangelist Catholic School (Plano)
- St. Thomas Aquinas School (Dallas)
- Strickland Middle School (Denton)
- Turner High School (Carrollton)
- Ursuline Academy (Dallas)
- Vivian Field Junior High School (Farmers Branch)

Source: Savageau, David, *Places Rated Almanac*, Macmillan General Reference, 6th ed., 1999.

★4121★
Outstanding secondary schools in Danbury, Connecticut

Ranking basis/background: Determined by each state's superintendent of instruction and the Council for American Private Education from evaluations of curricula and academic achievement, buildings and classrooms, classes and assemblies, cafeteria lunches, and interviews with students, parents, teachers, and administrators. **Number listed:** 2.

- Barlow High School (Redding)
- Shepaug Valley High School (Washington)

Source: Savageau, David, *Places Rated Almanac*, Macmillan General Reference, 6th ed., 1999.

★4122★
Outstanding secondary schools in Dayton-Springfield, Ohio

Ranking basis/background: Determined by each state's superintendent of instruction and the Council for American Private Education from evaluations of curricula and academic achievement, buildings and classrooms, classes and assemblies, cafeteria lunches, and interviews with students, parents, teachers, and administrators. **Number listed:** 7.

- Centerville High School (Centerville)
- Greene Academy (Dayton)
- Mad River Middle School (Dayton)
- Miamisburg High School (Miamisburg)
- Oakwood High School (Dayton)
- Tower Heights Middle School (Centerville)
- Yellow Springs High School (Yellow Springs)

Source: Savageau, David, *Places Rated Almanac*, Macmillan General Reference, 6th ed., 1999.

SCHOOLS, SECONDARY

★4123★
Outstanding secondary schools in Daytona Beach, Florida

Ranking basis/background: Determined by each state's superintendent of instruction and the Council for American Private Education from evaluations of curricula and academic achievement, buildings and classrooms, classes and assemblies, cafeteria lunches, and interviews with students, parents, teachers, and administrators. **Number listed:** 2.

 Mainland High School (Daytona Beach)
 Spruce Creek High School (Port Orange)

Source: Savageau, David, *Places Rated Almanac*, Macmillan General Reference, 6th ed., 1999.

★4124★
Outstanding secondary schools in Denver, Colorado

Ranking basis/background: Determined by each state's superintendent of instruction and the Council for American Private Education from evaluations of curricula and academic achievement, buildings and classrooms, classes and assemblies, cafeteria lunches, and interviews with students, parents, teachers, and administrators. **Number listed:** 11.

 Arapahoe High School (Littleton)
 Cherry Creek High School (Englewood)
 Cherry Creek West Middle School (Littleton)
 Flood Middle School (Englewood)
 Heritage High School (Littleton)
 Horizon High School (Thornton)
 Lutheran High School (Denver)
 Powell Middle School (Littleton)
 Regis Jesuit High School (Aurora)
 St. Mary's Academy (Englewood)
 Smoky Hill High School (Aurora)

Source: Savageau, David, *Places Rated Almanac*, Macmillan General Reference, 6th ed., 1999.

★4125★
Outstanding secondary schools in Detroit, Michigan

Ranking basis/background: Determined by each state's superintendent of instruction and the Council for American Private Education from evaluations of curricula and academic achievement, buildings and classrooms, classes and assemblies, cafeteria lunches, and interviews with students, parents, teachers, and administrators. **Number listed:** 19.

 Cass Technical High School (Detroit)
 Covington Middle School (Birmingham)
 De La Salle Collegiate High School (Warren)
 East Hills Middle School (Bloomfield Hills)
 The Grosse Pointe Academy (Grosse Pointe Farms)
 L'Anse Creuse Middle School Central (Harrison Township)
 L'Anse Creuse Middle School North (Macomb)
 L'Anse Creuse Middle School South (Harrison Township)
 North Farmington High School (Farmington Hills)
 Orchard Lake Middle School (West Bloomfield)
 Rochester Adams High School (Rochester Hills)
 St. Clare of Montefalco Catholic School (Grosse Pointe Park)
 St. Joan of Arc School (St. Clair Shores)
 Southfield Christian School (Southfield)
 Southfield-Lathrup High School (Lathrup Village)
 Troy Athens High School (Troy)
 Troy High School (Troy)
 Van Hoosen Middle School (Rochester)
 West Bloomfield High School (West Bloomfield)

Source: Savageau, David, *Places Rated Almanac*, Macmillan General Reference, 6th ed., 1999.

★4126★
Outstanding secondary schools in Dutchess County, New York

Ranking basis/background: Determined by each state's superintendent of instruction and the Council for American Private Education from evaluations of curricula and academic achievement, buildings and classrooms, classes and assemblies, cafeteria lunches, and interviews with students, parents, teachers, and administrators. **Number listed:** 1.

 Astor Learning Center (Rhinebeck)

Source: Savageau, David, *Places Rated Almanac*, Macmillan General Reference, 6th ed., 1999.

★4127★
Outstanding secondary schools in Eau Claire, Wisconsin

Ranking basis/background: Determined by each state's superintendent of instruction and the Council for American Private Education from evaluations of curricula and academic achievement, buildings and classrooms, classes and assemblies, cafeteria lunches, and interviews with students, parents, teachers, and administrators. **Number listed:** 1.

 Seymour Middle School (Seymour)

Source: Savageau, David, *Places Rated Almanac*, Macmillan General Reference, 6th ed., 1999.

★4128★
Outstanding secondary schools in El Paso, Texas

Ranking basis/background: Determined by each state's superintendent of instruction and the Council for American Private Education from evaluations of curricula and academic achievement, buildings and classrooms, classes and assemblies, cafeteria lunches, and interviews with students, parents, teachers, and administrators. **Number listed:** 4.

 Montwood High School
 St. Clement's Episcopal Parish School
 Slider Middle School
 Socorro High School

Source: Savageau, David, *Places Rated Almanac*, Macmillan General Reference, 6th ed., 1999.

★4129★
Outstanding secondary schools in Erie, Pennsylvania

Ranking basis/background: Determined by each state's superintendent of instruction and the Council for American Private Education from evaluations of curricula and academic achievement, buildings and classrooms, classes and assemblies, cafeteria lunches, and interviews with students, parents, teachers, and administrators. **Number listed:** 1.

 Mercyhurst Prep

Source: Savageau, David, *Places Rated Almanac*, Macmillan General Reference, 6th ed., 1999.

★4130★
Outstanding secondary schools in Evansville-Henderson, Indiana-Kentucky

Ranking basis/background: Determined by each state's superintendent of instruction and the Council for American Private Education from evaluations of curricula and academic achievement, buildings and classrooms, classes and assemblies, cafeteria lunches, and interviews with students, parents, teachers, and administrators. **Number listed:** 1.

 North High School (Evansville)

Source: Savageau, David, *Places Rated Almanac*, Macmillan General Reference, 6th ed., 1999.

★4131★
Outstanding secondary schools in Fayetteville-Springdale-Rogers, Arkansas

Ranking basis/background: Determined by each state's superintendent of instruction and the Council for American Private Education from evaluations of curricula and academic achievement, buildings and classrooms, classes and assemblies, cafeteria lunches, and interviews with students, parents, teachers, and administrators. **Number listed:** 1.

 Old High Middle School (Bentonville)

Source: Savageau, David, *Places Rated Almanac*, Macmillan General Reference, 6th ed., 1999.

★4132★
Outstanding secondary schools in Florence, Alabama

Ranking basis/background: Determined by each state's superintendent of instruction and the Council for American Private Education from evaluations of curricula and academic achievement, buildings and classrooms, classes and assemblies, cafeteria lunches, and interviews with students, parents, teachers, and administrators. **Number listed:** 2.

 Mars Hill Bible School (Florence)
 Muscle Shoals High School (Muscle Shoals)

Source: Savageau, David, *Places Rated Almanac*, Macmillan General Reference, 6th ed., 1999.

★4133★
Outstanding secondary schools in Fort Lauderdale, Florida

Ranking basis/background: Determined by each state's superintendent of instruction and the Council for American Private Education from evaluations of curricula and academic achievement, buildings and classrooms, classes and assemblies, cafeteria lunches, and interviews with students, parents, teachers, and administrators. **Number listed:** 11.

 Chaminade-Madonna Prep (Hollywood)
 Cooper City High School (Cooper City)
 Coral Springs Middle School (Coral Springs)
 Forest Glen Middle School (Coral Springs)
 Pompano Beach Middle School (Pompano Beach)
 Ramblewood Middle Springs (Coral Springs)
 Rogers Middle School (Fort Lauderdale)
 St. David Catholic School (Davie)
 St. Thomas Aquinas High School (Fort Lauderdale)
 Tequestra Trace Middle School (Fort Lauderdale)
 University School of Nova (Fort Lauderdale)

Source: Savageau, David, *Places Rated Almanac*, Macmillan General Reference, 6th ed., 1999.

★4134★
Outstanding secondary schools in Fort Myers-Cape Coral, Florida

Ranking basis/background: Determined by each state's superintendent of instruction and the Council for American Private Education from evaluations of curricula and academic achievement, buildings and classrooms, classes and assemblies, cafeteria lunches, and interviews with students, parents, teachers, and administrators. **Number listed:** 4.

Bonita Springs Middle School (Bonita Springs)
Caloosa Middle School (Cape Coral)
Fort Myers Middle School (Fort Myers)
St. Michael Lutheran School (Fort Myers)

Source: Savageau, David, *Places Rated Almanac*, Macmillan General Reference, 6th ed., 1999.

★4135★
Outstanding secondary schools in Fort Smith, Arkansas-Oklahoma

Ranking basis/background: Determined by each state's superintendent of instruction and the Council for American Private Education from evaluations of curricula and academic achievement, buildings and classrooms, classes and assemblies, cafeteria lunches, and interviews with students, parents, teachers, and administrators. **Number listed:** 1.

Northside High School

Source: Savageau, David, *Places Rated Almanac*, Macmillan General Reference, 6th ed., 1999.

★4136★
Outstanding secondary schools in Fort Walton Beach, Florida

Ranking basis/background: Determined by each state's superintendent of instruction and the Council for American Private Education from evaluations of curricula and academic achievement, buildings and classrooms, classes and assemblies, cafeteria lunches, and interviews with students, parents, teachers, and administrators. **Number listed:** 1.

Niceville High School (Niceville)

Source: Savageau, David, *Places Rated Almanac*, Macmillan General Reference, 6th ed., 1999.

★4137★
Outstanding secondary schools in Fort Worth-Arlington, Texas

Ranking basis/background: Determined by each state's superintendent of instruction and the Council for American Private Education from evaluations of curricula and academic achievement, buildings and classrooms, classes and assemblies, cafeteria lunches, and interviews with students, parents, teachers, and administrators. **Number listed:** 6.

Carroll High School (Southlake)
Carroll Middle School (Southlake)
Fort Worth Country Day (Fort Worth)
Grapevine Middle School (Grapevine)
Heritage Middle School (Colleyville)
Lawrence Bell High School (Hurst)

Source: Savageau, David, *Places Rated Almanac*, Macmillan General Reference, 6th ed., 1999.

★4138★
Outstanding secondary schools in Fresno, California

Ranking basis/background: Determined by each state's superintendent of instruction and the Council for American Private Education from evaluations of curricula and academic achievement, buildings and classrooms, classes and assemblies, cafeteria lunches, and interviews with students, parents, teachers, and administrators. **Number listed:** 5.

Buchanan High School (Clovis)
Clark Intermediate School (Clovis)
Clovis High School (Clovis)
Edison Computech Middle School (Fresno)
Kastner Intermediate School (Fresno)

Source: Savageau, David, *Places Rated Almanac*, Macmillan General Reference, 6th ed., 1999.

★4139★
Outstanding secondary schools in Gary, Indiana

Ranking basis/background: Determined by each state's superintendent of instruction and the Council for American Private Education from evaluations of curricula and academic achievement, buildings and classrooms, classes and assemblies, cafeteria lunches, and interviews with students, parents, teachers, and administrators. **Number listed:** 2.

Munster High School (Munster)
Wilbur Wright Middle School (Munster)

Source: Savageau, David, *Places Rated Almanac*, Macmillan General Reference, 6th ed., 1999.

★4140★
Outstanding secondary schools in Grand Rapids-Muskegon-Holland, Michigan

Ranking basis/background: Determined by each state's superintendent of instruction and the Council for American Private Education from evaluations of curricula and academic achievement, buildings and classrooms, classes and assemblies, cafeteria lunches, and interviews with students, parents, teachers, and administrators. **Number listed:** 6.

Caledonia High School (Caledonia)
East Grand Rapids High School (Grand Rapids)
East Grand Rapids Middle School (Grand Rapids)
Rockford High School (Rockford)
Rockford Middle School (Rockford)
Roguewood School (Rockford)

Source: Savageau, David, *Places Rated Almanac*, Macmillan General Reference, 6th ed., 1999.

★4141★
Outstanding secondary schools in Green Bay, Wisconsin

Ranking basis/background: Determined by each state's superintendent of instruction and the Council for American Private Education from evaluations of curricula and academic achievement, buildings and classrooms, classes and assemblies, cafeteria lunches, and interviews with students, parents, teachers, and administrators. **Number listed:** 1.

Bay View Middle School

Source: Savageau, David, *Places Rated Almanac*, Macmillan General Reference, 6th ed., 1999.

★4142★
Outstanding secondary schools in Greensboro-Winston-Salem-High Point, North Carolina

Ranking basis/background: Determined by each state's superintendent of instruction and the Council for American Private Education from evaluations of curricula and academic achievement, buildings and classrooms, classes and assemblies, cafeteria lunches, and interviews with students, parents, teachers, and administrators. **Number listed:** 1.

Williams High School (Burlington)

Source: Savageau, David, *Places Rated Almanac*, Macmillan General Reference, 6th ed., 1999.

★4143★
Outstanding secondary schools in Greenville-Spartanburg-Anderson, South Carolina

Ranking basis/background: Determined by each state's superintendent of instruction and the Council for American Private Education from evaluations of curricula and academic achievement, buildings and classrooms, classes and assemblies, cafeteria lunches, and interviews with students, parents, teachers, and administrators. **Number listed:** 2.

Hill Middle School (Duncan)
Spartanburg High School (Spartanburg)

Source: Savageau, David, *Places Rated Almanac*, Macmillan General Reference, 6th ed., 1999.

★4144★
Outstanding secondary schools in Hagerstown, Maryland

Ranking basis/background: Determined by each state's superintendent of instruction and the Council for American Private Education from evaluations of curricula and academic achievement, buildings and classrooms, classes and assemblies, cafeteria lunches, and interviews with students, parents, teachers, and administrators. **Number listed:** 1.

Hancock Middle Senior High School (Hancock)

Source: Savageau, David, *Places Rated Almanac*, Macmillan General Reference, 6th ed., 1999.

★4145★
Outstanding secondary schools in Hamilton-Middletown, Ohio

Ranking basis/background: Determined by each state's superintendent of instruction and the Council for American Private Education from evaluations of curricula and academic achievement, buildings and classrooms, classes and assemblies, cafeteria lunches, and interviews with students, parents, teachers, and administrators. **Number listed:** 1.

Lakota High School (West Chester)

Source: Savageau, David, *Places Rated Almanac*, Macmillan General Reference, 6th ed., 1999.

★4146★
Outstanding secondary schools in Harrisburg-Lebanon-Carlisle, Pennsylvania

Ranking basis/background: Determined by each state's superintendent of instruction and the Council for American Private Education from evaluations of curricula and academic achievement, buildings and classrooms, classes and assemblies, cafeteria lunches, and interviews with students, parents, teachers, and administrators. **Number listed:** 4.

Feaser Middle School (Middletown)
Harrisburg Academy (Wormleysburg)

SCHOOLS, SECONDARY

Hershey High School (Hershey)
Trinity High School (Camp Hill)
Source: Savageau, David, *Places Rated Almanac*, Macmillan General Reference, 6th ed., 1999.

★4147★
Outstanding secondary schools in Hartford, Connecticut

Ranking basis/background: Determined by each state's superintendent of instruction and the Council for American Private Education from evaluations of curricula and academic achievement, buildings and classrooms, classes and assemblies, cafeteria lunches, and interviews with students, parents, teachers, and administrators. **Number listed:** 10.

Edwin Smith High School (Storrs)
Granby Memorial Middle School (Granby)
John Wallace Middle School (Newington)
Mansfield Middle School (Storrs)
RHAM High School (Hebron)
Silas Deane Middle School (Wethersfield)
Southington High School (Southington)
Union School (Unionville)
West District School (Unionville)
Wethersfield High School (Wethersfield)
Source: Savageau, David, *Places Rated Almanac*, Macmillan General Reference, 6th ed., 1999.

★4148★
Outstanding secondary schools in Hattiesburg, Mississippi

Ranking basis/background: Determined by each state's superintendent of instruction and the Council for American Private Education from evaluations of curricula and academic achievement, buildings and classrooms, classes and assemblies, cafeteria lunches, and interviews with students, parents, teachers, and administrators. **Number listed:** 1.

Oak Grove School
Source: Savageau, David, *Places Rated Almanac*, Macmillan General Reference, 6th ed., 1999.

★4149★
Outstanding secondary schools in Honolulu, Hawaii

Ranking basis/background: Determined by each state's superintendent of instruction and the Council for American Private Education from evaluations of curricula and academic achievement, buildings and classrooms, classes and assemblies, cafeteria lunches, and interviews with students, parents, teachers, and administrators. **Number listed:** 7.

ASSETS School (Honolulu)
Governor Dole Intermediate School (Honolulu)
James Castle High School (Kaneohe)
Kailua Intermediate School (Kailua)
Kaimuki Intermediate School (Honolulu)
Kalaheo High School (Kailua)
Leilehua High School (Wahiawa)
Source: Savageau, David, *Places Rated Almanac*, Macmillan General Reference, 6th ed., 1999.

★4150★
Outstanding secondary schools in Houston, Texas

Ranking basis/background: Determined by each state's superintendent of instruction and the Council for American Private Education from evaluations of curricula and academic achievement, buildings and classrooms, classes and assemblies, cafeteria lunches, and interviews with students, parents, teachers, and administrators. **Number listed:** 25.

Arnold Junior High School (Cypress)
Bleyl Junior High School (Houston)
BT Washington Junior High School (Conroe)
Duchesne Academy (Houston)
James Taylor High School (Katy)
Klein Oak High School (Spring)
Labay Junior High School (Houston)
Langham Creek High School (Houston)
Mayde Creek High School (Houston)
Michael DeBakey High School (Houston)
Northbrook Middle School (Houston)
Olle Middle School (Houston)
River Oaks Baptist School (Houston)
Rogers Education Center (Houston)
St. Thomas More Parish School (Houston)
Spring Branch Middle School (Houston)
Spring Forest Middle School (Houston)
Spring High School (Spring)
Spring Oaks Middle School (Houston)
Spring Woods High School (Houston)
Strack Intermediate School (Klein)
Thomas Stovall Junior High School (Houston)
Woodlands High School (The Woodlands)
Source: Savageau, David, *Places Rated Almanac*, Macmillan General Reference, 6th ed., 1999.

★4151★
Outstanding secondary schools in Huntington-Ashland, West Virginia-Kentucky-Ohio

Ranking basis/background: Determined by each state's superintendent of instruction and the Council for American Private Education from evaluations of curricula and academic achievement, buildings and classrooms, classes and assemblies, cafeteria lunches, and interviews with students, parents, teachers, and administrators. **Number listed:** 1.

Our Lady of Fatima School (Huntington)
Source: Savageau, David, *Places Rated Almanac*, Macmillan General Reference, 6th ed., 1999.

★4152★
Outstanding secondary schools in Huntsville, Alabama

Ranking basis/background: Determined by each state's superintendent of instruction and the Council for American Private Education from evaluations of curricula and academic achievement, buildings and classrooms, classes and assemblies, cafeteria lunches, and interviews with students, parents, teachers, and administrators. **Number listed:** 1.

Bob Jones High School (Madison)
Source: Savageau, David, *Places Rated Almanac*, Macmillan General Reference, 6th ed., 1999.

★4153★
Outstanding secondary schools in Indianapolis, Indiana

Ranking basis/background: Determined by each state's superintendent of instruction and the Council for American Private Education from evaluations of curricula and academic achievement, buildings and classrooms, classes and assemblies, cafeteria lunches, and interviews with students, parents, teachers, and administrators. **Number listed:** 6.

Hebrew Academy
Craig Middle School
Lutheran High School
Roncalli High School
St. Jude Catholic School
St. Lawrence Catholic School
Source: Savageau, David, *Places Rated Almanac*, Macmillan General Reference, 6th ed., 1999.

★4154★
Outstanding secondary schools in Jackson, Mississippi

Ranking basis/background: Determined by each state's superintendent of instruction and the Council for American Private Education from evaluations of curricula and academic achievement, buildings and classrooms, classes and assemblies, cafeteria lunches, and interviews with students, parents, teachers, and administrators. **Number listed:** 1.

Pearl High School (Pearl)
Source: Savageau, David, *Places Rated Almanac*, Macmillan General Reference, 6th ed., 1999.

★4155★
Outstanding secondary schools in Jacksonville, Florida

Ranking basis/background: Determined by each state's superintendent of instruction and the Council for American Private Education from evaluations of curricula and academic achievement, buildings and classrooms, classes and assemblies, cafeteria lunches, and interviews with students, parents, teachers, and administrators. **Number listed:** 1.

Landrum Middle School (Ponte Vedrea Beach)
Source: Savageau, David, *Places Rated Almanac*, Macmillan General Reference, 6th ed., 1999.

★4156★
Outstanding secondary schools in Janesville-Beloit, Wisconsin

Ranking basis/background: Determined by each state's superintendent of instruction and the Council for American Private Education from evaluations of curricula and academic achievement, buildings and classrooms, classes and assemblies, cafeteria lunches, and interviews with students, parents, teachers, and administrators. **Number listed:** 1.

St. Paul's Lutheran School (Janesville)
Source: Savageau, David, *Places Rated Almanac*, Macmillan General Reference, 6th ed., 1999.

★4157★
Outstanding secondary schools in Johnson City-Kingsport-Bristol, Tennessee-Virginia

Ranking basis/background: Determined by each state's superintendent of instruction and the Council for American Private Education from evaluations of curricula and academic achievement, buildings and classrooms, classes and assemblies, cafeteria lunches, and interviews with students, parents, teachers, and administrators. **Number listed:** 1.

Science Hill High School (Johnson City)
Source: Savageau, David, *Places Rated Almanac*, Macmillan General Reference, 6th ed., 1999.

★4158★
Outstanding secondary schools in Kansas City, Missouri-Kansas

Ranking basis/background: Determined by each state's superintendent of instruction and the Council for American Private Education from evaluations of curricula and academic achievement, buildings and classrooms, classes and assemblies, cafeteria lunches, and interviews with students, parents, teachers, and administrators. **Number listed:** 12.

Blue Valley North High School (Overland Park)
Genesis School (Kansas City)
Mission Valley Middle School (Shawnee Mission)

Oak Grove Middle School (Oak Grove)
Olathe East High School (Olathe)
Olathe South High School (Olathe)
Oregon Trail Junior High School (Olathe)
Oxford Middle School (Overland Park)
Rogers Academy (Kansas City)
Shawnee Mission South High School (Overland Park)
Truman High School (Independence)
Volker Magnet School (Kansas City)
Source: Savageau, David, *Places Rated Almanac*, Macmillan General Reference, 6th ed., 1999.

★4159★
Outstanding secondary schools in Knoxville, Tennessee

Ranking basis/background: Determined by each state's superintendent of instruction and the Council for American Private Education from evaluations of curricula and academic achievement, buildings and classrooms, classes and assemblies, cafeteria lunches, and interviews with students, parents, teachers, and administrators. **Number listed:** 3.
Farragut High School (Knoxville)
Maryville Middle School (Maryville)
Sacred Heart Cathedral School (Knoxville)
Source: Savageau, David, *Places Rated Almanac*, Macmillan General Reference, 6th ed., 1999.

★4160★
Outstanding secondary schools in La Crosse, Wisconsin-Minnesota

Ranking basis/background: Determined by each state's superintendent of instruction and the Council for American Private Education from evaluations of curricula and academic achievement, buildings and classrooms, classes and assemblies, cafeteria lunches, and interviews with students, parents, teachers, and administrators. **Number listed:** 1.
Onalaska Middle School (Onalaska)
Source: Savageau, David, *Places Rated Almanac*, Macmillan General Reference, 6th ed., 1999.

★4161★
Outstanding secondary schools in Lafayette, Indiana

Ranking basis/background: Determined by each state's superintendent of instruction and the Council for American Private Education from evaluations of curricula and academic achievement, buildings and classrooms, classes and assemblies, cafeteria lunches, and interviews with students, parents, teachers, and administrators. **Number listed:** 1.
Jefferson High School
Source: Savageau, David, *Places Rated Almanac*, Macmillan General Reference, 6th ed., 1999.

★4162★
Outstanding secondary schools in Lafayette, Louisiana

Ranking basis/background: Determined by each state's superintendent of instruction and the Council for American Private Education from evaluations of curricula and academic achievement, buildings and classrooms, classes and assemblies, cafeteria lunches, and interviews with students, parents, teachers, and administrators. **Number listed:** 1.
St. Thomas More High School
Source: Savageau, David, *Places Rated Almanac*, Macmillan General Reference, 6th ed., 1999.

★4163★
Outstanding secondary schools in Lansing-East Lansing, Michigan

Ranking basis/background: Determined by each state's superintendent of instruction and the Council for American Private Education from evaluations of curricula and academic achievement, buildings and classrooms, classes and assemblies, cafeteria lunches, and interviews with students, parents, teachers, and administrators. **Number listed:** 2.
Everett High School (Lansing)
Holt High School (Holt)
Source: Savageau, David, *Places Rated Almanac*, Macmillan General Reference, 6th ed., 1999.

★4164★
Outstanding secondary schools in Las Vegas, Nevada-Arizona

Ranking basis/background: Determined by each state's superintendent of instruction and the Council for American Private Education from evaluations of curricula and academic achievement, buildings and classrooms, classes and assemblies, cafeteria lunches, and interviews with students, parents, teachers, and administrators. **Number listed:** 1.
O'Callaghan Middle School (Las Vegas)
Source: Savageau, David, *Places Rated Almanac*, Macmillan General Reference, 6th ed., 1999.

★4165★
Outstanding secondary schools in Long Island, New York

Ranking basis/background: Determined by each state's superintendent of instruction and the Council for American Private Education from evaluations of curricula and academic achievement, buildings and classrooms, classes and assemblies, cafeteria lunches, and interviews with students, parents, teachers, and administrators. **Number listed:** 19.
Baldwin High School (Baldwin)
Elmont Memorial High School (Elmont)
Floral Park Memorial High School (Floral Park)
Green Vale High School (Glen Head)
Herricks Middle School (Albertson)
Jericho High School (Jericho)
Longwood Middle School (Middle Island)
Lynbrook High School (Lynbrook)
New Hyde Park Memorial High School (New Hyde Park)
North Shore High School (Glen Head)
Our Lady of the Hamptons Regional (Southampton)
Sacred Heart Academy (Hempstead)
St. Joseph's School (Long Island)
Sewanhaka High School (Floral Park)
South Side High School (Rockville Centre)
Syosset High School (Syosset)
Wantagh High School (Wantagh)
Wantagh Middle School (Wantagh)
Source: Savageau, David, *Places Rated Almanac*, Macmillan General Reference, 6th ed., 1999.

★4166★
Outstanding secondary schools in Longview-Marshall, Texas

Ranking basis/background: Determined by each state's superintendent of instruction and the Council for American Private Education from evaluations of curricula and academic achievement, buildings and classrooms, classes and assemblies, cafeteria lunches, and interviews with students, parents, teachers, and administrators. **Number listed:** 4.
Forest Park Middle School (Longview)
Pine Tree High School (Longview)
Pine Tree Junior High School (Longview)
Pine Tree Middle School (Longview)
Source: Savageau, David, *Places Rated Almanac*, Macmillan General Reference, 6th ed., 1999.

★4167★
Outstanding secondary schools in Los Angeles-Long Beach, California

Ranking basis/background: Determined by each state's superintendent of instruction and the Council for American Private Education from evaluations of curricula and academic achievement, buildings and classrooms, classes and assemblies, cafeteria lunches, and interviews with students, parents, teachers, and administrators. **Number listed:** 31.
Alvarado Intermediate School (Rowland Heights)
Calle Mayor Middle School (Torrance)
Carmenita Junior High School (Cerritos)
Center for Enriched Studies (Los Angeles)
Chaminade Prep (Chatsworth)
Culver City High School (Culver City)
Dana Middle School (Arcadia)
El Monte High School (El Monte)
Flintridge Sacred Heart Academy (La Canada)
Harkham Hillel Hebrew Academy (Beverly Hills)
Huntington Middle School (San Marino)
La Canada High School (La Canada)
Louisville High School (Woodland Hills)
Manhattan Beach Intermediate School (Manhattan Beach)
Mayfield Junior High School of the Holy Child (Pasadena)
Medea Creek Middle School (Agoura)
Mira Costa High School (Manhattan Beach)
Notre Dame Academy (Los Angeles)
Notre Dame High School (Sherman Oaks)
Oak Park High School (Agoura)
Pacific School (Manhattan Beach)
Parras Middle School (Redondo Beach)
Providence High School (Burbank)
Ramona Convent High School (Alhambra)
Rosemont Middle School (La Crescenta)
Rowland High School (Rowland Heights)
St. James Episcopal School (Los Angeles)
St. Thomas the Apostle School (Los Angeles)
South Pasadena Middle School (South Pasadena)
Walnut High School (Walnut)
Whitney High School (Cerritos)
Source: Savageau, David, *Places Rated Almanac*, Macmillan General Reference, 6th ed., 1999.

★4168★
Outstanding secondary schools in Louisville, Kentucky-Indiana

Ranking basis/background: Determined by each state's superintendent of instruction and the Council for American Private Education from evaluations of curricula and academic achievement, buildings and classrooms, classes and assemblies, cafeteria lunches, and interviews with students, parents, teachers, and administrators. **Number listed:** 9.
Assumption High School (Louisville)
DuPont Manual Magnet High School (Louisville)
Floyd Central High School (Floyds Knobs)
Louisville Male High School (Louisville)
Sacred Heart Academy (Louisville)
St. Xavier High School (Louisville)

SCHOOLS, SECONDARY

St. Raphael the Archangel (Louisville)
South Oldham High School (Crestwood)
Trinity High School (Louisville)
Source: Savageau, David, *Places Rated Almanac*, Macmillan General Reference, 6th ed., 1999.

★4169★
Outstanding secondary schools in Lowell, Maine-New Hampshire
Ranking basis/background: Determined by each state's superintendent of instruction and the Council for American Private Education from evaluations of curricula and academic achievement, buildings and classrooms, classes and assemblies, cafeteria lunches, and interviews with students, parents, teachers, and administrators. **Number listed:** 1.
Lighthouse School (Chelmsford)
Source: Savageau, David, *Places Rated Almanac*, Macmillan General Reference, 6th ed., 1999.

★4170★
Outstanding secondary schools in Lubbock, Texas
Ranking basis/background: Determined by each state's superintendent of instruction and the Council for American Private Education from evaluations of curricula and academic achievement, buildings and classrooms, classes and assemblies, cafeteria lunches, and interviews with students, parents, teachers, and administrators. **Number listed:** 2.
Lubbock High School
All Saints Episcopal School
Source: Savageau, David, *Places Rated Almanac*, Macmillan General Reference, 6th ed., 1999.

★4171★
Outstanding secondary schools in Lynchburg, Virginia
Ranking basis/background: Determined by each state's superintendent of instruction and the Council for American Private Education from evaluations of curricula and academic achievement, buildings and classrooms, classes and assemblies, cafeteria lunches, and interviews with students, parents, teachers, and administrators. **Number listed:** 2.
Glass High School
Heritage High School
Source: Savageau, David, *Places Rated Almanac*, Macmillan General Reference, 6th ed., 1999.

★4172★
Outstanding secondary schools in Macon, Georgia
Ranking basis/background: Determined by each state's superintendent of instruction and the Council for American Private Education from evaluations of curricula and academic achievement, buildings and classrooms, classes and assemblies, cafeteria lunches, and interviews with students, parents, teachers, and administrators. **Number listed:** 3.
Houston County High School (Warner Robins)
Mount de Sales Academy (Macon)
Warner Robins High School (Warner Robins)
Source: Savageau, David, *Places Rated Almanac*, Macmillan General Reference, 6th ed., 1999.

★4173★
Outstanding secondary schools in Madison, Wisconsin
Ranking basis/background: Determined by each state's superintendent of instruction and the Council for American Private Education from evaluations of curricula and academic achievement, buildings and classrooms, classes and assemblies, cafeteria lunches, and interviews with students, parents, teachers, and administrators. **Number listed:** 1.
James Madison High School
Source: Savageau, David, *Places Rated Almanac*, Macmillan General Reference, 6th ed., 1999.

★4174★
Outstanding secondary schools in Mansfield, Ohio
Ranking basis/background: Determined by each state's superintendent of instruction and the Council for American Private Education from evaluations of curricula and academic achievement, buildings and classrooms, classes and assemblies, cafeteria lunches, and interviews with students, parents, teachers, and administrators. **Number listed:** 1.
St. Peter's High School
Source: Savageau, David, *Places Rated Almanac*, Macmillan General Reference, 6th ed., 1999.

★4175★
Outstanding secondary schools in McAllen-Edinburg-Mission, Texas
Ranking basis/background: Determined by each state's superintendent of instruction and the Council for American Private Education from evaluations of curricula and academic achievement, buildings and classrooms, classes and assemblies, cafeteria lunches, and interviews with students, parents, teachers, and administrators. **Number listed:** 1.
Travis Middle School (McAllen)
Source: Savageau, David, *Places Rated Almanac*, Macmillan General Reference, 6th ed., 1999.

★4176★
Outstanding secondary schools in Melbourne-Titusville-Palm Bay, Florida
Ranking basis/background: Determined by each state's superintendent of instruction and the Council for American Private Education from evaluations of curricula and academic achievement, buildings and classrooms, classes and assemblies, cafeteria lunches, and interviews with students, parents, teachers, and administrators. **Number listed:** 2.
Melbourne Central Catholic High School (Melbourne)
St. Joseph Catholic School (Palm Bay)
Source: Savageau, David, *Places Rated Almanac*, Macmillan General Reference, 6th ed., 1999.

★4177★
Outstanding secondary schools in Memphis, Tennessee-Arkansas-Mississippi
Ranking basis/background: Determined by each state's superintendent of instruction and the Council for American Private Education from evaluations of curricula and academic achievement, buildings and classrooms, classes and assemblies, cafeteria lunches, and interviews with students, parents, teachers, and administrators. **Number listed:** 3.
Craigmont High School (Memphis)
Germantown High School (Germantown)
St. Mary's Episcopal School (Memphis)
Source: Savageau, David, *Places Rated Almanac*, Macmillan General Reference, 6th ed., 1999.

★4178★
Outstanding secondary schools in Miami, Florida
Ranking basis/background: Determined by each state's superintendent of instruction and the Council for American Private Education from evaluations of curricula and academic achievement, buildings and classrooms, classes and assemblies, cafeteria lunches, and interviews with students, parents, teachers, and administrators. **Number listed:** 11.
Arvida Middle School (Miami)
The Cushman School (Miami)
Design and Architecture High School (Miami)
George Washington Carver Middle School (Miami)
Gulliver Academy (Coral Gables)
Gulliver Prep (Miami)
MAST Academy (Miami)
New World School of the Arts (Miami)
Our Lady of Lourdes Academy (Miami)
St. Rose of Lima (Miami Shores)
Thomas Jefferson Middle School (Miami)
Source: Savageau, David, *Places Rated Almanac*, Macmillan General Reference, 6th ed., 1999.

★4179★
Outstanding secondary schools in Middlesex-Somerset-Hunterdon, New Jersey
Ranking basis/background: Determined by each state's superintendent of instruction and the Council for American Private Education from evaluations of curricula and academic achievement, buildings and classrooms, classes and assemblies, cafeteria lunches, and interviews with students, parents, teachers, and administrators. **Number listed:** 14.
Churchill Junior High School (Brunswick)
Crossroads Middle School (Monmouth Junction)
East Brunswick High School (East Brunswick)
Hammarskjold Middle School (East Brunswick)
Hillcrest Magnet School (Somerset)
Hillsborough Middle School (Somerset)
Hunterdon Central Regional High School (Flemington)
Immaculata High School (Somerville)
Montgomery High School (Skillman)
Rutgers Prep (Somerset)
South Brunswick High School (Monmouth Junction)
Spotswood High School (Spotswood)
Midland School (North Branch)
Watchung Hills Regional High School (Warren)
Source: Savageau, David, *Places Rated Almanac*, Macmillan General Reference, 6th ed., 1999.

★4180★
Outstanding secondary schools in Milwaukee-Waukesha, Wisconsin
Ranking basis/background: Determined by each state's superintendent of instruction and the Council for American Private Education from evaluations of curricula and academic achievement, buildings and classrooms, classes and assemblies, cafeteria lunches, and interviews with students, parents, teachers, and administrators. **Number listed:** 13.
Bayside Middle School (Milwaukee)
Custer High School (Milwaukee)
Fritsche Middle School (Milwaukee)
Milwaukee Lutheran High School (Milwaukee)

Milwaukee Trade High School (Milwaukee)
Nicolet High School (Glendale)
Oconomowoc High School (Oconomowoc)
Pius XI High School (Milwaukee)
Rufus King High School (Milwaukee)
St. Alphonsus School (Greendale)
Samuel Morse Middle School (Milwaukee)
Thomas Jefferson Middle School (Port Washington)
Thomas More High School (Milwaukee)
Source: Savageau, David, *Places Rated Almanac*, Macmillan General Reference, 6th ed., 1999.

★4181★
Outstanding secondary schools in Minneapolis-St. Paul, Minnesota-Wisconsin

Ranking basis/background: Determined by each state's superintendent of instruction and the Council for American Private Education from evaluations of curricula and academic achievement, buildings and classrooms, classes and assemblies, cafeteria lunches, and interviews with students, parents, teachers, and administrators. **Number listed:** 26.
Academy of Holy Angels (Richfield)
Apple Valley High School (Apple Valley)
Benilde St. Margaret's High School (St. Louis Park)
The Blake Lower School (Minneapolis)
The Blake School (Minneapolis)
Breck School (Minneapolis)
Cedar Manor Intermediate School (St. Louis Park)
Central High School (St. Paul)
Cretin-Derham Hall School (St. Paul)
Dassel-Cokato High School (Cokato)
Eagan High School (Eagan)
Eden Prairie High School (Eden Prairie)
Farmington Middle School (Farmington)
Groves Academy (St. Louis Park)
Hastings Middle School (Hastings)
Highland Park High School (St. Paul)
Hosterman Middle School (New Hope)
Irondale High School (New Brighton)
Mounds Park Academy Lower School (St. Paul)
Oak Grove Intermediate School (Bloomington)
St. Anthony Middle School (St. Anthony Village)
Shakopee Junior High School (Shakopee)
Stillwater Junior High School (Stillwater)
Trinity School (Bloomington)
Valley Middle School (Apple Valley)
Wayzata High School (Plymouth)
Source: Savageau, David, *Places Rated Almanac*, Macmillan General Reference, 6th ed., 1999.

★4182★
Outstanding secondary schools in Mobile, Alabama

Ranking basis/background: Determined by each state's superintendent of instruction and the Council for American Private Education from evaluations of curricula and academic achievement, buildings and classrooms, classes and assemblies, cafeteria lunches, and interviews with students, parents, teachers, and administrators. **Number listed:** 3.
Davidson High School
Phillips Prep
St. Ignatius School
Source: Savageau, David, *Places Rated Almanac*, Macmillan General Reference, 6th ed., 1999.

★4183★
Outstanding secondary schools in Monmouth-Ocean, New Jersey

Ranking basis/background: Determined by each state's superintendent of instruction and the Council for American Private Education from evaluations of curricula and academic achievement, buildings and classrooms, classes and assemblies, cafeteria lunches, and interviews with students, parents, teachers, and administrators. **Number listed:** 2.
High Tech High School (Lincroft)
Marine Academy (Sandy Hook)
Source: Savageau, David, *Places Rated Almanac*, Macmillan General Reference, 6th ed., 1999.

★4184★
Outstanding secondary schools in Myrtle Beach, South Carolina

Ranking basis/background: Determined by each state's superintendent of instruction and the Council for American Private Education from evaluations of curricula and academic achievement, buildings and classrooms, classes and assemblies, cafeteria lunches, and interviews with students, parents, teachers, and administrators. **Number listed:** 3.
Conway Middle School (Conway)
Socastee High School (Myrtle Beach)
St. James Middle School (Surfside Beach)
Source: Savageau, David, *Places Rated Almanac*, Macmillan General Reference, 6th ed., 1999.

★4185★
Outstanding secondary schools in Nashua, New Hampshire

Ranking basis/background: Determined by each state's superintendent of instruction and the Council for American Private Education from evaluations of curricula and academic achievement, buildings and classrooms, classes and assemblies, cafeteria lunches, and interviews with students, parents, teachers, and administrators. **Number listed:** 1.
Amherst Middle School (Amherst)
Source: Savageau, David, *Places Rated Almanac*, Macmillan General Reference, 6th ed., 1999.

★4186★
Outstanding secondary schools in Nashville, Tennessee

Ranking basis/background: Determined by each state's superintendent of instruction and the Council for American Private Education from evaluations of curricula and academic achievement, buildings and classrooms, classes and assemblies, cafeteria lunches, and interviews with students, parents, teachers, and administrators. **Number listed:** 4.
Eagleville School (Eagleville)
Glendale Middle School (Nashville)
St. Cecilia Academy (Nashville)
Wright Middle School (Nashville)
Source: Savageau, David, *Places Rated Almanac*, Macmillan General Reference, 6th ed., 1999.

★4187★
Outstanding secondary schools in New Bedford, Massachusetts

Ranking basis/background: Determined by each state's superintendent of instruction and the Council for American Private Education from evaluations of curricula and academic achievement, buildings and classrooms, classes and assemblies, cafeteria lunches, and interviews with students, parents, teachers, and administrators. **Number listed:** 1.
Bishop Stang High School (North Dartmouth)
Source: Savageau, David, *Places Rated Almanac*, Macmillan General Reference, 6th ed., 1999.

★4188★
Outstanding secondary schools in New Haven-Meriden, Connecticut

Ranking basis/background: Determined by each state's superintendent of instruction and the Council for American Private Education from evaluations of curricula and academic achievement, buildings and classrooms, classes and assemblies, cafeteria lunches, and interviews with students, parents, teachers, and administrators. **Number listed:** 3.
Dodd Middle School (Cheshire)
Sacred Heart Academy (Hamden)
The Peck Place School (Orange)
Source: Savageau, David, *Places Rated Almanac*, Macmillan General Reference, 6th ed., 1999.

★4189★
Outstanding secondary schools in New London-Norwich, Connecticut-Rhode Island

Ranking basis/background: Determined by each state's superintendent of instruction and the Council for American Private Education from evaluations of curricula and academic achievement, buildings and classrooms, classes and assemblies, cafeteria lunches, and interviews with students, parents, teachers, and administrators. **Number listed:** 2.
Plainfield Central Middle School (Plainfield)
Old Saybrook Middle School (Old Saybrook)
Source: Savageau, David, *Places Rated Almanac*, Macmillan General Reference, 6th ed., 1999.

★4190★
Outstanding secondary schools in New Orleans, Louisiana

Ranking basis/background: Determined by each state's superintendent of instruction and the Council for American Private Education from evaluations of curricula and academic achievement, buildings and classrooms, classes and assemblies, cafeteria lunches, and interviews with students, parents, teachers, and administrators. **Number listed:** 16.
Archbishop Blenk High School (Gretna)
Archbishop Chapelle High School (Metairie)
De La Salle High School (New Orleans)
McDonogh High School (New Orleans)
McMain Magnet High School (New Orleans)
Mount Carmel Academy (New Orleans)
Our Lady of Divine Providence (Metairie)
St. Benilde (Metairie)
St. Christopher (Metairie)
St. Frances Xavier Cabrini (New Orleans)
St. Mary's Dominican High School (New Orleans)
St. Paul's Episcopal School (New Orleans)
St. Scholastica Academy (Covington)
Ursuline Academy (New Orleans)
Warren Easton Fundamental High School (New Orleans)
Xavier Prep (New Orleans)
Source: Savageau, David, *Places Rated Almanac*, Macmillan General Reference, 6th ed., 1999.

SCHOOLS, SECONDARY

★4191★
Outstanding secondary schools in New York, New York

Ranking basis/background: Determined by each state's superintendent of instruction and the Council for American Private Education from evaluations of curricula and academic achievement, buildings and classrooms, classes and assemblies, cafeteria lunches, and interviews with students, parents, teachers, and administrators. **Number listed:** 34.

- Alexander Hamilton High School (Elmsford)
- Berkeley Carroll School (Brooklyn)
- Bowne High School (Flushing)
- Bronxville High School (Bronxville)
- Catherine McAuley High School (Brooklyn)
- Covent Sacred Heart High School (New York)
- Dominican Academy (New York)
- Eastchester High School (Eastchester)
- Forest Hills High School (Forest Hills)
- Fox Lane High School (Bedford)
- Irvington High School (Irvington)
- Isaac Young Middle School (New Rochelle)
- Louis Klein Middle School (Harrison)
- Midwood High School at Brooklyn College (Brooklyn)
- Mother Cabrini High School (New York)
- Mount St. Michael Academy (Bronx)
- New Rochelle High School (New Rochelle)
- Pelham Memorial High School (Pelham)
- Pelham Middle School (Pelham)
- Pleasantville High School (Pleasantville)
- Rice High School (New York)
- Rye Neck High School (Mamaroneck)
- Sacred Heart/Mount Carmel (Mount Carmel)
- St. Catharine Academy (Bronx)
- St. Raymond High School for Boys (Bronx)
- Salanter Akiba Academy (Riverdale)
- Saunders Trades and Tech High School (Yonkers)
- Shenendehowa High School (Clifton Park)
- Shulamith High School for Girls (Brooklyn)
- Urban Academy (New York)
- The Ursuline School (New Rochelle)
- Webster Magnet School (New Rochelle)
- Xavier High School (New York)
- Yeshiva of Central Queens (Flushing)

Source: Savageau, David, *Places Rated Almanac*, Macmillan General Reference, 6th ed., 1999.

★4192★
Outstanding secondary schools in Newark, New Jersey

Ranking basis/background: Determined by each state's superintendent of instruction and the Council for American Private Education from evaluations of curricula and academic achievement, buildings and classrooms, classes and assemblies, cafeteria lunches, and interviews with students, parents, teachers, and administrators. **Number listed:** 5.

- Columbia High School (Maplewood)
- High Point Regional High School (Sussex)
- Kimberley Academy (Montclair)
- Kittatinny Regional High School (Newton)
- Livingston High School (Livingston)

Source: Savageau, David, *Places Rated Almanac*, Macmillan General Reference, 6th ed., 1999.

★4193★
Outstanding secondary schools in Newburgh, New York-Pennsylvania

Ranking basis/background: Determined by each state's superintendent of instruction and the Council for American Private Education from evaluations of curricula and academic achievement, buildings and classrooms, classes and assemblies, cafeteria lunches, and interviews with students, parents, teachers, and administrators. **Number listed:** 1.

- Horizons Magnet School

Source: Savageau, David, *Places Rated Almanac*, Macmillan General Reference, 6th ed., 1999.

★4194★
Outstanding secondary schools in Norfolk-Virginia Beach-Newport News, Virginia-North Carolina

Ranking basis/background: Determined by each state's superintendent of instruction and the Council for American Private Education from evaluations of curricula and academic achievement, buildings and classrooms, classes and assemblies, cafeteria lunches, and interviews with students, parents, teachers, and administrators. **Number listed:** 7.

- Cape Henry Collegiate (Virginia Beach)
- Gildersleeve Middle School (Newport News)
- Hampton Roads Academy (Newport News)
- Hines Middle School (Newport News)
- Norfolk Academy Lower School (Norfolk)
- Northside Middle School (Norfolk)
- Syms Middle School (Hampton)

Source: Savageau, David, *Places Rated Almanac*, Macmillan General Reference, 6th ed., 1999.

★4195★
Outstanding secondary schools in Oakland, California

Ranking basis/background: Determined by each state's superintendent of instruction and the Council for American Private Education from evaluations of curricula and academic achievement, buildings and classrooms, classes and assemblies, cafeteria lunches, and interviews with students, parents, teachers, and administrators. **Number listed:** 12.

- Alameda High School (Alameda)
- Alvarado Middle School (Union City)
- Bishop O'Dowd High School (Oakland)
- Charlotte Wood Middle School (Danville)
- Holy Names High School (Oakland)
- Irvington High School (Fremont)
- Miramonte High School (Orinda)
- Mission San Jose High School (Fremont)
- St. Isidore (Danville)
- St. Joseph (Fremont)
- San Lorenzo High School (San Lorenzo)
- Stone Valley Middle School (Alamo)

Source: Savageau, David, *Places Rated Almanac*, Macmillan General Reference, 6th ed., 1999.

★4196★
Outstanding secondary schools in Oklahoma City, Oklahoma

Ranking basis/background: Determined by each state's superintendent of instruction and the Council for American Private Education from evaluations of curricula and academic achievement, buildings and classrooms, classes and assemblies, cafeteria lunches, and interviews with students, parents, teachers, and administrators. **Number listed:** 3.

- Cimarron Middle School (Edmond)
- Sequoyah Middle School (Edmond)
- Summit Middle School (Edmond)

Source: Savageau, David, *Places Rated Almanac*, Macmillan General Reference, 6th ed., 1999.

★4197★
Outstanding secondary schools in Olympia, Washington

Ranking basis/background: Determined by each state's superintendent of instruction and the Council for American Private Education from evaluations of curricula and academic achievement, buildings and classrooms, classes and assemblies, cafeteria lunches, and interviews with students, parents, teachers, and administrators. **Number listed:** 2.

- Capital High School (Olympia)
- New Century High School (Lacey)

Source: Savageau, David, *Places Rated Almanac*, Macmillan General Reference, 6th ed., 1999.

★4198★
Outstanding secondary schools in Omaha, Nebraska-Iowa

Ranking basis/background: Determined by each state's superintendent of instruction and the Council for American Private Education from evaluations of curricula and academic achievement, buildings and classrooms, classes and assemblies, cafeteria lunches, and interviews with students, parents, teachers, and administrators. **Number listed:** 8.

- Duchesne Academy (Omaha)
- Gretna High School (Gretna)
- Marian High School (Omaha)
- Millard Central High School (Omaha)
- Ralston High School (Ralston)
- Valley Middle/High School (Valley)
- Westside High School (Omaha)
- Westside Middle School (Omaha)

Source: Savageau, David, *Places Rated Almanac*, Macmillan General Reference, 6th ed., 1999.

★4199★
Outstanding secondary schools in Orange County, California

Ranking basis/background: Determined by each state's superintendent of instruction and the Council for American Private Education from evaluations of curricula and academic achievement, buildings and classrooms, classes and assemblies, cafeteria lunches, and interviews with students, parents, teachers, and administrators. **Number listed:** 20.

- Brea Olinda High School (Brea)
- Corona del Mar High School (Newport Beach)
- Fairmont Junior High School (Anaheim)
- Foothill High School (Santa Ana)
- Hebrew Academy (Westminster)
- Hewes Middle School (La Habra)
- La Habra High School (La Habra)
- La Paz Intermediate School (Mission Viejo)
- Laguna Beach High School (Laguna Beach)
- Laguna Hills High School (Laguna Hills)
- Lakeside Middle School (Irvine)
- Los Alamitos High School (Los Alamitos)
- Los Alisos Intermediate School (Mission Viejo)
- Mission Viejo High School (Mission Viejo)
- Newhart Middle School (Mission Viejo)
- Rancho San Joaquin Middle School (Irvine)
- Santa Margarita High School (Rancho Santa)
- Venado Middle School (Irvine)
- Westminster High School (Westminster)

★4200★
Outstanding secondary schools in Orlando, Florida

Ranking basis/background: Determined by each state's superintendent of instruction and the Council for American Private Education from evaluations of curricula and academic achievement, buildings and classrooms, classes and assemblies, cafeteria lunches, and interviews with students, parents, teachers, and administrators. **Number listed:** 3.

   Apopka High School (Apopka)
   Neptune Middle School (Kissimmee)
   University High School (Orlando)

Source: Savageau, David, *Places Rated Almanac*, Macmillan General Reference, 6th ed., 1999.

★4201★
Outstanding secondary schools in Pensacola, Florida

Ranking basis/background: Determined by each state's superintendent of instruction and the Council for American Private Education from evaluations of curricula and academic achievement, buildings and classrooms, classes and assemblies, cafeteria lunches, and interviews with students, parents, teachers, and administrators. **Number listed:** 1.

   Pensacola Catholic High School

Source: Savageau, David, *Places Rated Almanac*, Macmillan General Reference, 6th ed., 1999.

★4202★
Outstanding secondary schools in Philadelphia, Pennsylvania-New Jersey

Ranking basis/background: Determined by each state's superintendent of instruction and the Council for American Private Education from evaluations of curricula and academic achievement, buildings and classrooms, classes and assemblies, cafeteria lunches, and interviews with students, parents, teachers, and administrators. **Number listed:** 28.

   Abington High School (Abington)
   Ancillae-Assumpta Academy (Wyncote)
   Arcola Intermediate School (Norristown)
   East High School (West Chester)
   Franklin Learning Center (Philadelphia)
   Fugett Middle School (West Chester)
   General Wayne Middle School (Malvern)
   Gordon Middle School (Coatesville)
   Gwynedd Mercy Academy (Gwynedd Valley)
   Harriton High School (Rosemont)
   Hatboro-Horsham High School (Horsham)
   Holy Ghost Prep (Bensalem)
   Indian Valley Middle School (Harleysville)
   Keith Valley Middle School (Horsham)
   Lower Moreland High School (Huntingdon Valley)
   Masterman School (Philadelphia)
   Merion Mercy Academy (Merion Station)
   Mount St. Joseph Academy (Flourtown)
   North Penn High School (Lansdale)
   Radnor High School (Radnor)
   South Brandywine Middle School (Coatesville)
   Tamanend Middle School (Warrington)
   Upper Dublin High School (Fort Washington)
   Upper Moreland Middle School (Hatboro)
   Upper Perkiomen High School (Pennsburg)
   Upper Perkiomen Middle School (East Greenville)
   Villa Joseph Marie High School (Holland)
   West Philadelphia Catholic High School (Philadelphia)

Source: Savageau, David, *Places Rated Almanac*, Macmillan General Reference, 6th ed., 1999.

★4203★
Outstanding secondary schools in Phoenix-Mesa, Arizona

Ranking basis/background: Determined by each state's superintendent of instruction and the Council for American Private Education from evaluations of curricula and academic achievement, buildings and classrooms, classes and assemblies, cafeteria lunches, and interviews with students, parents, teachers, and administrators. **Number listed:** 9.

   Desert Sky Middle School (Glendale)
   Greenway High School (Phoenix)
   Mohave Middle School (Scottsdale)
   Red Mountain High School (Mesa)
   Rhodes Junior High School (Mesa)
   Saguaro High School (Scottsdale)
   St. Thomas the Apostle School (Phoenix)
   Western Sky Middle School (Goodyear)
   Xavier Prep (Phoenix)

Source: Savageau, David, *Places Rated Almanac*, Macmillan General Reference, 6th ed., 1999.

★4204★
Outstanding secondary schools in Pittsburgh, Pennsylvania

Ranking basis/background: Determined by each state's superintendent of instruction and the Council for American Private Education from evaluations of curricula and academic achievement, buildings and classrooms, classes and assemblies, cafeteria lunches, and interviews with students, parents, teachers, and administrators. **Number listed:** 16.

   Boyce Middle School (Upper St. Clair)
   Carson Middle School (Pittsburgh)
   Dorseyville Middle School (Pittsburgh)
   Fort Couch Middle School (Upper St. Clair)
   Fox Chapel Area High School (Pittsburgh)
   Gateway High School (Monroeville)
   Hampton High School (Allison Park)
   Independence Middle School (Bethel Park)
   Ingomar Middle School (Pittsburgh)
   Mount Lebanon High School (Pittsburgh)
   Mount Lebanon Junior High School (Pittsburgh)
   North Allegheny High School (Wexford)
   Quaker Valley High School (Leetsdale)
   Sewickley Academy (Sewickley)
   Shaler Area Middle School (Glenshaw)
   Taylor Allderdice High School (Pittsburgh)

Source: Savageau, David, *Places Rated Almanac*, Macmillan General Reference, 6th ed., 1999.

★4205★
Outstanding secondary schools in Portland, Maine

Ranking basis/background: Determined by each state's superintendent of instruction and the Council for American Private Education from evaluations of curricula and academic achievement, buildings and classrooms, classes and assemblies, cafeteria lunches, and interviews with students, parents, teachers, and administrators. **Number listed:** 1.

   Old Orchard Beach High School (Old Orchard Beach)

Source: Savageau, David, *Places Rated Almanac*, Macmillan General Reference, 6th ed., 1999.

★4206★
Outstanding secondary schools in Portland-Vancouver, Oregon-Washington

Ranking basis/background: Determined by each state's superintendent of instruction and the Council for American Private Education from evaluations of curricula and academic achievement, buildings and classrooms, classes and assemblies, cafeteria lunches, and interviews with students, parents, teachers, and administrators. **Number listed:** 3.

   Jemtegaard Middle School (Washougal)
   Jesuit High School (Portland)
   St. Mary's Academy (Portland)

Source: Savageau, David, *Places Rated Almanac*, Macmillan General Reference, 6th ed., 1999.

★4207★
Outstanding secondary schools in Providence-Fall River-Warwick, Rhode Island-Maine

Ranking basis/background: Determined by each state's superintendent of instruction and the Council for American Private Education from evaluations of curricula and academic achievement, buildings and classrooms, classes and assemblies, cafeteria lunches, and interviews with students, parents, teachers, and administrators. **Number listed:** 8.

   Bishop Hendricken High School (Warwick)
   Davisville Middle School (North Kingstown)
   La Salle Academy (Providence)
   Mercymount Country Day School (Cumberland)
   Mount St. Charles Academy (Woonsocket)
   St. Luke School (Barrington)
   St. Mary Academy (Riverside)
   St. Rocco School (Johnston)

Source: Savageau, David, *Places Rated Almanac*, Macmillan General Reference, 6th ed., 1999.

★4208★
Outstanding secondary schools in Punta Gorda, Florida

Ranking basis/background: Determined by each state's superintendent of instruction and the Council for American Private Education from evaluations of curricula and academic achievement, buildings and classrooms, classes and assemblies, cafeteria lunches, and interviews with students, parents, teachers, and administrators. **Number listed:** 1.

   Murdock Middle School (Port Charlotte)

Source: Savageau, David, *Places Rated Almanac*, Macmillan General Reference, 6th ed., 1999.

★4209★
Outstanding secondary schools in Reading, Pennsylvania

Ranking basis/background: Determined by each state's superintendent of instruction and the Council for American Private Education from evaluations of curricula and academic achievement, buildings and classrooms, classes and assemblies, cafeteria lunches, and interviews with students, parents, teachers, and administrators. **Number listed:** 1.

   Wyomissing Area High School (Wyomissing)

Source: Savageau, David, *Places Rated Almanac*, Macmillan General Reference, 6th ed., 1999.

SCHOOLS, SECONDARY

★4210★
Outstanding secondary schools in Richmond-Petersburg, Virginia

Ranking basis/background: Determined by each state's superintendent of instruction and the Council for American Private Education from evaluations of curricula and academic achievement, buildings and classrooms, classes and assemblies, cafeteria lunches, and interviews with students, parents, teachers, and administrators. **Number listed:** 5.

- Freeman High School (Henrico County)
- Liberty Middle School (Asland)
- St. Gertrude High School (Richmond)
- Stonewall Jackson Middle School (Mechanicsville)
- Tuckahoe Middle School (Richmond)

Source: Savageau, David, *Places Rated Almanac*, Macmillan General Reference, 6th ed., 1999.

★4211★
Outstanding secondary schools in Riverside-San Bernardino, California

Ranking basis/background: Determined by each state's superintendent of instruction and the Council for American Private Education from evaluations of curricula and academic achievement, buildings and classrooms, classes and assemblies, cafeteria lunches, and interviews with students, parents, teachers, and administrators. **Number listed:** 3.

- Eisenhower High School (Rialto)
- University Heights Middle School (Riverside)
- Vineyard Junior High School (Alta Loma)

Source: Savageau, David, *Places Rated Almanac*, Macmillan General Reference, 6th ed., 1999.

★4212★
Outstanding secondary schools in Roanoke, Virginia

Ranking basis/background: Determined by each state's superintendent of instruction and the Council for American Private Education from evaluations of curricula and academic achievement, buildings and classrooms, classes and assemblies, cafeteria lunches, and interviews with students, parents, teachers, and administrators. **Number listed:** 1.

- Highland Park Magnet School

Source: Savageau, David, *Places Rated Almanac*, Macmillan General Reference, 6th ed., 1999.

★4213★
Outstanding secondary schools in Rochester, New York

Ranking basis/background: Determined by each state's superintendent of instruction and the Council for American Private Education from evaluations of curricula and academic achievement, buildings and classrooms, classes and assemblies, cafeteria lunches, and interviews with students, parents, teachers, and administrators. **Number listed:** 1.

- Canadaigua Academy (Canadaigua)

Source: Savageau, David, *Places Rated Almanac*, Macmillan General Reference, 6th ed., 1999.

★4214★
Outstanding secondary schools in Rockford, Illinois

Ranking basis/background: Determined by each state's superintendent of instruction and the Council for American Private Education from evaluations of curricula and academic achievement, buildings and classrooms, classes and assemblies, cafeteria lunches, and interviews with students, parents, teachers, and administrators. **Number listed:** 1.

- Boylan Central Catholic High School (Rockford)

Source: Savageau, David, *Places Rated Almanac*, Macmillan General Reference, 6th ed., 1999.

★4215★
Outstanding secondary schools in Sacramento, California

Ranking basis/background: Determined by each state's superintendent of instruction and the Council for American Private Education from evaluations of curricula and academic achievement, buildings and classrooms, classes and assemblies, cafeteria lunches, and interviews with students, parents, teachers, and administrators. **Number listed:** 2.

- Pliocene Ridge High School (North San Juan)
- Rio Americano High School (Sacramento)

Source: Savageau, David, *Places Rated Almanac*, Macmillan General Reference, 6th ed., 1999.

★4216★
Outstanding secondary schools in St. Louis, Missouri-Illinois

Ranking basis/background: Determined by each state's superintendent of instruction and the Council for American Private Education from evaluations of curricula and academic achievement, buildings and classrooms, classes and assemblies, cafeteria lunches, and interviews with students, parents, teachers, and administrators. **Number listed:** 18.

- Cor Jesu Academy (St. Louis)
- Crestview Middle School (Ellisville)
- Green Middle School (Richmond Heights)
- Hoech Middle School (St. Ann)
- LaSalle Springs Middle School (Glencoe)
- Lutheran High School South (St. Louis)
- Nerinx Hall High School (Webster Groves)
- North Kirkwood Middle School (Kirkwood)
- Oak Grove Middle School (Oak Grove)
- Parkway South High School (Manchester)
- Pattonville High School (Maryland Heights)
- Rockwood Eureka High School (Eureka)
- St. John Vianney High School (St. Louis)
- St. Joseph's Academy (St. Louis)
- Ste. Genevieve de Bois (St. Louis)
- Villa Duchesne School (St. Louis)
- Westminster Christian Academy (St. Louis)
- Wydown Middle School (Clayton)

Source: Savageau, David, *Places Rated Almanac*, Macmillan General Reference, 6th ed., 1999.

★4217★
Outstanding secondary schools in Salinas, California

Ranking basis/background: Determined by each state's superintendent of instruction and the Council for American Private Education from evaluations of curricula and academic achievement, buildings and classrooms, classes and assemblies, cafeteria lunches, and interviews with students, parents, teachers, and administrators. **Number listed:** 1.

- The York School (Monterey)

Source: Savageau, David, *Places Rated Almanac*, Macmillan General Reference, 6th ed., 1999.

★4218★
Outstanding secondary schools in Salt Lake City-Ogden, Utah

Ranking basis/background: Determined by each state's superintendent of instruction and the Council for American Private Education from evaluations of curricula and academic achievement, buildings and classrooms, classes and assemblies, cafeteria lunches, and interviews with students, parents, teachers, and administrators. **Number listed:** 4.

- Bryant Intermediate School (Salt Lake City)
- Granger High School (West Valley)
- Judge Memorial Catholic High School (Salt Lake City)
- Northwest Middle School (Salt Lake City)

Source: Savageau, David, *Places Rated Almanac*, Macmillan General Reference, 6th ed., 1999.

★4219★
Outstanding secondary schools in San Antonio, Texas

Ranking basis/background: Determined by each state's superintendent of instruction and the Council for American Private Education from evaluations of curricula and academic achievement, buildings and classrooms, classes and assemblies, cafeteria lunches, and interviews with students, parents, teachers, and administrators. **Number listed:** 6.

- Coke Stevenson Middle School
- Health Careers High School
- John Marshall High School
- Lackland Junior High School
- Robert Cole High School
- William Howard Taft High School

Source: Savageau, David, *Places Rated Almanac*, Macmillan General Reference, 6th ed., 1999.

★4220★
Outstanding secondary schools in San Diego, California

Ranking basis/background: Determined by each state's superintendent of instruction and the Council for American Private Education from evaluations of curricula and academic achievement, buildings and classrooms, classes and assemblies, cafeteria lunches, and interviews with students, parents, teachers, and administrators. **Number listed:** 19.

- Academy of Our Lady of Peace (San Diego)
- Black Mountain Middle School (San Diego)
- Cajon Park School (Santee)
- Coronado High School (Coronado)
- Diegueno Junior High School (Encinitas)
- Earl Warren Junior High School (Solana Beach)
- Hebrew Day School (San Diego)
- La Mesa Middle School (La Mesa)
- Oak Grove Middle School (Jamul)
- Olive Peirce Middle School (Ramona)
- Our Lady of Peace Academy (San Diego)
- Poway High School (Poway)
- Rancho Buena Vista High School (Vista)
- The Bishop's School (La Jolla)
- Torrey Pines High School (Encinitas)
- Torrey Pines High School (San Diego)
- Twin Peaks Middle School (Poway)
- University of San Diego High School (San Diego)
- Vista High School (Vista)

Source: Savageau, David, *Places Rated Almanac*, Macmillan General Reference, 6th ed., 1999.

★4221★
Outstanding secondary schools in San Francisco, California

Ranking basis/background: Determined by each state's superintendent of instruction and the Council for American Private Education from evaluations of curricula and academic achievement, buildings and classrooms, classes and assemblies, cafeteria lunches, and interviews with students, parents, teachers, and administrators. **Number listed:** 11.
- Convent Sacred Heart High School (San Francisco)
- Crocker School (Hillsborough)
- Davidson Middle School (San Rafael)
- Hall Middle School (Larkspur)
- Hillsdale High School (San Mateo)
- Lowell High School (San Francisco)
- Nathaniel Bowdith Middle School (Foster City)
- San Mateo High School (San Mateo)
- South Hillsborough School (Hillsborough)
- Taylor Middle School (Millbrae)
- West Hillsborough School (Hillsborough)

Source: Savageau, David, *Places Rated Almanac*, Macmillan General Reference, 6th ed., 1999.

★4222★
Outstanding secondary schools in San Jose, California

Ranking basis/background: Determined by each state's superintendent of instruction and the Council for American Private Education from evaluations of curricula and academic achievement, buildings and classrooms, classes and assemblies, cafeteria lunches, and interviews with students, parents, teachers, and administrators. **Number listed:** 13.
- Bullis Purissima School (Los Altos Hills)
- Cupertino High School (Cupertino)
- Davis Intermediate School (San Jose)
- Kennedy Junior High School (Cupertino)
- Lincoln Magnet School (San Jose)
- Los Gatos High School (Los Gatos)
- Monta Vista High School (Cupertino)
- Providence High School (Burbank)
- Rogers Middle School (San Jose)
- Rolling Hills Middle School (Los Gatos)
- St. Francis High School (Mountain View)
- St. Simon Catholic School (Los Altos)
- Westmont High School (Campbell)

Source: Savageau, David, *Places Rated Almanac*, Macmillan General Reference, 6th ed., 1999.

★4223★
Outstanding secondary schools in San Luis Obispo-Atascadero-Paso Robles, California

Ranking basis/background: Determined by each state's superintendent of instruction and the Council for American Private Education from evaluations of curricula and academic achievement, buildings and classrooms, classes and assemblies, cafeteria lunches, and interviews with students, parents, teachers, and administrators. **Number listed:** 1.
- Paulding Middle School (Arroyo Grande)

Source: Savageau, David, *Places Rated Almanac*, Macmillan General Reference, 6th ed., 1999.

★4224★
Outstanding secondary schools in Santa Barbara-Santa Maria-Lompoc, California

Ranking basis/background: Determined by each state's superintendent of instruction and the Council for American Private Education from evaluations of curricula and academic achievement, buildings and classrooms, classes and assemblies, cafeteria lunches, and interviews with students, parents, teachers, and administrators. **Number listed:** 4.
- Lakeview Junior High School (Santa Maria)
- Midland School (Los Olivos)
- Orcutt Junior High School (Orcutt)
- St. Joseph High School (Santa Maria)

Source: Savageau, David, *Places Rated Almanac*, Macmillan General Reference, 6th ed., 1999.

★4225★
Outstanding secondary schools in Santa Rosa, California

Ranking basis/background: Determined by each state's superintendent of instruction and the Council for American Private Education from evaluations of curricula and academic achievement, buildings and classrooms, classes and assemblies, cafeteria lunches, and interviews with students, parents, teachers, and administrators. **Number listed:** 1.
- Montgomery High School

Source: Savageau, David, *Places Rated Almanac*, Macmillan General Reference, 6th ed., 1999.

★4226★
Outstanding secondary schools in Savannah, Georgia

Ranking basis/background: Determined by each state's superintendent of instruction and the Council for American Private Education from evaluations of curricula and academic achievement, buildings and classrooms, classes and assemblies, cafeteria lunches, and interviews with students, parents, teachers, and administrators. **Number listed:** 3.
- Jenkins High School
- Myers Middle School
- Savannah Country Day School

Source: Savageau, David, *Places Rated Almanac*, Macmillan General Reference, 6th ed., 1999.

★4227★
Outstanding secondary schools in Seattle-Bellevue-Everett, Washington

Ranking basis/background: Determined by each state's superintendent of instruction and the Council for American Private Education from evaluations of curricula and academic achievement, buildings and classrooms, classes and assemblies, cafeteria lunches, and interviews with students, parents, teachers, and administrators. **Number listed:** 12.
- Blanchet High School (Seattle)
- Cedarcrest High School (Duvall)
- Chief Kanim Middle School (Fall City)
- Eton School (Bellevue)
- Holy Names Academy (Seattle)
- Holy Rosary (Seattle)
- Inglewood Junior High School (Redmond)
- Kent-Meridian High School (Kent)
- Liberty High School (Renton)
- The Northwest School (Seattle)
- St. Philomena (Des Moines)
- Shorewood High School (Shoreline)

Source: Savageau, David, *Places Rated Almanac*, Macmillan General Reference, 6th ed., 1999.

★4228★
Outstanding secondary schools in Sharon, Pennsylvania

Ranking basis/background: Determined by each state's superintendent of instruction and the Council for American Private Education from evaluations of curricula and academic achievement, buildings and classrooms, classes and assemblies, cafeteria lunches, and interviews with students, parents, teachers, and administrators. **Number listed:** 1.
- Hillview Intermediate Center (Grove City)

Source: Savageau, David, *Places Rated Almanac*, Macmillan General Reference, 6th ed., 1999.

★4229★
Outstanding secondary schools in Sheboygan, Wisconsin

Ranking basis/background: Determined by each state's superintendent of instruction and the Council for American Private Education from evaluations of curricula and academic achievement, buildings and classrooms, classes and assemblies, cafeteria lunches, and interviews with students, parents, teachers, and administrators. **Number listed:** 1.
- Horace Mann Middle School

Source: Savageau, David, *Places Rated Almanac*, Macmillan General Reference, 6th ed., 1999.

★4230★
Outstanding secondary schools in Shreveport-Bossier City, Louisiana

Ranking basis/background: Determined by each state's superintendent of instruction and the Council for American Private Education from evaluations of curricula and academic achievement, buildings and classrooms, classes and assemblies, cafeteria lunches, and interviews with students, parents, teachers, and administrators. **Number listed:** 3.
- Byrd High School (Shreveport)
- Christ the King School (Bossier City)
- Cope Middle School (Bossier City)

Source: Savageau, David, *Places Rated Almanac*, Macmillan General Reference, 6th ed., 1999.

★4231★
Outstanding secondary schools in South Bend, Indiana

Ranking basis/background: Determined by each state's superintendent of instruction and the Council for American Private Education from evaluations of curricula and academic achievement, buildings and classrooms, classes and assemblies, cafeteria lunches, and interviews with students, parents, teachers, and administrators. **Number listed:** 3.
- Trinity School (South Bend)
- John Young Middle School (Mishawaka)
- Penn High School (Mishawaka)

Source: Savageau, David, *Places Rated Almanac*, Macmillan General Reference, 6th ed., 1999.

★4232★
Outstanding secondary schools in Spokane, Washington

Ranking basis/background: Determined by each state's superintendent of instruction and the Council for American Private Education from evaluations of curricula and academic achievement, buildings and classrooms, classes and assemblies, cafeteria lunches, and interviews with students, parents, teachers, and administrators. **Number listed:** 1.
- Gonzaga Prep

Source: Savageau, David, *Places Rated Almanac*, Macmillan General Reference, 6th ed., 1999.

SCHOOLS, SECONDARY

★4233★
Outstanding secondary schools in Springfield, Maine

Ranking basis/background: Determined by each state's superintendent of instruction and the Council for American Private Education from evaluations of curricula and academic achievement, buildings and classrooms, classes and assemblies, cafeteria lunches, and interviews with students, parents, teachers, and administrators. **Number listed:** 1.

    Williston Northampton High School (Easthampton)

Source: Savageau, David, *Places Rated Almanac*, Macmillan General Reference, 6th ed., 1999.

★4234★
Outstanding secondary schools in Springfield, Missouri

Ranking basis/background: Determined by each state's superintendent of instruction and the Council for American Private Education from evaluations of curricula and academic achievement, buildings and classrooms, classes and assemblies, cafeteria lunches, and interviews with students, parents, teachers, and administrators. **Number listed:** 1.

    Kickapoo High School

Source: Savageau, David, *Places Rated Almanac*, Macmillan General Reference, 6th ed., 1999.

★4235★
Outstanding secondary schools in Stamford-Norwalk, Connecticut

Ranking basis/background: Determined by each state's superintendent of instruction and the Council for American Private Education from evaluations of curricula and academic achievement, buildings and classrooms, classes and assemblies, cafeteria lunches, and interviews with students, parents, teachers, and administrators. **Number listed:** 1.

    Weston High School (Weston)

Source: Savageau, David, *Places Rated Almanac*, Macmillan General Reference, 6th ed., 1999.

★4236★
Outstanding secondary schools in State College, Pennsylvania

Ranking basis/background: Determined by each state's superintendent of instruction and the Council for American Private Education from evaluations of curricula and academic achievement, buildings and classrooms, classes and assemblies, cafeteria lunches, and interviews with students, parents, teachers, and administrators. **Number listed:** 1.

    State College Area High School

Source: Savageau, David, *Places Rated Almanac*, Macmillan General Reference, 6th ed., 1999.

★4237★
Outstanding secondary schools in Steubenville-Weirton, Ohio-West Virginia

Ranking basis/background: Determined by each state's superintendent of instruction and the Council for American Private Education from evaluations of curricula and academic achievement, buildings and classrooms, classes and assemblies, cafeteria lunches, and interviews with students, parents, teachers, and administrators. **Number listed:** 2.

    Weir High School (Weirton)
    Weir Middle School (Weirton)

Source: Savageau, David, *Places Rated Almanac*, Macmillan General Reference, 6th ed., 1999.

★4238★
Outstanding secondary schools in Sumter, South Carolina

Ranking basis/background: Determined by each state's superintendent of instruction and the Council for American Private Education from evaluations of curricula and academic achievement, buildings and classrooms, classes and assemblies, cafeteria lunches, and interviews with students, parents, teachers, and administrators. **Number listed:** 2.

    Bates Middle School
    Sumter High School

Source: Savageau, David, *Places Rated Almanac*, Macmillan General Reference, 6th ed., 1999.

★4239★
Outstanding secondary schools in Syracuse, New York

Ranking basis/background: Determined by each state's superintendent of instruction and the Council for American Private Education from evaluations of curricula and academic achievement, buildings and classrooms, classes and assemblies, cafeteria lunches, and interviews with students, parents, teachers, and administrators. **Number listed:** 2.

    Skaneateles High School (Skaneateles)
    Westhill High School (Syracuse)

Source: Savageau, David, *Places Rated Almanac*, Macmillan General Reference, 6th ed., 1999.

★4240★
Outstanding secondary schools in Tampa-St. Petersburg-Clearwater, Florida

Ranking basis/background: Determined by each state's superintendent of instruction and the Council for American Private Education from evaluations of curricula and academic achievement, buildings and classrooms, classes and assemblies, cafeteria lunches, and interviews with students, parents, teachers, and administrators. **Number listed:** 4.

    Academy of the Holy Names
    Berkeley Prep
    Plant High School
    Woodrow Wilson Middle School

Source: Savageau, David, *Places Rated Almanac*, Macmillan General Reference, 6th ed., 1999.

★4241★
Outstanding secondary schools in Toledo, Ohio

Ranking basis/background: Determined by each state's superintendent of instruction and the Council for American Private Education from evaluations of curricula and academic achievement, buildings and classrooms, classes and assemblies, cafeteria lunches, and interviews with students, parents, teachers, and administrators. **Number listed:** 3.

    Central Catholic High School (Toledo)
    Notre Dame Academy (Park Hills)
    St. Ursula Academy (Toledo)

Source: Savageau, David, *Places Rated Almanac*, Macmillan General Reference, 6th ed., 1999.

★4242★
Outstanding secondary schools in Trenton, New Jersey

Ranking basis/background: Determined by each state's superintendent of instruction and the Council for American Private Education from evaluations of curricula and academic achievement, buildings and classrooms, classes and assemblies, cafeteria lunches, and interviews with students, parents, teachers, and administrators. **Number listed:** 1.

    West Windsor-Palainsboro High School (Princeton Junction)

Source: Savageau, David, *Places Rated Almanac*, Macmillan General Reference, 6th ed., 1999.

★4243★
Outstanding secondary schools in Tucson, Arizona

Ranking basis/background: Determined by each state's superintendent of instruction and the Council for American Private Education from evaluations of curricula and academic achievement, buildings and classrooms, classes and assemblies, cafeteria lunches, and interviews with students, parents, teachers, and administrators. **Number listed:** 2.

    Flowering Wells High School
    Magnet Middle School

Source: Savageau, David, *Places Rated Almanac*, Macmillan General Reference, 6th ed., 1999.

★4244★
Outstanding secondary schools in Tulsa, Oklahoma

Ranking basis/background: Determined by each state's superintendent of instruction and the Council for American Private Education from evaluations of curricula and academic achievement, buildings and classrooms, classes and assemblies, cafeteria lunches, and interviews with students, parents, teachers, and administrators. **Number listed:** 1.

    St. Pius X School

Source: Savageau, David, *Places Rated Almanac*, Macmillan General Reference, 6th ed., 1999.

★4245★
Outstanding secondary schools in Tyler, Texas

Ranking basis/background: Determined by each state's superintendent of instruction and the Council for American Private Education from evaluations of curricula and academic achievement, buildings and classrooms, classes and assemblies, cafeteria lunches, and interviews with students, parents, teachers, and administrators. **Number listed:** 1.

    Bishop Gorman High School

Source: Savageau, David, *Places Rated Almanac*, Macmillan General Reference, 6th ed., 1999.

★4246★
Outstanding secondary schools in Utica-Rome, New York

Ranking basis/background: Determined by each state's superintendent of instruction and the Council for American Private Education from evaluations of curricula and academic achievement, buildings and classrooms, classes and assemblies, cafeteria lunches, and interviews with students, parents, teachers, and administrators. **Number listed:** 1.

    Mount Markham Middle School (West Winfield)

Source: Savageau, David, *Places Rated Almanac*, Macmillan General Reference, 6th ed., 1999.

★4247★
Outstanding secondary schools in Vallejo-Fairfield-Napa, California

Ranking basis/background: Determined by each state's superintendent of instruction and the Council for American Private Education from evaluations of curricula and academic achievement, buildings and classrooms, classes and assemblies, cafeteria lunches, and interviews with students, parents, teachers, and administrators. **Number listed:** 1.

Benicia Middle School (Benicia)

Source: Savageau, David, *Places Rated Almanac*, Macmillan General Reference, 6th ed., 1999.

★4248★
Outstanding secondary schools in Ventura, California

Ranking basis/background: Determined by each state's superintendent of instruction and the Council for American Private Education from evaluations of curricula and academic achievement, buildings and classrooms, classes and assemblies, cafeteria lunches, and interviews with students, parents, teachers, and administrators. **Number listed:** 5.

Adolfo Camarillo High School (Camarillo)
Anacapa Middle School (Ventura)
Charles Blackstock Junior High School (Oxnard)
Green Junior High School (Oxnard)
The Thacher School (Ojai)

Source: Savageau, David, *Places Rated Almanac*, Macmillan General Reference, 6th ed., 1999.

★4249★
Outstanding secondary schools in Washington, District of Columbia-Maryland-Virginia-West Virginia

Ranking basis/background: Determined by each state's superintendent of instruction and the Council for American Private Education from evaluations of curricula and academic achievement, buildings and classrooms, classes and assemblies, cafeteria lunches, and interviews with students, parents, teachers, and administrators. **Number listed:** 29.

Academy of the Holy Cross (Kensington)
Banneker Academic High School (Washington)
Bishop O'Connell High School (Arlington)
DeMatha Catholic High School (Hyattsville)
Duke Ellington School of Arts (Washington)
Dunbar High School (Washington)
Eleanor Roosevelt High School (Greenbelt)
Frederick High School (Frederick)
George Mason Middle School (Falls Church)
Good Counsel High School (Wheaton)
Governor Johnson High School (Frederick)
Hebrew Academy (Silver Spring)
Herbert Hoover Middle School (Rockville)
Johnson High School (Bethesda)
Kettering Middle School (Upper Marlboro)
The Lab School of Washington (Washington)
Lemon Hine Junior High School (Washington)
Linganore High School (Frederick)
Martin Luther King Middle School (Beltsville)
Middletown Middle School (Middletown)
Montgomery High School (Rockville)
Redlands Middle School (Rockville)
School for Contemporary Education (Annandale)
St. Camillus (Silver Spring)
Stone Ridge Country Day School (Bethesda)
Stone Ridge-School of the Sacred Heart (Bethesda)
Washington Episcopal School (Bethesda)
Westland Intermediate School (Bethesda)
Winston Churchill High School (Potomac)

Source: Savageau, David, *Places Rated Almanac*, Macmillan General Reference, 6th ed., 1999.

★4250★
Outstanding secondary schools in Waterbury, Connecticut

Ranking basis/background: Determined by each state's superintendent of instruction and the Council for American Private Education from evaluations of curricula and academic achievement, buildings and classrooms, classes and assemblies, cafeteria lunches, and interviews with students, parents, teachers, and administrators. **Number listed:** 2.

Alcott Middle School (Wolcott)
Rochambeau Middle School (Southbury)

Source: Savageau, David, *Places Rated Almanac*, Macmillan General Reference, 6th ed., 1999.

★4251★
Outstanding secondary schools in West Palm Beach-Boca Raton, Florida

Ranking basis/background: Determined by each state's superintendent of instruction and the Council for American Private Education from evaluations of curricula and academic achievement, buildings and classrooms, classes and assemblies, cafeteria lunches, and interviews with students, parents, teachers, and administrators. **Number listed:** 3.

Boca Raton Christian School (Boca Raton)
Logger's Run Community Middle School (Boca Raton)
Suncoast Community High School (Riviera Beach)

Source: Savageau, David, *Places Rated Almanac*, Macmillan General Reference, 6th ed., 1999.

★4252★
Outstanding secondary schools in Wilmington-Newark, Delaware-Maryland

Ranking basis/background: Determined by each state's superintendent of instruction and the Council for American Private Education from evaluations of curricula and academic achievement, buildings and classrooms, classes and assemblies, cafeteria lunches, and interviews with students, parents, teachers, and administrators. **Number listed:** 3.

Padua Academy (Wilmington)
Perryville Middle School (Perryville)
St. Matthew School (Wilmington)

Source: Savageau, David, *Places Rated Almanac*, Macmillan General Reference, 6th ed., 1999.

★4253★
Outstanding secondary schools in Wilmington, North Carolina

Ranking basis/background: Determined by each state's superintendent of instruction and the Council for American Private Education from evaluations of curricula and academic achievement, buildings and classrooms, classes and assemblies, cafeteria lunches, and interviews with students, parents, teachers, and administrators. **Number listed:** 1.

Hoggard High School

Source: Savageau, David, *Places Rated Almanac*, Macmillan General Reference, 6th ed., 1999.

★4254★
Outstanding suburban public high schools in Metro Atlanta

Ranking basis/background: According to success ratios measuring number of Advanced Placement tests taken divided by number of seniors, percentage of students taking college-admissions tests, percentage of students passing the Georgia High School Graduation Test, and average colleges admissions test scores. **Number listed:** 10.

Avondale High School
Carrollton High School
Chamblee High School
Chattahoochee High School
Heritage High School
Jonesboro High School
Loganville High School
Milton High School
Parkview High School
Walton High School

Source: "Outstanding High Schools," *U.S. News & World Report*, January 18, 1999, pp. 46-82.

★4255★
Outstanding suburban public high schools in Metro Boston

Ranking basis/background: According to success ratios measuring number of Advanced Placement tests taken divided by number of seniors, percentage of students taking college-admissions tests, percentage of students passing the math and reading sections of the Massachusetts Educational Assessment Program, and average colleges admissions test scores. **Number listed:** 6.

Ashland High School
Dartmouth High School
Lexington High School
Saugus High School
Shepherd Hill Regional High School
Stoneham High School

Source: "Outstanding High Schools," *U.S. News & World Report*, January 18, 1999, pp. 46-82.

★4256★
Outstanding suburban public high schools in Metro Chicago

Ranking basis/background: According to success ratios measuring number of Advanced Placement tests taken divided by number of seniors, percentage of students taking college-admissions tests, percentage of students passing the math and reading sections of the Illinois Goal Assessment Program, and average colleges admissions test scores. **Number listed:** 12.

Adlai E. Stevenson High School
Buffalo Grove High School
Elk Grove High School
Glenbrook North High School
Glenbrook South High School
Maine West High School
Niles North High School
Palatine High School
Prospect High School
Rolling Meadows High School
Schaumburg High School
William Fremd High School

Source: "Outstanding High Schools," *U.S. News & World Report*, January 18, 1999, pp. 46-82.

SCHOOLS, SECONDARY

★4257★
Outstanding suburban public high schools in Metro Dallas-Ft. Worth

Ranking basis/background: According to success ratios measuring number of Advanced Placement tests taken divided by number of seniors, percentage of students taking college-admissions tests, percentage of students passing the math and reading sections of the Texas Assessment of Academic Skills test, and average colleges admissions test scores. **Number listed:** 6.
- Billy Ryan High School
- Cleburne High School
- Ennis High School
- Garland High School
- Plano East Senior High School
- Waxahachie High School

Source: "Outstanding High Schools," *U.S. News & World Report*, January 18, 1999, pp. 46-82.

★4258★
Outstanding suburban public high schools in Metro Detroit

Ranking basis/background: According to success ratios measuring number of Advanced Placement tests taken divided by number of seniors, percentage of students taking college-admissions tests, percentage of students passing the math and reading sections of Michigan's High School Proficiency Test, and average colleges admissions test scores. **Number listed:** 7.
- Churchill Senior High School
- Dwight D. Eisenhower High School
- Grosse Pointe South High School
- Henry Ford II High School
- Novi High School
- Troy High School
- Troy Athens High School

Source: "Outstanding High Schools," *U.S. News & World Report*, January 18, 1999, pp. 46-82.

★4259★
Outstanding suburban public high schools in Metro New York

Ranking basis/background: According to success ratios measuring number of Advanced Placement tests taken divided by number of seniors, percentage of students taking college-admissions tests, percentage of students passing the Regents Comprehensive English and Math III exams, and average colleges admissions test scores. **Number listed:** 3.
- Briarcliff High School
- Edgemont Junior/Senior High School
- Nyack High School

Source: "Outstanding High Schools," *U.S. News & World Report*, January 18, 1999, pp. 46-82.

★4260★
Outstanding urban public high schools in Metro Atlanta

Ranking basis/background: According to success ratios measuring number of Advanced Placement tests taken divided by number of seniors, percentage of students taking college-admissions tests, percentage of students passing the Georgia High School Graduation Test, and average colleges admissions test scores. **Number listed:** 3.
- Benjamin Mays High School
- Henry Grady High School
- North Springs High School

Source: "Outstanding High Schools," *U.S. News & World Report*, January 18, 1999, pp. 46-82.

★4261★
Outstanding urban public high schools in Metro Boston

Ranking basis/background: According to success ratios measuring number of Advanced Placement tests taken divided by number of seniors, percentage of students taking college-admissions tests, percentage of students passing the math and reading sections of the Massachusetts Educational Assessment Program, and average colleges admissions test scores. **Number listed:** 7.
- Boston Latin Academy
- Boston Latin School
- B.M.C. Durfee High School
- Lawrence High School
- Lowell High School
- Lynn Classical High School
- South High Community School

Source: "Outstanding High Schools," *U.S. News & World Report*, January 18, 1999, pp. 46-82.

★4262★
Outstanding urban public high schools in Metro Chicago

Ranking basis/background: According to success ratios measuring number of Advanced Placement tests taken divided by number of seniors, percentage of students taking college-admissions tests, percentage of students passing the math and reading sections of the Illinois Goal Assessment Program, and average colleges admissions test scores. **Number listed:** 4.
- Hyde Park Academy
- Kenwood Academy
- Von Steuben Metropolitan Science Center
- Whitney M. Young Magnet High School

Source: "Outstanding High Schools," *U.S. News & World Report*, January 18, 1999, pp. 46-82.

★4263★
Outstanding urban public high schools in Metro Dallas-Ft. Worth

Ranking basis/background: According to success ratios measuring number of Advanced Placement tests taken divided by number of seniors, percentage of students taking college-admissions tests, percentage of students passing the math and reading sections of the Texas Assessment of Academic Skills test, and average colleges admissions test scores. **Number listed:** 3.
- Lake Highlands High School
- Lamar High School
- Lincoln High School

Source: "Outstanding High Schools," *U.S. News & World Report*, January 18, 1999, pp. 46-82.

★4264★
Outstanding urban public high schools in Metro Detroit

Ranking basis/background: According to success ratios measuring number of Advanced Placement tests taken divided by number of seniors, percentage of students taking college-admissions tests, percentage of students passing the math and reading sections of Michigan's High School Proficiency Test, and average colleges admissions test scores. **Number listed:** 3.
- Cass Technical Senior High School
- Martin Luther King Jr. Senior High School
- Renaissance Senior High School

Source: "Outstanding High Schools," *U.S. News & World Report*, January 18, 1999, pp. 46-82.

★4265★
Outstanding urban public high schools in Metro New York

Ranking basis/background: According to success ratios measuring number of Advanced Placement tests taken divided by number of seniors, percentage of students taking college-admissions tests, percentage of students passing the Regents Comprehensive English and Math III exams, and average colleges admissions test scores. **Number listed:** 9.
- A. Philip Randolph Campus
- Bronx High School of Science
- Brooklyn Technical Senior High School
- DeWitt Clinton High School
- Frederick Douglass Academy
- John Bowne High School
- Manhattan Center for Science & Mathematics
- Midwood Senior High School
- Murry Bergtraum Senior High School

Source: "Outstanding High Schools," *U.S. News & World Report*, January 18, 1999, pp. 46-82.

★4266★
States with the highest percentage of high school freshmen enrolling in college within four years

Ranking basis/background: Percentage of high school freshmen in each state who enroll in college within four years. **Remarks:** Original source: The National Center for Public Policy and Higher Education. **Number listed:** 50.
1. North Dakota, with 63%
2. Iowa, 54%
2. Massachusetts, 54%
2. New Jersey, 54%
5. Nebraska, 51%
6. Illinois, 49%
7. Kansas, 47%
8. Hawaii, 46%
8. Minnesota, 46%
8. Montana, 46%
8. Rhode Island, 46%
8. Wisconsin, 46%

Source: "How Many Ninth Graders Make It to the Land of Higher Ed?," *U.S. News & World Report*, 129: 12, (December 11, 2000).

★4267★
States with the lowest percentage of high school freshmen enrolling in college within four years

Ranking basis/background: Percentage of high school freshmen who enroll in college within four years. **Remarks:** Original source: The National Center for Public Policy and Higher Education. **Number listed:** 50.
1. Nevada, with 25%
2. Alaska, 26%
3. Arizona, 28%
4. Florida, 29%
5. Louisiana, 31%
5. Georgia, 31%
7. Texas, 32%
7. South Carolina, 32%
9. Tennessee, 34%
9. North Carolina, 34%

Source: "How Many Ninth Graders Make It to the Land of Higher Ed?," *U.S. News & World Report*, 129: 12, (December 11, 2000).

Related Information

★4268★
Silver, Marc and Joellen Perry, "Grading a School: A Parent's Guide," *U.S. News & World Report*, January 18, 1999, pp. 84-87.
   Remarks: A comprehensive list of vital points to be examined when considering high schools, such as costs, curriculum, personnel, and how to conduct on-campus touring.

★4269★
"How We Identified Outstanding High Schools," *U.S. News & World Report*, January 18, 1999, pp. 50-51.
   Remarks: Provides an in-depth explanation for the scoring of state test results, percentage of student taking the SAT or ACT, Advanced Placement test taking, and persistence rates at outstanding high schools throughout the U.S.

★4270★
Daniel, Rod, "Performing and Visual Arts Schools," *Journal of Secondary Gifted Education*, 12: 43-48, (Fall).
   Remarks: Presents a guide to characteristics, options, and proven benefits of performing and visual arts schools. Also lists characteristics common among schools commended by the U.S. Department of Education and the National Endowment for the Arts for their excellence in arts education as well as academic programs.

SCHOOLS, SECONDARY–GRADUATES

★4271★
High school completion rates of Hispanic Americans, 1977 to 1997
Ranking basis/background: Completion rate percent. **Remarks:** Original source: American Council on Education, 2000. **Number listed:** 21.
   1977, with 54.7%
   1978, 55.9%
   1979, 55.2%
   1980, 54.1%
   1981, 55.8%
   1982, 57.6%
   1983, 54.8%
   1984, 60.1%
   1985, 62.9%
   1986, 59.9%
   1987, 61.6%
   1988, 55.2%
   1989, 55.9%
   1990, 54.5%
   1991, 52.1%
   1992, 57.3%
   1993, 60.9%
   1994, 56.6%
   1995, 58.6%
   1996, 57.5%
   1997, 62.0%
Source: Collison, Michele N-K, "Modest Gains in Enrollment, Says New ACE Report," *Black Issues in Higher Education*, 16: 18-20, (March 2, 2000).

★4272★
Percent of high school graduates in the U.S.
Ranking basis/background: Percent, by region, of people 25 and older who are high school graduates. **Remarks:** Original source: U.S. Census Bureau Current Population Survey. **Number listed:** 4.
   1. Midwest, with 86.2%
   2. Northeast, 84.6%
   3. West, 83.7%
   4. South, 80.7%
Source: Hall, Cindy and Genevieve Lynn, "Midwest Leads Graduation Rate," *USA Today*, October 12, 2000, Section C, p. 1C.

★4273★
Percentage of 18- to 24-year olds completing high school, by race, 1998
Ranking basis/background: High school graduation percentages by race in 1998. **Remarks:** Original source: Education Trust; Education Dept.; Census Bureau. **Number listed:** 4.
   Asian American, with 94%
   White, 90%
   African American, 81%
   Hispanic American/Latino, 63%
Source: Symonds, William C., "How to Fix America's Schools," *Business Week*, 3724: 66-72, (March 19, 2001).

★4274★
Projected number of high school graduates in midwest region public schools for the years 2001-02 to 2007-08
Ranking basis/background: Total number of high school graduates from public schools projected in the midwestern region of the U.S. for the years 2001-02 through 2007-08. **Remarks:** Original source: U.S. Department of Education, National Center for Education Statistics, Common Core of Data surveys. **Number listed:** 8.
   2001-02, with 652,650
   2002-03, 656,780
   2003-04, 671,960
   2004-05, 668,350
   2005-06, 660,460
   2006-07, 668,250
   2007-08, 678,240
Source: *Projections of Education Statistics to 2008*, NCES 98-016, U.S. Department of Education, National Center for Education Statistics (June 1998).

★4275★
Projected number of high school graduates in northeast region public schools for the years 2001-02 to 2007-08
Ranking basis/background: Total number of high school graduates from public schools projected in the northeast region of the U.S. for the years 2001-02 through 2007-08. **Remarks:** Original source: U.S. Department of Education, National Center for Education Statistics, Common Core of Data surveys. **Number listed:** 8.
   2001-02, with 461,650
   2002-03, 467,930
   2003-04, 480,260
   2004-05, 486,050
   2005-06, 492,620
   2006-07, 504,640
   2007-08, 509,480
Source: *Projections of Education Statistics to 2008*, NCES 98-016, U.S. Department of Education, National Center for Education Statistics (June 1998).

★4276★
Projected number of high school graduates in southern region public schools for the years 2001-02 to 2007-08
Ranking basis/background: Total number of high school graduates from public schools projected in the southern region of the U.S. for the years 2001-02 through 2007-08. **Remarks:** Original source: U.S. Department of Education, National Center for Education Statistics, Common Core of Data surveys. **Number listed:** 8.
   2001-02, with 873,080
   2002-03, 877,820
   2003-04, 896,030
   2004-05, 894,200
   2005-06, 900,490
   2006-07, 916,590
   2007-08, 935,270
Source: *Projections of Education Statistics to 2008*, NCES 98-016, U.S. Department of Education, National Center for Education Statistics (June 1998).

★4277★
Projected number of private high-school graduates for the years 2002-2008
Ranking basis/background: Based on data analysis conducted by the U.S. Department of Education. **Remarks:** Article contains projections on college enrollment, degree achievement, and high-school graduates. **Number listed:** 9.
   2002, with 299,000 graduates
   2003, 302,000
   2004, 308,000
   2005, 309,000
   2006, 310,000
   2007, 316,000
   2008, 321,000
Source: *Projections of Education Statistics to 2008*, NCES 98-016, U.S. Department of Education, National Center for Education Statistics (June 1998).

★4278★
Projected number of public high-school graduates for the years 2002-2008
Ranking basis/background: Based on data analysis conducted by the U.S. Department of Education. **Remarks:** Article contains projections on college enrollment, degree achievement, and high-school graduates. **Number listed:** 9.
   2002, with 2,587,000 graduates
   2003, 2,607,000
   2004, 2,664,000
   2005, 2,667,000
   2006, 2,675,000
   2007, 2,728,000
   2008, 2,772,000
Source: *Projections of Education Statistics to 2008*, NCES 98-016, U.S. Department of Education, National Center for Education Statistics (June 1998).

SCHOOLS OF EDUCATION
See: **Teacher Education**

SCIENCE PERIODICALS

★4279★
Immunology journals by impact factor, 1981 to 1997

Ranking basis/background: Current citations to a journal's published papers divided by total papers published over an 18-year period. **Remarks:** Original source: *Journal Citation Reports* and *Journal Performances Indicators on Diskette*. **Number listed:** 10.

1. *Annual Review of Immunology*, with 184.57
2. *Advances in Immunology*, 110.02
3. *Journal of Experimental Medicine*, 68.57
4. *Immunological Reviews*, 55.88
5. *Immunology Today*, 51.68
6. *Journal of Immunology*, 39.29
7. *CRC Current Review of Immunology*, 30.56
8. *Immunity*, 27.58
9. *Review of Infectious Diseases*, 26.71
10. *European Journal of Immunology*, 25.59

Source: "Journals Ranked by Impact: Immunology," *What's Hot in Research*, http://www.isinet.com/whatshot/whatshot.html, Institute for Scientific Information (February 8, 1999).

★4280★
Immunology journals by impact factor, 1993 to 1997

Ranking basis/background: Current citations to a journal's published papers divided by total papers published over the past five years. **Remarks:** Original source: *Journal Citation Reports* and *Journal Performances Indicators on Diskette*. **Number listed:** 10.

1. *Annual Review of Immunology*, with 95.97
2. *Advances in Immunology*, 42.84
3. *Immunology Today*, 33.24
4. *Journal of Experimental Medicine*, 30.40
5. *Immunity*, 27.58
6. *Current Opinion in Immunology*, 27.58
7. *Journal of Immunology*, 14.58
8. *Immunological Reviews*, 12.36
9. *European Journal of Immunology*, 12.08
10. *AIDS*, 9.30

Source: "Journals Ranked by Impact: Immunology," *What's Hot in Research*, http://www.isinet.com/whatshot/whatshot.html, Institute for Scientific Information (February 8, 1999).

★4281★
Top science journals by impact factor

Ranking basis/background: Five-year impact score, taken from citation data of 1984-1988 and two-year impact score is the mean from 1985 and 1986 impacts. **Number listed:** 25.

1. *Cell* (in the scientific subfield of biochemistry & molecular biology), with a two-year impact of 19.5; and a five-year impact of 77.4
2. *Journal of Experimental Medicine* (Immunology), 11.1; 44.2
3. *Proceedings National Academy of Sciences USA* (Multidisciplinary), 9.3; 38.5
4. *European Molecular Biology Organization Journal* (biochemistry & molecular biology), 7.7; 33.3
5. *Journal of Clinical Investigation* (Research & experimental medicine), 6.8; 31.1
6. *Archives of General Psychiatry* (Psychiatry), 8.1; 27.2
7. *Nucleic Acids Research* (Biochemistry & molecular biology), 6.1; 26.7
8. *Journal of Neuroscience* (Neuroscience), 6.2; 26.7
9. *Journal of Biological Chemistry* (biochemistry & molecular biology), 6.3; 25.7
10. *Circulation Research* (cardiovascular/hematology), 6.0; 25.4

Source: Klaic, B., "The Use of Scientometric Parameters for the Evaluation of Scientific Contributions," *Collegium Anthropologicum*, 23: 751-770, (December 1999).

SCIENCES

★4282★
Institute for Scientific Information's most cited papers, 1990-98

Ranking basis/background: Most cited papers of each year and number of citations received through December 1999. **Number listed:** 9.

1. 1990: "Basic Local Alignment Search Tool", *Journal of Molecular Biology*, by S.F. Altshul, et al, with 9,969 citations
2. 1991: "Nitric Oxide: Physiology, pathophysiology, and pharmacology", *Pharmacology Review*, S. Moncada, R.M.J. Palmer, and E.A. Higgs, 6,665
3. 1992: "Integrins: Versatility, modulation, and signaling in cell adhesion", *Cell*, R.O. Hynes, 4,610
4. 1993: "Inositol trisphosphate and calcium signaling", *Nature*, M.J. Berridge, 3,446
5. 1994: "Clustal W:Improving the sensitivity of prog. mult. sequence align. through sequence weighting, position-spec. gap penalties and weight matrix choice", *Nucleic Acid Res.*, J.D. Thompson, D.G. Higgins, T.J. Gibson, 3,352
6. 1995: "Apoptosis in the pathogenesis and treatment of disease", *Science*, C.B. Thompson, 1,745
7. 1996: "Particles and fields. 1. Review of particle physics", *Physics Review D*, R.M. Barnett, et al, 1,342
8. 1997: "Gapped BLAST and Psi-BLAST: A new generation of protein database search programs", *Nucleic Acid Research*, S.F. Altschul, et al, 1,534
9. 1998: "Cancer statistics, 1998", *CA-A Cancer Journal*, S.H. Landis, et al, 605

Source: "The Most-Cited Papers of 1990-98," *What's Hot in Research* (http://www.isinet.com/isi/hot/research) Institute for Scientific Information, May 29, 2000.

★4283★
United States' contribution of papers in the sciences, by field, 1995-99

Ranking basis/background: Percentage of science and social science papers from the United States over a five-year period. **Number listed:** 23.

1. Law, with 89.14%
2. Education, 62.36%
3. Economics and business, 58.31%
4. Social sciences, 58.16%
5. Psychology/psychiatry, 56.53%
6. Astrophysics, 48.91%
7. Molecular biology, 48.03%
8. Neuroscience, 45.88%
9. Immunology, 45.56%
10. Computer science, 41.73%

Source: "Science in United States of America, 1995-99," *What's Hot in Research* (http://www.isinet.com/isi/hot/research) Institute for Scientific Information, May 1, 2000.

★4284★
United States' contribution of papers in the sciences, by field, 1996-2000

Ranking basis/background: Percentage of science and social science papers from the United States over a five-year period. **Number listed:** 23.

1. Law, with 88.94%
2. Education, 61.29%
3. Social sciences, 57.11%
4. Economics and business, 56.68%
5. Psychology/psychiatry, 55.54%
6. Space science, 48.42%
7. Molecular biology, 47.57%
8. Neuroscience, 45.23%
9. Immunology, 45.12%
10. Computer science, 40.94%

Source: "Science in United States, 1996-2000," *What's Hot in Research* (http://www.isinet.com/isi/hot/research) Institute for Scientific Information.

★4285★
U.S. universities contributing the most papers in the field of neurosciences, 1993-97

Ranking basis/background: Average citations per paper. Also includes total number of papers. **Remarks:** Original source: *University Science Indicators of Diskette*, 1981-98. **Number listed:** 6.

1. Caltech, with 395 papers; and an average of 15.38 citations per paper
2. Stanford University, 911; 13.49
3. University of California, San Francisco, 1,257; 13.39
3. Johns Hopkins University, 1,558; 13.39
5. Harvard University, 2,419; 12.48
6. Rockefeller University, 529; 12.26

Source: "Neuroscience: High-Impact U.S. Universities, 1993-97," *What's Hot in Research*, http://www.isinet.com/whatshot/whatshot.html, Institute for Scientific Information, (March 8, 1999).

★4286★
U.S. universities publishing the most papers in the field of food science/nutrition, 1994-98

Ranking basis/background: Total number of papers published from each university. **Remarks:** Original source: *University Science Indicators on Diskette*, 1981-97. **Number listed:** 5.

1. Cornell University, with 360 papers
2. University of Wisconsin, Madison, 334
3. University of California, Davis, 318
4. University of Minnesota, 284
5. University of Georgia, 269

Source: "Food Science/Nutrition: Most Prolific U.S. Universities, 1994-98," *What's Hot in Research* (http://www.isinet.com/hot/research) Institute for Scientific Information, February 28, 2000.

★4287★
U.S. universities publishing the most papers in the field of neuroscience, 1994-98

Ranking basis/background: Number of papers published in the field of neuroscience over a five-year period, and percent of field based on each universities percentage of 130,614 papers entered in the ISI database from ISI-indexed neuroscience journals. **Number listed:** 5.
1. Harvard University, with 2,560 papers; 1.96% of field
2. University of California, Los Angeles, 1,891; 1.45%
3. Yale University, 1,732; 1.33%
4. Johns Hopkins University, 1,637; 1.25%
5. Columbia University, 1,590; 1.22%

Source: "Neuroscience: Most Prolific U.S. Universities, 1994-98," *What's Hot in Research* (http://www.isinet.com/isi/hot/research) *Institute for Scientific Information*, August 7, 2000.

★4288★
U.S. universities with the highest concentration of animal sciences papers published, 1994-98

Ranking basis/background: Total number of animal sciences papers published from each university and percentage they comprise of university's total papers between 1994 and 1998. **Remarks:** Original source: University Science Indicators on Diskette, 1981-98. **Number listed:** 5.
1. University of Alaska, with 123 animal sciences papers; 9.06% of university's total papers
2. University of Georgia, 442; 5.44%
3. Utah State University, 105; 4.82%
4. Colorado State University, 221; 4.35%
5. New Mexico State University, 75; 4.22%

Source: "U.S. Universities with Highest Concentrations in Animal Sciences, 1994-98," *What's Hot in Research* (http://www.isinet.com/hot/research) *Institute for Scientific Information*, January 24, 2000.

★4289★
U.S. universities with the highest concentration of papers published in the field of aquatic sciences, 1995-99

Ranking basis/background: Number of papers published in the field of aquatic sciences over a five-year period, and percentage they comprise of the university's total papers published. **Number listed:** 5.
1. University of Alaska, with 134 papers; 9.44% of university's total papers
2. University of Hawaii, 343; 6.66%
3. Oregon State University, 315; 6.35%
4. University of New Hampshire, 78; 4.27%
5. University of California, Santa Cruz, 127; 4.07%

Source: "U.S. Universities with Highest Concentrations in Aquatic Sciences, 1995-99," *What's Hot in Research* (http://www.isinet.com/isi/hot/research) *Institute for Scientific Information*, February 5, 2001.

★4290★
U.S. universities with the highest concentration of papers published in the field of materials science, 1995-99

Ranking basis/background: Number of papers published in the field of materials science over a five-year period, and percentage they comprise of the university's total papers published. **Number listed:** 5.
1. Lehigh University, with 276 papers; 16.27% of university's total papers
2. Georgia Institute of Technology, 485; 9.88%
3. North Carolina State University, 584; 7.88%
4. Virginia Polytechnic Institute, 374; 6.58%
5. University of California, Santa Barbara, 423; 6.35%

Source: "U.S. Universities with Highest Concentrations in Materials Science, 1995-99," *What's Hot in Research* (http://www.isinet.com/isi/hot/research) *Institute for Scientific Information*, October 9, 2000.

★4291★
U.S. universities with the highest relative citation impact, 1993-97

Ranking basis/background: Number of top ten appearances in 21 fields encompassing the physical, life and social sciences. Top tens figured according to each university's average number of cites per paper between 1993 and 1997 compared to a world-baseline figure of overall cites per paper in each field. **Remarks:** Original source: *National Science Indicators on Diskette, 1981-97* **Number listed:** 11.
1. Harvard University, with 17 top ten appearances
2. Stanford University, 13
3. Caltech, 11
4. Yale University, 9
4. University of Michigan, 9
6. Massachusetts Institute of Technology, 8
7. University of California, Berkeley, 7
8. University of Washington (WA), 6
8. University of California, Santa Barbara, 6
8. Cornell University, 6
8. University of California, San Diego, 6

Source: "Highest Impact U.S. Universities, 1993-97," *What's Hot*, November 23, 1998.

SCIENCES–AUSTRALIA

★4292★
Australia's contribution of papers in the sciences, by field, 1993-97

Ranking basis/background: Percentage of papers from Australia. **Remarks:** Original source: *National Science Indicators on Diskette, 1981-97* **Number listed:** 22.
1. Geosciences, with 5.08%
2. Plant and animal sciences, 4.85%
3. Education, 4.79%
4. Ecology/environmental, 4.33%
5. Agricultural sciences, 4.31%
6. Social sciences, 4.05%
7. Astrophysics, 3.62%
8. Psychology/psychiatry, 3.60%
9. Immunology, 3.38%
10. Microbiology, 3.22%

Source: "Science in Australia, 1993-97," *What's Hot*, November 6, 1998.

★4293★
Australia's contribution of papers in the sciences, by field, 1995-99

Ranking basis/background: Percentage of science and social science papers from Australia over a five-year period. **Number listed:** 22.
1. Geosciences, with 5.16%
2. Plant and animal sciences, 5.09%
3. Education, 4.61%
4. Social sciences, 4.51%
5. Agricultural sciences, 4.25%
6. Ecology/environmental, 4.22%
7. Astrophysics, 3.96%
8. Psychology/psychiatry, 3.82%
9. Economics and business, 3.64%
10. Immunology, 3.42%

Source: "Science in Australia, 1995-99," *What's Hot in Research* (http://www.isinet.com/isi/hot/research) *Institute for Scientific Information*, July 24, 2000.

SCIENCES, GRADUATE
See also: **Physical Sciences, Graduate**

★4294★
Private, 4-year undergraduate colleges and universities producing the most Ph.D.'s in the sciences, 1920-1990

Ranking basis/background: Number of doctoral degrees granted to graduates of 914 private, 4-year U.S. undergraduate colleges and universities. Medical, law, and other professional, non-doctoral degrees are not included. **Remarks:** Original source: Office of Scientific and Engineering Personnel of the National Research Council. Report contains 50 other tables detailing the distribution of doctoral recipients by field of study over various time frames. **Number listed:** 359.
1. Oberlin College, with 2,253 Ph.D.'s
2. Swarthmore College, 1,513
3. Reed College, 1,194
4. Polytechnic University, 1,191
5. Pomona College, 1,151
5. Carleton College, 1,151
7. Barnard College, 1,027
8. Amherst College, 984
9. Wesleyan University, 957
10. Union College, 944
11. Bucknell University, 909
12. Wellesley College, 894
13. Antioch College, 892
13. Franklin and Marshall College, 892
15. DePauw University, 884
16. Manhattan College, 854
17. Williams College, 841
18. College of Wooster, 817
19. Mount Holyoke College, 786
20. Smith College, 779

Source: *Baccalaureate Origins of Doctorate Recipients, 7th ed.,* Franklin & Marshall College, March 1993.

SCIENCES—GREAT BRITAIN

★4295★
Private, 4-year undergraduate colleges and universities producing the most Ph.D.'s in the sciences, 1981-1990

Ranking basis/background: Number of doctoral degrees granted to graduates of 914 private, 4-year U.S. undergraduate colleges and universities. Medical, law, and other professional, non-doctoral degrees are not included. **Remarks:** Original source: Office of Scientific and Engineering Personnel of the National Research Council. Report contains 50 other tables detailing the distribution of doctoral recipients by field of study over various time frames. **Number listed:** 355.
1. Oberlin College, with 517 Ph.D.'s
2. Carleton College, 404
3. Swarthmore College, 372
4. Barnard College, 314
5. Pomona College, 308
6. Wellesley College, 306
7. Reed College, 304
8. Wesleyan University, 303
9. Bucknell University, 300
10. Smith College, 298
11. Mount Holyoke College, 255
11. Clark University, 255
13. Williams College, 249
14. Vassar College, 248
15. St. Olaf College, 242
16. Franklin and Marshall College, 237
17. Union College, 228
17. Harvey Mudd College, 228
19. Colgate University, 224
20. Kalamazoo College, 215

Source: *Baccalaureate Origins of Doctorate Recipients, 7th ed.,* Franklin & Marshall College, March 1993.

★4296★
Radcliffe Institute for Advanced Study fellowship recipient in the field of cognitive and neural sciences, 2000-01

Ranking basis/background: Recipient and institutional affiliation of the Radcliffe Institute for Advanced study fellowship for pursuit of advanced work across a wide range of academic disciplines, professions, and creative arts. **Number listed:** 1.
   Ann Skoczenski, Smith-Kettlewell Eye Research Institute

Source: "The Radcliffe Institute for Advanced Study," *The Chronicle of Higher Education,* 46: A59, (June 2, 2000).

SCIENCES–GREAT BRITAIN

★4297★
United Kingdom's contribution of papers in the sciences, by field, 1995-99

Ranking basis/background: Percentage of science and social science papers from the United Kingdom over a five-year period. **Number listed:** 22.
1. Economics and business, 14.36%
2. Astrophysics, 14.02%
3. Social sciences, 13.78%
4. Education, 13.29%
5. Geosciences, 11.35%
6. Microbiology, 11.28%
7. Psychology/psychiatry, 10.94%
8. Molecular biology, 10.86%
9. Clinical medicine, 10.54%
10. Neuroscience, 10.26%

Source: "Science in the United Kingdom, 1995-99," *What's Hot in Research* (http://www.isinet.com/isi/hot/research) Institute for Scientific Information, December 11, 2000.

SCIENCES–INTERNATIONAL

★4298★
Austria's contribution of papers in the sciences by field, 1992-96

Ranking basis/background: Percent of papers from Austria. **Remarks:** Original source: ISI's *National Science Indicators on Diskette, 1981-96.* **Number listed:** 21.
1. Immunology, with 1.20%
2. Clinical medicine, 1.07%
3. Mathematics, 0.80%
3. Physics, 0.80%
5. Pharmacology, 0.75%
5. Molecular biology, 0.75%
7. Plant and animal sciences, 0.71%
7. Neuroscience, 0.71%
9. Microbiology, 0.69%
10. Biology and biochemistry, 0.68%

Source: "Science in Austria," *What's Hot,* January 26, 1998.

★4299★
Austria's contribution of papers in the sciences, by field, 1995-99

Ranking basis/background: Percentage of science and social science papers from Austria over a five-year period. **Number listed:** 21.
1. Immunology, with 1.32%
2. Clinical medicine, 1.23%
3. Physics, 0.93%
4. Neuroscience, 0.87%
4. Mathematics, 0.87%
6. Pharmacology, 0.86%
7. Microbiology, 0.85%
8. Molecular biology, 0.84%
9. Plant and animal science, 0.83%
9. Astrophysics, 0.83%

Source: "Science in Austria, 1995-99," *What's Hot in Research* (http://www.isinet.com/isi/hot/research) Institute for Scientific Information, January 8, 2001.

★4300★
Austria's relative impact in the sciences by field, 1992-96

Ranking basis/background: In percent, impact compared to the rest of the world of papers in the sciences. **Remarks:** Original source: ISI's *National Science Indicators on Diskette, 1981-96.* **Number listed:** 21.
1. Engineering, with 24%
2. Ecology/environmental, 16%
2. Materials science, 16%
4. Pharmacology, 14%
5. Molecular biology, 13%
6. Physics, 8%
7. Microbiology, 1%
8. Neuroscience, 5% decrease
8. Biology and biochemistry, 5% decrease
10. Chemistry, 6% decrease

Source: "Science in Austria," *What's Hot,* January 26, 1998.

★4301★
Belgium's contribution of papers in the sciences by field, 1992-96

Ranking basis/background: Percent of papers from Belgium. Also includes for each field of study the country's relative impact, in percent, compared to the rest of the world. **Remarks:** Original source: ISI's *National Science Indicators on Diskette, 1981-97.* **Number listed:** 21.
1. Microbiology, with 1.81%; relative impact of 13%
2. Immunology, 1.60%; 2% decrease
3. Pharmacology, 1.47%; 1% decrease
4. Clinical medicine, 1.45%; 16%
5. Molecular biology, 1.43%; 21% decrease
6. Biology and biochemistry, 1.38%; 7% decrease
7. Plant and animal sciences, 1.33%; 16%
8. Economics and business, 1.17%; 14% decrease
9. Astrophysics, 1.13%; 35% decrease
10. Mathematics, 1.11%; 23%
10. Physics, 1.11%; 15%

Source: "Science in Belgium, 1992-96," *What's Hot,* April 20, 1998.

★4302★
Belgium's contribution of papers in the sciences, by field, 1995-99

Ranking basis/background: Percentage of science and social science papers from Belgium over a five-year period. **Number listed:** 21.
1. Microbiology, with 1.94%
2. Immunology, 1.67%
3. Plant and animal sciences, 1.65%
4. Clinical medicine, 1.54%
5. Pharmacology, 1.53%
6. Molecular biology, 1.49%
7. Biology and biochemistry, 1.47%
8. Economics and business, 1.38%
9. Chemistry, 1.28%
10. Astrophysics, 1.26%

Source: "Science in Belgium, 1995-99," *What's Hot in Research* (http://www.isinet.com/isi/hot/research) Institute for Scientific Information, August 7, 2000.

★4303★
Canada's contribution of papers in the sciences, by field, 1995-99

Ranking basis/background: Percentage of science and social science papers from Canada over a five-year period. **Number listed:** 22.
1. Geosciences, with 8.59%
2. Ecology/environmental, 7.94%
3. Psychology/psychiatry, 7.64%
4. Plant and animal sciences, 7.10%
5. Economics and business, 6.77%
6. Neuroscience, 6.50%
7. Social sciences, 6.08%
8. Education, 5.98%
9. Molecular biology, 5.82%
10. Mathematics, 5.42%

Source: "Canadian Science, 1995-99," *What's Hot in Research* (http://www.isinet.com/isi/hot/research) Institute for Scientific Information, October 30, 2000.

★4304★
Canadian universities with the greatest impact in materials science, 1992-96

Ranking basis/background: For each university, total number of citations divided by number of published articles during the same time period. **Remarks:** Original source: *National Science Indicators on Diskette, 1981-97* **Number listed:** 5.
1. University of Toronto, with 2.92 citations per paper; 432 total papers
2. McMaster University, 2.83; 255
3. University of Montreal, 2.64; 268
4. Queen's University, 2.34; 228
5. University of Western Ontario, 2.26; 122

Source: "Canadian Universities: Highest Impact in Materials Science, 1992-96," *What's Hot*, July 27, 1998.

★4305★
Canadian universities with the greatest impact in neuroscience, 1993-97

Ranking basis/background: For each university, total number of citations divided by number of published articles during the same time period. **Remarks:** Original source: *National Science Indicators on Diskette, 1981-97* **Number listed:** 5.
1. University of British Columbia, with 9.03 citations per paper; 771 total papers
2. University of Ottawa, 8.41; 371
3. University of Toronto, 8.17; 1,617
4. McGill University, 7.91; 1,593
5. Laval University, 7.67; 383

Source: "Canadian Universities: Highest Impact in Neuroscience, 1993-97," *What's Hot*, November 30, 1998.

★4306★
Denmark's contribution of papers in the sciences, by field, 1994-98

Ranking basis/background: Percentage of papers from Denmark. **Remarks:** Original source: National Science Indicators on Diskette, 1981-98. **Number listed:** 21.
1. Ecology/environmental, with 1.66%
2. Biology and biochemistry, with 1.46%
3. Immunology, 1.45%
4. Microbiology, 1.44%
5. Plant and animal sciences, 1.33%
6. Clinical medicine, 1.31%
7. Astrophysics, 1.29%
8. Agricultural sciences, 1.19%
9. Molecular biology, 1.09%
10. Geosciences, 1.02%

Source: "Science in Denmark, 1994-98," *What's Hot in Research (http://www.isinet.com/hot/research) Institute for Scientific Information*, March 6, 2000.

★4307★
Denmark's contribution of papers in the sciences, by field, 1995-99

Ranking basis/background: Percentage of science and social science papers from Denmark over a five-year period. **Number listed:** 21.
1. Ecology/environmental, with 1.68%
2. Microbiology, 1.54%
3. Biology and biochemistry, 1.52%
4. Immunology, 1.44%
5. Plant and animal sciences, 1.40%
6. Astrophysics, 1.37%
7. Agricultural sciences, 1.30%
8. Clinical medicine, 1.28%
9. Geosciences, 1.11%
10. Molecular biology, 1.07%

Source: "Science in Denmark, 1995-99," *What's Hot in Research (http://www.isinet.com/isi/hot/research) Institute for Scientific Information*, December 25, 2000.

★4308★
England's contribution of papers in the sciences, by field, 1994-98

Ranking basis/background: Percentage of papers from England only and does not include Scotland, Wales, or Northern Ireland. **Remarks:** Original source: National Science Indicators on Diskette, 1981-98. **Number listed:** 23.
1. Economics and business, with 11.96%
2. Astrophysics, 11.70%
3. Education, 11.33%
4. Social sciences, 11.22%
5. Education, 10.47%
6. Geosciences, 9.65%
7. Psychology/psychiatry, 9.20%
7. Microbiology, 9.20%
9. Molecular biology, 9.16%
10. Clinical medicine, 9.10

Source: "Science in England, 1994-98," *What's Hot in Research (http://www.isinet.com/isi/hot/research) Institute for Scientific Information*, April 3, 2000.

★4309★
Finland's contribution of papers in the sciences by field, 1992-96

Ranking basis/background: Percent of papers from Finland. Also includes for each field of study the country's relative impact, in percent, compared to the rest of the world. **Remarks:** Original source: ISI's *National Science Indicators on Diskette, 1981-97*. **Number listed:** 21.
1. Ecology/environment, with 1.33%; a relative impact of 20%
2. Clinical medicine, 1.28%; 19%
3. Neuroscience, 1.21%; 24% decrease
4. Immunology, 1.18%; 39% decrease
5. Pharmacology, 1.06%; 3% decrease
6. Astrophysics, 0.98%; 19% decrease
7. Microbiology, 0.92%; 9%
7. Plant and animal sciences, 0.92%; 9% decrease
9. Molecular biology, 0.91%; 1%
10. Agricultural sciences, 0.89%; 17%

Source: "Science in Finland, 1992-96," *What's Hot*, March 23, 1998.

★4310★
Finland's contribution of papers in the sciences, by field, 1995-99

Ranking basis/background: Percentage of science and social science papers from Finland over a five-year period. **Number listed:** 21.
1. Ecology/environmental, with 1.61%
2. Neuroscience, 1.34%
3. Clinical medicine, 1.33%
4. Astrophysics, 1.17%
5. Immunology, 1.16%
6. Pharmacology, 1.15%
7. Plant and animal sciences, 1.11%
8. Molecular biology, 1.00%
9. Agricultural sciences, 0.98%
10. Biology and biochemistry, 0.97%

Source: "Science in Finland, 1995-99," *What's Hot in Research (http://www.isinet.com/isi/hot/research) Institute for Scientific Information*, June 26, 2000.

★4311★
France's contribution of papers in the sciences, by field, 1995-99

Ranking basis/background: Percentage of science and social science papers from France over a five-year period. **Number listed:** 21.
1. Mathematics, with 12.14%
2. Astrophysics, 10.05%
3. Geosciences, 9.19%
4. Physics, 8.50%
5. Microbiology, 8.12%
6. Molecular biology, 8.00%
7. Immunology, 7.23%
8. Biology and biochemistry, 6.97%
9. Chemistry, 6.84%
10. Pharmacology, 6.13%

Source: "Science in France, 1995-99," *What's Hot in Research (http://www.isinet.com/isi/hot/research) Institute for Scientific Information*, June 5, 2000.

★4312★
France's contribution of papers in the sciences, by field, 1996-2000

Ranking basis/background: Percentage of science and social science papers from France over a five-year period. **Number listed:** 21.
1. Mathematics, with 12.25%
2. Space science, 10.27%
3. Geosciences, 9.38%
4. Physics, 8.59%
5. Microbiology, 8.09%
6. Molecular biology, 7.99%
7. Immunology, 7.29%
8. Biology and biochemistry, 6.87%
9. Chemistry, 6.78%
10. Materials science, 6.12%

Source: "Science in France, 1996-2000," *What's Hot in Research (http://www.isinet.com/isi/hot/research) Institute for Scientific Information*.

★4313★
Germany's contribution of papers in the sciences, by field, 1995-99

Ranking basis/background: Percentage of science and social science papers from Germany over a five-year period. **Number listed:** 22.
1. Astrophysics, with 13.63%
2. Physics, 11.64%
3. Chemistry, 10.57%
4. Mathematics, 9.88%
5. Molecular biology, 9.72%
6. Microbiology, 9.62%
7. Materials science, 9.52%
8. Neuroscience, 8.33%
9. Clinical medicine, 8.32%
10. Biology and biochemistry, 7.89%

Source: "Science in Germany, 1995-99," *What's Hot in Research (http://www.isinet.com/isi/hot/research) Institute for Scientific Information*, September 18, 2000.

★4314★
Hong Kong's contribution of papers in the sciences, by field, 1995-99

Ranking basis/background: Percentage of science and social science papers from Hong Kong over a five-year period. **Number listed:** 20.
1. Economics and business, with 1.41%
2. Computer science, 1.37%
3. Engineering, 1.08%
4. Mathematics, 0.81%
5. Social sciences, 0.66%
6. Materials science, 0.63%

7. Psychology/psychiatry, 0.55%
8. Physics, 0.51%
9. Ecology/environmental, 0.45%
10. Clinical medicine, 0.43%

Source: "Science in Hong Kong, 1995-99," *What's Hot in Research* (http://www.isinet.com/isi/hot/research) Institute for Scientific Information.

★4315★
Ireland's contribution of papers in the sciences, by field, 1994-98

Ranking basis/background: Percentage of papers from Ireland. **Remarks:** Original source: National Science Indicators on Diskette, 1981-98. **Number listed:** 21.

1. Agricultural sciences, with 0.61%
2. Economics and business, 0.49%
3. Psychology/psychiatry, 0.48%
4. Microbiology, 0.45%
5. Clinical medicine, 0.38%
5. Plant and animal sciences, 0.38%
7. Mathematics, 0.36%
7. Biology and biochemistry, 0.36%
9. Neuroscience, 0.33%
9. Astrophysics, 0.33%

Source: "Science in Ireland, 1994-98," *What's Hot in Research* (http://www.isinet.com/hot/research) Institute for Scientific Information, December 6, 1999.

★4316★
Italy's contribution of papers in the sciences, by field, 1995-99

Ranking basis/background: Percentage of science and social science papers from Italy over a five-year period. **Number listed:** 21.

1. Astrophysics, with 8.43%
2. Pharmacology, 5.21%
3. Physics, 4.92%
4. Neuroscience, 4.87%
5. Computer science, 4.84%
6. Mathematics, 4.80%
7. Immunology, 4.78%
8. Clinical medicine, 4.73%
9. Molecular biology, 4.17%
10. Chemistry, 4.15%

Source: "Science in Italy, 1995-99," *What's Hot in Research* (http://www.isinet.com/isi/hot/research) Institute for Scientific Information, November 27, 2000.

★4317★
Italy's relative impact in the sciences by field, 1992-96

Ranking basis/background: In percent, impact compared to the rest of the world of papers in the sciences. **Remarks:** Original source: ISI's *National Science Indicators on Diskette, 1981-96.* **Number listed:** 21.

1. Physics, with 14%
2. Materials science, 11%
3. Chemistry, 3%
3. Engineering, 3%
5. Clinical medicine, 5% decrease
6. Computer science, 6% decrease
7. Agricultural sciences, 8% decrease
8. Astrophysics, 9% decrease
9. Mathematics, 10% decrease
10. Plant and animal sciences, 13% decrease

Source: "Science in Italy, 1992-96," *What's Hot,* February 10, 1998.

★4318★
Japan's contribution of papers in the sciences, by field, 1995-99

Ranking basis/background: Percentage of science and social science papers from Japan over a five-year period. **Number listed:** 21.

1. Materials science, with 15.04%
2. Physics, 13.96%
3. Pharmacology, 12.74%
4. Chemistry, 12.14%
5. Agricultural sciences, 11.53%
6. Biology and biochemistry, 11.03%
7. Computer science, 10.02%
8. Microbiology, 9.90%
9. Engineering, 9.83%
10. Neuroscience, 9.06%

Source: "Science in Japan, 1995-99," *What's Hot in Research* (http://www.isinet.com/isi/hot/research) Institute for Scientific Information, July 10, 2000.

★4319★
Japan's contribution of papers in the sciences, by field, 1996-2000

Ranking basis/background: Percentage of science and social science papers from Japan over a five-year period. **Number listed:** 21.

1. Materials science, with 15.17%
2. Physics, 14.18%
3. Pharmacology, 13.01%
4. Chemistry, 12.34%
5. Biology and biochemistry, 11.07%
6. Agricultural sciences, 10.90%
7. Microbiology, 10.00
8. Computer science, 9.62%
9. Engineering, 9.59%
10. Molecular biology, 9.45%

Source: "Science in Japan, 1996-2000," *What's Hot in Research* (http://www.isinet.com/isi/hot/research) Institute for Scientific Information.

★4320★
Nations with the most-cited papers in the sciences

Ranking basis/background: Number of paper and citations to papers based on a file of 838 papers indexed by ISI between May 1997 and April 1999. **Remarks:** Original source: Hot Paper Database from the ISI Research Services Group. **Number listed:** 5.

1. United States, with 581 papers; 30,724 citations to papers
2. England, 83; 4,520
3. Germany, 79; 3,190
4. Japan, 65; 2,987
5. Canada, 61; 2,999

Source: "Hot Papers: Prolific Nations," *What's Hot in Research* (http://www.isinet.com/hot/research) Institute for Scientific Information, July 5, 1999.

★4321★
Netherlands' contribution of papers in the sciences, by field, 1995-99

Ranking basis/background: Percentage of science and social science papers from the Netherlands over a five-year period. **Number listed:** 22.

1. Astrophysics, with 4.46%
2. Immunology, 4.02%
3. Microbiology, 3.87%
4. Ecology/environmental, 3.39%
5. Economics and business, 3.28%
6. Psychology/psychiatry, 3.21%
7. Clinical medicine, 3.21%
8. Molecular biology, 2.97%
9. Plant and animal sciences, 2.90%
10. Pharmacology, 2.69%

Source: "Science in the Netherlands, 1995-99," *What's Hot in Research* (http://www.isinet.com/isi/hot/research) Institute for Scientific Information, October 2, 2000.

★4322★
New Zealand's contribution of papers in the sciences, by field, 1994-98

Ranking basis/background: Percentage of papers from New Zealand. **Remarks:** Original source: National Science Indicators on Diskette, 1981-98. **Number listed:** 22.

1. Agricultural sciences, with 1.72%
2. Plant and animal sciences, 1.52%
3. Geosciences, 1.32%
4. Ecology/environmental, 1.21%
5. Education, 1.07%
6. Psychology/psychiatry, 0.87%
7. Economics and business, 0.82%
8. Social sciences, 0.72%
9. Pharmacology, 0.71%
10. Microbiology, 0.57%

Source: "Science in New Zealand, 1994-98," *What's Hot in Research* (http://www.isinet.com/hot/research) Institute for Scientific Information, April 17, 2000.

★4323★
Norway's contribution of papers in the sciences, by field, 1994-98

Ranking basis/background: Percentage of papers from Norway. **Remarks:** Original source: National Science Indicators on Diskette, 1981-98. **Number listed:** 20.

1. Geosciences, with 1.69%
2. Ecology/environmental, 1.27%
3. Plant and animal sciences, 1.10%
4. Immunology, 0.92%
5. Clinical medicine, 0.81%
6. Economics and business, 0.77%
7. Psychology/psychiatry, 0.74%
7. Social sciences, 0.74%
9. Microbiology, 0.59%
9. Molecular biology, 0.59%

Source: "Norwegian Science, 1994-98," *What's Hot in Research* (http://www.isinet.com/hot/research) Institute for Scientific Information, June 21, 1999.

★4324★
Poland's contribution of papers in the sciences, by field, 1993-97

Ranking basis/background: Percentage of papers from Poland. **Remarks:** Original source: *National Science Indicators on Diskette, 1981-97* **Number listed:** 21.

1. Physics, with 2.27%
2. Chemistry, 2.17%
3. Mathematics, 1.96%
4. Astrophysics, 1.62%
5. Engineering, 1.31%
6. Materials science, 1.27%
7. Biology and biochemistry, 0.91%
8. Plant and animal sciences, 0.87%
9. Pharmacology, 0.85%
10. Neuroscience, 0.66%

Source: "Science in Poland, 1993-97," *What's Hot,* September 28, 1998.

★4325★
Russia's contribution of papers in the sciences, by field, 1993-97

Ranking basis/background: Percentage of papers from Russia. **Remarks:** Original source: *National Science Indicators on Diskette, 1981-97* **Number listed:** 21.
1. Physics, with 9.73%
2. Chemistry, 7.43%
3. Geosciences, 7.17%
4. Astrophysics, 6.88%
5. Materials science, 4.57%
6. Engineering, 4.32%
7. Mathematics, 3.40%
8. Molecular biology, 2.94%
9. Microbiology, 2.17%
10. Biology and biochemistry, 2.05%

Source: "Russian Science, 1993-97," *What's Hot*, July 13, 1998.

★4326★
South Africa's contribution of papers in the sciences, by field, 1994-98

Ranking basis/background: Percentage of papers from South Africa. **Remarks:** Original source: National Science Indicators on Diskette, 1981-98. **Number listed:** 21.
1. Plant and animal sciences, with 1.55%
2. Geosciences, 1.16%
3. Astrophysics, 1.11%
4. Ecology/environmental, 1.10%
5. Education, 0.80%
6. Social sciences, 0.57%
7. Microbiology, 0.54%
8. Psychology/psychiatry, 0.52%
9. Agricultural sciences, 0.48%
10. Clinical medicine, 0.47%

Source: "Science in South Africa, 1994-98," *What's Hot in Research* (http://www.isinet.com/hot/research) Institute for Scientific Information, February 21, 2000.

★4327★
South Korea's contribution of papers in the sciences, by field, 1995-99

Ranking basis/background: Percentage of science and social science papers from South Korea over a five-year period. **Number listed:** 20.
1. Materials science, with 3.26%
2. Engineering, 2.53%
3. Physics, 2.51%
4. Computer science, 2.35%
5. Chemistry, 1.78
6. Pharmacology, 1.63%
7. Microbiology, 1.17%
8. Mathematics, 1.11%
9. Biology and biochemistry, 1.02%
10. Economics and business, 0.81%

Source: "South Korean Science, 1995-99," *What's Hot in Research* (http://www.isinet.com/isi/hot/research) Institute for Scientific Information, October 16, 2000.

★4328★
Spain's contribution of papers in the sciences, by field, 1993-97

Ranking basis/background: Percentage of papers from Spain. **Remarks:** Original source: *National Science Indicators on Diskette, 1981-97* **Number listed:** 21.
1. Astrophysics, with 4.13%
2. Agricultural sciences, 3.72%
3. Chemistry, 3.47%
4. Mathematics, 3.46%
5. Microbiology, 3.41%
6. Plant and animal sciences, 3.11%
7. Pharmacology, 2.84%
8. Ecology/environmental, 2.76%
9. Biology and biochemistry, 2.53%
10. Physics, 2.46%

Source: "Science in Spain, 1993-97," *What's Hot*, August 25, 1998.

★4329★
Spain's contribution of papers in the sciences, by field, 1995-99

Ranking basis/background: Percentage of science and social science papers from Spain over a five-year period. **Number listed:** 21.
1. Astrophysics, with 4.95%
2. Agricultural sciences, 4.41%
3. Microbiology, 4.00%
4. Mathematics, 3.88%
5. Chemistry, 3.82%
6. Plant and animal sciences, 3.50%
7. Ecology/environmental, 3.01%
8. Pharmacology, 2.88%
9. Physics, 2.71%
10. Biology and biochemistry, 2.70%

Source: "Science in Spain, 1995-99," *What's Hot in Research* (http://www.isinet.com/isi/hot/research) Institute for Scientific Information, May 15, 2000.

★4330★
Sweden's contribution of papers in the sciences by field, 1993-97

Ranking basis/background: Percent of papers from Sweden. Also includes for each field of study the country's relative impact, in percent, compared to the rest of the world. **Remarks:** Original source: National Science Indicators of Diskette, 1981-97. **Number listed:** 21.
1. Immunology, with 3.99%; relative impact of negative 34%
2. Neuroscience, 2.95%; 4%
3. Ecology/environmental, 2.93%; 35%
4. Clinical medicine, 2.68%; 15%
5. Biology and biochemistry, 2.56%; 3%
6. Pharmacology, 2.45%; 41%
7. Microbiology, 2.04%; 16%
8. Molecular biology, 1.99%; negative 15%
9. Plant and animal sciences, 1.87%; 36%
10. Geosciences, 1.70%; negative 4%

Source: "Science in Sweden, 1993-97," *What's Hot in Research*, http://www.isinet.com/whatshot/whatshot.html, Institute for Scientific Information (March 22, 1999).

★4331★
Sweden's contribution of papers in the sciences, by field, 1995-99

Ranking basis/background: Percentage of science and social science papers from Sweden over a five-year period. **Number listed:** 21.
1. Immunology, with 4.00%
2. Ecology/environmental, 3.16%
3. Neuroscience, 2.93%
4. Clinical medicine, 2.69%
5. Biology and biochemistry, 2.64%
6. Pharmacology, 2.50%
7. Microbiology, 2.08%
8. Molecular biology, 2.03%
9. Plant and animal sciences, 1.96%
10. Geosciences, 1.84%

Source: "Science in Sweden, 1995-99," *What's Hot in Research* (http://www.isinet.com/isi/hot/research) Institute for Scientific Information, November 13, 2000.

★4332★
Switzerland's contribution of papers in the sciences, by field, 1994-98

Ranking basis/background: Percentage of papers from Switzerland. **Remarks:** Original source: National Science Indicators on Diskette, 1981-98. **Number listed:** 21.
1. Immunology, with 3.26%
2. Molecular biology, 2.60%
3. Physics, 2.48%
4. Microbiology, 2.23%
5. Neuroscience, 2.04%
6. Biology and biochemistry, 2.02%
7. Clinical medicine, 1.96%
8. Geosciences, 1.90%
9. Chemistry, 1.84%
10. Pharmacology, 1.77%

Source: "Swiss Science, 1994-98," *What's Hot in Research* (http://www.isinet.com/hot/research) Institute for Scientific Information, March 20, 2000.

★4333★
Switzerland's contribution of papers in the sciences, by field, 1995-99

Ranking basis/background: Percentage of science and social science papers from Switzerland over a five-year period. **Number listed:** 21.
1. Immunology, with 3.31%
2. Molecular biology, 2.62%
3. Physics, 2.50%
4. Microbiology, 2.27%
5. Neuroscience, 2.12%
6. Geosciences, 2.05%
7. Clinical medicine, 2.02%
8. Biology and biochemistry, 2.00%
9. Chemistry, 1.87%
10. Pharmacology, 1.80%

Source: "Swiss Science, 1995-99," *What's Hot in Research* (http://www.isinet.com/isi/hot/research) Institute for Scientific Information, January 22, 2001.

★4334★
Taiwan contribution of papers in the sciences, by field, 1995-99

Ranking basis/background: Percentage of science and social science papers from Taiwan over a five-year period. **Number listed:** 21.
1. Computer science, with 3.72%
2. Engineering, 3.22%
3. Materials science, 2.37%
4. Physics, 1.50%
5. Pharmacology, 1.36%
6. Chemistry, 1.34%
7. Mathematics, 1.21%
8. Ecology/environmental, 1.14%
9. Clinical medicine, 0.92%
10. Microbiology, 0.90%

Source: "Science in Taiwan, 1995-99," *What's Hot in Research* (http://www.isinet.com/isi/hot/research) Institute for Scientific Information, February 5, 2001.

★4335★
Turkey's contribution of papers in the sciences, by field, 1995-99

Ranking basis/background: Percentage of science and social science papers from Turkey over a five-year period. **Number listed:** 21.
1. Pharmacology, with 0.88%
2. Clinical medicine, 0.82%
3. Engineering, 0.72%
4. Ecology/environmental, 0.69%
5. Agricultural science, 0.64%

SCIENTIFIC & TECHNOLOGICAL RESEARCH & DEVELOPMENT

6. Materials science, 0.59%
7. Chemistry, 0.58%
8. Geosciences, 0.57%
9. Computer science, 0.38%
10. Physics, 0.37%

Source: "Science in Turkey, 1995-99," *What's Hot in Research* (http://www.isinet.com/isi/hot/research) Institute for Scientific Information, August 21, 2000.

SCIENTIFIC & TECHNOLOGICAL RESEARCH & DEVELOPMENT FUNDING

★4336★
Stipend for entry-level postdoctoral researchers

Ranking basis/background: National Institutes of Health stipend for postdoctorate researchers receiving the National Research Service Award. **Number listed:** 5.
   2002, with $31,087
   2003, $34,195
   2004, $37,614
   2005, $41,375
   2006, $45,000

Source: Southwick, Ron, "NIH Offers Postdoctoral Scientists a Raise and Prospects for Better Treatment," *The Chronicle of Higher Education*, 47: A29-A30, (April 27, 2001).

SCIENTIFIC & TECHNOLOGICAL RESEARCH FUNDING

★4337★
National Science Foundation growth trends, 1997 to 2002

Ranking basis/background: Figures, in billions, from the U.S. government's fiscal appropriations for the National Science Foundation programs. **Number listed:** 6.
   1997, with $3.3 billion
   1998, $3.4
   1999, $3.7
   2000, $3.9
   2001, $4.4
   2002, $4.5 (proposed)

Source: Brainard, Jeffrey and Ron Southwick, "NIH Soars, Other Science Agencies Struggle in President's First Budget Plan," *The Chronicle of Higher Education*, 47: A35, A38-A39, (April 20, 2001).

★4338★
National Science Foundation research grants, 1998 to 2002

Ranking basis/background: Total number of new grants and continuing grants. **Number listed:** 5.
   1998, with 7,578 new grants; 19,782 continuing grants
   1999, 8,565; 20,163
   2000, 8,800; 21,789
   2001, 9,158; 23,246
   2002 (proposed), 9,158; 24,932

Source: Brainard, Jeffrey and Ron Southwick, "NIH Soars, Other Science Agencies Struggle in President's First Budget Plan," *The Chronicle of Higher Education*, 47: A35, A38-A39, (April 20, 2001).

★4339★
Proposed fiscal 2002 appropriations for science and technology research

Ranking basis/background: Percentage breakdown of the U.S. government's proposed fiscal 2002 appropriations for science and technology research, totaling $49.7-billion. **Number listed:** 8.
1. National Institutes of Health, with 46%
2. National Aeronautics and Space Administration, 14%
3. Defense, 10%
4. Energy, 9%
4. National Science Foundation, 9%
6. Agriculture, 4%
7. Interior, 2%
8. Other, 6%

Source: "Bush's Fiscal 2002 Budget Plan for Higher Education and Science," *The Chronicle of Higher Education*, 47: A36-A37, (April 20, 2001).

SKIING
See: **Athletics**

SOCIAL SCIENCES PERIODICALS

★4340★
Most-cited social sciences journals, 1981-97

Ranking basis/background: Total citations. **Remarks:** Original source: *National Science Indicators on Diskette, 1981-97* **Number listed:** 25.
1. *Archives of General Psychiatry*, with 23,238 citations
2. *American Journal of Psychiatry*, 22,478
3. *Journal of Personality and Social Psychology*, 17,864
4. *British Journal of Psychiatry*, 13,851
5. *American Journal of Public Health*, 12,217
6. *Psychological Bulletin*, 11,572
7. *Journal of Consulting and Clinical Psychology*, 10,333
8. *Child Development*, 9,372
9. *Psychological Review*, 9,005
10. *Physiology & Behavior*, 8,062

Source: "25 Most-Cited Social Sciences Journals," *What's Hot*, December 14, 1998.

★4341★
Social sciences journals with the greatest impact measure, 1981-97

Ranking basis/background: Average number of times recent journal articles were cited in 1997. **Remarks:** Original source: *National Science Indicators on Diskette, 1981-97* **Number listed:** 25.
1. *Archives of General Psychology*, with an impact factor of 10.751
2. *The Economist*, 9.167
3. *Behavioral and Brain Sciences*, 8.118
4. *Psychological Review*, 7.060
5. *American Journal of Psychiatry*, 6.501
6. *Harvard Law Review*, 6.325
7. *Psychological Bulletin*, 6.038
8. *Journal of Economic Literature*, 5.818
9. *Contemporary Sociology*, 5.667
10. *International Security*, 5.152

Source: "Social Sciences: The 25 Highest-Impact Journals," *What's Hot*, October 19, 1998.

SOCIAL WORK, GRADUATE

★4342★
Top recruiters for social work jobs for 2000-01 bachelor's degree recipients

Ranking basis/background: Projected number of college hires from on-campus recruitment for 2000-01. **Remarks:** Numbers reflect total expected hires, not just African American projected hires. **Number listed:** 2.
1. Eckerd Youth Alternatives, Inc., with 25 projected hires
2. ARAMARK Educational Resources, 10

Source: "The Top 100 Employers and the Majors in Demand for the Class of 2001," *The Black Collegian*, 31: 19-35, (February 2001).

★4343★
Top recruiters for social work jobs for 2000-01 master's degree recipients

Ranking basis/background: Projected number of college hires from on-campus recruitment for 2000-01. **Remarks:** Numbers reflect total expected hires, not just African American projected hires. **Number listed:** 3.
1. U.S. Air Force (Active Duty Hires), with 16 projected hires
2. Caddo Parish School Board, 5
2. Novant Health, 5

Source: "The Top 100 Employers and the Majors in Demand for the Class of 2001," *The Black Collegian*, 31: 19-35, (February 2001).

SOCIOLOGY

★4344★
Private, 4-year undergraduate colleges and universities producing the most Ph.D.'s in anthropology and sociology, 1920-1990

Ranking basis/background: Number of doctoral degrees granted to graduates of 914 private, 4-year U.S. undergraduate colleges and universities. Medical, law, and other professional, non-doctoral degrees are not included. **Remarks:** Original source: Office of Scientific and Engineering Personnel of the National Research Council. Report contains 50 other tables detailing the distribution of doctoral recipients by field of study over various time frames. **Number listed:** 357.
1. Oberlin College, with 149 Ph.D.'s
2. Reed College, 124
3. Barnard College, 121
4. Antioch College, 87
5. Swarthmore College, 82
6. Beloit College, 81
7. Vassar College, 80
8. Bryn Mawr College, 70
9. Pomona College, 66
9. Carleton College, 66
11. Wellesley College, 64
12. Smith College, 62
13. Wheaton College, 54
14. Franklin and Marshall College, 49
15. Wesleyan University, 47
16. Colgate University, 42
17. Mount Holyoke College, 39
18. DePauw University, 37
18. Grinnell College, 37
18. Roosevelt University, 37

SOCIOLOGY, GRADUATE

Source: *Baccalaureate Origins of Doctorate Recipients*, 7th ed., Franklin & Marshall College, March 1993.

★4345★
Private, 4-year undergraduate colleges and universities producing the most Ph.D.'s in anthropology and sociology, 1981-1990

Ranking basis/background: Number of doctoral degrees granted to graduates of 914 private, 4-year U.S. undergraduate colleges and universities. Medical, law, and other professionals, non-doctoral degrees are not included. **Remarks:** Original source: Office of Scientific and Engineering Personnel of the National Research Council. Report contains 50 other tables detailing the distribution of doctoral recipients by field of study over various time frames. **Number listed:** 257.

1. Barnard College, with 36 Ph.D.'s
2. Oberlin College, 35
3. Reed College, 32
4. Bryn Mawr College, 30
5. Beloit College, 25
6. Carleton College, 21
7. Swarthmore College, 20
7. Smith College, 20
7. Wellesley College, 20
7. Vassar College, 20
11. Wesleyan University, 18
12. Antioch College, 17
12. Mount Holyoke College, 17
14. Pomona College, 13
14. Colgate University, 13
14. Sarah Lawrence College, 13
14. Bucknell University, 13
14. Wheaton College, 13
19. Franklin and Marshall College, 12
19. Kalamazoo College, 12
19. Roosevelt University, 12

Source: *Baccalaureate Origins of Doctorate Recipients*, 7th ed., Franklin & Marshall College, March 1993.

★4346★
Radcliffe Institute for Advanced Study fellowship recipients in the field of sociology, 2000-01

Ranking basis/background: Recipient and institutional affiliation of the Radcliffe Institute for Advanced study fellowship for pursuit of advanced work across a wide range of academic disciplines, professions, and creative arts. **Number listed:** 4.

- Constance Ahrons, University of Southern California
- Cameron Macdonald, University of Connecticut
- Irene Padavic, Florida State University
- Phyllis Moen, Cornell University

Source: "The Radcliffe Institute for Advanced Study," *The Chronicle of Higher Education*, 46: A59, (June 2, 2000).

★4347★
Top recruiters for sociology jobs for 2000-01 bachelor's degree recipients

Ranking basis/background: Projected number of college hires from on-campus recruitment for 2000-01. **Remarks:** Numbers reflect total expected hires, not just African American projected hires. **Number listed:** 10.

1. Accenture, with 165 projected hires
2. Eckerd Youth Alternatives, Inc., 25
3. Federated Department Stores, 23
4. U.S. Air Force (Active Duty Hires), 20
5. Houghton Mifflin, 10
5. ARAMARK Educational Resources, 10
5. Macy's East, 10
8. Caddo Parish School Board, 5
8. Toys "R" Us, 5
8. Macy's West, 5

Source: "The Top 100 Employers and the Majors in Demand for the Class of 2001," *The Black Collegian*, 31: 19-35, (February 2001).

★4348★
U.S. universities publishing the most highly-cited papers, 1997-1999

Ranking basis/background: Number of "hot" papers and citations to "hot" papers based on a file of 961 papers indexed by ISI between March 1997 and February 1999. **Remarks:** Original source: Hot Papers Database from ISI Research Services Group. **Number listed:** 5.

1. Harvard University, with 65 "hot" papers; 4,741 citations to "hot" papers
2. University of California, San Diego, 29; 2,196
3. University of Texas System, 27; 2,635
4. Johns Hopkins University, 25; 1,559
4. University of California, San Francisco, 25; 1,119

Source: "Hot Papers, Hot Universities," *What's Hot in Research* (http://www.isinet.com/hot/research) Institute for Scientific Information, June 7, 1999.

★4349★
U.S. universities publishing the most papers in the field of sociology and anthropology, 1994-98

Ranking basis/background: Number of papers published in the field of sociology and anthropology over a five-year period, and percent of field based on each universities percentage of 22,114 papers entered in the ISI database from ISI-indexed sociology and anthropology journals. **Number listed:** 5.

1. University of Michigan, Ann Arbor, with 297 papers; 1.34% of field
2. University of Wisconsin, Madison, 276; 1.25%
3. Pennsylvania State University, 255; 1.15%
4. University of California, Los Angeles, 250; 1.13%
5. Harvard University, 240; 1.09%

Source: "Sociology & Anthropology: Most Prolific U.S. Universities, 1994-98," *What's Hot in Research* (http://www.isinet.com/isi/hot/research) Institute for Scientific Information, May 29, 2000.

★4350★
U.S. universities publishing the most papers in the fields of sociology and anthropology, 1993-97

Ranking basis/background: Total number of papers published from each university. **Remarks:** Original source: University Science Indicators on Diskette, 1981-97. **Number listed:** 6.

1. University of Michigan, with 263 papers
2. University of Wisconsin, Madison, 249
3. Pennsylvania State University, 226
4. Harvard University, 226
5. University of California, Los Angeles, 219
6. University of Chicago, 208

Source: "Sociology & Anthropology: Most Prolific U.S. Universities, 1993-97," *What's Hot in Research* (http://www.isinet.com/hot/research) Institute for Scientific Information, May 24, 1999.

★4351★
U.S. universities with the greatest impact in sociology and anthropology, 1995-99

Ranking basis/background: Average citations per paper from the top 100 federally funded U.S. universities that had at least 50 published papers in ISI indexed sociology and anthropology journals. Also includes total number of paper published during the five year period. **Number listed:** 5.

1. Duke University, with 159 papers; 4.21 citations per paper
2. Stanford University, 132; 3.39
3. University of Chicago, 211; 3.36
4. State University of New York, Stony Brook, 127; 3.35
5. Pennsylvania State University, 235; 3.29

Source: "Sociology & Anthropology: High Impact U.S. Universities, 1995-99," *What's Hot in Research* (http://www.isinet.com/isi/hot/research) Institute for Scientific Information, October 30, 2000.

SOCIOLOGY, GRADUATE

★4352★
Most effective sociology research-doctorate programs as evaluated by the National Research Council

Ranking basis/background: From a survey of nearly 8,000 faculty members conducted in the spring of 1993. Respondents were asked to rate programs in their field on "effectiveness of program in educating research scholars/scientists." **Remarks:** See *Chronicle* article for more details. Scores of 3.5-5.0 indicate "extremely effective;" 2.5-3.49 "reasonably effective;" 1.5-2.49 "minimally effective;" and 0.0-1.49 "not effective." Programs also ranked by "scholarly quality of program faculty." **Number listed:** 95.

1. University of Wisconsin, Madison, with an effectiveness rating of 4.61
2. University of Chicago, 4.26
3. University of Michigan, 4.08
4. University of North Carolina, Chapel Hill, 4.00
5. Indiana University, 3.85
6. Stanford University, 3.77
7. University of Washington (WA), 3.73
8. University of Pennsylvania, 3.66
9. Northwestern University, 3.61
10. University of California, Berkeley, 3.60

Source: "Rankings of Research-Doctorate Programs in 41 Disciplines at 274 Institutions," *The Chronicle of Higher Education* 42: A21-A30 (September 21, 1995).

★4353★
Top recruiters for sociology jobs for 2000-01 master's degree recipients

Ranking basis/background: Projected number of college hires from on-campus recruitment for 2000-01. **Remarks:** Numbers reflect total expected hires, not just African American projected hires. **Number listed:** 2.

1. Accenture, with 30 projected hires
2. Houghton Mifflin, 5

Source: "The Top 100 Employers and the Majors in Demand for the Class of 2001," *The Black Collegian*, 31: 19-35, (February 2001).

SOCIOLOGY PERIODICALS

★4354★
Top sociology research-doctorate programs as evaluated by the National Research Council

Ranking basis/background: From a survey of nearly 8,000 faculty members conducted in the spring of 1993. Respondents were asked to rate programs in their field on "scholarly quality of program faculty." When more than one program had the samescore, the council averaged the rank order and gave each program the same rank number (if three programs tied for the top position, each received a rank of 2). **Remarks:** See *Chronicle* article for more details. Scores of 4.01 and above indicate "distinguished;" 3.0-4.0 "strong;" 2.51-3.0 "good;" 2.0-2.5 "adequate;" 1.0-1.99 "marginal;" and 0.0-0.99 "not sufficient for doctoral education." Programs also ranked by "effectiveness of program in educating research scholars/scientists." **Number listed:** 95.

1. University of Chicago, with a quality rating of 4.77
2. University of Wisconsin, Madison, 4.74
3. University of California, Berkeley, 4.56
4. University of Michigan, 4.39
5. University of California, Los Angeles, 4.36
6. University of North Carolina, Chapel Hill, 4.31
7. Harvard University, 4.18
8. Stanford University, 4.08
9. Northwestern University, 4.07
10. University of Washington (WA), 4.03
11. University of Pennsylvania, 4.02
12. Indiana University, 3.94
13. Princeton University, 3.79
14. University of Arizona, 3.78
15. Columbia University, 3.76

Source: "Rankings of Research-Doctorate Programs in 41 Disciplines at 274 Institutions," *The Chronicle of Higher Education* 42: A21-A30 (September 21, 1995).

SOCIOLOGY PERIODICALS

★4355★
Sociology journals by impact factor, 1981 to 1997

Ranking basis/background: Current citations to a journal's published papers divided by total papers published over an 18-year period. **Remarks:** Original source: *Journal Citation Reports* and Journal Performances Indicators on Diskette. **Number listed:** 10.

1. *American Sociological Review*, with 24.36
2. *American Journal of Sociology*, 19.63
3. *Annual Review of Sociology*, 16.55
4. *Journal of Marriage and the Family*, 14.70
5. *Sociology of Education*, 11.11
6. *Population and Development Review*, 9.65
7. *Ethology and Sociobiology*, 9.59
8. *Social Problems*, 9.55
9. *Social Forces*, 8.81
10. *Law & Society Review*, 8.04

Source: "Journals Ranked by Impact: Sociology," *What's Hot in Research,* http://www.isinet.com/whatshot/whatshot.html, Institute for Scientific Information (March 15, 1999).

★4356★
Sociology journals by impact factor, 1993 to 1997

Ranking basis/background: Current citations to a journal's published papers divided by total papers published over the past five years. **Remarks:** Original source: *Journal Citation Reports* and Journal Performances Indicators on Diskette. **Number listed:** 10.

1. *American Sociological Review*, with 6.12
2. *American Journal of Sociology*, 6.09
3. *Annual Review of Sociology*, 3.88
4. *Ethology and Sociobiology*, 3.83
5. *Journal of Marriage and the Family*, 3.48
6. *Population and Development Review*, 2.86
7. *Social Forces*, 2.81
8. *Social Problems*, 2.36
9. *Journal of Leisure Research*, 2.28
10. *Law & Society Review*, 2.23

Source: "Journals Ranked by Impact: Sociology," *What's Hot in Research,* http://www.isinet.com/whatshot/whatshot.html, Institute for Scientific Information (March 15, 1999).

SPANISH LANGUAGE AND LITERATURE, GRADUATE

★4357★
Most effective Spanish and Portuguese language and literature research-doctorate programs as evaluated by the National Research Council

Ranking basis/background: From a survey of nearly 8,000 faculty members conducted in the spring of 1993. Respondents were asked to rate programs in their field on "effectiveness of program in educating research scholars/scientists." **Remarks:** See *Chronicle* article for more details. Scores of 3.5-5.0 indicate "extremely effective;" 2.5-3.49 "reasonably effective;" 1.5-2.49 "minimally effective;" and 0.0-1.49 "not effective." Programs also ranked by "scholarly quality of program faculty." **Number listed:** 54.

1. Brown University, with an effectiveness rating of 3.76
2. University of Kansas, 3.76
3. Cornell University, 3.69
4. University of Wisconsin, Madison, 3.66
5. Princeton University, 3.65
6. University of California, Berkeley, 3.61
7. University of Virginia, 3.55
8. University of Michigan, 3.53
9. University of Texas, Austin, 3.51
10. Columbia University, 3.46

Source: "Rankings of Research-Doctorate Programs in 41 Disciplines at 274 Institutions," *The Chronicle of Higher Education* 42: A21-A30 (September 21, 1995).

★4358★
Top Spanish and Portuguese language and literature research-doctorate programs as evaluated by the National Research Council

Ranking basis/background: From a survey of nearly 8,000 faculty members conducted in the spring of 1993. Respondents were asked to rate programs in their field on "scholarly quality of program faculty." When more than one program had the samescore, the council averaged the rank order and gave each program the same rank number (if three programs tied for the top position, each received a rank of 2). **Remarks:** See *Chronicle* article for more details. Scores of 4.01 and above indicate "distinguished;" 3.0-4.0 "strong;" 2.51-3.0 "good;" 2.0-2.5 "adequate;" 1.0-1.99 "marginal;" and 0.0-0.99 "not sufficient for doctoral education." Programs also ranked by "effectiveness of program in educating research scholars/scientists." **Number listed:** 54.

1. Columbia University, with a quality rating of 4.31
2. Duke University, 3.87
3. Brown University, 3.83
4. Princeton University, 3.80
5. University of Virginia, 3.76
6. University of Pennsylvania, 3.75
7. University of Wisconsin, Madison, 3.74
8. Cornell University, 3.73
9. University of California, Berkeley, 3.70
10. Harvard University, 3.63
11. University of Kansas, 3.60
12. University of Texas, Austin, 3.54
13. University of Michigan, 3.46
14. University of California, Davis, 3.43
15. University of California, Irvine, 3.41

Source: "Rankings of Research-Doctorate Programs in 41 Disciplines at 274 Institutions," *The Chronicle of Higher Education* 42: A21-A30 (September 21, 1995).

SPECTROSCOPY

★4359★
Spectroscopy journals by citation impact, 1981-99

Ranking basis/background: Impact factor calculated by taking the number of current citations to source items published and dividing it by the number of articles published in the journal during that time period. **Number listed:** 10.

1. *Progress in Analytical Atomic Spectroscopy*, with a 46.71 impact factor
2. *Progress in NMR Spectroscopy*, 45.04
3. *Mass Spectroscopy Review*, 36.82
4. *Spectrochimica Acta Reviews*, 22.60
5. *Progress in Analytical Spectroscopy*, 20.77
6. *Biomedical Mass Spectrometry*, 17.21
7. *Journal of Biomolecular NMR*, 15.23
8. *Applied Spectroscopy Reviews*, 14.27
9. *Spectrochimica Acta B*, 13.58
10. *Biomedical and Environmental Mass Spectrometry*, 13.12

Source: "Journals Ranked by Impact: Spectroscopy," *What's Hot in Research* (http://www.isinet.com/isi/hot/research) *Institute for Scientific Information*, December 4, 2000.

★4360★
Spectroscopy journals by citation impact, 1995-99

Ranking basis/background: Impact factor calculated by taking the number of current citations to source items published and dividing it by the number of articles published in the journal during that time period. **Number listed:** 10.
1. *Mass Spectroscopy Review*, with a 12.91 impact factor
2. *Journal of Biomolecular NMR*, 9.51
3. *Progress in NMR Spectroscopy*, 7.82
4. *Organic Mass Spectrometry*, 7.76
5. *Journal of the American Society of Mass Spectrometry*, 6.39
6. *Journal of Analytical Atomic Spectrometry*, 6.11
7. *Journal of Mass Spectrometry*, 5.48
8. *Biological Mass Spectrometry*, 5.27
9. *Spectrochimica Acta B*, 4.73
10. *Rapid Communications in Mass Spectrometry*, 4.67

Source: "Journals Ranked by Impact: Spectroscopy," *What's Hot in Research* (http://www.isinet.com/isi/hot/research) *Institute for Scientific Information*, December 4, 2000.

★4361★
Spectroscopy journals by citation impact, 1999

Ranking basis/background: Impact factor calculated by taking the number of current citations to source items published and dividing it by the number of articles published in the journal during that time period. **Number listed:** 10.
1. *Mass Spectroscopy Review*, with a 6.89 impact factor
2. *Progress in NMR Spectroscopy*, 4.43
3. *Journal of Analytical Atomic Spectrometry*, 3.68
4. *Journal of the American Society of Mass Spectrometry*, 3.46
5. *Journal of Biomolecular NMR*, 3.21
6. *Journal of Mass Spectrometry*, 3.17
7. *Rapid Communications in Mass Spectrometry*, 2.44
8. *Spectrochimica Acta B*, 2.42
9. *NMR in Biomedicine*, 2.18
10. *International Journal of Mass Spectrometry*, 2.09

Source: "Journals Ranked by Impact: Spectroscopy," *What's Hot in Research* (http://www.isinet.com/isi/hot/research) *Institute for Scientific Information*, December 4, 2000.

SPEECH COMMUNICATION
See also: **Mass Media**

★4362★
Speech communication's most published scholars between 1915-1985

Ranking basis/background: Number of published articles in the leading speech communication journals between 1915-1985. **Remarks:** This article contains three other tables on number of entries per author, articles published by author by journal, and impact of top authors on journal content by journal. **Number listed:** 25.
1. J. McCroskey (degree conferred by Pennsylvania State University; currently affiliated with West Virginia University), with 78
2. F. H. Knower (University of Minnesota; Ohio State University), 64
3. G. Miller (University of Iowa; Michigan State University), 55
4. L. Crocker (University of Michigan; Denison University), 54
5. W. Braden (University of Iowa; Louisiana State University), 45
6. B. Greenberg (University of Wisconsin; Michigan State University), 44
6. T. Clevenger (Florida State University; Florida State University), 44
8. L. Barker (Ohio University; Auburn University), 36
8. R. Oliver (University of Wisconsin; Pennsylvania State University), 36
10. S. Becker (University of Iowa; University of Iowa), 35

Source: Hickson, III, Mark, Don W. Stacks and Jonathan H. Amsbary, "An Analysis of Prolific Scholarship in Speech Communication, 1915-1985: Toward a Yardstick for Measuring Research Productivity," *Communication Education* 38: 230-236 (July 1989).

SPEECH COMMUNICATION-WOMEN

★4363★
Top published female authors (1915-1985) in the field of communication studies

Ranking basis/background: Ranked according to the number of authored and coauthored publications appearing in the *Index to Journals in Communication Studies Through 1985*. Only 6 women appeared on the complete list containing 99 authors. **Number listed:** 99.
1. V. Richmond, with 32 articles
2. J. Burgoon, 29
3. Patti Gillespie, 24
4. Laura Crowell, 21
4. Margaret McLaughlin 21
6. Ruth A. Clark, 18

Source: Burroughs, Nancy F., Diane Christophel, and J. Cole Ady, et al., "Top Published Authors in Communication Studies 1915-1985," *ACA Bulletin: Association for Communication Administration* 67: 37-45 (January 1989).

SPORTS
See: **Athletics**

STAFFORD LOANS
See: **Loan Repayment Student Financial Aid**

STATE AID TO EDUCATION
See: **Colleges & Universities–Financial Support & Expenditures Schools, Elementary & Secondary–Revenue Scientific & Technological Research & Development Funding Student Financial Aid**

STATISTICS
See: **Mathematics, Graduate–Statistics Mathematics–Statistics**

STUDENT COSTS
See: **Colleges & Universities, Liberal Arts–Student Costs Colleges & Universities–Student Costs**

STUDENT FINANCIAL AID

★4364★
Pell Grant award percentage at private 4-year institutions for selected years

Ranking basis/background: Maximum Pell Grant award as a percentage of cost of attendance. **Remarks:** Original source: U.S. Department of Education. **Number listed:** 5.
1975-76, 38%
1985-86, 26%
1995-96, 13%
1999-2000, 15%
2000-01, 15%

Source: Burd, Stephen, "Lack of Need-Based Financial Aid Still Impedes Access to College for Low-Income Students, Report Finds," *The Chronicle of Higher Education*, 47: A26, (March 2, 2001).

★4365★
Pell Grant award percentage at public 4-year institutions for selected years

Ranking basis/background: Maximum Pell Grant award as a percentage of cost of attendance. **Remarks:** Original source: U.S. Department of Education. **Number listed:** 5.
1975-76, with 84%
1985-86, 57%
1995-96, 34%
1999-2000, 39%
2000-01, 39%

Source: Burd, Stephen, "Lack of Need-Based Financial Aid Still Impedes Access to College for Low-Income Students, Report Finds," *The Chronicle of Higher Education*, 47: A26, (March 2, 2001).

★4366★
Proposed fiscal 2002 appropriations for student aid

Ranking basis/background: Percentage breakdown of the U.S. government's proposed fiscal 2002 appropriations for student aid, totaling $60.8-billion. **Number listed:** 5.
1. Guaranteed loans, with 41%
2. Direct loans, 19%
3. Pell Grants, 16%
4. Campus-based programs, 5%
5. Other loans, 19%

Source: "Bush's Fiscal 2002 Budget Plan for Higher Education and Science," *The Chronicle of Higher Education*, 47: A36-A37, (April 20, 2001).

STUDENT FINANCIAL AID—BLACKS

★4367★
States with the highest state support for need-based financial aid for students, 1999-2000

Ranking basis/background: Amount of state support for higher education. **Remarks:** Original source: National Association of State Student Grant and Aid Programs. **Number listed:** 52.
1. New York, with $602,311,000
2. California, $370,134,000
3. Illinois, $337,003,000
4. Pennsylvania, $280,402,000
5. New Jersey, $170,015,000
6. Texas, $161,178,000
7. Minnesota, $113,714,000
8. Indiana, $104,737,000
9. Massachusetts, $102,056,000
10. Ohio, $95,482,000

Source: Schmidt, Peter, "State Spending on Student Aid Spike 12.6% in 1999-2000, Study Finds," *The Chronicle of Higher Education*, 47: A34, (April 27, 2001).

★4368★
States with the highest state support for non need-based financial aid for students, 1999-2000

Ranking basis/background: Amount of state support for higher education. **Remarks:** Original source: National Association of State Student Grant and Aid Programs. **Number listed:** 52.
1. Georgia, with $240,458,000
2. Florida, $180,916,000
3. North Carolina, $82,390,000
4. Ohio, $68,815,000
5. Louisiana, $67,003,000
6. South Carolina, $55,624,000
7. Virginia, $50,946,000
8. Illinois, $23,174,000
9. New Jersey, $19,279,000
10. Mississippi, $18,618,000

Source: Schmidt, Peter, "State Spending on Student Aid Spike 12.6% in 1999-2000, Study Finds," *The Chronicle of Higher Education*, 47: A34, (April 27, 2001).

★4369★
Trends in student-loan default rates

Ranking basis/background: Student-loan default rates, in percent, from 1988 through 1998. **Remarks:** Original source: U.S. Department of Education. **Number listed:** 11.
- 1988, with 17.2%
- 1989, 21.4%
- 1990, 22.4%
- 1991, 17.8%
- 1992, 15.0%
- 1993, 11.6%
- 1994, 10.7%
- 1995, 10.4%
- 1996, 9.6%
- 1997, 8.8%
- 1998, 6.9%

Source: Burd, Stephen, "Rate of Student-Loan Defaults Drops for 8th Consecutive Year," *The Chronicle of Higher Education*, 47: A42, (October 13, 2000).

STUDENT FINANCIAL AID–BLACKS
See: **Black Students–Financial Aid**

STUDENT FINANCIAL AID–REPAYMENT ON LOANS
See: **Loan Repayment**

STUDENT-TEACHER RATIO
See: **Schools, Elementary & Secondary–Teacher-Student Ratio**

STUDENT TESTS
See: **Achievement Tests–Schools, Elementary & Secondary College Entrance Examinations**

SUBSTANCE ABUSE AND EDUCATION

★4370★
Percentage of 8th and 12th graders in the U.S. admitting to heavy alcohol use, 1999

Ranking basis/background: Percentage of usage determined from a survey of 14,100 high school seniors, 13,900 10th graders and 17,300 8th graders from 433 public and private secondary schools. **Remarks:** Original source: *Monitoring the Future*, University of Michigan Institute for Social Research and National Institute on Drug Abuse. **Number listed:** 2.

- 12th graders, with 38.1% male; 23.6% female; 34.8% white; 11.9% black
- 8th graders, 16.4%; 13.9%; 15.2%; 10.8%

Source: *The World Almanac and Book of Facts 2001*, World Almanac Books, 2001.

★4371★
Percentage of 8th and 12th graders in the U.S. that have used alcohol within the last month, 1999

Ranking basis/background: Percentage of usage determined from a survey of 14,100 high school seniors, 13,900 10th graders and 17,300 8th graders from 433 public and private secondary schools. **Remarks:** Original source: *Monitoring the Future*, University of Michigan Institute for Social Research and National Institute on Drug Abuse. **Number listed:** 2.

- 12th graders, with 55.3% male; 46.8% female; 54.9% white; 30.8% black
- 8th graders, 24.8%; 23.3%; 25.6%; 16.8%

Source: *The World Almanac and Book of Facts 2001*, World Almanac Books, 2001.

★4372★
Percentage of high school seniors in the U.S. admitting to experimenting with drugs at some point, 1999

Ranking basis/background: Percentage of usage determined from a survey of 14,100 high school seniors, 13,900 10th graders and 17,300 8th graders from 433 public and private secondary schools. **Remarks:** Original source: *Monitoring the Future*, University of Michigan Institute for Social Research and National Institute on Drug Abuse. **Number listed:** 18.

- Marijuana/hashish, with 49.7%
- Inhalants, 16.0%
- Amyl & butyl nitrites, 1.7%
- Hallucinogens, 14.2%
- LSD, 12.2%
- PCP, 3.4%
- Ecstasy, 8.0%
- Cocaine, 9.8%
- Crack, 4.6%
- Heroin, 2.0%
- Other opiates, 10.2%
- Stimulants, 16.3%
- Sedatives, 9.5%
- Barbiturates, 8.9%
- Methaqualone, 1.8%
- Tranquilizers, 9.3%
- Alcohol, 80.0%
- Cigarettes, 64.6%
- Steroids, 2.9%

Source: *The World Almanac and Book of Facts 2001*, World Almanac Books, 2001.

★4373★
Percentage of high school students using tobacco products by gender

Ranking basis/background: Percentage of high school boys and girls using tobacco products within 30 days of the National Youth Tobacco Survey. **Remarks:** Original source: Centers for Disease Control and Prevention. **Number listed:** 4.
1. Cigarettes, with 28.7% of boys using; 28.2% of girls using
2. Smokeless tobacco, 11.6%; 1.5%
3. Cigar, 20.3%; 10.2%
4. Pipe, 4.2%; 1.4%

Source: Wasson, Hillary and Sam Ward, "USA Today Snapshots: Teen Tobacco Use," *USA Today*, April 4, 2000, Section A, p. 1A.

★4374★
Percentage of middle school students using tobacco products by gender

Ranking basis/background: Percentage of middle school (grades 6-8) boys and girls using tobacco products within 30 days of the National Youth Tobacco Survey. **Remarks:** Original source: Centers for Disease Control and Prevention. **Number listed:** 4.
1. Cigarettes, with 9.6% of boys using; 8.8% of girls using
2. Smokeless tobacco, 4.2%; 1.3%
3. Cigar, 7.8%; 4.4%
4. Pipe, 3.5%; 1.4%

Source: Wasson, Hillary and Sam Ward, "USA Today Snapshots: Youth Tobacco Use," *USA Today*, April 3, 2000, Section A, p. 1A.

TEACHER BEHAVIOR

★4375★
States with the highest percentage of students struck by educators
Ranking basis/background: Percentage of students struck by educators. **Remarks:** Original source: U.S. Department of Education. **Number listed:** 10.
1. Mississippi, with 12.4%
2. Arkansas, 10.8%
3. Alabama, 6.3%
4. Tennessee, 4.7%
5. Texas, 3.1%
6. Georgia, 2.8%
7. Oklahoma, 2.7%
8. Louisiana, 2.6%
9. Missouri, 1.4%
10. South Carolina, 1.1%

Source: "Hitting Kids," *USA Today*, January 13, 2000, p. 9D.

TEACHER EDUCATION

★4376★
Teacher training effectiveness
Ranking basis/background: New teachers rate effectiveness of training programs for preparing them for the classroom. Note: Totals percent exceeds 100 due to rounding. **Remarks:** Original source: Public Agenda. **Number listed:** 4.

Excellent, with 28%
Good, 43%
Fair, 25%
Poor, 5%

Source: Hall, Cindy and Marcy E. Mullins, "Teacher Training Gets Good Grades," *USA Today*, October 12, 2000, Section D, p. 11D.

★4377★
Top recruiters for education jobs for 2000-01 bachelor's degree recipients
Ranking basis/background: Projected number of college hires from on-campus recruitment for 2000-01. **Remarks:** Numbers reflect total expected hires, not just African American projected hires. **Number listed:** 19.
1. Fairfax County Public Schools, with 1,091 projected hires
2. Footstar, 500
3. Chesapeake Public Schools, 322
4. Alief Independent School District, 300
4. Caddo Parish School Board, 300
6. Hurst-Euless-Bedford ISD, 132
7. Hanover County Public Schools, 129
8. Tyler Independent School District, 100
8. Gwinnett County Public Schools, 100
10. Fort Wayne Community Schools, 84

Source: "The Top 100 Employers and the Majors in Demand for the Class of 2001," *The Black Collegian*, 31: 19-35, (February 2001).

TEACHER EDUCATION, GRADUATE

★4378★
Academics' choices for best administration/supervision graduate programs, 2001
Ranking basis/background: From a *U.S. News & World Report* survey of education school deans and senior faculty. **Remarks:** Data collected by Market Facts, Inc. **Number listed:** 10.
1. University of Wisconsin, Madison
2. Harvard University
3. Stanford University
4. Ohio State University, Columbus
5. Vanderbilt University, Peabody College
6. University of Texas, Austin
7. Teachers College, Columbia University
8. University of Michigan, Ann Arbor
9. Indiana University, Bloomington
10. Penn State University, University Park

Source: "America's Best Graduate Schools: 2002 Annual Guide," *U.S. News & World Report*, 130: 60-97, (April 19, 2001).

★4379★
Academics' choices for best counseling/personnel services graduate programs, 2001
Ranking basis/background: From a *U.S. News & World Report* survey of education school deans and senior faculty. **Remarks:** Data collected by Market Facts, Inc. **Number listed:** 10.
1. University of Maryland, College Park
2. Ohio State University, Columbus
3. University of Minnesota, Twin Cities
4. University of Florida
5. Indiana University, Bloomington
6. Penn State University, University Park
7. University of North Carolina, Greensboro
8. University of Wisconsin, Madison
9. University of Missouri, Columbia
10. University of Georgia

Source: "America's Best Graduate Schools: 2002 Annual Guide," *U.S. News & World Report*, 130: 60-97, (April 19, 2001).

★4380★
Academics' choices for best curriculum/instruction graduate programs, 2001
Ranking basis/background: From a *U.S. News & World Report* survey of education school deans and senior faculty. **Remarks:** Data collected by Market Facts, Inc. **Number listed:** 10.
1. University of Wisconsin, Madison
2. Teachers College, Columbia University
3. Michigan State University
4. Stanford University
5. Ohio State University, Columbus
6. University of Michigan, Ann Arbor
7. University of Illinois, Urbana-Champaign
8. Indiana University, Bloomington
9. Vanderbilt University, Peabody College
10. Harvard University

Source: "America's Best Graduate Schools: 2002 Annual Guide," *U.S. News & World Report*, 130: 60-97, (April 19, 2001).

★4381★
Academics' choices for best education policy graduate programs, 2001
Ranking basis/background: From a *U.S. News & World Report* survey of education school deans and senior faculty. **Remarks:** Data collected by Market Facts, Inc. **Number listed:** 10.
1. Harvard University
2. Stanford University
3. University of Wisconsin, Madison
4. Teachers College, Columbia University
5. University of Michigan, Ann Arbor
6. University of California, Berkeley
7. Michigan State University
8. Vanderbilt University, Peabody College
9. University of Maryland, College Park
10. Indiana University, Bloomington

Source: "America's Best Graduate Schools: 2002 Annual Guide," *U.S. News & World Report*, 130: 60-97, (April 19, 2001).

★4382★
Academics' choices for best educational psychology graduate programs, 2001
Ranking basis/background: From a *U.S. News & World Report* survey of education school deans and senior faculty. **Remarks:** Data collected by Market Facts, Inc. **Number listed:** 10.
1. Stanford University
2. University of Wisconsin, Madison
3. Michigan State University
4. University of Illinois, Urbana-Champaign
5. University of Michigan, Ann Arbor
6. University of Minnesota, Twin Cities
7. Harvard University
8. University of California, Berkeley
9. University of California, Los Angeles
10. Teachers College, Columbia University

Source: "America's Best Graduate Schools: 2002 Annual Guide," *U.S. News & World Report*, 130: 60-97, (April 19, 2001).

★4383★
Academics' choices for best elementary education graduate programs, 2001
Ranking basis/background: From a *U.S. News & World Report* survey of education school deans and senior faculty. **Remarks:** Data collected by Market Facts, Inc. **Number listed:** 10.
1. Michigan State University
2. University of Wisconsin, Madison
3. Ohio State University, Columbus
4. University of Illinois, Urbana-Champaign
5. Vanderbilt University, Peabody College
6. Teachers College, Columbia University
7. Indiana University, Bloomington
8. University of Michigan, Ann Arbor
9. University of Virginia, Curry College

Source: "America's Best Graduate Schools: 2002 Annual Guide," *U.S. News & World Report*, 130: 60-97, (April 19, 2001).

★4384★
Academics' choices for best higher education administration graduate programs, 2001
Ranking basis/background: From a *U.S. News & World Report* survey of education school deans and senior faculty. **Remarks:** Data collected by Market Facts, Inc. **Number listed:** 10.
1. University of Michigan, Ann Arbor
2. Penn State University, University Park
3. University of California, Los Angeles
4. Michigan State University

TEACHER EDUCATION, GRADUATE

5. Harvard University
6. Indiana University, Bloomington
7. Stanford University
8. University of Arizona
9. Teachers College, Columbia University

Source: "America's Best Graduate Schools: 2002 Annual Guide," *U.S. News & World Report*, 130: 60-97, (April 19, 2001).

★4385★
Academics' choices for best secondary education graduate programs, 2001

Ranking basis/background: From a *U.S. News & World Report* survey of education school deans and senior faculty. **Remarks:** Data collected by Market Facts, Inc. **Number listed:** 10.
1. Michigan State University
2. Ohio State University, Columbus
3. University of Wisconsin, Madison
4. University of Georgia
5. Indiana University, Bloomington
6. Stanford University
7. University of Illinois, Urbana-Champaign
8. Teachers College, Columbia University
9. Vanderbilt University, Peabody College
10. University of Virginia, Curry College

Source: "America's Best Graduate Schools: 2002 Annual Guide," *U.S. News & World Report*, 130: 60-97, (April 19, 2001).

★4386★
Academics' choices for best special education graduate programs, 2001

Ranking basis/background: From a *U.S. News & World Report* survey of education school deans and senior faculty. **Remarks:** Data collected by Market Facts, Inc. **Number listed:** 10.
1. University of Kansas
2. Vanderbilt University, Peabody College
3. University of Oregon
4. University of Illinois, Urbana-Champaign
5. University of Virginia, Curry College
6. University of Wisconsin, Madison
7. University of Washington (WA)
8. University of Minnesota, Twin Cities
9. University of Texas, Austin
10. University of Maryland, College Park

Source: "America's Best Graduate Schools: 2002 Annual Guide," *U.S. News & World Report*, 130: 60-97, (April 19, 2001).

★4387★
Academics' choices for best vocational/technical graduate programs, 2001

Ranking basis/background: From a *U.S. News & World Report* survey of education school deans and senior faculty. **Remarks:** Data collected by Market Facts, Inc. **Number listed:** 10.
1. Ohio State University, Columbus
2. Penn State University, University Park
3. University of Minnesota, Twin Cities
4. University of Illinois, Urbana-Champaign
5. University of Georgia
6. Virginia Tech
7. Oklahoma State University
8. University of Missouri, Columbia
9. University of Wisconsin, Madison
10. Colorado State University

Source: "America's Best Graduate Schools: 2002 Annual Guide," *U.S. News & World Report*, 130: 60-97, (April 19, 2001).

★4388★
Acceptance rates at *U.S. News & World Report*'s top 10 graduate education schools, 2001

Ranking basis/background: From a *U.S. News & World Report* survey of acceptance rates for 2000. **Remarks:** Data collected by Market Facts, Inc. **Number listed:** 51.
1. University of Michigan, Ann Arbor, with 36.1%
2. University of California, Los Angeles, 34.8%
3. Teachers College, Columbia University, 29.7%
4. Vanderbilt University, 28.8%
5. University of Pennsylvania, 28.5%
6. University of Wisconsin, Madison, 24.7%
7. University of California, Berkeley, 21.1%
8. Northwestern University, 17.2%
9. Stanford University, 16.9%
10. Harvard University, 16.4%

Source: "America's Best Graduate Schools: 2002 Annual Guide," *U.S. News & World Report*, 130: 60-97, (April 19, 2001).

★4389★
Average quantitative GRE scores for *U.S. News & World Report*'s top 10 graduate education schools, 2001

Ranking basis/background: From a *U.S. News & World Report* survey of average GRE scores for 2000. **Remarks:** Data collected by Market Facts, Inc. **Number listed:** 51.
1. Northwestern University, with 732
2. University of Michigan, Ann Arbor, 667
3. Stanford University, 659
4. University of Pennsylvania, 653
5. University of California, Berkeley, 630
6. Teachers College, Columbia University, 628
7. Vanderbilt University, 622
8. Harvard University, 616
9. University of California, Los Angeles, 604
10. University of Wisconsin, Madison, 602

Source: "America's Best Graduate Schools: 2002 Annual Guide," *U.S. News & World Report*, 130: 60-97, (April 19, 2001).

★4390★
Average verbal GRE scores for *U.S. News & World Report*'s top 10 graduate education schools, 2001

Ranking basis/background: From a *U.S. News & World Report* survey of average GRE scores for 2000. **Remarks:** Data collected by Market Facts, Inc. **Number listed:** 51.
1. Northwestern University, with 657
2. Stanford University, 636
3. Harvard University, 608
4. University of Pennsylvania, 592
5. Vanderbilt University, 590
6. University of California, Berkeley, 585
7. University of Michigan, Ann Arbor, 581
8. Teachers College, Columbia University, 564
9. University of California, Los Angeles, 558
10. University of Wisconsin, Madison, 532

Source: "America's Best Graduate Schools: 2002 Annual Guide," *U.S. News & World Report*, 130: 60-97, (April 19, 2001).

★4391★
Doctoral students to faculty ratio at *U.S. News & World Report*'s top 10 graduate education schools, 2001

Ranking basis/background: From a *U.S. News & World Report* survey of student-faculty ratios for 2000. **Remarks:** Data collected by Market Facts, Inc. **Number listed:** 51.
1. Vanderbilt University, with 3.6 students per faculty member
2. University of Michigan, Ann Arbor, 5.8
3. University of Wisconsin, Madison, 6.1
4. University of Pennsylvania, 7.3
5. Stanford University, 8.5
6. Northwestern University, 8.6
7. Teachers College, Columbia University, 10.0
8. University of California, Los Angeles, 10.5
9. University of California, Berkeley, 12.2
10. Harvard University, 20.7

Source: "America's Best Graduate Schools: 2002 Annual Guide," *U.S. News & World Report*, 130: 60-97, (April 19, 2001).

★4392★
Ph.D.s and Ed.D.s granted at *U.S. News & World Report*'s top 10 graduate education schools, 2001

Ranking basis/background: From a *U.S. News & World Report* survey of total number of Ph.D.s and Ed.D.s granted during the 1999-2000 academic year. **Remarks:** Data collected by Market Facts, Inc. **Number listed:** 51.
1. Teachers College, Columbia University, with 175
2. University of Wisconsin, Madison, 157
3. University of California, Los Angeles, 72
4. Harvard University, 58
5. Vanderbilt University, 51
6. University of Pennsylvania, 49
7. University of California, Berkeley, 35
8. Stanford University, 29
9. University of Michigan, Ann Arbor, 22
10. Northwestern University, 12

Source: "America's Best Graduate Schools: 2002 Annual Guide," *U.S. News & World Report*, 130: 60-97, (April 19, 2001).

★4393★
Research expenditures for *U.S. News & World Report*'s top 10 graduate education schools, 2001

Ranking basis/background: From a *U.S. News & World Report* survey of research expenditures, in million of dollars, during 2000. **Remarks:** Data collected by Market Facts, Inc. **Number listed:** 51.
1. Teachers College, Columbia University, with $20.3 million
2. University of California, Los Angeles, $20.2
3. University of Pennsylvania, $16.7
4. Vanderbilt University, $16.1
5. University of Wisconsin, Madison, $15.5
6. Harvard University, $13.6
7. University of Michigan, Ann Arbor, $12.0
8. Stanford University, $11.2
9. University of California, Berkeley, $10.1
10. Northwestern University, $8.2

Source: "America's Best Graduate Schools: 2002 Annual Guide," *U.S. News & World Report*, 130: 60-97, (April 19, 2001).

★4394★
Research expenditures per faculty member at *U.S. News & World Report*'s top 10 graduate education schools, 2001

Ranking basis/background: From a *U.S. News & World Report* survey of research expenditures, in thousands of dollars, per faculty member during 2000. **Remarks:** Data collected by Market Facts, Inc. **Number listed:** 51.
1. University of California, Los Angeles, with $594.2 thousand
2. University of Michigan, Ann Arbor, $577.5
3. Harvard University, $503.6
4. Vanderbilt University, $474.9
5. Teachers College, Columbia University, $406.2
6. Stanford University, $385.1
7. University of Wisconsin, Madison, $355.4
8. University of Pennsylvania, $310.0
9. Northwestern University, $301.2
10. University of California, Berkeley, $223.1

Source: "America's Best Graduate Schools: 2002 Annual Guide," *U.S. News & World Report*, 130: 60-97, (April 19, 2001).

★4395★
Top graduate education schools, 2001

Ranking basis/background: From a *U.S. News & World Report* survey of teacher education programs based on academic reputation, student selectivity, research activity, and faculty resources. **Remarks:** Data collected by Market Facts, Inc. **Number listed:** 51.
1. Harvard University, with an overall score of 100
2. Stanford University, 99
3. Teachers College, Columbia University, 97
4. University of California, Los Angeles, 90
5. Vanderbilt University, 89
6. University of California, Berkeley, 88
7. University of Michigan, Ann Arbor, 87
8. University of Pennsylvania, 85
9. University of Wisconsin, Madison, 84
10. Northwestern University, 83

Source: "America's Best Graduate Schools: 2002 Annual Guide," *U.S. News & World Report*, 130: 60-97, (April 19, 2001).

★4396★
Top graduate education schools by reputation, as determined by academic personnel, 2001

Ranking basis/background: From a *U.S. News & World Report* survey of teacher education school deans and school superintendents in schools with more than 5,000 students. **Remarks:** Data collected by Market Facts, Inc. **Number listed:** 51.
1. Stanford University, 4.6
2. Harvard University, 4.4
2. Teachers College, Columbia University, 4.4
4. University of Michigan, Ann Arbor, 4.3
4. University of Wisconsin, Madison, 4.3
6. Vanderbilt University, 4.2
7. University of California, Berkeley, 4.2
8. University of California, Los Angeles, 4.1
8. Michigan State University, 4.1
8. University of Illinois, Urbana-Champaign, 4.1

Source: "America's Best Graduate Schools: 2002 Annual Guide," *U.S. News & World Report*, 130: 60-97, (April 19, 2001).

★4397★
Top graduate education schools by reputation, as determined by superintendents, 2001

Ranking basis/background: From a *U.S. News & World Report* survey of teacher education school deans and school superintendents in schools with more than 5,000 students. **Remarks:** Data collected by Market Facts, Inc. **Number listed:** 51.
1. Harvard University, 4.6
2. Teachers College, Columbia University, 4.4
3. Stanford University, 4.3
4. Vanderbilt University, 4.1
4. University of Michigan, Ann Arbor, 4.1
4. University of North Carolina, Chapel Hill, 4.1
7. University of California, Berkeley, 4.0
7. Ohio State University, Columbus, 4.0
9. University of California, Los Angeles, 3.8
9. University of Wisconsin, Madison, 3.8
9. Northwestern University, 3.8

Source: "America's Best Graduate Schools: 2002 Annual Guide," *U.S. News & World Report*, 130: 60-97, (April 19, 2001).

★4398★
Top recruiters for education jobs for 2000-01 master's degree recipients

Ranking basis/background: Projected number of college hires from on-campus recruitment for 2000-01. **Remarks:** Numbers reflect total expected hires, not just African American projected hires. **Number listed:** 19.
1. Gwinnett County Public Schools, with 1,100 projected hires
2. Fairfax County Public Schools, 944
3. Alief Independent School District, 200
4. Chesapeake Public Schools, 137
5. Tyler Independent School District, 100
6. Hanover County Public Schools, 71
7. Caddo Parish School Board, 50
8. Fort Wayne Community Schools, 41
9. Hurst-Euless-Bedford ISD, 25
10. Houghton Mifflin, 20

Source: "The Top 100 Employers and the Majors in Demand for the Class of 2001," *The Black Collegian*, 31: 19-35, (February 2001).

TEACHER-STUDENT RATIO
See: **Schools, Elementary & Secondary–Teacher-Student Ratio**

TEACHERS, COLLEGE
See: **College Faculty**

TEACHERS, ELEMENTARY AND SECONDARY

★4399★
All-USA Teacher Teams, First Team, 2000

Ranking basis/background: Educators name, school, and area of education, as selected by *USA Today*. **Number listed:** 10.

Lisa Arnold, Riverview Elementary School (Sioux City, IA), Music
Kelvin Chun, Nu'uanu Elementary School (Honolulu, HI), Technology
Betty Bigney, DuBois Area Middle and High School (DuBoise, PA), Gifted Grade 6-12
Michael Comeau, Waller Elementary School (Bossier City, IA), 4th grade
Harvey Burniston Jr., Johnson County Vocational School (Mountain City, TN), Agriculture
Beverly Gallagher, Princeton Day School (NJ), 3rd grade
Joseph Gaskin III, Richmond Senior High School (Rockingham, NC), Physics, chemistry
Norman Conard, Uniontown High School (KS), Social studies, video production
Shawn DeNight, Miami Edison Senior High School (FL), English, journalism
Marge Christensen Gould, Catalina High Magnet School (Tucson, AZ), English, literacy, workplace skills

Source: "All-USA Teacher Teams," *USA Today*, October 12, 2000, Section D, pp. 1D-10D.

★4400★
All-USA Teacher Teams, Second Team, 2000

Ranking basis/background: Educators name and school, as selected by *USA Today*. **Number listed:** 15.

Kathryn Howell Anders, Calabasas High School (CA), English, journalism
Judy Bieze, Hayden Meadows Elementary School (Hayden Lake, ID), 2nd grade
Darrel Brown, Excelsior High School (Aurora, CO), English, language arts
Debbie Bush, Academy Primary School (Buckhannon, WV), 2nd grade
Shawn Hardnett, Frederick Douglass Middle School (Rochester, NY), English, social studies, study skills
Leslie Lynch, Susick Elementary School (Troy, MI), 1st grade
Donna Matteson, G. Ray Badley High School (Fulton, NY), technology
Avis McEachen, Mesa High School (AZ), honors American studies, American literature
Mary Lee Muniz, Collinsville High School (IL), Latin
Luther Richardson, Pacelli Catholic High School, (Columbus, GA), physics
Carol Strickland, Emporia High School (KS), language arts
Gary Swalley, Edwardsville Middle School (IL), social studies
Christa Wise, Saugatuck High School (MI), art

Source: "All-USA Teacher Teams," *USA Today*, October 12, 2000, Section D, pp. 1D-10D.

★4401★
All-USA Teacher Teams, Third Team, 2000

Ranking basis/background: Educators name and school, as selected by *USA Today*. **Number listed:** 16.

Jenny Bernard, West Junior High Technology Magnet School (Richardson, TX), history

TEACHERS, ELEMENTARY AND SECONDARY

Judith Blood, Kearsarge Regional Elementary School (Bradford, NH), 3rd grade

C. June Bryant, Milton High School (Alpharetta, GA), U.S. history

Margaret Buley, Eisenhower Intermediate School (Bridgewater, NJ), 4th & 5th grade

Susan Cook, Applied Technology Center (Rock Hills, SC), commercial design

Lisa Goetz, Tripp Elementary School (Buffalo Grove, IL), 3rd grade

Jennifer Breaux Hebert, Strack Intermediate School (Klein, TX), American history and government

Sharon Lauber, West Lincoln School (NE), 4th grade

Nancy McIver, Lin-Wood Public School (Lincoln, NH), family and consumer science

Joan Jensen Moran, East Coloma School (Rock Falls, IL), physical education, health, discipline

Anthony Pattiz, Sandy Creek High School (Tyrone, GA), world history

Lindy Poling, Millbrook High School (Raleigh, NC), social studies

Kimberly Rauscher, Mechanicsburg Area Intermediate School (PA), social studies, science

Patricia Saltis, West Milford Elementary School (WV), 1st grade

Lois Kaplan Seaman, Richmond Heights Middle School (Miami, FL), language arts

Anthony Theille, Portsmouth Middle and High School (NH), theoretical linguistics

Source: "All-USA Teacher Teams," *USA Today*, October 12, 2000, Section D, pp. 1D-10D.

★4402★
High alternative projections for elementary and secondary school teachers for the years 2002-2008, by organizational level

Ranking basis/background: Number, in thousands, of classroom teachers in elementary and secondary schools for the years 2002-2008. **Remarks:** Original source: U.S. Department of Education, National Center for Education Statistics. Reports from various common core of Data surveys of Public and Private Elementary and Secondary Schools from 1983 through 1993. **Number listed:** 12.

2002, with 3,317 (K-12); 1,994 (Elementary); 1,323 (Secondary)
2003, 3,363; 2,014; 1,349
2004, 3,405; 2,029; 1,375
2005, 3,442; 2,043; 1,399
2006, 3,473; 2,056; 1,417
2007, 3,503; 2,073; 1,431
2008, 3,528; 2,090; 1,438

Source: *Projections of Education Statistics to 2008*, NCES 98-016, U.S. Department of Education, National Center for Education Statistics (June 1998).

★4403★
High alternative projections for private elementary and secondary school teachers for the years 2002-2008, by organizational level

Ranking basis/background: Number, in thousands, of classroom teachers in private elementary and secondary schools for the years 2002-2008. **Remarks:** Original source: U.S. Department of Education, National Center for Education Statistics. Reports from various common core of Data surveys of Public and Private Elementary and Secondary Schools from 1983 through 1993. **Number listed:** 12.

2002, with 422 (K-12); 296 (Elementary); 126 (Secondary)
2003, 427; 299; 128
2004, 432; 301; 131
2005, 437; 303; 133
2006, 440; 305; 135
2007, 444; 308; 136
2008, 447; 310; 137

Source: *Projections of Education Statistics to 2008*, NCES 98-016, U.S. Department of Education, National Center for Education Statistics (June 1998).

★4404★
High alternative projections for public elementary and secondary school teachers for the years 2002-2008, by organizational level

Ranking basis/background: Number, in thousands, of classroom teachers in public elementary and secondary schools for the years 2002-2008. **Remarks:** Original source: U.S. Department of Education, National Center for Education Statistics. Reports from various common core of Data surveys of Public and Private Elementary and Secondary Schools from 1983 through 1993. **Number listed:** 12.

2002, with 2,895 (K-12); 1,697 (Elementary); 1,197 (Secondary)
2003, 2,935; 1,715; 1,221
2004, 2,972; 1,728; 1,245
2005, 3,005; 1,740; 1,266
2006, 3,033; 1,751; 1,282
2007, 3,059; 1,765; 1,294
2008, 3,081; 1,780; 1,301

Source: *Projections of Education Statistics to 2008*, NCES 98-016, U.S. Department of Education, National Center for Education Statistics (June 1998).

★4405★
Low alternative projections for elementary and secondary school teachers for the years 2002-2008, by organizational level

Ranking basis/background: Number, in thousands, of classroom teachers in elementary and secondary schools for the years 2002-2008. **Remarks:** Original source: U.S. Department of Education, National Center for Education Statistics. Reports from various common core of Data surveys of Public and Private Elementary and Secondary Schools from 1983 through 1993. **Number listed:** 12.

2002, with 3,243 (K-12); 1,945 (Elementary); 1,298 (Secondary)
2003, 3,277; 1,957; 1,319
2004, 3,305; 1,965; 1,340
2005, 3,327; 1,970; 1,357
2006, 3,343; 1,974; 1,369
2007, 3,357; 1,980; 1,377
2008, 3,366; 1,988; 1,378

Source: *Projections of Education Statistics to 2008*, NCES 98-016, U.S. Department of Education, National Center for Education Statistics (June 1998).

★4406★
Low alternative projections for private elementary and secondary school teachers for the years 2002-2008, by organizational level

Ranking basis/background: Number, in thousands, of classroom teachers in private elementary and secondary schools for the years 2002-2008. **Remarks:** Original source: U.S. Department of Education, National Center for Education Statistics. Reports from various common core of Data surveys of Public and Private Elementary and Secondary Schools from 1983 through 1993. **Number listed:** 12.

2002, with 412 (K-12); 289 (Elementary); 124 (Secondary)
2003, 416; 291; 126
2004, 419; 292; 127
2005, 422; 293; 129
2006, 423; 293; 130
2007, 425; 294; 131
2008, 426; 295; 131

Source: *Projections of Education Statistics to 2008*, NCES 98-016, U.S. Department of Education, National Center for Education Statistics (June 1998).

★4407★
Low alternative projections for public elementary and secondary school teachers for the years 2002-2008, by organizational level

Ranking basis/background: Number, in thousands, of classroom teachers in public elementary and secondary schools for the years 2002-2008. **Remarks:** Original source: U.S. Department of Education, National Center for Education Statistics. Reports from various common core of Data surveys of Public and Private Elementary and Secondary Schools from 1983 through 1993. **Number listed:** 12.

2002, with 2,831 (K-12); 1,656 (Elementary); 1,175 (Secondary)
2003, 2,860; 1,667; 1,194
2004, 2,885; 1,673; 1,212
2005, 2,905; 1,678; 1,228
2006, 2,920; 1,681; 1,239
2007, 2,932; 1,686; 1,246
2008, 2,940; 1,693; 1,247

Source: *Projections of Education Statistics to 2008*, NCES 98-016, U.S. Department of Education, National Center for Education Statistics (June 1998).

★4408★
Middle alternative projections for elementary and secondary school teachers for the years 2002-2008, by organizational level

Ranking basis/background: Number, in thousands, of classroom teachers in elementary and secondary schools for the years 2002-2008. **Remarks:** Original source: U.S. Department of Education, National Center for Education Statistics. Reports from various common core of Data surveys of Public and Private Elementary and Secondary Schools from 1983 through 1993. **Number listed:** 12.

2002, with 3,284 (K-12); 1,972
  (Elementary); 1,312 (Secondary)
2003, 3,325; 1,989; 1,336
2004, 3,362; 2,001; 1,361
2005, 3,394; 2,012; 1,382
2006, 3,418; 2,021; 1,397
2007, 3,441; 2,033; 1,408
2008, 3,460; 2,047; 1,413

Source: *Projections of Education Statistics to 2008,* NCES 98-016, U.S. Department of Education, National Center for Education Statistics (June 1998).

★4409★
Middle alternative projections for private elementary and secondary school teachers for the years 2002-2008, by organizational level

Ranking basis/background: Number, in thousands, of classroom teachers in private elementary and secondary schools for the years 2002-2008. **Remarks:** Original source: U.S. Department of Education, National Center for Education Statistics. Reports from various common core of Data surveys of Public and Private Elementary and Secondary Schools from 1983 through 1993. **Number listed:** 12.

2002, with 418 (K-12); 293 (Elementary);
  125 (Secondary)
2003, 423; 295; 127
2004, 427; 297; 129
2005, 430; 299; 131
2006, 433; 300; 133
2007, 436; 302; 134
2008, 438; 304; 134

Source: *Projections of Education Statistics to 2008,* NCES 98-016, U.S. Department of Education, National Center for Education Statistics (June 1998).

★4410★
Middle alternative projections for public elementary and secondary school teachers for the years 2002-2008, by organizational level

Ranking basis/background: Number, in thousands, of classroom teachers in public elementary and secondary schools for the years 2002-2008. **Remarks:** Original source: U.S. Department of Education, National Center for Education Statistics. Reports from various common core of Data surveys of Public and Private Elementary and Secondary Schools from 1983 through 1993. **Number listed:** 12.

2002, with 2,866 (K-12); 1,679
  (Elementary); 1,187 (Secondary)
2003, 2,903; 1,693; 1,209
2004, 2,935; 1,704; 1,231
2005, 2,963; 1,713; 1,250
2006, 2,985; 1,721; 1,264
2007, 3,005; 1,731; 1,274
2008, 3,022; 1,743; 1,279

Source: *Projections of Education Statistics to 2008,* NCES 98-016, U.S. Department of Education, National Center for Education Statistics (June 1998).

★4411★
New teachers' opinions about teaching

Ranking basis/background: Percentage of new teachers citing each opinion. **Remarks:** Original source: Public Agenda. **Number listed:** 5.
1. Teaching is work they love to do, with 96%
2. They would choose teaching again if starting over, 80%
3. Teaching is a lifelong choice, 75%
4. They get a lot of satisfaction from teaching, 68%
5. They fell into teaching by chance, 12%

Source: Hall, Cindy and Suzy Parker, "New Teachers' Thoughts About Teaching," *USA Today*, October 16, 2000, Section D, p. 7D.

★4412★
Number of Illinois superintendents, by gender, 1999-2000

Ranking basis/background: Total number of male and female superintendents. **Remarks:** Original source: Illinois State Board of Education 1999-2000 figures. **Number listed:** 2.
1. Male superintendents, with 754
2. Female superintendents, 114

Source: Walters, Sabrina, "'Super' Job Eludes Women," *Chicago Sun-Times*, November 12, 2000, p. 6A.

★4413★
Number of Illinois teachers, by gender, 1999-2000

Ranking basis/background: Total number of male and female teachers. **Remarks:** Original source: Illinois State Board of Education 1999-2000 figures. **Number listed:** 2.
1. Female teachers, with 93,883
2. Male teachers, 30,396

Source: Walters, Sabrina, "'Super' Job Eludes Women," *Chicago Sun-Times*, November 12, 2000, p. 6A.

★4414★
Projected employment by general teaching specialty, through 2005

Ranking basis/background: For each specialty, projected employment, in thousands. Also includes projected change in employment, in percent, 1994-2005; projected change in employment, in thousands, 1994-2005; and projected annual average net replacement needs, in thousands, 1994-2005. **Number listed:** 2.

Preschool through grade 12 including special education, with 4,560 thousand; 26%; 87 thousand; 74 thousand
K-12 excluding special education, 3,541; 22%; 58; 65

Source: Barkume, Megan, "School Work: The Job Outlook for Teachers," *Occupational Outlook Quarterly*, pp. 22-31, (Spring 1997).

★4415★
Projected employment by specific teaching specialty, through 2005

Ranking basis/background: For each specialty, projected employment, in thousands. Also includes projected change in employment, in percent, 1994-2005; projected change in employment, in thousands, 1994-2005; and projected annual average net replacement needs, in thousands, 1994-2005. **Number listed:** 4.

Preschool and kindergarten teachers, with 602 thousand; 30%; 13 thousand; 7 thousand
Elementary school, 1,639; 16%; 20; 26
Secondary school, 1,726; 29%; 35; 36
Special education, 593; 53%; 19; 5

Source: Barkume, Megan, "School Work: The Job Outlook for Teachers," *Occupational Outlook Quarterly*, pp. 22-31, (Spring 1997).

TEACHERS, ELEMENTARY AND SECONDARY–SALARIES

See: **Salaries–Schools, Elementary & Secondary**

TECHNICAL COMMUNICATION

★4416★
Most cited applied arts serials in technical communication journals from 1988 to 1997

Ranking basis/background: Applied art serials receiving the most citations in four technical communications journals: *IEEE Transactions on Professional Communications, Journals of Business and Technical Communication, Journal of Technical Writing and Communication,* and *Technical Communication.* **Number listed:** 1.
  Information Design Journal

Source: Smith, Elizabeth Overman, "Strength in the Technical Communication Journals and Diversity in the Serials Cited," *Journal of Business and Technical Communication*, 14: 131-184, (April 2000).

★4417★
Most cited business serials in technical communication journals from 1988 to 1997

Ranking basis/background: Business serials receiving the most citations in four technical communications journals: *IEEE Transactions on Professional Communications, Journals of Business and Technical Communication, Journal of Technical Writing and Communication,* and *Technical Communication.* **Number listed:** 21.
  Human Relations
  Administrative Science Quarterly
  SIGCHI Bulletin
  Academy of Management Journal
  Academy of Management Review
  Management Science
  Journal of System Management
  Training & Development
  Management Communication Quarterly
  Business Week
  Fortune
  Harvard Business Review
  Journal of Marketing Research
  Journal of Marketing
  ACM Transactions on Information Systems
  MIS Quarterly
  Training
  Personnel Psychology
  Business Communication Quarterly
  Journal of Business Communication
  Journal of Advertising Research

Source: Smith, Elizabeth Overman, "Strength in the Technical Communication Journals and Diversity in the Serials Cited," *Journal of Business and Technical Communication*, 14: 131-184, (April 2000).

★4418★
Most cited education serials in technical communication journals from 1988 to 1997

Ranking basis/background: Education serials receiving the most citations in four technical communications journals: *IEEE Transactions on Professional Communications, Journals of Business and Technical Communication, Journal of Technical Writing and Communication,* and *Technical Communication.* **Number listed:** 13.

- American Educational Research Journal
- Instructional Science
- Reviews in Educational Research
- English Education
- Educational Technology
- Journal of Computer-Based Instruction
- Reading Research Quarterly
- Journal of Educational Psychology
- Contemporary Educational Psychology
- Journal of Experimental Psychology: Learning, Memory, Cognition
- Computers and Composition
- The Chronicle of Higher Education
- American Journal of Distance Education

Source: Smith, Elizabeth Overman, "Strength in the Technical Communication Journals and Diversity in the Serials Cited," *Journal of Business and Technical Communication,* 14: 131-184, (April 2000).

★4419★
Most cited general works serials in technical communication journals from 1988 to 1997

Ranking basis/background: General works serials receiving the most citations in four technical communications journals: *IEEE Transactions on Professional Communications, Journals of Business and Technical Communication, Journal of Technical Writing and Communication,* and *Technical Communication.* **Number listed:** 5.

- Los Angeles Times
- New York Times
- Newsweek
- Time
- The Wall Street Journal

Source: Smith, Elizabeth Overman, "Strength in the Technical Communication Journals and Diversity in the Serials Cited," *Journal of Business and Technical Communication,* 14: 131-184, (April 2000).

★4420★
Most cited language serials in technical communication journals from 1988 to 1997

Ranking basis/background: Language serials receiving the most citations in four technical communications journals: *IEEE Transactions on Professional Communications, Journals of Business and Technical Communication, Journal of Technical Writing and Communication,* and *Technical Communication.* **Number listed:** 18.

- Journal of Communication
- Communication Research
- Human Communication Research
- Written Communication
- PRE/TEXT
- College English
- English Journal
- College Composition Communication
- Research in Teaching English
- TESOL Quarterly
- Journal of Advanced Composition
- Journal of Business and Technical Communication
- Rhetoric Review
- Central States Speech Journal
- Quarterly Journal of Speech
- Communication Quarterly
- Communication Monographs
- Journalism Quarterly

Source: Smith, Elizabeth Overman, "Strength in the Technical Communication Journals and Diversity in the Serials Cited," *Journal of Business and Technical Communication,* 14: 131-184, (April 2000).

★4421★
Most cited philosophy serials in technical communication journals from 1988 to 1997

Ranking basis/background: Philosophy serials receiving the most citations in four technical communications journals: *IEEE Transactions on Professional Communications, Journals of Business and Technical Communication, Journal of Technical Writing and Communication,* and *Technical Communication.* **Number listed:** 1.

- Philosophy and Rhetoric

Source: Smith, Elizabeth Overman, "Strength in the Technical Communication Journals and Diversity in the Serials Cited," *Journal of Business and Technical Communication,* 14: 131-184, (April 2000).

★4422★
Most cited printing and publishing serials in technical communication journals from 1988 to 1997

Ranking basis/background: Printing and publishing serials receiving the most citations in four technical communications journals: *IEEE Transactions on Professional Communications, Journals of Business and Technical Communication, Journal of Technical Writing and Communication,* and *Technical Communication.* **Number listed:** 3.

- Visible Language
- Publish! The How-To Magazine of Desktop Publishing
- Scholarly Publishing

Source: Smith, Elizabeth Overman, "Strength in the Technical Communication Journals and Diversity in the Serials Cited," *Journal of Business and Technical Communication,* 14: 131-184, (April 2000).

★4423★
Most cited psychology serials in technical communication journals from 1988 to 1997

Ranking basis/background: Psychology serials receiving the most citations in four technical communications journals: *IEEE Transactions on Professional Communications, Journals of Business and Technical Communication, Journal of Technical Writing and Communication,* and *Technical Communication.* **Number listed:** 8.

- American Psychologist
- Journal of Applied Psychology
- Psychological Bulletin
- Psychology Review
- Cognitive Psychology
- Cognitive Science
- Memory and Cognition
- Journal of Memory and Language

Source: Smith, Elizabeth Overman, "Strength in the Technical Communication Journals and Diversity in the Serials Cited," *Journal of Business and Technical Communication,* 14: 131-184, (April 2000).

★4424★
Most cited science serials in technical communication journals from 1988 to 1997

Ranking basis/background: Science serials receiving the most citations in four technical communications journals: *IEEE Transactions on Professional Communications, Journal of Business and Technical Communication, Journal of Technical Writing and Communication,* and *Technical Communication.* **Number listed:** 10.

- Social Studies of Science
- Science
- Daedalus
- Behavior Information Technology
- Communications of the Association of Computing Machinery
- BYTE
- Computerworld
- Journal of Computer Documentation
- Human-Computer Interaction
- Quarterly Journal of Experimental Psychology

Source: Smith, Elizabeth Overman, "Strength in the Technical Communication Journals and Diversity in the Serials Cited," *Journal of Business and Technical Communication,* 14: 131-184, (April 2000).

★4425★
Most cited serials in technical communication journals from 1988 to 1997

Ranking basis/background: Total citations received between 1988 and 1997. **Number listed:** 100.

1. Technical Communication, with 894 total citations
2. Journal of Technical Writing and Communication, 624
3. IEEE Transactions on Professional Communication, 563
4. Journal of Business and Technical Communication, 454
5. Technical Communication Quarterly/Technical Writing Teacher, 453
6. College English, 418
7. College Composition Communication, 369
8. Journal of Business Communication, 357
9. Written Communication, 232
10. Business Communication Quarterly/Bulletin of the Association for Business Administration, 158
11. Research in Teaching English, 116
12. Communications of the Association of Computing Machinery, 94
13. Journal of Educational Psychology, 93
14. Journal of Advanced Composition, 88
15. Quarterly Journal of Speech, 84
16. Journal of Applied Psychology, 77
17. Journal of Memory and Language/Journal of Verbal Learning and Verbal Behavior, 76
18. Harvard Business Review, 75
19. New York Times, 69
20. Rhetoric Review, 68

Source: Smith, Elizabeth Overman, "Strength in the Technical Communication Journals and Diversity in the Serials Cited," *Journal of Business and Technical Communication*, 14: 131-184, (April 2000).

★4426★
Most cited sociology serials in technical communication journals from 1988 to 1997

Ranking basis/background: Sociology serials receiving the most citations in four technical communications journals: *IEEE Transactions on Professional Communications, Journals of Business and Technical Communication, Journal of Technical Writing and Communication*, and *Technical Communication*. **Number listed:** 3.
- American Sociological Review
- Journal of Personality and Social Psychology
- Public Opinion Quarterly

Source: Smith, Elizabeth Overman, "Strength in the Technical Communication Journals and Diversity in the Serials Cited," *Journal of Business and Technical Communication*, 14: 131-184, (April 2000).

★4427★
Most cited technology serials in technical communication journals from 1988 to 1997

Ranking basis/background: Technology serials receiving the most citations in four technical communications journals: *IEEE Transactions on Professional Communications, Jouurnals of Business and Technical Communication, Journal of Technical Writing and Communication*, and *Technical Communication*. **Number listed:** 16.
- Journal of Technical Writing and Communication
- Scientific American
- IEEE Transactions on Professional Communication
- Intercom
- Technostyle
- Technical Communication
- Technical Communication Quarterly
- Human Factors
- Engineering Education
- Datamation
- Computer Graphics World
- Ergonomics
- International Journal of Man-Machine Studies
- IEEE Computer
- IEEE Spectrum
- Industry Week

Source: Smith, Elizabeth Overman, "Strength in the Technical Communication Journals and Diversity in the Serials Cited," *Journal of Business and Technical Communication*, 14: 131-184, (April 2000).

TECHNOLOGICAL RESEARCH FUNDING
See: **Scientific & Technological Research & Development Funding**

TECHNOLOGY

★4428★
Information technology jobs most in demand, 2001

Ranking basis/background: Number of estimated openings in each job category. **Remarks:** Original source: ITAA. **Number listed:** 5.
1. Technical support, with 218,238
2. Database development/administration, 110,104
3. Programming/software engineering, 134,637
4. Network design/administration, 186,613
5. Web development/administration, 120,982

Source: Battey, Jim, "Demand for IT Workers by Job Category, 2000-2001," *Infoworld*, 23: 16, (April 16, 2001).

★4429★
Largest technology companies in the U.S. in terms of annual revenue, 2000

Ranking basis/background: Annual revenue, in billions of dollars, for 2000 and percent change from 1999. **Remarks:** Original source: Market Guide, Infoworld. **Number listed:** 10.
1. IBM, with $88.4 billion; a 1.0% change from 1999
2. Hewlett-Packard, $49.1; 12.1%
3. Compaq Computer, $42.4; 10.1%
4. Motorola, $37.6; 21.7%
5. Intel, $33.7; 14.6%
6. Dell Computer, $31.9; 26.1%
7. Cisco Systems, $24.0; 60.0%
8. Microsoft, $23.8; 8.7%
9. Sun Microsystems, $19.2; 45.5%
10. Oracle, $11.0; 13.4%

Source: "Largest Tech Companies," *Infoworld*, 23: 18, (April 2, 2001).

★4430★
Spending for E-marketplace services, by industry, 2001

Ranking basis/background: Figures, in millions of dollars, spent to develop, deploy and manage e-marketplaces. **Remarks:** Original source: IDC. **Number listed:** 10.
1. Manufacturing, with $1.26 billion
2. Financial services/insurance, $756.9 million
3. Transportation, $589.2
4. Communications/media, $426.4
5. Retail, $421.6
6. Government/education, $344.9
7. Health care, $282.6
8. Business services, $244.3
9. Utilities, $239.5
10. Wholesale, $124.6

Source: Battey, Jim, "E-Marketplace Industries," *Infoworld*, 23: 20, (April 9, 2001).

★4431★
Top future technologies

Ranking basis/background: Rapidly developing technologies according to scholars at George Washington University. **Remarks:** Identified by the GW Forecast; reported in The Futurist; published by the World Future Society. **Number listed:** 10.
1. Portable information devices
2. Cars powered by fuel cells
3. Computerized management of crops
4. Cybershopping will increase
5. "Teleliving"
6. Software "helpers" to handle routine chores
7. Genetically modified crops
8. Computerized health care
9. Alternative energy sources-wind, hydroelectric, solar-will show growth
10. Mobil robots that will perform more complex factory work and household chores

Source: Heylin, Michael, "Top Ten Future Technologies," *Association Management*, 52: 24, (November 2000).

TECHNOLOGY MANAGEMENT
See: **Business Administration–Technology Management**

TEEN PREGNANCY

★4432★
U.S. cities with the highest percentage of births to mothers with less than 12 years of education

Ranking basis/background: Percentage of births to mothers with less than 12 years of education. **Remarks:** Original source: National Center for Health Statistics, Alan Guttmacher Institute. **Number listed:** 10.
1. Los Angeles, with 45.3%
2. Dallas, 44.0%
3. Houston, 42.1%
4. Fresno, 40.9%
5. Phoenix, 39.9%
6. Long Beach, 38.1%
7. Fort Worth, 38.0%
8. El Paso, 36.6%
9. Chicago, 36.4%
10. Milwaukee, 34.9%

Source: "Sad But True: Teen Motherhood is as American as Apple Pie," *U.S. News & World Report*, 130: 8, (March 5, 2001).

★4433★
U.S. states with the highest percentage of births to teenagers who were already mothers

Ranking basis/background: Percentage of births to teenagers who already have a child(ren). **Remarks:** Original source: National Center for Health Statistics, Alan Guttmacher Institute. **Number listed:** 10.
1. Washington, DC, with 28.0%
2. Mississippi, 24.4%
3. Texas, 24.1%
4. Georgia, 24.0%
5. Arkansas, 23.5%
6. Illinois, 23.4%
7. Alabama, 23.0%
8. Nevada, 22.8%
9. Louisiana, 22.7%
10. Florida, 22.5%

Source: "Sad But True: Teen Motherhood is as American as Apple Pie," *U.S. News & World Report*, 130: 8, (March 5, 2001).

TESTS FOR COLLEGE ADMISSION
See: **College Entrance Examinations**

TESTS FOR STUDENT COMPETENCY

See: Achievement Tests–Schools, Elementary & Secondary Advanced Placement Tests College Entrance Examinations

TEXTILES

★4434★
Top recruiters for textiles/apparel jobs for 2000-01 bachelor's degree recipients

Ranking basis/background: Projected number of college hires from on-campus recruitment for 2000-01. **Remarks:** Numbers reflect total expected hires, not just African American projected hires. **Number listed:** 2.
1. SAKS Corporation, with 33 projected hires
2. Macy's West, 13

Source: "The Top 100 Employers and the Majors in Demand for the Class of 2001," *The Black Collegian*, 31: 19-35, (February 2001).

THEATRE ARTS

★4435★
Top plays of the twentieth century

Ranking basis/background: As selected by playwrights, actors, directors, journalists and other theater professional chosen by the Royal National Theater in London, to nominate ten English language, twentieth century plays they considered most "significant." **Number listed:** 377.
1. *Waiting for Godot*, by Samuel Beckett
2. *Death of a Salesman*, Arthur Miller
3. *A Streetcar Named Desire*, Tennessee Williams
4. *Look Back in Anger*, John Osborne
5. *Long Day's Journey into Night*, Eugene O'Neill
6. *The Crucible*, Arthur Miller
7. *Private Lives*, Noel Coward
7. *Rosencrantz & Guildenstern are Dead*, Tom Stoppard
9. *Angels in America*, Tony Kushner
9. *The Caretaker*, Harold Pinter

Source: http://spot.colorado.edu/~colemab./NT2000/NT2000.html#The Most Selected Plays.

★4436★
Top playwrights of the twentieth century

Ranking basis/background: As selected by playwrights, actors, directors, journalists and other theater professional chosen by the Royal National Theater in London, to nominate ten English language, twentieth century plays they considered most "significant." **Number listed:** 20.
1. Arthur Miller
2. Harold Pinter
3. Samuel Beckett
4. Tennessee Williams
5. John Osborne
6. George Bernard Shaw
7. Tom Stoppard
7. Eugene O'Neill
9. Noel Coward
10. David Hare
11. Sean O'Casey
12. Caryl Churchill
12. Edward Bond
14. Alan Ayckbourn
15. Terence Rattigan
16. Joe Orton
17. Brian Friel
17. Tony Kushner
19. J.B. Priestley
20. Edward Albee

Source: http://spot.colorado.edu/~colemab./NT2000/NT2000.html#The Most Selected Plays.

★4437★
U.S. universities publishing the most papers in the field of performing arts, 1994-98

Ranking basis/background: Total number of papers published from each university. **Remarks:** Original source: University Science Indicators on Diskette, 1981-97. **Number listed:** 5.
1. New York University, with 107 papers
2. City University of New York, 82
3. University of Wisconsin, Madison, 81
4. Yale University, 68
5. University of Texas, Austin, 59

Source: "Performing Arts: Most Prolific U.S. Universities, 1994-98," *What's Hot in Research* (http://www.isinet.com/hot/research) Institute for Scientific Information, August 16, 1999.

TUITION, COLLEGE

See: Colleges & Universities, Liberal Arts–Student Costs Colleges & Universities–Student Costs

TUITION SAVINGS PLANS

★4438★
States with the best college tuition savings plans

Ranking basis/background: As researched by *Kiplinger's*. **Number listed:** 5.
1. Utah, Educational Savings Plan
2. California, Golden State ScholarShare
3. Iowa, College Savings Iowa
4. Maine, NextGen
5. New Hampshire, Unique College Investing Plan

Source: Davis, Kristin, "College Bound," *Kiplinger's*, August 2000, pp. 111-117.

TWO-YEAR COLLEGES

★4439★
***Princeton Review*'s Deep Springs College Honor Roll**

Ranking basis/background: Title of lists that Deep Springs College, a unique two-year institution, ranked high or low on. **Remarks:** From a survey of nearly 60,000 students, answering 70 multiple choice question on school administration, quality of teaching, social life and campus life. Rankings from this survey are based purely on student opinion. Except for schools with less than 1,000 students enrolled, the Princeton Review heard from at least 100 students on each campus surveyed. **Number listed:** 19.
  Best Overall Academic Experience for Undergraduates
  The Toughest to Get Into
  Professors Bring Material to Life
  Professors Make Themselves Accessible
  Their Students Never Stop Studying
  School Runs Like Butter
  Students from Different Backgrounds Interact
  Gay Community Accepted
  This is a Library?
  Great Food on Campus
  Beautiful Campus
  Stone Cold Sober Schools
  Students Most Nostalgic for George McGovern
  Happy Students
  Election? What Election?
  Got Milk?
  Scotch and Soda, Hold the Scotch
  Don't Inhale
  Dodge-Ball Targets

Source: Franek, Robert, et. al., *The Best 311 Colleges, 2001 edition*, Princeton Review Publishing, 2000.

TWO-YEAR COLLEGES–ADMINISTRATION
See: College Administration

TWO-YEAR COLLEGES–ENROLLMENT
See: College Enrollment

TWO-YEAR COLLEGES–SALARIES
See: Salaries–Colleges & Universities

UNDERGRADUATE EDUCATION
See: Colleges & Universities

UNIVERSITIES
See: Colleges & Universities

URBAN ECONOMICS
See: **Economics Real Estate**

VETERANS' EDUCATIONAL BENEFITS
See: **Student Financial Aid**

VETERINARY–ANIMAL HEALTH

★4440★
U.S. universities with the greatest impact in veterinary medicine, 1995-99

Ranking basis/background: Average citations per paper from the top 100 federally funded U.S. universities that had at least 50 published papers in ISI indexed veterinary medicine and animal health journals. Also includes total number of paper published during the five year period. **Number listed:** 5.
1. University of California, Davis, with 916 papers; 2.54 citations per paper
2. Iowa State University, 256; 2.46
3. University of Kentucky, 118; 2.37
4. Washington State University, 348; 2.36
5. University of Wisconsin, Madison, 414; 2.34

Source: "Veterinary Medicine: High Impact U.S. Universities, 1995-99," *What's Hot in Research* (http://www.isinet.com/isi/hot/research) Institute for Scientific Information, December 25, 2000.

★4441★
U.S. universities with the highest concentration of papers published in the field of veterinary medicine, 1995-99

Ranking basis/background: Number of papers published in the field of veterinary medicine over a five-year period, and percentage they comprise of the university's total papers published. **Number listed:** 5.
1. Colorado State University, with 528 papers; 10.04% of university's total papers
2. Washington State University, 348; 6.92%
3. North Carolina State University, 504; 6.72%
4. University of California, Davis, 916; 6.51%
5. University of Georgia, 521; 6.40%

Source: "U.S. Universities with Highest Concentrations in Veterinary Medicine, 1995-99," *What's Hot in Research* (http://www.isinet.com/isi/hot/research) Institute for Scientific Information, December 4, 2000.

★4442★
Veterinary sciences journals with the greatest impact measure, 1981-98

Ranking basis/background: Citations-per-paper impact score is the total citations to a journal's published papers divided by total number of papers the journal has published over an eighteen year period. **Remarks:** Original source: *Journal Citation Reports* and Journal Performance Indicators on Diskette. **Number listed:** 10.
1. *Advances in Veterinary Sciences*, with an impact score of 12.38
2. *Canadian Journal of Comparative Medicine*, 10.95
3. *American Journal of Veterinary Research*, 8.99
4. *Animal Production*, 8.78
5. *Vaccine*, 8.29
6. *Theriogenology*, 8.18
7. *Animal Blood Groups*, 8.16
8. *Domestic Animal Endocrinology*, 8.12
9. *Journal of Fish Diseases*, 7.33
10. *Veterinary Pathology*, 7.24

Source: "Journals Ranked by Impact: Veterinary Sciences," *What's Hot in Research* (http://www.isinet.com/hot/research) Institute for Scientific Information, December 27, 1999.

★4443★
Veterinary sciences journals with the greatest impact measure, 1994-98

Ranking basis/background: Citations-per-paper impact score is the total citations to a journal's published papers divided by total number of papers the journal has published over a five year period. **Remarks:** Original source: *Journal Citation Reports* and Journal Performance Indicators on Diskette. **Number listed:** 10.
1. *Vaccine*, with an impact score of 4.10
2. *Animal Production*, 3.92
3. *Theriogenology*, 3.14
4. *Diseases of Aquatic Organisms*, 2.95
5. *British Veterinary Journal*, 2.94
6. *Veterinary Microbiology*, 2.79
7. *Advances in Veterinary Sciences*, 2.78
8. *Journal of Fish Diseases*, 2.70
9. *Veterinary Immunology Immunopathology*, 2.69
10. *Domestic Animal Endocrinology*, 2.67

Source: "Journals Ranked by Impact: Veterinary Sciences," *What's Hot in Research* (http://www.isinet.com/hot/research) Institute for Scientific Information, December 27, 1999.

VIOLENCE

★4444★
Adult opinions about the likelihood of school shootings in their community

Ranking basis/background: Percentage of adults stating the chances of a school shooting in their community, from a Gallup Poll of 1,015 adults in March of 2001. **Number listed:** 5.
  Very likely, with 31%
  Somewhat likely, 34%
  Somewhat unlikely, 20%
  Very unlikely, 13%
  No opinion, 2%

Source: Pompa, Frank, "Americans Fear School Shootings," *USA Today*, April 6, 2001, Section A, p. 1A.

★4445★
Number of students killed in school shootings, 1992-93 to 1998-99

Ranking basis/background: Number of school-related shooting deaths. **Remarks:** Original source: The National School Safety Center **Number listed:** 7.
  1992-93, with 32
  1993-94, 26
  1994-95, 13
  1995-96, 22
  1996-97, 11
  1997-98, 26
  1998-99, 19

Source: Kozakosr, Penny, "School-Related Shooting Deaths," *USA Today*, September 28, 1999, Section A, p. 1A.

WOMEN EXECUTIVES

★4446★
Best companies for working mothers

Ranking basis/background: Compiled from a rating system evaluating pay, opportunities for women to advance, child care, flexibility, other family friendly benefits, and work/life supports. List is alphabetical. **Number listed:** 10.
1. Allstate Insurance Company (10 years on the 100 Best List)
2. Bank of America (12)
3. Eli Lilly and Company, (6)
4. Fannie Mae, (7)
5. IBM (15)
6. Life Technologies, Inc. (5)
7. Lincoln Financial Group (14)
8. Merrill Lynch (5)
9. Novant Health, Inc. (1)
10. Prudential (11)

Source: "100 Best Companies for Working Mothers," *Working Mother*, 23: 94-170, (October 2000).

★4447★
Best companies for working mothers in offering advancement opportunities for women

Ranking basis/background: Compiled from a rating system evaluating pay, opportunities for women to advance, child care, flexibility, other family friendly benefits, and work/life supports. List is alphabetical. **Number listed:** 5.
  Baptist Health Systems of South Florida
  Benjamin Group/BSMG Worldwide
  CIGNA
  Northwestern Memorial Hospital
  Novant Health, Inc.

Source: "100 Best Companies for Working Mothers," *Working Mother*, 23: 94-170, (October 2000).

★4448★
Best companies for working mothers in offering flexible work hours

Ranking basis/background: Compiled from a rating system evaluating pay, opportunities for women to advance, child care, flexibility, other family friendly benefits, and work/life supports. List is alphabetical. **Number listed:** 5.
  Chase Manhattan Corporation
  Fannie Mae
  Pearson Education
  Prudential
  Valassis Communications, Inc.

Source: "100 Best Companies for Working Mothers," *Working Mother*, 23: 94-170, (October 2000).

WOMEN EXECUTIVES

★4449★
Best companies for working mothers in offering leave for new parents

Ranking basis/background: Compiled from a rating system evaluating pay, opportunities for women to advance, child care, flexibility, other family friendly benefits, and work/life supports. List is alphabetical. **Number listed:** 5.

- Bell Atlantic
- Eli Lilly and Company
- Ernst & Young LLP
- General Motors
- IBM

Source: "100 Best Companies for Working Mothers," *Working Mother*, 23: 94-170, (October 2000).

★4450★
Best companies for working mothers in terms of child care

Ranking basis/background: Compiled from a rating system evaluating pay, opportunities for women to advance, child care, flexibility, other family friendly benefits, and work/life supports. List is alphabetical. **Number listed:** 5.

- Fannie Mae
- GTE Corporation
- Merrill Lynch & Co., Inc.
- SAS
- Tom's of Maine

Source: "100 Best Companies for Working Mothers," *Working Mother*, 23: 94-170, (October 2000).

★4451★
Best companies for working mothers in terms of overall work/life support

Ranking basis/background: Compiled from a rating system evaluating pay, opportunities for women to advance, child care, flexibility, other family friendly benefits, and work/life supports. List is alphabetical. **Number listed:** 5.

- IBM
- Life Technologies, Inc.
- Marriott International
- Novant Health, Inc.
- Prudential

Source: "100 Best Companies for Working Mothers," *Working Mother*, 23: 94-170, (October 2000).

★4452★
Highest ranking women at the top public companies, 2000

Ranking basis/background: Based on *Working Woman*'s survey of publicly held companies with more than 3,000 employees and at least 2 women on the board of directors. Four categories were explored: female directors, women in senior management positions, women at the level of corporate vice president and above, and ratio of female managers to female employees. **Number listed:** 25.

1. Andrea Jung, CEO & President at Avon
2. Dawn Lepore, Vice Chair, CIO & Exec. VP at Charles Schwab
3. Barbara A. Marcus, President, Children's Book Publishing and Exec. VP at Scholastic
4. Deanna Watson Oppenheimer, President, Consumer Banking Group at Washington Mutual
5. Carly Fiorine, Chair, President, & CEO at Hewlett-Packard
6. Elease Wright, Sr. VP, Corporate Human Resources at Aetna
7. Kim Roy, Group President at Liz Claiborne
8. Mary Jean Connors, Sr. VP Human Resources at Knight Ridder
9. Joan Herman, Group President Senior, Specialty and State Sponsored Programs Division at WellPoint
10. Judy Lewent, Sr. VP & CFO at Merck

Source: Cleaver, Joanne, "Top Twenty Five Companies for Executive Women," *Working Woman*, 26: 58-70, (Dec. 2000/Jan. 2001).

★4453★
Highly recommended public companies for women executives, 2000

Ranking basis/background: Based on *Working Woman*'s survey of publicly held companies with more than 3,000 employees and at least 2 women on the board of directors. Four categories were explored: female directors, women in senior management positions, women at the level of corporate vice president and above, and ratio of female managers to female employees. **Number listed:** 16.

- Alliant Energy
- American Express
- Bank of America
- Baxter International
- Bristol-Myers Squibb
- Colgate-Palmolive
- Federated Department Stores
- Phoenix Home Life
- McDonald's
- Philip Morris
- Procter & Gamble
- Sallie Mae
- Sears, Roebuck
- Toys "R" Us
- Verizon Communications
- Xerox

Source: Cleaver, Joanne, "Top Twenty Five Companies for Executive Women," *Working Woman*, 26: 58-70, (Dec. 2000/Jan. 2001).

★4454★
Oldest women-owned companies

Ranking basis/background: Year company started. **Number listed:** 5.

1. Kiehl's, started in 1851
2. Jockey International, 1876
3. Witt Industries, 1887
4. Chas. Levy Companies, 1893
5. Tootsie Roll Industries, 1896

Source: "The Top 500 Women-Owned Businesses," *Working Woman*, 25: 51-94, (June 2000).

★4455★
States with the most women-owned companies

Ranking basis/background: Number of women-owned companies in each state. **Number listed:** 5.

1. California, with 94
2. New York, 54
3. Illinois, 43
4. Texas, 42
5. Michigan, 30

Source: "The Top 500 Women-Owned Businesses," *Working Woman*, 25: 51-94, (June 2000).

★4456★
Top industries for women-owned companies

Ranking basis/background: Number of women-owned companies in each industry. **Number listed:** 5.

1. Car dealership, with 48 companies
2. Personnel, 30
3. Computer products and services, 27
4. Apparel, 21
5. Real estate, 10

Source: "The Top 500 Women-Owned Businesses," *Working Woman*, 25: 51-94, (June 2000).

★4457★
Top public companies for women executives, 2000

Ranking basis/background: Based on *Working Woman*'s survey of publicly held companies with more than 3,000 employees and at least 2 women on the board of directors. Four categories were explored: female directors, women in senior management positions, women at the level of corporate vice president and above, and ratio of female managers to female employees. **Number listed:** 25.

1. Avon (rank in 1999 was No. 1)
2. Charles Schwab (No. 2)
3. Scholastic (No. 3)
4. Washington Mutual (Not ranked)
5. Hewlett-Packard (Honor Roll)
6. Aetna (No. 14)
7. Liz Claiborne (Not ranked)
8. Knight Ridder (No. 6)
9. WellPoint (No. 24)
10. Merck (No. 18)

Source: Cleaver, Joanne, "Top Twenty Five Companies for Executive Women," *Working Woman*, 26: 58-70, (Dec. 2000/Jan. 2001).

★4458★
Top public companies with the highest percentage of women board of directors, 2000

Ranking basis/background: Number and percentage of women Board of Directors. Based on *Working Woman*'s survey of publicly held companies with more than 3,000 employees and at least 2 women on the board of directors. Four categories were explored: female directors, women in senior management positions, women at the level of corporate vice pres. and above, and ratio of female managers to female employees. **Number listed:** 25.

1. Golden West, with 5 women on the Board (56% of total Board members)
2. Avon, 5 (45%)
3. WellPoint, 3 (43%)
4. Scholastic, 4 (33%)
4. Liz Claiborne, 4 (33%)
4. Aetna, 4 (33%)
4. Con Edison, 4 (33%)
8. Hewlett-Packard, 3 (30%)
9. Knight Ridder, 3 (27%)
9. SBC Communications, 6 (27%)
9. Pitney Bowes, 3 (27%)

Source: Cleaver, Joanne, "Top Twenty Five Companies for Executive Women," *Working Woman*, 26: 58-70, (Dec. 2000/Jan. 2001).

★4459★

Top public companies with the highest percentage of women employees, 2000

Ranking basis/background: Percentage of women employees worldwide. Based on *Working Woman*'s survey of publicly held companies with more than 3,000 employees and at least 2 women on the board of directors. Four categories were explored: female directors, women in senior management positions, women at the level of corporate vice president and above, and ratio of female managers to female employees. **Number listed:** 25.

1. Aetna, with 77% female employees
2. Lincoln National, 75%
3. Avon, 74%
4. WellPoint, 74%
5. Liz Claiborne, 72%
6. Gap, 69%
7. Washington Mutual, 68%
8. Scholastic, 67%
9. Target (Dayton Hudson), 67%
10. Golden West, 64%

Source: Cleaver, Joanne, "Top Twenty Five Companies for Executive Women," *Working Woman*, 26: 58-70, (Dec. 2000/Jan. 2001).

★4460★

Top women-owned companies

Ranking basis/background: Company name, location, owner and their title as listed in *Working Woman*'s Top 500 women-owned companies. **Number listed:** 500.

1. JM Family Enterprises (Deerfield Beach, FL), owner, Pat Moran, CEO, President
2. Fidelity Investments (Boston, MA), Abigail Johnson, Sr. VP, Equities
3. Carlson Companies (Minneapolis, MN), Marilyn Carlson Nelson, CEO
4. Golden West Financial (Oakland, CA), Marion O. Sandler, Chair, CEO
5. Raley's (W. Sacramento, CA), Jayce Raley Teel, Co-chair
6. Little Caesar Enterprises (Detroit, MI), Marian Ilitch, Secretary-Treasurer
7. Warnaco Group (New York, NY), Linda J. Wachner, Chair, CEO, President
8. Ingram Industries (Nashville, TN), Martha R. Ingram, Chair
9. Alberto-Culver (Melrose Park, IL), Bernice Lavin, V. Chair and Carol Bernick, V. Chair, Pres. N.A. Div.
10. 84 Lumber (Eighty-Four, PA), Maggie Hardy Magerko, COO, President
11. Roll International (Los Angeles, CA), Lynda R. Resnick, Vice Chair
12. Cumberland Farms (Canton, MA), Lily Bentas, CEO, President
13. Axel Johnson (Samford, CT), Antonia Axson Johnson, Chair
14. Minyard Food Stores (Coppel, TX), Liz Minyar, Co Chair & CEO and Gretchen M. Williams, Co-Chair & CEO
15. Charming Shoppes (Bensalem, PA), Dorrit J. Bern, Chair, CEO, President
16. Frank Consolidated Enterprises (Des Plains, IL), Elaine S. Frank, Chair
17. PC Connection (Merrimack, NH), Patricia Gallup, Chair, CEO, President
18. Helmsley Enterprises (New York, NY), Leona Helmsley, Owner
19. Printpack (Atlanta, GA), Gay Love, Chair
20. Software Spectrum (Garland, TX), Judy Odom Sims, Chair, CEO
21. Software House International (Somerset, NJ), Thai Lee, President
22. Longaberger Company (Newark, OH), Tami Longaberger, CEO, President
23. J. Crew (New York, NY), Emily Woods, Chair
24. Asia Source (Fremont, CA), Christine Liang, President
25. Golden Rule Insurance (Lawrenceville, IL), Therese A. Rooney, Chair

Source: "The Top 500 Women-Owned Businesses," *Working Woman*, 25: 51-94, (June 2000).

★4461★

Top women-owned companies in revenue growth since 1997

Ranking basis/background: Growth percentage for each women-owned company since 1997. **Number listed:** 3.

1. Reliance Technical Services, with 515%
2. Karen Neuburger, 477%
3. Allied Technology Group, 214%

Source: "The Top 500 Women-Owned Businesses," *Working Woman*, 25: 51-94, (June 2000).

★4462★

Top women-owned companies with the most employees

Ranking basis/background: Number of employees of each women-owned company. **Number listed:** 3.

1. Carlson Companies, with 44,000 employees
2. Fidelity Investments, 25,000
3. Warnaco Group, 20,000

Source: "The Top 500 Women-Owned Businesses," *Working Woman*, 25: 51-94, (June 2000).

Related Information

★4463★

"The Top 500 Women-Owned Businesses," *Working Woman*, 25: 51-94, (June 2000).

Remarks: Lists the top 500 women-owned companies; their owner with title; revenue, in millions, for 1997, 1998 and 1999; number of employees; type of business and web site, if any. Also includes articles about some selected women executives.

★4464★

"21st Annual Salary Survey," *Working Woman*, 25: 55-70, (July/August 2000).

Remarks: Presents an extensive survey conducted by *Working Woman* magazine comparing women's salaries to men's in each of 40 job fields.

★4465★

"100 Best Companies for Working Mothers," *Working Mother*, 23: 94-170, (October 2000).

Remarks: Directory of 100 companies evaluating pay, opportunities for women to advance, child care, flexibility, other family friendly benefits, and work/life supports.

WOMEN'S STUDIES

★4466★

Highly acknowledged individuals in the field of women's studies, 1975-94

Ranking basis/background: Number of acknowledgments received in articles in three women's studies journals. **Number listed:** 34.

1. Rayna Rapp, with 20 acknowledgements
2. Rosalind Petchesky, 17
3. Judy Stacey, 16
4. Marilyn B. Young, 15
5. Barrie Thorne, 14
6. Judy Walkowitz, 13
7. Heidi Hartmann, 12
8. Mary P. Ryan, 11
9. Estelle B. Freedman, 10
9. Linda Gordon, 10

Source: Cronin, Blaise, Elizabeth Davenport and Anna Martinson, "Women's Studies: Bibliometric and Content Analysis on the Formative Years," *Journal of Documentation*, March 1997, pp. 123-138.

Index

A

A Is for Salad
　Outstanding books for young readers, 2000　★328★

Aase; Craig H.
　Top pay and benefits for the chief executive and top paid employees at Macalester College　★3385★

ABA Journal
　Most frequently-cited law reviews and legal periodicals, according to *Shepard's Law Review Citations*, 1957-1986　★2620★

ABB
　Business Week's best companies in Switzerland　★405★

Abbott Laboratories
　Top recruiters for life sciences jobs for 2000-01 bachelor's degree recipients　★194★
　Top recruiters for biology/biological science jobs for 2000-01 bachelor's degree recipients　★198★
　Fortune's highest ranked pharmaceuticals companies, 2000　★485★
　Top recruiters for manufacturing management jobs for 2000-01 bachelor's degree recipients　★683★
　Top recruiters for chemistry jobs for 2000-01 bachelor's degree recipients　★792★
　Top recruiters for chemical engineering jobs for 2000-01 bachelor's degree recipients　★2343★
　Top recruiters for environmental engineering jobs for 2000-01 bachelor's degree recipients　★2357★
　Top recruiters for mechanical engineering jobs for 2000-01 bachelor's degree recipients　★2437★
　Most selective internships in the U.S., 2001　★2610★
　Top internships in the U.S. with the highest compensation, 2001　★2611★
　Top recruiters for medical technology jobs for 2000-01 bachelor's degree recipients　★2881★
　Top recruiters for pharmacology/pharmaceutical jobs for 2000-01 bachelor's degree recipients　★2934★

Abbott; Robert
　Most influential African Americans in business　★526★

Abene; Robert
　Top pay and benefits for the chief executive and top paid employees at Cardinal Stritch University　★3221★

Aberdeen; University of
　Top United Kingdom universities by total citations in the field of agricultural sciences, 1991-95　★2145★

Aberer; W.
　Most cited first authors in dermatology journals, 1981 to 1996　★1871★

Abernethy; Kenneth C.
　Top pay and benefits for the chief executive and top paid employees at Furman University　★3300★

Abilene Christian University
　U.S. News & World Report's best undergraduate fees among western regional universities by discount tuition, 2000　★1430★
　U.S. News & World Report's western regional universities with students most in debt, 1999　★1576★
　U.S. News & World Report's western regional universities with the highest percentage of full-time faculty, 2000-01　★1584★
　U.S. News & World Report's western regional universities with the lowest acceptance rates, 2000-01　★1586★
　Average faculty salaries for institutions of higher education in Texas, 2000-01　★3731★

Abingdon, VA
　America's most wired towns, 2001　★2575★

Abington High School
　Outstanding secondary schools in Philadelphia, Pennsylvania-New Jersey　★4202★

ABN Amro Holdings
　Business Week's best companies in the Netherlands　★410★

Abou-Gharbia; Magid A.
　American Chemical Society 2001 award winners (Group 1)　★751★

Abramson; Paul R.
　Authors most frequently published in *American Political Science Review*, 1974-94　★3047★

Abyssinian Chronicles
　Booklist's best first novels　★228★

The Academic Achievement Challenge: What Really Works in the Classroom?
　American School Board Journal's notable education books, 2000　★225★

Academic advisor
　African American college athletics administrators and staff, by gender, 1999-2000　★117★
　College athletics administrators and staff, by gender, 1999-2000　★121★
　Minority college athletics administrators and staff, by gender, 1999-2000　★132★
　Percentage of African American athletic administrators at NCAA Division I institutions, 1999　★138★
　Percentage of African American athletic administrators at NCAA Division II institutions, 1999　★139★
　Percentage of African American athletic administrators at NCAA Division III institutions, 1999　★140★

Academic Press
　Book publishers with the most citations (Class 3)　★2564★

Academy of Art College
　Professional or specialized institutions with the highest enrollment of foreign students, 1998-99　★2501★

The Academy for Advanced and Strategic Studies
　Most selective internships in the U.S., 2001　★2610★

Academy of Holy Angels
　Outstanding secondary schools in Minneapolis-St. Paul, Minnesota-Wisconsin　★4181★

Academy of the Holy Cross
　Outstanding secondary schools in Washington, District of Columbia-Maryland-Virginia-West Virginia　★4249★

Academy of the Holy Names
　Outstanding secondary schools in Albany-Schenectady-Troy, New York　★4079★
　Outstanding secondary schools in Tampa-St. Petersburg-Clearwater, Florida　★4240★

Academy of Management Journal
　Top management journals　★546★
　Top management journals by core impact　★547★
　Business journals by citation impact, 1981-98　★688★
　Business journals by citation impact, 1994-98　★689★
　Business journals by citation impact, 1998　★690★
　Journals with the highest impact factor in the field of management, 1981-96　★696★

ACADEMY

Most cited business serials in technical communication journals from 1988 to 1997 ★4417★

Academy of Management Review
Top management journals ★546★
Top management journals by core impact ★547★
Business journals by citation impact, 1981-98 ★688★
Business journals by citation impact, 1994-98 ★689★
Business journals by citation impact, 1998 ★690★
Journals with the highest impact factor in the field of management, 1981-96 ★696★
Journals and proceedings with the most citations (Class 2) ★2568★
Most cited business serials in technical communication journals from 1988 to 1997 ★4417★

Academy of Our Lady of Peace
Outstanding secondary schools in San Diego, California ★4220★

Academy Primary School
All-USA Teacher Teams, Second Team, 2000 ★4400★

Academy School District No. 20, Colorado
Comparison of 8th grade science achievement scores, U.S. and worldwide, 1999 ★6★

Academy of Television Arts & Sciences
Most selective internships in the U.S., 2001 ★2610★
Top internships in the U.S., 2001 ★2612★

Acadia University
Best Canadian universities for producing leaders of tomorrow, 2000 ★1148★
Best Canadian universities overall, 2000 ★1149★
Best Canadian universities that are the most innovative, 2000 ★1150★
Canadian primarily undergraduate universities best at producing leaders of tomorrow, 2000 ★1192★
Canadian primarily undergraduate universities by alumni support, 2000 ★1193★
Canadian primarily undergraduate universities by award-winning faculty members, 2000 ★1194★
Canadian primarily undergraduate universities by class size at the first and second-year level, 2000 ★1195★
Canadian primarily undergraduate universities by class size at the third and forth-year level, 2000 ★1196★
Canadian primarily undergraduate universities by classes taught by tenured faculty, 2000 ★1197★
Canadian primarily undergraduate universities by faculty members with Ph.D.'s, 2000 ★1198★
Canadian primarily undergraduate universities by library acquisitions, 2000 ★1199★
Canadian primarily undergraduate universities by library expenses, 2000 ★1200★
Canadian primarily undergraduate universities by library holdings per student, 2000 ★1201★
Canadian primarily undergraduate universities by medical/science grants per faculty member, 2000 ★1202★
Canadian primarily undergraduate universities by operating budget per student, 2000 ★1203★
Canadian primarily undergraduate universities by percentage of operating budget allocated to scholarships, 2000 ★1204★
Canadian primarily undergraduate universities by percentage of operating budget allocated to student services, 2000 ★1205★
Canadian primarily undergraduate universities by reputation, 2000 ★1206★
Canadian primarily undergraduate universities by social science/humanities grants per faculty member, 2000 ★1207★
Canadian primarily undergraduate universities by students from out of province, 2000 ★1208★
Canadian primarily undergraduate universities by students winning national awards, 2000 ★1209★
Canadian primarily undergraduate universities that are the best overall, 2000 ★1210★
Canadian primarily undergraduate universities that are the most innovative, 2000 ★1211★
Canadian primarily undergraduate universities with the highest quality, 2000 ★1212★
Canadian universities with the highest total cost, 2000 ★1217★
Top Canadian primarily undergraduate universities, 2000 ★1226★

Accenture
Top recruiters for biology/biological science jobs for 2000-01 bachelor's degree recipients ★198★
Top recruiters for biology/biological science jobs for 2000-01 master's degree recipients ★203★
Top recruiters for business administration jobs for 2000-01 bachelor's degree recipients ★554★
Top recruiters for accounting jobs for 2000-01 bachelor's degree recipients ★580★
Top recruiters for finance/banking jobs for 2000-01 bachelor's degree recipients ★582★
Top recruiters for business administration jobs for 2000-01 master's degree recipients ★652★
Top recruiters for accounting jobs for 2000-01 master's degree recipients ★661★
Top recruiters for finance/banking jobs for 2000-01 master's degree recipients ★664★
Top recruiters for manufacturing management jobs for 2000-01 master's degree recipients ★669★
Top recruiters for marketing jobs for 2000-01 master's degree recipients ★672★
Top recruiters for manufacturing management jobs for 2000-01 bachelor's degree recipients ★683★
Top recruiters for marketing jobs for 2000-01 bachelor's degree recipients ★684★
Top recruiters for chemistry jobs for 2000-01 bachelor's degree recipients ★792★
Top recruiters for chemistry jobs for 2000-01 master's degree recipients ★806★
Top recruiters for computer science jobs for 2000-01 bachelor's degree recipients ★1590★
Top recruiters for computer science jobs for 2000-01 master's degree recipients ★1598★
Top employers of college graduates, 2001 ★2325★
Top recruiters for systems engineer jobs for 2000-01 bachelor's degree recipients ★2336★
Top recruiters for aeronautical engineering jobs for 2000-01 bachelor's degree recipients ★2339★
Top recruiters for aerospace engineering jobs for 2000-01 bachelor's degree recipients ★2340★
Top recruiters for chemical engineering jobs for 2000-01 bachelor's degree recipients ★2343★
Top recruiters for civil engineering jobs for 2000-01 bachelor's degree recipients ★2346★
Top recruiters for computer engineering jobs for 2000-01 bachelor's degree recipients ★2352★
Top recruiters for electrical/electronic engineering jobs for 2000-01 bachelor's degree recipients ★2354★
Top recruiters for systems engineer jobs for 2000-01 master's degree recipients ★2371★
Top recruiters for aeronautical engineering jobs for 2000-01 master's degree recipients ★2373★
Top recruiters for aerospace engineering jobs for 2000-01 master's degree recipients ★2377★
Top recruiters for chemical engineering jobs for 2000-01 master's degree recipients ★2391★
Top recruiters for civil engineering jobs for 2000-01 master's degree recipients ★2397★
Top recruiters for computer engineering jobs for 2000-01 master's degree recipients ★2400★
Top recruiters for electrical/electronic engineering jobs for 2000-01 master's degree recipients ★2406★
Top recruiters for mechanical engineering jobs for 2000-01 master's degree recipients ★2424★
Top recruiters for nuclear engineering jobs for 2000-01 master's degree recipients ★2427★
Top recruiters for petroleum engineering jobs for 2000-01 master's degree recipients ★2430★
Top recruiters for mechanical engineering jobs for 2000-01 bachelor's degree recipients ★2437★
Top recruiters for nuclear engineering jobs for 2000-01 bachelor's degree recipients ★2440★
Top recruiters for petroleum engineering jobs for 2000-01 bachelor's degree recipients ★2441★
Top recruiters for language/literature jobs for 2000-01 bachelor's degree recipients ★2446★
Top recruiters for language/literature jobs for 2000-01 master's degree recipients ★2452★
Top recruiters for geology/geophysics jobs for 2000-01 bachelor's degree recipients ★2522★
Top recruiters for geology/geophysics jobs for 2000-01 master's degree recipients ★2524★
Top recruiters for health jobs for 2000-01 bachelor's degree recipients ★2541★
Top recruiters for health jobs for 2000-01 master's degree recipients ★2545★
Top recruiters for foreign language jobs for 2000-01 bachelor's degree recipients ★2614★
Top recruiters for foreign language jobs for 2000-01 master's degree recipients ★2615★
Top recruiters for liberal arts jobs for 2000-01 bachelor's degree recipients ★2675★
Top recruiters for liberal arts jobs for 2000-01 master's degree recipients ★2676★
Top recruiters for library science jobs for 2000-01 bachelor's degree recipients ★2716★
Top recruiters for library science jobs for 2000-01 master's degree recipients ★2717★
Top recruiters for information technology (MIS) jobs for 2000-01 bachelor's degree recipients ★2738★

Top recruiters for information technology (MIS) jobs for 2000-01 master's degree recipients ★2739★
Top recruiters for math/actuarial science jobs for 2000-01 bachelor's degree recipients ★2771★
Top recruiters for math/actuarial science jobs for 2000-01 master's degree recipients ★2779★
Top recruiters for statistics jobs for 2000-01 master's degree recipients ★2781★
Top recruiters for statistics jobs for 2000-01 bachelor's degree recipients ★2786★
Top recruiters for physics jobs for 2000-01 bachelor's degree recipients ★2974★
Top recruiters for physics jobs for 2000-01 master's degree recipients ★3016★
Top recruiters for psychology jobs for 2000-01 bachelor's degree recipients ★3063★
Top recruiters for psychology jobs for 2000-01 master's degree recipients ★3069★
Top recruiters for sociology jobs for 2000-01 bachelor's degree recipients ★4347★
Top recruiters for sociology jobs for 2000-01 master's degree recipients ★4353★

Access Pricing and Competition
Top cited energy papers from 1994 to 1998 ★2467★

AccessScience: The Online Encyclopedia of Science and Technology
Library Journal's best reference databases and discs, 2000 ★369★

Accountant
Jobs with the best physical demands scores ★2250★
Most desirable jobs in business/finance ★2270★

Accountants and auditors
Projected employment growth for selected occupations that require a bachelor's degree or more, 1998-2008 ★2317★

Accounting
Business and management doctorates awarded at U.S. colleges and universities, by subfield, 1999 ★1888★
Gender breakdown of business and management doctorate recipients, by subfield, 1999 ★1928★
Top bachelor's and master's degree majors in demand for employment, 2001 ★2323★
Top bachelor's degree majors in demand for employment, 2001 ★2324★
Top master's degree majors in demand for employment, 2001 ★2326★
Average starting salaries for college graduates, by field, 2000 ★3129★
Expected starting salaries of 2000-01 bachelor's degree recipients, by specific major ★3131★

Accounting Organizations and Society
Top accounting journals by half-life impact factor ★578★
Top accounting journals by mode impact factor ★579★

Accounting Review
Top accounting journals by half-life impact factor ★578★
Top accounting journals by mode impact factor ★579★
Top ranked business administration and business economics journals ★2188★

Accounts of Chemical Research
Chemistry journals by citation impact, 1981-99 ★808★
Chemistry journals by citation impact, 1995-99 ★809★
Chemistry journals by citation impact, 1999 ★810★

The Accunet/AP Photo Archive
Library Journal's best reference databases and discs, 2000 ★369★

Acdermann; Josef
European business moguls considered the best dealmakers ★440★

Achleitner; Paul
European business moguls considered the best dealmakers ★440★

Acker, S.J.; Rev. Thomas S.
Top pay and benefits for the chief executive and top paid employees at Wheeling Jesuit University ★3622★

Ackerman; Robert
Top pay and benefits for the chief executive and top paid employees at Willamette University ★3628★

Ackerman; Rudy
Top pay and benefits for the chief executive and top paid employees at Moravian College ★3407★

ACM Computing Surveys
Journals and proceedings with the most citations (Class 3) ★2569★

ACM SIGMOD Record
Journals and proceedings with the most citations (Class 3) ★2569★

ACM Transactions on Information Systems
Most cited business serials in technical communication journals from 1988 to 1997 ★4417★

ACM Transactions on Office Information Systems
Journals and proceedings with the most citations (Class 4) ★2570★
Information and library science journals by citation impact, 1981-99 ★2724★
Information and library science journals with the greatest impact measure, 1981-98 ★2727★

Acne
Leading categories of dermatologic disease covered by top articles in the field, 1945-1990 ★1869★

Acoustics
Gender breakdown of physics and astronomy doctorate recipients, by subfield, 1999 ★1939★
Physics and astronomy doctorates awarded at U.S. colleges and universities, by subfield, 1999 ★1994★

Acta Crystallography A
Crystallography journals by citation impact, 1981-98 ★1654★
Crystallography journals by citation impact, 1994-98 ★1655★
Crystallography journals by citation impact, 1998 ★1656★

Acta Crystallography B
Crystallography journals by citation impact, 1981-98 ★1654★
Crystallography journals by citation impact, 1994-98 ★1655★
Crystallography journals by citation impact, 1998 ★1656★

Acta Crystallography D
Crystallography journals by citation impact, 1994-98 ★1655★
Crystallography journals by citation impact, 1998 ★1656★

Acta Dermato-Venereologica
Number of citations and papers for original articles appearing in dermatology journals, 1981 to 1996 ★1873★
Number of citations and papers in dermatology journals, 1981 to 1996 ★1874★

Acta Mathematica
Mathematics journals by impact factor ★2783★
Mathematics journals by impact factor, 1981 to 1997 ★2784★
Mathematics journals by impact factor, 1993 to 1997 ★2785★

Actor
Jobs considered the most competitive ★2245★
Jobs with the worst income scores ★2261★
Most desirable jobs in the arts ★2277★

Actors, directors, and producers
Projected employment growth for selected occupations that require long-term on-the-job training, 1998-2008 ★2320★

Actors Theatre of Louisville
Most selective internships in the U.S., 2001 ★2610★

Actual Innocence: Five Days to Execution and Other Dispatches from the Wrongly Convicted
Library Journal's best nonfiction audiobooks, 2000 ★243★

Actuary
Jobs with the best environment scores ★2247★
Jobs with the best physical demands scores ★2250★
Jobs with the best stress scores ★2252★
Most desirable jobs in math/science ★2274★

Adams; Earl W.
Top pay and benefits for the chief executive and top paid employees at Allegheny College ★3170★

Adams; John
Top pay and benefits for the chief executive and top paid employees at Northeastern University ★3422★

Adams State College
Division II NCAA colleges with the lowest graduation rates for all sports, 1993-94 ★947★
U.S. colleges and universities awarding the most psychology master's degrees to Hispanic Americans ★1799★
Average faculty salaries for institutions of higher education in Colorado, 2000-01 ★3693★

Adams; Titus
All-American boy's high school football linemen, 2000 ★183★

Adams; William D.
Top pay and benefits for the chief executive and top paid employees at Bucknell University ★3213★

Adamski; M. Patricia
Top pay and benefits for the chief executive and top paid employees at Hofstra University ★3335★

ADC Telecommunications
Fortune's highest ranked network communications companies, 2000 ★482★
Top telecommunications companies in Standard & Poor's 500, 2001 ★559★

Addison-Wesley
Book publishers with the most citations (Class 1) ★2562★

Adelphi University
- Division II NCAA colleges with the 100% graduation rates for men's basketball players, 1993-94 ★943★
- Average faculty salaries for institutions of higher education in New York, 2000-01 ★3719★

Adirondack Community College
- Average faculty salaries for institutions of higher education in New York, 2000-01 ★3719★

Adjustment clerks
- Projected employment growth for selected occupations that require shorter moderate-term on-the-job training, 1998-2008 ★2321★

Adlai E. Stevenson 125
- Illinois high school districts with the highest teacher salaries, 1999 ★3985★

Adlai E. Stevenson High School
- Illinois high schools with the highest SAT scores ★874★
- Outstanding secondary schools in Chicago, Illinois ★4110★
- Outstanding suburban public high schools in Metro Chicago ★4256★

Adler School of Professional Psychology
- U.S. colleges and universities awarding the most psychology doctorate degrees to African Americans ★2120★

Administaff
- *Fortune*'s highest ranked outsourcing services companies, 2000 ★483★

Administration Science Quarterly
- Journals with the highest impact factor in the field of management, 1981-96 ★696★

Administrative Science Quarterly
- Top management journals ★546★
- Top management journals by core impact ★547★
- Business journals by citation impact, 1981-98 ★688★
- Business journals by citation impact, 1994-98 ★689★
- Business journals by citation impact, 1998 ★690★
- Journals and proceedings with the most citations (Class 2) ★2568★
- Most cited business serials in technical communication journals from 1988 to 1997 ★4417★

Administrative support
- Projected change in employment of college graduates, by occupational group, from 1998 to 2008 ★965★
- Projected employment of college graduates, by occupational group, 2008 ★966★
- Employment in college-level jobs, by occupational group, 2006 ★2295★
- Industries in Illinois with the highest projected worker increase through 2006 ★2304★
- Internet use by major occupational group, 1998 ★2587★

Administrative support, including clerical
- Employment change projections by major occupational group from 1998 to 2008 ★2288★
- Employment projections by major occupational group for 2008 ★2291★
- Percentages for projected employment growth by occupational group, 1998-2008 ★2314★
- Projected employment growth by occupational group, 1998-2008 ★2316★

Adobe Systems
- Software companies with the fastest growth, 2000 ★528★

Adolescence
- 'Outside' journals most frequently citing *Family Planning Perspectives*, 1991-95 ★1859★

Adolfo Camarillo High School
- Outstanding secondary schools in Ventura, California ★4248★

Adolph Coors
- *Fortune*'s highest ranked beverages companies, 2000 ★450★
- Top consumer products companies in Standard & Poor's 500, 2001 ★536★

Adrian College
- *U.S. News & World Report*'s midwestern regional liberal arts colleges with the best student/faculty ratios, 2000-01 ★1339★
- *U.S. News & World Report*'s midwestern regional liberal arts colleges with the lowest acceptance rates, 2000-01 ★1348★
- *U.S. News & World Report*'s best undergraduate fees among midwestern regional liberal arts colleges by discount tuition, 2000 ★1380★
- Highest undergraduate tuition and fees at colleges and universities in Michigan ★1518★
- Average faculty salaries for institutions of higher education in Michigan, 2000-01 ★3709★

Adult and continuing education
- Education doctorates awarded at U.S. colleges and universities, by subfield, 1999 ★1921★
- Gender breakdown of education doctorate recipients, by subfield, 1999 ★1933★

Advanced Digital Information
- Companies with the best two-year total returns since 1998 ★436★

Advanced Fibre Communications
- *Business Week*'s top companies in terms of earnings, 2000 ★428★
- Top companies in terms of growth, 2000 ★534★

Advanced Marketing Services
- Publishers with the best industry stocks, 2000 ★300★

Advanced Micro Devices
- *Fortune*'s highest ranked semiconductors companies, 2000 ★495★

Advanced scientific-computing research
- Energy Department research funding, 2001 ★3110★

Advances in Agronomy
- Agriculture journals by citation impact, 1981-96 ★50★
- Agriculture journals by citation impact, 1981-99 ★51★
- Agriculture journals by citation impact, 1992-96 ★52★
- Agriculture journals by citation impact, 1995-99 ★53★
- Agriculture journals by citation impact, 1999 ★54★

Advances in Atomic Molecular Optics
- Optics journals by citation impact, 1981-99 ★2906★
- Optics journals by citation impact, 1995-99 ★2907★
- Optics journals by citation impact, 1999 ★2908★
- Optics journals with the greatest impact measure, 1981-98 ★2909★
- Optics journals with the greatest impact measure, 1994-98 ★2910★

Advances in Ecological Research
- Ecology journals by citation impact, 1981-99 ★2136★
- Ecology journals by citation impact, 1995-99 ★2137★
- Ecology journals by citation impact, 1999 ★2138★

Advances in Immunology
- Immunology journals with the greatest impact measure, 1981-98 ★2810★
- Immunology journals with the greatest impact measure, 1994-98 ★2811★
- Immunology journals by impact factor, 1981 to 1997 ★4279★
- Immunology journals by impact factor, 1993 to 1997 ★4280★

Advances in Inorganic Chemistry
- Inorganic and nuclear chemistry journals by citation impact, 1981-99 ★811★
- Inorganic and nuclear chemistry journals by citation impact, 1999 ★813★

Advances in Insect Physiology
- Entomology journals by citation impact, 1981-98 ★2453★
- Entomology journals by citation impact, 1994-98 ★2454★
- Entomology journals by citation impact, 1998 ★2455★

Advances in International Comparative Management
- Business journals receiving the most citations in five core journals, 1995-97 ★691★

Advances in International Marketing
- Business journals receiving the most citations in five core journals, 1995-97 ★691★

Advances in Marine Biology
- Marine and freshwater biology journals with the greatest impact measure, 1981-98 ★196★
- Marine and freshwater biology journals with the greatest impact measure, 1994-98 ★197★

Advances in Mathematics
- Mathematics journals by impact factor, 1981 to 1997 ★2784★

Advances in Microbial Ecology
- Ecology journals by citation impact, 1981-99 ★2136★
- Ecology journals by citation impact, 1995-99 ★2137★

Advances in Organometallic Chemistry
- Inorganic and nuclear chemistry journals by citation impact, 1981-99 ★811★
- Inorganic and nuclear chemistry journals by citation impact, 1995-99 ★812★
- Inorganic and nuclear chemistry journals by citation impact, 1999 ★813★

Advances in Veterinary Sciences
- Veterinary sciences journals with the greatest impact measure, 1981-98 ★4442★
- Veterinary sciences journals with the greatest impact measure, 1994-98 ★4443★

Advantage Learning Systems
- Best small companies in the U.S. ★383★

Advantica
- *Fortune*'s highest ranked food services companies, 2000 ★465★

The Advent of the Algorithm: The Idea That Rules the World
- *Library Journal*'s most notable computer science books, 2000 ★255★
- Outstanding science books, 2000 ★291★
- *Booklist*'s best science and technology books ★366★

The Adventures of Huckleberry Finn
- American Library Association's most frequently challenged books of the decade ★224★
- American Library Associations most frequently challenged books for the 1990s ★742★
- Most frequently banned books in the 1990s ★745★

People for the American Way's list of most frequently challenged books, 1982-1992 ★747★

The Adventures of Tom Sawyer
Most frequently banned books in the 1990s ★745★

Advertising
Areas of specialization in journalism and mass communications programs with the highest enrollment, 1999 ★2740★

Advertising account executive
Jobs considered the most competitive ★2245★
Jobs with the best outlook scores ★2249★
Jobs with the best physical demands scores ★2250★
Most desirable jobs in communications ★2271★

Advertising, marketing, and public relations managers
Projected employment growth for selected occupations that require a bachelor's degree or more, 1998-2008 ★2317★

Advertising salesperson
Most desirable jobs in communications ★2271★

Advocacy Group
Lobbyist that billed the most to U.S. colleges and universities, 1999 ★1249★

Advocates for Children of New York
Most selective internships in the U.S., 2001 ★2610★

Aebersold; Robert N.
Top pay and benefits for the chief executive and top paid employees at Springfield College in Massachusetts ★3509★

Aegon
Business Week's best companies in the Netherlands ★410★

Aerospace, aeronautic., astronautic.
Engineering doctorates awarded at U.S. colleges and universities, by subfield, 1999 ★1923★
Gender breakdown of engineering doctorate recipients, by subfield, 1999 ★1934★

Aerospace engineer
Most desirable jobs in production/manufacturing ★2276★

AES
Top utilities companies in Standard & Poor's 500, 2001 ★561★

Aesop's Fables
Outstanding books for middle readers, 2000 ★326★
Outstanding children's picture books, 2000 ★331★

Aetna
Fortune's highest ranked health care companies, 2000 ★469★
Top public companies for women executives, 2000 ★4457★
Top public companies with the highest percentage of women board of directors, 2000 ★4458★
Top public companies with the highest percentage of women employees, 2000 ★4459★

Aetna Life Inc.
Top internships in the U.S. with the highest compensation, 2001 ★2611★

AFLAC
Fortune's highest ranked life and health insurance companies, 2000 ★472★

Africa
Region of origin of foreign students enrolled in U.S. institutions of higher education, 1998-99 ★2502★
World regions hosting U.S. students studying abroad, 1998-99 ★2515★
African periodical prices, 2001 ★2914★
First-year physics and astronomy graduate students from selected countries, 1997-98 ★2989★

African American
Percentage of Advanced Placement Exams taken, by race ethnicity, 2000 ★42★
College sports officials, by race, 1999-2000 ★124★
ACT composite scores, by race/ethnicity, 2000 ★871★
Graduation rates for female basketball players at Division I NCAA colleges, by race/ethnicity ★954★
Graduation rates for female basketball players at Division II NCAA colleges, 1993-94 ★955★
Graduation rates for female students and athletes at Division I NCAA colleges, by race/ethnicity ★956★
Graduation rates for female students at Division II NCAA colleges, 1993-94 ★957★
Graduation rates for football players at Division I NCAA colleges, by race/ethnicity ★958★
Graduation rates for football players at Division II NCAA colleges, 1993-94 ★959★
Graduation rates for male basketball players at Division I NCAA colleges, by race/ethnicity ★960★
Graduation rates for male basketball players at Division II NCAA colleges, 1993-94 ★961★
Graduation rates for male students and athletes at Division I NCAA colleges, by race/ethnicity ★962★
Graduation rates for male students at Division II NCAA colleges, 1993-94 ★963★
Racial and ethnic background of incoming freshmen, 2000 ★1058★
Age grouping of doctorate recipients, by race/ethnicity, 1999 ★1885★
Number of U.S. citizen/permanent resident doctorate recipients in all fields at U.S. colleges and universities, by race/ethnicity, 1999 ★1978★
Number of U.S. citizen/permanent resident doctorate recipients in education at U.S. colleges and universities, by race/ethnicity, 1999 ★1979★
Number of U.S. citizen/permanent resident doctorate recipients in engineering at U.S. colleges and universities, by race/ethnicity, 1999 ★1980★
Number of U.S. citizen/permanent resident doctorate recipients in humanities at U.S. colleges and universities, by race/ethnicity, 1999 ★1981★
Number of U.S. citizen/permanent resident doctorate recipients in life sciences at U.S. colleges and universities, by race/ethnicity, 1999 ★1982★
Number of U.S. citizen/permanent resident doctorate recipients in physical sciences, mathematics, and computer sciences at U.S. colleges and universities, by race/ethnicity, 1999 ★1983★
Number of U.S. citizen/permanent resident doctorate recipients in professional/other fields at U.S. colleges and universities, by race/ethnicity, 1999 ★1984★

Number of U.S. citizen/permanent resident doctorate recipients in social sciences at U.S. colleges and universities, by race/ethnicity, 1999 ★1985★
Percentage of doctoral degree recipients at U.S. universities, by race/ethnicity, 1999 ★1987★
Percentage of minority doctorate recipients in the U.S., 1999 ★1990★
Percentage of minority doctorate recipients in the U.S., by gender, 1999 ★1992★
High school dropouts in the U.S., by race and gender, 1999 ★2135★
Ethnic breakdown of executives and managers in Silicon Valley firms, 1997 ★2300★
Race/ethnicity profile of U.S. students studying abroad, 1998-99 ★2509★
Comparison data of internet use, by race/ethnicity for 1998 and 2000 ★2582★
Internet use, by race/ethnicity and gender breakdown, 2000 ★2588★
Bachelor's degrees granted in journalism and mass communications programs, by race/ethnicity, 1999 ★2742★
Bachelor's enrollments in journalism and mass communications programs, by race/ethnicity, 1999 ★2744★
Doctoral degrees granted in journalism and mass communications programs, by race/ethnicity, 1999 ★2759★
Doctoral enrollments in journalism and mass communications programs, by race/ethnicity, 1999 ★2761★
Master's degrees granted in journalism and mass communications programs, by race/ethnicity, 1999 ★2766★
Master's enrollments in journalism and mass communications programs, by race/ethnicity, 1999 ★2768★
U.S. medical school enrollment of U.S. citizens by racial/ethnic category, 1999-2000 ★2863★
National Society of Fund-Raising Executives, by race/ethnicity ★2942★
Physics faculty, by race/ethnicity, 2000 ★2965★
Average annual salaries for individuals obtaining a bachelor's degree, by race/ethnicity ★3115★
Average annual salaries for individuals obtaining a high school degree, by race/ethnicity ★3116★
Average annual salaries for individuals obtaining a master's degree, by race/ethnicity ★3117★
Average annual salaries for individuals without a high school degree, by race/ethnicity ★3118★
Average salaries for individuals with a bachelor's degree, by race/ethnicity ★3127★
Average salaries for individuals with a high school degree, by race/ethnicity ★3982★
Average salaries for individuals without a high school degree, by race/ethnicity ★3983★
Students participating in gifted and talented programs, by race ethnicity, 1997 ★4050★
Percentage of 18- to 24-year olds completing high school, by race, 1998 ★4273★

A.G. Edwards
Fortune's highest ranked securities companies, 2000 ★494★

Age
Geriatrics and gerontology journals with the greatest impact measure, 1998 ★2807★

Age and Aging
　Geriatrics and gerontology journals with the greatest impact measure, 1981-98 ★2805★
　Geriatrics and gerontology journals with the greatest impact measure, 1994-98 ★2806★
　Geriatrics and gerontology journals with the greatest impact measure, 1998 ★2807★

Agee; James
　Best U.S. works of journalism in the 20th century ★2769★

Agency director (nonprofit)
　Jobs with the best security scores ★2251★
　Jobs with the lowest unemployment ★2258★

Aggarwal; Mahesh C.
　Top pay and benefits for the chief executive and top paid employees at Gannon University ★3302★

Aggarwal; Raj
　Top pay and benefits for the chief executive and top paid employees at John Carroll University ★3353★

Agilent Technologies
　Top recruiters for finance/banking jobs for 2000-01 master's degree recipients ★664★
　Top recruiters for chemistry jobs for 2000-01 bachelor's degree recipients ★792★
　Top recruiters for chemistry jobs for 2000-01 master's degree recipients ★806★
　Top recruiters for computer science jobs for 2000-01 master's degree recipients ★1598★
　Top recruiters for systems engineer jobs for 2000-01 bachelor's degree recipients ★2336★
　Top recruiters for chemical engineering jobs for 2000-01 bachelor's degree recipients ★2343★
　Top recruiters for electrical/electronic engineering jobs for 2000-01 bachelor's degree recipients ★2354★
　Top recruiters for electrical/electronic engineering jobs for 2000-01 master's degree recipients ★2406★
　Top recruiters for industrial engineering jobs for 2000-01 bachelor's degree recipients ★2432★
　Top recruiters for information technology (MIS) jobs for 2000-01 master's degree recipients ★2739★
　Top recruiters for physics jobs for 2000-01 bachelor's degree recipients ★2974★

Agnes Scott College
　U.S. colleges and universities with the best financial aid programs ★1030★
　U.S. colleges and universities with the best quality of life ★1034★
　Highest undergraduate tuition and fees at colleges and universities in Georgia ★1496★
　Women's colleges granting physics bachelor's degrees, 2000 ★2982★
　Average faculty salaries for institutions of higher education in Georgia, 2000-01 ★3697★

Agnese Jr.; Louis J.
　Top pay and benefits for the chief executive and top paid employees at the University of the Incarnate Word ★3570★

Agresto; John
　Top pay and benefits for the chief executive and top paid employees at St. John's College in Maryland and New Mexico ★3473★

Agria; John
　Top pay and benefits for the chief executive and top paid employees at the University of Dubuque ★3542★

Agricultural
　Engineering doctorates awarded at U.S. colleges and universities, by subfield, 1999 ★1923★
　Gender breakdown of engineering doctorate recipients, by subfield, 1999 ★1934★

Agricultural and Biological Chemistry
　Agriculture journals by citation impact, 1981-96 ★50★
　Agriculture journals by citation impact, 1981-99 ★51★
　Agriculture journals by citation impact, 1992-96 ★52★

Agricultural business and management
　Agricultural sciences doctorates awarded at U.S. colleges and universities, by subfield, 1999 ★1886★
　Gender breakdown of agricultural sciences doctorate recipients, by subfield, 1999 ★1926★

Agricultural economics
　Agricultural sciences doctorates awarded at U.S. colleges and universities, by subfield, 1999 ★1886★
　Gender breakdown of agricultural sciences doctorate recipients, by subfield, 1999 ★1926★

Agricultural education
　Gender breakdown of teaching fields doctorate recipients, by subfield, 1999 ★1943★
　Teaching fields doctorates awarded at U.S. colleges and universities, by subfield, 1999 ★2046★

Agricultural and Forest Meteorology
　Agriculture journals by citation impact, 1981-96 ★50★
　Agriculture journals by citation impact, 1981-99 ★51★
　Agriculture journals by citation impact, 1992-96 ★52★
　Agriculture journals by citation impact, 1995-99 ★53★
　Agriculture journals by citation impact, 1999 ★54★

Agricultural History Review
　Top ranked economic history journals ★2190★

Agricultural Meteorology
　Agriculture journals by citation impact, 1981-96 ★50★
　Agriculture journals by citation impact, 1981-99 ★51★

Agricultural science
　Turkey's contribution of papers in the sciences, by field, 1995-99 ★4335★

Agricultural sciences
　Life sciences doctorates awarded to U.S. citizens/permanent residents at U.S. colleges and universities, by race/ethnicity and subfield, 1999 ★1950★
　Number of life sciences doctorate recipients at U.S. colleges and universities, by field, 1999 ★1974★
　Percentage of female doctorate recipients at U.S. colleges and universities, by subfield, 1999 ★1988★
　Australia's contribution of papers in the sciences, by field, 1993-97 ★4292★
　Australia's contribution of papers in the sciences, by field, 1995-99 ★4293★
　Denmark's contribution of papers in the sciences, by field, 1994-98 ★4306★
　Denmark's contribution of papers in the sciences, by field, 1995-99 ★4307★
　Finland's contribution of papers in the sciences by field, 1992-96 ★4309★
　Finland's contribution of papers in the sciences, by field, 1995-99 ★4310★
　Ireland's contribution of papers in the sciences, by field, 1994-98 ★4315★
　Italy's relative impact in the sciences by field, 1992-96 ★4317★
　Japan's contribution of papers in the sciences, by field, 1995-99 ★4318★
　Japan's contribution of papers in the sciences, by field, 1996-2000 ★4319★
　New Zealand's contribution of papers in the sciences, by field, 1994-98 ★4322★
　South Africa's contribution of papers in the sciences, by field, 1994-98 ★4326★
　Spain's contribution of papers in the sciences, by field, 1993-97 ★4328★
　Spain's contribution of papers in the sciences, by field, 1995-99 ★4329★

Agricultural sciences, general
　Agricultural sciences doctorates awarded at U.S. colleges and universities, by subfield, 1999 ★1886★
　Gender breakdown of agricultural sciences doctorate recipients, by subfield, 1999 ★1926★

Agricultural scientist
　Jobs with the lowest unemployment ★2258★
　Most desirable jobs in agriculture ★2268★

Agriculture
　Federal appropriations to colleges, by agency, 2000 ★1241★
　Industries in Illinois with the highest projected worker increase through 2006 ★2304★
　Fields of study profile of U.S. students studying abroad, 1998-99 ★2507★
　Average costs for Academic Search titles by subject, 2001 ★2918★
　Periodical prices by LC subject, 2001 ★2925★
　Proposed fiscal 2002 appropriations for science and technology research ★4339★

Agriculture Department
　Fiscal 2002 requested budget as compared with Fiscal 2001 budget for other agencies ★2230★

Agriculture and Environment
　Agriculture journals by citation impact, 1981-96 ★50★
　Agriculture journals by citation impact, 1981-99 ★51★

Agriculture/food science
　Median salary for B.S. chemists, by field ★781★
　Median salary for M.S. chemists, by field ★785★
　Median salary for Ph.D. chemists, by field ★786★

Agriculture, forestry, and fishing
　Internet use by industry, 1998 ★2586★

Agriculture, forestry, fishing, and related
　Employment change projections by major occupational group from 1998 to 2008 ★2288★
　Employment projections by major occupational group for 2008 ★2291★
　Percentages for projected employment growth by occupational group, 1998-2008 ★2314★
　Projected employment growth by occupational group, 1998-2008 ★2316★

Agro-Ecosystems
　Agriculture journals by citation impact, 1981-96 ★50★
　Agriculture journals by citation impact, 1981-99 ★51★

Agronomy and crop science
  Agricultural sciences doctorates awarded at U.S. colleges and universities, by subfield, 1999 ★1886★
  Gender breakdown of agricultural sciences doctorate recipients, by subfield, 1999 ★1926★

Agronomy Journal
  Agriculture journals by citation impact, 1981-96 ★50★
  Agriculture journals by citation impact, 1981-99 ★51★

Aguolu; C.C.
  Authors that most frequently cite *Libri* publications from 1972 to 1999 ★2723★

Agway
  Fortune's highest ranked food production companies, 2000 ★464★

Ahern; Joseph J.
  Top pay and benefits for the chief executive and top paid employees at College of Mount St. Joseph ★3244★

Ahladas; John A.
  Top pay and benefits for the chief executive and top paid employees at Randolph-Macon College ★3451★

Ahold USA
  Fortune's highest ranked food and drug stores, 2000 ★463★

Ahrens; Lisa
  All-USA College Academic Second Team, 2001 ★3★

Ahrons; Constance
  Radcliffe Institute for Advanced Study fellowship recipients in the field of sociology, 2000-01 ★4346★

AI Magazine
  Artificial intelligence journals by citation impact, 1999 ★96★
  Artificial intelligence journals with the greatest impact measure, 1998 ★99★

AIDS
  Immunology journals by impact factor, 1993 to 1997 ★4280★

AIDS Doctors: Voices from the Epidemic
  Library Journal's most notable health sciences books, 2000 ★262★

AIDS Education & Prevention
  Education and educational research journals by citation impact, 1995-99 ★2236★
  Education and educational research journals by citation impact, 1999 ★2237★
  Education and educational research journals with the greatest impact measure ★2238★

Aigner Associates
  Most selective internships in the U.S., 2001 ★2610★

Aiken Technical College
  Lowest undergraduate tuition and fees at colleges and universities in South Carolina ★1555★

Aims Community College
  Lowest undergraduate tuition and fees at colleges and universities in Colorado ★1489★

Air Force; Community College of the
  Largest degree-granting colleges and universities, by enrollment ★1068★

Air Products & Chemicals
  Fortune's highest ranked chemicals companies, 2000 ★452★
  Top chemical companies in Standard & Poor's 500, 2001 ★533★

Air traffic controller
  Jobs with the most stringent quotas ★2259★
  Jobs with the worst stress scores ★2265★

Airborne Freight
  Fortune's highest ranked mail, packaging, and freight delivery companies, 2000 ★473★

Airey; Sarah
  All-USA College Academic First Team, 2001 ★2★

Airplane pilot
  Jobs with the greatest potential income for beginners ★2253★
  Jobs with the lowest unemployment ★2258★
  Most desirable jobs in travel/food service ★2278★

Ait-Sahalia; Yacine
  Top pay and benefits for the chief executive and top paid employees at Princeton University ★3446★

AK Steel Holding
  Fortune's highest ranked metals companies, 2000 ★476★

Akin; William E.
  Top pay and benefits for the chief executive and top paid employees at Ursinus College ★3591★

Akron; University of
  U.S. colleges and universities with the lowest average football attendance, 1996-99 ★160★
  Division I NCAA colleges with that graduated less than 20% of their African American male athletes, 1990-91 to 1993-94 ★928★
  Division I NCAA colleges with the lowest graduation rates for football players, 1990-91 to 1993-94 ★938★
  State appropriations for Ohio's institutions of higher education, 2000-01 ★1288★
  Average faculty salaries for institutions of higher education in Ohio, 2000-01 ★3722★

Akron, Wayne College; University of
  Highest undergraduate tuition and fees at public 2-year colleges and universities ★1462★
  Average faculty salaries for institutions of higher education in Ohio, 2000-01 ★3722★

Aktan; Ahmet
  Top pay and benefits for the chief executive and top paid employees at Drexel University ★3274★

Al Collins Graphic Design School
  Highest undergraduate tuition and fees at colleges and universities in Arizona ★1482★

Alabama
  Mean composite ACT scores by state, 2000 ★895★
  Mean math SAT scores by state, 2000 ★900★
  Mean verbal SAT scores by state, 2000 ★903★
  States receiving the most in federal agency appropriations to colleges, 2000 ★1306★
  States receiving the most in federal agency appropriations to colleges, from 1996 to 2000 ★1307★
  Total doctorate recipients by state, 1999 ★2054★
  State grades for affordability of higher education for minority students, 2000 ★2883★
  State grades for benefits state receives for educating its minority students, 2000 ★2884★
  State grades for completion of higher education by minority students, 2000 ★2885★
  State grades for participation of minority students in higher education, 2000 ★2886★
  State grades for preparing minority students for higher education, 2000 ★2887★
  States expelling the highest ratio of students for violating the Gun-Free Schools Act, 1998-99 ★3993★
  States expelling the most students for violating the Gun-Free Schools Act, 1998-99 ★3994★
  States with the lowest per-pupil expenditures ★3998★
  U.S. states with the highest percentage of births to teenagers who were already mothers ★4433★

Alabama A&M University
  Colleges offering the Thurgood Marshall Scholarship Fund ★221★
  U.S. college campuses reporting murders or non-negligent manslaughters, 1999 ★728★
  State appropriations for Alabama's institutions of higher education, 2000-01 ★1254★
  Historically black colleges and universities awarding the most master's degrees to African Americans ★1670★
  Total baccalaureate education degrees awarded to African Americans from U.S. colleges and universities, 1997-98 ★1711★
  U.S. colleges and universities awarding the most computer and information sciences master's degrees to African Americans ★1766★
  U.S. colleges and universities awarding the most education master's degrees to African Americans ★1769★
  U.S. colleges and universities awarding the most physical sciences master's degrees to African Americans ★1793★
  U.S. colleges and universities awarding the most psychology master's degrees to African Americans ★1797★
  U.S. institutions awarding the most baccalaureate degrees to African Americans in agricultural sciences, 1998 ★1814★
  U.S. institutions awarding the most baccalaureate degrees to minorities in agricultural sciences, 1998 ★1820★
  U.S. institutions awarding the most master's degrees to African Americans in agribusiness and production, 1998 ★1824★
  U.S. institutions awarding the most master's degrees to African Americans in agricultural sciences, 1998 ★1825★
  U.S. institutions awarding the most master's degrees to minorities in agribusiness and production, 1998 ★1829★
  U.S. institutions awarding the most master's degrees to minorities in agricultural sciences, 1998 ★1830★
  U.S. colleges and universities awarding the most physical sciences doctorate degrees to African Americans ★2118★
  U.S. institutions awarding the most doctoral degrees to minorities in agricultural sciences, 1998 ★2131★

Alabama, Birmingham; University of
  All-USA College Academic First Team, 2001 ★2★
  Division I NCAA colleges with that graduated none of their African American male basketball players, 1990-91 to 1993-94 ★930★
  Division I NCAA colleges with the lowest graduation rates for female basketball players, 1990-91 to 1993-94 ★937★
  U.S. colleges and universities awarding the most health professions and related sciences master's degrees to African Americans ★1777★

ALABAMA

U.S. colleges and universities awarding the most health professions and related sciences first professional degrees to Native Americans ★1851★

U.S. colleges and universities awarding the most biological and life sciences doctorate degrees to Asian Americans ★2083★

U.S. colleges and universities awarding the most health professions and related sciences doctorate degrees to African Americans ★2114★

Academics' choices for best AIDS programs, 2001 ★2818★

Alabama Hospital at Birmingham; University of
Top rheumatology hospitals in the U.S., 2000 ★2802★

Alabama State University
Colleges offering the Thurgood Marshall Scholarship Fund ★221★

State appropriations for Alabama's institutions of higher education, 2000-01 ★1254★

U.S. News & World Report's southern regional universities with students most in debt, 1999 ★1432★

Historically black colleges and universities awarding the most master's degrees to African Americans ★1670★

Total baccalaureate computer and information science degrees awarded to African Americans from U.S. colleges and universities, 1997-98 ★1691★

Total baccalaureate education degrees awarded to African Americans from U.S. colleges and universities, 1997-98 ★1711★

Alabama System; University of
State appropriations for Alabama's institutions of higher education, 2000-01 ★1254★

Alabama, Tuscaloosa; University of
U.S. colleges and universities where students study the least ★1002★

U.S. colleges and universities with the most upper level courses taught by TAs ★1040★

Institutions receiving the most in federal agency appropriations to colleges, 2000 ★1245★

Alabama; University of
Division I-A all-time percentage leaders ★127★

U.S. universities with the greatest impact in microbiology, 1994-98 ★217★

U.S. colleges and universities where a large portion of the student body drink hard liquor ★992★

U.S. colleges and universities where fraternities and sororities are popular ★993★

U.S. colleges and universities where the general student body puts a strong emphasis on socializing ★1008★

U.S. colleges and universities with the worst financial aid programs ★1042★

Retention rates of African American students at traditionally white institutions, 1997-98 ★1121★

U.S. universities with the greatest impact in dentistry/oral surgery, 1994-98 ★1866★

Enrollment of students in the ten largest undergraduate journalism and mass communications programs, 1999 ★2746★

Degrees granted in the ten largest doctoral journalism and mass communications programs, 1999 ★2756★

Alamance Community College
Lowest undergraduate tuition and fees at colleges and universities in North Carolina ★1540★

Alameda; College of
Lowest undergraduate tuition and fees at public 2-year colleges and universities ★1465★

Alameda High School
Outstanding secondary schools in Oakland, California ★4195★

Alamo Community College, Palto Alto
Average faculty salaries for institutions of higher education in Texas, 2000-01 ★3731★

Alamo Community College, St. Philip's
Average faculty salaries for institutions of higher education in Texas, 2000-01 ★3731★

Alamo Community College, San Antonio
Average faculty salaries for institutions of higher education in Texas, 2000-01 ★3731★

Alaska
Mean composite ACT scores by state, 2000 ★895★

Mean math SAT scores by state, 2000 ★900★

Mean verbal SAT scores by state, 2000 ★903★

States allocating the smallest amount of state tax appropriations for higher education, 2000-01 ★1305★

States with the highest percentage increase in appropriations for higher education, 2000-01 ★1308★

Total doctorate recipients by state, 1999 ★2054★

State grades for affordability of higher education for minority students, 2000 ★2883★

State grades for benefits state receives for educating its minority students, 2000 ★2884★

State grades for completion of higher education by minority students, 2000 ★2885★

State grades for participation of minority students in higher education, 2000 ★2886★

State grades for preparing minority students for higher education, 2000 ★2887★

States expelling the highest ratio of students for violating the Gun-Free Schools Act, 1998-99 ★3993★

States with the highest per-pupil expenditures ★3996★

States with the lowest number of high school graduates, 1999-2000 ★3997★

States with the lowest percentage of high school freshmen enrolling in college within four years ★4267★

Alaska Air Group
Fortune's highest ranked airlines, 2000 ★447★

Alaska, Anchorage; University of
Division II NCAA colleges with the 100% graduation rates for women's basketball players, 1993-94 ★944★

Undergraduate tuition and fees at colleges and universities in Alaska ★1481★

Average faculty salaries for institutions of higher education in Alaska, 2000-01 ★3689★

Alaska Bible College
Undergraduate tuition and fees at colleges and universities in Alaska ★1481★

Alaska, Fairbanks; University of
Undergraduate tuition and fees at colleges and universities in Alaska ★1481★

Total baccalaureate education degrees awarded to Native Americans from U.S. colleges and universities, 1997-98 ★1714★

Average faculty salaries for institutions of higher education in Alaska, 2000-01 ★3689★

Alaska Pacific University
Institutions censured by the American Association of University Professors, 2001 ★1067★

Undergraduate tuition and fees at colleges and universities in Alaska ★1481★

Alaska, Southeast; University of
Undergraduate tuition and fees at colleges and universities in Alaska ★1481★

Average faculty salaries for institutions of higher education in Alaska, 2000-01 ★3689★

Alaska System; University of
State appropriations for Alaska's institutions of higher education, 2000-01 ★1255★

Alaska; University of
U.S. universities with the highest concentration of animal sciences papers published, 1994-98 ★4288★

U.S. universities with the highest concentration of papers published in the field of aquatic sciences, 1995-99 ★4289★

Albany College of Pharmacy
Average faculty salaries for institutions of higher education in New York, 2000-01 ★3719★

Albany Foundation; University of
Colleges and universities with the smallest endowments, 2000 ★1238★

Albany Law School
Average faculty salaries for institutions of higher education in New York, 2000-01 ★3719★

Albany Molecular Research
Best small companies in the U.S. ★383★

Top companies in terms of growth, 2000 ★534★

Albany-Schenectady-Troy, NY
Cities with the most Yahoo! listings per million residents ★2580★

Albany State College
Colleges offering the Thurgood Marshall Scholarship Fund ★221★

Albany State University
State appropriations for Georgia's institutions of higher education, 2000-01 ★1263★

Albee; Edward
Top playwrights of the twentieth century ★4436★

Albemarle; College of the
Average faculty salaries for institutions of higher education without academic ranks in North Carolina, 2000-01 ★3761★

Alberta
Canadian provinces by teaching days per year ★4058★

Alberta; University of
Canadian universities with the greatest impact in biology and biochemistry, 1993-97 ★195★

Canadian universities with the most citations per paper in the field of microbiology, 1992-96 ★214★

Best Canadian universities for producing leaders of tomorrow, 2000 ★1148★

Best Canadian universities overall, 2000 ★1149★

Best Canadian universities that are the most innovative, 2000 ★1150★

Best Canadian universities with the highest quality, 2000 ★1151★

Canadian medical/doctoral universities by alumni support, 2000 ★1172★

Canadian medical/doctoral universities by award-winning faculty members, 2000 ★1173★

Canadian medical/doctoral universities by class size at the first- and second-year level, 2000 ★1174★

Canadian medical/doctoral universities by class size at the third- and forth-year level, 2000 ★1175★

Canadian medical/doctoral universities by classes taught by tenured faculty, 2000 ★1176★

Canadian medical/doctoral universities by faculty members with Ph.D.'s, 2000 ★1177★

Canadian medical/doctoral universities by international graduate students, 2000 ★1178★

Canadian medical/doctoral universities by library acquisitions, 2000 ★1179★

Canadian medical/doctoral universities by library expenses, 2000 ★1180★

Canadian medical/doctoral universities by library holdings, 2000 ★1181★

Canadian medical/doctoral universities by library holdings per student, 2000 ★1182★

Canadian medical/doctoral universities by medical/science grants per faculty member, 2000 ★1184★

Canadian medical/doctoral universities by operating budget per student, 2000 ★1185★

Canadian medical/doctoral universities by percentage of operating budget allocated to scholarships, 2000 ★1186★

Canadian medical/doctoral universities by percentage of operating budget allocated to student services, 2000 ★1187★

Canadian medical/doctoral universities by reputation, 2000 ★1188★

Canadian medical/doctoral universities by social science/humanities grants per faculty member, 2000 ★1189★

Canadian medical/doctoral universities by students from out of province, 2000 ★1190★

Canadian medical/doctoral universities by students winning national awards, 2000 ★1191★

Top Canadian medical/doctoral universities, 2000 ★1221★

Top Canadian medical/doctoral universities best at producing leaders of tomorrow, 2000 ★1222★

Top Canadian medical/doctoral universities that are the best overall, 2000 ★1223★

Top Canadian medical/doctoral universities that are the most innovative, 2000 ★1224★

Top Canadian medical/doctoral universities with the highest quality, 2000 ★1225★

Canadian universities producing the most-cited papers in the field of computer science, 1992-96 ★1589★

University research libraries in the U.S. and Canada with the largest decreases in total expenditures from 1993-94 to 1998-99 ★2707★

Alberto-Culver
Fortune's highest ranked soaps and cosmetics companies, 2000 ★496★
Top women-owned companies ★4460★

Albertson College
U.S. colleges and universities where students and the local community relate well ★999★
U.S. colleges and universities with the best food service program ★1031★
U.S. News & World Report's best undergraduate fees among western regional liberal arts colleges by discount tuition, 2000 ★1384★

Academic reputation scores for U.S. News & World Report's top western regional liberal arts colleges, 2000-01 ★1387★

Acceptance rates for U.S. News & World Report's top western regional liberal arts colleges, 2000-01 ★1388★

Alumni giving rates at U.S. News & World Report's top western regional liberal arts colleges, 2000-01 ★1389★

Average freshmen retention rates for U.S. News & World Report's top western regional liberal arts colleges, 2000-01 ★1390★

Average graduation rates for U.S. News & World Report's top western regional liberal arts colleges, 2000-01 ★1391★

Percentage of freshmen in the top 25% of their high school class at U.S. News & World Report's top western regional liberal arts colleges, 2000-01 ★1392★

Percentage of full-time faculty at U.S. News & World Report's top western regional liberal arts colleges, 2000-01 ★1393★

Proportion of classes having 20 students or less at U.S. News & World Report's top western regional liberal arts colleges, 2000-01 ★1394★

Student/faculty ratios at U.S. News & World Report's top western regional liberal arts colleges, 2000-01 ★1395★

U.S. News & World Report's top western regional liberal arts colleges, 2000-01 ★1396★

Undergraduate tuition and fees at colleges and universities in Idaho ★1499★

Average faculty salaries for institutions of higher education in Idaho, 2000-01 ★3699★

Albertson's
Fortune's highest ranked food and drug stores, 2000 ★463★
Top food companies in Standard & Poor's 500, 2001 ★540★

Albertus Magnus College
Institutions censured by the American Association of University Professors, 2001 ★1067★
Average faculty salaries for institutions of higher education in Connecticut, 2000-01 ★3694★

Albion College
Highest undergraduate tuition and fees at colleges and universities in Michigan ★1518★
Most wired colleges, 2000 ★2595★
Institutions in the Worker Rights Consortium ★2913★
Average faculty salaries for institutions of higher education in Michigan, 2000-01 ★3709★

Albright College
Average faculty salaries for institutions of higher education in Pennsylvania, 2000-01 ★3725★

Albuquerque Technical Vocational Institute
Lowest undergraduate tuition and fees at colleges and universities in New Mexico ★1536★

Alcan
Top metals and mining companies in Standard & Poor's 500, 2001 ★549★

Alcatel
Business Week's best companies in France ★393★
Top recruiters for computer science jobs for 2000-01 bachelor's degree recipients ★1590★

Top recruiters for computer engineering jobs for 2000-01 bachelor's degree recipients ★2352★

Top recruiters for electrical/electronic engineering jobs for 2000-01 bachelor's degree recipients ★2354★

Alcoa
Fortune's highest ranked metals companies, 2000 ★476★
Top metals and mining companies in Standard & Poor's 500, 2001 ★549★

Alcorn; Sandy
Top pay and benefits for the chief executive and top paid employees at Aurora University ★3183★

Alcorn State University
Colleges offering the Thurgood Marshall Scholarship Fund ★221★
Division I NCAA colleges with the lowest graduation rates for female basketball players, 1990-91 to 1993-94 ★937★
State appropriations for Mississippi's institutions of higher education, 2000-01 ★1277★
Historically black colleges and universities awarding the most master's degrees to African Americans ★1670★
Total baccalaureate physical sciences degrees awarded to African Americans from U.S. colleges and universities, 1997-98 ★1733★
U.S. colleges and universities awarding the most biological and life sciences master's degrees to African Americans ★1756★
U.S. institutions awarding the most baccalaureate degrees to African Americans in agribusiness and production, 1998 ★1813★
U.S. institutions awarding the most baccalaureate degrees to African Americans in agricultural sciences, 1998 ★1814★
U.S. institutions awarding the most baccalaureate degrees to minorities in agribusiness and production, 1998 ★1819★
U.S. institutions awarding the most master's degrees to African Americans in agricultural sciences, 1998 ★1825★
U.S. institutions awarding the most master's degrees to minorities in agricultural sciences, 1998 ★1830★
Average faculty salaries for institutions of higher education in Mississippi, 2000-01 ★3711★

Alcott Middle School
Outstanding secondary schools in Waterbury, Connecticut ★4250★

Aldave; Barbara Bader
Top pay and benefits for the chief executive and top paid employees at Saint Mary's University in Texas ★3481★

Alderson-Broaddus College
Division II NCAA colleges with the lowest graduation rates for football players, 1993-94 ★948★
U.S. News & World Report's southern regional liberal arts colleges with students most in debt, 1999 ★1367★
Highest undergraduate tuition and fees at colleges and universities in West Virginia ★1568★

Alderson; Richard
Top pay and benefits for the chief executive and top paid employees at Point Loma Nazarene University ★3442★

Alexander; David
Top pay and benefits for the chief executive and top paid employees at Southern Nazarene University ★3503★

Alexander; George
Top pay and benefits for the chief executive and top paid employees at Santa Clara University in California ★3491★

Alexander Hamilton High School
Outstanding secondary schools in New York, New York ★4191★

Alexander; Hanan
Top pay and benefits for the chief executive and top paid employees at the University of Judaism ★3546★

Alexander; John
Top pay and benefits for the chief executive and top paid employees at Regis University in Colorado ★3454★

Alexander; Lorenzo
All-American boy's high school football linemen, 2000 ★183★

Alexander; Peter
Top pay and benefits for the chief executive and top paid employees at Saint Peter's College ★3485★

Alexander; Sue
Top pay and benefits for the chief executive and top paid employees at Wheaton College in Massachusetts ★3621★

Alexander; William R.
Top pay and benefits for the chief executive and top paid employees at Juniata College ★3357★

Alexandria Technical College
Lowest undergraduate tuition and fees at colleges and universities in Minnesota ★1521★
Average faculty salaries for institutions of higher education without academic ranks in Minnesota, 2000-01 ★3753★

Alexandria, VA
Counties with the highest per capita income ★2561★

Alford; R.
Top pay and benefits for the chief executive and top paid employees at University of Central Texas ★3589★

Alfred University
Radcliffe Institute for Advanced Study fellowship recipients in the field of visual arts, 2000-01 ★79★
U.S. News & World Report's northern regional universities with the best student/faculty ratios, 2000-01 ★1416★
U.S. News & World Report's northern regional universities with the highest acceptance rates, 2000-01 ★1417★
U.S. News & World Report's northern regional universities with the highest percentage of full-time faculty, 2000-01 ★1422★
U.S. News & World Report's northern regional universities with the highest proportion of classes with 20 students of less, 2000-01 ★1423★
U.S. News & World Report's best undergraduate fees among northern regional universities by discount tuition, 2000 ★1428★
Average faculty salaries for institutions of higher education in New York, 2000-01 ★3719★

Algebra
Gender breakdown of mathematics doctorate recipients, by subfield, 1999 ★1938★
Mathematics doctorates awarded at U.S. colleges and universities, by subfield, 1999 ★1951★

An Algonquian Year
Smithsonian's best books for children ages 6 to 10 ★364★

Ali; Muhammad
Most important African Americans in the twentieth century ★219★

Alice Lloyd College
U.S. News & World Report's southern regional liberal arts colleges with students least in debt, 1999 ★1366★

Alice's Tulips
Outstanding fiction books for young adults, 2000 ★333★

Alief Independent School District
Top recruiters for education jobs for 2000-01 bachelor's degree recipients ★4377★
Top recruiters for education jobs for 2000-01 master's degree recipients ★4398★

All Saints Episcopal School
Outstanding secondary schools in Lubbock, Texas ★4170★

Allar; Barbara
Top pay and benefits for the chief executive and top paid employees at Sarah Lawrence College ★3492★

Allegheny College
Average faculty salaries for institutions of higher education in Pennsylvania, 2000-01 ★3725★

Allegheny County; Community College of
Average faculty salaries for institutions of higher education in Pennsylvania, 2000-01 ★3725★

Allegheny Technologies
Business Week's best performing companies with the lowest 3-year sales performance ★423★
Fortune's highest ranked metals companies, 2000 ★476★
Top conglomerates in Standard & Poor's 500, 2001 ★535★

Allegheny University of the Health Sciences
U.S. colleges and universities awarding the most health professions and related sciences first professional degrees to African Americans ★1847★

Allen; Algia G.
Top pay and benefits for the chief executive and top paid employees at Amber University ★3172★

Allen; Alton P.
Top pay and benefits for the chief executive and top paid employees at Point Loma Nazarene University ★3442★

Allen; Bryce
Library and information science faculty with the most journal articles, 1993-1998 ★2711★

Allen County Community College
Lowest undergraduate tuition and fees at colleges and universities in Kansas ★1507★

Allen County Public Library
Highest Hennen's American Public Library Ratings for libraries serving a population of 250,000 to 499,999 ★2699★

Allen; John
All-America boys' high school basketball 2nd team, 2001 ★162★

Allen; Joseph
Top pay and benefits for the chief executive and top paid employees at Wheeling Jesuit University ★3622★

Allen Jr.; Clyde E.
Top pay and benefits for the chief executive and top paid employees at Concordia College-Moorhead ★3252★

Allen; Kathleen
Top pay and benefits for the chief executive and top paid employees at College of Saint Benedict ★3245★

Allen University
Historically black colleges and universities with major improvements in student loan default rates, 1998 ★2737★

Allentown College of St. Francis de Sales
U.S. News & World Report's northern regional liberal arts colleges with the highest freshmen retention rates, 2000-01 ★1357★
U.S. News & World Report's northern regional liberal arts colleges with the highest graduation rates, 2000-01 ★1358★
U.S. News & World Report's northern regional liberal arts colleges with the highest percentage of full-time faculty, 2000-01 ★1360★

Allerson; John E.
Top pay and benefits for the chief executive and top paid employees at Roosevelt University ★3466★

Alletto; Philip J.
Top pay and benefits for the chief executive and top paid employees at Westminster College in Utah ★3618★

Alliant Energy
Highly recommended public companies for women executives, 2000 ★4453★

Alliant Exchange
Largest private companies, 2000 ★523★

Allianz
Business Week's best companies in Germany ★394★

Allied health
Expected starting salaries of 2000-01 bachelor's degree recipients, by general major ★3130★

Allied Irish Banks
Business Week's best companies in Ireland ★396★

Allied Technology Group
Top women-owned companies in revenue growth since 1997 ★4461★

Allied Waste Industries
Business Week's best performing companies with the highest 1-year shareholder returns ★415★
Fortune's highest ranked waste management companies, 2000 ★504★
Top services industries in Standard & Poor's 500, 2001 ★558★

Allison; Graham T.
Most frequently downloaded *American Political Science Review* articles ★3039★

Allison; Linda G.
Top pay and benefits for the chief executive and top paid employees at Chatham College ★3230★

Allstate
Fortune's highest ranked property and casualty insurance companies, 2000 ★488★

Allstate Insurance Company
Best companies for working mothers ★4446★

ALLTEL
Fortune's highest ranked telecommunications companies, 2000 ★499★
Top telecommunications companies in Standard & Poor's 500, 2001 ★559★
Top recruiters for computer science jobs for 2000-01 master's degree recipients ★1598★
Top recruiters for computer engineering jobs for 2000-01 master's degree recipients ★2400★

Alma College
U.S. News & World Report's national liberal arts colleges with students least in debt, 1999 ★1385★
Highest undergraduate tuition and fees at colleges and universities in Michigan ★1518★
Average faculty salaries for institutions of higher education in Michigan, 2000-01 ★3709★

Almanij
Business Week's best companies in Belgium ★388★

Almond; David
Outstanding children's fiction books, 2000 ★329★

Almost Elvis: Elvis Impersonators and Their Quest for the Crown
Outstanding videos for library collections, 2000 ★2892★

Alpert; Geoffrey P.
Most-cited scholars in police studies articles/research notes ★2624★

Alston; Jerry
Top pay and benefits for the chief executive and top paid employees at National University in California ★3415★

Altadis
Business Week's best companies in Spain ★403★

AltaVista
Web sites where internet users spend the most time ★2609★

AltaVista Translations
Library Journal's best free reference websites, 2000 ★367★

Altera
Business Week's best performing companies with the highest net margin, 2000 ★419★
Top electrical and electronics companies in Standard & Poor's 500, 2001 ★539★

Alternate Research Paradigms: A Review and Teaching Proposal
Most frequently cited contribution articles in psychology journals from 1986 to 1996 ★3071★

Alvarado Intermediate School
Outstanding secondary schools in Los Angeles-Long Beach, California ★4167★

Alvarado Middle School
Outstanding secondary schools in Oakland, California ★4195★

Alvarez; Laurence
Top pay and benefits for the chief executive and top paid employees at the University of the South ★3572★

Alvernia College
Colleges and universities with the smallest endowments, 2000 ★1238★

Alverno College
U.S. News & World Report's midwestern regional liberal arts colleges with students most in debt, 1999 ★1338★
U.S. News & World Report's midwestern regional liberal arts colleges with the highest proportion of classes having 20 students or less, 2000-01 ★1347★
U.S. News & World Report's midwestern regional liberal arts colleges with the lowest acceptance rates, 2000-01 ★1348★
Average faculty salaries for institutions of higher education in Wisconsin, 2000-01 ★3738★

Alvin Community College
Average faculty salaries for institutions of higher education without academic ranks in Texas, 2000-01 ★3766★

Alza
Top health care companies in Standard & Poor's 500, 2001 ★542★

AMA Health Insight
Medical Library Association's top health related web sites ★2591★

Amadeus Global Travel Distribution
Business Week's best companies in Spain ★403★

Amaker; H. Tommy
Top pay and benefits for the chief executive and top paid employees at Seton Hall University ★3496★

Amarillo College
Institutions censured by the American Association of University Professors, 2001 ★1067★
Lowest undergraduate tuition and fees at colleges and universities in Texas ★1561★

The Amazing Adventures of Kavalier and Clay
Booklist's best fiction books for library collections, 2000 ★227★
Most notable fiction books, 2001 ★284★
Outstanding works of fiction, 2001 ★293★

The Amazing Life of Benjamin Franklin
Most notable books for middle readers, 2001 ★317★

Amazon.com
Top E-commerce web sites ★2603★

Ambac Financial Group
Business Week's best performing companies with the highest net margin, 2000 ★419★

The Amber Spyglass
Most notable books for older readers, 2001 ★318★
Publishers Weekly Off-the-Cuff Awards winner for best sequel, 2000 ★341★
Smithsonian's best books for children ages 10 and up ★365★

Amber University
U.S. colleges and universities awarding the most psychology master's degrees to African Americans ★1797★
Average faculty salaries for institutions of higher education in Texas, 2000-01 ★3731★

Ambrose; Charles M.
Top pay and benefits for the chief executive and top paid employees at Pfeiffer University ★3439★

Amdocs
Top information technology companies, 2000 ★544★

Amerada Hess
Business Week's best performing companies with the highest 3-year earnings growth ★416★
Top fuel companies in Standard & Poor's 500, 2001 ★541★

Amerco
Fortune's highest ranked automotive retailing services companies, 2000 ★449★
Fortune's least admired companies for social responsibility ★512★

America the Beautiful
Booklist's most recommended geography series for young people, 2000 ★313★

America Online
Business Week's best companies in the United States ★411★
Fortune's highest ranked computer and data services companies, 2000 ★453★

America West Holdings
Fortune's highest ranked airlines, 2000 ★447★
Fortune's least admired companies for innovation ★508★
Fortune's least admired companies for quality of products or services ★511★

American
Gender breakdown of language and literature doctorate recipients, by subfield, 1999 ★1937★
Language and literature doctorates awarded at U.S. colleges and universities, by subfield, 1999 ★1949★

American Academy of Religion
Scholarly societies with the highest membership, 1999 ★3052★

American Airlines
Top recruiters for finance/banking jobs for 2000-01 master's degree recipients ★664★
Top recruiters for marketing jobs for 2000-01 master's degree recipients ★672★

American Anthropologist
Anthropology journals by citation impact, 1994-98 ★64★

American Antiquity
Anthropology journals by citation impact, 1994-98 ★64★
Anthropology journals by citation impact, 1998 ★65★

American Association for the Advancement of Science
Scholarly societies with the highest membership, 1999 ★3052★

American Baptist College of ABT Seminary
Lowest undergraduate tuition and fees at private nonprofit, 4-year or above colleges and universities ★1464★

American Bar Association
Most selective internships in the U.S., 2001 ★2610★

American Cancer Society
Organizations with the most charitable contributions raised, 1999 ★2943★

American Civil Liberties Union
Most selective internships in the U.S., 2001 ★2610★

American Coin Merchandising
Companies with the worst two-year total returns since 1998 ★437★

American College
Average faculty salaries for institutions of higher education in Pennsylvania, 2000-01 ★3725★

American College (PA)
U.S. community colleges with the highest paid full professors, 2001 ★3976★

American Committee on Africa/The Africa Fund
Most selective internships in the U.S., 2001 ★2610★

American Criminal Law Review
Criminology and penology journals with the greatest impact measure, 1981-98 ★1611★

AMERICAN

Criminology and penology journals with the greatest impact measure, 1994-98 ★1612★

American Economic Review
Top accounting journals by half-life impact factor ★578★
Economics journals with the greatest impact measure, 1981-98 ★2161★
Economics journals with the greatest impact measure, 1994-98 ★2162★
Journals publishing the most articles on economic education research from 1963-1990 ★2170★
Alternative general economics journals, by non-uniform weighting of subdisciplinary impacts, including self-citations ★2180★
Alternative general economics journals, by uniform weighting of subdisciplinary impacts, including self-citations ★2181★
Economics journals by citation impact, 1981-98 ★2182★
Economics journals by citation impact, 1995-98 ★2183★
Economics journals by citation impact, 1998 ★2184★
Top ranked agricultural and natural resource economics journals ★2187★
Top ranked business administration and business economics journals ★2188★
Top ranked economic development, technological change, and growth journals ★2189★
Top ranked economic history journals ★2190★
Top ranked economic systems journals ★2191★
Top ranked financial economics journals ★2192★
Top ranked health, education, and welfare journals ★2193★
Top ranked industrial organization journals ★2194★
Top ranked international economics journals ★2195★
Top ranked labor and demographic economics journals ★2196★
Top ranked law and economics journals ★2197★
Top ranked mathematical and quantitative methods journals ★2198★
Top ranked microeconomics and monetary economics journals ★2199★
Top ranked microeconomics journals ★2200★
Top ranked public economics journals ★2201★
Top ranked urban, rural and regional economics journals ★2202★
Highest impact economics journals in energy from 1974 to 1979 ★2456★
Highest impact economics journals in energy from 1980 to 1989 ★2457★
Highest impact economics journals in energy from 1990 to 1998 ★2458★
Highest impact economics journals in exhaustible resources from 1974 to 1979 ★2459★
Highest impact economics journals in exhaustible resources from 1990 to 1998 ★2461★
Highly cited real estate journals, 1990 to 1995 ★3090★

American Economic Review (Proceedings)
Journals publishing the most articles on economic education research from 1963-1990 ★2170★

American Educational Research Journal
Education and educational research journals by citation impact, 1981-99 ★2235★
Education and educational research journals by citation impact, 1995-99 ★2236★
Education and educational research journals by citation impact, 1999 ★2237★
Education and educational research journals with the greatest impact measure ★2238★
Most cited education serials in technical communication journals from 1988 to 1997 ★4418★

American Electric Power
Fortune's highest ranked electric and gas utilities companies, 2000 ★459★

American and English language and literature
Humanities doctorates awarded to U.S. citizens/permanent residents at U.S. colleges and universities, by race/ethnicity and subfield, 1999 ★1947★

American Ethnologist
Anthropology journals by citation impact, 1991-98 ★63★
Anthropology journals by citation impact, 1998 ★65★

American Express
Fortune's highest ranked consumer credit companies, 2000 ★457★
Highly recommended public companies for women executives, 2000 ★4453★

American Forests
Most selective internships in the U.S., 2001 ★2610★

American Freightways
Fortune's highest ranked trucking companies, 2000 ★503★

American General
Fortune's highest ranked life and health insurance companies, 2000 ★472★

American Greetings
Business Week's best performing companies with the lowest 3-year shareholder returns ★424★
Fortune's highest ranked publishing companies, 2000 ★489★

American Heritage Talking Dictionary Classic
Top selling reference software, 2000 ★1601★

American Home Products
Business Week's best performing companies with the greatest decline in earnings growth ★412★
Fortune's highest ranked pharmaceuticals companies, 2000 ★485★

American Honda Motor
Fortune's highest ranked motor vehicles companies, 2000 ★481★

American Indian College of the Assemblies of God
Highest undergraduate tuition and fees at colleges and universities in Arizona ★1482★

American Indian History and Culture: An Online Encyclopedia
Outstanding reference sources, 2000 ★370★

American International College
Division II NCAA colleges with the 100% graduation rates for men's basketball players, 1993-94 ★943★
Division II NCAA colleges with the highest graduation rates for football players, 1993-94 ★946★
Institutions censured by the American Association of University Professors, 2001 ★1067★
U.S. News & World Report's northern regional universities with students most in debt, 1999 ★1414★

American International Group
Business Week's best companies in the United States ★411★
Business Week's top companies worldwide ★433★
Fortune's highest ranked property and casualty insurance companies, 2000 ★488★

American Journal of Agricultural Economics
Top ranked agricultural and natural resource economics journals ★2187★

American Journal of Dermatopathology
Number of citations and papers for original articles appearing in dermatology journals, 1981 to 1996 ★1873★

American Journal of Distance Education
Most cited education serials in technical communication journals from 1988 to 1997 ★4418★

American Journal of Education
Education and educational research journals with the greatest impact measure ★2238★

American Journal of Enology and Viticulture
Agriculture journals by citation impact, 1995-99 ★53★

American Journal of Kidney Diseases
Urology and nephrology journals with the greatest impact measure, 1981-98 ★2816★
Urology and nephrology journals with the greatest impact measure, 1994-98 ★2817★

American Journal of Physical Anthropology
Anthropology journals by citation impact, 1991-98 ★63★
Anthropology journals by citation impact, 1994-98 ★64★
Anthropology journals by citation impact, 1998 ★65★

American Journal of Political Science
Political science journals with the greatest impact measure, 1981-98 ★3049★
Political science journals with the greatest impact measure, 1994-98 ★3050★
Political science journals with the greatest percentage of articles by multiple authors, 1974-94 ★3051★

American Journal of Psychiatry
Psychiatry journals by citation impact, 1981-98 ★3054★
Psychiatry journals by citation impact, 1995-98 ★3055★
Psychiatry journals by citation impact, 1998 ★3056★
Psychiatry journals by impact factor, 1981 to 1998 ★3057★
Psychiatry journals by impact factor, 1994 to 1998 ★3058★
Most-cited social sciences journals, 1981-97 ★4340★
Social sciences journals with the greatest impact measure, 1981-97 ★4341★

American Journal of Public Health
'Outside' journals most frequently citing Family Planning Perspectives, 1991-95 ★1859★
Most-cited social sciences journals, 1981-97 ★4340★

American Journal of Sociology
Sociology journals by impact factor, 1981 to 1997 ★4355★

Sociology journals by impact factor, 1993 to 1997 ★4356★

American Journal of Surgery
Surgery journals with the greatest impact measure, 1981-98 ★2814★
Surgery journals with the greatest impact measure, 1994-98 ★2815★

American Journal of Surgical Pathology
Surgery journals with the greatest impact measure, 1981-98 ★2814★
Surgery journals with the greatest impact measure, 1994-98 ★2815★

American Journal of Veterinary Research
Veterinary sciences journals with the greatest impact measure, 1981-98 ★4442★

American Management Systems
Top recruiters for business administration jobs for 2000-01 master's degree recipients ★652★
Top recruiters for computer science jobs for 2000-01 bachelor's degree recipients ★1590★
Top recruiters for systems engineer jobs for 2000-01 bachelor's degree recipients ★2336★
Top recruiters for information technology (MIS) jobs for 2000-01 bachelor's degree recipients ★2738★
Top recruiters for math/actuarial science jobs for 2000-01 bachelor's degree recipients ★2771★

American Mathematical Society
Scholarly societies with the highest membership, 1999 ★3052★

American Movie: The Making of Northwestern
Most notable videos for adults, 2001 ★2891★

American National Biography
Library Journal's best reference databases and discs, 2000 ★369★

American Naturalist
Ecology journals by citation impact, 1981-99 ★2136★
Ecology journals by citation impact, 1995-99 ★2137★
Ecology journals by citation impact, 1999 ★2138★

American Naval History: A Guide
Selected new editions and supplements reference books, 2000 ★372★

American Physical Society
Scholarly societies with the highest membership, 1999 ★3052★

American Political Science Review
Top ranked law and economics journals ★2197★
Top ranked public economics journals ★2201★
Political science journals with the greatest impact measure, 1981-98 ★3049★
Political science journals with the greatest impact measure, 1994-98 ★3050★
Political science journals with the greatest percentage of articles by multiple authors, 1974-94 ★3051★

American Politics Quarterly
Political science journals with the greatest impact measure, 1981-98 ★3049★

American Potato Journal
Agriculture journals by citation impact, 1999 ★54★

American Psychological Association
Scholarly societies with the highest membership, 1999 ★3052★

American Psychologist
Most cited psychology serials in technical communication journals from 1988 to 1997 ★4423★

American Red Cross
Organizations with the most charitable contributions raised, 1999 ★2943★

American Rhapsody
Library Journal's best nonfiction audiobooks, 2000 ★243★

American River College
Lowest undergraduate tuition and fees at public 2-year colleges and universities ★1465★
Lowest undergraduate tuition and fees at colleges and universities in California ★1487★

American Sociological Review
Top management journals ★546★
'Outside' journals most frequently citing Demography, 1991-95 ★1858★
Political science journals with the greatest percentage of articles by multiple authors, 1974-94 ★3051★
Sociology journals by impact factor, 1981 to 1997 ★4355★
Sociology journals by impact factor, 1993 to 1997 ★4356★
Most cited sociology serials in technical communication journals from 1988 to 1997 ★4426★

American Standard
Fortune's highest ranked industrial and farm equipment companies, 2000 ★471★

An American Story
Booklist's most recommended African American nonfiction ★229★

American studies
Gender breakdown of humanities doctorate recipients, by subfield, 1999 ★1936★
Humanities doctorates awarded at U.S. colleges and universities, by subfield, 1999 ★1946★

American University
U.S. business schools with the slowest payback on MBA investments ★655★
Undergraduate tuition and fees at colleges and universities in the District of Columbia ★1493★
U.S. colleges and universities awarding the most communications master's degrees to African Americans ★1763★
U.S. colleges and universities awarding the most communications master's degrees to Hispanic Americans ★1765★
U.S. colleges and universities awarding the most computer and information sciences master's degrees to African Americans ★1766★
U.S. colleges and universities awarding the most computer and information sciences master's degrees to Hispanic Americans ★1768★
U.S. colleges and universities awarding the most law and legal studies master's degrees to Hispanic Americans ★1783★
U.S. colleges and universities awarding the most social sciences and history master's degrees to African Americans ★1801★
U.S. colleges and universities awarding the most social sciences and history master's degrees to Asian Americans ★1802★
U.S. colleges and universities awarding the most social sciences and history master's degrees to Hispanic Americans ★1803★
U.S. colleges and universities awarding the most law and legal studies first professional degrees to Asian Americans ★1853★
U.S. colleges and universities awarding the most law and legal studies first professional degrees to Native Americans ★1855★
U.S. colleges and universities awarding the most social sciences and history doctorate degrees to African Americans ★2124★
Doctoral institutions with the highest enrollment of foreign students, 1998-99 ★2494★
U.S. doctoral institutions with the largest number of students studying abroad, 1998-99 ★2512★
First-year student's choices for exemplary doctoral-extensive universities ★2534★
Academics' choices for best clinical law programs, 2001 ★2626★
Academics' choices for best international law programs, 2001 ★2631★
Enrollment of students in the ten largest master's journalism and mass communications programs, 1999 ★2763★
Presidents with the highest pay at Doctoral I and II universities, 1998-99 ★3160★
Average faculty salaries for institutions of higher education in the District of Columbia, 2000-01 ★3732★

American Women in Technology: An Encyclopedia
Selected reference books in the field of science and technology, 2000 ★381★

American Women's History: An Online Encyclopedia
Outstanding reference sources, 2000 ★370★

America's Champion Swimmer: Gertrude Ederle
Most notable books for young readers, 2001 ★319★
Outstanding books for young readers, 2000 ★328★

America's Crayfish: Crawling in Troubled Waters
Outstanding videos for library collections, 2000 ★2892★

America's Second Harvest
Organizations with the most charitable contributions raised, 1999 ★2943★

AmeriCorps
Fiscal 2002 requested budget as compared with Fiscal 2001 budget for other agencies ★2230★
Proposed fiscal 2002 appropriations for miscellaneous federal aid ★2487★

AmeriSource Health
Fortune's highest ranked wholesalers, 2000 ★505★

Amersley; Michael
All-America boys' high school soccer team midfielders, 2001 ★168★

Amerson; G. Malcolm
Top pay and benefits for the chief executive and top paid employees at Oglethorpe University ★3429★

Ames Public Library
Highest Hennen's American Public Library Ratings for libraries serving a population of 50,000 to 99,999 ★2697★

Amgen
Business Week's best performing companies with the highest 3-year shareholder returns ★418★
Fortune's highest ranked pharmaceuticals companies, 2000 ★485★

Amherst College
Private, 4-year undergraduate colleges and universities producing the most Ph.D.'s in the life sciences, 1920-1990 ★192★
Comparison of acceptance rates at the top 5 liberal arts colleges in the U.S., 1990 and 2001 ★844★
U.S. colleges and universities offering the best overall academic experience for undergraduates ★987★
U.S. colleges and universities that are the toughest to get into ★988★
U.S. News & World Report's best national liberal arts colleges, 2000-01 ★1320★
U.S. News & World Report's national liberal arts colleges with the best financial resources rank, 2000-01 ★1322★
U.S. News & World Report's national liberal arts colleges with the best freshmen retention rates, 2000-01 ★1323★
U.S. News & World Report's national liberal arts colleges with the best graduation and retention rank, 2000-01 ★1324★
U.S. News & World Report's national liberal arts colleges with the best selectivity rank, 2000-01 ★1325★
U.S. News & World Report's national liberal arts colleges with the best student/faculty ratios, 2000-01 ★1326★
U.S. News & World Report's national liberal arts colleges with the highest academic reputation scores, 2000-01 ★1327★
U.S. News & World Report's national liberal arts colleges with the highest alumni giving rank, 2000-01 ★1329★
U.S. News & World Report's national liberal arts colleges with the highest graduation rates, 2000-01 ★1330★
U.S. News & World Report's national liberal arts colleges with the highest percentage of alumni support, 2000-01 ★1331★
U.S. News & World Report's national liberal arts colleges with the highest percentage of freshmen in the top 10% of their high school class, 2000-01 ★1332★
U.S. News & World Report's national liberal arts colleges with the highest proportion of classes having 50 or more students, 2000-01 ★1334★
U.S. News & World Report's national liberal arts colleges with the lowest acceptance rates, 2000-01 ★1336★
U.S. News & World Report's best undergraduate fees among national liberal arts colleges by discount tuition, 2000 ★1381★
Highest undergraduate tuition and fees at private nonprofit, 4-year or above colleges and universities ★1461★
Private 4-year institutions with the highest tuition, 2000-01 ★1467★
Highest undergraduate tuition and fees at colleges and universities in Massachusetts ★1516★
Private, 4-year undergraduate colleges and universities producing the most Ph.D.'s in the computer sciences, 1920-1990 ★1595★
Private, 4-year undergraduate colleges and universities producing the most Ph.D.'s in the computer sciences, 1981-1990 ★1596★
Total baccalaureate law and legal studies degrees awarded to African Americans from U.S. colleges and universities, 1997-98 ★1725★
Private, 4-year undergraduate colleges and universities producing the most Ph.Ds in all fields of study, 1920-1990 ★2027★
Private, 4-year undergraduate colleges and universities producing the most Ph.D.'s in all fields of study, 1981-1990 ★2028★
Private, 4-year undergraduate colleges and universities producing the most Ph.D.'s in nonscience fields, 1920-1990 ★2030★
Private, 4-year undergraduate colleges and universities producing the most Ph.D.'s in the earth sciences, 1981-1990 ★2151★
Elite liberal arts colleges ranked by per capita quality adjusted scholarship articles in the field of economics, 1975-94 ★2164★
Top full professor economists at elite liberal arts colleges, 1975-94 ★2175★
Private, 4-year undergraduate colleges and universities producing the most Ph.D.'s in economics, 1920-1990 ★2211★
Private, 4-year undergraduate colleges and universities producing the most Ph.D.'s in economics, 1981-1990 ★2212★
Undergraduate institutions with the most graduates who received Ph.Ds in economics, 1920-1984 ★2214★
Private, 4-year undergraduate colleges and universities producing the most Ph.D.'s in English, 1920-1990 ★2449★
Private, 4-year undergraduate colleges and universities producing the most Ph.D.'s in English, 1981-1990 ★2450★
Private, 4-year undergraduate colleges and universities producing the most Ph.D.'s in history, 1920-1990 ★2552★
Private, 4-year undergraduate colleges and universities producing the most Ph.D.'s in history, 1981-1990 ★2553★
Private, 4-year undergraduate colleges and universities producing the most Ph.D.'s in mathematics, 1920-1990 ★2776★
Private, 4-year undergraduate colleges and universities producing the most Ph.D.'s in physics and astronomy, 1920-1990 ★2949★
Private, 4-year undergraduate colleges and universities producing the most Ph.D.'s in political science and international relations, 1920-1990 ★3044★
Private, 4-year undergraduate colleges and universities producing the most Ph.D.'s in political science and international relations, 1981-1990 ★3045★
Presidents with the highest pay at Baccalaureate I colleges, 1998-99 ★3159★
Average faculty salaries for institutions of higher education in Massachusetts, 2000-01 ★3708★
U.S. liberal arts colleges with the highest paid full professors, 2001 ★3980★
Private, 4-year undergraduate colleges and universities producing the most Ph.D.'s in the sciences, 1920-1990 ★4294★

Amherst Middle School
Outstanding secondary schools in Nashua, New Hampshire ★4185★

Amin; S.
Most cited authors in the journal *Social Justice*, 1990 to 1995 ★1631★

Amkor Technology
Fortune's highest ranked semiconductors companies, 2000 ★495★

Ammons; Richard A.
Top pay and benefits for the chief executive and top paid employees at Macalester College ★3385★

AMP Ltd.
Business Week's best companies in Australia ★386★

Amphibians: The World of Frogs, Toads, Salamanders, and Newts
Library Journal's best reference books, 2000 ★368★

AmphibiaWeb
Library Journal's best free reference websites, 2000 ★367★

AMR
Fortune's highest ranked airlines, 2000 ★447★
Top transportation companies in Standard & Poor's 500, 2001 ★560★

Amsterdam-Hague-Rotterdam-Utrecht
Cities with the highest productivity of paper in the discipline of cardiovascular systems, 1994-96 ★2869★
Cities with the highest productivity of paper in the discipline of hematology, 1994-96 ★2870★
Cities with the highest productivity of paper in the discipline of immunology, 1994-96 ★2871★

Anacapa Middle School
Outstanding secondary schools in Ventura, California ★4248★

Anadarko Petroleum
Best performing companies in Standard & Poor's 500, 2001 ★382★
Business Week's best performing companies with the highest 1-year earnings growth ★413★
Business Week's best performing companies with the highest 1-year sales performance ★414★
Business Week's best performing companies with the highest 3-year sales performance ★417★
Top fuel companies in Standard & Poor's 500, 2001 ★541★

Analog Devices
Fortune's highest ranked semiconductors companies, 2000 ★495★
Top electrical and electronics companies in Standard & Poor's 500, 2001 ★539★
Top information technology companies, 2000 ★544★

Analysis and functional analysis
Gender breakdown of mathematics doctorate recipients, by subfield, 1999 ★1938★
Mathematics doctorates awarded at U.S. colleges and universities, by subfield, 1999 ★1951★

Analytical
Chemistry doctorates awarded at U.S. colleges and universities, by subfield, 1999 ★1889★
Gender breakdown of chemistry doctorate recipients, by subfield, 1999 ★1929★

Anatomy
Biological sciences doctorates awarded at U.S. colleges and universities, by subfield, 1999 ★1887★
Gender breakdown of biological sciences doctorate recipients, by subfield, 1999 ★1927★
Average salaries for assistant professors at private institutions in preclinical department of medical schools, 2000-01 ★3785★
Average salaries for assistant professors at public and private institutions in preclinical department of medical schools, 2000-01 ★3786★
Average salaries for assistant professors at public institutions in preclinical department of medical schools, 2000-01 ★3787★
Average salaries for associate professors at private institutions in preclinical department of medical schools, 2000-01 ★3800★

Average salaries for associate professors at public and private institutions in preclinical department of medical schools, 2000-01 ★3801★

Average salaries for associate professors at public institutions in preclinical department of medical schools, 2000-01 ★3802★

Average salaries for full-time instructors at private institutions in preclinical department of medical schools, 2000-01 ★3854★

Average salaries for full-time instructors at public and private institutions in preclinical department of medical schools, 2000-01 ★3855★

Average salaries for full-time instructors at public institutions in preclinical department of medical schools, 2000-01 ★3856★

Average salaries for professors at private institutions in preclinical department of medical schools, 2000-01 ★3932★

Average salaries for professors at public and private institutions in preclinical department of medical schools, 2000-01 ★3933★

Average salaries for professors at public institutions in preclinical department of medical schools, 2000-01 ★3934★

Anchorage Daily News
Most selective internships in the U.S., 2001 ★2610★

Ancient Acid Flashes Back
Booklist's most recommended poetry books, 2001 ★231★

Ancient Civilizations
Outstanding reference sources, 2000 ★370★

Ancient Greece: Daily Life; Greek Theatre; The Original Olympics
Smithsonian's best books for children ages 6 to 10 ★364★

Ancillae-Assumpta Academy
Outstanding secondary schools in Philadelphia, Pennsylvania-New Jersey ★4202★

And This Too Shall Pass
Favorite books of African Americans ★238★

Anders; Kathryn Howell
All-USA Teacher Teams, Second Team, 2000 ★4400★

Andersen Consulting
Largest private companies, 2000 ★523★

Anderson; A.J.
Library and information science faculty with the most journal articles, 1993-1998 ★2711★

Anderson; Alan
All-America boys' high school basketball 4th team, 2001 ★164★

Anderson College (SC)
Division II NCAA colleges with the 0% graduation rates for men's basketball players, 1993-94 ★941★

Division II NCAA colleges with the lowest graduation rates for all sports, 1993-94 ★947★

Anderson; D.
Authors that most frequently cite *Libri* publications from 1972 to 1999 ★2723★

Anderson; David
Top pay and benefits for the chief executive and top paid employees at Allegheny College ★3170★

Anderson; David R.
Top pay and benefits for the chief executive and top paid employees at Luther College ★3383★

Anderson High School
Outstanding secondary schools in Cincinnati, Ohio-Kentucky-Indiana ★4112★

Anderson; Judith
Top pay and benefits for the chief executive and top paid employees at Andrews University ★3176★

Anderson; Kathleen
Top pay and benefits for the chief executive and top paid employees at Chestnut Hill College ★3231★

Anderson; Lester McTier
Top pay and benefits for the chief executive and top paid employees at Charleston Southern University ★3229★

Anderson; Loren J.
Top pay and benefits for the chief executive and top paid employees at Pacific Lutheran University ★3436★

Anderson; Marian
Most influential African American entertainers ★77★

Anderson; Patricia
Top pay and benefits for the chief executive and top paid employees at Azusa Pacific University ★3187★

Anderson; Paul S.
American Chemical Society 2001 award winners (Group 1) ★751★

Anderson; Richard L.
Top pay and benefits for the chief executive and top paid employees at Southwestern University in Texas ★3505★

Anderson; Robert L.
Top pay and benefits for the chief executive and top paid employees at Cardinal Stritch University ★3221★

Anderson; S. Cathy
Top pay and benefits for the chief executive and top paid employees at Queens College in North Carolina ★3448★

Anderson University
Average faculty salaries for institutions of higher education in Indiana, 2000-01 ★3701★

Anderson; William K.
Top pay and benefits for the chief executive and top paid employees at Hope College ★3339★

Andirondack Community College
Lowest undergraduate tuition and fees at colleges and universities in New York ★1538★

Andover College
Highest undergraduate tuition and fees at colleges and universities in Maine ★1512★

Average faculty salaries for institutions of higher education in Maine, 2000-01 ★3706★

Andover Newton Theological School
Average faculty salaries for institutions of higher education in Massachusetts, 2000-01 ★3708★

Andreasen; Niels-Erik A.
Top pay and benefits for the chief executive and top paid employees at Andrews University ★3176★

Andrews; D.A.
Most cited authors in the journal *Federal Probation*, 1990 to 1995 ★1623★

Andrews; Don A.
Most-cited scholars in *Canadian Journal of Criminology* ★1638★

Andrews; Ira
Top pay and benefits for the chief executive and top paid employees at Randolph-Macon College ★3451★

Andrews; Larry
Top pay and benefits for the chief executive and top paid employees at Brenau University ★3210★

Andrews; Lori
Top pay and benefits for the chief executive and top paid employees at Illinois Institute of Technology ★3346★

Andrews; Shawn
All-American boy's high school football linemen, 2000 ★183★

Andrews University
U.S. News & World Report's national universities with students most in debt, 1999 ★1476★

Angela's Ashes
Longest-running mass market paperback bestsellers, 2000 ★280★

Angeletti; Joseph
Top pay and benefits for the chief executive and top paid employees at Drew University ★3273★

Angelina Ballerina books
Publishers Weekly Off-the-Cuff Awards winner for book happiest to see back in print, 2000 ★345★

Angelina College
Lowest undergraduate tuition and fees at colleges and universities in Texas ★1561★

Angelo State University
U.S. colleges and universities awarding the most mathematics master's degrees to Hispanic Americans ★1792★

Angelou; Maya
Most influential African Americans in the arts ★78★

Favorite African American authors ★237★

Angels in America
Top plays of the twentieth century ★4435★

Angewandte Chemie International Edition
Chemistry journals by citation impact, 1981-99 ★808★

Chemistry journals by citation impact, 1995-99 ★809★

Chemistry journals by citation impact, 1999 ★810★

Anglo American
Business Week's top emerging-market companies worldwide ★434★

Angus, Thongs and Full-Frontal Snogging: Confessions of Georgia Nicolson
Booklist's best first novels for youths ★309★

Most notable fiction books for reluctant young adult readers, 2001 ★321★

Most notable fiction books for young adults, 2001 ★322★

Outstanding books for older readers, 2000 ★327★

Publishers Weekly Off-the-Cuff Awards winner for funniest novel, 2000 ★349★

Anheuser-Busch
Fortune's highest ranked beverages companies, 2000 ★450★

Top consumer products companies in Standard & Poor's 500, 2001 ★536★

Most selective internships in the U.S., 2001 ★2610★

Anil's Ghost
Most notable fiction books, 2001 ★284★

Outstanding works of fiction, 2001 ★293★

Animal Blood Groups
Veterinary sciences journals with the greatest impact measure, 1981-98 ★4442★

Animal breeding and genetics
  Agricultural sciences doctorates awarded at U.S. colleges and universities, by subfield, 1999 ★1886★
  Gender breakdown of agricultural sciences doctorate recipients, by subfield, 1999 ★1926★

Animal nutrition
  Agricultural sciences doctorates awarded at U.S. colleges and universities, by subfield, 1999 ★1886★
  Gender breakdown of agricultural sciences doctorate recipients, by subfield, 1999 ★1926★

Animal Production
  Veterinary sciences journals with the greatest impact measure, 1981-98 ★4442★
  Veterinary sciences journals with the greatest impact measure, 1994-98 ★4443★

Animal sciences
  Agricultural sciences doctorates awarded at U.S. colleges and universities, by subfield, 1999 ★1886★
  Gender breakdown of agricultural sciences doctorate recipients, by subfield, 1999 ★1926★

Anka; Paul
  Canada's best performing artists of the 20th century ★74★

Ann Arbor, MI
  Best college towns to live in ★3076★

Anna; Gary M.
  Top pay and benefits for the chief executive and top paid employees at Bradley University ★3208★

Anna Maria College
  U.S. News & World Report's northern regional universities with students least in debt, 1999 ★1413★

Anna Middle School
  Outstanding secondary schools in Dallas, Texas ★4120★

Annales Scientifiques de L'Ecole Normale Superieure
  Mathematics journals by impact factor ★2783★
  Mathematics journals by impact factor, 1981 to 1997 ★2784★
  Mathematics journals by impact factor, 1993 to 1997 ★2785★

Annals of Mathematical Statistics
  Top ranked mathematical and quantitative methods journals ★2198★

Annals of Mathematics
  Mathematics journals by impact factor ★2783★
  Mathematics journals by impact factor, 1981 to 1997 ★2784★
  Mathematics journals by impact factor, 1993 to 1997 ★2785★

Annals of Mathematics Studies
  Mathematics journals by impact factor, 1993 to 1997 ★2785★

Annals of Neurology
  Journals with the highest impact factor in the field of neuroscience, 1981-96 ★191★
  Neurosciences journals with the greatest impact measure, 1981-98 ★2812★
  Neurosciences journals with the greatest impact measure, 1994-98 ★2813★

Annals of Physics
  Physics journals with the greatest impact measure, 1981-98 ★3020★

Annals of Statistics
  Top ranked mathematical and quantitative methods journals ★2198★

Annals of Surgery
  Surgery journals with the greatest impact measure, 1981-98 ★2814★
  Surgery journals with the greatest impact measure, 1994-98 ★2815★

Annapolis, MD
  Best 'green & clean' places to live ★3077★

Anne Arundel Community College
  Lowest undergraduate tuition and fees at colleges and universities in Maryland ★1515★

Anne Arundel County Public Library
  Highest Hennen's American Public Library Ratings for libraries serving a population of 250,000 to 499,999 ★2699★

Anne Frank: A Hidden Life
  Outstanding children's nonfiction books, 2000 ★330★

The Annenberg/CPB Project Learner Online Home Page for Educators
  Top sites for educators ★2605★

Annie on My Mind
  Most frequently banned books in the 1990s ★745★

Annual Review of Anthropology
  Anthropology journals by citation impact, 1991-98 ★63★
  Anthropology journals by citation impact, 1994-98 ★64★
  Anthropology journals by citation impact, 1998 ★65★

Annual Review of Astronomy and Astrophysics
  Astronomy and astrophysics journals by citation impact, 1981-99 ★102★
  Astronomy and astrophysics journals by citation impact, 1995-99 ★103★
  Astronomy and astrophysics journals by citation impact, 1999 ★104★
  Astronomy and astrophysics journals by impact factor, 1981 to 1998 ★105★
  Astronomy and astrophysics journals by impact factor, 1994 to 1998 ★106★

Annual Review of Earth and Planetary Science
  Astronomy and astrophysics journals by citation impact, 1981-99 ★102★
  Astronomy and astrophysics journals by citation impact, 1995-99 ★103★
  Astronomy and astrophysics journals by citation impact, 1999 ★104★
  Astronomy and astrophysics journals by impact factor, 1981 to 1998 ★105★
  Astronomy and astrophysics journals by impact factor, 1994 to 1998 ★106★

Annual Review of Ecological Systems
  Ecology journals by citation impact, 1999 ★2138★

Annual Review of Entomology
  Entomology journals by citation impact, 1981-98 ★2453★
  Entomology journals by citation impact, 1994-98 ★2454★
  Entomology journals by citation impact, 1998 ★2455★

Annual Review of Immunology
  Immunology journals with the greatest impact measure, 1981-98 ★2810★
  Immunology journals with the greatest impact measure, 1994-98 ★2811★
  Immunology journals by impact factor, 1981 to 1997 ★4279★
  Immunology journals by impact factor, 1993 to 1997 ★4280★

Annual Review of Information Sciences
  Information and library science journals by citation impact, 1981-99 ★2724★
  Information and library science journals by citation impact, 1995-99 ★2725★
  Information and library science journals by citation impact, 1999 ★2726★
  Information and library science journals with the greatest impact measure, 1981-98 ★2727★

Annual Review of Neuroscience
  Journals with the highest impact factor in the field of neuroscience, 1981-96 ★191★
  Neurosciences journals with the greatest impact measure, 1981-98 ★2812★
  Neurosciences journals with the greatest impact measure, 1994-98 ★2813★

Annual Review of Psychology
  Journals and proceedings with the most citations (Class 4) ★2570★

Annual Review of Sociology
  'Outside' journals most frequently citing *Population and Development Review*, 1991-95 ★1860★
  Sociology journals by impact factor, 1981 to 1997 ★4355★
  Sociology journals by impact factor, 1993 to 1997 ★4356★

Annual Reviews of Ecological Systems
  Ecology journals by citation impact, 1981-99 ★2136★
  Ecology journals by citation impact, 1995-99 ★2137★

Anoka-Hennepin Tech College
  Average faculty salaries for institutions of higher education without academic ranks in Minnesota, 2000-01 ★3753★

Anoka-Ramsey Community College
  Average faculty salaries for institutions of higher education without academic ranks in Minnesota, 2000-01 ★3753★

Anolabehere, et al.; Stephen
  Most frequently downloaded *American Political Science Review* articles ★3039★

Another Beauty
  Outstanding arts and literature books, 2000 ★286★

L'Anse Creuse Middle School Central
  Outstanding secondary schools in Detroit, Michigan ★4125★

L'Anse Creuse Middle School North
  Outstanding secondary schools in Detroit, Michigan ★4125★

L'Anse Creuse Middle School South
  Outstanding secondary schools in Detroit, Michigan ★4125★

Antarctic Antics: A Book of Penguin Poems
  Most notable children's videos, 2001 ★2889★

Antecedents to Buyer-Seller Collaboration: An Analysis from the Buyer's Perspective
  Most influential articles in the *Journal of Business Research* from 1990 to 1994 ★699★

Antelope Valley College
  Lowest undergraduate tuition and fees at public 2-year colleges and universities ★1465★

Anthem Insurance
  Fortune's highest ranked health care companies, 2000 ★469★

Anthropologist
  Most desirable social sciences jobs ★2280★

Anthropology
Gender breakdown of social sciences doctorate recipients, by subfield, 1999 ★1942★
Number of social sciences doctorate recipients at U.S. colleges and universities, by field, 1999 ★1977★
Percentage of female doctorate recipients at U.S. colleges and universities, by subfield, 1999 ★1988★
Social sciences doctorates awarded at U.S. colleges and universities, by subfield, 1999 ★2044★
Top nonscience majors for accepted applicants to U.S. medical schools, 1999-2000 ★2854★
Average costs for Academic Search titles by subject, 2001 ★2918★
Periodical prices by LC subject, 2001 ★2925★

Anthropology and sociology
Social sciences doctorates awarded to U.S. citizens/permanent residents at U.S. colleges and universities, by race/ethnicity and subfield, 1999 ★2045★

Antioch College
Private, 4-year undergraduate colleges and universities producing the most Ph.D.'s in the life sciences, 1920-1990 ★192★
College freshmen's choices for exemplary liberal arts institutions ★1317★
College senior's choices for exemplary liberal arts institutions ★1318★
U.S. News & World Report's national liberal arts colleges with the highest proportion of classes with less than 20 students, 2000-01 ★1335★
Highest undergraduate tuition and fees at colleges and universities in Ohio ★1543★
Private, 4-year undergraduate colleges and universities producing the most Ph.D.'s in the computer sciences, 1920-1990 ★1595★
Private, 4-year undergraduate colleges and universities producing the most Ph.D.s in all fields of study, 1920-1990 ★2027★
Private, 4-year undergraduate colleges and universities producing the most Ph.D.'s in political science and international relations, 1920-1990 ★3044★
Private, 4-year undergraduate colleges and universities producing the most Ph.D.'s in political science and international relations, 1981-1990 ★3045★
Private, 4-year undergraduate colleges and universities producing the most Ph.D.'s in psychology, 1920-1990 ★3066★
Private, 4-year undergraduate colleges and universities producing the most Ph.D.'s in psychology, 1981-1990 ★3067★
Private, 4-year undergraduate colleges and universities producing the most Ph.D.'s in the sciences, 1920-1990 ★4294★
Private, 4-year undergraduate colleges and universities producing the most Ph.D.'s in anthropology and sociology, 1920-1990 ★4344★
Private, 4-year undergraduate colleges and universities producing the most Ph.D.'s in anthropology and sociology, 1981-1990 ★4345★

Antioch University
Average faculty salaries for institutions of higher education in Ohio, 2000-01 ★3722★

Antioch University, Los Angeles
U.S. colleges and universities awarding the most psychology master's degrees to Hispanic Americans ★1799★

Antioch University, McGregor
Average faculty salaries for institutions of higher education in Ohio, 2000-01 ★3722★
U.S. institutions with the lowest paid full professors, 2001 ★3979★

Antique dealer
Most desirable jobs in the arts ★2277★

Antone, R.S.M.; Sister M. Therese
Top pay and benefits for the chief executive and top paid employees at Salve Regina University ★3489★

...Any Advice?
Most notable nonfiction books for reluctant young adult readers, 2001 ★323★

AOL Time Warner
Business Week's best performing companies with the highest 3-year earnings growth ★416★
Business Week's best performing companies with the highest 3-year shareholder returns ★418★
Top office equipment and computers companies in Standard & Poor's 500, 2001 ★551★
Web sites where internet users spend the most time ★2609★

Apache
Best performing companies in Standard & Poor's 500, 2001 ★382★
Fortune's highest ranked mining and crude oil companies, 2000 ★477★
Top fuel companies in Standard & Poor's 500, 2001 ★541★

Apelian; Diran
Top pay and benefits for the chief executive and top paid employees at Worcester Polytechnic Institute ★3636★

Aperture Foundation
Most selective internships in the U.S., 2001 ★2610★

Apidologie
Agriculture journals by citation impact, 1995-99 ★53★
Agriculture journals by citation impact, 1999 ★54★

Apopka High School
Outstanding secondary schools in Orlando, Florida ★4200★

"Apoptosis in the pathogenesis and treatment of disease"
Institute for Scientific Information's most cited papers, 1990-98 ★4282★

Appalachian State University
State appropriations for North Carolina's institutions of higher education, 2000-01 ★1286★
U.S. News & World Report's best undergraduate fees among southern regional universities by discount tuition, 2000 ★1429★
U.S. News & World Report's southern regional universities with the best academic reputation scores, 2000-01 ★1433★
U.S. News & World Report's southern regional universities with the highest freshmen retention rates, 2000-01 ★1437★
U.S. News & World Report's southern regional universities with the highest graduation rates, 2000-01 ★1438★
U.S. News & World Report's southern regional universities with the highest percentage of full-time faculty, 2000-01 ★1440★
U.S. News & World Report's southern regional universities with the lowest acceptance rates, 2000-01 ★1442★
U.S. News & World Report's top public southern regional universities, 2000-01 ★1443★
U.S. News & World Report's top southern regional universities, 2000-01 ★1444★
U.S. master's institutions with the largest number of students studying abroad, 1998-99 ★2513★
Average faculty salaries for institutions of higher education in North Carolina, 2000-01 ★3720★

Appelbaum; Frederick R.
Most-cited researchers in oncology, 1981-1998 ★2877★

Apple Computer
Fortune's highest ranked computers and office equipment companies, 2000 ★456★
Most selective internships in the U.S., 2001 ★2610★

Apple Valley High School
Outstanding secondary schools in Minneapolis-St. Paul, Minnesota-Wisconsin ★4181★

Applebee's International
Top recruiters for marketing jobs for 2000-01 master's degree recipients ★672★
Top recruiters for health jobs for 2000-01 bachelor's degree recipients ★2541★
Top recruiters for hospitality/hotel/restaurant management jobs for 2000-01 bachelor's degree recipients ★2558★

Applera
Fortune's highest ranked scientific, photo and control equipment companies, 2000 ★493★

Appleton; James R.
Top pay and benefits for the chief executive and top paid employees at the University of Redlands ★3558★

Appleton, WI
U.S. cities with the lowest rate of violent crime ★3088★

Appliance repairer
'Blue-collar' jobs considered the least physically demanding ★2241★
Jobs with the best stress scores ★2252★

Applications in Soil Ecology
Soil science journals by citation impact, 1999 ★190★

Applied Materials
Best performing companies in Standard & Poor's 500, 2001 ★382★
Fortune's highest ranked scientific, photo and control equipment companies, 2000 ★493★
Top manufacturing companies in Standard & Poor's 500, 2001 ★548★

Applied mathematics
Gender breakdown of mathematics doctorate recipients, by subfield, 1999 ★1938★
Mathematics doctorates awarded at U.S. colleges and universities, by subfield, 1999 ★1951★

Applied Micro Circuits
Business Week's best companies in terms of share-price gain ★409★
Business Week's best performing companies with the highest 1-year sales performance ★414★
Business Week's best performing companies with the highest 3-year shareholder returns ★418★
Business Week's best performing companies with the lowest net margin, 2000 ★425★

Applied Optics
Optics journals with the greatest impact measure, 1981-98 ★2909★

Applied Physics B: Lasers and Optics
Optics journals with the greatest impact measure, 1994-98 ★2910★

Applied Psycholinguistics
  Language and linguistics journals with the greatest impact measure, 1981-98 ★2731★
Applied research
  Overall median salary for full-time chemists with a bachelor's degree, by work function, 2000 ★790★
  Overall median salary for full-time chemists with a doctoral degree, by work function, 2000 ★803★
  Overall median salary for full-time chemists with a master's degree, by work function, 2000 ★804★
Applied Spectroscopy Reviews
  Spectroscopy journals by citation impact, 1981-99 ★4359★
Applied Technology Center
  All-USA Teacher Teams, Third Team, 2000 ★4401★
Appraisal Journal
  Highly cited real estate journals, 1990 to 1995 ★3090★
The Apprenticeship of Duddy Kravitz
  Canada's best fiction selections of the 20th century ★233★
Aquatic Toxicology
  Marine and freshwater biology journals with the greatest impact measure, 1981-98 ★196★
  Marine and freshwater biology journals with the greatest impact measure, 1994-98 ★197★
Aquinas College
  Highest undergraduate tuition and fees at colleges and universities in Michigan ★1518★
  Average faculty salaries for institutions of higher education in Michigan, 2000-01 ★3709★
Arabic
  Gender breakdown of language and literature doctorate recipients, by subfield, 1999 ★1937★
  Language and literature doctorates awarded at U.S. colleges and universities, by subfield, 1999 ★1949★
Aram; Dorothy
  Top pay and benefits for the chief executive and top paid employees at Emerson College ★3287★
Aramark
  Fortune's highest ranked outsourcing services companies, 2000 ★483★
  Largest private companies, 2000 ★523★
ARAMARK Educational Resources
  Top recruiters for social work jobs for 2000-01 bachelor's degree recipients ★4342★
  Top recruiters for sociology jobs for 2000-01 bachelor's degree recipients ★4347★
Arapahoe Community College
  Lowest undergraduate tuition and fees at colleges and universities in Colorado ★1489★
Arapahoe High School
  Outstanding secondary schools in Denver, Colorado ★4124★
Arcadia Publishing
  Small publishers with the highest sales growth between 1997 and 1999 ★3073★
Arcadia University
  Average faculty salaries for institutions of higher education in Pennsylvania, 2000-01 ★3725★
Archaeological Method and Theory: An Encyclopedia
  Selected reference books in the field of archaeology, 2000 ★374★

Archangel
  Library Journal's best fiction audiobooks, 2000 ★241★
Archbishop Blenk High School
  Outstanding secondary schools in New Orleans, Louisiana ★4190★
Archbishop Chapelle High School
  Outstanding secondary schools in New Orleans, Louisiana ★4190★
Archbishop Hoban High School
  Outstanding secondary schools in Akron, Ohio ★4078★
Archbishop Molloy High School
  Outstanding Catholic high schools in Metro New York ★4076★
Archbishop Quigley Preparatory Seminary
  Outstanding Catholic high schools in Metro Chicago ★4074★
Archbishop Spalding High School
  Outstanding secondary schools in Baltimore, Maryland ★4092★
Archeologist
  Jobs with the lowest unemployment ★2258★
  Most desirable social sciences jobs ★2280★
Archeology
  Gender breakdown of humanities doctorate recipients, by subfield, 1999 ★1936★
  Humanities doctorates awarded at U.S. colleges and universities, by subfield, 1999 ★1946★
Archer Daniels Midland
  Fortune's highest ranked food production companies, 2000 ★464★
Archibald; Douglas
  Top pay and benefits for the chief executive and top paid employees at Colby College ★3241★
Architect
  Most desirable jobs in the arts ★2277★
Architectural drafter
  Most desirable jobs in the arts ★2277★
Architectural environmental design
  Gender breakdown of professional doctorate recipients, by subfield, 1999 ★1940★
  Professional doctorates awarded at U.S. colleges and universities, by subfield, 1999 ★2033★
Archives of Dermatology
  Number of citations and papers for original articles appearing in dermatology journals, 1981 to 1996 ★1873★
  Number of citations and papers in dermatology journals, 1981 to 1996 ★1874★
Archives of Dermatology Research
  Number of citations and papers for original articles appearing in dermatology journals, 1981 to 1996 ★1873★
  Number of citations and papers in dermatology journals, 1981 to 1996 ★1874★
Archives of General Psychiatry
  Psychiatry journals by citation impact, 1981-98 ★3054★
  Psychiatry journals by citation impact, 1995-98 ★3055★
  Psychiatry journals by citation impact, 1998 ★3056★
  Psychiatry journals by impact factor, 1981 to 1998 ★3057★
  Psychiatry journals by impact factor, 1994 to 1998 ★3058★
  Top science journals by impact factor ★4281★
  Most-cited social sciences journals, 1981-97 ★4340★

Archives of General Psychology
  Social sciences journals with the greatest impact measure, 1981-97 ★4341★
Archives of Insect Biochemistry
  Entomology journals by citation impact, 1981-98 ★2453★
  Entomology journals by citation impact, 1994-98 ★2454★
  Entomology journals by citation impact, 1998 ★2455★
Archives of Surgery
  Surgery journals with the greatest impact measure, 1981-98 ★2814★
  Surgery journals with the greatest impact measure, 1994-98 ★2815★
Archivists, curators, and conservators
  Projected employment growth for selected occupations that require advanced education, 1998-2008 ★2318★
Arcola Intermediate School
  Outstanding secondary schools in Philadelphia, Pennsylvania-New Jersey ★4202★
Ardolf, O.S.B.; Sister Miriam
  Top pay and benefits for the chief executive and top paid employees at College of Saint Benedict ★3245★
Area studies
  Gender breakdown of social sciences doctorate recipients, by subfield, 1999 ★1942★
  Social sciences doctorates awarded at U.S. colleges and universities, by subfield, 1999 ★2044★
Arends; Stewart
  Top pay and benefits for the chief executive and top paid employees at Madonna University ★3386★
Arendt; Hannah
  Best U.S. works of journalism in the 20th century ★2769★
Argentina
  Countries of origin for non-U.S. citizens awarded doctorates at U.S. colleges and universities, 1999 ★1901★
  Countries with the highest spending per student on higher education, 1997 ★2488★
  Percentage of internet usage for selected countries ★2599★
Aria of the Sea
  Most notable fiction books for young adults, 2001 ★322★
Arick; Bruce E.
  Top pay and benefits for the chief executive and top paid employees at Butler University ★3214★
Arinori; Mori
  Japan's ten great educators ★2234★
Arizona
  Mean composite ACT scores by state, 2000 ★895★
  Mean math SAT scores by state, 2000 ★900★
  Mean verbal SAT scores by state, 2000 ★903★
  Average class size at colleges and universities in the U.S., by state ★1064★
  Total doctorate recipients by state, 1999 ★2054★
  Hispanic American enrollment at Hispanic-serving institutions of higher education, by state, 1997 ★2547★
  State grades for affordability of higher education for minority students, 2000 ★2883★
  State grades for benefits state receives for educating its minority students, 2000 ★2884★

State grades for completion of higher education by minority students, 2000 ★2885★
State grades for participation of minority students in higher education, 2000 ★2886★
State grades for preparing minority students for higher education, 2000 ★2887★
States with the lowest per-pupil expenditures ★3998★
States with the highest average enrollment in public elementary schools ★4032★
States with the most charter schools ★4048★
States with the lowest percentage of high school freshmen enrolling in college within four years ★4267★

Arizona, Eller School MBA Program; University of
U.S. News & World Report's undergraduate business programs with the best management information systems departments, 2000-01 ★568★
Academics' choices for best graduate management information systems programs, 2001 ★585★

Arizona State University
All-USA College Academic Second Team, 2001 ★3★
Colleges with the highest number of freshman Merit Scholars, 2000 ★5★
U.S. universities publishing the most papers in the field of archaeology, 1994-98 ★66★
U.S. colleges and universities with the most alumni in the LPGA ★148★
Top business schools for within-discipline research performance in production/operations management, 1986-1998 ★648★
Institutions with the most full-time Hispanic American faculty ★923★
U.S. colleges and universities with the most full-time Hispanic American faculty ★925★
U.S. colleges and universities where students study the least ★1002★
U.S. colleges and universities with the least accessible instructors ★1036★
U.S. colleges and universities with the most upper level courses taught by TAs ★1040★
Largest degree-granting colleges and universities, by enrollment ★1068★
State appropriations for Arizona's institutions of higher education, 2000-01 ★1256★
Universities with the most-cited scholars in *Justice Quarterly* ★1652★
Total baccalaureate business management and administrative services degrees awarded to Native Americans from U.S. colleges and universities, 1997-98 ★1686★
Total baccalaureate communications degrees awarded to Hispanic Americans from U.S. colleges and universities, 1997-98 ★1689★
Total baccalaureate communications degrees awarded to Native Americans from U.S. colleges and universities, 1997-98 ★1690★
Total baccalaureate degrees awarded to Native Americans from U.S. colleges and universities, 1997-98 ★1710★
Total baccalaureate education degrees awarded to Hispanic Americans from U.S. colleges and universities, 1997-98 ★1713★
Total baccalaureate social sciences and history degrees awarded to Native Americans from U.S. colleges and universities, 1997-98 ★1744★
U.S. colleges and universities awarding the most business management and administrative services master's degrees to Native Americans ★1762★
U.S. colleges and universities awarding the most English language/literature/letters master's degrees to Hispanic Americans ★1775★
U.S. colleges and universities awarding the most master's degrees to Hispanic Americans ★1787★
U.S. colleges and universities awarding the most master's degrees to Native Americans ★1789★
U.S. colleges and universities awarding the most doctoral degrees to African Americans from 1995 to 1999 ★2091★
U.S. colleges and universities awarding the most doctorate degrees to Hispanic Americans ★2097★
U.S. colleges and universities awarding the most education doctorate degrees to Hispanic Americans ★2110★
Top geography research-doctorate programs as evaluated by the National Research Council ★2520★
U.S. universities with the greatest impact in astrophysics, 1994-98 ★2979★
Average faculty salaries for institutions of higher education in Arizona, 2000-01 ★3690★

Arizona State University, East
U.S. institutions awarding the most baccalaureate degrees to Hispanic Americans in agribusiness and production, 1998 ★1817★
Average faculty salaries for institutions of higher education in Arizona, 2000-01 ★3690★

Arizona State University, West
Average faculty salaries for institutions of higher education in Arizona, 2000-01 ★3690★

Arizona; University of
All-USA College Academic Third Team, 2001 ★4★
Most effective anthropology research-doctorate programs as evaluated by the National Research Council ★61★
Top anthropology research-doctorate programs as evaluated by the National Research Council ★62★
U.S. universities publishing the most papers in the field of archaeology, 1994-98 ★66★
U.S. colleges and universities with the most alumni in the LPGA ★148★
Top business schools for within-discipline research performance in marketing, 1986-1998 ★671★
Top business schools for within-discipline research performance in management information systems, 1986-1998 ★675★
U.S. college campuses with more than 5,000 students reporting murders or manslaughters, 1998 ★729★
U.S. colleges and universities reporting the most drug related arrests, 1998 ★731★
Institutions with the most full-time Hispanic American faculty ★923★
U.S. colleges and universities with the most full-time Hispanic American faculty ★925★
U.S. colleges and universities where intramural sports are popular ★997★
U.S. colleges and universities where the general student body puts a strong emphasis on athletic events ★1007★
State appropriations for Arizona's institutions of higher education, 2000-01 ★1256★
Highest undergraduate tuition and fees at colleges and universities in Arizona ★1482★
Total baccalaureate biology/life sciences degrees awarded to Hispanic Americans from U.S. colleges and universities, 1997-98 ★1681★
Total baccalaureate biology/life sciences degrees awarded to Native Americans from U.S. colleges and universities, 1997-98 ★1682★
Total baccalaureate education degrees awarded to Hispanic Americans from U.S. colleges and universities, 1997-98 ★1713★
Total baccalaureate physical sciences degrees awarded to Hispanic Americans from U.S. colleges and universities, 1997-98 ★1735★
Total baccalaureate social sciences and history degrees awarded to Native Americans from U.S. colleges and universities, 1997-98 ★1744★
Total ethnic/cultural studies master's degrees awarded to minorities from U.S. colleges and universities, 1997-98 ★1748★
U.S. colleges and universities awarding the most health professions and related sciences master's degrees to Native Americans ★1780★
U.S. colleges and universities awarding the most master's degrees to Native Americans ★1789★
U.S. institutions awarding the most baccalaureate degrees to Hispanic Americans in agricultural sciences, 1998 ★1818★
U.S. colleges and universities awarding the most first professional degrees to Native Americans ★1846★
U.S. colleges and universities awarding the most health professions and related sciences first professional degrees to Native Americans ★1851★
U.S. colleges and universities awarding the most doctoral degrees to American Indians and Alaskan Natives from 1995 to 1999 ★2092★
U.S. colleges and universities awarding the most education doctorate degrees to Asian Americans ★2109★
U.S. universities publishing the most papers in the field of civil engineering, 1994-98 ★2348★
U.S. universities publishing the most papers in the field of civil engineering, 1995-99 ★2349★
U.S. universities with the greatest impact in civil engineering, 1995-99 ★2350★
U.S. research institutions with the largest number of students studying abroad, 1998-99 ★2514★
Library and information science programs with the most journal articles per capita, 1993-1998 ★2714★
Most effective linguistics research-doctorate programs as evaluated by the National Research Council ★2732★
Top linguistics research-doctorate programs as evaluated by the National Research Council ★2733★
Institutions with the most prolific communication studies researchers ★2749★
Most effective philosophy research-doctorate programs as evaluated by the National Research Council ★2945★
Top philosophy research-doctorate programs as evaluated by the National Research Council ★2947★
U.S. universities publishing the most papers in the field of astrophysics, 1995-99 ★2978★
Most effective astrophysics and astronomy research-doctorate programs as evaluated by the National Research Council ★3006★
Top astrophysics and astronomy research-doctorate programs as evaluated by the National Research Council ★3014★

ARIZONA

Average faculty salaries for institutions of higher education in Arizona, 2000-01 ★3690★

Top sociology research-doctorate programs as evaluated by the National Research Council ★4354★

Academics' choices for best higher education administration graduate programs, 2001 ★4384★

Arizona Western College
Lowest undergraduate tuition and fees at colleges and universities in Arizona ★1483★

Average faculty salaries for institutions of higher education without academic ranks in Arizona, 2000-01 ★3741★

Arkansas
Mean composite ACT scores by state, 2000 ★895★

Mean math SAT scores by state, 2000 ★900★

Mean verbal SAT scores by state, 2000 ★903★

Total doctorate recipients by state, 1999 ★2054★

State grades for affordability of higher education for minority students, 2000 ★2883★

State grades for benefits state receives for educating its minority students, 2000 ★2884★

State grades for completion of higher education by minority students, 2000 ★2885★

State grades for participation of minority students in higher education, 2000 ★2886★

State grades for preparing minority students for higher education, 2000 ★2887★

States expelling the highest ratio of students for violating the Gun-Free Schools Act, 1998-99 ★3993★

States with the lowest per-pupil expenditures ★3998★

States with the smallest average class size ★4072★

U.S. states with the highest percentage of births to teenagers who were already mothers ★4433★

Arkansas Baptist College
U.S. colleges and universities with the highest percentage of African Americans enrolled, 1997 ★222★

Lowest undergraduate tuition and fees at private nonprofit, 4-year or above colleges and universities ★1464★

Private 4-year institutions with the lowest tuition, 2000-01 ★1468★

Arkansas Best
Fortune's highest ranked trucking companies, 2000 ★503★

Arkansas, Fayetteville; University of
Division I NCAA colleges with that graduated less than 20% of their African American male athletes, 1990-91 to 1993-94 ★928★

Division I NCAA colleges with that graduated none of their African American male basketball players, 1990-91 to 1993-94 ★930★

Division I NCAA colleges with the lowest graduation rates for football players, 1990-91 to 1993-94 ★938★

U.S. colleges and universities that devote the least course time to discussion ★989★

U.S. colleges and universities with the most upper level courses taught by TAs ★1040★

U.S. colleges and universities awarding the most doctoral degrees to American Indians and Alaskan Natives from 1995 to 1999 ★2092★

U.S. colleges and universities awarding the most doctorate degrees to Native Americans ★2099★

Arkansas, Little Rock; University of
Division I NCAA colleges with that graduated less than 20% of their African American male athletes, 1990-91 to 1993-94 ★928★

Division I NCAA colleges with the lowest graduation rates for female athletes, 1990-91 to 1993-94 ★936★

Division I NCAA colleges with the lowest graduation rates for male athletes, 1990-91 to 1993-94 ★939★

U.S. colleges and universities awarding the most mathematics master's degrees to African Americans ★1790★

Arkansas, Monticello; University of
Division II NCAA colleges with the 0% graduation rates for men's basketball players, 1993-94 ★941★

Division II NCAA colleges with the lowest graduation rates for all sports, 1993-94 ★947★

Division II NCAA colleges with the lowest graduation rates for football players, 1993-94 ★948★

Arkansas, Phillips Community College; University of
Lowest undergraduate tuition and fees at colleges and universities in Arkansas ★1485★

Arkansas, Pine Bluff; University of
Colleges offering the Thurgood Marshall Scholarship Fund ★221★

U.S. institutions awarding the most baccalaureate degrees to African Americans in agricultural sciences, 1998 ★1814★

U.S. institutions awarding the most baccalaureate degrees to minorities in agricultural sciences, 1998 ★1820★

Average faculty salaries for institutions of higher education in Arkansas, 2000-01 ★3691★

Arkansas State University
State appropriations for Arkansas's institutions of higher education, 2000-01 ★1257★

Average faculty salaries for institutions of higher education in Arkansas, 2000-01 ★3691★

Arkansas State University, Beebe Branch
Lowest undergraduate tuition and fees at colleges and universities in Arkansas ★1485★

Arkansas State University, Mountain Home
Lowest undergraduate tuition and fees at colleges and universities in Arkansas ★1485★

Arkansas System; University of
State appropriations for Arkansas's institutions of higher education, 2000-01 ★1257★

Arkansas Tech University
State appropriations for Arkansas's institutions of higher education, 2000-01 ★1257★

Average faculty salaries for institutions of higher education in Arkansas, 2000-01 ★3691★

Arkansas; University of
Division I all-time winningest college teams ★128★

Highest undergraduate tuition and fees at colleges and universities in Arkansas ★1484★

Average faculty salaries for institutions of higher education in Arkansas, 2000-01 ★3691★

Arlacchi; P.
Most cited authors in the journal *Crime, Law, and Social Change*, 1990 to 1995 ★1618★

Arlington Baptist College
Lowest undergraduate tuition and fees at private nonprofit, 4-year or above colleges and universities ★1464★

Arlington Heights High School, District 214
Illinois school districts with the most average years of teacher experience ★4012★

Arlington Heights Township 214
Illinois high school districts with the highest teacher salaries, 1999 ★3985★

Arlington, VA
Counties with the highest per capita income ★2561★

Armacost; Peter H.
Top pay and benefits for the chief executive and top paid employees at Eckerd College ★3282★

Armitage; Jacquelyn
Top pay and benefits for the chief executive and top paid employees at Emmanuel College in Massachusetts ★3288★

Armor; John N.
American Chemical Society 2001 award winners (Group 1) ★751★

Armstrong Atlantic State University
State appropriations for Georgia's institutions of higher education, 2000-01 ★1263★

Average faculty salaries for institutions of higher education in Georgia, 2000-01 ★3697★

Armstrong Holdings
Fortune's highest ranked building materials and glass companies, 2000 ★451★

Armstrong; Louis
Most influential African American entertainers ★77★

Armstrong Middle School
Outstanding secondary schools in Dallas, Texas ★4120★

Arnas; A. Ozer
Top pay and benefits for the chief executive and top paid employees at Wheeling Jesuit University ★3622★

Arnold; Donald
Top pay and benefits for the chief executive and top paid employees at Union College in New York ★3585★

Arnold; George F.
Top pay and benefits for the chief executive and top paid employees at Monmouth College in Illinois ★3405★

Arnold; J. David
Top pay and benefits for the chief executive and top paid employees at Saint John Fisher College in New York ★3472★

Arnold; Jasper
Top pay and benefits for the chief executive and top paid employees at Our Lady of the Lake University ★3434★

Arnold Junior High School
Outstanding secondary schools in Houston, Texas ★4150★

Arnold; Lisa
All-USA Teacher Teams, First Team, 2000 ★4399★

Arnott; David H.
Top pay and benefits for the chief executive and top paid employees at Dallas Baptist University ★3262★

Arons; Michael
Top pay and benefits for the chief executive and top paid employees at Long Island University ★3378★

Aronson; Marc
  Outstanding children's nonfiction books, 2000 ★330★
Arrington; Charles A.
  Top pay and benefits for the chief executive and top paid employees at Furman University ★3300★
Arrington; Frances
  Booklist's best first novels for youths ★309★
Arrow; Dennis
  Top pay and benefits for the chief executive and top paid employees at Oklahoma City University ★3431★
Arrow Electronics
  Fortune's highest ranked wholesalers, 2000 ★505★
Arslanian; Artin
  Top pay and benefits for the chief executive and top paid employees at Marist College ★3390★
Art and architecture
  Average costs for Academic Search titles by subject, 2001 ★2918★
  Periodical prices by LC subject, 2001 ★2925★
Art education
  Gender breakdown of teaching fields doctorate recipients, by subfield, 1999 ★1943★
  Teaching fields doctorates awarded at U.S. colleges and universities, by subfield, 1999 ★2046★
Art history
  Number of Advanced Placement Exams taken by African Americans, by subject, 2000 ★30★
  Number of Advanced Placement Exams taken by Asian Americans, by subject, 2000 ★31★
  Number of Advanced Placement Exams taken by Hispanic Americans, by subject, 2000 ★32★
  Percentage of female doctorate recipients at U.S. colleges and universities, by subfield, 1999 ★1988★
Art history/criticism/conservation
  Gender breakdown of humanities doctorate recipients, by subfield, 1999 ★1936★
  Humanities doctorates awarded at U.S. colleges and universities, by subfield, 1999 ★1946★
Art Institute of Atlanta
  U.S. colleges and universities with the lowest percentage of African Americans enrolled, 1997 ★223★
  Highest undergraduate tuition and fees at colleges and universities in Georgia ★1496★
Art Institute of Colorado
  Highest undergraduate tuition and fees at colleges and universities in Colorado ★1488★
The Art of Keeping Cool
  Booklist's most recommended historical fiction for youths, 2001 ★314★
  Most notable books for older readers, 2001 ★318★
The Art of Optical Illusions
  Most notable nonfiction books for reluctant young adult readers, 2001 ★323★
Art Technology Group
  Fast-growing information technology companies, 2000 ★444★
  Information technology companies giving the best returns, 2000 ★522★
Arteriosclerosis, Thrombosis and Vascular Biology
  Hematology journals with the greatest impact measure, 1994-98 ★2809★

Arthur Andersen
  Largest private companies, 2000 ★523★
Arthur Andersen LLP
  Top recruiters for accounting jobs for 2000-01 bachelor's degree recipients ★580★
  Top recruiters for finance/banking jobs for 2000-01 bachelor's degree recipients ★582★
  Top recruiters for accounting jobs for 2000-01 master's degree recipients ★661★
  Top recruiters for finance/banking jobs for 2000-01 master's degree recipients ★664★
  Top recruiters for marketing jobs for 2000-01 master's degree recipients ★672★
  Top recruiters for telecommunications jobs for 2000-01 master's degree recipients ★676★
  Top recruiters for telecommunications jobs for 2000-01 bachelor's degree recipients ★686★
  Top employers of college graduates, 2001 ★2325★
  Top recruiters for systems engineer jobs for 2000-01 bachelor's degree recipients ★2336★
  Top recruiters for systems engineer jobs for 2000-01 master's degree recipients ★2371★
  Top recruiters for computer engineering jobs for 2000-01 master's degree recipients ★2400★
  Top recruiters for health jobs for 2000-01 bachelor's degree recipients ★2541★
  Top recruiters for health jobs for 2000-01 master's degree recipients ★2545★
  Top recruiters for information technology (MIS) jobs for 2000-01 bachelor's degree recipients ★2738★
  Top recruiters for information technology (MIS) jobs for 2000-01 master's degree recipients ★2739★
  Top recruiters for math/actuarial science jobs for 2000-01 bachelor's degree recipients ★2771★
  Top recruiters for psychology jobs for 2000-01 bachelor's degree recipients ★3063★
Arthur D. Little School of Management
  U.S. colleges and universities awarding the most business management and administrative services master's degrees to Hispanic Americans ★1761★
Artificial Intelligence
  Artificial intelligence journals by citation impact, 1981-99 ★94★
  Artificial intelligence journals by citation impact, 1995-99 ★95★
  Artificial intelligence journals with the greatest impact measure, 1981-98 ★97★
  Artificial intelligence journals with the greatest impact measure, 1994-98 ★98★
  Artificial intelligence journals with the greatest impact measure, 1998 ★99★
  Journals and proceedings with the most citations (Class 2) ★2568★
Artist (commercial)
  Most desirable jobs in communications ★2271★
Artist (fine art)
  Most desirable jobs in the arts ★2277★
Artists and commercial artists
  Occupations with the highest number of self-employed workers, 1998 ★2311★
  Projected employment growth for selected occupations that require a bachelor's degree or more, 1998-2008 ★2317★
Arts/crafts/collectibles
  Subject areas with the highest library expenditures/circulation ★306★

Arts and humanities
  Expected majors for incoming freshmen, 2000 ★1050★
  Median age at conferral of doctoral degree from U.S. universities, by discipline, 1999 ★1952★
Arts; University of the
  Average faculty salaries for institutions of higher education in Pennsylvania, 2000-01 ★3725★
ArtStar.com
  Library Journal's best free reference websites, 2000 ★367★
Arvida Middle School
  Outstanding secondary schools in Miami, Florida ★4178★
Arvin Meritor
  Fortune's highest ranked motor vehicle parts companies, 2000 ★480★
As for Me and My House
  Canada's best fiction selections of the 20th century ★233★
Asbury College
  U.S. News & World Report's southern regional liberal arts colleges with the highest academic reputation scores, 2000-01 ★1369★
  U.S. News & World Report's southern regional liberal arts colleges with the highest acceptance rates, 2000-01 ★1370★
  U.S. News & World Report's southern regional liberal arts colleges with the highest alumni giving rates, 2000-01 ★1371★
  U.S. News & World Report's southern regional liberal arts colleges with the highest freshmen retention rates, 2000-01 ★1372★
  U.S. News & World Report's southern regional liberal arts colleges with the highest graduation rates, 2000-01 ★1373★
  U.S. News & World Report's southern regional liberal arts colleges with the highest proportion of freshmen in the top 25% of their high school class, 2000-01 ★1376★
  U.S. News & World Report's top southern regional liberal arts colleges, 2000-01 ★1379★
  Highest undergraduate tuition and fees at colleges and universities in Kentucky ★1508★
Asbury; Jacqueline W.
  Top pay and benefits for the chief executive and top paid employees at Lynchburg College ★3384★
Aschauer; D.
  Top full professor economists at elite liberal arts colleges, 1975-94 ★2175★
Asensio; Anne
  European business moguls considered the best innovators ★442★
Ash; James L.
  Top pay and benefits for the chief executive and top paid employees at Whittier College ★3624★
Ashbery; John
  Top pay and benefits for the chief executive and top paid employees at Bard College ★3190★
Ashbury College
  Average faculty salaries for institutions of higher education in Kentucky, 2000-01 ★3704★
Ashbury Theological Seminary
  Average faculty salaries for institutions of higher education in Kentucky, 2000-01 ★3704★

Asheville-Buncombe Tech Community College
Average faculty salaries for institutions of higher education without academic ranks in North Carolina, 2000-01 ★3761★

Asheville, NC
Best small towns to live in ★3085★

Ashland Community College
Lowest undergraduate tuition and fees at colleges and universities in Kentucky ★1509★

Ashland High School
Outstanding suburban public high schools in Metro Boston ★4255★

Ashland, OR
America's most wired towns, 2001 ★2575★
Best small towns to live in ★3085★

Ashley; Jeffrey
Top pay and benefits for the chief executive and top paid employees at Spalding University ★3506★

Ashman; H. Lowell
Top pay and benefits for the chief executive and top paid employees at Lenoir-Rhyne College ★3369★

Ashton-Savage; Audrey
Top pay and benefits for the chief executive and top paid employees at Emmanuel College in Massachusetts ★3288★

Asia
Region of origin of foreign students enrolled in U.S. institutions of higher education, 1998-99 ★2502★
World regions hosting U.S. students studying abroad, 1998-99 ★2515★

Asia Source
Top women-owned companies ★4460★

Asian American
ACT composite scores, by race/ethnicity, 2000 ★871★
Graduation rates for female basketball players at Division II NCAA colleges, 1993-94 ★955★
Graduation rates for female students at Division II NCAA colleges, 1993-94 ★957★
Graduation rates for football players at Division II NCAA colleges, 1993-94 ★959★
Graduation rates for male basketball players at Division II NCAA colleges, 1993-94 ★961★
Graduation rates for male students at Division II NCAA colleges, 1993-94 ★963★
Racial and ethnic background of incoming freshmen, 2000 ★1058★
Number of U.S. citizen/permanent resident doctorate recipients in all fields at U.S. colleges and universities, by race/ethnicity, 1999 ★1978★
Number of U.S. citizen/permanent resident doctorate recipients in education at U.S. colleges and universities, by race/ethnicity, 1999 ★1979★
Number of U.S. citizen/permanent resident doctorate recipients in engineering at U.S. colleges and universities, by race/ethnicity, 1999 ★1980★
Number of U.S. citizen/permanent resident doctorate recipients in humanities at U.S. colleges and universities, by race/ethnicity, 1999 ★1981★
Number of U.S. citizen/permanent resident doctorate recipients in life sciences at U.S. colleges and universities, by race/ethnicity, 1999 ★1982★
Number of U.S. citizen/permanent resident doctorate recipients in physical sciences, mathematics, and computer sciences at U.S. colleges and universities, by race/ethnicity, 1999 ★1983★
Number of U.S. citizen/permanent resident doctorate recipients in professional/other fields at U.S. colleges and universities, by race/ethnicity, 1999 ★1984★
Number of U.S. citizen/permanent resident doctorate recipients in social sciences at U.S. colleges and universities, by race/ethnicity, 1999 ★1985★
Percentage of doctoral degree recipients at U.S. universities, by race/ethnicity, 1999 ★1987★
Percentage of minority doctorate recipients in the U.S., 1999 ★1990★
Percentage of minority doctorate recipients in the U.S., by gender, 1999 ★1992★
Ethnic breakdown of executives and managers in Silicon Valley firms, 1997 ★2300★
Race/ethnicity profile of U.S. students studying abroad, 1998-99 ★2509★
Bachelor's degrees granted in journalism and mass communications programs, by race/ethnicity, 1999 ★2742★
Bachelor's enrollments in journalism and mass communications programs, by race/ethnicity, 1999 ★2744★
Doctoral degrees granted in journalism and mass communications programs, by race/ethnicity, 1999 ★2759★
Doctoral enrollments in journalism and mass communications programs, by race/ethnicity, 1999 ★2761★
Master's degrees granted in journalism and mass communications programs, by race/ethnicity, 1999 ★2766★
Master's enrollments in journalism and mass communications programs, by race/ethnicity, 1999 ★2768★
National Society of Fund-Raising Executives, by race/ethnicity ★2942★
Physics faculty, by race/ethnicity, 2000 ★2965★
Students participating in gifted and talented programs, by race ethnicity, 1997 ★4050★
Percentage of 18- to 24-year olds completing high school, by race, 1998 ★4273★

Asian American Experience On File Online
Library Journal's best reference databases and discs, 2000 ★369★

Asian American/Pacific Islander
Graduation rates for female basketball players at Division I NCAA colleges, by race/ethnicity ★954★
Graduation rates for female students and athletes at Division I NCAA colleges, by race/ethnicity ★956★
Graduation rates for football players at Division I NCAA colleges, by race/ethnicity ★958★
Graduation rates for male basketball players at Division I NCAA colleges, by race/ethnicity ★960★
Graduation rates for male students and athletes at Division I NCAA colleges, by race/ethnicity ★962★
Age grouping of doctorate recipients, by race/ethnicity, 1999 ★1885★
Comparison data of internet use, by race/ethnicity for 1998 and 2000 ★2582★
Internet use, by race/ethnicity and gender breakdown, 2000 ★2588★
U.S. medical school enrollment of U.S. citizens by racial/ethnic category, 1999-2000 ★2863★

Asian Institute of Management, Philippines
Asiaweek's best M.B.A. programs ★590★

Asian Institute of Technology, Thailand
Asiaweek's best M.B.A. programs ★590★

Asker; J.
Most cited authors in the journal *Social Justice*, 1990 to 1995 ★1631★

Askew; Thomas
Top pay and benefits for the chief executive and top paid employees at Gordon College in Massachusetts ★3312★

Aslanian; Paul J.
Top pay and benefits for the chief executive and top paid employees at Swarthmore College ★3514★

ASM Lithography Holding
Business Week's best companies in the Netherlands ★410★

Asnuntuck Community-Technical College
Lowest undergraduate tuition and fees at colleges and universities in Connecticut ★1491★

ASSETS School
Outstanding secondary schools in Honolulu, Hawaii ★4149★

Assicurazioni Generali
Business Week's best companies in Italy ★397★

Assistant athletics director
African American college athletics administrators and staff, by gender, 1999-2000 ★117★
College athletics administrators and staff, by gender, 1999-2000 ★121★
Minority college athletics administrators and staff, by gender, 1999-2000 ★132★

Assistant director of athletics
Percentage of African American athletic administrators at NCAA Division I institutions, 1999 ★138★
Percentage of African American athletic administrators at NCAA Division II institutions, 1999 ★139★
Percentage of African American athletic administrators at NCAA Division III institutions, 1999 ★140★

Assistant Directors Training Program
Most selective internships in the U.S., 2001 ★2610★

Associate athletics director
African American college athletics senior administrators, by gender, 1999-2000 ★119★
College athletics senior administrators, by gender, 1999-2000 ★123★
Minority college athletics senior administrators, by gender, 1999-2000 ★134★

Associate director of athletics
Percentage of African American athletic administrators at NCAA Division I institutions, 1999 ★138★
Percentage of African American athletic administrators at NCAA Division II institutions, 1999 ★139★
Percentage of African American athletic administrators at NCAA Division III institutions, 1999 ★140★

Associates First Capital
Fortune's highest ranked consumer credit companies, 2000 ★457★

Association of Trial Lawyers of America
Most selective internships in the U.S., 2001 ★2610★

Assumption College
U.S. News & World Report's northern regional universities with the highest average graduation rates, 2000-01 ★1419★

Assumption High School
Outstanding secondary schools in Louisville, Kentucky-Indiana ★4168★

Asteriod Impact
Booklist's best science books for children ★310★
Outstanding books for middle readers, 2000 ★326★

Astor Learning Center
Outstanding secondary schools in Dutchess County, New York ★4126★

Astrazeneca
Business Week's best companies in Britain ★389★

Astro; Richard A.
Top pay and benefits for the chief executive and top paid employees at Drexel University ★3274★

Astronaut
Jobs considered the most competitive ★2245★
Jobs with the worst environment scores ★2260★
Jobs with the worst stress scores ★2265★

Astronomer
Jobs with the lowest unemployment ★2258★
Most desirable jobs in math/science ★2274★

Astronomical Journal
Astronomy and astrophysics journals by citation impact, 1981-99 ★102★
Astronomy and astrophysics journals by citation impact, 1995-99 ★103★
Astronomy and astrophysics journals by citation impact, 1999 ★104★
Astronomy and astrophysics journals by impact factor, 1981 to 1998 ★105★
Astronomy and astrophysics journals by impact factor, 1994 to 1998 ★106★

Astronomy
Gender breakdown of physics and astronomy doctorate recipients, by subfield, 1999 ★1939★
Physics and astronomy doctorates awarded at U.S. colleges and universities, by subfield, 1999 ★1994★
Average costs for Academic Search titles by subject, 2001 ★2918★
Periodical prices by LC subject, 2001 ★2925★
Periodical prices by scientific discipline, 2001 ★2926★
Mean age of first and best contribution of scientists and inventors, by discipline ★3096★

Astronomy & Astrophysics
Astronomy and astrophysics journals by citation impact, 1995-99 ★103★

Astronomy/astrophysics
Major subfields of first-year physics and astronomy graduate students who are foreign citizens planning to receive a Ph.D., 1997-98 ★3004★
Major subfields of first-year physics and astronomy graduate students who are U.S. citizens planning to receive a Ph.D., 1997-98 ★3005★

Astronomy and Astrophysics Review
Astronomy and astrophysics journals by citation impact, 1981-99 ★102★
Astronomy and astrophysics journals by citation impact, 1995-99 ★103★
Astronomy and astrophysics journals by impact factor, 1981 to 1998 ★105★
Astronomy and astrophysics journals by impact factor, 1994 to 1998 ★106★

Astroparticle Physics
Astronomy and astrophysics journals by citation impact, 1999 ★104★

Astrophysical Journal
Astronomy and astrophysics journals by citation impact, 1981-99 ★102★
Astronomy and astrophysics journals by citation impact, 1995-99 ★103★
Astronomy and astrophysics journals by citation impact, 1999 ★104★
Astronomy and astrophysics journals by impact factor, 1981 to 1998 ★105★
Astronomy and astrophysics journals by impact factor, 1994 to 1998 ★106★

Astrophysical Journal Supplement Series
Astronomy and astrophysics journals by citation impact, 1981-99 ★102★
Astronomy and astrophysics journals by citation impact, 1995-99 ★103★
Astronomy and astrophysics journals by citation impact, 1999 ★104★
Astronomy and astrophysics journals by impact factor, 1981 to 1998 ★105★
Astronomy and astrophysics journals by impact factor, 1994 to 1998 ★106★

Astrophysics
Gender breakdown of physics and astronomy doctorate recipients, by subfield, 1999 ★1939★
Physics and astronomy doctorates awarded at U.S. colleges and universities, by subfield, 1999 ★1994★
United States' contribution of papers in the sciences, by field, 1995-99 ★4283★
Australia's contribution of papers in the sciences, by field, 1993-97 ★4292★
Australia's contribution of papers in the sciences, by field, 1995-99 ★4293★
United Kingdom's contribution of papers in the sciences, by field, 1995-99 ★4297★
Austria's contribution of papers in the sciences, by field, 1995-99 ★4299★
Belgium's contribution of papers in the sciences, by field, 1992-96 ★4301★
Belgium's contribution of papers in the sciences, by field, 1995-99 ★4302★
Denmark's contribution of papers in the sciences, by field, 1994-98 ★4306★
Denmark's contribution of papers in the sciences, by field, 1995-99 ★4307★
England's contribution of papers in the sciences, by field, 1994-98 ★4308★
Finland's contribution of papers in the sciences by field, 1992-96 ★4309★
Finland's contribution of papers in the sciences, by field, 1995-99 ★4310★
France's contribution of papers in the sciences, by field, 1995-99 ★4311★
Germany's contribution of papers in the sciences, by field, 1995-99 ★4313★
Ireland's contribution of papers in the sciences, by field, 1994-98 ★4315★
Italy's contribution of papers in the sciences, by field, 1995-99 ★4316★
Italy's relative impact in the sciences by field, 1992-96 ★4317★
Netherlands' contribution of papers in the sciences, by field, 1995-99 ★4321★
Poland's contribution of papers in the sciences, by field, 1993-97 ★4324★
Russia's contribution of papers in the sciences, by field, 1993-97 ★4325★
South Africa's contribution of papers in the sciences, by field, 1994-98 ★4326★
Spain's contribution of papers in the sciences, by field, 1993-97 ★4328★
Spain's contribution of papers in the sciences, by field, 1995-99 ★4329★

Asustek Computer
Business Week's top emerging-market companies worldwide ★434★
Most profitable information technology companies, 2000 ★527★

At the Sign of the Star
Booklist's most recommended historical fiction for youths, 2001 ★314★
Outstanding books for middle readers, 2000 ★326★

AT&T
Business Week's best companies in the United States ★411★
Fortune's highest ranked telecommunications companies, 2000 ★499★

Athens Area Technical Institute
Lowest undergraduate tuition and fees at colleges and universities in Georgia ★1497★

Athens Medical
Best small companies worldwide ★384★

Athens State College
State appropriations for Alabama's institutions of higher education, 2000-01 ★1254★

Athletics director
African American college athletics senior administrators, by gender, 1999-2000 ★119★
College athletics senior administrators, by gender, 1999-2000 ★123★
Minority college athletics senior administrators, by gender, 1999-2000 ★134★

Atholton High School
Outstanding secondary schools in Baltimore, Maryland ★4092★

Atificial Intelligence
Artificial intelligence journals by citation impact, 1999 ★96★

Atkinson; Jane
Top pay and benefits for the chief executive and top paid employees at Lewis and Clark College in Oregon ★3371★

Atlanta
U.S. cities with the highest number of high-tech employees, 1998 ★2284★
American cities with the highest percentage of people with Internet access ★2572★
U.S. market areas with the highest percentage of adults having internet access ★2607★

Atlanta College of Art
Highest undergraduate tuition and fees at colleges and universities in Georgia ★1496★

Atlanta, GA
U.S. cities considered to be the most affordable for IT professionals ★562★
Cities with the highest percentage of adults using the Internet at home ★2577★

Atlanta Metropolitan College
Average faculty salaries for institutions of higher education in Georgia, 2000-01 ★3697★

Atlantic Cape Community College
Lowest undergraduate tuition and fees at colleges and universities in New Jersey ★1534★

Atlantic; College of the
U.S. colleges and universities where students and the local community have strained relations ★998★
U.S. colleges and universities where students are very politically active ★1001★
U.S. colleges and universities with a large student body of liberal Democrats ★1017★
U.S. colleges and universities with the best food service program ★1031★
U.S. colleges and universities with the happiest students ★1035★
U.S. colleges and universities with the most accessible instructors ★1038★
U.S. colleges and universities with the most attractive campuses ★1039★
U.S. colleges and universities without a diverse student body ★1046★
Highest undergraduate tuition and fees at colleges and universities in Maine ★1512★
Highest undergraduate tuition and fees at colleges and universities in Puerto Rico ★1551★

Atmel
Fortune's highest ranked semiconductors companies, 2000 ★495★

Atmosphere-Ocean
Oceanography journals by citation impact, 1999 ★2141★

Atmospheric dynamics
Earth, atmosphere, and marine science doctorates awarded at U.S. colleges and universities, by subfield, 1999 ★1909★
Gender breakdown of earth, atmosphere, and marine science doctorate recipients, by subfield, 1999 ★1932★

Atmospheric physics and chemistry
Earth, atmosphere, and marine science doctorates awarded at U.S. colleges and universities, by subfield, 1999 ★1909★
Gender breakdown of earth, atmosphere, and marine science doctorate recipients, by subfield, 1999 ★1932★

Atmospheric science/meteorology, general
Earth, atmosphere, and marine science doctorates awarded at U.S. colleges and universities, by subfield, 1999 ★1909★
Gender breakdown of earth, atmosphere, and marine science doctorate recipients, by subfield, 1999 ★1932★

Atomic Fragments: A Daughter's Questions
Library Journal's most notable history of science books, 2000 ★263★

Atomic and molecular
Major subfields of first-year physics and astronomy graduate students who are foreign citizens planning to receive a Ph.D., 1997-98 ★3004★
Major subfields of first-year physics and astronomy graduate students who are U.S. citizens planning to receive a Ph.D., 1997-98 ★3005★

Attention Deficit/Hyperactivity Disorder: What Every Parent Wants To Know
Best selling small press releases, 2001 ★226★

Attorney
Jobs considered the most competitive ★2245★
Jobs with the best security scores ★2251★
Jobs with the lowest unemployment ★2258★

Atwood Heights, District 125
Illinois school districts with the most average years of teacher experience ★4012★

Aubrey; David
Top pay and benefits for the chief executive and top paid employees at Pacific Lutheran University ★3436★

Auburn University
U.S. colleges and universities with the highest average football attendance, 1996-99 ★159★
U.S. colleges and universities awarding the most mathematics master's degrees to African Americans ★1790★
Radcliffe Institute for Advanced Study fellowship recipient in the field of poetry, 2000-01 ★2444★

Auburn University System
State appropriations for Alabama's institutions of higher education, 2000-01 ★1254★

Audiologist
Jobs with the best security scores ★2251★
Jobs with the lowest unemployment ★2258★
Most desirable jobs in healthcare/medicine ★2273★

Auditing: A Journal of Practice & Theory
Top accounting journals by half-life impact factor ★578★
Top accounting journals by mode impact factor ★579★

Augsburg College
U.S. News & World Report's midwestern regional liberal arts colleges with students most in debt, 1999 ★1338★
U.S. News & World Report's midwestern regional liberal arts colleges with the highest academic reputation scores, 2000-01 ★1340★
U.S. News & World Report's midwestern regional liberal arts colleges with the lowest acceptance rates, 2000-01 ★1348★
Average faculty salaries for institutions of higher education in Minnesota, 2000-01 ★3710★

Augusta State University
Division II NCAA colleges with the 0% graduation rates for women's basketball players, 1993-94 ★942★
State appropriations for Georgia's institutions of higher education, 2000-01 ★1263★
Average faculty salaries for institutions of higher education in Georgia, 2000-01 ★3697★

Augustana College
U.S. News & World Report's midwestern regional liberal arts colleges with the best student/faculty ratios, 2000-01 ★1339★
U.S. News & World Report's midwestern regional liberal arts colleges with the highest academic reputation scores, 2000-01 ★1340★
U.S. News & World Report's midwestern regional liberal arts colleges with the highest freshmen retention rates, 2000-01 ★1343★
U.S. News & World Report's midwestern regional liberal arts colleges with the highest percentage of freshmen in the top 25% of their high school class, 2000-01 ★1345★
U.S. News & World Report's best undergraduate fees among midwestern regional liberal arts colleges by discount tuition, 2000 ★1380★
Highest undergraduate tuition and fees at colleges and universities in Illinois ★1500★
Highest undergraduate tuition and fees at colleges and universities in South Dakota ★1556★
Average faculty salaries for institutions of higher education in Illinois, 2000-01 ★3700★
Average faculty salaries for institutions of higher education in South Dakota, 2000-01 ★3729★

Augustus; Seimone
All-America girls' high school basketball 1st team, 2001 ★170★

Auinas High School
Outstanding Catholic high schools in Metro New York ★4076★

Aurely; Lorraine
Top pay and benefits for the chief executive and top paid employees at Chestnut Hill College ★3231★

Aurora High School
Outstanding secondary schools in Akron, Ohio ★4078★

Austensen; Roy A.
Top pay and benefits for the chief executive and top paid employees at Valparaiso University ★3592★

Austin College
U.S. colleges and universities where students are not very politically active ★1000★
U.S. colleges and universities with excellent instructors ★1024★
U.S. colleges and universities with the best overall administration ★1033★
U.S. News & World Report's national liberal arts colleges with students most in debt, 1999 ★1386★
Highest undergraduate tuition and fees at colleges and universities in Texas ★1560★
Average faculty salaries for institutions of higher education in Texas, 2000-01 ★3731★

Austin Community College
Average faculty salaries for institutions of higher education in Texas, 2000-01 ★3731★

Austin Peay State University
State appropriations for Tennessee's institutions of higher education, 2000-01 ★1295★
Average faculty salaries for institutions of higher education in Tennessee, 2000-01 ★3730★

Austin-San Marcos, TX
America's most wired cities, 2001 ★2573★
America's most wired cities with the highest domain density, 2001 ★2574★
Cities with the highest online spending per Internet user ★2576★
Cities with the highest percentage of adults using the Internet at home ★2577★
Cities with the most domains per 1,000 firms ★2579★

Austin, TX
U.S. cities considered to be the most affordable for IT professionals ★562★
Cities with the most Yahoo! listings per million residents ★2580★
Best college towns to live in ★3076★

Auston; David H.
Top pay and benefits for the chief executive and top paid employees at Rice University ★3457★

Australia
Eight grade science achievement scores from selected countries, 1999 ★14★
Math achievement test comparison ★19★
Percentage of enrollment at public institutions of higher education, by country, 1998 ★859★
Countries with the most computers, 2000 ★1603★
Countries with the most computers per capita, 2000 ★1604★
Countries of origin for non-U.S. citizens awarded doctorates at U.S. colleges and universities, 1999 ★1901★

Countries with the highest spending per student on higher education, 1997 ★2488★
Percentage of students enrolled in institutions of higher education that were not citizens of the country where they studied, 1998 ★2500★
Top countries of study for U.S. students studying abroad, 1998-99 ★2510★
Countries with the most Internet users ★2583★
Percentage of internet usage for selected countries ★2599★
Eighth grade mathematics achievement scores from selected countries, 1999 ★2773★
Australia and New Zealand periodical prices, 2001 ★2917★
Institute for Scientific Information periodical prices by country, 2001 ★2922★
Countries with the highest leader's salary ★3120★

Australia & New Zealand Banking Group
Business Week's best companies in Australia ★386★

Australia, New Zealand
First-year physics and astronomy graduate students from selected countries, 1997-98 ★2989★

Australian Journal of Agricultural Research
Agriculture journals by citation impact, 1992-96 ★52★

Australian Journal of Soil Science
Soil science journals by citation impact, 1981-99 ★188★
Soil science journals by citation impact, 1995-99 ★189★

Australian National University
Australian universities with the greatest impact in agricultural sciences, 1993-97 ★49★
Golden Key Scholar Award winners, 2000 ★1316★

Austria
Percentage of enrollment at public institutions of higher education, by country, 1998 ★859★
Annual leave days for employees in selected countries ★2239★
Percentage of students enrolled in institutions of higher education that were not citizens of the country where they studied, 1998 ★2500★
Institute for Scientific Information periodical prices by country, 2001 ★2922★

Author (books)
Jobs considered the loneliest ★2244★
Jobs with the greatest potential income for beginners ★2253★
Jobs with the most stringent quotas ★2259★
Most desirable jobs in communications ★2271★

Authorship Characteristics in Five International Library Journals
Most frequently cited *Libri* articles ★2730★

Autism
Disabled students served in U.S. public school programs, 1998-99 ★1877★

Autodesk
Business Week's best performing companies with the highest 1-year earnings growth ★413★

Autoliv
Fortune's highest ranked motor vehicle parts companies, 2000 ★480★

Automated Analysis Corporation
Top recruiters for computer engineering jobs for 2000-01 master's degree recipients ★2400★
Top recruiters for electrical/electronic engineering jobs for 2000-01 master's degree recipients ★2406★
Top recruiters for metallurgical/mining engineering jobs for 2000-01 master's degree recipients ★2420★
Top recruiters for mechanical engineering jobs for 2000-01 master's degree recipients ★2424★
Top recruiters for metallurgical/mining engineering jobs for 2000-01 bachelor's degree recipients ★2434★

Automatic Data Processing
Fortune's highest ranked computer and data services companies, 2000 ★453★

Automobile assembler
'Blue-collar' jobs considered the least physically demanding ★2241★
Jobs considered the loneliest ★2244★

Automobile painter
Jobs considered the loneliest ★2244★

Automobile salesperson
Jobs considered the most competitive ★2245★

Automotive body and related repairers
Projected employment growth for selected occupations that require long-term on-the-job training, 1998-2008 ★2320★

Automotive mechanics
Occupations with the highest number of self-employed workers, 1998 ★2311★

Automotive mechanics and service technicians
Projected employment growth for selected occupations that require an associate degree or less, 1998-2008 ★2319★

AutoNation
Fortune's highest ranked automotive retailing services companies, 2000 ★449★

Avalon Publishing
Small publishers with the highest sales growth between 1997 and 1999 ★3073★

Avaya
Business Week's best performing companies with the lowest return on equity, 2000 ★426★

Aventis
Business Week's best companies in France ★393★

Averett College
U.S. colleges and universities awarding the most business management and administrative services master's degrees to African Americans ★1759★
Average faculty salaries for institutions of higher education in Virginia, 2000-01 ★3735★

Avila College
Average faculty salaries for institutions of higher education in Missouri, 2000-01 ★3712★

Avis Rent A Car
Fortune's highest ranked automotive retailing services companies, 2000 ★449★

Avista
Fortune's highest ranked electric and gas utilities companies, 2000 ★459★

Avner; Ellis D.
Top pay and benefits for the chief executive and top paid employees at Case Western Reserve University ★3225★

Avoca Public School, District 37
Illinois school districts spending the most for elementary school education 1997-98 ★4009★

Avon
Mass market paperback bestsellers by publishing house, 2000 ★283★
Trade paperback bestsellers by publishing house, 2000 ★307★
Top public companies for women executives, 2000 ★4457★
Top public companies with the highest percentage of women board of directors, 2000 ★4458★
Top public companies with the highest percentage of women employees, 2000 ★4459★

Avon Products
Fortune's highest ranked soaps and cosmetics companies, 2000 ★496★

Avondale High School
Outstanding suburban public high schools in Metro Atlanta ★4254★

Awaken the Giant Within
Retail audiobook titles selling 400,000-500,000 copies ★304★

Axa
Business Week's best companies in France ★393★

AXA Financial
Fortune's highest ranked securities companies, 2000 ★494★

Axeen; David
Top pay and benefits for the chief executive and top paid employees at Occidental College ★3428★

Axel Johnson
Top women-owned companies ★4460★

Ayckbourn; Alan
Top playwrights of the twentieth century ★4436★

Ayn Rand: A Sense of Life
Most notable videos for adults, 2001 ★2891★

Ayres; Elizabeth
Top pay and benefits for the chief executive and top paid employees at American International College ★3173★

Ayres; J.
Highest ranked active communication studies researchers ★2747★

Azevedo; Holly
All-America girls' high school soccer team defenders, 2001 ★174★

Azordegan; Shahram
Top pay and benefits for the chief executive and top paid employees at National University in California ★3415★

Azusa Pacific University
U.S. colleges and universities awarding the most education master's degrees to Hispanic Americans ★1771★
U.S. colleges and universities awarding the most psychology master's degrees to Asian Americans ★1798★
Average faculty salaries for institutions of higher education in California, 2000-01 ★3692★

B

Baar; Stephen R.
Top pay and benefits for the chief executive and top paid employees at Westminster College in Utah ★3618★

Babakus; Emin
Highest impact authors in the *Journal of Business Research*, by adjusted number of citations in 12 journals, 1985-1999 ★692★
Highest impact authors in the *Journal of Business Research*, by number of citations in 12 journals, 1985-1999 ★693★

Babin; Barry J.
Authors with the most articles published in the *Journal of Business Research*, 1985 to 1999 ★687★

Babson College
Business Week's institutions with the best entrepreneurship programs ★594★
U.S. business schools with the slowest payback on MBA investments ★655★
U.S. colleges and universities where students and the local community have strained relations ★998★
U.S. colleges and universities where students are not very politically active ★1000★
U.S. colleges and universities with excellent instructors ★1024★
U.S. colleges and universities with harmonious race/class interaction ★1026★
U.S. colleges and universities with the most accessible instructors ★1038★
Professional or specialized institutions with the highest enrollment of foreign students, 1998-99 ★2501★
Average faculty salaries for institutions of higher education in Massachusetts, 2000-01 ★3708★
Private institutions of higher education that pay the highest salaries to female professors, 2000-01 ★3974★
U.S. institutions with the highest paid assistant professors, 2001 ★3977★

Babson College, F.W. Olin Graduate School of Business
U.S. News & World Report's undergraduate business programs with the best entrepreneurship departments, 2000-01 ★565★
Academics' choices for best graduate entrepreneurship programs, 2001 ★583★
Academics' choices for best part-time MBA programs, 2000 ★587★

Baby Steps
Smithsonian's best books for children ages 1 to 6 ★363★

Bachich; Frank J.
Top pay and benefits for the chief executive and top paid employees at Drexel University ★3274★

Bachner; David J.
Top pay and benefits for the chief executive and top paid employees at Hartwick College ★3326★

Backstreet Boys: The Official Book
Most notable nonfiction books for reluctant young adult readers, 2001 ★323★

Bacteriologic studies of necrotic dental pulps
Endodontic articles with the most citations, 1974 through 1999 ★1864★

Bacteriology
Biological sciences doctorates awarded at U.S. colleges and universities, by subfield, 1999 ★1887★
Gender breakdown of biological sciences doctorate recipients, by subfield, 1999 ★1927★

Baer; Elizabeth
Top pay and benefits for the chief executive and top paid employees at Gustavus Adolphus College ★3317★

Bagdasarian; Adam
Booklist's best first novels for youths ★309★

Bahls; Steven
Top pay and benefits for the chief executive and top paid employees at Capital University ★3220★

Bailey; Joan E.
Top pay and benefits for the chief executive and top paid employees at the College of New Rochelle ★3525★

Bailey; Leslie G.
Top pay and benefits for the chief executive and top paid employees at Saint Martin's College in Washington ★3479★

Bailey; Stephen
Top pay and benefits for the chief executive and top paid employees at Knox College ★3360★

Bainbridge College
Lowest undergraduate tuition and fees at colleges and universities in Georgia ★1497★

Baker College Center for Graduate Studies
U.S. colleges and universities awarding the most business management and administrative services master's degrees to Asian Americans ★1760★

Baker; George
Top pay and benefits for the chief executive and top paid employees at Xavier University of Louisiana ★3638★

Baker Hughes
Fortune's highest ranked industrial and farm equipment companies, 2000 ★471★

Baker; Jeffrey D.
Top pay and benefits for the chief executive and top paid employees at Luther College ★3383★

Baker; Raymond W.
Top pay and benefits for the chief executive and top paid employees at Trinity College in Connecticut ★3577★

Baker; Steve
Top pay and benefits for the chief executive and top paid employees at Westmont College ★3619★

Baker University
U.S. News & World Report's midwestern regional universities with the best student/faculty ratios, 2000-01 ★1403★
Highest undergraduate tuition and fees at colleges and universities in Kansas ★1506★
Average faculty salaries for institutions of higher education in Kansas, 2000-01 ★3703★

Bakersfield, CA
Cities with the highest percentage of broadband use and interest ★2578★

Bakersfield College
U.S. institutions awarding the most associate degrees to minorities in agribusiness and production, 1998 ★1808★

Bakken; Larry
Top pay and benefits for the chief executive and top paid employees at Hamline University ★3320★

Bala; Nicholas
Most-cited scholars in *Canadian Journal of Criminology* ★1638★

The "balanced force" concept for instrumentation of curved canals
Endodontic articles with the most citations, 1974 through 1999 ★1864★

Balch; Pamela
Top pay and benefits for the chief executive and top paid employees at Bethany College in West Virginia ★3202★

Baldasare; Paul
Top pay and benefits for the chief executive and top paid employees at St. Andrews Presbyterian College ★3469★

Baldeschwieler; John D.
American Chemical Society 2001 award winners (Group 1) ★751★

Baldwin High School
Outstanding secondary schools in Long Island, New York ★4165★

Baldwin; James
Most influential African Americans in the arts ★78★
Favorite African American authors ★237★

Baldwin; John C.
Top pay and benefits for the chief executive and top paid employees at Dartmouth College ★3263★

Baldwin; Lee E.
Top pay and benefits for the chief executive and top paid employees at the University of Mary Hardin-Baylor ★3549★

Baldwin-Wallace College
U.S. News & World Report's midwestern regional universities with students most in debt, 1999 ★1400★
U.S. News & World Report's midwestern regional universities with the best student/faculty ratios, 2000-01 ★1403★
U.S. News & World Report's midwestern regional universities with the highest freshmen retention rates, 2000-01 ★1405★
U.S. News & World Report's midwestern regional universities with the highest percentage of freshmen from the top 25% of their high school class, 2000-01 ★1407★
Average faculty salaries for institutions of higher education in Ohio, 2000-01 ★3722★

Ball
Fortune's highest ranked metal products companies, 2000 ★475★
Top containers and packaging companies in Standard & Poor's 500, 2001 ★537★

Ball State University
U.S. News & World Report's undergraduate business programs with the best entrepreneurship departments, 2000-01 ★565★
U.S. colleges and universities with the largest numerical increases in alcohol arrests, 1998 ★733★
Division I NCAA colleges with that graduated none of their African American male basketball players, 1990-91 to 1993-94 ★930★
State appropriations for Indiana's institutions of higher education, 2000-01 ★1267★
U.S. News & World Report's national universities with students least in debt, 1999 ★1475★
U.S. doctoral institutions with the largest number of students studying abroad, 1998-99 ★2512★
Enrollment of students in the ten largest undergraduate journalism and mass communications programs, 1999 ★2746★
Degrees granted in the ten largest master's journalism and mass communications programs, 1999 ★2757★
Enrollment of students in the ten largest master's journalism and mass communications programs, 1999 ★2763★
Average faculty salaries for institutions of higher education in Indiana, 2000-01 ★3701★

Balla; Ruth Ann
Top pay and benefits for the chief executive and top paid employees at Meredith College ★3399★

Ballantine
Mass market paperback bestsellers by publishing house, 2000 ★283★

Ballantyne of Omaha
Companies with the worst two-year total returns since 1998 ★437★

Ballweg; Jessica
All-America girls' high school soccer team defenders, 2001 ★174★

Baltes; Kenneth G.
Top pay and benefits for the chief executive and top paid employees at the College of St. Catherine ★3528★

Baltimore
U.S. school districts with the highest number of vacancies for K-12 teachers ★2331★

Baltimore City Community College
Institutions censured by the American Association of University Professors, 2001 ★1067★
Lowest undergraduate tuition and fees at colleges and universities in Maryland ★1515★

Baltimore; David
Top pay and benefits for the chief executive and top paid employees at the California Institute of Technology ★3521★

Baltimore School for the Arts
Outstanding secondary schools in Baltimore, Maryland ★4092★

Baltimore; University of
U.S. colleges and universities with the lowest percentage of African Americans enrolled, 1997 ★223★
U.S. colleges and universities awarding the most law and legal studies master's degrees to African Americans ★1781★
U.S. colleges and universities awarding the most psychology master's degrees to African Americans ★1797★
Traditionally white institutions awarding the most first professional degrees to African Americans ★1842★
U.S. colleges and universities awarding the most first professional degrees to African Americans ★1843★
U.S. colleges and universities awarding the most law and legal studies first professional degrees to African Americans ★1852★

Baltodano; Josefina
Top pay and benefits for the chief executive and top paid employees at John F. Kennedy University ★3354★

Banca Intesa
Business Week's best companies in Italy ★397★

Banco Bilbao Vizcaya Argentaria (BBVA)
Business Week's best companies in Spain ★403★

Banco Comercial Portugues (BCP)
Business Week's best companies in Portugal ★401★

Banco Popular Espanol
Business Week's best companies in Spain ★403★

Banco Santander Central Hispano
Business Week's best companies in Spain ★403★

Bank of America
Business Week's best companies in terms of profits ★406★
Fortune's highest ranked money center banks, 2000 ★478★
Best companies for working mothers ★4446★
Highly recommended public companies for women executives, 2000 ★4453★

Bank Austria
Business Week's best companies in Austria ★387★

Bank of Ireland
Business Week's best companies in Ireland ★396★

Bank of Montreal
Business Week's best companies in Canada ★390★

Bank of New York
Fortune's highest ranked money center banks, 2000 ★478★

Bank of Nova Scotia
Business Week's best companies in Canada ★390★

Bank officer
Jobs with the best physical demands scores ★2250★
Most desirable jobs in business/finance ★2270★

Bank One
Fortune's highest ranked super-regional banks, 2000 ★498★

Bank Street College of Education
Colleges and universities with the smallest endowments, 2000 ★1238★

Bank tellers
Occupations with the highest decline in employment, 1998-2008 ★2310★

Bank of Tokyo-Mitsubishi
Business Week's best companies in Japan ★398★

Banking/financial support services
Business and management doctorates awarded at U.S. colleges and universities, by subfield, 1999 ★1888★
Gender breakdown of business and management doctorate recipients, by subfield, 1999 ★1928★

Banks; John C.
Top pay and benefits for the chief executive and top paid employees at Andrews University ★3176★

Banneker Academic High School
Outstanding secondary schools in Washington, District of Columbia-Maryland-Virginia-West Virginia ★4249★

Banneker High School
Outstanding secondary schools in Atlanta, Georgia ★4087★

Bannister; Geoffrey
Top pay and benefits for the chief executive and top paid employees at Butler University ★3214★

Bannockburn School, District 106
Illinois school districts spending the most for elementary school education 1997-98 ★4009★
Illinois school districts spending the most per pupil for instruction ★4011★

Banta
Fortune's highest ranked printing companies, 2000 ★487★

Banta Corp.
Publishers with the best industry stocks, 2000 ★300★

Bantam
Hardcover bestsellers by publishing house, 2000 ★240★
Mass market paperback bestsellers by publishing house, 2000 ★283★

Baptist
Religious preference of incoming freshmen, 2000 ★1061★

Baptist Bible College
Lowest undergraduate tuition and fees at private nonprofit, 4-year or above colleges and universities ★1464★

Baptist Health Systems of South Florida
Best companies for working mothers in offering advancement opportunities for women ★4447★

Baptist Missionary Association Theological Seminary
Lowest undergraduate tuition and fees at private nonprofit, 4-year or above colleges and universities ★1464★

Baraka; Amiri
Most influential African Americans in the arts ★78★

Baraka; Kelly
All-American boy's high school football running backs, 2000 ★186★

Barat College
U.S. News & World Report's midwestern regional liberal arts colleges with students most in debt, 1999 ★1338★

Barazzone; Esther L.
Presidents with the highest pay at Baccalaureate I colleges, 1998-99 ★3159★
Top pay and benefits for the chief executive and top paid employees at Chatham College ★3230★

Barber
Most desirable jobs in personal services ★2275★

Barber-Scotia College
U.S. colleges and universities with the highest percentage of African Americans enrolled, 1997 ★222★
Historically black colleges and universities with high student loan default rates, 1998 ★2736★
Average faculty salaries for institutions of higher education in North Carolina, 2000-01 ★3720★

The Barber of Seville
Most frequently produced operas in North America, 1999-2000 ★2905★

Barbezat; D.
Top assistant professor economists at elite liberal arts colleges, 1975-94 ★2173★

Barbour, Griffith & Rogers
Lobbyist that billed the most to U.S. colleges and universities, 1999 ★1249★

Barclay; Devin
All-America boys' high school soccer team forwards, 2001 ★166★

Barclays Bank
Business Week's best companies in Britain ★389★

Bard College
U.S. colleges and universities where students are very politically active ★1001★
U.S. colleges and universities where the general student body puts little emphasis on athletic events ★1009★
U.S. colleges and universities with a generally liberal student body ★1015★

U.S. colleges and universities with a primarily non-religious student body ★1021★
U.S. colleges and universities with harmonious race/class interaction ★1026★
U.S. colleges and universities with the best food service program ★1031★
U.S. colleges and universities with the happiest students ★1035★
U.S. News & World Report's national liberal arts colleges with the best faculty resources rank, 2000-01 ★1321★
U.S. News & World Report's national liberal arts colleges with the best student/faculty ratios, 2000-01 ★1326★
U.S. News & World Report's national liberal arts colleges with the highest proportion of classes with less than 20 students, 2000-01 ★1335★
Highest undergraduate tuition and fees at private nonprofit, 4-year or above colleges and universities ★1461★
Highest undergraduate tuition and fees at colleges and universities in New York ★1537★
Institutions in the Worker Rights Consortium ★2913★
Average faculty salaries for institutions of higher education in New York, 2000-01 ★3719★

Bareikis; Robert
Top pay and benefits for the chief executive and top paid employees at the Centenary College of Louisiana ★3523★

Barker; L.
Highest ranked inactive communication studies researchers ★2748★
Speech communication's most published scholars between 1915-1985 ★4362★

Barletta; Frank J.
Top pay and benefits for the chief executive and top paid employees at Saint Peter's College ★3485★

Barlow High School
Outstanding secondary schools in Danbury, Connecticut ★4121★

Barnard College
Private, 4-year undergraduate colleges and universities producing the most Ph.D.'s in the life sciences, 1920-1990 ★192★
Private, 4-year undergraduate colleges and universities producing the most Ph.D.'s in the life sciences, 1981-1990 ★193★
U.S. News & World Report's national liberal arts colleges with the highest proportion of classes having 50 or more students, 2000-01 ★1334★
Private, 4-year undergraduate colleges and universities producing the most Ph.D.s in all fields of study, 1920-1990 ★2027★
Private, 4-year undergraduate colleges and universities producing the most Ph.D.'s in all fields of study, 1981-1990 ★2028★
Private, 4-year undergraduate colleges and universities producing the most Ph.D.'s in all fields of study, 1990 ★2029★
Private, 4-year undergraduate colleges and universities producing the most Ph.D.'s in nonscience fields, 1920-1990 ★2030★
Private, 4-year undergraduate colleges and universities producing the most Ph.D.'s in nonscience fields, 1981-1990 ★2031★
Private, 4-year undergraduate colleges and universities producing the most Ph.D.'s in nonscience fields, 1990 ★2032★
Elite liberal arts colleges ranked by per capita quality adjusted scholarship articles in the field of economics, 1975-94 ★2164★
Elite liberal arts colleges ranked by quality adjusted scholarship articles in the field of economics, 1975-94 ★2165★
Top assistant professor economists at elite liberal arts colleges, 1975-94 ★2173★
Top full professor economists at elite liberal arts colleges, 1975-94 ★2175★
Private, 4-year undergraduate colleges and universities producing the most Ph.D.'s in economics, 1920-1990 ★2211★
Private, 4-year undergraduate colleges and universities producing the most Ph.D.'s in English, 1920-1990 ★2449★
Private, 4-year undergraduate colleges and universities producing the most Ph.D.'s in English, 1981-1990 ★2450★
Private, 4-year undergraduate colleges and universities producing the most Ph.D.'s in history, 1920-1990 ★2552★
Private, 4-year undergraduate colleges and universities producing the most Ph.D.'s in history, 1981-1990 ★2553★
Women's colleges granting physics bachelor's degrees, 2000 ★2982★
Private, 4-year undergraduate colleges and universities producing the most Ph.D.'s in political science and international relations, 1920-1990 ★3044★
Private, 4-year undergraduate colleges and universities producing the most Ph.D.'s in political science and international relations, 1981-1990 ★3045★
Private, 4-year undergraduate colleges and universities producing the most Ph.D.'s in psychology, 1920-1990 ★3066★
Private, 4-year undergraduate colleges and universities producing the most Ph.D.'s in psychology, 1981-1990 ★3067★
U.S. liberal arts colleges with the highest paid full professors, 2001 ★3980★
Private, 4-year undergraduate colleges and universities producing the most Ph.D.'s in the sciences, 1920-1990 ★4294★
Private, 4-year undergraduate colleges and universities producing the most Ph.D.'s in the sciences, 1981-1990 ★4295★
Private, 4-year undergraduate colleges and universities producing the most Ph.D.'s in anthropology and sociology, 1920-1990 ★4344★
Private, 4-year undergraduate colleges and universities producing the most Ph.D.'s in anthropology and sociology, 1981-1990 ★4345★

Barnes & Noble
Publishers with the best industry stocks, 2000 ★300★

Barnes & Noble College Bookstores
Contractors managing the most college bookstores, 1999 ★846★

Barnes; Charlie
Top pay and benefits for the chief executive and top paid employees at the Maryville University of Saint Louis ★3534★

Barnes; James
Top pay and benefits for the chief executive and top paid employees at Indiana Wesleyan University ★3349★

Barnes; James A.
Top pay and benefits for the chief executive and top paid employees at Ashland University ★3180★

Barnes-Jewish Hospital
Top cardiology and heart surgery hospitals in the U.S., 2000 ★2788★
Top endocrinology hospitals in the U.S., 2000 ★2789★
Top hospitals in the U.S., 2000 ★2793★
Top nephrology hospitals in the U.S., 2000 ★2794★
Top neurology and neurosurgery hospitals in the U.S., 2000 ★2795★
Top ophthalmology hospitals in the U.S., 2000 ★2796★
Top ortolaryngology hospitals in the U.S., 2000 ★2798★
Top urology hospitals in the U.S., 2000 ★2803★

Barnes; Jodie
Top pay and benefits for the chief executive and top paid employees at Union College in Kentucky ★3584★

Barnes; Peter J.
Most-cited researchers in cardiology, 1981-1998 ★2874★

Barnesandnoble.com
Top E-commerce web sites ★2603★

Barnett; Gary L.
Top pay and benefits for the chief executive and top paid employees at Northwestern University ★3423★

Barney; Matthew
Best living artists ★73★

Baron; James
Top pay and benefits for the chief executive and top paid employees at Saint Bonaventure University ★3470★

Barquinero; James M.
Top pay and benefits for the chief executive and top paid employees at Sacred Heart University in Connecticut ★3467★

Barr Laboratories
Business Week's top companies in terms of sales, 2000 ★431★

Barra
Best small companies in the U.S. ★383★

Barrett; Sue
Top pay and benefits for the chief executive and top paid employees at Lewis University ★3372★

Barrick Gold
Business Week's best performing companies with the greatest decline in earnings growth ★412★
Business Week's best performing companies with the lowest net margin, 2000 ★425★
Business Week's best performing companies with the lowest return on equity, 2000 ★426★
Top metals and mining companies in Standard & Poor's 500, 2001 ★549★

Barrington Atlas of the Greek and Roman World
Library Journal's best reference books, 2000 ★368★
Selected reference books in the field of history, 2000 ★376★

Barrington High School
Illinois high schools with the highest SAT scores ★874★
Outstanding secondary schools in Chicago, Illinois ★4110★

Barro; Robert J.
U.S. academic economists by mean number of citations, 1971-92 ★2176★
U.S. academic economists by total citations, 1971-92 ★2177★

Barrow's Boys
Most notable nonfiction books, 2001 ★285★
Outstanding works of nonfiction, 2001 ★294★

Barry; James T.
 Top pay and benefits for the chief executive and top paid employees at Avila College ★3186★
Barry University
 Highest undergraduate tuition and fees at colleges and universities in Florida ★1494★
 Total baccalaureate education degrees awarded to Hispanic Americans from U.S. colleges and universities, 1997-98 ★1713★
 Total baccalaureate law and legal studies degrees awarded to Hispanic Americans from U.S. colleges and universities, 1997-98 ★1727★
 U.S. colleges and universities awarding the most biological and life sciences master's degrees to African Americans ★1756★
 U.S. colleges and universities awarding the most biological and life sciences master's degrees to Asian Americans ★1757★
 U.S. colleges and universities awarding the most biological and life sciences master's degrees to Hispanic Americans ★1758★
 U.S. colleges and universities awarding the most education master's degrees to Hispanic Americans ★1771★
 U.S. colleges and universities awarding the most health professions and related sciences master's degrees to African Americans ★1777★
 U.S. colleges and universities awarding the most health professions and related sciences master's degrees to Hispanic Americans ★1779★
 U.S. colleges and universities awarding the most master's degrees to Hispanic Americans ★1787★
 U.S. colleges and universities awarding the most psychology master's degrees to Hispanic Americans ★1799★
 Average faculty salaries for institutions of higher education in Florida, 2000-01 ★3696★
Barstow College
 Lowest undergraduate tuition and fees at public 2-year colleges and universities ★1465★
 Lowest undergraduate tuition and fees at colleges and universities in California ★1487★
Bartels; Larry M.
 Most frequently downloaded *American Political Science Review* articles ★3039★
Bartender
 Jobs with the worst income scores ★2261★
 Most desirable jobs in travel/food service ★2278★
Bartlesville Wesleyan College
 Highest undergraduate tuition and fees at colleges and universities in Oklahoma ★1545★
Barton College
 College senior's choices for exemplary undergraduate institutions ★1319★
 Average faculty salaries for institutions of higher education in North Carolina, 2000-01 ★3720★
Barton; Cornelius
 Top pay and benefits for the chief executive and top paid employees at Rensselaer Polytechnic Institute ★3455★
Bartrem; R.L.
 Top pay and benefits for the chief executive and top paid employees at Florida Institute of Technology ★3293★
Baseball player (Major League)
 Jobs considered the most competitive ★2245★
 Jobs that are potentially the highest paying ★2246★
 Jobs with the best income scores ★2248★
 Jobs with the greatest potential income for beginners ★2253★
 Jobs with the highest starting salaries ★2255★
 Jobs with the worst physical demands scores ★2263★
 Jobs with the worst security scores ★2264★
 Most desirable jobs in athletics ★2269★
Baseball umpire (Major League)
 Jobs with the best income scores ★2248★
 Jobs with the highest starting salaries ★2255★
 Jobs with the worst security scores ★2264★
 Most desirable jobs in athletics ★2269★
Baseball's Best Shots: The Greatest Baseball Photography of All Time
 Most notable nonfiction books for reluctant young adult readers, 2001 ★323★
Basel-Mulhouse-Freiburg
 Cities with the highest productivity of paper in the discipline of immunology, 1994-96 ★2871★
BASF
 Fortune's highest ranked chemicals companies, 2000 ★452★
Basho and the Fox
 Smithsonian's best books for children ages 6 to 10 ★364★
Basic energy sciences
 Energy Department research funding, 2001 ★3110★
"Basic Local Alignment Search Tool"
 Institute for Scientific Information's most cited papers, 1990-98 ★4282★
Basic research
 Overall median salary for full-time chemists with a bachelor's degree, by work function, 2000 ★790★
 Overall median salary for full-time chemists with a doctoral degree, by work function, 2000 ★803★
 Overall median salary for full-time chemists with a master's degree, by work function, 2000 ★804★
Basili; Victor R.
 Top published scholars in the field of systems and software engineering ★2333★
Basinger; Jeanine D.
 Top pay and benefits for the chief executive and top paid employees at Wesleyan University in Connecticut ★3612★
Basket Counts
 Most notable nonfiction books for reluctant young adult readers, 2001 ★323★
Basketball coach (NCAA)
 Jobs considered the most competitive ★2245★
 Most desirable jobs in athletics ★2269★
 'White-collar' jobs considered the most physically demanding ★2285★
Basketball player (NBA)
 Jobs considered the most competitive ★2245★
 Jobs that are potentially the highest paying ★2246★
 Jobs with the best income scores ★2248★
 Jobs with the greatest potential income for beginners ★2253★
 Jobs with the highest starting salaries ★2255★
 Jobs with the worst physical demands scores ★2263★
 Jobs with the worst security scores ★2264★
 Most desirable jobs in athletics ★2269★
Bass; Mistie
 All-America girls' high school basketball 2nd team, 2001 ★171★
Bassiouni; M. Cherif
 Top pay and benefits for the chief executive and top paid employees at DePaul University ★3266★
Batell; Susan
 Top pay and benefits for the chief executive and top paid employees at Viterbo University ★3597★
Bateman; B.
 Top associate professor economists at elite liberal arts colleges, 1975-94 ★2174★
Bates; Bruce P.
 Top pay and benefits for the chief executive and top paid employees at the University of New England ★3552★
Bates College
 U.S. colleges and universities with a popular radio station ★1019★
 U.S. colleges and universities with a primarily non-religious student body ★1021★
 U.S. News & World Report's national liberal arts colleges with the highest percentage of full-time faculty, 2000-01 ★1333★
 U.S. News & World Report's national liberal arts colleges with the highest proportion of classes having 50 or more students, 2000-01 ★1334★
 U.S. News & World Report's national liberal arts colleges with the lowest acceptance rates, 2000-01 ★1336★
 Elite liberal arts colleges ranked by per capita quality adjusted scholarship articles in the field of economics, 1975-94 ★2164★
 Elite liberal arts colleges ranked by quality adjusted scholarship articles in the field of economics, 1975-94 ★2165★
 Top full professor economists at elite liberal arts colleges, 1975-94 ★2175★
 U.S. bachelor's institutions with the largest number of students studying abroad, 1998-99 ★2511★
 Most wired colleges, 2000 ★2595★
 Average faculty salaries for institutions of higher education in Maine, 2000-01 ★3706★
Bates; Daisy
 Most influential African Americans in politics and civil rights ★3040★
Bates; Marcia J.
 Library and information science faculty with the most citations to journal articles, 1993-1998 ★2710★
 Library and information science faculty with the most journal articles, 1993-1998 ★2711★
Bates; Mark
 Top pay and benefits for the chief executive and top paid employees at the Maryville University of Saint Louis ★3534★
Bates Middle School
 Outstanding secondary schools in Sumter, South Carolina ★4238★
Batesko; Mary Lee
 Top pay and benefits for the chief executive and top paid employees at Georgian Court College ★3307★
Bateson; Mary Catherine
 Radcliffe Institute for Advanced Study fellowship recipients in the field of anthropology, 2000-01 ★60★
Bats! Strange and Wonderful
 Booklist's best science books for children ★310★
Batteast; Jacqueline
 All-America girls' high school basketball 1st team, 2001 ★170★

The Battle for God
Outstanding history books, 2000 ★289★

Battle of the Mad Scientists
Outstanding audio selections for young listeners, 2000 ★325★

Bauer; Cat
Booklist's best first novels for youths ★309★

Bauer; Richard L.
Top pay and benefits for the chief executive and top paid employees at Centre College ★3227★

Baugh; D. Matthew
All-USA College Academic First Team, 2001 ★2★

Bauman; Lorri
Division I women's career high scorers ★129★

Baumol; William
Authors most frequently contributing to the *American Economic Review* from 1911-1990 ★2156★
Authors most frequently contributing to the *American Economic Review* from 1951-1990 ★2157★

Bausch & Lomb
Fortune's highest ranked medical products and equipment companies, 2000 ★474★

Bawcom; Jerry G.
Top pay and benefits for the chief executive and top paid employees at the University of Mary Hardin-Baylor ★3549★

Baxter International
Fortune's highest ranked medical products and equipment companies, 2000 ★474★
Highly recommended public companies for women executives, 2000 ★4453★

Bay Mills Community College
U.S. tribal colleges ★1445★
U.S. institutions awarding the most associate degrees to minorities in ethnic/cultural studies, 1997-98 ★1810★

Bay View Middle School
Outstanding secondary schools in Green Bay, Wisconsin ★4141★

Bayer
Business Week's best companies in Germany ★394★
Fortune's highest ranked chemicals companies, 2000 ★452★

Bayer; Ernst
American Chemical Society 2001 award winners (Group 1) ★751★

Bayley; David H.
Most-cited scholars in police studies articles/research notes ★2624★

Bayley; D.H.
Most cited authors in the journal *Criminal Justice Review*, 1990 to 1995 ★1620★

Baylock; Sandra Kay
Top pay and benefits for the chief executive and top paid employees at Colorado Christian University ★3248★

Baylor College of Medicine
Top molecular and general genetics research-doctorate programs as evaluated by the National Research Council ★211★
U.S. universities with the greatest impact in cell and developmental biology, 1993-97 ★212★
State appropriations for Texas's institutions of higher education, 2000-01 ★1296★
U.S. colleges and universities awarding the most biological and life sciences doctorate degrees to Asian Americans ★2083★
U.S. colleges and universities awarding the most biological and life sciences doctorate degrees to Hispanic Americans ★2084★
Top primary-care medical schools by student selectivity rank, 2001 ★2858★
Top research-oriented medical schools by student selectivity, 2001 ★2862★
Most effective physiology research-doctorate programs as evaluated by the National Research Council ★3021★
Top physiology research-doctorate programs as evaluated by the National Research Council ★3022★

Baylor University
Division I NCAA colleges with that graduated none of their African American male basketball players, 1990-91 to 1993-94 ★930★
U.S. colleges and universities with a primarily religious student body ★1022★
Golden Key Scholar Award winners, 2000 ★1316★
Fiske Guide's best buys for private colleges and universities, 2001 ★1459★
U.S. doctoral institutions with the largest number of students studying abroad, 1998-99 ★2512★
Institutions with the most female physics bachelor's recipients, 1994-1998 ★2959★
U.S. institutions with more than 40% female bachelor's graduates in their physics departments, 1994-98 ★2977★
Average faculty salaries for institutions of higher education in Texas, 2000-01 ★3731★

Baylor University, Hankamer School of Business
U.S. News & World Report's undergraduate business programs with the best entrepreneurship departments, 2000-01 ★565★

Bayside Middle School
Outstanding secondary schools in Milwaukee-Waukesha, Wisconsin ★4180★

BB&T Corporation
Top recruiters for finance/banking jobs for 2000-01 bachelor's degree recipients ★582★
Top recruiters for business administration jobs for 2000-01 master's degree recipients ★652★
Top recruiters for finance/banking jobs for 2000-01 master's degree recipients ★664★

BCE (Bell Canada Enterprises)
Business Week's best companies in Canada ★390★

BEA Systems
Business Week's best companies in terms of share-price gain ★409★
Information technology companies giving the best returns, 2000 ★522★

Beachwood Middle School
Outstanding secondary schools in Cleveland-Lorain-Elyria, Ohio ★4114★

Beaird; Curtis
Top pay and benefits for the chief executive and top paid employees at the University of Mary Hardin-Baylor ★3549★

Beal College
Lowest undergraduate tuition and fees at colleges and universities in Maine ★1513★

Beal; Kathryn
All-America girls' high school soccer team defenders, 2001 ★174★

The Bear and the Dragon
Longest-running fiction hardcover bestsellers, 2000 ★279★

Bear Stearns
Fortune's highest ranked securities companies, 2000 ★494★

Bearden; William O.
Authors with the most articles published in the *Journal of Business Research*, 1985 to 1999 ★687★

Beasley Elementary
Chicago elementary magnet schools with the highest acceptance rates, 2000-01 ★4002★

Beast
Booklist's most recommended fantasy books for youth ★312★

The Beast God Forgot to Invent
Booklist's best fiction books for library collections, 2000 ★227★

Beatty; M.
Highest ranked active communication studies researchers ★2747★

Beaubien Elementary School
Chicago neighborhood schools with the highest ISAT scores in reading and math ★4004★

Beauchamp; Charles
Top pay and benefits for the chief executive and top paid employees at Holy Names College ★3337★

Beauchamp, C.S.C; Rev. E. William
Top pay and benefits for the chief executive and top paid employees at the University of Notre Dame ★3554★

Beaudoin; Ralph H.
Top pay and benefits for the chief executive and top paid employees at the Catholic University of America ★3522★

Beaufort County Community College
Lowest undergraduate tuition and fees at colleges and universities in North Carolina ★1540★
Average faculty salaries for institutions of higher education without academic ranks in North Carolina, 2000-01 ★3761★

Beaulieu Encyclopedia of the Automobile
Library Journal's best reference books, 2000 ★368★
Outstanding reference sources, 2001 ★371★

Beaumont Catholic High School
Outstanding secondary schools in Cleveland-Lorain-Elyria, Ohio ★4114★

Beaver College
U.S. News & World Report's northern regional universities with the best student/faculty ratios, 2000-01 ★1416★
U.S. News & World Report's northern regional universities with the highest proportion of classes with 20 students of less, 2000-01 ★1423★
U.S. News & World Report's northern regional universities with the lowest acceptance rates, 2000-01 ★1424★

Beaver County; Community College of
Lowest undergraduate tuition and fees at colleges and universities in Pennsylvania ★1550★
Average faculty salaries for institutions of higher education in Pennsylvania, 2000-01 ★3725★

Beaverton City Library
Highest Hennen's American Public Library Ratings for libraries serving a population of 100,000 to 249,999 ★2698★

Bebe Stores
Business Week's top companies in terms of earning growth, 2000 ★427★
Top companies in terms of growth, 2000 ★534★

Because of Winn-Dixie
  Most notable books for middle readers, 2001 ★317★
  Outstanding children's fiction books, 2000 ★329★
  Publishers Weekly Off-the-Cuff Awards winner for best opening line, 2000 ★339★
  Publishers Weekly Off-the-Cuff Awards winner for favorite novel of the year, 2000 ★346★
  Smithsonian's best books for children ages 10 and up ★365★
Bechtel National
  Top recruiters for multidisciplinary majors jobs for 2000-01 bachelor's degree recipients ★2327★
  Top recruiters for systems engineer jobs for 2000-01 bachelor's degree recipients ★2336★
  Top recruiters for chemical engineering jobs for 2000-01 bachelor's degree recipients ★2343★
  Top recruiters for civil engineering jobs for 2000-01 bachelor's degree recipients ★2346★
  Top recruiters for environmental engineering jobs for 2000-01 bachelor's degree recipients ★2357★
  Top recruiters for industrial engineering jobs for 2000-01 bachelor's degree recipients ★2432★
  Top recruiters for nuclear engineering jobs for 2000-01 bachelor's degree recipients ★2440★
Becker; Gary
  Most cited economists ★2185★
Becker; J.V.
  Most cited authors in the journal *International Journal of Offender Therapy and Comparative Criminology*, 1990 to 1995 ★1625★
Becker; S.
  Highest ranked active communication studies researchers ★2747★
  Speech communication's most published scholars between 1915-1985 ★4362★
Becker; Stephen
  Top pay and benefits for the chief executive and top paid employees at Whitman College ★3623★
Becker; William E.
  Individuals producing the most economic education research articles, 1963-1990 ★2166★
Beckett Baseball Card Monthly
  Best-selling youth magazines ★2920★
Beckett Basketball Card Monthly
  Best-selling youth magazines ★2920★
Beckett Football Card Monthly
  Best-selling youth magazines ★2920★
Beckett; Samuel
  Top playwrights of the twentieth century ★4436★
Beckman Coulter
  Fortune's highest ranked scientific, photo and control equipment companies, 2000 ★493★
Beckman; William E.
  Top pay and benefits for the chief executive and top paid employees at the Sage Colleges in New York ★3536★
Becoming Madame Mao
  Booklist's best fiction books for library collections, 2000 ★227★
Becton Dickinson
  Fortune's highest ranked medical products and equipment companies, 2000 ★474★

Bed Bath & Beyond
  Top consumer products companies in Standard & Poor's 500, 2001 ★536★
Bedard; Richard F.
  Top pay and benefits for the chief executive and top paid employees at American International College ★3173★
Bee County College
  Average faculty salaries for institutions of higher education without academic ranks in Texas, 2000-01 ★3766★
Beeler; Jesse D.
  Top pay and benefits for the chief executive and top paid employees at Millsaps College ★3403★
The Beet Field
  Outstanding books for older readers, 2000 ★327★
The Beet Fields: Memories of a Sixteenth Summer
  Most notable fiction books for young adults, 2001 ★322★
Beethoven Elementary School
  Illinois elementary schools chosen to be 'demonstration sites' for struggling schools ★4006★
The Beginner's Guide to Homeschooling
  Best selling small press releases, 2001 ★226★
Behavior Information Technology
  Most cited science serials in technical communication journals from 1988 to 1997 ★4424★
Behavioral and Brain Sciences
  Social sciences journals with the greatest impact measure, 1981-97 ★4341★
Behavioral sciences
  Subjects required by the most U.S. medical schools for the 2000-01 entering class ★2850★
Behrens; B. Lyn
  Top pay and benefits for the chief executive and top paid employees at Loma Linda University ★3377★
Behrs; David G.
  Top pay and benefits for the chief executive and top paid employees at Lynchburg College ★3384★
Beilein; John
  Top pay and benefits for the chief executive and top paid employees at the University of Richmond ★3559★
Being Dead
  Booklist's best fiction books for library collections, 2000 ★227★
  Most notable fiction books, 2001 ★284★
  Outstanding works of fiction, 2001 ★293★
Being with Henry
  Most notable fiction books for young adults, 2001 ★322★
Beitz; Charles R.
  Top pay and benefits for the chief executive and top paid employees at Bowdoin College ★3207★
Bekavac; Nancy Y.
  Top pay and benefits for the chief executive and top paid employees at Scripps College ★3493★
Belafonte; Harry
  Most influential African American entertainers ★77★
Belgium
  Annual leave days for employees in selected countries ★2239★
  Institute for Scientific Information periodical prices by country, 2001 ★2922★
  Countries spending the highest percentage of gross domestic product on education ★4060★
Belhaven College
  Highest undergraduate tuition and fees at colleges and universities in Mississippi ★1522★
Belkin; Nicholas
  Library and information science faculty with the most citations to journal articles, 1993-1998 ★2710★
Bell; Alexis T.
  American Chemical Society 2001 award winners (Group 1) ★751★
Bell Atlantic
  Best companies for working mothers in offering leave for new parents ★4449★
Bell; Diane
  Top pay and benefits for the chief executive and top paid employees at College of the Holy Cross ★3247★
Bell; Donald R.
  Top pay and benefits for the chief executive and top paid employees at Pacific Lutheran University ★3436★
Bell Elementary School
  Chicago neighborhood schools with the highest ISAT scores in reading and math ★4004★
Bell Journal of Economics
  Economics journals with the greatest impact measure, 1981-98 ★2161★
  Economics journals by citation impact, 1981-98 ★2182★
  Highest impact economics journals in energy from 1974 to 1979 ★2456★
  Highest impact economics journals in exhaustible resources from 1974 to 1979 ★2459★
Bell Labs, Lucent
  Top institutions in systems and software engineering publications ★2332★
Bell; Michael
  All-American boy's high school football all-purpose players, 2000 ★179★
Bell; Nora K.
  Top pay and benefits for the chief executive and top paid employees at Wesleyan College in Georgia ★3611★
Bellarmine College
  U.S. News & World Report's southern regional universities with the best alumni giving rates, 2000-01 ★1434★
  U.S. News & World Report's southern regional universities with the highest acceptance rates, 2000-01 ★1436★
  U.S. News & World Report's southern regional universities with the highest freshmen retention rates, 2000-01 ★1437★
  Highest undergraduate tuition and fees at colleges and universities in Kentucky ★1508★
Belle; Deborah
  Radcliffe Institute for Advanced Study fellowship recipients in the field of psychology, 2000-01 ★3062★
Bellevue University
  Private 4-year institutions with the lowest tuition, 2000-01 ★1468★
  U.S. colleges and universities awarding the most social sciences and history master's degrees to Native Americans ★1804★

BELLINGHAM

Bellingham, WA
Best 'green & clean' places to live ★3077★

Bellinzoni; Arthur
Top pay and benefits for the chief executive and top paid employees at Wells College ★3610★

Bellow
Outstanding biography books, 2000 ★288★

BellSouth
Fortune's highest ranked telecommunications companies, 2000 ★499★
Top telecommunications companies in Standard & Poor's 500, 2001 ★559★

Bellucci; Joseph T.
Top pay and benefits for the chief executive and top paid employees at Wilkes University ★3627★

Bellwood, District 88
Illinois elementary school districts with the highest teacher salaries, 1999 ★3984★

Belmont Abbey College
Average faculty salaries for institutions of higher education in North Carolina, 2000-01 ★3720★

Belmont University
All-USA College Academic First Team, 2001 ★2★
U.S. News & World Report's southern regional universities with the best student/faculty ratios, 2000-01 ★1435★
U.S. News & World Report's southern regional universities with the highest proportion of classes with 20 students or less, 2000-01 ★1441★
Highest undergraduate tuition and fees at colleges and universities in Tennessee ★1558★
Institutions with the most female physics bachelor's recipients, 1994-1998 ★2959★
U.S. institutions with more than 40% female bachelor's graduates in their physics departments, 1994-98 ★2977★
Average faculty salaries for institutions of higher education in Tennessee, 2000-01 ★3730★

Beloit College
U.S. colleges and universities with poor instructors ★1027★
U.S. News & World Report's national liberal arts colleges with the highest acceptance rates, 2000-01 ★1328★
Highest undergraduate tuition and fees at colleges and universities in Wisconsin ★1570★
Private, 4-year undergraduate colleges and universities producing the most Ph.D.'s in the earth sciences, 1981-1990 ★2151★
Average faculty salaries for institutions of higher education in Wisconsin, 2000-01 ★3738★
Private, 4-year undergraduate colleges and universities producing the most Ph.D.'s in anthropology and sociology, 1920-1990 ★4344★
Private, 4-year undergraduate colleges and universities producing the most Ph.D.'s in anthropology and sociology, 1981-1990 ★4345★

Beloved
Favorite books of African Americans ★238★

Bemidji State University
Average faculty salaries for institutions of higher education in Minnesota, 2000-01 ★3710★

Bemis
Top containers and packaging companies in Standard & Poor's 500, 2001 ★537★

Bemis; Susan A.
Top pay and benefits for the chief executive and top paid employees at Chatham College ★3230★

Ben Franklin Middle School
Outstanding secondary schools in Buffalo-Niagara Falls, New York ★4102★

Bend, OR
Best 'green & clean' places to live ★3077★

Bender; Aimee
Booklist's best first novels ★228★

Benedict College
U.S. colleges and universities with the highest percentage of African Americans enrolled, 1997 ★222★
Institutions censured by the American Association of University Professors, 2001 ★1067★
Total baccalaureate physical sciences degrees awarded to African Americans from U.S. colleges and universities, 1997-98 ★1733★

Benedictine College
Highest undergraduate tuition and fees at colleges and universities in Kansas ★1506★

Benedictine University
U.S. News & World Report's midwestern regional universities with the highest proportion of classes having 20 students or less, 2000-01 ★1409★
U.S. News & World Report's midwestern regional universities with the lowest acceptance rates, 2000-01 ★1410★

Beneduce; Ann Keay
Outstanding children's religion books, 2000 ★332★

Benet Academy
Outstanding Catholic high schools in Metro Chicago ★4074★

Benicia Middle School
Outstanding secondary schools in Vallejo-Fairfield-Napa, California ★4247★

Benilde St. Margaret's High School
Outstanding secondary schools in Minneapolis-St. Paul, Minnesota-Wisconsin ★4181★

Benjamin-Cummings
Book publishers with the most citations (Class 4) ★2565★

Benjamin Franklin Middle School
Outstanding secondary schools in Bergen-Passaic, New Jersey ★4096★

Benjamin Group/BSMG Worldwide
Best companies for working mothers in offering advancement opportunities for women ★4447★

Benjamin Mays High School
Outstanding urban public high schools in Metro Atlanta ★4260★

Benne; Kenneth G.
Top pay and benefits for the chief executive and top paid employees at Wittenberg University ★3633★

Bennet; Douglas J.
Top pay and benefits for the chief executive and top paid employees at Wesleyan University in Connecticut ★3612★

Bennett College
U.S. colleges and universities with the highest percentage of African Americans enrolled, 1997 ★222★

Bennett; Douglas
Top pay and benefits for the chief executive and top paid employees at Earlham College ★3279★

Bennett; John B.
Top pay and benefits for the chief executive and top paid employees at Quinnipiac University ★3449★

Bennett; Sean
All-USA College Academic Second Team, 2001 ★3★

Bennett; Sheila K.
Top pay and benefits for the chief executive and top paid employees at Hobart and William Smith Colleges ★3334★

Bennington College
U.S. colleges and universities where intercollegiate sports are not popular ★994★
U.S. colleges and universities where intramural sports are not popular ★996★
U.S. colleges and universities where students and the local community have strained relations ★998★
U.S. colleges and universities where students are not very politically active ★1000★
U.S. colleges and universities where the general student body puts little emphasis on athletic events ★1009★
U.S. colleges and universities with a generally liberal student body ★1015★
U.S. colleges and universities with strained race/class interaction ★1029★
U.S. colleges and universities with the best on-campus housing facilities ★1032★
U.S. colleges and universities with the happiest students ★1035★
Institutions censured by the American Association of University Professors, 2001 ★1067★
U.S. News & World Report's national liberal arts colleges with the highest proportion of classes with less than 20 students, 2000-01 ★1335★
U.S. News & World Report's national liberal arts colleges with students most in debt, 1999 ★1386★
Undergraduate tuition and fees at colleges and universities in Vermont ★1563★

Benoist; Howard
Top pay and benefits for the chief executive and top paid employees at Our Lady of the Lake University ★3434★

Benson; Cedric
All-American boy's high school football running backs, 2000 ★186★

Benson; Mark Birger
Top pay and benefits for the chief executive and top paid employees at Saint Michael's College ★3483★

Bentley College
Division II NCAA colleges with the 100% graduation rates for women's basketball players, 1993-94 ★944★
Division II NCAA colleges with the highest graduation rates for all sports, 1993-94 ★945★
Division II NCAA colleges with the highest graduation rates for football players, 1993-94 ★946★
Professional or specialized institutions with the highest enrollment of foreign students, 1998-99 ★2501★
Average faculty salaries for institutions of higher education in Massachusetts, 2000-01 ★3708★
U.S. institutions with the highest paid assistant professors, 2001 ★3977★

Benz; G. William
Top pay and benefits for the chief executive and top paid employees at Ashland University ★3180★

Beowulf
Outstanding works of poetry, 2001 ★295★

Berea College
Lowest undergraduate tuition and fees at private nonprofit, 4-year or above colleges and universities ★1464★
Private 4-year institutions with the lowest tuition, 2000-01 ★1468★
Lowest undergraduate tuition and fees at colleges and universities in Kentucky ★1509★
Private, 4-year undergraduate colleges and universities producing the most Ph.D.'s in economics, 1920-1990 ★2211★
Average faculty salaries for institutions of higher education in Kentucky, 2000-01 ★3704★

Berean Institute
Lowest undergraduate tuition and fees at colleges and universities in Pennsylvania ★1550★

Berek; Peter
Top pay and benefits for the chief executive and top paid employees at Mount Holyoke College ★3409★

Berenson; Jerry
Top pay and benefits for the chief executive and top paid employees at Bryn Mawr College ★3212★

Berg; Daniel
Top pay and benefits for the chief executive and top paid employees at Rensselaer Polytechnic Institute ★3455★

Bergdoll; James R.
Top pay and benefits for the chief executive and top paid employees at Virginia Wesleyan College ★3596★

Bergen Brunswig
Fortune's highest ranked wholesalers, 2000 ★505★

Bergen, NJ
Counties with the highest per capita income ★2561★

Berger; Allen
Top pay and benefits for the chief executive and top paid employees at Franklin College of Indiana ★3297★

Berger; Michael
Top pay and benefits for the chief executive and top paid employees at Beaver College ★3195★

Berger; Nathan A.
Top pay and benefits for the chief executive and top paid employees at Case Western Reserve University ★3225★

Berger; Thomas M.
Top pay and benefits for the chief executive and top paid employees at Hood College ★3338★

Berk; R.A.
Most cited authors in the journal *Crime and Delinquency*, 1990 to 1995 ★1616★

Berkeley; Alan
Top pay and benefits for the chief executive and top paid employees at New York University ★3419★

Berkeley Carroll School
Outstanding secondary schools in New York, New York ★4191★

Berkeley College
Average faculty salaries for institutions of higher education without academic ranks in New York, 2000-01 ★3760★

Berkeley College of Business
Average faculty salaries for institutions of higher education without academic ranks in New Jersey, 2000-01 ★3758★

Berkeley Prep
Outstanding secondary schools in Tampa-St. Petersburg-Clearwater, Florida ★4240★

Berklee College of Music
Professional or specialized institutions with the highest enrollment of foreign students, 1998-99 ★2501★
Average faculty salaries for institutions of higher education in Massachusetts, 2000-01 ★3708★

Berkley
Mass market paperback bestsellers by publishing house, 2000 ★283★

Berkshire Hathaway
Fortune's highest ranked property and casualty insurance companies, 2000 ★488★

Berkshire; Steven D.
Top pay and benefits for the chief executive and top paid employees at Alaska Pacific University ★3166★

Berlin
Cities with the highest productivity of paper in the discipline of cardiovascular systems, 1994-96 ★2869★
Cities with the highest productivity of paper in the discipline of hematology, 1994-96 ★2870★

Berlinski; David
Booklist's best science and technology books ★366★

Berman; Aaron
Top pay and benefits for the chief executive and top paid employees at Hampshire College ★3322★

Berman; Richard A.
Top pay and benefits for the chief executive and top paid employees at Manhattanville College ★3388★

Bernard; Daniel
European business moguls considered the best empire builders ★441★

Bernard; David M.
Top pay and benefits for the chief executive and top paid employees at Oral Roberts University ★3433★

Bernard; Jenny
All-USA Teacher Teams, Third Team, 2000 ★4401★

Bernardsville Public Library
Highest Hennen's American Public Library Ratings for libraries serving a population of 5,000 to 9,999 ★2694★

Bernhard; Durga
Booklist's best science books for children ★310★

Bernhardt; William
Top pay and benefits for the chief executive and top paid employees at Union College in Kentucky ★3584★

Bernstein; Carl
Best U.S. works of journalism in the 20th century ★2769★

Bernstein-Rein
Most selective internships in the U.S., 2001 ★2610★

Berquist; Marcus R.
Top pay and benefits for the chief executive and top paid employees at Thomas Aquinas College in California ★3574★

Berry College
U.S. News & World Report's southern regional liberal arts colleges with the best student/faculty ratios, 2000-01 ★1368★
U.S. News & World Report's southern regional liberal arts colleges with the highest academic reputation scores, 2000-01 ★1369★
U.S. News & World Report's southern regional liberal arts colleges with the highest freshmen retention rates, 2000-01 ★1372★
U.S. News & World Report's southern regional liberal arts colleges with the highest graduation rates, 2000-01 ★1373★
U.S. News & World Report's southern regional liberal arts colleges with the highest proportion of freshmen in the top 25% of their high school class, 2000-01 ★1376★
U.S. News & World Report's top southern regional liberal arts colleges, 2000-01 ★1379★
U.S. News & World Report's best undergraduate fees among southern regional liberal arts colleges by discount tuition, 2000 ★1383★
Average faculty salaries for institutions of higher education in Georgia, 2000-01 ★3697★

Berry; William S. Huddleston
Top pay and benefits for the chief executive and top paid employees at Webster University ★3608★

Berryman; Clifford
Top editorial cartoonists used in teaching journalism history ★2770★

Berson; Gail
Top pay and benefits for the chief executive and top paid employees at Wheaton College in Massachusetts ★3621★

Berte; Neal R.
Top pay and benefits for the chief executive and top paid employees at Birmingham-Southern College ★3204★

Bertozzi; Carolyn R.
American Chemical Society 2001 award winners (Group 1) ★751★

Bessemer State Technical College
Lowest undergraduate tuition and fees at colleges and universities in Alabama ★1480★

The Best American Science and Nature Writing, 2000
Library Journal's most notable general science books, 2000 ★260★

Best Buy
Fortune's highest ranked specialty retailers, 2000 ★497★
Top consumer products companies in Standard & Poor's 500, 2001 ★536★

The Best of Jackson Payne
Booklist's best fiction books for library collections, 2000 ★227★

Best; Sharon P.
Top pay and benefits for the chief executive and top paid employees at Hobart and William Smith Colleges ★3334★

Bestfoods
Fortune's highest ranked consumer food products companies, 2000 ★458★

Beston; Rose Marie
Top pay and benefits for the chief executive and top paid employees at Nazareth College of Rochester ★3416★

Beth Hatalmud Rabbinical College
Lowest undergraduate tuition and fees at private nonprofit, 4-year or above colleges and universities ★1464★

Bethany College
- Highest undergraduate tuition and fees at colleges and universities in Kansas ★1506★
- Highest undergraduate tuition and fees at colleges and universities in West Virginia ★1568★
- Average faculty salaries for institutions of higher education in Kansas, 2000-01 ★3703★
- Average faculty salaries for institutions of higher education in West Virginia, 2000-01 ★3737★

Bethany College (KS)
- U.S. institutions with the lowest paid full professors, 2001 ★3979★

Bethea; Phillip Osbourne
- Top pay and benefits for the chief executive and top paid employees at Occidental College ★3428★

Bethel College
- U.S. News & World Report's midwestern regional liberal arts colleges with the best student/faculty ratios, 2000-01 ★1339★
- U.S. News & World Report's midwestern regional liberal arts colleges with the highest academic reputation scores, 2000-01 ★1340★
- U.S. News & World Report's midwestern regional liberal arts colleges with the highest freshmen retention rates, 2000-01 ★1343★
- U.S. News & World Report's midwestern regional liberal arts colleges with the highest graduation rates, 2000-01 ★1344★
- U.S. News & World Report's midwestern regional liberal arts colleges with the highest proportion of classes having 20 students or less, 2000-01 ★1347★
- U.S. News & World Report's top midwestern regional liberal arts colleges, 2000-01 ★1349★
- Highest undergraduate tuition and fees at colleges and universities in Kansas ★1506★
- Average faculty salaries for institutions of higher education in Indiana, 2000-01 ★3701★
- Average faculty salaries for institutions of higher education in Kansas, 2000-01 ★3703★
- Average faculty salaries for institutions of higher education in Minnesota, 2000-01 ★3710★
- Average faculty salaries for institutions of higher education in Tennessee, 2000-01 ★3730★

Bethel College (KS)
- U.S. institutions with the lowest paid full professors, 2001 ★3979★

Bethel College (TN)
- U.S. institutions with the lowest paid full professors, 2001 ★3979★

Bethlehem Steel
- Fortune's highest ranked metals companies, 2000 ★476★

Bethune-Cookman College
- Average faculty salaries for institutions of higher education in Florida, 2000-01 ★3696★

Betrayal of Trust: The Collapse of Global Public Health
- Library Journal's most notable health sciences books, 2000 ★262★
- Outstanding social sciences books, 2000 ★292★

Betsey Johnson
- Most selective internships in the U.S., 2001 ★2610★

Better Homes and Gardens
- Magazines with the largest circulation ★2750★

Between the Lions
- Most notable children's web sites, 2001 ★2593★

Beutell; Nicholas J.
- Top pay and benefits for the chief executive and top paid employees at Iona College ★3350★

Beuys; Joseph
- Highly influential artists of the 20th century ★76★

Beveridge; David
- Top pay and benefits for the chief executive and top paid employees at Wesleyan University in Connecticut ★3612★

Bevilacqua, O.P.; Sister Linda M.
- Top pay and benefits for the chief executive and top paid employees at Gwynedd-Mercy College ★3318★

B.F. Goodrich
- Fortune's highest ranked aerospace companies, 2000 ★446★
- Top aerospace and defense companies in Standard & Poor's 500, 2001 ★529★

BFI Companion to Eastern European and Russian Cinema
- Selected reference books in the field of film, 2000 ★375★

Bhagwati; J.N.
- U.S. academic economists by mean number of citations, 1971-92 ★2176★
- U.S. academic economists by total citations, 1971-92 ★2177★

Bialik; Jeffrey V.
- Top pay and benefits for the chief executive and top paid employees at Dominican University of California ★3270★

Bibby; Charlie Henry
- Top pay and benefits for the chief executive and top paid employees at the University of Southern California ★3568★

Bibliometrics: Its Theoretical Foundations, Methods and Applications
- Most frequently cited Libri articles ★2730★

Bicycle Stunt Riding: Catch Air!
- Most notable nonfiction books for reluctant young adult readers, 2001 ★323★

Biemann; Klaus
- American Chemical Society 2001 award winners (Group 1) ★751★

Bienen; Henry S.
- Top pay and benefits for the chief executive and top paid employees at Northwestern University ★3423★

Bieze; Judy
- All-USA Teacher Teams, Second Team, 2000 ★4400★

Big Bend Community College
- Lowest undergraduate tuition and fees at colleges and universities in Washington ★1567★

Big Jabe
- Outstanding children's picture books, 2000 ★331★

The Big Six
- Smithsonian's best books for children ages 10 and up ★365★

Bigelow; Bruce E.
- Top pay and benefits for the chief executive and top paid employees at Hood College ★3338★

Biggs; William
- Top pay and benefits for the chief executive and top paid employees at Beaver College ★3195★

Bigham; Wanda
- Top pay and benefits for the chief executive and top paid employees at Huntingdon College ★3344★

Bigney; Betty
- All-USA Teacher Teams, First Team, 2000 ★4399★

Biles; David
- Most-cited scholars in Australian and New Zealand Journal of Criminology ★1636★

Bilik; Edward
- Top pay and benefits for the chief executive and top paid employees at Springfield College in Massachusetts ★3509★

Billings; Charles R.
- Top pay and benefits for the chief executive and top paid employees at Dominican University of California ★3270★

Bills; Daniel
- All-America boys' high school soccer team defenders, 2001 ★165★

Billups Jr.; Fred H.
- Top pay and benefits for the chief executive and top paid employees at St. John's College in Maryland and New Mexico ★3473★

Billy Ryan High School
- Outstanding suburban public high schools in Metro Dallas-Ft. Worth ★4257★

Biloxi/Gulfport, MS
- Best small towns to live in ★3085★

Binder; Kenneth
- Top pay and benefits for the chief executive and top paid employees at Rivier College ★3460★

Bingham; Kim
- All-America girls' high school soccer team goalkeepers, 2001 ★176★

Binghamton University (SUNY)
- U.S. colleges and universities with the most upper level courses taught by TAs ★1040★
- U.S. colleges and universities with the worst financial aid programs ★1042★

Biochemistry
- Biological sciences doctorates awarded at U.S. colleges and universities, by subfield, 1999 ★1887★
- Gender breakdown of biological sciences doctorate recipients, by subfield, 1999 ★1927★
- Percentage of female doctorate recipients at U.S. colleges and universities, by subfield, 1999 ★1988★
- Top physical science majors for accepted applicants to U.S. medical schools, 1999-2000 ★2855★
- Average salaries for assistant professors at private institutions in preclinical department of medical schools, 2000-01 ★3785★
- Average salaries for assistant professors at public and private institutions in preclinical department of medical schools, 2000-01 ★3786★
- Average salaries for assistant professors at public institutions in preclinical department of medical schools, 2000-01 ★3787★
- Average salaries for associate professors at private institutions in preclinical department of medical schools, 2000-01 ★3800★
- Average salaries for associate professors at public and private institutions in preclinical department of medical schools, 2000-01 ★3801★
- Average salaries for associate professors at public institutions in preclinical department of medical schools, 2000-01 ★3802★

Average salaries for full-time instructors at private institutions in preclinical department of medical schools, 2000-01 ★3854★

Average salaries for full-time instructors at public and private institutions in preclinical department of medical schools, 2000-01 ★3855★

Average salaries for full-time instructors at public institutions in preclinical department of medical schools, 2000-01 ★3856★

Average salaries for professors at private institutions in preclinical department of medical schools, 2000-01 ★3932★

Average salaries for professors at public and private institutions in preclinical department of medical schools, 2000-01 ★3933★

Average salaries for professors at public institutions in preclinical department of medical schools, 2000-01 ★3934★

Biodiversity Studies: A Bibliographic Review
Library Journal's best reference books, 2000 ★368★

Bioengineering and biomedical
Engineering doctorates awarded at U.S. colleges and universities, by subfield, 1999 ★1923★
Gender breakdown of engineering doctorate recipients, by subfield, 1999 ★1934★

Biogen
Business Week's best performing companies with the highest net margin, 2000 ★419★
Top health care companies in Standard & Poor's 500, 2001 ★542★

The Biographical Dictionary of Women in Science
Library Journal's best reference books, 2000 ★368★

The Biographical Dictionary of Women in Science: Pioneering Lives from Ancient Times to the Mid-20th Century
Outstanding reference sources, 2000 ★370★

Biography
Subject areas with the highest library expenditures/circulation ★306★

Biography.com
Library Journal's best free reference websites, 2000 ★367★

Biola University
Average faculty salaries for institutions of higher education in California, 2000-01 ★3692★

Biological Control
Agriculture journals by citation impact, 1995-99 ★53★
Agriculture journals by citation impact, 1999 ★54★
Entomology journals by citation impact, 1994-98 ★2454★
Entomology journals by citation impact, 1998 ★2455★

Biological and environmental research
Energy Department research funding, 2001 ★3110★

Biological immunology
Biological sciences doctorates awarded at U.S. colleges and universities, by subfield, 1999 ★1887★
Gender breakdown of biological sciences doctorate recipients, by subfield, 1999 ★1927★

Biological Mass Spectrometry
Spectroscopy journals by citation impact, 1995-99 ★4360★

Biological science
Proposed fiscal 2002 appropriations for the National Science Foundation ★3109★

Biological sciences
Median salary for B.S. chemists, by field ★781★
Median salary for M.S. chemists, by field ★785★
Median salary for Ph.D. chemists, by field ★786★
Expected majors for incoming freshmen, 2000 ★1050★
Life sciences doctorates awarded to U.S. citizens/permanent residents at U.S. colleges and universities, by race/ethnicity and subfield, 1999 ★1950★
Number of life sciences doctorate recipients at U.S. colleges and universities, by field, 1999 ★1974★

Biological sciences, general
Biological sciences doctorates awarded at U.S. colleges and universities, by subfield, 1999 ★1887★
Gender breakdown of biological sciences doctorate recipients, by subfield, 1999 ★1927★

Biological sciences/life sciences
Top bachelor's degree disciplines for African Americans, 1997-98 ★1672★
Top bachelor's degree disciplines for Asian Americans, 1997-98 ★1673★
Top bachelor's degree disciplines for Hispanic Americans, 1997-98 ★1674★
Top bachelor's degree disciplines for Native Americans, 1997-98 ★1675★
Top bachelor's degree disciplines for non-minorities, 1997-98 ★1676★

Biological scientists
Projections for the fastest growing occupations requiring a bachelor's degree or more from 1998 to 2008 ★2292★
Projected employment growth for selected occupations that require advanced education, 1998-2008 ★2318★

Biologist
Jobs with the best security scores ★2251★
Jobs with the lowest unemployment ★2258★
Most desirable jobs in math/science ★2274★

Biology
Number of Advanced Placement Exams taken by African Americans, by subject, 2000 ★30★
Number of Advanced Placement Exams taken by Asian Americans, by subject, 2000 ★31★
Number of Advanced Placement Exams taken by Hispanic Americans, by subject, 2000 ★32★
Subjects required by the most U.S. medical schools for the 2000-01 entering class ★2850★
Top biological science majors for accepted applicants to U.S. medical schools, 1999-2000 ★2851★
Average costs for Academic Search titles by subject, 2001 ★2918★
Periodical prices by LC subject, 2001 ★2925★
Periodical prices by scientific discipline, 2001 ★2926★
Mean age of first and best contribution of scientists and inventors, by discipline ★3096★

Biology and biochemistry
Austria's contribution of papers in the sciences by field, 1992-96 ★4298★
Austria's relative impact in the sciences by field, 1992-96 ★4300★
Belgium's contribution of papers in the sciences by field, 1992-96 ★4301★
Belgium's contribution of papers in the sciences, by field, 1995-99 ★4302★
Denmark's contribution of papers in the sciences, by field, 1994-98 ★4306★
Denmark's contribution of papers in the sciences, by field, 1995-99 ★4307★
Finland's contribution of papers in the sciences, by field, 1995-99 ★4310★
France's contribution of papers in the sciences, by field, 1995-99 ★4311★
France's contribution of papers in the sciences, by field, 1996-2000 ★4312★
Germany's contribution of papers in the sciences, by field, 1995-99 ★4313★
Ireland's contribution of papers in the sciences, by field, 1994-98 ★4315★
Japan's contribution of papers in the sciences, by field, 1995-99 ★4318★
Japan's contribution of papers in the sciences, by field, 1996-2000 ★4319★
Poland's contribution of papers in the sciences, by field, 1993-97 ★4324★
Russia's contribution of papers in the sciences, by field, 1993-97 ★4325★
South Korea's contribution of papers in the sciences, by field, 1995-99 ★4327★
Spain's contribution of papers in the sciences, by field, 1993-97 ★4328★
Spain's contribution of papers in the sciences, by field, 1995-99 ★4329★
Sweden's contribution of papers in the sciences by field, 1993-97 ★4330★
Sweden's contribution of papers in the sciences, by field, 1995-99 ★4331★
Switzerland's contribution of papers in the sciences, by field, 1994-98 ★4332★
Switzerland's contribution of papers in the sciences, by field, 1995-99 ★4333★

Biology and Fertility of Soils
Soil science journals by citation impact, 1981-99 ★188★
Soil science journals by citation impact, 1995-99 ★189★
Soil science journals by citation impact, 1999 ★190★

Biology or zoology
Subjects required by the most U.S. medical schools for the 2000-01 entering class ★2850★

Biomedical engineering
Top physical science majors for accepted applicants to U.S. medical schools, 1999-2000 ★2855★

Biomedical and Environmental Mass Spectrometry
Spectroscopy journals by citation impact, 1981-99 ★4359★

Biomedical Mass Spectrometry
Spectroscopy journals by citation impact, 1981-99 ★4359★

Biomedical sciences
Biological sciences doctorates awarded at U.S. colleges and universities, by subfield, 1999 ★1887★
Gender breakdown of biological sciences doctorate recipients, by subfield, 1999 ★1927★

Biometrics and biostatistics
Biological sciences doctorates awarded at U.S. colleges and universities, by subfield, 1999 ★1887★

Gender breakdown of biological sciences doctorate recipients, by subfield, 1999 ★1927★

Biondi, S.J.; Rev. Lawrence
Top pay and benefits for the chief executive and top paid employees at St. Louis University ★3478★

Biophysics
Biological sciences doctorates awarded at U.S. colleges and universities, by subfield, 1999 ★1887★
Gender breakdown of biological sciences doctorate recipients, by subfield, 1999 ★1927★
Major subfields of first-year physics and astronomy graduate students who are foreign citizens planning to receive a Ph.D., 1997-98 ★3004★
Major subfields of first-year physics and astronomy graduate students who are U.S. citizens planning to receive a Ph.D., 1997-98 ★3005★

Bioscience, Biotechnology and Biochemistry
Agriculture journals by citation impact, 1992-96 ★52★
Agriculture journals by citation impact, 1995-99 ★53★

Biotechnology Progress
Food science and technology journals by citation impact, 1995-99 ★2903★
Food science and technology journals by citation impact, 1999 ★2904★

Biotechnology research
Biological sciences doctorates awarded at U.S. colleges and universities, by subfield, 1999 ★1887★
Gender breakdown of biological sciences doctorate recipients, by subfield, 1999 ★1927★

Birch; Edward
Top pay and benefits for the chief executive and top paid employees at Westmont College ★3619★

Birgenheier; Raymond A.
Top pay and benefits for the chief executive and top paid employees at Gonzaga University ★3311★

Birkbeck College
United Kingdom universities with the greatest impact in chemistry, 1993-97 ★807★
United Kingdom universities contributing the most papers in the field of economics and business, 1993-97 ★2203★

Birkhead; William J.
Top pay and benefits for the chief executive and top paid employees at Westminster College in Pennsylvania ★3617★

Birmingham Southern College
U.S. colleges and universities where fraternities and sororities are popular ★993★
Fiske Guide's best buys for private colleges and universities, 2001 ★1459★
Highest undergraduate tuition and fees at colleges and universities in Alabama ★1479★

Birmingham; University of
United Kingdom universities with the greatest impact in chemistry, 1993-97 ★807★

Birrell; Stephen R.
Top pay and benefits for the chief executive and top paid employees at Williams College ★3631★

Bisbee, AZ
Best 'quirky' places to live ★3083★

Bishop Gorman High School
Outstanding secondary schools in Tyler, Texas ★4245★

Bishop Hendricken High School
Outstanding secondary schools in Providence-Fall River-Warwick, Rhode Island-Maine ★4207★

Bishop; Jeffrey
Top pay and benefits for the chief executive and top paid employees at St. John's College in Maryland and New Mexico ★3473★

Bishop; Jerry
Top pay and benefits for the chief executive and top paid employees at Lincoln Memorial University ★3374★

Bishop Lynch High School
Outstanding secondary schools in Dallas, Texas ★4120★

Bishop; Nic
Booklist's best science books for children ★310★

Bishop O'Connell High School
Outstanding secondary schools in Washington, District of Columbia-Maryland-Virginia-West Virginia ★4249★

Bishop O'Dowd High School
Outstanding secondary schools in Oakland, California ★4195★

Bishop Stang High School
Outstanding secondary schools in New Bedford, Massachusetts ★4187★

Bishop; Thomas B.
Top pay and benefits for the chief executive and top paid employees at Samford University ★3490★

The Bishop's School
Outstanding secondary schools in San Diego, California ★4220★

Bishop's University
Canadian primarily undergraduate universities by alumni support, 2000 ★1193★
Canadian primarily undergraduate universities by class size at the first and second-year level, 2000 ★1195★
Canadian primarily undergraduate universities by class size at the third and forth-year level, 2000 ★1196★
Canadian primarily undergraduate universities by classes taught by tenured faculty, 2000 ★1197★
Canadian primarily undergraduate universities by faculty members with Ph.D.'s, 2000 ★1198★
Canadian primarily undergraduate universities by library acquisitions, 2000 ★1199★
Canadian primarily undergraduate universities by library expenses, 2000 ★1200★
Canadian primarily undergraduate universities by library holdings per student, 2000 ★1201★
Canadian primarily undergraduate universities by medical/science grants per faculty member, 2000 ★1202★
Canadian primarily undergraduate universities by operating budget per student, 2000 ★1203★
Canadian primarily undergraduate universities by percentage of operating budget allocated to scholarships, 2000 ★1204★
Canadian primarily undergraduate universities by percentage of operating budget allocated to student services, 2000 ★1205★
Canadian primarily undergraduate universities by reputation, 2000 ★1206★
Canadian primarily undergraduate universities by social science/humanities grants per faculty member, 2000 ★1207★
Canadian primarily undergraduate universities by students from out of province, 2000 ★1208★
Canadian primarily undergraduate universities by students winning national awards, 2000 ★1209★
Canadian universities with the lowest total cost, 2000 ★1218★
Top Canadian primarily undergraduate universities, 2000 ★1226★

Bismarck State College
State appropriations for North Dakota's institutions of higher education, 2000-01 ★1287★
Lowest undergraduate tuition and fees at colleges and universities in North Dakota ★1542★
Average faculty salaries for institutions of higher education in North Dakota, 2000-01 ★3721★

Bissonnette; Paul E.
Top pay and benefits for the chief executive and top paid employees at the University of San Diego ★3565★

Black & Decker
Fortune's highest ranked industrial and farm equipment companies, 2000 ★471★

Black; Barbara Ellen
Top pay and benefits for the chief executive and top paid employees at Dowling College ★3271★

Black Cat
Most notable children's videos, 2001 ★2889★

Black; David
Top pay and benefits for the chief executive and top paid employees at Eastern College in Pennsylvania ★3280★

Black; Edward H.
Top pay and benefits for the chief executive and top paid employees at Union College in Kentucky ★3584★

Black Elementary
Chicago elementary magnet schools with the lowest acceptance rates, 2000-01 ★4003★

Black; Ellen
Top pay and benefits for the chief executive and top paid employees at Liberty University ★3373★

Black Enterprise
Most selective internships in the U.S., 2001 ★2610★

Black Hawk College
Average faculty salaries for institutions of higher education in Illinois, 2000-01 ★3700★

Black Hills State University
State appropriations for South Dakota's institutions of higher education, 2000-01 ★1294★
Average faculty salaries for institutions of higher education in South Dakota, 2000-01 ★3729★

Black; J.
Highest ranked inactive communication studies researchers ★2748★

Black Jack
Smithsonian's best books for children ages 10 and up ★365★

Black Mountain Middle School
Outstanding secondary schools in San Diego, California ★4220★

Black, White and Jewish: Autobiography of a Shifting Self
Booklist's most recommended African American nonfiction ★229★

Blackbird: A Childhood Lost
  Outstanding nonfiction books for young adults, 2000 ★334★
Blackfeet Community College
  U.S. tribal colleges ★1445★
  Lowest undergraduate tuition and fees at colleges and universities in Montana ★1527★
Blackhawk Technical College
  Lowest undergraduate tuition and fees at colleges and universities in Wisconsin ★1571★
Blackman; R. Craig
  Top pay and benefits for the chief executive and top paid employees at Christian Brothers University ★3233★
Blackmore; Josiah
  Top pay and benefits for the chief executive and top paid employees at Capital University ★3220★
Blackwell, Basil
  Book publishers with the most citations (Class 5) ★2566★
The Blade
  Most selective internships in the U.S., 2001 ★2610★
Bladen Community College
  Average faculty salaries for institutions of higher education without academic ranks in North Carolina, 2000-01 ★3761★
Blair; Norman
  Top pay and benefits for the chief executive and top paid employees at Saint Thomas University in Florida ★3486★
Blais; Roger N.
  Top pay and benefits for the chief executive and top paid employees at the University of Tulsa ★3573★
Blake; Bessie W.
  Top pay and benefits for the chief executive and top paid employees at the College of New Rochelle ★3525★
Blake; Diane
  Top pay and benefits for the chief executive and top paid employees at Union College in New York ★3585★
The Blake Lower School
  Outstanding secondary schools in Minneapolis-St. Paul, Minnesota-Wisconsin ★4181★
The Blake School
  Outstanding secondary schools in Minneapolis-St. Paul, Minnesota-Wisconsin ★4181★
Blake; Sylvia
  Top pay and benefits for the chief executive and top paid employees at Manhattanville College ★3388★
Blakey; G. C.
  Authors most frequently contributing to the *American Economic Review* from 1911-1990 ★2156★
Blakey; R. G.
  Authors most frequently contributing to the *American Economic Review* from 1911-1990 ★2156★
Blalack Junior High School
  Outstanding secondary schools in Dallas, Texas ★4120★
Blanca's Feather
  Smithsonian's best books for children ages 6 to 10 ★364★
Blanchet High School
  Outstanding secondary schools in Seattle-Bellevue-Everett, Washington ★4227★

Bland; Kirby Isaac
  Top pay and benefits for the chief executive and top paid employees at Brown University ★3211★
Blaney; George
  Top pay and benefits for the chief executive and top paid employees at Seton Hall University ★3496★
Blanshei; Sarah R.
  Top pay and benefits for the chief executive and top paid employees at Agnes Scott College ★3165★
Bleicher; Joel N.
  Top pay and benefits for the chief executive and top paid employees at Creighton University ★3259★
Blessed Sacrament School
  Outstanding secondary schools in Cincinnati, Ohio-Kentucky-Indiana ★4112★
Blessing the Boats: New and Selected Poems, 1988-2000
  Library Journal's best poetry books, 2000 ★244★
Bleyl Junior High School
  Outstanding secondary schools in Houston, Texas ★4150★
The Blind Assassin
  Booklist's best fiction books for library collections, 2000 ★227★
  Most notable fiction books, 2001 ★284★
  Outstanding works of fiction, 2001 ★293★
A Blind Man Can See How Much I Love You
  Booklist's best fiction books for library collections, 2000 ★227★
Blinder; David
  Top pay and benefits for the chief executive and top paid employees at Wellesley College ★3609★
Bling Blang; Howdi Do
  Outstanding children's picture books, 2000 ★331★
Blinn College
  Institutions censured by the American Association of University Professors, 2001 ★1067★
Blizzard! The Storm That Changed America
  Most notable books for older readers, 2001 ★318★
Block; Francesca Lia
  Outstanding children's fiction books, 2000 ★329★
Block; Herbert (Herblock)
  Top editorial cartoonists used in teaching journalism history ★2770★
Blockbuster Inc.
  Top recruiters for business administration jobs for 2000-01 bachelor's degree recipients ★554★
Blodgett; Cindy
  Division I women's career high scorers ★129★
Blood
  Hematology journals with the greatest impact measure, 1981-98 ★2808★
  Hematology journals with the greatest impact measure, 1994-98 ★2809★
Blood Cells
  Hematology journals with the greatest impact measure, 1994-98 ★2809★
Blood; Judith
  All-USA Teacher Teams, Third Team, 2000 ★4401★

The Blood Runs like a River through My Dreams: A Memoir
  Outstanding history books, 2000 ★289★
  Outstanding nonfiction books for young adults, 2000 ★334★
Blood and Smoke
  Library Journal's best fiction audiobooks, 2000 ★241★
Bloom; Alfred H.
  Top pay and benefits for the chief executive and top paid employees at Swarthmore College ★3514★
Bloomfield College
  Average faculty salaries for institutions of higher education in New Jersey, 2000-01 ★3717★
Bloomington, IN
  Best college towns to live in ★3076★
  U.S. cities with the most single people ★3089★
Bloomsburg University
  Average faculty salaries for institutions of higher education in Pennsylvania, 2000-01 ★3725★
Bloomsburg University of Pennsylvania
  U.S. News & World Report's top public northern regional universities, 2000-01 ★1426★
Blubber
  Most frequently banned books in the 1990s ★745★
  People for the American Way's list of most frequently challenged books, 1982-1992 ★747★
  People for the American Way's list of most frequently challenged books, 1991-1992 ★748★
Blue-collar worker supervisors
  Occupations with the highest number of self-employed workers, 1998 ★2311★
  Projected employment growth for selected occupations that require long-term on-the-job training, 1998-2008 ★2320★
Blue Deer Thaw
  Library Journal's best mystery titles, 2000 ★242★
Blue Mountain College
  Highest undergraduate tuition and fees at colleges and universities in Mississippi ★1522★
Blue Mountain Community College
  Lowest undergraduate tuition and fees at colleges and universities in Oregon ★1548★
Blue Ridge Community College
  Average faculty salaries for institutions of higher education without academic ranks in North Carolina, 2000-01 ★3761★
Blue Valley North High School
  Outstanding secondary schools in Kansas City, Missouri-Kansas ★4158★
Bluefield State College
  Division II NCAA colleges with the 0% graduation rates for men's basketball players, 1993-94 ★941★
  Division II NCAA colleges with the lowest graduation rates for all sports, 1993-94 ★947★
  State appropriations for West Virginia's institutions of higher education, 2000-01 ★1301★
  U.S. News & World Report's southern regional liberal arts colleges with students least in debt, 1999 ★1366★
  Lowest undergraduate tuition and fees at colleges and universities in West Virginia ★1569★

Average faculty salaries for institutions of higher education in West Virginia, 2000-01 ★3737★

The Bluest Eye
Longest-running trade paperback bestsellers, 2000 ★282★

Bluestem
Booklist's best first novels for youths ★309★
Booklist's most recommended historical fiction for youths, 2001 ★314★

Blufton College
U.S. News & World Report's midwestern regional liberal arts colleges with the best student/faculty ratios, 2000-01 ★1339★
U.S. News & World Report's midwestern regional liberal arts colleges with the highest alumni giving rates, 2000-01 ★1342★
U.S. News & World Report's midwestern regional liberal arts colleges with the highest proportion of classes having 20 students or less, 2000-01 ★1347★
Average faculty salaries for institutions of higher education in Ohio, 2000-01 ★3722★

Blume; Judy
Authors protested for more than one book between 1952 and 1989, according to the *Newsletter of Intellectual Freedom* ★743★
People for the American Way's list of most frequently challenged authors, 1982-1992 ★746★

Blume; Paul
Top pay and benefits for the chief executive and top paid employees at Hanover College ★3324★

Blumer; Jeffrey
Top pay and benefits for the chief executive and top paid employees at Case Western Reserve University ★3225★

Blumstein; Alfred
Most cited authors in the journal *Journal of Quantitative Criminology*, 1990 to 1995 ★1628★
Most cited authors in three criminal justice journals ★1633★
Most cited authors in three criminology journals ★1634★
Most-cited scholars in *British Journal of Criminology* ★1637★
Most-cited scholars in *Criminology* ★1639★

B.M.C. Durfee High School
Outstanding urban public high schools in Metro Boston ★4261★

BMC Software
Fortune's highest ranked computer software companies, 2000 ★455★
Software companies with the fastest growth, 2000 ★528★

BNP Paribas
Business Week's best companies in France ★393★

Board of Tech & Comprehensive Education
State appropriations for South Carolina's institutions of higher education, 2000-01 ★1293★

Board; Warren L.
Top pay and benefits for the chief executive and top paid employees at St. Andrews Presbyterian College ★3469★

Boatman; Sara
Top pay and benefits for the chief executive and top paid employees at Nebraska Wesleyan University ★3417★

Bob Jones High School
Outstanding secondary schools in Huntsville, Alabama ★4152★

Bobbi Brown Teenage Beauty: Everything You Need to Know to Look Pretty
Most notable nonfiction books for reluctant young adult readers, 2001 ★323★

Boca Raton Christian School
Outstanding secondary schools in West Palm Beach-Boca Raton, Florida ★4251★

Bode; Hank
Top pay and benefits for the chief executive and top paid employees at Azusa Pacific University ★3187★

Bodenhorn; H.
Top assistant professor economists at elite liberal arts colleges, 1975-94 ★2173★

The Body of Christopher Creed
Most notable fiction books for young adults, 2001 ★322★

Body for Life
Longest-running nonfiction hardcover bestsellers, 2000 ★281★

Boeheim; Jim
Coaches winning the most NCAA tournaments ★120★

Boeheim Jr.; James A.
Top pay and benefits for the chief executive and top paid employees at Syracuse University ★3516★

Boehms; Charles N.
Top pay and benefits for the chief executive and top paid employees at Georgetown College in Kentucky ★3305★

Boeing
Fortune's highest ranked aerospace companies, 2000 ★446★
Top aerospace and defense companies in Standard & Poor's 500, 2001 ★529★
Most selective internships in the U.S., 2001 ★2610★

Boelhower; Gary
Top pay and benefits for the chief executive and top paid employees at Marian College of Fond Du Lac ★3389★

The Boer War: Historiography and Annotated Bibliography
Selected reference books in the field of history, 2000 ★376★

Bohen; Frederick M.
Top pay and benefits for the chief executive and top paid employees at Rockefeller University ★3462★

Boise Bible College
Undergraduate tuition and fees at colleges and universities in Idaho ★1499★

Boise Cascade
Fortune's highest ranked forest and paper products companies, 2000 ★466★
Top paper and forest products companies in Standard & Poor's 500, 2001 ★552★

Boise, ID
Best 'green & clean' places to live ★3077★

Boise State University
Division I NCAA colleges with the lowest graduation rates for football players, 1990-91 to 1993-94 ★938★
Division I NCAA colleges with the lowest graduation rates for male athletes, 1990-91 to 1993-94 ★939★
State appropriations for Idaho's institutions of higher education, 2000-01 ★1265★
Undergraduate tuition and fees at colleges and universities in Idaho ★1499★

Average faculty salaries for institutions of higher education in Idaho, 2000-01 ★3699★

Bojar; Anthea
Top pay and benefits for the chief executive and top paid employees at Cardinal Stritch University ★3221★

Bolitt; Gabor
Top pay and benefits for the chief executive and top paid employees at Gettysburg College ★3308★

Boller; Gregory W.
Highest impact authors in the *Journal of Business Research*, by adjusted number of citations in 12 journals, 1985-1999 ★692★
Highest impact authors in the *Journal of Business Research*, by number of citations in 12 journals, 1985-1999 ★693★

Bombardier
Business Week's best companies in Canada ★390★

Bonaparte
Smithsonian's best books for children ages 1 to 6 ★363★

Bond; Edward
Top playwrights of the twentieth century ★4436★

Bond; James
Top pay and benefits for the chief executive and top paid employees at Seattle University ★3495★

Bond; John
European business moguls considered the best empire builders ★441★

Bonfini, I.H.M.; Sister Marie Roseanne
Top pay and benefits for the chief executive and top paid employees at Immaculata College ★3348★

Bonino; MaryAnn
Top pay and benefits for the chief executive and top paid employees at Mount Saint Mary's College in California ★3411★

Bonior; Rep. David E.
Members of Congress receiving the largest contributions from the Sallie Mae Inc. Political Action Committee ★3023★

Bonita Springs Middle School
Outstanding secondary schools in Fort Myers-Cape Coral, Florida ★4134★

Bonnel; Bruno
European business moguls considered the best innovators ★442★

Bonner; A. Frank
Top pay and benefits for the chief executive and top paid employees at Gardner-Webb University ★3303★

Bonnette; A. Kennerley
Top pay and benefits for the chief executive and top paid employees at Charleston Southern University ★3229★

Bonta; J.
Most cited authors in the journal *Federal Probation*, 1990 to 1995 ★1623★

Boogie Man: The Adventures of John Lee Hooker in the American Twentieth Century
Booklist's most recommended African American nonfiction ★229★

The Book of the Lion
Smithsonian's best books for children ages 10 and up ★365★

Book; Michael
Top pay and benefits for the chief executive and top paid employees at Wartburg College ★3603★

Bookkeeper
Jobs with the best stress scores ★2252★
Most desirable jobs in business/finance ★2270★

Bookkeeping, accounting, and auditing clerks
Occupations with the highest decline in employment, 1998-2008 ★2310★
Occupations with the highest number of self-employed workers, 1998 ★2311★

Bookman; Mark
Top pay and benefits for the chief executive and top paid employees at the University of Judaism ★3546★

Bookmarks/typed-in URLs
Web pages with the highest access percentages ★2608★

Boone; James Allen
Top pay and benefits for the chief executive and top paid employees at Rhodes College ★3456★

Boone; Tommy
Top pay and benefits for the chief executive and top paid employees at the College of St. Scholastica ★3530★

Booth; Frank
Top pay and benefits for the chief executive and top paid employees at Brenau University ★3210★

Booth; Jim
Top pay and benefits for the chief executive and top paid employees at the University of Saint Thomas in Texas ★3564★

Boothe; Fred D.
Top pay and benefits for the chief executive and top paid employees at University of Charleston ★3590★

Bop
Best-selling youth magazines ★2920★

Borden; Richard
Top pay and benefits for the chief executive and top paid employees at College of the Atlantic ★3246★

Borduas; Paul-Emile
Canada's best visual artists of the 20th century ★75★

Borek Jr.; John M.
Top pay and benefits for the chief executive and top paid employees at Liberty University ★3373★

Borgman; Christine
Library and information science faculty with the most citations to journal articles, 1993-1998 ★2710★

Bornstein; Rita
Top pay and benefits for the chief executive and top paid employees at Rollins College ★3465★

Borrowed Light
Most notable fiction books for young adults, 2001 ★322★

Borton; Teresa
All-America girls' high school basketball 2nd team, 2001 ★171★

Borum; Regina A.
Top pay and benefits for the chief executive and top paid employees at LaRoche College ★3364★

Boss Cupid
Booklist's most recommended poetry books, 2001 ★231★

Bosse; Patricia
Top pay and benefits for the chief executive and top paid employees at the College of Notre Dame in Maryland ★3527★

Bossier Parish Community College
Lowest undergraduate tuition and fees at colleges and universities in Louisiana ★1511★

Boston
U.S. cities with the highest number of high-tech employees, 1998 ★2284★
U.S. school districts with the highest number of vacancies for K-12 teachers ★2331★
American cities with the highest percentage of people with Internet access ★2572★
U.S. cities with the most wired households, 2001 ★2606★
U.S. market areas with the highest percentage of adults having internet access ★2607★

Boston College
U.S. catholic universities with the highest enrollment, 1999 ★864★
Division I NCAA colleges with the highest graduation rates for female athletes, 1990-91 to 1993-94 ★931★
Division I NCAA colleges with the highest graduation rates for female basketball players, 1990-91 to 1993-94 ★932★
U.S. colleges and universities least accepting of alternative lifestyles ★985★
U.S. colleges and universities that devote the most course time to discussion ★990★
U.S. colleges and universities without a diverse student body ★1046★
U.S. colleges and universities awarding the most psychology master's degrees to Asian Americans ★1798★
U.S. doctoral institutions with the largest number of students studying abroad, 1998-99 ★2512★
Institutions in the Worker Rights Consortium ★2913★
Average faculty salaries for institutions of higher education in Massachusetts, 2000-01 ★3708★
Outstanding Catholic high schools in Metro Boston ★4073★

The Boston Globe
Top internships in the U.S. with the highest compensation, 2001 ★2611★

Boston Latin Academy
Outstanding urban public high schools in Metro Boston ★4261★

Boston Latin School
Outstanding urban public high schools in Metro Boston ★4261★

Boston, MA
Cities with the highest online spending per Internet user ★2576★
Cities with the most Yahoo! listings per million residents ★2580★
Best big cities to live in ★3075★

Boston Scientific
Fortune's highest ranked medical products and equipment companies, 2000 ★474★

Boston University
U.S. business schools with the slowest payback on MBA investments ★655★
U.S. colleges and universities with a diverse student body ★1012★
U.S. colleges and universities with a favorable surrounding town or city ★1013★
U.S. colleges and universities spending the most on independent lobbyists, 1999 ★1310★
Highest undergraduate tuition and fees at colleges and universities in Massachusetts ★1516★
Total baccalaureate communications degrees awarded to Asian Americans from U.S. colleges and universities, 1997-98 ★1688★
U.S. colleges and universities awarding the most business management and administrative services master's degrees to Native Americans ★1762★
U.S. colleges and universities awarding the most communications master's degrees to African Americans ★1763★
U.S. colleges and universities awarding the most communications master's degrees to Asian Americans ★1764★
U.S. colleges and universities awarding the most health professions and related sciences master's degrees to Asian Americans ★1778★
U.S. colleges and universities awarding the most health professions and related sciences master's degrees to Native Americans ★1780★
U.S. colleges and universities awarding the most law and legal studies master's degrees to African Americans ★1781★
U.S. colleges and universities awarding the most master's degrees to Asian Americans ★1786★
U.S. colleges and universities awarding the most psychology master's degrees to Asian Americans ★1798★
U.S. colleges and universities awarding the most social sciences and history master's degrees to Asian Americans ★1802★
U.S. colleges and universities awarding the most first professional degrees to Asian Americans ★1844★
U.S. colleges and universities awarding the most law and legal studies first professional degrees to Asian Americans ★1853★
U.S. colleges and universities awarding the most law and legal studies first professional degrees to Native Americans ★1855★
U.S. colleges and universities awarding the most psychology doctorate degrees to Hispanic Americans ★2122★
Research institutions with the highest enrollment of foreign students, 1998-99 ★2503★
Academics' choices for best health law programs, 2001 ★2629★
Academics' choices for best intellectual property law programs, 2001 ★2630★
Academics' choices for best tax law programs, 2001 ★2632★
Law schools with the best intellectual property faculty, 1999-2000 ★2653★
Law schools with the best legal ethics, professional responsibility, and legal profession faculty, 1999-2000 ★2660★
Law schools with the best moral and political theory (Anglo-American traditions) faculty, 1999-2000 ★2662★
Degrees granted in the ten largest undergraduate journalism and mass communications programs, 1999 ★2745★
Enrollment of students in the ten largest undergraduate journalism and mass communications programs, 1999 ★2746★
Degrees granted in the ten largest master's journalism and mass communications programs, 1999 ★2757★
Enrollment of students in the ten largest master's journalism and mass communications programs, 1999 ★2763★

Radcliffe Institute for Advanced Study fellowship recipient in the field of physics, 2000-01 ★2970★
Radcliffe Institute for Advanced Study fellowship recipients in the field of psychology, 2000-01 ★3062★

Bota; Kofi
Top pay and benefits for the chief executive and top paid employees at Clark Atlanta University ★3237★

Botany
Biological sciences doctorates awarded at U.S. colleges and universities, by subfield, 1999 ★1887★
Gender breakdown of biological sciences doctorate recipients, by subfield, 1999 ★1927★
Average costs for Academic Search titles by subject, 2001 ★2918★
Periodical prices by LC subject, 2001 ★2925★
Periodical prices by scientific discipline, 2001 ★2926★

Botstein; Leon
Top pay and benefits for the chief executive and top paid employees at Bard College ★3190★

Bottoms; Anthony E.
Most-cited scholars in *British Journal of Criminology* ★1637★

Bottoms; Robert G.
Top pay and benefits for the chief executive and top paid employees at DePauw University ★3267★

Boulder, CO
Best 'green & clean' places to live ★3077★

Bound for the North Star: True Stories of Fugitive Slaves
Smithsonian's best books for children ages 10 and up ★365★

Bourgeois; Louise
Best living artists ★73★
Highly influential artists of the 20th century ★76★

Bourner; Susan
Top pay and benefits for the chief executive and top paid employees at Salem College ★3488★

Bourque, T.O.R.; Rev. Thomas
Top pay and benefits for the chief executive and top paid employees at the Franciscan University of Steubenville ★3532★

Bouton High School
Outstanding secondary schools in Albany-Schenectady-Troy, New York ★4079★

Boutros; Victor
Golden Key Scholar Award winners, 2000 ★1316★

Bove; Jose
European business moguls considered the best agenda setters ★438★

Bowden; Bobby
Division I-A all-time coaching victories ★126★

Bowden; Sandra T.
Top pay and benefits for the chief executive and top paid employees at Agnes Scott College ★3165★

Bowdoin College
U.S. colleges and universities with a primarily non-religious student body ★1021★
U.S. colleges and universities with the best food service program ★1031★
U.S. News & World Report's best national liberal arts colleges, 2000-01 ★1320★
U.S. News & World Report's national liberal arts colleges with the best financial resources rank, 2000-01 ★1322★
U.S. News & World Report's national liberal arts colleges with the best graduation and retention rank, 2000-01 ★1324★
U.S. News & World Report's national liberal arts colleges with the best selectivity rank, 2000-01 ★1325★
U.S. News & World Report's national liberal arts colleges with the highest academic reputation scores, 2000-01 ★1327★
U.S. News & World Report's national liberal arts colleges with the highest alumni giving rank, 2000-01 ★1329★
U.S. News & World Report's national liberal arts colleges with the highest graduation rates, 2000-01 ★1330★
U.S. News & World Report's national liberal arts colleges with the highest percentage of alumni support, 2000-01 ★1331★
U.S. News & World Report's national liberal arts colleges with the highest percentage of freshmen in the top 10% of their high school class, 2000-01 ★1332★
U.S. News & World Report's national liberal arts colleges with the highest proportion of classes having 50 or more students, 2000-01 ★1334★
U.S. News & World Report's national liberal arts colleges with the lowest acceptance rates, 2000-01 ★1336★
Highest undergraduate tuition and fees at private nonprofit, 4-year or above colleges and universities ★1461★
Highest undergraduate tuition and fees at colleges and universities in Maine ★1512★
Elite liberal arts colleges ranked by per capita quality adjusted scholarship articles in the field of economics, 1975-94 ★2164★
Elite liberal arts colleges ranked by quality adjusted scholarship articles in the field of economics, 1975-94 ★2165★
Top associate professor economists at elite liberal arts colleges, 1975-94 ★2174★
Private, 4-year undergraduate colleges and universities producing the most Ph.D.'s in economics, 1981-1990 ★2212★
Private, 4-year undergraduate colleges and universities producing the most Ph.D.'s in political science and international relations, 1920-1990 ★3044★
Private, 4-year undergraduate colleges and universities producing the most Ph.D.'s in political science and international relations, 1981-1990 ★3045★
Average faculty salaries for institutions of higher education in Maine, 2000-01 ★3706★
U.S. liberal arts colleges with the highest paid full professors, 2001 ★3980★

Bowen; Zeddie P.
Top pay and benefits for the chief executive and top paid employees at the University of Richmond ★3559★

Bower; Dolores
Top pay and benefits for the chief executive and top paid employees at Niagara University ★3420★

Bower; Sister Annette
Top pay and benefits for the chief executive and top paid employees at Mount Saint Mary's College in California ★3411★

Bowie State University
Colleges offering the Thurgood Marshall Scholarship Fund ★221★
Top college choices for Washington D.C. students ★847★
Four-year public institutions enrolling the highest number of students from the District of Columbia, 1998-99 ★855★
Division II NCAA colleges with the lowest graduation rates for all sports, 1993-94 ★947★
Division II NCAA colleges with the lowest graduation rates for football players, 1993-94 ★948★
Historically black colleges and universities awarding the most master's degrees to African Americans ★1670★
U.S. colleges and universities awarding the most business management and administrative services master's degrees to African Americans ★1759★
U.S. colleges and universities awarding the most communications master's degrees to African Americans ★1763★
U.S. colleges and universities awarding the most computer and information sciences master's degrees to African Americans ★1766★
U.S. colleges and universities awarding the most education master's degrees to African Americans ★1769★
U.S. colleges and universities awarding the most master's degrees to African Americans ★1785★
U.S. colleges and universities awarding the most psychology master's degrees to African Americans ★1797★
Average faculty salaries for institutions of higher education in Maryland, 2000-01 ★3707★

Bowles; S.
U.S. academic economists by total citations, 1971-92 ★2177★

Bowles; Sandra S.
Top pay and benefits for the chief executive and top paid employees at University of Charleston ★3590★

Bowling Green State University
U.S. colleges and universities with the lowest average football attendance, 1996-99 ★160★
Four-year institutions with the most liquor referrals reported, 1999 ★708★
State appropriations for Ohio's institutions of higher education, 2000-01 ★1288★
Average faculty salaries for institutions of higher education in Ohio, 2000-01 ★3722★

Bowling Green State University, Firelands College
Highest undergraduate tuition and fees at public 2-year colleges and universities ★1462★
Average faculty salaries for institutions of higher education in Ohio, 2000-01 ★3722★

Bowling; John C.
Top pay and benefits for the chief executive and top paid employees at Olivet Nazarene University ★3432★

Bowman; G. Timothy
Top pay and benefits for the chief executive and top paid employees at Chatham College ★3230★

Bowman; Kathleen G.
Top pay and benefits for the chief executive and top paid employees at Randolph-Macon Woman's College ★3452★

Bowman; Leonard
Top pay and benefits for the chief executive and top paid employees at the College of Notre Dame in Maryland ★3527★

Bowne High School
 Outstanding secondary schools in New York, New York ★4191★

Bowzer; Barbara
 Top pay and benefits for the chief executive and top paid employees at Central College in Iowa ★3226★

The Boxer
 Booklist's most recommended historical fiction for youths, 2001 ★314★
 Most notable fiction books for young adults, 2001 ★322★

Boyce Middle School
 Outstanding secondary schools in Pittsburgh, Pennsylvania ★4204★

Boyce; S.T.
 Most cited first authors in dermatology journals, 1981 to 1996 ★1871★

Boyd; Richard W.
 Top pay and benefits for the chief executive and top paid employees at Wesleyan University in Connecticut ★3612★

Boyd; Robert
 Top pay and benefits for the chief executive and top paid employees at the University of the Pacific ★3571★

Boyer; Benoit
 Top pay and benefits for the chief executive and top paid employees at Sacred Heart University in Connecticut ★3467★

The Boyfriend Clinic: The Final Word on Flirting, Dating, Guys and Love
 Most notable nonfiction books for reluctant young adult readers, 2001 ★323★

Boylan Central Catholic High School
 Outstanding secondary schools in Rockford, Illinois ★4214★

Boylan; Elizabeth S.
 Top pay and benefits for the chief executive and top paid employees at Barnard College ★3191★

Boyle; Marna E.
 Top pay and benefits for the chief executive and top paid employees at Cardinal Stritch University ★3221★

Boyle; Sister Agnes
 Top pay and benefits for the chief executive and top paid employees at Mount Saint Mary College in New York ★3410★

Boy's Life
 Best-selling youth magazines ★2920★

Bozell Public Relations
 Most selective internships in the U.S., 2001 ★2610★

Bozeman; Cedric
 All-America boys' high school basketball 2nd team, 2001 ★162★

Bozeman; Sylvia
 Top pay and benefits for the chief executive and top paid employees at Spelman College ★3507★

Bozik; Daniel S.
 Top pay and benefits for the chief executive and top paid employees at St. Ambrose University ★3468★

BP
 Top internships in the U.S. with the highest compensation, 2001 ★2611★

BP America
 Fortune's highest ranked petroleum refining companies, 2000 ★484★

BP Amoco
 Business Week's best companies in Britain ★389★
 Business Week's top companies worldwide ★433★

Braden; W.
 Highest ranked inactive communication studies researchers ★2748★
 Speech communication's most published scholars between 1915-1985 ★4362★

Bradford; Terry
 Top pay and benefits for the chief executive and top paid employees at Wheeling Jesuit University ★3622★

Bradley University
 U.S. News & World Report's midwestern regional universities with the best academic reputation scores, 2000-01 ★1401★
 U.S. News & World Report's midwestern regional universities with the best alumni giving rates, 2000-01 ★1402★
 U.S. News & World Report's midwestern regional universities with the highest graduation rates, 2000-01 ★1406★
 U.S. News & World Report's midwestern regional universities with the highest percentage of freshmen from the top 25% of their high school class, 2000-01 ★1407★
 U.S. News & World Report's top midwestern regional universities, 2000-01 ★1411★
 U.S. News & World Report's best undergraduate fees among midwestern regional universities by discount tuition, 2000 ★1427★
 U.S. News & World Report's undergraduate engineering programs with the best industrial manufacturing departments, 2000-01 ★2380★
 Presidents with the highest pay at Master's I and II colleges and universities, 1998-99 ★3161★
 Average faculty salaries for institutions of higher education in Illinois, 2000-01 ★3700★

Bradshaw; Mark
 All-USA College Academic Third Team, 2001 ★4★

Bradstreet; Clair
 Top pay and benefits for the chief executive and top paid employees at College of the Atlantic ★3246★

Brady; James
 Top pay and benefits for the chief executive and top paid employees at Jacksonville University ★3352★

Bragdon; Clifford R.
 Top pay and benefits for the chief executive and top paid employees at Dowling College ★3271★

Bragg; David B.
 Top pay and benefits for the chief executive and top paid employees at the University of Redlands ★3558★

Brahm; Gary
 Top pay and benefits for the chief executive and top paid employees at Chapman University ★3228★

Brain
 Journals with the highest impact factor in the field of neuroscience, 1981-96 ★191★
 Neurosciences journals with the greatest impact measure, 1981-98 ★2812★
 Neurosciences journals with the greatest impact measure, 1994-98 ★2813★

Brain and Language
 Language and linguistics journals with the greatest impact measure, 1981-98 ★2731★

Brain Research Review
 Journals with the highest impact factor in the field of neuroscience, 1981-96 ★191★
 Neurosciences journals with the greatest impact measure, 1981-98 ★2812★

Braithwaite; John
 Most cited authors in the journal *Australian and New Zealand Journals of Criminology*, 1990 to 1995 ★1613★
 Most-cited scholars in *Australian and New Zealand Journal of Criminology* ★1636★
 Most-cited scholars in *British Journal of Criminology* ★1637★

Brambles Industries
 Business Week's best companies in Australia ★386★

Branch Jr.; Charles L.
 Top pay and benefits for the chief executive and top paid employees at Wake Forest University ★3600★

Brancusi; Constantin
 Highly influential artists of the 20th century ★76★

Brandeis University
 Highest undergraduate tuition and fees at private nonprofit, 4-year or above colleges and universities ★1461★
 Private 4-year institutions with the highest tuition, 2000-01 ★1467★
 Highest undergraduate tuition and fees at colleges and universities in Massachusetts ★1516★
 U.S. universities with the highest concentration of papers published in the field of literary studies, 1994-98 ★2734★
 Most effective music research-doctorate programs as evaluated by the National Research Council ★2895★
 Top music research-doctorate programs as evaluated by the National Research Council ★2896★
 Average faculty salaries for institutions of higher education in Massachusetts, 2000-01 ★3708★

Brandon; Charles
 Top pay and benefits for the chief executive and top paid employees at Rollins College ★3465★

The Brandon Teena Story
 Most notable videos for adults, 2001 ★2891★

Brandon University
 Canadian primarily undergraduate universities by alumni support, 2000 ★1193★
 Canadian primarily undergraduate universities by class size at the first and second-year level, 2000 ★1195★
 Canadian primarily undergraduate universities by class size at the third and forth-year level, 2000 ★1196★
 Canadian primarily undergraduate universities by classes taught by tenured faculty, 2000 ★1197★
 Canadian primarily undergraduate universities by faculty members with Ph.D.'s, 2000 ★1198★
 Canadian primarily undergraduate universities by library acquisitions, 2000 ★1199★
 Canadian primarily undergraduate universities by library expenses, 2000 ★1200★
 Canadian primarily undergraduate universities by library holdings per student, 2000 ★1201★
 Canadian primarily undergraduate universities by medical/science grants per faculty member, 2000 ★1202★
 Canadian primarily undergraduate universities by operating budget per student, 2000 ★1203★

Branley; Franklyn M.
Booklist's best science books for children ★310★

Branson, MO
Best 'quirky' places to live ★3083★

Brasher; Kenton C.
Top pay and benefits for the chief executive and top paid employees at Charleston Southern University ★3229★

BrassRing
Top E-recruiting providers, 2000 ★2604★

Braunstein; John M.
Top pay and benefits for the chief executive and top paid employees at Iona College ★3350★

Braunwald; Eugene
Most-cited researchers in cardiology, 1981-1998 ★2874★
Most-cited researchers in clinical medicine, 1981-1998 ★2875★

Brazil
Percentage of enrollment at private institutions of higher education, by country, 1998 ★858★
Countries of origin for non-U.S. citizens awarded doctorates at U.S. colleges and universities, 1999 ★1901★
Annual leave days for employees in selected countries ★2239★
Countries with the highest spending per student on higher education, 1997 ★2488★
Percentage of internet usage for selected countries ★2599★

Brazil; John R.
Presidents with the highest pay at Master's I and II colleges and universities, 1998-99 ★3161★
Top pay and benefits for the chief executive and top paid employees at Bradley University ★3208★

Brazosport College
Lowest undergraduate tuition and fees at colleges and universities in Texas ★1561★

Brea Olinda High School
Outstanding secondary schools in Orange County, California ★4199★

Breaking and Entering: Policewomen on Patrol
Most-cited works in women and crime publications ★1646★

Breck School
Outstanding secondary schools in Minneapolis-St. Paul, Minnesota-Wisconsin ★4181★

Breckon; Donald J.
Top pay and benefits for the chief executive and top paid employees at Park University ★3438★

Breger; Nicole
All-America girls' high school soccer team midfielders, 2001 ★177★

Breiseth; Christopher N.
Top pay and benefits for the chief executive and top paid employees at Wilkes University ★3627★

Breit; William
Top pay and benefits for the chief executive and top paid employees at Trinity University in Texas ★3579★

Breitborde; Lawrence B.
Top pay and benefits for the chief executive and top paid employees at Knox College ★3360★

Bremner; Barron
Top pay and benefits for the chief executive and top paid employees at Coe College ★3240★

Brenau University
Average faculty salaries for institutions of higher education in Georgia, 2000-01 ★3697★

Brennan; John F.
Top pay and benefits for the chief executive and top paid employees at Suffolk University ★3513★

Brennan; Thomas M.
Top pay and benefits for the chief executive and top paid employees at LaSalle University ★3365★

Brennan; Z. Clara
Top pay and benefits for the chief executive and top paid employees at Park University ★3438★

Brennecke; Joan F.
American Chemical Society 2001 award winners (Group 1) ★751★

Brenner; Daeg S.
Top pay and benefits for the chief executive and top paid employees at Clark University ★3238★

Brerea College
U.S. News & World Report's southern regional liberal arts colleges with the best student/faculty ratios, 2000-01 ★1368★
U.S. News & World Report's southern regional liberal arts colleges with the highest academic reputation scores, 2000-01 ★1369★
U.S. News & World Report's southern regional liberal arts colleges with the highest percentage of full-time faculty, 2000-01 ★1374★
U.S. News & World Report's southern regional liberal arts colleges with the highest proportion of freshmen in the top 25% of their high school class, 2000-01 ★1376★
U.S. News & World Report's southern regional liberal arts colleges with the lowest acceptance rates, 2000-01 ★1377★
U.S. News & World Report's top southern regional liberal arts colleges, 2000-01 ★1379★

The Brethren
Longest-running fiction hardcover bestsellers, 2000 ★279★

Brevard College
Average faculty salaries for institutions of higher education in North Carolina, 2000-01 ★3720★

Brevard Community College
Lowest undergraduate tuition and fees at colleges and universities in Florida ★1495★
Average faculty salaries for institutions of higher education in Florida, 2000-01 ★3696★

Breznau; Thomas
Top pay and benefits for the chief executive and top paid employees at Kalamazoo College ★3358★

Briar Cliff College
Average faculty salaries for institutions of higher education in Iowa, 2000-01 ★3702★

Briarcliff High School
Outstanding suburban public high schools in Metro New York ★4259★

Bricklayer
Jobs with the highest unemployment ★2256★
Jobs with the worst security scores ★2264★
Most desirable jobs in construction trades ★2272★

Bricklayers, blockmasons, and stonemasons
Average salaries for occupations requiring on-the-job training ★3119★

Bride Again
Library Journal's notable new magazines, 1999 ★2923★

Bridge to Terabithia
American Library Association's most frequently challenged books of the decade ★224★
American Library Associations most frequently challenged books for the 1990s ★742★
Most frequently banned books in the 1990s ★745★
People for the American Way's list of most frequently challenged books, 1991-1992 ★748★

Bridgeport Public Library
Highest Hennen's American Public Library Ratings for libraries serving a population of 5,000 to 9,999 ★2694★

Bridgeport; University of
Division II NCAA colleges with the 0% graduation rates for men's basketball players, 1993-94 ★941★
Institutions censured by the American Association of University Professors, 2001 ★1067★
Master's institutions with the highest enrollment of foreign students, 1998-99 ★2499★

Bridgestone/Firestone
Fortune's highest ranked rubber and plastic products companies, 2000 ★492★
Fortune's least admired companies for long-term investment value ★509★

Bridgewater College
U.S. News & World Report's southern regional liberal arts colleges with the highest acceptance rates, 2000-01 ★1370★
U.S. News & World Report's southern regional liberal arts colleges with the highest freshmen retention rates, 2000-01 ★1372★
U.S. News & World Report's southern regional liberal arts colleges with the highest graduation rates, 2000-01 ★1373★
U.S. News & World Report's southern regional liberal arts colleges with the highest percentage of full-time faculty, 2000-01 ★1374★
U.S. News & World Report's best undergraduate fees among southern regional liberal arts colleges by discount tuition, 2000 ★1383★
Average faculty salaries for institutions of higher education in Virginia, 2000-01 ★3735★

Bridgewater State College
State appropriations for Massachusetts's institutions of higher education, 2000-01 ★1274★
U.S. News & World Report's northern regional universities with students least in debt, 1999 ★1413★
Average faculty salaries for institutions of higher education in Massachusetts, 2000-01 ★3708★

Briggs & Stratton
Business Week's best performing companies with the lowest 1-year sales performance ★421★

Brigham and Women's Hospital
Top cardiology and heart surgery hospitals in the U.S., 2000 ★2788★
Top endocrinology hospitals in the U.S., 2000 ★2789★
Top gynecology hospitals in the U.S., 2000 ★2792★
Top hospitals in the U.S., 2000 ★2793★
Top nephrology hospitals in the U.S., 2000 ★2794★
Top neurology and neurosurgery hospitals in the U.S., 2000 ★2795★
Top rheumatology hospitals in the U.S., 2000 ★2802★

Brigham Young University
Colleges with the highest number of freshman Merit Scholars, 2000 ★5★
U.S. business schools with the quickest payback on MBA investments ★654★
Division I NCAA colleges with that graduated less than 20% of their African American male athletes, 1990-91 to 1993-94 ★928★
Division I NCAA colleges with that graduated none of their African American male basketball players, 1990-91 to 1993-94 ★930★
U.S. colleges and universities where the general student body does not drink beer ★1004★
U.S. colleges and universities where the general student body does not drink hard liquor ★1005★
U.S. colleges and universities where the general student body does not smoke marijuana ★1006★
U.S. colleges and universities where the general student body puts little emphasis on socializing ★1010★
U.S. colleges and universities with a generally conservative student body ★1014★
U.S. colleges and universities with a primarily religious student body ★1022★
U.S. colleges and universities with the best quality of life ★1034★
Institutions censured by the American Association of University Professors, 2001 ★1067★
U.S. News & World Report's western regional liberal arts colleges with students least in debt, 1999 ★1397★
Fiske Guide's best buys for private colleges and universities, 2001 ★1459★
Lowest undergraduate tuition and fees at private nonprofit, 4-year or above colleges and universities ★1464★
Private 4-year institutions with the lowest tuition, 2000-01 ★1468★
Undergraduate tuition and fees at colleges and universities in Utah ★1562★
U.S. research institutions with the largest number of students studying abroad, 1998-99 ★2514★
College senior's choices for exemplary doctoral-extensive universities ★2531★

Brigham Young University (HI)
Academic reputation scores for *U.S. News & World Report*'s top western regional liberal arts colleges, 2000-01 ★1387★
Acceptance rates for *U.S. News & World Report*'s top western regional liberal arts colleges, 2000-01 ★1388★
Alumni giving rates at *U.S. News & World Report*'s top western regional liberal arts colleges, 2000-01 ★1389★
Average freshmen retention rates for *U.S. News & World Report*'s top western regional liberal arts colleges, 2000-01 ★1390★
Average graduation rates for *U.S. News & World Report*'s top western regional liberal arts colleges, 2000-01 ★1391★
Percentage of freshmen in the top 25% of their high school class at *U.S. News & World Report*'s top western regional liberal arts colleges, 2000-01 ★1392★
Percentage of full-time faculty at *U.S. News & World Report*'s top western regional liberal arts colleges, 2000-01 ★1393★
Proportion of classes having 20 students or less at *U.S. News & World Report*'s top western regional liberal arts colleges, 2000-01 ★1394★
Student/faculty ratios at *U.S. News & World Report*'s top western regional liberal arts colleges, 2000-01 ★1395★
U.S. News & World Report's top western regional liberal arts colleges, 2000-01 ★1396★
Lowest undergraduate tuition and fees at private nonprofit, 4-year or above colleges and universities ★1464★
Private 4-year institutions with the lowest tuition, 2000-01 ★1468★
Undergraduate tuition and fees at colleges and universities in Hawaii ★1498★

Brightly Burning
Booklist's most recommended science fiction/fantasy books ★232★

Brill; James R.
Top pay and benefits for the chief executive and top paid employees at the University of Tulsa ★3573★

Brill; Robert
Top pay and benefits for the chief executive and top paid employees at Hood College ★3338★

Brinker International
Fortune's highest ranked food services companies, 2000 ★465★

Brissette; Judith
Top pay and benefits for the chief executive and top paid employees at Western New England College ★3615★

Bristol Community College
Lowest undergraduate tuition and fees at colleges and universities in Massachusetts ★1517★

Bristol; Joan
Top pay and benefits for the chief executive and top paid employees at the College of New Rochelle ★3525★

Bristol-Myers Squibb
Business Week's best companies in the United States ★411★
Fortune's highest ranked pharmaceuticals companies, 2000 ★485★
Highly recommended public companies for women executives, 2000 ★4453★

Bristol; University of
Top United Kingdom universities by total citations in the field of plant and animal sciences, 1991-95 ★2148★
United Kingdom universities with the greatest impact in geosciences, 1993-97 ★2154★

Bristow; Michael R.
Authors with the greatest impact measure in cardiovascular research, 1993-98 ★2868★

Britain
Percentage of students enrolled in institutions of higher education that were not citizens of the country where they studied, 1998 ★2500★
Top countries of study for U.S. students studying abroad, 1998-99 ★2510★
Most wired countries, 2001 ★2596★

British Columbia
Canadian provinces by teaching days per year ★4058★

British Columbia, Canada; University of
Fiske Guide's best buys for public colleges and universities, 2001 ★1460★

British Columbia; University of
Canadian universities with the greatest impact in biology and biochemistry, 1993-97 ★195★
Canadian universities with the most citations per paper in the field of microbiology, 1992-96 ★214★
Best Canadian universities for producing leaders of tomorrow, 2000 ★1148★
Best Canadian universities overall, 2000 ★1149★
Best Canadian universities that are the most innovative, 2000 ★1150★
Best Canadian universities with the highest quality, 2000 ★1151★
Canadian medical/doctoral universities by award-winning faculty members, 2000 ★1173★
Canadian medical/doctoral universities by class size at the first- and second-year level, 2000 ★1174★
Canadian medical/doctoral universities by class size at the third- and forth-year level, 2000 ★1175★
Canadian medical/doctoral universities by classes taught by tenured faculty, 2000 ★1176★
Canadian medical/doctoral universities by faculty members with Ph.D.'s, 2000 ★1177★
Canadian medical/doctoral universities by international graduate students, 2000 ★1178★
Canadian medical/doctoral universities by library acquisitions, 2000 ★1179★
Canadian medical/doctoral universities by library expenses, 2000 ★1180★
Canadian medical/doctoral universities by library holdings, 2000 ★1181★
Canadian medical/doctoral universities by library holdings per student, 2000 ★1182★
Canadian medical/doctoral universities by medical/science grants per faculty member, 2000 ★1184★
Canadian medical/doctoral universities by operating budget per student, 2000 ★1185★
Canadian medical/doctoral universities by percentage of operating budget allocated to scholarships, 2000 ★1186★
Canadian medical/doctoral universities by percentage of operating budget allocated to student services, 2000 ★1187★
Canadian medical/doctoral universities by reputation, 2000 ★1188★

Canadian medical/doctoral universities by social science/humanities grants per faculty member, 2000 ★1189★
Canadian medical/doctoral universities by students from out of province, 2000 ★1190★
Canadian medical/doctoral universities by students winning national awards, 2000 ★1191★
Canadian universities by average entering grade, 2000 ★1213★
Canadian universities by students with 75% grade averages or higher, 2000 ★1215★
Canadian universities with the lowest total cost, 2000 ★1218★
Top Canadian medical/doctoral universities, 2000 ★1221★
Top Canadian medical/doctoral universities best at producing leaders of tomorrow, 2000 ★1222★
Top Canadian medical/doctoral universities that are the best overall, 2000 ★1223★
Top Canadian medical/doctoral universities that are the most innovative, 2000 ★1224★
Top Canadian medical/doctoral universities with the highest quality, 2000 ★1225★
Golden Key Scholar Award winners, 2000 ★1316★
Canadian universities producing the most-cited papers in the field of computer science, 1992-96 ★1589★
University research libraries in the U.S. and Canada with the largest decreases in total expenditures from 1993-94 to 1998-99 ★2707★
Canadian universities with the greatest impact in neuroscience, 1993-97 ★4305★

British Journal of Criminology
Criminology and penology journals with the greatest impact measure, 1981-98 ★1611★
Criminology and penology journals with the greatest impact measure, 1994-98 ★1612★

British Journal of Dermatology
Number of citations and papers for original articles appearing in dermatology journals, 1981 to 1996 ★1873★
Number of citations and papers in dermatology journals, 1981 to 1996 ★1874★

British Journal of Haematology
Hematology journals with the greatest impact measure, 1981-98 ★2808★

British Journal of Political Science
Political science journals with the greatest impact measure, 1981-98 ★3049★
Political science journals with the greatest impact measure, 1994-98 ★3050★

British Journal of Psychiatry
Psychiatry journals by citation impact, 1981-98 ★3054★
Psychiatry journals by citation impact, 1995-98 ★3055★
Psychiatry journals by citation impact, 1998 ★3056★
Psychiatry journals by impact factor, 1981 to 1998 ★3057★
Psychiatry journals by impact factor, 1994 to 1998 ★3058★
Most-cited social sciences journals, 1981-97 ★4340★

British Journal of Surgery
Surgery journals with the greatest impact measure, 1994-98 ★2815★

The British Monarchy
Library Journal's best free reference websites, 2000 ★367★

British Sky Broadcasting Group
Business Week's best companies in Britain ★389★

British Telecommunications
Business Week's best companies in Britain ★389★

British Veterinary Journal
Veterinary sciences journals with the greatest impact measure, 1994-98 ★4443★

Broad Meadows Middle School
Outstanding secondary schools in Boston, Massachusetts-New Hampshire ★4100★

Broadcast news
Areas of specialization in journalism and mass communications programs with the highest enrollment, 1999 ★2740★

Broadcast technician
Most desirable jobs in communications ★2271★

Broadcom
Business Week's best performing companies with the greatest decline in earnings growth ★412★
Business Week's best performing companies with the highest 3-year sales performance ★417★
Business Week's best performing companies with the lowest 1-year shareholder returns ★422★
Business Week's best performing companies with the lowest net margin, 2000 ★425★
Top information technology companies, 2000 ★544★

Broadvision
Business Week's best companies in terms of share-price gain ★409★
Business Week's best performing companies with the highest 1-year sales performance ★414★
Business Week's best performing companies with the highest 3-year sales performance ★417★
Business Week's best performing companies with the lowest 1-year shareholder returns ★422★
Business Week's best performing companies with the lowest net margin, 2000 ★425★
Business Week's best performing companies with the lowest return on equity, 2000 ★426★
Fast-growing information technology companies, 2000 ★444★
Information technology companies giving the best returns, 2000 ★522★

Brocade Communication Systems
Business Week's best companies in terms of share-price gain ★409★

Brock University
Canadian primarily undergraduate universities by alumni support, 2000 ★1193★
Canadian primarily undergraduate universities by class size at the first and second-year level, 2000 ★1195★
Canadian primarily undergraduate universities by class size at the third and forth-year level, 2000 ★1196★
Canadian primarily undergraduate universities by classes taught by tenured faculty, 2000 ★1197★
Canadian primarily undergraduate universities by faculty members with Ph.D.'s, 2000 ★1198★
Canadian primarily undergraduate universities by library acquisitions, 2000 ★1199★
Canadian primarily undergraduate universities by library expenses, 2000 ★1200★
Canadian primarily undergraduate universities by library holdings per student, 2000 ★1201★
Canadian primarily undergraduate universities by medical/science grants per faculty member, 2000 ★1202★
Canadian primarily undergraduate universities by operating budget per student, 2000 ★1203★
Canadian primarily undergraduate universities by percentage of operating budget allocated to scholarships, 2000 ★1204★
Canadian primarily undergraduate universities by percentage of operating budget allocated to student services, 2000 ★1205★
Canadian primarily undergraduate universities by reputation, 2000 ★1206★
Canadian primarily undergraduate universities by social science/humanities grants per faculty member, 2000 ★1207★
Canadian primarily undergraduate universities by students from out of province, 2000 ★1208★
Canadian primarily undergraduate universities by students winning national awards, 2000 ★1209★
Canadian universities chosen as being value added, 2000 ★1216★
Top Canadian primarily undergraduate universities, 2000 ★1226★

Brocks; Marion
Top pay and benefits for the chief executive and top paid employees at Loyola University of Chicago ★3382★

Brode; Joanna
Top pay and benefits for the chief executive and top paid employees at Radcliffe College ★3450★

Broderick; Mary E.
Top pay and benefits for the chief executive and top paid employees at the College of St. Catherine ★3528★

Brodie; Regis
Top pay and benefits for the chief executive and top paid employees at Skidmore College ★3500★

Brodnicki; Thomas
Top pay and benefits for the chief executive and top paid employees at the University of Saint Francis in Illinois ★3561★

Brody; William R.
Largest benefit packages awarded to presidents at institutions of higher education, 1998-99 ★3133★
Presidents with the highest pay at Research I and II universities, 1998-99 ★3162★
Top pay and benefits for the chief executive and top paid employees at Johns Hopkins University ★3355★

Broekhuizen; Karl
Top pay and benefits for the chief executive and top paid employees at Skidmore College ★3500★

Broken Hill Proprietary
Business Week's best companies in Australia ★386★

"Broken windows: the police and neighborhood safety"
Most-cited works in police studies articles/research notes ★2625★

Bromery; Randolph W.
Top pay and benefits for the chief executive and top paid employees at Springfield College in Massachusetts ★3509★

Bronx High School of Science
Outstanding urban public high schools in Metro New York ★4265★

Bronxville High School
Outstanding secondary schools in New York, New York ★4191★

Bronzino; Joseph
Top pay and benefits for the chief executive and top paid employees at Trinity College in Connecticut ★3577★

Brookes Publishing
Small publishers with the highest sales growth between 1997 and 1999 ★3073★

Brookhaven College
Lowest undergraduate tuition and fees at colleges and universities in Texas ★1561★
Average faculty salaries for institutions of higher education without academic ranks in Texas, 2000-01 ★3766★

Brookings Papers in Economics
Economics journals with the greatest impact measure, 1997 ★2163★

Brookings Papers on Economic Activity
Top ranked microeconomics and monetary economics journals ★2199★

Brooklyn Law School
U.S. colleges and universities awarding the most law and legal studies first professional degrees to Asian Americans ★1853★

Brooklyn Museum
Most selective internships in the U.S., 2001 ★2610★

Brooklyn Technical Senior High School
Outstanding urban public high schools in Metro New York ★4265★

Brooks-Gunn; Jeanne
Top pay and benefits for the chief executive and top paid employees at Teachers College, Columbia University ★3517★

Brooks; Gwendolyn
Most influential African Americans in the arts ★78★

Brooks; Lynn Alan
Top pay and benefits for the chief executive and top paid employees at Connecticut College ★3254★

Brookstein; David
Top pay and benefits for the chief executive and top paid employees at Philadelphia University ★3440★

Broome Community College
Average faculty salaries for institutions of higher education in New York, 2000-01 ★3719★

Brosnan; Joseph
Top pay and benefits for the chief executive and top paid employees at Teachers College, Columbia University ★3517★

Broward Community College
Community colleges in North America with the highest enrollment ★852★
Lowest undergraduate tuition and fees at colleges and universities in Florida ★1495★
Top colleges in terms of total associate degrees awarded to minorities, 1997-98 ★1677★

Broward County, FL
Superintendents' salaries at the largest U.S. schools districts, 1999-2000 ★3990★
Largest public school districts in the U.S. ★4016★

Brower; Bob
Top pay and benefits for the chief executive and top paid employees at Point Loma Nazarene University ★3442★

Brown; Darrel
All-USA Teacher Teams, Second Team, 2000 ★4400★

Brown Deer Public Library
Highest Hennen's American Public Library Ratings for libraries serving a population of 10,000 to 24,999 ★2695★

Brown; Dennis G.
Top pay and benefits for the chief executive and top paid employees at Clarkson University ★3239★

Brown; E.
Top associate professor economists at elite liberal arts colleges, 1975-94 ★2174★

Brown-Forman
Fortune's highest ranked beverages companies, 2000 ★450★

Brown; Judith
Top pay and benefits for the chief executive and top paid employees at Northeastern University ★3422★

Brown; Kwame
All-America boys' high school basketball 1st team, 2001 ★161★

Brown; Leslie Ellen
Top pay and benefits for the chief executive and top paid employees at Alma College ★3171★

Brown; Mark D.
Top pay and benefits for the chief executive and top paid employees at the University of Miami ★3550★

Brown; Michael J.
Top pay and benefits for the chief executive and top paid employees at the University of Saint Francis in Illinois ★3561★

Brown Miller Communications
Most selective internships in the U.S., 2001 ★2610★

Brown; R.
Authors with the most citations among authors published in *American Political Science Review*, 1974-94 ★3048★

Brown; Ray
Top pay and benefits for the chief executive and top paid employees at Christian Brothers University ★3233★

Brown; Robert A.
Top pay and benefits for the chief executive and top paid employees at Massachusetts Institute of Technology ★3397★

Brown University
Most effective classics research-doctorate programs as evaluated by the National Research Council ★815★
Top classics research-doctorate programs as evaluated by the National Research Council ★816★
U.S. colleges and universities with a popular radio station ★1019★
U.S. colleges and universities with a popular theater group ★1020★
U.S. News & World Report's national universities with the best freshmen retention rates, 2000-01 ★1128★
U.S. News & World Report's national universities with the best graduation and retention rank, 2000-01 ★1129★
U.S. News & World Report's national universities with the highest alumni giving rank, 2000-01 ★1132★
U.S. News & World Report's national universities with the highest graduation rate, 1999 ★1134★
U.S. News & World Report's national universities with the highest proportion of alumni support, 2000-01 ★1137★
U.S. News & World Report's national universities with the highest selectivity rank, 2000-01 ★1139★
U.S. News & World Report's national universities with the lowest acceptance rates, 2000-01 ★1140★
Highest undergraduate tuition and fees at private nonprofit, 4-year or above colleges and universities ★1461★
Private 4-year institutions with the highest tuition, 2000-01 ★1467★
U.S. News & World Report's national universities with students most in debt, 1999 ★1476★
Undergraduate tuition and fees at colleges and universities in Rhode Island ★1553★
Top computer science research-doctorate programs as evaluated by the National Research Council ★1597★
U.S. colleges and universities awarding the most biological and life sciences master's degrees to African Americans ★1756★
U.S. colleges and universities awarding the most English language/literature/letters master's degrees to African Americans ★1773★
Most effective geosciences research-doctorate programs as evaluated by the National Research Council ★2150★
Top geosciences research-doctorate programs as evaluated by the National Research Council ★2152★
U.S. universities with the greatest impact in mechanical engineering, 1994-98 ★2439★
Top English language and literature research-doctorate programs as evaluated by the National Research Council ★2451★
Top history research-doctorate programs as evaluated by the National Research Council ★2554★
Academics' choices for best drug and alcohol abuse programs, 2001 ★2819★
Institutions in the Worker Rights Consortium ★2913★
Top philosophy research-doctorate programs as evaluated by the National Research Council ★2947★
U.S. universities with the highest concentration of papers published in the field of psychiatry, 1994-98 ★3061★
Top religion research-doctorate programs as evaluated by the National Research Council ★3093★
Average faculty salaries for institutions of higher education in Rhode Island, 2000-01 ★3727★
Most effective Spanish and Portuguese language and literature research-doctorate programs as evaluated by the National Research Council ★4357★
Top Spanish and Portuguese language and literature research-doctorate programs as evaluated by the National Research Council ★4358★

Brown University Program in Applied Mathematics
Most effective mathematics research-doctorate programs as evaluated by the National Research Council ★2775★

Brown; Victor
Top pay and benefits for the chief executive and top paid employees at Walla Walla College ★3601★

Browne; A.
Most cited authors in the journal *Journal of Interpersonal Violence*, 1990 to 1995 ★1627★

Browne; John
European business moguls considered the best empire builders ★441★

Browne; Mark J.
Individual authors with the most published pages in *The Journal of Risk and Insurance*, 1987-1996 ★680★

Browning; Kenneth C.
Top pay and benefits for the chief executive and top paid employees at Illinois Wesleyan University ★3347★

Browning; Scott Wells
Top pay and benefits for the chief executive and top paid employees at Chestnut Hill College ★3231★

Brownsville Public Library
Highest Hennen's American Public Library Ratings for libraries serving a population of 999 and under ★2691★

Bruce Chatwin
Most notable nonfiction books, 2001 ★285★
Outstanding biography books, 2000 ★288★
Outstanding works of nonfiction, 2001 ★294★

Bruce; Robert J.
Top pay and benefits for the chief executive and top paid employees at Widener University ★3626★

Brum; Joseph P.
Top pay and benefits for the chief executive and top paid employees at Providence College ★3447★

Brunelle; Daniel J.
American Chemical Society 2001 award winners (Group 2) ★752★

Brunelleschi's Dome: How a Renaissance Genius Reinvented Architecture
Outstanding arts and literature books, 2000 ★286★

Bruno; Albert
Top pay and benefits for the chief executive and top paid employees at Santa Clara University in California ★3491★

Bruno; Dean
Top pay and benefits for the chief executive and top paid employees at Saint Bonaventure University ★3470★

Brunswick
Top leisure time industries in Standard & Poor's 500, 2001 ★545★

Brunswick College
Average faculty salaries for institutions of higher education in Georgia, 2000-01 ★3697★

Brunswick Community College
Average faculty salaries for institutions of higher education without academic ranks in North Carolina, 2000-01 ★3761★

Brunt; John
Top pay and benefits for the chief executive and top paid employees at Walla Walla College ★3601★

Brush; C. Beeler
Top pay and benefits for the chief executive and top paid employees at Hampden-Sydney College ★3321★

Brussels-Antwerp
Cities with the highest productivity of paper in the discipline of immunology, 1994-96 ★2871★

Bryan College
U.S. News & World Report's southern regional liberal arts colleges with the highest freshmen retention rates, 2000-01 ★1372★
U.S. News & World Report's southern regional liberal arts colleges with the highest proportion of classes having 20 students or less, 2000-01 ★1375★
U.S. News & World Report's southern regional liberal arts colleges with the highest proportion of freshmen in the top 25% of their high school class, 2000-01 ★1376★
U.S. News & World Report's southern regional liberal arts colleges with the lowest acceptance rates, 2000-01 ★1377★

Bryant; C. June
All-USA Teacher Teams, Third Team, 2000 ★4401★

Bryant College
Undergraduate tuition and fees at colleges and universities in Rhode Island ★1553★
Average faculty salaries for institutions of higher education in Rhode Island, 2000-01 ★3727★

Bryant College (RI)
Division II NCAA colleges with the highest graduation rates for all sports, 1993-94 ★945★

Bryant/College Station, TX
U.S. cities with the most single people ★3089★

Bryant Intermediate School
Outstanding secondary schools in Salt Lake City-Ogden, Utah ★4218★

Bryant; Paul "Bear"
Division I-A all-time coaching victories ★126★

Bryn Mawr College
Most effective classics research-doctorate programs as evaluated by the National Research Council ★815★
Top classics research-doctorate programs as evaluated by the National Research Council ★816★
U.S. colleges and universities where intramural sports are not popular ★996★
U.S. colleges and universities where students study the most ★1003★
U.S. colleges and universities with a generally liberal student body ★1015★
U.S. colleges and universities with the best on-campus housing facilities ★1032★
U.S. colleges and universities with the most attractive campuses ★1039★
U.S. News & World Report's national liberal arts colleges with the highest alumni giving rank, 2000-01 ★1329★
U.S. News & World Report's national liberal arts colleges with the highest percentage of alumni support, 2000-01 ★1331★
Highest undergraduate tuition and fees at colleges and universities in Pennsylvania ★1549★
Private, 4-year undergraduate colleges and universities producing the most Ph.D.'s in all fields of study, 1990 ★2029★
Private, 4-year undergraduate colleges and universities producing the most Ph.D.'s in nonscience fields, 1920-1990 ★2030★
Private, 4-year undergraduate colleges and universities producing the most Ph.D.'s in nonscience fields, 1981-1990 ★2031★
Private, 4-year undergraduate colleges and universities producing the most Ph.D.'s in nonscience fields, 1990 ★2032★
Private, 4-year undergraduate colleges and universities producing the most Ph.D.'s in English, 1920-1990 ★2449★
Private, 4-year undergraduate colleges and universities producing the most Ph.D.'s in English, 1981-1990 ★2450★
Private, 4-year undergraduate colleges and universities producing the most Ph.D.'s in history, 1920-1990 ★2552★
Private, 4-year undergraduate colleges and universities producing the most Ph.D.'s in history, 1981-1990 ★2553★
Women's colleges granting physics bachelor's degrees, 2000 ★2982★
Average faculty salaries for institutions of higher education in Pennsylvania, 2000-01 ★3725★
Private, 4-year undergraduate colleges and universities producing the most Ph.D.'s in anthropology and sociology, 1920-1990 ★4344★
Private, 4-year undergraduate colleges and universities producing the most Ph.D.'s in anthropology and sociology, 1981-1990 ★4345★

BT Washington Junior High School
Outstanding secondary schools in Houston, Texas ★4150★

BT Washington Performing Arts High School
Outstanding secondary schools in Dallas, Texas ★4120★

Buccino; Robert
Top pay and benefits for the chief executive and top paid employees at Oglethorpe University ★3429★

Buchanan High School
Outstanding secondary schools in Fresno, California ★4138★

Buchanan; James M.
Authors most frequently contributing to the *American Economic Review* from 1911-1990 ★2156★
Authors most frequently contributing to the *American Economic Review* from 1951-1990 ★2157★

Bucholz; Richard D.
Top pay and benefits for the chief executive and top paid employees at St. Louis University ★3478★

Buchowicz; Bruce
Top pay and benefits for the chief executive and top paid employees at Benedictine University ★3200★

Buck; Lawrence P.
Top pay and benefits for the chief executive and top paid employees at Widener University ★3626★

Buckholdt; David
Top pay and benefits for the chief executive and top paid employees at Marquette University ★3392★

Buckingham; David E.
Top pay and benefits for the chief executive and top paid employees at Virginia Wesleyan College ★3596★

Bucknell College
U.S. News & World Report's national liberal arts colleges with the highest proportion of classes having 50 or more students, 2000-01 ★1334★

Bucknell University
Private, 4-year undergraduate colleges and universities producing the most Ph.D.'s in the life sciences, 1920-1990 ★192★
Private, 4-year undergraduate colleges and universities producing the most Ph.D.'s in the life sciences, 1981-1990 ★193★

Division I NCAA colleges with that graduated all of their African American male basketball players, 1990-91 to 1993-94 ★927★

Division I NCAA colleges with the highest graduation rates for female athletes, 1990-91 to 1993-94 ★931★

Division I NCAA colleges with the highest graduation rates for male athletes, 1990-91 to 1993-94 ★934★

Division I NCAA colleges with the highest graduation rates for male basketball players, 1990-91 to 1993-94 ★935★

U.S. colleges and universities where a large portion of the student body drink hard liquor ★992★

U.S. News & World Report's national liberal arts colleges with the highest graduation rates, 2000-01 ★1330★

U.S. News & World Report's national liberal arts colleges with the highest percentage of full-time faculty, 2000-01 ★1333★

Private, 4-year undergraduate colleges and universities producing the most Ph.D.'s in the computer sciences, 1920-1990 ★1595★

Private, 4-year undergraduate colleges and universities producing the most Ph.D.'s in the computer sciences, 1981-1990 ★1596★

Private, 4-year undergraduate colleges and universities producing the most Ph.D.s in all fields of study, 1920-1990 ★2027★

Private, 4-year undergraduate colleges and universities producing the most Ph.D.'s in all fields of study, 1981-1990 ★2028★

Private, 4-year undergraduate colleges and universities producing the most Ph.D.'s in all fields of study, 1990 ★2029★

Private, 4-year undergraduate colleges and universities producing the most Ph.D.'s in nonscience fields, 1990 ★2032★

Private, 4-year undergraduate colleges and universities producing the most Ph.D.'s in the earth sciences, 1981-1990 ★2151★

Private, 4-year undergraduate colleges and universities producing the most Ph.D.'s in economics, 1981-1990 ★2212★

U.S. News & World Report's undergraduate engineering programs with the highest academic reputation scores, 2000-01 ★2337★

U.S. News & World Report's undergraduate engineering programs with the best chemical departments, 2000-01 ★2344★

U.S. News & World Report's undergraduate engineering programs with the best civil departments, 2000-01 ★2347★

U.S. News & World Report's undergraduate engineering programs with the best mechanical departments, 2000-01 ★2438★

Private, 4-year undergraduate colleges and universities producing the most Ph.D.'s in English, 1981-1990 ★2450★

Private, 4-year undergraduate colleges and universities producing the most Ph.D.'s in mathematics, 1920-1990 ★2776★

Private, 4-year undergraduate colleges and universities producing the most Ph.D.'s in mathematics, 1981-1990 ★2777★

Private, 4-year undergraduate colleges and universities producing the most Ph.D.'s in psychology, 1920-1990 ★3066★

Private, 4-year undergraduate colleges and universities producing the most Ph.D.'s in psychology, 1981-1990 ★3067★

Average faculty salaries for institutions of higher education in Pennsylvania, 2000-01 ★3725★

Private, 4-year undergraduate colleges and universities producing the most Ph.D.'s in the sciences, 1920-1990 ★4294★

Private, 4-year undergraduate colleges and universities producing the most Ph.D.'s in the sciences, 1981-1990 ★4295★

Private, 4-year undergraduate colleges and universities producing the most Ph.D.'s in anthropology and sociology, 1981-1990 ★4345★

Buckner; C. Dean
Most-cited researchers in oncology, 1981-1998 ★2877★

Bucks County Courier Times
Most selective internships in the U.S., 2001 ★2610★

Bucky; Jean-Bernard
Top pay and benefits for the chief executive and top paid employees at Williams College ★3631★

Bud, not Buddy
Most notable children's recordings, 2001 ★320★

Budd; John M.
Library and information science faculty with the most journal articles, 1993-1998 ★2711★

Buddhist
Religious preference of incoming freshmen, 2000 ★1061★

Budget Group
Fortune's highest ranked automotive retailing services companies, 2000 ★449★

Budiansky; Stephen
Booklist's best science books for children ★310★

Budlong Elementary School
Illinois elementary schools chosen to be 'demonstration sites' for struggling schools ★4006★

Buell; Denise
Radcliffe Institute for Advanced Study fellowship recipients in the field of religion, 2000-01 ★3092★

Buena Vista University
U.S. News & World Report's midwestern regional liberal arts colleges with the highest percentage of full-time faculty, 2000-01 ★1346★

U.S. News & World Report's best undergraduate fees among midwestern regional liberal arts colleges by discount tuition, 2000 ★1380★

Highest undergraduate tuition and fees at colleges and universities in Iowa ★1504★

Average faculty salaries for institutions of higher education in Iowa, 2000-01 ★3702★

Bueno de Mesquita; Bruce
Authors most frequently published in *American Political Science Review*, 1974-94 ★3047★

Buffalo Grove High School
Outstanding suburban public high schools in Metro Chicago ★4256★

Bufferd; Alan S.
Top pay and benefits for the chief executive and top paid employees at Massachusetts Institute of Technology ★3397★

Bugliarello; George
Top pay and benefits for the chief executive and top paid employees at Polytechnic University ★3443★

Building Big
Most notable books for older readers, 2001 ★318★

Outstanding books for older readers, 2000 ★327★

Outstanding children's nonfiction books, 2000 ★330★

Outstanding videos for library collections, 2000 ★2892★

Buley, I.H.M.; Sister Paula Marie
Top pay and benefits for the chief executive and top paid employees at Mount Saint Mary's College in Maryland ★3412★

Buley; Margaret
All-USA Teacher Teams, Third Team, 2000 ★4401★

Bulgaria
Eight grade science achievement scores from selected countries, 1999 ★14★

Eighth grade mathematics achievement scores from selected countries, 1999 ★2773★

Bull; Vivian A.
Top pay and benefits for the chief executive and top paid employees at Linfield College ★3376★

Bulletin of the American Mathematical Society
Mathematics journals by impact factor ★2783★

Mathematics journals by impact factor, 1981 to 1997 ★2784★

Mathematics journals by impact factor, 1993 to 1997 ★2785★

Bulletin of Entology Research
Entomology journals by citation impact, 1981-98 ★2453★

Bullis Purissima School
Outstanding secondary schools in San Jose, California ★4222★

Bullock; Mary Brown
Top pay and benefits for the chief executive and top paid employees at Agnes Scott College ★3165★

Bullock; Rev. Jeffrey
Top pay and benefits for the chief executive and top paid employees at the University of Dubuque ★3542★

Bullous dermatoses
Leading categories of dermatologic disease covered by top articles in the field, 1945-1990 ★1869★

Bully Dance
Most notable children's videos, 2001 ★2889★

Bunch; Katie
All-America girls' high school soccer team defenders, 2001 ★174★

Bundschuh; James E.
Top pay and benefits for the chief executive and top paid employees at Xavier University in Ohio ★3637★

Bunker Hill Community College
Lowest undergraduate tuition and fees at colleges and universities in Massachusetts ★1517★

Average faculty salaries for institutions of higher education in Massachusetts, 2000-01 ★3708★

Buntich; Paul
Top pay and benefits for the chief executive and top paid employees at Nazareth College of Rochester ★3416★

Burbridge; John C.
Top pay and benefits for the chief executive and top paid employees at Elon College ★3285★

Burchill; Thomas J.
Top pay and benefits for the chief executive and top paid employees at Saint Mary's University of Minnesota ★3482★

Burd; John S.
Top pay and benefits for the chief executive and top paid employees at Brenau University ★3210★

Burdekin; R.
Top associate professor economists at elite liberal arts colleges, 1975-94 ★2174★

Burdge; Robert E.
Top pay and benefits for the chief executive and top paid employees at St. Louis University ★3478★

Burgess; David R.
Top pay and benefits for the chief executive and top paid employees at Boston College ★3205★

Burgoon; J.
Highest ranked active communication studies researchers ★2747★
Top published female authors (1915-1985) in the field of communication studies ★4363★

Burgoon; M.
Highest ranked active communication studies researchers ★2747★

Burke; Deborah M.
Top pay and benefits for the chief executive and top paid employees at Pomona College ★3444★

Burke Jr.; Thomas
Top pay and benefits for the chief executive and top paid employees at the University of San Diego ★3565★

Burke; Maryalyce
Top pay and benefits for the chief executive and top paid employees at Dominican University in Illinois ★3269★

Burkette; D. Wayne
Top pay and benefits for the chief executive and top paid employees at Salem College ★3488★

Burkhart, et al.; Ross E.
Most frequently downloaded *American Political Science Review* articles ★3039★

Burley Elementary School
Illinois elementary schools chosen to be 'demonstration sites' for struggling schools ★4006★

Burlington College
Undergraduate tuition and fees at colleges and universities in Vermont ★1563★

Burlington County College
Lowest undergraduate tuition and fees at colleges and universities in New Jersey ★1534★

Burlington Industries
Fortune's highest ranked textiles companies, 2000 ★501★

Burlington Northern Santa Fe
Fortune's highest ranked railroads, 2000 ★490★
Top transportation companies in Standard & Poor's 500, 2001 ★560★

Burlington Resources
Business Week's best performing companies with the highest 1-year earnings growth ★413★
Fortune's highest ranked mining and crude oil companies, 2000 ★477★

Burlington, VT
Best 'green & clean' places to live ★3077★

The Burning Point
Library Journal's best romance titles, 2000 ★245★

Burniston Jr.; Harvey
All-USA Teacher Teams, First Team, 2000 ★4399★

Burns; Annina
All-USA College Academic First Team, 2001 ★2★

Burns; Kristine A.
Top pay and benefits for the chief executive and top paid employees at Whitworth College ★3625★

Burns; William A.
Top pay and benefits for the chief executive and top paid employees at Randolph-Macon Woman's College ★3452★

Burrows; Dave
Top pay and benefits for the chief executive and top paid employees at Beloit College ★3199★

Burton; Timothy
Top pay and benefits for the chief executive and top paid employees at Adelphi University ★3164★

Burwell; Elizabeth
Top pay and benefits for the chief executive and top paid employees at Mills College ★3402★

Burwick; Richard
Golden Key Scholar Award winners, 2000 ★1316★

Bus driver
'Blue-collar' jobs considered the least physically demanding ★2241★

Buser; Boyd
Top pay and benefits for the chief executive and top paid employees at the University of New England ★3552★

Bush; Debbie
All-USA Teacher Teams, Second Team, 2000 ★4400★

Bush; Jack
Canada's best visual artists of the 20th century ★75★

Bush; Mary T.
Top pay and benefits for the chief executive and top paid employees at Nazareth College of Rochester ★3416★

Business
Expected majors for incoming freshmen, 2000 ★1050★
Median age at conferral of doctoral degree from U.S. universities, by discipline, 1999 ★1952★
Fields of study profile of foreign students enrolled in U.S. institutions of higher education, 1998-99 ★2495★
Fields of study profile of U.S. students studying abroad, 1998-99 ★2507★
Expected starting salaries of 2000-01 bachelor's degree recipients, by general major ★3130★

Business administration
Expected starting salaries of 2000-01 bachelor's degree recipients, by specific major ★3131★

Business administration and management
Business and management doctorates awarded at U.S. colleges and universities, by subfield, 1999 ★1888★
Gender breakdown of business and management doctorate recipients, by subfield, 1999 ★1928★
Industries in Illinois with the highest projected worker increase through 2006 ★2304★
Top bachelor's and master's degree majors in demand for employment, 2001 ★2323★
Top bachelor's degree majors in demand for employment, 2001 ★2324★
Top master's degree majors in demand for employment, 2001 ★2326★

Business Communication Quarterly
Most cited business serials in technical communication journals from 1988 to 1997 ★4417★

Business Communication Quarterly/ Bulletin of the Association for Business Administration
Most cited serials in technical communication journals from 1988 to 1997 ★4425★

Business and economics
Average costs for Academic Search titles by subject, 2001 ★2918★
Periodical prices by LC subject, 2001 ★2925★

Business education
Gender breakdown of teaching fields doctorate recipients, by subfield, 1999 ★1943★
Teaching fields doctorates awarded at U.S. colleges and universities, by subfield, 1999 ★2046★

Business History Review
Top ranked economic history journals ★2190★

Business Lawyer
Most frequently-cited law reviews and legal periodicals, 1924-1986: a compilation ★2619★

Business and management
Number of professional/other doctorate recipients at U.S. colleges and universities, by field, 1999 ★1976★
Percentage of female doctorate recipients at U.S. colleges and universities, by subfield, 1999 ★1988★
Professional/other doctorates awarded to U.S. citizens/permanent residents at U.S. colleges and universities, by race/ethnicity and subfield, 1999 ★2034★

Business management and administrative services
Top bachelor's degree disciplines for African Americans, 1997-98 ★1672★
Top bachelor's degree disciplines for Asian Americans, 1997-98 ★1673★
Top bachelor's degree disciplines for Hispanic Americans, 1997-98 ★1674★
Top bachelor's degree disciplines for Native Americans, 1997-98 ★1675★
Top bachelor's degree disciplines for non-minorities, 1997-98 ★1676★

Business management/administrative services, general
Business and management doctorates awarded at U.S. colleges and universities, by subfield, 1999 ★1888★
Gender breakdown of business and management doctorate recipients, by subfield, 1999 ★1928★

Business manager
African American college athletics senior administrators, by gender, 1999-2000 ★119★
College athletics senior administrators, by gender, 1999-2000 ★123★
Minority college athletics senior administrators, by gender, 1999-2000 ★134★

Business/managerial economics
Business and management doctorates awarded at U.S. colleges and universities, by subfield, 1999 ★1888★
Gender breakdown of business and management doctorate recipients, by subfield, 1999 ★1928★

Business/personal finance
  Subject areas with the highest library expenditures/circulation ★306★
Business services
  Industries with the highest projected growth rate, 1994-2005 ★2306★
  Spending for E-marketplace services, by industry, 2001 ★4430★
Business Week
  Most cited business serials in technical communication journals from 1988 to 1997 ★4417★
Buskirk; Martha
  Radcliffe Institute for Advanced Study fellowship recipient in the field of art history, 2000-01 ★92★
But I Waaannt It!
  Publishers Weekly Off-the-Cuff Awards winner for most objectionable book, 2000 ★354★
Butchers and meatcutters
  Occupations with the highest decline in employment, 1998-2008 ★2310★
Butler County Community College
  Lowest undergraduate tuition and fees at colleges and universities in Pennsylvania ★1550★
  Average faculty salaries for institutions of higher education in Pennsylvania, 2000-01 ★3725★
Butler Elementary School, District 53
  Illinois school districts spending the most for elementary school education 1997-98 ★4009★
  Illinois school districts spending the most per pupil for instruction ★4011★
Butler; James C.
  Top pay and benefits for the chief executive and top paid employees at Tulane University ★3581★
Butler; Richard
  Individual authors with the most published pages in *The Journal of Risk and Insurance*, 1987-1996 ★680★
Butler University
  U.S. News & World Report's midwestern regional universities with the best academic reputation scores, 2000-01 ★1401★
  U.S. News & World Report's midwestern regional universities with the highest percentage of freshmen from the top 25% of their high school class, 2000-01 ★1407★
  U.S. News & World Report's top midwestern regional universities, 2000-01 ★1411★
  U.S. News & World Report's best undergraduate fees among midwestern regional universities by discount tuition, 2000 ★1427★
  Highest undergraduate tuition and fees at colleges and universities in Indiana ★1502★
  Average faculty salaries for institutions of higher education in Indiana, 2000-01 ★3701★
Butte College
  U.S. institutions awarding the most associate degrees to minorities in agribusiness and production, 1998 ★1808★
Butterfoss; Edwin
  Top pay and benefits for the chief executive and top paid employees at Hamline University ★3320★
Buttons
  Outstanding books for young readers, 2000 ★328★
  Smithsonian's best books for children ages 1 to 6 ★363★
Buy.com
  Top E-commerce web sites ★2603★

Buzzel; Sidney
  Top pay and benefits for the chief executive and top paid employees at Colorado Christian University ★3248★
Buzzwords: A Scientist Muses on Sex, Bugs, and Rock 'n' Roll
  Library Journal's most notable entomology books, 2000 ★258★
Byker; Gaylen J.
  Top pay and benefits for the chief executive and top paid employees at Calvin College ★3217★
Byrd High School
  Outstanding secondary schools in Shreveport-Bossier City, Louisiana ★4230★
Byrnes; Don R.
  Top pay and benefits for the chief executive and top paid employees at Houston Baptist University ★3342★
BYTE
  Most cited science serials in technical communication journals from 1988 to 1997 ★4424★

C

Cabin; Henry S.
  Top pay and benefits for the chief executive and top paid employees at Yale University ★3639★
Cable & Wireless
  Business Week's best companies in Britain ★389★
Cable & Wireless HKT
  Business Week's best companies in Hong Kong ★395★
Cable & Wireless Optus
  Business Week's best companies in Australia ★386★
Cabletron Systems
  Business Week's best performing companies with the highest 1-year earnings growth ★413★
  Business Week's best performing companies with the lowest 1-year sales performance ★421★
  Fortune's highest ranked network communications companies, 2000 ★482★
Cablevision Systems
  Fortune's highest ranked telecommunications companies, 2000 ★499★
Cabrini College
  Average faculty salaries for institutions of higher education in Pennsylvania, 2000-01 ★3725★
Caddo Parish School Board
  Top recruiters for biology/biological science jobs for 2000-01 bachelor's degree recipients ★198★
  Top recruiters for chemistry jobs for 2000-01 bachelor's degree recipients ★792★
  Top recruiters for criminal justice jobs for 2000-01 bachelor's degree recipients ★1647★
  Top recruiters for language/literature jobs for 2000-01 bachelor's degree recipients ★2446★
  Top recruiters for math/actuarial science jobs for 2000-01 bachelor's degree recipients ★2771★
  Top recruiters for music jobs for 2000-01 bachelor's degree recipients ★2894★
  Top recruiters for psychology jobs for 2000-01 bachelor's degree recipients ★3063★
  Top recruiters for social work jobs for 2000-01 master's degree recipients ★4343★

  Top recruiters for sociology jobs for 2000-01 bachelor's degree recipients ★4347★
  Top recruiters for education jobs for 2000-01 bachelor's degree recipients ★4377★
  Top recruiters for education jobs for 2000-01 master's degree recipients ★4398★
Cadence Design Systems
  Software companies with the fastest growth, 2000 ★528★
Cadwallader; Meaven
  Top pay and benefits for the chief executive and top paid employees at Union Institute ★3586★
Cafardi; Nicholas P.
  Top pay and benefits for the chief executive and top paid employees at Duquesne University ★3277★
Cajon Park School
  Outstanding secondary schools in San Diego, California ★4220★
Calabasas High School
  All-USA Teacher Teams, Second Team, 2000 ★4400★
Calculus
  Subjects required by the most U.S. medical schools for the 2000-01 entering class ★2850★
Calculus AB
  Number of Advanced Placement Exams taken by African Americans, by subject, 2000 ★30★
  Number of Advanced Placement Exams taken by Asian Americans, by subject, 2000 ★31★
  Number of Advanced Placement Exams taken by Hispanic Americans, by subject, 2000 ★32★
Calculus BC
  Number of Advanced Placement Exams taken by African Americans, by subject, 2000 ★30★
  Number of Advanced Placement Exams taken by Asian Americans, by subject, 2000 ★31★
  Number of Advanced Placement Exams taken by Hispanic Americans, by subject, 2000 ★32★
Caldwell College
  Average faculty salaries for institutions of higher education in New Jersey, 2000-01 ★3717★
Caldwell Community College and Technical Institute
  Average faculty salaries for institutions of higher education without academic ranks in North Carolina, 2000-01 ★3761★
Caldwell; Delmar R.
  Top pay and benefits for the chief executive and top paid employees at Tulane University ★3581★
Caldwell; Janis
  Radcliffe Institute for Advanced Study fellowship recipient in the field of English literature, 2000-01 ★2443★
Caledonia High School
  Outstanding secondary schools in Grand Rapids-Muskegon-Holland, Michigan ★4140★
Calgaard; Ronald
  Top pay and benefits for the chief executive and top paid employees at Trinity University in Texas ★3579★
Calgary; University of
  Canadian universities with the greatest impact in biology and biochemistry, 1993-97 ★195★
  Canadian universities with the most citations per paper in the field of microbiology, 1992-96 ★214★
  Best Canadian universities overall, 2000 ★1149★

Canadian medical/doctoral universities by alumni support, 2000 ★1172★
Canadian medical/doctoral universities by award-winning faculty members, 2000 ★1173★
Canadian medical/doctoral universities by class size at the first- and second-year level, 2000 ★1174★
Canadian medical/doctoral universities by class size at the third- and forth-year level, 2000 ★1175★
Canadian medical/doctoral universities by classes taught by tenured faculty, 2000 ★1176★
Canadian medical/doctoral universities by faculty members with Ph.D.'s, 2000 ★1177★
Canadian medical/doctoral universities by international graduate students, 2000 ★1178★
Canadian medical/doctoral universities by library acquisitions, 2000 ★1179★
Canadian medical/doctoral universities by library expenses, 2000 ★1180★
Canadian medical/doctoral universities by library holdings, 2000 ★1181★
Canadian medical/doctoral universities by library holdings per student, 2000 ★1182★
Canadian medical/doctoral universities by medical/science grants per faculty member, 2000 ★1184★
Canadian medical/doctoral universities by operating budget per student, 2000 ★1185★
Canadian medical/doctoral universities by percentage of operating budget allocated to scholarships, 2000 ★1186★
Canadian medical/doctoral universities by percentage of operating budget allocated to student services, 2000 ★1187★
Canadian medical/doctoral universities by reputation, 2000 ★1188★
Canadian medical/doctoral universities by social science/humanities grants per faculty member, 2000 ★1189★
Canadian medical/doctoral universities by students from out of province, 2000 ★1190★
Canadian medical/doctoral universities by students winning national awards, 2000 ★1191★
Top Canadian medical/doctoral universities, 2000 ★1221★

Califf; Robert M.
Authors with the greatest impact measure in cardiovascular research, 1993-98 ★2868★
Most-cited researchers in cardiology, 1981-1998 ★2874★

California
People for the American Way's list of states with the most challenges to library and school books, 1982-1992 ★750★
States with the highest enrollment in private 4-year institutions of higher education ★860★
States with the highest enrollment in public 4-year institutions of higher education ★861★
Mean composite ACT scores by state, 2000 ★895★
Mean math SAT scores by state, 2000 ★900★
Mean verbal SAT scores by state, 2000 ★903★
Average class size at colleges and universities in the U.S., by state ★1064★
States allocating the largest amount of state tax appropriations for higher education, 2000-01 ★1304★
States receiving the most in federal agency appropriations to colleges, 2000 ★1306★
States receiving the most in federal agency appropriations to colleges, from 1996 to 2000 ★1307★
States with the highest percentage increase in appropriations for higher education, 2000-01 ★1308★
Total doctorate recipients by state, 1999 ★2054★
Hispanic American enrollment at Hispanic-serving institutions of higher education, by state, 1997 ★2547★
States with the most law schools ★2668★
State library associations with most full-time staff ★2681★
State library associations with the highest annual revenue ★2682★
State library associations with the highest unrestricted net assets ★2684★
State library associations with the largest membership ★2685★
State grades for affordability of higher education for minority students, 2000 ★2883★
State grades for benefits state receives for educating its minority students, 2000 ★2884★
State grades for completion of higher education by minority students, 2000 ★2885★
State grades for participation of minority students in higher education, 2000 ★2886★
State grades for preparing minority students for higher education, 2000 ★2887★
States with the highest per capita income ★3123★
States with the largest growth in income ★3124★
States expelling the most students for violating the Gun-Free Schools Act, 1998-99 ★3994★
States with the highest number of high school graduates, 1999-2000 ★3995★
States with the most public school districts ★3999★
States with the highest average enrollment in public elementary schools ★4032★
States with the highest average enrollment in public secondary schools ★4033★
States with the highest K-12 public school enrollment ★4034★
States with the highest projected K-12 public school enrollment for 2010 ★4035★
States with the highest funding needs for school-building modernization ★4040★
States with the highest funding needs for school-technology modernization ★4041★
States with the most charter schools ★4048★
States with the most K-12 public schools ★4049★
States with the largest average class size ★4071★
States with the best college tuition savings plans ★4438★
States with the most women-owned companies ★4455★

California, Berkeley, Haas Graduate School of Business Administration; University of
U.S. News & World Report's undergraduate business programs with the best consulting departments, 2000-01 ★563★
U.S. News & World Report's undergraduate business programs with the best e-commerce departments, 2000-01 ★564★
U.S. News & World Report's undergraduate business programs with the best general management departments, 2000-01 ★566★
U.S. News & World Report's undergraduate business programs with the best real estate departments, 2000-01 ★570★
U.S. News & World Report's undergraduate business programs with the highest academic reputation scores, 2000-01 ★571★
Academics' choices for best graduate entrepreneurship programs, 2001 ★583★
Academics' choices for best graduate nonprofit organizations programs, 2001 ★586★
Academics' choices for best part-time MBA programs, 2000 ★587★
Acceptance rates for U.S. News & World Report's top 10 graduate business schools, 2001 ★588★
Average GMAT scores at U.S. News & World Report's top 10 graduate business schools, 2001 ★591★
Average undergraduate GPA at U.S. News & World Report's top 10 graduate business schools, 2001 ★593★
Business Week's top business schools with the highest percentage of women enrollees, 2000 ★614★
Business Week's top business schools with the lowest percentage of minority enrollment, 2000 ★616★
Median starting salaries of graduates from U.S. News & World Report's top 10 graduate business schools, 2001 ★636★
Out-of-state tuition and fees for U.S. News & World Report's top 10 graduate business schools, 2001 ★637★
Percentage of employed graduates at U.S. News & World Report's top 10 graduate business schools, 2001 ★639★
Percentage of graduates employed within 3 months of graduation from U.S. News & World Report's top 10 graduate business schools, 2001 ★641★
Top graduate business schools, 2001 ★649★
Top graduate business schools by reputation as determined by academic personnel, 2001 ★650★
Top graduate business schools by reputation, as determined by recruiters, 2001 ★651★
Academics' choices for best graduate finance programs, 2001 ★662★
U.S. News & World Report's undergraduate business programs with the best finance departments, 2000-01 ★665★
Academics' choices for best graduate general management programs, 2001 ★666★
Academics' choices for best graduate marketing programs, 2001 ★670★
Academics' choices for best graduate quantitative analysis programs, 2001 ★673★
U.S. News & World Report's undergraduate business programs with the best marketing departments, 2000-01 ★685★
Average GMAT scores for U.S. News & World Report's top 10 graduate business schools, 2000 ★2529★

California, Berkeley Program in Biostatistics; University of
Top statistics and biostatistics research-doctorate programs as evaluated by the National Research Council ★2782★

California, Berkeley Program in Statistics; University of
Top statistics and biostatistics research-doctorate programs as evaluated by the National Research Council ★2782★

California, Berkeley; University of
All-USA College Academic Third Team, 2001 ★4★
Colleges with the highest number of freshman Merit Scholars, 2000 ★5★
Most effective anthropology research-doctorate programs as evaluated by the National Research Council ★61★
Top anthropology research-doctorate programs as evaluated by the National Research Council ★62★
U.S. universities publishing the most papers in the field of archaeology, 1994-98 ★66★
U.S. universities publishing the most papers in the fields of art and architecture, 1994-98 ★70★
Most effective art history research-doctorate programs as evaluated by the National Research Council ★91★
Top art history research-doctorate programs as evaluated by the National Research Council ★93★
U.S. universities publishing the most papers in the field of artificial intelligence, 1995-99 ★100★
Most effective ecology, evolution, and behavior research-doctorate programs as evaluated by the National Research Council ★199★
Top ecology, evolution, and behavior research-doctorate programs as evaluated by the National Research Council ★201★
Top neurosciences research-doctorate programs as evaluated by the National Research Council ★202★
Most effective biochemistry and molecular biology research-doctorate programs as evaluated by the National Research Council ★205★
Most effective molecular and general genetics research-doctorate programs as evaluated by the National Research Council ★207★
Top biochemistry and molecular biology research-doctorate programs as evaluated by the National Research Council ★209★
Top cell and developmental biology research-doctorate programs as evaluated by the National Research Council ★210★
Top molecular and general genetics research-doctorate programs as evaluated by the National Research Council ★211★
U.S. News & World Report's universities with the best quantitative methods departments, 1999-2000 ★572★
Four-year institutions with the most drug arrests reported, 1999 ★705★
Four-year institutions with the most liquor arrests reported, 1999 ★707★
Four-year institutions with the most weapons arrests reported, 1999 ★709★
U.S. colleges and universities reporting the most alcohol related arrests, 1998 ★730★
U.S. colleges and universities reporting the most drug related arrests, 1998 ★731★
U.S. colleges and universities reporting the most weapons related arrests, 1998 ★732★
U.S. colleges and universities with the largest numerical increases in drug arrests, 1998 ★734★
Winner of the American Chemical Society's Arthur C. Cope Awards, 2001 ★795★
Most effective chemistry research-doctorate programs as evaluated by the National Research Council ★802★
Top chemistry research-doctorate programs as evaluated by the National Research Council ★805★
Most effective classics research-doctorate programs as evaluated by the National Research Council ★815★
Top classics research-doctorate programs as evaluated by the National Research Council ★816★
U.S. colleges and universities with a diverse student body ★1012★
U.S. colleges and universities with a favorable surrounding town or city ★1013★
U.S. News & World Report's best public national universities, 2000-01 ★1123★
U.S. News & World Report's national universities with the best academic reputation, 2000-01 ★1126★
U.S. News & World Report's national universities with the highest percentage of freshmen in the top 10% of their high school class, 2000-01 ★1135★
Most effective comparative literature research-doctorate programs as evaluated by the National Research Council ★1587★
Top comparative literature research-doctorate programs as evaluated by the National Research Council ★1588★
U.S. universities with the greatest impact in computer science, 1994-98 ★1592★
U.S. universities with the greatest impact in computer science, 1995-99 ★1593★
Most effective computer science research-doctorate programs as evaluated by the National Research Council ★1594★
Top computer science research-doctorate programs as evaluated by the National Research Council ★1597★
Top colleges in terms of total baccalaureate degrees awarded to minorities, 1997-98 ★1678★
Total baccalaureate biology/life sciences degrees awarded to Asian Americans from U.S. colleges and universities, 1997-98 ★1680★
Total baccalaureate communications degrees awarded to Asian Americans from U.S. colleges and universities, 1997-98 ★1688★
Total baccalaureate computer and information science degrees awarded to Asian Americans from U.S. colleges and universities, 1997-98 ★1692★
Total baccalaureate degrees awarded to Asian Americans from U.S. colleges and universities, 1997-98 ★1702★
Total baccalaureate education degrees awarded to Asian Americans from U.S. colleges and universities, 1997-98 ★1712★
Total baccalaureate English language, literature, and letters degrees awarded to Asian Americans from U.S. colleges and universities, 1997-98 ★1717★
Total baccalaureate English language, literature, and letters degrees awarded to Hispanic Americans from U.S. colleges and universities, 1997-98 ★1718★
Total baccalaureate English language, literature, and letters degrees awarded to Native Americans from U.S. colleges and universities, 1997-98 ★1719★
Total baccalaureate ethnic/cultural studies degrees awarded to African Americans from U.S. colleges and universities, 1997-98 ★1720★
Total baccalaureate law and legal studies degrees awarded to Asian Americans from U.S. colleges and universities, 1997-98 ★1726★
Total baccalaureate law and legal studies degrees awarded to Hispanic Americans from U.S. colleges and universities, 1997-98 ★1727★
Total baccalaureate mathematics degrees awarded to Asian Americans from U.S. colleges and universities, 1997-98 ★1730★
Total baccalaureate physical sciences degrees awarded to Asian Americans from U.S. colleges and universities, 1997-98 ★1734★
Total baccalaureate psychology degrees awarded to Asian Americans from U.S. colleges and universities, 1997-98 ★1738★
Total baccalaureate social sciences and history degrees awarded to Asian Americans from U.S. colleges and universities, 1997-98 ★1742★
Total baccalaureate social sciences and history degrees awarded to Hispanic Americans from U.S. colleges and universities, 1997-98 ★1743★
Total baccalaureate social sciences and history degrees awarded to Native Americans from U.S. colleges and universities, 1997-98 ★1744★
Total ethnic/cultural studies doctoral degrees awarded to minorities from U.S. colleges and universities, 1997-98 ★1746★
Total ethnic/cultural studies master's degrees awarded to minorities from U.S. colleges and universities, 1997-98 ★1748★
U.S. colleges and universities awarding the most business management and administrative services master's degrees to Asian Americans ★1760★
U.S. colleges and universities awarding the most communications master's degrees to Asian Americans ★1764★
U.S. colleges and universities awarding the most communications master's degrees to Hispanic Americans ★1765★
U.S. colleges and universities awarding the most education master's degrees to Asian Americans ★1770★
U.S. colleges and universities awarding the most English language/literature/letters master's degrees to Asian Americans ★1774★
U.S. colleges and universities awarding the most health professions and related sciences master's degrees to Asian Americans ★1778★
U.S. colleges and universities awarding the most health professions and related sciences master's degrees to Native Americans ★1780★
U.S. colleges and universities awarding the most master's degrees to Asian Americans ★1786★
U.S. colleges and universities awarding the most master's degrees to minorities ★1788★
U.S. colleges and universities awarding the most master's degrees to Native Americans ★1789★
U.S. colleges and universities awarding the most mathematics master's degrees to Asian Americans ★1791★
U.S. colleges and universities awarding the most physical sciences master's degrees to Asian Americans ★1794★
U.S. colleges and universities awarding the most social sciences and history master's degrees to Asian Americans ★1802★

CALIFORNIA

- U.S. colleges and universities awarding the most social sciences and history master's degrees to Hispanic Americans ★1803★
- U.S. institutions awarding the most baccalaureate degrees to minorities in ethnic/cultural studies, 1997-98 ★1821★
- U.S. colleges and universities awarding the most first professional degrees to Hispanic Americans ★1845★
- U.S. colleges and universities awarding the most law and legal studies first professional degrees to Asian Americans ★1853★
- U.S. colleges and universities awarding the most law and legal studies first professional degrees to Hispanic Americans ★1854★
- Top doctorate granting institutions, 1999 ★2047★
- U.S. colleges and universities awarding the most biological and life sciences doctorate degrees to Asian Americans ★2083★
- U.S. colleges and universities awarding the most biological and life sciences doctorate degrees to Hispanic Americans ★2084★
- U.S. colleges and universities awarding the most computer and information sciences doctorate degrees to Asian Americans ★2090★
- U.S. colleges and universities awarding the most doctoral degrees to African Americans from 1995 to 1999 ★2091★
- U.S. colleges and universities awarding the most doctoral degrees to Asian Americans and Pacific Islanders from 1995 to 1999 ★2093★
- U.S. colleges and universities awarding the most doctorate degrees to Asian Americans ★2096★
- U.S. colleges and universities awarding the most doctorate degrees to Hispanic Americans ★2097★
- U.S. colleges and universities awarding the most doctorate degrees to minorities ★2098★
- U.S. colleges and universities awarding the most doctorates in all fields, 1999 ★2100★
- U.S. colleges and universities awarding the most doctorates in engineering, 1999 ★2102★
- U.S. colleges and universities awarding the most doctorates in humanities, 1999 ★2103★
- U.S. colleges and universities awarding the most doctorates in life sciences, 1999 ★2104★
- U.S. colleges and universities awarding the most doctorates in physical sciences, mathematics, and computer sciences, 1999 ★2105★
- U.S. colleges and universities awarding the most doctorates in social sciences, 1999 ★2107★
- U.S. colleges and universities awarding the most English language/literature/letters doctorate degrees to African Americans ★2112★
- U.S. colleges and universities awarding the most English language/literature/letters doctorate degrees to Asian Americans ★2113★
- U.S. colleges and universities awarding the most health professions and related sciences doctorate degrees to Asian Americans ★2115★
- U.S. colleges and universities awarding the most health professions and related sciences doctorate degrees to Hispanic Americans ★2116★
- U.S. colleges and universities awarding the most physical sciences doctorate degrees to Asian Americans ★2119★
- U.S. colleges and universities awarding the most social sciences and history doctorate degrees to Asian Americans ★2125★
- U.S. colleges and universities awarding the most social sciences and history doctorate degrees to Hispanic Americans ★2126★
- U.S. institutions awarding the most doctorate degrees, 1999 ★2132★
- Most effective geosciences research-doctorate programs as evaluated by the National Research Council ★2150★
- Top geosciences research-doctorate programs as evaluated by the National Research Council ★2152★
- Economics departments by number of citations by top economists, 1971-92 ★2158★
- Economics departments by number of citations per top economist, 1971-92 ★2159★
- Economics departments by number of top economists, 1971-92 ★2160★
- Institutions most frequently contributing to the *American Economic Review* from 1911-1990 ★2168★
- Institutions most frequently contributing to the *American Economic Review* from 1951-1990 ★2169★
- U.S. universities publishing the most papers in the field of economics and business, 1995-99 ★2178★
- Economics Ph.D. programs by number of citations of top economist graduates, 1971-92 ★2204★
- Economics Ph.D. programs by number of citations per top economist graduate, 1971-92 ★2205★
- Economics Ph.D. programs by number of top economist graduates, 1971-92 ★2206★
- Most effective economics research-doctorate programs as evaluated by the National Research Council ★2207★
- Origin of doctorate for dissertation chairs in economics ★2208★
- Origin of doctorate for economics faculty at Ph.D.-granting institutions ★2209★
- Origin of doctorate for economics faculty at Ph.D.-granting institutions, by Ph.D. equivalents produced ★2210★
- Top economics research-doctorate programs as evaluated by the National Research Council ★2213★
- U.S. universities contributing the most papers in the field of AI, robotics, and auto control, 1993-97 ★2338★
- U.S. universities publishing the most papers in the field of civil engineering, 1994-98 ★2348★
- U.S. universities publishing the most papers in the field of civil engineering, 1995-99 ★2349★
- Acceptance rates for *U.S. News & World Report*'s top 10 graduate engineering schools, 2001 ★2358★
- Average analytic GRE scores for *U.S. News & World Report*'s top 10 graduate engineering schools, 2001 ★2359★
- Average quantitative GRE scores for *U.S. News & World Report*'s top 10 graduate engineering schools, 2001 ★2360★
- Doctoral student-faculty ratios at *U.S. News & World Report*'s top 10 graduate engineering schools, 2001 ★2361★
- Faculty membership in National Academy of Engineering at *U.S. News & World Report*'s top 10 graduate engineering schools, 2001 ★2362★
- Ph.D.s granted at *U.S. News & World Report*'s top 10 graduate engineering schools, 2001 ★2363★
- Research expenditures per faculty member at *U.S. News & World Report*'s top 10 graduate engineering schools, 2001 ★2364★
- Research funding allocated to *U.S. News & World Report*'s top 10 graduate engineering schools, 2001 ★2365★
- Top graduate engineering schools, 2001 ★2366★
- Top graduate engineering schools by reputation, as determined by academic personnel, 2001 ★2367★
- Top graduate engineering schools by reputation, as determined by engineers and recruiters, 2001 ★2368★
- *U.S. News & World Report*'s graduate engineering programs with the highest academic reputation scores, 2000-01 ★2372★
- Academics' choices for best graduate bioengineering/biomedical engineering programs, 2001 ★2381★
- Most effective biomedical engineering research-doctorate programs as evaluated by the National Research Council ★2383★
- Top biomedical engineering research-doctorate programs as evaluated by the National Research Council ★2384★
- Academics' choices for best graduate chemical engineering programs, 2001 ★2386★
- Most effective chemical engineering research-doctorate programs as evaluated by the National Research Council ★2389★
- Top chemical engineering research-doctorate programs as evaluated by the National Research Council ★2390★
- *U.S. News & World Report*'s graduate engineering programs with the best chemical departments, 2000-01 ★2392★
- Academics' choices for best graduate civil engineering programs, 2001 ★2394★
- Most effective civil engineering research-doctorate programs as evaluated by the National Research Council ★2395★
- Top civil engineering research-doctorate programs as evaluated by the National Research Council ★2396★
- *U.S. News & World Report*'s graduate engineering programs with the best civil departments, 2000-01 ★2398★
- Academics' choices for best graduate computer engineering programs, 2001 ★2399★
- *U.S. News & World Report*'s graduate engineering programs with the best computer departments, 2000-01 ★2401★
- Academics' choices for best graduate electrical/electronic/communications engineering programs, 2001 ★2403★
- Most effective electrical engineering research-doctorate programs as evaluated by the National Research Council ★2404★
- Top electrical engineering research-doctorate programs as evaluated by the National Research Council ★2405★
- *U.S. News & World Report*'s graduate engineering programs with the best electrical departments, 2000-01 ★2407★
- Academics' choices for best graduate environmental/environmental health engineering programs, 2001 ★2408★
- *U.S. News & World Report*'s graduate engineering programs with the best environmental departments, 2000-01 ★2410★
- Academics' choices for best graduate industrial/manufacturing engineering programs, 2001 ★2411★

Most effective industrial engineering research-doctorate programs as evaluated by the National Research Council ★2412★

Top industrial engineering research-doctorate programs as evaluated by the National Research Council ★2413★

U.S. News & World Report's graduate engineering programs with the best industrial manufacturing departments, 2000-01 ★2415★

Academics' choices for best graduate materials engineering programs, 2001 ★2417★

Most effective materials science research-doctorate programs as evaluated by the National Research Council ★2418★

Top materials science research-doctorate programs as evaluated by the National Research Council ★2419★

Academics' choices for best graduate mechanical engineering programs, 2001 ★2422★

Most effective mechanical engineering research-doctorate programs as evaluated by the National Research Council ★2423★

U.S. News & World Report's graduate engineering programs with the best mechanical departments, 2000-01 ★2425★

Academics' choices for best graduate nuclear engineering schools, 2000 ★2426★

U.S. News & World Report's graduate engineering programs with the best nuclear departments, 2000-01 ★2428★

U.S. universities publishing the most papers in the field of literature, 1994-98 ★2447★

Most effective English language and literature research-doctorate programs as evaluated by the National Research Council ★2448★

Top English language and literature research-doctorate programs as evaluated by the National Research Council ★2451★

U.S. universities publishing the most papers in the field of ecology/environmental sciences, 1994-98 ★2473★

Top French language and literature research-doctorate programs as evaluated by the National Research Council ★2516★

Faculty's scholarly reputation in the Ph.D.-granting departments of geography, 1925-1982 ★2518★

Most effective geography research-doctorate programs as evaluated by the National Research Council ★2519★

Top geography research-doctorate programs as evaluated by the National Research Council ★2520★

Top Ph.D.-granting departments of geography from 1925-1982 ★2521★

Most effective German language and literature research-doctorate programs as evaluated by the National Research Council ★2527★

Top German language and literature research-doctorate programs as evaluated by the National Research Council ★2528★

U.S. universities contributing the most papers in the field of history, 1993-97 ★2551★

Top history research-doctorate programs as evaluated by the National Research Council ★2554★

Academics' choices for best environmental law programs, 2001 ★2628★

Academics' choices for best intellectual property law programs, 2001 ★2630★

Academics' choices for best international law programs, 2001 ★2631★

Acceptance rates at U.S. News & World Report's top 10 law schools, 2001 ★2634★

Graduate employment after graduation percentage for U.S. News & World Report's top 10 law schools, 2001 ★2635★

Graduate employment percentage for U.S. News & World Report's top 10 law schools, 2001 ★2636★

Jurisdiction's overall bar passage rate for U.S. News & World Report's top 10 law schools, 2001 ★2637★

Law schools with the best constitutional law (freedom of religion) faculty, 1999-2000 ★2643★

Law schools with the best constitutional law (freedom of speech) faculty, 1999-2000 ★2644★

Law schools with the best criminal law (substantive) faculty, 1999-2000 ★2647★

Law schools with the best critical race theory faculty, 1999-2000 ★2649★

Law schools with the best environmental law faculty, 1999-2000 ★2650★

Law schools with the best intellectual property faculty, 1999-2000 ★2653★

Law schools with the best law and economics faculty, 1999-2000 ★2657★

Law schools with the best law and social science plus psychology and sociology faculty, 1999-2000 ★2659★

Law schools with the best moral and political theory (Anglo-American traditions) faculty, 1999-2000 ★2662★

Law schools with the highest quality, 1999-2000 ★2666★

School's bar passage rate in jurisdiction at U.S. News & World Report's top 10 law schools, 2001 ★2667★

Student-faculty ratios at U.S. News & World Report's top 10 law schools, 2001 ★2669★

Top law schools, 2001 ★2670★

Top law schools by reputation, as determined by academic personnel, 2001 ★2671★

Top law schools by reputation, as determined by lawyers and judges, 2001 ★2672★

Top law school student bodies, 1999-2000 ★2673★

Top university research libraries in the U.S. and Canada, 1998-99 ★2706★

Comparison of library and information science programs composite rankings with U.S. News & World Report survey ★2709★

Library and information science programs with the most citations to journal articles, 1993-1998 ★2712★

Library and information science programs with the most journal articles, 1993-1998 ★2713★

Library and information science programs with the most journal articles per capita, 1993-1998 ★2714★

Library and information science programs with the most per capita citations to journal articles, 1993-1998 ★2715★

Top linguistics research-doctorate programs as evaluated by the National Research Council ★2733★

Most effective mathematics research-doctorate programs as evaluated by the National Research Council ★2775★

Top mathematics research-doctorate programs as evaluated by the National Research Council ★2778★

Most effective statistics and biostatistics research-doctorate programs as evaluated by the National Research Council ★2780★

Most effective music research-doctorate programs as evaluated by the National Research Council ★2895★

Top music research-doctorate programs as evaluated by the National Research Council ★2896★

Institutions in the Worker Rights Consortium ★2913★

Top philosophy research-doctorate programs as evaluated by the National Research Council ★2947★

U.S. universities publishing the most papers in the field of astrophysics, 1995-99 ★2978★

Most effective astrophysics and astronomy research-doctorate programs as evaluated by the National Research Council ★3006★

Most effective physics research-doctorate programs as evaluated by the National Research Council ★3007★

Top astrophysics and astronomy research-doctorate programs as evaluated by the National Research Council ★3014★

Top physics research-doctorate programs as evaluated by the National Research Council ★3015★

Most effective political science research-doctorate programs as evaluated by the National Research Council ★3043★

Top political science research-doctorate programs as evaluated by the National Research Council ★3046★

Top psychology research-doctorate programs as evaluated by the National Research Council ★3068★

U.S. colleges and universities spending the most on chemical research and development, 1998 ★3099★

U.S. colleges and universities spending the most on chemical research equipment, 1998 ★3100★

U.S. colleges and universities with the most federal support for chemical research and development, 1998 ★3102★

U.S. colleges and universities with the most federal support for chemical research equipment, 1998 ★3103★

U.S. universities spending the most on research and development, 1998 ★3104★

Average faculty salaries for institutions of higher education in California, 2000-01 ★3692★

Public institutions of higher education that pay the highest salaries to female professors, 2000-01 ★3975★

U.S. universities with the highest relative citation impact, 1993-97 ★4291★

Most effective sociology research-doctorate programs as evaluated by the National Research Council ★4352★

Top sociology research-doctorate programs as evaluated by the National Research Council ★4354★

Most effective Spanish and Portuguese language and literature research-doctorate programs as evaluated by the National Research Council ★4357★

Top Spanish and Portuguese language and literature research-doctorate programs as evaluated by the National Research Council ★4358★

Academics' choices for best education policy graduate programs, 2001 ★4381★

Academics' choices for best educational psychology graduate programs, 2001 ★4382★

CALIFORNIA

Acceptance rates at *U.S. News & World Report*'s top 10 graduate education schools, 2001 ★4388★

Average quantitative GRE scores for *U.S. News & World Report*'s top 10 graduate education schools, 2001 ★4389★

Average verbal GRE scores for *U.S. News & World Report*'s top 10 graduate education schools, 2001 ★4390★

Doctoral students to faculty ratio at *U.S. News & World Report*'s top 10 graduate education schools, 2001 ★4391★

Ph.D.s and Ed.D.s granted at *U.S. News & World Report*'s top 10 graduate education schools, 2001 ★4392★

Research expenditures for *U.S. News & World Report*'s top 10 graduate education schools, 2001 ★4393★

Research expenditures per faculty member at *U.S. News & World Report*'s top 10 graduate education schools, 2001 ★4394★

Top graduate education schools, 2001 ★4395★

Top graduate education schools by reputation, as determined by academic personnel, 2001 ★4396★

Top graduate education schools by reputation, as determined by superintendents, 2001 ★4397★

California, Davis; University of

U.S. universities publishing the most papers in the fields of agriculture/agronomy, 1994-98 ★57★

Top anthropology research-doctorate programs as evaluated by the National Research Council ★62★

Most effective ecology, evolution, and behavior research-doctorate programs as evaluated by the National Research Council ★199★

Top ecology, evolution, and behavior research-doctorate programs as evaluated by the National Research Council ★201★

U.S. college campuses with more than 5,000 students reporting murders or manslaughters, 1998 ★729★

U.S. colleges and universities with the largest numerical increases in drug arrests, 1998 ★734★

Institutions with the most full-time Hispanic American faculty ★923★

U.S. colleges and universities with the most full-time Hispanic American faculty ★925★

U.S. News & World Report's best public national universities, 2000-01 ★1123★

U.S. News & World Report's national universities with the highest percentage of freshmen in the top 10% of their high school class, 2000-01 ★1135★

Top colleges in terms of total baccalaureate degrees awarded to minorities, 1997-98 ★1678★

Total baccalaureate biology/life sciences degrees awarded to Asian Americans from U.S. colleges and universities, 1997-98 ★1680★

Total baccalaureate biology/life sciences degrees awarded to Hispanic Americans from U.S. colleges and universities, 1997-98 ★1681★

Total baccalaureate biology/life sciences degrees awarded to Native Americans from U.S. colleges and universities, 1997-98 ★1682★

Total baccalaureate computer and information science degrees awarded to Asian Americans from U.S. colleges and universities, 1997-98 ★1692★

Total baccalaureate degrees awarded to Asian Americans from U.S. colleges and universities, 1997-98 ★1702★

Total baccalaureate education degrees awarded to Asian Americans from U.S. colleges and universities, 1997-98 ★1712★

Total baccalaureate English language, literature, and letters degrees awarded to Asian Americans from U.S. colleges and universities, 1997-98 ★1717★

Total baccalaureate mathematics degrees awarded to Asian Americans from U.S. colleges and universities, 1997-98 ★1730★

Total baccalaureate physical sciences degrees awarded to Hispanic Americans from U.S. colleges and universities, 1997-98 ★1735★

Total baccalaureate psychology degrees awarded to Asian Americans from U.S. colleges and universities, 1997-98 ★1738★

Total baccalaureate psychology degrees awarded to Hispanic Americans from U.S. colleges and universities, 1997-98 ★1739★

Total baccalaureate social sciences and history degrees awarded to Asian Americans from U.S. colleges and universities, 1997-98 ★1742★

U.S. colleges and universities awarding the most physical sciences master's degrees to Asian Americans ★1794★

U.S. institutions awarding the most baccalaureate degrees to Asian Americans in agribusiness and production, 1998 ★1815★

U.S. institutions awarding the most baccalaureate degrees to Asian Americans in agricultural sciences, 1998 ★1816★

U.S. institutions awarding the most baccalaureate degrees to Hispanic Americans in agribusiness and production, 1998 ★1817★

U.S. institutions awarding the most baccalaureate degrees to Hispanic Americans in agricultural sciences, 1998 ★1818★

U.S. institutions awarding the most baccalaureate degrees to minorities in agribusiness and production, 1998 ★1819★

U.S. institutions awarding the most baccalaureate degrees to minorities in agricultural sciences, 1998 ★1820★

U.S. institutions awarding the most master's degrees to Asian Americans in agribusiness and production, 1998 ★1826★

U.S. institutions awarding the most master's degrees to minorities in agribusiness and production, 1998 ★1829★

U.S. colleges and universities awarding the most first professional degrees to Hispanic Americans ★1845★

U.S. colleges and universities awarding the most law and legal studies first professional degrees to Asian Americans ★1853★

U.S. colleges and universities awarding the most biological and life sciences doctorate degrees to Asian Americans ★2083★

U.S. colleges and universities awarding the most biological and life sciences doctorate degrees to Hispanic Americans ★2084★

U.S. colleges and universities awarding the most doctoral degrees to Asian Americans and Pacific Islanders from 1995 to 1999 ★2093★

U.S. colleges and universities awarding the most doctorate degrees to Hispanic Americans ★2097★

U.S. colleges and universities awarding the most doctorates in life sciences, 1999 ★2104★

Academics' choices for best graduate agricultural engineering programs, 2001 ★2379★

U.S. universities publishing the most papers in the field of ecology/environmental sciences, 1994-98 ★2473★

Institutions with the most prolific communication studies researchers ★2749★

Institutions in the Worker Rights Consortium ★2913★

Women faculty in Ph.D. physics departments at U.S. institutions, 1998 ★2981★

Average faculty salaries for institutions of higher education in California, 2000-01 ★3692★

U.S. universities publishing the most papers in the field of food science/nutrition, 1994-98 ★4286★

Top Spanish and Portuguese language and literature research-doctorate programs as evaluated by the National Research Council ★4358★

U.S. universities with the greatest impact in veterinary medicine, 1995-99 ★4440★

U.S. universities with the highest concentration of papers published in the field of veterinary medicine, 1995-99 ★4441★

California, Hastings; University of

U.S. colleges and universities awarding the most law and legal studies first professional degrees to Asian Americans ★1853★

Law schools with the best civil procedure faculty, 1999-2000 ★2640★

California Institute of the Arts

Average faculty salaries for institutions of higher education without academic ranks in California, 2000-01 ★3743★

California Institute of Technology

Most effective neurosciences research-doctorate programs as evaluated by the National Research Council ★200★

Top neurosciences research-doctorate programs as evaluated by the National Research Council ★202★

Most effective biochemistry and molecular biology research-doctorate programs as evaluated by the National Research Council ★205★

Most effective cell and developmental biology research-doctorate programs as evaluated by the National Research Council ★206★

Most effective molecular and general genetics research-doctorate programs as evaluated by the National Research Council ★207★

Top biochemistry and molecular biology research-doctorate programs as evaluated by the National Research Council ★209★

Top cell and developmental biology research-doctorate programs as evaluated by the National Research Council ★210★

Top molecular and general genetics research-doctorate programs as evaluated by the National Research Council ★211★

Most effective chemistry research-doctorate programs as evaluated by the National Research Council ★802★

Top chemistry research-doctorate programs as evaluated by the National Research Council ★805★

Comparison of acceptance rates at the top 5 national universities in the U.S., 1990 and 2001 ★845★

U.S. colleges and universities where students study the most ★1003★

U.S. colleges and universities where the general student body does not drink hard liquor ★1005★

U.S. colleges and universities where the general student body does not smoke marijuana ★1006★

U.S. colleges and universities where the general student body puts little emphasis on socializing ★1010★

CALIFORNIA

U.S. colleges and universities with the least accessible instructors ★1036★
U.S. colleges and universities with the least attractive campuses ★1037★
U.S. News & World Report's national universities with the best academic reputation, 2000-01 ★1126★
U.S. News & World Report's national universities with the best faculty resources rank, 2000-01 ★1127★
U.S. News & World Report's national universities with the best student/faculty ratio, 2000-01 ★1130★
U.S. News & World Report's national universities with the highest alumni giving rank, 2000-01 ★1132★
U.S. News & World Report's national universities with the highest financial resources rank, 2000-01 ★1133★
U.S. News & World Report's national universities with the highest percentage of freshmen in the top 10% of their high school class, 2000-01 ★1135★
U.S. News & World Report's national universities with the highest percentage of full-time faculty, 2000-01 ★1136★
U.S. News & World Report's national universities with the highest proportion of alumni support, 2000-01 ★1137★
U.S. News & World Report's national universities with the highest proportion of classes with less than 20 students, 2000-01 ★1138★
U.S. News & World Report's national universities with the highest selectivity rank, 2000-01 ★1139★
U.S. News & World Report's national universities with the lowest acceptance rates, 2000-01 ★1140★
Fiske Guide's best buys for private colleges and universities, 2001 ★1459★
U.S. News & World Report's best undergraduate fees among national universities by discount tuition, 2000 ★1474★
Most effective computer science research-doctorate programs as evaluated by the National Research Council ★1594★
Top computer science research-doctorate programs as evaluated by the National Research Council ★1597★
U.S. colleges and universities awarding the most physical sciences doctorate degrees to Asian Americans ★2119★
Most effective geosciences research-doctorate programs as evaluated by the National Research Council ★2150★
Top geosciences research-doctorate programs as evaluated by the National Research Council ★2152★
Acceptance rates for *U.S. News & World Report*'s top 10 graduate engineering schools, 2001 ★2358★
Average analytic GRE scores for *U.S. News & World Report*'s top 10 graduate engineering schools, 2001 ★2359★
Average quantitative GRE scores for *U.S. News & World Report*'s top 10 graduate engineering schools, 2001 ★2360★
Doctoral student-faculty ratios at *U.S. News & World Report*'s top 10 graduate engineering schools, 2001 ★2361★
Faculty membership in National Academy of Engineering at *U.S. News & World Report*'s top 10 graduate engineering schools, 2001 ★2362★

Ph.D.s granted at *U.S. News & World Report*'s top 10 graduate engineering schools, 2001 ★2363★
Research expenditures per faculty member at *U.S. News & World Report*'s top 10 graduate engineering schools, 2001 ★2364★
Research funding allocated to *U.S. News & World Report*'s top 10 graduate engineering schools, 2001 ★2365★
Top graduate engineering schools, 2001 ★2366★
Top graduate engineering schools by reputation, as determined by academic personnel, 2001 ★2367★
Top graduate engineering schools by reputation, as determined by engineers and recruiters, 2001 ★2368★
U.S. News & World Report's graduate engineering programs with the highest academic reputation scores, 2000-01 ★2372★
Academics' choices for best graduate aerospace/aeronautical/astronautical engineering programs, 2001 ★2374★
Most effective aerospace engineering research-doctorate programs as evaluated by the National Research Council ★2375★
Top aerospace engineering research-doctorate programs as evaluated by the National Research Council ★2376★
Academics' choices for best graduate chemical engineering programs, 2001 ★2386★
Most effective chemical engineering research-doctorate programs as evaluated by the National Research Council ★2389★
Top chemical engineering research-doctorate programs as evaluated by the National Research Council ★2390★
Academics' choices for best graduate civil engineering programs, 2001 ★2394★
Most effective civil engineering research-doctorate programs as evaluated by the National Research Council ★2395★
Top civil engineering research-doctorate programs as evaluated by the National Research Council ★2396★
Academics' choices for best graduate electrical/electronic/communications engineering programs, 2001 ★2403★
Most effective electrical engineering research-doctorate programs as evaluated by the National Research Council ★2404★
Top electrical engineering research-doctorate programs as evaluated by the National Research Council ★2405★
Academics' choices for best graduate environmental/environmental health engineering programs, 2001 ★2408★
Top materials science research-doctorate programs as evaluated by the National Research Council ★2419★
Academics' choices for best graduate mechanical engineering programs, 2001 ★2422★
Most effective mechanical engineering research-doctorate programs as evaluated by the National Research Council ★2423★
Top mathematics research-doctorate programs as evaluated by the National Research Council ★2778★
Women faculty in Ph.D. physics departments at U.S. institutions, 1998 ★2981★
Most effective astrophysics and astronomy research-doctorate programs as evaluated by the National Research Council ★3006★

Most effective physics research-doctorate programs as evaluated by the National Research Council ★3007★
Top astrophysics and astronomy research-doctorate programs as evaluated by the National Research Council ★3014★
Top physics research-doctorate programs as evaluated by the National Research Council ★3015★
Top physiology research-doctorate programs as evaluated by the National Research Council ★3022★
U.S. colleges and universities spending the most on chemical research and development, 1998 ★3099★
U.S. colleges and universities spending the most on chemical research equipment, 1998 ★3100★
U.S. colleges and universities with the most federal support for chemical research and development, 1998 ★3102★
U.S. colleges and universities with the most federal support for chemical research equipment, 1998 ★3103★
Institutions receiving the most federal research and development expenditures, 1999 ★3105★
Institutions receiving the largest Energy Department research grants, 2000 ★3111★
Average faculty salaries for institutions of higher education in California, 2000-01 ★3692★
U.S. institutions with the highest paid assistant professors, 2001 ★3977★
U.S. institutions with the highest paid full professors, 2001 ★3978★

California, Irvine; University of
All-USA College Academic First Team, 2001 ★2★
All-USA College Academic Third Team, 2001 ★4★
U.S. business schools with the slowest payback on MBA investments ★655★
U.S. News & World Report's best public national universities, 2000-01 ★1123★
U.S. News & World Report's national universities with the highest percentage of freshmen in the top 10% of their high school class, 2000-01 ★1135★
U.S. News & World Report's national universities with the lowest graduation rates, 1999 ★1141★
Top comparative literature research-doctorate programs as evaluated by the National Research Council ★1588★
Universities with the most-cited scholars in *Criminology* ★1649★
Universities with the most-cited scholars in *Journal of Quantitative Criminology* ★1650★
Universities with the most-cited scholars in *Journal of Research in Crime and Delinquency* ★1651★
Universities with the most-cited scholars in *Justice Quarterly* ★1652★
Top colleges in terms of total baccalaureate degrees awarded to minorities, 1997-98 ★1678★
Total baccalaureate biology/life sciences degrees awarded to Asian Americans from U.S. colleges and universities, 1997-98 ★1680★
Total baccalaureate biology/life sciences degrees awarded to Hispanic Americans from U.S. colleges and universities, 1997-98 ★1681★

CALIFORNIA

Total baccalaureate computer and information science degrees awarded to Asian Americans from U.S. colleges and universities, 1997-98 ★1692★

Total baccalaureate degrees awarded to Asian Americans from U.S. colleges and universities, 1997-98 ★1702★

Total baccalaureate English language, literature, and letters degrees awarded to Asian Americans from U.S. colleges and universities, 1997-98 ★1717★

Total baccalaureate mathematics degrees awarded to Asian Americans from U.S. colleges and universities, 1997-98 ★1730★

Total baccalaureate physical sciences degrees awarded to Asian Americans from U.S. colleges and universities, 1997-98 ★1734★

Total baccalaureate physical sciences degrees awarded to Hispanic Americans from U.S. colleges and universities, 1997-98 ★1735★

Total baccalaureate psychology degrees awarded to Asian Americans from U.S. colleges and universities, 1997-98 ★1738★

Total baccalaureate social sciences and history degrees awarded to Asian Americans from U.S. colleges and universities, 1997-98 ★1742★

U.S. colleges and universities awarding the most English language/literature/letters master's degrees to Asian Americans ★1774★

U.S. colleges and universities awarding the most social sciences and history master's degrees to Asian Americans ★1802★

U.S. universities with the greatest impact in geosciences, 1994-98 ★2149★

U.S. universities with the greatest impact in geosciences, 1993-97 ★2155★

U.S. universities with the greatest impact in metallurgy, 1995-99 ★2435★

Top English language and literature research-doctorate programs as evaluated by the National Research Council ★2451★

Top French language and literature research-doctorate programs as evaluated by the National Research Council ★2516★

Top German language and literature research-doctorate programs as evaluated by the National Research Council ★2528★

Institutions in the Worker Rights Consortium ★2913★

Average faculty salaries for institutions of higher education in California, 2000-01 ★3692★

Top Spanish and Portuguese language and literature research-doctorate programs as evaluated by the National Research Council ★4358★

California Law Review

Most frequently-cited law reviews and legal periodicals, 1924-1986: a compilation ★2619★

Most frequently-cited law reviews and legal periodicals, according to *Shepard's Law Review Citations*, 1957-1986 ★2620★

California, Los Angeles, Anderson Graduate School of Management; University of

Academics' choices for best graduate entrepreneurship programs, 2001 ★583★

Academics' choices for best graduate executive MBA programs, 2001 ★584★

Academics' choices for best part-time MBA programs, 2000 ★587★

Business Week's top business schools as selected by recent MBA graduates, 2000 ★597★

Business Week's top business schools by intellectual capital, 2000 ★599★

Business Week's top business schools with the lowest percentage of international students, 2000 ★615★

Business Week's top business schools with the lowest percentage of minority enrollment, 2000 ★616★

Business Week's top business schools worst at responding to student concerns, 2000 ★621★

Highest post-MBA salaries for students enrolled in *Business Week*'s top business schools, 1999 ★631★

Highest pre-MBA salaries for students enrolled in *Business Week*'s top business schools, 1999 ★632★

Top graduate business schools by reputation, as determined by recruiters, 2001 ★651★

Academics' choices for best graduate finance programs, 2001 ★662★

Academics' choices for best graduate general management programs, 2001 ★666★

Academics' choices for best graduate international business programs, 2001 ★668★

Academics' choices for best graduate marketing programs, 2001 ★670★

Academics' choices for best graduate production/operations management programs, 2001 ★674★

California, Los Angeles; University of

Most effective anthropology research-doctorate programs as evaluated by the National Research Council ★61★

Top anthropology research-doctorate programs as evaluated by the National Research Council ★62★

Top art history research-doctorate programs as evaluated by the National Research Council ★93★

Division I all-time winningest college teams ★128★

NCAA men's gymnastics teams with the most individual champions ★137★

Women's Division I track and field programs with the most outdoor championships ★149★

Top neurosciences research-doctorate programs as evaluated by the National Research Council ★202★

Top biochemistry and molecular biology research-doctorate programs as evaluated by the National Research Council ★209★

Top business schools for within-discipline research performance in finance, 1986-1998 ★663★

Top chemistry research-doctorate programs as evaluated by the National Research Council ★805★

Top classics research-doctorate programs as evaluated by the National Research Council ★816★

Institutions with the most full-time Hispanic American faculty ★923★

U.S. colleges and universities with the most full-time Hispanic American faculty ★925★

Retention rates of African American students at traditionally white institutions, 1997-98 ★1121★

U.S. News & World Report's best public national universities, 2000-01 ★1123★

U.S. News & World Report's national universities with the best freshmen retention rates, 2000-01 ★1128★

U.S. News & World Report's national universities with the highest percentage of freshmen in the top 10% of their high school class, 2000-01 ★1135★

Institutions receiving the most gifts, 1999-2000 ★1244★

Fiske Guide's best buys for public colleges and universities, 2001 ★1460★

Top computer science research-doctorate programs as evaluated by the National Research Council ★1597★

Top colleges in terms of total baccalaureate degrees awarded to minorities, 1997-98 ★1678★

Total baccalaureate biology/life sciences degrees awarded to Asian Americans from U.S. colleges and universities, 1997-98 ★1680★

Total baccalaureate biology/life sciences degrees awarded to Hispanic Americans from U.S. colleges and universities, 1997-98 ★1681★

Total baccalaureate degrees awarded to Asian Americans from U.S. colleges and universities, 1997-98 ★1702★

Total baccalaureate degrees awarded to Hispanic Americans from U.S. colleges and universities, 1997-98 ★1705★

Total baccalaureate English language, literature, and letters degrees awarded to Asian Americans from U.S. colleges and universities, 1997-98 ★1717★

Total baccalaureate English language, literature, and letters degrees awarded to Hispanic Americans from U.S. colleges and universities, 1997-98 ★1718★

Total baccalaureate English language, literature, and letters degrees awarded to Native Americans from U.S. colleges and universities, 1997-98 ★1719★

Total baccalaureate mathematics degrees awarded to Asian Americans from U.S. colleges and universities, 1997-98 ★1730★

Total baccalaureate mathematics degrees awarded to Hispanic Americans from U.S. colleges and universities, 1997-98 ★1731★

Total baccalaureate physical sciences degrees awarded to Asian Americans from U.S. colleges and universities, 1997-98 ★1734★

Total baccalaureate psychology degrees awarded to Asian Americans from U.S. colleges and universities, 1997-98 ★1738★

Total baccalaureate psychology degrees awarded to Hispanic Americans from U.S. colleges and universities, 1997-98 ★1739★

Total baccalaureate social sciences and history degrees awarded to African Americans from U.S. colleges and universities, 1997-98 ★1741★

Total baccalaureate social sciences and history degrees awarded to Asian Americans from U.S. colleges and universities, 1997-98 ★1742★

Total baccalaureate social sciences and history degrees awarded to Hispanic Americans from U.S. colleges and universities, 1997-98 ★1743★

Total baccalaureate social sciences and history degrees awarded to Native Americans from U.S. colleges and universities, 1997-98 ★1744★

Total ethnic/cultural studies master's degrees awarded to African Americans from U.S. colleges and universities, 1997-98 ★1747★

Total ethnic/cultural studies master's degrees awarded to minorities from U.S. colleges and universities, 1997-98 ★1748★

U.S. colleges and universities awarding the most biological and life sciences master's degrees to Asian Americans ★1757★

U.S. colleges and universities awarding the most business management and administrative services master's degrees to Asian Americans ★1760★

U.S. colleges and universities awarding the most business management and administrative services master's degrees to Hispanic Americans ★1761★

U.S. colleges and universities awarding the most education master's degrees to Asian Americans ★1770★

U.S. colleges and universities awarding the most English language/literature/letters master's degrees to Asian Americans ★1774★

U.S. colleges and universities awarding the most English language/literature/letters master's degrees to Hispanic Americans ★1775★

U.S. colleges and universities awarding the most health professions and related sciences master's degrees to Asian Americans ★1778★

U.S. colleges and universities awarding the most health professions and related sciences master's degrees to Hispanic Americans ★1779★

U.S. colleges and universities awarding the most health professions and related sciences master's degrees to Native Americans ★1780★

U.S. colleges and universities awarding the most master's degrees to Asian Americans ★1786★

U.S. colleges and universities awarding the most master's degrees to Hispanic Americans ★1787★

U.S. colleges and universities awarding the most master's degrees to minorities ★1788★

U.S. colleges and universities awarding the most mathematics master's degrees to Asian Americans ★1791★

U.S. colleges and universities awarding the most psychology master's degrees to Asian Americans ★1798★

U.S. colleges and universities awarding the most social sciences and history master's degrees to Asian Americans ★1802★

U.S. institutions awarding the most baccalaureate degrees to minorities in ethnic/cultural studies, 1997-98 ★1821★

U.S. colleges and universities awarding the most first professional degrees to Asian Americans ★1844★

U.S. colleges and universities awarding the most first professional degrees to Hispanic Americans ★1845★

U.S. colleges and universities awarding the most health professions and related sciences first professional degrees to Hispanic Americans ★1849★

U.S. colleges and universities awarding the most law and legal studies first professional degrees to Asian Americans ★1853★

U.S. universities with the greatest impact in dermatology, 1995-99 ★1876★

Top doctorate granting institutions, 1999 ★2047★

U.S. colleges and universities awarding the most biological and life sciences doctorate degrees to Asian Americans ★2083★

U.S. colleges and universities awarding the most doctoral degrees to African Americans from 1995 to 1999 ★2091★

U.S. colleges and universities awarding the most doctoral degrees to American Indians and Alaskan Natives from 1995 to 1999 ★2092★

U.S. colleges and universities awarding the most doctoral degrees to Asian Americans and Pacific Islanders from 1995 to 1999 ★2093★

U.S. colleges and universities awarding the most doctorate degrees to African Americans ★2095★

U.S. colleges and universities awarding the most doctorate degrees to Asian Americans ★2096★

U.S. colleges and universities awarding the most doctorate degrees to Hispanic Americans ★2097★

U.S. colleges and universities awarding the most doctorate degrees to minorities ★2098★

U.S. colleges and universities awarding the most doctorate degrees to Native Americans ★2099★

U.S. colleges and universities awarding the most doctorates in all fields, 1999 ★2100★

U.S. colleges and universities awarding the most doctorates in humanities, 1999 ★2103★

U.S. colleges and universities awarding the most doctorates in social sciences, 1999 ★2107★

U.S. colleges and universities awarding the most education doctorate degrees to Asian Americans ★2109★

U.S. colleges and universities awarding the most education doctorate degrees to Hispanic Americans ★2110★

U.S. colleges and universities awarding the most health professions and related sciences doctorate degrees to Asian Americans ★2115★

U.S. colleges and universities awarding the most health professions and related sciences doctorate degrees to Hispanic Americans ★2116★

U.S. colleges and universities awarding the most mathematics doctorate degrees to Asian Americans ★2117★

U.S. colleges and universities awarding the most physical sciences doctorate degrees to Asian Americans ★2119★

U.S. colleges and universities awarding the most psychology doctorate degrees to Asian Americans ★2121★

U.S. colleges and universities awarding the most social sciences and history doctorate degrees to African Americans ★2124★

U.S. colleges and universities awarding the most social sciences and history doctorate degrees to Asian Americans ★2125★

U.S. colleges and universities awarding the most social sciences and history doctorate degrees to Hispanic Americans ★2126★

U.S. institutions awarding the most doctorate degrees, 1999 ★2132★

Top geosciences research-doctorate programs as evaluated by the National Research Council ★2152★

Economics departments by number of citations by top economists, 1971-92 ★2158★

Economics departments by number of citations per top economist, 1971-92 ★2159★

Economics departments by number of top economists, 1971-92 ★2160★

Institutions generating the most economic education research text, 1963-1990 ★2167★

Institutions most frequently contributing to the *American Economic Review* from 1951-1990 ★2169★

Top economics research-doctorate programs as evaluated by the National Research Council ★2213★

U.S. universities publishing the most papers in the field of education, 1994-98 ★2219★

U.S. universities with the greatest impact in education, 1994-98 ★2221★

Most effective aerospace engineering research-doctorate programs as evaluated by the National Research Council ★2375★

Top aerospace engineering research-doctorate programs as evaluated by the National Research Council ★2376★

Top electrical engineering research-doctorate programs as evaluated by the National Research Council ★2405★

U.S. universities publishing the most papers in the field of literature, 1994-98 ★2447★

Top English language and literature research-doctorate programs as evaluated by the National Research Council ★2451★

Faculty's scholarly reputation in the Ph.D.-granting departments of geography, 1925-1982 ★2518★

Top geography research-doctorate programs as evaluated by the National Research Council ★2520★

Top Ph.D.-granting departments of geography from 1925-1982 ★2521★

U.S. universities contributing the most papers in the field of history, 1993-97 ★2551★

Top history research-doctorate programs as evaluated by the National Research Council ★2554★

Most wired universities, 2000 ★2598★

Law schools with the best criminal law (substantive) faculty, 1999-2000 ★2647★

Law schools with the best feminist legal theory faculty, 1999-2000 ★2651★

Law schools with the best jurisprudence faculty, 1999-2000 ★2655★

Law schools with the best law and social science plus psychology and sociology faculty, 1999-2000 ★2659★

Law schools with the best Torts (including products liability) faculty, 1999-2000 ★2665★

Law schools with the highest quality, 1999-2000 ★2666★

Top university research libraries in the U.S. and Canada, 1998-99 ★2706★

Comparison of library and information science programs composite rankings with *U.S. News & World Report* survey ★2709★

Library and information science programs with the most citations to journal articles, 1993-1998 ★2712★

Library and information science programs with the most journal articles, 1993-1998 ★2713★

Library and information science programs with the most journal articles per capita, 1993-1998 ★2714★

Library and information science programs with the most per capita citations to journal articles, 1993-1998 ★2715★

Most effective linguistics research-doctorate programs as evaluated by the National Research Council ★2732★

Top linguistics research-doctorate programs as evaluated by the National Research Council ★2733★

Top mathematics research-doctorate programs as evaluated by the National Research Council ★2778★

Top statistics and biostatistics research-doctorate programs as evaluated by the National Research Council ★2782★

Academics' choices for best AIDS programs, 2001 ★2818★

Academics' choices for best drug and alcohol abuse programs, 2001 ★2819★

Academics' choices for best geriatrics programs, 2001 ★2821★

Academics' choices for best women's health medical programs, 2001 ★2825★

Institutions in the Worker Rights Consortium ★2913★

U.S. universities with the greatest impact in pharmacology, 1994-98 ★2936★

Most effective philosophy research-doctorate programs as evaluated by the National Research Council ★2945★

Top philosophy research-doctorate programs as evaluated by the National Research Council ★2947★

Top physics research-doctorate programs as evaluated by the National Research Council ★3015★

Most effective physiology research-doctorate programs as evaluated by the National Research Council ★3021★

Top physiology research-doctorate programs as evaluated by the National Research Council ★3022★

Top political science research-doctorate programs as evaluated by the National Research Council ★3046★

Top psychology research-doctorate programs as evaluated by the National Research Council ★3068★

U.S. colleges and universities with the most federal support for chemical research and development, 1998 ★3102★

U.S. universities spending the most on research and development, 1998 ★3104★

Institutions receiving the most federal research and development expenditures, 1999 ★3105★

Average faculty salaries for institutions of higher education in California, 2000-01 ★3692★

Public institutions of higher education that pay the highest salaries to female professors, 2000-01 ★3975★

U.S. universities publishing the most papers in the field of neuroscience, 1994-98 ★4287★

U.S. universities publishing the most papers in the field of sociology and anthropology, 1994-98 ★4349★

U.S. universities publishing the most papers in the fields of sociology and anthropology, 1993-97 ★4350★

Top sociology research-doctorate programs as evaluated by the National Research Council ★4354★

Academics' choices for best educational psychology graduate programs, 2001 ★4382★

Academics' choices for best higher education administration graduate programs, 2001 ★4384★

Acceptance rates at *U.S. News & World Report*'s top 10 graduate education schools, 2001 ★4388★

Average quantitative GRE scores for *U.S. News & World Report*'s top 10 graduate education schools, 2001 ★4389★

Average verbal GRE scores for *U.S. News & World Report*'s top 10 graduate education schools, 2001 ★4390★

Doctoral students to faculty ratio at *U.S. News & World Report*'s top 10 graduate education schools, 2001 ★4391★

Ph.D.s and Ed.D.s granted at *U.S. News & World Report*'s top 10 graduate education schools, 2001 ★4392★

Research expenditures for *U.S. News & World Report*'s top 10 graduate education schools, 2001 ★4393★

Research expenditures per faculty member at *U.S. News & World Report*'s top 10 graduate education schools, 2001 ★4394★

Top graduate education schools, 2001 ★4395★

Top graduate education schools by reputation, as determined by academic personnel, 2001 ★4396★

Top graduate education schools by reputation, as determined by superintendents, 2001 ★4397★

California Lutheran University

U.S. News & World Report's western regional universities with the lowest acceptance rates, 2000-01 ★1586★

Average faculty salaries for institutions of higher education in California, 2000-01 ★3692★

California Management Review

Business journals by citation impact, 1998 ★690★

California Maritime Academy

Average faculty salaries for institutions of higher education in California, 2000-01 ★3692★

California, Merced; University of

Institutions in the Worker Rights Consortium ★2913★

California Polytechnic State University

U.S. institutions awarding the most baccalaureate degrees to Asian Americans in agribusiness and production, 1998 ★1815★

U.S. institutions awarding the most baccalaureate degrees to Asian Americans in agricultural sciences, 1998 ★1816★

U.S. institutions awarding the most baccalaureate degrees to Hispanic Americans in agribusiness and production, 1998 ★1817★

U.S. institutions awarding the most baccalaureate degrees to Hispanic Americans in agricultural sciences, 1998 ★1818★

U.S. institutions awarding the most baccalaureate degrees to minorities in agribusiness and production, 1998 ★1819★

U.S. institutions awarding the most baccalaureate degrees to minorities in agricultural sciences, 1998 ★1820★

U.S. institutions awarding the most baccalaureate degrees to Native Americans in agribusiness and production, 1998 ★1822★

U.S. institutions awarding the most baccalaureate degrees to Native Americans in agricultural sciences, 1998 ★1823★

California Polytechnic State University, San Luis Obispo

U.S. colleges and universities with the worst on-campus housing facilities ★1044★

U.S. News & World Report's top public western regional universities, 2000-01 ★1573★

U.S. News & World Report's top western regional universities, 2000-01 ★1574★

U.S. News & World Report's western regional universities with the best academic reputation scores, 2000-01 ★1577★

U.S. News & World Report's western regional universities with the highest freshmen retention rates, 2000-01 ★1581★

U.S. News & World Report's western regional universities with the highest percentage of freshmen in the top 25% of their high school class, 2000-01 ★1583★

U.S. News & World Report's western regional universities with the lowest acceptance rates, 2000-01 ★1586★

U.S. News & World Report's undergraduate engineering programs with the highest academic reputation scores, 2000-01 ★2337★

U.S. News & World Report's undergraduate engineering programs with the best aerospace departments, 2000-01 ★2341★

U.S. News & World Report's undergraduate engineering programs with the best civil departments, 2000-01 ★2347★

U.S. News & World Report's undergraduate engineering programs with the best computer departments, 2000-01 ★2353★

U.S. News & World Report's undergraduate engineering programs with the best electrical departments, 2000-01 ★2355★

U.S. News & World Report's undergraduate engineering programs with the best industrial manufacturing departments, 2000-01 ★2380★

U.S. News & World Report's undergraduate engineering programs with the best mechanical departments, 2000-01 ★2438★

U.S. master's institutions with the largest number of students studying abroad, 1998-99 ★2513★

Average faculty salaries for institutions of higher education in California, 2000-01 ★3692★

California, Riverside; University of

All-USA College Academic First Team, 2001 ★2★

Division II NCAA colleges with the 0% graduation rates for men's basketball players, 1993-94 ★941★

U.S. colleges and universities with the unhappiest students ★1041★

Fiske Guide's best buys for public colleges and universities, 2001 ★1460★

Total baccalaureate biology/life sciences degrees awarded to Asian Americans from U.S. colleges and universities, 1997-98 ★1680★

U.S. colleges and universities awarding the most biological and life sciences master's degrees to Asian Americans ★1757★

U.S. colleges and universities awarding the most mathematics doctorate degrees to Asian Americans ★2117★

U.S. colleges and universities awarding the most social sciences and history doctorate degrees to Asian Americans ★2125★

U.S. universities with the highest concentration of papers published in the field of literary studies, 1994-98 ★2734★

U.S. universities with the highest concentrations in literary criticism, 1992-96 ★2735★

Institutions in the Worker Rights Consortium ★2913★

Average faculty salaries for institutions of higher education in California, 2000-01 ★3692★

California, San Diego; University of

Top anthropology research-doctorate programs as evaluated by the National Research Council ★62★

Most effective neurosciences research-doctorate programs as evaluated by the National Research Council ★200★

Top neurosciences research-doctorate programs as evaluated by the National Research Council ★202★

Most effective biochemistry and molecular biology research-doctorate programs as evaluated by the National Research Council ★205★

Most effective molecular and general genetics research-doctorate programs as evaluated by the National Research Council ★207★

Top biochemistry and molecular biology research-doctorate programs as evaluated by the National Research Council ★209★

Top cell and developmental biology research-doctorate programs as evaluated by the National Research Council ★210★

Top molecular and general genetics research-doctorate programs as evaluated by the National Research Council ★211★

U.S. universities with the greatest impact in chemistry, 1994-98 ★793★

Winner of the American Chemical Society's Arthur C. Cope Awards, 2001 ★795★

U.S. News & World Report's best public national universities, 2000-01 ★1123★

U.S. News & World Report's national universities with the highest percentage of freshmen in the top 10% of their high school class, 2000-01 ★1135★

Fiske Guide's best buys for public colleges and universities, 2001 ★1460★

Total baccalaureate biology/life sciences degrees awarded to Asian Americans from U.S. colleges and universities, 1997-98 ★1680★

Total baccalaureate biology/life sciences degrees awarded to Hispanic Americans from U.S. colleges and universities, 1997-98 ★1681★

Total baccalaureate communications degrees awarded to Asian Americans from U.S. colleges and universities, 1997-98 ★1688★

Total baccalaureate degrees awarded to Asian Americans from U.S. colleges and universities, 1997-98 ★1702★

Total baccalaureate physical sciences degrees awarded to Asian Americans from U.S. colleges and universities, 1997-98 ★1734★

Total baccalaureate psychology degrees awarded to Asian Americans from U.S. colleges and universities, 1997-98 ★1738★

Total baccalaureate psychology degrees awarded to Native Americans from U.S. colleges and universities, 1997-98 ★1740★

Total baccalaureate social sciences and history degrees awarded to Asian Americans from U.S. colleges and universities, 1997-98 ★1742★

U.S. colleges and universities awarding the most biological and life sciences master's degrees to Asian Americans ★1757★

U.S. colleges and universities awarding the most English language/literature/letters master's degrees to Asian Americans ★1774★

U.S. colleges and universities awarding the most physical sciences master's degrees to Asian Americans ★1794★

U.S. colleges and universities awarding the most social sciences and history master's degrees to Asian Americans ★1802★

U.S. colleges and universities awarding the most social sciences and history master's degrees to Hispanic Americans ★1803★

U.S. institutions awarding the most baccalaureate degrees to minorities in ethnic/cultural studies, 1997-98 ★1821★

U.S. colleges and universities awarding the most doctorate degrees to Asian Americans ★2096★

U.S. colleges and universities awarding the most health professions and related sciences doctorate degrees to Asian Americans ★2115★

U.S. colleges and universities awarding the most health professions and related sciences doctorate degrees to Hispanic Americans ★2116★

U.S. colleges and universities awarding the most physical sciences doctorate degrees to Asian Americans ★2119★

Most effective geosciences research-doctorate programs as evaluated by the National Research Council ★2150★

Top geosciences research-doctorate programs as evaluated by the National Research Council ★2152★

Top oceanography research-doctorate programs as evaluated by the National Research Council ★2153★

Top aerospace engineering research-doctorate programs as evaluated by the National Research Council ★2376★

Academics' choices for best graduate bioengineering/biomedical engineering programs, 2001 ★2381★

Most effective biomedical engineering research-doctorate programs as evaluated by the National Research Council ★2383★

Top biomedical engineering research-doctorate programs as evaluated by the National Research Council ★2384★

U.S. News & World Report's graduate engineering programs with the best biomedical departments, 2000-01 ★2385★

Top linguistics research-doctorate programs as evaluated by the National Research Council ★2733★

Academics' choices for best drug and alcohol abuse programs, 2001 ★2819★

U.S. universities with the greatest impact in optics and acoustics, 1994-98 ★2911★

Institutions in the Worker Rights Consortium ★2913★

Top pharmacology research-doctorate programs as evaluated by the National Research Council ★2939★

Top philosophy research-doctorate programs as evaluated by the National Research Council ★2947★

Most effective physiology research-doctorate programs as evaluated by the National Research Council ★3021★

Top physiology research-doctorate programs as evaluated by the National Research Council ★3022★

Top political science research-doctorate programs as evaluated by the National Research Council ★3046★

Most effective psychology research-doctorate programs as evaluated by the National Research Council ★3065★

Top psychology research-doctorate programs as evaluated by the National Research Council ★3068★

U.S. universities spending the most on research and development, 1998 ★3104★

Institutions receiving the most federal research and development expenditures, 1999 ★3105★

Average faculty salaries for institutions of higher education in California, 2000-01 ★3692★

U.S. universities with the highest relative citation impact, 1993-97 ★4291★

U.S. universities publishing the most highly-cited papers, 1997-1999 ★4348★

California, San Francisco Medical Center; University of
Top endocrinology hospitals in the U.S., 2000 ★2789★
Top gastroenterology hospitals in the U.S., 2000 ★2790★
Top hospitals in the U.S., 2000 ★2793★
Top neurology and neurosurgery hospitals in the U.S., 2000 ★2795★
Top ophthalmology hospitals in the U.S., 2000 ★2796★

California, San Francisco; University of
Most effective neurosciences research-doctorate programs as evaluated by the National Research Council ★200★

Top neurosciences research-doctorate programs as evaluated by the National Research Council ★202★

Most effective biochemistry and molecular biology research-doctorate programs as evaluated by the National Research Council ★205★

Most effective cell and developmental biology research-doctorate programs as evaluated by the National Research Council ★206★

Most effective molecular and general genetics research-doctorate programs as evaluated by the National Research Council ★207★

Top biochemistry and molecular biology research-doctorate programs as evaluated by the National Research Council ★209★

Top cell and developmental biology research-doctorate programs as evaluated by the National Research Council ★210★

Top molecular and general genetics research-doctorate programs as evaluated by the National Research Council ★211★

Institutions receiving the most corporate gifts, 1999-2000 ★1243★

Largest gifts to higher education, 1967-2000 ★1247★

Largest private gifts to higher education, 1967-2000 ★1248★

U.S. colleges and universities awarding the most health professions and related sciences master's degrees to Asian Americans ★1778★

U.S. colleges and universities awarding the most health professions and related sciences master's degrees to Hispanic Americans ★1779★

U.S. colleges and universities awarding the most first professional degrees to Asian Americans ★1844★

U.S. colleges and universities awarding the most first professional degrees to Native Americans ★1846★

U.S. colleges and universities awarding the most health professions and related sciences first professional degrees to Asian Americans ★1848★

U.S. colleges and universities awarding the most health professions and related sciences first professional degrees to Hispanic Americans ★1849★

U.S. colleges and universities awarding the most health professions and related sciences first professional degrees to minorities ★1850★

U.S. colleges and universities awarding the most health professions and related sciences first professional degrees to Native Americans ★1851★

U.S. colleges and universities awarding the most health professions and related sciences doctorate degrees to Asian Americans ★2115★

CALIFORNIA

U.S. colleges and universities awarding the most health professions and related sciences doctorate degrees to Hispanic Americans ★2116★

U.S. universities with the greatest impact in electrical and electronic engineering, 1994-99 ★2356★

Most effective biomedical engineering research-doctorate programs as evaluated by the National Research Council ★2383★

Top biomedical engineering research-doctorate programs as evaluated by the National Research Council ★2384★

U.S. universities with the greatest impact in metallurgy, 1995-99 ★2435★

U.S. universities with the greatest impact in mechanical engineering, 1994-98 ★2439★

Academics' choices for best AIDS programs, 2001 ★2818★

Academics' choices for best drug and alcohol abuse programs, 2001 ★2819★

Academics' choices for best internal medicine programs, 2001 ★2822★

Academics' choices for best pediatrics programs, 2001 ★2823★

Academics' choices for best women's health medical programs, 2001 ★2825★

Acceptance rates for *U.S. News & World Report*'s top 10 primary-care medical schools, 2001 ★2826★

Acceptance rates for *U.S. News & World Report*'s top 10 research-oriented medical schools, 2001 ★2827★

Average MCAT scores at *U.S. News & World Report*'s top 10 primary-care medical schools, 2001 ★2835★

Average MCAT scores at *U.S. News & World Report*'s top 10 research-oriented medical schools, 2001 ★2836★

Average undergraduate GPA at *U.S. News & World Report*'s top 10 primary-care medical schools, 2001 ★2837★

Average undergraduate GPA at *U.S. News & World Report*'s top 10 research-oriented medical schools, 2001 ★2838★

Faculty-student ratios at *U.S. News & World Report*'s top 10 primary-care medical schools, 2001 ★2841★

Faculty-student ratios at *U.S. News & World Report*'s top 10 research-oriented medical schools, 2001 ★2842★

NIH research grants for *U.S. News & World Report*'s top 10 research-oriented medical schools, 2001 ★2845★

Out-of-state tuition and fees at *U.S. News & World Report*'s top 10 primary-care medical schools, 2001 ★2846★

Out-of-state tuition and fees for *U.S. News & World Report*'s top 10 research-oriented medical schools, 2001 ★2847★

Percentage of graduates entering *U.S. News & World Report*'s top 10 primary-care medical schools, 2001 ★2848★

Top primary-care medical schools, 2001 ★2856★

Top primary-care medical schools by reputation, as determined by academic personnel, 2001 ★2857★

Top primary-care medical schools by student selectivity rank, 2001 ★2858★

Top research-oriented medical schools, 2001 ★2859★

Top research-oriented medical schools by reputation, as determined by academic personnel, 2001 ★2860★

Top research-oriented medical schools by reputation, as determined by intern/residency directors, 2001 ★2861★

Top research-oriented medical schools by student selectivity, 2001 ★2862★

Institutions in the Worker Rights Consortium ★2913★

U.S. universities with the greatest impact in physics, 1994-98 ★2980★

Most effective physiology research-doctorate programs as evaluated by the National Research Council ★3021★

Top physiology research-doctorate programs as evaluated by the National Research Council ★3022★

Institutions receiving the most federal research and development expenditures, 1999 ★3105★

Average faculty salaries for institutions of higher education in California, 2000-01 ★3692★

U.S. universities contributing the most papers in the field of neurosciences, 1993-97 ★4285★

U.S. universities publishing the most highly-cited papers, 1997-1999 ★4348★

California, Santa Barbara; University of

U.S. colleges and universities with strained race/class interaction ★1029★

U.S. colleges and universities with the most attractive campuses ★1039★

U.S. colleges and universities with the worst financial aid programs ★1042★

U.S. News & World Report's national universities with the highest percentage of freshmen in the top 10% of their high school class, 2000-01 ★1135★

U.S. News & World Report's national universities with the lowest graduation rates, 1999 ★1141★

Total baccalaureate communications degrees awarded to Asian Americans from U.S. colleges and universities, 1997-98 ★1688★

Total baccalaureate ethnic/cultural studies degrees awarded to African Americans from U.S. colleges and universities, 1997-98 ★1720★

Total baccalaureate law and legal studies degrees awarded to African Americans from U.S. colleges and universities, 1997-98 ★1725★

Total baccalaureate law and legal studies degrees awarded to Asian Americans from U.S. colleges and universities, 1997-98 ★1726★

Total baccalaureate law and legal studies degrees awarded to Hispanic Americans from U.S. colleges and universities, 1997-98 ★1727★

Total baccalaureate law and legal studies degrees awarded to Native Americans from U.S. colleges and universities, 1997-98 ★1728★

Total baccalaureate mathematics degrees awarded to Asian Americans from U.S. colleges and universities, 1997-98 ★1730★

Total baccalaureate social sciences and history degrees awarded to Hispanic Americans from U.S. colleges and universities, 1997-98 ★1743★

Total baccalaureate social sciences and history degrees awarded to Native Americans from U.S. colleges and universities, 1997-98 ★1744★

U.S. colleges and universities awarding the most physical sciences master's degrees to Asian Americans ★1794★

U.S. colleges and universities awarding the most social sciences and history master's degrees to Hispanic Americans ★1803★

U.S. institutions awarding the most baccalaureate degrees to minorities in ethnic/cultural studies, 1997-98 ★1821★

U.S. colleges and universities awarding the most doctorate degrees to Hispanic Americans ★2097★

U.S. colleges and universities awarding the most education doctorate degrees to Hispanic Americans ★2110★

U.S. colleges and universities awarding the most physical sciences doctorate degrees to Asian Americans ★2119★

U.S. universities with the greatest impact in electrical and electronic engineering, 1994-99 ★2356★

Top chemical engineering research-doctorate programs as evaluated by the National Research Council ★2390★

Academics' choices for best graduate materials engineering programs, 2001 ★2417★

Top materials science research-doctorate programs as evaluated by the National Research Council ★2419★

U.S. universities with the greatest impact in metallurgy, 1995-99 ★2435★

U.S. universities with the greatest impact in mechanical engineering, 1994-98 ★2439★

U.S. universities with the greatest impact in ecology/environmental sciences, 1994-98 ★2474★

Most effective geography research-doctorate programs as evaluated by the National Research Council ★2519★

Top geography research-doctorate programs as evaluated by the National Research Council ★2520★

Institutions with the most prolific communication studies researchers ★2749★

Institutions in the Worker Rights Consortium ★2913★

U.S. universities with the greatest impact in physics, 1994-98 ★2980★

Women faculty in Ph.D. physics departments at U.S. institutions, 1998 ★2981★

Top physics research-doctorate programs as evaluated by the National Research Council ★3015★

Top religion research-doctorate programs as evaluated by the National Research Council ★3093★

Average faculty salaries for institutions of higher education in California, 2000-01 ★3692★

U.S. universities with the highest concentration of papers published in the field of materials science, 1995-99 ★4290★

U.S. universities with the highest relative citation impact, 1993-97 ★4291★

California, Santa Cruz; University of

U.S. colleges and universities where the general student body puts a strong emphasis on socializing ★1008★

U.S. colleges and universities with the best quality of life ★1034★

U.S. colleges and universities with the most attractive campuses ★1039★

Total baccalaureate social sciences and history degrees awarded to Hispanic Americans from U.S. colleges and universities, 1997-98 ★1743★

U.S. colleges and universities awarding the most English language/literature/letters master's degrees to Asian Americans ★1774★

U.S. institutions awarding the most baccalaureate degrees to minorities in ethnic/cultural studies, 1997-98 ★1821★

Most effective linguistics research-doctorate programs as evaluated by the National Research Council ★2732★

Top linguistics research-doctorate programs as evaluated by the National Research Council ★2733★

Institutions in the Worker Rights Consortium ★2913★

U.S. universities with the greatest impact in astrophysics, 1994-98 ★2979★

U.S. universities with the greatest impact in physics, 1994-98 ★2980★

Most effective astrophysics and astronomy research-doctorate programs as evaluated by the National Research Council ★3006★

Top astrophysics and astronomy research-doctorate programs as evaluated by the National Research Council ★3014★

Average faculty salaries for institutions of higher education in California, 2000-01 ★3692★

U.S. universities with the highest concentration of papers published in the field of aquatic sciences, 1995-99 ★4289★

California School of Professional Psychology

U.S. colleges and universities awarding the most psychology master's degrees to Asian Americans ★1798★

U.S. colleges and universities awarding the most psychology master's degrees to Hispanic Americans ★1799★

U.S. colleges and universities awarding the most doctorate degrees to Hispanic Americans ★2097★

California School of Professional Psychology, Alameda

U.S. colleges and universities awarding the most psychology doctorate degrees to African Americans ★2120★

U.S. colleges and universities awarding the most psychology doctorate degrees to Asian Americans ★2121★

U.S. colleges and universities awarding the most psychology doctorate degrees to Hispanic Americans ★2122★

California School of Professional Psychology, Fresno

U.S. colleges and universities awarding the most psychology doctorate degrees to African Americans ★2120★

California School of Professional Psychology, Los Angeles

U.S. colleges and universities awarding the most psychology doctorate degrees to African Americans ★2120★

U.S. colleges and universities awarding the most psychology doctorate degrees to Asian Americans ★2121★

U.S. colleges and universities awarding the most psychology doctorate degrees to Hispanic Americans ★2122★

California School of Professional Psychology, San Diego

U.S. colleges and universities awarding the most psychology doctorate degrees to Asian Americans ★2121★

U.S. colleges and universities awarding the most psychology doctorate degrees to Hispanic Americans ★2122★

California State Polytechnic University

U.S. institutions awarding the most baccalaureate degrees to Asian Americans in agricultural sciences, 1998 ★1816★

U.S. institutions awarding the most baccalaureate degrees to Hispanic Americans in agricultural sciences, 1998 ★1818★

U.S. institutions awarding the most baccalaureate degrees to minorities in agricultural sciences, 1998 ★1820★

California State Polytechnic University, Pomona

Lowest undergraduate tuition and fees at public, 4-year or above colleges and universities ★1466★

U.S. News & World Report's top public western regional universities, 2000-01 ★1573★

U.S. News & World Report's western regional universities with the best academic reputation scores, 2000-01 ★1577★

U.S. News & World Report's western regional universities with the lowest acceptance rates, 2000-01 ★1586★

Total baccalaureate business management and administrative services degrees awarded to Asian Americans from U.S. colleges and universities, 1997-98 ★1684★

Total baccalaureate business management and administrative services degrees awarded to Hispanic Americans from U.S. colleges and universities, 1997-98 ★1685★

Total baccalaureate degrees awarded to Asian Americans from U.S. colleges and universities, 1997-98 ★1702★

Total baccalaureate physical sciences degrees awarded to Hispanic Americans from U.S. colleges and universities, 1997-98 ★1735★

U.S. News & World Report's undergraduate engineering programs with the best aerospace departments, 2000-01 ★2341★

Average faculty salaries for institutions of higher education in California, 2000-01 ★3692★

California State Senate

Most selective internships in the U.S., 2001 ★2610★

California State University

Division I NCAA colleges with that graduated none of their African American male basketball players, 1990-91 to 1993-94 ★930★

State appropriations for California's institutions of higher education, 2000-01 ★1258★

California State University, Bakersfield

Division II NCAA colleges with the 0% graduation rates for men's basketball players, 1993-94 ★941★

Average faculty salaries for institutions of higher education in California, 2000-01 ★3692★

California State University, Chico

U.S. News & World Report's top public western regional universities, 2000-01 ★1573★

Total baccalaureate communications degrees awarded to Native Americans from U.S. colleges and universities, 1997-98 ★1690★

U.S. institutions awarding the most baccalaureate degrees to Asian Americans in agribusiness and production, 1998 ★1815★

Average faculty salaries for institutions of higher education in California, 2000-01 ★3692★

California State University, Dominguez Hills

Division II NCAA colleges with the 0% graduation rates for men's basketball players, 1993-94 ★941★

Lowest undergraduate tuition and fees at public, 4-year or above colleges and universities ★1466★

U.S. colleges and universities awarding the most education master's degrees to Asian Americans ★1770★

U.S. colleges and universities awarding the most education master's degrees to Hispanic Americans ★1771★

U.S. colleges and universities awarding the most English language/literature/letters master's degrees to Hispanic Americans ★1775★

U.S. colleges and universities awarding the most psychology master's degrees to African Americans ★1797★

U.S. colleges and universities awarding the most psychology master's degrees to Asian Americans ★1798★

Average faculty salaries for institutions of higher education in California, 2000-01 ★3692★

California State University, Fresno

Division I NCAA colleges with that graduated less than 20% of their African American male athletes, 1990-91 to 1993-94 ★928★

Lowest undergraduate tuition and fees at public, 4-year or above colleges and universities ★1466★

U.S. News & World Report's top public western regional universities, 2000-01 ★1573★

Total baccalaureate health professions and related sciences degrees awarded to Native Americans from U.S. colleges and universities, 1997-98 ★1724★

Total baccalaureate social sciences and history degrees awarded to Hispanic Americans from U.S. colleges and universities, 1997-98 ★1743★

U.S. institutions awarding the most baccalaureate degrees to Asian Americans in agricultural sciences, 1998 ★1816★

U.S. institutions awarding the most baccalaureate degrees to Hispanic Americans in agribusiness and production, 1998 ★1817★

Average faculty salaries for institutions of higher education in California, 2000-01 ★3692★

California State University, Fullerton

Division I NCAA colleges with that graduated less than 20% of their African American male athletes, 1990-91 to 1993-94 ★928★

Division I NCAA colleges with the lowest graduation rates for female athletes, 1990-91 to 1993-94 ★936★

Division I NCAA colleges with the lowest graduation rates for football players, 1990-91 to 1993-94 ★938★

Division I NCAA colleges with the lowest graduation rates for male athletes, 1990-91 to 1993-94 ★939★

Top colleges in terms of total baccalaureate degrees awarded to minorities, 1997-98 ★1678★

Total baccalaureate business management and administrative services degrees awarded to Asian Americans from U.S. colleges and universities, 1997-98 ★1684★

Total baccalaureate business management and administrative services degrees awarded to Hispanic Americans from U.S. colleges and universities, 1997-98 ★1685★

Total baccalaureate communications degrees awarded to Asian Americans from U.S. colleges and universities, 1997-98 ★1688★

Total baccalaureate communications degrees awarded to Hispanic Americans from U.S. colleges and universities, 1997-98 ★1689★

Total baccalaureate communications degrees awarded to Native Americans from U.S. colleges and universities, 1997-98 ★1690★

CALIFORNIA

Total baccalaureate degrees awarded to Asian Americans from U.S. colleges and universities, 1997-98 ★1702★
Total baccalaureate degrees awarded to Hispanic Americans from U.S. colleges and universities, 1997-98 ★1705★
Total baccalaureate education degrees awarded to Asian Americans from U.S. colleges and universities, 1997-98 ★1712★
Total baccalaureate education degrees awarded to Hispanic Americans from U.S. colleges and universities, 1997-98 ★1713★
Total baccalaureate psychology degrees awarded to Native Americans from U.S. colleges and universities, 1997-98 ★1740★
U.S. colleges and universities awarding the most English language/literature/letters master's degrees to Asian Americans ★1774★
U.S. colleges and universities awarding the most psychology master's degrees to Hispanic Americans ★1799★
Master's institutions with the highest enrollment of foreign students, 1998-99 ★2499★
Degrees granted in the ten largest undergraduate journalism and mass communications programs, 1999 ★2745★
Enrollment of students in the ten largest undergraduate journalism and mass communications programs, 1999 ★2746★
Average faculty salaries for institutions of higher education in California, 2000-01 ★3692★

California State University, Hayward

U.S. college campuses with more than 5,000 students reporting murders or manslaughters, 1998 ★729★
Lowest undergraduate tuition and fees at public, 4-year or above colleges and universities ★1466★
Total baccalaureate business management and administrative services degrees awarded to Asian Americans from U.S. colleges and universities, 1997-98 ★1684★
U.S. colleges and universities awarding the most business management and administrative services master's degrees to Asian Americans ★1760★
U.S. colleges and universities awarding the most English language/literature/letters master's degrees to Asian Americans ★1774★
U.S. colleges and universities awarding the most mathematics master's degrees to Asian Americans ★1791★
Average faculty salaries for institutions of higher education in California, 2000-01 ★3692★

California State University, Long Beach

Division I NCAA colleges with that graduated less than 20% of their African American male athletes, 1990-91 to 1993-94 ★928★
Division I NCAA colleges with that graduated none of their African American male basketball players, 1990-91 to 1993-94 ★930★
Division I NCAA colleges with the lowest graduation rates for football players, 1990-91 to 1993-94 ★938★
Golden Key Scholar Award winners, 2000 ★1316★
Lowest undergraduate tuition and fees at public, 4-year or above colleges and universities ★1466★
U.S. News & World Report's western regional universities with students least in debt, 1999 ★1575★
Total baccalaureate education degrees awarded to Asian Americans from U.S. colleges and universities, 1997-98 ★1712★
Total baccalaureate English language, literature, and letters degrees awarded to Asian Americans from U.S. colleges and universities, 1997-98 ★1717★
Total baccalaureate English language, literature, and letters degrees awarded to Hispanic Americans from U.S. colleges and universities, 1997-98 ★1718★
Total baccalaureate English language, literature, and letters degrees awarded to Native Americans from U.S. colleges and universities, 1997-98 ★1719★
Total baccalaureate ethnic/cultural studies degrees awarded to African Americans from U.S. colleges and universities, 1997-98 ★1720★
Total baccalaureate health professions and related sciences degrees awarded to Asian Americans from U.S. colleges and universities, 1997-98 ★1722★
Total baccalaureate psychology degrees awarded to Hispanic Americans from U.S. colleges and universities, 1997-98 ★1739★
U.S. colleges and universities awarding the most computer and information sciences master's degrees to Asian Americans ★1767★
U.S. colleges and universities awarding the most education master's degrees to Asian Americans ★1770★
U.S. colleges and universities awarding the most health professions and related sciences master's degrees to Asian Americans ★1778★
U.S. colleges and universities awarding the most psychology master's degrees to Asian Americans ★1798★
Master's institutions with the highest enrollment of foreign students, 1998-99 ★2499★
Institutions with the most prolific communication studies researchers ★2749★
Average faculty salaries for institutions of higher education in California, 2000-01 ★3692★

California State University, Los Angeles

Lowest undergraduate tuition and fees at public, 4-year or above colleges and universities ★1466★
Total baccalaureate business management and administrative services degrees awarded to Asian Americans from U.S. colleges and universities, 1997-98 ★1684★
Total baccalaureate computer and information science degrees awarded to Asian Americans from U.S. colleges and universities, 1997-98 ★1692★
Total baccalaureate computer and information science degrees awarded to Hispanic Americans from U.S. colleges and universities, 1997-98 ★1693★
Total baccalaureate degrees awarded to Hispanic Americans from U.S. colleges and universities, 1997-98 ★1705★
Total baccalaureate education degrees awarded to Asian Americans from U.S. colleges and universities, 1997-98 ★1712★
Total baccalaureate education degrees awarded to Hispanic Americans from U.S. colleges and universities, 1997-98 ★1713★
Total baccalaureate psychology degrees awarded to Hispanic Americans from U.S. colleges and universities, 1997-98 ★1739★
U.S. colleges and universities awarding the most education master's degrees to Asian Americans ★1770★
U.S. colleges and universities awarding the most education master's degrees to Hispanic Americans ★1771★
U.S. colleges and universities awarding the most English language/literature/letters master's degrees to Asian Americans ★1774★
U.S. colleges and universities awarding the most English language/literature/letters master's degrees to Hispanic Americans ★1775★
U.S. colleges and universities awarding the most master's degrees to Hispanic Americans ★1787★
U.S. colleges and universities awarding the most mathematics master's degrees to Hispanic Americans ★1792★
U.S. colleges and universities awarding the most physical sciences master's degrees to Asian Americans ★1794★
U.S. colleges and universities awarding the most psychology master's degrees to Hispanic Americans ★1799★
Average faculty salaries for institutions of higher education in California, 2000-01 ★3692★

California State University, Monterey Bay

Average faculty salaries for institutions of higher education in California, 2000-01 ★3692★

California State University, Northridge

Total baccalaureate business management and administrative services degrees awarded to Asian Americans from U.S. colleges and universities, 1997-98 ★1684★
Total baccalaureate communications degrees awarded to Hispanic Americans from U.S. colleges and universities, 1997-98 ★1689★
Total baccalaureate education degrees awarded to Asian Americans from U.S. colleges and universities, 1997-98 ★1712★
Total baccalaureate English language, literature, and letters degrees awarded to Hispanic Americans from U.S. colleges and universities, 1997-98 ★1718★
Total baccalaureate ethnic/cultural studies degrees awarded to African Americans from U.S. colleges and universities, 1997-98 ★1720★
Total baccalaureate psychology degrees awarded to Hispanic Americans from U.S. colleges and universities, 1997-98 ★1739★
Total baccalaureate social sciences and history degrees awarded to Hispanic Americans from U.S. colleges and universities, 1997-98 ★1743★
U.S. colleges and universities awarding the most education master's degrees to Asian Americans ★1770★
U.S. institutions awarding the most baccalaureate degrees to minorities in ethnic/cultural studies, 1997-98 ★1821★
Average faculty salaries for institutions of higher education in California, 2000-01 ★3692★

California State University, Sacramento

U.S. college campuses reporting murders or non-negligent manslaughters, 1999 ★728★
Division I NCAA colleges with that graduated less than 20% of their African American male athletes, 1990-91 to 1993-94 ★928★
Division I NCAA colleges with that graduated none of their African American male basketball players, 1990-91 to 1993-94 ★930★
Division I NCAA colleges with the lowest graduation rates for male basketball players, 1990-91 to 1993-94 ★940★
Lowest undergraduate tuition and fees at public, 4-year or above colleges and universities ★1466★
Public 4-year institutions with the lowest tuition, 2000-01 ★1472★

U.S. News & World Report's top public western regional universities, 2000-01 ★1573★
Total baccalaureate communications degrees awarded to Native Americans from U.S. colleges and universities, 1997-98 ★1690★
Total baccalaureate education degrees awarded to Asian Americans from U.S. colleges and universities, 1997-98 ★1712★
Total baccalaureate social sciences and history degrees awarded to Native Americans from U.S. colleges and universities, 1997-98 ★1744★
U.S. colleges and universities awarding the most English language/literature/letters master's degrees to Hispanic Americans ★1775★
Average faculty salaries for institutions of higher education in California, 2000-01 ★3692★

California State University, San Bernardino
Lowest undergraduate tuition and fees at public, 4-year or above colleges and universities ★1466★
Average faculty salaries for institutions of higher education in California, 2000-01 ★3692★

California State University, San Marcos
Lowest undergraduate tuition and fees at public, 4-year or above colleges and universities ★1466★
Average faculty salaries for institutions of higher education in California, 2000-01 ★3692★

California State University, Stanislaus
Lowest undergraduate tuition and fees at public, 4-year or above colleges and universities ★1466★
Public 4-year institutions with the lowest tuition, 2000-01 ★1472★
Average faculty salaries for institutions of higher education in California, 2000-01 ★3692★

California System; University of
2000 endowment values of the 'wealthiest' U.S. universities ★1230★
2001 mid-year endowment values of the 'wealthiest' U.S. universities ★1234★
Endowment values for the wealthiest U.S. universities, 2000 ★1240★
Most patents issued to universities or research facilities, 1999 ★3097★
Institutions receiving the largest Energy Department research grants, 2000 ★3111★

California; University of
Colleges and universities with the largest endowments, 2000 ★1237★
State appropriations for California's institutions of higher education, 2000-01 ★1258★
Average faculty salaries for institutions of higher education in Pennsylvania, 2000-01 ★3725★

California's Untold Stories Gold Rush
Most notable children's web sites, 2001 ★2593★

The Callaghan Group
Most selective internships in the U.S., 2001 ★2610★

Callahan; Caryn
Top pay and benefits for the chief executive and top paid employees at the Chaminade University of Honolulu ★3524★

Callaway Advanced Technology
Most selective internships in the U.S., 2001 ★2610★

Calle Mayor Middle School
Outstanding secondary schools in Los Angeles-Long Beach, California ★4167★

Caloosa Middle School
Outstanding secondary schools in Fort Myers-Cape Coral, Florida ★4134★

Calpine
Best performing companies in Standard & Poor's 500, 2001 ★382★
Business Week's best performing companies with the highest 1-year sales performance ★414★
Business Week's best performing companies with the highest 3-year shareholder returns ★418★
Top utilities companies in Standard & Poor's 500, 2001 ★561★

Caltech
U.S. universities publishing the most papers in the field of artificial intelligence, 1995-99 ★100★
U.S. universities with the greatest impact in chemistry, 1994-98 ★793★
U.S. universities contributing the most papers in the field of AI, robotics, and auto control, 1993-97 ★2338★
U.S. universities with the greatest impact in mechanical engineering, 1994-98 ★2439★
U.S. universities with the greatest impact in ecology/environmental sciences, 1994-98 ★2474★
U.S. universities with the greatest impact in optics and acoustics, 1994-98 ★2911★
U.S. universities publishing the most papers in the field of astrophysics, 1995-99 ★2978★
U.S. universities contributing the most papers in the field of neurosciences, 1993-97 ★4285★
U.S. universities with the highest relative citation impact, 1993-97 ★4291★

Calumet College of St. Joseph
U.S. colleges and universities with the lowest percentage of African Americans enrolled, 1997 ★223★
Average faculty salaries for institutions of higher education in Indiana, 2000-01 ★3701★

Calvert; Kara
All-USA College Academic Second Team, 2001 ★3★

Calvin College
U.S. colleges and universities where the general student body does not drink beer ★1004★
U.S. colleges and universities where the general student body does not drink hard liquor ★1005★
U.S. colleges and universities where the general student body puts little emphasis on socializing ★1010★
U.S. News & World Report's midwestern regional universities with the best alumni giving rates, 2000-01 ★1402★
U.S. News & World Report's midwestern regional universities with the highest acceptance rates, 2000-01 ★1404★
U.S. News & World Report's midwestern regional universities with the highest freshmen retention rates, 2000-01 ★1405★
U.S. News & World Report's midwestern regional universities with the highest graduation rates, 2000-01 ★1406★
U.S. News & World Report's midwestern regional universities with the highest percentage of full-time faculty, 2000-01 ★1408★
U.S. News & World Report's top midwestern regional universities, 2000-01 ★1411★
U.S. News & World Report's best undergraduate fees among midwestern regional universities by discount tuition, 2000 ★1427★
Fiske Guide's best buys for private colleges and universities, 2001 ★1459★
Highest undergraduate tuition and fees at colleges and universities in Michigan ★1518★
Private, 4-year undergraduate colleges and universities producing the most Ph.D.'s in nonscience fields, 1920-1990 ★2030★
Private, 4-year undergraduate colleges and universities producing the most Ph.D.'s in nonscience fields, 1981-1990 ★2031★
Private, 4-year undergraduate colleges and universities producing the most Ph.D.'s in English, 1981-1990 ★2450★
U.S. master's institutions with the largest number of students studying abroad, 1998-99 ★2513★
Private, 4-year undergraduate colleges and universities producing the most Ph.D.'s in history, 1981-1990 ★2553★
Average faculty salaries for institutions of higher education in Michigan, 2000-01 ★3709★

Cambridge Bibliography of English Literature
Selected new editions and supplements reference books, 2000 ★372★

Cambridge College
Traditionally white institutions awarding the most master's degrees to African Americans ★1755★
U.S. colleges and universities awarding the most education master's degrees to African Americans ★1769★
U.S. colleges and universities awarding the most master's degrees to African Americans ★1785★

Cambridge; University of
United Kingdom universities with the greatest impact in chemistry, 1993-97 ★807★
Top United Kingdom universities by total citations in the field of geosciences, 1991-95 ★2147★
United Kingdom universities with the greatest impact in geosciences, 1993-97 ★2154★

Cambridge University Press
Book publishers with the most citations (Class 2) ★2563★

The Cambridge World History of Food
Library Journal's best reference books, 2000 ★368★
Outstanding reference sources, 2000 ★370★
Outstanding reference sources, 2001 ★371★

Camden County College
Lowest undergraduate tuition and fees at colleges and universities in New Jersey ★1534★

Camerer; Colin F.
Authors with the most published pages in impact-weighted insurance journals ★677★

Cameron; John L.
Top pay and benefits for the chief executive and top paid employees at Johns Hopkins University ★3355★

Cameron University
State appropriations for Oklahoma's institutions of higher education, 2000-01 ★1289★
U.S. colleges and universities awarding the most psychology master's degrees to African Americans ★1797★
Average faculty salaries for institutions of higher education in Oklahoma, 2000-01 ★3723★

Cameron University (OK)
Division II NCAA colleges with the lowest graduation rates for football players, 1993-94 ★948★

The Camino: A Journey of the Spirit
Library Journal's best nonfiction audiobooks, 2000 ★243★

Campanella; Francis B.
Top pay and benefits for the chief executive and top paid employees at Boston College ★3205★

Campanella; Linda S.
Top pay and benefits for the chief executive and top paid employees at Trinity College in Connecticut ★3577★

Campbell; C.
Top assistant professor economists at elite liberal arts colleges, 1975-94 ★2173★

Campbell; Carol N.
Top pay and benefits for the chief executive and top paid employees at Carleton College ★3222★

Campbell; Charles T.
American Chemical Society 2001 award winners (Group 2) ★752★

Campbell-Crane & Associates
Lobbyist that billed the most to U.S. colleges and universities, 1999 ★1249★

Campbell; D'Ann
Top pay and benefits for the chief executive and top paid employees at the Sage Colleges in New York ★3536★

Campbell; Evelyn S.
Top pay and benefits for the chief executive and top paid employees at Augustana College in Illinois ★3182★

Campbell; F. Gregory
Top pay and benefits for the chief executive and top paid employees at Carthage College ★3224★

Campbell; Frank
Top pay and benefits for the chief executive and top paid employees at Averett College ★3185★

Campbell; John W.
Top pay and benefits for the chief executive and top paid employees at Mount Saint Mary's College in Maryland ★3412★

Campbell; N.C.G.
Highest impact authors in the *Journal of Business Research*, by adjusted number of citations in 12 journals, 1985-1999 ★692★

Campbell Soup
Business Week's best companies in terms of return on equity ★407★
Fortune's highest ranked consumer food products companies, 2000 ★458★

Campilii; Anthony
Top pay and benefits for the chief executive and top paid employees at Marist College ★3390★

Campus Computing Survey
Top sites for educators ★2605★

Camus; Philippe
European business moguls considered the best challengers ★439★

Canada
Eight grade science achievement scores from selected countries, 1999 ★14★
Math achievement test comparison ★19★
Percentage of enrollment at public institutions of higher education, by country, 1998 ★859★
Countries with the most computers, 2000 ★1603★
Countries with the most computers per capita, 2000 ★1604★
Countries of origin for non-U.S. citizens awarded doctorates at U.S. colleges and universities, 1999 ★1901★
Annual leave days for employees in selected countries ★2239★
Countries with the highest spending per student on higher education, 1997 ★2488★
Foreign countries with the highest enrollment of foreign students, 1999-2000 ★2496★
Percentage of students enrolled in institutions of higher education that were not citizens of the country where they studied, 1998 ★2500★
Countries with the most Internet users ★2583★
Percentage of internet usage for selected countries ★2599★
Eighth grade mathematics achievement scores from selected countries, 1999 ★2773★
Institute for Scientific Information periodical prices by country, 2001 ★2922★
North American periodical prices by country, 2001 ★2924★
First-year physics and astronomy graduate students from the Americas, 1997-98 ★2990★
Countries with the highest leader's salary ★3120★
Countries spending the highest percentage of gross domestic product on education ★4060★
Nations with the most-cited papers in the sciences ★4320★

Canadaigua Academy
Outstanding secondary schools in Rochester, New York ★4213★

The Canadian Establishment
Canada's best nonfiction selections of the 20th century ★234★

Canadian Imperial Bank of Commerce
Business Week's best companies in Canada ★390★

Canadian Journal of Comparative Medicine
Veterinary sciences journals with the greatest impact measure, 1981-98 ★4442★

Canadian Journal of Criminology
Criminology and penology journals with the greatest impact measure, 1994-98 ★1612★

Canadian Journal of Economics
Top ranked international economics journals ★2195★

Canadian Journal of Fisheries and Aquatic Sciences
Marine and freshwater biology journals with the greatest impact measure, 1981-98 ★196★
Marine and freshwater biology journals with the greatest impact measure, 1994-98 ★197★

Canadian Journal of Soil Science
Soil science journals by citation impact, 1981-99 ★188★

Canavan; Thomas
Top pay and benefits for the chief executive and top paid employees at Providence College ★3447★

Cancer Institute
Proposed fiscal 2002 appropriations for National Institutes of Health scientific research ★3108★

"Cancer statistics, 1998"
Institute for Scientific Information's most cited papers, 1990-98 ★4282★

Candlewick
Top children's book publishers, 1999 ★3074★

C&S Wholesale Grocers
Largest private companies, 2000 ★523★

Caneris; Anthony T.
Top pay and benefits for the chief executive and top paid employees at Drexel University ★3274★

Canisius College
U.S. News & World Report's northern regional universities with students least in debt, 1999 ★1413★
U.S. News & World Report's northern regional universities with the highest acceptance rates, 2000-01 ★1417★
U.S. News & World Report's best undergraduate fees among northern regional universities by discount tuition, 2000 ★1428★
Average faculty salaries for institutions of higher education in New York, 2000-01 ★3719★

Cankdeska Cikana Community College
U.S. tribal colleges ★1445★

Canning; John R.
Top pay and benefits for the chief executive and top paid employees at Loyola University of Chicago ★3382★

Canon
Business Week's best companies in Japan ★398★

Canon U.S.A.
Fortune's highest ranked computers and office equipment companies, 2000 ★456★

Canton Country Day School
Outstanding secondary schools in Canton-Massillon, Ohio ★4103★

Cantu; Charles E.
Top pay and benefits for the chief executive and top paid employees at Saint Mary's University in Texas ★3481★

Canyon Vista Middle School
Outstanding secondary schools in Austin-San Marcos, Texas ★4090★

Cap Gemini Ernst & Young
Top recruiters for accounting jobs for 2000-01 bachelor's degree recipients ★580★
Top recruiters for computer science jobs for 2000-01 bachelor's degree recipients ★1590★
Top recruiters for electrical/electronic engineering jobs for 2000-01 bachelor's degree recipients ★2354★
Top recruiters for industrial engineering jobs for 2000-01 bachelor's degree recipients ★2432★
Top recruiters for health jobs for 2000-01 bachelor's degree recipients ★2541★
Top recruiters for information technology (MIS) jobs for 2000-01 bachelor's degree recipients ★2738★

Cap; Jean-Pierro
Top pay and benefits for the chief executive and top paid employees at Lafayette College ★3361★

Capano; Craig
All-America boys' high school soccer team midfielders, 2001 ★168★

Cape Breton; University College of
Canadian primarily undergraduate universities by alumni support, 2000 ★1193★
Canadian primarily undergraduate universities by class size at the firstand second-year level, 2000 ★1195★
Canadian primarily undergraduate universities by class size at the thirdand forth-year level, 2000 ★1196★

Canadian primarily undergraduate universities by classes taught by tenured faculty, 2000 ★1197★

Canadian primarily undergraduate universities by faculty members with Ph.D.'s, 2000 ★1198★

Canadian primarily undergraduate universities by library acquisitions, 2000 ★1199★

Canadian primarily undergraduate universities by library expenses, 2000 ★1200★

Canadian primarily undergraduate universities by library holdings per student, 2000 ★1201★

Canadian primarily undergraduate universities by medical/science grants per faculty member, 2000 ★1202★

Canadian primarily undergraduate universities by operating budget per student, 2000 ★1203★

Canadian primarily undergraduate universities by percentage of operating budget allocated to scholarships, 2000 ★1204★

Canadian primarily undergraduate universities by percentage of operating budget allocated to student services, 2000 ★1205★

Canadian primarily undergraduate universities by reputation, 2000 ★1206★

Canadian primarily undergraduate universities by social science/humanities grants per faculty member, 2000 ★1207★

Canadian primarily undergraduate universities by students from out of province, 2000 ★1208★

Canadian primarily undergraduate universities by students winning national awards, 2000 ★1209★

Top Canadian primarily undergraduate universities, 2000 ★1226★

Cape Cod Community College
Average faculty salaries for institutions of higher education in Massachusetts, 2000-01 ★3708★

Cape Fear Community College
Average faculty salaries for institutions of higher education without academic ranks in North Carolina, 2000-01 ★3761★

Cape Henry Collegiate
Outstanding secondary schools in Norfolk-Virginia Beach-Newport News, Virginia-North Carolina ★4194★

Capital Associates
Lobbyist that billed the most to U.S. colleges and universities, 1999 ★1249★

Capital Community College
Lowest undergraduate tuition and fees at colleges and universities in Connecticut ★1491★

Capital High School
Outstanding secondary schools in Charleston, West Virginia ★4107★

Outstanding secondary schools in Olympia, Washington ★4197★

Capital One Financial
Fortune's highest ranked consumer credit companies, 2000 ★457★

Top nonbank financial companies in Standard & Poor's 500, 2001 ★550★

Capital University
Average faculty salaries for institutions of higher education in Ohio, 2000-01 ★3722★

Capitalism, Patriarchy, and Crime: Toward a Socialist Feminist Criminology
Most-cited works in critical criminology publications ★1645★

Caplan; Gerald
Top pay and benefits for the chief executive and top paid employees at the University of the Pacific ★3571★

Capobianco; Salvatore
Top pay and benefits for the chief executive and top paid employees at Eckerd College ★3282★

Capote; Truman
Best U.S. works of journalism in the 20th century ★2769★

Capra; Daniel
Top pay and benefits for the chief executive and top paid employees at Fordham University ★3295★

Caprio; Anthony S.
Top pay and benefits for the chief executive and top paid employees at Western New England College ★3615★

Caputo; Peter
Top pay and benefits for the chief executive and top paid employees at Widener University ★3626★

Caraley; Demetrios
Top pay and benefits for the chief executive and top paid employees at Barnard College ★3191★

The Carbohydrate Addict's Diet
Longest-running mass market paperback bestsellers, 2000 ★280★

Carden; Allen
Top pay and benefits for the chief executive and top paid employees at Fresno Pacific University ★3298★

Cardinal Health
Business Week's best performing companies with the highest 1-year shareholder returns ★415★

Fortune's highest ranked wholesalers, 2000 ★505★

Top health care companies in Standard & Poor's 500, 2001 ★542★

Cardinal Stritch University
Average faculty salaries for institutions of higher education in Wisconsin, 2000-01 ★3738★

Cardiology
Clinical medicine subfields with the highest impact measure, 1981-1997 ★2873★

Cardozo-Yeshiva University
Academics' choices for best dispute resolution programs, 2001 ★2627★

Academics' choices for best intellectual property law programs, 2001 ★2630★

Career Point Business School
U.S. colleges and universities with the lowest percentage of African Americans enrolled, 1997 ★223★

CareerBuilder
Top career-related Web sites ★2602★

Top E-recruiting providers, 2000 ★2604★

The Caretaker
Top plays of the twentieth century ★4435★

Carey; Anthony J.
Top pay and benefits for the chief executive and top paid employees at St. John's College in Maryland and New Mexico ★3473★

Cargill
Largest private companies, 2000 ★523★

Caribbean Center for Advanced Studies
U.S. colleges and universities awarding the most psychology master's degrees to Hispanic Americans ★1799★

U.S. colleges and universities awarding the most doctorate degrees to Hispanic Americans ★2097★

U.S. colleges and universities awarding the most psychology doctorate degrees to Hispanic Americans ★2122★

Caribbean University
Highest undergraduate tuition and fees at colleges and universities in Puerto Rico ★1551★

Carignan; Robert
Top pay and benefits for the chief executive and top paid employees at Our Lady of the Lake University ★3434★

Carl Albert State College
Lowest undergraduate tuition and fees at colleges and universities in Oklahoma ★1546★

Carl Sandburg College
Average faculty salaries for institutions of higher education without academic ranks in Illinois, 2000-01 ★3747★

Carlberg; R. Judson
Top pay and benefits for the chief executive and top paid employees at Gordon College in Massachusetts ★3312★

Carleton College
All-USA College Academic First Team, 2001 ★2★

All-USA College Academic Second Team, 2001 ★3★

Private, 4-year undergraduate colleges and universities producing the most Ph.D.'s in the life sciences, 1920-1990 ★192★

Private, 4-year undergraduate colleges and universities producing the most Ph.D.'s in the life sciences, 1981-1990 ★193★

U.S. colleges and universities that devote the most course time to discussion ★990★

U.S. colleges and universities where intramural sports are popular ★997★

U.S. News & World Report's best national liberal arts colleges, 2000-01 ★1320★

U.S. News & World Report's national liberal arts colleges with the best faculty resources rank, 2000-01 ★1321★

U.S. News & World Report's national liberal arts colleges with the best freshmen retention rates, 2000-01 ★1323★

U.S. News & World Report's national liberal arts colleges with the best graduation and retention rank, 2000-01 ★1324★

U.S. News & World Report's national liberal arts colleges with the highest academic reputation scores, 2000-01 ★1327★

U.S. News & World Report's national liberal arts colleges with the highest alumni giving rank, 2000-01 ★1329★

U.S. News & World Report's national liberal arts colleges with the highest graduation rates, 2000-01 ★1330★

U.S. News & World Report's national liberal arts colleges with the highest percentage of alumni support, 2000-01 ★1331★

Highest undergraduate tuition and fees at colleges and universities in Minnesota ★1520★

Private, 4-year undergraduate colleges and universities producing the most Ph.D.'s in the computer sciences, 1920-1990 ★1595★

Private, 4-year undergraduate colleges and universities producing the most Ph.D.'s in the computer sciences, 1981-1990 ★1596★

Private, 4-year undergraduate colleges and universities producing the most Ph.Ds in all fields of study, 1920-1990 ★2027★

Private, 4-year undergraduate colleges and universities producing the most Ph.D.'s in all fields of study, 1981-1990 ★2028★

Private, 4-year undergraduate colleges and universities producing the most Ph.D.'s in all fields of study, 1990 ★2029★

CARLETON

Private, 4-year undergraduate colleges and universities producing the most Ph.D.'s in nonscience fields, 1920-1990 ★2030★

Private, 4-year undergraduate colleges and universities producing the most Ph.D.'s in nonscience fields, 1981-1990 ★2031★

Private, 4-year undergraduate colleges and universities producing the most Ph.D.'s in the earth sciences, 1981-1990 ★2151★

Private, 4-year undergraduate colleges and universities producing the most Ph.D.'s in economics, 1920-1990 ★2211★

Private, 4-year undergraduate colleges and universities producing the most Ph.D.'s in economics, 1981-1990 ★2212★

Undergraduate institutions with the most graduates who received Ph.D.s in economics, 1920-1984 ★2214★

Private, 4-year undergraduate colleges and universities producing the most Ph.D.'s in English, 1920-1990 ★2449★

Private, 4-year undergraduate colleges and universities producing the most Ph.D.'s in English, 1981-1990 ★2450★

Private, 4-year undergraduate colleges and universities producing the most Ph.D.'s in history, 1920-1990 ★2552★

Private, 4-year undergraduate colleges and universities producing the most Ph.D.'s in history, 1981-1990 ★2553★

Private, 4-year undergraduate colleges and universities producing the most Ph.D.'s in mathematics, 1920-1990 ★2776★

Private, 4-year undergraduate colleges and universities producing the most Ph.D.'s in mathematics, 1981-1990 ★2777★

Private, 4-year undergraduate colleges and universities producing the most Ph.D.'s in physics and astronomy, 1920-1990 ★2949★

Private, 4-year undergraduate colleges and universities producing the most Ph.D.'s in political science and international relations, 1920-1990 ★3044★

Private, 4-year undergraduate colleges and universities producing the most Ph.D.'s in political science and international relations, 1981-1990 ★3045★

Average faculty salaries for institutions of higher education in Minnesota, 2000-01 ★3710★

Private, 4-year undergraduate colleges and universities producing the most Ph.D.'s in the sciences, 1920-1990 ★4294★

Private, 4-year undergraduate colleges and universities producing the most Ph.D.'s in the sciences, 1981-1990 ★4295★

Private, 4-year undergraduate colleges and universities producing the most Ph.D.'s in anthropology and sociology, 1920-1990 ★4344★

Private, 4-year undergraduate colleges and universities producing the most Ph.D.'s in anthropology and sociology, 1981-1990 ★4345★

Carleton; University of

Canadian comprehensive universities by alumni support, 2000 ★1153★

Canadian comprehensive universities by award-winning faculty members, 2000 ★1154★

Canadian comprehensive universities by class size at the first- and second-year level, 2000 ★1155★

Canadian comprehensive universities by class size at the third- and forth-year level, 2000 ★1156★

Canadian comprehensive universities by classes taught by tenured faculty, 2000 ★1157★

Canadian comprehensive universities by faculty members with Ph.D.'s, 2000 ★1158★

Canadian comprehensive universities by international graduate students, 2000 ★1159★

Canadian comprehensive universities by library acquisitions, 2000 ★1160★

Canadian comprehensive universities by library expenses, 2000 ★1161★

Canadian comprehensive universities by library holdings per student, 2000 ★1162★

Canadian comprehensive universities by operating budget per student, 2000 ★1163★

Canadian comprehensive universities by percentage of operating budget allocated to scholarships, 2000 ★1164★

Canadian comprehensive universities by percentage of operating budget allocated to student services, 2000 ★1165★

Canadian comprehensive universities by social science/humanities grants per faculty member, 2000 ★1166★

Canadian comprehensive universities by students from out of province, 2000 ★1167★

Canadian comprehensive universities by students winning national awards, 2000 ★1168★

Canadian medical/doctoral universities by medical/science grants per faculty member, 2000 ★1183★

Canadian universities chosen as being value added, 2000 ★1216★

Top Canadian comprehensive universities, 2000 ★1219★

Top Canadian comprehensive universities by reputation, 2000 ★1220★

Radcliffe Institute for Advanced Study fellowship recipients in the field of psychology, 2000-01 ★3062★

Carlisle

Fortune's highest ranked rubber and plastic products companies, 2000 ★492★

Carlos Albizu University, San Juan

U.S. colleges and universities awarding the most doctoral degrees to African Americans from 1995 to 1999 ★2091★

Carlow College

U.S. News & World Report's northern regional liberal arts colleges with the best student/faculty ratios, 2000-01 ★1353★

U.S. News & World Report's northern regional liberal arts colleges with the highest proportion of classes having 20 students or less, 2000-01 ★1361★

U.S. News & World Report's northern regional liberal arts colleges with the lowest acceptance rates, 2000-01 ★1362★

Average faculty salaries for institutions of higher education in Pennsylvania, 2000-01 ★3725★

Carlsbad City Library

Highest Hennen's American Public Library Ratings for libraries serving a population of 50,000 to 99,999 ★2697★

Carlson Companies

Top women-owned companies ★4460★

Top women-owned companies with the most employees ★4462★

Carmel Clay Public Library

Highest Hennen's American Public Library Ratings for libraries serving a population of 25,000 to 49,999 ★2696★

Carmel High School

Outstanding secondary schools in Chicago, Illinois ★4110★

Carmenita Junior High School

Outstanding secondary schools in Los Angeles-Long Beach, California ★4167★

Carnal Innocence

Outstanding audiobooks, 2000 ★287★

Carnegie Elementary School

Illinois elementary schools chosen to be 'demonstration sites' for struggling schools ★4006★

Carnegie Mellon/SEI

Top institutions in systems and software engineering publications ★2332★

Carnegie Mellon University

All-USA College Academic Third Team, 2001 ★4★

U.S. universities publishing the most papers in the field of artificial intelligence, 1995-99 ★100★

U.S. News & World Report's universities with the best quantitative methods departments, 1999-2000 ★572★

Top business schools for within-discipline research performance in management science, 1986-1998 ★647★

Top business schools for within-discipline research performance in management information systems, 1986-1998 ★675★

U.S. colleges and universities where students are not very politically active ★1000★

U.S. colleges and universities where students study the most ★1003★

U.S. colleges and universities with harmonious race/class interaction ★1026★

U.S. News & World Report's national universities with the highest percentage of full-time faculty, 2000-01 ★1136★

Highest undergraduate tuition and fees at colleges and universities in Pennsylvania ★1549★

U.S. universities publishing the most papers in the field of computer science, 1994-98 ★1591★

Most effective computer science research-doctorate programs as evaluated by the National Research Council ★1594★

Top computer science research-doctorate programs as evaluated by the National Research Council ★1597★

Economics Ph.D. programs by number of citations of top economist graduates, 1971-92 ★2204★

Economics Ph.D. programs by number of citations per top economist graduate, 1971-92 ★2205★

Economics Ph.D. programs by number of top economist graduates, 1971-92 ★2206★

U.S. universities with the highest concentration of papers published in the field of chemical engineering, 1994-98 ★2345★

Acceptance rates for *U.S. News & World Report*'s top 10 graduate engineering schools, 2001 ★2358★

Average analytic GRE scores for *U.S. News & World Report*'s top 10 graduate engineering schools, 2001 ★2359★

Average quantitative GRE scores for *U.S. News & World Report*'s top 10 graduate engineering schools, 2001 ★2360★

Doctoral student-faculty ratios at *U.S. News & World Report*'s top 10 graduate engineering schools, 2001 ★2361★

Faculty membership in National Academy of Engineering at *U.S. News & World Report*'s top 10 graduate engineering schools, 2001 ★2362★

Ph.D.s granted at *U.S. News & World Report*'s top 10 graduate engineering schools, 2001 ★2363★

Research expenditures per faculty member at *U.S. News & World Report*'s top 10 graduate engineering schools, 2001 ★2364★

Research funding allocated to *U.S. News & World Report*'s top 10 graduate engineering schools, 2001 ★2365★

Top graduate engineering schools, 2001 ★2366★

Top graduate engineering schools by reputation, as determined by academic personnel, 2001 ★2367★

Top graduate engineering schools by reputation, as determined by engineers and recruiters, 2001 ★2368★

U.S. News & World Report's graduate engineering programs with the highest academic reputation scores, 2000-01 ★2372★

Top chemical engineering research-doctorate programs as evaluated by the National Research Council ★2390★

Most effective civil engineering research-doctorate programs as evaluated by the National Research Council ★2395★

Top civil engineering research-doctorate programs as evaluated by the National Research Council ★2396★

Academics' choices for best graduate computer engineering programs, 2001 ★2399★

U.S. News & World Report's graduate engineering programs with the best computer departments, 2000-01 ★2401★

U.S. universities with the highest concentrations in artificial intelligence, 1992-96 ★2402★

Academics' choices for best graduate electrical/electronic/communications engineering programs, 2001 ★2403★

Most effective electrical engineering research-doctorate programs as evaluated by the National Research Council ★2404★

Top electrical engineering research-doctorate programs as evaluated by the National Research Council ★2405★

Most effective materials science research-doctorate programs as evaluated by the National Research Council ★2418★

Top materials science research-doctorate programs as evaluated by the National Research Council ★2419★

U.S. universities with the highest concentration of metallurgy papers published, 1994-98 ★2436★

U.S. universities with the greatest impact in ecology/environmental sciences, 1994-98 ★2474★

Most wired universities, 2000 ★2598★

Most effective statistics and biostatistics research-doctorate programs as evaluated by the National Research Council ★2780★

U.S. universities with the greatest impact in psychology, 1995-99 ★3064★

Most effective psychology research-doctorate programs as evaluated by the National Research Council ★3065★

Top psychology research-doctorate programs as evaluated by the National Research Council ★3068★

Average faculty salaries for institutions of higher education in Pennsylvania, 2000-01 ★3725★

U.S. institutions with the highest paid assistant professors, 2001 ★3977★

Carnegie-Mellon University Graduate School of Industrial Administration

U.S. News & World Report's undergraduate business programs with the best e-commerce departments, 2000-01 ★564★

U.S. News & World Report's undergraduate business programs with the best management information systems departments, 2000-01 ★568★

U.S. News & World Report's undergraduate business programs with the best production/operations departments, 2000-01 ★569★

U.S. News & World Report's undergraduate business programs with the highest academic reputation scores, 2000-01 ★571★

Academics' choices for best graduate management information systems programs, 2001 ★585★

Business Week's top business schools for technology skills as selected by corporate recruiters, 2000 ★604★

Business Week's top business schools with the greatest decrease in MBA satisfaction, 2000 ★610★

Business Week's top business schools with the highest percentage of international students, 2000 ★612★

Business Week's top business schools with the lowest percentage of minority enrollment, 2000 ★616★

Business Week's top business schools with the lowest percentage of women enrollees, 2000 ★617★

Business Week's top business schools with the most improved program as selected by corporate recruiters, 2000 ★618★

Business Week's top business schools with the most innovative curriculum as selected by corporate recruiters, 2000 ★619★

Business Week's top business schools worst at responding to student concerns, 2000 ★621★

Lowest pre-MBA salaries for students enrolled in *Business Week*'s top business schools, 1999 ★635★

Top graduate business schools by reputation, as determined by recruiters, 2001 ★651★

Academics' choices for best graduate quantitative analysis programs, 2001 ★673★

Academics' choices for best graduate production/operations management programs, 2001 ★674★

Carnegie-Rochester Conference Series on Public Policy

Top ranked microeconomics and monetary economics journals ★2199★

Carney III; John F.

Top pay and benefits for the chief executive and top paid employees at Worcester Polytechnic Institute ★3636★

Carney; Rita

Top pay and benefits for the chief executive and top paid employees at Georgian Court College ★3307★

Carnival

Top leisure time industries in Standard & Poor's 500, 2001 ★545★

Carolina Ghost Woods

Library Journal's best poetry books, 2000 ★244★

Caron; Edward J.

Top pay and benefits for the chief executive and top paid employees at Providence College ★3447★

Carpenter

Jobs with the highest unemployment ★2256★

Most desirable jobs in construction trades ★2272★

Carpenter; Bernard R.

Top pay and benefits for the chief executive and top paid employees at Bates College ★3193★

Carpenter; Harold

Top pay and benefits for the chief executive and top paid employees at Bellevue University ★3197★

Carpenter; JoAnne

Top pay and benefits for the chief executive and top paid employees at College of the Atlantic ★3246★

Carpenter; Joel A.

Top pay and benefits for the chief executive and top paid employees at Calvin College ★3217★

Carpenter Middle School

Outstanding secondary schools in Dallas, Texas ★4120★

Carpenter; William

Top pay and benefits for the chief executive and top paid employees at College of the Atlantic ★3246★

Carpenters

Occupations with the highest number of self-employed workers, 1998 ★2311★

Projected employment growth for selected occupations that require long-term on-the-job training, 1998-2008 ★2320★

Carpentersville Unit, District 300

Illinois school districts with the highest paid superintendents, 1999-2000 ★3986★

Carpet installer

Jobs with the highest unemployment ★2256★

Most desirable jobs in construction trades ★2272★

Carr; Emily

Canada's best visual artists of the 20th century ★75★

Carr; Leland

Top pay and benefits for the chief executive and top paid employees at Pacific University in Oregon ★3437★

Carr; Marilyn

Radcliffe Institute for Advanced Study fellowship recipients in the field of economics, 2000-01 ★2172★

Carrado; Raymond R.

Most-cited scholars in *Canadian Journal of Criminology* ★1638★

Carrefour

Business Week's best companies in France ★393★

Carrier Access

Best small companies in the U.S. ★383★

Business Week's top companies in terms of earning growth, 2000 ★427★

Business Week's top companies in terms of sales growth, 2000 ★432★

Carrier; Jeffrey C.

Top pay and benefits for the chief executive and top paid employees at Albion College ★3167★

Carrocci; Noreen

Top pay and benefits for the chief executive and top paid employees at Spring Hill College ★3508★

Carroll; Ahmad

All-American boy's high school football defensive backs, 2000 ★180★

Carroll College
U.S. News & World Report's midwestern regional liberal arts colleges with the highest acceptance rates, 2000-01 ★1341★

U.S. News & World Report's best undergraduate fees among western regional liberal arts colleges by discount tuition, 2000 ★1384★

Academic reputation scores for *U.S. News & World Report*'s top western regional liberal arts colleges, 2000-01 ★1387★

Acceptance rates for *U.S. News & World Report*'s top western regional liberal arts colleges, 2000-01 ★1388★

Alumni giving rates at *U.S. News & World Report*'s top western regional liberal arts colleges, 2000-01 ★1389★

Average freshmen retention rates for *U.S. News & World Report*'s top western regional liberal arts colleges, 2000-01 ★1390★

Average graduation rates for *U.S. News & World Report*'s top western regional liberal arts colleges, 2000-01 ★1391★

Percentage of freshmen in the top 25% of their high school class at *U.S. News & World Report*'s top western regional liberal arts colleges, 2000-01 ★1392★

Percentage of full-time faculty at *U.S. News & World Report*'s top western regional liberal arts colleges, 2000-01 ★1393★

Proportion of classes having 20 students or less at *U.S. News & World Report*'s top western regional liberal arts colleges, 2000-01 ★1394★

Student/faculty ratios at *U.S. News & World Report*'s top western regional liberal arts colleges, 2000-01 ★1395★

U.S. News & World Report's top western regional liberal arts colleges, 2000-01 ★1396★

U.S. News & World Report's western regional liberal arts colleges with students most in debt, 1999 ★1398★

Highest undergraduate tuition and fees at colleges and universities in Montana ★1526★

Highest undergraduate tuition and fees at colleges and universities in Wisconsin ★1570★

Average faculty salaries for institutions of higher education in Montana, 2000-01 ★3713★

Average faculty salaries for institutions of higher education in Wisconsin, 2000-01 ★3738★

Carroll Community College
Lowest undergraduate tuition and fees at colleges and universities in Maryland ★1515★

Carroll; Diahann
Most influential African American entertainers ★77★

Carroll; Donna M.
Top pay and benefits for the chief executive and top paid employees at Dominican University in Illinois ★3269★

Carroll High School
Outstanding secondary schools in Fort Worth-Arlington, Texas ★4137★

Carroll Middle School
Outstanding secondary schools in Fort Worth-Arlington, Texas ★4137★

Carroll; Norman E.
Top pay and benefits for the chief executive and top paid employees at Dominican University in Illinois ★3269★

Carroll; William J.
Top pay and benefits for the chief executive and top paid employees at Benedictine University ★3200★

Carrollton High School
Outstanding suburban public high schools in Metro Atlanta ★4254★

Carruth; Rashaad
All-America boys' high school basketball 3rd team, 2001 ★163★

Carson; Ben
Most influential African Americans in medicine and science ★2879★

Carson Elementary School
Illinois elementary schools chosen to be 'demonstration sites' for struggling schools ★4006★

Carson; John L.
Top pay and benefits for the chief executive and top paid employees at Erskine College ★3290★

Carson Middle School
Outstanding secondary schools in Pittsburgh, Pennsylvania ★4204★

Carson-Newman College
U.S. News & World Report's southern regional liberal arts colleges with the highest academic reputation scores, 2000-01 ★1369★

U.S. News & World Report's southern regional liberal arts colleges with the highest acceptance rates, 2000-01 ★1370★

U.S. News & World Report's southern regional liberal arts colleges with the highest graduation rates, 2000-01 ★1373★

Average faculty salaries for institutions of higher education in Tennessee, 2000-01 ★3730★

Carson; Rachel
Best U.S. works of journalism in the 20th century ★2769★

Carter; Audry K.
Top pay and benefits for the chief executive and top paid employees at Ohio Wesleyan University ★3430★

Carter; Orwin L.
Top pay and benefits for the chief executive and top paid employees at Hamline University ★3320★

Carter; Stefani
All-USA College Academic Second Team, 2001 ★3★

Carthage College
U.S. News & World Report's midwestern regional universities with the best alumni giving rates, 2000-01 ★1402★

U.S. News & World Report's midwestern regional universities with the highest acceptance rates, 2000-01 ★1404★

U.S. News & World Report's midwestern regional universities with the highest proportion of classes having 20 students or less, 2000-01 ★1409★

Highest undergraduate tuition and fees at colleges and universities in Wisconsin ★1570★

Average faculty salaries for institutions of higher education in Wisconsin, 2000-01 ★3738★

Caruso; Joseph
Top pay and benefits for the chief executive and top paid employees at the College of Notre Dame in Maryland ★3527★

Carver; George Washington
Most important African Americans in the twentieth century ★219★

Cary Community, District 26
Illinois elementary school districts with the highest teacher salaries, 1999 ★3984★

Cary Memorial Library
Highest Hennen's American Public Library Ratings for libraries serving a population of 25,000 to 49,999 ★2696★

Casale; Rev. Msgr. Franklyn M.
Top pay and benefits for the chief executive and top paid employees at Saint Thomas University in Florida ★3486★

Casas; Ashley
All-America girls' high school soccer team midfielders, 2001 ★177★

A Case-Based Model of Searching Behavior
Journal of the American Society for Information Science's best papers, by total citations ★2729★

Case Western Reserve University
All-USA College Academic Second Team, 2001 ★3★

U.S. News & World Report's national universities with the highest acceptance rates, 2000-01 ★1131★

U.S. News & World Report's national universities with the highest percentage of full-time faculty, 2000-01 ★1136★

State appropriations for Ohio's institutions of higher education, 2000-01 ★1288★

U.S. News & World Report's best undergraduate fees among national universities by discount tuition, 2000 ★1474★

Highest undergraduate tuition and fees at colleges and universities in Ohio ★1543★

U.S. colleges and universities awarding the most law and legal studies master's degrees to African Americans ★1781★

U.S. universities with the greatest impact in dermatology, 1994-98 ★1875★

Academics' choices for best graduate bioengineering/biomedical engineering programs, 2001 ★2381★

Top biomedical engineering research-doctorate programs as evaluated by the National Research Council ★2384★

U.S. News & World Report's graduate engineering programs with the best biomedical departments, 2000-01 ★2385★

Academics' choices for best health law programs, 2001 ★2629★

Law schools with the best constitutional law (freedom of religion) faculty, 1999-2000 ★2643★

Academics' choices for best family medicine programs, 2001 ★2820★

U.S. universities with the greatest impact in psychiatry, 1995-99 ★3060★

U.S. colleges and universities spending the most on chemical engineering research and development, 1998 ★3098★

U.S. colleges and universities spending the most on chemical research equipment, 1998 ★3100★

U.S. colleges and universities with the most federal support for chemical engineering research and development, 1998 ★3101★

U.S. colleges and universities with the most federal support for chemical research equipment, 1998 ★3103★

Average faculty salaries for institutions of higher education in Ohio, 2000-01 ★3722★

Case Western Reserve University, Weatherhead School of Business
Academics' choices for best graduate nonprofit organizations programs, 2001 ★586★

Casey; Kevin
Top pay and benefits for the chief executive and top paid employees at National University in California ★3415★

Cash; Louise
Top pay and benefits for the chief executive and top paid employees at Emmanuel College in Massachusetts ★3288★

Cashier
Jobs with the worst income scores ★2261★

Cashiers
Occupations with the largest projected employment growth, 1998-2008 ★2312★
Projected employment growth for selected occupations that require shortor moderate-term on-the-job training, 1998-2008 ★2321★

Caskey; J.
Top associate professor economists at elite liberal arts colleges, 1975-94 ★2174★

Casper College
Undergraduate tuition and fees at colleges and universities in Wyoming ★1572★
Average faculty salaries for institutions of higher education without academic ranks in Wyoming, 2000-01 ★3769★

Casper; Gerhard
Top pay and benefits for the chief executive and top paid employees at Stanford University ★3510★

Cass Technical High School
Outstanding secondary schools in Detroit, Michigan ★4125★

Cass Technical Senior High School
Outstanding urban public high schools in Metro Detroit ★4264★

Cassidy & Associates
Lobbyist that billed the most to U.S. colleges and universities, 1999 ★1249★

Cassie Loves Beethoven
Smithsonian's best books for children ages 10 and up ★365★

Castelli; William P.
Most-cited researchers in epidemiology, 1981-1998 ★2876★

Castellino; Frank J.
Top pay and benefits for the chief executive and top paid employees at the University of Notre Dame ★3554★

Castleton State College
Undergraduate tuition and fees at colleges and universities in Vermont ★1563★
Average faculty salaries for institutions of higher education in Vermont, 2000-01 ★3734★

Catalina High Magnet School
All-USA Teacher Teams, First Team, 2000 ★4399★

Catawba College
U.S. colleges and universities with poor library facilities ★1028★
U.S. colleges and universities with the worst food service program ★1043★
Highest undergraduate tuition and fees at colleges and universities in North Carolina ★1539★
Average faculty salaries for institutions of higher education in North Carolina, 2000-01 ★3720★

Catawba Valley Community College
Average faculty salaries for institutions of higher education without academic ranks in North Carolina, 2000-01 ★3761★

The Catcher in the Rye
American Library Association's most frequently challenged books of the decade ★224★
American Library Associations most frequently challenged books for the 1990s ★742★
Most frequently banned books in the 1990s ★745★
People for the American Way's list of most frequently challenged books, 1982-1992 ★747★
People for the American Way's list of most frequently challenged books, 1991-1992 ★748★

Caterpillar Inc.
Fortune's highest ranked industrial and farm equipment companies, 2000 ★471★
Top recruiters for logistics jobs for 2000-01 bachelor's degree recipients ★555★
Top recruiters for manufacturing management jobs for 2000-01 bachelor's degree recipients ★683★
Top recruiters for chemical engineering jobs for 2000-01 bachelor's degree recipients ★2343★
Top recruiters for metallurgical/mining engineering jobs for 2000-01 bachelor's degree recipients ★2434★
Top recruiters for mechanical engineering jobs for 2000-01 bachelor's degree recipients ★2437★
Top recruiters for human resources jobs for 2000-01 bachelor's degree recipients ★2559★
Top recruiters for information technology (MIS) jobs for 2000-01 bachelor's degree recipients ★2738★

Cathay Life Insurance
Business Week's top emerging-market companies worldwide ★434★

Catherine McAuley High School
Outstanding secondary schools in New York, New York ★4191★

Catholic Central High School
Outstanding Catholic high schools in Metro Detroit ★4075★

Catholic High School
Outstanding secondary schools in Baton Rouge, Louisiana ★4093★

Catholic Medical Center School of Nursing
U.S. colleges and universities with the lowest percentage of African Americans enrolled, 1997 ★223★

Catholic priest
Jobs with the longest work weeks ★2257★
Jobs with the worst income scores ★2261★

Catholic University
U.S. institutions with more than 40% female bachelor's graduates in their physics departments, 1994-98 ★2977★

The Catholic University of America
Institutions censured by the American Association of University Professors, 2001 ★1067★
Undergraduate tuition and fees at colleges and universities in the District of Columbia ★1493★
Institutions with the most female physics bachelor's recipients, 1994-1998 ★2959★
Average faculty salaries for institutions of higher education in the District of Columbia, 2000-01 ★3732★

Caton; Gerald
Top pay and benefits for the chief executive and top paid employees at Rockford College in Illinois ★3463★

Catovsky; Daniel
Most-cited researchers in oncology, 1981-1998 ★2877★

Cauthron; Hal
Top pay and benefits for the chief executive and top paid employees at Southern Nazarene University ★3503★

Cavan; Michael
Top pay and benefits for the chief executive and top paid employees at Southern Methodist University ★3502★

Cavusgil; S. Tamer
Highest impact authors in the *Journal of Business Research*, by number of citations in 12 journals, 1985-1999 ★693★

Cawthon; David
Top pay and benefits for the chief executive and top paid employees at Oklahoma City University ★3431★

Cayuga County Community College
Highest undergraduate tuition and fees at public 2-year colleges and universities ★1462★
Average faculty salaries for institutions of higher education in New York, 2000-01 ★3719★

Cazenovia College
Average faculty salaries for institutions of higher education in New York, 2000-01 ★3719★

CBRL
Fortune's highest ranked food services companies, 2000 ★465★

CDI
Fortune's highest ranked temporary help companies, 2000 ★500★

Cdnow
Top E-commerce web sites ★2603★

CDW Computer Centers
Top information technology companies, 2000 ★544★

Cecil Community College
Lowest undergraduate tuition and fees at colleges and universities in Maryland ★1515★
Average faculty salaries for institutions of higher education in Maryland, 2000-01 ★3707★

Cedar Crest College
U.S. News & World Report's northern regional liberal arts colleges with the highest alumni giving rates, 2000-01 ★1356★
U.S. News & World Report's northern regional liberal arts colleges with the highest percentage of freshmen in the top 25% of their high school class, 2000-01 ★1359★
U.S. News & World Report's northern regional liberal arts colleges with the highest proportion of classes having 20 students or less, 2000-01 ★1361★
U.S. News & World Report's best undergraduate fees among northern regional liberal arts colleges by discount tuition, 2000 ★1382★
Average faculty salaries for institutions of higher education in Pennsylvania, 2000-01 ★3725★

Cedar Manor Intermediate School
Outstanding secondary schools in Minneapolis-St. Paul, Minnesota-Wisconsin ★4181★

Cedar Shoals High School
Outstanding secondary schools in Athens, Georgia ★4086★

Cedar Valley College
Lowest undergraduate tuition and fees at colleges and universities in Texas ★1561★
Average faculty salaries for institutions of higher education without academic ranks in Texas, 2000-01 ★3766★

Cedarcrest High School
Outstanding secondary schools in Seattle-Bellevue-Everett, Washington ★4227★

Cedarville College
U.S. News & World Report's midwestern regional liberal arts colleges with the highest freshmen retention rates, 2000-01 ★1343★
U.S. News & World Report's midwestern regional liberal arts colleges with the highest graduation rates, 2000-01 ★1344★
U.S. News & World Report's midwestern regional liberal arts colleges with the highest percentage of freshmen in the top 25% of their high school class, 2000-01 ★1345★
U.S. News & World Report's midwestern regional liberal arts colleges with the highest percentage of full-time faculty, 2000-01 ★1346★
U.S. News & World Report's midwestern regional liberal arts colleges with the lowest acceptance rates, 2000-01 ★1348★

Cedarville University
Average faculty salaries for institutions of higher education in Ohio, 2000-01 ★3722★

The Celestine Prophecy
Retail audiobook titles selling 300,000-400,000 copies ★303★

Cell
Molecular biology and genetics journals with the highest impact, 1992-96 ★204★
Top science journals by impact factor ★4281★

Cell biology
Biological sciences doctorates awarded at U.S. colleges and universities, by subfield, 1999 ★1887★
Gender breakdown of biological sciences doctorate recipients, by subfield, 1999 ★1927★
Percentage of female doctorate recipients at U.S. colleges and universities, by subfield, 1999 ★1988★

Cemera; Anthony J.
Presidents with the highest pay at Master's I and II colleges and universities, 1998-99 ★3161★

Cendant
Business Week's best performing companies with the lowest 3-year shareholder returns ★424★

Cendanta
Business Week's best performing companies with the lowest 1-year sales performance ★421★

Centenary College
Highest undergraduate tuition and fees at colleges and universities in New Jersey ★1533★

Centenary College of Louisiana
U.S. colleges and universities where the general student body does not smoke marijuana ★1006★
U.S. colleges and universities with the best financial aid programs ★1030★
U.S. News & World Report's best undergraduate fees among southern regional universities by discount tuition, 2000 ★1429★
U.S. News & World Report's southern regional universities with the best alumni giving rates, 2000-01 ★1434★
U.S. News & World Report's southern regional universities with the best student/faculty ratios, 2000-01 ★1435★
U.S. News & World Report's southern regional universities with the highest acceptance rates, 2000-01 ★1436★
U.S. News & World Report's southern regional universities with the highest percentage of full-time faculty, 2000-01 ★1440★
U.S. News & World Report's southern regional universities with the highest proportion of classes with 20 students or less, 2000-01 ★1441★
Highest undergraduate tuition and fees at colleges and universities in Louisiana ★1510★
Average faculty salaries for institutions of higher education in Louisiana, 2000-01 ★3705★

Center for Coastal Studies
Most selective internships in the U.S., 2001 ★2610★

Center for Creative Studies College of Art and Design
Highest undergraduate tuition and fees at colleges and universities in Michigan ★1518★

Center for Disease Control and Prevention
Library Journal's best free reference websites, 2000 ★367★

Center for Enriched Studies
Outstanding secondary schools in Los Angeles-Long Beach, California ★4167★

Center for Research Resources
Proposed fiscal 2002 appropriations for National Institutes of Health scientific research ★3108★

Centers for Disease Control and Prevention
Medical Library Association's top health related web sites ★2591★

Centerville High School
Outstanding secondary schools in Dayton-Springfield, Ohio ★4122★

Centex
Fortune's highest ranked engineering and construction companies, 2000 ★461★
Top housing and real estate companies in Standard & Poor's 500, 2001 ★543★

Centex Construction Products
Business Week's top companies in terms of earnings, 2000 ★428★

Centonze; Arthur L.
Top pay and benefits for the chief executive and top paid employees at Pace University ★3435★

Central Arizona College
Lowest undergraduate tuition and fees at colleges and universities in Arizona ★1483★
Average faculty salaries for institutions of higher education without academic ranks in Arizona, 2000-01 ★3741★

Central Arkansas; University of
Institutions censured by the American Association of University Professors, 2001 ★1067★
State appropriations for Arkansas's institutions of higher education, 2000-01 ★1257★
Average faculty salaries for institutions of higher education in Arkansas, 2000-01 ★3691★

Central Baptist College
Highest undergraduate tuition and fees at colleges and universities in Arkansas ★1484★

Central Carolina Community College
Average faculty salaries for institutions of higher education without academic ranks in North Carolina, 2000-01 ★3761★

Central Carolina Technical College
Lowest undergraduate tuition and fees at colleges and universities in South Carolina ★1555★

Central Catholic High School
Outstanding secondary schools in Allentown-Bethlehem-Easton, Pennsylvania ★4081★
Outstanding secondary schools in Toledo, Ohio ★4241★

Central City Public Library
Highest Hennen's American Public Library Ratings for libraries serving a population of 2,500 to 4,999 ★2693★

Central College
U.S. News & World Report's national liberal arts colleges with students most in debt, 1999 ★1386★
Average faculty salaries for institutions of higher education in Iowa, 2000-01 ★3702★

Central Community College
Lowest undergraduate tuition and fees at colleges and universities in Nebraska ★1529★
Average faculty salaries for institutions of higher education without academic ranks in Nebraska, 2000-01 ★3757★

Central Connecticut State University
Division I NCAA colleges with the lowest graduation rates for football players, 1990-91 to 1993-94 ★938★
Colleges and universities with the smallest endowments, 2000 ★1238★
Average faculty salaries for institutions of higher education in Connecticut, 2000-01 ★3694★

Central Connecticut University
State appropriations for Connecticut's institutions of higher education, 2000-01 ★1260★

Central Elementary School
Illinois elementary schools with the highest 5th grade writing scores ★15★
Illinois suburban elementary schools with the highest ISAT scores in reading and math ★18★

Central Florida; University of
Retention rates of African American students at traditionally white institutions, 1997-98 ★1121★
State appropriations for Florida's institutions of higher education, 2000-01 ★1262★
Total baccalaureate health professions and related sciences degrees awarded to Hispanic Americans from U.S. colleges and universities, 1997-98 ★1723★
Total baccalaureate law and legal studies degrees awarded to African Americans from U.S. colleges and universities, 1997-98 ★1725★
Total baccalaureate law and legal studies degrees awarded to Hispanic Americans from U.S. colleges and universities, 1997-98 ★1727★
U.S. colleges and universities awarding the most mathematics master's degrees to African Americans ★1790★
Degrees granted in the ten largest undergraduate journalism and mass communications programs, 1999 ★2745★
Average faculty salaries for institutions of higher education in Florida, 2000-01 ★3696★

Central High School
Outstanding secondary schools in Minneapolis-St. Paul, Minnesota-Wisconsin ★4181★

Central Lakes College
Average faculty salaries for institutions of higher education without academic ranks in Minnesota, 2000-01 ★3753★

Central Maine Medical Center School of Nursing
Highest undergraduate tuition and fees at colleges and universities in Maine ★1512★

Central Maine Technical College
Lowest undergraduate tuition and fees at colleges and universities in Maine ★1513★
Average faculty salaries for institutions of higher education without academic ranks in Maine, 2000-01 ★3749★

Central Michigan University
State appropriations for Michigan's institutions of higher education, 2000-01 ★1275★
U.S. News & World Report's top public midwestern regional universities, 2000-01 ★1412★
Traditionally white institutions awarding the most master's degrees to African Americans ★1755★
U.S. colleges and universities awarding the most business management and administrative services master's degrees to African Americans ★1759★
U.S. colleges and universities awarding the most business management and administrative services master's degrees to Hispanic Americans ★1761★
U.S. colleges and universities awarding the most business management and administrative services master's degrees to Native Americans ★1762★
U.S. colleges and universities awarding the most health professions and related sciences master's degrees to African Americans ★1777★
U.S. colleges and universities awarding the most master's degrees to African Americans ★1785★
U.S. colleges and universities awarding the most master's degrees to minorities ★1788★
U.S. colleges and universities awarding the most master's degrees to Native Americans ★1789★
Average faculty salaries for institutions of higher education in Michigan, 2000-01 ★3709★

Central Missouri State University
State appropriations for Missouri's institutions of higher education, 2000-01 ★1278★
Average faculty salaries for institutions of higher education in Missouri, 2000-01 ★3712★

Central Ohio Technical College
Lowest undergraduate tuition and fees at colleges and universities in Ohio ★1544★

Central Oklahoma; University of
Division II NCAA colleges with the 100% graduation rates for women's basketball players, 1993-94 ★944★
Division II NCAA colleges with the lowest graduation rates for football players, 1993-94 ★948★
State appropriations for Oklahoma's institutions of higher education, 2000-01 ★1289★
Total baccalaureate education degrees awarded to Native Americans from U.S. colleges and universities, 1997-98 ★1714★
U.S. colleges and universities awarding the most education master's degrees to Native Americans ★1772★
Master's institutions with the highest enrollment of foreign students, 1998-99 ★2499★

Average faculty salaries for institutions of higher education in Oklahoma, 2000-01 ★3723★

Central Piedmont Community College
Average faculty salaries for institutions of higher education without academic ranks in North Carolina, 2000-01 ★3761★

Central State University
Colleges offering the Thurgood Marshall Scholarship Fund ★221★
State appropriations for Ohio's institutions of higher education, 2000-01 ★1288★
Historically black colleges and universities with major improvements in student loan default rates, 1998 ★2737★
Average faculty salaries for institutions of higher education in Ohio, 2000-01 ★3722★

Central States Speech Journal
Most cited language serials in technical communication journals from 1988 to 1997 ★4420★

Central Texas College
Top colleges in terms of total associate degrees awarded to minorities, 1997-98 ★1677★

Central Virginia Community College
Lowest undergraduate tuition and fees at colleges and universities in Virginia ★1565★

Central Washington University
State appropriations for Washington's institutions of higher education, 2000-01 ★1300★
Average faculty salaries for institutions of higher education in Washington, 2000-01 ★3736★

Central Wyoming College
Undergraduate tuition and fees at colleges and universities in Wyoming ★1572★

Central Wyoming University
Average faculty salaries for institutions of higher education in Wyoming, 2000-01 ★3739★

Centralia College
Average faculty salaries for institutions of higher education without academic ranks in Washington, 2000-01 ★3768★

Centre College
College freshmen's choices for exemplary liberal arts institutions ★1317★
College senior's choices for exemplary liberal arts institutions ★1318★
U.S. News & World Report's national liberal arts colleges with the highest acceptance rates, 2000-01 ★1328★
U.S. News & World Report's national liberal arts colleges with the highest alumni giving rank, 2000-01 ★1329★
U.S. News & World Report's national liberal arts colleges with the highest percentage of alumni support, 2000-01 ★1331★
U.S. News & World Report's national liberal arts colleges with the highest percentage of full-time faculty, 2000-01 ★1333★
Fiske Guide's best buys for private colleges and universities, 2001 ★1459★
Highest undergraduate tuition and fees at colleges and universities in Kentucky ★1508★
Average faculty salaries for institutions of higher education in Kentucky, 2000-01 ★3704★

Century College
Average faculty salaries for institutions of higher education without academic ranks in Minnesota, 2000-01 ★3753★

Century High School
Outstanding secondary schools in Bismarck, North Dakota ★4099★

Centurytel
Top telecommunications companies in Standard & Poor's 500, 2001 ★559★

CEO of internet company
Careers college students considered most respected, 2000 ★740★

Ceramic sciences
Engineering doctorates awarded at U.S. colleges and universities, by subfield, 1999 ★1923★
Gender breakdown of engineering doctorate recipients, by subfield, 1999 ★1934★

Cerebrovascular and Brain Metabolism Reviews
Neurosciences journals with the greatest impact measure, 1981-98 ★2812★
Neurosciences journals with the greatest impact measure, 1994-98 ★2813★

Cernera; Anthony J.
Top pay and benefits for the chief executive and top paid employees at Sacred Heart University in Connecticut ★3467★

Cerro Coso Community College
Lowest undergraduate tuition and fees at public 2-year colleges and universities ★1465★
Lowest undergraduate tuition and fees at colleges and universities in California ★1487★

C.F. Menninger Memorial Hospital
Top psychiatric hospitals in the U.S., 2000 ★2800★

CGNU
Business Week's best companies in Britain ★389★

C.H. Robinson Worldwide
Fortune's highest ranked trucking companies, 2000 ★503★

Chabot College
Lowest undergraduate tuition and fees at public 2-year colleges and universities ★1465★
Lowest undergraduate tuition and fees at colleges and universities in California ★1487★

Chabotar; Kent John
Top pay and benefits for the chief executive and top paid employees at Bowdoin College ★3207★

Chace; William M.
Top pay and benefits for the chief executive and top paid employees at Emory University ★3289★

Chadron State College
State appropriations for Nebraska's institutions of higher education, 2000-01 ★1280★
Average faculty salaries for institutions of higher education in Nebraska, 2000-01 ★3714★

Chalupny; Lori
All-America girls' high school soccer team midfielders, 2001 ★177★

Chamberlain; Daniel R.
Top pay and benefits for the chief executive and top paid employees at Houghton College ★3341★

Chambers; Robert H.
Top pay and benefits for the chief executive and top paid employees at Western Maryland College ★3614★

Chamblee High School
Outstanding secondary schools in Atlanta, Georgia ★4087★
Outstanding suburban public high schools in Metro Atlanta ★4254★

Chambliss; William J.
Most cited scholars in critical criminology ★1640★
Most-cited scholars in critical criminology publications ★1641★

CHAMBON

Chambon; Pierre
Most-cited biomedical scientists, 1990-97 ★2382★

Chaminade-Madonna Prep
Outstanding secondary schools in Fort Lauderdale, Florida ★4133★

Chaminade Prep
Outstanding secondary schools in Los Angeles-Long Beach, California ★4167★

Chaminade University, Honolulu
Undergraduate tuition and fees at colleges and universities in Hawaii ★1498★
U.S. colleges and universities awarding the most psychology master's degrees to Asian Americans ★1798★

Champagne; Ronald
Top pay and benefits for the chief executive and top paid employees at Roosevelt University ★3466★

Champaign Central High School
Outstanding secondary schools in Champaign-Urbana, Illinois ★4105★

Champlain College
Undergraduate tuition and fees at colleges and universities in Vermont ★1563★
Average faculty salaries for institutions of higher education in Vermont, 2000-01 ★3734★

Chan; Lionel
Top pay and benefits for the chief executive and top paid employees at Saint Mary's College of California ★3480★

Chandler; Tyson
All-America boys' high school basketball 1st team, 2001 ★161★

Chang; David
Top pay and benefits for the chief executive and top paid employees at Polytechnic University ★3443★

Channahon School, District 17
Illinois school districts spending the least for elementary school education 1997-98 ★4007★

Chapin High School
Outstanding secondary schools in Columbia, South Carolina ★4117★

Chapin; Lloyd W.
Top pay and benefits for the chief executive and top paid employees at Eckerd College ★3282★

Chapin Middle School
Outstanding secondary schools in Columbia, South Carolina ★4117★

Chapman; Leslie T.
Top pay and benefits for the chief executive and top paid employees at Lake Forest College ★3363★

Chapman University
U.S. college campuses reporting murders or non-negligent manslaughters, 1999 ★728★
U.S. News & World Report's best undergraduate fees among western regional universities by discount tuition, 2000 ★1430★
Highest undergraduate tuition and fees at colleges and universities in California ★1486★
U.S. News & World Report's western regional universities with the best student/faculty ratios, 2000-01 ★1578★
U.S. News & World Report's western regional universities with the highest freshmen retention rates, 2000-01 ★1581★
U.S. News & World Report's western regional universities with the lowest acceptance rates, 2000-01 ★1586★

Total baccalaureate law and legal studies degrees awarded to Asian Americans from U.S. colleges and universities, 1997-98 ★1726★
Total baccalaureate law and legal studies degrees awarded to Hispanic Americans from U.S. colleges and universities, 1997-98 ★1727★
Average faculty salaries for institutions of higher education in California, 2000-01 ★3692★

Chapnick; Lisa
Top pay and benefits for the chief executive and top paid employees at Simmons College ★3499★

Charles Blackstock Junior High School
Outstanding secondary schools in Ventura, California ★4248★

Charles Schwab
Fortune's highest ranked securities companies, 2000 ★494★
Fortune's most admired companies for innovation ★516★
Top public companies for women executives, 2000 ★4457★

Charlesbridge Publishing
Small publishers with the highest sales growth between 1997 and 1999 ★3073★

Charleston; College of
Division I NCAA colleges with the highest graduation rates for female basketball players, 1990-91 to 1993-94 ★932★
State appropriations for South Carolina's institutions of higher education, 2000-01 ★1293★
U.S. News & World Report's southern regional universities with the best academic reputation scores, 2000-01 ★1433★
U.S. News & World Report's southern regional universities with the best alumni giving rates, 2000-01 ★1434★
U.S. News & World Report's southern regional universities with the lowest acceptance rates, 2000-01 ★1442★
U.S. News & World Report's top public southern regional universities, 2000-01 ★1443★
Average faculty salaries for institutions of higher education in South Carolina, 2000-01 ★3728★

Charleston, SC
Most polite cities in the U.S. ★3086★

Charleston Southern University
Division I NCAA colleges with the lowest graduation rates for female athletes, 1990-91 to 1993-94 ★936★
Highest undergraduate tuition and fees at colleges and universities in South Carolina ★1554★
Average faculty salaries for institutions of higher education in South Carolina, 2000-01 ★3728★

Charleston; University of
Highest undergraduate tuition and fees at colleges and universities in West Virginia ★1568★

Charlie Parker Played Be Bop!
Most notable children's recordings, 2001 ★320★

Charlotte Latin School
Outstanding secondary schools in Charlotte-Gastonia-Rock Hill, North Carolina-South Carolina ★4108★

Charlotte Wood Middle School
Outstanding secondary schools in Oakland, California ★4195★

Charlottesville, VA
Best college towns to live in ★3076★

Charming Shoppes
Top women-owned companies ★4460★

Charter Oak State College
Lowest undergraduate tuition and fees at colleges and universities in Connecticut ★1491★

Charter One Financial
Fortune's highest ranked mortgage finance companies, 2000 ★479★

Charter Schools in Action: Renewing Public Education
American School Board Journal's notable education books, 2000 ★225★

Chartered Semiconductor Manufacturing
Business Week's best companies in Singapore ★402★

Chas. Levy Companies
Oldest women-owned companies ★4454★

Chase Elementary School
Illinois elementary schools chosen to be 'demonstration sites' for struggling schools ★4006★

Chase Manhattan
Fortune's highest ranked money center banks, 2000 ★478★

Chase Manhattan Corporation
Best companies for working mothers in offering flexible work hours ★4448★

Chatham College
U.S. News & World Report's national liberal arts colleges with the highest proportion of classes with less than 20 students, 2000-01 ★1335★
Women's colleges granting physics bachelor's degrees, 2000 ★2982★
Presidents with the highest pay at Baccalaureate I colleges, 1998-99 ★3159★
Average faculty salaries for institutions of higher education in Pennsylvania, 2000-01 ★3725★

Chato and the Party Animals
Most notable books for young readers, 2001 ★319★

Chattahoochee High School
Outstanding suburban public high schools in Metro Atlanta ★4254★

Chattahoochee Technical Institute
Lowest undergraduate tuition and fees at colleges and universities in Georgia ★1497★

Chattahoochee Valley Community College
Average faculty salaries for institutions of higher education without academic ranks in Alabama, 2000-01 ★3740★

Chattanooga State Tech Community College
Average faculty salaries for institutions of higher education in Tennessee, 2000-01 ★3730★

Chauffeur
Most desirable jobs in personal services ★2275★

Cheaney; J.B.
Booklist's best first novels for youths ★309★

Check Point Software Technologies
Business Week's top emerging-market companies worldwide ★434★

Cheesman; Danielle
All-America girls' high school basketball 4th team, 2001 ★173★

Cheever Jr.; Daniel S.
Top pay and benefits for the chief executive and top paid employees at Simmons College ★3499★

Chemeketa Community College
  Lowest undergraduate tuition and fees at colleges and universities in Oregon ★1548★
Chemical
  Engineering doctorates awarded at U.S. colleges and universities, by subfield, 1999 ★1923★
  Gender breakdown of engineering doctorate recipients, by subfield, 1999 ★1934★
Chemical and atomic/molecular
  Gender breakdown of physics and astronomy doctorate recipients, by subfield, 1999 ★1939★
  Physics and astronomy doctorates awarded at U.S. colleges and universities, by subfield, 1999 ★1994★
Chemical Communications
  Chemistry journals by citation impact, 1999 ★810★
Chemical engineering
  Top physical science majors for accepted applicants to U.S. medical schools, 1999-2000 ★2855★
  Expected starting salaries of 2000-01 bachelor's degree recipients, by specific major ★3131★
Chemical engineers
  Median salary for B.S. chemists, by field ★781★
  Median salary for M.S. chemists, by field ★785★
  Median salary for Ph.D. chemists, by field ★786★
Chemical Research in Toxicology
  Chemistry journals by citation impact, 1995-99 ★809★
  Chemistry journals by citation impact, 1999 ★810★
Chemical Reviews
  Chemistry journals by citation impact, 1981-99 ★808★
  Chemistry journals by citation impact, 1995-99 ★809★
  Chemistry journals by citation impact, 1999 ★810★
Chemical Senses
  Food science and technology journals by citation impact, 1991-99 ★2902★
  Food science and technology journals by citation impact, 1995-99 ★2903★
  Food science and technology journals by citation impact, 1999 ★2904★
Chemical Society Reviews
  Chemistry journals by citation impact, 1981-99 ★808★
  Chemistry journals by citation impact, 1995-99 ★809★
  Chemistry journals by citation impact, 1999 ★810★
Chemist
  Jobs with the lowest unemployment ★2258★
  Most desirable jobs in math/science ★2274★
Chemistry
  Number of Advanced Placement Exams taken by African Americans, by subject, 2000 ★30★
  Number of Advanced Placement Exams taken by Asian Americans, by subject, 2000 ★31★
  Number of Advanced Placement Exams taken by Hispanic Americans, by subject, 2000 ★32★
  Median salary for B.S. chemists, by field ★781★
  Median salary for M.S. chemists, by field ★785★
  Median salary for Ph.D. chemists, by field ★786★

Comparative data of women receiving doctorate degrees in selected fields in 1950 and 1998 ★1899★
Number of physical sciences doctorate recipients at U.S. colleges and universities, by field, 1999 ★1975★
Percentage of female doctorate recipients at U.S. colleges and universities, by subfield, 1999 ★1988★
Physical sciences, mathematics, and computer sciences doctorates awarded to U.S. citizens/permanent residents at U.S. colleges and universities, by race/ethnicity and subfield, 1999 ★1993★
Top physical science majors for accepted applicants to U.S. medical schools, 1999-2000 ★2855★
Average costs for Academic Search titles by subject, 2001 ★2918★
Periodical prices by LC subject, 2001 ★2925★
Periodical prices by scientific discipline, 2001 ★2926★
Mean age of first and best contribution of scientists and inventors, by discipline ★3096★
Austria's relative impact in the sciences by field, 1992-96 ★4300★
Belgium's contribution of papers in the sciences, by field, 1995-99 ★4302★
France's contribution of papers in the sciences, by field, 1995-99 ★4311★
France's contribution of papers in the sciences, by field, 1996-2000 ★4312★
Germany's contribution of papers in the sciences, by field, 1995-99 ★4313★
Italy's contribution of papers in the sciences, by field, 1995-99 ★4316★
Italy's relative impact in the sciences by field, 1992-96 ★4317★
Japan's contribution of papers in the sciences, by field, 1995-99 ★4318★
Japan's contribution of papers in the sciences, by field, 1996-2000 ★4319★
Poland's contribution of papers in the sciences, by field, 1993-97 ★4324★
Russia's contribution of papers in the sciences, by field, 1993-97 ★4325★
South Korea's contribution of papers in the sciences, by field, 1995-99 ★4327★
Spain's contribution of papers in the sciences, by field, 1993-97 ★4328★
Spain's contribution of papers in the sciences, by field, 1995-99 ★4329★
Switzerland's contribution of papers in the sciences, by field, 1994-98 ★4332★
Switzerland's contribution of papers in the sciences, by field, 1995-99 ★4333★
Taiwan contribution of papers in the sciences, by field, 1995-99 ★4334★
Turkey's contribution of papers in the sciences, by field, 1995-99 ★4335★
Chemistry: A European Journal
  Chemistry journals by citation impact, 1995-99 ★809★
  Chemistry journals by citation impact, 1999 ★810★
Chemistry and biology
  Top physical science majors for accepted applicants to U.S. medical schools, 1999-2000 ★2855★
Chemistry, general
  Chemistry doctorates awarded at U.S. colleges and universities, by subfield, 1999 ★1889★
  Gender breakdown of chemistry doctorate recipients, by subfield, 1999 ★1929★

Chemometrics and Intelligent Laboratory Systems
  Artificial intelligence journals by citation impact, 1981-99 ★94★
  Artificial intelligence journals by citation impact, 1995-99 ★95★
  Artificial intelligence journals by citation impact, 1999 ★96★
  Artificial intelligence journals with the greatest impact measure, 1981-98 ★97★
  Artificial intelligence journals with the greatest impact measure, 1994-98 ★98★
  Artificial intelligence journals with the greatest impact measure, 1998 ★99★
Chen; Jen-Yen
  Top published scholars in the field of systems and software engineering ★2333★
Chenevert; Paul M.
  Top pay and benefits for the chief executive and top paid employees at Anna Maria College ★3177★
Cherry Creek High School
  Outstanding secondary schools in Denver, Colorado ★4124★
Cherry Creek West Middle School
  Outstanding secondary schools in Denver, Colorado ★4124★
Chesapeake College
  Lowest undergraduate tuition and fees at colleges and universities in Maryland ★1515★
  Average faculty salaries for institutions of higher education in Maryland, 2000-01 ★3707★
Chesapeake Public Schools
  Top recruiters for education jobs for 2000-01 bachelor's degree recipients ★4377★
  Top recruiters for education jobs for 2000-01 master's degree recipients ★4398★
Chesney-Lind; Meda
  Most cited authors in the journal *Justice Quarterly*, 1990 to 1995 ★1630★
  Most-cited scholars in women and crime publications ★1642★
Chesterfield-Marlboro Technical College
  Lowest undergraduate tuition and fees at colleges and universities in South Carolina ★1555★
Chestertown, MD
  Best small towns to live in ★3085★
Chestnut Hill College
  Average faculty salaries for institutions of higher education in Pennsylvania, 2000-01 ★3725★
Cheung Kong Holdings
  Business Week's best companies in Hong Kong ★395★
  Business Week's best companies in terms of profits ★406★
Chevron
  Fortune's highest ranked petroleum refining companies, 2000 ★484★
  Top fuel companies in Standard & Poor's 500, 2001 ★541★
  Top internships in the U.S. with the highest compensation, 2001 ★2611★
Chew; E. Byron
  Top pay and benefits for the chief executive and top paid employees at Birmingham-Southern College ★3204★
Cheyney University
  Average faculty salaries for institutions of higher education in Pennsylvania, 2000-01 ★3725★

Cheyney University of Pennsylvania
Division II NCAA colleges with the 0% graduation rates for men's basketball players, 1993-94 ★941★
U.S. colleges and universities awarding the most education master's degrees to African Americans ★1769★

Chicago
U.S. cities with the highest number of high-tech employees, 1998 ★2284★
U.S. school districts with the highest number of vacancies for K-12 teachers ★2331★
U.S. market areas with the highest percentage of adults having internet access ★2607★
Superintendents' salaries at the largest U.S. schools districts, 1999-2000 ★3990★
Largest public school districts in the U.S. ★4016★
U.S. cities with the highest percentage of births to mothers with less than 12 years of education ★4432★

Chicago Bulls
Most selective internships in the U.S., 2001 ★2610★

Chicago Graduate School of Business; University of
Academics' choices for best graduate executive MBA programs, 2001 ★584★
Academics' choices for best part-time MBA programs, 2000 ★587★
Acceptance rates for *U.S. News & World Report*'s top 10 graduate business schools, 2001 ★588★
Annual tuition at *Business Week*'s top business schools, 2000 ★589★
Average GMAT scores at *U.S. News & World Report*'s top 10 graduate business schools, 2001 ★591★
Average job offers received by graduates from *Business Week*'s top business schools, 1999 ★592★
Average undergraduate GPA at *U.S. News & World Report*'s top 10 graduate business schools, 2001 ★593★
Business Week's top business schools, 2000 ★595★
Business Week's top business schools as selected by corporate recruiters, 2000 ★596★
Business Week's top business schools by intellectual capital, 2000 ★599★
Business Week's top business schools for finance skills as selected by corporate recruiters, 2000 ★600★
Business Week's top business schools for general management skills as selected by corporate recruiters, 2000 ★601★
Business Week's top business schools for global scope skills as selected by corporate recruiters, 2000 ★602★
Business Week's top business schools for marketing skills as selected by corporate recruiters, 2000 ★603★
Business Week's top business schools for technology skills as selected by corporate recruiters, 2000 ★604★
Business Week's top business schools with the best placement offices, 2000 ★608★
Business Week's top business schools with the greatest decrease in MBA satisfaction, 2000 ★610★
Business Week's top business schools with the lowest percentage of minority enrollment, 2000 ★616★
Business Week's top business schools with the lowest percentage of women enrollees, 2000 ★617★
Business Week's top business schools with the most improved program as selected by corporate recruiters, 2000 ★618★
Highest post-MBA salaries for students enrolled in *Business Week*'s top business schools, 1999 ★631★
Highest pre-MBA salaries for students enrolled in *Business Week*'s top business schools, 1999 ★632★
Median starting salaries of graduates from *U.S. News & World Report*'s top 10 graduate business schools, 2001 ★636★
Out-of-state tuition and fees for *U.S. News & World Report*'s top 10 graduate business schools, 2001 ★637★
Percentage of applicants accepted at *Business Week*'s top business schools, 2000 ★638★
Percentage of employed graduates at *U.S. News & World Report*'s top 10 graduate business schools, 2001 ★639★
Percentage of graduates earning over $100,000 from *Business Week*'s top business schools, 1999 ★640★
Percentage of graduates employed within 3 months of graduation from *U.S. News & World Report*'s top 10 graduate business schools, 2001 ★641★
Top graduate business schools, 2001 ★649★
Top graduate business schools by reputation as determined by academic personnel, 2001 ★650★
Top graduate business schools by reputation, as determined by recruiters, 2001 ★651★
Academics' choices for best graduate accounting programs, 2001 ★659★
Academics' choices for best graduate finance programs, 2001 ★662★
Academics' choices for best graduate marketing programs, 2001 ★670★
Academics' choices for best graduate quantitative analysis programs, 2001 ★673★
Average GMAT scores for *U.S. News & World Report*'s top 10 graduate business schools, 2000 ★2529★

Chicago Hospitals; University of
Top cancer hospitals in the U.S., 2000 ★2787★
Top endocrinology hospitals in the U.S., 2000 ★2789★
Top gastroenterology hospitals in the U.S., 2000 ★2790★
Top hospitals in the U.S., 2000 ★2793★

Chicago, IL
Best big cities to live in ★3075★
Best place to live in the midwest U.S. ★3078★
Most polite cities in the U.S. ★3086★

Chicago-Kent College of Law, Illinois Institute of Technology
Law schools with the best environmental law faculty, 1999-2000 ★2650★

Chicago Law Review; University of
Law journals by citation impact, 1981-96 ★2617★
Most frequently-cited law reviews and legal periodicals, 1924-1986: a compilation ★2619★
Most frequently-cited law reviews and legal periodicals, according to *Shepard's Law Review Citations*, 1957-1986 ★2620★

Chicago State University
Fall enrollment at Chicago-area public universities, by minority percentages, 1999 ★868★
Division I NCAA colleges with the lowest graduation rates for female athletes, 1990-91 to 1993-94 ★936★
State appropriations for Illinois institutions of higher education, 2000-01 ★1266★
U.S. News & World Report's midwestern regional universities with students most in debt, 1999 ★1400★
Total baccalaureate degrees awarded to African Americans from traditionally white institutions, 1997-98 ★1698★
Total baccalaureate degrees awarded to African Americans from U.S. colleges and universities, 1997-98 ★1699★
Total baccalaureate education degrees awarded to African Americans from U.S. colleges and universities, 1997-98 ★1711★
Total baccalaureate psychology degrees awarded to African Americans from U.S. colleges and universities, 1997-98 ★1737★
Traditionally white institutions awarding the most master's degrees to African Americans ★1755★
U.S. colleges and universities awarding the most education master's degrees to African Americans ★1769★
U.S. colleges and universities awarding the most English language/literature/letters master's degrees to African Americans ★1773★
U.S. colleges and universities awarding the most master's degrees to African Americans ★1785★
U.S. colleges and universities awarding the most mathematics master's degrees to African Americans ★1790★

Chicago; University of
All-USA College Academic Second Team, 2001 ★3★
Colleges with the highest number of freshman Merit Scholars, 2000 ★5★
Most effective anthropology research-doctorate programs as evaluated by the National Research Council ★61★
Top anthropology research-doctorate programs as evaluated by the National Research Council ★62★
Most effective art history research-doctorate programs as evaluated by the National Research Council ★91★
Top art history research-doctorate programs as evaluated by the National Research Council ★93★
Most effective ecology, evolution, and behavior research-doctorate programs as evaluated by the National Research Council ★199★
Top ecology, evolution, and behavior research-doctorate programs as evaluated by the National Research Council ★201★
Most effective molecular and general genetics research-doctorate programs as evaluated by the National Research Council ★207★
Top cell and developmental biology research-doctorate programs as evaluated by the National Research Council ★210★
Top molecular and general genetics research-doctorate programs as evaluated by the National Research Council ★211★
Top business schools in research performance, 1986-1998 ★532★
Top business schools by average MBA rank, 1986-1998 ★644★
Top business schools for overall within-discipline research performance, 1986-1998 ★645★

Top business schools for within-discipline research performance in accounting, 1986-1998 ★660★
Top business schools for within-discipline research performance in finance, 1986-1998 ★663★
Top business schools for within-discipline research performance in marketing, 1986-1998 ★671★
Degree-granting institutions with the most published pages in *The Journal of Risk and Insurance*, 1987-1996 ★678★
Top chemistry research-doctorate programs as evaluated by the National Research Council ★805★
Top classics research-doctorate programs as evaluated by the National Research Council ★816★
Fall enrollment at the largest Chicago-area private institutions, by minority percentages, 1999 ★869★
U.S. News & World Report's national universities with the best academic reputation, 2000-01 ★1126★
U.S. News & World Report's national universities with the best faculty resources rank, 2000-01 ★1127★
U.S. News & World Report's national universities with the best student/faculty ratio, 2000-01 ★1130★
U.S. News & World Report's national universities with the highest percentage of full-time faculty, 2000-01 ★1136★
U.S. News & World Report's national universities with the lowest proportion of classes with 50 or more students, 2000-01 ★1142★
2001 mid-year endowment values of the 'wealthiest' U.S. universities ★1234★
Colleges and universities with the largest endowments, 2000 ★1237★
Highest undergraduate tuition and fees at private nonprofit, 4-year or above colleges and universities ★1461★
Highest undergraduate tuition and fees at colleges and universities in Illinois ★1500★
Top comparative literature research-doctorate programs as evaluated by the National Research Council ★1588★
Total baccalaureate social sciences and history degrees awarded to Asian Americans from U.S. colleges and universities, 1997-98 ★1742★
U.S. colleges and universities awarding the most business management and administrative services master's degrees to Asian Americans ★1760★
U.S. colleges and universities awarding the most mathematics master's degrees to Asian Americans ★1791★
U.S. colleges and universities awarding the most social sciences and history master's degrees to African Americans ★1801★
U.S. colleges and universities awarding the most social sciences and history master's degrees to Asian Americans ★1802★
U.S. colleges and universities awarding the most biological and life sciences doctorate degrees to Asian Americans ★2083★
U.S. colleges and universities awarding the most doctorates in humanities, 1999 ★2103★
U.S. colleges and universities awarding the most doctorates in social sciences, 1999 ★2107★
U.S. colleges and universities awarding the most physical sciences doctorate degrees to Asian Americans ★2119★

U.S. colleges and universities awarding the most social sciences and history doctorate degrees to African Americans ★2124★
U.S. colleges and universities awarding the most social sciences and history doctorate degrees to Asian Americans ★2125★
Most effective geosciences research-doctorate programs as evaluated by the National Research Council ★2150★
Top geosciences research-doctorate programs as evaluated by the National Research Council ★2152★
Economics departments by number of citations by top economists, 1971-92 ★2158★
Economics departments by number of citations per top economist, 1971-92 ★2159★
Economics departments by number of top economists, 1971-92 ★2160★
Institutions generating the most economic education research text, 1963-1990 ★2167★
Institutions most frequently contributing to the *American Economic Review* from 1911-1990 ★2168★
Institutions most frequently contributing to the *American Economic Review* from 1951-1990 ★2169★
U.S. universities with the greatest impact in economics, 1995-99 ★2179★
Economics Ph.D. programs by number of citations of top economist graduates, 1971-92 ★2204★
Economics Ph.D. programs by number of citations per top economist graduate, 1971-92 ★2205★
Economics Ph.D. programs by number of top economist graduates, 1971-92 ★2206★
Most effective economics research-doctorate programs as evaluated by the National Research Council ★2207★
Origin of doctorate for dissertation chairs in economics ★2208★
Origin of doctorate for economics faculty at Ph.D.-granting institutions ★2209★
Origin of doctorate for economics faculty at Ph.D.-granting institutions, by Ph.D. equivalents produced ★2210★
Top economics research-doctorate programs as evaluated by the National Research Council ★2213★
Most effective English language and literature research-doctorate programs as evaluated by the National Research Council ★2448★
Top English language and literature research-doctorate programs as evaluated by the National Research Council ★2451★
Faculty's scholarly reputation in the Ph.D.-granting departments of geography, 1925-1982 ★2518★
Top Ph.D.-granting departments of geography from 1925-1982 ★2521★
Top history research-doctorate programs as evaluated by the National Research Council ★2554★
U.S. universities publishing the most papers in the field of law, 1994-98 ★2623★
Academics' choices for best tax law programs, 2001 ★2632★
Acceptance rates at *U.S. News & World Report*'s top 10 law schools, 2001 ★2634★
Graduate employment after graduation percentage for *U.S. News & World Report*'s top 10 law schools, 2001 ★2635★
Graduate employment percentage for *U.S. News & World Report*'s top 10 law schools, 2001 ★2636★

Jurisdiction's overall bar passage rate for *U.S. News & World Report*'s top 10 law schools, 2001 ★2637★
Law schools with the best administrative law faculty, 1999-2000 ★2638★
Law schools with the best bankruptcy faculty, 1999-2000 ★2639★
Law schools with the best commercial law faculty, 1999-2000 ★2641★
Law schools with the best constitutional law (freedom of speech) faculty, 1999-2000 ★2644★
Law schools with the best constitutional law (general) faculty, 1999-2000 ★2645★
Law schools with the best corporate law and securities regulation faculty, 1999-2000 ★2646★
Law schools with the best criminal law (substantive) faculty, 1999-2000 ★2647★
Law schools with the best criminal procedure faculty, 1999-2000 ★2648★
Law schools with the best feminist legal theory faculty, 1999-2000 ★2651★
Law schools with the best law and economics faculty, 1999-2000 ★2657★
Law schools with the best moral and political theory (Continental traditions) faculty, 1999-2000 ★2663★
Law schools with the best tax faculty, 1999-2000 ★2664★
Law schools with the best Torts (including products liability) faculty, 1999-2000 ★2665★
Law schools with the highest quality, 1999-2000 ★2666★
School's bar passage rate in jurisdiction at *U.S. News & World Report*'s top 10 law schools, 2001 ★2667★
Student-faculty ratios at *U.S. News & World Report*'s top 10 law schools, 2001 ★2669★
Top law schools, 2001 ★2670★
Top law schools by reputation, as determined by academic personnel, 2001 ★2671★
Top law schools by reputation, as determined by lawyers and judges, 2001 ★2672★
Top law school student bodies, 1999-2000 ★2673★
Top university research libraries in the U.S. and Canada, 1998-99 ★2706★
Most effective linguistics research-doctorate programs as evaluated by the National Research Council ★2732★
Top linguistics research-doctorate programs as evaluated by the National Research Council ★2733★
Most effective mathematics research-doctorate programs as evaluated by the National Research Council ★2775★
Top mathematics research-doctorate programs as evaluated by the National Research Council ★2778★
Most effective statistics and biostatistics research-doctorate programs as evaluated by the National Research Council ★2780★
Top statistics and biostatistics research-doctorate programs as evaluated by the National Research Council ★2782★
Most effective music research-doctorate programs as evaluated by the National Research Council ★2895★
Top music research-doctorate programs as evaluated by the National Research Council ★2896★
U.S. universities with the greatest impact in pharmacology, 1994-98 ★2936★

Top philosophy research-doctorate programs as evaluated by the National Research Council ★2947★

Most effective astrophysics and astronomy research-doctorate programs as evaluated by the National Research Council ★3006★

Most effective physics research-doctorate programs as evaluated by the National Research Council ★3007★

Top astrophysics and astronomy research-doctorate programs as evaluated by the National Research Council ★3014★

Top physics research-doctorate programs as evaluated by the National Research Council ★3015★

Most effective physiology research-doctorate programs as evaluated by the National Research Council ★3021★

Top physiology research-doctorate programs as evaluated by the National Research Council ★3022★

Most effective political science research-doctorate programs as evaluated by the National Research Council ★3043★

Top political science research-doctorate programs as evaluated by the National Research Council ★3046★

Top religion research-doctorate programs as evaluated by the National Research Council ★3093★

U.S. universities with the highest concentrations in religion and theology, 1992-96 ★3094★

U.S. colleges and universities spending the most on chemical research equipment, 1998 ★3100★

U.S. colleges and universities with the most federal support for chemical research equipment, 1998 ★3103★

Average faculty salaries for institutions of higher education in Illinois, 2000-01 ★3700★

Private institutions of higher education that pay the highest salaries to female professors, 2000-01 ★3974★

U.S. institutions with the highest paid assistant professors, 2001 ★3977★

U.S. institutions with the highest paid full professors, 2001 ★3978★

U.S. universities publishing the most papers in the fields of sociology and anthropology, 1993-97 ★4350★

U.S. universities with the greatest impact in sociology and anthropology, 1995-99 ★4351★

Most effective sociology research-doctorate programs as evaluated by the National Research Council ★4352★

Top sociology research-doctorate programs as evaluated by the National Research Council ★4354★

Chicken Soup for the Teenage Soul III
Longest-running trade paperback bestsellers, 2000 ★282★

Chico High School
Outstanding secondary schools in Chico-Paradise, California ★4111★

Chico's FAS
Best small companies in the U.S. ★383★

Chief Buffalo Child Long Lance: The Glorious Impostor
Outstanding biography books, 2000 ★288★

Chief Kanim Middle School
Outstanding secondary schools in Seattle-Bellevue-Everett, Washington ★4227★

A Child Called "It"
Longest-running trade paperback bestsellers, 2000 ★282★

Child care worker
Jobs with the worst income scores ★2261★
Most desirable jobs in personal services ★2275★

Child-care workers, except private household
Occupations with the highest number of self-employed workers, 1998 ★2311★
Projected employment growth for selected occupations that require shorter moderate-term on-the-job training, 1998-2008 ★2321★

Child-care workers, private household
Occupations with the highest decline in employment, 1998-2008 ★2310★

Child day care services
Employment growth percentages for selected industries, 1998-2000 ★2294★
Industries with the highest projected growth rate, 1994-2005 ★2306★

Child Development
Most-cited social sciences journals, 1981-97 ★4340★

Child nutrition
Educational program activities expenditures, 2000 ★3992★

Childers; L. Dick
Top pay and benefits for the chief executive and top paid employees at Brenau University ★3210★

Children of the River
Outstanding audiobooks, 2000 ★287★

Children's Hospital, Boston
Top pediatrics hospitals in the U.S., 2000 ★2799★
Radcliffe Institute for Advanced Study fellowship recipients in the field of biomedicine, 2000-01 ★2880★

Children's Hospital, Denver
Top pediatrics hospitals in the U.S., 2000 ★2799★

Children's Hospital, Los Angeles
Top pediatrics hospitals in the U.S., 2000 ★2799★

Children's Hospital of Philadelphia
Top pediatrics hospitals in the U.S., 2000 ★2799★

Children's Hospital of Pittsburgh
Top pediatrics hospitals in the U.S., 2000 ★2799★

Children's Memorial Hospital, Chicago
Top pediatrics hospitals in the U.S., 2000 ★2799★

Childress; Josh
All-America boys' high school basketball 3rd team, 2001 ★163★

Chile
Eight grade science achievement scores from selected countries, 1999 ★14★
Eighth grade mathematics achievement scores from selected countries, 1999 ★2773★

China
CA journal literature abstracted, by country, 2000 ★757★
CA patents abstracted, by country, 2000 ★758★
Countries with the most computers, 2000 ★1603★
Countries with the lowest percentage of workers satisfied with their job ★2243★
Foreign countries with the highest enrollment of foreign students, 1999-2000 ★2496★
Countries with the most Internet users ★2583★
Countries with the lowest leader's salary ★3121★

China Telecom (Hong Kong)
Business Week's top emerging-market companies worldwide ★434★
Top information technology companies, 2000 ★544★

Chinese
Gender breakdown of language and literature doctorate recipients, by subfield, 1999 ★1937★
Language and literature doctorates awarded at U.S. colleges and universities, by subfield, 1999 ★1949★
Languages of requested materials from OCLC ILL, 1999 ★2679★

Chinese Taipei
Comparison of 8th grade science achievement scores, U.S. and worldwide, 1999 ★6★

Chipola Junior College
Lowest undergraduate tuition and fees at colleges and universities in Florida ★1495★

Chippewa Valley Technical College
Lowest undergraduate tuition and fees at colleges and universities in Wisconsin ★1571★

Chiquita Brands International
Fortune's highest ranked food production companies, 2000 ★464★

Chiropractor
Most desirable jobs in healthcare/medicine ★2273★

Chiropractors
Projected employment growth for selected occupations that require advanced education, 1998-2008 ★2318★

Chisholm; Shirley
Most influential African Americans in politics and civil rights ★3040★

Chisholm Trail Middle School
Outstanding secondary schools in Austin-San Marcos, Texas ★4090★

The Chocolate War
American Library Association's most frequently challenged books of the decade ★224★
American Library Associations most frequently challenged books for the 1990s ★742★
Most frequently banned books in the 1990s ★745★
People for the American Way's list of most frequently challenged books, 1982-1992 ★747★
People for the American Way's list of most frequently challenged books, 1991-1992 ★748★

Choice; Genesis
All-America girls' high school basketball 3rd team, 2001 ★172★

Chonko; Lawrence B.
Highest impact authors in the *Journal of Business Research*, by adjusted number of citations in 12 journals, 1985-1999 ★692★
Highest impact authors in the *Journal of Business Research*, by number of citations in 12 journals, 1985-1999 ★693★

Choppin State College
Historically black colleges and universities awarding the most master's degrees to African Americans ★1670★

Choreographer
Jobs considered the most competitive ★2245★

Most desirable jobs in the arts ★2277★
Chowan College
Average faculty salaries for institutions of higher education in North Carolina, 2000-01 ★3720★
Christ the King Catholic School
Outstanding secondary schools in Dallas, Texas ★4120★
Christ the King School
Outstanding secondary schools in Shreveport-Bossier City, Louisiana ★4230★
Christendom College
U.S. News & World Report's national liberal arts colleges with students least in debt, 1999 ★1385★
Christian Brothers University
U.S. News & World Report's southern regional universities with the best student/faculty ratios, 2000-01 ★1435★
Highest undergraduate tuition and fees at colleges and universities in Tennessee ★1558★
Christian Heritage College
U.S. News & World Report's western regional liberal arts colleges with students least in debt, 1999 ★1397★
Christiano; Paul
Top pay and benefits for the chief executive and top paid employees at Carnegie Mellon University ★3223★
Christiansen; David E.
Top pay and benefits for the chief executive and top paid employees at the University of Scranton ★3567★
Christiansen; J. Richard
Top pay and benefits for the chief executive and top paid employees at Assumption College ★3181★
Christine
Most frequently banned books in the 1990s ★745★
The Christmas Gift
Publishers Weekly Off-the-Cuff Awards winner for best treatment of a social issue, 2000 ★342★
Christofferson; Robert
Top pay and benefits for the chief executive and top paid employees at the University of the Pacific ★3571★
Christopher Newport University
State appropriations for Virginia's institutions of higher education, 2000-01 ★1299★
U.S. News & World Report's top public southern regional liberal arts colleges, 2000-01 ★1378★
Average faculty salaries for institutions of higher education in Virginia, 2000-01 ★3735★
The Chronicle of Higher Education
Most cited education serials in technical communication journals from 1988 to 1997 ★4418★
The Chronological Encyclopedia of Discoveries in Space
Outstanding reference sources, 2000 ★370★
Chun; David
All-America boys' high school soccer team defenders, 2001 ★165★
Chun; Kelvin
All-USA Teacher Teams, First Team, 2000 ★4399★
Church; Frank V.
Top pay and benefits for the chief executive and top paid employees at Connecticut College ★3254★

Churchill; Caryl
Top playwrights of the twentieth century ★4436★
Churchill; John
Top pay and benefits for the chief executive and top paid employees at Hendrix College ★3331★
Churchill Junior High School
Outstanding secondary schools in Middlesex-Somerset-Hunterdon, New Jersey ★4179★
Churchill Senior High School
Outstanding suburban public high schools in Metro Detroit ★4258★
Cicarelli; James S.
Top pay and benefits for the chief executive and top paid employees at Roosevelt University ★3466★
The Cider House Rules
Longest-running mass market paperback bestsellers, 2000 ★280★
Cigar
Percentage of high school students using tobacco products by gender ★4373★
Percentage of middle school students using tobacco products by gender ★4374★
Cigarettes
Percentage of high school students using tobacco products by gender ★4373★
Percentage of middle school students using tobacco products by gender ★4374★
Cigna
Fortune's highest ranked health care companies, 2000 ★469★
Top recruiters for finance/banking jobs for 2000-01 master's degree recipients ★664★
Top recruiters for industrial engineering jobs for 2000-01 master's degree recipients ★2414★
Top recruiters for math/actuarial science jobs for 2000-01 bachelor's degree recipients ★2771★
Best companies for working mothers in offering advancement opportunities for women ★4447★
Cimarron Middle School
Outstanding secondary schools in Oklahoma City, Oklahoma ★4196★
Cincinnati, Clermont College; University of
Highest undergraduate tuition and fees at public 2-year colleges and universities ★1462★
Cincinnati, Raymond Walters College; University of
Highest undergraduate tuition and fees at public 2-year colleges and universities ★1462★
Cincinnati; University of
Top business schools for within-discipline research performance in production/operations management, 1986-1998 ★648★
Division I NCAA colleges with that graduated none of their African American male basketball players, 1990-91 to 1993-94 ★930★
State appropriations for Ohio's institutions of higher education, 2000-01 ★1288★
Universities with the most-cited scholars in *Criminal Justice and Behavior* ★1648★
Universities with the most-cited scholars in *Criminology* ★1649★
Universities with the most-cited scholars in *Journal of Quantitative Criminology* ★1650★
Universities with the most-cited scholars in *Journal of Research in Crime and Delinquency* ★1651★

Universities with the most-cited scholars in *Justice Quarterly* ★1652★
U.S. colleges and universities awarding the most health professions and related sciences first professional degrees to African Americans ★1847★
U.S. colleges and universities awarding the most doctorate degrees to African Americans ★2095★
Academics' choices for best pediatrics programs, 2001 ★2823★
U.S. universities with the greatest impact in psychiatry, 1995-99 ★3060★
Average faculty salaries for institutions of higher education in Ohio, 2000-01 ★3722★
Cinema Verite: Defining the Moment
Most notable videos for adults, 2001 ★2891★
Cintas
Fortune's highest ranked outsourcing services companies, 2000 ★483★
Top services industries in Standard & Poor's 500, 2001 ★558★
Cipolla; Michael R.
Top pay and benefits for the chief executive and top paid employees at D'Youville College ★3278★
The Circle of Hanh
Outstanding biography books, 2000 ★288★
Circuit City Group
Fortune's highest ranked specialty retailers, 2000 ★497★
Circulation
Hematology journals with the greatest impact measure, 1981-98 ★2808★
Hematology journals with the greatest impact measure, 1994-98 ★2809★
Circulation Research
Hematology journals with the greatest impact measure, 1981-98 ★2808★
Hematology journals with the greatest impact measure, 1994-98 ★2809★
Top science journals by impact factor ★4281★
Circus Family Dog
Smithsonian's best books for children ages 1 to 6 ★363★
Cirner; Randall
Top pay and benefits for the chief executive and top paid employees at the Franciscan University of Steubenville ★3532★
Cisco Systems
Business Week's best companies in the United States ★411★
Business Week's top companies worldwide ★433★
Fortune's highest ranked network communications companies, 2000 ★482★
Top information technology companies, 2000 ★544★
Top office equipment and computers companies in Standard & Poor's 500, 2001 ★551★
Largest technology companies in the U.S. in terms of annual revenue, 2000 ★4429★
Ciskanik; John
Top pay and benefits for the chief executive and top paid employees at Christendom College ★3232★
Cisse; Ousmane
All-America boys' high school basketball 1st team, 2001 ★161★
The Citadel
State appropriations for South Carolina's institutions of higher education, 2000-01 ★1293★

U.S. News & World Report's southern regional universities with the best academic reputation scores, 2000-01 ★1433★
U.S. News & World Report's southern regional universities with the best alumni giving rates, 2000-01 ★1434★
U.S. News & World Report's southern regional universities with the highest graduation rates, 2000-01 ★1438★
U.S. News & World Report's southern regional universities with the highest percentage of full-time faculty, 2000-01 ★1440★
U.S. News & World Report's top public southern regional universities, 2000-01 ★1443★
U.S. News & World Report's top southern regional universities, 2000-01 ★1444★
Average faculty salaries for institutions of higher education in South Carolina, 2000-01 ★3728★

Citgo
Fortune's highest ranked petroleum refining companies, 2000 ★484★

Citibank
Top internships in the U.S. with the highest compensation, 2001 ★2611★

Citic Pacific
Business Week's best companies in Hong Kong ★395★

Citigroup
Business Week's best companies in terms of profits ★406★
Business Week's best companies in the United States ★411★
Business Week's top companies worldwide ★433★
Fortune's highest ranked money center banks, 2000 ★478★
Fortune's most admired companies for employee talent ★514★
Fortune's most admired companies for financial soundness ★515★
Fortune's most admired companies for innovation ★516★
Fortune's most admired companies for long-term investment value ★517★
Fortune's most admired companies for quality of management ★518★
Fortune's most admired companies for use of corporate assets ★521★
Top nonbank financial companies in Standard & Poor's 500, 2001 ★550★

The Citizens Network for Foreign Affairs
Most selective internships in the U.S., 2001 ★2610★

Citrix Systems
Business Week's best performing companies with the lowest 1-year shareholder returns ★422★
Business Week's top companies in terms of earnings, 2000 ★428★
Business Week's top companies in terms of market value, 2000 ★429★

City of Chicago School District 299 Cook
Illinois school districts with the highest paid superintendents, 1999-2000 ★3986★

City College of San Francisco
Community colleges in North America with the highest enrollment ★852★
Community colleges with the highest enrollment of foreign students, 1998-99 ★2493★

City University
U.S. colleges and universities awarding the most education master's degrees to Native Americans ★1772★
U.S. colleges and universities awarding the most master's degrees to Native Americans ★1789★
U.S. colleges and universities awarding the most psychology master's degrees to Asian Americans ★1798★
Average faculty salaries for institutions of higher education without academic ranks in Washington, 2000-01 ★3768★

City University of New York
U.S. universities with the highest concentrations in literary criticism, 1992-96 ★2735★

Civil
Engineering doctorates awarded at U.S. colleges and universities, by subfield, 1999 ★1923★
Gender breakdown of engineering doctorate recipients, by subfield, 1999 ★1934★

Civil engineer
Most desirable jobs in production/manufacturing ★2276★
Occupations with the highest average annual salaries for college graduates, 1998 ★3132★

Civil engineering
Expected starting salaries of 2000-01 bachelor's degree recipients, by specific major ★3131★

Cizadlo; Gerald
Top pay and benefits for the chief executive and top paid employees at the College of St. Scholastica ★3530★

CKE Restaurants
Fortune's highest ranked food services companies, 2000 ★465★
Fortune's least admired companies for social responsibility ★512★
Fortune's least admired companies for use of corporate assets ★513★

Claar; Joan M.
Top pay and benefits for the chief executive and top paid employees at Cornell College in Iowa ★3256★

Clackamas Community College
Lowest undergraduate tuition and fees at colleges and universities in Oregon ★1548★
Average faculty salaries for institutions of higher education without academic ranks in Oregon, 2000-01 ★3764★

Claflin College
U.S. colleges and universities with the highest percentage of African Americans enrolled, 1997 ★222★

Claflin University
U.S. News & World Report's southern regional liberal arts colleges with the highest alumni giving rates, 2000-01 ★1371★
U.S. News & World Report's southern regional liberal arts colleges with the highest freshmen retention rates, 2000-01 ★1372★
U.S. News & World Report's southern regional liberal arts colleges with the highest graduation rates, 2000-01 ★1373★
U.S. News & World Report's southern regional liberal arts colleges with the highest percentage of full-time faculty, 2000-01 ★1374★
U.S. News & World Report's southern regional liberal arts colleges with the lowest acceptance rates, 2000-01 ★1377★
U.S. News & World Report's best undergraduate fees among southern regional liberal arts colleges by discount tuition, 2000 ★1383★

Clapper; James M.
Top pay and benefits for the chief executive and top paid employees at Belmont University ★3198★

Clardy; Donald B.
Top pay and benefits for the chief executive and top paid employees at Baker University ★3188★

Claremont Graduate University
U.S. colleges and universities awarding the most mathematics master's degrees to Asian Americans ★1791★
U.S. colleges and universities awarding the most mathematics master's degrees to Hispanic Americans ★1792★
U.S. colleges and universities awarding the most social sciences and history master's degrees to Hispanic Americans ★1803★
Average faculty salaries for institutions of higher education in California, 2000-01 ★3692★

Claremont McKenna College
U.S. colleges and universities with the best quality of life ★1034★
U.S. News & World Report's national liberal arts colleges with the best selectivity rank, 2000-01 ★1325★
U.S. News & World Report's national liberal arts colleges with the best student/faculty ratios, 2000-01 ★1326★
U.S. News & World Report's national liberal arts colleges with the highest percentage of freshmen in the top 10% of their high school class, 2000-01 ★1332★
U.S. News & World Report's national liberal arts colleges with the lowest acceptance rates, 2000-01 ★1336★
U.S. News & World Report's best undergraduate fees among national liberal arts colleges by discount tuition, 2000 ★1381★
Highest undergraduate tuition and fees at colleges and universities in California ★1486★
Elite liberal arts colleges ranked by per capita quality adjusted scholarship articles in the field of economics, 1975-94 ★2164★
Elite liberal arts colleges ranked by quality adjusted scholarship articles in the field of economics, 1975-94 ★2165★
Top associate professor economists at elite liberal arts colleges, 1975-94 ★2174★
Top full professor economists at elite liberal arts colleges, 1975-94 ★2175★
U.S. liberal arts colleges with the highest paid full professors, 2001 ★3980★

Clarence Goes Out West and Meets a Purple Horse
Smithsonian's best books for children ages 1 to 6 ★363★

Clarendon Press
Publishers, journals and proceedings with the lowest citations (Class 6) ★2571★

Clarian Health Partners
Top cancer hospitals in the U.S., 2000 ★2787★

Clarion University
Average faculty salaries for institutions of higher education in Pennsylvania, 2000-01 ★3725★

Clark Atlanta University
U.S. colleges and universities with the highest percentage of African Americans enrolled, 1997 ★222★

Most dangerous college campuses in the U.S. ★712★
U.S. colleges and universities with the largest numerical increases in drug arrests, 1998 ★734★
Retention rates of African American students at historically black institutions, 1997-98 ★1120★
Historically black colleges and universities awarding the most master's degrees to African Americans ★1670★
Total baccalaureate biology/life sciences degrees awarded to African Americans from U.S. colleges and universities, 1997-98 ★1679★
Total baccalaureate communications degrees awarded to African Americans from U.S. colleges and universities, 1997-98 ★1687★
Total baccalaureate mathematics degrees awarded to African Americans from U.S. colleges and universities, 1997-98 ★1729★
Total baccalaureate psychology degrees awarded to African Americans from U.S. colleges and universities, 1997-98 ★1737★
Total ethnic/cultural studies master's degrees awarded to African Americans from U.S. colleges and universities, 1997-98 ★1747★
U.S. colleges and universities awarding the most business management and administrative services master's degrees to African Americans ★1759★
U.S. colleges and universities awarding the most computer and information sciences master's degrees to African Americans ★1766★
U.S. colleges and universities awarding the most education master's degrees to African Americans ★1769★
U.S. colleges and universities awarding the most master's degrees to African Americans ★1785★
U.S. colleges and universities awarding the most mathematics master's degrees to African Americans ★1790★
U.S. colleges and universities awarding the most physical sciences master's degrees to African Americans ★1793★
Historically black colleges and universities awarding the most doctorate degrees to African Americans ★1945★
Institutions awarding the most doctorate degrees to African Americans, 1997-98 ★1948★
U.S. colleges and universities awarding the most doctorate degrees to African Americans ★2095★
U.S. colleges and universities awarding the most education doctorate degrees to African Americans ★2108★
U.S. colleges and universities awarding the most social sciences and history doctorate degrees to African Americans ★2124★

Clark; Bobby Wayne
Top pay and benefits for the chief executive and top paid employees at Guilford College ★3316★

Clark County, NV
U.S. school districts with the highest number of vacancies for K-12 teachers ★2331★
Largest public school districts in the U.S. ★4016★

Clark High School
Outstanding secondary schools in Dallas, Texas ★4120★

Clark Intermediate School
Outstanding secondary schools in Fresno, California ★4138★

Clark; J. Maurice
Authors most frequently contributing to the *American Economic Review* from 1911-1990 ★2156★

Clark Jr.; Clifford E.
Top pay and benefits for the chief executive and top paid employees at Carleton College ★3222★

Clark Jr.; Leland C.
American Chemical Society 2001 award winners (Group 2) ★752★

Clark; Kim B.
Top pay and benefits for the chief executive and top paid employees at Harvard University ★3327★

Clark; Laron
Top pay and benefits for the chief executive and top paid employees at Morehouse College ★3408★

Clark; Leonard
Top pay and benefits for the chief executive and top paid employees at Earlham College ★3279★

Clark; Ricardo
All-America boys' high school soccer team midfielders, 2001 ★168★

Clark; Robert A.
Top pay and benefits for the chief executive and top paid employees at the University of Tampa ★3569★

Clark; Ruth A.
Top published female authors (1915-1985) in the field of communication studies ★4363★

Clark University
U.S. colleges and universities with a diverse student body ★1012★
Private, 4-year undergraduate colleges and universities producing the most Ph.D.'s in all fields of study, 1981-1990 ★2028★
Faculty's scholarly reputation in the Ph.D.-granting departments of geography, 1925-1982 ★2518★
Most effective geography research-doctorate programs as evaluated by the National Research Council ★2519★
Top geography research-doctorate programs as evaluated by the National Research Council ★2520★
Top Ph.D.-granting departments of geography from 1925-1982 ★2521★
Radcliffe Institute for Advanced Study fellowship recipient in the field of political science, 2000-01 ★3041★
Private, 4-year undergraduate colleges and universities producing the most Ph.D.'s in political science and international relations, 1981-1990 ★3045★
Private, 4-year undergraduate colleges and universities producing the most Ph.D.'s in psychology, 1920-1990 ★3066★
Private, 4-year undergraduate colleges and universities producing the most Ph.D.'s in psychology, 1981-1990 ★3067★
Average faculty salaries for institutions of higher education in Massachusetts, 2000-01 ★3708★
Private, 4-year undergraduate colleges and universities producing the most Ph.D.'s in the sciences, 1981-1990 ★4295★

Clarke College
U.S. News & World Report's midwestern regional liberal arts colleges with the best student/faculty ratios, 2000-01 ★1339★
U.S. News & World Report's midwestern regional liberal arts colleges with the highest proportion of classes having 20 students or less, 2000-01 ★1347★
U.S. News & World Report's midwestern regional liberal arts colleges with the lowest acceptance rates, 2000-01 ★1348★

Clarke Middle School
Outstanding secondary schools in Boston, Massachusetts-New Hampshire ★4100★

Clarke; Ronald V.G.
Most-cited scholars in *British Journal of Criminology* ★1637★

Clarke; R.V.G.
Most cited authors in the journal *Crime and Justice*, 1990 to 1995 ★1617★

Clarkson College
Institutions censured by the American Association of University Professors, 2001 ★1067★

Clarkson University
Private, 4-year undergraduate colleges and universities producing the most Ph.D.'s in the computer sciences, 1920-1990 ★1595★
Private, 4-year undergraduate colleges and universities producing the most Ph.D.'s in the computer sciences, 1981-1990 ★1596★
Doctorate-granting-institutions with the highest percentage of non-U.S. citizen doctoral degrees awarded, 1999 ★1907★
Average faculty salaries for institutions of higher education in New York, 2000-01 ★3719★

Clary; Donnie
Top pay and benefits for the chief executive and top paid employees at Gardner-Webb University ★3303★

Class Dismissed: A Year in the Life of an American High School, a Glimpse into the Heart of a Nation
American School Board Journal's notable education books, 2000 ★225★

Class, State, and Crime
Most-cited works in critical criminology publications ★1645★

Classics
Gender breakdown of humanities doctorate recipients, by subfield, 1999 ★1936★
Humanities doctorates awarded at U.S. colleges and universities, by subfield, 1999 ★1946★

Clatsop Community College
Lowest undergraduate tuition and fees at colleges and universities in Oregon ★1548★

Clay; David S.
Top pay and benefits for the chief executive and top paid employees at Grinnell College ★3315★

Clays & Clay Minerals
Soil science journals by citation impact, 1981-99 ★188★
Soil science journals by citation impact, 1995-99 ★189★
Soil science journals by citation impact, 1999 ★190★

Clayton College and State University
Division II NCAA colleges with the 0% graduation rates for men's basketball players, 1993-94 ★941★
Division II NCAA colleges with the lowest graduation rates for all sports, 1993-94 ★947★
State appropriations for Georgia's institutions of higher education, 2000-01 ★1263★

Clayton; Michael
All-American boy's high school football receivers, 2000 ★185★

Clayton; Ronnie
Top pay and benefits for the chief executive and top paid employees at Rollins College ★3465★

Clayville Library Association
Highest Hennen's American Public Library Ratings for libraries serving a population of 999 and under ★2691★

Cleaners and servants, private household
Occupations with the highest decline in employment, 1998-2008 ★2310★

Cleaning and shaping the root canal
Endodontic articles with the most citations, 1974 through 1999 ★1864★

Clear Channel Communications
Fortune's highest ranked entertainment companies, 2000 ★462★
Top publishing and broadcasting companies in Standard & Poor's 500, 2001 ★553★

Cleary College
Average faculty salaries for institutions of higher education in Michigan, 2000-01 ★3709★

Cleburne High School
Outstanding suburban public high schools in Metro Dallas-Ft. Worth ★4257★

Cleman; Michael W.
Top pay and benefits for the chief executive and top paid employees at Yale University ★3639★

Clemens; Kellen
All-American boy's high school football quarterbacks, 2000 ★184★

Clemson University
Institutions receiving the most corporate gifts, 1999-2000 ★1243★
State appropriations for South Carolina's institutions of higher education, 2000-01 ★1293★
Institutions generating the most economic education research text, 1963-1990 ★2167★
Average faculty salaries for institutions of higher education in South Carolina, 2000-01 ★3728★

Clendenning; Bonnie
Top pay and benefits for the chief executive and top paid employees at Radcliffe College ★3450★

Clergy
Projected employment growth for selected occupations that require advanced education, 1998-2008 ★2318★

Clerk, secretary, office manager
Occupational fields of tribal college graduates that are currently employed ★964★

Clermont College
Average faculty salaries for institutions of higher education in Ohio, 2000-01 ★3722★

Cleveland
U.S. market areas with the highest percentage of adults having internet access ★2607★

Cleveland; Charles E.
Top pay and benefits for the chief executive and top paid employees at Whitman College ★3623★

Cleveland Clinic
Top cardiology and heart surgery hospitals in the U.S., 2000 ★2788★
Top endocrinology hospitals in the U.S., 2000 ★2789★
Top gastroenterology hospitals in the U.S., 2000 ★2790★
Top geriatrics hospitals in the U.S., 2000 ★2791★
Top hospitals in the U.S., 2000 ★2793★
Top nephrology hospitals in the U.S., 2000 ★2794★
Top neurology and neurosurgery hospitals in the U.S., 2000 ★2795★
Top ophthalmology hospitals in the U.S., 2000 ★2796★
Top orthopedics hospitals in the U.S., 2000 ★2797★
Top ortolaryngology hospitals in the U.S., 2000 ★2798★
Top rheumatology hospitals in the U.S., 2000 ★2802★
Top urology hospitals in the U.S., 2000 ★2803★

Cleveland Heights-University Heights Public Library
Highest Hennen's American Public Library Ratings for libraries serving a population of 50,000 to 99,999 ★2697★

Cleveland Institute of Music
Highest undergraduate tuition and fees at colleges and universities in Ohio ★1543★

Cleveland Middle School
Outstanding secondary schools in Albuquerque, New Mexico ★4080★

Cleveland State Community College
Lowest undergraduate tuition and fees at colleges and universities in Tennessee ★1559★
Average faculty salaries for institutions of higher education in Tennessee, 2000-01 ★3730★

Cleveland State University
State appropriations for Ohio's institutions of higher education, 2000-01 ★1288★
U.S. News & World Report's national universities with students most in debt, 1999 ★1476★
Average faculty salaries for institutions of higher education in Ohio, 2000-01 ★3722★

Clevenger; T.
Highest ranked inactive communication studies researchers ★2748★
Speech communication's most published scholars between 1915-1985 ★4362★

Click, Clack, Moo: Cows That Type
Most notable books for young readers, 2001 ★319★
Outstanding children's picture books, 2000 ★331★
Publishers Weekly Off-the-Cuff Awards winner for best book title, 2000 ★338★
Publishers Weekly Off-the-Cuff Awards winner for funniest picture book, 2000 ★350★

Clicks and Mortar
Library Journal's most notable new economy books, 2000 ★271★

Climbing Back
Library Journal's best poetry books, 2000 ★244★

Cline; Erin
All-USA College Academic First Team, 2001 ★2★

Clinical
Gender breakdown of psychology doctorate recipients, by subfield, 1999 ★1941★
Psychology doctorates awarded at U.S. colleges and universities, by subfield, 1999 ★2043★

Clinical immunology and infectious diseases
Clinical medicine subfields with the highest impact measure, 1981-1997 ★2873★

Clinical medicine
United Kingdom's contribution of papers in the sciences, by field, 1995-99 ★4297★
Austria's contribution of papers in the sciences by field, 1992-96 ★4298★
Austria's contribution of papers in the sciences, by field, 1995-99 ★4299★
Belgium's contribution of papers in the sciences by field, 1992-96 ★4301★
Belgium's contribution of papers in the sciences, by field, 1995-99 ★4302★
Denmark's contribution of papers in the sciences, by field, 1994-98 ★4306★
Denmark's contribution of papers in the sciences, by field, 1995-99 ★4307★
England's contribution of papers in the sciences, by field, 1994-98 ★4308★
Finland's contribution of papers in the sciences by field, 1992-96 ★4309★
Finland's contribution of papers in the sciences, by field, 1995-99 ★4310★
Germany's contribution of papers in the sciences, by field, 1995-99 ★4313★
Hong Kong's contribution of papers in the sciences, by field, 1995-99 ★4314★
Ireland's contribution of papers in the sciences, by field, 1994-98 ★4315★
Italy's contribution of papers in the sciences, by field, 1995-99 ★4316★
Italy's relative impact in the sciences by field, 1992-96 ★4317★
Netherlands' contribution of papers in the sciences, by field, 1995-99 ★4321★
Norway's contribution of papers in the sciences, by field, 1994-98 ★4323★
South Africa's contribution of papers in the sciences, by field, 1994-98 ★4326★
Sweden's contribution of papers in the sciences by field, 1993-97 ★4330★
Sweden's contribution of papers in the sciences, by field, 1995-99 ★4331★
Switzerland's contribution of papers in the sciences, by field, 1994-98 ★4332★
Switzerland's contribution of papers in the sciences, by field, 1995-99 ★4333★
Taiwan contribution of papers in the sciences, by field, 1995-99 ★4334★
Turkey's contribution of papers in the sciences, by field, 1995-99 ★4335★

Clinical Nephrology
Urology and nephrology journals with the greatest impact measure, 1981-98 ★2816★

Clinical psychology and psychiatry
Clinical medicine subfields with the highest impact measure, 1981-1997 ★2873★

Clinics in Haematology
Hematology journals with the greatest impact measure, 1981-98 ★2808★

Clinton Community College
Lowest undergraduate tuition and fees at colleges and universities in Iowa ★1505★
Lowest undergraduate tuition and fees at colleges and universities in New York ★1538★
Average faculty salaries for institutions of higher education in New York, 2000-01 ★3719★

Clor; Harry
Top pay and benefits for the chief executive and top paid employees at Kenyon College ★3359★

Clorox
Fortune's highest ranked soaps and cosmetics companies, 2000 ★496★

Close; Lanny G.
Top pay and benefits for the chief executive and top paid employees at Columbia University ★3251★

Clovis Community College
Lowest undergraduate tuition and fees at colleges and universities in New Mexico ★1536★
Average faculty salaries for institutions of higher education without academic ranks in New Mexico, 2000-01 ★3759★

Clovis High School
Outstanding secondary schools in Fresno, California ★4138★

Cloyd; J. Timothy
Top pay and benefits for the chief executive and top paid employees at Hendrix College ★3331★

CLP Holdings
Business Week's best companies in Hong Kong ★395★

The Cluetrain Manifesto
Library Journal's most notable digital technology books, 2000 ★256★

"Clustal W:Improving the sensitivity of prog. mult. sequence align. through sequence weighting, position-spec. gap penalties and weight matrix choice"
Institute for Scientific Information's most cited papers, 1990-98 ★4282★

Clyne-Lindberg; Patricia
Top pay and benefits for the chief executive and top paid employees at Georgian Court College ★3307★

CNF Inc.
Top recruiters for systems engineer jobs for 2000-01 bachelor's degree recipients ★2336★
Top recruiters for computer engineering jobs for 2000-01 bachelor's degree recipients ★2352★
Top recruiters for systems engineer jobs for 2000-01 master's degree recipients ★2371★
Top recruiters for computer engineering jobs for 2000-01 master's degree recipients ★2400★

CNF Transportation
Fortune's highest ranked trucking companies, 2000 ★503★

CNN
Top internships in the U.S., 2001 ★2612★

Coase; Ronald H.
Most cited economists ★2185★

Coast Dental Services
Companies with the worst two-year total returns since 1998 ★437★

Coastal Carolina University
Division I NCAA colleges with that graduated less than 20% of their African American male athletes, 1990-91 to 1993-94 ★928★
State appropriations for South Carolina's institutions of higher education, 2000-01 ★1293★
Average faculty salaries for institutions of higher education in South Carolina, 2000-01 ★3728★

Coates; Geoffrey W.
Winner of the American Chemical Society's Arthur C. Cope Awards, 2001 ★795★

Coburn; Thomas B.
Top pay and benefits for the chief executive and top paid employees at St. Lawrence University ★3477★

Coca-Cola
Fortune's highest ranked beverages companies, 2000 ★450★

Coca-Cola Enterprises
Business Week's best companies in the United States ★411★
Fortune's highest ranked beverages companies, 2000 ★450★
Corporations making the most contributions to African American communities, 1995 ★2941★

Cochise College
Lowest undergraduate tuition and fees at colleges and universities in Arizona ★1483★
Average faculty salaries for institutions of higher education without academic ranks in Arizona, 2000-01 ★3741★

Cochran, Jr.; Johnnie L.
Most influential African Americans in politics and civil rights ★3040★

Cochrane; Ryan
All-America boys' high school soccer team defenders, 2001 ★165★

Code
Library Journal's notable new magazines, 1999 ★2923★

Cody; Shaun
All-American boy's high school football linemen, 2000 ★183★

Coe College
Highest undergraduate tuition and fees at colleges and universities in Iowa ★1504★
Average faculty salaries for institutions of higher education in Iowa, 2000-01 ★3702★

Coeur d'Alene, ID
Best 'green & clean' places to live ★3077★

Coffeyville Community College
Lowest undergraduate tuition and fees at colleges and universities in Kansas ★1507★

Cofield; Joseph
Top pay and benefits for the chief executive and top paid employees at Emerson College ★3287★

Cogan; Neil H.
Top pay and benefits for the chief executive and top paid employees at Quinnipiac University ★3449★

Cognitive Brain Research
Artificial intelligence journals by citation impact, 1981-99 ★94★
Artificial intelligence journals by citation impact, 1995-99 ★95★
Artificial intelligence journals by citation impact, 1999 ★96★
Artificial intelligence journals with the greatest impact measure, 1994-98 ★98★
Artificial intelligence journals with the greatest impact measure, 1998 ★99★

Cognitive and psycholinguistics
Gender breakdown of psychology doctorate recipients, by subfield, 1999 ★1941★
Psychology doctorates awarded at U.S. colleges and universities, by subfield, 1999 ★2043★

Cognitive Psychology
Most cited psychology serials in technical communication journals from 1988 to 1997 ★4423★

Cognitive Science
Most cited psychology serials in technical communication journals from 1988 to 1997 ★4423★

Cognizant Technology Solutions
Best small companies in the U.S. ★383★
Top companies in terms of growth, 2000 ★534★

Cohen; Arnold B.
Top pay and benefits for the chief executive and top paid employees at Villanova University ★3595★

Cohen; Elaine
Top pay and benefits for the chief executive and top paid employees at the College of Notre Dame in California ★3526★

Cohen; Jacqueline
Most cited authors in the journal *Journal of Quantitative Criminology*, 1990 to 1995 ★1628★
Most cited authors in three criminology journals ★1634★
Most-cited scholars in *Criminology* ★1639★

Cohen; Lawrence E.
Most cited authors in three criminal justice journals ★1633★
Most cited authors in three criminology journals ★1634★

Cohen; Leonard
Canada's best performing artists of the 20th century ★74★

Cohen; Mort
Top pay and benefits for the chief executive and top paid employees at Golden Gate University ★3310★

Cohen; Stanley
Most-cited scholars in *Australian and New Zealand Journal of Criminology* ★1636★
Most cited scholars in critical criminology ★1640★
Most-cited scholars in critical criminology publications ★1641★

Cohen; Warren
Top pay and benefits for the chief executive and top paid employees at Whittier College ★3624★

Cohon; Jared L.
Top pay and benefits for the chief executive and top paid employees at Carnegie Mellon University ★3223★

Coke Stevenson Middle School
Outstanding secondary schools in San Antonio, Texas ★4219★

Coker College
U.S. News & World Report's southern regional liberal arts colleges with the best student/faculty ratios, 2000-01 ★1368★
U.S. News & World Report's southern regional liberal arts colleges with the highest alumni giving rates, 2000-01 ★1371★
U.S. News & World Report's southern regional liberal arts colleges with the highest proportion of classes having 20 students or less, 2000-01 ★1375★
Highest undergraduate tuition and fees at colleges and universities in South Carolina ★1554★

Colby College
U.S. colleges and universities most accepting of alternative lifestyles ★986★
U.S. colleges and universities with the best food service program ★1031★
U.S. colleges and universities with the most attractive campuses ★1039★
U.S. News & World Report's national liberal arts colleges with the highest proportion of classes having 50 or more students, 2000-01 ★1334★
U.S. News & World Report's national liberal arts colleges with the lowest acceptance rates, 2000-01 ★1336★

Elite liberal arts colleges ranked by per capita quality adjusted scholarship articles in the field of economics, 1975-94 ★2164★
Top assistant professor economists at elite liberal arts colleges, 1975-94 ★2173★
U.S. bachelor's institutions with the largest number of students studying abroad, 1998-99 ★2511★
Average faculty salaries for institutions of higher education in Maine, 2000-01 ★3706★
U.S. liberal arts colleges with the highest paid full professors, 2001 ★3980★

Colby Community College
Lowest undergraduate tuition and fees at colleges and universities in Kansas ★1507★

Colby-Sawyer College
U.S. News & World Report's northern regional liberal arts colleges with the best student/faculty ratios, 2000-01 ★1353★
U.S. News & World Report's northern regional liberal arts colleges with the highest acceptance rates, 2000-01 ★1355★
Highest undergraduate tuition and fees at colleges and universities in New Hampshire ★1531★

Cold Little Duck, Duck, Duck
Most notable books for young readers, 2001 ★319★

Colditz; Graham A.
Most-cited researchers in epidemiology, 1981-1998 ★2876★

Cole; Charles D.
Top pay and benefits for the chief executive and top paid employees at Samford University ★3490★

Cole Jr.; Thomas W.
Top pay and benefits for the chief executive and top paid employees at Clark Atlanta University ★3237★

Cole; Nat "King"
Most influential African American entertainers ★77★

Colegio Universitario del Este
U.S. college campuses reporting murders or non-negligent manslaughters, 1999 ★728★
Highest undergraduate tuition and fees at colleges and universities in Puerto Rico ★1551★

Coleman; Carole T.
Top pay and benefits for the chief executive and top paid employees at Wheeling Jesuit University ★3622★

Coleman; Elizabeth
Top pay and benefits for the chief executive and top paid employees at Bennington College ★3201★

Coleman; Joseph F.
Top pay and benefits for the chief executive and top paid employees at Gwynedd-Mercy College ★3318★

Coleman; Winifred E.
Top pay and benefits for the chief executive and top paid employees at Saint Joseph College in Connecticut ★3475★

Colemon; Rev. Johnnie
Most influential African Americans in religion ★3091★

Coles; Julius
Top pay and benefits for the chief executive and top paid employees at Morehouse College ★3408★

Coley; Joan Develin
Top pay and benefits for the chief executive and top paid employees at Western Maryland College ★3614★

Colgate-Palmolive
Business Week's best performing companies with the highest return on equity, 2000 ★420★
Fortune's highest ranked soaps and cosmetics companies, 2000 ★496★
Top consumer products companies in Standard & Poor's 500, 2001 ★536★
Highly recommended public companies for women executives, 2000 ★4453★

Colgate University
Private, 4-year undergraduate colleges and universities producing the most Ph.D.'s in the life sciences, 1981-1990 ★193★
U.S. colleges and universities where intercollegiate sports are popular ★995★
U.S. colleges and universities where intramural sports are popular ★997★
U.S. colleges and universities where the general student body puts a strong emphasis on athletic events ★1007★
U.S. colleges and universities without a diverse student body ★1046★
U.S. News & World Report's national liberal arts colleges with the highest graduation rates, 2000-01 ★1330★
U.S. News & World Report's national liberal arts colleges with the highest percentage of full-time faculty, 2000-01 ★1333★
U.S. News & World Report's best undergraduate fees among national liberal arts colleges by discount tuition, 2000 ★1381★
Highest undergraduate tuition and fees at private nonprofit, 4-year or above colleges and universities ★1461★
Highest undergraduate tuition and fees at colleges and universities in New York ★1537★
Private, 4-year undergraduate colleges and universities producing the most Ph.D.'s in all fields of study, 1990 ★2029★
Private, 4-year undergraduate colleges and universities producing the most Ph.D.'s in the earth sciences, 1981-1990 ★2151★
Top assistant professor economists at elite liberal arts colleges, 1975-94 ★2173★
Private, 4-year undergraduate colleges and universities producing the most Ph.D.'s in English, 1920-1990 ★2449★
Private, 4-year undergraduate colleges and universities producing the most Ph.D.'s in English, 1981-1990 ★2450★
U.S. bachelor's institutions with the largest number of students studying abroad, 1998-99 ★2511★
Most wired colleges, 2000 ★2595★
Private, 4-year undergraduate colleges and universities producing the most Ph.D.'s in political science and international relations, 1920-1990 ★3044★
Average faculty salaries for institutions of higher education in New York, 2000-01 ★3719★
U.S. liberal arts colleges with the highest paid full professors, 2001 ★3980★
Private, 4-year undergraduate colleges and universities producing the most Ph.D.'s in the sciences, 1981-1990 ★4295★
Private, 4-year undergraduate colleges and universities producing the most Ph.D.'s in anthropology and sociology, 1920-1990 ★4344★
Private, 4-year undergraduate colleges and universities producing the most Ph.D.'s in anthropology and sociology, 1981-1990 ★4345★

Coll Jr.; Edward G.
Top pay and benefits for the chief executive and top paid employees at Alfred University ★3169★

Coll; Kathleen
Radcliffe Institute for Advanced Study fellowship recipient in the field of social anthropology, 2000-01 ★59★

The Collaborator: The Trial and Execution of Robert Brasillach
Most notable nonfiction books, 2001 ★285★
Outstanding works of nonfiction, 2001 ★294★

Collard; Sneed B.
Booklist's best science books for children ★310★

Collected Poems
Outstanding works of poetry, 2001 ★295★

The Collected Poems of Stanley Kunitz
Library Journal's best poetry books, 2000 ★244★

College of Aeronautics
Average faculty salaries for institutions of higher education in New York, 2000-01 ★3719★

College Bookstores of America
Contractors managing the most college bookstores, 1999 ★846★

College Composition Communication
Most cited language serials in technical communication journals from 1988 to 1997 ★4420★
Most cited serials in technical communication journals from 1988 to 1997 ★4425★

College English
Most cited language serials in technical communication journals from 1988 to 1997 ★4420★
Most cited serials in technical communication journals from 1988 to 1997 ★4425★

College for Lifelong Learning
Lowest undergraduate tuition and fees at colleges and universities in New Hampshire ★1532★

The College Fund/UNCF
Top recipients of corporate contributions to African American communities, 1995 ★2944★

College mathematics
Subjects required by the most U.S. medical schools for the 2000-01 entering class ★2850★

College Misericordia
Colleges and universities with the smallest endowments, 2000 ★1238★
Average faculty salaries for institutions of higher education in Pennsylvania, 2000-01 ★3725★

College of Mount St. Joseph
U.S. News & World Report's midwestern regional universities with the highest freshmen retention rates, 2000-01 ★1405★
U.S. News & World Report's midwestern regional universities with the highest graduation rates, 2000-01 ★1406★

College of New Jersey
U.S. colleges and universities where students and the local community have strained relations ★998★

College of New Rochelle
Total baccalaureate degrees awarded to African Americans from traditionally white institutions, 1997-98 ★1698★

College professor
Most desirable public sector jobs ★2279★

College and Research Libraries
Information and library science journals by citation impact, 1999 ★2726★

College teachers
Employment outlook for the year 2005 for selected occupations ★2297★

College and university faculty
Projected employment growth for selected occupations that require advanced education, 1998-2008 ★2318★

College Work-Study
Sources of financial aid for incoming freshmen, 2000 ★1062★

Collens; L.M.
Top pay and benefits for the chief executive and top paid employees at Illinois Institute of Technology ★3346★

Collier; Barry S.
Top pay and benefits for the chief executive and top paid employees at Butler University ★3214★

Collier; Mark H.
Top pay and benefits for the chief executive and top paid employees at Baldwin-Wallace College ★3189★

Colling; Richard
Top pay and benefits for the chief executive and top paid employees at Olivet Nazarene University ★3432★

Collins; Anthony G.
Top pay and benefits for the chief executive and top paid employees at Clarkson University ★3239★

Collins; James E.
Top pay and benefits for the chief executive and top paid employees at Clark University ★3238★

Collinsville High School
All-USA Teacher Teams, Second Team, 2000 ★4400★

Collis; John
Top pay and benefits for the chief executive and top paid employees at St. Ambrose University ★3468★

The Color of My Words
Booklist's best first novels for youths ★309★
Most notable books for older readers, 2001 ★318★

The Color Purple
Favorite books of African Americans ★238★
Most frequently banned books in the 1990s ★745★

Colorado
People for the American Way's list of states with the most challenges to library and school books, 1982-1992 ★750★
Mean composite ACT scores by state, 2000 ★895★
Mean math SAT scores by state, 2000 ★900★
Mean verbal SAT scores by state, 2000 ★903★
Average class size at colleges and universities in the U.S., by state ★1064★
Total doctorate recipients by state, 1999 ★2054★
Hispanic American enrollment at Hispanic-serving institutions of higher education, by state, 1997 ★2547★
State grades for affordability of higher education for minority students, 2000 ★2883★
State grades for benefits state receives for educating its minority students, 2000 ★2884★
State grades for completion of higher education by minority students, 2000 ★2885★
State grades for participation of minority students in higher education, 2000 ★2886★
State grades for preparing minority students for higher education, 2000 ★2887★
States with the highest per capita income ★3123★
States with the largest growth in income ★3124★
States expelling the highest ratio of students for violating the Gun-Free Schools Act, 1998-99 ★3993★
States with the most charter schools ★4048★

Colorado, Boulder; University of
Institutions, by adjusted authorship, with the most published authors in the *Journal of Business Research*, 1985 to 1999 ★694★
Institutions with the most full-time Hispanic American faculty ★923★
U.S. colleges and universities with the most full-time Hispanic American faculty ★925★
Division I NCAA colleges with that graduated none of their African American male basketball players, 1990-91 to 1993-94 ★930★
U.S. colleges and universities where the general student body puts a strong emphasis on socializing ★1008★
U.S. colleges and universities where the general student body smokes marijuana ★1011★
Fiske Guide's best buys for public colleges and universities, 2001 ★1460★
U.S. colleges and universities awarding the most English language/literature/letters master's degrees to Hispanic Americans ★1775★
U.S. colleges and universities awarding the most first professional degrees to Native Americans ★1846★
U.S. colleges and universities awarding the most law and legal studies first professional degrees to Native Americans ★1855★
U.S. research institutions with the largest number of students studying abroad, 1998-99 ★2514★
Academics' choices for best environmental law programs, 2001 ★2628★
Average faculty salaries for institutions of higher education in Colorado, 2000-01 ★3693★

Colorado Christian University
Division II NCAA colleges with the 0% graduation rates for men's basketball players, 1993-94 ★941★
Highest undergraduate tuition and fees at colleges and universities in Colorado ★1488★

Colorado College
U.S. colleges and universities that devote the most course time to discussion ★990★
U.S. colleges and universities with excellent instructors ★1024★
U.S. News & World Report's national liberal arts colleges with the best faculty resources rank, 2000-01 ★1321★
Highest undergraduate tuition and fees at colleges and universities in Colorado ★1488★
Private, 4-year undergraduate colleges and universities producing the most Ph.D.'s in all fields of study, 1990 ★2029★
Private, 4-year undergraduate colleges and universities producing the most Ph.D.'s in nonscience fields, 1990 ★2032★
Private, 4-year undergraduate colleges and universities producing the most Ph.D.'s in the earth sciences, 1981-1990 ★2151★
Private, 4-year undergraduate colleges and universities producing the most Ph.D.'s in economics, 1920-1990 ★2211★
U.S. bachelor's institutions with the largest number of students studying abroad, 1998-99 ★2511★
Private, 4-year undergraduate colleges and universities producing the most Ph.D.'s in history, 1981-1990 ★2553★
Private, 4-year undergraduate colleges and universities producing the most Ph.D.'s in political science and international relations, 1981-1990 ★3045★
Average faculty salaries for institutions of higher education in Colorado, 2000-01 ★3693★

Colorado, Colorado Springs; University of
Division II NCAA colleges with the 0% graduation rates for men's basketball players, 1993-94 ★941★
U.S. News & World Report's top public western regional universities, 2000-01 ★1573★
Average faculty salaries for institutions of higher education in Colorado, 2000-01 ★3693★

Colorado, Denver; University of
Average faculty salaries for institutions of higher education in Colorado, 2000-01 ★3693★

Colorado Health Sciences Center; University of
Four-year institutions with the most weapons arrests reported, 1999 ★709★
U.S. colleges and universities awarding the most health professions and related sciences first professional degrees to Hispanic Americans ★1849★
Academics' choices for best family medicine programs, 2001 ★2820★
Acceptance rates for *U.S. News & World Report*'s top 10 primary-care medical schools, 2001 ★2826★
Average MCAT scores at *U.S. News & World Report*'s top 10 primary-care medical schools, 2001 ★2835★
Average undergraduate GPA at *U.S. News & World Report*'s top 10 primary-care medical schools, 2001 ★2837★
Faculty-student ratios at *U.S. News & World Report*'s top 10 primary-care medical schools, 2001 ★2841★
Out-of-state tuition and fees at *U.S. News & World Report*'s top 10 primary-care medical schools, 2001 ★2846★
Percentage of graduates entering *U.S. News & World Report*'s top 10 primary-care medical schools, 2001 ★2848★
Top primary-care medical schools, 2001 ★2856★
Top primary-care medical schools by reputation, as determined by academic personnel, 2001 ★2857★

Colorado Mountain College, Alpine Campus
Lowest undergraduate tuition and fees at colleges and universities in Colorado ★1489★

Colorado Mountain College, Spring Valley Campus
Lowest undergraduate tuition and fees at colleges and universities in Colorado ★1489★

Colorado Mountain College, Timberline Campus
Lowest undergraduate tuition and fees at colleges and universities in Colorado ★1489★

COLORADO

Colorado Northwestern Community College
   Lowest undergraduate tuition and fees at colleges and universities in Colorado ★1489★

Colorado School of Mines
   Division II NCAA colleges with the highest graduation rates for football players, 1993-94 ★946★
   U.S. colleges and universities where students and the local community have strained relations ★998★
   U.S. colleges and universities where students are not very politically active ★1000★
   U.S. colleges and universities with strained race/class interaction ★1029★
   U.S. colleges and universities with the most accessible instructors ★1038★
   U.S. colleges and universities with the unhappiest students ★1041★
   U.S. colleges and universities with the worst food service program ★1043★
   State appropriations for Colorado's institutions of higher education, 2000-01 ★1259★
   Academics' choices for best graduate petroleum engineering schools, 2000 ★2429★
   U.S. News & World Report's graduate engineering programs with the best petroleum departments, 2000-01 ★2431★
   Average faculty salaries for institutions of higher education in Colorado, 2000-01 ★3693★

Colorado State University
   U.S. colleges and universities awarding the most English language/literature/letters master's degrees to Hispanic Americans ★1775★
   U.S. institutions awarding the most baccalaureate degrees to Hispanic Americans in agricultural sciences, 1998 ★1818★
   U.S. institutions awarding the most baccalaureate degrees to minorities in agricultural sciences, 1998 ★1820★
   U.S. institutions awarding the most baccalaureate degrees to Native Americans in agribusiness and production, 1998 ★1822★
   U.S. institutions awarding the most baccalaureate degrees to Native Americans in agricultural sciences, 1998 ★1823★
   U.S. colleges and universities awarding the most health professions and related sciences first professional degrees to Native Americans ★1851★
   U.S. colleges and universities awarding the most psychology doctorate degrees to Asian Americans ★2121★
   U.S. universities with the highest concentration of civil engineering papers published, 1994-98 ★2351★
   U.S. universities publishing the most papers in the field of ecology/environmental sciences, 1994-98 ★2473★
   Average faculty salaries for institutions of higher education in Colorado, 2000-01 ★3693★
   U.S. universities with the highest concentration of animal sciences papers published, 1994-98 ★4288★
   Academics' choices for best vocational/technical graduate programs, 2001 ★4387★
   U.S. universities with the highest concentration of papers published in the field of veterinary medicine, 1995-99 ★4441★

Colorado System; University of
   Largest gifts to higher education, 1967-2000 ★1247★
   Largest private gifts to higher education, 1967-2000 ★1248★

Colorado Technical University
   U.S. colleges and universities awarding the most computer and information sciences master's degrees to African Americans ★1766★

Colorado; University of
   NCAA Division I ski teams with the most championships ★135★
   Top biochemistry and molecular biology research-doctorate programs as evaluated by the National Research Council ★209★
   State appropriations for Colorado's institutions of higher education, 2000-01 ★1259★
   Institutions generating the most economic education research text, 1963-1990 ★2167★
   U.S. universities with the greatest impact in civil engineering, 1995-99 ★2350★
   Top aerospace engineering research-doctorate programs as evaluated by the National Research Council ★2376★
   Most effective geography research-doctorate programs as evaluated by the National Research Council ★2519★
   Top geography research-doctorate programs as evaluated by the National Research Council ★2520★
   Law schools with the best critical race theory faculty, 1999-2000 ★2649★
   Degrees granted in the ten largest doctoral journalism and mass communications programs, 1999 ★2756★
   Degrees granted in the ten largest master's journalism and mass communications programs, 1999 ★2757★
   Top astrophysics and astronomy research-doctorate programs as evaluated by the National Research Council ★3014★
   U.S. colleges and universities spending the most on chemical research and development, 1998 ★3099★
   U.S. colleges and universities spending the most on chemical research equipment, 1998 ★3100★
   U.S. colleges and universities with the most federal support for chemical research and development, 1998 ★3102★
   U.S. colleges and universities with the most federal support for chemical research equipment, 1998 ★3103★
   Institutions receiving the most federal research and development expenditures, 1999 ★3105★

Columbia College
   Fall enrollment at the largest Chicago-area private institutions, by minority percentages, 1999 ★869★
   U.S. News & World Report's southern regional liberal arts colleges with the best student/faculty ratios, 2000-01 ★1368★
   U.S. News & World Report's southern regional liberal arts colleges with the highest alumni giving rates, 2000-01 ★1371★
   U.S. News & World Report's southern regional liberal arts colleges with the highest graduation rates, 2000-01 ★1373★
   U.S. News & World Report's top southern regional liberal arts colleges, 2000-01 ★1379★
   Highest undergraduate tuition and fees at colleges and universities in Puerto Rico ★1551★
   Highest undergraduate tuition and fees at colleges and universities in South Carolina ★1554★
   Institutions most frequently contributing to the *American Economic Review* from 1911-1990 ★2168★

Average faculty salaries for institutions of higher education in Missouri, 2000-01 ★3712★
Average faculty salaries for institutions of higher education without academic ranks in Illinois, 2000-01 ★3747★

Columbia College (IL)
   Largest benefit packages awarded to presidents at institutions of higher education, 1998-99 ★3133★
   Presidents with the highest pay at Master's I and II colleges and universities, 1998-99 ★3161★

Columbia College of Nursing
   Highest undergraduate tuition and fees at colleges and universities in Wisconsin ★1570★

Columbia College (SC)
   College freshmen's choices for exemplary undergraduate institutions ★1065★
   College senior's choices for exemplary undergraduate institutions ★1319★

The Columbia Granger's World of Poetry
   Outstanding reference sources, 2000 ★370★

Columbia Granger's World of Poetry Online
   Library Journal's best reference databases and discs, 2000 ★369★

Columbia-Greene Community College
   Lowest undergraduate tuition and fees at colleges and universities in New York ★1538★
   Average faculty salaries for institutions of higher education in New York, 2000-01 ★3719★

Columbia High School
   Outstanding secondary schools in Newark, New Jersey ★4192★

Columbia Law Review
   Law journals by citation impact, 1981-96 ★2617★
   Law journals with the greatest impact measure, 1981-98 ★2618★
   Most frequently-cited law reviews and legal periodicals, 1924-1986: a compilation ★2619★
   Most frequently-cited law reviews and legal periodicals, according to *Shepard's Law Review Citations*, 1957-1986 ★2620★

Columbia, MO
   Best college towns to live in ★3076★

Columbia State Community College
   Lowest undergraduate tuition and fees at colleges and universities in Tennessee ★1559★

Columbia Theological Seminary
   Average faculty salaries for institutions of higher education in Georgia, 2000-01 ★3697★

Columbia Union College
   Average faculty salaries for institutions of higher education in Maryland, 2000-01 ★3707★

Columbia University
   U.S. universities publishing the most papers in the fields of art and architecture, 1994-98 ★70★
   Most effective art history research-doctorate programs as evaluated by the National Research Council ★91★
   Top art history research-doctorate programs as evaluated by the National Research Council ★93★
   Most effective neurosciences research-doctorate programs as evaluated by the National Research Council ★200★
   Top neurosciences research-doctorate programs as evaluated by the National Research Council ★202★

Top biochemistry and molecular biology research-doctorate programs as evaluated by the National Research Council ★209★
Top molecular and general genetics research-doctorate programs as evaluated by the National Research Council ★211★
U.S. universities with the greatest impact in cell and developmental biology, 1993-97 ★212★
U.S. universities with the greatest impact in cell and developmental biology, 1994-98 ★213★
U.S. universities with the greatest impact in microbiology, 1995-99 ★218★
Top business schools in research performance, 1986-1998 ★532★
U.S. universities with the greatest impact in management, 1994-98 ★575★
Comparisons of investment returns for entrepreneurship MBAs ★623★
Top business schools for overall within-discipline research performance, 1986-1998 ★645★
Top business schools for within-discipline research performance in management, 1986-1998 ★646★
Top business schools for within-discipline research performance in management science, 1986-1998 ★647★
Top business schools for within-discipline research performance in accounting, 1986-1998 ★660★
Top business schools for within-discipline research performance in finance, 1986-1998 ★663★
Top business schools for within-discipline research performance in marketing, 1986-1998 ★671★
U.S. college campuses with more than 5,000 students reporting murders or manslaughters, 1998 ★729★
Most effective chemistry research-doctorate programs as evaluated by the National Research Council ★802★
Top chemistry research-doctorate programs as evaluated by the National Research Council ★805★
Top classics research-doctorate programs as evaluated by the National Research Council ★816★
U.S. colleges and universities that are the toughest to get into ★988★
U.S. colleges and universities with a diverse student body ★1012★
U.S. News & World Report's national universities with the best academic reputation, 2000-01 ★1126★
U.S. News & World Report's national universities with the best freshmen retention rates, 2000-01 ★1128★
U.S. News & World Report's national universities with the best student/faculty ratio, 2000-01 ★1130★
U.S. News & World Report's national universities with the highest graduation rate, 1999 ★1134★
U.S. News & World Report's national universities with the highest selectivity rank, 2000-01 ★1139★
U.S. News & World Report's national universities with the lowest acceptance rates, 2000-01 ★1140★
Colleges and universities with the largest endowments, 2000 ★1237★
Institutions receiving the most gifts, 1999-2000 ★1244★

U.S. colleges and universities spending the most on independent lobbyists, 1999 ★1310★
Most effective comparative literature research-doctorate programs as evaluated by the National Research Council ★1587★
Top comparative literature research-doctorate programs as evaluated by the National Research Council ★1588★
U.S. universities with the greatest impact in computer science, 1995-99 ★1593★
Traditionally white institutions awarding the most master's degrees to African Americans ★1755★
U.S. colleges and universities awarding the most mathematics master's degrees to Asian Americans ★1791★
Traditionally white institutions awarding the most first professional degrees to African Americans ★1842★
U.S. universities with the greatest impact in geosciences, 1994-98 ★2149★
Most effective geosciences research-doctorate programs as evaluated by the National Research Council ★2150★
Top geosciences research-doctorate programs as evaluated by the National Research Council ★2152★
Top oceanography research-doctorate programs as evaluated by the National Research Council ★2153★
U.S. universities with the greatest impact in geosciences, 1993-97 ★2155★
Economics departments by number of citations by top economists, 1971-92 ★2158★
Economics departments by number of citations per top economist, 1971-92 ★2159★
Economics departments by number of top economists, 1971-92 ★2160★
Economics Ph.D. programs by number of citations of top economist graduates, 1971-92 ★2204★
Economics Ph.D. programs by number of citations per top economist graduate, 1971-92 ★2205★
Economics Ph.D. programs by number of top economist graduates, 1971-92 ★2206★
Origin of doctorate for dissertation chairs in economics ★2208★
Origin of doctorate for economics faculty at Ph.D.-granting institutions ★2209★
Origin of doctorate for economics faculty at Ph.D.-granting institutions, by Ph.D. equivalents produced ★2210★
Top economics research-doctorate programs as evaluated by the National Research Council ★2213★
Top electrical engineering research-doctorate programs as evaluated by the National Research Council ★2405★
U.S. universities publishing the most papers in the field of literature, 1994-98 ★2447★
Top English language and literature research-doctorate programs as evaluated by the National Research Council ★2451★
Research institutions with the highest enrollment of foreign students, 1998-99 ★2503★
Top French language and literature research-doctorate programs as evaluated by the National Research Council ★2516★
Top history research-doctorate programs as evaluated by the National Research Council ★2554★
Academics' choices for best international law programs, 2001 ★2631★
Acceptance rates at *U.S. News & World Report*'s top 10 law schools, 2001 ★2634★

Graduate employment after graduation percentage for *U.S. News & World Report*'s top 10 law schools, 2001 ★2635★
Graduate employment percentage for *U.S. News & World Report*'s top 10 law schools, 2001 ★2636★
Jurisdiction's overall bar passage rate for *U.S. News & World Report*'s top 10 law schools, 2001 ★2637★
Law schools with the best administrative law faculty, 1999-2000 ★2638★
Law schools with the best comparative law faculty, 1999-2000 ★2642★
Law schools with the best constitutional law (freedom of religion) faculty, 1999-2000 ★2643★
Law schools with the best constitutional law (freedom of speech) faculty, 1999-2000 ★2644★
Law schools with the best constitutional law (general) faculty, 1999-2000 ★2645★
Law schools with the best corporate law and securities regulation faculty, 1999-2000 ★2646★
Law schools with the best criminal law (substantive) faculty, 1999-2000 ★2647★
Law schools with the best critical race theory faculty, 1999-2000 ★2649★
Law schools with the best intellectual property faculty, 1999-2000 ★2653★
Law schools with the best international law faculty, 1999-2000 ★2654★
Law schools with the best jurisprudence faculty, 1999-2000 ★2655★
Law schools with the best labor law faculty, 1999-2000 ★2656★
Law schools with the best law and economics faculty, 1999-2000 ★2657★
Law schools with the best moral and political theory (Anglo-American traditions) faculty, 1999-2000 ★2662★
Law schools with the highest quality, 1999-2000 ★2666★
School's bar passage rate in jurisdiction at *U.S. News & World Report*'s top 10 law schools, 2001 ★2667★
Student-faculty ratios at *U.S. News & World Report*'s top 10 law schools, 2001 ★2669★
Top law schools, 2001 ★2670★
Top law schools by reputation, as determined by academic personnel, 2001 ★2671★
Top law schools by reputation, as determined by lawyers and judges, 2001 ★2672★
Top law school student bodies, 1999-2000 ★2673★
Top university research libraries in the U.S. and Canada, 1998-99 ★2706★
U.S. universities with the greatest impact in library and information science, 1994-98 ★2719★
Degrees granted in the ten largest master's journalism and mass communications programs, 1999 ★2757★
Enrollment of students in the ten largest master's journalism and mass communications programs, 1999 ★2763★
Top mathematics research-doctorate programs as evaluated by the National Research Council ★2778★
Top music research-doctorate programs as evaluated by the National Research Council ★2896★
Institutions in the Worker Rights Consortium ★2913★
Women faculty in Ph.D. physics departments at U.S. institutions, 1998 ★2981★

COLUMBIA

Top physics research-doctorate programs as evaluated by the National Research Council ★3015★

Top physiology research-doctorate programs as evaluated by the National Research Council ★3022★

U.S. institutions with the most citations in psychiatry research, 1990-98 ★3059★

U.S. universities with the highest concentration of papers published in the field of psychiatry, 1994-98 ★3061★

Top religion research-doctorate programs as evaluated by the National Research Council ★3093★

Most patents issued to universities or research facilities, 1999 ★3097★

Institutions receiving the most federal research and development expenditures, 1999 ★3105★

Presidents with the highest pay at Research I and II universities, 1998-99 ★3162★

Average faculty salaries for institutions of higher education in New York, 2000-01 ★3719★

Private institutions of higher education that pay the highest salaries to female professors, 2000-01 ★3974★

U.S. institutions with the highest paid full professors, 2001 ★3978★

U.S. universities publishing the most papers in the field of neuroscience, 1994-98 ★4287★

Top sociology research-doctorate programs as evaluated by the National Research Council ★4354★

Most effective Spanish and Portuguese language and literature research-doctorate programs as evaluated by the National Research Council ★4357★

Top Spanish and Portuguese language and literature research-doctorate programs as evaluated by the National Research Council ★4358★

Columbia University, Barnard College

Average faculty salaries for institutions of higher education in New York, 2000-01 ★3719★

Columbia University College of Physicians and Surgeons

Academics' choices for best AIDS programs, 2001 ★2818★

Academics' choices for best drug and alcohol abuse programs, 2001 ★2819★

Academics' choices for best women's health medical programs, 2001 ★2825★

Acceptance rates for *U.S. News & World Report*'s top 10 research-oriented medical schools, 2001 ★2827★

Average MCAT scores at *U.S. News & World Report*'s top 10 research-oriented medical schools, 2001 ★2836★

Average undergraduate GPA at *U.S. News & World Report*'s top 10 research-oriented medical schools, 2001 ★2838★

Faculty-student ratios at *U.S. News & World Report*'s top 10 research-oriented medical schools, 2001 ★2842★

NIH research grants for *U.S. News & World Report*'s top 10 research-oriented medical schools, 2001 ★2845★

Out-of-state tuition and fees for *U.S. News & World Report*'s top 10 research-oriented medical schools, 2001 ★2847★

Top research-oriented medical schools, 2001 ★2859★

Top research-oriented medical schools by reputation, as determined by academic personnel, 2001 ★2860★

Top research-oriented medical schools by reputation, as determined by intern/residency directors, 2001 ★2861★

Top research-oriented medical schools by student selectivity, 2001 ★2862★

Columbia University, Columbia College

Highest undergraduate tuition and fees at colleges and universities in New York ★1537★

Columbia University Foundation School of Engineering and Applied Science

Highest undergraduate tuition and fees at colleges and universities in New York ★1537★

Columbia University Graduate School of Business

Academics' choices for best graduate executive MBA programs, 2001 ★584★

Academics' choices for best graduate nonprofit organizations programs, 2001 ★586★

Acceptance rates for *U.S. News & World Report*'s top 10 graduate business schools, 2001 ★588★

Annual tuition at *Business Week*'s top business schools, 2000 ★589★

Average GMAT scores at *U.S. News & World Report*'s top 10 graduate business schools, 2001 ★591★

Average job offers received by graduates from *Business Week*'s top business schools, 1999 ★592★

Average undergraduate GPA at *U.S. News & World Report*'s top 10 graduate business schools, 2001 ★593★

Business Week's top business schools, 2000 ★595★

Business Week's top business schools as selected by corporate recruiters, 2000 ★596★

Business Week's top business schools by intellectual capital, 2000 ★599★

Business Week's top business schools for finance skills as selected by corporate recruiters, 2000 ★600★

Business Week's top business schools for general management skills as selected by corporate recruiters, 2000 ★601★

Business Week's top business schools for global scope skills as selected by corporate recruiters, 2000 ★602★

Business Week's top business schools for marketing skills as selected by corporate recruiters, 2000 ★603★

Business Week's top business schools with the highest percentage of minority enrollment, 2000 ★613★

Business Week's top business schools with the highest percentage of women enrollees, 2000 ★614★

Business Week's top business schools with the lowest percentage of international students, 2000 ★615★

Highest post-MBA salaries for students enrolled in *Business Week*'s top business schools, 1999 ★631★

Highest pre-MBA salaries for students enrolled in *Business Week*'s top business schools, 1999 ★632★

Median starting salaries of graduates from *U.S. News & World Report*'s top 10 graduate business schools, 2001 ★636★

Out-of-state tuition and fees for *U.S. News & World Report*'s top 10 graduate business schools, 2001 ★637★

Percentage of applicants accepted at *Business Week*'s top business schools, 2000 ★638★

Percentage of employed graduates at *U.S. News & World Report*'s top 10 graduate business schools, 2001 ★639★

Percentage of graduates earning over $100,000 from *Business Week*'s top business schools, 1999 ★640★

Percentage of graduates employed within 3 months of graduation from *U.S. News & World Report*'s top 10 graduate business schools, 2001 ★641★

Top graduate business schools, 2001 ★649★

Top graduate business schools by reputation as determined by academic personnel, 2001 ★650★

Top graduate business schools by reputation, as determined by recruiters, 2001 ★651★

Academics' choices for best graduate finance programs, 2001 ★662★

Academics' choices for best graduate international business programs, 2001 ★668★

Academics' choices for best graduate marketing programs, 2001 ★670★

Average GMAT scores for *U.S. News & World Report*'s top 10 graduate business schools, 2000 ★2529★

Columbia University, New York City

Institutions with the most full-time Hispanic American faculty ★923★

U.S. colleges and universities with the most full-time Hispanic American faculty ★925★

U.S. colleges and universities awarding the most biological and life sciences master's degrees to Asian Americans ★1757★

U.S. colleges and universities awarding the most communications master's degrees to African Americans ★1763★

U.S. colleges and universities awarding the most communications master's degrees to Asian Americans ★1764★

U.S. colleges and universities awarding the most communications master's degrees to Hispanic Americans ★1765★

U.S. colleges and universities awarding the most English language/literature/letters master's degrees to African Americans ★1773★

U.S. colleges and universities awarding the most English language/literature/letters master's degrees to Asian Americans ★1774★

U.S. colleges and universities awarding the most health professions and related sciences master's degrees to African Americans ★1777★

U.S. colleges and universities awarding the most health professions and related sciences master's degrees to Asian Americans ★1778★

U.S. colleges and universities awarding the most health professions and related sciences master's degrees to Hispanic Americans ★1779★

U.S. colleges and universities awarding the most master's degrees to Asian Americans ★1786★

U.S. colleges and universities awarding the most master's degrees to minorities ★1788★

U.S. colleges and universities awarding the most social sciences and history master's degrees to African Americans ★1801★

U.S. colleges and universities awarding the most social sciences and history master's degrees to Asian Americans ★1802★

U.S. colleges and universities awarding the most social sciences and history master's degrees to Hispanic Americans ★1803★

U.S. colleges and universities awarding the most first professional degrees to Asian Americans ★1844★

U.S. colleges and universities awarding the most health professions and related sciences first professional degrees to Asian Americans ★1848★

U.S. colleges and universities awarding the most law and legal studies first professional degrees to African Americans ★1852★

U.S. colleges and universities awarding the most biological and life sciences doctorate degrees to Asian Americans ★2083★

U.S. colleges and universities awarding the most doctoral degrees to Asian Americans and Pacific Islanders from 1995 to 1999 ★2093★

U.S. colleges and universities awarding the most doctorate degrees to Asian Americans ★2096★

U.S. colleges and universities awarding the most doctorates in humanities, 1999 ★2103★

U.S. colleges and universities awarding the most doctorates in social sciences, 1999 ★2107★

U.S. colleges and universities awarding the most English language/literature/letters doctorate degrees to African Americans ★2112★

U.S. colleges and universities awarding the most English language/literature/letters doctorate degrees to Asian Americans ★2113★

U.S. colleges and universities awarding the most social sciences and history doctorate degrees to Asian Americans ★2125★

Columbia University School of General Studies
Private 4-year institutions with the highest tuition, 2000-01 ★1467★
Highest undergraduate tuition and fees at colleges and universities in New York ★1537★

Columbia University, Teachers College
Institutions awarding the most doctorate degrees to African Americans, 1997-98 ★1948★

Columbus Metropolitan Library
Highest Hennen's American Public Library Ratings for libraries serving a population of over 500,000 ★2700★

Columbus School for Girls
Outstanding secondary schools in Columbus, Ohio ★4118★

Columbus State Community College
Lowest undergraduate tuition and fees at colleges and universities in Ohio ★1544★

Columbus State University
State appropriations for Georgia's institutions of higher education, 2000-01 ★1263★
U.S. colleges and universities awarding the most social sciences and history master's degrees to African Americans ★1801★
Average faculty salaries for institutions of higher education in Georgia, 2000-01 ★3697★

Columbus Technical Institute
Lowest undergraduate tuition and fees at colleges and universities in Georgia ★1497★

Comcast
Fortune's highest ranked telecommunications companies, 2000 ★499★
Top publishing and broadcasting companies in Standard & Poor's 500, 2001 ★553★

Comdisco
Fortune's highest ranked computer and data services companies, 2000 ★453★

Comeau; Michael
All-USA Teacher Teams, First Team, 2000 ★4399★

The Coming Internet
Library Journal's most notable new economy books, 2000 ★271★

Coming to Light: Edward S. Curtis and the North American Indians
Most notable videos for adults, 2001 ★2891★

Commerce
Federal appropriations to colleges, by agency, 2000 ★1241★

Commercial Metals
Fortune's highest ranked metals companies, 2000 ★476★

Commission on Civil Rights
Proposed fiscal 2002 appropriations for civil rights ★814★

Common Property as a Concept in Natural Resources Policy
Top cited nonrenewable resource papers from 1974 to 1978 ★2468★

Common Property Externalities-Isolation, Assurance, and Resource Depletion in a Traditional Grazing Context
Top cited nonrenewable resource papers from 1979 to 1983 ★2469★

Commonwealth Bank of Australia
Business Week's best companies in Australia ★386★

Communication Monographs
Most cited language serials in technical communication journals from 1988 to 1997 ★4420★

Communication Quarterly
Most cited language serials in technical communication journals from 1988 to 1997 ★4420★

Communication Research
Most cited language serials in technical communication journals from 1988 to 1997 ★4420★

Communication/telecommunication
Expected starting salaries of 2000-01 bachelor's degree recipients, by general major ★3130★

Communications
Top accounting journals by mode impact factor ★579★
Top bachelor's degree disciplines for African Americans, 1997-98 ★1672★
Top bachelor's degree disciplines for Asian Americans, 1997-98 ★1673★
Top bachelor's degree disciplines for Hispanic Americans, 1997-98 ★1674★
Top bachelor's degree disciplines for Native Americans, 1997-98 ★1675★
Top bachelor's degree disciplines for non-minorities, 1997-98 ★1676★
Engineering doctorates awarded at U.S. colleges and universities, by subfield, 1999 ★1923★
Gender breakdown of engineering doctorate recipients, by subfield, 1999 ★1934★
Number of professional/other doctorate recipients at U.S. colleges and universities, by field, 1999 ★1976★

Communications of the Association of Computing Machinery
Top ranked AACSB publications ★2186★
Journals and proceedings with the most citations (Class 1) ★2567★
Most cited science serials in technical communication journals from 1988 to 1997 ★4424★
Most cited serials in technical communication journals from 1988 to 1997 ★4425★

Communications equipment mechanic
'Blue-collar' jobs considered the least physically demanding ★2241★

Communications, general
Communications doctorates awarded at U.S. colleges and universities, by subfield, 1999 ★1898★
Gender breakdown of communications doctorate recipients, by subfield, 1999 ★1930★

Communications/media
Spending for E-marketplace services, by industry, 2001 ★4430★

Communications on Pure and Applied Mathematics
Mathematics journals by impact factor ★2783★
Mathematics journals by impact factor, 1981 to 1997 ★2784★
Mathematics journals by impact factor, 1993 to 1997 ★2785★

Communications research
Communications doctorates awarded at U.S. colleges and universities, by subfield, 1999 ★1898★
Gender breakdown of communications doctorate recipients, by subfield, 1999 ★1930★

Communications theory
Communications doctorates awarded at U.S. colleges and universities, by subfield, 1999 ★1898★
Gender breakdown of communications doctorate recipients, by subfield, 1999 ★1930★

Community College of Allegheny County
Lowest undergraduate tuition and fees at colleges and universities in Pennsylvania ★1550★

Community College of Aurora
Lowest undergraduate tuition and fees at colleges and universities in Colorado ★1489★

Community College of Baltimore County, Catonsville
Lowest undergraduate tuition and fees at colleges and universities in Maryland ★1515★

Community College of Baltimore County, Dundalk
Lowest undergraduate tuition and fees at colleges and universities in Maryland ★1515★

Community College of Baltimore County, Essex
Institutions censured by the American Association of University Professors, 2001 ★1067★
Lowest undergraduate tuition and fees at colleges and universities in Maryland ★1515★

Community High School
Outstanding secondary schools in Chicago, Illinois ★4110★

Community Mental Health Journal
Health policy and services journals by citation impact, 1981-99 ★2537★

Community Policing: A Contemporary Perspective
Most-cited works in police studies articles/research notes ★2625★

Companion Encyclopedia of Archaeology
Selected reference books in the field of archaeology, 2000 ★374★

Companion to African Literatures
Library Journal's best reference books, 2000 ★368★
Selected reference books in the field of literature, 2000 ★377★

Compaq Computer
Fortune's highest ranked computers and office equipment companies, 2000 ★456★

COMPARATIVE

Largest technology companies in the U.S. in terms of annual revenue, 2000 ★4429★

Comparative
Gender breakdown of psychology doctorate recipients, by subfield, 1999 ★1941★
Psychology doctorates awarded at U.S. colleges and universities, by subfield, 1999 ★2043★

Comparative literature
Gender breakdown of humanities doctorate recipients, by subfield, 1999 ★1936★
Humanities doctorates awarded at U.S. colleges and universities, by subfield, 1999 ★1946★

Comparative Political Studies
Political science journals with the greatest impact measure, 1981-98 ★3049★
Political science journals with the greatest impact measure, 1994-98 ★3050★
Political science journals with the greatest percentage of articles by multiple authors, 1974-94 ★3051★

The Complete Jacob Lawrence
Booklist's most recommended African American nonfiction ★229★
Outstanding arts and literature books, 2000 ★286★

Compliance coordinator
African American college athletics administrators and staff, by gender, 1999-2000 ★117★
College athletics administrators and staff, by gender, 1999-2000 ★121★
Minority college athletics administrators and staff, by gender, 1999-2000 ★132★

Compositor/typesetter
Jobs with the highest unemployment ★2256★
Jobs with the most stringent quotas ★2259★

Compton Community College
Lowest undergraduate tuition and fees at public 2-year colleges and universities ★1465★

Computer
Engineering doctorates awarded at U.S. colleges and universities, by subfield, 1999 ★1923★
Gender breakdown of engineering doctorate recipients, by subfield, 1999 ★1934★

Computer Associates
Software companies with the fastest growth, 2000 ★528★

Computer Associates International
Fortune's highest ranked computer software companies, 2000 ★455★

Computer books
Subject areas with the highest library expenditures/circulation ★306★

Computer consultant
Jobs that are potentially the highest paying ★2246★
Jobs with the best outlook scores ★2249★
Jobs with the best security scores ★2251★
Jobs with the highest employment growth ★2254★
Most desirable technical/repair jobs ★2281★

Computer and data processing
Industries with the highest percentage of projected employment growth from 1998 through 2008 ★2305★

Computer and data processing services
Employment growth percentages for selected industries, 1998-2000 ★2294★
Industries with the highest projected growth rate, 1994-2005 ★2306★

Computer engineering
Top master's degree majors in demand for employment, 2001 ★2326★
Average starting salaries for college graduates, by field, 2000 ★3129★
Expected starting salaries of 2000-01 bachelor's degree recipients, by specific major ★3131★

Computer engineers
Projections for the fastest growing occupations requiring a bachelor's degree or more from 1998 to 2008 ★2292★
Fastest growing occupations, 1998-2008 ★2302★
Occupations with the largest projected employment growth, 1998-2008 ★2312★
Projected employment growth for selected occupations that require a bachelor's degree or more, 1998-2008 ★2317★
Median annual earnings for computer technology jobs, 1998 ★3122★

Computer Graphics World
Most cited technology serials in technical communication journals from 1988 to 1997 ★4427★

Computer and information science
Top bachelor's degree disciplines for African Americans, 1997-98 ★1672★
Top bachelor's degree disciplines for Asian Americans, 1997-98 ★1673★
Top bachelor's degree disciplines for Hispanic Americans, 1997-98 ★1674★
Top bachelor's degree disciplines for Native Americans, 1997-98 ★1675★
Top bachelor's degree disciplines for non-minorities, 1997-98 ★1676★

Computer/math
Median salary for B.S. chemists, by field ★781★
Median salary for M.S. chemists, by field ★785★
Median salary for Ph.D. chemists, by field ★786★

Computer operator
Jobs considered the loneliest ★2244★
Jobs with the worst outlook scores ★2262★

Computer operators, except peripheral equipment
Occupations with the highest decline in employment, 1998-2008 ★2310★

Computer programmer
Jobs considered the loneliest ★2244★
Most desirable technical/repair jobs ★2281★

Computer programmers
Projected employment growth for selected occupations that require a bachelor's degree or more, 1998-2008 ★2317★

Computer science
Computer science doctorates awarded at U.S. colleges and universities, by subfield, 1999 ★1900★
Gender breakdown of computer science doctorate recipients, by subfield, 1999 ★1931★
Percentage of female doctorate recipients at U.S. colleges and universities, by subfield, 1999 ★1988★
Top bachelor's and master's degree majors in demand for employment, 2001 ★2323★
Top bachelor's degree majors in demand for employment, 2001 ★2324★
Top master's degree majors in demand for employment, 2001 ★2326★
Proposed fiscal 2002 appropriations for the National Science Foundation ★3109★
Average starting salaries for college graduates, by field, 2000 ★3129★
Expected starting salaries of 2000-01 bachelor's degree recipients, by specific major ★3131★
United States' contribution of papers in the sciences, by field, 1995-99 ★4283★
United States' contribution of papers in the sciences, by field, 1996-2000 ★4284★
Hong Kong's contribution of papers in the sciences, by field, 1995-99 ★4314★
Italy's contribution of papers in the sciences, by field, 1995-99 ★4316★
Italy's relative impact in the sciences by field, 1992-96 ★4317★
Japan's contribution of papers in the sciences, by field, 1995-99 ★4318★
Japan's contribution of papers in the sciences, by field, 1996-2000 ★4319★
South Korea's contribution of papers in the sciences, by field, 1995-99 ★4327★
Taiwan contribution of papers in the sciences, by field, 1995-99 ★4334★
Turkey's contribution of papers in the sciences, by field, 1995-99 ★4335★

Computer science A
Number of Advanced Placement Exams taken by African Americans, by subject, 2000 ★30★
Number of Advanced Placement Exams taken by Asian Americans, by subject, 2000 ★31★
Number of Advanced Placement Exams taken by Hispanic Americans, by subject, 2000 ★32★

Computer science AB
Number of Advanced Placement Exams taken by African Americans, by subject, 2000 ★30★
Number of Advanced Placement Exams taken by Asian Americans, by subject, 2000 ★31★
Number of Advanced Placement Exams taken by Hispanic Americans, by subject, 2000 ★32★

Computer Science Press
Publishers, journals and proceedings with the lowest citations (Class 6) ★2571★

Computer sciences
Fortune's highest ranked computer and data services companies, 2000 ★453★
Number of physical sciences doctorate recipients at U.S. colleges and universities, by field, 1999 ★1975★
Physical sciences, mathematics, and computer sciences doctorates awarded to U.S. citizens/permanent residents at U.S. colleges and universities, by race/ethnicity and subfield, 1999 ★1993★
Expected starting salaries of 2000-01 bachelor's degree recipients, by general major ★3130★

Computer service technician
Most desirable technical/repair jobs ★2281★

Computer Services
Best small companies worldwide ★384★

Computer support specialists
Fastest growing occupations, 1998-2008 ★2302★
Occupations with the largest projected employment growth, 1998-2008 ★2312★
Projected employment growth for selected occupations that require an associate degree or less, 1998-2008 ★2319★
Median annual earnings for computer technology jobs, 1998 ★3122★

Computer systems analyst
Jobs with the best environment scores ★2247★
Jobs with the best security scores ★2251★
Jobs with the highest employment growth ★2254★
Most desirable technical/repair jobs ★2281★

Occupations with the highest average annual salaries for college graduates, 1998 ★3132★

Computer systems analysts
Projections for the fastest growing occupations requiring a bachelor's degree or more from 1998 to 2008 ★2292★
Fastest growing occupations, 1998-2008 ★2302★
Occupations with the largest projected employment growth, 1998-2008 ★2312★
Projected employment growth for selected occupations that require a bachelor's degree or more, 1998-2008 ★2317★
Median annual earnings for computer technology jobs, 1998 ★3122★

Computers and Composition
Most cited education serials in technical communication journals from 1988 to 1997 ★4418★

Computerworld
Most cited science serials in technical communication journals from 1988 to 1997 ★4424★

Computing theory and practice
Gender breakdown of mathematics doctorate recipients, by subfield, 1999 ★1938★
Mathematics doctorates awarded at U.S. colleges and universities, by subfield, 1999 ★1951★

Compuware
Fortune's highest ranked computer software companies, 2000 ★455★
Software companies with the fastest growth, 2000 ★528★

Comtech Telecommunications
Business Week's top companies in terms of earning growth, 2000 ★427★

Comverse Technology
Software companies with the fastest growth, 2000 ★528★
Top telecommunications companies in Standard & Poor's 500, 2001 ★559★

Con Edison
Top public companies with the highest percentage of women board of directors, 2000 ★4458★

ConAgra
Fortune's highest ranked consumer food products companies, 2000 ★458★

Conant High School
Outstanding secondary schools in Chicago, Illinois ★4110★

Conard; Norman
All-USA Teacher Teams, First Team, 2000 ★4399★

Concepts and Measures of Natural Resource Scarcity with a Summary of Recent Trends
Journal of Environmental Economics and Management's best articles in depletable resources and energy ★2462★

Concord College
State appropriations for West Virginia's institutions of higher education, 2000-01 ★1301★
Average faculty salaries for institutions of higher education in West Virginia, 2000-01 ★3737★

Concord Pike Library
Highest Hennen's American Public Library Ratings for libraries serving a population of 25,000 to 49,999 ★2696★

Concordia College, Moorhead
U.S. News & World Report's national liberal arts colleges with students most in debt, 1999 ★1386★
Average faculty salaries for institutions of higher education in Minnesota, 2000-01 ★3710★

Concordia Seminary
Institutions censured by the American Association of University Professors, 2001 ★1067★

Concordia University
Canadian comprehensive universities by alumni support, 2000 ★1153★
Canadian comprehensive universities by award-winning faculty members, 2000 ★1154★
Canadian comprehensive universities by class size at the first- and second-year level, 2000 ★1155★
Canadian comprehensive universities by class size at the third- and forth-year level, 2000 ★1156★
Canadian comprehensive universities by classes taught by tenured faculty, 2000 ★1157★
Canadian comprehensive universities by faculty members with Ph.D.'s, 2000 ★1158★
Canadian comprehensive universities by international graduate students, 2000 ★1159★
Canadian comprehensive universities by library acquisitions, 2000 ★1160★
Canadian comprehensive universities by library expenses, 2000 ★1161★
Canadian comprehensive universities by library holdings per student, 2000 ★1162★
Canadian comprehensive universities by operating budget per student, 2000 ★1163★
Canadian comprehensive universities by percentage of operating budget allocated to scholarships, 2000 ★1164★
Canadian comprehensive universities by percentage of operating budget allocated to student services, 2000 ★1165★
Canadian comprehensive universities by social science/humanities grants per faculty member, 2000 ★1166★
Canadian comprehensive universities by students from out of province, 2000 ★1167★
Canadian comprehensive universities by students winning national awards, 2000 ★1168★
Canadian medical/doctoral universities by medical/science grants per faculty member, 2000 ★1183★
Canadian universities chosen as being value added, 2000 ★1216★
Canadian universities with the lowest total cost, 2000 ★1218★
Top Canadian comprehensive universities, 2000 ★1219★
Top Canadian comprehensive universities by reputation, 2000 ★1220★
U.S. News & World Report's best undergraduate fees among western regional liberal arts colleges by discount tuition, 2000 ★1384★
Academic reputation scores for *U.S. News & World Report*'s top western regional liberal arts colleges, 2000-01 ★1387★
Acceptance rates for *U.S. News & World Report*'s top western regional liberal arts colleges, 2000-01 ★1388★
Alumni giving rates at *U.S. News & World Report*'s top western regional liberal arts colleges, 2000-01 ★1389★
Average freshmen retention rates for *U.S. News & World Report*'s top western regional liberal arts colleges, 2000-01 ★1390★
Average graduation rates for *U.S. News & World Report*'s top western regional liberal arts colleges, 2000-01 ★1391★
Percentage of freshmen in the top 25% of their high school class at *U.S. News & World Report*'s top western regional liberal arts colleges, 2000-01 ★1392★
Percentage of full-time faculty at *U.S. News & World Report*'s top western regional liberal arts colleges, 2000-01 ★1393★
Proportion of classes having 20 students or less at *U.S. News & World Report*'s top western regional liberal arts colleges, 2000-01 ★1394★
Student/faculty ratios at *U.S. News & World Report*'s top western regional liberal arts colleges, 2000-01 ★1395★
U.S. News & World Report's top western regional liberal arts colleges, 2000-01 ★1396★
U.S. News & World Report's western regional liberal arts colleges with students least in debt, 1999 ★1397★
Highest undergraduate tuition and fees at colleges and universities in Nebraska ★1528★
Highest undergraduate tuition and fees at colleges and universities in Oregon ★1547★
Average faculty salaries for institutions of higher education in California, 2000-01 ★3692★
Average faculty salaries for institutions of higher education in Nebraska, 2000-01 ★3714★
Average faculty salaries for institutions of higher education in Wisconsin, 2000-01 ★3738★

Concordia University (NE)
U.S. institutions with the lowest paid full professors, 2001 ★3979★

Concordia University, River Forest (IL)
U.S. News & World Report's midwestern regional universities with the highest proportion of classes having 20 students or less, 2000-01 ★1409★
U.S. News & World Report's midwestern regional universities with the lowest acceptance rates, 2000-01 ★1410★

Condensed matter
Major subfields of first-year physics and astronomy graduate students who are foreign citizens planning to receive a Ph.D., 1997-98 ★3004★
Major subfields of first-year physics and astronomy graduate students who are U.S. citizens planning to receive a Ph.D., 1997-98 ★3005★

Conditional discrimination vs. matching-to-sample: An expansion of the testing paradigm
Most cited sources in experimental analyses of human behavior between 1990 and 1999 ★3070★

Condon; Jacquelyn
Top pay and benefits for the chief executive and top paid employees at Monmouth College in Illinois ★3405★

Conexant Systems
Business Week's best performing companies with the lowest 1-year shareholder returns ★422★
Business Week's best performing companies with the lowest net margin, 2000 ★425★
Business Week's best performing companies with the lowest return on equity, 2000 ★426★

Congenital dermatologic disease
Leading categories of dermatologic disease covered by top articles in the field, 1945-1990 ★1869★

Congreaves; Andrea
Division I women's career high scorers ★129★

Congressperson/Senator
Jobs considered the most competitive ★2245★
Jobs with the best income scores ★2248★
Jobs with the highest starting salaries ★2255★
Jobs with the lowest unemployment ★2258★

Coniglio; John U.
Top pay and benefits for the chief executive and top paid employees at the University of Rochester ★3560★

Conison; Jay
Top pay and benefits for the chief executive and top paid employees at Valparaiso University ★3592★

Conkright; John C.
Top pay and benefits for the chief executive and top paid employees at Randolph-Macon College ★3451★

Conley; Robert T.
Top pay and benefits for the chief executive and top paid employees at Union Institute ★3586★

Conlin; Kristina
Golden Key Scholar Award winners, 2000 ★1316★

Connecticut
Mean composite ACT scores by state, 2000 ★895★
Mean math SAT scores by state, 2000 ★900★
Mean verbal SAT scores by state, 2000 ★903★
Total doctorate recipients by state, 1999 ★2054★
Average Hennen's American Public Library Ratings, by state ★2690★
State grades for affordability of higher education for minority students, 2000 ★2883★
State grades for benefits state receives for educating its minority students, 2000 ★2884★
State grades for completion of higher education by minority students, 2000 ★2885★
State grades for participation of minority students in higher education, 2000 ★2886★
State grades for preparing minority students for higher education, 2000 ★2887★
States with the highest per capita income ★3123★
States with the highest per-pupil expenditures ★3996★

Connecticut College
U.S. colleges and universities most accepting of alternative lifestyles ★986★
U.S. colleges and universities where students and the local community have strained relations ★998★
U.S. colleges and universities where the general student body puts little emphasis on athletic events ★1009★
U.S. colleges and universities with a primarily non-religious student body ★1021★
U.S. News & World Report's national liberal arts colleges with the highest percentage of full-time faculty, 2000-01 ★1333★
Private, 4-year undergraduate colleges and universities producing the most Ph.D.'s in all fields of study, 1990 ★2029★
Private, 4-year undergraduate colleges and universities producing the most Ph.D.'s in nonscience fields, 1990 ★2032★
Presidents with the highest pay at Baccalaureate I colleges, 1998-99 ★3159★
Average faculty salaries for institutions of higher education in Connecticut, 2000-01 ★3694★

Connecticut; University of
NCAA Division I women's basketball teams with the best scoring margin ★156★
Women's basketball teams with the most appearances in the Final Four ★157★
Institutions, by adjusted authorship, with the most published authors in the *Journal of Business Research*, 1985 to 1999 ★694★
U.S. colleges and universities least accepting of alternative lifestyles ★985★
U.S. colleges and universities with the worst overall administration ★1045★
State appropriations for Connecticut's institutions of higher education, 2000-01 ★1260★
U.S. universities with the highest concentration of dentistry papers published, 1994-98 ★1868★
U.S. colleges and universities awarding the most biological and life sciences doctorate degrees to Hispanic Americans ★2084★
University research libraries in the U.S. and Canada with the largest increases in total expenditures from 1993-94 to 1998-99 ★2708★
Most effective linguistics research-doctorate programs as evaluated by the National Research Council ★2732★
Average faculty salaries for institutions of higher education in Connecticut, 2000-01 ★3694★
Radcliffe Institute for Advanced Study fellowship recipients in the field of sociology, 2000-01 ★4346★

Connective tissue disease
Leading categories of dermatologic disease covered by top articles in the field, 1945-1990 ★1869★

Connelly; R.
Top associate professor economists at elite liberal arts colleges, 1975-94 ★2174★

Conner; Laurence M.
Top pay and benefits for the chief executive and top paid employees at Marycrest International University ★3393★

Connolly; John
Top pay and benefits for the chief executive and top paid employees at Smith College ★3501★

Connors; Mary Jean
Highest ranking women at the top public companies, 2000 ★4452★

Connors State College
Lowest undergraduate tuition and fees at colleges and universities in Oklahoma ★1546★
U.S. institutions awarding the most associate degrees to minorities in agricultural sciences, 1998 ★1809★

Conoco
Fortune's highest ranked petroleum refining companies, 2000 ★484★
Top fuel companies in Standard & Poor's 500, 2001 ★541★

Conover; Catherine
Top pay and benefits for the chief executive and top paid employees at Wheaton College in Massachusetts ★3621★

Conquering the Beast Within: How I Fought Depression and Won...and How You Can, Too
Most notable nonfiction books for reluctant young adult readers, 2001 ★323★

Conrad; C.
Top assistant professor economists at elite liberal arts colleges, 1975-94 ★2173★

Conseco
Business Week's best performing companies with the greatest decline in earnings growth ★412★
Business Week's best performing companies with the lowest 3-year shareholder returns ★424★
Business Week's best performing companies with the lowest net margin, 2000 ★425★
Business Week's best performing companies with the lowest return on equity, 2000 ★426★

Conservation/renewable national resources
Agricultural sciences doctorates awarded at U.S. colleges and universities, by subfield, 1999 ★1886★
Gender breakdown of agricultural sciences doctorate recipients, by subfield, 1999 ★1926★

Conservationist
Jobs with the lowest unemployment ★2258★
Most desirable public sector jobs ★2279★
'White-collar' jobs considered the most physically demanding ★2285★

The Conservative Caucus
Most selective internships in the U.S., 2001 ★2610★

Conservatory of Music of Puerto Rico
Lowest undergraduate tuition and fees at public, 4-year or above colleges and universities ★1466★

Consolidated Edison
Fortune's highest ranked electric and gas utilities companies, 2000 ★459★

Consolidated Freightways
Fortune's highest ranked trucking companies, 2000 ★503★

Consolidated Stores
Business Week's best performing companies with the lowest 3-year sales performance ★423★

Constantine; Ruth
Top pay and benefits for the chief executive and top paid employees at Smith College ★3501★

Constellation Brands
Fortune's highest ranked beverages companies, 2000 ★450★

Construction
Employment change projections by major industry division from 1998 to 2008 ★2287★
Employment projections by major industry division for 2008 ★2290★
Expected starting salaries of 2000-01 bachelor's degree recipients, by specific major ★3131★

Construction and extracting
Industries in Illinois with the highest projected worker increase through 2006 ★2304★

Construction foreman
Most desirable jobs in construction trades ★2272★

Construction machinery operator
Jobs with the highest unemployment ★2256★
Most desirable jobs in construction trades ★2272★

Construction trades
Occupational fields of tribal college graduates that are currently employed ★964★

Construction worker (laborer)
Jobs with the highest unemployment ★2256★
Jobs with the worst physical demands scores ★2263★
Least desirable jobs ★2266★
Most desirable jobs in construction trades ★2272★

Consumer Price Index
2000 returns on university endowments and other comparative measures ★1231★

Contact Dermatitis
Number of citations and papers for original articles appearing in dermatology journals, 1981 to 1996 ★1873★
Number of citations and papers in dermatology journals, 1981 to 1996 ★1874★

Contact Kids
Best-selling youth magazines ★2920★

Contemporary Accounting Research
Top accounting journals by half-life impact factor ★578★
Top accounting journals by mode impact factor ★579★

Contemporary American Religion
Outstanding reference sources, 2001 ★371★

Contemporary Educational Psychology
Most cited education serials in technical communication journals from 1988 to 1997 ★4418★

Contemporary Sociology
Social sciences journals with the greatest impact measure, 1981-97 ★4341★

Contextual control of emergent equivalence relations
Most cited sources in experimental analyses of human behavior between 1990 and 1999 ★3070★

ContiGroup Cos
Largest private companies, 2000 ★523★

Continental Airlines
Fortune's highest ranked airlines, 2000 ★447★

Contra Costa College
Lowest undergraduate tuition and fees at public 2-year colleges and universities ★1465★
Lowest undergraduate tuition and fees at colleges and universities in California ★1487★

Contraception
'Outside' journals most frequently citing *Studies in Family Planning*, 1991-95 ★1862★

Contract Duration and Relationship-Specific Investments-Empirical Evidence from Coal Markets
Top cited energy papers from 1984 to 1988 ★2465★

Control Theory Applied to Natural and Environmental Resources-Exposition
Journal of Environmental Economics and Management's best articles in depletable resources and energy ★2462★

Convent Sacred Heart High School
Outstanding secondary schools in San Francisco, California ★4221★

Convergys
Fortune's highest ranked outsourcing services companies, 2000 ★483★
Top services industries in Standard & Poor's 500, 2001 ★558★

Converse College
U.S. News & World Report's best undergraduate fees among southern regional universities by discount tuition, 2000 ★1429★
U.S. News & World Report's southern regional universities with the best student/faculty ratios, 2000-01 ★1435★
U.S. News & World Report's southern regional universities with the highest graduation rates, 2000-01 ★1438★
U.S. News & World Report's southern regional universities with the highest percentage of freshmen in the top 25% of their high school class, 2000-01 ★1439★
U.S. News & World Report's southern regional universities with the highest percentage of full-time faculty, 2000-01 ★1440★
U.S. News & World Report's southern regional universities with the highest proportion of classes with 20 students or less, 2000-01 ★1441★
Highest undergraduate tuition and fees at colleges and universities in South Carolina ★1554★
Average faculty salaries for institutions of higher education in South Carolina, 2000-01 ★3728★

Convey Jr.; John J.
Top pay and benefits for the chief executive and top paid employees at the Catholic University of America ★3522★

Conway Middle School
Outstanding secondary schools in Myrtle Beach, South Carolina ★4184★

Cook/chef
Jobs considered the loneliest ★2244★
Most desirable jobs in travel/food service ★2278★

Cook; Clyde
Top pay and benefits for the chief executive and top paid employees at Biola University ★3203★

Cook County, IL
U.S. counties with the highest international enrollment, 1999-2000 ★2505★

Cook; Gary R.
Top pay and benefits for the chief executive and top paid employees at Dallas Baptist University ★3262★

Cook Memorial Public Library District
Highest Hennen's American Public Library Ratings for libraries serving a population of 25,000 to 49,999 ★2696★

Cook; Richard J.
Top pay and benefits for the chief executive and top paid employees at Allegheny College ★3170★

Cook; Susan
All-USA Teacher Teams, Third Team, 2000 ★4401★

Cook; William
Top pay and benefits for the chief executive and top paid employees at the University of La Verne ★3547★

Cookbooks
Subject areas with the highest library expenditures/circulation ★306★

Cooke, S.J.; Rev. Vincent M.
Top pay and benefits for the chief executive and top paid employees at Canisius College ★3219★

Cooks, restaurants
Projected employment growth for selected occupations that require long-term on-the-job training, 1998-2008 ★2320★

Cool, Calm & Collected Poems, 1960-2000
Booklist's most recommended poetry books, 2001 ★231★
Outstanding poetry books, 2000 ★290★

Cool in School
Most notable nonfiction books for reluctant young adult readers, 2001 ★323★

Cool; Linda
Top pay and benefits for the chief executive and top paid employees at Union College in New York ★3585★

Cooley; Martha H.
Top pay and benefits for the chief executive and top paid employees at Guilford College ★3316★

Cooley; Philip L.
Top pay and benefits for the chief executive and top paid employees at Trinity University in Texas ★3579★

Cooney; Terry A.
Top pay and benefits for the chief executive and top paid employees at the University of Puget Sound ★3557★

Cooper City High School
Outstanding secondary schools in Fort Lauderdale, Florida ★4133★

Cooper; J. California
Favorite African American authors ★237★

Cooper; Joel D.
Top pay and benefits for the chief executive and top paid employees at Washington University in Missouri ★3607★

Cooper; Michael E.
Top pay and benefits for the chief executive and top paid employees at Clarkson University ★3239★

Cooper; Robin
Top pay and benefits for the chief executive and top paid employees at the University of Evansville ★3543★

Cooper; S. L.
Top pay and benefits for the chief executive and top paid employees at Illinois Institute of Technology ★3346★

Cooper Tire & Rubber
Fortune's highest ranked rubber and plastic products companies, 2000 ★492★
Top automotive companies in Standard & Poor's 500, 2001 ★530★

Cooper Union
U.S. colleges and universities that are the toughest to get into ★988★
U.S. colleges and universities where intramural sports are not popular ★996★
U.S. colleges and universities where the general student body does not drink beer ★1004★
U.S. colleges and universities where the general student body does not drink hard liquor ★1005★
U.S. colleges and universities where the general student body puts little emphasis on athletic events ★1009★
U.S. colleges and universities where the general student body puts little emphasis on socializing ★1010★
U.S. colleges and universities with the least attractive campuses ★1037★
Fiske Guide's best buys for private colleges and universities, 2001 ★1459★
Private, 4-year undergraduate colleges and universities producing the most Ph.D.'s in the computer sciences, 1920-1990 ★1595★

U.S. News & World Report's undergraduate engineering programs with the highest academic reputation scores, 2000-01 ★2337★

U.S. News & World Report's undergraduate engineering programs with the best chemical departments, 2000-01 ★2344★

U.S. News & World Report's undergraduate engineering programs with the best civil departments, 2000-01 ★2347★

U.S. News & World Report's undergraduate engineering programs with the best computer departments, 2000-01 ★2353★

U.S. News & World Report's undergraduate engineering programs with the best electrical departments, 2000-01 ★2355★

U.S. News & World Report's undergraduate engineering programs with the best mechanical departments, 2000-01 ★2438★

Private, 4-year undergraduate colleges and universities producing the most Ph.D.'s in mathematics, 1920-1990 ★2776★

Private, 4-year undergraduate colleges and universities producing the most Ph.D.'s in physics and astronomy, 1920-1990 ★2949★

Average faculty salaries for institutions of higher education in New York, 2000-01 ★3719★

Cooper University
U.S. colleges and universities with a favorable surrounding town or city ★1013★

Cooper; William E.
Presidents with the highest pay at Master's I and II colleges and universities, 1998-99 ★3161★

Top pay and benefits for the chief executive and top paid employees at the University of Richmond ★3559★

Coordination Chemistry Reviews
Inorganic and nuclear chemistry journals by citation impact, 1981-99 ★811★

Cope Middle School
Outstanding secondary schools in Shreveport-Bossier City, Louisiana ★4230★

Copeland Jr.; W. James
Top pay and benefits for the chief executive and top paid employees at Southern Methodist University ★3502★

Copenhagen-Lund
Cities with the highest productivity of paper in the discipline of cardiovascular systems, 1994-96 ★2869★

Cities with the highest productivity of paper in the discipline of immunology, 1994-96 ★2871★

Copiah-Lincoln Community College
Average faculty salaries for institutions of higher education without academic ranks in Mississippi, 2000-01 ★3754★

Coppell Middle School
Outstanding secondary schools in Dallas, Texas ★4120★

Coppin State College
Colleges offering the Thurgood Marshall Scholarship Fund ★221★

Coppola; Leibert
Top pay and benefits for the chief executive and top paid employees at Saint Bonaventure University ★3470★

Coquillette; Daniel R.
Top pay and benefits for the chief executive and top paid employees at Boston College ★3205★

Cor Jesu Academy
Outstanding secondary schools in St. Louis, Missouri-Illinois ★4216★

Coral Springs Middle School
Outstanding secondary schools in Fort Lauderdale, Florida ★4133★

Corbett; William
Top pay and benefits for the chief executive and top paid employees at Suffolk University ★3513★

Corcoran; Christopher
All-America boys' high school soccer team midfielders, 2001 ★168★

Corcoran College of Art and Design
Undergraduate tuition and fees at colleges and universities in the District of Columbia ★1493★

Corey; Shana
Outstanding children's picture books, 2000 ★331★

Corinthian Schools National Institute of Technology
Highest undergraduate tuition and fees at colleges and universities in West Virginia ★1568★

Cormier; Robert
People for the American Way's list of most frequently challenged authors, 1982-1992 ★746★

Cornell College
Highest undergraduate tuition and fees at colleges and universities in Iowa ★1504★

Cornell Research Foundation
Most patents issued to universities or research facilities, 1999 ★3097★

Cornell University
Most effective ecology, evolution, and behavior research-doctorate programs as evaluated by the National Research Council ★199★

Top ecology, evolution, and behavior research-doctorate programs as evaluated by the National Research Council ★201★

U.S. universities publishing the most papers in the field of microbiology, 1994-98 ★215★

Winner of the American Chemical Society's Arthur C. Cope Awards, 2001 ★795★

Most effective chemistry research-doctorate programs as evaluated by the National Research Council ★802★

Top chemistry research-doctorate programs as evaluated by the National Research Council ★805★

Most effective classics research-doctorate programs as evaluated by the National Research Council ★815★

Top classics research-doctorate programs as evaluated by the National Research Council ★816★

U.S. News & World Report's national universities with the best academic reputation, 2000-01 ★1126★

U.S. News & World Report's national universities with the best freshmen retention rates, 2000-01 ★1128★

U.S. News & World Report's national universities with the highest graduation rate, 1999 ★1134★

U.S. News & World Report's national universities with the highest percentage of full-time faculty, 2000-01 ★1136★

U.S. News & World Report's national universities with the highest proportion of classes with less than 20 students, 2000-01 ★1138★

2001 mid-year endowment values of the 'wealthiest' U.S. universities ★1234★

Colleges and universities with the largest endowments, 2000 ★1237★

Institutions receiving the most alumni gifts, 1999-2000 ★1242★

Institutions receiving the most gifts, 1999-2000 ★1244★

Most effective comparative literature research-doctorate programs as evaluated by the National Research Council ★1587★

Top comparative literature research-doctorate programs as evaluated by the National Research Council ★1588★

Most effective computer science research-doctorate programs as evaluated by the National Research Council ★1594★

Top computer science research-doctorate programs as evaluated by the National Research Council ★1597★

Total baccalaureate physical sciences degrees awarded to Asian Americans from U.S. colleges and universities, 1997-98 ★1734★

U.S. colleges and universities awarding the most biological and life sciences master's degrees to Hispanic Americans ★1758★

U.S. institutions awarding the most baccalaureate degrees to African Americans in agribusiness and production, 1998 ★1813★

U.S. institutions awarding the most baccalaureate degrees to Asian Americans in agribusiness and production, 1998 ★1815★

U.S. institutions awarding the most baccalaureate degrees to Asian Americans in agricultural sciences, 1998 ★1816★

U.S. institutions awarding the most baccalaureate degrees to Hispanic Americans in agribusiness and production, 1998 ★1817★

U.S. institutions awarding the most baccalaureate degrees to minorities in agribusiness and production, 1998 ★1819★

U.S. institutions awarding the most master's degrees to African Americans in agricultural sciences, 1998 ★1825★

U.S. institutions awarding the most master's degrees to minorities in agribusiness and production, 1998 ★1829★

Top geosciences research-doctorate programs as evaluated by the National Research Council ★2152★

Origin of doctorate for economics faculty at Ph.D.-granting institutions ★2209★

Origin of doctorate for economics faculty at Ph.D.-granting institutions, by Ph.D. equivalents produced ★2210★

Acceptance rates for *U.S. News & World Report*'s top 10 graduate engineering schools, 2001 ★2358★

Average analytic GRE scores for *U.S. News & World Report*'s top 10 graduate engineering schools, 2001 ★2359★

Average quantitative GRE scores for *U.S. News & World Report*'s top 10 graduate engineering schools, 2001 ★2360★

Doctoral student-faculty ratios at *U.S. News & World Report*'s top 10 graduate engineering schools, 2001 ★2361★

Faculty membership in National Academy of Engineering at *U.S. News & World Report*'s top 10 graduate engineering schools, 2001 ★2362★

Ph.D.s granted at *U.S. News & World Report*'s top 10 graduate engineering schools, 2001 ★2363★

Research expenditures per faculty member at *U.S. News & World Report*'s top 10 graduate engineering schools, 2001 ★2364★

Research funding allocated to *U.S. News & World Report*'s top 10 graduate engineering schools, 2001 ★2365★

CORNELL

Top graduate engineering schools, 2001 ★2366★

Top graduate engineering schools by reputation, as determined by academic personnel, 2001 ★2367★

Top graduate engineering schools by reputation, as determined by engineers and recruiters, 2001 ★2368★

U.S. News & World Report's graduate engineering programs with the highest academic reputation scores, 2000-01 ★2372★

Academics' choices for best graduate aerospace/aeronautical/astronautical engineering programs, 2001 ★2374★

Most effective aerospace engineering research-doctorate programs as evaluated by the National Research Council ★2375★

Top aerospace engineering research-doctorate programs as evaluated by the National Research Council ★2376★

Academics' choices for best graduate agricultural engineering programs, 2001 ★2379★

Most effective chemical engineering research-doctorate programs as evaluated by the National Research Council ★2389★

Top chemical engineering research-doctorate programs as evaluated by the National Research Council ★2390★

Academics' choices for best graduate civil engineering programs, 2001 ★2394★

Most effective civil engineering research-doctorate programs as evaluated by the National Research Council ★2395★

Top civil engineering research-doctorate programs as evaluated by the National Research Council ★2396★

Academics' choices for best graduate computer engineering programs, 2001 ★2399★

Academics' choices for best graduate electrical/electronic/communications engineering programs, 2001 ★2403★

Most effective electrical engineering research-doctorate programs as evaluated by the National Research Council ★2404★

Top electrical engineering research-doctorate programs as evaluated by the National Research Council ★2405★

Academics' choices for best graduate materials engineering programs, 2001 ★2417★

Most effective materials science research-doctorate programs as evaluated by the National Research Council ★2418★

Top materials science research-doctorate programs as evaluated by the National Research Council ★2419★

Academics' choices for best graduate mechanical engineering programs, 2001 ★2422★

Most effective mechanical engineering research-doctorate programs as evaluated by the National Research Council ★2423★

Most effective English language and literature research-doctorate programs as evaluated by the National Research Council ★2448★

Top English language and literature research-doctorate programs as evaluated by the National Research Council ★2451★

U.S. universities publishing the most papers in the field of ecology/environmental sciences, 1994-98 ★2473★

Top French language and literature research-doctorate programs as evaluated by the National Research Council ★2516★

Most effective German language and literature research-doctorate programs as evaluated by the National Research Council ★2527★

Top German language and literature research-doctorate programs as evaluated by the National Research Council ★2528★

Top history research-doctorate programs as evaluated by the National Research Council ★2554★

Law schools with the best constitutional law (freedom of speech) faculty, 1999-2000 ★2644★

Law schools with the best feminist legal theory faculty, 1999-2000 ★2651★

Law schools with the best labor law faculty, 1999-2000 ★2656★

Law schools with the best Torts (including products liability) faculty, 1999-2000 ★2665★

Law schools with the highest quality, 1999-2000 ★2666★

Institutions with the most productive libraries, 1993-1997 ★2678★

Law library web sites, by visibility ★2687★

Top university research libraries in the U.S. and Canada, 1998-99 ★2706★

Most effective linguistics research-doctorate programs as evaluated by the National Research Council ★2732★

Top linguistics research-doctorate programs as evaluated by the National Research Council ★2733★

U.S. universities with the greatest impact in mathematics, 1995-99 ★2772★

Most effective mathematics research-doctorate programs as evaluated by the National Research Council ★2775★

Top mathematics research-doctorate programs as evaluated by the National Research Council ★2778★

Most effective statistics and biostatistics research-doctorate programs as evaluated by the National Research Council ★2780★

Top statistics and biostatistics research-doctorate programs as evaluated by the National Research Council ★2782★

Top primary-care medical schools by student selectivity rank, 2001 ★2858★

Most effective music research-doctorate programs as evaluated by the National Research Council ★2895★

Top music research-doctorate programs as evaluated by the National Research Council ★2896★

U.S. universities with the greatest impact in optics and acoustics, 1995-99 ★2912★

Institutions in the Worker Rights Consortium ★2913★

Most effective philosophy research-doctorate programs as evaluated by the National Research Council ★2945★

Top philosophy research-doctorate programs as evaluated by the National Research Council ★2947★

Most effective astrophysics and astronomy research-doctorate programs as evaluated by the National Research Council ★3006★

Most effective physics research-doctorate programs as evaluated by the National Research Council ★3007★

Top astrophysics and astronomy research-doctorate programs as evaluated by the National Research Council ★3014★

Top physics research-doctorate programs as evaluated by the National Research Council ★3015★

Top political science research-doctorate programs as evaluated by the National Research Council ★3046★

Top psychology research-doctorate programs as evaluated by the National Research Council ★3068★

U.S. colleges and universities spending the most on chemical research and development, 1998 ★3099★

Institutions receiving the most federal research and development expenditures, 1999 ★3105★

Largest benefit packages awarded to presidents at institutions of higher education, 1998-99 ★3133★

Average faculty salaries for institutions of higher education in Iowa, 2000-01 ★3702★

U.S. universities publishing the most papers in the field of food science/nutrition, 1994-98 ★4286★

U.S. universities with the highest relative citation impact, 1993-97 ★4291★

Radcliffe Institute for Advanced Study fellowship recipients in the field of sociology, 2000-01 ★4346★

Most effective Spanish and Portuguese language and literature research-doctorate programs as evaluated by the National Research Council ★4357★

Top Spanish and Portuguese language and literature research-doctorate programs as evaluated by the National Research Council ★4358★

Cornell University, Endowed Colleges

Doctorate-granting-institutions awarding the most non-U.S. citizen doctoral degrees, 1999 ★1906★

U.S. colleges and universities awarding the most doctorates in life sciences, 1999 ★2104★

Average faculty salaries for institutions of higher education in New York, 2000-01 ★3719★

U.S. institutions with the highest paid assistant professors, 2001 ★3977★

Cornell University, Johnson Graduate School of Business and Public Administration

Academics' choices for best graduate nonprofit organizations programs, 2001 ★586★

Annual tuition at *Business Week*'s top business schools, 2000 ★589★

Average job offers received by graduates from *Business Week*'s top business schools, 1999 ★592★

Business Week's top business schools, 2000 ★595★

Business Week's top business schools as selected by corporate recruiters, 2000 ★596★

Business Week's top business schools as selected by recent MBA graduates, 2000 ★597★

Business Week's top business schools best at responding to student concerns, 2000 ★598★

Business Week's top business schools by intellectual capital, 2000 ★599★

Business Week's top business schools for general management skills as selected by corporate recruiters, 2000 ★601★

Business Week's top business schools for marketing skills as selected by corporate recruiters, 2000 ★603★

Business Week's top business schools for technology skills as selected by corporate recruiters, 2000 ★604★

Business Week's top business schools with the best placement offices, 2000 ★608★

Business Week's top business schools with the best teachers, 2000 ★609★

Business Week's top business schools with the lowest percentage of international students, 2000 ★615★

Business Week's top business schools with the lowest percentage of minority enrollment, 2000 ★616★

Business Week's top business schools with the lowest percentage of women enrollees, 2000 ★617★

Business Week's top business schools with the most improved program as selected by corporate recruiters, 2000 ★618★

Percentage of applicants accepted at *Business Week*'s top business schools, 2000 ★638★

Percentage of graduates earning over $100,000 from *Business Week*'s top business schools, 1999 ★640★

Top graduate business schools by reputation, as determined by recruiters, 2001 ★651★

Cornell University Statutory Colleges
Average faculty salaries for institutions of higher education in New York, 2000-01 ★3719★

Cornerstone University
Average faculty salaries for institutions of higher education in Michigan, 2000-01 ★3709★

Corning
Fortune's highest ranked building materials and glass companies, 2000 ★451★

Top manufacturing companies in Standard & Poor's 500, 2001 ★548★

Top recruiters for engineering jobs for 2000-01 bachelor's degree recipients ★2334★

Top recruiters for systems engineer jobs for 2000-01 bachelor's degree recipients ★2336★

Top recruiters for chemical engineering jobs for 2000-01 bachelor's degree recipients ★2343★

Top recruiters for engineering jobs for 2000-01 master's degree recipients ★2369★

Top recruiters for systems engineer jobs for 2000-01 master's degree recipients ★2371★

Top recruiters for chemical engineering jobs for 2000-01 master's degree recipients ★2391★

Top recruiters for electrical/electronic engineering jobs for 2000-01 master's degree recipients ★2406★

Top recruiters for industrial engineering jobs for 2000-01 master's degree recipients ★2414★

Top recruiters for mechanical engineering jobs for 2000-01 master's degree recipients ★2424★

Top recruiters for industrial engineering jobs for 2000-01 bachelor's degree recipients ★2432★

Top recruiters for physics jobs for 2000-01 bachelor's degree recipients ★2974★

Top recruiters for physics jobs for 2000-01 master's degree recipients ★3016★

Corning Community College
Highest undergraduate tuition and fees at public 2-year colleges and universities ★1462★

Average faculty salaries for institutions of higher education in New York, 2000-01 ★3719★

Cornish College of the Arts
Highest undergraduate tuition and fees at colleges and universities in Washington ★1566★

The Coro Foundation
Top internships in the U.S., 2001 ★2612★

Corona del Mar High School
Outstanding secondary schools in Orange County, California ★4199★

Corona; Xavier
All-USA College Academic Third Team, 2001 ★4★

Coronado High School
Outstanding secondary schools in San Diego, California ★4220★

Corporate executive (senior)
Jobs considered the most competitive ★2245★
Jobs that are potentially the highest paying ★2246★
Jobs with the best income scores ★2248★
Jobs with the longest work weeks ★2257★
Jobs with the most stringent quotas ★2259★
Jobs with the worst stress scores ★2265★

Corporation for Public Broadcasting
Proposed fiscal 2002 appropriations for miscellaneous federal aid ★2487★

Corrarino; Mary
Top pay and benefits for the chief executive and top paid employees at Manhattanville College ★3388★

Correa; Peter C.
Top pay and benefits for the chief executive and top paid employees at Hampshire College ★3322★

Correction officer
'Blue-collar' jobs considered the least physically demanding ★2241★

Corrections officers
Projected employment growth for selected occupations that require long-term on-the-job training, 1998-2008 ★2320★

Cortina; Alfonsa
European business moguls considered the best turnaround artists ★443★

Corts; Thomas E.
Top pay and benefits for the chief executive and top paid employees at Samford University ★3490★

Cosby; Bill
Most influential African American entertainers ★77★

Cosmetologist
Most desirable jobs in personal services ★2275★

Costa Rica
Top countries of study for U.S. students studying abroad, 1998-99 ★2510★

Costco Wholesale
Fortune's highest ranked specialty retailers, 2000 ★497★

Top discount and fashion retailing companies in Standard & Poor's 500, 2001 ★538★

Cotter; James F.
Top pay and benefits for the chief executive and top paid employees at Mount Saint Mary College in New York ★3410★

Cotter; William R.
Top pay and benefits for the chief executive and top paid employees at Colby College ★3241★

Cottey College
Average faculty salaries for institutions of higher education in Missouri, 2000-01 ★3712★

Cotton; F. Albert
American Chemical Society 2001 award winners (Group 2) ★752★

Council on Hemispheric Affairs
Most selective internships in the U.S., 2001 ★2610★

Counseling
Gender breakdown of psychology doctorate recipients, by subfield, 1999 ★1941★

Psychology doctorates awarded at U.S. colleges and universities, by subfield, 1999 ★2043★

Counseling education/counseling and guidance
Education doctorates awarded at U.S. colleges and universities, by subfield, 1999 ★1921★
Gender breakdown of education doctorate recipients, by subfield, 1999 ★1933★

Counselors
Projected employment growth for selected occupations that require advanced education, 1998-2008 ★2318★

Counterfeit Son
Most notable fiction books for reluctant young adult readers, 2001 ★321★

Counting Coup: A True Story of Basketball and Honor on the Little Big Horn
Outstanding nonfiction books for young adults, 2000 ★334★

Country Insights
Booklist's most recommended geography series for young people, 2000 ★313★

Countrywide Credit Industries
Fortune's highest ranked mortgage finance companies, 2000 ★479★

Countrywide Home Loans
Top recruiters for language/literature jobs for 2000-01 bachelor's degree recipients ★2446★
Top recruiters for psychology jobs for 2000-01 bachelor's degree recipients ★3063★

County College of Morris
Lowest undergraduate tuition and fees at colleges and universities in New Jersey ★1534★

Courniotes; Harry J.
Top pay and benefits for the chief executive and top paid employees at American International College ★3173★

Courtice; Thomas B.
Top pay and benefits for the chief executive and top paid employees at Ohio Wesleyan University ★3430★

Covenant College
College senior's choices for exemplary undergraduate institutions ★1319★
U.S. News & World Report's southern regional liberal arts colleges with the highest freshmen retention rates, 2000-01 ★1372★
U.S. News & World Report's southern regional liberal arts colleges with the highest percentage of full-time faculty, 2000-01 ★1374★
U.S. News & World Report's southern regional liberal arts colleges with the lowest acceptance rates, 2000-01 ★1377★
Highest undergraduate tuition and fees at colleges and universities in Georgia ★1496★
Average faculty salaries for institutions of higher education in Georgia, 2000-01 ★3697★

Covenant Theological Seminary
Average faculty salaries for institutions of higher education in Missouri, 2000-01 ★3712★

Coveney; Kevin
Top pay and benefits for the chief executive and top paid employees at Washington College ★3606★

Covent Sacred Heart High School
Outstanding secondary schools in New York, New York ★4191★

Covington Middle School
Outstanding secondary schools in Detroit, Michigan ★4125★

Coward; Geoffrey
  Top pay and benefits for the chief executive and top paid employees at Wagner College ★3599★
Coward; Noel
  Top playwrights of the twentieth century ★4436★
Cowboy
  Jobs with the highest unemployment ★2256★
  Jobs with the worst outlook scores ★2262★
  Jobs with the worst physical demands scores ★2263★
  Least desirable jobs ★2266★
  Most desirable jobs in agriculture ★2268★
Cowdrey; Terry
  Top pay and benefits for the chief executive and top paid employees at St. Lawrence University ★3477★
Cowen; Scott S.
  Top pay and benefits for the chief executive and top paid employees at Tulane University ★3581★
Cowley County Community College
  Lowest undergraduate tuition and fees at colleges and universities in Kansas ★1507★
Cox; Gerard A.
  Top pay and benefits for the chief executive and top paid employees at Marist College ★3390★
Cox; James L.
  Top pay and benefits for the chief executive and top paid employees at Georgetown University ★3306★
Coyle and Cassidy High School
  Outstanding secondary schools in Boston, Massachusetts-New Hampshire ★4100★
CQ Researcher
  Library Journal's best reference databases and discs, 2000 ★369★
The Cradle of the Real Life
  Library Journal's best poetry books, 2000 ★244★
Craig Hospital
  Top rehabilitation hospitals in the U.S., 2000 ★2801★
Craig Middle School
  Outstanding secondary schools in Indianapolis, Indiana ★4153★
Craig; William G.
  Top pay and benefits for the chief executive and top paid employees at Monmouth University in New Jersey ★3406★
Craiglow; James
  Top pay and benefits for the chief executive and top paid employees at Antioch University ★3178★
Craigmont High School
  Outstanding secondary schools in Memphis, Tennessee-Arkansas-Mississippi ★4177★
Craigslist
  Top career-related Web sites ★2602★
Crampton; Stuart
  Top pay and benefits for the chief executive and top paid employees at Williams College ★3631★
Cranfield University School of Management
  European and Canadian business schools with the quickest payback on MBA investments ★628★
Crashboomlove: A Novel in Verse
  Most notable fiction books for reluctant young adult readers, 2001 ★321★

Craven Community College
  Average faculty salaries for institutions of higher education without academic ranks in North Carolina, 2000-01 ★3761★
Craven; Jordan
  All-American boy's high school football team, 2000 ★187★
Craven; Michael-Jordan
  All-American boy's high school football linebackers, 2000 ★182★
Crazy
  Most notable fiction books for young adults, 2001 ★322★
Crazy Horse's Vision
  Most notable books for middle readers, 2001 ★317★
CRC-Critical Review of Food Sciences
  Food science and technology journals by citation impact, 1991-99 ★2902★
CRC Critical Reviews in Immunology
  Immunology journals with the greatest impact measure, 1981-98 ★2810★
CRC Critical Reviews in Oncology and Hematology
  Hematology journals with the greatest impact measure, 1981-98 ★2808★
CRC Current Review of Immunology
  Immunology journals by impact factor, 1981 to 1997 ★4279★
Creamer Dickson Basford
  Most selective internships in the U.S., 2001 ★2610★
Credit reporting and collection
  Employment growth percentages for selected industries, 1998-2000 ★2294★
Credit Suisse Group
  Business Week's best companies in Switzerland ★405★
Creech; Sharon
  Outstanding children's fiction books, 2000 ★329★
  Outstanding children's picture books, 2000 ★331★
Creegan; Frank
  Top pay and benefits for the chief executive and top paid employees at Washington College ★3606★
Creighton; Joanne
  Top pay and benefits for the chief executive and top paid employees at Mount Holyoke College ★3409★
Creighton University
  U.S. News & World Report's midwestern regional universities with students most in debt, 1999 ★1400★
  U.S. News & World Report's midwestern regional universities with the best academic reputation scores, 2000-01 ★1401★
  U.S. News & World Report's midwestern regional universities with the highest acceptance rates, 2000-01 ★1404★
  U.S. News & World Report's midwestern regional universities with the highest freshmen retention rates, 2000-01 ★1405★
  U.S. News & World Report's midwestern regional universities with the highest graduation rates, 2000-01 ★1406★
  U.S. News & World Report's midwestern regional universities with the highest percentage of freshmen from the top 25% of their high school class, 2000-01 ★1407★
  U.S. News & World Report's top midwestern regional universities, 2000-01 ★1411★

  U.S. News & World Report's best undergraduate fees among midwestern regional universities by discount tuition, 2000 ★1427★
  Highest undergraduate tuition and fees at colleges and universities in Nebraska ★1528★
  Average faculty salaries for institutions of higher education in Nebraska, 2000-01 ★3714★
Cresco Public Library
  Highest Hennen's American Public Library Ratings for libraries serving a population of 5,000 to 9,999 ★2694★
Cress; Larry
  Top pay and benefits for the chief executive and top paid employees at Willamette University ★3628★
Crestline Capital
  Fortune's highest ranked hotels, casinos and resorts, 2000 ★470★
Crestview Middle School
  Outstanding secondary schools in St. Louis, Missouri-Illinois ★4216★
Crete-Monee Middle School
  Outstanding secondary schools in Chicago, Illinois ★4110★
Cretin-Derham Hall School
  Outstanding secondary schools in Minneapolis-St. Paul, Minnesota-Wisconsin ★4181★
Crews; James S.
  Top pay and benefits for the chief executive and top paid employees at the University of Evansville ★3543★
CRH
  Business Week's best companies in Ireland ★396★
Crichton College
  Average faculty salaries for institutions of higher education in Tennessee, 2000-01 ★3730★
Crickwing
  Publishers Weekly Off-the-Cuff Awards winner for most disappointing book by a favorite author (in terms of sales), 2000 ★352★
Crime & Delinquency
  Criminology and penology journals with the greatest impact measure, 1981-98 ★1611★
  Criminology and penology journals with the greatest impact measure, 1994-98 ★1612★
Crime & Justice
  Criminology and penology journals with the greatest impact measure, 1981-98 ★1611★
Criminal Justice and Behavior
  Criminology and penology journals with the greatest impact measure, 1981-98 ★1611★
  Criminology and penology journals with the greatest impact measure, 1994-98 ★1612★
Criminology
  Criminology and penology journals with the greatest impact measure, 1981-98 ★1611★
  Criminology and penology journals with the greatest impact measure, 1994-98 ★1612★
  Gender breakdown of social sciences doctorate recipients, by subfield, 1999 ★1942★
  Social sciences doctorates awarded at U.S. colleges and universities, by subfield, 1999 ★2044★
Crimmins; Michael T.
  Winner of the American Chemical Society's Arthur C. Cope Awards, 2001 ★795★
Crimmins; Robert J.
  Top pay and benefits for the chief executive and top paid employees at St. John's University in New York ★3474★

Criscillis; Arthur L.
Top pay and benefits for the chief executive and top paid employees at Rhodes College ★3456★

Crisp; Delmas
Top pay and benefits for the chief executive and top paid employees at Wesleyan College in Georgia ★3611★

Crist; Charles W.
Top pay and benefits for the chief executive and top paid employees at Hollins University ★3336★

Critical Review of Food Sciences
Food science and technology journals by citation impact, 1991-99 ★2902★
Food science and technology journals by citation impact, 1995-99 ★2903★
Food science and technology journals by citation impact, 1999 ★2904★

Critique of Legal Order: Crime Control in Capitalist Society
Most-cited works in critical criminology publications ★1645★

Crocetta; Alison
Radcliffe Institute for Advanced Study fellowship recipients in the field of visual arts, 2000-01 ★79★

Crocker; L.
Highest ranked inactive communication studies researchers ★2748★
Speech communication's most published scholars between 1915-1985 ★4362★

Crocker School
Outstanding secondary schools in San Francisco, California ★4221★

Crockett Jr.; Bennie
Top pay and benefits for the chief executive and top paid employees at William Carey College ★3629★

Crockett Middle School
Outstanding secondary schools in Amarillo, Texas ★4082★

Cronin; B.
Authors that most frequently cite *Libri* publications from 1972 to 1999 ★2723★

Cronin; Blaise
Library and information science faculty with the most citations to journal articles, 1993-1998 ★2710★
Library and information science faculty with the most journal articles, 1993-1998 ★2711★

Cronin; Doreen
Outstanding children's picture books, 2000 ★331★

Cronin; Paul
Top pay and benefits for the chief executive and top paid employees at Sweet Briar College ★3515★

Cronin; Steve
All-America boys' high school soccer team goalkeepers, 2001 ★167★
All-America boys' high school soccer team player of the year, 2001 ★169★

Cronin; Thomas E.
Top pay and benefits for the chief executive and top paid employees at Whitman College ★3623★

Cronk; Ronald
Top pay and benefits for the chief executive and top paid employees at Westmont College ★3619★

Cronkite Remembers
Library Journal's best nonfiction audiobooks, 2000 ★243★

Croom; Frederick
Top pay and benefits for the chief executive and top paid employees at the University of the South ★3572★

Crosby; Roscoe
All-American boy's high school football receivers, 2000 ★185★
All-American boy's high school football team, 2000 ★187★

Cross; Dennis
Top pay and benefits for the chief executive and top paid employees at Sarah Lawrence College ★3492★

Cross; William M.
Top pay and benefits for the chief executive and top paid employees at Illinois College ★3345★

Crossing Jordan
Most notable fiction books for young adults, 2001 ★322★

Crossroads Middle School
Outstanding secondary schools in Middlesex-Somerset-Hunterdon, New Jersey ★4179★

Crouch Jr.; William H.
Top pay and benefits for the chief executive and top paid employees at Georgetown College in Kentucky ★3305★

Crowder College
Lowest undergraduate tuition and fees at colleges and universities in Missouri ★1525★

Crowell; Laura
Top published female authors (1915-1985) in the field of communication studies ★4363★

Crown Capital
Most selective internships in the U.S., 2001 ★2610★

Crown Cork & Seal
Fortune's highest ranked metal products companies, 2000 ★475★

Crowpoint Institute of Technology
U.S. tribal colleges ★1445★

The Crucible
Top plays of the twentieth century ★4435★

Crucible of War: The Seven Years' War and the Faith of Empire in British North America
Outstanding history books, 2000 ★289★

Crum; Denny
Coaches winning the most NCAA tournaments ★120★

Crystal Lake Community 155
Illinois high school districts with the highest teacher salaries, 1999 ★3985★

Crystal Research and Technology
Crystallography journals by citation impact, 1998 ★1656★

Crystallography Lattice Defects
Crystallography journals by citation impact, 1981-98 ★1654★

CSX
Business Week's best performing companies with the lowest 1-year sales performance ★421★
Fortune's highest ranked railroads, 2000 ★490★
Top transportation companies in Standard & Poor's 500, 2001 ★560★

CTS
Most profitable information technology companies, 2000 ★527★
Top information technology companies, 2000 ★544★

Cucchi; Paolo
Top pay and benefits for the chief executive and top paid employees at Drew University ★3273★

Cuckoo, Mr. Edgar!
Most notable children's videos, 2001 ★2889★
Outstanding videos for library collections, 2000 ★2892★

Cuesta College
Average faculty salaries for institutions of higher education without academic ranks in California, 2000-01 ★3743★

Cujo
Most frequently banned books in the 1990s ★745★

Cullen Elementary School
Illinois elementary schools chosen to be 'demonstration sites' for struggling schools ★4006★

Cullen; Francis T.
Most cited authors in the journal *Federal Probation*, 1990 to 1995 ★1623★
Most cited authors in three criminal justice journals ★1633★

Cullen; F.T.
Most cited authors in the journal *International Journal of Comparative and Applied Criminal Justice*, 1990 to 1995 ★1624★

Cullen, Link, Wolfe, & Frank
Most cited works in academic literature dealing with corrections ★1643★

Cullen; Maureen
Top pay and benefits for the chief executive and top paid employees at Saint Joseph's University ★3476★

Cultural Anthropology
Anthropology journals by citation impact, 1998 ★65★

Culture, Medicine and Psychiatry
Anthropology journals by citation impact, 1991-98 ★63★
Anthropology journals by citation impact, 1994-98 ★64★

Cultures of the World
Booklist's most recommended geography series for young people, 2000 ★313★

Culver City High School
Outstanding secondary schools in Los Angeles-Long Beach, California ★4167★

Culver-Stockton College
U.S. News & World Report's midwestern regional liberal arts colleges with students least in debt, 1999 ★1337★
Average faculty salaries for institutions of higher education in Missouri, 2000-01 ★3712★

Cumberland County College
Average faculty salaries for institutions of higher education in New Jersey, 2000-01 ★3717★

Cumberland Farms
Top women-owned companies ★4460★

Cummings; J. David
Authors with the most published pages in impact-weighted insurance journals ★677★

Cummings; Robert
Top pay and benefits for the chief executive and top paid employees at Saint Xavier University ★3487★

Cummins; D. Duane
Top pay and benefits for the chief executive and top paid employees at Bethany College in West Virginia ★3202★

Cummins Engine
Fortune's highest ranked industrial and farm equipment companies, 2000 ★471★

Cummins; J. David
Individual authors with the most published pages in *The Journal of Risk and Insurance*, 1987-1996 ★680★

Cunneen; Chris
Most-cited scholars in *Australian and New Zealand Journal of Criminology* ★1636★

Cunningham Graphics International
Top companies in terms of growth, 2000 ★534★

Cupertino High School
Outstanding secondary schools in San Jose, California ★4222★

Curative Health Services
Companies with the worst two-year total returns since 1998 ★437★

Curran Jr.; Daniel J.
Top pay and benefits for the chief executive and top paid employees at Saint Joseph's University ★3476★

Current Anthropology
Anthropology journals by citation impact, 1991-98 ★63★
Anthropology journals by citation impact, 1994-98 ★64★
Anthropology journals by citation impact, 1998 ★65★

Current Opinion in Immunology
Immunology journals with the greatest impact measure, 1994-98 ★2811★
Immunology journals by impact factor, 1993 to 1997 ★4280★

Current Opinion in Neurobiology
Neurosciences journals with the greatest impact measure, 1994-98 ★2813★

Curriculum and instruction
Education doctorates awarded at U.S. colleges and universities, by subfield, 1999 ★1921★
Gender breakdown of education doctorate recipients, by subfield, 1999 ★1933★

Currie; Dean W.
Top pay and benefits for the chief executive and top paid employees at Rice University ★3457★

Currie; Monique
All-America girls' high school basketball 2nd team, 2001 ★171★

Currier; Barry A.
Top pay and benefits for the chief executive and top paid employees at Samford University ★3490★

Curry College
Average faculty salaries for institutions of higher education in Massachusetts, 2000-01 ★3708★

Curry; Eddy
All-America boys' high school basketball 1st team, 2001 ★161★

Curses, Hexes, and Spells
Most frequently banned books in the 1990s ★745★

Curtis; Monty
Top pay and benefits for the chief executive and top paid employees at Hiram College ★3333★

Curtis-Pierce; Ellen
Top pay and benefits for the chief executive and top paid employees at National University in California ★3415★

The Cushman School
Outstanding secondary schools in Miami, Florida ★4178★

Custer High School
Outstanding secondary schools in Milwaukee-Waukesha, Wisconsin ★4180★

Custodial accounts
Best ways to save for college ★843★

Cut
Most notable fiction books for reluctant young adult readers, 2001 ★321★

Cutler; B.L.
Most cited authors in the journal *Criminal Justice and Behavior*, 1990 to 1995 ★1619★

Cuyahoga Community College, Eastern
Lowest undergraduate tuition and fees at colleges and universities in Ohio ★1544★

Cuyahoga Community College, Metropolitan
Lowest undergraduate tuition and fees at colleges and universities in Ohio ★1544★

Cuyahoga Community College, Western
Lowest undergraduate tuition and fees at colleges and universities in Ohio ★1544★

CVS
Fortune's highest ranked food and drug stores, 2000 ★463★

Cypress Semiconductor
Top information technology companies, 2000 ★544★

Cyprus
Math achievement test comparison ★19★

Czech Republic
Eight grade science achievement scores from selected countries, 1999 ★14★
Math achievement test comparison ★19★
Percentage of enrollment at public institutions of higher education, by country, 1998 ★859★
Countries with the lowest percentage of workers satisfied with their job ★2243★
Countries with the lowest spending per student on higher education, 1997 ★2489★
Eighth grade mathematics achievement scores from selected countries, 1999 ★2773★
Institute for Scientific Information periodical prices by country, 2001 ★2922★

Czepiel; John A.
Highest impact authors in the *Journal of Business Research*, by adjusted number of citations in 12 journals, 1985-1999 ★692★

D

D-Q University
U.S. tribal colleges ★1445★

Dabney S. Lancaster Community College
Lowest undergraduate tuition and fees at colleges and universities in Virginia ★1565★

Dacey Jr.; Ralph G.
Top pay and benefits for the chief executive and top paid employees at Washington University in Missouri ★3607★

Daddy-Long-Legs
Most notable children's recordings, 2001 ★320★

Daddy's Roommate
American Library Association's most frequently challenged books of the decade ★224★
American Library Associations most frequently challenged books for the 1990s ★742★
Most frequently banned books in the 1990s ★745★

Dade Behring
Fortune's highest ranked medical products and equipment companies, 2000 ★474★

Dade County, FL
Superintendents' salaries at the largest U.S. schools districts, 1999-2000 ★3990★
Largest public school districts in the U.S. ★4016★

Daedalus
Most cited science serials in technical communication journals from 1988 to 1997 ★4424★

Daemen College
Average faculty salaries for institutions of higher education in New York, 2000-01 ★3719★

Dahl; Roald
People for the American Way's list of most frequently challenged authors, 1982-1992 ★746★

DaimlerChrysler
Business Week's best companies in Germany ★394★
Business Week's best companies in terms of sales ★408★
Fortune's highest ranked motor vehicles companies, 2000 ★481★

Dairy farmer
Jobs with the longest work weeks ★2257★
Most desirable jobs in agriculture ★2268★

Dairy science
Agricultural sciences doctorates awarded at U.S. colleges and universities, by subfield, 1999 ★1886★
Gender breakdown of agricultural sciences doctorate recipients, by subfield, 1999 ★1926★

Dakota County Library
Highest Hennen's American Public Library Ratings for libraries serving a population of 250,000 to 499,999 ★2699★

Dakota County Tech College
Average faculty salaries for institutions of higher education without academic ranks in Minnesota, 2000-01 ★3753★

Dakota State University
State appropriations for South Dakota's institutions of higher education, 2000-01 ★1294★
Highest undergraduate tuition and fees at colleges and universities in South Dakota ★1556★
Average faculty salaries for institutions of higher education in South Dakota, 2000-01 ★3729★

Dakota Wesleyan University
Highest undergraduate tuition and fees at colleges and universities in South Dakota ★1556★
Average faculty salaries for institutions of higher education in South Dakota, 2000-01 ★3729★

Dalby; Liza
Booklist's best first novels ★228★

Dalhousie University
Best Canadian universities overall, 2000 ★1149★
Canadian medical/doctoral universities by alumni support, 2000 ★1172★
Canadian medical/doctoral universities by award-winning faculty members, 2000 ★1173★
Canadian medical/doctoral universities by class size at the first- and second-year level, 2000 ★1174★
Canadian medical/doctoral universities by class size at the third- and forth-year level, 2000 ★1175★

Canadian medical/doctoral universities by classes taught by tenured faculty, 2000 ★1176★
Canadian medical/doctoral universities by faculty members with Ph.D.'s, 2000 ★1177★
Canadian medical/doctoral universities by international graduate students, 2000 ★1178★
Canadian medical/doctoral universities by library acquisitions, 2000 ★1179★
Canadian medical/doctoral universities by library expenses, 2000 ★1180★
Canadian medical/doctoral universities by library holdings, 2000 ★1181★
Canadian medical/doctoral universities by library holdings per student, 2000 ★1182★
Canadian medical/doctoral universities by medical/science grants per faculty member, 2000 ★1184★
Canadian medical/doctoral universities by operating budget per student, 2000 ★1185★
Canadian medical/doctoral universities by percentage of operating budget allocated to scholarships, 2000 ★1186★
Canadian medical/doctoral universities by percentage of operating budget allocated to student services, 2000 ★1187★
Canadian medical/doctoral universities by reputation, 2000 ★1188★
Canadian medical/doctoral universities by social science/humanities grants per faculty member, 2000 ★1189★
Canadian medical/doctoral universities by students from out of province, 2000 ★1190★
Canadian medical/doctoral universities by students winning national awards, 2000 ★1191★
Canadian universities by average entering grade, 2000 ★1213★
Canadian universities by graduation rate, 2000 ★1214★
Canadian universities by students with 75% grade averages or higher, 2000 ★1215★
Canadian universities with the highest total cost, 2000 ★1217★
Top Canadian medical/doctoral universities, 2000 ★1221★

Dali; Salvador
Highly influential artists of the 20th century ★76★

Dallas
U.S. cities with the highest number of high-tech employees, 1998 ★2284★
U.S. cities with the highest percentage of births to mothers with less than 12 years of education ★4432★

Dallas Baptist University
U.S. News & World Report's western regional universities with students least in debt, 1999 ★1575★

Dallas Cowboys
Most selective internships in the U.S., 2001 ★2610★

Dallas/Fort Worth
American cities with the highest percentage of people with Internet access ★2572★
U.S. market areas with the highest percentage of adults having internet access ★2607★

Dallas, TX
U.S. cities considered to be the most affordable for IT professionals ★562★
Cities with the highest online spending per Internet user ★2576★
Cities with the highest percentage of adults using the Internet at home ★2577★

Dallas; University of
U.S. colleges and universities with a generally conservative student body ★1014★
U.S. colleges and universities with a large student body of conservative Republicans ★1016★
U.S. colleges and universities with a primarily religious student body ★1022★
U.S. colleges and universities with the least attractive campuses ★1037★
Highest undergraduate tuition and fees at colleges and universities in Texas ★1560★
U.S. colleges and universities awarding the most business management and administrative services master's degrees to Native Americans ★1762★
Bachelor's institutions with the highest enrollment of foreign students, 1998-99 ★2492★

Dalrymple; Prudence
Top pay and benefits for the chief executive and top paid employees at Dominican University in Illinois ★3269★

Dalton State College
Lowest undergraduate tuition and fees at colleges and universities in Georgia ★1497★
Average faculty salaries for institutions of higher education in Georgia, 2000-01 ★3697★

Daly; Janis
Top pay and benefits for the chief executive and top paid employees at Walsh University ★3602★

Daly; Kathleen
Most-cited scholars in women and crime publications ★1642★

Daly; Thomas
Top pay and benefits for the chief executive and top paid employees at Marist College ★3390★

D'Amato; Paul H.
Top pay and benefits for the chief executive and top paid employees at Mercer University ★3398★

Dampskibsselskabet AF 1912
Business Week's best companies in Denmark ★391★

Dampskibsselskabet Svenborg
Business Week's best companies in Denmark ★391★

Dana
Business Week's best performing companies with the lowest 3-year shareholder returns ★424★
Fortune's highest ranked motor vehicle parts companies, 2000 ★480★
Top automotive companies in Standard & Poor's 500, 2001 ★530★

Dana College
Highest undergraduate tuition and fees at colleges and universities in Nebraska ★1528★

DANA-Journal of Fisheries and Marine Biology
Marine and freshwater biology journals with the greatest impact measure, 1981-98 ★196★

Dana Middle School
Outstanding secondary schools in Los Angeles-Long Beach, California ★4167★

Danahar; David C.
Top pay and benefits for the chief executive and top paid employees at Loyola University New Orleans ★3381★

Danaher
Fortune's highest ranked metal products companies, 2000 ★475★

Dancause; Elizabeth
All-America girls' high school basketball 3rd team, 2001 ★172★

A Dance for Three
Most notable fiction books for young adults, 2001 ★322★

Dance on a Moonbeam: A Collection of Songs and Poems
Most notable children's recordings, 2001 ★320★

Dancer
Jobs considered the most competitive ★2245★
Jobs with the greatest potential income for beginners ★2253★
Most desirable jobs in the arts ★2277★

Dances with Luigi: A Grandson's Determined Quest to Comprehend Italy and the Italians
Outstanding biography books, 2000 ★288★

Dancing With an Alien
Most notable fiction books for reluctant young adult readers, 2001 ★321★
Most notable fiction books for young adults, 2001 ★322★

Dandridge; William
Top pay and benefits for the chief executive and top paid employees at Lesley College ★3370★

Danheiser; Priscilla
Top pay and benefits for the chief executive and top paid employees at Wesleyan College in Georgia ★3611★

Daniel Webster College
Highest undergraduate tuition and fees at colleges and universities in New Hampshire ★1531★

Dant; Jenni
All-America girls' high school basketball 4th team, 2001 ★173★

Danville Area Community College
Lowest undergraduate tuition and fees at colleges and universities in Illinois ★1501★

Danville Community College
Lowest undergraduate tuition and fees at colleges and universities in Virginia ★1565★

D'Arcy; Stephen P.
Individual authors with the most published pages in *The Journal of Risk and Insurance*, 1987-1996 ★680★

Darden Restaurants
Fortune's highest ranked food services companies, 2000 ★465★
Top leisure time industries in Standard & Poor's 500, 2001 ★545★

Darden; William R.
Authors with the most articles published in the *Journal of Business Research*, 1985 to 1999 ★687★

Darien Library
Highest Hennen's American Public Library Ratings for libraries serving a population of 10,000 to 24,999 ★2695★

Daring to Resist: Three Women Face the Holocaust
Most notable DVDs and videos for young adults, 2001 ★2890★
Outstanding videos for library collections, 2000 ★2892★

Dark Matter
Library Journal's best science fiction and fantasy titles, 2000 ★246★

Dark Midnight When I Rise
  Christopher Awards winners for adult literature, 2000 ★235★
The Dark Portal
  Booklist's most recommended fantasy books for youth ★312★
  Outstanding books for middle readers, 2000 ★326★
Darkness in El Dorado: How Scientists and Journalist Devastated the Amazon
  Library Journal's most notable anthropology books, 2000 ★247★
Darkness over Denmark: The Danish Resistance and the Rescue of the Jews
  Most notable nonfiction books for young adults, 2001 ★324★
  Outstanding books for older readers, 2000 ★327★
Darkness Peering
  Library Journal's best fiction audiobooks, 2000 ★241★
Darling; J. Norwood "Ding"
  Top editorial cartoonists used in teaching journalism history ★2770★
Darling; Stanton
  Top pay and benefits for the chief executive and top paid employees at Capital University ★3220★
Darnell; James E.
  Top pay and benefits for the chief executive and top paid employees at Rockefeller University ★3462★
Dartmouth College
  NCAA Division I ski teams with the most championships ★135★
  U.S. colleges and universities with the best quality of life ★1034★
  U.S. News & World Report's national universities with the best freshmen retention rates, 2000-01 ★1128★
  U.S. News & World Report's national universities with the best graduation and retention rank, 2000-01 ★1129★
  U.S. News & World Report's national universities with the highest alumni giving rank, 2000-01 ★1132★
  U.S. News & World Report's national universities with the highest financial resources rank, 2000-01 ★1133★
  U.S. News & World Report's national universities with the highest graduation rate, 1999 ★1134★
  U.S. News & World Report's national universities with the highest proportion of alumni support, 2000-01 ★1137★
  U.S. News & World Report's national universities with the highest selectivity rank, 2000-01 ★1139★
  U.S. News & World Report's national universities with the lowest acceptance rates, 2000-01 ★1140★
  Colleges and universities with the largest endowments, 2000 ★1237★
  Institutions receiving the most in federal agency appropriations to colleges, 2000 ★1245★
  Highest undergraduate tuition and fees at private nonprofit, 4-year or above colleges and universities ★1461★
  U.S. News & World Report's best undergraduate fees among national universities by discount tuition, 2000 ★1474★
  Highest undergraduate tuition and fees at colleges and universities in New Hampshire ★1531★
  U.S. doctoral institutions with the largest number of students studying abroad, 1998-99 ★2512★
  Radcliffe Institute for Advanced Study fellowship recipient in the field of geography, 2000-01 ★2517★
  Presidents with the highest pay at Doctoral I and II universities, 1998-99 ★3160★
  Average faculty salaries for institutions of higher education in New Hampshire, 2000-01 ★3716★
Dartmouth College, Amos Tuck School of Business Administration
  Business Week's institutions with the best entrepreneurship programs ★594★
  Business Week's top business schools with the greatest decrease in MBA satisfaction, 2000 ★610★
  Business Week's top business schools with the highest percentage of women enrollees, 2000 ★614★
  Highest post-MBA salaries for students enrolled in Business Week's top business schools, 1999 ★631★
  Highest pre-MBA salaries for students enrolled in Business Week's top business schools, 1999 ★632★
  Top graduate business schools by reputation, as determined by recruiters, 2001 ★651★
  Academics' choices for best graduate general management programs, 2001 ★666★
Dartmouth High School
  Outstanding suburban public high schools in Metro Boston ★4255★
Dartmouth Medical Grant Program
  State appropriations for New Hampshire's institutions of higher education, 2000-01 ★1282★
Dartmouth University
  Top business schools by average MBA rank, 1986-1998 ★644★
  Most wired universities, 2000 ★2598★
Darwin's Ghost: "The Origin of Species" Updated
  Library Journal's most notable biology books, 2000 ★250★
Dassel-Cokato High School
  Outstanding secondary schools in Minneapolis-St. Paul, Minnesota-Wisconsin ★4181★
Dassler; Brian
  All-USA College Academic Third Team, 2001 ★4★
Data Mining and Knowledge Discovery
  Artificial intelligence journals by citation impact, 1999 ★96★
Data processing equipment repairers
  Fastest growing occupations, 1998-2008 ★2302★
  Projected employment growth for selected occupations that require an associate degree or less, 1998-2008 ★2319★
Database administrators
  Projections for the fastest growing occupations requiring a bachelor's degree or more from 1998 to 2008 ★2292★
  Fastest growing occupations, 1998-2008 ★2302★
  Median annual earnings for computer technology jobs, 1998 ★3122★
Database development
  Job openings for high-tech workers ★2330★
Database development/administration
  Information technology jobs most in demand, 2001 ★4428★
Datalink
  Business Week's top companies in terms of return on capital, 2000 ★430★
Datamation
  Most cited technology serials in technical communication journals from 1988 to 1997 ★4427★
Daughdrill Jr.; James H.
  Presidents with the highest pay at Baccalaureate I colleges, 1998-99 ★3159★
  Top pay and benefits for the chief executive and top paid employees at Rhodes College ★3456★
Daughter of the Forest
  Booklist's most recommended science fiction/fantasy books ★232★
  Most notable fiction books for young adults, 2001 ★322★
  Outstanding fiction books for young adults, 2000 ★333★
Daughter of the Moon
  Most notable fiction books for reluctant young adult readers, 2001 ★321★
Daughter of the Shining Isles
  Booklist's most recommended science fiction/fantasy books ★232★
Davenport, Bettendorf, IA-Moline, Rock Island, IL
  Most polite cities in the U.S. ★3086★
Davey; Richard J.
  Top pay and benefits for the chief executive and top paid employees at Santa Clara University in California ★3491★
David Lipscomb University
  U.S. News & World Report's southern regional liberal arts colleges with the highest acceptance rates, 2000-01 ★1370★
Davidson College
  U.S. colleges and universities where students study the most ★1003★
  U.S. colleges and universities with the best quality of life ★1034★
  U.S. News & World Report's national liberal arts colleges with the best freshmen retention rates, 2000-01 ★1323★
  U.S. News & World Report's national liberal arts colleges with the best selectivity rank, 2000-01 ★1325★
  U.S. News & World Report's national liberal arts colleges with the highest alumni giving rank, 2000-01 ★1329★
  U.S. News & World Report's national liberal arts colleges with the highest graduation rates, 2000-01 ★1330★
  U.S. News & World Report's national liberal arts colleges with the highest percentage of alumni support, 2000-01 ★1331★
  U.S. News & World Report's national liberal arts colleges with the highest percentage of freshmen in the top 10% of their high school class, 2000-01 ★1332★
  U.S. News & World Report's national liberal arts colleges with the highest percentage of full-time faculty, 2000-01 ★1333★
  Highest undergraduate tuition and fees at colleges and universities in North Carolina ★1539★
  Private, 4-year undergraduate colleges and universities producing the most Ph.D.'s in history, 1920-1990 ★2552★
  Private, 4-year undergraduate colleges and universities producing the most Ph.D.'s in mathematics, 1920-1990 ★2776★

DAVIDSON

Davidson
Average faculty salaries for institutions of higher education in North Carolina, 2000-01 ★3720★

Davidson High School
Outstanding secondary schools in Mobile, Alabama ★4182★

Davidson; James M.
American Chemical Society 2001 award winners (Group 2) ★752★

Davidson Middle School
Outstanding secondary schools in San Francisco, California ★4221★

Davila; Robert R.
Top pay and benefits for the chief executive and top paid employees at Rochester Institute of Technology ★3461★

Davis; Angela
Most influential African Americans in politics and civil rights ★3040★

Davis; Anita P.
Top pay and benefits for the chief executive and top paid employees at Converse College ★3255★

Davis; Benjamin
Most influential African Americans in the military ★2882★

Davis; Chauncy
All-American boy's high school football linebackers, 2000 ★182★

Davis and Elkins College
Highest undergraduate tuition and fees at colleges and universities in West Virginia ★1568★
Average faculty salaries for institutions of higher education in West Virginia, 2000-01 ★3737★

Davis Hays & Co.
Most selective internships in the U.S., 2001 ★2610★

Davis; Howard E.
Top pay and benefits for the chief executive and top paid employees at Randolph-Macon College ★3451★

Davis III; Rep. Thomas M.
Members of Congress receiving the largest contributions from the Sallie Mae Inc. Political Action Committee ★3023★

Davis Intermediate School
Outstanding secondary schools in San Jose, California ★4222★

Davis; Jabari
All-American boy's high school football running backs, 2000 ★186★

Davis; James A.
Top pay and benefits for the chief executive and top paid employees at Shenandoah University ★3497★

Davis; Kathy
Radcliffe Institute for Advanced Study fellowship recipients in the field of history, 2000-01 ★2549★

Davis; Miles
Most influential African American entertainers ★77★

Davis; Owen
Top pay and benefits for the chief executive and top paid employees at Cornell University ★3257★

Davis; Richard
Top pay and benefits for the chief executive and top paid employees at the College of St. Scholastica ★3530★

Davis-Taylor; Linda
Top pay and benefits for the chief executive and top paid employees at Scripps College ★3493★

Davis; Wylie H.
Top pay and benefits for the chief executive and top paid employees at Texas Wesleyan University ★3519★

Davisville Middle School
Outstanding secondary schools in Providence-Fall River-Warwick, Rhode Island-Maine ★4207★

Dawson Community College
Lowest undergraduate tuition and fees at colleges and universities in Montana ★1527★
Average faculty salaries for institutions of higher education without academic ranks in Montana, 2000-01 ★3756★

Day; Fran
Top pay and benefits for the chief executive and top paid employees at College of the Atlantic ★3246★

A Day No Pigs Would Die
Most frequently banned books in the 1990s ★745★
People for the American Way's list of most frequently challenged books, 1991-1992 ★748★

The Day the Rabbi Disappeared: Jewish Holiday Tales of Magic
Smithsonian's best books for children ages 10 and up ★365★

Day; Teresa M.
Top pay and benefits for the chief executive and top paid employees at Loma Linda University ★3377★

Days Like This: A Collection of Small Poems
Booklist's most recommended poetry for youths, 2001 ★315★
Most notable books for young readers, 2001 ★319★

Dayton & Montgomery County Public Library
Highest Hennen's American Public Library Ratings for libraries serving a population of 250,000 to 499,999 ★2699★

Dayton; University of
U.S. catholic universities with the highest enrollment, 1999 ★864★
U.S. News & World Report's midwestern regional universities with the best academic reputation scores, 2000-01 ★1401★
U.S. News & World Report's midwestern regional universities with the highest freshmen retention rates, 2000-01 ★1405★
U.S. News & World Report's midwestern regional universities with the highest graduation rates, 2000-01 ★1406★
U.S. News & World Report's top midwestern regional universities, 2000-01 ★1411★
U.S. News & World Report's best undergraduate fees among midwestern regional universities by discount tuition, 2000 ★1427★
Private, 4-year undergraduate colleges and universities producing the most Ph.D.'s in the computer sciences, 1920-1990 ★1595★
Private, 4-year undergraduate colleges and universities producing the most Ph.D.'s in the computer sciences, 1981-1990 ★1596★
Private, 4-year undergraduate colleges and universities producing the most Ph.D.'s in all fields of study, 1981-1990 ★2028★

Private, 4-year undergraduate colleges and universities producing the most Ph.D.'s in mathematics, 1920-1990 ★2776★
Average faculty salaries for institutions of higher education in Ohio, 2000-01 ★3722★

DBS Group Holdings
Business Week's best companies in Singapore ★402★

De Imperatoribus Romanis: An Online Encyclopedia of Roman Emperors
Library Journal's best free reference websites, 2000 ★367★

de la Camara; Maria
Top pay and benefits for the chief executive and top paid employees at Lake Erie College ★3362★

De La Salle Collegiate High School
Outstanding Catholic high schools in Metro Detroit ★4075★
Outstanding secondary schools in Detroit, Michigan ★4125★

De La Salle High School
Outstanding secondary schools in New Orleans, Louisiana ★4190★

De Mol; John
European business moguls considered the best innovators ★442★

Deaf-blindness
Disabled students served in U.S. public school programs, 1998-99 ★1877★

Deal With It: A Whole New Approach to Your Body, Brain and Life as a Girl
Most notable nonfiction books for reluctant young adult readers, 2001 ★323★

Dean College
Institutions censured by the American Association of University Professors, 2001 ★1067★

Dean Foods
Fortune's highest ranked food production companies, 2000 ★464★

Dease; Rev. Dennis
Top pay and benefits for the chief executive and top paid employees at the University of St. Thomas in Minnesota ★3563★

Death of a Salesman
Top plays of the twentieth century ★4435★

The Debt: What America Owes to Blacks
Outstanding social sciences books, 2000 ★292★

Decaro; Frank
Top pay and benefits for the chief executive and top paid employees at Georgian Court College ★3307★

Decatur Classical
Chicago elementary magnet schools with the lowest acceptance rates, 2000-01 ★4003★

Decision Sciences
Top ranked AACSB publications ★2186★

Deeg; H. Joachim
Most-cited researchers in surgery/transplantation, 1981-1998 ★2878★

Deegan Jr.; John
Top pay and benefits for the chief executive and top paid employees at Westminster College in Pennsylvania ★3617★

Deep-Sea Research Part A
Oceanography journals by citation impact, 1981-99 ★2139★

Deep-Sea Research, Part I
Oceanography journals by citation impact, 1995-99 ★2140★
Oceanography journals by citation impact, 1999 ★2141★

Educational Rankings Annual • 2002 DELOITTE

Deep Sea Research, Part II
Oceanography journals by citation impact, 1995-99 ★2140★

Deep Springs College
Fiske Guide's best buys for private colleges and universities, 2001 ★1459★

Deer Path Junior High School
Outstanding secondary schools in Chicago, Illinois ★4110★

Deere
Fortune's highest ranked industrial and farm equipment companies, 2000 ★471★

Deerfield High School
Illinois high schools with the highest SAT scores ★874★
Outstanding secondary schools in Chicago, Illinois ★4110★

Dees; Gerald T.
Top pay and benefits for the chief executive and top paid employees at Elmira College ★3284★

Dees Jr.; Charles R.
Top pay and benefits for the chief executive and top paid employees at Fairleigh Dickinson University ★3292★

Defenders of the Truth: The Battle for Science in the Sociobiology Debate and Beyond
Library Journal's most notable general science books, 2000 ★260★

Defending the Cavewoman: And Other Tales of Clinical Neurology
Library Journal's most notable psychology books, 2000 ★275★

Defense
Federal appropriations to colleges, by agency, 2000 ★1241★
Proposed fiscal 2002 appropriations for science and technology research ★4339★

Deffenbacher; Mark
Top pay and benefits for the chief executive and top paid employees at Fresno Pacific University ★3298★

Defiance College
Average faculty salaries for institutions of higher education in Ohio, 2000-01 ★3722★

Define "Normal"
Most notable fiction books for reluctant young adult readers, 2001 ★321★
Most notable fiction books for young adults, 2001 ★322★

DeHeer; David
Top pay and benefits for the chief executive and top paid employees at Calvin College ★3217★

Deisher; Phylis J.
Top pay and benefits for the chief executive and top paid employees at Midamerica Nazarene University ★3400★

DeKalb Technical Institute
Lowest undergraduate tuition and fees at colleges and universities in Georgia ★1497★

Del Carmen; R.V.
Most cited authors in the journal *Journal of Criminal Justice*, 1990 to 1995 ★1626★

Del Mar College
Institutions with the most part-time Hispanic American faculty ★924★
Average faculty salaries for institutions of higher education in Texas, 2000-01 ★3731★

Del Webb
Fortune's highest ranked real estate companies, 2000 ★491★

Delacorte
Hardcover bestsellers by publishing house, 2000 ★240★

Delaware
Mean composite ACT scores by state, 2000 ★895★
Mean math SAT scores by state, 2000 ★900★
Mean verbal SAT scores by state, 2000 ★903★
States allocating the smallest amount of state tax appropriations for higher education, 2000-01 ★1305★
Total doctorate recipients by state, 1999 ★2054★
State grades for affordability of higher education for minority students, 2000 ★2883★
State grades for benefits state receives for educating its minority students, 2000 ★2884★
State grades for completion of higher education by minority students, 2000 ★2885★
State grades for participation of minority students in higher education, 2000 ★2886★
State grades for preparing minority students for higher education, 2000 ★2887★
States with the highest per-pupil expenditures ★3996★
States with the lowest number of high school graduates, 1999-2000 ★3997★
States with the highest average enrollment in public elementary schools ★4032★
States with the highest average enrollment in public secondary schools ★4033★

Delaware County Community College
Lowest undergraduate tuition and fees at colleges and universities in Pennsylvania ★1550★

Delaware State College
Colleges offering the Thurgood Marshall Scholarship Fund ★221★
State appropriations for Delaware's institutions of higher education, 2000-01 ★1261★

Delaware State University
Four-year public institutions enrolling the highest number of students from the District of Columbia, 1998-99 ★855★
Undergraduate tuition and fees at colleges and universities in Delaware ★1492★
U.S. colleges and universities awarding the most physical sciences master's degrees to African Americans ★1793★
U.S. institutions awarding the most baccalaureate degrees to African Americans in agribusiness and production, 1998 ★1813★
Average faculty salaries for institutions of higher education in Delaware, 2000-01 ★3695★

Delaware Technical and Community College, Owens Campus
Undergraduate tuition and fees at colleges and universities in Delaware ★1492★

Delaware Technical and Community College, Stanton/Wilmington Campus
Undergraduate tuition and fees at colleges and universities in Delaware ★1492★

Delaware Technical and Community College, Terry Campus
Undergraduate tuition and fees at colleges and universities in Delaware ★1492★

Delaware; University of
All-USA College Academic First Team, 2001 ★2★
Top art history research-doctorate programs as evaluated by the National Research Council ★93★
Four-year institutions with the most liquor referrals reported, 1999 ★708★
U.S. universities with the highest concentration of papers published in the field of chemistry, 1994-98 ★794★
State appropriations for Delaware's institutions of higher education, 2000-01 ★1261★
Undergraduate tuition and fees at colleges and universities in Delaware ★1492★
Universities with the most-cited scholars in *Criminal Justice and Behavior* ★1648★
U.S. universities with the highest concentration of papers published in the field of chemical engineering, 1994-98 ★2345★
U.S. universities with the highest concentration of civil engineering papers published, 1994-98 ★2351★
Academics' choices for best graduate chemical engineering programs, 2001 ★2386★
Most effective chemical engineering research-doctorate programs as evaluated by the National Research Council ★2389★
Top chemical engineering research-doctorate programs as evaluated by the National Research Council ★2390★
U.S. News & World Report's graduate engineering programs with the best chemical departments, 2000-01 ★2392★
U.S. universities with the greatest impact in chemical engineering, 1994-98 ★2393★
Most wired universities, 2000 ★2598★
U.S. colleges and universities spending the most on chemical engineering research and development, 1998 ★3098★
U.S. colleges and universities with the most federal support for chemical engineering research and development, 1998 ★3101★
Average faculty salaries for institutions of higher education in Delaware, 2000-01 ★3695★

Delaware Valley College
Average faculty salaries for institutions of higher education in Pennsylvania, 2000-01 ★3725★

Delgado Community College
Lowest undergraduate tuition and fees at colleges and universities in Louisiana ★1511★

Delhaize America
Fortune's highest ranked food and drug stores, 2000 ★463★

The Delinquent Virgin
Most notable fiction books, 2001 ★284★
Outstanding works of fiction, 2001 ★293★

Dell
Mass market paperback bestsellers by publishing house, 2000 ★283★

Dell Computer
Biggest information technology companies, 2000 ★385★
Business Week's best companies in the United States ★411★
Fortune's highest ranked computers and office equipment companies, 2000 ★456★
Most profitable information technology companies, 2000 ★527★
Top information technology companies, 2000 ★544★
Top office equipment and computers companies in Standard & Poor's 500, 2001 ★551★
Largest technology companies in the U.S. in terms of annual revenue, 2000 ★4429★

Dell.com
Top E-commerce web sites ★2603★

Deloitte & Touche
Top recruiters for business administration jobs for 2000-01 bachelor's degree recipients ★554★

DELOITTE

Top recruiters for accounting jobs for 2000-01 bachelor's degree recipients ★580★
Top recruiters for finance/banking jobs for 2000-01 bachelor's degree recipients ★582★
Top recruiters for business administration jobs for 2000-01 master's degree recipients ★652★
Top recruiters for accounting jobs for 2000-01 master's degree recipients ★661★
Top recruiters for finance/banking jobs for 2000-01 master's degree recipients ★664★
Top recruiters for computer science jobs for 2000-01 bachelor's degree recipients ★1590★
Top recruiters for multidisciplinary majors jobs for 2000-01 master's degree recipients ★2328★
Top recruiters for computer engineering jobs for 2000-01 bachelor's degree recipients ★2352★
Top recruiters for computer engineering jobs for 2000-01 master's degree recipients ★2400★
Top internships in the U.S. with the highest compensation, 2001 ★2611★
Top recruiters for liberal arts jobs for 2000-01 master's degree recipients ★2676★
Top recruiters for information technology (MIS) jobs for 2000-01 bachelor's degree recipients ★2738★
Top recruiters for information technology (MIS) jobs for 2000-01 master's degree recipients ★2739★
Top recruiters for math/actuarial science jobs for 2000-01 bachelor's degree recipients ★2771★
Top recruiters for math/actuarial science jobs for 2000-01 master's degree recipients ★2779★

Deloitte & Touche LLP
Top employers of college graduates, 2001 ★2325★

Deloitte Touche Tomatsu
Largest private companies, 2000 ★523★

Delphi Automotive Systems
Fortune's highest ranked motor vehicle parts companies, 2000 ★480★
Top automotive companies in Standard & Poor's 500, 2001 ★530★

Delphos Public Library
Highest Hennen's American Public Library Ratings for libraries serving a population of 10,000 to 24,999 ★2695★

Delta Air Lines
Fortune's highest ranked airlines, 2000 ★447★
Top transportation companies in Standard & Poor's 500, 2001 ★560★

Delta College
Colleges and universities with the smallest endowments, 2000 ★1238★

Delta College (MI)
Community colleges receiving the most gifts, 1999-2000 ★1239★

Delta State University
State appropriations for Mississippi's institutions of higher education, 2000-01 ★1277★
Average faculty salaries for institutions of higher education in Mississippi, 2000-01 ★3711★

DeLuca; Frank S.
Top pay and benefits for the chief executive and top paid employees at Mount Saint Mary's College in Maryland ★3412★

Deluxe
Business Week's best performing companies with the highest return on equity, 2000 ★420★
Business Week's best performing companies with the lowest 3-year sales performance ★423★
Fortune's highest ranked printing companies, 2000 ★487★

DeMatha Catholic High School
Outstanding secondary schools in Washington, District of Columbia-Maryland-Virginia-West Virginia ★4249★

DeMeis; Debra K.
Top pay and benefits for the chief executive and top paid employees at Hobart and William Smith Colleges ★3334★

Dement; Michael D.
Top pay and benefits for the chief executive and top paid employees at Southern Methodist University ★3502★

Dementia
Psychiatry journals by citation impact, 1995-98 ★3055★
Psychiatry journals by impact factor, 1994 to 1998 ★3058★

Demography
Demography journals with the highest average citations after 5 years ★1856★
Most cited demography journals, 1991-95 ★1857★
Top demography journals by average impact factor, 1991-95 ★1863★

Demography/population studies
Gender breakdown of social sciences doctorate recipients, by subfield, 1999 ★1942★
Social sciences doctorates awarded at U.S. colleges and universities, by subfield, 1999 ★2044★

Demon in My View
Most notable fiction books for reluctant young adult readers, 2001 ★321★

Dempsey; William M.
Top pay and benefits for the chief executive and top paid employees at Rochester Institute of Technology ★3461★

Demszky; Gabor
European business moguls considered the best agenda setters ★438★

Den Danske Bank
Business Week's best companies in Denmark ★391★

DeNardis; Lawrence J.
Top pay and benefits for the chief executive and top paid employees at the University of New Haven ★3553★

DeNicola; Daniel
Top pay and benefits for the chief executive and top paid employees at Gettysburg College ★3308★

DeNight; Shawn
All-USA Teacher Teams, First Team, 2000 ★4399★

Denison University
All-USA College Academic First Team, 2001 ★2★
U.S. colleges and universities least accepting of alternative lifestyles ★985★
U.S. colleges and universities with a popular radio station ★1019★
U.S. colleges and universities with strained race/class interaction ★1029★
College freshmen's choices for exemplary liberal arts institutions ★1317★
U.S. News & World Report's national liberal arts colleges with the highest acceptance rates, 2000-01 ★1328★
U.S. News & World Report's national liberal arts colleges with the highest percentage of full-time faculty, 2000-01 ★1333★
Highest undergraduate tuition and fees at colleges and universities in Ohio ★1543★
Private, 4-year undergraduate colleges and universities producing the most Ph.D.'s in psychology, 1920-1990 ★3066★
Private, 4-year undergraduate colleges and universities producing the most Ph.D.'s in psychology, 1981-1990 ★3067★
Average faculty salaries for institutions of higher education in Ohio, 2000-01 ★3722★

Denmark
Countries with the most computers per capita, 2000 ★1604★
Countries with the highest percentage of workers satisfied with their job ★2242★
Percentage of students enrolled in institutions of higher education that were not citizens of the country where they studied, 1998 ★2500★
Most wired countries, 2001 ★2596★
Institute for Scientific Information periodical prices by country, 2001 ★2922★

Denmark Technical College
Lowest undergraduate tuition and fees at colleges and universities in South Carolina ★1555★

Dennis; Marguerite J.
Top pay and benefits for the chief executive and top paid employees at Suffolk University ★3513★

Dent Middle School
Outstanding secondary schools in Columbia, South Carolina ★4117★

Dental assistants
Fastest growing occupations, 1998-2008 ★2302★

Dental hygienist
Jobs with the highest employment growth ★2254★
Most desirable jobs in healthcare/medicine ★2273★

Dental hygienists
Projected employment growth for selected occupations that require an associate degree or less, 1998-2008 ★2319★

Dental laboratory technician
Jobs considered the loneliest ★2244★

Dentist
Jobs with the highest starting salaries ★2255★
Occupations with the highest average annual salaries for college graduates, 1998 ★3132★

Dentists
Projected employment growth for selected occupations that require advanced education, 1998-2008 ★2318★

Denver
American cities with the highest percentage of people with Internet access ★2572★
U.S. cities with the most wired households, 2001 ★2606★
U.S. market areas with the highest percentage of adults having internet access ★2607★

Denver; Community College of
Average faculty salaries for institutions of higher education in Colorado, 2000-01 ★3693★

Denver Conservative Baptist Seminary
U.S. colleges and universities with the highest percentage of African Americans enrolled, 1997 ★222★

Denver Public Library
Highest Hennen's American Public Library Ratings for libraries serving a population of over 500,000 ★2700★

Denver; University of
- NCAA Division I ski teams with the most championships ★135★
- Highest undergraduate tuition and fees at colleges and universities in Colorado ★1488★
- U.S. colleges and universities awarding the most communications master's degrees to Asian Americans ★1764★
- U.S. colleges and universities awarding the most communications master's degrees to Hispanic Americans ★1765★
- U.S. colleges and universities awarding the most computer and information sciences master's degrees to African Americans ★1766★
- Institutions with the most female physics bachelor's recipients, 1994-1998 ★2959★
- U.S. institutions with more than 40% female bachelor's graduates in their physics departments, 1994-98 ★2977★
- Average faculty salaries for institutions of higher education in Colorado, 2000-01 ★3693★

Department of Energy
- Proposed fiscal 2002 appropriations for Department of Commerce research ★3107★

DePaul University
- U.S. catholic universities with the highest enrollment, 1999 ★864★
- Fall enrollment at the largest Chicago-area private institutions, by minority percentages, 1999 ★869★
- U.S. colleges and universities with a popular radio station ★1019★
- U.S. colleges and universities awarding the most business management and administrative services master's degrees to Asian Americans ★1760★
- U.S. colleges and universities awarding the most computer and information sciences master's degrees to Asian Americans ★1767★
- Academics' choices for best health law programs, 2001 ★2629★
- Academics' choices for best intellectual property law programs, 2001 ★2630★
- Institutions in the Worker Rights Consortium ★2913★
- Radcliffe Institute for Advanced Study fellowship recipients in the field of philosophy, 2000-01 ★2946★
- Average faculty salaries for institutions of higher education in Illinois, 2000-01 ★3700★

DePaul University, Charles H. Kellstadt Graduate School of Business
- Academics' choices for best part-time MBA programs, 2000 ★587★

DePauw University
- Private, 4-year undergraduate colleges and universities producing the most Ph.D.'s in the life sciences, 1920-1990 ★192★
- U.S. colleges and universities where fraternities and sororities are popular ★993★
- U.S. colleges and universities with a favorable surrounding town or city ★1013★
- *U.S. News & World Report*'s national liberal arts colleges with the highest acceptance rates, 2000-01 ★1328★
- *U.S. News & World Report*'s national liberal arts colleges with students least in debt, 1999 ★1385★
- Highest undergraduate tuition and fees at colleges and universities in Indiana ★1502★
- Private, 4-year undergraduate colleges and universities producing the most Ph.D.s in all fields of study, 1920-1990 ★2027★
- Private, 4-year undergraduate colleges and universities producing the most Ph.D.'s in nonscience fields, 1920-1990 ★2030★
- U.S. bachelor's institutions with the largest number of students studying abroad, 1998-99 ★2511★
- Private, 4-year undergraduate colleges and universities producing the most Ph.D.'s in history, 1920-1990 ★2552★
- Private, 4-year undergraduate colleges and universities producing the most Ph.D.'s in political science and international relations, 1920-1990 ★3044★
- Private, 4-year undergraduate colleges and universities producing the most Ph.D.'s in psychology, 1920-1990 ★3066★
- Average faculty salaries for institutions of higher education in Indiana, 2000-01 ★3701★
- Private, 4-year undergraduate colleges and universities producing the most Ph.D.'s in the sciences, 1920-1990 ★4294★
- Private, 4-year undergraduate colleges and universities producing the most Ph.D.'s in anthropology and sociology, 1920-1990 ★4344★

deRegnier; Mary M.
- Top pay and benefits for the chief executive and top paid employees at Ripon College ★3459★

Dermatitis
- Leading categories of dermatologic disease covered by top articles in the field, 1945-1990 ★1869★

Dermatologic Clinics
- Number of citations and papers for original articles appearing in dermatology journals, 1981 to 1996 ★1873★
- Number of citations and papers in dermatology journals, 1981 to 1996 ★1874★

Dermatologic Surgery
- Number of citations and papers for original articles appearing in dermatology journals, 1981 to 1996 ★1873★
- Number of citations and papers in dermatology journals, 1981 to 1996 ★1874★

DeRosa; Donald V.
- Top pay and benefits for the chief executive and top paid employees at the University of the Pacific ★3571★

DeRose; Robert
- Top pay and benefits for the chief executive and top paid employees at Lewis University ★3372★

Derring; Richard A.
- Authors with the most published pages in impact-weighted insurance journals ★677★
- Individual authors with the most published pages in *The Journal of Risk and Insurance*, 1987-1996 ★680★

Derryberry; Bob R.
- Top pay and benefits for the chief executive and top paid employees at Southwest Baptist University ★3504★

Des Moines Area Community College
- Lowest undergraduate tuition and fees at colleges and universities in Iowa ★1505★

Des Moines University Osteopathic Medical Center
- Institutions censured by the American Association of University Professors, 2001 ★1067★

DeSales University
- Average faculty salaries for institutions of higher education in Pennsylvania, 2000-01 ★3725★

DeSalle; R. Michael
- Top pay and benefits for the chief executive and top paid employees at Columbia College in Illinois ★3250★

Descoteaux, C.S.C.; Sister Carol J. J.
- Top pay and benefits for the chief executive and top paid employees at Notre Dame College in New Hampshire ★3425★

Desert Sky Middle School
- Outstanding secondary schools in Phoenix-Mesa, Arizona ★4203★

DeSieno; Robert
- Top pay and benefits for the chief executive and top paid employees at Skidmore College ★3500★

Design and Architecture High School
- Outstanding secondary schools in Miami, Florida ★4178★

Design Tech International
- Most selective internships in the U.S., 2001 ★2610★

Designers, except interior designers
- Occupations with the highest number of self-employed workers, 1998 ★2311★
- Projected employment growth for selected occupations that require a bachelor's degree or more, 1998-2008 ★2317★

DeSimone; Albert J.
- Top pay and benefits for the chief executive and top paid employees at Augustana College in Illinois ★3182★

Desktop publishing specialists
- Fastest growing occupations, 1998-2008 ★2302★

Desmond; John
- Top pay and benefits for the chief executive and top paid employees at Whitman College ★3623★

Desroches; J.I.
- Most cited authors in the journal *Criminologie*, 1990 to 1995 ★1621★

Determining the Optimal Number of Volumes for a Library's Core Collection
- Most frequently cited *Libri* articles ★2730★

DeThomasis, F.S.C.; Bro. Louis
- Top pay and benefits for the chief executive and top paid employees at Saint Mary's University of Minnesota ★3482★

Detroit
- U.S. market areas with the highest percentage of adults having internet access ★2607★
- Largest public school districts in the U.S. ★4016★

Detroit Mercy; University of
- Highest undergraduate tuition and fees at colleges and universities in Michigan ★1518★
- Total baccalaureate law and legal studies degrees awarded to African Americans from U.S. colleges and universities, 1997-98 ★1725★
- U.S. colleges and universities awarding the most psychology master's degrees to African Americans ★1797★
- U.S. colleges and universities awarding the most psychology doctorate degrees to African Americans ★2120★

Detweiler; Richard A.
- Top pay and benefits for the chief executive and top paid employees at Hartwick College ★3326★

Deutsche Bank
- *Business Week*'s best companies in Germany ★394★

Deutsche Telekom
Business Week's best companies in Germany ★394★
Business Week's top companies worldwide ★433★

Developing Understanding of Self and Others (DUSO)
People for the American Way's list of most frequently challenged materials, 1982-1992 ★749★

Developmental biology/embryology
Biological sciences doctorates awarded at U.S. colleges and universities, by subfield, 1999 ★1887★
Gender breakdown of biological sciences doctorate recipients, by subfield, 1999 ★1927★

Developmental and child
Gender breakdown of psychology doctorate recipients, by subfield, 1999 ★1941★
Psychology doctorates awarded at U.S. colleges and universities, by subfield, 1999 ★2043★

Devine; Robert
Top pay and benefits for the chief executive and top paid employees at Antioch University ★3178★

Devlin; Brian
All-America boys' high school soccer team midfielders, 2001 ★168★

Devlin; Victoria
Top pay and benefits for the chief executive and top paid employees at Bates College ★3193★

Devon Energy
Business Week's best performing companies with the highest 3-year sales performance ★417★

DeVries II; Henry E.
Top pay and benefits for the chief executive and top paid employees at Calvin College ★3217★

Devry Institute of Technology
U.S. colleges and universities with the lowest percentage of African Americans enrolled, 1997 ★223★

DeVry Institute of Technology, Chicago
Fall enrollment at Chicago-area proprietary institutions, by minority percentages, 1999 ★866★
Total baccalaureate computer and information science degrees awarded to Hispanic Americans from U.S. colleges and universities, 1997-98 ★1693★

DeVry Institute of Technology, Decatur
Total baccalaureate computer and information science degrees awarded to African Americans from U.S. colleges and universities, 1997-98 ★1691★

DeVry Institute of Technology, DuPage
Fall enrollment at Chicago-area proprietary institutions, by minority percentages, 1999 ★866★

DeVry Institute of Technology, Phoenix
Highest undergraduate tuition and fees at colleges and universities in Arizona ★1482★

DeVry Institute of Technology, Pomona
Total baccalaureate computer and information science degrees awarded to Hispanic Americans from U.S. colleges and universities, 1997-98 ★1693★

Dewberry & Davis LLC
Top recruiters for civil engineering jobs for 2000-01 bachelor's degree recipients ★2346★
Top recruiters for environmental engineering jobs for 2000-01 bachelor's degree recipients ★2357★
Top recruiters for civil engineering jobs for 2000-01 master's degree recipients ★2397★
Top recruiters for environmental engineering jobs for 2000-01 master's degree recipients ★2409★
Top recruiters for geology/geophysics jobs for 2000-01 bachelor's degree recipients ★2522★

DeWitt Clinton High School
Outstanding urban public high schools in Metro New York ★4265★

DeWitt; Helen
Booklist's best first novels ★228★

Dexia
Business Week's best companies in Belgium ★388★

DeYoung; Robert
Top pay and benefits for the chief executive and top paid employees at Hope College ★3339★

Diablo Valley College
Lowest undergraduate tuition and fees at public 2-year colleges and universities ★1465★
Lowest undergraduate tuition and fees at colleges and universities in California ★1487★

The Diagnosis
Booklist's best fiction books for library collections, 2000 ★227★

Dial
Fortune's highest ranked soaps and cosmetics companies, 2000 ★496★

Diamond Dogs
Outstanding fiction books for young adults, 2000 ★333★

Diary farmer
Jobs with the highest unemployment ★2256★

DiBiaggio; John
Top pay and benefits for the chief executive and top paid employees at Tufts University ★3580★

DiCamillo; Kate
Outstanding children's fiction books, 2000 ★329★
Publishers Weekly Off-the-Cuff Awards winner for most promising new author, 2000 ★357★

Diccionario de la musica espanola e hispanoamericana
Selected reference books in the field of music, 2000 ★378★

Dice.com
Top career-related Web sites ★2602★
Top E-recruiting providers, 2000 ★2604★

Dickerman; Richard M.
Top pay and benefits for the chief executive and top paid employees at Mount Saint Mary College in New York ★3410★

Dickey; Elizabeth
Top pay and benefits for the chief executive and top paid employees at New School University ★3418★

Dickinson College
U.S. colleges and universities with the best food service program ★1031★
Highest undergraduate tuition and fees at colleges and universities in Pennsylvania ★1549★
Private, 4-year undergraduate colleges and universities producing the most Ph.D.'s in the earth sciences, 1981-1990 ★2151★
Institutions with the most female physics bachelor's recipients, 1994-1998 ★2959★
U.S. institutions with more than 40% female bachelor's graduates in their physics departments, 1994-98 ★2977★
Presidents with the highest pay at Baccalaureate I colleges, 1998-99 ★3159★
Average faculty salaries for institutions of higher education in Pennsylvania, 2000-01 ★3725★

Dickinson School of Law
U.S. colleges and universities awarding the most law and legal studies master's degrees to Asian Americans ★1782★

Dickinson State University
State appropriations for North Dakota's institutions of higher education, 2000-01 ★1287★
Lowest undergraduate tuition and fees at colleges and universities in North Dakota ★1542★
Average faculty salaries for institutions of higher education in North Dakota, 2000-01 ★3721★

Dickson Jr.; David A.
Top pay and benefits for the chief executive and top paid employees at St. Edward's University ★3471★

Dicovitsky; Gary
Top pay and benefits for the chief executive and top paid employees at Pomona College ★3444★

Dictionary of Archaeology
Selected reference books in the field of archaeology, 2000 ★374★

Dictionnaire historique de la France sous l'Occupation
Selected reference books in the field of history, 2000 ★376★

Didion; Joan
Top essayists from 1946-1996 ★2445★
Best U.S. works of journalism in the 20th century ★2769★

Die; Ann H.
Top pay and benefits for the chief executive and top paid employees at Hendrix College ★3331★

Diedriech; Dan
Top pay and benefits for the chief executive and top paid employees at Westminster College in Missouri ★3616★

Diegueno Junior High School
Outstanding secondary schools in San Diego, California ★4220★

Diener; Travis
All-America boys' high school basketball 4th team, 2001 ★164★

Dietician
Jobs with the lowest unemployment ★2258★
Most desirable jobs in healthcare/medicine ★2273★

DiFeliciantonio; Richard
Top pay and benefits for the chief executive and top paid employees at Ursinus College ★3591★

Diffley; George E.
Top pay and benefits for the chief executive and top paid employees at Fairfield University ★3291★

DiFilippo Jr.; Eugene B.
  Top pay and benefits for the chief executive and top paid employees at Boston College ★3205★
Digging for Bird-Dinosaurs: An Expedition to Madagascar
  Booklist's best science books for children ★310★
  Most notable books for middle readers, 2001 ★317★
  Outstanding books for middle readers, 2000 ★326★
  Smithsonian's best books for children ages 10 and up ★365★
Digital media
  Job openings for high-tech workers ★2330★
Digital Transition Fund
  Proposed fiscal 2002 appropriations for miscellaneous federal aid ★2487★
Dilendik Jr.; John R.
  Top pay and benefits for the chief executive and top paid employees at Moravian College ★3407★
Diles; David
  Top pay and benefits for the chief executive and top paid employees at Saint Bonaventure University ★3470★
Dillard University
  U.S. colleges and universities with the highest percentage of African Americans enrolled, 1997 ★222★
  Highest undergraduate tuition and fees at colleges and universities in Louisiana ★1510★
  Total baccalaureate health professions and related sciences degrees awarded to African Americans from U.S. colleges and universities, 1997-98 ★1721★
  Institutions with the most female physics bachelor's recipients, 1994-1998 ★2959★
  U.S. institutions with more than 40% female bachelor's graduates in their physics departments, 1994-98 ★2977★
Dillard's
  Fortune's highest ranked general merchandisers, 2000 ★468★
  Fortune's least admired companies for innovation ★508★
Dillon; Joseph
  Top pay and benefits for the chief executive and top paid employees at Manhattan College ★3387★
Dillon; R. Mark
  Top pay and benefits for the chief executive and top paid employees at Wheaton College in Illinois ★3620★
Dillon; Thomas E.
  Top pay and benefits for the chief executive and top paid employees at Thomas Aquinas College in California ★3574★
Dilulio
  Most cited works in academic literature dealing with corrections ★1643★
Dime Bancorp
  Fortune's highest ranked mortgage finance companies, 2000 ★479★
Dimenna; Grey
  Top pay and benefits for the chief executive and top paid employees at Monmouth University in New Jersey ★3406★
Dimitroff; Alexandra
  Library and information science faculty with the most journal articles, 1993-1998 ★2711★

Dimon
  Fortune's highest ranked tobacco companies, 2000 ★502★
Dine College
  U.S. tribal colleges ★1445★
  Lowest undergraduate tuition and fees at colleges and universities in Arizona ★1483★
  U.S. institutions awarding the most associate degrees to minorities in ethnic/cultural studies, 1997-98 ★1810★
Dinkel; Dianne
  Top pay and benefits for the chief executive and top paid employees at Concordia University in Illinois ★3253★
Dion; Celine
  Canada's best performing artists of the 20th century ★74★
Diop; De Sagana
  All-America boys' high school basketball 1st team, 2001 ★161★
Direct Focus
  Business Week's top companies in terms of earning growth, 2000 ★427★
  Business Week's top companies in terms of return on capital, 2000 ★430★
  Business Week's top companies in terms of sales growth, 2000 ★432★
  Top companies in terms of growth, 2000 ★534★
Director of athletics
  Percentage of African American athletic administrators at NCAA Division I institutions, 1999 ★138★
  Percentage of African American athletic administrators at NCAA Division II institutions, 1999 ★139★
  Percentage of African American athletic administrators at NCAA Division III institutions, 1999 ★140★
Directory of University Libraries in Europe
  Selected new editions and supplements reference books, 2000 ★372★
DISCovering Multicultural America
  Library Journal's best reference databases and discs, 2000 ★369★
Discovery School's Puzzlemaker
  Most notable children's web sites, 2001 ★2593★
Diseases of Aquatic Organisms
  Veterinary sciences journals with the greatest impact measure, 1994-98 ★4443★
Disgrace
  Most notable fiction books, 2001 ★284★
  Outstanding works of fiction, 2001 ★293★
Dishwasher
  Jobs considered the loneliest ★2244★
  Jobs with the highest unemployment ★2256★
  Jobs with the worst income scores ★2261★
  Most desirable jobs in travel/food service ★2278★
DiSibio; Robert A.
  Top pay and benefits for the chief executive and top paid employees at D'Youville College ★3278★
Disk jockey
  Jobs considered the loneliest ★2244★
  Jobs considered the most competitive ★2245★
  Most desirable jobs in communications ★2271★
Disney Juvenile Pub.
  Top children's book publishers, 1999 ★3074★

Disobedience
  Library Journal's best fiction audiobooks, 2000 ★241★
DiSpigno; Anthony J.
  Top pay and benefits for the chief executive and top paid employees at the University of Portland ★3556★
Dissappearing Acts
  Favorite books of African Americans ★238★
District of Columbia
  Mean composite ACT scores by state, 2000 ★895★
  Mean math SAT scores by state, 2000 ★900★
  Mean verbal SAT scores by state, 2000 ★903★
  Total doctorate recipients by state, 1999 ★2054★
  States with the most law schools ★2668★
  States expelling the highest ratio of students for violating the Gun-Free Schools Act, 1998-99 ★3993★
  States with the highest per-pupil expenditures ★3996★
  States with the lowest number of high school graduates, 1999-2000 ★3997★
District of Columbia; University of the
  Colleges offering the Thurgood Marshall Scholarship Fund ★221★
  Division II NCAA colleges with the lowest graduation rates for all sports, 1993-94 ★947★
  Institutions censured by the American Association of University Professors, 2001 ★1067★
  Undergraduate tuition and fees at colleges and universities in the District of Columbia ★1493★
  Total baccalaureate law and legal studies degrees awarded to African Americans from U.S. colleges and universities, 1997-98 ★1725★
Dittus; Robert
  Top pay and benefits for the chief executive and top paid employees at Carthage College ★3224★
Diversity Your World
  Library Journal's best reference databases and discs, 2000 ★369★
Dixie State College
  Undergraduate tuition and fees at colleges and universities in Utah ★1562★
Dixon Elementary School
  Illinois elementary schools chosen to be 'demonstration sites' for struggling schools ★4006★
Dixon; Ralph
  Top pay and benefits for the chief executive and top paid employees at Gardner-Webb University ★3303★
Dixon; Thomas E.
  Top pay and benefits for the chief executive and top paid employees at DePauw University ★3267★
Dixon; W. J.
  Authors with the most citations among authors published in *American Political Science Review*, 1974-94 ★3048★
D.I.Y. Beauty
  Most notable nonfiction books for reluctant young adult readers, 2001 ★323★
DK Publishing
  Top children's book publishers, 1999 ★3074★

Doane College
- *U.S. News & World Report*'s midwestern regional liberal arts colleges with the highest acceptance rates, 2000-01 ★1341★
- *U.S. News & World Report*'s midwestern regional liberal arts colleges with the highest alumni giving rates, 2000-01 ★1342★
- *U.S. News & World Report*'s best undergraduate fees among midwestern regional liberal arts colleges by discount tuition, 2000 ★1380★
- Highest undergraduate tuition and fees at colleges and universities in Nebraska ★1528★
- U.S. colleges and universities awarding the most education master's degrees to Native Americans ★1772★
- U.S. colleges and universities awarding the most master's degrees to Native Americans ★1789★
- Average faculty salaries for institutions of higher education in Nebraska, 2000-01 ★3714★

Dobash; R.E.
- Most cited authors in the journal *Canadian Journal of Criminology*, 1990 to 1995 ★1615★
- Most cited authors in the journal *Crime and Delinquency*, 1990 to 1995 ★1616★

Dobash; Russell P.
- Most cited authors in the journal *Canadian Journal of Criminology*, 1990 to 1995 ★1615★
- Most cited authors in the journal *Crime and Delinquency*, 1990 to 1995 ★1616★
- Most-cited scholars in women and crime publications ★1642★

Dobbin, O.S.A.; Rev. Edmund J.
- Top pay and benefits for the chief executive and top paid employees at Villanova University ★3595★

Dobelle; Evan S.
- Top pay and benefits for the chief executive and top paid employees at Trinity College in Connecticut ★3577★

Doberstein; Audrey K.
- Presidents with the highest pay at Master's I and II colleges and universities, 1998-99 ★3161★
- Top pay and benefits for the chief executive and top paid employees at Wilmington College in Delaware ★3632★

Dobranski; Bernard
- Top pay and benefits for the chief executive and top paid employees at the Catholic University of America ★3522★

Doctor
- Careers college students considered most respected, 2000 ★740★

Dr. Atkins' New Diet Revolution
- Longest-running mass market paperback bestsellers, 2000 ★280★

Dr. Martin Luther King Jr. College Prep
- Admissions to college prep schools in Chicago that are the toughest to get into, 2001 ★4001★
- College prep schools in Chicago that are the toughest to get into ★4005★

Dodd; Glenn W.
- Top pay and benefits for the chief executive and top paid employees at Cornell College in Iowa ★3256★

Dodd Middle School
- Outstanding secondary schools in New Haven-Meriden, Connecticut ★4188★

Dodge; Linda L.
- Top pay and benefits for the chief executive and top paid employees at Anna Maria College ★3177★

Dodson; Lisa
- Radcliffe Institute for Advanced Study fellowship recipients in the field of public policy, 2000-01 ★2622★

Dodson; Robert K.
- Top pay and benefits for the chief executive and top paid employees at Lawrence University ★3367★

Doerksen; Randall C.
- Top pay and benefits for the chief executive and top paid employees at Friends University ★3299★

Doerr; Roger
- Top pay and benefits for the chief executive and top paid employees at Hastings College ★3328★

Dogs Have the Strangest Friends & Other True Stories of Animal Feelings
- *Smithsonian*'s best books for children ages 6 to 10 ★364★

Doherty; Berlie
- Outstanding children's picture books, 2000 ★331★

Dolan; Robert
- Top pay and benefits for the chief executive and top paid employees at City University in Washington ★3234★

Dolinsky; Paul
- All-America boys' high school soccer team midfielders, 2001 ★168★

The Doll People
- Most notable books for middle readers, 2001 ★317★
- Outstanding children's fiction books, 2000 ★329★

Dollinger; Ron
- Top pay and benefits for the chief executive and top paid employees at John F. Kennedy University ★3354★

Domanski; Tomasz
- Most published authors, adjusted for coauthorship, in the *Journal of Business Research*, 1985 to 1999 ★701★

Domenico; Chelsea
- All-America girls' high school basketball 4th team, 2001 ★173★

Domestic Animal Endocrinology
- Veterinary sciences journals with the greatest impact measure, 1981-98 ★4442★
- Veterinary sciences journals with the greatest impact measure, 1994-98 ★4443★

Dominguez; Luis V.
- Most published authors, adjusted for coauthorship, in the *Journal of Business Research*, 1985 to 1999 ★701★

Dominican Academy
- Outstanding secondary schools in New York, New York ★4191★

Dominican College, Blauvelt
- Average faculty salaries for institutions of higher education in New York, 2000-01 ★3719★

Dominican College of San Rafael
- Average faculty salaries for institutions of higher education in California, 2000-01 ★3692★

Dominican University
- *U.S. News & World Report*'s midwestern regional universities with the best student/faculty ratios, 2000-01 ★1403★
- *U.S. News & World Report*'s midwestern regional universities with the highest proportion of classes having 20 students or less, 2000-01 ★1409★
- Average faculty salaries for institutions of higher education in Illinois, 2000-01 ★3700★

Dominick; Charles A.
- Top pay and benefits for the chief executive and top paid employees at Wittenberg University ★3633★

Don Giovanni
- Most frequently produced operas in North America, 1999-2000 ★2905★

Dona Ana Branch Community College
- Lowest undergraduate tuition and fees at colleges and universities in New Mexico ★1536★

Donaldson; Robert H.
- Top pay and benefits for the chief executive and top paid employees at the University of Tulsa ★3573★

Done Deals: Venture Capitalists Tell Their Stories
- *Library Journal*'s most notable books about venture capital, 2000 ★252★

Donnelley
- Publishers with the best industry stocks, 2000 ★300★

Donnelly; Eileen
- Top pay and benefits for the chief executive and top paid employees at Salve Regina University ★3489★

Donnithorne; Larry
- Top pay and benefits for the chief executive and top paid employees at Colorado Christian University ★3248★

Donor; Albert E.
- Top pay and benefits for the chief executive and top paid employees at Dowling College ★3271★

Don't Tell Anyone
- Most notable fiction books, 2001 ★284★
- Outstanding works of fiction, 2001 ★293★

Doob; Anthony N.
- Most-cited scholars in *Canadian Journal of Criminology* ★1638★

Doohan; Leonard
- Top pay and benefits for the chief executive and top paid employees at Gonzaga University ★3311★

Doolittle; Phillip L.
- Top pay and benefits for the chief executive and top paid employees at the University of Redlands ★3558★

Dopp; Dale R.
- Top pay and benefits for the chief executive and top paid employees at Albion College ★3167★

Doppke; James
- Top pay and benefits for the chief executive and top paid employees at the University of Saint Francis in Illinois ★3561★

Dordt College
- *U.S. News & World Report*'s midwestern regional liberal arts colleges with the highest acceptance rates, 2000-01 ★1341★
- *U.S. News & World Report*'s midwestern regional liberal arts colleges with the highest alumni giving rates, 2000-01 ★1342★
- *U.S. News & World Report*'s midwestern regional liberal arts colleges with the highest freshmen retention rates, 2000-01 ★1343★
- Average faculty salaries for institutions of higher education in Iowa, 2000-01 ★3702★

Dorger; John
Top pay and benefits for the chief executive and top paid employees at Claremont Graduate University ★3235★

Dorman; Jay A.
Top pay and benefits for the chief executive and top paid employees at Huntingdon College ★3344★

Dornbusch; R.W.
U.S. academic economists by mean number of citations, 1971-92 ★2176★
U.S. academic economists by total citations, 1971-92 ★2177★

Dorsey; Stuart B.
Top pay and benefits for the chief executive and top paid employees at Baker University ★3188★

Dorsey; Thomas A.
Most influential African Americans in religion ★3091★

Dorseyville Middle School
Outstanding secondary schools in Pittsburgh, Pennsylvania ★4204★

Dortmund-Dusseldorf-Cologne
Cities with the highest productivity of paper in the discipline of cardiovascular systems, 1994-96 ★2869★

Doshi; Hetal
All-USA College Academic Third Team, 2001 ★4★

Dostal; Robert J.
Top pay and benefits for the chief executive and top paid employees at Bryn Mawr College ★3212★

Doti; James L.
Top pay and benefits for the chief executive and top paid employees at Chapman University ★3228★

Double major science
Top mixed discipline majors for accepted applicants to U.S. medical schools, 1999-2000 ★2853★

Double major science/nonscience
Top mixed discipline majors for accepted applicants to U.S. medical schools, 1999-2000 ★2853★

Doubleday
Hardcover bestsellers by publishing house, 2000 ★240★

Doud; Jacqueline P.
Top pay and benefits for the chief executive and top paid employees at Mount Saint Mary's College in California ★3411★

Douglas MacArthur State Technical College
Lowest undergraduate tuition and fees at colleges and universities in Alabama ★1480★

Douglas; Stan
Canada's best visual artists of the 20th century ★75★

DOUGLASS: Archives of American Public Address
Library Journal's best free reference websites, 2000 ★367★

Dove; G. Robert
Top pay and benefits for the chief executive and top paid employees at Friends University ★3299★

Dover
Fortune's highest ranked industrial and farm equipment companies, 2000 ★471★
Top manufacturing companies in Standard & Poor's 500, 2001 ★548★

Dovre; Paul J.
Top pay and benefits for the chief executive and top paid employees at Concordia College-Moorhead ★3252★

Dow Chemical Co.
Fortune's highest ranked chemicals companies, 2000 ★452★
Top chemical companies in Standard & Poor's 500, 2001 ★533★
Top internships in the U.S. with the highest compensation, 2001 ★2611★

Dow Jones
Business Week's best performing companies with the highest 3-year earnings growth ★416★
Fortune's highest ranked publishing companies, 2000 ★489★
Top publishing and broadcasting companies in Standard & Poor's 500, 2001 ★553★

Dow; Richard W.
Top pay and benefits for the chief executive and top paid employees at Dartmouth College ★3263★

Dowdell; Karen
Top pay and benefits for the chief executive and top paid employees at City University in Washington ★3234★

Dowling; Keeley
All-America girls' high school soccer team forwards, 2001 ★175★

Downers Grove Public Library
Highest Hennen's American Public Library Ratings for libraries serving a population of 25,000 to 49,999 ★2696★

Downing College
Presidents with the highest pay at Master's I and II colleges and universities, 1998-99 ★3161★

Doyle; Luke P.
Top pay and benefits for the chief executive and top paid employees at Sacred Heart University in Connecticut ★3467★

Drachman; Virginia
Radcliffe Institute for Advanced Study fellowship recipients in the field of history, 2000-01 ★2549★

Drafters
Projected employment growth for selected occupations that require an associate degree or less, 1998-2008 ★2319★

Drake University
U.S. News & World Report's midwestern regional universities with the best academic reputation scores, 2000-01 ★1401★
U.S. News & World Report's midwestern regional universities with the best student/faculty ratios, 2000-01 ★1403★
U.S. News & World Report's midwestern regional universities with the highest acceptance rates, 2000-01 ★1404★
U.S. News & World Report's midwestern regional universities with the highest graduation rates, 2000-01 ★1406★
U.S. News & World Report's midwestern regional universities with the highest percentage of freshmen from the top 25% of their high school class, 2000-01 ★1407★
U.S. News & World Report's midwestern regional universities with the highest proportion of classes having 20 students or less, 2000-01 ★1409★
U.S. News & World Report's top midwestern regional universities, 2000-01 ★1411★
U.S. News & World Report's best undergraduate fees among midwestern regional universities by discount tuition, 2000 ★1427★
Highest undergraduate tuition and fees at colleges and universities in Iowa ★1504★
Private, 4-year undergraduate colleges and universities producing the most Ph.D.'s in nonscience fields, 1981-1990 ★2031★
Average faculty salaries for institutions of higher education in Iowa, 2000-01 ★3702★

Drama/theater arts
Gender breakdown of humanities doctorate recipients, by subfield, 1999 ★1936★
Humanities doctorates awarded at U.S. colleges and universities, by subfield, 1999 ★1946★

Draudt; Wayne J.
Top pay and benefits for the chief executive and top paid employees at Lewis University ★3372★

Drawing Lessons from a Bear
Booklist's best first novels for youths ★309★
Smithsonian's best books for children ages 1 to 6 ★363★

Dream Freedom
Smithsonian's best books for children ages 10 and up ★365★

Dream of the Walled City
Booklist's most recommended historical novels, 2001 ★230★

Dreamland
Most notable fiction books for young adults, 2001 ★322★
Outstanding books for older readers, 2000 ★327★

Dreams: Explore the You That You Can't Control
Most notable nonfiction books for reluctant young adult readers, 2001 ★323★

Dreisbach; Joseph H.
Top pay and benefits for the chief executive and top paid employees at the University of Scranton ★3567★

Dressler; Joshua
Top pay and benefits for the chief executive and top paid employees at the University of the Pacific ★3571★

Dressmaker
Jobs considered the loneliest ★2244★
Jobs with the worst income scores ★2261★
Jobs with the worst outlook scores ★2262★

Dretsch; Curtis
Top pay and benefits for the chief executive and top paid employees at Muhlenberg College ★3413★

Drew; Charles
Most important African Americans in the twentieth century ★219★
Most influential African Americans in medicine and science ★2879★

Drew; David
Top pay and benefits for the chief executive and top paid employees at Claremont Graduate University ★3235★

Drew; Homer W.
Top pay and benefits for the chief executive and top paid employees at Valparaiso University ★3592★

Drew; Lewis H.
Top pay and benefits for the chief executive and top paid employees at Hampden-Sydney College ★3321★

Drew University
U.S. colleges and universities with a large student body of liberal Democrats ★1017★
Highest undergraduate tuition and fees at colleges and universities in New Jersey ★1533★

Institutions with the most female physics bachelor's recipients, 1994-1998 ★2959★
U.S. institutions with more than 40% female bachelor's graduates in their physics departments, 1994-98 ★2977★
Average faculty salaries for institutions of higher education in New Jersey, 2000-01 ★3717★

Drexel University
Division I NCAA colleges with the highest graduation rates for male basketball players, 1990-91 to 1993-94 ★935★
U.S. colleges and universities with the least attractive campuses ★1037★
U.S. colleges and universities awarding the most computer and information sciences master's degrees to African Americans ★1766★
Doctoral institutions with the highest enrollment of foreign students, 1998-99 ★2494★
Library and information science programs with the most citations to journal articles, 1993-1998 ★2712★
Library and information science programs with the most per capita citations to journal articles, 1993-1998 ★2715★
Presidents with the highest pay at Doctoral I and II universities, 1998-99 ★3160★
Average faculty salaries for institutions of higher education in Pennsylvania, 2000-01 ★3725★

Drill-press operator
Jobs considered the loneliest ★2244★
Jobs with the highest unemployment ★2256★
Jobs with the worst outlook scores ★2262★
Jobs with the worst security scores ★2264★

Drinkwater Jr.; Davis
Top pay and benefits for the chief executive and top paid employees at Vanderbilt University ★3593★

Droesch; Clare
All-America girls' high school basketball 1st team, 2001 ★170★

The Drowning People
Library Journal's best fiction audiobooks, 2000 ★241★

Drucker; Sheldon
Top pay and benefits for the chief executive and top paid employees at Fairleigh Dickinson University ★3292★

Drug reaction
Leading categories of dermatologic disease covered by top articles in the field, 1945-1990 ★1869★

Drugovich; Margaret
Top pay and benefits for the chief executive and top paid employees at Ohio Wesleyan University ★3430★

Drugs and Aging
Geriatrics and gerontology journals with the greatest impact measure, 1998 ★2807★

Drum; Alice
Top pay and benefits for the chief executive and top paid employees at Franklin and Marshall College ★3296★

Drummond; Robert K.
Top pay and benefits for the chief executive and top paid employees at Midamerica Nazarene University ★3400★

Drumsticks
Library Journal's best mystery titles, 2000 ★242★

Drury College
Average faculty salaries for institutions of higher education in Missouri, 2000-01 ★3712★

Drury University
U.S. News & World Report's midwestern regional universities with the best alumni giving rates, 2000-01 ★1402★
U.S. News & World Report's midwestern regional universities with the best student/faculty ratios, 2000-01 ★1403★
U.S. News & World Report's midwestern regional universities with the highest acceptance rates, 2000-01 ★1404★
U.S. News & World Report's best undergraduate fees among midwestern regional universities by discount tuition, 2000 ★1427★

Drushal; Mary Ellen
Top pay and benefits for the chief executive and top paid employees at Ashland University ★3180★

Drywall applicator/finisher
Jobs with the highest unemployment ★2256★
Jobs with the worst security scores ★2264★
Most desirable jobs in construction trades ★2272★

Du Page (Glen Ellyn, IL); College of
Community colleges in North America with the highest enrollment ★852★

Du Pont
Fortune's highest ranked chemicals companies, 2000 ★452★
Fortune's most admired companies for social responsibility ★520★

Dubinsky; Alan J.
Authors with the most articles published in the *Journal of Business Research*, 1985 to 1999 ★687★

DuBois Area Middle and High School
All-USA Teacher Teams, First Team, 2000 ★4399★

DuBois; W.E.B.
Most important African Americans in the twentieth century ★219★
Best U.S. works of journalism in the 20th century ★2769★
Most influential African Americans in politics and civil rights ★3040★

Duchesne Academy
Outstanding secondary schools in Houston, Texas ★4150★
Outstanding secondary schools in Omaha, Nebraska-Iowa ★4198★

Dudley; Phillip
Top pay and benefits for the chief executive and top paid employees at Hastings College ★3328★

Duff; John B.
Largest benefit packages awarded to presidents at institutions of higher education, 1998-99 ★3133★
Presidents with the highest pay at Master's I and II colleges and universities, 1998-99 ★3161★
Top pay and benefits for the chief executive and top paid employees at Columbia College in Illinois ★3250★

Duffy; Edmund
Top editorial cartoonists used in teaching journalism history ★2770★

Dugoni; Arthur
Top pay and benefits for the chief executive and top paid employees at the University of the Pacific ★3571★

Duhlstine; G. E.
Top pay and benefits for the chief executive and top paid employees at Lenoir-Rhyne College ★3369★

DUI: Dead in 5 Seconds
Most notable DVDs and videos for young adults, 2001 ★2890★

Duke; Charles L.
Top pay and benefits for the chief executive and top paid employees at Grinnell College ★3315★

Duke Ellington
Most notable children's recordings, 2001 ★320★
Most notable children's videos, 2001 ★2889★

Duke Ellington School of Arts
Outstanding secondary schools in Washington, District of Columbia-Maryland-Virginia-West Virginia ★4249★

Duke Ellington: The Piano Prince and His Orchestra
Outstanding videos for library collections, 2000 ★2892★

Duke Energy
Business Week's best performing companies with the highest 1-year sales performance ★414★
Fortune's highest ranked electric and gas utilities companies, 2000 ★459★
Top utilities companies in Standard & Poor's 500, 2001 ★561★

Duke Mathematical Journal
Mathematics journals by impact factor, 1993 to 1997 ★2785★

Duke University
All-USA College Academic First Team, 2001 ★2★
Division I all-time winningest college teams ★128★
Most effective ecology, evolution, and behavior research-doctorate programs as evaluated by the National Research Council ★199★
Top ecology, evolution, and behavior research-doctorate programs as evaluated by the National Research Council ★201★
Top biochemistry and molecular biology research-doctorate programs as evaluated by the National Research Council ★209★
Top cell and developmental biology research-doctorate programs as evaluated by the National Research Council ★210★
Top molecular and general genetics research-doctorate programs as evaluated by the National Research Council ★211★
Top business schools by average MBA rank, 1986-1998 ★644★
Top business schools for within-discipline research performance in management science, 1986-1998 ★647★
Top business schools for within-discipline research performance in finance, 1986-1998 ★663★
Top classics research-doctorate programs as evaluated by the National Research Council ★816★
Division I NCAA colleges with that graduated more than 80% of their African American male athletes, 1990-91 to 1993-94 ★929★
Division I NCAA colleges with the highest graduation rates for female athletes, 1990-91 to 1993-94 ★931★
Division I NCAA colleges with the highest graduation rates for football players, 1990-91 to 1993-94 ★933★
Division I NCAA colleges with the highest graduation rates for male athletes, 1990-91 to 1993-94 ★934★
U.S. colleges and universities least accepting of alternative lifestyles ★985★

U.S. colleges and universities where students and the local community have strained relations ★998★

U.S. News & World Report's national universities with the best academic reputation, 2000-01 ★1126★

U.S. News & World Report's national universities with the best faculty resources rank, 2000-01 ★1127★

U.S. News & World Report's national universities with the best freshmen retention rates, 2000-01 ★1128★

U.S. News & World Report's national universities with the best graduation and retention rank, 2000-01 ★1129★

U.S. News & World Report's national universities with the best student/faculty ratio, 2000-01 ★1130★

U.S. News & World Report's national universities with the highest alumni giving rank, 2000-01 ★1132★

U.S. News & World Report's national universities with the highest graduation rate, 1999 ★1134★

U.S. News & World Report's national universities with the highest percentage of full-time faculty, 2000-01 ★1136★

U.S. News & World Report's national universities with the highest proportion of alumni support, 2000-01 ★1137★

U.S. News & World Report's national universities with the lowest proportion of classes with 50 or more students, 2000-01 ★1142★

Colleges and universities with the largest endowments, 2000 ★1237★

Institutions receiving the most corporate gifts, 1999-2000 ★1243★

Institutions receiving the most gifts, 1999-2000 ★1244★

Highest undergraduate tuition and fees at private nonprofit, 4-year or above colleges and universities ★1461★

Highest undergraduate tuition and fees at colleges and universities in North Carolina ★1539★

Most effective comparative literature research-doctorate programs as evaluated by the National Research Council ★1587★

Top comparative literature research-doctorate programs as evaluated by the National Research Council ★1588★

U.S. colleges and universities awarding the most social sciences and history doctorate degrees to Asian Americans ★2125★

Top oceanography research-doctorate programs as evaluated by the National Research Council ★2153★

Institutions generating the most economic education research text, 1963-1990 ★2167★

Academics' choices for best graduate bioengineering/biomedical engineering programs, 2001 ★2381★

Top biomedical engineering research-doctorate programs as evaluated by the National Research Council ★2384★

U.S. News & World Report's graduate engineering programs with the best biomedical departments, 2000-01 ★2385★

Most effective English language and literature research-doctorate programs as evaluated by the National Research Council ★2448★

Top English language and literature research-doctorate programs as evaluated by the National Research Council ★2451★

Top French language and literature research-doctorate programs as evaluated by the National Research Council ★2516★

Top history research-doctorate programs as evaluated by the National Research Council ★2554★

Acceptance rates at *U.S. News & World Report*'s top 10 law schools, 2001 ★2634★

Graduate employment after graduation percentage for *U.S. News & World Report*'s top 10 law schools, 2001 ★2635★

Graduate employment percentage for *U.S. News & World Report*'s top 10 law schools, 2001 ★2636★

Jurisdiction's overall bar passage rate for *U.S. News & World Report*'s top 10 law schools, 2001 ★2637★

Law schools with the best civil procedure faculty, 1999-2000 ★2640★

Law schools with the best constitutional law (general) faculty, 1999-2000 ★2645★

Law schools with the best critical race theory faculty, 1999-2000 ★2649★

Law schools with the best feminist legal theory faculty, 1999-2000 ★2651★

Law schools with the best health law (excluding medical ethics) faculty, 1999-2000 ★2652★

Law schools with the best law and religion (excluding First Amendment issues) faculty, 1999-2000 ★2658★

Law schools with the highest quality, 1999-2000 ★2666★

School's bar passage rate in jurisdiction at *U.S. News & World Report*'s top 10 law schools, 2001 ★2667★

Student-faculty ratios at *U.S. News & World Report*'s top 10 law schools, 2001 ★2669★

Top law schools, 2001 ★2670★

Top law schools by reputation, as determined by lawyers and judges, 2001 ★2672★

Academics' choices for best geriatrics programs, 2001 ★2821★

Academics' choices for best internal medicine programs, 2001 ★2822★

Academics' choices for best pediatrics programs, 2001 ★2823★

Academics' choices for best women's health medical programs, 2001 ★2825★

Acceptance rates for *U.S. News & World Report*'s top 10 research-oriented medical schools, 2001 ★2827★

Average MCAT scores at *U.S. News & World Report*'s top 10 research-oriented medical schools, 2001 ★2836★

Average undergraduate GPA at *U.S. News & World Report*'s top 10 research-oriented medical schools, 2001 ★2838★

Faculty-student ratios at *U.S. News & World Report*'s top 10 research-oriented medical schools, 2001 ★2842★

NIH research grants for *U.S. News & World Report*'s top 10 research-oriented medical schools, 2001 ★2845★

Out-of-state tuition and fees for *U.S. News & World Report*'s top 10 research-oriented medical schools, 2001 ★2847★

Top primary-care medical schools by student selectivity rank, 2001 ★2858★

Top research-oriented medical schools, 2001 ★2859★

Top research-oriented medical schools by reputation, as determined by academic personnel, 2001 ★2860★

Top research-oriented medical schools by reputation, as determined by intern/residency directors, 2001 ★2861★

Top research-oriented medical schools by student selectivity, 2001 ★2862★

U.S. universities with the greatest impact in pharmacology, 1994-98 ★2936★

Most effective pharmacology research-doctorate programs as evaluated by the National Research Council ★2938★

Top pharmacology research-doctorate programs as evaluated by the National Research Council ★2939★

Top political science research-doctorate programs as evaluated by the National Research Council ★3046★

Top religion research-doctorate programs as evaluated by the National Research Council ★3093★

U.S. universities with the highest concentrations in religion and theology, 1992-96 ★3094★

Average faculty salaries for institutions of higher education in North Carolina, 2000-01 ★3720★

U.S. universities with the greatest impact in sociology and anthropology, 1995-99 ★4351★

Top Spanish and Portuguese language and literature research-doctorate programs as evaluated by the National Research Council ★4358★

Duke University, Fuqua School of Business

Academics' choices for best graduate executive MBA programs, 2001 ★584★

Acceptance rates for *U.S. News & World Report*'s top 10 graduate business schools, 2001 ★588★

Annual tuition at *Business Week*'s top business schools, 2000 ★589★

Average GMAT scores at *U.S. News & World Report*'s top 10 graduate business schools, 2001 ★591★

Average job offers received by graduates from *Business Week*'s top business schools, 1999 ★592★

Average undergraduate GPA at *U.S. News & World Report*'s top 10 graduate business schools, 2001 ★593★

Business Week's top business schools, 2000 ★595★

Business Week's top business schools as selected by corporate recruiters, 2000 ★596★

Business Week's top business schools as selected by recent MBA graduates, 2000 ★597★

Business Week's top business schools best at responding to student concerns, 2000 ★598★

Business Week's top business schools by intellectual capital, 2000 ★599★

Business Week's top business schools for finance skills as selected by corporate recruiters, 2000 ★600★

Business Week's top business schools for general management skills as selected by corporate recruiters, 2000 ★601★

Business Week's top business schools for global scope skills as selected by corporate recruiters, 2000 ★602★

Business Week's top business schools for marketing skills as selected by corporate recruiters, 2000 ★603★

Business Week's top business schools for technology skills as selected by corporate recruiters, 2000 ★604★

Business Week's top business schools with the best placement offices, 2000 ★608★

Business Week's top business schools with the highest percentage of minority enrollment, 2000 ★613★

Business Week's top business schools with the highest percentage of women enrollees, 2000 ★614★

Business Week's top business schools with the lowest percentage of international students, 2000 ★615★

Business Week's top business schools with the most improved program as selected by corporate recruiters, 2000 ★618★

Median starting salaries of graduates from *U.S. News & World Report*'s top 10 graduate business schools, 2001 ★636★

Out-of-state tuition and fees for *U.S. News & World Report*'s top 10 graduate business schools, 2001 ★637★

Percentage of applicants accepted at *Business Week*'s top business schools, 2000 ★638★

Percentage of employed graduates at *U.S. News & World Report*'s top 10 graduate business schools, 2001 ★639★

Percentage of graduates earning over $100,000 from *Business Week*'s top business schools, 1999 ★640★

Percentage of graduates employed within 3 months of graduation from *U.S. News & World Report*'s top 10 graduate business schools, 2001 ★641★

Top graduate business schools, 2001 ★649★

Top graduate business schools by reputation as determined by academic personnel, 2001 ★650★

Top graduate business schools by reputation, as determined by recruiters, 2001 ★651★

Academics' choices for best graduate general management programs, 2001 ★666★

Academics' choices for best graduate international business programs, 2001 ★668★

Academics' choices for best graduate marketing programs, 2001 ★670★

Academics' choices for best graduate quantitative analysis programs, 2001 ★673★

Average GMAT scores for *U.S. News & World Report*'s top 10 graduate business schools, 2000 ★2529★

Duke University Medical Center
Top cancer hospitals in the U.S., 2000 ★2787★
Top cardiology and heart surgery hospitals in the U.S., 2000 ★2788★
Top gastroenterology hospitals in the U.S., 2000 ★2790★
Top geriatrics hospitals in the U.S., 2000 ★2791★
Top gynecology hospitals in the U.S., 2000 ★2792★
Top hospitals in the U.S., 2000 ★2793★
Top nephrology hospitals in the U.S., 2000 ★2794★
Top ophthalmology hospitals in the U.S., 2000 ★2796★
Top orthopedics hospitals in the U.S., 2000 ★2797★
Top psychiatric hospitals in the U.S., 2000 ★2800★
Top rheumatology hospitals in the U.S., 2000 ★2802★
Top urology hospitals in the U.S., 2000 ★2803★

Dull Knife Memorial College
U.S. tribal colleges ★1445★

Lowest undergraduate tuition and fees at colleges and universities in Montana ★1527★

Dull; Richard
Top pay and benefits for the chief executive and top paid employees at Moravian College ★3407★

Duluth High School
Outstanding secondary schools in Atlanta, Georgia ★4087★

Dumas; Jocques
All-American boy's high school football linemen, 2000 ★183★

Dumbarton Middle School
Outstanding secondary schools in Baltimore, Maryland ★4092★

Dun & Bradstreet
Fortune's highest ranked computer and data services companies, 2000 ★453★

Dunbar High School
Outstanding secondary schools in Washington, District of Columbia-Maryland-Virginia-West Virginia ★4249★

Dune: House Harkonnen
Library Journal's best science fiction and fantasy titles, 2000 ★246★

Dunham; David
Top pay and benefits for the chief executive and top paid employees at Walsh University ★3602★

Dunlap; Benjamin
Top pay and benefits for the chief executive and top paid employees at Wofford College ★3634★

Dunlop; Wayne
Top pay and benefits for the chief executive and top paid employees at Eastern Nazarene College ★3281★

Dunn; Donald
Top pay and benefits for the chief executive and top paid employees at Western New England College ★3615★

Dunn; Douglas
Top pay and benefits for the chief executive and top paid employees at Carnegie Mellon University ★3223★

Dunn; Joe P.
Top pay and benefits for the chief executive and top paid employees at Converse College ★3255★

Dunn; Mary Maples
Top pay and benefits for the chief executive and top paid employees at Radcliffe College ★3450★

Dunnington; Don W.
Top pay and benefits for the chief executive and top paid employees at Southern Nazarene University ★3503★

Dunphy; Linda
Top pay and benefits for the chief executive and top paid employees at Saint Joseph's University ★3476★

Dunton; Susan
Top pay and benefits for the chief executive and top paid employees at Fontbonne College ★3294★

DuPage Community College
Fall enrollment at Chicago-area public community colleges, by minority percentages, 1999 ★867★

DuPont
Business Week's best performing companies with the highest 1-year earnings growth ★413★
Top chemical companies in Standard & Poor's 500, 2001 ★533★

Most selective internships in the U.S., 2001 ★2610★
Top internships in the U.S. with the highest compensation, 2001 ★2611★

DuPont Junior High School
Outstanding secondary schools in Charleston, West Virginia ★4107★

DuPont Manual Magnet High School
Outstanding secondary schools in Louisville, Kentucky-Indiana ★4168★

Dupuy; George
Top pay and benefits for the chief executive and top paid employees at Presbyterian College ★3445★

Duquesne University
U.S. colleges and universities with the least attractive campuses ★1037★
Private, 4-year undergraduate colleges and universities producing the most Ph.D.'s in nonscience fields, 1920-1990 ★2030★
Private, 4-year undergraduate colleges and universities producing the most Ph.D.'s in nonscience fields, 1981-1990 ★2031★
Private, 4-year undergraduate colleges and universities producing the most Ph.D.'s in nonscience fields, 1990 ★2032★
Private, 4-year undergraduate colleges and universities producing the most Ph.D.'s in English, 1981-1990 ★2450★
Presidents with the highest pay at Doctoral I and II universities, 1998-99 ★3160★
Average faculty salaries for institutions of higher education in Pennsylvania, 2000-01 ★3725★

Durgin; William R.
Top pay and benefits for the chief executive and top paid employees at College of the Holy Cross ★3247★

Durham Tech Community College
Average faculty salaries for institutions of higher education without academic ranks in North Carolina, 2000-01 ★3761★

Duryea; William
Top pay and benefits for the chief executive and top paid employees Saint Francis College in Pennsylvania ★3641★

Dutch Fork High School
Outstanding secondary schools in Columbia, South Carolina ★4117★

Dutchess Community College
Lowest undergraduate tuition and fees at colleges and universities in New York ★1538★
Average faculty salaries for institutions of higher education in New York, 2000-01 ★3719★

Dutton
Hardcover bestsellers by publishing house, 2000 ★240★

Dwight D. Eisenhower High School
Outstanding suburban public high schools in Metro Detroit ★4258★

Dye; Nancy S.
Top pay and benefits for the chief executive and top paid employees at Oberlin College ★3427★

Dyersburg State Community College
Lowest undergraduate tuition and fees at colleges and universities in Tennessee ★1559★
Average faculty salaries for institutions of higher education in Tennessee, 2000-01 ★3730★

Dykeman Associates
Most selective internships in the U.S., 2001 ★2610★

Dynegy
  Best performing companies in Standard & Poor's 500, 2001 ★382★
  Fortune's highest ranked pipelines and energy companies, 2000 ★486★
  Top services industries in Standard & Poor's 500, 2001 ★558★

E

E-Tek Dynamics
  Business Week's top companies in terms of market value, 2000 ★429★
  Top companies in terms of growth, 2000 ★534★
Eagan High School
  Outstanding secondary schools in Minneapolis-St. Paul, Minnesota-Wisconsin ★4181★
Eagleville School
  Outstanding secondary schools in Nashville, Tennessee ★4186★
Eagon; Madeleine R.
  Top pay and benefits for the chief executive and top paid employees at DePauw University ★3267★
Earhart Opt for Knowledge
  Chicago neighborhood schools with the highest ISAT scores in reading and math ★4004★
Earl Warren Junior High School
  Outstanding secondary schools in San Diego, California ★4220★
Earley; Ashley
  All-America girls' high school basketball 1st team, 2001 ★170★
Earlham College
  Private, 4-year undergraduate colleges and universities producing the most Ph.D.'s in the life sciences, 1920-1990 ★192★
  U.S. colleges and universities where students and the local community relate well ★999★
  U.S. colleges and universities where students are very politically active ★1001★
  U.S. News & World Report's national liberal arts colleges with students least in debt, 1999 ★1385★
  Highest undergraduate tuition and fees at colleges and universities in Indiana ★1502★
  Private, 4-year undergraduate colleges and universities producing the most Ph.D.'s in the earth sciences, 1981-1990 ★2151★
  Institutions in the Worker Rights Consortium ★2913★
  Average faculty salaries for institutions of higher education in Indiana, 2000-01 ★3701★
Early Childhood Classics: Old Favorites with a New Twist
  Outstanding audio selections for young listeners, 2000 ★325★
Early; Joseph E.
  Top pay and benefits for the chief executive and top paid employees at Cumberland College ★3260★
Earth, atmosphere, and marine science
  Number of physical sciences doctorate recipients at U.S. colleges and universities, by field, 1999 ★1975★
  Percentage of female doctorate recipients at U.S. colleges and universities, by subfield, 1999 ★1988★
  Physical sciences, mathematics, and computer sciences doctorates awarded to U.S. citizens/permanent residents at U.S. colleges and universities, by race/ethnicity and subfield, 1999 ★1993★

Earth sciences
  Median salary for B.S. chemists, by field ★781★
  Median salary for M.S. chemists, by field ★785★
  Median salary for Ph.D. chemists, by field ★786★
  Mean age of first and best contribution of scientists and inventors, by discipline ★3096★
Earth, Sky, Wet, Dry: A Book of Nature Opposites
  Booklist's best science books for children ★310★
Eason; Rick
  Top pay and benefits for the chief executive and top paid employees at Southwestern University in Texas ★3505★
East Anchorage High School
  Outstanding secondary schools in Anchorage, Alaska ★4083★
East Anglia; University of
  Top United Kingdom universities by citation impact in the field of geosciences, 1991-95 ★2143★
  Top United Kingdom universities by citation impact in the field of plant and animal sciences, 1991-95 ★2144★
  Top United Kingdom universities by total citations in the field of agricultural sciences, 1991-95 ★2145★
  Top United Kingdom universities by total citations in the field of plant and animal sciences, 1991-95 ★2148★
  United Kingdom universities with the greatest impact in geosciences, 1993-97 ★2154★
East Arkansas Community College
  Lowest undergraduate tuition and fees at colleges and universities in Arkansas ★1485★
East Brunswick High School
  Outstanding secondary schools in Middlesex-Somerset-Hunterdon, New Jersey ★4179★
East Carolina University
  State appropriations for North Carolina's institutions of higher education, 2000-01 ★1286★
  U.S. News & World Report's best undergraduate fees among southern regional universities by discount tuition, 2000 ★1429★
  U.S. News & World Report's southern regional universities with the highest percentage of full-time faculty, 2000-01 ★1440★
  U.S. News & World Report's top public southern regional universities, 2000-01 ★1443★
  Academics' choices for best rural medicine programs, 2001 ★2824★
  Top primary-care medical schools by reputation, as determined by academic personnel, 2001 ★2857★
  Average faculty salaries for institutions of higher education in North Carolina, 2000-01 ★3720★
East Central Community College
  U.S. colleges and universities with the lowest percentage of African Americans enrolled, 1997 ★223★
  Lowest undergraduate tuition and fees at colleges and universities in Mississippi ★1523★
East Central University
  State appropriations for Oklahoma's institutions of higher education, 2000-01 ★1289★
  Total baccalaureate business management and administrative services degrees awarded to Native Americans from U.S. colleges and universities, 1997-98 ★1686★

Total baccalaureate degrees awarded to Native Americans from U.S. colleges and universities, 1997-98 ★1710★
  Total baccalaureate education degrees awarded to Native Americans from U.S. colleges and universities, 1997-98 ★1714★
  Total baccalaureate English language, literature, and letters degrees awarded to Native Americans from U.S. colleges and universities, 1997-98 ★1719★
  Total baccalaureate health professions and related sciences degrees awarded to Native Americans from U.S. colleges and universities, 1997-98 ★1724★
  Total baccalaureate law and legal studies degrees awarded to Native Americans from U.S. colleges and universities, 1997-98 ★1728★
  U.S. colleges and universities awarding the most business management and administrative services master's degrees to Native Americans ★1762★
  U.S. colleges and universities awarding the most education master's degrees to Native Americans ★1772★
  U.S. colleges and universities awarding the most master's degrees to Native Americans ★1789★
  Average faculty salaries for institutions of higher education in Oklahoma, 2000-01 ★3723★
East Coloma School
  All-USA Teacher Teams, Third Team, 2000 ★4401★
East Georgia College
  Lowest undergraduate tuition and fees at colleges and universities in Georgia ★1497★
East Grand Rapids High School
  Outstanding secondary schools in Grand Rapids-Muskegon-Holland, Michigan ★4140★
East Grand Rapids Middle School
  Outstanding secondary schools in Grand Rapids-Muskegon-Holland, Michigan ★4140★
East High School
  Outstanding secondary schools in Philadelphia, Pennsylvania-New Jersey ★4202★
East Hills Middle School
  Outstanding secondary schools in Detroit, Michigan ★4125★
East Middle School
  Outstanding secondary schools in Binghamton, New York ★4097★
East Mississippi Community College
  Lowest undergraduate tuition and fees at colleges and universities in Mississippi ★1523★
East Syracuse Free Library
  Highest Hennen's American Public Library Ratings for libraries serving a population of 2,500 to 4,999 ★2693★
East Tennessee State University
  State appropriations for Tennessee's institutions of higher education, 2000-01 ★1295★
  Academics' choices for best rural medicine programs, 2001 ★2824★
  Average faculty salaries for institutions of higher education in Tennessee, 2000-01 ★3730★
East Texas Baptist University
  Average faculty salaries for institutions of higher education in Texas, 2000-01 ★3731★
Eastchester High School
  Outstanding secondary schools in New York, New York ★4191★
Eastern Arizona College
  Lowest undergraduate tuition and fees at colleges and universities in Arizona ★1483★

Eastern Baptist Theological Seminary
  Average faculty salaries for institutions of higher education in Pennsylvania, 2000-01 ★3725★

Eastern and Central Europe
  First-year physics and astronomy graduate students from Europe, 1997-98 ★2988★

Eastern College
  Average faculty salaries for institutions of higher education in Pennsylvania, 2000-01 ★3725★

Eastern Connecticut State University
  Average faculty salaries for institutions of higher education in Connecticut, 2000-01 ★3694★

Eastern Connecticut University
  State appropriations for Connecticut's institutions of higher education, 2000-01 ★1260★

Eastern Idaho Technical College
  Undergraduate tuition and fees at colleges and universities in Idaho ★1499★

Eastern Illinois University
  State appropriations for Illinois institutions of higher education, 2000-01 ★1266★
  U.S. News & World Report's top public midwestern regional universities, 2000-01 ★1412★
  Average faculty salaries for institutions of higher education in Illinois, 2000-01 ★3700★

Eastern Kentucky University
  Division I NCAA colleges with that graduated none of their African American male basketball players, 1990-91 to 1993-94 ★930★
  State appropriations for Kentucky's institutions of higher education, 2000-01 ★1270★
  Average faculty salaries for institutions of higher education in Kentucky, 2000-01 ★3704★

Eastern Maine Technical College
  Lowest undergraduate tuition and fees at colleges and universities in Maine ★1513★

Eastern Mennonite University
  U.S. News & World Report's southern regional liberal arts colleges with the highest alumni giving rates, 2000-01 ★1371★
  U.S. News & World Report's southern regional liberal arts colleges with the highest graduation rates, 2000-01 ★1373★
  Average faculty salaries for institutions of higher education in Virginia, 2000-01 ★3735★

Eastern Michigan University
  U.S. colleges and universities with the lowest average football attendance, 1996-99 ★160★
  State appropriations for Michigan's institutions of higher education, 2000-01 ★1275★
  Total baccalaureate English language, literature, and letters degrees awarded to Native Americans from U.S. colleges and universities, 1997-98 ★1719★
  U.S. colleges and universities awarding the most mathematics master's degrees to Asian Americans ★1791★

Eastern New Mexico University
  Division II NCAA colleges with the lowest graduation rates for football players, 1993-94 ★948★
  State appropriations for New Mexico's institutions of higher education, 2000-01 ★1284★
  Highest undergraduate tuition and fees at colleges and universities in New Mexico ★1535★
  Average faculty salaries for institutions of higher education in New Mexico, 2000-01 ★3718★

Eastern New Mexico University, Roswell
  Lowest undergraduate tuition and fees at colleges and universities in New Mexico ★1536★

Eastern Oklahoma State College
  U.S. institutions awarding the most associate degrees to minorities in agricultural sciences, 1998 ★1809★
  U.S. institutions awarding the most associate degrees to Native Americans in agricultural sciences, 1998 ★1812★
  Average faculty salaries for institutions of higher education without academic ranks in Oklahoma, 2000-01 ★3763★

Eastern Oregon University
  U.S. News & World Report's top public western regional liberal arts colleges, 2000-01 ★1365★
  Average faculty salaries for institutions of higher education in Oregon, 2000-01 ★3724★

Eastern Orthodox
  Religious preference of incoming freshmen, 2000 ★1061★

Eastern Utah; College of
  Undergraduate tuition and fees at colleges and universities in Utah ★1562★

Eastern Washington University
  Division I NCAA colleges with that graduated none of their African American male basketball players, 1990-91 to 1993-94 ★930★
  State appropriations for Washington's institutions of higher education, 2000-01 ★1300★
  Average faculty salaries for institutions of higher education in Washington, 2000-01 ★3736★

Eastern Wyoming College
  Undergraduate tuition and fees at colleges and universities in Wyoming ★1572★
  Average faculty salaries for institutions of higher education without academic ranks in Wyoming, 2000-01 ★3769★

Eastfield College
  Lowest undergraduate tuition and fees at colleges and universities in Texas ★1561★
  Average faculty salaries for institutions of higher education without academic ranks in Texas, 2000-01 ★3766★

Eastman Chemical Company
  Business Week's best performing companies with the highest 1-year earnings growth ★413★
  Top chemical companies in Standard & Poor's 500, 2001 ★533★
  Top recruiters for chemical engineering jobs for 2000-01 bachelor's degree recipients ★2343★

Eastman Kodak Company
  Business Week's best performing companies with the highest 3-year earnings growth ★416★
  Fortune's highest ranked scientific, photo and control equipment companies, 2000 ★493★
  Top leisure time industries in Standard & Poor's 500, 2001 ★545★
  Top internships in the U.S. with the highest compensation, 2001 ★2611★

Easton Library
  Highest Hennen's American Public Library Ratings for libraries serving a population of 999 and under ★2691★

Easy CD Creator Deluxe 4.0
  Top selling personal productivity software, 2000 ★1600★

Eating Well for Optimum Health
  Longest-running nonfiction hardcover bestsellers, 2000 ★281★

Eaton
  Fortune's highest ranked electronics and electrical equipment companies, 2000 ★460★
  Top automotive companies in Standard & Poor's 500, 2001 ★530★

Eaton; Philip
  Top pay and benefits for the chief executive and top paid employees at Seattle Pacific University ★3494★

eBay
  Top E-commerce web sites ★2603★
  Web sites where internet users spend the most time ★2609★

eBay Magazine
  Library Journal's notable new magazines, 1999 ★2923★

Ebben; James A.
  Top pay and benefits for the chief executive and top paid employees at Edgewood College ★3283★

Ebbs; George
  Top pay and benefits for the chief executive and top paid employees at Embry-Riddle Aeronautical University ★3286★

Ebell; Tyler
  All-American boy's high school football running backs, 2000 ★186★
  All-American boy's high school football team, 2000 ★187★

Eber; John
  Top pay and benefits for the chief executive and top paid employees at Saint Xavier University ★3487★

Eberlein; Timothy J.
  Top pay and benefits for the chief executive and top paid employees at Washington University in Missouri ★3607★

Ebner; Stephanie
  All-America girls' high school soccer team defenders, 2001 ★174★

eBoys: The First Inside Account of Venture Capitalists at Work
  Library Journal's most notable books about venture capital, 2000 ★252★

Eckard III; W. David
  Top pay and benefits for the chief executive and top paid employees at Widener University ★3626★

Eckerd College
  Highest undergraduate tuition and fees at colleges and universities in Florida ★1494★
  Bachelor's institutions with the highest enrollment of foreign students, 1998-99 ★2492★
  Average faculty salaries for institutions of higher education in Florida, 2000-01 ★3696★

Eckerd Youth Alternatives, Inc.
  Top recruiters for criminal justice jobs for 2000-01 bachelor's degree recipients ★1647★
  Top recruiters for language/literature jobs for 2000-01 bachelor's degree recipients ★2446★
  Top recruiters for history jobs for 2000-01 bachelor's degree recipients ★2550★
  Top recruiters for psychology jobs for 2000-01 bachelor's degree recipients ★3063★
  Top recruiters for social work jobs for 2000-01 bachelor's degree recipients ★4342★
  Top recruiters for sociology jobs for 2000-01 bachelor's degree recipients ★4347★

Ecolab
Top consumer products companies in Standard & Poor's 500, 2001 ★536★

Ecological Entomology
Entomology journals by citation impact, 1981-98 ★2453★
Entomology journals by citation impact, 1994-98 ★2454★
Entomology journals by citation impact, 1998 ★2455★

Ecological Monographs
Ecology journals by citation impact, 1981-99 ★2136★
Ecology journals by citation impact, 1995-99 ★2137★
Ecology journals by citation impact, 1999 ★2138★

Ecologist
Ecology journals by citation impact, 1995-99 ★2137★

Ecology
Biological sciences doctorates awarded at U.S. colleges and universities, by subfield, 1999 ★1887★
Gender breakdown of biological sciences doctorate recipients, by subfield, 1999 ★1927★
Percentage of female doctorate recipients at U.S. colleges and universities, by subfield, 1999 ★1988★
Ecology journals by citation impact, 1981-99 ★2136★
Ecology journals by citation impact, 1999 ★2138★

Ecology/environment
Finland's contribution of papers in the sciences by field, 1992-96 ★4309★

Ecology/environmental
Australia's contribution of papers in the sciences, by field, 1993-97 ★4292★
Australia's contribution of papers in the sciences, by field, 1995-99 ★4293★
Austria's relative impact in the sciences by field, 1992-96 ★4300★
Canada's contribution of papers in the sciences, by field, 1995-99 ★4303★
Denmark's contribution of papers in the sciences, by field, 1994-98 ★4306★
Denmark's contribution of papers in the sciences, by field, 1995-99 ★4307★
Finland's contribution of papers in the sciences, by field, 1995-99 ★4310★
Hong Kong's contribution of papers in the sciences, by field, 1995-99 ★4314★
Netherlands' contribution of papers in the sciences, by field, 1995-99 ★4321★
New Zealand's contribution of papers in the sciences, by field, 1994-98 ★4322★
Norway's contribution of papers in the sciences, by field, 1994-98 ★4323★
South Africa's contribution of papers in the sciences, by field, 1994-98 ★4326★
Spain's contribution of papers in the sciences, by field, 1993-97 ★4328★
Spain's contribution of papers in the sciences, by field, 1995-99 ★4329★
Sweden's contribution of papers in the sciences by field, 1993-97 ★4330★
Sweden's contribution of papers in the sciences, by field, 1995-99 ★4331★
Taiwan contribution of papers in the sciences, by field, 1995-99 ★4334★
Turkey's contribution of papers in the sciences, by field, 1995-99 ★4335★

Econometrica
Economics journals with the greatest impact measure, 1981-98 ★2161★
Economics journals with the greatest impact measure, 1994-98 ★2162★
Economics journals with the greatest impact measure, 1997 ★2163★
Alternative general economics journals, by non-uniform weighting of subdisciplinary impacts, including self-citations ★2180★
Alternative general economics journals, by uniform weighting of subdisciplinary impacts, including self-citations ★2181★
Economics journals by citation impact, 1981-98 ★2182★
Economics journals by citation impact, 1995-98 ★2183★
Economics journals by citation impact, 1998 ★2184★
Top ranked agricultural and natural resource economics journals ★2187★
Top ranked business administration and business economics journals ★2188★
Top ranked economic development, technological change, and growth journals ★2189★
Top ranked economic systems journals ★2191★
Top ranked financial economics journals ★2192★
Top ranked health, education, and welfare journals ★2193★
Top ranked industrial organization journals ★2194★
Top ranked international economics journals ★2195★
Top ranked labor and demographic economics journals ★2196★
Top ranked law and economics journals ★2197★
Top ranked mathematical and quantitative methods journals ★2198★
Top ranked microeconomics and monetary economics journals ★2199★
Top ranked microeconomics journals ★2200★
Top ranked public economics journals ★2201★
Highest impact economics journals in energy from 1980 to 1989 ★2457★
Highest impact economics journals in exhaustible resources from 1980 to 1989 ★2460★
Journals and proceedings with the most citations (Class 2) ★2568★

Econometrics
Gender breakdown of social sciences doctorate recipients, by subfield, 1999 ★1942★
Social sciences doctorates awarded at U.S. colleges and universities, by subfield, 1999 ★2044★

Econometrika
Highly cited real estate journals, 1990 to 1995 ★3090★

Economic Development and Cultural Change
Top ranked economic development, technological change, and growth journals ★2189★

Economic Geography
Economics journals by citation impact, 1998 ★2184★

Economic Geology
Geology journals with the greatest impact measure, 1981-98 ★2525★

Economic History Review
Top ranked economic history journals ★2190★

Economic Inquiry
Top ranked health, education, and welfare journals ★2193★

Economic Inquiry/Western Economic Journal
Journals publishing the most articles on economic education research from 1963-1990 ★2170★

Economic Journal
Top ranked economic development, technological change, and growth journals ★2189★
Top ranked economic history journals ★2190★
Top ranked economic systems journals ★2191★
Top ranked international economics journals ★2195★
Highest impact economics journals in energy from 1990 to 1998 ★2458★

Economic and Political Weekly
'Outside' journals most frequently citing Population and Development Review, 1991-95 ★1860★

Economica
Top ranked economic systems journals ★2191★

Economics
Gender breakdown of social sciences doctorate recipients, by subfield, 1999 ★1942★
Number of social sciences doctorate recipients at U.S. colleges and universities, by field, 1999 ★1977★
Percentage of female doctorate recipients at U.S. colleges and universities, by subfield, 1999 ★1988★
Social sciences doctorates awarded at U.S. colleges and universities, by subfield, 1999 ★2044★
Social sciences doctorates awarded to U.S. citizens/permanent residents at U.S. colleges and universities, by race/ethnicity and subfield, 1999 ★2045★
Journals publishing the most articles on economic education research from 1963-1990 ★2170★
Top nonscience majors for accepted applicants to U.S. medical schools, 1999-2000 ★2854★
Expected starting salaries of 2000-01 bachelor's degree recipients, by specific major ★3131★

Economics and business
United States' contribution of papers in the sciences, by field, 1995-99 ★4283★
United States' contribution of papers in the sciences, by field, 1996-2000 ★4284★
Australia's contribution of papers in the sciences, by field, 1995-99 ★4293★
United Kingdom's contribution of papers in the sciences, by field, 1995-99 ★4297★
Belgium's contribution of papers in the sciences by field, 1992-96 ★4301★
Belgium's contribution of papers in the sciences, by field, 1995-99 ★4302★
Canada's contribution of papers in the sciences, by field, 1995-99 ★4303★
England's contribution of papers in the sciences, by field, 1994-98 ★4308★
Hong Kong's contribution of papers in the sciences, by field, 1995-99 ★4314★
Ireland's contribution of papers in the sciences, by field, 1994-98 ★4315★
Netherlands' contribution of papers in the sciences, by field, 1995-99 ★4321★

ECONOMICS

New Zealand's contribution of papers in the sciences, by field, 1994-98 ★4322★
Norway's contribution of papers in the sciences, by field, 1994-98 ★4323★
South Korea's contribution of papers in the sciences, by field, 1995-99 ★4327★

Economics macro
Number of Advanced Placement Exams taken by African Americans, by subject, 2000 ★30★
Number of Advanced Placement Exams taken by Asian Americans, by subject, 2000 ★31★
Number of Advanced Placement Exams taken by Hispanic Americans, by subject, 2000 ★32★

Economics micro
Number of Advanced Placement Exams taken by African Americans, by subject, 2000 ★30★
Number of Advanced Placement Exams taken by Asian Americans, by subject, 2000 ★31★
Number of Advanced Placement Exams taken by Hispanic Americans, by subject, 2000 ★32★

Economics or finance
Average starting salaries for college graduates, by field, 2000 ★3129★

Economics of Resources or Resources of Economics
Top cited nonrenewable resource papers from 1974 to 1978 ★2468★

Economics and Sustainability-Balancing Trade-Offs and Imperatives
Top cited nonrenewable resource papers from 1994 to 1998 ★2472★

The Economist
Economics journals with the greatest impact measure, 1997 ★2163★
Economics journals by citation impact, 1998 ★2184★
Jobs with the best physical demands scores ★2250★
Most desirable jobs in business/finance ★2270★
Social sciences journals with the greatest impact measure, 1981-97 ★4341★

Economy and Society
Economics journals with the greatest impact measure, 1997 ★2163★

ECTJ-Education, Communication, Technology Journal
Education and educational research journals by citation impact, 1981-99 ★2235★

EDC
Highest revenues of publicly held book publishers, 1999 ★3072★

Edelin; Billy
All-America boys' high school basketball 3rd team, 2001 ★163★

Edelman Public Relations Worldwide
Most selective internships in the U.S., 2001 ★2610★

Eden Prairie High School
Outstanding secondary schools in Minneapolis-St. Paul, Minnesota-Wisconsin ★4181★

The Edge
Library Journal's best fiction audiobooks, 2000 ★241★
Most notable fiction books for reluctant young adult readers, 2001 ★321★

Edgebrook Elementary School
Illinois elementary schools with the highest 5th grade writing scores ★15★
Chicago neighborhood schools with the highest ISAT scores in reading and math ★4004★

Edgecombe Community College
Average faculty salaries for institutions of higher education without academic ranks in North Carolina, 2000-01 ★3761★

Edgemont Junior/Senior High School
Outstanding suburban public high schools in Metro New York ★4259★

Edgewood College
Average faculty salaries for institutions of higher education in Wisconsin, 2000-01 ★3738★

Edinboro University
Average faculty salaries for institutions of higher education in Pennsylvania, 2000-01 ★3725★

Edinboro University of Pennsylvania
Division II NCAA colleges with the 0% graduation rates for men's basketball players, 1993-94 ★941★

Edinburgh-Glasgow
Cities with the highest productivity of paper in the discipline of cardiovascular systems, 1994-96 ★2869★

Edinburgh; University of
Top United Kingdom universities by total citations in the field of geosciences, 1991-95 ★2147★

Edison Computech Middle School
Outstanding secondary schools in Fresno, California ★4138★

Edison Gifted Elementary School
Illinois elementary schools with the highest 5th grade writing scores ★15★
Illinois schools with the highest 7th grade science scores ★17★
Chicago elementary magnet schools with the lowest acceptance rates, 2000-01 ★4003★

Edison International
Fortune's highest ranked electric and gas utilities companies, 2000 ★459★

Editor
Most desirable jobs in communications ★2271★

Edman; Neal A.
Top pay and benefits for the chief executive and top paid employees at Westminster College in Pennsylvania ★3617★

Edmondson; Charles
Top pay and benefits for the chief executive and top paid employees at Rollins College ★3465★

EDS
Top recruiters for business administration jobs for 2000-01 bachelor's degree recipients ★554★
Top recruiters for accounting jobs for 2000-01 bachelor's degree recipients ★580★
Top recruiters for finance/banking jobs for 2000-01 bachelor's degree recipients ★582★
Top recruiters for business administration jobs for 2000-01 master's degree recipients ★652★
Top recruiters for accounting jobs for 2000-01 master's degree recipients ★661★
Top recruiters for finance/banking jobs for 2000-01 master's degree recipients ★664★
Top recruiters for marketing jobs for 2000-01 bachelor's degree recipients ★684★
Top recruiters for computer science jobs for 2000-01 bachelor's degree recipients ★1590★
Top recruiters for computer science jobs for 2000-01 master's degree recipients ★1598★
Top employers of college graduates, 2001 ★2325★
Top recruiters for systems engineer jobs for 2000-01 bachelor's degree recipients ★2336★
Top recruiters for systems engineer jobs for 2000-01 master's degree recipients ★2371★
Top recruiters for liberal arts jobs for 2000-01 bachelor's degree recipients ★2675★
Top recruiters for information technology (MIS) jobs for 2000-01 bachelor's degree recipients ★2738★
Top recruiters for information technology (MIS) jobs for 2000-01 master's degree recipients ★2739★

Education
Top fields of study for college and university presidents, 1998 ★839★
Expected majors for incoming freshmen, 2000 ★1050★
Federal appropriations to colleges, by agency, 2000 ★1241★
Top bachelor's degree disciplines for African Americans, 1997-98 ★1672★
Top bachelor's degree disciplines for Asian Americans, 1997-98 ★1673★
Top bachelor's degree disciplines for Hispanic Americans, 1997-98 ★1674★
Top bachelor's degree disciplines for Native Americans, 1997-98 ★1675★
Top bachelor's degree disciplines for non-minorities, 1997-98 ★1676★
Age grouping of doctorate recipients, by broad field, 1999 ★1882★
Comparative data of women receiving doctorate degrees in selected fields in 1950 and 1998 ★1899★
Doctoral degree distribution by broad field, 1999 ★1902★
Median age at conferral of doctoral degree from U.S. universities, by discipline, 1999 ★1952★
Number of doctorate recipients at U.S. colleges and universities, by field, 1999 ★1969★
Percentage of female doctorate recipients, by broad field, 1999 ★1989★
Percentage of minority doctorate recipients in the U.S., by broad field, 1999 ★1991★
Top bachelor's and master's degree majors in demand for employment, 2001 ★2323★
Top bachelor's degree majors in demand for employment, 2001 ★2324★
Top master's degree majors in demand for employment, 2001 ★2326★
Fields of study profile of foreign students enrolled in U.S. institutions of higher education, 1998-99 ★2495★
Fields of study profile of U.S. students studying abroad, 1998-99 ★2507★
Average costs for Academic Search titles by subject, 2001 ★2918★
Periodical prices by LC subject, 2001 ★2925★
United States' contribution of papers in the sciences, by field, 1995-99 ★4283★
United States' contribution of papers in the sciences, by field, 1996-2000 ★4284★
Australia's contribution of papers in the sciences, by field, 1993-97 ★4292★
Australia's contribution of papers in the sciences, by field, 1995-99 ★4293★
United Kingdom's contribution of papers in the sciences, by field, 1995-99 ★4297★
Canada's contribution of papers in the sciences, by field, 1995-99 ★4303★
England's contribution of papers in the sciences, by field, 1994-98 ★4308★
New Zealand's contribution of papers in the sciences, by field, 1994-98 ★4322★

South Africa's contribution of papers in the sciences, by field, 1994-98 ★4326★

Education administrators
Employment outlook for the year 2005 for selected occupations ★2297★

Education for the disadvantaged
Educational program activities expenditures, 2000 ★3992★

Education, general
Gender breakdown of teaching fields doctorate recipients, by subfield, 1999 ★1943★
Teaching fields doctorates awarded at U.S. colleges and universities, by subfield, 1999 ★2046★

Education IRAs
Best ways to save for college ★843★

Education reforms–Goals 2000
Educational program activities expenditures, 2000 ★3992★

Education research
2002 budget request for education research and statistics ★2228★

Education statistics
2002 budget request for education research and statistics ★2228★

Educational
Gender breakdown of psychology doctorate recipients, by subfield, 1999 ★1941★
Psychology doctorates awarded at U.S. colleges and universities, by subfield, 1999 ★2043★

Educational administration and supervision
Education doctorates awarded at U.S. colleges and universities, by subfield, 1999 ★1921★
Gender breakdown of education doctorate recipients, by subfield, 1999 ★1933★

Educational assessment, testing and measures
Education doctorates awarded at U.S. colleges and universities, by subfield, 1999 ★1921★
Gender breakdown of education doctorate recipients, by subfield, 1999 ★1933★

Educational/instructional media design
Education doctorates awarded at U.S. colleges and universities, by subfield, 1999 ★1921★
Gender breakdown of education doctorate recipients, by subfield, 1999 ★1933★

Educational leadership
Education doctorates awarded at U.S. colleges and universities, by subfield, 1999 ★1921★
Gender breakdown of education doctorate recipients, by subfield, 1999 ★1933★

Educational psychology
Education doctorates awarded at U.S. colleges and universities, by subfield, 1999 ★1921★
Gender breakdown of education doctorate recipients, by subfield, 1999 ★1933★

Educational Research
Education and educational research journals with the greatest impact measure ★2238★

Educational statistics/research methods
Education doctorates awarded at U.S. colleges and universities, by subfield, 1999 ★1921★
Gender breakdown of education doctorate recipients, by subfield, 1999 ★1933★

Educational Technology
Most cited education serials in technical communication journals from 1988 to 1997 ★4418★

Edward Waters College
Most dangerous college campuses in the U.S. ★712★

Edwards; LaVell
Division I-A all-time coaching victories ★126★

Edwards; Mark U.
Top pay and benefits for the chief executive and top paid employees at St. Olaf College ★3484★

Edwards Middle School
Outstanding secondary schools in Atlanta, Georgia ★4087★

Edwards; Robert H.
Top pay and benefits for the chief executive and top paid employees at Bowdoin College ★3207★

Edwards; Thomas L.
Top pay and benefits for the chief executive and top paid employees at Hollins University ★3336★

Edwardsville Middle School
All-USA Teacher Teams, Second Team, 2000 ★4400★

EdWeb
Top sites for educators ★2605★

Edwin Smith High School
Outstanding secondary schools in Hartford, Connecticut ★4147★

The effects of surgical exposures of dental pulps in germ-free and conventional laboratory rats
Endodontic articles with the most citations, 1974 through 1999 ★1864★

Egypt
Countries of origin for non-U.S. citizens awarded doctorates at U.S. colleges and universities, 1999 ★1901★

Ehrlich Martin; Susan
Most-cited scholars in women and crime publications ★1642★

The Eighth Continent: Life, Death, and Discovery in the Lost World of Madagascar
Library Journal's most notable natural history books, 2000 ★269★

84 Lumber
Top women-owned companies ★4460★

Einstein's Unfinished Symphony: Listening to the Sounds of Space-Time
Library Journal's most notable astronomy books, 2000 ★248★

Eircom
Business Week's best companies in Ireland ★396★

Eisenberg; Howard B.
Top pay and benefits for the chief executive and top paid employees at Marquette University ★3392★

Eisenhower High School
Outstanding secondary schools in Riverside-San Bernardino, California ★4211★

Eisenhower Intermediate School
All-USA Teacher Teams, Third Team, 2000 ★4401★

Eisenstein; J.
Most cited authors in the journal *International Journal of Comparative and Applied Criminal Justice*, 1990 to 1995 ★1624★

Eismeier; Elizabeth
Top pay and benefits for the chief executive and top paid employees at Colgate University ★3242★

Eisner; Robert
Authors most frequently contributing to the *American Economic Review* from 1951-1990 ★2157★

Eisner, S.N.D.; Sister Janet
Top pay and benefits for the chief executive and top paid employees at Emmanuel College in Massachusetts ★3288★

El Centro College
Lowest undergraduate tuition and fees at colleges and universities in Texas ★1561★
Average faculty salaries for institutions of higher education without academic ranks in Texas, 2000-01 ★3766★

El Monte High School
Outstanding secondary schools in Los Angeles-Long Beach, California ★4167★

El Paso
Top utilities companies in Standard & Poor's 500, 2001 ★561★
U.S. cities with the highest percentage of births to mothers with less than 12 years of education ★4432★

El Paso Community College
Institutions with the most full-time Hispanic American faculty ★923★
Institutions with the most part-time Hispanic American faculty ★924★
U.S. colleges and universities with the most full-time Hispanic American faculty ★925★

El Paso Energy
Fortune's highest ranked pipelines and energy companies, 2000 ★486★

El Sierra Elementary School
Illinois elementary schools with the highest 5th grade writing scores ★15★

Elaine Nunez Community College
Average faculty salaries for institutions of higher education in Louisiana, 2000-01 ★3705★

Elan
Business Week's best companies in Ireland ★396★

Eleanor
Most notable children's recordings, 2001 ★320★

Eleanor Roosevelt High School
Outstanding secondary schools in Washington, District of Columbia-Maryland-Virginia-West Virginia ★4249★

Electrabel
Business Week's best companies in Belgium ★388★

Electrafina
Business Week's best companies in Belgium ★388★

Electrical/electrical engineering
Top bachelor's and master's degree majors in demand for employment, 2001 ★2323★
Top bachelor's degree majors in demand for employment, 2001 ★2324★
Top master's degree majors in demand for employment, 2001 ★2326★

Electrical and electronic engineer
Occupations with the highest average annual salaries for college graduates, 1998 ★3132★

Electrical and electronic technicians and technologists
Projected employment growth for selected occupations that require an associate degree or less, 1998-2008 ★2319★

Electrical, electronics
Engineering doctorates awarded at U.S. colleges and universities, by subfield, 1999 ★1923★

ELECTRICAL

Gender breakdown of engineering doctorate recipients, by subfield, 1999 ★1934★

Electrical engineer
Most desirable jobs in production/manufacturing ★2276★

Electrical engineering
Top physical science majors for accepted applicants to U.S. medical schools, 1999-2000 ★2855★
Average starting salaries for college graduates, by field, 2000 ★3129★
Expected starting salaries of 2000-01 bachelor's degree recipients, by specific major ★3131★

Electrical engineers
Projected employment growth for selected occupations that require a bachelor's degree or more, 1998-2008 ★2317★

Electrical equipment repairer
'Blue-collar' jobs considered the least physically demanding ★2241★

Electrical powerline installers and repairers
Average salaries for occupations requiring on-the-job training ★3119★

Electrical technician
Most desirable technical/repair jobs ★2281★

Electrician
Jobs with the highest unemployment ★2256★

Electricians
Projected employment growth for selected occupations that require long-term on-the-job training, 1998-2008 ★2320★
Average salaries for occupations requiring on-the-job training ★3119★

Electricidade de Portugal (EDP)
Business Week's best companies in Portugal ★401★

Electronic Arts
Fortune's highest ranked computer software companies, 2000 ★455★

The Electronic B@zaar: From the Silk Road to the eRoad
Library Journal's most notable books on capitalism, 2000 ★253★

Electronic Data Systems
Fortune's highest ranked computer and data services companies, 2000 ★453★

Electronic semiconductor processors
Fastest growing occupations, 1998-2008 ★2302★

Electronics Arts
Software companies with the fastest growth, 2000 ★528★

Elefteriades; John A.
Top pay and benefits for the chief executive and top paid employees at Yale University ★3639★

Elementary education
Education doctorates awarded at U.S. colleges and universities, by subfield, 1999 ★1921★
Gender breakdown of education doctorate recipients, by subfield, 1999 ★1933★

The Elementary Particles
Booklist's best fiction books for library collections, 2000 ★227★
Gender breakdown of physics and astronomy doctorate recipients, by subfield, 1999 ★1939★
Physics and astronomy doctorates awarded at U.S. colleges and universities, by subfield, 1999 ★1994★

Elementary and secondary education
State tax expenditures, 1999-2000 ★2233★

Elementary teachers
Employment outlook for the year 2005 for selected occupations ★2297★

Elevator installers and repairers
Average salaries for occupations requiring on-the-job training ★3119★

Elgin Community College
Fall enrollment at Chicago-area public community colleges, by minority percentages, 1999 ★867★

Eli Lilly and Company
Fortune's highest ranked pharmaceuticals companies, 2000 ★485★
Best companies for working mothers ★4446★
Best companies for working mothers in offering leave for new parents ★4449★

Elias; P.M.
Most cited authors in dermatology journals, 1981 to 1996 ★1870★

Elizabeth City State University
Colleges offering the Thurgood Marshall Scholarship Fund ★221★
U.S. college campuses reporting murders or non-negligent manslaughters, 1999 ★728★
State appropriations for North Carolina's institutions of higher education, 2000-01 ★1286★
Lowest undergraduate tuition and fees at public, 4-year or above colleges and universities ★1466★
Public 4-year institutions with the lowest tuition, 2000-01 ★1472★
Average faculty salaries for institutions of higher education in North Carolina, 2000-01 ★3720★

Elizabeth State University
Retention rates of African American students at historically black institutions, 1997-98 ★1120★

Elizabethtown College
U.S. News & World Report's northern regional liberal arts colleges with the best student/faculty ratios, 2000-01 ★1353★
U.S. News & World Report's northern regional liberal arts colleges with the highest academic reputation scores, 2000-01 ★1354★
U.S. News & World Report's northern regional liberal arts colleges with the highest alumni giving rates, 2000-01 ★1356★
U.S. News & World Report's northern regional liberal arts colleges with the highest freshmen retention rates, 2000-01 ★1357★
U.S. News & World Report's northern regional liberal arts colleges with the highest graduation rates, 2000-01 ★1358★
U.S. News & World Report's northern regional liberal arts colleges with the highest percentage of freshmen in the top 25% of their high school class, 2000-01 ★1359★
U.S. News & World Report's northern regional liberal arts colleges with the highest percentage of full-time faculty, 2000-01 ★1360★
U.S. News & World Report's northern regional liberal arts colleges with the highest proportion of classes having 20 students or less, 2000-01 ★1361★
U.S. News & World Report's top northern regional liberal arts colleges, 2000-01 ★1363★
U.S. News & World Report's best undergraduate fees among northern regional liberal arts colleges by discount tuition, 2000 ★1382★

Average faculty salaries for institutions of higher education in Pennsylvania, 2000-01 ★3725★

Elizabethtown Community College
Lowest undergraduate tuition and fees at colleges and universities in Kentucky ★1509★

Elk Grove High School
Outstanding secondary schools in Chicago, Illinois ★4110★
Outstanding suburban public high schools in Metro Chicago ★4256★

Ellington; Edward "Duke"
Most influential African American entertainers ★77★

Elliot; Frank W.
Top pay and benefits for the chief executive and top paid employees at Texas Wesleyan University ★3519★

Elliott; Delbert S.
Most cited authors in the journal *Journal of Research in Crime and Delinquency*, 1990 to 1995 ★1629★
Most cited authors in three criminology journals ★1634★
Most-cited scholars in *Criminology* ★1639★

Ellisburg Free Library
Highest Hennen's American Public Library Ratings for libraries serving a population of 999 and under ★2691★

Elliston; Edgar J.
Top pay and benefits for the chief executive and top paid employees at Hope International University ★3340★

Ellsworth; David J.
Top pay and benefits for the chief executive and top paid employees at Oral Roberts University ★3433★

Elm Elementary School
Illinois elementary schools with the highest 5th grade writing scores ★15★

Elmhurst College
U.S. News & World Report's midwestern regional liberal arts colleges with the highest freshmen retention rates, 2000-01 ★1343★
U.S. News & World Report's midwestern regional liberal arts colleges with the lowest acceptance rates, 2000-01 ★1348★
Average faculty salaries for institutions of higher education in Illinois, 2000-01 ★3700★

Elmhurst Public Library
Highest Hennen's American Public Library Ratings for libraries serving a population of 25,000 to 49,999 ★2696★

Elmira College
U.S. News & World Report's northern regional universities with students most in debt, 1999 ★1414★
U.S. News & World Report's northern regional universities with the best student/faculty ratios, 2000-01 ★1416★
U.S. News & World Report's northern regional universities with the highest alumni giving rates, 2000-01 ★1418★
U.S. News & World Report's northern regional universities with the highest percentage of full-time faculty, 2000-01 ★1422★
U.S. News & World Report's northern regional universities with the highest proportion of classes with 20 students of less, 2000-01 ★1423★
U.S. News & World Report's best undergraduate fees among northern regional universities by discount tuition, 2000 ★1428★
Average faculty salaries for institutions of higher education in New York, 2000-01 ★3719★

Elmont Memorial High School
Outstanding secondary schools in Long Island, New York ★4165★

Elms College
Average faculty salaries for institutions of higher education in Massachusetts, 2000-01 ★3708★

Elnicky; Sarah
All-America girls' high school soccer team defenders, 2001 ★174★

Elon College
U.S. News & World Report's southern regional universities with the highest freshmen retention rates, 2000-01 ★1437★
U.S. News & World Report's southern regional universities with the highest percentage of full-time faculty, 2000-01 ★1440★
U.S. News & World Report's southern regional universities with the lowest acceptance rates, 2000-01 ★1442★
Highest undergraduate tuition and fees at colleges and universities in North Carolina ★1539★
U.S. master's institutions with the largest number of students studying abroad, 1998-99 ★2513★
Average faculty salaries for institutions of higher education in North Carolina, 2000-01 ★3720★

Elrod; John
Top pay and benefits for the chief executive and top paid employees at Washington and Lee University ★3605★

Elsbeck; George J.
Top pay and benefits for the chief executive and top paid employees at Ohio Wesleyan University ★3430★

Elsevier
Book publishers with the most citations (Class 3) ★2564★

Elwood Community Consolidated School, District 203
Illinois school districts spending the least for elementary school education 1997-98 ★4007★

Ely; Shyra
All-America girls' high school basketball 1st team, 2001 ★170★

Elyria Catholic High School
Outstanding secondary schools in Cleveland-Lorain-Elyria, Ohio ★4114★

EMBO Journal
Molecular biology and genetics journals with the highest impact, 1992-96 ★204★

Embry-Riddle Aeronautical University
Highest undergraduate tuition and fees at colleges and universities in Arizona ★1482★
U.S. News & World Report's undergraduate engineering programs with the best aerospace departments, 2000-01 ★2341★
Average faculty salaries for institutions of higher education in Florida, 2000-01 ★3696★

EMC
Business Week's best companies in the United States ★411★
Companies that have been on Business Week's top 50 list the longest ★435★
Fortune's highest ranked computer peripherals companies, 2000 ★454★
Top office equipment and computers companies in Standard & Poor's 500, 2001 ★551★

E=mc2: A Biography of the World's Most Famous Equation
Library Journal's most notable physics books, 2000 ★274★

Emcor Group
Fortune's highest ranked engineering and construction companies, 2000 ★461★

Emergency medical technicians
Projected employment growth for selected occupations that require an associate degree or less, 1998-2008 ★2319★

Emerick; Betsy K.
Top pay and benefits for the chief executive and top paid employees at Dickinson College ★3268★

Emerson College
U.S. colleges and universities where intercollegiate sports are not popular ★994★
U.S. colleges and universities where intramural sports are not popular ★996★
U.S. colleges and universities where students and the local community relate well ★999★
U.S. colleges and universities with a favorable surrounding town or city ★1013★
U.S. colleges and universities with a popular radio station ★1019★
U.S. colleges and universities with a popular theater group ★1020★
U.S. colleges and universities with the best food service program ★1031★
U.S. News & World Report's northern regional universities with the highest acceptance rates, 2000-01 ★1417★
Average faculty salaries for institutions of higher education in Massachusetts, 2000-01 ★3708★

Emerson Dobash; Rebecca
Most-cited scholars in women and crime publications ★1642★

Emerson Electric
Fortune's highest ranked electronics and electrical equipment companies, 2000 ★460★

Emory and Henry College
U.S. News & World Report's southern regional liberal arts colleges with the highest academic reputation scores, 2000-01 ★1369★
U.S. News & World Report's southern regional liberal arts colleges with the highest alumni giving rates, 2000-01 ★1371★
U.S. News & World Report's southern regional liberal arts colleges with the highest graduation rates, 2000-01 ★1373★
U.S. News & World Report's southern regional liberal arts colleges with the highest percentage of full-time faculty, 2000-01 ★1374★
U.S. News & World Report's top southern regional liberal arts colleges, 2000-01 ★1379★
U.S. News & World Report's best undergraduate fees among southern regional liberal arts colleges by discount tuition, 2000 ★1383★
Average faculty salaries for institutions of higher education in Virginia, 2000-01 ★3735★

Emory University
All-USA College Academic Third Team, 2001 ★4★
U.S. universities with the greatest impact in chemistry, 1994-98 ★793★
U.S. colleges and universities with a favorable surrounding town or city ★1013★
U.S. colleges and universities with strained race/class interaction ★1029★
U.S. News & World Report's national universities with the best faculty resources rank, 2000-01 ★1127★
U.S. News & World Report's national universities with the best student/faculty ratio, 2000-01 ★1130★
U.S. News & World Report's national universities with the lowest proportion of classes with 50 or more students, 2000-01 ★1142★
2000 endowment values of the 'wealthiest' U.S. universities ★1230★
2001 mid-year endowment values of the 'wealthiest' U.S. universities ★1234★
Colleges and universities with the largest endowments, 2000 ★1237★
Endowment values for the wealthiest U.S. universities, 2000 ★1240★
Largest gifts to higher education, 1967-2000 ★1247★
Largest private gifts to higher education, 1967-2000 ★1248★
Highest undergraduate tuition and fees at colleges and universities in Georgia ★1496★
U.S. colleges and universities awarding the most health professions and related sciences master's degrees to African Americans ★1777★
U.S. colleges and universities awarding the most health professions and related sciences master's degrees to Asian Americans ★1778★
Traditionally white institutions awarding the most first professional degrees to African Americans ★1842★
U.S. universities with the greatest impact in dermatology, 1994-98 ★1875★
Top French language and literature research-doctorate programs as evaluated by the National Research Council ★2516★
Academics' choices for best trial advocacy programs, 2001 ★2633★
Law schools with the best law and religion (excluding First Amendment issues) faculty, 1999-2000 ★2658★
Law library web sites, by visibility ★2687★
Top pharmacology research-doctorate programs as evaluated by the National Research Council ★2939★
U.S. universities with the greatest impact in psychiatry, 1995-99 ★3060★
Top religion research-doctorate programs as evaluated by the National Research Council ★3093★
U.S. universities with the highest concentrations in religion and theology, 1992-96 ★3094★
Average faculty salaries for institutions of higher education in Georgia, 2000-01 ★3697★

Emory University, Goizueta Graduate School of Business
Academics' choices for best graduate executive MBA programs, 2001 ★584★
Business Week's top business schools with the lowest percentage of minority enrollment, 2000 ★616★
Lowest post-MBA salaries for students enrolled in Business Week's top business schools, 1999 ★634★
Lowest pre-MBA salaries for students enrolled in Business Week's top business schools, 1999 ★635★

Emory University Hospital
Top cardiology and heart surgery hospitals in the U.S., 2000 ★2788★

Top ophthalmology hospitals in the U.S., 2000 ★2796★

Emotional disturbance
Disabled students served in U.S. public school programs, 1998-99 ★1877★

Empire State College
Average faculty salaries for institutions of higher education in New York, 2000-01 ★3719★

An Empirical Assessment of the SERVQUAL Scale
Most influential articles in the *Journal of Business Research*, 1985-1999 ★697★
Most influential articles in the *Journal of Business Research* from 1990 to 1994 ★699★

Emporia High School
All-USA Teacher Teams, Second Team, 2000 ★4400★

Emporia State University
Division II NCAA colleges with the 100% graduation rates for men's basketball players, 1993-94 ★943★
Division II NCAA colleges with the 100% graduation rates for women's basketball players, 1993-94 ★944★
State appropriations for Kansas institutions of higher education, 2000-01 ★1269★
Average faculty salaries for institutions of higher education in Kansas, 2000-01 ★3703★

Encyclopedia of the American Civil War: A Political, Social, and Military History
Outstanding reference sources, 2000 ★370★
Outstanding reference sources, 2001 ★371★

Encyclopedia of the American Civil War: A Political, Social, and MilitaryHistory
Library Journal's best reference books, 2000 ★368★

Encyclopedia of the American Constitution
Library Journal's best reference books, 2000 ★368★
Selected new editions and supplements reference books, 2000 ★372★

Encyclopedia of American Radio, 1920-1960
Outstanding reference sources, 2000 ★370★

Encyclopedia of American Radio: An A to Z Guide to Radio from Jack Benny to Howard Stern
Selected new editions and supplements reference books, 2000 ★372★

Encyclopedia of Aquaculture
Outstanding reference sources, 2001 ★371★

Encyclopedia of Archaeology: The Great Archaeologists
Selected reference books in the field of archaeology, 2000 ★374★

Encyclopedia of Biodiversity
Library Journal's best reference books, 2000 ★368★
Outstanding reference sources, 2001 ★371★

Encyclopedia of British Columbia
Library Journal's best reference books, 2000 ★368★

Encyclopedia of Contemporary Italian Culture
Library Journal's best reference books, 2000 ★368★
Selected reference books in the field of history, 2000 ★376★

The Encyclopedia of the Dead Sea Scrolls
Outstanding reference sources, 2000 ★370★

Encyclopedia of Eastern Europe
Library Journal's best reference books, 2000 ★368★

Encyclopedia of Eastern Europe: From the Congress of Vienna to the Fall of Communism
Outstanding reference sources, 2000 ★370★
Selected reference books in the field of history, 2000 ★376★

Encyclopedia of ED Statistics
Library Journal's best free reference websites, 2000 ★367★

The Encyclopedia of Ephemera
Library Journal's best reference books, 2000 ★368★

Encyclopedia of Ephemera: A Guide to the Fragmentary Documents of Everyday Life for the Collector, Curator, and Historian
Outstanding reference sources, 2001 ★371★

Encyclopedia of European Social History from 1350 to 2000
Outstanding reference sources, 2001 ★371★

Encyclopedia of German Literature
Library Journal's best reference books, 2000 ★368★
Outstanding reference sources, 2001 ★371★
Selected reference books in the field of literature, 2000 ★377★

Encyclopedia of Human Evolution and Prehistory
Selected new editions and supplements reference books, 2000 ★372★

Encyclopedia of Judaism
Outstanding reference sources, 2001 ★371★

Encyclopedia of the Korean War: A Political, Social, and Military History
Library Journal's best reference books, 2000 ★368★
Outstanding reference sources, 2000 ★370★

Encyclopedia of Lesbian and Gay Histories and Cultures
Outstanding reference sources, 2001 ★371★

The Encyclopedia of Louisville
Library Journal's best reference books, 2000 ★368★

Encyclopedia of Major Marketing Campaigns
Outstanding reference sources, 2000 ★370★

Encyclopedia of Modern Separatist Movements
Selected reference books in the field of political science, 2000 ★379★

Encyclopedia of Monasticism
Outstanding reference sources, 2000 ★370★
Outstanding reference sources, 2001 ★371★

Encyclopedia of Movie Special Effects
Outstanding reference sources, 2001 ★371★

Encyclopedia of Paleontology
Outstanding reference sources, 2001 ★371★

Encyclopedia of the Palestinians
Outstanding reference sources, 2000 ★370★
Outstanding reference sources, 2001 ★371★

Encyclopedia of Psychology
Library Journal's best reference books, 2000 ★368★
Outstanding reference sources, 2000 ★370★
Outstanding reference sources, 2001 ★371★

Encyclopedia of the Scientific Revolution
Outstanding reference sources, 2001 ★371★

Encyclopedia of Stress
Library Journal's best reference books, 2000 ★368★

Encyclopedia of Third Parties in America
Library Journal's best reference books, 2000 ★368★
Outstanding reference sources, 2000 ★370★

Encyclopedia of Twentieth Century American Humor
Outstanding reference sources, 2001 ★371★

Encyclopedia of the United States Cabinet
Library Journal's best reference books, 2000 ★368★
Outstanding reference sources, 2001 ★371★

Encyclopedia of the U.S. Census
Library Journal's best reference books, 2000 ★368★

Encyclopedia of the Vietnam War
Selected new editions and supplements reference books, 2000 ★372★

Encyclopedia of World History
Library Journal's best reference books, 2000 ★368★

Endesa
Business Week's best companies in Spain ★403★

Endicott College
Average faculty salaries for institutions of higher education in Massachusetts, 2000-01 ★3708★

Endocrinology
Biological sciences doctorates awarded at U.S. colleges and universities, by subfield, 1999 ★1887★
Gender breakdown of biological sciences doctorate recipients, by subfield, 1999 ★1927★

Endocrinology, metabolism and nutrition
Clinical medicine subfields with the highest impact measure, 1981-1997 ★2873★

Endodontic success-who's reading the radiograph?
Endodontic articles with the most citations, 1974 through 1999 ★1864★

Endsley; Douglas B.
Top pay and benefits for the chief executive and top paid employees at the University of the Incarnate Word ★3570★

ENEL
Business Week's best companies in Italy ★397★

Energy
Federal appropriations to colleges, by agency, 2000 ★1241★
Proposed fiscal 2002 appropriations for science and technology research ★4339★

Energy Department
Fiscal 2002 requested budget as compared with Fiscal 2001 budget for other agencies ★2230★

Enfield; Michael
All-America boys' high school soccer team midfielders, 2001 ★168★

Engdahl; David
Top pay and benefits for the chief executive and top paid employees at Seattle University ★3495★

Engdahl; George
Top pay and benefits for the chief executive and top paid employees at California Lutheran University ★3216★

Engelhard
Top metals and mining companies in Standard & Poor's 500, 2001 ★549★

Engineering
Expected majors for incoming freshmen, 2000 ★1050★

Top bachelor's degree disciplines for African Americans, 1997-98 ★1672★
Top bachelor's degree disciplines for Asian Americans, 1997-98 ★1673★
Top bachelor's degree disciplines for Hispanic Americans, 1997-98 ★1674★
Top bachelor's degree disciplines for Native Americans, 1997-98 ★1675★
Top bachelor's degree disciplines for non-minorities, 1997-98 ★1676★
Age grouping of doctorate recipients, by broad field, 1999 ★1882★
Comparative data of women receiving doctorate degrees in selected fields in 1950 and 1998 ★1899★
Doctoral degree distribution by broad field, 1999 ★1902★
Median age at conferral of doctoral degree from U.S. universities, by discipline, 1999 ★1952★
Number of doctorate recipients at U.S. colleges and universities, by field, 1999 ★1969★
Number of engineering doctorate recipients at U.S. colleges and universities, by field, 1999 ★1972★
Percentage of female doctorate recipients, by broad field, 1999 ★1989★
Percentage of minority doctorate recipients in the U.S., by broad field, 1999 ★1991★
Fields of study profile of foreign students enrolled in U.S. institutions of higher education, 1998-99 ★2495★
Fields of study profile of U.S. students studying abroad, 1998-99 ★2507★
Average costs for Academic Search titles by subject, 2001 ★2918★
Periodical prices by LC subject, 2001 ★2925★
Periodical prices by scientific discipline, 2001 ★2926★
Proposed fiscal 2002 appropriations for the National Science Foundation ★3109★
Expected starting salaries of 2000-01 bachelor's degree recipients, by general major ★3130★
Austria's relative impact in the sciences by field, 1992-96 ★4300★
Hong Kong's contribution of papers in the sciences, by field, 1995-99 ★4314★
Italy's relative impact in the sciences by field, 1992-96 ★4317★
Japan's contribution of papers in the sciences, by field, 1995-99 ★4318★
Japan's contribution of papers in the sciences, by field, 1996-2000 ★4319★
Poland's contribution of papers in the sciences, by field, 1993-97 ★4324★
Russia's contribution of papers in the sciences, by field, 1993-97 ★4325★
South Korea's contribution of papers in the sciences, by field, 1995-99 ★4327★
Taiwan contribution of papers in the sciences, by field, 1995-99 ★4334★
Turkey's contribution of papers in the sciences, by field, 1995-99 ★4335★

Engineering and Econometric Interpretation of Energy-Capital Complementarity
Top cited energy papers from 1979 to 1983 ★2464★

Engineering Education
Most cited technology serials in technical communication journals from 1988 to 1997 ★4427★

Engineering, general
Engineering doctorates awarded at U.S. colleges and universities, by subfield, 1999 ★1923★
Gender breakdown of engineering doctorate recipients, by subfield, 1999 ★1934★

Engineering, mechanics
Engineering doctorates awarded at U.S. colleges and universities, by subfield, 1999 ★1923★
Gender breakdown of engineering doctorate recipients, by subfield, 1999 ★1934★

Engineering, natural science, and computer systems managers
Projections for the fastest growing occupations requiring a bachelor's degree or more from 1998 to 2008 ★2292★
Projected employment growth for selected occupations that require a bachelor's degree or more, 1998-2008 ★2317★

Engineering physics
Engineering doctorates awarded at U.S. colleges and universities, by subfield, 1999 ★1923★
Gender breakdown of engineering doctorate recipients, by subfield, 1999 ★1934★

Engineering science
Engineering doctorates awarded at U.S. colleges and universities, by subfield, 1999 ★1923★
Gender breakdown of engineering doctorate recipients, by subfield, 1999 ★1934★

Engineering, science, and computer systems managers
Fastest growing occupations, 1998-2008 ★2302★

Engineering technician
Most desirable jobs in production/manufacturing ★2276★

Engineering technology
Expected starting salaries of 2000-01 bachelor's degree recipients, by specific major ★3131★

England
Eight grade science achievement scores from selected countries, 1999 ★14★
Math achievement test comparison ★19★
Eighth grade mathematics achievement scores from selected countries, 1999 ★2773★
Institute for Scientific Information periodical prices by country, 2001 ★2922★
Nations with the most-cited papers in the sciences ★4320★

English
Gender breakdown of language and literature doctorate recipients, by subfield, 1999 ★1937★
Language and literature doctorates awarded at U.S. colleges and universities, by subfield, 1999 ★1949★
Subjects required by the most U.S. medical schools for the 2000-01 entering class ★2850★
Top nonscience majors for accepted applicants to U.S. medical schools, 1999-2000 ★2854★

English education
Gender breakdown of teaching fields doctorate recipients, by subfield, 1999 ★1943★
Teaching fields doctorates awarded at U.S. colleges and universities, by subfield, 1999 ★2046★
Most cited education serials in technical communication journals from 1988 to 1997 ★4418★

English Journal
Most cited language serials in technical communication journals from 1988 to

English language
Number of Advanced Placement Exams taken by African Americans, by subject, 2000 ★30★
Number of Advanced Placement Exams taken by Asian Americans, by subject, 2000 ★31★
Number of Advanced Placement Exams taken by Hispanic Americans, by subject, 2000 ★32★

English language and literature
Number of humanities doctorate recipients at U.S. colleges and universities, by field, 1999 ★1973★
Average starting salaries for college graduates, by field, 2000 ★3129★

English language, literature, and letters
Top bachelor's degree disciplines for African Americans, 1997-98 ★1672★
Top bachelor's degree disciplines for Asian Americans, 1997-98 ★1673★
Top bachelor's degree disciplines for Hispanic Americans, 1997-98 ★1674★
Top bachelor's degree disciplines for Native Americans, 1997-98 ★1675★
Top bachelor's degree disciplines for non-minorities, 1997-98 ★1676★

English literature
Number of Advanced Placement Exams taken by African Americans, by subject, 2000 ★30★
Number of Advanced Placement Exams taken by Asian Americans, by subject, 2000 ★31★
Number of Advanced Placement Exams taken by Hispanic Americans, by subject, 2000 ★32★

English Novel, 1770-1829: A Bibliographical Survey of Prose Fiction Published in the British Isles
Selected reference books in the field of literature, 2000 ★377★

English Passengers
Booklist's best fiction books for library collections, 2000 ★227★
Most notable fiction books, 2001 ★284★
Outstanding works of fiction, 2001 ★293★

The English Patient
Canada's best fiction selections of the 20th century ★233★

ENI
Business Week's best companies in Italy ★397★

Eniger; Carol B.
Top pay and benefits for the chief executive and top paid employees at Rockefeller University ★3462★

Enloe; Cynthia
Radcliffe Institute for Advanced Study fellowship recipient in the field of political science, 2000-01 ★3041★

Ennis High School
Outstanding suburban public high schools in Metro Dallas-Ft. Worth ★4257★

Enron
Business Week's best performing companies with the highest 1-year sales performance ★414★
Fortune's highest ranked pipelines and energy companies, 2000 ★486★
Fortune's most admired companies for innovation ★516★
Fortune's most admired companies for quality of management ★518★
Top services industries in Standard & Poor's 500, 2001 ★558★

Entergy
Fortune's highest ranked electric and gas utilities companies, 2000 ★459★

Enterprise analysis
Job openings for high-tech workers ★2330★

Enterprise Rent-A-Car
 Largest private companies, 2000 ★523★
 Top recruiters for business administration jobs for 2000-01 bachelor's degree recipients ★554★
 Top recruiters for marketing jobs for 2000-01 bachelor's degree recipients ★684★
 Top employers of college graduates, 2001 ★2325★
 Top recruiters for liberal arts jobs for 2000-01 bachelor's degree recipients ★2675★

Enterprise State Junior College
 Average faculty salaries for institutions of higher education without academic ranks in Alabama, 2000-01 ★3740★

Entomologia Experiments and Applications
 Entomology journals by citation impact, 1981-98 ★2453★

Entomology
 Biological sciences doctorates awarded at U.S. colleges and universities, by subfield, 1999 ★1887★
 Gender breakdown of biological sciences doctorate recipients, by subfield, 1999 ★1927★

Entrepreneur America: Lessons from Inside Bob Ryan's High-Tech Start-Up boot Camp
 Library Journal's most notable books about entrepreneurship, 2000 ★251★

The Environment as a Factor of Production-The Effects of Economic Growth and Trade Liberalization
 Top cited nonrenewable resource papers from 1994 to 1998 ★2472★

Environmental health
 Gender breakdown of health sciences doctorate recipients, by subfield, 1999 ★1935★
 Health sciences doctorates awarded at U.S. colleges and universities, by subfield, 1999 ★1944★

Environmental health engineering
 Engineering doctorates awarded at U.S. colleges and universities, by subfield, 1999 ★1923★
 Gender breakdown of engineering doctorate recipients, by subfield, 1999 ★1934★

Environmental life sciences
 Median salary for B.S. chemists, by field ★781★
 Median salary for M.S. chemists, by field ★785★
 Median salary for Ph.D. chemists, by field ★786★

Environmental Protection Agency Science and technology
 Proposed fiscal 2002 appropriations for Department of Commerce research ★3107★

Environmental science
 Number of Advanced Placement Exams taken by African Americans, by subject, 2000 ★30★
 Number of Advanced Placement Exams taken by Asian Americans, by subject, 2000 ★31★
 Number of Advanced Placement Exams taken by Hispanic Americans, by subject, 2000 ★32★
 Earth, atmosphere, and marine science doctorates awarded at U.S. colleges and universities, by subfield, 1999 ★1909★
 Gender breakdown of earth, atmosphere, and marine science doctorate recipients, by subfield, 1999 ★1932★

EOG Resources
 Business Week's best performing companies with the highest 1-year shareholder returns ★415★
 Top fuel companies in Standard & Poor's 500, 2001 ★541★

Eonometrica
 Top ranked urban, rural and regional economics journals ★2202★

EPA
 Federal appropriations to colleges, by agency, 2000 ★1241★

Epidemiology
 Gender breakdown of health sciences doctorate recipients, by subfield, 1999 ★1935★
 Health sciences doctorates awarded at U.S. colleges and universities, by subfield, 1999 ★1944★

Episcopal
 Religious preference of incoming freshmen, 2000 ★1061★

Episcopal High School
 Outstanding secondary schools in Baton Rouge, Louisiana ★4093★

Epp; Helmut P.
 Top pay and benefits for the chief executive and top paid employees at DePaul University ★3266★

Epstein; Irving R.
 Top pay and benefits for the chief executive and top paid employees at Brandeis University ★3209★

Epstein; Michael
 Top pay and benefits for the chief executive and top paid employees at Rider University ★3458★

Epstein; Stephen E.
 Most-cited researchers in cardiology, 1981-1998 ★2874★

Equal Employment Opportunity Commission
 Proposed fiscal 2002 appropriations for civil rights ★814★

Equestrian
 Fastest growing men's collegiate athletics teams ★130★
 Fastest growing women's collegiate athletics teams ★131★

Equifax
 Business Week's best performing companies with the highest return on equity, 2000 ★420★

Equipment rental and leasing
 Industries with the highest percentage of projected employment growth from 1998 through 2008 ★2305★
 Industries with the highest projected growth rate, 1994-2005 ★2306★

Equity Office Properties
 Fortune's highest ranked real estate companies, 2000 ★491★

Equity Residential Properties
 Fortune's highest ranked real estate companies, 2000 ★491★

Equivalence class formation in language-able and language-disabled children
 Most cited sources in experimental analyses of human behavior between 1990 and 1999 ★3070★

Equivalence relations: Where do they come from?
 Most cited sources in experimental analyses of human behavior between 1990 and 1999 ★3070★

Eraslan; Arsev
 Top pay and benefits for the chief executive and top paid employees at Wheeling Jesuit University ★3622★

Ergonomics
 Most cited technology serials in technical communication journals from 1988 to 1997 ★4427★

Ericson; R.V.
 Most cited authors in the journal *Australian and New Zealand Journals of Criminology*, 1990 to 1995 ★1613★

Ericson Scholastic
 Chicago elementary magnet schools with the highest acceptance rates, 2000-01 ★4002★

Ericsson
 Biggest information technology companies, 2000 ★385★

Erikson; Robert S.
 Authors most frequently published in *American Political Science Review*, 1974-94 ★3047★

Ernest L. Thayer's Casey at the Bat: A Ballad of the Republic Sung in the Year 1888
 Most notable books for young readers, 2001 ★319★

Ernst & Young
 Largest private companies, 2000 ★523★

Ernst & Young LLP
 Best companies for working mothers in offering leave for new parents ★4449★

Erskine College
 Highest undergraduate tuition and fees at colleges and universities in South Carolina ★1554★
 Average faculty salaries for institutions of higher education in South Carolina, 2000-01 ★3728★

Erwin; Christina Bodurow
 American Chemical Society 2001 award winners (Group 1) ★751★

Erwin; John
 Top pay and benefits for the chief executive and top paid employees at Mount Holyoke College ★3409★

Escuela Superior de Administracion y Direccion de Empresas (ESADE)
 European and Canadian business schools with the slowest payback on MBA investments ★629★

Eshelman; John
 Top pay and benefits for the chief executive and top paid employees at Seattle University ★3495★

Esperanza Rising
 Most notable fiction books for young adults, 2001 ★322★
 Outstanding children's fiction books, 2000 ★329★
 Publishers Weekly Off-the-Cuff Awards winner for favorite novel of the year, 2000 ★346★
 Smithsonian's best books for children ages 10 and up ★365★

Estee Lauder
 Fortune's highest ranked soaps and cosmetics companies, 2000 ★496★

Estonia
 Countries with the lowest percentage of workers satisfied with their job ★2243★
 Countries with the lowest leader's salary ★3121★

Estuarine and Coastal Marine Science
 Oceanography journals by citation impact, 1981-99 ★2139★

Estuarine and Coastal Shelf Science
 Oceanography journals by citation impact, 1999 ★2141★

The Eternal Darkness: A Personal History of Deep Sea Exploration
 Library Journal's most notable oceanography books, 2000 ★272★

Ethics and Marketing Management: An Empirical Examination
 Most influential articles in the *Journal of Business Research*, 1985-1999 ★697★
 Most influential articles in the *Journal of Business Research* from 1985 to 1989 ★698★

Ethology and Sociobiology
 Sociology journals by impact factor, 1981 to 1997 ★4355★
 Sociology journals by impact factor, 1993 to 1997 ★4356★

Eti Technical College
 U.S. colleges and universities with the lowest percentage of African Americans enrolled, 1997 ★223★

Etling; William
 Top pay and benefits for the chief executive and top paid employees at Ashland University ★3180★

Eton School
 Outstanding secondary schools in Seattle-Bellevue-Everett, Washington ★4227★

eToys
 Top E-commerce web sites ★2603★

Eubanks; Audrey
 Top pay and benefits for the chief executive and top paid employees at the University of Mobile ★3551★

Eugene Lang College
 U.S. colleges and universities where intramural sports are not popular ★996★
 U.S. colleges and universities where the general student body puts little emphasis on athletic events ★1009★

Eureka College
 Average faculty salaries for institutions of higher education in Illinois, 2000-01 ★3700★

Europe
 Region of origin of foreign students enrolled in U.S. institutions of higher education, 1998-99 ★2502★
 World regions hosting U.S. students studying abroad, 1998-99 ★2515★

European history
 Number of Advanced Placement Exams taken by African Americans, by subject, 2000 ★30★
 Number of Advanced Placement Exams taken by Asian Americans, by subject, 2000 ★31★
 Number of Advanced Placement Exams taken by Hispanic Americans, by subject, 2000 ★32★

European Institute of Business Administration (INSEAD)
 Business Week's top business schools outside the U.S. as selected by corporate recruiters, 2000 ★605★
 Business Week's top business schools outside the U.S. as selected by recent MBA graduates, 2000 ★606★
 Business Week's top business schools outside the U.S. for intellectual capital, 2000 ★607★
 European and Canadian business schools with the quickest payback on MBA investments ★628★

 Post-MBA salaries for graduates from *Business Week*'s top business schools outside the U.S., 2000 ★642★
 Pre-MBA salaries for students at *Business Week*'s top business schools outside the U.S., 2000 ★643★

European Journal of Immunology
 Immunology journals with the greatest impact measure, 1981-98 ★2810★
 Immunology journals with the greatest impact measure, 1994-98 ★2811★
 Immunology journals by impact factor, 1981 to 1997 ★4279★
 Immunology journals by impact factor, 1993 to 1997 ★4280★

European Journal of Operational Research
 Journals and proceedings with the most citations (Class 2) ★2568★

European Journal of Plant Pathology
 Agriculture journals by citation impact, 1995-99 ★53★

European Journal of Soil Science
 Soil science journals by citation impact, 1995-99 ★189★
 Soil science journals by citation impact, 1999 ★190★

European Molecular Biology Organization Journal
 Top science journals by impact factor ★4281★

European Patent Organization
 CA patents abstracted, by country, 2000 ★758★

Europolitan Holdings
 Business Week's best companies in terms of return on equity ★407★

Evaluating Natural Resource Investment
 Top cited nonrenewable resource papers from 1984 to 1988 ★2470★

Evans; Andrew B.
 Top pay and benefits for the chief executive and top paid employees at Oberlin College ★3427★

Evans; Chester
 Top pay and benefits for the chief executive and top paid employees at Barry University ★3192★

Evans; Frances E.
 Top pay and benefits for the chief executive and top paid employees at the University of Dayton ★3539★

Evans; Gary A.
 Top pay and benefits for the chief executive and top paid employees at Lafayette College ★3361★

Evans; James D.
 Top pay and benefits for the chief executive and top paid employees at Lindenwood University ★3375★

Evans; Marshawn
 All-USA College Academic First Team, 2001 ★2★

Evans; Tom
 Top pay and benefits for the chief executive and top paid employees at Hanover College ★3324★

Evans; Walker
 Best U.S. works of journalism in the 20th century ★2769★

Evanston Community, District 65
 Illinois elementary school districts with the highest teacher salaries, 1999 ★3984★

Evanston Township High School, District 202
 Illinois school districts spending the most for high school education 1997-98 ★4010★

Evansville; University of
 U.S. News & World Report's midwestern regional universities with the best student/faculty ratios, 2000-01 ★1403★
 U.S. News & World Report's midwestern regional universities with the highest acceptance rates, 2000-01 ★1404★
 U.S. News & World Report's midwestern regional universities with the highest percentage of freshmen from the top 25% of their high school class, 2000-01 ★1407★
 U.S. News & World Report's midwestern regional universities with the highest percentage of full-time faculty, 2000-01 ★1408★
 U.S. News & World Report's best undergraduate fees among midwestern regional universities by discount tuition, 2000 ★1427★
 Highest undergraduate tuition and fees at colleges and universities in Indiana ★1502★
 Average faculty salaries for institutions of higher education in Indiana, 2000-01 ★3701★

Event planner
 Monster.com's most searched job listings ★2308★

Everest: The Death Zone
 Most notable DVDs and videos for young adults, 2001 ★2890★

Everett Community College
 Lowest undergraduate tuition and fees at colleges and universities in Washington ★1567★

Everett High School
 Outstanding secondary schools in Lansing-East Lansing, Michigan ★4163★

Evergreen State College
 U.S. colleges and universities where intramural sports are not popular ★996★
 U.S. colleges and universities where students are very politically active ★1001★
 U.S. colleges and universities with a popular theater group ★1020★
 State appropriations for Washington's institutions of higher education, 2000-01 ★1300★
 College senior's choices for exemplary liberal arts institutions ★1318★
 U.S. News & World Report's top public western regional liberal arts colleges, 2000-01 ★1365★
 Academic reputation scores for *U.S. News & World Report*'s top western regional liberal arts colleges, 2000-01 ★1387★
 Acceptance rates for *U.S. News & World Report*'s top western regional liberal arts colleges, 2000-01 ★1388★
 Alumni giving rates at *U.S. News & World Report*'s top western regional liberal arts colleges, 2000-01 ★1389★
 Average freshmen retention rates for *U.S. News & World Report*'s top western regional liberal arts colleges, 2000-01 ★1390★
 Average graduation rates for *U.S. News & World Report*'s top western regional liberal arts colleges, 2000-01 ★1391★
 Percentage of full-time faculty at *U.S. News & World Report*'s top western regional liberal arts colleges, 2000-01 ★1393★
 Proportion of classes having 20 students or less at *U.S. News & World Report*'s top western regional liberal arts colleges, 2000-01 ★1394★

Student/faculty ratios at *U.S. News & World Report*'s top western regional liberal arts colleges, 2000-01 ★1395★

U.S. News & World Report's top western regional liberal arts colleges, 2000-01 ★1396★

Fiske Guide's best buys for public colleges and universities, 2001 ★1460★

Evers; Medgar
Most influential African Americans in politics and civil rights ★3040★

Everyday Math Made E-Z
Best selling small press releases, 2001 ★226★

The Everything Book
Outstanding children's picture books, 2000 ★331★

Evolution
Ecology journals by citation impact, 1981-99 ★2136★
Ecology journals by citation impact, 1995-99 ★2137★
Ecology journals by citation impact, 1999 ★2138★

The Evolution of Policy Responses to Stratospheric Ozone Depletion
Top cited nonrenewable resource papers from 1989 to 1993 ★2471★

Ewen; Gary
Top pay and benefits for the chief executive and top paid employees at Colorado Christian University ★3248★

Excelsior High School
All-USA Teacher Teams, Second Team, 2000 ★4400★

Excite@Home
Web sites where internet users spend the most time ★2609★

Executive, administrative, and managerial
College graduates in the labor force, by occupational group, 1998 ★926★
Projected change in employment of college graduates, by occupational group, from 1998 to 2008 ★965★
Projected employment of college graduates, by occupational group, 2008 ★966★
Employment change projections by major occupational group from 1998 to 2008 ★2288★
Employment projections by major occupational group for 2008 ★2291★
Employment in college-level jobs, by occupational group, 2006 ★2295★
Percentages for projected employment growth by occupational group, 1998-2008 ★2314★
Projected employment growth by occupational group, 1998-2008 ★2316★

Executive search consultant
Jobs with the best physical demands scores ★2250★
Most desirable jobs in business/finance ★2270★

Exelon
Top utilities companies in Standard & Poor's 500, 2001 ★561★
Top recruiters for electrical/electronic engineering jobs for 2000-01 bachelor's degree recipients ★2354★

Exercise physiology/science, kinesiology
Gender breakdown of health sciences doctorate recipients, by subfield, 1999 ★1935★
Health sciences doctorates awarded at U.S. colleges and universities, by subfield, 1999 ★1944★

Exile
Booklist's best fiction books for library collections, 2000 ★227★

Exotic Paper Airplanes
Best selling small press releases, 2001 ★226★

Expedia
Top E-commerce web sites ★2603★

Expeditors International of Washington
Fortune's highest ranked mail, packaging, and freight delivery companies, 2000 ★473★

Experimental
Gender breakdown of psychology doctorate recipients, by subfield, 1999 ★1941★
Psychology doctorates awarded at U.S. colleges and universities, by subfield, 1999 ★2043★

An Experimental Comparison of the Effectiveness of Computers and Humans as Search Intermediaries
Journal of the American Society for Information Science's best papers, by total citations ★2729★

Experimental Gerontology
Geriatrics and gerontology journals with the greatest impact measure, 1981-98 ★2805★
Geriatrics and gerontology journals with the greatest impact measure, 1994-98 ★2806★
Geriatrics and gerontology journals with the greatest impact measure, 1998 ★2807★

Experimental Hematology
Hematology journals with the greatest impact measure, 1994-98 ★2809★

Experiments in Aging Research
Geriatrics and gerontology journals with the greatest impact measure, 1981-98 ★2805★

Explorations in Economic History
Top ranked economic history journals ★2190★

Exploring the Concept of Affective Quality: Expanding the Concept of Retail Personality
Most influential articles in the *Journal of Business Research* from 1990 to 1994 ★699★

Exploring Cultures of the World
Booklist's most recommended geography series for young people, 2000 ★313★

Exploring Life Sciences
Outstanding reference sources, 2000 ★370★

Exploring World Art
Booklist's best art books for young people ★308★

Exports, Policy Choices, and Economic Growth in Developing Countries after 1973 Oil Shock
Top cited energy papers from 1984 to 1988 ★2465★

Extinct Humans
Library Journal's most notable paleontology books, 2000 ★273★

Exxon
Top internships in the U.S. with the highest compensation, 2001 ★2611★
Corporations making the most contributions to African American communities, 1995 ★2941★

Exxon Mobil
Business Week's best companies in terms of profits ★406★
Business Week's best companies in terms of sales ★408★
Business Week's best companies in the United States ★411★
Business Week's top companies worldwide ★433★

Fortune's highest ranked petroleum refining companies, 2000 ★484★
Fortune's most admired companies for financial soundness ★515★
Fortune's most admired companies for long-term investment value ★517★
Fortune's most admired companies for use of corporate assets ★521★
Top fuel companies in Standard & Poor's 500, 2001 ★541★

Eye Institute
Proposed fiscal 2002 appropriations for National Institutes of Health scientific research ★3108★

F

Fabrizio; Jamie
All-America girls' high school soccer team defenders, 2001 ★174★

Fackler; John P.
American Chemical Society 2001 award winners (Group 2) ★752★

Fackler; Peter C.
Top pay and benefits for the chief executive and top paid employees at Bates College ★3193★

Facts On File Companion to the American Short Story
Outstanding reference sources, 2001 ★371★

Faculty athletics representative
African American college athletics senior administrators, by gender, 1999-2000 ★119★
College athletics senior administrators, by gender, 1999-2000 ★123★
Minority college athletics senior administrators, by gender, 1999-2000 ★134★

Fagan; Joseph A.
Top pay and benefits for the chief executive and top paid employees at Rivier College ★3460★

Fagan; Stuart I.
Top pay and benefits for the chief executive and top paid employees at Roosevelt University ★3466★

Fagin; James
Top pay and benefits for the chief executive and top paid employees at the Chaminade University of Honolulu ★3524★

Fagin; Ralph
Top pay and benefits for the chief executive and top paid employees at Oral Roberts University ★3433★

Fahl; Charles
Top pay and benefits for the chief executive and top paid employees at Alaska Pacific University ★3166★

Fainstein; Norman
Top pay and benefits for the chief executive and top paid employees at Vassar College ★3594★

Fair Lawn High School
Outstanding secondary schools in Bergen-Passaic, New Jersey ★4096★

Fairfax Community Library
Highest Hennen's American Public Library Ratings for libraries serving a population of 1,000 to 2,499 ★2692★

Fairfax County Public Library
Highest Hennen's American Public Library Ratings for libraries serving a population of over 500,000 ★2700★

Fairfax County Public Schools
Top employers of college graduates, 2001 ★2325★
Top recruiters for education jobs for 2000-01 bachelor's degree recipients ★4377★
Top recruiters for education jobs for 2000-01 master's degree recipients ★4398★

Fairfax, VA
Counties with the highest per capita income ★2561★

Fairfield, CT
Counties with the highest per capita income ★2561★

Fairfield University
Division I NCAA colleges with that graduated more than 80% of their African American male athletes, 1990-91 to 1993-94 ★929★
U.S. colleges and universities that devote the most course time to discussion ★990★
U.S. colleges and universities without a diverse student body ★1046★
U.S. News & World Report's northern regional universities with the best academic reputation scores, 2000-01 ★1415★
U.S. News & World Report's northern regional universities with the highest alumni giving rates, 2000-01 ★1418★
U.S. News & World Report's northern regional universities with the highest average graduation rates, 2000-01 ★1419★
U.S. News & World Report's northern regional universities with the highest freshmen retention rates, 2000-01 ★1420★
U.S. News & World Report's northern regional universities with the highest percentage of freshmen in the top 25% of their high school class, 2000-01 ★1421★
U.S. News & World Report's northern regional universities with the lowest acceptance rates, 2000-01 ★1424★
U.S. News & World Report's top northern regional universities, 2000-01 ★1425★
Highest undergraduate tuition and fees at colleges and universities in Connecticut ★1490★
Average faculty salaries for institutions of higher education in Connecticut, 2000-01 ★3694★

Fairleigh Dickinson University
Highest undergraduate tuition and fees at colleges and universities in New Jersey ★1533★
U.S. colleges and universities awarding the most psychology master's degrees to Hispanic Americans ★1799★

Fairmont Junior High School
Outstanding secondary schools in Orange County, California ★4199★

Fairmont State College
State appropriations for West Virginia's institutions of higher education, 2000-01 ★1301★
U.S. News & World Report's southern regional liberal arts colleges with students least in debt, 1999 ★1366★
Lowest undergraduate tuition and fees at colleges and universities in West Virginia ★1569★
Average faculty salaries for institutions of higher education in West Virginia, 2000-01 ★3737★

Fairy Tales
Outstanding children's picture books, 2000 ★331★

Faith Baptist Bible College and Seminary
Average faculty salaries for institutions of higher education in Iowa, 2000-01 ★3702★

Faith Baptist Bible College and Theological Seminary
U.S. institutions with the lowest paid full professors, 2001 ★3979★

Falabella; Daniel
Top pay and benefits for the chief executive and top paid employees at Albright College ★3168★

Falconer; Etta Z.
Top pay and benefits for the chief executive and top paid employees at Spelman College ★3507★

Falconer; Ian
Outstanding children's picture books, 2000 ★331★
Publishers Weekly Off-the-Cuff Awards winner for most promising new illustrator, 2000 ★358★

Falconer Public Library
Highest Hennen's American Public Library Ratings for libraries serving a population of 2,500 to 4,999 ★2693★

Fallen Angels
Most frequently banned books in the 1990s ★745★

Falley; Peter
Top pay and benefits for the chief executive and top paid employees at Fairleigh Dickinson University ★3292★

Falls City Public Library
Highest Hennen's American Public Library Ratings for libraries serving a population of 999 and under ★2691★

False Pretenses
Library Journal's best fiction audiobooks, 2000 ★241★

Falwell; Jerry
Top pay and benefits for the chief executive and top paid employees at Liberty University ★3373★

Fama; E.F.
U.S. academic economists by mean number of citations, 1971-92 ★2176★
U.S. academic economists by total citations, 1971-92 ★2177★

Fama; Eugene
Authors most frequently contributing to the American Economic Review from 1951-1990 ★2157★

Families around the World (A Family From...)
Booklist's most recommended geography series for young people, 2000 ★313★

Family Circle
Magazines with the largest circulation ★2750★

Family and marriage counseling
Gender breakdown of psychology doctorate recipients, by subfield, 1999 ★1941★
Psychology doctorates awarded at U.S. colleges and universities, by subfield, 1999 ★2043★

Family Planning Perspectives
Demography journals with the highest average citations after 5 years ★1856★
Most cited demography journals, 1991-95 ★1857★
Top demography journals by average impact factor, 1991-95 ★1863★

FAMU/FSU College of Engineering
Total baccalaureate engineering degrees awarded to minorities from U.S. colleges and universities, 1997-98 ★1715★

Fannie Mae
Fortune's highest ranked mortgage finance companies, 2000 ★479★
Best companies for working mothers ★4446★
Best companies for working mothers in offering flexible work hours ★4448★

Fantasy
Publishers Weekly Off-the-Cuff Awards winner for most overdone subject, 2000 ★356★

Fanton; Jonathan F.
Presidents with the highest pay at Doctoral I and II universities, 1998-99 ★3160★
Top pay and benefits for the chief executive and top paid employees at New School University ★3418★

Faria; Pamela F.
Top pay and benefits for the chief executive and top paid employees at Knox College ★3360★

Farm workers
Occupations with the highest decline in employment, 1998-2008 ★2310★

Farmer
Jobs with the highest unemployment ★2256★
Jobs with the longest work weeks ★2257★
Most desirable jobs in agriculture ★2268★

Farmers
Occupations with the highest decline in employment, 1998-2008 ★2310★
Occupations with the highest number of self-employed workers, 1998 ★2311★

Farming, forestry, and fishing
Internet use by major occupational group, 1998 ★2587★

Farmington Middle School
Outstanding secondary schools in Minneapolis-St. Paul, Minnesota-Wisconsin ★4181★

Farmland Industries
Fortune's highest ranked consumer food products companies, 2000 ★458★

Farragut High School
Outstanding secondary schools in Knoxville, Tennessee ★4159★

Farrakhan; Louis
Most influential African Americans in religion ★3091★

Farrington; David P.
Most cited authors in the journal British Journal of Criminology, 1990 to 1995 ★1614★
Most cited authors in the journal Crime and Justice, 1990 to 1995 ★1617★
Most cited authors in the journal Journal of Quantitative Criminology, 1990 to 1995 ★1628★
Most cited authors in the journal Journal of Research in Crime and Delinquency, 1990 to 1995 ★1629★
Most cited authors in three criminology journals ★1634★
Most-cited scholars in British Journal of Criminology ★1637★
Most-cited scholars in Criminology ★1639★

Farrington; Gregory
Top pay and benefits for the chief executive and top paid employees at Lehigh University ★3368★

Fashion designer
Most desirable jobs in the arts ★2277★

FASHION

Fashion Institute of Technology
Professional or specialized institutions with the highest enrollment of foreign students, 1998-99 ★2501★
Average faculty salaries for institutions of higher education in New York, 2000-01 ★3719★
U.S. community colleges with the highest paid full professors, 2001 ★3976★

Fashion model
Jobs considered the most competitive ★2245★
Jobs with the greatest potential income for beginners ★2253★
Most desirable jobs in the arts ★2277★

Fass; Richard A.
Top pay and benefits for the chief executive and top paid employees at Pomona College ★3444★

Fauci; Anthony S.
Most-cited researchers in clinical medicine, 1981-1998 ★2875★

Faulkner College
Highest undergraduate tuition and fees at colleges and universities in Alabama ★1479★

Fay III; Cornelius R.
Top pay and benefits for the chief executive and top paid employees at Hood College ★3338★

Fay, O.P.; Sister Maureen A.
Top pay and benefits for the chief executive and top paid employees at the University of Detroit Mercy ★3541★

Fay School
Outstanding secondary schools in Boston, Massachusetts-New Hampshire ★4100★

Fayetteville Free Library
Highest Hennen's American Public Library Ratings for libraries serving a population of 5,000 to 9,999 ★2694★

Fayetteville State University
Colleges offering the Thurgood Marshall Scholarship Fund ★221★
State appropriations for North Carolina's institutions of higher education, 2000-01 ★1286★
Lowest undergraduate tuition and fees at public, 4-year or above colleges and universities ★1466★
Public 4-year institutions with the lowest tuition, 2000-01 ★1472★
U.S. colleges and universities awarding the most mathematics master's degrees to African Americans ★1790★
Average faculty salaries for institutions of higher education in North Carolina, 2000-01 ★3720★

Fayetteville Technical Community College
Lowest undergraduate tuition and fees at colleges and universities in North Carolina ★1540★
Average faculty salaries for institutions of higher education without academic ranks in North Carolina, 2000-01 ★3761★

Fayrewood
Best small companies worldwide ★384★

Fazio; Amy
All-America girls' high school soccer team defenders, 2001 ★174★

Fearful Symmetry
Canada's best nonfiction selections of the 20th century ★234★

Fearless
Most notable fiction books for reluctant young adult readers, 2001 ★321★

Feaser Middle School
Outstanding secondary schools in Allentown-Bethlehem-Easton, Pennsylvania ★4081★
Outstanding secondary schools in Harrisburg-Lebanon-Carlisle, Pennsylvania ★4146★

Featherman; Sandra
Top pay and benefits for the chief executive and top paid employees at the University of New England ★3552★

Feber; Michel
Booklist's best first novels ★228★

Federal Administration Direct Loan Program
Proposed fiscal 2002 appropriations for student assistance ★1251★
Fiscal 2002 requested budget as compared with Fiscal 2001 budget for the Education Department ★2231★

Federal Bureau of Investigation
Most selective internships in the U.S., 2001 ★2610★

Federal and business credit institutions
Employment growth percentages for selected industries, 1998-2000 ★2294★

Federal Deposit Insurance Company
Top recruiters for accounting jobs for 2000-01 bachelor's degree recipients ★580★
Top recruiters for finance/banking jobs for 2000-01 bachelor's degree recipients ★582★
Top recruiters for accounting jobs for 2000-01 master's degree recipients ★661★
Top recruiters for finance/banking jobs for 2000-01 master's degree recipients ★664★
Top recruiters for computer science jobs for 2000-01 master's degree recipients ★1598★
Top recruiters for computer engineering jobs for 2000-01 master's degree recipients ★2400★
Top recruiters for liberal arts jobs for 2000-01 master's degree recipients ★2676★
Top recruiters for math/actuarial science jobs for 2000-01 bachelor's degree recipients ★2771★
Top recruiters for statistics jobs for 2000-01 bachelor's degree recipients ★2786★

Federal government
Employment change projections by major industry division from 1998 to 2008 ★2287★
Employment projections by major industry division for 2008 ★2290★

Federal-Mogul
Fortune's highest ranked motor vehicle parts companies, 2000 ★480★
Fortune's least admired companies for financial soundness ★507★
Fortune's least admired companies for long-term investment value ★509★
Fortune's least admired companies for quality of management ★510★
Fortune's least admired companies for use of corporate assets ★513★

Federal Reserve Bank of New York
Most selective internships in the U.S., 2001 ★2610★

Federal Reserve System, Board of Governors
Library Journal's best free reference websites, 2000 ★367★

Federal Work-Study
Proposed fiscal 2002 appropriations for student assistance ★1251★

Federated Department Stores
Fortune's highest ranked general merchandisers, 2000 ★468★
Top recruiters for logistics jobs for 2000-01 bachelor's degree recipients ★555★
Top recruiters for retail merchandising jobs for 2000-01 bachelor's degree recipients ★556★
Top recruiters for finance/banking jobs for 2000-01 bachelor's degree recipients ★582★
Top recruiters for marketing jobs for 2000-01 bachelor's degree recipients ★684★
Top recruiters for hospitality/hotel/restaurant management jobs for 2000-01 bachelor's degree recipients ★2558★
Top recruiters for foreign language jobs for 2000-01 bachelor's degree recipients ★2614★
Top recruiters for liberal arts jobs for 2000-01 bachelor's degree recipients ★2675★
Top recruiters for psychology jobs for 2000-01 bachelor's degree recipients ★3063★
Top recruiters for sociology jobs for 2000-01 bachelor's degree recipients ★4347★
Highly recommended public companies for women executives, 2000 ★4453★

FedEx
Fortune's highest ranked mail, packaging, and freight delivery companies, 2000 ★473★
Top transportation companies in Standard & Poor's 500, 2001 ★560★

Feeny; Curtis
Top pay and benefits for the chief executive and top paid employees at Stanford University ★3510★

Feerick; John
Top pay and benefits for the chief executive and top paid employees at Fordham University ★3295★

Fein; Alan
Top pay and benefits for the chief executive and top paid employees at Lesley College ★3370★

Feldman; Howard
Top pay and benefits for the chief executive and top paid employees at the University of Portland ★3556★

Feldstein; Martin S.
Authors most frequently contributing to the *American Economic Review* from 1951-1990 ★2157★
U.S. academic economists by mean number of citations, 1971-92 ★2176★
U.S. academic economists by total citations, 1971-92 ★2177★
Most cited economists ★2185★

Felician College
Average faculty salaries for institutions of higher education in New Jersey, 2000-01 ★3717★

Felix; Richard
Top pay and benefits for the chief executive and top paid employees at Azusa Pacific University ★3187★

Fellowships/dissertation grants
Primary sources of financial support for doctorate recipients, by citizenship, 1999 ★2003★
Primary sources of financial support for doctorate recipients, by gender, 1999 ★2004★
Primary sources of financial support for doctorate recipients, by race/ethnicity, 1999 ★2005★
Primary sources of financial support for education doctorate recipients, by citizenship, 1999 ★2006★

Primary sources of financial support for education doctorate recipients, by gender, 1999 ★2007★
Primary sources of financial support for education doctorate recipients, by race/ethnicity, 1999 ★2008★
Primary sources of financial support for engineering doctorate recipients, by citizenship, 1999 ★2009★
Primary sources of financial support for engineering doctorate recipients, by gender, 1999 ★2010★
Primary sources of financial support for engineering doctorate recipients, by race/ethnicity, 1999 ★2011★
Primary sources of financial support for humanities doctorate recipients, by citizenship, 1999 ★2012★
Primary sources of financial support for humanities doctorate recipients, by gender, 1999 ★2013★
Primary sources of financial support for humanities doctorate recipients, by race/ethnicity, 1999 ★2014★
Primary sources of financial support for life sciences doctorate recipients, by citizenship, 1999 ★2015★
Primary sources of financial support for life sciences doctorate recipients, by gender, 1999 ★2016★
Primary sources of financial support for life sciences doctorate recipients, by race/ethnicity, 1999 ★2017★
Primary sources of financial support for physical sciences, mathematics, and computer sciences doctorate recipients, by citizenship, 1999 ★2018★
Primary sources of financial support for physical sciences, mathematics, and computer sciences doctorate recipients, by gender, 1999 ★2019★
Primary sources of financial support for physical sciences, mathematics, and computer sciences doctorate recipients, by race/ethnicity, 1999 ★2020★
Primary sources of financial support for professional/other doctorate recipients, by citizenship, 1999 ★2021★
Primary sources of financial support for professional/other doctorate recipients, by gender, 1999 ★2022★
Primary sources of financial support for professional/other doctorate recipients, by race/ethnicity, 1999 ★2023★
Primary sources of financial support for social sciences doctorate recipients, by citizenship, 1999 ★2024★
Primary sources of financial support for social sciences doctorate recipients, by gender, 1999 ★2025★
Primary sources of financial support for social sciences doctorate recipients, by race/ethnicity, 1999 ★2026★

Fell's Official Know-It-All Guide: Magic for Beginners
Best selling small press releases, 2001 ★226★

Fell's Official Know-It-All Guide: Wedding Planner
Best selling small press releases, 2001 ★226★

Felton; Raymond
All-America boys' high school basketball 3rd team, 2001 ★163★

"Feminism and Criminology"
Most-cited works in women and crime publications ★1646★

Fendler; Janos H.
Top pay and benefits for the chief executive and top paid employees at Clarkson University ★3239★

Fennell; Francis
Top pay and benefits for the chief executive and top paid employees at Western Maryland College ★3614★

Fenton Jr.; John E.
Top pay and benefits for the chief executive and top paid employees at Suffolk University ★3513★

Fenton; Norman
Top published scholars in the field of systems and software engineering ★2333★

Fenton; Norman P.
Top pay and benefits for the chief executive and top paid employees at Averett College ★3185★

Fenwick High School
Outstanding Catholic high schools in Metro Chicago ★4074★

Ferejohn; John A.
Authors most frequently published in *American Political Science Review*, 1974-94 ★3047★

Fergus Falls Community College
Average faculty salaries for institutions of higher education without academic ranks in Minnesota, 2000-01 ★3753★

Fergus Falls Public Library
Highest Hennen's American Public Library Ratings for libraries serving a population of 10,000 to 24,999 ★2695★

Ferguson; Pamela A.
Top pay and benefits for the chief executive and top paid employees at Grinnell College ★3315★

Fergusson; Frances D.
Presidents with the highest pay at Baccalaureate I colleges, 1998-99 ★3159★
Top pay and benefits for the chief executive and top paid employees at Vassar College ★3594★

Ferin; Michael
Top pay and benefits for the chief executive and top paid employees at the University of Indianapolis ★3545★

Fernandes; Jane
Top pay and benefits for the chief executive and top paid employees at Gallaudet University ★3301★

Ferrall Jr.; Victor E.
Top pay and benefits for the chief executive and top paid employees at Beloit College ★3199★

Ferralli; Michael
Top pay and benefits for the chief executive and top paid employees at Gannon University ★3302★

Ferrari; Michael R.
Presidents with the highest pay at Doctoral I and II universities, 1998-99 ★3160★
Top pay and benefits for the chief executive and top paid employees at Drake University ★3272★
Top pay and benefits for the chief executive and top paid employees at Texas Christian University ★3518★

Ferraro; K.J.
Most cited authors in the journal *Crime and Delinquency*, 1990 to 1995 ★1616★

Ferrell; O.C.
Authors with the most articles published in the *Journal of Business Research*, 1985 to 1999 ★687★

Ferrero Jr.; Ray
Top pay and benefits for the chief executive and top paid employees at Nova Southeastern University ★3426★

Ferrier; Richard D.
Top pay and benefits for the chief executive and top paid employees at Thomas Aquinas College in California ★3574★

Ferrigno; Michael
Top pay and benefits for the chief executive and top paid employees at Saint Mary's College of California ★3480★

Ferris State University
State appropriations for Michigan's institutions of higher education, 2000-01 ★1275★
Average faculty salaries for institutions of higher education in Michigan, 2000-01 ★3709★

Fetter; Frank
Authors most frequently contributing to the *American Economic Review* from 1911-1990 ★2156★

Fever 1793
Booklist's most recommended historical fiction for youths, 2001 ★314★
Most notable fiction books for young adults, 2001 ★322★

Fiacco; Norene
Top pay and benefits for the chief executive and top paid employees at Eastern Nazarene College ★3281★

Fickess; Douglas
Top pay and benefits for the chief executive and top paid employees at Westminster College in Missouri ★3616★

Fiction
Subject areas with the highest library expenditures/circulation ★306★

Fidelity Investments
Largest private companies, 2000 ★523★
Top women-owned companies ★4460★
Top women-owned companies with the most employees ★4462★

Fidelity Investments Charitable Gift Fund
Organizations with the most charitable contributions raised, 1999 ★2943★

Field Park Elementary School
Illinois suburban elementary schools with the highest ISAT scores in reading and math ★18★

The Fielding Institute
U.S. colleges and universities awarding the most social sciences and history doctorate degrees to African Americans ★2124★

Fifth Business
Canada's best fiction selections of the 20th century ★233★

Fifth Third Bancorp
Top banks in Standard & Poor's 500, 2001 ★531★

The Fifth Woman
Library Journal's best mystery titles, 2000 ★242★

Fight Club
Outstanding audiobooks, 2000 ★287★

The Figure in the Shadows
Most frequently banned books in the 1990s ★745★

Fike; David
Top pay and benefits for the chief executive and top paid employees at Holy Names College ★3337★

Filling root canals in three dimensions
Endodontic articles with the most citations, 1974 through 1999 ★1864★

Finance
Expected starting salaries of 2000-01 bachelor's degree recipients, by specific major ★3131★

Finance/banking
Top bachelor's and master's degree majors in demand for employment, 2001 ★2323★
Top bachelor's degree majors in demand for employment, 2001 ★2324★
Top master's degree majors in demand for employment, 2001 ★2326★

Finance, insurance, and real estate
Employment change projections by major industry division from 1998 to 2008 ★2287★
Employment projections by major industry division for 2008 ★2290★
Internet use by industry, 1998 ★2586★

Financial manager
Occupations with the highest average annual salaries for college graduates, 1998 ★3132★

Financial managers
Projected employment growth for selected occupations that require a bachelor's degree or more, 1998-2008 ★2317★

Financial planner
Jobs with the best outlook scores ★2249★
Most desirable jobs in business/finance ★2270★

Financial services/insurance
Spending for E-marketplace services, by industry, 2001 ★4430★

Finch University of Health Science, Chicago
U.S. colleges and universities awarding the most biological and life sciences master's degrees to Asian Americans ★1757★

Finding My Way
People for the American Way's list of most frequently challenged materials, 1982-1992 ★749★

Findlay-Hancock County Public Library
Highest Hennen's American Public Library Ratings for libraries serving a population of 50,000 to 99,999 ★2697★

Findlay; University of
U.S. News & World Report's midwestern regional liberal arts colleges with students most in debt, 1999 ★1338★
U.S. colleges and universities awarding the most business management and administrative services master's degrees to Native Americans ★1762★
Average faculty salaries for institutions of higher education in Ohio, 2000-01 ★3722★

Findley; Roger
Top pay and benefits for the chief executive and top paid employees at Loyola Marymount University ★3380★

Fine; J.D.
Most cited first authors in dermatology journals, 1981 to 1996 ★1871★

Fine or applied arts
Fields of study profile of foreign students enrolled in U.S. institutions of higher education, 1998-99 ★2495★
Fields of study profile of U.S. students studying abroad, 1998-99 ★2507★

Fineberg; Harvey V.
Top pay and benefits for the chief executive and top paid employees at Harvard University ★3327★

Finger Lakes Community College
Lowest undergraduate tuition and fees at colleges and universities in New York ★1538★
Average faculty salaries for institutions of higher education in New York, 2000-01 ★3719★

Finisar
Top companies in terms of growth, 2000 ★534★

Fink; Joseph R.
Top pay and benefits for the chief executive and top paid employees at Dominican University of California ★3270★

Finkelhor; D.
Most cited authors in the journal *Journal of Interpersonal Violence*, 1990 to 1995 ★1627★

Finks; Frederick
Top pay and benefits for the chief executive and top paid employees at Ashland University ★3180★

Finland
Eight grade science achievement scores from selected countries, 1999 ★14★
Countries with the most computers per capita, 2000 ★1604★
Most wired countries, 2001 ★2596★
Eighth grade mathematics achievement scores from selected countries, 1999 ★2773★

Finlandia University
Average faculty salaries for institutions of higher education in Michigan, 2000-01 ★3709★

Finley; Robert L.
Top pay and benefits for the chief executive and top paid employees at Queens College in North Carolina ★3448★

Finn; Alicia
Top pay and benefits for the chief executive and top paid employees at Notre Dame College in New Hampshire ★3425★

Fiorine; Carly
Highest ranking women at the top public companies, 2000 ★4452★

Fire Bringer
Booklist's most recommended fantasy books for youth ★312★
Outstanding books for older readers, 2000 ★327★

Firefighter
Jobs with the longest work weeks ★2257★
Jobs with the worst environment scores ★2260★
Jobs with the worst physical demands scores ★2263★
Jobs with the worst stress scores ★2265★

Fireflies in the Dark: The Story of Friedl Dicker-Brandeis and the Children of Terezin
Booklist's best art books for young people ★308★

Firm and Management Characteristics as Discriminators of Export Marketing Activity
Most influential articles in the *Journal of Business Research*, 1985-1999 ★697★
Most influential articles in the *Journal of Business Research* from 1985 to 1989 ★698★

First American Financial
Fortune's highest ranked mortgage finance companies, 2000 ★479★

First Data
Fortune's highest ranked computer and data services companies, 2000 ★453★

First in the World Consortium, Illinois
Comparison of 8th grade science achievement scores, U.S. and worldwide, 1999 ★6★

First Lady
Library Journal's best romance titles, 2000 ★245★

First They Killed My Father: A Daughter of Cambodia Remembers
Outstanding history books, 2000 ★289★
Most notable nonfiction books for young adults, 2001 ★324★

First Things First
Retail audiobook titles selling 300,000-400,000 copies ★303★

First Union
Fortune's highest ranked super-regional banks, 2000 ★498★

First Word Book
Smithsonian's best books for children ages 1 to 6 ★363★

Firstar
Fortune's highest ranked super-regional banks, 2000 ★498★

Fischer; Elizabeth
Top pay and benefits for the chief executive and top paid employees at Lake Forest College ★3363★

Fischer; Jerry
Top pay and benefits for the chief executive and top paid employees at the University of Mary ★3548★

Fischer; Michael
Top pay and benefits for the chief executive and top paid employees at Saint Bonaventure University ★3470★

A Fish Caught in Time: The Search for the Coelacanth
Library Journal's most notable zoology books, 2000 ★278★

Fishburn; Peter C.
Authors with the most published pages in impact-weighted insurance journals ★677★

Fisher; Irving
Authors most frequently contributing to the *American Economic Review* from 1911-1990 ★2156★

Fisher; John
Top pay and benefits for the chief executive and top paid employees at Lehigh University ★3368★

Fisheries Oceanography
Oceanography journals by citation impact, 1999 ★2141★

Fisheries science and management
Agricultural sciences doctorates awarded at U.S. colleges and universities, by subfield, 1999 ★1886★
Gender breakdown of agricultural sciences doctorate recipients, by subfield, 1999 ★1926★

Fisherman
Jobs with the highest unemployment ★2256★
Jobs with the worst outlook scores ★2262★
Jobs with the worst security scores ★2264★
Least desirable jobs ★2266★
Most desirable jobs in agriculture ★2268★
Occupations with the highest decline in employment, 1998-2008 ★2310★

Fishing in the Air
  Outstanding children's picture books, 2000 ★331★
Fisk University
  Historically black institutions with the highest number of National Achievement Scholars, 1998 ★8★
  U.S. colleges and universities with the highest percentage of African Americans enrolled, 1997 ★222★
  U.S. News & World Report's southern regional liberal arts colleges with students most in debt, 1999 ★1367★
  U.S. News & World Report's southern regional liberal arts colleges with the highest acceptance rates, 2000-01 ★1370★
  U.S. News & World Report's southern regional liberal arts colleges with the highest freshmen retention rates, 2000-01 ★1372★
  U.S. News & World Report's southern regional liberal arts colleges with the highest percentage of full-time faculty, 2000-01 ★1374★
  U.S. colleges and universities awarding the most physical sciences master's degrees to African Americans ★1793★
  Institutions with the most female physics bachelor's recipients, 1994-1998 ★2959★
  U.S. institutions with more than 40% female bachelor's graduates in their physics departments, 1994-98 ★2977★
  Average faculty salaries for institutions of higher education in Tennessee, 2000-01 ★3730★
Fisse; Brent
  Most cited authors in the journal *Australian and New Zealand Journals of Criminology*, 1990 to 1995 ★1613★
  Most-cited scholars in *Australian and New Zealand Journal of Criminology* ★1636★
Fitchburg State College
  State appropriations for Massachusetts's institutions of higher education, 2000-01 ★1274★
Fitz, S.M.; Bro. Raymond L.
  Top pay and benefits for the chief executive and top paid employees at the University of Dayton ★3539★
Fitzgerald; Ella
  Most influential African American entertainers ★77★
Fitzgibbons Jr.; Robert J.
  Top pay and benefits for the chief executive and top paid employees at Creighton University ★3259★
Fitzkee; Nicholas
  All-USA College Academic Third Team, 2001 ★4★
Fitzpatrick; Daniel R.
  Top editorial cartoonists used in teaching journalism history ★2770★
Fitzpatrick; P.
  Most cited authors in the journal *Criminologie*, 1990 to 1995 ★1621★
Fitzrandolph; John
  Top pay and benefits for the chief executive and top paid employees at Whittier College ★3624★
Fixman; Carol
  Top pay and benefits for the chief executive and top paid employees at Philadelphia University ★3440★
Flagler College
  U.S. News & World Report's southern regional liberal arts colleges with the lowest acceptance rates, 2000-01 ★1377★

Flags of Our Fathers
  Christopher Awards winners for adult literature, 2000 ★235★
  Longest-running nonfiction hardcover bestsellers, 2000 ★281★
Flagstaff, AZ
  Best 'green & clean' places to live ★3077★
Flamini; Sue
  All-America girls' high school soccer team midfielders, 2001 ★177★
Flanagan; Jerry E.
  Top pay and benefits for the chief executive and top paid employees at Saint Michael's College ★3483★
Flanagan; Patrick
  Top pay and benefits for the chief executive and top paid employees at Stevens Institute of Technology ★3512★
Flanagan; Thomas
  Top pay and benefits for the chief executive and top paid employees at Salve Regina University ★3489★
Flanigan Jr.; Robert D.
  Top pay and benefits for the chief executive and top paid employees at Spelman College ★3507★
Flanigan; Matthew G.
  Top pay and benefits for the chief executive and top paid employees at Jacksonville University ★3352★
Flannery; Francis X.
  Top pay and benefits for the chief executive and top paid employees at Suffolk University ★3513★
Flashman and the Tiger
  Booklist's most recommended historical novels, 2001 ★230★
Flat Rock Middle School
  Outstanding secondary schools in Atlanta, Georgia ★4087★
Flathead Valley Community College
  Lowest undergraduate tuition and fees at colleges and universities in Montana ★1527★
Flaumenhaft; Harvey
  Top pay and benefits for the chief executive and top paid employees at St. John's College in Maryland and New Mexico ★3473★
Flecky; Katy
  All-America girls' high school basketball 3rd team, 2001 ★172★
FleetBoston
  Fortune's highest ranked super-regional banks, 2000 ★498★
Fleetboston Financial
  Top banks in Standard & Poor's 500, 2001 ★531★
Fleetwood Enterprises
  Fortune's highest ranked motor vehicle parts companies, 2000 ★480★
Fleischman; Richard
  Top pay and benefits for the chief executive and top paid employees at John Carroll University ★3353★
Fleming
  Fortune's highest ranked wholesalers, 2000 ★505★
Fleming; David C.
  Top pay and benefits for the chief executive and top paid employees at LaSalle University ★3365★
Fleming; Denise
  Outstanding children's picture books, 2000 ★331★

Fletcher; Jim
  Top pay and benefits for the chief executive and top paid employees at Morehouse College ★3408★
Fletcher; Richard
  Top pay and benefits for the chief executive and top paid employees at Baldwin-Wallace College ★3189★
Flight attendant
  Most desirable jobs in travel/food service ★2278★
Flight attendants
  Average salaries for occupations requiring on-the-job training ★3119★
Flintridge Sacred Heart Academy
  Outstanding secondary schools in Los Angeles-Long Beach, California ★4167★
FlipDog.com
  Top career-related Web sites ★2602★
The Floating Girl
  Outstanding fiction books for young adults, 2000 ★333★
Flood Middle School
  Outstanding secondary schools in Denver, Colorado ★4124★
Floral Park Memorial High School
  Outstanding secondary schools in Long Island, New York ★4165★
Florence-Darlington Tech College
  Average faculty salaries for institutions of higher education without academic ranks in South Carolina, 2000-01 ★3765★
Florida
  People for the American Way's list of states with the most challenges to library and school books, 1982-1992 ★750★
  States with the highest enrollment in private 4-year institutions of higher education ★860★
  States with the highest enrollment in public 4-year institutions of higher education ★861★
  Mean composite ACT scores by state, 2000 ★895★
  Mean math SAT scores by state, 2000 ★900★
  Mean verbal SAT scores by state, 2000 ★903★
  Average class size at colleges and universities in the U.S., by state ★1064★
  States allocating the largest amount of state tax appropriations for higher education, 2000-01 ★1304★
  States receiving the most in federal agency appropriations to colleges, 2000 ★1306★
  States receiving the most in federal agency appropriations to colleges, from 1996 to 2000 ★1307★
  Total doctorate recipients by state, 1999 ★2054★
  Hispanic American enrollment at Hispanic-serving institutions of higher education, by state, 1997 ★2547★
  States with the most law schools ★2668★
  State library associations with the highest annual revenue ★2682★
  State library associations with the highest conference attendance ★2683★
  State library associations with the highest unrestricted net assets ★2684★
  State library associations with the largest membership ★2685★
  State grades for affordability of higher education for minority students, 2000 ★2883★
  State grades for benefits state receives for educating its minority students, 2000 ★2884★

FLORIDA

State grades for completion of higher education by minority students, 2000 ★2885★

State grades for participation of minority students in higher education, 2000 ★2886★

State grades for preparing minority students for higher education, 2000 ★2887★

States with the highest number of high school graduates, 1999-2000 ★3995★

States with the highest average enrollment in public elementary schools ★4032★

States with the highest average enrollment in public secondary schools ★4033★

States with the highest K-12 public school enrollment ★4034★

States with the highest projected K-12 public school enrollment for 2010 ★4035★

States with the highest funding needs for school-technology modernization ★4041★

States with the most charter schools ★4048★

States with the most K-12 public schools ★4049★

States with the largest average class size ★4071★

States with the lowest percentage of high school freshmen enrolling in college within four years ★4267★

States with the highest state support for non need-based financial aid for students, 1999-2000 ★4368★

U.S. states with the highest percentage of births to teenagers who were already mothers ★4433★

Florida A&M State University

Retention rates of African American students at historically black institutions, 1997-98 ★1120★

Historically black colleges and universities awarding the most master's degrees to African Americans ★1670★

Total baccalaureate communications degrees awarded to African Americans from U.S. colleges and universities, 1997-98 ★1687★

Total baccalaureate education degrees awarded to African Americans from U.S. colleges and universities, 1997-98 ★1711★

Total baccalaureate health professions and related sciences degrees awarded to African Americans from U.S. colleges and universities, 1997-98 ★1721★

Total baccalaureate mathematics degrees awarded to African Americans from U.S. colleges and universities, 1997-98 ★1729★

U.S. colleges and universities awarding the most physical sciences master's degrees to African Americans ★1793★

U.S. institutions awarding the most baccalaureate degrees to African Americans in agribusiness and production, 1998 ★1813★

U.S. institutions awarding the most baccalaureate degrees to African Americans in agricultural sciences, 1998 ★1814★

U.S. institutions awarding the most baccalaureate degrees to minorities in agribusiness and production, 1998 ★1819★

Historically black colleges and universities awarding the most first professional degrees to African Americans ★1835★

U.S. colleges and universities awarding the most health professions and related sciences first professional degrees to African Americans ★1847★

Florida A&M University

Historically black institutions with the highest number of National Achievement Scholars, 1998 ★8★

U.S. universities enrolling the most National Achievement Scholars, 1994 ★9★

U.S. universities enrolling the most National Achievement Scholars, 1995 ★10★

U.S. universities enrolling the most National Achievement Scholars, 1996 ★11★

U.S. universities enrolling the most National Achievement Scholars, 1997 ★12★

U.S. universities enrolling the most National Achievement Scholars, 1998 ★13★

Colleges offering the Thurgood Marshall Scholarship Fund ★221★

Four-year public institutions enrolling the highest number of students from the District of Columbia, 1998-99 ★855★

U.S. colleges and universities with a popular theater group ★1020★

U.S. colleges and universities with the worst on-campus housing facilities ★1044★

State appropriations for Florida's institutions of higher education, 2000-01 ★1262★

Total baccalaureate business management and administrative services degrees awarded to African Americans from U.S. colleges and universities, 1997-98 ★1683★

Total baccalaureate computer and information science degrees awarded to African Americans from U.S. colleges and universities, 1997-98 ★1691★

Total baccalaureate degrees awarded to African Americans from historically black colleges, 1997-98 ★1697★

Total baccalaureate degrees awarded to African Americans from U.S. colleges and universities, 1997-98 ★1699★

Total baccalaureate psychology degrees awarded to African Americans from U.S. colleges and universities, 1997-98 ★1737★

U.S. colleges and universities awarding the most education master's degrees to African Americans ★1769★

U.S. colleges and universities awarding the most master's degrees to African Americans ★1785★

U.S. colleges and universities awarding the most social sciences and history master's degrees to African Americans ★1801★

U.S. colleges and universities awarding the most first professional degrees to African Americans ★1843★

Florida Atlantic University

Division I NCAA colleges with the lowest graduation rates for female athletes, 1990-91 to 1993-94 ★936★

Division I NCAA colleges with the lowest graduation rates for female basketball players, 1990-91 to 1993-94 ★937★

Division I NCAA colleges with the lowest graduation rates for male athletes, 1990-91 to 1993-94 ★939★

State appropriations for Florida's institutions of higher education, 2000-01 ★1262★

U.S. colleges and universities awarding the most physical sciences master's degrees to Asian Americans ★1794★

U.S. colleges and universities awarding the most physical sciences master's degrees to Hispanic Americans ★1795★

Average faculty salaries for institutions of higher education in Florida, 2000-01 ★3696★

Florida Gulf Coast University

State appropriations for Florida's institutions of higher education, 2000-01 ★1262★

Average faculty salaries for institutions of higher education in Florida, 2000-01 ★3696★

Florida Institute of Technology

U.S. News & World Report's national universities with students most in debt, 1999 ★1476★

Highest undergraduate tuition and fees at colleges and universities in Florida ★1494★

U.S. colleges and universities awarding the most business management and administrative services master's degrees to African Americans ★1759★

U.S. colleges and universities awarding the most business management and administrative services master's degrees to Native Americans ★1762★

Florida International University

Institutions with the most full-time Hispanic American faculty ★923★

U.S. colleges and universities with the most full-time Hispanic American faculty ★925★

State appropriations for Florida's institutions of higher education, 2000-01 ★1262★

U.S. News & World Report's national universities with students least in debt, 1999 ★1475★

Top colleges in terms of total baccalaureate degrees awarded to minorities, 1997-98 ★1678★

Total baccalaureate biology/life sciences degrees awarded to Hispanic Americans from U.S. colleges and universities, 1997-98 ★1681★

Total baccalaureate business management and administrative services degrees awarded to Hispanic Americans from U.S. colleges and universities, 1997-98 ★1685★

Total baccalaureate communications degrees awarded to Hispanic Americans from U.S. colleges and universities, 1997-98 ★1689★

Total baccalaureate computer and information science degrees awarded to Hispanic Americans from U.S. colleges and universities, 1997-98 ★1693★

Total baccalaureate degrees awarded to African Americans from traditionally white institutions, 1997-98 ★1698★

Total baccalaureate degrees awarded to Hispanic Americans from U.S. colleges and universities, 1997-98 ★1705★

Total baccalaureate education degrees awarded to Hispanic Americans from U.S. colleges and universities, 1997-98 ★1713★

Total baccalaureate engineering degrees awarded to minorities from U.S. colleges and universities, 1997-98 ★1715★

Total baccalaureate English language, literature, and letters degrees awarded to Hispanic Americans from U.S. colleges and universities, 1997-98 ★1718★

Total baccalaureate health professions and related sciences degrees awarded to African Americans from U.S. colleges and universities, 1997-98 ★1721★

Total baccalaureate health professions and related sciences degrees awarded to Hispanic Americans from U.S. colleges and universities, 1997-98 ★1723★

Total baccalaureate physical sciences degrees awarded to Hispanic Americans from U.S. colleges and universities, 1997-98 ★1735★

Total baccalaureate psychology degrees awarded to Hispanic Americans from U.S. colleges and universities, 1997-98 ★1739★

Total baccalaureate social sciences and history degrees awarded to Hispanic Americans from U.S. colleges and universities, 1997-98 ★1743★

Traditionally white institutions awarding the most master's degrees to African Americans ★1755★

U.S. colleges and universities awarding the most business management and administrative services master's degrees to Hispanic Americans ★1761★

U.S. colleges and universities awarding the most communications master's degrees to Hispanic Americans ★1765★

U.S. colleges and universities awarding the most education master's degrees to Hispanic Americans ★1771★

U.S. colleges and universities awarding the most health professions and related sciences master's degrees to African Americans ★1777★

U.S. colleges and universities awarding the most health professions and related sciences master's degrees to Hispanic Americans ★1779★

U.S. colleges and universities awarding the most master's degrees to Hispanic Americans ★1787★

U.S. colleges and universities awarding the most master's degrees to minorities ★1788★

U.S. colleges and universities awarding the most physical sciences master's degrees to Hispanic Americans ★1795★

U.S. colleges and universities awarding the most social sciences and history master's degrees to Hispanic Americans ★1803★

U.S. colleges and universities awarding the most psychology doctorate degrees to Hispanic Americans ★2122★

U.S. doctoral institutions with the largest number of students studying abroad, 1998-99 ★2512★

Florida Southern College

U.S. News & World Report's southern regional liberal arts colleges with the lowest acceptance rates, 2000-01 ★1377★

U.S. News & World Report's best undergraduate fees among southern regional liberal arts colleges by discount tuition, 2000 ★1383★

Average faculty salaries for institutions of higher education in Florida, 2000-01 ★3696★

Florida State University

U.S. colleges and universities with the highest average football attendance, 1996-99 ★159★

Institutions with the most published authors in the *Journal of Business Research*, 1985 to 1999 ★695★

U.S. colleges and universities with the largest numerical increases in alcohol arrests, 1998 ★733★

U.S. colleges and universities where a large portion of the student body drink beer ★991★

U.S. colleges and universities where a large portion of the student body drink hard liquor ★992★

U.S. colleges and universities where fraternities and sororities are popular ★993★

U.S. colleges and universities where intercollegiate sports are popular ★995★

U.S. colleges and universities where the general student body puts a strong emphasis on socializing ★1008★

U.S. colleges and universities with poor library facilities ★1028★

U.S. colleges and universities with the least accessible instructors ★1036★

Retention rates of African American students at traditionally white institutions, 1997-98 ★1121★

State appropriations for Florida's institutions of higher education, 2000-01 ★1262★

Universities with the most-cited scholars in *Criminology* ★1649★

Universities with the most-cited scholars in *Journal of Research in Crime and Delinquency* ★1651★

U.S. colleges and universities awarding the most communications master's degrees to Hispanic Americans ★1765★

U.S. colleges and universities awarding the most social sciences and history master's degrees to African Americans ★1801★

Institutions awarding the most doctorate degrees to African Americans, 1997-98 ★1948★

Traditionally white institutions awarding the most doctorate degrees to African Americans ★2079★

U.S. colleges and universities awarding the most business management and administrative services doctorate degrees to African Americans ★2085★

U.S. colleges and universities awarding the most doctoral degrees to Hispanic Americans from 1995 to 1999 ★2094★

U.S. colleges and universities awarding the most doctorate degrees to African Americans ★2095★

Top oceanography research-doctorate programs as evaluated by the National Research Council ★2153★

Women faculty in Ph.D. physics departments at U.S. institutions, 1998 ★2981★

Average faculty salaries for institutions of higher education in Florida, 2000-01 ★3696★

Radcliffe Institute for Advanced Study fellowship recipients in the field of sociology, 2000-01 ★4346★

Florida; University of

All-USA College Academic Third Team, 2001 ★4★

Colleges with the highest number of freshman Merit Scholars, 2000 ★5★

U.S. universities enrolling the most National Achievement Scholars, 1994 ★9★

U.S. universities enrolling the most National Achievement Scholars, 1997 ★12★

U.S. universities enrolling the most National Achievement Scholars, 1998 ★13★

U.S. universities publishing the most papers in the fields of agriculture/agronomy, 1994-98 ★57★

Top anthropology research-doctorate programs as evaluated by the National Research Council ★62★

NCAA Division I women's swimming teams with the most individual championships ★136★

U.S. colleges and universities with the highest average football attendance, 1996-99 ★159★

U.S. News & World Report's universities with the best taxation departments, 1999-2000 ★573★

Comparisons of investment returns for consulting MBAs ★622★

Comparisons of investment returns for finance MBAs ★624★

U.S. business schools with the slowest payback on MBA investments ★655★

Top business schools for within-discipline research performance in marketing, 1986-1998 ★671★

Institutions with the most full-time Hispanic American faculty ★923★

U.S. colleges and universities with the most full-time Hispanic American faculty ★925★

U.S. colleges and universities where the general student body puts a strong emphasis on athletic events ★1007★

U.S. colleges and universities with a popular newspaper ★1018★

U.S. colleges and universities with the most upper level courses taught by TAs ★1040★

U.S. colleges and universities with the worst on-campus housing facilities ★1044★

Largest degree-granting colleges and universities, by enrollment ★1068★

State appropriations for Florida's institutions of higher education, 2000-01 ★1262★

Golden Key Scholar Award winners, 2000 ★1316★

Total baccalaureate communications degrees awarded to African Americans from U.S. colleges and universities, 1997-98 ★1687★

Total baccalaureate communications degrees awarded to Hispanic Americans from U.S. colleges and universities, 1997-98 ★1689★

Total baccalaureate engineering degrees awarded to minorities from U.S. colleges and universities, 1997-98 ★1715★

U.S. colleges and universities awarding the most communications master's degrees to Hispanic Americans ★1765★

U.S. colleges and universities awarding the most law and legal studies master's degrees to African Americans ★1781★

U.S. institutions awarding the most baccalaureate degrees to African Americans in agribusiness and production, 1998 ★1813★

U.S. institutions awarding the most baccalaureate degrees to African Americans in agricultural sciences, 1998 ★1814★

U.S. institutions awarding the most baccalaureate degrees to Asian Americans in agribusiness and production, 1998 ★1815★

U.S. institutions awarding the most baccalaureate degrees to Asian Americans in agricultural sciences, 1998 ★1816★

U.S. institutions awarding the most baccalaureate degrees to Hispanic Americans in agribusiness and production, 1998 ★1817★

U.S. institutions awarding the most baccalaureate degrees to Hispanic Americans in agricultural sciences, 1998 ★1818★

U.S. institutions awarding the most baccalaureate degrees to minorities in agribusiness and production, 1998 ★1819★

U.S. institutions awarding the most baccalaureate degrees to minorities in agricultural sciences, 1998 ★1820★

Traditionally white institutions awarding the most first professional degrees to African Americans ★1842★

U.S. colleges and universities awarding the most first professional degrees to African Americans ★1843★

U.S. colleges and universities awarding the most first professional degrees to Hispanic Americans ★1845★

U.S. colleges and universities awarding the most health professions and related sciences first professional degrees to Hispanic Americans ★1849★

U.S. colleges and universities awarding the most law and legal studies first professional degrees to African Americans ★1852★

U.S. colleges and universities awarding the most law and legal studies first professional degrees to Hispanic Americans ★1854★

U.S. colleges and universities awarding the most doctorates in life sciences, 1999 ★2104★

U.S. colleges and universities awarding the most health professions and related sciences doctorate degrees to Asian Americans ★2115★

U.S. colleges and universities awarding the most health professions and related sciences doctorate degrees to Hispanic Americans ★2116★

U.S. colleges and universities awarding the most physical sciences doctorate degrees to African Americans ★2118★

U.S. institutions awarding the most doctoral degrees to minorities in agricultural sciences, 1998 ★2131★

Academics' choices for best graduate agricultural engineering programs, 2001 ★2379★

Academics' choices for best graduate materials engineering programs, 2001 ★2417★

Academics' choices for best graduate nuclear engineering schools, 2000 ★2426★

U.S. universities publishing the most papers in the field of ecology/environmental sciences, 1994-98 ★2473★

Academics' choices for best tax law programs, 2001 ★2632★

Law schools with the best criminal procedure faculty, 1999-2000 ★2648★

Institutions with the most productive libraries, 1993-1997 ★2678★

Degrees granted in the ten largest undergraduate journalism and mass communications programs, 1999 ★2745★

Enrollment of students in the ten largest undergraduate journalism and mass communications programs, 1999 ★2746★

Degrees granted in the ten largest doctoral journalism and mass communications programs, 1999 ★2756★

Degrees granted in the ten largest master's journalism and mass communications programs, 1999 ★2757★

Enrollment of students in the ten largest doctoral journalism and mass communications programs, 1999 ★2762★

Enrollment of students in the ten largest master's journalism and mass communications programs, 1999 ★2763★

Average faculty salaries for institutions of higher education in Florida, 2000-01 ★3696★

Academics' choices for best counseling/personnel services graduate programs, 2001 ★4379★

Florist
Jobs with the best stress scores ★2252★

Flossmoor High School
Outstanding secondary schools in Chicago, Illinois ★4110★

Flowering Wells High School
Outstanding secondary schools in Tucson, Arizona ★4243★

Floyd Central High School
Outstanding secondary schools in Louisville, Kentucky-Indiana ★4168★

Floyd College
Average faculty salaries for institutions of higher education in Georgia, 2000-01 ★3697★

Floyd; Samuel A.
Top pay and benefits for the chief executive and top paid employees at Columbia College in Illinois ★3250★

Fluids
Gender breakdown of physics and astronomy doctorate recipients, by subfield, 1999 ★1939★
Physics and astronomy doctorates awarded at U.S. colleges and universities, by subfield, 1999 ★1994★

Fluker; Walter
Top pay and benefits for the chief executive and top paid employees at Morehouse College ★3408★

Fluor
Fortune's highest ranked engineering and construction companies, 2000 ★461★

Flynn Jr.; Charles L.
Top pay and benefits for the chief executive and top paid employees at Assumption College ★3181★

Flynn; Richard B.
Top pay and benefits for the chief executive and top paid employees at Springfield College in Massachusetts ★3509★

Foamex International
Fortune's highest ranked rubber and plastic products companies, 2000 ★492★

Foereningssparbanken
Business Week's best companies in Sweden ★404★

Foldberg; H.J.
Top pay and benefits for the chief executive and top paid employees at the University of San Francisco ★3566★

Foley; D.
Top full professor economists at elite liberal arts colleges, 1975-94 ★2175★

Foley; Mark
Top pay and benefits for the chief executive and top paid employees at the University of Mobile ★3551★

The Folk Keeper
Most notable children's recordings, 2001 ★320★

Follett College Stores
Contractors managing the most college bookstores, 1999 ★846★

Fond du Lac Tribal and Community College
U.S. tribal colleges ★1445★
Average faculty salaries for institutions of higher education without academic ranks in Minnesota, 2000-01 ★3753★

Fong; Bobby
Top pay and benefits for the chief executive and top paid employees at Hamilton College ★3319★

Food/Cosmetics Toxicology
Food science and technology journals by citation impact, 1991-99 ★2902★

Food counter and related workers
Occupations with the largest projected employment growth, 1998-2008 ★2312★
Projected employment growth for selected occupations that require shorter moderate-term on-the-job training, 1998-2008 ★2321★

Food engineering
Agricultural sciences doctorates awarded at U.S. colleges and universities, by subfield, 1999 ★1886★
Gender breakdown of agricultural sciences doctorate recipients, by subfield, 1999 ★1926★

Food Microstructure
Food science and technology journals by citation impact, 1991-99 ★2902★

Food preparation workers
Projected employment growth for selected occupations that require shorter moderate-term on-the-job training, 1998-2008 ★2321★

Food science
Average costs for Academic Search titles by subject, 2001 ★2918★
Periodical prices by LC subject, 2001 ★2925★
Periodical prices by scientific discipline, 2001 ★2926★

Food service and lodging managers
Occupations with the highest number of self-employed workers, 1998 ★2311★
Projected employment growth for selected occupations that require long-term on-the-job training, 1998-2008 ★2320★

Football
African American college athletics head coaches, by gender, 1999-2000 ★118★
College athletics head coaches, by gender, 1999-2000 ★122★
Minority college athletics head coaches, by gender, 1999-2000 ★133★

Football player (NFL)
Jobs considered the most competitive ★2245★
Jobs that are potentially the highest paying ★2246★
Jobs with the best income scores ★2248★
Jobs with the greatest potential income for beginners ★2253★
Jobs with the highest starting salaries ★2255★
Jobs with the worst environment scores ★2260★
Jobs with the worst physical demands scores ★2263★
Jobs with the worst security scores ★2264★
Jobs with the worst stress scores ★2265★
Most desirable jobs in athletics ★2269★

Foote II; Edward T.
Presidents with the highest pay at Research I and II universities, 1998-99 ★3162★
Top pay and benefits for the chief executive and top paid employees at the University of Miami ★3550★

Foothill High School
Outstanding secondary schools in Orange County, California ★4199★

Footstar
Top recruiters for business administration jobs for 2000-01 bachelor's degree recipients ★554★
Top recruiters for accounting jobs for 2000-01 bachelor's degree recipients ★580★
Top recruiters for finance/banking jobs for 2000-01 bachelor's degree recipients ★582★
Top employers of college graduates, 2001 ★2325★
Top recruiters for systems engineer jobs for 2000-01 bachelor's degree recipients ★2336★
Top recruiters for language/literature jobs for 2000-01 bachelor's degree recipients ★2446★
Top recruiters for human resources jobs for 2000-01 bachelor's degree recipients ★2559★
Top recruiters for human resources jobs for 2000-01 master's degree recipients ★2560★
Top recruiters for liberal arts jobs for 2000-01 bachelor's degree recipients ★2675★

Top recruiters for information technology (MIS) jobs for 2000-01 bachelor's degree recipients ★2738★
Top recruiters for information technology (MIS) jobs for 2000-01 master's degree recipients ★2739★
Top recruiters for psychology jobs for 2000-01 bachelor's degree recipients ★3063★
Top recruiters for education jobs for 2000-01 bachelor's degree recipients ★4377★

Forbes
Most selective internships in the U.S., 2001 ★2610★

Forbes; Geraldine
Top pay and benefits for the chief executive and top paid employees at Woodbury University ★3635★

Ford; Andrew T.
Top pay and benefits for the chief executive and top paid employees at Wabash College ★3598★

The Ford Foundation
Most selective internships in the U.S., 2001 ★2610★
Top internships in the U.S. with the highest compensation, 2001 ★2611★

Ford Heights, District 169
Illinois school districts with the most average years of teacher experience ★4012★

Ford Motor Company
Business Week's best companies in terms of sales ★408★
Fortune's highest ranked motor vehicles companies, 2000 ★481★
Top automotive companies in Standard & Poor's 500, 2001 ★530★
Top employers of college graduates, 2001 ★2325★
Top recruiters for multidisciplinary majors jobs for 2000-01 bachelor's degree recipients ★2327★
Top internships in the U.S. with the highest compensation, 2001 ★2611★
Corporations making the most contributions to African American communities, 1995 ★2941★

Ford; Thomas P.
Top pay and benefits for the chief executive and top paid employees at Immaculata College ★3348★

Ford; T.J.
All-America boys' high school basketball 2nd team, 2001 ★162★

Fordham University
U.S. catholic universities with the highest enrollment, 1999 ★864★
U.S. colleges and universities where intercollegiate sports are not popular ★994★
U.S. colleges and universities where intramural sports are not popular ★996★
U.S. colleges and universities with a popular radio station ★1019★
Total baccalaureate computer and information science degrees awarded to Hispanic Americans from U.S. colleges and universities, 1997-98 ★1693★
Traditionally white institutions awarding the most first professional degrees to African Americans ★1842★
U.S. colleges and rankings awarding the most law and legal studies first professional degrees to African Americans ★1852★
U.S. colleges and universities awarding the most law and legal studies first professional degrees to Asian Americans ★1853★
U.S. colleges and universities awarding the most law and legal studies first professional degrees to Hispanic Americans ★1854★
Radcliffe Institute for Advanced Study fellowship recipients in the field of philosophy, 2000-01 ★2946★
Institutions with the most female physics bachelor's recipients, 1994-1998 ★2959★
U.S. institutions with more than 40% female bachelor's graduates in their physics departments, 1994-98 ★2977★
Average faculty salaries for institutions of higher education in New York, 2000-01 ★3719★

Foreign government
Primary sources of financial support for doctorate recipients, by citizenship, 1999 ★2003★
Primary sources of financial support for doctorate recipients, by gender, 1999 ★2004★
Primary sources of financial support for doctorate recipients, by race/ethnicity, 1999 ★2005★
Primary sources of financial support for education doctorate recipients, by citizenship, 1999 ★2006★
Primary sources of financial support for education doctorate recipients, by gender, 1999 ★2007★
Primary sources of financial support for education doctorate recipients, by race/ethnicity, 1999 ★2008★
Primary sources of financial support for engineering doctorate recipients, by citizenship, 1999 ★2009★
Primary sources of financial support for engineering doctorate recipients, by gender, 1999 ★2010★
Primary sources of financial support for engineering doctorate recipients, by race/ethnicity, 1999 ★2011★
Primary sources of financial support for humanities doctorate recipients, by citizenship, 1999 ★2012★
Primary sources of financial support for humanities doctorate recipients, by gender, 1999 ★2013★
Primary sources of financial support for humanities doctorate recipients, by race/ethnicity, 1999 ★2014★
Primary sources of financial support for life sciences doctorate recipients, by citizenship, 1999 ★2015★
Primary sources of financial support for life sciences doctorate recipients, by gender, 1999 ★2016★
Primary sources of financial support for life sciences doctorate recipients, by race/ethnicity, 1999 ★2017★
Primary sources of financial support for physical sciences, mathematics, and computer sciences doctorate recipients, by citizenship, 1999 ★2018★
Primary sources of financial support for physical sciences, mathematics, and computer sciences doctorate recipients, by gender, 1999 ★2019★
Primary sources of financial support for physical sciences, mathematics, and computer sciences doctorate recipients, by race/ethnicity, 1999 ★2020★
Primary sources of financial support for professional/other doctorate recipients, by citizenship, 1999 ★2021★
Primary sources of financial support for professional/other doctorate recipients, by gender, 1999 ★2022★
Primary sources of financial support for professional/other doctorate recipients, by race/ethnicity, 1999 ★2023★
Primary sources of financial support for social sciences doctorate recipients, by citizenship, 1999 ★2024★
Primary sources of financial support for social sciences doctorate recipients, by gender, 1999 ★2025★
Primary sources of financial support for social sciences doctorate recipients, by race/ethnicity, 1999 ★2026★

Foreign Language
Top nonscience majors for accepted applicants to U.S. medical schools, 1999-2000 ★2854★

Foreign language education
Gender breakdown of teaching fields doctorate recipients, by subfield, 1999 ★1943★
Teaching fields doctorates awarded at U.S. colleges and universities, by subfield, 1999 ★2046★

Foreign language and literature
Humanities doctorates awarded to U.S. citizens/permanent residents at U.S. colleges and universities, by race/ethnicity and subfield, 1999 ★1947★
Number of humanities doctorate recipients at U.S. colleges and universities, by field, 1999 ★1973★

Foreign languages
Fields of study profile of U.S. students studying abroad, 1998-99 ★2507★

Forest biology
Agricultural sciences doctorates awarded at U.S. colleges and universities, by subfield, 1999 ★1886★
Gender breakdown of agricultural sciences doctorate recipients, by subfield, 1999 ★1926★

Forest engineering
Agricultural sciences doctorates awarded at U.S. colleges and universities, by subfield, 1999 ★1886★
Gender breakdown of agricultural sciences doctorate recipients, by subfield, 1999 ★1926★

Forest Glen Middle School
Outstanding secondary schools in Fort Lauderdale, Florida ★4133★

Forest Hills High School
Outstanding secondary schools in New York, New York ★4191★

The Forest in the Clouds
Booklist's best science books for children ★310★

Forest Laboratories
Top health care companies in Standard & Poor's 500, 2001 ★542★

Forest management
Agricultural sciences doctorates awarded at U.S. colleges and universities, by subfield, 1999 ★1886★
Gender breakdown of agricultural sciences doctorate recipients, by subfield, 1999 ★1926★

Forest Meadow Junior High School
Outstanding secondary schools in Dallas, Texas ★4120★

Forest Park Middle School
Outstanding secondary schools in Longview-Marshall, Texas ★4166★

Forestry and related sciences
Agricultural sciences doctorates awarded at U.S. colleges and universities, by subfield, 1999 ★1886★
Gender breakdown of agricultural sciences doctorate recipients, by subfield, 1999 ★1926★

Forever
American Library Association's most frequently challenged books of the decade ★224★
American Library Associations most frequently challenged books for the 1990s ★742★
People for the American Way's list of most frequently challenged books, 1982-1992 ★747★

Forget; Thomas
Top pay and benefits for the chief executive and top paid employees at Sacred Heart University in Connecticut ★3467★

Forgotten Fire
Booklist's best first novels for youths ★309★
Most notable fiction books for young adults, 2001 ★322★
Outstanding books for older readers, 2000 ★327★

Forklift operator
'Blue-collar' jobs considered the least physically demanding ★2241★
Jobs with the best stress scores ★2252★
Jobs with the highest unemployment ★2256★

Forman; Jan
Top pay and benefits for the chief executive and top paid employees at Trevecca Nazarene University ★3576★

Forschner Jr.; Robert E.
Top pay and benefits for the chief executive and top paid employees at the University of Tampa ★3569★

Forster; Jerry
Top pay and benefits for the chief executive and top paid employees at University of Charleston ★3590★

Forsyth Technical Community College
Lowest undergraduate tuition and fees at colleges and universities in North Carolina ★1540★

Fort Belknap College
U.S. tribal colleges ★1445★

Fort Berthold Community College
U.S. tribal colleges ★1445★
Highest undergraduate tuition and fees at colleges and universities in North Dakota ★1541★

Fort Campbell High School
Outstanding secondary schools in Clarkesville-Hoplinsville, Tennessee-Kentucky ★4113★

Fort Collins, CO
Best small towns to live in ★3085★

Fort Counch Middle School
Outstanding secondary schools in Pittsburgh, Pennsylvania ★4204★

Fort Hays State University
State appropriations for Kansas institutions of higher education, 2000-01 ★1269★
U.S. colleges and universities awarding the most communications master's degrees to Asian Americans ★1764★
Average faculty salaries for institutions of higher education in Kansas, 2000-01 ★3703★

Fort James
Fortune's highest ranked forest and paper products companies, 2000 ★466★

Fort Lewis College
Total baccalaureate computer and information science degrees awarded to Native Americans from U.S. colleges and universities, 1997-98 ★1694★
Total baccalaureate degrees awarded to Native Americans from U.S. colleges and universities, 1997-98 ★1710★
Total baccalaureate English language, literature, and letters degrees awarded to Native Americans from U.S. colleges and universities, 1997-98 ★1719★
Total baccalaureate social sciences and history degrees awarded to Native Americans from U.S. colleges and universities, 1997-98 ★1744★
Average faculty salaries for institutions of higher education in Colorado, 2000-01 ★3693★

Fort Myers Middle School
Outstanding secondary schools in Fort Myers-Cape Coral, Florida ★4134★

Fort Oglethorpe High School
Outstanding secondary schools in Chattanooga, Tennessee-Georgia ★4109★

Fort Peck Community College
U.S. tribal colleges ★1445★
Lowest undergraduate tuition and fees at colleges and universities in Montana ★1527★

Fort Scott Community College
Lowest undergraduate tuition and fees at colleges and universities in Kansas ★1507★

Fort Valley State College
Historically black institutions with the highest number of National Achievement Scholars, 1998 ★8★
Colleges offering the Thurgood Marshall Scholarship Fund ★221★

Fort Valley State University
State appropriations for Georgia's institutions of higher education, 2000-01 ★1263★
Historically black colleges and universities awarding the most master's degrees to African Americans ★1670★
U.S. colleges and universities awarding the most education master's degrees to African Americans ★1769★
U.S. institutions awarding the most baccalaureate degrees to African Americans in agribusiness and production, 1998 ★1813★

Fort Wayne Community Schools
Top recruiters for education jobs for 2000-01 bachelor's degree recipients ★4377★
Top recruiters for education jobs for 2000-01 master's degree recipients ★4398★

Fort Worth
U.S. cities with the highest percentage of births to mothers with less than 12 years of education ★4432★

Fort Worth-Arlington, TX
Cities with the highest percentage of broadband use and interest ★2578★

Fort Worth Country Day
Outstanding secondary schools in Fort Worth-Arlington, Texas ★4137★

Fortis
Business Week's best companies in Belgium ★388★

Fortune
Most cited business serials in technical communication journals from 1988 to 1997 ★4417★

Fortune Brands
Fortune's highest ranked metal products companies, 2000 ★475★

Forty Acres and a Mule Filmworks
Most selective internships in the U.S., 2001 ★2610★

42 Up
Most notable videos for adults, 2001 ★2891★

Foss; Howard
Top pay and benefits for the chief executive and top paid employees at Whittier College ★3624★

Foster; Andrew
Top pay and benefits for the chief executive and top paid employees at George Washington University ★3304★

Foster; James
Top pay and benefits for the chief executive and top paid employees at Walsh University ★3602★

Foster Wheeler
Fortune's highest ranked engineering and construction companies, 2000 ★461★

Foucault; Michael
Most cited authors in the journal *Social Justice*, 1990 to 1995 ★1631★
Most cited scholars in critical criminology ★1640★
Most-cited scholars in critical criminology publications ★1641★
Most cited works in critical criminology ★1644★

Fouhy; Edward M.
Top pay and benefits for the chief executive and top paid employees at the University of Richmond ★3559★

Foundation Center's Guide to Grantseeking on the Web
Selected new editions and supplements reference books, 2000 ★372★

Fountain; Jane
Radcliffe Institute for Advanced Study fellowship recipients in the field of public policy, 2000-01 ★2622★

The Four Agreements
Longest-running trade paperback bestsellers, 2000 ★282★

4 Fantastic Novels
Smithsonian's best books for children ages 10 and up ★365★

Fowler; Jack
Top pay and benefits for the chief executive and top paid employees at Judson College in Alabama ★3356★

Fox Chapel Area High School
Outstanding secondary schools in Pittsburgh, Pennsylvania ★4204★

Fox; Geoffrey
Top pay and benefits for the chief executive and top paid employees at Syracuse University ★3516★

Fox Lane High School
Outstanding secondary schools in New York, New York ★4191★

Frakt; Phyllis M.
Top pay and benefits for the chief executive and top paid employees at Rider University ★3458★

Framingham State College
State appropriations for Massachusetts's institutions of higher education, 2000-01 ★1274★

France
Percentage of enrollment at private institutions of higher education, by country, 1998 ★858★
Percentage of enrollment at public institutions of higher education, by country, 1998 ★859★

Countries with the most computers, 2000 ★1603★
Countries of origin for non-U.S. citizens awarded doctorates at U.S. colleges and universities, 1999 ★1901★
Percentage of students enrolled in institutions of higher education that were not citizens of the country where they studied, 1998 ★2500★
Top countries of study for U.S. students studying abroad, 1998-99 ★2510★
Countries with the most Internet users ★2583★
European periodical prices by country, 2001 ★2921★
Institute for Scientific Information periodical prices by country, 2001 ★2922★
Countries spending the highest percentage of gross domestic product on education ★4060★

France Telecom
Business Week's best companies in France ★393★

Franchione; Dennis W.
Top pay and benefits for the chief executive and top paid employees at Texas Christian University ★3518★

Francilene, C.S.S.F.; Sister Mary
Top pay and benefits for the chief executive and top paid employees at Madonna University ★3386★

Francis; Gerald L.
Top pay and benefits for the chief executive and top paid employees at Elon College ★3285★

Francis; Kim
All-America girls' high school soccer team midfielders, 2001 ★177★

Francis Marion University
State appropriations for South Carolina's institutions of higher education, 2000-01 ★1293★
Average faculty salaries for institutions of higher education in South Carolina, 2000-01 ★3728★

Francis; Norman C.
Top pay and benefits for the chief executive and top paid employees at Xavier University of Louisiana ★3638★

Franciscan University of Steubenville
U.S. News & World Report's midwestern regional universities with students most in debt, 1999 ★1400★
Average faculty salaries for institutions of higher education in Ohio, 2000-01 ★3722★

Frank Consolidated Enterprises
Top women-owned companies ★4460★

Frank; E.R.
Booklist's best first novels for youths ★309★

Frank; Lawrence
Top pay and benefits for the chief executive and top paid employees at Saint Xavier University ★3487★

Frank O. Gehry: Outside In
Most notable books for middle readers, 2001 ★317★
Outstanding books for older readers, 2000 ★327★
Smithsonian's best books for children ages 10 and up ★365★

Frank Phillips College
Institutions censured by the American Association of University Professors, 2001 ★1067★

Frankfort Junior High School
Outstanding secondary schools in Chicago, Illinois ★4110★

Frankino; Steven P.
Top pay and benefits for the chief executive and top paid employees at Villanova University ★3595★

Franklin; Aretha
Most influential African American entertainers ★77★

Franklin Fine Arts
Chicago elementary magnet schools with the lowest acceptance rates, 2000-01 ★4003★

Franklin Institute of Boston
Highest undergraduate tuition and fees at public, 4-year or above colleges and universities ★1463★

Franklin Learning Center
Outstanding secondary schools in Philadelphia, Pennsylvania-New Jersey ★4202★

Franklin and Marshall College
Highest undergraduate tuition and fees at colleges and universities in Pennsylvania ★1549★
Private, 4-year undergraduate colleges and universities producing the most Ph.D.'s in the earth sciences, 1981-1990 ★2151★
Private, 4-year undergraduate colleges and universities producing the most Ph.D.'s in political science and international relations, 1981-1990 ★3045★
Private, 4-year undergraduate colleges and universities producing the most Ph.D.'s in psychology, 1920-1990 ★3066★
Private, 4-year undergraduate colleges and universities producing the most Ph.D.'s in psychology, 1981-1990 ★3067★
Average faculty salaries for institutions of higher education in Pennsylvania, 2000-01 ★3725★
Private, 4-year undergraduate colleges and universities producing the most Ph.D.'s in the sciences, 1920-1990 ★4294★
Private, 4-year undergraduate colleges and universities producing the most Ph.D.'s in the sciences, 1981-1990 ★4295★
Private, 4-year undergraduate colleges and universities producing the most Ph.D.'s in anthropology and sociology, 1920-1990 ★4344★
Private, 4-year undergraduate colleges and universities producing the most Ph.D.'s in anthropology and sociology, 1981-1990 ★4345★

Franklin Pierce College
Division II NCAA colleges with the 100% graduation rates for men's basketball players, 1993-94 ★943★
Division II NCAA colleges with the 100% graduation rates for women's basketball players, 1993-94 ★944★
Division II NCAA colleges with the highest graduation rates for all sports, 1993-94 ★945★
Highest undergraduate tuition and fees at colleges and universities in New Hampshire ★1531★

Franklin Pierce Law Center
Academics' choices for best intellectual property law programs, 2001 ★2630★
Average faculty salaries for institutions of higher education in New Hampshire, 2000-01 ★3716★

Franklin Resources
Fortune's highest ranked securities companies, 2000 ★494★

Franklin W. Olin College of Engineering
Largest gifts to higher education, 1967-2000 ★1247★
Largest private gifts to higher education, 1967-2000 ★1248★

Frantz; Eugene G.
Top pay and benefits for the chief executive and top paid employees at Lynchburg College ★3384★

Franz; Bro. Craig
Top pay and benefits for the chief executive and top paid employees at Saint Mary's College of California ★3480★

Franz; Laurence W.
Top pay and benefits for the chief executive and top paid employees at Canisius College ★3219★

Fraschilla; Fran
Top pay and benefits for the chief executive and top paid employees at St. John's University in New York ★3474★

Fraumeni; Joseph F.
Most-cited researchers in epidemiology, 1981-1998 ★2876★

Frazier; Michael V.
Top pay and benefits for the chief executive and top paid employees at Providence College ★3447★

Frechet; Jean M.J.
Winner of the American Chemical Society's Arthur C. Cope Awards, 2001 ★795★

Freddie Mac
Fortune's highest ranked mortgage finance companies, 2000 ★479★
Top nonbank financial companies in Standard & Poor's 500, 2001 ★550★

Freddy the Pilot
Most notable children's recordings, 2001 ★320★

Frederick; Charles
All-American boy's high school football receivers, 2000 ★185★

Frederick Douglass Academy
Outstanding urban public high schools in Metro New York ★4265★

Frederick Douglass Middle School
All-USA Teacher Teams, Second Team, 2000 ★4400★

Frederick High School
Outstanding secondary schools in Washington, District of Columbia-Maryland-Virginia-West Virginia ★4249★

Fredericton Social Library
North America's first ten public libraries ★2680★

Free a Man to Fight: Women Soldiers of WWII
Outstanding videos for library collections, 2000 ★2892★

Free Press
Book publishers with the most citations (Class 4) ★2565★

Freed-Hardeman University
Average faculty salaries for institutions of higher education in Tennessee, 2000-01 ★3730★

Freedman; Estelle B.
Most-cited scholars in women and crime publications ★1642★
Highly acknowledged individuals in the field of women's studies, 1975-94 ★4466★

Freedman; James O.
Top pay and benefits for the chief executive and top paid employees at Dartmouth College ★3263★

Freedom Like Sunlight: Praisesongs for Black Americans
Most notable books for older readers, 2001 ★318★

Freedom River
Most notable books for middle readers, 2001 ★317★

Freeland; Richard M.
Top pay and benefits for the chief executive and top paid employees at Northeastern University ★3422★

Freelen; Robert E.
Top pay and benefits for the chief executive and top paid employees at Dickinson College ★3268★

Freeman
Book publishers with the most citations (Class 5) ★2566★

Freeman; Brian
Top pay and benefits for the chief executive and top paid employees at Capital University ★3220★

Freeman High School
Outstanding secondary schools in Richmond-Petersburg, Virginia ★4210★

Freeman; Hunter
All-America boys' high school soccer team defenders, 2001 ★165★

Freeman; R.B.
U.S. academic economists by mean number of citations, 1971-92 ★2176★
U.S. academic economists by total citations, 1971-92 ★2177★

Freeport-McMoran Copper & Gold
Fortune's highest ranked mining and crude oil companies, 2000 ★477★
Top metals and mining companies in Standard & Poor's 500, 2001 ★549★

Freidberg; Susanne
Radcliffe Institute for Advanced Study fellowship recipient in the field of geography, 2000-01 ★2517★

Freight transportation arrangement
Employment growth percentages for selected industries, 1998-2000 ★2294★

Freitas; David
Top pay and benefits for the chief executive and top paid employees at National-Louis University in Illinois ★3414★

French
Gender breakdown of language and literature doctorate recipients, by subfield, 1999 ★1937★
Language and literature doctorates awarded at U.S. colleges and universities, by subfield, 1999 ★1949★
Languages of requested materials from OCLC ILL, 1999 ★2679★

French language
Number of Advanced Placement Exams taken by African Americans, by subject, 2000 ★30★
Number of Advanced Placement Exams taken by Asian Americans, by subject, 2000 ★31★
Number of Advanced Placement Exams taken by Hispanic Americans, by subject, 2000 ★32★

French literature
Number of Advanced Placement Exams taken by African Americans, by subject, 2000 ★30★
Number of Advanced Placement Exams taken by Asian Americans, by subject, 2000 ★31★
Number of Advanced Placement Exams taken by Hispanic Americans, by subject, 2000 ★32★

French; Peter B.
Top pay and benefits for the chief executive and top paid employees at Brandeis University ★3209★

French; Roderick
Top pay and benefits for the chief executive and top paid employees at American University ★3174★

Freshour; Brett
Top pay and benefits for the chief executive and top paid employees at Walsh University ★3602★

Fresno
U.S. cities with the highest percentage of births to mothers with less than 12 years of education ★4432★

Fretwell; Gary L.
Top pay and benefits for the chief executive and top paid employees at Millsaps College ★3403★

Frey; Robert L.
Top pay and benefits for the chief executive and top paid employees at University of Charleston ★3590★

Friberg; Stig
Top pay and benefits for the chief executive and top paid employees at Clarkson University ★3239★

Friedman; Milton
Most cited economists ★2185★

Friedman; Phillip
Top pay and benefits for the chief executive and top paid employees at Golden Gate University ★3310★

Friel; Brian
Top playwrights of the twentieth century ★4436★

A Friend of the Earth
Booklist's best fiction books for library collections, 2000 ★227★

Friendly; Fred
Best U.S. works of journalism in the 20th century ★2769★

Friends University
Average faculty salaries for institutions of higher education in Kansas, 2000-01 ★3703★

Frisch; Ivan
Top pay and benefits for the chief executive and top paid employees at Polytechnic University ★3443★

Frito-Lay
Top internships in the U.S. with the highest compensation, 2001 ★2611★

Fritsche Middle School
Outstanding secondary schools in Milwaukee-Waukesha, Wisconsin ★4180★

Fritschler; A. Lee
Presidents with the highest pay at Baccalaureate I colleges, 1998-99 ★3159★
Top pay and benefits for the chief executive and top paid employees at Dickinson College ★3268★

Fritz
Fortune's highest ranked mail, packaging, and freight delivery companies, 2000 ★473★

Fritze; Barbara
Top pay and benefits for the chief executive and top paid employees at Goucher College ★3314★

From Dawn to Decadence: 500 Years of Western Cultural Life, 1500 to the Present
Most notable nonfiction books, 2001 ★285★
Outstanding history books, 2000 ★289★
Outstanding works of nonfiction, 2001 ★294★

From Third World to First: The Singapore Story 1965-2000
Library Journal's most notable biography books, 2000 ★249★

Fromm; E.
Most cited authors in the journal *Crime, Law, and Social Change*, 1990 to 1995 ★1618★

Frontal Neuroendocrinology
Neurosciences journals with the greatest impact measure, 1994-98 ★2813★

Frontier Community College
Lowest undergraduate tuition and fees at colleges and universities in Illinois ★1501★

Frost; Douglas
Top pay and benefits for the chief executive and top paid employees at Bellevue University ★3197★

Frostburg State University
Average faculty salaries for institutions of higher education in Maryland, 2000-01 ★3707★

Fruitvale High School
Outstanding secondary schools in Bakersfield, California ★4091★

Fry; Hayden
Division I-A all-time coaching victories ★126★

Frye; Channing
All-America boys' high school basketball 4th team, 2001 ★164★

Frye; Randy
Top pay and benefits for the chief executive and top paid employees Saint Francis College in Pennsylvania ★3641★

Fucaloro; Anthony
Top pay and benefits for the chief executive and top paid employees at Claremont McKenna College ★3236★

Fugett Middle School
Outstanding secondary schools in Philadelphia, Pennsylvania-New Jersey ★4202★

Fuggetta; Alfonso
Top published scholars in the field of systems and software engineering ★2333★

Fujitsu
Business Week's best companies in Japan ★398★

Fuller; Richard M.
Top pay and benefits for the chief executive and top paid employees at Hamilton College ★3319★

Fuller Theological Seminary
Average faculty salaries for institutions of higher education in California, 2000-01 ★3692★

Fuller; Timothy
Top pay and benefits for the chief executive and top paid employees at Colorado College ★3249★

Fulton; Leroy M.
Top pay and benefits for the chief executive and top paid employees at Hope International University ★3340★

Fulton-Montgomery Community College
Average faculty salaries for institutions of higher education in New York, 2000-01 ★3719★

Functional analysis of emergent verbal classes
  Most cited sources in experimental analyses of human behavior between 1990 and 1999 ★3070★
Funk; Robert N.
  Top pay and benefits for the chief executive and top paid employees at St. Edward's University ★3471★
The Fur Trade in Canada
  Canada's best nonfiction selections of the 20th century ★234★
Furman University
  All-USA College Academic Third Team, 2001 ★4★
  U.S. colleges and universities with the most alumni in the LPGA ★148★
  U.S. colleges and universities where the general student body does not smoke marijuana ★1006★
  U.S. colleges and universities with a generally conservative student body ★1014★
  Largest gifts to higher education, 1967-2000 ★1247★
  Largest private gifts to higher education, 1967-2000 ★1248★
  U.S. News & World Report's national liberal arts colleges with the highest percentage of full-time faculty, 2000-01 ★1333★
  U.S. News & World Report's national liberal arts colleges with students least in debt, 1999 ★1385★
  Highest undergraduate tuition and fees at colleges and universities in South Carolina ★1554★
  Private, 4-year undergraduate colleges and universities producing the most Ph.D.'s in the computer sciences, 1920-1990 ★1595★
  Average faculty salaries for institutions of higher education in South Carolina, 2000-01 ★3728★
Furniture Brands International
  Fortune's highest ranked furniture companies, 2000 ★467★
Furrow; Barry R.
  Top pay and benefits for the chief executive and top paid employees at Widener University ★3626★
Fusion energy sciences
  Energy Department research funding, 2001 ★3110★
Fuster; Valentin
  Authors with the greatest impact measure in cardiovascular research, 1993-98 ★2868★
  Most-cited researchers in cardiology, 1981-1998 ★2874★
Futrell; Charles M.
  Authors with the most articles published in the *Journal of Business Research*, 1985 to 1999 ★687★
  Highest impact authors in the *Journal of Business Research*, by number of citations in 12 journals, 1985-1999 ★693★
Future of Children
  Health policy and services journals by citation impact, 1995-99 ★2538★
Futurestep
  Top E-recruiting providers, 2000 ★2604★
Fyfe; J.J.
  Most cited authors in the journal *Criminal Justice Review*, 1990 to 1995 ★1620★

G

G. Ray Badley High School
  All-USA Teacher Teams, Second Team, 2000 ★4400★
Gabelnick; Faith
  Top pay and benefits for the chief executive and top paid employees at Pacific University in Oregon ★3437★
Gaede; Stan
  Top pay and benefits for the chief executive and top paid employees at Westmont College ★3619★
Gaffney, F.S.C.; Bro. James
  Top pay and benefits for the chief executive and top paid employees at Lewis University ★3372★
Gagarin; Alexandra
  All-America girls' high school soccer team goalkeepers, 2001 ★176★
Gailey; William E.
  Top pay and benefits for the chief executive and top paid employees at Agnes Scott College ★3165★
Gainesville College
  Lowest undergraduate tuition and fees at colleges and universities in Georgia ★1497★
Gainesville, FL
  U.S. cities with the most single people ★3089★
Gainey; Kathryn
  Golden Key Scholar Award winners, 2000 ★1316★
Galbraith; John K.
  Most cited economists ★2185★
Gale; Robert P.
  Most-cited researchers in oncology, 1981-1998 ★2877★
Galecke; Robert M.
  Top pay and benefits for the chief executive and top paid employees at the University of Dallas ★3538★
Galileo Scholastic
  Chicago elementary magnet schools with the highest acceptance rates, 2000-01 ★4002★
Galileo and the Stargazers
  Outstanding audio selections for young listeners, 2000 ★325★
Gall; Albert C.
  Top pay and benefits for the chief executive and top paid employees at Columbia College in Illinois ★3250★
Gallagher; Beverly
  All-USA Teacher Teams, First Team, 2000 ★4399★
Gallagher; James P.
  Top pay and benefits for the chief executive and top paid employees at Philadelphia University ★3440★
Gallagher; John A.
  Top pay and benefits for the chief executive and top paid employees at Rockford College in Illinois ★3463★
Gallagher, R.S.H.M.; Sister Eymard
  Top pay and benefits for the chief executive and top paid employees at Marymount University ★3395★
Gallaudet University
  2002 budget request for aid to individual institutions ★1235★
  U.S. News & World Report's northern regional universities with the best academic reputation scores, 2000-01 ★1415★
  U.S. News & World Report's northern regional universities with the best student/faculty ratios, 2000-01 ★1416★
  U.S. News & World Report's northern regional universities with the highest percentage of full-time faculty, 2000-01 ★1422★
  Undergraduate tuition and fees at colleges and universities in the District of Columbia ★1493★
  Average faculty salaries for institutions of higher education in the District of Columbia, 2000-01 ★3732★
Gallman; Robert E.
  Top pay and benefits for the chief executive and top paid employees at the University of Evansville ★3543★
Gallo; Robert C.
  Most-cited researchers in clinical medicine, 1981-1998 ★2875★
Gallopade International
  Small publishers with the highest sales growth between 1997 and 1999 ★3073★
Galovich; Steven P.
  Top pay and benefits for the chief executive and top paid employees at Lake Forest College ★3363★
Gamber; E.
  Top assistant professor economists at elite liberal arts colleges, 1975-94 ★2173★
Gammon; W.R.
  Most cited first authors in dermatology journals, 1981 to 1996 ★1871★
Ganev; Stoyan
  Top pay and benefits for the chief executive and top paid employees at University of Bridgeport ★3588★
Gannett
  Fortune's highest ranked publishing companies, 2000 ★489★
  Top publishing and broadcasting companies in Standard & Poor's 500, 2001 ★553★
Gannett Fleming, Inc.
  Top recruiters for civil engineering jobs for 2000-01 bachelor's degree recipients ★2346★
  Top recruiters for environmental engineering jobs for 2000-01 bachelor's degree recipients ★2357★
  Top recruiters for civil engineering jobs for 2000-01 master's degree recipients ★2397★
  Top recruiters for environmental engineering jobs for 2000-01 master's degree recipients ★2409★
Gannon University
  Average faculty salaries for institutions of higher education in Pennsylvania, 2000-01 ★3725★
Gantos; Jack
  Outstanding children's fiction books, 2000 ★329★
Gap
  Fortune's highest ranked specialty retailers, 2000 ★497★
  Top discount and fashion retailing companies in Standard & Poor's 500, 2001 ★538★
  Top public companies with the highest percentage of women employees, 2000 ★4459★
GAP Inc.
  Top recruiters for liberal arts jobs for 2000-01 bachelor's degree recipients ★2675★
Gapp; Jerry B.
  Top pay and benefits for the chief executive and top paid employees at Elmira College ★3284★

"Gapped BLAST and Psi-BLAST: A new generation of protein database search programs"
Institute for Scientific Information's most cited papers, 1990-98 ★4282★

GAR Memorial Library
Highest Hennen's American Public Library Ratings for libraries serving a population of 2,500 to 4,999 ★2693★

Garafola; David
Top pay and benefits for the chief executive and top paid employees at Webster University ★3608★

Garbage collector
Jobs with the highest unemployment ★2256★
Jobs with the worst physical demands scores ★2263★
Jobs with the worst security scores ★2264★
Least desirable jobs ★2266★

Garbs; Cindy
Top pay and benefits for the chief executive and top paid employees at Houston Baptist University ★3342★

Garden City Community College
Lowest undergraduate tuition and fees at colleges and universities in Kansas ★1507★

Garden Escape
Library Journal's notable new magazines, 1999 ★2923★

A Gardener's Alphabet
Smithsonian's best books for children ages 1 to 6 ★363★

Gardner-Webb University
U.S. News & World Report's southern regional universities with students least in debt, 1999 ★1431★
Average faculty salaries for institutions of higher education in North Carolina, 2000-01 ★3720★

Garell; Dale Clinton
Top pay and benefits for the chief executive and top paid employees at the University of Southern California ★3568★

Garfield; Alan
Top pay and benefits for the chief executive and top paid employees at Marycrest International University ★3393★

Garfield; E.
Authors that most frequently cite *Libri* publications from 1972 to 1999 ★2723★

Garland; Anita
Top pay and benefits for the chief executive and top paid employees at Hampden-Sydney College ★3321★

Garland County Community College
Institutions censured by the American Association of University Professors, 2001 ★1067★
Lowest undergraduate tuition and fees at colleges and universities in Arkansas ★1485★

Garland High School
Outstanding suburban public high schools in Metro Dallas-Ft. Worth ★4257★

Garlett; Fred
Top pay and benefits for the chief executive and top paid employees at Azusa Pacific University ★3187★

Garner Jr.; Leslie H.
Top pay and benefits for the chief executive and top paid employees at Cornell College in Iowa ★3256★

Garofalo; James
Top pay and benefits for the chief executive and top paid employees at Aquinas College in Michigan ★3179★

Garrett; Dan
Top pay and benefits for the chief executive and top paid employees at Abilene Christian University ★3163★

Garrison; R. Bruce
Top pay and benefits for the chief executive and top paid employees at Houston Baptist University ★3342★

Garrow; T.S.
Top pay and benefits for the chief executive and top paid employees at Illinois Institute of Technology ★3346★

Garton; Christine
All-USA College Academic First Team, 2001 ★2★

Garven; James R.
Individual authors with the most published pages in *The Journal of Risk and Insurance*, 1987-1996 ★680★

Gas Natural SDG
Business Week's best companies in Spain ★403★

Gaskin III; Joseph
All-USA Teacher Teams, First Team, 2000 ★4399★

Gass; Wayne
Top pay and benefits for the chief executive and top paid employees at Mount Holyoke College ★3409★

Gaston College
Average faculty salaries for institutions of higher education without academic ranks in North Carolina, 2000-01 ★3761★

Gastroenterology and hepatology
Clinical medicine subfields with the highest impact measure, 1981-1997 ★2873★

Gates Jr.; Henry Louis
Most influential African Americans in education ★2216★

Gates Millennium Scholars program
Largest gifts to higher education, 1967-2000 ★1247★

Gateway
Business Week's best performing companies with the lowest 1-year shareholder returns ★422★
Fortune's highest ranked computers and office equipment companies, 2000 ★456★

Gateway Community College
Lowest undergraduate tuition and fees at colleges and universities in Arizona ★1483★
Lowest undergraduate tuition and fees at colleges and universities in Connecticut ★1491★

Gateway High School
Outstanding secondary schools in Pittsburgh, Pennsylvania ★4204★

Gateway Technical College
Lowest undergraduate tuition and fees at colleges and universities in Wisconsin ★1571★

Gathering Blue
Outstanding books for middle readers, 2000 ★326★

Gatley; Ian
Top pay and benefits for the chief executive and top paid employees at Rochester Institute of Technology ★3461★

Gaudiani; Claire
Presidents with the highest pay at Baccalaureate I colleges, 1998-99 ★3159★
Top pay and benefits for the chief executive and top paid employees at Connecticut College ★3254★

Gault; Paul H.
Top pay and benefits for the chief executive and top paid employees at Park University ★3438★

Gauly; Stephen K.
Top pay and benefits for the chief executive and top paid employees at DePauw University ★3267★

Gay Histories and Cultures: An Encyclopedia
Outstanding reference sources, 2000 ★370★

Gazprom
Business Week's top emerging-market companies worldwide ★434★

Gazzerro Jr.; Paul
Top pay and benefits for the chief executive and top paid employees at Albright College ★3168★

GEAR UP
Proposed fiscal 2002 appropriations for aid to the disadvantaged ★1879★
Fiscal 2002 requested budget as compared with Fiscal 2001 budget for the Education Department ★2231★

Gearhart; William H.
Top pay and benefits for the chief executive and top paid employees at St. Andrews Presbyterian College ★3469★

Gedeon; Donald S.
Top pay and benefits for the chief executive and top paid employees at Hawaii Pacific University ★3330★

Gee; E. Gordon
Top pay and benefits for the chief executive and top paid employees at Brown University ★3211★

Gee; Jayson
Top pay and benefits for the chief executive and top paid employees at University of Charleston ★3590★

Geeks: How Two Lost Boys Rode the Internet out of Idaho
Most notable nonfiction books for young adults, 2001 ★324★
Outstanding nonfiction books for young adults, 2000 ★334★

Geil; Peter Gus
Top pay and benefits for the chief executive and top paid employees at Wittenberg University ★3633★

Gelbart; William M.
American Chemical Society 2001 award winners (Group 2) ★752★

Geller; W.A.
Most cited authors in the journal *Criminal Justice Review*, 1990 to 1995 ★1620★

Gelles; R.J.
Most cited authors in the journal *Canadian Journal of Criminology*, 1990 to 1995 ★1615★
Most cited authors in the journal *Violence and Victims*, 1990 to 1995 ★1632★

Gemini: The Eighth Book of the House of Niccolo
Booklist's most recommended historical novels, 2001 ★230★

Genardi; Dick
Top pay and benefits for the chief executive and top paid employees at Union Institute ★3586★

GenCorp
  Fortune's highest ranked rubber and plastic products companies, 2000 ★492★
Gendreau; P.
  Most cited authors in the journal *Federal Probation*, 1990 to 1995 ★1623★
Genentech, Inc.
  Top recruiters for biology/biological science jobs for 2000-01 bachelor's degree recipients ★198★
General Cable
  Fortune's highest ranked metal products companies, 2000 ★475★
General Dynamics
  Fortune's highest ranked aerospace companies, 2000 ★446★
  Top aerospace and defense companies in Standard & Poor's 500, 2001 ★529★
General Dynamics Land Systems
  Top recruiters for supplier chain management jobs for 2000-01 bachelor's degree recipients ★557★
  Top recruiters for computer engineering jobs for 2000-01 bachelor's degree recipients ★2352★
General Electric
  Business Week's best companies in terms of profits ★406★
  Business Week's best companies in terms of sales ★408★
  Business Week's best companies in the United States ★411★
  Business Week's top companies worldwide ★433★
  Fortune's highest ranked electronics and electrical equipment companies, 2000 ★460★
  Top conglomerates in Standard & Poor's 500, 2001 ★535★
General and internal medicine
  Clinical medicine subfields with the highest impact measure, 1981-1997 ★2873★
General management
  Overall median salary for full-time chemists with a bachelor's degree, by work function, 2000 ★790★
  Overall median salary for full-time chemists with a doctoral degree, by work function, 2000 ★803★
  Overall median salary for full-time chemists with a master's degree, by work function, 2000 ★804★
General managers and top executives
  Occupations with the largest projected employment growth, 1998-2008 ★2312★
  Projected employment growth for selected occupations that require a bachelor's degree or more, 1998-2008 ★2317★
General Mills
  Business Week's best companies in terms of return on equity ★407★
  Fortune's highest ranked consumer food products companies, 2000 ★458★
  Top food companies in Standard & Poor's 500, 2001 ★540★
  Top internships in the U.S. with the highest compensation, 2001 ★2611★
General Motors
  Top recruiters for art jobs for 2000-01 bachelor's degree recipients ★80★
  Business Week's best companies in terms of sales ★408★
  Fortune's highest ranked motor vehicles companies, 2000 ★481★
  Top automotive companies in Standard & Poor's 500, 2001 ★530★
  Top recruiters for business administration jobs for 2000-01 bachelor's degree recipients ★554★
  Top recruiters for business administration jobs for 2000-01 master's degree recipients ★652★
  Top recruiters for accounting jobs for 2000-01 master's degree recipients ★661★
  Top recruiters for electrical/electronic engineering jobs for 2000-01 bachelor's degree recipients ★2354★
  Top recruiters for environmental engineering jobs for 2000-01 bachelor's degree recipients ★2357★
  Top recruiters for electrical/electronic engineering jobs for 2000-01 master's degree recipients ★2406★
  Top recruiters for mechanical engineering jobs for 2000-01 master's degree recipients ★2424★
  Top recruiters for metallurgical/mining engineering jobs for 2000-01 bachelor's degree recipients ★2434★
  Top recruiters for mechanical engineering jobs for 2000-01 bachelor's degree recipients ★2437★
  Corporations making the most contributions to African American communities, 1995 ★2941★
  Best companies for working mothers in offering leave for new parents ★4449★
General science
  Average costs for Academic Search titles by subject, 2001 ★2918★
  Periodical prices by LC subject, 2001 ★2925★
  Periodical prices by scientific discipline, 2001 ★2926★
General Wayne Middle School
  Outstanding secondary schools in Philadelphia, Pennsylvania-New Jersey ★4202★
General works
  Average costs for Academic Search titles by subject, 2001 ★2918★
  Periodical prices by LC subject, 2001 ★2925★
Genes & Development
  Molecular biology and genetics journals with the highest impact, 1992-96 ★204★
Genesee Community College
  Average faculty salaries for institutions of higher education in New York, 2000-01 ★3719★
Genesis School
  Outstanding secondary schools in Kansas City, Missouri-Kansas ★4158★
Genetics
  Average salaries for assistant professors at private institutions in preclinical department of medical schools, 2000-01 ★3785★
  Average salaries for assistant professors at public and private institutions in preclinical department of medical schools, 2000-01 ★3786★
  Average salaries for assistant professors at public institutions in preclinical department of medical schools, 2000-01 ★3787★
  Average salaries for associate professors at private institutions in preclinical department of medical schools, 2000-01 ★3800★
  Average salaries for associate professors at public and private institutions in preclinical department of medical schools, 2000-01 ★3801★
  Average salaries for associate professors at public institutions in preclinical department of medical schools, 2000-01 ★3802★
  Average salaries for full-time instructors at private institutions in preclinical department of medical schools, 2000-01 ★3854★
  Average salaries for full-time instructors at public and private institutions in preclinical department of medical schools, 2000-01 ★3855★
  Average salaries for full-time instructors at public institutions in preclinical department of medical schools, 2000-01 ★3856★
  Average salaries for professors at private institutions in preclinical department of medical schools, 2000-01 ★3932★
  Average salaries for professors at public and private institutions in preclinical department of medical schools, 2000-01 ★3933★
  Average salaries for professors at public institutions in preclinical department of medical schools, 2000-01 ★3934★
Geneva College
  Average faculty salaries for institutions of higher education in Pennsylvania, 2000-01 ★3725★
Genitourinary Medicine
  Urology and nephrology journals with the greatest impact measure, 1994-98 ★2817★
The Genius of Leonardo
  Booklist's best art books for young people ★308★
Genome: The Autobiography of a Species in 23 Chapters
  Library Journal's most notable genetics books, 2000 ★261★
  Most notable nonfiction books, 2001 ★285★
  Outstanding science books, 2000 ★291★
  Outstanding works of nonfiction, 2001 ★294★
  Booklist's best science and technology books ★366★
Genre fiction
  Subject areas with the highest library expenditures/circulation ★306★
Gensler
  Most selective internships in the U.S., 2001 ★2610★
Gent; Chris
  European business moguls considered the best empire builders ★441★
Gentzler; Randall D.
  Top pay and benefits for the chief executive and top paid employees at Philadelphia University ★3440★
Geochemistry
  Earth, atmosphere, and marine science doctorates awarded at U.S. colleges and universities, by subfield, 1999 ★1909★
  Gender breakdown of earth, atmosphere, and marine science doctorate recipients, by subfield, 1999 ★1932★
Geoderma
  Soil science journals by citation impact, 1981-99 ★188★
  Soil science journals by citation impact, 1995-99 ★189★
  Soil science journals by citation impact, 1999 ★190★
Geography
  Gender breakdown of social sciences doctorate recipients, by subfield, 1999 ★1942★
  Social sciences doctorates awarded at U.S. colleges and universities, by subfield, 1999 ★2044★

Average costs for Academic Search titles by subject, 2001 ★2918★
Periodical prices by LC subject, 2001 ★2925★
Periodical prices by scientific discipline, 2001 ★2926★

Geological and related science, general
Earth, atmosphere, and marine science doctorates awarded at U.S. colleges and universities, by subfield, 1999 ★1909★
Gender breakdown of earth, atmosphere, and marine science doctorate recipients, by subfield, 1999 ★1932★

Geologist
Jobs with the lowest unemployment ★2258★
Most desirable jobs in math/science ★2274★

Geology
Earth, atmosphere, and marine science doctorates awarded at U.S. colleges and universities, by subfield, 1999 ★1909★
Gender breakdown of earth, atmosphere, and marine science doctorate recipients, by subfield, 1999 ★1932★
Geology journals with the greatest impact measure, 1981-98 ★2525★
Geology journals with the greatest impact measure, 1994-98 ★2526★
Periodical prices by LC subject, 2001 ★2925★
Periodical prices by scientific discipline, 2001 ★2926★

Geometry
Gender breakdown of mathematics doctorate recipients, by subfield, 1999 ★1938★
Mathematics doctorates awarded at U.S. colleges and universities, by subfield, 1999 ★1951★

Geomorphology and glacial geology
Earth, atmosphere, and marine science doctorates awarded at U.S. colleges and universities, by subfield, 1999 ★1909★
Gender breakdown of earth, atmosphere, and marine science doctorate recipients, by subfield, 1999 ★1932★

Geophysics and seismology
Earth, atmosphere, and marine science doctorates awarded at U.S. colleges and universities, by subfield, 1999 ★1909★
Gender breakdown of earth, atmosphere, and marine science doctorate recipients, by subfield, 1999 ★1932★

George C. Wallace State Community College
Lowest undergraduate tuition and fees at colleges and universities in Alabama ★1480★

George; Carol
Top pay and benefits for the chief executive and top paid employees at Hobart and William Smith Colleges ★3334★

George F. Johnson Memorial Library
Highest Hennen's American Public Library Ratings for libraries serving a population of 10,000 to 24,999 ★2695★

George Fox University
U.S. News & World Report's best undergraduate fees among western regional liberal arts colleges by discount tuition, 2000 ★1384★
Academic reputation scores for *U.S. News & World Report*'s top western regional liberal arts colleges, 2000-01 ★1387★
Acceptance rates for *U.S. News & World Report*'s top western regional liberal arts colleges, 2000-01 ★1388★
Alumni giving rates at *U.S. News & World Report*'s top western regional liberal arts colleges, 2000-01 ★1389★

Average freshmen retention rates for *U.S. News & World Report*'s top western regional liberal arts colleges, 2000-01 ★1390★
Average graduation rates for *U.S. News & World Report*'s top western regional liberal arts colleges, 2000-01 ★1391★
Percentage of freshmen in the top 25% of their high school class at *U.S. News & World Report*'s top western regional liberal arts colleges, 2000-01 ★1392★
Percentage of full-time faculty at *U.S. News & World Report*'s top western regional liberal arts colleges, 2000-01 ★1393★
Proportion of classes having 20 students or less at *U.S. News & World Report*'s top western regional liberal arts colleges, 2000-01 ★1394★
Student/faculty ratios at *U.S. News & World Report*'s top western regional liberal arts colleges, 2000-01 ★1395★
U.S. News & World Report's top western regional liberal arts colleges, 2000-01 ★1396★
Highest undergraduate tuition and fees at colleges and universities in Oregon ★1547★
Average faculty salaries for institutions of higher education in Oregon, 2000-01 ★3724★

George; James P.
Top pay and benefits for the chief executive and top paid employees at Texas Wesleyan University ★3519★

George Lucas in Love
Most notable DVDs and videos for young adults, 2001 ★2890★

George and Martha
Most notable children's videos, 2001 ★2889★

George Mason Middle School
Outstanding secondary schools in Washington, District of Columbia-Maryland-Virginia-West Virginia ★4249★

George Mason University
Radcliffe Institute for Advanced Study fellowship recipients in the field of anthropology, 2000-01 ★60★
U.S. colleges and universities where students study the least ★1002★
State appropriations for Virginia's institutions of higher education, 2000-01 ★1299★
Total baccalaureate computer and information science degrees awarded to Asian Americans from U.S. colleges and universities, 1997-98 ★1692★
Total baccalaureate English language, literature, and letters degrees awarded to Asian Americans from U.S. colleges and universities, 1997-98 ★1717★
U.S. colleges and universities awarding the most computer and information sciences master's degrees to Asian Americans ★1767★
U.S. colleges and universities awarding the most computer and information sciences master's degrees to Hispanic Americans ★1768★
U.S. colleges and universities awarding the most education master's degrees to Asian Americans ★1770★
U.S. colleges and universities awarding the most social sciences and history master's degrees to Asian Americans ★1802★
U.S. colleges and universities awarding the most social sciences and history master's degrees to Hispanic Americans ★1803★
U.S. doctoral institutions with the largest number of students studying abroad, 1998-99 ★2512★
Average faculty salaries for institutions of higher education in Virginia, 2000-01 ★3735★

George; Neil J.
Top pay and benefits for the chief executive and top paid employees at Webster University ★3608★

George Washington Carver Middle School
Outstanding secondary schools in Miami, Florida ★4178★

George Washington Elementary School
Chicago neighborhood schools with the highest ISAT scores in reading and math ★4004★

George Washington University
U.S. business schools with the slowest payback on MBA investments ★655★
Undergraduate tuition and fees at colleges and universities in the District of Columbia ★1493★
U.S. colleges and universities awarding the most biological and life sciences master's degrees to Asian Americans ★1757★
U.S. colleges and universities awarding the most computer and information sciences master's degrees to African Americans ★1766★
U.S. colleges and universities awarding the most health professions and related sciences master's degrees to African Americans ★1777★
U.S. colleges and universities awarding the most health professions and related sciences master's degrees to Asian Americans ★1778★
U.S. colleges and universities awarding the most law and legal studies master's degrees to African Americans ★1781★
U.S. colleges and universities awarding the most law and legal studies master's degrees to Asian Americans ★1782★
U.S. colleges and universities awarding the most master's degrees to Asian Americans ★1786★
U.S. colleges and universities awarding the most master's degrees to minorities ★1788★
U.S. colleges and universities awarding the most physical sciences master's degrees to African Americans ★1793★
U.S. colleges and universities awarding the most physical sciences master's degrees to Asian Americans ★1794★
U.S. colleges and universities awarding the most physical sciences master's degrees to Hispanic Americans ★1795★
U.S. colleges and universities awarding the most social sciences and history master's degrees to Asian Americans ★1802★
U.S. colleges and universities awarding the most social sciences and history master's degrees to Hispanic Americans ★1803★
Traditionally white institutions awarding the most first professional degrees to African Americans ★1842★
U.S. colleges and universities awarding the most first professional degrees to African Americans ★1843★
U.S. colleges and universities awarding the most first professional degrees to Hispanic Americans ★1845★
U.S. colleges and universities awarding the most law and legal studies first professional degrees to African Americans ★1852★
U.S. colleges and universities awarding the most law and legal studies first professional degrees to Asian Americans ★1853★
U.S. colleges and universities awarding the most law and legal studies first professional degrees to Hispanic Americans ★1854★

U.S. colleges and universities awarding the most doctorate degrees to African Americans ★2095★

U.S. colleges and universities awarding the most doctorate degrees to Native Americans ★2099★

U.S. colleges and universities awarding the most education doctorate degrees to African Americans ★2108★

Academics' choices for best environmental law programs, 2001 ★2628★

Academics' choices for best intellectual property law programs, 2001 ★2630★

Academics' choices for best international law programs, 2001 ★2631★

Law schools with the best administrative law faculty, 1999-2000 ★2638★

Law schools with the best constitutional law (freedom of religion) faculty, 1999-2000 ★2643★

Presidents with the highest pay at Research I and II universities, 1998-99 ★3162★

Average faculty salaries for institutions of higher education in the District of Columbia, 2000-01 ★3732★

George Washington's Mother
Most notable children's recordings, 2001 ★320★

George; William
Highest impact authors in the *Journal of Business Research*, by adjusted number of citations in 12 journals, 1985-1999 ★692★

Georgetown College
Highest undergraduate tuition and fees at colleges and universities in Kentucky ★1508★

Average faculty salaries for institutions of higher education in Kentucky, 2000-01 ★3704★

Georgetown High School
Outstanding secondary schools in Austin-San Marcos, Texas ★4090★

Georgetown University
U.S. catholic universities with the highest enrollment, 1999 ★864★

Division I NCAA colleges with the highest graduation rates for female athletes, 1990-91 to 1993-94 ★931★

Division I NCAA colleges with the highest graduation rates for male athletes, 1990-91 to 1993-94 ★934★

U.S. colleges and universities that devote the most course time to discussion ★990★

U.S. colleges and universities with a favorable surrounding town or city ★1013★

U.S. News & World Report's national universities with the best freshmen retention rates, 2000-01 ★1128★

U.S. News & World Report's national universities with the lowest acceptance rates, 2000-01 ★1140★

Undergraduate tuition and fees at colleges and universities in the District of Columbia ★1493★

Total ethnic/cultural studies master's degrees awarded to African Americans from U.S. colleges and universities, 1997-98 ★1747★

U.S. colleges and universities awarding the most biological and life sciences master's degrees to Asian Americans ★1757★

U.S. colleges and universities awarding the most law and legal studies master's degrees to African Americans ★1781★

U.S. colleges and universities awarding the most law and legal studies master's degrees to Asian Americans ★1782★

U.S. colleges and universities awarding the most law and legal studies master's degrees to Hispanic Americans ★1783★

U.S. colleges and universities awarding the most law and legal studies master's degrees to Native Americans ★1784★

U.S. colleges and universities awarding the most social sciences and history master's degrees to Hispanic Americans ★1803★

Traditionally white institutions awarding the most first professional degrees to African Americans ★1842★

U.S. colleges and universities awarding the most first professional degrees to African Americans ★1843★

U.S. colleges and universities awarding the most first professional degrees to Hispanic Americans ★1845★

U.S. colleges and universities awarding the most first professional degrees to Native Americans ★1846★

U.S. colleges and universities awarding the most health professions and related sciences first professional degrees to African Americans ★1847★

U.S. colleges and universities awarding the most law and legal studies first professional degrees to African Americans ★1852★

U.S. colleges and universities awarding the most law and legal studies first professional degrees to Asian Americans ★1853★

U.S. colleges and universities awarding the most law and legal studies first professional degrees to Hispanic Americans ★1854★

U.S. colleges and universities awarding the most law and legal studies first professional degrees to Native Americans ★1855★

U.S. universities publishing the most papers in the field of law, 1994-98 ★2623★

Academics' choices for best clinical law programs, 2001 ★2626★

Academics' choices for best dispute resolution programs, 2001 ★2627★

Academics' choices for best environmental law programs, 2001 ★2628★

Academics' choices for best international law programs, 2001 ★2631★

Academics' choices for best tax law programs, 2001 ★2632★

Academics' choices for best trial advocacy programs, 2001 ★2633★

Law schools with the best constitutional law (general) faculty, 1999-2000 ★2645★

Law schools with the best critical race theory faculty, 1999-2000 ★2649★

Law schools with the best environmental law faculty, 1999-2000 ★2650★

Law schools with the best feminist legal theory faculty, 1999-2000 ★2651★

Law schools with the best health law (excluding medical ethics) faculty, 1999-2000 ★2652★

Law schools with the best international law faculty, 1999-2000 ★2654★

Law schools with the best legal ethics, professional responsibility, and legal profession faculty, 1999-2000 ★2660★

Law schools with the highest quality, 1999-2000 ★2666★

Top law school student bodies, 1999-2000 ★2673★

Law library web sites, by visibility ★2687★

Institutions in the Worker Rights Consortium ★2913★

Average faculty salaries for institutions of higher education in the District of Columbia, 2000-01 ★3732★

Georgetown University, McDonough School of Business
Business Week's top business schools with the highest percentage of international students, 2000 ★612★

Business Week's top business schools with the highest percentage of women enrollees, 2000 ★614★

Business Week's top business schools with the lowest percentage of minority enrollment, 2000 ★616★

Business Week's top business schools with the worst placement offices, 2000 ★620★

Georgia
Mean composite ACT scores by state, 2000 ★895★

Mean math SAT scores by state, 2000 ★900★

Mean verbal SAT scores by state, 2000 ★903★

Total doctorate recipients by state, 1999 ★2054★

State grades for affordability of higher education for minority students, 2000 ★2883★

State grades for benefits state receives for educating its minority students, 2000 ★2884★

State grades for completion of higher education by minority students, 2000 ★2885★

State grades for participation of minority students in higher education, 2000 ★2886★

State grades for preparing minority students for higher education, 2000 ★2887★

States expelling the highest ratio of students for violating the Gun-Free Schools Act, 1998-99 ★3993★

States expelling the most students for violating the Gun-Free Schools Act, 1998-99 ★3994★

States with the highest average enrollment in public elementary schools ★4032★

States with the highest average enrollment in public secondary schools ★4033★

States with the highest K-12 public school enrollment ★4034★

States with the highest projected K-12 public school enrollment for 2010 ★4035★

States with the highest funding needs for school-technology modernization ★4041★

States with the lowest percentage of high school freshmen enrolling in college within four years ★4267★

States with the highest state support for non need-based financial aid for students, 1999-2000 ★4368★

U.S. states with the highest percentage of births to teenagers who were already mothers ★4433★

Georgia College and State University
State appropriations for Georgia's institutions of higher education, 2000-01 ★1263★

Average faculty salaries for institutions of higher education in Georgia, 2000-01 ★3697★

Georgia Institute of Technology
Institutions, by adjusted authorship, with the most published authors in the *Journal of Business Research*, 1985 to 1999 ★694★

Division I NCAA colleges with that graduated none of their African American male basketball players, 1990-91 to 1993-94 ★930★

U.S. colleges and universities with an unfavorable surrounding town or city ★1023★

U.S. colleges and universities with poor instructors ★1027★

GEORGIA

U.S. News & World Report's best public national universities, 2000-01 ★1123★

U.S. News & World Report's national universities with the highest acceptance rates, 2000-01 ★1131★

U.S. News & World Report's national universities with the highest percentage of full-time faculty, 2000-01 ★1136★

U.S. News & World Report's national universities with the lowest graduation rates, 1999 ★1141★

State appropriations for Georgia's institutions of higher education, 2000-01 ★1263★

Fiske Guide's best buys for public colleges and universities, 2001 ★1460★

Total baccalaureate engineering degrees awarded to minorities from U.S. colleges and universities, 1997-98 ★1715★

U.S. colleges and universities awarding the most physical sciences master's degrees to African Americans ★1793★

U.S. colleges and universities awarding the most doctorates in engineering, 1999 ★2102★

U.S. universities with the greatest impact in geosciences, 1994-98 ★2149★

U.S. universities with the greatest impact in geosciences, 1993-97 ★2155★

U.S. universities with the highest concentration of papers published in the field of chemical engineering, 1994-98 ★2345★

U.S. universities with the highest concentration of civil engineering papers published, 1994-98 ★2351★

Acceptance rates for *U.S. News & World Report*'s top 10 graduate engineering schools, 2001 ★2358★

Average analytic GRE scores for *U.S. News & World Report*'s top 10 graduate engineering schools, 2001 ★2359★

Average quantitative GRE scores for *U.S. News & World Report*'s top 10 graduate engineering schools, 2001 ★2360★

Doctoral student-faculty ratios at *U.S. News & World Report*'s top 10 graduate engineering schools, 2001 ★2361★

Faculty membership in National Academy of Engineering at *U.S. News & World Report*'s top 10 graduate engineering schools, 2001 ★2362★

Ph.D.s granted at *U.S. News & World Report*'s top 10 graduate engineering schools, 2001 ★2363★

Research expenditures per faculty member at *U.S. News & World Report*'s top 10 graduate engineering schools, 2001 ★2364★

Research funding allocated to *U.S. News & World Report*'s top 10 graduate engineering schools, 2001 ★2365★

Top graduate engineering schools, 2001 ★2366★

Top graduate engineering schools by reputation, as determined by academic personnel, 2001 ★2367★

Top graduate engineering schools by reputation, as determined by engineers and recruiters, 2001 ★2368★

U.S. News & World Report's graduate engineering programs with the highest academic reputation scores, 2000-01 ★2372★

Academics' choices for best graduate aerospace/aeronautical/astronautical engineering programs, 2001 ★2374★

Most effective aerospace engineering research-doctorate programs as evaluated by the National Research Council ★2375★

Top aerospace engineering research-doctorate programs as evaluated by the National Research Council ★2376★

U.S. News & World Report's graduate engineering programs with the best aerospace departments, 2000-01 ★2378★

Academics' choices for best graduate bioengineering/biomedical engineering programs, 2001 ★2381★

Academics' choices for best graduate civil engineering programs, 2001 ★2394★

U.S. News & World Report's graduate engineering programs with the best civil departments, 2000-01 ★2398★

Academics' choices for best graduate electrical/electronic/communications engineering programs, 2001 ★2403★

Top electrical engineering research-doctorate programs as evaluated by the National Research Council ★2405★

Academics' choices for best graduate environmental/environmental health engineering programs, 2001 ★2408★

Academics' choices for best graduate industrial/manufacturing engineering programs, 2001 ★2411★

Most effective industrial engineering research-doctorate programs as evaluated by the National Research Council ★2412★

Top industrial engineering research-doctorate programs as evaluated by the National Research Council ★2413★

U.S. News & World Report's graduate engineering programs with the best industrial manufacturing departments, 2000-01 ★2415★

Academics' choices for best graduate mechanical engineering programs, 2001 ★2422★

University research libraries in the U.S. and Canada with the largest increases in total expenditures from 1993-94 to 1998-99 ★2708★

Average faculty salaries for institutions of higher education in Georgia, 2000-01 ★3697★

Public institutions of higher education that pay the highest salaries to female professors, 2000-01 ★3975★

U.S. universities with the highest concentration of papers published in the field of materials science, 1995-99 ★4290★

Georgia Military College

Highest undergraduate tuition and fees at public 2-year colleges and universities ★1462★

Georgia-Pacific

Fortune's highest ranked forest and paper products companies, 2000 ★466★

Top paper and forest products companies in Standard & Poor's 500, 2001 ★552★

Georgia Perimeter College

Average faculty salaries for institutions of higher education in Georgia, 2000-01 ★3697★

Georgia Southern University

Division I NCAA colleges with that graduated none of their African American male basketball players, 1990-91 to 1993-94 ★930★

State appropriations for Georgia's institutions of higher education, 2000-01 ★1263★

U.S. colleges and universities awarding the most biological and life sciences master's degrees to African Americans ★1756★

Average faculty salaries for institutions of higher education in Georgia, 2000-01 ★3697★

Georgia Southwestern State University

State appropriations for Georgia's institutions of higher education, 2000-01 ★1263★

U.S. News & World Report's southern regional universities with students most in debt, 1999 ★1432★

Georgia State University

Top business schools for within-discipline research performance in insurance, international business and real estate, 1986-1998 ★667★

Top business schools for within-discipline research performance in management information systems, 1986-1998 ★675★

Employing institutions with the most published pages in *The Journal of Risk and Insurance*, 1987-1996 ★679★

U.S. News & World Report's universities with the best insurance departments, 1999-2000 ★681★

Institutions with the most published authors in the *Journal of Business Research*, 1985 to 1999 ★695★

State appropriations for Georgia's institutions of higher education, 2000-01 ★1263★

Total baccalaureate business management and administrative services degrees awarded to African Americans from U.S. colleges and universities, 1997-98 ★1683★

Total baccalaureate computer and information science degrees awarded to African Americans from U.S. colleges and universities, 1997-98 ★1691★

Total baccalaureate degrees awarded to African Americans from traditionally white institutions, 1997-98 ★1698★

Total baccalaureate mathematics degrees awarded to African Americans from U.S. colleges and universities, 1997-98 ★1729★

Traditionally white institutions awarding the most master's degrees to African Americans ★1755★

U.S. colleges and universities awarding the most business management and administrative services master's degrees to African Americans ★1759★

U.S. colleges and universities awarding the most computer and information sciences master's degrees to Asian Americans ★1767★

U.S. colleges and universities awarding the most physical sciences master's degrees to African Americans ★1793★

U.S. colleges and universities awarding the most law and legal studies first professional degrees to African Americans ★1852★

Doctoral institutions with the highest enrollment of foreign students, 1998-99 ★2494★

Average faculty salaries for institutions of higher education in Georgia, 2000-01 ★3697★

Public institutions of higher education that pay the highest salaries to female professors, 2000-01 ★3975★

Georgia State University, J. Mack Robinson College of Business

Academics' choices for best part-time MBA programs, 2000 ★587★

Georgia Tech

U.S. business schools with the quickest payback on MBA investments ★654★

Georgia Tech, DuPree College of Management

Business Week's top business schools with the highest percentage of minority enrollment, 2000 ★613★

Business Week's top business schools with the lowest percentage of international students, 2000 ★615★

Business Week's top business schools worst at responding to student concerns, 2000 ★621★

Lowest post-MBA salaries for students enrolled in Business Week's top business schools, 1999 ★634★

Lowest pre-MBA salaries for students enrolled in Business Week's top business schools, 1999 ★635★

Georgia; University of
NCAA Division I women's swimming teams with the most individual championships ★136★

U.S. colleges and universities with the most alumni in the LPGA ★148★

Women's basketball teams with the most appearances in the Final Four ★157★

U.S. colleges and universities with the highest average football attendance, 1996-99 ★159★

Top business schools for within-discipline research performance in insurance, international business and real estate, 1986-1998 ★667★

Top business schools for within-discipline research performance in management information systems, 1986-1998 ★675★

Degree-granting institutions with the most published pages in The Journal of Risk and Insurance, 1987-1996 ★678★

Employing institutions with the most published pages in The Journal of Risk and Insurance, 1987-1996 ★679★

U.S. News & World Report's universities with the best insurance departments, 1999-2000 ★681★

U.S. colleges and universities that devote the least course time to discussion ★989★

U.S. colleges and universities where fraternities and sororities are popular ★993★

U.S. colleges and universities where students study the least ★1002★

U.S. colleges and universities where the general student body puts a strong emphasis on athletic events ★1007★

U.S. colleges and universities with a favorable surrounding town or city ★1013★

U.S. colleges and universities with the worst on-campus housing facilities ★1044★

State appropriations for Georgia's institutions of higher education, 2000-01 ★1263★

U.S. universities with the greatest impact in communication, 1995-99 ★1657★

U.S. colleges and universities awarding the most doctorate degrees to Native Americans ★2099★

U.S. colleges and universities awarding the most doctorates in education, 1999 ★2101★

U.S. colleges and universities awarding the most psychology doctorate degrees to African Americans ★2120★

Institutions generating the most economic education research text, 1963-1990 ★2167★

U.S. universities publishing the most papers in the field of education, 1994-98 ★2219★

U.S. universities with the highest concentration of education papers published, 1994-98 ★2223★

Faculty's scholarly reputation in the Ph.D.-granting departments of geography, 1925-1982 ★2518★

Law schools with the best law and religion (excluding First Amendment issues) faculty, 1999-2000 ★2658★

University research libraries in the U.S. and Canada with the largest increases in total expenditures from 1993-94 to 1998-99 ★2708★

Degrees granted in the ten largest undergraduate journalism and mass communications programs, 1999 ★2745★

Institutions with the most prolific communication studies researchers ★2749★

U.S. universities publishing the most papers in the field of communication, 1994-98 ★2755★

Degrees granted in the ten largest doctoral journalism and mass communications programs, 1999 ★2756★

Average faculty salaries for institutions of higher education in Georgia, 2000-01 ★3697★

U.S. universities publishing the most papers in the field of food science/nutrition, 1994-98 ★4286★

U.S. universities with the highest concentration of animal sciences papers published, 1994-98 ★4288★

Academics' choices for best counseling/personnel services graduate programs, 2001 ★4379★

Academics' choices for best secondary education graduate programs, 2001 ★4385★

Academics' choices for best vocational/technical graduate programs, 2001 ★4387★

U.S. universities with the highest concentration of papers published in the field of veterinary medicine, 1995-99 ★4441★

Georgian Court College
Women's colleges granting physics bachelor's degrees, 2000 ★2982★

Average faculty salaries for institutions of higher education in New Jersey, 2000-01 ★3717★

Georgiana: Duchess of Devonshire
Outstanding biography books, 2000 ★288★

Geosciences
Proposed fiscal 2002 appropriations for the National Science Foundation ★3109★

Australia's contribution of papers in the sciences, by field, 1993-97 ★4292★

Australia's contribution of papers in the sciences, by field, 1995-99 ★4293★

United Kingdom's contribution of papers in the sciences, by field, 1995-99 ★4297★

Canada's contribution of papers in the sciences, by field, 1995-99 ★4303★

Denmark's contribution of papers in the sciences, by field, 1994-98 ★4306★

Denmark's contribution of papers in the sciences, by field, 1995-99 ★4307★

England's contribution of papers in the sciences, by field, 1994-98 ★4308★

France's contribution of papers in the sciences, by field, 1995-99 ★4311★

France's contribution of papers in the sciences, by field, 1996-2000 ★4312★

New Zealand's contribution of papers in the sciences, by field, 1994-98 ★4322★

Norway's contribution of papers in the sciences, by field, 1994-98 ★4323★

Russia's contribution of papers in the sciences, by field, 1993-97 ★4325★

South Africa's contribution of papers in the sciences, by field, 1994-98 ★4326★

Sweden's contribution of papers in the sciences by field, 1993-97 ★4330★

Sweden's contribution of papers in the sciences, by field, 1995-99 ★4331★

Switzerland's contribution of papers in the sciences, by field, 1994-98 ★4332★

Switzerland's contribution of papers in the sciences, by field, 1995-99 ★4333★

Turkey's contribution of papers in the sciences, by field, 1995-99 ★4335★

Gerard; Gregory
Top pay and benefits for the chief executive and top paid employees at LaSierra University ★3366★

Geraty; Lawrence T.
Top pay and benefits for the chief executive and top paid employees at LaSierra University ★3366★

Gerety; Tom
Presidents with the highest pay at Baccalaureate I colleges, 1998-99 ★3159★

Top pay and benefits for the chief executive and top paid employees at Amherst College ★3175★

Gerhart; Norman
Top pay and benefits for the chief executive and top paid employees at Avila College ★3186★

Gerhart; Philip M.
Top pay and benefits for the chief executive and top paid employees at the University of Evansville ★3543★

German
Gender breakdown of language and literature doctorate recipients, by subfield, 1999 ★1937★

Language and literature doctorates awarded at U.S. colleges and universities, by subfield, 1999 ★1949★

Languages of requested materials from OCLC ILL, 1999 ★2679★

German literature
Number of Advanced Placement Exams taken by African Americans, by subject, 2000 ★30★

Number of Advanced Placement Exams taken by Asian Americans, by subject, 2000 ★31★

Number of Advanced Placement Exams taken by Hispanic Americans, by subject, 2000 ★32★

Germanna Community College
Average faculty salaries for institutions of higher education in Virginia, 2000-01 ★3735★

Germantown High School
Outstanding secondary schools in Memphis, Tennessee-Arkansas-Mississippi ★4177★

Germany
CA journal literature abstracted, by country, 2000 ★757★

Countries with the most computers, 2000 ★1603★

Countries of origin for non-U.S. citizens awarded doctorates at U.S. colleges and universities, 1999 ★1901★

Annual leave days for employees in selected countries ★2239★

Percentage of students enrolled in institutions of higher education that were not citizens of the country where they studied, 1998 ★2500★

Top countries of study for U.S. students studying abroad, 1998-99 ★2510★

Countries with the most Internet users ★2583★

European periodical prices by country, 2001 ★2921★

Institute for Scientific Information periodical prices by country, 2001 ★2922★

Nations with the most-cited papers in the sciences ★4320★

Gerontologist
Geriatrics and gerontology journals with the greatest impact measure, 1981-98 ★2805★

GERONTOLOGY

Geriatrics and gerontology journals with the greatest impact measure, 1994-98 ★2806★

Gerontology
Geriatrics and gerontology journals with the greatest impact measure, 1998 ★2807★

Gershon's Monster: A Story for the Jewish New Year
Outstanding children's religion books, 2000 ★332★

Gesu Catholic School
Outstanding secondary schools in Cleveland-Lorain-Elyria, Ohio ★4114★

Gettys; Jim
Top pay and benefits for the chief executive and top paid employees at Erskine College ★3290★

Gettysburg College
Highest undergraduate tuition and fees at colleges and universities in Pennsylvania ★1549★
Average faculty salaries for institutions of higher education in Pennsylvania, 2000-01 ★3725★

Gewertz; Bruce
Top pay and benefits for the chief executive and top paid employees at the University of Chicago ★3537★

Geysbeek; Lee
Top pay and benefits for the chief executive and top paid employees at Cornerstone University ★3258★

Ghost Boy
Most notable books for older readers, 2001 ★318★
Most notable fiction books for young adults, 2001 ★322★
Outstanding children's fiction books, 2000 ★329★

Ghostwritten
Booklist's best fiction books for library collections, 2000 ★227★
Booklist's best first novels ★228★

Giamartino; Gary
Top pay and benefits for the chief executive and top paid employees at the University of Detroit Mercy ★3541★

Giant Steps: The New Generation of African American Writers
Outstanding nonfiction books for young adults, 2000 ★334★

Gibbons; Robert E.
Top pay and benefits for the chief executive and top paid employees at Our Lady of the Lake University ★3434★

Gibbs College
Highest undergraduate tuition and fees at colleges and universities in Connecticut ★1490★

Gibbs, Smith Publisher
Small publishers with the highest sales growth between 1997 and 1999 ★3073★

Gibson; Sheila
Top pay and benefits for the chief executive and top paid employees at Holy Names College ★3337★

Gibson; Terry G.
Top pay and benefits for the chief executive and top paid employees at Cornell College in Iowa ★3256★

Giese; Richard F.
Top pay and benefits for the chief executive and top paid employees at Monmouth College in Illinois ★3405★

Gifford; Duncan P.
Top pay and benefits for the chief executive and top paid employees at the University of New Haven ★3553★

The Giggler Treatment
Publishers Weekly Off-the-Cuff Awards winner for biggest flop, per publisher's expectations, 2000 ★344★

Gilbert; Charlene
Radcliffe Institute for Advanced Study fellowship recipient in the field of film making, 2000-01 ★2751★

Gilbert; Joanna
Radcliffe Institute for Advanced Study fellowship recipients in the field of biomedicine, 2000-01 ★2880★

Gilbert; Zelda
Top pay and benefits for the chief executive and top paid employees at Woodbury University ★3635★

Gildersleeve Middle School
Outstanding secondary schools in Norfolk-Virginia Beach-Newport News, Virginia-North Carolina ★4194★

Giles; Zachary
All-American boy's high school football linemen, 2000 ★183★

Gillespie; J. David
Top pay and benefits for the chief executive and top paid employees at Presbyterian College ★3445★

Gillespie; James
Top pay and benefits for the chief executive and top paid employees at the New York Institute of Technology ★3535★

Gillespie; P.
Highest ranked inactive communication studies researchers ★2748★

Gillespie; Patti
Top published female authors (1915-1985) in the field of communication studies ★4363★

Gillette
Fortune's highest ranked soaps and cosmetics companies, 2000 ★496★

Gillette; Dennis
Top pay and benefits for the chief executive and top paid employees at California Lutheran University ★3216★

Gillis; Arthur L.
Top pay and benefits for the chief executive and top paid employees at Guilford College ★3316★

Gillis; Malcolm
Presidents with the highest pay at Research I and II universities, 1998-99 ★3162★
Top pay and benefits for the chief executive and top paid employees at Rice University ★3457★

Gilmore; Glenda
Radcliffe Institute for Advanced Study fellowship recipients in the field of history, 2000-01 ★2549★

Gines; David L.
Top pay and benefits for the chief executive and top paid employees at Brenau University ★3210★

Ginevan; David W.
Top pay and benefits for the chief executive and top paid employees at Middlebury College ★3401★

Ginsburg; Herbert
Top pay and benefits for the chief executive and top paid employees at Teachers College, Columbia University ★3517★

Giordano; Nicholas A.
Top pay and benefits for the chief executive and top paid employees at LaSalle University ★3365★

Girl, Interrupted
Longest-running trade paperback bestsellers, 2000 ★282★

The Girl Who Spun Gold
Booklist's most recommended black history books for youth ★311★
Outstanding books for young readers, 2000 ★328★

Girl with a Pearl Earring
Most notable fiction books for young adults, 2001 ★322★
Outstanding fiction books for young adults, 2000 ★333★

The Girls
Most notable fiction books for reluctant young adult readers, 2001 ★321★
Most notable fiction books for young adults, 2001 ★322★

The Girls' Guide to Hunting and Fishing
Longest-running trade paperback bestsellers, 2000 ★282★

Girls Prep
Outstanding secondary schools in Chattanooga, Tennessee-Georgia ★4109★

The Girls of Summer: The U.S. Women's Soccer Team and How It Changed the World
Outstanding nonfiction books for young adults, 2000 ★334★

Girls Think of Everything: Stories of Ingenious Inventions by Women
Smithsonian's best books for children ages 6 to 10 ★364★

Gitenstein; R. Barbara
Top pay and benefits for the chief executive and top paid employees at Drake University ★3272★

Give Me Liberty: The Story of the Declaration of Independence
Most notable nonfiction books for young adults, 2001 ★324★

Givens; Douglas
Top pay and benefits for the chief executive and top paid employees at Kenyon College ★3359★

Gladfelter; Donald
Top pay and benefits for the chief executive and top paid employees at Monmouth College in Illinois ★3405★

Glaeser; Janet A.
Top pay and benefits for the chief executive and top paid employees at Westminster College in Utah ★3618★

Glasgow, MT
America's most wired towns, 2001 ★2575★

Glasgow; Terry L.
Top pay and benefits for the chief executive and top paid employees at Monmouth College in Illinois ★3405★

Glass High School
Outstanding secondary schools in Lynchburg, Virginia ★4171★

Glass; Robert L.
Top published scholars in the field of systems and software engineering ★2333★

Glasser; Charles E.
Top pay and benefits for the chief executive and top paid employees at John F. Kennedy University ★3354★

Glassick; Charles
Top pay and benefits for the chief executive and top paid employees at Converse College ★3255★

Glaxo Wellcome
Business Week's best companies in Britain ★389★

Glazer; Frank
Top pay and benefits for the chief executive and top paid employees at Philadelphia University ★3440★

Glazer; Penina M.
Top pay and benefits for the chief executive and top paid employees at Hampshire College ★3322★

Glazier
Jobs with the highest unemployment ★2256★
Most desirable jobs in construction trades ★2272★

Glazier; Steven S.
Top pay and benefits for the chief executive and top paid employees at Wake Forest University ★3600★

Glen Oaks Community College
Lowest undergraduate tuition and fees at colleges and universities in Michigan ★1519★

Glenbrook North High School
Illinois high schools with the highest SAT scores ★874★
Outstanding suburban public high schools in Metro Chicago ★4256★

Glenbrook South High School
Outstanding suburban public high schools in Metro Chicago ★4256★

Glendale Community College
Lowest undergraduate tuition and fees at colleges and universities in Arizona ★1483★

Glendale Middle School
Outstanding secondary schools in Nashville, Tennessee ★4186★

Glenville State College
State appropriations for West Virginia's institutions of higher education, 2000-01 ★1301★
Lowest undergraduate tuition and fees at colleges and universities in West Virginia ★1569★
Average faculty salaries for institutions of higher education in West Virginia, 2000-01 ★3737★

Glick; Robert
Top pay and benefits for the chief executive and top paid employees at St. John's College in Maryland and New Mexico ★3473★

Glickman; Robert M.
Top pay and benefits for the chief executive and top paid employees at New York University ★3419★

Glicksman; Martin
Top pay and benefits for the chief executive and top paid employees at Rensselaer Polytechnic Institute ★3455★

Global Codes of Conduct
Library Journal's most notable management books, 2000 ★265★

Global Crossing
Business Week's best performing companies with the greatest decline in earnings growth ★412★
Business Week's best performing companies with the highest 1-year sales performance ★414★
Business Week's best performing companies with the highest 3-year sales performance ★417★
Business Week's best performing companies with the lowest net margin, 2000 ★425★

A Glossary of Contemporary Literary Theory
Selected new editions and supplements reference books, 2000 ★372★

Glotzbach; Philip A.
Top pay and benefits for the chief executive and top paid employees at the University of Redlands ★3558★

Gloucester County College
Lowest undergraduate tuition and fees at colleges and universities in New Jersey ★1534★
Average faculty salaries for institutions of higher education in New Jersey, 2000-01 ★3717★
U.S. community colleges with the highest paid full professors, 2001 ★3976★
U.S. institutions with the highest paid assistant professors, 2001 ★3977★

Glynn, S.J.; Rev. Edward
Top pay and benefits for the chief executive and top paid employees at John Carroll University ★3353★

GMC Truck
Top internships in the U.S. with the highest compensation, 2001 ★2611★

Go Ask Alice
People for the American Way's list of most frequently challenged authors, 1982-1992 ★746★
People for the American Way's list of most frequently challenged books, 1982-1992 ★747★

Gober; Jerald R.
Top pay and benefits for the chief executive and top paid employees at Lenoir-Rhyne College ★3369★

Goddard College
U.S. colleges and universities where intercollegiate sports are not popular ★994★
U.S. colleges and universities with a popular radio station ★1019★
U.S. colleges and universities with the best quality of life ★1034★
Undergraduate tuition and fees at colleges and universities in Vermont ★1563★

God's Name in Vain: The Wrongs and Rights of Religion in Politics
Outstanding social sciences books, 2000 ★292★

Godsey; R. Kirby
Top pay and benefits for the chief executive and top paid employees at Mercer University ★3398★

Goebel; Steven R.
Top pay and benefits for the chief executive and top paid employees at St. Ambrose University ★3468★

Goethals II; George R.
Top pay and benefits for the chief executive and top paid employees at Williams College ★3631★

Goetz; Lisa
All-USA Teacher Teams, Third Team, 2000 ★4401★

Gogebic Community College
Lowest undergraduate tuition and fees at colleges and universities in Michigan ★1519★

Goins; G. Michael
Top pay and benefits for the chief executive and top paid employees at West Virginia Wesleyan College ★3613★

Gold Dust
Most notable books for older readers, 2001 ★318★
Most notable fiction books for young adults, 2001 ★322★

Gold Kist
Fortune's highest ranked food production companies, 2000 ★464★

Gold Zack
Best small companies worldwide ★384★

Goldberg; Morton F.
Top pay and benefits for the chief executive and top paid employees at Johns Hopkins University ★3355★

The Golden Age
Booklist's best fiction books for library collections, 2000 ★227★
Booklist's most recommended historical novels, 2001 ★230★

Golden; Andrew K.
Top pay and benefits for the chief executive and top paid employees at Princeton University ★3446★

Golden Books
Highest revenues of publicly held book publishers, 1999 ★3072★
Top children's book publishers, 1999 ★3074★

Golden, C.M.; Rev. Paul L.
Top pay and benefits for the chief executive and top paid employees at Niagara University ★3420★

Golden; Dennis C.
Top pay and benefits for the chief executive and top paid employees at Fontbonne College ★3294★

Golden Gate College
U.S. colleges and universities where intercollegiate sports are not popular ★994★

Golden Gate University
U.S. colleges and universities where the general student body does not drink beer ★1004★
U.S. colleges and universities where the general student body does not smoke marijuana ★1006★

Golden Gate University, San Francisco
U.S. colleges and universities awarding the most business management and administrative services master's degrees to Asian Americans ★1760★
U.S. colleges and universities awarding the most business management and administrative services master's degrees to Hispanic Americans ★1761★
U.S. colleges and universities awarding the most computer and information sciences master's degrees to African Americans ★1766★
U.S. colleges and universities awarding the most computer and information sciences master's degrees to Asian Americans ★1767★
U.S. colleges and universities awarding the most law and legal studies master's degrees to Asian Americans ★1782★
U.S. colleges and universities awarding the most master's degrees to Asian Americans ★1786★
U.S. colleges and universities awarding the most psychology master's degrees to Asian Americans ★1798★

Golden Rule Insurance
Top women-owned companies ★4460★

Golden State Bancorp
Fortune's highest ranked mortgage finance companies, 2000 ★479★

Golden West
 Top public companies with the highest percentage of women board of directors, 2000 ★4458★
 Top public companies with the highest percentage of women employees, 2000 ★4459★

Golden West Financial
 Fortune's highest ranked mortgage finance companies, 2000 ★479★
 Top women-owned companies ★4460★

Goldey-Beacom College
 Undergraduate tuition and fees at colleges and universities in Delaware ★1492★

Goldgar; Bertrand
 Top pay and benefits for the chief executive and top paid employees at Lawrence University ★3367★

Goldman; I. David
 Top pay and benefits for the chief executive and top paid employees at Yeshiva University ★3640★

Goldman Sachs
 Fortune's highest ranked securities companies, 2000 ★494★
 Fortune's most admired companies for employee talent ★514★

Goldsby; Richard
 Top pay and benefits for the chief executive and top paid employees at Amherst College ★3175★

Goldsmith; Ronald E.
 Authors with the most articles published in the *Journal of Business Research*, 1985 to 1999 ★687★
 Most published authors, adjusted for coauthorship, in the *Journal of Business Research*, 1985 to 1999 ★701★

Goldson; Alfred
 Top pay and benefits for the chief executive and top paid employees at Howard University ★3343★

Goldstein; Alan H.
 Top pay and benefits for the chief executive and top paid employees at Alfred University ★3169★

Goldstein; Herman
 Most-cited scholars in police studies articles/research notes ★2624★

Goldstein; Matthew
 Top pay and benefits for the chief executive and top paid employees at Adelphi University ★3164★

Goldstein; Nancy
 Radcliffe Institute for Advanced Study fellowship recipients in the field of economics, 2000-01 ★2172★

Goldstein; T.
 Most cited authors in the journal *Crime, Law, and Social Change*, 1990 to 1995 ★1618★

Golf
 Fastest growing women's collegiate athletics teams ★131★

Gollier; Christian
 Authors with the most published pages in impact-weighted insurance journals ★677★

Gollub; Jerry P.
 Top pay and benefits for the chief executive and top paid employees at Haverford College ★3329★

Golub; S.
 Top associate professor economists at elite liberal arts colleges, 1975-94 ★2174★

Goncalves; Diane
 Top pay and benefits for the chief executive and top paid employees at Saint Joseph College in Connecticut ★3475★

Gonzaga Prep
 Outstanding secondary schools in Spokane, Washington ★4232★

Gonzaga University
 U.S. News & World Report's best undergraduate fees among western regional universities by discount tuition, 2000 ★1430★
 Highest undergraduate tuition and fees at colleges and universities in Washington ★1566★
 U.S. News & World Report's top western regional universities, 2000-01 ★1574★
 U.S. News & World Report's western regional universities with the best academic reputation scores, 2000-01 ★1577★
 U.S. News & World Report's western regional universities with the best student/faculty ratios, 2000-01 ★1578★
 U.S. News & World Report's western regional universities with the highest acceptance rates, 2000-01 ★1579★
 U.S. News & World Report's western regional universities with the highest alumni giving rates, 2000-01 ★1580★
 U.S. News & World Report's western regional universities with the highest freshmen retention rates, 2000-01 ★1581★
 U.S. News & World Report's western regional universities with the highest graduation rates, 2000-01 ★1582★
 U.S. News & World Report's western regional universities with the highest percentage of full-time faculty, 2000-01 ★1584★
 U.S. colleges and universities awarding the most education master's degrees to Native Americans ★1772★
 U.S. colleges and universities awarding the most law and legal studies first professional degrees to Native Americans ★1855★
 Law library web sites, by visibility ★2687★

Gooch; Walter
 Top pay and benefits for the chief executive and top paid employees at Centre College ★3227★

Good Counsel High School
 Outstanding secondary schools in Washington, District of Columbia-Maryland-Virginia-West Virginia ★4249★

Good Housekeeping
 Magazines with the largest circulation ★2750★

Good Night, Good Knight
 Most notable books for young readers, 2001 ★319★

Good Night Mr. Snoozleberg
 Most notable children's web sites, 2001 ★2593★

Good Shepherd Episcopal School
 Outstanding secondary schools in Dallas, Texas ★4120★

Good; Stephen H.
 Top pay and benefits for the chief executive and top paid employees at Drury University ★3275★

Goodman; Murray
 Winner of the American Chemical Society's Arthur C. Cope Awards, 2001 ★795★

Goodpaster; Kenneth
 Top pay and benefits for the chief executive and top paid employees at the University of St. Thomas in Minnesota ★3563★

Goodwin; Larry
 Top pay and benefits for the chief executive and top paid employees at the College of St. Scholastica ★3530★

Goodyear Tire & Rubber
 Fortune's highest ranked rubber and plastic products companies, 2000 ★492★
 Top automotive companies in Standard & Poor's 500, 2001 ★530★

Google
 Web sites where internet users spend the most time ★2609★

Goplerud; Peter
 Top pay and benefits for the chief executive and top paid employees at Drake University ★3272★

Goplin; Scott J.
 Top pay and benefits for the chief executive and top paid employees at Ripon College ★3459★

Gorcum, Van
 Publishers, journals and proceedings with the lowest citations (Class 6) ★2571★

Gordis; Daniel
 Top pay and benefits for the chief executive and top paid employees at the University of Judaism ★3546★

Gordon; Bonnie
 Top pay and benefits for the chief executive and top paid employees at Ithaca College ★3351★

Gordon; Bridgette
 NCAA Division I female basketball scoring leaders ★155★

Gordon College
 U.S. News & World Report's national liberal arts colleges with students least in debt, 1999 ★1385★
 Institutions with the most female physics bachelor's recipients, 1994-1998 ★2959★
 U.S. institutions with more than 40% female bachelor's graduates in their physics departments, 1994-98 ★2977★
 Average faculty salaries for institutions of higher education in Massachusetts, 2000-01 ★3708★

Gordon; David
 Top pay and benefits for the chief executive and top paid employees at the University of Dallas ★3538★

Gordon; Linda
 Highly acknowledged individuals in the field of women's studies, 1975-94 ★4466★

Gordon Middle School
 Outstanding secondary schools in Philadelphia, Pennsylvania-New Jersey ★4202★

Gordy; Berry
 Most influential African Americans in business ★526★

Gore; Frank
 All-American boy's high school football running backs, 2000 ★186★

Gore; R. J.
 Top pay and benefits for the chief executive and top paid employees at Erskine College ★3290★

Gores; Connie
 Top pay and benefits for the chief executive and top paid employees at Randolph-Macon Woman's College ★3452★

Goring; Gillian
 All-America girls' high school basketball 2nd team, 2001 ★171★

Gorman; Richard
Top pay and benefits for the chief executive and top paid employees at New School University ★3418★

Gorton; Kenneth E.
Top pay and benefits for the chief executive and top paid employees at Eastern Nazarene College ★3281★

Goshen College
Average faculty salaries for institutions of higher education in Indiana, 2000-01 ★3701★

Gospel Birds
Retail audiobook titles selling 300,000-400,000 copies ★303★

Gotsch; Susan
Top pay and benefits for the chief executive and top paid employees at Hartwick College ★3326★

Gotsmanov; Sasha
All-America boys' high school soccer team forwards, 2001 ★166★

Gottfredson; Michael R.
Most cited authors in the journal *Criminology*, 1990 to 1995 ★1622★
Most cited authors in the journal *Journal of Criminal Justice*, 1990 to 1995 ★1626★
Most cited authors in three criminal justice journals ★1633★
Most cited authors in three criminology journals ★1634★
Most-cited scholars in *Criminology* ★1639★

Goucher College
Highest undergraduate tuition and fees at colleges and universities in Maryland ★1514★
Average faculty salaries for institutions of higher education in Maryland, 2000-01 ★3707★

Gould; Glenn
Canada's best performing artists of the 20th century ★74★

Gould; Marge Christensen
All-USA Teacher Teams, First Team, 2000 ★4399★

Gould; Stephen Jay
Booklist's best science and technology books ★366★

Gould; William
Top pay and benefits for the chief executive and top paid employees at Hardin-Simmons University ★3325★

Goveia; John
Top pay and benefits for the chief executive and top paid employees at the University of Portland ★3556★

Government
Employment change projections by major industry division from 1998 to 2008 ★2287★
Employment projections by major industry division for 2008 ★2290★

Government/education
Spending for E-marketplace services, by industry, 2001 ★4430★

Government and politics comp.
Number of Advanced Placement Exams taken by African Americans, by subject, 2000 ★30★
Number of Advanced Placement Exams taken by Asian Americans, by subject, 2000 ★31★
Number of Advanced Placement Exams taken by Hispanic Americans, by subject, 2000 ★32★

Governor Dole Intermediate School
Outstanding secondary schools in Honolulu, Hawaii ★4149★

Governor Johnson High School
Outstanding secondary schools in Washington, District of Columbia-Maryland-Virginia-West Virginia ★4249★

Governors State University
Fall enrollment at Chicago-area public universities, by minority percentages, 1999 ★868★
State appropriations for Illinois institutions of higher education, 2000-01 ★1266★
U.S. colleges and universities awarding the most communications master's degrees to African Americans ★1763★
U.S. colleges and universities awarding the most health professions and related sciences master's degrees to African Americans ★1777★
U.S. colleges and universities awarding the most psychology master's degrees to African Americans ★1797★
U.S. colleges and universities awarding the most psychology master's degrees to Hispanic Americans ★1799★
Average faculty salaries for institutions of higher education without academic ranks in Illinois, 2000-01 ★3747★

Govindarajan; Vijay
Top pay and benefits for the chief executive and top paid employees at Dartmouth College ★3263★

Goyal; Lipika
All-USA College Academic Third Team, 2001 ★4★

Grabavoy; Ned
All-America boys' high school soccer team midfielders, 2001 ★168★

Graber; Harlan D.
Top pay and benefits for the chief executive and top paid employees at Cornell College in Iowa ★3256★

Grabois; Neil R.
Top pay and benefits for the chief executive and top paid employees at Colgate University ★3242★

Grabosky; Peter
Most-cited scholars in *Australian and New Zealand Journal of Criminology* ★1636★

Grace College
Average faculty salaries for institutions of higher education in Indiana, 2000-01 ★3701★

Grace; Marcellus
Top pay and benefits for the chief executive and top paid employees at Xavier University of Louisiana ★3638★

Grace University
Average faculty salaries for institutions of higher education in Nebraska, 2000-01 ★3714★

Graceland University
Average faculty salaries for institutions of higher education in Iowa, 2000-01 ★3702★

Graduate assistant
African American college athletics administrators and staff, by gender, 1999-2000 ★117★
College athletics administrators and staff, by gender, 1999-2000 ★121★
Minority college athletics administrators and staff, by gender, 1999-2000 ★132★

Graham; Bernard W.
Top pay and benefits for the chief executive and top paid employees at Wilkes University ★3627★

Graham; Bob
Outstanding children's picture books, 2000 ★331★

Graham; Bruce
Top pay and benefits for the chief executive and top paid employees at the University of Detroit Mercy ★3541★

Graham; Karen
Top pay and benefits for the chief executive and top paid employees at Andrews University ★3176★

Grajek; Michael
Top pay and benefits for the chief executive and top paid employees at Hiram College ★3333★

Gramatica; Bill
Longest field goals in college football ★158★

Gramatica; Martin
Longest field goals in college football ★158★

Grambling State University
Colleges offering the Thurgood Marshall Scholarship Fund ★221★
State appropriations for Louisiana institutions of higher education, 2000-01 ★1271★
Historically black colleges and universities awarding the most master's degrees to African Americans ★1670★
Total baccalaureate biology/life sciences degrees awarded to African Americans from U.S. colleges and universities, 1997-98 ★1679★
Total baccalaureate business management and administrative services degrees awarded to African Americans from U.S. colleges and universities, 1997-98 ★1683★
Total baccalaureate communications degrees awarded to African Americans from U.S. colleges and universities, 1997-98 ★1687★
Total baccalaureate computer and information science degrees awarded to African Americans from U.S. colleges and universities, 1997-98 ★1691★
Total baccalaureate degrees awarded to African Americans from historically black colleges, 1997-98 ★1697★
Total baccalaureate degrees awarded to African Americans from U.S. colleges and universities, 1997-98 ★1699★
Total baccalaureate psychology degrees awarded to African Americans from U.S. colleges and universities, 1997-98 ★1737★
Institutions with the most female physics bachelor's recipients, 1994-1998 ★2959★
U.S. institutions with more than 40% female bachelor's graduates in their physics departments, 1994-98 ★2977★
Average faculty salaries for institutions of higher education in Louisiana, 2000-01 ★3705★

Granby Memorial Middle School
Outstanding secondary schools in Hartford, Connecticut ★4147★

Grand Canyon University
Highest undergraduate tuition and fees at colleges and universities in Arizona ★1482★
Average faculty salaries for institutions of higher education in Arizona, 2000-01 ★3690★

Grand Valley State University
State appropriations for Michigan's institutions of higher education, 2000-01 ★1275★
Average faculty salaries for institutions of higher education in Michigan, 2000-01 ★3709★

Grand View College
U.S. News & World Report's midwestern regional liberal arts colleges with students least in debt, 1999 ★1337★

Grande dizionario italiano dell'uso
  Selected reference books-dictionaries, 2000 ★373★
Granger; C.W.J.
  U.S. academic economists by mean number of citations, 1971-92 ★2176★
  U.S. academic economists by total citations, 1971-92 ★2177★
Granger High School
  Outstanding secondary schools in Salt Lake City-Ogden, Utah ★4218★
Grant
  Booklist's most recommended historical novels, 2001 ★230★
Grant; Erin
  All-America girls' high school basketball 3rd team, 2001 ★172★
Grant; Michael J.
  Top pay and benefits for the chief executive and top paid employees at University of Bridgeport ★3588★
Grantham College of Engineering
  Highest undergraduate tuition and fees at colleges and universities in Louisiana ★1510★
Grantswood Community School
  Outstanding secondary schools in Birmingham, Alabama ★4098★
Granville High School
  Outstanding secondary schools in Columbus, Ohio ★4118★
The Grapes of Wrath
  Most frequently banned books in the 1990s ★745★
Grapevine Middle School
  Outstanding secondary schools in Fort Worth-Arlington, Texas ★4137★
Grasmick; H.G.
  Most cited authors in the journal *Criminology*, 1990 to 1995 ★1622★
Gray; Edward
  Top pay and benefits for the chief executive and top paid employees at the University of Hartford ★3544★
Gray; Harry B.
  American Chemical Society 2001 award winners (Group 2) ★752★
Graybar Electric, Inc.
  Top recruiters for industrial engineering jobs for 2000-01 bachelor's degree recipients ★2432★
Grayslake High School, District 127
  Illinois school districts spending the least for high school education 1997-98 ★4008★
Grayslake Middle School
  Outstanding secondary schools in Chicago, Illinois ★4110★
The Great Arc: The Dramatic Tale of How India Was Mapped and Everest Was Named
  Outstanding history books, 2000 ★289★
  Booklist's best science and technology books ★366★
Great Basin College
  Undergraduate tuition and fees at colleges and universities in Nevada ★1530★
  Average faculty salaries for institutions of higher education in Nevada, 2000-01 ★3715★
Great Britain
  Countries with the highest leader's salary ★3120★

The Great Crash, the Oil Price Shock, and The Unit-Root Hypothesis
  Top cited energy papers from 1989 to 1993 ★2466★
Great Falls; University of
  U.S. News & World Report's western regional liberal arts colleges with students most in debt, 1999 ★1398★
  Highest undergraduate tuition and fees at colleges and universities in Montana ★1526★
The Great Gilly Hopkins
  Most frequently banned books in the 1990s ★745★
Great Lakes Chemical
  Top chemical companies in Standard & Poor's 500, 2001 ★533★
The Great Turkey Walk
  Most notable children's recordings, 2001 ★320★
The Great War: Breakthroughs
  Booklist's most recommended science fiction/fantasy books ★232★
The Greatest Generation
  Longest-running nonfiction hardcover bestsellers, 2000 ★281★
Greathouse; Kelly
  All-America girls' high school basketball 4th team, 2001 ★173★
Greece
  Countries of origin for non-U.S. citizens awarded doctorates at U.S. colleges and universities, 1999 ★1901★
  Countries with the lowest spending per student on higher education, 1997 ★2489★
Greeley Elementary School
  Illinois suburban elementary schools with the highest ISAT scores in reading and math ★18★
Green; Barth A.
  Top pay and benefits for the chief executive and top paid employees at the University of Miami ★3550★
Green Junior High School
  Outstanding secondary schools in Ventura, California ★4248★
Green Middle School
  Outstanding secondary schools in St. Louis, Missouri-Illinois ★4216★
Green; Mott T.
  Top pay and benefits for the chief executive and top paid employees at the University of Puget Sound ★3557★
Green Mountain College
  Undergraduate tuition and fees at colleges and universities in Vermont ★1563★
Green; Phillip K.
  Top pay and benefits for the chief executive and top paid employees at Friends University ★3299★
Green; Richard M.
  Top pay and benefits for the chief executive and top paid employees at the University of Rochester ★3560★
Green; Ronald G.
  Top pay and benefits for the chief executive and top paid employees at Albright College ★3168★
Green Vale High School
  Outstanding secondary schools in Long Island, New York ★4165★

Greenaway; Frederick
  Top pay and benefits for the chief executive and top paid employees at Clark University ★3238★
Greenberg; B.
  Highest ranked active communication studies researchers ★2747★
  Speech communication's most published scholars between 1915-1985 ★4362★
Greene Academy
  Outstanding secondary schools in Dayton-Springfield, Ohio ★4122★
Greene Jr.; Charles E.
  Top pay and benefits for the chief executive and top paid employees at the College of St. Rose ★3529★
Greengard; Paul
  Top pay and benefits for the chief executive and top paid employees at Rockefeller University ★3462★
Greensboro College
  Average faculty salaries for institutions of higher education in North Carolina, 2000-01 ★3720★
Greenville College
  Average faculty salaries for institutions of higher education in Illinois, 2000-01 ★3700★
Greenville-Spartanburg-Anderson, SC
  Cities with the most Yahoo! listings per million residents ★2580★
Greenville Technical College
  Community colleges receiving the most gifts, 1999-2000 ★1239★
Greenwald; J. Patrick
  Top pay and benefits for the chief executive and top paid employees at Canisius College ★3219★
Greenwalt; Cisti
  All-America girls' high school basketball 4th team, 2001 ★173★
Greenway High School
  Outstanding secondary schools in Phoenix-Mesa, Arizona ★4203★
Greenwood Press
  Publishers, journals and proceedings with the lowest citations (Class 6) ★2571★
Greenwood; Zoe
  Golden Key Scholar Award winners, 2000 ★1316★
Greer Jr.; William T.
  Top pay and benefits for the chief executive and top paid employees at Virginia Wesleyan College ★3596★
Greer; Quemont
  All-America boys' high school basketball 4th team, 2001 ★164★
Greer; Sammye
  Top pay and benefits for the chief executive and top paid employees at Wittenberg University ★3633★
Gregorian; Vartan
  Top pay and benefits for the chief executive and top paid employees at Brown University ★3211★
Gregory; Eugene
  Top pay and benefits for the chief executive and top paid employees at the Centenary College of Louisiana ★3523★
Greiner; Stephen
  Top pay and benefits for the chief executive and top paid employees at the University of Evansville ★3543★

Grendel
Most frequently banned books in the 1990s ★745★

Gresham; Loren
Top pay and benefits for the chief executive and top paid employees at Southern Nazarene University ★3503★

Gress; Edward
Top pay and benefits for the chief executive and top paid employees at Canisius College ★3219★

Gretna High School
Outstanding secondary schools in Omaha, Nebraska-Iowa ★4198★

Gribbin; Daniel
Top pay and benefits for the chief executive and top paid employees at Goddard College ★3309★

Griesemer; James R.
Top pay and benefits for the chief executive and top paid employees at the University of Denver ★3540★

Griffin; Gray
All-America boys' high school soccer team defenders, 2001 ★165★

Griffin; Walter J.
Top pay and benefits for the chief executive and top paid employees at Gwynedd-Mercy College ★3318★

Griffis Jr.; Frank E.
Top pay and benefits for the chief executive and top paid employees at Norwich University in Vermont ★3424★

Griffith; John V.
Top pay and benefits for the chief executive and top paid employees at Presbyterian College ★3445★

Griffith; Larry
Top pay and benefits for the chief executive and top paid employees at Franklin College of Indiana ★3297★

Griffiths; C.E.M.
Most cited first authors in dermatology journals, 1981 to 1996 ★1871★

Grifo; James A.
Top pay and benefits for the chief executive and top paid employees at New York University ★3419★

Griggs; Jack
Top pay and benefits for the chief executive and top paid employees at Abilene Christian University ★3163★

Griliches; Z.
U.S. academic economists by total citations, 1971-92 ★2177★

Grinnell College
Private, 4-year undergraduate colleges and universities producing the most Ph.D.'s in the life sciences, 1981-1990 ★193★
U.S. colleges and universities where students are very politically active ★1001★
U.S. News & World Report's national liberal arts colleges with the best faculty resources rank, 2000-01 ★1321★
U.S. News & World Report's national liberal arts colleges with the highest percentage of full-time faculty, 2000-01 ★1333★
U.S. News & World Report's best undergraduate fees among national liberal arts colleges by discount tuition, 2000 ★1381★
Fiske Guide's best buys for private colleges and universities, 2001 ★1459★
Highest undergraduate tuition and fees at colleges and universities in Iowa ★1504★
Private, 4-year undergraduate colleges and universities producing the most Ph.D.'s in all fields of study, 1990 ★2029★
Elite liberal arts colleges ranked by per capita quality adjusted scholarship articles in the field of economics, 1975-94 ★2164★
Elite liberal arts colleges ranked by quality adjusted scholarship articles in the field of economics, 1975-94 ★2165★
Top associate professor economists at elite liberal arts colleges, 1975-94 ★2174★
Top full professor economists at elite liberal arts colleges, 1975-94 ★2175★
Private, 4-year undergraduate colleges and universities producing the most Ph.D.'s in economics, 1920-1990 ★2211★
Private, 4-year undergraduate colleges and universities producing the most Ph.D.'s in economics, 1981-1990 ★2212★
Undergraduate institutions with the most graduates who received Ph.D.s in economics, 1920-1984 ★2214★
Private, 4-year undergraduate colleges and universities producing the most Ph.D.'s in history, 1920-1990 ★2552★
Private, 4-year undergraduate colleges and universities producing the most Ph.D.'s in history, 1981-1990 ★2553★
Private, 4-year undergraduate colleges and universities producing the most Ph.D.'s in political science and international relations, 1920-1990 ★3044★
Presidents with the highest pay at Baccalaureate I colleges, 1998-99 ★3159★
Average faculty salaries for institutions of higher education in Iowa, 2000-01 ★3702★
Private, 4-year undergraduate colleges and universities producing the most Ph.D.'s in anthropology and sociology, 1920-1990 ★4344★

Grisham Middle School
Outstanding secondary schools in Austin-San Marcos, Texas ★4090★

Grissom; Jason
All-USA College Academic Second Team, 2001 ★3★

Groff; David
Top pay and benefits for the chief executive and top paid employees at Linfield College ★3376★

Grolier Multimedia Encyclopedia 2.0
Library Journal's best reference databases and discs, 2000 ★369★

Gronroos; Christian
Highest impact authors in the *Journal of Business Research*, by adjusted number of citations in 12 journals, 1985-1999 ★692★

Groopman; Jerome E.
Most-cited researchers in oncology, 1981-1998 ★2877★

Gross; Rhonda I.
Top pay and benefits for the chief executive and top paid employees at Lehigh University ★3368★

Gross; Theodore L.
Top pay and benefits for the chief executive and top paid employees at Roosevelt University ★3466★

The Grosse Pointe Academy
Outstanding secondary schools in Detroit, Michigan ★4125★

Grosse Pointe South High School
Outstanding suburban public high schools in Metro Detroit ★4258★

Grossman; Claudio
Top pay and benefits for the chief executive and top paid employees at American University ★3174★

Grossman; R.
Top assistant professor economists at elite liberal arts colleges, 1975-94 ★2173★

Grossman; S.J.
U.S. academic economists by mean number of citations, 1971-92 ★2176★

Group 1 Automotive
Fortune's highest ranked automotive retailing services companies, 2000 ★449★

Groupe Bruxelles Lambert
Business Week's best companies in Belgium ★388★

Groupe UCB
Business Week's best companies in Belgium ★388★

Grove City College
U.S. colleges and universities least accepting of alternative lifestyles ★985★
U.S. colleges and universities where the general student body does not drink hard liquor ★1005★
U.S. colleges and universities where the general student body does not smoke marijuana ★1006★
U.S. colleges and universities with a generally conservative student body ★1014★
U.S. colleges and universities with a large student body of conservative Republicans ★1016★
U.S. colleges and universities with a primarily religious student body ★1022★
U.S. colleges and universities without a diverse student body ★1046★
Institutions censured by the American Association of University Professors, 2001 ★1067★
U.S. News & World Report's northern regional liberal arts colleges with the highest academic reputation scores, 2000-01 ★1354★
U.S. News & World Report's northern regional liberal arts colleges with the highest freshmen retention rates, 2000-01 ★1357★
U.S. News & World Report's northern regional liberal arts colleges with the highest graduation rates, 2000-01 ★1358★
U.S. News & World Report's northern regional liberal arts colleges with the highest percentage of freshmen in the top 25% of their high school class, 2000-01 ★1359★
U.S. News & World Report's northern regional liberal arts colleges with the highest percentage of full-time faculty, 2000-01 ★1360★
U.S. News & World Report's northern regional liberal arts colleges with the lowest acceptance rates, 2000-01 ★1362★
U.S. News & World Report's top northern regional liberal arts colleges, 2000-01 ★1363★
U.S. News & World Report's best undergraduate fees among northern regional liberal arts colleges by discount tuition, 2000 ★1382★

Groves Academy
Outstanding secondary schools in Minneapolis-St. Paul, Minnesota-Wisconsin ★4181★

Groves; Richard
Top pay and benefits for the chief executive and top paid employees at the University of Saint Francis in Indiana ★3562★

Growing Seasons
   Smithsonian's best books for children ages 6 to 10 ★364★

Grubbs; Robert H.
   American Chemical Society 2001 award winners (Group 2) ★752★

Grugle; Roger
   Top pay and benefits for the chief executive and top paid employees at Baldwin-Wallace College ★3189★

GTE
   Most selective internships in the U.S., 2001 ★2610★
   Top internships in the U.S. with the highest compensation, 2001 ★2611★

Guarasci; Richard
   Top pay and benefits for the chief executive and top paid employees at Wagner College ★3599★

Guard
   'Blue-collar' jobs considered the least physically demanding ★2241★
   Jobs considered the loneliest ★2244★

Guardian Life of America
   Fortune's highest ranked life and health insurance companies, 2000 ★472★

Guards
   Occupations with the largest projected employment growth, 1998-2008 ★2312★
   Projected employment growth for selected occupations that require shorter moderate-term on-the-job training, 1998-2008 ★2321★

Guelph; University of
   Best Canadian universities for producing leaders of tomorrow, 2000 ★1148★
   Best Canadian universities overall, 2000 ★1149★
   Best Canadian universities that are the most innovative, 2000 ★1150★
   Best Canadian universities with the highest quality, 2000 ★1151★
   Canadian comprehensive universities best at producing leaders of tomorrow, 2000 ★1152★
   Canadian comprehensive universities by alumni support, 2000 ★1153★
   Canadian comprehensive universities by award-winning faculty members, 2000 ★1154★
   Canadian comprehensive universities by class size at the first- and second-year level, 2000 ★1155★
   Canadian comprehensive universities by class size at the third- and forth-year level, 2000 ★1156★
   Canadian comprehensive universities by classes taught by tenured faculty, 2000 ★1157★
   Canadian comprehensive universities by faculty members with Ph.D.'s, 2000 ★1158★
   Canadian comprehensive universities by international graduate students, 2000 ★1159★
   Canadian comprehensive universities by library acquisitions, 2000 ★1160★
   Canadian comprehensive universities by library expenses, 2000 ★1161★
   Canadian comprehensive universities by library holdings per student, 2000 ★1162★
   Canadian comprehensive universities by operating budget per student, 2000 ★1163★
   Canadian comprehensive universities by percentage of operating budget allocated to scholarships, 2000 ★1164★
   Canadian comprehensive universities by percentage of operating budget allocated to student services, 2000 ★1165★
   Canadian comprehensive universities by social science/humanities grants per faculty member, 2000 ★1166★
   Canadian comprehensive universities by students from out of province, 2000 ★1167★
   Canadian comprehensive universities by students winning national awards, 2000 ★1168★
   Canadian comprehensive universities that are the best overall, 2000 ★1169★
   Canadian comprehensive universities that are the most innovative, 2000 ★1170★
   Canadian comprehensive universities with the highest quality, 2000 ★1171★
   Canadian medical/doctoral universities by medical/science grants per faculty member, 2000 ★1183★
   Canadian universities by average entering grade, 2000 ★1213★
   Canadian universities by graduation rate, 2000 ★1214★
   Canadian universities by students with 75% grade averages or higher, 2000 ★1215★
   Top Canadian comprehensive universities, 2000 ★1219★
   Top Canadian comprehensive universities by reputation, 2000 ★1220★
   University research libraries in the U.S. and Canada with the largest decreases in total expenditures from 1993-94 to 1998-99 ★2707★

Guelzo; Allen
   Top pay and benefits for the chief executive and top paid employees at Eastern College in Pennsylvania ★3280★

Guest; Elissa Haden
   Outstanding children's fiction books, 2000 ★329★

Guidant
   Fortune's highest ranked medical products and equipment companies, 2000 ★474★

Guilford College
   Highest undergraduate tuition and fees at colleges and universities in North Carolina ★1539★
   Average faculty salaries for institutions of higher education in North Carolina, 2000-01 ★3720★

Guiliano; Edward
   Top pay and benefits for the chief executive and top paid employees at the New York Institute of Technology ★3535★

Guillermin; A. Pierre
   Top pay and benefits for the chief executive and top paid employees at Liberty University ★3373★

Guinn; David M.
   Top pay and benefits for the chief executive and top paid employees at Baylor University ★3194★

Guinness World Records 2001
   Longest-running nonfiction hardcover bestsellers, 2000 ★281★

Gulliver Academy
   Outstanding secondary schools in Miami, Florida ★4178★

Gulliver Prep
   Outstanding secondary schools in Miami, Florida ★4178★

Gundersheimer; Werner L.
   Top pay and benefits for the chief executive and top paid employees at Amherst College ★3175★

Gunsaulus Scholastic
   Chicago elementary magnet schools with the highest acceptance rates, 2000-01 ★4002★

Gunshin; Hiromi
   Radcliffe Institute for Advanced Study fellowship recipients in the field of biomedicine, 2000-01 ★2880★

Gunter-Smith; Pamela
   Top pay and benefits for the chief executive and top paid employees at Spelman College ★3507★

Gupta; Pranav
   All-USA College Academic Second Team, 2001 ★3★

Gura; Daniel T.
   Top pay and benefits for the chief executive and top paid employees at the University of Tampa ★3569★

Gurley; Francis P.
   Top pay and benefits for the chief executive and top paid employees at Assumption College ★3181★

Gurnee, District 56
   Illinois elementary school districts with the highest teacher salaries, 1999 ★3984★

Gusick; Lindsay
   All-America girls' high school soccer team forwards, 2001 ★175★

Guskin; Alan E.
   Top pay and benefits for the chief executive and top paid employees at Antioch University ★3178★

Gustav Klimt: Silver, Gold, and Precious Stone
   Booklist's best art books for young people ★308★

Gustavus Adolphus College
   U.S. colleges and universities with the worst food service program ★1043★
   Highest undergraduate tuition and fees at colleges and universities in Minnesota ★1520★
   U.S. bachelor's institutions with the largest number of students studying abroad, 1998-99 ★2511★
   Average faculty salaries for institutions of higher education in Minnesota, 2000-01 ★3710★

Guthrie; Woody
   Outstanding children's picture books, 2000 ★331★

Gutierrez; Carlos G.
   American Chemical Society 2001 award winners (Group 3) ★753★

Gutman; John
   Top pay and benefits for the chief executive and top paid employees at Saint Michael's College ★3483★

Guy; Laurie
   Top pay and benefits for the chief executive and top paid employees at Queens College in North Carolina ★3448★

Guy-Sheftall; Beverly
   Top pay and benefits for the chief executive and top paid employees at Spelman College ★3507★

Gwendolyn Brooks (Southside) College Prep
   Admissions to college prep schools in Chicago that are the toughest to get into, 2001 ★4001★
   College prep schools in Chicago that are the toughest to get into ★4005★

Gwinnett County Public Library System
Highest Hennen's American Public Library Ratings for libraries serving a population of over 500,000 ★2700★

Gwinnett County Public Schools
Top recruiters for education jobs for 2000-01 bachelor's degree recipients ★4377★
Top recruiters for education jobs for 2000-01 master's degree recipients ★4398★

Gwinnett Technical Institute
Lowest undergraduate tuition and fees at colleges and universities in Georgia ★1497★

Gwynedd Mercy Academy
Outstanding secondary schools in Philadelphia, Pennsylvania-New Jersey ★4202★

Gwynedd-Mercy College
Average faculty salaries for institutions of higher education in Pennsylvania, 2000-01 ★3725★

H

Haaland; Gordon A.
Top pay and benefits for the chief executive and top paid employees at Gettysburg College ★3308★

Haas-Wilson; D.
Top associate professor economists at elite liberal arts colleges, 1975-94 ★2174★

Habenicht; Charles W.
Top pay and benefits for the chief executive and top paid employees at Andrews University ★3176★

Habermas; J.
Most cited authors in the journal *Journal of Criminal Justice*, 1990 to 1995 ★1626★

Habitat for Humanity International
Organizations with the most charitable contributions raised, 1999 ★2943★

Habtermariam; Tsegaye
Top pay and benefits for the chief executive and top paid employees at Tuskegee University ★3583★

Hackett; Paul R.
Top pay and benefits for the chief executive and top paid employees at the University of Southern California ★3568★

Haden; William R.
Top pay and benefits for the chief executive and top paid employees at West Virginia Wesleyan College ★3613★

Hader; Sandra M.
Top pay and benefits for the chief executive and top paid employees at William Jewell College ★3630★

Hagan; John L.
Most cited authors in the journal *Criminology*, 1990 to 1995 ★1622★
Most cited authors in the journal *Justice Quarterly*, 1990 to 1995 ★1630★
Most cited authors in three criminal justice journals ★1633★

Hagan; Joseph H.
Top pay and benefits for the chief executive and top paid employees at Assumption College ★3181★

Hagelin; John
Top pay and benefits for the chief executive and top paid employees at the Maharishi University of Management ★3533★

Hagerstown College
Average faculty salaries for institutions of higher education in Maryland, 2000-01 ★3707★

Hagerstown Community College
Lowest undergraduate tuition and fees at colleges and universities in Maryland ★1515★

Hagerstown-Jefferson Township Public Library
Highest Hennen's American Public Library Ratings for libraries serving a population of 2,500 to 4,999 ★2693★

Hagler Bailly
Companies with the worst two-year total returns since 1998 ★437★

Hahn Rafter; Nicole
Most-cited scholars in women and crime publications ★1642★

Haider; S.J.
Authors that most frequently cite *Libri* publications from 1972 to 1999 ★2723★

Hainer; Peter C.
Top pay and benefits for the chief executive and top paid employees at Curry College ★3261★

Haines Elementary School
Illinois elementary schools chosen to be 'demonstration sites' for struggling schools ★4006★

Haines; Terrel W.
Top pay and benefits for the chief executive and top paid employees at Huntingdon College ★3344★

Hairstylists and cosmetologists
Occupations with the highest number of self-employed workers, 1998 ★2311★
Projected employment growth for selected occupations that require an associate degree or less, 1998-2008 ★2319★

Hale; Clara
Most influential African Americans in medicine and science ★2879★

Hales; R. Stanton
Top pay and benefits for the chief executive and top paid employees at the College of Wooster ★3531★

Haley; Alex
Most influential African Americans in the arts ★78★

Halifax Community College
Average faculty salaries for institutions of higher education without academic ranks in North Carolina, 2000-01 ★3761★

Halifax Library
North America's first ten public libraries ★2680★

Halifax Public Library
North America's first ten public libraries ★2680★

Hall; Alvin
Top pay and benefits for the chief executive and top paid employees at Union Institute ★3586★

Hall; David
Top pay and benefits for the chief executive and top paid employees at Northeastern University ★3422★

Hall; Ellen
Top pay and benefits for the chief executive and top paid employees at Wells College ★3610★

Hall; James W.
Top pay and benefits for the chief executive and top paid employees at Antioch University ★3178★

Hall; Lanny
Top pay and benefits for the chief executive and top paid employees at Hardin-Simmons University ★3325★

Hall; Maurice
All-American boy's high school football running backs, 2000 ★186★

Hall Middle School
Outstanding secondary schools in San Francisco, California ★4221★

Hall; R.E.
U.S. academic economists by mean number of citations, 1971-92 ★2176★

Hall; William B.
Top pay and benefits for the chief executive and top paid employees at Salve Regina University ★3489★

Halliburton
Business Week's best performing companies with the lowest 3-year sales performance ★423★
Fortune's highest ranked engineering and construction companies, 2000 ★461★

Hallmark Cards
Most selective internships in the U.S., 2001 ★2610★
Top internships in the U.S. with the highest compensation, 2001 ★2611★

Hallmark Institute of Technology
Highest undergraduate tuition and fees at colleges and universities in Texas ★1560★

Halloran; William S.
Top pay and benefits for the chief executive and top paid employees at the College of St. Catherine ★3528★

Halloween ABC
Most frequently banned books in the 1990s ★745★

Hameline; Walter L.
Top pay and benefits for the chief executive and top paid employees at Wagner College ★3599★

Hamer; Fannie Lou
Most influential African Americans in politics and civil rights ★3040★

Hamilton College
U.S. colleges and universities with a popular theater group ★1020★
U.S. colleges and universities with excellent library facilities ★1025★
U.S. News & World Report's national liberal arts colleges with the highest percentage of alumni support, 2000-01 ★1331★
Private 4-year institutions with the highest tuition, 2000-01 ★1467★
Highest undergraduate tuition and fees at colleges and universities in New York ★1537★
Top full professor economists at elite liberal arts colleges, 1975-94 ★2175★
Private, 4-year undergraduate colleges and universities producing the most Ph.D.'s in English, 1920-1990 ★2449★
Average faculty salaries for institutions of higher education in New York, 2000-01 ★3719★

Hamilton; Harry
Top pay and benefits for the chief executive and top paid employees at Chapman University ★3228★

Hamilton Jr.; Kenneth N.
Top pay and benefits for the chief executive and top paid employees at Walsh University ★3602★

Hamilton Public Library
Highest Hennen's American Public Library Ratings for libraries serving a population of 2,500 to 4,999 ★2693★

Hamlin; James
Top pay and benefits for the chief executive and top paid employees at Central College in Iowa ★3226★

Hamline University
U.S. News & World Report's national liberal arts colleges with students most in debt, 1999 ★1386★
Highest undergraduate tuition and fees at colleges and universities in Minnesota ★1520★
U.S. colleges and universities awarding the most law and legal studies first professional degrees to Native Americans ★1855★
Academics' choices for best dispute resolution programs, 2001 ★2627★
Average faculty salaries for institutions of higher education in Minnesota, 2000-01 ★3710★

Hamlow; Clifford
Top pay and benefits for the chief executive and top paid employees at Azusa Pacific University ★3187★

Hammarskjold Middle School
Outstanding secondary schools in Middlesex-Somerset-Hunterdon, New Jersey ★4179★

Hammerschmidt; Peter K.
Top pay and benefits for the chief executive and top paid employees at Eckerd College ★3282★

Hammett, Harrold, Gross, & Epstein
Most cited works in academic literature dealing with corrections ★1643★

Hammon; Craig
Top pay and benefits for the chief executive and top paid employees at Gordon College in Massachusetts ★3312★

Hampden-Sydney College
All-USA College Academic Third Team, 2001 ★4★
U.S. News & World Report's national liberal arts colleges with students least in debt, 1999 ★1385★
Highest undergraduate tuition and fees at colleges and universities in Virginia ★1564★
Average faculty salaries for institutions of higher education in Virginia, 2000-01 ★3735★

Hampshire College
U.S. colleges and universities where intercollegiate sports are not popular ★994★
U.S. colleges and universities where students are very politically active ★1001★
U.S. colleges and universities with a generally liberal student body ★1015★
U.S. colleges and universities with a large student body of liberal Democrats ★1017★
U.S. colleges and universities with a popular theater group ★1020★
Highest undergraduate tuition and fees at private nonprofit, 4-year or above colleges and universities ★1461★
Private 4-year institutions with the highest tuition, 2000-01 ★1467★
Highest undergraduate tuition and fees at colleges and universities in Massachusetts ★1516★
Average faculty salaries for institutions of higher education in Massachusetts, 2000-01 ★3708★

Hampton; Clark
Top pay and benefits for the chief executive and top paid employees at United States International University ★3587★

Hampton College
U.S. News & World Report's southern regional universities with the highest freshmen retention rates, 2000-01 ★1437★

Hampton; Henry
Best U.S. works of journalism in the 20th century ★2769★

Hampton High School
Outstanding secondary schools in Pittsburgh, Pennsylvania ★4204★

Hampton Roads Academy
Outstanding secondary schools in Norfolk-Virginia Beach-Newport News, Virginia-North Carolina ★4194★

Hampton University
Four-year institutions with the most weapons referrals reported, 1999 ★710★
Top college choices for Washington D.C. students ★847★
U.S. colleges and universities least accepting of alternative lifestyles ★985★
U.S. colleges and universities with a popular radio station ★1019★
U.S. colleges and universities with poor library facilities ★1028★
U.S. colleges and universities with the worst financial aid programs ★1042★
U.S. colleges and universities with the worst food service program ★1043★
U.S. colleges and universities with the worst overall administration ★1045★
Retention rates of African American students at historically black institutions, 1997-98 ★1120★
U.S. News & World Report's southern regional universities with students most in debt, 1999 ★1432★
U.S. News & World Report's southern regional universities with the highest percentage of freshmen in the top 25% of their high school class, 2000-01 ★1439★
U.S. News & World Report's southern regional universities with the lowest acceptance rates, 2000-01 ★1442★
Total baccalaureate biology/life sciences degrees awarded to African Americans from U.S. colleges and universities, 1997-98 ★1679★
Total baccalaureate business management and administrative services degrees awarded to African Americans from U.S. colleges and universities, 1997-98 ★1683★
Total baccalaureate communications degrees awarded to African Americans from U.S. colleges and universities, 1997-98 ★1687★
Total baccalaureate degrees awarded to African Americans from historically black colleges, 1997-98 ★1697★
Total baccalaureate degrees awarded to African Americans from U.S. colleges and universities, 1997-98 ★1699★
Total baccalaureate English language, literature, and letters degrees awarded to African Americans from U.S. colleges and universities, 1997-98 ★1716★
Total baccalaureate psychology degrees awarded to African Americans from U.S. colleges and universities, 1997-98 ★1737★
U.S. colleges and universities awarding the most biological and life sciences master's degrees to African Americans ★1756★
U.S. colleges and universities awarding the most physical sciences master's degrees to African Americans ★1793★
Private, 4-year undergraduate colleges and universities producing the most Ph.D.'s in nonscience fields, 1990 ★2032★
Most wired historically black colleges and universities, 2000 ★2597★

Hanchrow; Gracie
Top pay and benefits for the chief executive and top paid employees at Huntingdon College ★3344★

Hancock Jr.; Ben E.
Top pay and benefits for the chief executive and top paid employees at Albion College ★3167★

Hancock Middle Senior High School
Outstanding secondary schools in Hagerstown, Maryland ★4144★

Hand packers and packagers
Projected employment growth for selected occupations that require shorter moderate-term on-the-job training, 1998-2008 ★2321★

Handbook of Dates for Students of British History
Selected new editions and supplements reference books, 2000 ★372★

The Handmaid's Tale
Canada's best fiction selections of the 20th century ★233★
Most frequently banned books in the 1990s ★745★

Hang Seng Bank
Business Week's best companies in Hong Kong ★395★

Hanifin; Leo
Top pay and benefits for the chief executive and top paid employees at the University of Detroit Mercy ★3541★

Hankin; Jo Ann
Top pay and benefits for the chief executive and top paid employees at Whittier College ★3624★

Hankinson; Mel
Top pay and benefits for the chief executive and top paid employees at Liberty University ★3373★

Hanna Sacks Bais Yaakov High School
Outstanding independent high schools in Metro Chicago ★4077★

Hannah's Collections
Outstanding books for young readers, 2000 ★328★

Hanover College
U.S. colleges and universities where intramural sports are popular ★997★
U.S. colleges and universities with poor library facilities ★1028★
U.S. News & World Report's national liberal arts colleges with students least in debt, 1999 ★1385★
Average faculty salaries for institutions of higher education in Indiana, 2000-01 ★3701★

Hanover County Public Schools
Top recruiters for education jobs for 2000-01 bachelor's degree recipients ★4377★
Top recruiters for education jobs for 2000-01 master's degree recipients ★4398★

Hansberry; Lorraine
Most influential African Americans in the arts ★78★

Hansen; Elaine
Top pay and benefits for the chief executive and top paid employees at Haverford College ★3329★

Hansen; G. Holger
Top pay and benefits for the chief executive and top paid employees at Haverford College ★3329★

Hansen; Richard S.
Top pay and benefits for the chief executive and top paid employees at Norwich University in Vermont ★3424★

Hansen; Terrence A.
Top pay and benefits for the chief executive and top paid employees at Loma Linda University ★3377★

Hansen; W. Lee
Individuals producing the most economic education research articles, 1963-1990 ★2166★

Hanson; Janet
Top pay and benefits for the chief executive and top paid employees at Marian College of Fond Du Lac ★3389★

Hanson; Jason
Longest field goals in college football ★158★

Hanson; Linda
Top pay and benefits for the chief executive and top paid employees at Seattle University ★3495★

The Happy Bottom Riding Club: The Life and Times of Pancho Barnes
Outstanding biography books, 2000 ★288★

Harbaugh; Joseph
Top pay and benefits for the chief executive and top paid employees at Nova Southeastern University ★3426★

Harborview Medical Center
Top orthopedics hospitals in the U.S., 2000 ★2797★

Harcourt
Highest revenues of publicly held book publishers, 1999 ★3072★
Top children's book publishers, 1999 ★3074★

Harcourt General
Publishers with the best industry stocks, 2000 ★300★

Harcum College
Average faculty salaries for institutions of higher education in Pennsylvania, 2000-01 ★3725★

Hardin; Brian
Top pay and benefits for the chief executive and top paid employees at Willamette University ★3628★

Hardin-Simmons University
Average faculty salaries for institutions of higher education in Texas, 2000-01 ★3731★

Harding Middle School
Outstanding secondary schools in Cedar Rapids, Iowa ★4104★

Harding University
Division II NCAA colleges with the highest graduation rates for football players, 1993-94 ★946★
U.S. News & World Report's best undergraduate fees among southern regional universities by discount tuition, 2000 ★1429★
U.S. News & World Report's southern regional universities with students most in debt, 1999 ★1432★
U.S. News & World Report's southern regional universities with the best alumni giving rates, 2000-01 ★1434★
U.S. News & World Report's southern regional universities with the highest acceptance rates, 2000-01 ★1436★
Highest undergraduate tuition and fees at colleges and universities in Arkansas ★1484★

Hardnett; Shawn
All-USA Teacher Teams, Second Team, 2000 ★4400★

Hare; David
Top playwrights of the twentieth century ★4436★

Hare; R.D.
Most cited authors in the journal *Criminal Justice and Behavior*, 1990 to 1995 ★1619★

Harford Community College
Lowest undergraduate tuition and fees at colleges and universities in Maryland ★1515★
Average faculty salaries for institutions of higher education in Maryland, 2000-01 ★3707★

Hargadon; Kristian
All-USA College Academic Third Team, 2001 ★4★

Harkham Hillel Hebrew Academy
Outstanding secondary schools in Los Angeles-Long Beach, California ★4167★

Harley-Davidson
Top leisure time industries in Standard & Poor's 500, 2001 ★545★

Harley, Like a Person
Booklist's best first novels for youths ★309★
Most notable fiction books for reluctant young adult readers, 2001 ★321★
Most notable fiction books for young adults, 2001 ★322★

Harlow; David L.
Top pay and benefits for the chief executive and top paid employees at Rhodes College ★3456★

Harmon; George M.
Top pay and benefits for the chief executive and top paid employees at Millsaps College ★3403★

Harmon; Karlie
Top pay and benefits for the chief executive and top paid employees at Oklahoma City University ★3431★

Harms; Clarence
Top pay and benefits for the chief executive and top paid employees at Westminster College in Pennsylvania ★3617★

Harnichar; Andrew
Top pay and benefits for the chief executive and top paid employees at the College of St. Rose ★3529★

Harold Washington College
Fall enrollment at Chicago-area city colleges, by minority percentages, 1999 ★865★

Harper Community College
Fall enrollment at Chicago-area public community colleges, by minority percentages, 1999 ★867★

Harper and Row
Book publishers with the most citations (Class 5) ★2566★

HarperCollins
Hardcover bestsellers by corporation, 2000 ★239★
Hardcover bestsellers by publishing house, 2000 ★240★
Paperback bestsellers by corporation, 2000 ★296★
Highest revenues of publicly held book publishers, 1999 ★3072★
Top children's book publishers, 1999 ★3074★

HarperPaperbacks
Mass market paperback bestsellers by publishing house, 2000 ★283★

Harrah's Entertainment
Fortune's highest ranked hotels, casinos and resorts, 2000 ★470★

Harre; Alan F.
Top pay and benefits for the chief executive and top paid employees at Valparaiso University ★3592★

Harrington, C.M.; Rev. Donald J.
Top pay and benefits for the chief executive and top paid employees at St. John's University in New York ★3474★

Harrington; John
Top pay and benefits for the chief executive and top paid employees at Tufts University ★3580★

Harrington; Scott E.
Authors with the most published pages in impact-weighted insurance journals ★677★
Individual authors with the most published pages in *The Journal of Risk and Insurance*, 1987-1996 ★680★

Harris; Ashlyn
All-America girls' high school soccer team goalkeepers, 2001 ★176★

Harris; E. Lynn
Favorite African American authors ★237★

Harris; Lawren
Canada's best visual artists of the 20th century ★75★

Harris; Orien
All-American boy's high school football linemen, 2000 ★183★

Harris; Robin
Top pay and benefits for the chief executive and top paid employees at Rockhurst University ★3464★

Harris; Stephen
Top pay and benefits for the chief executive and top paid employees at Trevecca Nazarene University ★3576★

Harris-Stowe State College
State appropriations for Missouri's institutions of higher education, 2000-01 ★1278★
Average faculty salaries for institutions of higher education in Missouri, 2000-01 ★3712★

Harris; Tommie
All-American boy's high school football linemen, 2000 ★183★

Harris; Winfred
Top pay and benefits for the chief executive and top paid employees at Clark Atlanta University ★3237★

Harrisburg Academy
Outstanding secondary schools in Harrisburg-Lebanon-Carlisle, Pennsylvania ★4146★

Harrisburg Area Community College
Lowest undergraduate tuition and fees at colleges and universities in Pennsylvania ★1550★
Average faculty salaries for institutions of higher education in Pennsylvania, 2000-01 ★3725★

Harrisburg-Lebanon-Carlisle, PA
Cities with the most Yahoo! listings per million residents ★2580★

Harrison; David
All-America boys' high school basketball 1st team, 2001 ★161★

Harrison; Walter
Top pay and benefits for the chief executive and top paid employees at the University of Hartford ★3544★

Harriton High School
Outstanding secondary schools in Philadelphia, Pennsylvania-New Jersey ★4202★

Harry Potter
Publishers Weekly Off-the-Cuff Awards winner for most often requested title, 2000 ★355★
Most notable children's web sites, 2001 ★2593★

Harry Potter and the Goblet of Fire
Outstanding audiobooks, 2000 ★287★
Booklist's most recommended fantasy books for youth ★312★
Most notable children's recordings, 2001 ★320★
Outstanding books for middle readers, 2000 ★326★
Outstanding children's fiction books, 2000 ★329★
Publishers Weekly Off-the-Cuff Awards winner for best audiobook, 2000 ★336★
Smithsonian's best books for children ages 10 and up ★365★

Harry Potter and the Prisoner of Azkaban
Most notable children's recordings, 2001 ★320★
Publishers Weekly Off-the-Cuff Awards winner for hottest selling book to go out of stock, 2000 ★351★

Harry S. Truman College
Fall enrollment at Chicago-area city colleges, by minority percentages, 1999 ★865★

Harry's Home
Smithsonian's best books for children ages 1 to 6 ★363★

Hartford Financial Services Group
Fortune's highest ranked property and casualty insurance companies, 2000 ★488★

Hartford/New Haven, CT
U.S. cities with the most wired households, 2001 ★2606★

Hartford; University of
Division I NCAA colleges with that graduated more than 80% of their African American male athletes, 1990-91 to 1993-94 ★929★
Highest undergraduate tuition and fees at colleges and universities in Connecticut ★1490★
Average faculty salaries for institutions of higher education in Connecticut, 2000-01 ★3694★

Hartland High School
Outstanding secondary schools in Ann Arbor, Michigan ★4084★

Hartley; Alan
Top pay and benefits for the chief executive and top paid employees at Scripps College ★3493★

Hartman; Paul W.
Top pay and benefits for the chief executive and top paid employees at DePauw University ★3267★

Hartmann; Heidi
Highly acknowledged individuals in the field of women's studies, 1975-94 ★4466★

Hartnell College
Lowest undergraduate tuition and fees at public 2-year colleges and universities ★1465★

Hartshorn; Liz
Top pay and benefits for the chief executive and top paid employees at Alaska Pacific University ★3166★

Hartwick College
Average faculty salaries for institutions of higher education in New York, 2000-01 ★3719★

Harvard Business Review
Top management journals ★546★
Top management journals by core impact ★547★
Top ranked AACSB publications ★2186★
Journals and proceedings with the most citations (Class 2) ★2568★
Most cited business serials in technical communication journals from 1988 to 1997 ★4417★
Most cited serials in technical communication journals from 1988 to 1997 ★4425★

Harvard Business School Press
Book publishers with the most citations (Class 5) ★2566★

Harvard College
U.S. colleges and universities offering the best overall academic experience for undergraduates ★987★
U.S. colleges and universities that are the toughest to get into ★988★
U.S. colleges and universities with excellent library facilities ★1025★
U.S. colleges and universities with the best overall administration ★1033★
U.S. colleges and universities with the best quality of life ★1034★
Highest undergraduate tuition and fees at colleges and universities in Massachusetts ★1516★

Harvard Education Review
Education and educational research journals by citation impact, 1981-99 ★2235★
Education and educational research journals by citation impact, 1995-99 ★2236★
Education and educational research journals by citation impact, 1999 ★2237★
Education and educational research journals with the greatest impact measure ★2238★

Harvard Law Review
Law journals by citation impact, 1981-96 ★2617★
Law journals with the greatest impact measure, 1981-98 ★2618★
Most frequently-cited law reviews and legal periodicals, 1924-1986: a compilation ★2619★
Most frequently-cited law reviews and legal periodicals, according to *Shepard's Law Review Citations*, 1957-1986 ★2620★
Social sciences journals with the greatest impact measure, 1981-97 ★4341★

Harvard Medical School
Radcliffe Institute for Advanced Study fellowship recipients in the field of molecular biology, 2000-01 ★208★
Radcliffe Institute for Advanced Study fellowship recipients in the field of biomedicine, 2000-01 ★2880★

Harvard University
All-USA College Academic First Team, 2001 ★2★
All-USA College Academic Second Team, 2001 ★3★
Colleges with the highest number of freshman Merit Scholars, 2000 ★5★
U.S. universities enrolling the most National Achievement Scholars, 1994 ★9★
U.S. universities enrolling the most National Achievement Scholars, 1995 ★10★
U.S. universities enrolling the most National Achievement Scholars, 1996 ★11★
U.S. universities enrolling the most National Achievement Scholars, 1997 ★12★
U.S. universities enrolling the most National Achievement Scholars, 1998 ★13★
Most effective anthropology research-doctorate programs as evaluated by the National Research Council ★61★
Top anthropology research-doctorate programs as evaluated by the National Research Council ★62★
U.S. universities publishing the most papers in the field of archaeology, 1994-98 ★66★
U.S. universities publishing the most papers in the fields of art and architecture, 1994-98 ★70★
Most effective art history research-doctorate programs as evaluated by the National Research Council ★91★
Top art history research-doctorate programs as evaluated by the National Research Council ★93★
Most effective neurosciences research-doctorate programs as evaluated by the National Research Council ★200★
Top neurosciences research-doctorate programs as evaluated by the National Research Council ★202★
Most effective biochemistry and molecular biology research-doctorate programs as evaluated by the National Research Council ★205★
Most effective cell and developmental biology research-doctorate programs as evaluated by the National Research Council ★206★
Most effective molecular and general genetics research-doctorate programs as evaluated by the National Research Council ★207★
Radcliffe Institute for Advanced Study fellowship recipients in the field of molecular biology, 2000-01 ★208★
Top biochemistry and molecular biology research-doctorate programs as evaluated by the National Research Council ★209★
Top cell and developmental biology research-doctorate programs as evaluated by the National Research Council ★210★
Top molecular and general genetics research-doctorate programs as evaluated by the National Research Council ★211★
U.S. universities with the greatest impact in cell and developmental biology, 1993-97 ★212★
U.S. universities with the greatest impact in cell and developmental biology, 1994-98 ★213★
U.S. universities publishing the most papers in the field of microbiology, 1994-98 ★215★
U.S. universities with the greatest impact in biotechnology and applied microbiology, 1995-99 ★216★
U.S. universities with the greatest impact in microbiology, 1994-98 ★217★
Top business schools in research performance, 1986-1998 ★532★
U.S. universities publishing the most papers in the field of management, 1995-99 ★574★
Top business schools by average MBA rank, 1986-1998 ★644★
Top business schools for overall within-discipline research performance, 1986-1998 ★645★

Top business schools for within-discipline research performance in management, 1986-1998 ★646★

Top business schools for within-discipline research performance in finance, 1986-1998 ★663★

Top business schools for within-discipline research performance in management information systems, 1986-1998 ★675★

Degree-granting institutions with the most published pages in *The Journal of Risk and Insurance*, 1987-1996 ★678★

U.S. universities with the greatest impact in chemistry, 1994-98 ★793★

Most effective chemistry research-doctorate programs as evaluated by the National Research Council ★802★

Top chemistry research-doctorate programs as evaluated by the National Research Council ★805★

Most effective classics research-doctorate programs as evaluated by the National Research Council ★815★

Top classics research-doctorate programs as evaluated by the National Research Council ★816★

Comparison of acceptance rates at the top 5 national universities in the U.S., 1990 and 2001 ★845★

U.S. News & World Report's national universities with the best academic reputation, 2000-01 ★1126★

U.S. News & World Report's national universities with the best faculty resources rank, 2000-01 ★1127★

U.S. News & World Report's national universities with the best freshmen retention rates, 2000-01 ★1128★

U.S. News & World Report's national universities with the best graduation and retention rank, 2000-01 ★1129★

U.S. News & World Report's national universities with the best student/faculty ratio, 2000-01 ★1130★

U.S. News & World Report's national universities with the highest alumni giving rank, 2000-01 ★1132★

U.S. News & World Report's national universities with the highest financial resources rank, 2000-01 ★1133★

U.S. News & World Report's national universities with the highest graduation rate, 1999 ★1134★

U.S. News & World Report's national universities with the highest proportion of alumni support, 2000-01 ★1137★

U.S. News & World Report's national universities with the highest selectivity rank, 2000-01 ★1139★

U.S. News & World Report's national universities with the lowest acceptance rates, 2000-01 ★1140★

2000 endowment values of the 'wealthiest' U.S. universities ★1230★

Colleges and universities with the largest endowments, 2000 ★1237★

Endowment values for the wealthiest U.S. universities, 2000 ★1240★

Institutions receiving the most alumni gifts, 1999-2000 ★1242★

Institutions receiving the most gifts, 1999-2000 ★1244★

U.S. News & World Report's best undergraduate fees among national universities by discount tuition, 2000 ★1474★

Most effective comparative literature research-doctorate programs as evaluated by the National Research Council ★1587★

Top comparative literature research-doctorate programs as evaluated by the National Research Council ★1588★

Top computer science research-doctorate programs as evaluated by the National Research Council ★1597★

Total baccalaureate physical sciences degrees awarded to Asian Americans from U.S. colleges and universities, 1997-98 ★1734★

U.S. colleges and universities awarding the most business management and administrative services master's degrees to Asian Americans ★1760★

U.S. colleges and universities awarding the most education master's degrees to Asian Americans ★1770★

U.S. colleges and universities awarding the most education master's degrees to Native Americans ★1772★

U.S. colleges and universities awarding the most health professions and related sciences master's degrees to Asian Americans ★1778★

U.S. colleges and universities awarding the most master's degrees to Asian Americans ★1786★

U.S. colleges and universities awarding the most master's degrees to minorities ★1788★

U.S. colleges and universities awarding the most master's degrees to Native Americans ★1789★

Traditionally white institutions awarding the most first professional degrees to African Americans ★1842★

U.S. colleges and universities awarding the most first professional degrees to African Americans ★1843★

U.S. colleges and universities awarding the most first professional degrees to Asian Americans ★1844★

U.S. colleges and universities awarding the most first professional degrees to Hispanic Americans ★1845★

U.S. colleges and universities awarding the most health professions and related sciences first professional degrees to African Americans ★1847★

U.S. colleges and universities awarding the most health professions and related sciences first professional degrees to Asian Americans ★1848★

U.S. colleges and universities awarding the most health professions and related sciences first professional degrees to minorities ★1850★

U.S. colleges and universities awarding the most law and legal studies first professional degrees to African Americans ★1852★

U.S. colleges and universities awarding the most law and legal studies first professional degrees to Asian Americans ★1853★

U.S. universities with the greatest impact in dermatology, 1995-99 ★1876★

Institutions awarding the most doctorate degrees to African Americans, 1997-98 ★1948★

Top doctorate granting institutions, 1999 ★2047★

Traditionally white institutions awarding the most doctorate degrees to African Americans ★2079★

U.S. colleges and universities awarding the most biological and life sciences doctorate degrees to African Americans ★2082★

U.S. colleges and universities awarding the most doctoral degrees to African Americans from 1995 to 1999 ★2091★

U.S. colleges and universities awarding the most doctoral degrees to Asian Americans and Pacific Islanders from 1995 to 1999 ★2093★

U.S. colleges and universities awarding the most doctorate degrees to African Americans ★2095★

U.S. colleges and universities awarding the most doctorate degrees to Asian Americans ★2096★

U.S. colleges and universities awarding the most doctorate degrees to minorities ★2098★

U.S. colleges and universities awarding the most doctorate degrees to Native Americans ★2099★

U.S. colleges and universities awarding the most doctorates in all fields, 1999 ★2100★

U.S. colleges and universities awarding the most doctorates in humanities, 1999 ★2103★

U.S. colleges and universities awarding the most doctorates in life sciences, 1999 ★2104★

U.S. colleges and universities awarding the most doctorates in social sciences, 1999 ★2107★

U.S. colleges and universities awarding the most health professions and related sciences doctorate degrees to African Americans ★2114★

U.S. colleges and universities awarding the most health professions and related sciences doctorate degrees to Asian Americans ★2115★

U.S. colleges and universities awarding the most health professions and related sciences doctorate degrees to Hispanic Americans ★2116★

U.S. colleges and universities awarding the most social sciences and history doctorate degrees to African Americans ★2124★

U.S. colleges and universities awarding the most social sciences and history doctorate degrees to Asian Americans ★2125★

U.S. colleges and universities awarding the most social sciences and history doctorate degrees to Hispanic Americans ★2126★

U.S. colleges and universities awarding the most social sciences and history doctorate degrees to Native Americans ★2127★

U.S. institutions awarding the most doctorate degrees, 1999 ★2132★

U.S. universities with the greatest impact in geosciences, 1994-98 ★2149★

Top geosciences research-doctorate programs as evaluated by the National Research Council ★2152★

U.S. universities with the greatest impact in geosciences, 1993-97 ★2155★

Economics departments by number of citations by top economists, 1971-92 ★2158★

Economics departments by number of citations per top economist, 1971-92 ★2159★

Economics departments by number of top economists, 1971-92 ★2160★

Institutions most frequently contributing to the *American Economic Review* from 1911-1990 ★2168★

Institutions most frequently contributing to the *American Economic Review* from 1951-1990 ★2169★

U.S. universities publishing the most papers in the field of economics and business, 1995-99 ★2178★

U.S. universities with the greatest impact in economics, 1995-99 ★2179★

HARVARD

Economics Ph.D. programs by number of citations of top economist graduates, 1971-92 ★2204★

Economics Ph.D. programs by number of citations per top economist graduate, 1971-92 ★2205★

Economics Ph.D. programs by number of top economist graduates, 1971-92 ★2206★

Most effective economics research-doctorate programs as evaluated by the National Research Council ★2207★

Origin of doctorate for dissertation chairs in economics ★2208★

Origin of doctorate for economics faculty at Ph.D.-granting institutions ★2209★

Origin of doctorate for economics faculty at Ph.D.-granting institutions, by Ph.D. equivalents produced ★2210★

Top economics research-doctorate programs as evaluated by the National Research Council ★2213★

Radcliffe Institute for Advanced Study fellowship recipient in the field of education, 2000-01 ★2218★

Most effective English language and literature research-doctorate programs as evaluated by the National Research Council ★2448★

Top English language and literature research-doctorate programs as evaluated by the National Research Council ★2451★

Most effective German language and literature research-doctorate programs as evaluated by the National Research Council ★2527★

Top German language and literature research-doctorate programs as evaluated by the National Research Council ★2528★

Average GMAT scores for *U.S. News & World Report*'s top 10 graduate business schools, 2000 ★2529★

U.S. universities contributing the most papers in the field of history, 1993-97 ★2551★

Top history research-doctorate programs as evaluated by the National Research Council ★2554★

Radcliffe Institute for Advanced Study fellowship recipients in the field of public policy, 2000-01 ★2622★

U.S. universities publishing the most papers in the field of law, 1994-98 ★2623★

Academics' choices for best dispute resolution programs, 2001 ★2627★

Academics' choices for best international law programs, 2001 ★2631★

Academics' choices for best tax law programs, 2001 ★2632★

Acceptance rates at *U.S. News & World Report*'s top 10 law schools, 2001 ★2634★

Graduate employment percentage for *U.S. News & World Report*'s top 10 law schools, 2001 ★2636★

Jurisdiction's overall bar passage rate for *U.S. News & World Report*'s top 10 law schools, 2001 ★2637★

Law schools with the best bankruptcy faculty, 1999-2000 ★2639★

Law schools with the best civil procedure faculty, 1999-2000 ★2640★

Law schools with the best commercial law faculty, 1999-2000 ★2641★

Law schools with the best comparative law faculty, 1999-2000 ★2642★

Law schools with the best constitutional law (general) faculty, 1999-2000 ★2645★

Law schools with the best corporate law and securities regulation faculty, 1999-2000 ★2646★

Law schools with the best criminal procedure faculty, 1999-2000 ★2648★

Law schools with the best feminist legal theory faculty, 1999-2000 ★2651★

Law schools with the best international law faculty, 1999-2000 ★2654★

Law schools with the best labor law faculty, 1999-2000 ★2656★

Law schools with the best law and economics faculty, 1999-2000 ★2657★

Law schools with the best legal history faculty, 1999-2000 ★2661★

Law schools with the best tax faculty, 1999-2000 ★2664★

Law schools with the highest quality, 1999-2000 ★2666★

School's bar passage rate in jurisdiction at *U.S. News & World Report*'s top 10 law schools, 2001 ★2667★

Student-faculty ratios at *U.S. News & World Report*'s top 10 law schools, 2001 ★2669★

Top law schools, 2001 ★2670★

Top law schools by reputation, as determined by academic personnel, 2001 ★2671★

Top law schools by reputation, as determined by lawyers and judges, 2001 ★2672★

Top law school student bodies, 1999-2000 ★2673★

Law library web sites, by visibility ★2687★

Top university research libraries in the U.S. and Canada, 1998-99 ★2706★

U.S. universities with the greatest impact in library and information science, 1994-98 ★2719★

U.S. universities with the greatest impact in mathematics, 1995-99 ★2772★

Most effective mathematics research-doctorate programs as evaluated by the National Research Council ★2775★

Top mathematics research-doctorate programs as evaluated by the National Research Council ★2778★

Top statistics and biostatistics research-doctorate programs as evaluated by the National Research Council ★2782★

Academics' choices for best AIDS programs, 2001 ★2818★

Academics' choices for best drug and alcohol abuse programs, 2001 ★2819★

Academics' choices for best geriatrics programs, 2001 ★2821★

Academics' choices for best internal medicine programs, 2001 ★2822★

Academics' choices for best pediatrics programs, 2001 ★2823★

Academics' choices for best women's health medical programs, 2001 ★2825★

Acceptance rates for *U.S. News & World Report*'s top 10 research-oriented medical schools, 2001 ★2827★

Average MCAT scores at *U.S. News & World Report*'s top 10 research-oriented medical schools, 2001 ★2836★

Average undergraduate GPA at *U.S. News & World Report*'s top 10 research-oriented medical schools, 2001 ★2838★

Faculty-student ratios at *U.S. News & World Report*'s top 10 research-oriented medical schools, 2001 ★2842★

NIH research grants for *U.S. News & World Report*'s top 10 research-oriented medical schools, 2001 ★2845★

Out-of-state tuition and fees for *U.S. News & World Report*'s top 10 research-oriented medical schools, 2001 ★2847★

Top primary-care medical schools by student selectivity rank, 2001 ★2858★

Top research-oriented medical schools, 2001 ★2859★

Top research-oriented medical schools by reputation, as determined by academic personnel, 2001 ★2860★

Top research-oriented medical schools by reputation, as determined by intern/residency directors, 2001 ★2861★

Top research-oriented medical schools by student selectivity, 2001 ★2862★

Most effective music research-doctorate programs as evaluated by the National Research Council ★2895★

Top music research-doctorate programs as evaluated by the National Research Council ★2896★

U.S. universities with the greatest impact in optics and acoustics, 1995-99 ★2912★

Most effective pharmacology research-doctorate programs as evaluated by the National Research Council ★2938★

Top pharmacology research-doctorate programs as evaluated by the National Research Council ★2939★

Organizations with the most charitable contributions raised, 1999 ★2943★

Most effective philosophy research-doctorate programs as evaluated by the National Research Council ★2945★

Top philosophy research-doctorate programs as evaluated by the National Research Council ★2947★

U.S. universities publishing the most papers in the field of philosophy, 1995-99 ★2948★

Radcliffe Institute for Advanced Study fellowship recipient in the field of geophysics, 2000-01 ★2969★

Most effective astrophysics and astronomy research-doctorate programs as evaluated by the National Research Council ★3006★

Most effective physics research-doctorate programs as evaluated by the National Research Council ★3007★

Top astrophysics and astronomy research-doctorate programs as evaluated by the National Research Council ★3014★

Top physics research-doctorate programs as evaluated by the National Research Council ★3015★

Most effective political science research-doctorate programs as evaluated by the National Research Council ★3043★

Top political science research-doctorate programs as evaluated by the National Research Council ★3046★

U.S. institutions with the most citations in psychiatry research, 1990-98 ★3059★

Most effective psychology research-doctorate programs as evaluated by the National Research Council ★3065★

Top psychology research-doctorate programs as evaluated by the National Research Council ★3068★

Radcliffe Institute for Advanced Study fellowship recipients in the field of religion, 2000-01 ★3092★

Top religion research-doctorate programs as evaluated by the National Research Council ★3093★

U.S. universities with the highest concentrations in religion and theology, 1992-96 ★3094★

Most patents issued to universities or research facilities, 1999 ★3097★

U.S. colleges and universities with the most federal support for chemical research and development, 1998 ★3102★

Institutions receiving the most federal research and development expenditures, 1999 ★3105★

Average faculty salaries for institutions of higher education in Massachusetts, 2000-01 ★3708★

Private institutions of higher education that pay the highest salaries to female professors, 2000-01 ★3974★

U.S. institutions with the highest paid assistant professors, 2001 ★3977★

U.S. institutions with the highest paid full professors, 2001 ★3978★

U.S. universities contributing the most papers in the field of neurosciences, 1993-97 ★4285★

U.S. universities publishing the most papers in the field of neuroscience, 1994-98 ★4287★

U.S. universities with the highest relative citation impact, 1993-97 ★4291★

U.S. universities publishing the most highly-cited papers, 1997-1999 ★4348★

U.S. universities publishing the most papers in the field of sociology and anthropology, 1994-98 ★4349★

U.S. universities publishing the most papers in the fields of sociology and anthropology, 1993-97 ★4350★

Top sociology research-doctorate programs as evaluated by the National Research Council ★4354★

Top Spanish and Portuguese language and literature research-doctorate programs as evaluated by the National Research Council ★4358★

Academics' choices for best administration/supervision graduate programs, 2001 ★4378★

Academics' choices for best curriculum/instruction graduate programs, 2001 ★4380★

Academics' choices for best education policy graduate programs, 2001 ★4381★

Academics' choices for best educational psychology graduate programs, 2001 ★4382★

Academics' choices for best higher education administration graduate programs, 2001 ★4384★

Acceptance rates at *U.S. News & World Report*'s top 10 graduate education schools, 2001 ★4388★

Average quantitative GRE scores for *U.S. News & World Report*'s top 10 graduate education schools, 2001 ★4389★

Average verbal GRE scores for *U.S. News & World Report*'s top 10 graduate education schools, 2001 ★4390★

Doctoral students to faculty ratio at *U.S. News & World Report*'s top 10 graduate education schools, 2001 ★4391★

Ph.D.s and Ed.D.s granted at *U.S. News & World Report*'s top 10 graduate education schools, 2001 ★4392★

Research expenditures for *U.S. News & World Report*'s top 10 graduate education schools, 2001 ★4393★

Research expenditures per faculty member at *U.S. News & World Report*'s top 10 graduate education schools, 2001 ★4394★

Top graduate education schools, 2001 ★4395★

Top graduate education schools by reputation, as determined by academic personnel, 2001 ★4396★

Top graduate education schools by reputation, as determined by superintendents, 2001 ★4397★

Harvard University Graduate School of Business Administration

Academics' choices for best graduate entrepreneurship programs, 2001 ★583★

Academics' choices for best graduate nonprofit organizations programs, 2001 ★586★

Acceptance rates for *U.S. News & World Report*'s top 10 graduate business schools, 2001 ★588★

Annual tuition at *Business Week*'s top business schools, 2000 ★589★

Average GMAT scores at *U.S. News & World Report*'s top 10 graduate business schools, 2001 ★591★

Average job offers received by graduates from *Business Week*'s top business schools, 1999 ★592★

Average undergraduate GPA at *U.S. News & World Report*'s top 10 graduate business schools, 2001 ★593★

Business Week's institutions with the best entrepreneurship programs ★594★

Business Week's top business schools, 2000 ★595★

Business Week's top business schools as selected by corporate recruiters, 2000 ★596★

Business Week's top business schools as selected by recent MBA graduates, 2000 ★597★

Business Week's top business schools for finance skills as selected by corporate recruiters, 2000 ★600★

Business Week's top business schools for general management skills as selected by corporate recruiters, 2000 ★601★

Business Week's top business schools for global scope skills as selected by corporate recruiters, 2000 ★602★

Business Week's top business schools for marketing skills as selected by corporate recruiters, 2000 ★603★

Business Week's top business schools for technology skills as selected by corporate recruiters, 2000 ★604★

Business Week's top business schools with the greatest rise in MBA satisfaction, 2000 ★611★

Business Week's top business schools with the highest percentage of minority enrollment, 2000 ★613★

Business Week's top business schools with the highest percentage of women enrollees, 2000 ★614★

Business Week's top business schools with the most innovative curriculum as selected by corporate recruiters, 2000 ★619★

Business Week's top business schools worst at responding to student concerns, 2000 ★621★

Highest post-MBA salaries for students enrolled in *Business Week*'s top business schools, 1999 ★631★

Highest pre-MBA salaries for students enrolled in *Business Week*'s top business schools, 1999 ★632★

Median starting salaries of graduates from *U.S. News & World Report*'s top 10 graduate business schools, 2001 ★636★

Out-of-state tuition and fees for *U.S. News & World Report*'s top 10 graduate business schools, 2001 ★637★

Percentage of applicants accepted at *Business Week*'s top business schools, 2000 ★638★

Percentage of employed graduates at *U.S. News & World Report*'s top 10 graduate business schools, 2001 ★639★

Percentage of graduates earning over $100,000 from *Business Week*'s top business schools, 1999 ★640★

Percentage of graduates employed within 3 months of graduation from *U.S. News & World Report*'s top 10 graduate business schools, 2001 ★641★

Top graduate business schools, 2001 ★649★

Top graduate business schools by reputation as determined by academic personnel, 2001 ★650★

Top graduate business schools by reputation, as determined by recruiters, 2001 ★651★

Academics' choices for best graduate accounting programs, 2001 ★659★

Academics' choices for best graduate finance programs, 2001 ★662★

Academics' choices for best graduate general management programs, 2001 ★666★

Academics' choices for best graduate international business programs, 2001 ★668★

Academics' choices for best graduate marketing programs, 2001 ★670★

Academics' choices for best graduate production/operations management programs, 2001 ★674★

Harvard University Press

Book publishers with the most citations (Class 5) ★2566★

Harvey; Jordan

All-America boys' high school soccer team defenders, 2001 ★165★

Harvey Mudd College

U.S. colleges and universities offering the best overall academic experience for undergraduates ★987★

Highest undergraduate tuition and fees at colleges and universities in California ★1486★

Private, 4-year undergraduate colleges and universities producing the most Ph.D.'s in the computer sciences, 1920-1990 ★1595★

Private, 4-year undergraduate colleges and universities producing the most Ph.D.'s in the computer sciences, 1981-1990 ★1596★

Private, 4-year undergraduate colleges and universities producing the most Ph.D.'s in the earth sciences, 1981-1990 ★2151★

U.S. News & World Report's undergraduate engineering programs with the highest academic reputation scores, 2000-01 ★2337★

U.S. News & World Report's undergraduate engineering programs with the best civil departments, 2000-01 ★2347★

U.S. News & World Report's undergraduate engineering programs with the best electrical departments, 2000-01 ★2355★

U.S. News & World Report's undergraduate engineering programs with the best mechanical departments, 2000-01 ★2438★

Private, 4-year undergraduate colleges and universities producing the most Ph.D.'s in mathematics, 1920-1990 ★2776★

Private, 4-year undergraduate colleges and universities producing the most Ph.D.'s in mathematics, 1981-1990 ★2777★

Private, 4-year undergraduate colleges and universities producing the most Ph.D.'s in physics and astronomy, 1920-1990 ★2949★

Average faculty salaries for institutions of higher education in California, 2000-01 ★3692★

U.S. liberal arts colleges with the highest paid full professors, 2001 ★3980★
Private, 4-year undergraduate colleges and universities producing the most Ph.D.'s in the sciences, 1981-1990 ★4295★

Harvey; Peter
Top pay and benefits for the chief executive and top paid employees at Whitman College ★3623★

Harvey; William R.
Top pay and benefits for the chief executive and top paid employees at Hampton University ★3323★

Harward; Donald W.
Top pay and benefits for the chief executive and top paid employees at Bates College ★3193★

Hash; Dorothy E.
Top pay and benefits for the chief executive and top paid employees at Southwest Baptist University ★3504★

Hasi; Rudolph
Top pay and benefits for the chief executive and top paid employees at St. John's University in New York ★3474★

Haskell Indian Nations University
U.S. tribal colleges ★1445★

Haskins; Richard T.
Top pay and benefits for the chief executive and top paid employees at Eckerd College ★3282★

Hastings College
Highest undergraduate tuition and fees at colleges and universities in Nebraska ★1528★
Average faculty salaries for institutions of higher education in Nebraska, 2000-01 ★3714★

Hastings College of Law
State appropriations for California's institutions of higher education, 2000-01 ★1258★

Hastings Middle School
Outstanding secondary schools in Minneapolis-St. Paul, Minnesota-Wisconsin ★4181★

Hatboro-Horsham High School
Outstanding secondary schools in Philadelphia, Pennsylvania-New Jersey ★4202★

Hatch; Nathan O.
Top pay and benefits for the chief executive and top paid employees at the University of Notre Dame ★3554★

Hatfield; Kenneth W.
Top pay and benefits for the chief executive and top paid employees at Rice University ★3457★

Haugen; Clifford
All-USA College Academic Second Team, 2001 ★3★

Haverford College
U.S. colleges and universities offering the best overall academic experience for undergraduates ★987★
U.S. colleges and universities with a generally liberal student body ★1015★
U.S. colleges and universities with excellent instructors ★1024★
U.S. colleges and universities with excellent library facilities ★1025★
U.S. colleges and universities with the best overall administration ★1033★
U.S. News & World Report's best national liberal arts colleges, 2000-01 ★1320★
U.S. News & World Report's national liberal arts colleges with the best freshmen retention rates, 2000-01 ★1323★
U.S. News & World Report's national liberal arts colleges with the best graduation and retention rank, 2000-01 ★1324★
U.S. News & World Report's national liberal arts colleges with the best selectivity rank, 2000-01 ★1325★
U.S. News & World Report's national liberal arts colleges with the best student/faculty ratios, 2000-01 ★1326★
U.S. News & World Report's national liberal arts colleges with the highest academic reputation scores, 2000-01 ★1327★
U.S. News & World Report's national liberal arts colleges with the highest percentage of alumni support, 2000-01 ★1331★
U.S. News & World Report's national liberal arts colleges with the highest percentage of freshmen in the top 10% of their high school class, 2000-01 ★1332★
U.S. News & World Report's national liberal arts colleges with the highest proportion of classes having 50 or more students, 2000-01 ★1334★
U.S. News & World Report's national liberal arts colleges with the lowest acceptance rates, 2000-01 ★1336★
Highest undergraduate tuition and fees at colleges and universities in Pennsylvania ★1549★
Private, 4-year undergraduate colleges and universities producing the most Ph.D.'s in economics, 1920-1990 ★2211★
Private, 4-year undergraduate colleges and universities producing the most Ph.D.'s in economics, 1981-1990 ★2212★
Private, 4-year undergraduate colleges and universities producing the most Ph.D.'s in English, 1920-1990 ★2449★
Private, 4-year undergraduate colleges and universities producing the most Ph.D.'s in mathematics, 1920-1990 ★2776★
Private, 4-year undergraduate colleges and universities producing the most Ph.D.'s in mathematics, 1981-1990 ★2777★
Institutions in the Worker Rights Consortium ★2913★
Private, 4-year undergraduate colleges and universities producing the most Ph.D.'s in physics and astronomy, 1920-1990 ★2949★
Private, 4-year undergraduate colleges and universities producing the most Ph.D.'s in political science and international relations, 1920-1990 ★3044★
Private, 4-year undergraduate colleges and universities producing the most Ph.D.'s in political science and international relations, 1981-1990 ★3045★
Average faculty salaries for institutions of higher education in Pennsylvania, 2000-01 ★3725★

Havertape; John
Top pay and benefits for the chief executive and top paid employees at Viterbo University ★3597★

Havre de Grace High School
Outstanding secondary schools in Baltimore, Maryland ★4092★

Hawaii
Mean composite ACT scores by state, 2000 ★895★
Mean math SAT scores by state, 2000 ★900★
Mean verbal SAT scores by state, 2000 ★903★
Average class size at colleges and universities in the U.S., by state ★1064★
States receiving the most in federal agency appropriations to colleges, 2000 ★1306★
States receiving the most in federal agency appropriations to colleges, from 1996 to 2000 ★1307★
Total doctorate recipients by state, 1999 ★2054★
State grades for affordability of higher education for minority students, 2000 ★2883★
State grades for benefits state receives for educating its minority students, 2000 ★2884★
State grades for completion of higher education by minority students, 2000 ★2885★
State grades for participation of minority students in higher education, 2000 ★2886★
State grades for preparing minority students for higher education, 2000 ★2887★
States with the lowest number of high school graduates, 1999-2000 ★3997★
Largest public school districts in the U.S. ★4016★
States with the highest average enrollment in public elementary schools ★4032★
States with the highest average enrollment in public secondary schools ★4033★
States with the highest percentage of high school freshmen enrolling in college within four years ★4266★

Hawaii Community College
Average faculty salaries for institutions of higher education in Hawaii, 2000-01 ★3698★

Hawaii, Hawaii Community College; University of
Undergraduate tuition and fees at colleges and universities in Hawaii ★1498★

Hawaii, Hilo; University of
Division II NCAA colleges with the 0% graduation rates for men's basketball players, 1993-94 ★941★
Division II NCAA colleges with the lowest graduation rates for all sports, 1993-94 ★947★
U.S. News & World Report's top public western regional liberal arts colleges, 2000-01 ★1365★
U.S. News & World Report's western regional liberal arts colleges with students least in debt, 1999 ★1397★
Lowest undergraduate tuition and fees at public, 4-year or above colleges and universities ★1466★
Public 4-year institutions with the lowest tuition, 2000-01 ★1472★
Undergraduate tuition and fees at colleges and universities in Hawaii ★1498★
U.S. institutions awarding the most baccalaureate degrees to Asian Americans in agricultural sciences, 1998 ★1816★
Average faculty salaries for institutions of higher education in Hawaii, 2000-01 ★3698★

Hawaii, Honolulu Community College; University of
Undergraduate tuition and fees at colleges and universities in Hawaii ★1498★

Hawaii, Kapiolani Community College; University of
Undergraduate tuition and fees at colleges and universities in Hawaii ★1498★

Hawaii, Kauai Community College; University of
Undergraduate tuition and fees at colleges and universities in Hawaii ★1498★

Hawaii, Leeward Community College; University of
Undergraduate tuition and fees at colleges and universities in Hawaii ★1498★

Hawaii, Manoa; University of
Division I NCAA colleges with that graduated none of their African American male basketball players, 1990-91 to 1993-94 ★930★
U.S. colleges and universities where students study the least ★1002★
U.S. colleges and universities with the most upper level courses taught by TAs ★1040★
U.S. colleges and universities with the worst financial aid programs ★1042★
Institutions receiving the most in federal agency appropriations to colleges, 2000 ★1245★
Undergraduate tuition and fees at colleges and universities in Hawaii ★1498★
Top colleges in terms of total baccalaureate degrees awarded to minorities, 1997-98 ★1678★
Total baccalaureate business management and administrative services degrees awarded to Asian Americans from U.S. colleges and universities, 1997-98 ★1684★
Total baccalaureate communications degrees awarded to Asian Americans from U.S. colleges and universities, 1997-98 ★1688★
Total baccalaureate degrees awarded to Asian Americans from U.S. colleges and universities, 1997-98 ★1702★
Total baccalaureate education degrees awarded to Asian Americans from U.S. colleges and universities, 1997-98 ★1712★
Total baccalaureate English language, literature, and letters degrees awarded to Asian Americans from U.S. colleges and universities, 1997-98 ★1717★
Total baccalaureate health professions and related sciences degrees awarded to Asian Americans from U.S. colleges and universities, 1997-98 ★1722★
Total baccalaureate physical sciences degrees awarded to Asian Americans from U.S. colleges and universities, 1997-98 ★1734★
Total baccalaureate psychology degrees awarded to Asian Americans from U.S. colleges and universities, 1997-98 ★1738★
Total baccalaureate social sciences and history degrees awarded to Asian Americans from U.S. colleges and universities, 1997-98 ★1742★
Total ethnic/cultural studies master's degrees awarded to minorities from U.S. colleges and universities, 1997-98 ★1748★
U.S. colleges and universities awarding the most biological and life sciences master's degrees to Asian Americans ★1757★
U.S. colleges and universities awarding the most business management and administrative services master's degrees to Asian Americans ★1760★
U.S. colleges and universities awarding the most communications master's degrees to Asian Americans ★1764★
U.S. colleges and universities awarding the most education master's degrees to Asian Americans ★1770★
U.S. colleges and universities awarding the most English language/literature/letters master's degrees to Asian Americans ★1774★
U.S. colleges and universities awarding the most health professions and related sciences master's degrees to Asian Americans ★1778★
U.S. colleges and universities awarding the most health professions and related sciences master's degrees to Native Americans ★1780★
U.S. colleges and universities awarding the most master's degrees to Asian Americans ★1786★
U.S. colleges and universities awarding the most physical sciences master's degrees to Asian Americans ★1794★
U.S. colleges and universities awarding the most psychology master's degrees to Asian Americans ★1798★
U.S. colleges and universities awarding the most social sciences and history master's degrees to Asian Americans ★1802★
U.S. institutions awarding the most baccalaureate degrees to Asian Americans in agricultural sciences, 1998 ★1816★
U.S. institutions awarding the most baccalaureate degrees to minorities in ethnic/cultural studies, 1997-98 ★1821★
U.S. institutions awarding the most master's degrees to Asian Americans in agricultural sciences, 1998 ★1827★
U.S. institutions awarding the most master's degrees to minorities in agricultural sciences, 1998 ★1830★
U.S. colleges and universities awarding the most first professional degrees to Asian Americans ★1844★
U.S. colleges and universities awarding the most law and legal studies first professional degrees to Asian Americans ★1853★
U.S. colleges and universities awarding the most biological and life sciences doctorate degrees to Asian Americans ★2083★
U.S. colleges and universities awarding the most doctorate degrees to Asian Americans ★2096★
U.S. colleges and universities awarding the most doctorate degrees to minorities ★2098★
U.S. colleges and universities awarding the most physical sciences doctorate degrees to Asian Americans ★2119★
U.S. colleges and universities awarding the most social sciences and history doctorate degrees to Asian Americans ★2125★
U.S. institutions awarding the most doctoral degrees to Asian Americans in agribusiness and production, 1998 ★2128★
U.S. institutions awarding the most doctoral degrees to Asian Americans in agricultural sciences, 1998 ★2129★
U.S. institutions awarding the most doctoral degrees to minorities in agribusiness and production, 1998 ★2130★
U.S. institutions awarding the most doctoral degrees to minorities in agricultural sciences, 1998 ★2131★
Top oceanography research-doctorate programs as evaluated by the National Research Council ★2153★
Top astrophysics and astronomy research-doctorate programs as evaluated by the National Research Council ★3014★
Average faculty salaries for institutions of higher education in Hawaii, 2000-01 ★3698★

Hawaii, Maui Community College; University of
Undergraduate tuition and fees at colleges and universities in Hawaii ★1498★

Hawaii Pacific University
Undergraduate tuition and fees at colleges and universities in Hawaii ★1498★

Total baccalaureate computer and information science degrees awarded to Native Americans from U.S. colleges and universities, 1997-98 ★1694★
U.S. colleges and universities awarding the most computer and information sciences master's degrees to African Americans ★1766★
U.S. colleges and universities awarding the most computer and information sciences master's degrees to Asian Americans ★1767★
Master's institutions with the highest enrollment of foreign students, 1998-99 ★2499★

Hawaii; University of
State appropriations for Hawaii's institutions of higher education, 2000-01 ★1264★
U.S. colleges and universities spending the most on independent lobbyists, 1999 ★1310★
U.S. colleges and universities awarding the most master's degrees to minorities ★1788★
University research libraries in the U.S. and Canada with the largest decreases in total expenditures from 1993-94 to 1998-99 ★2707★
Library and information science programs with the most journal articles, 1993-1998 ★2713★
Library and information science programs with the most journal articles per capita, 1993-1998 ★2714★
Library and information science programs with the most per capita citations to journal articles, 1993-1998 ★2715★
U.S. universities with the highest concentration of papers published in the field of aquatic sciences, 1995-99 ★4289★

Hawaii, West Oahu; University of
Undergraduate tuition and fees at colleges and universities in Hawaii ★1498★
Average faculty salaries for institutions of higher education in Hawaii, 2000-01 ★3698★

Hawaii, Windward Community College; University of
Undergraduate tuition and fees at colleges and universities in Hawaii ★1498★

Hawk: Occupation: Skateboarder
Most notable nonfiction books for reluctant young adult readers, 2001 ★323★

Hawkey; Philip
Top pay and benefits for the chief executive and top paid employees at the University of La Verne ★3547★

Hawsey; David
Top pay and benefits for the chief executive and top paid employees at Juniata College ★3357★

Hawthorne; Anttaj
All-American boy's high school football linemen, 2000 ★183★

Hay House
Small publishers with the highest sales growth between 1997 and 1999 ★3073★

Hayden; John
All-America boys' high school soccer team midfielders, 2001 ★168★

Hayden Meadows Elementary School
All-USA Teacher Teams, Second Team, 2000 ★4400★

Hayes; Alice B.
Top pay and benefits for the chief executive and top paid employees at the University of San Diego ★3565★

Hayes; Chuck
All-America boys' high school basketball 4th team, 2001 ★164★

Hayes; Elvin
Division I NCAA men's basketball players with the highest tournament scores ★154★

Hayes; Gilbert
Top pay and benefits for the chief executive and top paid employees at College of Saint Benedict ★3245★

Hayes; Robert
Top pay and benefits for the chief executive and top paid employees at Concordia University in Illinois ★3253★

Hayes; Woody
Division I-A all-time coaching victories ★126★

Haynes; Gale Stevens
Top pay and benefits for the chief executive and top paid employees at Long Island University ★3378★

Hays; Garry D.
Top pay and benefits for the chief executive and top paid employees at United States International University ★3587★

Hays; John C.
Top pay and benefits for the chief executive and top paid employees at Oberlin College ★3427★

Hays; Larry
Top pay and benefits for the chief executive and top paid employees at the Maryville University of Saint Louis ★3534★

Hays Public Library
Highest Hennen's American Public Library Ratings for libraries serving a population of 10,000 to 24,999 ★2695★

Hayt Elementary School
Illinois elementary schools chosen to be 'demonstration sites' for struggling schools ★4006★

Haywood Community College
Lowest undergraduate tuition and fees at colleges and universities in North Carolina ★1540★
Average faculty salaries for institutions of higher education without academic ranks in North Carolina, 2000-01 ★3761★

Hazard Community College
Lowest undergraduate tuition and fees at colleges and universities in Kentucky ★1509★

Hazel L. Meyer Memorial Library
Highest Hennen's American Public Library Ratings for libraries serving a population of 1,000 to 2,499 ★2692★

Hazeur; Camille
Top pay and benefits for the chief executive and top paid employees at Trinity College in Washington D.C. ★3578★

H.C. Andersen Elementary School
Illinois elementary schools chosen to be 'demonstration sites' for struggling schools ★4006★

HCA
Fortune's highest ranked health care companies, 2000 ★469★

HE Butt Grocery
Largest private companies, 2000 ★523★

Head; Robert
Top pay and benefits for the chief executive and top paid employees at Benedictine University ★3200★

Head start
Educational program activities expenditures, 2000 ★3992★

Headhunter.net
Top career-related Web sites ★2602★
Top E-recruiting providers, 2000 ★2604★

The Headless Cupid
Most frequently banned books in the 1990s ★745★

Heald Business College, Honolulu
Undergraduate tuition and fees at colleges and universities in Hawaii ★1498★

Health Affairs
Health policy and services journals by citation impact, 1981-99 ★2537★
Health policy and services journals by citation impact, 1995-99 ★2538★
Health policy and services journals by citation impact, 1999 ★2539★

Health care
Spending for E-marketplace services, by industry, 2001 ★4430★

Health Care Financial Review
Health policy and services journals by citation impact, 1995-99 ★2538★

Health care/nursing
Occupational fields of tribal college graduates that are currently employed ★964★

Health Careers High School
Outstanding secondary schools in San Antonio, Texas ★4219★

Health Communications
Paperback bestsellers by corporation, 2000 ★296★
Trade paperback bestsellers by publishing house, 2000 ★307★

Health Economics
Economics journals by citation impact, 1998 ★2184★
Health policy and services journals by citation impact, 1999 ★2539★

Health education
Gender breakdown of teaching fields doctorate recipients, by subfield, 1999 ★1943★
Teaching fields doctorates awarded at U.S. colleges and universities, by subfield, 1999 ★2046★

Health and human services
Federal appropriations to colleges, by agency, 2000 ★1241★

Health information technicians
Fastest growing occupations, 1998-2008 ★2302★
Projected employment growth for selected occupations that require an associate degree or less, 1998-2008 ★2319★

Health Net
Fortune's highest ranked health care companies, 2000 ★469★

Health professional and related sciences
Top bachelor's degree disciplines for African Americans, 1997-98 ★1672★
Top bachelor's degree disciplines for Asian Americans, 1997-98 ★1673★
Top bachelor's degree disciplines for Hispanic Americans, 1997-98 ★1674★
Top bachelor's degree disciplines for Native Americans, 1997-98 ★1675★
Top bachelor's degree disciplines for non-minorities, 1997-98 ★1676★

Health professions
Fields of study profile of foreign students enrolled in U.S. institutions of higher education, 1998-99 ★2495★

Health sciences
Life sciences doctorates awarded to U.S. citizens/permanent residents at U.S. colleges and universities, by race/ethnicity and subfield, 1999 ★1950★
Number of life sciences doctorate recipients at U.S. colleges and universities, by field, 1999 ★1974★
Percentage of female doctorate recipients at U.S. colleges and universities, by subfield, 1999 ★1988★
Fields of study profile of U.S. students studying abroad, 1998-99 ★2507★
Average costs for Academic Search titles by subject, 2001 ★2918★
Periodical prices by LC subject, 2001 ★2925★
Periodical prices by scientific discipline, 2001 ★2926★

Health sciences, general
Gender breakdown of health sciences doctorate recipients, by subfield, 1999 ★1935★
Health sciences doctorates awarded at U.S. colleges and universities, by subfield, 1999 ★1944★

Health services
Industries in Illinois with the highest projected worker increase through 2006 ★2304★
Industries with the highest percentage of projected employment growth from 1998 through 2008 ★2305★
Industries with the highest projected growth rate, 1994-2005 ★2306★

Health Services Research
Health policy and services journals by citation impact, 1981-99 ★2537★
Health policy and services journals by citation impact, 1995-99 ★2538★
Health policy and services journals by citation impact, 1999 ★2539★

Health systems/services administration
Gender breakdown of health sciences doctorate recipients, by subfield, 1999 ★1935★
Health sciences doctorates awarded at U.S. colleges and universities, by subfield, 1999 ★1944★

Health Web
Medical Library Association's top health related web sites ★2591★

Healthfinder
Medical Library Association's top health related web sites ★2591★

Healthsouth
Business Week's best performing companies with the highest 1-year shareholder returns ★415★

Healy Elementary School
Illinois elementary schools chosen to be 'demonstration sites' for struggling schools ★4006★

Healy Jr.; Nicholas
Top pay and benefits for the chief executive and top paid employees at the Franciscan University of Steubenville ★3532★

Healy; Michael
Top pay and benefits for the chief executive and top paid employees at the Franciscan University of Steubenville ★3532★

Healy; Patrick J.
Top pay and benefits for the chief executive and top paid employees at Quinnipiac University ★3449★

Hearing impairments
Disabled students served in U.S. public school programs, 1998-99 ★1877★

Hearn Jr.; Thomas K.
Largest benefit packages awarded to presidents at institutions of higher education, 1998-99 ★3133★
Presidents with the highest pay at Doctoral I and II universities, 1998-99 ★3160★

Top pay and benefits for the chief executive and top paid employees at Wake Forest University ★3600★

Heart, Lung, and Blood Institute
Proposed fiscal 2002 appropriations for National Institutes of Health scientific research ★3108★

The Heart of the Sea: The Tragedy of the Whaleship Essex
Outstanding nonfiction books for young adults, 2000 ★334★

A Heartbreaking Work of Staggering Genius
Most notable nonfiction books, 2001 ★285★
Outstanding works of nonfiction, 2001 ★294★

Heaston; Patrick
Top pay and benefits for the chief executive and top paid employees at Drake University ★3272★

Heath; Raymond P.
Top pay and benefits for the chief executive and top paid employees at Marywood University ★3396★

Heath; Ron
Top pay and benefits for the chief executive and top paid employees at the University of Dubuque ★3542★

Heather Has Two Mommies
American Library Association's most frequently challenged books of the decade ★224★
American Library Associations most frequently challenged books for the 1990s ★742★
Most frequently banned books in the 1990s ★745★

Heathwood Hall Episcopal School
Outstanding secondary schools in Columbia, South Carolina ★4117★

Heating, air conditioning, and refrigeration mechanics
Projected employment growth for selected occupations that require long-term on-the-job training, 1998-2008 ★2320★

Hebert; Jennifer Breaux
All-USA Teacher Teams, Third Team, 2000 ★4401★

Hebert; Stephen J.
Top pay and benefits for the chief executive and top paid employees at Worcester Polytechnic Institute ★3636★

Hebrew
Gender breakdown of language and literature doctorate recipients, by subfield, 1999 ★1937★
Language and literature doctorates awarded at U.S. colleges and universities, by subfield, 1999 ★1949★

Hebrew Academy
Outstanding secondary schools in Indianapolis, Indiana ★4153★
Outstanding secondary schools in Orange County, California ★4199★
Outstanding secondary schools in Washington, District of Columbia-Maryland-Virginia-West Virginia ★4249★

Hebrew Day School
Outstanding secondary schools in San Diego, California ★4220★

Hebrew Union College
Top religion research-doctorate programs as evaluated by the National Research Council ★3093★

Heckeba; Jeb
All-American boy's high school football linebackers, 2000 ★182★

Heckman; J.J.
U.S. academic economists by mean number of citations, 1971-92 ★2176★
U.S. academic economists by total citations, 1971-92 ★2177★

Hedtke; James
Top pay and benefits for the chief executive and top paid employees at Cabrini College ★3215★

Hegman; John
Top pay and benefits for the chief executive and top paid employees at Converse College ★3255★

Hegranes; Colleen
Top pay and benefits for the chief executive and top paid employees at the College of St. Catherine ★3528★

Heidelberg College
U.S. News & World Report's midwestern regional liberal arts colleges with the best student/faculty ratios, 2000-01 ★1339★
U.S. News & World Report's midwestern regional liberal arts colleges with the highest alumni giving rates, 2000-01 ★1342★
U.S. News & World Report's midwestern regional liberal arts colleges with the highest proportion of classes having 20 students or less, 2000-01 ★1347★
U.S. News & World Report's best undergraduate fees among midwestern regional liberal arts colleges by discount tuition, 2000 ★1380★
Average faculty salaries for institutions of higher education in Ohio, 2000-01 ★3722★

Heider; George C.
Top pay and benefits for the chief executive and top paid employees at Concordia University in Illinois ★3253★

Height; Dorothy
Most influential African Americans in politics and civil rights ★3040★

Heineken
Business Week's best companies in the Netherlands ★410★

Heinemann
Book publishers with the most citations (Class 5) ★2566★

Heinrichs; Ruth
Top pay and benefits for the chief executive and top paid employees at Fresno Pacific University ★3298★

Heitmann; George
Top pay and benefits for the chief executive and top paid employees at Muhlenberg College ★3413★

Helena College of Technology
Lowest undergraduate tuition and fees at colleges and universities in Montana ★1527★

Hellenic Telecommunications Organization
Business Week's top emerging-market companies worldwide ★434★

Hellister; Peter
Top pay and benefits for the chief executive and top paid employees at Union Institute ★3586★

Hellman; Lawrence
Top pay and benefits for the chief executive and top paid employees at Oklahoma City University ★3431★

Hello U.S.A.
Booklist's most recommended geography series for young people, 2000 ★313★

Helm; Peyton R.
Top pay and benefits for the chief executive and top paid employees at Colby College ★3241★

Helming; Jared
All-American boy's high school football linemen, 2000 ★183★

Helmsley Enterprises
Top women-owned companies ★4460★

Helpman; Elhanan
Authors most frequently contributing to the *American Economic Review* from 1951-1990 ★2157★

Helton; J. Tom
Top pay and benefits for the chief executive and top paid employees at Judson College in Alabama ★3356★

Hely; John L.
Top pay and benefits for the chief executive and top paid employees at Worcester Polytechnic Institute ★3636★

Hematology
Clinical medicine subfields with the highest impact measure, 1981-1997 ★2873★

Hemp; Richard E.
Top pay and benefits for the chief executive and top paid employees at Luther College ★3383★

Henberg; Marvin
Top pay and benefits for the chief executive and top paid employees at Linfield College ★3376★

Henderson; Brian E.
Top pay and benefits for the chief executive and top paid employees at the University of Southern California ★3568★

Henderson Community College
Lowest undergraduate tuition and fees at colleges and universities in Kentucky ★1509★

Henderson; Doug
Booklist's best science books for children ★310★

Henderson State University
State appropriations for Arkansas's institutions of higher education, 2000-01 ★1257★
Average faculty salaries for institutions of higher education in Arkansas, 2000-01 ★3691★

Hendley; Clark
Top pay and benefits for the chief executive and top paid employees at College of Saint Benedict ★3245★

Hendrix College
U.S. colleges and universities with a popular theater group ★1020★
Fiske Guide's best buys for private colleges and universities, 2001 ★1459★
Highest undergraduate tuition and fees at colleges and universities in Arkansas ★1484★
Average faculty salaries for institutions of higher education in Arkansas, 2000-01 ★3691★

Henggeler; S.W.
Most cited authors in the journal *International Journal of Offender Therapy and Comparative Criminology*, 1990 to 1995 ★1625★

Henkelmann; Reinhold
Top pay and benefits for the chief executive and top paid employees at Cumberland College ★3260★

Henkes; Kevin
Outstanding children's picture books, 2000 ★331★

Henkhaus; Edward
Top pay and benefits for the chief executive and top paid employees at St. Ambrose University ★3468★

Hennekens; Charles H.
Authors with the greatest impact measure in cardiovascular research, 1993-98 ★2868★
Most-cited researchers in clinical medicine, 1981-1998 ★2875★
Most-cited researchers in epidemiology, 1981-1998 ★2876★

Hennepin County Library
Highest Hennen's American Public Library Ratings for libraries serving a population of over 500,000 ★2700★

Hennepin Technical College
Lowest undergraduate tuition and fees at colleges and universities in Minnesota ★1521★
Average faculty salaries for institutions of higher education without academic ranks in Minnesota, 2000-01 ★3753★

Hennes & Mauritz
Business Week's best companies in Sweden ★404★

Hennessy; Catherine
Top pay and benefits for the chief executive and top paid employees at Adelphi University ★3164★

Hennig; Margaret
Top pay and benefits for the chief executive and top paid employees at Simmons College ★3499★

Henning; Douglas D.
Top pay and benefits for the chief executive and top paid employees at Midamerica Nazarene University ★3400★

Henning; Kent
Top pay and benefits for the chief executive and top paid employees at Carthage College ★3224★

Henrico County Public Schools
Top recruiters for art jobs for 2000-01 bachelor's degree recipients ★80★
Top recruiters for art jobs for 2000-01 master's degree recipients ★81★
Top recruiters for biology/biological science jobs for 2000-01 bachelor's degree recipients ★198★
Top recruiters for biology/biological science jobs for 2000-01 master's degree recipients ★203★
Top recruiters for language/literature jobs for 2000-01 bachelor's degree recipients ★2446★
Top recruiters for language/literature jobs for 2000-01 master's degree recipients ★2452★
Top recruiters for history jobs for 2000-01 bachelor's degree recipients ★2550★
Top recruiters for history jobs for 2000-01 master's degree recipients ★2555★
Top recruiters for foreign language jobs for 2000-01 bachelor's degree recipients ★2614★
Top recruiters for math/actuarial science jobs for 2000-01 bachelor's degree recipients ★2771★
Top recruiters for math/actuarial science jobs for 2000-01 master's degree recipients ★2779★

Henry Ford II High School
Outstanding suburban public high schools in Metro Detroit ★4258★

Henry Grady High School
Outstanding urban public high schools in Metro Atlanta ★4260★

Henry Hikes to Fitchburg
Outstanding books for young readers, 2000 ★328★
Outstanding children's picture books, 2000 ★331★
Publishers Weekly Off-the-Cuff Awards winner for hottest selling book to go out of stock, 2000 ★351★

Henry Sr.; John D.
Top pay and benefits for the chief executive and top paid employees at Emory University ★3289★

Henry; Thad A.
Top pay and benefits for the chief executive and top paid employees at William Jewell College ★3630★

Heppner; Benn
Canada's best performing artists of the 20th century ★74★

Herbert Hoover Middle School
Outstanding secondary schools in Washington, District of Columbia-Maryland-Virginia-West Virginia ★4249★

Herbst; George
Top pay and benefits for the chief executive and top paid employees at Rollins College ★3465★

Hercules
Business Week's best performing companies with the lowest 3-year shareholder returns ★424★
Top chemical companies in Standard & Poor's 500, 2001 ★533★

Here Comes Pontus!
Smithsonian's best books for children ages 6 to 10 ★364★

Heriot-Watt
Institutions generating the most economic education research text, 1963-1990 ★2167★

Heritage College
U.S. colleges and universities awarding the most education master's degrees to Native Americans ★1772★

Heritage High School
Outstanding secondary schools in Denver, Colorado ★4124★
Outstanding secondary schools in Lynchburg, Virginia ★4171★
Outstanding suburban public high schools in Metro Atlanta ★4254★

Heritage Middle School
Outstanding secondary schools in Fort Worth-Arlington, Texas ★4137★

Herkimer County Community College
Lowest undergraduate tuition and fees at colleges and universities in New York ★1538★
Average faculty salaries for institutions of higher education in New York, 2000-01 ★3719★

Herman; Joan
Highest ranking women at the top public companies, 2000 ★4452★

Herman Miller
Fortune's highest ranked furniture companies, 2000 ★467★

Hernon; Peter
Library and information science faculty with the most citations to journal articles, 1993-1998 ★2710★
Library and information science faculty with the most journal articles, 1993-1998 ★2711★

Hero: The Magazine for the Rest of Us
Library Journal's notable new magazines, 1999 ★2923★

Heros; Roberto C.
Top pay and benefits for the chief executive and top paid employees at the University of Miami ★3550★

Herr; Michael
Best U.S. works of journalism in the 20th century ★2769★

Herricks Middle School
Outstanding secondary schools in Long Island, New York ★4165★

Herring; Carol
Top pay and benefits for the chief executive and top paid employees at Barnard College ★3191★

Herring; P. Donald
Top pay and benefits for the chief executive and top paid employees at Wabash College ★3598★

Herron; Orley R.
Top pay and benefits for the chief executive and top paid employees at National-Louis University in Illinois ★3414★

Herschbach; Lisa
Radcliffe Institute for Advanced Study fellowship recipients in the field of history, 2000-01 ★2549★

Hersen; Michel
Top pay and benefits for the chief executive and top paid employees at Pacific University in Oregon ★3437★

Hersey; John
Best U.S. works of journalism in the 20th century ★2769★

Hersh; Richard H.
Top pay and benefits for the chief executive and top paid employees at Hobart and William Smith Colleges ★3334★

Hersh; Seymour
Best U.S. works of journalism in the 20th century ★2769★

Hershey High School
Outstanding secondary schools in Harrisburg-Lebanon-Carlisle, Pennsylvania ★4146★

Hesston College
Highest undergraduate tuition and fees at colleges and universities in Kansas ★1506★

Hetrick; Barbara
Top pay and benefits for the chief executive and top paid employees at the College of Wooster ★3531★

Hetrick; Patrick
Top pay and benefits for the chief executive and top paid employees at Campbell University ★3218★

Hetrick; William M.
Top pay and benefits for the chief executive and top paid employees at William Carey College ★3629★

Hewes Middle School
Outstanding secondary schools in Orange County, California ★4199★

Hewitt Associates
Top internships in the U.S. with the highest compensation, 2001 ★2611★

Hewitt; Harold W.
Top pay and benefits for the chief executive and top paid employees at Occidental College ★3428★

Hewitt; Patricia
European business moguls considered the best agenda setters ★438★

Hewitt; Paul H.
Top pay and benefits for the chief executive and top paid employees at Siena College ★3498★

Hewitt-Trussville High School
Outstanding secondary schools in Birmingham, Alabama ★4098★

Hewlett-Packard
Biggest information technology companies, 2000 ★385★
Business Week's best companies in the United States ★411★
Fortune's highest ranked computers and office equipment companies, 2000 ★456★
Top internships in the U.S. with the highest compensation, 2001 ★2611★
Top internships in the U.S., 2001 ★2612★
Largest technology companies in the U.S. in terms of annual revenue, 2000 ★4429★
Top public companies for women executives, 2000 ★4457★
Top public companies with the highest percentage of women board of directors, 2000 ★4458★

Hibbing Community College Agricultural Technical and Community College
Lowest undergraduate tuition and fees at colleges and universities in Minnesota ★1521★

Hibbing Community College Tech and Community College
Average faculty salaries for institutions of higher education without academic ranks in Minnesota, 2000-01 ★3753★

Hickey; Thomas
Top pay and benefits for the chief executive and top paid employees at Spring Hill College ★3508★

Hickman High School
Outstanding secondary schools in Columbia, Missouri ★4116★

Hicks; Lyle
Top pay and benefits for the chief executive and top paid employees at the University of Saint Francis in Illinois ★3561★

Hidden Evidence: Forty True Crime Stories and How Forensic Science Helped to Solve Them
Most notable nonfiction books for reluctant young adult readers, 2001 ★323★

Hidden Value: How Great Companies Achieve Extraordinary Results with Ordinary People
Library Journal's most notable management books, 2000 ★265★

Hietpas; Quentin J.
Top pay and benefits for the chief executive and top paid employees at the University of St. Thomas in Minnesota ★3563★

Higginbotham, Jr.; Leon
Most influential African Americans in politics and civil rights ★3040★

High-energy physics
Energy Department research funding, 2001 ★3110★

High Point Regional High School
Outstanding secondary schools in Newark, New Jersey ★4192★

High Point University
U.S. News & World Report's southern regional liberal arts colleges with the highest acceptance rates, 2000-01 ★1370★

U.S. News & World Report's southern regional liberal arts colleges with the highest proportion of classes having 20 students or less, 2000-01 ★1375★
Average faculty salaries for institutions of higher education in North Carolina, 2000-01 ★3720★

High Tech High School
Outstanding secondary schools in Monmouth-Ocean, New Jersey ★4183★

Higher education/evaluation and research
Education doctorates awarded at U.S. colleges and universities, by subfield, 1999 ★1921★
Gender breakdown of education doctorate recipients, by subfield, 1999 ★1933★

Highland Community College
Average faculty salaries for institutions of higher education without academic ranks in Illinois, 2000-01 ★3747★

Highland High School
Outstanding secondary schools in Bakersfield, California ★4091★

Highland Middle School
Outstanding secondary schools in Chicago, Illinois ★4110★

Highland Park High School
Illinois high schools with the highest SAT scores ★874★
Outstanding secondary schools in Minneapolis-St. Paul, Minnesota-Wisconsin ★4181★

Highland Park Magnet School
Outstanding secondary schools in Roanoke, Virginia ★4212★

Highlands Elementary School
Illinois suburban elementary schools with the highest ISAT scores in reading and math ★18★

Highline Community College
Lowest undergraduate tuition and fees at colleges and universities in Washington ★1567★

Highs! Over 150 Ways to Feel Really, Really Good...without Alcohol or Other Drugs
Most notable nonfiction books for reluctant young adult readers, 2001 ★323★

Hightower; Jami
All-American boy's high school football linemen, 2000 ★183★

Highum; Anne C.
Top pay and benefits for the chief executive and top paid employees at Luther College ★3383★

Highway patrol officer
Jobs with the best outlook scores ★2249★

Hilbert College
U.S. News & World Report's northern regional liberal arts colleges with students least in debt, 1999 ★1351★
Average faculty salaries for institutions of higher education in New York, 2000-01 ★3719★

Hilden; Delores
Top pay and benefits for the chief executive and top paid employees at Marycrest International University ★3393★

Hilgardia
Agriculture journals by citation impact, 1981-96 ★50★
Agriculture journals by citation impact, 1981-99 ★51★

Hill; Alan
Top pay and benefits for the chief executive and top paid employees at Alma College ★3171★

The Hill Bachelors
Booklist's best fiction books for library collections, 2000 ★227★

Hill; Carolyn
Top pay and benefits for the chief executive and top paid employees at Notre Dame College in New Hampshire ★3425★

Hill Country Middle School
Outstanding secondary schools in Austin-San Marcos, Texas ★4090★

Hill and Holiday Advertising, Inc.
Most selective internships in the U.S., 2001 ★2610★

Hill; Jerome
Top pay and benefits for the chief executive and top paid employees at University of Central Texas ★3589★

Hill; Kent R.
Top pay and benefits for the chief executive and top paid employees at Eastern Nazarene College ★3281★

Hill; Lawrence
Top pay and benefits for the chief executive and top paid employees at Lewis University ★3372★

Hill; Michael B.
Top pay and benefits for the chief executive and top paid employees at Tuskegee University ★3583★

Hill Middle School
Outstanding secondary schools in Greenville-Spartanburg-Anderson, South Carolina ★4143★

Hill; Ronald P.
Top pay and benefits for the chief executive and top paid employees at the University of Portland ★3556★

Hill; Timothy J.
Top pay and benefits for the chief executive and top paid employees at Hendrix College ★3331★

Hillcrest Magnet School
Outstanding secondary schools in Middlesex-Somerset-Hunterdon, New Jersey ★4179★

Hillenbrand Industries
Fortune's highest ranked medical products and equipment companies, 2000 ★474★

Hillenmeyer; Susan
Top pay and benefits for the chief executive and top paid employees at Belmont University ★3198★

Hillman; Pamela
Top pay and benefits for the chief executive and top paid employees at Mount Saint Mary's College in California ★3411★

Hillsborough Middle School
Outstanding secondary schools in Middlesex-Somerset-Hunterdon, New Jersey ★4179★

Hillsdale College
Division II NCAA colleges with the highest graduation rates for football players, 1993-94 ★946★
Institutions censured by the American Association of University Professors, 2001 ★1067★
U.S. News & World Report's midwestern regional liberal arts colleges with the best student/faculty ratios, 2000-01 ★1339★
U.S. News & World Report's midwestern regional liberal arts colleges with the highest freshmen retention rates, 2000-01 ★1343★
U.S. News & World Report's midwestern regional liberal arts colleges with the highest graduation rates, 2000-01 ★1344★

HILLSDALE

U.S. News & World Report's midwestern regional liberal arts colleges with the highest percentage of freshmen in the top 25% of their high school class, 2000-01 ★1345★

U.S. News & World Report's midwestern regional liberal arts colleges with the highest proportion of classes having 20 students or less, 2000-01 ★1347★

U.S. News & World Report's top midwestern regional liberal arts colleges, 2000-01 ★1349★

Hillsdale High School
Outstanding secondary schools in San Francisco, California ★4221★

Hillview Intermediate Center
Outstanding secondary schools in Sharon, Pennsylvania ★4228★

Hilton Hotels
Fortune's highest ranked hotels, casinos and resorts, 2000 ★470★

Hinds; Carol
Top pay and benefits for the chief executive and top paid employees at Mount Saint Mary's College in Maryland ★3412★

Hinds Community College
Average faculty salaries for institutions of higher education without academic ranks in Mississippi, 2000-01 ★3754★

Hindustan Lever
Business Week's top emerging-market companies worldwide ★434★

Hine; Suzanne
Top pay and benefits for the chief executive and top paid employees at Tusculum College ★3582★

Hines Middle School
Outstanding secondary schools in Norfolk-Virginia Beach-Newport News, Virginia-North Carolina ★4194★

Hinkle; Bryan
All-America boys' high school soccer team midfielders, 2001 ★168★

Hiram College
U.S. colleges and universities with the worst food service program ★1043★
Institutions with the most female physics bachelor's recipients, 1994-1998 ★2959★
U.S. institutions with more than 40% female bachelor's graduates in their physics departments, 1994-98 ★2977★
Average faculty salaries for institutions of higher education in Ohio, 2000-01 ★3722★

Hirmanpour; Iraj
Top pay and benefits for the chief executive and top paid employees at Embry-Riddle Aeronautical University ★3286★

Hirohito and the Making of Modern Japan
Outstanding biography books, 2000 ★288★

Hirsch; Jerry A.
Top pay and benefits for the chief executive and top paid employees at Western New England College ★3615★

Hirschi; Travis
Most cited authors in the journal *Criminology*, 1990 to 1995 ★1622★
Most cited authors in the journal *Journal of Criminal Justice*, 1990 to 1995 ★1626★
Most cited authors in the journal *Journal of Quantitative Criminology*, 1990 to 1995 ★1628★
Most cited authors in the journal *Journal of Research in Crime and Delinquency*, 1990 to 1995 ★1629★

Most cited authors in the journal *Justice Quarterly*, 1990 to 1995 ★1630★
Most cited authors in three criminal justice journals ★1633★
Most cited authors in three criminology journals ★1634★
Most-cited scholars in *British Journal of Criminology* ★1637★
Most-cited scholars in *Canadian Journal of Criminology* ★1638★
Most-cited scholars in *Criminology* ★1639★

Hirte; J. Richard
Top pay and benefits for the chief executive and top paid employees at Xavier University in Ohio ★3637★

Hispanic American
ACT composite scores, by race/ethnicity, 2000 ★871★
Graduation rates for female basketball players at Division I NCAA colleges, by race/ethnicity ★954★
Graduation rates for female basketball players at Division II NCAA colleges, 1993-94 ★955★
Graduation rates for female students and athletes at Division I NCAA colleges, by race/ethnicity ★956★
Graduation rates for female students at Division II NCAA colleges, 1993-94 ★957★
Graduation rates for football players at Division I NCAA colleges, by race/ethnicity ★958★
Graduation rates for football players at Division II NCAA colleges, 1993-94 ★959★
Graduation rates for male basketball players at Division I NCAA colleges, by race/ethnicity ★960★
Graduation rates for male basketball players at Division II NCAA colleges, 1993-94 ★961★
Graduation rates for male students and athletes at Division I NCAA colleges, by race/ethnicity ★962★
Graduation rates for male students at Division II NCAA colleges, 1993-94 ★963★
Racial and ethnic background of incoming freshmen, 2000 ★1058★
Bachelor's degree recipients by race/ethnicity ★1669★
Age grouping of doctorate recipients, by race/ethnicity, 1999 ★1885★
Number of U.S. citizen/permanent resident doctorate recipients in all fields at U.S. colleges and universities, by race/ethnicity, 1999 ★1978★
Number of U.S. citizen/permanent resident doctorate recipients in education at U.S. colleges and universities, by race/ethnicity, 1999 ★1979★
Number of U.S. citizen/permanent resident doctorate recipients in engineering at U.S. colleges and universities, by race/ethnicity, 1999 ★1980★
Number of U.S. citizen/permanent resident doctorate recipients in humanities at U.S. colleges and universities, by race/ethnicity, 1999 ★1981★
Number of U.S. citizen/permanent resident doctorate recipients in life sciences at U.S. colleges and universities, by race/ethnicity, 1999 ★1982★
Number of U.S. citizen/permanent resident doctorate recipients in physical sciences, mathematics, and computer sciences at U.S. colleges and universities, by race/ethnicity, 1999 ★1983★

Number of U.S. citizen/permanent resident doctorate recipients in professional/other fields at U.S. colleges and universities, by race/ethnicity, 1999 ★1984★
Number of U.S. citizen/permanent resident doctorate recipients in social sciences at U.S. colleges and universities, by race/ethnicity, 1999 ★1985★
Percentage of doctoral degree recipients at U.S. universities, by race/ethnicity, 1999 ★1987★
Percentage of minority doctorate recipients in the U.S., 1999 ★1990★
Percentage of minority doctorate recipients in the U.S., by gender, 1999 ★1992★
High school dropouts in the U.S., by race and gender, 1999 ★2135★
Ethnic breakdown of executives and managers in Silicon Valley firms, 1997 ★2300★
Race/ethnicity profile of U.S. students studying abroad, 1998-99 ★2509★
Comparison data of internet use, by race/ethnicity for 1998 and 2000 ★2582★
Internet use, by race/ethnicity and gender breakdown, 2000 ★2588★
Bachelor's degrees granted in journalism and mass communications programs, by race/ethnicity, 1999 ★2742★
Bachelor's enrollments in journalism and mass communications programs, by race/ethnicity, 1999 ★2744★
Doctoral degrees granted in journalism and mass communications programs, by race/ethnicity, 1999 ★2759★
Doctoral enrollments in journalism and mass communications programs, by race/ethnicity, 1999 ★2761★
Master's degrees granted in journalism and mass communications programs, by race/ethnicity, 1999 ★2766★
Master's enrollments in journalism and mass communications programs, by race/ethnicity, 1999 ★2768★
National Society of Fund-Raising Executives, by race/ethnicity ★2942★
Physics faculty, by race/ethnicity, 2000 ★2965★
Average annual salaries for individuals obtaining a bachelor's degree, by race/ethnicity ★3115★
Average annual salaries for individuals obtaining a high school degree, by race/ethnicity ★3116★
Average annual salaries for individuals obtaining a master's degree, by race/ethnicity ★3117★
Average annual salaries for individuals without a high school degree, by race/ethnicity ★3118★
Average salaries for individuals with a bachelor's degree, by race/ethnicity ★3127★
Average salaries for individuals with a high school degree, by race/ethnicity ★3982★
Average salaries for individuals without a high school degree, by race/ethnicity ★3983★
Students participating in gifted and talented programs, by race ethnicity, 1997 ★4050★

Hispanic American/Latino
Percentage of 18- to 24-year olds completing high school, by race, 1998 ★4273★

Historian
Jobs with the best environment scores ★2247★
Most desirable social sciences jobs ★2280★

HOLY

Historical Dictionary of the 1950s
  Selected new editions and supplements reference books, 2000 ★372★
Historical Encyclopedia of Atomic Energy
  Outstanding reference sources, 2000 ★370★

History
  Subject areas with the highest library expenditures/circulation ★306★
  Humanities doctorates awarded to U.S. citizens/permanent residents at U.S. colleges and universities, by race/ethnicity and subfield, 1999 ★1947★
  Number of humanities doctorate recipients at U.S. colleges and universities, by field, 1999 ★1973★
  Percentage of female doctorate recipients at U.S. colleges and universities, by subfield, 1999 ★1988★
  Top nonscience majors for accepted applicants to U.S. medical schools, 1999-2000 ★2854★
  Average costs for Academic Search titles by subject, 2001 ★2918★
  Periodical prices by LC subject, 2001 ★2925★
  Average starting salaries for college graduates, by field, 2000 ★3129★
  Subjects students most want to see on classroom TV ★4051★

History, American
  Gender breakdown of humanities doctorate recipients, by subfield, 1999 ★1936★
  Humanities doctorates awarded at U.S. colleges and universities, by subfield, 1999 ★1946★

History, Asian
  Gender breakdown of humanities doctorate recipients, by subfield, 1999 ★1936★
  Humanities doctorates awarded at U.S. colleges and universities, by subfield, 1999 ★1946★

History, European
  Gender breakdown of humanities doctorate recipients, by subfield, 1999 ★1936★
  Humanities doctorates awarded at U.S. colleges and universities, by subfield, 1999 ★1946★

History, general
  Gender breakdown of humanities doctorate recipients, by subfield, 1999 ★1936★
  Humanities doctorates awarded at U.S. colleges and universities, by subfield, 1999 ★1946★

History/philosophy of science and technology
  Gender breakdown of humanities doctorate recipients, by subfield, 1999 ★1936★
  Humanities doctorates awarded at U.S. colleges and universities, by subfield, 1999 ★1946★

History Resource Center: U.S.
  Library Journal's best reference databases and discs, 2000 ★369★

History Today Who's Who in British History
  Selected new editions and supplements reference books, 2000 ★372★

Hitachi Ltd.
  Business Week's best companies in Japan ★398★

Hite; Robert D.
  Top pay and benefits for the chief executive and top paid employees at Holy Names College ★3337★

Hite; Robert E.
  Most published authors, adjusted for coauthorship, in the *Journal of Business Research*, 1985 to 1999 ★701★

Hitler, 1936-1945: Nemesis
  Outstanding biography books, 2000 ★288★

Hittinger; William
  Top pay and benefits for the chief executive and top paid employees at Lehigh University ★3368★

HIV InSite
  Medical Library Association's top health related web sites ★2591★

H.J. Heinz
  Fortune's highest ranked consumer food products companies, 2000 ★458★
  Top food companies in Standard & Poor's 500, 2001 ★540★

Hlede; Korie
  Division I women's career high scorers ★129★

Ho Chi Minh
  Outstanding biography books, 2000 ★288★

Ho; Yhi-Min
  Top pay and benefits for the chief executive and top paid employees at the University of Saint Thomas in Texas ★3564★

Hoagland, Jr.; Laurance R.
  Top pay and benefits for the chief executive and top paid employees at Stanford University ★3510★

Hobart and William Smith College
  Highest undergraduate tuition and fees at colleges and universities in New York ★1537★
  Average faculty salaries for institutions of higher education in New York, 2000-01 ★3719★

Hochberg; L. Jim
  Top pay and benefits for the chief executive and top paid employees at Hawaii Pacific University ★3330★

Hodge; Julius
  All-America boys' high school basketball 2nd team, 2001 ★162★

Hodge; Sandra
  Division I women's career high scorers ★129★

Hodgkiss; William F.
  Top pay and benefits for the chief executive and top paid employees at Lawrence University ★3367★

Hodo; E. D.
  Top pay and benefits for the chief executive and top paid employees at Houston Baptist University ★3342★

Hoech Middle School
  Outstanding secondary schools in St. Louis, Missouri-Illinois ★4216★

Hoek; Christine
  Top pay and benefits for the chief executive and top paid employees at Skidmore College ★3500★

Hoff, S.J.; Rev. James E.
  Top pay and benefits for the chief executive and top paid employees at Xavier University in Ohio ★3637★

Hoffman-La Roche
  Most selective internships in the U.S., 2001 ★2610★

Hoffmann; Michael R.
  American Chemical Society 2001 award winners (Group 3) ★753★

Hofreiter; Trina
  All-USA College Academic Third Team, 2001 ★4★

Hofstra University
  U.S. colleges and universities with poor instructors ★1027★
  U.S. colleges and universities with the unhappiest students ★1041★
  U.S. colleges and universities with the worst overall administration ★1045★
  Presidents with the highest pay at Doctoral I and II universities, 1998-99 ★3160★
  Average faculty salaries for institutions of higher education in New York, 2000-01 ★3719★

Hoggard High School
  Outstanding secondary schools in Wilmington, North Carolina ★4253★

Holding Up the Earth
  Most notable fiction books for young adults, 2001 ★322★

Holdsclaw; Chamique
  NCAA Division I female basketball scoring leaders ★155★

Holes
  Publishers Weekly Off-the-Cuff Awards winner for best audiobook, 2000 ★336★

Holiday; Billie
  Most influential African American entertainers ★77★

Holland; Justin
  All-American boy's high school football quarterbacks, 2000 ★184★

Hollingsworth; A.T.
  Top pay and benefits for the chief executive and top paid employees at Florida Institute of Technology ★3293★

Hollins University
  U.S. colleges and universities where the general student body puts little emphasis on athletic events ★1009★
  U.S. colleges and universities with poor library facilities ★1028★
  Highest undergraduate tuition and fees at colleges and universities in Virginia ★1564★
  Women's colleges granting physics bachelor's degrees, 2000 ★2982★
  Average faculty salaries for institutions of higher education in Virginia, 2000-01 ★3735★

Hollis; Tarcha
  Division I women's career high scorers ★129★

Hollywood Elementary School
  Illinois suburban elementary schools with the highest ISAT scores in reading and math ★18★

Holm; Margo
  Top pay and benefits for the chief executive and top paid employees at College Misericordia ★3243★

Holmes; David R.
  Most-cited researchers in cardiology, 1981-1998 ★2874★

Holmgren; Janet L.
  Top pay and benefits for the chief executive and top paid employees at Mills College ★3402★

Holt High School
  Outstanding secondary schools in Lansing-East Lansing, Michigan ★4163★

Holtzbrinck
  Top children's book publishers, 1999 ★3074★

Holy Cross; College of the
  Division I NCAA colleges with that graduated all of their African American male basketball players, 1990-91 to 1993-94 ★927★
  Division I NCAA colleges with the highest graduation rates for football players, 1990-91 to 1993-94 ★933★
  U.S. colleges and universities with a primarily religious student body ★1022★

HOLY

U.S. colleges and universities with the worst financial aid programs ★1042★

U.S. colleges and universities without a diverse student body ★1046★

U.S. News & World Report's national liberal arts colleges with the best graduation and retention rank, 2000-01 ★1324★

U.S. News & World Report's national liberal arts colleges with the highest graduation rates, 2000-01 ★1330★

Private, 4-year undergraduate colleges and universities producing the most Ph.D.'s in English, 1920-1990 ★2449★

Private, 4-year undergraduate colleges and universities producing the most Ph.D.'s in history, 1920-1990 ★2552★

Private, 4-year undergraduate colleges and universities producing the most Ph.D.'s in history, 1981-1990 ★2553★

Private, 4-year undergraduate colleges and universities producing the most Ph.D.'s in mathematics, 1920-1990 ★2776★

Institutions in the Worker Rights Consortium ★2913★

Average faculty salaries for institutions of higher education in Massachusetts, 2000-01 ★3708★

Holy Family College
Average faculty salaries for institutions of higher education in Pennsylvania, 2000-01 ★3725★

Holy Ghost Prep
Outstanding secondary schools in Philadelphia, Pennsylvania-New Jersey ★4202★

Holy Names Academy
Outstanding secondary schools in Seattle-Bellevue-Everett, Washington ★4227★

Holy Names High School
Outstanding secondary schools in Oakland, California ★4195★

Holy Rosary
Outstanding secondary schools in Seattle-Bellevue-Everett, Washington ★4227★

Holyoke Community College
Lowest undergraduate tuition and fees at colleges and universities in Massachusetts ★1517★

Average faculty salaries for institutions of higher education in Massachusetts, 2000-01 ★3708★

Holzman; Alice
Top pay and benefits for the chief executive and top paid employees at Pitzer College ★3441★

Home Depot
Business Week's best companies in the United States ★411★

Fortune's highest ranked specialty retailers, 2000 ★497★

Top discount and fashion retailing companies in Standard & Poor's 500, 2001 ★538★

Home economics
Gender breakdown of professional doctorate recipients, by subfield, 1999 ★1940★

Professional doctorates awarded at U.S. colleges and universities, by subfield, 1999 ★2033★

Home economics education
Gender breakdown of teaching fields doctorate recipients, by subfield, 1999 ★1943★

Teaching fields doctorates awarded at U.S. colleges and universities, by subfield, 1999 ★2046★

Home economist
Most desirable social sciences jobs ★2280★

Home health care services
Employment growth percentages for selected industries, 1998-2000 ★2294★

Homecoming: The Story of African-American Farmers
Booklist's most recommended African American nonfiction ★229★

Outstanding social sciences books, 2000 ★292★

Homeless Bird
Most notable books for older readers, 2001 ★318★

Most notable fiction books for young adults, 2001 ★322★

Outstanding books for older readers, 2000 ★327★

Homestake Mining
Business Week's best performing companies with the lowest 3-year sales performance ★423★

Top metals and mining companies in Standard & Poor's 500, 2001 ★549★

Homewood-Flossmoor Community 233
Illinois high school districts with the highest teacher salaries, 1999 ★3985★

Homewood-Flossmoor High School, District 233
Illinois school districts with the most average years of teacher experience ★4012★

Homewood Middle School
Outstanding secondary schools in Birmingham, Alabama ★4098★

Hon Industries
Fortune's highest ranked furniture companies, 2000 ★467★

Honda of America Manufacturing Inc.
Top recruiters for chemical engineering jobs for 2000-01 bachelor's degree recipients ★2343★

Top recruiters for industrial engineering jobs for 2000-01 bachelor's degree recipients ★2432★

Top recruiters for mechanical engineering jobs for 2000-01 bachelor's degree recipients ★2437★

Honda Motor
Business Week's best companies in Japan ★398★

Honeywell International
Fortune's highest ranked aerospace companies, 2000 ★446★

Top conglomerates in Standard & Poor's 500, 2001 ★535★

Hong Kong
Math achievement test comparison ★19★

Countries of origin for non-U.S. citizens awarded doctorates at U.S. colleges and universities, 1999 ★1901★

Percentage of internet usage for selected countries ★2599★

Countries with the highest leader's salary ★3120★

HongKong Electric Holdings
Business Week's best companies in Hong Kong ★395★

Honky
Outstanding nonfiction books for young adults, 2000 ★334★

Honolulu Community College
Average faculty salaries for institutions of higher education in Hawaii, 2000-01 ★3698★

Honolulu, HI
U.S. cities with the highest home prices ★3087★

Honorable Company
Booklist's most recommended historical novels, 2001 ★230★

Hontas; Mark J.
Top pay and benefits for the chief executive and top paid employees at Tulane University ★3581★

Hood College
U.S. News & World Report's northern regional universities with the best student/faculty ratios, 2000-01 ★1416★

U.S. News & World Report's northern regional universities with the highest acceptance rates, 2000-01 ★1417★

U.S. News & World Report's northern regional universities with the highest percentage of freshmen in the top 25% of their high school class, 2000-01 ★1421★

U.S. News & World Report's northern regional universities with the highest percentage of full-time faculty, 2000-01 ★1422★

U.S. News & World Report's northern regional universities with the highest proportion of classes with 20 students of less, 2000-01 ★1423★

U.S. News & World Report's best undergraduate fees among northern regional universities by discount tuition, 2000 ★1428★

Highest undergraduate tuition and fees at colleges and universities in Maryland ★1514★

Average faculty salaries for institutions of higher education in Maryland, 2000-01 ★3707★

Hoover; Richard E.
Top pay and benefits for the chief executive and top paid employees at Hastings College ★3328★

Hope College
Fiske Guide's best buys for private colleges and universities, 2001 ★1459★

Highest undergraduate tuition and fees at colleges and universities in Michigan ★1518★

Average faculty salaries for institutions of higher education in Michigan, 2000-01 ★3709★

Hope Franklin; John
Most influential African Americans in education ★2216★

Hope Is the Thing with Feathers: A Personal Chronicle of Vanished Birds
Library Journal's most notable zoology books, 2000 ★278★

Hope Was Here
Christopher Awards winners for youth literature, 2000 ★316★

Most notable books for older readers, 2001 ★318★

Most notable fiction books for young adults, 2001 ★322★

Hopke; Philip K.
Top pay and benefits for the chief executive and top paid employees at Clarkson University ★3239★

Hopkins; Richard S.
Top pay and benefits for the chief executive and top paid employees at Niagara University ★3420★

Hopkinsville Community College
Lowest undergraduate tuition and fees at colleges and universities in Kentucky ★1509★

Hopps; John
Top pay and benefits for the chief executive and top paid employees at Morehouse College ★3408★

Horace Mann Middle School
  Outstanding secondary schools in Sheboygan, Wisconsin ★4229★
Horizon High School
  Outstanding secondary schools in Denver, Colorado ★4124★
Horizons Magnet School
  Outstanding secondary schools in Newburgh, New York-Pennsylvania ★4193★
Horn; David
  Top pay and benefits for the chief executive and top paid employees at Goucher College ★3314★
Horne; Lena
  Most influential African American entertainers ★77★
Horowitz; Helen
  Radcliffe Institute for Advanced Study fellowship recipients in the field of history, 2000-01 ★2549★
Horse Heaven
  Library Journal's best fiction audiobooks, 2000 ★241★
Horticulture science
  Agricultural sciences doctorates awarded at U.S. colleges and universities, by subfield, 1999 ★1886★
  Gender breakdown of agricultural sciences doctorate recipients, by subfield, 1999 ★1926★
Horton; D.R.
  Fortune's highest ranked engineering and construction companies, 2000 ★461★
Hortonville Middle School
  Outstanding secondary schools in Appleton-Oshkosh-Neenah, Wisconsin ★4085★
Horvath; Csaba
  American Chemical Society 2001 award winners (Group 3) ★753★
Horwitch; Mel
  Top pay and benefits for the chief executive and top paid employees at Polytechnic University ★3443★
Hoskins; Patricia
  Division I women's career high scorers ★129★
Hospital administrator
  Jobs with the best environment scores ★2247★
  Jobs with the best outlook scores ★2249★
  Most desirable jobs in healthcare/medicine ★2273★
Hospital for Special Surgery
  Top orthopedics hospitals in the U.S., 2000 ★2797★
  Top rheumatology hospitals in the U.S., 2000 ★2802★
Hospitality
  Expected starting salaries of 2000-01 bachelor's degree recipients, by specific major ★3131★
Hosterman Middle School
  Outstanding secondary schools in Minneapolis-St. Paul, Minnesota-Wisconsin ★4181★
Hot Springs, AZ
  Best 'quirky' places to live ★3083★
Hotel manager
  Most desirable jobs in travel/food service ★2278★
HotJobs.com
  Top career-related Web sites ★2602★
  Top E-recruiting providers, 2000 ★2604★

Hottell; Kendall L.
  Top pay and benefits for the chief executive and top paid employees at the University of Indianapolis ★3545★
Hough; J. Michael
  Most-cited scholars in *British Journal of Criminology* ★1637★
Houghton College
  Average faculty salaries for institutions of higher education in New York, 2000-01 ★3719★
Houghton; John G.
  Top pay and benefits for the chief executive and top paid employees at St. Edward's University ★3471★
Houghton Mifflin
  Top recruiters for art jobs for 2000-01 bachelor's degree recipients ★80★
  Top recruiters for art jobs for 2000-01 master's degree recipients ★81★
  Publishers with the best industry stocks, 2000 ★300★
  Top recruiters for accounting jobs for 2000-01 master's degree recipients ★661★
  Top recruiters for marketing jobs for 2000-01 master's degree recipients ★672★
  Top recruiters for chemistry jobs for 2000-01 bachelor's degree recipients ★792★
  Top recruiters for chemistry jobs for 2000-01 master's degree recipients ★806★
  Top recruiters for language/literature jobs for 2000-01 bachelor's degree recipients ★2446★
  Top recruiters for language/literature jobs for 2000-01 master's degree recipients ★2452★
  Top recruiters for history jobs for 2000-01 bachelor's degree recipients ★2550★
  Book publishers with the most citations (Class 4) ★2565★
  Top recruiters for foreign language jobs for 2000-01 bachelor's degree recipients ★2614★
  Top recruiters for foreign language jobs for 2000-01 master's degree recipients ★2615★
  Top recruiters for liberal arts jobs for 2000-01 bachelor's degree recipients ★2675★
  Top recruiters for information technology (MIS) jobs for 2000-01 bachelor's degree recipients ★2738★
  Top recruiters for information technology (MIS) jobs for 2000-01 master's degree recipients ★2739★
  Top recruiters for math/actuarial science jobs for 2000-01 bachelor's degree recipients ★2771★
  Top recruiters for statistics jobs for 2000-01 master's degree recipients ★2781★
  Top recruiters for statistics jobs for 2000-01 bachelor's degree recipients ★2786★
  Top recruiters for psychology jobs for 2000-01 bachelor's degree recipients ★3063★
  Top recruiters for psychology jobs for 2000-01 master's degree recipients ★3069★
  Highest revenues of publicly held book publishers, 1999 ★3072★
  Top children's book publishers, 1999 ★3074★
  Top recruiters for sociology jobs for 2000-01 bachelor's degree recipients ★4347★
  Top recruiters for sociology jobs for 2000-01 master's degree recipients ★4353★
  Top recruiters for education jobs for 2000-01 master's degree recipients ★4398★
Houlihan; Francis M.
  American Chemical Society 2001 award winners (Group 2) ★752★

The Hours
  Longest-running trade paperback bestsellers, 2000 ★282★
Housatonic Community-Technical College
  Lowest undergraduate tuition and fees at colleges and universities in Connecticut ★1491★
The House of Blue Light
  Booklist's most recommended poetry books, 2001 ★231★
House; Ray S.
  Top pay and benefits for the chief executive and top paid employees at Christian Brothers University ★3233★
Household International
  Fortune's highest ranked consumer credit companies, 2000 ★457★
  Top nonbank financial companies in Standard & Poor's 500, 2001 ★550★
Housing and urban development
  Federal appropriations to colleges, by agency, 2000 ★1241★
Houston
  U.S. school districts with the highest number of vacancies for K-12 teachers ★2331★
  U.S. market areas with the highest percentage of adults having internet access ★2607★
  Largest public school districts in the U.S. ★4016★
  U.S. cities with the highest percentage of births to mothers with less than 12 years of education ★4432★
Houston Baptist University
  Institutions censured by the American Association of University Professors, 2001 ★1067★
  Average faculty salaries for institutions of higher education in Texas, 2000-01 ★3731★
Houston; Cedric
  All-American boy's high school football running backs, 2000 ★186★
Houston, Clear Lake; University of
  Total baccalaureate law and legal studies degrees awarded to Hispanic Americans from U.S. colleges and universities, 1997-98 ★1727★
  Average faculty salaries for institutions of higher education in Texas, 2000-01 ★3731★
Houston Community College System
  Community colleges in North America with the highest enrollment ★852★
  Institutions with the most part-time Hispanic American faculty ★924★
  Community colleges with the highest enrollment of foreign students, 1998-99 ★2493★
  Average faculty salaries for institutions of higher education without academic ranks in Texas, 2000-01 ★3766★
Houston County High School
  Outstanding secondary schools in Macon, Georgia ★4172★
Houston, Downtown; University of
  Average faculty salaries for institutions of higher education in Texas, 2000-01 ★3731★
Houston; George
  Top pay and benefits for the chief executive and top paid employees at Mount Saint Mary's College in Maryland ★3412★
Houston System; University of
  State appropriations for Texas's institutions of higher education, 2000-01 ★1296★
Houston, TX
  U.S. cities considered to be the most affordable for IT professionals ★562★

Houston; University of
Division I NCAA colleges with the lowest graduation rates for female athletes, 1990-91 to 1993-94 ★936★

Division I NCAA colleges with the lowest graduation rates for female basketball players, 1990-91 to 1993-94 ★937★

Division I NCAA colleges with the lowest graduation rates for male athletes, 1990-91 to 1993-94 ★939★

U.S. colleges and universities awarding the most doctorate degrees to Hispanic Americans ★2097★

Academics' choices for best health law programs, 2001 ★2629★

Academics' choices for best intellectual property law programs, 2001 ★2630★

Law schools with the best health law (excluding medical ethics) faculty, 1999-2000 ★2652★

Houston, University Park; University of
Total baccalaureate business management and administrative services degrees awarded to Hispanic Americans from U.S. colleges and universities, 1997-98 ★1685★

Total baccalaureate mathematics degrees awarded to Hispanic Americans from U.S. colleges and universities, 1997-98 ★1731★

U.S. colleges and universities awarding the most social sciences and history master's degrees to Hispanic Americans ★1803★

U.S. colleges and universities awarding the most first professional degrees to Native Americans ★1846★

U.S. colleges and universities awarding the most law and legal studies first professional degrees to Native Americans ★1855★

U.S. colleges and universities awarding the most education doctorate degrees to Hispanic Americans ★2110★

Average faculty salaries for institutions of higher education in Texas, 2000-01 ★3731★

Houston, Victoria; University of
Average faculty salaries for institutions of higher education in Texas, 2000-01 ★3731★

How All This Started
Outstanding fiction books for young adults, 2000 ★333★

How Digital Is Your Business?
Library Journal's most notable digital technology books, 2000 ★256★

How Do Dinosaurs Say Good Night?
Christopher Awards winners for youth literature, 2000 ★316★

Most notable books for young readers, 2001 ★319★

Outstanding books for young readers, 2000 ★328★

How God Fix Jonah
Most notable books for older readers, 2001 ★318★

How to Be Gorgeous: The Ultimate Beauty Guide to Hair, Makeup and More
Most notable nonfiction books for reluctant young adult readers, 2001 ★323★

How to Eat Fried Worms
Most frequently banned books in the 1990s ★745★

How-to/home repair
Subject areas with the highest library expenditures/circulation ★306★

How to Know God
Longest-running nonfiction hardcover bestsellers, 2000 ★281★

How to Pick Stocks Like Warren Buffett
Library Journal's most notable investing books, 2000 ★264★

Howard Community College
Average faculty salaries for institutions of higher education in Maryland, 2000-01 ★3707★

Howard; H. Wendall
Top pay and benefits for the chief executive and top paid employees at Saint John Fisher College in New York ★3472★

Howard; Harold C.
Top pay and benefits for the chief executive and top paid employees at Eastern College in Pennsylvania ★3280★

Howard High School
Outstanding secondary schools in Baltimore, Maryland ★4092★

Howard; Lee N.
Top pay and benefits for the chief executive and top paid employees at Linfield College ★3376★

Howard; Margaret E. L.
Top pay and benefits for the chief executive and top paid employees at Drew University ★3273★

Howard University
Historically black institutions with the highest number of National Achievement Scholars, 1998 ★8★

U.S. universities enrolling the most National Achievement Scholars, 1994 ★9★

U.S. universities enrolling the most National Achievement Scholars, 1995 ★10★

U.S. universities enrolling the most National Achievement Scholars, 1996 ★11★

U.S. universities enrolling the most National Achievement Scholars, 1997 ★12★

U.S. universities enrolling the most National Achievement Scholars, 1998 ★13★

Four-year institutions with the most weapons referrals reported, 1999 ★710★

U.S. college campuses reporting murders or non-negligent manslaughters, 1999 ★728★

Top college choices for Washington D.C. students ★847★

U.S. colleges and universities with the worst financial aid programs ★1042★

U.S. colleges and universities with the worst on-campus housing facilities ★1044★

U.S. colleges and universities with the worst overall administration ★1045★

Retention rates of African American students at historically black institutions, 1997-98 ★1120★

U.S. News & World Report's national universities with the highest proportion of classes with less than 20 students, 2000-01 ★1138★

2002 budget request for aid to individual institutions ★1235★

Undergraduate tuition and fees at colleges and universities in the District of Columbia ★1493★

Historically black colleges and universities awarding the most master's degrees to African Americans ★1670★

Total baccalaureate biology/life sciences degrees awarded to African Americans from U.S. colleges and universities, 1997-98 ★1679★

Total baccalaureate business management and administrative services degrees awarded to African Americans from U.S. colleges and universities, 1997-98 ★1683★

Total baccalaureate communications degrees awarded to African Americans from U.S. colleges and universities, 1997-98 ★1687★

Total baccalaureate degrees awarded to African Americans from historically black colleges, 1997-98 ★1697★

Total baccalaureate degrees awarded to African Americans from U.S. colleges and universities, 1997-98 ★1699★

Total baccalaureate English language, literature, and letters degrees awarded to African Americans from U.S. colleges and universities, 1997-98 ★1716★

Total baccalaureate health professions and related sciences degrees awarded to African Americans from U.S. colleges and universities, 1997-98 ★1721★

Total baccalaureate physical sciences degrees awarded to African Americans from U.S. colleges and universities, 1997-98 ★1733★

Total baccalaureate psychology degrees awarded to African Americans from U.S. colleges and universities, 1997-98 ★1737★

Total baccalaureate social sciences and history degrees awarded to African Americans from U.S. colleges and universities, 1997-98 ★1741★

U.S. colleges and universities awarding the most biological and life sciences master's degrees to African Americans ★1756★

U.S. colleges and universities awarding the most communications master's degrees to African Americans ★1763★

U.S. colleges and universities awarding the most English language/literature/letters master's degrees to African Americans ★1773★

U.S. colleges and universities awarding the most health professions and related sciences master's degrees to Native Americans ★1780★

U.S. colleges and universities awarding the most law and legal studies master's degrees to African Americans ★1781★

U.S. colleges and universities awarding the most master's degrees to African Americans ★1785★

U.S. colleges and universities awarding the most physical sciences master's degrees to African Americans ★1793★

U.S. colleges and universities awarding the most social sciences and history master's degrees to African Americans ★1801★

Historically black colleges and universities awarding the most first professional degrees to African Americans ★1835★

U.S. colleges and universities awarding the most first professional degrees to African Americans ★1843★

U.S. colleges and universities awarding the most health professions and related sciences first professional degrees to African Americans ★1847★

U.S. colleges and universities awarding the most health professions and related sciences first professional degrees to minorities ★1850★

U.S. colleges and universities awarding the most law and legal studies first professional degrees to African Americans ★1852★

Historically black colleges and universities awarding the most doctorate degrees to African Americans ★1945★

Institutions awarding the most doctorate degrees to African Americans, 1997-98 ★1948★

U.S. colleges and universities awarding the most biological and life sciences doctorate degrees to African Americans ★2082★

U.S. colleges and universities awarding the most communications doctorate degrees to African Americans ★2088★

U.S. colleges and universities awarding the most doctoral degrees to Hispanic Americans from 1995 to 1999 ★2094★

U.S. colleges and universities awarding the most doctorate degrees to African Americans ★2095★

U.S. colleges and universities awarding the most doctorate degrees to minorities ★2098★

U.S. colleges and universities awarding the most health professions and related sciences doctorate degrees to African Americans ★2114★

U.S. colleges and universities awarding the most physical sciences doctorate degrees to African Americans ★2118★

U.S. colleges and universities awarding the most psychology doctorate degrees to African Americans ★2120★

U.S. colleges and universities awarding the most social sciences and history doctorate degrees to African Americans ★2124★

University research libraries in the U.S. and Canada with the largest increases in total expenditures from 1993-94 to 1998-99 ★2708★

Degrees granted in the ten largest doctoral journalism and mass communications programs, 1999 ★2756★

Enrollment of students in the ten largest doctoral journalism and mass communications programs, 1999 ★2762★

Top recipients of corporate contributions to African American communities, 1995 ★2944★

Average faculty salaries for institutions of higher education in the District of Columbia, 2000-01 ★3732★

Howland; John L.
Top pay and benefits for the chief executive and top paid employees at Bowdoin College ★3207★

Howliday Inn
Most notable children's recordings, 2001 ★320★

Hoyle; Joe B.
Top pay and benefits for the chief executive and top paid employees at the University of Richmond ★3559★

HSBC Holdings
Business Week's best companies in Britain ★389★

http://193.135.156.15
Law library web sites with the most visible external hostnames ★2688★

http://law.house.gov
Law library web sites with the most visible external hostnames ★2688★
Law library web sites with the most visible external URLs ★2689★

http://lawlib.wuacc.edu
Law library web sites with the most visible external hostnames ★2688★

http://members.aol.com
Most frequently referenced web sites ★2592★

http://member.tripod.com
Most frequently referenced web sites ★2592★

http://thomas.loc.gov
Law library web sites with the most visible external URLs ★2689★

http://www.abanet.org
Law library web sites with the most visible external hostnames ★2688★

Law library web sites with the most visible external URLs ★2689★

http://www.access.gpo.gov
Law library web sites with the most visible external hostnames ★2688★

http://www.access.gpo.gov/su_docs/aces/aces140.html
Law library web sites with the most visible external URLs ★2689★

http://www.adobe.com
Most frequently referenced web sites ★2592★

http://www.altavista.com
Most frequently referenced web sites ★2592★

http://www.amazon.com
Most frequently referenced web sites ★2592★

http://www.aol.com
Most visited websites, 2000 ★2594★

http://www.excite.com
Most visited websites, 2000 ★2594★

http://www.findlaw.com
Law library web sites with the most visible external hostnames ★2688★
Law library web sites with the most visible external URLs ★2689★

http://www.geocities.com (geocities.yahoo.com/home/)
Most frequently referenced web sites ★2592★

http://www.go.com
Most visited websites, 2000 ★2594★

http://www.hotmail.com
Most visited websites, 2000 ★2594★

http://www.house.gov
Law library web sites with the most visible external hostnames ★2688★

http://www.law.cornell.edu
Law library web sites with the most visible external hostnames ★2688★
Law library web sites with the most visible external URLs ★2689★

http://www.law.cornell.edu/uscode
Law library web sites with the most visible external URLs ★2689★

http://www.law.emory.edu
Law library web sites with the most visible external hostnames ★2688★

http://www.lycos.com
Most visited websites, 2000 ★2594★

http://www.macromedia.com
Most frequently referenced web sites ★2592★

http://www.microsoft.com
Most frequently referenced web sites ★2592★
Most visited websites, 2000 ★2594★

http://www.msn.com
Most visited websites, 2000 ★2594★

http://www.netscape.com
Most frequently referenced web sites ★2592★
Most visited websites, 2000 ★2594★

http://www.passport.com
Most visited websites, 2000 ★2594★

http://www.senate.gov
Law library web sites with the most visible external URLs ★2689★

http://www.un.org
Law library web sites with the most visible external URLs ★2689★

http://www.yahoo.com
Most frequently referenced web sites ★2592★
Most visited websites, 2000 ★2594★
Law library web sites with the most visible external hostnames ★2688★
Law library web sites with the most visible external URLs ★2689★

Hu; Michael Y.
Most published authors, adjusted for coauthorship, in the *Journal of Business Research*, 1985 to 1999 ★701★

Hubbell; Loren Loomis
Top pay and benefits for the chief executive and top paid employees at Hobart and William Smith Colleges ★3334★

Huber; Margaret A.
Top pay and benefits for the chief executive and top paid employees at the College of Notre Dame in California ★3526★

Huckabee; Roy M.
Top pay and benefits for the chief executive and top paid employees at Mount Saint Mary College in New York ★3410★

Hudson; Gue
Top pay and benefits for the chief executive and top paid employees at Agnes Scott College ★3165★

Hudson Valley Community College
Average faculty salaries for institutions of higher education in New York, 2000-01 ★3719★

Huenerfauth; Matthew
All-USA College Academic First Team, 2001 ★2★

Huff; Archie V.
Top pay and benefits for the chief executive and top paid employees at Furman University ★3300★

Huffman; James L.
Top pay and benefits for the chief executive and top paid employees at Lewis and Clark College in Oregon ★3371★

Huffman; Sarah
All-America girls' high school soccer team midfielders, 2001 ★177★

Hughes; Langston
Most influential African Americans in the arts ★78★
Favorite African American authors ★237★

Hughes; Paula Ann
Top pay and benefits for the chief executive and top paid employees at the University of Dallas ★3538★

Hughes; Rhonda
Top pay and benefits for the chief executive and top paid employees at Bryn Mawr College ★3212★

Huizinga; David
Most cited authors in the journal *Journal of Research in Crime and Delinquency*, 1990 to 1995 ★1629★
Most cited authors in three criminology journals ★1634★
Most-cited scholars in *Criminology* ★1639★

Hull; J. Webster
Top pay and benefits for the chief executive and top paid employees at Eckerd College ★3282★

Hull; Roger H.
Top pay and benefits for the chief executive and top paid employees at Union College in New York ★3585★

Hullett; John W.
Top pay and benefits for the chief executive and top paid employees at Augustana College in Illinois ★3182★

Human and animal genetics
Biological sciences doctorates awarded at U.S. colleges and universities, by subfield, 1999 ★1887★

Gender breakdown of biological sciences doctorate recipients, by subfield, 1999 ★1927★

Human and animal pathology
Biological sciences doctorates awarded at U.S. colleges and universities, by subfield, 1999 ★1887★
Gender breakdown of biological sciences doctorate recipients, by subfield, 1999 ★1927★

Human and animal pharmacology
Biological sciences doctorates awarded at U.S. colleges and universities, by subfield, 1999 ★1887★
Gender breakdown of biological sciences doctorate recipients, by subfield, 1999 ★1927★

Human and animal physiology
Biological sciences doctorates awarded at U.S. colleges and universities, by subfield, 1999 ★1887★
Gender breakdown of biological sciences doctorate recipients, by subfield, 1999 ★1927★

Human Communication Research
Most cited language serials in technical communication journals from 1988 to 1997 ★4420★

Human-Computer Interaction
Most cited science serials in technical communication journals from 1988 to 1997 ★4424★

Human Factors
Most cited technology serials in technical communication journals from 1988 to 1997 ★4427★

Human Genome Research Institute
Proposed fiscal 2002 appropriations for National Institutes of Health scientific research ★3108★

Human/individual and family counseling
Gender breakdown of psychology doctorate recipients, by subfield, 1999 ★1941★
Psychology doctorates awarded at U.S. colleges and universities, by subfield, 1999 ★2043★

Human Nature: An Interdisciplinary Biosocial Perspective
Anthropology journals by citation impact, 1994-98 ★64★
Anthropology journals by citation impact, 1998 ★65★

Human Relations
Top management journals ★546★
Top management journals by core impact ★547★
Most cited business serials in technical communication journals from 1988 to 1997 ★4417★

Human resources
Expected starting salaries of 2000-01 bachelor's degree recipients, by specific major ★3131★

Human resources assistant
Monster.com's most searched job listings ★2308★

Humana
Fortune's highest ranked health care companies, 2000 ★469★

Humanities
Top fields of study for college and university presidents, 1998 ★839★
Age grouping of doctorate recipients, by broad field, 1999 ★1882★
Doctoral degree distribution by broad field, 1999 ★1902★
Number of doctorate recipients at U.S. colleges and universities, by field, 1999 ★1969★
Percentage of female doctorate recipients, by broad field, 1999 ★1989★
Percentage of minority doctorate recipients in the U.S., by broad field, 1999 ★1991★
Fields of study profile of foreign students enrolled in U.S. institutions of higher education, 1998-99 ★2495★
Fields of study profile of U.S. students studying abroad, 1998-99 ★2507★
Subjects required by the most U.S. medical schools for the 2000-01 entering class ★2850★

Humanities/social science
Expected starting salaries of 2000-01 bachelor's degree recipients, by general major ★3130★

Humboldt State University
U.S. News & World Report's top public western regional universities, 2000-01 ★1573★
Average faculty salaries for institutions of higher education in California, 2000-01 ★3692★

Humphrey; David
Top pay and benefits for the chief executive and top paid employees at Westminster College in Missouri ★3616★

Hunady; Ronald
Top pay and benefits for the chief executive and top paid employees at Pfeiffer University ★3439★

Hungary
Comparison of 8th grade science achievement scores, U.S. and worldwide, 1999 ★6★
Eight grade science achievement scores from selected countries, 1999 ★14★
Math achievement test comparison ★19★
Percentage of enrollment at private institutions of higher education, by country, 1998 ★858★
Countries with the lowest percentage of workers satisfied with their job ★2243★
Countries with the lowest spending per student on higher education, 1997 ★2489★
Eighth grade mathematics achievement scores from selected countries, 1999 ★2773★
Institute for Scientific Information periodical prices by country, 2001 ★2922★

Hunt; Gary C.
Top pay and benefits for the chief executive and top paid employees at Southwest Baptist University ★3504★

Hunt; Hayley
All-America girls' high school soccer team defenders, 2001 ★174★

Hunt; Richard
Most influential African Americans in the arts ★78★

Hunt; Shelby D.
Highest impact authors in the Journal of Business Research, by number of citations in 12 journals, 1985-1999 ★693★

The Hunter: A Chinese Folktale
Outstanding books for young readers, 2000 ★328★

Hunter; Janet C.
Top pay and benefits for the chief executive and top paid employees at Knox College ★3360★

Hunter Jr.; Jairy C.
Top pay and benefits for the chief executive and top paid employees at Charleston Southern University ★3229★

Hunterdon Central Regional High School
Outstanding secondary schools in Middlesex-Somerset-Hunterdon, New Jersey ★4179★

Huntington College
U.S. News & World Report's midwestern regional liberal arts colleges with the best student/faculty ratios, 2000-01 ★1339★
U.S. News & World Report's midwestern regional liberal arts colleges with the highest acceptance rates, 2000-01 ★1341★
U.S. News & World Report's midwestern regional liberal arts colleges with the highest alumni giving rates, 2000-01 ★1342★
Highest undergraduate tuition and fees at colleges and universities in Alabama ★1479★
Average faculty salaries for institutions of higher education in Indiana, 2000-01 ★3701★

Huntington Middle School
Outstanding secondary schools in Los Angeles-Long Beach, California ★4167★

Huntington; S. P.
Authors with the most citations among authors published in American Political Science Review, 1974-94 ★3048★

Huntsman
Largest private companies, 2000 ★523★

Huron University
Highest undergraduate tuition and fees at colleges and universities in South Dakota ★1556★

Hurst-Euless-Bedford ISD
Top recruiters for education jobs for 2000-01 bachelor's degree recipients ★4377★
Top recruiters for education jobs for 2000-01 master's degree recipients ★4398★

Hurston; Zora Neale
Most influential African Americans in the arts ★78★

Hurt; Carlas
All-America boys' high school basketball 3rd team, 2001 ★163★

Hurwitz; Ellen S.
Top pay and benefits for the chief executive and top paid employees at Albright College ★3168★

Huskey; Peter
All-USA College Academic Third Team, 2001 ★4★

Husson College
Institutions censured by the American Association of University Professors, 2001 ★1067★
Highest undergraduate tuition and fees at colleges and universities in Maine ★1512★
Average faculty salaries for institutions of higher education in Maine, 2000-01 ★3706★

Husted; Stewart W.
Top pay and benefits for the chief executive and top paid employees at Lynchburg College ★3384★

Huston-Tillotson College
Historically black colleges and universities with major improvements in student loan default rates, 1998 ★2737★

Hutchinson; Diane L.
Top pay and benefits for the chief executive and top paid employees at Wells College ★3610★

Hutchison Whampoa
Business Week's best companies in Hong Kong ★395★

Business Week's best companies in terms of profits ★406★
Hyatt Hotels & Resorts
Top recruiters for hospitality/hotel/restaurant management jobs for 2000-01 bachelor's degree recipients ★2558★
Hyble; Carol
Top pay and benefits for the chief executive and top paid employees at Alma College ★3171★
Hyde; Michael E.
Top pay and benefits for the chief executive and top paid employees at Alfred University ★3169★
Hyde Park Academy
Outstanding urban public high schools in Metro Chicago ★4262★
The hydrodynamics of the dentine; its possible relationship to dentinal pain
Endodontic articles with the most citations, 1974 through 1999 ★1864★
Hydrology and water resources
Earth, atmosphere, and marine science doctorates awarded at U.S. colleges and universities, by subfield, 1999 ★1909★
Gender breakdown of earth, atmosphere, and marine science doctorate recipients, by subfield, 1999 ★1932★
Hyman; Eric C.
Top pay and benefits for the chief executive and top paid employees at Texas Christian University ★3518★
Hynes; William
Top pay and benefits for the chief executive and top paid employees at Saint Mary's College of California ★3480★
Hyperion
Hardcover bestsellers by corporation, 2000 ★239★
Hardcover bestsellers by publishing house, 2000 ★240★
Paperback bestsellers by corporation, 2000 ★296★
Trade paperback bestsellers by publishing house, 2000 ★307★
Hypovereinsbank
Business Week's best companies in Germany ★394★

I

I Have to Go
Most frequently banned books in the 1990s ★745★
I Know Why the Caged Bird Sings
American Library Association's most frequently challenged books of the decade ★224★
Favorite books of African Americans ★238★
American Library Associations most frequently challenged books for the 1990s ★742★
Most frequently banned books in the 1990s ★745★
I Love You Like Crazy Cakes
Publishers Weekly Off-the-Cuff Awards winner for best treatment of a social issue, 2000 ★342★
I May Not Get There with You: The True Martin Luther King, Jr
Outstanding social sciences books, 2000 ★292★
I Was a Sixth Grade Alien
Most notable children's recordings, 2001 ★320★

I2 Technologies
Business Week's best companies in terms of share-price gain ★409★
Iadarola; Antoinette
Top pay and benefits for the chief executive and top paid employees at Cabrini College ★3215★
Iberdrola
Business Week's best companies in Spain ★403★
IBM
Business Week's best companies in terms of profits ★406★
Business Week's best companies in the United States ★411★
Business Week's top companies worldwide ★433★
Fortune's highest ranked computers and office equipment companies, 2000 ★456★
Largest technology companies in the U.S. in terms of annual revenue, 2000 ★4429★
Best companies for working mothers ★4446★
Best companies for working mothers in offering leave for new parents ★4449★
Best companies for working mothers in terms of overall work/life support ★4451★
IBP
Fortune's highest ranked food production companies, 2000 ★464★
Icarus
Astronomy and astrophysics journals by citation impact, 1981-99 ★102★
Astronomy and astrophysics journals by citation impact, 1999 ★104★
Icarus: International Journal of Solar System Studies
Astronomy and astrophysics journals by impact factor, 1981 to 1998 ★105★
The Ice Master: The Doomed 1913 Voyage of the Karluk
Outstanding nonfiction books for young adults, 2000 ★334★
Ickes; Jeffrey
Top pay and benefits for the chief executive and top paid employees at Alaska Pacific University ★3166★
ICPR Junior College
Highest undergraduate tuition and fees at colleges and universities in Puerto Rico ★1551★
ICT Automatisering
Best small companies worldwide ★384★
Ida B. Wells: Mother of the Civil Rights Movement
Booklist's most recommended black history books for youth ★311★
Most notable books for older readers, 2001 ★318★
Most notable nonfiction books for young adults, 2001 ★324★
Outstanding books for older readers, 2000 ★327★
Idaho
Mean composite ACT scores by state, 2000 ★895★
Mean math SAT scores by state, 2000 ★900★
Mean verbal SAT scores by state, 2000 ★903★
Total doctorate recipients by state, 1999 ★2054★
State grades for affordability of higher education for minority students, 2000 ★2883★

State grades for benefits state receives for educating its minority students, 2000 ★2884★
State grades for completion of higher education by minority students, 2000 ★2885★
State grades for participation of minority students in higher education, 2000 ★2886★
State grades for preparing minority students for higher education, 2000 ★2887★
States with the largest growth in income ★3124★
States with the lowest per-pupil expenditures ★3998★
Idaho State University
Division I NCAA colleges with that graduated less than 20% of their African American male athletes, 1990-91 to 1993-94 ★928★
Division I NCAA colleges with the lowest graduation rates for football players, 1990-91 to 1993-94 ★938★
Division I NCAA colleges with the lowest graduation rates for male athletes, 1990-91 to 1993-94 ★939★
State appropriations for Idaho's institutions of higher education, 2000-01 ★1265★
Undergraduate tuition and fees at colleges and universities in Idaho ★1499★
Idaho; University of
Division I NCAA colleges with that graduated none of their African American male basketball players, 1990-91 to 1993-94 ★930★
Division I NCAA colleges with the lowest graduation rates for male basketball players, 1990-91 to 1993-94 ★940★
U.S. colleges and universities that devote the least course time to discussion ★989★
U.S. colleges and universities where students are not very politically active ★1000★
State appropriations for Idaho's institutions of higher education, 2000-01 ★1265★
Undergraduate tuition and fees at colleges and universities in Idaho ★1499★
Average faculty salaries for institutions of higher education in Idaho, 2000-01 ★3699★
IDG Books
Highest revenues of publicly held book publishers, 1999 ★3072★
IEE Proceedings-Optoelectronics
Optics journals with the greatest impact measure, 1994-98 ★2910★
IEEE
Top ranked AACSB publications ★2186★
IEEE Computer
Most cited technology serials in technical communication journals from 1988 to 1997 ★4427★
IEEE Journal of Selected Topics in Quantum Electronics
Optics journals by citation impact, 1995-99 ★2907★
Optics journals by citation impact, 1999 ★2908★
IEEE Photonics Technology
Optics journals by citation impact, 1995-99 ★2907★
Optics journals by citation impact, 1999 ★2908★
Optics journals with the greatest impact measure, 1994-98 ★2910★
IEEE Spectrum
Most cited technology serials in technical communication journals from 1988 to 1997 ★4427★

IEEE Transactions of Neural Networks
Artificial intelligence journals by citation impact, 1981-99 ★94★

IEEE Transactions on Fuzzy Systems
Artificial intelligence journals by citation impact, 1995-99 ★95★
Artificial intelligence journals by citation impact, 1999 ★96★
Artificial intelligence journals with the greatest impact measure, 1994-98 ★98★

IEEE Transactions on Knowledge and Data Engineering
Journals and proceedings with the most citations (Class 3) ★2569★

IEEE Transactions on Neural Networks
Artificial intelligence journals with the greatest impact measure, 1981-98 ★97★
Artificial intelligence journals with the greatest impact measure, 1994-98 ★98★
Artificial intelligence journals with the greatest impact measure, 1998 ★99★

IEEE Transactions on Pattern Analysis
Artificial intelligence journals by citation impact, 1981-99 ★94★
Artificial intelligence journals by citation impact, 1995-99 ★95★
Artificial intelligence journals by citation impact, 1999 ★96★

IEEE Transactions on Pattern Analysis and Machine Intelligence
Artificial intelligence journals with the greatest impact measure, 1981-98 ★97★
Artificial intelligence journals with the greatest impact measure, 1994-98 ★98★
Artificial intelligence journals with the greatest impact measure, 1998 ★99★

IEEE Transactions on Professional Communication
Most cited serials in technical communication journals from 1988 to 1997 ★4425★
Most cited technology serials in technical communication journals from 1988 to 1997 ★4427★

IEEE Transactions on Software Engineering
Journals and proceedings with the most citations (Class 2) ★2568★

IEEE Transactions on Systems, Man and Cybernetics
Journals and proceedings with the most citations (Class 3) ★2569★

IEEE Transcripts on Information Theory
Information and library science journals with the greatest impact measure, 1981-98 ★2727★

If You Take a Mouse to the Movies
Publishers Weekly Off-the-Cuff Awards winner for hottest selling book to go out of stock, 2000 ★351★

Il nuovo etimologico: DELI: Dizionario etimologico della lingua italiano
Selected reference books-dictionaries, 2000 ★373★

Ilchman; Alice Stone
Top pay and benefits for the chief executive and top paid employees at Sarah Lawrence College ★3492★

Iliff School of Theology
Average faculty salaries for institutions of higher education in Colorado, 2000-01 ★3693★

Illinois
People for the American Way's list of states with the most challenges to library and school books, 1982-1992 ★750★
States with the highest enrollment in private 4-year institutions of higher education ★860★
States with the highest enrollment in public 4-year institutions of higher education ★861★
Mean composite ACT scores by state, 2000 ★895★
Mean math SAT scores by state, 2000 ★900★
Mean verbal SAT scores by state, 2000 ★903★
States allocating the largest amount of state tax appropriations for higher education, 2000-01 ★1304★
Total doctorate recipients by state, 1999 ★2054★
Hispanic American enrollment at Hispanic-serving institutions of higher education, by state, 1997 ★2547★
States with the most law schools ★2668★
State library associations with most full-time staff ★2681★
State library associations with the highest annual revenue ★2682★
State library associations with the highest conference attendance ★2683★
State library associations with the highest unrestricted net assets ★2684★
State library associations with the largest membership ★2685★
State grades for affordability of higher education for minority students, 2000 ★2883★
State grades for benefits state receives for educating its minority students, 2000 ★2884★
State grades for completion of higher education by minority students, 2000 ★2885★
State grades for participation of minority students in higher education, 2000 ★2886★
State grades for preparing minority students for higher education, 2000 ★2887★
States with the highest per capita income ★3123★
States with the highest number of high school graduates, 1999-2000 ★3995★
States with the most public school districts ★3999★
States with the highest K-12 public school enrollment ★4034★
States with the highest projected K-12 public school enrollment for 2010 ★4035★
States with the highest funding needs for school-building modernization ★4040★
States with the highest funding needs for school-technology modernization ★4041★
States with the most K-12 public schools ★4049★
States with the highest percentage of high school freshmen enrolling in college within four years ★4266★
States with the highest state support for non need-based financial aid for students, 1999-2000 ★4368★
States with the most women-owned companies ★4455★

Illinois Central College
Average faculty salaries for institutions of higher education in Illinois, 2000-01 ★3700★

Illinois, Chicago; University of
All-USA College Academic Second Team, 2001 ★3★
Fall enrollment at Chicago-area public universities, by minority percentages, 1999 ★868★
U.S. colleges and universities awarding the most English language/literature/letters master's degrees to Asian Americans ★1774★
U.S. colleges and universities awarding the most health professions and related sciences master's degrees to Hispanic Americans ★1779★
U.S. colleges and universities awarding the most physical sciences master's degrees to Asian Americans ★1794★
Traditionally white institutions awarding the most first professional degrees to African Americans ★1842★
U.S. colleges and universities awarding the most first professional degrees to Asian Americans ★1844★
U.S. colleges and universities awarding the most first professional degrees to Hispanic Americans ★1845★
U.S. colleges and universities awarding the most health professions and related sciences first professional degrees to African Americans ★1847★
U.S. colleges and universities awarding the most health professions and related sciences first professional degrees to Asian Americans ★1848★
U.S. colleges and universities awarding the most health professions and related sciences first professional degrees to Hispanic Americans ★1849★
U.S. colleges and universities awarding the most health professions and related sciences first professional degrees to minorities ★1850★
U.S. universities with the greatest impact in education, 1995-99 ★2222★
Illinois institutions with the highest article output ★2677★
Institutions with the most productive libraries, 1993-1997 ★2678★
U.S. universities with the highest concentration of papers published in the field of pharmacology, 1995-99 ★2937★
Average faculty salaries for institutions of higher education in Illinois, 2000-01 ★3700★

Illinois College
U.S. News & World Report's national liberal arts colleges with students least in debt, 1999 ★1385★
Average faculty salaries for institutions of higher education in Illinois, 2000-01 ★3700★

Illinois College of Optometry
Institutions censured by the American Association of University Professors, 2001 ★1067★

Illinois Department of Transportation
Top recruiters for civil engineering jobs for 2000-01 bachelor's degree recipients ★2346★

Illinois Hospital and Clinics; University of
Top ophthalmology hospitals in the U.S., 2000 ★2796★

Illinois Institute of Technology
Most dangerous college campuses in the U.S. ★712★
Fall enrollment at the largest Chicago-area private institutions, by minority percentages, 1999 ★869★
U.S. colleges and universities that devote the least course time to discussion ★989★
U.S. News & World Report's national universities with the highest proportion of classes with less than 20 students, 2000-01 ★1138★
Highest undergraduate tuition and fees at colleges and universities in Illinois ★1500★

U.S. colleges and universities awarding the most computer and information sciences master's degrees to African Americans ★1766★

U.S. colleges and universities awarding the most computer and information sciences master's degrees to Asian Americans ★1767★

U.S. colleges and universities awarding the most computer and information sciences master's degrees to Hispanic Americans ★1768★

U.S. colleges and universities awarding the most law and legal studies first professional degrees to Asian Americans ★1853★

Doctorate-granting-institutions with the highest percentage of non-U.S. citizen doctoral degrees awarded, 1999 ★1907★

U.S. colleges and universities awarding the most computer and information sciences doctorate degrees to Asian Americans ★2090★

Doctoral institutions with the highest enrollment of foreign students, 1998-99 ★2494★

Average faculty salaries for institutions of higher education in Illinois, 2000-01 ★3700★

Illinois School of Professional Psychology

U.S. colleges and universities awarding the most psychology doctorate degrees to Asian Americans ★2121★

U.S. colleges and universities awarding the most psychology doctorate degrees to Hispanic Americans ★2122★

Illinois, Springfield; University of

Average faculty salaries for institutions of higher education in Illinois, 2000-01 ★3700★

Illinois State University

Four-year institutions with the most weapons referrals reported, 1999 ★710★

State appropriations for Illinois institutions of higher education, 2000-01 ★1266★

U.S. News & World Report's national universities with students least in debt, 1999 ★1475★

Institutions generating the most economic education research text, 1963-1990 ★2167★

Illinois institutions with the highest article output ★2677★

Average faculty salaries for institutions of higher education in Illinois, 2000-01 ★3700★

Illinois System; University of

Institutions receiving the largest Energy Department research grants, 2000 ★3111★

Illinois Tool Works

Fortune's highest ranked metal products companies, 2000 ★475★

Top manufacturing companies in Standard & Poor's 500, 2001 ★548★

Illinois; University of

NCAA men's gymnastics teams with the most individual champions ★137★

Top business schools for within-discipline research performance in management, 1986-1998 ★646★

Top business schools for within-discipline research performance in insurance, international business and real estate, 1986-1998 ★667★

Degree-granting institutions with the most published pages in The Journal of Risk and Insurance, 1987-1996 ★678★

Employing institutions with the most published pages in The Journal of Risk and Insurance, 1987-1996 ★679★

Institutions receiving the most corporate gifts, 1999-2000 ★1243★

State appropriations for Illinois institutions of higher education, 2000-01 ★1266★

Institutions generating the most economic education research text, 1963-1990 ★2167★

Top institutions in systems and software engineering publications ★2332★

Faculty's scholarly reputation in the Ph.D.-granting departments of geography, 1925-1982 ★2518★

Law schools with the best labor law faculty, 1999-2000 ★2656★

Comparison of library and information science programs composite rankings with U.S. News & World Report survey ★2709★

Library and information science programs with the most citations to journal articles, 1993-1998 ★2712★

Library and information science programs with the most journal articles, 1993-1998 ★2713★

Library and information science programs with the most journal articles per capita, 1993-1998 ★2714★

Library and information science programs with the most per capita citations to journal articles, 1993-1998 ★2715★

Illinois, Urbana-Champaign College of Commerce and Business Administration; University of

U.S. News & World Report's undergraduate business programs with the best human resources departments, 2000-01 ★567★

U.S. News & World Report's undergraduate business programs with the highest academic reputation scores, 2000-01 ★571★

U.S. News & World Report's undergraduate business programs with the best accounting departments, 2000-01 ★581★

Academics' choices for best graduate accounting programs, 2001 ★659★

Illinois, Urbana-Champaign; University of

Most effective anthropology research-doctorate programs as evaluated by the National Research Council ★61★

Top anthropology research-doctorate programs as evaluated by the National Research Council ★62★

U.S. News & World Report's universities with the best taxation departments, 1999-2000 ★573★

Institutions, by adjusted authorship, with the most published authors in the Journal of Business Research, 1985 to 1999 ★694★

Four-year institutions with the most weapons referrals reported, 1999 ★710★

U.S. college campuses with more than 5,000 students reporting murders or manslaughters, 1998 ★729★

Most effective chemistry research-doctorate programs as evaluated by the National Research Council ★802★

Top chemistry research-doctorate programs as evaluated by the National Research Council ★805★

Retention rates of African American students at traditionally white institutions, 1997-98 ★1121★

U.S. News & World Report's best public national universities, 2000-01 ★1123★

U.S. News & World Report's national universities with the highest acceptance rates, 2000-01 ★1131★

U.S. universities publishing the most papers in the field of computer science, 1994-98 ★1591★

U.S. universities with the greatest impact in computer science, 1994-98 ★1592★

U.S. universities with the greatest impact in computer science, 1995-99 ★1593★

Most effective computer science research-doctorate programs as evaluated by the National Research Council ★1594★

Top computer science research-doctorate programs as evaluated by the National Research Council ★1597★

Total baccalaureate biology/life sciences degrees awarded to Asian Americans from U.S. colleges and universities, 1997-98 ★1680★

Total baccalaureate English language, literature, and letters degrees awarded to African Americans from U.S. colleges and universities, 1997-98 ★1716★

Total baccalaureate English language, literature, and letters degrees awarded to Asian Americans from U.S. colleges and universities, 1997-98 ★1717★

Total baccalaureate psychology degrees awarded to Asian Americans from U.S. colleges and universities, 1997-98 ★1738★

U.S. colleges and universities awarding the most biological and life sciences master's degrees to African Americans ★1756★

U.S. colleges and universities awarding the most biological and life sciences master's degrees to Asian Americans ★1757★

U.S. colleges and universities awarding the most biological and life sciences master's degrees to Hispanic Americans ★1758★

U.S. colleges and universities awarding the most business management and administrative services master's degrees to Native Americans ★1762★

U.S. colleges and universities awarding the most physical sciences master's degrees to Asian Americans ★1794★

U.S. institutions awarding the most baccalaureate degrees to Asian Americans in agricultural sciences, 1998 ★1816★

U.S. institutions awarding the most master's degrees to African Americans in agribusiness and production, 1998 ★1824★

U.S. institutions awarding the most master's degrees to African Americans in agricultural sciences, 1998 ★1825★

U.S. institutions awarding the most master's degrees to minorities in agribusiness and production, 1998 ★1829★

U.S. institutions awarding the most master's degrees to minorities in agricultural sciences, 1998 ★1830★

Doctorate-granting-institutions awarding the most non-U.S. citizen doctoral degrees, 1999 ★1906★

Top doctorate granting institutions, 1999 ★2047★

U.S. colleges and universities awarding the most computer and information sciences doctorate degrees to Asian Americans ★2090★

U.S. colleges and universities awarding the most doctoral degrees to Asian Americans and Pacific Islanders from 1995 to 1999 ★2093★

U.S. colleges and universities awarding the most doctorate degrees to Asian Americans ★2096★

U.S. colleges and universities awarding the most doctorate degrees to minorities ★2098★

U.S. colleges and universities awarding the most doctorate degrees to Native Americans ★2099★

U.S. colleges and universities awarding the most doctorates in all fields, 1999 ★2100★

ILLINOIS

U.S. colleges and universities awarding the most doctorates in engineering, 1999 ★2102★
U.S. colleges and universities awarding the most doctorates in physical sciences, mathematics, and computer sciences, 1999 ★2105★
U.S. colleges and universities awarding the most doctorates in social sciences, 1999 ★2107★
U.S. colleges and universities awarding the most education doctorate degrees to African Americans ★2108★
U.S. colleges and universities awarding the most physical sciences doctorate degrees to Asian Americans ★2119★
U.S. institutions awarding the most doctorate degrees, 1999 ★2132★
U.S. universities with the greatest impact in education, 1993-97 ★2220★
U.S. universities contributing the most papers in the field of AI, robotics, and auto control, 1993-97 ★2338★
U.S. universities with the greatest impact in electrical and electronic engineering, 1994-99 ★2356★
Acceptance rates for *U.S. News & World Report*'s top 10 graduate engineering schools, 2001 ★2358★
Average analytic GRE scores for *U.S. News & World Report*'s top 10 graduate engineering schools, 2001 ★2359★
Average quantitative GRE scores for *U.S. News & World Report*'s top 10 graduate engineering schools, 2001 ★2360★
Doctoral student-faculty ratios at *U.S. News & World Report*'s top 10 graduate engineering schools, 2001 ★2361★
Faculty membership in National Academy of Engineering at *U.S. News & World Report*'s top 10 graduate engineering schools, 2001 ★2362★
Ph.D.s granted at *U.S. News & World Report*'s top 10 graduate engineering schools, 2001 ★2363★
Research expenditures per faculty member at *U.S. News & World Report*'s top 10 graduate engineering schools, 2001 ★2364★
Research funding allocated to *U.S. News & World Report*'s top 10 graduate engineering schools, 2001 ★2365★
Top graduate engineering schools, 2001 ★2366★
Top graduate engineering schools by reputation, as determined by academic personnel, 2001 ★2367★
Top graduate engineering schools by reputation, as determined by engineers and recruiters, 2001 ★2368★
U.S. News & World Report's graduate engineering programs with the highest academic reputation scores, 2000-01 ★2372★
Academics' choices for best graduate aerospace/aeronautical/astronautical engineering programs, 2001 ★2374★
Top aerospace engineering research-doctorate programs as evaluated by the National Research Council ★2376★
Academics' choices for best graduate agricultural engineering programs, 2001 ★2379★
Academics' choices for best graduate chemical engineering programs, 2001 ★2386★
Most effective chemical engineering research-doctorate programs as evaluated by the National Research Council ★2389★
Top chemical engineering research-doctorate programs as evaluated by the National Research Council ★2390★
Academics' choices for best graduate civil engineering programs, 2001 ★2394★
Most effective civil engineering research-doctorate programs as evaluated by the National Research Council ★2395★
Top civil engineering research-doctorate programs as evaluated by the National Research Council ★2396★
U.S. News & World Report's graduate engineering programs with the best civil departments, 2000-01 ★2398★
Academics' choices for best graduate computer engineering programs, 2001 ★2399★
U.S. News & World Report's graduate engineering programs with the best computer departments, 2000-01 ★2401★
Academics' choices for best graduate electrical/electronic/communications engineering programs, 2001 ★2403★
Most effective electrical engineering research-doctorate programs as evaluated by the National Research Council ★2404★
Top electrical engineering research-doctorate programs as evaluated by the National Research Council ★2405★
U.S. News & World Report's graduate engineering programs with the best electrical departments, 2000-01 ★2407★
Academics' choices for best graduate environmental/environmental health engineering programs, 2001 ★2408★
U.S. News & World Report's graduate engineering programs with the best environmental departments, 2000-01 ★2410★
Top industrial engineering research-doctorate programs as evaluated by the National Research Council ★2413★
Academics' choices for best graduate materials engineering programs, 2001 ★2417★
Most effective materials science research-doctorate programs as evaluated by the National Research Council ★2418★
Top materials science research-doctorate programs as evaluated by the National Research Council ★2419★
U.S. News & World Report's graduate engineering programs with the best materials departments, 2000-01 ★2421★
Academics' choices for best graduate mechanical engineering programs, 2001 ★2422★
Most effective mechanical engineering research-doctorate programs as evaluated by the National Research Council ★2423★
U.S. News & World Report's graduate engineering programs with the best mechanical departments, 2000-01 ★2425★
Academics' choices for best graduate nuclear engineering schools, 2000 ★2426★
Research institutions with the highest enrollment of foreign students, 1998-99 ★2503★
U.S. research institutions with the largest number of students studying abroad, 1998-99 ★2514★
Illinois institutions with the highest article output ★2677★
Institutions with the most productive libraries, 1993-1997 ★2678★
Top university research libraries in the U.S. and Canada, 1998-99 ★2706★
U.S. universities publishing the most papers in the field of library and information science, 1995-99 ★2718★
Top music research-doctorate programs as evaluated by the National Research Council ★2896★
Institutions in the Worker Rights Consortium ★2913★
Most effective physics research-doctorate programs as evaluated by the National Research Council ★3007★
Top astrophysics and astronomy research-doctorate programs as evaluated by the National Research Council ★3014★
Top physics research-doctorate programs as evaluated by the National Research Council ★3015★
Most effective physiology research-doctorate programs as evaluated by the National Research Council ★3021★
Most effective psychology research-doctorate programs as evaluated by the National Research Council ★3065★
Top psychology research-doctorate programs as evaluated by the National Research Council ★3068★
U.S. colleges and universities spending the most on chemical research and development, 1998 ★3099★
Average faculty salaries for institutions of higher education in Illinois, 2000-01 ★3700★
Academics' choices for best curriculum/instruction graduate programs, 2001 ★4380★
Academics' choices for best educational psychology graduate programs, 2001 ★4382★
Academics' choices for best elementary education graduate programs, 2001 ★4383★
Academics' choices for best secondary education graduate programs, 2001 ★4385★
Academics' choices for best special education graduate programs, 2001 ★4386★
Academics' choices for best vocational/technical graduate programs, 2001 ★4387★
Top graduate education schools by reputation, as determined by academic personnel, 2001 ★4396★

Illinois Wesleyan University
Highest undergraduate tuition and fees at colleges and universities in Illinois ★1500★
Most wired colleges, 2000 ★2595★
Average faculty salaries for institutions of higher education in Illinois, 2000-01 ★3700★

Imation
Fortune's highest ranked computer peripherals companies, 2000 ★454★

Imler; David
Top pay and benefits for the chief executive and top paid employees at Fontbonne College ★3294★

Immaculata High School
Outstanding secondary schools in Middlesex-Somerset-Hunterdon, New Jersey ★4179★

Immaculate College
Average faculty salaries for institutions of higher education in Pennsylvania, 2000-01 ★3725★

Immaculate Conception School
Outstanding secondary schools in Columbus, Ohio ★4118★

Immaculate Conception Ukrainian Catholic High School
Outstanding Catholic high schools in Metro Detroit ★4075★

Immaculate Heart Academy
Outstanding secondary schools in Bergen-Passaic, New Jersey ★4096★

Immaculate Heart of Mary High School
Outstanding secondary schools in Chicago, Illinois ★4110★

Immigration and Naturalization Service
  Top employers of college graduates, 2001 ★2325★
  Top recruiters for multidisciplinary majors jobs for 2000-01 bachelor's degree recipients ★2327★
Immunity
  Immunology journals with the greatest impact measure, 1981-98 ★2810★
  Immunology journals with the greatest impact measure, 1994-98 ★2811★
  Immunology journals by impact factor, 1981 to 1997 ★4279★
  Immunology journals by impact factor, 1993 to 1997 ★4280★
Immunological Reviews
  Immunology journals with the greatest impact measure, 1981-98 ★2810★
  Immunology journals with the greatest impact measure, 1994-98 ★2811★
  Immunology journals by impact factor, 1981 to 1997 ★4279★
  Immunology journals by impact factor, 1993 to 1997 ★4280★
Immunology
  United States' contribution of papers in the sciences, by field, 1995-99 ★4283★
  United States' contribution of papers in the sciences, by field, 1996-2000 ★4284★
  Australia's contribution of papers in the sciences, by field, 1993-97 ★4292★
  Australia's contribution of papers in the sciences, by field, 1995-99 ★4293★
  Austria's contribution of papers in the sciences, by field, 1992-96 ★4298★
  Austria's contribution of papers in the sciences, by field, 1995-99 ★4299★
  Belgium's contribution of papers in the sciences by field, 1992-96 ★4301★
  Belgium's contribution of papers in the sciences, by field, 1995-99 ★4302★
  Denmark's contribution of papers in the sciences, by field, 1994-98 ★4306★
  Denmark's contribution of papers in the sciences, by field, 1995-99 ★4307★
  Finland's contribution of papers in the sciences, by field, 1992-96 ★4309★
  Finland's contribution of papers in the sciences, by field, 1995-99 ★4310★
  France's contribution of papers in the sciences, by field, 1995-99 ★4311★
  France's contribution of papers in the sciences, by field, 1996-2000 ★4312★
  Italy's contribution of papers in the sciences, by field, 1995-99 ★4316★
  Netherlands' contribution of papers in the sciences, by field, 1995-99 ★4321★
  Norway's contribution of papers in the sciences, by field, 1994-98 ★4323★
  Sweden's contribution of papers in the sciences by field, 1993-97 ★4330★
  Sweden's contribution of papers in the sciences, by field, 1995-99 ★4331★
  Switzerland's contribution of papers in the sciences, by field, 1994-98 ★4332★
  Switzerland's contribution of papers in the sciences, by field, 1995-99 ★4333★
Immunology Today
  Immunology journals with the greatest impact measure, 1981-98 ★2810★
  Immunology journals with the greatest impact measure, 1994-98 ★2811★
  Immunology journals by impact factor, 1981 to 1997 ★4279★
  Immunology journals by impact factor, 1993 to 1997 ★4280★

Immutable Laws of Internet Branding
  Library Journal's most notable digital technology books, 2000 ★256★
Impact aid
  Educational program activities expenditures, 2000 ★3992★
The Impact of Global Warming on Agriculture-A Ricardian Analysis
  Top cited energy papers from 1994 to 1998 ★2467★
Imperial Chemical Industries
  Business Week's best companies in terms of return on equity ★407★
Imperial College
  Top United Kingdom universities by total citations in the field of ecology/environmental, 1991-95 ★2146★
Imperial Sugar
  Fortune's highest ranked food production companies, 2000 ★464★
Imperial Valley College
  Lowest undergraduate tuition and fees at public 2-year colleges and universities ★1465★
  Lowest undergraduate tuition and fees at colleges and universities in California ★1487★
Impressions
  Most frequently banned books in the 1990s ★745★
  People for the American Way's list of most frequently challenged materials, 1982-1992 ★749★
In a Different Voice: Psychological Theory and Women's Development
  Most-cited works in women and crime publications ★1646★
In a Sunburned Country
  Library Journal's best nonfiction audiobooks, 2000 ★243★
  Outstanding audiobooks, 2000 ★287★
  Outstanding history books, 2000 ★289★
In America
  Booklist's best fiction books for library collections, 2000 ★227★
In Every Tiny Grain of Sand: A Child's Book of Prayers and Praise
  Booklist's most recommended poetry for youths, 2001 ★315★
  Most notable books for young readers, 2001 ★319★
  Outstanding books for middle readers, 2000 ★326★
In the Fall
  Booklist's best first novels ★228★
In the Heart of the Sea: The Tragedy of the Whaleship Essex
  Outstanding history books, 2000 ★289★
In the Line of Fire: Presidents' Lives at Stake
  Most notable nonfiction books for young adults, 2001 ★324★
In the Midnight Rain
  Library Journal's best romance titles, 2000 ★245★
In the Night Kitchen
  Most frequently banned books in the 1990s ★745★
In Real Life: Six Women Photographers
  Booklist's best art books for young people ★308★
  Outstanding books for older readers, 2000 ★327★

In Search of Moby Dick: The Quest for the Great White Whale
  Outstanding arts and literature books, 2000 ★286★
In Siberia
  Most notable nonfiction books, 2001 ★285★
  Outstanding works of nonfiction, 2001 ★294★
In Touch
  Library Journal's notable new magazines, 1999 ★2923★
Inazo; Nitobe
  Japan's ten great educators ★2234★
Incarnate Word; University of the
  U.S. colleges and universities awarding the most biological and life sciences master's degrees to Hispanic Americans ★1758★
  Average faculty salaries for institutions of higher education in Texas, 2000-01 ★3731★
Inco
  Business Week's best performing companies with the highest 1-year earnings growth ★413★
  Top metals and mining companies in Standard & Poor's 500, 2001 ★549★
Incropera; Frank
  Top pay and benefits for the chief executive and top paid employees at the University of Notre Dame ★3554★
Independence Community College
  Lowest undergraduate tuition and fees at colleges and universities in Kansas ★1507★
Independence Middle School
  Outstanding secondary schools in Pittsburgh, Pennsylvania ★4204★
Index to Twentieth-Century Spanish Plays: In Collections, Anthologies, and Periodicals
  Selected reference books in the field of literature, 2000 ★377★
India
  Countries of origin for non-U.S. citizens awarded doctorates at U.S. colleges and universities, 1999 ★1901★
  Countries with the highest percentage of workers satisfied with their job ★2242★
  Foreign countries with the highest enrollment of foreign students, 1999-2000 ★2496★
  Institute for Scientific Information periodical prices by country, 2001 ★2922★
  First-year physics and astronomy graduate students from Asia, 1997-98 ★2987★
  Countries with the lowest leader's salary ★3121★
Indian Hills Community College
  Lowest undergraduate tuition and fees at colleges and universities in Iowa ★1505★
  Average faculty salaries for institutions of higher education without academic ranks in Iowa, 2000-01 ★3748★
Indian Institute of Management at Ahmadabad
  Asiaweek's best M.B.A. programs ★590★
Indian River Community College
  Lowest undergraduate tuition and fees at colleges and universities in Florida ★1495★
Indian Valley Middle School
  Outstanding secondary schools in Philadelphia, Pennsylvania-New Jersey ★4202★
Indiana
  States with the highest enrollment in public 4-year institutions of higher education ★861★
  Mean composite ACT scores by state, 2000 ★895★
  Mean math SAT scores by state, 2000 ★900★

INDIANA

Mean verbal SAT scores by state, 2000 ★903★
Total doctorate recipients by state, 1999 ★2054★
Average Hennen's American Public Library Ratings, by state ★2690★
State grades for affordability of higher education for minority students, 2000 ★2883★
State grades for benefits state receives for educating its minority students, 2000 ★2884★
State grades for completion of higher education by minority students, 2000 ★2885★
State grades for participation of minority students in higher education, 2000 ★2886★
State grades for preparing minority students for higher education, 2000 ★2887★

Indiana State University
U.S. News & World Report's national universities with students least in debt, 1999 ★1475★
Average faculty salaries for institutions of higher education in Indiana, 2000-01 ★3701★

Indiana State University, Terre Haute
State appropriations for Indiana's institutions of higher education, 2000-01 ★1267★

Indiana University
All-USA College Academic First Team, 2001 ★2★
Degree-granting institutions with the most published pages in *The Journal of Risk and Insurance*, 1987-1996 ★678★
State appropriations for Indiana's institutions of higher education, 2000-01 ★1267★
Institutions generating the most economic education research text, 1963-1990 ★2167★
U.S. universities publishing the most papers in the field of education, 1994-98 ★2219★
U.S. universities publishing the most papers in the field of literature, 1994-98 ★2447★
Top German language and literature research-doctorate programs as evaluated by the National Research Council ★2528★
Top university research libraries in the U.S. and Canada, 1998-99 ★2706★
U.S. universities publishing the most papers in the field of library and information science, 1995-99 ★2718★
U.S. universities with the highest concentrations in literary criticism, 1992-96 ★2735★
U.S. universities publishing the most papers in the field of communication, 1994-98 ★2755★
Degrees granted in the ten largest doctoral journalism and mass communications programs, 1999 ★2756★
U.S. universities with the highest concentrations in religion and theology, 1992-96 ★3094★
Most effective sociology research-doctorate programs as evaluated by the National Research Council ★4352★
Top sociology research-doctorate programs as evaluated by the National Research Council ★4354★

Indiana University, Bloomington
Four-year institutions with the most drug arrests reported, 1999 ★705★
Four-year institutions with the most liquor referrals reported, 1999 ★708★
U.S. colleges and universities awarding the most doctorates in humanities, 1999 ★2103★
U.S. colleges and universities awarding the most doctorates in professional and other fields, 1999 ★2106★

U.S. colleges and universities awarding the most education doctorate degrees to Asian Americans ★2109★
First-year student's choices for exemplary doctoral-extensive universities ★2534★
Most wired universities, 2000 ★2598★
Institutions in the Worker Rights Consortium ★2913★
Average faculty salaries for institutions of higher education in Indiana, 2000-01 ★3701★
Academics' choices for best administration/supervision graduate programs, 2001 ★4378★
Academics' choices for best counseling/personnel services graduate programs, 2001 ★4379★
Academics' choices for best curriculum/instruction graduate programs, 2001 ★4380★
Academics' choices for best education policy graduate programs, 2001 ★4381★
Academics' choices for best elementary education graduate programs, 2001 ★4383★
Academics' choices for best higher education administration graduate programs, 2001 ★4384★
Academics' choices for best secondary education graduate programs, 2001 ★4385★

Indiana University, East
Average faculty salaries for institutions of higher education in Indiana, 2000-01 ★3701★

Indiana University, Indianapolis
Academics' choices for best health law programs, 2001 ★2629★

Indiana University, Kelley Graduate School of Business
U.S. News & World Report's undergraduate business programs with the best general management departments, 2000-01 ★566★
U.S. News & World Report's undergraduate business programs with the best human resources departments, 2000-01 ★567★
U.S. News & World Report's undergraduate business programs with the best production/operations departments, 2000-01 ★569★
U.S. News & World Report's undergraduate business programs with the highest academic reputation scores, 2000-01 ★571★
Business Week's top business schools best at responding to student concerns, 2000 ★598★
Business Week's top business schools with the best teachers, 2000 ★609★
Business Week's top business schools with the lowest percentage of women enrollees, 2000 ★617★
Lowest post-MBA salaries for students enrolled in *Business Week*'s top business schools, 1999 ★634★
Lowest pre-MBA salaries for students enrolled in *Business Week*'s top business schools, 1999 ★635★
Top graduate business schools by reputation, as determined by recruiters, 2001 ★651★
Academics' choices for best graduate production/operations management programs, 2001 ★674★
U.S. News & World Report's undergraduate business programs with the best marketing departments, 2000-01 ★685★

Indiana University, Kokomo
Average faculty salaries for institutions of higher education in Indiana, 2000-01 ★3701★

Educational Rankings Annual • 2002

Indiana University, Northwest
Average faculty salaries for institutions of higher education in Indiana, 2000-01 ★3701★

Indiana University (PA)
Division II NCAA colleges with the 100% graduation rates for women's basketball players, 1993-94 ★944★
U.S. colleges and universities awarding the most English language/literature/letters doctorate degrees to African Americans ★2112★
U.S. colleges and universities awarding the most English language/literature/letters doctorate degrees to Asian Americans ★2113★
Average faculty salaries for institutions of higher education in Pennsylvania, 2000-01 ★3725★

Indiana University-Purdue University
U.S. colleges and universities awarding the most health professions and related sciences first professional degrees to Native Americans ★1851★

Indiana University-Purdue University, Fort Wayne
Average faculty salaries for institutions of higher education in Indiana, 2000-01 ★3701★

Indiana University-Purdue University, Indianapolis
U.S. college campuses reporting murders or non-negligent manslaughters, 1999 ★728★
U.S. college campuses with more than 5,000 students reporting murders or manslaughters, 1998 ★729★
Average faculty salaries for institutions of higher education in Indiana, 2000-01 ★3701★

Indiana University, South Bend
Average faculty salaries for institutions of higher education in Indiana, 2000-01 ★3701★

Indiana University, Southeast
Average faculty salaries for institutions of higher education in Indiana, 2000-01 ★3701★

Indianapolis-Marion County Public Library
Highest Hennen's American Public Library Ratings for libraries serving a population of over 500,000 ★2700★

Indianapolis; University of
Average faculty salaries for institutions of higher education in Indiana, 2000-01 ★3701★

Individual Discount Rates and the Purchase and Utilization of Energy-Using Durables
Top cited energy papers from 1979 to 1983 ★2464★

Individual, family, and other social services
Employment growth percentages for selected industries, 1998-2000 ★2294★

Indonesia
Eight grade science achievement scores from selected countries, 1999 ★14★
Percentage of enrollment at private institutions of higher education, by country, 1998 ★858★
Countries of origin for non-U.S. citizens awarded doctorates at U.S. colleges and universities, 1999 ★1901★
Foreign countries with the highest enrollment of foreign students, 1999-2000 ★2496★
Eighth grade mathematics achievement scores from selected countries, 1999 ★2773★
Countries with the lowest leader's salary ★3121★

Industrial designer
Jobs with the best environment scores ★2247★

Most desirable jobs in production/manufacturing ★2276★

Industrial engineer
Most desirable jobs in math/science ★2274★

Industrial engineering
Average starting salaries for college graduates, by field, 2000 ★3129★
Expected starting salaries of 2000-01 bachelor's degree recipients, by specific major ★3131★

Industrial and Labor Relations Review
Top management journals ★546★
Top management journals by core impact ★547★
Top ranked health, education, and welfare journals ★2193★
Top ranked labor and demographic economics journals ★2196★

Industrial/manufacturing
Engineering doctorates awarded at U.S. colleges and universities, by subfield, 1999 ★1923★
Gender breakdown of engineering doctorate recipients, by subfield, 1999 ★1934★

Industrial and organizational
Gender breakdown of psychology doctorate recipients, by subfield, 1999 ★1941★
Psychology doctorates awarded at U.S. colleges and universities, by subfield, 1999 ★2043★

Industrial Relations
Top ranked labor and demographic economics journals ★2196★

Industry Week
Most cited technology serials in technical communication journals from 1988 to 1997 ★4427★

Inet Technologies
Best small companies in the U.S. ★383★
Top companies in terms of growth, 2000 ★534★

Infante; D.
Highest ranked active communication studies researchers ★2747★

Infectious dermatologic disease
Leading categories of dermatologic disease covered by top articles in the field, 1945-1990 ★1869★

Influence of Firm Size on Export Planning and Performance
Most influential articles in the *Journal of Business Research*, 1985-1999 ★697★
Most influential articles in the *Journal of Business Research* from 1990 to 1994 ★699★

Information Design Journal
Most cited applied arts serials in technical communication journals from 1988 to 1997 ★4416★

Information and Information Science in Context
Most frequently cited *Libri* articles ★2730★

Information and Management
Journals and proceedings with the most citations (Class 3) ★2569★

Information Processing and Management
Journals and proceedings with the most citations (Class 4) ★2570★
Information and library science journals by citation impact, 1981-99 ★2724★

An Information-Procession Approach to Personal Problem Solving
Most frequently cited contribution articles in psychology journals from 1986 to 1996 ★3071★

Information sciences (MIS)
Expected starting salaries of 2000-01 bachelor's degree recipients, by specific major ★3131★

Information sciences and systems
Computer science doctorates awarded at U.S. colleges and universities, by subfield, 1999 ★1900★
Gender breakdown of computer science doctorate recipients, by subfield, 1999 ★1931★

Information Search Tactics
Journal of the American Society for Information Science's best papers, by citations per year ★2728★
Journal of the American Society for Information Science's best papers, by total citations ★2729★

Information-Seeking Strategies of Novices Using a Full-Text Encyclopedia
Journal of the American Society for Information Science's best papers, by citations per year ★2728★

Information systems
Average starting salaries for college graduates, by field, 2000 ★3129★

Information Systems Research
Top ranked AACSB publications ★2186★
Information and library science journals by citation impact, 1995-99 ★2725★

Information technology (MIS)
Top bachelor's and master's degree majors in demand for employment, 2001 ★2323★
Top bachelor's degree majors in demand for employment, 2001 ★2324★
Top master's degree majors in demand for employment, 2001 ★2326★

Information Technology R&D Applications
Information and library science journals by citation impact, 1981-99 ★2724★
Information and library science journals with the greatest impact measure, 1981-98 ★2727★

Infospace
Fast-growing information technology companies, 2000 ★444★

ING Groep
Business Week's best companies in the Netherlands ★410★

Ingalls Shipbuilding
Top recruiters for Naval architecture jobs for 2000-01 bachelor's degree recipients ★69★
Top recruiters for Naval architecture jobs for 2000-01 master's degree recipients ★72★
Top recruiters for civil engineering jobs for 2000-01 bachelor's degree recipients ★2346★
Top recruiters for civil engineering jobs for 2000-01 master's degree recipients ★2397★
Top recruiters for electrical/electronic engineering jobs for 2000-01 master's degree recipients ★2406★
Top recruiters for marine engineering jobs for 2000-01 master's degree recipients ★2416★
Top recruiters for mechanical engineering jobs for 2000-01 master's degree recipients ★2424★
Top recruiters for marine engineering jobs for 2000-01 bachelor's degree recipients ★2433★

Inge; M. Thomas
Top pay and benefits for the chief executive and top paid employees at Randolph-Macon College ★3451★

Ingersoll-Rand
Fortune's highest ranked industrial and farm equipment companies, 2000 ★471★

Inglewood Junior High School
Outstanding secondary schools in Seattle-Bellevue-Everett, Washington ★4227★

Ingomar Middle School
Outstanding secondary schools in Pittsburgh, Pennsylvania ★4204★

Ingram; Denny O.
Top pay and benefits for the chief executive and top paid employees at Texas Wesleyan University ★3519★

Ingram Industries
Top women-owned companies ★4460★

Ingram Micro
Fortune's highest ranked wholesalers, 2000 ★505★

Inkster; Lawrence
Top pay and benefits for the chief executive and top paid employees at Union College in Kentucky ★3584★

Inorganic
Chemistry doctorates awarded at U.S. colleges and universities, by subfield, 1999 ★1889★
Gender breakdown of chemistry doctorate recipients, by subfield, 1999 ★1929★

Inorganic Chemistry
Inorganic and nuclear chemistry journals by citation impact, 1981-99 ★811★
Inorganic and nuclear chemistry journals by citation impact, 1995-99 ★812★
Inorganic and nuclear chemistry journals by citation impact, 1999 ★813★

Inorganic (general) chemistry
Subjects required by the most U.S. medical schools for the 2000-01 entering class ★2850★

Inorganica Chimica Acta
Inorganic and nuclear chemistry journals by citation impact, 1981-99 ★811★

"Inositol trisphosphate and calcium signaling"
Institute for Scientific Information's most cited papers, 1990-98 ★4282★

Inquiry-Journal of Health Care
Health policy and services journals by citation impact, 1981-99 ★2537★
Health policy and services journals by citation impact, 1995-99 ★2538★

Inroads
Top internships in the U.S. with the highest compensation, 2001 ★2611★
Top internships in the U.S., 2001 ★2612★

Insect Biochemistry
Entomology journals by citation impact, 1981-98 ★2453★

Insect Biochemistry and Molecular Biology
Entomology journals by citation impact, 1994-98 ★2454★
Entomology journals by citation impact, 1998 ★2455★

Insect Molecular Biology
Entomology journals by citation impact, 1994-98 ★2454★
Entomology journals by citation impact, 1998 ★2455★

Instituto de Estudios Superiors de la Empresa-International Graduate School of Management
Business Week's top business schools outside the U.S. as selected by corporate recruiters, 2000 ★605★

INSPECTORS

Business Week's top business schools outside the U.S. as selected by recent MBA graduates, 2000 ★606★

Business Week's top business schools outside the U.S. for intellectual capital, 2000 ★607★

Post-MBA salaries for graduates from *Business Week*'s top business schools outside the U.S., 2000 ★642★

Pre-MBA salaries for students at *Business Week*'s top business schools outside the U.S., 2000 ★643★

Inspectors, testers, and graders, precision
Occupations with the highest decline in employment, 1998-2008 ★2310★

Institute of Advanced Studies
Australian universities with the greatest impact in agricultural sciences, 1993-97 ★49★

Australian universities with the greatest impact in mathematics, 1993-97 ★2774★

Institute of Allergy and Infectious Diseases
Proposed fiscal 2002 appropriations for National Institutes of Health scientific research ★3108★

Institute of American Indian Arts
U.S. tribal colleges ★1445★

Highest undergraduate tuition and fees at colleges and universities in New Mexico ★1535★

Institute of Arthritis and Musculoskeletal and Skin Diseases
Proposed fiscal 2002 appropriations for National Institutes of Health scientific research ★3108★

Institute of Child Health and Human Development
Proposed fiscal 2002 appropriations for National Institutes of Health scientific research ★3108★

Institute of Dental and Craniofacial Research
Proposed fiscal 2002 appropriations for National Institutes of Health scientific research ★3108★

Institute of Diabetes and Digestive and Kidney Diseases
Proposed fiscal 2002 appropriations for National Institutes of Health scientific research ★3108★

Institute of Environmental Health Sciences
Proposed fiscal 2002 appropriations for National Institutes of Health scientific research ★3108★

Institute for Christian Studies
Lowest undergraduate tuition and fees at private nonprofit, 4-year or above colleges and universities ★1464★

The Institute for Rehabilitation and Research
Top rehabilitation hospitals in the U.S., 2000 ★2801★

Institute of General Medical Sciences
Proposed fiscal 2002 appropriations for National Institutes of Health scientific research ★3108★

Institute of Mental Health
Proposed fiscal 2002 appropriations for National Institutes of Health scientific research ★3108★

Institute of Museum and Library Services
Proposed fiscal 2002 appropriations for arts and humanities ★101★

Institute of Neurological Disorders and Stroke
Proposed fiscal 2002 appropriations for National Institutes of Health scientific research ★3108★

Institute of Nursing Research
Proposed fiscal 2002 appropriations for National Institutes of Health scientific research ★3108★

Institute on Aging
Proposed fiscal 2002 appropriations for National Institutes of Health scientific research ★3108★

Institute on Alcohol Abuse and Alcoholism
Proposed fiscal 2002 appropriations for National Institutes of Health scientific research ★3108★

Institute on Deafness and Other Communication Disorders
Proposed fiscal 2002 appropriations for National Institutes of Health scientific research ★3108★

Institute on Drug Abuse
Proposed fiscal 2002 appropriations for National Institutes of Health scientific research ★3108★

Institute of Paper Science & Technology
Average faculty salaries for institutions of higher education in Georgia, 2000-01 ★3697★

Instructional control of human operant behavior
Most cited sources in experimental analyses of human behavior between 1990 and 1999 ★3070★

Instructional Science
Most cited education serials in technical communication journals from 1988 to 1997 ★4418★

Instructors, adults (nonvocational) education
Projected employment growth for selected occupations that require long-term on-the-job training, 1998-2008 ★2320★

Insurance adjusters, examiners, and investigators
Projected employment growth for selected occupations that require long-term on-the-job training, 1998-2008 ★2320★

Average salaries for occupations requiring on-the-job training ★3119★

Insurance Services Office
Most selective internships in the U.S., 2001 ★2610★

Insurance underwriter
Jobs with the most stringent quotas ★2259★

Most desirable jobs in business/finance ★2270★

Integrated Device Technology
Business Week's best companies in terms of share-price gain ★409★

Information technology companies giving the best returns, 2000 ★522★

"Integrins: Versatility, modulation, and signaling in cell adhesion"
Institute for Scientific Information's most cited papers, 1990-98 ★4282★

Intel
Business Week's best companies in the United States ★411★

Business Week's top companies worldwide ★433★

Fortune's highest ranked semiconductors companies, 2000 ★495★

Fortune's most admired companies for financial soundness ★515★

Top internships in the U.S. with the highest compensation, 2001 ★2611★

Largest technology companies in the U.S. in terms of annual revenue, 2000 ★4429★

Intensive English language
Fields of study profile of foreign students enrolled in U.S. institutions of higher education, 1998-99 ★2495★

Inter-American
Chicago elementary magnet schools with the highest acceptance rates, 2000-01 ★4002★

An Interaction Approach to Organizational Buying Behavior
Most influential articles in the *Journal of Business Research*, 1985-1999 ★697★

Most influential articles in the *Journal of Business Research* from 1985 to 1989 ★698★

Intercom
Most cited technology serials in technical communication journals from 1988 to 1997 ★4427★

Intercountry Translog Model of Energy Substitution Responses
Top cited energy papers from 1974 to 1978 ★2463★

Interdenominational Theological Center
Historically black colleges and universities awarding the most first professional degrees to African Americans ★1835★

U.S. colleges and universities awarding the most first professional degrees to African Americans ★1843★

Historically black colleges and universities awarding the most doctorate degrees to African Americans ★1945★

Interdisciplinary studies
Top mixed discipline majors for accepted applicants to U.S. medical schools, 1999-2000 ★2853★

Interface
Fortune's highest ranked textiles companies, 2000 ★501★

Interfaces
Journals and proceedings with the most citations (Class 4) ★2570★

Intergenerational Equity and Exhaustible Resources
Top cited nonrenewable resource papers from 1974 to 1978 ★2468★

Intern
African American college athletics administrators and staff, by gender, 1999-2000 ★117★

College athletics administrators and staff, by gender, 1999-2000 ★121★

Minority college athletics administrators and staff, by gender, 1999-2000 ★132★

Internal links
Web pages with the highest access percentages ★2608★

Internal Marketing and Organizational Behavior: A Partnership in Developing Customer-Conscious Employees at Every Level
  Most influential articles in the *Journal of Business Research*, 1985-1999 ★697★
  Most influential articles in the *Journal of Business Research* from 1990 to 1994 ★699★

International business
  Business and management doctorates awarded at U.S. colleges and universities, by subfield, 1999 ★1888★
  Gender breakdown of business and management doctorate recipients, by subfield, 1999 ★1928★

International Business Review
  Business journals receiving the most citations in five core journals, 1995-97 ★691★

International Center
  Proposed fiscal 2002 appropriations for National Institutes of Health scientific research ★3108★

International Creative Management
  Most selective internships in the U.S., 2001 ★2610★

International Economic Review
  Top ranked agricultural and natural resource economics journals ★2187★
  Top ranked international economics journals ★2195★
  Top ranked mathematical and quantitative methods journals ★2198★
  Top ranked microeconomics journals ★2200★
  Highest impact economics journals in energy from 1980 to 1989 ★2457★

International Encyclopedia of Women and Sports
  Outstanding reference sources, 2001 ★371★

International English language
  Number of Advanced Placement Exams taken by African Americans, by subject, 2000 ★30★
  Number of Advanced Placement Exams taken by Asian Americans, by subject, 2000 ★31★
  Number of Advanced Placement Exams taken by Hispanic Americans, by subject, 2000 ★32★

International Flavors & Fragrances
  Top chemical companies in Standard & Poor's 500, 2001 ★533★

The International Foundation for Education & Self-Help
  Most selective internships in the U.S., 2001 ★2610★

International Institute for Management Development (IMD)
  Business Week's top business schools outside the U.S. as selected by corporate recruiters, 2000 ★605★
  Business Week's top business schools outside the U.S. as selected by recent MBA graduates, 2000 ★606★
  Business Week's top business schools outside the U.S. for intellectual capital, 2000 ★607★
  European and Canadian business schools with the quickest payback on MBA investments ★628★
  Post-MBA salaries for graduates from *Business Week*'s top business schools outside the U.S., 2000 ★642★
  Pre-MBA salaries for students at *Business Week*'s top business schools outside the U.S., 2000 ★643★

International Journal of Computer Vision
  Artificial intelligence journals by citation impact, 1981-99 ★94★
  Artificial intelligence journals by citation impact, 1995-99 ★95★
  Artificial intelligence journals by citation impact, 1999 ★96★
  Artificial intelligence journals with the greatest impact measure, 1981-98 ★97★
  Artificial intelligence journals with the greatest impact measure, 1994-98 ★98★
  Artificial intelligence journals with the greatest impact measure, 1998 ★99★

International Journal of Dermatology
  Number of citations and papers in dermatology journals, 1981 to 1996 ★1874★

International Journal of Food Microbiology
  Food science and technology journals by citation impact, 1995-99 ★2903★
  Food science and technology journals by citation impact, 1999 ★2904★

International Journal of Game Theory
  Top ranked microeconomics journals ★2200★

International Journal of Geographical Information Systems
  Information and library science journals by citation impact, 1981-99 ★2724★
  Information and library science journals by citation impact, 1995-99 ★2725★
  Information and library science journals by citation impact, 1999 ★2726★

International Journal of Gynecology and Obstetrics
  'Outside' journals most frequently citing *Studies in Family Planning*, 1991-95 ★1862★

International Journal of Health Services
  Health policy and services journals by citation impact, 1981-99 ★2537★

International Journal of Man-Machine Studies
  Most cited technology serials in technical communication journals from 1988 to 1997 ★4427★

International Journal of Mass Spectrometry
  Spectroscopy journals by citation impact, 1999 ★4361★

International Journal of Production Research
  Journals and proceedings with the most citations (Class 4) ★2570★

International Journal of Research in Marketing
  Business journals receiving the most citations in five core journals, 1995-97 ★691★

International Marketing Review
  Business journals receiving the most citations in five core journals, 1995-97 ★691★

International Migration Review
  Demography journals with the highest average citations after 5 years ★1856★
  Most cited demography journals, 1991-95 ★1857★
  Top demography journals by average impact factor, 1991-95 ★1863★

International Paper
  Fortune's highest ranked forest and paper products companies, 2000 ★466★
  Top paper and forest products companies in Standard & Poor's 500, 2001 ★552★
  Top recruiters for chemical engineering jobs for 2000-01 bachelor's degree recipients ★2343★
  Top recruiters for civil engineering jobs for 2000-01 bachelor's degree recipients ★2346★
  Top recruiters for environmental engineering jobs for 2000-01 bachelor's degree recipients ★2357★
  Top recruiters for environmental engineering jobs for 2000-01 master's degree recipients ★2409★
  Top recruiters for mechanical engineering jobs for 2000-01 bachelor's degree recipients ★2437★
  Top recruiters for human resources jobs for 2000-01 bachelor's degree recipients ★2559★
  Top recruiters for human resources jobs for 2000-01 master's degree recipients ★2560★

International relations/affairs
  Gender breakdown of social sciences doctorate recipients, by subfield, 1999 ★1942★
  Social sciences doctorates awarded at U.S. colleges and universities, by subfield, 1999 ★2044★

International Review of Neurobiology
  Journals with the highest impact factor in the field of neuroscience, 1981-96 ★191★

International Security
  Social sciences journals with the greatest impact measure, 1981-97 ★4341★

The International Space Station
  Booklist's best science books for children ★310★

International Studies of Management and Organization
  Business journals receiving the most citations in five core journals, 1995-97 ★691★

Internet Basics Without Fear!
  Best selling small press releases, 2001 ★226★

Internet Resources for Technology Education
  Top sites for educators ★2605★

Interpublic Group
  Fortune's highest ranked advertising and marketing companies, 2000 ★445★
  Top services industries in Standard & Poor's 500, 2001 ★558★

Intest
  Companies with the best two-year total returns since 1998 ★436★

Intuit
  Business Week's best performing companies with the highest 3-year earnings growth ★416★

Intuition, Critical Evaluation and Ethical Principles: The Foundation for Ethical Decisions in Counseling Psychology
  Most frequently cited contribution articles in psychology journals from 1986 to 1996 ★3071★

Inventiones Mathematical
  Mathematics journals by impact factor ★2783★
  Mathematics journals by impact factor, 1981 to 1997 ★2784★
  Mathematics journals by impact factor, 1993 to 1997 ★2785★

Inver Hills Community College
  Average faculty salaries for institutions of higher education without academic ranks in Minnesota, 2000-01 ★3753★

An Investigation of Relationalism across a Range of Marketing Relationships and Alliances
  Most influential articles in the *Journal of Business Research* from 1995 to 1999 ★700★

INVESTIGATIVE

Investigative Urology
Urology and nephrology journals with the greatest impact measure, 1981-98 ★2816★

Investment Titans
Library Journal's most notable investing books, 2000 ★264★

Investor
Business Week's best companies in Sweden ★404★

Invisible Man
Favorite books of African Americans ★238★

Invisible Revolution: A Youth Subculture of Hate
Most notable DVDs and videos for young adults, 2001 ★2890★

An Invisible Sign of My Own
Booklist's best first novels ★228★

Iomega
Fortune's highest ranked computer peripherals companies, 2000 ★454★

Iona College
Average faculty salaries for institutions of higher education in New York, 2000-01 ★3719★

Iowa
People for the American Way's list of states with the most challenges to library and school books, 1982-1992 ★750★
Mean composite ACT scores by state, 2000 ★895★
Mean math SAT scores by state, 2000 ★900★
Mean verbal SAT scores by state, 2000 ★903★
Total doctorate recipients by state, 1999 ★2054★
State library associations with most full-time staff ★2681★
State library associations with the highest annual revenue ★2682★
State library associations with the highest unrestricted net assets ★2684★
State library associations with the largest membership ★2685★
State grades for affordability of higher education for minority students, 2000 ★2883★
State grades for benefits state receives for educating its minority students, 2000 ★2884★
State grades for completion of higher education by minority students, 2000 ★2885★
State grades for participation of minority students in higher education, 2000 ★2886★
State grades for preparing minority students for higher education, 2000 ★2887★
States with the highest percentage of high school freshmen enrolling in college within four years ★4266★
States with the best college tuition savings plans ★4438★

Iowa Central Community College
Lowest undergraduate tuition and fees at colleges and universities in Iowa ★1505★

Iowa City, IA
Best college towns to live in ★3076★

Iowa Hospitals and Clinics; University of
Top ophthalmology hospitals in the U.S., 2000 ★2796★
Top orthopedics hospitals in the U.S., 2000 ★2797★
Top ortolaryngology hospitals in the U.S., 2000 ★2798★

Iowa State University
All-USA College Academic Second Team, 2001 ★3★
Colleges with the highest number of freshman Merit Scholars, 2000 ★5★
U.S. universities publishing the most papers in the fields of agriculture/agronomy, 1994-98 ★57★
U.S. universities with the highest concentration of papers published in the field of chemistry, 1994-98 ★794★
State appropriations for Iowa's institutions of higher education, 2000-01 ★1268★
U.S. colleges and universities awarding the most English language/literature/letters master's degrees to African Americans ★1773★
U.S. institutions awarding the most baccalaureate degrees to Hispanic Americans in agricultural sciences, 1998 ★1818★
Top institutions in systems and software engineering publications ★2332★
Academics' choices for best graduate agricultural engineering programs, 2001 ★2379★
Institutions with the most productive libraries, 1993-1997 ★2678★
Most effective statistics and biostatistics research-doctorate programs as evaluated by the National Research Council ★2780★
Top statistics and biostatistics research-doctorate programs as evaluated by the National Research Council ★2782★
Average faculty salaries for institutions of higher education in Iowa, 2000-01 ★3702★
U.S. universities with the greatest impact in veterinary medicine, 1995-99 ★4440★

Iowa; University of
U.S. universities publishing the most papers in the field of microbiology, 1994-98 ★215★
U.S. business schools with the quickest payback on MBA investments ★654★
Top business schools for within-discipline research performance in accounting, 1986-1998 ★660★
U.S. colleges and universities with poor instructors ★1027★
U.S. colleges and universities with the most upper level courses taught by TAs ★1040★
State appropriations for Iowa's institutions of higher education, 2000-01 ★1268★
Fiske Guide's best buys for public colleges and universities, 2001 ★1460★
Total ethnic/cultural studies master's degrees awarded to African Americans from U.S. colleges and universities, 1997-98 ★1747★
U.S. colleges and universities awarding the most English language/literature/letters master's degrees to Asian Americans ★1774★
U.S. colleges and universities awarding the most English language/literature/letters master's degrees to Hispanic Americans ★1775★
U.S. universities publishing the most papers in the field of dentistry/oral surgery and medicine, 1995-99 ★1865★
U.S. universities with the highest concentration of dentistry papers published, 1994-98 ★1868★
Faculty's scholarly reputation in the Ph.D.-granting departments of geography, 1925-1982 ★2518★
Enrollment of students in the ten largest doctoral journalism and mass communications programs, 1999 ★2762★
Academics' choices for best family medicine programs, 2001 ★2820★
Academics' choices for best rural medicine programs, 2001 ★2824★
Acceptance rates for *U.S. News & World Report*'s top 10 primary-care medical schools, 2001 ★2826★
Average MCAT scores at *U.S. News & World Report*'s top 10 primary-care medical schools, 2001 ★2835★
Average undergraduate GPA at *U.S. News & World Report*'s top 10 primary-care medical schools, 2001 ★2837★
Faculty-student ratios at *U.S. News & World Report*'s top 10 primary-care medical schools, 2001 ★2841★
Out-of-state tuition and fees at *U.S. News & World Report*'s top 10 primary-care medical schools, 2001 ★2846★
Percentage of graduates entering *U.S. News & World Report*'s top 10 primary-care medical schools, 2001 ★2848★
Top primary-care medical schools, 2001 ★2856★
Top primary-care medical schools by reputation, as determined by academic personnel, 2001 ★2857★
Institutions in the Worker Rights Consortium ★2913★
Women faculty in Ph.D. physics departments at U.S. institutions, 1998 ★2981★
Top physiology research-doctorate programs as evaluated by the National Research Council ★3022★
Average faculty salaries for institutions of higher education in Iowa, 2000-01 ★3702★

Iran
Eight grade science achievement scores from selected countries, 1999 ★14★
Math achievement test comparison ★19★
Countries of origin for non-U.S. citizens awarded doctorates at U.S. colleges and universities, 1999 ★1901★
Eighth grade mathematics achievement scores from selected countries, 1999 ★2773★

Ireland
Percentage of enrollment at public institutions of higher education, by country, 1998 ★859★
Annual leave days for employees in selected countries ★2239★
Countries with the highest percentage of workers satisfied with their job ★2242★
Percentage of students enrolled in institutions of higher education that were not citizens of the country where they studied, 1998 ★2500★
European periodical prices by country, 2001 ★2921★
Institute for Scientific Information periodical prices by country, 2001 ★2922★

Iris and Walter
Most notable books for young readers, 2001 ★319★
Outstanding children's fiction books, 2000 ★329★

Irmo High School
Outstanding secondary schools in Columbia, South Carolina ★4117★

Irmo Middle School
Outstanding secondary schools in Columbia, South Carolina ★4117★

The Iron-Blue Vault: Selected Poems
Booklist's most recommended poetry books, 2001 ★231★

Irondale High School
Outstanding secondary schools in Minneapolis-St. Paul, Minnesota-Wisconsin ★4181★

Ironworker
Jobs with the highest unemployment ★2256★
Jobs with the worst physical demands scores ★2263★
Least desirable jobs ★2266★

Most desirable jobs in construction trades ★2272★

Irrational Exuberance
Library Journal's most notable investing books, 2000 ★264★

The Irreducible Needs of Children: What Every Child Must Have to Grow, Learn, and Flourish
American School Board Journal's notable education books, 2000 ★225★

IRS agent
Careers college students considered least respected, 2000 ★739★

Irvin; Sandora
All-America girls' high school basketball 2nd team, 2001 ★171★

Irvine; John C.
Top pay and benefits for the chief executive and top paid employees at Lincoln Memorial University ★3374★

Irvington High School
Outstanding secondary schools in New York, New York ★4191★
Outstanding secondary schools in Oakland, California ★4195★

A Is for Salad
Publishers Weekly Off-the-Cuff Awards winner for best book title, 2000 ★338★

Isaac Young Middle School
Outstanding secondary schools in New York, New York ★4191★

Isegawa; Moses
Booklist's best first novels ★228★

Isenberg; Steven
Top pay and benefits for the chief executive and top paid employees at Adelphi University ★3164★

Islamic
Religious preference of incoming freshmen, 2000 ★1061★

The Island of the Skog
Outstanding videos for library collections, 2000 ★2892★

The Islington Crime Survey: Crime Victimization, and Policing in Inner-City London
Most-cited works in critical criminology publications ★1645★

Isom; O. Wayne
Top pay and benefits for the chief executive and top paid employees at Cornell University ★3257★

Isotope Geoscience
Geology journals with the greatest impact measure, 1981-98 ★2525★

Israel
Eight grade science achievement scores from selected countries, 1999 ★14★
Top countries of study for U.S. students studying abroad, 1998-99 ★2510★
Eighth grade mathematics achievement scores from selected countries, 1999 ★2773★
Institute for Scientific Information periodical prices by country, 2001 ★2922★

Israel; Jerry
Top pay and benefits for the chief executive and top paid employees at the University of Indianapolis ★3545★

It Takes a City: Getting Serious about Urban School Reform
American School Board Journal's notable education books, 2000 ★225★

Italian
Gender breakdown of language and literature doctorate recipients, by subfield, 1999 ★1937★
Language and literature doctorates awarded at U.S. colleges and universities, by subfield, 1999 ★1949★
Languages of requested materials from OCLC ILL, 1999 ★2679★

Italy
Eight grade science achievement scores from selected countries, 1999 ★14★
Math achievement test comparison ★19★
Countries with the most computers, 2000 ★1603★
Countries of origin for non-U.S. citizens awarded doctorates at U.S. colleges and universities, 1999 ★1901★
College dropout rates for selected countries ★2134★
Countries with the lowest spending per student on higher education, 1997 ★2489★
Top countries of study for U.S. students studying abroad, 1998-99 ★2510★
Countries with the most Internet users ★2583★
Percentage of internet usage for selected countries ★2599★
Eighth grade mathematics achievement scores from selected countries, 1999 ★2773★
European periodical prices by country, 2001 ★2921★
Institute for Scientific Information periodical prices by country, 2001 ★2922★

Itawamba Community College
Lowest undergraduate tuition and fees at colleges and universities in Mississippi ★1523★

Ithaca College
U.S. colleges and universities with a popular theater group ★1020★
U.S. News & World Report's northern regional universities with the best academic reputation scores, 2000-01 ★1415★
U.S. News & World Report's northern regional universities with the best student/faculty ratios, 2000-01 ★1416★
U.S. News & World Report's northern regional universities with the highest average graduation rates, 2000-01 ★1419★
U.S. News & World Report's northern regional universities with the highest percentage of full-time faculty, 2000-01 ★1422★
U.S. News & World Report's northern regional universities with the highest proportion of classes with 20 students of less, 2000-01 ★1423★
U.S. News & World Report's top northern regional universities, 2000-01 ★1425★
U.S. News & World Report's best undergraduate fees among northern regional universities by discount tuition, 2000 ★1428★
U.S. colleges and universities awarding the most communications master's degrees to Asian Americans ★1764★
Degrees granted in the ten largest undergraduate journalism and mass communications programs, 1999 ★2745★
Average faculty salaries for institutions of higher education in New York, 2000-01 ★3719★

Itochu
Business Week's best companies in terms of sales ★408★

It's Not About the Bike: My Journey Back to Life
Christopher Awards winners for adult literature, 2000 ★235★
Longest-running nonfiction hardcover bestsellers, 2000 ★281★
Most notable nonfiction books for young adults, 2001 ★324★

It's Raining Pigs & Noodles
Publishers Weekly Off-the-Cuff Awards winner for best book of poetry, 2000 ★337★

ITT Industries
Business Week's best performing companies with the highest 3-year earnings growth ★416★
Fortune's highest ranked industrial and farm equipment companies, 2000 ★471★
Top manufacturing companies in Standard & Poor's 500, 2001 ★548★

Iverson; Thomas
Top pay and benefits for the chief executive and top paid employees at Central College in Iowa ★3226★

Ivy Tech State College
State appropriations for Indiana's institutions of higher education, 2000-01 ★1267★
Average faculty salaries for institutions of higher education in Indiana, 2000-01 ★3701★

Ivy Tech State College, Central Indiana
Lowest undergraduate tuition and fees at colleges and universities in Indiana ★1503★

Ivy Tech State College, Columbus
Lowest undergraduate tuition and fees at colleges and universities in Indiana ★1503★

Ivy Tech State College, Eastcentral
Lowest undergraduate tuition and fees at colleges and universities in Indiana ★1503★

Ivy Tech State College, Kokomo
Lowest undergraduate tuition and fees at colleges and universities in Indiana ★1503★

Ivy Tech State College, Lafayette
Lowest undergraduate tuition and fees at colleges and universities in Indiana ★1503★

Ivy Tech State College, Northcentral
Lowest undergraduate tuition and fees at colleges and universities in Indiana ★1503★

Ivy Tech State College, Northeast
Lowest undergraduate tuition and fees at colleges and universities in Indiana ★1503★

Ivy Tech State College, Northwest
Lowest undergraduate tuition and fees at colleges and universities in Indiana ★1503★

Ivy Tech State College, Southcentral
Lowest undergraduate tuition and fees at colleges and universities in Indiana ★1503★

Ivy Tech State College, Southeast
Lowest undergraduate tuition and fees at colleges and universities in Indiana ★1503★

Ivy Tech State College, Southwest
Lowest undergraduate tuition and fees at colleges and universities in Indiana ★1503★

Ivy Tech State College, Wabash Valley
Lowest undergraduate tuition and fees at colleges and universities in Indiana ★1503★

Ivy Tech. State College, Whitewater
Lowest undergraduate tuition and fees at colleges and universities in Indiana ★1503★

Iwatsuki; Shunzabora
Most-cited researchers in surgery/transplantation, 1981-1998 ★2878★

J

J. Crew
Top women-owned companies ★4460★

J. F. Drake State Technical College
Lowest undergraduate tuition and fees at colleges and universities in Alabama ★1480★

Jackson; Gordon
Top pay and benefits for the chief executive and top paid employees at Whitworth College ★3625★

Jackson; Jesse
Most important African Americans in the twentieth century ★219★

Jackson; Mahalia
Most influential African Americans in religion ★3091★

Jackson; Michael
Top pay and benefits for the chief executive and top paid employees at Loma Linda University ★3377★

Jackson Middle School
Outstanding secondary schools in Charleston, West Virginia ★4107★

Jackson; Nancy Jean
Top pay and benefits for the chief executive and top paid employees at Meredith College ★3399★

Jackson, Sr.; Rev. Jesse L.
Most influential African Americans in politics and civil rights ★3040★

Jackson State Community College
Lowest undergraduate tuition and fees at colleges and universities in Tennessee ★1559★

Jackson State University
Colleges offering the Thurgood Marshall Scholarship Fund ★221★
State appropriations for Mississippi's institutions of higher education, 2000-01 ★1277★
Historically black colleges and universities awarding the most master's degrees to African Americans ★1670★
Total baccalaureate biology/life sciences degrees awarded to African Americans from U.S. colleges and universities, 1997-98 ★1679★
Total baccalaureate degrees awarded to African Americans from historically black colleges, 1997-98 ★1697★
Total baccalaureate English language, literature, and letters degrees awarded to African Americans from U.S. colleges and universities, 1997-98 ★1716★
Total baccalaureate mathematics degrees awarded to African Americans from U.S. colleges and universities, 1997-98 ★1729★
Total baccalaureate physical sciences degrees awarded to African Americans from U.S. colleges and universities, 1997-98 ★1733★
U.S. colleges and universities awarding the most biological and life sciences master's degrees to African Americans ★1756★
U.S. colleges and universities awarding the most education master's degrees to African Americans ★1769★
U.S. colleges and universities awarding the most English language/literature/letters master's degrees to African Americans ★1773★
U.S. colleges and universities awarding the most master's degrees to African Americans ★1785★
U.S. colleges and universities awarding the most social sciences and history master's degrees to African Americans ★1801★
Historically black colleges and universities awarding the most doctorate degrees to African Americans ★1945★
U.S. colleges and universities awarding the most doctorate degrees to African Americans ★2095★
U.S. colleges and universities awarding the most education doctorate degrees to African Americans ★2108★
Institutions with the most female physics bachelor's recipients, 1994-1998 ★2959★
U.S. institutions with more than 40% female bachelor's graduates in their physics departments, 1994-98 ★2977★
Average faculty salaries for institutions of higher education in Mississippi, 2000-01 ★3711★

Jackson; Thomas H.
Top pay and benefits for the chief executive and top paid employees at the University of Rochester ★3560★

Jackson; Weldon
Top pay and benefits for the chief executive and top paid employees at Manhattan College ★3387★

Jacksonville State University
Division I NCAA colleges with that graduated none of their African American male basketball players, 1990-91 to 1993-94 ★930★
State appropriations for Alabama's institutions of higher education, 2000-01 ★1254★
U.S. colleges and universities awarding the most English language/literature/letters master's degrees to African Americans ★1773★

Jacksonville University
Highest undergraduate tuition and fees at colleges and universities in Florida ★1494★
Average faculty salaries for institutions of higher education in Florida, 2000-01 ★3696★

Jacob; Bernard
Top pay and benefits for the chief executive and top paid employees at Hofstra University ★3335★

Jacobs; J. Thomas
Top pay and benefits for the chief executive and top paid employees at Marycrest International University ★3393★

Jacobs; Jeffrey
Golden Key Scholar Award winners, 2000 ★1316★

Jacobsen; Eric N.
American Chemical Society 2001 award winners (Group 3) ★753★

Jacobsen; J.
Top assistant professor economists at elite liberal arts colleges, 1975-94 ★2173★

Jacobson; Harry R.
Top pay and benefits for the chief executive and top paid employees at Vanderbilt University ★3593★

Jacobson; Ira D.
Top pay and benefits for the chief executive and top paid employees at Embry-Riddle Aeronautical University ★3286★

Jacobson; John H.
Top pay and benefits for the chief executive and top paid employees at Hope College ★3339★

Jacso; Peter
Library and information science faculty with the most journal articles, 1993-1998 ★2711★

Jade Green: A Ghost Story
Most notable fiction books for reluctant young adult readers, 2001 ★321★

Jaffe; Elaine S.
Most-cited researchers in oncology, 1981-1998 ★2877★

Jaffe; Peter G.
Most-cited scholars in *Canadian Journal of Criminology* ★1638★

Jaffe-Ruiz; Marilyn
Top pay and benefits for the chief executive and top paid employees at Pace University ★3435★

JAI Press
Book publishers with the most citations (Class 4) ★2565★

Jain; Dipak C.
Top pay and benefits for the chief executive and top paid employees at Northwestern University ★3423★

Jain; Jiya
Top pay and benefits for the chief executive and top paid employees at the University of Saint Francis in Indiana ★3562★

Jakks Pacific
Business Week's top companies in terms of sales growth, 2000 ★432★

Jakoubek; Jane
Top pay and benefits for the chief executive and top paid employees at Hanover College ★3324★

James Bond: The Secret World of 007
Most notable nonfiction books for reluctant young adult readers, 2001 ★323★

James Bowie High School
Outstanding secondary schools in Austin-San Marcos, Texas ★4090★

James Castle High School
Outstanding secondary schools in Honolulu, Hawaii ★4149★

James; Daniel "Chappie"
Most influential African Americans in the military ★2882★

James and the Giant Peach
Most frequently banned books in the 1990s ★745★

James Hart Middle School
Outstanding secondary schools in Chicago, Illinois ★4110★

James; LeBron
All-America boys' high school basketball 2nd team, 2001 ★162★

James; Linda
Top pay and benefits for the chief executive and top paid employees at Georgian Court College ★3307★

James Madison High School
Outstanding secondary schools in Madison, Wisconsin ★4173★

James Madison University
Division I NCAA colleges with that graduated none of their African American male basketball players, 1990-91 to 1993-94 ★930★
State appropriations for Virginia's institutions of higher education, 2000-01 ★1299★
U.S. News & World Report's best undergraduate fees among southern regional universities by discount tuition, 2000 ★1429★
U.S. News & World Report's southern regional universities with the best academic reputation scores, 2000-01 ★1433★
U.S. News & World Report's southern regional universities with the highest freshmen retention rates, 2000-01 ★1437★
U.S. News & World Report's southern regional universities with the highest graduation rates, 2000-01 ★1438★
U.S. News & World Report's southern regional universities with the highest percentage of freshmen in the top 25% of their high school class, 2000-01 ★1439★

U.S. News & World Report's southern regional universities with the highest percentage of full-time faculty, 2000-01 ★1440★
U.S. News & World Report's southern regional universities with the lowest acceptance rates, 2000-01 ★1442★
U.S. News & World Report's top public southern regional universities, 2000-01 ★1443★
U.S. News & World Report's top southern regional universities, 2000-01 ★1444★
U.S. master's institutions with the largest number of students studying abroad, 1998-99 ★2513★
Average faculty salaries for institutions of higher education in Virginia, 2000-01 ★3735★

James Prendergast Library Association
Highest Hennen's American Public Library Ratings for libraries serving a population of 25,000 to 49,999 ★2696★

James R. Bekkering
Top pay and benefits for the chief executive and top paid employees at Hope College ★3339★

James Taylor High School
Outstanding secondary schools in Houston, Texas ★4150★

Jamestown College
Highest undergraduate tuition and fees at colleges and universities in North Dakota ★1541★
Average faculty salaries for institutions of higher education in North Dakota, 2000-01 ★3721★

Jamestown Community College
Highest undergraduate tuition and fees at public 2-year colleges and universities ★1462★
Average faculty salaries for institutions of higher education in New York, 2000-01 ★3719★

Janet; Jerome
All-American boy's high school football receivers, 2000 ★185★

Janitor
Jobs with the best stress scores ★2252★
Jobs with the highest unemployment ★2256★

Janitors and cleaners
Occupations with the highest number of self-employed workers, 1998 ★2311★
Occupations with the largest projected employment growth, 1998-2008 ★2312★
Projected employment growth for selected occupations that require shorter moderate-term on-the-job training, 1998-2008 ★2321★

Jansky; Lynn
Top pay and benefits for the chief executive and top paid employees at Rivier College ★3460★

Japan
Comparison of 8th grade science achievement scores, U.S. and worldwide, 1999 ★6★
Eight grade science achievement scores from selected countries, 1999 ★14★
Math achievement test comparison ★19★
CA journal literature abstracted, by country, 2000 ★757★
CA patents abstracted, by country, 2000 ★758★
Percentage of enrollment at private institutions of higher education, by country, 1998 ★858★
Countries with the most computers, 2000 ★1603★
Countries of origin for non-U.S. citizens awarded doctorates at U.S. colleges and universities, 1999 ★1901★
College dropout rates for selected countries ★2134★
Annual leave days for employees in selected countries ★2239★
Countries with the highest spending per student on higher education, 1997 ★2488★
Foreign countries with the highest enrollment of foreign students, 1999-2000 ★2496★
Countries with the most Internet users ★2583★
Percentage of internet usage for selected countries ★2599★
Eighth grade mathematics achievement scores from selected countries, 1999 ★2773★
Asian periodical prices by country, 2001 ★2916★
Institute for Scientific Information periodical prices by country, 2001 ★2922★
First-year physics and astronomy graduate students from Asia, 1997-98 ★2987★
Countries with the highest leader's salary ★3120★
Nations with the most-cited papers in the sciences ★4320★

Japanese
Gender breakdown of language and literature doctorate recipients, by subfield, 1999 ★1937★
Language and literature doctorates awarded at U.S. colleges and universities, by subfield, 1999 ★1949★
Languages of requested materials from OCLC ILL, 1999 ★2679★

Japin; Arthur
Booklist's best first novels ★228★

Jardim; Anne
Top pay and benefits for the chief executive and top paid employees at Simmons College ★3499★

Jariwala; Sunit
All-USA College Academic Second Team, 2001 ★3★

Jarvis; Michael
Top pay and benefits for the chief executive and top paid employees at St. John's University in New York ★3474★

Javits Fellowships
Proposed fiscal 2002 appropriations for graduate support ★1250★

Jayber Crow: The Life Story of Jayber Crow, Barber, of the Port William Membership, as Written by Himself
Booklist's best fiction books for library collections, 2000 ★227★

The Jazz Fly
Smithsonian's best books for children ages 1 to 6 ★363★

J.B. Hunt Transport Services
Fortune's highest ranked trucking companies, 2000 ★503★

JC Penney
Business Week's best performing companies with the lowest 3-year shareholder returns ★424★
Fortune's highest ranked general merchandisers, 2000 ★468★
Fortune's least admired companies for innovation ★508★

JCEE
Institutions generating the most economic education research text, 1963-1990 ★2167★

JCPenney Company
Top recruiters for retail merchandising jobs for 2000-01 bachelor's degree recipients ★556★
Top recruiters for health jobs for 2000-01 bachelor's degree recipients ★2541★

JCPenney.com
Top E-commerce web sites ★2603★

JDS Uniphase
Business Week's best performing companies with the greatest decline in earnings growth ★412★
Business Week's best performing companies with the highest 1-year sales performance ★414★
Business Week's best performing companies with the highest 3-year sales performance ★417★
Business Week's best performing companies with the lowest 1-year shareholder returns ★422★
Business Week's best performing companies with the lowest net margin, 2000 ★425★
Fast-growing information technology companies, 2000 ★444★
Top information technology companies, 2000 ★544★

Jeelani; Shalk
Top pay and benefits for the chief executive and top paid employees at Tuskegee University ★3583★

Jeevanandam; Valluvan
Top pay and benefits for the chief executive and top paid employees at the University of Chicago ★3537★

Jefferson College
Lowest undergraduate tuition and fees at colleges and universities in Missouri ★1525★

Jefferson Community College
Lowest undergraduate tuition and fees at colleges and universities in Kentucky ★1509★
Lowest undergraduate tuition and fees at colleges and universities in Ohio ★1544★
Average faculty salaries for institutions of higher education in New York, 2000-01 ★3719★

Jefferson Government Relations
Lobbyist that billed the most to U.S. colleges and universities, 1999 ★1249★

Jefferson High School
Outstanding secondary schools in Lafayette, Indiana ★4161★

Jefferson Junior High School
Outstanding secondary schools in Columbia, Missouri ★4116★

Jefferson State College
Average faculty salaries for institutions of higher education without academic ranks in Alabama, 2000-01 ★3740★

Jefferson's Children: The Story of One American Family
Most notable nonfiction books for young adults, 2001 ★324★

Jeffords; Sen. James M.
Members of Congress receiving the largest contributions from the Sallie Mae Inc. Political Action Committee ★3023★

Jeffrey; W. Stephen
Top pay and benefits for the chief executive and top paid employees at the University of Hartford ★3544★

Jemison; Mae
Most influential African Americans in medicine and science ★2879★

Jemtegaard Middle School
Outstanding secondary schools in Portland-Vancouver, Oregon-Washington ★4206★

Jeni LeGon: Living in a Great Big Way
Most notable videos for adults, 2001 ★2891★

Jenkins High School
  Outstanding secondary schools in Savannah, Georgia ★4226★
Jennings; Paul C.
  Top pay and benefits for the chief executive and top paid employees at the California Institute of Technology ★3521★
Jennings; Stephen
  Top pay and benefits for the chief executive and top paid employees at Oklahoma City University ★3431★
Jensen; M.C.
  U.S. academic economists by mean number of citations, 1971-92 ★2176★
  U.S. academic economists by total citations, 1971-92 ★2177★
Jensen; Robert E.
  Top pay and benefits for the chief executive and top paid employees at Trinity University in Texas ★3579★
Jepson; Alvin
  Top pay and benefits for the chief executive and top paid employees at Eastern College in Pennsylvania ★3280★
Jericho High School
  Outstanding secondary schools in Long Island, New York ★4165★
Jersey City State College
  Total baccalaureate mathematics degrees awarded to Hispanic Americans from U.S. colleges and universities, 1997-98 ★1731★
Jesuit High School
  Outstanding secondary schools in Portland-Vancouver, Oregon-Washington ★4206★
Jesuit Prep
  Outstanding secondary schools in Dallas, Texas ★4120★
Jeweler
  Jobs with the worst outlook scores ★2262★
Jewish
  Religious preference of incoming freshmen, 2000 ★1061★
Jewish Theological Seminary
  Top religion research-doctorate programs as evaluated by the National Research Council ★3093★
J.F. Drake State Tech College
  Average faculty salaries for institutions of higher education without academic ranks in Alabama, 2000-01 ★3740★
Ji; Niuniu
  All-USA College Academic Second Team, 2001 ★3★
Jim, the Boy
  Outstanding fiction books for young adults, 2000 ★333★
The Jim Henson Company
  Most selective internships in the U.S., 2001 ★2610★
Jinzo; Naruse
  Japan's ten great educators ★2234★
JLA: Earth 2
  Most notable nonfiction books for reluctant young adult readers, 2001 ★323★
JM Family Enterprises
  Largest private companies, 2000 ★523★
  Top women-owned companies ★4460★
Job Corps
  Educational program activities expenditures, 2000 ★3992★
Jobe; Carol A.
  Top pay and benefits for the chief executive and top paid employees at American International College ★3173★

Jobline International
  Top E-recruiting providers, 2000 ★2604★
JobPilot
  Top E-recruiting providers, 2000 ★2604★
JobsOnline
  Top career-related Web sites ★2602★
Jockey
  Jobs considered the most competitive ★2245★
  Jobs that are potentially the highest paying ★2246★
  Jobs with the greatest potential income for beginners ★2253★
  Jobs with the worst environment scores ★2260★
  Most desirable jobs in athletics ★2269★
Jockey International
  Oldest women-owned companies ★4454★
Joey Pigza Loses Control
  Most notable books for middle readers, 2001 ★317★
  Outstanding books for middle readers, 2000 ★326★
  Outstanding children's fiction books, 2000 ★329★
Joey Pigza Swallowed the Key
  Outstanding audiobooks, 2000 ★287★
John A. Logan College
  Average faculty salaries for institutions of higher education in Illinois, 2000-01 ★3700★
John A. Macdonald
  Canada's best nonfiction selections of the 20th century ★234★
John Bogle on Investing
  Library Journal's most notable investing books, 2000 ★264★
John Bowne High School
  Outstanding urban public high schools in Metro New York ★4265★
John Brown University
  U.S. News & World Report's southern regional liberal arts colleges with the highest freshmen retention rates, 2000-01 ★1372★
  U.S. News & World Report's southern regional liberal arts colleges with the highest percentage of full-time faculty, 2000-01 ★1374★
  Highest undergraduate tuition and fees at colleges and universities in Arkansas ★1484★
  Average faculty salaries for institutions of higher education in Arkansas, 2000-01 ★3691★
John Carroll High School
  Outstanding secondary schools in Baltimore, Maryland ★4092★
John Carroll University
  U.S. News & World Report's midwestern regional universities with the best academic reputation scores, 2000-01 ★1401★
  U.S. News & World Report's midwestern regional universities with the best alumni giving rates, 2000-01 ★1402★
  U.S. News & World Report's midwestern regional universities with the best student/faculty ratios, 2000-01 ★1403★
  U.S. News & World Report's midwestern regional universities with the highest freshmen retention rates, 2000-01 ★1405★
  U.S. News & World Report's midwestern regional universities with the highest graduation rates, 2000-01 ★1406★
  U.S. News & World Report's top midwestern regional universities, 2000-01 ★1411★
  U.S. News & World Report's best undergraduate fees among midwestern regional universities by discount tuition, 2000 ★1427★

Institutions generating the most economic education research text, 1963-1990 ★2167★
Average faculty salaries for institutions of higher education in Ohio, 2000-01 ★3722★
John F. Kennedy University
  U.S. colleges and universities awarding the most psychology master's degrees to Asian Americans ★1798★
John Hopkins University
  Institutions receiving the most gifts, 1999-2000 ★1244★
  Women faculty in Ph.D. physics departments at U.S. institutions, 1998 ★2981★
  Largest benefit packages awarded to presidents at institutions of higher education, 1998-99 ★3133★
John M Patterson State Tech College
  Average faculty salaries for institutions of higher education without academic ranks in Alabama, 2000-01 ★3740★
John M. Patterson State Technical College
  Lowest undergraduate tuition and fees at colleges and universities in Alabama ★1480★
John Marshall High School
  Outstanding secondary schools in San Antonio, Texas ★4219★
John Marshall Law School
  U.S. colleges and universities awarding the most law and legal studies master's degrees to Hispanic Americans ★1783★
  Academics' choices for best trial advocacy programs, 2001 ★2633★
John Tyler Community College
  Lowest undergraduate tuition and fees at colleges and universities in Virginia ★1565★
John Wallace Middle School
  Outstanding secondary schools in Hartford, Connecticut ★4147★
John Wiley
  Publishers with the best industry stocks, 2000 ★300★
  Highest revenues of publicly held book publishers, 1999 ★3072★
John Wiley & Sons
  Most selective internships in the U.S., 2001 ★2610★
John Young Middle School
  Outstanding secondary schools in South Bend, Indiana ★4231★
Johns Hopkins Hospital
  Top cancer hospitals in the U.S., 2000 ★2787★
  Top cardiology and heart surgery hospitals in the U.S., 2000 ★2788★
  Top endocrinology hospitals in the U.S., 2000 ★2789★
  Top gastroenterology hospitals in the U.S., 2000 ★2790★
  Top geriatrics hospitals in the U.S., 2000 ★2791★
  Top gynecology hospitals in the U.S., 2000 ★2792★
  Top hospitals in the U.S., 2000 ★2793★
  Top nephrology hospitals in the U.S., 2000 ★2794★
  Top neurology and neurosurgery hospitals in the U.S., 2000 ★2795★
  Top orthopedics hospitals in the U.S., 2000 ★2797★
  Top ortolaryngology hospitals in the U.S., 2000 ★2798★
  Top pediatrics hospitals in the U.S., 2000 ★2799★

Top psychiatric hospitals in the U.S., 2000 ★2800★

Top rheumatology hospitals in the U.S., 2000 ★2802★

Top urology hospitals in the U.S., 2000 ★2803★

Johns Hopkins Hospital (Wilmer Eye Institute)

Top ophthalmology hospitals in the U.S., 2000 ★2796★

Johns Hopkins University

All-USA College Academic Third Team, 2001 ★4★

Most effective anthropology research-doctorate programs as evaluated by the National Research Council ★61★

Top art history research-doctorate programs as evaluated by the National Research Council ★93★

Most effective neurosciences research-doctorate programs as evaluated by the National Research Council ★200★

Top neurosciences research-doctorate programs as evaluated by the National Research Council ★202★

Most effective biochemistry and molecular biology research-doctorate programs as evaluated by the National Research Council ★205★

Most effective molecular and general genetics research-doctorate programs as evaluated by the National Research Council ★207★

Top biochemistry and molecular biology research-doctorate programs as evaluated by the National Research Council ★209★

Top molecular and general genetics research-doctorate programs as evaluated by the National Research Council ★211★

U.S. universities publishing the most papers in the field of microbiology, 1994-98 ★215★

U.S. News & World Report's national universities with the best academic reputation, 2000-01 ★1126★

U.S. News & World Report's national universities with the highest financial resources rank, 2000-01 ★1133★

Institutions receiving the most alumni gifts, 1999-2000 ★1242★

U.S. colleges and universities spending the most on independent lobbyists, 1999 ★1310★

Golden Key Scholar Award winners, 2000 ★1316★

Highest undergraduate tuition and fees at private nonprofit, 4-year or above colleges and universities ★1461★

Highest undergraduate tuition and fees at colleges and universities in Maryland ★1514★

Most effective comparative literature research-doctorate programs as evaluated by the National Research Council ★1587★

Top comparative literature research-doctorate programs as evaluated by the National Research Council ★1588★

Traditionally white institutions awarding the most master's degrees to African Americans ★1755★

U.S. colleges and universities awarding the most biological and life sciences master's degrees to African Americans ★1756★

U.S. colleges and universities awarding the most biological and life sciences master's degrees to Asian Americans ★1757★

U.S. colleges and universities awarding the most business management and administrative services master's degrees to African Americans ★1759★

U.S. colleges and universities awarding the most computer and information sciences master's degrees to African Americans ★1766★

U.S. colleges and universities awarding the most computer and information sciences master's degrees to Asian Americans ★1767★

U.S. colleges and universities awarding the most health professions and related sciences master's degrees to African Americans ★1777★

U.S. colleges and universities awarding the most health professions and related sciences master's degrees to Asian Americans ★1778★

U.S. colleges and universities awarding the most health professions and related sciences master's degrees to Hispanic Americans ★1779★

U.S. colleges and universities awarding the most master's degrees to Asian Americans ★1786★

U.S. colleges and universities awarding the most mathematics master's degrees to African Americans ★1790★

U.S. colleges and universities awarding the most physical sciences master's degrees to African Americans ★1793★

U.S. colleges and universities awarding the most physical sciences master's degrees to Asian Americans ★1794★

U.S. colleges and universities awarding the most psychology master's degrees to African Americans ★1797★

U.S. colleges and universities awarding the most social sciences and history master's degrees to Asian Americans ★1802★

U.S. colleges and universities awarding the most social sciences and history master's degrees to Hispanic Americans ★1803★

U.S. colleges and universities awarding the most biological and life sciences doctorate degrees to African Americans ★2082★

U.S. colleges and universities awarding the most doctorates in life sciences, 1999 ★2104★

U.S. colleges and universities awarding the most health professions and related sciences doctorate degrees to African Americans ★2114★

U.S. colleges and universities awarding the most health professions and related sciences doctorate degrees to Asian Americans ★2115★

U.S. colleges and universities awarding the most health professions and related sciences doctorate degrees to Hispanic Americans ★2116★

Most effective geosciences research-doctorate programs as evaluated by the National Research Council ★2150★

Economics Ph.D. programs by number of citations of top economist graduates, 1971-92 ★2204★

Economics Ph.D. programs by number of citations per top economist graduate, 1971-92 ★2205★

Economics Ph.D. programs by number of top economist graduates, 1971-92 ★2206★

Academics' choices for best graduate bioengineering/biomedical engineering programs, 2001 ★2381★

Most effective biomedical engineering research-doctorate programs as evaluated by the National Research Council ★2383★

Top biomedical engineering research-doctorate programs as evaluated by the National Research Council ★2384★

U.S. News & World Report's graduate engineering programs with the best biomedical departments, 2000-01 ★2385★

Academics' choices for best graduate environmental/environmental health engineering programs, 2001 ★2408★

Most effective English language and literature research-doctorate programs as evaluated by the National Research Council ★2448★

Top English language and literature research-doctorate programs as evaluated by the National Research Council ★2451★

Faculty's scholarly reputation in the Ph.D.-granting departments of geography, 1925-1982 ★2518★

Top German language and literature research-doctorate programs as evaluated by the National Research Council ★2528★

Top history research-doctorate programs as evaluated by the National Research Council ★2554★

Academics' choices for best AIDS programs, 2001 ★2818★

Academics' choices for best drug and alcohol abuse programs, 2001 ★2819★

Academics' choices for best geriatrics programs, 2001 ★2821★

Academics' choices for best internal medicine programs, 2001 ★2822★

Academics' choices for best pediatrics programs, 2001 ★2823★

Academics' choices for best women's health medical programs, 2001 ★2825★

Acceptance rates for *U.S. News & World Report*'s top 10 research-oriented medical schools, 2001 ★2827★

Average MCAT scores at *U.S. News & World Report*'s top 10 research-oriented medical schools, 2001 ★2836★

Average undergraduate GPA at *U.S. News & World Report*'s top 10 research-oriented medical schools, 2001 ★2838★

Faculty-student ratios at *U.S. News & World Report*'s top 10 research-oriented medical schools, 2001 ★2842★

NIH research grants for *U.S. News & World Report*'s top 10 research-oriented medical schools, 2001 ★2845★

Out-of-state tuition and fees for *U.S. News & World Report*'s top 10 research-oriented medical schools, 2001 ★2847★

Top primary-care medical schools by student selectivity rank, 2001 ★2858★

Top research-oriented medical schools, 2001 ★2859★

Top research-oriented medical schools by reputation, as determined by academic personnel, 2001 ★2860★

Top research-oriented medical schools by reputation, as determined by intern/residency directors, 2001 ★2861★

Top research-oriented medical schools by student selectivity, 2001 ★2862★

Most effective pharmacology research-doctorate programs as evaluated by the National Research Council ★2938★

Top pharmacology research-doctorate programs as evaluated by the National Research Council ★2939★

U.S. universities publishing the most papers in the field of astrophysics, 1995-99 ★2978★
Most patents issued to universities or research facilities, 1999 ★3097★
U.S. colleges and universities spending the most on chemical research and development, 1998 ★3099★
U.S. colleges and universities with the most federal support for chemical engineering research and development, 1998 ★3101★
U.S. colleges and universities with the most federal support for chemical research and development, 1998 ★3102★
U.S. universities spending the most on research and development, 1998 ★3104★
Institutions receiving the most federal research and development expenditures, 1999 ★3105★
Presidents with the highest pay at Research I and II universities, 1998-99 ★3162★
U.S. universities contributing the most papers in the field of neurosciences, 1993-97 ★4285★
U.S. universities publishing the most papers in the field of neuroscience, 1994-98 ★4287★
U.S. universities publishing the most highly-cited papers, 1997-1999 ★4348★

Johns Hopkins University, Peabody Conservatory of Music
Highest undergraduate tuition and fees at colleges and universities in Maryland ★1514★

Johns; Jasper
Best living artists ★73★

Johns Manville
Fortune's highest ranked building materials and glass companies, 2000 ★451★

Johns; Michael M.E.
Top pay and benefits for the chief executive and top paid employees at Emory University ★3289★

Johnson & Johnson
Business Week's best companies in the United States ★411★
Fortune's highest ranked pharmaceuticals companies, 2000 ★485★

Johnson & Wales University
Institutions censured by the American Association of University Professors, 2001 ★1067★
Professional or specialized institutions with the highest enrollment of foreign students, 1998-99 ★2501★

Johnson C. Smith University
U.S. colleges and universities with the highest percentage of African Americans enrolled, 1997 ★222★

Johnson; Christine
All-America girls' high school soccer team midfielders, 2001 ★177★

Johnson; Colton
Top pay and benefits for the chief executive and top paid employees at Vassar College ★3594★

Johnson Controls
Fortune's highest ranked motor vehicle parts companies, 2000 ★480★
Top manufacturing companies in Standard & Poor's 500, 2001 ★548★

Johnson County Community College
Average faculty salaries for institutions of higher education in Kansas, 2000-01 ★3703★

Johnson County Library
Highest Hennen's American Public Library Ratings for libraries serving a population of 250,000 to 499,999 ★2699★

Johnson County Vocational School
All-USA Teacher Teams, First Team, 2000 ★4399★

Johnson; D. B.
Outstanding children's picture books, 2000 ★331★

Johnson; David
All-America boys' high school soccer team midfielders, 2001 ★168★

Johnson; D.B.
Publishers Weekly Off-the-Cuff Awards winner for most promising new illustrator, 2000 ★358★

Johnson; Dennis
Top pay and benefits for the chief executive and top paid employees at Gustavus Adolphus College ★3317★

Johnson; Derrick
All-American boy's high school football linebackers, 2000 ★182★

Johnson; Edward
All-America boys' high school soccer team forwards, 2001 ★166★

Johnson; Geneva R.
Top pay and benefits for the chief executive and top paid employees at the University of Mobile ★3551★

Johnson High School
Outstanding secondary schools in Washington, District of Columbia-Maryland-Virginia-West Virginia ★4249★

Johnson; Jacqueline
Top pay and benefits for the chief executive and top paid employees at Saint Martin's College in Washington ★3479★

Johnson; John H.
Most influential African Americans in business ★526★

Johnson; Johnny A.
Top pay and benefits for the chief executive and top paid employees at Birmingham-Southern College ★3204★

Johnson; Karen
Top pay and benefits for the chief executive and top paid employees at Walla Walla College ★3601★

Johnson; Ken
Top pay and benefits for the chief executive and top paid employees at Amber University ★3172★

Johnson; Kenneth W.
Top pay and benefits for the chief executive and top paid employees at the University of Mary Hardin-Baylor ★3549★

Johnson; Marjorie
Top pay and benefits for the chief executive and top paid employees at Seattle Pacific University ★3494★

Johnson; Paul
All-America boys' high school soccer team forwards, 2001 ★166★

Johnson; Richard
Top pay and benefits for the chief executive and top paid employees at Bucknell University ★3213★

Johnson; Robert
Most influential African Americans in business ★526★
Top pay and benefits for the chief executive and top paid employees at Albion College ★3167★

Johnson; Ronald
Top pay and benefits for the chief executive and top paid employees at the University of Scranton ★3567★

Johnson State College
Undergraduate tuition and fees at colleges and universities in Vermont ★1563★
Average faculty salaries for institutions of higher education in Vermont, 2000-01 ★3734★

Johnson; Thomas
Top pay and benefits for the chief executive and top paid employees at the University of Mary ★3548★

Johnson; Thomas A.
Top pay and benefits for the chief executive and top paid employees at the University of New Haven ★3553★
Top pay and benefits for the chief executive and top paid employees at Whitworth College ★3625★

Johnston and Associates
Lobbyist that billed the most to U.S. colleges and universities, 1999 ★1249★

Johnston; Bryan
Top pay and benefits for the chief executive and top paid employees at Willamette University ★3628★

Johnston Community College
Average faculty salaries for institutions of higher education without academic ranks in North Carolina, 2000-01 ★3761★

Johnston; Dale
Top pay and benefits for the chief executive and top paid employees at Antioch University ★3178★

Johnston; David E.
Top pay and benefits for the chief executive and top paid employees at Wheaton College in Illinois ★3620★

Johnston; Jeff (J.D.)
All-America boys' high school soccer team forwards, 2001 ★166★

Johnston; Mark W.
Highest impact authors in the *Journal of Business Research*, by number of citations in 12 journals, 1985-1999 ★693★

Johnston; Wesley J.
Authors with the most articles published in the *Journal of Business Research*, 1985 to 1999 ★687★
Most published authors, adjusted for coauthorship, in the *Journal of Business Research*, 1985 to 1999 ★701★

The Joint Commission Journal on Quality Improvement
Health policy and services journals by citation impact, 1999 ★2539★

Jolicoeur; Pam
Top pay and benefits for the chief executive and top paid employees at California Lutheran University ★3216★

Joliet Community College
Fall enrollment at Chicago-area public community colleges, by minority percentages, 1999 ★867★

Joliet Junior College
Average faculty salaries for institutions of higher education in Illinois, 2000-01 ★3700★

Jones Academic College Prep
Admissions to college prep schools in Chicago that are the toughest to get into, 2001 ★4001★
College prep schools in Chicago that are the toughest to get into ★4005★

Jones Apparel Group
Fortune's highest ranked apparel companies, 2000 ★448★

Jones College Prep
Acceptance rates at Chicago college prep magnet schools, 2000-01 ★4000★

Jones County Junior College
Lowest undergraduate tuition and fees at colleges and universities in Mississippi ★1523★

Jones; D.
Top full professor economists at elite liberal arts colleges, 1975-94 ★2175★

Jones; Derek
Top pay and benefits for the chief executive and top paid employees at Hamilton College ★3319★

Jones; Diana Wynne
Outstanding children's fiction books, 2000 ★329★

Jones; Dwayne
All-America boys' high school soccer team forwards, 2001 ★166★

Jones; E.
Authors with the most citations among authors published in *American Political Science Review*, 1974-94 ★3048★

Jones; J. Brooks
Top pay and benefits for the chief executive and top paid employees at West Virginia Wesleyan College ★3613★

Jones Jr.; James F.
Top pay and benefits for the chief executive and top paid employees at Kalamazoo College ★3358★

Jones; Kevin
All-American boy's high school football running backs, 2000 ★186★

Jones; M.
Top associate professor economists at elite liberal arts colleges, 1975-94 ★2174★

Jones; Mark W.
Top pay and benefits for the chief executive and top paid employees at Goucher College ★3314★

Jones Memorial Library
Highest Hennen's American Public Library Ratings for libraries serving a population of 1,000 to 2,499 ★2692★

Jones; Phillip D.
Top pay and benefits for the chief executive and top paid employees at Xavier University in Ohio ★3637★

Jones; Quincy
Most influential African Americans in business ★526★

Jones; Ray
Top pay and benefits for the chief executive and top paid employees at William Jewell College ★3630★

Jones; Rev. Rock
Top pay and benefits for the chief executive and top paid employees at Hendrix College ★3331★

Jones; Shirley
Top pay and benefits for the chief executive and top paid employees at Mississippi College ★3404★

Jones; Stanton L.
Top pay and benefits for the chief executive and top paid employees at Wheaton College in Illinois ★3620★

Jones; Trevor
Most cited scholars in critical criminology ★1640★

Most-cited scholars in critical criminology publications ★1641★
Most cited works in critical criminology ★1644★

Jones; William B.
Top pay and benefits for the chief executive and top paid employees at Southwestern University in Texas ★3505★

Jonesboro High School
Outstanding suburban public high schools in Metro Atlanta ★4254★

Jordan
Eight grade science achievement scores from selected countries, 1999 ★14★
Countries of origin for non-U.S. citizens awarded doctorates at U.S. colleges and universities, 1999 ★1901★
Eighth grade mathematics achievement scores from selected countries, 1999 ★2773★

Jordan; Barbara
Most influential African Americans in politics and civil rights ★3040★

Jordan; David
Top pay and benefits for the chief executive and top paid employees at Austin College ★3184★

Jordan; I. King
Top pay and benefits for the chief executive and top paid employees at Gallaudet University ★3301★

Jorden, Burt, Boros, Cicchetti, Berenson & Johnson
Lobbyist that billed the most to U.S. colleges and universities, 1999 ★1249★

Jorgensen; Lennard
Top pay and benefits for the chief executive and top paid employees at LaSierra University ★3366★

Joseph; Lynn
Booklist's best first novels for youths ★309★

Joseph; Michael
Top pay and benefits for the chief executive and top paid employees at North Central College in Illinois ★3421★

Joseph; Msgr. Milam J.
Top pay and benefits for the chief executive and top paid employees at the University of Dallas ★3538★

Joseph Sears Elementary School
Illinois suburban elementary schools with the highest ISAT scores in reading and math ★18★

Joseph; William T.
Top pay and benefits for the chief executive and top paid employees at Virginia Wesleyan College ★3596★

Jossey-Bass
Book publishers with the most citations (Class 4) ★2565★

Jost; Robert A.
Top pay and benefits for the chief executive and top paid employees at Embry-Riddle Aeronautical University ★3286★

Journal of Accounting and Economics
Top accounting journals by half-life impact factor ★578★
Top accounting journals by mode impact factor ★579★
Top ranked business administration and business economics journals ★2188★

Journal of Accounting Research
Top accounting journals by half-life impact factor ★578★
Top accounting journals by mode impact factor ★579★
Top ranked business administration and business economics journals ★2188★
Journals and proceedings with the most citations (Class 2) ★2568★

Journal of the ACM
Top ranked AACSB publications ★2186★
Journals and proceedings with the most citations (Class 2) ★2568★

Journal of Adolescent Health
'Outside' journals most frequently citing *Family Planning Perspectives*, 1991-95 ★1859★

Journal of Advanced Composition
Most cited language serials in technical communication journals from 1988 to 1997 ★4420★
Most cited serials in technical communication journals from 1988 to 1997 ★4425★

Journal of Advertising Research
Most cited business serials in technical communication journals from 1988 to 1997 ★4417★

Journal of Agricultural and Resource Economics
Top ranked agricultural and natural resource economics journals ★2187★

Journal of Agriculture and Food Chemistry
Agriculture journals by citation impact, 1981-96 ★50★
Agriculture journals by citation impact, 1992-96 ★52★
Agriculture journals by citation impact, 1995-99 ★53★
Agriculture journals by citation impact, 1999 ★54★
Food science and technology journals by citation impact, 1995-99 ★2903★
Food science and technology journals by citation impact, 1999 ★2904★

Journal of the American Academy of Child and Adolescent Psychiatry
Psychiatry journals by citation impact, 1981-98 ★3054★
Psychiatry journals by citation impact, 1998 ★3056★
Psychiatry journals by impact factor, 1981 to 1998 ★3057★
Psychiatry journals by impact factor, 1994 to 1998 ★3058★

Journal of the American Academy of Child And Adolescent Psychiatry
Psychiatry journals by citation impact, 1995-98 ★3055★

Journal of American Academy of Dermatology
Number of citations and papers for original articles appearing in dermatology journals, 1981 to 1996 ★1873★
Number of citations and papers in dermatology journals, 1981 to 1996 ★1874★

Journal of the American Chemical Society
Chemistry journals by citation impact, 1981-99 ★808★
Chemistry journals by citation impact, 1995-99 ★809★
Chemistry journals by citation impact, 1999 ★810★

Journal of American College Health
Education and educational research journals by citation impact, 1999 ★2237★

Journal of the American Geriatric Society
- Geriatrics and gerontology journals with the greatest impact measure, 1981-98 ★2805★
- Geriatrics and gerontology journals with the greatest impact measure, 1994-98 ★2806★
- Geriatrics and gerontology journals with the greatest impact measure, 1998 ★2807★

Journal of the American Mathematical Society
- Mathematics journals by impact factor ★2783★

Journal of American Medical Informatics Association
- Information and library science journals by citation impact, 1995-99 ★2725★
- Information and library science journals by citation impact, 1999 ★2726★

Journal of American Society of Information Sciences
- Information and library science journals by citation impact, 1981-99 ★2724★
- Information and library science journals by citation impact, 1995-99 ★2725★
- Information and library science journals by citation impact, 1999 ★2726★
- Information and library science journals with the greatest impact measure, 1981-98 ★2727★

Journal of the American Society of Mass Spectrometry
- Spectroscopy journals by citation impact, 1995-99 ★4360★
- Spectroscopy journals by citation impact, 1999 ★4361★

Journal of the American Society of Nephrology
- Urology and nephrology journals with the greatest impact measure, 1981-98 ★2816★
- Urology and nephrology journals with the greatest impact measure, 1994-98 ★2817★

Journal of American Statistical Assn.
- Top ranked mathematical and quantitative methods journals ★2198★

Journal of Analytical Atomic Spectrometry
- Spectroscopy journals by citation impact, 1995-99 ★4360★
- Spectroscopy journals by citation impact, 1999 ★4361★

Journal of Animal Ecology
- Ecology journals by citation impact, 1981-99 ★2136★
- Ecology journals by citation impact, 1995-99 ★2137★

Journal of Anthropology and Archaeology
- Anthropology journals by citation impact, 1991-98 ★63★

Journal of Applied Crystallography
- Crystallography journals by citation impact, 1981-98 ★1654★
- Crystallography journals by citation impact, 1994-98 ★1655★
- Crystallography journals by citation impact, 1998 ★1656★

Journal of Applied Psychology
- Top management journals ★546★
- Top management journals by core impact ★547★
- Most cited psychology serials in technical communication journals from 1988 to 1997 ★4423★
- Most cited serials in technical communication journals from 1988 to 1997 ★4425★

Journal of Biological Chemistry
- Top science journals by impact factor ★4281★

Journal of Biology and Inorganic Chemistry
- Inorganic and nuclear chemistry journals by citation impact, 1995-99 ★812★
- Inorganic and nuclear chemistry journals by citation impact, 1999 ★813★

Journal of Biomolecular NMR
- Spectroscopy journals by citation impact, 1981-99 ★4359★
- Spectroscopy journals by citation impact, 1995-99 ★4360★
- Spectroscopy journals by citation impact, 1999 ★4361★

Journal of Biosocial Science
- Demography journals with the highest average citations after 5 years ★1856★
- Most cited demography journals, 1991-95 ★1857★
- Top demography journals by average impact factor, 1991-95 ★1863★

Journal of Business
- Business journals by citation impact, 1981-98 ★688★
- Top ranked business administration and business economics journals ★2188★
- Top ranked financial economics journals ★2192★
- Highest impact economics journals in exhaustible resources from 1980 to 1989 ★2460★

Journal of Business Communication
- Most cited business serials in technical communication journals from 1988 to 1997 ★4417★
- Most cited serials in technical communication journals from 1988 to 1997 ★4425★

Journal of Business and Technical Communication
- Most cited language serials in technical communication journals from 1988 to 1997 ★4420★
- Most cited serials in technical communication journals from 1988 to 1997 ★4425★

Journal of Cereal Science
- Food science and technology journals by citation impact, 1991-99 ★2902★
- Food science and technology journals by citation impact, 1995-99 ★2903★
- Food science and technology journals by citation impact, 1999 ★2904★

Journal of Cerebral Blood Flow
- Journals with the highest impact factor in the field of neuroscience, 1981-96 ★191★
- Hematology journals with the greatest impact measure, 1981-98 ★2808★
- Hematology journals with the greatest impact measure, 1994-98 ★2809★

Journal of Cerebral Blood Flow and Metabolism
- Neurosciences journals with the greatest impact measure, 1981-98 ★2812★

Journal of Chemical Information and Computer Sciences
- Information and library science journals with the greatest impact measure, 1981-98 ★2727★

Journal of the Chemical Society-Chemical Communications
- Chemistry journals by citation impact, 1981-99 ★808★
- Chemistry journals by citation impact, 1995-99 ★809★

Journal Chemical Society (London)-Dalton Transactions
- Inorganic and nuclear chemistry journals by citation impact, 1995-99 ★812★

Journal of Child Language
- Language and linguistics journals with the greatest impact measure, 1981-98 ★2731★

Journal of Child Psychology, Psychiatry and Allied Disciplines
- Psychiatry journals by citation impact, 1998 ★3056★

Journal of Clinical Investigation
- Top science journals by impact factor ★4281★

Journal of Clinical Psychiatry
- Psychiatry journals by citation impact, 1981-98 ★3054★
- Psychiatry journals by citation impact, 1995-98 ★3055★
- Psychiatry journals by citation impact, 1998 ★3056★
- Psychiatry journals by impact factor, 1981 to 1998 ★3057★
- Psychiatry journals by impact factor, 1994 to 1998 ★3058★

Journal of Clinical Psychopharmacology
- Psychiatry journals by impact factor, 1981 to 1998 ★3057★
- Psychiatry journals by impact factor, 1994 to 1998 ★3058★

Journal of Clinical Psychopharmacy
- Psychiatry journals by citation impact, 1981-98 ★3054★
- Psychiatry journals by citation impact, 1995-98 ★3055★

Journal of Common Market Studies
- Business journals by citation impact, 1998 ★690★

Journal of Communication
- Most cited language serials in technical communication journals from 1988 to 1997 ★4420★

Journal of Comparative Economics
- Top ranked economic systems journals ★2191★

Journal of Comparative Neurology
- Journals with the highest impact factor in the field of neuroscience, 1981-96 ★191★

Journal of Computational Chemistry
- Chemistry journals by citation impact, 1981-99 ★808★

Journal of Computer-Based Instruction
- Most cited education serials in technical communication journals from 1988 to 1997 ★4418★

Journal of Computer Documentation
- Most cited science serials in technical communication journals from 1988 to 1997 ★4424★

Journal of Conflict Resolution
- Political science journals with the greatest impact measure, 1981-98 ★3049★
- Political science journals with the greatest impact measure, 1994-98 ★3050★

Journal of Consulting and Clinical Psychology
- Most-cited social sciences journals, 1981-97 ★4340★

Journal of Consumer Research
- Business journals by citation impact, 1981-98 ★688★
- Business journals by citation impact, 1994-98 ★689★
- Business journals by citation impact, 1998 ★690★

Journal of Criminal Law and Criminology
Criminology and penology journals with the greatest impact measure, 1981-98 ★1611★
Criminology and penology journals with the greatest impact measure, 1994-98 ★1612★

Journal of Crystal Growth
Crystallography journals by citation impact, 1981-98 ★1654★
Crystallography journals by citation impact, 1994-98 ★1655★
Crystallography journals by citation impact, 1998 ★1656★

Journal of Crystallographic and Spectroscopal Research
Crystallography journals by citation impact, 1994-98 ★1655★

Journal of Crystallography and Molecular Structures
Crystallography journals by citation impact, 1981-98 ★1654★

Journal of Dairy Research
Food science and technology journals by citation impact, 1991-99 ★2902★
Food science and technology journals by citation impact, 1995-99 ★2903★

Journal of Dairy Science
Food science and technology journals by citation impact, 1991-99 ★2902★
Food science and technology journals by citation impact, 1999 ★2904★

Journal de Physique Letters
Physics journals with the greatest impact measure, 1981-98 ★3020★

Journal des Mathematiques Pures et Appliquees
Mathematics journals by impact factor ★2783★

Journal of Development Economics
Top ranked economic development, technological change, and growth journals ★2189★
Highest impact economics journals in exhaustible resources from 1990 to 1998 ★2461★

Journal of Development Studies
Top ranked economic development, technological change, and growth journals ★2189★

Journal of Differential Geometry
Mathematics journals by impact factor ★2783★
Mathematics journals by impact factor, 1981 to 1997 ★2784★
Mathematics journals by impact factor, 1993 to 1997 ★2785★

Journal of Documentation
Information and library science journals by citation impact, 1981-99 ★2724★
Information and library science journals by citation impact, 1995-99 ★2725★
Information and library science journals by citation impact, 1999 ★2726★
Information and library science journals with the greatest impact measure, 1981-98 ★2727★

Journal of Ecology
Ecology journals by citation impact, 1995-99 ★2137★

Journal of Econometrics
Top ranked agricultural and natural resource economics journals ★2187★
Top ranked mathematical and quantitative methods journals ★2198★

Journal of Economic Education
Journals publishing the most articles on economic education research from 1963-1990 ★2170★
Top ranked health, education, and welfare journals ★2193★

Journal of Economic Entomology
Agriculture journals by citation impact, 1992-96 ★52★

Journal of Economic History
Top ranked economic history journals ★2190★

Journal of Economic Literature
Economics journals with the greatest impact measure, 1981-98 ★2161★
Economics journals with the greatest impact measure, 1994-98 ★2162★
Economics journals with the greatest impact measure, 1997 ★2163★
Economics journals by citation impact, 1981-98 ★2182★
Economics journals by citation impact, 1995-98 ★2183★
Economics journals by citation impact, 1998 ★2184★
Top ranked health, education, and welfare journals ★2193★
Social sciences journals with the greatest impact measure, 1981-97 ★4341★

Journal of Economic Perspectives
Economics journals with the greatest impact measure, 1994-98 ★2162★
Economics journals with the greatest impact measure, 1997 ★2163★
Economics journals by citation impact, 1995-98 ★2183★
Economics journals by citation impact, 1998 ★2184★

Journal of Economic Theory
Alternative general economics journals, by non-uniform weighting of subdisciplinary impacts, including self-citations ★2180★
Alternative general economics journals, by uniform weighting of subdisciplinary impacts, including self-citations ★2181★
Top ranked financial economics journals ★2192★
Top ranked industrial organization journals ★2194★
Top ranked mathematical and quantitative methods journals ★2198★
Top ranked microeconomics and monetary economics journals ★2199★
Top ranked microeconomics journals ★2200★

Journal of Educational Psychology
Most cited education serials in technical communication journals from 1988 to 1997 ★4418★
Most cited serials in technical communication journals from 1988 to 1997 ★4425★

Journal of Educational Statistics
Education and educational research journals by citation impact, 1981-99 ★2235★
Education and educational research journals with the greatest impact measure ★2238★

Journal of Environmental Economics and Management
Business journals by citation impact, 1994-98 ★689★
Economics journals by citation impact, 1995-98 ★2183★
Highest impact economics journals in exhaustible resources from 1980 to 1989 ★2460★

Journal of Evolutionary Biology
Ecology journals by citation impact, 1999 ★2138★

Journal of Experimental Medicine
Immunology journals with the greatest impact measure, 1981-98 ★2810★
Immunology journals with the greatest impact measure, 1994-98 ★2811★
Immunology journals by impact factor, 1981 to 1997 ★4279★
Immunology journals by impact factor, 1993 to 1997 ★4280★
Top science journals by impact factor ★4281★

Journal of Experimental Psychology: Learning, Memory, Cognition
Most cited education serials in technical communication journals from 1988 to 1997 ★4418★

Journal of Family History
'Outside' journals most frequently citing *Population Studies*, 1991-95 ★1861★

Journal of Finance
Top accounting journals by half-life impact factor ★578★
Top accounting journals by mode impact factor ★579★
Alternative general economics journals, by non-uniform weighting of subdisciplinary impacts, including self-citations ★2180★
Alternative general economics journals, by uniform weighting of subdisciplinary impacts, including self-citations ★2181★
Top ranked business administration and business economics journals ★2188★
Top ranked financial economics journals ★2192★
Top ranked microeconomics and monetary economics journals ★2199★
Highest impact economics journals in energy from 1990 to 1998 ★2458★
Highly cited real estate journals, 1990 to 1995 ★3090★

Journal of Financial Economics
Top accounting journals by half-life impact factor ★578★
Top accounting journals by mode impact factor ★579★
Economics journals with the greatest impact measure, 1981-98 ★2161★
Economics journals with the greatest impact measure, 1994-98 ★2162★
Economics journals with the greatest impact measure, 1997 ★2163★
Alternative general economics journals, by non-uniform weighting of subdisciplinary impacts, including self-citations ★2180★
Alternative general economics journals, by uniform weighting of subdisciplinary impacts, including self-citations ★2181★
Economics journals by citation impact, 1981-98 ★2182★
Economics journals by citation impact, 1995-98 ★2183★
Top ranked business administration and business economics journals ★2188★
Top ranked financial economics journals ★2192★
Top ranked industrial organization journals ★2194★
Highly cited real estate journals, 1990 to 1995 ★3090★

Journal of Financial and Quantitative Analysis
Top ranked financial economics journals ★2192★

Journal of Fish Diseases
  Veterinary sciences journals with the greatest impact measure, 1981-98 ★4442★
  Veterinary sciences journals with the greatest impact measure, 1994-98 ★4443★
Journal of Food Protection
  Food science and technology journals by citation impact, 1999 ★2904★
Journal of Forecasting
  Journals with the highest impact factor in the field of management, 1981-96 ★696★
Journal of Functional Analysis
  Mathematics journals by impact factor, 1993 to 1997 ★2785★
Journal of Futures Markets
  Top ranked financial economics journals ★2192★
Journal of the Geological Society of Australia
  Geology journals with the greatest impact measure, 1981-98 ★2525★
Journal of Geology
  Geology journals with the greatest impact measure, 1981-98 ★2525★
  Geology journals with the greatest impact measure, 1994-98 ★2526★
Journal of Geophysical Research-Atmosphere
  Oceanography journals by citation impact, 1981-99 ★2139★
  Oceanography journals by citation impact, 1995-99 ★2140★
Journal of Geophysical Research-Oceans
  Oceanography journals by citation impact, 1995-99 ★2140★
Journal of Geophysical Research-Oceans and Atmospheres
  Oceanography journals by citation impact, 1981-99 ★2139★
Journal of Geophysical Research, Section D-Atmospheres
  Astronomy and astrophysics journals by citation impact, 1981-99 ★102★
  Astronomy and astrophysics journals by citation impact, 1995-99 ★103★
  Astronomy and astrophysics journals by impact factor, 1981 to 1998 ★105★
  Astronomy and astrophysics journals by impact factor, 1994 to 1998 ★106★
Journal of Geophysical Research-Solid
  Oceanography journals by citation impact, 1995-99 ★2140★
Journal of Geophysical Research-Solid Earth
  Astronomy and astrophysics journals by citation impact, 1995-99 ★103★
  Astronomy and astrophysics journals by impact factor, 1994 to 1998 ★106★
Journal of Geophysical Research-Space Physics
  Astronomy and astrophysics journals by citation impact, 1981-99 ★102★
  Astronomy and astrophysics journals by impact factor, 1981 to 1998 ★105★
  Oceanography journals by citation impact, 1981-99 ★2139★
Journal of Geriatric Psychology and Neurology
  Geriatrics and gerontology journals with the greatest impact measure, 1994-98 ★2806★
Journal of Gerontology
  Geriatrics and gerontology journals with the greatest impact measure, 1981-98 ★2805★
  Geriatrics and gerontology journals with the greatest impact measure, 1994-98 ★2806★
Journal of the Great Lakes
  Marine and freshwater biology journals with the greatest impact measure, 1994-98 ★197★
Journal of Health Economics
  Economics journals with the greatest impact measure, 1994-98 ★2162★
  Economics journals with the greatest impact measure, 1997 ★2163★
  Economics journals by citation impact, 1995-98 ★2183★
  Economics journals by citation impact, 1998 ★2184★
  Health policy and services journals by citation impact, 1981-99 ★2537★
  Health policy and services journals by citation impact, 1995-99 ★2538★
  Health policy and services journals by citation impact, 1999 ★2539★
Journal of Health Politics and Policy
  Health policy and services journals by citation impact, 1981-99 ★2537★
  Health policy and services journals by citation impact, 1999 ★2539★
Journal of Higher Education
  Education and educational research journals with the greatest impact measure ★2238★
Journal of Human Evolution
  Anthropology journals by citation impact, 1991-98 ★63★
  Anthropology journals by citation impact, 1994-98 ★64★
  Anthropology journals by citation impact, 1998 ★65★
Journal of Human Resources
  Top ranked health, education, and welfare journals ★2193★
  Top ranked labor and demographic economics journals ★2196★
Journal of Immunology
  Immunology journals with the greatest impact measure, 1981-98 ★2810★
  Immunology journals with the greatest impact measure, 1994-98 ★2811★
  Immunology journals by impact factor, 1981 to 1997 ★4279★
  Immunology journals by impact factor, 1993 to 1997 ★4280★
Journal Inclusion Phenomena and Molecular Recognition
  Crystallography journals by citation impact, 1981-98 ★1654★
  Crystallography journals by citation impact, 1994-98 ★1655★
  Crystallography journals by citation impact, 1998 ★1656★
Journal of Inflammation
  Hematology journals with the greatest impact measure, 1994-98 ★2809★
Journal of Insect Physiology
  Entomology journals by citation impact, 1981-98 ★2453★
  Entomology journals by citation impact, 1994-98 ★2454★
  Entomology journals by citation impact, 1998 ★2455★
Journal of the International Association of Mathematical Geology
  Geology journals with the greatest impact measure, 1981-98 ★2525★
Journal of International Business Studies
  Top management journals ★546★
  Top management journals by core impact ★547★
  Business journals receiving the most citations in five core journals, 1995-97 ★691★
Journal of International Economics
  Top ranked international economics journals ★2195★
Journal of International Marketing
  Business journals receiving the most citations in five core journals, 1995-97 ★691★
Journal of Interpersonal Violence
  Criminology and penology journals with the greatest impact measure, 1981-98 ★1611★
  Criminology and penology journals with the greatest impact measure, 1994-98 ★1612★
Journal of Investigative Dermatology
  Number of citations and papers for original articles appearing in dermatology journals, 1981 to 1996 ★1873★
  Number of citations and papers in dermatology journals, 1981 to 1996 ★1874★
Journal of Labor Research
  Top ranked labor and demographic economics journals ★2196★
Journal of Law and Economics
  Economics journals with the greatest impact measure, 1981-98 ★2161★
  Economics journals by citation impact, 1981-98 ★2182★
  Top ranked industrial organization journals ★2194★
  Top ranked law and economics journals ★2197★
  Highest impact economics journals in energy from 1980 to 1989 ★2457★
  Law journals by citation impact, 1981-96 ★2617★
  Law journals with the greatest impact measure, 1981-98 ★2618★
Journal of Law of Economics
  Top ranked public economics journals ★2201★
Journal of Learning Sciences
  Education and educational research journals by citation impact, 1995-99 ★2236★
  Education and educational research journals by citation impact, 1999 ★2237★
Journal of Legal Studies
  Law journals by citation impact, 1981-96 ★2617★
  Law journals with the greatest impact measure, 1981-98 ★2618★
Journal of Leisure Research
  Sociology journals by impact factor, 1993 to 1997 ★4356★
Journal of Leukocyte Biology
  Hematology journals with the greatest impact measure, 1981-98 ★2808★
  Hematology journals with the greatest impact measure, 1994-98 ★2809★
  Immunology journals with the greatest impact measure, 1994-98 ★2811★
Journal of Lightwave Technology
  Optics journals by citation impact, 1981-99 ★2906★
  Optics journals by citation impact, 1995-99 ★2907★
  Optics journals by citation impact, 1999 ★2908★
  Optics journals with the greatest impact measure, 1981-98 ★2909★
  Optics journals with the greatest impact measure, 1994-98 ★2910★
Journal of Management
  Top management journals by core impact ★547★

Business journals by citation impact, 1981-98 ★688★
Business journals by citation impact, 1994-98 ★689★
Journals with the highest impact factor in the field of management, 1981-96 ★696★
Journals and proceedings with the most citations (Class 4) ★2570★

Journal of Management Information Systems
Top ranked AACSB publications ★2186★
Journals and proceedings with the most citations (Class 2) ★2568★

Journal of Marine Research
Oceanography journals by citation impact, 1981-99 ★2139★
Oceanography journals by citation impact, 1999 ★2141★

Journal of Marketing
Business journals by citation impact, 1981-98 ★688★
Business journals by citation impact, 1994-98 ★689★
Business journals by citation impact, 1998 ★690★
Journals and proceedings with the most citations (Class 4) ★2570★
Most cited business serials in technical communication journals from 1988 to 1997 ★4417★

Journal of Marketing Research
Business journals by citation impact, 1981-98 ★688★
Business journals by citation impact, 1994-98 ★689★
Business journals by citation impact, 1998 ★690★
Most cited business serials in technical communication journals from 1988 to 1997 ★4417★

Journal of Marriage and the Family
'Outside' journals most frequently citing *Demography*, 1991-95 ★1858★
Sociology journals by impact factor, 1981 to 1997 ★4355★
Sociology journals by impact factor, 1993 to 1997 ★4356★

Journal of Mass Spectrometry
Spectroscopy journals by citation impact, 1995-99 ★4360★
Spectroscopy journals by citation impact, 1999 ★4361★

Journal of Mathematical Economics
Top ranked microeconomics journals ★2200★

Journal of Medical Entomology
Entomology journals by citation impact, 1998 ★2455★

Journal of Memory and Language
Language and linguistics journals with the greatest impact measure, 1981-98 ★2731★
Most cited psychology serials in technical communication journals from 1988 to 1997 ★4423★

Journal of Memory and Language/ Journal of Verbal Learning and Verbal Behavior
Most cited serials in technical communication journals from 1988 to 1997 ★4425★

Journal of Mental Health Administration
Health policy and services journals by citation impact, 1995-99 ★2538★

Journal of Metamorphic Geology
Geology journals with the greatest impact measure, 1981-98 ★2525★
Geology journals with the greatest impact measure, 1994-98 ★2526★

Journal of Molecular Graphics/Models
Crystallography journals by citation impact, 1981-98 ★1654★
Crystallography journals by citation impact, 1994-98 ★1655★
Crystallography journals by citation impact, 1998 ★1656★

Journal of Monetary Economics
Economics journals with the greatest impact measure, 1981-98 ★2161★
Economics journals with the greatest impact measure, 1994-98 ★2162★
Alternative general economics journals, by non-uniform weighting of subdisciplinary impacts, including self-citations ★2180★
Economics journals by citation impact, 1981-98 ★2182★
Top ranked international economics journals ★2195★
Top ranked microeconomics and monetary economics journals ★2199★

Journal of Money, Credit & Banking
Top ranked microeconomics and monetary economics journals ★2199★

Journal of Neurology Neurosurgery and Psychiatry
Surgery journals with the greatest impact measure, 1981-98 ★2814★
Surgery journals with the greatest impact measure, 1994-98 ★2815★

Journal of Neuroscience
Neurosciences journals with the greatest impact measure, 1981-98 ★2812★
Neurosciences journals with the greatest impact measure, 1994-98 ★2813★
Top science journals by impact factor ★4281★

Journal of Neurosurgery
Surgery journals with the greatest impact measure, 1981-98 ★2814★
Surgery journals with the greatest impact measure, 1994-98 ★2815★

Journal of the Optical Society of America
Optics journals by citation impact, 1981-99 ★2906★
Optics journals with the greatest impact measure, 1981-98 ★2909★

Journal of the Optical Society of America A-Optics Image Science and Vision
Optics journals by citation impact, 1981-99 ★2906★
Optics journals by citation impact, 1995-99 ★2907★
Optics journals by citation impact, 1999 ★2908★
Optics journals with the greatest impact measure, 1981-98 ★2909★
Optics journals with the greatest impact measure, 1994-98 ★2910★

Journal of the Optical Society of America B
Optics journals by citation impact, 1981-99 ★2906★
Optics journals by citation impact, 1995-99 ★2907★
Optics journals by citation impact, 1999 ★2908★
Optics journals with the greatest impact measure, 1981-98 ★2909★
Optics journals with the greatest impact measure, 1994-98 ★2910★

Journal of Personality and Social Psychology
Top management journals ★546★
Journals and proceedings with the most citations (Class 2) ★2568★
Most-cited social sciences journals, 1981-97 ★4340★
Most cited sociology serials in technical communication journals from 1988 to 1997 ★4426★

Journal of Phycology
Marine and freshwater biology journals with the greatest impact measure, 1994-98 ★197★

Journal of Physical Chemistry
Chemistry journals by citation impact, 1999 ★810★

Journal of Physical Oceanography
Oceanography journals by citation impact, 1981-99 ★2139★
Oceanography journals by citation impact, 1999 ★2141★

Journal of Physics B
Optics journals by citation impact, 1981-99 ★2906★
Optics journals with the greatest impact measure, 1981-98 ★2909★
Optics journals with the greatest impact measure, 1994-98 ★2910★

Journal of Physics B-Atomic Molecular Optics
Optics journals by citation impact, 1995-99 ★2907★
Optics journals by citation impact, 1999 ★2908★

Journal of Police Science & Administration
Criminology and penology journals with the greatest impact measure, 1981-98 ★1611★

Journal of Political Economics
Economics journals with the greatest impact measure, 1981-98 ★2161★
Economics journals with the greatest impact measure, 1994-98 ★2162★
Economics journals with the greatest impact measure, 1997 ★2163★
Alternative general economics journals, by non-uniform weighting of subdisciplinary impacts, including self-citations ★2180★
Alternative general economics journals, by uniform weighting of subdisciplinary impacts, including self-citations ★2181★
Economics journals by citation impact, 1981-98 ★2182★
Economics journals by citation impact, 1995-98 ★2183★
Economics journals by citation impact, 1998 ★2184★
Top ranked agricultural and natural resource economics journals ★2187★
Top ranked business administration and business economics journals ★2188★
Top ranked economic development, technological change, and growth journals ★2189★
Top ranked economic history journals ★2190★
Top ranked economic systems journals ★2191★
Top ranked financial economics journals ★2192★
Top ranked health, education, and welfare journals ★2193★
Top ranked industrial organization journals ★2194★
Top ranked international economics journals ★2195★

Top ranked labor and demographic economics journals ★2196★
Top ranked law and economics journals ★2197★
Top ranked mathematical and quantitative methods journals ★2198★
Top ranked microeconomics and monetary economics journals ★2199★
Top ranked microeconomics journals ★2200★
Top ranked public economics journals ★2201★
Top ranked urban, rural and regional economics journals ★2202★
Highest impact economics journals in energy from 1974 to 1979 ★2456★
Highest impact economics journals in energy from 1980 to 1989 ★2457★
Highest impact economics journals in energy from 1990 to 1998 ★2458★
Highest impact economics journals in exhaustible resources from 1974 to 1979 ★2459★
Highest impact economics journals in exhaustible resources from 1980 to 1989 ★2460★
Highly cited real estate journals, 1990 to 1995 ★3090★

Journal of Politics
Political science journals with the greatest impact measure, 1981-98 ★3049★
Political science journals with the greatest impact measure, 1994-98 ★3050★
Political science journals with the greatest percentage of articles by multiple authors, 1974-94 ★3051★

Journal of Population Economics
Demography journals with the highest average citations after 5 years ★1856★

Journal of Public Economics
Top ranked law and economics journals ★2197★
Top ranked public economics journals ★2201★
Top ranked urban, rural and regional economics journals ★2202★
Highest impact economics journals in exhaustible resources from 1990 to 1998 ★2461★

Journal of Quantitative Criminology
Criminology and penology journals with the greatest impact measure, 1994-98 ★1612★

Journal of Reading Behavior
Education and educational research journals by citation impact, 1981-99 ★2235★
Education and educational research journals by citation impact, 1995-99 ★2236★

Journal of Real Estate Finance & Economics
Highly cited real estate journals, 1990 to 1995 ★3090★

Journal of Regional Science
Top ranked urban, rural and regional economics journals ★2202★

Journal of Research in Crime and Delinquency
Criminology and penology journals with the greatest impact measure, 1981-98 ★1611★
Criminology and penology journals with the greatest impact measure, 1994-98 ★1612★

Journal of Research and Science Teaching
Education and educational research journals by citation impact, 1995-99 ★2236★
Education and educational research journals by citation impact, 1999 ★2237★

Journal of Sedimentary Petrology
Geology journals with the greatest impact measure, 1981-98 ★2525★
Geology journals with the greatest impact measure, 1994-98 ★2526★

Journal of Sedimentology Research
Geology journals with the greatest impact measure, 1994-98 ★2526★

Journal of Sedimentology Research Part A
Geology journals with the greatest impact measure, 1994-98 ★2526★

Journal of Soil Science
Soil science journals by citation impact, 1981-99 ★188★

Journal of Soil and Water Conservation
Soil science journals by citation impact, 1995-99 ★189★

Journal of Speech and Hearing Disorders
Language and linguistics journals with the greatest impact measure, 1981-98 ★2731★

Journal of Speech and Hearing Research
Language and linguistics journals with the greatest impact measure, 1981-98 ★2731★

Journal of System Management
Most cited business serials in technical communication journals from 1988 to 1997 ★4417★

Journal of Technical Writing and Communication
Most cited serials in technical communication journals from 1988 to 1997 ★4425★
Most cited technology serials in technical communication journals from 1988 to 1997 ★4427★

Journal of Thoracic and Cardiovascular Surgery
Surgery journals with the greatest impact measure, 1981-98 ★2814★
Surgery journals with the greatest impact measure, 1994-98 ★2815★

Journal of Urban Economics
Top ranked urban, rural and regional economics journals ★2202★
Highly cited real estate journals, 1990 to 1995 ★3090★

Journal of Urology
Urology and nephrology journals with the greatest impact measure, 1981-98 ★2816★
Urology and nephrology journals with the greatest impact measure, 1994-98 ★2817★

Journal of Vascular Surgery
Surgery journals with the greatest impact measure, 1981-98 ★2814★
Surgery journals with the greatest impact measure, 1994-98 ★2815★

Journal of Verbal Learning and Behavior
Language and linguistics journals with the greatest impact measure, 1981-98 ★2731★

Journal of World Business
Business journals receiving the most citations in five core journals, 1995-97 ★691★

Journalism
Areas of specialization in journalism and mass communications programs with the highest enrollment, 1999 ★2740★

Journalism Quarterly
Most cited language serials in technical communication journals from 1988 to 1997 ★4420★

Journalist
Careers college students considered least respected, 2000 ★739★

Journals of Gerontology, Series B: Psychological Sciences & Social Sciences
Geriatrics and gerontology journals with the greatest impact measure, 1994-98 ★2806★
Geriatrics and gerontology journals with the greatest impact measure, 1998 ★2807★

Journey of the Pink Dolphins: An Amazon Quest
Outstanding science books, 2000 ★291★
Booklist's best science and technology books ★366★

Journey; R. Bruce
Top pay and benefits for the chief executive and top paid employees at Massachusetts Institute of Technology ★3397★

Jove
Mass market paperback bestsellers by publishing house, 2000 ★283★

Joy to the World: A Family Christmas Treasury
Outstanding children's religion books, 2000 ★332★

Joyce; David C.
Top pay and benefits for the chief executive and top paid employees at Union College in Kentucky ★3584★

Joyce; Timothy W.
Top pay and benefits for the chief executive and top paid employees at Saint Joseph's University ★3476★

J.P. Morgan & Co.
Fortune's highest ranked money center banks, 2000 ★478★
Top internships in the U.S. with the highest compensation, 2001 ★2611★

Judd; Donald
Highly influential artists of the 20th century ★76★

Judge (Federal)
Jobs with the best income scores ★2248★
Jobs with the highest starting salaries ★2255★
Jobs with the lowest unemployment ★2258★
Most desirable public sector jobs ★2279★

Judge Memorial Catholic High School
Outstanding secondary schools in Salt Lake City-Ogden, Utah ★4218★

Judson College
U.S. News & World Report's national liberal arts colleges with the highest proportion of classes with less than 20 students, 2000-01 ★1335★
U.S. News & World Report's national liberal arts colleges with students least in debt, 1999 ★1385★
Average faculty salaries for institutions of higher education in Illinois, 2000-01 ★3700★

Judy Moody
Most notable books for middle readers, 2001 ★317★
Outstanding children's fiction books, 2000 ★329★

Juhl; Donald
Top pay and benefits for the chief executive and top paid employees at Wartburg College ★3603★

The Jumbo Book of Gardening
Smithsonian's best books for children ages 6 to 10 ★364★

Jumpstart First Grade
Top selling home education software, 2000 ★1599★

Jumpstart Phonics
Top selling home education software, 2000 ★1599★

Jumpstart Preschool
Top selling home education software, 2000 ★1599★

Jumpstart Second Grade
Top selling home education software, 2000 ★1599★

Juneteenth
Library Journal's best fiction audiobooks, 2000 ★241★

Jung; Andrea
Highest ranking women at the top public companies, 2000 ★4452★

Jung; Laramie
Top pay and benefits for the chief executive and top paid employees at Cardinal Stritch University ★3221★

Jungck; John
Top pay and benefits for the chief executive and top paid employees at Beloit College ★3199★

Juniata College
Average faculty salaries for institutions of higher education in Pennsylvania, 2000-01 ★3725★

Junior Great Books Series
People for the American Way's list of most frequently challenged materials, 1982-1992 ★749★

Jurasek; Richard T.
Top pay and benefits for the chief executive and top paid employees at Augustana College in Illinois ★3182★

Jurenovich; David M.
Top pay and benefits for the chief executive and top paid employees at the University of the Incarnate Word ★3570★

Jurick, S.N.D.; Sister Donna M.
Top pay and benefits for the chief executive and top paid employees at St. Edward's University ★3471★

Just Six Numbers: The Deep Forces That Shape Our Universe
Library Journal's most notable astronomy books, 2000 ★248★

Justice
Federal appropriations to colleges, by agency, 2000 ★1241★

Justice Without Trial: Law Enforcement in a Democratic Society
Most-cited works in police studies articles/research notes ★2625★

K

Kabakov; Ilya
Best living artists ★73★

Kahneman; Daniel
Top pay and benefits for the chief executive and top paid employees at Princeton University ★3446★

Kailua Intermediate School
Outstanding secondary schools in Honolulu, Hawaii ★4149★

Kaimuki Intermediate School
Outstanding secondary schools in Honolulu, Hawaii ★4149★

Kain; Karen
Canada's best performing artists of the 20th century ★74★

Kaiser; Thomas J.
Top pay and benefits for the chief executive and top paid employees at Thomas Aquinas College in California ★3574★

Kalaheo High School
Outstanding secondary schools in Honolulu, Hawaii ★4149★

Kalamazoo College
Private, 4-year undergraduate colleges and universities producing the most Ph.D.'s in the life sciences, 1981-1990 ★193★
U.S. college campuses reporting murders or non-negligent manslaughters, 1999 ★728★
Highest undergraduate tuition and fees at colleges and universities in Michigan ★1518★
Private, 4-year undergraduate colleges and universities producing the most Ph.D.'s in economics, 1981-1990 ★2212★
Private, 4-year undergraduate colleges and universities producing the most Ph.D.'s in mathematics, 1981-1990 ★2777★
Average faculty salaries for institutions of higher education in Michigan, 2000-01 ★3709★
Private, 4-year undergraduate colleges and universities producing the most Ph.D.'s in the sciences, 1981-1990 ★4295★
Private, 4-year undergraduate colleges and universities producing the most Ph.D.'s in anthropology and sociology, 1981-1990 ★4345★

Kalamazoo Valley Community College
Lowest undergraduate tuition and fees at colleges and universities in Michigan ★1519★

Kalberer; Neal
Top pay and benefits for the chief executive and top paid employees at the University of Mary ★3548★

Kale; David
Top pay and benefits for the chief executive and top paid employees at Eastern Nazarene College ★3281★

Kalodner; Howard
Top pay and benefits for the chief executive and top paid employees at Western New England College ★3615★

Kalyon; Dilhan
Top pay and benefits for the chief executive and top paid employees at Stevens Institute of Technology ★3512★

Kamenar; Frank
Top pay and benefits for the chief executive and top paid employees at Wagner College ★3599★

Kandel; David
Top pay and benefits for the chief executive and top paid employees at Lindenwood University ★3375★

Kandinsky; Vasily
Highly influential artists of the 20th century ★76★

Kang; Han
All-USA College Academic First Team, 2001 ★2★

Kanjorski; Rep. Paul E.
Members of Congress receiving the largest contributions from the Sallie Mae Inc. Political Action Committee ★3023★

Kankakee Community College
Lowest undergraduate tuition and fees at colleges and universities in Illinois ★1501★

Kannel; William B.
Most-cited researchers in cardiology, 1981-1998 ★2874★

Kansas
Mean composite ACT scores by state, 2000 ★895★
Mean math SAT scores by state, 2000 ★900★
Mean verbal SAT scores by state, 2000 ★903★
Total doctorate recipients by state, 1999 ★2054★
Hispanic American enrollment at Hispanic-serving institutions of higher education, by state, 1997 ★2547★
Average Hennen's American Public Library Ratings, by state ★2690★
State grades for affordability of higher education for minority students, 2000 ★2883★
State grades for benefits state receives for educating its minority students, 2000 ★2884★
State grades for completion of higher education by minority students, 2000 ★2885★
State grades for participation of minority students in higher education, 2000 ★2886★
State grades for preparing minority students for higher education, 2000 ★2887★
States with the smallest average class size ★4072★
States with the highest percentage of high school freshmen enrolling in college within four years ★4266★

Kansas City Art Institute
Highest undergraduate tuition and fees at colleges and universities in Missouri ★1524★
Average faculty salaries for institutions of higher education in Missouri, 2000-01 ★3712★

Kansas City Kansas Community College
Lowest undergraduate tuition and fees at colleges and universities in Kansas ★1507★
Average faculty salaries for institutions of higher education in Kansas, 2000-01 ★3703★

Kansas City, MO
U.S. cities with the most wired households, 2001 ★2606★

Kansas City So. Industries
Fortune's highest ranked railroads, 2000 ★490★

Kansas State University
Longest field goals in college football ★158★
U.S. colleges and universities where the general student body puts a strong emphasis on athletic events ★1007★
State appropriations for Kansas institutions of higher education, 2000-01 ★1269★
Average faculty salaries for institutions of higher education in Kansas, 2000-01 ★3703★

Kansas; University of
All-USA College Academic First Team, 2001 ★2★
All-USA College Academic Third Team, 2001 ★4★
Colleges with the highest number of freshman Merit Scholars, 2000 ★5★
Division I all-time winningest college teams ★128★
State appropriations for Kansas institutions of higher education, 2000-01 ★1269★
Fiske Guide's best buys for public colleges and universities, 2001 ★1460★
U.S. colleges and universities awarding the most master's degrees to Native Americans ★1789★
Faculty's scholarly reputation in the Ph.D.-granting departments of geography, 1925-1982 ★2518★
U.S. universities with the highest concentration of papers published in the field of pharmacology, 1995-99 ★2937★
Women faculty in Ph.D. physics departments at U.S. institutions, 1998 ★2981★

Average faculty salaries for institutions of higher education in Kansas, 2000-01 ★3703★

Most effective Spanish and Portuguese language and literature research-doctorate programs as evaluated by the National Research Council ★4357★

Top Spanish and Portuguese language and literature research-doctorate programs as evaluated by the National Research Council ★4358★

Academics' choices for best special education graduate programs, 2001 ★4386★

Kansas Wesleyan University
Highest undergraduate tuition and fees at colleges and universities in Kansas ★1506★
Average faculty salaries for institutions of higher education in Kansas, 2000-01 ★3703★
U.S. institutions with the lowest paid full professors, 2001 ★3979★

Kanter; Stephen
Top pay and benefits for the chief executive and top paid employees at Lewis and Clark College in Oregon ★3371★

Kantor; Paul
Library and information science faculty with the most journal articles, 1993-1998 ★2711★

Kantz; Paul
Top pay and benefits for the chief executive and top paid employees at John Carroll University ★3353★

Kanzo; Uchimura
Japan's ten great educators ★2234★

Kapiolani Community College
Average faculty salaries for institutions of higher education in Hawaii, 2000-01 ★3698★

Kaplan; Barbara
Top pay and benefits for the chief executive and top paid employees at Sarah Lawrence College ★3492★

Kaplan; Shirley
Top pay and benefits for the chief executive and top paid employees at Sarah Lawrence College ★3492★

Kaplan; Steve
Top pay and benefits for the chief executive and top paid employees at Butler University ★3214★

Karakitsos; Demetri
Top pay and benefits for the chief executive and top paid employees at Park University ★3438★

Karcher; Steven D.
Top pay and benefits for the chief executive and top paid employees at Marywood University ★3396★

Karen Neuburger
Top women-owned companies in revenue growth since 1997 ★4461★

Kargleder; Charles
Top pay and benefits for the chief executive and top paid employees at Spring Hill College ★3508★

Karns; Julie
Top pay and benefits for the chief executive and top paid employees at Rider University ★3458★

Karoff; Paul
Top pay and benefits for the chief executive and top paid employees at Lesley College ★3370★

Karolinska Institute
Institutions with the highest impact in psychiatry research, 1990-98 ★3053★

Karplus; Martin
American Chemical Society 2001 award winners (Group 3) ★753★

Kaskaskia College
Lowest undergraduate tuition and fees at colleges and universities in Illinois ★1501★

Kasperson; Roger E.
Top pay and benefits for the chief executive and top paid employees at Clark University ★3238★

Kastner Intermediate School
Outstanding secondary schools in Fresno, California ★4138★

Kate and the Beanstalk
Most notable books for young readers, 2001 ★319★
Outstanding books for young readers, 2000 ★328★
Outstanding children's picture books, 2000 ★331★

Katie.com: My Story
Most notable nonfiction books for reluctant young adult readers, 2001 ★323★

Katona; Steven K.
Top pay and benefits for the chief executive and top paid employees at College of the Atlantic ★3246★

Katsoris; Constantine
Top pay and benefits for the chief executive and top paid employees at Fordham University ★3295★

Katz; S.I.
Most cited authors in dermatology journals, 1981 to 1996 ★1870★

Kauai Community College
Average faculty salaries for institutions of higher education in Hawaii, 2000-01 ★3698★

Kaufman & Broad
Fortune's highest ranked engineering and construction companies, 2000 ★461★

Kaufman; Barry
Top pay and benefits for the chief executive and top paid employees at Barnard College ★3191★

Kayne; Jon
Top pay and benefits for the chief executive and top paid employees at Bellevue University ★3197★

KB Home
Top housing and real estate companies in Standard & Poor's 500, 2001 ★543★

KBC Bancassurance Holding
Business Week's best companies in Belgium ★388★

KCSA Public Relations
Most selective internships in the U.S., 2001 ★2610★

Kean; Thomas H.
Top pay and benefits for the chief executive and top paid employees at Drew University ★3273★

Kean University
State appropriations for New Jersey's institutions of higher education, 2000-01 ★1283★

Kearsarge Regional Elementary School
All-USA Teacher Teams, Third Team, 2000 ★4401★

Keates; Jon C.
Top pay and benefits for the chief executive and top paid employees at Claremont McKenna College ★3236★

Keay; John
Booklist's best science and technology books ★366★

Keef; Patrick
Top pay and benefits for the chief executive and top paid employees at Whitman College ★3623★

Keene State College
State appropriations for New Hampshire's institutions of higher education, 2000-01 ★1282★
Average faculty salaries for institutions of higher education in New Hampshire, 2000-01 ★3716★

Keeney; Terry
Top pay and benefits for the chief executive and top paid employees at Goddard College ★3309★

The Keeper of Dreams
Outstanding fiction books for young adults, 2000 ★333★

Keffer; Charles
Top pay and benefits for the chief executive and top paid employees at the University of St. Thomas in Minnesota ★3563★

Keiser College
U.S. colleges and universities with the lowest percentage of African Americans enrolled, 1997 ★223★

Keith; Jennie
Top pay and benefits for the chief executive and top paid employees at Swarthmore College ★3514★

Keith; Kenneth
Top pay and benefits for the chief executive and top paid employees at Nebraska Wesleyan University ★3417★

Keith Valley Middle School
Outstanding secondary schools in Philadelphia, Pennsylvania-New Jersey ★4202★

Keller; Donald
Top pay and benefits for the chief executive and top paid employees at D'Youville College ★3278★

Keller Gifted
Illinois schools with the highest 7th grade science scores ★17★
Chicago elementary magnet schools with the highest acceptance rates, 2000-01 ★4002★

Keller Graduate School of Management, Inc.(GA)
U.S. colleges and universities awarding the most business management and administrative services master's degrees to African Americans ★1759★

Keller Graduate School of Management, Inc. (IL)
U.S. colleges and universities awarding the most business management and administrative services master's degrees to African Americans ★1759★

Keller; Martin B.
Top pay and benefits for the chief executive and top paid employees at Brown University ★3211★

Keller; Michael
Top pay and benefits for the chief executive and top paid employees at Aquinas College in Michigan ★3179★

Kelley; Allen C.
Individuals producing the most economic education research articles, 1963-1990 ★2166★

Kelley Jr.; F. William
Top pay and benefits for the chief executive and top paid employees at the University of Saint Francis in Illinois ★3561★

Kelley, S.J.; Rev. Aloysius P.
Top pay and benefits for the chief executive and top paid employees at Fairfield University ★3291★

Kelley; William N.
Top pay and benefits for the chief executive and top paid employees at the University of Pennsylvania ★3555★

Kelling; George L.
Most-cited scholars in police studies articles/research notes ★2624★

Kellman Elementary School
Illinois elementary schools chosen to be 'demonstration sites' for struggling schools ★4006★

Kellogg
Business Week's best performing companies with the highest return on equity, 2000 ★420★
Fortune's highest ranked consumer food products companies, 2000 ★458★

Kellogg Community College
Lowest undergraduate tuition and fees at colleges and universities in Michigan ★1519★

Kellwood
Fortune's highest ranked apparel companies, 2000 ★448★

Kelly; Jeffrey W.
Winner of the American Chemical Society's Arthur C. Cope Awards, 2001 ★795★

Kelly Jr.; David L.
Top pay and benefits for the chief executive and top paid employees at Wake Forest University ★3600★

Kelly; L. Thomas
Top pay and benefits for the chief executive and top paid employees at the University of St. Thomas in Minnesota ★3563★

Kelly; Lynn
Top pay and benefits for the chief executive and top paid employees at Madonna University ★3386★

Kelly; Marci
Top pay and benefits for the chief executive and top paid employees at Golden Gate University ★3310★

Kelly; Paul
Top pay and benefits for the chief executive and top paid employees at Gallaudet University ★3301★

Kelly Services
Fortune's highest ranked temporary help companies, 2000 ★500★

Kelly; Stephen
Top pay and benefits for the chief executive and top paid employees at Carleton College ★3222★

Kemet
Information technology companies giving the best returns, 2000 ★522★

Ken Schultz's Fishing Encyclopedia: Worldwide Angling Guide
Outstanding reference sources, 2001 ★371★

Kenderdine; Nancy
Top pay and benefits for the chief executive and top paid employees at Oklahoma City University ★3431★

Kenig; M. Jerry
Top pay and benefits for the chief executive and top paid employees at the University of New Haven ★3553★

Kenilworth School, District 38
Illinois school districts spending the most per pupil for instruction ★4011★

Kenmore East High School
Outstanding secondary schools in Buffalo-Niagara Falls, New York ★4102★

Kennebec Valley Technical College
Lowest undergraduate tuition and fees at colleges and universities in Maine ★1513★

Kennedy Drieger Middle School
Outstanding secondary schools in Baltimore, Maryland ★4092★

Kennedy; Joseph P.
Top pay and benefits for the chief executive and top paid employees at DePaul University ★3266★

Kennedy Junior High School
Outstanding secondary schools in San Jose, California ★4222★

Kennedy, Jr.; Kenneth W.
Top pay and benefits for the chief executive and top paid employees at Rice University ★3457★

Kennedy King College
Fall enrollment at Chicago-area city colleges, by minority percentages, 1999 ★865★

Kennedy; Larry W.
Top pay and benefits for the chief executive and top paid employees at William Carey College ★3629★

Kennedy; Sen. Edward M.
Members of Congress receiving the largest contributions from the Sallie Mae Inc. Political Action Committee ★3023★

Kennedy; Thomas
Top pay and benefits for the chief executive and top paid employees at National-Louis University in Illinois ★3414★

Kennedy; Tom
Top pay and benefits for the chief executive and top paid employees at Regis University in Colorado ★3454★

Kennelly, C.S.J.; Sister Karen
Top pay and benefits for the chief executive and top paid employees at Mount Saint Mary's College in California ★3411★

Kennesaw State University
State appropriations for Georgia's institutions of higher education, 2000-01 ★1263★
Average faculty salaries for institutions of higher education in Georgia, 2000-01 ★3697★

Kenston High School
Outstanding secondary schools in Cleveland-Lorain-Elyria, Ohio ★4114★

Kent-Meridian High School
Outstanding secondary schools in Seattle-Bellevue-Everett, Washington ★4227★

Kent State University
U.S. colleges and universities with the lowest average football attendance, 1996-99 ★160★
State appropriations for Ohio's institutions of higher education, 2000-01 ★1288★
Institutions with the most prolific communication studies researchers ★2749★
Average faculty salaries for institutions of higher education in Ohio, 2000-01 ★3722★

Kent State University, Ashtabula
Highest undergraduate tuition and fees at public 2-year colleges and universities ★1462★
Average faculty salaries for institutions of higher education in Ohio, 2000-01 ★3722★

Kent State University, East Liverpool
Highest undergraduate tuition and fees at public 2-year colleges and universities ★1462★
Average faculty salaries for institutions of higher education in Ohio, 2000-01 ★3722★

Kent State University, Geauga
Average faculty salaries for institutions of higher education in Ohio, 2000-01 ★3722★

Kent State University, Salem
Highest undergraduate tuition and fees at public 2-year colleges and universities ★1462★
Average faculty salaries for institutions of higher education in Ohio, 2000-01 ★3722★

Kent State University, Stark
Highest undergraduate tuition and fees at public 2-year colleges and universities ★1462★
Average faculty salaries for institutions of higher education in Ohio, 2000-01 ★3722★

Kent State University, Trumbull
Highest undergraduate tuition and fees at public 2-year colleges and universities ★1462★
Average faculty salaries for institutions of higher education in Ohio, 2000-01 ★3722★

Kent State University, Tuscarawas
Highest undergraduate tuition and fees at public 2-year colleges and universities ★1462★
Average faculty salaries for institutions of higher education in Ohio, 2000-01 ★3722★

Kentucky
Mean composite ACT scores by state, 2000 ★895★
Mean math SAT scores by state, 2000 ★900★
Mean verbal SAT scores by state, 2000 ★903★
States with the highest percentage increase in appropriations for higher education, 2000-01 ★1308★
Total doctorate recipients by state, 1999 ★2054★
State library associations with the highest annual revenue ★2682★
State library associations with the highest conference attendance ★2683★
State library associations with the largest membership ★2685★
State grades for affordability of higher education for minority students, 2000 ★2883★
State grades for benefits state receives for educating its minority students, 2000 ★2884★
State grades for completion of higher education by minority students, 2000 ★2885★
State grades for participation of minority students in higher education, 2000 ★2886★
State grades for preparing minority students for higher education, 2000 ★2887★

Kentucky Christian College
Average faculty salaries for institutions of higher education in Kentucky, 2000-01 ★3704★

Kentucky State University
Colleges offering the Thurgood Marshall Scholarship Fund ★221★
State appropriations for Kentucky's institutions of higher education, 2000-01 ★1270★
Average faculty salaries for institutions of higher education in Kentucky, 2000-01 ★3704★

Kentucky; University of
Division I all-time winningest college teams ★128★
State appropriations for Kentucky's institutions of higher education, 2000-01 ★1270★
University research libraries in the U.S. and Canada with the largest increases in total expenditures from 1993-94 to 1998-99 ★2708★
Average faculty salaries for institutions of higher education in Kentucky, 2000-01 ★3704★
U.S. universities with the greatest impact in veterinary medicine, 1995-99 ★4440★

KENTUCKY

Kentucky Wesleyan College
  Highest undergraduate tuition and fees at colleges and universities in Kentucky ★1508★
  Average faculty salaries for institutions of higher education in Kentucky, 2000-01 ★3704★

Kenwood Academy
  Outstanding urban public high schools in Metro Chicago ★4262★

Kenwood Academy High School
  Illinois schools with the highest 7th grade science scores ★17★

Kenya
  Countries with the lowest leader's salary ★3121★

Kenyon College
  U.S. News & World Report's national liberal arts colleges with the highest acceptance rates, 2000-01 ★1328★
  U.S. News & World Report's national liberal arts colleges with the highest percentage of full-time faculty, 2000-01 ★1333★
  Highest undergraduate tuition and fees at private nonprofit, 4-year or above colleges and universities ★1461★
  Private 4-year institutions with the highest tuition, 2000-01 ★1467★
  Highest undergraduate tuition and fees at colleges and universities in Ohio ★1543★
  Private, 4-year undergraduate colleges and universities producing the most Ph.D.'s in English, 1920-1990 ★2449★
  Private, 4-year undergraduate colleges and universities producing the most Ph.D.'s in English, 1981-1990 ★2450★
  Average faculty salaries for institutions of higher education in Ohio, 2000-01 ★3722★

Keohane; Nannerl O.
  Top pay and benefits for the chief executive and top paid employees at Duke University ★3276★

Keough; Katherine E.
  Top pay and benefits for the chief executive and top paid employees at Saint John Fisher College in New York ★3472★

Kepple Jr.; Thomas R.
  Top pay and benefits for the chief executive and top paid employees at Juniata College ★3357★

Keppler; Joseph
  Top editorial cartoonists used in teaching journalism history ★2770★

Keratinocyte biology
  Leading categories of dermatologic disease covered by top articles in the field, 1945-1990 ★1869★

Kerr-McGee
  Best performing companies in Standard & Poor's 500, 2001 ★382★
  Top fuel companies in Standard & Poor's 500, 2001 ★541★

Kerr; Msgr. William A.
  Top pay and benefits for the chief executive and top paid employees at LaRoche College ★3364★

Kerr; Nancy
  Top pay and benefits for the chief executive and top paid employees at Oglethorpe University ★3429★

Kerwin; Cornelius
  Top pay and benefits for the chief executive and top paid employees at American University ★3174★

Keselica; Noelle
  All-America girls' high school soccer team midfielders, 2001 ★177★

Kessen; John J.
  Top pay and benefits for the chief executive and top paid employees at the University of Saint Francis in Indiana ★3562★

Kessler Institute for Rehabilitation
  Top rehabilitation hospitals in the U.S., 2000 ★2801★

Kessler; Lawrence
  Top pay and benefits for the chief executive and top paid employees at Hofstra University ★3335★

Kessler; Paul
  Top pay and benefits for the chief executive and top paid employees at the University of Dubuque ★3542★

Kettering Middle School
  Outstanding secondary schools in Washington, District of Columbia-Maryland-Virginia-West Virginia ★4249★

Kettering University
  Highest undergraduate tuition and fees at colleges and universities in Michigan ★1518★
  U.S. News & World Report's undergraduate engineering programs with the best industrial manufacturing departments, 2000-01 ★2380★

Keuka College
  U.S. News & World Report's northern regional liberal arts colleges with students most in debt, 1999 ★1352★
  Average faculty salaries for institutions of higher education in New York, 2000-01 ★3719★

The Key Is Lost
  Booklist's most recommended historical fiction for youths, 2001 ★314★

Key West, FL
  Best 'quirky' places to live ★3083★

KeyCorp
  Fortune's highest ranked super-regional banks, 2000 ★498★

Keynes; John Maynard
  Most cited economists ★2185★

Kickapoo High School
  Outstanding secondary schools in Springfield, Missouri ★4234★

Kid City Magazine
  Best-selling youth magazines ★2920★

Kidney International
  Urology and nephrology journals with the greatest impact measure, 1981-98 ★2816★
  Urology and nephrology journals with the greatest impact measure, 1994-98 ★2817★

Kids on Strike!
  Most notable nonfiction books for young adults, 2001 ★324★

Kidtopia: 'Round the Country and Back Through Time in 60 Projects
  Smithsonian's best books for children ages 6 to 10 ★364★

Kief; Richard
  Top pay and benefits for the chief executive and top paid employees at Western Maryland College ★3614★

Kiefer; Michael
  Top pay and benefits for the chief executive and top paid employees at Amherst College ★3175★

Kiehl's
  Oldest women-owned companies ★4454★

Kiely; Colleen
  Radcliffe Institute for Advanced Study fellowship recipients in the field of visual arts, 2000-01 ★79★

Kierstead; Raymond
  Top pay and benefits for the chief executive and top paid employees at Reed College ★3453★

Kilbourne High School
  Outstanding secondary schools in Columbus, Ohio ★4118★

Kildee; Rep. Dale E.
  Members of Congress receiving the largest contributions from the Sallie Mae Inc. Political Action Committee ★3023★

Kilian Community College
  Highest undergraduate tuition and fees at colleges and universities in South Dakota ★1556★

Killing Us Softly III: Advertising's Image of Women
  Most notable DVDs and videos for young adults, 2001 ★2890★

Kim; Sung Kyu
  Top pay and benefits for the chief executive and top paid employees at Macalester College ★3385★

Kimberley Academy
  Outstanding secondary schools in Newark, New Jersey ★4192★

Kimberly-Clark
  Fortune's highest ranked forest and paper products companies, 2000 ★466★
  Top paper and forest products companies in Standard & Poor's 500, 2001 ★552★

Kimmel; Eric A.
  Outstanding children's religion books, 2000 ★332★

Kind of Blue: The Making of the Miles Davis Masterpiece
  Booklist's most recommended African American nonfiction ★229★

Kindelsperger; Kris
  Top pay and benefits for the chief executive and top paid employees at Hanover College ★3324★

Kinder Morgan
  Fortune's highest ranked pipelines and energy companies, 2000 ★486★

King; Carolyn
  Top pay and benefits for the chief executive and top paid employees at the Maharishi University of Management ★3533★

King College
  U.S. News & World Report's southern regional liberal arts colleges with the best student/faculty ratios, 2000-01 ★1368★
  U.S. News & World Report's southern regional liberal arts colleges with the highest proportion of classes having 20 students or less, 2000-01 ★1375★
  U.S. News & World Report's southern regional liberal arts colleges with the highest proportion of freshmen in the top 25% of their high school class, 2000-01 ★1376★
  U.S. News & World Report's best undergraduate fees among southern regional liberal arts colleges by discount tuition, 2000 ★1383★
  Highest undergraduate tuition and fees at colleges and universities in Tennessee ★1558★

King of the Dragons
  Outstanding audiobooks, 2000 ★287★

King; John
 Top pay and benefits for the chief executive and top paid employees at Ursinus College ★3591★

King, Jr.; Rev. Martin Luther
 Most important African Americans in the twentieth century ★219★
 Top essayists from 1946-1996 ★2445★
 Most influential African Americans in politics and civil rights ★3040★

King Pharmaceuticals
 Business Week's best performing companies with the highest 3-year sales performance ★417★

King; Richard
 Top pay and benefits for the chief executive and top paid employees at Woodbury University ★3635★

King; Stephen
 People for the American Way's list of most frequently challenged authors, 1982-1992 ★746★
 Top pay and benefits for the chief executive and top paid employees at College of the Holy Cross ★3247★

The Kingfisher Book of Fairy Tales
 Smithsonian's best books for children ages 6 to 10 ★364★

The Kingfisher Science Encyclopedia
 Smithsonian's best books for children ages 10 and up ★365★

King's College
 U.S. News & World Report's northern regional liberal arts colleges with the highest academic reputation scores, 2000-01 ★1354★
 U.S. News & World Report's northern regional liberal arts colleges with the highest acceptance rates, 2000-01 ★1355★
 U.S. News & World Report's northern regional liberal arts colleges with the highest alumni giving rates, 2000-01 ★1356★
 U.S. News & World Report's northern regional liberal arts colleges with the highest freshmen retention rates, 2000-01 ★1357★
 U.S. News & World Report's northern regional liberal arts colleges with the highest graduation rates, 2000-01 ★1358★
 U.S. News & World Report's northern regional liberal arts colleges with the highest percentage of full-time faculty, 2000-01 ★1360★
 U.S. News & World Report's northern regional liberal arts colleges with the highest proportion of classes having 20 students or less, 2000-01 ★1361★
 U.S. News & World Report's top northern regional liberal arts colleges, 2000-01 ★1363★
 Average faculty salaries for institutions of higher education in Pennsylvania, 2000-01 ★3725★

Kingston; Thomas J.
 Top pay and benefits for the chief executive and top paid employees at Franklin and Marshall College ★3296★

Kinkead; Mary Ann
 Top pay and benefits for the chief executive and top paid employees at Mills College ★3402★

Kinsey; Richard H.
 Top pay and benefits for the chief executive and top paid employees at St. Edward's University ★3471★

Kirby; Rollin
 Top editorial cartoonists used in teaching journalism history ★2770★

Kirgis; Frederic
 Top pay and benefits for the chief executive and top paid employees at Washington and Lee University ★3605★

Kirk; Wesley
 All-America boys' high school soccer team forwards, 2001 ★166★

Kirkland Community College
 Average faculty salaries for institutions of higher education without academic ranks in Michigan, 2000-01 ★3752★

Kirkwood Community College
 Lowest undergraduate tuition and fees at colleges and universities in Iowa ★1505★
 U.S. institutions awarding the most associate degrees to minorities in agribusiness and production, 1998 ★1808★
 Average faculty salaries for institutions of higher education in Iowa, 2000-01 ★3702★

Kirkwood; Donald
 Top pay and benefits for the chief executive and top paid employees at Albright College ★3168★

Kirtland Middle School
 Outstanding secondary schools in Cleveland-Lorain-Elyria, Ohio ★4114★

Kishel; Shannon
 All-USA College Academic First Team, 2001 ★2★

Kishi; Yoshito
 American Chemical Society 2001 award winners (Group 5) ★755★

Kishore; Vimal
 Top pay and benefits for the chief executive and top paid employees at Xavier University of Louisiana ★3638★

Kissing Tennessee and Other Stories from the Stardust Dance
 Most notable fiction books for reluctant young adult readers, 2001 ★321★
 Most notable fiction books for young adults, 2001 ★322★

Kissing: The Complete Guide
 Most notable nonfiction books for reluctant young adult readers, 2001 ★323★

Kitchens; Terance
 Longest field goals in college football ★158★

Kit's Wilderness
 Most notable books for older readers, 2001 ★318★
 Most notable children's recordings, 2001 ★320★
 Most notable fiction books for young adults, 2001 ★322★
 Outstanding books for older readers, 2000 ★327★
 Outstanding children's fiction books, 2000 ★329★

Kittatinny Regional High School
 Outstanding secondary schools in Newark, New Jersey ★4192★

Kla-Tencor
 Top electrical and electronics companies in Standard & Poor's 500, 2001 ★539★

Klaas; C.J.
 All-America boys' high school soccer team defenders, 2001 ★165★

Klaus; Allen R.
 Top pay and benefits for the chief executive and top paid employees at Our Lady of the Lake University ★3434★

Klebba; James
 Top pay and benefits for the chief executive and top paid employees at Loyola University New Orleans ★3381★

Kleckner; Richard C.
 Top pay and benefits for the chief executive and top paid employees at Aurora University ★3183★

Klein; Elizabeth
 Top pay and benefits for the chief executive and top paid employees at the University of Hartford ★3544★

Klein; Norman
 Authors protested for more than one book between 1952 and 1989, according to the *Newsletter of Intellectual Freedom* ★743★

Klein Oak High School
 Outstanding secondary schools in Houston, Texas ★4150★

Klemperer; William A.
 American Chemical Society 2001 award winners (Group 3) ★753★

Klotzbach; Daniel
 Top pay and benefits for the chief executive and top paid employees at Edgewood College ★3283★

Klukoff; Philip J.
 Top pay and benefits for the chief executive and top paid employees at Columbia College in Illinois ★3250★

Kluwer
 Book publishers with the most citations (Class 4) ★2565★

Klyczek; James P.
 Top pay and benefits for the chief executive and top paid employees at D'Youville College ★3278★

Kmart
 Fortune's highest ranked general merchandisers, 2000 ★468★
 Fortune's least admired companies for quality of products or services ★511★

Knauf; Noah
 All-USA College Academic Third Team, 2001 ★4★

Kneedler; Richard
 Top pay and benefits for the chief executive and top paid employees at Franklin and Marshall College ★3296★

Kneten; Norval
 Top pay and benefits for the chief executive and top paid employees at Nebraska Wesleyan University ★3417★

Knight; Bob
 Coaches winning the most NCAA tournaments ★120★

Knight Jr.; Lon B.
 Top pay and benefits for the chief executive and top paid employees at Furman University ★3300★

Knight Ridder
 Fortune's highest ranked publishing companies, 2000 ★489★
 Top publishing and broadcasting companies in Standard & Poor's 500, 2001 ★553★
 Top public companies for women executives, 2000 ★4457★
 Top public companies with the highest percentage of women board of directors, 2000 ★4458★

Knobel; Dale T.
 Top pay and benefits for the chief executive and top paid employees at Denison University ★3265★

Knopf
  Hardcover bestsellers by publishing house, 2000 ★240★
Knopke; Harry J.
  Top pay and benefits for the chief executive and top paid employees at Aquinas College in Michigan ★3179★
Knoth, S.J.; Rev. Bernard P.
  Top pay and benefits for the chief executive and top paid employees at Loyola University New Orleans ★3381★
Knott III; John B.
  Top pay and benefits for the chief executive and top paid employees at Oglethorpe University ★3429★
Knott; Robert E.
  Top pay and benefits for the chief executive and top paid employees at Tusculum College ★3582★
Knower; F. H.
  Speech communication's most published scholars between 1915-1985 ★4362★
Knowledge Acquisition
  Artificial intelligence journals by citation impact, 1981-99 ★94★
  Artificial intelligence journals by citation impact, 1995-99 ★95★
  Artificial intelligence journals with the greatest impact measure, 1981-98 ★97★
  Artificial intelligence journals with the greatest impact measure, 1994-98 ★98★
  Information and library science journals by citation impact, 1981-99 ★2724★
  Information and library science journals by citation impact, 1995-99 ★2725★
  Information and library science journals with the greatest impact measure, 1981-98 ★2727★
Knowledge Engineering Review
  Artificial intelligence journals with the greatest impact measure, 1998 ★99★
Knox College
  U.S. colleges and universities that devote the most course time to discussion ★990★
  U.S. colleges and universities with excellent library facilities ★1025★
  U.S. colleges and universities with the best financial aid programs ★1030★
  U.S. News & World Report's best undergraduate fees among national liberal arts colleges by discount tuition, 2000 ★1381★
  Highest undergraduate tuition and fees at colleges and universities in Illinois ★1500★
  Private, 4-year undergraduate colleges and universities producing the most Ph.D.'s in mathematics, 1920-1990 ★2776★
  Private, 4-year undergraduate colleges and universities producing the most Ph.D.'s in mathematics, 1981-1990 ★2777★
  Average faculty salaries for institutions of higher education in Illinois, 2000-01 ★3700★
Knox; Edward
  Top pay and benefits for the chief executive and top paid employees at Middlebury College ★3401★
Koblik; Steven S.
  Top pay and benefits for the chief executive and top paid employees at Reed College ★3453★
Kobuszewski; Jeanne
  Top pay and benefits for the chief executive and top paid employees at the College of St. Rose ★3529★
Koch Industries
  Largest private companies, 2000 ★523★

Kochersperger; Richard
  Top pay and benefits for the chief executive and top paid employees at Saint Joseph's University ★3476★
Koehler; William H.
  Top pay and benefits for the chief executive and top paid employees at Texas Christian University ★3518★
Koeneman; Alvin B.
  Top pay and benefits for the chief executive and top paid employees at Wartburg College ★3603★
Kohl's
  Top discount and fashion retailing companies in Standard & Poor's 500, 2001 ★538★
Kohls; Winfred A.
  Top pay and benefits for the chief executive and top paid employees at Moravian College ★3407★
Kolbeck; Kevin D.
  Top pay and benefits for the chief executive and top paid employees at Thomas Aquinas College in California ★3574★
Kolodny; Nancy H.
  Top pay and benefits for the chief executive and top paid employees at Wellesley College ★3609★
Konigsburg; E. L.
  Outstanding children's fiction books, 2000 ★329★
Koninkluke Ahold
  Business Week's best companies in the Netherlands ★410★
Koninkluke KPN
  Business Week's best companies in the Netherlands ★410★
Konow; Gary
  Top pay and benefits for the chief executive and top paid employees at Aquinas College in Michigan ★3179★
Koonin; Steven E.
  Top pay and benefits for the chief executive and top paid employees at the California Institute of Technology ★3521★
Kopera; Kerry
  Top pay and benefits for the chief executive and top paid employees at National-Louis University in Illinois ★3414★
Kopf; Gary S.
  Top pay and benefits for the chief executive and top paid employees at Yale University ★3639★
Koppes; Clayton R.
  Top pay and benefits for the chief executive and top paid employees at Oberlin College ★3427★
Korea
  Countries of origin for non-U.S. citizens awarded doctorates at U.S. colleges and universities, 1999 ★1901★
Korea Electric Power (KEPCO)
  Business Week's top emerging-market companies worldwide ★434★
Korea Telecom
  Business Week's top emerging-market companies worldwide ★434★
Korea: Yu Sings Pansori
  Most notable children's videos, 2001 ★2889★
Koss; M.P.
  Most cited authors in the journal *Journal of Interpersonal Violence*, 1990 to 1995 ★1627★
  Most cited authors in the journal *Violence and Victims*, 1990 to 1995 ★1632★

Kossiakoff; Anthony A.
  Top pay and benefits for the chief executive and top paid employees at the University of Chicago ★3537★
Kourilsky; Marilyn
  Individuals producing the most economic education research articles, 1963-1990 ★2166★
Kowpak; Corinne P.
  Top pay and benefits for the chief executive and top paid employees at Springfield College in Massachusetts ★3509★
KPMG International
  Largest private companies, 2000 ★523★
Kraai; James
  Top pay and benefits for the chief executive and top paid employees at Calvin College ★3217★
Kraemer; Irene
  Top pay and benefits for the chief executive and top paid employees at Carthage College ★3224★
Kraft Foods, Inc.
  Top internships in the U.S. with the highest compensation, 2001 ★2611★
Kragballe; K.
  Most cited first authors in dermatology journals, 1981 to 1996 ★1871★
Kramer; Larry
  Top pay and benefits for the chief executive and top paid employees at Avila College ★3186★
Krasij; Victor
  All-America boys' high school soccer team midfielders, 2001 ★168★
Krieg; Richard
  Top pay and benefits for the chief executive and top paid employees at Roosevelt University ★3466★
Kriegbaum; Ward A.
  Top pay and benefits for the chief executive and top paid employees at Wheaton College in Illinois ★3620★
Krieger; Karl H.
  Top pay and benefits for the chief executive and top paid employees at Cornell University ★3257★
Krienert; Dennis
  Top pay and benefits for the chief executive and top paid employees at Hastings College ★3328★
Kriss, O.S.F.; Sister Mary Elise
  Top pay and benefits for the chief executive and top paid employees at the University of Saint Francis in Indiana ★3562★
Kritsky; Gene
  Top pay and benefits for the chief executive and top paid employees at College of Mount St. Joseph ★3244★
Kroger
  Fortune's highest ranked food and drug stores, 2000 ★463★
  Top food companies in Standard & Poor's 500, 2001 ★540★
  Top recruiters for multidisciplinary majors jobs for 2000-01 bachelor's degree recipients ★2327★
  Top recruiters for multidisciplinary majors jobs for 2000-01 master's degree recipients ★2328★
Kroger; Elizabeth
  Top pay and benefits for the chief executive and top paid employees at Chestnut Hill College ★3231★

Kronholm; Mark E.
Top pay and benefits for the chief executive and top paid employees at Carleton College ★3222★

Krueger; C. Norman
Top pay and benefits for the chief executive and top paid employees at Hampden-Sydney College ★3321★

Kryzewski; Mike
Coaches winning the most NCAA tournaments ★120★
Top pay and benefits for the chief executive and top paid employees at Duke University ★3276★

Kucia; John F.
Top pay and benefits for the chief executive and top paid employees at Xavier University in Ohio ★3637★

Kughn Jr.; James C.
Top pay and benefits for the chief executive and top paid employees at Randolph-Macon Woman's College ★3452★

Kugler; Jacek
Top pay and benefits for the chief executive and top paid employees at Claremont Graduate University ★3235★

Kuhlthau; Carol
Library and information science faculty with the most citations to journal articles, 1993-1998 ★2710★

Kuhn; Sarah
Radcliffe Institute for Advanced Study fellowship recipient in the field of economic and social development, 2000-01 ★2171★

Kuhns; William
Top pay and benefits for the chief executive and top paid employees at Cabrini College ★3215★

Kumar; Pooja
All-USA College Academic First Team, 2001 ★2★

Kunard; Ramona
Top pay and benefits for the chief executive and top paid employees at United States International University ★3587★

Kung; David
Top pay and benefits for the chief executive and top paid employees at the University of La Verne ★3547★

Kunhardt; Erich E.
Top pay and benefits for the chief executive and top paid employees at Stevens Institute of Technology ★3512★

Kunreuther; Howard
Authors with the most published pages in impact-weighted insurance journals ★677★

Kunzel; Regina
Radcliffe Institute for Advanced Study fellowship recipients in the field of history, 2000-01 ★2549★

Kurey; Joseph M.
Top pay and benefits for the chief executive and top paid employees at Bethany College in West Virginia ★3202★

Kushner; Tony
Top playwrights of the twentieth century ★4436★

Kutztown University
Average faculty salaries for institutions of higher education in Pennsylvania, 2000-01 ★3725★

Kuykendall; John W.
Top pay and benefits for the chief executive and top paid employees at Davidson College ★3264★

Kuznets; Simon
Most cited economists ★2185★

Kyocera
Business Week's best companies in Japan ★398★

Kytle; Jackson
Top pay and benefits for the chief executive and top paid employees at Norwich University in Vermont ★3424★

L

La Boheme
Most frequently produced operas in North America, 1999-2000 ★2905★

La Canada High School
Outstanding secondary schools in Los Angeles-Long Beach, California ★4167★

La Grange College
Average faculty salaries for institutions of higher education in Georgia, 2000-01 ★3697★

La Grange School, District 105 (South)
Illinois school districts spending the most per pupil for instruction ★4011★

La Habra High School
Outstanding secondary schools in Orange County, California ★4199★

La Mesa Middle School
Outstanding secondary schools in San Diego, California ★4220★

La Paz Intermediate School
Outstanding secondary schools in Orange County, California ★4199★

La Roche College
Average faculty salaries for institutions of higher education in Pennsylvania, 2000-01 ★3725★

La Salle Academy
Outstanding secondary schools in Providence-Fall River-Warwick, Rhode Island-Maine ★4207★

La Salle Institute
Outstanding secondary schools in Albany-Schenectady-Troy, New York ★4079★

La Salle University
Division I NCAA colleges with the highest graduation rates for male athletes, 1990-91 to 1993-94 ★934★
U.S. News & World Report's northern regional universities with the highest acceptance rates, 2000-01 ★1417★
U.S. News & World Report's northern regional universities with the highest average graduation rates, 2000-01 ★1419★
Private, 4-year undergraduate colleges and universities producing the most Ph.D.'s in economics, 1981-1990 ★2212★
Average faculty salaries for institutions of higher education in Pennsylvania, 2000-01 ★3725★

La Sierra University
Average faculty salaries for institutions of higher education in California, 2000-01 ★3692★

La Trobe University
Australian universities with the greatest impact in agricultural sciences, 1993-97 ★49★
Australian universities with the greatest impact in mathematics, 1993-97 ★2774★

La-Z-Boy
Fortune's highest ranked furniture companies, 2000 ★467★

The Lab School of Washington
Outstanding secondary schools in Washington, District of Columbia-Maryland-Virginia-West Virginia ★4249★

Labat; Deidre D.
Top pay and benefits for the chief executive and top paid employees at Xavier University of Louisiana ★3638★

Labay Junior High School
Outstanding secondary schools in Houston, Texas ★4150★

Labette Community College
Lowest undergraduate tuition and fees at colleges and universities in Kansas ★1507★

Labor; Earle
Top pay and benefits for the chief executive and top paid employees at the Centenary College of Louisiana ★3523★

Laborers, landscaping and groundskeeping
Occupations with the highest number of self-employed workers, 1998 ★2311★
Projected employment growth for selected occupations that require shorter moderate-term on-the-job training, 1998-2008 ★2321★

Lac Courte Oreilles Ojibwa Community College
U.S. tribal colleges ★1445★

Lacey; Paul A.
Top pay and benefits for the chief executive and top paid employees at Earlham College ★3279★

Lackland Junior High School
Outstanding secondary schools in San Antonio, Texas ★4219★

Lackner; James R.
Top pay and benefits for the chief executive and top paid employees at Brandeis University ★3209★

Lacrosse
Fastest growing men's collegiate athletics teams ★130★

Ladies' Home Journal
Magazines with the largest circulation ★2750★

Ladner; Benjamin
Top pay and benefits for the chief executive and top paid employees at American University ★3174★

Ladysmith
Booklist's most recommended historical novels, 2001 ★230★

Ladywood High School
Outstanding Catholic high schools in Metro Detroit ★4075★

Laettner; Christian
Division I NCAA men's basketball players with the highest tournament scores ★154★

Lafayette College
Division I NCAA colleges with the highest graduation rates for female basketball players, 1990-91 to 1993-94 ★932★
U.S. colleges and universities where a large portion of the student body drink beer ★991★
Highest undergraduate tuition and fees at colleges and universities in Pennsylvania ★1549★
Top assistant professor economists at elite liberal arts colleges, 1975-94 ★2173★

LAGRANGE

Average faculty salaries for institutions of higher education in Pennsylvania, 2000-01 ★3725★

LaGrange College
U.S. News & World Report's best undergraduate fees among southern regional liberal arts colleges by discount tuition, 2000 ★1383★

Laguna Beach High School
Outstanding secondary schools in Orange County, California ★4199★

Laguna Hills High School
Outstanding secondary schools in Orange County, California ★4199★

Lahey; John L.
Presidents with the highest pay at Master's I and II colleges and universities, 1998-99 ★3161★
Top pay and benefits for the chief executive and top paid employees at Quinnipiac University ★3449★

Lahey; Richard
Top pay and benefits for the chief executive and top paid employees at Rensselaer Polytechnic Institute ★3455★

LaHurd; Ryan A.
Top pay and benefits for the chief executive and top paid employees at Lenoir-Rhyne College ★3369★

Lai; Mary M.
Top pay and benefits for the chief executive and top paid employees at Long Island University ★3378★

Lai; Richard
Top published scholars in the field of systems and software engineering ★2333★

Lait
Food science and technology journals by citation impact, 1999 ★2904★

Lake Area Technical Institute
Lowest undergraduate tuition and fees at colleges and universities in South Dakota ★1557★

Lake Bluff Junior High School
Outstanding secondary schools in Chicago, Illinois ★4110★

Lake Charles American Press
Most selective internships in the U.S., 2001 ★2610★

Lake City Community College
Lowest undergraduate tuition and fees at colleges and universities in Florida ★1495★

Lake County Community College
Fall enrollment at Chicago-area public community colleges, by minority percentages, 1999 ★867★

Lake Forest College
U.S. colleges and universities with the best financial aid programs ★1030★
Highest undergraduate tuition and fees at colleges and universities in Illinois ★1500★
Average faculty salaries for institutions of higher education in Illinois, 2000-01 ★3700★

Lake Forest Community High School, District 115
Illinois school districts spending the most for high school education 1997-98 ★4010★

Lake Forest Country Day School
Outstanding secondary schools in Chicago, Illinois ★4110★

Lake Forest High School
Illinois high schools with the highest SAT scores ★874★

Lake Highlands High School
Outstanding urban public high schools in Metro Dallas-Ft. Worth ★4263★

Lake, IL
Counties with the highest per capita income ★2561★

Lake Michigan College
Lowest undergraduate tuition and fees at colleges and universities in Michigan ★1519★

Lake Region State College
State appropriations for North Dakota's institutions of higher education, 2000-01 ★1287★
Lowest undergraduate tuition and fees at colleges and universities in North Dakota ★1542★

Lake Superior College
Average faculty salaries for institutions of higher education without academic ranks in Minnesota, 2000-01 ★3753★

Lake Superior State University
State appropriations for Michigan's institutions of higher education, 2000-01 ★1275★
Average faculty salaries for institutions of higher education in Michigan, 2000-01 ★3709★

Lake Tahoe Community College
Lowest undergraduate tuition and fees at public 2-year colleges and universities ★1465★
Lowest undergraduate tuition and fees at colleges and universities in California ★1487★

Lake Washington Technical College
Lowest undergraduate tuition and fees at colleges and universities in Washington ★1567★

Lake Wobegon Days
Retail audiobook titles selling 300,000-400,000 copies ★303★

Lakehead University
Canadian primarily undergraduate universities by alumni support, 2000 ★1193★
Canadian primarily undergraduate universities by award-winning faculty members, 2000 ★1194★
Canadian primarily undergraduate universities by class size at the first and second-year level, 2000 ★1195★
Canadian primarily undergraduate universities by class size at the third and forth-year level, 2000 ★1196★
Canadian primarily undergraduate universities by classes taught by tenured faculty, 2000 ★1197★
Canadian primarily undergraduate universities by faculty members with Ph.D.'s, 2000 ★1198★
Canadian primarily undergraduate universities by library acquisitions, 2000 ★1199★
Canadian primarily undergraduate universities by library expenses, 2000 ★1200★
Canadian primarily undergraduate universities by library holdings per student, 2000 ★1201★
Canadian primarily undergraduate universities by medical/science grants per faculty member, 2000 ★1202★
Canadian primarily undergraduate universities by operating budget per student, 2000 ★1203★
Canadian primarily undergraduate universities by percentage of operating budget allocated to scholarships, 2000 ★1204★
Canadian primarily undergraduate universities by percentage of operating budget allocated to student services, 2000 ★1205★
Canadian primarily undergraduate universities by reputation, 2000 ★1206★
Canadian primarily undergraduate universities by social science/humanities grants per faculty member, 2000 ★1207★
Canadian primarily undergraduate universities by students from out of province, 2000 ★1208★
Canadian primarily undergraduate universities by students winning national awards, 2000 ★1209★
Canadian universities chosen as being value added, 2000 ★1216★
Top Canadian primarily undergraduate universities, 2000 ★1226★

Lakeland College
Average faculty salaries for institutions of higher education in Wisconsin, 2000-01 ★3738★

Lakeland Community College
Lowest undergraduate tuition and fees at colleges and universities in Ohio ★1544★

Lakeshore Technical College
Lowest undergraduate tuition and fees at colleges and universities in Wisconsin ★1571★

Lakeside Middle School
Outstanding secondary schools in Orange County, California ★4199★

Lakeview Junior High School
Outstanding secondary schools in Santa Barbara-Santa Maria-Lompoc, California ★4224★

Lakner; Benjamin
Presidents with the highest pay at Doctoral I and II universities, 1998-99 ★3160★

Lakota High School
Outstanding secondary schools in Hamilton-Middletown, Ohio ★4145★

Lakso; James
Top pay and benefits for the chief executive and top paid employees at Juniata College ★3357★

LaMagra; Anthony J.
Top pay and benefits for the chief executive and top paid employees at Manhattanville College ★3388★

Lamar High School
Outstanding urban public high schools in Metro Dallas-Ft. Worth ★4263★

Lamar State College
Average faculty salaries for institutions of higher education in Texas, 2000-01 ★3731★

Lamar University
Division I NCAA colleges with that graduated less than 20% of their African American male athletes, 1990-91 to 1993-94 ★928★

Lambert; Daniel M.
Top pay and benefits for the chief executive and top paid employees at Baker University ★3188★

Lambuth University
Average faculty salaries for institutions of higher education in Tennessee, 2000-01 ★3730★

Lament for a Nation
Canada's best nonfiction selections of the 20th century ★234★

Lamkin; Michael
Top pay and benefits for the chief executive and top paid employees at Scripps College ★3493★

Lamm; Norman
Top pay and benefits for the chief executive and top paid employees at Yeshiva University ★3640★

Lammers; Michael
Top pay and benefits for the chief executive and top paid employees at Marylhurst University ★3394★

LaMonte; Edward S.
Top pay and benefits for the chief executive and top paid employees at Birmingham-Southern College ★3204★

LaMothe; Kimerer
Radcliffe Institute for Advanced Study fellowship recipients in the field of religion, 2000-01 ★3092★

Lancaster Bible College
Average faculty salaries for institutions of higher education in Pennsylvania, 2000-01 ★3725★

Lancaster; University of
Top United Kingdom universities by citation impact in the field of plant and animal sciences, 1991-95 ★2144★
Top United Kingdom universities by total citations in the field of ecology/environmental, 1991-95 ★2146★

Lancos; Chris
All-America boys' high school soccer team defenders, 2001 ★165★

Land Economics
Top ranked agricultural and natural resource economics journals ★2187★
Top ranked urban, rural and regional economics journals ★2202★
Highly cited real estate journals, 1990 to 1995 ★3090★

LandAmerica Financial Group
Fortune's highest ranked mortgage finance companies, 2000 ★479★

Lander University
State appropriations for South Carolina's institutions of higher education, 2000-01 ★1293★
Average faculty salaries for institutions of higher education in South Carolina, 2000-01 ★3728★

Landis; Dennis
Top pay and benefits for the chief executive and top paid employees at Case Western Reserve University ★3225★

Landman; Bette E.
Top pay and benefits for the chief executive and top paid employees at Beaver College ★3195★

Landmark College
Undergraduate tuition and fees at colleges and universities in Vermont ★1563★
Average faculty salaries for institutions of higher education in Vermont, 2000-01 ★3734★

Landoll's
Top children's book publishers, 1999 ★3074★

Landreville; P.
Most cited authors in the journal *Criminologie*, 1990 to 1995 ★1621★

Landroche; Gregory
Top pay and benefits for the chief executive and top paid employees at Notre Dame College in New Hampshire ★3425★

Landrum Middle School
Outstanding secondary schools in Jacksonville, Florida ★4155★

Landstar
Fortune's highest ranked trucking companies, 2000 ★503★

Lane College
U.S. colleges and universities with the highest percentage of African Americans enrolled, 1997 ★222★
Historically black colleges and universities with major improvements in student loan default rates, 1998 ★2737★
Average faculty salaries for institutions of higher education in Tennessee, 2000-01 ★3730★

Lane Community College
Lowest undergraduate tuition and fees at colleges and universities in Oregon ★1548★
Average faculty salaries for institutions of higher education without academic ranks in Oregon, 2000-01 ★3764★

Lane; Robert J.
Top pay and benefits for the chief executive and top paid employees at Illinois College ★3345★

Lane Technical
Acceptance rates at Chicago college prep magnet schools, 2000-01 ★4000★
Admissions to college prep schools in Chicago that are the toughest to get into, 2001 ★4001★
College prep schools in Chicago that are the toughest to get into ★4005★

Lanegran; David A.
Top pay and benefits for the chief executive and top paid employees at Macalester College ★3385★

Laney College
Lowest undergraduate tuition and fees at public 2-year colleges and universities ★1465★

Lang; Samuel J.
Top pay and benefits for the chief executive and top paid employees at Cornell University ★3257★

Langerhan's cell
Leading categories of dermatologic disease covered by top articles in the field, 1945-1990 ★1869★

Langham Creek High School
Outstanding secondary schools in Houston, Texas ★4150★

Langlois; Emile
Top pay and benefits for the chief executive and top paid employees at Sweet Briar College ★3515★

Langston Hughes Reads
Library Journal's best nonfiction audiobooks, 2000 ★243★

Langston University
Colleges offering the Thurgood Marshall Scholarship Fund ★221★
State appropriations for Oklahoma's institutions of higher education, 2000-01 ★1289★

Language
Language and linguistics journals with the greatest impact measure, 1981-98 ★2731★

Language and literature
Percentage of female doctorate recipients at U.S. colleges and universities, by subfield, 1999 ★1988★
Average costs for Academic Search titles by subject, 2001 ★2918★
Periodical prices by LC subject, 2001 ★2925★

Lanier High School
Outstanding secondary schools in Austin-San Marcos, Texas ★4090★

Lansing Community College
Lowest undergraduate tuition and fees at colleges and universities in Michigan ★1519★

Lant; Theresa K.
Highest impact authors in the *Journal of Business Research*, by adjusted number of citations in 12 journals, 1985-1999 ★692★

Lantz; Duane L.
Top pay and benefits for the chief executive and top paid employees at Washington and Jefferson College ★3604★

Lantz Jr.; G. Benjamin
Top pay and benefits for the chief executive and top paid employees at the University of Indianapolis ★3545★

Lapovsky; Lucie
Top pay and benefits for the chief executive and top paid employees at Goucher College ★3314★

Lappas; Stephen
Top pay and benefits for the chief executive and top paid employees at Villanova University ★3595★

Laragh; John H.
Most-cited researchers in cardiology, 1981-1998 ★2874★

Laramie County Community College
Undergraduate tuition and fees at colleges and universities in Wyoming ★1572★
Average faculty salaries for institutions of higher education without academic ranks in Wyoming, 2000-01 ★3769★

Laredo Community College
Institutions with the most full-time Hispanic American faculty ★923★
Institutions with the most part-time Hispanic American faculty ★924★
U.S. colleges and universities with the most full-time Hispanic American faculty ★925★
Average faculty salaries for institutions of higher education without academic ranks in Texas, 2000-01 ★3766★

Large; Larry D.
Top pay and benefits for the chief executive and top paid employees at Oglethorpe University ★3429★
Top pay and benefits for the chief executive and top paid employees at Reed College ★3453★

Larrey; Martin
Top pay and benefits for the chief executive and top paid employees at the University of Saint Francis in Illinois ★3561★

Larsen; Blake
All-American boy's high school football linemen, 2000 ★183★
All-American boy's high school football team, 2000 ★187★

Larsen; David C.
Top pay and benefits for the chief executive and top paid employees at Beaver College ★3195★

Las Cruces, NM
Best college towns to live in ★3076★

Las Mamis: Favorite Latino Authors Remember Their Mothers
Outstanding nonfiction books for young adults, 2000 ★334★

Las Vegas College
Undergraduate tuition and fees at colleges and universities in Nevada ★1530★

Las Vegas, NV
America's most wired cities, 2001 ★2573★
America's most wired cities with the highest domain density, 2001 ★2574★
Cities with the highest percentage of broadband use and interest ★2578★
Cities with the most Yahoo! listings per million residents ★2580★
Most polite cities in the U.S. ★3086★

LaSalle Language
Chicago elementary magnet schools with the lowest acceptance rates, 2000-01 ★4003★

LaSalle Springs Middle School
Outstanding secondary schools in St. Louis, Missouri-Illinois ★4216★

LaSalle; Stephen C.
Top pay and benefits for the chief executive and top paid employees at Nazareth College of Rochester ★3416★

LaSasso; Carol J.
Top pay and benefits for the chief executive and top paid employees at Gallaudet University ★3301★

Lasley; Steven T.
Top pay and benefits for the chief executive and top paid employees at Belmont University ★3198★

Lassus; Marc
European business moguls considered the best innovators ★442★

The Last Book in the Universe
Most notable fiction books for young adults, 2001 ★322★

The Last Good Man
Library Journal's best romance titles, 2000 ★245★

The Last Man Standing: The Tragedy and Triumph of Geronimo Pratt
Outstanding biography books, 2000 ★288★

The Last Samurai
Booklist's best first novels ★228★
Most notable fiction books, 2001 ★284★
Outstanding works of fiction, 2001 ★293★

The Last Spike
Canada's best nonfiction selections of the 20th century ★234★

Lastoria; Michael D.
Top pay and benefits for the chief executive and top paid employees at Houghton College ★3341★

Late Show with David Letterman
Most selective internships in the U.S., 2001 ★2610★

Latin America
Region of origin of foreign students enrolled in U.S. institutions of higher education, 1998-99 ★2502★
World regions hosting U.S. students studying abroad, 1998-99 ★2515★

Latin American Network Information Center (LANIC)
Library Journal's best free reference websites, 2000 ★367★

Latin literature
Number of Advanced Placement Exams taken by African Americans, by subject, 2000 ★30★
Number of Advanced Placement Exams taken by Asian Americans, by subject, 2000 ★31★
Number of Advanced Placement Exams taken by Hispanic Americans, by subject, 2000 ★32★

Latin virgil
Number of Advanced Placement Exams taken by African Americans, by subject, 2000 ★30★
Number of Advanced Placement Exams taken by Asian Americans, by subject, 2000 ★31★
Number of Advanced Placement Exams taken by Hispanic Americans, by subject, 2000 ★32★

Latter-day Saints (Mormon)
Religious preference of incoming freshmen, 2000 ★1061★

Latvia
Math achievement test comparison ★19★

Lauber; Sharon
All-USA Teacher Teams, Third Team, 2000 ★4401★

Lauper; Russell T.
Top pay and benefits for the chief executive and top paid employees at Dowling College ★3271★

Laureman; William C.
Top pay and benefits for the chief executive and top paid employees at Georgetown University ★3306★

Laurentian University of Sudbury
Canadian primarily undergraduate universities by alumni support, 2000 ★1193★
Canadian primarily undergraduate universities by award-winning faculty members, 2000 ★1194★
Canadian primarily undergraduate universities by class size at the first and second-year level, 2000 ★1195★
Canadian primarily undergraduate universities by class size at the third and forth-year level, 2000 ★1196★
Canadian primarily undergraduate universities by classes taught by tenured faculty, 2000 ★1197★
Canadian primarily undergraduate universities by faculty members with Ph.D.'s, 2000 ★1198★
Canadian primarily undergraduate universities by library acquisitions, 2000 ★1199★
Canadian primarily undergraduate universities by library expenses, 2000 ★1200★
Canadian primarily undergraduate universities by library holdings per student, 2000 ★1201★
Canadian primarily undergraduate universities by medical/science grants per faculty member, 2000 ★1202★
Canadian primarily undergraduate universities by operating budget per student, 2000 ★1203★
Canadian primarily undergraduate universities by percentage of operating budget allocated to scholarships, 2000 ★1204★
Canadian primarily undergraduate universities by percentage of operating budget allocated to student services, 2000 ★1205★
Canadian primarily undergraduate universities by reputation, 2000 ★1206★
Canadian primarily undergraduate universities by students from out of province, 2000 ★1208★
Canadian primarily undergraduate universities by students winning national awards, 2000 ★1209★
Canadian universities chosen as being value added, 2000 ★1216★
Top Canadian primarily undergraduate universities, 2000 ★1226★

Laval University
Best Canadian universities overall, 2000 ★1149★
Canadian medical/doctoral universities by alumni support, 2000 ★1172★
Canadian medical/doctoral universities by award-winning faculty members, 2000 ★1173★
Canadian medical/doctoral universities by class size at the first- and second-year level, 2000 ★1174★
Canadian medical/doctoral universities by class size at the third- and forth-year level, 2000 ★1175★
Canadian medical/doctoral universities by classes taught by tenured faculty, 2000 ★1176★
Canadian medical/doctoral universities by faculty members with Ph.D.'s, 2000 ★1177★
Canadian medical/doctoral universities by international graduate students, 2000 ★1178★
Canadian medical/doctoral universities by library acquisitions, 2000 ★1179★
Canadian medical/doctoral universities by library expenses, 2000 ★1180★
Canadian medical/doctoral universities by library holdings, 2000 ★1181★
Canadian medical/doctoral universities by library holdings per student, 2000 ★1182★
Canadian medical/doctoral universities by medical/science grants per faculty member, 2000 ★1184★
Canadian medical/doctoral universities by operating budget per student, 2000 ★1185★
Canadian medical/doctoral universities by percentage of operating budget allocated to scholarships, 2000 ★1186★
Canadian medical/doctoral universities by percentage of operating budget allocated to student services, 2000 ★1187★
Canadian medical/doctoral universities by reputation, 2000 ★1188★
Canadian medical/doctoral universities by social science/humanities grants per faculty member, 2000 ★1189★
Canadian medical/doctoral universities by students from out of province, 2000 ★1190★
Canadian medical/doctoral universities by students winning national awards, 2000 ★1191★
Canadian universities by average entering grade, 2000 ★1213★
Canadian universities with the lowest total cost, 2000 ★1218★
Top Canadian medical/doctoral universities, 2000 ★1221★
University research libraries in the U.S. and Canada with the largest decreases in total expenditures from 1993-94 to 1998-99 ★2707★
Canadian universities with the greatest impact in neuroscience, 1993-97 ★4305★

LaVerne; University of
U.S. colleges and universities awarding the most education doctorate degrees to Hispanic Americans ★2110★
Average faculty salaries for institutions of higher education in California, 2000-01 ★3692★

Law
Comparative data of women receiving doctorate degrees in selected fields in 1950 and 1998 ★1899★
Gender breakdown of professional doctorate recipients, by subfield, 1999 ★1940★
Professional doctorates awarded at U.S. colleges and universities, by subfield, 1999 ★2033★
Average costs for Academic Search titles by subject, 2001 ★2918★
Periodical prices by LC subject, 2001 ★2925★
United States' contribution of papers in the sciences, by field, 1995-99 ★4283★
United States' contribution of papers in the sciences, by field, 1996-2000 ★4284★

Law & Society Review
Sociology journals by impact factor, 1981 to 1997 ★4355★
Sociology journals by impact factor, 1993 to 1997 ★4356★

Lawless; Robert W.
Top pay and benefits for the chief executive and top paid employees at the University of Tulsa ★3573★

Lawrence Bell High School
Outstanding secondary schools in Fort Worth-Arlington, Texas ★4137★

Lawrence; Denis G.
Top pay and benefits for the chief executive and top paid employees at Marylhurst University ★3394★

Lawrence Erlbaum Associates
Book publishers with the most citations (Class 3) ★2564★

Lawrence High School
Outstanding urban public high schools in Metro Boston ★4261★

Lawrence; Iain
Outstanding children's fiction books, 2000 ★329★

Lawrence; Janice
NCAA Division I female basketball scoring leaders ★155★

Lawrence, KS
U.S. cities with the most single people ★3089★

Lawrence Livermore National Laboratory
Top internships in the U.S. with the highest compensation, 2001 ★2611★

Lawrence Pfleeger; Shari
Top published scholars in the field of systems and software engineering ★2333★

Lawrence; Sally
Top pay and benefits for the chief executive and top paid employees at the Sage Colleges in New York ★3536★

Lawrence Technological University
Institutions censured by the American Association of University Professors, 2001 ★1067★

Lawrence University
U.S. News & World Report's national liberal arts colleges with the highest acceptance rates, 2000-01 ★1328★
Highest undergraduate tuition and fees at colleges and universities in Wisconsin ★1570★
Average faculty salaries for institutions of higher education in Wisconsin, 2000-01 ★3738★

Laws; Priscilla W.
Top pay and benefits for the chief executive and top paid employees at Dickinson College ★3268★

Lawson; E. LeRoy
Top pay and benefits for the chief executive and top paid employees at Hope International University ★3340★

Lawson State Community College
U.S. colleges and universities with the highest percentage of African Americans enrolled, 1997 ★222★

Lawyer
Careers college students considered least respected, 2000 ★739★
Occupations with the highest average annual salaries for college graduates, 1998 ★3132★

Lawyers
Occupations with the highest number of self-employed workers, 1998 ★2311★
Projected employment growth for selected occupations that require advanced education, 1998-2008 ★2318★

Laydon; Harold F.
Top pay and benefits for the chief executive and top paid employees at Lake Erie College ★3362★

Layton; Robert A.
Top pay and benefits for the chief executive and top paid employees at Baker University ★3188★

Lazaro; Tony de Sam
Top pay and benefits for the chief executive and top paid employees at Saint Martin's College in Washington ★3479★

Lazarus; Francis M.
Top pay and benefits for the chief executive and top paid employees at the University of San Diego ★3565★

LDS Business College
Undergraduate tuition and fees at colleges and universities in Utah ★1562★

Le Corbusier
Highly influential artists of the 20th century ★76★

Le Moyne College
U.S. News & World Report's northern regional liberal arts colleges with the highest academic reputation scores, 2000-01 ★1354★
U.S. News & World Report's northern regional liberal arts colleges with the highest alumni giving rates, 2000-01 ★1356★
U.S. News & World Report's northern regional liberal arts colleges with the highest freshmen retention rates, 2000-01 ★1357★
U.S. News & World Report's northern regional liberal arts colleges with the highest graduation rates, 2000-01 ★1358★
U.S. News & World Report's top northern regional liberal arts colleges, 2000-01 ★1363★
U.S. News & World Report's best undergraduate fees among northern regional liberal arts colleges by discount tuition, 2000 ★1382★
Average faculty salaries for institutions of higher education in New York, 2000-01 ★3719★

Le Moyne-Owen College
U.S. colleges and universities with the highest percentage of African Americans enrolled, 1997 ★222★

Lea; John
Most cited scholars in critical criminology ★1640★
Most-cited scholars in critical criminology publications ★1641★
Most cited works in critical criminology ★1644★

Leading the Revolution
Library Journal's most notable management books, 2000 ★265★

Leahy, S.J.; Rev. William P.
Top pay and benefits for the chief executive and top paid employees at Boston College ★3205★

Leap
Outstanding history books, 2000 ★289★

The Leap: A Memoir of Love and Madness in the Internet Gold Rush
Library Journal's most notable biography books, 2000 ★249★

Lear
Fortune's highest ranked motor vehicle parts companies, 2000 ★480★

Learning disabilities
Disabled students served in U.S. public school programs, 1998-99 ★1877★

Learning Human: Selected Poems
Outstanding works of poetry, 2001 ★295★

Learning to Swim: A Memoir
Most notable nonfiction books for young adults, 2001 ★324★

The Learning Tree
Most frequently banned books in the 1990s ★745★

Lebanon Valley College
U.S. News & World Report's northern regional liberal arts colleges with the best student/faculty ratios, 2000-01 ★1353★
U.S. News & World Report's northern regional liberal arts colleges with the highest alumni giving rates, 2000-01 ★1356★
U.S. News & World Report's northern regional liberal arts colleges with the highest percentage of freshmen in the top 25% of their high school class, 2000-01 ★1359★
U.S. News & World Report's northern regional liberal arts colleges with the highest proportion of classes having 20 students or less, 2000-01 ★1361★
U.S. News & World Report's northern regional liberal arts colleges with the lowest acceptance rates, 2000-01 ★1362★
U.S. News & World Report's top northern regional liberal arts colleges, 2000-01 ★1363★
U.S. News & World Report's best undergraduate fees among northern regional liberal arts colleges by discount tuition, 2000 ★1382★
Average faculty salaries for institutions of higher education in Pennsylvania, 2000-01 ★3725★

LeBlanc; Paul J.
Top pay and benefits for the chief executive and top paid employees at Marlboro College ★3391★

Ledewitz; Jeffrey H.
Top pay and benefits for the chief executive and top paid employees at Embry-Riddle Aeronautical University ★3286★

The Ledge
Library Journal's best poetry books, 2000 ★244★

Lee; Chae-Jin
Top pay and benefits for the chief executive and top paid employees at Claremont McKenna College ★3236★

Lee; David
All-America boys' high school basketball 1st team, 2001 ★161★

Lee; E. Joseph
Top pay and benefits for the chief executive and top paid employees at Manhattan College ★3387★

Lee; H. Douglas
Top pay and benefits for the chief executive and top paid employees at Stetson University ★3511★

Lee, I.H.M.; Andrea J.
Top pay and benefits for the chief executive and top paid employees at the College of St. Catherine ★3528★

Lee; J. Larry
Top pay and benefits for the chief executive and top paid employees at Mississippi College ★3404★

Lee; J. Patrick
Top pay and benefits for the chief executive and top paid employees at Barry University ★3192★

Lee; Jerry
Top pay and benefits for the chief executive and top paid employees at Albright College ★3168★

Lee; Jerry C.
Presidents with the highest pay at Master's I and II colleges and universities, 1998-99 ★3161★
Top pay and benefits for the chief executive and top paid employees at National University in California ★3415★

Lee; Lawrence W.
Top pay and benefits for the chief executive and top paid employees at Bennington College ★3201★

Lee; Michael E.
Top pay and benefits for the chief executive and top paid employees at Wilmington College in Delaware ★3632★

Lee Public Library
Highest Hennen's American Public Library Ratings for libraries serving a population of 2,500 to 4,999 ★2693★

Lee; Spike
Most influential African American entertainers ★77★

Lee; Steve
Top pay and benefits for the chief executive and top paid employees at the University of Mobile ★3551★

Lee University
Average faculty salaries for institutions of higher education in Tennessee, 2000-01 ★3730★

Lee; Yuan Chuan
American Chemical Society 2001 award winners (Group 3) ★753★

Leech Lake Tribal College
U.S. tribal colleges ★1445★

Lees-McRae College
Average faculty salaries for institutions of higher education in North Carolina, 2000-01 ★3720★
U.S. institutions with the lowest paid full professors, 2001 ★3979★

Leete Jr.; William M.
Top pay and benefits for the chief executive and top paid employees at the University of New Haven ★3553★

Leeward Community College
Average faculty salaries for institutions of higher education in Hawaii, 2000-01 ★3698★

Lefkowitz; Mary
Top pay and benefits for the chief executive and top paid employees at Wellesley College ★3609★

Left Back: A Century of Failed School Reforms
American School Board Journal's notable education books, 2000 ★225★

Left Behind
Longest-running trade paperback bestsellers, 2000 ★282★

The Legacy: Murder and Media Politics and Prison
Most notable videos for adults, 2001 ★2891★

Legal secretaries
Projected employment growth for selected occupations that require an associate degree or less, 1998-2008 ★2319★

Legend Holdings
Information technology companies giving the best returns, 2000 ★522★
Top information technology companies, 2000 ★544★

The Legend of Sleepy Hollow
Outstanding audiobooks, 2000 ★287★

Leggett & Platt
Fortune's highest ranked furniture companies, 2000 ★467★

Legislative Studies Quarterly
Political science journals with the greatest impact measure, 1981-98 ★3049★

Legoza; Janice
Top pay and benefits for the chief executive and top paid employees at Colorado College ★3249★

Lehigh Carbon Community College
Lowest undergraduate tuition and fees at colleges and universities in Pennsylvania ★1550★
Average faculty salaries for institutions of higher education in Pennsylvania, 2000-01 ★3725★

Lehigh University
U.S. universities with the highest concentration of papers published in the field of chemistry, 1994-98 ★794★
Division I NCAA colleges with the highest graduation rates for female athletes, 1990-91 to 1993-94 ★931★
Division I NCAA colleges with the highest graduation rates for female basketball players, 1990-91 to 1993-94 ★932★
Division I NCAA colleges with the highest graduation rates for football players, 1990-91 to 1993-94 ★933★
Division I NCAA colleges with the highest graduation rates for male athletes, 1990-91 to 1993-94 ★934★
U.S. colleges and universities where a large portion of the student body drink beer ★991★
U.S. colleges and universities where a large portion of the student body drink hard liquor ★992★
U.S. colleges and universities where the general student body smokes marijuana ★1011★
U.S. colleges and universities with a large student body of conservative Republicans ★1016★
U.S. News & World Report's national universities with the lowest proportion of classes with 50 or more students, 2000-01 ★1142★
Highest undergraduate tuition and fees at colleges and universities in Pennsylvania ★1549★
U.S. universities with the highest concentration of education papers published, 1994-98 ★2223★
U.S. universities with the highest concentration of papers published in the field of chemical engineering, 1994-98 ★2345★
U.S. universities with the greatest impact in chemical engineering, 1994-98 ★2393★
Top industrial engineering research-doctorate programs as evaluated by the National Research Council ★2413★
U.S. universities with the highest concentration of metallurgy papers published, 1994-98 ★2436★
Average faculty salaries for institutions of higher education in Pennsylvania, 2000-01 ★3725★
U.S. universities with the highest concentration of papers published in the field of materials science, 1995-99 ★4290★

Lehman Brothers Aggregate Bond Index
2000 returns on university endowments and other comparative measures ★1231★

Lehman Brothers Holdings
Fortune's highest ranked securities companies, 2000 ★494★
Top nonbank financial companies in Standard & Poor's 500, 2001 ★550★

Leicester; University of
Top United Kingdom universities by citation impact in the field of plant and animal sciences, 1991-95 ★2144★

Leilehua High School
Outstanding secondary schools in Honolulu, Hawaii ★4149★

Leinart; Matt
All-American boy's high school football quarterbacks, 2000 ★184★

Leischner; Ralph P.
Top pay and benefits for the chief executive and top paid employees at Loyola University of Chicago ★3382★

Leitzel; Thomas C.
Top pay and benefits for the chief executive and top paid employees at Pfeiffer University ★3439★

Lemon Hine Junior High School
Outstanding secondary schools in Washington, District of Columbia-Maryland-Virginia-West Virginia ★4249★

LeMoyne College (NY)
Division II NCAA colleges with the 100% graduation rates for men's basketball players, 1993-94 ★943★

LeMoyne-Owen College
Most dangerous college campuses in the U.S. ★712★
Average faculty salaries for institutions of higher education in Tennessee, 2000-01 ★3730★

LeMoyne-Owen College (TN)
Division II NCAA colleges with the lowest graduation rates for all sports, 1993-94 ★947★

Lenart Gifted
Illinois schools with the highest 7th grade science scores ★17★
Chicago elementary magnet schools with the highest acceptance rates, 2000-01 ★4002★

Lenglet; Isadore R.
Top pay and benefits for the chief executive and top paid employees at Duquesne University ★3277★

Lennar
Fortune's highest ranked engineering and construction companies, 2000 ★461★

Lennon; J. Michael
Top pay and benefits for the chief executive and top paid employees at Wilkes University ★3627★

Lenoir Community College
Average faculty salaries for institutions of higher education without academic ranks in North Carolina, 2000-01 ★3761★

Lenoir-Rhyne College
Division II NCAA colleges with the highest graduation rates for football players, 1993-94 ★946★
U.S. News & World Report's southern regional universities with students least in debt, 1999 ★1431★
Average faculty salaries for institutions of higher education in North Carolina, 2000-01 ★3720★

Lent; Jeffrey
Booklist's best first novels ★228★

Lenz; George
Top pay and benefits for the chief executive and top paid employees at Sweet Briar College ★3515★

Leopold; Aloysius A.
Top pay and benefits for the chief executive and top paid employees at Saint Mary's University in Texas ★3481★

Lepage; Robert
Canada's best performing artists of the 20th century ★74★

Lepore; Dawn
Highest ranking women at the top public companies, 2000 ★4452★

Lerman; Paul
Top pay and benefits for the chief executive and top paid employees at Fairleigh Dickinson University ★3292★

Lerman; Zafra
Top pay and benefits for the chief executive and top paid employees at Columbia College in Illinois ★3250★

Lerner; Laurence M.
Top pay and benefits for the chief executive and top paid employees at Manhattan College ★3387★

Lesbian Histories and Cultures: An Encyclopedia
Outstanding reference sources, 2000 ★370★

Leschied; Alan W.
Most-cited scholars in *Canadian Journal of Criminology* ★1638★

Lesesne Jr.; Joab M.
Top pay and benefits for the chief executive and top paid employees at Wofford College ★3634★

Leshin; Berry
Top pay and benefits for the chief executive and top paid employees at Wake Forest University ★3600★

Lesko; Wayne A.
Top pay and benefits for the chief executive and top paid employees at Marymount University ★3395★

Lesley College
U.S. colleges and universities awarding the most education master's degrees to Asian Americans ★1770★
U.S. colleges and universities awarding the most education master's degrees to Native Americans ★1772★
U.S. colleges and universities awarding the most master's degrees to Native Americans ★1789★

Leslie's Journal
Most notable fiction books for reluctant young adult readers, 2001 ★321★

Lester; Julius
Outstanding children's fiction books, 2000 ★329★

Lester; William L.
Top pay and benefits for the chief executive and top paid employees at Tuskegee University ★3583★

LeSueur; Bethany
All-America girls' high school basketball 3rd team, 2001 ★172★

Let It Shine: Stories of Black Women Freedom Fighters
Most notable books for middle readers, 2001 ★317★
Smithsonian's best books for children ages 10 and up ★365★

Lethbridge; University of
Canadian primarily undergraduate universities best at producing leaders of tomorrow, 2000 ★1192★
Canadian primarily undergraduate universities by alumni support, 2000 ★1193★
Canadian primarily undergraduate universities by award-winning faculty members, 2000 ★1194★
Canadian primarily undergraduate universities by class size at the first and second-year level, 2000 ★1195★
Canadian primarily undergraduate universities by class size at the third and forth-year level, 2000 ★1196★
Canadian primarily undergraduate universities by classes taught by tenured faculty, 2000 ★1197★
Canadian primarily undergraduate universities by faculty members with Ph.D.'s, 2000 ★1198★
Canadian primarily undergraduate universities by library acquisitions, 2000 ★1199★
Canadian primarily undergraduate universities by library expenses, 2000 ★1200★
Canadian primarily undergraduate universities by library holdings per student, 2000 ★1201★
Canadian primarily undergraduate universities by medical/science grants per faculty member, 2000 ★1202★
Canadian primarily undergraduate universities by operating budget per student, 2000 ★1203★
Canadian primarily undergraduate universities by percentage of operating budget allocated to scholarships, 2000 ★1204★
Canadian primarily undergraduate universities by percentage of operating budget allocated to student services, 2000 ★1205★
Canadian primarily undergraduate universities by reputation, 2000 ★1206★
Canadian primarily undergraduate universities by social science/humanities grants per faculty member, 2000 ★1207★
Canadian primarily undergraduate universities by students from out of province, 2000 ★1208★
Canadian primarily undergraduate universities by students winning national awards, 2000 ★1209★
Top Canadian primarily undergraduate universities, 2000 ★1226★

LeTourneau University
Academic reputation scores for *U.S. News & World Report*'s top western regional liberal arts colleges, 2000-01 ★1387★
Acceptance rates for *U.S. News & World Report*'s top western regional liberal arts colleges, 2000-01 ★1388★
Alumni giving rates at *U.S. News & World Report*'s top western regional liberal arts colleges, 2000-01 ★1389★
Average freshmen retention rates for *U.S. News & World Report*'s top western regional liberal arts colleges, 2000-01 ★1390★
Average graduation rates for *U.S. News & World Report*'s top western regional liberal arts colleges, 2000-01 ★1391★
Percentage of freshmen in the top 25% of their high school class at *U.S. News & World Report*'s top western regional liberal arts colleges, 2000-01 ★1392★
Percentage of full-time faculty at *U.S. News & World Report*'s top western regional liberal arts colleges, 2000-01 ★1393★
Proportion of classes having 20 students or less at *U.S. News & World Report*'s top western regional liberal arts colleges, 2000-01 ★1394★
Student/faculty ratios at *U.S. News & World Report*'s top western regional liberal arts colleges, 2000-01 ★1395★
U.S. News & World Report's top western regional liberal arts colleges, 2000-01 ★1396★
Average faculty salaries for institutions of higher education in Texas, 2000-01 ★3731★

Letters from the Editor: The New Yorker's Harold Ross
Outstanding arts and literature books, 2000 ★286★

Letters, general
Gender breakdown of humanities doctorate recipients, by subfield, 1999 ★1936★
Humanities doctorates awarded at U.S. colleges and universities, by subfield, 1999 ★1946★

Leuhan; David
Authors most frequently contributing to the *American Economic Review* from 1951-1990 ★2157★

Levant; Ronald
Top pay and benefits for the chief executive and top paid employees at Nova Southeastern University ★3426★

Leveraging Educational Assistance Partnership
Proposed fiscal 2002 appropriations for student assistance ★1251★
Fiscal 2002 requested budget as compared with Fiscal 2001 budget for the Education Department ★2231★

Levi Strauss & Company
Largest private companies, 2000 ★523★

Levin; Richard C.
Largest benefit packages awarded to presidents at institutions of higher education, 1998-99 ★3133★
Presidents with the highest pay at Research I and II universities, 1998-99 ★3162★
Top pay and benefits for the chief executive and top paid employees at Yale University ★3639★

Levine; Alan
Top pay and benefits for the chief executive and top paid employees at Marywood University ★3396★

Levine; Arnold
Top pay and benefits for the chief executive and top paid employees at Rockefeller University ★3462★

Levine; Arthur
Top pay and benefits for the chief executive and top paid employees at Teachers College, Columbia University ★3517★

Levine; Stuart
Top pay and benefits for the chief executive and top paid employees at Bard College ★3190★

Levinson; Ronald
Top pay and benefits for the chief executive and top paid employees at John F. Kennedy University ★3354★

LeVoir; Mark
All-American boy's high school football linemen, 2000 ★183★

Levy; David
Top pay and benefits for the chief executive and top paid employees at Bard College ★3190★

Levy; Judith
  Top pay and benefits for the chief executive and top paid employees at Ursinus College ★3591★
Lewando; Carol Ann
  Top pay and benefits for the chief executive and top paid employees at the University of Mobile ★3551★
Lewent; Judy
  Highest ranking women at the top public companies, 2000 ★4452★
Lewis and Clark College
  U.S. colleges and universities where students are very politically active ★1001★
  U.S. colleges and universities where the general student body smokes marijuana ★1011★
  U.S. colleges and universities with a large student body of liberal Democrats ★1017★
  U.S. colleges and universities with a primarily non-religious student body ★1021★
  Highest undergraduate tuition and fees at colleges and universities in Oregon ★1547★
  U.S. colleges and universities awarding the most psychology master's degrees to Asian Americans ★1798★
  U.S. colleges and universities awarding the most psychology master's degrees to Native Americans ★1800★
  Academics' choices for best environmental law programs, 2001 ★2628★
Lewis-Clark State College
  State appropriations for Idaho's institutions of higher education, 2000-01 ★1265★
  Undergraduate tuition and fees at colleges and universities in Idaho ★1499★
Lewis College of Business
  U.S. colleges and universities with the highest percentage of African Americans enrolled, 1997 ★222★
Lewis; David K.
  Top pay and benefits for the chief executive and top paid employees at Connecticut College ★3254★
Lewis; Jim
  Top pay and benefits for the chief executive and top paid employees at Austin College ★3184★
Lewis; John
  Most influential African Americans in politics and civil rights ★3040★
Lewis Jr.; Stephen R.
  Top pay and benefits for the chief executive and top paid employees at Carleton College ★3222★
Lewis; Reginald
  Most influential African Americans in business ★526★
Lewis University
  Fall enrollment at the largest Chicago-area private institutions, by minority percentages, 1999 ★869★
Lexington Community College
  Average faculty salaries for institutions of higher education in Kentucky, 2000-01 ★3704★
Lexington High School
  Outstanding suburban public high schools in Metro Boston ★4255★
Lexington Middle School
  Outstanding secondary schools in Columbia, South Carolina ★4117★
Lexmark International Group
  Fortune's highest ranked computer peripherals companies, 2000 ★454★

Most profitable information technology companies, 2000 ★527★
Liberal arts
  Top bachelor's and master's degree majors in demand for employment, 2001 ★2323★
  Top bachelor's degree majors in demand for employment, 2001 ★2324★
Liberal arts and general studies
  Fields of study profile of foreign students enrolled in U.S. institutions of higher education, 1998-99 ★2495★
Liberal arts, general studies, humanities
  Top bachelor's degree disciplines for African Americans, 1997-98 ★1672★
  Top bachelor's degree disciplines for Asian Americans, 1997-98 ★1673★
  Top bachelor's degree disciplines for Hispanic Americans, 1997-98 ★1674★
  Top bachelor's degree disciplines for Native Americans, 1997-98 ★1675★
  Top bachelor's degree disciplines for non-minorities, 1997-98 ★1676★
Liberty
  Most notable books for middle readers, 2001 ★317★
Liberty High School
  Outstanding secondary schools in Seattle-Bellevue-Everett, Washington ★4227★
Liberty Middle School
  Outstanding secondary schools in Richmond-Petersburg, Virginia ★4210★
Liberty Mutual Insurance Group
  Fortune's highest ranked property and casualty insurance companies, 2000 ★488★
Liberty; Stan
  Top pay and benefits for the chief executive and top paid employees at Bradley University ★3208★
Liberty University
  Average faculty salaries for institutions of higher education in Virginia, 2000-01 ★3735★
Libertyville High School
  Illinois high schools with the highest SAT scores ★874★
  Outstanding secondary schools in Chicago, Illinois ★4110★
Librarian
  Jobs with the best stress scores ★2252★
  Most desirable public sector jobs ★2279★
Librarians
  Projected employment growth for selected occupations that require advanced education, 1998-2008 ★2318★
The Library of Congress
  Most selective internships in the U.S., 2001 ★2610★
The Library of Congress: An Architectural Alphabet
  Smithsonian's best books for children ages 6 to 10 ★364★
Library of Congress Presents America's Story from America's Library
  Most notable children's web sites, 2001 ★2593★
Library and information science
  Average costs for Academic Search titles by subject, 2001 ★2918★
  Periodical prices by LC subject, 2001 ★2925★
Library and Information Science Research
  Information and library science journals by citation impact, 1999 ★2726★

Library of Medicine
  Proposed fiscal 2002 appropriations for National Institutes of Health scientific research ★3108★
Library Quarterly
  Information and library science journals by citation impact, 1995-99 ★2725★
  Information and library science journals by citation impact, 1999 ★2726★
Library science
  Gender breakdown of professional doctorate recipients, by subfield, 1999 ★1940★
  Professional doctorates awarded at U.S. colleges and universities, by subfield, 1999 ★2033★
Licciardi; Frederick
  Top pay and benefits for the chief executive and top paid employees at New York University ★3419★
Licensed practical nurses
  Projected employment growth for selected occupations that require an associate degree or less, 1998-2008 ★2319★
Liebergott; Jacqueline
  Top pay and benefits for the chief executive and top paid employees at Emerson College ★3287★
Lieberman; Erez
  All-USA College Academic Second Team, 2001 ★3★
Liebigs Annalen der Chemie
  Chemistry journals by citation impact, 1995-99 ★809★
Liebowitz; Ronald D.
  Top pay and benefits for the chief executive and top paid employees at Middlebury College ★3401★
Life Chiropractic College, West
  U.S. colleges and universities awarding the most health professions and related sciences first professional degrees to Native Americans ★1851★
A Life in the Twentieth Century: Innocent Beginnings, 1917-1950
  Outstanding biography books, 2000 ★288★
Life is Funny
  Booklist's best first novels for youths ★309★
  Booklist's most recommended black history books for youth ★311★
  Most notable fiction books for reluctant young adult readers, 2001 ★321★
  Outstanding books for older readers, 2000 ★327★
Life Is So Good
  Christopher Awards winners for adult literature, 2000 ★235★
LIFE: Our Century in Pictures for Young People
  Outstanding children's nonfiction books, 2000 ★330★
  Smithsonian's best books for children ages 10 and up ★365★
Life-related science
  Median salary for B.S. chemists, by field ★781★
  Median salary for M.S. chemists, by field ★785★
  Median salary for Ph.D. chemists, by field ★786★
Life Scan
  Top recruiters for chemical engineering jobs for 2000-01 bachelor's degree recipients ★2343★
  Top recruiters for chemical engineering jobs for 2000-01 master's degree recipients ★2391★

Life sciences
Age grouping of doctorate recipients, by broad field, 1999 ★1882★
Comparative data of women receiving doctorate degrees in selected fields in 1950 and 1998 ★1899★
Doctoral degree distribution by broad field, 1999 ★1902★
Median age at conferral of doctoral degree from U.S. universities, by discipline, 1999 ★1952★
Number of doctorate recipients at U.S. colleges and universities, by field, 1999 ★1969★
Percentage of female doctorate recipients, by broad field, 1999 ★1989★
Percentage of minority doctorate recipients in the U.S., by broad field, 1999 ★1991★

Life Strategies
Longest-running trade paperback bestsellers, 2000 ★282★

Life Technologies, Inc.
Best companies for working mothers ★4446★
Best companies for working mothers in terms of overall work/life support ★4451★

Life University
U.S. colleges and universities awarding the most first professional degrees to Native Americans ★1846★
U.S. colleges and universities awarding the most health professions and related sciences first professional degrees to African Americans ★1847★
U.S. colleges and universities awarding the most health professions and related sciences first professional degrees to Hispanic Americans ★1849★
U.S. colleges and universities awarding the most health professions and related sciences first professional degrees to Native Americans ★1851★

Lifelong Learning; College of
State appropriations for New Hampshire's institutions of higher education, 2000-01 ★1282★

Light; Alfred
Top pay and benefits for the chief executive and top paid employees at Saint Thomas University in Florida ★3486★

Light Gathering Poems
Booklist's most recommended poetry for youths, 2001 ★315★

Light House
Booklist's best first novels ★228★

A Light in the Attic
People for the American Way's list of most frequently challenged books, 1982-1992 ★747★

Light; Leah
Top pay and benefits for the chief executive and top paid employees at Pitzer College ★3441★

Lightcap; Stephen J.
Top pay and benefits for the chief executive and top paid employees at Cabrini College ★3215★

Lightfoot; Gordon
Canada's best performing artists of the 20th century ★74★

Lighthouse School
Outstanding secondary schools in Lowell, Maine-New Hampshire ★4169★

Liguori, C.F.C.; Bro. James A.
Top pay and benefits for the chief executive and top paid employees at Iona College ★3350★

The Likes of Me
Most notable fiction books for young adults, 2001 ★322★

Lillis; John R.
Top pay and benefits for the chief executive and top paid employees at Cornerstone University ★3258★

Lilly; Deona M.
Top pay and benefits for the chief executive and top paid employees at Southwest Baptist University ★3504★

Lilly's Purple Plastic Purse
Most notable children's recordings, 2001 ★320★

Lim; Andrew
Golden Key Scholar Award winners, 2000 ★1316★

Limestone College
U.S. News & World Report's southern regional liberal arts colleges with students least in debt, 1999 ★1366★
Average faculty salaries for institutions of higher education in South Carolina, 2000-01 ★3728★

Limited
Fortune's highest ranked specialty retailers, 2000 ★497★

Limnology & Oceanography
Oceanography journals by citation impact, 1981-99 ★2139★
Oceanography journals by citation impact, 1995-99 ★2140★
Oceanography journals by citation impact, 1999 ★2141★

Lin-Wood Public School
All-USA Teacher Teams, Third Team, 2000 ★4401★

Linam; Gail G.
Top pay and benefits for the chief executive and top paid employees at Dallas Baptist University ★3262★

Linamen; Larry H.
Top pay and benefits for the chief executive and top paid employees at Dallas Baptist University ★3262★

Lincoln: A Foreigner's Quest
Outstanding biography books, 2000 ★288★

Lincoln Center for the Performing Arts
Most selective internships in the U.S., 2001 ★2610★
Top internships in the U.S. with the highest compensation, 2001 ★2611★

Lincoln Christian College and Seminary
Average faculty salaries for institutions of higher education in Illinois, 2000-01 ★3700★

Lincoln College
Average faculty salaries for institutions of higher education without academic ranks in Illinois, 2000-01 ★3747★

Lincoln Elementary School
Chicago neighborhood schools with the highest ISAT scores in reading and math ★4004★
Illinois elementary schools chosen to be 'demonstration sites' for struggling schools ★4006★

Lincoln Financial Group
Best companies for working mothers ★4446★

Lincoln High School
Outstanding urban public high schools in Metro Dallas-Ft. Worth ★4263★

Lincoln; James
Top pay and benefits for the chief executive and top paid employees at DePauw University ★3267★

Lincoln Junior High
Illinois schools with the highest 7th grade science scores ★17★

Lincoln Magnet School
Outstanding secondary schools in San Jose, California ★4222★

Lincoln Memorial University
Division II NCAA colleges with the 0% graduation rates for women's basketball players, 1993-94 ★942★
Average faculty salaries for institutions of higher education in Tennessee, 2000-01 ★3730★
U.S. institutions with the lowest paid full professors, 2001 ★3979★

Lincoln National
Top public companies with the highest percentage of women employees, 2000 ★4459★

Lincoln Trail College
Lowest undergraduate tuition and fees at colleges and universities in Illinois ★1501★

Lincoln University
Historically black institutions with the highest number of National Achievement Scholars, 1998 ★8★
State appropriations for Missouri's institutions of higher education, 2000-01 ★1278★
State appropriations for Pennsylvania's institutions of higher education, 2000-01 ★1291★
Historically black colleges and universities awarding the most master's degrees to African Americans ★1670★
Total baccalaureate physical sciences degrees awarded to African Americans from U.S. colleges and universities, 1997-98 ★1733★
U.S. colleges and universities awarding the most business management and administrative services master's degrees to African Americans ★1759★
Average faculty salaries for institutions of higher education in Missouri, 2000-01 ★3712★
Average faculty salaries for institutions of higher education in Pennsylvania, 2000-01 ★3725★

Lincoln University (MO)
Colleges offering the Thurgood Marshall Scholarship Fund ★221★

Lincoln University (PA)
Colleges offering the Thurgood Marshall Scholarship Fund ★221★
Institutions with the most female physics bachelor's recipients, 1994-1998 ★2959★
U.S. institutions with more than 40% female bachelor's graduates in their physics departments, 1994-98 ★2977★

Lincoln-Way Community High School, District 210
Illinois school districts spending the least for high school education 1997-98 ★4008★

Lincolnwood School, District 74
Illinois school districts spending the most per pupil for instruction ★4011★

Lindblom; C. E.
Authors with the most citations among authors published in *American Political Science Review*, 1974-94 ★3048★

Lindblom College Prep
Acceptance rates at Chicago college prep magnet schools, 2000-01 ★4000★
Admissions to college prep schools in Chicago that are the toughest to get into, 2001 ★4001★
College prep schools in Chicago that are the toughest to get into ★4005★

Lindsey Wilson College
Average faculty salaries for institutions of higher education in Kentucky, 2000-01 ★3704★

Lindstrom; Stacy
All-America girls' high school soccer team midfielders, 2001 ★177★

Line; M.B.
Authors that most frequently cite *Libri* publications from 1972 to 1999 ★2723★

Linear Technology
Business Week's best performing companies with the highest net margin, 2000 ★419★
Top electrical and electronics companies in Standard & Poor's 500, 2001 ★539★

Lineback; Donald J.
Top pay and benefits for the chief executive and top paid employees at Furman University ★3300★

Linfield College
U.S. News & World Report's best undergraduate fees among western regional universities by discount tuition, 2000 ★1430★
Highest undergraduate tuition and fees at colleges and universities in Oregon ★1547★
U.S. News & World Report's top western regional universities, 2000-01 ★1574★
U.S. News & World Report's western regional universities with the best academic reputation scores, 2000-01 ★1577★
U.S. News & World Report's western regional universities with the best student/faculty ratios, 2000-01 ★1578★
U.S. News & World Report's western regional universities with the highest acceptance rates, 2000-01 ★1579★
U.S. News & World Report's western regional universities with the highest alumni giving rates, 2000-01 ★1580★
U.S. News & World Report's western regional universities with the highest graduation rates, 2000-01 ★1582★
U.S. News & World Report's western regional universities with the highest percentage of full-time faculty, 2000-01 ★1584★
U.S. News & World Report's western regional universities with the highest proportion of classes with 20 students or less, 2000-01 ★1585★
Average faculty salaries for institutions of higher education in Oregon, 2000-01 ★3724★

Linganore High School
Outstanding secondary schools in Washington, District of Columbia-Maryland-Virginia-West Virginia ★4249★

Lingenfelter; Sherwood
Top pay and benefits for the chief executive and top paid employees at Biola University ★3203★

Lingg; Jodey
Top pay and benefits for the chief executive and top paid employees at City University in Washington ★3234★

Linguistic Inquiry
Language and linguistics journals with the greatest impact measure, 1981-98 ★2731★

Linguistics
Gender breakdown of humanities doctorate recipients, by subfield, 1999 ★1936★
Humanities doctorates awarded at U.S. colleges and universities, by subfield, 1999 ★1946★
Percentage of female doctorate recipients at U.S. colleges and universities, by subfield, 1999 ★1988★

Link; James C.
Top pay and benefits for the chief executive and top paid employees at Hartwick College ★3326★

Linn-Benton Community College
Lowest undergraduate tuition and fees at colleges and universities in Oregon ★1548★
Average faculty salaries for institutions of higher education without academic ranks in Oregon, 2000-01 ★3764★

Linn State Technical College
State appropriations for Missouri's institutions of higher education, 2000-01 ★1278★

Linskey; Gerard F.
Top pay and benefits for the chief executive and top paid employees at Curry College ★3261★

The Lion's Game
Longest-running fiction hardcover bestsellers, 2000 ★279★

Lipscomb University
Average faculty salaries for institutions of higher education in Tennessee, 2000-01 ★3730★

Liquid Crystals
Crystallography journals by citation impact, 1981-98 ★1654★
Crystallography journals by citation impact, 1994-98 ★1655★
Crystallography journals by citation impact, 1998 ★1656★

Literature
Subject areas with the highest library expenditures/circulation ★306★

Literature in Context Online
Library Journal's best reference databases and discs, 2000 ★369★

Litfin; A. Duane
Top pay and benefits for the chief executive and top paid employees at Wheaton College in Illinois ★3620★

Lithia Motors
Fortune's highest ranked automotive retailing services companies, 2000 ★449★

Lithographer/photoengraver
Most desirable jobs in production/manufacturing ★2276★

Lithuania
Eight grade science achievement scores from selected countries, 1999 ★14★
Eighth grade mathematics achievement scores from selected countries, 1999 ★2773★

Little Big Horn College
U.S. tribal colleges ★1445★

Little; Bill F.
Top pay and benefits for the chief executive and top paid employees at Southwest Baptist University ★3504★

Little; Brian
Radcliffe Institute for Advanced Study fellowship recipients in the field of psychology, 2000-01 ★3062★

Little, Brown
Hardcover bestsellers by publishing house, 2000 ★240★
Top children's book publishers, 1999 ★3074★

Little Caesar Enterprises
Top women-owned companies ★4460★

Little; Daniel
Top pay and benefits for the chief executive and top paid employees at Bucknell University ★3213★

Little Hoop Community College
Lowest undergraduate tuition and fees at colleges and universities in North Dakota ★1542★

Little; Lester
Top pay and benefits for the chief executive and top paid employees at Smith College ★3501★

Little Lit
Outstanding children's picture books, 2000 ★331★
Publishers Weekly Off-the-Cuff Awards winner for most unusual picture book, 2000 ★359★

Little; Phyllis
Top pay and benefits for the chief executive and top paid employees at Benedictine University ★3200★

Little Priest Tribal College
U.S. tribal colleges ★1445★

Little Puppy, Little Lamb, Little Calf
Smithsonian's best books for children ages 1 to 6 ★363★

Little Red Riding Hood
Most frequently banned books in the 1990s ★745★

Little; Richard
Top pay and benefits for the chief executive and top paid employees at Baldwin-Wallace College ★3189★

Litton Industries
Top recruiters for accounting jobs for 2000-01 bachelor's degree recipients ★580★
Top recruiters for accounting jobs for 2000-01 master's degree recipients ★661★
Top recruiters for manufacturing management jobs for 2000-01 bachelor's degree recipients ★683★
Top recruiters for computer science jobs for 2000-01 master's degree recipients ★1598★
Top recruiters for aerospace engineering jobs for 2000-01 bachelor's degree recipients ★2340★
Top recruiters for computer engineering jobs for 2000-01 bachelor's degree recipients ★2352★
Top recruiters for aerospace engineering jobs for 2000-01 master's degree recipients ★2377★
Top recruiters for computer engineering jobs for 2000-01 master's degree recipients ★2400★

Living on the Fault Line: Managing for Shareholder Value in the Age of the Internet
Library Journal's most notable management books, 2000 ★265★

Living to Tell
Most notable fiction books, 2001 ★284★
Outstanding works of fiction, 2001 ★293★

Livingston College
Division II NCAA colleges with the highest graduation rates for football players, 1993-94 ★946★
Historically black colleges and universities with high student loan default rates, 1998 ★2736★

Livingston High School
Outstanding secondary schools in Newark, New Jersey ★4192★

Livingstone College
Division II NCAA colleges with the 0% graduation rates for men's basketball players, 1993-94 ★941★
Division II NCAA colleges with the 0% graduation rates for women's basketball players, 1993-94 ★942★

Liz Claiborne
Fortune's highest ranked apparel companies, 2000 ★448★

Ljungquist; Gary
Top pay and benefits for the chief executive and top paid employees at Salem College ★3488★

Lloyd; Carli
All-America girls' high school soccer team midfielders, 2001 ★177★

Lloyd; David
Top pay and benefits for the chief executive and top paid employees at Scripps College ★3493★

Lloyds TSB Group
Business Week's best companies in Britain ★389★

LM Ericsson
Business Week's best companies in Sweden ★404★

Local and suburban transportation
Employment growth percentages for selected industries, 1998-2000 ★2294★

Locatelli, S.J.; Rev. Paul L.
Top pay and benefits for the chief executive and top paid employees at Santa Clara University in California ★3491★

Lock Haven University
Average faculty salaries for institutions of higher education in Pennsylvania, 2000-01 ★3725★

Lockaby; Kayla
All-America girls' high school soccer team midfielders, 2001 ★177★

Lockheed Martin
Fortune's highest ranked aerospace companies, 2000 ★446★
Top aerospace and defense companies in Standard & Poor's 500, 2001 ★529★

Lockport Township High School, District 205
Illinois school districts spending the least for high school education 1997-98 ★4008★

Lockport Township School, District 91
Illinois school districts spending the least for elementary school education 1997-98 ★4007★

Lodz, Poland; University of
Institutions, by adjusted authorship, with the most published authors in the *Journal of Business Research*, 1985 to 1999 ★694★
Institutions with the most published authors in the *Journal of Business Research*, 1985 to 1999 ★695★

Loevy; Robert D.
Top pay and benefits for the chief executive and top paid employees at Colorado College ★3249★

Loewen; Howard J.
Top pay and benefits for the chief executive and top paid employees at Fresno Pacific University ★3298★

Loews
Business Week's best performing companies with the highest 1-year shareholder returns ★415★
Fortune's highest ranked property and casualty insurance companies, 2000 ★488★

Logan; Lee
Top pay and benefits for the chief executive and top paid employees at Erskine College ★3290★

Loganville High School
Outstanding suburban public high schools in Metro Atlanta ★4254★

Logger's Run Community Middle School
Outstanding secondary schools in West Palm Beach-Boca Raton, Florida ★4251★

Logic
Gender breakdown of mathematics doctorate recipients, by subfield, 1999 ★1938★
Mathematics doctorates awarded at U.S. colleges and universities, by subfield, 1999 ★1951★

Logistics/supply chain management
Expected starting salaries of 2000-01 bachelor's degree recipients, by specific major ★3131★

Lohman; David
Top pay and benefits for the chief executive and top paid employees at Hawaii Pacific University ★3330★

Lois Lenski titles
Publishers Weekly Off-the-Cuff Awards winner for book happiest to see back in print, 2000 ★345★

Loken; Barbara
Highest impact authors in the *Journal of Business Research*, by adjusted number of citations in 12 journals, 1985-1999 ★692★

Loma Linda University
Institutions censured by the American Association of University Professors, 2001 ★1067★
Institutions receiving the most in federal agency appropriations to colleges, 2000 ★1245★
Total baccalaureate health professions and related sciences degrees awarded to Asian Americans from U.S. colleges and universities, 1997-98 ★1722★
U.S. colleges and universities awarding the most health professions and related sciences master's degrees to Asian Americans ★1778★
U.S. colleges and universities awarding the most health professions and related sciences master's degrees to Hispanic Americans ★1779★
U.S. colleges and universities awarding the most first professional degrees to Asian Americans ★1844★
U.S. colleges and universities awarding the most health professions and related sciences first professional degrees to Asian Americans ★1848★

Lombard, District 44
Illinois elementary school districts with the highest teacher salaries, 1999 ★3984★

Lombardo; Guy
Canada's best performing artists of the 20th century ★74★

Lonchyna; Vassyl A.
Top pay and benefits for the chief executive and top paid employees at Tulane University ★3581★

London
Cities with the highest productivity of paper in the discipline of cardiovascular systems, 1994-96 ★2869★
Cities with the highest productivity of paper in the discipline of hematology, 1994-96 ★2870★
Cities with the highest productivity of paper in the discipline of immunology, 1994-96 ★2871★

London Business School
Business Week's top business schools outside the U.S. as selected by corporate recruiters, 2000 ★605★
Business Week's top business schools outside the U.S. as selected by recent MBA graduates, 2000 ★606★
Business Week's top business schools outside the U.S. for intellectual capital, 2000 ★607★
Post-MBA salaries for graduates from *Business Week*'s top business schools outside the U.S., 2000 ★642★
Pre-MBA salaries for students at *Business Week*'s top business schools outside the U.S., 2000 ★643★

London University
Institutions generating the most economic education research text, 1963-1990 ★2167★
United Kingdom universities contributing the most papers in the field of economics and business, 1993-97 ★2203★

Long Beach
U.S. cities with the highest percentage of births to mothers with less than 12 years of education ★4432★

Long Day's Journey into Night
Top plays of the twentieth century ★4435★

Long Island University
Presidents with the highest pay at Master's I and II colleges and universities, 1998-99 ★3161★
Average faculty salaries for institutions of higher education in New York, 2000-01 ★3719★

Long Island University, Brooklyn
Total baccalaureate health professions and related sciences degrees awarded to Asian Americans from U.S. colleges and universities, 1997-98 ★1722★
Traditionally white institutions awarding the most master's degrees to African Americans ★1755★
U.S. colleges and universities awarding the most biological and life sciences master's degrees to African Americans ★1756★
U.S. colleges and universities awarding the most education master's degrees to African Americans ★1769★
U.S. colleges and universities awarding the most English language/literature/letters master's degrees to African Americans ★1773★
U.S. colleges and universities awarding the most health professions and related sciences master's degrees to African Americans ★1777★
U.S. colleges and universities awarding the most master's degrees to African Americans ★1785★
U.S. colleges and universities awarding the most physical sciences master's degrees to Asian Americans ★1794★
U.S. colleges and universities awarding the most psychology master's degrees to African Americans ★1797★
U.S. colleges and universities awarding the most psychology master's degrees to Asian Americans ★1798★
U.S. colleges and universities awarding the most psychology master's degrees to Hispanic Americans ★1799★

Long Island University, Southhampton College
Private, 4-year undergraduate colleges and universities producing the most Ph.D.'s in the earth sciences, 1981-1990 ★2151★

Long Night's Journey into Day
Outstanding videos for library collections, 2000 ★2892★

Long Range Planning
Top management journals by core impact ★547★

Longaberger Company
Top women-owned companies ★4460★

Longfellow Elementary School
Illinois elementary schools with the highest 5th grade writing scores ★15★

Longfield; Bradley
Top pay and benefits for the chief executive and top paid employees at the University of Dubuque ★3542★

The Longitude Prize
Most notable books for older readers, 2001 ★318★

Longview Community College
Lowest undergraduate tuition and fees at colleges and universities in Missouri ★1525★
Average faculty salaries for institutions of higher education without academic ranks in Missouri, 2000-01 ★3755★

Longwood College
State appropriations for Virginia's institutions of higher education, 2000-01 ★1299★
U.S. News & World Report's top public southern regional universities, 2000-01 ★1443★
Average faculty salaries for institutions of higher education in Virginia, 2000-01 ★3735★

Longwood Middle School
Outstanding secondary schools in Long Island, New York ★4165★

Look Back in Anger
Top plays of the twentieth century ★4435★

Loomer; Glenn
Top pay and benefits for the chief executive and top paid employees at Queens College in North Carolina ★3448★

Looser; Don
Top pay and benefits for the chief executive and top paid employees at Houston Baptist University ★3342★

Lorain County Community College
Average faculty salaries for institutions of higher education in Ohio, 2000-01 ★3722★

Loras College
U.S. News & World Report's midwestern regional liberal arts colleges with the best student/faculty ratios, 2000-01 ★1339★
U.S. News & World Report's midwestern regional liberal arts colleges with the highest freshmen retention rates, 2000-01 ★1343★
U.S. News & World Report's midwestern regional liberal arts colleges with the highest proportion of classes having 20 students or less, 2000-01 ★1347★
Highest undergraduate tuition and fees at colleges and universities in Iowa ★1504★
Average faculty salaries for institutions of higher education in Iowa, 2000-01 ★3702★

Lord Brocktree
Booklist's most recommended fantasy books for youth ★312★

Lord Emsworth and Others
Outstanding audiobooks, 2000 ★287★

Lord Fairfax Community College
Average faculty salaries for institutions of higher education in Virginia, 2000-01 ★3735★

Lord of the Flies
Most frequently banned books in the 1990s ★745★

Lord; Richard
Top pay and benefits for the chief executive and top paid employees at Campbell University ★3218★

Lorenzi; Peter
Top pay and benefits for the chief executive and top paid employees at Loyola College in Maryland ★3379★

Loritz; Daniel
Top pay and benefits for the chief executive and top paid employees at Hamline University ★3320★

Los Alamitos High School
Outstanding secondary schools in Orange County, California ★4199★

Los Alisos Intermediate School
Outstanding secondary schools in Orange County, California ★4199★

Los Angeles
U.S. cities with the highest number of high-tech employees, 1998 ★2284★
U.S. school districts with the highest number of vacancies for K-12 teachers ★2331★
American cities with the highest percentage of people with Internet access ★2572★
U.S. market areas with the highest percentage of adults having internet access ★2607★
Superintendents' salaries at the largest U.S. schools districts, 1999-2000 ★3990★
Largest public school districts in the U.S. ★4016★
U.S. cities with the highest percentage of births to mothers with less than 12 years of education ★4432★

Los Angeles College of Chiropractic
U.S. colleges and universities awarding the most health professions and related sciences first professional degrees to Asian Americans ★1848★
U.S. colleges and universities awarding the most health professions and related sciences first professional degrees to Hispanic Americans ★1849★
Average faculty salaries for institutions of higher education in California, 2000-01 ★3692★

Los Angeles County
U.S. counties with the highest international enrollment, 1999-2000 ★2505★

Los Angeles-Long Beach, CA
America's most wired cities with the highest domain density, 2001 ★2574★
Cities with the most domains per 1,000 firms ★2579★

Los Angeles Times
Most cited general works serials in technical communication journals from 1988 to 1997 ★4419★

Los Gatos High School
Outstanding secondary schools in San Jose, California ★4222★

Los Medanos College
Lowest undergraduate tuition and fees at public 2-year colleges and universities ★1465★

Losada; Luis A.
Top pay and benefits for the chief executive and top paid employees at Manhattanville College ★3388★

Loscheider; Paul H.
Top pay and benefits for the chief executive and top paid employees at North Central College in Illinois ★3421★

Losee; Robert
Library and information science faculty with the most journal articles, 1993-1998 ★2711★

Losing the Fight against Crime
Most-cited works in critical criminology publications ★1645★

Lost Mountain Middle School
Outstanding secondary schools in Atlanta, Georgia ★4087★

Lotze; Michael T.
Most-cited researchers in oncology, 1981-1998 ★2877★

Loudoun County Public Library
Highest Hennen's American Public Library Ratings for libraries serving a population of 100,000 to 249,999 ★2698★

Loughran, S.J.; Rev. James N.
Top pay and benefits for the chief executive and top paid employees at Saint Peter's College ★3485★

Louis Klein Middle School
Outstanding secondary schools in New York, New York ★4191★

Louis Pizitz Middle School
Outstanding secondary schools in Birmingham, Alabama ★4098★

Louisiana
Mean composite ACT scores by state, 2000 ★895★
Mean math SAT scores by state, 2000 ★900★
Mean verbal SAT scores by state, 2000 ★903★
Average class size at colleges and universities in the U.S., by state ★1064★
States receiving the most in federal agency appropriations to colleges, from 1996 to 2000 ★1307★
Total doctorate recipients by state, 1999 ★2054★
State library associations with most full-time staff ★2681★
State library associations with the highest annual revenue ★2682★
State library associations with the highest conference attendance ★2683★
State library associations with the highest unrestricted net assets ★2684★
State library associations with the largest membership ★2685★
State grades for affordability of higher education for minority students, 2000 ★2883★
State grades for benefits state receives for educating its minority students, 2000 ★2884★
State grades for completion of higher education by minority students, 2000 ★2885★
State grades for participation of minority students in higher education, 2000 ★2886★
State grades for preparing minority students for higher education, 2000 ★2887★
States with the lowest percentage of high school freshmen enrolling in college within four years ★4267★
States with the highest state support for non need-based financial aid for students, 1999-2000 ★4368★
U.S. states with the highest percentage of births to teenagers who were already mothers ★4433★

Louisiana College
U.S. News & World Report's southern regional liberal arts colleges with the highest proportion of classes having 20 students or less, 2000-01 ★1375★
U.S. News & World Report's southern regional liberal arts colleges with the highest proportion of freshmen in the top 25% of their high school class, 2000-01 ★1376★
U.S. News & World Report's southern regional liberal arts colleges with the lowest acceptance rates, 2000-01 ★1377★
Highest undergraduate tuition and fees at colleges and universities in Louisiana ★1510★
Average faculty salaries for institutions of higher education in Louisiana, 2000-01 ★3705★

Louisiana, Lafayette; University of
U.S. college campuses reporting murders or non-negligent manslaughters, 1999 ★728★
Division I NCAA colleges with that graduated less than 20% of their African American male athletes, 1990-91 to 1993-94 ★928★
State appropriations for Louisiana institutions of higher education, 2000-01 ★1271★
Lowest undergraduate tuition and fees at colleges and universities in Louisiana ★1511★
Average faculty salaries for institutions of higher education in Louisiana, 2000-01 ★3705★

Louisiana, Monroe; University of
State appropriations for Louisiana institutions of higher education, 2000-01 ★1271★
Average faculty salaries for institutions of higher education in Louisiana, 2000-01 ★3705★

Louisiana-Pacific
Top paper and forest products companies in Standard & Poor's 500, 2001 ★552★

Louisiana State University
Women's Division I track and field programs with the most outdoor championships ★149★
Institutions with the most published authors in the *Journal of Business Research*, 1985 to 1999 ★695★
Division I NCAA colleges with that graduated none of their African American male basketball players, 1990-91 to 1993-94 ★930★
Institutions receiving the most in federal agency appropriations to colleges, 2000 ★1245★
Institutions generating the most economic education research text, 1963-1990 ★2167★
Faculty's scholarly reputation in the Ph.D.-granting departments of geography, 1925-1982 ★2518★

Louisiana State University and A&M College
U.S. institutions awarding the most baccalaureate degrees to Hispanic Americans in agricultural sciences, 1998 ★1818★
Average faculty salaries for institutions of higher education in Louisiana, 2000-01 ★3705★

Louisiana State University, Alexandria
Lowest undergraduate tuition and fees at colleges and universities in Louisiana ★1511★

Louisiana State University, Baton Rouge
U.S. colleges and universities with the highest average football attendance, 1996-99 ★159★
U.S. colleges and universities where a large portion of the student body drink beer ★991★
U.S. colleges and universities where a large portion of the student body drink hard liquor ★992★
U.S. colleges and universities where fraternities and sororities are popular ★993★
U.S. colleges and universities where the general student body puts a strong emphasis on socializing ★1008★
U.S. colleges and universities with a large student body of conservative Republicans ★1016★
U.S. colleges and universities with a popular radio station ★1019★
Academics' choices for best graduate petroleum engineering schools, 2000 ★2429★

Louisiana State University, Eunice
Lowest undergraduate tuition and fees at colleges and universities in Louisiana ★1511★

Louisiana State University Medical Center
U.S. colleges and universities awarding the most biological and life sciences master's degrees to African Americans ★1756★
U.S. colleges and universities awarding the most health professions and related sciences first professional degrees to African Americans ★1847★
U.S. colleges and universities awarding the most biological and life sciences doctorate degrees to Asian Americans ★2083★

Louisiana State University, Shreveport
Lowest undergraduate tuition and fees at colleges and universities in Louisiana ★1511★
Average faculty salaries for institutions of higher education in Louisiana, 2000-01 ★3705★

Louisiana State University System
State appropriations for Louisiana institutions of higher education, 2000-01 ★1271★

Louisiana Tech
NCAA Division I women's basketball teams with the best scoring margin ★156★
Women's basketball teams with the most appearances in the Final Four ★157★
State appropriations for Louisiana institutions of higher education, 2000-01 ★1271★
Average faculty salaries for institutions of higher education in Louisiana, 2000-01 ★3705★

Louisville High School
Outstanding secondary schools in Los Angeles-Long Beach, California ★4167★

Louisville Male High School
Outstanding secondary schools in Louisville, Kentucky-Indiana ★4168★

Louisville Technical Institute
Highest undergraduate tuition and fees at colleges and universities in Kentucky ★1508★

Louisville; University of
Division I NCAA colleges with that graduated none of their African American male basketball players, 1990-91 to 1993-94 ★930★
State appropriations for Kentucky's institutions of higher education, 2000-01 ★1270★
Average faculty salaries for institutions of higher education in Kentucky, 2000-01 ★3704★

Louthan; William C.
Top pay and benefits for the chief executive and top paid employees at Ohio Wesleyan University ★3430★

Love Him Forever
Most notable fiction books for reluctant young adult readers, 2001 ★321★

Love and Other Four Letter Words
Most notable fiction books for reluctant young adult readers, 2001 ★321★

Love; Peter
All-USA College Academic First Team, 2001 ★2★

Lovell; M.
Top full professor economists at elite liberal arts colleges, 1975-94 ★2175★

Lovell; Michael
Top pay and benefits for the chief executive and top paid employees at Wesleyan University in Connecticut ★3612★

Lovin; Keith
Top pay and benefits for the chief executive and top paid employees at the Maryville University of Saint Louis ★3534★

Lowe; Calvin
Top pay and benefits for the chief executive and top paid employees at Hampton University ★3323★

Lowe; David
Best U.S. works of journalism in the 20th century ★2769★

Lowe; William
Top pay and benefits for the chief executive and top paid employees at the College of St. Rose ★3529★

Lowell High School
Outstanding secondary schools in San Francisco, California ★4221★
Outstanding urban public high schools in Metro Boston ★4261★

Lower Merion Library System
Highest Hennen's American Public Library Ratings for libraries serving a population of 50,000 to 99,999 ★2697★

Lower Moreland High School
Outstanding secondary schools in Philadelphia, Pennsylvania-New Jersey ★4202★

Lowe's
Fortune's highest ranked specialty retailers, 2000 ★497★
Top discount and fashion retailing companies in Standard & Poor's 500, 2001 ★538★

Loyd; Jo Lynn
Top pay and benefits for the chief executive and top paid employees at Amber University ★3172★

Loyola College
U.S. News & World Report's northern regional universities with the best academic reputation scores, 2000-01 ★1415★
U.S. News & World Report's northern regional universities with the highest alumni giving rates, 2000-01 ★1418★
U.S. News & World Report's northern regional universities with the highest average graduation rates, 2000-01 ★1419★
U.S. News & World Report's northern regional universities with the highest freshmen retention rates, 2000-01 ★1420★
U.S. News & World Report's northern regional universities with the highest percentage of freshmen in the top 25% of their high school class, 2000-01 ★1421★
U.S. News & World Report's top northern regional universities, 2000-01 ★1425★

Loyola College (MD)
Division I NCAA colleges with the highest graduation rates for male athletes, 1990-91 to 1993-94 ★934★
U.S. News & World Report's best undergraduate fees among northern regional universities by discount tuition, 2000 ★1428★
Highest undergraduate tuition and fees at colleges and universities in Maryland ★1514★

Loyola

First-year student's choices for exemplary master's institutions ★2536★
Average faculty salaries for institutions of higher education in Maryland, 2000-01 ★3707★

Loyola Law School
Academics' choices for best trial advocacy programs, 2001 ★2633★

Loyola Marymount University
U.S. colleges and universities with a popular newspaper ★1018★
U.S. colleges and universities with a popular radio station ★1019★
U.S. News & World Report's best undergraduate fees among western regional universities by discount tuition, 2000 ★1430★
U.S. News & World Report's top western regional universities, 2000-01 ★1574★
U.S. News & World Report's western regional universities with the best academic reputation scores, 2000-01 ★1577★
U.S. News & World Report's western regional universities with the best student/faculty ratios, 2000-01 ★1578★
U.S. News & World Report's western regional universities with the highest freshmen retention rates, 2000-01 ★1581★
U.S. News & World Report's western regional universities with the highest graduation rates, 2000-01 ★1582★
U.S. News & World Report's western regional universities with the lowest acceptance rates, 2000-01 ★1586★
U.S. colleges and universities awarding the most communications master's degrees to Hispanic Americans ★1765★
U.S. colleges and universities awarding the most first professional degrees to Asian Americans ★1844★
U.S. colleges and universities awarding the most first professional degrees to Hispanic Americans ★1845★
U.S. colleges and universities awarding the most law and legal studies first professional degrees to Asian Americans ★1853★
U.S. colleges and universities awarding the most law and legal studies first professional degrees to Hispanic Americans ★1854★
Average faculty salaries for institutions of higher education in California, 2000-01 ★3692★

Loyola University
All-USA College Academic First Team, 2001 ★2★
Illinois institutions with the highest article output ★2677★
U.S. universities with the highest concentration of papers published in the field of literary studies, 1994-98 ★2734★

Loyola University, Chicago
U.S. catholic universities with the highest enrollment, 1999 ★864★
Fall enrollment at the largest Chicago-area private institutions, by minority percentages, 1999 ★869★
Division I NCAA colleges with the highest graduation rates for female basketball players, 1990-91 to 1993-94 ★932★
Highest undergraduate tuition and fees at colleges and universities in Illinois ★1500★
U.S. colleges and universities awarding the most law and legal studies master's degrees to African Americans ★1781★
U.S. colleges and universities awarding the most law and legal studies master's degrees to Asian Americans ★1782★
U.S. colleges and universities awarding the most doctorates in education, 1999 ★2101★

College senior's choices for exemplary doctoral-extensive universities ★2531★
Academics' choices for best health law programs, 2001 ★2629★
Institutions in the Worker Rights Consortium ★2913★
Average faculty salaries for institutions of higher education in Illinois, 2000-01 ★3700★

Loyola University, New Orleans
U.S. News & World Report's best undergraduate fees among southern regional universities by discount tuition, 2000 ★1429★
U.S. News & World Report's southern regional universities with the best academic reputation scores, 2000-01 ★1433★
U.S. News & World Report's southern regional universities with the best student/faculty ratios, 2000-01 ★1435★
U.S. News & World Report's southern regional universities with the highest acceptance rates, 2000-01 ★1436★
U.S. News & World Report's top southern regional universities, 2000-01 ★1444★
Highest undergraduate tuition and fees at colleges and universities in Louisiana ★1510★
Institutions in the Worker Rights Consortium ★2913★
Average faculty salaries for institutions of higher education in Louisiana, 2000-01 ★3705★

LSI Logic
Fortune's highest ranked semiconductors companies, 2000 ★495★

LTV
Fortune's highest ranked metals companies, 2000 ★476★
Fortune's least admired companies for employee talent ★506★
Fortune's least admired companies for quality of management ★510★

Lubbock Christian University
Average faculty salaries for institutions of higher education in Texas, 2000-01 ★3731★

Lubbock High School
Outstanding secondary schools in Lubbock, Texas ★4170★

Lucas; Robert E.
U.S. academic economists by mean number of citations, 1971-92 ★2176★
U.S. academic economists by total citations, 1971-92 ★2177★
Most cited economists ★2185★

Lucas; William J.
Top pay and benefits for the chief executive and top paid employees at Fairfield University ★3291★

Lucasfilm/LucasDigital
Most selective internships in the U.S., 2001 ★2610★

Lucent Technologies
Business Week's best companies in the United States ★411★
Business Week's best performing companies with the lowest 1-year shareholder returns ★422★
Business Week's top companies worldwide ★433★
Fortune's highest ranked network communications companies, 2000 ★482★
Top recruiters for business administration jobs for 2000-01 master's degree recipients ★652★
Top recruiters for accounting jobs for 2000-01 master's degree recipients ★661★

Top recruiters for manufacturing management jobs for 2000-01 master's degree recipients ★669★
Top recruiters for marketing jobs for 2000-01 master's degree recipients ★672★
Top recruiters for manufacturing management jobs for 2000-01 bachelor's degree recipients ★683★
Top recruiters for chemistry jobs for 2000-01 master's degree recipients ★806★
Top recruiters for computer science jobs for 2000-01 bachelor's degree recipients ★1590★
Top recruiters for computer science jobs for 2000-01 master's degree recipients ★1598★
Top employers of college graduates, 2001 ★2325★
Top recruiters for systems engineer jobs for 2000-01 bachelor's degree recipients ★2336★
Top recruiters for computer engineering jobs for 2000-01 bachelor's degree recipients ★2352★
Top recruiters for electrical/electronic engineering jobs for 2000-01 bachelor's degree recipients ★2354★
Top recruiters for systems engineer jobs for 2000-01 master's degree recipients ★2371★
Top recruiters for chemical engineering jobs for 2000-01 master's degree recipients ★2391★
Top recruiters for computer engineering jobs for 2000-01 master's degree recipients ★2400★
Top recruiters for electrical/electronic engineering jobs for 2000-01 master's degree recipients ★2406★
Top recruiters for liberal arts jobs for 2000-01 bachelor's degree recipients ★2675★
Top recruiters for liberal arts jobs for 2000-01 master's degree recipients ★2676★
Top recruiters for library science jobs for 2000-01 master's degree recipients ★2717★
Top recruiters for information technology (MIS) jobs for 2000-01 bachelor's degree recipients ★2738★
Top recruiters for information technology (MIS) jobs for 2000-01 master's degree recipients ★2739★
Top recruiters for math/actuarial science jobs for 2000-01 bachelor's degree recipients ★2771★
Top recruiters for math/actuarial science jobs for 2000-01 master's degree recipients ★2779★
Top recruiters for statistics jobs for 2000-01 master's degree recipients ★2781★
Top recruiters for statistics jobs for 2000-01 bachelor's degree recipients ★2786★
Top recruiters for physics jobs for 2000-01 master's degree recipients ★3016★

Lucey, S.J.; Rev. Gregory F.
Top pay and benefits for the chief executive and top paid employees at Spring Hill College ★3508★

Lucia; Donald J.
Top pay and benefits for the chief executive and top paid employees at Colorado College ★3249★

Lucifer's Legacy: The Meaning of Asymmetry
Library Journal's most notable physics books, 2000 ★274★

Luckhardt; John L.
Top pay and benefits for the chief executive and top paid employees at Washington and Jefferson College ★3604★

Lucy; Denise M.
Top pay and benefits for the chief executive and top paid employees at Dominican University of California ★3270★

Ludovic: The Snow Gift
Outstanding videos for library collections, 2000 ★2892★

Luebbert; Karen
Top pay and benefits for the chief executive and top paid employees at Webster University ★3608★

Luedeke; J. Barton
Top pay and benefits for the chief executive and top paid employees at Rider University ★3458★

Luedtke; Luther
Top pay and benefits for the chief executive and top paid employees at California Lutheran University ★3216★

Luftman; Jerry
Top pay and benefits for the chief executive and top paid employees at Stevens Institute of Technology ★3512★

Lukoil Holding
Business Week's top emerging-market companies worldwide ★434★

Lumberjack
Jobs with the highest unemployment ★2256★
Jobs with the worst environment scores ★2260★
Jobs with the worst outlook scores ★2262★
Jobs with the worst physical demands scores ★2263★
Least desirable jobs ★2266★

Lumpkin; James R.
Authors with the most articles published in the *Journal of Business Research*, 1985 to 1999 ★687★

Lumsden; Keith G.
Individuals producing the most economic education research articles, 1963-1990 ★2166★

Lundquist; Dan
Top pay and benefits for the chief executive and top paid employees at Union College in New York ★3585★

Luo; Robert
All-USA College Academic Second Team, 2001 ★3★

Lurleen B Wallace Junior College
Average faculty salaries for institutions of higher education without academic ranks in Alabama, 2000-01 ★3740★

Lusardi; Robert
Top pay and benefits for the chief executive and top paid employees at Western New England College ★3615★

Luther College
Highest undergraduate tuition and fees at colleges and universities in Iowa ★1504★
Average faculty salaries for institutions of higher education in Iowa, 2000-01 ★3702★

Lutheran
Religious preference of incoming freshmen, 2000 ★1061★

Lutheran High School
Outstanding secondary schools in Denver, Colorado ★4124★
Outstanding secondary schools in Indianapolis, Indiana ★4153★

Lutheran High School South
Outstanding secondary schools in St. Louis, Missouri-Illinois ★4216★

Lutheran Services in America
Organizations with the most charitable contributions raised, 1999 ★2943★

Lutheran Theological Southern Seminary
Average faculty salaries for institutions of higher education in South Carolina, 2000-01 ★3728★

Luzerne County Community College
Lowest undergraduate tuition and fees at colleges and universities in Pennsylvania ★1550★
Average faculty salaries for institutions of higher education in Pennsylvania, 2000-01 ★3725★

Lycoming College
U.S. News & World Report's northern regional liberal arts colleges with the best student/faculty ratios, 2000-01 ★1353★
U.S. News & World Report's northern regional liberal arts colleges with the highest acceptance rates, 2000-01 ★1355★
U.S. News & World Report's northern regional liberal arts colleges with the highest freshmen retention rates, 2000-01 ★1357★
U.S. News & World Report's northern regional liberal arts colleges with the highest percentage of full-time faculty, 2000-01 ★1360★
Average faculty salaries for institutions of higher education in Pennsylvania, 2000-01 ★3725★

Lyddy; James P.
Top pay and benefits for the chief executive and top paid employees at Marquette University ★3392★

The Lying Stones of Marrakech: Penultimate Reflections in Natural History
Booklist's best science and technology books ★366★

Lyles Middle School
Outstanding secondary schools in Dallas, Texas ★4120★

Lynbrook High School
Outstanding secondary schools in Long Island, New York ★4165★

Lynch; Dennis
Top pay and benefits for the chief executive and top paid employees at the University of Denver ★3540★

Lynch; Leslie
All-USA Teacher Teams, Second Team, 2000 ★4400★

Lynch; Robert G.
Top pay and benefits for the chief executive and top paid employees at the University of Dallas ★3538★

Lynchburg College
Highest undergraduate tuition and fees at colleges and universities in Virginia ★1564★
Average faculty salaries for institutions of higher education in Virginia, 2000-01 ★3735★

Lyndon Johnson Middle School
Outstanding secondary schools in Albuquerque, New Mexico ★4080★

Lyndon State College
Undergraduate tuition and fees at colleges and universities in Vermont ★1563★
Average faculty salaries for institutions of higher education in Vermont, 2000-01 ★3734★

Lynn Classical High School
Outstanding urban public high schools in Metro Boston ★4261★

Lynn University
Highest undergraduate tuition and fees at colleges and universities in Florida ★1494★

Lynnville Public Library
Highest Hennen's American Public Library Ratings for libraries serving a population of 999 and under ★2691★

Lyon; B. J.
Top pay and benefits for the chief executive and top paid employees at University of Central Texas ★3589★

Lyon College
U.S. News & World Report's southern regional liberal arts colleges with the best student/faculty ratios, 2000-01 ★1368★
U.S. News & World Report's southern regional liberal arts colleges with the highest academic reputation scores, 2000-01 ★1369★
U.S. News & World Report's southern regional liberal arts colleges with the highest percentage of full-time faculty, 2000-01 ★1374★
U.S. News & World Report's southern regional liberal arts colleges with the highest proportion of classes having 20 students or less, 2000-01 ★1375★
U.S. News & World Report's southern regional liberal arts colleges with the highest proportion of freshmen in the top 25% of their high school class, 2000-01 ★1376★
U.S. News & World Report's top southern regional liberal arts colleges, 2000-01 ★1379★
U.S. News & World Report's best undergraduate fees among southern regional liberal arts colleges by discount tuition, 2000 ★1383★
Highest undergraduate tuition and fees at colleges and universities in Arkansas ★1484★
Average faculty salaries for institutions of higher education in Arkansas, 2000-01 ★3691★

Lyon Jr.; Thomas L.
Top pay and benefits for the chief executive and top paid employees at Rockhurst University ★3464★

Lyons; Donald
Top pay and benefits for the chief executive and top paid employees at Hampton University ★3323★

Lyons; Mary E.
Top pay and benefits for the chief executive and top paid employees at College of Saint Benedict ★3245★

Lyons Press
Small publishers with the highest sales growth between 1997 and 1999 ★3073★

Lyons Township High School, District 204
Illinois school districts with the most average years of teacher experience ★4012★

M

Macalester College
U.S. colleges and universities with a favorable surrounding town or city ★1013★
U.S. colleges and universities with a primarily non-religious student body ★1021★
Highest undergraduate tuition and fees at colleges and universities in Minnesota ★1520★
Private, 4-year undergraduate colleges and universities producing the most Ph.D.'s in all fields of study, 1990 ★2029★

Bachelor's institutions with the highest enrollment of foreign students, 1998-99 ★2492★
Institutions in the Worker Rights Consortium ★2913★
Private, 4-year undergraduate colleges and universities producing the most Ph.D.'s in political science and international relations, 1920-1990 ★3044★
Private, 4-year undergraduate colleges and universities producing the most Ph.D.'s in political science and international relations, 1981-1990 ★3045★
Average faculty salaries for institutions of higher education in Minnesota, 2000-01 ★3710★

Macaulay; David
Outstanding children's nonfiction books, 2000 ★330★

Macdonald; Cameron
Radcliffe Institute for Advanced Study fellowship recipients in the field of sociology, 2000-01 ★4346★

MacDonald; D.M.
Most cited authors in dermatology journals, 1981 to 1996 ★1870★

MacDowell-Boyer; Grace
All-USA College Academic First Team, 2001 ★2★

MacDowell; Michael
Top pay and benefits for the chief executive and top paid employees at College Misericordia ★3243★

Machado; Duarte
All-USA College Academic Third Team, 2001 ★4★

Machine Learning
Artificial intelligence journals by citation impact, 1981-99 ★94★
Artificial intelligence journals by citation impact, 1995-99 ★95★
Artificial intelligence journals by citation impact, 1999 ★96★
Artificial intelligence journals with the greatest impact measure, 1981-98 ★97★

Machine tool cutting operators
Occupations with the highest decline in employment, 1998-2008 ★2310★

Machine tool operator
Jobs considered the loneliest ★2244★

Machinist
Jobs considered the loneliest ★2244★

Macias; Anthony
Top pay and benefits for the chief executive and top paid employees at the College of Notre Dame in California ★3526★

Maciumas; Robert J.
Top pay and benefits for the chief executive and top paid employees at the University of Rochester ★3560★

Mack; Tracy
Booklist's best first novels for youths ★309★

Mackin, O.F.M.; Rev. Kevin E.
Top pay and benefits for the chief executive and top paid employees at Siena College ★3498★

MacLean; Brian D.
Most cited scholars in critical criminology ★1640★
Most-cited scholars in critical criminology publications ★1641★

MacLean; Richard
Top pay and benefits for the chief executive and top paid employees at Benedictine University ★3200★

MacLeod; Stephen
Top pay and benefits for the chief executive and top paid employees at Gordon College in Massachusetts ★3312★

Macmillan
Book publishers with the most citations (Class 4) ★2565★

Macon State College
Lowest undergraduate tuition and fees at public, 4-year or above colleges and universities ★1466★
Public 4-year institutions with the lowest tuition, 2000-01 ★1472★
Average faculty salaries for institutions of higher education in Georgia, 2000-01 ★3697★

Macro; Dennis C.
Top pay and benefits for the chief executive and top paid employees at Monmouth University in New Jersey ★3406★

Macy's East
Top recruiters for marketing jobs for 2000-01 bachelor's degree recipients ★684★
Top recruiters for hospitality/hotel/restaurant management jobs for 2000-01 bachelor's degree recipients ★2558★
Top recruiters for psychology jobs for 2000-01 bachelor's degree recipients ★3063★
Top recruiters for sociology jobs for 2000-01 bachelor's degree recipients ★4347★

Macy's West
Top recruiters for biology/biological science jobs for 2000-01 bachelor's degree recipients ★198★
Top recruiters for biology/biological science jobs for 2000-01 master's degree recipients ★203★
Top recruiters for psychology jobs for 2000-01 bachelor's degree recipients ★3063★
Top recruiters for sociology jobs for 2000-01 bachelor's degree recipients ★4347★
Top recruiters for textiles/apparel jobs for 2000-01 bachelor's degree recipients ★4434★

Mad River Middle School
Outstanding secondary schools in Dayton-Springfield, Ohio ★4122★

Madame Butterfly
Most frequently produced operas in North America, 1999-2000 ★2905★

Maddox; Ronald
Top pay and benefits for the chief executive and top paid employees at Campbell University ★3218★

Made for Each Other
Publishers Weekly Off-the-Cuff Awards winners for books for adults, not for children, 2000 ★362★

Madeira High School
Outstanding secondary schools in Cincinnati, Ohio-Kentucky-Indiana ★4112★

Madison Elementary School
Illinois suburban elementary schools with the highest ISAT scores in reading and math ★18★

Madison, WI
Best college towns to live in ★3076★

Madisonville Community College
Lowest undergraduate tuition and fees at colleges and universities in Kentucky ★1509★

Madlenka
Outstanding children's picture books, 2000 ★331★
Smithsonian's best books for children ages 1 to 6 ★363★

Madonna High School
Outstanding secondary schools in Chicago, Illinois ★4110★

Madonna; Paul K.
Top pay and benefits for the chief executive and top paid employees at Sacred Heart University in Connecticut ★3467★

Madonna University
U.S. colleges and universities awarding the most education master's degrees to Asian Americans ★1770★
Average faculty salaries for institutions of higher education in Michigan, 2000-01 ★3709★

Maestro: Greenspan's Fed and the American Boom
Library Journal's most notable biography books, 2000 ★249★

Magee; Michael
All-America boys' high school soccer team forwards, 2001 ★166★

The Magic of M.C. Escher
Most notable nonfiction books for reluctant young adult readers, 2001 ★323★

Magic Terror: Seven Tales
Booklist's most recommended science fiction/fantasy books ★232★

Magida; David
Top pay and benefits for the chief executive and top paid employees at Norwich University in Vermont ★3424★

Magnet Middle School
Outstanding secondary schools in Tucson, Arizona ★4243★

Magnolia Bible College
Highest undergraduate tuition and fees at colleges and universities in Mississippi ★1522★

Magnus Holdings
Best small companies worldwide ★384★

Maguire; John
Top pay and benefits for the chief executive and top paid employees at Claremont Graduate University ★3235★

Maguire, Pastore, & Flanagan
Most cited works in academic literature dealing with corrections ★1643★

Mahaffey Middle School
Outstanding secondary schools in Clarkesville-Hoplinsville, Tennessee-Kentucky ★4113★

Mahan; Robert A.
Top pay and benefits for the chief executive and top paid employees at Manhattan College ★3387★

Maharishi University of Management
Highest undergraduate tuition and fees at colleges and universities in Iowa ★1504★

Maher; Julianne
Top pay and benefits for the chief executive and top paid employees at Elon College ★3285★

Mahler; Gregory S.
Top pay and benefits for the chief executive and top paid employees at Kalamazoo College ★3358★

Mahmood; Ausif
Top pay and benefits for the chief executive and top paid employees at University of Bridgeport ★3588★

Mahon; Malachy
Top pay and benefits for the chief executive and top paid employees at Hofstra University ★3335★

Mahoney; Sally
  Top pay and benefits for the chief executive and top paid employees at Our Lady of the Lake University ★3434★
Maid
  Jobs with the highest unemployment ★2256★
  Jobs with the worst income scores ★2261★
  Most desirable jobs in personal services ★2275★
Maier; David
  All-America boys' high school soccer team forwards, 2001 ★166★
Mail-Well
  Fortune's highest ranked printing companies, 2000 ★487★
Mailer; Kathleen
  Top pay and benefits for the chief executive and top paid employees at Marian College of Fond Du Lac ★3389★
Mailer; Norman
  Best U.S. works of journalism in the 20th century ★2769★
Maine
  Mean composite ACT scores by state, 2000 ★895★
  Mean math SAT scores by state, 2000 ★900★
  Mean verbal SAT scores by state, 2000 ★903★
  States allocating the smallest amount of state tax appropriations for higher education, 2000-01 ★1305★
  Total doctorate recipients by state, 1999 ★2054★
  State grades for affordability of higher education for minority students, 2000 ★2883★
  State grades for benefits state receives for educating its minority students, 2000 ★2884★
  State grades for completion of higher education by minority students, 2000 ★2885★
  State grades for participation of minority students in higher education, 2000 ★2886★
  State grades for preparing minority students for higher education, 2000 ★2887★
  States with the best college tuition savings plans ★4438★
Maine, Augusta; University of
  U.S. News & World Report's northern regional liberal arts colleges with students least in debt, 1999 ★1351★
  Lowest undergraduate tuition and fees at colleges and universities in Maine ★1513★
  Average faculty salaries for institutions of higher education in Maine, 2000-01 ★3706★
Maine College of Art
  Highest undergraduate tuition and fees at colleges and universities in Maine ★1512★
Maine, Farmington; University of
  U.S. News & World Report's northern regional liberal arts colleges with the highest percentage of full-time faculty, 2000-01 ★1360★
  U.S. News & World Report's northern regional liberal arts colleges with the lowest acceptance rates, 2000-01 ★1362★
  U.S. News & World Report's top public northern regional liberal arts colleges, 2000-01 ★1364★
  Average faculty salaries for institutions of higher education in Maine, 2000-01 ★3706★
Maine, Fort Kent; University of
  Lowest undergraduate tuition and fees at colleges and universities in Maine ★1513★
  Average faculty salaries for institutions of higher education in Maine, 2000-01 ★3706★

Maine, Manchias; University of
  Average faculty salaries for institutions of higher education in Maine, 2000-01 ★3706★
Maine Maritime Academy
  State appropriations for Maine's institutions of higher education, 2000-01 ★1272★
Maine, Presque Isle; University of
  Lowest undergraduate tuition and fees at colleges and universities in Maine ★1513★
  Average faculty salaries for institutions of higher education in Maine, 2000-01 ★3706★
Maine Public Broadcasting Corp.
  State appropriations for Maine's institutions of higher education, 2000-01 ★1272★
Maine State Music Theater
  Most selective internships in the U.S., 2001 ★2610★
Maine System; University of
  State appropriations for Maine's institutions of higher education, 2000-01 ★1272★
Maine Technical College System
  State appropriations for Maine's institutions of higher education, 2000-01 ★1272★
Maine Township High School West
  Outstanding secondary schools in Chicago, Illinois ★4110★
Maine; University of
  Four-year institutions with the most drug arrests reported, 1999 ★705★
  Average faculty salaries for institutions of higher education in Maine, 2000-01 ★3706★
Maine West High School
  Outstanding suburban public high schools in Metro Chicago ★4256★
Mainland; College of the
  Lowest undergraduate tuition and fees at colleges and universities in Texas ★1561★
  Average faculty salaries for institutions of higher education in Texas, 2000-01 ★3731★
Mainland High School
  Outstanding secondary schools in Daytona Beach, Florida ★4123★
Mainland Regional High School
  Outstanding secondary schools in Atlantic-Cape May, New Jersey ★4088★
Maintenance repairers, general utility
  Projected employment growth for selected occupations that require long-term on-the-job training, 1998-2008 ★2320★
Makdisi; John
  Top pay and benefits for the chief executive and top paid employees at Loyola University New Orleans ★3381★
Makovsky & Company
  Most selective internships in the U.S., 2001 ★2610★
Maksin; Beverly
  Top pay and benefits for the chief executive and top paid employees at the University of Hartford ★3544★
Malaysia
  Percentage of enrollment at private institutions of higher education, by country, 1998 ★858★
  Percentage of enrollment at public institutions of higher education, by country, 1998 ★859★
  Countries of origin for non-U.S. citizens awarded doctorates at U.S. colleges and universities, 1999 ★1901★
Malcolm X
  Most important African Americans in the twentieth century ★219★
  Most influential African Americans in politics and civil rights ★3040★

Malcolm X College
  Fall enrollment at Chicago-area city colleges, by minority percentages, 1999 ★865★
Malden Catholic High School
  Outstanding Catholic high schools in Metro Boston ★4073★
Malevich; Kazimir
  Highly influential artists of the 20th century ★76★
Malhotra; Amit
  All-USA College Academic Third Team, 2001 ★4★
Malicky; Neal
  Top pay and benefits for the chief executive and top paid employees at Baldwin-Wallace College ★3189★
Mallinckrodt
  Fortune's highest ranked medical products and equipment companies, 2000 ★474★
Mallory; Frank
  Top pay and benefits for the chief executive and top paid employees at Bryn Mawr College ★3212★
Malloy, C.S.C.; Rev. Edward A.
  Top pay and benefits for the chief executive and top paid employees at the University of Notre Dame ★3554★
Malone College
  Average faculty salaries for institutions of higher education in Ohio, 2000-01 ★3722★
Maloney; Daniel
  Top pay and benefits for the chief executive and top paid employees at Saint Mary's University of Minnesota ★3482★
Malpass; Scott C.
  Top pay and benefits for the chief executive and top paid employees at the University of Notre Dame ★3554★
Malthus; Thomas
  Most cited economists ★2185★
Malveaux; Floyd
  Top pay and benefits for the chief executive and top paid employees at Howard University ★3343★
Mammalabilia
  Publishers Weekly Off-the-Cuff Awards winner for best book of poetry, 2000 ★337★
  Smithsonian's best books for children ages 6 to 10 ★364★
Man
  Anthropology journals by citation impact, 1991-98 ★63★
  Anthropology journals by citation impact, 1994-98 ★64★
Man; Bryan
  Top pay and benefits for the chief executive and top paid employees at the Chaminade University of Honolulu ★3524★
Man Ray
  Highly influential artists of the 20th century ★76★
The Man That Corrupted Hadleyburg
  Outstanding videos for library collections, 2000 ★2892★
Management analysts
  Occupations with the highest number of self-employed workers, 1998 ★2311★
  Projected employment growth for selected occupations that require a bachelor's degree or more, 1998-2008 ★2317★
Management Communication Quarterly
  Most cited business serials in technical communication journals from 1988 to 1997 ★4417★

MANAGEMENT

Management information systems/ business data processing
- Business and management doctorates awarded at U.S. colleges and universities, by subfield, 1999 ★1888★
- Gender breakdown of business and management doctorate recipients, by subfield, 1999 ★1928★

Management International Review
- Business journals receiving the most citations in five core journals, 1995-97 ★691★

Management and public relations
- Employment growth percentages for selected industries, 1998-2000 ★2294★
- Industries with the highest percentage of projected employment growth from 1998 through 2008 ★2305★

Management Science
- Top management journals ★546★
- Top management journals by core impact ★547★
- Top ranked AACSB publications ★2186★
- Journals and proceedings with the most citations (Class 1) ★2567★
- Most cited business serials in technical communication journals from 1988 to 1997 ★4417★

Managerial and professional specialty
- Internet use by major occupational group, 1998 ★2587★

Managing Six Sigma
- *Library Journal*'s most notable management books, 2000 ★265★

Manche; Edward
- Top pay and benefits for the chief executive and top paid employees at Stanford University ★3510★

Manchester College
- *U.S. News & World Report*'s midwestern regional liberal arts colleges with the highest percentage of full-time faculty, 2000-01 ★1346★
- *U.S. News & World Report*'s best undergraduate fees among midwestern regional liberal arts colleges by discount tuition, 2000 ★1380★
- Average faculty salaries for institutions of higher education in Indiana, 2000-01 ★3701★

Manchester Community-Technical College
- Lowest undergraduate tuition and fees at colleges and universities in Connecticut ★1491★

Mandalay Resort Group
- *Fortune*'s highest ranked hotels, casinos and resorts, 2000 ★470★

Manhattan
- U.S. counties with the highest international enrollment, 1999-2000 ★2505★

Manhattan Beach Intermediate School
- Outstanding secondary schools in Los Angeles-Long Beach, California ★4167★

Manhattan Center for Science & Mathematics
- Outstanding urban public high schools in Metro New York ★4265★

Manhattan College
- Division I NCAA colleges with that graduated all of their African American male basketball players, 1990-91 to 1993-94 ★927★
- Division I NCAA colleges that graduated more than 80% of their African American male athletes, 1990-91 to 1993-94 ★929★
- Division I NCAA colleges with the highest graduation rates for male athletes, 1990-91 to 1993-94 ★934★
- Division I NCAA colleges with the highest graduation rates for male basketball players, 1990-91 to 1993-94 ★935★
- *U.S. News & World Report*'s northern regional universities with the highest average graduation rates, 2000-01 ★1419★
- Private, 4-year undergraduate colleges and universities producing the most Ph.D.'s in the computer sciences, 1920-1990 ★1595★
- Private, 4-year undergraduate colleges and universities producing the most Ph.D.'s in the computer sciences, 1981-1990 ★1596★
- *U.S. News & World Report*'s undergraduate engineering programs with the best chemical departments, 2000-01 ★2344★
- Private, 4-year undergraduate colleges and universities producing the most Ph.D.'s in mathematics, 1920-1990 ★2776★
- Private, 4-year undergraduate colleges and universities producing the most Ph.D.'s in physics and astronomy, 1920-1990 ★2949★
- Average faculty salaries for institutions of higher education in New York, 2000-01 ★3719★
- Private, 4-year undergraduate colleges and universities producing the most Ph.D.'s in the sciences, 1920-1990 ★4294★

Manhattan Eye, Ear and Throat Hospital
- Top ophthalmology hospitals in the U.S., 2000 ★2796★

Manhattan, NY
- Counties with the highest per capita income ★2561★

Manhattan Theater Club
- Most selective internships in the U.S., 2001 ★2610★

Maniaci; Vincent M.
- Top pay and benefits for the chief executive and top paid employees at Bellarmine University ★3196★

Manifold; James H.
- Top pay and benefits for the chief executive and top paid employees at Scripps College ★3493★

Manitoba
- Canadian provinces by teaching days per year ★4058★

Manitoba; University of
- Canadian medical/doctoral universities by alumni support, 2000 ★1172★
- Canadian medical/doctoral universities by award-winning faculty members, 2000 ★1173★
- Canadian medical/doctoral universities by class size at the first- and second-year level, 2000 ★1174★
- Canadian medical/doctoral universities by class size at the third- and forth-year level, 2000 ★1175★
- Canadian medical/doctoral universities by classes taught by tenured faculty, 2000 ★1176★
- Canadian medical/doctoral universities by faculty members with Ph.D.'s, 2000 ★1177★
- Canadian medical/doctoral universities by international graduate students, 2000 ★1178★
- Canadian medical/doctoral universities by library acquisitions, 2000 ★1179★
- Canadian medical/doctoral universities by library expenses, 2000 ★1180★
- Canadian medical/doctoral universities by library holdings, 2000 ★1181★
- Canadian medical/doctoral universities by library holdings per student, 2000 ★1182★
- Canadian medical/doctoral universities by medical/science grants per faculty member, 2000 ★1184★
- Canadian medical/doctoral universities by operating budget per student, 2000 ★1185★
- Canadian medical/doctoral universities by percentage of operating budget allocated to scholarships, 2000 ★1186★
- Canadian medical/doctoral universities by percentage of operating budget allocated to student services, 2000 ★1187★
- Canadian medical/doctoral universities by reputation, 2000 ★1188★
- Canadian medical/doctoral universities by social science/humanities grants per faculty member, 2000 ★1189★
- Canadian medical/doctoral universities by students from out of province, 2000 ★1190★
- Canadian medical/doctoral universities by students winning national awards, 2000 ★1191★
- Canadian universities chosen as being value added, 2000 ★1216★
- Top Canadian medical/doctoral universities, 2000 ★1221★

Mankato State University
- U.S. colleges and universities awarding the most English language/literature/letters master's degrees to Asian Americans ★1774★

Mankekar; Purnima
- Radcliffe Institute for Advanced Study fellowship recipients in the field of anthropology, 2000-01 ★60★

Manley; Audrey F.
- Top pay and benefits for the chief executive and top paid employees at Spelman College ★3507★

Manlius Library
- Highest Hennen's American Public Library Ratings for libraries serving a population of 5,000 to 9,999 ★2694★

Mann; D.
- Top assistant professor economists at elite liberal arts colleges, 1975-94 ★2173★

Mannheim-Heidelberg
- Cities with the highest productivity of paper in the discipline of hematology, 1994-96 ★2870★

Manning; Brooke
- All-USA College Academic Second Team, 2001 ★3★

Manning; Danny
- Division I NCAA men's basketball players with the highest tournament scores ★154★

Manning; Kevin
- Top pay and benefits for the chief executive and top paid employees at Immaculata College ★3348★

Manning; Peter K.
- Most-cited scholars in police studies articles/research notes ★2624★

Manor Care
- *Business Week*'s best performing companies with the highest 1-year shareholder returns ★415★

Manos; Steven
- Top pay and benefits for the chief executive and top paid employees at Tufts University ★3580★

Manpower
- *Fortune*'s highest ranked temporary help companies, 2000 ★500★

Mansfield High School
 Outstanding secondary schools in Boston, Massachusetts-New Hampshire ★4100★

Mansfield; Joseph
 Top pay and benefits for the chief executive and top paid employees at Loyola University New Orleans ★3381★

Mansfield Middle School
 Outstanding secondary schools in Hartford, Connecticut ★4147★

Mansfield; Stephen S.
 Top pay and benefits for the chief executive and top paid employees at Virginia Wesleyan College ★3596★

Mansfield University
 Average faculty salaries for institutions of higher education in Pennsylvania, 2000-01 ★3725★

Manufacturing
 Employment change projections by major industry division from 1998 to 2008 ★2287★
 Employment projections by major industry division for 2008 ★2290★
 Spending for E-marketplace services, by industry, 2001 ★4430★

Manufacturing, construction, and mining
 Internet use by industry, 1998 ★2586★

Many Stones
 Most notable fiction books for young adults, 2001 ★322★
 Outstanding books for older readers, 2000 ★327★

Maple Woods Community College
 Lowest undergraduate tuition and fees at colleges and universities in Missouri ★1525★
 Average faculty salaries for institutions of higher education without academic ranks in Missouri, 2000-01 ★3755★

Mapp; Justin
 All-America boys' high school soccer team midfielders, 2001 ★168★

Mapping Our World
 Booklist's most recommended geography series for young people, 2000 ★313★

Marathon Oil
 Top recruiters for environmental engineering jobs for 2000-01 bachelor's degree recipients ★2357★
 Top recruiters for petroleum engineering jobs for 2000-01 bachelor's degree recipients ★2441★
 Top recruiters for geology/geophysics jobs for 2000-01 bachelor's degree recipients ★2522★

Marblehead Middle School
 Outstanding secondary schools in Boston, Massachusetts-New Hampshire ★4100★

Marcel Proust
 Outstanding biography books, 2000 ★288★

Marcell; David W.
 Top pay and benefits for the chief executive and top paid employees at the Sage Colleges in New York ★3536★

March; J. G.
 Authors with the most citations among authors published in *American Political Science Review*, 1974-94 ★3048★

March; James G.
 Most frequently downloaded *American Political Science Review* articles ★3039★

March; Tamar
 Top pay and benefits for the chief executive and top paid employees at Radcliffe College ★3450★

Marchionini; Gary
 Library and information science faculty with the most citations to journal articles, 1993-1998 ★2710★

Marcoccia; Louis G.
 Top pay and benefits for the chief executive and top paid employees at Syracuse University ★3516★

Marconi
 Business Week's best companies in Britain ★389★

Marcotte; Paul J.
 Top pay and benefits for the chief executive and top paid employees at the University of Pennsylvania ★3555★

Marcus; Barbara A.
 Highest ranking women at the top public companies, 2000 ★4452★

Marcus High School
 Outstanding secondary schools in Dallas, Texas ★4120★

Marengo Community High School, District 154
 Illinois school districts spending the least for high school education 1997-98 ★4008★

Margaret Mead Junior High School
 Outstanding secondary schools in Chicago, Illinois ★4110★

Margenthaler; Charles R.
 Top pay and benefits for the chief executive and top paid employees at Loyola College in Maryland ★3379★

Margulies; Martin B.
 Top pay and benefits for the chief executive and top paid employees at Quinnipiac University ★3449★

Marian Catholic High School
 Outstanding Catholic high schools in Metro Chicago ★4074★
 Outstanding secondary schools in Chicago, Illinois ★4110★

Marian College of Fond du Lac
 Average faculty salaries for institutions of higher education in Wisconsin, 2000-01 ★3738★

Marian High School
 Outstanding secondary schools in Omaha, Nebraska-Iowa ★4198★

Maricopa County Community College
 Average faculty salaries for institutions of higher education without academic ranks in Arizona, 2000-01 ★3741★

Maricopa County Community College District
 Community colleges receiving the most gifts, 1999-2000 ★1239★

Marie Antoinette: The Last Queen of France
 Outstanding biography books, 2000 ★288★

Marie Murphy Middle School
 Illinois schools with the highest 7th grade science scores ★17★

Marietta College
 U.S. News & World Report's midwestern regional liberal arts colleges with the best student/faculty ratios, 2000-01 ★1339★
 U.S. News & World Report's midwestern regional liberal arts colleges with the highest acceptance rates, 2000-01 ★1341★
 U.S. News & World Report's midwestern regional liberal arts colleges with the highest proportion of classes having 20 students or less, 2000-01 ★1347★
 Average faculty salaries for institutions of higher education in Ohio, 2000-01 ★3722★

Marik; Margaret
 Top pay and benefits for the chief executive and top paid employees at Heritage College ★3332★

Marin, CA
 Counties with the highest per capita income ★2561★

Marin Kentfield; College of
 Lowest undergraduate tuition and fees at public 2-year colleges and universities ★1465★

Marine Academy
 Outstanding secondary schools in Monmouth-Ocean, New Jersey ★4183★

Marine Biology
 Marine and freshwater biology journals with the greatest impact measure, 1981-98 ★196★

Marine Biology Letters
 Marine and freshwater biology journals with the greatest impact measure, 1981-98 ★196★

Marine Chemistry
 Oceanography journals by citation impact, 1995-99 ★2140★
 Oceanography journals by citation impact, 1999 ★2141★

Marine Ecology-Progress
 Marine and freshwater biology journals with the greatest impact measure, 1981-98 ★196★
 Marine and freshwater biology journals with the greatest impact measure, 1994-98 ★197★

Marine sciences
 Earth, atmosphere, and marine science doctorates awarded at U.S. colleges and universities, by subfield, 1999 ★1909★
 Gender breakdown of earth, atmosphere, and marine science doctorate recipients, by subfield, 1999 ★1932★

Marinelli; Noe A.
 Top pay and benefits for the chief executive and top paid employees at Rockford College in Illinois ★3463★

Marion Military Institute
 Highest undergraduate tuition and fees at colleges and universities in Alabama ★1479★

Marion; Paul
 Top pay and benefits for the chief executive and top paid employees at Franklin College of Indiana ★3297★

Marist College
 U.S. News & World Report's northern regional universities with the highest freshmen retention rates, 2000-01 ★1420★
 U.S. News & World Report's northern regional universities with the lowest acceptance rates, 2000-01 ★1424★
 Average faculty salaries for institutions of higher education in New York, 2000-01 ★3719★

Maritime College
 Average faculty salaries for institutions of higher education in New York, 2000-01 ★3719★

Mark IV Industries
 Fortune's highest ranked rubber and plastic products companies, 2000 ★492★

Market; L. Wayne
 Top pay and benefits for the chief executive and top paid employees at Hollins University ★3336★

MARKET

Market research analyst
  Jobs with the best physical demands scores ★2250★
  Most desirable jobs in business/finance ★2270★

Marketing
  Top bachelor's and master's degree majors in demand for employment, 2001 ★2323★
  Top bachelor's degree majors in demand for employment, 2001 ★2324★
  Expected starting salaries of 2000-01 bachelor's degree recipients, by specific major ★3131★

Marketing, advertising, and public relations manager
  Occupations with the highest average annual salaries for college graduates, 1998 ★3132★

Marketing management
  Business and management doctorates awarded at U.S. colleges and universities, by subfield, 1999 ★1888★
  Gender breakdown of business and management doctorate recipients, by subfield, 1999 ★1928★
  Average starting salaries for college graduates, by field, 2000 ★3129★

Marketing and sales
  Overall median salary for full-time chemists with a bachelor's degree, by work function, 2000 ★790★
  Overall median salary for full-time chemists with a doctoral degree, by work function, 2000 ★803★
  Overall median salary for full-time chemists with a master's degree, by work function, 2000 ★804★
  College graduates in the labor force, by occupational group, 1998 ★926★
  Projected change in employment of college graduates, by occupational group, from 1998 to 2008 ★965★
  Projected employment of college graduates, by occupational group, 2008 ★966★
  Employment change projections by major occupational group from 1998 to 2008 ★2288★
  Employment projections by major occupational group for 2008 ★2291★
  Employment in college-level jobs, by occupational group, 2006 ★2295★
  Industries in Illinois with the highest projected worker increase through 2006 ★2304★
  Percentages for projected employment growth by occupational group, 1998-2008 ★2314★
  Projected employment growth by occupational group, 1998-2008 ★2316★

Marketing and sales manager
  Monster.com's most searched job listings ★2308★

Marketing and sales worker supervisors
  Occupations with the highest number of self-employed workers, 1998 ★2311★
  Occupations with the largest projected employment growth, 1998-2008 ★2312★
  Projected employment growth for selected occupations that require long-term on-the-job training, 1998-2008 ★2320★

Marketing Science
  Business journals by citation impact, 1981-98 ★688★
  Business journals by citation impact, 1994-98 ★689★
  Business journals by citation impact, 1998 ★690★

Markley; Nelson G.
  Top pay and benefits for the chief executive and top paid employees at Lehigh University ★3368★

Marks Jr.; Thomas
  Top pay and benefits for the chief executive and top paid employees at Stetson University ★3511★

Marks; Tobin J.
  American Chemical Society 2001 award winners (Group 3) ★753★

Markwart; Alan E.
  Most-cited scholars in *Canadian Journal of Criminology* ★1638★

Marlboro College
  U.S. colleges and universities with the best on-campus housing facilities ★1032★
  U.S. News & World Report's national liberal arts colleges with the highest proportion of classes with less than 20 students, 2000-01 ★1335★
  Undergraduate tuition and fees at colleges and universities in Vermont ★1563★

Marmon Group
  Largest private companies, 2000 ★523★

Maroon; Joseph
  Top pay and benefits for the chief executive and top paid employees at the Allegheny University of the Health Sciences ★3520★

Marquette University
  U.S. catholic universities with the highest enrollment, 1999 ★864★
  Highest undergraduate tuition and fees at colleges and universities in Wisconsin ★1570★
  U.S. colleges and universities awarding the most health professions and related sciences first professional degrees to Native Americans ★1851★
  Average faculty salaries for institutions of higher education in Wisconsin, 2000-01 ★3738★

Marriott International
  Fortune's highest ranked hotels, casinos and resorts, 2000 ★470★
  Top leisure time industries in Standard & Poor's 500, 2001 ★545★
  Top recruiters for accounting jobs for 2000-01 bachelor's degree recipients ★580★
  Top recruiters for finance/banking jobs for 2000-01 master's degree recipients ★664★
  Top recruiters for hospitality/hotel/restaurant management jobs for 2000-01 bachelor's degree recipients ★2558★
  Best companies for working mothers in terms of overall work/life support ★4451★

Marron; Joseph M.
  Top pay and benefits for the chief executive and top paid employees at United States International University ★3587★

Mars
  Largest private companies, 2000 ★523★

Mars Hill Bible School
  Outstanding secondary schools in Florence, Alabama ★4132★

Mars Hill College
  Average faculty salaries for institutions of higher education in North Carolina, 2000-01 ★3720★

Marseille; Myrna S.
  Top pay and benefits for the chief executive and top paid employees at Concordia University in Illinois ★3253★

Marsh & McLennan
  Top nonbank financial companies in Standard & Poor's 500, 2001 ★550★

Marsh Elementary School
  Illinois elementary schools chosen to be 'demonstration sites' for struggling schools ★4006★

Marshall; Alfred
  Most cited economists ★2185★

Marshall; Chad
  All-America boys' high school soccer team defenders, 2001 ★165★

Marshall; Dale Rogers
  Top pay and benefits for the chief executive and top paid employees at Wheaton College in Massachusetts ★3621★

Marshall; Thurgood
  Most important African Americans in the twentieth century ★219★
  Most influential African Americans in politics and civil rights ★3040★

Marshall University
  State appropriations for West Virginia's institutions of higher education, 2000-01 ★1301★
  Average faculty salaries for institutions of higher education in West Virginia, 2000-01 ★3737★

Martha Stewart Living
  Business Week's top companies in terms of sales growth, 2000 ★432★

Martha Stewart Living Omnimedia
  Top companies in terms of growth, 2000 ★534★

Martin; Agnes
  Best living artists ★73★

Martin; Ann M.
  Outstanding children's fiction books, 2000 ★329★

Martin; B. J.
  Top pay and benefits for the chief executive and top paid employees at William Carey College ★3629★

Martin Community College
  Average faculty salaries for institutions of higher education without academic ranks in North Carolina, 2000-01 ★3761★

Martin; Edward E.
  Top pay and benefits for the chief executive and top paid employees at the University of Mary Hardin-Baylor ★3549★

Martin; George
  Top pay and benefits for the chief executive and top paid employees at Saint Peter's College ★3485★

Martin; Glenn
  Top pay and benefits for the chief executive and top paid employees at Indiana Wesleyan University ★3349★

Martin; Ingle
  All-American boy's high school football quarterbacks, 2000 ★184★

Martin; Joseph B.
  Top pay and benefits for the chief executive and top paid employees at Harvard University ★3327★

Martin; Judy
  Top pay and benefits for the chief executive and top paid employees at Drury University ★3275★

Martin; Kira
  All-USA College Academic First Team, 2001 ★2★

Martin; Lawrence H.
  Top pay and benefits for the chief executive and top paid employees at Hampden-Sydney College ★3321★

Martin Luther King: A Concise Biography
Library Journal's best nonfiction audiobooks, 2000 ★243★

Martin Luther King Jr. Senior High School
Outstanding urban public high schools in Metro Detroit ★4264★

Martin Luther King Middle School
Outstanding secondary schools in Washington, District of Columbia-Maryland-Virginia-West Virginia ★4249★

Martin Marietta Materials
Fortune's highest ranked mining and crude oil companies, 2000 ★477★

Martin; Michael
Top pay and benefits for the chief executive and top paid employees at Fordham University ★3295★

Martin; Roger H.
Top pay and benefits for the chief executive and top paid employees at Randolph-Macon College ★3451★

Martin; Scott
All-USA College Academic Third Team, 2001 ★4★

Martin University
U.S. colleges and universities awarding the most psychology master's degrees to African Americans ★1797★

Martin; William Bryan
Top pay and benefits for the chief executive and top paid employees at Franklin College of Indiana ★3297★

Marx; Karl
Most cited economists ★2185★

Mary Baldwin College
U.S. News & World Report's southern regional liberal arts colleges with the best student/faculty ratios, 2000-01 ★1368★
U.S. News & World Report's southern regional liberal arts colleges with the highest academic reputation scores, 2000-01 ★1369★
U.S. News & World Report's southern regional liberal arts colleges with the highest acceptance rates, 2000-01 ★1370★
U.S. News & World Report's southern regional liberal arts colleges with the highest alumni giving rates, 2000-01 ★1371★
U.S. News & World Report's southern regional liberal arts colleges with the highest graduation rates, 2000-01 ★1373★
U.S. News & World Report's top southern regional liberal arts colleges, 2000-01 ★1379★
Women's colleges granting physics bachelor's degrees, 2000 ★2982★
Average faculty salaries for institutions of higher education in Virginia, 2000-01 ★3735★

Mary Cassatt: American Impressionist
Most notable children's videos, 2001 ★2889★

Mary Cotton Public Library
Highest Hennen's American Public Library Ratings for libraries serving a population of 1,000 to 2,499 ★2692★

Mary Holmes College
Highest undergraduate tuition and fees at colleges and universities in Mississippi ★1522★
Historically black colleges and universities with major improvements in student loan default rates, 1998 ★2737★

Mary; University of
Highest undergraduate tuition and fees at colleges and universities in North Dakota ★1541★

Mary Washington College
State appropriations for Virginia's institutions of higher education, 2000-01 ★1299★
U.S. News & World Report's southern regional universities with the best academic reputation scores, 2000-01 ★1433★
U.S. News & World Report's southern regional universities with the best alumni giving rates, 2000-01 ★1434★
U.S. News & World Report's southern regional universities with the highest freshmen retention rates, 2000-01 ★1437★
U.S. News & World Report's southern regional universities with the highest graduation rates, 2000-01 ★1438★
U.S. News & World Report's southern regional universities with the highest percentage of freshmen in the top 25% of their high school class, 2000-01 ★1439★
U.S. News & World Report's southern regional universities with the highest percentage of full-time faculty, 2000-01 ★1440★
U.S. News & World Report's southern regional universities with the lowest acceptance rates, 2000-01 ★1442★
U.S. News & World Report's top public southern regional universities, 2000-01 ★1443★
U.S. News & World Report's top southern regional universities, 2000-01 ★1444★
Fiske Guide's best buys for public colleges and universities, 2001 ★1460★
Institutions with the most female physics bachelor's recipients, 1994-1998 ★2959★
U.S. institutions with more than 40% female bachelor's graduates in their physics departments, 1994-98 ★2977★
Average faculty salaries for institutions of higher education in Virginia, 2000-01 ★3735★

Marygrove College
Traditionally white institutions awarding the most master's degrees to African Americans ★1755★
U.S. colleges and universities awarding the most education master's degrees to African Americans ★1769★

Maryland
Mean composite ACT scores by state, 2000 ★895★
Mean math SAT scores by state, 2000 ★900★
Mean verbal SAT scores by state, 2000 ★903★
States with the highest percentage increase in appropriations for higher education, 2000-01 ★1308★
Total doctorate recipients by state, 1999 ★2054★
State grades for affordability of higher education for minority students, 2000 ★2883★
State grades for benefits state receives for educating its minority students, 2000 ★2884★
State grades for completion of higher education by minority students, 2000 ★2885★
State grades for participation of minority students in higher education, 2000 ★2886★
State grades for preparing minority students for higher education, 2000 ★2887★
States with the highest per capita income ★3123★
States with the highest average enrollment in public elementary schools ★4032★
States with the highest average enrollment in public secondary schools ★4033★
States with the largest average class size ★4071★

Maryland, Baltimore; University of
U.S. universities with the greatest impact in biotechnology and applied microbiology, 1995-99 ★216★
U.S. college campuses with more than 5,000 students reporting murders or manslaughters, 1998 ★729★
U.S. colleges and universities with a diverse student body ★1012★
U.S. colleges and universities with the least accessible instructors ★1036★
Total baccalaureate computer and information science degrees awarded to African Americans from U.S. colleges and universities, 1997-98 ★1691★
Traditionally white institutions awarding the most first professional degrees to African Americans ★1842★
U.S. colleges and universities awarding the most first professional degrees to African Americans ★1843★
U.S. colleges and universities awarding the most first professional degrees to Asian Americans ★1844★
U.S. colleges and universities awarding the most health professions and related sciences first professional degrees to African Americans ★1847★
U.S. colleges and universities awarding the most health professions and related sciences first professional degrees to Asian Americans ★1848★
U.S. colleges and universities awarding the most health professions and related sciences first professional degrees to minorities ★1850★
U.S. colleges and universities awarding the most law and legal studies first professional degrees to African Americans ★1852★
Average faculty salaries for institutions of higher education in Maryland, 2000-01 ★3707★

Maryland, College Park; University of
U.S. universities publishing the most papers in the field of artificial intelligence, 1995-99 ★100★
Four-year public institutions enrolling the highest number of students from the District of Columbia, 1998-99 ★855★
U.S. universities publishing the most papers in the field of computer science, 1994-98 ★1591★
Total baccalaureate biology/life sciences degrees awarded to African Americans from U.S. colleges and universities, 1997-98 ★1679★
Total baccalaureate computer and information science degrees awarded to Asian Americans from U.S. colleges and universities, 1997-98 ★1692★
Total baccalaureate degrees awarded to African Americans from traditionally white institutions, 1997-98 ★1698★
Total baccalaureate English language, literature, and letters degrees awarded to African Americans from U.S. colleges and universities, 1997-98 ★1716★
Total baccalaureate social sciences and history degrees awarded to African Americans from U.S. colleges and universities, 1997-98 ★1741★
Traditionally white institutions awarding the most master's degrees to African Americans ★1755★

MARYLAND

Maryland
- U.S. colleges and universities awarding the most communications master's degrees to African Americans ★1763★
- U.S. colleges and universities awarding the most mathematics master's degrees to African Americans ★1790★
- U.S. institutions awarding the most baccalaureate degrees to African Americans in agribusiness and production, 1998 ★1813★
- U.S. colleges and universities awarding the most doctoral degrees to Hispanic Americans from 1995 to 1999 ★2094★
- U.S. colleges and universities awarding the most doctorate degrees to Asian Americans ★2096★
- U.S. colleges and universities awarding the most doctorates in physical sciences, mathematics, and computer sciences, 1999 ★2105★
- U.S. colleges and universities awarding the most doctorates in social sciences, 1999 ★2107★
- Top oceanography research-doctorate programs as evaluated by the National Research Council ★2153★
- U.S. universities with the greatest impact in education, 1993-97 ★2220★
- U.S. universities with the highest concentrations in artificial intelligence, 1992-96 ★2402★
- U.S. universities publishing the most papers in the field of astrophysics, 1995-99 ★2978★
- Average faculty salaries for institutions of higher education in Maryland, 2000-01 ★3707★
- Academics' choices for best counseling/personnel services graduate programs, 2001 ★4379★
- Academics' choices for best education policy graduate programs, 2001 ★4381★
- Academics' choices for best special education graduate programs, 2001 ★4386★

Maryland, Eastern Shore; University of
- Colleges offering the Thurgood Marshall Scholarship Fund ★221★
- Four-year public institutions enrolling the highest number of students from the District of Columbia, 1998-99 ★855★
- U.S. institutions awarding the most baccalaureate degrees to African Americans in agribusiness and production, 1998 ★1813★
- Average faculty salaries for institutions of higher education in Maryland, 2000-01 ★3707★

Maryland Institute, College of Art
- Institutions censured by the American Association of University Professors, 2001 ★1067★
- Highest undergraduate tuition and fees at colleges and universities in Maryland ★1514★

Maryland, Smith Graduate School of Management and Technology; University of
- Academics' choices for best graduate management information systems programs, 2001 ★585★
- *Business Week*'s top business schools with the highest percentage of international students, 2000 ★612★
- *Business Week*'s top business schools with the highest percentage of women enrollees, 2000 ★614★
- *Business Week*'s top business schools with the worst placement offices, 2000 ★620★
- Lowest post-MBA salaries for students enrolled in *Business Week*'s top business schools, 1999 ★634★
- Lowest pre-MBA salaries for students enrolled in *Business Week*'s top business schools, 1999 ★635★

Maryland System; University of
- State appropriations for Maryland's institutions of higher education, 2000-01 ★1273★
- Institutions receiving the largest Energy Department research grants, 2000 ★3111★

Maryland; University of
- Top college choices for Washington D.C. students ★847★
- Universities with the most-cited scholars in *Criminal Justice and Behavior* ★1648★
- Universities with the most-cited scholars in *Criminology* ★1649★
- Universities with the most-cited scholars in *Journal of Quantitative Criminology* ★1650★
- Universities with the most-cited scholars in *Journal of Research in Crime and Delinquency* ★1651★
- Universities with the most-cited scholars in *Justice Quarterly* ★1652★
- Economics departments by number of citations by top economists, 1971-92 ★2158★
- Economics departments by number of citations per top economist, 1971-92 ★2159★
- Economics departments by number of top economists, 1971-92 ★2160★
- Top institutions in systems and software engineering publications ★2332★
- Academics' choices for best clinical law programs, 2001 ★2626★
- Academics' choices for best environmental law programs, 2001 ★2628★
- Academics' choices for best health law programs, 2001 ★2629★
- Law schools with the best health law (excluding medical ethics) faculty, 1999-2000 ★2652★
- Comparison of library and information science programs composite rankings with *U.S. News & World Report* survey ★2709★
- Library and information science programs with the most citations to journal articles, 1993-1998 ★2712★
- Library and information science programs with the most journal articles, 1993-1998 ★2713★
- Library and information science programs with the most journal articles per capita, 1993-1998 ★2714★
- Library and information science programs with the most per capita citations to journal articles, 1993-1998 ★2715★

Maryland, University College; University of
- Four-year public institutions enrolling the highest number of students from the District of Columbia, 1998-99 ★855★
- Total baccalaureate degrees awarded to African Americans from traditionally white institutions, 1997-98 ★1698★
- U.S. colleges and universities awarding the most business management and administrative services master's degrees to African Americans ★1759★
- U.S. colleges and universities awarding the most business management and administrative services master's degrees to Asian Americans ★1760★
- U.S. colleges and universities awarding the most business management and administrative services master's degrees to Hispanic Americans ★1761★
- Average faculty salaries for institutions of higher education without academic ranks in Maryland, 2000-01 ★3750★

Marylhurst University
- *U.S. News & World Report*'s western regional universities with the best student/faculty ratios, 2000-01 ★1578★
- *U.S. News & World Report*'s western regional universities with the highest acceptance rates, 2000-01 ★1579★
- *U.S. News & World Report*'s western regional universities with the highest alumni giving rates, 2000-01 ★1580★
- *U.S. News & World Report*'s western regional universities with the highest percentage of freshmen in the top 25% of their high school class, 2000-01 ★1583★
- *U.S. News & World Report*'s western regional universities with the highest proportion of classes with 20 students or less, 2000-01 ★1585★

Marymount College
- Average faculty salaries for institutions of higher education in New York, 2000-01 ★3719★

Marymount College (NY)
- College freshmen's choices for exemplary undergraduate institutions ★1065★

Marymount College, Tarrytown
- *U.S. News & World Report*'s northern regional liberal arts colleges with the best student/faculty ratios, 2000-01 ★1353★
- *U.S. News & World Report*'s northern regional liberal arts colleges with the highest acceptance rates, 2000-01 ★1355★
- *U.S. News & World Report*'s northern regional liberal arts colleges with the highest proportion of classes having 20 students or less, 2000-01 ★1361★

Marymount Manhattan College
- *U.S. News & World Report*'s northern regional liberal arts colleges with the highest academic reputation scores, 2000-01 ★1354★
- *U.S. News & World Report*'s northern regional liberal arts colleges with the highest percentage of freshmen in the top 25% of their high school class, 2000-01 ★1359★
- *U.S. News & World Report*'s northern regional liberal arts colleges with the highest proportion of classes having 20 students or less, 2000-01 ★1361★
- *U.S. News & World Report*'s northern regional liberal arts colleges with the lowest acceptance rates, 2000-01 ★1362★
- Average faculty salaries for institutions of higher education in New York, 2000-01 ★3719★

Marymount University
- U.S. colleges and universities awarding the most law and legal studies master's degrees to African Americans ★1781★
- U.S. colleges and universities awarding the most psychology master's degrees to African Americans ★1797★
- Average faculty salaries for institutions of higher education in Virginia, 2000-01 ★3735★

Maryville College
- *U.S. News & World Report*'s southern regional liberal arts colleges with the highest academic reputation scores, 2000-01 ★1369★
- *U.S. News & World Report*'s southern regional liberal arts colleges with the highest alumni giving rates, 2000-01 ★1371★
- *U.S. News & World Report*'s southern regional liberal arts colleges with the highest freshmen retention rates, 2000-01 ★1372★
- *U.S. News & World Report*'s southern regional liberal arts colleges with the highest proportion of freshmen in the top 25% of their high school class, 2000-01 ★1376★

U.S. News & World Report's top southern regional liberal arts colleges, 2000-01 ★1379★
U.S. News & World Report's best undergraduate fees among southern regional liberal arts colleges by discount tuition, 2000 ★1383★
Highest undergraduate tuition and fees at colleges and universities in Tennessee ★1558★
Average faculty salaries for institutions of higher education in Tennessee, 2000-01 ★3730★

Maryville Middle School
Outstanding secondary schools in Knoxville, Tennessee ★4159★

Maryville University, St. Louis
Average faculty salaries for institutions of higher education in Missouri, 2000-01 ★3712★

Marywood University
Average faculty salaries for institutions of higher education in Pennsylvania, 2000-01 ★3725★

Masataro; Sawayanagi
Japan's ten great educators ★2234★

Masco
Fortune's highest ranked metal products companies, 2000 ★475★
Top housing and real estate companies in Standard & Poor's 500, 2001 ★543★

Mason; David Y.
Most-cited researchers in oncology, 1981-1998 ★2877★

Mason H
Outstanding secondary schools in Cincinnati, Ohio-Kentucky-Indiana ★4112★

Mason; Susan E.
Top pay and benefits for the chief executive and top paid employees at Niagara University ★3420★

Mass communications
Communications doctorates awarded at U.S. colleges and universities, by subfield, 1999 ★1898★
Gender breakdown of communications doctorate recipients, by subfield, 1999 ★1930★
Areas of specialization in journalism and mass communications programs with the highest enrollment, 1999 ★2740★

Mass; Daniel P.
Top pay and benefits for the chief executive and top paid employees at the University of Chicago ★3537★

Mass Spectroscopy Review
Spectroscopy journals by citation impact, 1981-99 ★4359★
Spectroscopy journals by citation impact, 1995-99 ★4360★
Spectroscopy journals by citation impact, 1999 ★4361★

Massachusetts
States with the highest enrollment in private 4-year institutions of higher education ★860★
Mean composite ACT scores by state, 2000 ★895★
Mean math SAT scores by state, 2000 ★900★
Mean verbal SAT scores by state, 2000 ★903★
States receiving the most in federal agency appropriations to colleges, 2000 ★1306★
States with the highest percentage increase in appropriations for higher education, 2000-01 ★1308★
Total doctorate recipients by state, 1999 ★2054★
States with the most law schools ★2668★
Average Hennen's American Public Library Ratings, by state ★2690★
State grades for affordability of higher education for minority students, 2000 ★2883★
State grades for benefits state receives for educating its minority students, 2000 ★2884★
State grades for completion of higher education by minority students, 2000 ★2885★
State grades for participation of minority students in higher education, 2000 ★2886★
State grades for preparing minority students for higher education, 2000 ★2887★
States with the highest per capita income ★3123★
States with the largest growth in income ★3124★
States with the highest per-pupil expenditures ★3996★
States with the highest funding needs for school-building modernization ★4040★
States with the highest percentage of high school freshmen enrolling in college within four years ★4266★

Massachusetts, Amherst; University of
U.S. colleges and universities with a popular newspaper ★1018★
U.S. colleges and universities with the worst overall administration ★1045★
Total baccalaureate law and legal studies degrees awarded to African Americans from U.S. colleges and universities, 1997-98 ★1725★
Total baccalaureate law and legal studies degrees awarded to Asian Americans from U.S. colleges and universities, 1997-98 ★1726★
Total baccalaureate law and legal studies degrees awarded to Hispanic Americans from U.S. colleges and universities, 1997-98 ★1727★
U.S. institutions awarding the most associate degrees to minorities in agribusiness and production, 1998 ★1808★
U.S. colleges and universities awarding the most health professions and related sciences doctorate degrees to African Americans ★2114★
U.S. colleges and universities awarding the most psychology doctorate degrees to Hispanic Americans ★2122★
Most effective materials science research-doctorate programs as evaluated by the National Research Council ★2418★
Top materials science research-doctorate programs as evaluated by the National Research Council ★2419★
Most effective linguistics research-doctorate programs as evaluated by the National Research Council ★2732★
Top linguistics research-doctorate programs as evaluated by the National Research Council ★2733★
Women faculty in Ph.D. physics departments at U.S. institutions, 1998 ★2981★
Average faculty salaries for institutions of higher education in Massachusetts, 2000-01 ★3708★

Massachusetts Bay Community College
Lowest undergraduate tuition and fees at colleges and universities in Massachusetts ★1517★

Massachusetts, Boston; University of
Radcliffe Institute for Advanced Study fellowship recipient in the field of architectural history, 2000-01 ★67★
Radcliffe Institute for Advanced Study fellowship recipients in the field of religion, 2000-01 ★3092★
Average faculty salaries for institutions of higher education in Massachusetts, 2000-01 ★3708★

Massachusetts College of Art
Radcliffe Institute for Advanced Study fellowship recipients in the field of visual arts, 2000-01 ★79★
State appropriations for Massachusetts's institutions of higher education, 2000-01 ★1274★

Massachusetts College of Liberal Arts
State appropriations for Massachusetts's institutions of higher education, 2000-01 ★1274★
U.S. News & World Report's top public northern regional liberal arts colleges, 2000-01 ★1364★

Massachusetts, Dartmouth; University of
U.S. News & World Report's northern regional universities with the highest percentage of full-time faculty, 2000-01 ★1422★
U.S. News & World Report's top public northern regional universities, 2000-01 ★1426★
Average faculty salaries for institutions of higher education in Massachusetts, 2000-01 ★3708★

Massachusetts Eye and Ear Infirmary
Top ophthalmology hospitals in the U.S., 2000 ★2796★
Top ortolaryngology hospitals in the U.S., 2000 ★2798★

Massachusetts General Hospital
Top cancer hospitals in the U.S., 2000 ★2787★
Top cardiology and heart surgery hospitals in the U.S., 2000 ★2788★
Top endocrinology hospitals in the U.S., 2000 ★2789★
Top gastroenterology hospitals in the U.S., 2000 ★2790★
Top geriatrics hospitals in the U.S., 2000 ★2791★
Top gynecology hospitals in the U.S., 2000 ★2792★
Top hospitals in the U.S., 2000 ★2793★
Top nephrology hospitals in the U.S., 2000 ★2794★
Top neurology and neurosurgery hospitals in the U.S., 2000 ★2795★
Top orthopedics hospitals in the U.S., 2000 ★2797★
Top rheumatology hospitals in the U.S., 2000 ★2802★
Top urology hospitals in the U.S., 2000 ★2803★

Massachusetts General Hospital, Boston
Top psychiatric hospitals in the U.S., 2000 ★2800★

Massachusetts Institute of Technology
Colleges with the highest number of freshman Merit Scholars, 2000 ★5★
U.S. universities enrolling the most National Achievement Scholars, 1994 ★9★
U.S. universities publishing the most papers in the field of artificial intelligence, 1995-99 ★100★
Top neurosciences research-doctorate programs as evaluated by the National Research Council ★202★
Most effective biochemistry and molecular biology research-doctorate programs as evaluated by the National Research Council ★205★

MASSACHUSETTS

Most effective cell and developmental biology research-doctorate programs as evaluated by the National Research Council ★206★

Most effective molecular and general genetics research-doctorate programs as evaluated by the National Research Council ★207★

Top biochemistry and molecular biology research-doctorate programs as evaluated by the National Research Council ★209★

Top cell and developmental biology research-doctorate programs as evaluated by the National Research Council ★210★

Top molecular and general genetics research-doctorate programs as evaluated by the National Research Council ★211★

U.S. universities with the greatest impact in cell and developmental biology, 1993-97 ★212★

U.S. universities with the greatest impact in cell and developmental biology, 1994-98 ★213★

U.S. universities with the greatest impact in biotechnology and applied microbiology, 1995-99 ★216★

U.S. News & World Report's universities with the best quantitative methods departments, 1999-2000 ★572★

U.S. universities publishing the most papers in the field of management, 1995-99 ★574★

U.S. universities with the greatest impact in management, 1994-98 ★575★

Top business schools by average MBA rank, 1986-1998 ★644★

Top business schools for within-discipline research performance in management science, 1986-1998 ★647★

Top business schools for within-discipline research performance in management information systems, 1986-1998 ★675★

Winner of the American Chemical Society's Arthur C. Cope Awards, 2001 ★795★

Most effective chemistry research-doctorate programs as evaluated by the National Research Council ★802★

Top chemistry research-doctorate programs as evaluated by the National Research Council ★805★

Comparison of acceptance rates at the top 5 national universities in the U.S., 1990 and 2001 ★845★

U.S. colleges and universities where students study the most ★1003★

U.S. colleges and universities with a diverse student body ★1012★

U.S. News & World Report's national universities with the best academic reputation, 2000-01 ★1126★

U.S. News & World Report's national universities with the best freshmen retention rates, 2000-01 ★1128★

U.S. News & World Report's national universities with the best graduation and retention rank, 2000-01 ★1129★

U.S. News & World Report's national universities with the best student/faculty ratio, 2000-01 ★1130★

U.S. News & World Report's national universities with the highest alumni giving rank, 2000-01 ★1132★

U.S. News & World Report's national universities with the highest financial resources rank, 2000-01 ★1133★

U.S. News & World Report's national universities with the highest graduation rate, 1999 ★1134★

U.S. News & World Report's national universities with the highest percentage of freshmen in the top 10% of their high school class, 2000-01 ★1135★

U.S. News & World Report's national universities with the highest proportion of alumni support, 2000-01 ★1137★

U.S. News & World Report's national universities with the highest selectivity rank, 2000-01 ★1139★

U.S. News & World Report's national universities with the lowest acceptance rates, 2000-01 ★1140★

2000 endowment values of the 'wealthiest' U.S. universities ★1230★

Colleges and universities with the largest endowments, 2000 ★1237★

Endowment values for the wealthiest U.S. universities, 2000 ★1240★

Institutions receiving the most alumni gifts, 1999-2000 ★1242★

Institutions receiving the most corporate gifts, 1999-2000 ★1243★

Largest gifts to higher education, 1967-2000 ★1247★

Largest private gifts to higher education, 1967-2000 ★1248★

Highest undergraduate tuition and fees at private nonprofit, 4-year or above colleges and universities ★1461★

Private 4-year institutions with the highest tuition, 2000-01 ★1467★

U.S. News & World Report's best undergraduate fees among national universities by discount tuition, 2000 ★1474★

U.S. News & World Report's national universities with students most in debt, 1999 ★1476★

Highest undergraduate tuition and fees at colleges and universities in Massachusetts ★1516★

U.S. universities publishing the most papers in the field of computer science, 1994-98 ★1591★

U.S. universities with the greatest impact in computer science, 1994-98 ★1592★

Most effective computer science research-doctorate programs as evaluated by the National Research Council ★1594★

Top computer science research-doctorate programs as evaluated by the National Research Council ★1597★

Total baccalaureate physical sciences degrees awarded to Asian Americans from U.S. colleges and universities, 1997-98 ★1734★

U.S. colleges and universities awarding the most doctoral degrees to Asian Americans and Pacific Islanders from 1995 to 1999 ★2093★

U.S. colleges and universities awarding the most doctorates in engineering, 1999 ★2102★

U.S. colleges and universities awarding the most doctorates in physical sciences, mathematics, and computer sciences, 1999 ★2105★

U.S. colleges and universities awarding the most physical sciences doctorate degrees to African Americans ★2118★

Most effective geosciences research-doctorate programs as evaluated by the National Research Council ★2150★

Top geosciences research-doctorate programs as evaluated by the National Research Council ★2152★

Top oceanography research-doctorate programs as evaluated by the National Research Council ★2153★

Economics departments by number of citations by top economists, 1971-92 ★2158★

Economics departments by number of citations per top economist, 1971-92 ★2159★

Economics departments by number of top economists, 1971-92 ★2160★

Institutions most frequently contributing to the *American Economic Review* from 1911-1990 ★2168★

Institutions most frequently contributing to the *American Economic Review* from 1951-1990 ★2169★

U.S. universities publishing the most papers in the field of economics and business, 1995-99 ★2178★

U.S. universities with the greatest impact in economics, 1995-99 ★2179★

Economics Ph.D. programs by number of citations of top economist graduates, 1971-92 ★2204★

Economics Ph.D. programs by number of citations per top economist graduate, 1971-92 ★2205★

Economics Ph.D. programs by number of top economist graduates, 1971-92 ★2206★

Most effective economics research-doctorate programs as evaluated by the National Research Council ★2207★

Origin of doctorate for dissertation chairs in economics ★2208★

Origin of doctorate for economics faculty at Ph.D.-granting institutions ★2209★

Origin of doctorate for economics faculty at Ph.D.-granting institutions, by Ph.D. equivalents produced ★2210★

Top economics research-doctorate programs as evaluated by the National Research Council ★2213★

U.S. universities publishing the most papers in the field of civil engineering, 1994-98 ★2348★

U.S. universities publishing the most papers in the field of civil engineering, 1995-99 ★2349★

U.S. universities with the greatest impact in electrical and electronic engineering, 1994-99 ★2356★

Acceptance rates for *U.S. News & World Report*'s top 10 graduate engineering schools, 2001 ★2358★

Average analytic GRE scores for *U.S. News & World Report*'s top 10 graduate engineering schools, 2001 ★2359★

Average quantitative GRE scores for *U.S. News & World Report*'s top 10 graduate engineering schools, 2001 ★2360★

Doctoral student-faculty ratios at *U.S. News & World Report*'s top 10 graduate engineering schools, 2001 ★2361★

Faculty membership in National Academy of Engineering at *U.S. News & World Report*'s top 10 graduate engineering schools, 2001 ★2362★

Ph.D.s granted at *U.S. News & World Report*'s top 10 graduate engineering schools, 2001 ★2363★

Research expenditures per faculty member at *U.S. News & World Report*'s top 10 graduate engineering schools, 2001 ★2364★

Research funding allocated to *U.S. News & World Report*'s top 10 graduate engineering schools, 2001 ★2365★

Top graduate engineering schools, 2001 ★2366★

Top graduate engineering schools by reputation, as determined by academic personnel, 2001 ★2367★

Top graduate engineering schools by reputation, as determined by engineers and recruiters, 2001 ★2368★

U.S. News & World Report's graduate engineering programs with the highest academic reputation scores, 2000-01 ★2372★

Academics' choices for best graduate aerospace/aeronautical/astronautical engineering programs, 2001 ★2374★

Most effective aerospace engineering research-doctorate programs as evaluated by the National Research Council ★2375★

Top aerospace engineering research-doctorate programs as evaluated by the National Research Council ★2376★

U.S. News & World Report's graduate engineering programs with the best aerospace departments, 2000-01 ★2378★

Academics' choices for best graduate bioengineering/biomedical engineering programs, 2001 ★2381★

Most effective biomedical engineering research-doctorate programs as evaluated by the National Research Council ★2383★

Top biomedical engineering research-doctorate programs as evaluated by the National Research Council ★2384★

U.S. News & World Report's graduate engineering programs with the best biomedical departments, 2000-01 ★2385★

Academics' choices for best graduate chemical engineering programs, 2001 ★2386★

Most effective chemical engineering research-doctorate programs as evaluated by the National Research Council ★2389★

Top chemical engineering research-doctorate programs as evaluated by the National Research Council ★2390★

U.S. News & World Report's graduate engineering programs with the best chemical departments, 2000-01 ★2392★

Academics' choices for best graduate civil engineering programs, 2001 ★2394★

Most effective civil engineering research-doctorate programs as evaluated by the National Research Council ★2395★

Top civil engineering research-doctorate programs as evaluated by the National Research Council ★2396★

U.S. News & World Report's graduate engineering programs with the best civil departments, 2000-01 ★2398★

Academics' choices for best graduate computer engineering programs, 2001 ★2399★

U.S. News & World Report's graduate engineering programs with the best computer departments, 2000-01 ★2401★

U.S. universities with the highest concentrations in artificial intelligence, 1992-96 ★2402★

Academics' choices for best graduate electrical/electronic/communications engineering programs, 2001 ★2403★

Most effective electrical engineering research-doctorate programs as evaluated by the National Research Council ★2404★

Top electrical engineering research-doctorate programs as evaluated by the National Research Council ★2405★

U.S. News & World Report's graduate engineering programs with the best electrical departments, 2000-01 ★2407★

Academics' choices for best graduate environmental/environmental health engineering programs, 2001 ★2408★

U.S. News & World Report's graduate engineering programs with the best environmental departments, 2000-01 ★2410★

Academics' choices for best graduate materials engineering programs, 2001 ★2417★

Most effective materials science research-doctorate programs as evaluated by the National Research Council ★2418★

Top materials science research-doctorate programs as evaluated by the National Research Council ★2419★

U.S. News & World Report's graduate engineering programs with the best materials departments, 2000-01 ★2421★

Academics' choices for best graduate mechanical engineering programs, 2001 ★2422★

Most effective mechanical engineering research-doctorate programs as evaluated by the National Research Council ★2423★

U.S. News & World Report's graduate engineering programs with the best mechanical departments, 2000-01 ★2425★

Academics' choices for best graduate nuclear engineering schools, 2000 ★2426★

U.S. News & World Report's graduate engineering programs with the best nuclear departments, 2000-01 ★2428★

U.S. universities with the highest concentration of metallurgy papers published, 1994-98 ★2436★

Most wired universities, 2000 ★2598★

Most effective linguistics research-doctorate programs as evaluated by the National Research Council ★2732★

Top linguistics research-doctorate programs as evaluated by the National Research Council ★2733★

Most effective mathematics research-doctorate programs as evaluated by the National Research Council ★2775★

Top mathematics research-doctorate programs as evaluated by the National Research Council ★2778★

U.S. universities with the greatest impact in optics and acoustics, 1994-98 ★2911★

Top pharmacology research-doctorate programs as evaluated by the National Research Council ★2939★

Most effective philosophy research-doctorate programs as evaluated by the National Research Council ★2945★

Top philosophy research-doctorate programs as evaluated by the National Research Council ★2947★

Women faculty in Ph.D. physics departments at U.S. institutions, 1998 ★2981★

Most effective astrophysics and astronomy research-doctorate programs as evaluated by the National Research Council ★3006★

Most effective physics research-doctorate programs as evaluated by the National Research Council ★3007★

Top astrophysics and astronomy research-doctorate programs as evaluated by the National Research Council ★3014★

Top physics research-doctorate programs as evaluated by the National Research Council ★3015★

Top political science research-doctorate programs as evaluated by the National Research Council ★3046★

U.S. universities with the greatest impact in psychology, 1995-99 ★3064★

Most patents issued to universities or research facilities, 1999 ★3097★

U.S. colleges and universities spending the most on chemical engineering research and development, 1998 ★3098★

U.S. colleges and universities with the most federal support for chemical engineering research and development, 1998 ★3101★

U.S. colleges and universities with the most federal support for chemical research and development, 1998 ★3102★

U.S. colleges and universities with the most federal support for chemical research equipment, 1998 ★3103★

U.S. universities spending the most on research and development, 1998 ★3104★

Institutions receiving the most federal research and development expenditures, 1999 ★3105★

Institutions receiving the largest Energy Department research grants, 2000 ★3111★

Average faculty salaries for institutions of higher education in Massachusetts, 2000-01 ★3708★

U.S. institutions with the highest paid assistant professors, 2001 ★3977★

U.S. universities with the highest relative citation impact, 1993-97 ★4291★

Massachusetts Institute of Technology, Alfred P. Sloan School of Management

U.S. News & World Report's undergraduate business programs with the best consulting departments, 2000-01 ★563★

U.S. News & World Report's undergraduate business programs with the best e-commerce departments, 2000-01 ★564★

U.S. News & World Report's undergraduate business programs with the best general management departments, 2000-01 ★566★

U.S. News & World Report's undergraduate business programs with the best management information systems departments, 2000-01 ★568★

U.S. News & World Report's undergraduate business programs with the best production/operations departments, 2000-01 ★569★

U.S. News & World Report's undergraduate business programs with the highest academic reputation scores, 2000-01 ★571★

Academics' choices for best graduate entrepreneurship programs, 2001 ★583★

Academics' choices for best graduate management information systems programs, 2001 ★585★

Acceptance rates for *U.S. News & World Report*'s top 10 graduate business schools, 2001 ★588★

Annual tuition at *Business Week*'s top business schools, 2000 ★589★

Average GMAT scores at *U.S. News & World Report*'s top 10 graduate business schools, 2001 ★591★

Average job offers received by graduates from *Business Week*'s top business schools, 1999 ★592★

Average undergraduate GPA at *U.S. News & World Report*'s top 10 graduate business schools, 2001 ★593★

Business Week's top business schools, 2000 ★595★

Business Week's top business schools as selected by corporate recruiters, 2000 ★596★

Business Week's top business schools as selected by recent MBA graduates, 2000 ★597★

MASSACHUSETTS

Business Week's top business schools by intellectual capital, 2000 ★599★
Business Week's top business schools for finance skills as selected by corporate recruiters, 2000 ★600★
Business Week's top business schools for global scope skills as selected by corporate recruiters, 2000 ★602★
Business Week's top business schools for technology skills as selected by corporate recruiters, 2000 ★604★
Business Week's top business schools with the greatest rise in MBA satisfaction, 2000 ★611★
Business Week's top business schools with the highest percentage of international students, 2000 ★612★
Business Week's top business schools with the highest percentage of minority enrollment, 2000 ★613★
Business Week's top business schools with the lowest percentage of women enrollees, 2000 ★617★
Highest post-MBA salaries for students enrolled in *Business Week*'s top business schools, 1999 ★631★
Highest pre-MBA salaries for students enrolled in *Business Week*'s top business schools, 1999 ★632★
Median starting salaries of graduates from *U.S. News & World Report*'s top 10 graduate business schools, 2001 ★636★
Out-of-state tuition and fees for *U.S. News & World Report*'s top 10 graduate business schools, 2001 ★637★
Percentage of applicants accepted at *Business Week*'s top business schools, 2000 ★638★
Percentage of employed graduates at *U.S. News & World Report*'s top 10 graduate business schools, 2001 ★639★
Percentage of graduates earning over $100,000 from *Business Week*'s top business schools, 1999 ★640★
Percentage of graduates employed within 3 months of graduation from *U.S. News & World Report*'s top 10 graduate business schools, 2001 ★641★
Top graduate business schools, 2001 ★649★
Top graduate business schools by reputation as determined by academic personnel, 2001 ★650★
Top graduate business schools by reputation, as determined by recruiters, 2001 ★651★
Academics' choices for best graduate finance programs, 2001 ★662★
U.S. News & World Report's undergraduate business programs with the best finance departments, 2000-01 ★665★
Academics' choices for best graduate quantitative analysis programs, 2001 ★673★
Academics' choices for best graduate production/operations management programs, 2001 ★674★
Average GMAT scores for *U.S. News & World Report*'s top 10 graduate business schools, 2000 ★2529★

Massachusetts, Lowell; University of
Doctorate-granting-institutions with the highest percentage of non-U.S. citizen doctoral degrees awarded, 1999 ★1907★
Radcliffe Institute for Advanced Study fellowship recipient in the field of economic and social development, 2000-01 ★2171★

Average faculty salaries for institutions of higher education in Massachusetts, 2000-01 ★3708★

Massachusetts Maritime Academy
State appropriations for Massachusetts's institutions of higher education, 2000-01 ★1274★

Massachusetts Mutual Life Insurance
Fortune's highest ranked life and health insurance companies, 2000 ★472★

Massachusetts; University of
State appropriations for Massachusetts's institutions of higher education, 2000-01 ★1274★

Massachusetts, Worcester; University of
Acceptance rates for *U.S. News & World Report*'s top 10 primary-care medical schools, 2001 ★2826★
Average MCAT scores at *U.S. News & World Report*'s top 10 primary-care medical schools, 2001 ★2835★
Average undergraduate GPA at *U.S. News & World Report*'s top 10 primary-care medical schools, 2001 ★2837★
Faculty-student ratios at *U.S. News & World Report*'s top 10 primary-care medical schools, 2001 ★2841★
Out-of-state tuition and fees at *U.S. News & World Report*'s top 10 primary-care medical schools, 2001 ★2846★
Percentage of graduates entering *U.S. News & World Report*'s top 10 primary-care medical schools, 2001 ★2848★
Top primary-care medical schools, 2001 ★2856★

Massasoit Community College
Lowest undergraduate tuition and fees at colleges and universities in Massachusetts ★1517★
Average faculty salaries for institutions of higher education in Massachusetts, 2000-01 ★3708★

Massey; Marilyn Chapin
Top pay and benefits for the chief executive and top paid employees at Pitzer College ★3441★

Massey; Walter E.
Top pay and benefits for the chief executive and top paid employees at Morehouse College ★3408★

Massingill; Nan
Top pay and benefits for the chief executive and top paid employees at Austin College ★3184★

MAST Academy
Outstanding secondary schools in Miami, Florida ★4178★

Mast; Sarah
All-USA College Academic Third Team, 2001 ★4★

Master of the Crossroads
Booklist's best fiction books for library collections, 2000 ★227★
Booklist's most recommended historical novels, 2001 ★230★

Masterman School
Outstanding secondary schools in Philadelphia, Pennsylvania-New Jersey ★4202★

Master's College and Seminary
U.S. News & World Report's best undergraduate fees among western regional liberal arts colleges by discount tuition, 2000 ★1384★
Academic reputation scores for *U.S. News & World Report*'s top western regional liberal arts colleges, 2000-01 ★1387★

Acceptance rates for *U.S. News & World Report*'s top western regional liberal arts colleges, 2000-01 ★1388★
Alumni giving rates at *U.S. News & World Report*'s top western regional liberal arts colleges, 2000-01 ★1389★
Average freshmen retention rates for *U.S. News & World Report*'s top western regional liberal arts colleges, 2000-01 ★1390★
Average graduation rates for *U.S. News & World Report*'s top western regional liberal arts colleges, 2000-01 ★1391★
Percentage of freshmen in the top 25% of their high school class at *U.S. News & World Report*'s top western regional liberal arts colleges, 2000-01 ★1392★
Percentage of full-time faculty at *U.S. News & World Report*'s top western regional liberal arts colleges, 2000-01 ★1393★
Proportion of classes having 20 students or less at *U.S. News & World Report*'s top western regional liberal arts colleges, 2000-01 ★1394★
Student/faculty ratios at *U.S. News & World Report*'s top western regional liberal arts colleges, 2000-01 ★1395★
U.S. News & World Report's top western regional liberal arts colleges, 2000-01 ★1396★

Materials science
Engineering doctorates awarded at U.S. colleges and universities, by subfield, 1999 ★1923★
Gender breakdown of engineering doctorate recipients, by subfield, 1999 ★1934★
Major subfields of first-year physics and astronomy graduate students who are foreign citizens planning to receive a Ph.D., 1997-98 ★3004★
Major subfields of first-year physics and astronomy graduate students who are U.S. citizens planning to receive a Ph.D., 1997-98 ★3005★
Austria's relative impact in the sciences by field, 1992-96 ★4300★
France's contribution of papers in the sciences, by field, 1996-2000 ★4312★
Germany's contribution of papers in the sciences, by field, 1995-99 ★4313★
Hong Kong's contribution of papers in the sciences, by field, 1995-99 ★4314★
Italy's relative impact in the sciences by field, 1992-96 ★4317★
Japan's contribution of papers in the sciences, by field, 1995-99 ★4318★
Japan's contribution of papers in the sciences, by field, 1996-2000 ★4319★
Poland's contribution of papers in the sciences, by field, 1993-97 ★4324★
Russia's contribution of papers in the sciences, by field, 1993-97 ★4325★
South Korea's contribution of papers in the sciences, by field, 1995-99 ★4327★
Taiwan contribution of papers in the sciences, by field, 1995-99 ★4334★
Turkey's contribution of papers in the sciences, by field, 1995-99 ★4335★

Math
Academic Achievement comparison of 12th graders, 1998 ★1★
Eighth grade students' proficiency ★7★
Comparative data of women receiving doctorate degrees in selected fields in 1950 and 1998 ★1899★
Subjects students most want to see on classroom TV ★4051★

Math/actuarial science
　Top master's degree majors in demand for employment, 2001 ★2326★

Math and computer science
　Fields of study profile of foreign students enrolled in U.S. institutions of higher education, 1998-99 ★2495★
　Fields of study profile of U.S. students studying abroad, 1998-99 ★2507★
　Average costs for Academic Search titles by subject, 2001 ★2918★
　Periodical prices by LC subject, 2001 ★2925★
　Periodical prices by scientific discipline, 2001 ★2926★

The Math Gene: How Mathematical Thinking Evolved and Why Number Are Like Gossip
　Library Journal's most notable mathematics books, 2000 ★266★

Mathematical and physical sciences
　Proposed fiscal 2002 appropriations for the National Science Foundation ★3109★

Mathematical statistics
　Gender breakdown of mathematics doctorate recipients, by subfield, 1999 ★1938★
　Mathematics doctorates awarded at U.S. colleges and universities, by subfield, 1999 ★1951★

Mathematician
　Jobs with the best environment scores ★2247★
　Jobs with the best physical demands scores ★2250★
　Most desirable jobs in math/science ★2274★

Mathematics
　Number of physical sciences doctorate recipients at U.S. colleges and universities, by field, 1999 ★1975★
　Percentage of female doctorate recipients at U.S. colleges and universities, by subfield, 1999 ★1988★
　Physical sciences, mathematics, and computer sciences doctorates awarded to U.S. citizens/permanent residents at U.S. colleges and universities, by race/ethnicity and subfield, 1999 ★1993★
　Top physical science majors for accepted applicants to U.S. medical schools, 1999-2000 ★2855★
　Mean age of first and best contribution of scientists and inventors, by discipline ★3096★
　Austria's contribution of papers in the sciences by field, 1992-96 ★4298★
　Austria's contribution of papers in the sciences, by field, 1995-99 ★4299★
　Belgium's contribution of papers in the sciences by field, 1992-96 ★4301★
　Canada's contribution of papers in the sciences, by field, 1995-99 ★4303★
　France's contribution of papers in the sciences, by field, 1995-99 ★4311★
　France's contribution of papers in the sciences, by field, 1996-2000 ★4312★
　Germany's contribution of papers in the sciences, by field, 1995-99 ★4313★
　Hong Kong's contribution of papers in the sciences, by field, 1995-99 ★4314★
　Ireland's contribution of papers in the sciences, by field, 1994-98 ★4315★
　Italy's contribution of papers in the sciences, by field, 1995-99 ★4316★
　Italy's relative impact in the sciences by field, 1992-96 ★4317★
　Poland's contribution of papers in the sciences, by field, 1993-97 ★4324★
　Russia's contribution of papers in the sciences, by field, 1993-97 ★4325★
　South Korea's contribution of papers in the sciences, by field, 1995-99 ★4327★
　Spain's contribution of papers in the sciences, by field, 1993-97 ★4328★
　Spain's contribution of papers in the sciences, by field, 1995-99 ★4329★
　Taiwan contribution of papers in the sciences, by field, 1995-99 ★4334★

Mathematics education
　Gender breakdown of teaching fields doctorate recipients, by subfield, 1999 ★1943★
　Teaching fields doctorates awarded at U.S. colleges and universities, by subfield, 1999 ★2046★

Mathematics, general
　Gender breakdown of mathematics doctorate recipients, by subfield, 1999 ★1938★
　Mathematics doctorates awarded at U.S. colleges and universities, by subfield, 1999 ★1951★

Matheny; Nancy
　Top pay and benefits for the chief executive and top paid employees at Lindenwood University ★3375★

Mathews; Keith
　Top pay and benefits for the chief executive and top paid employees at Baldwin-Wallace College ★3189★

Matilda Bone
　Most notable children's recordings, 2001 ★320★

Matisse; Henri
　Highly influential artists of the 20th century ★76★

Matsushita Electric Industrial
　Business Week's best companies in Japan ★398★

Mattel Toys
　Top internships in the U.S. with the highest compensation, 2001 ★2611★

Matteson; Donna
　All-USA Teacher Teams, Second Team, 2000 ★4400★

Matthaus Schmidt; Karl
　European business moguls considered the best challengers ★439★

Matthews; Claire
　Top pay and benefits for the chief executive and top paid employees at Connecticut College ★3254★

Matthews; George
　Top pay and benefits for the chief executive and top paid employees at Saint Xavier University ★3487★

Matthews; Roger
　Most cited scholars in critical criminology ★1640★
　Most-cited scholars in critical criminology publications ★1641★

Mattox; Douglas E.
　Top pay and benefits for the chief executive and top paid employees at Emory University ★3289★

Maturitas
　Geriatrics and gerontology journals with the greatest impact measure, 1981-98 ★2805★
　Geriatrics and gerontology journals with the greatest impact measure, 1994-98 ★2806★
　Geriatrics and gerontology journals with the greatest impact measure, 1998 ★2807★

Matzek; Richard
　Top pay and benefits for the chief executive and top paid employees at Nazareth College of Rochester ★3416★

Mauer; Joe
　All-American boy's high school football quarterbacks, 2000 ★184★
　All-American boy's high school football team, 2000 ★187★

Maui Community College
　Average faculty salaries for institutions of higher education in Hawaii, 2000-01 ★3698★

Mauldin; Bill
　Top editorial cartoonists used in teaching journalism history ★2770★

Maultsby; Dan
　Top pay and benefits for the chief executive and top paid employees at Wofford College ★3634★

Maultsby; Hubert D.
　Top pay and benefits for the chief executive and top paid employees at Norwich University in Vermont ★3424★

Maurer; M.
　Most cited authors in the journal *Social Justice*, 1990 to 1995 ★1631★

Mavis Beacon Teaches Typing 10.0
　Top selling home education software, 2000 ★1599★

Max
　Most notable books for young readers, 2001 ★319★
　Outstanding children's picture books, 2000 ★331★
　Smithsonian's best books for children ages 1 to 6 ★363★

Max Planck Institute of Psychiatry
　Institutions with the highest impact in psychiatry research, 1990-98 ★3053★

Maxim Integrated Products
　Business Week's best performing companies with the highest net margin, 2000 ★419★
　Top electrical and electronics companies in Standard & Poor's 500, 2001 ★539★

Maxtor
　Fortune's highest ranked computer peripherals companies, 2000 ★454★

Maxwell; Barry
　Top pay and benefits for the chief executive and top paid employees at Bucknell University ★3213★

Maxwell; David E.
　Top pay and benefits for the chief executive and top paid employees at Drake University ★3272★

Maxxam
　Fortune's highest ranked metals companies, 2000 ★476★

May Department Stores
　Fortune's highest ranked general merchandisers, 2000 ★468★
　Top recruiters for retail merchandising jobs for 2000-01 bachelor's degree recipients ★556★
　Top recruiters for finance/banking jobs for 2000-01 bachelor's degree recipients ★582★
　Top recruiters for marketing jobs for 2000-01 bachelor's degree recipients ★684★
　Top recruiters for multidisciplinary majors jobs for 2000-01 bachelor's degree recipients ★2327★

May Jr.; James W.
Top pay and benefits for the chief executive and top paid employees at Davidson College ★3264★

Maybury; Greg J.
Top pay and benefits for the chief executive and top paid employees at Hope College ★3339★

Mayde Creek High School
Outstanding secondary schools in Houston, Texas ★4150★

Maydew; Mary Jo
Top pay and benefits for the chief executive and top paid employees at Mount Holyoke College ★3409★

Mayer; Lisa
Top pay and benefits for the chief executive and top paid employees at Simmons College ★3499★

Mayfield Junior High School of the Holy Child
Outstanding secondary schools in Los Angeles-Long Beach, California ★4167★

Mayhew; Patricia M.
Most-cited scholars in *British Journal of Criminology* ★1637★

Mayhew; P.M.
Most cited authors in the journal *British Journal of Criminology*, 1990 to 1995 ★1614★
Most cited authors in the journal *Crime and Justice*, 1990 to 1995 ★1617★

Mayo Clinic
Top cancer hospitals in the U.S., 2000 ★2787★
Top cardiology and heart surgery hospitals in the U.S., 2000 ★2788★
Top endocrinology hospitals in the U.S., 2000 ★2789★
Top gastroenterology hospitals in the U.S., 2000 ★2790★
Top geriatrics hospitals in the U.S., 2000 ★2791★
Top gynecology hospitals in the U.S., 2000 ★2792★
Top hospitals in the U.S., 2000 ★2793★
Top nephrology hospitals in the U.S., 2000 ★2794★
Top neurology and neurosurgery hospitals in the U.S., 2000 ★2795★
Top ophthalmology hospitals in the U.S., 2000 ★2796★
Top orthopedics hospitals in the U.S., 2000 ★2797★
Top ortolaryngology hospitals in the U.S., 2000 ★2798★
Top psychiatric hospitals in the U.S., 2000 ★2800★
Top rehabilitation hospitals in the U.S., 2000 ★2801★
Top rheumatology hospitals in the U.S., 2000 ★2802★
Top urology hospitals in the U.S., 2000 ★2803★

Mayo Clinic Health Oasis
Medical Library Association's top health related web sites ★2591★

Mayo Medical School
State appropriations for Minnesota's institutions of higher education, 2000-01 ★1276★
Top primary-care medical schools by student selectivity rank, 2001 ★2858★
Top research-oriented medical schools by student selectivity, 2001 ★2862★

Mayor
Jobs considered the most competitive ★2245★
Jobs with the best security scores ★2251★
Jobs with the lowest unemployment ★2258★

Mays; Benjamin
Most influential African Americans in education ★2216★

Mays; John E.
Top pay and benefits for the chief executive and top paid employees at Tusculum College ★3582★

Maysville Community College
Lowest undergraduate tuition and fees at colleges and universities in Kentucky ★1509★

Maytag
Business Week's best performing companies with the highest return on equity, 2000 ★420★

Mayville State University
State appropriations for North Dakota's institutions of higher education, 2000-01 ★1287★
Highest undergraduate tuition and fees at colleges and universities in North Dakota ★1541★
Average faculty salaries for institutions of higher education in North Dakota, 2000-01 ★3721★

Mazurak; Stephen
Top pay and benefits for the chief executive and top paid employees at the University of Detroit Mercy ★3541★

MBIA
Business Week's best performing companies with the highest net margin, 2000 ★419★

MBNA
Fortune's highest ranked consumer credit companies, 2000 ★457★
Top banks in Standard & Poor's 500, 2001 ★531★

McAllister; Eugene J.
Top pay and benefits for the chief executive and top paid employees at Jacksonville University ★3352★

McArthur; Robert L.
Top pay and benefits for the chief executive and top paid employees at Colby College ★3241★

McBride; Duane
Top pay and benefits for the chief executive and top paid employees at Andrews University ★3176★

McBride; Lawrence R.
Top pay and benefits for the chief executive and top paid employees at St. Louis University ★3478★

McCall's
Magazines with the largest circulation ★2750★

McCandless; John O.
Top pay and benefits for the chief executive and top paid employees at Allegheny College ★3170★

McCants; Rashad
All-America boys' high school basketball 4th team, 2001 ★164★

McCardell Jr.; John M.
Top pay and benefits for the chief executive and top paid employees at Middlebury College ★3401★

McCarthy; Walter
Top pay and benefits for the chief executive and top paid employees at the College of New Rochelle ★3525★

McCay; Skelly
All-USA College Academic First Team, 2001 ★2★

McClennen; Charles E.
Top pay and benefits for the chief executive and top paid employees at Colgate University ★3242★

McCleskey Middle School
Outstanding secondary schools in Atlanta, Georgia ★4087★

McClure; Charles
Library and information science faculty with the most citations to journal articles, 1993-1998 ★2710★
Library and information science faculty with the most journal articles, 1993-1998 ★2711★

McConnell; H. Keith
Top pay and benefits for the chief executive and top paid employees at John F. Kennedy University ★3354★

McCord Renaissance Center
Outstanding secondary schools in Benton Harbor, Michigan ★4095★

McCormack; Amy
Top pay and benefits for the chief executive and top paid employees at Dominican University in Illinois ★3269★

McCormick; Deana S.
Top pay and benefits for the chief executive and top paid employees at Wabash College ★3598★

McCormick; M. Patrick
Top pay and benefits for the chief executive and top paid employees at Hampton University ★3323★

McCormick Theological Seminary
U.S. colleges and universities awarding the most doctorate degrees to Asian Americans ★2096★
U.S. colleges and universities awarding the most doctorate degrees to Hispanic Americans ★2097★
Average faculty salaries for institutions of higher education in Illinois, 2000-01 ★3700★

McCoy; Roger
Top pay and benefits for the chief executive and top paid employees at Rockhurst University ★3464★

McCray; Curtis L.
Top pay and benefits for the chief executive and top paid employees at National-Louis University in Illinois ★3414★

McCroskey; J.
Highest ranked active communication studies researchers ★2747★
Speech communication's most published scholars between 1915-1985 ★4362★

McCue; Harold
Top pay and benefits for the chief executive and top paid employees at Trevecca Nazarene University ★3576★

McCulloch; Dave
Top pay and benefits for the chief executive and top paid employees at National-Louis University in Illinois ★3414★

McCulloch Middle School
Outstanding secondary schools in Dallas, Texas ★4120★

McCune; James
Top pay and benefits for the chief executive and top paid employees at Lincoln Memorial University ★3374★

McDade Classical
Chicago elementary magnet schools with the lowest acceptance rates, 2000-01 ★4003★

McDaniel; Thomas
Top pay and benefits for the chief executive and top paid employees at Converse College ★3255★

McDermott International
Business Week's best performing companies with the lowest 1-year sales performance ★421★
Business Week's best performing companies with the lowest 3-year sales performance ★423★
Business Week's best performing companies with the lowest 3-year shareholder returns ★424★

McDonald; Eugene J.
Top pay and benefits for the chief executive and top paid employees at Duke University ★3276★

McDonald; Kelly
All-America girls' high school soccer team forwards, 2001 ★175★

McDonald; Mary Jane
Top pay and benefits for the chief executive and top paid employees at Denison University ★3265★

McDonald; Megan
Outstanding children's fiction books, 2000 ★329★

McDonald's
Fortune's highest ranked food services companies, 2000 ★465★
Fortune's most admired companies for social responsibility ★520★
Top leisure time industries in Standard & Poor's 500, 2001 ★545★
Highly recommended public companies for women executives, 2000 ★4453★

McDonogh High School
Outstanding secondary schools in New Orleans, Louisiana ★4190★

McDowell; Mary
All-America girls' high school soccer team forwards, 2001 ★175★

McDowell; Richard
Top pay and benefits for the chief executive and top paid employees at Chapman University ★3228★

McDowell Technical Community College
Lowest undergraduate tuition and fees at colleges and universities in North Carolina ★1540★
Average faculty salaries for institutions of higher education without academic ranks in North Carolina, 2000-01 ★3761★

McDuffee; Paul
Top pay and benefits for the chief executive and top paid employees at Embry-Riddle Aeronautical University ★3286★

McEachen; Avis
All-USA Teacher Teams, Second Team, 2000 ★4400★

McElderry; Christina
All-USA College Academic Third Team, 2001 ★4★

McElwain; Hugh
Top pay and benefits for the chief executive and top paid employees at Dominican University in Illinois ★3269★

McFarlane; Edwin O.
Top pay and benefits for the chief executive and top paid employees at Reed College ★3453★

McGarry; William D.
Top pay and benefits for the chief executive and top paid employees at Springfield College in Massachusetts ★3509★

McGee; Glenn "Max"
Illinois school districts with the highest paid superintendents, 1999-2000 ★3986★

McGehee; Larry T.
Top pay and benefits for the chief executive and top paid employees at Wofford College ★3634★

McGill University
Canadian universities with the greatest impact in biology and biochemistry, 1993-97 ★195★
Canadian universities with the most citations per paper in the field of microbiology, 1992-96 ★214★
U.S. colleges and universities that devote the least course time to discussion ★989★
Best Canadian universities for producing leaders of tomorrow, 2000 ★1148★
Best Canadian universities overall, 2000 ★1149★
Best Canadian universities that are the most innovative, 2000 ★1150★
Best Canadian universities with the highest quality, 2000 ★1151★
Canadian medical/doctoral universities by alumni support, 2000 ★1172★
Canadian medical/doctoral universities by award-winning faculty members, 2000 ★1173★
Canadian medical/doctoral universities by class size at the first- and second-year level, 2000 ★1174★
Canadian medical/doctoral universities by class size at the third- and forth-year level, 2000 ★1175★
Canadian medical/doctoral universities by classes taught by tenured faculty, 2000 ★1176★
Canadian medical/doctoral universities by faculty members with Ph.D.'s, 2000 ★1177★
Canadian medical/doctoral universities by international graduate students, 2000 ★1178★
Canadian medical/doctoral universities by library acquisitions, 2000 ★1179★
Canadian medical/doctoral universities by library expenses, 2000 ★1180★
Canadian medical/doctoral universities by library holdings, 2000 ★1181★
Canadian medical/doctoral universities by library holdings per student, 2000 ★1182★
Canadian medical/doctoral universities by medical/science grants per faculty member, 2000 ★1184★
Canadian medical/doctoral universities by operating budget per student, 2000 ★1185★
Canadian medical/doctoral universities by percentage of operating budget allocated to scholarships, 2000 ★1186★
Canadian medical/doctoral universities by percentage of operating budget allocated to student services, 2000 ★1187★
Canadian medical/doctoral universities by reputation, 2000 ★1188★
Canadian medical/doctoral universities by social science/humanities grants per faculty member, 2000 ★1189★
Canadian medical/doctoral universities by students from out of province, 2000 ★1190★
Canadian medical/doctoral universities by students winning national awards, 2000 ★1191★
Canadian universities by average entering grade, 2000 ★1213★
Canadian universities by graduation rate, 2000 ★1214★
Canadian universities by students with 75% grade averages or higher, 2000 ★1215★
Canadian universities chosen as being value added, 2000 ★1216★
Canadian universities with the highest total cost, 2000 ★1217★
Top Canadian medical/doctoral universities, 2000 ★1221★
Top Canadian medical/doctoral universities best at producing leaders of tomorrow, 2000 ★1222★
Top Canadian medical/doctoral universities that are the best overall, 2000 ★1223★
Top Canadian medical/doctoral universities with the highest quality, 2000 ★1225★
Fiske Guide's best buys for public colleges and universities, 2001 ★1460★
University research libraries in the U.S. and Canada with the largest decreases in total expenditures from 1993-94 to 1998-99 ★2707★
Canadian universities with the greatest impact in neuroscience, 1993-97 ★4305★

McGinniss, F.S.C.; Bro. Michael J.
Top pay and benefits for the chief executive and top paid employees at Christian Brothers University ★3233★

McGowan; James A.
Top pay and benefits for the chief executive and top paid employees at Texas Christian University ★3518★

McGowan Jr.; Joseph J.
Top pay and benefits for the chief executive and top paid employees at Bellarmine University ★3196★

McGowan; Robert P.
Top pay and benefits for the chief executive and top paid employees at the University of Denver ★3540★

McGraw-Hill
Publishers with the best industry stocks, 2000 ★300★
Fortune's highest ranked publishing companies, 2000 ★489★
Top publishing and broadcasting companies in Standard & Poor's 500, 2001 ★553★
Book publishers with the most citations (Class 3) ★2564★
Highest revenues of publicly held book publishers, 1999 ★3072★

McGregor; Katie
All-America girls' high school soccer team forwards, 2001 ★175★

McGuire; Michael H.
Top pay and benefits for the chief executive and top paid employees at Creighton University ★3259★

McGuire; Patricia A.
Top pay and benefits for the chief executive and top paid employees at Trinity College in Washington D.C. ★3578★

McGuire; Thomas
Top pay and benefits for the chief executive and top paid employees at the University of La Verne ★3547★

McHenry Community College
Fall enrollment at Chicago-area public community colleges, by minority percentages, 1999 ★867★

McHenry Community High School, District 156
Illinois school districts spending the least for high school education 1997-98 ★4008★

McHenry County College
Average faculty salaries for institutions of higher education without academic ranks in Illinois, 2000-01 ★3747★

McHugh; Kenneth A.
Top pay and benefits for the chief executive and top paid employees at DePaul University ★3266★

McIntosh College
Highest undergraduate tuition and fees at colleges and universities in New Hampshire ★1531★

McIntosh; Robert
Top pay and benefits for the chief executive and top paid employees at Seattle Pacific University ★3494★

McIver; Nancy
All-USA Teacher Teams, Third Team, 2000 ★4401★

McKane; Joseph
Top pay and benefits for the chief executive and top paid employees at Aurora University ★3183★

McKay; Alan
Top pay and benefits for the chief executive and top paid employees at Shenandoah University ★3497★

McKay North; Douglas
Top pay and benefits for the chief executive and top paid employees at Alaska Pacific University ★3166★

McKendree College
Colleges and universities with the smallest endowments, 2000 ★1238★
U.S. News & World Report's midwestern regional liberal arts colleges with the highest percentage of freshmen in the top 25% of their high school class, 2000-01 ★1345★
U.S. News & World Report's midwestern regional liberal arts colleges with the lowest acceptance rates, 2000-01 ★1348★
Average faculty salaries for institutions of higher education in Illinois, 2000-01 ★3700★

McKenna; Margaret A.
Top pay and benefits for the chief executive and top paid employees at Lesley College ★3370★

McKenzie; Peter C.
Top pay and benefits for the chief executive and top paid employees at Boston College ★3205★

McKenzie; Stanley D.
Top pay and benefits for the chief executive and top paid employees at Rochester Institute of Technology ★3461★

McKeon; Rep. Howard P. (Buck)
Members of Congress receiving the largest contributions from the Sallie Mae Inc. Political Action Committee ★3023★

McKesson HBOC
Fortune's highest ranked wholesalers, 2000 ★505★

McKinley Middle School
Outstanding secondary schools in Albuquerque, New Mexico ★4080★

McKinney; Paul
Top pay and benefits for the chief executive and top paid employees at Wabash College ★3598★

McKinsey; Elizabeth
Top pay and benefits for the chief executive and top paid employees at Carleton College ★3222★

McKitish; Michael B.
Top pay and benefits for the chief executive and top paid employees at Drew University ★3273★

McKone; Harold
Top pay and benefits for the chief executive and top paid employees at Saint Joseph College in Connecticut ★3475★

McLaughlin; Gerald T.
Top pay and benefits for the chief executive and top paid employees at Loyola Marymount University ★3380★

McLaughlin; James B.
Top pay and benefits for the chief executive and top paid employees at Campbell University ★3218★

McLaughlin; Kelly
Radcliffe Institute for Advanced Study fellowship recipients in the field of molecular biology, 2000-01 ★208★

McLaughlin; Margaret
Top published female authors (1915-1985) in the field of communication studies ★4363★

McLean Hospital
Top psychiatric hospitals in the U.S., 2000 ★2800★

McLeod Bethune; Mary
Most influential African Americans in education ★2216★

McLeod; Kim
Radcliffe Institute for Advanced Study fellowship recipient in the field of astronomy, 2000-01 ★109★

McLeod; William
Top pay and benefits for the chief executive and top paid employees at Saint Mary's College of California ★3480★

McMahon; Linda
Top pay and benefits for the chief executive and top paid employees at Marymount University ★3395★

McMain Magnet High School
Outstanding secondary schools in New Orleans, Louisiana ★4190★

McMaste; James
Top pay and benefits for the chief executive and top paid employees at the Allegheny University of the Health Sciences ★3520★

McMaster University
Canadian universities with the most citations per paper in the field of microbiology, 1992-96 ★214★
Best Canadian universities for producing leaders of tomorrow, 2000 ★1148★
Best Canadian universities overall, 2000 ★1149★
Best Canadian universities that are the most innovative, 2000 ★1150★
Best Canadian universities with the highest quality, 2000 ★1151★
Canadian medical/doctoral universities by alumni support, 2000 ★1172★
Canadian medical/doctoral universities by award-winning faculty members, 2000 ★1173★
Canadian medical/doctoral universities by class size at the first- and second-year level, 2000 ★1174★
Canadian medical/doctoral universities by class size at the third- and forth-year level, 2000 ★1175★
Canadian medical/doctoral universities by classes taught by tenured faculty, 2000 ★1176★
Canadian medical/doctoral universities by faculty members with Ph.D.'s, 2000 ★1177★
Canadian medical/doctoral universities by international graduate students, 2000 ★1178★
Canadian medical/doctoral universities by library acquisitions, 2000 ★1179★
Canadian medical/doctoral universities by library expenses, 2000 ★1180★
Canadian medical/doctoral universities by library holdings, 2000 ★1181★
Canadian medical/doctoral universities by library holdings per student, 2000 ★1182★
Canadian medical/doctoral universities by medical/science grants per faculty member, 2000 ★1184★
Canadian medical/doctoral universities by operating budget per student, 2000 ★1185★
Canadian medical/doctoral universities by percentage of operating budget allocated to scholarships, 2000 ★1186★
Canadian medical/doctoral universities by percentage of operating budget allocated to student services, 2000 ★1187★
Canadian medical/doctoral universities by reputation, 2000 ★1188★
Canadian medical/doctoral universities by social science/humanities grants per faculty member, 2000 ★1189★
Canadian medical/doctoral universities by students from out of province, 2000 ★1190★
Canadian medical/doctoral universities by students winning national awards, 2000 ★1191★
Canadian universities by graduation rate, 2000 ★1214★
Canadian universities chosen as being value added, 2000 ★1216★
Top Canadian medical/doctoral universities, 2000 ★1221★
Top Canadian medical/doctoral universities that are the most innovative, 2000 ★1224★
Canadian universities publishing the most papers in the fields of economics and business, 1992-96 ★2215★
University research libraries in the U.S. and Canada with the largest decreases in total expenditures from 1993-94 to 1998-99 ★2707★
Canadian universities with the greatest impact in materials science, 1992-96 ★4304★

McMillan; Lex O.
Top pay and benefits for the chief executive and top paid employees at Gettysburg College ★3308★

McMillan; Terry
Favorite African American authors ★237★

McMorrow; Kyle
All-America boys' high school soccer team forwards, 2001 ★166★

McMurry University
U.S. News & World Report's best undergraduate fees among western regional liberal arts colleges by discount tuition, 2000 ★1384★
Academic reputation scores for U.S. News & World Report's top western regional liberal arts colleges, 2000-01 ★1387★
Acceptance rates for U.S. News & World Report's top western regional liberal arts colleges, 2000-01 ★1388★
Alumni giving rates at U.S. News & World Report's top western regional liberal arts colleges, 2000-01 ★1389★

Average freshmen retention rates for *U.S. News & World Report*'s top western regional liberal arts colleges, 2000-01 ★1390★

Average graduation rates for *U.S. News & World Report*'s top western regional liberal arts colleges, 2000-01 ★1391★

Percentage of freshmen in the top 25% of their high school class at *U.S. News & World Report*'s top western regional liberal arts colleges, 2000-01 ★1392★

Percentage of full-time faculty at *U.S. News & World Report*'s top western regional liberal arts colleges, 2000-01 ★1393★

Proportion of classes having 20 students or less at *U.S. News & World Report*'s top western regional liberal arts colleges, 2000-01 ★1394★

Student/faculty ratios at *U.S. News & World Report*'s top western regional liberal arts colleges, 2000-01 ★1395★

U.S. News & World Report's top western regional liberal arts colleges, 2000-01 ★1396★

Average faculty salaries for institutions of higher education in Texas, 2000-01 ★3731★

McNamara; John G.
Top pay and benefits for the chief executive and top paid employees at the University of San Diego ★3565★

McNeese State University
Division I NCAA colleges with that graduated none of their African American male basketball players, 1990-91 to 1993-94 ★930★

Division I NCAA colleges with the lowest graduation rates for female athletes, 1990-91 to 1993-94 ★936★

Division I NCAA colleges with the lowest graduation rates for female basketball players, 1990-91 to 1993-94 ★937★

State appropriations for Louisiana institutions of higher education, 2000-01 ★1271★

Average faculty salaries for institutions of higher education in Louisiana, 2000-01 ★3705★

McNemar; Donald W.
Top pay and benefits for the chief executive and top paid employees at Guilford College ★3316★

McNew; Janet
Top pay and benefits for the chief executive and top paid employees at Illinois Wesleyan University ★3347★

MCP Hahnemann University
U.S. News & World Report's national universities with the highest proportion of classes with less than 20 students, 2000-01 ★1138★

McPherson College
Highest undergraduate tuition and fees at colleges and universities in Kansas ★1506★

Average faculty salaries for institutions of higher education in Kansas, 2000-01 ★3703★

U.S. institutions with the lowest paid full professors, 2001 ★3979★

McPherson; Michael S.
Top pay and benefits for the chief executive and top paid employees at Macalester College ★3385★

McShane, S.J.; Rev. Joseph
Top pay and benefits for the chief executive and top paid employees at the University of Scranton ★3567★

McShane; William
Top pay and benefits for the chief executive and top paid employees at Polytechnic University ★3443★

McShurley; Mark
Top pay and benefits for the chief executive and top paid employees at Christendom College ★3232★

McTague; Kieran
Top pay and benefits for the chief executive and top paid employees at Emmanuel College in Massachusetts ★3288★

McThenia; Andrew
Top pay and benefits for the chief executive and top paid employees at Washington and Lee University ★3605★

Me Talk Pretty One Day
Library Journal's best nonfiction audiobooks, 2000 ★243★

Mead
Fortune's highest ranked forest and paper products companies, 2000 ★466★

Top paper and forest products companies in Standard & Poor's 500, 2001 ★552★

Meade Instruments
Companies with the best two-year total returns since 1998 ★436★

Meadow Glens Elementary School
Illinois suburban elementary schools with the highest ISAT scores in reading and math ★18★

The Meaning of Work in Women's Lives: A Sociopsychological Model of Career Choice and Work Behavior
Most frequently cited contribution articles in psychology journals from 1986 to 1996 ★3071★

The Measure of a Man: A Spiritual Autobiography
Booklist's most recommended African American nonfiction ★229★

Measuring Natural Resource Scarcity-Theory and Practice
Journal of Environmental Economics and Management's best articles in depletable resources and energy ★2462★

Mechanical
Engineering doctorates awarded at U.S. colleges and universities, by subfield, 1999 ★1923★

Gender breakdown of engineering doctorate recipients, by subfield, 1999 ★1934★

Mechanical engineer
Most desirable jobs in production/manufacturing ★2276★

Occupations with the highest average annual salaries for college graduates, 1998 ★3132★

Mechanical engineering
Average starting salaries for college graduates, by field, 2000 ★3129★

Expected starting salaries of 2000-01 bachelor's degree recipients, by specific major ★3131★

Mechanicsburg Area Intermediate School
All-USA Teacher Teams, Third Team, 2000 ★4401★

Mechanisms of Ageing and Development
Geriatrics and gerontology journals with the greatest impact measure, 1981-98 ★2805★

Geriatrics and gerontology journals with the greatest impact measure, 1998 ★2807★

Medaille College
Average faculty salaries for institutions of higher education in New York, 2000-01 ★3719★

Medcenter One College of Nursing
Lowest undergraduate tuition and fees at private nonprofit, 4-year or above colleges and universities ★1464★

Private 4-year institutions with the lowest tuition, 2000-01 ★1468★

Highest undergraduate tuition and fees at colleges and universities in North Dakota ★1541★

Medea Creek Middle School
Outstanding secondary schools in Los Angeles-Long Beach, California ★4167★

Medical Anthropology Quarterly
Anthropology journals by citation impact, 1998 ★65★

Medical assistants
Fastest growing occupations, 1998-2008 ★2302★

Projected employment growth for selected occupations that require shorter moderate-term on-the-job training, 1998-2008 ★2321★

Medical Care
Health policy and services journals by citation impact, 1981-99 ★2537★

Health policy and services journals by citation impact, 1995-99 ★2538★

Health policy and services journals by citation impact, 1999 ★2539★

Medical College of Georgia
State appropriations for Georgia's institutions of higher education, 2000-01 ★1263★

U.S. colleges and universities awarding the most biological and life sciences doctorate degrees to African Americans ★2082★

Medical College of Ohio
State appropriations for Ohio's institutions of higher education, 2000-01 ★1288★

Medical College of Wisconsin
State appropriations for Wisconsin's institutions of higher education, 2000-01 ★1302★

Medical laboratory technician
Jobs considered the loneliest ★2244★

Medical records technician
Jobs with the best environment scores ★2247★

Jobs with the best stress scores ★2252★

Jobs with the highest employment growth ★2254★

Most desirable jobs in healthcare/medicine ★2273★

Medical Research Council (UK)
Institutions with the highest impact in psychiatry research, 1990-98 ★3053★

Medical scientists
Projected employment growth for selected occupations that require advanced education, 1998-2008 ★2318★

Medical secretaries
Projected employment growth for selected occupations that require an associate degree or less, 1998-2008 ★2319★

Medical secretary
Jobs with the best stress scores ★2252★

Medical technologist
Most desirable jobs in healthcare/medicine ★2273★

Medical technology
Top health professions majors for accepted applicants to U.S. medical schools, 1999-2000 ★2852★

Medical University of South Carolina
Institutions receiving the most in federal agency appropriations to colleges, 2000 ★1245★

MEDICINAL

State appropriations for South Carolina's institutions of higher education, 2000-01 ★1293★

U.S. colleges and universities awarding the most health professions and related sciences first professional degrees to African Americans ★1847★

Medicinal/pharmaceutical
Chemistry doctorates awarded at U.S. colleges and universities, by subfield, 1999 ★1889★

Gender breakdown of chemistry doctorate recipients, by subfield, 1999 ★1929★

Medicine
Mean age of first and best contribution of scientists and inventors, by discipline ★3096★

Medicine and Dentistry of New Jersey; University of
State appropriations for New Jersey's institutions of higher education, 2000-01 ★1283★

U.S. colleges and universities awarding the most first professional degrees to Asian Americans ★1844★

U.S. colleges and universities awarding the most first professional degrees to Hispanic Americans ★1845★

U.S. colleges and universities awarding the most health professions and related sciences first professional degrees to African Americans ★1847★

U.S. colleges and universities awarding the most health professions and related sciences first professional degrees to Asian Americans ★1848★

U.S. colleges and universities awarding the most health professions and related sciences first professional degrees to Hispanic Americans ★1849★

U.S. colleges and universities awarding the most health professions and related sciences first professional degrees to minorities ★1850★

U.S. colleges and universities awarding the most biological and life sciences doctorate degrees to Asian Americans ★2083★

Medicine/health
Subject areas with the highest library expenditures/circulation ★306★

Medieval Folklore: An Encyclopedia of Myths, Legends, Tales, Beliefs, and Customs
Outstanding reference sources, 2000 ★370★

Medimmune
Top health care companies in Standard & Poor's 500, 2001 ★542★

Medina; Arturo N.
American Chemical Society 2001 award winners (Group 2) ★752★

Medland; William J.
Top pay and benefits for the chief executive and top paid employees at Viterbo University ★3597★

MEDLINEplus
Medical Library Association's top health related web sites ★2591★

Medtronic
Fortune's highest ranked medical products and equipment companies, 2000 ★474★

Top health care companies in Standard & Poor's 500, 2001 ★542★

Meely LaBauve
Most notable fiction books for young adults, 2001 ★322★

Meets the Eye
Most notable fiction books for reluctant young adult readers, 2001 ★321★

Meharry Medical College
Historically black colleges and universities awarding the most first professional degrees to African Americans ★1835★

U.S. colleges and universities awarding the most first professional degrees to African Americans ★1843★

U.S. colleges and universities awarding the most health professions and related sciences first professional degrees to African Americans ★1847★

U.S. colleges and universities awarding the most health professions and related sciences first professional degrees to minorities ★1850★

Historically black colleges and universities awarding the most doctorate degrees to African Americans ★1945★

U.S. colleges and universities awarding the most biological and life sciences doctorate degrees to African Americans ★2082★

Mehrling; P.
Top assistant professor economists at elite liberal arts colleges, 1975-94 ★2173★

Mehrotra; Chandra
Top pay and benefits for the chief executive and top paid employees at the College of St. Scholastica ★3530★

Mehta; D. Paul
Top pay and benefits for the chief executive and top paid employees at Bradley University ★3208★

Mehta; Naushirwan R.
Top pay and benefits for the chief executive and top paid employees at Tufts University ★3580★

Meier; Thomas K.
Top pay and benefits for the chief executive and top paid employees at Elmira College ★3284★

Meijer
Largest private companies, 2000 ★523★

Meister; Richard J.
Top pay and benefits for the chief executive and top paid employees at DePaul University ★3266★

Meisterling; Richard
Top pay and benefits for the chief executive and top paid employees at Coe College ★3240★

Melbourne Business School
Asiaweek's best M.B.A. programs ★590★

Melbourne Central Catholic High School
Outstanding secondary schools in Melbourne-Titusville-Palm Bay, Florida ★4176★

Melbourne; University of
Australian universities with the greatest impact in agricultural sciences, 1993-97 ★49★

Australian universities with the greatest impact in mathematics, 1993-97 ★2774★

Melton II; William F.
Top pay and benefits for the chief executive and top paid employees at Middlebury College ★3401★

Melton; L. Joseph
Most-cited researchers in epidemiology, 1981-1998 ★2876★

Melton; Loyd
Top pay and benefits for the chief executive and top paid employees at Erskine College ★3290★

Meltzer; Allan
Top pay and benefits for the chief executive and top paid employees at Carnegie Mellon University ★3223★

Memoirs of a Geisha
Longest-running trade paperback bestsellers, 2000 ★282★

Memoirs of the American Mathematical Society
Mathematics journals by impact factor ★2783★

Memorial Sloan-Kettering Cancer Center
Top cancer hospitals in the U.S., 2000 ★2787★

Top gynecology hospitals in the U.S., 2000 ★2792★

Top urology hospitals in the U.S., 2000 ★2803★

Memorial University
Canadian comprehensive universities by alumni support, 2000 ★1153★

Canadian comprehensive universities by award-winning faculty members, 2000 ★1154★

Canadian comprehensive universities by class size at the first- and second-year level, 2000 ★1155★

Canadian comprehensive universities by class size at the third- and forth-year level, 2000 ★1156★

Canadian comprehensive universities by classes taught by tenured faculty, 2000 ★1157★

Canadian comprehensive universities by faculty members with Ph.D.'s, 2000 ★1158★

Canadian comprehensive universities by international graduate students, 2000 ★1159★

Canadian comprehensive universities by library acquisitions, 2000 ★1160★

Canadian comprehensive universities by library expenses, 2000 ★1161★

Canadian comprehensive universities by library holdings per student, 2000 ★1162★

Canadian comprehensive universities by operating budget per student, 2000 ★1163★

Canadian comprehensive universities by percentage of operating budget allocated to scholarships, 2000 ★1164★

Canadian comprehensive universities by percentage of operating budget allocated to student services, 2000 ★1165★

Canadian comprehensive universities by social science/humanities grants per faculty member, 2000 ★1166★

Canadian comprehensive universities by students from out of province, 2000 ★1167★

Canadian comprehensive universities by students winning national awards, 2000 ★1168★

Canadian medical/doctoral universities by medical/science grants per faculty member, 2000 ★1183★

Top Canadian comprehensive universities, 2000 ★1219★

Top Canadian comprehensive universities by reputation, 2000 ★1220★

Memories of Summer
Most notable fiction books for young adults, 2001 ★322★

Memory and Cognition
Most cited psychology serials in technical communication journals from 1988 to 1997 ★4423★

Memphis College of Art
Highest undergraduate tuition and fees at colleges and universities in Tennessee ★1558★

Memphis; University of
Institutions with the most published authors in the *Journal of Business Research*, 1985 to 1999 ★695★
Division I NCAA colleges with that graduated none of their African American male basketball players, 1990-91 to 1993-94 ★930★
State appropriations for Tennessee's institutions of higher education, 2000-01 ★1295★
U.S. colleges and universities awarding the most social sciences and history master's degrees to African Americans ★1801★
Average faculty salaries for institutions of higher education in Tennessee, 2000-01 ★3730★

Men Are from Mars, Women Are from Venus
Retail audiobook titles selling 1 million copies ★301★

Men in the Off Hours
Library Journal's best poetry books, 2000 ★244★

Mencken; H.L.
Best U.S. works of journalism in the 20th century ★2769★

Menlo College
Average faculty salaries for institutions of higher education in California, 2000-01 ★3692★

Menominee Nations; College of the
U.S. tribal colleges ★1445★

Men's basketball
African American college athletics head coaches, by gender, 1999-2000 ★118★
College athletics head coaches, by gender, 1999-2000 ★122★
Minority college athletics head coaches, by gender, 1999-2000 ★133★

Mental retardation
Disabled students served in U.S. public school programs, 1998-99 ★1877★

Mentor Shore Junior High School
Outstanding secondary schools in Cleveland-Lorain-Elyria, Ohio ★4114★

Menzel; Paul T.
Top pay and benefits for the chief executive and top paid employees at Pacific Lutheran University ★3436★

Mercer University
Division I NCAA colleges with that graduated less than 20% of their African American male athletes, 1990-91 to 1993-94 ★928★
U.S. News & World Report's best undergraduate fees among southern regional universities by discount tuition, 2000 ★1429★
U.S. News & World Report's southern regional universities with the best academic reputation scores, 2000-01 ★1433★
U.S. News & World Report's southern regional universities with the highest percentage of freshmen in the top 25% of their high school class, 2000-01 ★1439★
U.S. News & World Report's southern regional universities with the highest proportion of classes with 20 students or less, 2000-01 ★1441★
U.S. News & World Report's top southern regional universities, 2000-01 ★1444★
Highest undergraduate tuition and fees at colleges and universities in Georgia ★1496★
U.S. colleges and universities awarding the most business management and administrative services master's degrees to African Americans ★1759★
Average faculty salaries for institutions of higher education in Georgia, 2000-01 ★3697★

Merck
Business Week's best companies in the United States ★411★
Business Week's top companies worldwide ★433★
Companies that have been on *Business Week*'s top 50 list the longest ★435★
Fortune's highest ranked pharmaceuticals companies, 2000 ★485★
Top health care companies in Standard & Poor's 500, 2001 ★542★
Most selective internships in the U.S., 2001 ★2610★
Top internships in the U.S. with the highest compensation, 2001 ★2611★
Top public companies for women executives, 2000 ★4457★

Merck; Edwin J.
Top pay and benefits for the chief executive and top paid employees at Wheaton College in Massachusetts ★3621★

Mercury Interactive
Business Week's best performing companies with the highest 3-year shareholder returns ★418★
Top office equipment and computers companies in Standard & Poor's 500, 2001 ★551★

Mercy College
Average faculty salaries for institutions of higher education in New York, 2000-01 ★3719★

Mercyhurst College
Colleges and universities with the smallest endowments, 2000 ★1238★
U.S. News & World Report's northern regional liberal arts colleges with the highest percentage of full-time faculty, 2000-01 ★1360★
Average faculty salaries for institutions of higher education in Pennsylvania, 2000-01 ★3725★

Mercyhurst Prep
Outstanding secondary schools in Erie, Pennsylvania ★4129★

Mercymount Country Day School
Outstanding secondary schools in Providence-Fall River-Warwick, Rhode Island-Maine ★4207★

Meredith
Top publishing and broadcasting companies in Standard & Poor's 500, 2001 ★553★

Meredith College
U.S. News & World Report's southern regional universities with the best alumni giving rates, 2000-01 ★1434★
U.S. News & World Report's southern regional universities with the highest acceptance rates, 2000-01 ★1436★
U.S. News & World Report's southern regional universities with the highest freshmen retention rates, 2000-01 ★1437★
U.S. News & World Report's southern regional universities with the highest graduation rates, 2000-01 ★1438★
Average faculty salaries for institutions of higher education in North Carolina, 2000-01 ★3720★

The merger of equivalence classes by unreinforced conditional section of comparison stimuli
Most cited sources in experimental analyses of human behavior between 1990 and 1999 ★3070★

Merino; Donald N.
Top pay and benefits for the chief executive and top paid employees at Stevens Institute of Technology ★3512★

Merion Mercy Academy
Outstanding secondary schools in Philadelphia, Pennsylvania-New Jersey ★4202★

Merkatz; Irwin R.
Top pay and benefits for the chief executive and top paid employees at Yeshiva University ★3640★

Merkel; Angela
European business moguls considered the best agenda setters ★438★

Merkt; Mary Lou
Top pay and benefits for the chief executive and top paid employees at Sweet Briar College ★3515★

Merolli; Roy
Top pay and benefits for the chief executive and top paid employees at Marist College ★3390★

Merrill Lynch
Fortune's highest ranked securities companies, 2000 ★494★
Top nonbank financial companies in Standard & Poor's 500, 2001 ★550★
Most selective internships in the U.S., 2001 ★2610★
Best companies for working mothers ★4446★

Merrill; Thomas
Top pay and benefits for the chief executive and top paid employees at Barry University ★3192★

Merrimack College
Division II NCAA colleges with the 100% graduation rates for men's basketball players, 1993-94 ★943★
Division II NCAA colleges with the 100% graduation rates for women's basketball players, 1993-94 ★944★
Division II NCAA colleges with the highest graduation rates for all sports, 1993-94 ★945★
U.S. News & World Report's northern regional liberal arts colleges with students most in debt, 1999 ★1352★
U.S. News & World Report's northern regional liberal arts colleges with the highest percentage of full-time faculty, 2000-01 ★1360★
U.S. News & World Report's northern regional liberal arts colleges with the lowest acceptance rates, 2000-01 ★1362★
Average faculty salaries for institutions of higher education in Massachusetts, 2000-01 ★3708★

Merritt College
Lowest undergraduate tuition and fees at public 2-year colleges and universities ★1465★
Lowest undergraduate tuition and fees at colleges and universities in California ★1487★

Mertz; Francis J.
Top pay and benefits for the chief executive and top paid employees at Fairleigh Dickinson University ★3292★

Mesa Community College
Lowest undergraduate tuition and fees at colleges and universities in Arizona ★1483★

Mesa High School
All-USA Teacher Teams, Second Team, 2000 ★4400★

Mesa State College
Average faculty salaries for institutions of higher education in Colorado, 2000-01 ★3693★

Meskill; Victor P.
- Presidents with the highest pay at Master's I and II colleges and universities, 1998-99 ★3161★
- Top pay and benefits for the chief executive and top paid employees at Dowling College ★3271★

Messenger, Messenger
- *Booklist*'s most recommended black history books for youth ★311★
- Outstanding books for young readers, 2000 ★328★

Messiah College
- *U.S. News & World Report*'s northern regional liberal arts colleges with the highest academic reputation scores, 2000-01 ★1354★
- *U.S. News & World Report*'s northern regional liberal arts colleges with the highest acceptance rates, 2000-01 ★1355★
- *U.S. News & World Report*'s northern regional liberal arts colleges with the highest freshmen retention rates, 2000-01 ★1357★
- *U.S. News & World Report*'s northern regional liberal arts colleges with the highest graduation rates, 2000-01 ★1358★
- *U.S. News & World Report*'s northern regional liberal arts colleges with the highest percentage of freshmen in the top 25% of their high school class, 2000-01 ★1359★
- *U.S. News & World Report*'s northern regional liberal arts colleges with the highest percentage of full-time faculty, 2000-01 ★1360★
- *U.S. News & World Report*'s top northern regional liberal arts colleges, 2000-01 ★1363★
- U.S. bachelor's institutions with the largest number of students studying abroad, 1998-99 ★2511★
- Average faculty salaries for institutions of higher education in Pennsylvania, 2000-01 ★3725★

Messner; Ann
- Radcliffe Institute for Advanced Study fellowship recipients in the field of visual arts, 2000-01 ★79★

Metal Ions/Biological Systems
- Inorganic and nuclear chemistry journals by citation impact, 1981-99 ★811★
- Inorganic and nuclear chemistry journals by citation impact, 1995-99 ★812★
- Inorganic and nuclear chemistry journals by citation impact, 1999 ★813★

Metallurgical
- Engineering doctorates awarded at U.S. colleges and universities, by subfield, 1999 ★1923★
- Gender breakdown of engineering doctorate recipients, by subfield, 1999 ★1934★

Meteorologist
- Jobs with the best outlook scores ★2249★
- Jobs with the lowest unemployment ★2258★
- Most desirable jobs in math/science ★2274★

Meteorology
- Earth, atmosphere, and marine science doctorates awarded at U.S. colleges and universities, by subfield, 1999 ★1909★
- Gender breakdown of earth, atmosphere, and marine science doctorate recipients, by subfield, 1999 ★1932★

Methodist
- Religious preference of incoming freshmen, 2000 ★1061★

Methodist College
- Highest undergraduate tuition and fees at colleges and universities in North Carolina ★1539★
- Average faculty salaries for institutions of higher education in North Carolina, 2000-01 ★3720★

Methodist Hospital (Cullen Eye Institute)
- Top ophthalmology hospitals in the U.S., 2000 ★2796★

Methodist Theological School Ohio
- Average faculty salaries for institutions of higher education in Ohio, 2000-01 ★3722★

MetLife
- *Fortune*'s highest ranked life and health insurance companies, 2000 ★472★

Metro Catholic Parish School
- Outstanding secondary schools in Cleveland-Lorain-Elyria, Ohio ★4114★

Metro High School
- Outstanding secondary schools in Cedar Rapids, Iowa ★4104★

Metropolitan Community College
- Institutions censured by the American Association of University Professors, 2001 ★1067★
- Lowest undergraduate tuition and fees at colleges and universities in Nebraska ★1529★

Metropolitan State College, Devner
- Total baccalaureate computer and information science degrees awarded to Hispanic Americans from U.S. colleges and universities, 1997-98 ★1693★

Metropolitan State University
- Average faculty salaries for institutions of higher education in Minnesota, 2000-01 ★3710★

Mexican American/Chicano
- U.S. medical school enrollment of U.S. citizens by racial/ethnic category, 1999-2000 ★2863★

Mexico
- Countries of origin for non-U.S. citizens awarded doctorates at U.S. colleges and universities, 1999 ★1901★
- Countries with the lowest spending per student on higher education, 1997 ★2489★
- Foreign countries with the highest enrollment of foreign students, 1999-2000 ★2496★
- Top countries of study for U.S. students studying abroad, 1998-99 ★2510★
- Institute for Scientific Information periodical prices by country, 2001 ★2922★

Mexico, South and Central America
- First-year physics and astronomy graduate students from the Americas, 1997-98 ★2990★

Meyer; Donald
- Top pay and benefits for the chief executive and top paid employees at Central College in Iowa ★3226★

Meyer; J. Barton
- Top pay and benefits for the chief executive and top paid employees at Transylvania University ★3575★

Meyer; Sharon
- Top pay and benefits for the chief executive and top paid employees at Golden Gate University ★3310★

Meyers; Richard S.
- Top pay and benefits for the chief executive and top paid employees at Webster University ★3608★

MGIC Investment
- *Business Week*'s best performing companies with the highest net margin, 2000 ★419★

MGM Mirage
- *Fortune*'s highest ranked hotels, casinos and resorts, 2000 ★470★

Miabach; H.I.
- Most cited authors in dermatology journals, 1981 to 1996 ★1870★

Miami (Bascom Palmer Eye Institute); University of
- Top ophthalmology hospitals in the U.S., 2000 ★2796★

Miami-Dade
- U.S. school districts with the highest number of vacancies for K-12 teachers ★2331★

Miami-Dade Community College
- Community colleges in North America with the highest enrollment ★852★
- Institutions with the most full-time Hispanic American faculty ★923★
- Institutions with the most part-time Hispanic American faculty ★924★
- U.S. colleges and universities with the most full-time Hispanic American faculty ★925★
- Largest degree-granting colleges and universities, by enrollment ★1068★
- Top colleges in terms of total associate degrees awarded to minorities, 1997-98 ★1677★
- Community colleges with the highest enrollment of foreign students, 1998-99 ★2493★
- Average faculty salaries for institutions of higher education in Florida, 2000-01 ★3696★

Miami Edison Senior High School
- All-USA Teacher Teams, First Team, 2000 ★4399★

Miami/Fort Lauderdale, FL
- U.S. market areas with the highest percentage of adults having internet access ★2607★

Miami; University of
- Institutions with the most full-time Hispanic American faculty ★923★
- U.S. colleges and universities with the most full-time Hispanic American faculty ★925★
- U.S. colleges and universities with an unfavorable surrounding town or city ★1023★
- U.S. colleges and universities spending the most on independent lobbyists, 1999 ★1310★
- Highest undergraduate tuition and fees at colleges and universities in Florida ★1494★
- Total baccalaureate communications degrees awarded to Hispanic Americans from U.S. colleges and universities, 1997-98 ★1689★
- Total baccalaureate health professions and related sciences degrees awarded to Hispanic Americans from U.S. colleges and universities, 1997-98 ★1723★
- Total baccalaureate physical sciences degrees awarded to Hispanic Americans from U.S. colleges and universities, 1997-98 ★1735★
- U.S. colleges and universities awarding the most biological and life sciences master's degrees to Hispanic Americans ★1758★
- U.S. colleges and universities awarding the most business management and administrative services master's degrees to Hispanic Americans ★1761★
- U.S. colleges and universities awarding the most communications master's degrees to Hispanic Americans ★1765★
- U.S. colleges and universities awarding the most English language/literature/letters master's degrees to Hispanic Americans ★1775★

U.S. colleges and universities awarding the most health professions and related sciences master's degrees to Hispanic Americans ★1779★

U.S. colleges and universities awarding the most law and legal studies master's degrees to Hispanic Americans ★1783★

U.S. colleges and universities awarding the most master's degrees to Hispanic Americans ★1787★

U.S. colleges and universities awarding the most psychology master's degrees to Hispanic Americans ★1799★

Traditionally white institutions awarding the most first professional degrees to African Americans ★1842★

U.S. colleges and universities awarding the most first professional degrees to African Americans ★1843★

U.S. colleges and universities awarding the most first professional degrees to Hispanic Americans ★1845★

U.S. colleges and universities awarding the most law and legal studies first professional degrees to African Americans ★1852★

U.S. colleges and universities awarding the most law and legal studies first professional degrees to Hispanic Americans ★1854★

U.S. colleges and universities awarding the most doctorate degrees to Hispanic Americans ★2097★

U.S. colleges and universities awarding the most psychology doctorate degrees to Hispanic Americans ★2122★

Top oceanography research-doctorate programs as evaluated by the National Research Council ★2153★

Academics' choices for best tax law programs, 2001 ★2632★

Law schools with the best constitutional law (general) faculty, 1999-2000 ★2645★

University research libraries in the U.S. and Canada with the largest decreases in total expenditures from 1993-94 to 1998-99 ★2707★

Academics' choices for best AIDS programs, 2001 ★2818★

Presidents with the highest pay at Research I and II universities, 1998-99 ★3162★

Average faculty salaries for institutions of higher education in Florida, 2000-01 ★3696★

Miami University, Hamilton
Average faculty salaries for institutions of higher education in Ohio, 2000-01 ★3722★

Miami University, Middletown
Average faculty salaries for institutions of higher education in Ohio, 2000-01 ★3722★
U.S. community colleges with the highest paid full professors, 2001 ★3976★

Miami University (OH)
U.S. colleges and universities with poor instructors ★1027★
U.S. colleges and universities with poor library facilities ★1028★
State appropriations for Ohio's institutions of higher education, 2000-01 ★1288★
Fiske Guide's best buys for public colleges and universities, 2001 ★1460★
U.S. doctoral institutions with the largest number of students studying abroad, 1998-99 ★2512★
College senior's choices for exemplary doctoral-intensive universities ★2532★
Institutions in the Worker Rights Consortium ★2913★

Miami University, Oxford
Average faculty salaries for institutions of higher education in Ohio, 2000-01 ★3722★

Miamisburg High School
Outstanding secondary schools in Dayton-Springfield, Ohio ★4122★

Michael DeBakey High School
Outstanding secondary schools in Houston, Texas ★4150★

Micheaux; Oscar
Most influential African American entertainers ★77★

Michelangelo
Booklist's best art books for young people ★308★
Outstanding books for middle readers, 2000 ★326★

Michell; Peter
Top pay and benefits for the chief executive and top paid employees at Mills College ★3402★

Michigan
People for the American Way's list of states with the most challenges to library and school books, 1982-1992 ★750★
States with the highest enrollment in private 4-year institutions of higher education ★860★
States with the highest enrollment in public 4-year institutions of higher education ★861★
Mean composite ACT scores by state, 2000 ★895★
Mean math SAT scores by state, 2000 ★900★
Mean verbal SAT scores by state, 2000 ★903★
Average class size at colleges and universities in the U.S., by state ★1064★
States allocating the largest amount of state tax appropriations for higher education, 2000-01 ★1304★
Total doctorate recipients by state, 1999 ★2054★
State library associations with most full-time staff ★2681★
State library associations with the highest annual revenue ★2682★
State library associations with the highest conference attendance ★2683★
State library associations with the highest unrestricted net assets ★2684★
State library associations with the largest membership ★2685★
State grades for affordability of higher education for minority students, 2000 ★2883★
State grades for benefits state receives for educating its minority students, 2000 ★2884★
State grades for completion of higher education by minority students, 2000 ★2885★
State grades for participation of minority students in higher education, 2000 ★2886★
State grades for preparing minority students for higher education, 2000 ★2887★
States with the highest number of high school graduates, 1999-2000 ★3995★
States with the most public school districts ★3999★
States with the highest K-12 public school enrollment ★4034★
States with the highest projected K-12 public school enrollment for 2010 ★4035★
States with the highest funding needs for school-building modernization ★4040★
States with the highest funding needs for school-technology modernization ★4041★
States with the most charter schools ★4048★
States with the most K-12 public schools ★4049★
States with the most women-owned companies ★4455★

Michigan, Ann Arbor; University of
U.S. universities publishing the most papers in the field of artificial intelligence, 1995-99 ★100★
U.S. colleges and universities with the highest average football attendance, 1996-99 ★159★
U.S. universities publishing the most papers in the field of management, 1995-99 ★574★
Academics' choices for best part-time MBA programs, 2000 ★587★
Four-year institutions with the most liquor arrests reported, 1999 ★707★
Four-year public institutions enrolling the highest number of students from the District of Columbia, 1998-99 ★855★
U.S. colleges and universities where intercollegiate sports are popular ★995★
U.S. colleges and universities with excellent library facilities ★1025★
Retention rates of African American students at traditionally white institutions, 1997-98 ★1121★
U.S. News & World Report's best public national universities, 2000-01 ★1123★
U.S. News & World Report's national universities with the highest acceptance rates, 2000-01 ★1131★
Total baccalaureate English language, literature, and letters degrees awarded to Asian Americans from U.S. colleges and universities, 1997-98 ★1717★
Total baccalaureate English language, literature, and letters degrees awarded to Native Americans from U.S. colleges and universities, 1997-98 ★1719★
Total baccalaureate psychology degrees awarded to Asian Americans from U.S. colleges and universities, 1997-98 ★1738★
Traditionally white institutions awarding the most master's degrees to African Americans ★1755★
U.S. colleges and universities awarding the most biological and life sciences master's degrees to Asian Americans ★1757★
U.S. colleges and universities awarding the most business management and administrative services master's degrees to African Americans ★1759★
U.S. colleges and universities awarding the most business management and administrative services master's degrees to Hispanic Americans ★1761★
U.S. colleges and universities awarding the most English language/literature/letters master's degrees to Asian Americans ★1774★
U.S. colleges and universities awarding the most health professions and related sciences master's degrees to African Americans ★1777★
U.S. colleges and universities awarding the most health professions and related sciences master's degrees to Asian Americans ★1778★
U.S. colleges and universities awarding the most master's degrees to African Americans ★1785★
U.S. colleges and universities awarding the most master's degrees to Asian Americans ★1786★
U.S. colleges and universities awarding the most master's degrees to minorities ★1788★

MICHIGAN

U.S. colleges and universities awarding the most physical sciences master's degrees to Asian Americans ★1794★

U.S. colleges and universities awarding the most social sciences and history master's degrees to African Americans ★1801★

Traditionally white institutions awarding the most first professional degrees to African Americans ★1842★

U.S. colleges and universities awarding the most first professional degrees to African Americans ★1843★

U.S. colleges and universities awarding the most first professional degrees to Asian Americans ★1844★

U.S. colleges and universities awarding the most health professions and related sciences first professional degrees to African Americans ★1847★

U.S. colleges and universities awarding the most health professions and related sciences first professional degrees to Asian Americans ★1848★

U.S. colleges and universities awarding the most health professions and related sciences first professional degrees to minorities ★1850★

Doctorate-granting-institutions awarding the most non-U.S. citizen doctoral degrees, 1999 ★1906★

Top doctorate granting institutions, 1999 ★2047★

Traditionally white institutions awarding the most doctorate degrees to African Americans ★2079★

U.S. colleges and universities awarding the most doctoral degrees to African Americans from 1995 to 1999 ★2091★

U.S. colleges and universities awarding the most doctoral degrees to American Indians and Alaskan Natives from 1995 to 1999 ★2092★

U.S. colleges and universities awarding the most doctoral degrees to Asian Americans and Pacific Islanders from 1995 to 1999 ★2093★

U.S. colleges and universities awarding the most doctoral degrees to Hispanic Americans from 1995 to 1999 ★2094★

U.S. colleges and universities awarding the most doctorate degrees to African Americans ★2095★

U.S. colleges and universities awarding the most doctorate degrees to Asian Americans ★2096★

U.S. colleges and universities awarding the most doctorate degrees to Hispanic Americans ★2097★

U.S. colleges and universities awarding the most doctorate degrees to minorities ★2098★

U.S. colleges and universities awarding the most doctorates in all fields, 1999 ★2100★

U.S. colleges and universities awarding the most doctorates in engineering, 1999 ★2102★

U.S. colleges and universities awarding the most doctorates in humanities, 1999 ★2103★

U.S. colleges and universities awarding the most doctorates in physical sciences, mathematics, and computer sciences, 1999 ★2105★

U.S. colleges and universities awarding the most doctorates in social sciences, 1999 ★2107★

U.S. colleges and universities awarding the most physical sciences doctorate degrees to African Americans ★2118★

U.S. colleges and universities awarding the most psychology doctorate degrees to Hispanic Americans ★2122★

U.S. colleges and universities awarding the most social sciences and history doctorate degrees to Hispanic Americans ★2126★

U.S. institutions awarding the most doctorate degrees, 1999 ★2132★

U.S. universities publishing the most papers in the field of education, 1994-98 ★2219★

Acceptance rates for *U.S. News & World Report*'s top 10 graduate engineering schools, 2001 ★2358★

Average analytic GRE scores for *U.S. News & World Report*'s top 10 graduate engineering schools, 2001 ★2359★

Average quantitative GRE scores for *U.S. News & World Report*'s top 10 graduate engineering schools, 2001 ★2360★

Doctoral student-faculty ratios at *U.S. News & World Report*'s top 10 graduate engineering schools, 2001 ★2361★

Faculty membership in National Academy of Engineering at *U.S. News & World Report*'s top 10 graduate engineering schools, 2001 ★2362★

Ph.D.s granted at *U.S. News & World Report*'s top 10 graduate engineering schools, 2001 ★2363★

Research expenditures per faculty member at *U.S. News & World Report*'s top 10 graduate engineering schools, 2001 ★2364★

Research funding allocated to *U.S. News & World Report*'s top 10 graduate engineering schools, 2001 ★2365★

Top graduate engineering schools, 2001 ★2366★

Top graduate engineering schools by reputation, as determined by academic personnel, 2001 ★2367★

Top graduate engineering schools by reputation, as determined by engineers and recruiters, 2001 ★2368★

U.S. News & World Report's graduate engineering programs with the highest academic reputation scores, 2000-01 ★2372★

Academics' choices for best graduate aerospace/aeronautical/astronautical engineering programs, 2001 ★2374★

U.S. News & World Report's graduate engineering programs with the best aerospace departments, 2000-01 ★2378★

Academics' choices for best graduate bioengineering/biomedical engineering programs, 2001 ★2381★

Academics' choices for best graduate civil engineering programs, 2001 ★2394★

Academics' choices for best graduate computer engineering programs, 2001 ★2399★

Academics' choices for best graduate electrical/electronic/communications engineering programs, 2001 ★2403★

U.S. News & World Report's graduate engineering programs with the best electrical departments, 2000-01 ★2407★

Academics' choices for best graduate environmental/environmental health engineering programs, 2001 ★2408★

U.S. News & World Report's graduate engineering programs with the best environmental departments, 2000-01 ★2410★

Academics' choices for best graduate industrial/manufacturing engineering programs, 2001 ★2411★

U.S. News & World Report's graduate engineering programs with the best industrial manufacturing departments, 2000-01 ★2415★

Academics' choices for best graduate materials engineering programs, 2001 ★2417★

U.S. News & World Report's graduate engineering programs with the best materials departments, 2000-01 ★2421★

Academics' choices for best graduate mechanical engineering programs, 2001 ★2422★

U.S. News & World Report's graduate engineering programs with the best mechanical departments, 2000-01 ★2425★

Academics' choices for best graduate nuclear engineering schools, 2000 ★2426★

U.S. News & World Report's graduate engineering programs with the best nuclear departments, 2000-01 ★2428★

U.S. universities publishing the most papers in the field of literature, 1994-98 ★2447★

Research institutions with the highest enrollment of foreign students, 1998-99 ★2503★

Average GMAT scores for *U.S. News & World Report*'s top 10 graduate business schools, 2000 ★2529★

College senior's choices for exemplary doctoral-extensive universities ★2531★

First-year student's choices for exemplary doctoral-extensive universities ★2534★

Academics' choices for best clinical law programs, 2001 ★2626★

Academics' choices for best international law programs, 2001 ★2631★

Acceptance rates at *U.S. News & World Report*'s top 10 law schools, 2001 ★2634★

Graduate employment after graduation percentage for *U.S. News & World Report*'s top 10 law schools, 2001 ★2635★

Graduate employment percentage for *U.S. News & World Report*'s top 10 law schools, 2001 ★2636★

Jurisdiction's overall bar passage rate for *U.S. News & World Report*'s top 10 law schools, 2001 ★2637★

School's bar passage rate in jurisdiction at *U.S. News & World Report*'s top 10 law schools, 2001 ★2667★

Student-faculty ratios at *U.S. News & World Report*'s top 10 law schools, 2001 ★2669★

Top law schools, 2001 ★2670★

Top law schools by reputation, as determined by academic personnel, 2001 ★2671★

Top law schools by reputation, as determined by lawyers and judges, 2001 ★2672★

Academics' choices for best family medicine programs, 2001 ★2820★

Academics' choices for best geriatrics programs, 2001 ★2821★

Academics' choices for best internal medicine programs, 2001 ★2822★

Acceptance rates for *U.S. News & World Report*'s top 10 research-oriented medical schools, 2001 ★2827★

Average MCAT scores at *U.S. News & World Report*'s top 10 research-oriented medical schools, 2001 ★2836★

Average undergraduate GPA at *U.S. News & World Report*'s top 10 research-oriented medical schools, 2001 ★2838★

Faculty-student ratios at *U.S. News & World Report*'s top 10 research-oriented medical schools, 2001 ★2842★

NIH research grants for *U.S. News & World Report*'s top 10 research-oriented medical schools, 2001 ★2845★

Out-of-state tuition and fees for *U.S. News & World Report*'s top 10 research-oriented medical schools, 2001 ★2847★
Top research-oriented medical schools, 2001 ★2859★
Top research-oriented medical schools by reputation, as determined by academic personnel, 2001 ★2860★
Top research-oriented medical schools by reputation, as determined by intern/residency directors, 2001 ★2861★
Institutions in the Worker Rights Consortium ★2913★
Average faculty salaries for institutions of higher education in Michigan, 2000-01 ★3709★
Public institutions of higher education that pay the highest salaries to female professors, 2000-01 ★3975★
U.S. universities publishing the most papers in the field of sociology and anthropology, 1994-98 ★4349★
Academics' choices for best administration/supervision graduate programs, 2001 ★4378★
Academics' choices for best curriculum/instruction graduate programs, 2001 ★4380★
Academics' choices for best education policy graduate programs, 2001 ★4381★
Academics' choices for best educational psychology graduate programs, 2001 ★4382★
Academics' choices for best elementary education graduate programs, 2001 ★4383★
Academics' choices for best higher education administration graduate programs, 2001 ★4384★
Acceptance rates at *U.S. News & World Report*'s top 10 graduate education schools, 2001 ★4388★
Average quantitative GRE scores for *U.S. News & World Report*'s top 10 graduate education schools, 2001 ★4389★
Average verbal GRE scores for *U.S. News & World Report*'s top 10 graduate education schools, 2001 ★4390★
Doctoral students to faculty ratio at *U.S. News & World Report*'s top 10 graduate education schools, 2001 ★4391★
Ph.D.s and Ed.D.s granted at *U.S. News & World Report*'s top 10 graduate education schools, 2001 ★4392★
Research expenditures for *U.S. News & World Report*'s top 10 graduate education schools, 2001 ★4393★
Research expenditures per faculty member at *U.S. News & World Report*'s top 10 graduate education schools, 2001 ★4394★
Top graduate education schools, 2001 ★4395★
Top graduate education schools by reputation, as determined by academic personnel, 2001 ★4396★
Top graduate education schools by reputation, as determined by superintendents, 2001 ★4397★

Michigan Business School; University of
U.S. News & World Report's undergraduate business programs with the best consulting departments, 2000-01 ★563★
U.S. News & World Report's undergraduate business programs with the best general management departments, 2000-01 ★566★
U.S. News & World Report's undergraduate business programs with the best human resources departments, 2000-01 ★567★
U.S. News & World Report's undergraduate business programs with the best production/operations departments, 2000-01 ★569★
U.S. News & World Report's undergraduate business programs with the highest academic reputation scores, 2000-01 ★571★
U.S. News & World Report's undergraduate business programs with the best accounting departments, 2000-01 ★581★
Academics' choices for best graduate entrepreneurship programs, 2001 ★583★
Academics' choices for best graduate executive MBA programs, 2001 ★584★
Academics' choices for best graduate management information systems programs, 2001 ★585★
Academics' choices for best graduate nonprofit organizations programs, 2001 ★586★
Acceptance rates for *U.S. News & World Report*'s top 10 graduate business schools, 2001 ★588★
Annual tuition at *Business Week*'s top business schools, 2000 ★589★
Average GMAT scores at *U.S. News & World Report*'s top 10 graduate business schools, 2001 ★591★
Average job offers received by graduates from *Business Week*'s top business schools, 1999 ★592★
Average undergraduate GPA at *U.S. News & World Report*'s top 10 graduate business schools, 2001 ★593★
Business Week's top business schools, 2000 ★595★
Business Week's top business schools as selected by corporate recruiters, 2000 ★596★
Business Week's top business schools as selected by recent MBA graduates, 2000 ★597★
Business Week's top business schools for finance skills as selected by corporate recruiters, 2000 ★600★
Business Week's top business schools for general management skills as selected by corporate recruiters, 2000 ★601★
Business Week's top business schools for global scope skills as selected by corporate recruiters, 2000 ★602★
Business Week's top business schools for marketing skills as selected by corporate recruiters, 2000 ★603★
Business Week's top business schools with the highest percentage of minority enrollment, 2000 ★613★
Highest pre-MBA salaries for students enrolled in *Business Week*'s top business schools, 1999 ★632★
Median starting salaries of graduates from *U.S. News & World Report*'s top 10 graduate business schools, 2001 ★636★
Out-of-state tuition and fees for *U.S. News & World Report*'s top 10 graduate business schools, 2001 ★637★
Percentage of applicants accepted at *Business Week*'s top business schools, 2000 ★638★
Percentage of employed graduates at *U.S. News & World Report*'s top 10 graduate business schools, 2001 ★639★
Percentage of graduates earning over $100,000 from *Business Week*'s top business schools, 1999 ★640★
Percentage of graduates employed within 3 months of graduation from *U.S. News & World Report*'s top 10 graduate business schools, 2001 ★641★
Top graduate business schools, 2001 ★649★
Top graduate business schools by reputation as determined by academic personnel, 2001 ★650★
Top graduate business schools by reputation, as determined by recruiters, 2001 ★651★
Academics' choices for best graduate accounting programs, 2001 ★659★
U.S. News & World Report's undergraduate business programs with the best finance departments, 2000-01 ★665★
Academics' choices for best graduate general management programs, 2001 ★666★
Academics' choices for best graduate international business programs, 2001 ★668★
Academics' choices for best graduate marketing programs, 2001 ★670★
Academics' choices for best graduate quantitative analysis programs, 2001 ★673★
Academics' choices for best graduate production/operations management programs, 2001 ★674★
U.S. News & World Report's undergraduate business programs with the best international business departments, 2000-01 ★682★
U.S. News & World Report's undergraduate business programs with the best marketing departments, 2000-01 ★685★

Michigan, Dearborn; University of
U.S. News & World Report's top public midwestern regional universities, 2000-01 ★1412★
Institutions with the most female physics bachelor's recipients, 1994-1998 ★2959★
U.S. institutions with more than 40% female bachelor's graduates in their physics departments, 1994-98 ★2977★
Average faculty salaries for institutions of higher education in Michigan, 2000-01 ★3709★

Michigan, Flint; University of
Average faculty salaries for institutions of higher education in Michigan, 2000-01 ★3709★

Michigan Invitational Group
Comparison of 8th grade science achievement scores, U.S. and worldwide, 1999 ★6★

Michigan Law Review
Law journals by citation impact, 1981-96 ★2617★
Law journals with the greatest impact measure, 1981-98 ★2618★
Most frequently-cited law reviews and legal periodicals, 1924-1986: a compilation ★2619★
Most frequently-cited law reviews and legal periodicals, according to *Shepard's Law Review Citations*, 1957-1986 ★2620★

Michigan Medical Center; University of
Top endocrinology hospitals in the U.S., 2000 ★2789★
Top geriatrics hospitals in the U.S., 2000 ★2791★
Top hospitals in the U.S., 2000 ★2793★
Top otolaryngology hospitals in the U.S., 2000 ★2798★
Top rehabilitation hospitals in the U.S., 2000 ★2801★
Top pharmacology research-doctorate programs as evaluated by the National Research Council ★2939★

Michigan Model for Comprehensive School Health Education
People for the American Way's list of most frequently challenged materials, 1982-1992 ★749★

MICHIGAN

Michigan State University
- Top business schools for within-discipline research performance in production/operations management, 1986-1998 ★648★
- U.S. business schools with the quickest payback on MBA investments ★654★
- Institutions with the most published authors in the *Journal of Business Research*, 1985 to 1999 ★695★
- Four-year institutions with the most drug arrests reported, 1999 ★705★
- Four-year institutions with the most liquor arrests reported, 1999 ★707★
- Four-year institutions with the most weapons arrests reported, 1999 ★709★
- U.S. college campuses with more than 5,000 students reporting murders or manslaughters, 1998 ★729★
- U.S. colleges and universities reporting the most alcohol related arrests, 1998 ★730★
- U.S. colleges and universities reporting the most weapons related arrests, 1998 ★732★
- U.S. colleges and universities with the largest numerical increases in weapons arrests, 1998 ★735★
- U.S. colleges and universities where intercollegiate sports are popular ★995★
- U.S. colleges and universities with a popular newspaper ★1018★
- U.S. colleges and universities with the most upper level courses taught by TAs ★1040★
- Largest degree-granting colleges and universities, by enrollment ★1068★
- State appropriations for Michigan's institutions of higher education, 2000-01 ★1275★
- Universities with the most-cited scholars in *Criminal Justice and Behavior* ★1648★
- U.S. colleges and universities awarding the most communications master's degrees to African Americans ★1763★
- U.S. colleges and universities awarding the most communications master's degrees to Asian Americans ★1764★
- U.S. colleges and universities awarding the most education master's degrees to Native Americans ★1772★
- U.S. institutions awarding the most baccalaureate degrees to African Americans in agribusiness and production, 1998 ★1813★
- U.S. institutions awarding the most baccalaureate degrees to Asian Americans in agribusiness and production, 1998 ★1815★
- U.S. institutions awarding the most baccalaureate degrees to minorities in agribusiness and production, 1998 ★1819★
- U.S. institutions awarding the most master's degrees to minorities in agribusiness and production, 1998 ★1829★
- U.S. colleges and universities awarding the most health professions and related sciences first professional degrees to Hispanic Americans ★1849★
- U.S. colleges and universities awarding the most health professions and related sciences first professional degrees to Native Americans ★1851★
- Traditionally white institutions awarding the most doctorate degrees to African Americans ★2079★
- U.S. colleges and universities awarding the most doctorate degrees to African Americans ★2095★
- U.S. colleges and universities awarding the most doctorate degrees to minorities ★2098★
- U.S. colleges and universities awarding the most doctorate degrees to Native Americans ★2099★
- U.S. colleges and universities awarding the most doctorates in professional and other fields, 1999 ★2106★
- U.S. colleges and universities awarding the most social sciences and history doctorate degrees to African Americans ★2124★
- U.S. institutions awarding the most doctoral degrees to minorities in agricultural sciences, 1998 ★2131★
- U.S. universities with the greatest impact in education, 1993-97 ★2220★
- U.S. universities with the greatest impact in education, 1994-98 ★2221★
- U.S. research institutions with the largest number of students studying abroad, 1998-99 ★2514★
- Institutions with the most prolific communication studies researchers ★2749★
- U.S. universities publishing the most papers in the field of communication, 1994-98 ★2755★
- Academics' choices for best family medicine programs, 2001 ★2820★
- Academics' choices for best rural medicine programs, 2001 ★2824★
- Acceptance rates for *U.S. News & World Report*'s top 10 primary-care medical schools, 2001 ★2826★
- Average MCAT scores at *U.S. News & World Report*'s top 10 primary-care medical schools, 2001 ★2835★
- Average undergraduate GPA at *U.S. News & World Report*'s top 10 primary-care medical schools, 2001 ★2837★
- Faculty-student ratios at *U.S. News & World Report*'s top 10 primary-care medical schools, 2001 ★2841★
- Out-of-state tuition and fees at *U.S. News & World Report*'s top 10 primary-care medical schools, 2001 ★2846★
- Percentage of graduates entering *U.S. News & World Report*'s top 10 primary-care medical schools, 2001 ★2848★
- Top primary-care medical schools, 2001 ★2856★
- Top primary-care medical schools by reputation, as determined by academic personnel, 2001 ★2857★
- Women faculty in Ph.D. physics departments at U.S. institutions, 1998 ★2981★
- Most patents issued to universities or research facilities, 1999 ★3097★
- Average faculty salaries for institutions of higher education in Michigan, 2000-01 ★3709★
- Academics' choices for best curriculum/instruction graduate programs, 2001 ★4380★
- Academics' choices for best education policy graduate programs, 2001 ★4381★
- Academics' choices for best educational psychology graduate programs, 2001 ★4382★
- Academics' choices for best elementary education graduate programs, 2001 ★4383★
- Academics' choices for best higher education administration graduate programs, 2001 ★4384★
- Academics' choices for best secondary education graduate programs, 2001 ★4385★
- Top graduate education schools by reputation, as determined by academic personnel, 2001 ★4396★

Michigan State University, Eli Broad College of Business
- *Business Week*'s top business schools with the highest percentage of international students, 2000 ★612★
- *Business Week*'s top business schools with the lowest percentage of minority enrollment, 2000 ★616★
- Lowest post-MBA salaries for students enrolled in *Business Week*'s top business schools, 1999 ★634★
- Lowest pre-MBA salaries for students enrolled in *Business Week*'s top business schools, 1999 ★635★

Michigan Technological University
- U.S. colleges and universities that devote the least course time to discussion ★989★
- State appropriations for Michigan's institutions of higher education, 2000-01 ★1275★
- Doctorate-granting-institutions with the highest percentage of non-U.S. citizen doctoral degrees awarded, 1999 ★1907★
- Average faculty salaries for institutions of higher education in Michigan, 2000-01 ★3709★

Michigan; University of
- Most effective anthropology research-doctorate programs as evaluated by the National Research Council ★61★
- Top anthropology research-doctorate programs as evaluated by the National Research Council ★62★
- Most effective art history research-doctorate programs as evaluated by the National Research Council ★91★
- Top art history research-doctorate programs as evaluated by the National Research Council ★93★
- Division I-A all-time percentage leaders ★127★
- Most effective ecology, evolution, and behavior research-doctorate programs as evaluated by the National Research Council ★199★
- Top ecology, evolution, and behavior research-doctorate programs as evaluated by the National Research Council ★201★
- Top business schools in research performance, 1986-1998 ★532★
- Top business schools by average MBA rank, 1986-1998 ★644★
- Top business schools for overall within-discipline research performance, 1986-1998 ★645★
- Top business schools for within-discipline research performance in management, 1986-1998 ★646★
- Top business schools for within-discipline research performance in management science, 1986-1998 ★647★
- Top business schools for within-discipline research performance in accounting, 1986-1998 ★660★
- Top business schools for within-discipline research performance in finance, 1986-1998 ★663★
- Most effective classics research-doctorate programs as evaluated by the National Research Council ★815★
- Top classics research-doctorate programs as evaluated by the National Research Council ★816★
- Division I NCAA colleges with that graduated none of their African American male basketball players, 1990-91 to 1993-94 ★930★
- U.S. colleges and universities where fraternities and sororities are popular ★993★

2001 mid-year endowment values of the 'wealthiest' U.S. universities ★1234★
Colleges and universities with the largest endowments, 2000 ★1237★
Institutions receiving the most alumni gifts, 1999-2000 ★1242★
State appropriations for Michigan's institutions of higher education, 2000-01 ★1275★
Top comparative literature research-doctorate programs as evaluated by the National Research Council ★1588★
U.S. universities with the greatest impact in communication, 1995-99 ★1657★
U.S. universities publishing the most papers in the field of dentistry/oral surgery and medicine, 1995-99 ★1865★
U.S. universities with the greatest impact in dermatology, 1994-98 ★1875★
U.S. universities with the greatest impact in dermatology, 1995-99 ★1876★
Economics departments by number of citations by top economists, 1971-92 ★2158★
Economics departments by number of citations per top economist, 1971-92 ★2159★
Economics departments by number of top economists, 1971-92 ★2160★
Economics Ph.D. programs by number of citations of top economist graduates, 1971-92 ★2204★
Economics Ph.D. programs by number of citations per top economist graduate, 1971-92 ★2205★
Economics Ph.D. programs by number of top economist graduates, 1971-92 ★2206★
Origin of doctorate for economics faculty at Ph.D.-granting institutions ★2209★
Origin of doctorate for economics faculty at Ph.D.-granting institutions, by Ph.D. equivalents produced ★2210★
Top economics research-doctorate programs as evaluated by the National Research Council ★2213★
U.S. universities with the greatest impact in education, 1993-97 ★2220★
U.S. universities with the greatest impact in education, 1994-98 ★2221★
Most effective aerospace engineering research-doctorate programs as evaluated by the National Research Council ★2375★
Top aerospace engineering research-doctorate programs as evaluated by the National Research Council ★2376★
Top biomedical engineering research-doctorate programs as evaluated by the National Research Council ★2384★
Most effective civil engineering research-doctorate programs as evaluated by the National Research Council ★2395★
Top civil engineering research-doctorate programs as evaluated by the National Research Council ★2396★
U.S. universities with the highest concentrations in artificial intelligence, 1992-96 ★2402★
Most effective electrical engineering research-doctorate programs as evaluated by the National Research Council ★2404★
Top electrical engineering research-doctorate programs as evaluated by the National Research Council ★2405★
Most effective industrial engineering research-doctorate programs as evaluated by the National Research Council ★2412★
Top industrial engineering research-doctorate programs as evaluated by the National Research Council ★2413★

Top materials science research-doctorate programs as evaluated by the National Research Council ★2419★
Most effective mechanical engineering research-doctorate programs as evaluated by the National Research Council ★2423★
U.S. universities with the greatest impact in metallurgy, 1995-99 ★2435★
Top French language and literature research-doctorate programs as evaluated by the National Research Council ★2516★
Top Ph.D.-granting departments of geography from 1925-1982 ★2521★
U.S. universities contributing the most papers in the field of history, 1993-97 ★2551★
Top history research-doctorate programs as evaluated by the National Research Council ★2554★
Publishers, journals and proceedings with the lowest citations (Class 6) ★2571★
Law schools with the best commercial law faculty, 1999-2000 ★2641★
Law schools with the best comparative law faculty, 1999-2000 ★2642★
Law schools with the best criminal procedure faculty, 1999-2000 ★2648★
Law schools with the best feminist legal theory faculty, 1999-2000 ★2651★
Law schools with the best jurisprudence faculty, 1999-2000 ★2655★
Law schools with the best law and social science plus psychology and sociology faculty, 1999-2000 ★2659★
Law schools with the best legal history faculty, 1999-2000 ★2661★
Law schools with the best moral and political theory (Anglo-American traditions) faculty, 1999-2000 ★2662★
Law schools with the highest quality, 1999-2000 ★2666★
Top law school student bodies, 1999-2000 ★2673★
Top university research libraries in the U.S. and Canada, 1998-99 ★2706★
Comparison of library and information science programs composite rankings with *U.S. News & World Report* survey ★2709★
Library and information science programs with the most citations to journal articles, 1993-1998 ★2712★
Library and information science programs with the most journal articles per capita, 1993-1998 ★2714★
Library and information science programs with the most per capita citations to journal articles, 1993-1998 ★2715★
Top mathematics research-doctorate programs as evaluated by the National Research Council ★2778★
Most effective music research-doctorate programs as evaluated by the National Research Council ★2895★
Top music research-doctorate programs as evaluated by the National Research Council ★2896★
U.S. universities with the greatest impact in optics and acoustics, 1994-98 ★2911★
Most effective philosophy research-doctorate programs as evaluated by the National Research Council ★2945★
Top philosophy research-doctorate programs as evaluated by the National Research Council ★2947★
U.S. universities with the greatest impact in astrophysics, 1994-98 ★2979★

Top physiology research-doctorate programs as evaluated by the National Research Council ★3022★
Most effective political science research-doctorate programs as evaluated by the National Research Council ★3043★
Top political science research-doctorate programs as evaluated by the National Research Council ★3046★
Institutions with the highest impact in psychiatry research, 1990-98 ★3053★
U.S. universities with the greatest impact in psychiatry, 1995-99 ★3060★
Most effective psychology research-doctorate programs as evaluated by the National Research Council ★3065★
Top psychology research-doctorate programs as evaluated by the National Research Council ★3068★
U.S. universities spending the most on research and development, 1998 ★3104★
Institutions receiving the most federal research and development expenditures, 1999 ★3105★
Institutions receiving the largest Energy Department research grants, 2000 ★3111★
U.S. universities with the highest relative citation impact, 1993-97 ★4291★
U.S. universities publishing the most papers in the fields of sociology and anthropology, 1993-97 ★4350★
Most effective sociology research-doctorate programs as evaluated by the National Research Council ★4352★
Top sociology research-doctorate programs as evaluated by the National Research Council ★4354★
Most effective Spanish and Portuguese language and literature research-doctorate programs as evaluated by the National Research Council ★4357★
Top Spanish and Portuguese language and literature research-doctorate programs as evaluated by the National Research Council ★4358★

Michl; Josef
American Chemical Society 2001 award winners (Group 3) ★753★

Mickens; Ronald
Top pay and benefits for the chief executive and top paid employees at Clark Atlanta University ★3237★

Micrel
Best small companies in the U.S. ★383★
Companies with the best two-year total returns since 1998 ★436★

Micro Warehouse
Fortune's highest ranked computer and data services companies, 2000 ★453★

Microbial Ecology
Marine and freshwater biology journals with the greatest impact measure, 1981-98 ★196★
Marine and freshwater biology journals with the greatest impact measure, 1994-98 ★197★

Microbiology
Biological sciences doctorates awarded at U.S. colleges and universities, by subfield, 1999 ★1887★
Gender breakdown of biological sciences doctorate recipients, by subfield, 1999 ★1927★
Percentage of female doctorate recipients at U.S. colleges and universities, by subfield, 1999 ★1988★

MICRON

Top biological science majors for accepted applicants to U.S. medical schools, 1999-2000 ★2851★

Average salaries for assistant professors at private institutions in preclinical department of medical schools, 2000-01 ★3785★

Average salaries for assistant professors at public and private institutions in preclinical department of medical schools, 2000-01 ★3786★

Average salaries for assistant professors at public institutions in preclinical department of medical schools, 2000-01 ★3787★

Average salaries for associate professors at private institutions in preclinical department of medical schools, 2000-01 ★3800★

Average salaries for associate professors at public and private institutions in preclinical department of medical schools, 2000-01 ★3801★

Average salaries for associate professors at public institutions in preclinical department of medical schools, 2000-01 ★3802★

Average salaries for full-time instructors at private institutions in preclinical department of medical schools, 2000-01 ★3854★

Average salaries for full-time instructors at public and private institutions in preclinical department of medical schools, 2000-01 ★3855★

Average salaries for full-time instructors at public institutions in preclinical department of medical schools, 2000-01 ★3856★

Average salaries for professors at private institutions in preclinical department of medical schools, 2000-01 ★3932★

Average salaries for professors at public and private institutions in preclinical department of medical schools, 2000-01 ★3933★

Average salaries for professors at public institutions in preclinical department of medical schools, 2000-01 ★3934★

Australia's contribution of papers in the sciences, by field, 1993-97 ★4292★

United Kingdom's contribution of papers in the sciences, by field, 1995-99 ★4297★

Austria's contribution of papers in the sciences by field, 1992-96 ★4298★

Austria's contribution of papers in the sciences, by field, 1995-99 ★4299★

Austria's relative impact in the sciences by field, 1992-96 ★4300★

Belgium's contribution of papers in the sciences by field, 1992-96 ★4301★

Belgium's contribution of papers in the sciences, by field, 1995-99 ★4302★

Denmark's contribution of papers in the sciences, by field, 1994-98 ★4306★

Denmark's contribution of papers in the sciences, by field, 1995-99 ★4307★

England's contribution of papers in the sciences, by field, 1994-98 ★4308★

Finland's contribution of papers in the sciences, by field, 1992-96 ★4309★

France's contribution of papers in the sciences, by field, 1995-99 ★4311★

France's contribution of papers in the sciences, by field, 1996-2000 ★4312★

Germany's contribution of papers in the sciences, by field, 1995-99 ★4313★

Ireland's contribution of papers in the sciences, by field, 1994-98 ★4315★

Japan's contribution of papers in the sciences, by field, 1995-99 ★4318★

Japan's contribution of papers in the sciences, by field, 1996-2000 ★4319★

Netherlands' contribution of papers in the sciences, by field, 1995-99 ★4321★

New Zealand's contribution of papers in the sciences, by field, 1994-98 ★4322★

Norway's contribution of papers in the sciences, by field, 1994-98 ★4323★

Russia's contribution of papers in the sciences, by field, 1993-97 ★4325★

South Africa's contribution of papers in the sciences, by field, 1994-98 ★4326★

South Korea's contribution of papers in the sciences, by field, 1995-99 ★4327★

Spain's contribution of papers in the sciences, by field, 1993-97 ★4328★

Spain's contribution of papers in the sciences, by field, 1995-99 ★4329★

Sweden's contribution of papers in the sciences by field, 1993-97 ★4330★

Sweden's contribution of papers in the sciences, by field, 1995-99 ★4331★

Switzerland's contribution of papers in the sciences, by field, 1994-98 ★4332★

Switzerland's contribution of papers in the sciences, by field, 1995-99 ★4333★

Taiwan contribution of papers in the sciences, by field, 1995-99 ★4334★

Micron Technology

Top electrical and electronics companies in Standard & Poor's 500, 2001 ★539★

Top information technology companies, 2000 ★544★

Microscopic investigation of root apexes

Endodontic articles with the most citations, 1974 through 1999 ★1864★

Microsoft

Biggest information technology companies, 2000 ★385★

Business Week's best companies in terms of profits ★406★

Business Week's best companies in the United States ★411★

Business Week's best performing companies with the highest net margin, 2000 ★419★

Business Week's top companies worldwide ★433★

Fortune's highest ranked computer software companies, 2000 ★455★

Top office equipment and computers companies in Standard & Poor's 500, 2001 ★551★

Top internships in the U.S. with the highest compensation, 2001 ★2611★

Largest technology companies in the U.S. in terms of annual revenue, 2000 ★4429★

Microsoft Encarta Encyclopedia

Top selling reference software, 2000 ★1601★

Microsoft Encarta Encyclopedia Deluxe

Top selling reference software, 2000 ★1601★

Microsoft Encarta Reference Suite

Top selling reference software, 2000 ★1601★

Microsoft Expedia Streets

Top selling personal productivity software, 2000 ★1600★

Microsoft Greetings

Top selling personal productivity software, 2000 ★1600★

Microsoft Home Publishing

Top selling personal productivity software, 2000 ★1600★

Microsoft Home Publishing Suite

Top selling personal productivity software, 2000 ★1600★

Microsoft Picture It

Top selling personal productivity software, 2000 ★1600★

Microsoft Works Suite

Top selling personal productivity software, 2000 ★1600★

Mid-America Bible College

Highest undergraduate tuition and fees at colleges and universities in Oklahoma ★1545★

Mid-Continent Consolidated Library District

Highest Hennen's American Public Library Ratings for libraries serving a population of over 500,000 ★2700★

Mid Plains Community College Area

Lowest undergraduate tuition and fees at colleges and universities in Nebraska ★1529★

Mid-State Technical College

Lowest undergraduate tuition and fees at colleges and universities in Wisconsin ★1571★

MidAmerican Energy Holdings

Fortune's highest ranked pipelines and energy companies, 2000 ★486★

Middelhof; Thomas

European business moguls considered the best agenda setters ★438★

Middle East

Region of origin of foreign students enrolled in U.S. institutions of higher education, 1998-99 ★2502★

World regions hosting U.S. students studying abroad, 1998-99 ★2515★

First-year physics and astronomy graduate students from selected countries, 1997-98 ★2989★

Middle Tennessee State University

U.S. colleges and universities with the lowest average football attendance, 1996-99 ★160★

State appropriations for Tennessee's institutions of higher education, 2000-01 ★1295★

Degrees granted in the ten largest undergraduate journalism and mass communications programs, 1999 ★2745★

Enrollment of students in the ten largest undergraduate journalism and mass communications programs, 1999 ★2746★

Average faculty salaries for institutions of higher education in Tennessee, 2000-01 ★3730★

Middlebury College

U.S. colleges and universities with the best on-campus housing facilities ★1032★

U.S. News & World Report's best national liberal arts colleges, 2000-01 ★1320★

U.S. News & World Report's national liberal arts colleges with the best financial resources rank, 2000-01 ★1322★

U.S. News & World Report's national liberal arts colleges with the best freshmen retention rates, 2000-01 ★1323★

U.S. News & World Report's national liberal arts colleges with the best graduation and retention rank, 2000-01 ★1324★

U.S. News & World Report's national liberal arts colleges with the best selectivity rank, 2000-01 ★1325★

U.S. News & World Report's national liberal arts colleges with the highest graduation rates, 2000-01 ★1330★

U.S. News & World Report's national liberal arts colleges with the highest percentage of freshmen in the top 10% of their high school class, 2000-01 ★1332★

U.S. News & World Report's national liberal arts colleges with the highest percentage of full-time faculty, 2000-01 ★1333★

U.S. News & World Report's national liberal arts colleges with the lowest acceptance rates, 2000-01 ★1336★
Private, 4-year undergraduate colleges and universities producing the most Ph.D.'s in the earth sciences, 1981-1990 ★2151★
Private, 4-year undergraduate colleges and universities producing the most Ph.D.'s in English, 1920-1990 ★2449★
Private, 4-year undergraduate colleges and universities producing the most Ph.D.'s in English, 1981-1990 ★2450★
Private, 4-year undergraduate colleges and universities producing the most Ph.D.'s in mathematics, 1981-1990 ★2777★
Institutions in the Worker Rights Consortium ★2913★
Average faculty salaries for institutions of higher education in Vermont, 2000-01 ★3734★
U.S. liberal arts colleges with the highest paid full professors, 2001 ★3980★

Middlesex Community-Technical College
Lowest undergraduate tuition and fees at colleges and universities in Connecticut ★1491★

Middlesex County, MA
U.S. counties with the highest international enrollment, 1999-2000 ★2505★

Middlesex-Somerset-Hunterdon, NJ
America's most wired cities, 2001 ★2573★
Cities with the highest online spending per Internet user ★2576★
Cities with the highest percentage of adults using the Internet at home ★2577★

Middletown Middle School
Outstanding secondary schools in Washington, District of Columbia-Maryland-Virginia-West Virginia ★4249★

Middletown Public Library
Highest Hennen's American Public Library Ratings for libraries serving a population of 100,000 to 249,999 ★2698★

Midland College
Average faculty salaries for institutions of higher education without academic ranks in Texas, 2000-01 ★3766★

Midland Lutheran College
Highest undergraduate tuition and fees at colleges and universities in Nebraska ★1528★
Average faculty salaries for institutions of higher education in Nebraska, 2000-01 ★3714★

Midland School
Outstanding secondary schools in Middlesex-Somerset-Hunterdon, New Jersey ★4179★
Outstanding secondary schools in Santa Barbara-Santa Maria-Lompoc, California ★4224★

Midlands Tech College
Average faculty salaries for institutions of higher education without academic ranks in South Carolina, 2000-01 ★3765★

Midnight Math: Twelve Terrific Math Games
Smithsonian's best books for children ages 6 to 10 ★364★

Midway College
Average faculty salaries for institutions of higher education in Kentucky, 2000-01 ★3704★

Midwestern State University
State appropriations for Texas's institutions of higher education, 2000-01 ★1296★
Average faculty salaries for institutions of higher education in Texas, 2000-01 ★3731★

Midwood High School at Brooklyn College
Outstanding secondary schools in New York, New York ★4191★

Midwood Senior High School
Outstanding urban public high schools in Metro New York ★4265★

Milan
Cities with the highest productivity of paper in the discipline of cardiovascular systems, 1994-96 ★2869★
Cities with the highest productivity of paper in the discipline of hematology, 1994-96 ★2870★
Cities with the highest productivity of paper in the discipline of immunology, 1994-96 ★2871★

Milbank Members Fund Quarterly
Health policy and services journals by citation impact, 1981-99 ★2537★

Milbank Quarterly
Health policy and services journals by citation impact, 1981-99 ★2537★
Health policy and services journals by citation impact, 1995-99 ★2538★
Health policy and services journals by citation impact, 1999 ★2539★

The Mildenhall Treasure
Smithsonian's best books for children ages 10 and up ★365★

Miles; Aaron
All-America boys' high school basketball 2nd team, 2001 ★162★

Miles College
U.S. colleges and universities with the highest percentage of African Americans enrolled, 1997 ★222★
Historically black colleges and universities with major improvements in student loan default rates, 1998 ★2737★

Miles Community College
Lowest undergraduate tuition and fees at colleges and universities in Montana ★1527★

Miles; L. William
Top pay and benefits for the chief executive and top paid employees at Fairfield University ★3291★

Miles; Vernon
Top pay and benefits for the chief executive and top paid employees at Union College in Kentucky ★3584★

Military (commissioned officer)
Most desirable public sector jobs ★2279★

Military and Naval science
Average costs for Academic Search titles by subject, 2001 ★2918★
Periodical prices by LC subject, 2001 ★2925★

Milki; Amin A.
Top pay and benefits for the chief executive and top paid employees at Stanford University ★3510★

Mill Pond Public Library
Highest Hennen's American Public Library Ratings for libraries serving a population of 999 and under ★2691★

Millard Central High School
Outstanding secondary schools in Omaha, Nebraska-Iowa ★4198★

Millbrook
Highest revenues of publicly held book publishers, 1999 ★3072★

Millbrook High School
All-USA Teacher Teams, Third Team, 2000 ★4401★

Millennials Rising: The Next Great Generation
American School Board Journal's notable education books, 2000 ★225★

Miller; Arthur
Top playwrights of the twentieth century ★4436★

Miller; Arthur H.
Authors most frequently published in *American Political Science Review,* 1974-94 ★3047★

Miller Brewing Company
Most selective internships in the U.S., 2001 ★2610★
Top internships in the U.S. with the highest compensation, 2001 ★2611★

Miller; Carlene
Top pay and benefits for the chief executive and top paid employees at Pomona College ★3444★

Miller; Cheryl
NCAA Division I female basketball scoring leaders ★155★

Miller; G.
Highest ranked inactive communication studies researchers ★2748★
Speech communication's most published scholars between 1915-1985 ★4362★

Miller; Gail L.
Top pay and benefits for the chief executive and top paid employees at Westminster College in Pennsylvania ★3617★

Miller; Harold
Top pay and benefits for the chief executive and top paid employees at the University of Mary ★3548★

Miller; James E.
Top pay and benefits for the chief executive and top paid employees at Transylvania University ★3575★

Miller; Keith
Top pay and benefits for the chief executive and top paid employees at Niagara University ★3420★

Miller; Merrill L.
Top pay and benefits for the chief executive and top paid employees at Colgate University ★3242★

Miller; Reuben
Top pay and benefits for the chief executive and top paid employees at Sweet Briar College ★3515★

Miller; Rev. Michael
Top pay and benefits for the chief executive and top paid employees at the University of Saint Thomas in Texas ★3564★

Miller; Richard
Top pay and benefits for the chief executive and top paid employees at Oberlin College ★3427★

Miller; Robert A.
Top pay and benefits for the chief executive and top paid employees at Nazareth College of Rochester ★3416★

Millersville University
Average faculty salaries for institutions of higher education in Pennsylvania, 2000-01 ★3725★

Millersville University of Pennsylvania
U.S. News & World Report's top public northern regional universities, 2000-01 ★1426★

Milligan College
U.S. News & World Report's southern regional liberal arts colleges with the highest proportion of classes having 20 students or less, 2000-01 ★1375★

U.S. News & World Report's southern regional liberal arts colleges with the lowest acceptance rates, 2000-01 ★1377★

Highest undergraduate tuition and fees at colleges and universities in Tennessee ★1558★

Average faculty salaries for institutions of higher education in Tennessee, 2000-01 ★3730★

Milligan; Wayne
Top pay and benefits for the chief executive and top paid employees at Spalding University ★3506★

Milliken Middle School
Outstanding secondary schools in Dallas, Texas ★4120★

Millikin University
U.S. News & World Report's midwestern regional liberal arts colleges with the best student/faculty ratios, 2000-01 ★1339★

U.S. News & World Report's midwestern regional liberal arts colleges with the highest academic reputation scores, 2000-01 ★1340★

U.S. News & World Report's midwestern regional liberal arts colleges with the highest graduation rates, 2000-01 ★1344★

U.S. News & World Report's midwestern regional liberal arts colleges with the lowest acceptance rates, 2000-01 ★1348★

U.S. News & World Report's top midwestern regional liberal arts colleges, 2000-01 ★1349★

Average faculty salaries for institutions of higher education in Illinois, 2000-01 ★3700★

The Millionaire Mind
Library Journal's most notable biography books, 2000 ★249★

Longest-running nonfiction hardcover bestsellers, 2000 ★281★

Millipore
Business Week's best performing companies with the highest 3-year earnings growth ★416★

Millman; Richard S.
Top pay and benefits for the chief executive and top paid employees at Knox College ★3360★

Mills College
U.S. colleges and universities awarding the most English language/literature/letters master's degrees to Asian Americans ★1774★

Mills; Esther
Top pay and benefits for the chief executive and top paid employees at Avila College ★3186★

Mills; George H.
Top pay and benefits for the chief executive and top paid employees at the University of Puget Sound ★3557★

Mills II; Ernest R.
Top pay and benefits for the chief executive and top paid employees at Mount Saint Mary College in New York ★3410★

Millsaps College
U.S. colleges and universities with a popular theater group ★1020★

U.S. colleges and universities with excellent instructors ★1024★

U.S. colleges and universities with the best overall administration ★1033★

U.S. News & World Report's national liberal arts colleges with students most in debt, 1999 ★1386★

Fiske Guide's best buys for private colleges and universities, 2001 ★1459★

Highest undergraduate tuition and fees at colleges and universities in Mississippi ★1522★

Average faculty salaries for institutions of higher education in Mississippi, 2000-01 ★3711★

Milne; David
Canada's best visual artists of the 20th century ★75★

Milton High School
Outstanding suburban public high schools in Metro Atlanta ★4254★

All-USA Teacher Teams, Third Team, 2000 ★4401★

Milwaukee
U.S. cities with the highest percentage of births to mothers with less than 12 years of education ★4432★

Milwaukee Institute of Art & Design
Highest undergraduate tuition and fees at colleges and universities in Wisconsin ★1570★

The Milwaukee Journal Sentinel
Most selective internships in the U.S., 2001 ★2610★

Milwaukee Lutheran High School
Outstanding secondary schools in Milwaukee-Waukesha, Wisconsin ★4180★

Milwaukee School of Engineering
Highest undergraduate tuition and fees at colleges and universities in Wisconsin ★1570★

U.S. News & World Report's undergraduate engineering programs with the best computer departments, 2000-01 ★2353★

Average faculty salaries for institutions of higher education in Wisconsin, 2000-01 ★3738★

Milwaukee Trade High School
Outstanding secondary schools in Milwaukee-Waukesha, Wisconsin ★4180★

Milwaukee, WI
Most polite cities in the U.S. ★3086★

Mineral Area College
Lowest undergraduate tuition and fees at colleges and universities in Missouri ★1525★

Mineral Depletion with Cost as the Extraction Limit...
Journal of Environmental Economics and Management's best articles in depletable resources and energy ★2462★

Mineral Depletion, with Special Reference to Petroleum
Top cited nonrenewable resource papers from 1989 to 1993 ★2471★

Mineralogy, petrology
Earth, atmosphere, and marine science doctorates awarded at U.S. colleges and universities, by subfield, 1999 ★1909★

Gender breakdown of earth, atmosphere, and marine science doctorate recipients, by subfield, 1999 ★1932★

Mingolelli; Jennie L.
Top pay and benefits for the chief executive and top paid employees at Gettysburg College ★3308★

Mining
Employment change projections by major industry division from 1998 to 2008 ★2287★

Employment projections by major industry division for 2008 ★2290★

Mining and mineral
Engineering doctorates awarded at U.S. colleges and universities, by subfield, 1999 ★1923★

Gender breakdown of engineering doctorate recipients, by subfield, 1999 ★1934★

Minneapolis College of Art and Design
Institutions censured by the American Association of University Professors, 2001 ★1067★

Highest undergraduate tuition and fees at colleges and universities in Minnesota ★1520★

Average faculty salaries for institutions of higher education in Minnesota, 2000-01 ★3710★

Minneapolis Community and Technical College
Average faculty salaries for institutions of higher education without academic ranks in Minnesota, 2000-01 ★3753★

Minneapolis/St. Paul
U.S. cities with the highest number of high-tech employees, 1998 ★2284★

U.S. market areas with the highest percentage of adults having internet access ★2607★

Minneapolis/St. Paul, MN
Cities with the most Yahoo! listings per million residents ★2580★

Best big cities to live in ★3075★

Minnesota
Mean composite ACT scores by state, 2000 ★895★

Mean math SAT scores by state, 2000 ★900★

Mean verbal SAT scores by state, 2000 ★903★

Total doctorate recipients by state, 1999 ★2054★

Average Hennen's American Public Library Ratings, by state ★2690★

State grades for affordability of higher education for minority students, 2000 ★2883★

State grades for benefits state receives for educating its minority students, 2000 ★2884★

State grades for completion of higher education by minority students, 2000 ★2885★

State grades for participation of minority students in higher education, 2000 ★2886★

State grades for preparing minority students for higher education, 2000 ★2887★

States with the highest per capita income ★3123★

States with the most charter schools ★4048★

States with the highest percentage of high school freshmen enrolling in college within four years ★4266★

Minnesota, Carlson School of Management; University of
U.S. News & World Report's undergraduate business programs with the best management information systems departments, 2000-01 ★568★

Academics' choices for best graduate management information systems programs, 2001 ★585★

Minnesota, Crookston; University of
U.S. News & World Report's top public midwestern regional liberal arts colleges, 2000-01 ★1350★

Average faculty salaries for institutions of higher education in Minnesota, 2000-01 ★3710★

Minnesota, Duluth; University of
U.S. News & World Report's top public midwestern regional universities, 2000-01 ★1412★

U.S. News & World Report's undergraduate engineering programs with the best chemical departments, 2000-01 ★2344★

Academics' choices for best rural medicine programs, 2001 ★2824★
Acceptance rates for *U.S. News & World Report*'s top 10 primary-care medical schools, 2001 ★2826★
Average MCAT scores at *U.S. News & World Report*'s top 10 primary-care medical schools, 2001 ★2835★
Average undergraduate GPA at *U.S. News & World Report*'s top 10 primary-care medical schools, 2001 ★2837★
Faculty-student ratios at *U.S. News & World Report*'s top 10 primary-care medical schools, 2001 ★2841★
Out-of-state tuition and fees at *U.S. News & World Report*'s top 10 primary-care medical schools, 2001 ★2846★
Percentage of graduates entering *U.S. News & World Report*'s top 10 primary-care medical schools, 2001 ★2848★
Top primary-care medical schools, 2001 ★2856★
Average faculty salaries for institutions of higher education in Minnesota, 2000-01 ★3710★

Minnesota Mining & Manufacturing
Fortune's highest ranked scientific, photo and control equipment companies, 2000 ★493★
Top manufacturing companies in Standard & Poor's 500, 2001 ★548★

Minnesota, Morris; University of
Institutions with the most female physics bachelor's recipients, 1994-1998 ★2959★
U.S. institutions with more than 40% female bachelor's graduates in their physics departments, 1994-98 ★2977★
Average faculty salaries for institutions of higher education in Minnesota, 2000-01 ★3710★

Minnesota Program in Statistics; University of
Top statistics and biostatistics research-doctorate programs as evaluated by the National Research Council ★2782★

Minnesota School of Professional Psychology
U.S. colleges and universities awarding the most doctorate degrees to Native Americans ★2099★
U.S. colleges and universities awarding the most psychology doctorate degrees to Native Americans ★2123★

Minnesota State College Southeast Tech
Average faculty salaries for institutions of higher education without academic ranks in Minnesota, 2000-01 ★3753★

Minnesota State University, Mankato
Average faculty salaries for institutions of higher education in Minnesota, 2000-01 ★3710★

Minnesota State University, Moorhead
Average faculty salaries for institutions of higher education in Minnesota, 2000-01 ★3710★

Minnesota System; University of
Institutions receiving the largest Energy Department research grants, 2000 ★3111★

Minnesota, Twin Cities; University of
Four-year institutions with the most liquor arrests reported, 1999 ★707★
U.S. colleges and universities reporting the most alcohol related arrests, 1998 ★730★
Division I NCAA colleges with that graduated none of their African American male basketball players, 1990-91 to 1993-94 ★930★
U.S. colleges and universities with a popular newspaper ★1018★
Largest degree-granting colleges and universities, by enrollment ★1068★
U.S. colleges and universities awarding the most health professions and related sciences master's degrees to Native Americans ★1780★
U.S. institutions awarding the most baccalaureate degrees to Asian Americans in agricultural sciences, 1998 ★1816★
U.S. colleges and universities awarding the most first professional degrees to Native Americans ★1846★
U.S. colleges and universities awarding the most health professions and related sciences first professional degrees to Native Americans ★1851★
Doctorate-granting-institutions awarding the most non-U.S. citizen doctoral degrees, 1999 ★1906★
Top doctorate granting institutions, 1999 ★2047★
U.S. colleges and universities awarding the most biological and life sciences doctorate degrees to Asian Americans ★2083★
U.S. colleges and universities awarding the most doctoral degrees to American Indians and Alaskan Natives from 1995 to 1999 ★2092★
U.S. colleges and universities awarding the most doctorates in all fields, 1999 ★2100★
U.S. colleges and universities awarding the most doctorates in education, 1999 ★2101★
U.S. colleges and universities awarding the most doctorates in life sciences, 1999 ★2104★
U.S. colleges and universities awarding the most doctorates in professional and other fields, 1999 ★2106★
U.S. institutions awarding the most doctorate degrees, 1999 ★2132★
Academics' choices for best graduate chemical engineering programs, 2001 ★2386★
U.S. News & World Report's graduate engineering programs with the best chemical departments, 2000-01 ★2392★
Academics' choices for best graduate mechanical engineering programs, 2001 ★2422★
Academics' choices for best family medicine programs, 2001 ★2820★
Institutions in the Worker Rights Consortium ★2913★
Average faculty salaries for institutions of higher education in Minnesota, 2000-01 ★3710★
Academics' choices for best counseling/personnel services graduate programs, 2001 ★4379★
Academics' choices for best educational psychology graduate programs, 2001 ★4382★
Academics' choices for best special education graduate programs, 2001 ★4386★
Academics' choices for best vocational/technical graduate programs, 2001 ★4387★

Minnesota; University of
U.S. universities publishing the most papers in the fields of agriculture/agronomy, 1994-98 ★57★
Top ecology, evolution, and behavior research-doctorate programs as evaluated by the National Research Council ★201★
Top business schools in research performance, 1986-1998 ★532★
Top business schools by average MBA rank, 1986-1998 ★644★
Top business schools for overall within-discipline research performance, 1986-1998 ★645★
Top business schools for within-discipline research performance in management, 1986-1998 ★646★
Top business schools for within-discipline research performance in production/operations management, 1986-1998 ★648★
Top business schools for within-discipline research performance in marketing, 1986-1998 ★671★
Top business schools for within-discipline research performance in management information systems, 1986-1998 ★675★
Employing institutions with the most published pages in *The Journal of Risk and Insurance*, 1987-1996 ★679★
Institutions receiving the most corporate gifts, 1999-2000 ★1243★
State appropriations for Minnesota's institutions of higher education, 2000-01 ★1276★
U.S. universities with the greatest impact in dentistry/oral surgery, 1994-98 ★1866★
U.S. colleges and universities awarding the most doctorate degrees to Native Americans ★2099★
Economics departments by number of citations by top economists, 1971-92 ★2158★
Economics departments by number of citations per top economist, 1971-92 ★2159★
Economics departments by number of top economists, 1971-92 ★2160★
Institutions generating the most economic education research text, 1963-1990 ★2167★
Economics Ph.D. programs by number of citations of top economist graduates, 1971-92 ★2204★
Economics Ph.D. programs by number of citations per top economist graduate, 1971-92 ★2205★
Economics Ph.D. programs by number of top economist graduates, 1971-92 ★2206★
Most effective economics research-doctorate programs as evaluated by the National Research Council ★2207★
Origin of doctorate for dissertation chairs in economics ★2208★
Origin of doctorate for economics faculty at Ph.D.-granting institutions ★2209★
Origin of doctorate for economics faculty at Ph.D.-granting institutions, by Ph.D. equivalents produced ★2210★
Top economics research-doctorate programs as evaluated by the National Research Council ★2213★
Top aerospace engineering research-doctorate programs as evaluated by the National Research Council ★2376★
Most effective chemical engineering research-doctorate programs as evaluated by the National Research Council ★2389★
Top chemical engineering research-doctorate programs as evaluated by the National Research Council ★2390★
Top civil engineering research-doctorate programs as evaluated by the National Research Council ★2396★
U.S. universities publishing the most papers in the field of ecology/environmental sciences, 1994-98 ★2473★
Faculty's scholarly reputation in the Ph.D.-granting departments of geography, 1925-1982 ★2518★
Most effective geography research-doctorate programs as evaluated by the National Research Council ★2519★

MINNESOTA

Top geography research-doctorate programs as evaluated by the National Research Council ★2520★

Top Ph.D.-granting departments of geography from 1925-1982 ★2521★

Most effective German language and literature research-doctorate programs as evaluated by the National Research Council ★2527★

Top German language and literature research-doctorate programs as evaluated by the National Research Council ★2528★

Institutions with the most productive libraries, 1993-1997 ★2678★

Top university research libraries in the U.S. and Canada, 1998-99 ★2706★

U.S. universities publishing the most papers in the field of communication, 1994-98 ★2755★

Enrollment of students in the ten largest doctoral journalism and mass communications programs, 1999 ★2762★

U.S. universities with the greatest impact in mathematics, 1995-99 ★2772★

Top mathematics research-doctorate programs as evaluated by the National Research Council ★2778★

Most effective political science research-doctorate programs as evaluated by the National Research Council ★3043★

Top political science research-doctorate programs as evaluated by the National Research Council ★3046★

Most effective psychology research-doctorate programs as evaluated by the National Research Council ★3065★

Top psychology research-doctorate programs as evaluated by the National Research Council ★3068★

U.S. colleges and universities spending the most on chemical engineering research and development, 1998 ★3098★

U.S. colleges and universities with the most federal support for chemical engineering research and development, 1998 ★3101★

Institutions receiving the most federal research and development expenditures, 1999 ★3105★

U.S. universities publishing the most papers in the field of food science/nutrition, 1994-98 ★4286★

Minnesota West Community and Technical College

Lowest undergraduate tuition and fees at colleges and universities in Minnesota ★1521★

Average faculty salaries for institutions of higher education without academic ranks in Minnesota, 2000-01 ★3753★

Minogue, C.M.; Rev. John P.

Top pay and benefits for the chief executive and top paid employees at DePaul University ★3266★

Minot State University

State appropriations for North Dakota's institutions of higher education, 2000-01 ★1287★

U.S. News & World Report's midwestern regional universities with students least in debt, 1999 ★1399★

Lowest undergraduate tuition and fees at colleges and universities in North Dakota ★1542★

Average faculty salaries for institutions of higher education in North Dakota, 2000-01 ★3721★

Minot State University, Bottineau

Lowest undergraduate tuition and fees at colleges and universities in North Dakota ★1542★

Minyard Food Stores

Top women-owned companies ★4460★

The Miocene Arrow

Booklist's most recommended science fiction/fantasy books ★232★

Mira Costa High School

Outstanding secondary schools in Los Angeles-Long Beach, California ★4167★

Miracle's Boys

Most notable fiction books for young adults, 2001 ★322★

Smithsonian's best books for children ages 10 and up ★365★

Miramonte High School

Outstanding secondary schools in Oakland, California ★4195★

Mirrer Yeshiva Central Institute

Lowest undergraduate tuition and fees at private nonprofit, 4-year or above colleges and universities ★1464★

The Mirror Lied

Most notable DVDs and videos for young adults, 2001 ★2890★

Mirsepassi; Ali

Top pay and benefits for the chief executive and top paid employees at Hampshire College ★3322★

MIS Quarterly

Journals with the highest impact factor in the field of management, 1981-96 ★696★

Top ranked AACSB publications ★2186★

Journals and proceedings with the most citations (Class 1) ★2567★

Information and library science journals by citation impact, 1981-99 ★2724★

Information and library science journals by citation impact, 1995-99 ★2725★

Information and library science journals by citation impact, 1999 ★2726★

Information and library science journals with the greatest impact measure, 1981-98 ★2727★

Most cited business serials in technical communication journals from 1988 to 1997 ★4417★

Misner; Robert

Top pay and benefits for the chief executive and top paid employees at Willamette University ★3628★

Miss Alaineus

Publishers Weekly Off-the-Cuff Awards winner for best book title, 2000 ★338★

Miss Porter's School

Most selective internships in the U.S., 2001 ★2610★

Mission San Jose High School

Outstanding secondary schools in Oakland, California ★4195★

Mission Valley Middle School

Outstanding secondary schools in Kansas City, Missouri-Kansas ★4158★

Mission Viejo High School

Outstanding secondary schools in Orange County, California ★4199★

Mississippi

Mean composite ACT scores by state, 2000 ★895★

Mean math SAT scores by state, 2000 ★900★

Mean verbal SAT scores by state, 2000 ★903★

States receiving the most in federal agency appropriations to colleges, 2000 ★1306★

States receiving the most in federal agency appropriations to colleges, from 1996 to 2000 ★1307★

Total doctorate recipients by state, 1999 ★2054★

State grades for affordability of higher education for minority students, 2000 ★2883★

State grades for benefits state receives for educating its minority students, 2000 ★2884★

State grades for completion of higher education by minority students, 2000 ★2885★

State grades for participation of minority students in higher education, 2000 ★2886★

State grades for preparing minority students for higher education, 2000 ★2887★

States with the lowest per-pupil expenditures ★3998★

States with the highest state support for non need-based financial aid for students, 1999-2000 ★4368★

U.S. states with the highest percentage of births to teenagers who were already mothers ★4433★

Mississippi College

U.S. News & World Report's southern regional universities with the highest acceptance rates, 2000-01 ★1436★

U.S. News & World Report's southern regional universities with the highest freshmen retention rates, 2000-01 ★1437★

U.S. News & World Report's southern regional universities with the highest proportion of classes with 20 students or less, 2000-01 ★1441★

Highest undergraduate tuition and fees at colleges and universities in Mississippi ★1522★

Private, 4-year undergraduate colleges and universities producing the most Ph.D.'s in nonscience fields, 1981-1990 ★2031★

Private, 4-year undergraduate colleges and universities producing the most Ph.D.'s in nonscience fields, 1990 ★2032★

Mississippi County Community College

Lowest undergraduate tuition and fees at colleges and universities in Arkansas ★1485★

Mississippi Delta Community College

Lowest undergraduate tuition and fees at colleges and universities in Mississippi ★1523★

U.S. institutions awarding the most associate degrees to African Americans in agribusiness and production, 1998 ★1805★

U.S. institutions awarding the most associate degrees to minorities in agribusiness and production, 1998 ★1808★

Mississippi Gulf Coast Community College, Jackson County Campus

Lowest undergraduate tuition and fees at colleges and universities in Mississippi ★1523★

Mississippi Gulf Coast Community College, Jefferson Davis Campus

Lowest undergraduate tuition and fees at colleges and universities in Mississippi ★1523★

Mississippi Gulf Coast Community College, Perkinston

Lowest undergraduate tuition and fees at colleges and universities in Mississippi ★1523★

Mississippi State University

Institutions, by adjusted authorship, with the most published authors in the Journal of Business Research, 1985 to 1999 ★694★

State appropriations for Mississippi's institutions of higher education, 2000-01 ★1277★

Average faculty salaries for institutions of higher education in Mississippi, 2000-01 ★3711★

Mississippi; University of
U.S. colleges and universities with an unfavorable surrounding town or city ★1023★
Institutions receiving the most in federal agency appropriations to colleges, 2000 ★1245★
State appropriations for Mississippi's institutions of higher education, 2000-01 ★1277★
Average faculty salaries for institutions of higher education in Mississippi, 2000-01 ★3711★

Mississippi University for Women
State appropriations for Mississippi's institutions of higher education, 2000-01 ★1277★
U.S. News & World Report's southern regional liberal arts colleges with the highest academic reputation scores, 2000-01 ★1369★
U.S. News & World Report's southern regional liberal arts colleges with the highest proportion of freshmen in the top 25% of their high school class, 2000-01 ★1376★
U.S. News & World Report's southern regional liberal arts colleges with the lowest acceptance rates, 2000-01 ★1377★
U.S. News & World Report's top public southern regional liberal arts colleges, 2000-01 ★1378★
U.S. News & World Report's best undergraduate fees among southern regional liberal arts colleges by discount tuition, 2000 ★1383★
Total baccalaureate law and legal studies degrees awarded to African Americans from U.S. colleges and universities, 1997-98 ★1725★
Average faculty salaries for institutions of higher education in Mississippi, 2000-01 ★3711★

Mississippi Valley State University
Colleges offering the Thurgood Marshall Scholarship Fund ★221★
U.S. colleges and universities with the highest percentage of African Americans enrolled, 1997 ★222★
Division I NCAA colleges with the lowest graduation rates for female athletes, 1990-91 to 1993-94 ★936★
State appropriations for Mississippi's institutions of higher education, 2000-01 ★1277★

Missouri
States with the highest enrollment in private 4-year institutions of higher education ★860★
Mean composite ACT scores by state, 2000 ★895★
Mean math SAT scores by state, 2000 ★900★
Mean verbal SAT scores by state, 2000 ★903★
States receiving the most in federal agency appropriations to colleges, 2000 ★1306★
Total doctorate recipients by state, 1999 ★2054★
State grades for affordability of higher education for minority students, 2000 ★2883★
State grades for benefits state receives for educating its minority students, 2000 ★2884★
State grades for completion of higher education by minority students, 2000 ★2885★
State grades for participation of minority students in higher education, 2000 ★2886★
State grades for preparing minority students for higher education, 2000 ★2887★
States expelling the highest ratio of students for violating the Gun-Free Schools Act, 1998-99 ★3993★
States expelling the most students for violating the Gun-Free Schools Act, 1998-99 ★3994★
States with the most public school districts ★3999★
States with the most K-12 public schools ★4049★

Missouri Baptist College
Average faculty salaries for institutions of higher education in Missouri, 2000-01 ★3712★

Missouri, Columbia; University of
Institutions receiving the most in federal agency appropriations to colleges, 2000 ★1245★
U.S. colleges and universities awarding the most communications master's degrees to African Americans ★1763★
U.S. colleges and universities awarding the most communications master's degrees to Asian Americans ★1764★
Academics' choices for best dispute resolution programs, 2001 ★2627★
Academics' choices for best family medicine programs, 2001 ★2820★
Average faculty salaries for institutions of higher education in Missouri, 2000-01 ★3712★
Academics' choices for best counseling/personnel services graduate programs, 2001 ★4379★
Academics' choices for best vocational/technical graduate programs, 2001 ★4387★

Missouri, Kansas City; University of
Division I NCAA colleges with the lowest graduation rates for female basketball players, 1990-91 to 1993-94 ★937★
U.S. News & World Report's national universities with students most in debt, 1999 ★1476★
Average faculty salaries for institutions of higher education in Missouri, 2000-01 ★3712★

Missouri, Rolla; University of
U.S. colleges and universities with the least accessible instructors ★1036★
U.S. colleges and universities with the unhappiest students ★1041★
Doctorate-granting-institutions with the highest percentage of non-U.S. citizen doctoral degrees awarded, 1999 ★1907★
Average faculty salaries for institutions of higher education in Missouri, 2000-01 ★3712★

Missouri, St. Louis; University of
Universities with the most-cited scholars in *Criminology* ★1649★
Universities with the most-cited scholars in *Journal of Quantitative Criminology* ★1650★
Universities with the most-cited scholars in *Journal of Research in Crime and Delinquency* ★1651★
Universities with the most-cited scholars in *Justice Quarterly* ★1652★
U.S. colleges and universities awarding the most biological and life sciences master's degrees to Hispanic Americans ★1758★
Average faculty salaries for institutions of higher education in Missouri, 2000-01 ★3712★

Missouri Southern State College
Division II NCAA colleges with the 0% graduation rates for women's basketball players, 1993-94 ★942★
State appropriations for Missouri's institutions of higher education, 2000-01 ★1278★
Average faculty salaries for institutions of higher education in Missouri, 2000-01 ★3712★

Missouri; University of
State appropriations for Missouri's institutions of higher education, 2000-01 ★1278★
Library and information science programs with the most journal articles, 1993-1998 ★2713★
Library and information science programs with the most journal articles per capita, 1993-1998 ★2714★
Library and information science programs with the most per capita citations to journal articles, 1993-1998 ★2715★
Degrees granted in the ten largest master's journalism and mass communications programs, 1999 ★2757★
Enrollment of students in the ten largest master's journalism and mass communications programs, 1999 ★2763★

Missouri Western State College
State appropriations for Missouri's institutions of higher education, 2000-01 ★1278★
Average faculty salaries for institutions of higher education in Missouri, 2000-01 ★3712★

MIT Press
Book publishers with the most citations (Class 2) ★2563★

Mitchell; Arthur
Most influential African American entertainers ★77★

Mitchell; Brian
Top pay and benefits for the chief executive and top paid employees at Washington and Jefferson College ★3604★

Mitchell Community College
Average faculty salaries for institutions of higher education without academic ranks in North Carolina, 2000-01 ★3761★

Mitchell; David
Booklist's best first novels ★228★

Mitchell; Edna
Top pay and benefits for the chief executive and top paid employees at Mills College ★3402★

Mitchell; Helena
Top pay and benefits for the chief executive and top paid employees at Clark Atlanta University ★3237★

Mitchell; John T.
Top pay and benefits for the chief executive and top paid employees at Mercer University ★3398★

Mitchell; Joni
Canada's best performing artists of the 20th century ★74★

Mitchell; Peter T.
Top pay and benefits for the chief executive and top paid employees at Albion College ★3167★

Mitchell Technical Institute
Lowest undergraduate tuition and fees at colleges and universities in South Dakota ★1557★

Mitsakos; Charles L.
Top pay and benefits for the chief executive and top paid employees at Rivier College ★3460★

Mitsubishi Corp.
Business Week's best companies in terms of sales ★408★

Mitsui
Business Week's best companies in terms of sales ★408★

Moberly Area Community College
Lowest undergraduate tuition and fees at colleges and universities in Missouri ★1525★

Mobile, AL
Most polite cities in the U.S. ★3086★

Mobile; University of
Highest undergraduate tuition and fees at colleges and universities in Alabama ★1479★

A Model for Analyzing Human Adaptation to Transition
  Most frequently cited contribution articles in psychology journals from 1986 to 1996 ★3071★

Model of Mining and Exploring for Exhaustible Resources
  Journal of Environmental Economics and Management's best articles in depletable resources and energy ★2462★

Moder, S.M.; Rev. John
  Top pay and benefits for the chief executive and top paid employees at Saint Mary's University in Texas ★3481★

Modern Language Association of America
  Scholarly societies with the highest membership, 1999 ★3052★

Modern Nations of the World
  Booklist's most recommended geography series for young people, 2000 ★313★

Moderson; Chris
  Top pay and benefits for the chief executive and top paid employees at Rockford College in Illinois ★3463★

Modigliani; Franco
  Authors most frequently contributing to the *American Economic Review* from 1911-1990 ★2156★
  Authors most frequently contributing to the *American Economic Review* from 1951-1990 ★2157★

Modis Professional Services
  Fortune's highest ranked temporary help companies, 2000 ★500★

Moeller; Donald J.
  Top pay and benefits for the chief executive and top paid employees at St. Ambrose University ★3468★

Moen; Phyllis
  Radcliffe Institute for Advanced Study fellowship recipients in the field of sociology, 2000-01 ★4346★

Mohave Community College
  Lowest undergraduate tuition and fees at colleges and universities in Arizona ★1483★

Mohave Middle School
  Outstanding secondary schools in Phoenix-Mesa, Arizona ★4203★

Mohawk Industries
  Fortune's highest ranked textiles companies, 2000 ★501★

Mohawk Valley Community College
  Average faculty salaries for institutions of higher education in New York, 2000-01 ★3719★

Mohr; John R.
  Top pay and benefits for the chief executive and top paid employees at Knox College ★3360★

Mohraz; Judy Jolley
  Top pay and benefits for the chief executive and top paid employees at Goucher College ★3314★

Mohrman; Kathryn
  Top pay and benefits for the chief executive and top paid employees at Colorado College ★3249★

Mol; Robert
  Top pay and benefits for the chief executive and top paid employees at Cornerstone University ★3258★

Molecular biology
  Biological sciences doctorates awarded at U.S. colleges and universities, by subfield, 1999 ★1887★
  Gender breakdown of biological sciences doctorate recipients, by subfield, 1999 ★1927★
  Percentage of female doctorate recipients at U.S. colleges and universities, by subfield, 1999 ★1988★
  United States' contribution of papers in the sciences, by field, 1995-99 ★4283★
  United States' contribution of papers in the sciences, by field, 1996-2000 ★4284★
  United Kingdom's contribution of papers in the sciences, by field, 1995-99 ★4297★
  Austria's contribution of papers in the sciences by field, 1992-96 ★4298★
  Austria's contribution of papers in the sciences, by field, 1995-99 ★4299★
  Austria's relative impact in the sciences by field, 1992-96 ★4300★
  Belgium's contribution of papers in the sciences by field, 1992-96 ★4301★
  Belgium's contribution of papers in the sciences, by field, 1995-99 ★4302★
  Canada's contribution of papers in the sciences, by field, 1995-99 ★4303★
  Denmark's contribution of papers in the sciences, by field, 1994-98 ★4306★
  Denmark's contribution of papers in the sciences, by field, 1995-99 ★4307★
  England's contribution of papers in the sciences, by field, 1994-98 ★4308★
  Finland's contribution of papers in the sciences by field, 1992-96 ★4309★
  Finland's contribution of papers in the sciences, by field, 1995-99 ★4310★
  France's contribution of papers in the sciences, by field, 1995-99 ★4311★
  France's contribution of papers in the sciences, by field, 1996-2000 ★4312★
  Germany's contribution of papers in the sciences, by field, 1995-99 ★4313★
  Italy's contribution of papers in the sciences, by field, 1995-99 ★4316★
  Japan's contribution of papers in the sciences, by field, 1996-2000 ★4319★
  Netherlands' contribution of papers in the sciences, by field, 1995-99 ★4321★
  Norway's contribution of papers in the sciences, by field, 1994-98 ★4323★
  Russia's contribution of papers in the sciences, by field, 1993-97 ★4325★
  Sweden's contribution of papers in the sciences by field, 1993-97 ★4330★
  Sweden's contribution of papers in the sciences, by field, 1995-99 ★4331★
  Switzerland's contribution of papers in the sciences, by field, 1994-98 ★4332★
  Switzerland's contribution of papers in the sciences, by field, 1995-99 ★4333★

Molecular Breeding
  Agriculture journals by citation impact, 1999 ★54★

Molecular Cellular Biology
  Molecular biology and genetics journals with the highest impact, 1992-96 ★204★
  Average salaries for assistant professors at private institutions in preclinical department of medical schools, 2000-01 ★3785★
  Average salaries for assistant professors at public and private institutions in preclinical department of medical schools, 2000-01 ★3786★
  Average salaries for assistant professors at public institutions in preclinical department of medical schools, 2000-01 ★3787★
  Average salaries for associate professors at private institutions in preclinical department of medical schools, 2000-01 ★3800★
  Average salaries for associate professors at public and private institutions in preclinical department of medical schools, 2000-01 ★3801★
  Average salaries for associate professors at public institutions in preclinical department of medical schools, 2000-01 ★3802★
  Average salaries for full-time instructors at private institutions in preclinical department of medical schools, 2000-01 ★3854★
  Average salaries for full-time instructors at public and private institutions in preclinical department of medical schools, 2000-01 ★3855★
  Average salaries for full-time instructors at public institutions in preclinical department of medical schools, 2000-01 ★3856★
  Average salaries for professors at private institutions in preclinical department of medical schools, 2000-01 ★3932★
  Average salaries for professors at public and private institutions in preclinical department of medical schools, 2000-01 ★3933★
  Average salaries for professors at public institutions in preclinical department of medical schools, 2000-01 ★3934★

Molecular Crystallography and Liquid Crystals
  Crystallography journals by citation impact, 1981-98 ★1654★

Molecular Ecology
  Ecology journals by citation impact, 1999 ★2138★

Molecular Psychiatry
  Psychiatry journals by citation impact, 1995-98 ★3055★

Molinari; Jim
  Top pay and benefits for the chief executive and top paid employees at Bradley University ★3208★

Moller; Sidney L.
  Top pay and benefits for the chief executive and top paid employees at Mississippi College ★3404★

Mollica; Albert C.
  Top pay and benefits for the chief executive and top paid employees at Cabrini College ★3215★

Molloy College
  Average faculty salaries for institutions of higher education in New York, 2000-01 ★3719★

Monahan; Joseph
  Top pay and benefits for the chief executive and top paid employees at Dowling College ★3271★

Monahan; William
  Booklist's best first novels ★228★

Monan, S.J.; J. Donald
  Top pay and benefits for the chief executive and top paid employees at Boston College ★3205★

Monarch Dental
  Companies with the worst two-year total returns since 1998 ★437★

Monash University
  Australian universities with the greatest impact in agricultural sciences, 1993-97 ★49★
  Australian universities with the greatest impact in mathematics, 1993-97 ★2774★

Moncada; Salvador
Most-cited biomedical scientists, 1990-97 ★2382★

Monet; Claude
Highly influential artists of the 20th century ★76★

Money; Royce L.
Top pay and benefits for the chief executive and top paid employees at Abilene Christian University ★3163★

Monk Camps Out
Smithsonian's best books for children ages 1 to 6 ★363★

The Monk in the Garden: The Lost and Found Genius of Gregor Mendel, the Father of Genetics
Library Journal's most notable scientific biography books, 2000 ★276★

Monmouth College
Average faculty salaries for institutions of higher education in Illinois, 2000-01 ★3700★

Monmouth University
Highest undergraduate tuition and fees at colleges and universities in New Jersey ★1533★
Average faculty salaries for institutions of higher education in New Jersey, 2000-01 ★3717★

Monmouth University (NJ)
Presidents with the highest pay at Master's I and II colleges and universities, 1998-99 ★3161★

Monroe College
Top colleges in terms of total associate degrees awarded to minorities, 1997-98 ★1677★

Monroe Community College
Average faculty salaries for institutions of higher education in New York, 2000-01 ★3719★
U.S. community colleges with the highest paid full professors, 2001 ★3976★

Monroe County Community College
Lowest undergraduate tuition and fees at colleges and universities in Michigan ★1519★

Monroe Elementary School
Illinois suburban elementary schools with the highest ISAT scores in reading and math ★18★

Monsignor Farrell High School
Outstanding Catholic high schools in Metro New York ★4076★

Monsignor Kelly High School
Outstanding secondary schools in Beaumont-Port Arthur, Texas ★4094★

Monster.com
Top career-related Web sites ★2602★
Top E-recruiting providers, 2000 ★2604★

Monta Vista High School
Outstanding secondary schools in San Jose, California ★4222★

Montana
Mean composite ACT scores by state, 2000 ★895★
Mean math SAT scores by state, 2000 ★900★
Mean verbal SAT scores by state, 2000 ★903★
States allocating the smallest amount of state tax appropriations for higher education, 2000-01 ★1305★
Total doctorate recipients by state, 1999 ★2054★
State grades for affordability of higher education for minority students, 2000 ★2883★
State grades for benefits state receives for educating its minority students, 2000 ★2884★
State grades for completion of higher education by minority students, 2000 ★2885★
State grades for participation of minority students in higher education, 2000 ★2886★
State grades for preparing minority students for higher education, 2000 ★2887★
States with the lowest number of high school graduates, 1999-2000 ★3997★
States with the smallest average class size ★4072★
States with the highest percentage of high school freshmen enrolling in college within four years ★4266★

Montana, Missoula; University of
U.S. colleges and universities where students study the least ★1002★
U.S. colleges and universities with the least accessible instructors ★1036★
U.S. colleges and universities with the worst on-campus housing facilities ★1044★
Highest undergraduate tuition and fees at colleges and universities in Montana ★1526★

Montana State University
State appropriations for Montana's institutions of higher education, 2000-01 ★1279★

Montana State University, Billings
Highest undergraduate tuition and fees at colleges and universities in Montana ★1526★
Average faculty salaries for institutions of higher education in Montana, 2000-01 ★3713★

Montana State University, Billings College of Technology
Highest undergraduate tuition and fees at colleges and universities in Montana ★1526★

Montana State University, Bozeman
Highest undergraduate tuition and fees at colleges and universities in Montana ★1526★
Average faculty salaries for institutions of higher education in Montana, 2000-01 ★3713★

Montana State University, College of Technology, Billings
Highest undergraduate tuition and fees at public 2-year colleges and universities ★1462★

Montana State University College of Technology, Great Falls
Lowest undergraduate tuition and fees at colleges and universities in Montana ★1527★

Montana State University, Northern
Highest undergraduate tuition and fees at colleges and universities in Montana ★1526★

Montana Tech
Highest undergraduate tuition and fees at colleges and universities in Montana ★1526★
Average faculty salaries for institutions of higher education in Montana, 2000-01 ★3713★

Montana Tech of the University of Montana
Lowest undergraduate tuition and fees at colleges and universities in Montana ★1527★
U.S. News & World Report's top public western regional universities, 2000-01 ★1573★
U.S. News & World Report's western regional universities with the highest acceptance rates, 2000-01 ★1579★
U.S. News & World Report's western regional universities with the highest alumni giving rates, 2000-01 ★1580★
U.S. News & World Report's western regional universities with the highest percentage of full-time faculty, 2000-01 ★1584★
U.S. News & World Report's western regional universities with the highest proportion of classes with 20 students or less, 2000-01 ★1585★

Montana; University of
Division I NCAA colleges with that graduated less than 20% of their African American male athletes, 1990-91 to 1993-94 ★928★
State appropriations for Montana's institutions of higher education, 2000-01 ★1279★
Average faculty salaries for institutions of higher education in Montana, 2000-01 ★3713★

Montclair State College
State appropriations for New Jersey's institutions of higher education, 2000-01 ★1283★

Montclair State University
U.S. News & World Report's northern regional universities with students most in debt, 1999 ★1414★
U.S. News & World Report's top public northern regional universities, 2000-01 ★1426★
Average faculty salaries for institutions of higher education in New Jersey, 2000-01 ★3717★

Montegomery College
Average faculty salaries for institutions of higher education in Maryland, 2000-01 ★3707★

Montevallo; University of
State appropriations for Alabama's institutions of higher education, 2000-01 ★1254★

Montgomery College
Top college choices for Washington D.C. students ★847★
Colleges and universities with the smallest endowments, 2000 ★1238★
Community colleges receiving the most gifts, 1999-2000 ★1239★

Montgomery College, Rockville
Community colleges with the highest enrollment of foreign students, 1998-99 ★2493★

Montgomery Community College
Average faculty salaries for institutions of higher education without academic ranks in North Carolina, 2000-01 ★3761★

Montgomery High School
Outstanding secondary schools in Middlesex-Somerset-Hunterdon, New Jersey ★4179★
Outstanding secondary schools in Santa Rosa, California ★4225★
Outstanding secondary schools in Washington, District of Columbia-Maryland-Virginia-West Virginia ★4249★

Montgomery; John
Winner of the American Chemical Society's Arthur C. Cope Awards, 2001 ★795★

Montgomery; M.
Top associate professor economists at elite liberal arts colleges, 1975-94 ★2174★

Montgomery, MD
Counties with the highest per capita income ★2561★

Montgomery, PA
Counties with the highest per capita income ★2561★

Montgomery; Sy
Booklist's best science and technology books ★366★

Monthly Labor Review
Top ranked labor and demographic economics journals ★2196★

Monthly Notices of the Royal Astronomy Society
- Astronomy and astrophysics journals by citation impact, 1981-99 ★102★
- Astronomy and astrophysics journals by citation impact, 1995-99 ★103★
- Astronomy and astrophysics journals by citation impact, 1999 ★104★
- Astronomy and astrophysics journals by impact factor, 1981 to 1998 ★105★
- Astronomy and astrophysics journals by impact factor, 1994 to 1998 ★106★

Montreal Public Library
- North America's first ten public libraries ★2680★

Montreal; University of
- Best Canadian universities overall, 2000 ★1149★
- Canadian medical/doctoral universities by alumni support, 2000 ★1172★
- Canadian medical/doctoral universities by award-winning faculty members, 2000 ★1173★
- Canadian medical/doctoral universities by class size at the first- and second-year level, 2000 ★1174★
- Canadian medical/doctoral universities by class size at the third- and forth-year level, 2000 ★1175★
- Canadian medical/doctoral universities by classes taught by tenured faculty, 2000 ★1176★
- Canadian medical/doctoral universities by faculty members with Ph.D.'s, 2000 ★1177★
- Canadian medical/doctoral universities by international graduate students, 2000 ★1178★
- Canadian medical/doctoral universities by library acquisitions, 2000 ★1179★
- Canadian medical/doctoral universities by library expenses, 2000 ★1180★
- Canadian medical/doctoral universities by library holdings, 2000 ★1181★
- Canadian medical/doctoral universities by library holdings per student, 2000 ★1182★
- Canadian medical/doctoral universities by medical/science grants per faculty member, 2000 ★1184★
- Canadian medical/doctoral universities by operating budget per student, 2000 ★1185★
- Canadian medical/doctoral universities by percentage of operating budget allocated to scholarships, 2000 ★1186★
- Canadian medical/doctoral universities by percentage of operating budget allocated to student services, 2000 ★1187★
- Canadian medical/doctoral universities by reputation, 2000 ★1188★
- Canadian medical/doctoral universities by social science/humanities grants per faculty member, 2000 ★1189★
- Canadian medical/doctoral universities by students from out of province, 2000 ★1190★
- Canadian medical/doctoral universities by students winning national awards, 2000 ★1191★
- Canadian universities by graduation rate, 2000 ★1214★
- Canadian universities chosen as being value added, 2000 ★1216★
- Canadian universities with the lowest total cost, 2000 ★1218★
- Top Canadian medical/doctoral universities, 2000 ★1221★
- Canadian universities publishing the most papers in the fields of economics and business, 1992-96 ★2215★
- Canadian universities with the greatest impact in materials science, 1992-96 ★4304★

Montreat College
- Average faculty salaries for institutions of higher education in North Carolina, 2000-01 ★3720★

Montserrat College of Art
- Radcliffe Institute for Advanced Study fellowship recipient in the field of art history, 2000-01 ★92★

Montwood High School
- Outstanding secondary schools in El Paso, Texas ★4128★

Moody; Lizabeth A.
- Top pay and benefits for the chief executive and top paid employees at Stetson University ★3511★

Moody; Merri
- Top pay and benefits for the chief executive and top paid employees at Saint Mary's University of Minnesota ★3482★

Mooney; James
- Top pay and benefits for the chief executive and top paid employees at Immaculata College ★3348★

Mooney; Michael
- Top pay and benefits for the chief executive and top paid employees at Lewis and Clark College in Oregon ★3371★

Moore; Bruce
- Top pay and benefits for the chief executive and top paid employees at Gardner-Webb University ★3303★

Moore Campbell; Bebe
- Favorite African American authors ★237★

Moore; D.B.
- Most cited authors in the journal *Australian and New Zealand Journals of Criminology*, 1990 to 1995 ★1613★

Moore; Dennis D.
- Top pay and benefits for the chief executive and top paid employees at Cornell College in Iowa ★3256★

Moore; Dontrel
- All-American boy's high school football all-purpose players, 2000 ★179★

Moore; Edward G.
- Top pay and benefits for the chief executive and top paid employees at Randolph-Macon College ★3451★

Moore; Frank
- Top pay and benefits for the chief executive and top paid employees at New School University ★3418★

Moore; Franklin M.
- Top pay and benefits for the chief executive and top paid employees at Midamerica Nazarene University ★3400★

Moore Jr.; John E.
- Top pay and benefits for the chief executive and top paid employees at Drury University ★3275★

Moore; Loree
- All-America girls' high school basketball 1st team, 2001 ★170★

Moore; Steve L.
- Top pay and benefits for the chief executive and top paid employees at the College of Wooster ★3531★

Moore; William M.
- Top pay and benefits for the chief executive and top paid employees at Valparaiso University ★3592★

Moorhead; J. David
- Top pay and benefits for the chief executive and top paid employees at Loma Linda University ★3377★

Moorpark College
- U.S. institutions awarding the most associate degrees to minorities in agribusiness and production, 1998 ★1808★

Moose Lake Public Library
- Highest Hennen's American Public Library Ratings for libraries serving a population of 1,000 to 2,499 ★2692★

Moraine Park Technical College
- Lowest undergraduate tuition and fees at colleges and universities in Wisconsin ★1571★

Moraine Valley Community College
- Fall enrollment at Chicago-area public community colleges, by minority percentages, 1999 ★867★
- Community colleges with the highest enrollment of foreign students, 1998-99 ★2493★
- Average faculty salaries for institutions of higher education in Illinois, 2000-01 ★3700★
- U.S. community colleges with the highest paid full professors, 2001 ★3976★

Moral Intensity and Ethical Decision-Making of Marketing Professionals
- Most influential articles in the *Journal of Business Research* from 1995 to 1999 ★700★

Moran; Joan Jensen
- All-USA Teacher Teams, Third Team, 2000 ★4401★

Moran; Rep. James P.
- Members of Congress receiving the largest contributions from the Sallie Mae Inc. Political Action Committee ★3023★

Moravian College
- Private, 4-year undergraduate colleges and universities producing the most Ph.D.'s in the computer sciences, 1920-1990 ★1595★
- Private, 4-year undergraduate colleges and universities producing the most Ph.D.'s in the computer sciences, 1981-1990 ★1596★
- Average faculty salaries for institutions of higher education in Pennsylvania, 2000-01 ★3725★

More; Ellen
- Radcliffe Institute for Advanced Study fellowship recipients in the field of history, 2000-01 ★2549★

More News from Lake Wobegon
- Retail audiobook titles selling 300,000-400,000 copies ★303★

More Scary Stories to Tell in the Dark
- Most frequently banned books in the 1990s ★745★
- People for the American Way's list of most frequently challenged books, 1991-1992 ★748★

Morehead State University
- State appropriations for Kentucky's institutions of higher education, 2000-01 ★1270★
- Average faculty salaries for institutions of higher education in Kentucky, 2000-01 ★3704★

Morehead State University (KY)
- Division I NCAA colleges with that graduated none of their African American male basketball players, 1990-91 to 1993-94 ★930★

Morehouse College
Historically black institutions with the highest number of National Achievement Scholars, 1998 ★8★
U.S. colleges and universities with the highest percentage of African Americans enrolled, 1997 ★222★
Most dangerous college campuses in the U.S. ★712★
Division II NCAA colleges with the highest graduation rates for all sports, 1993-94 ★945★
Division II NCAA colleges with the highest graduation rates for football players, 1993-94 ★946★
U.S. colleges and universities with a primarily religious student body ★1022★
Retention rates of African American students at historically black institutions, 1997-98 ★1120★
Fiske Guide's best buys for private colleges and universities, 2001 ★1459★
Total baccalaureate biology/life sciences degrees awarded to African Americans from U.S. colleges and universities, 1997-98 ★1679★
Total baccalaureate business management and administrative services degrees awarded to African Americans from U.S. colleges and universities, 1997-98 ★1683★
Total baccalaureate English language, literature, and letters degrees awarded to African Americans from U.S. colleges and universities, 1997-98 ★1716★
Total baccalaureate mathematics degrees awarded to African Americans from U.S. colleges and universities, 1997-98 ★1729★
Total baccalaureate psychology degrees awarded to African Americans from U.S. colleges and universities, 1997-98 ★1737★
Total baccalaureate social sciences and history degrees awarded to African Americans from U.S. colleges and universities, 1997-98 ★1741★
Most wired historically black colleges and universities, 2000 ★2597★
Average faculty salaries for institutions of higher education in Georgia, 2000-01 ★3697★

Morehouse School of Medicine
Historically black colleges and universities awarding the most first professional degrees to African Americans ★1835★
U.S. colleges and universities awarding the most health professions and related sciences first professional degrees to African Americans ★1847★

Moreland; James
Top pay and benefits for the chief executive and top paid employees at Biola University ★3203★

Morgan Community College
Lowest undergraduate tuition and fees at colleges and universities in Colorado ★1489★
Average faculty salaries for institutions of higher education without academic ranks in Colorado, 2000-01 ★3744★

Morgan; Daniel
Top pay and benefits for the chief executive and top paid employees at Oklahoma City University ★3431★

Morgan; Donnie
Top pay and benefits for the chief executive and top paid employees at Randolph-Macon Woman's College ★3452★

Morgan Kaufmann Publishers
Book publishers with the most citations (Class 3) ★2564★

Morgan Stanley Dean Witter
Companies that have been on *Business Week*'s top 50 list the longest ★435★
Fortune's highest ranked securities companies, 2000 ★494★
Top nonbank financial companies in Standard & Poor's 500, 2001 ★550★

Morgan State University
Colleges offering the Thurgood Marshall Scholarship Fund ★221★
U.S. college campuses with more than 5,000 students reporting murders or manslaughters, 1998 ★729★
Top college choices for Washington D.C. students ★847★
Four-year public institutions enrolling the highest number of students from the District of Columbia, 1998-99 ★855★
State appropriations for Maryland's institutions of higher education, 2000-01 ★1273★
Total baccalaureate communications degrees awarded to African Americans from U.S. colleges and universities, 1997-98 ★1687★
Total baccalaureate computer and information science degrees awarded to African Americans from U.S. colleges and universities, 1997-98 ★1691★
Total baccalaureate degrees awarded to African Americans from historically black colleges, 1997-98 ★1697★
Total baccalaureate degrees awarded to African Americans from U.S. colleges and universities, 1997-98 ★1699★
Total baccalaureate physical sciences degrees awarded to African Americans from U.S. colleges and universities, 1997-98 ★1733★
U.S. colleges and universities awarding the most English language/literature/letters master's degrees to African Americans ★1773★
Average faculty salaries for institutions of higher education in Maryland, 2000-01 ★3707★

Morgan; Stephen C.
Top pay and benefits for the chief executive and top paid employees at the University of La Verne ★3547★

Morgan; Stephen R.
Top pay and benefits for the chief executive and top paid employees at Westminster College in Utah ★3618★

Morley; David
Top pay and benefits for the chief executive and top paid employees at Westmont College ★3619★

Morningside College
Average faculty salaries for institutions of higher education in Iowa, 2000-01 ★3702★

Morocco; Patricia
Top pay and benefits for the chief executive and top paid employees at Bellevue University ★3197★

Morrell; Robynn Anne
All-America girls' high school soccer team forwards, 2001 ★175★

Morrill; Richard L.
Top pay and benefits for the chief executive and top paid employees at the University of Richmond ★3559★

Morris; Allison
Most-cited scholars in women and crime publications ★1642★

Morris; Bevan
Top pay and benefits for the chief executive and top paid employees at the Maharishi University of Management ★3533★

Morris Brown College
Most dangerous college campuses in the U.S. ★712★
Division II NCAA colleges with the lowest graduation rates for football players, 1993-94 ★948★
Total baccalaureate law and legal studies degrees awarded to African Americans from U.S. colleges and universities, 1997-98 ★1725★

Morris; Charles J.
Top pay and benefits for the chief executive and top paid employees at Denison University ★3265★

Morris College
U.S. colleges and universities with the highest percentage of African Americans enrolled, 1997 ★222★

Morris; Grant
Top pay and benefits for the chief executive and top paid employees at the University of San Diego ★3565★

Morris, NJ
Counties with the highest per capita income ★2561★

Morris Public Library
Highest Hennen's American Public Library Ratings for libraries serving a population of 5,000 to 9,999 ★2694★

Morris; Robert C.
Top pay and benefits for the chief executive and top paid employees at Loyola University of Chicago ★3382★

Morrison & Foerster
Top internships in the U.S. with the highest compensation, 2001 ★2611★

Morrison; Daniel B.
Top pay and benefits for the chief executive and top paid employees at Wofford College ★3634★

Morrison, S.J.; Rev. Michael G.
Top pay and benefits for the chief executive and top paid employees at Creighton University ★3259★

Morrison; Toni
Most influential African Americans in the arts ★78★
Favorite African American authors ★237★

Morrissey; Daniel
Top pay and benefits for the chief executive and top paid employees at Saint Thomas University in Florida ★3486★

Morrow
Hardcover bestsellers by publishing house, 2000 ★240★

Mortal Sins
Library Journal's best fiction audiobooks, 2000 ★241★

Mortenson; Donald
Top pay and benefits for the chief executive and top paid employees at Seattle Pacific University ★3494★

Morton Community College
Fall enrollment at Chicago-area public community colleges, by minority percentages, 1999 ★867★

Morton; Terry
Top pay and benefits for the chief executive and top paid employees at Nova Southeastern University ★3426★

Moseley; Pauline S.
Top pay and benefits for the chief executive and top paid employees at University of Central Texas ★3589★

Mosely; James G.
Top pay and benefits for the chief executive and top paid employees at Transylvania University ★3575★

Moses; Edward A.
Top pay and benefits for the chief executive and top paid employees at Rollins College ★3465★

Moses; William A.
Top pay and benefits for the chief executive and top paid employees at Gallaudet University ★3301★

Moss; Harold G.
Top pay and benefits for the chief executive and top paid employees at Washington and Jefferson College ★3604★

Mossberg; Barbara
Top pay and benefits for the chief executive and top paid employees at Goddard College ★3309★

Mother Cabrini High School
Outstanding secondary schools in New York, New York ★4191★

Mother Jones
Most selective internships in the U.S., 2001 ★2610★

Mother McAuley High School
Outstanding secondary schools in Chicago, Illinois ★4110★

MotherKind
Booklist's best fiction books for library collections, 2000 ★227★

Motion picture editor
Jobs with the most stringent quotas ★2259★
Most desirable jobs in the arts ★2277★

Motlow State Community College
Lowest undergraduate tuition and fees at colleges and universities in Tennessee ★1559★
Average faculty salaries for institutions of higher education in Tennessee, 2000-01 ★3730★

Motorola
Fortune's highest ranked electronics and electrical equipment companies, 2000 ★460★
Largest technology companies in the U.S. in terms of annual revenue, 2000 ★4429★

Moulton; Susan
Top pay and benefits for the chief executive and top paid employees at Lesley College ★3370★

Mounds Park Academy Lower School
Outstanding secondary schools in Minneapolis-St. Paul, Minnesota-Wisconsin ★4181★

Mount Allison University
Best Canadian universities overall, 2000 ★1149★
Canadian primarily undergraduate universities best at producing leaders of tomorrow, 2000 ★1192★
Canadian primarily undergraduate universities by alumni support, 2000 ★1193★
Canadian primarily undergraduate universities by award-winning faculty members, 2000 ★1194★
Canadian primarily undergraduate universities by class size at the firstand second-year level, 2000 ★1195★
Canadian primarily undergraduate universities by class size at the thirdand forth-year level, 2000 ★1196★
Canadian primarily undergraduate universities by classes taught by tenured faculty, 2000 ★1197★
Canadian primarily undergraduate universities by faculty members with Ph.D.'s, 2000 ★1198★
Canadian primarily undergraduate universities by library acquisitions, 2000 ★1199★
Canadian primarily undergraduate universities by library expenses, 2000 ★1200★
Canadian primarily undergraduate universities by library holdings per student, 2000 ★1201★
Canadian primarily undergraduate universities by medical/science grants per faculty member, 2000 ★1202★
Canadian primarily undergraduate universities by operating budget per student, 2000 ★1203★
Canadian primarily undergraduate universities by percentage of operating budget allocated to scholarships, 2000 ★1204★
Canadian primarily undergraduate universities by percentage of operating budget allocated to student services, 2000 ★1205★
Canadian primarily undergraduate universities by reputation, 2000 ★1206★
Canadian primarily undergraduate universities by social science/humanities grants per faculty member, 2000 ★1207★
Canadian primarily undergraduate universities by students from out of province, 2000 ★1208★
Canadian primarily undergraduate universities by students winning national awards, 2000 ★1209★
Canadian primarily undergraduate universities that are the best overall, 2000 ★1210★
Canadian primarily undergraduate universities that are the most innovative, 2000 ★1211★
Canadian primarily undergraduate universities with the highest quality, 2000 ★1212★
Canadian universities by average entering grade, 2000 ★1213★
Canadian universities with the highest total cost, 2000 ★1217★
Top Canadian primarily undergraduate universities, 2000 ★1226★

Mount Aloysius College
U.S. News & World Report's northern regional liberal arts colleges with students least in debt, 1999 ★1351★

Mount Carmel Academy
Outstanding secondary schools in New Orleans, Louisiana ★4190★

Mount de Sales Academy
Outstanding secondary schools in Macon, Georgia ★4172★

Mount Holyoke College
Private, 4-year undergraduate colleges and universities producing the most Ph.D.'s in the life sciences, 1920-1990 ★192★
Private, 4-year undergraduate colleges and universities producing the most Ph.D.'s in the life sciences, 1981-1990 ★193★
U.S. colleges and universities most accepting of alternative lifestyles ★986★
U.S. colleges and universities where the general student body does not drink beer ★1004★
U.S. colleges and universities where the general student body does not drink hard liquor ★1005★
U.S. colleges and universities where the general student body puts little emphasis on socializing ★1010★
U.S. colleges and universities with a diverse student body ★1012★
U.S. colleges and universities with excellent library facilities ★1025★
U.S. colleges and universities with the most attractive campuses ★1039★
U.S. News & World Report's national liberal arts colleges with the best financial resources rank, 2000-01 ★1322★
U.S. News & World Report's national liberal arts colleges with the highest percentage of alumni support, 2000-01 ★1331★
Highest undergraduate tuition and fees at private nonprofit, 4-year or above colleges and universities ★1461★
Highest undergraduate tuition and fees at colleges and universities in Massachusetts ★1516★
Private, 4-year undergraduate colleges and universities producing the most Ph.D.s in all fields of study, 1920-1990 ★2027★
Private, 4-year undergraduate colleges and universities producing the most Ph.D.'s in all fields of study, 1981-1990 ★2028★
Private, 4-year undergraduate colleges and universities producing the most Ph.D.'s in all fields of study, 1990 ★2029★
Private, 4-year undergraduate colleges and universities producing the most Ph.D.'s in nonscience fields, 1920-1990 ★2030★
Private, 4-year undergraduate colleges and universities producing the most Ph.D.'s in nonscience fields, 1981-1990 ★2031★
Private, 4-year undergraduate colleges and universities producing the most Ph.D.'s in English, 1920-1990 ★2449★
Private, 4-year undergraduate colleges and universities producing the most Ph.D.'s in English, 1981-1990 ★2450★
Bachelor's institutions with the highest enrollment of foreign students, 1998-99 ★2492★
Private, 4-year undergraduate colleges and universities producing the most Ph.D.'s in history, 1920-1990 ★2552★
Private, 4-year undergraduate colleges and universities producing the most Ph.D.'s in history, 1981-1990 ★2553★
Women's colleges granting physics bachelor's degrees, 2000 ★2982★
Private, 4-year undergraduate colleges and universities producing the most Ph.D.'s in political science and international relations, 1981-1990 ★3045★
Private, 4-year undergraduate colleges and universities producing the most Ph.D.'s in psychology, 1920-1990 ★3066★
Private, 4-year undergraduate colleges and universities producing the most Ph.D.'s in psychology, 1981-1990 ★3067★
Average faculty salaries for institutions of higher education in Massachusetts, 2000-01 ★3708★
U.S. liberal arts colleges with the highest paid full professors, 2001 ★3980★
Private, 4-year undergraduate colleges and universities producing the most Ph.D.'s in the sciences, 1920-1990 ★4294★
Private, 4-year undergraduate colleges and universities producing the most Ph.D.'s in the sciences, 1981-1990 ★4295★
Private, 4-year undergraduate colleges and universities producing the most Ph.D.'s in anthropology and sociology, 1920-1990 ★4344★

Private, 4-year undergraduate colleges and universities producing the most Ph.D.'s in anthropology and sociology, 1981-1990 ★4345★

Mount Hood Community College
Lowest undergraduate tuition and fees at colleges and universities in Oregon ★1548★

Mount Ida College
Colleges and universities with the smallest endowments, 2000 ★1238★

Mount Lebanon High School
Outstanding secondary schools in Pittsburgh, Pennsylvania ★4204★

Mount Lebanon Junior High School
Outstanding secondary schools in Pittsburgh, Pennsylvania ★4204★

Mount Markham Middle School
Outstanding secondary schools in Utica-Rome, New York ★4246★

Mount Marty College
Institutions censured by the American Association of University Professors, 2001 ★1067★
Highest undergraduate tuition and fees at colleges and universities in South Dakota ★1556★

Mount Mary College
U.S. News & World Report's midwestern regional liberal arts colleges with students most in debt, 1999 ★1338★
Average faculty salaries for institutions of higher education in Wisconsin, 2000-01 ★3738★

Mount Mercy College
Average faculty salaries for institutions of higher education in Iowa, 2000-01 ★3702★

Mount Olive College
U.S. News & World Report's southern regional liberal arts colleges with students least in debt, 1999 ★1366★

Mount St. Charles Academy
Outstanding secondary schools in Providence-Fall River-Warwick, Rhode Island-Maine ★4207★

Mount St. Joseph Academy
Outstanding secondary schools in Philadelphia, Pennsylvania-New Jersey ★4202★

Mount St. Joseph; College of
U.S. News & World Report's midwestern regional universities with the best alumni giving rates, 2000-01 ★1402★
U.S. News & World Report's midwestern regional universities with the highest proportion of classes having 20 students or less, 2000-01 ★1409★
U.S. News & World Report's best undergraduate fees among midwestern regional universities by discount tuition, 2000 ★1427★
Average faculty salaries for institutions of higher education in Ohio, 2000-01 ★3722★

Mount St. Mary College
Average faculty salaries for institutions of higher education in New York, 2000-01 ★3719★

Mount St. Mary's College and Seminary
U.S. News & World Report's northern regional universities with the highest acceptance rates, 2000-01 ★1417★
U.S. News & World Report's best undergraduate fees among northern regional universities by discount tuition, 2000 ★1428★
Highest undergraduate tuition and fees at colleges and universities in Maryland ★1514★
U.S. News & World Report's western regional universities with students most in debt, 1999 ★1576★

U.S. News & World Report's western regional universities with the highest freshmen retention rates, 2000-01 ★1581★
U.S. News & World Report's western regional universities with the highest graduation rates, 2000-01 ★1582★
U.S. News & World Report's western regional universities with the lowest acceptance rates, 2000-01 ★1586★
Average faculty salaries for institutions of higher education in California, 2000-01 ★3692★
Average faculty salaries for institutions of higher education in Maryland, 2000-01 ★3707★

Mount St. Michael Academy
Outstanding secondary schools in New York, New York ★4191★

Mount St. Vincent University
Canadian primarily undergraduate universities by alumni support, 2000 ★1193★
Canadian primarily undergraduate universities by class size at the first and second-year level, 2000 ★1195★
Canadian primarily undergraduate universities by class size at the third and forth-year level, 2000 ★1196★
Canadian primarily undergraduate universities by classes taught by tenured faculty, 2000 ★1197★
Canadian primarily undergraduate universities by faculty members with Ph.D.'s, 2000 ★1198★
Canadian primarily undergraduate universities by library acquisitions, 2000 ★1199★
Canadian primarily undergraduate universities by library expenses, 2000 ★1200★
Canadian primarily undergraduate universities by library holdings per student, 2000 ★1201★
Canadian primarily undergraduate universities by medical/science grants per faculty member, 2000 ★1202★
Canadian primarily undergraduate universities by operating budget per student, 2000 ★1203★
Canadian primarily undergraduate universities by percentage of operating budget allocated to scholarships, 2000 ★1204★
Canadian primarily undergraduate universities by percentage of operating budget allocated to student services, 2000 ★1205★
Canadian primarily undergraduate universities by reputation, 2000 ★1206★
Canadian primarily undergraduate universities by social science/humanities grants per faculty member, 2000 ★1207★
Canadian primarily undergraduate universities by students from out of province, 2000 ★1208★
Canadian primarily undergraduate universities by students winning national awards, 2000 ★1209★
Top Canadian primarily undergraduate universities, 2000 ★1226★

Mount Sinai Medical Center
Top gastroenterology hospitals in the U.S., 2000 ★2790★
Top geriatrics hospitals in the U.S., 2000 ★2791★

Mount Sinai School of Medicine
Academics' choices for best geriatrics programs, 2001 ★2821★

Mount Union College
U.S. News & World Report's midwestern regional liberal arts colleges with the highest acceptance rates, 2000-01 ★1341★

U.S. News & World Report's midwestern regional liberal arts colleges with the highest percentage of freshmen in the top 25% of their high school class, 2000-01 ★1345★
U.S. News & World Report's midwestern regional liberal arts colleges with the highest percentage of full-time faculty, 2000-01 ★1346★
U.S. News & World Report's best undergraduate fees among midwestern regional liberal arts colleges by discount tuition, 2000 ★1380★
Average faculty salaries for institutions of higher education in Ohio, 2000-01 ★3722★

Mount Wachusett Community College
Lowest undergraduate tuition and fees at colleges and universities in Massachusetts ★1517★
Average faculty salaries for institutions of higher education in Massachusetts, 2000-01 ★3708★

Mountain Biking: Get on the Trail
Most notable nonfiction books for reluctant young adult readers, 2001 ★323★

Mountain Brook High School
Outstanding secondary schools in Birmingham, Alabama ★4098★

Mountain State College
Highest undergraduate tuition and fees at colleges and universities in West Virginia ★1568★

Mountain View College
U.S. colleges and universities with the lowest percentage of African Americans enrolled, 1997 ★223★
Lowest undergraduate tuition and fees at colleges and universities in Texas ★1561★
Average faculty salaries for institutions of higher education without academic ranks in Texas, 2000-01 ★3766★

Mountain West College
Undergraduate tuition and fees at colleges and universities in Utah ★1562★

The Mousery
Christopher Awards winners for youth literature, 2000 ★316★

MP Roller Coaster Tycoon
Top selling software in all categories, 2000 ★1602★

Mr. Bear to the Rescue
Smithsonian's best books for children ages 1 to 6 ★363★

Mr. Bear's Vacation
Smithsonian's best books for children ages 1 to 6 ★363★

Mr. Popper's Penguins
Most notable children's recordings, 2001 ★320★

Mr. Willowby's Christmas Tree
Publishers Weekly Off-the-Cuff Awards winner for book happiest to see back in print, 2000 ★345★

MS Windows 98 2nd Edition Upgrade
Top selling software in all categories, 2000 ★1602★

MTV's Celebrity Deathmatch Companion
Most notable nonfiction books for reluctant young adult readers, 2001 ★323★

MTV's the Real World New Orleans: Unmasked
Most notable nonfiction books for reluctant young adult readers, 2001 ★323★

Mucciolo; Laurence F.
Top pay and benefits for the chief executive and top paid employees at Northeastern University ★3422★

Muhammad; Elijah
Most influential African Americans in religion ★3091★

Muhlenberg College
Private, 4-year undergraduate colleges and universities producing the most Ph.D.'s in the life sciences, 1981-1990 ★193★
Average faculty salaries for institutions of higher education in Pennsylvania, 2000-01 ★3725★

Muhlenfeld; Elisabeth
Top pay and benefits for the chief executive and top paid employees at Sweet Briar College ★3515★

Muhlfelder; Leslie F.
Top pay and benefits for the chief executive and top paid employees at Lafayette College ★3361★

Mukwonago Community Library
Highest Hennen's American Public Library Ratings for libraries serving a population of 5,000 to 9,999 ★2694★

Mulford; William J.
Top pay and benefits for the chief executive and top paid employees at Anna Maria College ★3177★

Mulhall; Gary
Top pay and benefits for the chief executive and top paid employees at Saint Martin's College in Washington ★3479★

Mullahy; J.
Top associate professor economists at elite liberal arts colleges, 1975-94 ★2174★

Mullaney; Kathryn
Top pay and benefits for the chief executive and top paid employees at St. Lawrence University ★3477★

Muller; Edward N.
Authors most frequently published in *American Political Science Review*, 1974-94 ★3047★

Muller; John
Top pay and benefits for the chief executive and top paid employees at Bellevue University ★3197★

Mullins; Terry W.
Top pay and benefits for the chief executive and top paid employees at Jacksonville University ★3352★

Multi-cultural/interdisciplinary studies
Top bachelor's degree disciplines for African Americans, 1997-98 ★1672★
Top bachelor's degree disciplines for Asian Americans, 1997-98 ★1673★
Top bachelor's degree disciplines for Hispanic Americans, 1997-98 ★1674★
Top bachelor's degree disciplines for Native Americans, 1997-98 ★1675★
Top bachelor's degree disciplines for non-minorities, 1997-98 ★1676★

Multidisciplinary major
Top bachelor's and master's degree majors in demand for employment, 2001 ★2323★
Top bachelor's degree majors in demand for employment, 2001 ★2324★
Top master's degree majors in demand for employment, 2001 ★2326★

Multilingual
Languages of requested materials from OCLC ILL, 1999 ★2679★

Multiple disabilities
Disabled students served in U.S. public school programs, 1998-99 ★1877★

Multiple Streams of Income
Library Journal's most notable investing books, 2000 ★264★

Multnomah Bible College and Biblical Seminary
Average faculty salaries for institutions of higher education in Oregon, 2000-01 ★3724★

Multnomah County Library
Highest Hennen's American Public Library Ratings for libraries serving a population of over 500,000 ★2700★

Mummies, Bones & Body Parts
Most notable nonfiction books for reluctant young adult readers, 2001 ★323★

Munchener Rueck.
Business Week's best companies in Germany ★394★

Munday; Terry
Top pay and benefits for the chief executive and top paid employees at Indiana Wesleyan University ★3349★

Mundelein, District 75
Illinois elementary school districts with the highest teacher salaries, 1999 ★3984★

Mundelein High School
Outstanding secondary schools in Chicago, Illinois ★4110★

Mundy's Mill Middle School
Outstanding secondary schools in Atlanta, Georgia ★4087★

Munich
Cities with the highest productivity of paper in the discipline of cardiovascular systems, 1994-96 ★2869★
Cities with the highest productivity of paper in the discipline of hematology, 1994-96 ★2870★

Muniz; Mary Lee
All-USA Teacher Teams, Second Team, 2000 ★4400★

Munoz; Michelle
All-America girls' high school basketball 3rd team, 2001 ★172★

Munoz; Pam
Outstanding children's fiction books, 2000 ★329★

Munster High School
Outstanding secondary schools in Gary, Indiana ★4139★

Muraka; Shyam
Top pay and benefits for the chief executive and top paid employees at Rensselaer Polytechnic Institute ★3455★

Murata Manufacturing
Business Week's best companies in Japan ★398★

Murdock Middle School
Outstanding secondary schools in Punta Gorda, Florida ★4208★

Murfin; Ross C.
Top pay and benefits for the chief executive and top paid employees at Southern Methodist University ★3502★

Murnane; Thomas
Top pay and benefits for the chief executive and top paid employees at Tufts University ★3580★

Murphy; Bruce
Top pay and benefits for the chief executive and top paid employees at Seattle Pacific University ★3494★

Murphy; Charles J.
Top pay and benefits for the chief executive and top paid employees at Gonzaga University ★3311★

Murphy; John F.
Top pay and benefits for the chief executive and top paid employees at Villanova University ★3595★

Murphy; M. Janice
Top pay and benefits for the chief executive and top paid employees at Spalding University ★3506★

Murphy; Robert P.
Top pay and benefits for the chief executive and top paid employees at D'Youville College ★3278★

Murphy, R.S.H.M.; Sister Michelle
Top pay and benefits for the chief executive and top paid employees at Marymount University ★3395★

Murphy; Thomas E.
Top pay and benefits for the chief executive and top paid employees at Hamilton College ★3319★

Murray; Anne
Canada's best performing artists of the 20th century ★74★

Murray; Dennis J.
Top pay and benefits for the chief executive and top paid employees at Marist College ★3390★

Murray Jr.; John E.
Presidents with the highest pay at Doctoral I and II universities, 1998-99 ★3160★
Top pay and benefits for the chief executive and top paid employees at Duquesne University ★3277★

Murray, KY
America's most wired towns, 2001 ★2575★

Murray Language
Chicago elementary magnet schools with the lowest acceptance rates, 2000-01 ★4003★

Murray; M.
Top full professor economists at elite liberal arts colleges, 1975-94 ★2175★

Murray; Michael P.
Top pay and benefits for the chief executive and top paid employees at Bates College ★3193★

Murray State College
Lowest undergraduate tuition and fees at colleges and universities in Oklahoma ★1546★

Murray State University
U.S. college campuses with more than 5,000 students reporting murders or manslaughters, 1998 ★729★
Institutions censured by the American Association of University Professors, 2001 ★1067★
State appropriations for Kentucky's institutions of higher education, 2000-01 ★1270★
U.S. News & World Report's best undergraduate fees among southern regional universities by discount tuition, 2000 ★1429★
U.S. News & World Report's southern regional universities with the highest percentage of freshmen in the top 25% of their high school class, 2000-01 ★1439★
U.S. News & World Report's southern regional universities with the highest percentage of full-time faculty, 2000-01 ★1440★
U.S. News & World Report's southern regional universities with the lowest acceptance rates, 2000-01 ★1442★

U.S. News & World Report's top public southern regional universities, 2000-01 ★1443★
Average faculty salaries for institutions of higher education in Kentucky, 2000-01 ★3704★

Murrin; Thomas J.
Top pay and benefits for the chief executive and top paid employees at Duquesne University ★3277★

Murrow; Edward R.
Best U.S. works of journalism in the 20th century ★2769★

Murrow; Wayne
Top pay and benefits for the chief executive and top paid employees at Southern Nazarene University ★3503★

Murry Bergtraum Senior High School
Outstanding urban public high schools in Metro New York ★4265★

Murtha; James
Top pay and benefits for the chief executive and top paid employees at New School University ★3418★

Muscatine Community College
Lowest undergraduate tuition and fees at colleges and universities in Iowa ★1505★

Muscle Shoals High School
Outstanding secondary schools in Florence, Alabama ★4132★

Museum curator
Most desirable jobs in the arts ★2277★

Museums
Industries with the highest percentage of projected employment growth from 1998 through 2008 ★2305★

Museums and botanical and zoological gardens
Employment growth percentages for selected industries, 1998-2000 ★2294★

Mushlin; Michael B.
Top pay and benefits for the chief executive and top paid employees at Pace University ★3435★

Music
Gender breakdown of humanities doctorate recipients, by subfield, 1999 ★1936★
Humanities doctorates awarded at U.S. colleges and universities, by subfield, 1999 ★1946★
Percentage of female doctorate recipients at U.S. colleges and universities, by subfield, 1999 ★1988★
Average costs for Academic Search titles by subject, 2001 ★2918★
Periodical prices by LC subject, 2001 ★2925★

Music of the American Colonies
Most notable children's recordings, 2001 ★320★

Music education
Gender breakdown of teaching fields doctorate recipients, by subfield, 1999 ★1943★
Teaching fields doctorates awarded at U.S. colleges and universities, by subfield, 1999 ★2046★

Music theory
Number of Advanced Placement Exams taken by African Americans, by subject, 2000 ★30★
Number of Advanced Placement Exams taken by Asian Americans, by subject, 2000 ★31★
Number of Advanced Placement Exams taken by Hispanic Americans, by subject, 2000 ★32★

Musical instrument repairer
Jobs with the best stress scores ★2252★
Most desirable technical/repair jobs ★2281★

Musical instrument repairers
Jobs with the worst outlook scores ★2262★

Musician
Most desirable jobs in the arts ★2277★
'White-collar' jobs considered the most physically demanding ★2285★

Musicians, singers, and related workers
Projected employment growth for selected occupations that require long-term on-the-job training, 1998-2008 ★2320★

Muskegon Community College
Lowest undergraduate tuition and fees at colleges and universities in Michigan ★1519★

Muskingum College
U.S. News & World Report's midwestern regional liberal arts colleges with the highest percentage of full-time faculty, 2000-01 ★1346★
U.S. News & World Report's best undergraduate fees among midwestern regional liberal arts colleges by discount tuition, 2000 ★1380★
Average faculty salaries for institutions of higher education in Ohio, 2000-01 ★3722★

Mutongi; Kenda
Radcliffe Institute for Advanced Study fellowship recipients in the field of history, 2000-01 ★2549★

Mutti; John H.
Top full professor economists at elite liberal arts colleges, 1975-94 ★2175★
Top pay and benefits for the chief executive and top paid employees at Grinnell College ★3315★

Muzina; Dario
Top pay and benefits for the chief executive and top paid employees at Lake Erie College ★3362★

My America: A Poetry Atlas of the United States
Booklist's most recommended poetry for youths, 2001 ★315★

My Brother Sam Is Dead
Most frequently banned books in the 1990s ★745★

My Favorite Things: 75 Works of Art from Around the World
Most notable nonfiction books for young adults, 2001 ★324★

My First Garden
Smithsonian's best books for children ages 1 to 6 ★363★

My First Oxford Book of Stories
Smithsonian's best books for children ages 1 to 6 ★363★

My House
Most frequently banned books in the 1990s ★745★

My Little Red Toolbox
Publishers Weekly Off-the-Cuff Awards winners for best activity book/kit, 2000 ★360★

My Mother's Ghost
Outstanding biography books, 2000 ★288★

My Season with Penguins: An Antarctic Journal
Most notable books for middle readers, 2001 ★317★
Smithsonian's best books for children ages 10 and up ★365★

Myers; Christopher
Outstanding children's picture books, 2000 ★331★

Myers; Donald L.
Top pay and benefits for the chief executive and top paid employees at American University ★3174★

Myers Jr.; Minor
Top pay and benefits for the chief executive and top paid employees at Illinois Wesleyan University ★3347★

Myers; Mark William
Top pay and benefits for the chief executive and top paid employees at Trevecca Nazarene University ★3576★

Myers; Michele Tolela
Top pay and benefits for the chief executive and top paid employees at Denison University ★3265★
Top pay and benefits for the chief executive and top paid employees at Sarah Lawrence College ★3492★

Myers Middle School
Outstanding secondary schools in Savannah, Georgia ★4226★

Myerson; Alan
Top pay and benefits for the chief executive and top paid employees at Polytechnic University ★3443★

Mysteries
Subject areas with the highest library expenditures/circulation ★306★

The Mysteries Within: A Surgeon Reflects on Medical Myths
Library Journal's most notable health sciences books, 2000 ★262★
Outstanding science books, 2000 ★291★
Booklist's best science and technology books ★366★

The Mystery of Capital
Library Journal's most notable books on capitalism, 2000 ★253★

N

NAACP
Top recipients of corporate contributions to African American communities, 1995 ★2944★

Nabisco
Top internships in the U.S. with the highest compensation, 2001 ★2611★

Nabisco Group Holdings
Fortune's highest ranked consumer food products companies, 2000 ★458★

Nagel; Roger N.
Top pay and benefits for the chief executive and top paid employees at Lehigh University ★3368★

Nagler; Arnold
Top pay and benefits for the chief executive and top paid employees at the New York Institute of Technology ★3535★

Naidorf; Louis
Top pay and benefits for the chief executive and top paid employees at Woodbury University ★3635★

Naik; Haley
All-USA College Academic Second Team, 2001 ★3★

Naik; Nitin
Top pay and benefits for the chief executive and top paid employees at Wheeling Jesuit University ★3622★

Najarlan; John S.
Most-cited researchers in surgery/transplantation, 1981-1998 ★2878★

Nalamasu; Omkaram
American Chemical Society 2001 award winners (Group 2) ★752★

Nance; Marcia K.
Top pay and benefits for the chief executive and top paid employees at St. Andrews Presbyterian College ★3469★

Nantucket, MA
Counties with the highest per capita income ★2561★

Naor; Jacob
Highest impact authors in the *Journal of Business Research*, by adjusted number of citations in 12 journals, 1985-1999 ★692★

Napa Valley College
Lowest undergraduate tuition and fees at public 2-year colleges and universities ★1465★

Naperville Central High School
Illinois high schools with the highest SAT scores ★874★

Naperville, IL
Best small towns to live in ★3085★

Naperville North High School
Illinois high schools with the highest SAT scores ★874★

Naperville Public Libraries
Highest Hennen's American Public Library Ratings for libraries serving a population of 100,000 to 249,999 ★2698★

Naperville School District No. 203, Illinois
Comparison of 8th grade science achievement scores, U.S. and worldwide, 1999 ★6★

Narnia
Most notable children's web sites, 2001 ★2593★

Naropa University
Highest undergraduate tuition and fees at colleges and universities in Colorado ★1488★

NASA
Federal appropriations to colleges, by agency, 2000 ★1241★

NASA Headquarters
Top recruiters for multidisciplinary majors jobs for 2000-01 bachelor's degree recipients ★2327★
Top recruiters for multidisciplinary engineers jobs for 2000-01 bachelor's degree recipients ★2335★

Nash Community College
Average faculty salaries for institutions of higher education without academic ranks in North Carolina, 2000-01 ★3761★

Nashua, NH
U.S. cities with the lowest rate of violent crime ★3088★

Nashville State Technical Institute
Lowest undergraduate tuition and fees at colleges and universities in Tennessee ★1559★
Average faculty salaries for institutions of higher education in Tennessee, 2000-01 ★3730★

Naso; Mary Ann
Top pay and benefits for the chief executive and top paid employees at Lake Erie College ★3362★

Nassau Community College
Lowest undergraduate tuition and fees at colleges and universities in New York ★1538★
Average faculty salaries for institutions of higher education in New York, 2000-01 ★3719★
U.S. community colleges with the highest paid full professors, 2001 ★3976★

Nassau, NY
Counties with the highest per capita income ★2561★

Nassif, S.N.D.; Rosemarie
Top pay and benefits for the chief executive and top paid employees at Holy Names College ★3337★

Nast; Thomas
Top editorial cartoonists used in teaching journalism history ★2770★

Nathaniel Bowdith Middle School
Outstanding secondary schools in San Francisco, California ★4221★

The Nation
Most selective internships in the U.S., 2001 ★2610★

National Aeronautics and Space Administration
Proposed fiscal 2002 appropriations for Department of Commerce research ★3107★
Proposed fiscal 2002 appropriations for science and technology research ★4339★

National American University, Denver
Highest undergraduate tuition and fees at colleges and universities in Colorado ★1488★

National American University, Rapid City
Highest undergraduate tuition and fees at colleges and universities in South Dakota ★1556★

National Archives and Records Administration
Proposed fiscal 2002 appropriations for arts and humanities ★101★

The National Audobon Society
Most selective internships in the U.S., 2001 ★2610★

National Australia Bank
Business Week's best companies in Australia ★386★

National Center for Fair and Open Testing
Most selective internships in the U.S., 2001 ★2610★

National Chiao Tung University
Top institutions in systems and software engineering publications ★2332★

National City
Fortune's highest ranked super-regional banks, 2000 ★498★

National Collegiate Athletic Association
Most selective internships in the U.S., 2001 ★2610★

National Consortium for Graduate Degrees for Minorities in Engineering and Science
Top internships in the U.S. with the highest compensation, 2001 ★2611★

National Education Center Spartan School of Aeronautics
Highest undergraduate tuition and fees at colleges and universities in Oklahoma ★1545★

National Endowment for the Arts
Proposed fiscal 2002 appropriations for arts and humanities ★101★
Fiscal 2002 requested budget as compared with Fiscal 2001 budget for other agencies ★2230★

National Endowment for the Humanities
Proposed fiscal 2002 appropriations for arts and humanities ★101★

Fiscal 2002 requested budget as compared with Fiscal 2001 budget for other agencies ★2230★
Most selective internships in the U.S., 2001 ★2610★

National Football League
Most selective internships in the U.S., 2001 ★2610★

National Geographic Adventure
Library Journal's notable new magazines, 1999 ★2923★

National Geographic Magazine
Magazines with the largest circulation ★2750★

National Historical Publications and Records Commission
Proposed fiscal 2002 appropriations for arts and humanities ★101★

National Institute of Mental Health
U.S. institutions with the most citations in psychiatry research, 1990-98 ★3059★

National Institute on Disability and Rehabilitation Research
2002 budget request for education of the handicapped ★1878★

National Institute of Standards and Technology
Proposed fiscal 2002 appropriations for Department of Commerce research ★3107★

National Institutes of Health
Fiscal 2002 requested budget as compared with Fiscal 2001 budget for other agencies ★2230★
Proposed fiscal 2002 appropriations for science and technology research ★4339★

National Journal
Most selective internships in the U.S., 2001 ★2610★

National-Louis University
Fall enrollment at the largest Chicago-area private institutions, by minority percentages, 1999 ★869★
Traditionally white institutions awarding the most master's degrees to African Americans ★1755★
U.S. colleges and universities awarding the most business management and administrative services master's degrees to African Americans ★1759★
U.S. colleges and universities awarding the most education master's degrees to African Americans ★1769★
U.S. colleges and universities awarding the most education master's degrees to Hispanic Americans ★1771★
U.S. colleges and universities awarding the most master's degrees to African Americans ★1785★
Average faculty salaries for institutions of higher education in Illinois, 2000-01 ★3700★

National Oceanic and Atmospheric Administration
Proposed fiscal 2002 appropriations for Department of Commerce research ★3107★

National Review
Most selective internships in the U.S., 2001 ★2610★

National Science Foundation
Fiscal 2002 requested budget as compared with Fiscal 2001 budget for other agencies ★2230★
Proposed fiscal 2002 appropriations for science and technology research ★4339★

National Science Foundation Research
Proposed fiscal 2002 appropriations for the National Science Foundation ★3109★

National Security Agency
Top internships in the U.S. with the highest compensation, 2001 ★2611★

National Semiconductor
Fortune's highest ranked semiconductors companies, 2000 ★495★

National Tax Journal
Top accounting journals by half-life impact factor ★578★
Top accounting journals by mode impact factor ★579★
Top ranked law and economics journals ★2197★
Top ranked public economics journals ★2201★

National Technical Institute for the Deaf
2002 budget request for aid to individual institutions ★1235★

National Telecommunications and Information Administration Information Infrastructure Grants
Proposed fiscal 2002 appropriations for Department of Commerce research ★3107★

The National Transportation Safety Board
Library Journal's best free reference websites, 2000 ★367★

National University
U.S. colleges and universities awarding the most business management and administrative services master's degrees to Hispanic Americans ★1761★
U.S. colleges and universities awarding the most education master's degrees to Asian Americans ★1770★
U.S. colleges and universities awarding the most education master's degrees to Hispanic Americans ★1771★
U.S. colleges and universities awarding the most education master's degrees to Native Americans ★1772★
U.S. colleges and universities awarding the most master's degrees to Hispanic Americans ★1787★
U.S. colleges and universities awarding the most master's degrees to minorities ★1788★
U.S. colleges and universities awarding the most psychology master's degrees to African Americans ★1797★
U.S. colleges and universities awarding the most psychology master's degrees to Asian Americans ★1798★
U.S. colleges and universities awarding the most psychology master's degrees to Hispanic Americans ★1799★
Average faculty salaries for institutions of higher education in California, 2000-01 ★3692★

National University (CA)
Presidents with the highest pay at Master's I and II colleges and universities, 1998-99 ★3161★

National Wildlife Federation
Most selective internships in the U.S., 2001 ★2610★

National Women's Health Information Center
Medical Library Association's top health related web sites ★2591★

National Women's Health Network
Most selective internships in the U.S., 2001 ★2610★

Nationwide Insurance Enterprise
Fortune's highest ranked property and casualty insurance companies, 2000 ★488★

Native American
ACT composite scores, by race/ethnicity, 2000 ★871★
Racial and ethnic background of incoming freshmen, 2000 ★1058★
Number of U.S. citizen/permanent resident doctorate recipients in all fields at U.S. colleges and universities, by race/ethnicity, 1999 ★1978★
Number of U.S. citizen/permanent resident doctorate recipients in education at U.S. colleges and universities, by race/ethnicity, 1999 ★1979★
Number of U.S. citizen/permanent resident doctorate recipients in engineering at U.S. colleges and universities, by race/ethnicity, 1999 ★1980★
Number of U.S. citizen/permanent resident doctorate recipients in humanities at U.S. colleges and universities, by race/ethnicity, 1999 ★1981★
Number of U.S. citizen/permanent resident doctorate recipients in life sciences at U.S. colleges and universities, by race/ethnicity, 1999 ★1982★
Number of U.S. citizen/permanent resident doctorate recipients in physical sciences, mathematics, and computer sciences at U.S. colleges and universities, by race/ethnicity, 1999 ★1983★
Number of U.S. citizen/permanent resident doctorate recipients in professional/other fields at U.S. colleges and universities, by race/ethnicity, 1999 ★1984★
Number of U.S. citizen/permanent resident doctorate recipients in social sciences at U.S. colleges and universities, by race/ethnicity, 1999 ★1985★
Percentage of doctoral degree recipients at U.S. universities, by race/ethnicity, 1999 ★1987★
Percentage of minority doctorate recipients in the U.S., 1999 ★1990★
Percentage of minority doctorate recipients in the U.S., by gender, 1999 ★1992★
Ethnic breakdown of executives and managers in Silicon Valley firms, 1997 ★2300★
Race/ethnicity profile of U.S. students studying abroad, 1998-99 ★2509★
Bachelor's degrees granted in journalism and mass communications programs, by race/ethnicity, 1999 ★2742★
Bachelor's enrollments in journalism and mass communications programs, by race/ethnicity, 1999 ★2744★
Doctoral degrees granted in journalism and mass communications programs, by race/ethnicity, 1999 ★2759★
Doctoral enrollments in journalism and mass communications programs, by race/ethnicity, 1999 ★2761★
Master's degrees granted in journalism and mass communications programs, by race/ethnicity, 1999 ★2766★
Master's enrollments in journalism and mass communications programs, by race/ethnicity, 1999 ★2768★
U.S. medical school enrollment of U.S. citizens by racial/ethnic category, 1999-2000 ★2863★
National Society of Fund-Raising Executives, by race/ethnicity ★2942★
Students participating in gifted and talented programs, by race ethnicity, 1997 ★4050★

Native American/Alaskan Native
Graduation rates for female basketball players at Division I NCAA colleges, by race/ethnicity ★954★
Graduation rates for female basketball players at Division II NCAA colleges, 1993-94 ★955★
Graduation rates for female students and athletes at Division I NCAA colleges, by race/ethnicity ★956★
Graduation rates for female students at Division II NCAA colleges, 1993-94 ★957★
Graduation rates for football players at Division I NCAA colleges, by race/ethnicity ★958★
Graduation rates for football players at Division II NCAA colleges, 1993-94 ★959★
Graduation rates for male basketball players at Division I NCAA colleges, by race/ethnicity ★960★
Graduation rates for male basketball players at Division II NCAA colleges, 1993-94 ★961★
Graduation rates for male students and athletes at Division I NCAA colleges, by race/ethnicity ★962★
Graduation rates for male students at Division II NCAA colleges, 1993-94 ★963★
Age grouping of doctorate recipients, by race/ethnicity, 1999 ★1885★

Native American Crafts & Skills: A Fully Illustrated Guide to Wilderness Living and Survival
Best selling small press releases, 2001 ★226★

Native Son
Favorite books of African Americans ★238★

Natural Language & Linguistics Theory
Language and linguistics journals with the greatest impact measure, 1981-98 ★2731★

Natural Resource Scarcity-Empirical Evidence and Public Policy
Journal of Environmental Economics and Management's best articles in depletable resources and energy ★2462★

Natural Resources, National Accounting, and Economic Depreciation
Top cited nonrenewable resource papers from 1989 to 1993 ★2471★

Natural sciences
Top physical science majors for accepted applicants to U.S. medical schools, 1999-2000 ★2855★

Nature
Molecular biology and genetics journals with the highest impact, 1992-96 ★204★

Nature Genetics
Molecular biology and genetics journals with the highest impact, 1992-96 ★204★

Naugatuck Valley Community-Technical College
Lowest undergraduate tuition and fees at colleges and universities in Connecticut ★1491★

Nauman; Bruce
Best living artists ★73★
Highly influential artists of the 20th century ★76★

Navistar International
Business Week's best performing companies with the lowest 1-year sales performance ★421★
Fortune's highest ranked motor vehicles companies, 2000 ★481★
Top automotive companies in Standard & Poor's 500, 2001 ★530★

Navratil; Frank
  Top pay and benefits for the chief executive and top paid employees at John Carroll University ★3353★

Nazareth College of Rochester
  U.S. News & World Report's northern regional universities with the best student/faculty ratios, 2000-01 ★1416★
  U.S. News & World Report's northern regional universities with the highest percentage of freshmen in the top 25% of their high school class, 2000-01 ★1421★
  U.S. News & World Report's best undergraduate fees among northern regional universities by discount tuition, 2000 ★1428★
  Average faculty salaries for institutions of higher education in New York, 2000-01 ★3719★

The Nazi Olympics: Berlin, 1936
  Most notable nonfiction books for young adults, 2001 ★324★

NCR
  Business Week's best performing companies with the highest 3-year earnings growth ★416★
  Fortune's highest ranked computers and office equipment companies, 2000 ★456★

Neale Hurston; Zora
  Favorite African American authors ★237★

Nebraska
  Mean composite ACT scores by state, 2000 ★895★
  Mean math SAT scores by state, 2000 ★900★
  Mean verbal SAT scores by state, 2000 ★903★
  States with the highest percentage increase in appropriations for higher education, 2000-01 ★1308★
  Total doctorate recipients by state, 1999 ★2054★
  State grades for affordability of higher education for minority students, 2000 ★2883★
  State grades for benefits state receives for educating its minority students, 2000 ★2884★
  State grades for completion of higher education by minority students, 2000 ★2885★
  State grades for participation of minority students in higher education, 2000 ★2886★
  State grades for preparing minority students for higher education, 2000 ★2887★
  States with the most public school districts ★3999★
  States with the highest percentage of high school freshmen enrolling in college within four years ★4266★

Nebraska College of Technical Agriculture
  Lowest undergraduate tuition and fees at colleges and universities in Nebraska ★1529★

Nebraska Indian Community College
  U.S. tribal colleges ★1445★

Nebraska, Kearney; University of
  Average faculty salaries for institutions of higher education in Nebraska, 2000-01 ★3714★

Nebraska, Lincoln; University of
  Academics' choices for best graduate agricultural engineering programs, 2001 ★2379★
  Average faculty salaries for institutions of higher education in Nebraska, 2000-01 ★3714★

Nebraska Medical Center; University of
  U.S. colleges and universities awarding the most health professions and related sciences master's degrees to Hispanic Americans ★1779★
  U.S. colleges and universities awarding the most health professions and related sciences master's degrees to Native Americans ★1780★

Nebraska Methodist College of Nursing and Allied Health
  Highest undergraduate tuition and fees at colleges and universities in Nebraska ★1528★

Nebraska, Omaha; University of
  Universities with the most-cited scholars in *Criminal Justice and Behavior* ★1648★
  Universities with the most-cited scholars in *Journal of Quantitative Criminology* ★1650★
  Universities with the most-cited scholars in *Justice Quarterly* ★1652★
  Average faculty salaries for institutions of higher education in Nebraska, 2000-01 ★3714★

Nebraska; University of
  U.S. universities publishing the most papers in the fields of agriculture/agronomy, 1994-98 ★57★
  Division I-A all-time percentage leaders ★127★
  NCAA men's gymnastics teams with the most individual champions ★137★
  Women's Division I track and field programs with the most outdoor championships ★149★
  State appropriations for Nebraska's institutions of higher education, 2000-01 ★1280★
  Institutions generating the most economic education research text, 1963-1990 ★2167★

Nebraska Wesleyan University
  Highest undergraduate tuition and fees at colleges and universities in Nebraska ★1528★
  Average faculty salaries for institutions of higher education in Nebraska, 2000-01 ★3714★

NEC
  Business Week's best companies in Japan ★398★

Neely; Walter
  Top pay and benefits for the chief executive and top paid employees at Millsaps College ★3403★

Neff; Jeanne H.
  Top pay and benefits for the chief executive and top paid employees at the Sage Colleges in New York ★3536★

Neff; Robert W.
  Top pay and benefits for the chief executive and top paid employees at Juniata College ★3357★

Neice; Joan
  Top pay and benefits for the chief executive and top paid employees at Marylhurst University ★3394★

Neitzel; Ann
  Top pay and benefits for the chief executive and top paid employees at Muhlenberg College ★3413★

Nejib; Umid
  Top pay and benefits for the chief executive and top paid employees at Wilkes University ★3627★

Nel; Stanley
  Top pay and benefits for the chief executive and top paid employees at the University of San Francisco ★3566★

Nelson; Christopher B.
  Top pay and benefits for the chief executive and top paid employees at St. John's College in Maryland and New Mexico ★3473★

Nelson; Herbert J.
  Top pay and benefits for the chief executive and top paid employees at Canisius College ★3219★

Nelson III; Leonard
  Top pay and benefits for the chief executive and top paid employees at Chapman University ★3228★

Nelson; John P.
  Top pay and benefits for the chief executive and top paid employees at Barry University ★3192★

Nelson; Joseph G.
  Top pay and benefits for the chief executive and top paid employees at Kenyon College ★3359★

Nelson; Karen
  Top pay and benefits for the chief executive and top paid employees at Austin College ★3184★

Nelson; W. G.
  Top pay and benefits for the chief executive and top paid employees at Walla Walla College ★3601★

Nelson; William H.
  Top pay and benefits for the chief executive and top paid employees at Mercer University ★3398★

Nemeroff; Charles B.
  Top pay and benefits for the chief executive and top paid employees at Emory University ★3289★

Neon Systems
  Top companies in terms of growth, 2000 ★534★

Neoplasia
  Leading categories of dermatologic disease covered by top articles in the field, 1945-1990 ★1869★

Neosho County Community College
  Lowest undergraduate tuition and fees at colleges and universities in Kansas ★1507★

Nepal
  Countries with the lowest leader's salary ★3121★

Nephron
  Urology and nephrology journals with the greatest impact measure, 1981-98 ★2816★

Neptune Middle School
  Outstanding secondary schools in Orlando, Florida ★4200★

Nerinx Hall High School
  Outstanding secondary schools in St. Louis, Missouri-Illinois ★4216★

Nestle
  Business Week's best companies in Switzerland ★405★

Nestle USA
  Fortune's highest ranked consumer food products companies, 2000 ★458★

Net National Product as an Indicator of Sustainability
  Top cited nonrenewable resource papers from 1994 to 1998 ★2472★

Net-Temps
  Top career-related Web sites ★2602★

Netcom
  Most profitable information technology companies, 2000 ★527★

Netcreations
  Fast-growing information technology companies, 2000 ★444★

Netherlands
Eight grade science achievement scores from selected countries, 1999 ★14★
Math achievement test comparison ★19★
Countries with the most computers per capita, 2000 ★1604★
Eighth grade mathematics achievement scores from selected countries, 1999 ★2773★
European periodical prices by country, 2001 ★2921★
Institute for Scientific Information periodical prices by country, 2001 ★2922★

Netherlands Journal of Plant Pathology
Agriculture journals by citation impact, 1992-96 ★52★

Netherlands Journal of Sea Research
Marine and freshwater biology journals with the greatest impact measure, 1981-98 ★196★
Marine and freshwater biology journals with the greatest impact measure, 1994-98 ★197★
Oceanography journals by citation impact, 1995-99 ★2140★

Netherlands Milk/Dairy Journal
Food science and technology journals by citation impact, 1991-99 ★2902★
Food science and technology journals by citation impact, 1995-99 ★2903★

Netherton; James S.
Top pay and benefits for the chief executive and top paid employees at Samford University ★3490★

Netscout Systems
Top companies in terms of growth, 2000 ★534★

Network Appliance
Business Week's best performing companies with the highest 3-year shareholder returns ★418★
Business Week's top companies in terms of earning growth, 2000 ★427★
Business Week's top companies in terms of market value, 2000 ★429★
Business Week's top companies in terms of sales, 2000 ★431★
Top companies in terms of growth, 2000 ★534★
Top information technology companies, 2000 ★544★
Top office equipment and computers companies in Standard & Poor's 500, 2001 ★551★

Network: Computation in Neural Systems
Artificial intelligence journals by citation impact, 1995-99 ★95★

Network design
Job openings for high-tech workers ★2330★

Network design/administration
Information technology jobs most in demand, 2001 ★4428★

Network-Neural Computations
Artificial intelligence journals with the greatest impact measure, 1994-98 ★98★
Artificial intelligence journals with the greatest impact measure, 1998 ★99★

Network Solutions
Business Week's top companies in terms of market value, 2000 ★429★

Neuhauser; Charlotte
Top pay and benefits for the chief executive and top paid employees at Madonna University ★3386★

Neumann College
U.S. News & World Report's northern regional liberal arts colleges with students most in debt, 1999 ★1352★

Average faculty salaries for institutions of higher education in Pennsylvania, 2000-01 ★3725★

Neural Computation
Artificial intelligence journals by citation impact, 1981-99 ★94★
Artificial intelligence journals by citation impact, 1995-99 ★95★
Artificial intelligence journals by citation impact, 1999 ★96★
Artificial intelligence journals with the greatest impact measure, 1981-98 ★97★
Artificial intelligence journals with the greatest impact measure, 1994-98 ★98★
Artificial intelligence journals with the greatest impact measure, 1998 ★99★
Journals and proceedings with the most citations (Class 4) ★2570★

Neural Networks
Artificial intelligence journals by citation impact, 1981-99 ★94★
Artificial intelligence journals with the greatest impact measure, 1981-98 ★97★

Neurobiology of Aging
Geriatrics and gerontology journals with the greatest impact measure, 1981-98 ★2805★
Geriatrics and gerontology journals with the greatest impact measure, 1994-98 ★2806★
Geriatrics and gerontology journals with the greatest impact measure, 1998 ★2807★

Neurology
Clinical medicine subfields with the highest impact measure, 1981-1997 ★2873★

Neuron
Journals with the highest impact factor in the field of neuroscience, 1981-96 ★191★
Neurosciences journals with the greatest impact measure, 1981-98 ★2812★
Neurosciences journals with the greatest impact measure, 1994-98 ★2813★

Neuropsychopharmacology
Psychiatry journals by citation impact, 1995-98 ★3055★
Psychiatry journals by impact factor, 1994 to 1998 ★3058★

Neuroscience
Biological sciences doctorates awarded at U.S. colleges and universities, by subfield, 1999 ★1887★
Gender breakdown of biological sciences doctorate recipients, by subfield, 1999 ★1927★
Percentage of female doctorate recipients at U.S. colleges and universities, by subfield, 1999 ★1988★
United States' contribution of papers in the sciences, by field, 1995-99 ★4283★
United States' contribution of papers in the sciences, by field, 1996-2000 ★4284★
United Kingdom's contribution of papers in the sciences, by field, 1995-99 ★4297★
Austria's contribution of papers in the sciences by field, 1992-96 ★4298★
Austria's contribution of papers in the sciences, by field, 1995-99 ★4299★
Austria's relative impact in the sciences by field, 1992-96 ★4300★
Canada's contribution of papers in the sciences, by field, 1995-99 ★4303★
Finland's contribution of papers in the sciences by field, 1992-96 ★4309★
Finland's contribution of papers in the sciences, by field, 1995-99 ★4310★
Germany's contribution of papers in the sciences, by field, 1995-99 ★4313★

Ireland's contribution of papers in the sciences, by field, 1994-98 ★4315★
Italy's contribution of papers in the sciences, by field, 1995-99 ★4316★
Japan's contribution of papers in the sciences, by field, 1995-99 ★4318★
Poland's contribution of papers in the sciences, by field, 1993-97 ★4324★
Sweden's contribution of papers in the sciences by field, 1993-97 ★4330★
Sweden's contribution of papers in the sciences, by field, 1995-99 ★4331★
Switzerland's contribution of papers in the sciences, by field, 1994-98 ★4332★
Switzerland's contribution of papers in the sciences, by field, 1995-99 ★4333★

Nevada
Mean composite ACT scores by state, 2000 ★895★
Mean math SAT scores by state, 2000 ★900★
Mean verbal SAT scores by state, 2000 ★903★
Average class size at colleges and universities in the U.S., by state ★1064★
Total doctorate recipients by state, 1999 ★2054★
State grades for affordability of higher education for minority students, 2000 ★2883★
State grades for benefits state receives for educating its minority students, 2000 ★2884★
State grades for completion of higher education by minority students, 2000 ★2885★
State grades for participation of minority students in higher education, 2000 ★2886★
State grades for preparing minority students for higher education, 2000 ★2887★
States expelling the highest ratio of students for violating the Gun-Free Schools Act, 1998-99 ★3993★
States with the highest average enrollment in public elementary schools ★4032★
States with the highest average enrollment in public secondary schools ★4033★
States with the lowest percentage of high school freshmen enrolling in college within four years ★4267★
U.S. states with the highest percentage of births to teenagers who were already mothers ★4433★

Nevada, Las Vegas; University of
Division I all-time winningest college teams ★128★
Division I NCAA colleges with that graduated less than 20% of their African American male athletes, 1990-91 to 1993-94 ★928★
Division I NCAA colleges with that graduated none of their African American male basketball players, 1990-91 to 1993-94 ★930★
Undergraduate tuition and fees at colleges and universities in Nevada ★1530★
U.S. News & World Report's top public western regional universities, 2000-01 ★1573★
Average faculty salaries for institutions of higher education in Nevada, 2000-01 ★3715★

Nevada, Reno; University of
U.S. college campuses with more than 5,000 students reporting murders or manslaughters, 1998 ★729★
Division I NCAA colleges with that graduated less than 20% of their African American male athletes, 1990-91 to 1993-94 ★928★

Division I NCAA colleges with that graduated none of their African American male basketball players, 1990-91 to 1993-94 ★930★

Division I NCAA colleges with the lowest graduation rates for female basketball players, 1990-91 to 1993-94 ★937★

Division I NCAA colleges with the lowest graduation rates for football players, 1990-91 to 1993-94 ★938★

Division I NCAA colleges with the lowest graduation rates for male athletes, 1990-91 to 1993-94 ★939★

Undergraduate tuition and fees at colleges and universities in Nevada ★1530★

Average faculty salaries for institutions of higher education in Nevada, 2000-01 ★3715★

Nevada System; University of
State appropriations for Nevada's institutions of higher education, 2000-01 ★1281★

Never Cry Wolf
Canada's best nonfiction selections of the 20th century ★234★

New Astronomy
Astronomy and astrophysics journals by citation impact, 1999 ★104★

The New Blue Line: Police Innovation in Six American Cities
Most-cited works in police studies articles/research notes ★2625★

New Brunswick
Canadian provinces by teaching days per year ★4058★

New Brunswick, Canada; University of
Canadian primarily undergraduate universities by award-winning faculty members, 2000 ★1194★

Canadian primarily undergraduate universities by class size at the first and second-year level, 2000 ★1195★

Canadian primarily undergraduate universities by class size at the third and forth-year level, 2000 ★1196★

Canadian primarily undergraduate universities by classes taught by tenured faculty, 2000 ★1197★

Canadian primarily undergraduate universities by faculty members with Ph.D.'s, 2000 ★1198★

Canadian primarily undergraduate universities by library acquisitions, 2000 ★1199★

Canadian primarily undergraduate universities by library expenses, 2000 ★1200★

Canadian primarily undergraduate universities by library holdings per student, 2000 ★1201★

Canadian primarily undergraduate universities by medical/science grants per faculty member, 2000 ★1202★

Canadian primarily undergraduate universities by operating budget per student, 2000 ★1203★

Canadian primarily undergraduate universities by percentage of operating budget allocated to scholarships, 2000 ★1204★

Canadian primarily undergraduate universities by percentage of operating budget allocated to student services, 2000 ★1205★

Canadian primarily undergraduate universities by reputation, 2000 ★1206★

Canadian primarily undergraduate universities by social science/humanities grants per faculty member, 2000 ★1207★

Canadian primarily undergraduate universities by students from out of province, 2000 ★1208★

Canadian primarily undergraduate universities by students winning national awards, 2000 ★1209★

Canadian universities with the lowest total cost, 2000 ★1218★

Top Canadian primarily undergraduate universities, 2000 ★1226★

New Brunswick; University of
Best Canadian universities overall, 2000 ★1149★

Canadian comprehensive universities best at producing leaders of tomorrow, 2000 ★1152★

Canadian comprehensive universities by alumni support, 2000 ★1153★

Canadian comprehensive universities by award-winning faculty members, 2000 ★1154★

Canadian comprehensive universities by class size at the first- and second-year level, 2000 ★1155★

Canadian comprehensive universities by class size at the third- and forth-year level, 2000 ★1156★

Canadian comprehensive universities by classes taught by tenured faculty, 2000 ★1157★

Canadian comprehensive universities by faculty members with Ph.D.'s, 2000 ★1158★

Canadian comprehensive universities by international graduate students, 2000 ★1159★

Canadian comprehensive universities by library acquisitions, 2000 ★1160★

Canadian comprehensive universities by library expenses, 2000 ★1161★

Canadian comprehensive universities by library holdings per student, 2000 ★1162★

Canadian comprehensive universities by operating budget per student, 2000 ★1163★

Canadian comprehensive universities by percentage of operating budget allocated to scholarships, 2000 ★1164★

Canadian comprehensive universities by percentage of operating budget allocated to student services, 2000 ★1165★

Canadian comprehensive universities by social science/humanities grants per faculty member, 2000 ★1166★

Canadian comprehensive universities by students from out of province, 2000 ★1167★

Canadian comprehensive universities by students winning national awards, 2000 ★1168★

Canadian medical/doctoral universities by medical/science grants per faculty member, 2000 ★1183★

Top Canadian comprehensive universities, 2000 ★1219★

Top Canadian comprehensive universities by reputation, 2000 ★1220★

New Century High School
Outstanding secondary schools in Olympia, Washington ★4197★

New College of the University of South Florida
All-USA College Academic Third Team, 2001 ★4★

U.S. colleges and universities where the general student body puts little emphasis on athletic events ★1009★

U.S. colleges and universities where the general student body smokes marijuana ★1011★

U.S. colleges and universities with a large student body of liberal Democrats ★1017★

Fiske Guide's best buys for public colleges and universities, 2001 ★1460★

The New Criminology: For a Social Theory of Deviance
Most-cited works in critical criminology publications ★1645★

New England College
Highest undergraduate tuition and fees at colleges and universities in New Hampshire ★1531★

Average faculty salaries for institutions of higher education in New Hampshire, 2000-01 ★3716★

New England College of Optometry
Average faculty salaries for institutions of higher education in Massachusetts, 2000-01 ★3708★

New England Culinary Institute
Undergraduate tuition and fees at colleges and universities in Vermont ★1563★

New England Institute of Technology
Undergraduate tuition and fees at colleges and universities in Rhode Island ★1553★

New England School of Law
Average faculty salaries for institutions of higher education in Massachusetts, 2000-01 ★3708★

New England; University of
Highest undergraduate tuition and fees at colleges and universities in Maine ★1512★

Average faculty salaries for institutions of higher education in Maine, 2000-01 ★3706★

New Hampshire
Mean composite ACT scores by state, 2000 ★895★

Mean math SAT scores by state, 2000 ★900★

Mean verbal SAT scores by state, 2000 ★903★

States allocating the smallest amount of state tax appropriations for higher education, 2000-01 ★1305★

Total doctorate recipients by state, 1999 ★2054★

State grades for affordability of higher education for minority students, 2000 ★2883★

State grades for benefits state receives for educating its minority students, 2000 ★2884★

State grades for completion of higher education by minority students, 2000 ★2885★

State grades for participation of minority students in higher education, 2000 ★2886★

State grades for preparing minority students for higher education, 2000 ★2887★

States with the highest per capita income ★3123★

States with the largest growth in income ★3124★

States with the best college tuition savings plans ★4438★

New Hampshire College
Highest undergraduate tuition and fees at colleges and universities in New Hampshire ★1531★

Professional or specialized institutions with the highest enrollment of foreign students, 1998-99 ★2501★

Average faculty salaries for institutions of higher education in New Hampshire, 2000-01 ★3716★

New Hampshire Community Tech College Berlin/Laconia
Average faculty salaries for institutions of higher education in New Hampshire, 2000-01 ★3716★

New Hampshire Community Tech College Manchester/Stratham
Average faculty salaries for institutions of higher education in New Hampshire, 2000-01 ★3716★

New Hampshire Community Tech College Nashua/Claremont
Average faculty salaries for institutions of higher education in New Hampshire, 2000-01 ★3716★

New Hampshire Community Technical College, Berline
Lowest undergraduate tuition and fees at colleges and universities in New Hampshire ★1532★

New Hampshire Community Technical College, Claremont
Lowest undergraduate tuition and fees at colleges and universities in New Hampshire ★1532★

New Hampshire Community Technical College, Laconia
Lowest undergraduate tuition and fees at colleges and universities in New Hampshire ★1532★

New Hampshire Community Technical College, Manchester
Lowest undergraduate tuition and fees at colleges and universities in New Hampshire ★1532★

New Hampshire Community Technical College, Nashua
Lowest undergraduate tuition and fees at colleges and universities in New Hampshire ★1532★

New Hampshire Community Technical College, Stratham
Lowest undergraduate tuition and fees at colleges and universities in New Hampshire ★1532★

New Hampshire, Durham; University of
State appropriations for New Hampshire's institutions of higher education, 2000-01 ★1282★

New Hampshire, Manchester; University of
State appropriations for New Hampshire's institutions of higher education, 2000-01 ★1282★
Lowest undergraduate tuition and fees at colleges and universities in New Hampshire ★1532★

New Hampshire Technical Institute
State appropriations for New Hampshire's institutions of higher education, 2000-01 ★1282★
Highest undergraduate tuition and fees at public 2-year colleges and universities ★1462★
Lowest undergraduate tuition and fees at colleges and universities in New Hampshire ★1532★
Average faculty salaries for institutions of higher education in New Hampshire, 2000-01 ★3716★

New Hampshire; University of
Division I NCAA colleges with the highest graduation rates for football players, 1990-91 to 1993-94 ★933★
Highest undergraduate tuition and fees at public, 4-year or above colleges and universities ★1463★
Public 4-year institutions with the highest tuition, 2000-01 ★1471★
U.S. universities with the greatest impact in geosciences, 1994-98 ★2149★
U.S. universities with the greatest impact in geosciences, 1993-97 ★2155★
U.S. universities with the highest concentration of education papers published, 1994-98 ★2223★
U.S. universities with the greatest impact in ecology/environmental sciences, 1994-98 ★2474★
U.S. doctoral institutions with the largest number of students studying abroad, 1998-99 ★2512★
U.S. universities with the highest concentration of papers published in the field of literary studies, 1994-98 ★2734★
U.S. universities with the highest concentrations in literary criticism, 1992-96 ★2735★
Average faculty salaries for institutions of higher education in New Hampshire, 2000-01 ★3716★
U.S. universities with the highest concentration of papers published in the field of aquatic sciences, 1995-99 ★4289★

New Haven; University of
Highest undergraduate tuition and fees at colleges and universities in Connecticut ★1490★
Average faculty salaries for institutions of higher education in Connecticut, 2000-01 ★3694★

New Historical Atlas of Religion in America
Library Journal's best reference books, 2000 ★368★

New Hyde Park Memorial High School
Outstanding secondary schools in Long Island, New York ★4165★

New Jersey
Mean composite ACT scores by state, 2000 ★895★
Mean math SAT scores by state, 2000 ★900★
Mean verbal SAT scores by state, 2000 ★903★
States allocating the largest amount of state tax appropriations for higher education, 2000-01 ★1304★
Total doctorate recipients by state, 1999 ★2054★
Hispanic American enrollment at Hispanic-serving institutions of higher education, by state, 1997 ★2547★
State library associations with most full-time staff ★2681★
State library associations with the highest annual revenue ★2682★
State library associations with the highest conference attendance ★2683★
State library associations with the highest unrestricted net assets ★2684★
State library associations with the largest membership ★2685★
State grades for affordability of higher education for minority students, 2000 ★2883★
State grades for benefits state receives for educating its minority students, 2000 ★2884★
State grades for completion of higher education by minority students, 2000 ★2885★
State grades for participation of minority students in higher education, 2000 ★2886★
State grades for preparing minority students for higher education, 2000 ★2887★
States with the highest per capita income ★3123★
States with the highest number of high school graduates, 1999-2000 ★3995★
States with the highest per-pupil expenditures ★3996★
States with the most public school districts ★3999★
States with the highest K-12 public school enrollment ★4034★
States with the highest funding needs for school-building modernization ★4040★
States with the highest funding needs for school-technology modernization ★4041★
States with the most K-12 public schools ★4049★
States with the highest percentage of high school freshmen enrolling in college within four years ★4266★
States with the highest state support for non need-based financial aid for students, 1999-2000 ★4368★

New Jersey City University
State appropriations for New Jersey's institutions of higher education, 2000-01 ★1283★

New Jersey; College of
U.S. colleges and universities where students are not very politically active ★1000★
State appropriations for New Jersey's institutions of higher education, 2000-01 ★1283★
U.S. News & World Report's northern regional universities with the best academic reputation scores, 2000-01 ★1415★
U.S. News & World Report's northern regional universities with the highest average graduation rates, 2000-01 ★1419★
U.S. News & World Report's northern regional universities with the highest freshmen retention rates, 2000-01 ★1420★
U.S. News & World Report's northern regional universities with the highest percentage of freshmen in the top 25% of their high school class, 2000-01 ★1421★
U.S. News & World Report's northern regional universities with the lowest acceptance rates, 2000-01 ★1424★
U.S. News & World Report's top northern regional universities, 2000-01 ★1425★
U.S. News & World Report's top public northern regional universities, 2000-01 ★1426★
U.S. News & World Report's best undergraduate fees among northern regional universities by discount tuition, 2000 ★1428★
Average faculty salaries for institutions of higher education in New Jersey, 2000-01 ★3717★

New Jersey Institute of Technology
U.S. colleges and universities with the least attractive campuses ★1037★
U.S. colleges and universities with the unhappiest students ★1041★
State appropriations for New Jersey's institutions of higher education, 2000-01 ★1283★
Highest undergraduate tuition and fees at public, 4-year or above colleges and universities ★1463★
U.S. News & World Report's national universities with students least in debt, 1999 ★1475★
U.S. colleges and universities awarding the most computer and information sciences master's degrees to Asian Americans ★1767★
U.S. colleges and universities awarding the most computer and information sciences master's degrees to Hispanic Americans ★1768★
Doctorate-granting-institutions with the highest percentage of non-U.S. citizen doctoral degrees awarded, 1999 ★1907★
Most wired universities, 2000 ★2598★

New Left Review
Political science journals with the greatest impact measure, 1994-98 ★3050★

New Lenox School, District 122
Illinois school districts spending the least for elementary school education 1997-98 ★4007★

New Media Centers
Top sites for educators ★2605★

New Mexico
Mean composite ACT scores by state, 2000 ★895★
Mean math SAT scores by state, 2000 ★900★
Mean verbal SAT scores by state, 2000 ★903★
Average class size at colleges and universities in the U.S., by state ★1064★
Total doctorate recipients by state, 1999 ★2054★
Hispanic American enrollment at Hispanic-serving institutions of higher education, by state, 1997 ★2547★
State grades for affordability of higher education for minority students, 2000 ★2883★
State grades for benefits state receives for educating its minority students, 2000 ★2884★
State grades for completion of higher education by minority students, 2000 ★2885★
State grades for participation of minority students in higher education, 2000 ★2886★
State grades for preparing minority students for higher education, 2000 ★2887★
States expelling the highest ratio of students for violating the Gun-Free Schools Act, 1998-99 ★3993★
States with the lowest per-pupil expenditures ★3998★

New Mexico, Gallup; University of
Average faculty salaries for institutions of higher education in New Mexico, 2000-01 ★3718★

New Mexico Highlands University
State appropriations for New Mexico's institutions of higher education, 2000-01 ★1284★
Highest undergraduate tuition and fees at colleges and universities in New Mexico ★1535★
U.S. colleges and universities awarding the most health professions and related sciences master's degrees to Hispanic Americans ★1779★
U.S. colleges and universities awarding the most health professions and related sciences master's degrees to Native Americans ★1780★

New Mexico Institute of Mining and Technology
State appropriations for New Mexico's institutions of higher education, 2000-01 ★1284★
Highest undergraduate tuition and fees at colleges and universities in New Mexico ★1535★
Academics' choices for best graduate petroleum engineering schools, 2000 ★2429★

New Mexico Junior College
Lowest undergraduate tuition and fees at colleges and universities in New Mexico ★1536★
Average faculty salaries for institutions of higher education without academic ranks in New Mexico, 2000-01 ★3759★

New Mexico Military Institute
Highest undergraduate tuition and fees at colleges and universities in New Mexico ★1535★

New Mexico State University
U.S. colleges and universities with the lowest average football attendance, 1996-99 ★160★
State appropriations for New Mexico's institutions of higher education, 2000-01 ★1284★
Highest undergraduate tuition and fees at colleges and universities in New Mexico ★1535★
Total baccalaureate education degrees awarded to Hispanic Americans from U.S. colleges and universities, 1997-98 ★1713★
U.S. colleges and universities awarding the most biological and life sciences master's degrees to Hispanic Americans ★1758★
U.S. colleges and universities awarding the most education master's degrees to Hispanic Americans ★1771★
U.S. institutions awarding the most baccalaureate degrees to Hispanic Americans in agricultural sciences, 1998 ★1818★
U.S. institutions awarding the most baccalaureate degrees to minorities in agricultural sciences, 1998 ★1820★
U.S. institutions awarding the most baccalaureate degrees to Native Americans in agricultural sciences, 1998 ★1823★
U.S. colleges and universities spending the most on chemical engineering research and development, 1998 ★3098★
U.S. colleges and universities with the most federal support for chemical engineering research and development, 1998 ★3101★
Average faculty salaries for institutions of higher education in New Mexico, 2000-01 ★3718★
U.S. universities with the highest concentration of animal sciences papers published, 1994-98 ★4288★

New Mexico State University, Alamogordo
Lowest undergraduate tuition and fees at colleges and universities in New Mexico ★1536★
Average faculty salaries for institutions of higher education in New Mexico, 2000-01 ★3718★

New Mexico State University, Carlsbad
Lowest undergraduate tuition and fees at colleges and universities in New Mexico ★1536★
Average faculty salaries for institutions of higher education in New Mexico, 2000-01 ★3718★

New Mexico State University, Dona Ana
Average faculty salaries for institutions of higher education in New Mexico, 2000-01 ★3718★

New Mexico State University, Grants
Average faculty salaries for institutions of higher education in New Mexico, 2000-01 ★3718★

New Mexico; University of
U.S. college campuses with more than 5,000 students reporting murders or manslaughters, 1998 ★729★
Institutions with the most full-time Hispanic American faculty ★923★
U.S. colleges and universities with the most full-time Hispanic American faculty ★925★
State appropriations for New Mexico's institutions of higher education, 2000-01 ★1284★
Highest undergraduate tuition and fees at colleges and universities in New Mexico ★1535★
Total baccalaureate biology/life sciences degrees awarded to Hispanic Americans from U.S. colleges and universities, 1997-98 ★1681★
Total baccalaureate biology/life sciences degrees awarded to Native Americans from U.S. colleges and universities, 1997-98 ★1682★
Total baccalaureate business management and administrative services degrees awarded to Native Americans from U.S. colleges and universities, 1997-98 ★1686★
Total baccalaureate degrees awarded to Hispanic Americans from U.S. colleges and universities, 1997-98 ★1705★
Total baccalaureate degrees awarded to Native Americans from U.S. colleges and universities, 1997-98 ★1710★
Total baccalaureate education degrees awarded to Hispanic Americans from U.S. colleges and universities, 1997-98 ★1713★
Total baccalaureate education degrees awarded to Native Americans from U.S. colleges and universities, 1997-98 ★1714★
Total baccalaureate English language, literature, and letters degrees awarded to Native Americans from U.S. colleges and universities, 1997-98 ★1719★
Total baccalaureate health professions and related sciences degrees awarded to Hispanic Americans from U.S. colleges and universities, 1997-98 ★1723★
Total baccalaureate health professions and related sciences degrees awarded to Native Americans from U.S. colleges and universities, 1997-98 ★1724★
Total baccalaureate physical sciences degrees awarded to Native Americans from U.S. colleges and universities, 1997-98 ★1736★
Total baccalaureate psychology degrees awarded to Native Americans from U.S. colleges and universities, 1997-98 ★1740★
Total baccalaureate social sciences and history degrees awarded to Native Americans from U.S. colleges and universities, 1997-98 ★1744★
Total ethnic/cultural studies master's degrees awarded to minorities from U.S. colleges and universities, 1997-98 ★1748★
U.S. colleges and universities awarding the most education master's degrees to Hispanic Americans ★1771★
U.S. colleges and universities awarding the most education master's degrees to Native Americans ★1772★
U.S. colleges and universities awarding the most English language/literature/letters master's degrees to Hispanic Americans ★1775★
U.S. colleges and universities awarding the most master's degrees to Hispanic Americans ★1787★
U.S. colleges and universities awarding the most master's degrees to Native Americans ★1789★
U.S. colleges and universities awarding the most first professional degrees to Hispanic Americans ★1845★
U.S. colleges and universities awarding the most first professional degrees to Native Americans ★1846★
U.S. colleges and universities awarding the most health professions and related sciences first professional degrees to Native Americans ★1851★
U.S. colleges and universities awarding the most law and legal studies first professional degrees to Hispanic Americans ★1854★
U.S. colleges and universities awarding the most law and legal studies first professional degrees to Native Americans ★1855★

U.S. colleges and universities awarding the most doctorate degrees to Hispanic Americans ★2097★

U.S. colleges and universities awarding the most education doctorate degrees to Hispanic Americans ★2110★

Academics' choices for best clinical law programs, 2001 ★2626★

Academics' choices for best family medicine programs, 2001 ★2820★

Academics' choices for best rural medicine programs, 2001 ★2824★

Acceptance rates for *U.S. News & World Report*'s top 10 primary-care medical schools, 2001 ★2826★

Average MCAT scores at *U.S. News & World Report*'s top 10 primary-care medical schools, 2001 ★2835★

Average undergraduate GPA at *U.S. News & World Report*'s top 10 primary-care medical schools, 2001 ★2837★

Faculty-student ratios at *U.S. News & World Report*'s top 10 primary-care medical schools, 2001 ★2841★

Out-of-state tuition and fees at *U.S. News & World Report*'s top 10 primary-care medical schools, 2001 ★2846★

Percentage of graduates entering *U.S. News & World Report*'s top 10 primary-care medical schools, 2001 ★2848★

Top primary-care medical schools, 2001 ★2856★

Top primary-care medical schools by reputation, as determined by academic personnel, 2001 ★2857★

Average faculty salaries for institutions of higher education in New Mexico, 2000-01 ★3718★

New Mexico, Valencia; University of
Average faculty salaries for institutions of higher education in New Mexico, 2000-01 ★3718★

New Orleans Public Library
North America's first ten public libraries ★2680★

New Orleans; University of
Division I NCAA colleges with that graduated none of their African American male basketball players, 1990-91 to 1993-94 ★930★

U.S. colleges and universities spending the most on independent lobbyists, 1999 ★1310★

The New Republic
Most selective internships in the U.S., 2001 ★2610★

New Rochelle; College of
U.S. colleges and universities awarding the most communications master's degrees to Hispanic Americans ★1765★

Average faculty salaries for institutions of higher education in New York, 2000-01 ★3719★

New Rochelle High School
Outstanding secondary schools in New York, New York ★4191★

New School for Social Research
U.S. colleges and universities awarding the most communications master's degrees to African Americans ★1763★

U.S. colleges and universities awarding the most communications master's degrees to Hispanic Americans ★1765★

U.S. colleges and universities awarding the most social sciences and history master's degrees to African Americans ★1801★

U.S. colleges and universities awarding the most social sciences and history master's degrees to Asian Americans ★1802★

U.S. colleges and universities awarding the most social sciences and history master's degrees to Hispanic Americans ★1803★

New School University
U.S. News & World Report's national universities with the highest proportion of classes with less than 20 students, 2000-01 ★1138★

U.S. News & World Report's national universities with students most in debt, 1999 ★1476★

Doctoral institutions with the highest enrollment of foreign students, 1998-99 ★2494★

Presidents with the highest pay at Doctoral I and II universities, 1998-99 ★3160★

The New Teenage Body Book
Most frequently banned books in the 1990s ★745★

New Trier High School, District 203
Illinois school districts spending the most for high school education 1997-98 ★4010★

New Trier Township 203
Illinois high school districts with the highest teacher salaries, 1999 ★3985★

New Trier Township High School
Illinois high schools with the highest SAT scores ★874★

Outstanding secondary schools in Chicago, Illinois ★4110★

New World School of the Arts
Outstanding secondary schools in Miami, Florida ★4178★

New York
People for the American Way's list of states with the most challenges to library and school books, 1982-1992 ★750★

States with the highest enrollment in private 4-year institutions of higher education ★860★

States with the highest enrollment in public 4-year institutions of higher education ★861★

Mean composite ACT scores by state, 2000 ★895★

Mean math SAT scores by state, 2000 ★900★

Mean verbal SAT scores by state, 2000 ★903★

States allocating the largest amount of state tax appropriations for higher education, 2000-01 ★1304★

States receiving the most in federal agency appropriations to colleges, 2000 ★1306★

States receiving the most in federal agency appropriations to colleges, from 1996 to 2000 ★1307★

Total doctorate recipients by state, 1999 ★2054★

U.S. cities with the highest number of high-tech employees, 1998 ★2284★

Hispanic American enrollment at Hispanic-serving institutions of higher education, by state, 1997 ★2547★

U.S. market areas with the highest percentage of adults having internet access ★2607★

States with the most law schools ★2668★

State library associations with most full-time staff ★2681★

State library associations with the highest annual revenue ★2682★

State library associations with the highest conference attendance ★2683★

State library associations with the highest unrestricted net assets ★2684★

State library associations with the largest membership ★2685★

Average Hennen's American Public Library Ratings, by state ★2690★

State grades for affordability of higher education for minority students, 2000 ★2883★

State grades for benefits state receives for educating its minority students, 2000 ★2884★

State grades for completion of higher education by minority students, 2000 ★2885★

State grades for participation of minority students in higher education, 2000 ★2886★

State grades for preparing minority students for higher education, 2000 ★2887★

States with the highest per capita income ★3123★

States expelling the most students for violating the Gun-Free Schools Act, 1998-99 ★3994★

States with the highest number of high school graduates, 1999-2000 ★3995★

States with the highest per-pupil expenditures ★3996★

States with the most public school districts ★3999★

States with the highest average enrollment in public elementary schools ★4032★

States with the highest average enrollment in public secondary schools ★4033★

States with the highest K-12 public school enrollment ★4034★

States with the highest projected K-12 public school enrollment for 2010 ★4035★

States with the highest funding needs for school-building modernization ★4040★

States with the highest funding needs for school-technology modernization ★4041★

States with the most K-12 public schools ★4049★

States with the most women-owned companies ★4455★

Outstanding videos for library collections, 2000 ★2892★

New York, Albany; State University of
U.S. colleges and universities with the worst financial aid programs ★1042★

Universities with the most-cited scholars in *Criminal Justice and Behavior* ★1648★

Universities with the most-cited scholars in *Criminology* ★1649★

Universities with the most-cited scholars in *Journal of Quantitative Criminology* ★1650★

Universities with the most-cited scholars in *Journal of Research in Crime and Delinquency* ★1651★

Universities with the most-cited scholars in *Justice Quarterly* ★1652★

Total baccalaureate English language, literature, and letters degrees awarded to African Americans from U.S. colleges and universities, 1997-98 ★1716★

Total baccalaureate English language, literature, and letters degrees awarded to Asian Americans from U.S. colleges and universities, 1997-98 ★1717★

Total baccalaureate ethnic/cultural studies degrees awarded to African Americans from U.S. colleges and universities, 1997-98 ★1720★

Average faculty salaries for institutions of higher education in New York, 2000-01 ★3719★

New York, Bernard M. Baruch College; City University of
U.S. News & World Report's northern regional universities with students least in debt, 1999 ★1413★

Total baccalaureate business management and administrative services degrees awarded to African Americans from U.S. colleges and universities, 1997-98 ★1683★

Total baccalaureate business management and administrative services degrees awarded to Asian Americans from U.S. colleges and universities, 1997-98 ★1684★

Total baccalaureate business management and administrative services degrees awarded to Hispanic Americans from U.S. colleges and universities, 1997-98 ★1685★

Total baccalaureate computer and information science degrees awarded to African Americans from U.S. colleges and universities, 1997-98 ★1691★

Total baccalaureate computer and information science degrees awarded to Asian Americans from U.S. colleges and universities, 1997-98 ★1692★

Total baccalaureate computer and information science degrees awarded to Hispanic Americans from U.S. colleges and universities, 1997-98 ★1693★

U.S. colleges and universities awarding the most business management and administrative services master's degrees to Asian Americans ★1760★

U.S. colleges and universities awarding the most computer and information sciences master's degrees to African Americans ★1766★

U.S. colleges and universities awarding the most computer and information sciences master's degrees to Asian Americans ★1767★

Master's institutions with the highest enrollment of foreign students, 1998-99 ★2499★

New York, Binghamton; State University of
Average faculty salaries for institutions of higher education in New York, 2000-01 ★3719★

New York, Borough of Manhattan Community College; City University of
Top colleges in terms of total associate degrees awarded to minorities, 1997-98 ★1677★

Community colleges with the highest enrollment of foreign students, 1998-99 ★2493★

New York, Bronx Community College; City University of
Top colleges in terms of total associate degrees awarded to minorities, 1997-98 ★1677★

New York, Brooklyn College; City University of
Traditionally white institutions awarding the most master's degrees to African Americans ★1755★

U.S. colleges and universities awarding the most communications master's degrees to African Americans ★1763★

U.S. colleges and universities awarding the most computer and information sciences master's degrees to African Americans ★1766★

U.S. colleges and universities awarding the most education master's degrees to African Americans ★1769★

U.S. colleges and universities awarding the most master's degrees to African Americans ★1785★

U.S. colleges and universities awarding the most social sciences and history master's degrees to African Americans ★1801★

New York, Buffalo; State University of
U.S. colleges and universities with the lowest average football attendance, 1996-99 ★160★

U.S. colleges and universities with poor instructors ★1027★

U.S. colleges and universities with the least accessible instructors ★1036★

U.S. colleges and universities with the most upper level courses taught by TAs ★1040★

U.S. colleges and universities with the unhappiest students ★1041★

U.S. colleges and universities with the worst on-campus housing facilities ★1044★

U.S. universities with the greatest impact in dentistry/oral surgery, 1994-98 ★1866★

U.S. universities with the greatest impact in dentistry/oral surgery and medicine, 1995-99 ★1867★

Faculty's scholarly reputation in the Ph.D.-granting departments of geography, 1925-1982 ★2518★

Top geography research-doctorate programs as evaluated by the National Research Council ★2520★

Radcliffe Institute for Advanced Study fellowship recipient in the field of film making, 2000-01 ★2751★

Average faculty salaries for institutions of higher education in New York, 2000-01 ★3719★

New York City
U.S. school districts with the highest number of vacancies for K-12 teachers ★2331★

U.S. cities with the most single people ★3089★

Superintendents' salaries at the largest U.S. schools districts, 1999-2000 ★3990★

Largest public school districts in the U.S. ★4016★

New York, City College; City University of
Most dangerous college campuses in the U.S. ★712★

Total baccalaureate degrees awarded to African Americans from traditionally white institutions, 1997-98 ★1698★

Total baccalaureate education degrees awarded to Hispanic Americans from U.S. colleges and universities, 1997-98 ★1713★

Total baccalaureate engineering degrees awarded to minorities from U.S. colleges and universities, 1997-98 ★1715★

Traditionally white institutions awarding the most master's degrees to African Americans ★1755★

U.S. colleges and universities awarding the most computer and information sciences master's degrees to Asian Americans ★1767★

U.S. colleges and universities awarding the most education master's degrees to African Americans ★1769★

U.S. colleges and universities awarding the most education master's degrees to Asian Americans ★1770★

U.S. colleges and universities awarding the most education master's degrees to Hispanic Americans ★1771★

U.S. colleges and universities awarding the most English language/literature/letters master's degrees to African Americans ★1773★

U.S. colleges and universities awarding the most master's degrees to African Americans ★1785★

U.S. colleges and universities awarding the most master's degrees to Hispanic Americans ★1787★

U.S. colleges and universities awarding the most master's degrees to minorities ★1788★

U.S. colleges and universities awarding the most psychology master's degrees to Hispanic Americans ★1799★

U.S. colleges and universities awarding the most social sciences and history master's degrees to African Americans ★1801★

Master's institutions with the highest enrollment of foreign students, 1998-99 ★2499★

New York; City University of
State appropriations for New York's institutions of higher education, 2000-01 ★1285★

U.S. universities publishing the most papers in the field of literature, 1994-98 ★2447★

U.S. universities contributing the most papers in the field of history, 1993-97 ★2551★

U.S. universities with the highest concentration of papers published in the field of literary studies, 1994-98 ★2734★

U.S. universities publishing the most papers in the field of philosophy, 1995-99 ★2948★

U.S. universities publishing the most papers in the field of performing arts, 1994-98 ★4437★

New York, College of A&T, Cobleskill; State University of
U.S. institutions awarding the most associate degrees to minorities in agricultural sciences, 1998 ★1809★

Average faculty salaries for institutions of higher education in New York, 2000-01 ★3719★

New York, College of A&T, Morrisville; State University of
Highest undergraduate tuition and fees at public 2-year colleges and universities ★1462★

U.S. institutions awarding the most associate degrees to minorities in agricultural sciences, 1998 ★1809★

Average faculty salaries for institutions of higher education in New York, 2000-01 ★3719★

New York, College of Arts & Sciences, Geneseo; State University of
U.S. News & World Report's northern regional universities with the best academic reputation scores, 2000-01 ★1415★

U.S. News & World Report's northern regional universities with the highest average graduation rates, 2000-01 ★1419★

U.S. News & World Report's northern regional universities with the highest freshmen retention rates, 2000-01 ★1420★

U.S. News & World Report's northern regional universities with the highest percentage of freshmen in the top 25% of their high school class, 2000-01 ★1421★

U.S. News & World Report's northern regional universities with the lowest acceptance rates, 2000-01 ★1424★

U.S. News & World Report's top northern regional universities, 2000-01 ★1425★

U.S. News & World Report's top public northern regional universities, 2000-01 ★1426★

New York, College at Brockport; State University of
Average faculty salaries for institutions of higher education in New York, 2000-01 ★3719★

New York, College at Buffalo; State University of
Average faculty salaries for institutions of higher education in New York, 2000-01 ★3719★

New York, College at Cortland; State University of
Average faculty salaries for institutions of higher education in New York, 2000-01 ★3719★

New York, College at Fredonia; State University of
Average faculty salaries for institutions of higher education in New York, 2000-01 ★3719★

New York, College at Geneseo; State University of
Average faculty salaries for institutions of higher education in New York, 2000-01 ★3719★

New York, College at Old Westbury; State University of
Total baccalaureate ethnic/cultural studies degrees awarded to African Americans from U.S. colleges and universities, 1997-98 ★1720★
Average faculty salaries for institutions of higher education in New York, 2000-01 ★3719★

New York, College at Oneonta; State University of
Four-year institutions with the most drug referrals reported, 1999 ★706★
Average faculty salaries for institutions of higher education in New York, 2000-01 ★3719★

New York, College at Oswego; State University of
Average faculty salaries for institutions of higher education in New York, 2000-01 ★3719★

New York, College at Plattsburgh; State University of
Average faculty salaries for institutions of higher education in New York, 2000-01 ★3719★

New York, College at Potsdam; State University of
Average faculty salaries for institutions of higher education in New York, 2000-01 ★3719★

New York, College at Purchase; State University of
Average faculty salaries for institutions of higher education in New York, 2000-01 ★3719★

New York College of Environmental Science and Forestry; State University of
College senior's choices for exemplary doctoral-intensive universities ★2532★
Average faculty salaries for institutions of higher education in New York, 2000-01 ★3719★

New York, College of Optometry; State University of
Average faculty salaries for institutions of higher education in New York, 2000-01 ★3719★

New York College and Schools; State University of
State appropriations for New York's institutions of higher education, 2000-01 ★1285★

New York College of Technology, Alfred; State University of
Community colleges receiving the most gifts, 1999-2000 ★1239★
Average faculty salaries for institutions of higher education in New York, 2000-01 ★3719★

New York College of Technology, Canton; State University of
Highest undergraduate tuition and fees at public 2-year colleges and universities ★1462★
Average faculty salaries for institutions of higher education in New York, 2000-01 ★3719★

New York College of Technology, Delhi; State University of
Highest undergraduate tuition and fees at public 2-year colleges and universities ★1462★
Average faculty salaries for institutions of higher education in New York, 2000-01 ★3719★

New York College of Technology, Utica-Rome; State University of
Average faculty salaries for institutions of higher education in New York, 2000-01 ★3719★

New York Eye and Ear Infirmary
Top ophthalmology hospitals in the U.S., 2000 ★2796★

New York, Farmingdale; State University of
Average faculty salaries for institutions of higher education in New York, 2000-01 ★3719★

New York, Geneseo Foundation; State University of
Colleges and universities with the smallest endowments, 2000 ★1238★

New York, Graduate School and University Center; City University of
Top art history research-doctorate programs as evaluated by the National Research Council ★93★
Colleges and universities with the smallest endowments, 2000 ★1238★
U.S. colleges and universities awarding the most biological and life sciences doctorate degrees to Asian Americans ★2083★
U.S. colleges and universities awarding the most psychology doctorate degrees to Hispanic Americans ★2122★
U.S. colleges and universities awarding the most social sciences and history doctorate degrees to African Americans ★2124★
Top French language and literature research-doctorate programs as evaluated by the National Research Council ★2516★
Top linguistics research-doctorate programs as evaluated by the National Research Council ★2733★
Most effective music research-doctorate programs as evaluated by the National Research Council ★2895★
Top music research-doctorate programs as evaluated by the National Research Council ★2896★

New York, Health Science Center, Brooklyn; State University of
Total baccalaureate health professions and related sciences degrees awarded to African Americans from U.S. colleges and universities, 1997-98 ★1721★
U.S. colleges and universities awarding the most health professions and related sciences first professional degrees to Asian Americans ★1848★
U.S. colleges and universities awarding the most health professions and related sciences first professional degrees to minorities ★1850★

New York, Hostos Community College; City University of
Institutions with the most part-time Hispanic American faculty ★924★

New York, Hunter College; City University of
U.S. colleges and universities that devote the least course time to discussion ★989★
U.S. colleges and universities with the least attractive campuses ★1037★
U.S. colleges and universities with the worst overall administration ★1045★
Total baccalaureate English language, literature, and letters degrees awarded to Hispanic Americans from U.S. colleges and universities, 1997-98 ★1718★
Total baccalaureate ethnic/cultural studies degrees awarded to African Americans from U.S. colleges and universities, 1997-98 ★1720★
Total baccalaureate psychology degrees awarded to Hispanic Americans from U.S. colleges and universities, 1997-98 ★1739★
Total baccalaureate social sciences and history degrees awarded to African Americans from U.S. colleges and universities, 1997-98 ★1741★
Total baccalaureate social sciences and history degrees awarded to Hispanic Americans from U.S. colleges and universities, 1997-98 ★1743★
U.S. colleges and universities awarding the most education master's degrees to Asian Americans ★1770★
U.S. colleges and universities awarding the most education master's degrees to Hispanic Americans ★1771★
U.S. colleges and universities awarding the most health professions and related sciences master's degrees to African Americans ★1777★
U.S. colleges and universities awarding the most master's degrees to Hispanic Americans ★1787★

New York Institute of Technology
Average faculty salaries for institutions of higher education in New York, 2000-01 ★3719★

New York Institute of Technology, Manhattan
U.S. colleges and universities with the lowest percentage of African Americans enrolled, 1997 ★223★

New York Institute of Technology, Old Westbury
U.S. colleges and universities awarding the most health professions and related sciences first professional degrees to Hispanic Americans ★1849★

New York, John Jay College of Criminal Justice; City University of
Top colleges in terms of total associate degrees awarded to minorities, 1997-98 ★1677★
Total baccalaureate psychology degrees awarded to African Americans from U.S. colleges and universities, 1997-98 ★1737★
U.S. colleges and universities awarding the most psychology master's degrees to African Americans ★1797★
U.S. colleges and universities awarding the most psychology master's degrees to Hispanic Americans ★1799★
U.S. colleges and universities awarding the most psychology master's degrees to Native Americans ★1800★

New York, Laguardia Community College; City University of
Top colleges in terms of total associate degrees awarded to minorities, 1997-98 ★1677★

New York Law School
U.S. colleges and universities awarding the most law and legal studies first professional degrees to African Americans ★1852★

New York, Lehman College; City University of
Total baccalaureate computer and information science degrees awarded to Hispanic Americans from U.S. colleges and universities, 1997-98 ★1693★

Total baccalaureate health professions and related sciences degrees awarded to African Americans from U.S. colleges and universities, 1997-98 ★1721★

Total baccalaureate health professions and related sciences degrees awarded to Hispanic Americans from U.S. colleges and universities, 1997-98 ★1723★

Total baccalaureate psychology degrees awarded to Hispanic Americans from U.S. colleges and universities, 1997-98 ★1739★

U.S. colleges and universities awarding the most education master's degrees to Hispanic Americans ★1771★

New York Life Insurance
Fortune's highest ranked life and health insurance companies, 2000 ★472★

New York; Medgar Evers College of the City University of
College freshmen's choices for exemplary undergraduate institutions ★1065★

New York Medical College
U.S. colleges and universities awarding the most biological and life sciences master's degrees to African Americans ★1756★

U.S. colleges and universities awarding the most health professions and related sciences first professional degrees to Asian Americans ★1848★

New York, New Paltz; State University of
Average faculty salaries for institutions of higher education in New York, 2000-01 ★3719★

New York, New York City Technical College; City University of
Top colleges in terms of total associate degrees awarded to minorities, 1997-98 ★1677★

New York, NY
Cities with the most domains per 1,000 firms ★2579★
Best big cities to live in ★3075★

New York, Potsdam College Foundation; State University of
Colleges and universities with the smallest endowments, 2000 ★1238★

New York Presbyterian Hospital
Top gynecology hospitals in the U.S., 2000 ★2792★
Top nephrology hospitals in the U.S., 2000 ★2794★
Top neurology and neurosurgery hospitals in the U.S., 2000 ★2795★
Top psychiatric hospitals in the U.S., 2000 ★2800★
Top urology hospitals in the U.S., 2000 ★2803★

New York Presbyterian Hospital (Babies & Children's Hospital)
Top pediatrics hospitals in the U.S., 2000 ★2799★

New York, Purchase College; State University of
U.S. News & World Report's top public northern regional liberal arts colleges, 2000-01 ★1364★

New York, Queens College; City University of
U.S. colleges and universities where the general student body does not drink beer ★1004★
U.S. colleges and universities with the unhappiest students ★1041★
U.S. News & World Report's top public northern regional universities, 2000-01 ★1426★
U.S. colleges and universities awarding the most English language/literature/letters master's degrees to Hispanic Americans ★1775★
U.S. colleges and universities awarding the most social sciences and history master's degrees to African Americans ★1801★
Academics' choices for best clinical law programs, 2001 ★2626★

New York, Queensborough Community College; City University of
U.S. colleges and universities with the lowest percentage of African Americans enrolled, 1997 ★223★

New York State College of Ceramics, Alfred University
Highest undergraduate tuition and fees at public, 4-year or above colleges and universities ★1463★
Public 4-year institutions with the highest tuition, 2000-01 ★1471★
Average faculty salaries for institutions of higher education in New York, 2000-01 ★3719★

New York State Psychiatric Institute
U.S. institutions with the most citations in psychiatry research, 1990-98 ★3059★

New York; State University of
Institutions censured by the American Association of University Professors, 2001 ★1067★
Colleges and universities with the smallest endowments, 2000 ★1238★

New York, Stony Brook; State University of
Top ecology, evolution, and behavior research-doctorate programs as evaluated by the National Research Council ★201★
Winner of the American Chemical Society's Arthur C. Cope Awards, 2001 ★795★
U.S. colleges and universities with poor instructors ★1027★
U.S. colleges and universities with the least attractive campuses ★1037★
U.S. colleges and universities with the worst on-campus housing facilities ★1044★
Total baccalaureate mathematics degrees awarded to Asian Americans from U.S. colleges and universities, 1997-98 ★1730★
Total baccalaureate mathematics degrees awarded to Hispanic Americans from U.S. colleges and universities, 1997-98 ★1731★
U.S. colleges and universities awarding the most mathematics master's degrees to Hispanic Americans ★1792★
U.S. colleges and universities awarding the most physical sciences master's degrees to Asian Americans ★1794★
U.S. universities with the greatest impact in dermatology, 1995-99 ★1876★
U.S. colleges and universities awarding the most biological and life sciences doctorate degrees to Asian Americans ★2083★
U.S. colleges and universities awarding the most biological and life sciences doctorate degrees to Hispanic Americans ★2084★
U.S. colleges and universities awarding the most doctorate degrees to Asian Americans ★2096★
U.S. colleges and universities awarding the most social sciences and history doctorate degrees to Asian Americans ★2125★
Top oceanography research-doctorate programs as evaluated by the National Research Council ★2153★
Top music research-doctorate programs as evaluated by the National Research Council ★2896★
Average faculty salaries for institutions of higher education in New York, 2000-01 ★3719★
U.S. universities with the greatest impact in sociology and anthropology, 1995-99 ★4351★

New York Times
Fortune's highest ranked publishing companies, 2000 ★489★
Fortune's most admired companies for quality of products or services ★519★
Top publishing and broadcasting companies in Standard & Poor's 500, 2001 ★553★
Most selective internships in the U.S., 2001 ★2610★
Top internships in the U.S. with the highest compensation, 2001 ★2611★
Best U.S. works of journalism in the 20th century ★2769★
Most cited general works serials in technical communication journals from 1988 to 1997 ★4419★
Most cited serials in technical communication journals from 1988 to 1997 ★4425★

New York University
Colleges with the highest number of freshman Merit Scholars, 2000 ★5★
Top anthropology research-doctorate programs as evaluated by the National Research Council ★62★
U.S. universities publishing the most papers in the fields of art and architecture, 1994-98 ★70★
Most effective art history research-doctorate programs as evaluated by the National Research Council ★91★
Top art history research-doctorate programs as evaluated by the National Research Council ★93★
U.S. universities with the greatest impact in microbiology, 1994-98 ★217★
U.S. universities with the greatest impact in microbiology, 1995-99 ★218★
Top business schools in research performance, 1986-1998 ★532★
U.S. News & World Report's universities with the best taxation departments, 1999-2000 ★573★
Top business schools for overall within-discipline research performance, 1986-1998 ★645★
Top business schools for within-discipline research performance in management, 1986-1998 ★646★
Top business schools for within-discipline research performance in finance, 1986-1998 ★663★
Top business schools for within-discipline research performance in insurance, international business and real estate, 1986-1998 ★667★
Top business schools for within-discipline research performance in marketing, 1986-1998 ★671★
Top business schools for within-discipline research performance in management information systems, 1986-1998 ★675★
U.S. colleges and universities most accepting of alternative lifestyles ★986★
U.S. colleges and universities where the general student body smokes marijuana ★1011★
U.S. colleges and universities with a diverse student body ★1012★

U.S. colleges and universities with a favorable surrounding town or city ★1013★
U.S. colleges and universities with a large student body of liberal Democrats ★1017★
U.S. colleges and universities with excellent library facilities ★1025★
Institutions censured by the American Association of University Professors, 2001 ★1067★
Retention rates of African American students at traditionally white institutions, 1997-98 ★1121★
U.S. News & World Report's national universities with the lowest graduation rates, 1999 ★1141★
Institutions receiving the most alumni gifts, 1999-2000 ★1242★
Largest gifts to higher education, 1967-2000 ★1247★
Largest private gifts to higher education, 1967-2000 ★1248★
U.S. colleges and universities spending the most on independent lobbyists, 1999 ★1310★
Top comparative literature research-doctorate programs as evaluated by the National Research Council ★1588★
Total baccalaureate computer and information science degrees awarded to Asian Americans from U.S. colleges and universities, 1997-98 ★1692★
Total baccalaureate mathematics degrees awarded to Asian Americans from U.S. colleges and universities, 1997-98 ★1730★
Total baccalaureate social sciences and history degrees awarded to Asian Americans from U.S. colleges and universities, 1997-98 ★1742★
Traditionally white institutions awarding the most master's degrees to African Americans ★1755★
U.S. colleges and universities awarding the most biological and life sciences master's degrees to African Americans ★1756★
U.S. colleges and universities awarding the most biological and life sciences master's degrees to Asian Americans ★1757★
U.S. colleges and universities awarding the most business management and administrative services master's degrees to Asian Americans ★1760★
U.S. colleges and universities awarding the most business management and administrative services master's degrees to Hispanic Americans ★1761★
U.S. colleges and universities awarding the most communications master's degrees to African Americans ★1763★
U.S. colleges and universities awarding the most communications master's degrees to Asian Americans ★1764★
U.S. colleges and universities awarding the most communications master's degrees to Hispanic Americans ★1765★
U.S. colleges and universities awarding the most computer and information sciences master's degrees to Asian Americans ★1767★
U.S. colleges and universities awarding the most computer and information sciences master's degrees to Hispanic Americans ★1768★
U.S. colleges and universities awarding the most education master's degrees to Asian Americans ★1770★
U.S. colleges and universities awarding the most English language/literature/letters master's degrees to African Americans ★1773★
U.S. colleges and universities awarding the most English language/literature/letters master's degrees to Asian Americans ★1774★
U.S. colleges and universities awarding the most English language/literature/letters master's degrees to Hispanic Americans ★1775★
U.S. colleges and universities awarding the most health professions and related sciences master's degrees to African Americans ★1777★
U.S. colleges and universities awarding the most health professions and related sciences master's degrees to Asian Americans ★1778★
U.S. colleges and universities awarding the most health professions and related sciences master's degrees to Hispanic Americans ★1779★
U.S. colleges and universities awarding the most law and legal studies master's degrees to African Americans ★1781★
U.S. colleges and universities awarding the most law and legal studies master's degrees to Asian Americans ★1782★
U.S. colleges and universities awarding the most law and legal studies master's degrees to Hispanic Americans ★1783★
U.S. colleges and universities awarding the most master's degrees to African Americans ★1785★
U.S. colleges and universities awarding the most master's degrees to Asian Americans ★1786★
U.S. colleges and universities awarding the most master's degrees to Hispanic Americans ★1787★
U.S. colleges and universities awarding the most master's degrees to minorities ★1788★
U.S. colleges and universities awarding the most psychology master's degrees to Asian Americans ★1798★
U.S. colleges and universities awarding the most social sciences and history master's degrees to Asian Americans ★1802★
U.S. colleges and universities awarding the most social sciences and history master's degrees to Hispanic Americans ★1803★
U.S. colleges and universities awarding the most first professional degrees to Asian Americans ★1844★
U.S. colleges and universities awarding the most first professional degrees to Hispanic Americans ★1845★
U.S. colleges and universities awarding the most health professions and related sciences first professional degrees to Asian Americans ★1848★
U.S. colleges and universities awarding the most health professions and related sciences first professional degrees to Hispanic Americans ★1849★
U.S. colleges and universities awarding the most health professions and related sciences first professional degrees to minorities ★1850★
U.S. colleges and universities awarding the most law and legal studies first professional degrees to Asian Americans ★1853★
U.S. colleges and universities awarding the most business management and administrative services doctorate degrees to Asian Americans ★2086★
U.S. colleges and universities awarding the most doctorate degrees to Asian Americans ★2096★
U.S. colleges and universities awarding the most doctorate degrees to Hispanic Americans ★2097★
U.S. colleges and universities awarding the most doctorate degrees to minorities ★2098★
U.S. colleges and universities awarding the most doctorates in humanities, 1999 ★2103★
U.S. colleges and universities awarding the most doctorates in professional and other fields, 1999 ★2106★
U.S. colleges and universities awarding the most education doctorate degrees to Asian Americans ★2109★
U.S. colleges and universities awarding the most psychology doctorate degrees to Asian Americans ★2121★
U.S. colleges and universities awarding the most social sciences and history doctorate degrees to Asian Americans ★2125★
Research institutions with the highest enrollment of foreign students, 1998-99 ★2503★
U.S. research institutions with the largest number of students studying abroad, 1998-99 ★2514★
Top French language and literature research-doctorate programs as evaluated by the National Research Council ★2516★
Academics' choices for best clinical law programs, 2001 ★2626★
Academics' choices for best intellectual property law programs, 2001 ★2630★
Academics' choices for best international law programs, 2001 ★2631★
Academics' choices for best tax law programs, 2001 ★2632★
Academics' choices for best trial advocacy programs, 2001 ★2633★
Acceptance rates at *U.S. News & World Report*'s top 10 law schools, 2001 ★2634★
Graduate employment after graduation percentage for *U.S. News & World Report*'s top 10 law schools, 2001 ★2635★
Graduate employment percentage for *U.S. News & World Report*'s top 10 law schools, 2001 ★2636★
Jurisdiction's overall bar passage rate for *U.S. News & World Report*'s top 10 law schools, 2001 ★2637★
Law schools with the best administrative law faculty, 1999-2000 ★2638★
Law schools with the best bankruptcy faculty, 1999-2000 ★2639★
Law schools with the best commercial law faculty, 1999-2000 ★2641★
Law schools with the best constitutional law (freedom of religion) faculty, 1999-2000 ★2643★
Law schools with the best corporate law and securities regulation faculty, 1999-2000 ★2646★
Law schools with the best critical race theory faculty, 1999-2000 ★2649★
Law schools with the best environmental law faculty, 1999-2000 ★2650★
Law schools with the best intellectual property faculty, 1999-2000 ★2653★
Law schools with the best international law faculty, 1999-2000 ★2654★
Law schools with the best jurisprudence faculty, 1999-2000 ★2655★
Law schools with the best law and economics faculty, 1999-2000 ★2657★
Law schools with the best legal history faculty, 1999-2000 ★2661★

Law schools with the best moral and political theory (Anglo-American traditions) faculty, 1999-2000 ★2662★

Law schools with the best tax faculty, 1999-2000 ★2664★

Law schools with the highest quality, 1999-2000 ★2666★

School's bar passage rate in jurisdiction at *U.S. News & World Report*'s top 10 law schools, 2001 ★2667★

Student-faculty ratios at *U.S. News & World Report*'s top 10 law schools, 2001 ★2669★

Top law schools, 2001 ★2670★

Top law schools by reputation, as determined by academic personnel, 2001 ★2671★

Top law schools by reputation, as determined by lawyers and judges, 2001 ★2672★

Top law school student bodies, 1999-2000 ★2673★

Enrollment of students in the ten largest master's journalism and mass communications programs, 1999 ★2763★

U.S. universities with the greatest impact in mathematics, 1995-99 ★2772★

Most effective mathematics research-doctorate programs as evaluated by the National Research Council ★2775★

Top mathematics research-doctorate programs as evaluated by the National Research Council ★2778★

Academics' choices for best AIDS programs, 2001 ★2818★

Academics' choices for best drug and alcohol abuse programs, 2001 ★2819★

Institutions in the Worker Rights Consortium ★2913★

Top pharmacology research-doctorate programs as evaluated by the National Research Council ★2939★

Top physiology research-doctorate programs as evaluated by the National Research Council ★3022★

Presidents with the highest pay at Research I and II universities, 1998-99 ★3162★

Average faculty salaries for institutions of higher education in New York, 2000-01 ★3719★

Private institutions of higher education that pay the highest salaries to female professors, 2000-01 ★3974★

U.S. institutions with the highest paid assistant professors, 2001 ★3977★

U.S. institutions with the highest paid full professors, 2001 ★3978★

U.S. universities publishing the most papers in the field of performing arts, 1994-98 ★4437★

New York University Law Review

Most frequently-cited law reviews and legal periodicals, 1924-1986: a compilation ★2619★

Most frequently-cited law reviews and legal periodicals, according to *Shepard's Law Review Citations*, 1957-1986 ★2620★

New York University, Leonard N. Stern School of Business

U.S. News & World Report's undergraduate business programs with the best consulting departments, 2000-01 ★563★

U.S. News & World Report's undergraduate business programs with the best entrepreneurship departments, 2000-01 ★565★

U.S. News & World Report's undergraduate business programs with the best real estate departments, 2000-01 ★570★

U.S. News & World Report's undergraduate business programs with the highest academic reputation scores, 2000-01 ★571★

Academics' choices for best graduate executive MBA programs, 2001 ★584★

Academics' choices for best graduate management information systems programs, 2001 ★585★

Academics' choices for best part-time MBA programs, 2000 ★587★

Business Week's top business schools for finance skills as selected by corporate recruiters, 2000 ★600★

Business Week's top business schools with the highest percentage of international students, 2000 ★612★

Business Week's top business schools with the highest percentage of women enrollees, 2000 ★614★

Highest post-MBA salaries for students enrolled in *Business Week*'s top business schools, 1999 ★631★

Lowest pre-MBA salaries for students enrolled in *Business Week*'s top business schools, 1999 ★635★

Top graduate business schools by reputation, as determined by recruiters, 2001 ★651★

Academics' choices for best graduate accounting programs, 2001 ★659★

Academics' choices for best graduate finance programs, 2001 ★662★

U.S. News & World Report's undergraduate business programs with the best finance departments, 2000-01 ★665★

Academics' choices for best graduate international business programs, 2001 ★668★

U.S. News & World Report's undergraduate business programs with the best international business departments, 2000-01 ★682★

New York University Medical Center (Rusk Institute)

Top rehabilitation hospitals in the U.S., 2000 ★2801★

New York, York College; City University of

Total baccalaureate degrees awarded to African Americans from traditionally white institutions, 1997-98 ★1698★

Total baccalaureate mathematics degrees awarded to African Americans from U.S. colleges and universities, 1997-98 ★1729★

Total baccalaureate mathematics degrees awarded to Hispanic Americans from U.S. colleges and universities, 1997-98 ★1731★

Total baccalaureate psychology degrees awarded to African Americans from U.S. colleges and universities, 1997-98 ★1737★

The New Young American Poets

Booklist's most recommended poetry books, 2001 ★231★

New Zealand

Eight grade science achievement scores from selected countries, 1999 ★14★

Math achievement test comparison ★19★

Percentage of enrollment at public institutions of higher education, by country, 1998 ★859★

Countries with the most computers per capita, 2000 ★1604★

Eighth grade mathematics achievement scores from selected countries, 1999 ★2773★

Australia and New Zealand periodical prices, 2001 ★2917★

Institute for Scientific Information periodical prices by country, 2001 ★2922★

Countries spending the highest percentage of gross domestic product on education ★4060★

Newark, NJ

U.S. school districts with the highest number of vacancies for K-12 teachers ★2331★

Cities with the highest online spending per Internet user ★2576★

Cities with the highest percentage of adults using the Internet at home ★2577★

Newberry College

Highest undergraduate tuition and fees at colleges and universities in South Carolina ★1554★

Newell; Alton E.

Top pay and benefits for the chief executive and top paid employees at Guilford College ★3316★

Newell Rubbermaid

Fortune's highest ranked metal products companies, 2000 ★475★

Top manufacturing companies in Standard & Poor's 500, 2001 ★548★

Newfoundland

Canadian provinces by teaching days per year ★4058★

Newhart Middle School

Outstanding secondary schools in Orange County, California ★4199★

Newman Smith High School

Outstanding secondary schools in Dallas, Texas ★4120★

Newmont Mining

Fortune's highest ranked mining and crude oil companies, 2000 ★477★

Top metals and mining companies in Standard & Poor's 500, 2001 ★549★

Newport Beach Public Library

Highest Hennen's American Public Library Ratings for libraries serving a population of 50,000 to 99,999 ★2697★

Newport Library

North America's first ten public libraries ★2680★

Newport News Shipbuilding

Top recruiters for civil engineering jobs for 2000-01 bachelor's degree recipients ★2346★

Top recruiters for mechanical engineering jobs for 2000-01 bachelor's degree recipients ★2437★

Top recruiters for nuclear engineering jobs for 2000-01 bachelor's degree recipients ★2440★

News America

Fortune's highest ranked entertainment companies, 2000 ★462★

News Corp.

Business Week's best companies in Australia ★386★

News editorial

Areas of specialization in journalism and mass communications programs with the highest enrollment, 1999 ★2740★

News from Lake Wobegon

Retail audiobook titles selling 500,000-600,000 copies ★305★

Newscaster

Jobs considered the most competitive ★2245★

Most desirable jobs in communications ★2271★

Newsday/New York Newsday

Top internships in the U.S. with the highest compensation, 2001 ★2611★

The Newshour with Jim Lehrer
  Most selective internships in the U.S., 2001 ★2610★
Newsweek
  Most selective internships in the U.S., 2001 ★2610★
  Top internships in the U.S. with the highest compensation, 2001 ★2611★
  Most cited general works serials in technical communication journals from 1988 to 1997 ★4419★
Newswriter (radio/TV)
  Most desirable jobs in communications ★2271★
Newton; Chelsea
  All-America girls' high school basketball 3rd team, 2001 ★172★
Newton; Huey
  Most influential African Americans in politics and civil rights ★3040★
Newton; Neil J.
  Top pay and benefits for the chief executive and top paid employees at the University of Denver ★3540★
Newtown Free Library
  Highest Hennen's American Public Library Ratings for libraries serving a population of 50,000 to 99,999 ★2697★
Nextel Communications
  Business Week's best performing companies with the greatest decline in earnings growth ★412★
  Business Week's best performing companies with the lowest return on equity, 2000 ★426★
Nguyen; My Hanh
  Golden Key Scholar Award winners, 2000 ★1316★
Niagara County Community College
  Average faculty salaries for institutions of higher education in New York, 2000-01 ★3719★
  U.S. community colleges with the highest paid full professors, 2001 ★3976★
Niagara Library
  North America's first ten public libraries ★2680★
Niagara University
  Average faculty salaries for institutions of higher education in New York, 2000-01 ★3719★
Niceville High School
  Outstanding secondary schools in Fort Walton Beach, Florida ★4136★
Nicholas; John
  Top pay and benefits for the chief executive and top paid employees at Beloit College ★3199★
Nicholls State University
  Division I NCAA colleges with that graduated less than 20% of their African American male athletes, 1990-91 to 1993-94 ★928★
  Division I NCAA colleges with that graduated none of their African American male basketball players, 1990-91 to 1993-94 ★930★
  Division I NCAA colleges with the lowest graduation rates for football players, 1990-91 to 1993-94 ★938★
  Division I NCAA colleges with the lowest graduation rates for male athletes, 1990-91 to 1993-94 ★939★
  Division I NCAA colleges with the lowest graduation rates for male basketball players, 1990-91 to 1993-94 ★940★
  State appropriations for Louisiana institutions of higher education, 2000-01 ★1271★
  Average faculty salaries for institutions of higher education in Louisiana, 2000-01 ★3705★
Nichols College
  Institutions censured by the American Association of University Professors, 2001 ★1067★
Nichols; Russell
  Top pay and benefits for the chief executive and top paid employees at Hanover College ★3324★
Nickoloff; B.J.
  Most cited authors in dermatology journals, 1981 to 1996 ★1870★
  Most cited first authors in dermatology journals, 1981 to 1996 ★1871★
Nicolet Area Technical College
  Lowest undergraduate tuition and fees at colleges and universities in Wisconsin ★1571★
Nicolet High School
  Outstanding secondary schools in Milwaukee-Waukesha, Wisconsin ★4180★
Nie; N. H.
  Authors with the most citations among authors published in *American Political Science Review*, 1974-94 ★3048★
Nielsen; Kenneth R.
  Top pay and benefits for the chief executive and top paid employees at Woodbury University ★3635★
Niemi Jr.; Albert
  Top pay and benefits for the chief executive and top paid employees at Southern Methodist University ★3502★
Niemi; Richard G.
  Authors most frequently published in *American Political Science Review*, 1974-94 ★3047★
Nienhuis; Robert
  Top pay and benefits for the chief executive and top paid employees at Cornerstone University ★3258★
Nigeria
  Countries with the lowest leader's salary ★3121★
Night Chills
  Most frequently banned books in the 1990s ★745★
Night Flying
  Most notable fiction books for young adults, 2001 ★322★
  Smithsonian's best books for children ages 10 and up ★365★
Night Hoops
  Most notable fiction books for young adults, 2001 ★322★
The Night My Mother Met Bruce Lee: Observations on Not Fitting In
  Outstanding nonfiction books for young adults, 2000 ★334★
Night of the Pompon
  Most notable fiction books for reluctant young adult readers, 2001 ★321★
Night Worker
  Most notable books for young readers, 2001 ★319★
  Outstanding books for young readers, 2000 ★328★
Nightline
  Most selective internships in the U.S., 2001 ★2610★
Nigro; Richard A.
  Top pay and benefits for the chief executive and top paid employees at LaSalle University ★3365★
Nike
  Fortune's highest ranked apparel companies, 2000 ★448★
  Most selective internships in the U.S., 2001 ★2610★
Niles Elementary School, District 71
  Illinois school districts spending the most per pupil for instruction ★4011★
Niles North High School
  Outstanding secondary schools in Chicago, Illinois ★4110★
  Outstanding suburban public high schools in Metro Chicago ★4256★
Niles West High School
  Outstanding secondary schools in Chicago, Illinois ★4110★
Ninos Heros Elementary School
  Illinois elementary schools chosen to be 'demonstration sites' for struggling schools ★4006★
Nipissing; University of
  Canadian primarily undergraduate universities by alumni support, 2000 ★1193★
  Canadian primarily undergraduate universities by class size at the firstand second-year level, 2000 ★1195★
  Canadian primarily undergraduate universities by class size at the thirdand forth-year level, 2000 ★1196★
  Canadian primarily undergraduate universities by classes taught by tenured faculty, 2000 ★1197★
  Canadian primarily undergraduate universities by faculty members with Ph.D.'s, 2000 ★1198★
  Canadian primarily undergraduate universities by library acquisitions, 2000 ★1199★
  Canadian primarily undergraduate universities by library expenses, 2000 ★1200★
  Canadian primarily undergraduate universities by library holdings per student, 2000 ★1201★
  Canadian primarily undergraduate universities by medical/science grants per faculty member, 2000 ★1202★
  Canadian primarily undergraduate universities by operating budget per student, 2000 ★1203★
  Canadian primarily undergraduate universities by percentage of operating budget allocated to scholarships, 2000 ★1204★
  Canadian primarily undergraduate universities by percentage of operating budget allocated to student services, 2000 ★1205★
  Canadian primarily undergraduate universities by reputation, 2000 ★1206★
  Canadian primarily undergraduate universities by social science/humanities grants per faculty member, 2000 ★1207★
  Canadian primarily undergraduate universities by students from out of province, 2000 ★1208★
  Canadian primarily undergraduate universities by students winning national awards, 2000 ★1209★
  Top Canadian primarily undergraduate universities, 2000 ★1226★
Nippon Telegraph & Telephone
  Business Week's best companies in Japan ★398★
  Business Week's top companies worldwide ★433★
"Nitric Oxide: Physiology, pathophysiology, and pharmacology"
  Institute for Scientific Information's most cited papers, 1990-98 ★4282★

NMR-Basic Principles and Progress
Physics journals with the greatest impact measure, 1981-98 ★3020★

NMR in Biomedicine
Spectroscopy journals by citation impact, 1999 ★4361★

No Condition Is Permanent
Most notable fiction books for young adults, 2001 ★322★

No Crystal Stair
Library Journal's best romance titles, 2000 ★245★

NOAH: New York Online Access to Health
Medical Library Association's top health related web sites ★2591★

Noah; Phyliss B.
Top pay and benefits for the chief executive and top paid employees at Lincoln Memorial University ★3374★

Noble; Kimberly
Golden Key Scholar Award winners, 2000 ★1316★

Nokia
Biggest information technology companies, 2000 ★385★
Business Week's best companies in Finland ★392★
Business Week's top companies worldwide ★433★
Most profitable information technology companies, 2000 ★527★
Top information technology companies, 2000 ★544★

Nolan; Ernest
Top pay and benefits for the chief executive and top paid employees at Madonna University ★3386★

Nolan; James
Top pay and benefits for the chief executive and top paid employees at Siena College ★3498★

Nolen; Jerdine
Outstanding children's picture books, 2000 ★331★

Nolon; John R.
Top pay and benefits for the chief executive and top paid employees at Pace University ★3435★

Nomura Securities
Business Week's best companies in Japan ★398★

Nonstore retailers, including mail order
Employment growth percentages for selected industries, 1998-2000 ★2294★

Nonzero: The Logic of Human Destiny
Library Journal's most notable general science books, 2000 ★260★

Norberg; Scott F.
Top pay and benefits for the chief executive and top paid employees at Mississippi College ★3404★

Nordic Baltic Holding
Business Week's best companies in Sweden ★404★

Nordstrom
Fortune's highest ranked general merchandisers, 2000 ★468★

Norfleet; Robert C.
Top pay and benefits for the chief executive and top paid employees at Davidson College ★3264★

Norfolk Academy Lower School
Outstanding secondary schools in Norfolk-Virginia Beach-Newport News, Virginia-North Carolina ★4194★

Norfolk Southern
Fortune's highest ranked railroads, 2000 ★490★
Top transportation companies in Standard & Poor's 500, 2001 ★560★

Norfolk State University
Colleges offering the Thurgood Marshall Scholarship Fund ★221★
Top college choices for Washington D.C. students ★847★
State appropriations for Virginia's institutions of higher education, 2000-01 ★1299★
Historically black colleges and universities awarding the most master's degrees to African Americans ★1670★
Total baccalaureate communications degrees awarded to African Americans from U.S. colleges and universities, 1997-98 ★1687★
Total baccalaureate degrees awarded to African Americans from historically black colleges, 1997-98 ★1697★
Total baccalaureate degrees awarded to African Americans from U.S. colleges and universities, 1997-98 ★1699★
Total baccalaureate social sciences and history degrees awarded to African Americans from U.S. colleges and universities, 1997-98 ★1741★
U.S. colleges and universities awarding the most communications master's degrees to African Americans ★1763★
U.S. colleges and universities awarding the most education master's degrees to African Americans ★1769★

Norman Rockwell: Storyteller with a Brush
Most notable books for middle readers, 2001 ★317★
Outstanding books for middle readers, 2000 ★326★
Smithsonian's best books for children ages 10 and up ★365★

Normandale Community College
Average faculty salaries for institutions of higher education without academic ranks in Minnesota, 2000-01 ★3753★

Norris; Harold E.
Top pay and benefits for the chief executive and top paid employees at Dallas Baptist University ★3262★

Norsk Hydro
Business Week's best companies in Norway ★400★

Nortel Networks
Biggest information technology companies, 2000 ★385★
Business Week's best companies in Canada ★390★
Business Week's best performing companies with the greatest decline in earnings growth ★412★
Business Week's best performing companies with the lowest return on equity, 2000 ★426★
Fortune's highest ranked network communications companies, 2000 ★482★

North Alabama; University of
Division II NCAA colleges with the 0% graduation rates for women's basketball players, 1993-94 ★942★
State appropriations for Alabama's institutions of higher education, 2000-01 ★1254★

North Allegheny High School
Outstanding secondary schools in Pittsburgh, Pennsylvania ★4204★

North America
Region of origin of foreign students enrolled in U.S. institutions of higher education, 1998-99 ★2502★
World regions hosting U.S. students studying abroad, 1998-99 ★2515★

North American Scientific
Best small companies in the U.S. ★383★

North Arkansas College
Lowest undergraduate tuition and fees at colleges and universities in Arkansas ★1485★
Average faculty salaries for institutions of higher education without academic ranks in Arkansas, 2000-01 ★3742★

North Carolina
Mean composite ACT scores by state, 2000 ★895★
Mean math SAT scores by state, 2000 ★900★
Mean verbal SAT scores by state, 2000 ★903★
States allocating the largest amount of state tax appropriations for higher education, 2000-01 ★1304★
Total doctorate recipients by state, 1999 ★2054★
State grades for affordability of higher education for minority students, 2000 ★2883★
State grades for benefits state receives for educating its minority students, 2000 ★2884★
State grades for completion of higher education by minority students, 2000 ★2885★
State grades for participation of minority students in higher education, 2000 ★2886★
State grades for preparing minority students for higher education, 2000 ★2887★
States expelling the most students for violating the Gun-Free Schools Act, 1998-99 ★3994★
States with the highest number of high school graduates, 1999-2000 ★3995★
States with the highest projected K-12 public school enrollment for 2010 ★4035★
States with the most charter schools ★4048★
States with the lowest percentage of high school freshmen enrolling in college within four years ★4267★
States with the highest state support for non need-based financial aid for students, 1999-2000 ★4368★

North Carolina A&T State University
Historically black institutions with the highest number of National Achievement Scholars, 1998 ★8★
Colleges offering the Thurgood Marshall Scholarship Fund ★221★
State appropriations for North Carolina's institutions of higher education, 2000-01 ★1286★
Historically black colleges and universities awarding the most master's degrees to African Americans ★1670★
Total baccalaureate business management and administrative services degrees awarded to African Americans from U.S. colleges and universities, 1997-98 ★1683★
Total baccalaureate computer and information science degrees awarded to African Americans from U.S. colleges and universities, 1997-98 ★1691★

Total baccalaureate degrees awarded to African Americans from historically black colleges, 1997-98 ★1697★
Total baccalaureate degrees awarded to African Americans from U.S. colleges and universities, 1997-98 ★1699★
Total baccalaureate education degrees awarded to African Americans from U.S. colleges and universities, 1997-98 ★1711★
Total baccalaureate engineering degrees awarded to minorities from U.S. colleges and universities, 1997-98 ★1715★
U.S. colleges and universities awarding the most computer and information sciences master's degrees to African Americans ★1766★
U.S. colleges and universities awarding the most mathematics master's degrees to African Americans ★1790★
U.S. institutions awarding the most baccalaureate degrees to African Americans in agricultural sciences, 1998 ★1814★
U.S. institutions awarding the most master's degrees to African Americans in agribusiness and production, 1998 ★1824★
U.S. institutions awarding the most master's degrees to African Americans in agricultural sciences, 1998 ★1825★
U.S. institutions awarding the most master's degrees to minorities in agribusiness and production, 1998 ★1829★
U.S. institutions awarding the most master's degrees to minorities in agricultural sciences, 1998 ★1830★
Average faculty salaries for institutions of higher education in North Carolina, 2000-01 ★3720★

North Carolina, Asheville; University of
All-USA College Academic Third Team, 2001 ★4★
State appropriations for North Carolina's institutions of higher education, 2000-01 ★1286★
Fiske Guide's best buys for public colleges and universities, 2001 ★1460★
Average faculty salaries for institutions of higher education in North Carolina, 2000-01 ★3720★

North Carolina Central University
Colleges offering the Thurgood Marshall Scholarship Fund ★221★
Retention rates of African American students at historically black institutions, 1997-98 ★1120★
State appropriations for North Carolina's institutions of higher education, 2000-01 ★1286★
Historically black colleges and universities awarding the most master's degrees to African Americans ★1670★
Total baccalaureate degrees awarded to African Americans from historically black colleges, 1997-98 ★1697★
Total baccalaureate social sciences and history degrees awarded to African Americans from U.S. colleges and universities, 1997-98 ★1741★
U.S. colleges and universities awarding the most biological and life sciences master's degrees to African Americans ★1756★
U.S. colleges and universities awarding the most computer and information sciences master's degrees to African Americans ★1766★
Historically black colleges and universities awarding the most first professional degrees to African Americans ★1835★

U.S. colleges and universities awarding the most first professional degrees to African Americans ★1843★
U.S. colleges and universities awarding the most law and legal studies first professional degrees to African Americans ★1852★
Average faculty salaries for institutions of higher education in North Carolina, 2000-01 ★3720★

North Carolina, Chapel Hill interdisciplinary with the Schools of Medicine, Pharmacology, and Public Health; University of
Most effective pharmacology research-doctorate programs as evaluated by the National Research Council ★2938★

North Carolina, Chapel Hill Program in Statistics; University of
Top statistics and biostatistics research-doctorate programs as evaluated by the National Research Council ★2782★

North Carolina, Chapel Hill School of Arts and Sciences; University of
Most effective pharmacology research-doctorate programs as evaluated by the National Research Council ★2938★
Top pharmacology research-doctorate programs as evaluated by the National Research Council ★2939★

North Carolina, Chapel Hill; University of
Colleges with the highest number of freshman Merit Scholars, 2000 ★5★
Top business schools for within-discipline research performance in production/operations management, 1986-1998 ★648★
Top business schools for within-discipline research performance in accounting, 1986-1998 ★660★
Top business schools for within-discipline research performance in insurance, international business and real estate, 1986-1998 ★667★
Winner of the American Chemical Society's Arthur C. Cope Awards, 2001 ★795★
Most effective classics research-doctorate programs as evaluated by the National Research Council ★815★
Top classics research-doctorate programs as evaluated by the National Research Council ★816★
U.S. colleges and universities where intercollegiate sports are popular ★995★
U.S. colleges and universities where the general student body puts a strong emphasis on athletic events ★1007★
U.S. colleges and universities with a popular newspaper ★1018★
Retention rates of African American students at traditionally white institutions, 1997-98 ★1121★
U.S. News & World Report's best public national universities, 2000-01 ★1123★
U.S. News & World Report's national universities with the highest percentage of full-time faculty, 2000-01 ★1136★
State appropriations for North Carolina's institutions of higher education, 2000-01 ★1286★
Fiske Guide's best buys for public colleges and universities, 2001 ★1460★
Total baccalaureate communications degrees awarded to African Americans from U.S. colleges and universities, 1997-98 ★1687★

Total baccalaureate communications degrees awarded to Native Americans from U.S. colleges and universities, 1997-98 ★1690★
Total baccalaureate physical sciences degrees awarded to Asian Americans from U.S. colleges and universities, 1997-98 ★1734★
U.S. colleges and universities awarding the most health professions and related sciences master's degrees to African Americans ★1777★
U.S. colleges and universities awarding the most physical sciences master's degrees to African Americans ★1793★
Traditionally white institutions awarding the most first professional degrees to African Americans ★1842★
U.S. colleges and universities awarding the most first professional degrees to African Americans ★1843★
U.S. colleges and universities awarding the most first professional degrees to Native Americans ★1846★
U.S. colleges and universities awarding the most health professions and related sciences first professional degrees to African Americans ★1847★
U.S. colleges and universities awarding the most health professions and related sciences first professional degrees to Native Americans ★1851★
U.S. colleges and universities awarding the most law and legal studies first professional degrees to Native Americans ★1855★
U.S. universities publishing the most papers in the field of dentistry/oral surgery and medicine, 1995-99 ★1865★
U.S. universities with the greatest impact in dentistry/oral surgery, 1994-98 ★1866★
U.S. universities with the greatest impact in dentistry/oral surgery and medicine, 1995-99 ★1867★
U.S. universities with the highest concentration of dentistry papers published, 1994-98 ★1868★
U.S. colleges and universities awarding the most biological and life sciences doctorate degrees to Asian Americans ★2083★
U.S. colleges and universities awarding the most physical sciences doctorate degrees to African Americans ★2118★
Top oceanography research-doctorate programs as evaluated by the National Research Council ★2153★
Top civil engineering research-doctorate programs as evaluated by the National Research Council ★2396★
Academics' choices for best graduate environmental/environmental health engineering programs, 2001 ★2408★
U.S. research institutions with the largest number of students studying abroad, 1998-99 ★2514★
U.S. universities publishing the most papers in the field of library and information science, 1995-99 ★2718★
U.S. universities with the greatest impact in library and information science, 1994-98 ★2719★
Academics' choices for best family medicine programs, 2001 ★2820★
Academics' choices for best rural medicine programs, 2001 ★2824★
Acceptance rates for U.S. News & World Report's top 10 primary-care medical schools, 2001 ★2826★

NORTH

- Average MCAT scores at *U.S. News & World Report*'s top 10 primary-care medical schools, 2001 ★2835★
- Average undergraduate GPA at *U.S. News & World Report*'s top 10 primary-care medical schools, 2001 ★2837★
- Faculty-student ratios at *U.S. News & World Report*'s top 10 primary-care medical schools, 2001 ★2841★
- Out-of-state tuition and fees at *U.S. News & World Report*'s top 10 primary-care medical schools, 2001 ★2846★
- Percentage of graduates entering *U.S. News & World Report*'s top 10 primary-care medical schools, 2001 ★2848★
- Top primary-care medical schools, 2001 ★2856★
- Top primary-care medical schools by reputation, as determined by academic personnel, 2001 ★2857★
- Institutions in the Worker Rights Consortium ★2913★
- U.S. universities with the highest concentration of papers published in the field of pharmacology, 1995-99 ★2937★
- Average faculty salaries for institutions of higher education in North Carolina, 2000-01 ★3720★
- Public institutions of higher education that pay the highest salaries to female professors, 2000-01 ★3975★
- Most effective sociology research-doctorate programs as evaluated by the National Research Council ★4352★
- Top sociology research-doctorate programs as evaluated by the National Research Council ★4354★
- Top graduate education schools by reputation, as determined by superintendents, 2001 ★4397★

North Carolina, Charlotte; University of
- Four-year institutions with the most weapons arrests reported, 1999 ★709★
- U.S. colleges and universities reporting the most weapons related arrests, 1998 ★732★
- State appropriations for North Carolina's institutions of higher education, 2000-01 ★1286★
- *U.S. News & World Report*'s southern regional universities with the best academic reputation scores, 2000-01 ★1433★
- *U.S. News & World Report*'s southern regional universities with the lowest acceptance rates, 2000-01 ★1442★
- *U.S. News & World Report*'s top public southern regional universities, 2000-01 ★1443★
- Average faculty salaries for institutions of higher education in North Carolina, 2000-01 ★3720★

North Carolina, Greensboro; University of
- U.S. colleges and universities reporting the most drug related arrests, 1998 ★731★
- U.S. colleges and universities reporting the most weapons related arrests, 1998 ★732★
- U.S. colleges and universities with the largest numerical increases in drug arrests, 1998 ★734★
- U.S. colleges and universities with the largest numerical increases in weapons arrests, 1998 ★735★
- State appropriations for North Carolina's institutions of higher education, 2000-01 ★1286★
- *U.S. News & World Report*'s national universities with students least in debt, 1999 ★1475★
- Average faculty salaries for institutions of higher education in North Carolina, 2000-01 ★3720★
- Academics' choices for best counseling/personnel services graduate programs, 2001 ★4379★

North Carolina Hospitals at Chapel Hill; University of
- State appropriations for North Carolina's institutions of higher education, 2000-01 ★1286★

North Carolina, Kenan Flagler Business School; University of
- *U.S. News & World Report*'s undergraduate business programs with the highest academic reputation scores, 2000-01 ★571★
- Academics' choices for best graduate executive MBA programs, 2001 ★584★
- *Business Week*'s top business schools best at responding to student concerns, 2000 ★598★
- *Business Week*'s top business schools with the greatest rise in MBA satisfaction, 2000 ★611★
- *Business Week*'s top business schools with the highest percentage of minority enrollment, 2000 ★613★
- *Business Week*'s top business schools with the highest percentage of women enrollees, 2000 ★614★
- *Business Week*'s top business schools with the lowest percentage of international students, 2000 ★615★
- Top graduate business schools by reputation, as determined by recruiters, 2001 ★651★

North Carolina, Pembroke; University of
- Division II NCAA colleges with the 100% graduation rates for men's basketball players, 1993-94 ★943★
- State appropriations for North Carolina's institutions of higher education, 2000-01 ★1286★
- *U.S. News & World Report*'s southern regional universities with students least in debt, 1999 ★1431★
- Total baccalaureate biology/life sciences degrees awarded to Native Americans from U.S. colleges and universities, 1997-98 ★1682★
- Total baccalaureate business management and administrative services degrees awarded to Native Americans from U.S. colleges and universities, 1997-98 ★1686★
- Total baccalaureate degrees awarded to Native Americans from U.S. colleges and universities, 1997-98 ★1710★
- Total baccalaureate education degrees awarded to Native Americans from U.S. colleges and universities, 1997-98 ★1714★
- Total baccalaureate English language, literature, and letters degrees awarded to Native Americans from U.S. colleges and universities, 1997-98 ★1719★
- Total baccalaureate mathematics degrees awarded to Native Americans from U.S. colleges and universities, 1997-98 ★1732★
- Total baccalaureate social sciences and history degrees awarded to Native Americans from U.S. colleges and universities, 1997-98 ★1744★
- Average faculty salaries for institutions of higher education in North Carolina, 2000-01 ★3720★

North Carolina School of the Arts
- State appropriations for North Carolina's institutions of higher education, 2000-01 ★1286★

North Carolina State University
- All-USA College Academic Second Team, 2001 ★3★
- State appropriations for North Carolina's institutions of higher education, 2000-01 ★1286★
- U.S. colleges and universities awarding the most biological and life sciences master's degrees to African Americans ★1756★
- U.S. colleges and universities awarding the most English language/literature/letters master's degrees to African Americans ★1773★
- U.S. colleges and universities awarding the most mathematics master's degrees to African Americans ★1790★
- U.S. colleges and universities awarding the most doctorate degrees to African Americans ★2095★
- Academics' choices for best graduate agricultural engineering programs, 2001 ★2379★
- Top industrial engineering research-doctorate programs as evaluated by the National Research Council ★2413★
- Academics' choices for best graduate nuclear engineering schools, 2000 ★2426★
- University research libraries in the U.S. and Canada with the largest increases in total expenditures from 1993-94 to 1998-99 ★2708★
- U.S. colleges and universities spending the most on chemical engineering research and development, 1998 ★3098★
- U.S. colleges and universities with the most federal support for chemical engineering research and development, 1998 ★3101★
- Average faculty salaries for institutions of higher education in North Carolina, 2000-01 ★3720★
- U.S. universities with the highest concentration of papers published in the field of materials science, 1995-99 ★4290★
- U.S. universities with the highest concentration of papers published in the field of veterinary medicine, 1995-99 ★4441★

North Carolina State University, Raleigh
- U.S. colleges and universities awarding the most doctoral degrees to American Indians and Alaskan Natives from 1995 to 1999 ★2092★
- U.S. colleges and universities awarding the most doctorates in engineering, 1999 ★2102★

North Carolina; University of
- Division I all-time winningest college teams ★128★
- Degree-granting institutions with the most published pages in *The Journal of Risk and Insurance*, 1987-1996 ★678★
- Total baccalaureate physical sciences degrees awarded to Native Americans from U.S. colleges and universities, 1997-98 ★1736★
- Top university research libraries in the U.S. and Canada, 1998-99 ★2706★
- Comparison of library and information science programs composite rankings with *U.S. News & World Report* survey ★2709★
- Library and information science programs with the most citations to journal articles, 1993-1998 ★2712★
- Library and information science programs with the most journal articles, 1993-1998 ★2713★

Library and information science programs with the most journal articles per capita, 1993-1998 ★2714★

Library and information science programs with the most per capita citations to journal articles, 1993-1998 ★2715★

Degrees granted in the ten largest doctoral journalism and mass communications programs, 1999 ★2756★

Enrollment of students in the ten largest doctoral journalism and mass communications programs, 1999 ★2762★

North Carolina Wesleyan College
Average faculty salaries for institutions of higher education in North Carolina, 2000-01 ★3720★

North Carolina, Wilmington; University of
State appropriations for North Carolina's institutions of higher education, 2000-01 ★1286★
U.S. News & World Report's southern regional universities with the lowest acceptance rates, 2000-01 ★1442★
U.S. News & World Report's top public southern regional universities, 2000-01 ★1443★
Average faculty salaries for institutions of higher education in North Carolina, 2000-01 ★3720★

North Central College
U.S. News & World Report's midwestern regional universities with the best alumni giving rates, 2000-01 ★1402★
U.S. News & World Report's midwestern regional universities with the best student/faculty ratios, 2000-01 ★1403★
U.S. News & World Report's midwestern regional universities with the highest proportion of classes having 20 students or less, 2000-01 ★1409★
U.S. News & World Report's midwestern regional universities with the lowest acceptance rates, 2000-01 ★1410★
U.S. News & World Report's best undergraduate fees among midwestern regional universities by discount tuition, 2000 ★1427★
Average faculty salaries for institutions of higher education in Illinois, 2000-01 ★3700★

North Central Michigan College
Lowest undergraduate tuition and fees at colleges and universities in Michigan ★1519★
Average faculty salaries for institutions of higher education in Michigan, 2000-01 ★3709★

North Central Missouri College
Lowest undergraduate tuition and fees at colleges and universities in Missouri ★1525★

North Central State College
Average faculty salaries for institutions of higher education in Ohio, 2000-01 ★3722★

North Central Texas
Average faculty salaries for institutions of higher education without academic ranks in Texas, 2000-01 ★3766★

North Country Community College
Average faculty salaries for institutions of higher education in New York, 2000-01 ★3719★

North Dakota
Mean composite ACT scores by state, 2000 ★895★
Mean math SAT scores by state, 2000 ★900★
Mean verbal SAT scores by state, 2000 ★903★
States allocating the smallest amount of state tax appropriations for higher education, 2000-01 ★1305★

Total doctorate recipients by state, 1999 ★2054★
State grades for affordability of higher education for minority students, 2000 ★2883★
State grades for benefits state receives for educating its minority students, 2000 ★2884★
State grades for completion of higher education by minority students, 2000 ★2885★
State grades for participation of minority students in higher education, 2000 ★2886★
State grades for preparing minority students for higher education, 2000 ★2887★
States with the lowest number of high school graduates, 1999-2000 ★3997★
States with the highest percentage of high school freshmen enrolling in college within four years ★4266★

North Dakota State College of Science
Lowest undergraduate tuition and fees at colleges and universities in North Dakota ★1542★
Average faculty salaries for institutions of higher education in North Dakota, 2000-01 ★3721★

North Dakota State University
State appropriations for North Dakota's institutions of higher education, 2000-01 ★1287★
Highest undergraduate tuition and fees at colleges and universities in North Dakota ★1541★
Average faculty salaries for institutions of higher education in North Dakota, 2000-01 ★3721★

North Dakota; University of
U.S. colleges and universities with poor library facilities ★1028★
U.S. colleges and universities with the least accessible instructors ★1036★
State appropriations for North Dakota's institutions of higher education, 2000-01 ★1287★
Highest undergraduate tuition and fees at colleges and universities in North Dakota ★1541★
Total baccalaureate health professions and related sciences degrees awarded to Native Americans from U.S. colleges and universities, 1997-98 ★1724★
Total baccalaureate psychology degrees awarded to Native Americans from U.S. colleges and universities, 1997-98 ★1740★
U.S. colleges and universities awarding the most first professional degrees to Native Americans ★1846★
U.S. colleges and universities awarding the most health professions and related sciences first professional degrees to Native Americans ★1851★
U.S. colleges and universities awarding the most doctorate degrees to Native Americans ★2099★
Academics' choices for best rural medicine programs, 2001 ★2824★
Average faculty salaries for institutions of higher education in North Dakota, 2000-01 ★3721★

North Farmington High School
Outstanding secondary schools in Detroit, Michigan ★4125★

North Florida Community College
Lowest undergraduate tuition and fees at colleges and universities in Florida ★1495★

North Florida; University of
State appropriations for Florida's institutions of higher education, 2000-01 ★1262★
U.S. News & World Report's top public southern regional universities, 2000-01 ★1443★

North Georgia College and State University
State appropriations for Georgia's institutions of higher education, 2000-01 ★1263★
Average faculty salaries for institutions of higher education in Georgia, 2000-01 ★3697★

North Greenville College
Institutions censured by the American Association of University Professors, 2001 ★1067★

North Harford Middle School
Outstanding secondary schools in Baltimore, Maryland ★4092★

North Hennepin Community College
Average faculty salaries for institutions of higher education without academic ranks in Minnesota, 2000-01 ★3753★

North High School
Outstanding secondary schools in Evansville-Henderson, Indiana-Kentucky ★4130★

North-Holland
Book publishers with the most citations (Class 4) ★2565★

North Idaho College
Undergraduate tuition and fees at colleges and universities in Idaho ★1499★

North Iowa Area Community College
Average faculty salaries for institutions of higher education without academic ranks in Iowa, 2000-01 ★3748★

North Kirkwood Middle School
Outstanding secondary schools in St. Louis, Missouri-Illinois ★4216★

North Lake College
Lowest undergraduate tuition and fees at colleges and universities in Texas ★1561★
Average faculty salaries for institutions of higher education without academic ranks in Texas, 2000-01 ★3766★

North Liberty Community Library
Highest Hennen's American Public Library Ratings for libraries serving a population of 2,500 to 4,999 ★2693★

North Park College & Theological Seminary
Private, 4-year undergraduate colleges and universities producing the most Ph.D.'s in the computer sciences, 1920-1990 ★1595★
Private, 4-year undergraduate colleges and universities producing the most Ph.D.'s in the computer sciences, 1981-1990 ★1596★

North Park University
U.S. News & World Report's midwestern regional liberal arts colleges with the highest alumni giving rates, 2000-01 ★1342★
Highest undergraduate tuition and fees at colleges and universities in Illinois ★1500★

North Penn High School
Outstanding secondary schools in Philadelphia, Pennsylvania-New Jersey ★4202★

North Shore Community College
Lowest undergraduate tuition and fees at colleges and universities in Massachusetts ★1517★

North Shore High School
Outstanding secondary schools in Long Island, New York ★4165★

North Springs High School
Outstanding urban public high schools in Metro Atlanta ★4260★

North Texas Health Science Center, Fort Worth; University of
U.S. colleges and universities awarding the most health professions and related sciences first professional degrees to Native Americans ★1851★

North Texas System; University of
State appropriations for Texas's institutions of higher education, 2000-01 ★1296★

North Texas; University of
Institutions, by adjusted authorship, with the most published authors in the *Journal of Business Research*, 1985 to 1999 ★694★
Total baccalaureate communications degrees awarded to Hispanic Americans from U.S. colleges and universities, 1997-98 ★1689★
Doctoral institutions with the highest enrollment of foreign students, 1998-99 ★2494★
Library and information science programs with the most citations to journal articles, 1993-1998 ★2712★
Library and information science programs with the most journal articles, 1993-1998 ★2713★
Library and information science programs with the most journal articles per capita, 1993-1998 ★2714★
Library and information science programs with the most per capita citations to journal articles, 1993-1998 ★2715★
Average faculty salaries for institutions of higher education in Texas, 2000-01 ★3731★

Northampton County Area Community College
Average faculty salaries for institutions of higher education in Pennsylvania, 2000-01 ★3725★

Northbrook Junior High School
Outstanding secondary schools in Chicago, Illinois ★4110★

Northbrook Middle School
Outstanding secondary schools in Houston, Texas ★4150★

Northbrook School, District 27
Illinois school districts spending the most for elementary school education 1997-98 ★4009★

Northbrook School, District 28
Illinois elementary school districts with the highest teacher salaries, 1999 ★3984★
Illinois school districts spending the most per pupil for instruction ★4011★

Northeast Alabama Community College
Lowest undergraduate tuition and fees at colleges and universities in Alabama ★1480★

Northeast Community College
Lowest undergraduate tuition and fees at colleges and universities in Nebraska ★1529★
Average faculty salaries for institutions of higher education without academic ranks in Nebraska, 2000-01 ★3757★

Northeast Louisiana University
Total baccalaureate health professions and related sciences degrees awarded to Native Americans from U.S. colleges and universities, 1997-98 ★1724★

Northeast State Tech Community College
Average faculty salaries for institutions of higher education in Tennessee, 2000-01 ★3730★

Northeast Wisconsin Technical College
Lowest undergraduate tuition and fees at colleges and universities in Wisconsin ★1571★

Northeastern Illinois University
Fall enrollment at Chicago-area public universities, by minority percentages, 1999 ★868★
State appropriations for Illinois institutions of higher education, 2000-01 ★1266★
Total ethnic/cultural studies master's degrees awarded to African Americans from U.S. colleges and universities, 1997-98 ★1747★
Total ethnic/cultural studies master's degrees awarded to minorities from U.S. colleges and universities, 1997-98 ★1748★
Average faculty salaries for institutions of higher education in Illinois, 2000-01 ★3700★

Northeastern Ohio University's College of Medicine
State appropriations for Ohio's institutions of higher education, 2000-01 ★1288★

Northeastern Oklahoma A&M College
Lowest undergraduate tuition and fees at colleges and universities in Oklahoma ★1546★

Northeastern State University
State appropriations for Oklahoma's institutions of higher education, 2000-01 ★1289★
U.S. News & World Report's western regional universities with students least in debt, 1999 ★1575★
Total baccalaureate biology/life sciences degrees awarded to Native Americans from U.S. colleges and universities, 1997-98 ★1682★
Total baccalaureate business management and administrative services degrees awarded to Native Americans from U.S. colleges and universities, 1997-98 ★1686★
Total baccalaureate communications degrees awarded to Native Americans from U.S. colleges and universities, 1997-98 ★1690★
Total baccalaureate degrees awarded to Native Americans from U.S. colleges and universities, 1997-98 ★1710★
Total baccalaureate education degrees awarded to Native Americans from U.S. colleges and universities, 1997-98 ★1714★
Total baccalaureate English language, literature, and letters degrees awarded to Native Americans from U.S. colleges and universities, 1997-98 ★1719★
Total baccalaureate health professions and related sciences degrees awarded to Native Americans from U.S. colleges and universities, 1997-98 ★1724★
Total baccalaureate psychology degrees awarded to Native Americans from U.S. colleges and universities, 1997-98 ★1740★
U.S. colleges and universities awarding the most business management and administrative services master's degrees to Native Americans ★1762★
U.S. colleges and universities awarding the most education master's degrees to Native Americans ★1772★
U.S. colleges and universities awarding the most master's degrees to Native Americans ★1789★
Average faculty salaries for institutions of higher education in Oklahoma, 2000-01 ★3723★

Northeastern University
Universities with the most-cited scholars in *Criminology* ★1649★
Universities with the most-cited scholars in *Journal of Quantitative Criminology* ★1650★
Universities with the most-cited scholars in *Journal of Research in Crime and Delinquency* ★1651★
Law schools with the best labor law faculty, 1999-2000 ★2656★
Average faculty salaries for institutions of higher education in Massachusetts, 2000-01 ★3708★

Northern Arizona University
State appropriations for Arizona's institutions of higher education, 2000-01 ★1256★
Total baccalaureate business management and administrative services degrees awarded to Native Americans from U.S. colleges and universities, 1997-98 ★1686★
Total baccalaureate computer and information science degrees awarded to Native Americans from U.S. colleges and universities, 1997-98 ★1694★
Total baccalaureate degrees awarded to Native Americans from U.S. colleges and universities, 1997-98 ★1710★
Total baccalaureate education degrees awarded to Native Americans from U.S. colleges and universities, 1997-98 ★1714★
Total baccalaureate psychology degrees awarded to Native Americans from U.S. colleges and universities, 1997-98 ★1740★
U.S. colleges and universities awarding the most education master's degrees to Hispanic Americans ★1771★
U.S. colleges and universities awarding the most education master's degrees to Native Americans ★1772★
U.S. colleges and universities awarding the most master's degrees to Hispanic Americans ★1787★
U.S. colleges and universities awarding the most master's degrees to Native Americans ★1789★
U.S. colleges and universities awarding the most physical sciences master's degrees to Native Americans ★1796★
Average faculty salaries for institutions of higher education in Arizona, 2000-01 ★3690★

Northern Colorado; University of
State appropriations for Colorado's institutions of higher education, 2000-01 ★1259★
U.S. colleges and universities awarding the most education master's degrees to Native Americans ★1772★
Average faculty salaries for institutions of higher education in Colorado, 2000-01 ★3693★

Northern Essex Community College
Lowest undergraduate tuition and fees at colleges and universities in Massachusetts ★1517★
Average faculty salaries for institutions of higher education in Massachusetts, 2000-01 ★3708★

Northern Illinois University
U.S. colleges and universities with the lowest average football attendance, 1996-99 ★160★
State appropriations for Illinois institutions of higher education, 2000-01 ★1266★
U.S. colleges and universities awarding the most English language/literature/letters master's degrees to African Americans ★1773★
U.S. colleges and universities awarding the most education doctorate degrees to Asian Americans ★2109★
Illinois institutions with the highest article output ★2677★
Institutions in the Worker Rights Consortium ★2913★
Average faculty salaries for institutions of higher education in Illinois, 2000-01 ★3700★

Northern Iowa; University of
State appropriations for Iowa's institutions of higher education, 2000-01 ★1268★
U.S. News & World Report's midwestern regional universities with the highest percentage of full-time faculty, 2000-01 ★1408★
U.S. News & World Report's top public midwestern regional universities, 2000-01 ★1412★
U.S. master's institutions with the largest number of students studying abroad, 1998-99 ★2513★
Average faculty salaries for institutions of higher education in Iowa, 2000-01 ★3702★

Northern Kentucky University
State appropriations for Kentucky's institutions of higher education, 2000-01 ★1270★
U.S. News & World Report's southern regional universities with students most in debt, 1999 ★1432★
Average faculty salaries for institutions of higher education in Kentucky, 2000-01 ★3704★

Northern Maine Technical College
Lowest undergraduate tuition and fees at colleges and universities in Maine ★1513★
Average faculty salaries for institutions of higher education without academic ranks in Maine, 2000-01 ★3749★

Northern Michigan University
State appropriations for Michigan's institutions of higher education, 2000-01 ★1275★
Average faculty salaries for institutions of higher education in Michigan, 2000-01 ★3709★

Northern New Mexico Community College
Lowest undergraduate tuition and fees at colleges and universities in New Mexico ★1536★

Northern Oklahoma College
Lowest undergraduate tuition and fees at colleges and universities in Oklahoma ★1546★

Northern State University
State appropriations for South Dakota's institutions of higher education, 2000-01 ★1294★
Lowest undergraduate tuition and fees at colleges and universities in South Dakota ★1557★

Northern Trust
Top banks in Standard & Poor's 500, 2001 ★531★

Northern Valley Regional High School
Outstanding secondary schools in Bergen-Passaic, New Jersey ★4096★

Northern Virginia Community College
Community colleges in North America with the highest enrollment ★852★
Community colleges with the highest enrollment of foreign students, 1998-99 ★2493★

Northland College
Average faculty salaries for institutions of higher education in Wisconsin, 2000-01 ★3738★

Northland Community and Technical College
Average faculty salaries for institutions of higher education without academic ranks in Minnesota, 2000-01 ★3753★

Northland Pioneer College
Lowest undergraduate tuition and fees at colleges and universities in Arizona ★1483★

Northridge Preparatory High School
Outstanding independent high schools in Metro Chicago ★4077★

Northrop Grumman
Fortune's highest ranked aerospace companies, 2000 ★446★
Top aerospace and defense companies in Standard & Poor's 500, 2001 ★529★

Northside College Prep
Acceptance rates at Chicago college prep magnet schools, 2000-01 ★4000★
Admissions to college prep schools in Chicago that are the toughest to get into, 2001 ★4001★
College prep schools in Chicago that are the toughest to get into ★4005★

Northside High School
Outstanding secondary schools in Fort Smith, Arkansas-Oklahoma ★4135★

Northside Middle School
Outstanding secondary schools in Norfolk-Virginia Beach-Newport News, Virginia-North Carolina ★4194★

Northwest Airlines
Fortune's highest ranked airlines, 2000 ★447★

Northwest Arkansas Community College
Lowest undergraduate tuition and fees at colleges and universities in Arkansas ★1485★

Northwest Christian College
U.S. News & World Report's western regional liberal arts colleges with students most in debt, 1999 ★1398★
Highest undergraduate tuition and fees at colleges and universities in Oregon ★1547★

Northwest College
Undergraduate tuition and fees at colleges and universities in Wyoming ★1572★
Average faculty salaries for institutions of higher education in Washington, 2000-01 ★3736★
Average faculty salaries for institutions of higher education in Wyoming, 2000-01 ★3739★

Northwest Indian College
U.S. tribal colleges ★1445★

Northwest Iowa Community College
Lowest undergraduate tuition and fees at colleges and universities in Iowa ★1505★

Northwest Middle School
Outstanding secondary schools in Salt Lake City-Ogden, Utah ★4218★

Northwest Mississippi Community College
Lowest undergraduate tuition and fees at colleges and universities in Mississippi ★1523★

Northwest Missouri State University
State appropriations for Missouri's institutions of higher education, 2000-01 ★1278★
Average faculty salaries for institutions of higher education in Missouri, 2000-01 ★3712★

Northwest Nazarene University
Academic reputation scores for *U.S. News & World Report*'s top western regional liberal arts colleges, 2000-01 ★1387★
Acceptance rates for *U.S. News & World Report*'s top western regional liberal arts colleges, 2000-01 ★1388★
Alumni giving rates at *U.S. News & World Report*'s top western regional liberal arts colleges, 2000-01 ★1389★
Average freshmen retention rates for *U.S. News & World Report*'s top western regional liberal arts colleges, 2000-01 ★1390★
Average graduation rates for *U.S. News & World Report*'s top western regional liberal arts colleges, 2000-01 ★1391★
Percentage of freshmen in the top 25% of their high school class at *U.S. News & World Report*'s top western regional liberal arts colleges, 2000-01 ★1392★
Percentage of full-time faculty at *U.S. News & World Report*'s top western regional liberal arts colleges, 2000-01 ★1393★
Proportion of classes having 20 students or less at *U.S. News & World Report*'s top western regional liberal arts colleges, 2000-01 ★1394★
Student/faculty ratios at *U.S. News & World Report*'s top western regional liberal arts colleges, 2000-01 ★1395★
U.S. News & World Report's top western regional liberal arts colleges, 2000-01 ★1396★
Undergraduate tuition and fees at colleges and universities in Idaho ★1499★
Average faculty salaries for institutions of higher education without academic ranks in Idaho, 2000-01 ★3746★

The Northwest School
Outstanding secondary schools in Seattle-Bellevue-Everett, Washington ★4227★

Northwest Shoals Community College
Average faculty salaries for institutions of higher education without academic ranks in Alabama, 2000-01 ★3740★

Northwest Technical College
Lowest undergraduate tuition and fees at colleges and universities in Minnesota ★1521★
Average faculty salaries for institutions of higher education without academic ranks in Minnesota, 2000-01 ★3753★

NorthWestern
Fortune's highest ranked pipelines and energy companies, 2000 ★486★

Northwestern College
U.S. News & World Report's midwestern regional liberal arts colleges with the highest acceptance rates, 2000-01 ★1341★
U.S. News & World Report's midwestern regional liberal arts colleges with the highest alumni giving rates, 2000-01 ★1342★
U.S. News & World Report's best undergraduate fees among midwestern regional liberal arts colleges by discount tuition, 2000 ★1380★
Average faculty salaries for institutions of higher education in Iowa, 2000-01 ★3702★
Average faculty salaries for institutions of higher education in Minnesota, 2000-01 ★3710★

Northwestern Connecticut Community-Technical College
Lowest undergraduate tuition and fees at colleges and universities in Connecticut ★1491★

Northwestern Memorial Hospital
Best companies for working mothers in offering advancement opportunities for women ★4447★

Northwestern Mutual Financial Network
Top recruiters for accounting jobs for 2000-01 bachelor's degree recipients ★580★
Top recruiters for marketing jobs for 2000-01 bachelor's degree recipients ★684★
Most selective internships in the U.S., 2001 ★2610★

Northwestern Mutual Life Insurance
Fortune's highest ranked life and health insurance companies, 2000 ★472★
Top internships in the U.S., 2001 ★2612★

Northwestern Oklahoma State University
State appropriations for Oklahoma's institutions of higher education, 2000-01 ★1289★

NORTHWESTERN

Northwestern State University
State appropriations for Louisiana institutions of higher education, 2000-01 ★1271★
Average faculty salaries for institutions of higher education in Louisiana, 2000-01 ★3705★

Northwestern State University of Louisiana
U.S. News & World Report's southern regional universities with students least in debt, 1999 ★1431★

Northwestern University
Most effective art history research-doctorate programs as evaluated by the National Research Council ★91★
Top art history research-doctorate programs as evaluated by the National Research Council ★93★
Top business schools in research performance, 1986-1998 ★532★
U.S. universities with the greatest impact in management, 1994-98 ★575★
Top business schools by average MBA rank, 1986-1998 ★644★
Top business schools for overall within-discipline research performance, 1986-1998 ★645★
Top business schools for within-discipline research performance in management, 1986-1998 ★646★
Top business schools for within-discipline research performance in accounting, 1986-1998 ★660★
Top business schools for within-discipline research performance in finance, 1986-1998 ★663★
Top business schools for within-discipline research performance in marketing, 1986-1998 ★671★
Top chemistry research-doctorate programs as evaluated by the National Research Council ★805★
Fall enrollment at the largest Chicago-area private institutions, by minority percentages, 1999 ★869★
Division I NCAA colleges with that graduated all of their African American male basketball players, 1990-91 to 1993-94 ★927★
Division I NCAA colleges with that graduated more than 80% of their African American male athletes, 1990-91 to 1993-94 ★929★
Division I NCAA colleges with the highest graduation rates for female athletes, 1990-91 to 1993-94 ★931★
Division I NCAA colleges with the highest graduation rates for football players, 1990-91 to 1993-94 ★933★
Division I NCAA colleges with the highest graduation rates for male athletes, 1990-91 to 1993-94 ★934★
Division I NCAA colleges with the highest graduation rates for male basketball players, 1990-91 to 1993-94 ★935★
U.S. News & World Report's national universities with the best graduation and retention rank, 2000-01 ★1129★
U.S. News & World Report's national universities with the best student/faculty ratio, 2000-01 ★1130★
U.S. News & World Report's national universities with the highest graduation rate, 1999 ★1134★
Colleges and universities with the largest endowments, 2000 ★1237★
U.S. colleges and universities spending the most on independent lobbyists, 1999 ★1310★
Highest undergraduate tuition and fees at colleges and universities in Illinois ★1500★
U.S. universities with the greatest impact in communication, 1995-99 ★1657★
U.S. colleges and universities awarding the most biological and life sciences master's degrees to Asian Americans ★1757★
U.S. colleges and universities awarding the most business management and administrative services master's degrees to African Americans ★1759★
U.S. colleges and universities awarding the most business management and administrative services master's degrees to Asian Americans ★1760★
U.S. colleges and universities awarding the most business management and administrative services master's degrees to Native Americans ★1762★
U.S. colleges and universities awarding the most communications master's degrees to African Americans ★1763★
U.S. colleges and universities awarding the most communications master's degrees to Asian Americans ★1764★
U.S. colleges and universities awarding the most communications master's degrees to Hispanic Americans ★1765★
U.S. colleges and universities awarding the most master's degrees to Asian Americans ★1786★
U.S. colleges and universities awarding the most first professional degrees to Asian Americans ★1844★
U.S. colleges and universities awarding the most health professions and related sciences first professional degrees to Asian Americans ★1848★
U.S. colleges and universities awarding the most health professions and related sciences first professional degrees to minorities ★1850★
U.S. colleges and universities awarding the most social sciences and history doctorate degrees to Asian Americans ★2125★
Economics departments by number of citations by top economists, 1971-92 ★2158★
Economics departments by number of citations per top economist, 1971-92 ★2159★
Economics departments by number of top economists, 1971-92 ★2160★
Economics Ph.D. programs by number of citations of top economist graduates, 1971-92 ★2204★
Economics Ph.D. programs by number of citations per top economist graduate, 1971-92 ★2205★
Economics Ph.D. programs by number of top economist graduates, 1971-92 ★2206★
Most effective economics research-doctorate programs as evaluated by the National Research Council ★2207★
Origin of doctorate for dissertation chairs in economics ★2208★
Origin of doctorate for economics faculty at Ph.D.-granting institutions ★2209★
Origin of doctorate for economics faculty at Ph.D.-granting institutions, by Ph.D. equivalents produced ★2210★
Top economics research-doctorate programs as evaluated by the National Research Council ★2213★
Top biomedical engineering research-doctorate programs as evaluated by the National Research Council ★2384★
Top chemical engineering research-doctorate programs as evaluated by the National Research Council ★2390★
U.S. universities with the greatest impact in chemical engineering, 1994-98 ★2393★
Top civil engineering research-doctorate programs as evaluated by the National Research Council ★2396★
Academics' choices for best graduate industrial/manufacturing engineering programs, 2001 ★2411★
Most effective industrial engineering research-doctorate programs as evaluated by the National Research Council ★2412★
Top industrial engineering research-doctorate programs as evaluated by the National Research Council ★2413★
Academics' choices for best graduate materials engineering programs, 2001 ★2417★
Most effective materials science research-doctorate programs as evaluated by the National Research Council ★2418★
Top materials science research-doctorate programs as evaluated by the National Research Council ★2419★
U.S. News & World Report's graduate engineering programs with the best materials departments, 2000-01 ★2421★
Most effective mechanical engineering research-doctorate programs as evaluated by the National Research Council ★2423★
Top Ph.D.-granting departments of geography from 1925-1982 ★2521★
Academics' choices for best clinical law programs, 2001 ★2626★
Academics' choices for best trial advocacy programs, 2001 ★2633★
Law schools with the best administrative law faculty, 1999-2000 ★2638★
Law schools with the best criminal law (substantive) faculty, 1999-2000 ★2647★
Law schools with the best law and social science plus psychology and sociology faculty, 1999-2000 ★2659★
Law schools with the highest quality, 1999-2000 ★2666★
Illinois institutions with the highest article output ★2677★
Degrees granted in the ten largest master's journalism and mass communications programs, 1999 ★2757★
Enrollment of students in the ten largest master's journalism and mass communications programs, 1999 ★2763★
Academics' choices for best women's health medical programs, 2001 ★2825★
Women faculty in Ph.D. physics departments at U.S. institutions, 1998 ★2981★
Average faculty salaries for institutions of higher education in Illinois, 2000-01 ★3700★
U.S. institutions with the highest paid assistant professors, 2001 ★3977★
Most effective sociology research-doctorate programs as evaluated by the National Research Council ★4352★
Top sociology research-doctorate programs as evaluated by the National Research Council ★4354★
Acceptance rates at *U.S. News & World Report*'s top 10 graduate education schools, 2001 ★4388★
Average quantitative GRE scores for *U.S. News & World Report*'s top 10 graduate education schools, 2001 ★4389★

Average verbal GRE scores for *U.S. News & World Report*'s top 10 graduate education schools, 2001 ★4390★
Doctoral students to faculty ratio at *U.S. News & World Report*'s top 10 graduate education schools, 2001 ★4391★
Ph.D.s and Ed.D.s granted at *U.S. News & World Report*'s top 10 graduate education schools, 2001 ★4392★
Research expenditures for *U.S. News & World Report*'s top 10 graduate education schools, 2001 ★4393★
Research expenditures per faculty member at *U.S. News & World Report*'s top 10 graduate education schools, 2001 ★4394★
Top graduate education schools, 2001 ★4395★
Top graduate education schools by reputation, as determined by superintendents, 2001 ★4397★

Northwestern University, Kellogg Graduate School of Management
Academics' choices for best graduate entrepreneurship programs, 2001 ★583★
Academics' choices for best graduate executive MBA programs, 2001 ★584★
Academics' choices for best graduate nonprofit organizations programs, 2001 ★586★
Academics' choices for best part-time MBA programs, 2000 ★587★
Acceptance rates for *U.S. News & World Report*'s top 10 graduate business schools, 2001 ★588★
Annual tuition at *Business Week*'s top business schools, 2000 ★589★
Average GMAT scores at *U.S. News & World Report*'s top 10 graduate business schools, 2001 ★591★
Average job offers received by graduates from *Business Week*'s top business schools, 1999 ★592★
Average undergraduate GPA at *U.S. News & World Report*'s top 10 graduate business schools, 2001 ★593★
Business Week's top business schools, 2000 ★595★
Business Week's top business schools as selected by corporate recruiters, 2000 ★596★
Business Week's top business schools as selected by recent MBA graduates, 2000 ★597★
Business Week's top business schools for finance skills as selected by corporate recruiters, 2000 ★600★
Business Week's top business schools for general management skills as selected by corporate recruiters, 2000 ★601★
Business Week's top business schools for global scope skills as selected by corporate recruiters, 2000 ★602★
Business Week's top business schools for marketing skills as selected by corporate recruiters, 2000 ★603★
Business Week's top business schools for technology skills as selected by corporate recruiters, 2000 ★604★
Business Week's top business schools with the best placement offices, 2000 ★608★
Business Week's top business schools with the highest percentage of minority enrollment, 2000 ★613★
Business Week's top business schools with the highest percentage of women enrollees, 2000 ★614★
Business Week's top business schools with the most improved program as selected by corporate recruiters, 2000 ★618★
Business Week's top business schools with the most innovative curriculum as selected by corporate recruiters, 2000 ★619★
Highest post-MBA salaries for students enrolled in *Business Week*'s top business schools, 1999 ★631★
Highest pre-MBA salaries for students enrolled in *Business Week*'s top business schools, 1999 ★632★
Median starting salaries of graduates from *U.S. News & World Report*'s top 10 graduate business schools, 2001 ★636★
Out-of-state tuition and fees for *U.S. News & World Report*'s top 10 graduate business schools, 2001 ★637★
Percentage of applicants accepted at *Business Week*'s top business schools, 2000 ★638★
Percentage of employed graduates at *U.S. News & World Report*'s top 10 graduate business schools, 2001 ★639★
Percentage of graduates earning over $100,000 from *Business Week*'s top business schools, 1999 ★640★
Percentage of graduates employed within 3 months of graduation from *U.S. News & World Report*'s top 10 graduate business schools, 2001 ★641★
Top graduate business schools, 2001 ★649★
Top graduate business schools by reputation as determined by academic personnel, 2001 ★650★
Top graduate business schools by reputation, as determined by recruiters, 2001 ★651★
Academics' choices for best graduate accounting programs, 2001 ★659★
Academics' choices for best graduate finance programs, 2001 ★662★
Academics' choices for best graduate general management programs, 2001 ★666★
Academics' choices for best graduate international business programs, 2001 ★668★
Academics' choices for best graduate marketing programs, 2001 ★670★
Academics' choices for best graduate quantitative analysis programs, 2001 ★673★
Academics' choices for best graduate production/operations management programs, 2001 ★674★
Average GMAT scores for *U.S. News & World Report*'s top 10 graduate business schools, 2000 ★2529★

Northwood Middle School
Outstanding secondary schools in Chicago, Illinois ★4110★

Norton
Publishers, journals and proceedings with the lowest citations (Class 6) ★2571★

Norton; Alan
Top pay and benefits for the chief executive and top paid employees at St. Olaf College ★3484★

Norton Antivirus 2000 6.0
Top selling software in all categories, 2000 ★1602★

Norwalk Community-Technical College
Lowest undergraduate tuition and fees at colleges and universities in Connecticut ★1491★

Norway
Countries with the most computers per capita, 2000 ★1604★
Countries with the highest percentage of workers satisfied with their job ★2242★
Countries with the highest spending per student on higher education, 1997 ★2488★
Most wired countries, 2001 ★2596★
Institute for Scientific Information periodical prices by country, 2001 ★2922★
Countries spending the highest percentage of gross domestic product on education ★4060★

Norwich University
Undergraduate tuition and fees at colleges and universities in Vermont ★1563★

Norwood Park Elementary School
Chicago neighborhood schools with the highest ISAT scores in reading and math ★4004★
Illinois elementary schools chosen to be 'demonstration sites' for struggling schools ★4006★

Nory Ryan's Song
Booklist's most recommended historical fiction for youths, 2001 ★314★
Most notable books for middle readers, 2001 ★317★
Most notable children's recordings, 2001 ★320★
Most notable fiction books for young adults, 2001 ★322★

Not for Ourselves Alone: The Story of Elizabeth Cady Stanton and Susan B. Anthony
Outstanding videos for library collections, 2000 ★2892★

Nothing Like It in the World
Longest-running nonfiction hardcover bestsellers, 2000 ★281★

Notre Dame Academy
Outstanding secondary schools in Cincinnati, Ohio-Kentucky-Indiana ★4112★
Outstanding secondary schools in Los Angeles-Long Beach, California ★4167★
Outstanding secondary schools in Toledo, Ohio ★4241★

Notre Dame College
U.S. News & World Report's northern regional universities with the highest percentage of full-time faculty, 2000-01 ★1422★
U.S. News & World Report's northern regional universities with the highest proportion of classes with 20 students of less, 2000-01 ★1423★
Highest undergraduate tuition and fees at colleges and universities in New Hampshire ★1531★
U.S. News & World Report's western regional universities with the highest proportion of classes with 20 students or less, 2000-01 ★1585★
U.S. colleges and universities awarding the most psychology master's degrees to Asian Americans ★1798★
Average faculty salaries for institutions of higher education in California, 2000-01 ★3692★
Average faculty salaries for institutions of higher education in New Hampshire, 2000-01 ★3716★
Average faculty salaries for institutions of higher education in Ohio, 2000-01 ★3722★

Notre Dame High School
Outstanding secondary schools in Los Angeles-Long Beach, California ★4167★

Notre Dame (MD); College of
First-year student's choices for exemplary master's institutions ★2536★
Women's colleges granting physics bachelor's degrees, 2000 ★2982★

Average faculty salaries for institutions of higher education in Maryland, 2000-01 ★3707★

Notre Dame School
Outstanding Catholic high schools in Metro New York ★4076★

Notre Dame; University of
Division I-A all-time percentage leaders ★127★
U.S. catholic universities with the highest enrollment, 1999 ★864★
Division I NCAA colleges with the highest graduation rates for female athletes, 1990-91 to 1993-94 ★931★
Division I NCAA colleges with the highest graduation rates for football players, 1990-91 to 1993-94 ★933★
Division I NCAA colleges with the highest graduation rates for male athletes, 1990-91 to 1993-94 ★934★
Division I NCAA colleges with the highest graduation rates for male basketball players, 1990-91 to 1993-94 ★935★
U.S. colleges and universities least accepting of alternative lifestyles ★985★
U.S. colleges and universities where intercollegiate sports are popular ★995★
U.S. colleges and universities where intramural sports are popular ★997★
U.S. colleges and universities where the general student body puts a strong emphasis on athletic events ★1007★
U.S. colleges and universities without a diverse student body ★1046★
U.S. News & World Report's national universities with the best freshmen retention rates, 2000-01 ★1128★
U.S. News & World Report's national universities with the best graduation and retention rank, 2000-01 ★1129★
U.S. News & World Report's national universities with the highest alumni giving rank, 2000-01 ★1132★
U.S. News & World Report's national universities with the highest graduation rate, 1999 ★1134★
U.S. News & World Report's national universities with the highest proportion of alumni support, 2000-01 ★1137★
Colleges and universities with the largest endowments, 2000 ★1237★
Highest undergraduate tuition and fees at colleges and universities in Indiana ★1502★
Academics' choices for best trial advocacy programs, 2001 ★2633★
Law schools with the best law and religion (excluding First Amendment issues) faculty, 1999-2000 ★2658★
University research libraries in the U.S. and Canada with the largest increases in total expenditures from 1993-94 to 1998-99 ★2708★
Women faculty in Ph.D. physics departments at U.S. institutions, 1998 ★2981★
Top religion research-doctorate programs as evaluated by the National Research Council ★3093★
Average faculty salaries for institutions of higher education in Indiana, 2000-01 ★3701★

Nouveau Journal de Chemie
Chemistry journals by citation impact, 1981-99 ★808★

Nova Scotia
Canadian provinces by teaching days per year ★4058★

Nova Southeastern University
U.S. News & World Report's national universities with the highest proportion of classes with less than 20 students, 2000-01 ★1138★
Total baccalaureate education degrees awarded to African Americans from U.S. colleges and universities, 1997-98 ★1711★
Total baccalaureate education degrees awarded to Hispanic Americans from U.S. colleges and universities, 1997-98 ★1713★
Traditionally white institutions awarding the most master's degrees to African Americans ★1755★
U.S. colleges and universities awarding the most business management and administrative services master's degrees to African Americans ★1759★
U.S. colleges and universities awarding the most business management and administrative services master's degrees to Hispanic Americans ★1761★
U.S. colleges and universities awarding the most education master's degrees to African Americans ★1769★
U.S. colleges and universities awarding the most education master's degrees to Hispanic Americans ★1771★
U.S. colleges and universities awarding the most health professions and related sciences master's degrees to Hispanic Americans ★1779★
U.S. colleges and universities awarding the most master's degrees to African Americans ★1785★
U.S. colleges and universities awarding the most master's degrees to Hispanic Americans ★1787★
U.S. colleges and universities awarding the most master's degrees to minorities ★1788★
U.S. colleges and universities awarding the most psychology master's degrees to Hispanic Americans ★1799★
Traditionally white institutions awarding the most first professional degrees to African Americans ★1842★
U.S. colleges and universities awarding the most first professional degrees to Hispanic Americans ★1845★
U.S. colleges and universities awarding the most health professions and related sciences first professional degrees to Hispanic Americans ★1849★
U.S. colleges and universities awarding the most health professions and related sciences first professional degrees to minorities ★1850★
U.S. colleges and universities awarding the most law and legal studies first professional degrees to Hispanic Americans ★1854★
Top doctorate granting institutions, 1999 ★2047★
Traditionally white institutions awarding the most doctorate degrees to African Americans ★2079★
U.S. colleges and universities awarding the most computer and information sciences doctorate degrees to African Americans ★2089★
U.S. colleges and universities awarding the most doctoral degrees to Hispanic Americans from 1995 to 1999 ★2094★
U.S. colleges and universities awarding the most doctorate degrees to African Americans ★2095★
U.S. colleges and universities awarding the most doctorate degrees to Hispanic Americans ★2097★
U.S. colleges and universities awarding the most doctorate degrees to minorities ★2098★
U.S. colleges and universities awarding the most doctorates in all fields, 1999 ★2100★
U.S. colleges and universities awarding the most doctorates in education, 1999 ★2101★
U.S. colleges and universities awarding the most doctorates in professional and other fields, 1999 ★2106★
U.S. colleges and universities awarding the most education doctorate degrees to African Americans ★2108★
U.S. colleges and universities awarding the most education doctorate degrees to Asian Americans ★2109★
U.S. colleges and universities awarding the most psychology doctorate degrees to Hispanic Americans ★2122★
U.S. institutions awarding the most doctorate degrees, 1999 ★2132★
Average faculty salaries for institutions of higher education in Florida, 2000-01 ★3696★

Nova Southern University
Institutions awarding the most doctorate degrees to African Americans, 1997-98 ★1948★

Novant Health
Top recruiters for biology/biological science jobs for 2000-01 bachelor's degree recipients ★198★
Top recruiters for accounting jobs for 2000-01 master's degree recipients ★661★
Top recruiters for chemistry jobs for 2000-01 bachelor's degree recipients ★792★
Top recruiters for chemistry jobs for 2000-01 master's degree recipients ★806★
Top recruiters for computer engineering jobs for 2000-01 master's degree recipients ★2400★
Top recruiters for health jobs for 2000-01 bachelor's degree recipients ★2541★
Top recruiters for allied health/biomedical science jobs for 2000-01 master's degree recipients ★2544★
Top recruiters for health jobs for 2000-01 master's degree recipients ★2545★
Top recruiters for medical technology jobs for 2000-01 bachelor's degree recipients ★2881★
Top recruiters for nursing jobs for 2000-01 bachelor's degree recipients ★2898★
Top recruiters for pharmacology/pharmaceutical jobs for 2000-01 bachelor's degree recipients ★2934★
Top recruiters for pharmacology/pharmaceutical jobs for 2000-01 master's degree recipients ★2940★
Top recruiters for social work jobs for 2000-01 master's degree recipients ★4343★

Novant Health, Inc.
Best companies for working mothers ★4446★
Best companies for working mothers in offering advancement opportunities for women ★4447★
Best companies for working mothers in terms of overall work/life support ★4451★

Novartis
Business Week's best companies in Switzerland ★405★

Novell
Business Week's best performing companies with the lowest 1-year sales performance ★421★
Business Week's best performing companies with the lowest 1-year shareholder returns ★422★
Fortune's highest ranked computer software companies, 2000 ★455★

Novi High School
 Outstanding suburban public high schools in Metro Detroit ★4258★
Novo-Nordisk
 Business Week's best companies in Denmark ★391★
NOW Legal Defense and Education Fund
 Most selective internships in the U.S., 2001 ★2610★
Nowak; Paul J.
 Top pay and benefits for the chief executive and top paid employees at Drury University ★3275★
Nowhere Else of Earth
 Booklist's most recommended historical novels, 2001 ★230★
Noyes; Nicole
 Top pay and benefits for the chief executive and top paid employees at New York University ★3419★
Noyori; Ryoji
 American Chemical Society 2001 award winners (Group 4) ★754★
NTT Docomo
 Biggest information technology companies, 2000 ★385★
 Business Week's best companies in Japan ★398★
 Business Week's top companies worldwide ★433★
Nuclear
 Chemistry doctorates awarded at U.S. colleges and universities, by subfield, 1999 ★1889★
 Engineering doctorates awarded at U.S. colleges and universities, by subfield, 1999 ★1923★
 Gender breakdown of chemistry doctorate recipients, by subfield, 1999 ★1929★
 Gender breakdown of engineering doctorate recipients, by subfield, 1999 ★1934★
 Gender breakdown of physics and astronomy doctorate recipients, by subfield, 1999 ★1939★
 Physics and astronomy doctorates awarded at U.S. colleges and universities, by subfield, 1999 ★1994★
 Major subfields of first-year physics and astronomy graduate students who are foreign citizens planning to receive a Ph.D., 1997-98 ★3004★
 Major subfields of first-year physics and astronomy graduate students who are U.S. citizens planning to receive a Ph.D., 1997-98 ★3005★
Nuclear engineer
 Most desirable jobs in production/manufacturing ★2276★
Nuclear physics
 Energy Department research funding, 2001 ★3110★
Nucleic Acids Research
 Top science journals by impact factor ★4281★
Nucor
 Fortune's highest ranked metals companies, 2000 ★476★
 Top metals and mining companies in Standard & Poor's 500, 2001 ★549★
Nueva Enciclopedia Cumbre en Linea
 Outstanding reference sources, 2000 ★370★
Nuland; Sherwin B.
 Booklist's best science and technology books ★366★

Number theory
 Gender breakdown of mathematics doctorate recipients, by subfield, 1999 ★1938★
 Mathematics doctorates awarded at U.S. colleges and universities, by subfield, 1999 ★1951★
Nunez Community College
 Lowest undergraduate tuition and fees at colleges and universities in Louisiana ★1511★
Nunnally; Jerry E.
 Top pay and benefits for the chief executive and top paid employees at the California Institute of Technology ★3521★
Nurse (registered)
 Jobs with the most stringent quotas ★2259★
Nurse's aide
 Jobs with the worst income scores ★2261★
Nursing
 Gender breakdown of health sciences doctorate recipients, by subfield, 1999 ★1935★
 Health sciences doctorates awarded at U.S. colleges and universities, by subfield, 1999 ★1944★
 Top health professions majors for accepted applicants to U.S. medical schools, 1999-2000 ★2852★
Nursing aides and attendants
 Occupations with the largest projected employment growth, 1998-2008 ★2312★
 Projected employment growth for selected occupations that require shorter moderate-term on-the-job training, 1998-2008 ★2321★
Nursing education
 Gender breakdown of teaching fields doctorate recipients, by subfield, 1999 ★1943★
 Teaching fields doctorates awarded at U.S. colleges and universities, by subfield, 1999 ★2046★
NUS Business School, Singapore
 Asiaweek's best M.B.A. programs ★590★
Nutritional sciences
 Biological sciences doctorates awarded at U.S. colleges and universities, by subfield, 1999 ★1887★
 Gender breakdown of biological sciences doctorate recipients, by subfield, 1999 ★1927★
Nutting; Willard H.
 Top pay and benefits for the chief executive and top paid employees at the University of San Francisco ★3566★
Nu'uanu Elementary School
 All-USA Teacher Teams, First Team, 2000 ★4399★
Nuzzo; Angelica
 Radcliffe Institute for Advanced Study fellowship recipients in the field of philosophy, 2000-01 ★2946★
Nvidia
 Most profitable information technology companies, 2000 ★527★
 Top information technology companies, 2000 ★544★
Nyack College
 Institutions censured by the American Association of University Professors, 2001 ★1067★
Nyack High School
 Outstanding suburban public high schools in Metro New York ★4259★
Nyenhuis; Jacob E.
 Top pay and benefits for the chief executive and top paid employees at Hope College ★3339★

O

O.A. Thorp Scholastic
 Chicago elementary magnet schools with the highest acceptance rates, 2000-01 ★4002★
Oak Grove Intermediate School
 Outstanding secondary schools in Minneapolis-St. Paul, Minnesota-Wisconsin ★4181★
Oak Grove Middle School
 Outstanding secondary schools in Kansas City, Missouri-Kansas ★4158★
 Outstanding secondary schools in St. Louis, Missouri-Illinois ★4216★
 Outstanding secondary schools in San Diego, California ★4220★
Oak Grove School
 Outstanding secondary schools in Hattiesburg, Mississippi ★4148★
Oak Lawn High School, District 218
 Illinois school districts with the most average years of teacher experience ★4012★
Oak Lawn-Hometown, District 123
 Illinois elementary school districts with the highest teacher salaries, 1999 ★3984★
Oak Park High School
 Outstanding secondary schools in Los Angeles-Long Beach, California ★4167★
Oak Park and River Forest District 200
 Illinois high school districts with the highest teacher salaries, 1999 ★3985★
 Illinois school districts spending the most for high school education 1997-98 ★4010★
Oakland, CA
 America's most wired cities with the highest domain density, 2001 ★2574★
 Cities with the highest online spending per Internet user ★2576★
 Cities with the most domains per 1,000 firms ★2579★
Oakland Community College
 Lowest undergraduate tuition and fees at colleges and universities in Michigan ★1519★
Oakland Community College (MI)
 Community colleges in North America with the highest enrollment ★852★
Oakland, MI
 Counties with the highest per capita income ★2561★
Oakland University
 State appropriations for Michigan's institutions of higher education, 2000-01 ★1275★
 Average faculty salaries for institutions of higher education in Michigan, 2000-01 ★3709★
Oakton Community College
 Fall enrollment at Chicago-area public community colleges, by minority percentages, 1999 ★867★
Oakwood College
 Highest undergraduate tuition and fees at colleges and universities in Alabama ★1479★
Oakwood High School
 Outstanding secondary schools in Dayton-Springfield, Ohio ★4122★
Oates; Thomas R.
 Top pay and benefits for the chief executive and top paid employees at Spalding University ★3506★
Oberlin College
 Private, 4-year undergraduate colleges and universities producing the most Ph.D.'s in the life sciences, 1920-1990 ★192★

Private, 4-year undergraduate colleges and universities producing the most Ph.D.'s in the life sciences, 1981-1990 ★193★
U.S. colleges and universities that devote the most course time to discussion ★990★
U.S. colleges and universities where the general student body smokes marijuana ★1011★
U.S. News & World Report's national liberal arts colleges with the highest proportion of classes having 50 or more students, 2000-01 ★1334★
Highest undergraduate tuition and fees at private nonprofit, 4-year or above colleges and universities ★1461★
Highest undergraduate tuition and fees at colleges and universities in Ohio ★1543★
Private, 4-year undergraduate colleges and universities producing the most Ph.D.'s in the computer sciences, 1920-1990 ★1595★
Private, 4-year undergraduate colleges and universities producing the most Ph.D.'s in the computer sciences, 1981-1990 ★1596★
Private, 4-year undergraduate colleges and universities producing the most Ph.D.s in all fields of study, 1920-1990 ★2027★
Private, 4-year undergraduate colleges and universities producing the most Ph.D.'s in all fields of study, 1981-1990 ★2028★
Private, 4-year undergraduate colleges and universities producing the most Ph.D.'s in all fields of study, 1990 ★2029★
Private, 4-year undergraduate colleges and universities producing the most Ph.D.'s in nonscience fields, 1920-1990 ★2030★
Private, 4-year undergraduate colleges and universities producing the most Ph.D.'s in nonscience fields, 1981-1990 ★2031★
Private, 4-year undergraduate colleges and universities producing the most Ph.D.'s in nonscience fields, 1990 ★2032★
Private, 4-year undergraduate colleges and universities producing the most Ph.D.'s in the earth sciences, 1981-1990 ★2151★
Private, 4-year undergraduate colleges and universities producing the most Ph.D.'s in economics, 1920-1990 ★2211★
Private, 4-year undergraduate colleges and universities producing the most Ph.D.'s in economics, 1981-1990 ★2212★
Undergraduate institutions with the most graduates who received Ph.D.s in economics, 1920-1984 ★2214★
Private, 4-year undergraduate colleges and universities producing the most Ph.D.'s in English, 1920-1990 ★2449★
Private, 4-year undergraduate colleges and universities producing the most Ph.D.'s in English, 1981-1990 ★2450★
Bachelor's institutions with the highest enrollment of foreign students, 1998-99 ★2492★
Private, 4-year undergraduate colleges and universities producing the most Ph.D.'s in history, 1920-1990 ★2552★
Private, 4-year undergraduate colleges and universities producing the most Ph.D.'s in history, 1981-1990 ★2553★
Most wired colleges, 2000 ★2595★
Private, 4-year undergraduate colleges and universities producing the most Ph.D.'s in mathematics, 1920-1990 ★2776★
Private, 4-year undergraduate colleges and universities producing the most Ph.D.'s in mathematics, 1981-1990 ★2777★
Institutions in the Worker Rights Consortium ★2913★
Private, 4-year undergraduate colleges and universities producing the most Ph.D.'s in physics and astronomy, 1920-1990 ★2949★
Private, 4-year undergraduate colleges and universities producing the most Ph.D.'s in political science and international relations, 1920-1990 ★3044★
Private, 4-year undergraduate colleges and universities producing the most Ph.D.'s in political science and international relations, 1981-1990 ★3045★
Private, 4-year undergraduate colleges and universities producing the most Ph.D.'s in psychology, 1920-1990 ★3066★
Private, 4-year undergraduate colleges and universities producing the most Ph.D.'s in psychology, 1981-1990 ★3067★
Average faculty salaries for institutions of higher education in Ohio, 2000-01 ★3722★
Private, 4-year undergraduate colleges and universities producing the most Ph.D.'s in the sciences, 1920-1990 ★4294★
Private, 4-year undergraduate colleges and universities producing the most Ph.D.'s in the sciences, 1981-1990 ★4295★
Private, 4-year undergraduate colleges and universities producing the most Ph.D.'s in anthropology and sociology, 1920-1990 ★4344★
Private, 4-year undergraduate colleges and universities producing the most Ph.D.'s in anthropology and sociology, 1981-1990 ★4345★

Oblak; John
Top pay and benefits for the chief executive and top paid employees at Ithaca College ★3351★

O'Brien Academy
Outstanding secondary schools in Albany-Schenectady-Troy, New York ★4079★

O'Brien; Patricia
Top pay and benefits for the chief executive and top paid employees at Simmons College ★3499★

O'Callaghan Middle School
Outstanding secondary schools in Las Vegas, Nevada-Arizona ★4164★

O'Casey; Sean
Top playwrights of the twentieth century ★4436★

OCBC Overseas Chinese Bank
Business Week's best companies in Singapore ★402★

Occidental College
U.S. colleges and universities that devote the most course time to discussion ★990★
U.S. colleges and universities where the general student body puts little emphasis on athletic events ★1009★
Highest undergraduate tuition and fees at colleges and universities in California ★1486★
Private, 4-year undergraduate colleges and universities producing the most Ph.D.'s in the computer sciences, 1920-1990 ★1595★
Private, 4-year undergraduate colleges and universities producing the most Ph.D.'s in the earth sciences, 1981-1990 ★2151★
Private, 4-year undergraduate colleges and universities producing the most Ph.D.'s in economics, 1920-1990 ★2211★
Most wired colleges, 2000 ★2595★
Private, 4-year undergraduate colleges and universities producing the most Ph.D.'s in political science and international relations, 1920-1990 ★3044★
Private, 4-year undergraduate colleges and universities producing the most Ph.D.'s in political science and international relations, 1981-1990 ★3045★
Private, 4-year undergraduate colleges and universities producing the most Ph.D.'s in psychology, 1920-1990 ★3066★
Average faculty salaries for institutions of higher education in California, 2000-01 ★3692★

Occidental Petroleum
Best performing companies in Standard & Poor's 500, 2001 ★382★
Fortune's highest ranked mining and crude oil companies, 2000 ★477★
Top fuel companies in Standard & Poor's 500, 2001 ★541★

Occupational safety/health inspector
'White-collar' jobs considered the most physically demanding ★2285★

Occupational therapist
Jobs with the lowest unemployment ★2258★
Most desirable jobs in healthcare/medicine ★2273★

Ocean
Engineering doctorates awarded at U.S. colleges and universities, by subfield, 1999 ★1923★
Gender breakdown of engineering doctorate recipients, by subfield, 1999 ★1934★

Ocean County College
Lowest undergraduate tuition and fees at colleges and universities in New Jersey ★1534★

Oceania
Region of origin of foreign students enrolled in U.S. institutions of higher education, 1998-99 ★2502★
World regions hosting U.S. students studying abroad, 1998-99 ★2515★

Oceanographer
Jobs with the lowest unemployment ★2258★
Most desirable jobs in math/science ★2274★

Oceanography
Earth, atmosphere, and marine science doctorates awarded at U.S. colleges and universities, by subfield, 1999 ★1909★
Gender breakdown of earth, atmosphere, and marine science doctorate recipients, by subfield, 1999 ★1932★

Oceanography & Marine Biology
Marine and freshwater biology journals with the greatest impact measure, 1981-98 ★196★
Marine and freshwater biology journals with the greatest impact measure, 1994-98 ★197★
Oceanography journals by citation impact, 1981-99 ★2139★
Oceanography journals by citation impact, 1995-99 ★2140★

O'Connell; Heather A.
Top pay and benefits for the chief executive and top paid employees at Wilmington College in Delaware ★3632★

O'Connell; Rev. David M.
Top pay and benefits for the chief executive and top paid employees at the Catholic University of America ★3522★

Oconomowoc High School
Outstanding secondary schools in Milwaukee-Waukesha, Wisconsin ★4180★

Octel Communications
Most selective internships in the U.S., 2001 ★2610★

Top internships in the U.S. with the highest compensation, 2001 ★2611★

Oden; Robert A.
Top pay and benefits for the chief executive and top paid employees at Kenyon College ★3359★

Odessa College
Average faculty salaries for institutions of higher education in Texas, 2000-01 ★3731★

Odon Winkelpleck Memorial Library
Highest Hennen's American Public Library Ratings for libraries serving a population of 1,000 to 2,499 ★2692★

O'Donnell Ewers; Patricia
Top pay and benefits for the chief executive and top paid employees at Pace University ★3435★

O'Donnell; Timothy
Top pay and benefits for the chief executive and top paid employees at Christendom College ★3232★

O'Donovan, S.J.; Reverend Leo J.
Top pay and benefits for the chief executive and top paid employees at Georgetown University ★3306★

Oehling; Richard
Top pay and benefits for the chief executive and top paid employees at Assumption College ★3181★

Oester; John R.
Top pay and benefits for the chief executive and top paid employees at Loyola Marymount University ★3380★

Of Mice and Men
American Library Association's most frequently challenged books of the decade ★224★
American Library Associations most frequently challenged books for the 1990s ★742★
Most frequently banned books in the 1990s ★745★
People for the American Way's list of most frequently challenged books, 1982-1992 ★747★
People for the American Way's list of most frequently challenged books, 1991-1992 ★748★

Ofe; Suellen
Top pay and benefits for the chief executive and top paid employees at Huntingdon College ★3344★

Off to the Sweet Shores of Africa and Other Talking Drum Rhymes
Most notable books for young readers, 2001 ★319★

Office and administrative support supervisors and managers
Occupations with the largest projected employment growth, 1998-2008 ★2312★
Projected employment growth for selected occupations that require long-term on-the-job training, 1998-2008 ★2320★

Office clerks, general
Occupations with the largest projected employment growth, 1998-2008 ★2312★
Projected employment growth for selected occupations that require shorter moderate-term on-the-job training, 1998-2008 ★2321★

Office Depot
Fortune's highest ranked specialty retailers, 2000 ★497★
Top recruiters for business administration jobs for 2000-01 bachelor's degree recipients ★554★

Top recruiters for retail merchandising jobs for 2000-01 bachelor's degree recipients ★556★
Top recruiters for marketing jobs for 2000-01 bachelor's degree recipients ★684★

Office for Civil Rights
2002 budget request for miscellaneous education programs ★2229★
Fiscal 2002 requested budget as compared with Fiscal 2001 budget for the Education Department ★2231★

Office of Job Corps
Top internships in the U.S. with the highest compensation, 2001 ★2611★

Office machine repairer
'Blue-collar' jobs considered the least physically demanding ★2241★
Most desirable technical/repair jobs ★2281★

Offices of physicians
Employment growth percentages for selected industries, 1998-2000 ★2294★

Offner; Elliot M.
Top pay and benefits for the chief executive and top paid employees at Smith College ★3501★

Offset lithographic press operators
Occupations with the highest decline in employment, 1998-2008 ★2310★

Ogden
Fortune's highest ranked outsourcing services companies, 2000 ★483★

Oglala Lakota College
U.S. tribal colleges ★1445★
Lowest undergraduate tuition and fees at colleges and universities in South Dakota ★1557★
Total baccalaureate social sciences and history degrees awarded to Native Americans from U.S. colleges and universities, 1997-98 ★1744★
U.S. institutions awarding the most associate degrees to minorities in ethnic/cultural studies, 1997-98 ★1810★

Ogle; Jeff
Top pay and benefits for the chief executive and top paid employees at Oral Roberts University ★3433★

Oglethorpe University
U.S. colleges and universities with the best financial aid programs ★1030★
U.S. colleges and universities with the worst food service program ★1043★
U.S. News & World Report's national liberal arts colleges with students most in debt, 1999 ★1386★
Highest undergraduate tuition and fees at colleges and universities in Georgia ★1496★
Average faculty salaries for institutions of higher education in Georgia, 2000-01 ★3697★

O'Gorman; James
Top pay and benefits for the chief executive and top paid employees at Wellesley College ★3609★

O'Hara; Heather
All-USA College Academic Second Team, 2001 ★3★

O'Hara; Leo
Top pay and benefits for the chief executive and top paid employees at Woodbury University ★3635★

O'Hara, S.J.; Rev. Joseph A.
Top pay and benefits for the chief executive and top paid employees at Fordham University ★3295★

O'Hare; William T.
Top pay and benefits for the chief executive and top paid employees at Rockford College in Illinois ★3463★

Ohio
People for the American Way's list of states with the most challenges to library and school books, 1982-1992 ★750★
States with the highest enrollment in private 4-year institutions of higher education ★860★
States with the highest enrollment in public 4-year institutions of higher education ★861★
Mean composite ACT scores by state, 2000 ★895★
Mean math SAT scores by state, 2000 ★900★
Mean verbal SAT scores by state, 2000 ★903★
States allocating the largest amount of state tax appropriations for higher education, 2000-01 ★1304★
Total doctorate recipients by state, 1999 ★2054★
States with the most law schools ★2668★
State library associations with most full-time staff ★2681★
State library associations with the highest annual revenue ★2682★
State library associations with the highest conference attendance ★2683★
State library associations with the highest unrestricted net assets ★2684★
State library associations with the largest membership ★2685★
Average Hennen's American Public Library Ratings, by state ★2690★
State grades for affordability of higher education for minority students, 2000 ★2883★
State grades for benefits state receives for educating its minority students, 2000 ★2884★
State grades for completion of higher education by minority students, 2000 ★2885★
State grades for participation of minority students in higher education, 2000 ★2886★
State grades for preparing minority students for higher education, 2000 ★2887★
States with the highest number of high school graduates, 1999-2000 ★3995★
States with the most public school districts ★3999★
States with the highest K-12 public school enrollment ★4034★
States with the highest projected K-12 public school enrollment for 2010 ★4035★
States with the highest funding needs for school-building modernization ★4040★
States with the highest funding needs for school-technology modernization ★4041★
States with the most charter schools ★4048★
States with the most K-12 public schools ★4049★
States with the highest state support for non need-based financial aid for students, 1999-2000 ★4368★

Ohio Dominican College
Average faculty salaries for institutions of higher education in Ohio, 2000-01 ★3722★

Ohio Northern University
U.S. News & World Report's midwestern regional liberal arts colleges with the best student/faculty ratios, 2000-01 ★1339★
U.S. News & World Report's midwestern regional liberal arts colleges with the highest academic reputation scores, 2000-01 ★1340★

OHIO

- *U.S. News & World Report*'s midwestern regional liberal arts colleges with the highest acceptance rates, 2000-01 ★1341★
- *U.S. News & World Report*'s midwestern regional liberal arts colleges with the highest freshmen retention rates, 2000-01 ★1343★
- *U.S. News & World Report*'s midwestern regional liberal arts colleges with the highest percentage of freshmen in the top 25% of their high school class, 2000-01 ★1345★
- *U.S. News & World Report*'s midwestern regional liberal arts colleges with the highest percentage of full-time faculty, 2000-01 ★1346★
- *U.S. News & World Report*'s top midwestern regional liberal arts colleges, 2000-01 ★1349★
- Highest undergraduate tuition and fees at colleges and universities in Ohio ★1543★
- Average faculty salaries for institutions of higher education in Ohio, 2000-01 ★3722★

Ohio State University
- Colleges with the highest number of freshman Merit Scholars, 2000 ★5★
- Division I-A all-time percentage leaders ★127★
- U.S. colleges and universities with the highest average football attendance, 1996-99 ★159★
- Top business schools for within-discipline research performance in production/operations management, 1986-1998 ★648★
- Top business schools for within-discipline research performance in finance, 1986-1998 ★663★
- Degree-granting institutions with the most published pages in *The Journal of Risk and Insurance*, 1987-1996 ★678★
- Four-year institutions with the most drug referrals reported, 1999 ★706★
- Winner of the American Chemical Society's Arthur C. Cope Awards, 2001 ★795★
- Division I NCAA colleges with that graduated less than 20% of their African American male athletes, 1990-91 to 1993-94 ★928★
- Largest degree-granting colleges and universities, by enrollment ★1068★
- Institutions receiving the most corporate gifts, 1999-2000 ★1243★
- State appropriations for Ohio's institutions of higher education, 2000-01 ★1288★
- Total baccalaureate ethnic/cultural studies degrees awarded to African Americans from U.S. colleges and universities, 1997-98 ★1720★
- Total ethnic/cultural studies master's degrees awarded to African Americans from U.S. colleges and universities, 1997-98 ★1747★
- Total ethnic/cultural studies master's degrees awarded to minorities from U.S. colleges and universities, 1997-98 ★1748★
- U.S. institutions awarding the most baccalaureate degrees to African Americans in agribusiness and production, 1998 ★1813★
- U.S. institutions awarding the most baccalaureate degrees to minorities in agribusiness and production, 1998 ★1819★
- Traditionally white institutions awarding the most first professional degrees to African Americans ★1842★
- U.S. colleges and universities awarding the most first professional degrees to African Americans ★1843★
- U.S. colleges and universities awarding the most first professional degrees to Asian Americans ★1844★
- U.S. colleges and universities awarding the most health professions and related sciences first professional degrees to African Americans ★1847★
- U.S. colleges and universities awarding the most health professions and related sciences first professional degrees to Asian Americans ★1848★
- U.S. colleges and universities awarding the most health professions and related sciences first professional degrees to minorities ★1850★
- Doctorate-granting-institutions awarding the most non-U.S. citizen doctoral degrees, 1999 ★1906★
- Traditionally white institutions awarding the most doctorate degrees to African Americans ★2079★
- U.S. colleges and universities awarding the most biological and life sciences doctorate degrees to African Americans ★2082★
- U.S. colleges and universities awarding the most doctoral degrees to Hispanic Americans from 1995 to 1999 ★2094★
- U.S. colleges and universities awarding the most doctorate degrees to African Americans ★2095★
- U.S. colleges and universities awarding the most doctorate degrees to minorities ★2098★
- U.S. colleges and universities awarding the most doctorates in education, 1999 ★2101★
- U.S. colleges and universities awarding the most doctorates in life sciences, 1999 ★2104★
- U.S. colleges and universities awarding the most doctorates in professional and other fields, 1999 ★2106★
- U.S. colleges and universities awarding the most education doctorate degrees to African Americans ★2108★
- Top institutions in systems and software engineering publications ★2332★
- Top industrial engineering research-doctorate programs as evaluated by the National Research Council ★2413★
- Research institutions with the highest enrollment of foreign students, 1998-99 ★2503★
- Faculty's scholarly reputation in the Ph.D.-granting departments of geography, 1925-1982 ★2518★
- Most effective geography research-doctorate programs as evaluated by the National Research Council ★2519★
- Top geography research-doctorate programs as evaluated by the National Research Council ★2520★
- Academics' choices for best dispute resolution programs, 2001 ★2627★
- Law schools with the best health law (excluding medical ethics) faculty, 1999-2000 ★2652★
- Law schools with the best labor law faculty, 1999-2000 ★2656★
- Institutions with the most productive libraries, 1993-1997 ★2678★
- Top linguistics research-doctorate programs as evaluated by the National Research Council ★2733★
- Degrees granted in the ten largest undergraduate journalism and mass communications programs, 1999 ★2745★
- Degrees granted in the ten largest doctoral journalism and mass communications programs, 1999 ★2756★
- U.S. colleges and universities spending the most on chemical research equipment, 1998 ★3100★
- Average faculty salaries for institutions of higher education in Ohio, 2000-01 ★3722★

Ohio State University A&T Institute
- Highest undergraduate tuition and fees at public 2-year colleges and universities ★1462★
- U.S. institutions awarding the most associate degrees to African Americans in agribusiness and production, 1998 ★1805★
- Average faculty salaries for institutions of higher education in Ohio, 2000-01 ★3722★

Ohio State University, Columbus
- U.S. colleges and universities with excellent library facilities ★1025★
- Academics' choices for best administration/supervision graduate programs, 2001 ★4378★
- Academics' choices for best counseling/personnel services graduate programs, 2001 ★4379★
- Academics' choices for best curriculum/instruction graduate programs, 2001 ★4380★
- Academics' choices for best elementary education graduate programs, 2001 ★4383★
- Academics' choices for best secondary education graduate programs, 2001 ★4385★
- Academics' choices for best vocational/technical graduate programs, 2001 ★4387★
- Top graduate education schools by reputation, as determined by superintendents, 2001 ★4397★

Ohio State University, Fisher School of Business
- *U.S. News & World Report*'s undergraduate business programs with the best human resources departments, 2000-01 ★567★
- *U.S. News & World Report*'s undergraduate business programs with the best real estate departments, 2000-01 ★570★

Ohio State University, Lima
- Average faculty salaries for institutions of higher education in Ohio, 2000-01 ★3722★

Ohio State University, Mansfield
- Average faculty salaries for institutions of higher education in Ohio, 2000-01 ★3722★

Ohio State University, Marion
- Average faculty salaries for institutions of higher education in Ohio, 2000-01 ★3722★

Ohio State University Medical Center
- Top rehabilitation hospitals in the U.S., 2000 ★2801★

Ohio State University, Newark
- Average faculty salaries for institutions of higher education in Ohio, 2000-01 ★3722★

Ohio University
- State appropriations for Ohio's institutions of higher education, 2000-01 ★1288★
- U.S. colleges and universities awarding the most social sciences and history master's degrees to African Americans ★1801★
- Average faculty salaries for institutions of higher education in Ohio, 2000-01 ★3722★

Ohio University A&T Institute
- U.S. institutions awarding the most associate degrees to minorities in agribusiness and production, 1998 ★1808★

Ohio University, Athens
- U.S. colleges and universities where fraternities and sororities are popular ★993★
- U.S. colleges and universities where the general student body puts a strong emphasis on socializing ★1008★

Ohio University, Chillicothe
- Average faculty salaries for institutions of higher education in Ohio, 2000-01 ★3722★

Ohio University, Eastern
Average faculty salaries for institutions of higher education in Ohio, 2000-01 ★3722★

Ohio University, Lancaster
Average faculty salaries for institutions of higher education in Ohio, 2000-01 ★3722★

Ohio University, Zanesville
Average faculty salaries for institutions of higher education in Ohio, 2000-01 ★3722★

Ohio Valley College
Division II NCAA colleges with the 0% graduation rates for men's basketball players, 1993-94 ★941★

Division II NCAA colleges with the 0% graduation rates for women's basketball players, 1993-94 ★942★

Division II NCAA colleges with the lowest graduation rates for all sports, 1993-94 ★947★

Highest undergraduate tuition and fees at colleges and universities in West Virginia ★1568★

Average faculty salaries for institutions of higher education in West Virginia, 2000-01 ★3737★

Ohio Wesleyan University
U.S. colleges and universities where students and the local community relate well ★999★

U.S. News & World Report's national liberal arts colleges with students most in debt, 1999 ★1386★

Highest undergraduate tuition and fees at colleges and universities in Ohio ★1543★

Private, 4-year undergraduate colleges and universities producing the most Ph.D.'s in nonscience fields, 1920-1990 ★2030★

Private, 4-year undergraduate colleges and universities producing the most Ph.D.'s in economics, 1920-1990 ★2211★

Undergraduate institutions with the most graduates who received Ph.D.s in economics, 1920-1984 ★2214★

Bachelor's institutions with the highest enrollment of foreign students, 1998-99 ★2492★

Private, 4-year undergraduate colleges and universities producing the most Ph.D.'s in political science and international relations, 1920-1990 ★3044★

Average faculty salaries for institutions of higher education in Ohio, 2000-01 ★3722★

Ohle; John R.
Top pay and benefits for the chief executive and top paid employees at Wartburg College ★3603★

Ohles; Frederik F.
Top pay and benefits for the chief executive and top paid employees at Illinois College ★3345★

O'Hop; Paul A.
Top pay and benefits for the chief executive and top paid employees at Wilkes University ★3627★

Oil and the Macroeconomy Since World War II
Top cited energy papers from 1979 to 1983 ★2464★

Ojima; Iwao
American Chemical Society 2001 award winners (Group 4) ★754★

Okaloosa-Walton Community College
Lowest undergraduate tuition and fees at colleges and universities in Florida ★1495★

Average faculty salaries for institutions of higher education without academic ranks in Florida, 2000-01 ★3745★

Oklahoma
Mean composite ACT scores by state, 2000 ★895★

Mean math SAT scores by state, 2000 ★900★

Mean verbal SAT scores by state, 2000 ★903★

Total doctorate recipients by state, 1999 ★2054★

State grades for affordability of higher education for minority students, 2000 ★2883★

State grades for benefits state receives for educating its minority students, 2000 ★2884★

State grades for completion of higher education by minority students, 2000 ★2885★

State grades for participation of minority students in higher education, 2000 ★2886★

State grades for preparing minority students for higher education, 2000 ★2887★

States with the lowest per-pupil expenditures ★3998★

States with the most public school districts ★3999★

Oklahoma Baptist University
U.S. News & World Report's best undergraduate fees among western regional liberal arts colleges by discount tuition, 2000 ★1384★

Academic reputation scores for *U.S. News & World Report*'s top western regional liberal arts colleges, 2000-01 ★1387★

Acceptance rates for *U.S. News & World Report*'s top western regional liberal arts colleges, 2000-01 ★1388★

Alumni giving rates at *U.S. News & World Report*'s top western regional liberal arts colleges, 2000-01 ★1389★

Average freshmen retention rates for *U.S. News & World Report*'s top western regional liberal arts colleges, 2000-01 ★1390★

Average graduation rates for *U.S. News & World Report*'s top western regional liberal arts colleges, 2000-01 ★1391★

Percentage of freshmen in the top 25% of their high school class at *U.S. News & World Report*'s top western regional liberal arts colleges, 2000-01 ★1392★

Percentage of full-time faculty at *U.S. News & World Report*'s top western regional liberal arts colleges, 2000-01 ★1393★

Proportion of classes having 20 students or less at *U.S. News & World Report*'s top western regional liberal arts colleges, 2000-01 ★1394★

Student/faculty ratios at *U.S. News & World Report*'s top western regional liberal arts colleges, 2000-01 ★1395★

U.S. News & World Report's top western regional liberal arts colleges, 2000-01 ★1396★

Highest undergraduate tuition and fees at colleges and universities in Oklahoma ★1545★

Average faculty salaries for institutions of higher education in Oklahoma, 2000-01 ★3723★

Oklahoma Christian University
Academic reputation scores for *U.S. News & World Report*'s top western regional liberal arts colleges, 2000-01 ★1387★

Acceptance rates for *U.S. News & World Report*'s top western regional liberal arts colleges, 2000-01 ★1388★

Alumni giving rates at *U.S. News & World Report*'s top western regional liberal arts colleges, 2000-01 ★1389★

Average freshmen retention rates for *U.S. News & World Report*'s top western regional liberal arts colleges, 2000-01 ★1390★

Average graduation rates for *U.S. News & World Report*'s top western regional liberal arts colleges, 2000-01 ★1391★

Percentage of full-time faculty at *U.S. News & World Report*'s top western regional liberal arts colleges, 2000-01 ★1393★

Proportion of classes having 20 students or less at *U.S. News & World Report*'s top western regional liberal arts colleges, 2000-01 ★1394★

Student/faculty ratios at *U.S. News & World Report*'s top western regional liberal arts colleges, 2000-01 ★1395★

U.S. News & World Report's top western regional liberal arts colleges, 2000-01 ★1396★

Average faculty salaries for institutions of higher education in Oklahoma, 2000-01 ★3723★

Oklahoma Christian University of Science and Arts
Highest undergraduate tuition and fees at colleges and universities in Oklahoma ★1545★

Oklahoma City Community College
Lowest undergraduate tuition and fees at colleges and universities in Oklahoma ★1546★

Average faculty salaries for institutions of higher education without academic ranks in Oklahoma, 2000-01 ★3763★

Oklahoma City, OK
Cities with the highest percentage of broadband use and interest ★2578★

Oklahoma City University
U.S. News & World Report's best undergraduate fees among western regional universities by discount tuition, 2000 ★1430★

Highest undergraduate tuition and fees at colleges and universities in Oklahoma ★1545★

U.S. News & World Report's western regional universities with the highest proportion of classes with 20 students or less, 2000-01 ★1585★

U.S. News & World Report's western regional universities with the lowest acceptance rates, 2000-01 ★1586★

U.S. colleges and universities awarding the most business management and administrative services master's degrees to Native Americans ★1762★

U.S. colleges and universities awarding the most master's degrees to Native Americans ★1789★

U.S. colleges and universities awarding the most first professional degrees to Native Americans ★1846★

U.S. colleges and universities awarding the most law and legal studies first professional degrees to Native Americans ★1855★

Average faculty salaries for institutions of higher education in Oklahoma, 2000-01 ★3723★

Oklahoma Health Sciences Center; University of
Total baccalaureate health professions and related sciences degrees awarded to Native Americans from U.S. colleges and universities, 1997-98 ★1724★

OKLAHOMA

U.S. colleges and universities awarding the most health professions and related sciences master's degrees to Native Americans ★1780★

U.S. colleges and universities awarding the most master's degrees to Native Americans ★1789★

U.S. colleges and universities awarding the most first professional degrees to Native Americans ★1846★

U.S. colleges and universities awarding the most health professions and related sciences first professional degrees to Native Americans ★1851★

U.S. colleges and universities awarding the most health professions and related sciences doctorate degrees to African Americans ★2114★

U.S. colleges and universities awarding the most health professions and related sciences doctorate degrees to Asian Americans ★2115★

U.S. colleges and universities awarding the most health professions and related sciences doctorate degrees to Hispanic Americans ★2116★

Oklahoma, Norman; University of

Total baccalaureate biology/life sciences degrees awarded to Native Americans from U.S. colleges and universities, 1997-98 ★1682★

Total baccalaureate business management and administrative services degrees awarded to Native Americans from U.S. colleges and universities, 1997-98 ★1686★

Total baccalaureate communications degrees awarded to Native Americans from U.S. colleges and universities, 1997-98 ★1690★

Total baccalaureate degrees awarded to Native Americans from U.S. colleges and universities, 1997-98 ★1710★

Total baccalaureate English language, literature, and letters degrees awarded to Native Americans from U.S. colleges and universities, 1997-98 ★1719★

Total baccalaureate physical sciences degrees awarded to Native Americans from U.S. colleges and universities, 1997-98 ★1736★

Total baccalaureate psychology degrees awarded to Native Americans from U.S. colleges and universities, 1997-98 ★1740★

U.S. colleges and universities awarding the most education master's degrees to Native Americans ★1772★

U.S. colleges and universities awarding the most master's degrees to Native Americans ★1789★

U.S. colleges and universities awarding the most social sciences and history master's degrees to African Americans ★1801★

U.S. colleges and universities awarding the most social sciences and history master's degrees to Asian Americans ★1802★

U.S. colleges and universities awarding the most social sciences and history master's degrees to Hispanic Americans ★1803★

U.S. colleges and universities awarding the most social sciences and history master's degrees to Native Americans ★1804★

U.S. colleges and universities awarding the most first professional degrees to Native Americans ★1846★

U.S. colleges and universities awarding the most law and legal studies first professional degrees to Native Americans ★1855★

Oklahoma Panhandle State University

State appropriations for Oklahoma's institutions of higher education, 2000-01 ★1289★

U.S. News & World Report's western regional liberal arts colleges with students least in debt, 1999 ★1397★

Oklahoma Redhawks Baseball Club

Most selective internships in the U.S., 2001 ★2610★

Oklahoma State University

State appropriations for Oklahoma's institutions of higher education, 2000-01 ★1289★

Total baccalaureate biology/life sciences degrees awarded to Native Americans from U.S. colleges and universities, 1997-98 ★1682★

Total baccalaureate business management and administrative services degrees awarded to Native Americans from U.S. colleges and universities, 1997-98 ★1686★

Total baccalaureate communications degrees awarded to Native Americans from U.S. colleges and universities, 1997-98 ★1690★

Total baccalaureate degrees awarded to Native Americans from U.S. colleges and universities, 1997-98 ★1710★

Total baccalaureate education degrees awarded to Native Americans from U.S. colleges and universities, 1997-98 ★1714★

Total baccalaureate psychology degrees awarded to Native Americans from U.S. colleges and universities, 1997-98 ★1740★

U.S. colleges and universities awarding the most English language/literature/letters master's degrees to Native Americans ★1776★

U.S. colleges and universities awarding the most master's degrees to Native Americans ★1789★

U.S. institutions awarding the most baccalaureate degrees to Native Americans in agribusiness and production, 1998 ★1822★

U.S. institutions awarding the most baccalaureate degrees to Native Americans in agricultural sciences, 1998 ★1823★

U.S. institutions awarding the most master's degrees to minorities in agricultural sciences, 1998 ★1830★

U.S. institutions awarding the most master's degrees to Native Americans in agricultural sciences, 1998 ★1831★

U.S. colleges and universities awarding the most health professions and related sciences first professional degrees to Native Americans ★1851★

U.S. colleges and universities awarding the most doctoral degrees to American Indians and Alaskan Natives from 1995 to 1999 ★2092★

U.S. colleges and universities awarding the most doctorate degrees to Native Americans ★2099★

U.S. colleges and universities awarding the most doctorates in education, 1999 ★2101★

Average faculty salaries for institutions of higher education in Oklahoma, 2000-01 ★3723★

Academics' choices for best vocational/technical graduate programs, 2001 ★4387★

Oklahoma State University, Oklahoma City

Average faculty salaries for institutions of higher education in Oklahoma, 2000-01 ★3723★

Oklahoma State University, Tech

Average faculty salaries for institutions of higher education in Oklahoma, 2000-01 ★3723★

Educational Rankings Annual • 2002

Oklahoma; University of

Colleges with the highest number of freshman Merit Scholars, 2000 ★5★

U.S. universities enrolling the most National Achievement Scholars, 1995 ★10★

Division I-A all-time percentage leaders ★127★

Division I NCAA colleges with that graduated none of their African American male basketball players, 1990-91 to 1993-94 ★930★

State appropriations for Oklahoma's institutions of higher education, 2000-01 ★1289★

U.S. colleges and universities awarding the most doctoral degrees to American Indians and Alaskan Natives from 1995 to 1999 ★2092★

Academics' choices for best graduate petroleum engineering schools, 2000 ★2429★

U.S. News & World Report's graduate engineering programs with the best petroleum departments, 2000-01 ★2431★

Average faculty salaries for institutions of higher education in Oklahoma, 2000-01 ★3723★

Okun; Arthur

Most cited economists ★2185★

Olah; George A.

Winner of the American Chemical Society's Arthur C. Cope Awards, 2001 ★795★

Olathe East High School

Outstanding secondary schools in Kansas City, Missouri-Kansas ★4158★

Olathe South High School

Outstanding secondary schools in Kansas City, Missouri-Kansas ★4158★

O'Laughlin, O.P.; Sister Jeanne

Top pay and benefits for the chief executive and top paid employees at Barry University ★3192★

Old Dominion University

NCAA Division I women's basketball teams with the best scoring margin ★156★

State appropriations for Virginia's institutions of higher education, 2000-01 ★1299★

Total baccalaureate English language, literature, and letters degrees awarded to Native Americans from U.S. colleges and universities, 1997-98 ★1719★

Total baccalaureate health professions and related sciences degrees awarded to Native Americans from U.S. colleges and universities, 1997-98 ★1724★

U.S. colleges and universities awarding the most education master's degrees to African Americans ★1769★

U.S. colleges and universities awarding the most education master's degrees to Native Americans ★1772★

U.S. colleges and universities awarding the most English language/literature/letters master's degrees to African Americans ★1773★

U.S. colleges and universities awarding the most social sciences and history doctorate degrees to African Americans ★2124★

Average faculty salaries for institutions of higher education in Virginia, 2000-01 ★3735★

Old High Middle School

Outstanding secondary schools in Fayetteville-Springdale-Rogers, Arkansas ★4131★

Old Orchard Beach High School

Outstanding secondary schools in Portland, Maine ★4205★

Old Saybrook Middle School
Outstanding secondary schools in New London-Norwich, Connecticut-Rhode Island ★4189★

Oldsmobile
Top internships in the U.S. with the highest compensation, 2001 ★2611★

O'Leary; Daniel J.
Top pay and benefits for the chief executive and top paid employees at Hamilton College ★3319★

O'Leary; K.D.
Most cited authors in the journal *Violence and Victims*, 1990 to 1995 ★1632★

O'Leary; Michael
European business moguls considered the best challengers ★439★

Oligopoly Extraction of a Common Property Natural Resource-The Importance of the Period of Commitment in Dynamic Games
Top cited nonrenewable resource papers from 1984 to 1988 ★2470★

Oliphant; Pat
Top editorial cartoonists used in teaching journalism history ★2770★

Oliphant; Van
Top pay and benefits for the chief executive and top paid employees at William Carey College ★3629★

Oliva; L. Jay
Presidents with the highest pay at Research I and II universities, 1998-99 ★3162★
Top pay and benefits for the chief executive and top paid employees at New York University ★3419★

Olive; David
Top pay and benefits for the chief executive and top paid employees at Pfeiffer University ★3439★

Olive-Harvey College
Fall enrollment at Chicago-area city colleges, by minority percentages, 1999 ★865★

Olive Peirce Middle School
Outstanding secondary schools in San Diego, California ★4220★

Oliver; G. Benjamin
Top pay and benefits for the chief executive and top paid employees at Hiram College ★3333★

Oliver; R.
Highest ranked inactive communication studies researchers ★2748★
Speech communication's most published scholars between 1915-1985 ★4362★

Olivet College
Institutions censured by the American Association of University Professors, 2001 ★1067★
Average faculty salaries for institutions of higher education in Michigan, 2000-01 ★3709★

Olivet Nazarene University
Average faculty salaries for institutions of higher education in Illinois, 2000-01 ★3700★

Olivia
Publishers Weekly Off-the-Cuff Awards winner for most memorable character in a lead role, 2000 ★353★
Most notable books for young readers, 2001 ★319★
Outstanding books for young readers, 2000 ★328★
Outstanding children's picture books, 2000 ★331★
Publishers Weekly Off-the-Cuff Awards winner for favorite picture book of the year, 2000 ★347★

Olle Middle School
Outstanding secondary schools in Houston, Texas ★4150★

Olmsted Falls High School
Outstanding secondary schools in Cleveland-Lorain-Elyria, Ohio ★4114★

Olney Central College
Lowest undergraduate tuition and fees at colleges and universities in Illinois ★1501★

Ology
Most notable children's web sites, 2001 ★2593★

Olsen; Johan P.
Most frequently downloaded *American Political Science Review* articles ★3039★

Olsen; John
Top pay and benefits for the chief executive and top paid employees at Central College in Iowa ★3226★

Olson; Donald
Top pay and benefits for the chief executive and top paid employees at Saint Mary's University of Minnesota ★3482★

Olson; Lute
Coaches winning the most NCAA tournaments ★120★

Olson; M.
U.S. academic economists by mean number of citations, 1971-92 ★2176★
U.S. academic economists by total citations, 1971-92 ★2177★
Authors with the most citations among authors published in *American Political Science Review*, 1974-94 ★3048★

Olympic College
Lowest undergraduate tuition and fees at colleges and universities in Washington ★1567★

Omaha, NE-Council Bluffs, IA
Most polite cities in the U.S. ★3086★

O'Malley; Pat
Most-cited scholars in *Australian and New Zealand Journal of Criminology* ★1636★

O'Malley, S.J.; Rev. Thomas P.
Top pay and benefits for the chief executive and top paid employees at Loyola Marymount University ★3380★

O'Malley; Timothy
Top pay and benefits for the chief executive and top paid employees at Pacific University in Oregon ★3437★

Oman; Michael
Top pay and benefits for the chief executive and top paid employees at the University of Puget Sound ★3557★

Omni Energy Services
Companies with the worst two-year total returns since 1998 ★437★

Omnicom Group
Fortune's highest ranked advertising and marketing companies, 2000 ★445★
Fortune's most admired companies for employee talent ★514★
Fortune's most admired companies for financial soundness ★515★
Fortune's most admired companies for long-term investment value ★517★
Fortune's most admired companies for quality of management ★518★
Fortune's most admired companies for quality of products or services ★519★
Fortune's most admired companies for use of corporate assets ★521★
Top services industries in Standard & Poor's 500, 2001 ★558★

On the Horizon
Top sites for educators ★2605★

On the Intergenerational Allocation of Natural Resources
Top cited nonrenewable resource papers from 1984 to 1988 ★2470★

On-line
Average class size at colleges and universities in the U.S., by state ★1064★

On Money and Markets: A Wall Street Memoir
Library Journal's most notable investing books, 2000 ★264★

On My Honor
Most frequently banned books in the 1990s ★745★

On Our Own Terms: Moyers on Death and Dying in America
Most notable videos for adults, 2001 ★2891★
Outstanding videos for library collections, 2000 ★2892★

On the Same Day in March: A Tour of the World's Weather
Booklist's best science books for children ★310★

On Selecting a Measure of Retrieval Effectiveness
Journal of the American Society for Information Science's best papers, by total citations ★2729★

Onalaska Middle School
Outstanding secondary schools in La Crosse, Wisconsin-Minnesota ★4160★

Oncolink
Medical Library Association's top health related web sites ★2591★

Oncology
Clinical medicine subfields with the highest impact measure, 1981-1997 ★2873★

One Day Longer: Story of the Frontier Strike
Most notable videos for adults, 2001 ★2891★

One Good Turn: A Natural History of the Screwdriver and the Screw
Library Journal's most notable technology books, 2000 ★277★

145th Street: Short Stories
Most notable fiction books for reluctant young adult readers, 2001 ★321★
Most notable fiction books for young adults, 2001 ★322★

One Hundred Years of Solitude
Most frequently banned books in the 1990s ★745★

O'Neill; Eugene
Top playwrights of the twentieth century ★4436★

O'Neill; Kristen
All-America girls' high school basketball 4th team, 2001 ★173★

Oneok
Business Week's best performing companies with the highest 1-year sales performance ★414★
Top utilities companies in Standard & Poor's 500, 2001 ★561★

ONLINE! A Reference Guide to Using Internet Sources
Library Journal's best free reference websites, 2000 ★367★

Online Adventures of Captain Underpants
Most notable children's web sites, 2001 ★2593★

Only Passing Through: The Story of Sojourner Truth
Most notable books for middle readers, 2001 ★317★

Onondaga Community College
Average faculty salaries for institutions of higher education in New York, 2000-01 ★3719★

Ontario
Canadian provinces by teaching days per year ★4058★

Open City Films
Most selective internships in the U.S., 2001 ★2610★

Open University
Top United Kingdom universities by citation impact in the field of geosciences, 1991-95 ★2143★
United Kingdom universities with the greatest impact in geosciences, 1993-97 ★2154★

Operating engineers
Average salaries for occupations requiring on-the-job training ★3119★

Operations Research
Journals with the highest impact factor in the field of management, 1981-96 ★696★
Business and management doctorates awarded at U.S. colleges and universities, by subfield, 1999 ★1888★
Engineering doctorates awarded at U.S. colleges and universities, by subfield, 1999 ★1923★
Gender breakdown of business and management doctorate recipients, by subfield, 1999 ★1928★
Gender breakdown of engineering doctorate recipients, by subfield, 1999 ★1934★
Gender breakdown of mathematics doctorate recipients, by subfield, 1999 ★1938★
Mathematics doctorates awarded at U.S. colleges and universities, by subfield, 1999 ★1951★

Operations research analysts
Projected employment growth for selected occupations that require advanced education, 1998-2008 ★2318★

Operators, fabricators, and laborers
Employment change projections by major occupational group from 1998 to 2008 ★2288★
Employment projections by major occupational group for 2008 ★2291★
Percentages for projected employment growth by occupational group, 1998-2008 ★2314★
Projected employment growth by occupational group, 1998-2008 ★2316★
Internet use by major occupational group, 1998 ★2587★

Oppelt; John A.
Top pay and benefits for the chief executive and top paid employees at Bellarmine University ★3196★

Oppenheimer; Deanna Watson
Highest ranking women at the top public companies, 2000 ★4452★

Optica Acta
Optics journals by citation impact, 1981-99 ★2906★
Optics journals with the greatest impact measure, 1981-98 ★2909★

Optics
Gender breakdown of physics and astronomy doctorate recipients, by subfield, 1999 ★1939★
Physics and astronomy doctorates awarded at U.S. colleges and universities, by subfield, 1999 ★1994★

Optics Letters
Optics journals by citation impact, 1981-99 ★2906★
Optics journals by citation impact, 1995-99 ★2907★
Optics journals by citation impact, 1999 ★2908★
Optics journals with the greatest impact measure, 1981-98 ★2909★
Optics journals with the greatest impact measure, 1994-98 ★2910★

Optics/photonics
Major subfields of first-year physics and astronomy graduate students who are foreign citizens planning to receive a Ph.D., 1997-98 ★3004★
Major subfields of first-year physics and astronomy graduate students who are U.S. citizens planning to receive a Ph.D., 1997-98 ★3005★

Optimal Pricing, Use, and Exploration of Uncertain Natural ChangResource Stocks
Journal of Environmental Economics and Management's best articles in depletable resources and energy ★2462★

Optimal Use of Non-Renewable Resources-Theory of Extraction
Journal of Environmental Economics and Management's best articles in depletable resources and energy ★2462★

Optometrist
Jobs with the lowest unemployment ★2258★

Optometrists
Projected employment growth for selected occupations that require advanced education, 1998-2008 ★2318★

Oracle
Best performing companies in Standard & Poor's 500, 2001 ★382★
Business Week's best companies in terms of share-price gain ★409★
Business Week's best companies in the United States ★411★
Business Week's best performing companies with the highest net margin, 2000 ★419★
Business Week's best performing companies with the highest return on equity, 2000 ★420★
Business Week's top companies worldwide ★433★
Fortune's highest ranked computer software companies, 2000 ★455★
Information technology companies giving the best returns, 2000 ★522★
Most profitable information technology companies, 2000 ★527★
Top information technology companies, 2000 ★544★
Top office equipment and computers companies in Standard & Poor's 500, 2001 ★551★
Largest technology companies in the U.S. in terms of annual revenue, 2000 ★4429★

Oral Roberts University
Division I NCAA colleges with the lowest graduation rates for male athletes, 1990-91 to 1993-94 ★939★

Highest undergraduate tuition and fees at colleges and universities in Oklahoma ★1545★
U.S. News & World Report's western regional universities with students most in debt, 1999 ★1576★
Average faculty salaries for institutions of higher education in Oklahoma, 2000-01 ★3723★

Orange Coast College
Community colleges with the highest enrollment of foreign students, 1998-99 ★2493★

Orange County, CA
U.S. cities with the highest number of high-tech employees, 1998 ★2284★
America's most wired cities, 2001 ★2573★
America's most wired cities with the highest domain density, 2001 ★2574★
Cities with the highest online spending per Internet user ★2576★
Cities with the highest percentage of adults using the Internet at home ★2577★
Cities with the most domains per 1,000 firms ★2579★

Orange County Community College
Lowest undergraduate tuition and fees at colleges and universities in New York ★1538★
Average faculty salaries for institutions of higher education in New York, 2000-01 ★3719★

Orange High School
Outstanding secondary schools in Cleveland-Lorain-Elyria, Ohio ★4114★

Orangeburg-Calhoun Technical College
Lowest undergraduate tuition and fees at colleges and universities in South Carolina ★1555★

Oravec, T.O.R.; Rev. Christian
Top pay and benefits for the chief executive and top paid employees Saint Francis College in Pennsylvania ★3641★

Orchard Lake Middle School
Outstanding secondary schools in Detroit, Michigan ★4125★

Orcutt Junior High School
Outstanding secondary schools in Santa Barbara-Santa Maria-Lompoc, California ★4224★

Order, Law, and Crime: An Introduction to Criminology
Most-cited works in critical criminology publications ★1645★

Ordeshook; Peter C.
Authors most frequently published in *American Political Science Review*, 1974-94 ★3047★

Ordina
Best small companies worldwide ★384★

Ordinary People
People for the American Way's list of most frequently challenged books, 1982-1992 ★747★

Ordinary Resurrections: Children in the Years of Hope
American School Board Journal's notable education books, 2000 ★225★
Christopher Awards winners for adult literature, 2000 ★235★
Outstanding social sciences books, 2000 ★292★

Ore Geology Reviews
Geology journals with the greatest impact measure, 1994-98 ★2526★

L'Oreal
Business Week's best companies in France ★393★

Oregon
- People for the American Way's list of states with the most challenges to library and school books, 1982-1992 ★750★
- Mean composite ACT scores by state, 2000 ★895★
- Mean math SAT scores by state, 2000 ★900★
- Mean verbal SAT scores by state, 2000 ★903★
- Average class size at colleges and universities in the U.S., by state ★1064★
- Total doctorate recipients by state, 1999 ★2054★
- Hispanic American enrollment at Hispanic-serving institutions of higher education, by state, 1997 ★2547★
- State grades for affordability of higher education for minority students, 2000 ★2883★
- State grades for benefits state receives for educating its minority students, 2000 ★2884★
- State grades for completion of higher education by minority students, 2000 ★2885★
- State grades for participation of minority students in higher education, 2000 ★2886★
- State grades for preparing minority students for higher education, 2000 ★2887★

Oregon Health Sciences University
- U.S. universities with the greatest impact in microbiology, 1994-98 ★217★
- State appropriations for Oregon's institutions of higher education, 2000-01 ★1290★
- Academics' choices for best family medicine programs, 2001 ★2820★
- Academics' choices for best rural medicine programs, 2001 ★2824★
- Acceptance rates for *U.S. News & World Report*'s top 10 primary-care medical schools, 2001 ★2826★
- Average MCAT scores at *U.S. News & World Report*'s top 10 primary-care medical schools, 2001 ★2835★
- Average undergraduate GPA at *U.S. News & World Report*'s top 10 primary-care medical schools, 2001 ★2837★
- Faculty-student ratios at *U.S. News & World Report*'s top 10 primary-care medical schools, 2001 ★2841★
- Out-of-state tuition and fees at *U.S. News & World Report*'s top 10 primary-care medical schools, 2001 ★2846★
- Percentage of graduates entering *U.S. News & World Report*'s top 10 primary-care medical schools, 2001 ★2848★
- Top primary-care medical schools, 2001 ★2856★
- Top primary-care medical schools by reputation, as determined by academic personnel, 2001 ★2857★
- U.S. universities with the greatest impact in pharmacology, 1994-98 ★2936★

Oregon Institute of Technology
- Average faculty salaries for institutions of higher education in Oregon, 2000-01 ★3724★

Oregon State University
- Division I NCAA colleges with that graduated none of their African American male basketball players, 1990-91 to 1993-94 ★930★
- U.S. institutions awarding the most baccalaureate degrees to Asian Americans in agribusiness and production, 1998 ★1815★
- Top oceanography research-doctorate programs as evaluated by the National Research Council ★2153★
- Women faculty in Ph.D. physics departments at U.S. institutions, 1998 ★2981★
- Average faculty salaries for institutions of higher education in Oregon, 2000-01 ★3724★
- U.S. universities with the highest concentration of papers published in the field of aquatic sciences, 1995-99 ★4289★

Oregon Trail Junior High School
- Outstanding secondary schools in Kansas City, Missouri-Kansas ★4158★

Oregon; University of
- Institutions, by adjusted authorship, with the most published authors in the *Journal of Business Research*, 1985 to 1999 ★694★
- Four-year institutions with the most drug referrals reported, 1999 ★706★
- *Fiske Guide*'s best buys for public colleges and universities, 2001 ★1460★
- U.S. colleges and universities awarding the most doctorate degrees to Native Americans ★2099★
- U.S. universities with the highest concentration of education papers published, 1994-98 ★2223★
- U.S. universities with the highest concentrations in literary criticism, 1992-96 ★2735★
- Institutions in the Worker Rights Consortium ★2913★
- Average faculty salaries for institutions of higher education in Oregon, 2000-01 ★3724★
- Academics' choices for best special education graduate programs, 2001 ★4386★

Oregon University System
- State appropriations for Oregon's institutions of higher education, 2000-01 ★1290★

Organ. Behavior
- Journals with the highest impact factor in the field of management, 1981-96 ★696★

Organic
- Chemistry doctorates awarded at U.S. colleges and universities, by subfield, 1999 ★1889★
- Gender breakdown of chemistry doctorate recipients, by subfield, 1999 ★1929★

Organic chemistry
- Subjects required by the most U.S. medical schools for the 2000-01 entering class ★2850★

Organic Mass Spectrometry
- Spectroscopy journals by citation impact, 1995-99 ★4360★

Organization of American Historians
- Scholarly societies with the highest membership, 1999 ★3052★

Organization Science
- Top management journals by core impact ★547★

Organizational behavior
- Business and management doctorates awarded at U.S. colleges and universities, by subfield, 1999 ★1888★
- Gender breakdown of business and management doctorate recipients, by subfield, 1999 ★1928★

Organizational Behavior and Human Decision Processes
- Top management journals ★546★
- Top management journals by core impact ★547★

Organizational communication
- Areas of specialization in journalism and mass communications programs with the highest enrollment, 1999 ★2740★

Organometallics
- Inorganic and nuclear chemistry journals by citation impact, 1981-99 ★811★
- Inorganic and nuclear chemistry journals by citation impact, 1995-99 ★812★
- Inorganic and nuclear chemistry journals by citation impact, 1999 ★813★

Oriole Park Elementary School
- Chicago neighborhood schools with the highest ISAT scores in reading and math ★4004★
- Illinois elementary schools chosen to be 'demonstration sites' for struggling schools ★4006★

Orlando, FL
- Cities with the most Yahoo! listings per million residents ★2580★
- U.S. cities with the most wired households, 2001 ★2606★

O'Rourke; Joseph
- Top pay and benefits for the chief executive and top paid employees at Smith College ★3501★

Orozco Elementary School
- Illinois elementary schools chosen to be 'demonstration sites' for struggling schools ★4006★

Orthopedic impairments
- Disabled students served in U.S. public school programs, 1998-99 ★1877★

Orton; Joe
- Top playwrights of the twentieth century ★4436★

Orwell; George
- Top essayists from 1946-1996 ★2445★

Orwell's Luck
- *Booklist*'s most recommended fantasy books for youth ★312★
- Outstanding books for middle readers, 2000 ★326★

Osborne; John
- Top playwrights of the twentieth century ★4436★

Osborne Jr.; Murphy M.
- Top pay and benefits for the chief executive and top paid employees at Meredith College ★3399★

Osborne Jr.; Robert H.
- Top pay and benefits for the chief executive and top paid employees at Georgetown College in Kentucky ★3305★

Osborne; Leslie
- All-America girls' high school soccer team midfielders, 2001 ★177★

Osborne; Mary Pope
- Outstanding children's picture books, 2000 ★331★

Osborne; Tom
- Division I-A all-time coaching victories ★126★

Oscar Meyer Wienermobile
- Most selective internships in the U.S., 2001 ★2610★
- Top internships in the U.S. with the highest compensation, 2001 ★2611★

Oscar Wilde: A Certain Genius
- Outstanding biography books, 2000 ★288★

Osceola: Memories of a Sharecropper's Daughter
- *Booklist*'s most recommended black history books for youth ★311★
- Most notable books for middle readers, 2001 ★317★
- *Smithsonian*'s best books for children ages 10 and up ★365★

Osgood; Russell K.
- Presidents with the highest pay at Baccalaureate I colleges, 1998-99 ★3159★

Top pay and benefits for the chief executive and top paid employees at Grinnell College ★3315★

O'Shea; Donald
Top pay and benefits for the chief executive and top paid employees at Mount Holyoke College ★3409★

Oshkosh Truck
Fortune's highest ranked motor vehicles companies, 2000 ★481★

Osnes; Larry
Top pay and benefits for the chief executive and top paid employees at Hamline University ★3320★

Osteopath
Jobs with the longest work weeks ★2257★
'White-collar' jobs considered the most physically demanding ★2285★

Osteopathic Medicine; College of
U.S. colleges and universities awarding the most first professional degrees to Native Americans ★1846★

Osteopathic Medicine of Oklahoma; College of
U.S. colleges and universities awarding the most health professions and related sciences first professional degrees to Native Americans ★1851★

Ostriker; Jeremiah P.
Top pay and benefits for the chief executive and top paid employees at Princeton University ★3446★

Ostrom; Charles W.
Authors most frequently published in *American Political Science Review*, 1974-94 ★3047★

Ostrowski; Thomas S.
Top pay and benefits for the chief executive and top paid employees at Gannon University ★3302★

Otero Junior College
Lowest undergraduate tuition and fees at colleges and universities in Colorado ★1489★

Ott; W. Richard
Top pay and benefits for the chief executive and top paid employees at Alfred University ★3169★

Ottawa; University of
Canadian medical/doctoral universities by alumni support, 2000 ★1172★
Canadian medical/doctoral universities by award-winning faculty members, 2000 ★1173★
Canadian medical/doctoral universities by class size at the first- and second-year level, 2000 ★1174★
Canadian medical/doctoral universities by class size at the third- and forth-year level, 2000 ★1175★
Canadian medical/doctoral universities by classes taught by tenured faculty, 2000 ★1176★
Canadian medical/doctoral universities by faculty members with Ph.D.'s, 2000 ★1177★
Canadian medical/doctoral universities by international graduate students, 2000 ★1178★
Canadian medical/doctoral universities by library acquisitions, 2000 ★1179★
Canadian medical/doctoral universities by library expenses, 2000 ★1180★
Canadian medical/doctoral universities by library holdings, 2000 ★1181★
Canadian medical/doctoral universities by library holdings per student, 2000 ★1182★
Canadian medical/doctoral universities by medical/science grants per faculty member, 2000 ★1184★
Canadian medical/doctoral universities by operating budget per student, 2000 ★1185★
Canadian medical/doctoral universities by percentage of operating budget allocated to scholarships, 2000 ★1186★
Canadian medical/doctoral universities by percentage of operating budget allocated to student services, 2000 ★1187★
Canadian medical/doctoral universities by reputation, 2000 ★1188★
Canadian medical/doctoral universities by social science/humanities grants per faculty member, 2000 ★1189★
Canadian medical/doctoral universities by students from out of province, 2000 ★1190★
Canadian medical/doctoral universities by students winning national awards, 2000 ★1191★
Canadian universities by graduation rate, 2000 ★1214★
Canadian universities chosen as being value added, 2000 ★1216★
Top Canadian medical/doctoral universities, 2000 ★1221★
Average faculty salaries for institutions of higher education in Kansas, 2000-01 ★3703★
Canadian universities with the greatest impact in neuroscience, 1993-97 ★4305★

Otterbein College
U.S. News & World Report's midwestern regional liberal arts colleges with the highest academic reputation scores, 2000-01 ★1340★
U.S. News & World Report's midwestern regional liberal arts colleges with the highest acceptance rates, 2000-01 ★1341★
U.S. News & World Report's midwestern regional liberal arts colleges with the highest alumni giving rates, 2000-01 ★1342★
U.S. News & World Report's midwestern regional liberal arts colleges with the highest freshmen retention rates, 2000-01 ★1343★
U.S. News & World Report's midwestern regional liberal arts colleges with the highest graduation rates, 2000-01 ★1344★
U.S. News & World Report's top midwestern regional liberal arts colleges, 2000-01 ★1349★
Average faculty salaries for institutions of higher education in Ohio, 2000-01 ★3722★

Otwell Middle School
Outstanding secondary schools in Atlanta, Georgia ★4087★

Ouachita Baptist University
U.S. News & World Report's southern regional liberal arts colleges with the highest alumni giving rates, 2000-01 ★1371★
U.S. News & World Report's southern regional liberal arts colleges with the lowest acceptance rates, 2000-01 ★1377★
U.S. News & World Report's best undergraduate fees among southern regional liberal arts colleges by discount tuition, 2000 ★1383★
Highest undergraduate tuition and fees at colleges and universities in Arkansas ★1484★
Average faculty salaries for institutions of higher education in Arkansas, 2000-01 ★3691★

Ouch!
Most notable children's recordings, 2001 ★320★

Our Lady of Divine Providence
Outstanding secondary schools in New Orleans, Louisiana ★4190★

Our Lady of Fatima School
Outstanding secondary schools in Huntington-Ashland, West Virginia-Kentucky-Ohio ★4151★

Our Lady of the Hamptons Regional
Outstanding secondary schools in Long Island, New York ★4165★

Our Lady of Holy Cross College
U.S. News & World Report's southern regional liberal arts colleges with students most in debt, 1999 ★1367★
Highest undergraduate tuition and fees at colleges and universities in Louisiana ★1510★

Our Lady of the Lake University, San Antonio
Total baccalaureate computer and information science degrees awarded to Hispanic Americans from U.S. colleges and universities, 1997-98 ★1693★
U.S. colleges and universities awarding the most business management and administrative services master's degrees to Hispanic Americans ★1761★
U.S. colleges and universities awarding the most English language/literature/letters master's degrees to Hispanic Americans ★1775★
Average faculty salaries for institutions of higher education in Texas, 2000-01 ★3731★

Our Lady of Lourdes Academy
Outstanding secondary schools in Miami, Florida ★4178★

Our Lady of Peace Academy
Outstanding secondary schools in San Diego, California ★4220★

Our Lady of Perpetual Help School
Outstanding secondary schools in Columbus, Ohio ★4118★

Our Lady Star of the Sea School
Outstanding secondary schools in Atlantic-Cape May, New Jersey ★4088★

Our Lady of the Wayside School
Outstanding secondary schools in Chicago, Illinois ★4110★

Outback Steakhouse
Fortune's highest ranked food services companies, 2000 ★465★

Ove Arup & Partners
Most selective internships in the U.S., 2001 ★2610★

Overlook Press
Small publishers with the highest sales growth between 1997 and 1999 ★3073★

Owada; Yasuyuki
Top pay and benefits for the chief executive and top paid employees at the University of Redlands ★3558★

Owens; Billy R.
Top pay and benefits for the chief executive and top paid employees at Tuskegee University ★3583★

Owens Community College, Findlay
Lowest undergraduate tuition and fees at colleges and universities in Ohio ★1544★

Owens Community College, Toledo
Lowest undergraduate tuition and fees at colleges and universities in Ohio ★1544★

Owens Corning
Fortune's highest ranked building materials and glass companies, 2000 ★451★

Fortune's least admired companies for financial soundness ★507★
Fortune's least admired companies for long-term investment value ★509★
Owens-Illinois
Fortune's highest ranked building materials and glass companies, 2000 ★451★
Owens; Kathleen
Top pay and benefits for the chief executive and top paid employees Saint Francis College in Pennsylvania ★3641★
Owensboro Community College
Lowest undergraduate tuition and fees at colleges and universities in Kentucky ★1509★
Owensboro, KY
U.S. cities with the lowest rate of violent crime ★3088★
Oxford College of Emory University
Highest undergraduate tuition and fees at colleges and universities in Georgia ★1496★
Oxford Companion to Crime and Mystery Writing
Outstanding reference sources, 2001 ★371★
Oxford Companion to English Literature
Selected new editions and supplements reference books, 2000 ★372★
Oxford Companion to Fairy Tales
Outstanding reference sources, 2000 ★370★
Outstanding reference sources, 2001 ★371★
Oxford Dictionary for Writers and Editors
Selected new editions and supplements reference books, 2000 ★372★
Oxford English Dictionary Online
Outstanding reference sources, 2000 ★370★
Oxford First Book of Art
Booklist's best art books for young people ★308★
Oxford Middle School
Outstanding secondary schools in Kansas City, Missouri-Kansas ★4158★
Oxford, MS
Best small towns to live in ★3085★
Oxford-Reading
Cities with the highest productivity of paper in the discipline of immunology, 1994-96 ★2871★
Oxford; University of
United Kingdom universities with the greatest impact in chemistry, 1993-97 ★807★
Top United Kingdom universities by citation impact in the field of geosciences, 1991-95 ★2143★
Top United Kingdom universities by total citations in the field of ecology/environmental, 1991-95 ★2146★
Top United Kingdom universities by total citations in the field of geosciences, 1991-95 ★2147★
Top United Kingdom universities by total citations in the field of plant and animal sciences, 1991-95 ★2148★
United Kingdom universities contributing the most papers in the field of economics and business, 1993-97 ★2203★
Oxford University Press
Book publishers with the most citations (Class 4) ★2565★
Oxnard-Ventura, CA
America's most wired cities, 2001 ★2573★
Cities with the highest percentage of broadband use and interest ★2578★

Cities with the most domains per 1,000 firms ★2579★
Oyewole; Sandra
Top pay and benefits for the chief executive and top paid employees at Trinity College in Washington D.C. ★3578★
Oz; Mehmet C.
Top pay and benefits for the chief executive and top paid employees at Columbia University ★3251★
Ozarks; College of the
U.S. colleges and universities where the general student body does not drink beer ★1004★
U.S. colleges and universities where the general student body does not smoke marijuana ★1006★
U.S. colleges and universities with a large student body of conservative Republicans ★1016★
U.S. News & World Report's midwestern regional liberal arts colleges with students least in debt, 1999 ★1337★
U.S. News & World Report's midwestern regional liberal arts colleges with the highest percentage of full-time faculty, 2000-01 ★1346★
U.S. News & World Report's midwestern regional liberal arts colleges with the lowest acceptance rates, 2000-01 ★1348★
Average faculty salaries for institutions of higher education in Missouri, 2000-01 ★3712★
Ozarks; University of the
U.S. News & World Report's southern regional liberal arts colleges with the highest percentage of full-time faculty, 2000-01 ★1374★
U.S. News & World Report's southern regional liberal arts colleges with the highest proportion of classes having 20 students or less, 2000-01 ★1375★
U.S. News & World Report's southern regional liberal arts colleges with the lowest acceptance rates, 2000-01 ★1377★
U.S. News & World Report's best undergraduate fees among southern regional liberal arts colleges by discount tuition, 2000 ★1383★
Highest undergraduate tuition and fees at colleges and universities in Arkansas ★1484★
Average faculty salaries for institutions of higher education in Arkansas, 2000-01 ★3691★

P

PA Dept. Environmental Protection
Top recruiters for biology/biological science jobs for 2000-01 bachelor's degree recipients ★198★
Top recruiters for chemistry jobs for 2000-01 bachelor's degree recipients ★792★
Top recruiters for chemical engineering jobs for 2000-01 bachelor's degree recipients ★2343★
Top recruiters for environmental engineering jobs for 2000-01 bachelor's degree recipients ★2357★
Top recruiters for geology/geophysics jobs for 2000-01 bachelor's degree recipients ★2522★
PA Department of Transportation
Top recruiters for multidisciplinary engineers jobs for 2000-01 bachelor's degree recipients ★2335★

Top recruiters for civil engineering jobs for 2000-01 bachelor's degree recipients ★2346★
Paccar
Business Week's best performing companies with the lowest 1-year sales performance ★421★
Fortune's highest ranked motor vehicles companies, 2000 ★481★
Top automotive companies in Standard & Poor's 500, 2001 ★530★
Pace University
Division II NCAA colleges with the 100% graduation rates for women's basketball players, 1993-94 ★944★
Division II NCAA colleges with the highest graduation rates for all sports, 1993-94 ★945★
U.S. colleges and universities awarding the most communications master's degrees to Asian Americans ★1764★
U.S. colleges and universities awarding the most computer and information sciences master's degrees to African Americans ★1766★
U.S. colleges and universities awarding the most computer and information sciences master's degrees to Hispanic Americans ★1768★
Academics' choices for best environmental law programs, 2001 ★2628★
Law library web sites, by visibility ★2687★
Average faculty salaries for institutions of higher education in New York, 2000-01 ★3719★
Pace University, White Plains
U.S. colleges and universities awarding the most computer and information sciences master's degrees to African Americans ★1766★
U.S. colleges and universities awarding the most computer and information sciences master's degrees to Hispanic Americans ★1768★
Pacelli Catholic High School
All-USA Teacher Teams, Second Team, 2000 ★4400★
Pacific Century Cyberworks
Business Week's best companies in Hong Kong ★395★
Business Week's best companies in terms of return on equity ★407★
The Pacific-Islands: An Encyclopedia
Library Journal's best reference books, 2000 ★368★
Pacific Lutheran University
U.S. News & World Report's best undergraduate fees among western regional universities by discount tuition, 2000 ★1430★
Highest undergraduate tuition and fees at colleges and universities in Washington ★1566★
U.S. News & World Report's top western regional universities, 2000-01 ★1574★
U.S. News & World Report's western regional universities with the best academic reputation scores, 2000-01 ★1577★
U.S. News & World Report's western regional universities with the highest freshmen retention rates, 2000-01 ★1581★
U.S. News & World Report's western regional universities with the highest graduation rates, 2000-01 ★1582★
U.S. News & World Report's western regional universities with the highest percentage of freshmen in the top 25% of their high school class, 2000-01 ★1583★
U.S. News & World Report's western regional universities with the highest percentage of full-time faculty, 2000-01 ★1584★

U.S. master's institutions with the largest number of students studying abroad, 1998-99 ★2513★
Average faculty salaries for institutions of higher education in Washington, 2000-01 ★3736★

Pacific School
Outstanding secondary schools in Los Angeles-Long Beach, California ★4167★

Pacific School of Religion
Average faculty salaries for institutions of higher education in California, 2000-01 ★3692★

Pacific Union College
U.S. News & World Report's best undergraduate fees among western regional liberal arts colleges by discount tuition, 2000 ★1384★
Academic reputation scores for U.S. News & World Report's top western regional liberal arts colleges, 2000-01 ★1387★
Acceptance rates for U.S. News & World Report's top western regional liberal arts colleges, 2000-01 ★1388★
Alumni giving rates at U.S. News & World Report's top western regional liberal arts colleges, 2000-01 ★1389★
Average freshmen retention rates for U.S. News & World Report's top western regional liberal arts colleges, 2000-01 ★1390★
Average graduation rates for U.S. News & World Report's top western regional liberal arts colleges, 2000-01 ★1391★
Percentage of freshmen in the top 25% of their high school class at U.S. News & World Report's top western regional liberal arts colleges, 2000-01 ★1392★
Percentage of full-time faculty at U.S. News & World Report's top western regional liberal arts colleges, 2000-01 ★1393★
Proportion of classes having 20 students or less at U.S. News & World Report's top western regional liberal arts colleges, 2000-01 ★1394★
Student/faculty ratios at U.S. News & World Report's top western regional liberal arts colleges, 2000-01 ★1395★
U.S. News & World Report's top western regional liberal arts colleges, 2000-01 ★1396★
U.S. News & World Report's western regional liberal arts colleges with students least in debt, 1999 ★1397★
Average faculty salaries for institutions of higher education in California, 2000-01 ★3692★

Pacific; University of the
Division I NCAA colleges with that graduated none of their African American male basketball players, 1990-91 to 1993-94 ★930★
U.S. colleges and universities awarding the most law and legal studies master's degrees to Asian Americans ★1782★
U.S. colleges and universities awarding the most law and legal studies master's degrees to Hispanic Americans ★1783★
U.S. colleges and universities awarding the most first professional degrees to Asian Americans ★1844★
U.S. colleges and universities awarding the most first professional degrees to Hispanic Americans ★1845★
U.S. colleges and universities awarding the most first professional degrees to Native Americans ★1846★
U.S. colleges and universities awarding the most health professions and related sciences first professional degrees to Asian Americans ★1848★

U.S. colleges and universities awarding the most health professions and related sciences first professional degrees to minorities ★1850★
U.S. colleges and universities awarding the most law and legal studies first professional degrees to Asian Americans ★1853★
U.S. colleges and universities awarding the most law and legal studies first professional degrees to Hispanic Americans ★1854★
U.S. colleges and universities awarding the most law and legal studies first professional degrees to Native Americans ★1855★
Average faculty salaries for institutions of higher education in California, 2000-01 ★3692★

Pacific University (OR)
U.S. News & World Report's best undergraduate fees among western regional universities by discount tuition, 2000 ★1430★
Highest undergraduate tuition and fees at colleges and universities in Oregon ★1547★
U.S. News & World Report's western regional universities with the best student/faculty ratios, 2000-01 ★1578★
U.S. News & World Report's western regional universities with the highest acceptance rates, 2000-01 ★1579★
U.S. News & World Report's western regional universities with the highest alumni giving rates, 2000-01 ★1580★
U.S. News & World Report's western regional universities with the highest percentage of freshmen in the top 25% of their high school class, 2000-01 ★1583★
U.S. News & World Report's western regional universities with the highest proportion of classes with 20 students or less, 2000-01 ★1585★
Average faculty salaries for institutions of higher education in Oregon, 2000-01 ★3724★

PacifiCare Health Systems
Fortune's highest ranked health care companies, 2000 ★469★

Pactiv
Fortune's highest ranked rubber and plastic products companies, 2000 ★492★
Top containers and packaging companies in Standard & Poor's 500, 2001 ★537★

Padavic; Irene
Radcliffe Institute for Advanced Study fellowship recipients in the field of sociology, 2000-01 ★4346★

Padberg; Lawrence
Top pay and benefits for the chief executive and top paid employees at Marymount University ★3395★

Paderon; Eduardo S.
Top pay and benefits for the chief executive and top paid employees at the University of the Incarnate Word ★3570★

Padua Academy
Outstanding secondary schools in Wilmington-Newark, Delaware-Maryland ★4252★

Paducah Community College
Lowest undergraduate tuition and fees at colleges and universities in Kentucky ★1509★

Pagano; Anthony J.
Top pay and benefits for the chief executive and top paid employees at Golden Gate University ★3310★

Page; Alfred
Top pay and benefits for the chief executive and top paid employees at the University of Tampa ★3569★

Page, et al.; Benjamin I.
Most frequently downloaded American Political Science Review articles ★3039★

Page; Oscar C.
Top pay and benefits for the chief executive and top paid employees at Austin College ★3184★

Page; William H.
Top pay and benefits for the chief executive and top paid employees at Mississippi College ★3404★

Paik; Nam June
Highly influential artists of the 20th century ★76★

The Pain Tree and Other Teenage Angst-Ridden Poetry
Most notable nonfiction books for reluctant young adult readers, 2001 ★323★

Paine College
U.S. News & World Report's southern regional liberal arts colleges with students most in debt, 1999 ★1367★

Paine Webber Group
Fortune's highest ranked securities companies, 2000 ★494★

Painter
Most desirable jobs in construction trades ★2272★

Painters and paperhangers
Occupations with the highest number of self-employed workers, 1998 ★2311★

Pak; Kirk
All-USA College Academic Third Team, 2001 ★4★

Pakistan
Countries of origin for non-U.S. citizens awarded doctorates at U.S. colleges and universities, 1999 ★1901★
First-year physics and astronomy graduate students from Asia, 1997-98 ★2987★

Palaios
Geology journals with the greatest impact measure, 1994-98 ★2526★

Palatine Consolidated, District 15
Illinois school districts with the highest paid superintendents, 1999-2000 ★3986★

Palatine High School
Outstanding secondary schools in Chicago, Illinois ★4110★
Outstanding suburban public high schools in Metro Chicago ★4256★

Palatine High School, District 211
Illinois school districts with the highest paid superintendents, 1999-2000 ★3986★
Illinois school districts with the most average years of teacher experience ★4012★

Palatine Public Library District
Highest Hennen's American Public Library Ratings for libraries serving a population of 50,000 to 99,999 ★2697★

Palatine Township 211
Illinois high school districts with the highest teacher salaries, 1999 ★3985★

Palchick; Bernard S.
Top pay and benefits for the chief executive and top paid employees at Kalamazoo College ★3358★

Paleoceanography
Oceanography journals by citation impact, 1995-99 ★2140★
Oceanography journals by citation impact, 1999 ★2141★

Paleontology
  Earth, atmosphere, and marine science doctorates awarded at U.S. colleges and universities, by subfield, 1999 ★1909★
  Gender breakdown of earth, atmosphere, and marine science doctorate recipients, by subfield, 1999 ★1932★

Pall
  Top conglomerates in Standard & Poor's 500, 2001 ★535★

Palm Beach Atlantic College
  Average faculty salaries for institutions of higher education in Florida, 2000-01 ★3696★

Palm Beach Community College
  Lowest undergraduate tuition and fees at colleges and universities in Florida ★1495★

Palm Reading for Beginners
  Best selling small press releases, 2001 ★226★

Palmer College of Chiropractic
  U.S. colleges and universities awarding the most health professions and related sciences first professional degrees to Native Americans ★1851★
  Average faculty salaries for institutions of higher education in Iowa, 2000-01 ★3702★

Palmer; Hans C.
  Top pay and benefits for the chief executive and top paid employees at Pomona College ★3444★

Palmstierna; Carl
  European business moguls considered the best dealmakers ★440★

Palmucci; John A.
  Top pay and benefits for the chief executive and top paid employees at Loyola College in Maryland ★3379★

Palo Verde College
  Lowest undergraduate tuition and fees at public 2-year colleges and universities ★1465★
  Lowest undergraduate tuition and fees at colleges and universities in California ★1487★
  Average faculty salaries for institutions of higher education without academic ranks in California, 2000-01 ★3743★

Palos East Elementary School
  Illinois elementary schools with the highest 5th grade writing scores ★15★

Pamlico Community College
  Lowest undergraduate tuition and fees at colleges and universities in North Carolina ★1540★
  Average faculty salaries for institutions of higher education without academic ranks in North Carolina, 2000-01 ★3761★

Panasyuk; Svetlana
  Radcliffe Institute for Advanced Study fellowship recipient in the field of geophysics, 2000-01 ★2969★

Pandian; R. Devadoss
  Top pay and benefits for the chief executive and top paid employees at North Central College in Illinois ★3421★

Papadakis; Constantine N.
  Presidents with the highest pay at Doctoral I and II universities, 1998-99 ★3160★
  Top pay and benefits for the chief executive and top paid employees at Drexel University ★3274★

Papadimitriou; Dimitri
  Top pay and benefits for the chief executive and top paid employees at Bard College ★3190★

Papageorge; Maria
  Top pay and benefits for the chief executive and top paid employees at Tufts University ★3580★

Paper Shadow: A Memoir of a Past Lost and Found
  Outstanding nonfiction books for young adults, 2000 ★334★

Paradise Valley Community College
  Lowest undergraduate tuition and fees at colleges and universities in Arizona ★1483★

Paraguay
  Countries with the highest spending per student on higher education, 1997 ★2488★

Paralegal assistant
  Jobs with the highest employment growth ★2254★
  Most desirable jobs in business/finance ★2270★

Paralegals and legal assistants
  Fastest growing occupations, 1998-2008 ★2302★
  Projected employment growth for selected occupations that require an associate degree or less, 1998-2008 ★2319★

Parametric Technology
  Business Week's best performing companies with the lowest 1-year sales performance ★421★

Parasite Rex: Inside the Bizarre World of Nature's Most Dangerous Creatures
  Library Journal's most notable microbiology books, 2000 ★268★

Parasitology
  Biological sciences doctorates awarded at U.S. colleges and universities, by subfield, 1999 ★1887★
  Gender breakdown of biological sciences doctorate recipients, by subfield, 1999 ★1927★

Pareto; Elizabeth
  Top pay and benefits for the chief executive and top paid employees at Marian College of Fond Du Lac ★3389★

Paris
  Cities with the highest productivity of paper in the discipline of cardiovascular systems, 1994-96 ★2869★
  Cities with the highest productivity of paper in the discipline of hematology, 1994-96 ★2870★
  Cities with the highest productivity of paper in the discipline of immunology, 1994-96 ★2871★

The Paris Review
  Most selective internships in the U.S., 2001 ★2610★

Parish Jr.; Albert E.
  Top pay and benefits for the chief executive and top paid employees at Charleston Southern University ★3229★

Park College
  Total baccalaureate business management and administrative services degrees awarded to African Americans from U.S. colleges and universities, 1997-98 ★1683★

Park Place Entertainment
  Fortune's highest ranked hotels, casinos and resorts, 2000 ★470★

Park; Richard M.
  Top pay and benefits for the chief executive and top paid employees at Franklin College of Indiana ★3297★

Parker; Annette S.
  Top pay and benefits for the chief executive and top paid employees at Dickinson College ★3268★

Parker; Bernard S.
  Top pay and benefits for the chief executive and top paid employees at Anna Maria College ★3177★

Parker Hannifin
  Top recruiters for agribusiness jobs for 2000-01 bachelor's degree recipients ★55★
  Fortune's highest ranked industrial and farm equipment companies, 2000 ★471★
  Top manufacturing companies in Standard & Poor's 500, 2001 ★548★
  Top recruiters for industrial engineering jobs for 2000-01 bachelor's degree recipients ★2432★
  Top recruiters for mechanical engineering jobs for 2000-01 bachelor's degree recipients ★2437★

Parker; Mathew
  All-USA College Academic Third Team, 2001 ★4★

Parker; Richard D.
  Top pay and benefits for the chief executive and top paid employees at Houston Baptist University ★3342★

Parkhill Junior High School
  Outstanding secondary schools in Dallas, Texas ★4120★

Parkland Memorial Hospitals
  Top gynecology hospitals in the U.S., 2000 ★2792★

Parks/recreation/leisure/fitness
  Gender breakdown of professional doctorate recipients, by subfield, 1999 ★1940★
  Professional doctorates awarded at U.S. colleges and universities, by subfield, 1999 ★2033★

Parks; Rosa
  Most important African Americans in the twentieth century ★219★
  Most influential African Americans in politics and civil rights ★3040★

Parkview High School
  Outstanding suburban public high schools in Metro Atlanta ★4254★

Parkway South High School
  Outstanding secondary schools in St. Louis, Missouri-Illinois ★4216★

Parole officer
  Most desirable public sector jobs ★2279★

Parra; Carlos
  All-America boys' high school soccer team defenders, 2001 ★165★

Parras Middle School
  Outstanding secondary schools in Los Angeles-Long Beach, California ★4167★

Parrinello; Michele
  American Chemical Society 2001 award winners (Group 4) ★754★

Parrish; Edward A.
  Top pay and benefits for the chief executive and top paid employees at Worcester Polytechnic Institute ★3636★

Parsons; Yvonne
  Radcliffe Institute for Advanced Study fellowship recipients in the field of molecular biology, 2000-01 ★208★

Partial Justice: Women, Prisons, and Social Control
  Most-cited works in women and crime publications ★1646★

Particles and fields
  Major subfields of first-year physics and astronomy graduate students who are foreign citizens planning to receive a Ph.D., 1997-98 ★3004★
  Major subfields of first-year physics and astronomy graduate students who are U.S. citizens planning to receive a Ph.D., 1997-98 ★3005★

"Particles and fields. 1. Review of particle physics"
  Institute for Scientific Information's most cited papers, 1990-98 ★4282★

Partridge; Bruce
  Top pay and benefits for the chief executive and top paid employees at Haverford College ★3329★

Pasadena City College
  Lowest undergraduate tuition and fees at public 2-year colleges and universities ★1465★
  Lowest undergraduate tuition and fees at colleges and universities in California ★1487★
  Community colleges with the highest enrollment of foreign students, 1998-99 ★2493★

Pasqualoni; Paul L.
  Top pay and benefits for the chief executive and top paid employees at Syracuse University ★3516★

Pasquaraello; George J.
  Top pay and benefits for the chief executive and top paid employees at the University of New England ★3552★

Passage to Freedom: The Sugihara Story
  Most notable children's recordings, 2001 ★320★

Passaic County Community College
  Lowest undergraduate tuition and fees at colleges and universities in New Jersey ★1534★
  Average faculty salaries for institutions of higher education in New Jersey, 2000-01 ★3717★
  U.S. community colleges with the highest paid full professors, 2001 ★3976★

Passon; Richard H.
  Top pay and benefits for the chief executive and top paid employees at the University of Scranton ★3567★

Past Present
  Top ranked economic history journals ★2190★

Pasternack; Robert
  American Chemical Society 2001 award winners (Group 4) ★754★

Pasternack; Robert F.
  Top pay and benefits for the chief executive and top paid employees at Swarthmore College ★3514★

Pastore; Christopher
  Top pay and benefits for the chief executive and top paid employees at Philadelphia University ★3440★

Patent; Dorothy Hinshaw
  Booklist's best science books for children ★310★

Paterno; Joe
  Division I-A all-time coaching victories ★126★

Paternoster; Raymond
  Most-cited scholars in *Criminology* ★1639★

Paterson; John A.
  Top pay and benefits for the chief executive and top paid employees at Seton Hall University ★3496★

Paterson; Katherine
  People for the American Way's list of most frequently challenged authors, 1982-1992 ★746★

Patouhas; Zoy
  Golden Key Scholar Award winners, 2000 ★1316★

Patrick Henry Community College
  Lowest undergraduate tuition and fees at colleges and universities in Virginia ★1565★

Pattern Recognition
  Artificial intelligence journals with the greatest impact measure, 1981-98 ★97★

Patterson; Ben J.
  Top pay and benefits for the chief executive and top paid employees at Hope College ★3339★

Patterson; Charles
  Top pay and benefits for the chief executive and top paid employees at Guilford College ★3316★

Patterson; Cynthia M.
  Top pay and benefits for the chief executive and top paid employees at Anna Maria College ★3177★

Pattiz; Anthony
  All-USA Teacher Teams, Third Team, 2000 ★4401★

Patton; Sara L.
  Top pay and benefits for the chief executive and top paid employees at the College of Wooster ★3531★

Patton; Seth H.
  Top pay and benefits for the chief executive and top paid employees at Denison University ★3265★

Patton; William
  Top pay and benefits for the chief executive and top paid employees at Whittier College ★3624★

Pattonville High School
  Outstanding secondary schools in St. Louis, Missouri-Illinois ★4216★

Paul D. Camp Community College
  Lowest undergraduate tuition and fees at colleges and universities in Virginia ★1565★

Paul Quinn College
  Historically black colleges and universities with major improvements in student loan default rates, 1998 ★2737★

Paulding Middle School
  Outstanding secondary schools in San Luis Obispo-Atascadero-Paso Robles, California ★4223★

Pavlovich; Mark
  Top pay and benefits for the chief executive and top paid employees at College of Mount St. Joseph ★3244★

Pavsek; Daniel
  Top pay and benefits for the chief executive and top paid employees at Shenandoah University ★3497★

Pay It Forward
  Most notable fiction books for young adults, 2001 ★322★

Paychex
  Top services industries in Standard & Poor's 500, 2001 ★558★

Payne; David
  Top pay and benefits for the chief executive and top paid employees at College Misericordia ★3243★

Payne; Harry C.
  Largest benefit packages awarded to presidents at institutions of higher education, 1998-99 ★3133★
  Presidents with the highest pay at Baccalaureate I colleges, 1998-99 ★3159★
  Top pay and benefits for the chief executive and top paid employees at Williams College ★3631★

Payroll and timekeeping clerks
  Occupations with the highest decline in employment, 1998-2008 ★2310★

Payseur; Victoria F.
  Top pay and benefits for the chief executive and top paid employees at Drake University ★3272★

Payton; Benjamin F.
  Top pay and benefits for the chief executive and top paid employees at Tuskegee University ★3583★

Payton College Prep
  Acceptance rates at Chicago college prep magnet schools, 2000-01 ★4000★

PC Connection
  Top information technology companies, 2000 ★544★
  Top women-owned companies ★4460★

Peace Corps
  Top internships in the U.S. with the highest compensation, 2001 ★2611★

Pearl High School
  Outstanding secondary schools in Jackson, Mississippi ★4154★

Pearson Education
  Best companies for working mothers in offering flexible work hours ★4448★

Pearson; Paul D.
  Top pay and benefits for the chief executive and top paid employees at Augustana College in Illinois ★3182★

Pearson; Thomas S.
  Top pay and benefits for the chief executive and top paid employees at Monmouth University in New Jersey ★3406★

Pearson; Wesley
  Top pay and benefits for the chief executive and top paid employees at St. Olaf College ★3484★

Pease; K.
  Most cited authors in the journal *British Journal of Criminology*, 1990 to 1995 ★1614★
  Most cited authors in the journal *Crime and Justice*, 1990 to 1995 ★1617★

Pease; Ken
  Most-cited scholars in *British Journal of Criminology* ★1637★

The Peck Place School
  Outstanding secondary schools in New Haven-Meriden, Connecticut ★4188★

Pedemonti; Robert A.
  Top pay and benefits for the chief executive and top paid employees at Trinity College in Connecticut ★3577★

Pederson; Wayne D.
  Top pay and benefits for the chief executive and top paid employees at Lewis and Clark College in Oregon ★3371★

Pedro and Me: Friendship, Loss, and What I Learned
  Most notable books for older readers, 2001 ★318★
  Most notable nonfiction books for reluctant young adult readers, 2001 ★323★

Most notable nonfiction books for young adults, 2001 ★324★
Outstanding children's nonfiction books, 2000 ★330★

Peg and the Whale
Outstanding books for young readers, 2000 ★328★

Peggy Guggenheim Collection
Top internships in the U.S. with the highest compensation, 2001 ★2611★

Pelham Memorial High School
Outstanding secondary schools in New York, New York ★4191★

Pelham Middle School
Outstanding secondary schools in New York, New York ★4191★

Pell Grants
Sources of financial aid for incoming freshmen, 2000 ★1062★
Proposed fiscal 2002 appropriations for student assistance ★1251★
Fiscal 2002 requested budget as compared with Fiscal 2001 budget for the Education Department ★2231★
Proposed fiscal 2002 appropriations for student aid ★4366★

Pella
Most selective internships in the U.S., 2001 ★2610★
Top internships in the U.S. with the highest compensation, 2001 ★2611★

Pellissippi State Tech Community College
Average faculty salaries for institutions of higher education in Tennessee, 2000-01 ★3730★

Pelnar-Zaiko; Ivana
Top pay and benefits for the chief executive and top paid employees at Wagner College ★3599★

Pelphrey; Karen
Division I women's career high scorers ★129★

Pelton; M. Lee
Top pay and benefits for the chief executive and top paid employees at Willamette University ★3628★

Pena; Elsa
Top pay and benefits for the chief executive and top paid employees at Agnes Scott College ★3165★

Pence; Jim
Top pay and benefits for the chief executive and top paid employees at St. Olaf College ★3484★

Penders; Thomas
Top pay and benefits for the chief executive and top paid employees at George Washington University ★3304★

Pendleton; Cynthia Joy
Top pay and benefits for the chief executive and top paid employees at Salem College ★3488★

Penfield; Henry Irvin
Top pay and benefits for the chief executive and top paid employees at Birmingham-Southern College ★3204★

Penguin
Trade paperback bestsellers by publishing house, 2000 ★307★

Penguin Putnam
Hardcover bestsellers by corporation, 2000 ★239★
Top children's book publishers, 1999 ★3074★

Penguin Putnam Inc.
Paperback bestsellers by corporation, 2000 ★296★

Peninsula College
Average faculty salaries for institutions of higher education in Washington, 2000-01 ★3736★

Penland; Roger G.
Top pay and benefits for the chief executive and top paid employees at Elmira College ★3284★

Penn High School
Outstanding secondary schools in South Bend, Indiana ★4231★

Penn State, Commonwealth College
Bachelor's institutions with the highest enrollment of foreign students, 1998-99 ★2492★

Penn State University
Division I-A all-time percentage leaders ★127★
NCAA men's gymnastics teams with the most individual champions ★137★
U.S. business schools with the quickest payback on MBA investments ★654★

Penn State University, Abington
Highest undergraduate tuition and fees at public, 4-year or above colleges and universities ★1463★

Penn State University, Altoona
Highest undergraduate tuition and fees at public, 4-year or above colleges and universities ★1463★

Penn State University, Beaver
Highest undergraduate tuition and fees at public, 4-year or above colleges and universities ★1463★

Penn State University, Behrend College
Highest undergraduate tuition and fees at public, 4-year or above colleges and universities ★1463★

Penn State University, Berks
Highest undergraduate tuition and fees at public, 4-year or above colleges and universities ★1463★

Penn State University, Capital College
Highest undergraduate tuition and fees at public, 4-year or above colleges and universities ★1463★

Penn State University, Delaware County
Highest undergraduate tuition and fees at public, 4-year or above colleges and universities ★1463★

Penn State University, Dubois
Highest undergraduate tuition and fees at public, 4-year or above colleges and universities ★1463★

Penn State University, Erie
Public 4-year institutions with the highest tuition, 2000-01 ★1471★

Penn State University, Fayette
Highest undergraduate tuition and fees at public, 4-year or above colleges and universities ★1463★

Penn State University, Harrisburg
Highest undergraduate tuition and fees at public, 4-year or above colleges and universities ★1463★
Public 4-year institutions with the highest tuition, 2000-01 ★1471★

Penn State University, Hazleton
Highest undergraduate tuition and fees at public, 4-year or above colleges and universities ★1463★

Penn State University, Lehigh Valley
Highest undergraduate tuition and fees at public, 4-year or above colleges and universities ★1463★

Penn State University, McKeesport
Highest undergraduate tuition and fees at public, 4-year or above colleges and universities ★1463★

Penn State University, Mont Alto
Highest undergraduate tuition and fees at public, 4-year or above colleges and universities ★1463★

Penn State University, New Kensington
Highest undergraduate tuition and fees at public, 4-year or above colleges and universities ★1463★

Penn State University, Shenango
Highest undergraduate tuition and fees at public, 4-year or above colleges and universities ★1463★

Penn State University, University Park
Highest undergraduate tuition and fees at public, 4-year or above colleges and universities ★1463★
Public 4-year institutions with the highest tuition, 2000-01 ★1471★
Top graduate engineering schools by reputation, as determined by engineers and recruiters, 2001 ★2368★
Academics' choices for best graduate agricultural engineering programs, 2001 ★2379★
Academics' choices for best graduate industrial/manufacturing engineering programs, 2001 ★2411★
Academics' choices for best graduate materials engineering programs, 2001 ★2417★
Academics' choices for best graduate nuclear engineering schools, 2000 ★2426★
Academics' choices for best graduate petroleum engineering schools, 2000 ★2429★
Academics' choices for best administration/supervision graduate programs, 2001 ★4378★
Academics' choices for best counseling/personnel services graduate programs, 2001 ★4379★
Academics' choices for best higher education administration graduate programs, 2001 ★4384★
Academics' choices for best vocational/technical graduate programs, 2001 ★4387★

Penn State University, Wilkes-Barre
Highest undergraduate tuition and fees at public, 4-year or above colleges and universities ★1463★

Penn State University, Worthington Scranton
Highest undergraduate tuition and fees at public, 4-year or above colleges and universities ★1463★

Penn State University, York
Highest undergraduate tuition and fees at public, 4-year or above colleges and universities ★1463★

Penn Valley Community College
Lowest undergraduate tuition and fees at colleges and universities in Missouri ★1525★
Average faculty salaries for institutions of higher education without academic ranks in Missouri, 2000-01 ★3755★

Penneys; N.S.
Most cited first authors in dermatology journals, 1981 to 1996 ★1871★

PENNSYLVANIA

Pennsylvania
States with the highest enrollment in private 4-year institutions of higher education ★860★
States with the highest enrollment in public 4-year institutions of higher education ★861★
Mean composite ACT scores by state, 2000 ★895★
Mean math SAT scores by state, 2000 ★900★
Mean verbal SAT scores by state, 2000 ★903★
States allocating the largest amount of state tax appropriations for higher education, 2000-01 ★1304★
States receiving the most in federal agency appropriations to colleges, from 1996 to 2000 ★1307★
Total doctorate recipients by state, 1999 ★2054★
States with the most law schools ★2668★
State library associations with most full-time staff ★2681★
State library associations with the highest annual revenue ★2682★
State library associations with the highest conference attendance ★2683★
State library associations with the highest unrestricted net assets ★2684★
State library associations with the largest membership ★2685★
State grades for affordability of higher education for minority students, 2000 ★2883★
State grades for benefits state receives for educating its minority students, 2000 ★2884★
State grades for completion of higher education by minority students, 2000 ★2885★
State grades for participation of minority students in higher education, 2000 ★2886★
State grades for preparing minority students for higher education, 2000 ★2887★
States expelling the most students for violating the Gun-Free Schools Act, 1998-99 ★3994★
States with the highest number of high school graduates, 1999-2000 ★3995★
States with the highest per-pupil expenditures ★3996★
States with the highest K-12 public school enrollment ★4034★
States with the highest projected K-12 public school enrollment for 2010 ★4035★
States with the highest funding needs for school-building modernization ★4040★
States with the highest funding needs for school-technology modernization ★4041★
States with the most K-12 public schools ★4049★

Pennsylvania, Cheyney; University of
Colleges offering the Thurgood Marshall Scholarship Fund ★221★

Pennsylvania College of Technology
Highest undergraduate tuition and fees at public, 4-year or above colleges and universities ★1463★
Public 4-year institutions with the highest tuition, 2000-01 ★1471★

Pennsylvania; Hospital of the University of
Top hospitals in the U.S., 2000 ★2793★
Top neurology and neurosurgery hospitals in the U.S., 2000 ★2795★
Top ortolaryngology hospitals in the U.S., 2000 ★2798★

Pennsylvania Law Review
Law journals by citation impact, 1981-96 ★2617★
Most frequently-cited law reviews and legal periodicals, 1924-1986: a compilation ★2619★
Most frequently-cited law reviews and legal periodicals, according to *Shepard's Law Review Citations*, 1957-1986 ★2620★

Pennsylvania State University
All-USA College Academic First Team, 2001 ★2★
Employing institutions with the most published pages in *The Journal of Risk and Insurance*, 1987-1996 ★679★
U.S. colleges and universities where intercollegiate sports are popular ★995★
U.S. colleges and universities where intramural sports are popular ★997★
U.S. colleges and universities where the general student body puts a strong emphasis on athletic events ★1007★
Largest degree-granting colleges and universities, by enrollment ★1068★
State appropriations for Pennsylvania's institutions of higher education, 2000-01 ★1291★
Universities with the most-cited scholars in *Criminal Justice and Behavior* ★1648★
Universities with the most-cited scholars in *Criminology* ★1649★
Universities with the most-cited scholars in *Journal of Quantitative Criminology* ★1650★
Universities with the most-cited scholars in *Journal of Research in Crime and Delinquency* ★1651★
Universities with the most-cited scholars in *Justice Quarterly* ★1652★
Doctorate-granting-institutions awarding the most non-U.S. citizen doctoral degrees, 1999 ★1906★
Top doctorate granting institutions, 1999 ★2047★
U.S. colleges and universities awarding the most doctoral degrees to American Indians and Alaskan Natives from 1995 to 1999 ★2092★
U.S. colleges and universities awarding the most doctorates in all fields, 1999 ★2100★
U.S. colleges and universities awarding the most doctorates in education, 1999 ★2101★
U.S. colleges and universities awarding the most doctorates in engineering, 1999 ★2102★
U.S. colleges and universities awarding the most doctorates in professional and other fields, 1999 ★2106★
U.S. institutions awarding the most doctorate degrees, 1999 ★2132★
Top geosciences research-doctorate programs as evaluated by the National Research Council ★2152★
Most effective industrial engineering research-doctorate programs as evaluated by the National Research Council ★2412★
Top industrial engineering research-doctorate programs as evaluated by the National Research Council ★2413★
Most effective materials science research-doctorate programs as evaluated by the National Research Council ★2418★
Top materials science research-doctorate programs as evaluated by the National Research Council ★2419★
U.S. universities publishing the most papers in the field of literature, 1994-98 ★2447★

Educational Rankings Annual • 2002

Faculty's scholarly reputation in the Ph.D.-granting departments of geography, 1925-1982 ★2518★
Most effective geography research-doctorate programs as evaluated by the National Research Council ★2519★
Top geography research-doctorate programs as evaluated by the National Research Council ★2520★
Institutions with the most productive libraries, 1993-1997 ★2678★
Top university research libraries in the U.S. and Canada, 1998-99 ★2706★
University research libraries in the U.S. and Canada with the largest increases in total expenditures from 1993-94 to 1998-99 ★2708★
U.S. universities publishing the most papers in the field of library and information science, 1995-99 ★2718★
Degrees granted in the ten largest undergraduate journalism and mass communications programs, 1999 ★2745★
Enrollment of students in the ten largest undergraduate journalism and mass communications programs, 1999 ★2746★
Enrollment of students in the ten largest doctoral journalism and mass communications programs, 1999 ★2762★
U.S. colleges and universities spending the most on chemical research and development, 1998 ★3099★
U.S. colleges and universities spending the most on chemical research equipment, 1998 ★3100★
U.S. colleges and universities with the most federal support for chemical research and development, 1998 ★3102★
U.S. colleges and universities with the most federal support for chemical research equipment, 1998 ★3103★
Institutions receiving the most federal research and development expenditures, 1999 ★3105★
U.S. community colleges with the highest paid full professors, 2001 ★3976★
U.S. universities publishing the most papers in the field of sociology and anthropology, 1994-98 ★4349★
U.S. universities publishing the most papers in the fields of sociology and anthropology, 1993-97 ★4350★
U.S. universities with the greatest impact in sociology and anthropology, 1995-99 ★4351★

Pennsylvania State University, University Park
U.S. colleges and universities with the highest average football attendance, 1996-99 ★159★
U.S. News & World Report's national universities with the highest percentage of full-time faculty, 2000-01 ★1136★
U.S. colleges and universities awarding the most English language/literature/letters master's degrees to African Americans ★1773★
U.S. colleges and universities awarding the most doctorate degrees to African Americans ★2095★
U.S. colleges and universities awarding the most doctorate degrees to minorities ★2098★
U.S. colleges and universities awarding the most doctorate degrees to Native Americans ★2099★

U.S. colleges and universities awarding the most education doctorate degrees to Asian Americans ★2109★

U.S. colleges and universities awarding the most education doctorate degrees to Native Americans ★2111★

U.S. News & World Report's graduate engineering programs with the best materials departments, 2000-01 ★2421★

U.S. News & World Report's graduate engineering programs with the best nuclear departments, 2000-01 ★2428★

Average faculty salaries for institutions of higher education in Pennsylvania, 2000-01 ★3725★

Pennsylvania; University of

All-USA College Academic Second Team, 2001 ★3★

All-USA College Academic Third Team, 2001 ★4★

Most effective anthropology research-doctorate programs as evaluated by the National Research Council ★61★

Top anthropology research-doctorate programs as evaluated by the National Research Council ★62★

U.S. universities publishing the most papers in the field of archaeology, 1994-98 ★66★

Most effective art history research-doctorate programs as evaluated by the National Research Council ★91★

Top art history research-doctorate programs as evaluated by the National Research Council ★93★

Top ecology, evolution, and behavior research-doctorate programs as evaluated by the National Research Council ★201★

Top neurosciences research-doctorate programs as evaluated by the National Research Council ★202★

U.S. universities with the greatest impact in microbiology, 1995-99 ★218★

Top business schools in research performance, 1986-1998 ★532★

U.S. News & World Report's universities with the best quantitative methods departments, 1999-2000 ★572★

U.S. universities publishing the most papers in the field of management, 1995-99 ★574★

U.S. universities with the greatest impact in management, 1994-98 ★575★

Top business schools by average MBA rank, 1986-1998 ★644★

Top business schools for overall within-discipline research performance, 1986-1998 ★645★

Top business schools for within-discipline research performance in management, 1986-1998 ★646★

Top business schools for within-discipline research performance in management science, 1986-1998 ★647★

Top business schools for within-discipline research performance in accounting, 1986-1998 ★660★

Top business schools for within-discipline research performance in finance, 1986-1998 ★663★

Top business schools for within-discipline research performance in insurance, international business and real estate, 1986-1998 ★667★

Top business schools for within-discipline research performance in marketing, 1986-1998 ★671★

Degree-granting institutions with the most published pages in *The Journal of Risk and Insurance*, 1987-1996 ★678★

Employing institutions with the most published pages in *The Journal of Risk and Insurance*, 1987-1996 ★679★

U.S. News & World Report's universities with the best insurance departments, 1999-2000 ★681★

U.S. college campuses with more than 5,000 students reporting murders or manslaughters, 1998 ★729★

Top classics research-doctorate programs as evaluated by the National Research Council ★816★

U.S. colleges and universities with a popular newspaper ★1018★

U.S. News & World Report's national universities with the best faculty resources rank, 2000-01 ★1127★

U.S. News & World Report's national universities with the best freshmen retention rates, 2000-01 ★1128★

U.S. News & World Report's national universities with the best student/faculty ratio, 2000-01 ★1130★

U.S. News & World Report's national universities with the highest alumni giving rank, 2000-01 ★1132★

U.S. News & World Report's national universities with the highest financial resources rank, 2000-01 ★1133★

U.S. News & World Report's national universities with the highest proportion of alumni support, 2000-01 ★1137★

U.S. News & World Report's national universities with the highest selectivity rank, 2000-01 ★1139★

U.S. News & World Report's national universities with the lowest proportion of classes with 50 or more students, 2000-01 ★1142★

Colleges and universities with the largest endowments, 2000 ★1237★

Institutions receiving the most gifts, 1999-2000 ★1244★

U.S. News & World Report's national universities with students most in debt, 1999 ★1476★

Highest undergraduate tuition and fees at colleges and universities in Pennsylvania ★1549★

Top comparative literature research-doctorate programs as evaluated by the National Research Council ★1588★

Total ethnic/cultural studies master's degrees awarded to minorities from U.S. colleges and universities, 1997-98 ★1748★

U.S. colleges and universities awarding the most first professional degrees to Asian Americans ★1844★

U.S. colleges and universities awarding the most health professions and related sciences first professional degrees to Asian Americans ★1848★

U.S. colleges and universities awarding the most law and legal studies first professional degrees to Hispanic Americans ★1854★

U.S. colleges and universities awarding the most doctorates in professional and other fields, 1999 ★2106★

U.S. colleges and universities awarding the most English language/literature/letters doctorate degrees to African Americans ★2112★

Economics departments by number of citations by top economists, 1971-92 ★2158★

Economics departments by number of citations per top economist, 1971-92 ★2159★

Economics departments by number of top economists, 1971-92 ★2160★

Institutions most frequently contributing to the *American Economic Review* from 1911-1990 ★2168★

Institutions most frequently contributing to the *American Economic Review* from 1951-1990 ★2169★

U.S. universities publishing the most papers in the field of economics and business, 1995-99 ★2178★

U.S. universities with the greatest impact in economics, 1995-99 ★2179★

Economics Ph.D. programs by number of citations of top economist graduates, 1971-92 ★2204★

Economics Ph.D. programs by number of citations per top economist graduate, 1971-92 ★2205★

Economics Ph.D. programs by number of top economist graduates, 1971-92 ★2206★

Origin of doctorate for economics faculty at Ph.D.-granting institutions ★2209★

Origin of doctorate for economics faculty at Ph.D.-granting institutions, by Ph.D. equivalents produced ★2210★

Top economics research-doctorate programs as evaluated by the National Research Council ★2213★

Academics' choices for best graduate bioengineering/biomedical engineering programs, 2001 ★2381★

Most effective biomedical engineering research-doctorate programs as evaluated by the National Research Council ★2383★

Top biomedical engineering research-doctorate programs as evaluated by the National Research Council ★2384★

Most effective chemical engineering research-doctorate programs as evaluated by the National Research Council ★2389★

Top chemical engineering research-doctorate programs as evaluated by the National Research Council ★2390★

Top materials science research-doctorate programs as evaluated by the National Research Council ★2419★

Most effective English language and literature research-doctorate programs as evaluated by the National Research Council ★2448★

Top English language and literature research-doctorate programs as evaluated by the National Research Council ★2451★

U.S. research institutions with the largest number of students studying abroad, 1998-99 ★2514★

Top French language and literature research-doctorate programs as evaluated by the National Research Council ★2516★

Top history research-doctorate programs as evaluated by the National Research Council ★2554★

Acceptance rates at *U.S. News & World Report*'s top 10 law schools, 2001 ★2634★

Graduate employment after graduation percentage for *U.S. News & World Report*'s top 10 law schools, 2001 ★2635★

Graduate employment percentage for *U.S. News & World Report*'s top 10 law schools, 2001 ★2636★

Jurisdiction's overall bar passage rate for *U.S. News & World Report*'s top 10 law schools, 2001 ★2637★

PENNSYLVANIA

Law schools with the best civil procedure faculty, 1999-2000 ★2640★

Law schools with the best comparative law faculty, 1999-2000 ★2642★

Law schools with the best constitutional law (freedom of speech) faculty, 1999-2000 ★2644★

Law schools with the best criminal law (substantive) faculty, 1999-2000 ★2647★

Law schools with the best jurisprudence faculty, 1999-2000 ★2655★

Law schools with the best labor law faculty, 1999-2000 ★2656★

Law schools with the best law and social science plus psychology and sociology faculty, 1999-2000 ★2659★

Law schools with the best legal ethics, professional responsibility, and legal profession faculty, 1999-2000 ★2660★

Law schools with the highest quality, 1999-2000 ★2666★

School's bar passage rate in jurisdiction at *U.S. News & World Report*'s top 10 law schools, 2001 ★2667★

Student-faculty ratios at *U.S. News & World Report*'s top 10 law schools, 2001 ★2669★

Top law schools, 2001 ★2670★

Top law schools by reputation, as determined by academic personnel, 2001 ★2671★

Top law schools by reputation, as determined by lawyers and judges, 2001 ★2672★

Top law school student bodies, 1999-2000 ★2673★

Law library web sites, by visibility. ★2687★

Top university research libraries in the U.S. and Canada, 1998-99 ★2706★

University research libraries in the U.S. and Canada with the largest increases in total expenditures from 1993-94 to 1998-99 ★2708★

Most effective linguistics research-doctorate programs as evaluated by the National Research Council ★2732★

Top linguistics research-doctorate programs as evaluated by the National Research Council ★2733★

Academics' choices for best drug and alcohol abuse programs, 2001 ★2819★

Academics' choices for best geriatrics programs, 2001 ★2821★

Academics' choices for best internal medicine programs, 2001 ★2822★

Academics' choices for best pediatrics programs, 2001 ★2823★

Academics' choices for best women's health medical programs, 2001 ★2825★

Acceptance rates for *U.S. News & World Report*'s top 10 research-oriented medical schools, 2001 ★2827★

Average MCAT scores at *U.S. News & World Report*'s top 10 research-oriented medical schools, 2001 ★2836★

Average undergraduate GPA at *U.S. News & World Report*'s top 10 research-oriented medical schools, 2001 ★2838★

Faculty-student ratios at *U.S. News & World Report*'s top 10 research-oriented medical schools, 2001 ★2842★

NIH research grants for *U.S. News & World Report*'s top 10 research-oriented medical schools, 2001 ★2845★

Out-of-state tuition and fees for *U.S. News & World Report*'s top 10 research-oriented medical schools, 2001 ★2847★

Top primary-care medical schools by student selectivity rank, 2001 ★2858★

Top research-oriented medical schools, 2001 ★2859★

Top research-oriented medical schools by reputation, as determined by academic personnel, 2001 ★2860★

Top research-oriented medical schools by reputation, as determined by intern/residency directors, 2001 ★2861★

Top research-oriented medical schools by student selectivity, 2001 ★2862★

Top music research-doctorate programs as evaluated by the National Research Council ★2896★

U.S. universities with the greatest impact in optics and acoustics, 1995-99 ★2912★

Most effective pharmacology research-doctorate programs as evaluated by the National Research Council ★2938★

Top pharmacology research-doctorate programs as evaluated by the National Research Council ★2939★

Women faculty in Ph.D. physics departments at U.S. institutions, 1998 ★2981★

Most effective physiology research-doctorate programs as evaluated by the National Research Council ★3021★

Top physiology research-doctorate programs as evaluated by the National Research Council ★3022★

Most effective psychology research-doctorate programs as evaluated by the National Research Council ★3065★

Top psychology research-doctorate programs as evaluated by the National Research Council ★3068★

Top religion research-doctorate programs as evaluated by the National Research Council ★3093★

Most patents issued to universities or research facilities, 1999 ★3097★

U.S. colleges and universities spending the most on chemical research equipment, 1998 ★3100★

U.S. colleges and universities with the most federal support for chemical research and development, 1998 ★3102★

U.S. colleges and universities with the most federal support for chemical research equipment, 1998 ★3103★

Institutions receiving the most federal research and development expenditures, 1999 ★3105★

Presidents with the highest pay at Research I and II universities, 1998-99 ★3162★

Average faculty salaries for institutions of higher education in Pennsylvania, 2000-01 ★3725★

Private institutions of higher education that pay the highest salaries to female professors, 2000-01 ★3974★

U.S. institutions with the highest paid assistant professors, 2001 ★3977★

U.S. institutions with the highest paid full professors, 2001 ★3978★

Most effective sociology research-doctorate programs as evaluated by the National Research Council ★4352★

Top sociology research-doctorate programs as evaluated by the National Research Council ★4354★

Top Spanish and Portuguese language and literature research-doctorate programs as evaluated by the National Research Council ★4358★

Acceptance rates at *U.S. News & World Report*'s top 10 graduate education schools, 2001 ★4388★

Average quantitative GRE scores for *U.S. News & World Report*'s top 10 graduate education schools, 2001 ★4389★

Average verbal GRE scores for *U.S. News & World Report*'s top 10 graduate education schools, 2001 ★4390★

Doctoral students to faculty ratio at *U.S. News & World Report*'s top 10 graduate education schools, 2001 ★4391★

Ph.D.s and Ed.D.s granted at *U.S. News & World Report*'s top 10 graduate education schools, 2001 ★4392★

Research expenditures for *U.S. News & World Report*'s top 10 graduate education schools, 2001 ★4393★

Research expenditures per faculty member at *U.S. News & World Report*'s top 10 graduate education schools, 2001 ★4394★

Top graduate education schools, 2001 ★4395★

Pennsylvania, Wharton School of Business; University of

U.S. News & World Report's undergraduate business programs with the best consulting departments, 2000-01 ★563★

U.S. News & World Report's undergraduate business programs with the best e-commerce departments, 2000-01 ★564★

U.S. News & World Report's undergraduate business programs with the best entrepreneurship departments, 2000-01 ★565★

U.S. News & World Report's undergraduate business programs with the best general management departments, 2000-01 ★566★

U.S. News & World Report's undergraduate business programs with the best human resources departments, 2000-01 ★567★

U.S. News & World Report's undergraduate business programs with the best production/operations departments, 2000-01 ★569★

U.S. News & World Report's undergraduate business programs with the best real estate departments, 2000-01 ★570★

U.S. News & World Report's undergraduate business programs with the highest academic reputation scores, 2000-01 ★571★

U.S. News & World Report's undergraduate business programs with the best accounting departments, 2000-01 ★581★

Academics' choices for best graduate entrepreneurship programs, 2001 ★583★

Academics' choices for best graduate executive MBA programs, 2001 ★584★

Academics' choices for best graduate management information systems programs, 2001 ★585★

Academics' choices for best graduate nonprofit organizations programs, 2001 ★586★

Acceptance rates for *U.S. News & World Report*'s top 10 graduate business schools, 2001 ★588★

Annual tuition at *Business Week*'s top business schools, 2000 ★589★

Average GMAT scores at *U.S. News & World Report*'s top 10 graduate business schools, 2001 ★591★

Average job offers received by graduates from *Business Week*'s top business schools, 1999 ★592★

Average undergraduate GPA at *U.S. News & World Report*'s top 10 graduate business schools, 2001 ★593★

Business Week's institutions with the best entrepreneurship programs ★594★
Business Week's top business schools, 2000 ★595★
Business Week's top business schools as selected by corporate recruiters, 2000 ★596★
Business Week's top business schools as selected by recent MBA graduates, 2000 ★597★
Business Week's top business schools by intellectual capital, 2000 ★599★
Business Week's top business schools for finance skills as selected by corporate recruiters, 2000 ★600★
Business Week's top business schools for general management skills as selected by corporate recruiters, 2000 ★601★
Business Week's top business schools for global scope skills as selected by corporate recruiters, 2000 ★602★
Business Week's top business schools for marketing skills as selected by corporate recruiters, 2000 ★603★
Business Week's top business schools for technology skills as selected by corporate recruiters, 2000 ★604★
Business Week's top business schools with the highest percentage of international students, 2000 ★612★
Business Week's top business schools with the most innovative curriculum as selected by corporate recruiters, 2000 ★619★
Business Week's top business schools with the worst placement offices, 2000 ★620★
Highest post-MBA salaries for students enrolled in *Business Week*'s top business schools, 1999 ★631★
Highest pre-MBA salaries for students enrolled in *Business Week*'s top business schools, 1999 ★632★
Median starting salaries of graduates from *U.S. News & World Report*'s top 10 graduate business schools, 2001 ★636★
Out-of-state tuition and fees for *U.S. News & World Report*'s top 10 graduate business schools, 2001 ★637★
Percentage of applicants accepted at *Business Week*'s top business schools, 2000 ★638★
Percentage of employed graduates at *U.S. News & World Report*'s top 10 graduate business schools, 2001 ★639★
Percentage of graduates earning over $100,000 from *Business Week*'s top business schools, 1999 ★640★
Percentage of graduates employed within 3 months of graduation from *U.S. News & World Report*'s top 10 graduate business schools, 2001 ★641★
Top graduate business schools, 2001 ★649★
Top graduate business schools by reputation as determined by academic personnel, 2001 ★650★
Top graduate business schools by reputation, as determined by recruiters, 2001 ★651★
Academics' choices for best graduate accounting programs, 2001 ★659★
Academics' choices for best graduate finance programs, 2001 ★662★
U.S. News & World Report's undergraduate business programs with the best finance departments, 2000-01 ★665★
Academics' choices for best graduate general management programs, 2001 ★666★
Academics' choices for best graduate international business programs, 2001 ★668★

Academics' choices for best graduate marketing programs, 2001 ★670★
Academics' choices for best graduate quantitative analysis programs, 2001 ★673★
Academics' choices for best graduate production/operations management programs, 2001 ★674★
U.S. News & World Report's undergraduate business programs with the best international business departments, 2000-01 ★682★
U.S. News & World Report's undergraduate business programs with the best marketing departments, 2000-01 ★685★
Average GMAT scores for *U.S. News & World Report*'s top 10 graduate business schools, 2000 ★2529★

Pensacola Catholic High School
Outstanding secondary schools in Pensacola, Florida ★4201★

People's Republic of China
Countries of origin for non-U.S. citizens awarded doctorates at U.S. colleges and universities, 1999 ★1901★
First-year physics and astronomy graduate students from Asia, 1997-98 ★2987★

PeopleSoft
Fortune's highest ranked computer software companies, 2000 ★455★
Software companies with the fastest growth, 2000 ★528★

Pepose; Jay S.
Top pay and benefits for the chief executive and top paid employees at Washington University in Missouri ★3607★

Pepperdine University
U.S. colleges and universities with a primarily religious student body ★1022★
U.S. News & World Report's national universities with the lowest graduation rates, 1999 ★1141★
U.S. News & World Report's national universities with the lowest proportion of classes with 50 or more students, 2000-01 ★1142★
U.S. News & World Report's national universities with students most in debt, 1999 ★1476★
Highest undergraduate tuition and fees at colleges and universities in California ★1486★
U.S. colleges and universities awarding the most business management and administrative services master's degrees to Asian Americans ★1760★
U.S. colleges and universities awarding the most business management and administrative services master's degrees to Hispanic Americans ★1761★
U.S. colleges and universities awarding the most psychology master's degrees to African Americans ★1797★
U.S. colleges and universities awarding the most psychology master's degrees to Asian Americans ★1798★
U.S. colleges and universities awarding the most psychology master's degrees to Hispanic Americans ★1799★
U.S. colleges and universities awarding the most psychology master's degrees to Native Americans ★1800★
U.S. doctoral institutions with the largest number of students studying abroad, 1998-99 ★2512★
College senior's choices for exemplary doctoral-intensive universities ★2532★

First-year student's choices for exemplary doctoral-intensive universities ★2535★
Academics' choices for best dispute resolution programs, 2001 ★2627★
Average faculty salaries for institutions of higher education in California, 2000-01 ★3692★

Peppers; Larry
Top pay and benefits for the chief executive and top paid employees at Washington and Lee University ★3605★

PepsiCo
Fortune's highest ranked beverages companies, 2000 ★450★
Top consumer products companies in Standard & Poor's 500, 2001 ★536★

Peralta Community College
Average faculty salaries for institutions of higher education without academic ranks in California, 2000-01 ★3743★

The Perceived Importance of the Ethical Decision-Making of Ad Managers
Most influential articles in the *Journal of Business Research* from 1995 to 1999 ★700★

Pereira; Paulo
European business moguls considered the best dealmakers ★440★

Perez-Lopez; Rene
Top pay and benefits for the chief executive and top paid employees at Virginia Wesleyan College ★3596★

Perfect Family
Most notable fiction books for young adults, 2001 ★322★

The Perfect Storm
Longest-running mass market paperback bestsellers, 2000 ★280★

Performance and Job Satisfaction Effects on Salesperson Turnover: A Replication and Extension
Most influential articles in the *Journal of Business Research*, 1985-1999 ★697★
Most influential articles in the *Journal of Business Research* from 1985 to 1989 ★698★

Performance Technologies
Companies with the best two-year total returns since 1998 ★436★

Pergamon Press
Publishers, journals and proceedings with the lowest citations (Class 6) ★2571★

Perham Area Public Library
Highest Hennen's American Public Library Ratings for libraries serving a population of 1,000 to 2,499 ★2692★

Perillo; Joseph M.
Top pay and benefits for the chief executive and top paid employees at Fordham University ★3295★

Peripheral computer equipment operators
Occupations with the highest decline in employment, 1998-2008 ★2310★

Perkins Loans
Sources of financial aid for incoming freshmen, 2000 ★1062★
Proposed fiscal 2002 appropriations for student assistance ★1251★
Fiscal 2002 requested budget as compared with Fiscal 2001 budget for the Education Department ★2231★

Perlman; David
American Chemical Society 2001 award winners (Group 4) ★754★

Perlmann; Joel
Top pay and benefits for the chief executive and top paid employees at Bard College ★3190★

Perna; Richard P.
Top pay and benefits for the chief executive and top paid employees at the University of Dayton ★3539★

Perrin; Kathy
Top pay and benefits for the chief executive and top paid employees at the University of Mary ★3548★

Perritt; H.H.
Top pay and benefits for the chief executive and top paid employees at Illinois Institute of Technology ★3346★

Perry; Douglas
Top pay and benefits for the chief executive and top paid employees at Olivet Nazarene University ★3432★

Perry High School
Outstanding secondary schools in Cleveland-Lorain-Elyria, Ohio ★4114★

Perryville Middle School
Outstanding secondary schools in Wilmington-Newark, Delaware-Maryland ★4252★

Persian Mirrors: The Elusive Face of Iran
Most notable nonfiction books, 2001 ★285★
Outstanding works of nonfiction, 2001 ★294★

Persico; Sebastian
Top pay and benefits for the chief executive and top paid employees at Manhattanville College ★3388★

Personal care and home health aides
Fastest growing occupations, 1998-2008 ★2302★
Occupations with the largest projected employment growth, 1998-2008 ★2312★
Projected employment growth for selected occupations that require shorter moderate-term on-the-job training, 1998-2008 ★2321★

Personal credit institutions
Employment growth percentages for selected industries, 1998-2000 ★2294★

Personality
Gender breakdown of psychology doctorate recipients, by subfield, 1999 ★1941★
Psychology doctorates awarded at U.S. colleges and universities, by subfield, 1999 ★2043★

Personnel Psychology
Top management journals ★546★
Top management journals by core impact ★547★
Journals and proceedings with the most citations (Class 4) ★2570★
Most cited business serials in technical communication journals from 1988 to 1997 ★4417★

Personnel supply services
Employment growth percentages for selected industries, 1998-2000 ★2294★
Industries with the highest percentage of projected employment growth from 1998 through 2008 ★2305★
Industries with the highest projected growth rate, 1994-2005 ★2306★

Peru State College
State appropriations for Nebraska's institutions of higher education, 2000-01 ★1280★
Lowest undergraduate tuition and fees at colleges and universities in Nebraska ★1529★

Average faculty salaries for institutions of higher education in Nebraska, 2000-01 ★3714★

Pesticide Biochemistry and Physiology
Entomology journals by citation impact, 1981-98 ★2453★
Entomology journals by citation impact, 1994-98 ★2454★

Pesticide Science
Agriculture journals by citation impact, 1992-96 ★52★
Entomology journals by citation impact, 1998 ★2455★

Pesticides Monitoring Journal
Agriculture journals by citation impact, 1981-96 ★50★
Agriculture journals by citation impact, 1981-99 ★51★

Petchesky; Rosalind
Highly acknowledged individuals in the field of women's studies, 1975-94 ★4466★

Peter Kiewit Sons'
Fortune's highest ranked engineering and construction companies, 2000 ★461★

Peter Pan
Most notable children's videos, 2001 ★2889★

Peterboro Public Library
North America's first ten public libraries ★2680★

Peters Township Public Library
Highest Hennen's American Public Library Ratings for libraries serving a population of 10,000 to 24,999 ★2695★

Petersilia; J.
Most cited authors in the journal *Federal Probation*, 1990 to 1995 ★1623★
Most cited authors in three criminal justice journals ★1633★

Peterson; Bruce
Top pay and benefits for the chief executive and top paid employees at Middlebury College ★3401★

Peterson, O.P.; Very Rev. Thomas R.
Top pay and benefits for the chief executive and top paid employees at Seton Hall University ★3496★

Peterson; Oscar
Canada's best performing artists of the 20th century ★74★

Peterson; Shirley D.
Top pay and benefits for the chief executive and top paid employees at Hood College ★3338★

Peterson; Walter
Top pay and benefits for the chief executive and top paid employees at the University of Dubuque ★3542★

Peto; Richard
Most-cited researchers in epidemiology, 1981-1998 ★2876★

Petri; Rep. Thomas E.
Members of Congress receiving the largest contributions from the Sallie Mae Inc. Political Action Committee ★3023★

Petrobras
Business Week's top emerging-market companies worldwide ★434★

Petroleum
Engineering doctorates awarded at U.S. colleges and universities, by subfield, 1999 ★1923★
Gender breakdown of engineering doctorate recipients, by subfield, 1999 ★1934★

Petroleum engineer
Most desirable jobs in production/manufacturing ★2276★

Petruska; Christina
Top pay and benefits for the chief executive and top paid employees at Rider University ★3458★

Petsko; Greg
Top pay and benefits for the chief executive and top paid employees at Brandeis University ★3209★

Pettit; Linda R.
Top pay and benefits for the chief executive and top paid employees at St. Lawrence University ★3477★

Petunia
Publishers Weekly Off-the-Cuff Awards winner for book happiest to see back in print, 2000 ★345★

Pfau; Richard A.
Top pay and benefits for the chief executive and top paid employees at Illinois College ★3345★

Pfeiffer University
Average faculty salaries for institutions of higher education in North Carolina, 2000-01 ★3720★

Pfizer
Business Week's best companies in the United States ★411★
Business Week's top companies worldwide ★433★
Fortune's highest ranked pharmaceuticals companies, 2000 ★485★
Top health care companies in Standard & Poor's 500, 2001 ★542★
Top internships in the U.S. with the highest compensation, 2001 ★2611★

PG&E
Fortune's highest ranked electric and gas utilities companies, 2000 ★459★

Pharaoh's Daughter
Outstanding children's fiction books, 2000 ★329★

Pharmacia
Fortune's highest ranked pharmaceuticals companies, 2000 ★485★

Pharmacist
Jobs with the lowest unemployment ★2258★
Occupations with the highest average annual salaries for college graduates, 1998 ★3132★

Pharmacists
Projected employment growth for selected occupations that require advanced education, 1998-2008 ★2318★

Pharmacology
Average salaries for assistant professors at private institutions in preclinical department of medical schools, 2000-01 ★3785★
Average salaries for assistant professors at public and private institutions in preclinical department of medical schools, 2000-01 ★3786★
Average salaries for assistant professors at public institutions in preclinical department of medical schools, 2000-01 ★3787★
Average salaries for associate professors at private institutions in preclinical department of medical schools, 2000-01 ★3800★
Average salaries for associate professors at public and private institutions in preclinical department of medical schools, 2000-01 ★3801★
Average salaries for associate professors at public institutions in preclinical department of medical schools, 2000-01 ★3802★

Average salaries for full-time instructors at private institutions in preclinical department of medical schools, 2000-01 ★3854★

Average salaries for full-time instructors at public and private institutions in preclinical department of medical schools, 2000-01 ★3855★

Average salaries for full-time instructors at public institutions in preclinical department of medical schools, 2000-01 ★3856★

Average salaries for professors at private institutions in preclinical department of medical schools, 2000-01 ★3932★

Average salaries for professors at public and private institutions in preclinical department of medical schools, 2000-01 ★3933★

Average salaries for professors at public institutions in preclinical department of medical schools, 2000-01 ★3934★

Austria's contribution of papers in the sciences by field, 1992-96 ★4298★

Austria's contribution of papers in the sciences, by field, 1995-99 ★4299★

Austria's relative impact in the sciences by field, 1992-96 ★4300★

Belgium's contribution of papers in the sciences by field, 1992-96 ★4301★

Belgium's contribution of papers in the sciences, by field, 1995-99 ★4302★

Finland's contribution of papers in the sciences by field, 1992-96 ★4309★

Finland's contribution of papers in the sciences, by field, 1995-99 ★4310★

France's contribution of papers in the sciences, by field, 1995-99 ★4311★

Italy's contribution of papers in the sciences, by field, 1995-99 ★4316★

Japan's contribution of papers in the sciences, by field, 1995-99 ★4318★

Japan's contribution of papers in the sciences, by field, 1996-2000 ★4319★

Netherlands' contribution of papers in the sciences, by field, 1995-99 ★4321★

New Zealand's contribution of papers in the sciences, by field, 1994-98 ★4322★

Poland's contribution of papers in the sciences, by field, 1993-97 ★4324★

South Korea's contribution of papers in the sciences, by field, 1995-99 ★4327★

Spain's contribution of papers in the sciences, by field, 1993-97 ★4328★

Spain's contribution of papers in the sciences, by field, 1995-99 ★4329★

Sweden's contribution of papers in the sciences by field, 1993-97 ★4330★

Sweden's contribution of papers in the sciences, by field, 1995-99 ★4331★

Switzerland's contribution of papers in the sciences, by field, 1994-98 ★4332★

Switzerland's contribution of papers in the sciences, by field, 1995-99 ★4333★

Taiwan contribution of papers in the sciences, by field, 1995-99 ★4334★

Turkey's contribution of papers in the sciences, by field, 1995-99 ★4335★

Pharmacy
Gender breakdown of health sciences doctorate recipients, by subfield, 1999 ★1935★
Health sciences doctorates awarded at U.S. colleges and universities, by subfield, 1999 ★1944★
Top health professions majors for accepted applicants to U.S. medical schools, 1999-2000 ★2852★

Pheasant; Clayton N.
Top pay and benefits for the chief executive and top paid employees at Marywood University ★3396★

Phelan; James
Top pay and benefits for the chief executive and top paid employees at Mount Saint Mary's College in Maryland ★3412★

Phelps Dodge
Fortune's highest ranked metals companies, 2000 ★476★
Top metals and mining companies in Standard & Poor's 500, 2001 ★549★

Phifer; James
Top pay and benefits for the chief executive and top paid employees at Coe College ★3240★

Philadelphia
U.S. school districts with the highest number of vacancies for K-12 teachers ★2331★
U.S. market areas with the highest percentage of adults having internet access ★2607★
Largest public school districts in the U.S. ★4016★

Philadelphia College of Bible
Average faculty salaries for institutions of higher education in Pennsylvania, 2000-01 ★3725★

Philadelphia College of Pharmacy and Science
Private, 4-year undergraduate colleges and universities producing the most Ph.D.'s in the life sciences, 1920-1990 ★192★

The Philadelphia Inquirer
Top internships in the U.S. with the highest compensation, 2001 ★2611★

Philadelphia University
Average faculty salaries for institutions of higher education in Pennsylvania, 2000-01 ★3725★

Philander Smith College
Private 4-year institutions with the lowest tuition, 2000-01 ★1468★
Highest undergraduate tuition and fees at colleges and universities in Arkansas ★1484★

Philip Morris
Business Week's best companies in terms of profits ★406★
Business Week's best performing companies with the highest 1-year shareholder returns ★415★
Fortune's highest ranked tobacco companies, 2000 ★502★
Top consumer products companies in Standard & Poor's 500, 2001 ★536★
Highly recommended public companies for women executives, 2000 ★4453★

Philip Randolph Campus; A.
Outstanding urban public high schools in Metro New York ★4265★

Philippines
Eight grade science achievement scores from selected countries, 1999 ★14★
Percentage of enrollment at private institutions of higher education, by country, 1998 ★858★
Countries with the lowest spending per student on higher education, 1997 ★2489★
Eighth grade mathematics achievement scores from selected countries, 1999 ★2773★
Countries with the lowest leader's salary ★3121★

Philips Electronics N.A.
Fortune's highest ranked electronics and electrical equipment companies, 2000 ★460★

Phillips Community College of the University of Arkansas
Institutions censured by the American Association of University Professors, 2001 ★1067★

Phillips; G.
Highest ranked inactive communication studies researchers ★2748★

Phillips Petroleum
Fortune's highest ranked petroleum refining companies, 2000 ★484★
Top fuel companies in Standard & Poor's 500, 2001 ★541★

Phillips Prep
Outstanding secondary schools in Mobile, Alabama ★4182★

Phillips-Van Heusen
Fortune's highest ranked apparel companies, 2000 ★448★

Philosopher
Most desirable social sciences jobs ★2280★

Philosophy
Gender breakdown of humanities doctorate recipients, by subfield, 1999 ★1936★
Humanities doctorates awarded at U.S. colleges and universities, by subfield, 1999 ★1946★
Percentage of female doctorate recipients at U.S. colleges and universities, by subfield, 1999 ★1988★
Top nonscience majors for accepted applicants to U.S. medical schools, 1999-2000 ★2854★

Philosophy and religion
Average costs for Academic Search titles by subject, 2001 ★2918★
Periodical prices by LC subject, 2001 ★2925★

Philosophy and Rhetoric
Most cited philosophy serials in technical communication journals from 1988 to 1997 ★4421★

Phizacklea; Thomas
Top pay and benefits for the chief executive and top paid employees at the Centenary College of Louisiana ★3523★

Phoenix
U.S. market areas with the highest percentage of adults having internet access ★2607★
U.S. cities with the highest percentage of births to mothers with less than 12 years of education ★4432★

Phoenix, Albuquerque; University of
U.S. colleges and universities awarding the most computer and information sciences master's degrees to Hispanic Americans ★1768★

Phoenix, AZ
Cities with the most Yahoo! listings per million residents ★2580★

Phoenix College
Lowest undergraduate tuition and fees at colleges and universities in Arizona ★1483★

Phoenix Home Life
Highly recommended public companies for women executives, 2000 ★4453★

Phoenix-Mesa, AZ
America's most wired cities with the highest domain density, 2001 ★2574★

Phoenix (MI); University of
U.S. colleges and universities awarding the most health professions and related sciences master's degrees to African Americans ★1777★

Phoenix; University of
  Highest undergraduate tuition and fees at colleges and universities in Arizona ★1482★
  U.S. colleges and universities awarding the most business management and administrative services master's degrees to African Americans ★1759★
  U.S. colleges and universities awarding the most business management and administrative services master's degrees to Hispanic Americans ★1761★
  U.S. colleges and universities awarding the most business management and administrative services master's degrees to Native Americans ★1762★
  U.S. colleges and universities awarding the most business management and administrative services doctorate degrees to Hispanic Americans ★2087★

Phonics Pathways
  Best selling small press releases, 2001 ★226★

Photographer
  Most desirable jobs in communications ★2271★

Photographic process worker
  Jobs considered the loneliest ★2244★
  Most desirable jobs in production/manufacturing ★2276★

Photojournalist
  Jobs considered the most competitive ★2245★
  Jobs with the most stringent quotas ★2259★
  Most desirable jobs in communications ★2271★
  'White-collar' jobs considered the most physically demanding ★2285★

Physica D
  Physics journals with the greatest impact measure, 1981-98 ★3020★

Physical
  Chemistry doctorates awarded at U.S. colleges and universities, by subfield, 1999 ★1889★
  Gender breakdown of chemistry doctorate recipients, by subfield, 1999 ★1929★

Physical education and coaching
  Gender breakdown of teaching fields doctorate recipients, by subfield, 1999 ★1943★
  Teaching fields doctorates awarded at U.S. colleges and universities, by subfield, 1999 ★2046★

Physical and life sciences
  Fields of study profile of foreign students enrolled in U.S. institutions of higher education, 1998-99 ★2495★

Physical Review A
  Optics journals by citation impact, 1981-99 ★2906★
  Optics journals by citation impact, 1995-99 ★2907★
  Optics journals by citation impact, 1999 ★2908★
  Physics journals with the greatest impact measure, 1981-98 ★3020★

Physical Review Letters
  Physics journals with the greatest impact measure, 1981-98 ★3020★

Physical science/math
  Doctoral degree distribution by broad field, 1999 ★1902★

Physical sciences
  Median salary for B.S. chemists, by field ★781★
  Median salary for M.S. chemists, by field ★785★
  Median salary for Ph.D. chemists, by field ★786★
  Expected majors for incoming freshmen, 2000 ★1050★
  Age grouping of doctorate recipients, by broad field, 1999 ★1882★
  Comparative data of women receiving doctorate degrees in selected fields in 1950 and 1998 ★1899★
  Median age at conferral of doctoral degree from U.S. universities, by discipline, 1999 ★1952★
  Number of doctorate recipients at U.S. colleges and universities, by field, 1999 ★1969★
  Percentage of female doctorate recipients, by broad field, 1999 ★1989★
  Percentage of minority doctorate recipients in the U.S., by broad field, 1999 ★1991★
  Fields of study profile of U.S. students studying abroad, 1998-99 ★2507★

Physical therapist
  Jobs with the lowest unemployment ★2258★
  'White-collar' jobs considered the most physically demanding ★2285★

Physical therapists
  Projected employment growth for selected occupations that require advanced education, 1998-2008 ★2318★

Physical therapy assistants and aides
  Fastest growing occupations, 1998-2008 ★2302★
  Projected employment growth for selected occupations that require an associate degree or less, 1998-2008 ★2319★

Physician
  Occupations with the highest average annual salaries for college graduates, 1998 ★3132★

Physician assistant
  Jobs with the best outlook scores ★2249★
  Jobs with the highest employment growth ★2254★
  Jobs with the lowest unemployment ★2258★

Physician assistants
  Projections for the fastest growing occupations requiring a bachelor's degree or more from 1998 to 2008 ★2292★
  Fastest growing occupations, 1998-2008 ★2302★

Physician (general practice)
  Jobs with the best outlook scores ★2249★
  Jobs with the longest work weeks ★2257★
  Jobs with the lowest unemployment ★2258★

Physicians
  Projected employment growth for selected occupations that require advanced education, 1998-2008 ★2318★

Physicist
  Most desirable jobs in math/science ★2274★

Physics
  Comparative data of women receiving doctorate degrees in selected fields in 1950 and 1998 ★1899★
  Subjects required by the most U.S. medical schools for the 2000-01 entering class ★2850★
  Top physical science majors for accepted applicants to U.S. medical schools, 1999-2000 ★2855★
  Average costs for Academic Search titles by subject, 2001 ★2918★
  Periodical prices by LC subject, 2001 ★2925★
  Periodical prices by scientific discipline, 2001 ★2926★
  Mean age of first and best contribution of scientists and inventors, by discipline ★3096★
  Austria's contribution of papers in the sciences by field, 1992-96 ★4298★
  Austria's contribution of papers in the sciences, by field, 1995-99 ★4299★
  Austria's relative impact in the sciences by field, 1992-96 ★4300★
  Belgium's contribution of papers in the sciences by field, 1992-96 ★4301★
  France's contribution of papers in the sciences, by field, 1995-99 ★4311★
  France's contribution of papers in the sciences, by field, 1996-2000 ★4312★
  Germany's contribution of papers in the sciences, by field, 1995-99 ★4313★
  Hong Kong's contribution of papers in the sciences, by field, 1995-99 ★4314★
  Italy's contribution of papers in the sciences, by field, 1995-99 ★4316★
  Italy's relative impact in the sciences by field, 1992-96 ★4317★
  Japan's contribution of papers in the sciences, by field, 1995-99 ★4318★
  Japan's contribution of papers in the sciences, by field, 1996-2000 ★4319★
  Poland's contribution of papers in the sciences, by field, 1993-97 ★4324★
  Russia's contribution of papers in the sciences, by field, 1993-97 ★4325★
  South Korea's contribution of papers in the sciences, by field, 1995-99 ★4327★
  Spain's contribution of papers in the sciences, by field, 1993-97 ★4328★
  Spain's contribution of papers in the sciences, by field, 1995-99 ★4329★
  Switzerland's contribution of papers in the sciences, by field, 1994-98 ★4332★
  Switzerland's contribution of papers in the sciences, by field, 1995-99 ★4333★
  Taiwan contribution of papers in the sciences, by field, 1995-99 ★4334★
  Turkey's contribution of papers in the sciences, by field, 1995-99 ★4335★

Physics/astronomy
  Median salary for B.S. chemists, by field ★781★
  Median salary for M.S. chemists, by field ★785★
  Median salary for Ph.D. chemists, by field ★786★
  Number of physical sciences doctorate recipients at U.S. colleges and universities, by field, 1999 ★1975★
  Percentage of female doctorate recipients at U.S. colleges and universities, by subfield, 1999 ★1988★
  Physical sciences, mathematics, and computer sciences doctorates awarded to U.S. citizens/permanent residents at U.S. colleges and universities, by race/ethnicity and subfield, 1999 ★1993★

Physics B
  Number of Advanced Placement Exams taken by African Americans, by subject, 2000 ★30★
  Number of Advanced Placement Exams taken by Asian Americans, by subject, 2000 ★31★
  Number of Advanced Placement Exams taken by Hispanic Americans, by subject, 2000 ★32★

Physics B E&M
  Number of Advanced Placement Exams taken by African Americans, by subject, 2000 ★30★
  Number of Advanced Placement Exams taken by Asian Americans, by subject, 2000 ★31★

Number of Advanced Placement Exams taken by Hispanic Americans, by subject, 2000 ★32★

Physics C mech
Number of Advanced Placement Exams taken by African Americans, by subject, 2000 ★30★
Number of Advanced Placement Exams taken by Asian Americans, by subject, 2000 ★31★
Number of Advanced Placement Exams taken by Hispanic Americans, by subject, 2000 ★32★

Physics, general
Gender breakdown of physics and astronomy doctorate recipients, by subfield, 1999 ★1939★
Physics and astronomy doctorates awarded at U.S. colleges and universities, by subfield, 1999 ★1994★

Physics Letters B
Physics journals with the greatest impact measure, 1981-98 ★3020★

Physics Reports
Physics journals with the greatest impact measure, 1981-98 ★3020★

Physiological Entomology
Entomology journals by citation impact, 1981-98 ★2453★
Entomology journals by citation impact, 1994-98 ★2454★

Physiological/psychobiology
Gender breakdown of psychology doctorate recipients, by subfield, 1999 ★1941★
Psychology doctorates awarded at U.S. colleges and universities, by subfield, 1999 ★2043★

Physiologist
Jobs with the lowest unemployment ★2258★
Most desirable jobs in healthcare/medicine ★2273★

Physiology
Top biological science majors for accepted applicants to U.S. medical schools, 1999-2000 ★2851★
Average salaries for assistant professors at private institutions in preclinical department of medical schools, 2000-01 ★3785★
Average salaries for assistant professors at public and private institutions in preclinical department of medical schools, 2000-01 ★3786★
Average salaries for assistant professors at public institutions in preclinical department of medical schools, 2000-01 ★3787★
Average salaries for associate professors at private institutions in preclinical department of medical schools, 2000-01 ★3800★
Average salaries for associate professors at public and private institutions in preclinical department of medical schools, 2000-01 ★3801★
Average salaries for associate professors at public institutions in preclinical department of medical schools, 2000-01 ★3802★
Average salaries for full-time instructors at private institutions in preclinical department of medical schools, 2000-01 ★3854★
Average salaries for full-time instructors at public and private institutions in preclinical department of medical schools, 2000-01 ★3855★
Average salaries for full-time instructors at public institutions in preclinical department of medical schools, 2000-01 ★3856★
Average salaries for professors at private institutions in preclinical department of medical schools, 2000-01 ★3932★

Average salaries for professors at public and private institutions in preclinical department of medical schools, 2000-01 ★3933★
Average salaries for professors at public institutions in preclinical department of medical schools, 2000-01 ★3934★

Physiology & Behavior
Most-cited social sciences journals, 1981-97 ★4340★

Piatt; Robert William
Top pay and benefits for the chief executive and top paid employees at Saint Mary's University in Texas ★3481★

Picasso; Pablo
Highly influential artists of the 20th century ★76★

The Picture of Dorian Gray
Outstanding audiobooks, 2000 ★287★

Piderit, S.J.; Rev. John
Top pay and benefits for the chief executive and top paid employees at Loyola University of Chicago ★3382★

Piedmont College
Average faculty salaries for institutions of higher education in Georgia, 2000-01 ★3697★

Piedmont Community College
Average faculty salaries for institutions of higher education without academic ranks in North Carolina, 2000-01 ★3761★

Piedmont Middle School
Outstanding secondary schools in Charlotte-Gastonia-Rock Hill, North Carolina-South Carolina ★4108★

Piedmont Open Middle School
Outstanding secondary schools in Charlotte-Gastonia-Rock Hill, North Carolina-South Carolina ★4108★

Piedmont Virginia Community College
Lowest undergraduate tuition and fees at colleges and universities in Virginia ★1565★

Pieken; Russell W.
Top pay and benefits for the chief executive and top paid employees at Baker University ★3188★

Piepenburg; Kurt
Top pay and benefits for the chief executive and top paid employees at Carthage College ★3224★

Pierce; Lillian
All-USA College Academic First Team, 2001 ★2★

Pierce; Susan Resneck
Top pay and benefits for the chief executive and top paid employees at the University of Puget Sound ★3557★

Pierre Pierce
All-America boys' high school basketball 3rd team, 2001 ★163★

Pierson; Carol Anne
Top pay and benefits for the chief executive and top paid employees at Saint Bonaventure University ★3470★

The Pigman
Most frequently banned books in the 1990s ★745★

Piker; Steven I.
Top pay and benefits for the chief executive and top paid employees at Swarthmore College ★3514★

Pikes Peak Community College
Lowest undergraduate tuition and fees at colleges and universities in Colorado ★1489★

Average faculty salaries for institutions of higher education without academic ranks in Colorado, 2000-01 ★3744★

Pikeville College
Average faculty salaries for institutions of higher education in Kentucky, 2000-01 ★3704★

Pilcher; Webster H.
Top pay and benefits for the chief executive and top paid employees at the University of Rochester ★3560★

Pilgrim; John
Top pay and benefits for the chief executive and top paid employees at Millsaps College ★3403★

Pillowtex
Fortune's highest ranked textiles companies, 2000 ★501★

Pima Community College
Community colleges in North America with the highest enrollment ★852★
Institutions with the most part-time Hispanic American faculty ★924★
Lowest undergraduate tuition and fees at colleges and universities in Arizona ★1483★

Pinchin; Jane L.
Top pay and benefits for the chief executive and top paid employees at Colgate University ★3242★

Pinckney Middle School
Outstanding secondary schools in Ann Arbor, Michigan ★4084★

Pinckneyville Middle School
Outstanding secondary schools in Atlanta, Georgia ★4087★

Pinder; Margaret
Top pay and benefits for the chief executive and top paid employees at Amber University ★3172★

Pine Manor College
Average faculty salaries for institutions of higher education in Massachusetts, 2000-01 ★3708★

Pine Technical College
Lowest undergraduate tuition and fees at colleges and universities in Minnesota ★1521★
Average faculty salaries for institutions of higher education without academic ranks in Minnesota, 2000-01 ★3753★

Pine Tree High School
Outstanding secondary schools in Longview-Marshall, Texas ★4166★

Pine Tree Junior High School
Outstanding secondary schools in Longview-Marshall, Texas ★4166★

Pine Tree Middle School
Outstanding secondary schools in Longview-Marshall, Texas ★4166★

Pinkney; Jerry
Outstanding children's picture books, 2000 ★331★

Pinter; Harold
Top playwrights of the twentieth century ★4436★

Pipe
Percentage of high school students using tobacco products by gender ★4373★
Percentage of middle school students using tobacco products by gender ★4374★

Pipes; P. Bruce
Top pay and benefits for the chief executive and top paid employees at Franklin and Marshall College ★3296★

Pirie Elementary School
Illinois elementary schools chosen to be 'demonstration sites' for struggling schools ★4006★

Piros; Susan
Top pay and benefits for the chief executive and top paid employees at Saint Xavier University ★3487★

Pitkin, CO
Counties with the highest per capita income ★2561★

Pitman
Book publishers with the most citations (Class 5) ★2566★

Pitney Bowes
Top public companies with the highest percentage of women board of directors, 2000 ★4458★

Pitt Community College
Average faculty salaries for institutions of higher education without academic ranks in North Carolina, 2000-01 ★3761★

Pitter; Keiko
Top pay and benefits for the chief executive and top paid employees at Whitman College ★3623★

Pittsburgh
U.S. market areas with the highest percentage of adults having internet access ★2607★

Pittsburgh, Bradford; University of
Average faculty salaries for institutions of higher education in Pennsylvania, 2000-01 ★3725★

Pittsburgh, Greensburg; University of
Average faculty salaries for institutions of higher education in Pennsylvania, 2000-01 ★3725★

Pittsburgh, Johnstown; University of
Average faculty salaries for institutions of higher education in Pennsylvania, 2000-01 ★3725★

Pittsburgh Medical Center; University of
Top gastroenterology hospitals in the U.S., 2000 ★2790★
Top hospitals in the U.S., 2000 ★2793★
Top ortolaryngology hospitals in the U.S., 2000 ★2798★
Top psychiatric hospitals in the U.S., 2000 ★2800★

Pittsburgh Post-Gazette
Most selective internships in the U.S., 2001 ★2610★

Pittsburgh, Program in History and Philosophy of Science; University of
Most effective philosophy research-doctorate programs as evaluated by the National Research Council ★2945★
Top philosophy research-doctorate programs as evaluated by the National Research Council ★2947★

Pittsburgh State University
State appropriations for Kansas institutions of higher education, 2000-01 ★1269★
Average faculty salaries for institutions of higher education in Kansas, 2000-01 ★3703★

Pittsburgh Theological Seminary
Average faculty salaries for institutions of higher education in Pennsylvania, 2000-01 ★3725★

Pittsburgh, Titusville; University of
Average faculty salaries for institutions of higher education in Pennsylvania, 2000-01 ★3725★

Pittsburgh; University of
Comparisons of investment returns for finance MBAs ★624★
U.S. business schools with the quickest payback on MBA investments ★654★
Top business schools for within-discipline research performance in management information systems, 1986-1998 ★675★
Four-year public institutions enrolling the highest number of students from the District of Columbia, 1998-99 ★855★
U.S. colleges and universities with an unfavorable surrounding town or city ★1023★
U.S. colleges and universities with poor instructors ★1027★
U.S. colleges and universities with strained race/class interaction ★1029★
U.S. colleges and universities with the most upper level courses taught by TAs ★1040★
State appropriations for Pennsylvania's institutions of higher education, 2000-01 ★1291★
Highest undergraduate tuition and fees at public, 4-year or above colleges and universities ★1463★
Public 4-year institutions with the highest tuition, 2000-01 ★1471★
U.S. colleges and universities awarding the most communications master's degrees to Asian Americans ★1764★
U.S. colleges and universities awarding the most computer and information sciences master's degrees to Hispanic Americans ★1768★
U.S. colleges and universities awarding the most English language/literature/letters master's degrees to African Americans ★1773★
U.S. colleges and universities awarding the most health professions and related sciences master's degrees to African Americans ★1777★
U.S. colleges and universities awarding the most education doctorate degrees to Asian Americans ★2109★
U.S. colleges and universities awarding the most health professions and related sciences doctorate degrees to African Americans ★2114★
U.S. colleges and universities awarding the most health professions and related sciences doctorate degrees to Asian Americans ★2115★
U.S. colleges and universities awarding the most health professions and related sciences doctorate degrees to Hispanic Americans ★2116★
U.S. universities with the greatest impact in education, 1995-99 ★2222★
U.S. universities with the greatest impact in chemical engineering, 1994-98 ★2393★
Library and information science programs with the most citations to journal articles, 1993-1998 ★2712★
Library and information science programs with the most journal articles, 1993-1998 ★2713★
U.S. universities with the greatest impact in library and information science, 1994-98 ★2719★
Most effective philosophy research-doctorate programs as evaluated by the National Research Council ★2945★
Top philosophy research-doctorate programs as evaluated by the National Research Council ★2947★
U.S. universities publishing the most papers in the field of philosophy, 1995-99 ★2948★
U.S. universities with the highest concentration of papers published in the field of psychiatry, 1994-98 ★3061★
U.S. universities with the greatest impact in psychology, 1995-99 ★3064★
Average faculty salaries for institutions of higher education in Pennsylvania, 2000-01 ★3725★

Pittston
Fortune's highest ranked mail, packaging, and freight delivery companies, 2000 ★473★

Pitzer College
U.S. colleges and universities most accepting of alternative lifestyles ★986★
U.S. colleges and universities with excellent instructors ★1024★
U.S. colleges and universities with harmonious race/class interaction ★1026★
U.S. colleges and universities with the happiest students ★1035★
U.S. News & World Report's national liberal arts colleges with students most in debt, 1999 ★1386★
Highest undergraduate tuition and fees at private nonprofit, 4-year or above colleges and universities ★1461★
Highest undergraduate tuition and fees at colleges and universities in California ★1486★
Average faculty salaries for institutions of higher education in California, 2000-01 ★3692★

Pius XI High School
Outstanding secondary schools in Milwaukee-Waukesha, Wisconsin ★4180★

Pizarro; Alejo
Top pay and benefits for the chief executive and top paid employees at LaSierra University ★3366★

Placer Dome
Top metals and mining companies in Standard & Poor's 500, 2001 ★549★

Plainfield Central Middle School
Outstanding secondary schools in New London-Norwich, Connecticut-Rhode Island ★4189★

Plains Resources
Fortune's highest ranked mining and crude oil companies, 2000 ★477★

Plainsong
Longest-running trade paperback bestsellers, 2000 ★282★
Most notable fiction books for young adults, 2001 ★322★

Planchon; John
Top pay and benefits for the chief executive and top paid employees at Rhodes College ★3456★

Plano East Senior High School
Outstanding secondary schools in Dallas, Texas ★4120★
Outstanding suburban public high schools in Metro Dallas-Ft. Worth ★4257★

Plano High School
Outstanding secondary schools in Dallas, Texas ★4120★

Plant and animal science
Austria's contribution of papers in the sciences, by field, 1995-99 ★4299★

Plant and animal sciences
Australia's contribution of papers in the sciences, by field, 1993-97 ★4292★
Australia's contribution of papers in the sciences, by field, 1995-99 ★4293★

Austria's contribution of papers in the sciences by field, 1992-96 ★4298★
Belgium's contribution of papers in the sciences by field, 1992-96 ★4301★
Belgium's contribution of papers in the sciences, by field, 1995-99 ★4302★
Canada's contribution of papers in the sciences, by field, 1995-99 ★4303★
Denmark's contribution of papers in the sciences by field, 1994-98 ★4306★
Denmark's contribution of papers in the sciences, by field, 1995-99 ★4307★
Finland's contribution of papers in the sciences by field, 1992-96 ★4309★
Finland's contribution of papers in the sciences, by field, 1995-99 ★4310★
Ireland's contribution of papers in the sciences by field, 1994-98 ★4315★
Italy's relative impact in the sciences by field, 1992-96 ★4317★
Netherlands' contribution of papers in the sciences, by field, 1995-99 ★4321★
New Zealand's contribution of papers in the sciences, by field, 1994-98 ★4322★
Norway's contribution of papers in the sciences by field, 1994-98 ★4323★
Poland's contribution of papers in the sciences, by field, 1993-97 ★4324★
South Africa's contribution of papers in the sciences, by field, 1994-98 ★4326★
Spain's contribution of papers in the sciences, by field, 1993-97 ★4328★
Spain's contribution of papers in the sciences, by field, 1995-99 ★4329★
Sweden's contribution of papers in the sciences by field, 1993-97 ★4330★
Sweden's contribution of papers in the sciences, by field, 1995-99 ★4331★

Plant breeding and genetics
Agricultural sciences doctorates awarded at U.S. colleges and universities, by subfield, 1999 ★1886★
Gender breakdown of agricultural sciences doctorate recipients, by subfield, 1999 ★1926★

Plant genetics
Biological sciences doctorates awarded at U.S. colleges and universities, by subfield, 1999 ★1887★
Gender breakdown of biological sciences doctorate recipients, by subfield, 1999 ★1927★

Plant High School
Outstanding secondary schools in Tampa-St. Petersburg-Clearwater, Florida ★4240★

Plant manager
Monster.com's most searched job listings ★2308★

Plant pathology
Agricultural sciences doctorates awarded at U.S. colleges and universities, by subfield, 1999 ★1886★
Biological sciences doctorates awarded at U.S. colleges and universities, by subfield, 1999 ★1887★
Gender breakdown of agricultural sciences doctorate recipients, by subfield, 1999 ★1926★
Gender breakdown of biological sciences doctorate recipients, by subfield, 1999 ★1927★

Plant physiology
Biological sciences doctorates awarded at U.S. colleges and universities, by subfield, 1999 ★1887★

Gender breakdown of biological sciences doctorate recipients, by subfield, 1999 ★1927★

Plant sciences
Agricultural sciences doctorates awarded at U.S. colleges and universities, by subfield, 1999 ★1886★
Gender breakdown of agricultural sciences doctorate recipients, by subfield, 1999 ★1926★

Plant and Soil
Agriculture journals by citation impact, 1992-96 ★52★
Agriculture journals by citation impact, 1995-99 ★53★
Agriculture journals by citation impact, 1999 ★54★
Soil science journals by citation impact, 1981-99 ★188★
Soil science journals by citation impact, 1995-99 ★189★
Soil science journals by citation impact, 1999 ★190★

Plantinga Jr.; Cornelius
Top pay and benefits for the chief executive and top paid employees at Calvin College ★3217★

Plantronics
Business Week's top companies in terms of return on capital, 2000 ★430★

Plasma and high-temperature
Gender breakdown of physics and astronomy doctorate recipients, by subfield, 1999 ★1939★
Physics and astronomy doctorates awarded at U.S. colleges and universities, by subfield, 1999 ★1994★

Plasterer
Most desirable jobs in construction trades ★2272★

Platz; Matthew S.
Winner of the American Chemical Society's Arthur C. Cope Awards, 2001 ★795★

Play Like a Man, Win Like a Woman
Library Journal's most notable books on job performance, 2000 ★254★

Player; Mark A.
Top pay and benefits for the chief executive and top paid employees at Santa Clara University in California ★3491★

Players
Most notable fiction books for reluctant young adult readers, 2001 ★321★

Playhouse on the Square
Most selective internships in the U.S., 2001 ★2610★

Playing Without the Ball
Most notable fiction books for reluctant young adult readers, 2001 ★321★
Most notable fiction books for young adults, 2001 ★322★

The Playmaker
Booklist's best first novels for youths ★309★

Pleasantville High School
Outstanding secondary schools in New York, New York ★4191★

Pliocene Ridge High School
Outstanding secondary schools in Sacramento, California ★4215★

Plofchan; Thomas K.
Top pay and benefits for the chief executive and top paid employees at the University of the Incarnate Word ★3570★

Plough; Thomas
Top pay and benefits for the chief executive and top paid employees at Assumption College ★3181★

Plum Grove Junior High School
Outstanding secondary schools in Chicago, Illinois ★4110★

Plumb; Robert
Top pay and benefits for the chief executive and top paid employees at Heritage College ★3332★

Plumber
Jobs with the highest unemployment ★2256★

Plume
Trade paperback bestsellers by publishing house, 2000 ★307★

Pluta; Joseph E.
Top pay and benefits for the chief executive and top paid employees at St. Edward's University ★3471★

PLX Technology
Best small companies in the U.S. ★383★
Top companies in terms of growth, 2000 ★534★

Plymouth State College
State appropriations for New Hampshire's institutions of higher education, 2000-01 ★1282★
Lowest undergraduate tuition and fees at colleges and universities in New Hampshire ★1532★
Average faculty salaries for institutions of higher education in New Hampshire, 2000-01 ★3716★

Plympton; Margaret
Top pay and benefits for the chief executive and top paid employees at Bucknell University ★3213★

PMC-Sierra
Business Week's best companies in terms of share-price gain ★409★

PMK Public Relations
Most selective internships in the U.S., 2001 ★2610★

PNAS
Molecular biology and genetics journals with the highest impact, 1992-96 ★204★

PNC Financial Services Group
Fortune's highest ranked super-regional banks, 2000 ★498★

Pochard; Steve
Top pay and benefits for the chief executive and top paid employees at Spring Hill College ★3508★

Pocket
Trade paperback bestsellers by publishing house, 2000 ★307★

Pocket Books
Mass market paperback bestsellers by publishing house, 2000 ★283★

Podiatrist
Jobs with the lowest unemployment ★2258★

Podiatrists
Projected employment growth for selected occupations that require advanced education, 1998-2008 ★2318★

Poe Classical
Chicago elementary magnet schools with the lowest acceptance rates, 2000-01 ★4003★

Poggendorf; Brenda
Top pay and benefits for the chief executive and top paid employees at Carthage College ★3224★

Pohlman; Randolph
Top pay and benefits for the chief executive and top paid employees at Nova Southeastern University ★3426★

Point Loma Nazarene College
Average faculty salaries for institutions of higher education in California, 2000-01 ★3692★

Point Park College
U.S. News & World Report's northern regional liberal arts colleges with students least in debt, 1999 ★1351★

The Poisonwood Bible
Longest-running trade paperback bestsellers, 2000 ★282★

Poitier; Sidney
Most influential African American entertainers ★77★

Pokemon Studio Blue
Top selling home education software, 2000 ★1599★

Pokemon Studio Red
Top selling home education software, 2000 ★1599★

Poland
Countries with the lowest spending per student on higher education, 1997 ★2489★

Poland Public Library
Highest Hennen's American Public Library Ratings for libraries serving a population of 999 and under ★2691★

Polaroid
Fortune's highest ranked scientific, photo and control equipment companies, 2000 ★493★

Polcyn; Laura J.
Top pay and benefits for the chief executive and top paid employees at Pacific Lutheran University ★3436★

Police officer
Careers college students considered most respected, 2000 ★740★
Jobs with the worst environment scores ★2260★
Jobs with the worst stress scores ★2265★

Police patrol officers
Projected employment growth for selected occupations that require long-term on-the-job training, 1998-2008 ★2320★
Average salaries for occupations requiring on-the-job training ★3119★

Police: Streetcorner Politicians
Most-cited works in police studies articles/research notes ★2625★

Policing a Free Society
Most-cited works in police studies articles/research notes ★2625★

Poling; Lindy
All-USA Teacher Teams, Third Team, 2000 ★4401★

Political Geography
Political science journals with the greatest impact measure, 1994-98 ★3050★

Political Research Quarterly
Political science journals with the greatest impact measure, 1994-98 ★3050★

Political science
Top nonscience majors for accepted applicants to U.S. medical schools, 1999-2000 ★2854★
Average costs for Academic Search titles by subject, 2001 ★2918★
Periodical prices by LC subject, 2001 ★2925★
Average starting salaries for college graduates, by field, 2000 ★3129★

Political science and government
Gender breakdown of social sciences doctorate recipients, by subfield, 1999 ★1942★
Percentage of female doctorate recipients at U.S. colleges and universities, by subfield, 1999 ★1988★
Social sciences doctorates awarded at U.S. colleges and universities, by subfield, 1999 ★2044★

Political science and international relations
Number of social sciences doctorate recipients at U.S. colleges and universities, by field, 1999 ★1977★
Social sciences doctorates awarded to U.S. citizens/permanent residents at U.S. colleges and universities, by race/ethnicity and subfield, 1999 ★2045★

Political scientist
Most desirable social sciences jobs ★2280★

Politician
Careers college students considered least respected, 2000 ★739★

Politics & Society
Political science journals with the greatest impact measure, 1981-98 ★3049★

The Politics of the Police
Most-cited works in police studies articles/research notes ★2625★

Polk; Shawntinice
All-America girls' high school basketball 1st team, 2001 ★170★

Polke; Sigmar
Best living artists ★73★

Pollard; Nina
Top pay and benefits for the chief executive and top paid employees at William Jewell College ★3630★

Pollard; William F.
Top pay and benefits for the chief executive and top paid employees at Huntingdon College ★3344★

Pollock; Jackson
Highly influential artists of the 20th century ★76★

Polo Ralph Lauren
Fortune's highest ranked apparel companies, 2000 ★448★

Polyhedron
Crystallography journals by citation impact, 1994-98 ★1655★
Crystallography journals by citation impact, 1998 ★1656★

Polymer
Chemistry doctorates awarded at U.S. colleges and universities, by subfield, 1999 ★1889★
Gender breakdown of chemistry doctorate recipients, by subfield, 1999 ★1929★
Gender breakdown of physics and astronomy doctorate recipients, by subfield, 1999 ★1939★
Physics and astronomy doctorates awarded at U.S. colleges and universities, by subfield, 1999 ★1994★

Polymer/plastics
Engineering doctorates awarded at U.S. colleges and universities, by subfield, 1999 ★1923★
Gender breakdown of engineering doctorate recipients, by subfield, 1999 ★1934★

PolyOne
Fortune's highest ranked rubber and plastic products companies, 2000 ★492★

Polytechnic University
Private, 4-year undergraduate colleges and universities producing the most Ph.D.'s in the computer sciences, 1920-1990 ★1595★
Private, 4-year undergraduate colleges and universities producing the most Ph.D.'s in the computer sciences, 1981-1990 ★1596★
Doctorate-granting-institutions with the highest percentage of non-U.S. citizen doctoral degrees awarded, 1999 ★1907★
Private, 4-year undergraduate colleges and universities producing the most Ph.D.s in all fields of study, 1920-1990 ★2027★
Private, 4-year undergraduate colleges and universities producing the most Ph.D.'s in mathematics, 1920-1990 ★2776★
Private, 4-year undergraduate colleges and universities producing the most Ph.D.'s in mathematics, 1981-1990 ★2777★
Private, 4-year undergraduate colleges and universities producing the most Ph.D.'s in physics and astronomy, 1920-1990 ★2949★
Average faculty salaries for institutions of higher education in New York, 2000-01 ★3719★
Private, 4-year undergraduate colleges and universities producing the most Ph.D.'s in the sciences, 1920-1990 ★4294★

Polytechnic University (NY)
First-year student's choices for exemplary doctoral-intensive universities ★2535★

Pomona College
Private, 4-year undergraduate colleges and universities producing the most Ph.D.'s in the life sciences, 1920-1990 ★192★
Private, 4-year undergraduate colleges and universities producing the most Ph.D.'s in the life sciences, 1981-1990 ★193★
Comparison of acceptance rates at the top 5 liberal arts colleges in the U.S., 1990 and 2001 ★844★
U.S. colleges and universities with the best overall administration ★1033★
U.S. colleges and universities with the happiest students ★1035★
U.S. News & World Report's best national liberal arts colleges, 2000-01 ★1320★
U.S. News & World Report's national liberal arts colleges with the best faculty resources rank, 2000-01 ★1321★
U.S. News & World Report's national liberal arts colleges with the best financial resources rank, 2000-01 ★1322★
U.S. News & World Report's national liberal arts colleges with the best freshmen retention rates, 2000-01 ★1323★
U.S. News & World Report's national liberal arts colleges with the best graduation and retention rank, 2000-01 ★1324★
U.S. News & World Report's national liberal arts colleges with the best selectivity rank, 2000-01 ★1325★
U.S. News & World Report's national liberal arts colleges with the best student/faculty ratios, 2000-01 ★1326★
U.S. News & World Report's national liberal arts colleges with the highest academic reputation scores, 2000-01 ★1327★
U.S. News & World Report's national liberal arts colleges with the highest graduation rates, 2000-01 ★1330★
U.S. News & World Report's national liberal arts colleges with the highest percentage of freshmen in the top 10% of their high school class, 2000-01 ★1332★

U.S. News & World Report's national liberal arts colleges with the lowest acceptance rates, 2000-01 ★1336★

U.S. News & World Report's best undergraduate fees among national liberal arts colleges by discount tuition, 2000 ★1381★

Highest undergraduate tuition and fees at colleges and universities in California ★1486★

Private, 4-year undergraduate colleges and universities producing the most Ph.D.'s in the computer sciences, 1920-1990 ★1595★

Private, 4-year undergraduate colleges and universities producing the most Ph.D.'s in the computer sciences, 1981-1990 ★1596★

Private, 4-year undergraduate colleges and universities producing the most Ph.D.s in all fields of study, 1920-1990 ★2027★

Private, 4-year undergraduate colleges and universities producing the most Ph.D.'s in all fields of study, 1981-1990 ★2028★

Private, 4-year undergraduate colleges and universities producing the most Ph.D.'s in all fields of study, 1990 ★2029★

Private, 4-year undergraduate colleges and universities producing the most Ph.D.'s in nonscience fields, 1920-1990 ★2030★

Private, 4-year undergraduate colleges and universities producing the most Ph.D.'s in nonscience fields, 1981-1990 ★2031★

Private, 4-year undergraduate colleges and universities producing the most Ph.D.'s in nonscience fields, 1990 ★2032★

Private, 4-year undergraduate colleges and universities producing the most Ph.D.'s in the earth sciences, 1981-1990 ★2151★

Elite liberal arts colleges ranked by per capita quality adjusted scholarship articles in the field of economics, 1975-94 ★2164★

Elite liberal arts colleges ranked by quality adjusted scholarship articles in the field of economics, 1975-94 ★2165★

Top associate professor economists at elite liberal arts colleges, 1975-94 ★2174★

Top full professor economists at elite liberal arts colleges, 1975-94 ★2175★

Private, 4-year undergraduate colleges and universities producing the most Ph.D.'s in economics, 1920-1990 ★2211★

Private, 4-year undergraduate colleges and universities producing the most Ph.D.'s in economics, 1981-1990 ★2212★

Undergraduate institutions with the most graduates who received Ph.D.s in economics, 1920-1984 ★2214★

Private, 4-year undergraduate colleges and universities producing the most Ph.D.'s in English, 1981-1990 ★2450★

Private, 4-year undergraduate colleges and universities producing the most Ph.D.'s in history, 1920-1990 ★2552★

Private, 4-year undergraduate colleges and universities producing the most Ph.D.'s in history, 1981-1990 ★2553★

Private, 4-year undergraduate colleges and universities producing the most Ph.D.'s in mathematics, 1920-1990 ★2776★

Private, 4-year undergraduate colleges and universities producing the most Ph.D.'s in mathematics, 1981-1990 ★2777★

Private, 4-year undergraduate colleges and universities producing the most Ph.D.'s in physics and astronomy, 1920-1990 ★2949★

Private, 4-year undergraduate colleges and universities producing the most Ph.D.'s in political science and international relations, 1920-1990 ★3044★

Private, 4-year undergraduate colleges and universities producing the most Ph.D.'s in political science and international relations, 1981-1990 ★3045★

Private, 4-year undergraduate colleges and universities producing the most Ph.D.'s in psychology, 1920-1990 ★3066★

Private, 4-year undergraduate colleges and universities producing the most Ph.D.'s in psychology, 1981-1990 ★3067★

Average faculty salaries for institutions of higher education in California, 2000-01 ★3692★

U.S. liberal arts colleges with the highest paid full professors, 2001 ★3980★

Private, 4-year undergraduate colleges and universities producing the most Ph.D.'s in the sciences, 1920-1990 ★4294★

Private, 4-year undergraduate colleges and universities producing the most Ph.D.'s in the sciences, 1981-1990 ★4295★

Private, 4-year undergraduate colleges and universities producing the most Ph.D.'s in anthropology and sociology, 1920-1990 ★4344★

Private, 4-year undergraduate colleges and universities producing the most Ph.D.'s in anthropology and sociology, 1981-1990 ★4345★

Pompano Beach Middle School
Outstanding secondary schools in Fort Lauderdale, Florida ★4133★

Ponchione; Raymond
Top pay and benefits for the chief executive and top paid employees Saint Francis College in Pennsylvania ★3641★

Pondexter; Cappie
All-America girls' high school basketball 1st team, 2001 ★170★

Pondillo; Anthony G.
Top pay and benefits for the chief executive and top paid employees at Siena College ★3498★

Pontifical Catholic University
Average faculty salaries for institutions of higher education in Puerto Rico, 2000-01 ★3726★

Pontifical Catholic University of Puerto Rico
Institutions censured by the American Association of University Professors, 2001 ★1067★

Highest undergraduate tuition and fees at colleges and universities in Puerto Rico ★1551★

Pontius Jr.; John M.
Top pay and benefits for the chief executive and top paid employees at Hartwick College ★3326★

Ponto; Thomas M.
Top pay and benefits for the chief executive and top paid employees at Kalamazoo College ★3358★

Pool; Tabitha
All-America girls' high school basketball 2nd team, 2001 ★171★

Pop-Up Book of Phobias
Most notable nonfiction books for reluctant young adult readers, 2001 ★323★

PopNet
Library Journal's best free reference websites, 2000 ★367★

Poppenberg; Mary Kay
Top pay and benefits for the chief executive and top paid employees at Chatham College ★3230★

Popper; Edward T.L.
Top pay and benefits for the chief executive and top paid employees at Bellarmine University ★3196★

Population
Most cited demography journals, 1991-95 ★1857★

Population Bulletin
Demography journals with the highest average citations after 5 years ★1856★
Most cited demography journals, 1991-95 ★1857★
Top demography journals by average impact factor, 1991-95 ★1863★

Population and Development Review
Demography journals with the highest average citations after 5 years ★1856★
Most cited demography journals, 1991-95 ★1857★
Top demography journals by average impact factor, 1991-95 ★1863★
Sociology journals by impact factor, 1981 to 1997 ★4355★
Sociology journals by impact factor, 1993 to 1997 ★4356★

Population and Environment
Top demography journals by average impact factor, 1991-95 ★1863★

Population Research and Policy Review
Top demography journals by average impact factor, 1991-95 ★1863★

Population Studies
Demography journals with the highest average citations after 5 years ★1856★
Most cited demography journals, 1991-95 ★1857★
Top demography journals by average impact factor, 1991-95 ★1863★

Porter County Public Library System
Highest Hennen's American Public Library Ratings for libraries serving a population of 100,000 to 249,999 ★2698★

Porter; David
Top pay and benefits for the chief executive and top paid employees at Skidmore College ★3500★

Porter; Hugh
Top pay and benefits for the chief executive and top paid employees at Reed College ★3453★

Porter; Judith
Top pay and benefits for the chief executive and top paid employees at Bryn Mawr College ★3212★

Porter; M.E.
U.S. academic economists by mean number of citations, 1971-92 ★2176★

Portland Community College
Community colleges in North America with the highest enrollment ★852★
Lowest undergraduate tuition and fees at colleges and universities in Oregon ★1548★

Portland, OR
American cities with the highest percentage of people with Internet access ★2572★
U.S. cities with the most wired households, 2001 ★2606★
Best place to live in the U.S. ★3081★

Portland, OR/Vancouver, WA
Best 'green & clean' places to live ★3077★

Portland State University
Radcliffe Institute for Advanced Study fellowship recipient in the field of American literature, 2000-01 ★2442★
Average faculty salaries for institutions of higher education in Oregon, 2000-01 ★3724★

Portland; University of
U.S. News & World Report's best undergraduate fees among western regional universities by discount tuition, 2000 ★1430★
Highest undergraduate tuition and fees at colleges and universities in Oregon ★1547★
U.S. News & World Report's top western regional universities, 2000-01 ★1574★
U.S. News & World Report's western regional universities with the best academic reputation scores, 2000-01 ★1577★
U.S. News & World Report's western regional universities with the best student/faculty ratios, 2000-01 ★1578★
U.S. News & World Report's western regional universities with the highest acceptance rates, 2000-01 ★1579★
U.S. News & World Report's western regional universities with the highest alumni giving rates, 2000-01 ★1580★
U.S. News & World Report's western regional universities with the highest graduation rates, 2000-01 ★1582★
U.S. News & World Report's western regional universities with the highest percentage of freshmen in the top 25% of their high school class, 2000-01 ★1583★
U.S. News & World Report's western regional universities with the highest percentage of full-time faculty, 2000-01 ★1584★

Portrait in Paradox: Commitment and Ambivalence in American Librarianship, 1876-1976
Most frequently cited *Libri* articles ★2730★

Portsmouth Middle and High School
All-USA Teacher Teams, Third Team, 2000 ★4401★

Portsmouth, NH
U.S. cities with the lowest rate of violent crime ★3088★

Portugal
Countries spending the highest percentage of gross domestic product on education ★4060★

Portugal Telecom
Business Week's best companies in Portugal ★401★

Portuguese
Languages of requested materials from OCLC ILL, 1999 ★2679★

Posner; Jessica
All-USA College Academic Third Team, 2001 ★4★

Postal inspector
Most desirable public sector jobs ★2279★

Postal mail carriers
Average salaries for occupations requiring on-the-job training ★3119★

Potlatch
Top containers and packaging companies in Standard & Poor's 500, 2001 ★537★

Potolicchio; Samuel
Top pay and benefits for the chief executive and top paid employees at George Washington University ★3304★

Potomac State College
Lowest undergraduate tuition and fees at colleges and universities in West Virginia ★1569★

Potter; Patricia
Top pay and benefits for the chief executive and top paid employees at National University in California ★3415★

Potts; David E.
Top pay and benefits for the chief executive and top paid employees at Judson College in Alabama ★3356★

Poultry science
Agricultural sciences doctorates awarded at U.S. colleges and universities, by subfield, 1999 ★1886★
Gender breakdown of agricultural sciences doctorate recipients, by subfield, 1999 ★1926★

Pounder; Robert
Top pay and benefits for the chief executive and top paid employees at Vassar College ★3594★

Poway High School
Outstanding secondary schools in San Diego, California ★4220★

Powell; Adam Clayton
Most influential African Americans in politics and civil rights ★3040★

Powell; Colin
Most influential African Americans in the military ★2882★

Powell; Jack P.
Top pay and benefits for the chief executive and top paid employees at Cornerstone University ★3258★

Powell, Jr.; G. Bingham
Most frequently downloaded *American Political Science Review* articles ★3039★

Powell Middle School
Outstanding secondary schools in Denver, Colorado ★4124★

Power, Bureaucracy, Influence and Performance: Their Relationships in Industrial Distribution Channels
Most influential articles in the *Journal of Business Research* from 1995 to 1999 ★700★

The Power of Gold: The History of an Obsession
Library Journal's most notable investing books, 2000 ★264★

Power Integrations
Top companies in terms of growth, 2000 ★534★

The Power of Positive Thinking
Retail audiobook titles selling 300,000-400,000 copies ★303★

Powers; Kathleen
Top pay and benefits for the chief executive and top paid employees at Saint John Fisher College in New York ★3472★

Powers; Richard W.
Top pay and benefits for the chief executive and top paid employees at Hiram College ★3333★

Powerwave Technologies
Companies with the best two-year total returns since 1998 ★436★
Information technology companies giving the best returns, 2000 ★522★
Top information technology companies, 2000 ★544★

PPG Industries
Fortune's highest ranked chemicals companies, 2000 ★452★
Top housing and real estate companies in Standard & Poor's 500, 2001 ★543★

PPL
Top utilities companies in Standard & Poor's 500, 2001 ★561★

Prairie State Community College
Fall enrollment at Chicago-area public community colleges, by minority percentages, 1999 ★867★

Prairie View A&M University
Colleges offering the Thurgood Marshall Scholarship Fund ★221★
Historically black colleges and universities awarding the most master's degrees to African Americans ★1670★
Total baccalaureate biology/life sciences degrees awarded to African Americans from U.S. colleges and universities, 1997-98 ★1679★
Total baccalaureate engineering degrees awarded to minorities from U.S. colleges and universities, 1997-98 ★1715★
U.S. colleges and universities awarding the most education master's degrees to African Americans ★1769★
U.S. colleges and universities awarding the most master's degrees to African Americans ★1785★
U.S. colleges and universities awarding the most social sciences and history master's degrees to African Americans ★1801★
U.S. institutions awarding the most baccalaureate degrees to African Americans in agricultural sciences, 1998 ★1814★
U.S. institutions awarding the most master's degrees to African Americans in agribusiness and production, 1998 ★1824★
U.S. institutions awarding the most master's degrees to African Americans in agricultural sciences, 1998 ★1825★
U.S. institutions awarding the most master's degrees to minorities in agribusiness and production, 1998 ★1829★
U.S. institutions awarding the most master's degrees to minorities in agricultural sciences, 1998 ★1830★
Average faculty salaries for institutions of higher education in Texas, 2000-01 ★3731★

Prall; Bruce
Top pay and benefits for the chief executive and top paid employees at Marian College of Fond Du Lac ★3389★

Pratt Institute
Radcliffe Institute for Advanced Study fellowship recipients in the field of visual arts, 2000-01 ★79★
Professional or specialized institutions with the highest enrollment of foreign students, 1998-99 ★2501★
Average faculty salaries for institutions of higher education in New York, 2000-01 ★3719★

Praxair
Fortune's highest ranked chemicals companies, 2000 ★452★
Top chemical companies in Standard & Poor's 500, 2001 ★533★

Pre-elementary/early childhood
Education doctorates awarded at U.S. colleges and universities, by subfield, 1999 ★1921★
Gender breakdown of education doctorate recipients, by subfield, 1999 ★1933★

Pre-Paid Legal Services
Best small companies in the U.S. ★383★

Pre-school, kindergarten teachers
Employment outlook for the year 2005 for selected occupations ★2297★

PRE/TEXT
    Most cited language serials in technical communication journals from 1988 to 1997 ★4420★
PRECIS in a Multilingual Context
    Most frequently cited *Libri* articles ★2730★
Precision assembler
    'Blue-collar' jobs considered the least physically demanding ★2241★
    Jobs considered the loneliest ★2244★
Precision production, craft, and repair
    Employment change projections by major occupational group from 1998 to 2008 ★2288★
    Employment projections by major occupational group for 2008 ★2291★
    Percentages for projected employment growth by occupational group, 1998-2008 ★2314★
    Projected employment growth by occupational group, 1998-2008 ★2316★
    Internet use by major occupational group, 1998 ★2587★
Premcor
    Largest private companies, 2000 ★523★
Premedical
    Top mixed discipline majors for accepted applicants to U.S. medical schools, 1999-2000 ★2853★
Prentice Hall
    Book publishers with the most citations (Class 2) ★2563★
Prepaid college tuition plans
    Best ways to save for college ★843★
Preprofessional
    Top mixed discipline majors for accepted applicants to U.S. medical schools, 1999-2000 ★2853★
Presbyterian
    Religious preference of incoming freshmen, 2000 ★1061★
Presbyterian College
    Fiske Guide's best buys for private colleges and universities, 2001 ★1459★
    Highest undergraduate tuition and fees at colleges and universities in South Carolina ★1554★
    Average faculty salaries for institutions of higher education in South Carolina, 2000-01 ★3728★
Prescott, AZ
    Best small towns to live in ★3085★
Prescott College
    Highest undergraduate tuition and fees at colleges and universities in Arizona ★1482★
    Total baccalaureate education degrees awarded to Native Americans from U.S. colleges and universities, 1997-98 ★1714★
Prescott; Loren
    Top pay and benefits for the chief executive and top paid employees at Widener University ★3626★
Presentation College
    Highest undergraduate tuition and fees at colleges and universities in South Dakota ★1556★
    Average faculty salaries for institutions of higher education in South Dakota, 2000-01 ★3729★
President (U.S.)
    Jobs considered the most competitive ★2245★
    Jobs that are potentially the highest paying ★2246★
    Jobs with the best income scores ★2248★
    Jobs with the highest starting salaries ★2255★
    Jobs with the longest work weeks ★2257★
    Jobs with the lowest unemployment ★2258★
    Jobs with the most stringent quotas ★2259★
    Jobs with the worst environment scores ★2260★
    Jobs with the worst stress scores ★2265★
Pressler; Mirjam
    Outstanding children's nonfiction books, 2000 ★330★
Preston; Fannie
    Top pay and benefits for the chief executive and top paid employees at Saint Mary's College of California ★3480★
Preston; Harold
    Top pay and benefits for the chief executive and top paid employees at Hardin-Simmons University ★3325★
Prestonsburg Community College
    Lowest undergraduate tuition and fees at colleges and universities in Kentucky ★1509★
Prezeau; Maryse
    Top pay and benefits for the chief executive and top paid employees at the New York Institute of Technology ★3535★
Pribbenow; Paul P.
    Top pay and benefits for the chief executive and top paid employees at Wabash College ★3598★
Price; John E.
    Top pay and benefits for the chief executive and top paid employees at Anna Maria College ★3177★
Price; Leontyne
    Most influential African American entertainers ★77★
PricewaterhouseCoopers
    Largest private companies, 2000 ★523★
Priestley; J.B.
    Top playwrights of the twentieth century ★4436★
Primedia
    Fortune's highest ranked publishing companies, 2000 ★489★
Prince Edward Island
    Canadian provinces by teaching days per year ★4058★
Prince Edward Island; University of
    Canadian primarily undergraduate universities by alumni support, 2000 ★1193★
    Canadian primarily undergraduate universities by class size at the first and second-year level, 2000 ★1195★
    Canadian primarily undergraduate universities by class size at the third and forth-year level, 2000 ★1196★
    Canadian primarily undergraduate universities by classes taught by tenured faculty, 2000 ★1197★
    Canadian primarily undergraduate universities by faculty members with Ph.D.'s, 2000 ★1198★
    Canadian primarily undergraduate universities by library acquisitions, 2000 ★1199★
    Canadian primarily undergraduate universities by library expenses, 2000 ★1200★
    Canadian primarily undergraduate universities by library holdings per student, 2000 ★1201★
    Canadian primarily undergraduate universities by medical/science grants per faculty member, 2000 ★1202★
    Canadian primarily undergraduate universities by operating budget per student, 2000 ★1203★
    Canadian primarily undergraduate universities by percentage of operating budget allocated to scholarships, 2000 ★1204★
    Canadian primarily undergraduate universities by percentage of operating budget allocated to student services, 2000 ★1205★
    Canadian primarily undergraduate universities by reputation, 2000 ★1206★
    Canadian primarily undergraduate universities by social science/humanities grants per faculty member, 2000 ★1207★
    Canadian primarily undergraduate universities by students from out of province, 2000 ★1208★
    Canadian primarily undergraduate universities by students winning national awards, 2000 ★1209★
    Top Canadian primarily undergraduate universities, 2000 ★1226★
Prince George's Community College
    Top college choices for Washington D.C. students ★847★
    Average faculty salaries for institutions of higher education in Maryland, 2000-01 ★3707★
Prince Jr.; Gregory S.
    Top pay and benefits for the chief executive and top paid employees at Hampshire College ★3322★
Prince William Public Library System
    Highest Hennen's American Public Library Ratings for libraries serving a population of 250,000 to 499,999 ★2699★
Prince William Sound Community College
    Undergraduate tuition and fees at colleges and universities in Alaska ★1481★
The Princess Diaries
    Most notable fiction books for reluctant young adult readers, 2001 ★321★
    Most notable fiction books for young adults, 2001 ★322★
Princeton Day School
    All-USA Teacher Teams, First Team, 2000 ★4399★
Princeton High School
    Outstanding secondary schools in Cincinnati, Ohio-Kentucky-Indiana ★4112★
Princeton Junior High School
    Outstanding secondary schools in Cincinnati, Ohio-Kentucky-Indiana ★4112★
Princeton, NJ
    Best college towns to live in ★3076★
Princeton Theological Seminary
    Top religion research-doctorate programs as evaluated by the National Research Council ★3093★
Princeton University
    All-USA College Academic First Team, 2001 ★2★
    All-USA College Academic Second Team, 2001 ★3★
    U.S. universities enrolling the most National Achievement Scholars, 1998 ★13★
    Most effective art history research-doctorate programs as evaluated by the National Research Council ★91★
    Top art history research-doctorate programs as evaluated by the National Research Council ★93★
    Most effective ecology, evolution, and behavior research-doctorate programs as evaluated by the National Research Council ★199★
    Top ecology, evolution, and behavior research-doctorate programs as evaluated by the National Research Council ★201★

Most effective cell and developmental biology research-doctorate programs as evaluated by the National Research Council ★206★
Top cell and developmental biology research-doctorate programs as evaluated by the National Research Council ★210★
Most effective classics research-doctorate programs as evaluated by the National Research Council ★815★
Top classics research-doctorate programs as evaluated by the National Research Council ★816★
Comparison of acceptance rates at the top 5 national universities in the U.S., 1990 and 2001 ★845★
U.S. colleges and universities offering the best overall academic experience for undergraduates ★987★
U.S. colleges and universities that are the toughest to get into ★988★
U.S. News & World Report's national universities with the best academic reputation, 2000-01 ★1126★
U.S. News & World Report's national universities with the best faculty resources rank, 2000-01 ★1127★
U.S. News & World Report's national universities with the best freshmen retention rates, 2000-01 ★1128★
U.S. News & World Report's national universities with the best graduation and retention rank, 2000-01 ★1129★
U.S. News & World Report's national universities with the best student/faculty ratio, 2000-01 ★1130★
U.S. News & World Report's national universities with the highest alumni giving rank, 2000-01 ★1132★
U.S. News & World Report's national universities with the highest graduation rate, 1999 ★1134★
U.S. News & World Report's national universities with the highest percentage of freshmen in the top 10% of their high school class, 2000-01 ★1135★
U.S. News & World Report's national universities with the highest proportion of alumni support, 2000-01 ★1137★
U.S. News & World Report's national universities with the highest selectivity rank, 2000-01 ★1139★
U.S. News & World Report's national universities with the lowest acceptance rates, 2000-01 ★1140★
2000 endowment values of the 'wealthiest' U.S. universities ★1230★
2001 mid-year endowment values of the 'wealthiest' U.S. universities ★1234★
Colleges and universities with the largest endowments, 2000 ★1237★
Endowment values for the wealthiest U.S. universities, 2000 ★1240★
Institutions receiving the most alumni gifts, 1999-2000 ★1242★
Highest undergraduate tuition and fees at private nonprofit, 4-year or above colleges and universities ★1461★
U.S. News & World Report's best undergraduate fees among national universities by discount tuition, 2000 ★1474★
Highest undergraduate tuition and fees at colleges and universities in New Jersey ★1533★
Most effective comparative literature research-doctorate programs as evaluated by the National Research Council ★1587★
Top comparative literature research-doctorate programs as evaluated by the National Research Council ★1588★
U.S. universities with the greatest impact in computer science, 1994-98 ★1592★
U.S. universities with the greatest impact in computer science, 1995-99 ★1593★
Most effective computer science research-doctorate programs as evaluated by the National Research Council ★1594★
Top computer science research-doctorate programs as evaluated by the National Research Council ★1597★
Top geosciences research-doctorate programs as evaluated by the National Research Council ★2152★
Economics departments by number of citations by top economists, 1971-92 ★2158★
Economics departments by number of citations per top economist, 1971-92 ★2159★
Economics departments by number of top economists, 1971-92 ★2160★
Institutions most frequently contributing to the American Economic Review from 1911-1990 ★2168★
Institutions most frequently contributing to the American Economic Review from 1951-1990 ★2169★
U.S. universities with the greatest impact in economics, 1995-99 ★2179★
Economics Ph.D. programs by number of citations of top economist graduates, 1971-92 ★2204★
Economics Ph.D. programs by number of citations per top economist graduate, 1971-92 ★2205★
Economics Ph.D. programs by number of top economist graduates, 1971-92 ★2206★
Most effective economics research-doctorate programs as evaluated by the National Research Council ★2207★
Origin of doctorate for dissertation chairs in economics ★2208★
Origin of doctorate for economics faculty at Ph.D.-granting institutions ★2209★
Origin of doctorate for economics faculty at Ph.D.-granting institutions, by Ph.D. equivalents produced ★2210★
Top economics research-doctorate programs as evaluated by the National Research Council ★2213★
U.S. universities with the greatest impact in civil engineering, 1995-99 ★2350★
Top graduate engineering schools by reputation, as determined by academic personnel, 2001 ★2367★
Academics' choices for best graduate aerospace/aeronautical/astronautical engineering programs, 2001 ★2374★
Most effective aerospace engineering research-doctorate programs as evaluated by the National Research Council ★2375★
Top aerospace engineering research-doctorate programs as evaluated by the National Research Council ★2376★
Academics' choices for best graduate chemical engineering programs, 2001 ★2386★
Most effective chemical engineering research-doctorate programs as evaluated by the National Research Council ★2389★
Top chemical engineering research-doctorate programs as evaluated by the National Research Council ★2390★
Most effective civil engineering research-doctorate programs as evaluated by the National Research Council ★2395★
Top civil engineering research-doctorate programs as evaluated by the National Research Council ★2396★
Academics' choices for best graduate computer engineering programs, 2001 ★2399★
Most effective electrical engineering research-doctorate programs as evaluated by the National Research Council ★2404★
Top electrical engineering research-doctorate programs as evaluated by the National Research Council ★2405★
Most effective mechanical engineering research-doctorate programs as evaluated by the National Research Council ★2423★
Top English language and literature research-doctorate programs as evaluated by the National Research Council ★2451★
Top French language and literature research-doctorate programs as evaluated by the National Research Council ★2516★
Most effective German language and literature research-doctorate programs as evaluated by the National Research Council ★2527★
Top German language and literature research-doctorate programs as evaluated by the National Research Council ★2528★
Top history research-doctorate programs as evaluated by the National Research Council ★2554★
Top university research libraries in the U.S. and Canada, 1998-99 ★2706★
Most effective mathematics research-doctorate programs as evaluated by the National Research Council ★2775★
Top mathematics research-doctorate programs as evaluated by the National Research Council ★2778★
Radcliffe Institute for Advanced Study fellowship recipient in the field of music composition, 2000-01 ★2893★
Most effective music research-doctorate programs as evaluated by the National Research Council ★2895★
Top music research-doctorate programs as evaluated by the National Research Council ★2896★
U.S. universities with the greatest impact in optics and acoustics, 1995-99 ★2912★
Most effective philosophy research-doctorate programs as evaluated by the National Research Council ★2945★
Top philosophy research-doctorate programs as evaluated by the National Research Council ★2947★
U.S. universities publishing the most papers in the field of philosophy, 1995-99 ★2948★
U.S. universities with the greatest impact in astrophysics, 1994-98 ★2979★
Most effective astrophysics and astronomy research-doctorate programs as evaluated by the National Research Council ★3006★
Most effective physics research-doctorate programs as evaluated by the National Research Council ★3007★
Top astrophysics and astronomy research-doctorate programs as evaluated by the National Research Council ★3014★
Top physics research-doctorate programs as evaluated by the National Research Council ★3015★
Most effective political science research-doctorate programs as evaluated by the National Research Council ★3043★
Top political science research-doctorate programs as evaluated by the National Research Council ★3046★

Most effective psychology research-doctorate programs as evaluated by the National Research Council ★3065★

Top psychology research-doctorate programs as evaluated by the National Research Council ★3068★

Top religion research-doctorate programs as evaluated by the National Research Council ★3093★

U.S. universities with the highest concentrations in religion and theology, 1992-96 ★3094★

Presidents with the highest pay at Research I and II universities, 1998-99 ★3162★

Average faculty salaries for institutions of higher education in New Jersey, 2000-01 ★3717★

Private institutions of higher education that pay the highest salaries to female professors, 2000-01 ★3974★

U.S. institutions with the highest paid full professors, 2001 ★3978★

Top sociology research-doctorate programs as evaluated by the National Research Council ★4354★

Most effective Spanish and Portuguese language and literature research-doctorate programs as evaluated by the National Research Council ★4357★

Top Spanish and Portuguese language and literature research-doctorate programs as evaluated by the National Research Council ★4358★

Principal Financial Group
Top recruiters for information technology (MIS) jobs for 2000-01 bachelor's degree recipients ★2738★

Top recruiters for math/actuarial science jobs for 2000-01 bachelor's degree recipients ★2771★

Principia College
U.S. News & World Report's midwestern regional liberal arts colleges with students least in debt, 1999 ★1337★

U.S. News & World Report's midwestern regional liberal arts colleges with the best student/faculty ratios, 2000-01 ★1339★

U.S. News & World Report's midwestern regional liberal arts colleges with the highest freshmen retention rates, 2000-01 ★1343★

U.S. News & World Report's midwestern regional liberal arts colleges with the highest graduation rates, 2000-01 ★1344★

U.S. News & World Report's midwestern regional liberal arts colleges with the highest proportion of classes having 20 students or less, 2000-01 ★1347★

U.S. News & World Report's top midwestern regional liberal arts colleges, 2000-01 ★1349★

Average faculty salaries for institutions of higher education in Illinois, 2000-01 ★3700★

Pringle; Laurence
Booklist's best science books for children ★310★

Print Shop Deluxe
Top selling personal productivity software, 2000 ★1600★

Printmaster Gold
Top selling personal productivity software, 2000 ★1600★

Printmaster Silver
Top selling personal productivity software, 2000 ★1600★

Printpack
Top women-owned companies ★4460★

Prisco; Dorothy A.
Top pay and benefits for the chief executive and top paid employees at Gwynedd-Mercy College ★3318★

Private Lives
Top plays of the twentieth century ★4435★

Pro-Found Software
Most selective internships in the U.S., 2001 ★2610★

Top internships in the U.S. with the highest compensation, 2001 ★2611★

Problem-Oriented Policing
Most-cited works in police studies articles/research notes ★2625★

The Problem-Solving Approach to Negotiations in Industrial Marketing
Most influential articles in the *Journal of Business Research*, 1985-1999 ★697★

Most influential articles in the *Journal of Business Research* from 1985 to 1989 ★698★

Probstfeld; Carol
Top pay and benefits for the chief executive and top paid employees at the College of Notre Dame in California ★3526★

Proceedings of the ACM Conference on Management of Data (SIGMOD)
Journals and proceedings with the most citations (Class 1) ★2567★

Proceedings of the ACM Symposium on the Theory of Computing (STOC)
Journals and proceedings with the most citations (Class 3) ★2569★

Proceedings of the IEEE
Journals and proceedings with the most citations (Class 4) ★2570★

Proceedings of the IEEE International Computer Conference (COMPCON)
Journals and proceedings with the most citations (Class 4) ★2570★

Proceedings of the IEEE International Conference on Data Engineering (ICDE)
Journals and proceedings with the most citations (Class 3) ★2569★

Proceedings of the IEEE Real-Time Systems Symposium
Journals and proceedings with the most citations (Class 4) ★2570★

Proceedings of the IEEE Symposium on Foundations of Computer Science (FOCS)
Journals and proceedings with the most citations (Class 4) ★2570★

Proceedings of the International Conference on Information Systems (ICIS)
Journals and proceedings with the most citations (Class 3) ★2569★

Proceedings of the International Conference on Logic Programming (ICLP)
Journals and proceedings with the most citations (Class 3) ★2569★

Proceedings of the International Conference on Machine Learning (ICML)
Journals and proceedings with the most citations (Class 4) ★2570★

Proceedings of the International Conference on Principles of Knowledge
Journals and proceedings with the most citations (Class 4) ★2570★

Proceedings of the International Conference on Very Large Databases (VLDB)
Journals and proceedings with the most citations (Class 1) ★2567★

Proceedings of the International Joint Conference on Artificial Intelligence (IJCAI)
Journals and proceedings with the most citations (Class 3) ★2569★

Proceedings of the International Symposium on Computer Architecture
Journals and proceedings with the most citations (Class 4) ★2570★

Proceedings of the London Mathematical Society
Mathematics journals by impact factor, 1981 to 1997 ★2784★

Proceedings National Academy of Sciences USA
Top science journals by impact factor ★4281★

Proceedings of the National Conference on Artificial Intelligence (AAAI)
Journals and proceedings with the most citations (Class 2) ★2568★

Procom Technology
Companies with the best two-year total returns since 1998 ★436★

Procter & Gamble
Fortune's highest ranked soaps and cosmetics companies, 2000 ★496★

Top recruiters for business administration jobs for 2000-01 master's degree recipients ★652★

Top recruiters for computer science jobs for 2000-01 master's degree recipients ★1598★

Top recruiters for jobs requiring a graduate professional degree (attorney-JD) ★1836★

Top recruiters for chemical engineering jobs for 2000-01 bachelor's degree recipients ★2343★

Top recruiters for chemical engineering jobs for 2000-01 master's degree recipients ★2391★

Top recruiters for electrical/electronic engineering jobs for 2000-01 master's degree recipients ★2406★

Top recruiters for mechanical engineering jobs for 2000-01 master's degree recipients ★2424★

Top recruiters for mechanical engineering jobs for 2000-01 bachelor's degree recipients ★2437★

Top recruiters for jobs requiring a graduate professional degree (Ph.D.) ★2523★

Top internships in the U.S., 2001 ★2612★

Highly recommended public companies for women executives, 2000 ★4453★

Proctor; Samuel
Most influential African Americans in religion ★3091★

Procurement clerks
Occupations with the highest decline in employment, 1998-2008 ★2310★

Production
Overall median salary for full-time chemists with a bachelor's degree, by work function, 2000 ★790★

Overall median salary for full-time chemists with a doctoral degree, by work function, 2000 ★803★

Overall median salary for full-time chemists with a master's degree, by work function, 2000 ★804★

Production and manufacturing
   Industries in Illinois with the highest projected worker increase through 2006 ★2304★

Production supervisor
   Monster.com's most searched job listings ★2308★

Professional
   Expected majors for incoming freshmen, 2000 ★1050★

Professional fields
   Median age at conferral of doctoral degree from U.S. universities, by discipline, 1999 ★1952★

Professional fields, general
   Gender breakdown of professional doctorate recipients, by subfield, 1999 ★1940★
   Professional doctorates awarded at U.S. colleges and universities, by subfield, 1999 ★2033★

Professional specialty
   College graduates in the labor force, by occupational group, 1998 ★926★
   Projected change in employment of college graduates, by occupational group, from 1998 to 2008 ★965★
   Projected employment of college graduates, by occupational group, 2008 ★966★
   Employment change projections by major occupational group from 1998 to 2008 ★2288★
   Employment projections by major occupational group for 2008 ★2291★
   Employment in college-level jobs, by occupational group, 2006 ★2295★
   Percentages for projected employment growth by occupational group, 1998-2008 ★2314★
   Projected employment growth by occupational group, 1998-2008 ★2316★

Professional and technical
   Industries in Illinois with the highest projected worker increase through 2006 ★2304★

Program administrator
   Occupational fields of tribal college graduates that are currently employed ★964★

Programming
   Expected starting salaries of 2000-01 bachelor's degree recipients, by specific major ★3131★

Programming/software engineering
   Job openings for high-tech workers ★2330★
   Information technology jobs most in demand, 2001 ★4428★

Progress in Analytical Atomic Spectroscopy
   Spectroscopy journals by citation impact, 1981-99 ★4359★

Progress in Analytical Spectroscopy
   Spectroscopy journals by citation impact, 1981-99 ★4359★

Progress in Inorganic Chemistry
   Inorganic and nuclear chemistry journals by citation impact, 1981-99 ★811★
   Inorganic and nuclear chemistry journals by citation impact, 1995-99 ★812★
   Inorganic and nuclear chemistry journals by citation impact, 1999 ★813★

Progress in Neurobiology
   Journals with the highest impact factor in the field of neuroscience, 1981-96 ★191★
   Neurosciences journals with the greatest impact measure, 1981-98 ★2812★
   Neurosciences journals with the greatest impact measure, 1994-98 ★2813★

Progress in NMR Spectroscopy
   Spectroscopy journals by citation impact, 1981-99 ★4359★
   Spectroscopy journals by citation impact, 1995-99 ★4360★
   Spectroscopy journals by citation impact, 1999 ★4361★

Progress in Oceanography
   Oceanography journals by citation impact, 1981-99 ★2139★
   Oceanography journals by citation impact, 1999 ★2141★

Progress in Optics
   Optics journals by citation impact, 1981-99 ★2906★
   Optics journals by citation impact, 1995-99 ★2907★
   Optics journals by citation impact, 1999 ★2908★
   Optics journals with the greatest impact measure, 1981-98 ★2909★
   Optics journals with the greatest impact measure, 1994-98 ★2910★

Progress in Solid State Chemistry
   Inorganic and nuclear chemistry journals by citation impact, 1981-99 ★811★
   Inorganic and nuclear chemistry journals by citation impact, 1995-99 ★812★
   Inorganic and nuclear chemistry journals by citation impact, 1999 ★813★

Project manager
   Monster.com's most searched job listings ★2308★

Project manager (entry level)
   Monster.com's most searched job listings ★2308★

Property and real estate managers
   Occupations with the highest number of self-employed workers, 1998 ★2311★

Prospect Elementary School
   Illinois suburban elementary schools with the highest ISAT scores in reading and math ★18★

Prospect High School
   Outstanding secondary schools in Chicago, Illinois ★4110★
   Outstanding suburban public high schools in Metro Chicago ★4256★

Prospero's Children
   Library Journal's best science fiction and fantasy titles, 2000 ★246★
   Outstanding fiction books for young adults, 2000 ★333★

Prosser; George E.
   Top pay and benefits for the chief executive and top paid employees at Xavier University in Ohio ★3637★

Prostate
   Urology and nephrology journals with the greatest impact measure, 1981-98 ★2816★
   Urology and nephrology journals with the greatest impact measure, 1994-98 ★2817★

Protective services
   Top bachelor's degree disciplines for African Americans, 1997-98 ★1672★
   Top bachelor's degree disciplines for Asian Americans, 1997-98 ★1673★
   Top bachelor's degree disciplines for Hispanic Americans, 1997-98 ★1674★
   Top bachelor's degree disciplines for Native Americans, 1997-98 ★1675★
   Top bachelor's degree disciplines for non-minorities, 1997-98 ★1676★

Protestant minister
   Jobs with the longest work weeks ★2257★

Proto; Angelo B.
   Top pay and benefits for the chief executive and top paid employees at Adelphi University ★3164★

Providence College
   Division I NCAA colleges with that graduated all of their African American male basketball players, 1990-91 to 1993-94 ★927★
   Division I NCAA colleges with that graduated more than 80% of their African American male athletes, 1990-91 to 1993-94 ★929★
   U.S. colleges and universities where students study the least ★1002★
   U.S. colleges and universities with a generally conservative student body ★1014★
   U.S. News & World Report's northern regional universities with the best academic reputation scores, 2000-01 ★1415★
   U.S. News & World Report's northern regional universities with the highest alumni giving rates, 2000-01 ★1418★
   U.S. News & World Report's northern regional universities with the highest average graduation rates, 2000-01 ★1419★
   U.S. News & World Report's northern regional universities with the highest freshmen retention rates, 2000-01 ★1420★
   U.S. News & World Report's northern regional universities with the highest percentage of freshmen in the top 25% of their high school class, 2000-01 ★1421★
   U.S. News & World Report's northern regional universities with the highest percentage of full-time faculty, 2000-01 ★1422★
   U.S. News & World Report's northern regional universities with the lowest acceptance rates, 2000-01 ★1424★
   U.S. News & World Report's top northern regional universities, 2000-01 ★1425★
   Undergraduate tuition and fees at colleges and universities in Rhode Island ★1553★
   Average faculty salaries for institutions of higher education in Rhode Island, 2000-01 ★3727★

Providence High School
   Outstanding secondary schools in Los Angeles-Long Beach, California ★4167★
   Outstanding secondary schools in San Jose, California ★4222★

Providence, RI
   Best place to live in the northeastern U.S. ★3079★

Providence Senior High School
   Outstanding secondary schools in Charlotte-Gastonia-Rock Hill, North Carolina-South Carolina ★4108★

Providian Financial
   Best performing companies in Standard & Poor's 500, 2001 ★382★
   Fortune's highest ranked consumer credit companies, 2000 ★457★
   Top banks in Standard & Poor's 500, 2001 ★531★

Proviso High School, District 209 (Maywood)
   Illinois school districts with the highest paid superintendents, 1999-2000 ★3986★

Proviso Township 209
   Illinois high school districts with the highest teacher salaries, 1999 ★3985★

Prudential
   Best companies for working mothers ★4446★
   Best companies for working mothers in offering flexible work hours ★4448★

Best companies for working mothers in terms of overall work/life support ★4451★

Prudential Insurance of America
Fortune's highest ranked life and health insurance companies, 2000 ★472★

Pryor; F.
Top full professor economists at elite liberal arts colleges, 1975-94 ★2175★

Prystowsky; Michael B.
Top pay and benefits for the chief executive and top paid employees at Yeshiva University ★3640★

Psoriasis
Leading categories of dermatologic disease covered by top articles in the field, 1945-1990 ★1869★

Psychiatric Services
Health policy and services journals by citation impact, 1999 ★2539★

Psychiatrist
Jobs with the highest starting salaries ★2255★
Jobs with the longest work weeks ★2257★
Jobs with the lowest unemployment ★2258★

Psychobiology
Top nonscience majors for accepted applicants to U.S. medical schools, 1999-2000 ★2854★

Psychological Bulletin
Top management journals ★546★
Most-cited social sciences journals, 1981-97 ★4340★
Social sciences journals with the greatest impact measure, 1981-97 ★4341★
Most cited psychology serials in technical communication journals from 1988 to 1997 ★4423★

Psychological Medicine
Psychiatry journals by citation impact, 1981-98 ★3054★
Psychiatry journals by citation impact, 1998 ★3056★
Psychiatry journals by impact factor, 1981 to 1998 ★3057★

Psychological Review
Journals and proceedings with the most citations (Class 3) ★2569★
Most-cited social sciences journals, 1981-97 ★4340★
Social sciences journals with the greatest impact measure, 1981-97 ★4341★

Psychologists
Projected employment growth for selected occupations that require advanced education, 1998-2008 ★2318★

Psychology
Number of Advanced Placement Exams taken by African Americans, by subject, 2000 ★30★
Number of Advanced Placement Exams taken by Asian Americans, by subject, 2000 ★31★
Number of Advanced Placement Exams taken by Hispanic Americans, by subject, 2000 ★32★
Top bachelor's degree disciplines for African Americans, 1997-98 ★1672★
Top bachelor's degree disciplines for Asian Americans, 1997-98 ★1673★
Top bachelor's degree disciplines for Hispanic Americans, 1997-98 ★1674★
Top bachelor's degree disciplines for Native Americans, 1997-98 ★1675★
Top bachelor's degree disciplines for non-minorities, 1997-98 ★1676★
Number of social sciences doctorate recipients at U.S. colleges and universities, by field, 1999 ★1977★
Percentage of female doctorate recipients at U.S. colleges and universities, by subfield, 1999 ★1988★
Social sciences doctorates awarded to U.S. citizens/permanent residents at U.S. colleges and universities, by race/ethnicity and subfield, 1999 ★2045★
Top nonscience majors for accepted applicants to U.S. medical schools, 1999-2000 ★2854★
Average costs for Academic Search titles by subject, 2001 ★2918★
Periodical prices by LC subject, 2001 ★2925★
Average starting salaries for college graduates, by field, 2000 ★3129★
Expected starting salaries of 2000-01 bachelor's degree recipients, by specific major ★3131★

Psychology and Aging
Geriatrics and gerontology journals with the greatest impact measure, 1981-98 ★2805★
Geriatrics and gerontology journals with the greatest impact measure, 1994-98 ★2806★

Psychology, general
Gender breakdown of psychology doctorate recipients, by subfield, 1999 ★1941★
Psychology doctorates awarded at U.S. colleges and universities, by subfield, 1999 ★2043★

Psychology/psychiatry
United States' contribution of papers in the sciences, by field, 1995-99 ★4283★
United States' contribution of papers in the sciences, by field, 1996-2000 ★4284★
Australia's contribution of papers in the sciences, by field, 1993-97 ★4292★
Australia's contribution of papers in the sciences, by field, 1995-99 ★4293★
United Kingdom's contribution of papers in the sciences, by field, 1995-99 ★4297★
Canada's contribution of papers in the sciences, by field, 1995-99 ★4303★
England's contribution of papers in the sciences, by field, 1994-98 ★4308★
Hong Kong's contribution of papers in the sciences, by field, 1995-99 ★4314★
Ireland's contribution of papers in the sciences, by field, 1994-98 ★4315★
Netherlands' contribution of papers in the sciences, by field, 1995-99 ★4321★
New Zealand's contribution of papers in the sciences, by field, 1994-98 ★4322★
Norway's contribution of papers in the sciences, by field, 1994-98 ★4323★
South Africa's contribution of papers in the sciences, by field, 1994-98 ★4326★

Psychology, Public Policy, and Law
Health policy and services journals by citation impact, 1995-99 ★2538★
Health policy and services journals by citation impact, 1999 ★2539★

Psychology Review
Most cited psychology serials in technical communication journals from 1988 to 1997 ★4423★

Psychometrics
Gender breakdown of psychology doctorate recipients, by subfield, 1999 ★1941★
Psychology doctorates awarded at U.S. colleges and universities, by subfield, 1999 ★2043★

Psychopharmacology
Psychiatry journals by citation impact, 1981-98 ★3054★
Psychiatry journals by impact factor, 1981 to 1998 ★3057★
Psychiatry journals by impact factor, 1994 to 1998 ★3058★

Psychopharmacology Bulletin
Psychiatry journals by citation impact, 1998 ★3056★

Psychosomatic Medicine
Psychiatry journals by citation impact, 1981-98 ★3054★
Psychiatry journals by citation impact, 1998 ★3056★
Psychiatry journals by impact factor, 1981 to 1998 ★3057★

Public administration
Gender breakdown of professional doctorate recipients, by subfield, 1999 ★1940★
Professional doctorates awarded at U.S. colleges and universities, by subfield, 1999 ★2033★
Internet use by industry, 1998 ★2586★

Public administration and services
Top bachelor's degree disciplines for African Americans, 1997-98 ★1672★
Top bachelor's degree disciplines for Asian Americans, 1997-98 ★1673★
Top bachelor's degree disciplines for Hispanic Americans, 1997-98 ★1674★
Top bachelor's degree disciplines for Native Americans, 1997-98 ★1675★
Top bachelor's degree disciplines for non-minorities, 1997-98 ★1676★

Public Choice
Alternative general economics journals, by uniform weighting of subdisciplinary impacts, including self-citations ★2181★
Top ranked law and economics journals ★2197★
Top ranked public economics journals ★2201★

Public health
Gender breakdown of health sciences doctorate recipients, by subfield, 1999 ★1935★
Health sciences doctorates awarded at U.S. colleges and universities, by subfield, 1999 ★1944★

Public Library of Charlotte & Mecklenburg Co.
Highest Hennen's American Public Library Ratings for libraries serving a population of over 500,000 ★2700★

Public Opinion Quarterly
Political science journals with the greatest impact measure, 1981-98 ★3049★
Political science journals with the greatest impact measure, 1994-98 ★3050★
Most cited sociology serials in technical communication journals from 1988 to 1997 ★4426★

Public policy analysis
Gender breakdown of social sciences doctorate recipients, by subfield, 1999 ★1942★
Social sciences doctorates awarded at U.S. colleges and universities, by subfield, 1999 ★2044★

Public relations
Areas of specialization in journalism and mass communications programs with the highest enrollment, 1999 ★2740★

Public relations/advertising combined
Areas of specialization in journalism and mass communications programs with the highest enrollment, 1999 ★2740★

Public relations executive
Jobs with the most stringent quotas ★2259★
Most desirable jobs in communications ★2271★

PUBLICATIONS

Publications of the Astronomical Society of Japan
Astronomy and astrophysics journals by impact factor, 1994 to 1998 ★106★

Publish! The How-To Magazine of Desktop Publishing
Most cited printing and publishing serials in technical communication journals from 1988 to 1997 ★4422★

Publix Super Markets
Fortune's highest ranked food and drug stores, 2000 ★463★
Largest private companies, 2000 ★523★

Puerto Rican
Racial and ethnic background of incoming freshmen, 2000 ★1058★
U.S. medical school enrollment of U.S. citizens by racial/ethnic category, 1999-2000 ★2863★

Puerto Rico
Average class size at colleges and universities in the U.S., by state ★1064★
Total doctorate recipients by state, 1999 ★2054★
Hispanic American enrollment at Hispanic-serving institutions of higher education, by state, 1997 ★2547★

Puerto Rico, Aguadilla; University of
Lowest undergraduate tuition and fees at private nonprofit, 4-year or above colleges and universities ★1464★
Highest undergraduate tuition and fees at colleges and universities in Puerto Rico ★1551★
Lowest undergraduate tuition and fees at colleges and universities in Puerto Rico ★1552★

Puerto Rico, Arecibo; University of
Lowest undergraduate tuition and fees at private nonprofit, 4-year or above colleges and universities ★1464★
Highest undergraduate tuition and fees at colleges and universities in Puerto Rico ★1551★
Lowest undergraduate tuition and fees at colleges and universities in Puerto Rico ★1552★

Puerto Rico, Barranquitas; University of
Lowest undergraduate tuition and fees at private nonprofit, 4-year or above colleges and universities ★1464★
Highest undergraduate tuition and fees at colleges and universities in Puerto Rico ★1551★
Lowest undergraduate tuition and fees at colleges and universities in Puerto Rico ★1552★

Puerto Rico, Bayamon; University of
Lowest undergraduate tuition and fees at private nonprofit, 4-year or above colleges and universities ★1464★
Highest undergraduate tuition and fees at colleges and universities in Puerto Rico ★1551★
Lowest undergraduate tuition and fees at colleges and universities in Puerto Rico ★1552★

Puerto Rico, Carolina Regional College; University of
Lowest undergraduate tuition and fees at colleges and universities in Puerto Rico ★1552★

Puerto Rico, Cayey University; University of
Lowest undergraduate tuition and fees at public, 4-year or above colleges and universities ★1466★
Lowest undergraduate tuition and fees at colleges and universities in Puerto Rico ★1552★

Puerto Rico, Fajardo; University of
Highest undergraduate tuition and fees at colleges and universities in Puerto Rico ★1551★

Puerto Rico, Guayama; University of
Highest undergraduate tuition and fees at colleges and universities in Puerto Rico ★1551★

Puerto Rico, Humacao University; University of
Lowest undergraduate tuition and fees at public, 4-year or above colleges and universities ★1466★
Lowest undergraduate tuition and fees at colleges and universities in Puerto Rico ★1552★
Average faculty salaries for institutions of higher education in Puerto Rico, 2000-01 ★3726★

Puerto Rico, Mayaguez; University of
Lowest undergraduate tuition and fees at public, 4-year or above colleges and universities ★1466★
Lowest undergraduate tuition and fees at colleges and universities in Puerto Rico ★1552★

Puerto Rico Medical Sciences Campus; University of
Lowest undergraduate tuition and fees at colleges and universities in Puerto Rico ★1552★

Puerto Rico, Metropolitan; University of
Lowest undergraduate tuition and fees at private nonprofit, 4-year or above colleges and universities ★1464★
Highest undergraduate tuition and fees at colleges and universities in Puerto Rico ★1551★

Puerto Rico, Ponce; University of
Lowest undergraduate tuition and fees at private nonprofit, 4-year or above colleges and universities ★1464★
Highest undergraduate tuition and fees at colleges and universities in Puerto Rico ★1551★
Lowest undergraduate tuition and fees at colleges and universities in Puerto Rico ★1552★
Average faculty salaries for institutions of higher education in Puerto Rico, 2000-01 ★3726★

Puerto Rico, Rio Piedras; University of
Lowest undergraduate tuition and fees at public, 4-year or above colleges and universities ★1466★
Lowest undergraduate tuition and fees at colleges and universities in Puerto Rico ★1552★
U.S. colleges and universities awarding the most doctoral degrees to African Americans from 1995 to 1999 ★2091★

Puerto Rico, San German; University of
Lowest undergraduate tuition and fees at private nonprofit, 4-year or above colleges and universities ★1464★
Highest undergraduate tuition and fees at colleges and universities in Puerto Rico ★1551★

Puerto Rico, Utuado; University of
Lowest undergraduate tuition and fees at colleges and universities in Puerto Rico ★1552★

The Puffin Book of Nonsense Stories
Smithsonian's best books for children ages 10 and up ★365★

Puget Sound; University of
U.S. News & World Report's national liberal arts colleges with students most in debt, 1999 ★1386★
Highest undergraduate tuition and fees at colleges and universities in Washington ★1566★

U.S. colleges and universities awarding the most education master's degrees to Native Americans ★1772★
Average faculty salaries for institutions of higher education in Washington, 2000-01 ★3736★

Pulitzer Prizes
Library Journal's best free reference websites, 2000 ★367★

Pulte
Fortune's highest ranked engineering and construction companies, 2000 ★461★
Top housing and real estate companies in Standard & Poor's 500, 2001 ★543★

Pumsy: In Pursuit of Excellence
People for the American Way's list of most frequently challenged materials, 1982-1992 ★749★

Punish: Birth of the Prison
Most-cited works in critical criminology publications ★1645★

Purchasing agent
Jobs with the most stringent quotas ★2259★
Most desirable jobs in business/finance ★2270★

Purdue University
Comparisons of investment returns for operations MBAs ★627★
Top business schools for within-discipline research performance in management science, 1986-1998 ★647★
U.S. business schools with the quickest payback on MBA investments ★654★
U.S. universities with the highest concentration of papers published in the field of chemistry, 1994-98 ★794★
State appropriations for Indiana's institutions of higher education, 2000-01 ★1267★
U.S. universities with the greatest impact in communication, 1995-99 ★1657★
Total baccalaureate communications degrees awarded to Native Americans from U.S. colleges and universities, 1997-98 ★1690★
Doctorate-granting-institutions awarding the most non-U.S. citizen doctoral degrees, 1999 ★1906★
U.S. colleges and universities awarding the most doctorate degrees to Asian Americans ★2096★
U.S. colleges and universities awarding the most doctorates in engineering, 1999 ★2102★
Institutions generating the most economic education research text, 1963-1990 ★2167★
U.S. universities with the greatest impact in education, 1993-97 ★2220★
U.S. universities with the greatest impact in education, 1995-99 ★2222★
U.S. universities publishing the most papers in the field of civil engineering, 1994-98 ★2348★
Most effective aerospace engineering research-doctorate programs as evaluated by the National Research Council ★2375★
Top aerospace engineering research-doctorate programs as evaluated by the National Research Council ★2376★
Top civil engineering research-doctorate programs as evaluated by the National Research Council ★2396★
U.S. universities with the highest concentrations in artificial intelligence, 1992-96 ★2402★
Most effective electrical engineering research-doctorate programs as evaluated by the National Research Council ★2404★

Top electrical engineering research-doctorate programs as evaluated by the National Research Council ★2405★
Most effective industrial engineering research-doctorate programs as evaluated by the National Research Council ★2412★
Top industrial engineering research-doctorate programs as evaluated by the National Research Council ★2413★
Most effective mechanical engineering research-doctorate programs as evaluated by the National Research Council ★2423★
Research institutions with the highest enrollment of foreign students, 1998-99 ★2503★
Institutions with the most prolific communication studies researchers ★2749★
Enrollment of students in the ten largest doctoral journalism and mass communications programs, 1999 ★2762★
Top statistics and biostatistics research-doctorate programs as evaluated by the National Research Council ★2782★
U.S. colleges and universities spending the most on chemical research and development, 1998 ★3099★
U.S. colleges and universities spending the most on chemical research equipment, 1998 ★3100★
U.S. colleges and universities with the most federal support for chemical research equipment, 1998 ★3103★
Average faculty salaries for institutions of higher education in Indiana, 2000-01 ★3701★

Purdue University, Calumet
Average faculty salaries for institutions of higher education in Indiana, 2000-01 ★3701★

Purdue University, Krannert School of Management
U.S. News & World Report's undergraduate business programs with the best production/operations departments, 2000-01 ★569★
Business Week's top business schools with the highest percentage of international students, 2000 ★612★
Business Week's top business schools with the lowest percentage of women enrollees, 2000 ★617★
Lowest post-MBA salaries for students enrolled in *Business Week*'s top business schools, 1999 ★634★
Lowest pre-MBA salaries for students enrolled in *Business Week*'s top business schools, 1999 ★635★
Academics' choices for best graduate quantitative analysis programs, 2001 ★673★
Academics' choices for best graduate production/operations management programs, 2001 ★674★

Purdue University, North Central
U.S. News & World Report's top public midwestern regional liberal arts colleges, 2000-01 ★1350★
Average faculty salaries for institutions of higher education in Indiana, 2000-01 ★3701★
U.S. community colleges with the highest paid full professors, 2001 ★3976★

Purdue University, West Lafayette
U.S. News & World Report's universities with the best quantitative methods departments, 1999-2000 ★572★
Top graduate engineering schools by reputation, as determined by academic personnel, 2001 ★2367★
Top graduate engineering schools by reputation, as determined by engineers and recruiters, 2001 ★2368★
U.S. News & World Report's graduate engineering programs with the highest academic reputation scores, 2000-01 ★2372★
Academics' choices for best graduate aerospace/aeronautical/astronautical engineering programs, 2001 ★2374★
U.S. News & World Report's graduate engineering programs with the best aerospace departments, 2000-01 ★2378★
Academics' choices for best graduate agricultural engineering programs, 2001 ★2379★
Academics' choices for best graduate civil engineering programs, 2001 ★2394★
Academics' choices for best graduate electrical/electronic/communications engineering programs, 2001 ★2403★
Academics' choices for best graduate industrial/manufacturing engineering programs, 2001 ★2411★
U.S. News & World Report's graduate engineering programs with the best industrial manufacturing departments, 2000-01 ★2415★
Academics' choices for best graduate mechanical engineering programs, 2001 ★2422★
Academics' choices for best graduate nuclear engineering schools, 2000 ★2426★

Purnell Jr.; Oliver G.
Top pay and benefits for the chief executive and top paid employees at the University of Dayton ★3539★

Purpura; Dominick
Top pay and benefits for the chief executive and top paid employees at Yeshiva University ★3640★

Pusey; Stephen M.
Top pay and benefits for the chief executive and top paid employees at Trevecca Nazarene University ★3576★

Putnam
Hardcover bestsellers by publishing house, 2000 ★240★

Pyle; Ernie
Best U.S. works of journalism in the 20th century ★2769★

Pytte; Agnar
Top pay and benefits for the chief executive and top paid employees at Case Western Reserve University ★3225★

Q

Qlogic
Best small companies in the U.S. ★383★
Business Week's best performing companies with the highest 3-year shareholder returns ★418★
Business Week's best performing companies with the lowest 1-year shareholder returns ★422★

Quaegebeaur; Jan Modest
Top pay and benefits for the chief executive and top paid employees at Columbia University ★3251★

Quah; J.S.T.
Most cited authors in the journal *International Journal of Comparative and Applied Criminal Justice*, 1990 to 1995 ★1624★

Quah; S.
Most cited authors in the journal *International Journal of Comparative and Applied Criminal Justice*, 1990 to 1995 ★1624★

Quaker
Religious preference of incoming freshmen, 2000 ★1061★

Quaker Oats
Business Week's best companies in terms of return on equity ★407★
Business Week's best performing companies with the highest return on equity, 2000 ★420★
Top food companies in Standard & Poor's 500, 2001 ★540★

Quaker United National Office
Most selective internships in the U.S., 2001 ★2610★

Quaker Valley High School
Outstanding secondary schools in Pittsburgh, Pennsylvania ★4204★

Qualcomm
Business Week's best performing companies with the highest 3-year shareholder returns ★418★
Business Week's best performing companies with the lowest 1-year sales performance ★421★
Top recruiters for computer science jobs for 2000-01 master's degree recipients ★1598★
Top recruiters for electrical/electronic engineering jobs for 2000-01 master's degree recipients ★2406★

Quantitative
Gender breakdown of psychology doctorate recipients, by subfield, 1999 ★1941★
Psychology doctorates awarded at U.S. colleges and universities, by subfield, 1999 ★2043★

Quantum
Fortune's highest ranked computer peripherals companies, 2000 ★454★
Top recruiters for marketing jobs for 2000-01 master's degree recipients ★672★

Quaranta; Santino
All-America boys' high school soccer team midfielders, 2001 ★168★

Quarterly Journal of Economics
Economics journals with the greatest impact measure, 1981-98 ★2161★
Economics journals with the greatest impact measure, 1994-98 ★2162★
Economics journals with the greatest impact measure, 1997 ★2163★
Alternative general economics journals, by non-uniform weighting of subdisciplinary impacts, including self-citations ★2180★
Alternative general economics journals, by uniform weighting of subdisciplinary impacts, including self-citations ★2181★
Economics journals by citation impact, 1981-98 ★2182★
Economics journals by citation impact, 1995-98 ★2183★
Economics journals by citation impact, 1998 ★2184★
Top ranked economic development, technological change, and growth journals ★2189★
Top ranked economic systems journals ★2191★
Top ranked industrial organization journals ★2194★
Top ranked international economics journals ★2195★
Top ranked labor and demographic economics journals ★2196★

Top ranked law and economics journals ★2197★
Top ranked microeconomics and monetary economics journals ★2199★
Top ranked microeconomics journals ★2200★
Top ranked public economics journals ★2201★

Quarterly Journal of Experimental Psychology
Most cited science serials in technical communication journals from 1988 to 1997 ★4424★

Quarterly Journal of Speech
Most cited language serials in technical communication journals from 1988 to 1997 ★4420★
Most cited serials in technical communication journals from 1988 to 1997 ★4425★

Quarternary Science Review
Geology journals with the greatest impact measure, 1981-98 ★2525★
Geology journals with the greatest impact measure, 1994-98 ★2526★

Quay; H.C.
Most cited authors in the journal *Criminal Justice and Behavior*, 1990 to 1995 ★1619★

Quebec
Canadian provinces by teaching days per year ★4058★

Quebec City Library
North America's first ten public libraries ★2680★

The Queen of Attolia
Booklist's most recommended fantasy books for youth ★312★

Queen of Peace High School
Outstanding secondary schools in Bergen-Passaic, New Jersey ★4096★

Queen's College
Division II NCAA colleges with the 100% graduation rates for women's basketball players, 1993-94 ★944★
U.S. News & World Report's best undergraduate fees among southern regional universities by discount tuition, 2000 ★1429★
U.S. News & World Report's southern regional universities with the best student/faculty ratios, 2000-01 ★1435★
U.S. News & World Report's southern regional universities with the highest proportion of classes with 20 students or less, 2000-01 ★1441★
Average faculty salaries for institutions of higher education in North Carolina, 2000-01 ★3720★

Queen's Own Fool
Booklist's most recommended historical fiction for youths, 2001 ★314★
Most notable fiction books for young adults, 2001 ★322★

Queen's University
Best Canadian universities for producing leaders of tomorrow, 2000 ★1148★
Best Canadian universities overall, 2000 ★1149★
Best Canadian universities that are the most innovative, 2000 ★1150★
Best Canadian universities with the highest quality, 2000 ★1151★
Canadian medical/doctoral universities by alumni support, 2000 ★1172★
Canadian medical/doctoral universities by award-winning faculty members, 2000 ★1173★
Canadian medical/doctoral universities by class size at the first- and second-year level, 2000 ★1174★
Canadian medical/doctoral universities by class size at the third- and forth-year level, 2000 ★1175★
Canadian medical/doctoral universities by classes taught by tenured faculty, 2000 ★1176★
Canadian medical/doctoral universities by faculty members with Ph.D.'s, 2000 ★1177★
Canadian medical/doctoral universities by international graduate students, 2000 ★1178★
Canadian medical/doctoral universities by library acquisitions, 2000 ★1179★
Canadian medical/doctoral universities by library expenses, 2000 ★1180★
Canadian medical/doctoral universities by library holdings, 2000 ★1181★
Canadian medical/doctoral universities by library holdings per student, 2000 ★1182★
Canadian medical/doctoral universities by medical/science grants per faculty member, 2000 ★1184★
Canadian medical/doctoral universities by operating budget per student, 2000 ★1185★
Canadian medical/doctoral universities by percentage of operating budget allocated to scholarships, 2000 ★1186★
Canadian medical/doctoral universities by percentage of operating budget allocated to student services, 2000 ★1187★
Canadian medical/doctoral universities by reputation, 2000 ★1188★
Canadian medical/doctoral universities by social science/humanities grants per faculty member, 2000 ★1189★
Canadian medical/doctoral universities by students from out of province, 2000 ★1190★
Canadian medical/doctoral universities by students winning national awards, 2000 ★1191★
Canadian universities by average entering grade, 2000 ★1213★
Canadian universities by graduation rate, 2000 ★1214★
Canadian universities by students with 75% grade averages or higher, 2000 ★1215★
Top Canadian medical/doctoral universities, 2000 ★1221★
Top Canadian medical/doctoral universities best at producing leaders of tomorrow, 2000 ★1222★
Top Canadian medical/doctoral universities that are the best overall, 2000 ★1223★
Top Canadian medical/doctoral universities that are the most innovative, 2000 ★1224★
Top Canadian medical/doctoral universities with the highest quality, 2000 ★1225★
Canadian universities producing the most-cited papers in the field of computer science, 1992-96 ★1589★
Canadian universities publishing the most papers in the fields of economics and business, 1992-96 ★2215★
Canadian universities with the greatest impact in materials science, 1992-96 ★4304★

Queens University of Belfast
United Kingdom universities with the greatest impact in geosciences, 1993-97 ★2154★

Queen's University (ON)
Winner of the American Chemical Society's Arthur C. Cope Awards, 2001 ★795★

Queensland; University of
Australian universities with the greatest impact in mathematics, 1993-97 ★2774★

Quest
People for the American Way's list of most frequently challenged materials, 1982-1992 ★749★

The Quick and the Dead
Most notable fiction books, 2001 ★284★
Outstanding works of fiction, 2001 ★293★

Quigley Jr.; Kenneth K.
Top pay and benefits for the chief executive and top paid employees at Curry College ★3261★

Quincy College
Highest undergraduate tuition and fees at public 2-year colleges and universities ★1462★

Quincy University
Average faculty salaries for institutions of higher education in Illinois, 2000-01 ★3700★

Quinebaug Valley Community College
Lowest undergraduate tuition and fees at colleges and universities in Connecticut ★1491★

Quinney; Richard
Most cited scholars in critical criminology ★1640★
Most-cited scholars in critical criminology publications ★1641★
Most cited works in critical criminology ★1644★

Quinnipiac College
Average faculty salaries for institutions of higher education in Connecticut, 2000-01 ★3694★

Quinnipiac University
U.S. News & World Report's northern regional universities with the highest alumni giving rates, 2000-01 ★1418★
U.S. News & World Report's northern regional universities with the highest average graduation rates, 2000-01 ★1419★
U.S. News & World Report's northern regional universities with the highest freshmen retention rates, 2000-01 ★1420★
Highest undergraduate tuition and fees at colleges and universities in Connecticut ★1490★
Presidents with the highest pay at Master's I and II colleges and universities, 1998-99 ★3161★

Quinsigamond Community College
Lowest undergraduate tuition and fees at colleges and universities in Massachusetts ★1517★

Quintiles Transnational
Business Week's best performing companies with the lowest 3-year shareholder returns ★424★

Quivey; Frederick J.
Top pay and benefits for the chief executive and top paid employees at Lafayette College ★3361★

Qwest Communications
Fortune's highest ranked telecommunications companies, 2000 ★499★

R

Rabbi
Jobs with the longest work weeks ★2257★

Rabbinical College Bobover Yeshiva B'nei Zion
Lowest undergraduate tuition and fees at private nonprofit, 4-year or above colleges and universities ★1464★

Rabbit in the Moon
  Most notable videos for adults, 2001 ★2891★
Rabinowitz; Stuart
  Top pay and benefits for the chief executive and top paid employees at Hofstra University ★3335★
Race car driver (Indy Class)
  Jobs considered the most competitive ★2245★
  Jobs that are potentially the highest paying ★2246★
  Jobs with the best income scores ★2248★
  Jobs with the greatest potential income for beginners ★2253★
  Jobs with the worst environment scores ★2260★
  Jobs with the worst stress scores ★2265★
  Most desirable jobs in athletics ★2269★
Rader; James D.
  Top pay and benefits for the chief executive and top paid employees at the University of Tulsa ★3573★
Radford University
  State appropriations for Virginia's institutions of higher education, 2000-01 ★1299★
  U.S. News & World Report's top public southern regional universities, 2000-01 ★1443★
  Average faculty salaries for institutions of higher education in Virginia, 2000-01 ★3735★
Radio Rescue
  Most notable books for young readers, 2001 ★319★
  Smithsonian's best books for children ages 6 to 10 ★364★
Radio Shack
  Top consumer products companies in Standard & Poor's 500, 2001 ★536★
Radiographic and direct observations of experimental lesions in bone 1
  Endodontic articles with the most citations, 1974 through 1999 ★1864★
Radiologic technologists and technicians
  Projected employment growth for selected occupations that require an associate degree or less, 1998-2008 ★2319★
Radnor High School
  Outstanding secondary schools in Philadelphia, Pennsylvania-New Jersey ★4202★
Railroad conductor
  Jobs with the highest unemployment ★2256★
  Jobs with the worst outlook scores ★2262★
  Most desirable jobs in travel/food service ★2278★
Rainy River Community College
  Average faculty salaries for institutions of higher education without academic ranks in Minnesota, 2000-01 ★3753★
Raleigh-Durham-Chapel Hill, NC
  America's most wired cities, 2001 ★2573★
  Cities with the highest percentage of adults using the Internet at home ★2577★
  Cities with the highest percentage of broadband use and interest ★2578★
  Best big cities to live in ★3075★
  Best place to live in the southern U.S. ★3080★
Raley's
  Top women-owned companies ★4460★
Ralph Bunche Middle School
  Outstanding secondary schools in Atlanta, Georgia ★4087★
Ralston High School
  Outstanding secondary schools in Omaha, Nebraska-Iowa ★4198★

Ralston Purina
  Business Week's best performing companies with the highest return on equity, 2000 ★420★
  Business Week's best performing companies with the lowest 3-year sales performance ★423★
  Top food companies in Standard & Poor's 500, 2001 ★540★
Ramapo College
  Average faculty salaries for institutions of higher education in New Jersey, 2000-01 ★3717★
Ramapo College of New Jersey
  State appropriations for New Jersey's institutions of higher education, 2000-01 ★1283★
  U.S. News & World Report's top public northern regional liberal arts colleges, 2000-01 ★1364★
Ramblewood Middle Springs
  Outstanding secondary schools in Fort Lauderdale, Florida ★4133★
Ramey; George G.
  Top pay and benefits for the chief executive and top paid employees at Cumberland College ★3260★
Ramirez; Julio J.
  Top pay and benefits for the chief executive and top paid employees at Davidson College ★3264★
Ramona Convent High School
  Outstanding secondary schools in Los Angeles-Long Beach, California ★4167★
Ramos; Tammy K.
  Top pay and benefits for the chief executive and top paid employees at Creighton University ★3259★
Rampart High School
  Outstanding secondary schools in Colorado Springs, Colorado ★4115★
Ramsay; Carol
  Top pay and benefits for the chief executive and top paid employees at Lake Erie College ★3362★
Ramsey; Julie L.
  Top pay and benefits for the chief executive and top paid employees at Gettysburg College ★3308★
Rancho Buena Vista High School
  Outstanding secondary schools in San Diego, California ★4220★
Rancho San Joaquin Middle School
  Outstanding secondary schools in Orange County, California ★4199★
Rancho Santiago Community College District
  Institutions with the most part-time Hispanic American faculty ★924★
Rand
  Top internships in the U.S. with the highest compensation, 2001 ★2611★
Rand Journal of Economics
  Alternative general economics journals, by non-uniform weighting of subdisciplinary impacts, including self-citations ★2180★
  Alternative general economics journals, by uniform weighting of subdisciplinary impacts, including self-citations ★2181★
  Top ranked business administration and business economics journals ★2188★
  Top ranked economic systems journals ★2191★
  Top ranked financial economics journals ★2192★
  Top ranked industrial organization journals ★2194★
  Top ranked law and economics journals ★2197★
  Top ranked microeconomics journals ★2200★
Randall; Bryan
  All-American boy's high school football all-purpose players, 2000 ★179★
  All-American boy's high school football team, 2000 ★187★
Randall; Gary
  Top pay and benefits for the chief executive and top paid employees at Gonzaga University ★3311★
R&D management
  Overall median salary for full-time chemists with a bachelor's degree, by work function, 2000 ★790★
  Overall median salary for full-time chemists with a doctoral degree, by work function, 2000 ★803★
  Overall median salary for full-time chemists with a master's degree, by work function, 2000 ★804★
Randel; Sally
  Top pay and benefits for the chief executive and top paid employees at Mills College ★3402★
Randolph; A. Philip
  Most influential African Americans in politics and civil rights ★3040★
Randolph Community College
  Average faculty salaries for institutions of higher education without academic ranks in North Carolina, 2000-01 ★3761★
Randolph-Macon College
  Highest undergraduate tuition and fees at colleges and universities in Virginia ★1564★
  Average faculty salaries for institutions of higher education in Virginia, 2000-01 ★3735★
Randolph-Macon Woman's College
  U.S. colleges and universities with the best on-campus housing facilities ★1032★
  Fiske Guide's best buys for private colleges and universities, 2001 ★1459★
  Highest undergraduate tuition and fees at colleges and universities in Virginia ★1564★
  Women's colleges granting physics bachelor's degrees, 2000 ★2982★
  Average faculty salaries for institutions of higher education in Virginia, 2000-01 ★3735★
Randolph; Sara
  All-America girls' high school soccer team midfielders, 2001 ★177★
Randolph; Shavlik
  All-America boys' high school basketball 2nd team, 2001 ★162★
Random House
  Hardcover bestsellers by corporation, 2000 ★239★
  Hardcover bestsellers by publishing house, 2000 ★240★
  Paperback bestsellers by corporation, 2000 ★296★
  Top children's book publishers, 1999 ★3074★
Rankin; Richard
  Top pay and benefits for the chief executive and top paid employees at Queens College in North Carolina ★3448★
Ranney; Gipsie
  Top pay and benefits for the chief executive and top paid employees at Belmont University ★3198★

Ranslow; Paul B.
Top pay and benefits for the chief executive and top paid employees at Ripon College ★3459★

Ransmeier; Denis
Top pay and benefits for the chief executive and top paid employees at Seattle University ★3495★

Rapid Communications in Mass Spectrometry
Spectroscopy journals by citation impact, 1995-99 ★4360★
Spectroscopy journals by citation impact, 1999 ★4361★

Rapp; Rayna
Highly acknowledged individuals in the field of women's studies, 1975-94 ★4466★

Raquette Lake Free Library
Highest Hennen's American Public Library Ratings for libraries serving a population of 999 and under ★2691★

Raritan Valley Community College
Lowest undergraduate tuition and fees at colleges and universities in New Jersey ★1534★

Rasch; Edgar O.
Top pay and benefits for the chief executive and top paid employees at the Maryville University of Saint Louis ★3534★

Rashford, S.J.; Rev. Nicholas S.
Top pay and benefits for the chief executive and top paid employees at Saint Joseph's University ★3476★

Raskin; Lisa R.
Top pay and benefits for the chief executive and top paid employees at Amherst College ★3175★

Rasmussen; Janet
Top pay and benefits for the chief executive and top paid employees at Hollins University ★3336★

Rasp; Kenneth
Top pay and benefits for the chief executive and top paid employees at Immaculata College ★3348★

Rattigan; Terence
Top playwrights of the twentieth century ★4436★

Rauchut; Ed
Top pay and benefits for the chief executive and top paid employees at Bellevue University ★3197★

Rauschenberg; Robert
Highly influential artists of the 20th century ★76★

Rauscher; Kimberly
All-USA Teacher Teams, Third Team, 2000 ★4401★

Raveche; Harold J.
Presidents with the highest pay at Doctoral I and II universities, 1998-99 ★3160★
Top pay and benefits for the chief executive and top paid employees at Stevens Institute of Technology ★3512★

Ravelstein
Booklist's best fiction books for library collections, 2000 ★227★

Raviv; Artur
Top pay and benefits for the chief executive and top paid employees at Northwestern University ★3423★

Rawles; Scott
Top pay and benefits for the chief executive and top paid employees at Converse College ★3255★

Rawlings III; Hunter R.
Largest benefit packages awarded to presidents at institutions of higher education, 1998-99 ★3133★
Top pay and benefits for the chief executive and top paid employees at Cornell University ★3257★

Rawls; Brent
All-American boy's high school football quarterbacks, 2000 ★184★

Ray Elementary School
Illinois elementary schools chosen to be 'demonstration sites' for struggling schools ★4006★

Ray; Helen C.
Top pay and benefits for the chief executive and top paid employees at Brenau University ★3210★

Ray; Jerry
Top pay and benefits for the chief executive and top paid employees at Transylvania University ★3575★

Ray; Robert D.
Top pay and benefits for the chief executive and top paid employees at Drake University ★3272★

Raychem
Most selective internships in the U.S., 2001 ★2610★
Top internships in the U.S. with the highest compensation, 2001 ★2611★

Rayman; Paula
Top pay and benefits for the chief executive and top paid employees at Radcliffe College ★3450★

Raymond Waters College
Average faculty salaries for institutions of higher education in Ohio, 2000-01 ★3722★

Raytheon
Fortune's highest ranked aerospace companies, 2000 ★446★
Top aerospace and defense companies in Standard & Poor's 500, 2001 ★529★

Reaction of rat connective tissue to polyethylene tube implants. Parts I and II
Endodontic articles with the most citations, 1974 through 1999 ★1864★

Reader's Digest
Publishers with the best industry stocks, 2000 ★300★
Highest revenues of publicly held book publishers, 1999 ★3072★
Magazines with the largest circulation ★2750★

Reader's Digest Association
Fortune's highest ranked publishing companies, 2000 ★489★

Reading
Eighth grade students' proficiency ★7★

Reading Area Community College
Lowest undergraduate tuition and fees at colleges and universities in Pennsylvania ★1550★

Reading and auditory-visual equivalencies
Most cited sources in experimental analyses of human behavior between 1990 and 1999 ★3070★

Reading Central Community School
Outstanding secondary schools in Cincinnati, Ohio-Kentucky-Indiana ★4112★

Reading education
Gender breakdown of teaching fields doctorate recipients, by subfield, 1999 ★1943★
Teaching fields doctorates awarded at U.S. colleges and universities, by subfield, 1999 ★2046★

Reading and literacy grants
2002 budget request for miscellaneous education programs ★2229★

Reading Research Quarterly
Education and educational research journals by citation impact, 1981-99 ★2235★
Education and educational research journals by citation impact, 1995-99 ★2236★
Education and educational research journals by citation impact, 1999 ★2237★
Most cited education serials in technical communication journals from 1988 to 1997 ★4418★

Reading; University of
Top United Kingdom universities by total citations in the field of agricultural sciences, 1991-95 ★2145★

Reagan; Melinda H.
Top pay and benefits for the chief executive and top paid employees at Amber University ★3172★

Real Boys' Voices
Outstanding nonfiction books for young adults, 2000 ★334★

Real estate agent
Jobs with the most stringent quotas ★2259★

Real Estate Economics
Highly cited real estate journals, 1990 to 1995 ★3090★

Real Rules for Girls
Most notable nonfiction books for reluctant young adult readers, 2001 ★323★

Reap, I.H.M.; Sister Mary
Top pay and benefits for the chief executive and top paid employees at Marywood University ★3396★

Reardon, R.S.M.; Sister Maureen
Top pay and benefits for the chief executive and top paid employees at Saint Joseph College in Connecticut ★3475★

Rebecca
Outstanding audiobooks, 2000 ★287★

Reboul; A. Duane
Top pay and benefits for the chief executive and top paid employees at Birmingham-Southern College ★3204★

Recent Developments in Cognitive Approaches to Counseling and Psychotherapy
Most frequently cited contribution articles in psychology journals from 1986 to 1996 ★3071★

Receptionists and information clerks
Occupations with the largest projected employment growth, 1998-2008 ★2312★
Projected employment growth for selected occupations that require shorter moderate-term on-the-job training, 1998-2008 ★2321★

Recovering the Gifted Child
Chicago neighborhood schools with the highest ISAT scores in reading and math ★4004★

Recreation
Average costs for Academic Search titles by subject, 2001 ★2918★
Periodical prices by LC subject, 2001 ★2925★

Recreation worker
Most desirable social sciences jobs ★2280★

Red Bank High School
Outstanding secondary schools in Chattanooga, Tennessee-Georgia ★4109★

Red Mountain High School
Outstanding secondary schools in Phoenix-Mesa, Arizona ★4203★

Red Rocks Community College
Average faculty salaries for institutions of higher education without academic ranks in Colorado, 2000-01 ★3744★

The Red Tent
Longest-running trade paperback bestsellers, 2000 ★282★

Reddick; Bryan D.
Top pay and benefits for the chief executive and top paid employees at Elmira College ★3284★

Reddy; Ashok T.
American Chemical Society 2001 award winners (Group 2) ★752★

Reddy; Raj
Top pay and benefits for the chief executive and top paid employees at Carnegie Mellon University ★3223★

Redlands Community College
Lowest undergraduate tuition and fees at colleges and universities in Oklahoma ★1546★
Average faculty salaries for institutions of higher education without academic ranks in Oklahoma, 2000-01 ★3763★

Redlands Middle School
Outstanding secondary schools in Washington, District of Columbia-Maryland-Virginia-West Virginia ★4249★

Redlands; University of
U.S. News & World Report's best undergraduate fees among western regional universities by discount tuition, 2000 ★1430★
U.S. News & World Report's top western regional universities, 2000-01 ★1574★
U.S. News & World Report's western regional universities with students most in debt, 1999 ★1576★
U.S. News & World Report's western regional universities with the best academic reputation scores, 2000-01 ★1577★
U.S. News & World Report's western regional universities with the highest alumni giving rates, 2000-01 ★1580★
U.S. News & World Report's western regional universities with the highest percentage of freshmen in the top 25% of their high school class, 2000-01 ★1583★
U.S. News & World Report's western regional universities with the highest proportion of classes with 20 students or less, 2000-01 ★1585★
Average faculty salaries for institutions of higher education in California, 2000-01 ★3692★

Redman; Margaret
Top pay and benefits for the chief executive and top paid employees at the University of La Verne ★3547★

Redwood Falls Public Library
Highest Hennen's American Public Library Ratings for libraries serving a population of 5,000 to 9,999 ★2694★

Redwoods; College of the
Average faculty salaries for institutions of higher education without academic ranks in California, 2000-01 ★3743★

Reebok
Most selective internships in the U.S., 2001 ★2610★
Top internships in the U.S. with the highest compensation, 2001 ★2611★

Reebok International
Business Week's best performing companies with the highest 1-year earnings growth ★413★
Business Week's best performing companies with the highest 1-year shareholder returns ★415★
Fortune's highest ranked apparel companies, 2000 ★448★

Reed College
Private, 4-year undergraduate colleges and universities producing the most Ph.D.'s in the life sciences, 1920-1990 ★192★
Private, 4-year undergraduate colleges and universities producing the most Ph.D.'s in the life sciences, 1981-1990 ★193★
U.S. colleges and universities most accepting of alternative lifestyles ★986★
U.S. colleges and universities where intercollegiate sports are not popular ★994★
U.S. colleges and universities where the general student body puts little emphasis on athletic events ★1009★
U.S. colleges and universities where the general student body smokes marijuana ★1011★
U.S. colleges and universities with a generally liberal student body ★1015★
U.S. colleges and universities with a large student body of liberal Democrats ★1017★
U.S. colleges and universities with a primarily non-religious student body ★1021★
U.S. colleges and universities without a diverse student body ★1046★
Highest undergraduate tuition and fees at colleges and universities in Oregon ★1547★
Private, 4-year undergraduate colleges and universities producing the most Ph.D.'s in the computer sciences, 1920-1990 ★1595★
Private, 4-year undergraduate colleges and universities producing the most Ph.D.'s in the computer sciences, 1981-1990 ★1596★
Private, 4-year undergraduate colleges and universities producing the most Ph.Ds in all fields of study, 1920-1990 ★2027★
Private, 4-year undergraduate colleges and universities producing the most Ph.D.'s in all fields of study, 1981-1990 ★2028★
Private, 4-year undergraduate colleges and universities producing the most Ph.D.'s in all fields of study, 1990 ★2029★
Private, 4-year undergraduate colleges and universities producing the most Ph.D.'s in economics, 1920-1990 ★2211★
Private, 4-year undergraduate colleges and universities producing the most Ph.D.'s in economics, 1981-1990 ★2212★
Private, 4-year undergraduate colleges and universities producing the most Ph.D.'s in English, 1981-1990 ★2450★
Private, 4-year undergraduate colleges and universities producing the most Ph.D.'s in history, 1920-1990 ★2552★
Private, 4-year undergraduate colleges and universities producing the most Ph.D.'s in history, 1981-1990 ★2553★
Private, 4-year undergraduate colleges and universities producing the most Ph.D.'s in mathematics, 1920-1990 ★2776★
Private, 4-year undergraduate colleges and universities producing the most Ph.D.'s in mathematics, 1981-1990 ★2777★
Private, 4-year undergraduate colleges and universities producing the most Ph.D.'s in physics and astronomy, 1920-1990 ★2949★
Private, 4-year undergraduate colleges and universities producing the most Ph.D.'s in political science and international relations, 1920-1990 ★3044★
Private, 4-year undergraduate colleges and universities producing the most Ph.D.'s in psychology, 1920-1990 ★3066★
Average faculty salaries for institutions of higher education in Oregon, 2000-01 ★3724★
Private, 4-year undergraduate colleges and universities producing the most Ph.D.'s in the sciences, 1920-1990 ★4294★
Private, 4-year undergraduate colleges and universities producing the most Ph.D.'s in the sciences, 1981-1990 ★4295★
Private, 4-year undergraduate colleges and universities producing the most Ph.D.'s in anthropology and sociology, 1920-1990 ★4344★
Private, 4-year undergraduate colleges and universities producing the most Ph.D.'s in anthropology and sociology, 1981-1990 ★4345★

Reed; John
Best U.S. works of journalism in the 20th century ★2769★
Top pay and benefits for the chief executive and top paid employees at Linfield College ★3376★

Reed; Millard
Top pay and benefits for the chief executive and top paid employees at Trevecca Nazarene University ★3576★

Reed; William S.
Top pay and benefits for the chief executive and top paid employees at Wellesley College ★3609★

Rees; David
Top pay and benefits for the chief executive and top paid employees at Bennington College ★3201★

Reference
Subject areas with the highest library expenditures/circulation ★306★

Reflections of a Siamese Twin
Canada's best nonfiction selections of the 20th century ★234★

Regeneration series
Most notable fiction books for reluctant young adult readers, 2001 ★321★

Regina Dominican High School
Outstanding secondary schools in Chicago, Illinois ★4110★

Regina High School
Outstanding secondary schools in Cleveland-Lorain-Elyria, Ohio ★4114★

Regina; University of
Canadian comprehensive universities by alumni support, 2000 ★1153★
Canadian comprehensive universities by award-winning faculty members, 2000 ★1154★
Canadian comprehensive universities by class size at the first- and second-year level, 2000 ★1155★
Canadian comprehensive universities by class size at the third- and forth-year level, 2000 ★1156★
Canadian comprehensive universities by classes taught by tenured faculty, 2000 ★1157★
Canadian comprehensive universities by faculty members with Ph.D.'s, 2000 ★1158★
Canadian comprehensive universities by international graduate students, 2000 ★1159★

REGIONAL

Canadian comprehensive universities by library acquisitions, 2000 ★1160★
Canadian comprehensive universities by library expenses, 2000 ★1161★
Canadian comprehensive universities by library holdings per student, 2000 ★1162★
Canadian comprehensive universities by operating budget per student, 2000 ★1163★
Canadian comprehensive universities by percentage of operating budget allocated to scholarships, 2000 ★1164★
Canadian comprehensive universities by percentage of operating budget allocated to student services, 2000 ★1165★
Canadian comprehensive universities by social science/humanities grants per faculty member, 2000 ★1166★
Canadian comprehensive universities by students from out of province, 2000 ★1167★
Canadian comprehensive universities by students winning national awards, 2000 ★1168★
Canadian medical/doctoral universities by medical/science grants per faculty member, 2000 ★1183★
Top Canadian comprehensive universities, 2000 ★1219★
Top Canadian comprehensive universities by reputation, 2000 ★1220★

A Regional Dynamic General-Equilibrium Model of Alternative Climate Change Strategies
Top cited energy papers from 1994 to 1998 ★2467★

Regional Science and Urban Economics
Top ranked urban, rural and regional economics journals ★2202★

Regis College
U.S. News & World Report's northern regional liberal arts colleges with the best student/faculty ratios, 2000-01 ★1353★
U.S. News & World Report's northern regional liberal arts colleges with the highest academic reputation scores, 2000-01 ★1354★
U.S. News & World Report's northern regional liberal arts colleges with the highest acceptance rates, 2000-01 ★1355★
U.S. News & World Report's northern regional liberal arts colleges with the highest alumni giving rates, 2000-01 ★1356★
U.S. News & World Report's northern regional liberal arts colleges with the highest freshmen retention rates, 2000-01 ★1357★
U.S. News & World Report's northern regional liberal arts colleges with the highest proportion of classes having 20 students or less, 2000-01 ★1361★
U.S. News & World Report's top northern regional liberal arts colleges, 2000-01 ★1363★
Average faculty salaries for institutions of higher education in Massachusetts, 2000-01 ★3708★

Regis College (MA)
College senior's choices for exemplary master's institutions ★2533★
First-year student's choices for exemplary master's institutions ★2536★

Regis Jesuit High School
Outstanding secondary schools in Denver, Colorado ★4124★

Regis University
Division II NCAA colleges with the 100% graduation rates for men's basketball players, 1993-94 ★943★

Highest undergraduate tuition and fees at colleges and universities in Colorado ★1488★
U.S. News & World Report's western regional universities with the highest freshmen retention rates, 2000-01 ★1581★
U.S. News & World Report's western regional universities with the highest proportion of classes with 20 students or less, 2000-01 ★1585★
U.S. colleges and universities awarding the most computer and information sciences master's degrees to Hispanic Americans ★1768★
Average faculty salaries for institutions of higher education in Colorado, 2000-01 ★3693★

Registered nurses
Occupations with the largest projected employment growth, 1998-2008 ★2312★
Projected employment growth for selected occupations that require an associate degree or less, 1998-2008 ★2319★

Rehabilitation Institute of Chicago
Top rehabilitation hospitals in the U.S., 2000 ★2801★

Rehabilitation/therapeutic services
Gender breakdown of health sciences doctorate recipients, by subfield, 1999 ★1935★
Health sciences doctorates awarded at U.S. colleges and universities, by subfield, 1999 ★1944★

Reichblum; William
Top pay and benefits for the chief executive and top paid employees at Bennington College ★3201★

Reid; James F.
Top pay and benefits for the chief executive and top paid employees at Tusculum College ★3582★

Reid State Technical College
Lowest undergraduate tuition and fees at colleges and universities in Alabama ★1480★

Reid; Tammy A.
Top pay and benefits for the chief executive and top paid employees at Whitworth College ★3625★

Reigelman; Milton
Top pay and benefits for the chief executive and top paid employees at Centre College ★3227★

Reinhardt College
Average faculty salaries for institutions of higher education in Georgia, 2000-01 ★3697★

Reinharz; Jehuda
Top pay and benefits for the chief executive and top paid employees at Brandeis University ★3209★

Reiss; A.J.
Most cited authors in the journal Criminal Justice Review, 1990 to 1995 ★1620★

Relationship Approach to Marketing in Service Contexts: The Marketing and Organizational Behavior Interface
Most influential articles in the Journal of Business Research, 1985-1999 ★697★
Most influential articles in the Journal of Business Research from 1990 to 1994 ★699★

The Relationship in Counseling and Psychotherapy: Components, Consequences, and Theoretical Antecedents
Most frequently cited contribution articles in psychology journals from 1986 to 1996 ★3071★

Relationship Management: Managing the Selling and the Buying Interface
Most influential articles in the Journal of Business Research, 1985-1999 ★697★
Most influential articles in the Journal of Business Research from 1985 to 1989 ★698★

Relationship Rescue
Longest-running nonfiction hardcover bestsellers, 2000 ★281★

Reliance Technical Services
Top women-owned companies in revenue growth since 1997 ★4461★

Reliant Energy
Fortune's highest ranked electric and gas utilities companies, 2000 ★459★
Top utilities companies in Standard & Poor's 500, 2001 ★561★

Religion
Gender breakdown of humanities doctorate recipients, by subfield, 1999 ★1936★
Humanities doctorates awarded at U.S. colleges and universities, by subfield, 1999 ★1946★

Relland; Lance
All-USA College Academic First Team, 2001 ★2★

Rembert; G. Andrew
Top pay and benefits for the chief executive and top paid employees at Washington and Jefferson College ★3604★

Remembering Blue
Library Journal's best fiction audiobooks, 2000 ★241★

Remick; Oscar E.
Top pay and benefits for the chief executive and top paid employees at Westminster College in Pennsylvania ★3617★

Remington; Brodie
Top pay and benefits for the chief executive and top paid employees at Trinity College in Connecticut ★3577★

Remington College-Education American, Inc.
Highest undergraduate tuition and fees at colleges and universities in Louisiana ★1510★

Renaissance Senior High School
Outstanding urban public high schools in Metro Detroit ★4264★

Renal Physiology & Biochemistry
Urology and nephrology journals with the greatest impact measure, 1981-98 ★2816★
Urology and nephrology journals with the greatest impact measure, 1994-98 ★2817★

Rend Lake College
Lowest undergraduate tuition and fees at colleges and universities in Illinois ★1501★

Rendleman; Doug
Top pay and benefits for the chief executive and top paid employees at Washington and Lee University ★3605★

Renew America
Most selective internships in the U.S., 2001 ★2610★
Top internships in the U.S. with the highest compensation, 2001 ★2611★

Renner Middle School
Outstanding secondary schools in Dallas, Texas ★4120★

Rennison; Louise
Booklist's best first novels for youths ★309★

Reno, NV
Best 'quirky' places to live ★3083★

Rensselaer Polytechnic Institute
  U.S. colleges and universities where students and the local community relate well ★999★
  U.S. colleges and universities where students are not very politically active ★1000★
  U.S. colleges and universities with an unfavorable surrounding town or city ★1023★
  U.S. colleges and universities with the most accessible instructors ★1038★
  U.S. News & World Report's national universities with the highest acceptance rates, 2000-01 ★1131★
  U.S. News & World Report's national universities with the lowest graduation rates, 1999 ★1141★
  Largest private gifts to higher education, 1967-2000 ★1248★
  Top industrial engineering research-doctorate programs as evaluated by the National Research Council ★2413★
  Most effective materials science research-doctorate programs as evaluated by the National Research Council ★2418★
  Top materials science research-doctorate programs as evaluated by the National Research Council ★2419★
  Most wired universities, 2000 ★2598★
  Average faculty salaries for institutions of higher education in New York, 2000-01 ★3719★

Reporter (newspaper)
  Jobs with the most stringent quotas ★2259★
  Most desirable jobs in communications ★2271★

Reports on Progress in Physics
  Physics journals with the greatest impact measure, 1981-98 ★3020★

Representation and Reasoning
  Journals and proceedings with the most citations (Class 4) ★2570★

Repsol YPF
  Business Week's best companies in Spain ★403★

Republic of China (Taiwan)
  Countries of origin for non-U.S. citizens awarded doctorates at U.S. colleges and universities, 1999 ★1901★

Republic of Korea
  Comparison of 8th grade science achievement scores, U.S. and worldwide, 1999 ★6★
  Math achievement test comparison ★19★
  Foreign countries with the highest enrollment of foreign students, 1999-2000 ★2496★

Republic Services
  Fortune's highest ranked waste management companies, 2000 ★504★

Research assistantships/traineeships
  Primary sources of financial support for doctorate recipients, by citizenship, 1999 ★2003★
  Primary sources of financial support for doctorate recipients, by gender, 1999 ★2004★
  Primary sources of financial support for doctorate recipients, by race/ethnicity, 1999 ★2005★
  Primary sources of financial support for education doctorate recipients, by citizenship, 1999 ★2006★
  Primary sources of financial support for education doctorate recipients, by gender, 1999 ★2007★
  Primary sources of financial support for education doctorate recipients, by race/ethnicity, 1999 ★2008★
  Primary sources of financial support for engineering doctorate recipients, by citizenship, 1999 ★2009★
  Primary sources of financial support for engineering doctorate recipients, by gender, 1999 ★2010★
  Primary sources of financial support for engineering doctorate recipients, by race/ethnicity, 1999 ★2011★
  Primary sources of financial support for humanities doctorate recipients, by citizenship, 1999 ★2012★
  Primary sources of financial support for humanities doctorate recipients, by gender, 1999 ★2013★
  Primary sources of financial support for humanities doctorate recipients, by race/ethnicity, 1999 ★2014★
  Primary sources of financial support for life sciences doctorate recipients, by citizenship, 1999 ★2015★
  Primary sources of financial support for life sciences doctorate recipients, by gender, 1999 ★2016★
  Primary sources of financial support for life sciences doctorate recipients, by race/ethnicity, 1999 ★2017★
  Primary sources of financial support for physical sciences, mathematics, and computer sciences doctorate recipients, by citizenship, 1999 ★2018★
  Primary sources of financial support for physical sciences, mathematics, and computer sciences doctorate recipients, by gender, 1999 ★2019★
  Primary sources of financial support for physical sciences, mathematics, and computer sciences doctorate recipients, by race/ethnicity, 1999 ★2020★
  Primary sources of financial support for professional/other doctorate recipients, by citizenship, 1999 ★2021★
  Primary sources of financial support for professional/other doctorate recipients, by gender, 1999 ★2022★
  Primary sources of financial support for professional/other doctorate recipients, by race/ethnicity, 1999 ★2023★
  Primary sources of financial support for social sciences doctorate recipients, by citizenship, 1999 ★2024★
  Primary sources of financial support for social sciences doctorate recipients, by gender, 1999 ★2025★
  Primary sources of financial support for social sciences doctorate recipients, by race/ethnicity, 1999 ★2026★

Research College of Nursing
  Highest undergraduate tuition and fees at colleges and universities in Missouri ★1524★

Research in Counseling: Methodological and Professional Issues
  Most frequently cited contribution articles in psychology journals from 1986 to 1996 ★3071★

Research in Teaching English
  Most cited language serials in technical communication journals from 1988 to 1997 ★4420★
  Most cited serials in technical communication journals from 1988 to 1997 ★4425★

Research and testing services
  Employment growth percentages for selected industries, 1998-2000 ★2294★
  Industries with the highest percentage of projected employment growth from 1998 through 2008 ★2305★

Residential care
  Industries with the highest percentage of projected employment growth from 1998 through 2008 ★2305★
  Industries with the highest projected growth rate, 1994-2005 ★2306★

Residential care facilities
  Employment growth percentages for selected industries, 1998-2000 ★2294★

Residential counselors
  Projections for the fastest growing occupations requiring a bachelor's degree or more from 1998 to 2008 ★2292★
  Fastest growing occupations, 1998-2008 ★2302★
  Projected employment growth for selected occupations that require a bachelor's degree or more, 1998-2008 ★2317★

Resource for Teaching of English
  Education and educational research journals by citation impact, 1981-99 ★2235★

Respiratory therapist
  Jobs with the highest employment growth ★2254★
  Jobs with the lowest unemployment ★2258★

Respiratory therapists
  Fastest growing occupations, 1998-2008 ★2302★
  Projected employment growth for selected occupations that require an associate degree or less, 1998-2008 ★2319★

Restaino; Katherine
  Top pay and benefits for the chief executive and top paid employees at Saint Peter's College ★3485★

Resurrection High School
  Outstanding Catholic high schools in Metro Chicago ★4074★

Retail
  Spending for E-marketplace services, by industry, 2001 ★4430★

Retail salesperson
  Projected employment growth for selected occupations that require shortor moderate-term on-the-job training, 1998-2008 ★2321★

Retail salespersons
  Occupations with the highest number of self-employed workers, 1998 ★2311★
  Occupations with the largest projected employment growth, 1998-2008 ★2312★

Retail trade
  Employment change projections by major industry division from 1998 to 2008 ★2287★
  Employment projections by major industry division for 2008 ★2290★

Retrospetiva
  Companies with the worst two-year total returns since 1998 ★437★

Return to Wholeness: Embracing Body, Mind, and Spirit in the Face of Cancer
  Library Journal's best nonfiction audiobooks, 2000 ★243★

Reuter; Edward W.
  Top pay and benefits for the chief executive and top paid employees at Saint Peter's College ★3485★

Reuters Group
  Business Week's best companies in terms of return on equity ★407★

Revay; A.R.
   Top pay and benefits for the chief executive and top paid employees at Florida Institute of Technology ★3293★

Revere High School
   Outstanding secondary schools in Akron, Ohio ★4078★

Review of Economic Studies
   Economics journals with the greatest impact measure, 1981-98 ★2161★
   Economics journals with the greatest impact measure, 1994-98 ★2162★
   Alternative general economics journals, by non-uniform weighting of subdisciplinary impacts, including self-citations ★2180★
   Alternative general economics journals, by uniform weighting of subdisciplinary impacts, including self-citations ★2181★
   Economics journals by citation impact, 1981-98 ★2182★
   Top ranked agricultural and natural resource economics journals ★2187★
   Top ranked economic systems journals ★2191★
   Top ranked health, education, and welfare journals ★2193★
   Top ranked industrial organization journals ★2194★
   Top ranked international economics journals ★2195★
   Top ranked mathematical and quantitative methods journals ★2198★
   Top ranked microeconomics journals ★2200★
   Top ranked public economics journals ★2201★
   Highest impact economics journals in energy from 1990 to 1998 ★2458★
   Highest impact economics journals in exhaustible resources from 1974 to 1979 ★2459★
   Highest impact economics journals in exhaustible resources from 1990 to 1998 ★2461★

Review of Economics and Statistics
   Top ranked agricultural and natural resource economics journals ★2187★
   Top ranked economic development, technological change, and growth journals ★2189★
   Top ranked economic systems journals ★2191★
   Top ranked health, education, and welfare journals ★2193★
   Top ranked industrial organization journals ★2194★
   Top ranked labor and demographic economics journals ★2196★
   Top ranked urban, rural and regional economics journals ★2202★
   Highest impact economics journals in energy from 1974 to 1979 ★2456★
   Highest impact economics journals in exhaustible resources from 1974 to 1979 ★2459★
   Highest impact economics journals in exhaustible resources from 1990 to 1998 ★2461★

Review of Infectious Diseases
   Immunology journals by impact factor, 1981 to 1997 ★4279★

Review of Modern Physics
   Physics journals with the greatest impact measure, 1981-98 ★3020★

Review of Research in Education
   Education and educational research journals with the greatest impact measure ★2238★

Reviews of Chemical Intermediates
   Chemistry journals by citation impact, 1981-99 ★808★

Reviews in Computational Chemistry
   Chemistry journals by citation impact, 1995-99 ★809★

Reviews in Educational Research
   Education and educational research journals by citation impact, 1981-99 ★2235★
   Education and educational research journals by citation impact, 1995-99 ★2236★
   Education and educational research journals by citation impact, 1999 ★2237★
   Education and educational research journals with the greatest impact measure ★2238★
   Most cited education serials in technical communication journals from 1988 to 1997 ★4418★

Reviews in Fish Biology and Fisheries
   Marine and freshwater biology journals with the greatest impact measure, 1994-98 ★197★

Reviews of Infectious Diseases
   Immunology journals with the greatest impact measure, 1981-98 ★2810★

Reviews of Research in Education
   Education and educational research journals by citation impact, 1981-99 ★2235★
   Education and educational research journals by citation impact, 1995-99 ★2236★
   Education and educational research journals by citation impact, 1999 ★2237★

Revlon
   Fortune's highest ranked soaps and cosmetics companies, 2000 ★496★

Revolting Rhymes
   Most frequently banned books in the 1990s ★745★
   People for the American Way's list of most frequently challenged books, 1991-1992 ★748★

Rex; Ronald W.
   Top pay and benefits for the chief executive and top paid employees at the Chaminade University of Honolulu ★3524★

Rey; Margret and H. A.
   Outstanding children's picture books, 2000 ★331★

Reynders; John C.
   Top pay and benefits for the chief executive and top paid employees at Allegheny College ★3170★

Reynolds & Reynolds
   Fortune's highest ranked printing companies, 2000 ★487★

Reynolds; Herbert H.
   Top pay and benefits for the chief executive and top paid employees at Baylor University ★3194★

Reynolds; J. T.
   Top pay and benefits for the chief executive and top paid employees at University of Central Texas ★3589★

Reynolds; John M.
   Top pay and benefits for the chief executive and top paid employees at Biola University ★3203★

Reynolds; Thomas E.
   Top pay and benefits for the chief executive and top paid employees at Regis University in Colorado ★3454★

RHAM High School
   Outstanding secondary schools in Hartford, Connecticut ★4147★

Rheem; Joe
   All-American boy's high school football kicker, 2000 ★181★
   All-American boy's high school football team, 2000 ★187★

Rheins; Carl
   Top pay and benefits for the chief executive and top paid employees at Adelphi University ★3164★

Rheinschmidt; Richard
   Top pay and benefits for the chief executive and top paid employees at Coe College ★3240★

Rhetoric Review
   Most cited language serials in technical communication journals from 1988 to 1997 ★4420★
   Most cited serials in technical communication journals from 1988 to 1997 ★4425★

Rheumatology
   Clinical medicine subfields with the highest impact measure, 1981-1997 ★2873★

Rhode Island
   Mean composite ACT scores by state, 2000 ★895★
   Mean math SAT scores by state, 2000 ★900★
   Mean verbal SAT scores by state, 2000 ★903★
   States allocating the smallest amount of state tax appropriations for higher education, 2000-01 ★1305★
   Total doctorate recipients by state, 1999 ★2054★
   State grades for affordability of higher education for minority students, 2000 ★2883★
   State grades for benefits state receives for educating its minority students, 2000 ★2884★
   State grades for completion of higher education by minority students, 2000 ★2885★
   State grades for participation of minority students in higher education, 2000 ★2886★
   State grades for preparing minority students for higher education, 2000 ★2887★
   States with the highest per-pupil expenditures ★3996★
   States with the lowest number of high school graduates, 1999-2000 ★3997★
   States with the highest percentage of high school freshmen enrolling in college within four years ★4266★

Rhode Island College
   State appropriations for Rhode Island's institutions of higher education, 2000-01 ★1292★
   Undergraduate tuition and fees at colleges and universities in Rhode Island ★1553★
   Average faculty salaries for institutions of higher education in Rhode Island, 2000-01 ★3727★

Rhode Island; Community College of
   State appropriations for Rhode Island's institutions of higher education, 2000-01 ★1292★
   Undergraduate tuition and fees at colleges and universities in Rhode Island ★1553★
   Average faculty salaries for institutions of higher education in Rhode Island, 2000-01 ★3727★

Rhode Island School of Design
   First-year student's choices for exemplary special mission institutions ★1066★

Undergraduate tuition and fees at colleges and universities in Rhode Island ★1553★
Average faculty salaries for institutions of higher education in Rhode Island, 2000-01 ★3727★

Rhode Island; University of
U.S. colleges and universities where students study the least ★1002★
State appropriations for Rhode Island's institutions of higher education, 2000-01 ★1292★
Undergraduate tuition and fees at colleges and universities in Rhode Island ★1553★
Top oceanography research-doctorate programs as evaluated by the National Research Council ★2153★
Average faculty salaries for institutions of higher education in Rhode Island, 2000-01 ★3727★

Rhodes College
U.S. colleges and universities with the best quality of life ★1034★
U.S. News & World Report's national liberal arts colleges with the highest acceptance rates, 2000-01 ★1328★
Highest undergraduate tuition and fees at colleges and universities in Tennessee ★1558★
Presidents with the highest pay at Baccalaureate I colleges, 1998-99 ★3159★
Average faculty salaries for institutions of higher education in Tennessee, 2000-01 ★3730★

Rhodes; Fred W.
Top pay and benefits for the chief executive and top paid employees at Bellarmine University ★3196★

Rhodes Junior High School
Outstanding secondary schools in Phoenix-Mesa, Arizona ★4203★

Rhodes School, District 84-5
Illinois school districts spending the most per pupil for instruction ★4011★

Rhodus; Kenneth
Top pay and benefits for the chief executive and top paid employees at Hastings College ★3328★

Rhythm in My Shoes
Most notable children's recordings, 2001 ★320★
Outstanding audio selections for young listeners, 2000 ★325★

Ricardo; David
Most cited economists ★2185★

Riccio; Ronald J.
Top pay and benefits for the chief executive and top paid employees at Seton Hall University ★3496★

Rice; Glen
Division I NCAA men's basketball players with the highest tournament scores ★154★

Rice High School
Outstanding secondary schools in New York, New York ★4191★

Rice; Robert
Top pay and benefits for the chief executive and top paid employees at Christendom College ★3232★

Rice University
Colleges with the highest number of freshman Merit Scholars, 2000 ★5★
U.S. universities with the highest concentration of papers published in the field of chemistry, 1994-98 ★794★
U.S. colleges and universities where intramural sports are popular ★997★

U.S. colleges and universities where students study the most ★1003★
U.S. colleges and universities with the best on-campus housing facilities ★1032★
U.S. News & World Report's national universities with the best faculty resources rank, 2000-01 ★1127★
Colleges and universities with the largest endowments, 2000 ★1237★
Fiske Guide's best buys for private colleges and universities, 2001 ★1459★
U.S. News & World Report's best undergraduate fees among national universities by discount tuition, 2000 ★1474★
U.S. News & World Report's national universities with students least in debt, 1999 ★1475★
Highest undergraduate tuition and fees at colleges and universities in Texas ★1560★
Most effective biomedical engineering research-doctorate programs as evaluated by the National Research Council ★2383★
Top biomedical engineering research-doctorate programs as evaluated by the National Research Council ★2384★
First-year student's choices for exemplary doctoral-extensive universities ★2534★
U.S. universities with the greatest impact in physics, 1994-98 ★2980★
Presidents with the highest pay at Research I and II universities, 1998-99 ★3162★
Average faculty salaries for institutions of higher education in Texas, 2000-01 ★3731★
U.S. institutions with the highest paid assistant professors, 2001 ★3977★

Rich Dad Poor Dad
Longest-running trade paperback bestsellers, 2000 ★282★

Rich; Jack W.
Top pay and benefits for the chief executive and top paid employees at Abilene Christian University ★3163★

Rich Mountain Community College
Lowest undergraduate tuition and fees at colleges and universities in Arkansas ★1485★

Rich Township, District 227
Illinois school districts with the most average years of teacher experience ★4012★

Richard Bland College
Average faculty salaries for institutions of higher education in Virginia, 2000-01 ★3735★

Richard J. Daley College
Fall enrollment at Chicago-area city colleges, by minority percentages, 1999 ★865★

Richard Stockton College of New Jersey
State appropriations for New Jersey's institutions of higher education, 2000-01 ★1283★

Richards; B. Stephen
Top pay and benefits for the chief executive and top paid employees at Franklin College of Indiana ★3297★

Richardson; Anthony
All-America boys' high school basketball 3rd team, 2001 ★163★

Richardson; Barrie
Top pay and benefits for the chief executive and top paid employees at the Centenary College of Louisiana ★3523★

Richardson, C.M.; Rev. John T.
Top pay and benefits for the chief executive and top paid employees at DePaul University ★3266★

Richardson; David
Top pay and benefits for the chief executive and top paid employees at St. Lawrence University ★3477★

Richardson Junior High School
Outstanding secondary schools in Dallas, Texas ★4120★

Richardson; Luther
All-USA Teacher Teams, Second Team, 2000 ★4400★

Richardson; Walter
Top pay and benefits for the chief executive and top paid employees at Oral Roberts University ★3433★

Richer and the Poor Get Prison: Ideology, Crime, and Criminal Justice
Most-cited works in critical criminology publications ★1645★

Richey; Melody
Top pay and benefits for the chief executive and top paid employees at Rhodes College ★3456★

Richland College
Lowest undergraduate tuition and fees at colleges and universities in Texas ★1561★
Average faculty salaries for institutions of higher education without academic ranks in Texas, 2000-01 ★3766★

Richland County Public Library
Highest Hennen's American Public Library Ratings for libraries serving a population of 250,000 to 499,999 ★2699★

Richland Northeast High School
Outstanding secondary schools in Columbia, South Carolina ★4117★

Richmond Community College
Average faculty salaries for institutions of higher education in North Carolina, 2000-01 ★3720★

Richmond Heights Middle School
All-USA Teacher Teams, Third Team, 2000 ★4401★

Richmond Senior High School
All-USA Teacher Teams, First Team, 2000 ★4399★

Richmond; University of
All-USA College Academic Second Team, 2001 ★3★
Division I NCAA colleges with the highest graduation rates for female athletes, 1990-91 to 1993-94 ★931★
Division I NCAA colleges with the highest graduation rates for football players, 1990-91 to 1993-94 ★933★
U.S. colleges and universities with the best quality of life ★1034★
U.S. colleges and universities with the most attractive campuses ★1039★
U.S. News & World Report's best undergraduate fees among southern regional universities by discount tuition, 2000 ★1429★
U.S. News & World Report's southern regional universities with the best academic reputation scores, 2000-01 ★1433★
U.S. News & World Report's southern regional universities with the best alumni giving rates, 2000-01 ★1434★
U.S. News & World Report's southern regional universities with the best student/faculty ratios, 2000-01 ★1435★
U.S. News & World Report's southern regional universities with the highest freshmen retention rates, 2000-01 ★1437★

U.S. News & World Report's southern regional universities with the highest graduation rates, 2000-01 ★1438★

U.S. News & World Report's southern regional universities with the highest percentage of freshmen in the top 25% of their high school class, 2000-01 ★1439★

U.S. News & World Report's southern regional universities with the highest percentage of full-time faculty, 2000-01 ★1440★

U.S. News & World Report's southern regional universities with the lowest acceptance rates, 2000-01 ★1442★

U.S. News & World Report's top southern regional universities, 2000-01 ★1444★

Highest undergraduate tuition and fees at colleges and universities in Virginia ★1564★

Private, 4-year undergraduate colleges and universities producing the most Ph.D.'s in economics, 1920-1990 ★2211★

College senior's choices for exemplary master's institutions ★2533★

First-year student's choices for exemplary master's institutions ★2536★

Presidents with the highest pay at Master's I and II colleges and universities, 1998-99 ★3161★

Average faculty salaries for institutions of higher education in Virginia, 2000-01 ★3735★

Richmond; V.
Highest ranked active communication studies researchers ★2747★
Top published female authors (1915-1985) in the field of communication studies ★4363★

Rich's Lazarus Goldsmiths
Top recruiters for retail merchandising jobs for 2000-01 bachelor's degree recipients ★556★

Richter; Gerhard
Best living artists ★73★

Richton International
Best small companies in the U.S. ★383★

Rickert; Rick
All-America boys' high school basketball 1st team, 2001 ★161★

Rickey; Jeffrey
Top pay and benefits for the chief executive and top paid employees at Earlham College ★3279★

Ricks College
Undergraduate tuition and fees at colleges and universities in Idaho ★1499★

Ridenour; Richard I.
Top pay and benefits for the chief executive and top paid employees at Marian College of Fond Du Lac ★3389★

Rider; B.A.K.
Most cited authors in the journal *International Journal of Comparative and Applied Criminal Justice*, 1990 to 1995 ★1624★

Rider University
U.S. News & World Report's northern regional universities with the highest acceptance rates, 2000-01 ★1417★
Highest undergraduate tuition and fees at colleges and universities in New Jersey ★1533★
Average faculty salaries for institutions of higher education in New Jersey, 2000-01 ★3717★

Ridgewater College
Average faculty salaries for institutions of higher education without academic ranks in Minnesota, 2000-01 ★3753★

Ridley; Matt
Booklist's best science and technology books ★366★

Ridley, S.J.; Rev. Harold
Top pay and benefits for the chief executive and top paid employees at Loyola College in Maryland ★3379★

Riemann; Mike M.
Top pay and benefits for the chief executive and top paid employees at Pfeiffer University ★3439★

Rigos; Chris
Top pay and benefits for the chief executive and top paid employees at City University in Washington ★3234★

Rimbaud
Outstanding biography books, 2000 ★288★

Ringling School of Art and Design
Highest undergraduate tuition and fees at colleges and universities in Florida ★1494★

Rinker; Meryle G.
Top pay and benefits for the chief executive and top paid employees at Illinois College ★3345★

Rio Americano High School
Outstanding secondary schools in Sacramento, California ★4215★

Rio Grande; University of
Lowest undergraduate tuition and fees at private nonprofit, 4-year or above colleges and universities ★1464★
Private 4-year institutions with the lowest tuition, 2000-01 ★1468★
Average faculty salaries for institutions of higher education in Ohio, 2000-01 ★3722★

Rio Salado College
Lowest undergraduate tuition and fees at colleges and universities in Arizona ★1483★

Ripon College
U.S. colleges and universities with the best financial aid programs ★1030★
Highest undergraduate tuition and fees at colleges and universities in Wisconsin ★1570★
Average faculty salaries for institutions of higher education in Wisconsin, 2000-01 ★3738★

Risboskin; John
Top pay and benefits for the chief executive and top paid employees at College Misericordia ★3243★

Risinger; Edward
Top pay and benefits for the chief executive and top paid employees at National-Louis University in Illinois ★3414★

Rist; Boyd C.
Top pay and benefits for the chief executive and top paid employees at Liberty University ★3373★

Ritchie; Daniel
Top pay and benefits for the chief executive and top paid employees at the University of Denver ★3540★

Rite Aid
Fortune's highest ranked food and drug stores, 2000 ★463★

River Dell Regional High School
Outstanding secondary schools in Bergen-Passaic, New Jersey ★4096★

River Oaks Baptist School
Outstanding secondary schools in Houston, Texas ★4150★

Rivera; Katie
All-America girls' high school soccer team forwards, 2001 ★175★

Riverland Community College
Average faculty salaries for institutions of higher education without academic ranks in Minnesota, 2000-01 ★3753★

Riverland Community College Agricultural Technical and Community College
Lowest undergraduate tuition and fees at colleges and universities in Minnesota ★1521★

Riverview Elementary School
All-USA Teacher Teams, First Team, 2000 ★4399★

Rivier College
Highest undergraduate tuition and fees at colleges and universities in New Hampshire ★1531★
Average faculty salaries for institutions of higher education in New Hampshire, 2000-01 ★3716★

R.J. Reynolds Tobacco
Fortune's highest ranked tobacco companies, 2000 ★502★

Roadway Express
Fortune's highest ranked trucking companies, 2000 ★503★

Roane State Community College
Lowest undergraduate tuition and fees at colleges and universities in Tennessee ★1559★
Average faculty salaries for institutions of higher education in Tennessee, 2000-01 ★3730★

Roanoke-Chowan Community College
Average faculty salaries for institutions of higher education without academic ranks in North Carolina, 2000-01 ★3761★

Roanoke College
U.S. News & World Report's southern regional liberal arts colleges with the highest academic reputation scores, 2000-01 ★1369★
U.S. News & World Report's southern regional liberal arts colleges with the highest alumni giving rates, 2000-01 ★1371★
U.S. News & World Report's southern regional liberal arts colleges with the highest freshmen retention rates, 2000-01 ★1372★
U.S. News & World Report's southern regional liberal arts colleges with the highest graduation rates, 2000-01 ★1373★
U.S. News & World Report's top southern regional liberal arts colleges, 2000-01 ★1379★
Highest undergraduate tuition and fees at colleges and universities in Virginia ★1564★
Average faculty salaries for institutions of higher education in Virginia, 2000-01 ★3735★

Robb; Sen. Charles S.
Members of Congress receiving the largest contributions from the Sallie Mae Inc. Political Action Committee ★3023★

Roberson; Anthony
All-America boys' high school basketball 3rd team, 2001 ★163★

Robert C. Byrd honors scholarships
Proposed fiscal 2002 appropriations for graduate support ★1250★

Robert Cole High School
Outstanding secondary schools in San Antonio, Texas ★4219★

Robert Half International
Fortune's highest ranked temporary help companies, 2000 ★500★
Top services industries in Standard & Poor's 500, 2001 ★558★

Robert; P.
Most cited authors in the journal *Criminologie*, 1990 to 1995 ★1621★

Roberto: The Insect Architect
Smithsonian's best books for children ages 1 to 6 ★363★

Roberts; A. Wayne
Top pay and benefits for the chief executive and top paid employees at Macalester College ★3385★

Roberts; Edward B.
Top pay and benefits for the chief executive and top paid employees at Massachusetts Institute of Technology ★3397★

Roberts; G. Oral
Top pay and benefits for the chief executive and top paid employees at Oral Roberts University ★3433★

Roberts; John D.
American Chemical Society 2001 award winners (Group 4) ★754★

Roberts; Joseph
Top pay and benefits for the chief executive and top paid employees at Reed College ★3453★

Roberts; Judith
Top pay and benefits for the chief executive and top paid employees at Judson College in Alabama ★3356★

Roberts; Richard L.
Top pay and benefits for the chief executive and top paid employees at Oral Roberts University ★3433★

Robertson; Harold
Top pay and benefits for the chief executive and top paid employees at Hendrix College ★3331★

Robertson; Jesse
Top pay and benefits for the chief executive and top paid employees at Jacksonville University ★3352★

Robertson; Oscar
Division I NCAA men's basketball players with the highest tournament scores ★154★

Robeson Community College
Average faculty salaries for institutions of higher education without academic ranks in North Carolina, 2000-01 ★3761★

Robeson; Paul
Most influential African American entertainers ★77★

Robfogel; Nathan
Top pay and benefits for the chief executive and top paid employees at Rochester Institute of Technology ★3461★

Robinette; Katie
All-America girls' high school basketball 1st team, 2001 ★170★

Robinson; William P.
Top pay and benefits for the chief executive and top paid employees at Whitworth College ★3625★

Robo Sapiens: Evolution of a New Species
Library Journal's most notable technology books, 2000 ★277★

Robotics: Sensing-Thinking-Acting
Most notable children's web sites, 2001 ★2593★

Rocha; Mark W.
Top pay and benefits for the chief executive and top paid employees at Seton Hall University ★3496★

Rochambeau Middle School
Outstanding secondary schools in Waterbury, Connecticut ★4250★

Roche Holding
Business Week's best companies in Switzerland ★405★

Roche; Sister Denise A.
Top pay and benefits for the chief executive and top paid employees at D'Youville College ★3278★

Rochester Adams High School
Outstanding secondary schools in Detroit, Michigan ★4125★

Rochester Community and Technical College
Average faculty salaries for institutions of higher education without academic ranks in Minnesota, 2000-01 ★3753★

Rochester Institute of Technology
U.S. colleges and universities with the least attractive campuses ★1037★
U.S. News & World Report's northern regional universities with the best academic reputation scores, 2000-01 ★1415★
U.S. News & World Report's northern regional universities with the highest acceptance rates, 2000-01 ★1417★
U.S. News & World Report's top northern regional universities, 2000-01 ★1425★
U.S. News & World Report's best undergraduate fees among northern regional universities by discount tuition, 2000 ★1428★
U.S. News & World Report's undergraduate engineering programs with the highest academic reputation scores, 2000-01 ★2337★
U.S. News & World Report's undergraduate engineering programs with the best computer departments, 2000-01 ★2353★
U.S. News & World Report's undergraduate engineering programs with the best electrical departments, 2000-01 ★2355★
U.S. News & World Report's undergraduate engineering programs with the best industrial manufacturing departments, 2000-01 ★2380★
Average faculty salaries for institutions of higher education in New York, 2000-01 ★3719★

Rochester, Simon Graduate School of Management; University of
Business Week's top business schools with the best teachers, 2000 ★609★
Business Week's top business schools with the highest percentage of international students, 2000 ★612★
Business Week's top business schools with the highest percentage of minority enrollment, 2000 ★613★
Business Week's top business schools with the lowest percentage of women enrollees, 2000 ★617★
Lowest post-MBA salaries for students enrolled in *Business Week*'s top business schools, 1999 ★634★
Lowest pre-MBA salaries for students enrolled in *Business Week*'s top business schools, 1999 ★635★

Rochester; University of
Top business schools for within-discipline research performance in accounting, 1986-1998 ★660★
U.S. News & World Report's national universities with the highest acceptance rates, 2000-01 ★1131★
U.S. News & World Report's national universities with the lowest graduation rates, 1999 ★1141★
U.S. News & World Report's best undergraduate fees among national universities by discount tuition, 2000 ★1474★
Most effective economics research-doctorate programs as evaluated by the National Research Council ★2207★
Origin of doctorate for economics faculty at Ph.D.-granting institutions ★2209★
Origin of doctorate for economics faculty at Ph.D.-granting institutions, by Ph.D. equivalents produced ★2210★
Top economics research-doctorate programs as evaluated by the National Research Council ★2213★
Top biomedical engineering research-doctorate programs as evaluated by the National Research Council ★2384★
Most effective music research-doctorate programs as evaluated by the National Research Council ★2895★
Top music research-doctorate programs as evaluated by the National Research Council ★2896★
Most effective political science research-doctorate programs as evaluated by the National Research Council ★3043★
Top political science research-doctorate programs as evaluated by the National Research Council ★3046★
U.S. universities with the greatest impact in psychology, 1995-99 ★3064★
Average faculty salaries for institutions of higher education in New York, 2000-01 ★3719★

Rock and Ice Climbing: Top the Tower!
Most notable nonfiction books for reluctant young adult readers, 2001 ★323★

Rock; John A.
Top pay and benefits for the chief executive and top paid employees at Emory University ★3289★

The Rock Says
Longest-running nonfiction hardcover bestsellers, 2000 ★281★
Most notable nonfiction books for reluctant young adult readers, 2001 ★323★

Rockefeller University
Most effective neurosciences research-doctorate programs as evaluated by the National Research Council ★200★
Top neurosciences research-doctorate programs as evaluated by the National Research Council ★202★
Most effective cell and developmental biology research-doctorate programs as evaluated by the National Research Council ★206★
Top cell and developmental biology research-doctorate programs as evaluated by the National Research Council ★210★
U.S. universities with the greatest impact in cell and developmental biology, 1993-97 ★212★
U.S. universities with the greatest impact in cell and developmental biology, 1994-98 ★213★
U.S. universities with the greatest impact in microbiology, 1994-98 ★217★
U.S. universities with the greatest impact in microbiology, 1995-99 ★218★
Doctorate-granting-institutions with the highest percentage of non-U.S. citizen doctoral degrees awarded, 1999 ★1907★

Largest benefit packages awarded to presidents at institutions of higher education, 1998-99 ★3133★

Average faculty salaries for institutions of higher education in New York, 2000-01 ★3719★

Private institutions of higher education that pay the highest salaries to female professors, 2000-01 ★3974★

U.S. institutions with the highest paid full professors, 2001 ★3978★

U.S. universities contributing the most papers in the field of neurosciences, 1993-97 ★4285★

Rockford College

U.S. News & World Report's midwestern regional universities with the best alumni giving rates, 2000-01 ★1402★

U.S. News & World Report's midwestern regional universities with the best student/faculty ratios, 2000-01 ★1403★

U.S. News & World Report's midwestern regional universities with the highest percentage of full-time faculty, 2000-01 ★1408★

U.S. News & World Report's midwestern regional universities with the lowest acceptance rates, 2000-01 ★1410★

Average faculty salaries for institutions of higher education in Illinois, 2000-01 ★3700★

Rockford High School

Outstanding secondary schools in Grand Rapids-Muskegon-Holland, Michigan ★4140★

Rockford Middle School

Outstanding secondary schools in Grand Rapids-Muskegon-Holland, Michigan ★4140★

Rockhurst University

U.S. News & World Report's midwestern regional universities with the best student/faculty ratios, 2000-01 ★1403★

U.S. News & World Report's midwestern regional universities with the highest acceptance rates, 2000-01 ★1404★

Highest undergraduate tuition and fees at colleges and universities in Missouri ★1524★

Average faculty salaries for institutions of higher education in Missouri, 2000-01 ★3712★

Rockingham Community College

Average faculty salaries for institutions of higher education without academic ranks in North Carolina, 2000-01 ★3761★

Rockland Community College

Lowest undergraduate tuition and fees at colleges and universities in New York ★1538★

Rockwell Collins

Top recruiters for aerospace engineering jobs for 2000-01 bachelor's degree recipients ★2340★

Top recruiters for electrical/electronic engineering jobs for 2000-01 bachelor's degree recipients ★2354★

Rockwell International

Fortune's highest ranked electronics and electrical equipment companies, 2000 ★460★

Rockwood Eureka High School

Outstanding secondary schools in St. Louis, Missouri-Illinois ★4216★

Rocky Mountain College

U.S. News & World Report's western regional liberal arts colleges with students most in debt, 1999 ★1398★

Highest undergraduate tuition and fees at colleges and universities in Montana ★1526★

Rocky Mountain College of Art & Design

Highest undergraduate tuition and fees at colleges and universities in Colorado ★1488★

Rocky River High School

Outstanding secondary schools in Cleveland-Lorain-Elyria, Ohio ★4114★

Rocky River Middle School

Outstanding secondary schools in Cleveland-Lorain-Elyria, Ohio ★4114★

Rodin; Judith

Presidents with the highest pay at Research I and II universities, 1998-99 ★3162★

Top pay and benefits for the chief executive and top paid employees at the University of Pennsylvania ★3555★

Rodriguez; Arnaldo

Top pay and benefits for the chief executive and top paid employees at Pitzer College ★3441★

Roe; David

Top pay and benefits for the chief executive and top paid employees at Central College in Iowa ★3226★

Roeder; Robert G.

Top pay and benefits for the chief executive and top paid employees at Rockefeller University ★3462★

Roessler; Philip

All-USA College Academic First Team, 2001 ★2★

Roffers; David

Top pay and benefits for the chief executive and top paid employees at Saint Mary's University of Minnesota ★3482★

Rogalski; Edward

Top pay and benefits for the chief executive and top paid employees at St. Ambrose University ★3468★

Roger Williams University

U.S. News & World Report's northern regional liberal arts colleges with the highest acceptance rates, 2000-01 ★1355★

Undergraduate tuition and fees at colleges and universities in Rhode Island ★1553★

Rogers Academy

Outstanding secondary schools in Kansas City, Missouri-Kansas ★4158★

Rogers; Annie

Radcliffe Institute for Advanced Study fellowship recipient in the field of education, 2000-01 ★2218★

Rogers; Brian

Top pay and benefits for the chief executive and top paid employees at Connecticut College ★3254★

Rogers Education Center

Outstanding secondary schools in Houston, Texas ★4150★

Rogers; Elizabeth A.

Top pay and benefits for the chief executive and top paid employees at Elon College ★3285★

Rogers Middle School

Outstanding secondary schools in Fort Lauderdale, Florida ★4133★

Outstanding secondary schools in San Jose, California ★4222★

Rogers; R.

Most cited authors in the journal *Criminal Justice and Behavior*, 1990 to 1995 ★1619★

Rogers; Rex M.

Top pay and benefits for the chief executive and top paid employees at Cornerstone University ★3258★

Rogers State University

State appropriations for Oklahoma's institutions of higher education, 2000-01 ★1289★

Rogers University, Claremore

U.S. institutions awarding the most associate degrees to minorities in agribusiness and production, 1998 ★1808★

U.S. institutions awarding the most associate degrees to Native Americans in agribusiness and production, 1998 ★1811★

Roguewood School

Outstanding secondary schools in Grand Rapids-Muskegon-Holland, Michigan ★4140★

Roh; Mark

Top pay and benefits for the chief executive and top paid employees at the Allegheny University of the Health Sciences ★3520★

Rohan; Patrick

Top pay and benefits for the chief executive and top paid employees at St. John's University in New York ★3474★

Rohm

Business Week's best companies in Japan ★398★

Rohm & Haas

Fortune's highest ranked chemicals companies, 2000 ★452★

Top chemical companies in Standard & Poor's 500, 2001 ★533★

Rohner; Ralph J.

Top pay and benefits for the chief executive and top paid employees at the Catholic University of America ★3522★

Rokach; Joshua

Top pay and benefits for the chief executive and top paid employees at Florida Institute of Technology ★3293★

Rokke; Ervin

Top pay and benefits for the chief executive and top paid employees at Moravian College ★3407★

The Role of Employee Effort in Satisfaction with Service Transactions

Most influential articles in the *Journal of Business Research* from 1995 to 1999 ★700★

Roll International

Top women-owned companies ★4460★

Rolle; Antrel

All-American boy's high school football defensive backs, 2000 ★180★

Rolling Hills Middle School

Outstanding secondary schools in San Jose, California ★4222★

Rolling Meadows High School

Outstanding secondary schools in Chicago, Illinois ★4110★

Outstanding suburban public high schools in Metro Chicago ★4256★

Rolling Stone

Most selective internships in the U.S., 2001 ★2610★

Rollins College

U.S. News & World Report's best undergraduate fees among southern regional universities by discount tuition, 2000 ★1429★

U.S. News & World Report's southern regional universities with the best academic reputation scores, 2000-01 ★1433★

U.S. News & World Report's southern regional universities with the best student/faculty ratios, 2000-01 ★1435★

U.S. News & World Report's southern regional universities with the highest graduation rates, 2000-01 ★1438★

U.S. News & World Report's southern regional universities with the highest percentage of freshmen in the top 25% of their high school class, 2000-01 ★1439★

U.S. News & World Report's southern regional universities with the highest proportion of classes with 20 students or less, 2000-01 ★1441★

U.S. News & World Report's top southern regional universities, 2000-01 ★1444★

Highest undergraduate tuition and fees at colleges and universities in Florida ★1494★

Average faculty salaries for institutions of higher education in Florida, 2000-01 ★3696★

Roman Catholic
Religious preference of incoming freshmen, 2000 ★1061★

Romania
Eight grade science achievement scores from selected countries, 1999 ★14★

Countries of origin for non-U.S. citizens awarded doctorates at U.S. colleges and universities, 1999 ★1901★

Eighth grade mathematics achievement scores from selected countries, 1999 ★2773★

Romano; C. Renee
Top pay and benefits for the chief executive and top paid employees at Hollins University ★3336★

Romano; Joseph J.
Top pay and benefits for the chief executive and top paid employees at Cabrini College ★3215★

Rome
Cities with the highest productivity of paper in the discipline of cardiovascular systems, 1994-96 ★2869★

Cities with the highest productivity of paper in the discipline of hematology, 1994-96 ★2870★

Cities with the highest productivity of paper in the discipline of immunology, 1994-96 ★2871★

Romeo and Juliet
People for the American Way's list of most frequently challenged materials, 1982-1992 ★749★

Romig; James
Top pay and benefits for the chief executive and top paid employees at Drake University ★3272★

Ronayne; Michael R.
Top pay and benefits for the chief executive and top paid employees at Suffolk University ★3513★

Roncalli High School
Outstanding secondary schools in Indianapolis, Indiana ★4153★

Rondout Elementary School, District 72
Illinois school districts spending the most for elementary school education 1997-98 ★4009★

Rondout School, District 72
Illinois school districts spending the most per pupil for instruction ★4011★

Roofer
Jobs with the highest unemployment ★2256★

Most desirable jobs in construction trades ★2272★

Rookie: Tamika Whitmore's First Year in the WNBA
Most notable nonfiction books for reluctant young adult readers, 2001 ★323★

Roomkin; Myron
Top pay and benefits for the chief executive and top paid employees at American University ★3174★

Rooney; Gerard J.
Top pay and benefits for the chief executive and top paid employees at Saint John Fisher College in New York ★3472★

Roosevelt Middle School
Illinois schools with the highest 7th grade science scores ★17★

Outstanding secondary schools in Albuquerque, New Mexico ★4080★

Roosevelt University
U.S. colleges and universities with the lowest percentage of African Americans enrolled, 1997 ★223★

Fall enrollment at the largest Chicago-area private institutions, by minority percentages, 1999 ★869★

U.S. colleges and universities awarding the most business management and administrative services master's degrees to African Americans ★1759★

Degrees granted in the ten largest master's journalism and mass communications programs, 1999 ★2757★

Enrollment of students in the ten largest master's journalism and mass communications programs, 1999 ★2763★

Private, 4-year undergraduate colleges and universities producing the most Ph.D.'s in psychology, 1920-1990 ★3066★

Average faculty salaries for institutions of higher education in Illinois, 2000-01 ★3700★

Private, 4-year undergraduate colleges and universities producing the most Ph.D.'s in anthropology and sociology, 1920-1990 ★4344★

Private, 4-year undergraduate colleges and universities producing the most Ph.D.'s in anthropology and sociology, 1981-1990 ★4345★

Rose; Eric Allen
Top pay and benefits for the chief executive and top paid employees at Columbia University ★3251★

Rose-Hulman Institute of Technology
U.S. colleges and universities with a large student body of conservative Republicans ★1016★

First-year student's choices for exemplary special mission institutions ★1066★

Highest undergraduate tuition and fees at colleges and universities in Indiana ★1502★

U.S. News & World Report's undergraduate engineering programs with the highest academic reputation scores, 2000-01 ★2337★

U.S. News & World Report's undergraduate engineering programs with the best chemical departments, 2000-01 ★2344★

U.S. News & World Report's undergraduate engineering programs with the best civil departments, 2000-01 ★2347★

U.S. News & World Report's undergraduate engineering programs with the best computer departments, 2000-01 ★2353★

U.S. News & World Report's undergraduate engineering programs with the best electrical departments, 2000-01 ★2355★

U.S. News & World Report's undergraduate engineering programs with the best mechanical departments, 2000-01 ★2438★

Average faculty salaries for institutions of higher education in Indiana, 2000-01 ★3701★

Rose State College
Lowest undergraduate tuition and fees at colleges and universities in Oklahoma ★1546★

Average faculty salaries for institutions of higher education without academic ranks in Oklahoma, 2000-01 ★3763★

The Rose That Grew from Concrete
Most notable nonfiction books for reluctant young adult readers, 2001 ★323★

Rosemont College
U.S. News & World Report's northern regional liberal arts colleges with the best student/faculty ratios, 2000-01 ★1353★

U.S. News & World Report's northern regional liberal arts colleges with the highest acceptance rates, 2000-01 ★1355★

U.S. News & World Report's northern regional liberal arts colleges with the highest alumni giving rates, 2000-01 ★1356★

U.S. News & World Report's northern regional liberal arts colleges with the highest freshmen retention rates, 2000-01 ★1357★

U.S. News & World Report's northern regional liberal arts colleges with the highest graduation rates, 2000-01 ★1358★

U.S. News & World Report's northern regional liberal arts colleges with the highest proportion of classes having 20 students or less, 2000-01 ★1361★

U.S. News & World Report's best undergraduate fees among northern regional liberal arts colleges by discount tuition, 2000 ★1382★

Rosemont, District 78
Illinois elementary school districts with the highest teacher salaries, 1999 ★3984★

Rosemont Middle School
Outstanding secondary schools in Los Angeles-Long Beach, California ★4167★

Rosen; Roslyn
Top pay and benefits for the chief executive and top paid employees at Gallaudet University ★3301★

Rosenberg; Steven A.
Most-cited researchers in clinical medicine, 1981-1998 ★2875★

Most-cited researchers in oncology, 1981-1998 ★2877★

Rosenberg; Warren
Top pay and benefits for the chief executive and top paid employees at Iona College ★3350★

Rosenbluth International
Most selective internships in the U.S., 2001 ★2610★

Rosencrantz & Guildenstern are Dead
Top plays of the twentieth century ★4435★

Rosenfeld; L.
Highest ranked active communication studies researchers ★2747★

Rosenman; Mark
Top pay and benefits for the chief executive and top paid employees at Union Institute ★3586★

Rosenwaks; Zev
Top pay and benefits for the chief executive and top paid employees at Cornell University ★3257★

The Roses and the Beast: Fairy Tales Retold
Outstanding children's fiction books, 2000 ★329★

Roslien; David J.
Top pay and benefits for the chief executive and top paid employees at Luther College ★3383★

Rosner; Bernard
Most-cited researchers in epidemiology, 1981-1998 ★2876★

Ross; Clark G.
Top pay and benefits for the chief executive and top paid employees at Davidson College ★3264★

Ross; John
American Chemical Society 2001 award winners (Group 4) ★754★

Ross; Sam
Top pay and benefits for the chief executive and top paid employees at Benedictine University ★3200★

Ross, S.N.J.M.; Kathleen A.
Top pay and benefits for the chief executive and top paid employees at Heritage College ★3332★

Rossum; Ralph
Top pay and benefits for the chief executive and top paid employees at Claremont McKenna College ★3236★

Roswell High School
Outstanding secondary schools in Atlanta, Georgia ★4087★

Roswell Park Cancer Institute
Top cancer hospitals in the U.S., 2000 ★2787★

Roth; Alvin E.
Top pay and benefits for the chief executive and top paid employees at Harvard University ★3327★

Roth IRAs
Best ways to save for college ★843★

Roth; Phyllis
Top pay and benefits for the chief executive and top paid employees at Skidmore College ★3500★

Rothblatt; Daniel
Top pay and benefits for the chief executive and top paid employees at the University of Judaism ★3546★

Rothkopf; Arthur J.
Top pay and benefits for the chief executive and top paid employees at Lafayette College ★3361★

Rothman; Michael
Top pay and benefits for the chief executive and top paid employees at the University of Puget Sound ★3557★

Rothschild; Michael
Top pay and benefits for the chief executive and top paid employees at Princeton University ★3446★

Rotterdam School of Management
Business Week's top business schools outside the U.S. as selected by corporate recruiters, 2000 ★605★
Business Week's top business schools outside the U.S. as selected by recent MBA graduates, 2000 ★606★
Business Week's top business schools outside the U.S. for intellectual capital, 2000 ★607★
Post-MBA salaries for graduates from *Business Week*'s top business schools outside the U.S., 2000 ★642★
Pre-MBA salaries for students at *Business Week*'s top business schools outside the U.S., 2000 ★643★

Rounds; Paul A.
Top pay and benefits for the chief executive and top paid employees at Park University ★3438★

Rouse; Albert J.
Top pay and benefits for the chief executive and top paid employees at Edgewood College ★3283★

Roush; John
Top pay and benefits for the chief executive and top paid employees at Centre College ★3227★

Roustabout
Jobs with the highest unemployment ★2256★
Jobs with the worst physical demands scores ★2263★
Jobs with the worst security scores ★2264★
Least desirable jobs ★2266★

Routledge
Book publishers with the most citations (Class 5) ★2566★

Routledge Encyclopedia of Philosophy Online
Library Journal's best reference databases and discs, 2000 ★369★

Rover; Stefan
European business moguls considered the best innovators ★442★

Rowan University
State appropriations for New Jersey's institutions of higher education, 2000-01 ★1283★
U.S. News & World Report's northern regional universities with the lowest acceptance rates, 2000-01 ★1424★
U.S. News & World Report's top public northern regional universities, 2000-01 ★1426★
U.S. colleges and universities awarding the most communications master's degrees to African Americans ★1763★

Rowe; B. David
Top pay and benefits for the chief executive and top paid employees at Wesleyan College in Georgia ★3611★

Rowell; LaMarcus
All-American boy's high school football linebackers, 2000 ★182★

Rowing
Fastest growing men's collegiate athletics teams ★130★
Fastest growing women's collegiate athletics teams ★131★

Rowland; George
Top pay and benefits for the chief executive and top paid employees at Austin College ★3184★

Rowland High School
Outstanding secondary schools in Los Angeles-Long Beach, California ★4167★

Rowling; J. K.
Outstanding children's fiction books, 2000 ★329★

Roy; Edward C.
Top pay and benefits for the chief executive and top paid employees at Trinity University in Texas ★3579★

Roy; Kim
Highest ranking women at the top public companies, 2000 ★4452★

Roy; Rabindra
Top pay and benefits for the chief executive and top paid employees at Drury University ★3275★

Roy; Wayne
Top pay and benefits for the chief executive and top paid employees at Hardin-Simmons University ★3325★

Royal Bank of Canada
Business Week's best companies in Canada ★390★

Royal Bank of Scotland Group
Business Week's best companies in Britain ★389★

Royal Dutch Electronics
Business Week's best companies in the Netherlands ★410★

Royal Dutch Petroleum
Business Week's best companies in the Netherlands ★410★

Royal Dutch/Shell
Business Week's best companies in terms of profits ★406★
Business Week's top companies worldwide ★433★

R.R. Donnelley & Sons
Fortune's highest ranked printing companies, 2000 ★487★
Top services industries in Standard & Poor's 500, 2001 ★558★

RTV/telecommunications
Areas of specialization in journalism and mass communications programs with the highest enrollment, 1999 ★2740★

Rubenstein; Richard L.
Top pay and benefits for the chief executive and top paid employees at University of Bridgeport ★3588★

Rubino; Msgr. David A.
Top pay and benefits for the chief executive and top paid employees at Gannon University ★3302★

Rudenstine; Neil L.
Top pay and benefits for the chief executive and top paid employees at Harvard University ★3327★

Ruder-Finn
Most selective internships in the U.S., 2001 ★2610★

Rueter; Ken
Top pay and benefits for the chief executive and top paid employees at Westminster College in Missouri ★3616★

Rufus King High School
Outstanding secondary schools in Milwaukee-Waukesha, Wisconsin ★4180★

A Rum Affair: A True Story of Botanical Fraud
Library Journal's most notable history of science books, 2000 ★263★

Runals Memorial Library
Highest Hennen's American Public Library Ratings for libraries serving a population of 1,000 to 2,499 ★2692★

Runtz; M.
Most cited authors in the journal *Journal of Interpersonal Violence*, 1990 to 1995 ★1627★

Runyon; Mary
Top pay and benefits for the chief executive and top paid employees at Bennington College ★3201★

Ruoti; James
Top pay and benefits for the chief executive and top paid employees at Illinois Wesleyan University ★3347★

Rupp; Adolph
Coaches winning the most NCAA tournaments ★120★

Rupp; George
Presidents with the highest pay at Research I and II universities, 1998-99 ★3162★
Top pay and benefits for the chief executive and top paid employees at Columbia University ★3251★

Ruscio Jr.; Thomas J.
Top pay and benefits for the chief executive and top paid employees at Springfield College in Massachusetts ★3509★

Rush; Charles
All-American boy's high school football linemen, 2000 ★183★

Rush University
U.S. colleges and universities awarding the most health professions and related sciences doctorate degrees to Asian Americans ★2115★
U.S. colleges and universities awarding the most health professions and related sciences doctorate degrees to Hispanic Americans ★2116★

Russell 3000 Index
2000 returns on university endowments and other comparative measures ★1231★

Russell; D.E.H.
Most cited authors in the journal *Journal of Interpersonal Violence*, 1990 to 1995 ★1627★

Russell; James
Top pay and benefits for the chief executive and top paid employees at Hampton University ★3323★

Russia
Eight grade science achievement scores from selected countries, 1999 ★14★
CA patents abstracted, by country, 2000 ★758★
Countries of origin for non-U.S. citizens awarded doctorates at U.S. colleges and universities, 1999 ★1901★
Eighth grade mathematics achievement scores from selected countries, 1999 ★2773★
Institute for Scientific Information periodical prices by country, 2001 ★2922★

Russian
Gender breakdown of language and literature doctorate recipients, by subfield, 1999 ★1937★
Language and literature doctorates awarded at U.S. colleges and universities, by subfield, 1999 ★1949★
Languages of requested materials from OCLC ILL, 1999 ★2679★

Rust College
Highest undergraduate tuition and fees at colleges and universities in Mississippi ★1522★

Rutan; Thomas K.
Top pay and benefits for the chief executive and top paid employees at Elmira College ★3284★

Rutgers Prep
Outstanding secondary schools in Middlesex-Somerset-Hunterdon, New Jersey ★4179★

Rutgers State University, Newark
Academics' choices for best clinical law programs, 2001 ★2626★

Rutgers University
All-USA College Academic Second Team, 2001 ★3★
All-USA College Academic Third Team, 2001 ★4★
U.S. universities with the greatest impact in biotechnology and applied microbiology, 1995-99 ★216★
U.S. business schools with the slowest payback on MBA investments ★655★
Top business schools for within-discipline research performance in insurance, international business and real estate, 1986-1998 ★667★
State appropriations for New Jersey's institutions of higher education, 2000-01 ★1283★
Radcliffe Institute for Advanced Study fellowship recipients in the field of history, 2000-01 ★2549★
Institutions with the most productive libraries, 1993-1997 ★2678★
Comparison of library and information science programs composite rankings with *U.S. News & World Report* survey ★2709★
Library and information science programs with the most citations to journal articles, 1993-1998 ★2712★
Library and information science programs with the most journal articles, 1993-1998 ★2713★
Library and information science programs with the most journal articles per capita, 1993-1998 ★2714★
Library and information science programs with the most per capita citations to journal articles, 1993-1998 ★2715★
U.S. universities publishing the most papers in the field of library and information science, 1995-99 ★2718★
U.S. universities with the greatest impact in physics, 1994-98 ★2980★
Women faculty in Ph.D. physics departments at U.S. institutions, 1998 ★2981★

Rutgers University, Camden
U.S. News & World Report's northern regional universities with the lowest acceptance rates, 2000-01 ★1424★
U.S. News & World Report's top public northern regional universities, 2000-01 ★1426★
Average faculty salaries for institutions of higher education in New Jersey, 2000-01 ★3717★

Rutgers University, New Brunswick
U.S. colleges and universities reporting the most drug related arrests, 1998 ★731★
Division I NCAA colleges with that graduated none of their African American male basketball players, 1990-91 to 1993-94 ★930★
Retention rates of African American students at traditionally white institutions, 1997-98 ★1121★
Total baccalaureate biology/life sciences degrees awarded to Asian Americans from U.S. colleges and universities, 1997-98 ★1680★
Total baccalaureate communications degrees awarded to Hispanic Americans from U.S. colleges and universities, 1997-98 ★1689★
Total baccalaureate education degrees awarded to Asian Americans from U.S. colleges and universities, 1997-98 ★1712★
Total baccalaureate English language, literature, and letters degrees awarded to Asian Americans from U.S. colleges and universities, 1997-98 ★1717★
Total baccalaureate ethnic/cultural studies degrees awarded to African Americans from U.S. colleges and universities, 1997-98 ★1720★
Total baccalaureate health professions and related sciences degrees awarded to Asian Americans from U.S. colleges and universities, 1997-98 ★1722★
Total baccalaureate mathematics degrees awarded to Asian Americans from U.S. colleges and universities, 1997-98 ★1730★
Total baccalaureate psychology degrees awarded to Asian Americans from U.S. colleges and universities, 1997-98 ★1738★
Total baccalaureate social sciences and history degrees awarded to Asian Americans from U.S. colleges and universities, 1997-98 ★1742★
U.S. colleges and universities awarding the most biological and life sciences master's degrees to Asian Americans ★1757★
U.S. colleges and universities awarding the most physical sciences master's degrees to Asian Americans ★1794★
U.S. institutions awarding the most baccalaureate degrees to minorities in ethnic/cultural studies, 1997-98 ★1821★
U.S. institutions awarding the most master's degrees to Asian Americans in agricultural sciences, 1998 ★1827★
U.S. institutions awarding the most master's degrees to minorities in agricultural sciences, 1998 ★1830★
U.S. colleges and universities awarding the most doctorate degrees to Asian Americans ★2096★
U.S. colleges and universities awarding the most doctorate degrees to minorities ★2098★
U.S. colleges and universities awarding the most mathematics doctorate degrees to Asian Americans ★2117★
U.S. colleges and universities awarding the most psychology doctorate degrees to Hispanic Americans ★2122★
Top geography research-doctorate programs as evaluated by the National Research Council ★2520★
Top philosophy research-doctorate programs as evaluated by the National Research Council ★2947★
Average faculty salaries for institutions of higher education in New Jersey, 2000-01 ★3717★
Public institutions of higher education that pay the highest salaries to female professors, 2000-01 ★3975★

Rutgers University, Newark
Universities with the most-cited scholars in *Criminal Justice and Behavior* ★1648★
Universities with the most-cited scholars in *Criminology* ★1649★
Universities with the most-cited scholars in *Journal of Quantitative Criminology* ★1650★
Universities with the most-cited scholars in *Journal of Research in Crime and Delinquency* ★1651★
Universities with the most-cited scholars in *Justice Quarterly* ★1652★
U.S. colleges and universities awarding the most business management and administrative services master's degrees to Asian Americans ★1760★

U.S. colleges and universities awarding the most law and legal studies first professional degrees to Hispanic Americans ★1854★

Doctorate-granting-institutions with the highest percentage of non-U.S. citizen doctoral degrees awarded, 1999 ★1907★

Average faculty salaries for institutions of higher education in New Jersey, 2000-01 ★3717★

Public institutions of higher education that pay the highest salaries to female professors, 2000-01 ★3975★

Rutgers University, Rutgers College
U.S. colleges and universities with the worst on-campus housing facilities ★1044★
U.S. colleges and universities with the worst overall administration ★1045★

Ryan; Barry
Top pay and benefits for the chief executive and top paid employees at Point Loma Nazarene University ★3442★

Ryan; Carole Ann
Top pay and benefits for the chief executive and top paid employees at Illinois College ★3345★

Ryan Jr.; Stephen J.
Top pay and benefits for the chief executive and top paid employees at the University of Southern California ★3568★

Ryan; Mary P.
Highly acknowledged individuals in the field of women's studies, 1975-94 ★4466★

Ryan-Mosley; Calvin N.
Top pay and benefits for the chief executive and top paid employees at the College of St. Catherine ★3528★

Ryba Jr.; Walter
Top pay and benefits for the chief executive and top paid employees at Fairfield University ★3291★

Ryder System
Fortune's highest ranked automotive retailing services companies, 2000 ★449★
Top transportation companies in Standard & Poor's 500, 2001 ★560★

Rye Neck High School
Outstanding secondary schools in New York, New York ★4191★

Ryerson; Lisa Marsh
Top pay and benefits for the chief executive and top paid employees at Wells College ★3610★

Ryerson University
Best Canadian universities overall, 2000 ★1149★
Canadian primarily undergraduate universities best at producing leaders of tomorrow, 2000 ★1192★
Canadian primarily undergraduate universities by alumni support, 2000 ★1193★
Canadian primarily undergraduate universities by class size at the first and second-year level, 2000 ★1195★
Canadian primarily undergraduate universities by class size at the third and forth-year level, 2000 ★1196★
Canadian primarily undergraduate universities by classes taught by tenured faculty, 2000 ★1197★
Canadian primarily undergraduate universities by faculty members with Ph.D.'s, 2000 ★1198★
Canadian primarily undergraduate universities by library acquisitions, 2000 ★1199★
Canadian primarily undergraduate universities by library expenses, 2000 ★1200★
Canadian primarily undergraduate universities by library holdings per student, 2000 ★1201★
Canadian primarily undergraduate universities by medical/science grants per faculty member, 2000 ★1202★
Canadian primarily undergraduate universities by operating budget per student, 2000 ★1203★
Canadian primarily undergraduate universities by percentage of operating budget allocated to scholarships, 2000 ★1204★
Canadian primarily undergraduate universities by percentage of operating budget allocated to student services, 2000 ★1205★
Canadian primarily undergraduate universities by reputation, 2000 ★1206★
Canadian primarily undergraduate universities by students from out of province, 2000 ★1208★
Canadian primarily undergraduate universities by students winning national awards, 2000 ★1209★
Canadian primarily undergraduate universities that are the best overall, 2000 ★1210★
Canadian primarily undergraduate universities that are the most innovative, 2000 ★1211★
Canadian primarily undergraduate universities with the highest quality, 2000 ★1212★
Top Canadian primarily undergraduate universities, 2000 ★1226★

S

S3
Most profitable information technology companies, 2000 ★527★
Top information technology companies, 2000 ★544★

Saber; Al
Top pay and benefits for the chief executive and top paid employees at Friends University ★3299★

Sabin Bicultural
Chicago elementary magnet schools with the highest acceptance rates, 2000-01 ★4002★

Sacramento, CA
Cities with the highest percentage of broadband use and interest ★2578★

Sacramento City College
Lowest undergraduate tuition and fees at public 2-year colleges and universities ★1465★
Lowest undergraduate tuition and fees at colleges and universities in California ★1487★

Sacramento/Stockton/Modesto, CA
U.S. market areas with the highest percentage of adults having internet access ★2607★

Sacred Heart Academy
Outstanding secondary schools in Long Island, New York ★4165★
Outstanding secondary schools in Louisville, Kentucky-Indiana ★4168★
Outstanding secondary schools in New Haven-Meriden, Connecticut ★4188★

Sacred Heart Cathedral School
Outstanding secondary schools in Knoxville, Tennessee ★4159★

Sacred Heart Major Seminary
Average faculty salaries for institutions of higher education in Michigan, 2000-01 ★3709★

Sacred Heart/Mount Carmel
Outstanding secondary schools in New York, New York ★4191★

Sacred Heart (PR); University of
Highest undergraduate tuition and fees at colleges and universities in Puerto Rico ★1551★

Enrollment of students in the ten largest undergraduate journalism and mass communications programs, 1999 ★2746★

Sacred Heart University
Highest undergraduate tuition and fees at colleges and universities in Connecticut ★1490★
Average faculty salaries for institutions of higher education in Connecticut, 2000-01 ★3694★

Sacred Heart University (CT)
Presidents with the highest pay at Master's I and II colleges and universities, 1998-99 ★3161★

Sadler; Bill
Top pay and benefits for the chief executive and top paid employees at Holy Names College ★3337★

Safety-Kleen
Fortune's highest ranked waste management companies, 2000 ★504★

Safeway
Fortune's highest ranked food and drug stores, 2000 ★463★
Top food companies in Standard & Poor's 500, 2001 ★540★

Sagamore Associates
Lobbyist that billed the most to U.S. colleges and universities, 1999 ★1249★

Sage Publications
Book publishers with the most citations (Class 3) ★2564★

Sager; Jeffrey K.
Highest impact authors in the *Journal of Business Research*, by number of citations in 12 journals, 1985-1999 ★693★

Saginaw Valley State University
State appropriations for Michigan's institutions of higher education, 2000-01 ★1275★
U.S. News & World Report's midwestern regional universities with students least in debt, 1999 ★1399★

Saguaro High School
Outstanding secondary schools in Phoenix-Mesa, Arizona ★4203★

Sailer; Julie
All-America girls' high school basketball 2nd team, 2001 ★171★

Sailing
Fastest growing men's collegiate athletics teams ★130★

St. Alphonsus School
Outstanding secondary schools in Milwaukee-Waukesha, Wisconsin ★4180★

St. Ambrose University
Average faculty salaries for institutions of higher education in Iowa, 2000-01 ★3702★

St. Andres Social Library
North America's first ten public libraries ★2680★

St. Andrew School
Outstanding secondary schools in Columbus, Ohio ★4118★

St. Andrews Presbyterian College
Highest undergraduate tuition and fees at colleges and universities in North Carolina ★1539★
Average faculty salaries for institutions of higher education in North Carolina, 2000-01 ★3720★

St. Anselm College
Division II NCAA colleges with the 100% graduation rates for men's basketball players, 1993-94 ★943★

Division II NCAA colleges with the highest graduation rates for all sports, 1993-94 ★945★

U.S. News & World Report's northern regional liberal arts colleges with the highest academic reputation scores, 2000-01 ★1354★

U.S. News & World Report's northern regional liberal arts colleges with the highest alumni giving rates, 2000-01 ★1356★

U.S. News & World Report's northern regional liberal arts colleges with the highest freshmen retention rates, 2000-01 ★1357★

U.S. News & World Report's northern regional liberal arts colleges with the highest graduation rates, 2000-01 ★1358★

U.S. News & World Report's northern regional liberal arts colleges with the highest percentage of freshmen in the top 25% of their high school class, 2000-01 ★1359★

U.S. News & World Report's northern regional liberal arts colleges with the highest percentage of full-time faculty, 2000-01 ★1360★

U.S. News & World Report's northern regional liberal arts colleges with the lowest acceptance rates, 2000-01 ★1362★

U.S. News & World Report's top northern regional liberal arts colleges, 2000-01 ★1363★

Highest undergraduate tuition and fees at colleges and universities in New Hampshire ★1531★

Average faculty salaries for institutions of higher education in New Hampshire, 2000-01 ★3716★

St. Anthony Middle School
Outstanding secondary schools in Minneapolis-St. Paul, Minnesota-Wisconsin ★4181★

St. Benedict; College of
Highest undergraduate tuition and fees at colleges and universities in Minnesota ★1520★

Average faculty salaries for institutions of higher education in Minnesota, 2000-01 ★3710★

St. Benedict/St. John (MN); College of
U.S. bachelor's institutions with the largest number of students studying abroad, 1998-99 ★2511★

St. Benilde
Outstanding secondary schools in New Orleans, Louisiana ★4190★

St. Bonaventure University
U.S. colleges and universities where a large portion of the student body drink beer ★991★

U.S. colleges and universities where a large portion of the student body drink hard liquor ★992★

U.S. colleges and universities where students are not very politically active ★1000★

U.S. colleges and universities where students study the least ★1002★

U.S. colleges and universities with strained race/class interaction ★1029★

U.S. colleges and universities with the happiest students ★1035★

U.S. colleges and universities with the most accessible instructors ★1038★

U.S. colleges and universities with the worst food service program ★1043★

Institutions censured by the American Association of University Professors, 2001 ★1067★

U.S. News & World Report's northern regional universities with the highest acceptance rates, 2000-01 ★1417★

U.S. News & World Report's northern regional universities with the highest alumni giving rates, 2000-01 ★1418★

U.S. News & World Report's best undergraduate fees among northern regional universities by discount tuition, 2000 ★1428★

Average faculty salaries for institutions of higher education in New York, 2000-01 ★3719★

St. Camillus
Outstanding secondary schools in Washington, District of Columbia-Maryland-Virginia-West Virginia ★4249★

St. Catharine Academy
Outstanding secondary schools in New York, New York ★4191★

St. Catherine; College of
All-USA College Academic Third Team, 2001 ★4★

U.S. News & World Report's midwestern regional universities with the best student/faculty ratios, 2000-01 ★1403★

U.S. News & World Report's midwestern regional universities with the highest proportion of classes having 20 students or less, 2000-01 ★1409★

Highest undergraduate tuition and fees at colleges and universities in Minnesota ★1520★

Women's colleges granting physics bachelor's degrees, 2000 ★2982★

St. Catherine (MN); College of
College senior's choices for exemplary master's institutions ★2533★

St. Cecilia Academy
Outstanding secondary schools in Nashville, Tennessee ★4186★

St. Charles City-County Library District
Highest Hennen's American Public Library Ratings for libraries serving a population of 100,000 to 249,999 ★2698★

St. Charles County Community College
Lowest undergraduate tuition and fees at colleges and universities in Missouri ★1525★

Average faculty salaries for institutions of higher education in Missouri, 2000-01 ★3712★

St. Charles High School
Outstanding secondary schools in Chicago, Illinois ★4110★

St. Christopher
Outstanding secondary schools in New Orleans, Louisiana ★4190★

St. Clare of Montefalco Catholic School
Outstanding secondary schools in Detroit, Michigan ★4125★

St. Clement's Episcopal Parish School
Outstanding secondary schools in El Paso, Texas ★4128★

St. Cloud State University
Institutions in the Worker Rights Consortium ★2913★

Average faculty salaries for institutions of higher education in Minnesota, 2000-01 ★3710★

St. Cloud Technical College
Lowest undergraduate tuition and fees at colleges and universities in Minnesota ★1521★

Average faculty salaries for institutions of higher education without academic ranks in Minnesota, 2000-01 ★3753★

St. Damian School
Outstanding secondary schools in Chicago, Illinois ★4110★

St. David Catholic School
Outstanding secondary schools in Fort Lauderdale, Florida ★4133★

St. Edward High School
Outstanding secondary schools in Cleveland-Lorain-Elyria, Ohio ★4114★

St. Edward's University
U.S. News & World Report's western regional universities with students most in debt, 1999 ★1576★

Average faculty salaries for institutions of higher education in Texas, 2000-01 ★3731★

St. Elizabeth; College of
U.S. News & World Report's northern regional liberal arts colleges with the best student/faculty ratios, 2000-01 ★1353★

U.S. News & World Report's northern regional liberal arts colleges with the highest acceptance rates, 2000-01 ★1355★

U.S. News & World Report's northern regional liberal arts colleges with the highest alumni giving rates, 2000-01 ★1356★

U.S. News & World Report's northern regional liberal arts colleges with the highest proportion of classes having 20 students or less, 2000-01 ★1361★

U.S. News & World Report's best undergraduate fees among northern regional liberal arts colleges by discount tuition, 2000 ★1382★

Average faculty salaries for institutions of higher education in New Jersey, 2000-01 ★3717★

St. Frances Xavier Cabrini
Outstanding secondary schools in New Orleans, Louisiana ★4190★

St. Francis College
Average faculty salaries for institutions of higher education in New York, 2000-01 ★3719★

St. Francis College (PA)
Division I NCAA colleges with that graduated more than 80% of their African American male athletes, 1990-91 to 1993-94 ★929★

St. Francis DeSales High School
Outstanding secondary schools in Columbus, Ohio ★4118★

St. Francis High School
Outstanding secondary schools in San Jose, California ★4222★

St. Francis Preparatory School
Outstanding Catholic high schools in Metro New York ★4076★

St. Francis; University of
Fall enrollment at the largest Chicago-area private institutions, by minority percentages, 1999 ★869★

U.S. News & World Report's midwestern regional universities with students least in debt, 1999 ★1399★

U.S. News & World Report's midwestern regional universities with the best student/faculty ratios, 2000-01 ★1403★

U.S. News & World Report's midwestern regional universities with the lowest acceptance rates, 2000-01 ★1410★

Average faculty salaries for institutions of higher education in Illinois, 2000-01 ★3700★

St. Francis Xavier University
Best Canadian universities overall, 2000 ★1149★

Canadian primarily undergraduate universities by alumni support, 2000 ★1193★

Canadian primarily undergraduate universities by class size at the first and second-year level, 2000 ★1195★

Canadian primarily undergraduate universities by class size at the third and forth-year level, 2000 ★1196★

SAINT

Canadian primarily undergraduate universities by classes taught by tenured faculty, 2000 ★1197★
Canadian primarily undergraduate universities by faculty members with Ph.D.'s, 2000 ★1198★
Canadian primarily undergraduate universities by library acquisitions, 2000 ★1199★
Canadian primarily undergraduate universities by library expenses, 2000 ★1200★
Canadian primarily undergraduate universities by library holdings per student, 2000 ★1201★
Canadian primarily undergraduate universities by medical/science grants per faculty member, 2000 ★1202★
Canadian primarily undergraduate universities by operating budget per student, 2000 ★1203★
Canadian primarily undergraduate universities by percentage of operating budget allocated to scholarships, 2000 ★1204★
Canadian primarily undergraduate universities by percentage of operating budget allocated to student services, 2000 ★1205★
Canadian primarily undergraduate universities by reputation, 2000 ★1206★
Canadian primarily undergraduate universities by social science/humanities grants per faculty member, 2000 ★1207★
Canadian primarily undergraduate universities by students from out of province, 2000 ★1208★
Canadian primarily undergraduate universities by students winning national awards, 2000 ★1209★
Canadian primarily undergraduate universities that are the best overall, 2000 ★1210★
Canadian primarily undergraduate universities with the highest quality, 2000 ★1212★
Canadian universities by graduation rate, 2000 ★1214★
Canadian universities chosen as being value added, 2000 ★1216★
Canadian universities with the highest total cost, 2000 ★1217★
Top Canadian primarily undergraduate universities, 2000 ★1226★

Ste. Genevieve de Bois
Outstanding secondary schools in St. Louis, Missouri-Illinois ★4216★

St. George; Judith
Outstanding children's nonfiction books, 2000 ★330★

St. Gertrude High School
Outstanding secondary schools in Richmond-Petersburg, Virginia ★4210★

St. Gregory's University
Highest undergraduate tuition and fees at colleges and universities in Oklahoma ★1545★

St. Ignatius School
Outstanding secondary schools in Mobile, Alabama ★4182★

St. Isidore
Outstanding secondary schools in Oakland, California ★4195★

St. James Encyclopedia of Popular Culture
Library Journal's best reference books, 2000 ★368★
Outstanding reference sources, 2000 ★370★

St. James Episcopal School
Outstanding secondary schools in Corpus Christi, Texas ★4119★
Outstanding secondary schools in Los Angeles-Long Beach, California ★4167★

St. James Middle School
Outstanding secondary schools in Myrtle Beach, South Carolina ★4184★

St. James White Oak School
Outstanding secondary schools in Cincinnati, Ohio-Kentucky-Indiana ★4112★

St. Joan of Arc School
Outstanding secondary schools in Detroit, Michigan ★4125★

St. John Bosco School
Outstanding secondary schools in Cleveland-Lorain-Elyria, Ohio ★4114★

St. John the Evangelist High School
Outstanding secondary schools in Atlanta, Georgia ★4087★

St. John Fisher College
Average faculty salaries for institutions of higher education in New York, 2000-01 ★3719★

St. John Neumann High School
Outstanding secondary schools in Atlanta, Georgia ★4087★

St. John Vianney High School
Outstanding secondary schools in St. Louis, Missouri-Illinois ★4216★

St. John's College
Highest undergraduate tuition and fees at colleges and universities in Maryland ★1514★
Highest undergraduate tuition and fees at colleges and universities in New Mexico ★1535★

St. John's College (NM)
U.S. colleges and universities where intercollegiate sports are not popular ★994★

St. Johns River Community College
Lowest undergraduate tuition and fees at colleges and universities in Florida ★1495★

St. John's University
U.S. catholic universities with the highest enrollment, 1999 ★864★
Highest undergraduate tuition and fees at colleges and universities in Minnesota ★1520★
Average faculty salaries for institutions of higher education in Minnesota, 2000-01 ★3710★

St. John's University and College of St. Benedict
Fiske Guide's best buys for private colleges and universities, 2001 ★1459★

St. John's University (NY)
Division I all-time winningest college teams ★128★
Division I NCAA colleges with the highest graduation rates for female basketball players, 1990-91 to 1993-94 ★932★
Retention rates of African American students at traditionally white institutions, 1997-98 ★1121★
Total baccalaureate health professions and related sciences degrees awarded to Asian Americans from U.S. colleges and universities, 1997-98 ★1722★
U.S. colleges and universities awarding the most mathematics master's degrees to African Americans ★1790★
U.S. colleges and universities awarding the most psychology master's degrees to Asian Americans ★1798★
U.S. colleges and universities awarding the most social sciences and history master's degrees to African Americans ★1801★
U.S. colleges and universities awarding the most first professional degrees to Hispanic Americans ★1845★
U.S. colleges and universities awarding the most law and legal studies first professional degrees to Hispanic Americans ★1854★
Average faculty salaries for institutions of higher education in New York, 2000-01 ★3719★

St. Joseph
Outstanding secondary schools in Oakland, California ★4195★

St. Joseph Academy
Outstanding secondary schools in Cleveland-Lorain-Elyria, Ohio ★4114★

St. Joseph Catholic School
Outstanding secondary schools in Melbourne-Titusville-Palm Bay, Florida ★4176★

St. Joseph College
U.S. News & World Report's northern regional universities with the highest percentage of full-time faculty, 2000-01 ★1422★
Highest undergraduate tuition and fees at colleges and universities in Connecticut ★1490★
Average faculty salaries for institutions of higher education in Connecticut, 2000-01 ★3694★

St. Joseph College (CT)
U.S. News & World Report's northern regional universities with students least in debt, 1999 ★1413★
U.S. News & World Report's northern regional universities with the best student/faculty ratios, 2000-01 ★1416★
U.S. News & World Report's northern regional universities with the highest acceptance rates, 2000-01 ★1417★
U.S. News & World Report's northern regional universities with the highest alumni giving rates, 2000-01 ★1418★
U.S. News & World Report's northern regional universities with the highest proportion of classes with 20 students of less, 2000-01 ★1423★
U.S. News & World Report's best undergraduate fees among northern regional universities by discount tuition, 2000 ★1428★

St. Joseph County Public Library
Highest Hennen's American Public Library Ratings for libraries serving a population of 100,000 to 249,999 ★2698★

St. Joseph High School
Outstanding secondary schools in Santa Barbara-Santa Maria-Lompoc, California ★4224★

St. Joseph Montessori School
Outstanding secondary schools in Columbus, Ohio ★4118★

St. Joseph Seminary College
Highest undergraduate tuition and fees at colleges and universities in Louisiana ★1510★

St. Joseph (VT); College of
Undergraduate tuition and fees at colleges and universities in Vermont ★1563★

St. Joseph's Academy
Outstanding secondary schools in Baton Rouge, Louisiana ★4093★
Outstanding secondary schools in St. Louis, Missouri-Illinois ★4216★

St. Joseph's College
Highest undergraduate tuition and fees at colleges and universities in Maine ★1512★
Average faculty salaries for institutions of higher education in New York, 2000-01 ★3719★

St. Joseph's College (IN)
Average faculty salaries for institutions of higher education in Indiana, 2000-01 ★3701★

St. Joseph's College (ME)
Average faculty salaries for institutions of higher education in Maine, 2000-01 ★3706★

St. Joseph's College (NY)
U.S. News & World Report's northern regional liberal arts colleges with the highest freshmen retention rates, 2000-01 ★1357★
U.S. News & World Report's northern regional liberal arts colleges with the lowest acceptance rates, 2000-01 ★1362★
Total baccalaureate health professions and related sciences degrees awarded to African Americans from U.S. colleges and universities, 1997-98 ★1721★

St. Joseph's School
Outstanding secondary schools in Long Island, New York ★4165★

St. Joseph's University
U.S. colleges and universities awarding the most computer and information sciences master's degrees to Asian Americans ★1767★
Private, 4-year undergraduate colleges and universities producing the most Ph.D.'s in physics and astronomy, 1920-1990 ★2949★

St. Joseph's University (PA)
U.S. News & World Report's northern regional universities with the best academic reputation scores, 2000-01 ★1415★
U.S. News & World Report's northern regional universities with the highest average graduation rates, 2000-01 ★1419★
U.S. News & World Report's northern regional universities with the highest freshmen retention rates, 2000-01 ★1420★
U.S. News & World Report's northern regional universities with the highest percentage of freshmen in the top 25% of their high school class, 2000-01 ★1421★
U.S. News & World Report's northern regional universities with the lowest acceptance rates, 2000-01 ★1424★
U.S. News & World Report's top northern regional universities, 2000-01 ★1425★
Average faculty salaries for institutions of higher education in Pennsylvania, 2000-01 ★3725★

St. Jude Catholic School
Outstanding secondary schools in Indianapolis, Indiana ★4153★

St. Lawrence Catholic School
Outstanding secondary schools in Indianapolis, Indiana ★4153★

St. Lawrence University
U.S. colleges and universities where a large portion of the student body drink beer ★991★
U.S. colleges and universities where students and the local community relate well ★999★
U.S. colleges and universities with an unfavorable surrounding town or city ★1023★
U.S. colleges and universities with harmonious race/class interaction ★1026★
U.S. colleges and universities with poor library facilities ★1028★
U.S. colleges and universities with the happiest students ★1035★
Average faculty salaries for institutions of higher education in New York, 2000-01 ★3719★

St. Leo College
Total baccalaureate business management and administrative services degrees awarded to African Americans from U.S. colleges and universities, 1997-98 ★1683★
Total baccalaureate social sciences and history degrees awarded to African Americans from U.S. colleges and universities, 1997-98 ★1741★

St. Leo University
Average faculty salaries for institutions of higher education in Florida, 2000-01 ★3696★

St. Louis College of Pharmacy
Highest undergraduate tuition and fees at colleges and universities in Missouri ★1524★
Average faculty salaries for institutions of higher education in Missouri, 2000-01 ★3712★

St. Louis Community College, Florissant Valley
Lowest undergraduate tuition and fees at colleges and universities in Missouri ★1525★

St. Louis Community College, Forest Park
Lowest undergraduate tuition and fees at colleges and universities in Missouri ★1525★

St. Louis Community College, Meramec
Lowest undergraduate tuition and fees at colleges and universities in Missouri ★1525★

St. Louis County Library
Highest Hennen's American Public Library Ratings for libraries serving a population of over 500,000 ★2700★

St. Louis University
U.S. catholic universities with the highest enrollment, 1999 ★864★
Highest undergraduate tuition and fees at colleges and universities in Missouri ★1524★
U.S. News & World Report's undergraduate engineering programs with the best aerospace departments, 2000-01 ★2341★
Academics' choices for best health law programs, 2001 ★2629★
Average faculty salaries for institutions of higher education in Missouri, 2000-01 ★3712★

St. Louis University Hospital
Top geriatrics hospitals in the U.S., 2000 ★2791★

St. Luke School
Outstanding secondary schools in Chicago, Illinois ★4110★
Outstanding secondary schools in Providence-Fall River-Warwick, Rhode Island-Maine ★4207★

St. Mark the Evangelist Catholic School
Outstanding secondary schools in Dallas, Texas ★4120★

St. Martin of Tours School
Outstanding secondary schools in Cleveland-Lorain-Elyria, Ohio ★4114★

St. Martin's
Hardcover bestsellers by publishing house, 2000 ★240★

St. Martin's College
Highest undergraduate tuition and fees at colleges and universities in Washington ★1566★
Average faculty salaries for institutions of higher education in Washington, 2000-01 ★3736★

St. Mary Academy
Outstanding secondary schools in Providence-Fall River-Warwick, Rhode Island-Maine ★4207★

St. Mary College (KS)
Highest undergraduate tuition and fees at colleges and universities in Kansas ★1506★
Average faculty salaries for institutions of higher education in Kansas, 2000-01 ★3703★

St. Mary (NE); College of
Highest undergraduate tuition and fees at colleges and universities in Nebraska ★1528★

St. Mary-of-the-Woods College
Average faculty salaries for institutions of higher education in Indiana, 2000-01 ★3701★

St. Mary School
Outstanding secondary schools in Cincinnati, Ohio-Kentucky-Indiana ★4112★

St. Mary's Academy
Outstanding secondary schools in Denver, Colorado ★4124★
Outstanding secondary schools in Portland-Vancouver, Oregon-Washington ★4206★

St. Mary's College
Institutions in the Worker Rights Consortium ★2913★

St. Mary's College (CA)
U.S. News & World Report's best undergraduate fees among western regional universities by discount tuition, 2000 ★1430★
U.S. News & World Report's top western regional universities, 2000-01 ★1574★
U.S. News & World Report's western regional universities with the best academic reputation scores, 2000-01 ★1577★
U.S. News & World Report's western regional universities with the best student/faculty ratios, 2000-01 ★1578★
U.S. News & World Report's western regional universities with the highest freshmen retention rates, 2000-01 ★1581★
U.S. News & World Report's western regional universities with the highest graduation rates, 2000-01 ★1582★
Average faculty salaries for institutions of higher education in California, 2000-01 ★3692★

St. Mary's College (IN)
U.S. News & World Report's midwestern regional liberal arts colleges with the best student/faculty ratios, 2000-01 ★1339★
U.S. News & World Report's midwestern regional liberal arts colleges with the highest academic reputation scores, 2000-01 ★1340★
U.S. News & World Report's midwestern regional liberal arts colleges with the highest alumni giving rates, 2000-01 ★1342★
U.S. News & World Report's midwestern regional liberal arts colleges with the highest freshmen retention rates, 2000-01 ★1343★
U.S. News & World Report's midwestern regional liberal arts colleges with the highest graduation rates, 2000-01 ★1344★
U.S. News & World Report's midwestern regional liberal arts colleges with the highest percentage of freshmen in the top 25% of their high school class, 2000-01 ★1345★
U.S. News & World Report's top midwestern regional liberal arts colleges, 2000-01 ★1349★
Highest undergraduate tuition and fees at colleges and universities in Indiana ★1502★
Average faculty salaries for institutions of higher education in Indiana, 2000-01 ★3701★

St. Mary's College (MD)
State appropriations for Maryland's institutions of higher education, 2000-01 ★1273★

Highest undergraduate tuition and fees at public, 4-year or above colleges and universities ★1463★
Public 4-year institutions with the highest tuition, 2000-01 ★1471★
Average faculty salaries for institutions of higher education in Maryland, 2000-01 ★3707★

St. Mary's Dominican High School
Outstanding secondary schools in New Orleans, Louisiana ★4190★

St. Mary's Episcopal School
Outstanding secondary schools in Memphis, Tennessee-Arkansas-Mississippi ★4177★

St. Mary's University (MN)
Average faculty salaries for institutions of higher education in Minnesota, 2000-01 ★3710★

St. Mary's University (NS)
Best Canadian universities overall, 2000 ★1149★
Canadian primarily undergraduate universities by alumni support, 2000 ★1193★
Canadian primarily undergraduate universities by class size at the first and second-year level, 2000 ★1195★
Canadian primarily undergraduate universities by class size at the third and forth-year level, 2000 ★1196★
Canadian primarily undergraduate universities by classes taught by tenured faculty, 2000 ★1197★
Canadian primarily undergraduate universities by faculty members with Ph.D.'s, 2000 ★1198★
Canadian primarily undergraduate universities by library acquisitions, 2000 ★1199★
Canadian primarily undergraduate universities by library expenses, 2000 ★1200★
Canadian primarily undergraduate universities by library holdings per student, 2000 ★1201★
Canadian primarily undergraduate universities by medical/science grants per faculty member, 2000 ★1202★
Canadian primarily undergraduate universities by operating budget per student, 2000 ★1203★
Canadian primarily undergraduate universities by percentage of operating budget allocated to scholarships, 2000 ★1204★
Canadian primarily undergraduate universities by percentage of operating budget allocated to student services, 2000 ★1205★
Canadian primarily undergraduate universities by reputation, 2000 ★1206★
Canadian primarily undergraduate universities by social science/humanities grants per faculty member, 2000 ★1207★
Canadian primarily undergraduate universities by students from out of province, 2000 ★1208★
Canadian primarily undergraduate universities by students winning national awards, 2000 ★1209★
Canadian primarily undergraduate universities that are the most innovative, 2000 ★1211★
Canadian universities with the highest total cost, 2000 ★1217★
Top Canadian primarily undergraduate universities, 2000 ★1226★

St. Mary's University, San Antonio
U.S. News & World Report's western regional universities with the highest percentage of full-time faculty, 2000-01 ★1584★

St. Mary's University (TX)
U.S. News & World Report's best undergraduate fees among western regional universities by discount tuition, 2000 ★1430★
Highest undergraduate tuition and fees at colleges and universities in Texas ★1560★
U.S. News & World Report's western regional universities with the best student/faculty ratios, 2000-01 ★1578★
U.S. News & World Report's western regional universities with the highest acceptance rates, 2000-01 ★1579★
U.S. News & World Report's western regional universities with the highest alumni giving rates, 2000-01 ★1580★
U.S. News & World Report's western regional universities with the highest freshmen retention rates, 2000-01 ★1581★
U.S. colleges and universities awarding the most communications master's degrees to Hispanic Americans ★1765★
U.S. colleges and universities awarding the most computer and information sciences master's degrees to Hispanic Americans ★1768★
U.S. colleges and universities awarding the most psychology master's degrees to Hispanic Americans ★1799★
U.S. colleges and universities awarding the most social sciences and history master's degrees to Hispanic Americans ★1803★
U.S. colleges and universities awarding the most law and legal studies first professional degrees to Hispanic Americans ★1854★
Private, 4-year undergraduate colleges and universities producing the most Ph.D.'s in political science and international relations, 1981-1990 ★3045★
Average faculty salaries for institutions of higher education in Texas, 2000-01 ★3731★

St. Matthew School
Outstanding secondary schools in Wilmington-Newark, Delaware-Maryland ★4252★

St. Meinrad School of Theology
Institutions censured by the American Association of University Professors, 2001 ★1067★

St. Michael Lutheran School
Outstanding secondary schools in Fort Myers-Cape Coral, Florida ★4134★

St. Michael's College
Division II NCAA colleges with the 100% graduation rates for men's basketball players, 1993-94 ★943★
Division II NCAA colleges with the 100% graduation rates for women's basketball players, 1993-94 ★944★
Division II NCAA colleges with the highest graduation rates for all sports, 1993-94 ★945★
U.S. News & World Report's best undergraduate fees among northern regional universities by discount tuition, 2000 ★1428★
Undergraduate tuition and fees at colleges and universities in Vermont ★1563★
College senior's choices for exemplary master's institutions ★2533★

St. Norbert College
U.S. News & World Report's midwestern regional liberal arts colleges with the highest academic reputation scores, 2000-01 ★1340★
U.S. News & World Report's midwestern regional liberal arts colleges with the highest acceptance rates, 2000-01 ★1341★
U.S. News & World Report's midwestern regional liberal arts colleges with the highest freshmen retention rates, 2000-01 ★1343★
U.S. News & World Report's midwestern regional liberal arts colleges with the highest graduation rates, 2000-01 ★1344★
U.S. News & World Report's midwestern regional liberal arts colleges with the highest percentage of freshmen in the top 25% of their high school class, 2000-01 ★1345★
U.S. News & World Report's midwestern regional liberal arts colleges with the highest percentage of full-time faculty, 2000-01 ★1346★
U.S. News & World Report's top midwestern regional liberal arts colleges, 2000-01 ★1349★
Highest undergraduate tuition and fees at colleges and universities in Wisconsin ★1570★

St. Olaf College
Private, 4-year undergraduate colleges and universities producing the most Ph.D.'s in the life sciences, 1920-1990 ★192★
Private, 4-year undergraduate colleges and universities producing the most Ph.D.'s in the life sciences, 1981-1990 ★193★
Highest undergraduate tuition and fees at colleges and universities in Minnesota ★1520★
Private, 4-year undergraduate colleges and universities producing the most Ph.D.'s in the computer sciences, 1920-1990 ★1595★
Private, 4-year undergraduate colleges and universities producing the most Ph.D.s in all fields of study, 1920-1990 ★2027★
Private, 4-year undergraduate colleges and universities producing the most Ph.D.'s in all fields of study, 1981-1990 ★2028★
Private, 4-year undergraduate colleges and universities producing the most Ph.D.'s in all fields of study, 1990 ★2029★
Private, 4-year undergraduate colleges and universities producing the most Ph.D.'s in nonscience fields, 1920-1990 ★2030★
Private, 4-year undergraduate colleges and universities producing the most Ph.D.'s in nonscience fields, 1981-1990 ★2031★
Private, 4-year undergraduate colleges and universities producing the most Ph.D.'s in nonscience fields, 1990 ★2032★
U.S. bachelor's institutions with the largest number of students studying abroad, 1998-99 ★2511★
Private, 4-year undergraduate colleges and universities producing the most Ph.D.'s in mathematics, 1920-1990 ★2776★
Private, 4-year undergraduate colleges and universities producing the most Ph.D.'s in mathematics, 1981-1990 ★2777★
Private, 4-year undergraduate colleges and universities producing the most Ph.D.'s in physics and astronomy, 1920-1990 ★2949★
Average faculty salaries for institutions of higher education in Minnesota, 2000-01 ★3710★
Private, 4-year undergraduate colleges and universities producing the most Ph.D.'s in the sciences, 1981-1990 ★4295★

St. Patrick's Gargoyle
Booklist's most recommended science fiction/fantasy books ★232★

St. Paul
Fortune's highest ranked property and casualty insurance companies, 2000 ★488★

St. Paul Technical College
Lowest undergraduate tuition and fees at colleges and universities in Minnesota ★1521★
Average faculty salaries for institutions of higher education without academic ranks in Minnesota, 2000-01 ★3753★

St. Paul's College
Average faculty salaries for institutions of higher education in Virginia, 2000-01 ★3735★

St. Paul's Episcopal School
Outstanding secondary schools in New Orleans, Louisiana ★4190★

St. Paul's Lutheran School
Outstanding secondary schools in Janesville-Beloit, Wisconsin ★4156★

St. Paul's School
Top internships in the U.S. with the highest compensation, 2001 ★2611★

St. Peter's College
Highest undergraduate tuition and fees at colleges and universities in New Jersey ★1533★
Average faculty salaries for institutions of higher education in New Jersey, 2000-01 ★3717★

St. Peter's High School
Outstanding secondary schools in Mansfield, Ohio ★4174★

St. Philomena
Outstanding secondary schools in Seattle-Bellevue-Everett, Washington ★4227★

St. Pius X School
Outstanding secondary schools in Tulsa, Oklahoma ★4244★

St. Raphael the Archangel
Outstanding secondary schools in Louisville, Kentucky-Indiana ★4168★

St. Raymond High School for Boys
Outstanding secondary schools in New York, New York ★4191★

St. Rita of Cascia High School
Outstanding Catholic high schools in Metro Chicago ★4074★

St. Rocco School
Outstanding secondary schools in Providence-Fall River-Warwick, Rhode Island-Maine ★4207★

St. Rose; College of
Division II NCAA colleges with the 100% graduation rates for women's basketball players, 1993-94 ★944★
Average faculty salaries for institutions of higher education in New York, 2000-01 ★3719★

St. Rose of Lima
Outstanding secondary schools in Miami, Florida ★4178★

St. Saviour High School
Outstanding Catholic high schools in Metro New York ★4076★

St. Scholastica Academy
Outstanding secondary schools in New Orleans, Louisiana ★4190★

St. Scholastica; College of
U.S. News & World Report's midwestern regional universities with students most in debt, 1999 ★1400★
U.S. News & World Report's midwestern regional universities with the best student/faculty ratios, 2000-01 ★1403★
U.S. News & World Report's midwestern regional universities with the highest acceptance rates, 2000-01 ★1404★
U.S. News & World Report's midwestern regional universities with the highest percentage of freshmen from the top 25% of their high school class, 2000-01 ★1407★
U.S. News & World Report's midwestern regional universities with the highest percentage of full-time faculty, 2000-01 ★1408★

U.S. News & World Report's midwestern regional universities with the highest proportion of classes having 20 students or less, 2000-01 ★1409★
U.S. News & World Report's best undergraduate fees among midwestern regional universities by discount tuition, 2000 ★1427★
Average faculty salaries for institutions of higher education in Minnesota, 2000-01 ★3710★

St. Simon Catholic School
Outstanding secondary schools in San Jose, California ★4222★

St. Thomas the Apostle School
Outstanding secondary schools in Los Angeles-Long Beach, California ★4167★
Outstanding secondary schools in Phoenix-Mesa, Arizona ★4203★

St. Thomas Aquinas College
U.S. News & World Report's northern regional liberal arts colleges with the highest freshmen retention rates, 2000-01 ★1357★
Average faculty salaries for institutions of higher education in New York, 2000-01 ★3719★

St. Thomas Aquinas High School
Outstanding secondary schools in Fort Lauderdale, Florida ★4133★

St. Thomas Aquinas School
Outstanding secondary schools in Dallas, Texas ★4120★

St. Thomas (MN); University of
U.S. master's institutions with the largest number of students studying abroad, 1998-99 ★2513★

St. Thomas More High School
Outstanding secondary schools in Lafayette, Louisiana ★4162★

St. Thomas More Parish School
Outstanding secondary schools in Houston, Texas ★4150★

St. Thomas More School
Outstanding secondary schools in Cleveland-Lorain-Elyria, Ohio ★4114★

St. Thomas; University of
U.S. News & World Report's midwestern regional universities with the best academic reputation scores, 2000-01 ★1401★
U.S. News & World Report's midwestern regional universities with the highest freshmen retention rates, 2000-01 ★1405★
U.S. News & World Report's midwestern regional universities with the highest graduation rates, 2000-01 ★1406★
U.S. News & World Report's midwestern regional universities with the highest percentage of freshmen from the top 25% of their high school class, 2000-01 ★1407★
U.S. News & World Report's top midwestern regional universities, 2000-01 ★1411★
U.S. News & World Report's best undergraduate fees among midwestern regional universities by discount tuition, 2000 ★1427★
Highest undergraduate tuition and fees at colleges and universities in Minnesota ★1520★
U.S. colleges and universities awarding the most computer and information sciences master's degrees to African Americans ★1766★
Average faculty salaries for institutions of higher education in Minnesota, 2000-01 ★3710★
Average faculty salaries for institutions of higher education in Texas, 2000-01 ★3731★

St. Thomas University (FL)
U.S. colleges and universities awarding the most business management and administrative services master's degrees to Hispanic Americans ★1761★

U.S. colleges and universities awarding the most psychology master's degrees to Hispanic Americans ★1799★
U.S. colleges and universities awarding the most law and legal studies first professional degrees to Hispanic Americans ★1854★

St. Thomas University (NB)
Canadian primarily undergraduate universities by alumni support, 2000 ★1193★
Canadian primarily undergraduate universities by class size at the first and second-year level, 2000 ★1195★
Canadian primarily undergraduate universities by class size at the third and forth-year level, 2000 ★1196★
Canadian primarily undergraduate universities by classes taught by tenured faculty, 2000 ★1197★
Canadian primarily undergraduate universities by faculty members with Ph.D.'s, 2000 ★1198★
Canadian primarily undergraduate universities by library acquisitions, 2000 ★1199★
Canadian primarily undergraduate universities by library expenses, 2000 ★1200★
Canadian primarily undergraduate universities by library holdings per student, 2000 ★1201★
Canadian primarily undergraduate universities by operating budget per student, 2000 ★1203★
Canadian primarily undergraduate universities by percentage of operating budget allocated to scholarships, 2000 ★1204★
Canadian primarily undergraduate universities by percentage of operating budget allocated to student services, 2000 ★1205★
Canadian primarily undergraduate universities by reputation, 2000 ★1206★
Canadian primarily undergraduate universities by social science/humanities grants per faculty member, 2000 ★1207★
Canadian primarily undergraduate universities by students from out of province, 2000 ★1208★
Canadian primarily undergraduate universities by students winning national awards, 2000 ★1209★
Top Canadian primarily undergraduate universities, 2000 ★1226★

St. Ursula Academy
Outstanding secondary schools in Toledo, Ohio ★4241★

St. Vincent College
U.S. News & World Report's northern regional liberal arts colleges with students most in debt, 1999 ★1352★
U.S. News & World Report's northern regional liberal arts colleges with the best student/faculty ratios, 2000-01 ★1353★
U.S. News & World Report's northern regional liberal arts colleges with the highest acceptance rates, 2000-01 ★1355★
U.S. News & World Report's northern regional liberal arts colleges with the highest alumni giving rates, 2000-01 ★1356★
U.S. News & World Report's northern regional liberal arts colleges with the highest freshmen retention rates, 2000-01 ★1357★
U.S. News & World Report's northern regional liberal arts colleges with the highest percentage of full-time faculty, 2000-01 ★1360★
U.S. News & World Report's best undergraduate fees among northern regional liberal arts colleges by discount tuition, 2000 ★1382★

Average faculty salaries for institutions of higher education in Pennsylvania, 2000-01 ★3725★

St. Xavier High School
Outstanding secondary schools in Louisville, Kentucky-Indiana ★4168★

St. Xavier University
Fall enrollment at the largest Chicago-area private institutions, by minority percentages, 1999 ★869★
U.S. News & World Report's midwestern regional universities with the lowest acceptance rates, 2000-01 ★1410★
Total baccalaureate health professions and related sciences degrees awarded to Native Americans from U.S. colleges and universities, 1997-98 ★1724★
Average faculty salaries for institutions of higher education in Illinois, 2000-01 ★3700★

St. Xavier University (IL)
U.S. News & World Report's best undergraduate fees among midwestern regional universities by discount tuition, 2000 ★1427★

Sakac; Sister Ann
Top pay and benefits for the chief executive and top paid employees at Mount Saint Mary College in New York ★3410★

Saks Corporation
Fortune's highest ranked general merchandisers, 2000 ★468★
Top recruiters for marketing jobs for 2000-01 master's degree recipients ★672★
Top recruiters for textiles/apparel jobs for 2000-01 bachelor's degree recipients ★4434★

Salanter Akiba Academy
Outstanding secondary schools in New York, New York ★4191★

Saleh; Kassem
Top published scholars in the field of systems and software engineering ★2333★

Salem College
Highest undergraduate tuition and fees at colleges and universities in North Carolina ★1539★
Average faculty salaries for institutions of higher education in North Carolina, 2000-01 ★3720★

Salem Community College
Lowest undergraduate tuition and fees at colleges and universities in New Jersey ★1534★
Average faculty salaries for institutions of higher education in New Jersey, 2000-01 ★3717★

Salem State College
State appropriations for Massachusetts's institutions of higher education, 2000-01 ★1274★

Salem-Teikyo University
U.S. News & World Report's southern regional liberal arts colleges with students most in debt, 1999 ★1367★
Highest undergraduate tuition and fees at colleges and universities in West Virginia ★1568★
Average faculty salaries for institutions of higher education in West Virginia, 2000-01 ★3737★

Sales
Internet use by major occupational group, 1998 ★2587★

Sales agents, real estate
Occupations with the highest number of self-employed workers, 1998 ★2311★
Projected employment growth for selected occupations that require an associate degree or less, 1998-2008 ★2319★

Sales/medical
Monster.com's most searched job listings ★2308★

Salesperson
Careers college students considered least respected, 2000 ★739★

Salinger; J. D.
Authors protested for more than one book between 1952 and 1989, according to the *Newsletter of Intellectual Freedom* ★743★
People for the American Way's list of most frequently challenged authors, 1982-1992 ★746★

Salisbury State University
U.S. News & World Report's top public northern regional universities, 2000-01 ★1426★
Average faculty salaries for institutions of higher education in Maryland, 2000-01 ★3707★

Salish Kootenai College
U.S. tribal colleges ★1445★
Lowest undergraduate tuition and fees at private nonprofit, 4-year or above colleges and universities ★1464★

Sallee; David L.
Top pay and benefits for the chief executive and top paid employees at Luther College ★3383★

Sallie Mae
Highly recommended public companies for women executives, 2000 ★4453★

Salm; Thomas R.
Top pay and benefits for the chief executive and top paid employees at Ithaca College ★3351★

Salt Creek School, District 48
Illinois elementary school districts with the highest teacher salaries, 1999 ★3984★
Illinois school districts spending the most per pupil for instruction ★4011★

Salt Lake City-Ogden, UT
Cities with the highest percentage of broadband use and interest ★2578★
Cities with the most Yahoo! listings per million residents ★2580★

Salt Lake City, UT
Best place to live in the western U.S. ★3082★

Salt Lake Community College
Undergraduate tuition and fees at colleges and universities in Utah ★1562★
Average faculty salaries for institutions of higher education in Utah, 2000-01 ★3733★

Salting the Ocean: 100 Poems by Young Poets
Booklist's most recommended poetry for youths, 2001 ★315★

Saltis; Patricia
All-USA Teacher Teams, Third Team, 2000 ★4401★

Salvation Army
Organizations with the most charitable contributions raised, 1999 ★2943★

Salve Regina University
Undergraduate tuition and fees at colleges and universities in Rhode Island ★1553★
Average faculty salaries for institutions of higher education in Rhode Island, 2000-01 ★3727★

Salvucci; James
Top pay and benefits for the chief executive and top paid employees at Curry College ★3261★

Sam Houston State University
Universities with the most-cited scholars in *Criminal Justice and Behavior* ★1648★

Average faculty salaries for institutions of higher education in Texas, 2000-01 ★3731★

Samet; Tom
Top pay and benefits for the chief executive and top paid employees at Hood College ★3338★

Samford University
Division I NCAA colleges with that graduated none of their African American male basketball players, 1990-91 to 1993-94 ★930★
U.S. colleges and universities where the general student body does not drink beer ★1004★
U.S. colleges and universities where the general student body does not smoke marijuana ★1006★
U.S. colleges and universities where the general student body puts little emphasis on socializing ★1010★
U.S. colleges and universities with a primarily religious student body ★1022★
U.S. News & World Report's best undergraduate fees among southern regional universities by discount tuition, 2000 ★1429★
U.S. News & World Report's southern regional universities with the best academic reputation scores, 2000-01 ★1433★
U.S. News & World Report's southern regional universities with the highest acceptance rates, 2000-01 ★1436★
U.S. News & World Report's southern regional universities with the highest freshmen retention rates, 2000-01 ★1437★
U.S. News & World Report's southern regional universities with the highest graduation rates, 2000-01 ★1438★
U.S. News & World Report's southern regional universities with the highest percentage of freshmen in the top 25% of their high school class, 2000-01 ★1439★
U.S. News & World Report's southern regional universities with the highest proportion of classes with 20 students or less, 2000-01 ★1441★
U.S. News & World Report's top southern regional universities, 2000-01 ★1444★
Highest undergraduate tuition and fees at colleges and universities in Alabama ★1479★

Samiee; Saeed
Most published authors, adjusted for coauthorship, in the *Journal of Business Research*, 1985 to 1999 ★701★

Samir and Yonatan
Most notable books for older readers, 2001 ★318★

Sammelson; Owen
Top pay and benefits for the chief executive and top paid employees at Gustavus Adolphus College ★3317★

Sammy Keyes
Publishers Weekly Off-the-Cuff Awards winner for favorite series, 2000 ★348★

Sample; Steven B.
Top pay and benefits for the chief executive and top paid employees at the University of Southern California ★3568★

Sampson Community College
Average faculty salaries for institutions of higher education without academic ranks in North Carolina, 2000-01 ★3761★

Sampson; Jamal
All-America boys' high school basketball 3rd team, 2001 ★163★

Sampson; Nicole S.
  Winner of the American Chemical Society's Arthur C. Cope Awards, 2001 ★795★

Sampson; R.J.
  Most cited authors in the journal *International Journal of Comparative and Applied Criminal Justice*, 1990 to 1995 ★1624★
  Most cited authors in the journal *Journal of Quantitative Criminology*, 1990 to 1995 ★1628★

Sampson; Robert J.
  Most cited authors in the journal *Criminology*, 1990 to 1995 ★1622★
  Most cited authors in three criminology journals ★1634★
  Most-cited scholars in *Criminology* ★1639★

Samsung Electronics
  Business Week's top emerging-market companies worldwide ★434★

Samuel Inman Middle School
  Outstanding secondary schools in Atlanta, Georgia ★4087★

Samuel Morse Middle School
  Outstanding secondary schools in Milwaukee-Waukesha, Wisconsin ★4180★

Samuelson; Paul
  Authors most frequently contributing to the *American Economic Review* from 1911-1990 ★2156★
  Authors most frequently contributing to the *American Economic Review* from 1951-1990 ★2157★

San Antonio, TX
  Best big cities to live in ★3075★

San Diego
  American cities with the highest percentage of people with Internet access ★2572★
  U.S. cities with the most wired households, 2001 ★2606★

San Diego, CA
  America's most wired cities with the highest domain density, 2001 ★2574★
  Cities with the most domains per 1,000 firms ★2579★
  Best big cities to live in ★3075★

San Diego City College
  U.S. institutions awarding the most associate degrees to African Americans in ethnic/cultural studies, 1997-98 ★1806★
  U.S. institutions awarding the most associate degrees to minorities in ethnic/cultural studies, 1997-98 ★1810★

San Diego Mesa College
  U.S. institutions awarding the most associate degrees to African Americans in ethnic/cultural studies, 1997-98 ★1806★
  U.S. institutions awarding the most associate degrees to minorities in ethnic/cultural studies, 1997-98 ★1810★

San Diego State University
  U.S. colleges and universities with the largest numerical increases in alcohol arrests, 1998 ★733★
  U.S. colleges and universities with the largest numerical increases in drug arrests, 1998 ★734★
  Division I NCAA colleges with that graduated less than 20% of their African American male athletes, 1990-91 to 1993-94 ★928★
  Lowest undergraduate tuition and fees at public, 4-year or above colleges and universities ★1466★
  Top colleges in terms of total baccalaureate degrees awarded to minorities, 1997-98 ★1678★
  Total baccalaureate business management and administrative services degrees awarded to Hispanic Americans from U.S. colleges and universities, 1997-98 ★1685★
  Total baccalaureate degrees awarded to Hispanic Americans from U.S. colleges and universities, 1997-98 ★1705★
  Total baccalaureate education degrees awarded to Asian Americans from U.S. colleges and universities, 1997-98 ★1712★
  Total baccalaureate English language, literature, and letters degrees awarded to Hispanic Americans from U.S. colleges and universities, 1997-98 ★1718★
  Total baccalaureate English language, literature, and letters degrees awarded to Native Americans from U.S. colleges and universities, 1997-98 ★1719★
  Total baccalaureate mathematics degrees awarded to Hispanic Americans from U.S. colleges and universities, 1997-98 ★1731★
  Total baccalaureate psychology degrees awarded to Hispanic Americans from U.S. colleges and universities, 1997-98 ★1739★
  Total baccalaureate social sciences and history degrees awarded to Hispanic Americans from U.S. colleges and universities, 1997-98 ★1743★
  U.S. colleges and universities awarding the most business management and administrative services master's degrees to Hispanic Americans ★1761★
  U.S. colleges and universities awarding the most communications master's degrees to Asian Americans ★1764★
  U.S. colleges and universities awarding the most education master's degrees to Asian Americans ★1770★
  U.S. colleges and universities awarding the most education master's degrees to Hispanic Americans ★1771★
  U.S. colleges and universities awarding the most education master's degrees to Native Americans ★1772★
  U.S. colleges and universities awarding the most English language/literature/letters master's degrees to Asian Americans ★1774★
  U.S. colleges and universities awarding the most English language/literature/letters master's degrees to Hispanic Americans ★1775★
  U.S. colleges and universities awarding the most health professions and related sciences master's degrees to Asian Americans ★1778★
  U.S. colleges and universities awarding the most health professions and related sciences master's degrees to Hispanic Americans ★1779★
  U.S. colleges and universities awarding the most master's degrees to Asian Americans ★1786★
  U.S. colleges and universities awarding the most master's degrees to Hispanic Americans ★1787★
  U.S. colleges and universities awarding the most master's degrees to minorities ★1788★
  U.S. colleges and universities awarding the most mathematics master's degrees to Asian Americans ★1791★
  U.S. colleges and universities awarding the most mathematics master's degrees to Hispanic Americans ★1792★
  U.S. colleges and universities awarding the most physical sciences master's degrees to Asian Americans ★1794★
  U.S. colleges and universities awarding the most physical sciences master's degrees to Hispanic Americans ★1795★
  U.S. colleges and universities awarding the most doctorate degrees to Hispanic Americans ★2097★
  U.S. colleges and universities awarding the most education doctorate degrees to Hispanic Americans ★2110★
  U.S. colleges and universities awarding the most psychology doctorate degrees to Hispanic Americans ★2122★
  Average faculty salaries for institutions of higher education in California, 2000-01 ★3692★

San Diego; University of
  Division I NCAA colleges with the highest graduation rates for male basketball players, 1990-91 to 1993-94 ★935★
  U.S. News & World Report's national universities with students most in debt, 1999 ★1476★
  U.S. colleges and universities awarding the most law and legal studies master's degrees to Asian Americans ★1782★
  U.S. colleges and universities awarding the most law and legal studies master's degrees to Hispanic Americans ★1783★
  U.S. colleges and universities awarding the most law and legal studies first professional degrees to Asian Americans ★1853★

San Diego Zoo
  Most selective internships in the U.S., 2001 ★2610★

San Francisco
  U.S. cities with the most wired households, 2001 ★2606★

San Francisco 49ers
  Most selective internships in the U.S., 2001 ★2610★

San Francisco, CA
  Counties with the highest per capita income ★2561★
  America's most wired cities, 2001 ★2573★
  America's most wired cities with the highest domain density, 2001 ★2574★
  Cities with the highest online spending per Internet user ★2576★
  Cities with the highest percentage of adults using the Internet at home ★2577★
  Cities with the most domains per 1,000 firms ★2579★
  Best big cities to live in ★3075★
  Most polite cities in the U.S. ★3086★
  U.S. cities with the highest home prices ★3087★

San Francisco Chronicle
  Most selective internships in the U.S., 2001 ★2610★
  Top internships in the U.S. with the highest compensation, 2001 ★2611★

San Francisco Community College District
  Institutions with the most full-time Hispanic American faculty ★923★
  U.S. colleges and universities with the most full-time Hispanic American faculty ★925★

San Francisco/Oakland/San Jose
  American cities with the highest percentage of people with Internet access ★2572★
  U.S. market areas with the highest percentage of adults having internet access ★2607★

San Francisco State University
  Total baccalaureate business management and administrative services degrees awarded to Asian Americans from U.S. colleges and universities, 1997-98 ★1684★

Total baccalaureate degrees awarded to Asian Americans from U.S. colleges and universities, 1997-98 ★1702★
Total baccalaureate education degrees awarded to Asian Americans from U.S. colleges and universities, 1997-98 ★1712★
Total baccalaureate health professions and related sciences degrees awarded to Asian Americans from U.S. colleges and universities, 1997-98 ★1722★
U.S. colleges and universities awarding the most business management and administrative services master's degrees to Asian Americans ★1760★
U.S. colleges and universities awarding the most communications master's degrees to Asian Americans ★1764★
U.S. colleges and universities awarding the most communications master's degrees to Hispanic Americans ★1765★
U.S. colleges and universities awarding the most education master's degrees to Asian Americans ★1770★
U.S. colleges and universities awarding the most English language/literature/letters master's degrees to Asian Americans ★1774★
U.S. colleges and universities awarding the most English language/literature/letters master's degrees to Hispanic Americans ★1775★
U.S. colleges and universities awarding the most master's degrees to Asian Americans ★1786★
U.S. colleges and universities awarding the most psychology master's degrees to Native Americans ★1800★
U.S. colleges and universities awarding the most social sciences and history master's degrees to Asian Americans ★1802★
Master's institutions with the highest enrollment of foreign students, 1998-99 ★2499★
Institutions in the Worker Rights Consortium ★2913★
Average faculty salaries for institutions of higher education in California, 2000-01 ★3692★

San Francisco; University of
U.S. News & World Report's national universities with students most in debt, 1999 ★1476★
U.S. colleges and universities awarding the most law and legal studies first professional degrees to Asian Americans ★1853★
U.S. colleges and universities awarding the most education doctorate degrees to Asian Americans ★2109★

San Jacinto College, Central
Lowest undergraduate tuition and fees at colleges and universities in Texas ★1561★

San Jacinto College, North
Lowest undergraduate tuition and fees at colleges and universities in Texas ★1561★

San Joaquin Delta College
Lowest undergraduate tuition and fees at public 2-year colleges and universities ★1465★
Lowest undergraduate tuition and fees at colleges and universities in California ★1487★

San Jose, CA
U.S. cities with the highest number of high-tech employees, 1998 ★2284★
America's most wired cities, 2001 ★2573★
America's most wired cities with the highest domain density, 2001 ★2574★
Cities with the highest online spending per Internet user ★2576★
Cities with the highest percentage of adults using the Internet at home ★2577★
Cities with the highest percentage of broadband use and interest ★2578★
Cities with the most domains per 1,000 firms ★2579★
U.S. cities with the highest home prices ★3087★

San Jose State University
U.S. colleges and universities with the lowest average football attendance, 1996-99 ★160★
U.S. colleges and universities reporting the most weapons related arrests, 1998 ★732★
U.S. News & World Report's top public western regional universities, 2000-01 ★1573★
Top colleges in terms of total baccalaureate degrees awarded to minorities, 1997-98 ★1678★
Total baccalaureate business management and administrative services degrees awarded to Asian Americans from U.S. colleges and universities, 1997-98 ★1684★
Total baccalaureate communications degrees awarded to Asian Americans from U.S. colleges and universities, 1997-98 ★1688★
Total baccalaureate computer and information science degrees awarded to Asian Americans from U.S. colleges and universities, 1997-98 ★1692★
Total baccalaureate degrees awarded to Asian Americans from U.S. colleges and universities, 1997-98 ★1702★
Total baccalaureate education degrees awarded to Asian Americans from U.S. colleges and universities, 1997-98 ★1712★
Total baccalaureate health professions and related sciences degrees awarded to Asian Americans from U.S. colleges and universities, 1997-98 ★1722★
Total baccalaureate physical sciences degrees awarded to Asian Americans from U.S. colleges and universities, 1997-98 ★1734★
U.S. colleges and universities awarding the most communications master's degrees to Asian Americans ★1764★
U.S. colleges and universities awarding the most education master's degrees to Asian Americans ★1770★
U.S. colleges and universities awarding the most master's degrees to Asian Americans ★1786★
U.S. colleges and universities awarding the most physical sciences master's degrees to Asian Americans ★1794★
Master's institutions with the highest enrollment of foreign students, 1998-99 ★2499★
Average faculty salaries for institutions of higher education in California, 2000-01 ★3692★

San Juan College
Lowest undergraduate tuition and fees at colleges and universities in New Mexico ★1536★

San Lorenzo High School
Outstanding secondary schools in Oakland, California ★4195★

San Mateo, CA
Counties with the highest per capita income ★2561★

San Mateo High School
Outstanding secondary schools in San Francisco, California ★4221★

San Paolo-IMI
Business Week's best companies in Italy ★397★

Sandberg; Mark E.
Top pay and benefits for the chief executive and top paid employees at Rider University ★3458★

Sanderson; Natalie
All-America girls' high school soccer team forwards, 2001 ★175★
All-America girls' high school soccer team player of the year, 2001 ★178★

Sandhills Community College
Average faculty salaries for institutions of higher education in North Carolina, 2000-01 ★3720★

Sands; Kathleen
Radcliffe Institute for Advanced Study fellowship recipients in the field of religion, 2000-01 ★3092★

Sandy Creek High School
All-USA Teacher Teams, Third Team, 2000 ★4401★

Sanmina
Top electrical and electronics companies in Standard & Poor's 500, 2001 ★539★

Sansing; Lucille
Top pay and benefits for the chief executive and top paid employees at the College of Notre Dame in California ★3526★

Santa Barbara City College
Community colleges receiving the most gifts, 1999-2000 ★1239★

Santa Clara City Library
Highest Hennen's American Public Library Ratings for libraries serving a population of 100,000 to 249,999 ★2698★

Santa Clara County Free Library
Highest Hennen's American Public Library Ratings for libraries serving a population of 250,000 to 499,999 ★2699★

Santa Clara University
Division I NCAA colleges with the highest graduation rates for female basketball players, 1990-91 to 1993-94 ★932★
U.S. News & World Report's best undergraduate fees among western regional universities by discount tuition, 2000 ★1430★
U.S. News & World Report's top western regional universities, 2000-01 ★1574★
U.S. News & World Report's western regional universities with the best academic reputation scores, 2000-01 ★1577★
U.S. News & World Report's western regional universities with the best student/faculty ratios, 2000-01 ★1578★
U.S. News & World Report's western regional universities with the highest alumni giving rates, 2000-01 ★1580★
U.S. News & World Report's western regional universities with the highest freshmen retention rates, 2000-01 ★1581★
U.S. News & World Report's western regional universities with the highest graduation rates, 2000-01 ★1582★
U.S. News & World Report's western regional universities with the highest percentage of freshmen in the top 25% of their high school class, 2000-01 ★1583★
U.S. News & World Report's western regional universities with the highest percentage of full-time faculty, 2000-01 ★1584★
U.S. News & World Report's western regional universities with the lowest acceptance rates, 2000-01 ★1586★
Private, 4-year undergraduate colleges and universities producing the most Ph.D.'s in the computer sciences, 1920-1990 ★1595★

U.S. colleges and universities awarding the most business management and administrative services master's degrees to Asian Americans ★1760★

U.S. colleges and universities awarding the most master's degrees to Asian Americans ★1786★

U.S. colleges and universities awarding the most law and legal studies first professional degrees to Asian Americans ★1853★

Private, 4-year undergraduate colleges and universities producing the most Ph.D.'s in economics, 1920-1990 ★2211★

U.S. master's institutions with the largest number of students studying abroad, 1998-99 ★2513★

Academics' choices for best intellectual property law programs, 2001 ★2630★

Private, 4-year undergraduate colleges and universities producing the most Ph.D.'s in mathematics, 1981-1990 ★2777★

Average faculty salaries for institutions of higher education in California, 2000-01 ★3692★

Santa Cruz, CA
Best 'quirky' places to live ★3083★

Santa Fe; College of
Highest undergraduate tuition and fees at colleges and universities in New Mexico ★1535★

Santa Fe Community College
Lowest undergraduate tuition and fees at colleges and universities in New Mexico ★1536★

Santa Fe Community College, Gainesville
U.S. institutions awarding the most associate degrees to Hispanic Americans in agricultural sciences, 1998 ★1807★

U.S. institutions awarding the most associate degrees to minorities in agricultural sciences, 1998 ★1809★

Santa Margarita High School
Outstanding secondary schools in Orange County, California ★4199★

Santa Monica College
Community colleges with the highest enrollment of foreign students, 1998-99 ★2493★

Santa Rosa, CA
U.S. cities with the highest home prices ★3087★

Santa Rosa Junior College
Community colleges receiving the most gifts, 1999-2000 ★1239★

Sante Fe; College of
Academic reputation scores for U.S. News & World Report's top western regional liberal arts colleges, 2000-01 ★1387★

Acceptance rates for U.S. News & World Report's top western regional liberal arts colleges, 2000-01 ★1388★

Alumni giving rates at U.S. News & World Report's top western regional liberal arts colleges, 2000-01 ★1389★

Average freshmen retention rates for U.S. News & World Report's top western regional liberal arts colleges, 2000-01 ★1390★

Average graduation rates for U.S. News & World Report's top western regional liberal arts colleges, 2000-01 ★1391★

Percentage of freshmen in the top 25% of their high school class at U.S. News & World Report's top western regional liberal arts colleges, 2000-01 ★1392★

Percentage of full-time faculty at U.S. News & World Report's top western regional liberal arts colleges, 2000-01 ★1393★

Proportion of classes having 20 students or less at U.S. News & World Report's top western regional liberal arts colleges, 2000-01 ★1394★

Student/faculty ratios at U.S. News & World Report's top western regional liberal arts colleges, 2000-01 ★1395★

U.S. News & World Report's top western regional liberal arts colleges, 2000-01 ★1396★

Average faculty salaries for institutions of higher education in New Mexico, 2000-01 ★3718★

Santee; Robert
Top pay and benefits for the chief executive and top paid employees at the Chaminade University of Honolulu ★3524★

Sanzo; Anthony
Top pay and benefits for the chief executive and top paid employees at the Allegheny University of the Health Sciences ★3520★

SAP
Business Week's best companies in Germany ★394★

Sapient
Companies with the best two-year total returns since 1998 ★436★

Sara Lee
Business Week's best companies in terms of return on equity ★407★

Fortune's highest ranked consumer food products companies, 2000 ★458★

Saracevic; Tefko
Library and information science faculty with the most citations to journal articles, 1993-1998 ★2710★

Library and information science faculty with the most journal articles, 1993-1998 ★2711★

Sarah Lawrence
U.S. colleges and universities with a generally liberal student body ★1015★

Sarah Lawrence College
U.S. colleges and universities most accepting of alternative lifestyles ★986★

U.S. colleges and universities that devote the most course time to discussion ★990★

U.S. colleges and universities where intercollegiate sports are not popular ★994★

U.S. colleges and universities where intramural sports are not popular ★996★

U.S. colleges and universities where students and the local community have strained relations ★998★

U.S. colleges and universities with a large student body of liberal Democrats ★1017★

U.S. colleges and universities with the best on-campus housing facilities ★1032★

U.S. News & World Report's national liberal arts colleges with the best student/faculty ratios, 2000-01 ★1326★

U.S. News & World Report's national liberal arts colleges with the highest proportion of classes with less than 20 students, 2000-01 ★1335★

Highest undergraduate tuition and fees at private nonprofit, 4-year or above colleges and universities ★1461★

Private 4-year institutions with the highest tuition, 2000-01 ★1467★

Highest undergraduate tuition and fees at colleges and universities in New York ★1537★

Private, 4-year undergraduate colleges and universities producing the most Ph.D.'s in psychology, 1981-1990 ★3067★

Average faculty salaries for institutions of higher education in New York, 2000-01 ★3719★

Private, 4-year undergraduate colleges and universities producing the most Ph.D.'s in anthropology and sociology, 1981-1990 ★4345★

Sarasota County Library System
Highest Hennen's American Public Library Ratings for libraries serving a population of 250,000 to 499,999 ★2699★

Sarasota, FL
Best big cities to live in ★3075★
Best small city in the U.S. ★3084★

Sargent; David J.
Top pay and benefits for the chief executive and top paid employees at Suffolk University ★3513★

Sargent; Gordon A.
Top pay and benefits for the chief executive and top paid employees at the University of Dayton ★3539★

Sargent; Mark
Top pay and benefits for the chief executive and top paid employees at Gordon College in Massachusetts ★3312★

Top pay and benefits for the chief executive and top paid employees at Villanova University ★3595★

Sargent; T.J.
U.S. academic economists by mean number of citations, 1971-92 ★2176★

U.S. academic economists by total citations, 1971-92 ★2177★

Saskatchewan
Canadian provinces by teaching days per year ★4058★

Saskatchewan; University of
Best Canadian universities overall, 2000 ★1149★

Canadian medical/doctoral universities by alumni support, 2000 ★1172★

Canadian medical/doctoral universities by award-winning faculty members, 2000 ★1173★

Canadian medical/doctoral universities by class size at the first- and second-year level, 2000 ★1174★

Canadian medical/doctoral universities by class size at the third- and forth-year level, 2000 ★1175★

Canadian medical/doctoral universities by classes taught by tenured faculty, 2000 ★1176★

Canadian medical/doctoral universities by faculty members with Ph.D.'s, 2000 ★1177★

Canadian medical/doctoral universities by international graduate students, 2000 ★1178★

Canadian medical/doctoral universities by library acquisitions, 2000 ★1179★

Canadian medical/doctoral universities by library expenses, 2000 ★1180★

Canadian medical/doctoral universities by library holdings, 2000 ★1181★

Canadian medical/doctoral universities by library holdings per student, 2000 ★1182★

Canadian medical/doctoral universities by medical/science grants per faculty member, 2000 ★1184★

Canadian medical/doctoral universities by operating budget per student, 2000 ★1185★

Canadian medical/doctoral universities by percentage of operating budget allocated to scholarships, 2000 ★1186★

SATCHEL

Satchel (continued)
Canadian medical/doctoral universities by percentage of operating budget allocated to student services, 2000 ★1187★
Canadian medical/doctoral universities by reputation, 2000 ★1188★
Canadian medical/doctoral universities by social science/humanities grants per faculty member, 2000 ★1189★
Canadian medical/doctoral universities by students from out of province, 2000 ★1190★
Canadian medical/doctoral universities by students winning national awards, 2000 ★1191★
Top Canadian medical/doctoral universities, 2000 ★1221★

Satchel Paige
Most notable books for middle readers, 2001 ★317★
Outstanding books for middle readers, 2000 ★326★

Satija; M.P.
Authors that most frequently cite *Libri* publications from 1972 to 1999 ★2723★

Satterlee; Brian
Top pay and benefits for the chief executive and top paid employees at Averett College ★3185★

Satyam Computer
Best small companies worldwide ★384★

Saucedo Elementary School
Illinois elementary schools chosen to be 'demonstration sites' for struggling schools ★4006★

Saucedo Scholastic
Chicago elementary magnet schools with the highest acceptance rates, 2000-01 ★4002★

Sauder; D.N.
Most cited first authors in dermatology journals, 1981 to 1996 ★1871★

Saudi Arabia
Countries of origin for non-U.S. citizens awarded doctorates at U.S. colleges and universities, 1999 ★1901★

Saugatuck High School
All-USA Teacher Teams, Second Team, 2000 ★4400★

Saugus High School
Outstanding suburban public high schools in Metro Boston ★4255★

Saunders; Philip
Individuals producing the most economic education research articles, 1963-1990 ★2166★

Saunders Trades and Tech High School
Outstanding secondary schools in New York, New York ★4191★

Sauter; Marcia
Top pay and benefits for the chief executive and top paid employees at the University of Saint Francis in Indiana ★3562★

The Savage Damsel and the Dwarf
Most notable fiction books for young adults, 2001 ★322★

Savannah College of Art and Design
Institutions censured by the American Association of University Professors, 2001 ★1067★
Highest undergraduate tuition and fees at colleges and universities in Georgia ★1496★

Savannah Country Day School
Outstanding secondary schools in Savannah, Georgia ★4226★

Savannah, GA
Most polite cities in the U.S. ★3086★

Savannah State University
Colleges offering the Thurgood Marshall Scholarship Fund ★221★
State appropriations for Georgia's institutions of higher education, 2000-01 ★1263★

Savannah Technical Institute
Lowest undergraduate tuition and fees at colleges and universities in Georgia ★1497★

The Saving Graces
Longest-running mass market paperback bestsellers, 2000 ★280★

Savion: My Life in Tap
Most notable nonfiction books for young adults, 2001 ★324★

Savvy Management
Most selective internships in the U.S., 2001 ★2610★

Sawaya; Francesca
Radcliffe Institute for Advanced Study fellowship recipient in the field of American literature, 2000-01 ★2442★

Sawtek
Best small companies in the U.S. ★383★

Say; Allen
Outstanding children's picture books, 2000 ★331★

Sayre; April Pulley
Booklist's best science books for children ★310★

Sayre; Philip R.
Top pay and benefits for the chief executive and top paid employees at Western Maryland College ★3614★

SBC Communications
Biggest information technology companies, 2000 ★385★
Business Week's best companies in the United States ★411★
Fortune's highest ranked telecommunications companies, 2000 ★499★
Top telecommunications companies in Standard & Poor's 500, 2001 ★559★
Top public companies with the highest percentage of women board of directors, 2000 ★4458★

Scandalmonger
Booklist's best fiction books for library collections, 2000 ★227★

Scandinavian Journal of Economics
Highest impact economics journals in exhaustible resources from 1980 to 1989 ★2460★
Highest impact economics journals in exhaustible resources from 1990 to 1998 ★2461★

Scanlan, F.S.C.; Bro. Thomas J.
Top pay and benefits for the chief executive and top paid employees at Manhattan College ★3387★

Scanlan, T.O.R.; Rev. Michael
Top pay and benefits for the chief executive and top paid employees at the Franciscan University of Steubenville ★3532★

Scanning the Century: The Penguin Book of the Twentieth Century in Poetry
Booklist's most recommended poetry books, 2001 ★231★

Scar Vegas
Most notable fiction books, 2001 ★284★
Outstanding works of fiction, 2001 ★293★

Scardino; Marjorie
European business moguls considered the best turnaround artists ★443★

Scary Stories 3: More Tales to Chill Your Bones
Most frequently banned books in the 1990s ★745★

Scary Stories Series
American Library Association's most frequently challenged books of the decade ★224★
American Library Associations most frequently challenged books for the 1990s ★742★
People for the American Way's list of most frequently challenged books, 1982-1992 ★747★

Scary Stories to Tell in the Dark
Most frequently banned books in the 1990s ★745★
People for the American Way's list of most frequently challenged books, 1991-1992 ★748★

Scattergood; Hudson B.
Top pay and benefits for the chief executive and top paid employees at Ursinus College ★3591★

Schaafsma; Dianne
Top pay and benefits for the chief executive and top paid employees at Olivet Nazarene University ★3432★

Schaedler; N. John
Top pay and benefits for the chief executive and top paid employees at United States International University ★3587★

Schaefer; Arthur M.
Top pay and benefits for the chief executive and top paid employees at the University of the South ★3572★

Schaefer; Kristina
Top pay and benefits for the chief executive and top paid employees at Simmons College ★3499★

Schaffer; Andrew C.
Top pay and benefits for the chief executive and top paid employees at Dallas Baptist University ★3262★

Schall; Lawrence M.
Top pay and benefits for the chief executive and top paid employees at Swarthmore College ★3514★

Schappert; Phil
Booklist's best science and technology books ★366★

Schar; Stuart
Top pay and benefits for the chief executive and top paid employees at the University of Hartford ★3544★

Schaumburg Community, District 54
Illinois elementary school districts with the highest teacher salaries, 1999 ★3984★

Schaumburg High School
Outstanding secondary schools in Chicago, Illinois ★4110★
Outstanding suburban public high schools in Metro Chicago ★4256★

Schaumburg Township District Library
Highest Hennen's American Public Library Ratings for libraries serving a population of 100,000 to 249,999 ★2698★

Schauss; John A.
Top pay and benefits for the chief executive and top paid employees at Eastern College in Pennsylvania ★3280★

Schechter; Stephen L.
  Top pay and benefits for the chief executive and top paid employees at the Sage Colleges in New York ★3536★
Schembechler; Bo
  Division I-A all-time coaching victories ★126★
Schenectady County Community College
  Lowest undergraduate tuition and fees at colleges and universities in New York ★1538★
  Average faculty salaries for institutions of higher education in New York, 2000-01 ★3719★
Scherer; F.M.
  U.S. academic economists by mean number of citations, 1971-92 ★2176★
  U.S. academic economists by total citations, 1971-92 ★2177★
Schering-Plough
  Fortune's highest ranked pharmaceuticals companies, 2000 ★485★
Schermer; Tracy W.
  Top pay and benefits for the chief executive and top paid employees at Kenyon College ★3359★
Scheuer; James
  Top pay and benefits for the chief executive and top paid employees at Yeshiva University ★3640★
Scheye; Thomas E.
  Top pay and benefits for the chief executive and top paid employees at Loyola College in Maryland ★3379★
Schiffgens; Michelle
  Top pay and benefits for the chief executive and top paid employees at Marycrest International University ★3393★
Schilling; W. A. Hayden
  Top pay and benefits for the chief executive and top paid employees at the College of Wooster ★3531★
Schillo; Stephen A.
  Top pay and benefits for the chief executive and top paid employees at Gannon University ★3302★
Schiowitz; Stanley
  Top pay and benefits for the chief executive and top paid employees at the New York Institute of Technology ★3535★
Schizophrenia Bulletin
  Psychiatry journals by citation impact, 1981-98 ★3054★
  Psychiatry journals by citation impact, 1995-98 ★3055★
  Psychiatry journals by citation impact, 1998 ★3056★
  Psychiatry journals by impact factor, 1981 to 1998 ★3057★
  Psychiatry journals by impact factor, 1994 to 1998 ★3058★
Schlessinger; Joseph
  Most-cited biomedical scientists, 1990-97 ★2382★
Schlogel, S.J.; Rev. J.
  Top pay and benefits for the chief executive and top paid employees at the University of San Francisco ★3566★
Schlueter; David A.
  Top pay and benefits for the chief executive and top paid employees at Saint Mary's University in Texas ★3481★
Schlueter; June
  Top pay and benefits for the chief executive and top paid employees at Lafayette College ★3361★

Schlumberger
  Top recruiters for multidisciplinary engineers jobs for 2000-01 bachelor's degree recipients ★2335★
  Top recruiters for multidisciplinary engineers jobs for 2000-01 master's degree recipients ★2370★
Schmeltekopt; Donald D.
  Top pay and benefits for the chief executive and top paid employees at Baylor University ★3194★
Schmidmaier; D.
  Authors that most frequently cite *Libri* publications from 1972 to 1999 ★2723★
Schmidt; Adeny
  Top pay and benefits for the chief executive and top paid employees at LaSierra University ★3366★
Schmiedicke; Joseph E.
  Top pay and benefits for the chief executive and top paid employees at Edgewood College ★3283★
Schneider, O.S.F.; Sister Mary Lea
  Top pay and benefits for the chief executive and top paid employees at Cardinal Stritch University ★3221★
Schneider; Richard W.
  Top pay and benefits for the chief executive and top paid employees at Norwich University in Vermont ★3424★
Schneider; Robert
  Top pay and benefits for the chief executive and top paid employees at the Maharishi University of Management ★3533★
Schnur; Fred A.
  Top pay and benefits for the chief executive and top paid employees at Teachers College, Columbia University ★3517★
Schoemer; James R.
  Top pay and benefits for the chief executive and top paid employees at Regis University in Colorado ★3454★
Scholarly Publishing
  Most cited printing and publishing serials in technical communication journals from 1988 to 1997 ★4422★
Scholastic
  Publishers with the best industry stocks, 2000 ★300★
  Highest revenues of publicly held book publishers, 1999 ★3072★
  Top children's book publishers, 1999 ★3074★
  Top public companies for women executives, 2000 ★4457★
  Top public companies with the highest percentage of women board of directors, 2000 ★4458★
  Top public companies with the highest percentage of women employees, 2000 ★4459★
Scholz; Joachim
  Top pay and benefits for the chief executive and top paid employees at Washington College ★3606★
School
  Gender breakdown of psychology doctorate recipients, by subfield, 1999 ★1941★
  Psychology doctorates awarded at U.S. colleges and universities, by subfield, 1999 ★2043★
School of the Art Institute of Chicago
  Highest undergraduate tuition and fees at colleges and universities in Illinois ★1500★

U.S. colleges and universities awarding the most English language/literature/letters master's degrees to Asian Americans ★1774★
School bus operation
  Employment growth percentages for selected industries, 1998-2000 ★2294★
School for Contemporary Education
  Outstanding secondary schools in Washington, District of Columbia-Maryland-Virginia-West Virginia ★4249★
School-improvement programs
  Educational program activities expenditures, 2000 ★3992★
School principal
  Most desirable public sector jobs ★2279★
School psychology
  Education doctorates awarded at U.S. colleges and universities, by subfield, 1999 ★1921★
  Gender breakdown of education doctorate recipients, by subfield, 1999 ★1933★
Schoolcraft College
  Average faculty salaries for institutions of higher education without academic ranks in Michigan, 2000-01 ★3752★
Schott; Sally B.
  Top pay and benefits for the chief executive and top paid employees at Georgetown College in Kentucky ★3305★
Schramm; Peter W.
  Top pay and benefits for the chief executive and top paid employees at Ashland University ★3180★
Schreiber; Carl W.
  Top pay and benefits for the chief executive and top paid employees at Biola University ★3203★
Schreiber; Heather
  All-America girls' high school basketball 4th team, 2001 ★173★
Schreiner College
  U.S. News & World Report's best undergraduate fees among western regional liberal arts colleges by discount tuition, 2000 ★1384★
  Academic reputation scores for *U.S. News & World Report*'s top western regional liberal arts colleges, 2000-01 ★1387★
  Acceptance rates for *U.S. News & World Report*'s top western regional liberal arts colleges, 2000-01 ★1388★
  Alumni giving rates at *U.S. News & World Report*'s top western regional liberal arts colleges, 2000-01 ★1389★
  Average freshmen retention rates for *U.S. News & World Report*'s top western regional liberal arts colleges, 2000-01 ★1390★
  Average graduation rates for *U.S. News & World Report*'s top western regional liberal arts colleges, 2000-01 ★1391★
  Percentage of freshmen in the top 25% of their high school class at *U.S. News & World Report*'s top western regional liberal arts colleges, 2000-01 ★1392★
  Percentage of full-time faculty at *U.S. News & World Report*'s top western regional liberal arts colleges, 2000-01 ★1393★
  Proportion of classes having 20 students or less at *U.S. News & World Report*'s top western regional liberal arts colleges, 2000-01 ★1394★
  Student/faculty ratios at *U.S. News & World Report*'s top western regional liberal arts colleges, 2000-01 ★1395★
  U.S. News & World Report's top western regional liberal arts colleges, 2000-01 ★1396★

Average faculty salaries for institutions of higher education in Texas, 2000-01 ★3731★

Schrock; Richard R.
Winner of the American Chemical Society's Arthur C. Cope Awards, 2001 ★795★

Schroeder; John
Top pay and benefits for the chief executive and top paid employees at Viterbo University ★3597★

Schrum; Jake B.
Top pay and benefits for the chief executive and top paid employees at Texas Wesleyan University ★3519★

Schubert; A.
Authors that most frequently cite *Libri* publications from 1972 to 1999 ★2723★

Schuerman; Adam
All-America boys' high school soccer team goalkeepers, 2001 ★167★

Schulman; Mark
Top pay and benefits for the chief executive and top paid employees at Antioch University ★3178★

Schultz; Carl
Top pay and benefits for the chief executive and top paid employees at Houghton College ★3341★

Schultz; John
Top pay and benefits for the chief executive and top paid employees at Westminster College in Missouri ★3616★

Schultz; Peter G.
American Chemical Society 2001 award winners (Group 4) ★754★

Schultz; Vicki
Radcliffe Institute for Advanced Study fellowship recipient in the field of law, 2000-01 ★2621★

Schulumberger
Top internships in the U.S. with the highest compensation, 2001 ★2611★

Schulz; Lawrence E.
Top pay and benefits for the chief executive and top paid employees at St. Andrews Presbyterian College ★3469★

Schumpeter; Joseph
Most cited economists ★2185★

Schure; Matthew
Top pay and benefits for the chief executive and top paid employees at the New York Institute of Technology ★3535★

Schwab; Kenneth L.
Top pay and benefits for the chief executive and top paid employees at the Centenary College of Louisiana ★3523★

Schwartz; Alvin
People for the American Way's list of most frequently challenged authors, 1982-1992 ★746★

Schwartz; Kevin
All-USA College Academic First Team, 2001 ★2★

Schwartz; Murray
Top pay and benefits for the chief executive and top paid employees at Emerson College ★3287★

Schwarz; Helmut
American Chemical Society 2001 award winners (Group 4) ★754★

Science
Academic Achievement comparison of 12th graders, 1998 ★1★

Top biological science majors for accepted applicants to U.S. medical schools, 1999-2000 ★2851★
Top physical science majors for accepted applicants to U.S. medical schools, 1999-2000 ★2855★
Molecular biology and genetics journals with the highest impact, 1992-96 ★204★
Most cited science serials in technical communication journals from 1988 to 1997 ★4424★

Science & Arts; University of
State appropriations for Oklahoma's institutions of higher education, 2000-01 ★1289★

Science Applications International
Fortune's highest ranked computer and data services companies, 2000 ★453★
Largest private companies, 2000 ★523★

Science and Arts of Oklahoma; University of
Average faculty salaries for institutions of higher education in Oklahoma, 2000-01 ★3723★

Science education
Gender breakdown of teaching fields doctorate recipients, by subfield, 1999 ★1943★
Teaching fields doctorates awarded at U.S. colleges and universities, by subfield, 1999 ★2046★
Education and educational research journals by citation impact, 1999 ★2237★

Science and engineering education
Proposed fiscal 2002 appropriations for the National Science Foundation ★3109★

Science Hill High School
Outstanding secondary schools in Johnson City-Kingsport-Bristol, Tennessee-Virginia ★4157★

Science and Its Times: Understanding the Social Significance of Scientific Discovery
Outstanding reference sources, 2000 ★370★
Outstanding reference sources, 2001 ★371★

Science/nature
Subjects students most want to see on classroom TV ★4051★

Science News
Most selective internships in the U.S., 2001 ★2610★

Science/technology
Subject areas with the highest library expenditures/circulation ★306★

Sciences
Expected starting salaries of 2000-01 bachelor's degree recipients, by general major ★3130★

Sciences in Philadelphia; University of the
Average faculty salaries for institutions of higher education in Pennsylvania, 2000-01 ★3725★

Scientific American
Most cited technology serials in technical communication journals from 1988 to 1997 ★4427★

Scientific American Desk Reference
Outstanding reference sources, 2001 ★371★

Scientific-Atlanta
Business Week's best performing companies with the highest 3-year shareholder returns ★418★
Top telecommunications companies in Standard & Poor's 500, 2001 ★559★

Scientist
Information and library science journals by citation impact, 1995-99 ★2725★

Scientometrics
Information and library science journals by citation impact, 1999 ★2726★

Scoby; Jerry L.
Top pay and benefits for the chief executive and top paid employees at Alma College ★3171★

Scotland
Institute for Scientific Information periodical prices by country, 2001 ★2922★

Scott; Arthur
Top pay and benefits for the chief executive and top paid employees at Marlboro College ★3391★

Scott Community College
Lowest undergraduate tuition and fees at colleges and universities in Iowa ★1505★

Scott; H. Denman
Top pay and benefits for the chief executive and top paid employees at Brown University ★3211★

Scott; Hazel
Top pay and benefits for the chief executive and top paid employees at Occidental College ★3428★

Scott; Leon L.
Top pay and benefits for the chief executive and top paid employees at Hampton University ★3323★

Scott; Richard D.
Top pay and benefits for the chief executive and top paid employees at Baylor University ★3194★

Scott; Sylvester
Top pay and benefits for the chief executive and top paid employees at Wheeling Jesuit University ★3622★

Scottsdale Community College
Lowest undergraduate tuition and fees at colleges and universities in Arizona ★1483★

The Scrambled States of America
Most notable children's videos, 2001 ★2889★

Scranton; University of
U.S. News & World Report's northern regional universities with the highest alumni giving rates, 2000-01 ★1418★
U.S. News & World Report's northern regional universities with the highest average graduation rates, 2000-01 ★1419★
U.S. News & World Report's northern regional universities with the highest freshmen retention rates, 2000-01 ★1420★
U.S. News & World Report's northern regional universities with the highest percentage of freshmen in the top 25% of their high school class, 2000-01 ★1421★
U.S. News & World Report's top northern regional universities, 2000-01 ★1425★
U.S. News & World Report's best undergraduate fees among northern regional universities by discount tuition, 2000 ★1428★
Average faculty salaries for institutions of higher education in Pennsylvania, 2000-01 ★3725★

Scripps College
U.S. colleges and universities where students study the most ★1003★
U.S. News & World Report's national liberal arts colleges with the best financial resources rank, 2000-01 ★1322★
U.S. News & World Report's national liberal arts colleges with the highest acceptance rates, 2000-01 ★1328★

U.S. News & World Report's national liberal arts colleges with the highest alumni giving rank, 2000-01 ★1329★

U.S. News & World Report's national liberal arts colleges with the highest percentage of alumni support, 2000-01 ★1331★

U.S. News & World Report's national liberal arts colleges with the highest proportion of classes having 50 or more students, 2000-01 ★1334★

U.S. News & World Report's national liberal arts colleges with students most in debt, 1999 ★1386★

Highest undergraduate tuition and fees at colleges and universities in California ★1486★

Women's colleges granting physics bachelor's degrees, 2000 ★2982★

Average faculty salaries for institutions of higher education in California, 2000-01 ★3692★

Scripps Research Institute
Winner of the American Chemical Society's Arthur C. Cope Awards, 2001 ★795★

Scully; Nicholas W.
Top pay and benefits for the chief executive and top paid employees at Christian Brothers University ★3233★

SDL
Business Week's best companies in terms of share-price gain ★409★

Sea Soup: Zooplankton
Smithsonian's best books for children ages 10 and up ★365★

Seaboard
Fortune's highest ranked food production companies, 2000 ★464★

Seagate Technology
Fortune's highest ranked computer peripherals companies, 2000 ★454★

Seagram
Business Week's best companies in Canada ★390★

Sealed Air
Fortune's highest ranked rubber and plastic products companies, 2000 ★492★

Top containers and packaging companies in Standard & Poor's 500, 2001 ★537★

Seaman
Most desirable jobs in agriculture ★2268★

Seaman; Lois Kaplan
All-USA Teacher Teams, Third Team, 2000 ★4401★

Search engines
Web pages with the highest access percentages ★2608★

Searchers' Selection of Search Keys
Journal of the American Society for Information Science's best papers, by citations per year ★2728★

Sears, Roebuck
Fortune's highest ranked general merchandisers, 2000 ★468★

Highly recommended public companies for women executives, 2000 ★4453★

Seaside, FL
Best 'quirky' places to live ★3083★

A Season on the Reservation: My Sojourn with the White Mountain Apache
Library Journal's best nonfiction audiobooks, 2000 ★243★

Seat Pagine Gialle
Business Week's best companies in Italy ★397★

The Seat of the Soul
Longest-running trade paperback bestsellers, 2000 ★282★

Seattle Pacific University
Highest undergraduate tuition and fees at colleges and universities in Washington ★1566★

U.S. News & World Report's western regional universities with the highest acceptance rates, 2000-01 ★1579★

U.S. News & World Report's western regional universities with the highest percentage of freshmen in the top 25% of their high school class, 2000-01 ★1583★

Average faculty salaries for institutions of higher education in Washington, 2000-01 ★3736★

Seattle/Tacoma
American cities with the highest percentage of people with Internet access ★2572★

U.S. market areas with the highest percentage of adults having internet access ★2607★

The Seattle Times
Most selective internships in the U.S., 2001 ★2610★

Seattle University
Highest undergraduate tuition and fees at colleges and universities in Washington ★1566★

U.S. News & World Report's western regional universities with the best academic reputation scores, 2000-01 ★1577★

U.S. News & World Report's western regional universities with the highest percentage of full-time faculty, 2000-01 ★1584★

U.S. colleges and universities awarding the most first professional degrees to Native Americans ★1846★

U.S. colleges and universities awarding the most law and legal studies first professional degrees to Native Americans ★1855★

U.S. colleges and universities awarding the most education doctorate degrees to Asian Americans ★2109★

Average faculty salaries for institutions of higher education in Washington, 2000-01 ★3736★

Seattle, WA
America's most wired cities, 2001 ★2573★

U.S. cities with the most wired households, 2001 ★2606★

Best big cities to live in ★3075★

Most polite cities in the U.S. ★3086★

The Second Escape of Arthur Cooper
Smithsonian's best books for children ages 6 to 10 ★364★

Secondary education
Education doctorates awarded at U.S. colleges and universities, by subfield, 1999 ★1921★

Gender breakdown of education doctorate recipients, by subfield, 1999 ★1933★

Secondary teachers
Employment outlook for the year 2005 for selected occupations ★2297★

The Secret Handshake: Mastering the Politics of the Business Inner Circle
Library Journal's most notable books on job performance, 2000 ★254★

The Secret Life of Fishes: From Angels to Zebras on the Coral Reef
Smithsonian's best books for children ages 6 to 10 ★364★

The Secret Life of Teens: Young People Speak Out about Their Lives
Most notable nonfiction books for reluctant young adult readers, 2001 ★323★

Secretary
Jobs with the most stringent quotas ★2259★

Section 529 Plans
Best ways to save for college ★843★

Securitas
Business Week's best companies in Sweden ★404★

Securities, commodities, and financial services sales agents
Projections for the fastest growing occupations requiring a bachelor's degree or more from 1998 to 2008 ★2292★

Securities and financial services sales agents
Fastest growing occupations, 1998-2008 ★2302★

Projected employment growth for selected occupations that require a bachelor's degree or more, 1998-2008 ★2317★

Security and commodity brokers
Employment growth percentages for selected industries, 1998-2000 ★2294★

Industries with the highest percentage of projected employment growth from 1998 through 2008 ★2305★

Security and commodity exchanges and services
Employment growth percentages for selected industries, 1998-2000 ★2294★

Sedimentology
Geology journals with the greatest impact measure, 1981-98 ★2525★

Geology journals with the greatest impact measure, 1994-98 ★2526★

Sedlik; Earl
Top pay and benefits for the chief executive and top paid employees at City University in Washington ★3234★

Seibert; Mary Lee
Top pay and benefits for the chief executive and top paid employees at Ithaca College ★3351★

Seidel; Ethan
Top pay and benefits for the chief executive and top paid employees at Western Maryland College ★3614★

Seidelman; James E.
Top pay and benefits for the chief executive and top paid employees at Westminster College in Utah ★3618★

Seifert; Werner
European business moguls considered the best empire builders ★441★

Seiya; Munakata
Japan's ten great educators ★2234★

Sekhar; Lalaigam N.
Top pay and benefits for the chief executive and top paid employees at George Washington University ★3304★

Selected Stories
Canada's best fiction selections of the 20th century ★233★

The Selected Stories of Mavis Gallant
Canada's best fiction selections of the 20th century ★233★

Self; Bill E.
Top pay and benefits for the chief executive and top paid employees at the University of Tulsa ★3573★

Selfe; Charles
Booklist's best science and technology books ★366★

Seligman; David B.
Top pay and benefits for the chief executive and top paid employees at Ripon College ★3459★

Selk; Vicke
Top pay and benefits for the chief executive and top paid employees at Pitzer College ★3441★

Sellitto; Anthony
Top pay and benefits for the chief executive and top paid employees at Hawaii Pacific University ★3330★

Sellman Middle School
Outstanding secondary schools in Cincinnati, Ohio-Kentucky-Indiana ★4112★

Semenza; Michael
Top pay and benefits for the chief executive and top paid employees at Salve Regina University ★3489★

Seminars in Hematology
Hematology journals with the greatest impact measure, 1981-98 ★2808★

Seminars in Nephrology
Urology and nephrology journals with the greatest impact measure, 1994-98 ★2817★

Seminole State College
Lowest undergraduate tuition and fees at colleges and universities in Oklahoma ★1546★
Average faculty salaries for institutions of higher education without academic ranks in Oklahoma, 2000-01 ★3763★

Semtech
Best small companies in the U.S. ★383★
Companies with the best two-year total returns since 1998 ★436★

Sen; A.K.
U.S. academic economists by mean number of citations, 1971-92 ★2176★
U.S. academic economists by total citations, 1971-92 ★2177★

Send One Angel Down
Most notable fiction books for young adults, 2001 ★322★

Seneca Free Library
Highest Hennen's American Public Library Ratings for libraries serving a population of 1,000 to 2,499 ★2692★

Senior woman administrator
African American college athletics senior administrators, by gender, 1999-2000 ★119★
College athletics senior administrators, by gender, 1999-2000 ★123★
Minority college athletics senior administrators, by gender, 1999-2000 ★134★
Percentage of African American athletic administrators at NCAA Division I institutions, 1999 ★138★
Percentage of African American athletic administrators at NCAA Division II institutions, 1999 ★139★
Percentage of African American athletic administrators at NCAA Division III institutions, 1999 ★140★

Senuys; Patrick W.
Most-cited researchers in cardiology, 1981-1998 ★2874★

A Separate Peace
Most frequently banned books in the 1990s ★745★

Sepe; James
Top pay and benefits for the chief executive and top paid employees at Santa Clara University in California ★3491★

Sequa
Fortune's highest ranked aerospace companies, 2000 ★446★

Sequoyah Middle School
Outstanding secondary schools in Oklahoma City, Oklahoma ★4196★

Serena Software
Best small companies in the U.S. ★383★
Top companies in terms of growth, 2000 ★534★

A Series of Unfortunate Events
Publishers Weekly Off-the-Cuff Awards winner for favorite series, 2000 ★348★

Serletti; Joseph M.
Top pay and benefits for the chief executive and top paid employees at the University of Rochester ★3560★

Serono
Business Week's best companies in Switzerland ★405★

The Serpent Slayer and Other Stories of Strong Women
Publishers Weekly Off-the-Cuff Awards winner for best anthology or collection, 2000 ★335★

Service
Employment change projections by major occupational group from 1998 to 2008 ★2288★
Employment projections by major occupational group for 2008 ★2291★
Percentages for projected employment growth by occupational group, 1998-2008 ★2314★
Projected employment growth by occupational group, 1998-2008 ★2316★
Internet use by major occupational group, 1998 ★2587★

Service; Allan L.
Top pay and benefits for the chief executive and top paid employees at Regis University in Colorado ★3454★

Service Encounters and Service Relationships: Implications for Research
Most influential articles in the *Journal of Business Research*, 1985-1999 ★697★
Most influential articles in the *Journal of Business Research* from 1990 to 1994 ★699★

ServiceMaster
Fortune's highest ranked outsourcing services companies, 2000 ★483★

Services
Internet use by industry, 1998 ★2586★

Services (excluding health)
Industries in Illinois with the highest projected worker increase through 2006 ★2304★

Set designer
Most desirable jobs in the arts ★2277★

Set in Darkness
Library Journal's best mystery titles, 2000 ★242★

Seton Hall University
U.S. catholic universities with the highest enrollment, 1999 ★864★
U.S. colleges and universities least accepting of alternative lifestyles ★985★
U.S. colleges and universities where a large portion of the student body drink beer ★991★
U.S. colleges and universities where students and the local community relate well ★999★
U.S. colleges and universities where students study the least ★1002★
U.S. colleges and universities with a diverse student body ★1012★
U.S. colleges and universities with harmonious race/class interaction ★1026★
U.S. colleges and universities with poor library facilities ★1028★
U.S. colleges and universities with the least attractive campuses ★1037★
Highest undergraduate tuition and fees at colleges and universities in New Jersey ★1533★
U.S. colleges and universities awarding the most communications master's degrees to African Americans ★1763★
First-year student's choices for exemplary doctoral-intensive universities ★2535★
Academics' choices for best health law programs, 2001 ★2629★

Seton Hill College
Average faculty salaries for institutions of higher education in Pennsylvania, 2000-01 ★3725★

Seurkamp; Mary Pat
Top pay and benefits for the chief executive and top paid employees at the College of Notre Dame in Maryland ★3527★

The Seven Continents
Booklist's most recommended geography series for young people, 2000 ★313★

Seven-Eleven Japan
Business Week's best companies in Japan ★398★

The Seven Habits of Highly Effective People
Retail audiobook titles selling 1.5 million copies ★302★

Seven Spools of Thread: A Kwanzaa Story
Most notable books for young readers, 2001 ★319★

Seven Stories Press
Small publishers with the highest sales growth between 1997 and 1999 ★3073★

Seventh-day Adventist
Religious preference of incoming freshmen, 2000 ★1061★

Severtson; Erving S.
Top pay and benefits for the chief executive and top paid employees at Pacific Lutheran University ★3436★

Sewanhaka High School
Outstanding secondary schools in Long Island, New York ★4165★

Seward County Community College
Lowest undergraduate tuition and fees at colleges and universities in Kansas ★1507★

Seward Elementary School
Illinois elementary schools chosen to be 'demonstration sites' for struggling schools ★4006★

Sewickley Academy
Outstanding secondary schools in Pittsburgh, Pennsylvania ★4204★

Sewing machine operators, garment
Occupations with the highest decline in employment, 1998-2008 ★2310★

Seymour Middle School
Outstanding secondary schools in Appleton-Oshkosh-Neenah, Wisconsin ★4085★
Outstanding secondary schools in Eau Claire, Wisconsin ★4127★

Seymour; Susan
Top pay and benefits for the chief executive and top paid employees at Pitzer College ★3441★

SGI
Top internships in the U.S. with the highest compensation, 2001 ★2611★

Sgrecci; Carl
Top pay and benefits for the chief executive and top paid employees at Ithaca College ★3351★

Shack; Bruce R.
Top pay and benefits for the chief executive and top paid employees at Vanderbilt University ★3593★

Shackelford; Jeanette
Top pay and benefits for the chief executive and top paid employees at Wesleyan College in Georgia ★3611★

Shah; Grishma
All-USA College Academic Third Team, 2001 ★4★

Shaker Junior High School
Outstanding secondary schools in Albany-Schenectady-Troy, New York ★4079★

Shakespeare's Scribe
Most notable fiction books for young adults, 2001 ★322★
Smithsonian's best books for children ages 10 and up ★365★

Shakopee Junior High School
Outstanding secondary schools in Minneapolis-St. Paul, Minnesota-Wisconsin ★4181★

Shaler Area Middle School
Outstanding secondary schools in Pittsburgh, Pennsylvania ★4204★

Shaler; Michael D.
Top pay and benefits for the chief executive and top paid employees at Marywood University ★3396★

Shannon; Stephen
Top pay and benefits for the chief executive and top paid employees at the University of New England ★3552★

Shaping the Earth
Booklist's best science books for children ★310★

Shapiro; Harold T.
Presidents with the highest pay at Research I and II universities, 1998-99 ★3162★
Top pay and benefits for the chief executive and top paid employees at Princeton University ★3446★

Shapiro; Judith R.
Top pay and benefits for the chief executive and top paid employees at Barnard College ★3191★

Shaughnessy; Mary Angela
Top pay and benefits for the chief executive and top paid employees at Spalding University ★3506★

Shaver; Judson
Top pay and benefits for the chief executive and top paid employees at Iona College ★3350★

Shaw; Byers W.
Most-cited researchers in surgery/transplantation, 1981-1998 ★2878★

Shaw; George Bernard
Top playwrights of the twentieth century ★4436★

Shaw Industries
Fortune's highest ranked textiles companies, 2000 ★501★

Shaw; Kenneth A.
Top pay and benefits for the chief executive and top paid employees at Syracuse University ★3516★

Shaw; Susanne I.
Top pay and benefits for the chief executive and top paid employees at Moravian College ★3407★

Shaw University
Division II NCAA colleges with the 100% graduation rates for men's basketball players, 1993-94 ★943★
Average faculty salaries for institutions of higher education in North Carolina, 2000-01 ★3720★

Shawnee Community College
Lowest undergraduate tuition and fees at colleges and universities in Illinois ★1501★

Shawnee Mission South High School
Outstanding secondary schools in Kansas City, Missouri-Kansas ★4158★

Shawnee State University
State appropriations for Ohio's institutions of higher education, 2000-01 ★1288★
Average faculty salaries for institutions of higher education in Ohio, 2000-01 ★3722★

Shazor; Ernest
All-American boy's high school football defensive backs, 2000 ★180★
All-American boy's high school football team, 2000 ★187★

Shearer; Charles L.
Top pay and benefits for the chief executive and top paid employees at Transylvania University ★3575★

Sheeran; Janet A.
Top pay and benefits for the chief executive and top paid employees at Saint Michael's College ★3483★

Sheeran, S.J.; Rev. Michael J.
Top pay and benefits for the chief executive and top paid employees at Regis University in Colorado ★3454★

Sheeran, S.T.D.; Msgr. Robert
Top pay and benefits for the chief executive and top paid employees at Seton Hall University ★3496★

Sheet metal worker
Jobs with the highest unemployment ★2256★
Most desirable jobs in construction trades ★2272★

Sheff; Paul
Top pay and benefits for the chief executive and top paid employees at College of the Holy Cross ★3247★

Shefferly; William G.
Top pay and benefits for the chief executive and top paid employees at Aquinas College in Michigan ★3179★

Shelby State Community College
Lowest undergraduate tuition and fees at colleges and universities in Tennessee ★1559★

Sheldon Jackson College
Undergraduate tuition and fees at colleges and universities in Alaska ★1481★

Shell Oil
Fortune's highest ranked petroleum refining companies, 2000 ★484★

Shell Transport & Trading
Business Week's best companies in Britain ★389★
Business Week's best companies in terms of return on equity ★407★

Shelley; L.I.
Most cited authors in the journal *Crime, Law, and Social Change*, 1990 to 1995 ★1618★

Shellhamer; Samuel A.
Top pay and benefits for the chief executive and top paid employees at Wheaton College in Illinois ★3620★

Shelton; Earnest
All-America boys' high school basketball 4th team, 2001 ★164★

Shelton; Eric
All-American boy's high school football running backs, 2000 ★186★

Shelton; Robert D.
Top pay and benefits for the chief executive and top paid employees at Loyola College in Maryland ★3379★

Shelton State Community College
Lowest undergraduate tuition and fees at colleges and universities in Alabama ★1480★

Shenandoah University
Highest undergraduate tuition and fees at colleges and universities in Virginia ★1564★
Average faculty salaries for institutions of higher education in Virginia, 2000-01 ★3735★

Shenendehowa High School
Outstanding secondary schools in New York, New York ★4191★

Shenker; Joseph
Top pay and benefits for the chief executive and top paid employees at Long Island University ★3378★

Shepaug Valley High School
Outstanding secondary schools in Danbury, Connecticut ★4121★

Shepherd College
State appropriations for West Virginia's institutions of higher education, 2000-01 ★1301★
Lowest undergraduate tuition and fees at colleges and universities in West Virginia ★1569★

Shepherd Hill Regional High School
Outstanding suburban public high schools in Metro Boston ★4255★

Shepsle; Kenneth A.
Authors most frequently published in *American Political Science Review*, 1974-94 ★3047★

Sher; Alvin I.
Top pay and benefits for the chief executive and top paid employees at Ohio Wesleyan University ★3430★

Sherbrooke; University of
Best Canadian universities overall, 2000 ★1149★
Canadian medical/doctoral universities by alumni support, 2000 ★1172★
Canadian medical/doctoral universities by award-winning faculty members, 2000 ★1173★
Canadian medical/doctoral universities by class size at the first- and second-year level, 2000 ★1174★
Canadian medical/doctoral universities by class size at the third- and forth-year level, 2000 ★1175★
Canadian medical/doctoral universities by classes taught by tenured faculty, 2000 ★1176★
Canadian medical/doctoral universities by faculty members with Ph.D.'s, 2000 ★1177★

Canadian medical/doctoral universities by international graduate students, 2000 ★1178★
Canadian medical/doctoral universities by library acquisitions, 2000 ★1179★
Canadian medical/doctoral universities by library expenses, 2000 ★1180★
Canadian medical/doctoral universities by library holdings, 2000 ★1181★
Canadian medical/doctoral universities by library holdings per student, 2000 ★1182★
Canadian medical/doctoral universities by medical/science grants per faculty member, 2000 ★1184★
Canadian medical/doctoral universities by operating budget per student, 2000 ★1185★
Canadian medical/doctoral universities by percentage of operating budget allocated to scholarships, 2000 ★1186★
Canadian medical/doctoral universities by percentage of operating budget allocated to student services, 2000 ★1187★
Canadian medical/doctoral universities by reputation, 2000 ★1188★
Canadian medical/doctoral universities by social science/humanities grants per faculty member, 2000 ★1189★
Canadian medical/doctoral universities by students from out of province, 2000 ★1190★
Canadian medical/doctoral universities by students winning national awards, 2000 ★1191★
Canadian universities with the lowest total cost, 2000 ★1218★
Top Canadian medical/doctoral universities, 2000 ★1221★

Sheridan College
Undergraduate tuition and fees at colleges and universities in Wyoming ★1572★

Sheriffs and deputy sheriffs
Projected employment growth for selected occupations that require long-term on-the-job training, 1998-2008 ★2320★

Sherman; Cindy
Best living artists ★73★
Highly influential artists of the 20th century ★76★

Sherman; Gary L.
Top pay and benefits for the chief executive and top paid employees at Averett College ★3185★

Sherman; Lawrence W.
Most-cited scholars in police studies articles/research notes ★2624★

Sherman; L.W.
Most cited authors in the journal *Australian and New Zealand Journals of Criminology*, 1990 to 1995 ★1613★
Most cited authors in the journal *Crime and Delinquency*, 1990 to 1995 ★1616★
Most cited authors in the journal *Crime and Justice*, 1990 to 1995 ★1617★
Most cited authors in the journal *Criminal Justice Review*, 1990 to 1995 ★1620★
Most cited authors in the journal *Journal of Research in Crime and Delinquency*, 1990 to 1995 ★1629★
Most cited authors in the journal *Justice Quarterly*, 1990 to 1995 ★1630★
Most cited authors in three criminal justice journals ★1633★

Sherwin-Williams
Top recruiters for art jobs for 2000-01 bachelor's degree recipients ★80★

Fortune's highest ranked chemicals companies, 2000 ★452★
Top housing and real estate companies in Standard & Poor's 500, 2001 ★543★
Top recruiters for business administration jobs for 2000-01 bachelor's degree recipients ★554★
Top recruiters for manufacturing management jobs for 2000-01 bachelor's degree recipients ★683★
Top recruiters for marketing jobs for 2000-01 bachelor's degree recipients ★684★
Top recruiters for health jobs for 2000-01 bachelor's degree recipients ★2541★
Top recruiters for hospitality/hotel/restaurant management jobs for 2000-01 bachelor's degree recipients ★2558★
Top recruiters for liberal arts jobs for 2000-01 bachelor's degree recipients ★2675★

Shi; David E.
Top pay and benefits for the chief executive and top paid employees at Furman University ★3300★

Shick; Richard
Top pay and benefits for the chief executive and top paid employees at Canisius College ★3219★

Shickle; Richard C.
Top pay and benefits for the chief executive and top paid employees at Shenandoah University ★3497★

Shields; William A.
Top pay and benefits for the chief executive and top paid employees at Rockford College in Illinois ★3463★

Shigeru; Nambara
Japan's ten great educators ★2234★

Shilling Jr.; Roy B.
Presidents with the highest pay at Baccalaureate I colleges, 1998-99 ★3159★
Top pay and benefits for the chief executive and top paid employees at Southwestern University in Texas ★3505★

Shingler; Arthur L.
Top pay and benefits for the chief executive and top paid employees at Point Loma Nazarene University ★3442★

Ship of Destiny
Booklist's most recommended science fiction/fantasy books ★232★

Shippensburg University
Average faculty salaries for institutions of higher education in Pennsylvania, 2000-01 ★3725★

Shippensburg University of Pennsylvania
U.S. News & World Report's northern regional universities with the highest alumni giving rates, 2000-01 ★1418★
U.S. News & World Report's northern regional universities with the highest percentage of full-time faculty, 2000-01 ★1422★
U.S. News & World Report's top public northern regional universities, 2000-01 ★1426★

Shirer; William
Best U.S. works of journalism in the 20th century ★2769★

Shirvani; Hassan
Top pay and benefits for the chief executive and top paid employees at the University of Saint Thomas in Texas ★3564★

Shiva's Fire
Outstanding children's fiction books, 2000 ★329★

Shockley; D.J.
All-American boy's high school football quarterbacks, 2000 ★184★

Shoe maker/repairer
Jobs considered the loneliest ★2244★
Jobs with the worst outlook scores ★2262★

Shoe Pavilion
Companies with the worst two-year total returns since 1998 ★437★

Shoemaker; Herman
Top pay and benefits for the chief executive and top paid employees at the University of Mobile ★3551★

Shorewood High School
Outstanding secondary schools in Seattle-Bellevue-Everett, Washington ★4227★

Shorter College
Average faculty salaries for institutions of higher education in Georgia, 2000-01 ★3697★

Shoup; Robert
Top pay and benefits for the chief executive and top paid employees at California Lutheran University ★3216★

Showalter; Shirley H.
Top pay and benefits for the chief executive and top paid employees at Goshen College ★3313★

Shpunt; Loretta
Top pay and benefits for the chief executive and top paid employees at Trinity College in Washington D.C. ★3578★

Shropshire; William O.
Top pay and benefits for the chief executive and top paid employees at Oglethorpe University ★3429★

Shuart; James M.
Presidents with the highest pay at Doctoral I and II universities, 1998-99 ★3160★
Top pay and benefits for the chief executive and top paid employees at Hofstra University ★3335★

Shuck; Jerry M.
Top pay and benefits for the chief executive and top paid employees at Case Western Reserve University ★3225★

Shuker Jr.; Arthur T.
Top pay and benefits for the chief executive and top paid employees at LaRoche College ★3364★

Shulamith High School for Girls
Outstanding secondary schools in New York, New York ★4191★

Si Tanka College
U.S. tribal colleges ★1445★

Sidlin; Murry
Top pay and benefits for the chief executive and top paid employees at Pacific University in Oregon ★3437★

Siebel Systems
Business Week's best performing companies with the highest 1-year sales performance ★414★
Information technology companies giving the best returns, 2000 ★522★
Software companies with the fastest growth, 2000 ★528★
Top information technology companies, 2000 ★544★
Top office equipment and computers companies in Standard & Poor's 500, 2001 ★551★

Siegel; Sharon G.
Top pay and benefits for the chief executive and top paid employees at Amherst College ★3175★

Siegfried; J. J.
Individuals producing the most economic education research articles, 1963-1990 ★2166★

Siemens
Business Week's best companies in Germany ★394★
Fortune's highest ranked electronics and electrical equipment companies, 2000 ★460★

Siena College
Division I NCAA colleges with the highest graduation rates for female athletes, 1990-91 to 1993-94 ★931★
Division I NCAA colleges with the highest graduation rates for female basketball players, 1990-91 to 1993-94 ★932★
Average faculty salaries for institutions of higher education in New York, 2000-01 ★3719★

Siena Heights University
Average faculty salaries for institutions of higher education in Michigan, 2000-01 ★3709★

Sierra Nevada College
Undergraduate tuition and fees at colleges and universities in Nevada ★1530★

Sievert; MaryEllen
Library and information science faculty with the most journal articles, 1993-1998 ★2711★

SIGCHI Bulletin
Most cited business serials in technical communication journals from 1988 to 1997 ★4417★

Sigethy; Robert
Top pay and benefits for the chief executive and top paid employees at Marymount University ★3395★

Sigmen; Mary
Top pay and benefits for the chief executive and top paid employees at Saint Martin's College in Washington ★3479★

The Sign Painter
Booklist's best art books for young people ★308★
Outstanding children's picture books, 2000 ★331★

Signature Eyewear
Companies with the worst two-year total returns since 1998 ★437★

Signet
Mass market paperback bestsellers by publishing house, 2000 ★283★

Silas Deane Middle School
Outstanding secondary schools in Hartford, Connecticut ★4147★

Silber; Cathy
Radcliffe Institute for Advanced Study fellowship recipient in the field of Asian literature, 2000-01 ★2613★

Silberman; Joellen
Top pay and benefits for the chief executive and top paid employees at Kalamazoo College ★3358★

Silent Sentinels
Outstanding videos for library collections, 2000 ★2892★

Silent to the Bone
Most notable fiction books for young adults, 2001 ★322★
Outstanding books for older readers, 2000 ★327★
Outstanding children's fiction books, 2000 ★329★
Publishers Weekly Off-the-Cuff Awards winners for best novel for older teens, 2000 ★361★

Silhouette
Paperback bestsellers by corporation, 2000 ★296★

Silva; Dennis
Top pay and benefits for the chief executive and top paid employees at Nazareth College of Rochester ★3416★

Silvagni; Anthony
Top pay and benefits for the chief executive and top paid employees at Nova Southeastern University ★3426★

Silver City, NM
Best small towns to live in ★3085★

Silver; Jay
Top pay and benefits for the chief executive and top paid employees at Saint Thomas University in Florida ★3486★

Silver Lake College
Average faculty salaries for institutions of higher education in Wisconsin, 2000-01 ★3738★

Silver; Rae
Top pay and benefits for the chief executive and top paid employees at Barnard College ★3191★

Silverman; Robert
Top pay and benefits for the chief executive and top paid employees at Emerson College ★3287★

Silverstein; Shel
People for the American Way's list of most frequently challenged authors, 1982-1992 ★746★

Simcock; Manford
Top pay and benefits for the chief executive and top paid employees at Walla Walla College ★3601★

Simien; Wayne
All-America boys' high school basketball 2nd team, 2001 ★162★

Simmons College
U.S. News & World Report's northern regional universities with the best student/faculty ratios, 2000-01 ★1416★
U.S. News & World Report's northern regional universities with the highest proportion of classes with 20 students of less, 2000-01 ★1423★
U.S. News & World Report's best undergraduate fees among northern regional universities by discount tuition, 2000 ★1428★
Average faculty salaries for institutions of higher education in Massachusetts, 2000-01 ★3708★

Simmons; Elizabeth
Radcliffe Institute for Advanced Study fellowship recipient in the field of physics, 2000-01 ★2970★

Simmons; Marvin
All-American boy's high school football linebackers, 2000 ★182★

Simmons; Richard L.
Most-cited researchers in surgery/transplantation, 1981-1998 ★2878★

Simmons; Russell
Most influential African Americans in business ★526★

Simmons; Ruth
Presidents with the highest pay at Baccalaureate I colleges, 1998-99 ★3159★
Top pay and benefits for the chief executive and top paid employees at Smith College ★3501★

Simmons University
Comparison of library and information science programs composite rankings with *U.S. News & World Report* survey ★2709★
Library and information science programs with the most citations to journal articles, 1993-1998 ★2712★
Library and information science programs with the most journal articles, 1993-1998 ★2713★
Library and information science programs with the most journal articles per capita, 1993-1998 ★2714★
Library and information science programs with the most per capita citations to journal articles, 1993-1998 ★2715★

Simo; Chefik
All-America boys' high school soccer team defenders, 2001 ★165★

Simon; Albert
Top pay and benefits for the chief executive and top paid employees Saint Francis College in Pennsylvania ★3641★

Simon & Schuster
Hardcover bestsellers by corporation, 2000 ★239★
Hardcover bestsellers by publishing house, 2000 ★240★
Paperback bestsellers by corporation, 2000 ★296★
Publishers, journals and proceedings with the lowest citations (Class 6) ★2571★
Highest revenues of publicly held book publishers, 1999 ★3072★
Top children's book publishers, 1999 ★3074★

Simon & Schuster/Fireside
Trade paperback bestsellers by publishing house, 2000 ★307★

Simon Fraser University
Best Canadian universities for producing leaders of tomorrow, 2000 ★1148★
Best Canadian universities overall, 2000 ★1149★
Best Canadian universities that are the most innovative, 2000 ★1150★
Best Canadian universities with the highest quality, 2000 ★1151★
Canadian comprehensive universities best at producing leaders of tomorrow, 2000 ★1152★
Canadian comprehensive universities by alumni support, 2000 ★1153★
Canadian comprehensive universities by award-winning faculty members, 2000 ★1154★
Canadian comprehensive universities by class size at the first- and second-year level, 2000 ★1155★
Canadian comprehensive universities by class size at the third- and forth-year level, 2000 ★1156★
Canadian comprehensive universities by classes taught by tenured faculty, 2000 ★1157★
Canadian comprehensive universities by faculty members with Ph.D.'s, 2000 ★1158★
Canadian comprehensive universities by international graduate students, 2000 ★1159★
Canadian comprehensive universities by library acquisitions, 2000 ★1160★
Canadian comprehensive universities by library expenses, 2000 ★1161★
Canadian comprehensive universities by library holdings per student, 2000 ★1162★
Canadian comprehensive universities by operating budget per student, 2000 ★1163★

SIMON

Canadian comprehensive universities by percentage of operating budget allocated to scholarships, 2000 ★1164★
Canadian comprehensive universities by percentage of operating budget allocated to student services, 2000 ★1165★
Canadian comprehensive universities by social science/humanities grants per faculty member, 2000 ★1166★
Canadian comprehensive universities by students from out of province, 2000 ★1167★
Canadian comprehensive universities by students winning national awards, 2000 ★1168★
Canadian comprehensive universities that are the best overall, 2000 ★1169★
Canadian comprehensive universities that are the most innovative, 2000 ★1170★
Canadian comprehensive universities with the highest quality, 2000 ★1171★
Canadian medical/doctoral universities by medical/science grants per faculty member, 2000 ★1183★
Canadian universities by average entering grade, 2000 ★1213★
Canadian universities by students with 75% grade averages or higher, 2000 ★1215★
Canadian universities with the lowest total cost, 2000 ★1218★
Top Canadian comprehensive universities, 2000 ★1219★
Top Canadian comprehensive universities by reputation, 2000 ★1220★
Canadian universities producing the most-cited papers in the field of computer science, 1992-96 ★1589★
Canadian universities publishing the most papers in the fields of economics and business, 1992-96 ★2215★

Simon; Kevin
All-American boy's high school football linebackers, 2000 ★182★

Simon Property Group
Fortune's highest ranked real estate companies, 2000 ★491★

Simonds Middle School
Outstanding secondary schools in Boston, Massachusetts-New Hampshire ★4100★

Simone; Albert J.
Top pay and benefits for the chief executive and top paid employees at Rochester Institute of Technology ★3461★

Simon's Rock College of Bard
U.S. colleges and universities most accepting of alternative lifestyles ★986★
U.S. colleges and universities where intercollegiate sports are not popular ★994★
U.S. colleges and universities where intramural sports are not popular ★996★
U.S. colleges and universities where students are very politically active ★1001★
U.S. colleges and universities where the general student body does not drink hard liquor ★1005★
U.S. colleges and universities where the general student body puts little emphasis on athletic events ★1009★
U.S. colleges and universities with an unfavorable surrounding town or city ★1023★
U.S. colleges and universities with harmonious race/class interaction ★1026★
U.S. colleges and universities with the best food service program ★1031★

U.S. News & World Report's national liberal arts colleges with the highest proportion of classes with less than 20 students, 2000-01 ★1335★
Highest undergraduate tuition and fees at colleges and universities in Massachusetts ★1516★
Average faculty salaries for institutions of higher education without academic ranks in Massachusetts, 2000-01 ★3751★

Simple Gifts
Outstanding audio selections for young listeners, 2000 ★325★

Simpson College
U.S. News & World Report's midwestern regional liberal arts colleges with the highest academic reputation scores, 2000-01 ★1340★
U.S. News & World Report's midwestern regional liberal arts colleges with the highest freshmen retention rates, 2000-01 ★1343★
U.S. News & World Report's midwestern regional liberal arts colleges with the highest graduation rates, 2000-01 ★1344★
U.S. News & World Report's top midwestern regional liberal arts colleges, 2000-01 ★1349★
U.S. News & World Report's best undergraduate fees among midwestern regional liberal arts colleges by discount tuition, 2000 ★1380★
Highest undergraduate tuition and fees at colleges and universities in Iowa ★1504★
Average faculty salaries for institutions of higher education in Iowa, 2000-01 ★3702★

Simpson; David
Top pay and benefits for the chief executive and top paid employees at the University of the South ★3572★

Simpson's Comics a Go-Go
Most notable fiction books for reluctant young adult readers, 2001 ★321★

The Sims
Top selling software in all categories, 2000 ★1602★

Sinak; Christine
All-America girls' high school soccer team defenders, 2001 ★174★

Sinclair Community College
Average faculty salaries for institutions of higher education in Ohio, 2000-01 ★3722★

Sinel; Kathleen
Top pay and benefits for the chief executive and top paid employees at the College of St. Rose ★3529★

Sing, Dance 'n Sign!
Outstanding videos for library collections, 2000 ★2892★

Sing Faster: The Stagehand's Ring Cycle
Most notable videos for adults, 2001 ★2891★

Singapore
Comparison of 8th grade science achievement scores, U.S. and worldwide, 1999 ★6★
Eight grade science achievement scores from selected countries, 1999 ★14★
Math achievement test comparison ★19★
Eighth grade mathematics achievement scores from selected countries, 1999 ★2773★
Institute for Scientific Information periodical prices by country, 2001 ★2922★
Countries with the highest leader's salary ★3120★

Singapore Airlines
Business Week's best companies in Singapore ★402★

Singapore; National University of
Top institutions in systems and software engineering publications ★2332★

Singapore Press Holdings
Business Week's best companies in Singapore ★402★

Singapore Telecommunications
Business Week's best companies in Singapore ★402★

Singer
Most desirable jobs in the arts ★2277★

Singer; Marilyn
Booklist's best science books for children ★310★

Sinte Gleska University
U.S. tribal colleges ★1445★
Lowest undergraduate tuition and fees at colleges and universities in South Dakota ★1557★

Sioux Falls, SD
Best 'quirky' places to live ★3083★

Sioux Falls; University of
Highest undergraduate tuition and fees at colleges and universities in South Dakota ★1556★
Average faculty salaries for institutions of higher education in South Dakota, 2000-01 ★3729★

Sippel; Leonard C.
Top pay and benefits for the chief executive and top paid employees at Pace University ★3435★

Sir Walter Raleigh and the Quest for El Dorado
Most notable books for older readers, 2001 ★318★
Outstanding children's nonfiction books, 2000 ★330★

Sis; Peter
Outstanding children's picture books, 2000 ★331★

Sisseton-Wahpeton Community College
U.S. tribal colleges ★1445★
Highest undergraduate tuition and fees at public 2-year colleges and universities ★1462★
Lowest undergraduate tuition and fees at colleges and universities in South Dakota ★1557★

Sitting Bull College
U.S. tribal colleges ★1445★
Highest undergraduate tuition and fees at colleges and universities in North Dakota ★1541★
Average faculty salaries for institutions of higher education without academic ranks in North Dakota, 2000-01 ★3762★

Sitting Bull and His World
Most notable nonfiction books for young adults, 2001 ★324★

Sitzman; Barbara Pressey
American Chemical Society 2001 award winners (Group 4) ★754★

Six-member stimulus classes generated by conditional-discrimination procedures
Most cited sources in experimental analyses of human behavior between 1990 and 1999 ★3070★

The Six Sigma Way
Library Journal's most notable management books, 2000 ★265★

16 Magazine
Best-selling youth magazines ★2920★

Sizemore; W. Christian
Top pay and benefits for the chief executive and top paid employees at William Jewell College ★3630★

SK Telecom
Business Week's top emerging-market companies worldwide ★434★

Skagit Valley College
Lowest undergraduate tuition and fees at colleges and universities in Washington ★1567★

Skandia Forsakring
Business Week's best companies in Sweden ★404★

Skandinaviska Enskilda Banken
Business Week's best companies in Sweden ★404★

Skaneateles High School
Outstanding secondary schools in Syracuse, New York ★4239★

Skechers U.S.A.
Business Week's top companies in terms of return on capital, 2000 ★430★
Business Week's top companies in terms of sales, 2000 ★431★
Top companies in terms of growth, 2000 ★534★

Skelton; W. Douglas
Top pay and benefits for the chief executive and top paid employees at Mercer University ★3398★

Skidmore College
U.S. colleges and universities with excellent library facilities ★1025★
U.S. News & World Report's national liberal arts colleges with the highest percentage of full-time faculty, 2000-01 ★1333★
Highest undergraduate tuition and fees at private nonprofit, 4-year or above colleges and universities ★1461★
Highest undergraduate tuition and fees at colleges and universities in New York ★1537★
Average faculty salaries for institutions of higher education in New York, 2000-01 ★3719★

Skinner Elementary School
Illinois elementary schools with the highest 5th grade writing scores ★15★

Skiviat; David
Top pay and benefits for the chief executive and top paid employees at the Franciscan University of Steubenville ★3532★

Skoczenski; Ann
Radcliffe Institute for Advanced Study fellowship recipient in the field of cognitive and neural sciences, 2000-01 ★4296★

Skogan; Wesley G.
Most-cited scholars in *Canadian Journal of Criminology* ★1638★

Skolnick; Jerome H.
Most-cited scholars in police studies articles/research notes ★2624★

Skooglund; Richard D.
Top pay and benefits for the chief executive and top paid employees at Butler University ★3214★

Skorheim; Mary
Top pay and benefits for the chief executive and top paid employees at St. Olaf College ★3484★

Skotko; Brian
All-USA College Academic First Team, 2001 ★2★

Skullcrack
Most notable fiction books for reluctant young adult readers, 2001 ★321★

Sladich; Harry H.
Top pay and benefits for the chief executive and top paid employees at Gonzaga University ★3311★

SLAM
Most notable nonfiction books for reluctant young adult readers, 2001 ★323★

Slane; Alton
Top pay and benefits for the chief executive and top paid employees at Muhlenberg College ★3413★

Slaughter; John B.
Top pay and benefits for the chief executive and top paid employees at Occidental College ★3428★

Slaughterhouse-Five
Most frequently banned books in the 1990s ★745★

Slave Narratives
Booklist's most recommended African American nonfiction ★229★

Slavic
Gender breakdown of language and literature doctorate recipients, by subfield, 1999 ★1937★
Language and literature doctorates awarded at U.S. colleges and universities, by subfield, 1999 ★1949★

Sleds on Boston Common
Smithsonian's best books for children ages 6 to 10 ★364★

Slender Existence
Most notable DVDs and videos for young adults, 2001 ★2890★

Slider Middle School
Outstanding secondary schools in El Paso, Texas ★4128★

Slippery Rock University (PA)
Division II NCAA colleges with the 100% graduation rates for women's basketball players, 1993-94 ★944★

Sliwa; Steven M.
Top pay and benefits for the chief executive and top paid employees at Embry-Riddle Aeronautical University ★3286★

Sloan Jr.; Robert B.
Top pay and benefits for the chief executive and top paid employees at Baylor University ★3194★

Sloan Management Review
Business journals by citation impact, 1998 ★690★
Top ranked AACSB publications ★2186★

Slovenia
Math achievement test comparison ★19★

Smalley; Richard E.
Top pay and benefits for the chief executive and top paid employees at Rice University ★3457★

Smart; Carol
Most-cited scholars in women and crime publications ★1642★

Smerek; Edward
Top pay and benefits for the chief executive and top paid employees at Hiram College ★3333★

Smiddy; William E.
Top pay and benefits for the chief executive and top paid employees at the University of Miami ★3550★

Smith
Smithsonian's best books for children ages 10 and up ★365★

Smith; Adam
Most cited economists ★2185★

Smith; Alexander F.
Top pay and benefits for the chief executive and top paid employees at Wartburg College ★3603★

Smith; Bruce J.
Top pay and benefits for the chief executive and top paid employees at Allegheny College ★3170★

Smith; Charles Thomas
Top pay and benefits for the chief executive and top paid employees at LaSierra University ★3366★

Smith College
Private, 4-year undergraduate colleges and universities producing the most Ph.D.'s in the life sciences, 1920-1990 ★192★
Private, 4-year undergraduate colleges and universities producing the most Ph.D.'s in the life sciences, 1981-1990 ★193★
U.S. colleges and universities most accepting of alternative lifestyles ★986★
U.S. colleges and universities offering the best overall academic experience for undergraduates ★987★
U.S. colleges and universities with a generally liberal student body ★1015★
U.S. colleges and universities with excellent instructors ★1024★
U.S. colleges and universities with the best on-campus housing facilities ★1032★
U.S. News & World Report's national liberal arts colleges with the best graduation and retention rank, 2000-01 ★1324★
U.S. News & World Report's national liberal arts colleges with the highest academic reputation scores, 2000-01 ★1327★
U.S. News & World Report's national liberal arts colleges with the highest percentage of full-time faculty, 2000-01 ★1333★
U.S. News & World Report's national liberal arts colleges with the highest proportion of classes having 50 or more students, 2000-01 ★1334★
Private, 4-year undergraduate colleges and universities producing the most Ph.D.s in all fields of study, 1920-1990 ★2027★
Private, 4-year undergraduate colleges and universities producing the most Ph.D.'s in all fields of study, 1981-1990 ★2028★
Private, 4-year undergraduate colleges and universities producing the most Ph.D.'s in all fields of study, 1990 ★2029★
Private, 4-year undergraduate colleges and universities producing the most Ph.D.'s in nonscience fields, 1920-1990 ★2030★
Private, 4-year undergraduate colleges and universities producing the most Ph.D.'s in nonscience fields, 1981-1990 ★2031★
Private, 4-year undergraduate colleges and universities producing the most Ph.D.'s in nonscience fields, 1990 ★2032★
Elite liberal arts colleges ranked by quality adjusted scholarship articles in the field of economics, 1975-94 ★2165★
Top associate professor economists at elite liberal arts colleges, 1975-94 ★2174★
Private, 4-year undergraduate colleges and universities producing the most Ph.D.'s in economics, 1920-1990 ★2211★

Private, 4-year undergraduate colleges and universities producing the most Ph.D.'s in economics, 1981-1990 ★2212★
Private, 4-year undergraduate colleges and universities producing the most Ph.D.'s in English, 1920-1990 ★2449★
Private, 4-year undergraduate colleges and universities producing the most Ph.D.'s in English, 1981-1990 ★2450★
Bachelor's institutions with the highest enrollment of foreign students, 1998-99 ★2492★
Radcliffe Institute for Advanced Study fellowship recipients in the field of history, 2000-01 ★2549★
Private, 4-year undergraduate colleges and universities producing the most Ph.D.'s in history, 1920-1990 ★2552★
Private, 4-year undergraduate colleges and universities producing the most Ph.D.'s in history, 1981-1990 ★2553★
Most wired colleges, 2000 ★2595★
Institutions in the Worker Rights Consortium ★2913★
Women's colleges granting physics bachelor's degrees, 2000 ★2982★
Private, 4-year undergraduate colleges and universities producing the most Ph.D.'s in political science and international relations, 1920-1990 ★3044★
Private, 4-year undergraduate colleges and universities producing the most Ph.D.'s in political science and international relations, 1981-1990 ★3045★
Private, 4-year undergraduate colleges and universities producing the most Ph.D.'s in psychology, 1920-1990 ★3066★
Private, 4-year undergraduate colleges and universities producing the most Ph.D.'s in psychology, 1981-1990 ★3067★
Presidents with the highest pay at Baccalaureate I colleges, 1998-99 ★3159★
Average faculty salaries for institutions of higher education in Massachusetts, 2000-01 ★3708★
Private, 4-year undergraduate colleges and universities producing the most Ph.D.'s in the sciences, 1920-1990 ★4294★
Private, 4-year undergraduate colleges and universities producing the most Ph.D.'s in the sciences, 1981-1990 ★4295★
Private, 4-year undergraduate colleges and universities producing the most Ph.D.'s in anthropology and sociology, 1920-1990 ★4344★
Private, 4-year undergraduate colleges and universities producing the most Ph.D.'s in anthropology and sociology, 1981-1990 ★4345★

Smith; Craig Richey
Top pay and benefits for the chief executive and top paid employees at Columbia University ★3251★

Smith; David B.
Top pay and benefits for the chief executive and top paid employees at Siena College ★3498★

Smith; Dean
Coaches winning the most NCAA tournaments ★120★

Smith; Erica
All-America girls' high school basketball 4th team, 2001 ★173★

Smith; G.
Top full professor economists at elite liberal arts colleges, 1975-94 ★2175★

Smith; Gary
Top pay and benefits for the chief executive and top paid employees at Johns Hopkins University ★3355★

Smith; Gregory D.
Top pay and benefits for the chief executive and top paid employees at Polytechnic University ★3443★

Smith; Joseph A.
Top pay and benefits for the chief executive and top paid employees at Vanderbilt University ★3593★

Smith-Kettlewell Eye Research Institute
Radcliffe Institute for Advanced Study fellowship recipient in the field of cognitive and neural sciences, 2000-01 ★4296★

Smith; Lawrence
Top pay and benefits for the chief executive and top paid employees at Mount Saint Mary's College in California ★3411★

Smith; Linda C.
Library and information science faculty with the most journal articles, 1993-1998 ★2711★

Smith; Mark
Top pay and benefits for the chief executive and top paid employees at Christian Brothers University ★3233★

Smith; M.D.
Most cited authors in the journal *Canadian Journal of Criminology*, 1990 to 1995 ★1615★

Smith; Norman R.
Top pay and benefits for the chief executive and top paid employees at Wagner College ★3599★

Smith, O.P.; Rev. Philip A.
Top pay and benefits for the chief executive and top paid employees at Providence College ★3447★

Smith; Richard A.
Top pay and benefits for the chief executive and top paid employees at Millsaps College ★3403★

Smith; Richard K.
Top pay and benefits for the chief executive and top paid employees at Earlham College ★3279★

Smith; Robert
Top pay and benefits for the chief executive and top paid employees at Washington College ★3606★

Smith; Roger M.
Most frequently downloaded *American Political Science Review* articles ★3039★

Smith; Vernon
Authors most frequently contributing to the *American Economic Review* from 1911-1990 ★2156★
Authors most frequently contributing to the *American Economic Review* from 1951-1990 ★2157★

Smith; Zadie
Booklist's best first novels ★228★

Smithkline Beecham
Business Week's best companies in Britain ★389★

Smithson; Robert
Highly influential artists of the 20th century ★76★

Smits; Kenneth H.
Top pay and benefits for the chief executive and top paid employees at Marquette University ★3392★

Smokeless tobacco
Percentage of high school students using tobacco products by gender ★4373★
Percentage of middle school students using tobacco products by gender ★4374★

Smoky Hill High School
Outstanding secondary schools in Denver, Colorado ★4124★

Smolowitz; Ira A.
Top pay and benefits for the chief executive and top paid employees at American International College ★3173★

Smolskis; Joseph W.
Top pay and benefits for the chief executive and top paid employees at Trinity College in Washington D.C. ★3578★

Smorynski; Henry W.
Top pay and benefits for the chief executive and top paid employees at Lewis University ★3372★

Smurfit-Stone Container
Fortune's highest ranked forest and paper products companies, 2000 ★466★

Snail Mail No More
Most notable fiction books for reluctant young adult readers, 2001 ★321★

Snapp; Terry
Top pay and benefits for the chief executive and top paid employees at Park University ★3438★

Snead State Community College
Lowest undergraduate tuition and fees at colleges and universities in Alabama ★1480★

Snide; James A.
Top pay and benefits for the chief executive and top paid employees at the University of Dayton ★3539★

Snider; Thomas R.
Top pay and benefits for the chief executive and top paid employees at Butler University ★3214★

Snieckus; Victor A.
Winner of the American Chemical Society's Arthur C. Cope Awards, 2001 ★795★

Sniteman; Steve
Top pay and benefits for the chief executive and top paid employees at Erskine College ★3290★

Snoddy; William H.
Top pay and benefits for the chief executive and top paid employees at the College of Wooster ★3531★

Snow
Most notable children's recordings, 2001 ★320★
Outstanding audio selections for young listeners, 2000 ★325★

Snow College
Undergraduate tuition and fees at colleges and universities in Utah ★1562★

Snow Falling on Cedars
Outstanding audiobooks, 2000 ★287★

Snow; Michael
Canada's best visual artists of the 20th century ★75★

Snyder; Solomon H.
Most-cited biomedical scientists, 1990-97 ★2382★

Snyderman; Ralph
Top pay and benefits for the chief executive and top paid employees at Duke University ★3276★

So You Want to Be President?
  Most notable books for middle readers, 2001 ★317★
  Outstanding books for middle readers, 2000 ★326★
  Outstanding children's nonfiction books, 2000 ★330★
  Publishers Weekly Off-the-Cuff Awards winner for best work of nonfiction, 2000 ★343★

Sobh; Tarek M.
  Top pay and benefits for the chief executive and top paid employees at University of Bridgeport ★3588★

Socastee High School
  Outstanding secondary schools in Myrtle Beach, South Carolina ★4184★

Soccer
  Fastest growing men's collegiate athletics teams ★130★
  Fastest growing women's collegiate athletics teams ★131★

Socci; Al
  Top pay and benefits for the chief executive and top paid employees at Eastern Nazarene College ★3281★

Social
  Gender breakdown of psychology doctorate recipients, by subfield, 1999 ★1941★
  Psychology doctorates awarded at U.S. colleges and universities, by subfield, 1999 ★2043★

Social, behavioral, and economic science
  Proposed fiscal 2002 appropriations for the National Science Foundation ★3109★

Social Biology
  Demography journals with the highest average citations after 5 years ★1856★
  Most cited demography journals, 1991-95 ★1857★

Social Education
  Journals publishing the most articles on economic education research from 1963-1990 ★2170★

Social Forces
  'Outside' journals most frequently citing *Demography*, 1991-95 ★1858★
  Sociology journals by impact factor, 1981 to 1997 ★4355★
  Sociology journals by impact factor, 1993 to 1997 ★4356★

Social History
  Top ranked economic history journals ★2190★

Social History of Medicine
  'Outside' journals most frequently citing *Population Studies*, 1991-95 ★1861★

Social and human service assistants
  Fastest growing occupations, 1998-2008 ★2302★
  Projected employment growth for selected occupations that require shortor moderate-term on-the-job training, 1998-2008 ★2321★

Social Networks
  Anthropology journals by citation impact, 1991-98 ★63★

Social/philosophical foundations of education
  Education doctorates awarded at U.S. colleges and universities, by subfield, 1999 ★1921★
  Gender breakdown of education doctorate recipients, by subfield, 1999 ★1933★

Social Problems
  Sociology journals by impact factor, 1981 to 1997 ★4355★
  Sociology journals by impact factor, 1993 to 1997 ★4356★

Social science
  Subject areas with the highest library expenditures/circulation ★306★

Social Science Computer Review
  Journals publishing the most articles on economic education research from 1963-1990 ★2170★

Social science education
  Gender breakdown of teaching fields doctorate recipients, by subfield, 1999 ★1943★
  Teaching fields doctorates awarded at U.S. colleges and universities, by subfield, 1999 ★2046★

Social Science Information Studies
  Information and library science journals by citation impact, 1981-99 ★2724★

Social Science and Medicine
  'Outside' journals most frequently citing *Population and Development Review*, 1991-95 ★1860★
  'Outside' journals most frequently citing *Population Studies*, 1991-95 ★1861★
  'Outside' journals most frequently citing *Studies in Family Planning*, 1991-95 ★1862★

Social sciences
  Median salary for B.S. chemists, by field ★781★
  Median salary for M.S. chemists, by field ★785★
  Median salary for Ph.D. chemists, by field ★786★
  Top fields of study for college and university presidents, 1998 ★839★
  Expected majors for incoming freshmen, 2000 ★1050★
  Age grouping of doctorate recipients, by broad field, 1999 ★1882★
  Comparative data of women receiving doctorate degrees in selected fields in 1950 and 1998 ★1899★
  Doctoral degree distribution by broad field, 1999 ★1902★
  Median age at conferral of doctoral degree from U.S. universities, by discipline, 1999 ★1952★
  Number of doctorate recipients at U.S. colleges and universities, by field, 1999 ★1969★
  Percentage of female doctorate recipients, by broad field, 1999 ★1989★
  Percentage of minority doctorate recipients in the U.S., by broad field, 1999 ★1991★
  Fields of study profile of foreign students enrolled in U.S. institutions of higher education, 1998-99 ★2495★
  Fields of study profile of U.S. students studying abroad, 1998-99 ★2507★
  Subjects required by the most U.S. medical schools for the 2000-01 entering class ★2850★
  United States' contribution of papers in the sciences, by field, 1995-99 ★4283★
  United States' contribution of papers in the sciences, by field, 1996-2000 ★4284★
  Australia's contribution of papers in the sciences, by field, 1993-97 ★4292★
  Australia's contribution of papers in the sciences, by field, 1995-99 ★4293★
  United Kingdom's contribution of papers in the sciences, by field, 1995-99 ★4297★
  Canada's contribution of papers in the sciences, by field, 1995-99 ★4303★
  England's contribution of papers in the sciences, by field, 1994-98 ★4308★
  Hong Kong's contribution of papers in the sciences, by field, 1995-99 ★4314★
  New Zealand's contribution of papers in the sciences, by field, 1994-98 ★4322★
  Norway's contribution of papers in the sciences, by field, 1994-98 ★4323★
  South Africa's contribution of papers in the sciences, by field, 1994-98 ★4326★

Social sciences, general
  Gender breakdown of social sciences doctorate recipients, by subfield, 1999 ★1942★
  Social sciences doctorates awarded at U.S. colleges and universities, by subfield, 1999 ★2044★

Social sciences and history
  Top bachelor's degree disciplines for African Americans, 1997-98 ★1672★
  Top bachelor's degree disciplines for Asian Americans, 1997-98 ★1673★
  Top bachelor's degree disciplines for Hispanic Americans, 1997-98 ★1674★
  Top bachelor's degree disciplines for Native Americans, 1997-98 ★1675★
  Top bachelor's degree disciplines for non-minorities, 1997-98 ★1676★

Social services
  Industries with the highest projected growth rate, 1994-2005 ★2306★

Social studies
  Subjects students most want to see on classroom TV ★4051★

Social Studies of Science
  Most cited science serials in technical communication journals from 1988 to 1997 ★4424★

Social work
  Gender breakdown of professional doctorate recipients, by subfield, 1999 ★1940★
  Professional doctorates awarded at U.S. colleges and universities, by subfield, 1999 ★2033★
  Expected starting salaries of 2000-01 bachelor's degree recipients, by specific major ★3131★

Social worker
  Careers college students considered most respected, 2000 ★740★
  Jobs with the most stringent quotas ★2259★
  Most desirable public sector jobs ★2279★

Social workers
  Projections for the fastest growing occupations requiring a bachelor's degree or more from 1998 to 2008 ★2292★
  Projected employment growth for selected occupations that require a bachelor's degree or more, 1998-2008 ★2317★

Societe Europeenne Des Satellites
  Business Week's best companies in Belgium ★388★

Sociologist
  Most desirable social sciences jobs ★2280★

Sociology
  Gender breakdown of social sciences doctorate recipients, by subfield, 1999 ★1942★
  Number of social sciences doctorate recipients at U.S. colleges and universities, by field, 1999 ★1977★
  Percentage of female doctorate recipients at U.S. colleges and universities, by subfield, 1999 ★1988★
  Social sciences doctorates awarded at U.S. colleges and universities, by subfield, 1999 ★2044★
  Top nonscience majors for accepted applicants to U.S. medical schools, 1999-2000 ★2854★

SOCIOLOGY

Average costs for Academic Search titles by subject, 2001 ★2918★
Periodical prices by LC subject, 2001 ★2925★

Sociology of Education
Education and educational research journals by citation impact, 1981-99 ★2235★
Education and educational research journals by citation impact, 1995-99 ★2236★
Education and educational research journals with the greatest impact measure ★2238★
Sociology journals by impact factor, 1981 to 1997 ★4355★

The Sociopolitical Nature of Counseling
Most frequently cited contribution articles in psychology journals from 1986 to 1996 ★3071★

Socorro High School
Outstanding secondary schools in El Paso, Texas ★4128★

Soda; Dominic
Top pay and benefits for the chief executive and top paid employees at Lindenwood University ★3375★

Sodexho Marriott Services
Fortune's highest ranked outsourcing services companies, 2000 ★483★

Soenksen; Gordon
Top pay and benefits for the chief executive and top paid employees at St. Olaf College ★3484★

Softbank
Business Week's best companies in Japan ★398★

Software engineer
Jobs considered the loneliest ★2244★
Jobs with the best environment scores ★2247★
Jobs with the best security scores ★2251★
Jobs with the highest employment growth ★2254★
Most desirable technical/repair jobs ★2281★

Software House International
Top women-owned companies ★4460★

Software Spectrum
Top women-owned companies ★4460★

Soil Biology & Biochemistry
Soil science journals by citation impact, 1981-99 ★188★
Soil science journals by citation impact, 1995-99 ★189★
Soil science journals by citation impact, 1999 ★190★

Soil chemistry/microbiology
Agricultural sciences doctorates awarded at U.S. colleges and universities, by subfield, 1999 ★1886★
Gender breakdown of agricultural sciences doctorate recipients, by subfield, 1999 ★1926★

Soil Science
Soil science journals by citation impact, 1981-99 ★188★
Soil science journals by citation impact, 1995-99 ★189★
Soil science journals by citation impact, 1999 ★190★

Soil Science Society of America Journal
Soil science journals by citation impact, 1981-99 ★188★
Soil science journals by citation impact, 1995-99 ★189★
Soil science journals by citation impact, 1999 ★190★

Soil sciences
Agricultural sciences doctorates awarded at U.S. colleges and universities, by subfield, 1999 ★1886★
Gender breakdown of agricultural sciences doctorate recipients, by subfield, 1999 ★1926★

Soil Use & Management
Soil science journals by citation impact, 1999 ★190★

Sojka; Gary
Top pay and benefits for the chief executive and top paid employees at Bucknell University ★3213★

Sojourner-Douglass College
Private 4-year institutions with the lowest tuition, 2000-01 ★1468★

Solar Physics
Astronomy and astrophysics journals by citation impact, 1999 ★104★

Solectron
Fortune's highest ranked electronics and electrical equipment companies, 2000 ★460★

Solid state and low-temperature
Gender breakdown of physics and astronomy doctorate recipients, by subfield, 1999 ★1939★
Physics and astronomy doctorates awarded at U.S. colleges and universities, by subfield, 1999 ★1994★

Soliday; Joanne C.
Top pay and benefits for the chief executive and top paid employees at West Virginia Wesleyan College ★3613★

Soller; Dan S.
Top pay and benefits for the chief executive and top paid employees at LaRoche College ★3364★

Solomon; Edward I.
American Chemical Society 2001 award winners (Group 5) ★755★

Solomon Elementary School
Chicago neighborhood schools with the highest ISAT scores in reading and math ★4004★

Solon High School
Outstanding secondary schools in Cleveland-Lorain-Elyria, Ohio ★4114★

Solow; Anita
Top pay and benefits for the chief executive and top paid employees at Randolph-Macon Woman's College ★3452★

Soloway; Mark S.
Top pay and benefits for the chief executive and top paid employees at the University of Miami ★3550★

Solum; Lawrence B.
Top pay and benefits for the chief executive and top paid employees at Loyola Marymount University ★3380★

Solvay
Business Week's best companies in Belgium ★388★

Some Economics of Global Warming
Top cited energy papers from 1989 to 1993 ★2466★

Some Ether
Booklist's most recommended poetry books, 2001 ★231★
Library Journal's best poetry books, 2000 ★244★

Some Love, Some Pain, Some Time: Stories
Favorite books of African Americans ★238★

Some Things Are Scary
Publishers Weekly Off-the-Cuff Awards winners for books for adults, not for children, 2000 ★362★

Somera Communications
Business Week's top companies in terms of return on capital, 2000 ★430★
Business Week's top companies in terms of sales growth, 2000 ★432★
Top companies in terms of growth, 2000 ★534★

Somerset Community College
Community colleges receiving the most gifts, 1999-2000 ★1239★
Lowest undergraduate tuition and fees at colleges and universities in Kentucky ★1509★

Somerset, NJ
Counties with the highest per capita income ★2561★

Something New Under the Sun: An Environmental History of the Twentieth Century World
Library Journal's most notable environmental sciences books, 2000 ★259★

Sonera
Business Week's best companies in Finland ★392★

Song of Solomon
Favorite books of African Americans ★238★

Sonic Automotive
Fortune's highest ranked automotive retailing services companies, 2000 ★449★

Sonnenberg; Eugene
Top pay and benefits for the chief executive and top paid employees at Hope International University ★3340★

Sonnenschein; Hugo
Top pay and benefits for the chief executive and top paid employees at the University of Chicago ★3537★

Sonoma County, CA
Best 'quirky' places to live ★3083★

Sonoma State University
U.S. colleges and universities with poor instructors ★1027★
U.S. colleges and universities with the least accessible instructors ★1036★
U.S. colleges and universities with the unhappiest students ★1041★
U.S. News & World Report's top public western regional universities, 2000-01 ★1573★
Average faculty salaries for institutions of higher education in California, 2000-01 ★3692★

Sony
Business Week's best companies in Japan ★398★

Soper; John C.
Individuals producing the most economic education research articles, 1963-1990 ★2166★

Sophie and the New Baby
Smithsonian's best books for children ages 1 to 6 ★363★

Sosa: An Autobiography
Library Journal's best nonfiction audiobooks, 2000 ★243★

Sosso; Michael
All-USA College Academic Second Team, 2001 ★3★

Sourcebook of Criminal Justice Statistics, 1994
Most-cited works in police studies articles/research notes ★2625★

South Africa
Eight grade science achievement scores from selected countries, 1999 ★14★

Eighth grade mathematics achievement scores from selected countries, 1999 ★2773★

Institute for Scientific Information periodical prices by country, 2001 ★2922★

South Alabama; University of
Division I NCAA colleges with the lowest graduation rates for female basketball players, 1990-91 to 1993-94 ★937★

State appropriations for Alabama's institutions of higher education, 2000-01 ★1254★

U.S. News & World Report's southern regional universities with students least in debt, 1999 ★1431★

South America
South American periodical prices, 2001 ★2933★

South Baylo University
U.S. colleges and universities awarding the most health professions and related sciences master's degrees to Asian Americans ★1778★

U.S. colleges and universities awarding the most master's degrees to Asian Americans ★1786★

U.S. colleges and universities awarding the most master's degrees to minorities ★1788★

South Brandywine Middle School
Outstanding secondary schools in Philadelphia, Pennsylvania-New Jersey ★4202★

South Brunswick High School
Outstanding secondary schools in Middlesex-Somerset-Hunterdon, New Jersey ★4179★

South Carolina
Mean composite ACT scores by state, 2000 ★895★

Mean math SAT scores by state, 2000 ★900★

Mean verbal SAT scores by state, 2000 ★903★

States with the highest percentage increase in appropriations for higher education, 2000-01 ★1308★

Total doctorate recipients by state, 1999 ★2054★

State grades for affordability of higher education for minority students, 2000 ★2883★

State grades for benefits state receives for educating its minority students, 2000 ★2884★

State grades for completion of higher education by minority students, 2000 ★2885★

State grades for participation of minority students in higher education, 2000 ★2886★

State grades for preparing minority students for higher education, 2000 ★2887★

States with the lowest percentage of high school freshmen enrolling in college within four years ★4267★

States with the highest state support for non need-based financial aid for students, 1999-2000 ★4368★

South Carolina, Aiken; University of
U.S. News & World Report's top public southern regional liberal arts colleges, 2000-01 ★1378★

Average faculty salaries for institutions of higher education in South Carolina, 2000-01 ★3728★

South Carolina, Beaufort; University of
Average faculty salaries for institutions of higher education in South Carolina, 2000-01 ★3728★

South Carolina, Columbia; University of
U.S. colleges and universities with the highest average football attendance, 1996-99 ★159★

U.S. News & World Report's universities with the best insurance departments, 1999-2000 ★681★

Total baccalaureate English language, literature, and letters degrees awarded to African Americans from U.S. colleges and universities, 1997-98 ★1716★

Traditionally white institutions awarding the most master's degrees to African Americans ★1755★

U.S. colleges and universities awarding the most education master's degrees to African Americans ★1769★

U.S. colleges and universities awarding the most health professions and related sciences master's degrees to African Americans ★1777★

U.S. colleges and universities awarding the most physical sciences master's degrees to African Americans ★1793★

Average faculty salaries for institutions of higher education in South Carolina, 2000-01 ★3728★

South Carolina, Darla Moore School of Business; University of
Academics' choices for best graduate international business programs, 2001 ★668★

U.S. News & World Report's undergraduate business programs with the best international business departments, 2000-01 ★682★

South Carolina, Lancaster; University of
Average faculty salaries for institutions of higher education in South Carolina, 2000-01 ★3728★

South Carolina, Salkehatchie; University of
Average faculty salaries for institutions of higher education in South Carolina, 2000-01 ★3728★

South Carolina, Spartanburg; University of
Average faculty salaries for institutions of higher education in South Carolina, 2000-01 ★3728★

South Carolina State University
Colleges offering the Thurgood Marshall Scholarship Fund ★221★

Four-year institutions with the most weapons arrests reported, 1999 ★709★

Retention rates of African American students at historically black institutions, 1997-98 ★1120★

State appropriations for South Carolina's institutions of higher education, 2000-01 ★1293★

Historically black colleges and universities awarding the most master's degrees to African Americans ★1670★

Total baccalaureate mathematics degrees awarded to African Americans from U.S. colleges and universities, 1997-98 ★1729★

U.S. colleges and universities awarding the most health professions and related sciences master's degrees to African Americans ★1777★

U.S. institutions awarding the most baccalaureate degrees to African Americans in agribusiness and production, 1998 ★1813★

U.S. institutions awarding the most master's degrees to African Americans in agribusiness and production, 1998 ★1824★

U.S. institutions awarding the most master's degrees to minorities in agribusiness and production, 1998 ★1829★

Historically black colleges and universities awarding the most doctorate degrees to African Americans ★1945★

U.S. colleges and universities awarding the most education doctorate degrees to African Americans ★2108★

South Carolina, Sumter; University of
Average faculty salaries for institutions of higher education in South Carolina, 2000-01 ★3728★

South Carolina; University of
All-USA College Academic Third Team, 2001 ★4★

Comparisons of investment returns for information technology MBAs ★625★

Top business schools for within-discipline research performance in production/operations management, 1986-1998 ★648★

Top business schools for within-discipline research performance in insurance, international business and real estate, 1986-1998 ★667★

Employing institutions with the most published pages in *The Journal of Risk and Insurance*, 1987-1996 ★679★

Institutions with the most published authors in the *Journal of Business Research*, 1985 to 1999 ★695★

State appropriations for South Carolina's institutions of higher education, 2000-01 ★1293★

University research libraries in the U.S. and Canada with the largest increases in total expenditures from 1993-94 to 1998-99 ★2708★

South Central Technical College
Lowest undergraduate tuition and fees at colleges and universities in Minnesota ★1521★

Average faculty salaries for institutions of higher education without academic ranks in Minnesota, 2000-01 ★3753★

South Cobb High School
Outstanding secondary schools in Atlanta, Georgia ★4087★

South Dakota
Mean composite ACT scores by state, 2000 ★895★

Mean math SAT scores by state, 2000 ★900★

Mean verbal SAT scores by state, 2000 ★903★

States allocating the smallest amount of state tax appropriations for higher education, 2000-01 ★1305★

Total doctorate recipients by state, 1999 ★2054★

State grades for affordability of higher education for minority students, 2000 ★2883★

State grades for benefits state receives for educating its minority students, 2000 ★2884★

State grades for completion of higher education by minority students, 2000 ★2885★

State grades for participation of minority students in higher education, 2000 ★2886★

State grades for preparing minority students for higher education, 2000 ★2887★

States with the lowest number of high school graduates, 1999-2000 ★3997★

States with the lowest per-pupil expenditures ★3998★

States with the smallest average class size ★4072★

South Dakota School of Mines and Technology
State appropriations for South Dakota's institutions of higher education, 2000-01 ★1294★
Lowest undergraduate tuition and fees at colleges and universities in South Dakota ★1557★
Average faculty salaries for institutions of higher education in South Dakota, 2000-01 ★3729★

South Dakota State University
Division II NCAA colleges with the highest graduation rates for football players, 1993-94 ★946★
State appropriations for South Dakota's institutions of higher education, 2000-01 ★1294★
U.S. News & World Report's midwestern regional universities with the highest acceptance rates, 2000-01 ★1404★
U.S. News & World Report's midwestern regional universities with the highest percentage of full-time faculty, 2000-01 ★1408★
U.S. News & World Report's top public midwestern regional universities, 2000-01 ★1412★
U.S. News & World Report's best undergraduate fees among midwestern regional universities by discount tuition, 2000 ★1427★
Lowest undergraduate tuition and fees at colleges and universities in South Dakota ★1557★
U.S. institutions awarding the most baccalaureate degrees to Native Americans in agricultural sciences, 1998 ★1823★
Average faculty salaries for institutions of higher education in South Dakota, 2000-01 ★3729★

South Dakota; University of
State appropriations for South Dakota's institutions of higher education, 2000-01 ★1294★
Highest undergraduate tuition and fees at colleges and universities in South Dakota ★1556★
Academics' choices for best rural medicine programs, 2001 ★2824★
Average faculty salaries for institutions of higher education in South Dakota, 2000-01 ★3729★

South Florida Community College
Average faculty salaries for institutions of higher education without academic ranks in Florida, 2000-01 ★3745★

South Florida University
Longest field goals in college football ★158★
State appropriations for Florida's institutions of higher education, 2000-01 ★1262★
U.S. colleges and universities awarding the most health professions and related sciences master's degrees to Hispanic Americans ★1779★
U.S. colleges and universities awarding the most health professions and related sciences first professional degrees to Native Americans ★1851★
Top oceanography research-doctorate programs as evaluated by the National Research Council ★2153★
Average faculty salaries for institutions of higher education in Florida, 2000-01 ★3696★

South High Community School
Outstanding urban public high schools in Metro Boston ★4261★

South Hillsborough School
Outstanding secondary schools in San Francisco, California ★4221★

South Holland, District 151
Illinois elementary school districts with the highest teacher salaries, 1999 ★3984★

South Korea
Eight grade science achievement scores from selected countries, 1999 ★14★
Percentage of enrollment at private institutions of higher education, by country, 1998 ★858★
Countries with the most computers, 2000 ★1603★
Countries with the most Internet users ★2583★
Eighth grade mathematics achievement scores from selected countries, 1999 ★2773★
First-year physics and astronomy graduate students from Asia, 1997-98 ★2987★
Countries with the highest leader's salary ★3120★

South Mountain Community College
Lowest undergraduate tuition and fees at colleges and universities in Arizona ★1483★

South Oldham High School
Outstanding secondary schools in Louisville, Kentucky-Indiana ★4168★

South Pasadena Middle School
Outstanding secondary schools in Los Angeles-Long Beach, California ★4167★

South, Sewanee; University of the
Fiske Guide's best buys for private colleges and universities, 2001 ★1459★

South Side High School
Outstanding secondary schools in Long Island, New York ★4165★

South Suburban Community College
Fall enrollment at Chicago-area public community colleges, by minority percentages, 1999 ★867★

South Texas College of Law
U.S. colleges and universities awarding the most law and legal studies first professional degrees to Hispanic Americans ★1854★
Academics' choices for best trial advocacy programs, 2001 ★2633★

South Texas Community College
Institutions with the most part-time Hispanic American faculty ★924★

South; University of the
U.S. News & World Report's national liberal arts colleges with the best faculty resources rank, 2000-01 ★1321★
U.S. News & World Report's national liberal arts colleges with the highest acceptance rates, 2000-01 ★1328★
U.S. News & World Report's best undergraduate fees among national liberal arts colleges by discount tuition, 2000 ★1381★
Highest undergraduate tuition and fees at colleges and universities in Tennessee ★1558★
Private, 4-year undergraduate colleges and universities producing the most Ph.D.'s in English, 1920-1990 ★2449★
Average faculty salaries for institutions of higher education in Tennessee, 2000-01 ★3730★

Southdown
Fortune's highest ranked building materials and glass companies, 2000 ★451★

Southeast Community College
Lowest undergraduate tuition and fees at colleges and universities in Kentucky ★1509★

Southeast Community College, Beatrice Campus
Lowest undergraduate tuition and fees at colleges and universities in Nebraska ★1529★

Southeast Community College, Lincoln Campus
Lowest undergraduate tuition and fees at colleges and universities in Nebraska ★1529★

Southeast Community College, Milford Campus
Lowest undergraduate tuition and fees at colleges and universities in Nebraska ★1529★

Southeast Missouri State University
State appropriations for Missouri's institutions of higher education, 2000-01 ★1278★
Average faculty salaries for institutions of higher education in Missouri, 2000-01 ★3712★

Southeast Technical Institute
Lowest undergraduate tuition and fees at colleges and universities in South Dakota ★1557★

Southeastern Baptist College
Lowest undergraduate tuition at private nonprofit, 4-year or above colleges and universities ★1464★

Southeastern Baptist Theological Seminary
Institutions censured by the American Association of University Professors, 2001 ★1067★

Southeastern Community College
U.S. colleges and universities with the lowest percentage of African Americans enrolled, 1997 ★223★
Average faculty salaries for institutions of higher education without academic ranks in Iowa, 2000-01 ★3748★

Southeastern Community College, North Campus
Lowest undergraduate tuition and fees at colleges and universities in Iowa ★1505★

Southeastern Community College, South Campus
Lowest undergraduate tuition and fees at colleges and universities in Iowa ★1505★

Southeastern Illinois College
Lowest undergraduate tuition and fees at colleges and universities in Illinois ★1501★

Southeastern Louisiana University
U.S. college campuses with more than 5,000 students reporting murders or manslaughters, 1998 ★729★
Division I NCAA colleges with the lowest graduation rates for female basketball players, 1990-91 to 1993-94 ★937★
State appropriations for Louisiana institutions of higher education, 2000-01 ★1271★
Average faculty salaries for institutions of higher education in Louisiana, 2000-01 ★3705★

Southeastern Oklahoma State University
State appropriations for Oklahoma's institutions of higher education, 2000-01 ★1289★
Total baccalaureate biology/life sciences degrees awarded to Native Americans from U.S. colleges and universities, 1997-98 ★1682★
Total baccalaureate business management and administrative services degrees awarded to Native Americans from U.S. colleges and universities, 1997-98 ★1686★
Total baccalaureate communications degrees awarded to Native Americans from U.S. colleges and universities, 1997-98 ★1690★

Total baccalaureate computer and information science degrees awarded to Native Americans from U.S. colleges and universities, 1997-98 ★1694★

Total baccalaureate degrees awarded to Native Americans from U.S. colleges and universities, 1997-98 ★1710★

Total baccalaureate education degrees awarded to Native Americans from U.S. colleges and universities, 1997-98 ★1714★

Total baccalaureate physical sciences degrees awarded to Native Americans from U.S. colleges and universities, 1997-98 ★1736★

Total baccalaureate psychology degrees awarded to Native Americans from U.S. colleges and universities, 1997-98 ★1740★

U.S. colleges and universities awarding the most business management and administrative services master's degrees to Native Americans ★1762★

U.S. colleges and universities awarding the most education master's degrees to Native Americans ★1772★

U.S. colleges and universities awarding the most master's degrees to Native Americans ★1789★

U.S. colleges and universities awarding the most psychology master's degrees to Native Americans ★1800★

Average faculty salaries for institutions of higher education in Oklahoma, 2000-01 ★3723★

Southeastern University
Undergraduate tuition and fees at colleges and universities in the District of Columbia ★1493★

U.S. colleges and universities awarding the most business management and administrative services master's degrees to Asian Americans ★1760★

U.S. colleges and universities awarding the most computer and information sciences master's degrees to Asian Americans ★1767★

Southerland; Charles
Top pay and benefits for the chief executive and top paid employees at Barry University ★3192★

Southern
Fortune's highest ranked electric and gas utilities companies, 2000 ★459★

Top utilities companies in Standard & Poor's 500, 2001 ★561★

Southern Adventist University
Average faculty salaries for institutions of higher education in Tennessee, 2000-01 ★3730★

U.S. institutions with the lowest paid full professors, 2001 ★3979★

Southern Arkansas University
State appropriations for Arkansas's institutions of higher education, 2000-01 ★1257★

Average faculty salaries for institutions of higher education in Arkansas, 2000-01 ★3691★

Southern Arkansas University Tech
U.S. colleges and universities with the lowest percentage of African Americans enrolled, 1997 ★223★

Southern California, Marshall Graduate School of Business; University of
Academics' choices for best part-time MBA programs, 2000 ★587★

Southern California, Marshall School of Business; University of
U.S. News & World Report's undergraduate business programs with the best entrepreneurship departments, 2000-01 ★565★

U.S. News & World Report's undergraduate business programs with the best accounting departments, 2000-01 ★581★

Academics' choices for best graduate entrepreneurship programs, 2001 ★583★

Business Week's top business schools with the highest percentage of minority enrollment, 2000 ★613★

Business Week's top business schools with the highest percentage of women enrollees, 2000 ★614★

Business Week's top business schools with the lowest percentage of international students, 2000 ★615★

Lowest post-MBA salaries for students enrolled in Business Week's top business schools, 1999 ★634★

Academics' choices for best graduate accounting programs, 2001 ★659★

U.S. News & World Report's undergraduate business programs with the best international business departments, 2000-01 ★682★

Southern California; University of
All-USA College Academic Third Team, 2001 ★4★

Colleges with the highest number of freshman Merit Scholars, 2000 ★5★

Division I-A all-time percentage leaders ★127★

NCAA men's gymnastics teams with the most individual champions ★137★

U.S. News & World Report's universities with the best taxation departments, 1999-2000 ★573★

Comparisons of investment returns for entrepreneurship MBAs ★623★

U.S. business schools with the slowest payback on MBA investments ★655★

Institutions, by adjusted authorship, with the most published authors in the Journal of Business Research, 1985 to 1999 ★694★

Institutions with the most published authors in the Journal of Business Research, 1985 to 1999 ★695★

Winner of the American Chemical Society's Arthur C. Cope Awards, 2001 ★795★

Institutions with the most part-time Hispanic American faculty ★924★

U.S. News & World Report's national universities with the lowest graduation rates, 1999 ★1141★

Golden Key Scholar Award winners, 2000 ★1316★

Highest undergraduate tuition and fees at colleges and universities in California ★1486★

Total baccalaureate business management and administrative services degrees awarded to Asian Americans from U.S. colleges and universities, 1997-98 ★1684★

Total baccalaureate business management and administrative services degrees awarded to Hispanic Americans from U.S. colleges and universities, 1997-98 ★1685★

Total baccalaureate communications degrees awarded to Asian Americans from U.S. colleges and universities, 1997-98 ★1688★

Total baccalaureate health professions and related sciences degrees awarded to Asian Americans from U.S. colleges and universities, 1997-98 ★1722★

U.S. colleges and universities awarding the most business management and administrative services master's degrees to Asian Americans ★1760★

U.S. colleges and universities awarding the most business management and administrative services master's degrees to Hispanic Americans ★1761★

U.S. colleges and universities awarding the most business management and administrative services master's degrees to Native Americans ★1762★

U.S. colleges and universities awarding the most communications master's degrees to Asian Americans ★1764★

U.S. colleges and universities awarding the most computer and information sciences master's degrees to Asian Americans ★1767★

U.S. colleges and universities awarding the most health professions and related sciences master's degrees to Asian Americans ★1778★

U.S. colleges and universities awarding the most master's degrees to Asian Americans ★1786★

U.S. colleges and universities awarding the most master's degrees to Hispanic Americans ★1787★

U.S. colleges and universities awarding the most master's degrees to minorities ★1788★

U.S. colleges and universities awarding the most social sciences and history master's degrees to Asian Americans ★1802★

Traditionally white institutions awarding the most first professional degrees to African Americans ★1842★

U.S. colleges and universities awarding the most first professional degrees to Asian Americans ★1844★

U.S. colleges and universities awarding the most first professional degrees to Hispanic Americans ★1845★

U.S. colleges and universities awarding the most health professions and related sciences first professional degrees to Asian Americans ★1848★

U.S. colleges and universities awarding the most health professions and related sciences first professional degrees to Hispanic Americans ★1849★

U.S. colleges and universities awarding the most health professions and related sciences first professional degrees to minorities ★1850★

U.S. colleges and universities awarding the most health professions and related sciences first professional degrees to Native Americans ★1851★

U.S. colleges and universities awarding the most law and legal studies first professional degrees to Hispanic Americans ★1854★

U.S. universities with the greatest impact in dentistry/oral surgery, 1994-98 ★1866★

U.S. universities with the greatest impact in dentistry/oral surgery and medicine, 1995-99 ★1867★

U.S. colleges and universities awarding the most biological and life sciences doctorate degrees to Asian Americans ★2083★

U.S. colleges and universities awarding the most doctoral degrees to Asian Americans and Pacific Islanders from 1995 to 1999 ★2093★

U.S. colleges and universities awarding the most doctorate degrees to Asian Americans ★2096★

U.S. colleges and universities awarding the most doctorate degrees to Hispanic Americans ★2097★

U.S. colleges and universities awarding the most doctorate degrees to minorities ★2098★

SOUTHERN

U.S. colleges and universities awarding the most doctorates in professional and other fields, 1999 ★2106★

U.S. colleges and universities awarding the most education doctorate degrees to Asian Americans ★2109★

U.S. colleges and universities awarding the most education doctorate degrees to Hispanic Americans ★2110★

U.S. colleges and universities awarding the most health professions and related sciences doctorate degrees to Asian Americans ★2115★

U.S. colleges and universities awarding the most health professions and related sciences doctorate degrees to Hispanic Americans ★2116★

U.S. colleges and universities awarding the most social sciences and history doctorate degrees to Asian Americans ★2125★

U.S. universities contributing the most papers in the field of AI, robotics, and auto control, 1993-97 ★2338★

Top electrical engineering research-doctorate programs as evaluated by the National Research Council ★2405★

U.S. universities with the greatest impact in metallurgy, 1995-99 ★2435★

Research institutions with the highest enrollment of foreign students, 1998-99 ★2503★

Law library web sites, by visibility ★2687★

Top linguistics research-doctorate programs as evaluated by the National Research Council ★2733★

Institutions receiving the most federal research and development expenditures, 1999 ★3105★

Average faculty salaries for institutions of higher education in California, 2000-01 ★3692★

Radcliffe Institute for Advanced Study fellowship recipients in the field of sociology, 2000-01 ★4346★

Southern Christian University

Highest undergraduate tuition and fees at colleges and universities in Alabama ★1479★

Southern Colorado; University of

Average faculty salaries for institutions of higher education in Colorado, 2000-01 ★3693★

Southern Connecticut State University

Average faculty salaries for institutions of higher education in Connecticut, 2000-01 ★3694★

Southern Connecticut University

State appropriations for Connecticut's institutions of higher education, 2000-01 ★1260★

Southern Economic Journal

Journals publishing the most articles on economic education research from 1963-1990 ★2170★

Highest impact economics journals in energy from 1974 to 1979 ★2456★

Southern Idaho; College of

Community colleges receiving the most gifts, 1999-2000 ★1239★

Undergraduate tuition and fees at colleges and universities in Idaho ★1499★

Southern Illinois University

State appropriations for Illinois institutions of higher education, 2000-01 ★1266★

Illinois institutions with the highest article output ★2677★

Enrollment of students in the ten largest doctoral journalism and mass communications programs, 1999 ★2762★

Southern Illinois University, Carbondale

Four-year institutions with the most drug referrals reported, 1999 ★706★

Division I NCAA colleges with that graduated none of their African American male basketball players, 1990-91 to 1993-94 ★930★

U.S. News & World Report's national universities with students least in debt, 1999 ★1475★

Total baccalaureate degrees awarded to African Americans from traditionally white institutions, 1997-98 ★1698★

Total baccalaureate education degrees awarded to African Americans from U.S. colleges and universities, 1997-98 ★1711★

Total baccalaureate education degrees awarded to Asian Americans from U.S. colleges and universities, 1997-98 ★1712★

Total baccalaureate health professions and related sciences degrees awarded to African Americans from U.S. colleges and universities, 1997-98 ★1721★

U.S. colleges and universities awarding the most psychology doctorate degrees to Asian Americans ★2121★

Average faculty salaries for institutions of higher education in Illinois, 2000-01 ★3700★

Southern Illinois University, Edwardsville

U.S. colleges and universities awarding the most English language/literature/letters master's degrees to African Americans ★1773★

Average faculty salaries for institutions of higher education in Illinois, 2000-01 ★3700★

Southern Indiana; University of

Four-year institutions with the most liquor referrals reported, 1999 ★708★

Four-year institutions with the most weapons referrals reported, 1999 ★710★

State appropriations for Indiana's institutions of higher education, 2000-01 ★1267★

Average faculty salaries for institutions of higher education in Indiana, 2000-01 ★3701★

Southern Lehigh Middle School

Outstanding secondary schools in Allentown-Bethlehem-Easton, Pennsylvania ★4081★

Southern Maine Technical College

Lowest undergraduate tuition and fees at colleges and universities in Maine ★1513★

Average faculty salaries for institutions of higher education without academic ranks in Maine, 2000-01 ★3749★

Southern Maine; University of

Radcliffe Institute for Advanced Study fellowship recipients in the field of economics, 2000-01 ★2172★

Average faculty salaries for institutions of higher education in Maine, 2000-01 ★3706★

Southern Methodist University

NCAA Division I women's swimming teams with the most individual championships ★136★

Division I NCAA colleges with the highest graduation rates for male basketball players, 1990-91 to 1993-94 ★935★

U.S. colleges and universities with a large student body of conservative Republicans ★1016★

Highest undergraduate tuition and fees at colleges and universities in Texas ★1560★

U.S. colleges and universities awarding the most computer and information sciences master's degrees to Hispanic Americans ★1768★

U.S. colleges and universities awarding the most English language/literature/letters master's degrees to Hispanic Americans ★1775★

U.S. colleges and universities awarding the most law and legal studies master's degrees to Asian Americans ★1782★

U.S. colleges and universities awarding the most mathematics master's degrees to Asian Americans ★1791★

Presidents with the highest pay at Doctoral I and II universities, 1998-99 ★3160★

Average faculty salaries for institutions of higher education in Texas, 2000-01 ★3731★

Southern Mississippi; University of

State appropriations for Mississippi's institutions of higher education, 2000-01 ★1277★

U.S. colleges and universities awarding the most communications master's degrees to African Americans ★1763★

U.S. colleges and universities awarding the most education doctorate degrees to African Americans ★2108★

Enrollment of students in the ten largest doctoral journalism and mass communications programs, 1999 ★2762★

Average faculty salaries for institutions of higher education in Mississippi, 2000-01 ★3711★

Southern Nazarene University

Institutions censured by the American Association of University Professors, 2001 ★1067★

Highest undergraduate tuition and fees at colleges and universities in Oklahoma ★1545★

Southern Nevada; Community College of

Undergraduate tuition and fees at colleges and universities in Nevada ★1530★

Southern Oregon University

Average faculty salaries for institutions of higher education in Oregon, 2000-01 ★3724★

Southern Polytechnic State University

State appropriations for Georgia's institutions of higher education, 2000-01 ★1263★

U.S. colleges and universities awarding the most English language/literature/letters master's degrees to African Americans ★1773★

Professional or specialized institutions with the highest enrollment of foreign students, 1998-99 ★2501★

Average faculty salaries for institutions of higher education in Georgia, 2000-01 ★3697★

Southern State Community College

Average faculty salaries for institutions of higher education in Ohio, 2000-01 ★3722★

Southern Union State Community College

Average faculty salaries for institutions of higher education without academic ranks in Alabama, 2000-01 ★3740★

Southern University

Colleges offering the Thurgood Marshall Scholarship Fund ★221★

U.S. college campuses reporting murders or non-negligent manslaughters, 1999 ★728★

Lowest undergraduate tuition and fees at colleges and universities in Louisiana ★1511★

U.S. institutions with more than 40% female bachelor's graduates in their physics departments, 1994-98 ★2977★

Southern University and A&M College

Most dangerous college campuses in the U.S. ★712★

Lowest undergraduate tuition and fees at colleges and universities in Louisiana ★1511★

Historically black colleges and universities awarding the most master's degrees to African Americans ★1670★
Total baccalaureate degrees awarded to African Americans from historically black colleges, 1997-98 ★1697★
Total baccalaureate degrees awarded to African Americans from U.S. colleges and universities, 1997-98 ★1699★
Total baccalaureate education degrees awarded to African Americans from U.S. colleges and universities, 1997-98 ★1711★
Total baccalaureate health professions and related sciences degrees awarded to African Americans from U.S. colleges and universities, 1997-98 ★1721★
Total baccalaureate mathematics degrees awarded to African Americans from U.S. colleges and universities, 1997-98 ★1729★
Total baccalaureate physical sciences degrees awarded to African Americans from U.S. colleges and universities, 1997-98 ★1733★
Total baccalaureate social sciences and history degrees awarded to African Americans from U.S. colleges and universities, 1997-98 ★1741★
U.S. colleges and universities awarding the most communications master's degrees to African Americans ★1763★
U.S. colleges and universities awarding the most computer and information sciences master's degrees to African Americans ★1766★
U.S. colleges and universities awarding the most health professions and related sciences master's degrees to African Americans ★1777★
U.S. colleges and universities awarding the most master's degrees to African Americans ★1785★
U.S. colleges and universities awarding the most mathematics master's degrees to African Americans ★1790★
U.S. colleges and universities awarding the most psychology master's degrees to African Americans ★1797★
U.S. colleges and universities awarding the most social sciences and history master's degrees to African Americans ★1801★
U.S. institutions awarding the most baccalaureate degrees to African Americans in agribusiness and production, 1998 ★1813★
U.S. institutions awarding the most baccalaureate degrees to African Americans in agricultural sciences, 1998 ★1814★
U.S. institutions awarding the most baccalaureate degrees to minorities in agribusiness and production, 1998 ★1819★
Historically black colleges and universities awarding the most first professional degrees to African Americans ★1835★
U.S. colleges and universities awarding the most first professional degrees to African Americans ★1843★
U.S. colleges and universities awarding the most law and legal studies first professional degrees to African Americans ★1852★

Southern University, Baton Rouge
Division I NCAA colleges with that graduated none of their African American male basketball players, 1990-91 to 1993-94 ★930★
Division I NCAA colleges with the lowest graduation rates for male basketball players, 1990-91 to 1993-94 ★940★
Average faculty salaries for institutions of higher education in Louisiana, 2000-01 ★3705★

Southern University (LA)
Institutions with the most female physics bachelor's recipients, 1994-1998 ★2959★

Southern University, New Orleans
Lowest undergraduate tuition and fees at colleges and universities in Louisiana ★1511★
Total baccalaureate education degrees awarded to African Americans from U.S. colleges and universities, 1997-98 ★1711★

Southern University System
State appropriations for Louisiana institutions of higher education, 2000-01 ★1271★

Southern Utah University
All-USA College Academic First Team, 2001 ★2★
Division I NCAA colleges with that graduated all of their African American male basketball players, 1990-91 to 1993-94 ★927★
State appropriations for Utah's institutions of higher education, 2000-01 ★1297★
Undergraduate tuition and fees at colleges and universities in Utah ★1562★

Southern Vermont College
Undergraduate tuition and fees at colleges and universities in Vermont ★1563★

Southern Wesleyan University
Highest undergraduate tuition and fees at colleges and universities in South Carolina ★1554★
Average faculty salaries for institutions of higher education in South Carolina, 2000-01 ★3728★

Southern West Virginia Community and Technical College
State appropriations for West Virginia's institutions of higher education, 2000-01 ★1301★
Lowest undergraduate tuition and fees at colleges and universities in West Virginia ★1569★
Average faculty salaries for institutions of higher education in West Virginia, 2000-01 ★3737★

Southfield Christian School
Outstanding secondary schools in Detroit, Michigan ★4125★

Southfield-Lathrup High School
Outstanding secondary schools in Detroit, Michigan ★4125★

Southington High School
Outstanding secondary schools in Hartford, Connecticut ★4147★

Southside College Prep
Acceptance rates at Chicago college prep magnet schools, 2000-01 ★4000★

Southwest Airlines
Fortune's highest ranked airlines, 2000 ★447★
Top transportation companies in Standard & Poor's 500, 2001 ★560★

Southwest; College of the
Private 4-year institutions with the lowest tuition, 2000-01 ★1468★
Highest undergraduate tuition and fees at colleges and universities in New Mexico ★1535★

Southwest Mississippi Community College
Lowest undergraduate tuition and fees at colleges and universities in Mississippi ★1523★

Southwest Missouri State University
Division I NCAA colleges with that graduated none of their African American male basketball players, 1990-91 to 1993-94 ★930★

Division I NCAA colleges with the lowest graduation rates for male basketball players, 1990-91 to 1993-94 ★940★
State appropriations for Missouri's institutions of higher education, 2000-01 ★1278★
Average faculty salaries for institutions of higher education in Missouri, 2000-01 ★3712★

Southwest School of Electronics
Highest undergraduate tuition and fees at colleges and universities in Texas ★1560★

Southwest State University
U.S. News & World Report's top public midwestern regional liberal arts colleges, 2000-01 ★1350★
Average faculty salaries for institutions of higher education in Minnesota, 2000-01 ★3710★

Southwest Tennessee Community College
Average faculty salaries for institutions of higher education in Tennessee, 2000-01 ★3730★

Southwest Texas Junior College
Average faculty salaries for institutions of higher education without academic ranks in Texas, 2000-01 ★3766★

Southwest Texas State University
Average faculty salaries for institutions of higher education in Texas, 2000-01 ★3731★

Southwest Wisconsin Technical College
Lowest undergraduate tuition and fees at colleges and universities in Wisconsin ★1571★

Southwestern Adventist University
Institutions censured by the American Association of University Professors, 2001 ★1067★

Southwestern Christian College
Historically black colleges and universities with high student loan default rates, 1998 ★2736★

Southwestern College
Highest undergraduate tuition and fees at colleges and universities in Arizona ★1482★
Highest undergraduate tuition and fees at colleges and universities in Kansas ★1506★
Average faculty salaries for institutions of higher education in Kansas, 2000-01 ★3703★

Southwestern Community College
Average faculty salaries for institutions of higher education without academic ranks in North Carolina, 2000-01 ★3761★

The Southwestern Company
Top internships in the U.S. with the highest compensation, 2001 ★2611★

Southwestern Illinois College
Average faculty salaries for institutions of higher education in Illinois, 2000-01 ★3700★

Southwestern Indian Polytechnic Institute
U.S. tribal colleges ★1445★

Southwestern Louisiana; University of
U.S. colleges and universities awarding the most computer and information sciences master's degrees to Asian Americans ★1767★
U.S. colleges and universities awarding the most mathematics master's degrees to Asian Americans ★1791★
U.S. colleges and universities awarding the most mathematics doctorate degrees to Asian Americans ★2117★

Southwestern Oklahoma State University
State appropriations for Oklahoma's institutions of higher education, 2000-01 ★1289★
U.S. News & World Report's western regional universities with students least in debt, 1999 ★1575★

SOUTHWESTERN

Total baccalaureate health professions and related sciences degrees awarded to Native Americans from U.S. colleges and universities, 1997-98 ★1724★

Total baccalaureate physical sciences degrees awarded to Native Americans from U.S. colleges and universities, 1997-98 ★1736★

Southwestern Oklahoma State University, Syre
Average faculty salaries for institutions of higher education in Oklahoma, 2000-01 ★3723★

Southwestern Oklahoma State University, Weatherford
Average faculty salaries for institutions of higher education in Oklahoma, 2000-01 ★3723★

Southwestern Oregon Community College
Lowest undergraduate tuition and fees at colleges and universities in Oregon ★1548★

Southwestern University
U.S. News & World Report's national liberal arts colleges with students most in debt, 1999 ★1386★
Highest undergraduate tuition and fees at colleges and universities in Texas ★1560★
Average faculty salaries for institutions of higher education in Texas, 2000-01 ★3731★

Southwestern University School of Law
U.S. colleges and universities awarding the most law and legal studies first professional degrees to Asian Americans ★1853★
U.S. colleges and universities awarding the most law and legal studies first professional degrees to Hispanic Americans ★1854★

Southwestern University (TX)
Presidents with the highest pay at Baccalaureate I colleges, 1998-99 ★3159★

Space Race
Most notable books for middle readers, 2001 ★317★

Space science
United States' contribution of papers in the sciences, by field, 1996-2000 ★4284★
France's contribution of papers in the sciences, by field, 1996-2000 ★4312★

Spadafora; David
Top pay and benefits for the chief executive and top paid employees at Lake Forest College ★3363★

Spain
Percentage of enrollment at private institutions of higher education, by country, 1998 ★858★
Percentage of enrollment at public institutions of higher education, by country, 1998 ★859★
Countries of origin for non-U.S. citizens awarded doctorates at U.S. colleges and universities, 1999 ★1901★
Countries with the lowest spending per student on higher education, 1997 ★2489★
Top countries of study for U.S. students studying abroad, 1998-99 ★2510★
Institute for Scientific Information periodical prices by country, 2001 ★2922★
Countries spending the highest percentage of gross domestic product on education ★4060★

Spalding University
Highest undergraduate tuition and fees at colleges and universities in Kentucky ★1508★

Spangler; David R.
Top pay and benefits for the chief executive and top paid employees at Saint Martin's College in Washington ★3479★

Spanish
Gender breakdown of language and literature doctorate recipients, by subfield, 1999 ★1937★
Language and literature doctorates awarded at U.S. colleges and universities, by subfield, 1999 ★1949★
Languages of requested materials from OCLC ILL, 1999 ★2679★

Spanish language
Number of Advanced Placement Exams taken by African Americans, by subject, 2000 ★30★
Number of Advanced Placement Exams taken by Asian Americans, by subject, 2000 ★31★
Number of Advanced Placement Exams taken by Hispanic Americans, by subject, 2000 ★32★

Spanish literature
Number of Advanced Placement Exams taken by African Americans, by subject, 2000 ★30★
Number of Advanced Placement Exams taken by Asian Americans, by subject, 2000 ★31★
Number of Advanced Placement Exams taken by Hispanic Americans, by subject, 2000 ★32★

Spartanburg High School
Outstanding secondary schools in Greenville-Spartanburg-Anderson, South Carolina ★4143★

Spartz; James L.
Top pay and benefits for the chief executive and top paid employees at Wilmington College in Delaware ★3632★

Spatt; Chester S.
Top pay and benefits for the chief executive and top paid employees at Carnegie Mellon University ★3223★

Spear; Jeffrey B.
Top pay and benefits for the chief executive and top paid employees at Houghton College ★3341★

Spear; Scott L.
Top pay and benefits for the chief executive and top paid employees at Georgetown University ★3306★

Spears; Marcus
All-American boy's high school football receivers, 2000 ★185★

Special education
Education doctorates awarded at U.S. colleges and universities, by subfield, 1999 ★1921★
Gender breakdown of education doctorate recipients, by subfield, 1999 ★1933★
Educational program activities expenditures, 2000 ★3992★

Special education teachers
Employment outlook for the year 2005 for selected occupations ★2297★

Spectrochimica Acta B
Spectroscopy journals by citation impact, 1981-99 ★4359★
Spectroscopy journals by citation impact, 1995-99 ★4360★
Spectroscopy journals by citation impact, 1999 ★4361★

Spectrochimica Acta Reviews
Spectroscopy journals by citation impact, 1981-99 ★4359★

Speech
Areas of specialization in journalism and mass communications programs with the highest enrollment, 1999 ★2740★

Educational Rankings Annual • 2002

Speech impairments
Disabled students served in U.S. public school programs, 1998-99 ★1877★

Speech-language pathologists and audiologists
Projections for the fastest growing occupations requiring a bachelor's degree or more from 1998 to 2008 ★2292★
Projected employment growth for selected occupations that require advanced education, 1998-2008 ★2318★

Speech-language pathology and audiology
Gender breakdown of health sciences doctorate recipients, by subfield, 1999 ★1935★
Health sciences doctorates awarded at U.S. colleges and universities, by subfield, 1999 ★1944★

Speech pathologist
Jobs with the lowest unemployment ★2258★
Most desirable jobs in healthcare/medicine ★2273★

Speech and rhetorical studies
Gender breakdown of humanities doctorate recipients, by subfield, 1999 ★1936★
Humanities doctorates awarded at U.S. colleges and universities, by subfield, 1999 ★1946★

Speizer; Frank E.
Most-cited researchers in epidemiology, 1981-1998 ★2876★

Spekman; Robert E.
Authors with the most articles published in the *Journal of Business Research*, 1985 to 1999 ★687★
Highest impact authors in the *Journal of Business Research*, by number of citations in 12 journals, 1985-1999 ★693★

Spellbinder: The Life of Harry Houdini
Most notable nonfiction books for young adults, 2001 ★324★

Speller; Richard
Top pay and benefits for the chief executive and top paid employees at Beaver College ★3195★

Spellmann; Dennis C.
Top pay and benefits for the chief executive and top paid employees at Lindenwood University ★3375★

Spelman College
Historically black institutions with the highest number of National Achievement Scholars, 1998 ★8★
Most dangerous college campuses in the U.S. ★712★
U.S. colleges and universities with the unhappiest students ★1041★
U.S. colleges and universities with the worst overall administration ★1045★
Retention rates of African American students at historically black institutions, 1997-98 ★1120★
Fiske Guide's best buys for private colleges and universities, 2001 ★1459★
Total baccalaureate English language, literature, and letters degrees awarded to African Americans from U.S. colleges and universities, 1997-98 ★1716★
Total baccalaureate mathematics degrees awarded to African Americans from U.S. colleges and universities, 1997-98 ★1729★
Total baccalaureate physical sciences degrees awarded to African Americans from U.S. colleges and universities, 1997-98 ★1733★

Total baccalaureate psychology degrees awarded to African Americans from U.S. colleges and universities, 1997-98 ★1737★

Total baccalaureate social sciences and history degrees awarded to African Americans from U.S. colleges and universities, 1997-98 ★1741★

Private, 4-year undergraduate colleges and universities producing the most Ph.D.'s in nonscience fields, 1990 ★2032★

Women's colleges granting physics bachelor's degrees, 2000 ★2982★

Spencer; Brock
Top pay and benefits for the chief executive and top paid employees at Beloit College ★3199★

Spencer; Chris
All-American boy's high school football linemen, 2000 ★183★

Spencer; Rick E.
Top pay and benefits for the chief executive and top paid employees at North Central College in Illinois ★3421★

Speros; George L.
Top pay and benefits for the chief executive and top paid employees at Lake Forest College ★3363★

Speth; Gerald L.
Top pay and benefits for the chief executive and top paid employees at the University of Indianapolis ★3545★

Speziali; Helen J.
Top pay and benefits for the chief executive and top paid employees at College Misericordia ★3243★

Spherion
Fortune's highest ranked temporary help companies, 2000 ★500★

Spider Sparrow
Most notable children's recordings, 2001 ★320★

Spiegelman; Art
Outstanding children's picture books, 2000 ★331★

Spindle; Richard L.
Top pay and benefits for the chief executive and top paid employees at Midamerica Nazarene University ★3400★

Spindle's End
Booklist's most recommended fantasy books for youth ★312★

Spinelli; Jerry
Outstanding children's fiction books, 2000 ★329★

Spink; Amanda
Library and information science faculty with the most journal articles, 1993-1998 ★2711★

Spiro; Barbara S.
Top pay and benefits for the chief executive and top paid employees at Drexel University ★3274★

Spitzer, S.J.; Robert
Top pay and benefits for the chief executive and top paid employees at Gonzaga University ★3311★

Spivak; Michael
Top pay and benefits for the chief executive and top paid employees at the Maharishi University of Management ★3533★

Spivey; Oscar S.
Top pay and benefits for the chief executive and top paid employees at Mercer University ★3398★

Splish! Splash! Animal Baths
Booklist's best science books for children ★310★

Split Image
Most notable fiction books for young adults, 2001 ★322★

Spokane Community College
Lowest undergraduate tuition and fees at colleges and universities in Washington ★1567★
Average faculty salaries for institutions of higher education without academic ranks in Washington, 2000-01 ★3768★

Spokane Falls Community College
Lowest undergraduate tuition and fees at colleges and universities in Washington ★1567★
Average faculty salaries for institutions of higher education without academic ranks in Washington, 2000-01 ★3768★

Sponsors for Educational Opportunity
Top internships in the U.S. with the highest compensation, 2001 ★2611★

Spooner; LaRose F.
Top pay and benefits for the chief executive and top paid employees at Meredith College ★3399★

Sports agents mentorship
Monster.com's most searched job listings ★2308★

Sports Illustrated
People for the American Way's list of most frequently challenged materials, 1982-1992 ★749★

Sports instructor
Most desirable jobs in athletics ★2269★

Sports: The Complete Visual Reference
Library Journal's best reference books, 2000 ★368★
Outstanding reference sources, 2001 ★371★

Spotswood High School
Outstanding secondary schools in Middlesex-Somerset-Hunterdon, New Jersey ★4179★

Spray; Thomas L.
Top pay and benefits for the chief executive and top paid employees at the University of Pennsylvania ★3555★

Sprayberry High School
Outstanding secondary schools in Atlanta, Georgia ★4087★

Spring Arbor College
Average faculty salaries for institutions of higher education in Michigan, 2000-01 ★3709★

Spring Branch Middle School
Outstanding secondary schools in Houston, Texas ★4150★

Spring Forest Middle School
Outstanding secondary schools in Houston, Texas ★4150★

Spring High School
Outstanding secondary schools in Houston, Texas ★4150★

Spring Hill College
U.S. News & World Report's best undergraduate fees among southern regional universities by discount tuition, 2000 ★1429★
U.S. News & World Report's southern regional universities with the best alumni giving rates, 2000-01 ★1434★
U.S. News & World Report's southern regional universities with the highest acceptance rates, 2000-01 ★1436★
Highest undergraduate tuition and fees at colleges and universities in Alabama ★1479★

Spring Oaks Middle School
Outstanding secondary schools in Houston, Texas ★4150★

Spring Valley High School
Outstanding secondary schools in Columbia, South Carolina ★4117★

Spring Woods High School
Outstanding secondary schools in Houston, Texas ★4150★

Springer-Verlag
Book publishers with the most citations (Class 1) ★2562★

Springfield College
U.S. News & World Report's northern regional universities with the best student/faculty ratios, 2000-01 ★1416★
U.S. News & World Report's northern regional universities with the highest alumni giving rates, 2000-01 ★1418★
Average faculty salaries for institutions of higher education in Massachusetts, 2000-01 ★3708★
Average faculty salaries for institutions of higher education without academic ranks in Illinois, 2000-01 ★3747★

Springfield Technical Community College
Lowest undergraduate tuition and fees at colleges and universities in Massachusetts ★1517★
Average faculty salaries for institutions of higher education in Massachusetts, 2000-01 ★3708★

Springs Industries
Fortune's highest ranked textiles companies, 2000 ★501★

Sprint
Fortune's highest ranked telecommunications companies, 2000 ★499★

Sprint PCS Group
Business Week's best performing companies with the greatest decline in earnings growth ★412★
Business Week's best performing companies with the highest 3-year sales performance ★417★
Business Week's best performing companies with the lowest net margin, 2000 ★425★
Business Week's best performing companies with the lowest return on equity, 2000 ★426★

Sprinthall; Richard
Top pay and benefits for the chief executive and top paid employees at American International College ★3173★

Spruce Creek High School
Outstanding secondary schools in Daytona Beach, Florida ★4123★

Spuller; Robert L.
Top pay and benefits for the chief executive and top paid employees at Lenoir-Rhyne College ★3369★

Squandering Aimlessly: My Adventures in the American Marketplace
Library Journal's best nonfiction audiobooks, 2000 ★243★

Squeaking of Art: The Mice Go to the Museum
Booklist's best art books for young people ★308★

Stabile; Paul F.
Top pay and benefits for the chief executive and top paid employees at LaRoche College ★3364★

Stacey; Judy
Highly acknowledged individuals in the field of women's studies, 1975-94 ★4466★

Stackhouse; Janifer
Top pay and benefits for the chief executive and top paid employees at the College of Notre Dame in California ★3526★

Staff Leasing
Fortune's highest ranked outsourcing services companies, 2000 ★483★

Staff; Scott
Top pay and benefits for the chief executive and top paid employees at Lewis and Clark College in Oregon ★3371★

Stafford; Elizabeth A.
Top pay and benefits for the chief executive and top paid employees at Spring Hill College ★3508★

Stafford Loans
Sources of financial aid for incoming freshmen, 2000 ★1062★

Stafford; Rebecca
Presidents with the highest pay at Master's I and II colleges and universities, 1998-99 ★3161★
Top pay and benefits for the chief executive and top paid employees at Monmouth University in New Jersey ★3406★

Stagg; Amos Alonzo
Division I-A all-time coaching victories ★126★

Stagg High School
Outstanding secondary schools in Chicago, Illinois ★4110★

Stahl; Gregory
Top pay and benefits for the chief executive and top paid employees at Siena College ★3498★

Staisloff; Richard L.
Top pay and benefits for the chief executive and top paid employees at the College of Notre Dame in Maryland ★3527★

Stamford, CT
U.S. cities with the highest home prices ★3087★

Stamos; Nickolas
Top pay and benefits for the chief executive and top paid employees at Dickinson College ★3268★

Stamper; Ernie W.
Top pay and benefits for the chief executive and top paid employees at Georgetown College in Kentucky ★3305★

Stampfer; Meir J.
Authors with the greatest impact measure in cardiovascular research, 1993-98 ★2868★
Most-cited researchers in clinical medicine, 1981-1998 ★2875★
Most-cited researchers in epidemiology, 1981-1998 ★2876★

Standard & Poor's 500 Index
2000 returns on university endowments and other comparative measures ★1231★

Standard Register
Fortune's highest ranked printing companies, 2000 ★487★

Stanford Law Review
Law journals by citation impact, 1981-96 ★2617★
Law journals with the greatest impact measure, 1981-98 ★2618★

Stanford University
Colleges with the highest number of freshman Merit Scholars, 2000 ★5★
U.S. universities enrolling the most National Achievement Scholars, 1995 ★10★
U.S. universities enrolling the most National Achievement Scholars, 1997 ★12★
Radcliffe Institute for Advanced Study fellowship recipient in the field of social anthropology, 2000-01 ★59★
Radcliffe Institute for Advanced Study fellowship recipients in the field of anthropology, 2000-01 ★60★
Most effective anthropology research-doctorate programs as evaluated by the National Research Council ★61★
Top anthropology research-doctorate programs as evaluated by the National Research Council ★62★
Top art history research-doctorate programs as evaluated by the National Research Council ★93★
NCAA Division I women's swimming teams with the most individual championships ★136★
Women's basketball teams with the most appearances in the Final Four ★157★
Most effective ecology, evolution, and behavior research-doctorate programs as evaluated by the National Research Council ★199★
Most effective neurosciences research-doctorate programs as evaluated by the National Research Council ★200★
Top ecology, evolution, and behavior research-doctorate programs as evaluated by the National Research Council ★201★
Top neurosciences research-doctorate programs as evaluated by the National Research Council ★202★
Most effective biochemistry and molecular biology research-doctorate programs as evaluated by the National Research Council ★205★
Most effective molecular and general genetics research-doctorate programs as evaluated by the National Research Council ★207★
Top biochemistry and molecular biology research-doctorate programs as evaluated by the National Research Council ★209★
Top molecular and general genetics research-doctorate programs as evaluated by the National Research Council ★211★
U.S. universities with the greatest impact in microbiology, 1995-99 ★218★
Top business schools in research performance, 1986-1998 ★532★
U.S. universities publishing the most papers in the field of management, 1995-99 ★574★
U.S. universities with the greatest impact in management, 1994-98 ★575★
Comparisons of investment returns for information technology MBAs ★625★
Comparisons of investment returns for marketing MBAs ★626★
Top business schools by average MBA rank, 1986-1998 ★644★
Top business schools for overall within-discipline research performance, 1986-1998 ★645★
Top business schools for within-discipline research performance in management, 1986-1998 ★646★
Top business schools for within-discipline research performance in management science, 1986-1998 ★647★
U.S. business schools with the slowest payback on MBA investments ★655★
Top business schools for within-discipline research performance in accounting, 1986-1998 ★660★
U.S. universities with the greatest impact in chemistry, 1994-98 ★793★
Most effective chemistry research-doctorate programs as evaluated by the National Research Council ★802★
Top chemistry research-doctorate programs as evaluated by the National Research Council ★805★
Division I NCAA colleges with that graduated all of their African American male basketball players, 1990-91 to 1993-94 ★927★
Division I NCAA colleges with that graduated more than 80% of their African American male athletes, 1990-91 to 1993-94 ★929★
Division I NCAA colleges with the highest graduation rates for football players, 1990-91 to 1993-94 ★933★
Division I NCAA colleges with the highest graduation rates for male athletes, 1990-91 to 1993-94 ★934★
Division I NCAA colleges with the highest graduation rates for male basketball players, 1990-91 to 1993-94 ★935★
U.S. colleges and universities that are the toughest to get into ★988★
U.S. colleges and universities with the most attractive campuses ★1039★
U.S. News & World Report's national universities with the best academic reputation, 2000-01 ★1126★
U.S. News & World Report's national universities with the best freshmen retention rates, 2000-01 ★1128★
U.S. News & World Report's national universities with the best graduation and retention rank, 2000-01 ★1129★
U.S. News & World Report's national universities with the best student/faculty ratio, 2000-01 ★1130★
U.S. News & World Report's national universities with the highest financial resources rank, 2000-01 ★1133★
U.S. News & World Report's national universities with the highest selectivity rank, 2000-01 ★1139★
U.S. News & World Report's national universities with the lowest acceptance rates, 2000-01 ★1140★
2000 endowment values of the 'wealthiest' U.S. universities ★1230★
2001 mid-year endowment values of the 'wealthiest' U.S. universities ★1234★
Colleges and universities with the largest endowments, 2000 ★1237★
Endowment values for the wealthiest U.S. universities, 2000 ★1240★
Institutions receiving the most alumni gifts, 1999-2000 ★1242★
Institutions receiving the most corporate gifts, 1999-2000 ★1243★
Institutions receiving the most gifts, 1999-2000 ★1244★
Largest gifts to higher education, 1967-2000 ★1247★
Largest private gifts to higher education, 1967-2000 ★1248★
U.S. News & World Report's best undergraduate fees among national universities by discount tuition, 2000 ★1474★
Highest undergraduate tuition and fees at colleges and universities in California ★1486★

Most effective comparative literature research-doctorate programs as evaluated by the National Research Council ★1587★

Top comparative literature research-doctorate programs as evaluated by the National Research Council ★1588★

U.S. universities publishing the most papers in the field of computer science, 1994-98 ★1591★

U.S. universities with the greatest impact in computer science, 1994-98 ★1592★

Most effective computer science research-doctorate programs as evaluated by the National Research Council ★1594★

Top computer science research-doctorate programs as evaluated by the National Research Council ★1597★

Total ethnic/cultural studies master's degrees awarded to minorities from U.S. colleges and universities, 1997-98 ★1748★

U.S. colleges and universities awarding the most biological and life sciences master's degrees to Asian Americans ★1757★

U.S. colleges and universities awarding the most communications master's degrees to Asian Americans ★1764★

U.S. colleges and universities awarding the most computer and information sciences master's degrees to Asian Americans ★1767★

U.S. colleges and universities awarding the most education master's degrees to Asian Americans ★1770★

U.S. colleges and universities awarding the most English language/literature/letters master's degrees to Asian Americans ★1774★

U.S. colleges and universities awarding the most master's degrees to Asian Americans ★1786★

U.S. colleges and universities awarding the most master's degrees to minorities ★1788★

U.S. colleges and universities awarding the most mathematics master's degrees to Asian Americans ★1791★

U.S. colleges and universities awarding the most physical sciences master's degrees to Asian Americans ★1794★

U.S. colleges and universities awarding the most psychology master's degrees to Asian Americans ★1798★

U.S. colleges and universities awarding the most social sciences and history master's degrees to African Americans ★1801★

U.S. colleges and universities awarding the most social sciences and history master's degrees to Asian Americans ★1802★

U.S. colleges and universities awarding the most social sciences and history master's degrees to Hispanic Americans ★1803★

U.S. colleges and universities awarding the most first professional degrees to Hispanic Americans ★1845★

U.S. colleges and universities awarding the most law and legal studies first professional degrees to Hispanic Americans ★1854★

U.S. colleges and universities awarding the most biological and life sciences doctorate degrees to Hispanic Americans ★2084★

U.S. colleges and universities awarding the most computer and information sciences doctorate degrees to Asian Americans ★2090★

U.S. colleges and universities awarding the most doctoral degrees to African Americans from 1995 to 1999 ★2091★

U.S. colleges and universities awarding the most doctoral degrees to American Indians and Alaskan Natives from 1995 to 1999 ★2092★

U.S. colleges and universities awarding the most doctoral degrees to Asian Americans and Pacific Islanders from 1995 to 1999 ★2093★

U.S. colleges and universities awarding the most doctoral degrees to Asian Americans ★2096★

U.S. colleges and universities awarding the most doctoral degrees to Hispanic Americans ★2097★

U.S. colleges and universities awarding the most doctoral degrees to minorities ★2098★

U.S. colleges and universities awarding the most doctoral degrees to Native Americans ★2099★

U.S. colleges and universities awarding the most doctorates in engineering, 1999 ★2102★

U.S. colleges and universities awarding the most doctorates in physical sciences, mathematics, and computer sciences, 1999 ★2105★

U.S. colleges and universities awarding the most physical sciences doctorate degrees to Asian Americans ★2119★

U.S. colleges and universities awarding the most social sciences and history doctorate degrees to Asian Americans ★2125★

Most effective geosciences research-doctorate programs as evaluated by the National Research Council ★2150★

Top geosciences research-doctorate programs as evaluated by the National Research Council ★2152★

Economics departments by number of citations by top economists, 1971-92 ★2158★

Economics departments by number of citations per top economist, 1971-92 ★2159★

Economics departments by number of top economists, 1971-92 ★2160★

Institutions generating the most economic education research text, 1963-1990 ★2167★

Institutions most frequently contributing to the *American Economic Review* from 1911-1990 ★2168★

Institutions most frequently contributing to the *American Economic Review* from 1951-1990 ★2169★

U.S. universities publishing the most papers in the field of economics and business, 1995-99 ★2178★

Economics Ph.D. programs by number of citations of top economist graduates, 1971-92 ★2204★

Economics Ph.D. programs by number of citations per top economist graduate, 1971-92 ★2205★

Economics Ph.D. programs by number of top economist graduates, 1971-92 ★2206★

Most effective economics research-doctorate programs as evaluated by the National Research Council ★2207★

Origin of doctorate for dissertation chairs in economics ★2208★

Origin of doctorate for economics faculty at Ph.D.-granting institutions ★2209★

Origin of doctorate for economics faculty at Ph.D.-granting institutions, by Ph.D. equivalents produced ★2210★

Top economics research-doctorate programs as evaluated by the National Research Council ★2213★

U.S. universities with the greatest impact in education, 1993-97 ★2220★

U.S. universities with the greatest impact in education, 1994-98 ★2221★

U.S. universities with the greatest impact in civil engineering, 1995-99 ★2350★

U.S. universities with the greatest impact in electrical and electronic engineering, 1994-99 ★2356★

Acceptance rates for *U.S. News & World Report*'s top 10 graduate engineering schools, 2001 ★2358★

Average analytic GRE scores for *U.S. News & World Report*'s top 10 graduate engineering schools, 2001 ★2359★

Average quantitative GRE scores for *U.S. News & World Report*'s top 10 graduate engineering schools, 2001 ★2360★

Doctoral student-faculty ratios at *U.S. News & World Report*'s top 10 graduate engineering schools, 2001 ★2361★

Faculty membership in National Academy of Engineering at *U.S. News & World Report*'s top 10 graduate engineering schools, 2001 ★2362★

Ph.D.s granted at *U.S. News & World Report*'s top 10 graduate engineering schools, 2001 ★2363★

Research expenditures per faculty member at *U.S. News & World Report*'s top 10 graduate engineering schools, 2001 ★2364★

Research funding allocated to *U.S. News & World Report*'s top 10 graduate engineering schools, 2001 ★2365★

Top graduate engineering schools, 2001 ★2366★

Top graduate engineering schools by reputation, as determined by academic personnel, 2001 ★2367★

Top graduate engineering schools by reputation, as determined by engineers and recruiters, 2001 ★2368★

U.S. News & World Report's graduate engineering programs with the highest academic reputation scores, 2000-01 ★2372★

Academics' choices for best graduate aerospace/aeronautical/astronautical engineering programs, 2001 ★2374★

Most effective aerospace engineering research-doctorate programs as evaluated by the National Research Council ★2375★

Top aerospace engineering research-doctorate programs as evaluated by the National Research Council ★2376★

U.S. News & World Report's graduate engineering programs with the best aerospace departments, 2000-01 ★2378★

Most effective biomedical engineering research-doctorate programs as evaluated by the National Research Council ★2383★

Top biomedical engineering research-doctorate programs as evaluated by the National Research Council ★2384★

Academics' choices for best graduate chemical engineering programs, 2001 ★2386★

Most effective chemical engineering research-doctorate programs as evaluated by the National Research Council ★2389★

Top chemical engineering research-doctorate programs as evaluated by the National Research Council ★2390★

Academics' choices for best graduate civil engineering programs, 2001 ★2394★

Most effective civil engineering research-doctorate programs as evaluated by the National Research Council ★2395★

STANFORD

Top civil engineering research-doctorate programs as evaluated by the National Research Council ★2396★

Academics' choices for best graduate computer engineering programs, 2001 ★2399★

U.S. News & World Report's graduate engineering programs with the best computer departments, 2000-01 ★2401★

Academics' choices for best graduate electrical/electronic/communications engineering programs, 2001 ★2403★

Most effective electrical engineering research-doctorate programs as evaluated by the National Research Council ★2404★

Top electrical engineering research-doctorate programs as evaluated by the National Research Council ★2405★

U.S. News & World Report's graduate engineering programs with the best electrical departments, 2000-01 ★2407★

Academics' choices for best graduate environmental/environmental health engineering programs, 2001 ★2408★

U.S. News & World Report's graduate engineering programs with the best environmental departments, 2000-01 ★2410★

Academics' choices for best graduate industrial/manufacturing engineering programs, 2001 ★2411★

Most effective industrial engineering research-doctorate programs as evaluated by the National Research Council ★2412★

Top industrial engineering research-doctorate programs as evaluated by the National Research Council ★2413★

Academics' choices for best graduate materials engineering programs, 2001 ★2417★

Most effective materials science research-doctorate programs as evaluated by the National Research Council ★2418★

Top materials science research-doctorate programs as evaluated by the National Research Council ★2419★

U.S. News & World Report's graduate engineering programs with the best materials departments, 2000-01 ★2421★

Academics' choices for best graduate mechanical engineering programs, 2001 ★2422★

Most effective mechanical engineering research-doctorate programs as evaluated by the National Research Council ★2423★

U.S. News & World Report's graduate engineering programs with the best mechanical departments, 2000-01 ★2425★

Academics' choices for best graduate petroleum engineering schools, 2000 ★2429★

U.S. universities with the greatest impact in mechanical engineering, 1994-98 ★2439★

Most effective English language and literature research-doctorate programs as evaluated by the National Research Council ★2448★

Top English language and literature research-doctorate programs as evaluated by the National Research Council ★2451★

U.S. universities with the greatest impact in ecology/environmental sciences, 1994-98 ★2474★

Top French language and literature research-doctorate programs as evaluated by the National Research Council ★2516★

Most effective German language and literature research-doctorate programs as evaluated by the National Research Council ★2527★

Top German language and literature research-doctorate programs as evaluated by the National Research Council ★2528★

Average GMAT scores for *U.S. News & World Report*'s top 10 graduate business schools, 2000 ★2529★

Top history research-doctorate programs as evaluated by the National Research Council ★2554★

Academics' choices for best dispute resolution programs, 2001 ★2627★

Academics' choices for best environmental law programs, 2001 ★2628★

Academics' choices for best intellectual property law programs, 2001 ★2630★

Academics' choices for best tax law programs, 2001 ★2632★

Acceptance rates at *U.S. News & World Report*'s top 10 law schools, 2001 ★2634★

Graduate employment after graduation percentage for *U.S. News & World Report*'s top 10 law schools, 2001 ★2635★

Graduate employment percentage for *U.S. News & World Report*'s top 10 law schools, 2001 ★2636★

Jurisdiction's overall bar passage rate for *U.S. News & World Report*'s top 10 law schools, 2001 ★2637★

Law schools with the best commercial law faculty, 1999-2000 ★2641★

Law schools with the best constitutional law (general) faculty, 1999-2000 ★2645★

Law schools with the best corporate law and securities regulation faculty, 1999-2000 ★2646★

Law schools with the best feminist legal theory faculty, 1999-2000 ★2651★

Law schools with the best intellectual property faculty, 1999-2000 ★2653★

Law schools with the best law and economics faculty, 1999-2000 ★2657★

Law schools with the best legal ethics, professional responsibility, and legal profession faculty, 1999-2000 ★2660★

Law schools with the best legal history faculty, 1999-2000 ★2661★

Law schools with the best tax faculty, 1999-2000 ★2664★

Law schools with the highest quality, 1999-2000 ★2666★

School's bar passage rate in jurisdiction at *U.S. News & World Report*'s top 10 law schools, 2001 ★2667★

Student-faculty ratios at *U.S. News & World Report*'s top 10 law schools, 2001 ★2669★

Top law schools, 2001 ★2670★

Top law schools by reputation, as determined by academic personnel, 2001 ★2671★

Top law schools by reputation, as determined by lawyers and judges, 2001 ★2672★

Top law school student bodies, 1999-2000 ★2673★

Top university research libraries in the U.S. and Canada, 1998-99 ★2706★

University research libraries in the U.S. and Canada with the largest increases in total expenditures from 1993-94 to 1998-99 ★2708★

U.S. universities with the greatest impact in library and information science, 1994-98 ★2719★

Most effective linguistics research-doctorate programs as evaluated by the National Research Council ★2732★

Top linguistics research-doctorate programs as evaluated by the National Research Council ★2733★

U.S. universities with the greatest impact in mathematics, 1995-99 ★2772★

Most effective mathematics research-doctorate programs as evaluated by the National Research Council ★2775★

Top mathematics research-doctorate programs as evaluated by the National Research Council ★2778★

Most effective statistics and biostatistics research-doctorate programs as evaluated by the National Research Council ★2780★

Top statistics and biostatistics research-doctorate programs as evaluated by the National Research Council ★2782★

Academics' choices for best AIDS programs, 2001 ★2818★

Academics' choices for best internal medicine programs, 2001 ★2822★

Academics' choices for best pediatrics programs, 2001 ★2823★

Acceptance rates for *U.S. News & World Report*'s top 10 research-oriented medical schools, 2001 ★2827★

Average MCAT scores at *U.S. News & World Report*'s top 10 research-oriented medical schools, 2001 ★2836★

Average undergraduate GPA at *U.S. News & World Report*'s top 10 research-oriented medical schools, 2001 ★2838★

Faculty-student ratios at *U.S. News & World Report*'s top 10 research-oriented medical schools, 2001 ★2842★

NIH research grants for *U.S. News & World Report*'s top 10 research-oriented medical schools, 2001 ★2845★

Out-of-state tuition and fees for *U.S. News & World Report*'s top 10 research-oriented medical schools, 2001 ★2847★

Top research-oriented medical schools, 2001 ★2859★

Top research-oriented medical schools by reputation, as determined by academic personnel, 2001 ★2860★

Top research-oriented medical schools by reputation, as determined by intern/residency directors, 2001 ★2861★

Top research-oriented medical schools by student selectivity, 2001 ★2862★

Top music research-doctorate programs as evaluated by the National Research Council ★2896★

U.S. universities with the greatest impact in optics and acoustics, 1994-98 ★2911★

U.S. universities with the greatest impact in optics and acoustics, 1995-99 ★2912★

Most effective philosophy research-doctorate programs as evaluated by the National Research Council ★2945★

Top philosophy research-doctorate programs as evaluated by the National Research Council ★2947★

Most effective physics research-doctorate programs as evaluated by the National Research Council ★3007★

Top physics research-doctorate programs as evaluated by the National Research Council ★3015★

Most effective physiology research-doctorate programs as evaluated by the National Research Council ★3021★

Top physiology research-doctorate programs as evaluated by the National Research Council ★3022★

Most effective political science research-doctorate programs as evaluated by the National Research Council ★3043★
Top political science research-doctorate programs as evaluated by the National Research Council ★3046★
Most effective psychology research-doctorate programs as evaluated by the National Research Council ★3065★
Top psychology research-doctorate programs as evaluated by the National Research Council ★3068★
Most patents issued to universities or research facilities, 1999 ★3097★
U.S. colleges and universities spending the most on chemical engineering research and development, 1998 ★3098★
U.S. colleges and universities spending the most on chemical research and development, 1998 ★3099★
U.S. colleges and universities spending the most on chemical research equipment, 1998 ★3100★
U.S. colleges and universities with the most federal support for chemical engineering research and development, 1998 ★3101★
U.S. colleges and universities with the most federal support for chemical research and development, 1998 ★3102★
U.S. colleges and universities with the most federal support for chemical research equipment, 1998 ★3103★
U.S. universities spending the most on research and development, 1998 ★3104★
Institutions receiving the most federal research and development expenditures, 1999 ★3105★
Average faculty salaries for institutions of higher education in California, 2000-01 ★3692★
Private institutions of higher education that pay the highest salaries to female professors, 2000-01 ★3974★
U.S. institutions with the highest paid assistant professors, 2001 ★3977★
U.S. institutions with the highest paid full professors, 2001 ★3978★
U.S. universities contributing the most papers in the field of neurosciences, 1993-97 ★4285★
U.S. universities with the highest relative citation impact, 1993-97 ★4291★
U.S. universities with the greatest impact in sociology and anthropology, 1995-99 ★4351★
Most effective sociology research-doctorate programs as evaluated by the National Research Council ★4352★
Top sociology research-doctorate programs as evaluated by the National Research Council ★4354★
Academics' choices for best administration/supervision graduate programs, 2001 ★4378★
Academics' choices for best curriculum/instruction graduate programs, 2001 ★4380★
Academics' choices for best education policy graduate programs, 2001 ★4381★
Academics' choices for best educational psychology graduate programs, 2001 ★4382★
Academics' choices for best higher education administration graduate programs, 2001 ★4384★
Academics' choices for best secondary education graduate programs, 2001 ★4385★

Acceptance rates at *U.S. News & World Report*'s top 10 graduate education schools, 2001 ★4388★
Average quantitative GRE scores for *U.S. News & World Report*'s top 10 graduate education schools, 2001 ★4389★
Average verbal GRE scores for *U.S. News & World Report*'s top 10 graduate education schools, 2001 ★4390★
Doctoral students to faculty ratio at *U.S. News & World Report*'s top 10 graduate education schools, 2001 ★4391★
Ph.Ds and Ed.D.s granted at *U.S. News & World Report*'s top 10 graduate education schools, 2001 ★4392★
Research expenditures for *U.S. News & World Report*'s top 10 graduate education schools, 2001 ★4393★
Research expenditures per faculty member at *U.S. News & World Report*'s top 10 graduate education schools, 2001 ★4394★
Top graduate education schools, 2001 ★4395★
Top graduate education schools by reputation, as determined by academic personnel, 2001 ★4396★
Top graduate education schools by reputation, as determined by superintendents, 2001 ★4397★

Stanford University Graduate School of Business
Academics' choices for best graduate entrepreneurship programs, 2001 ★583★
Academics' choices for best graduate management information systems programs, 2001 ★585★
Academics' choices for best graduate nonprofit organizations programs, 2001 ★586★
Acceptance rates for *U.S. News & World Report*'s top 10 graduate business schools, 2001 ★588★
Average GMAT scores at *U.S. News & World Report*'s top 10 graduate business schools, 2001 ★591★
Average undergraduate GPA at *U.S. News & World Report*'s top 10 graduate business schools, 2001 ★593★
Business Week's institutions with the best entrepreneurship programs ★594★
Business Week's top business schools by intellectual capital, 2000 ★599★
Business Week's top business schools for general management skills as selected by corporate recruiters, 2000 ★601★
Business Week's top business schools for global scope skills as selected by corporate recruiters, 2000 ★602★
Business Week's top business schools for marketing skills as selected by corporate recruiters, 2000 ★603★
Business Week's top business schools for technology skills as selected by corporate recruiters, 2000 ★604★
Business Week's top business schools with the greatest decrease in MBA satisfaction, 2000 ★610★
Business Week's top business schools with the highest percentage of women enrollees, 2000 ★614★
Business Week's top business schools with the worst placement offices, 2000 ★620★
Business Week's top business schools worst at responding to student concerns, 2000 ★621★
Highest post-MBA salaries for students enrolled in *Business Week*'s top business schools, 1999 ★631★

Highest pre-MBA salaries for students enrolled in *Business Week*'s top business schools, 1999 ★632★
Median starting salaries of graduates from *U.S. News & World Report*'s top 10 graduate business schools, 2001 ★636★
Out-of-state tuition and fees for *U.S. News & World Report*'s top 10 graduate business schools, 2001 ★637★
Percentage of employed graduates at *U.S. News & World Report*'s top 10 graduate business schools, 2001 ★639★
Percentage of graduates employed within 3 months of graduation from *U.S. News & World Report*'s top 10 graduate business schools, 2001 ★641★
Top graduate business schools, 2001 ★649★
Top graduate business schools by reputation as determined by academic personnel, 2001 ★650★
Top graduate business schools by reputation, as determined by recruiters, 2001 ★651★
Academics' choices for best graduate accounting programs, 2001 ★659★
Academics' choices for best graduate finance programs, 2001 ★662★
Academics' choices for best graduate general management programs, 2001 ★666★
Academics' choices for best graduate marketing programs, 2001 ★670★
Academics' choices for best graduate quantitative analysis programs, 2001 ★673★
Academics' choices for best graduate production/operations management programs, 2001 ★674★

Stanford University Hospital
Top cardiology and heart surgery hospitals in the U.S., 2000 ★2788★
Top hospitals in the U.S., 2000 ★2793★
Top rheumatology hospitals in the U.S., 2000 ★2802★
Top urology hospitals in the U.S., 2000 ★2803★

Stanford University Program in Geophysics
Most effective geosciences research-doctorate programs as evaluated by the National Research Council ★2150★

Stanford University School of Arts and Sciences
Top cell and developmental biology research-doctorate programs as evaluated by the National Research Council ★210★

Stanford University School of Medicine
Most effective cell and developmental biology research-doctorate programs as evaluated by the National Research Council ★206★
Top cell and developmental biology research-doctorate programs as evaluated by the National Research Council ★210★

Stanko; E.A.
Most cited authors in the journal *Canadian Journal of Criminology*, 1990 to 1995 ★1615★

Stanley Community College
Average faculty salaries for institutions of higher education without academic ranks in North Carolina, 2000-01 ★3761★

Stanley; Peter W.
Top pay and benefits for the chief executive and top paid employees at Pomona College ★3444★

Stanley Works
  Fortune's highest ranked metal products companies, 2000 ★475★
Stanton; Donald S.
  Top pay and benefits for the chief executive and top paid employees at Oglethorpe University ★3429★
Staples
  Fortune's highest ranked specialty retailers, 2000 ★497★
  Top discount and fashion retailing companies in Standard & Poor's 500, 2001 ★538★
Staples; Suzanne Fisher
  Outstanding children's fiction books, 2000 ★329★
Starbucks
  Fortune's highest ranked food services companies, 2000 ★465★
  Top food companies in Standard & Poor's 500, 2001 ★540★
Stargirl
  Most notable fiction books for young adults, 2001 ★322★
  Outstanding children's fiction books, 2000 ★329★
  Publishers Weekly Off-the-Cuff Awards winner for favorite novel of the year, 2000 ★346★
  Publishers Weekly Off-the-Cuff Awards winners for best novel for older teens, 2000 ★361★
Stark; Jack L.
  Top pay and benefits for the chief executive and top paid employees at Claremont McKenna College ★3236★
Stark; Judy
  Top pay and benefits for the chief executive and top paid employees at Marycrest International University ★3393★
Stark; Louis
  Top pay and benefits for the chief executive and top paid employees at Coe College ★3240★
Stark; Walter Jackson
  Top pay and benefits for the chief executive and top paid employees at Johns Hopkins University ★3355★
Starke
  Food science and technology journals by citation impact, 1991-99 ★2902★
Starkey; Armstrong
  Top pay and benefits for the chief executive and top paid employees at Adelphi University ★3164★
Start Small, Finish Big: Fifteen Key Lessons to Start-and Run-Your Own Successful Business
  Library Journal's most notable books about entrepreneurship, 2000 ★251★
Starwood Hotels & Resorts
  Fortune's highest ranked hotels, casinos and resorts, 2000 ★470★
  Top leisure time industries in Standard & Poor's 500, 2001 ★545★
Starzi; Thomas E.
  Most-cited researchers in clinical medicine, 1981-1998 ★2875★
  Most-cited researchers in surgery/transplantation, 1981-1998 ★2878★
State Board of Agriculture
  State appropriations for Colorado's institutions of higher education, 2000-01 ★1259★
State College Area High School
  Outstanding secondary schools in State College, Pennsylvania ★4236★
State College, PA
  Best college towns to live in ★3076★

U.S. cities with the lowest rate of violent crime ★3088★
State College of Science
  State appropriations for North Dakota's institutions of higher education, 2000-01 ★1287★
State Fair Community College
  Lowest undergraduate tuition and fees at colleges and universities in Missouri ★1525★
  Average faculty salaries for institutions of higher education without academic ranks in Missouri, 2000-01 ★3755★
State Farm Insurance Company
  Fortune's highest ranked property and casualty insurance companies, 2000 ★488★
  Top recruiters for computer science jobs for 2000-01 bachelor's degree recipients ★1590★
  Top recruiters for systems engineer jobs for 2000-01 bachelor's degree recipients ★2336★
  Top recruiters for math/actuarial science jobs for 2000-01 bachelor's degree recipients ★2771★
State and local government
  Employment change projections by major industry division from 1998 to 2008 ★2287★
  Employment projections by major industry division for 2008 ★2290★
State Street
  Top banks in Standard & Poor's 500, 2001 ★531★
State System of Higher Education
  State appropriations for Pennsylvania's institutions of higher education, 2000-01 ★1291★
State Teachers Retirement System of Ohio
  Top internships in the U.S. with the highest compensation, 2001 ★2611★
State University of West Georgia
  State appropriations for Georgia's institutions of higher education, 2000-01 ★1263★
Statistician
  Jobs with the best environment scores ★2247★
  Jobs with the best physical demands scores ★2250★
  Most desirable jobs in math/science ★2274★
Statistics
  Number of Advanced Placement Exams taken by African Americans, by subject, 2000 ★30★
  Number of Advanced Placement Exams taken by Asian Americans, by subject, 2000 ★31★
  Number of Advanced Placement Exams taken by Hispanic Americans, by subject, 2000 ★32★
  Gender breakdown of social sciences doctorate recipients, by subfield, 1999 ★1942★
  Social sciences doctorates awarded at U.S. colleges and universities, by subfield, 1999 ★2044★
Staton; Knofel
  Top pay and benefits for the chief executive and top paid employees at Hope International University ★3340★
Staudinger; W. Leonard
  Top pay and benefits for the chief executive and top paid employees at Nebraska Wesleyan University ★3417★
Stauffer; Thomas M.
  Top pay and benefits for the chief executive and top paid employees at Golden Gate University ★3310★

Staunton Public Library
  Highest Hennen's American Public Library Ratings for libraries serving a population of 10,000 to 24,999 ★2695★
Stavenga; Mink
  Top pay and benefits for the chief executive and top paid employees at United States International University ★3587★
Steadman; Amy
  All-America girls' high school soccer team defenders, 2001 ★174★
Stebbings; Timothy
  Top pay and benefits for the chief executive and top paid employees at Gordon College in Massachusetts ★3312★
Steelcase
  Fortune's highest ranked furniture companies, 2000 ★467★
Steele; Anne C.
  Top pay and benefits for the chief executive and top paid employees at Chatham College ★3230★
Steele, Jr.; Glenn D.
  Top pay and benefits for the chief executive and top paid employees at the University of Chicago ★3537★
Steele; Richard E.
  Top pay and benefits for the chief executive and top paid employees at Bowdoin College ★3207★
Stefansson; Kari
  European business moguls considered the best innovators ★442★
Steffens; Lincoln
  Best U.S. works of journalism in the 20th century ★2769★
Steffy; James
  Top pay and benefits for the chief executive and top paid employees at Muhlenberg College ★3413★
Stegall; Joel R.
  Top pay and benefits for the chief executive and top paid employees at Shenandoah University ★3497★
Stein; Jeremy C.
  Top pay and benefits for the chief executive and top paid employees at Massachusetts Institute of Technology ★3397★
Stein; Jerome
  Authors most frequently contributing to the *American Economic Review* from 1951-1990 ★2157★
Steinbeck; John
  Authors protested for more than one book between 1952 and 1989, according to the *Newsletter of Intellectual Freedom* ★743★
  People for the American Way's list of most frequently challenged authors, 1982-1992 ★746★
Steinberg; Bruce D.
  Top pay and benefits for the chief executive and top paid employees at Curry College ★3261★
Steinberg; David J.
  Presidents with the highest pay at Master's I and II colleges and universities, 1998-99 ★3161★
  Top pay and benefits for the chief executive and top paid employees at Long Island University ★3378★
Steinberg; Gary
  Top pay and benefits for the chief executive and top paid employees at Stanford University ★3510★

Steinberger; Peter
Top pay and benefits for the chief executive and top paid employees at Reed College ★3453★

Stellato; Anthony C.
Top pay and benefits for the chief executive and top paid employees at Vassar College ★3594★

Stenographer/court reporter
Jobs with the most stringent quotas ★2259★

Stephany; Ronald J.
Top pay and benefits for the chief executive and top paid employees at the University of Redlands ★3558★

Stephen F. Austin State University
State appropriations for Texas's institutions of higher education, 2000-01 ★1296★
Total baccalaureate law and legal studies degrees awarded to Hispanic Americans from U.S. colleges and universities, 1997-98 ★1727★
Average faculty salaries for institutions of higher education in Texas, 2000-01 ★3731★

Stephens College
U.S. colleges and universities where intramural sports are not popular ★996★
U.S. News & World Report's midwestern regional liberal arts colleges with the best student/faculty ratios, 2000-01 ★1339★
U.S. News & World Report's midwestern regional liberal arts colleges with the highest percentage of freshmen in the top 25% of their high school class, 2000-01 ★1345★
U.S. News & World Report's midwestern regional liberal arts colleges with the highest percentage of full-time faculty, 2000-01 ★1346★
U.S. News & World Report's midwestern regional liberal arts colleges with the highest proportion of classes having 20 students or less, 2000-01 ★1347★
Highest undergraduate tuition and fees at colleges and universities in Missouri ★1524★

Stephens; John W.
Top pay and benefits for the chief executive and top paid employees at Midamerica Nazarene University ★3400★

StepStone
Top E-recruiting providers, 2000 ★2604★

Sterbak; Jana
Canada's best visual artists of the 20th century ★75★

Sterling College
Highest undergraduate tuition and fees at colleges and universities in Kansas ★1506★
Undergraduate tuition and fees at colleges and universities in Vermont ★1563★
Average faculty salaries for institutions of higher education in Kansas, 2000-01 ★3703★

Stern's
Top recruiters for retail merchandising jobs for 2000-01 bachelor's degree recipients ★556★

Stetson University
U.S. News & World Report's best undergraduate fees among southern regional universities by discount tuition, 2000 ★1429★
U.S. News & World Report's southern regional universities with the best academic reputation scores, 2000-01 ★1433★
U.S. News & World Report's southern regional universities with the best alumni giving rates, 2000-01 ★1434★
U.S. News & World Report's southern regional universities with the best student/faculty ratios, 2000-01 ★1435★
U.S. News & World Report's southern regional universities with the highest graduation rates, 2000-01 ★1438★
U.S. News & World Report's southern regional universities with the highest percentage of freshmen in the top 25% of their high school class, 2000-01 ★1439★
U.S. News & World Report's southern regional universities with the highest percentage of full-time faculty, 2000-01 ★1440★
U.S. News & World Report's southern regional universities with the highest proportion of classes with 20 students or less, 2000-01 ★1441★
U.S. News & World Report's top southern regional universities, 2000-01 ★1444★
Highest undergraduate tuition and fees at colleges and universities in Florida ★1494★
Academics' choices for best trial advocacy programs, 2001 ★2633★
Average faculty salaries for institutions of higher education in Florida, 2000-01 ★3696★

Stettler III; H. Louis
Top pay and benefits for the chief executive and top paid employees at Washington College ★3606★

Steuer; Axel
Top pay and benefits for the chief executive and top paid employees at Gustavus Adolphus College ★3317★

Stevedore
Jobs with the highest unemployment ★2256★
Jobs with the most stringent quotas ★2259★
Least desirable jobs ★2266★

Steven Institute of Technology
Presidents with the highest pay at Doctoral I and II universities, 1998-99 ★3160★

Stevens-Henager College of Business
Undergraduate tuition and fees at colleges and universities in Utah ★1562★

Stevens Institute of Technology
U.S. colleges and universities with the worst food service program ★1043★
U.S. colleges and universities with the worst overall administration ★1045★
Highest undergraduate tuition and fees at colleges and universities in New Jersey ★1533★
Private, 4-year undergraduate colleges and universities producing the most Ph.D.'s in the computer sciences, 1920-1990 ★1595★
Private, 4-year undergraduate colleges and universities producing the most Ph.D.'s in the computer sciences, 1981-1990 ★1596★
U.S. colleges and universities awarding the most business management and administrative services master's degrees to Hispanic Americans ★1761★
U.S. colleges and universities awarding the most computer and information sciences master's degrees to Hispanic Americans ★1768★
Doctorate-granting-institutions with the highest percentage of non-U.S. citizen doctoral degrees awarded, 1999 ★1907★
Private, 4-year undergraduate colleges and universities producing the most Ph.D.'s in mathematics, 1920-1990 ★2776★
Private, 4-year undergraduate colleges and universities producing the most Ph.D.'s in mathematics, 1981-1990 ★2777★
Private, 4-year undergraduate colleges and universities producing the most Ph.D.'s in physics and astronomy, 1920-1990 ★2949★

Stevens; Robert N.
Top pay and benefits for the chief executive and top paid employees at Charleston Southern University ★3229★

Stevenson; Dan
All-American boy's high school football linemen, 2000 ★183★

Stick Figure: A Diary of My Former Self
Most notable nonfiction books for reluctant young adult readers, 2001 ★323★
Most notable nonfiction books for young adults, 2001 ★324★

Stick and Whittle
Smithsonian's best books for children ages 10 and up ★365★

Stickel; Scott E.
Top pay and benefits for the chief executive and top paid employees at LaSalle University ★3365★

Stidham; Ann B.
Top pay and benefits for the chief executive and top paid employees at Presbyterian College ★3445★

Stieber; Nancy
Radcliffe Institute for Advanced Study fellowship recipient in the field of architectural history, 2000-01 ★67★

Stieglitz; Alfred
Highly influential artists of the 20th century ★76★

Stigler; George J.
Authors most frequently contributing to the *American Economic Review* from 1911-1990 ★2156★
Most cited economists ★2185★

Stiglitz; Joseph
Authors most frequently contributing to the *American Economic Review* from 1911-1990 ★2156★
Authors most frequently contributing to the *American Economic Review* from 1951-1990 ★2157★
U.S. academic economists by mean number of citations, 1971-92 ★2176★
U.S. academic economists by total citations, 1971-92 ★2177★

Still the Same Me
Most notable children's recordings, 2001 ★320★

Stillwater Junior High School
Outstanding secondary schools in Minneapolis-St. Paul, Minnesota-Wisconsin ★4181★

Stilwell Financial
Business Week's best performing companies with the highest return on equity, 2000 ★420★
Top nonbank financial companies in Standard & Poor's 500, 2001 ★550★

Stingl; G.
Most cited authors in dermatology journals, 1981 to 1996 ★1870★

STMicroelectronics
Business Week's best companies in France ★393★
Top information technology companies, 2000 ★544★

Stock clerks and order fillers
Projected employment growth for selected occupations that require shortor moderate-term on-the-job training, 1998-2008 ★2321★

Stock; Peggy A.
Largest benefit packages awarded to presidents at institutions of higher education, 1998-99 ★3133★
Top pay and benefits for the chief executive and top paid employees at Westminster College in Utah ★3618★

Stockbroker
Jobs with the highest employment growth ★2254★
Jobs with the most stringent quotas ★2259★

Stockholm-Uppsala
Cities with the highest productivity of paper in the discipline of immunology, 1994-96 ★2871★

Stockton Elementary School
Illinois elementary schools chosen to be 'demonstration sites' for struggling schools ★4006★

Stockton-Lodi, CA
Cities with the highest percentage of broadband use and interest ★2578★

Stokes; Mark A.
Top pay and benefits for the chief executive and top paid employees at Tusculum College ★3582★

Stolley; Richard B.
Outstanding children's nonfiction books, 2000 ★330★

Stone; Alan J.
Top pay and benefits for the chief executive and top paid employees at Alma College ★3171★

The Stone Angel
Canada's best fiction selections of the 20th century ★233★

Stone Bench in an Empty Park
Booklist's most recommended poetry for youths, 2001 ★315★

Stone; Bradford
Top pay and benefits for the chief executive and top paid employees at Stetson University ★3511★

Stone Child College
U.S. tribal colleges ★1445★
Lowest undergraduate tuition and fees at colleges and universities in Montana ★1527★

Stone; Edward C.
Top pay and benefits for the chief executive and top paid employees at the California Institute of Technology ★3521★

Stone; I.F.
Best U.S. works of journalism in the 20th century ★2769★

Stone; Jordan
All-America boys' high school soccer team midfielders, 2001 ★168★

Stone Ridge Country Day School
Outstanding secondary schools in Washington, District of Columbia-Maryland-Virginia-West Virginia ★4249★

Stone Ridge-School of the Sacred Heart
Outstanding secondary schools in Washington, District of Columbia-Maryland-Virginia-West Virginia ★4249★

Stone Valley Middle School
Outstanding secondary schools in Oakland, California ★4195★

Stone; William
Top pay and benefits for the chief executive and top paid employees at Trinity University in Texas ★3579★

Stoneham High School
Outstanding suburban public high schools in Metro Boston ★4255★

Stonehill College
Division II NCAA colleges with the highest graduation rates for all sports, 1993-94 ★945★
U.S. News & World Report's northern regional liberal arts colleges with the best student/faculty ratios, 2000-01 ★1353★
U.S. News & World Report's northern regional liberal arts colleges with the highest academic reputation scores, 2000-01 ★1354★
U.S. News & World Report's northern regional liberal arts colleges with the highest freshmen retention rates, 2000-01 ★1357★
U.S. News & World Report's northern regional liberal arts colleges with the highest graduation rates, 2000-01 ★1358★
U.S. News & World Report's northern regional liberal arts colleges with the highest percentage of freshmen in the top 25% of their high school class, 2000-01 ★1359★
U.S. News & World Report's northern regional liberal arts colleges with the lowest acceptance rates, 2000-01 ★1362★
U.S. News & World Report's top northern regional liberal arts colleges, 2000-01 ★1363★
Average faculty salaries for institutions of higher education in Massachusetts, 2000-01 ★3708★

Stonewall Jackson Middle School
Outstanding secondary schools in Richmond-Petersburg, Virginia ★4210★

Stoppard; Tom
Top playwrights of the twentieth century ★4436★

Stopsky; Fred H.
Top pay and benefits for the chief executive and top paid employees at Webster University ★3608★

Stora Enso
Business Week's best companies in Finland ★392★

Storage Technology
Fortune's highest ranked computer peripherals companies, 2000 ★454★

Storb; Rainer
Most-cited researchers in clinical medicine, 1981-1998 ★2875★
Most-cited researchers in oncology, 1981-1998 ★2877★

Storm; Kathy H.
Top pay and benefits for the chief executive and top paid employees at Whitworth College ★3625★

StormWatch: Force of Nature
Most notable nonfiction books for reluctant young adult readers, 2001 ★323★

Strabbing; Timothy
All-USA College Academic Second Team, 2001 ★3★

Strack Intermediate School
Outstanding secondary schools in Houston, Texas ★4150★
All-USA Teacher Teams, Third Team, 2000 ★4401★

Strange Fruit: Billie Holiday, Cafe Society, and an Early Call for Civil Rights
Booklist's most recommended African American nonfiction ★229★

Stranger with a Camera
Most notable videos for adults, 2001 ★2891★
Outstanding videos for library collections, 2000 ★2892★

Stranges; John
Top pay and benefits for the chief executive and top paid employees at Niagara University ★3420★

Strasheim; Dwayne
Top pay and benefits for the chief executive and top paid employees at Hastings College ★3328★

Strassburger; John
Top pay and benefits for the chief executive and top paid employees at Ursinus College ★3591★

Strategic Management Journal
Top management journals ★546★
Top management journals by core impact ★547★
Business journals by citation impact, 1981-98 ★688★
Business journals by citation impact, 1994-98 ★689★
Journals with the highest impact factor in the field of management, 1981-96 ★696★

The Strategy-Focused Organization
Library Journal's most notable management books, 2000 ★265★

Stratfield School
Outstanding secondary schools in Bridgeport, Connecticut ★4101★

Stratigraphy, sedimentation
Earth, atmosphere, and marine science doctorates awarded at U.S. colleges and universities, by subfield, 1999 ★1909★
Gender breakdown of earth, atmosphere, and marine science doctorate recipients, by subfield, 1999 ★1932★

Straub; Carl
Top pay and benefits for the chief executive and top paid employees at Bates College ★3193★

Straus; M.A.
Most cited authors in the journal *Canadian Journal of Criminology*, 1990 to 1995 ★1615★
Most cited authors in the journal *Journal of Interpersonal Violence*, 1990 to 1995 ★1627★
Most cited authors in the journal *Violence and Victims*, 1990 to 1995 ★1632★
Most-cited scholars in *Canadian Journal of Criminology* ★1638★

Strayer College, Alexandria
Total baccalaureate computer and information science degrees awarded to African Americans from U.S. colleges and universities, 1997-98 ★1691★
U.S. colleges and universities awarding the most computer and information sciences master's degrees to African Americans ★1766★
U.S. colleges and universities awarding the most computer and information sciences master's degrees to Hispanic Americans ★1768★

Strayer University
Average faculty salaries for institutions of higher education without academic ranks in the District of Columbia, 2000-01 ★3767★

A Streetcar Named Desire
Top plays of the twentieth century ★4435★

Strega Nona
Most notable children's videos, 2001 ★2889★

Streit; Carol
Top pay and benefits for the chief executive and top paid employees at Lesley College ★3370★

Streit; Gary W.
Top pay and benefits for the chief executive and top paid employees at Olivet Nazarene University ★3432★

Strickland; Carol
All-USA Teacher Teams, Second Team, 2000 ★4400★

Strickland; Lewis Randy
Top pay and benefits for the chief executive and top paid employees at Spalding University ★3506★

Strickland Middle School
Outstanding secondary schools in Dallas, Texas ★4120★

Strickler; Barbara
Top pay and benefits for the chief executive and top paid employees at the University of Tampa ★3569★

Strobel; James W.
Top pay and benefits for the chief executive and top paid employees at Erskine College ★3290★

Stroh; Janice M.
Top pay and benefits for the chief executive and top paid employees at Alfred University ★3169★

Strong; Michael
Top pay and benefits for the chief executive and top paid employees at the Allegheny University of the Health Sciences ★3520★

Strong; Susan R.
Top pay and benefits for the chief executive and top paid employees at Alfred University ★3169★

Strother; Ann
All-America girls' high school basketball 2nd team, 2001 ★171★

Stroud; Jonathan
Top pay and benefits for the chief executive and top paid employees at Wesleyan College in Georgia ★3611★

Stryker
Business Week's best performing companies with the highest 1-year earnings growth ★413★
Fortune's highest ranked scientific, photo and control equipment companies, 2000 ★493★
Top health care companies in Standard & Poor's 500, 2001 ★542★

Stuck in Neutral
Booklist's best first novels for youths ★309★
Most notable fiction books for reluctant young adult readers, 2001 ★321★
Most notable fiction books for young adults, 2001 ★322★
Outstanding books for older readers, 2000 ★327★

Stucture & Bonding
Inorganic and nuclear chemistry journals by citation impact, 1981-99 ★811★
Inorganic and nuclear chemistry journals by citation impact, 1995-99 ★812★
Inorganic and nuclear chemistry journals by citation impact, 1999 ★813★

Student Resource Center
Outstanding reference sources, 2000 ★370★

Student Works Painting
Most selective internships in the U.S., 2001 ★2610★
Top internships in the U.S. with the highest compensation, 2001 ★2611★

Studies in Family Planning
Demography journals with the highest average citations after 5 years ★1856★
Most cited demography journals, 1991-95 ★1857★
Top demography journals by average impact factor, 1991-95 ★1863★

Studio art-drawing
Number of Advanced Placement Exams taken by African Americans, by subject, 2000 ★30★
Number of Advanced Placement Exams taken by Asian Americans, by subject, 2000 ★31★
Number of Advanced Placement Exams taken by Hispanic Americans, by subject, 2000 ★32★

Studio art-general
Number of Advanced Placement Exams taken by African Americans, by subject, 2000 ★30★
Number of Advanced Placement Exams taken by Asian Americans, by subject, 2000 ★31★
Number of Advanced Placement Exams taken by Hispanic Americans, by subject, 2000 ★32★

A Study of Information Seeking and Retrieving, Parts I-III
Journal of the American Society for Information Science's best papers, by citations per year ★2728★
Journal of the American Society for Information Science's best papers, by total citations ★2729★

Stuller; Adam
All-America boys' high school soccer team forwards, 2001 ★166★

The Subject Specialist in National and University Libraries with Special Reference to Book Selection
Most frequently cited *Libri* articles ★2730★

The Subject Specialist on the Academic Library Staff
Most frequently cited *Libri* articles ★2730★

Subject Specialization in Three British University Libraries
Most frequently cited *Libri* articles ★2730★

The Subtle Knife
Most notable children's recordings, 2001 ★320★

Suffolk County Community College, Ammerman
Average faculty salaries for institutions of higher education in New York, 2000-01 ★3719★
U.S. community colleges with the highest paid full professors, 2001 ★3976★

Suffolk County Community College, Eastern
Average faculty salaries for institutions of higher education in New York, 2000-01 ★3719★
U.S. community colleges with the highest paid full professors, 2001 ★3976★

Suffolk County Community College, Western
Average faculty salaries for institutions of higher education in New York, 2000-01 ★3719★
U.S. community colleges with the highest paid full professors, 2001 ★3976★

Suffolk University
U.S. News & World Report's northern regional universities with students most in debt, 1999 ★1414★
Average faculty salaries for institutions of higher education in Massachusetts, 2000-01 ★3708★

Sugar Busters!
Longest-running nonfiction hardcover bestsellers, 2000 ★281★

Sugimoto; Jeffrey T.
Top pay and benefits for the chief executive and top paid employees at Creighton University ★3259★

Suiza Foods
Fortune's highest ranked food production companies, 2000 ★464★

Sul Ross State University
U.S. colleges and universities awarding the most education master's degrees to Hispanic Americans ★1771★
Average faculty salaries for institutions of higher education in Texas, 2000-01 ★3731★

Sullivan; Barry
Top pay and benefits for the chief executive and top paid employees at Washington and Lee University ★3605★

Sullivan County Community College
Average faculty salaries for institutions of higher education in New York, 2000-01 ★3719★

Sullivan; Daniel F.
Top pay and benefits for the chief executive and top paid employees at St. Lawrence University ★3477★

Sullivan; R. Mark
Top pay and benefits for the chief executive and top paid employees at the College of St. Rose ★3529★

Sullivan; Robert
Booklist's best science and technology books ★366★

Sullivan; Robert L.
Top pay and benefits for the chief executive and top paid employees at Florida Institute of Technology ★3293★

Sullivan; William J.
Top pay and benefits for the chief executive and top paid employees at Springfield College in Massachusetts ★3509★

Sumitomo Bank
Business Week's best companies in Japan ★398★

Summerbridge International
Top internships in the U.S., 2001 ★2612★

Summit Middle School
Outstanding secondary schools in Oklahoma City, Oklahoma ★4196★

Summit Parkway Middle School
Outstanding secondary schools in Columbia, South Carolina ★4117★

Sumter High School
Outstanding secondary schools in Sumter, South Carolina ★4238★

Sun Hung Kai Properties
Business Week's best companies in Hong Kong ★395★

Sun Microsystems
Business Week's best companies in the United States ★411★
Companies that have been on *Business Week*'s top 50 list the longest ★435★
Fortune's highest ranked computers and office equipment companies, 2000 ★456★
Top information technology companies, 2000 ★544★
Top office equipment and computers companies in Standard & Poor's 500, 2001 ★551★
Largest technology companies in the U.S. in terms of annual revenue, 2000 ★4429★

Suncoast Community High School
　Outstanding secondary schools in West Palm Beach-Boca Raton, Florida ★4251★

Sunday You Learn How to Box
　Outstanding fiction books for young adults, 2000 ★333★

Sundborg, S.J.; Rev. Steven
　Top pay and benefits for the chief executive and top paid employees at Seattle University ★3495★

Sunshine; Eugene S.
　Top pay and benefits for the chief executive and top paid employees at Northwestern University ★3423★

SunTrust Banks
　Fortune's highest ranked super-regional banks, 2000 ★498★
　Top banks in Standard & Poor's 500, 2001 ★531★

Sunwing
　Smithsonian's best books for children ages 10 and up ★365★

Super Teen
　Best-selling youth magazines ★2920★

Supernatural Love: Poems 1976-1992
　Library Journal's best poetry books, 2000 ★244★

Supervalu
　Fortune's highest ranked wholesalers, 2000 ★505★

Supervision: A Conceptual Model
　Most frequently cited contribution articles in psychology journals from 1986 to 1996 ★3071★

Supplemental Educational Opportunity Grants
　Sources of financial aid for incoming freshmen, 2000 ★1062★

Supplemental Grants
　Proposed fiscal 2002 appropriations for student assistance ★1251★
　Fiscal 2002 requested budget as compared with Fiscal 2001 budget for the Education Department ★2231★

Supreme Court of the United States
　Most selective internships in the U.S., 2001 ★2610★
　Top internships in the U.S., 2001 ★2612★

Surfing the Edge of Chaos
　Library Journal's most notable new economy books, 2000 ★271★

Surgeon
　Jobs that are potentially the highest paying ★2246★
　Jobs with the best income scores ★2248★
　Jobs with the highest starting salaries ★2255★
　Jobs with the longest work weeks ★2257★
　Jobs with the lowest unemployment ★2258★
　Jobs with the worst environment scores ★2260★
　Jobs with the worst stress scores ★2265★
　'White-collar' jobs considered the most physically demanding ★2285★

Surgery
　Surgery journals with the greatest impact measure, 1981-98 ★2814★

Surgical technologists
　Fastest growing occupations, 1998-2008 ★2302★
　Projected employment growth for selected occupations that require an associate degree or less, 1998-2008 ★2319★

Surry Community College
　Average faculty salaries for institutions of higher education without academic ranks in North Carolina, 2000-01 ★3761★

Surveyor
　Most desirable jobs in construction trades ★2272★

Surviving Brick Johnson
　Most notable books for middle readers, 2001 ★317★

Susanka Jr.; Thomas J.
　Top pay and benefits for the chief executive and top paid employees at Thomas Aquinas College in California ★3574★

Susick Elementary School
　All-USA Teacher Teams, Second Team, 2000 ★4400★

Susquehanna University
　U.S. colleges and universities with the best financial aid programs ★1030★
　U.S. colleges and universities with the most attractive campuses ★1039★
　U.S. News & World Report's northern regional liberal arts colleges with the highest academic reputation scores, 2000-01 ★1354★
　U.S. News & World Report's northern regional liberal arts colleges with the highest alumni giving rates, 2000-01 ★1356★
　U.S. News & World Report's northern regional liberal arts colleges with the highest freshmen retention rates, 2000-01 ★1357★
　U.S. News & World Report's northern regional liberal arts colleges with the highest graduation rates, 2000-01 ★1358★
　U.S. News & World Report's northern regional liberal arts colleges with the highest percentage of freshmen in the top 25% of their high school class, 2000-01 ★1359★
　U.S. News & World Report's northern regional liberal arts colleges with the highest percentage of full-time faculty, 2000-01 ★1360★
　U.S. News & World Report's top northern regional liberal arts colleges, 2000-01 ★1363★
　U.S. News & World Report's best undergraduate fees among northern regional liberal arts colleges by discount tuition, 2000 ★1382★
　Average faculty salaries for institutions of higher education in Pennsylvania, 2000-01 ★3725★

Sussex; University of
　United Kingdom universities with the greatest impact in chemistry, 1993-97 ★807★
　United Kingdom universities contributing the most papers in the field of economics and business, 1993-97 ★2203★

Sutherland; David E.R.
　Most-cited researchers in surgery/transplantation, 1981-1998 ★2878★

Sutherland Elementary School
　Illinois elementary schools chosen to be 'demonstration sites' for struggling schools ★4006★

Sutton; George
　Top pay and benefits for the chief executive and top paid employees at Long Island University ★3378★

Sutton; Leslie
　Top pay and benefits for the chief executive and top paid employees at the University of Pennsylvania ★3555★

Svenska Handelsbanken
　Business Week's best companies in Sweden ★404★

Swalley; Gary
　All-USA Teacher Teams, Second Team, 2000 ★4400★

Swannack; Patricia
　Top pay and benefits for the chief executive and top paid employees at Monmouth University in New Jersey ★3406★

Swanson; Carl
　Top pay and benefits for the chief executive and top paid employees at California Lutheran University ★3216★

Swarm
　Outstanding poetry books, 2000 ★290★

Swarthmore College
　Private, 4-year undergraduate colleges and universities producing the most Ph.D.'s in the life sciences, 1920-1990 ★192★
　Private, 4-year undergraduate colleges and universities producing the most Ph.D.'s in the life sciences, 1981-1990 ★193★
　Comparison of acceptance rates at the top 5 liberal arts colleges in the U.S., 1990 and 2001 ★844★
　U.S. colleges and universities offering the best overall academic experience for undergraduates ★987★
　U.S. colleges and universities where students are very politically active ★1001★
　U.S. colleges and universities where students study the most ★1003★
　U.S. colleges and universities with harmonious race/class interaction ★1026★
　U.S. colleges and universities with the best on-campus housing facilities ★1032★
　U.S. colleges and universities with the happiest students ★1035★
　U.S. News & World Report's best national liberal arts colleges, 2000-01 ★1320★
　U.S. News & World Report's national liberal arts colleges with the best faculty resources rank, 2000-01 ★1321★
　U.S. News & World Report's national liberal arts colleges with the best financial resources rank, 2000-01 ★1322★
　U.S. News & World Report's national liberal arts colleges with the best freshmen retention rates, 2000-01 ★1323★
　U.S. News & World Report's national liberal arts colleges with the best graduation and retention rank, 2000-01 ★1324★
　U.S. News & World Report's national liberal arts colleges with the best selectivity rank, 2000-01 ★1325★
　U.S. News & World Report's national liberal arts colleges with the best student/faculty ratios, 2000-01 ★1326★
　U.S. News & World Report's national liberal arts colleges with the highest academic reputation scores, 2000-01 ★1327★
　U.S. News & World Report's national liberal arts colleges with the highest alumni giving rank, 2000-01 ★1329★
　U.S. News & World Report's national liberal arts colleges with the highest graduation rates, 2000-01 ★1330★
　U.S. News & World Report's national liberal arts colleges with the highest percentage of alumni support, 2000-01 ★1331★
　U.S. News & World Report's national liberal arts colleges with the highest percentage of freshmen in the top 10% of their high school class, 2000-01 ★1332★
　U.S. News & World Report's national liberal arts colleges with the lowest acceptance rates, 2000-01 ★1336★

U.S. News & World Report's best undergraduate fees among national liberal arts colleges by discount tuition, 2000 ★1381★

Highest undergraduate tuition and fees at private nonprofit, 4-year or above colleges and universities ★1461★

Highest undergraduate tuition and fees at colleges and universities in Pennsylvania ★1549★

Private, 4-year undergraduate colleges and universities producing the most Ph.D.'s in the computer sciences, 1920-1990 ★1595★

Private, 4-year undergraduate colleges and universities producing the most Ph.D.'s in the computer sciences, 1981-1990 ★1596★

Private, 4-year undergraduate colleges and universities producing the most Ph.D.s in all fields of study, 1920-1990 ★2027★

Private, 4-year undergraduate colleges and universities producing the most Ph.D.'s in all fields of study, 1981-1990 ★2028★

Private, 4-year undergraduate colleges and universities producing the most Ph.D.'s in all fields of study, 1990 ★2029★

Private, 4-year undergraduate colleges and universities producing the most Ph.D.'s in nonscience fields, 1920-1990 ★2030★

Private, 4-year undergraduate colleges and universities producing the most Ph.D.'s in nonscience fields, 1981-1990 ★2031★

Private, 4-year undergraduate colleges and universities producing the most Ph.D.'s in the earth sciences, 1981-1990 ★2151★

Elite liberal arts colleges ranked by per capita quality adjusted scholarship articles in the field of economics, 1975-94 ★2164★

Elite liberal arts colleges ranked by quality adjusted scholarship articles in the field of economics, 1975-94 ★2165★

Top associate professor economists at elite liberal arts colleges, 1975-94 ★2174★

Top full professor economists at elite liberal arts colleges, 1975-94 ★2175★

Private, 4-year undergraduate colleges and universities producing the most Ph.D.'s in economics, 1920-1990 ★2211★

Private, 4-year undergraduate colleges and universities producing the most Ph.D.'s in economics, 1981-1990 ★2212★

Undergraduate institutions with the most graduates who received Ph.D.s in economics, 1920-1984 ★2214★

U.S. News & World Report's undergraduate engineering programs with the highest academic reputation scores, 2000-01 ★2337★

Private, 4-year undergraduate colleges and universities producing the most Ph.D.'s in English, 1920-1990 ★2449★

Private, 4-year undergraduate colleges and universities producing the most Ph.D.'s in English, 1981-1990 ★2450★

Private, 4-year undergraduate colleges and universities producing the most Ph.D.'s in history, 1920-1990 ★2552★

Private, 4-year undergraduate colleges and universities producing the most Ph.D.'s in history, 1981-1990 ★2553★

Private, 4-year undergraduate colleges and universities producing the most Ph.D.'s in mathematics, 1920-1990 ★2776★

Private, 4-year undergraduate colleges and universities producing the most Ph.D.'s in mathematics, 1981-1990 ★2777★

Private, 4-year undergraduate colleges and universities producing the most Ph.D.'s in physics and astronomy, 1920-1990 ★2949★

Private, 4-year undergraduate colleges and universities producing the most Ph.D.'s in political science and international relations, 1920-1990 ★3044★

Private, 4-year undergraduate colleges and universities producing the most Ph.D.'s in political science and international relations, 1981-1990 ★3045★

Private, 4-year undergraduate colleges and universities producing the most Ph.D.'s in psychology, 1920-1990 ★3066★

Private, 4-year undergraduate colleges and universities producing the most Ph.D.'s in psychology, 1981-1990 ★3067★

Average faculty salaries for institutions of higher education in Pennsylvania, 2000-01 ★3725★

U.S. liberal arts colleges with the highest paid full professors, 2001 ★3980★

Private, 4-year undergraduate colleges and universities producing the most Ph.D.'s in the sciences, 1920-1990 ★4294★

Private, 4-year undergraduate colleges and universities producing the most Ph.D.'s in the sciences, 1981-1990 ★4295★

Private, 4-year undergraduate colleges and universities producing the most Ph.D.'s in anthropology and sociology, 1920-1990 ★4344★

Private, 4-year undergraduate colleges and universities producing the most Ph.D.'s in anthropology and sociology, 1981-1990 ★4345★

Swartz; James E.
Top pay and benefits for the chief executive and top paid employees at Grinnell College ★3315★

Sweden
Countries with the most computers per capita, 2000 ★1604★
Annual leave days for employees in selected countries ★2239★
Countries with the highest spending per student on higher education, 1997 ★2488★
Percentage of students enrolled in institutions of higher education that were not citizens of the country where they studied, 1998 ★2500★
Most wired countries, 2001 ★2596★
Percentage of internet usage for selected countries ★2599★
Institute for Scientific Information periodical prices by country, 2001 ★2922★
Countries spending the highest percentage of gross domestic product on education ★4060★

Sweeny; Stephen J.
Top pay and benefits for the chief executive and top paid employees at the College of New Rochelle ★3525★

Sweet Briar College
U.S. colleges and universities with a generally conservative student body ★1014★
College senior's choices for exemplary liberal arts institutions ★1318★
U.S. News & World Report's national liberal arts colleges with the highest proportion of classes with less than 20 students, 2000-01 ★1335★
Highest undergraduate tuition and fees at colleges and universities in Virginia ★1564★
Most wired colleges, 2000 ★2595★
Women's colleges granting physics bachelor's degrees, 2000 ★2982★

Average faculty salaries for institutions of higher education in Virginia, 2000-01 ★3735★

Sweet Dreams of Hope
Outstanding audio selections for young listeners, 2000 ★325★

Sweet; Leonard V.
Top pay and benefits for the chief executive and top paid employees at Drew University ★3273★

Swensen; David F.
Top pay and benefits for the chief executive and top paid employees at Yale University ★3639★

Swift; Jonathan
Top essayists from 1946-1996 ★2445★

Swindle; Richard
Top pay and benefits for the chief executive and top paid employees at Franklin College of Indiana ★3297★

Swinney; Alvis
Top pay and benefits for the chief executive and top paid employees at Duke University ★3276★

Swire Pacific
Business Week's best companies in Hong Kong ★395★

Swiss RE
Business Week's best companies in Switzerland ★405★

Swisscom
Business Week's best companies in Switzerland ★405★

Switchboard operators
Occupations with the highest decline in employment, 1998-2008 ★2310★

Switzerland
Countries with the highest spending per student on higher education, 1997 ★2488★
Percentage of students enrolled in institutions of higher education that were not citizens of the country where they studied, 1998 ★2500★
European periodical prices by country, 2001 ★2921★
Institute for Scientific Information periodical prices by country, 2001 ★2922★
Countries spending the highest percentage of gross domestic product on education ★4060★

Swope; Suzanne
Top pay and benefits for the chief executive and top paid employees at Emerson College ★3287★

Swygert; H. Patrick
Top pay and benefits for the chief executive and top paid employees at Howard University ★3343★

Swygert; Michael I.
Top pay and benefits for the chief executive and top paid employees at Stetson University ★3511★

Sylvester; John
Top pay and benefits for the chief executive and top paid employees at Golden Gate University ★3310★

Sylvester; Robert J.
Top pay and benefits for the chief executive and top paid employees at the University of Scranton ★3567★

Symantec Corporation
Most selective internships in the U.S., 2001 ★2610★
Top internships in the U.S. with the highest compensation, 2001 ★2611★

SYMPHONY

Symphony conductor
  Jobs that are potentially the highest paying ★2246★
  Jobs with the greatest potential income for beginners ★2253★
  Most desirable jobs in the arts ★2277★
Syms Middle School
  Outstanding secondary schools in Norfolk-Virginia Beach-Newport News, Virginia-North Carolina ★4194★
Synovus Financial
  Top banks in Standard & Poor's 500, 2001 ★531★
Syosset High School
  Outstanding secondary schools in Long Island, New York ★4165★
Syracuse University
  Division I all-time winningest college teams ★128★
  U.S. colleges and universities where intercollegiate sports are popular ★995★
  U.S. colleges and universities where the general student body puts a strong emphasis on athletic events ★1007★
  U.S. colleges and universities with a popular newspaper ★1018★
  U.S. colleges and universities with harmonious race/class interaction ★1026★
  U.S. colleges and universities with poor library facilities ★1028★
  U.S. colleges and universities with the least accessible instructors ★1036★
  U.S. colleges and universities awarding the most communications master's degrees to African Americans ★1763★
  U.S. colleges and universities awarding the most communications master's degrees to Asian Americans ★1764★
  U.S. colleges and universities awarding the most communications master's degrees to Hispanic Americans ★1765★
  U.S. colleges and universities awarding the most computer and information sciences master's degrees to African Americans ★1766★
  Faculty's scholarly reputation in the Ph.D.-granting departments of geography, 1925-1982 ★2518★
  Most effective geography research-doctorate programs as evaluated by the National Research Council ★2519★
  Top geography research-doctorate programs as evaluated by the National Research Council ★2520★
  Top Ph.D.-granting departments of geography from 1925-1982 ★2521★
  Library and information science programs with the most citations to journal articles, 1993-1998 ★2712★
  Library and information science programs with the most journal articles, 1993-1998 ★2713★
  Degrees granted in the ten largest undergraduate journalism and mass communications programs, 1999 ★2745★
  Enrollment of students in the ten largest undergraduate journalism and mass communications programs, 1999 ★2746★
  Degrees granted in the ten largest master's journalism and mass communications programs, 1999 ★2757★
  Enrollment of students in the ten largest master's journalism and mass communications programs, 1999 ★2763★
  Average faculty salaries for institutions of higher education in New York, 2000-01 ★3719★

Sysco
  Fortune's highest ranked wholesalers, 2000 ★505★
  Top food companies in Standard & Poor's 500, 2001 ★540★
Systemic dermatologic disease
  Leading categories of dermatologic disease covered by top articles in the field, 1945-1990 ★1869★
Systems
  Engineering doctorates awarded at U.S. colleges and universities, by subfield, 1999 ★1923★
  Gender breakdown of engineering doctorate recipients, by subfield, 1999 ★1934★
Syverson; Steven T.
  Top pay and benefits for the chief executive and top paid employees at Lawrence University ★3367★
Szelistowski; Warren
  Top pay and benefits for the chief executive and top paid employees at the College of Notre Dame in Maryland ★3527★

T

Tabor College
  Highest undergraduate tuition and fees at colleges and universities in Kansas ★1506★
  Average faculty salaries for institutions of higher education in Kansas, 2000-01 ★3703★
  U.S. institutions with the lowest paid full professors, 2001 ★3979★
Tacke; Diane L.
  Top pay and benefits for the chief executive and top paid employees at Luther College ★3383★
Tacoma Community College
  Average faculty salaries for institutions of higher education without academic ranks in Washington, 2000-01 ★3768★
Tactics for Thinking
  People for the American Way's list of most frequently challenged materials, 1982-1992 ★749★
Tahmassian; Taline
  All-America girls' high school soccer team forwards, 2001 ★175★
Taiwan
  Eight grade science achievement scores from selected countries, 1999 ★14★
  Foreign countries with the highest enrollment of foreign students, 1999-2000 ★2496★
  Eighth grade mathematics achievement scores from selected countries, 1999 ★2773★
  Institute for Scientific Information periodical prices by country, 2001 ★2922★
  First-year physics and astronomy graduate students from Asia, 1997-98 ★2987★
  Countries with the highest leader's salary ★3120★
Taiwan Semiconductor Manufacturing
  Business Week's top emerging-market companies worldwide ★434★
  Top information technology companies, 2000 ★544★
Take Time for Your Life
  Longest-running trade paperback bestsellers, 2000 ★282★
Takeda Chemical Industries
  Business Week's best companies in Japan ★398★
The Tale of Murasaki
  Booklist's best first novels ★228★

Tales of an Empty Cabin
  Canada's best nonfiction selections of the 20th century ★234★
Talk
  Library Journal's notable new magazines, 1999 ★2923★
Talking Dirty to the Gods
  Booklist's most recommended poetry books, 2001 ★231★
Tall Tales: Six Amazing Basketball Dreams
  Most notable fiction books for reluctant young adult readers, 2001 ★321★
Talladega College
  U.S. colleges and universities with the highest percentage of African Americans enrolled, 1997 ★222★
  Institutions censured by the American Association of University Professors, 2001 ★1067★
Tallahassee Community College
  Lowest undergraduate tuition and fees at colleges and universities in Florida ★1495★
Tamanend Middle School
  Outstanding secondary schools in Philadelphia, Pennsylvania-New Jersey ★4202★
Tampa/St. Petersburg/Sarasota, FL
  U.S. market areas with the highest percentage of adults having internet access ★2607★
Tampa; University of
  Highest undergraduate tuition and fees at colleges and universities in Florida ★1494★
  Average faculty salaries for institutions of higher education in Florida, 2000-01 ★3696★
Tantillo; Richard C.
  Top pay and benefits for the chief executive and top paid employees at Hamilton College ★3319★
Tape; Carl
  All-USA College Academic First Team, 2001 ★2★
Taplin Barrow; Willie
  Most influential African Americans in religion ★3091★
Tarbell; Ida
  Best U.S. works of journalism in the 20th century ★2769★
Tarbert; Foard H.
  Top pay and benefits for the chief executive and top paid employees at Presbyterian College ★3445★
Target
  Fortune's highest ranked general merchandisers, 2000 ★468★
  Top discount and fashion retailing companies in Standard & Poor's 500, 2001 ★538★
Target (Dayton Hudson)
  Top public companies with the highest percentage of women employees, 2000 ★4459★
Tarkanian; Jerry
  Coaches winning the most NCAA tournaments ★120★
Tarleton State University
  Average faculty salaries for institutions of higher education in Texas, 2000-01 ★3731★
Tarpley; Linsay
  All-America girls' high school soccer team forwards, 2001 ★175★
Tarrant County College District
  Average faculty salaries for institutions of higher education in Texas, 2000-01 ★3731★

Tarrant County Junior College (Ft. Worth)
Community colleges in North America with the highest enrollment ★852★

Tasca; Jules
Top pay and benefits for the chief executive and top paid employees at Gwynedd-Mercy College ★3318★

Tasler; Vi
Top pay and benefits for the chief executive and top paid employees at City University in Washington ★3234★

Tavana; Madjid
Top pay and benefits for the chief executive and top paid employees at LaSalle University ★3365★

Tax-deferred retirement plans
Best ways to save for college ★843★

Taxation of Non-Replenishable Natural Resources
Journal of Environmental Economics and Management's best articles in depletable resources and energy ★2462★

Taxcut 1000 Federal Filling Edition Deluxe
Top selling software in all categories, 2000 ★1602★

Taxcut 1999 Federal Filling Edition
Top selling software in all categories, 2000 ★1602★

Taxi driver
Jobs with the worst environment scores ★2260★
Jobs with the worst stress scores ★2265★
Least desirable jobs ★2266★
Most desirable jobs in personal services ★2275★

Taylor Allderdice High School
Outstanding secondary schools in Pittsburgh, Pennsylvania ★4204★

Taylor & Francis
Publishers, journals and proceedings with the lowest citations (Class 6) ★2571★

Taylor; Arthur R.
Top pay and benefits for the chief executive and top paid employees at Muhlenberg College ★3413★

Taylor; C. Pat
Top pay and benefits for the chief executive and top paid employees at Southwest Baptist University ★3504★

Taylor; Cecelia
Top pay and benefits for the chief executive and top paid employees at the College of St. Scholastica ★3530★

Taylor; Greg
Authors with the most published pages in impact-weighted insurance journals ★677★
Individual authors with the most published pages in *The Journal of Risk and Insurance*, 1987-1996 ★680★

Taylor; Ian
Most cited scholars in critical criminology ★1640★
Most-cited scholars in critical criminology publications ★1641★
Most cited works in critical criminology ★1644★

Taylor; James H.
Top pay and benefits for the chief executive and top paid employees at Cumberland College ★3260★

Taylor Jr.; Charles E.
Top pay and benefits for the chief executive and top paid employees at Meredith College ★3399★

Taylor Middle School
Outstanding secondary schools in Albuquerque, New Mexico ★4080★
Outstanding secondary schools in San Francisco, California ★4221★

Taylor; Robert
All-American boy's high school football linemen, 2000 ★183★

Taylor; Robert B.
Top pay and benefits for the chief executive and top paid employees at Wesleyan University in Connecticut ★3612★

Taylor; Susan
Most influential African Americans in the arts ★78★

Taylor; Susan S.
American Chemical Society 2001 award winners (Group 5) ★755★

Taylor University
U.S. News & World Report's midwestern regional liberal arts colleges with the highest academic reputation scores, 2000-01 ★1340★
U.S. News & World Report's midwestern regional liberal arts colleges with the highest alumni giving rates, 2000-01 ★1342★
U.S. News & World Report's midwestern regional liberal arts colleges with the highest freshmen retention rates, 2000-01 ★1343★
U.S. News & World Report's midwestern regional liberal arts colleges with the highest graduation rates, 2000-01 ★1344★
U.S. News & World Report's midwestern regional liberal arts colleges with the highest percentage of freshmen in the top 25% of their high school class, 2000-01 ★1345★
U.S. News & World Report's midwestern regional liberal arts colleges with the highest percentage of full-time faculty, 2000-01 ★1346★
U.S. News & World Report's midwestern regional liberal arts colleges with the lowest acceptance rates, 2000-01 ★1348★
U.S. News & World Report's top midwestern regional liberal arts colleges, 2000-01 ★1349★
Highest undergraduate tuition and fees at colleges and universities in Indiana ★1502★

Taylor University, Fort Wayne
Average faculty salaries for institutions of higher education in Indiana, 2000-01 ★3701★

Taylor University, Upland
Average faculty salaries for institutions of higher education in Indiana, 2000-01 ★3701★

Teacher
Careers college students considered most respected, 2000 ★740★
Occupational fields of tribal college graduates that are currently employed ★964★
Jobs with the most stringent quotas ★2259★

Teacher aides
Employment outlook for the year 2005 for selected occupations ★2297★

Teacher assistants
Occupations with the largest projected employment growth, 1998-2008 ★2312★
Projected employment growth for selected occupations that require shorter moderate-term on-the-job training, 1998-2008 ★2321★

Teacher education
Education doctorates awarded to U.S. citizens/permanent residents at U.S. colleges and universities, by race/ethnicity and subfield, 1999 ★1922★
Number of education doctorate recipients at U.S. colleges and universities, by field, 1999 ★1971★

Teacher education/special academics and vocations
Gender breakdown of teaching fields doctorate recipients, by subfield, 1999 ★1943★
Teaching fields doctorates awarded at U.S. colleges and universities, by subfield, 1999 ★2046★

Teacher Quality Enhancement Grants
2002 budget request for miscellaneous education programs ★2229★
Fiscal 2002 requested budget as compared with Fiscal 2001 budget for the Education Department ★2231★

Teachers College, Columbia University
U.S. colleges and universities awarding the most education master's degrees to Asian Americans ★1770★
U.S. colleges and universities awarding the most English language/literature/letters master's degrees to African Americans ★1773★
U.S. colleges and universities awarding the most psychology master's degrees to African Americans ★1797★
U.S. colleges and universities awarding the most psychology master's degrees to Asian Americans ★1798★
U.S. colleges and universities awarding the most psychology master's degrees to Hispanic Americans ★1799★
Traditionally white institutions awarding the most doctorate degrees to African Americans ★2079★
U.S. colleges and universities awarding the most doctoral degrees to Hispanic Americans from 1995 to 1999 ★2094★
U.S. colleges and universities awarding the most doctorate degrees to African Americans ★2095★
U.S. colleges and universities awarding the most doctorates in education, 1999 ★2101★
U.S. colleges and universities awarding the most education doctorate degrees to African Americans ★2108★
U.S. colleges and universities awarding the most education doctorate degrees to Asian Americans ★2109★
U.S. colleges and universities awarding the most psychology doctorate degrees to Asian Americans ★2121★
Academics' choices for best administration/supervision graduate programs, 2001 ★4378★
Academics' choices for best curriculum/instruction graduate programs, 2001 ★4380★
Academics' choices for best education policy graduate programs, 2001 ★4381★
Academics' choices for best educational psychology graduate programs, 2001 ★4382★
Academics' choices for best elementary education graduate programs, 2001 ★4383★
Academics' choices for best higher education administration graduate programs, 2001 ★4384★
Academics' choices for best secondary education graduate programs, 2001 ★4385★

Acceptance rates at *U.S. News & World Report*'s top 10 graduate education schools, 2001 ★4388★

Average quantitative GRE scores for *U.S. News & World Report*'s top 10 graduate education schools, 2001 ★4389★

Average verbal GRE scores for *U.S. News & World Report*'s top 10 graduate education schools, 2001 ★4390★

Doctoral students to faculty ratio at *U.S. News & World Report*'s top 10 graduate education schools, 2001 ★4391★

Ph.D.s and Ed.D.s granted at *U.S. News & World Report*'s top 10 graduate education schools, 2001 ★4392★

Research expenditures for *U.S. News & World Report*'s top 10 graduate education schools, 2001 ★4393★

Research expenditures per faculty member at *U.S. News & World Report*'s top 10 graduate education schools, 2001 ★4394★

Top graduate education schools, 2001 ★4395★

Top graduate education schools by reputation, as determined by academic personnel, 2001 ★4396★

Top graduate education schools by reputation, as determined by superintendents, 2001 ★4397★

Teachers, elementary school
Projected employment growth for selected occupations that require a bachelor's degree or more, 1998-2008 ★2317★

Teachers and instructors, vocational education
Projected employment growth for selected occupations that require long-term on-the-job training, 1998-2008 ★2320★

Teachers, preschool
Projected employment growth for selected occupations that require a bachelor's degree or more, 1998-2008 ★2317★

Teachers, secondary school
Occupations with the largest projected employment growth, 1998-2008 ★2312★

Projected employment growth for selected occupations that require a bachelor's degree or more, 1998-2008 ★2317★

Teachers, special education
Projected employment growth for selected occupations that require a bachelor's degree or more, 1998-2008 ★2317★

Teaching assistantships
Primary sources of financial support for doctorate recipients, by citizenship, 1999 ★2003★

Primary sources of financial support for doctorate recipients, by gender, 1999 ★2004★

Primary sources of financial support for doctorate recipients, by race/ethnicity, 1999 ★2005★

Primary sources of financial support for education doctorate recipients, by citizenship, 1999 ★2006★

Primary sources of financial support for education doctorate recipients, by gender, 1999 ★2007★

Primary sources of financial support for education doctorate recipients, by race/ethnicity, 1999 ★2008★

Primary sources of financial support for engineering doctorate recipients, by citizenship, 1999 ★2009★

Primary sources of financial support for engineering doctorate recipients, by gender, 1999 ★2010★

Primary sources of financial support for engineering doctorate recipients, by race/ethnicity, 1999 ★2011★

Primary sources of financial support for humanities doctorate recipients, by citizenship, 1999 ★2012★

Primary sources of financial support for humanities doctorate recipients, by gender, 1999 ★2013★

Primary sources of financial support for humanities doctorate recipients, by race/ethnicity, 1999 ★2014★

Primary sources of financial support for life sciences doctorate recipients, by citizenship, 1999 ★2015★

Primary sources of financial support for life sciences doctorate recipients, by gender, 1999 ★2016★

Primary sources of financial support for life sciences doctorate recipients, by race/ethnicity, 1999 ★2017★

Primary sources of financial support for physical sciences, mathematics, and computer sciences doctorate recipients, by citizenship, 1999 ★2018★

Primary sources of financial support for physical sciences, mathematics, and computer sciences doctorate recipients, by gender, 1999 ★2019★

Primary sources of financial support for physical sciences, mathematics, and computer sciences doctorate recipients, by race/ethnicity, 1999 ★2020★

Primary sources of financial support for professional/other doctorate recipients, by citizenship, 1999 ★2021★

Primary sources of financial support for professional/other doctorate recipients, by gender, 1999 ★2022★

Primary sources of financial support for professional/other doctorate recipients, by race/ethnicity, 1999 ★2023★

Primary sources of financial support for social sciences doctorate recipients, by citizenship, 1999 ★2024★

Primary sources of financial support for social sciences doctorate recipients, by gender, 1999 ★2025★

Primary sources of financial support for social sciences doctorate recipients, by race/ethnicity, 1999 ★2026★

Teaching fields
Education doctorates awarded to U.S. citizens/permanent residents at U.S. colleges and universities, by race/ethnicity and subfield, 1999 ★1922★

Number of education doctorate recipients at U.S. colleges and universities, by field, 1999 ★1971★

Teamer; Charles
Top pay and benefits for the chief executive and top paid employees at Clark Atlanta University ★3237★

Tech Data
Biggest information technology companies, 2000 ★385★

Fortune's highest ranked wholesalers, 2000 ★505★

Tech support
Job openings for high-tech workers ★2330★

Technical
Expected majors for incoming freshmen, 2000 ★1050★

Technical College of the Lowcountry
Lowest undergraduate tuition and fees at colleges and universities in South Carolina ★1555★

Average faculty salaries for institutions of higher education without academic ranks in South Carolina, 2000-01 ★3765★

Technical Communication
Most cited serials in technical communication journals from 1988 to 1997 ★4425★

Most cited technology serials in technical communication journals from 1988 to 1997 ★4427★

Technical Communication Quarterly
Most cited technology serials in technical communication journals from 1988 to 1997 ★4427★

Technical Communication Quarterly/Technical Writing Teacher
Most cited serials in technical communication journals from 1988 to 1997 ★4425★

Technical consultant
Monster.com's most searched job listings ★2308★

Technical education
Gender breakdown of teaching fields doctorate recipients, by subfield, 1999 ★1943★

Teaching fields doctorates awarded at U.S. colleges and universities, by subfield, 1999 ★2046★

Technical/industrial arts education
Gender breakdown of teaching fields doctorate recipients, by subfield, 1999 ★1943★

Teaching fields doctorates awarded at U.S. colleges and universities, by subfield, 1999 ★2046★

Technical support
Information technology jobs most in demand, 2001 ★4428★

Technical Trades Institute
Highest undergraduate tuition and fees at colleges and universities in Colorado ★1488★

Technical writer
Jobs with the most stringent quotas ★2259★

Most desirable jobs in communications ★2271★

Technical writing
Job openings for high-tech workers ★2330★

Technicians and related
College graduates in the labor force, by occupational group, 1998 ★926★

Projected change in employment of college graduates, by occupational group, from 1998 to 2008 ★965★

Projected employment of college graduates, by occupational group, 2008 ★966★

Technicians and related support
Employment change projections by major occupational group from 1998 to 2008 ★2288★

Employment projections by major occupational group for 2008 ★2291★

Employment in college-level jobs, by occupational group, 2006 ★2295★

Percentages for projected employment growth by occupational group, 1998-2008 ★2314★

Projected employment growth by occupational group, 1998-2008 ★2316★

Internet use by major occupational group, 1998 ★2587★

Technology
Average costs for Academic Search titles by subject, 2001 ★2918★

Periodical prices by LC subject, 2001 ★2925★

Periodical prices by scientific discipline, 2001 ★2926★
Mean age of first and best contribution of scientists and inventors, by discipline ★3096★

The Technology Coordinator's Web Site
Top sites for educators ★2605★

Technology, Prices and the Derived Demand for Energy
Top cited energy papers from 1974 to 1978 ★2463★

Technostyle
Most cited technology serials in technical communication journals from 1988 to 1997 ★4427★

Tecnost
Business Week's best companies in Italy ★397★

Teen Beat
Best-selling youth magazines ★2920★

Teen Love: On Relationships, a Book for Teenagers
Most notable nonfiction books for reluctant young adult readers, 2001 ★323★

Teikyo Loretto Height University
Bachelor's institutions with the highest enrollment of foreign students, 1998-99 ★2492★

Teitelman Middle School
Outstanding secondary schools in Atlantic-Cape May, New Jersey ★4088★

Tektronix
Business Week's best performing companies with the lowest 3-year sales performance ★423★
Fortune's highest ranked scientific, photo and control equipment companies, 2000 ★493★

Telcordia Technologies
Top recruiters for computer science jobs for 2000-01 bachelor's degree recipients ★1590★
Top recruiters for computer science jobs for 2000-01 master's degree recipients ★1598★
Top recruiters for electrical/electronic engineering jobs for 2000-01 bachelor's degree recipients ★2354★
Top recruiters for electrical/electronic engineering jobs for 2000-01 master's degree recipients ★2406★

Tele Danmark
Business Week's best companies in Denmark ★391★

Telecom Corp. of New Zealand
Business Week's best companies in New Zealand ★399★

Telecom Italia
Business Week's best companies in Italy ★397★

Telefonica
Business Week's best companies in Spain ★403★

Telefonos de Mexico (Telmex)
Business Week's top emerging-market companies worldwide ★434★

Telekom Malaysia
Business Week's top emerging-market companies worldwide ★434★

Telephone/cable TV installers and repairers
Projected employment growth for selected occupations that require long-term on-the-job training, 1998-2008 ★2320★

Tell Me
Library Journal's best poetry books, 2000 ★244★

Tellabs
Companies that have been on *Business Week*'s top 50 list the longest ★435★
Fortune's highest ranked network communications companies, 2000 ★482★
Top telecommunications companies in Standard & Poor's 500, 2001 ★559★
Top recruiters for computer science jobs for 2000-01 master's degree recipients ★1598★
Top recruiters for computer engineering jobs for 2000-01 bachelor's degree recipients ★2352★
Top recruiters for electrical/electronic engineering jobs for 2000-01 master's degree recipients ★2406★
Most selective internships in the U.S., 2001 ★2610★
Top internships in the U.S. with the highest compensation, 2001 ★2611★
Top recruiters for information technology (MIS) jobs for 2000-01 master's degree recipients ★2739★

The Telling
Library Journal's best science fiction and fantasy titles, 2000 ★246★

Telstra
Business Week's best companies in Australia ★386★

Temple-Inland
Fortune's highest ranked forest and paper products companies, 2000 ★466★
Top containers and packaging companies in Standard & Poor's 500, 2001 ★537★

Temple University
U.S. colleges and universities with the lowest average football attendance, 1996-99 ★160★
Employing institutions with the most published pages in *The Journal of Risk and Insurance*, 1987-1996 ★679★
U.S. college campuses with more than 5,000 students reporting murders or manslaughters, 1998 ★729★
Four-year public institutions enrolling the highest number of students from the District of Columbia, 1998-99 ★855★
U.S. colleges and universities with a diverse student body ★1012★
U.S. colleges and universities with the unhappiest students ★1041★
U.S. colleges and universities with the worst financial aid programs ★1042★
U.S. colleges and universities with the worst overall administration ★1045★
State appropriations for Pennsylvania's institutions of higher education, 2000-01 ★1291★
U.S. colleges and universities spending the most on independent lobbyists, 1999 ★1310★
Highest undergraduate tuition and fees at public, 4-year or above colleges and universities ★1463★
Public 4-year institutions with the highest tuition, 2000-01 ★1471★
Universities with the most-cited scholars in *Criminal Justice and Behavior* ★1648★
Universities with the most-cited scholars in *Criminology* ★1649★
Universities with the most-cited scholars in *Journal of Quantitative Criminology* ★1650★
Universities with the most-cited scholars in *Journal of Research in Crime and Delinquency* ★1651★
Universities with the most-cited scholars in *Justice Quarterly* ★1652★

Total baccalaureate communications degrees awarded to African Americans from U.S. colleges and universities, 1997-98 ★1687★
Total baccalaureate degrees awarded to African Americans from traditionally white institutions, 1997-98 ★1698★
Total baccalaureate degrees awarded to African Americans from U.S. colleges and universities, 1997-98 ★1699★
Total baccalaureate education degrees awarded to African Americans from U.S. colleges and universities, 1997-98 ★1711★
Total baccalaureate health professions and related sciences degrees awarded to Asian Americans from U.S. colleges and universities, 1997-98 ★1722★
Total ethnic/cultural studies doctoral degrees awarded to African Americans from U.S. colleges and universities, 1997-98 ★1745★
Total ethnic/cultural studies doctoral degrees awarded to minorities from U.S. colleges and universities, 1997-98 ★1746★
Total ethnic/cultural studies master's degrees awarded to African Americans from U.S. colleges and universities, 1997-98 ★1747★
Total ethnic/cultural studies master's degrees awarded to minorities from U.S. colleges and universities, 1997-98 ★1748★
Traditionally white institutions awarding the most master's degrees to African Americans ★1755★
U.S. colleges and universities awarding the most communications master's degrees to African Americans ★1763★
U.S. colleges and universities awarding the most computer and information sciences master's degrees to Hispanic Americans ★1768★
U.S. colleges and universities awarding the most health professions and related sciences master's degrees to Native Americans ★1780★
U.S. colleges and universities awarding the most law and legal studies master's degrees to African Americans ★1781★
U.S. colleges and universities awarding the most master's degrees to African Americans ★1785★
Traditionally white institutions awarding the most first professional degrees to African Americans ★1842★
U.S. colleges and universities awarding the most first professional degrees to African Americans ★1843★
U.S. colleges and universities awarding the most first professional degrees to Asian Americans ★1844★
U.S. colleges and universities awarding the most first professional degrees to Hispanic Americans ★1845★
U.S. colleges and universities awarding the most health professions and related sciences first professional degrees to African Americans ★1847★
U.S. colleges and universities awarding the most health professions and related sciences first professional degrees to Asian Americans ★1848★
U.S. colleges and universities awarding the most health professions and related sciences first professional degrees to Hispanic Americans ★1849★
U.S. colleges and universities awarding the most health professions and related sciences first professional degrees to minorities ★1850★

TEN

U.S. colleges and universities awarding the most law and legal studies first professional degrees to African Americans ★1852★
Traditionally white institutions awarding the most doctorate degrees to African Americans ★2079★
U.S. colleges and universities awarding the most business management and administrative services doctorate degrees to Asian Americans ★2086★
U.S. colleges and universities awarding the most doctoral degrees to Hispanic Americans from 1995 to 1999 ★2094★
U.S. colleges and universities awarding the most doctorate degrees to African Americans ★2095★
U.S. colleges and universities awarding the most doctorate degrees to minorities ★2098★
U.S. colleges and universities awarding the most psychology doctorate degrees to African Americans ★2120★
Academics' choices for best trial advocacy programs, 2001 ★2633★
Average faculty salaries for institutions of higher education in Pennsylvania, 2000-01 ★3725★

Ten Things I Wish I'd Known-Before I Went Out into the Real World
Longest-running nonfiction hardcover bestsellers, 2000 ★281★

Tenaga Nasional
Business Week's top emerging-market companies worldwide ★434★

Tenet Healthcare
Business Week's best performing companies with the highest 1-year shareholder returns ★415★
Fortune's highest ranked health care companies, 2000 ★469★

Tenneco Automotive
Fortune's highest ranked motor vehicle parts companies, 2000 ★480★

Tennessee
Mean composite ACT scores by state, 2000 ★895★
Mean math SAT scores by state, 2000 ★900★
Mean verbal SAT scores by state, 2000 ★903★
Total doctorate recipients by state, 1999 ★2054★
State grades for affordability of higher education for minority students, 2000 ★2883★
State grades for benefits state receives for educating its minority students, 2000 ★2884★
State grades for completion of higher education by minority students, 2000 ★2885★
State grades for participation of minority students in higher education, 2000 ★2886★
State grades for preparing minority students for higher education, 2000 ★2887★
States expelling the highest ratio of students for violating the Gun-Free Schools Act, 1998-99 ★3993★
States expelling the most students for violating the Gun-Free Schools Act, 1998-99 ★3994★
States with the lowest per-pupil expenditures ★3998★
States with the lowest percentage of high school freshmen enrolling in college within four years ★4267★

Tennessee, Chattanooga; University of
Average faculty salaries for institutions of higher education in Tennessee, 2000-01 ★3730★

Tennessee Institute of Agriculture; University of
Average faculty salaries for institutions of higher education in Tennessee, 2000-01 ★3730★

Tennessee, Knoxville; University of
U.S. colleges and universities with the highest average football attendance, 1996-99 ★159★
U.S. business schools with the quickest payback on MBA investments ★654★
U.S. colleges and universities where a large portion of the student body drink beer ★991★
U.S. colleges and universities where the general student body puts a strong emphasis on socializing ★1008★
Average faculty salaries for institutions of higher education in Tennessee, 2000-01 ★3730★

Tennessee, Martin; University of
Average faculty salaries for institutions of higher education in Tennessee, 2000-01 ★3730★

Tennessee, Memphis; University of
U.S. colleges and universities awarding the most health professions and related sciences first professional degrees to African Americans ★1847★
Average faculty salaries for institutions of higher education in Tennessee, 2000-01 ★3730★

Tennessee State University
Colleges offering the Thurgood Marshall Scholarship Fund ★221★
State appropriations for Tennessee's institutions of higher education, 2000-01 ★1295★
Historically black colleges and universities awarding the most master's degrees to African Americans ★1670★
Total baccalaureate biology/life sciences degrees awarded to African Americans from U.S. colleges and universities, 1997-98 ★1679★
U.S. colleges and universities awarding the most biological and life sciences master's degrees to African Americans ★1756★
U.S. colleges and universities awarding the most mathematics master's degrees to African Americans ★1790★
U.S. institutions awarding the most baccalaureate degrees to African Americans in agricultural sciences, 1998 ★1814★
U.S. institutions awarding the most master's degrees to African Americans in agricultural sciences, 1998 ★1825★
U.S. institutions awarding the most master's degrees to minorities in agricultural sciences, 1998 ★1830★
Historically black colleges and universities awarding the most doctorate degrees to African Americans ★1945★
Most wired historically black colleges and universities, 2000 ★2597★

Tennessee Tech University
Average faculty salaries for institutions of higher education in Tennessee, 2000-01 ★3730★

Tennessee Technological University
State appropriations for Tennessee's institutions of higher education, 2000-01 ★1295★

Tennessee; University of
Women's basketball teams with the most appearances in the Final Four ★157★
State appropriations for Tennessee's institutions of higher education, 2000-01 ★1295★
Comparison of library and information science programs composite rankings with *U.S. News & World Report* survey ★2709★

Library and information science programs with the most citations to journal articles, 1993-1998 ★2712★
Library and information science programs with the most journal articles, 1993-1998 ★2713★
Library and information science programs with the most journal articles per capita, 1993-1998 ★2714★
Library and information science programs with the most per capita citations to journal articles, 1993-1998 ★2715★
Degrees granted in the ten largest doctoral journalism and mass communications programs, 1999 ★2756★

Tennessee Wesleyan College
Average faculty salaries for institutions of higher education in Tennessee, 2000-01 ★3730★
U.S. institutions with the lowest paid full professors, 2001 ★3979★

Tenopir; Carol
Library and information science faculty with the most journal articles, 1993-1998 ★2711★

Tequestra Trace Middle School
Outstanding secondary schools in Fort Lauderdale, Florida ★4133★

Teradyne
Fortune's highest ranked scientific, photo and control equipment companies, 2000 ★493★
Top electrical and electronics companies in Standard & Poor's 500, 2001 ★539★

Termini; John
Top pay and benefits for the chief executive and top paid employees at Averett College ★3185★

Terra Community College
Lowest undergraduate tuition and fees at colleges and universities in Ohio ★1544★

Terra Networks
Business Week's best companies in Spain ★403★

Terra State Community College
Average faculty salaries for institutions of higher education in Ohio, 2000-01 ★3722★

Terry; Charles D.
Top pay and benefits for the chief executive and top paid employees at Averett College ★3185★

TESOL Quarterly
Most cited language serials in technical communication journals from 1988 to 1997 ★4420★

The Testament
Longest-running mass market paperback bestsellers, 2000 ★280★

Testing for the Effects of Oil-Price Rises Using Vector Autoregression
Top cited energy papers from 1984 to 1988 ★2465★

Teton, WY
Counties with the highest per capita income ★2561★

Tetrahedron-Asymmetry
Inorganic and nuclear chemistry journals by citation impact, 1995-99 ★812★
Inorganic and nuclear chemistry journals by citation impact, 1999 ★813★

Tew; Mark
Top pay and benefits for the chief executive and top paid employees at Judson College in Alabama ★3356★

Texaco
Fortune's highest ranked petroleum refining companies, 2000 ★484★

Top recruiters for chemical engineering jobs for 2000-01 bachelor's degree recipients ★2343★
Top recruiters for geology/geophysics jobs for 2000-01 master's degree recipients ★2524★

Texas

People for the American Way's list of states with the most challenges to library and school books, 1982-1992 ★750★
States with the highest enrollment in private 4-year institutions of higher education ★860★
States with the highest enrollment in public 4-year institutions of higher education ★861★
Mean composite ACT scores by state, 2000 ★895★
Mean math SAT scores by state, 2000 ★900★
Mean verbal SAT scores by state, 2000 ★903★
States allocating the largest amount of state tax appropriations for higher education, 2000-01 ★1304★
States receiving the most in federal agency appropriations to colleges, 2000 ★1306★
States receiving the most in federal agency appropriations to colleges, from 1996 to 2000 ★1307★
Total doctorate recipients by state, 1999 ★2054★
Hispanic American enrollment at Hispanic-serving institutions of higher education, by state, 1997 ★2547★
States with the most law schools ★2668★
State library associations with most full-time staff ★2681★
State library associations with the highest annual revenue ★2682★
State library associations with the highest conference attendance ★2683★
State library associations with the highest unrestricted net assets ★2684★
State library associations with the largest membership ★2685★
State grades for affordability of higher education for minority students, 2000 ★2883★
State grades for benefits state receives for educating its minority students, 2000 ★2884★
State grades for completion of higher education by minority students, 2000 ★2885★
State grades for participation of minority students in higher education, 2000 ★2886★
State grades for preparing minority students for higher education, 2000 ★2887★
States expelling the most students for violating the Gun-Free Schools Act, 1998-99 ★3994★
States with the highest number of high school graduates, 1999-2000 ★3995★
States with the most public school districts ★3999★
States with the highest average enrollment in public elementary schools ★4032★
States with the highest K-12 public school enrollment ★4034★
States with the highest projected K-12 public school enrollment for 2010 ★4035★
States with the highest funding needs for school-building modernization ★4040★
States with the highest funding needs for school-technology modernization ★4041★
States with the most charter schools ★4048★
States with the most K-12 public schools ★4049★
States with the lowest percentage of high school freshmen enrolling in college within four years ★4267★
U.S. states with the highest percentage of births to teenagers who were already mothers ★4433★
States with the most women-owned companies ★4455★

Texas A&M International University

Total baccalaureate mathematics degrees awarded to Hispanic Americans from U.S. colleges and universities, 1997-98 ★1731★
U.S. colleges and universities awarding the most business management and administrative services master's degrees to Hispanic Americans ★1761★
U.S. colleges and universities awarding the most English language/literature/letters master's degrees to Hispanic Americans ★1775★
U.S. colleges and universities awarding the most psychology master's degrees to Hispanic Americans ★1799★
U.S. colleges and universities awarding the most social sciences and history master's degrees to Hispanic Americans ★1803★
Average faculty salaries for institutions of higher education in Texas, 2000-01 ★3731★

Texas A&M University

Colleges with the highest number of freshman Merit Scholars, 2000 ★5★
Longest field goals in college football ★158★
Comparisons of investment returns for marketing MBAs ★626★
U.S. business schools with the quickest payback on MBA investments ★654★
Institutions with the most published authors in the *Journal of Business Research*, 1985 to 1999 ★695★
Top chemistry research-doctorate programs as evaluated by the National Research Council ★805★
Largest degree-granting colleges and universities, by enrollment ★1068★
Total baccalaureate engineering degrees awarded to minorities from U.S. colleges and universities, 1997-98 ★1715★
Total baccalaureate mathematics degrees awarded to African Americans from U.S. colleges and universities, 1997-98 ★1729★
Total baccalaureate mathematics degrees awarded to Asian Americans from U.S. colleges and universities, 1997-98 ★1730★
Total baccalaureate mathematics degrees awarded to Hispanic Americans from U.S. colleges and universities, 1997-98 ★1731★
Total baccalaureate physical sciences degrees awarded to Hispanic Americans from U.S. colleges and universities, 1997-98 ★1735★
U.S. institutions awarding the most baccalaureate degrees to Hispanic Americans in agribusiness and production, 1998 ★1817★
U.S. institutions awarding the most baccalaureate degrees to Hispanic Americans in agricultural sciences, 1998 ★1818★
U.S. institutions awarding the most baccalaureate degrees to minorities in agribusiness and production, 1998 ★1819★
U.S. institutions awarding the most baccalaureate degrees to minorities in agricultural sciences, 1998 ★1820★
U.S. institutions awarding the most master's degrees to Hispanic Americans in agricultural sciences, 1998 ★1828★
U.S. institutions awarding the most master's degrees to minorities in agricultural sciences, 1998 ★1830★
Doctorate-granting-institutions awarding the most non-U.S. citizen doctoral degrees, 1999 ★1906★

U.S. colleges and universities awarding the most doctoral degrees to African Americans from 1995 to 1999 ★2091★
U.S. colleges and universities awarding the most doctorate degrees to Asian Americans ★2096★
U.S. colleges and universities awarding the most doctorate degrees to Hispanic Americans ★2097★
U.S. colleges and universities awarding the most doctorates in physical sciences, mathematics, and computer sciences, 1999 ★2105★
U.S. colleges and universities awarding the most social sciences and history doctorate degrees to Asian Americans ★2125★
U.S. institutions awarding the most doctoral degrees to minorities in agricultural sciences, 1998 ★2131★
Top oceanography research-doctorate programs as evaluated by the National Research Council ★2153★
U.S. universities publishing the most papers in the field of civil engineering, 1995-99 ★2349★
Most effective industrial engineering research-doctorate programs as evaluated by the National Research Council ★2412★
Top industrial engineering research-doctorate programs as evaluated by the National Research Council ★2413★
Institutions with the most productive libraries, 1993-1997 ★2678★
University research libraries in the U.S. and Canada with the largest increases in total expenditures from 1993-94 to 1998-99 ★2708★
Top statistics and biostatistics research-doctorate programs as evaluated by the National Research Council ★2782★
U.S. colleges and universities spending the most on chemical engineering research and development, 1998 ★3098★
U.S. universities spending the most on research and development, 1998 ★3104★

Texas A&M University, College Station

Top business schools for within-discipline research performance in management, 1986-1998 ★646★
Top business schools for within-discipline research performance in production/operations management, 1986-1998 ★648★
Academics' choices for best graduate agricultural engineering programs, 2001 ★2379★
Academics' choices for best graduate civil engineering programs, 2001 ★2394★
Academics' choices for best graduate industrial/manufacturing engineering programs, 2001 ★2411★
U.S. News & World Report's graduate engineering programs with the best industrial manufacturing departments, 2000-01 ★2415★
Academics' choices for best graduate nuclear engineering schools, 2000 ★2426★
Academics' choices for best graduate petroleum engineering schools, 2000 ★2429★
U.S. News & World Report's graduate engineering programs with the best petroleum departments, 2000-01 ★2431★
Average faculty salaries for institutions of higher education in Texas, 2000-01 ★3731★

Texas A&M University, Commerce

U.S. colleges and universities awarding the most education doctorate degrees to Asian Americans ★2109★

TEXAS — Educational Rankings Annual • 2002

Average faculty salaries for institutions of higher education in Texas, 2000-01 ★3731★

Texas A&M University, Corpus Christi
U.S. colleges and universities awarding the most education master's degrees to Hispanic Americans ★1771★
U.S. colleges and universities awarding the most health professions and related sciences master's degrees to Hispanic Americans ★1779★
U.S. colleges and universities awarding the most master's degrees to Hispanic Americans ★1787★
Average faculty salaries for institutions of higher education in Texas, 2000-01 ★3731★

Texas A&M University, Galveston
U.S. News & World Report's top public western regional liberal arts colleges, 2000-01 ★1365★
Academic reputation scores for U.S. News & World Report's top western regional liberal arts colleges, 2000-01 ★1387★
Acceptance rates for U.S. News & World Report's top western regional liberal arts colleges, 2000-01 ★1388★
Average freshmen retention rates for U.S. News & World Report's top western regional liberal arts colleges, 2000-01 ★1390★
Average graduation rates for U.S. News & World Report's top western regional liberal arts colleges, 2000-01 ★1391★
Percentage of freshmen in the top 25% of their high school class at U.S. News & World Report's top western regional liberal arts colleges, 2000-01 ★1392★
Percentage of full-time faculty at U.S. News & World Report's top western regional liberal arts colleges, 2000-01 ★1393★
Proportion of classes having 20 students or less at U.S. News & World Report's top western regional liberal arts colleges, 2000-01 ★1394★
Student/faculty ratios at U.S. News & World Report's top western regional liberal arts colleges, 2000-01 ★1395★
U.S. News & World Report's top western regional liberal arts colleges, 2000-01 ★1396★

Texas A&M University, Kingsville
Division II NCAA colleges with the lowest graduation rates for football players, 1993-94 ★948★
U.S. colleges and universities awarding the most education master's degrees to Hispanic Americans ★1771★
U.S. colleges and universities awarding the most psychology master's degrees to Hispanic Americans ★1799★
U.S. institutions awarding the most baccalaureate degrees to Hispanic Americans in agribusiness and production, 1998 ★1817★
U.S. colleges and universities awarding the most doctorate degrees to Hispanic Americans ★2097★
U.S. colleges and universities awarding the most education doctorate degrees to Hispanic Americans ★2110★
Average faculty salaries for institutions of higher education in Texas, 2000-01 ★3731★

Texas A&M University System
Colleges and universities with the largest endowments, 2000 ★1237★
State appropriations for Texas's institutions of higher education, 2000-01 ★1296★

Texas A&M University System and Foundations
2000 endowment values of the 'wealthiest' U.S. universities ★1230★
2001 mid-year endowment values of the 'wealthiest' U.S. universities ★1234★
Endowment values for the wealthiest U.S. universities, 2000 ★1240★

Texas, Arlington; University of
Division I NCAA colleges with that graduated less than 20% of their African American male athletes, 1990-91 to 1993-94 ★928★
U.S. colleges and universities awarding the most business management and administrative services doctorate degrees to Asian Americans ★2086★
Doctoral institutions with the highest enrollment of foreign students, 1998-99 ★2494★
Average faculty salaries for institutions of higher education in Texas, 2000-01 ★3731★

Texas, Austin, McCombs School of Business; University of
U.S. News & World Report's undergraduate business programs with the best e-commerce departments, 2000-01 ★564★
U.S. News & World Report's undergraduate business programs with the best entrepreneurship departments, 2000-01 ★565★
U.S. News & World Report's undergraduate business programs with the best management information systems departments, 2000-01 ★568★
U.S. News & World Report's undergraduate business programs with the highest academic reputation scores, 2000-01 ★571★
U.S. News & World Report's undergraduate business programs with the best accounting departments, 2000-01 ★581★
Academics' choices for best graduate entrepreneurship programs, 2001 ★583★
Academics' choices for best graduate management information systems programs, 2001 ★585★
Business Week's top business schools with the lowest percentage of international students, 2000 ★615★
Business Week's top business schools with the lowest percentage of minority enrollment, 2000 ★616★
Business Week's top business schools with the lowest percentage of women enrollees, 2000 ★617★
Business Week's top business schools with the worst placement offices, 2000 ★620★
Lowest post-MBA salaries for students enrolled in Business Week's top business schools, 1999 ★634★
Lowest pre-MBA salaries for students enrolled in Business Week's top business schools, 1999 ★635★
Top graduate business schools by reputation, as determined by recruiters, 2001 ★651★
Academics' choices for best graduate accounting programs, 2001 ★659★
U.S. News & World Report's undergraduate business programs with the best marketing departments, 2000-01 ★685★

Texas, Austin; University of
All-USA College Academic Second Team, 2001 ★3★
Colleges with the highest number of freshman Merit Scholars, 2000 ★5★
Top anthropology research-doctorate programs as evaluated by the National Research Council ★62★
Top ecology, evolution, and behavior research-doctorate programs as evaluated by the National Research Council ★201★
Top business schools in research performance, 1986-1998 ★532★
U.S. News & World Report's universities with the best taxation departments, 1999-2000 ★573★
Top business schools for overall within-discipline research performance, 1986-1998 ★645★
Top business schools for within-discipline research performance in management science, 1986-1998 ★647★
Top business schools for within-discipline research performance in insurance, international business and real estate, 1986-1998 ★667★
Top business schools for within-discipline research performance in marketing, 1986-1998 ★671★
Top business schools for within-discipline research performance in management information systems, 1986-1998 ★675★
Institutions with the most published authors in the Journal of Business Research, 1985 to 1999 ★695★
Top chemistry research-doctorate programs as evaluated by the National Research Council ★805★
Most effective classics research-doctorate programs as evaluated by the National Research Council ★815★
Top classics research-doctorate programs as evaluated by the National Research Council ★816★
Institutions with the most full-time Hispanic American faculty ★923★
U.S. colleges and universities with the most full-time Hispanic American faculty ★925★
U.S. colleges and universities where a large portion of the student body drink beer ★991★
U.S. colleges and universities where fraternities and sororities are popular ★993★
U.S. colleges and universities where the general student body puts a strong emphasis on socializing ★1008★
Largest degree-granting colleges and universities, by enrollment ★1068★
U.S. News & World Report's national universities with the highest percentage of full-time faculty, 2000-01 ★1136★
U.S. News & World Report's national universities with the lowest graduation rates, 1999 ★1141★
Institutions receiving the most corporate gifts, 1999-2000 ★1243★
Fiske Guide's best buys for public colleges and universities, 2001 ★1460★
Top computer science research-doctorate programs as evaluated by the National Research Council ★1597★
Top colleges in terms of total baccalaureate degrees awarded to minorities, 1997-98 ★1678★
Total baccalaureate biology/life sciences degrees awarded to Asian Americans from U.S. colleges and universities, 1997-98 ★1680★
Total baccalaureate biology/life sciences degrees awarded to Hispanic Americans from U.S. colleges and universities, 1997-98 ★1681★

900

Total baccalaureate communications degrees awarded to Asian Americans from U.S. colleges and universities, 1997-98 ★1688★

Total baccalaureate communications degrees awarded to Hispanic Americans from U.S. colleges and universities, 1997-98 ★1689★

Total baccalaureate communications degrees awarded to Native Americans from U.S. colleges and universities, 1997-98 ★1690★

Total baccalaureate computer and information science degrees awarded to Hispanic Americans from U.S. colleges and universities, 1997-98 ★1693★

Total baccalaureate computer and information science degrees awarded to Native Americans from U.S. colleges and universities, 1997-98 ★1694★

Total baccalaureate degrees awarded to Hispanic Americans from U.S. colleges and universities, 1997-98 ★1705★

Total baccalaureate engineering degrees awarded to minorities from U.S. colleges and universities, 1997-98 ★1715★

Total baccalaureate English language, literature, and letters degrees awarded to Hispanic Americans from U.S. colleges and universities, 1997-98 ★1718★

Total baccalaureate health professions and related sciences degrees awarded to Hispanic Americans from U.S. colleges and universities, 1997-98 ★1723★

Total baccalaureate mathematics degrees awarded to Hispanic Americans from U.S. colleges and universities, 1997-98 ★1731★

Total baccalaureate physical sciences degrees awarded to Hispanic Americans from U.S. colleges and universities, 1997-98 ★1735★

Total baccalaureate psychology degrees awarded to Hispanic Americans from U.S. colleges and universities, 1997-98 ★1739★

Total baccalaureate social sciences and history degrees awarded to Hispanic Americans from U.S. colleges and universities, 1997-98 ★1743★

U.S. colleges and universities awarding the most business management and administrative services master's degrees to Hispanic Americans ★1761★

U.S. colleges and universities awarding the most communications master's degrees to Hispanic Americans ★1765★

U.S. colleges and universities awarding the most English language/literature/letters master's degrees to Hispanic Americans ★1775★

U.S. colleges and universities awarding the most master's degrees to Hispanic Americans ★1787★

U.S. colleges and universities awarding the most master's degrees to minorities ★1788★

U.S. colleges and universities awarding the most first professional degrees to Hispanic Americans ★1845★

U.S. colleges and universities awarding the most law and legal studies first professional degrees to African Americans ★1852★

U.S. colleges and universities awarding the most law and legal studies first professional degrees to Hispanic Americans ★1854★

U.S. universities publishing the most papers in the field of dentistry/oral surgery and medicine, 1995-99 ★1865★

Doctorate-granting-institutions awarding the most non-U.S. citizen doctoral degrees, 1999 ★1906★

Top doctorate granting institutions, 1999 ★2047★

U.S. colleges and universities awarding the most biological and life sciences doctorate degrees to Asian Americans ★2083★

U.S. colleges and universities awarding the most doctoral degrees to African Americans from 1995 to 1999 ★2091★

U.S. colleges and universities awarding the most doctoral degrees to American Indians and Alaskan Natives from 1995 to 1999 ★2092★

U.S. colleges and universities awarding the most doctorate degrees to Asian Americans ★2096★

U.S. colleges and universities awarding the most doctorate degrees to Hispanic Americans ★2097★

U.S. colleges and universities awarding the most doctorate degrees to minorities ★2098★

U.S. colleges and universities awarding the most doctorates in all fields, 1999 ★2100★

U.S. colleges and universities awarding the most doctorates in education, 1999 ★2101★

U.S. colleges and universities awarding the most doctorates in engineering, 1999 ★2102★

U.S. colleges and universities awarding the most doctorates in humanities, 1999 ★2103★

U.S. colleges and universities awarding the most doctorates in physical sciences, mathematics, and computer sciences, 1999 ★2105★

U.S. colleges and universities awarding the most doctorates in professional and other fields, 1999 ★2106★

U.S. colleges and universities awarding the most doctorates in social sciences, 1999 ★2107★

U.S. colleges and universities awarding the most education doctorate degrees to Asian Americans ★2109★

U.S. colleges and universities awarding the most education doctorate degrees to Hispanic Americans ★2110★

U.S. institutions awarding the most doctorate degrees, 1999 ★2132★

Top geosciences research-doctorate programs as evaluated by the National Research Council ★2152★

U.S. universities contributing the most papers in the field of AI, robotics, and auto control, 1993-97 ★2338★

U.S. universities publishing the most papers in the field of civil engineering, 1994-98 ★2348★

U.S. universities publishing the most papers in the field of civil engineering, 1995-99 ★2349★

Acceptance rates for *U.S. News & World Report*'s top 10 graduate engineering schools, 2001 ★2358★

Average analytic GRE scores for *U.S. News & World Report*'s top 10 graduate engineering schools, 2001 ★2359★

Average quantitative GRE scores for *U.S. News & World Report*'s top 10 graduate engineering schools, 2001 ★2360★

Doctoral student-faculty ratios at *U.S. News & World Report*'s top 10 graduate engineering schools, 2001 ★2361★

Faculty membership in National Academy of Engineering at *U.S. News & World Report*'s top 10 graduate engineering schools, 2001 ★2362★

Ph.D.s granted at *U.S. News & World Report*'s top 10 graduate engineering schools, 2001 ★2363★

Research expenditures per faculty member at *U.S. News & World Report*'s top 10 graduate engineering schools, 2001 ★2364★

Research funding allocated to *U.S. News & World Report*'s top 10 graduate engineering schools, 2001 ★2365★

Top graduate engineering schools, 2001 ★2366★

Top graduate engineering schools by reputation, as determined by academic personnel, 2001 ★2367★

Top graduate engineering schools by reputation, as determined by engineers and recruiters, 2001 ★2368★

U.S. News & World Report's graduate engineering programs with the highest academic reputation scores, 2000-01 ★2372★

Academics' choices for best graduate aerospace/aeronautical/astronautical engineering programs, 2001 ★2374★

Most effective aerospace engineering research-doctorate programs as evaluated by the National Research Council ★2375★

Top aerospace engineering research-doctorate programs as evaluated by the National Research Council ★2376★

Academics' choices for best graduate chemical engineering programs, 2001 ★2386★

Top chemical engineering research-doctorate programs as evaluated by the National Research Council ★2390★

Academics' choices for best graduate civil engineering programs, 2001 ★2394★

Most effective civil engineering research-doctorate programs as evaluated by the National Research Council ★2395★

Top civil engineering research-doctorate programs as evaluated by the National Research Council ★2396★

U.S. News & World Report's graduate engineering programs with the best civil departments, 2000-01 ★2398★

Academics' choices for best graduate computer engineering programs, 2001 ★2399★

Top electrical engineering research-doctorate programs as evaluated by the National Research Council ★2405★

Academics' choices for best graduate environmental/environmental health engineering programs, 2001 ★2408★

Academics' choices for best graduate mechanical engineering programs, 2001 ★2422★

Academics' choices for best graduate petroleum engineering schools, 2000 ★2429★

U.S. News & World Report's graduate engineering programs with the best petroleum departments, 2000-01 ★2431★

Research institutions with the highest enrollment of foreign students, 1998-99 ★2503★

U.S. research institutions with the largest number of students studying abroad, 1998-99 ★2514★

Top geography research-doctorate programs as evaluated by the National Research Council ★2520★

Top German language and literature research-doctorate programs as evaluated by the National Research Council ★2528★

Academics' choices for best dispute resolution programs, 2001 ★2627★

Academics' choices for best tax law programs, 2001 ★2632★

Academics' choices for best trial advocacy programs, 2001 ★2633★

Law schools with the best bankruptcy faculty, 1999-2000 ★2639★

Law schools with the best civil procedure faculty, 1999-2000 ★2640★

TEXAS

Law schools with the best comparative law faculty, 1999-2000 ★2642★
Law schools with the best constitutional law (freedom of religion) faculty, 1999-2000 ★2643★
Law schools with the best constitutional law (freedom of speech) faculty, 1999-2000 ★2644★
Law schools with the best constitutional law (general) faculty, 1999-2000 ★2645★
Law schools with the best environmental law faculty, 1999-2000 ★2650★
Law schools with the best intellectual property faculty, 1999-2000 ★2653★
Law schools with the best jurisprudence faculty, 1999-2000 ★2655★
Law schools with the best labor law faculty, 1999-2000 ★2656★
Law schools with the best legal ethics, professional responsibility, and legal profession faculty, 1999-2000 ★2660★
Law schools with the best legal history faculty, 1999-2000 ★2661★
Law schools with the best moral and political theory (Continental traditions) faculty, 1999-2000 ★2663★
Law schools with the best tax faculty, 1999-2000 ★2664★
Law schools with the best Torts (including products liability) faculty, 1999-2000 ★2665★
Law schools with the highest quality, 1999-2000 ★2666★
Law library web sites, by visibility ★2687★
Top linguistics research-doctorate programs as evaluated by the National Research Council ★2733★
U.S. universities publishing the most papers in the field of communication, 1994-98 ★2755★
Degrees granted in the ten largest doctoral journalism and mass communications programs, 1999 ★2756★
Top astrophysics and astronomy research-doctorate programs as evaluated by the National Research Council ★3014★
Top physics research-doctorate programs as evaluated by the National Research Council ★3015★
U.S. colleges and universities spending the most on chemical engineering research and development, 1998 ★3098★
U.S. colleges and universities with the most federal support for chemical engineering research and development, 1998 ★3101★
Average faculty salaries for institutions of higher education in Texas, 2000-01 ★3731★
Most effective Spanish and Portuguese language and literature research-doctorate programs as evaluated by the National Research Council ★4357★
Top Spanish and Portuguese language and literature research-doctorate programs as evaluated by the National Research Council ★4358★
Academics' choices for best administration/supervision graduate programs, 2001 ★4378★
Academics' choices for best special education graduate programs, 2001 ★4386★
U.S. universities publishing the most papers in the field of performing arts, 1994-98 ★4437★

Texas, Brownsville; University of
Institutions with the most full-time Hispanic American faculty ★923★
U.S. colleges and universities with the most full-time Hispanic American faculty ★925★
Lowest undergraduate tuition and fees at public, 4-year or above colleges and universities ★1466★
Public 4-year institutions with the lowest tuition, 2000-01 ★1472★
Average faculty salaries for institutions of higher education in Texas, 2000-01 ★3731★

Texas Center for Educational Technology
Top sites for educators ★2605★

Texas Children's Hospital, Houston
Top pediatrics hospitals in the U.S., 2000 ★2799★

Texas Christian University
All-USA College Academic First Team, 2001 ★2★
U.S. colleges and universities where students are not very politically active ★1000★
U.S. colleges and universities with a generally conservative student body ★1014★
U.S. colleges and universities with the best overall administration ★1033★
Highest undergraduate tuition and fees at colleges and universities in Texas ★1560★
Presidents with the highest pay at Doctoral I and II universities, 1998-99 ★3160★
Average faculty salaries for institutions of higher education in Texas, 2000-01 ★3731★

Texas College
Historically black colleges and universities with high student loan default rates, 1998 ★2736★

Texas, Dallas; University of
U.S. universities with the greatest impact in cell and developmental biology, 1994-98 ★213★
Total baccalaureate computer and information science degrees awarded to Asian Americans from U.S. colleges and universities, 1997-98 ★1692★
U.S. colleges and universities awarding the most computer and information sciences master's degrees to Asian Americans ★1767★
Doctoral institutions with the highest enrollment of foreign students, 1998-99 ★2494★
Average faculty salaries for institutions of higher education in Texas, 2000-01 ★3731★
U.S. institutions with the highest paid assistant professors, 2001 ★3977★

Texas, El Paso; University of
Institutions with the most full-time Hispanic American faculty ★923★
U.S. colleges and universities with the most full-time Hispanic American faculty ★925★
Division I NCAA colleges with that graduated none of their African American male basketball players, 1990-91 to 1993-94 ★930★
Division I NCAA colleges with the lowest graduation rates for female basketball players, 1990-91 to 1993-94 ★937★
U.S. News & World Report's western regional universities with students least in debt, 1999 ★1575★
Total baccalaureate biology/life sciences degrees awarded to Hispanic Americans from U.S. colleges and universities, 1997-98 ★1681★
Total baccalaureate business management and administrative services degrees awarded to Hispanic Americans from U.S. colleges and universities, 1997-98 ★1685★
Total baccalaureate communications degrees awarded to Hispanic Americans from U.S. colleges and universities, 1997-98 ★1689★
Total baccalaureate degrees awarded to Hispanic Americans from U.S. colleges and universities, 1997-98 ★1705★
Total baccalaureate engineering degrees awarded to minorities from U.S. colleges and universities, 1997-98 ★1715★
Total baccalaureate English language, literature, and letters degrees awarded to Hispanic Americans from U.S. colleges and universities, 1997-98 ★1718★
Total baccalaureate health professions and related sciences degrees awarded to Hispanic Americans from U.S. colleges and universities, 1997-98 ★1723★
Total baccalaureate physical sciences degrees awarded to Hispanic Americans from U.S. colleges and universities, 1997-98 ★1735★
U.S. colleges and universities awarding the most communications master's degrees to Hispanic Americans ★1765★
U.S. colleges and universities awarding the most education master's degrees to Hispanic Americans ★1771★
U.S. colleges and universities awarding the most English language/literature/letters master's degrees to Hispanic Americans ★1775★
U.S. colleges and universities awarding the most health professions and related sciences master's degrees to Hispanic Americans ★1779★
U.S. colleges and universities awarding the most master's degrees to Hispanic Americans ★1787★
Master's institutions with the highest enrollment of foreign students, 1998-99 ★2499★
Average faculty salaries for institutions of higher education in Texas, 2000-01 ★3731★

Texas Health Science Center, Houston; University of
U.S. colleges and universities awarding the most first professional degrees to Hispanic Americans ★1845★
U.S. colleges and universities awarding the most health professions and related sciences first professional degrees to Hispanic Americans ★1849★
U.S. colleges and universities awarding the most health professions and related sciences first professional degrees to minorities ★1850★
U.S. colleges and universities awarding the most health professions and related sciences doctorate degrees to Asian Americans ★2115★
U.S. colleges and universities awarding the most health professions and related sciences doctorate degrees to Hispanic Americans ★2116★

Texas Health Science Center, San Antonio; University of
Institutions with the most full-time Hispanic American faculty ★923★
U.S. colleges and universities with the most full-time Hispanic American faculty ★925★
Total baccalaureate health professions and related sciences degrees awarded to Hispanic Americans from U.S. colleges and universities, 1997-98 ★1723★
U.S. colleges and universities awarding the most first professional degrees to Hispanic Americans ★1845★

U.S. colleges and universities awarding the most health professions and related sciences first professional degrees to Asian Americans ★1848★

U.S. colleges and universities awarding the most health professions and related sciences first professional degrees to Hispanic Americans ★1849★

U.S. colleges and universities awarding the most health professions and related sciences first professional degrees to minorities ★1850★

Texas Health Science Center; University of

U.S. colleges and universities awarding the most health professions and related sciences master's degrees to Asian Americans ★1778★

U.S. colleges and universities awarding the most health professions and related sciences master's degrees to Hispanic Americans ★1779★

Texas Heart Institute-St. Luke's Episcopal Hospital

Top cardiology and heart surgery hospitals in the U.S., 2000 ★2788★

Texas Hill Country

Best small towns to live in ★3085★

Texas, Houston; University of

U.S. universities with the greatest impact in dentistry/oral surgery and medicine, 1995-99 ★1867★

U.S. universities with the highest concentration of dentistry papers published, 1994-98 ★1868★

Texas Instruments

Business Week's best companies in the United States ★411★

Fortune's highest ranked semiconductors companies, 2000 ★495★

Top electrical and electronics companies in Standard & Poor's 500, 2001 ★539★

Top internships in the U.S. with the highest compensation, 2001 ★2611★

Texas Lutheran University

U.S. News & World Report's best undergraduate fees among western regional liberal arts colleges by discount tuition, 2000 ★1384★

Academic reputation scores for *U.S. News & World Report*'s top western regional liberal arts colleges, 2000-01 ★1387★

Acceptance rates for *U.S. News & World Report*'s top western regional liberal arts colleges, 2000-01 ★1388★

Alumni giving rates at *U.S. News & World Report*'s top western regional liberal arts colleges, 2000-01 ★1389★

Average freshmen retention rates for *U.S. News & World Report*'s top western regional liberal arts colleges, 2000-01 ★1390★

Average graduation rates for *U.S. News & World Report*'s top western regional liberal arts colleges, 2000-01 ★1391★

Percentage of freshmen in the top 25% of their high school class at *U.S. News & World Report*'s top western regional liberal arts colleges, 2000-01 ★1392★

Percentage of full-time faculty at *U.S. News & World Report*'s top western regional liberal arts colleges, 2000-01 ★1393★

Proportion of classes having 20 students or less at *U.S. News & World Report*'s top western regional liberal arts colleges, 2000-01 ★1394★

Student/faculty ratios at *U.S. News & World Report*'s top western regional liberal arts colleges, 2000-01 ★1395★

U.S. News & World Report's top western regional liberal arts colleges, 2000-01 ★1396★

U.S. News & World Report's western regional liberal arts colleges with students most in debt, 1999 ★1398★

Average faculty salaries for institutions of higher education in Texas, 2000-01 ★3731★

Texas, M.D. Anderson Cancer Center; University of

Top cancer hospitals in the U.S., 2000 ★2787★

Top gynecology hospitals in the U.S., 2000 ★2792★

Texas Medical Branch, Galveston; University of

Lowest undergraduate tuition and fees at public, 4-year or above colleges and universities ★1466★

Public 4-year institutions with the lowest tuition, 2000-01 ★1472★

Total baccalaureate health professions and related sciences degrees awarded to Hispanic Americans from U.S. colleges and universities, 1997-98 ★1723★

U.S. colleges and universities awarding the most first professional degrees to Hispanic Americans ★1845★

U.S. colleges and universities awarding the most health professions and related sciences first professional degrees to Hispanic Americans ★1849★

U.S. colleges and universities awarding the most health professions and related sciences first professional degrees to Native Americans ★1851★

Texas, Pan American; University of

Institutions with the most full-time Hispanic American faculty ★923★

U.S. colleges and universities with the most full-time Hispanic American faculty ★925★

Division I NCAA colleges with that graduated less than 20% of their African American male athletes, 1990-91 to 1993-94 ★928★

Division I NCAA colleges with that graduated none of their African American male basketball players, 1990-91 to 1993-94 ★930★

Division I NCAA colleges with the lowest graduation rates for female athletes, 1990-91 to 1993-94 ★936★

Division I NCAA colleges with the lowest graduation rates for male athletes, 1990-91 to 1993-94 ★939★

Total baccalaureate business management and administrative services degrees awarded to Hispanic Americans from U.S. colleges and universities, 1997-98 ★1685★

Total baccalaureate computer and information science degrees awarded to Hispanic Americans from U.S. colleges and universities, 1997-98 ★1693★

Total baccalaureate degrees awarded to Hispanic Americans from U.S. colleges and universities, 1997-98 ★1705★

Total baccalaureate English language, literature, and letters degrees awarded to Hispanic Americans from U.S. colleges and universities, 1997-98 ★1718★

Total baccalaureate health professions and related sciences degrees awarded to Hispanic Americans from U.S. colleges and universities, 1997-98 ★1723★

Total baccalaureate mathematics degrees awarded to Hispanic Americans from U.S. colleges and universities, 1997-98 ★1731★

U.S. colleges and universities awarding the most English language/literature/letters master's degrees to Hispanic Americans ★1775★

U.S. colleges and universities awarding the most master's degrees to Hispanic Americans ★1787★

Average faculty salaries for institutions of higher education in Texas, 2000-01 ★3731★

Texas, Permian Basin; University of

Average faculty salaries for institutions of higher education in Texas, 2000-01 ★3731★

Texas, San Antonio; University of

Division I NCAA colleges with the lowest graduation rates for female basketball players, 1990-91 to 1993-94 ★937★

Golden Key Scholar Award winners, 2000 ★1316★

Total baccalaureate biology/life sciences degrees awarded to Hispanic Americans from U.S. colleges and universities, 1997-98 ★1681★

Total baccalaureate business management and administrative services degrees awarded to Hispanic Americans from U.S. colleges and universities, 1997-98 ★1685★

Total baccalaureate degrees awarded to Hispanic Americans from U.S. colleges and universities, 1997-98 ★1705★

Total baccalaureate mathematics degrees awarded to Hispanic Americans from U.S. colleges and universities, 1997-98 ★1731★

U.S. colleges and universities awarding the most biological and life sciences master's degrees to Asian Americans ★1757★

U.S. colleges and universities awarding the most biological and life sciences master's degrees to Hispanic Americans ★1758★

U.S. universities publishing the most papers in the field of dentistry/oral surgery and medicine, 1995-99 ★1865★

U.S. universities with the highest concentration of dentistry papers published, 1994-98 ★1868★

Texas Southern University

Colleges offering the Thurgood Marshall Scholarship Fund ★221★

Division I NCAA colleges with that graduated less than 20% of their African American male athletes, 1990-91 to 1993-94 ★928★

Division I NCAA colleges with the lowest graduation rates for football players, 1990-91 to 1993-94 ★938★

Division I NCAA colleges with the lowest graduation rates for male athletes, 1990-91 to 1993-94 ★939★

State appropriations for Texas's institutions of higher education, 2000-01 ★1296★

Total baccalaureate health professions and related sciences degrees awarded to African Americans from U.S. colleges and universities, 1997-98 ★1721★

U.S. colleges and universities awarding the most biological and life sciences master's degrees to African Americans ★1756★

Historically black colleges and universities awarding the most first professional degrees to African Americans ★1835★

U.S. colleges and universities awarding the most first professional degrees to African Americans ★1843★

U.S. colleges and universities awarding the most first professional degrees to Hispanic Americans ★1845★

TEXAS

Texas Southmost College
U.S. colleges and universities awarding the most law and legal studies first professional degrees to African Americans ★1852★
U.S. colleges and universities awarding the most law and legal studies first professional degrees to Hispanic Americans ★1854★
Historically black colleges and universities awarding the most doctorate degrees to African Americans ★1945★
Historically black colleges and universities with major improvements in student loan default rates, 1998 ★2737★

Texas Southmost College
Highest undergraduate tuition and fees at public 2-year colleges and universities ★1462★

Texas Southwest Medical Center; University of
U.S. colleges and universities awarding the most health professions and related sciences first professional degrees to Hispanic Americans ★1849★
U.S. colleges and universities awarding the most biological and life sciences doctorate degrees to Asian Americans ★2083★
Most effective pharmacology research-doctorate programs as evaluated by the National Research Council ★2938★
Top pharmacology research-doctorate programs as evaluated by the National Research Council ★2939★

Texas State Technical College
State appropriations for Texas's institutions of higher education, 2000-01 ★1296★

Texas State Technical College, Harlingen
U.S. institutions awarding the most associate degrees to Hispanic Americans in agricultural sciences, 1998 ★1807★
U.S. institutions awarding the most associate degrees to minorities in agricultural sciences, 1998 ★1809★

Texas State University System
State appropriations for Texas's institutions of higher education, 2000-01 ★1296★

Texas System; University of
2000 endowment values of the 'wealthiest' U.S. universities ★1230★
2001 mid-year endowment values of the 'wealthiest' U.S. universities ★1234★
Colleges and universities with the largest endowments, 2000 ★1237★
Endowment values for the wealthiest U.S. universities, 2000 ★1240★
State appropriations for Texas's institutions of higher education, 2000-01 ★1296★
U.S. universities publishing the most highly-cited papers, 1997-1999 ★4348★

Texas Tech University
Division I NCAA colleges with that graduated none of their African American male basketball players, 1990-91 to 1993-94 ★930★
U.S. colleges and universities awarding the most first professional degrees to Native Americans ★1846★
U.S. colleges and universities awarding the most law and legal studies first professional degrees to Native Americans ★1855★
Academics' choices for best graduate petroleum engineering schools, 2000 ★2429★
Average faculty salaries for institutions of higher education in Texas, 2000-01 ★3731★

Texas Tech University Health Sciences Center
U.S. colleges and universities awarding the most health professions and related sciences first professional degrees to Hispanic Americans ★1849★

Texas Tech University System
State appropriations for Texas's institutions of higher education, 2000-01 ★1296★

Texas, Tyler; University of
Average faculty salaries for institutions of higher education in Texas, 2000-01 ★3731★

Texas; University of
Division I-A all-time percentage leaders ★127★
NCAA Division I women's swimming teams with the most individual championships ★136★
U.S. colleges and universities with the most alumni in the LPGA ★148★
Women's Division I track and field programs with the most outdoor championships ★149★
Comparisons of investment returns for consulting MBAs ★622★
Degree-granting institutions with the most published pages in *The Journal of Risk and Insurance*, 1987-1996 ★678★
Employing institutions with the most published pages in *The Journal of Risk and Insurance*, 1987-1996 ★679★
U.S. colleges and universities awarding the most education master's degrees to Hispanic Americans ★1771★
Top institutions in systems and software engineering publications ★2332★
Radcliffe Institute for Advanced Study fellowship recipients in the field of history, 2000-01 ★2549★
Top university research libraries in the U.S. and Canada, 1998-99 ★2706★
Institutions with the most prolific communication studies researchers ★2749★

Texas Wesleyan University
Average faculty salaries for institutions of higher education in Texas, 2000-01 ★3731★

Texas Weslyan University
Total baccalaureate law and legal studies degrees awarded to Hispanic Americans from U.S. colleges and universities, 1997-98 ★1727★

Texas Woman's University
State appropriations for Texas's institutions of higher education, 2000-01 ★1296★
U.S. colleges and universities awarding the most health professions and related sciences master's degrees to Hispanic Americans ★1779★
U.S. colleges and universities awarding the most health professions and related sciences master's degrees to Native Americans ★1780★
Average faculty salaries for institutions of higher education in Texas, 2000-01 ★3731★

Textile draw-out and winding machine operators
Occupations with the highest decline in employment, 1998-2008 ★2310★

Textron
Fortune's highest ranked aerospace companies, 2000 ★446★
Top conglomerates in Standard & Poor's 500, 2001 ★535★

The Thacher School
Outstanding secondary schools in Ventura, California ★4248★

Thaddeus Stevens College of Technology
State appropriations for Pennsylvania's institutions of higher education, 2000-01 ★1291★

Thaddeus Stevens State School of Technology
Highest undergraduate tuition and fees at public 2-year colleges and universities ★1462★

Thailand
Eight grade science achievement scores from selected countries, 1999 ★14★
Countries of origin for non-U.S. citizens awarded doctorates at U.S. colleges and universities, 1999 ★1901★
Foreign countries with the highest enrollment of foreign students, 1999-2000 ★2496★
Eighth grade mathematics achievement scores from selected countries, 1999 ★2773★
Countries with the lowest leader's salary ★3121★

That's a Family!
Outstanding videos for library collections, 2000 ★2892★

The; Siu
Radcliffe Institute for Advanced Study fellowship recipients in the field of molecular biology, 2000-01 ★208★

Theall; David
Top pay and benefits for the chief executive and top paid employees at Saint Joseph College in Connecticut ★3475★

Theil; H.
U.S. academic economists by mean number of citations, 1971-92 ★2176★
U.S. academic economists by total citations, 1971-92 ★2177★

Theil; T'Nae
All-America girls' high school basketball 3rd team, 2001 ★172★

Theille; Anthony
All-USA Teacher Teams, Third Team, 2000 ★4401★

Their Eyes Were Watching God
Favorite books of African Americans ★238★

Their Sisters' Keepers: Women's Prison Reform in America, 1830-1930
Most-cited works in women and crime publications ★1646★

Then Again, Maybe I Won't
Most frequently banned books in the 1990s ★745★
People for the American Way's list of most frequently challenged books, 1982-1992 ★747★

Theology/religious education
Gender breakdown of professional doctorate recipients, by subfield, 1999 ★1940★
Professional doctorates awarded at U.S. colleges and universities, by subfield, 1999 ★2033★

Theoretical
Chemistry doctorates awarded at U.S. colleges and universities, by subfield, 1999 ★1889★
Gender breakdown of chemistry doctorate recipients, by subfield, 1999 ★1929★

Theoretical and Applied Genetics
Agriculture journals by citation impact, 1981-99 ★51★
Agriculture journals by citation impact, 1995-99 ★53★
Agriculture journals by citation impact, 1999 ★54★

Theory into Practice
  Journals publishing the most articles on economic education research from 1963-1990 ★2170★

Theory and Research in Social Education
  Journals publishing the most articles on economic education research from 1963-1990 ★2170★

Theriogenology
  Veterinary sciences journals with the greatest impact measure, 1981-98 ★4442★
  Veterinary sciences journals with the greatest impact measure, 1994-98 ★4443★

Thermo Electron
  Business Week's best performing companies with the lowest 3-year sales performance ★423★
  Fortune's highest ranked scientific, photo and control equipment companies, 2000 ★493★

Thibeault; Dennis M.
  Top pay and benefits for the chief executive and top paid employees at Curry College ★3261★

Thibodeau, P.M.; Sister Lucille
  Top pay and benefits for the chief executive and top paid employees at Rivier College ★3460★

Thibodeau; Thomas
  Top pay and benefits for the chief executive and top paid employees at Viterbo University ★3597★

Thiel College
  U.S. News & World Report's northern regional liberal arts colleges with students most in debt, 1999 ★1352★
  Average faculty salaries for institutions of higher education in Pennsylvania, 2000-01 ★3725★

Thios; Samuel J.
  Top pay and benefits for the chief executive and top paid employees at Denison University ★3265★

This Book Really Sucks
  Most notable nonfiction books for reluctant young adult readers, 2001 ★323★

Thivolet; J.
  Most cited authors in dermatology journals, 1981 to 1996 ★1870★

Thobum; Crawford
  Top pay and benefits for the chief executive and top paid employees at Wells College ★3610★

Thomas & Betts
  Business Week's best performing companies with the lowest 3-year shareholder returns ★424★

Thomas; Chris
  All-America boys' high school basketball 4th team, 2001 ★164★

Thomas College
  Colleges and universities with the smallest endowments, 2000 ★1238★
  Highest undergraduate tuition and fees at colleges and universities in Maine ★1512★
  Average faculty salaries for institutions of higher education in Maine, 2000-01 ★3706★
  U.S. institutions with the lowest paid full professors, 2001 ★3979★

Thomas; E. Donnall
  Most-cited researchers in clinical medicine, 1981-1998 ★2875★
  Most-cited researchers in surgery/transplantation, 1981-1998 ★2878★

Thomas Edison State College
  State appropriations for New Jersey's institutions of higher education, 2000-01 ★1283★

Thomas; James Regan
  Top pay and benefits for the chief executive and top paid employees at St. Louis University ★3478★

Thomas Jefferson Middle School
  Outstanding secondary schools in Miami, Florida ★4178★
  Outstanding secondary schools in Milwaukee-Waukesha, Wisconsin ★4180★

Thomas Jefferson University
  U.S. colleges and universities awarding the most biological and life sciences master's degrees to Asian Americans ★1757★

Thomas Jefferson University Hospital
  Top rehabilitation hospitals in the U.S., 2000 ★2801★

Thomas; Lewis
  Top essayists from 1946-1996 ★2445★

Thomas More College
  U.S. News & World Report's southern regional liberal arts colleges with the best student/faculty ratios, 2000-01 ★1368★
  U.S. News & World Report's southern regional liberal arts colleges with the highest acceptance rates, 2000-01 ★1370★
  U.S. News & World Report's southern regional liberal arts colleges with the highest proportion of classes having 20 students or less, 2000-01 ★1375★
  Highest undergraduate tuition and fees at colleges and universities in Kentucky ★1508★

Thomas More High School
  Outstanding secondary schools in Milwaukee-Waukesha, Wisconsin ★4180★

Thomas Nelson
  Highest revenues of publicly held book publishers, 1999 ★3072★
  Top pay and benefits for the chief executive and top paid employees at Walla Walla College ★3601★

Thomas Nelson Community College
  Average faculty salaries for institutions of higher education in Virginia, 2000-01 ★3735★

Thomas; Robert L.
  Top pay and benefits for the chief executive and top paid employees at Xavier University of Louisiana ★3638★

Thomas Stovall Junior High School
  Outstanding secondary schools in Houston, Texas ★4150★

Thompson; Alexander
  Top pay and benefits for the chief executive and top paid employees at Vassar College ★3594★

Thompson; Carey
  Top pay and benefits for the chief executive and top paid employees at Centre College ★3227★

Thompson; D. D.
  Top pay and benefits for the chief executive and top paid employees at Lincoln Memorial University ★3374★

Thompson; James P.
  Top pay and benefits for the chief executive and top paid employees at Earlham College ★3279★

Thompson; John
  Coaches winning the most NCAA tournaments ★120★

Thompson; John R.
  Top pay and benefits for the chief executive and top paid employees at Georgetown University ★3306★

Thompson; John W.
  Top pay and benefits for the chief executive and top paid employees at the University of New England ★3552★

Thompson; Peter
  Top pay and benefits for the chief executive and top paid employees at Hamline University ★3320★

Thompson; W.
  Highest ranked inactive communication studies researchers ★2748★

Thomson
  Business Week's best companies in Canada ★390★

Thomson High School
  Outstanding secondary schools in Augusta-Aiken, Georgia-South Carolina ★4089★

Thomson; M. Kay
  Top pay and benefits for the chief executive and top paid employees at Oberlin College ★3427★

Thomson; Tom
  Canada's best visual artists of the 20th century ★75★

Thoreau; Henry David
  Top essayists from 1946-1996 ★2445★

Thorne; Barrie
  Highly acknowledged individuals in the field of women's studies, 1975-94 ★4466★

Thornton Township 205
  Illinois high school districts with the highest teacher salaries, 1999 ★3985★

Thornton Township High School, District 205
  Illinois school districts with the most average years of teacher experience ★4012★

Thrailkill, O.S.U.; Sister Francis Marie
  Top pay and benefits for the chief executive and top paid employees at College of Mount St. Joseph ★3244★

300Incredible.com
  Small publishers with the highest sales growth between 1997 and 1999 ★3073★

Three Rivers Community-Technical College
  Lowest undergraduate tuition and fees at colleges and universities in Connecticut ★1491★

3Com
  Fortune's highest ranked network communications companies, 2000 ★482★

Thrift; Julianne Still
  Top pay and benefits for the chief executive and top paid employees at Salem College ★3488★

Thro; Patricia
  Top pay and benefits for the chief executive and top paid employees at the Maryville University of Saint Louis ★3534★

Thrombosis and Haemostasis
  Hematology journals with the greatest impact measure, 1981-98 ★2808★
  Hematology journals with the greatest impact measure, 1994-98 ★2809★

Through the Burning Steppe: A Wartime Memoir
  Smithsonian's best books for children ages 10 and up ★365★

Thunderbird, American Graduate School of International Management
Business Week's top business schools for global scope skills as selected by corporate recruiters, 2000 ★602★
Comparisons of investment returns for operations MBAs ★627★
U.S. business schools with the slowest payback on MBA investments ★655★
Academics' choices for best graduate international business programs, 2001 ★668★
Professional or specialized institutions with the highest enrollment of foreign students, 1998-99 ★2501★

Thurber; James
Top essayists from 1946-1996 ★2445★

Thurman; Howard
Most influential African Americans in religion ★3091★

Thurow; Glen E.
Top pay and benefits for the chief executive and top paid employees at the University of Dallas ★3538★

TIAA-CREF
Fortune's highest ranked life and health insurance companies, 2000 ★472★

Ticket agent
Most desirable jobs in travel/food service ★2278★

The Tidal Poole
Library Journal's best mystery titles, 2000 ★242★

Tiffany
Top discount and fashion retailing companies in Standard & Poor's 500, 2001 ★538★

Tiffin University
Colleges and universities with the smallest endowments, 2000 ★1238★
Average faculty salaries for institutions of higher education in Ohio, 2000-01 ★3722★

Tightrope
Most notable fiction books for young adults, 2001 ★322★

TIM
Business Week's best companies in Italy ★397★

Time
Magazines with the largest circulation ★2750★
Most cited general works serials in technical communication journals from 1988 to 1997 ★4419★

Time Warner
Hardcover bestsellers by corporation, 2000 ★239★
Paperback bestsellers by corporation, 2000 ★296★
Fortune's highest ranked entertainment companies, 2000 ★462★

Timeline
Longest-running fiction hardcover bestsellers, 2000 ★279★
Most notable fiction books for young adults, 2001 ★322★

The Times They Used to Be
Booklist's most recommended black history books for youth ★311★

Timilty Middle School
Outstanding secondary schools in Boston, Massachusetts-New Hampshire ★4100★

Timothy Christian High School
Outstanding independent high schools in Metro Chicago ★4077★

The Tin Flute
Canada's best fiction selections of the 20th century ★233★

Tin House
Library Journal's notable new magazines, 1999 ★2923★

Tingley; William D.
Top pay and benefits for the chief executive and top paid employees at Occidental College ★3428★

Tinsley; Charlotte P.
Top pay and benefits for the chief executive and top paid employees at Wofford College ★3634★

Tiny's Hat
Most notable children's videos, 2001 ★2889★

Tippecanoe County Public Library
Highest Hennen's American Public Library Ratings for libraries serving a population of 100,000 to 249,999 ★2698★

Tipson; Baird
Top pay and benefits for the chief executive and top paid employees at Wittenberg University ★3633★

Tipton; Paul S.
Top pay and benefits for the chief executive and top paid employees at Jacksonville University ★3352★

Tirrell; David A.
American Chemical Society 2001 award winners (Group 5) ★755★

'Tis
Longest-running nonfiction hardcover bestsellers, 2000 ★281★

Tittle; C.R.
Most cited authors in the journal *Journal of Criminal Justice*, 1990 to 1995 ★1626★
Most-cited scholars in *Criminology* ★1639★

TJX
Top discount and fashion retailing companies in Standard & Poor's 500, 2001 ★538★

To Slow or Not to Slow-The Economics of the Greenhouse Effect
Top cited energy papers from 1989 to 1993 ★2466★

Toben; Bradley J.B.
Top pay and benefits for the chief executive and top paid employees at Baylor University ★3194★

Tobin; Eugene M.
Top pay and benefits for the chief executive and top paid employees at Hamilton College ★3319★

Tobin; Rosemary
Top pay and benefits for the chief executive and top paid employees at Emmanuel College in Massachusetts ★3288★

Tobin; Zachary
All-America boys' high school soccer team forwards, 2001 ★166★

Tocco; Anthony
Top pay and benefits for the chief executive and top paid employees at Rockhurst University ★3464★

Todd; Howell W.
Top pay and benefits for the chief executive and top paid employees at Mississippi College ★3404★

Todo; Satoru
Most-cited researchers in surgery/transplantation, 1981-1998 ★2878★

Tokyo Electric Power
Business Week's best companies in Japan ★398★

Toledo-Lucas County Public Library
Highest Hennen's American Public Library Ratings for libraries serving a population of 250,000 to 499,999 ★2699★

Toledo; University of
Institutions, by adjusted authorship, with the most published authors in the *Journal of Business Research*, 1985 to 1999 ★694★
Division I NCAA colleges with that graduated none of their African American male basketball players, 1990-91 to 1993-94 ★930★
State appropriations for Ohio's institutions of higher education, 2000-01 ★1288★
Doctoral institutions with the highest enrollment of foreign students, 1998-99 ★2494★

Toler; Penny
NCAA Division I female basketball scoring leaders ★155★

Toll; John S.
Top pay and benefits for the chief executive and top paid employees at Washington College ★3606★

Tom Strong, Book 1
Most notable nonfiction books for reluctant young adult readers, 2001 ★323★

Tomball, TX
America's most wired towns, 2001 ★2575★

Tommy Nelson
Top children's book publishers, 1999 ★3074★

Tompkins-Cortland Community College
Average faculty salaries for institutions of higher education in New York, 2000-01 ★3719★

Too Inc.
Business Week's top companies in terms of sales, 2000 ★431★

Tooch; H.
Most cited authors in the journal *Criminal Justice Review*, 1990 to 1995 ★1620★

Tool-and-die maker
Jobs considered the loneliest ★2244★

Tool and die makers
Average salaries for occupations requiring on-the-job training ★3119★

Tootsie Roll Industries
Oldest women-owned companies ★4454★

Topics in Current Chemistry
Chemistry journals by citation impact, 1981-99 ★808★
Chemistry journals by citation impact, 1999 ★810★

Topol; Eric J.
Authors with the greatest impact measure in cardiovascular research, 1993-98 ★2868★
Most-cited researchers in cardiology, 1981-1998 ★2874★

Topology
Gender breakdown of mathematics doctorate recipients, by subfield, 1999 ★1938★
Mathematics doctorates awarded at U.S. colleges and universities, by subfield, 1999 ★1951★
Mathematics journals by impact factor, 1981 to 1997 ★2784★

Torab; Hamid
Top pay and benefits for the chief executive and top paid employees at Gannon University ★3302★

Torbert; Kelvin
All-America boys' high school basketball 1st team, 2001 ★161★

Torgerson; Richard L.
Top pay and benefits for the chief executive and top paid employees at Gustavus Adolphus College ★3317★

Torn Thread
  Most notable fiction books for young adults, 2001 ★322★
  Smithsonian's best books for children ages 10 and up ★365★

Toronto-Dominion Bank
  Business Week's best companies in Canada ★390★

Toronto; University of
  Canadian universities with the greatest impact in biology and biochemistry, 1993-97 ★195★
  Business Week's top business schools outside the U.S. as selected by corporate recruiters, 2000 ★605★
  Business Week's top business schools outside the U.S. as selected by recent MBA graduates, 2000 ★606★
  Business Week's top business schools outside the U.S. for intellectual capital, 2000 ★607★
  European and Canadian business schools with the slowest payback on MBA investments ★629★
  Post-MBA salaries for graduates from *Business Week*'s top business schools outside the U.S., 2000 ★642★
  Pre-MBA salaries for students at *Business Week*'s top business schools outside the U.S., 2000 ★643★
  U.S. colleges and universities that devote the least course time to discussion ★989★
  U.S. colleges and universities with poor instructors ★1027★
  Best Canadian universities for producing leaders of tomorrow, 2000 ★1148★
  Best Canadian universities overall, 2000 ★1149★
  Best Canadian universities that are the most innovative, 2000 ★1150★
  Best Canadian universities with the highest quality, 2000 ★1151★
  Canadian medical/doctoral universities by alumni support, 2000 ★1172★
  Canadian medical/doctoral universities by award-winning faculty members, 2000 ★1173★
  Canadian medical/doctoral universities by class size at the first- and second-year level, 2000 ★1174★
  Canadian medical/doctoral universities by class size at the third- and forth-year level, 2000 ★1175★
  Canadian medical/doctoral universities by classes taught by tenured faculty, 2000 ★1176★
  Canadian medical/doctoral universities by faculty members with Ph.D.'s, 2000 ★1177★
  Canadian medical/doctoral universities by international graduate students, 2000 ★1178★
  Canadian medical/doctoral universities by library acquisitions, 2000 ★1179★
  Canadian medical/doctoral universities by library expenses, 2000 ★1180★
  Canadian medical/doctoral universities by library holdings, 2000 ★1181★
  Canadian medical/doctoral universities by library holdings per student, 2000 ★1182★
  Canadian medical/doctoral universities by medical/science grants per faculty member, 2000 ★1184★
  Canadian medical/doctoral universities by operating budget per student, 2000 ★1185★
  Canadian medical/doctoral universities by percentage of operating budget allocated to scholarships, 2000 ★1186★
  Canadian medical/doctoral universities by percentage of operating budget allocated to student services, 2000 ★1187★
  Canadian medical/doctoral universities by reputation, 2000 ★1188★
  Canadian medical/doctoral universities by social science/humanities grants per faculty member, 2000 ★1189★
  Canadian medical/doctoral universities by students from out of province, 2000 ★1190★
  Canadian medical/doctoral universities by students winning national awards, 2000 ★1191★
  Canadian universities by average entering grade, 2000 ★1213★
  Canadian universities by graduation rate, 2000 ★1214★
  Canadian universities by students with 75% grade averages or higher, 2000 ★1215★
  Canadian universities with the highest total cost, 2000 ★1217★
  Top Canadian medical/doctoral universities, 2000 ★1221★
  Top Canadian medical/doctoral universities best at producing leaders of tomorrow, 2000 ★1222★
  Top Canadian medical/doctoral universities that are the best overall, 2000 ★1223★
  Top Canadian medical/doctoral universities that are the most innovative, 2000 ★1224★
  Top Canadian medical/doctoral universities with the highest quality, 2000 ★1225★
  Fiske Guide's best buys for public colleges and universities, 2001 ★1460★
  Canadian universities producing the most-cited papers in the field of computer science, 1992-96 ★1589★
  Top university research libraries in the U.S. and Canada, 1998-99 ★2706★
  Canadian universities with the greatest impact in materials science, 1992-96 ★4304★
  Canadian universities with the greatest impact in neuroscience, 1993-97 ★4305★

Torres; Aurelio
  Top pay and benefits for the chief executive and top paid employees at Wells College ★3610★

Torrey Pines High School
  Outstanding secondary schools in San Diego, California ★4220★

Torrey; William A.
  Top pay and benefits for the chief executive and top paid employees at Bowdoin College ★3207★

Tosca
  Most frequently produced operas in North America, 1999-2000 ★2905★

Tosco
  Fortune's highest ranked petroleum refining companies, 2000 ★484★

Total Astrology: What the Stars Say about Life and Love
  Most notable nonfiction books for reluctant young adult readers, 2001 ★323★

Totalfinaelf
  Business Week's best companies in France ★393★

TOTALInternational Paper
  Top recruiters for manufacturing management jobs for 2000-01 bachelor's degree recipients ★683★

Tougaloo College
  U.S. colleges and universities with the highest percentage of African Americans enrolled, 1997 ★222★
  Highest undergraduate tuition and fees at colleges and universities in Mississippi ★1522★
  Institutions with the most female physics bachelor's recipients, 1994-1998 ★2959★
  U.S. institutions with more than 40% female bachelor's graduates in their physics departments, 1994-98 ★2977★

Touro College
  U.S. colleges and universities awarding the most law and legal studies master's degrees to Asian Americans ★1782★
  U.S. colleges and universities awarding the most law and legal studies first professional degrees to African Americans ★1852★

Tower Heights Middle School
  Outstanding secondary schools in Dayton-Springfield, Ohio ★4122★

Town House Mouse and Country Mouse Cottage: How We Lived One Hundred Years Ago
  Smithsonian's best books for children ages 1 to 6 ★363★

Township High School, District 113
  Illinois school districts spending the most for high school education 1997-98 ★4010★

Towson State University
  U.S. News & World Report's top public northern regional universities, 2000-01 ★1426★
  U.S. colleges and universities awarding the most psychology master's degrees to African Americans ★1797★
  Enrollment of students in the ten largest undergraduate journalism and mass communications programs, 1999 ★2746★
  Average faculty salaries for institutions of higher education in Maryland, 2000-01 ★3707★

Toxicology
  Biological sciences doctorates awarded at U.S. colleges and universities, by subfield, 1999 ★1887★
  Gender breakdown of biological sciences doctorate recipients, by subfield, 1999 ★1927★

Toyota Motor
  Business Week's best companies in Japan ★398★
  Business Week's best companies in terms of sales ★408★

Toyota Motor Sales USA
  Fortune's highest ranked motor vehicles companies, 2000 ★481★
  Fortune's most admired companies for quality of products or services ★519★

Toys "R" Us
  Fortune's highest ranked specialty retailers, 2000 ★497★
  Top recruiters for logistics jobs for 2000-01 bachelor's degree recipients ★555★
  Top recruiters for logistics jobs for 2000-01 master's degree recipients ★653★
  Top recruiters for accounting jobs for 2000-01 master's degree recipients ★661★
  Top recruiters for psychology jobs for 2000-01 bachelor's degree recipients ★3063★
  Top recruiters for sociology jobs for 2000-01 bachelor's degree recipients ★4347★
  Highly recommended public companies for women executives, 2000 ★4453★

Trachtenberg; Stephen J.
  Presidents with the highest pay at Research I and II universities, 1998-99 ★3162★
  Top pay and benefits for the chief executive and top paid employees at George Washington University ★3304★
Tracy Memorial Library
  Highest Hennen's American Public Library Ratings for libraries serving a population of 2,500 to 4,999 ★2693★
Trade and industrial education
  Gender breakdown of teaching fields doctorate recipients, by subfield, 1999 ★1943★
  Teaching fields doctorates awarded at U.S. colleges and universities, by subfield, 1999 ★2046★
Trade, Travel, and Exploration in the Middle Ages: An Encyclopedia
  Library Journal's best reference books, 2000 ★368★
Traer; James F.
  Top pay and benefits for the chief executive and top paid employees at Westminster College in Missouri ★3616★
Traina; Richard P.
  Top pay and benefits for the chief executive and top paid employees at Clark University ★3238★
Training
  Most cited business serials in technical communication journals from 1988 to 1997 ★4417★
Training & Development
  Most cited business serials in technical communication journals from 1988 to 1997 ★4417★
Training programs
  Educational program activities expenditures, 2000 ★3992★
Trainor; Steven
  Top pay and benefits for the chief executive and top paid employees at Rivier College ★3460★
Trammell; Alan
  All-USA College Academic Second Team, 2001 ★3★
The Trans-Atlantic Slave Trade (CD-ROM)
  Library Journal's best reference databases and discs, 2000 ★369★
Trans World Airlines
  Fortune's highest ranked airlines, 2000 ★447★
  Fortune's least admired companies for employee talent ★506★
  Fortune's least admired companies for financial soundness ★507★
Transaction on Information Systems
  Information and library science journals with the greatest impact measure, 1981-98 ★2727★
Transfer of a conditional ordering response through conditional equivalence classes
  Most cited sources in experimental analyses of human behavior between 1990 and 1999 ★3070★
TransMontaigne Oil
  Fortune's highest ranked pipelines and energy companies, 2000 ★486★
TransPacific Hawaii College
  Undergraduate tuition and fees at colleges and universities in Hawaii ★1498★

Transplantation
  Surgery journals with the greatest impact measure, 1981-98 ★2814★
  Surgery journals with the greatest impact measure, 1994-98 ★2815★
Transportation
  Federal appropriations to colleges, by agency, 2000 ★1241★
  Spending for E-marketplace services, by industry, 2001 ★4430★
Transportation, communications, and utilities
  Employment change projections by major industry division from 1998 to 2008 ★2287★
  Employment projections by major industry division for 2008 ★2290★
  Internet use by industry, 1998 ★2586★
Transportation, material handling
  Industries in Illinois with the highest projected worker increase through 2006 ★2304★
Transportation services
  Industries with the highest percentage of projected employment growth from 1998 through 2008 ★2305★
Transylvania University
  Highest undergraduate tuition and fees at colleges and universities in Kentucky ★1508★
  Institutions in the Worker Rights Consortium ★2913★
  Average faculty salaries for institutions of higher education in Kentucky, 2000-01 ★3704★
Trask III; Tallman
  Top pay and benefits for the chief executive and top paid employees at Duke University ★3276★
Traumatic brain injury
  Disabled students served in U.S. public school programs, 1998-99 ★1877★
Travel
  Subject areas with the highest library expenditures/circulation ★306★
Travel agent
  Most desirable jobs in travel/food service ★2278★
Travel agents
  Projected employment growth for selected occupations that require an associate degree or less, 1998-2008 ★2319★
Travelocity
  Top E-commerce web sites ★2603★
Travis; Frederick
  Top pay and benefits for the chief executive and top paid employees at John Carroll University ★3353★
Travis Middle School
  Outstanding secondary schools in McAllen-Edinburg-Mission, Texas ★4175★
Traylor; Donald R.
  Top pay and benefits for the chief executive and top paid employees at the University of the Incarnate Word ★3570★
Treacherous Love: The Diary of an Anonymous Teenager
  Most notable fiction books for reluctant young adult readers, 2001 ★321★
Tredway; Thomas
  Top pay and benefits for the chief executive and top paid employees at Augustana College in Illinois ★3182★

Trelka; Dennis G.
  Top pay and benefits for the chief executive and top paid employees at Washington and Jefferson College ★3604★
Trends in Ecology/Evolution
  Ecology journals by citation impact, 1981-99 ★2136★
  Ecology journals by citation impact, 1995-99 ★2137★
  Ecology journals by citation impact, 1999 ★2138★
Trends in Food Science and Technology
  Food science and technology journals by citation impact, 1995-99 ★2903★
  Food science and technology journals by citation impact, 1999 ★2904★
Trends in Natural Resource Commodity Prices-An Analysis of the Time Domain
  Journal of Environmental Economics and Management's best articles in depletable resources and energy ★2462★
  Top cited nonrenewable resource papers from 1979 to 1983 ★2469★
Trends in Neuroscience
  Journals with the highest impact factor in the field of neuroscience, 1981-96 ★191★
  Neurosciences journals with the greatest impact measure, 1981-98 ★2812★
  Neurosciences journals with the greatest impact measure, 1994-98 ★2813★
Trenholm State Technical College
  Lowest undergraduate tuition and fees at colleges and universities in Alabama ★1480★
  U.S. institutions awarding the most associate degrees to African Americans in agribusiness and production, 1998 ★1805★
  U.S. institutions awarding the most associate degrees to minorities in agribusiness and production, 1998 ★1808★
Trent University
  Canadian primarily undergraduate universities by alumni support, 2000 ★1193★
  Canadian primarily undergraduate universities by award-winning faculty members, 2000 ★1194★
  Canadian primarily undergraduate universities by class size at the first and second-year level, 2000 ★1195★
  Canadian primarily undergraduate universities by class size at the third and forth-year level, 2000 ★1196★
  Canadian primarily undergraduate universities by classes taught by tenured faculty, 2000 ★1197★
  Canadian primarily undergraduate universities by faculty members with Ph.D.'s, 2000 ★1198★
  Canadian primarily undergraduate universities by library acquisitions, 2000 ★1199★
  Canadian primarily undergraduate universities by library expenses, 2000 ★1200★
  Canadian primarily undergraduate universities by library holdings per student, 2000 ★1201★
  Canadian primarily undergraduate universities by medical/science grants per faculty member, 2000 ★1202★
  Canadian primarily undergraduate universities by operating budget per student, 2000 ★1203★
  Canadian primarily undergraduate universities by percentage of operating budget allocated to scholarships, 2000 ★1204★
  Canadian primarily undergraduate universities by percentage of operating budget allocated to student services, 2000 ★1205★

Canadian primarily undergraduate universities by reputation, 2000 ★1206★
Canadian primarily undergraduate universities by social science/humanities grants per faculty member, 2000 ★1207★
Canadian primarily undergraduate universities by students from out of province, 2000 ★1208★
Canadian primarily undergraduate universities by students winning national awards, 2000 ★1209★
Canadian universities chosen as being value added, 2000 ★1216★
Top Canadian primarily undergraduate universities, 2000 ★1226★

Tress; Daryl
Radcliffe Institute for Advanced Study fellowship recipients in the field of philosophy, 2000-01 ★2946★

Trethewey; Natasha
Radcliffe Institute for Advanced Study fellowship recipient in the field of poetry, 2000-01 ★2444★

Trevecca Nazarene University
Average faculty salaries for institutions of higher education in Tennessee, 2000-01 ★3730★

Trex
Best small companies in the U.S. ★383★

Tri-County Community College
Lowest undergraduate tuition and fees at colleges and universities in North Carolina ★1540★
Average faculty salaries for institutions of higher education without academic ranks in North Carolina, 2000-01 ★3761★

Tri-County Technical College
Lowest undergraduate tuition and fees at colleges and universities in South Carolina ★1555★

Tribal colleges
Proposed fiscal 2002 appropriations for institutional assistance ★2232★

Tribune
Fortune's highest ranked publishing companies, 2000 ★489★
Top publishing and broadcasting companies in Standard & Poor's 500, 2001 ★553★

Tribune Ed.
Highest revenues of publicly held book publishers, 1999 ★3072★

Trickum Middle School
Outstanding secondary schools in Atlanta, Georgia ★4087★

Tricon Global Restaurants
Business Week's best performing companies with the lowest 3-year sales performance ★423★
Fortune's highest ranked food services companies, 2000 ★465★

Trident Technical College
Lowest undergraduate tuition and fees at colleges and universities in South Carolina ★1555★

Trilobite!: Eyewitness to Evolution
Library Journal's most notable paleontology books, 2000 ★273★

Trimble; Joseph
Radcliffe Institute for Advanced Study fellowship recipients in the field of psychology, 2000-01 ★3062★

Trinity Bible College
Highest undergraduate tuition and fees at colleges and universities in North Dakota ★1541★

Trinity College
All-USA College Academic Third Team, 2001 ★4★

U.S. colleges and universities where a large portion of the student body drink hard liquor ★992★
U.S. colleges and universities where the general student body smokes marijuana ★1011★
U.S. colleges and universities with strained race/class interaction ★1029★
U.S. colleges and universities without a diverse student body ★1046★
U.S. News & World Report's national liberal arts colleges with the best financial resources rank, 2000-01 ★1322★
U.S. News & World Report's national liberal arts colleges with the highest proportion of classes having 50 or more students, 2000-01 ★1334★
U.S. News & World Report's northern regional universities with students most in debt, 1999 ★1414★
Highest undergraduate tuition and fees at private nonprofit, 4-year or above colleges and universities ★1461★
Highest undergraduate tuition and fees at colleges and universities in Connecticut ★1490★
Undergraduate tuition and fees at colleges and universities in the District of Columbia ★1493★
Top associate professor economists at elite liberal arts colleges, 1975-94 ★2174★
Most wired colleges, 2000 ★2595★
Average faculty salaries for institutions of higher education in Connecticut, 2000-01 ★3694★
Average faculty salaries for institutions of higher education in the District of Columbia, 2000-01 ★3732★

Trinity College (CT)
U.S. bachelor's institutions with the largest number of students studying abroad, 1998-99 ★2511★
U.S. liberal arts colleges with the highest paid full professors, 2001 ★3980★

Trinity College (VT)
Undergraduate tuition and fees at colleges and universities in Vermont ★1563★

Trinity High School
Outstanding secondary schools in Harrisburg-Lebanon-Carlisle, Pennsylvania ★4146★
Outstanding secondary schools in Louisville, Kentucky-Indiana ★4168★

Trinity International University
Average faculty salaries for institutions of higher education in Illinois, 2000-01 ★3700★

Trinity Lutheran School
Outstanding secondary schools in Chicago, Illinois ★4110★

Trinity School
Outstanding secondary schools in Minneapolis-St. Paul, Minnesota-Wisconsin ★4181★
Outstanding secondary schools in South Bend, Indiana ★4231★

Trinity University
U.S. News & World Report's best undergraduate fees among western regional universities by discount tuition, 2000 ★1430★
Fiske Guide's best buys for private colleges and universities, 2001 ★1459★
Highest undergraduate tuition and fees at colleges and universities in Texas ★1560★
U.S. News & World Report's top western regional universities, 2000-01 ★1574★
U.S. News & World Report's western regional universities with the best academic reputation scores, 2000-01 ★1577★

U.S. News & World Report's western regional universities with the best student/faculty ratios, 2000-01 ★1578★
U.S. News & World Report's western regional universities with the highest freshmen retention rates, 2000-01 ★1581★
U.S. News & World Report's western regional universities with the highest graduation rates, 2000-01 ★1582★
U.S. News & World Report's western regional universities with the highest percentage of freshmen in the top 25% of their high school class, 2000-01 ★1583★
U.S. News & World Report's western regional universities with the highest percentage of full-time faculty, 2000-01 ★1584★
U.S. News & World Report's western regional universities with the lowest acceptance rates, 2000-01 ★1586★
U.S. colleges and universities awarding the most social sciences and history master's degrees to Hispanic Americans ★1803★
Average faculty salaries for institutions of higher education in Texas, 2000-01 ★3731★

Trinity Valley Community College
Lowest undergraduate tuition and fees at colleges and universities in Texas ★1561★

TRIO programs
Proposed fiscal 2002 appropriations for aid to the disadvantaged ★1879★
Fiscal 2002 requested budget as compared with Fiscal 2001 budget for the Education Department ★2231★

Tripp Elementary School
All-USA Teacher Teams, Third Team, 2000 ★4401★

Triton Community College
Fall enrollment at Chicago-area public community colleges, by minority percentages, 1999 ★867★

Tritton; Thomas
Top pay and benefits for the chief executive and top paid employees at Haverford College ★3329★

Trojanowicz; Robert J.
Most-cited scholars in police studies articles/research notes ★2624★

Trollinger; Richard
Top pay and benefits for the chief executive and top paid employees at Centre College ★3227★

The Trolls
Outstanding audiobooks, 2000 ★287★
Most notable children's recordings, 2001 ★320★

Trombley; Laura Skandera
Top pay and benefits for the chief executive and top paid employees at Coe College ★3240★

Tronchetti Provera; Marco
European business moguls considered the best turnaround artists ★443★

Trotter; JoAnne
Top pay and benefits for the chief executive and top paid employees at Gwynedd-Mercy College ★3318★

Trouble on Thunder Mountain
Smithsonian's best books for children ages 6 to 10 ★364★

Troutt; William T.
Top pay and benefits for the chief executive and top paid employees at Belmont University ★3198★

Troy Athens High School
Outstanding secondary schools in Detroit, Michigan ★4125★

TROY

Outstanding suburban public high schools in Metro Detroit ★4258★

Troy High School
Outstanding secondary schools in Detroit, Michigan ★4125★
Outstanding suburban public high schools in Metro Detroit ★4258★

Troy State University
U.S. colleges and universities awarding the most psychology master's degrees to African Americans ★1797★

Troy State University, Montgomery
U.S. colleges and universities awarding the most computer and information sciences master's degrees to African Americans ★1766★
U.S. colleges and universities awarding the most psychology master's degrees to African Americans ★1797★

Troy State University System
State appropriations for Alabama's institutions of higher education, 2000-01 ★1254★

Truck driver
Most desirable jobs in travel/food service ★2278★

Truck drivers, except driver/salesworkers
Occupations with the highest number of self-employed workers, 1998 ★2311★
Occupations with the largest projected employment growth, 1998-2008 ★2312★
Projected employment growth for selected occupations that require shorter moderate-term on-the-job training, 1998-2008 ★2321★

Truckee Meadows Community College
Undergraduate tuition and fees at colleges and universities in Nevada ★1530★

Trudge; Colin
Booklist's best science and technology books ★366★

True Believer
Booklist's most recommended black history books for youth ★311★

True North Communications
Fortune's highest ranked advertising and marketing companies, 2000 ★445★

Trueman; Terry
Booklist's best first novels for youths ★309★

Truett-McConnell College
Average faculty salaries for institutions of higher education in Georgia, 2000-01 ★3697★
U.S. institutions with the lowest paid full professors, 2001 ★3979★

The Truly Tasteless Scratch & Sniff Book
Most notable nonfiction books for reluctant young adult readers, 2001 ★323★

Truman High School
Outstanding secondary schools in Kansas City, Missouri-Kansas ★4158★

Truman State University
Division II NCAA colleges with the highest graduation rates for football players, 1993-94 ★946★
State appropriations for Missouri's institutions of higher education, 2000-01 ★1278★
U.S. News & World Report's midwestern regional universities with the best academic reputation scores, 2000-01 ★1401★
U.S. News & World Report's midwestern regional universities with the highest freshmen retention rates, 2000-01 ★1405★
U.S. News & World Report's midwestern regional universities with the highest percentage of freshmen from the top 25% of their high school class, 2000-01 ★1407★
U.S. News & World Report's midwestern regional universities with the highest percentage of full-time faculty, 2000-01 ★1408★
U.S. News & World Report's top public midwestern regional universities, 2000-01 ★1412★
Average faculty salaries for institutions of higher education in Missouri, 2000-01 ★3712★

Trump Hotels & Casino Resorts
Fortune's highest ranked hotels, casinos and resorts, 2000 ★470★

Trump Hotels and Casino Resorts
Fortune's least admired companies for social responsibility ★512★

Trust and Risk in Internet Commerce
Library Journal's most notable digital technology books, 2000 ★256★

The Truth About Violence
Most notable DVDs and videos for young adults, 2001 ★2890★

Truth and Bright Water
Most notable fiction books, 2001 ★284★
Outstanding works of fiction, 2001 ★293★

TRW
Fortune's highest ranked motor vehicle parts companies, 2000 ★480★
Top conglomerates in Standard & Poor's 500, 2001 ★535★

Trzyna; Thomas
Top pay and benefits for the chief executive and top paid employees at Seattle Pacific University ★3494★

Tubbs; Billy D.
Top pay and benefits for the chief executive and top paid employees at Texas Christian University ★3518★

Tuckahoe Middle School
Outstanding secondary schools in Richmond-Petersburg, Virginia ★4210★

Tucson, AZ
Best 'green & clean' places to live ★3077★

Tuesdays with Morrie
Longest-running nonfiction hardcover bestsellers, 2000 ★281★

Tufts University
U.S. colleges and universities where students and the local community have strained relations ★998★
U.S. colleges and universities with a popular newspaper ★1018★
U.S. colleges and universities with an unfavorable surrounding town or city ★1023★
U.S. colleges and universities with excellent instructors ★1024★
U.S. colleges and universities with strained race/class interaction ★1029★
U.S. colleges and universities with the happiest students ★1035★
U.S. colleges and universities with the most accessible instructors ★1038★
U.S. News & World Report's national universities with the best freshmen retention rates, 2000-01 ★1128★
U.S. News & World Report's national universities with the best student/faculty ratio, 2000-01 ★1130★

Educational Rankings Annual • 2002

U.S. News & World Report's national universities with the lowest proportion of classes with 50 or more students, 2000-01 ★1142★
Highest undergraduate tuition and fees at private nonprofit, 4-year or above colleges and universities ★1461★
Highest undergraduate tuition and fees at colleges and universities in Massachusetts ★1516★
U.S. colleges and universities awarding the most social sciences and history master's degrees to Asian Americans ★1802★
U.S. colleges and universities awarding the most social sciences and history master's degrees to Hispanic Americans ★1803★
U.S. colleges and universities awarding the most first professional degrees to Asian Americans ★1844★
U.S. colleges and universities awarding the most health professions and related sciences first professional degrees to Asian Americans ★1848★
U.S. colleges and universities awarding the most health professions and related sciences first professional degrees to Hispanic Americans ★1849★
U.S. colleges and universities awarding the most health professions and related sciences first professional degrees to minorities ★1850★
U.S. colleges and universities awarding the most health professions and related sciences first professional degrees to Native Americans ★1851★
Radcliffe Institute for Advanced Study fellowship recipients in the field of history, 2000-01 ★2549★
Average faculty salaries for institutions of higher education in Massachusetts, 2000-01 ★3708★

Tulane University
U.S. colleges and universities where a large portion of the student body drink hard liquor ★992★
U.S. colleges and universities where the general student body puts a strong emphasis on socializing ★1008★
U.S. News & World Report's national universities with the highest acceptance rates, 2000-01 ★1131★
U.S. News & World Report's national universities with the lowest graduation rates, 1999 ★1141★
U.S. colleges and universities spending the most on independent lobbyists, 1999 ★1310★
Highest undergraduate tuition and fees at private nonprofit, 4-year or above colleges and universities ★1461★
Highest undergraduate tuition and fees at colleges and universities in Louisiana ★1510★
U.S. colleges and universities awarding the most health professions and related sciences master's degrees to African Americans ★1777★
U.S. colleges and universities awarding the most health professions and related sciences master's degrees to Hispanic Americans ★1779★
U.S. colleges and universities awarding the most law and legal studies master's degrees to Hispanic Americans ★1783★
U.S. colleges and universities awarding the most first professional degrees to Native Americans ★1846★

U.S. colleges and universities awarding the most health professions and related sciences first professional degrees to Native Americans ★1851★

U.S. colleges and universities awarding the most law and legal studies first professional degrees to African Americans ★1852★

Academics' choices for best environmental law programs, 2001 ★2628★

Average faculty salaries for institutions of higher education in Louisiana, 2000-01 ★3705★

Tullock; G.
Authors with the most citations among authors published in *American Political Science Review*, 1974-94 ★3048★

Tulsa; University of
U.S. News & World Report's national universities with students most in debt, 1999 ★1476★

Highest undergraduate tuition and fees at colleges and universities in Oklahoma ★1545★

U.S. colleges and universities awarding the most health professions and related sciences master's degrees to Native Americans ★1780★

U.S. colleges and universities awarding the most first professional degrees to Native Americans ★1846★

U.S. colleges and universities awarding the most law and legal studies first professional degrees to Native Americans ★1855★

Academics' choices for best graduate petroleum engineering schools, 2000 ★2429★

U.S. News & World Report's graduate engineering programs with the best petroleum departments, 2000-01 ★2431★

Average faculty salaries for institutions of higher education in Oklahoma, 2000-01 ★3723★

Tunisia
Eight grade science achievement scores from selected countries, 1999 ★14★

Eighth grade mathematics achievement scores from selected countries, 1999 ★2773★

Tunxis Community College
Lowest undergraduate tuition and fees at colleges and universities in Connecticut ★1491★

Turabo University
Highest undergraduate tuition and fees at colleges and universities in Puerto Rico ★1551★

Turack; Daniel
Top pay and benefits for the chief executive and top paid employees at Capital University ★3220★

Turbo Tax
Top selling software in all categories, 2000 ★1602★

Turbo Tax Deluxe
Top selling software in all categories, 2000 ★1602★

Turbo Tax Multi State
Top selling software in all categories, 2000 ★1602★

Turkey
Eight grade science achievement scores from selected countries, 1999 ★14★

Percentage of enrollment at public institutions of higher education, by country, 1998 ★859★

Countries of origin for non-U.S. citizens awarded doctorates at U.S. colleges and universities, 1999 ★1901★

Countries with the lowest spending per student on higher education, 1997 ★2489★

Foreign countries with the highest enrollment of foreign students, 1999-2000 ★2496★

Eighth grade mathematics achievement scores from selected countries, 1999 ★2773★

Turkiye Is Bankasi
Business Week's top emerging-market companies worldwide ★434★

Turner; Cheryl
Top pay and benefits for the chief executive and top paid employees at Fontbonne College ★3294★

Turner; Craig
Top pay and benefits for the chief executive and top paid employees at Hardin-Simmons University ★3325★

Turner Drew Language
Chicago elementary magnet schools with the lowest acceptance rates, 2000-01 ★4003★

Turner High School
Outstanding secondary schools in Dallas, Texas ★4120★

Turner; R. Gerald
Presidents with the highest pay at Doctoral I and II universities, 1998-99 ★3160★

Top pay and benefits for the chief executive and top paid employees at Southern Methodist University ★3502★

Turning Seventeen series
Most notable fiction books for reluctant young adult readers, 2001 ★321★

Turtle Mountain Community College
U.S. tribal colleges ★1445★

Tusculum College
Highest undergraduate tuition and fees at colleges and universities in Tennessee ★1558★

Average faculty salaries for institutions of higher education in Tennessee, 2000-01 ★3730★

Tuskegee University
Private, 4-year undergraduate colleges and universities producing the most Ph.D.'s in the life sciences, 1981-1990 ★193★

Colleges offering the Thurgood Marshall Scholarship Fund ★221★

U.S. colleges and universities with the worst food service program ★1043★

Highest undergraduate tuition and fees at colleges and universities in Alabama ★1479★

U.S. institutions awarding the most baccalaureate degrees to African Americans in agricultural sciences, 1998 ★1814★

U.S. institutions awarding the most baccalaureate degrees to minorities in agricultural sciences, 1998 ★1820★

Historically black colleges and universities awarding the most first professional degrees to African Americans ★1835★

U.S. colleges and universities awarding the most health professions and related sciences first professional degrees to African Americans ★1847★

TV Guide
Magazines with the largest circulation ★2750★

Twain; Mark
People for the American Way's list of most frequently challenged authors, 1982-1992 ★746★

Top essayists from 1946-1996 ★2445★

12 Technologies
Information technology companies giving the best returns, 2000 ★522★

Twentieth-Century Literary Movements Dictionary
Selected reference books in the field of literature, 2000 ★377★

Twin Cities, MN
U.S. cities considered to be the most affordable for IT professionals ★562★

Twin Peaks Middle School
Outstanding secondary schools in San Diego, California ★4220★

Twinsburg Public Library
Highest Hennen's American Public Library Ratings for libraries serving a population of 10,000 to 24,999 ★2695★

The Two Hearts of Kwasi Boachi
Booklist's best first novels ★228★

TXU
Fortune's highest ranked electric and gas utilities companies, 2000 ★459★

Tyburski; Robert L.
Top pay and benefits for the chief executive and top paid employees at Colgate University ★3242★

Tyce; Sarah J.
Top pay and benefits for the chief executive and top paid employees at Howard University ★3343★

Tychsen; Robert L.
Top pay and benefits for the chief executive and top paid employees at Washington University in Missouri ★3607★

Tyco International
Best performing companies in Standard & Poor's 500, 2001 ★382★

Business Week's best performing companies with the highest 3-year earnings growth ★416★

Fortune's highest ranked electronics and electrical equipment companies, 2000 ★460★

Top manufacturing companies in Standard & Poor's 500, 2001 ★548★

Tyco Toys
Most selective internships in the U.S., 2001 ★2610★

Tying Down the Wind: Adventures in the Worst Weather on Earth
Library Journal's most notable meteorology books, 2000 ★267★

Tyler Independent School District
Top recruiters for education jobs for 2000-01 bachelor's degree recipients ★4377★

Top recruiters for education jobs for 2000-01 master's degree recipients ★4398★

Tyler Junior College
Average faculty salaries for institutions of higher education without academic ranks in Texas, 2000-01 ★3766★

Tyler Junior College Foundation
Colleges and universities with the smallest endowments, 2000 ★1238★

Tyndale
Hardcover bestsellers by corporation, 2000 ★239★

Paperback bestsellers by corporation, 2000 ★296★

Trade paperback bestsellers by publishing house, 2000 ★307★

Typist/work processor
Jobs with the best environment scores ★2247★
Jobs with the most stringent quotas ★2259★

Typists/word processors
Occupations with the highest decline in employment, 1998-2008 ★2310★

Tyson, C.S.C.; Rev. David T.
Top pay and benefits for the chief executive and top paid employees at the University of Portland ★3556★

Tyson Foods
Fortune's highest ranked food production companies, 2000 ★464★

Tyson; John
Top pay and benefits for the chief executive and top paid employees at Abilene Christian University ★3163★

U

UAL
Fortune's highest ranked airlines, 2000 ★447★

UBS
Business Week's best companies in Switzerland ★405★

UCC Groep
Best small companies worldwide ★384★

UCLA Medical Center
Top cancer hospitals in the U.S., 2000 ★2787★
Top gastroenterology hospitals in the U.S., 2000 ★2790★
Top geriatrics hospitals in the U.S., 2000 ★2791★
Top gynecology hospitals in the U.S., 2000 ★2792★
Top hospitals in the U.S., 2000 ★2793★
Top neurology and neurosurgery hospitals in the U.S., 2000 ★2795★
Top orthopedics hospitals in the U.S., 2000 ★2797★
Top ortolaryngology hospitals in the U.S., 2000 ★2798★
Top rheumatology hospitals in the U.S., 2000 ★2802★
Top urology hospitals in the U.S., 2000 ★2803★

UCLA Medical Center (Jules Stein Eye Institute)
Top ophthalmology hospitals in the U.S., 2000 ★2796★

UCLA Neuropsychiatric Hospital
Top psychiatric hospitals in the U.S., 2000 ★2800★

Uebelacker; James W.
Top pay and benefits for the chief executive and top paid employees at the University of New Haven ★3553★

Ukraine
Countries with the lowest percentage of workers satisfied with their job ★2243★

Ulster County Community College
Average faculty salaries for institutions of higher education in New York, 2000-01 ★3719★

Ultima Thule
Library Journal's best poetry books, 2000 ★244★

Ultimate Game
Most notable books for older readers, 2001 ★318★

Ume; Tsuda
Japan's ten great educators ★2234★

Ummel; Vern
Top pay and benefits for the chief executive and top paid employees at Dominican University of California ★3270★

Umpqua Community College
Lowest undergraduate tuition and fees at colleges and universities in Oregon ★1548★

Uncertainty and Exhaustible Resource Markets
Top cited nonrenewable resource papers from 1979 to 1983 ★2469★

Uncommon Traveler: Mary Kingsley in Africa
Most notable books for young readers, 2001 ★319★

Under the Skin
Booklist's best first novels ★228★
Booklist's most recommended science fiction/fantasy books ★232★

Understanding Media
Canada's best nonfiction selections of the 20th century ★234★

Undertaker
Most desirable jobs in personal services ★2275★
'White-collar' jobs considered the most physically demanding ★2285★

Underwood; William D.
Top pay and benefits for the chief executive and top paid employees at Baylor University ★3194★

Unicredito Italiano
Business Week's best companies in Italy ★397★

Unifi
Fortune's highest ranked textiles companies, 2000 ★501★

Unilever NV
Business Week's best companies in the Netherlands ★410★

Unilever U.S.
Fortune's highest ranked soaps and cosmetics companies, 2000 ★496★

Union Carbide
Fortune's highest ranked chemicals companies, 2000 ★452★
Top internships in the U.S. with the highest compensation, 2001 ★2611★

Union College
Private, 4-year undergraduate colleges and universities producing the most Ph.D.'s in the life sciences, 1920-1990 ★192★
Private, 4-year undergraduate colleges and universities producing the most Ph.D.'s in the life sciences, 1981-1990 ★193★
U.S. colleges and universities where a large portion of the student body drink beer ★991★
U.S. colleges and universities where a large portion of the student body drink hard liquor ★992★
Highest undergraduate tuition and fees at colleges and universities in Kentucky ★1508★
Highest undergraduate tuition and fees at colleges and universities in Nebraska ★1528★
Highest undergraduate tuition and fees at colleges and universities in New York ★1537★
Private, 4-year undergraduate colleges and universities producing the most Ph.D.'s in the computer sciences, 1920-1990 ★1595★
Private, 4-year undergraduate colleges and universities producing the most Ph.D.'s in the computer sciences, 1981-1990 ★1596★
Private, 4-year undergraduate colleges and universities producing the most Ph.D.'s in mathematics, 1920-1990 ★2776★
Private, 4-year undergraduate colleges and universities producing the most Ph.D.'s in physics and astronomy, 1920-1990 ★2949★
Private, 4-year undergraduate colleges and universities producing the most Ph.D.'s in psychology, 1920-1990 ★3066★
Private, 4-year undergraduate colleges and universities producing the most Ph.D.'s in psychology, 1981-1990 ★3067★
Average faculty salaries for institutions of higher education in New York, 2000-01 ★3719★
Private, 4-year undergraduate colleges and universities producing the most Ph.D.'s in the sciences, 1920-1990 ★4294★
Private, 4-year undergraduate colleges and universities producing the most Ph.D.'s in the sciences, 1981-1990 ★4295★

Union Electrica Fenosa
Business Week's best companies in Spain ★403★

Union Institute
U.S. News & World Report's national universities with the highest proportion of classes with less than 20 students, 2000-01 ★1138★
U.S. News & World Report's national universities with students most in debt, 1999 ★1476★
Institutions awarding the most doctorate degrees to African Americans, 1997-98 ★1948★

Union Institute, Cincinnati
Traditionally white institutions awarding the most doctorate degrees to African Americans ★2079★
U.S. colleges and universities awarding the most doctorate degrees to African Americans ★2095★
U.S. colleges and universities awarding the most doctorate degrees to Hispanic Americans ★2097★
U.S. colleges and universities awarding the most psychology doctorate degrees to African Americans ★2120★

Union Pacific
Fortune's highest ranked railroads, 2000 ★490★
Top transportation companies in Standard & Poor's 500, 2001 ★560★

Union Public Library
Highest Hennen's American Public Library Ratings for libraries serving a population of 1,000 to 2,499 ★2692★

Union Ridge School District 86
Illinois school districts with the most average years of teacher experience ★4012★

Union School
Outstanding secondary schools in Hartford, Connecticut ★4147★

Union Theological Seminary (VA)
Average faculty salaries for institutions of higher education in Virginia, 2000-01 ★3735★

Union University
U.S. News & World Report's southern regional liberal arts colleges with the best student/faculty ratios, 2000-01 ★1368★
U.S. News & World Report's southern regional liberal arts colleges with the highest acceptance rates, 2000-01 ★1370★
U.S. News & World Report's southern regional liberal arts colleges with the highest graduation rates, 2000-01 ★1373★
U.S. News & World Report's southern regional liberal arts colleges with the highest proportion of freshmen in the top 25% of their high school class, 2000-01 ★1376★
U.S. News & World Report's top southern regional liberal arts colleges, 2000-01 ★1379★

Average faculty salaries for institutions of higher education in Tennessee, 2000-01 ★3730★

Uniontown High School
All-USA Teacher Teams, First Team, 2000 ★4399★

Unisys
Fortune's highest ranked computer and data services companies, 2000 ★453★
Top recruiters for computer science jobs for 2000-01 bachelor's degree recipients ★1590★
Top recruiters for systems engineer jobs for 2000-01 bachelor's degree recipients ★2336★
Top recruiters for computer engineering jobs for 2000-01 bachelor's degree recipients ★2352★

Unit 4
Best small companies worldwide ★384★

United Auto Group
Fortune's highest ranked automotive retailing services companies, 2000 ★449★

United Church of Christ
Religious preference of incoming freshmen, 2000 ★1061★

United HealthCare
Fortune's highest ranked health care companies, 2000 ★469★

United Jewish Communities
Organizations with the most charitable contributions raised, 1999 ★2943★

United Kingdom
CA journal literature abstracted, by country, 2000 ★757★
Countries with the most computers, 2000 ★1603★
Countries with the most computers per capita, 2000 ★1604★
Countries of origin for non-U.S. citizens awarded doctorates at U.S. colleges and universities, 1999 ★1901★
Annual leave days for employees in selected countries ★2239★
Countries with the most Internet users ★2583★
Percentage of internet usage for selected countries ★2599★
European periodical prices by country, 2001 ★2921★

United Microelectronics
Business Week's top emerging-market companies worldwide ★434★

United Overseas Bank
Business Week's best companies in Singapore ★402★

United Parcel Service of America
Fortune's highest ranked mail, packaging, and freight delivery companies, 2000 ★473★
Fortune's most admired companies for financial soundness ★515★

United States
Eight grade science achievement scores from selected countries, 1999 ★14★
Math achievement test comparison ★19★
CA journal literature abstracted, by country, 2000 ★757★
CA patents abstracted, by country, 2000 ★758★
Percentage of enrollment at private institutions of higher education, by country, 1998 ★858★
Countries with the most computers, 2000 ★1603★
Countries with the most computers per capita, 2000 ★1604★

College dropout rates for selected countries ★2134★
Annual leave days for employees in selected countries ★2239★
Countries with the highest percentage of workers satisfied with their job ★2242★
Countries with the highest spending per student on higher education, 1997 ★2488★
Countries with the most Internet users ★2583★
Most wired countries, 2001 ★2596★
Percentage of internet usage for selected countries ★2599★
Eighth grade mathematics achievement scores from selected countries, 1999 ★2773★
Institute for Scientific Information periodical prices by country, 2001 ★2922★
North American periodical prices by country, 2001 ★2924★
Countries with the highest leader's salary ★3120★
Countries spending the highest percentage of gross domestic product on education ★4060★
Nations with the most-cited papers in the sciences ★4320★

United States Air Force Academy
U.S. colleges and universities offering the best overall academic experience for undergraduates ★987★
U.S. colleges and universities that are the toughest to get into ★988★
U.S. colleges and universities with the best overall administration ★1033★
U.S. News & World Report's undergraduate engineering programs with the highest academic reputation scores, 2000-01 ★2337★
U.S. News & World Report's undergraduate engineering programs with the best aerospace departments, 2000-01 ★2341★
U.S. News & World Report's undergraduate engineering programs with the best civil departments, 2000-01 ★2347★
U.S. News & World Report's undergraduate engineering programs with the best electrical departments, 2000-01 ★2355★

U.S. Air Force (Active Duty Hires)
Top recruiters for architecture jobs for 2000-01 bachelor's degree recipients ★68★
Top recruiters for chemistry jobs for 2000-01 bachelor's degree recipients ★792★
Top recruiters for criminal justice jobs for 2000-01 bachelor's degree recipients ★1647★
Top recruiters for multidisciplinary majors jobs for 2000-01 bachelor's degree recipients ★2327★
Top recruiters for aeronautical engineering jobs for 2000-01 bachelor's degree recipients ★2339★
Top recruiters for aerospace engineering jobs for 2000-01 bachelor's degree recipients ★2340★
Top recruiters for chemical engineering jobs for 2000-01 bachelor's degree recipients ★2343★
Top recruiters for computer engineering jobs for 2000-01 bachelor's degree recipients ★2352★
Top recruiters for electrical/electronic engineering jobs for 2000-01 bachelor's degree recipients ★2354★
Top recruiters for environmental engineering jobs for 2000-01 bachelor's degree recipients ★2357★

Top recruiters for aeronautical engineering jobs for 2000-01 master's degree recipients ★2373★
Top recruiters for metallurgical/mining engineering jobs for 2000-01 bachelor's degree recipients ★2434★
Top recruiters for mechanical engineering jobs for 2000-01 bachelor's degree recipients ★2437★
Top recruiters for nuclear engineering jobs for 2000-01 bachelor's degree recipients ★2440★
Top recruiters for geology/geophysics jobs for 2000-01 bachelor's degree recipients ★2522★
Top recruiters for allied health/biomedical science jobs for 2000-01 bachelor's degree recipients ★2540★
Top recruiters for allied health/biomedical science jobs for 2000-01 master's degree recipients ★2544★
Top recruiters for health jobs for 2000-01 master's degree recipients ★2545★
Top recruiters for foreign language jobs for 2000-01 bachelor's degree recipients ★2614★
Top recruiters for math/actuarial science jobs for 2000-01 bachelor's degree recipients ★2771★
Top recruiters for statistics jobs for 2000-01 bachelor's degree recipients ★2786★
Top recruiters for medical technology jobs for 2000-01 bachelor's degree recipients ★2881★
Top recruiters for nursing jobs for 2000-01 bachelor's degree recipients ★2898★
Top recruiters for pharmacology/pharmaceutical jobs for 2000-01 master's degree recipients ★2940★
Top recruiters for physics jobs for 2000-01 bachelor's degree recipients ★2974★
Top recruiters for social work jobs for 2000-01 master's degree recipients ★4343★
Top recruiters for sociology jobs for 2000-01 bachelor's degree recipients ★4347★

U.S. Air Force (Civilian Hires)
Top recruiters for criminal justice jobs for 2000-01 bachelor's degree recipients ★1647★
Top recruiters for aeronautical engineering jobs for 2000-01 bachelor's degree recipients ★2339★
Top recruiters for civil engineering jobs for 2000-01 bachelor's degree recipients ★2346★
Top recruiters for psychology jobs for 2000-01 bachelor's degree recipients ★3063★

U.S. Air Force Randolph AFB
Top recruiters for meteorology jobs for 2000-01 bachelor's degree recipients ★2142★

U.S. Bancorp
Fortune's highest ranked super-regional banks, 2000 ★498★
Top banks in Standard & Poor's 500, 2001 ★531★

United States Coast Guard Academy
U.S. colleges and universities offering the best overall academic experience for undergraduates ★987★
U.S. colleges and universities where students and the local community relate well ★999★
U.S. colleges and universities where students study the most ★1003★
U.S. colleges and universities where the general student body does not drink hard liquor ★1005★

UNITED

U.S. colleges and universities where the general student body puts little emphasis on socializing ★1010★

U.S. colleges and universities with a generally conservative student body ★1014★

U.S. colleges and universities with a primarily religious student body ★1022★

U.S. colleges and universities with the most accessible instructors ★1038★

U.S. Concrete
Top companies in terms of growth, 2000 ★534★

U.S. Energy Policy and Economic Growth, 1975-2000
Top cited energy papers from 1974 to 1978 ★2463★

U.S. Forest Services
Top recruiters for biology/biological science jobs for 2000-01 bachelor's degree recipients ★198★

Top recruiters for biology/biological science jobs for 2000-01 master's degree recipients ★203★

Top recruiters for civil engineering jobs for 2000-01 bachelor's degree recipients ★2346★

U.S. government and politics
Number of Advanced Placement Exams taken by African Americans, by subject, 2000 ★30★

Number of Advanced Placement Exams taken by Asian Americans, by subject, 2000 ★31★

Number of Advanced Placement Exams taken by Hispanic Americans, by subject, 2000 ★32★

U.S. Government Savings Bonds
Best ways to save for college ★843★

U.S. history
Number of Advanced Placement Exams taken by African Americans, by subject, 2000 ★30★

Number of Advanced Placement Exams taken by Asian Americans, by subject, 2000 ★31★

Number of Advanced Placement Exams taken by Hispanic Americans, by subject, 2000 ★32★

U.S. Industries
Fortune's highest ranked metal products companies, 2000 ★475★

U.S. International University
U.S. colleges and universities awarding the most psychology doctorate degrees to African Americans ★2120★

U.S. Marine Corps
Top recruiters for multidisciplinary majors jobs for 2000-01 bachelor's degree recipients ★2327★

Top recruiters for multidisciplinary majors jobs for 2000-01 master's degree recipients ★2328★

United States Military Academy
U.S. colleges and universities that are the toughest to get into ★988★

U.S. colleges and universities with the most accessible instructors ★1038★

U.S. News & World Report's undergraduate engineering programs with the highest academic reputation scores, 2000-01 ★2337★

U.S. News & World Report's undergraduate engineering programs with the best civil departments, 2000-01 ★2347★

U.S. News & World Report's undergraduate engineering programs with the best mechanical departments, 2000-01 ★2438★

United States Naval Academy
All-USA College Academic Second Team, 2001 ★3★

U.S. colleges and universities that are the toughest to get into ★988★

U.S. colleges and universities where the general student body puts little emphasis on socializing ★1010★

U.S. colleges and universities with the best overall administration ★1033★

U.S. colleges and universities with the most accessible instructors ★1038★

Total baccalaureate physical sciences degrees awarded to African Americans from U.S. colleges and universities, 1997-98 ★1733★

Total baccalaureate physical sciences degrees awarded to Hispanic Americans from U.S. colleges and universities, 1997-98 ★1735★

U.S. News & World Report's undergraduate engineering programs with the highest academic reputation scores, 2000-01 ★2337★

U.S. News & World Report's undergraduate engineering programs with the best aerospace departments, 2000-01 ★2341★

Average faculty salaries for institutions of higher education in Maryland, 2000-01 ★3707★

United States Senate Youth Program
Top internships in the U.S. with the highest compensation, 2001 ★2611★

United Talent Agency
Most selective internships in the U.S., 2001 ★2610★

United Technologies
Fortune's highest ranked aerospace companies, 2000 ★446★

Top aerospace and defense companies in Standard & Poor's 500, 2001 ★529★

United Theological Seminary
Institutions awarding the most doctorate degrees to African Americans, 1997-98 ★1948★

United Theological Seminary, Dayton
Traditionally white institutions awarding the most doctorate degrees to African Americans ★2079★

U.S. colleges and universities awarding the most doctorate degrees to African Americans ★2095★

U.S. colleges and universities awarding the most doctorate degrees to minorities ★2098★

United Tribes Technical College
U.S. tribal colleges ★1445★

Highest undergraduate tuition and fees at colleges and universities in North Dakota ★1541★

Unity College
Highest undergraduate tuition and fees at colleges and universities in Maine ★1512★

Universal
Fortune's highest ranked tobacco companies, 2000 ★502★

Universidad Metropolitana
Lowest undergraduate tuition and fees at private nonprofit, 4-year or above colleges and universities ★1464★

Universidad Politecnica de Puerta Rico
Highest undergraduate tuition and fees at colleges and universities in Puerto Rico ★1551★

Universite de Moncton
Canadian primarily undergraduate universities by alumni support, 2000 ★1193★

Canadian primarily undergraduate universities by class size at the first and second-year level, 2000 ★1195★

Canadian primarily undergraduate universities by class size at the third and forth-year level, 2000 ★1196★

Canadian primarily undergraduate universities by classes taught by tenured faculty, 2000 ★1197★

Canadian primarily undergraduate universities by faculty members with Ph.D.'s, 2000 ★1198★

Canadian primarily undergraduate universities by library acquisitions, 2000 ★1199★

Canadian primarily undergraduate universities by library expenses, 2000 ★1200★

Canadian primarily undergraduate universities by library holdings per student, 2000 ★1201★

Canadian primarily undergraduate universities by medical/science grants per faculty member, 2000 ★1202★

Canadian primarily undergraduate universities by operating budget per student, 2000 ★1203★

Canadian primarily undergraduate universities by percentage of operating budget allocated to scholarships, 2000 ★1204★

Canadian primarily undergraduate universities by percentage of operating budget allocated to student services, 2000 ★1205★

Canadian primarily undergraduate universities by reputation, 2000 ★1206★

Canadian primarily undergraduate universities by social science/humanities grants per faculty member, 2000 ★1207★

Canadian primarily undergraduate universities by students from out of province, 2000 ★1208★

Canadian primarily undergraduate universities by students winning national awards, 2000 ★1209★

Canadian universities by graduation rate, 2000 ★1214★

Canadian universities chosen as being value added, 2000 ★1216★

Top Canadian primarily undergraduate universities, 2000 ★1226★

University of California Press
Book publishers with the most citations (Class 5) ★2566★

University of Chicago Law Review
Law journals with the greatest impact measure, 1981-98 ★2618★

University of Chicago Press
Book publishers with the most citations (Class 5) ★2566★

University College London
United Kingdom universities contributing the most papers in the field of economics and business, 1993-97 ★2203★

University Heights Middle School
Outstanding secondary schools in Riverside-San Bernardino, California ★4211★

University High School
Outstanding secondary schools in Orlando, Florida ★4200★

University Hospital
Top nephrology hospitals in the U.S., 2000 ★2794★

University Hospitals of Cleveland (Rainbow Babies & Children's Hospital)
Top pediatrics hospitals in the U.S., 2000 ★2799★

University of Indiana
Top business schools for within-discipline research performance in production/operations management, 1986-1998 ★648★

Comparison of library and information science programs composite rankings with *U.S. News & World Report* survey ★2709★

Library and information science programs with the most citations to journal articles, 1993-1998 ★2712★

Library and information science programs with the most journal articles, 1993-1998 ★2713★

Library and information science programs with the most journal articles per capita, 1993-1998 ★2714★

Library and information science programs with the most per capita citations to journal articles, 1993-1998 ★2715★

Institutions with the most prolific communication studies researchers ★2749★

University of Pennsylvania Law Review
Law journals with the greatest impact measure, 1981-98 ★2618★

University of San Diego High School
Outstanding secondary schools in San Diego, California ★4220★

University School of Nova
Outstanding secondary schools in Fort Lauderdale, Florida ★4133★

University System of West Virginia Institute of Tech
Average faculty salaries for institutions of higher education in West Virginia, 2000-01 ★3737★

Univision Communications
Top publishing and broadcasting companies in Standard & Poor's 500, 2001 ★553★

Unocal
Business Week's best performing companies with the highest 1-year earnings growth ★413★
Fortune's highest ranked mining and crude oil companies, 2000 ★477★

UnumProvident
Fortune's highest ranked life and health insurance companies, 2000 ★472★

Upham; Steadman
Top pay and benefits for the chief executive and top paid employees at Claremont Graduate University ★3235★

UPM-Kymmene
Business Week's best companies in Finland ★392★

Upper Dublin High School
Outstanding secondary schools in Philadelphia, Pennsylvania-New Jersey ★4202★

Upper Iowa University
Average faculty salaries for institutions of higher education in Iowa, 2000-01 ★3702★

Upper Moreland Middle School
Outstanding secondary schools in Philadelphia, Pennsylvania-New Jersey ★4202★

Upper Perkiomen High School
Outstanding secondary schools in Philadelphia, Pennsylvania-New Jersey ★4202★

Upper Perkiomen Middle School
Outstanding secondary schools in Philadelphia, Pennsylvania-New Jersey ★4202★

Uproar
Web sites where internet users spend the most time ★2609★

Upshaw; Charles R.
Top pay and benefits for the chief executive and top paid employees at Pacific Lutheran University ★3436★

The Upside Down Boy; El Nino de Cabeza
Smithsonian's best books for children ages 6 to 10 ★364★

Urban Academy
Outstanding secondary schools in New York, New York ★4191★

Urban affairs/studies
Gender breakdown of social sciences doctorate recipients, by subfield, 1999 ★1942★
Social sciences doctorates awarded at U.S. colleges and universities, by subfield, 1999 ★2044★

Urban League
Top recipients of corporate contributions to African American communities, 1995 ★2944★

Urban/regional planner
Most desirable public sector jobs ★2279★

Urban/regional planners
Projected employment growth for selected occupations that require advanced education, 1998-2008 ★2318★

Urban Studies
Top ranked urban, rural and regional economics journals ★2202★

Urbana Free Library
Highest Hennen's American Public Library Ratings for libraries serving a population of 25,000 to 49,999 ★2696★

Urbana University
Average faculty salaries for institutions of higher education in Ohio, 2000-01 ★3722★

Urologic Clinics of North America
Urology and nephrology journals with the greatest impact measure, 1981-98 ★2816★
Urology and nephrology journals with the greatest impact measure, 1994-98 ★2817★

Urology
Urology and nephrology journals with the greatest impact measure, 1994-98 ★2817★

Ursinus College
U.S. colleges and universities with the best financial aid programs ★1030★
Average faculty salaries for institutions of higher education in Pennsylvania, 2000-01 ★3725★

Ursuline Academy
Outstanding secondary schools in Dallas, Texas ★4120★
Outstanding secondary schools in New Orleans, Louisiana ★4190★

Ursuline College
Average faculty salaries for institutions of higher education in Ohio, 2000-01 ★3722★

The Ursuline School
Outstanding secondary schools in New York, New York ★4191★

Uruguay
Countries with the lowest spending per student on higher education, 1997 ★2489★

US Airways Group
Fortune's highest ranked airlines, 2000 ★447★
Fortune's least admired companies for quality of products or services ★511★
Top transportation companies in Standard & Poor's 500, 2001 ★560★

US International University
Average faculty salaries for institutions of higher education in California, 2000-01 ★3692★

US West
Business Week's best companies in terms of return on equity ★407★

USA Education
Fortune's highest ranked consumer credit companies, 2000 ★457★

USA Networks
Fortune's highest ranked entertainment companies, 2000 ★462★

USAA
Fortune's highest ranked property and casualty insurance companies, 2000 ★488★

USC Medical Center (Doheny Eye Institute)
Top ophthalmology hospitals in the U.S., 2000 ★2796★

USEC
Fortune's highest ranked pipelines and energy companies, 2000 ★486★

USFreightways
Fortune's highest ranked trucking companies, 2000 ★503★

USG
Fortune's highest ranked building materials and glass companies, 2000 ★451★

UST
Business Week's best performing companies with the highest return on equity, 2000 ★420★
Fortune's highest ranked tobacco companies, 2000 ★502★
Top consumer products companies in Standard & Poor's 500, 2001 ★536★

USX
Fortune's highest ranked petroleum refining companies, 2000 ★484★

USX-U.S. Steel Group
Top metals and mining companies in Standard & Poor's 500, 2001 ★549★

Utah
Mean composite ACT scores by state, 2000 ★895★
Mean math SAT scores by state, 2000 ★900★
Mean verbal SAT scores by state, 2000 ★903★
Average class size at colleges and universities in the U.S., by state ★1064★
Total doctorate recipients by state, 1999 ★2054★
Average Hennen's American Public Library Ratings, by state ★2690★
State grades for affordability of higher education for minority students, 2000 ★2883★
State grades for benefits state receives for educating its minority students, 2000 ★2884★
State grades for completion of higher education by minority students, 2000 ★2885★
State grades for participation of minority students in higher education, 2000 ★2886★
State grades for preparing minority students for higher education, 2000 ★2887★
States with the lowest per-pupil expenditures ★3998★
States with the highest average enrollment in public secondary schools ★4033★
States with the highest funding needs for school-building modernization ★4040★
States with the largest average class size ★4071★
States with the best college tuition savings plans ★4438★

Utah State University
Division I NCAA colleges with that graduated none of their African American male basketball players, 1990-91 to 1993-94 ★930★
State appropriations for Utah's institutions of higher education, 2000-01 ★1297★

Golden Key Scholar Award winners, 2000 ★1316★
Undergraduate tuition and fees at colleges and universities in Utah ★1562★
U.S. colleges and universities awarding the most psychology master's degrees to Native Americans ★1800★
U.S. universities with the highest concentration of education papers published, 1994-98 ★2223★
U.S. universities with the greatest impact in civil engineering, 1995-99 ★2350★
U.S. universities with the highest concentration of civil engineering papers published, 1994-98 ★2351★
Average faculty salaries for institutions of higher education in Utah, 2000-01 ★3733★
U.S. universities with the highest concentration of animal sciences papers published, 1994-98 ★4288★

Utah; University of
NCAA Division I ski teams with the most championships ★135★
Top molecular and general genetics research-doctorate programs as evaluated by the National Research Council ★211★
State appropriations for Utah's institutions of higher education, 2000-01 ★1297★
Undergraduate tuition and fees at colleges and universities in Utah ★1562★
U.S. colleges and universities awarding the most master's degrees to Native Americans ★1789★
Most effective biomedical engineering research-doctorate programs as evaluated by the National Research Council ★2383★
Top biomedical engineering research-doctorate programs as evaluated by the National Research Council ★2384★
Law schools with the best constitutional law (freedom of religion) faculty, 1999-2000 ★2643★
University research libraries in the U.S. and Canada with the largest increases in total expenditures from 1993-94 to 1998-99 ★2708★
Degrees granted in the ten largest doctoral journalism and mass communications programs, 1999 ★2756★
Enrollment of students in the ten largest doctoral journalism and mass communications programs, 1999 ★2762★
Average faculty salaries for institutions of higher education in Utah, 2000-01 ★3733★

Utah Valley State College
Lowest undergraduate tuition and fees at public, 4-year or above colleges and universities ★1466★
Public 4-year institutions with the lowest tuition, 2000-01 ★1472★
Undergraduate tuition and fees at colleges and universities in Utah ★1562★

UtiliCorp United
Fortune's highest ranked electric and gas utilities companies, 2000 ★459★

Utilities
Spending for E-marketplace services, by industry, 2001 ★4430★

Utrecht University
Radcliffe Institute for Advanced Study fellowship recipients in the field of history, 2000-01 ★2549★

V

Vaccine
Veterinary sciences journals with the greatest impact measure, 1981-98 ★4442★
Veterinary sciences journals with the greatest impact measure, 1994-98 ★4443★

Vagt; Robert F.
Top pay and benefits for the chief executive and top paid employees at Davidson College ★3264★

Vaill; Peter B.
Top pay and benefits for the chief executive and top paid employees at the University of St. Thomas in Minnesota ★3563★

Vaillancourt; Ross
All-America boys' high school soccer team midfielders, 2001 ★168★

Vairo; Georgene M.
Top pay and benefits for the chief executive and top paid employees at Loyola Marymount University ★3380★

Valassis Communications, Inc.
Best companies for working mothers in offering flexible work hours ★4448★

Valdosta State University
State appropriations for Georgia's institutions of higher education, 2000-01 ★1263★
Total baccalaureate law and legal studies degrees awarded to African Americans from U.S. colleges and universities, 1997-98 ★1725★
Average faculty salaries for institutions of higher education in Georgia, 2000-01 ★3697★

Vale, S.S.J.; Sister Carol Jean
Top pay and benefits for the chief executive and top paid employees at Chestnut Hill College ★3231★

Valencia Community College
Top colleges in terms of total associate degrees awarded to minorities, 1997-98 ★1677★
Average faculty salaries for institutions of higher education without academic ranks in Florida, 2000-01 ★3745★

Valenti; Christine
Top pay and benefits for the chief executive and top paid employees at Viterbo University ★3597★

Valentine; Bryan
Top pay and benefits for the chief executive and top paid employees at St. John's College in Maryland and New Mexico ★3473★

Valentine; Richard
Top pay and benefits for the chief executive and top paid employees at Monmouth College in Illinois ★3405★

Valley City State University
State appropriations for North Dakota's institutions of higher education, 2000-01 ★1287★
U.S. News & World Report's top public midwestern regional liberal arts colleges, 2000-01 ★1350★
Highest undergraduate tuition and fees at colleges and universities in North Dakota ★1541★
Average faculty salaries for institutions of higher education in North Dakota, 2000-01 ★3721★

Valley Forge Christian College
Average faculty salaries for institutions of higher education in Pennsylvania, 2000-01 ★3725★

Valley Middle/High School
Outstanding secondary schools in Omaha, Nebraska-Iowa ★4198★

Valley Middle School
Outstanding secondary schools in Minneapolis-St. Paul, Minnesota-Wisconsin ★4181★

Valley View, District 365
Illinois school districts with the most average years of teacher experience ★4012★

Valparaiso University
U.S. News & World Report's midwestern regional universities with the best academic reputation scores, 2000-01 ★1401★
U.S. News & World Report's midwestern regional universities with the best alumni giving rates, 2000-01 ★1402★
U.S. News & World Report's midwestern regional universities with the best student/faculty ratios, 2000-01 ★1403★
U.S. News & World Report's midwestern regional universities with the highest freshmen retention rates, 2000-01 ★1405★
U.S. News & World Report's midwestern regional universities with the highest graduation rates, 2000-01 ★1406★
U.S. News & World Report's midwestern regional universities with the highest percentage of freshmen from the top 25% of their high school class, 2000-01 ★1407★
U.S. News & World Report's midwestern regional universities with the highest percentage of full-time faculty, 2000-01 ★1408★
U.S. News & World Report's top midwestern regional universities, 2000-01 ★1411★
U.S. News & World Report's best undergraduate fees among midwestern regional universities by discount tuition, 2000 ★1427★
Highest undergraduate tuition and fees at colleges and universities in Indiana ★1502★

Van Buren Middle School
Outstanding secondary schools in Albuquerque, New Mexico ★4080★

Van Gogh and Gauguin: The Search for Sacred Art
Outstanding arts and literature books, 2000 ★286★

Van Hoosen Middle School
Outstanding secondary schools in Detroit, Michigan ★4125★

Van Horn; Drew
Top pay and benefits for the chief executive and top paid employees at Gardner-Webb University ★3303★

Van Scoyoc Associates
Lobbyist that billed the most to U.S. colleges and universities, 1999 ★1249★

Van Sickle; Fred
Top pay and benefits for the chief executive and top paid employees at Lake Forest College ★3363★

Van Thiel; David
Most-cited researchers in surgery/transplantation, 1981-1998 ★2878★

Van Voorhis; Jerry
Top pay and benefits for the chief executive and top paid employees at Shenandoah University ★3497★

Vance; Carl B.
Top pay and benefits for the chief executive and top paid employees at Linfield College ★3376★

Vance; Connie N.
Top pay and benefits for the chief executive and top paid employees at the College of New Rochelle ★3525★

Vance-Granville Community College
Average faculty salaries for institutions of higher education without academic ranks in North Carolina, 2000-01 ★3761★

Vander Heyden; Marc A.
Top pay and benefits for the chief executive and top paid employees at Saint Michael's College ★3483★

Vanderbilt University
Division I NCAA colleges with that graduated more than 80% of their African American male athletes, 1990-91 to 1993-94 ★929★
U.S. News & World Report's national universities with the best faculty resources rank, 2000-01 ★1127★
U.S. News & World Report's national universities with the lowest proportion of classes with 50 or more students, 2000-01 ★1142★
Largest gifts to higher education, 1967-2000 ★1247★
Largest private gifts to higher education, 1967-2000 ★1248★
Highest undergraduate tuition and fees at colleges and universities in Tennessee ★1558★
Institutions generating the most economic education research text, 1963-1990 ★2167★
U.S. universities with the greatest impact in education, 1994-98 ★2221★
U.S. universities with the greatest impact in education, 1995-99 ★2222★
Law schools with the best bankruptcy faculty, 1999-2000 ★2639★
U.S. universities with the greatest impact in pharmacology, 1994-98 ★2936★
Most effective pharmacology research-doctorate programs as evaluated by the National Research Council ★2938★
Top pharmacology research-doctorate programs as evaluated by the National Research Council ★2939★
Top physiology research-doctorate programs as evaluated by the National Research Council ★3022★
Top religion research-doctorate programs as evaluated by the National Research Council ★3093★
Presidents with the highest pay at Research I and II universities, 1998-99 ★3162★
Average faculty salaries for institutions of higher education in Tennessee, 2000-01 ★3730★
Acceptance rates at *U.S. News & World Report*'s top 10 graduate education schools, 2001 ★4388★
Average quantitative GRE scores for *U.S. News & World Report*'s top 10 graduate education schools, 2001 ★4389★
Average verbal GRE scores for *U.S. News & World Report*'s top 10 graduate education schools, 2001 ★4390★
Doctoral students to faculty ratio at *U.S. News & World Report*'s top 10 graduate education schools, 2001 ★4391★
Ph.D.s and Ed.D.s granted at *U.S. News & World Report*'s top 10 graduate education schools, 2001 ★4392★
Research expenditures for *U.S. News & World Report*'s top 10 graduate education schools, 2001 ★4393★
Research expenditures per faculty member at *U.S. News & World Report*'s top 10 graduate education schools, 2001 ★4394★
Top graduate education schools, 2001 ★4395★
Top graduate education schools by reputation, as determined by academic personnel, 2001 ★4396★
Top graduate education schools by reputation, as determined by superintendents, 2001 ★4397★

Vanderbilt University Hospital and Clinic
Top nephrology hospitals in the U.S., 2000 ★2794★

Vanderbilt University, Owen Graduate School of Management
Business Week's top business schools by intellectual capital, 2000 ★599★
Business Week's top business schools with the lowest percentage of international students, 2000 ★615★
Business Week's top business schools with the lowest percentage of minority enrollment, 2000 ★616★
Business Week's top business schools with the lowest percentage of women enrollees, 2000 ★617★
Lowest pre-MBA salaries for students enrolled in *Business Week*'s top business schools, 1999 ★635★

Vanderbilt University, Peabody College
Academics' choices for best administration/supervision graduate programs, 2001 ★4378★
Academics' choices for best curriculum/instruction graduate programs, 2001 ★4380★
Academics' choices for best education policy graduate programs, 2001 ★4381★
Academics' choices for best elementary education graduate programs, 2001 ★4383★
Academics' choices for best secondary education graduate programs, 2001 ★4385★
Academics' choices for best special education graduate programs, 2001 ★4386★

VanderCook College of Music
Most dangerous college campuses in the U.S. ★712★

Vandercoy; David E.
Top pay and benefits for the chief executive and top paid employees at Valparaiso University ★3592★

VanDerhei; Jack L.
Individual authors with the most published pages in *The Journal of Risk and Insurance*, 1987-1996 ★680★

Vanderpoel Humanities
Chicago elementary magnet schools with the lowest acceptance rates, 2000-01 ★4003★

Vanguard University of Southern California
Average faculty salaries for institutions of higher education in California, 2000-01 ★3692★

VanRheenen; Dwayne
Top pay and benefits for the chief executive and top paid employees at Abilene Christian University ★3163★

VanWicklin; John F.
Top pay and benefits for the chief executive and top paid employees at Houghton College ★3341★

Varadarajan; P. Rajan
Authors with the most articles published in the *Journal of Business Research*, 1985 to 1999 ★687★
Highest impact authors in the *Journal of Business Research*, by number of citations in 12 journals, 1985-1999 ★693★

Varian; Hal
Library and information science faculty with the most citations to journal articles, 1993-1998 ★2710★
Library and information science faculty with the most journal articles, 1993-1998 ★2711★

Variations in Relevance Assessments and the Measurements of Retrieval Effectiveness
Journal of the American Society for Information Science's best papers, by citations per year ★2728★

Varieties of Police Behavior: The Management of Law and Order in Eight Communities
Most-cited works in police studies articles/research notes ★2625★

The Variety of Life: A Survey and a Celebration of All the Creatures That Have Ever Lived
Library Journal's most notable biology books, 2000 ★250★

The Variety of Life: The Meaning of Biodiversity
Outstanding science books, 2000 ★291★
Booklist's best science and technology books ★366★

Varisco; Dominic
Top pay and benefits for the chief executive and top paid employees at Salve Regina University ★3489★

Varney; Thomas
Top pay and benefits for the chief executive and top paid employees at Colorado Christian University ★3248★

Varsalona; Jack P.
Top pay and benefits for the chief executive and top paid employees at Wilmington College in Delaware ★3632★

Varsity Student Painters
Most selective internships in the U.S., 2001 ★2610★
Top internships in the U.S. with the highest compensation, 2001 ★2611★

Varvis; Stephen
Top pay and benefits for the chief executive and top paid employees at Fresno Pacific University ★3298★

Vassar College
Private, 4-year undergraduate colleges and universities producing the most Ph.D.'s in the life sciences, 1920-1990 ★192★
Private, 4-year undergraduate colleges and universities producing the most Ph.D.'s in the life sciences, 1981-1990 ★193★
U.S. colleges and universities where students are very politically active ★1001★
U.S. colleges and universities where the general student body smokes marijuana ★1011★
U.S. colleges and universities with a large student body of liberal Democrats ★1017★
U.S. colleges and universities with a primarily non-religious student body ★1021★
U.S. colleges and universities with harmonious race/class interaction ★1026★
U.S. colleges and universities with the most attractive campuses ★1039★
U.S. News & World Report's national liberal arts colleges with the best student/faculty ratios, 2000-01 ★1326★

Private, 4-year undergraduate colleges and universities producing the most Ph.D.s in all fields of study, 1920-1990 ★2027★
Private, 4-year undergraduate colleges and universities producing the most Ph.D.'s in all fields of study, 1981-1990 ★2028★
Private, 4-year undergraduate colleges and universities producing the most Ph.D.'s in all fields of study, 1990 ★2029★
Private, 4-year undergraduate colleges and universities producing the most Ph.D.'s in nonscience fields, 1920-1990 ★2030★
Private, 4-year undergraduate colleges and universities producing the most Ph.D.'s in nonscience fields, 1981-1990 ★2031★
Private, 4-year undergraduate colleges and universities producing the most Ph.D.'s in nonscience fields, 1990 ★2032★
Private, 4-year undergraduate colleges and universities producing the most Ph.D.'s in economics, 1920-1990 ★2211★
Private, 4-year undergraduate colleges and universities producing the most Ph.D.'s in economics, 1981-1990 ★2212★
Private, 4-year undergraduate colleges and universities producing the most Ph.D.'s in English, 1920-1990 ★2449★
Private, 4-year undergraduate colleges and universities producing the most Ph.D.'s in English, 1981-1990 ★2450★
Private, 4-year undergraduate colleges and universities producing the most Ph.D.'s in history, 1920-1990 ★2552★
Private, 4-year undergraduate colleges and universities producing the most Ph.D.'s in history, 1981-1990 ★2553★
Private, 4-year undergraduate colleges and universities producing the most Ph.D.'s in mathematics, 1981-1990 ★2777★
Private, 4-year undergraduate colleges and universities producing the most Ph.D.'s in psychology, 1920-1990 ★3066★
Private, 4-year undergraduate colleges and universities producing the most Ph.D.'s in psychology, 1981-1990 ★3067★
Presidents with the highest pay at Baccalaureate I colleges, 1998-99 ★3159★
Average faculty salaries for institutions of higher education in New York, 2000-01 ★3719★
U.S. liberal arts colleges with the highest paid full professors, 2001 ★3980★
Private, 4-year undergraduate colleges and universities producing the most Ph.D.'s in the sciences, 1981-1990 ★4295★
Private, 4-year undergraduate colleges and universities producing the most Ph.D.'s in anthropology and sociology, 1920-1990 ★4344★
Private, 4-year undergraduate colleges and universities producing the most Ph.D.'s in anthropology and sociology, 1981-1990 ★4345★

Vaughn; Ronald L.
Top pay and benefits for the chief executive and top paid employees at the University of Tampa ★3569★

Vault.com
Top career-related Web sites ★2602★

Vause; W. Gary
Top pay and benefits for the chief executive and top paid employees at Stetson University ★3511★

Veba
Business Week's best companies in Germany ★394★

Veber; Daniel F.
American Chemical Society 2001 award winners (Group 5) ★755★

Veena; Sneh
Top pay and benefits for the chief executive and top paid employees at Heritage College ★3332★

Veler; Richard
Top pay and benefits for the chief executive and top paid employees at Wittenberg University ★3633★

Vellaccio; Frank
Top pay and benefits for the chief executive and top paid employees at College of the Holy Cross ★3247★

Venado Middle School
Outstanding secondary schools in Orange County, California ★4199★

Vending machine repairer
'Blue-collar' jobs considered the least physically demanding ★2241★

Venezuela
Countries of origin for non-U.S. citizens awarded doctorates at U.S. colleges and universities, 1999 ★1901★

Ventura County Community College
Average faculty salaries for institutions of higher education without academic ranks in California, 2000-01 ★3743★

Ventus
Booklist's most recommended science fiction/fantasy books ★232★

Verba, et al.; Sidney
Most frequently downloaded American Political Science Review articles ★3039★

Veritas Software
Business Week's best companies in terms of share-price gain ★409★
Business Week's best performing companies with the greatest decline in earnings growth ★412★
Business Week's best performing companies with the highest 3-year sales performance ★417★
Business Week's best performing companies with the highest 3-year shareholder returns ★418★
Business Week's best performing companies with the lowest net margin, 2000 ★425★
Business Week's best performing companies with the lowest return on equity, 2000 ★426★
Companies with the best two-year total returns since 1998 ★436★
Fast-growing information technology companies, 2000 ★444★
Software companies with the fastest growth, 2000 ★528★

Verizon Communications
Fortune's highest ranked telecommunications companies, 2000 ★499★
Top telecommunications companies in Standard & Poor's 500, 2001 ★559★
Highly recommended public companies for women executives, 2000 ★4453★

Vermont
Mean composite ACT scores by state, 2000 ★895★
Mean math SAT scores by state, 2000 ★900★
Mean verbal SAT scores by state, 2000 ★903★
States allocating the smallest amount of state tax appropriations for higher education, 2000-01 ★1305★
Total doctorate recipients by state, 1999 ★2054★
State grades for affordability of higher education for minority students, 2000 ★2883★
State grades for benefits state receives for educating its minority students, 2000 ★2884★
State grades for completion of higher education by minority students, 2000 ★2885★
State grades for participation of minority students in higher education, 2000 ★2886★
State grades for preparing minority students for higher education, 2000 ★2887★
States with the lowest number of high school graduates, 1999-2000 ★3997★
States with the smallest average class size ★4072★

Vermont; Community College of
Highest undergraduate tuition and fees at public 2-year colleges and universities ★1462★
Undergraduate tuition and fees at colleges and universities in Vermont ★1563★

Vermont Law School
Academics' choices for best environmental law programs, 2001 ★2628★

Vermont Technical College
Undergraduate tuition and fees at colleges and universities in Vermont ★1563★
Average faculty salaries for institutions of higher education in Vermont, 2000-01 ★3734★

Vermont; University of
All-USA College Academic Second Team, 2001 ★3★
NCAA Division I ski teams with the most championships ★135★
Four-year institutions with the most drug referrals reported, 1999 ★706★
Four-year institutions with the most liquor referrals reported, 1999 ★708★
U.S. college campuses with more than 5,000 students reporting murders or manslaughters, 1998 ★729★
U.S. colleges and universities with a primarily non-religious student body ★1021★
State appropriations for Vermont's institutions of higher education, 2000-01 ★1298★
Highest undergraduate tuition and fees at public, 4-year or above colleges and universities ★1463★
Public 4-year institutions with the highest tuition, 2000-01 ★1471★
U.S. News & World Report's national universities with students most in debt, 1999 ★1476★
Undergraduate tuition and fees at colleges and universities in Vermont ★1563★
Average faculty salaries for institutions of higher education in Vermont, 2000-01 ★3734★

Vernon Regional Junior College
Average faculty salaries for institutions of higher education without academic ranks in Texas, 2000-01 ★3766★

Vest; Charles M.
Top pay and benefits for the chief executive and top paid employees at Massachusetts Institute of Technology ★3397★

Vestavia Hills High School
Outstanding secondary schools in Birmingham, Alabama ★4098★

Veteran Administration Medical Center School of Radiology Technology (CA)
U.S. college campuses reporting murders or non-negligent manslaughters, 1999 ★728★

Veterinarian
Jobs with the best outlook scores ★2249★
'White-collar' jobs considered the most physically demanding ★2285★

Veterinarians
  Projected employment growth for selected occupations that require advanced education, 1998-2008 ★2318★
Veterinary Immunology Immunopathology
  Veterinary sciences journals with the greatest impact measure, 1994-98 ★4443★
Veterinary medicine
  Gender breakdown of health sciences doctorate recipients, by subfield, 1999 ★1935★
  Health sciences doctorates awarded at U.S. colleges and universities, by subfield, 1999 ★1944★
Veterinary Microbiology
  Veterinary sciences journals with the greatest impact measure, 1994-98 ★4443★
Veterinary Pathology
  Veterinary sciences journals with the greatest impact measure, 1981-98 ★4442★
Vetter; Bernard
  Top pay and benefits for the chief executive and top paid employees at Loyola University New Orleans ★3381★
Vetter; Michael
  Top pay and benefits for the chief executive and top paid employees at Transylvania University ★3575★
VF
  Fortune's highest ranked apparel companies, 2000 ★448★
Viacom
  Fortune's highest ranked entertainment companies, 2000 ★462★
  Top leisure time industries in Standard & Poor's 500, 2001 ★545★
  Web sites where internet users spend the most time ★2609★
Viad
  Fortune's highest ranked outsourcing services companies, 2000 ★483★
Viant
  Fast-growing information technology companies, 2000 ★444★
Vickers; Joel
  Top pay and benefits for the chief executive and top paid employees at Pfeiffer University ★3439★
Vickers; Jon
  Canada's best performing artists of the 20th century ★74★
Vickers; Nancy
  Top pay and benefits for the chief executive and top paid employees at Bryn Mawr College ★3212★
Victor Valley College
  Lowest undergraduate tuition and fees at public 2-year colleges and universities ★1465★
Victoria; University of
  Best Canadian universities overall, 2000 ★1149★
  Canadian comprehensive universities by alumni support, 2000 ★1153★
  Canadian comprehensive universities by award-winning faculty members, 2000 ★1154★
  Canadian comprehensive universities by class size at the first- and second-year level, 2000 ★1155★
  Canadian comprehensive universities by class size at the third- and forth-year level, 2000 ★1156★
  Canadian comprehensive universities by classes taught by tenured faculty, 2000 ★1157★
  Canadian comprehensive universities by faculty members with Ph.D.'s, 2000 ★1158★
  Canadian comprehensive universities by international graduate students, 2000 ★1159★
  Canadian comprehensive universities by library acquisitions, 2000 ★1160★
  Canadian comprehensive universities by library expenses, 2000 ★1161★
  Canadian comprehensive universities by library holdings per student, 2000 ★1162★
  Canadian comprehensive universities by operating budget per student, 2000 ★1163★
  Canadian comprehensive universities by percentage of operating budget allocated to scholarships, 2000 ★1164★
  Canadian comprehensive universities by percentage of operating budget allocated to student services, 2000 ★1165★
  Canadian comprehensive universities by social science/humanities grants per faculty member, 2000 ★1166★
  Canadian comprehensive universities by students from out of province, 2000 ★1167★
  Canadian comprehensive universities by students winning national awards, 2000 ★1168★
  Canadian comprehensive universities that are the best overall, 2000 ★1169★
  Canadian comprehensive universities that are the most innovative, 2000 ★1170★
  Canadian comprehensive universities with the highest quality, 2000 ★1171★
  Canadian medical/doctoral universities by medical/science grants per faculty member, 2000 ★1183★
  Canadian universities by students with 75% grade averages or higher, 2000 ★1215★
  Canadian universities with the lowest total cost, 2000 ★1218★
  Top Canadian comprehensive universities, 2000 ★1219★
  Top Canadian comprehensive universities by reputation, 2000 ★1220★
Viehmann; Russ
  Top pay and benefits for the chief executive and top paid employees at Webster University ★3608★
Vienna
  Cities with the highest productivity of paper in the discipline of hematology, 1994-96 ★2870★
Vigneault; Gilles
  Canada's best performing artists of the 20th century ★74★
Vignette
  Fast-growing information technology companies, 2000 ★444★
Viking
  Hardcover bestsellers by publishing house, 2000 ★240★
Villa Duchesne School
  Outstanding secondary schools in St. Louis, Missouri-Illinois ★4216★
Villa Joseph Marie High School
  Outstanding secondary schools in Philadelphia, Pennsylvania-New Jersey ★4202★
Villa Park High School, District 88
  Illinois school districts with the highest paid superintendents, 1999-2000 ★3986★
Villa; Vincent
  Top pay and benefits for the chief executive and top paid employees at Southwestern University in Texas ★3505★
Villalobos; Josh
  All-America boys' high school soccer team forwards, 2001 ★166★
Villanova University
  Private, 4-year undergraduate colleges and universities producing the most Ph.D.'s in the life sciences, 1981-1990 ★193★
  U.S. catholic universities with the highest enrollment, 1999 ★864★
  U.S. colleges and universities where intercollegiate sports are popular ★995★
  U.S. colleges and universities where students and the local community have strained relations ★998★
  U.S. colleges and universities where the general student body puts a strong emphasis on athletic events ★1007★
  U.S. colleges and universities with a generally conservative student body ★1014★
  U.S. colleges and universities with a large student body of conservative Republicans ★1016★
  U.S. colleges and universities with an unfavorable surrounding town or city ★1023★
  U.S. colleges and universities with excellent instructors ★1024★
  U.S. colleges and universities with strained race/class interaction ★1029★
  U.S. colleges and universities with the best overall administration ★1033★
  U.S. colleges and universities with the most accessible instructors ★1038★
  U.S. News & World Report's northern regional universities with the best academic reputation scores, 2000-01 ★1415★
  U.S. News & World Report's northern regional universities with the highest average graduation rates, 2000-01 ★1419★
  U.S. News & World Report's northern regional universities with the highest freshmen retention rates, 2000-01 ★1420★
  U.S. News & World Report's northern regional universities with the highest percentage of freshmen in the top 25% of their high school class, 2000-01 ★1421★
  U.S. News & World Report's northern regional universities with the lowest acceptance rates, 2000-01 ★1424★
  U.S. News & World Report's top northern regional universities, 2000-01 ★1425★
  U.S. colleges and universities awarding the most computer and information sciences master's degrees to Asian Americans ★1767★
  U.S. colleges and universities awarding the most physical sciences master's degrees to Asian Americans ★1794★
  Private, 4-year undergraduate colleges and universities producing the most Ph.D.'s in all fields of study, 1981-1990 ★2028★
  Private, 4-year undergraduate colleges and universities producing the most Ph.D.'s in nonscience fields, 1981-1990 ★2031★
  Private, 4-year undergraduate colleges and universities producing the most Ph.D.'s in nonscience fields, 1990 ★2032★
  U.S. master's institutions with the largest number of students studying abroad, 1998-99 ★2513★
  Private, 4-year undergraduate colleges and universities producing the most Ph.D.'s in physics and astronomy, 1920-1990 ★2949★
  Average faculty salaries for institutions of higher education in Pennsylvania, 2000-01 ★3725★
Villette; Charles J.
  Top pay and benefits for the chief executive and top paid employees at College of Saint Benedict ★3245★

Vincennes University
  State appropriations for Indiana's institutions of higher education, 2000-01 ★1267★
  Average faculty salaries for institutions of higher education in Indiana, 2000-01 ★3701★

Vincow; Gershon
  Top pay and benefits for the chief executive and top paid employees at Syracuse University ★3516★

Vineyard Haven Public Library
  Highest Hennen's American Public Library Ratings for libraries serving a population of 2,500 to 4,999 ★2693★

Vineyard Junior High School
  Outstanding secondary schools in Riverside-San Bernardino, California ★4211★

Vinson; James S.
  Top pay and benefits for the chief executive and top paid employees at the University of Evansville ★3543★

Vintage
  Trade paperback bestsellers by publishing house, 2000 ★307★

Viola; Carl
  Top pay and benefits for the chief executive and top paid employees at Fairleigh Dickinson University ★3292★

Virgie Goes to School with Us Boys
  Most notable books for young readers, 2001 ★319★

Virgin Islands; University of the
  Colleges offering the Thurgood Marshall Scholarship Fund ★221★

Virginia
  States with the highest enrollment in public 4-year institutions of higher education ★861★
  Mean composite ACT scores by state, 2000 ★895★
  Mean math SAT scores by state, 2000 ★900★
  Mean verbal SAT scores by state, 2000 ★903★
  States with the highest percentage increase in appropriations for higher education, 2000-01 ★1308★
  Total doctorate recipients by state, 1999 ★2054★
  States with the most law schools ★2668★
  State grades for affordability of higher education for minority students, 2000 ★2883★
  State grades for benefits state receives for educating its minority students, 2000 ★2884★
  State grades for completion of higher education by minority students, 2000 ★2885★
  State grades for participation of minority students in higher education, 2000 ★2886★
  State grades for preparing minority students for higher education, 2000 ★2887★
  States with the highest average enrollment in public secondary schools ★4033★
  States with the highest state support for non need-based financial aid for students, 1999-2000 ★4368★

Virginia, College at Wise; University of
  Average faculty salaries for institutions of higher education in Virginia, 2000-01 ★3735★

Virginia Commonwealth University
  U.S. colleges and universities reporting the most drug related arrests, 1998 ★731★
  Division I NCAA colleges with that graduated none of their African American male basketball players, 1990-91 to 1993-94 ★930★
  State appropriations for Virginia's institutions of higher education, 2000-01 ★1299★

  U.S. News & World Report's national universities with students most in debt, 1999 ★1476★
  U.S. colleges and universities awarding the most communications master's degrees to African Americans ★1763★
  U.S. colleges and universities awarding the most health professions and related sciences first professional degrees to African Americans ★1847★
  U.S. colleges and universities awarding the most biological and life sciences doctorate degrees to Asian Americans ★2083★
  Degrees granted in the ten largest master's journalism and mass communications programs, 1999 ★2757★
  U.S. universities with the highest concentration of papers published in the field of pharmacology, 1995-99 ★2937★
  Institutions with the highest impact in psychiatry research, 1990-98 ★3053★
  U.S. universities with the highest concentration of papers published in the field of psychiatry, 1994-98 ★3061★
  Average faculty salaries for institutions of higher education in Virginia, 2000-01 ★3735★

Virginia Community College System
  Institutions censured by the American Association of University Professors, 2001 ★1067★

Virginia, Curry College; University of
  Academics' choices for best elementary education graduate programs, 2001 ★4383★
  Academics' choices for best secondary education graduate programs, 2001 ★4385★
  Academics' choices for best special education graduate programs, 2001 ★4386★

Virginia, Darden Graduate School of Business Administration; University of
  Annual tuition at *Business Week*'s top business schools, 2000 ★589★
  Average job offers received by graduates from *Business Week*'s top business schools, 1999 ★592★
  Business Week's top business schools, 2000 ★595★
  Business Week's top business schools as selected by corporate recruiters, 2000 ★596★
  Business Week's top business schools as selected by recent MBA graduates, 2000 ★597★
  Business Week's top business schools for finance skills as selected by corporate recruiters, 2000 ★600★
  Business Week's top business schools for general management skills as selected by corporate recruiters, 2000 ★601★
  Business Week's top business schools for marketing skills as selected by corporate recruiters, 2000 ★603★
  Business Week's top business schools for technology skills as selected by corporate recruiters, 2000 ★604★
  Business Week's top business schools with the best placement offices, 2000 ★608★
  Business Week's top business schools with the best teachers, 2000 ★609★
  Business Week's top business schools with the greatest rise in MBA satisfaction, 2000 ★611★
  Business Week's top business schools with the highest percentage of minority enrollment, 2000 ★613★
  Business Week's top business schools with the lowest percentage of international students, 2000 ★615★

  Business Week's top business schools with the most innovative curriculum as selected by corporate recruiters, 2000 ★619★
  Highest pre-MBA salaries for students enrolled in *Business Week*'s top business schools, 1999 ★632★
  Percentage of applicants accepted at *Business Week*'s top business schools, 2000 ★638★
  Percentage of graduates earning over $100,000 from *Business Week*'s top business schools, 1999 ★640★
  Top graduate business schools by reputation, as determined by recruiters, 2001 ★651★
  Academics' choices for best graduate general management programs, 2001 ★666★

Virginia Health Sciences Center; University of
  Top endocrinology hospitals in the U.S., 2000 ★2789★

Virginia Highlands Community College
  Lowest undergraduate tuition and fees at colleges and universities in Virginia ★1565★

Virginia Intermont College
  Average faculty salaries for institutions of higher education in Virginia, 2000-01 ★3735★

Virginia Law Review
  Law journals by citation impact, 1981-96 ★2617★
  Law journals with the greatest impact measure, 1981-98 ★2618★
  Most frequently-cited law reviews and legal periodicals, 1924-1986: a compilation ★2619★
  Most frequently-cited law reviews and legal periodicals, according to *Shepard's Law Review Citations*, 1957-1986 ★2620★

Virginia, McIntire Graduate School of Business Administration; University of
  U.S. News & World Report's undergraduate business programs with the highest academic reputation scores, 2000-01 ★571★

Virginia Military Institute
  State appropriations for Virginia's institutions of higher education, 2000-01 ★1299★
  Average faculty salaries for institutions of higher education in Virginia, 2000-01 ★3735★

Virginia Polytechnic Institute
  U.S. universities with the highest concentration of papers published in the field of materials science, 1995-99 ★4290★

Virginia Polytechnic Institute and State University
  Institutions awarding the most doctorate degrees to African Americans, 1997-98 ★1948★
  Traditionally white institutions awarding the most doctorate degrees to African Americans ★2079★
  U.S. colleges and universities awarding the most doctoral degrees to Hispanic Americans from 1995 to 1999 ★2094★
  U.S. colleges and universities awarding the most doctorate degrees to African Americans ★2095★
  U.S. colleges and universities awarding the most doctorates in education, 1999 ★2101★
  U.S. colleges and universities awarding the most doctorates in professional and other fields, 1999 ★2106★
  U.S. colleges and universities awarding the most education doctorate degrees to African Americans ★2108★
  U.S. universities with the highest concentration of civil engineering papers published, 1994-98 ★2351★

Top aerospace engineering research-doctorate programs as evaluated by the National Research Council ★2376★
Most effective industrial engineering research-doctorate programs as evaluated by the National Research Council ★2412★
Top industrial engineering research-doctorate programs as evaluated by the National Research Council ★2413★

Virginia State University
Colleges offering the Thurgood Marshall Scholarship Fund ★221★
Top college choices for Washington D.C. students ★847★
State appropriations for Virginia's institutions of higher education, 2000-01 ★1299★
Historically black colleges and universities awarding the most master's degrees to African Americans ★1670★
Total baccalaureate English language, literature, and letters degrees awarded to African Americans from U.S. colleges and universities, 1997-98 ★1716★
Total baccalaureate social sciences and history degrees awarded to African Americans from U.S. colleges and universities, 1997-98 ★1741★
U.S. colleges and universities awarding the most biological and life sciences master's degrees to African Americans ★1756★
U.S. colleges and universities awarding the most mathematics master's degrees to African Americans ★1790★
Average faculty salaries for institutions of higher education in Virginia, 2000-01 ★3735★

Virginia Tech
All-USA College Academic First Team, 2001 ★2★
State appropriations for Virginia's institutions of higher education, 2000-01 ★1299★
U.S. institutions awarding the most associate degrees to African Americans in agribusiness and production, 1998 ★1805★
U.S. institutions awarding the most associate degrees to minorities in agribusiness and production, 1998 ★1808★
Academics' choices for best graduate industrial/manufacturing engineering programs, 2001 ★2411★
Average faculty salaries for institutions of higher education in Virginia, 2000-01 ★3735★
Academics' choices for best vocational/technical graduate programs, 2001 ★4387★

Virginia Union University
U.S. colleges and universities with the highest percentage of African Americans enrolled, 1997 ★222★
Historically black colleges and universities awarding the most doctorate degrees to African Americans ★1945★
Institutions awarding the most doctorate degrees to African Americans, 1997-98 ★1948★
U.S. colleges and universities awarding the most doctorate degrees to African Americans ★2095★
U.S. colleges and universities awarding the most doctorate degrees to minorities ★2098★
Average faculty salaries for institutions of higher education in Virginia, 2000-01 ★3735★

Virginia; University of
U.S. universities enrolling the most National Achievement Scholars, 1994 ★9★
U.S. universities enrolling the most National Achievement Scholars, 1996 ★11★

Four-year public institutions enrolling the highest number of students from the District of Columbia, 1998-99 ★855★
U.S. colleges and universities with excellent library facilities ★1025★
Retention rates of African American students at traditionally white institutions, 1997-98 ★1121★
U.S. News & World Report's best public national universities, 2000-01 ★1123★
U.S. News & World Report's national universities with the best freshmen retention rates, 2000-01 ★1128★
U.S. News & World Report's national universities with the best graduation and retention rank, 2000-01 ★1129★
U.S. News & World Report's national universities with the highest graduation rate, 1999 ★1134★
U.S. News & World Report's national universities with the highest percentage of full-time faculty, 2000-01 ★1136★
Institutions receiving the most alumni gifts, 1999-2000 ★1242★
State appropriations for Virginia's institutions of higher education, 2000-01 ★1299★
U.S. universities with the greatest impact in computer science, 1995-99 ★1593★
Total baccalaureate English language, literature, and letters degrees awarded to African Americans from U.S. colleges and universities, 1997-98 ★1716★
Traditionally white institutions awarding the most first professional degrees to African Americans ★1842★
U.S. colleges and universities awarding the most first professional degrees to African Americans ★1843★
U.S. colleges and universities awarding the most health professions and related sciences first professional degrees to African Americans ★1847★
U.S. colleges and universities awarding the most law and legal studies first professional degrees to African Americans ★1852★
U.S. universities with the highest concentration of metallurgy papers published, 1994-98 ★2436★
Most effective English language and literature research-doctorate programs as evaluated by the National Research Council ★2448★
Top English language and literature research-doctorate programs as evaluated by the National Research Council ★2451★
Top French language and literature research-doctorate programs as evaluated by the National Research Council ★2516★
Most effective German language and literature research-doctorate programs as evaluated by the National Research Council ★2527★
Top German language and literature research-doctorate programs as evaluated by the National Research Council ★2528★
College senior's choices for exemplary doctoral-extensive universities ★2531★
Most wired universities, 2000 ★2598★
U.S. universities publishing the most papers in the field of law, 1994-98 ★2623★
Academics' choices for best international law programs, 2001 ★2631★
Academics' choices for best tax law programs, 2001 ★2632★
Acceptance rates at *U.S. News & World Report*'s top 10 law schools, 2001 ★2634★

Graduate employment after graduation percentage for *U.S. News & World Report*'s top 10 law schools, 2001 ★2635★
Graduate employment percentage for *U.S. News & World Report*'s top 10 law schools, 2001 ★2636★
Jurisdiction's overall bar passage rate for *U.S. News & World Report*'s top 10 law schools, 2001 ★2637★
Law schools with the best administrative law faculty, 1999-2000 ★2638★
Law schools with the best commercial law faculty, 1999-2000 ★2641★
Law schools with the best constitutional law (freedom of speech) faculty, 1999-2000 ★2644★
Law schools with the best law and social science plus psychology and sociology faculty, 1999-2000 ★2659★
Law schools with the best legal history faculty, 1999-2000 ★2661★
Law schools with the best Torts (including products liability) faculty, 1999-2000 ★2665★
Law schools with the highest quality, 1999-2000 ★2666★
School's bar passage rate in jurisdiction at *U.S. News & World Report*'s top 10 law schools, 2001 ★2667★
Student-faculty ratios at *U.S. News & World Report*'s top 10 law schools, 2001 ★2669★
Top law schools, 2001 ★2670★
Top law schools by reputation, as determined by academic personnel, 2001 ★2671★
Top law schools by reputation, as determined by lawyers and judges, 2001 ★2672★
Top law school student bodies, 1999-2000 ★2673★
University research libraries in the U.S. and Canada with the largest increases in total expenditures from 1993-94 to 1998-99 ★2708★
Top physiology research-doctorate programs as evaluated by the National Research Council ★3022★
Top religion research-doctorate programs as evaluated by the National Research Council ★3093★
Average faculty salaries for institutions of higher education in Virginia, 2000-01 ★3735★
Public institutions of higher education that pay the highest salaries to female professors, 2000-01 ★3975★
Most effective Spanish and Portuguese language and literature research-doctorate programs as evaluated by the National Research Council ★4357★
Top Spanish and Portuguese language and literature research-doctorate programs as evaluated by the National Research Council ★4358★

Virginia/Washington
States expelling the most students for violating the Gun-Free Schools Act, 1998-99 ★3994★

Virginia Wesleyan College
Average faculty salaries for institutions of higher education in Virginia, 2000-01 ★3735★

Virginia Western Community College
Lowest undergraduate tuition and fees at colleges and universities in Virginia ★1565★

Virginia, Wise; University of
State appropriations for Virginia's institutions of higher education, 2000-01 ★1299★

VIRTUAL

U.S. News & World Report's top public southern regional liberal arts colleges, 2000-01 ★1378★

Virtual Classroom
Top sites for educators ★2605★

The Virtual Library for Information Technology
Top sites for educators ★2605★

Viscione; Jerry A.
Top pay and benefits for the chief executive and top paid employees at Marquette University ★3392★

Viscusi; W. Kip
Authors with the most published pages in impact-weighted insurance journals ★677★

Visible Language
Most cited printing and publishing serials in technical communication journals from 1988 to 1997 ★4422★

Vista Community College
Lowest undergraduate tuition and fees at public 2-year colleges and universities ★1465★
Lowest undergraduate tuition and fees at colleges and universities in California ★1487★

Vista High School
Outstanding secondary schools in San Diego, California ★4220★

Visteon
Top automotive companies in Standard & Poor's 500, 2001 ★530★

Visual impairments
Disabled students served in U.S. public school programs, 1998-99 ★1877★

Visual and performing arts
Top bachelor's degree disciplines for African Americans, 1997-98 ★1672★
Top bachelor's degree disciplines for Asian Americans, 1997-98 ★1673★
Top bachelor's degree disciplines for Hispanic Americans, 1997-98 ★1674★
Top bachelor's degree disciplines for Native Americans, 1997-98 ★1675★
Top bachelor's degree disciplines for non-minorities, 1997-98 ★1676★

Vitell; Scott J.
Authors with the most articles published in the *Journal of Business Research*, 1985 to 1999 ★687★

Viterbo College
Average faculty salaries for institutions of higher education in Wisconsin, 2000-01 ★3738★

Vitesse Semiconductor
Business Week's top companies in terms of market value, 2000 ★429★

Vivendi
Business Week's best companies in France ★393★

Vivian Field Junior High School
Outstanding secondary schools in Dallas, Texas ★4120★

Vocational and adult education
Educational program activities expenditures, 2000 ★3992★

Vocational education
2002 budget request for adult and vocational education ★2227★

Vodafone Airtouch
Business Week's best companies in Britain ★389★
Business Week's top companies worldwide ★433★

Voelker; Cathleen
Top pay and benefits for the chief executive and top paid employees at Franklin and Marshall College ★3296★

Vogel; Frank C.
Top pay and benefits for the chief executive and top paid employees at Beaver College ★3195★

Vogel; Mark A.
Top pay and benefits for the chief executive and top paid employees at the University of Denver ★3540★

Vogel; Robert L.
Top pay and benefits for the chief executive and top paid employees at Wartburg College ★3603★

Vogelstein; Bert
Most-cited biomedical scientists, 1990-97 ★2382★

Vogt; Richard
Top pay and benefits for the chief executive and top paid employees at Nebraska Wesleyan University ★3417★

Voices: Poetry and Art from Around the World
Booklist's most recommended poetry for youths, 2001 ★315★
Most notable books for older readers, 2001 ★318★

Voices of the Shoah: Remembrances of the Holocaust
Outstanding audio selections for young listeners, 2000 ★325★

Voicestream Wireless
Fast-growing information technology companies, 2000 ★444★

Volcano Cowboys: The Rocky Evolution of a Dangerous Science
Library Journal's most notable earth sciences books, 2000 ★257★

Volk; Gregory A.
Top pay and benefits for the chief executive and top paid employees at Lawrence University ★3367★

Volk; Sherry
Top pay and benefits for the chief executive and top paid employees at Dominican University of California ★3270★

Volker Magnet School
Outstanding secondary schools in Kansas City, Missouri-Kansas ★4158★

Volpe; Ronald
Top pay and benefits for the chief executive and top paid employees at Capital University ★3220★

Volt Information Sciences
Fortune's highest ranked temporary help companies, 2000 ★500★

Volunteer State Community College
Lowest undergraduate tuition and fees at colleges and universities in Tennessee ★1559★
Average faculty salaries for institutions of higher education in Tennessee, 2000-01 ★3730★

Volvo
Business Week's best companies in Sweden ★404★

Von Holtzbrinck
Hardcover bestsellers by corporation, 2000 ★239★
Paperback bestsellers by corporation, 2000 ★296★

Von Steuben Metropolitan Science Center
Outstanding urban public high schools in Metro Chicago ★4262★

Voorhees College
U.S. colleges and universities with the highest percentage of African Americans enrolled, 1997 ★222★

Voorhees; J.J.
Most cited authors in dermatology journals, 1981 to 1996 ★1870★

Voss; Todd
Top pay and benefits for the chief executive and top paid employees at Indiana Wesleyan University ★3349★

Vulcan Materials
Fortune's highest ranked building materials and glass companies, 2000 ★451★
Top housing and real estate companies in Standard & Poor's 500, 2001 ★543★

W

Wabash
Average faculty salaries for institutions of higher education in Indiana, 2000-01 ★3701★

Wabash College
U.S. colleges and universities where intramural sports are popular ★997★
U.S. colleges and universities with a large student body of conservative Republicans ★1016★
U.S. colleges and universities with a popular newspaper ★1018★
U.S. colleges and universities with excellent instructors ★1024★
U.S. colleges and universities with the happiest students ★1035★
College freshmen's choices for exemplary liberal arts institutions ★1317★
U.S. News & World Report's best undergraduate fees among national liberal arts colleges by discount tuition, 2000 ★1381★
Highest undergraduate tuition and fees at colleges and universities in Indiana ★1502★

Wabash Valley College
Lowest undergraduate tuition and fees at colleges and universities in Illinois ★1501★

Wachovia
Top recruiters for business administration jobs for 2000-01 master's degree recipients ★652★

Wackenhut
Fortune's highest ranked outsourcing services companies, 2000 ★483★

Wackenhut Corrections
Business Week's top companies in terms of sales, 2000 ★431★

Wagner; Anne Marie
Top pay and benefits for the chief executive and top paid employees at College of Mount St. Joseph ★3244★

Wagner College
Division I NCAA colleges with the highest graduation rates for female basketball players, 1990-91 to 1993-94 ★932★
U.S. News & World Report's northern regional universities with the highest average graduation rates, 2000-01 ★1419★
U.S. News & World Report's northern regional universities with the highest proportion of classes with 20 students of less, 2000-01 ★1423★

Average faculty salaries for institutions of higher education in New York, 2000-01 ★3719★

Wagner; Dajuan
All-America boys' high school basketball 1st team, 2001 ★161★

Wagner; David L.
Top pay and benefits for the chief executive and top paid employees at Northwestern University ★3423★

Wagner; Tracy A.
Top pay and benefits for the chief executive and top paid employees at the University of Dubuque ★3542★

Waiter/waitress
Jobs with the worst income scores ★2261★
Most desirable jobs in travel/food service ★2278★

Waiters and waitresses
Occupations with the largest projected employment growth, 1998-2008 ★2312★
Projected employment growth for selected occupations that require shorter moderate-term on-the-job training, 1998-2008 ★2321★

Waiting for Godot
Top plays of the twentieth century ★4435★

Wajert; Susan C.
Top pay and benefits for the chief executive and top paid employees at College of Mount St. Joseph ★3244★

Wake Forest University
All-USA College Academic Second Team, 2001 ★3★
All-USA College Academic Third Team, 2001 ★4★
Private, 4-year undergraduate colleges and universities producing the most Ph.D.'s in the life sciences, 1981-1990 ★193★
U.S. colleges and universities where intercollegiate sports are popular ★995★
U.S. colleges and universities where students study the most ★1003★
U.S. News & World Report's national universities with the highest financial resources rank, 2000-01 ★1133★
U.S. News & World Report's national universities with the lowest proportion of classes with 50 or more students, 2000-01 ★1142★
Highest undergraduate tuition and fees at colleges and universities in North Carolina ★1539★
U.S. colleges and universities awarding the most communications master's degrees to Asian Americans ★1764★
Private, 4-year undergraduate colleges and universities producing the most Ph.D.'s in all fields of study, 1981-1990 ★2028★
Private, 4-year undergraduate colleges and universities producing the most Ph.D.'s in nonscience fields, 1920-1990 ★2030★
Private, 4-year undergraduate colleges and universities producing the most Ph.D.'s in nonscience fields, 1981-1990 ★2031★
Private, 4-year undergraduate colleges and universities producing the most Ph.D.'s in nonscience fields, 1990 ★2032★
Radcliffe Institute for Advanced Study fellowship recipient in the field of English literature, 2000-01 ★2443★
Private, 4-year undergraduate colleges and universities producing the most Ph.D.'s in English, 1981-1990 ★2450★
Private, 4-year undergraduate colleges and universities producing the most Ph.D.'s in history, 1981-1990 ★2553★
Law schools with the best law and religion (excluding First Amendment issues) faculty, 1999-2000 ★2658★
Academics' choices for best geriatrics programs, 2001 ★2821★
Private, 4-year undergraduate colleges and universities producing the most Ph.D.'s in political science and international relations, 1981-1990 ★3045★
Private, 4-year undergraduate colleges and universities producing the most Ph.D.'s in psychology, 1981-1990 ★3067★
Largest benefit packages awarded to presidents at institutions of higher education, 1998-99 ★3133★
Presidents with the highest pay at Doctoral I and II universities, 1998-99 ★3160★
Average faculty salaries for institutions of higher education in North Carolina, 2000-01 ★3720★

Wake; Sue
Top pay and benefits for the chief executive and top paid employees at Cumberland College ★3260★

Wake Technical Community College
Lowest undergraduate tuition and fees at colleges and universities in North Carolina ★1540★
Average faculty salaries for institutions of higher education without academic ranks in North Carolina, 2000-01 ★3761★

Wal-Mart Stores
Business Week's best companies in terms of sales ★408★
Business Week's best companies in the United States ★411★
Business Week's top companies worldwide ★433★
Fortune's highest ranked general merchandisers, 2000 ★468★
Top discount and fashion retailing companies in Standard & Poor's 500, 2001 ★538★

Walden University
U.S. colleges and universities awarding the most business management and administrative services doctorate degrees to African Americans ★2085★

Waldman; Robert
Top pay and benefits for the chief executive and top paid employees at Bennington College ★3201★

Waldorf College
Average faculty salaries for institutions of higher education in Iowa, 2000-01 ★3702★

Waldstein; Fredric A.
Top pay and benefits for the chief executive and top paid employees at Wartburg College ★3603★

Walford's Guide to Reference Material
Selected new editions and supplements reference books, 2000 ★372★

Walgreen
Fortune's highest ranked food and drug stores, 2000 ★463★
Top health care companies in Standard & Poor's 500, 2001 ★542★

Walker; Albertina
Most influential African Americans in religion ★3091★

Walker; Alice
Most influential African Americans in the arts ★78★
Favorite African American authors ★237★

Walker; Homer
Top pay and benefits for the chief executive and top paid employees at Worcester Polytechnic Institute ★3636★

Walker; Jerald
Top pay and benefits for the chief executive and top paid employees at Oklahoma City University ★3431★

Walker; John
Most-cited scholars in *Australian and New Zealand Journal of Criminology* ★1636★

Walker; Joyce
Division I women's career high scorers ★129★

Walker; L.E.
Most cited authors in the journal *Violence and Victims*, 1990 to 1995 ★1632★

Walker; Madame C.J.
Most influential African Americans in business ★526★

Walker; Sally J.
Top pay and benefits for the chief executive and top paid employees at Albion College ★3167★

Walker; Samuel
Most-cited scholars in police studies articles/research notes ★2624★

Walker; W. Earl
Top pay and benefits for the chief executive and top paid employees at Rockhurst University ★3464★

Walker; William
Top pay and benefits for the chief executive and top paid employees at Chestnut Hill College ★3231★

Walkin' the Dog
Library Journal's best fiction audiobooks, 2000 ★241★

Walking with Dinosaurs
Most notable videos for adults, 2001 ★2891★

Walkowitz; Judy
Highly acknowledged individuals in the field of women's studies, 1975-94 ★4466★

Wall; Jeff
Best living artists ★73★

Wall; Robert E.
Top pay and benefits for the chief executive and top paid employees at Fairfield University ★3291★

The Wall Street Journal
Most selective internships in the U.S., 2001 ★2610★
Top internships in the U.S. with the highest compensation, 2001 ★2611★
Most cited general works serials in technical communication journals from 1988 to 1997 ★4419★

Wall Street Music
Most selective internships in the U.S., 2001 ★2610★

Walla Walla College
Highest undergraduate tuition and fees at colleges and universities in Washington ★1566★
Average faculty salaries for institutions of higher education in Washington, 2000-01 ★3736★

Wallace; Andrew G.
Top pay and benefits for the chief executive and top paid employees at Dartmouth College ★3263★

Wallace Community College
Lowest undergraduate tuition and fees at colleges and universities in Alabama ★1480★

Wallace Computer Services
Fortune's highest ranked printing companies, 2000 ★487★

Wallace; Dana
All-USA College Academic Second Team, 2001 ★3★

Wallace; Jon
Top pay and benefits for the chief executive and top paid employees at Azusa Pacific University ★3187★

Wallace; Keith
Top pay and benefits for the chief executive and top paid employees at the Maharishi University of Management ★3533★

Wallace State Community College
Lowest undergraduate tuition and fees at colleges and universities in Alabama ★1480★

Wallace's Bookstores
Contractors managing the most college bookstores, 1999 ★846★

Waller Elementary School
All-USA Teacher Teams, First Team, 2000 ★4399★

Wallerstein; I.
Most cited authors in the journal *Social Justice*, 1990 to 1995 ★1631★

Walnut High School
Outstanding secondary schools in Los Angeles-Long Beach, California ★4167★

Walser; Joseph D.
Top pay and benefits for the chief executive and top paid employees at Alma College ★3171★

Walsh; Diana Chapman
Top pay and benefits for the chief executive and top paid employees at Wellesley College ★3609★

Walsh Elementary School
Illinois elementary schools chosen to be 'demonstration sites' for struggling schools ★4006★

Walsh University
Average faculty salaries for institutions of higher education in Ohio, 2000-01 ★3722★

Walstad; William B.
Individuals producing the most economic education research articles, 1963-1990 ★2166★

Walt Disney
Fortune's highest ranked entertainment companies, 2000 ★462★
Top publishing and broadcasting companies in Standard & Poor's 500, 2001 ★553★
Web sites where internet users spend the most time ★2609★

Walter; Jane
Top pay and benefits for the chief executive and top paid employees at Notre Dame College in New Hampshire ★3425★

Walter Payton College Prep
Admissions to college prep schools in Chicago that are the toughest to get into, 2001 ★4001★
College prep schools in Chicago that are the toughest to get into ★4005★

Walter R. Sundling Junior High School
Outstanding secondary schools in Chicago, Illinois ★4110★

Walters; Cynthia A.
Top pay and benefits for the chief executive and top paid employees at John F. Kennedy University ★3354★

Walters State Community College
Lowest undergraduate tuition and fees at colleges and universities in Tennessee ★1559★
Average faculty salaries for institutions of higher education in Tennessee, 2000-01 ★3730★

Walters; William B.
American Chemical Society 2001 award winners (Group 5) ★755★

Walthall; Howard P.
Top pay and benefits for the chief executive and top paid employees at Samford University ★3490★

Walton High School
Outstanding suburban public high schools in Metro Atlanta ★4254★

Walwer; Frank K.
Top pay and benefits for the chief executive and top paid employees at Texas Wesleyan University ★3519★

Walzer; Judith
Top pay and benefits for the chief executive and top paid employees at New School University ★3418★

Wampler; Dale L.
Top pay and benefits for the chief executive and top paid employees at Juniata College ★3357★

The Wanderer
Christopher Awards winners for youth literature, 2000 ★316★
Most notable books for older readers, 2001 ★318★
Most notable fiction books for young adults, 2001 ★322★
Outstanding books for older readers, 2000 ★327★
Outstanding children's fiction books, 2000 ★329★
Publishers Weekly Off-the-Cuff Awards winner for favorite novel of the year, 2000 ★346★

Wang; Ming X.
Top pay and benefits for the chief executive and top paid employees at Vanderbilt University ★3593★

Wang; Yun Chow
Top pay and benefits for the chief executive and top paid employees at the Catholic University of America ★3522★

Wantagh High School
Outstanding secondary schools in Long Island, New York ★4165★

Wantagh Middle School
Outstanding secondary schools in Long Island, New York ★4165★

Warburg Theological Seminary
Average faculty salaries for institutions of higher education in Iowa, 2000-01 ★3702★

Warch; Richard
Top pay and benefits for the chief executive and top paid employees at Lawrence University ★3367★

Ward; John
Top pay and benefits for the chief executive and top paid employees at Centre College ★3227★

Wardrop; Maribeth
Top pay and benefits for the chief executive and top paid employees at Aquinas College in Michigan ★3179★

Ware; Mary
Top pay and benefits for the chief executive and top paid employees at William Carey College ★3629★

Ware; Matt
All-American boy's high school football all-purpose players, 2000 ★179★

Warhol; Andy
Highly influential artists of the 20th century ★76★

Warnaco Group
Fortune's highest ranked apparel companies, 2000 ★448★
Fortune's least admired companies for employee talent ★506★
Fortune's least admired companies for quality of management ★510★
Fortune's least admired companies for use of corporate assets ★513★
Top women-owned companies ★4460★
Top women-owned companies with the most employees ★4462★

Warner
Hardcover bestsellers by publishing house, 2000 ★240★
Mass market paperback bestsellers by publishing house, 2000 ★283★
Trade paperback bestsellers by publishing house, 2000 ★307★

Warner; Glenn "Pop"
Division I-A all-time coaching victories ★126★

Warner Pacific College
Highest undergraduate tuition and fees at colleges and universities in Oregon ★1547★
Average faculty salaries for institutions of higher education in Oregon, 2000-01 ★3724★

Warner; Rev. Douglas W.
Top pay and benefits for the chief executive and top paid employees at Amber University ★3172★

Warner Robins High School
Outstanding secondary schools in Macon, Georgia ★4172★

Warren; Charles O.
Top pay and benefits for the chief executive and top paid employees at Lynchburg College ★3384★

Warren County Community College
Lowest undergraduate tuition and fees at colleges and universities in New Jersey ★1534★

Warren Easton Fundamental High School
Outstanding secondary schools in New Orleans, Louisiana ★4190★

Warren; Jerry L.
Top pay and benefits for the chief executive and top paid employees at Belmont University ★3198★

Warren; Robert R.
Top pay and benefits for the chief executive and top paid employees at Lenoir-Rhyne College ★3369★

Warren Wilson College
U.S. colleges and universities where the general student body smokes marijuana ★1011★
U.S. colleges and universities with a generally liberal student body ★1015★
U.S. colleges and universities with the best financial aid programs ★1030★
U.S. News & World Report's southern regional liberal arts colleges with the best student/faculty ratios, 2000-01 ★1368★
U.S. News & World Report's southern regional liberal arts colleges with the highest percentage of full-time faculty, 2000-01 ★1374★

U.S. News & World Report's southern regional liberal arts colleges with the lowest acceptance rates, 2000-01 ★1377★
Highest undergraduate tuition and fees at colleges and universities in North Carolina ★1539★
Average faculty salaries for institutions of higher education in North Carolina, 2000-01 ★3720★

The Wars
Canada's best fiction selections of the 20th century ★233★

Wartburg College
Highest undergraduate tuition and fees at colleges and universities in Iowa ★1504★
Average faculty salaries for institutions of higher education in Iowa, 2000-01 ★3702★

Wasan; Darsh T.
Top pay and benefits for the chief executive and top paid employees at Illinois Institute of Technology ★3346★

Washburn University
State appropriations for Kansas institutions of higher education, 2000-01 ★1269★
U.S. News & World Report's top public midwestern regional universities, 2000-01 ★1412★
Law library web sites, by visibility ★2687★
Average faculty salaries for institutions of higher education in Kansas, 2000-01 ★3703★

Washburne Junior High
Illinois schools with the highest 7th grade science scores ★17★

Washington
People for the American Way's list of states with the most challenges to library and school books, 1982-1992 ★750★
Mean composite ACT scores by state, 2000 ★895★
Mean math SAT scores by state, 2000 ★900★
Mean verbal SAT scores by state, 2000 ★903★
Average class size at colleges and universities in the U.S., by state ★1064★
Total doctorate recipients by state, 1999 ★2054★
U.S. cities with the highest number of high-tech employees, 1998 ★2284★
Hispanic American enrollment at Hispanic-serving institutions of higher education, by state, 1997 ★2547★
U.S. cities with the most wired households, 2001 ★2606★
Average Hennen's American Public Library Ratings, by state ★2690★
State grades for affordability of higher education for minority students, 2000 ★2883★
State grades for benefits state receives for educating its minority students, 2000 ★2884★
State grades for completion of higher education by minority students, 2000 ★2885★
State grades for participation of minority students in higher education, 2000 ★2886★
State grades for preparing minority students for higher education, 2000 ★2887★
States with the largest average class size ★4071★

Washington; Booker T.
Most influential African Americans in education ★2216★

Washington, Bothell; University of
Average faculty salaries for institutions of higher education in Washington, 2000-01 ★3736★

Washington Carver; George
Most influential African Americans in medicine and science ★2879★

Washington-Centerville Public Library
Highest Hennen's American Public Library Ratings for libraries serving a population of 25,000 to 49,999 ★2696★

Washington College
Highest undergraduate tuition and fees at colleges and universities in Maryland ★1514★
Average faculty salaries for institutions of higher education in Maryland, 2000-01 ★3707★

Washington County Technical College
Lowest undergraduate tuition and fees at colleges and universities in Maine ★1513★

Washington, DC
American cities with the highest percentage of people with Internet access ★2572★
America's most wired cities, 2001 ★2573★
America's most wired cities with the highest domain density, 2001 ★2574★
Cities with the highest online spending per Internet user ★2576★
Cities with the highest percentage of adults using the Internet at home ★2577★
Cities with the most domains per 1,000 firms ★2579★
U.S. market areas with the highest percentage of adults having internet access ★2607★
States with the highest per capita income ★3123★
U.S. states with the highest percentage of births to teenagers who were already mothers ★4433★

Washington Episcopal School
Outstanding secondary schools in Washington, District of Columbia-Maryland-Virginia-West Virginia ★4249★

Washington; Harold
Most influential African Americans in politics and civil rights ★3040★

Washington High School
Outstanding secondary schools in Cedar Rapids, Iowa ★4104★

Washington and Jefferson College
Average faculty salaries for institutions of higher education in Pennsylvania, 2000-01 ★3725★

Washington and Lee University
U.S. colleges and universities where fraternities and sororities are popular ★993★
U.S. colleges and universities without a diverse student body ★1046★
U.S. News & World Report's national liberal arts colleges with the best faculty resources rank, 2000-01 ★1321★
U.S. News & World Report's national liberal arts colleges with the best student/faculty ratios, 2000-01 ★1326★
U.S. News & World Report's national liberal arts colleges with the highest alumni giving rank, 2000-01 ★1329★
U.S. News & World Report's national liberal arts colleges with the highest percentage of alumni support, 2000-01 ★1331★
U.S. News & World Report's national liberal arts colleges with the highest percentage of full-time faculty, 2000-01 ★1333★
Fiske Guide's best buys for private colleges and universities, 2001 ★1459★
Highest undergraduate tuition and fees at colleges and universities in Virginia ★1564★

Average faculty salaries for institutions of higher education in Virginia, 2000-01 ★3735★

Washington Medical Center; University of
Top hospitals in the U.S., 2000 ★2793★
Top orthopedics hospitals in the U.S., 2000 ★2797★
Top rehabilitation hospitals in the U.S., 2000 ★2801★

Washington Mutual
Business Week's best performing companies with the highest 1-year shareholder returns ★415★
Fortune's highest ranked mortgage finance companies, 2000 ★479★
Top nonbank financial companies in Standard & Poor's 500, 2001 ★550★
Top public companies for women executives, 2000 ★4457★
Top public companies with the highest percentage of women employees, 2000 ★4459★

Washington Office on Latin America
Most selective internships in the U.S., 2001 ★2610★

The Washington Post
Fortune's highest ranked publishing companies, 2000 ★489★
Most selective internships in the U.S., 2001 ★2610★
Top internships in the U.S. with the highest compensation, 2001 ★2611★
Top internships in the U.S., 2001 ★2612★

Washington Program in Biostatistics; University of
Most effective statistics and biostatistics research-doctorate programs as evaluated by the National Research Council ★2780★
Top statistics and biostatistics research-doctorate programs as evaluated by the National Research Council ★2782★

Washington Program in Statistics; University of
Most effective statistics and biostatistics research-doctorate programs as evaluated by the National Research Council ★2780★
Top statistics and biostatistics research-doctorate programs as evaluated by the National Research Council ★2782★

Washington, Seattle; University of
Top business schools for within-discipline research performance in management science, 1986-1998 ★647★
Top business schools for within-discipline research performance in accounting, 1986-1998 ★660★
Top Ph.D.-granting departments of geography from 1925-1982 ★2521★
Law schools with the best environmental law faculty, 1999-2000 ★2650★
Average faculty salaries for institutions of higher education in Washington, 2000-01 ★3736★

Washington State University
Longest field goals in college football ★158★
U.S. college campuses with more than 5,000 students reporting murders or manslaughters, 1998 ★729★
U.S. colleges and universities with the largest numerical increases in alcohol arrests, 1998 ★733★
U.S. colleges and universities with the largest numerical increases in weapons arrests, 1998 ★735★
U.S. colleges and universities with the worst financial aid programs ★1042★

WASHINGTON

State appropriations for Washington's institutions of higher education, 2000-01 ★1300★

Total baccalaureate biology/life sciences degrees awarded to Native Americans from U.S. colleges and universities, 1997-98 ★1682★

U.S. universities with the highest concentration of metallurgy papers published, 1994-98 ★2436★

Most wired universities, 2000 ★2598★

Women faculty in Ph.D. physics departments at U.S. institutions, 1998 ★2981★

Average faculty salaries for institutions of higher education in Washington, 2000-01 ★3736★

U.S. universities with the greatest impact in veterinary medicine, 1995-99 ★4440★

U.S. universities with the highest concentration of papers published in the field of veterinary medicine, 1995-99 ★4441★

Washington, Tacoma; University of

Average faculty salaries for institutions of higher education in Washington, 2000-01 ★3736★

Washington University

Most effective neurosciences research-doctorate programs as evaluated by the National Research Council ★200★

Top ecology, evolution, and behavior research-doctorate programs as evaluated by the National Research Council ★201★

Top neurosciences research-doctorate programs as evaluated by the National Research Council ★202★

Most effective cell and developmental biology research-doctorate programs as evaluated by the National Research Council ★206★

Top biochemistry and molecular biology research-doctorate programs as evaluated by the National Research Council ★209★

Top cell and developmental biology research-doctorate programs as evaluated by the National Research Council ★210★

U.S. colleges and universities with the best food service program ★1031★

Highest undergraduate tuition and fees at colleges and universities in Missouri ★1524★

U.S. colleges and universities awarding the most biological and life sciences master's degrees to Asian Americans ★1757★

U.S. colleges and universities awarding the most physical sciences master's degrees to African Americans ★1793★

U.S. colleges and universities awarding the most biological and life sciences doctorate degrees to Asian Americans ★2083★

Most effective German language and literature research-doctorate programs as evaluated by the National Research Council ★2527★

Top German language and literature research-doctorate programs as evaluated by the National Research Council ★2528★

U.S. universities with the greatest impact in psychiatry, 1995-99 ★3060★

Washington University in St. Louis

U.S. News & World Report's national universities with the highest financial resources rank, 2000-01 ★1133★

U.S. News & World Report's national universities with the highest proportion of classes with less than 20 students, 2000-01 ★1138★

Washington University, John M. Olin School of Business

Business Week's top business schools as selected by recent MBA graduates, 2000 ★597★

Business Week's top business schools best at responding to student concerns, 2000 ★598★

Business Week's top business schools with the best teachers, 2000 ★609★

Business Week's top business schools with the greatest rise in MBA satisfaction, 2000 ★611★

Business Week's top business schools with the highest percentage of international students, 2000 ★612★

Business Week's top business schools with the lowest percentage of women enrollees, 2000 ★617★

Lowest post-MBA salaries for students enrolled in *Business Week*'s top business schools, 1999 ★634★

Lowest pre-MBA salaries for students enrolled in *Business Week*'s top business schools, 1999 ★635★

Washington University (MO)

Colleges with the highest number of freshman Merit Scholars, 2000 ★5★

2000 endowment values of the 'wealthiest' U.S. universities ★1230★

2001 mid-year endowment values of the 'wealthiest' U.S. universities ★1234★

Colleges and universities with the largest endowments, 2000 ★1237★

Endowment values for the wealthiest U.S. universities, 2000 ★1240★

University research libraries in the U.S. and Canada with the largest increases in total expenditures from 1993-94 to 1998-99 ★2708★

Academics' choices for best drug and alcohol abuse programs, 2001 ★2819★

Academics' choices for best internal medicine programs, 2001 ★2822★

Academics' choices for best pediatrics programs, 2001 ★2823★

Academics' choices for best women's health medical programs, 2001 ★2825★

Acceptance rates for *U.S. News & World Report*'s top 10 research-oriented medical schools, 2001 ★2827★

Average MCAT scores at *U.S. News & World Report*'s top 10 research-oriented medical schools, 2001 ★2836★

Average undergraduate GPA at *U.S. News & World Report*'s top 10 research-oriented medical schools, 2001 ★2838★

Faculty-student ratios at *U.S. News & World Report*'s top 10 research-oriented medical schools, 2001 ★2842★

NIH research grants for *U.S. News & World Report*'s top 10 research-oriented medical schools, 2001 ★2845★

Out-of-state tuition and fees for *U.S. News & World Report*'s top 10 research-oriented medical schools, 2001 ★2847★

Top primary-care medical schools by student selectivity rank, 2001 ★2858★

Top research-oriented medical schools, 2001 ★2859★

Top research-oriented medical schools by reputation, as determined by academic personnel, 2001 ★2860★

Top research-oriented medical schools by reputation, as determined by intern/residency directors, 2001 ★2861★

Top research-oriented medical schools by student selectivity, 2001 ★2862★

Institutions receiving the most federal research and development expenditures, 1999 ★3105★

Average faculty salaries for institutions of higher education in Missouri, 2000-01 ★3712★

Washington (WA); University of

Most effective ecology, evolution, and behavior research-doctorate programs as evaluated by the National Research Council ★199★

Top neurosciences research-doctorate programs as evaluated by the National Research Council ★202★

Most effective cell and developmental biology research-doctorate programs as evaluated by the National Research Council ★206★

Four-year institutions with the most drug arrests reported, 1999 ★705★

Institutions with the most full-time Hispanic American faculty ★923★

U.S. colleges and universities with the most full-time Hispanic American faculty ★925★

U.S. colleges and universities that devote the least course time to discussion ★989★

U.S. colleges and universities with the worst on-campus housing facilities ★1044★

U.S. News & World Report's national universities with the highest acceptance rates, 2000-01 ★1131★

U.S. News & World Report's national universities with the lowest graduation rates, 1999 ★1141★

Institutions receiving the most corporate gifts, 1999-2000 ★1243★

State appropriations for Washington's institutions of higher education, 2000-01 ★1300★

U.S. News & World Report's national universities with students least in debt, 1999 ★1475★

Top comparative literature research-doctorate programs as evaluated by the National Research Council ★1588★

Most effective computer science research-doctorate programs as evaluated by the National Research Council ★1594★

Top computer science research-doctorate programs as evaluated by the National Research Council ★1597★

Total baccalaureate biology/life sciences degrees awarded to Asian Americans from U.S. colleges and universities, 1997-98 ★1680★

Total baccalaureate biology/life sciences degrees awarded to Native Americans from U.S. colleges and universities, 1997-98 ★1682★

Total baccalaureate business management and administrative services degrees awarded to Native Americans from U.S. colleges and universities, 1997-98 ★1686★

Total baccalaureate communications degrees awarded to Asian Americans from U.S. colleges and universities, 1997-98 ★1688★

Total baccalaureate degrees awarded to Asian Americans from U.S. colleges and universities, 1997-98 ★1702★

Total baccalaureate English language, literature, and letters degrees awarded to Asian Americans from U.S. colleges and universities, 1997-98 ★1717★

Total baccalaureate English language, literature, and letters degrees awarded to Native Americans from U.S. colleges and universities, 1997-98 ★1719★

Total baccalaureate health professions and related sciences degrees awarded to Native Americans from U.S. colleges and universities, 1997-98 ★1724★

Total baccalaureate mathematics degrees awarded to Asian Americans from U.S. colleges and universities, 1997-98 ★1730★

Total baccalaureate psychology degrees awarded to Asian Americans from U.S. colleges and universities, 1997-98 ★1738★
Total baccalaureate psychology degrees awarded to Native Americans from U.S. colleges and universities, 1997-98 ★1740★
Total baccalaureate social sciences and history degrees awarded to Asian Americans from U.S. colleges and universities, 1997-98 ★1742★
Total baccalaureate social sciences and history degrees awarded to Native Americans from U.S. colleges and universities, 1997-98 ★1744★
U.S. colleges and universities awarding the most health professions and related sciences master's degrees to Asian Americans ★1778★
U.S. colleges and universities awarding the most health professions and related sciences master's degrees to Native Americans ★1780★
U.S. colleges and universities awarding the most master's degrees to Native Americans ★1789★
U.S. colleges and universities awarding the most physical sciences master's degrees to Asian Americans ★1794★
U.S. institutions awarding the most baccalaureate degrees to minorities in ethnic/cultural studies, 1997-98 ★1821★
U.S. colleges and universities awarding the most first professional degrees to Native Americans ★1846★
U.S. colleges and universities awarding the most health professions and related sciences first professional degrees to Native Americans ★1851★
U.S. colleges and universities awarding the most law and legal studies first professional degrees to Native Americans ★1855★
U.S. universities publishing the most papers in the field of dentistry/oral surgery and medicine, 1995-99 ★1865★
U.S. universities with the greatest impact in dentistry/oral surgery and medicine, 1995-99 ★1867★
U.S. universities with the greatest impact in dermatology, 1994-98 ★1875★
U.S. universities with the greatest impact in dermatology, 1995-99 ★1876★
U.S. colleges and universities awarding the most doctoral degrees to American Indians and Alaskan Natives from 1995 to 1999 ★2092★
U.S. colleges and universities awarding the most doctorate degrees to Asian Americans ★2096★
U.S. colleges and universities awarding the most doctorates in life sciences, 1999 ★2104★
U.S. colleges and universities awarding the most doctorates in physical sciences, mathematics, and computer sciences, 1999 ★2105★
U.S. colleges and universities awarding the most education doctorate degrees to Asian Americans ★2109★
U.S. colleges and universities awarding the most health professions and related sciences doctorate degrees to Asian Americans ★2115★
U.S. colleges and universities awarding the most health professions and related sciences doctorate degrees to Hispanic Americans ★2116★
U.S. colleges and universities awarding the most physical sciences doctorate degrees to Asian Americans ★2119★
Top oceanography research-doctorate programs as evaluated by the National Research Council ★2153★
Academics' choices for best graduate bioengineering/biomedical engineering programs, 2001 ★2381★
Most effective biomedical engineering research-doctorate programs as evaluated by the National Research Council ★2383★
Top biomedical engineering research-doctorate programs as evaluated by the National Research Council ★2384★
Top civil engineering research-doctorate programs as evaluated by the National Research Council ★2396★
Academics' choices for best graduate computer engineering programs, 2001 ★2399★
Faculty's scholarly reputation in the Ph.D.-granting departments of geography, 1925-1982 ★2518★
Most effective geography research-doctorate programs as evaluated by the National Research Council ★2519★
Top geography research-doctorate programs as evaluated by the National Research Council ★2520★
Top German language and literature research-doctorate programs as evaluated by the National Research Council ★2528★
Top university research libraries in the U.S. and Canada, 1998-99 ★2706★
Library and information science programs with the most citations to journal articles, 1993-1998 ★2712★
Library and information science programs with the most per capita citations to journal articles, 1993-1998 ★2715★
Academics' choices for best AIDS programs, 2001 ★2818★
Academics' choices for best family medicine programs, 2001 ★2820★
Academics' choices for best geriatrics programs, 2001 ★2821★
Academics' choices for best internal medicine programs, 2001 ★2822★
Academics' choices for best pediatrics programs, 2001 ★2823★
Academics' choices for best rural medicine programs, 2001 ★2824★
Academics' choices for best women's health medical programs, 2001 ★2825★
Acceptance rates for *U.S. News & World Report*'s top 10 primary-care medical schools, 2001 ★2826★
Average MCAT scores at *U.S. News & World Report*'s top 10 primary-care medical schools, 2001 ★2835★
Average undergraduate GPA at *U.S. News & World Report*'s top 10 primary-care medical schools, 2001 ★2837★
Faculty-student ratios at *U.S. News & World Report*'s top 10 primary-care medical schools, 2001 ★2841★
Out-of-state tuition and fees at *U.S. News & World Report*'s top 10 primary-care medical schools, 2001 ★2846★
Percentage of graduates entering *U.S. News & World Report*'s top 10 primary-care medical schools, 2001 ★2848★
Top primary-care medical schools, 2001 ★2856★
Top primary-care medical schools by reputation, as determined by academic personnel, 2001 ★2857★
Top research-oriented medical schools by reputation, as determined by academic personnel, 2001 ★2860★
Most effective pharmacology research-doctorate programs as evaluated by the National Research Council ★2938★
Top pharmacology research-doctorate programs as evaluated by the National Research Council ★2939★
Top physics research-doctorate programs as evaluated by the National Research Council ★3015★
Most effective physiology research-doctorate programs as evaluated by the National Research Council ★3021★
Top physiology research-doctorate programs as evaluated by the National Research Council ★3022★
Top psychology research-doctorate programs as evaluated by the National Research Council ★3068★
U.S. universities spending the most on research and development, 1998 ★3104★
Institutions receiving the most federal research and development expenditures, 1999 ★3105★
Institutions receiving the largest Energy Department research grants, 2000 ★3111★
U.S. universities with the highest relative citation impact, 1993-97 ★4291★
Most effective sociology research-doctorate programs as evaluated by the National Research Council ★4352★
Top sociology research-doctorate programs as evaluated by the National Research Council ★4354★
Academics' choices for best special education graduate programs, 2001 ★4386★

Wasicko; Mark
Top pay and benefits for the chief executive and top paid employees at Aurora University ★3183★

Waste Management
Fortune's highest ranked waste management companies, 2000 ★504★
Fortune's most admired companies for social responsibility ★520★

Watchung Hills Regional High School
Outstanding secondary schools in Middlesex-Somerset-Hunterdon, New Jersey ★4179★

Water polo
Fastest growing women's collegiate athletics teams ★131★

Water supply and sanitary services
Employment growth percentages for selected industries, 1998-2000 ★2294★

Water: The Fate of Our Most Precious Resource
Library Journal's most notable natural history books, 2000 ★269★

Water Torture, The Barking Mouse, and Other Tales of Wonder
Most notable children's recordings, 2001 ★320★

Waterloo; University of
Best Canadian universities for producing leaders of tomorrow, 2000 ★1148★
Best Canadian universities overall, 2000 ★1149★
Best Canadian universities that are the most innovative, 2000 ★1150★

Best Canadian universities with the highest quality, 2000 ★1151★
Canadian comprehensive universities best at producing leaders of tomorrow, 2000 ★1152★
Canadian comprehensive universities by alumni support, 2000 ★1153★
Canadian comprehensive universities by award-winning faculty members, 2000 ★1154★
Canadian comprehensive universities by class size at the first- and second-year level, 2000 ★1155★
Canadian comprehensive universities by class size at the third- and forth-year level, 2000 ★1156★
Canadian comprehensive universities by classes taught by tenured faculty, 2000 ★1157★
Canadian comprehensive universities by faculty members with Ph.D.'s, 2000 ★1158★
Canadian comprehensive universities by international graduate students, 2000 ★1159★
Canadian comprehensive universities by library acquisitions, 2000 ★1160★
Canadian comprehensive universities by library expenses, 2000 ★1161★
Canadian comprehensive universities by library holdings per student, 2000 ★1162★
Canadian comprehensive universities by operating budget per student, 2000 ★1163★
Canadian comprehensive universities by percentage of operating budget allocated to scholarships, 2000 ★1164★
Canadian comprehensive universities by percentage of operating budget allocated to student services, 2000 ★1165★
Canadian comprehensive universities by social science/humanities grants per faculty member, 2000 ★1166★
Canadian comprehensive universities by students from out of province, 2000 ★1167★
Canadian comprehensive universities by students winning national awards, 2000 ★1168★
Canadian comprehensive universities that are the best overall, 2000 ★1169★
Canadian comprehensive universities that are the most innovative, 2000 ★1170★
Canadian comprehensive universities with the highest quality, 2000 ★1171★
Canadian medical/doctoral universities by medical/science grants per faculty member, 2000 ★1183★
Canadian universities by average entering grade, 2000 ★1213★
Canadian universities by students with 75% grade averages or higher, 2000 ★1215★
Canadian universities with the highest total cost, 2000 ★1217★
Top Canadian comprehensive universities, 2000 ★1219★
Top Canadian comprehensive universities by reputation, 2000 ★1220★
Canadian universities producing the most-cited papers in the field of computer science, 1992-96 ★1589★
University research libraries in the U.S. and Canada with the largest decreases in total expenditures from 1993-94 to 1998-99 ★2707★

Watkins III; Millard J.
Top pay and benefits for the chief executive and top paid employees at Howard University ★3343★

Watkins; Levi
All-America boys' high school basketball 4th team, 2001 ★164★

Watson; Jeanie
Top pay and benefits for the chief executive and top paid employees at Nebraska Wesleyan University ★3417★

Watson; Perry
Top pay and benefits for the chief executive and top paid employees at the University of Detroit Mercy ★3541★

Watson; Tommy G.
Top pay and benefits for the chief executive and top paid employees at the University of the South ★3572★

Watts; Glenn
Top pay and benefits for the chief executive and top paid employees at Antioch University ★3178★

Watts; Michael W.
Individuals producing the most economic education research articles, 1963-1990 ★2166★

Waubonsee Community College
Fall enrollment at Chicago-area public community colleges, by minority percentages, 1999 ★867★

Waxahachie High School
Outstanding suburban public high schools in Metro Dallas-Ft. Worth ★4257★

The Way Things Work Kit
Publishers Weekly Off-the-Cuff Awards winners for best activity book/kit, 2000 ★360★

Wayne Community College
Average faculty salaries for institutions of higher education without academic ranks in North Carolina, 2000-01 ★3761★

Wayne County Community College
Average faculty salaries for institutions of higher education without academic ranks in Michigan, 2000-01 ★3752★

Wayne State College
State appropriations for Nebraska's institutions of higher education, 2000-01 ★1280★
Average faculty salaries for institutions of higher education in Nebraska, 2000-01 ★3714★

Wayne State University
U.S. college campuses with more than 5,000 students reporting murders or manslaughters, 1998 ★729★
Winner of the American Chemical Society's Arthur C. Cope Awards, 2001 ★795★
Division II NCAA colleges with the lowest graduation rates for football players, 1993-94 ★948★
State appropriations for Michigan's institutions of higher education, 2000-01 ★1275★
Golden Key Scholar Award winners, 2000 ★1316★
Traditionally white institutions awarding the most master's degrees to African Americans ★1755★
U.S. colleges and universities awarding the most biological and life sciences master's degrees to Asian Americans ★1757★
U.S. colleges and universities awarding the most communications master's degrees to African Americans ★1763★
U.S. colleges and universities awarding the most computer and information sciences master's degrees to Asian Americans ★1767★
U.S. colleges and universities awarding the most education master's degrees to African Americans ★1769★
U.S. colleges and universities awarding the most master's degrees to African Americans ★1785★

U.S. colleges and universities awarding the most master's degrees to Asian Americans ★1786★
U.S. colleges and universities awarding the most master's degrees to minorities ★1788★
U.S. colleges and universities awarding the most physical sciences master's degrees to Asian Americans ★1794★
Traditionally white institutions awarding the most first professional degrees to African Americans ★1842★
U.S. colleges and universities awarding the most health professions and related sciences first professional degrees to African Americans ★1847★
U.S. colleges and universities awarding the most health professions and related sciences first professional degrees to Native Americans ★1851★
U.S. colleges and universities awarding the most communications doctorate degrees to African Americans ★2088★
U.S. colleges and universities awarding the most computer and information sciences doctorate degrees to Asian Americans ★2090★
U.S. colleges and universities awarding the most doctoral degrees to Hispanic Americans from 1995 to 1999 ★2094★
U.S. colleges and universities awarding the most doctorate degrees to minorities ★2098★
U.S. colleges and universities awarding the most health professions and related sciences doctorate degrees to Asian Americans ★2115★
U.S. colleges and universities awarding the most health professions and related sciences doctorate degrees to Hispanic Americans ★2116★
U.S. colleges and universities awarding the most social sciences and history doctorate degrees to African Americans ★2124★
Average faculty salaries for institutions of higher education in Michigan, 2000-01 ★3709★

Wayne Thomas Elementary School
Illinois elementary schools with the highest 5th grade writing scores ★15★

Wayne University
U.S. colleges and universities awarding the most doctorate degrees to Asian Americans ★2096★
U.S. colleges and universities awarding the most education doctorate degrees to Asian Americans ★2109★

Waynesburg College
Average faculty salaries for institutions of higher education in Pennsylvania, 2000-01 ★3725★

Wayzata High School
Outstanding secondary schools in Minneapolis-St. Paul, Minnesota-Wisconsin ★4181★

WCW: The Ultimate Guide
Most notable nonfiction books for reluctant young adult readers, 2001 ★323★

We, the People
Booklist's most recommended poetry for youths, 2001 ★315★

Weaver-Hart; Ann
Top pay and benefits for the chief executive and top paid employees at Claremont Graduate University ★3235★

Weaver; Lynn Edward
Top pay and benefits for the chief executive and top paid employees at Florida Institute of Technology ★3293★

Web developer
  Jobs with the best security scores ★2251★
  Jobs with the highest employment growth ★2254★
  Most desirable technical/repair jobs ★2281★
Web development
  Job openings for high-tech workers ★2330★
Web development/administration
  Information technology jobs most in demand, 2001 ★4428★
W.E.B. Du Bois: The Fight for Equality and the American Century, 1919-63
  Booklist's most recommended African American nonfiction ★229★
W.E.B. DuBois: The Fight for Equality and the American Century, 1919-63
  Outstanding biography books, 2000 ★288★
Weber; Michael P.
  Top pay and benefits for the chief executive and top paid employees at Duquesne University ★3277★
Weber State University
  Division I NCAA colleges with that graduated less than 20% of their African American male athletes, 1990-91 to 1993-94 ★928★
  Division I NCAA colleges with the lowest graduation rates for female athletes, 1990-91 to 1993-94 ★936★
  State appropriations for Utah's institutions of higher education, 2000-01 ★1297★
  Undergraduate tuition and fees at colleges and universities in Utah ★1562★
  U.S. News & World Report's top public western regional universities, 2000-01 ★1573★
  Average faculty salaries for institutions of higher education in Utah, 2000-01 ★3733★
Website manager
  Jobs with the best outlook scores ★2249★
  Jobs with the best physical demands scores ★2250★
  Jobs with the best security scores ★2251★
  Jobs with the highest employment growth ★2254★
  Most desirable technical/repair jobs ★2281★
Webster; Cynthia
  Most published authors, adjusted for coauthorship, in the *Journal of Business Research*, 1985 to 1999 ★701★
Webster Magnet School
  Outstanding secondary schools in New York, New York ★4191★
Webster University
  U.S. News & World Report's midwestern regional universities with the highest proportion of classes having 20 students or less, 2000-01 ★1409★
  U.S. News & World Report's midwestern regional universities with the lowest acceptance rates, 2000-01 ★1410★
  Traditionally white institutions awarding the most master's degrees to African Americans ★1755★
  U.S. colleges and universities awarding the most business management and administrative services master's degrees to African Americans ★1759★
  U.S. colleges and universities awarding the most business management and administrative services master's degrees to Asian Americans ★1760★
  U.S. colleges and universities awarding the most business management and administrative services master's degrees to Hispanic Americans ★1761★

U.S. colleges and universities awarding the most business management and administrative services master's degrees to Native Americans ★1762★
U.S. colleges and universities awarding the most communications master's degrees to African Americans ★1763★
U.S. colleges and universities awarding the most health professions and related sciences master's degrees to African Americans ★1777★
U.S. colleges and universities awarding the most law and legal studies master's degrees to African Americans ★1781★
U.S. colleges and universities awarding the most master's degrees to African Americans ★1785★
U.S. colleges and universities awarding the most master's degrees to Hispanic Americans ★1787★
U.S. colleges and universities awarding the most master's degrees to minorities ★1788★
U.S. colleges and universities awarding the most master's degrees to Native Americans ★1789★
U.S. colleges and universities awarding the most psychology master's degrees to African Americans ★1797★
U.S. colleges and universities awarding the most psychology master's degrees to Asian Americans ★1798★
U.S. colleges and universities awarding the most psychology master's degrees to Hispanic Americans ★1799★
U.S. colleges and universities awarding the most psychology master's degrees to Native Americans ★1800★
Average faculty salaries for institutions of higher education in Missouri, 2000-01 ★3712★
Webster's Gold Encyclopedia 2000
  Top selling reference software, 2000 ★1601★
WebTrends
  Best small companies in the U.S. ★383★
Weed Science
  Agriculture journals by citation impact, 1999 ★54★
Weeking the Collection: A Review of Research on Identifying Obsolete Stock
  Most frequently cited *Libri* articles ★2730★
Weeks Jr.; Richard G.
  Top pay and benefits for the chief executive and top paid employees at West Virginia Wesleyan College ★3613★
Weems; John E.
  Top pay and benefits for the chief executive and top paid employees at Meredith College ★3399★
Weil; Gordon
  Top pay and benefits for the chief executive and top paid employees at Wheaton College in Massachusetts ★3621★
Weingand; Darlene
  Library and information science faculty with the most journal articles, 1993-1998 ★2711★
Weinstein; Robert
  Top pay and benefits for the chief executive and top paid employees at Bradley University ★3208★
Weir High School
  Outstanding secondary schools in Steubenville-Weirton, Ohio-West Virginia ★4237★
Weir Middle School
  Outstanding secondary schools in Steubenville-Weirton, Ohio-West Virginia ★4237★

Weis; Frederick M.
  Top pay and benefits for the chief executive and top paid employees at Claremont McKenna College ★3236★
Weisburd; D.
  Most cited authors in the journal *Justice Quarterly*, 1990 to 1995 ★1630★
Weisler; Steve
  Top pay and benefits for the chief executive and top paid employees at Hampshire College ★3322★
Weiss; Dorothy
  All-USA College Academic Second Team, 2001 ★3★
Weiss; Everett
  Golden Key Scholar Award winners, 2000 ★1316★
Weiss; Ira R.
  Top pay and benefits for the chief executive and top paid employees at Northeastern University ★3422★
Weiss; Kristen
  All-America girls' high school soccer team forwards, 2001 ★175★
Weiss; Mary A.
  Individual authors with the most published pages in *The Journal of Risk and Insurance*, 1987-1996 ★680★
Weissman; Neil
  Top pay and benefits for the chief executive and top paid employees at Dickinson College ★3268★
Weitzel-O'Neill; Patricia
  Top pay and benefits for the chief executive and top paid employees at Trinity College in Washington D.C. ★3578★
Welch; Edwin H.
  Top pay and benefits for the chief executive and top paid employees at University of Charleston ★3590★
Welch; Robert S.
  Top pay and benefits for the chief executive and top paid employees at Goucher College ★3314★
Welder
  Least desirable jobs ★2266★
Welder; Sister Thomas
  Top pay and benefits for the chief executive and top paid employees at the University of Mary ★3548★
Welders and cutters
  Projected employment growth for selected occupations that require long-term on-the-job training, 1998-2008 ★2320★
Well-Founded Fear
  Most notable videos for adults, 2001 ★2891★
Wellesley College
  Radcliffe Institute for Advanced Study fellowship recipient in the field of astronomy, 2000-01 ★109★
  Private, 4-year undergraduate colleges and universities producing the most Ph.D.'s in the life sciences, 1920-1990 ★192★
  Private, 4-year undergraduate colleges and universities producing the most Ph.D.'s in the life sciences, 1981-1990 ★193★
  Comparison of acceptance rates at the top 5 liberal arts colleges in the U.S., 1990 and 2001 ★844★
  U.S. colleges and universities where the general student body puts little emphasis on socializing ★1010★
  U.S. colleges and universities with the most attractive campuses ★1039★

U.S. News & World Report's best national liberal arts colleges, 2000-01 ★1320★

U.S. News & World Report's national liberal arts colleges with the best financial resources rank, 2000-01 ★1322★

U.S. News & World Report's national liberal arts colleges with the best freshmen retention rates, 2000-01 ★1323★

U.S. News & World Report's national liberal arts colleges with the highest academic reputation scores, 2000-01 ★1327★

U.S. News & World Report's national liberal arts colleges with the highest graduation rates, 2000-01 ★1330★

Private, 4-year undergraduate colleges and universities producing the most Ph.D.s in all fields of study, 1920-1990 ★2027★

Private, 4-year undergraduate colleges and universities producing the most Ph.D.'s in all fields of study, 1981-1990 ★2028★

Private, 4-year undergraduate colleges and universities producing the most Ph.D.'s in all fields of study, 1990 ★2029★

Private, 4-year undergraduate colleges and universities producing the most Ph.D.'s in nonscience fields, 1920-1990 ★2030★

Private, 4-year undergraduate colleges and universities producing the most Ph.D.'s in nonscience fields, 1981-1990 ★2031★

Private, 4-year undergraduate colleges and universities producing the most Ph.D.'s in nonscience fields, 1990 ★2032★

Private, 4-year undergraduate colleges and universities producing the most Ph.D.'s in the earth sciences, 1981-1990 ★2151★

Private, 4-year undergraduate colleges and universities producing the most Ph.D.'s in economics, 1920-1990 ★2211★

Private, 4-year undergraduate colleges and universities producing the most Ph.D.'s in economics, 1981-1990 ★2212★

Undergraduate institutions with the most graduates who received Ph.D.s in economics, 1920-1984 ★2214★

Private, 4-year undergraduate colleges and universities producing the most Ph.D.'s in English, 1920-1990 ★2449★

Private, 4-year undergraduate colleges and universities producing the most Ph.D.'s in English, 1981-1990 ★2450★

Private, 4-year undergraduate colleges and universities producing the most Ph.D.'s in history, 1920-1990 ★2552★

Private, 4-year undergraduate colleges and universities producing the most Ph.D.'s in history, 1981-1990 ★2553★

Women's colleges granting physics bachelor's degrees, 2000 ★2982★

Private, 4-year undergraduate colleges and universities producing the most Ph.D.'s in political science and international relations, 1920-1990 ★3044★

Private, 4-year undergraduate colleges and universities producing the most Ph.D.'s in political science and international relations, 1981-1990 ★3045★

Private, 4-year undergraduate colleges and universities producing the most Ph.D.'s in psychology, 1920-1990 ★3066★

Private, 4-year undergraduate colleges and universities producing the most Ph.D.'s in psychology, 1981-1990 ★3067★

Average faculty salaries for institutions of higher education in Massachusetts, 2000-01 ★3708★

U.S. liberal arts colleges with the highest paid full professors, 2001 ★3980★

Private, 4-year undergraduate colleges and universities producing the most Ph.D.'s in the sciences, 1920-1990 ★4294★

Private, 4-year undergraduate colleges and universities producing the most Ph.D.'s in the sciences, 1981-1990 ★4295★

Private, 4-year undergraduate colleges and universities producing the most Ph.D.'s in anthropology and sociology, 1920-1990 ★4344★

Private, 4-year undergraduate colleges and universities producing the most Ph.D.'s in anthropology and sociology, 1981-1990 ★4345★

WellPoint
Top public companies for women executives, 2000 ★4457★

Top public companies with the highest percentage of women board of directors, 2000 ★4458★

Top public companies with the highest percentage of women employees, 2000 ★4459★

WellPoint Health Networks
Fortune's highest ranked health care companies, 2000 ★469★

Wells College
U.S. colleges and universities most accepting of alternative lifestyles ★986★

U.S. colleges and universities that devote the most course time to discussion ★990★

U.S. colleges and universities where students and the local community relate well ★999★

U.S. colleges and universities where the general student body does not smoke marijuana ★1006★

U.S. colleges and universities with the best on-campus housing facilities ★1032★

U.S. News & World Report's national liberal arts colleges with the highest proportion of classes with less than 20 students, 2000-01 ★1335★

Average faculty salaries for institutions of higher education in New York, 2000-01 ★3719★

Wells Fargo
Fortune's highest ranked super-regional banks, 2000 ★498★

Top banks in Standard & Poor's 500, 2001 ★531★

Wells Fargo Bank
Most selective internships in the U.S., 2001 ★2610★

Wells Fargo Financial
Top recruiters for business administration jobs for 2000-01 bachelor's degree recipients ★554★

Top recruiters for finance/banking jobs for 2000-01 bachelor's degree recipients ★582★

Top recruiters for business administration jobs for 2000-01 master's degree recipients ★652★

Top recruiters for finance/banking jobs for 2000-01 master's degree recipients ★664★

Top recruiters for marketing jobs for 2000-01 master's degree recipients ★672★

Top recruiters for criminal justice jobs for 2000-01 bachelor's degree recipients ★1647★

Top recruiters for history jobs for 2000-01 bachelor's degree recipients ★2550★

Top recruiters for liberal arts jobs for 2000-01 bachelor's degree recipients ★2675★

Wells; G.L.
Most cited authors in the journal *Criminal Justice and Behavior*, 1990 to 1995 ★1619★

Welsh; Timothy J.
Top pay and benefits for the chief executive and top paid employees at Providence College ★3447★

Wemberly Worried
Most notable books for young readers, 2001 ★319★

Outstanding children's picture books, 2000 ★331★

Wenatchee Valley College
Lowest undergraduate tuition and fees at colleges and universities in Washington ★1567★

Average faculty salaries for institutions of higher education without academic ranks in Washington, 2000-01 ★3768★

Wendy's International
Fortune's highest ranked food services companies, 2000 ★465★

Top leisure time industries in Standard & Poor's 500, 2001 ★545★

Wesley College
U.S. News & World Report's northern regional liberal arts colleges with students least in debt, 1999 ★1351★

Lowest undergraduate tuition and fees at private nonprofit, 4-year or above colleges and universities ★1464★

Undergraduate tuition and fees at colleges and universities in Delaware ★1492★

Average faculty salaries for institutions of higher education in Delaware, 2000-01 ★3695★

Wesleyan College
U.S. colleges and universities where the general student body does not drink beer ★1004★

U.S. colleges and universities where the general student body does not drink hard liquor ★1005★

U.S. News & World Report's national liberal arts colleges with the highest proportion of classes with less than 20 students, 2000-01 ★1335★

Highest undergraduate tuition and fees at colleges and universities in Georgia ★1496★

Wesleyan College (GA)
College senior's choices for exemplary liberal arts institutions ★1318★

Wesleyan University
Private, 4-year undergraduate colleges and universities producing the most Ph.D.'s in the life sciences, 1920-1990 ★192★

Private, 4-year undergraduate colleges and universities producing the most Ph.D.'s in the life sciences, 1981-1990 ★193★

U.S. colleges and universities with a generally liberal student body ★1015★

U.S. colleges and universities with a large student body of liberal Democrats ★1017★

U.S. colleges and universities with a primarily non-religious student body ★1021★

U.S. News & World Report's best national liberal arts colleges, 2000-01 ★1320★

U.S. News & World Report's national liberal arts colleges with the best freshmen retention rates, 2000-01 ★1323★

U.S. News & World Report's national liberal arts colleges with the best selectivity rank, 2000-01 ★1325★

U.S. News & World Report's national liberal arts colleges with the best student/faculty ratios, 2000-01 ★1326★

U.S. News & World Report's national liberal arts colleges with the highest academic reputation scores, 2000-01 ★1327★

U.S. News & World Report's national liberal arts colleges with the highest percentage of freshmen in the top 10% of their high school class, 2000-01 ★1332★

U.S. News & World Report's national liberal arts colleges with the highest proportion of classes having 50 or more students, 2000-01 ★1334★

U.S. News & World Report's national liberal arts colleges with the lowest acceptance rates, 2000-01 ★1336★

U.S. News & World Report's national liberal arts colleges with students most in debt, 1999 ★1386★

Highest undergraduate tuition and fees at private nonprofit, 4-year or above colleges and universities ★1461★

Private 4-year institutions with the highest tuition, 2000-01 ★1467★

Highest undergraduate tuition and fees at colleges and universities in Connecticut ★1490★

Private, 4-year undergraduate colleges and universities producing the most Ph.D.'s in the computer sciences, 1920-1990 ★1595★

Private, 4-year undergraduate colleges and universities producing the most Ph.D.'s in the computer sciences, 1981-1990 ★1596★

Total baccalaureate ethnic/cultural studies degrees awarded to African Americans from U.S. colleges and universities, 1997-98 ★1720★

U.S. institutions awarding the most baccalaureate degrees to minorities in ethnic/cultural studies, 1997-98 ★1821★

Private, 4-year undergraduate colleges and universities producing the most Ph.D.s in all fields of study, 1920-1990 ★2027★

Private, 4-year undergraduate colleges and universities producing the most Ph.D.'s in all fields of study, 1981-1990 ★2028★

Private, 4-year undergraduate colleges and universities producing the most Ph.D.'s in all fields of study, 1990 ★2029★

Private, 4-year undergraduate colleges and universities producing the most Ph.D.'s in nonscience fields, 1920-1990 ★2030★

Private, 4-year undergraduate colleges and universities producing the most Ph.D.'s in nonscience fields, 1981-1990 ★2031★

Private, 4-year undergraduate colleges and universities producing the most Ph.D.'s in nonscience fields, 1990 ★2032★

Private, 4-year undergraduate colleges and universities producing the most Ph.D.'s in the earth sciences, 1981-1990 ★2151★

Elite liberal arts colleges ranked by per capita quality adjusted scholarship articles in the field of economics, 1975-94 ★2164★

Elite liberal arts colleges ranked by quality adjusted scholarship articles in the field of economics, 1975-94 ★2165★

Top assistant professor economists at elite liberal arts colleges, 1975-94 ★2173★

Top full professor economists at elite liberal arts colleges, 1975-94 ★2175★

Private, 4-year undergraduate colleges and universities producing the most Ph.D.'s in economics, 1920-1990 ★2211★

Private, 4-year undergraduate colleges and universities producing the most Ph.D.'s in economics, 1981-1990 ★2212★

Undergraduate institutions with the most graduates who received Ph.D.s in economics, 1920-1984 ★2214★

Private, 4-year undergraduate colleges and universities producing the most Ph.D.'s in English, 1920-1990 ★2449★

Private, 4-year undergraduate colleges and universities producing the most Ph.D.'s in English, 1981-1990 ★2450★

Bachelor's institutions with the highest enrollment of foreign students, 1998-99 ★2492★

Private, 4-year undergraduate colleges and universities producing the most Ph.D.'s in history, 1920-1990 ★2552★

Private, 4-year undergraduate colleges and universities producing the most Ph.D.'s in history, 1981-1990 ★2553★

Private, 4-year undergraduate colleges and universities producing the most Ph.D.'s in mathematics, 1920-1990 ★2776★

Private, 4-year undergraduate colleges and universities producing the most Ph.D.'s in mathematics, 1981-1990 ★2777★

Private, 4-year undergraduate colleges and universities producing the most Ph.D.'s in physics and astronomy, 1920-1990 ★2949★

Private, 4-year undergraduate colleges and universities producing the most Ph.D.'s in political science and international relations, 1920-1990 ★3044★

Private, 4-year undergraduate colleges and universities producing the most Ph.D.'s in political science and international relations, 1981-1990 ★3045★

Private, 4-year undergraduate colleges and universities producing the most Ph.D.'s in psychology, 1920-1990 ★3066★

Private, 4-year undergraduate colleges and universities producing the most Ph.D.'s in psychology, 1981-1990 ★3067★

Private, 4-year undergraduate colleges and universities producing the most Ph.D.'s in the sciences, 1920-1990 ★4294★

Private, 4-year undergraduate colleges and universities producing the most Ph.D.'s in the sciences, 1981-1990 ★4295★

Private, 4-year undergraduate colleges and universities producing the most Ph.D.'s in anthropology and sociology, 1920-1990 ★4344★

Private, 4-year undergraduate colleges and universities producing the most Ph.D.'s in anthropology and sociology, 1981-1990 ★4345★

Wesolowski; Mitchell
Top pay and benefits for the chief executive and top paid employees at Lynchburg College ★3384★

Wessel; Barbara M.
Top pay and benefits for the chief executive and top paid employees at Saint Michael's College ★3483★

Wesselkamper; Mary C.
Top pay and benefits for the chief executive and top paid employees at the Chaminade University of Honolulu ★3524★

West Alabama; University of
Division II NCAA colleges with the 0% graduation rates for women's basketball players, 1993-94 ★942★
State appropriations for Alabama's institutions of higher education, 2000-01 ★1254★

West Anchorage High School
Outstanding secondary schools in Anchorage, Alaska ★4083★

West Bloomfield High School
Outstanding secondary schools in Detroit, Michigan ★4125★

West Chester University
Average faculty salaries for institutions of higher education in Pennsylvania, 2000-01 ★3725★

West Chester University of Pennsylvania
Colleges and universities with the smallest endowments, 2000 ★1238★

West; Cornel
Most influential African Americans in education ★2216★

West District School
Outstanding secondary schools in Hartford, Connecticut ★4147★

West Florida; University of
Division II NCAA colleges with the 0% graduation rates for men's basketball players, 1993-94 ★941★
State appropriations for Florida's institutions of higher education, 2000-01 ★1262★
Total baccalaureate law and legal studies degrees awarded to Asian Americans from U.S. colleges and universities, 1997-98 ★1726★
Average faculty salaries for institutions of higher education in Florida, 2000-01 ★3696★

West Hills Community College
Lowest undergraduate tuition and fees at public 2-year colleges and universities ★1465★

West Hillsborough School
Outstanding secondary schools in San Francisco, California ★4221★

West Junior High Technology Magnet School
All-USA Teacher Teams, Third Team, 2000 ★4401★

West Liberty State College
Division II NCAA colleges with the 100% graduation rates for women's basketball players, 1993-94 ★944★
State appropriations for West Virginia's institutions of higher education, 2000-01 ★1301★
Lowest undergraduate tuition and fees at colleges and universities in West Virginia ★1569★
Average faculty salaries for institutions of higher education in West Virginia, 2000-01 ★3737★

West Lincoln School
All-USA Teacher Teams, Third Team, 2000 ★4401★

West Los Angeles; University of
Total baccalaureate law and legal studies degrees awarded to African Americans from U.S. colleges and universities, 1997-98 ★1725★

West; Michael P.
Top pay and benefits for the chief executive and top paid employees at the University of Mary Hardin-Baylor ★3549★

West Milford Elementary School
All-USA Teacher Teams, Third Team, 2000 ★4401★

West Philadelphia Catholic High School
Outstanding secondary schools in Philadelphia, Pennsylvania-New Jersey ★4202★

West Ridge Middle School
Outstanding secondary schools in Austin-San Marcos, Texas ★4090★

West Rowan High School
Outstanding secondary schools in Charlotte-Gastonia-Rock Hill, North Carolina-South Carolina ★4108★

West Texas A&M University
Average faculty salaries for institutions of higher education in Texas, 2000-01 ★3731★

West Virginia
Mean composite ACT scores by state, 2000 ★895★
Mean math SAT scores by state, 2000 ★900★
Mean verbal SAT scores by state, 2000 ★903★
States receiving the most in federal agency appropriations to colleges, 2000 ★1306★
States receiving the most in federal agency appropriations to colleges, from 1996 to 2000 ★1307★
Total doctorate recipients by state, 1999 ★2054★
State grades for affordability of higher education for minority students, 2000 ★2883★
State grades for benefits state receives for educating its minority students, 2000 ★2884★
State grades for completion of higher education by minority students, 2000 ★2885★
State grades for participation of minority students in higher education, 2000 ★2886★
State grades for preparing minority students for higher education, 2000 ★2887★

West Virginia Northern Community College
State appropriations for West Virginia's institutions of higher education, 2000-01 ★1301★
Lowest undergraduate tuition and fees at colleges and universities in West Virginia ★1569★

West Virginia School of Osteopathic Medicine
State appropriations for West Virginia's institutions of higher education, 2000-01 ★1301★

West Virginia State College
Division II NCAA colleges with the lowest graduation rates for football players, 1993-94 ★948★
State appropriations for West Virginia's institutions of higher education, 2000-01 ★1301★
Lowest undergraduate tuition and fees at colleges and universities in West Virginia ★1569★

West Virginia University
All-USA College Academic First Team, 2001 ★2★
Institutions receiving the most in federal agency appropriations to colleges, 2000 ★1245★
State appropriations for West Virginia's institutions of higher education, 2000-01 ★1301★
U.S. universities with the highest concentration of papers published in the field of chemical engineering, 1994-98 ★2345★
Institutions with the most prolific communication studies researchers ★2749★
U.S. universities with the highest concentration of papers published in the field of pharmacology, 1995-99 ★2937★
Average faculty salaries for institutions of higher education in West Virginia, 2000-01 ★3737★

West Virginia University, Parkersburg
Lowest undergraduate tuition and fees at public, 4-year or above colleges and universities ★1466★
Public 4-year institutions with the lowest tuition, 2000-01 ★1472★
Lowest undergraduate tuition and fees at colleges and universities in West Virginia ★1569★

West Virginia Wesleyan College
Highest undergraduate tuition and fees at colleges and universities in West Virginia ★1568★
Average faculty salaries for institutions of higher education in West Virginia, 2000-01 ★3737★

West Windsor-Palainsboro High School
Outstanding secondary schools in Trenton, New Jersey ★4242★

Westark College
Community colleges receiving the most gifts, 1999-2000 ★1239★
Lowest undergraduate tuition and fees at colleges and universities in Arkansas ★1485★

Westchester Community College
Average faculty salaries for institutions of higher education in New York, 2000-01 ★3719★
U.S. community colleges with the highest paid full professors, 2001 ★3976★

Westchester, NY
Counties with the highest per capita income ★2561★

Western Baptist College
Average faculty salaries for institutions of higher education in Oregon, 2000-01 ★3724★

Western Carolina University
State appropriations for North Carolina's institutions of higher education, 2000-01 ★1286★
Average faculty salaries for institutions of higher education in North Carolina, 2000-01 ★3720★

Western Connecticut State University
Average faculty salaries for institutions of higher education in Connecticut, 2000-01 ★3694★

Western Connecticut University
State appropriations for Connecticut's institutions of higher education, 2000-01 ★1260★

Western Dakota Technical Institute
Lowest undergraduate tuition and fees at colleges and universities in South Dakota ★1557★

Western Europe
First-year physics and astronomy graduate students from Europe, 1997-98 ★2988★

Western Gas Resources
Fortune's highest ranked pipelines and energy companies, 2000 ★486★

Western Illinois University
Division I NCAA colleges with that graduated none of their African American male basketball players, 1990-91 to 1993-94 ★930★
State appropriations for Illinois institutions of higher education, 2000-01 ★1266★
Illinois institutions with the highest article output ★2677★
Average faculty salaries for institutions of higher education in Illinois, 2000-01 ★3700★

Western International University
Highest undergraduate tuition and fees at colleges and universities in Arizona ★1482★

Western Interstate Commission for Higher Education
State appropriations for Hawaii's institutions of higher education, 2000-01 ★1264★

Western Kentucky; University of
Division I all-time winningest college teams ★128★
State appropriations for Kentucky's institutions of higher education, 2000-01 ★1270★
Average faculty salaries for institutions of higher education in Kentucky, 2000-01 ★3704★

Western Maryland College
Highest undergraduate tuition and fees at colleges and universities in Maryland ★1514★
Average faculty salaries for institutions of higher education in Maryland, 2000-01 ★3707★

Western Michigan University
Four-year institutions with the most liquor arrests reported, 1999 ★707★
U.S. colleges and universities reporting the most alcohol related arrests, 1998 ★730★
State appropriations for Michigan's institutions of higher education, 2000-01 ★1275★
Doctoral institutions with the highest enrollment of foreign students, 1998-99 ★2494★
Institutions in the Worker Rights Consortium ★2913★
Average faculty salaries for institutions of higher education in Michigan, 2000-01 ★3709★

Western Michigan University Foundation
Colleges and universities with the smallest endowments, 2000 ★1238★

Western Montana College
Highest undergraduate tuition and fees at colleges and universities in Montana ★1526★
Average faculty salaries for institutions of higher education in Montana, 2000-01 ★3713★

Western Nebraska Community College
Lowest undergraduate tuition and fees at colleges and universities in Nebraska ★1529★
Average faculty salaries for institutions of higher education without academic ranks in Nebraska, 2000-01 ★3757★

Western Nevada Community College
Undergraduate tuition and fees at colleges and universities in Nevada ★1530★

Western New England College
Average faculty salaries for institutions of higher education in Massachusetts, 2000-01 ★3708★

Western New Mexico University
State appropriations for New Mexico's institutions of higher education, 2000-01 ★1284★
U.S. colleges and universities awarding the most education master's degrees to Native Americans ★1772★
Average faculty salaries for institutions of higher education in New Mexico, 2000-01 ★3718★

Western Oklahoma State College
Lowest undergraduate tuition and fees at colleges and universities in Oklahoma ★1546★

Western Ontario; University of
Business Week's top business schools outside the U.S. as selected by corporate recruiters, 2000 ★605★
Business Week's top business schools outside the U.S. as selected by recent MBA graduates, 2000 ★606★
Business Week's top business schools outside the U.S. for intellectual capital, 2000 ★607★
Post-MBA salaries for graduates from *Business Week*'s top business schools outside the U.S., 2000 ★642★
Pre-MBA salaries for students at *Business Week*'s top business schools outside the U.S., 2000 ★643★
Canadian universities publishing the most papers in the fields of economics and business, 1992-96 ★2215★

Western Oregon University
Division II NCAA colleges with the 0% graduation rates for men's basketball players, 1993-94 ★941★
Division II NCAA colleges with the lowest graduation rates for football players, 1993-94 ★948★
Average faculty salaries for institutions of higher education in Oregon, 2000-01 ★3724★

Western Piedmont Community College
Average faculty salaries for institutions of higher education without academic ranks in North Carolina, 2000-01 ★3761★

Western Sky Middle School
Outstanding secondary schools in Phoenix-Mesa, Arizona ★4203★

Western Southern Life
Top recruiters for finance/banking jobs for 2000-01 bachelor's degree recipients ★582★
Top recruiters for marketing jobs for 2000-01 bachelor's degree recipients ★684★

Western Springs, District 101
Illinois elementary school districts with the highest teacher salaries, 1999 ★3984★

Western State College of Colorado
Average faculty salaries for institutions of higher education in Colorado, 2000-01 ★3693★

Western; University of
Best Canadian universities overall, 2000 ★1149★
Best Canadian universities with the highest quality, 2000 ★1151★
Canadian medical/doctoral universities by alumni support, 2000 ★1172★
Canadian medical/doctoral universities by award-winning faculty members, 2000 ★1173★
Canadian medical/doctoral universities by class size at the first- and second-year level, 2000 ★1174★
Canadian medical/doctoral universities by class size at the third- and forth-year level, 2000 ★1175★
Canadian medical/doctoral universities by classes taught by tenured faculty, 2000 ★1176★
Canadian medical/doctoral universities by faculty members with Ph.D.'s, 2000 ★1177★
Canadian medical/doctoral universities by international graduate students, 2000 ★1178★
Canadian medical/doctoral universities by library acquisitions, 2000 ★1179★
Canadian medical/doctoral universities by library expenses, 2000 ★1180★
Canadian medical/doctoral universities by library holdings, 2000 ★1181★
Canadian medical/doctoral universities by library holdings per student, 2000 ★1182★
Canadian medical/doctoral universities by medical/science grants per faculty member, 2000 ★1184★
Canadian medical/doctoral universities by operating budget per student, 2000 ★1185★
Canadian medical/doctoral universities by percentage of operating budget allocated to scholarships, 2000 ★1186★
Canadian medical/doctoral universities by percentage of operating budget allocated to student services, 2000 ★1187★
Canadian medical/doctoral universities by reputation, 2000 ★1188★
Canadian medical/doctoral universities by social science/humanities grants per faculty member, 2000 ★1189★
Canadian medical/doctoral universities by students from out of province, 2000 ★1190★
Canadian medical/doctoral universities by students winning national awards, 2000 ★1191★
Canadian universities by average entering grade, 2000 ★1213★
Canadian universities by students with 75% grade averages or higher, 2000 ★1215★
Top Canadian medical/doctoral universities, 2000 ★1221★

Western Washington University
State appropriations for Washington's institutions of higher education, 2000-01 ★1300★
U.S. News & World Report's top public western regional universities, 2000-01 ★1573★
U.S. News & World Report's western regional universities with the highest graduation rates, 2000-01 ★1582★
U.S. News & World Report's western regional universities with the highest percentage of full-time faculty, 2000-01 ★1584★
Total baccalaureate social sciences and history degrees awarded to Native Americans from U.S. colleges and universities, 1997-98 ★1744★
Radcliffe Institute for Advanced Study fellowship recipients in the field of psychology, 2000-01 ★3062★
Average faculty salaries for institutions of higher education in Washington, 2000-01 ★3736★

Western Wyoming Community College
Undergraduate tuition and fees at colleges and universities in Wyoming ★1572★

Westerville Public Library
Highest Hennen's American Public Library Ratings for libraries serving a population of 50,000 to 99,999 ★2697★

Westfield Public Library
Highest Hennen's American Public Library Ratings for libraries serving a population of 5,000 to 9,999 ★2694★

Westfield State College
State appropriations for Massachusetts's institutions of higher education, 2000-01 ★1274★
Average faculty salaries for institutions of higher education in Massachusetts, 2000-01 ★3708★

Westhill High School
Outstanding secondary schools in Syracuse, New York ★4239★

Westinghouse
Top recruiters for chemical engineering jobs for 2000-01 bachelor's degree recipients ★2343★
Top recruiters for mechanical engineering jobs for 2000-01 bachelor's degree recipients ★2437★
Top recruiters for nuclear engineering jobs for 2000-01 bachelor's degree recipients ★2440★

Westland Intermediate School
Outstanding secondary schools in Washington, District of Columbia-Maryland-Virginia-West Virginia ★4249★

Westminster Choir College of Rider University
Highest undergraduate tuition and fees at colleges and universities in New Jersey ★1533★

Westminster Christian Academy
Outstanding secondary schools in St. Louis, Missouri-Illinois ★4216★

Westminster College
U.S. colleges and universities with the worst food service program ★1043★
U.S. News & World Report's best undergraduate fees among western regional universities by discount tuition, 2000 ★1430★
Highest undergraduate tuition and fees at colleges and universities in Missouri ★1524★
Undergraduate tuition and fees at colleges and universities in Utah ★1562★
U.S. News & World Report's western regional universities with the highest acceptance rates, 2000-01 ★1579★
U.S. News & World Report's western regional universities with the highest proportion of classes with 20 students or less, 2000-01 ★1585★
Average faculty salaries for institutions of higher education in Missouri, 2000-01 ★3712★
Average faculty salaries for institutions of higher education in Pennsylvania, 2000-01 ★3725★
Average faculty salaries for institutions of higher education in Utah, 2000-01 ★3733★

Westminster College (PA)
Division II NCAA colleges with the highest graduation rates for all sports, 1993-94 ★945★
Division II NCAA colleges with the highest graduation rates for football players, 1993-94 ★946★

Westminster College (UT)
Institutions censured by the American Association of University Professors, 2001 ★1067★
Largest benefit packages awarded to presidents at institutions of higher education, 1998-99 ★3133★

Westminster High School
Outstanding secondary schools in Orange County, California ★4199★

Westmont College
U.S. News & World Report's national liberal arts colleges with students most in debt, 1999 ★1386★
Average faculty salaries for institutions of higher education in California, 2000-01 ★3692★

Westmont High School
Outstanding secondary schools in San Jose, California ★4222★

Westmoreland County Community College
Lowest undergraduate tuition and fees at colleges and universities in Pennsylvania ★1550★
Average faculty salaries for institutions of higher education in Pennsylvania, 2000-01 ★3725★

Weston High School
Outstanding secondary schools in Stamford-Norwalk, Connecticut ★4235★

Westpac Banking
Business Week's best companies in Australia ★386★

Westphal; Kenneth
Top pay and benefits for the chief executive and top paid employees at Gustavus Adolphus College ★3317★

WestPoint Stevens
Fortune's highest ranked textiles companies, 2000 ★501★

Westside High School
Outstanding secondary schools in Omaha, Nebraska-Iowa ★4198★

Westside Middle School
Outstanding secondary schools in Omaha, Nebraska-Iowa ★4198★

Westvaco
Top containers and packaging companies in Standard & Poor's 500, 2001 ★537★

Westwood College of Aviation Technology
Highest undergraduate tuition and fees at colleges and universities in Colorado ★1488★

Westwood High School
Outstanding secondary schools in Austin-San Marcos, Texas ★4090★

Wethersfield High School
Outstanding secondary schools in Hartford, Connecticut ★4147★

Wetzel; James R.
Top pay and benefits for the chief executive and top paid employees at Franklin and Marshall College ★3296★

Wexler; Rabbi Robert
Top pay and benefits for the chief executive and top paid employees at the University of Judaism ★3546★

Weyerhauser
Fortune's highest ranked forest and paper products companies, 2000 ★466★
Top paper and forest products companies in Standard & Poor's 500, 2001 ★552★
Top internships in the U.S. with the highest compensation, 2001 ★2611★

Weyuker; Elaine J.
Top published scholars in the field of systems and software engineering ★2333★

WGN-Chicago
Most selective internships in the U.S., 2001 ★2610★

A Whale Hunt
Booklist's best science and technology books ★366★

What the Ice Gets: Shakleton's Antarctic Expedition, 1914-1916
Booklist's most recommended poetry books, 2001 ★231★

What Is to Be Done About Law and Order?
Most-cited works in critical criminology publications ★1645★

Whatcom Community College
Lowest undergraduate tuition and fees at colleges and universities in Washington ★1567★
Average faculty salaries for institutions of higher education without academic ranks in Washington, 2000-01 ★3768★

What's in a Name?
Most notable fiction books for young adults, 2001 ★322★

What's in the Meadow?
Smithsonian's best books for children ages 1 to 6 ★363★

What's in the Tide Pool?
Smithsonian's best books for children ages 1 to 6 ★363★

Wheaton College
U.S. colleges and universities awarding the most communications master's degrees to Asian Americans ★1764★
Private, 4-year undergraduate colleges and universities producing the most Ph.Ds in all fields of study, 1920-1990 ★2027★
Private, 4-year undergraduate colleges and universities producing the most Ph.D.'s in all fields of study, 1981-1990 ★2028★
Private, 4-year undergraduate colleges and universities producing the most Ph.D.'s in all fields of study, 1990 ★2029★
Private, 4-year undergraduate colleges and universities producing the most Ph.D.'s in nonscience fields, 1920-1990 ★2030★
Private, 4-year undergraduate colleges and universities producing the most Ph.D.'s in nonscience fields, 1981-1990 ★2031★
Private, 4-year undergraduate colleges and universities producing the most Ph.D.'s in nonscience fields, 1990 ★2032★
Private, 4-year undergraduate colleges and universities producing the most Ph.D.'s in English, 1920-1990 ★2449★
Private, 4-year undergraduate colleges and universities producing the most Ph.D.'s in English, 1981-1990 ★2450★
Private, 4-year undergraduate colleges and universities producing the most Ph.D.'s in history, 1920-1990 ★2552★
Private, 4-year undergraduate colleges and universities producing the most Ph.D.'s in history, 1981-1990 ★2553★
Private, 4-year undergraduate colleges and universities producing the most Ph.D.'s in mathematics, 1981-1990 ★2777★
Private, 4-year undergraduate colleges and universities producing the most Ph.D.'s in psychology, 1920-1990 ★3066★
Private, 4-year undergraduate colleges and universities producing the most Ph.D.'s in psychology, 1981-1990 ★3067★
Average faculty salaries for institutions of higher education in Illinois, 2000-01 ★3700★
Average faculty salaries for institutions of higher education in Massachusetts, 2000-01 ★3708★
Private, 4-year undergraduate colleges and universities producing the most Ph.D.'s in anthropology and sociology, 1920-1990 ★4344★
Private, 4-year undergraduate colleges and universities producing the most Ph.D.'s in anthropology and sociology, 1981-1990 ★4345★

Wheaton College (IL)
U.S. colleges and universities least accepting of alternative lifestyles ★985★
U.S. colleges and universities where students and the local community relate well ★999★
U.S. colleges and universities where the general student body does not drink beer ★1004★
U.S. colleges and universities where the general student body does not drink hard liquor ★1005★
U.S. colleges and universities where the general student body does not smoke marijuana ★1006★
U.S. colleges and universities where the general student body puts little emphasis on socializing ★1010★
U.S. colleges and universities with a generally conservative student body ★1014★
U.S. colleges and universities with a primarily religious student body ★1022★
U.S. colleges and universities with the best food service program ★1031★

Wheaton Public Library
Highest Hennen's American Public Library Ratings for libraries serving a population of 50,000 to 99,999 ★2697★

Wheel of the Infinite
Library Journal's best science fiction and fantasy titles, 2000 ★246★

Wheeling Jesuit University
Division II NCAA colleges with the 100% graduation rates for men's basketball players, 1993-94 ★943★
Institutions receiving the most in federal agency appropriations to colleges, 2000 ★1245★
U.S. News & World Report's southern regional universities with the best alumni giving rates, 2000-01 ★1434★
U.S. News & World Report's southern regional universities with the best student/faculty ratios, 2000-01 ★1435★
U.S. News & World Report's southern regional universities with the highest acceptance rates, 2000-01 ★1436★
U.S. News & World Report's southern regional universities with the highest proportion of classes with 20 students or less, 2000-01 ★1441★
Highest undergraduate tuition and fees at colleges and universities in West Virginia ★1568★
Average faculty salaries for institutions of higher education in West Virginia, 2000-01 ★3737★

Wheelock College
Average faculty salaries for institutions of higher education in Massachusetts, 2000-01 ★3708★

Whelan; W. James
Top pay and benefits for the chief executive and top paid employees at Saint John Fisher College in New York ★3472★

When Battered Women Kill
Most-cited works in women and crime publications ★1646★

When Genius Failed: The Rise and Fall of Long-Term Capital Management
Library Journal's most notable investing books, 2000 ★264★

When Jeff Comes Home
Most notable fiction books for reluctant young adult readers, 2001 ★321★

When Kambia Elaine Flew in from Neptune
Booklist's best first novels for youths ★309★
Booklist's most recommended black history books for youth ★311★
Most notable fiction books for young adults, 2001 ★322★

When Mack Came Back
Smithsonian's best books for children ages 6 to 10 ★364★

When Night Time Comes Near
Smithsonian's best books for children ages 1 to 6 ★363★

When Schools Compete: A Cautionary Tale
American School Board Journal's notable education books, 2000 ★225★

When Zachary Beaver Came to Town
  Most notable children's recordings, 2001 ★320★
Where Did It All Go Right?
  Outstanding biography books, 2000 ★288★
Where the Heart Is
  Longest-running trade paperback bestsellers, 2000 ★282★
Where's Wallace?
  Publishers Weekly Off-the-Cuff Awards winner for book happiest to see back in print, 2000 ★345★
  Smithsonian's best books for children ages 1 to 6 ★363★
Whichard; Willis P.
  Top pay and benefits for the chief executive and top paid employees at Campbell University ★3218★
While I Was Gone
  Longest-running trade paperback bestsellers, 2000 ★282★
Whirlpool
  Fortune's highest ranked electronics and electrical equipment companies, 2000 ★460★
White; Barbara
  Radcliffe Institute for Advanced Study fellowship recipient in the field of music composition, 2000-01 ★2893★
White Earth Tribal College
  U.S. tribal colleges ★1445★
White; E.B.
  Top essayists from 1946-1996 ★2445★
White Hotel
  Outstanding videos for library collections, 2000 ★2892★
White; James
  All-America boys' high school basketball 2nd team, 2001 ★162★
White; James J.
  Top pay and benefits for the chief executive and top paid employees at Lake Erie College ★3362★
White; J.M.
  American Chemical Society 2001 award winners (Group 5) ★755★
White; John
  Top pay and benefits for the chief executive and top paid employees at Colorado Christian University ★3248★
White Jr.; John
  Top pay and benefits for the chief executive and top paid employees at Nebraska Wesleyan University ★3417★
White; M. Christopher
  Top pay and benefits for the chief executive and top paid employees at Gardner-Webb University ★3303★
White; Tan
  All-America girls' high school basketball 4th team, 2001 ★173★
White Teeth
  Booklist's best first novels ★228★
  Most notable fiction books, 2001 ★284★
  Outstanding works of fiction, 2001 ★293★
White; Walter
  Most influential African Americans in politics and civil rights ★3040★
Whiteblack the Penguin Sees the World
  Outstanding children's picture books, 2000 ★331★

Whitecloud, III; Thomas S.
  Top pay and benefits for the chief executive and top paid employees at Tulane University ★3581★
Whitehead & Lindquist
  Most cited works in academic literature dealing with corrections ★1643★
Whitehorn; Michael
  Top pay and benefits for the chief executive and top paid employees at Hardin-Simmons University ★3325★
Whiteside; Valorie
  Division I women's career high scorers ★129★
Whitfield; Patricia
  Top pay and benefits for the chief executive and top paid employees at Heritage College ★3332★
Whitley; Wynter
  All-America girls' high school basketball 2nd team, 2001 ★171★
Whitlock; Richard
  Top pay and benefits for the chief executive and top paid employees at Illinois Wesleyan University ★3347★
Whitman
  Fortune's highest ranked beverages companies, 2000 ★450★
Whitman College
  U.S. colleges and universities where intramural sports are popular ★997★
  U.S. colleges and universities with a popular theater group ★1020★
  U.S. News & World Report's national liberal arts colleges with the best faculty resources rank, 2000-01 ★1321★
  Highest undergraduate tuition and fees at colleges and universities in Washington ★1566★
  Average faculty salaries for institutions of higher education in Washington, 2000-01 ★3736★
Whitney High School
  Outstanding secondary schools in Los Angeles-Long Beach, California ★4167★
Whitney M. Young Magnet High School
  Outstanding urban public high schools in Metro Chicago ★4262★
Whitney Young
  Acceptance rates at Chicago college prep magnet schools, 2000-01 ★4000★
Whitney Young High School
  Illinois high schools with the highest SAT scores ★874★
Whitney Young Magnet
  Admissions to college prep schools in Chicago that are the toughest to get into, 2001 ★4001★
  College prep schools in Chicago that are the toughest to get into ★4005★
Whitney Young Middle School
  Outstanding secondary schools in Cleveland-Lorain-Elyria, Ohio ★4114★
Whitt; Cynthia
  Top pay and benefits for the chief executive and top paid employees at Lincoln Memorial University ★3374★
Whittier College
  Average faculty salaries for institutions of higher education in California, 2000-01 ★3692★
Whittington; Gerald O.
  Top pay and benefits for the chief executive and top paid employees at Elon College ★3285★

Whitworth College
  U.S. News & World Report's best undergraduate fees among western regional universities by discount tuition, 2000 ★1430★
  Highest undergraduate tuition and fees at colleges and universities in Washington ★1566★
  U.S. News & World Report's top western regional universities, 2000-01 ★1574★
  U.S. News & World Report's western regional universities with the best academic reputation scores, 2000-01 ★1577★
  U.S. News & World Report's western regional universities with the highest acceptance rates, 2000-01 ★1579★
  U.S. News & World Report's western regional universities with the highest alumni giving rates, 2000-01 ★1580★
  U.S. News & World Report's western regional universities with the highest freshmen retention rates, 2000-01 ★1581★
  U.S. News & World Report's western regional universities with the highest percentage of freshmen in the top 25% of their high school class, 2000-01 ★1583★
  U.S. News & World Report's western regional universities with the highest percentage of full-time faculty, 2000-01 ★1584★
  U.S. News & World Report's western regional universities with the highest proportion of classes with 20 students or less, 2000-01 ★1585★
  Average faculty salaries for institutions of higher education in Washington, 2000-01 ★3736★
Who Moved My Cheese?
  Longest-running nonfiction hardcover bestsellers, 2000 ★281★
Who Wants To Be A Millionaire
  Top selling software in all categories, 2000 ★1602★
Wholesale
  Spending for E-marketplace services, by industry, 2001 ★4430★
Wholesale and retail trade
  Internet use by industry, 1998 ★2586★
Wholesale trade
  Employment change projections by major industry division from 1998 to 2008 ★2287★
  Employment projections by major industry division for 2008 ★2290★
Why We Hurt: The Natural History of Pain
  Library Journal's most notable neurology books, 2000 ★270★
Wichita State University
  State appropriations for Kansas institutions of higher education, 2000-01 ★1269★
  Average faculty salaries for institutions of higher education in Kansas, 2000-01 ★3703★
Wicked
  Library Journal's notable new magazines, 1999 ★2923★
Wickenheiser; Robert J.
  Top pay and benefits for the chief executive and top paid employees at Saint Bonaventure University ★3470★
Wickliffe Public Library
  Highest Hennen's American Public Library Ratings for libraries serving a population of 10,000 to 24,999 ★2695★
Wicks; Frank E.
  Top pay and benefits for the chief executive and top paid employees at Union College in New York ★3585★

Wide-Awake Club Library
  Highest Hennen's American Public Library Ratings for libraries serving a population of 999 and under ★2691★
Widener University
  U.S. News & World Report's northern regional universities with the best student/faculty ratios, 2000-01 ★1416★
  U.S. News & World Report's northern regional universities with the highest acceptance rates, 2000-01 ★1417★
  U.S. News & World Report's northern regional universities with the highest proportion of classes with 20 students of less, 2000-01 ★1423★
  U.S. colleges and universities awarding the most law and legal studies master's degrees to African Americans ★1781★
  Academics' choices for best health law programs, 2001 ★2629★
  Average faculty salaries for institutions of higher education in Pennsylvania, 2000-01 ★3725★
The Widmeyer Baker Group
  Most selective internships in the U.S., 2001 ★2610★
Wiedeking; Wendelin
  European business moguls considered the best turnaround artists ★443★
Wiegand; W.A.
  Authors that most frequently cite *Libri* publications from 1972 to 1999 ★2723★
Wieland; Joyce
  Canada's best visual artists of the 20th century ★75★
Wiesel; Sam W.
  Top pay and benefits for the chief executive and top paid employees at Georgetown University ★3306★
Wiesel; Torsten N.
  Largest benefit packages awarded to presidents at institutions of higher education, 1998-99 ★3133★
  Top pay and benefits for the chief executive and top paid employees at Rockefeller University ★3462★
Wiesner; Brett
  All-America boys' high school soccer team forwards, 2001 ★166★
Wiest; Joseph E.
  Top pay and benefits for the chief executive and top paid employees at West Virginia Wesleyan College ★3613★
Wiggins; Norman A.
  Top pay and benefits for the chief executive and top paid employees at Campbell University ★3218★
Wilbur Wright College
  Fall enrollment at Chicago-area city colleges, by minority percentages, 1999 ★865★
Wilbur Wright Middle School
  Outstanding secondary schools in Gary, Indiana ★4139★
Wild Life
  Booklist's most recommended historical novels, 2001 ★230★
Wild Minds: What Animals Really Think
  Library Journal's most notable zoology books, 2000 ★278★
Wild, S.J.; Rev. Robert A.
  Top pay and benefits for the chief executive and top paid employees at Marquette University ★3392★

Wildavsky; A.
  Authors with the most citations among authors published in *American Political Science Review*, 1974-94 ★3048★
Wilde; Harold R.
  Top pay and benefits for the chief executive and top paid employees at North Central College in Illinois ★3421★
Wilders; Richard
  Top pay and benefits for the chief executive and top paid employees at North Central College in Illinois ★3421★
Wilderson; Ben
  All-American boy's high school football linemen, 2000 ★183★
Wildlife Monographs
  Ecology journals by citation impact, 1999 ★2138★
Wildlife/range management
  Agricultural sciences doctorates awarded at U.S. colleges and universities, by subfield, 1999 ★1886★
  Gender breakdown of agricultural sciences doctorate recipients, by subfield, 1999 ★1926★
Wiley
  Book publishers with the most citations (Class 1) ★2562★
Wiley and the Hairy Man: Adapted from an American Folktale
  Most notable children's recordings, 2001 ★320★
Wilfrid Laurier University
  Best Canadian universities overall, 2000 ★1149★
  Canadian primarily undergraduate universities best at producing leaders of tomorrow, 2000 ★1192★
  Canadian primarily undergraduate universities by alumni support, 2000 ★1193★
  Canadian primarily undergraduate universities by class size at the first and second-year level, 2000 ★1195★
  Canadian primarily undergraduate universities by class size at the third and forth-year level, 2000 ★1196★
  Canadian primarily undergraduate universities by classes taught by tenured faculty, 2000 ★1197★
  Canadian primarily undergraduate universities by faculty members with Ph.D.'s, 2000 ★1198★
  Canadian primarily undergraduate universities by library acquisitions, 2000 ★1199★
  Canadian primarily undergraduate universities by library expenses, 2000 ★1200★
  Canadian primarily undergraduate universities by library holdings per student, 2000 ★1201★
  Canadian primarily undergraduate universities by medical/science grants per faculty member, 2000 ★1202★
  Canadian primarily undergraduate universities by operating budget per student, 2000 ★1203★
  Canadian primarily undergraduate universities by percentage of operating budget allocated to scholarships, 2000 ★1204★
  Canadian primarily undergraduate universities by percentage of operating budget allocated to student services, 2000 ★1205★
  Canadian primarily undergraduate universities by reputation, 2000 ★1206★
  Canadian primarily undergraduate universities by social science/humanities grants per faculty member, 2000 ★1207★
  Canadian primarily undergraduate universities by students from out of province, 2000 ★1208★
  Canadian primarily undergraduate universities by students winning national awards, 2000 ★1209★
  Canadian primarily undergraduate universities that are the best overall, 2000 ★1210★
  Canadian primarily undergraduate universities that are the most innovative, 2000 ★1211★
  Canadian primarily undergraduate universities with the highest quality, 2000 ★1212★
  Top Canadian primarily undergraduate universities, 2000 ★1226★
Wilgenbusch; Nancy
  Top pay and benefits for the chief executive and top paid employees at Marylhurst University ★3394★
Wilhelm; Leonard
  Top pay and benefits for the chief executive and top paid employees at Madonna University ★3386★
Wilkes University
  Average faculty salaries for institutions of higher education in Pennsylvania, 2000-01 ★3725★
Wilkins; Roy
  Most influential African Americans in politics and civil rights ★3040★
Wilkinson; Catherine
  Top pay and benefits for the chief executive and top paid employees at College Misericordia ★3243★
Will County School, District 92
  Illinois school districts spending the least for elementary school education 1997-98 ★4007★
Will; Katherine H.
  Top pay and benefits for the chief executive and top paid employees at Kenyon College ★3359★
Willamette Industries
  Fortune's highest ranked forest and paper products companies, 2000 ★466★
  Top paper and forest products companies in Standard & Poor's 500, 2001 ★552★
Willamette University
  U.S. News & World Report's national liberal arts colleges with the best faculty resources rank, 2000-01 ★1321★
  U.S. News & World Report's national liberal arts colleges with the highest acceptance rates, 2000-01 ★1328★
  Academics' choices for best dispute resolution programs, 2001 ★2627★
Willard; Timothy
  Top pay and benefits for the chief executive and top paid employees at Fontbonne College ★3294★
Willa's New World
  Booklist's most recommended historical fiction for youths, 2001 ★314★
Willemze; R.
  Most cited first authors in dermatology journals, 1981 to 1996 ★1871★
Willett; T.
  Top full professor economists at elite liberal arts colleges, 1975-94 ★2175★
Willett; Walter C.
  Most-cited researchers in clinical medicine, 1981-1998 ★2875★
  Most-cited researchers in epidemiology, 1981-1998 ★2876★

Willey; William
Top pay and benefits for the chief executive and top paid employees at Pacific University in Oregon ★3437★

William Carey College
Highest undergraduate tuition and fees at colleges and universities in Mississippi ★1522★

William Fremd High School
Outstanding suburban public high schools in Metro Chicago ★4256★

William Henry Harrison High School
Outstanding secondary schools in Cincinnati, Ohio-Kentucky-Indiana ★4112★

William Howard Taft High School
Outstanding secondary schools in San Antonio, Texas ★4219★

William Jewell College
Highest undergraduate tuition and fees at colleges and universities in Missouri ★1524★
Average faculty salaries for institutions of higher education in Missouri, 2000-01 ★3712★

William and Mary; College of
Division I NCAA colleges with the highest graduation rates for football players, 1990-91 to 1993-94 ★933★
U.S. News & World Report's best public national universities, 2000-01 ★1123★
U.S. News & World Report's national universities with the best freshmen retention rates, 2000-01 ★1128★
U.S. News & World Report's national universities with the lowest proportion of classes with 50 or more students, 2000-01 ★1142★
State appropriations for Virginia's institutions of higher education, 2000-01 ★1299★
Average faculty salaries for institutions of higher education in Virginia, 2000-01 ★3735★
Public institutions of higher education that pay the highest salaries to female professors, 2000-01 ★3975★

William Mitchell College of Law
Academics' choices for best trial advocacy programs, 2001 ★2633★

William Paterson University
Average faculty salaries for institutions of higher education in New Jersey, 2000-01 ★3717★

William Paterson University of New Jersey
State appropriations for New Jersey's institutions of higher education, 2000-01 ★1283★

William Tyndale College
U.S. News & World Report's midwestern regional liberal arts colleges with students least in debt, 1999 ★1337★

William Woods University
Highest undergraduate tuition and fees at colleges and universities in Missouri ★1524★

Williamette University
Highest undergraduate tuition and fees at colleges and universities in Oregon ★1547★

Williams
Fortune's highest ranked pipelines and energy companies, 2000 ★486★

Williams; Alan L.
Top pay and benefits for the chief executive and top paid employees at St. Louis University ★3478★

Williams; Angelina
All-America girls' high school basketball 3rd team, 2001 ★172★

Williams Baptist College
Highest undergraduate tuition and fees at colleges and universities in Arkansas ★1484★
Average faculty salaries for institutions of higher education in Arkansas, 2000-01 ★3691★

Williams; Carnell
All-American boy's high school football running backs, 2000 ★186★

Williams College
Comparison of acceptance rates at the top 5 liberal arts colleges in the U.S., 1990 and 2001 ★844★
U.S. colleges and universities offering the best overall academic experience for undergraduates ★987★
U.S. colleges and universities where intramural sports are popular ★997★
U.S. colleges and universities with the best overall administration ★1033★
U.S. News & World Report's best national liberal arts colleges, 2000-01 ★1320★
U.S. News & World Report's national liberal arts colleges with the best financial resources rank, 2000-01 ★1322★
U.S. News & World Report's national liberal arts colleges with the best freshmen retention rates, 2000-01 ★1323★
U.S. News & World Report's national liberal arts colleges with the best graduation and retention rank, 2000-01 ★1324★
U.S. News & World Report's national liberal arts colleges with the best selectivity rank, 2000-01 ★1325★
U.S. News & World Report's national liberal arts colleges with the best student/faculty ratios, 2000-01 ★1326★
U.S. News & World Report's national liberal arts colleges with the highest academic reputation scores, 2000-01 ★1327★
U.S. News & World Report's national liberal arts colleges with the highest alumni giving rank, 2000-01 ★1329★
U.S. News & World Report's national liberal arts colleges with the highest graduation rates, 2000-01 ★1330★
U.S. News & World Report's national liberal arts colleges with the highest percentage of alumni support, 2000-01 ★1331★
U.S. News & World Report's national liberal arts colleges with the highest percentage of freshmen in the top 10% of their high school class, 2000-01 ★1332★
U.S. News & World Report's national liberal arts colleges with the highest percentage of full-time faculty, 2000-01 ★1333★
U.S. News & World Report's national liberal arts colleges with the highest proportion of classes having 50 or more students, 2000-01 ★1334★
U.S. News & World Report's national liberal arts colleges with the lowest acceptance rates, 2000-01 ★1336★
U.S. News & World Report's best undergraduate fees among national liberal arts colleges by discount tuition, 2000 ★1381★
Highest undergraduate tuition and fees at colleges and universities in Massachusetts ★1516★
Private, 4-year undergraduate colleges and universities producing the most Ph.D.'s in the computer sciences, 1920-1990 ★1595★
Private, 4-year undergraduate colleges and universities producing the most Ph.D.'s in the computer sciences, 1981-1990 ★1596★
Private, 4-year undergraduate colleges and universities producing the most Ph.D.s in all fields of study, 1920-1990 ★2027★
Private, 4-year undergraduate colleges and universities producing the most Ph.D.'s in all fields of study, 1981-1990 ★2028★
Private, 4-year undergraduate colleges and universities producing the most Ph.D.'s in the earth sciences, 1981-1990 ★2151★
Elite liberal arts colleges ranked by quality adjusted scholarship articles in the field of economics, 1975-94 ★2165★
Top assistant professor economists at elite liberal arts colleges, 1975-94 ★2173★
Private, 4-year undergraduate colleges and universities producing the most Ph.D.'s in economics, 1920-1990 ★2211★
Private, 4-year undergraduate colleges and universities producing the most Ph.D.'s in economics, 1981-1990 ★2212★
Undergraduate institutions with the most graduates who received Ph.D.s in economics, 1920-1984 ★2214★
Private, 4-year undergraduate colleges and universities producing the most Ph.D.'s in English, 1920-1990 ★2449★
Private, 4-year undergraduate colleges and universities producing the most Ph.D.'s in English, 1981-1990 ★2450★
Radcliffe Institute for Advanced Study fellowship recipients in the field of history, 2000-01 ★2549★
Private, 4-year undergraduate colleges and universities producing the most Ph.D.'s in history, 1920-1990 ★2552★
Private, 4-year undergraduate colleges and universities producing the most Ph.D.'s in history, 1981-1990 ★2553★
Most wired colleges, 2000 ★2595★
Radcliffe Institute for Advanced Study fellowship recipient in the field of Asian literature, 2000-01 ★2613★
Private, 4-year undergraduate colleges and universities producing the most Ph.D.'s in mathematics, 1981-1990 ★2777★
Private, 4-year undergraduate colleges and universities producing the most Ph.D.'s in physics and astronomy, 1920-1990 ★2949★
Private, 4-year undergraduate colleges and universities producing the most Ph.D.'s in political science and international relations, 1920-1990 ★3044★
Private, 4-year undergraduate colleges and universities producing the most Ph.D.'s in political science and international relations, 1981-1990 ★3045★
Private, 4-year undergraduate colleges and universities producing the most Ph.D.'s in psychology, 1981-1990 ★3067★
Radcliffe Institute for Advanced Study fellowship recipients in the field of religion, 2000-01 ★3092★
Largest benefit packages awarded to presidents at institutions of higher education, 1998-99 ★3133★
Presidents with the highest pay at Baccalaureate I colleges, 1998-99 ★3159★
Average faculty salaries for institutions of higher education in Massachusetts, 2000-01 ★3708★
U.S. liberal arts colleges with the highest paid full professors, 2001 ★3980★
Private, 4-year undergraduate colleges and universities producing the most Ph.D.'s in the sciences, 1920-1990 ★4294★

Private, 4-year undergraduate colleges and universities producing the most Ph.D.'s in the sciences, 1981-1990 ★4295★

Williams; Daniel Hale
Most influential African Americans in medicine and science ★2879★

Williams; David K.
Top pay and benefits for the chief executive and top paid employees at Ripon College ★3459★

Williams; David R.
Top pay and benefits for the chief executive and top paid employees at Lindenwood University ★3375★

Williams; Ford
All-America boys' high school soccer team goalkeepers, 2001 ★167★

Williams; Frank
Top pay and benefits for the chief executive and top paid employees at Hanover College ★3324★

Williams; Gary G.
Top pay and benefits for the chief executive and top paid employees at the University of San Francisco ★3566★

Williams; Gerald B.
Top pay and benefits for the chief executive and top paid employees at William Jewell College ★3630★

Williams High School
Outstanding secondary schools in Greensboro-Winston-Salem-High Point, North Carolina ★4142★

Williams; Janet
Top pay and benefits for the chief executive and top paid employees at Marylhurst University ★3394★

Williams; Jawad
All-America boys' high school basketball 2nd team, 2001 ★162★

Williams; John F.
Top pay and benefits for the chief executive and top paid employees at George Washington University ★3304★

Williams; Lee J.
Top pay and benefits for the chief executive and top paid employees at the University of Saint Thomas in Texas ★3564★

Williams; Leon
All-American boy's high school football linebackers, 2000 ★182★

Williams; Lori Aurelia
Booklist's best first novels for youths ★309★

Williams; Martha E.
Library and information science faculty with the most journal articles, 1993-1998 ★2711★

Williams; Maurice
All-America boys' high school basketball 3rd team, 2001 ★163★

Williams Middle School
Outstanding secondary schools in Charleston-North Charleston, South Carolina ★4106★

Williams; Parham
Top pay and benefits for the chief executive and top paid employees at Chapman University ★3228★

Williams; Peggy R.
Top pay and benefits for the chief executive and top paid employees at Ithaca College ★3351★

Williams; Raymond B.
Top pay and benefits for the chief executive and top paid employees at Wabash College ★3598★

Williams; Reggie
All-American boy's high school football receivers, 2000 ★185★

Williams, R.S.M.; Sister Barbara
Top pay and benefits for the chief executive and top paid employees at Georgian Court College ★3307★

Williams; Shelden
All-America boys' high school basketball 4th team, 2001 ★164★

Williams; Tennessee
Top playwrights of the twentieth century ★4436★

Williams; Warrington
Top pay and benefits for the chief executive and top paid employees at Westminster College in Missouri ★3616★

Williamsburg Technical College
Lowest undergraduate tuition and fees at colleges and universities in South Carolina ★1555★

Williamson Free Public Library
Highest Hennen's American Public Library Ratings for libraries serving a population of 5,000 to 9,999 ★2694★

Williamson Jr.; R. Thomas
Top pay and benefits for the chief executive and top paid employees at Westminster College in Pennsylvania ★3617★

Williamson; O.E.
U.S. academic economists by mean number of citations, 1971-92 ★2176★
U.S. academic economists by total citations, 1971-92 ★2177★

Williamson; Samuel
Top pay and benefits for the chief executive and top paid employees at the University of the South ★3572★

Williston Northampton High School
Outstanding secondary schools in Springfield, Maine ★4233★

Williston State College
State appropriations for North Dakota's institutions of higher education, 2000-01 ★1287★
Lowest undergraduate tuition and fees at colleges and universities in North Dakota ★1542★
Average faculty salaries for institutions of higher education in North Dakota, 2000-01 ★3721★

Willoughby South High School
Outstanding secondary schools in Cleveland-Lorain-Elyria, Ohio ★4114★

Wills Eye Hospital
Top ophthalmology hospitals in the U.S., 2000 ★2796★

Wilmer; Wesley
Top pay and benefits for the chief executive and top paid employees at Biola University ★3203★

Wilmette Junior High School
Illinois schools with the highest 7th grade science scores ★17★
Outstanding secondary schools in Chicago, Illinois ★4110★

Wilmington College
Undergraduate tuition and fees at colleges and universities in Delaware ★1492★
Average faculty salaries for institutions of higher education in Delaware, 2000-01 ★3695★
Average faculty salaries for institutions of higher education in Ohio, 2000-01 ★3722★

Wilmington College (DE)
Presidents with the highest pay at Master's I and II colleges and universities, 1998-99 ★3161★

Wilmington College, New Castle
U.S. colleges and universities awarding the most business management and administrative services master's degrees to African Americans ★1759★

Wilmington, NC
Best 'quirky' places to live ★3083★

Wilson; August
Most influential African Americans in the arts ★78★

Wilson; David T.
Most published authors, adjusted for coauthorship, in the *Journal of Business Research*, 1985 to 1999 ★701★

Wilson; Don
Top pay and benefits for the chief executive and top paid employees at Colorado College ★3249★

Wilson; Jack
Top pay and benefits for the chief executive and top paid employees at Rensselaer Polytechnic Institute ★3455★

Wilson; James Q.
Most cited authors in three criminal justice journals ★1633★
Most-cited scholars in police studies articles/research notes ★2624★

Wilson; John A.
Top pay and benefits for the chief executive and top paid employees at Wake Forest University ★3600★

Wilson; Kelly
All-America girls' high school soccer team forwards, 2001 ★175★

Wilson; Linda
Top pay and benefits for the chief executive and top paid employees at Radcliffe College ★3450★

Wilson-Oyelaran; Eileen
Top pay and benefits for the chief executive and top paid employees at Salem College ★3488★

Wilson; Paul R.
Most-cited scholars in *Australian and New Zealand Journal of Criminology* ★1636★

The Wilson Quarterly
Most selective internships in the U.S., 2001 ★2610★

Wilson; Samuel V.
Top pay and benefits for the chief executive and top paid employees at Hampden-Sydney College ★3321★

Wilson; Sheryl C.
Top pay and benefits for the chief executive and top paid employees at Friends University ★3299★

Wilson Technical Community College
Lowest undergraduate tuition and fees at colleges and universities in North Carolina ★1540★
Average faculty salaries for institutions of higher education without academic ranks in North Carolina, 2000-01 ★3761★

Wimmer; Judith
Top pay and benefits for the chief executive and top paid employees at Edgewood College ★3283★

The Wind Singer
Most notable books for older readers, 2001 ★318★

Windham, NH
America's most wired towns, 2001 ★2575★
Windsor; University of
Canadian comprehensive universities by alumni support, 2000 ★1153★
Canadian comprehensive universities by award-winning faculty members, 2000 ★1154★
Canadian comprehensive universities by class size at the first- and second-year level, 2000 ★1155★
Canadian comprehensive universities by class size at the third- and forth-year level, 2000 ★1156★
Canadian comprehensive universities by classes taught by tenured faculty, 2000 ★1157★
Canadian comprehensive universities by faculty members with Ph.D.'s, 2000 ★1158★
Canadian comprehensive universities by international graduate students, 2000 ★1159★
Canadian comprehensive universities by library acquisitions, 2000 ★1160★
Canadian comprehensive universities by library expenses, 2000 ★1161★
Canadian comprehensive universities by library holdings per student, 2000 ★1162★
Canadian comprehensive universities by operating budget per student, 2000 ★1163★
Canadian comprehensive universities by percentage of operating budget allocated to scholarships, 2000 ★1164★
Canadian comprehensive universities by percentage of operating budget allocated to student services, 2000 ★1165★
Canadian comprehensive universities by social science/humanities grants per faculty member, 2000 ★1166★
Canadian comprehensive universities by students from out of province, 2000 ★1167★
Canadian comprehensive universities by students winning national awards, 2000 ★1168★
Canadian medical/doctoral universities by medical/science grants per faculty member, 2000 ★1183★
Canadian universities chosen as being value added, 2000 ★1216★
Top Canadian comprehensive universities, 2000 ★1219★
Top Canadian comprehensive universities by reputation, 2000 ★1220★
Windward Community College
Average faculty salaries for institutions of higher education in Hawaii, 2000-01 ★3698★
Winfield High School
Outstanding secondary schools in Charleston, West Virginia ★4107★
Winfrey; Oprah
Most influential African Americans in business ★526★
Wing; Edward
Top pay and benefits for the chief executive and top paid employees at Brown University ★3211★
Wingate University
Institutions censured by the American Association of University Professors, 2001 ★1067★
U.S. News & World Report's southern regional liberal arts colleges with the best student/faculty ratios, 2000-01 ★1368★
U.S. News & World Report's southern regional liberal arts colleges with the highest acceptance rates, 2000-01 ★1370★

U.S. News & World Report's southern regional liberal arts colleges with the highest percentage of full-time faculty, 2000-01 ★1374★
U.S. News & World Report's southern regional liberal arts colleges with the highest proportion of classes having 20 students or less, 2000-01 ★1375★
Average faculty salaries for institutions of higher education in North Carolina, 2000-01 ★3720★
Wingood; Harold M.
Top pay and benefits for the chief executive and top paid employees at Clark University ★3238★
Wings
Booklist's most recommended black history books for youth ★311★
Most notable books for middle readers, 2001 ★317★
Outstanding books for young readers, 2000 ★328★
Outstanding children's picture books, 2000 ★331★
The Wings of Merlin
Booklist's most recommended fantasy books for youth ★312★
Winick; Judd
Outstanding children's nonfiction books, 2000 ★330★
Winkelmann; R.K.
Most cited authors in dermatology journals, 1981 to 1996 ★1870★
Winn-Dixie Stores
Business Week's best performing companies with the lowest return on equity, 2000 ★426★
Fortune's highest ranked food and drug stores, 2000 ★463★
Winnie The Pooh Kindergarten
Top selling home education software, 2000 ★1599★
Winnie The Pooh Preschool
Top selling home education software, 2000 ★1599★
Winnie The Pooh Toddler
Top selling home education software, 2000 ★1599★
Winnipeg; University of
Canadian primarily undergraduate universities by alumni support, 2000 ★1193★
Canadian primarily undergraduate universities by award-winning faculty members, 2000 ★1194★
Canadian primarily undergraduate universities by class size at the first and second-year level, 2000 ★1195★
Canadian primarily undergraduate universities by class size at the third and forth-year level, 2000 ★1196★
Canadian primarily undergraduate universities by classes taught by tenured faculty, 2000 ★1197★
Canadian primarily undergraduate universities by faculty members with Ph.D.'s, 2000 ★1198★
Canadian primarily undergraduate universities by library acquisitions, 2000 ★1199★
Canadian primarily undergraduate universities by library expenses, 2000 ★1200★
Canadian primarily undergraduate universities by library holdings per student, 2000 ★1201★
Canadian primarily undergraduate universities by medical/science grants per faculty member, 2000 ★1202★

Canadian primarily undergraduate universities by operating budget per student, 2000 ★1203★
Canadian primarily undergraduate universities by percentage of operating budget allocated to scholarships, 2000 ★1204★
Canadian primarily undergraduate universities by percentage of operating budget allocated to student services, 2000 ★1205★
Canadian primarily undergraduate universities by reputation, 2000 ★1206★
Canadian primarily undergraduate universities by social science/humanities grants per faculty member, 2000 ★1207★
Canadian primarily undergraduate universities by students from out of province, 2000 ★1208★
Canadian primarily undergraduate universities by students winning national awards, 2000 ★1209★
Canadian universities with the lowest total cost, 2000 ★1218★
Top Canadian primarily undergraduate universities, 2000 ★1226★
Winona State University
Average faculty salaries for institutions of higher education in Minnesota, 2000-01 ★3710★
Winschel; Sister Carolyn
Top pay and benefits for the chief executive and top paid employees at LaRoche College ★3364★
Winship; Daniel H.
Top pay and benefits for the chief executive and top paid employees at Loyola University of Chicago ★3382★
Winship; Nancy
Top pay and benefits for the chief executive and top paid employees at Brandeis University ★3209★
Winslow Homer: An American Original
Most notable children's videos, 2001 ★2889★
Outstanding videos for library collections, 2000 ★2892★
Winston Campus Elementary School
Illinois elementary schools with the highest 5th grade writing scores ★15★
Winston Churchill High School
Outstanding secondary schools in Washington, District of Columbia-Maryland-Virginia-West Virginia ★4249★
Winston; Gordon C.
Top pay and benefits for the chief executive and top paid employees at Williams College ★3631★
Winston-Salem State University
Colleges offering the Thurgood Marshall Scholarship Fund ★221★
Retention rates of African American students at historically black institutions, 1997-98 ★1120★
State appropriations for North Carolina's institutions of higher education, 2000-01 ★1286★
Lowest undergraduate tuition and fees at public, 4-year or above colleges and universities ★1466★
Average faculty salaries for institutions of higher education in North Carolina, 2000-01 ★3720★
Winter; David K.
Top pay and benefits for the chief executive and top paid employees at Westmont College ★3619★

Winters; Ronald
Top pay and benefits for the chief executive and top paid employees at Denison University ★3265★

Winthrop University
State appropriations for South Carolina's institutions of higher education, 2000-01 ★1293★
U.S. News & World Report's top public southern regional universities, 2000-01 ★1443★
U.S. colleges and universities awarding the most English language/literature/letters master's degrees to African Americans ★1773★
Average faculty salaries for institutions of higher education in South Carolina, 2000-01 ★3728★

Wireman; Billy O.
Top pay and benefits for the chief executive and top paid employees at Queens College in North Carolina ★3448★

Wirtz; Virginia H.
Top pay and benefits for the chief executive and top paid employees at Edgewood College ★3283★

Wisconsin
Mean composite ACT scores by state, 2000 ★895★
Mean math SAT scores by state, 2000 ★900★
Mean verbal SAT scores by state, 2000 ★903★
States with the highest percentage increase in appropriations for higher education, 2000-01 ★1308★
Total doctorate recipients by state, 1999 ★2054★
Average Hennen's American Public Library Ratings, by state ★2690★
State grades for affordability of higher education for minority students, 2000 ★2883★
State grades for benefits state receives for educating its minority students, 2000 ★2884★
State grades for completion of higher education by minority students, 2000 ★2885★
State grades for participation of minority students in higher education, 2000 ★2886★
State grades for preparing minority students for higher education, 2000 ★2887★
States with the highest per-pupil expenditures ★3996★
States with the most charter schools ★4048★
States with the highest percentage of high school freshmen enrolling in college within four years ★4266★

Wisconsin Alumni Research Foundation, University of Wisconsin, Madison
Most patents issued to universities or research facilities, 1999 ★3097★

Wisconsin, Eau Claire; University of
U.S. News & World Report's midwestern regional universities with the highest percentage of full-time faculty, 2000-01 ★1408★
U.S. News & World Report's midwestern regional universities with the lowest acceptance rates, 2000-01 ★1410★
U.S. News & World Report's top public midwestern regional universities, 2000-01 ★1412★
Average faculty salaries for institutions of higher education in Wisconsin, 2000-01 ★3738★

Wisconsin, Green Bay; University of
Division I NCAA colleges with that graduated less than 20% of their African American male athletes, 1990-91 to 1993-94 ★928★
Division I NCAA colleges with that graduated none of their African American male basketball players, 1990-91 to 1993-94 ★930★
Average faculty salaries for institutions of higher education in Wisconsin, 2000-01 ★3738★

Wisconsin Hospital and Clinics; University of
Top ophthalmology hospitals in the U.S., 2000 ★2796★

Wisconsin Indianhead Technical College
Lowest undergraduate tuition and fees at colleges and universities in Wisconsin ★1571★

Wisconsin, La Crosse; University of
U.S. News & World Report's midwestern regional universities with the lowest acceptance rates, 2000-01 ★1410★
U.S. News & World Report's top public midwestern regional universities, 2000-01 ★1412★
Average faculty salaries for institutions of higher education in Wisconsin, 2000-01 ★3738★

Wisconsin, Madison; University of
Most effective ecology, evolution, and behavior research-doctorate programs as evaluated by the National Research Council ★199★
Top ecology, evolution, and behavior research-doctorate programs as evaluated by the National Research Council ★201★
Most effective biochemistry and molecular biology research-doctorate programs as evaluated by the National Research Council ★205★
Most effective molecular and general genetics research-doctorate programs as evaluated by the National Research Council ★207★
Top biochemistry and molecular biology research-doctorate programs as evaluated by the National Research Council ★209★
Top molecular and general genetics research-doctorate programs as evaluated by the National Research Council ★211★
U.S. universities publishing the most papers in the field of microbiology, 1994-98 ★215★
U.S. universities with the greatest impact in biotechnology and applied microbiology, 1995-99 ★216★
U.S. News & World Report's undergraduate business programs with the best real estate departments, 2000-01 ★570★
U.S. News & World Report's undergraduate business programs with the highest academic reputation scores, 2000-01 ★571★
Top business schools for within-discipline research performance in production/operations management, 1986-1998 ★648★
Top business schools for within-discipline research performance in insurance, international business and real estate, 1986-1998 ★667★
Top business schools for within-discipline research performance in marketing, 1986-1998 ★671★
U.S. News & World Report's universities with the best insurance departments, 1999-2000 ★681★
U.S. colleges and universities reporting the most alcohol related arrests, 1998 ★730★
U.S. colleges and universities with the largest numerical increases in alcohol arrests, 1998 ★733★
U.S. colleges and universities with the largest numerical increases in weapons arrests, 1998 ★735★
Most effective chemistry research-doctorate programs as evaluated by the National Research Council ★802★
Top chemistry research-doctorate programs as evaluated by the National Research Council ★805★
Four-year public institutions enrolling the highest number of students from the District of Columbia, 1998-99 ★855★
Division I NCAA colleges with the highest graduation rates for female basketball players, 1990-91 to 1993-94 ★932★
U.S. colleges and universities where a large portion of the student body drink hard liquor ★992★
U.S. colleges and universities where the general student body puts a strong emphasis on socializing ★1008★
U.S. News & World Report's best public national universities, 2000-01 ★1123★
U.S. News & World Report's national universities with the highest acceptance rates, 2000-01 ★1131★
Institutions receiving the most gifts, 1999-2000 ★1244★
Golden Key Scholar Award winners, 2000 ★1316★
Fiske Guide's best buys for public colleges and universities, 2001 ★1460★
Most effective computer science research-doctorate programs as evaluated by the National Research Council ★1594★
Top computer science research-doctorate programs as evaluated by the National Research Council ★1597★
U.S. universities with the greatest impact in communication, 1995-99 ★1657★
Traditionally white institutions awarding the most first professional degrees to African Americans ★1842★
U.S. colleges and universities awarding the most first professional degrees to Hispanic Americans ★1845★
U.S. colleges and universities awarding the most first professional degrees to Native Americans ★1846★
U.S. colleges and universities awarding the most health professions and related sciences first professional degrees to Native Americans ★1851★
U.S. colleges and universities awarding the most law and legal studies first professional degrees to African Americans ★1852★
Doctorate-granting-institutions awarding the most non-U.S. citizen doctoral degrees, 1999 ★1906★
Top doctorate granting institutions, 1999 ★2047★
U.S. colleges and universities awarding the most doctorate degrees to Hispanic Americans ★2097★
U.S. colleges and universities awarding the most doctorates in all fields, 1999 ★2100★
U.S. colleges and universities awarding the most doctorates in life sciences, 1999 ★2104★
U.S. colleges and universities awarding the most doctorates in physical sciences, mathematics, and computer sciences, 1999 ★2105★
U.S. colleges and universities awarding the most doctorates in social sciences, 1999 ★2107★
U.S. colleges and universities awarding the most education doctorate degrees to Hispanic Americans ★2110★

U.S. colleges and universities awarding the most health professions and related sciences doctorate degrees to Hispanic Americans ★2116★

U.S. institutions awarding the most doctorate degrees, 1999 ★2132★

Top economics research-doctorate programs as evaluated by the National Research Council ★2213★

U.S. universities publishing the most papers in the field of education, 1994-98 ★2219★

U.S. universities with the greatest impact in education, 1995-99 ★2222★

Top graduate engineering schools by reputation, as determined by engineers and recruiters, 2001 ★2368★

Academics' choices for best graduate chemical engineering programs, 2001 ★2386★

Most effective chemical engineering research-doctorate programs as evaluated by the National Research Council ★2389★

Top chemical engineering research-doctorate programs as evaluated by the National Research Council ★2390★

U.S. News & World Report's graduate engineering programs with the best chemical departments, 2000-01 ★2392★

U.S. universities with the greatest impact in chemical engineering, 1994-98 ★2393★

Academics' choices for best graduate industrial/manufacturing engineering programs, 2001 ★2411★

Most effective industrial engineering research-doctorate programs as evaluated by the National Research Council ★2412★

Top industrial engineering research-doctorate programs as evaluated by the National Research Council ★2413★

Top materials science research-doctorate programs as evaluated by the National Research Council ★2419★

Academics' choices for best graduate nuclear engineering schools, 2000 ★2426★

U.S. News & World Report's graduate engineering programs with the best nuclear departments, 2000-01 ★2428★

Research institutions with the highest enrollment of foreign students, 1998-99 ★2503★

U.S. research institutions with the largest number of students studying abroad, 1998-99 ★2514★

Top French language and literature research-doctorate programs as evaluated by the National Research Council ★2516★

Faculty's scholarly reputation in the Ph.D.-granting departments of geography, 1925-1982 ★2518★

Most effective geography research-doctorate programs as evaluated by the National Research Council ★2519★

Top geography research-doctorate programs as evaluated by the National Research Council ★2520★

Most effective German language and literature research-doctorate programs as evaluated by the National Research Council ★2527★

Top German language and literature research-doctorate programs as evaluated by the National Research Council ★2528★

Top history research-doctorate programs as evaluated by the National Research Council ★2554★

Law schools with the best law and social science plus psychology and sociology faculty, 1999-2000 ★2659★

Law schools with the best legal ethics, professional responsibility, and legal profession faculty, 1999-2000 ★2660★

U.S. universities publishing the most papers in the field of communication, 1994-98 ★2755★

Degrees granted in the ten largest doctoral journalism and mass communications programs, 1999 ★2756★

Enrollment of students in the ten largest doctoral journalism and mass communications programs, 1999 ★2762★

Top mathematics research-doctorate programs as evaluated by the National Research Council ★2778★

Most effective statistics and biostatistics research-doctorate programs as evaluated by the National Research Council ★2780★

Top statistics and biostatistics research-doctorate programs as evaluated by the National Research Council ★2782★

Top primary-care medical schools by reputation, as determined by academic personnel, 2001 ★2857★

Institutions in the Worker Rights Consortium ★2913★

Top pharmacology research-doctorate programs as evaluated by the National Research Council ★2939★

U.S. universities publishing the most papers in the field of philosophy, 1995-99 ★2948★

U.S. universities with the greatest impact in astrophysics, 1994-98 ★2979★

Most effective astrophysics and astronomy research-doctorate programs as evaluated by the National Research Council ★3006★

Top astrophysics and astronomy research-doctorate programs as evaluated by the National Research Council ★3014★

Most effective political science research-doctorate programs as evaluated by the National Research Council ★3043★

Top political science research-doctorate programs as evaluated by the National Research Council ★3046★

Top psychology research-doctorate programs as evaluated by the National Research Council ★3068★

U.S. colleges and universities spending the most on chemical engineering research and development, 1998 ★3098★

U.S. colleges and universities spending the most on chemical research and development, 1998 ★3099★

U.S. colleges and universities with the most federal support for chemical engineering research and development, 1998 ★3101★

U.S. universities spending the most on research and development, 1998 ★3104★

Institutions receiving the most federal research and development expenditures, 1999 ★3105★

Average faculty salaries for institutions of higher education in Wisconsin, 2000-01 ★3738★

U.S. universities publishing the most papers in the field of food science/nutrition, 1994-98 ★4286★

U.S. universities publishing the most papers in the field of sociology and anthropology, 1994-98 ★4349★

U.S. universities publishing the most papers in the fields of sociology and anthropology, 1993-97 ★4350★

Most effective sociology research-doctorate programs as evaluated by the National Research Council ★4352★

Top sociology research-doctorate programs as evaluated by the National Research Council ★4354★

Most effective Spanish and Portuguese language and literature research-doctorate programs as evaluated by the National Research Council ★4357★

Top Spanish and Portuguese language and literature research-doctorate programs as evaluated by the National Research Council ★4358★

Academics' choices for best administration/supervision graduate programs, 2001 ★4378★

Academics' choices for best counseling/personnel services graduate programs, 2001 ★4379★

Academics' choices for best curriculum/instruction graduate programs, 2001 ★4380★

Academics' choices for best education policy graduate programs, 2001 ★4381★

Academics' choices for best educational psychology graduate programs, 2001 ★4382★

Academics' choices for best elementary education graduate programs, 2001 ★4383★

Academics' choices for best secondary education graduate programs, 2001 ★4385★

Academics' choices for best special education graduate programs, 2001 ★4386★

Academics' choices for best vocational/technical graduate programs, 2001 ★4387★

Acceptance rates at *U.S. News & World Report*'s top 10 graduate education schools, 2001 ★4388★

Average quantitative GRE scores for *U.S. News & World Report*'s top 10 graduate education schools, 2001 ★4389★

Average verbal GRE scores for *U.S. News & World Report*'s top 10 graduate education schools, 2001 ★4390★

Doctoral students to faculty ratio at *U.S. News & World Report*'s top 10 graduate education schools, 2001 ★4391★

Ph.D.s and Ed.D.s granted at *U.S. News & World Report*'s top 10 graduate education schools, 2001 ★4392★

Research expenditures for *U.S. News & World Report*'s top 10 graduate education schools, 2001 ★4393★

Research expenditures per faculty member at *U.S. News & World Report*'s top 10 graduate education schools, 2001 ★4394★

Top graduate education schools, 2001 ★4395★

Top graduate education schools by reputation, as determined by academic personnel, 2001 ★4396★

Top graduate education schools by reputation, as determined by superintendents, 2001 ★4397★

U.S. universities publishing the most papers in the field of performing arts, 1994-98 ★4437★

U.S. universities with the greatest impact in veterinary medicine, 1995-99 ★4440★

Wisconsin, Milwaukee; University of

Division I NCAA colleges with that graduated less than 20% of their African American male athletes, 1990-91 to 1993-94 ★928★

Division I NCAA colleges with that graduated none of their African American male basketball players, 1990-91 to 1993-94 ★930★

WISCONSIN

Library and information science programs with the most journal articles, 1993-1998 ★2713★

Library and information science programs with the most journal articles per capita, 1993-1998 ★2714★

Average faculty salaries for institutions of higher education in Wisconsin, 2000-01 ★3738★

Wisconsin, Oshkosh; University of
U.S. colleges and universities with the largest numerical increases in weapons arrests, 1998 ★735★

Average faculty salaries for institutions of higher education in Wisconsin, 2000-01 ★3738★

Wisconsin, Parkside; University of
U.S. News & World Report's midwestern regional universities with students least in debt, 1999 ★1399★

Average faculty salaries for institutions of higher education in Wisconsin, 2000-01 ★3738★

Wisconsin, Platteville; University of
U.S. News & World Report's midwestern regional universities with students least in debt, 1999 ★1399★

U.S. News & World Report's undergraduate engineering programs with the best industrial manufacturing departments, 2000-01 ★2380★

Average faculty salaries for institutions of higher education in Wisconsin, 2000-01 ★3738★

Wisconsin, River Falls; University of
Average faculty salaries for institutions of higher education in Wisconsin, 2000-01 ★3738★

Wisconsin, Stevens Point; University of
U.S. News & World Report's midwestern regional universities with the highest percentage of full-time faculty, 2000-01 ★1408★

U.S. News & World Report's midwestern regional universities with the lowest acceptance rates, 2000-01 ★1410★

U.S. News & World Report's top public midwestern regional universities, 2000-01 ★1412★

Institutions in the Worker Rights Consortium ★2913★

Average faculty salaries for institutions of higher education in Wisconsin, 2000-01 ★3738★

Wisconsin, Stout; University of
Average faculty salaries for institutions of higher education in Wisconsin, 2000-01 ★3738★

Wisconsin, Superior; University of
Average faculty salaries for institutions of higher education in Wisconsin, 2000-01 ★3738★

Wisconsin System; University of
State appropriations for Wisconsin's institutions of higher education, 2000-01 ★1302★

Institutions receiving the largest Energy Department research grants, 2000 ★3111★

Wisconsin Tech System
State appropriations for Wisconsin's institutions of higher education, 2000-01 ★1302★

Wisconsin; University of
Women's Division I track and field programs with the most outdoor championships ★149★

Degree-granting institutions with the most published pages in *The Journal of Risk and Insurance*, 1987-1996 ★678★

Employing institutions with the most published pages in *The Journal of Risk and Insurance*, 1987-1996 ★679★

U.S. colleges and universities awarding the most health professions and related sciences doctorate degrees to Asian Americans ★2115★

Economics departments by number of citations by top economists, 1971-92 ★2158★

Economics departments by number of citations per top economist, 1971-92 ★2159★

Economics departments by number of top economists, 1971-92 ★2160★

Institutions generating the most economic education research text, 1963-1990 ★2167★

Institutions most frequently contributing to the *American Economic Review* from 1911-1990 ★2168★

Institutions most frequently contributing to the *American Economic Review* from 1951-1990 ★2169★

Economics Ph.D. programs by number of citations of top economist graduates, 1971-92 ★2204★

Economics Ph.D. programs by number of citations per top economist graduate, 1971-92 ★2205★

Economics Ph.D. programs by number of top economist graduates, 1971-92 ★2206★

Origin of doctorate for economics faculty at Ph.D.-granting institutions ★2209★

Origin of doctorate for economics faculty at Ph.D.-granting institutions, by Ph.D. equivalents produced ★2210★

Top Ph.D.-granting departments of geography from 1925-1982 ★2521★

Top university research libraries in the U.S. and Canada, 1998-99 ★2706★

Institutions with the most prolific communication studies researchers ★2749★

Wisconsin, Whitewater; University of
Colleges and universities with the smallest endowments, 2000 ★1238★

U.S. News & World Report's top public midwestern regional universities, 2000-01 ★1412★

Average faculty salaries for institutions of higher education in Wisconsin, 2000-01 ★3738★

Wise; Christa
All-USA Teacher Teams, Second Team, 2000 ★4400★

Wiser; James
Top pay and benefits for the chief executive and top paid employees at the University of San Francisco ★3566★

The Witches
Most frequently banned books in the 1990s ★745★

People for the American Way's list of most frequently challenged books, 1982-1992 ★747★

People for the American Way's list of most frequently challenged books, 1991-1992 ★748★

Witches, Pumpkins, and Grinning Ghosts: The Story of the Halloween Symbols
Most frequently banned books in the 1990s ★745★

The Witches of Worm
Most frequently banned books in the 1990s ★745★

With Love and Prayers
Christopher Awards winners for adult literature, 2000 ★235★

Witt Industries
Oldest women-owned companies ★4454★

Wittenberg University
Highest undergraduate tuition and fees at colleges and universities in Ohio ★1543★

Average faculty salaries for institutions of higher education in Ohio, 2000-01 ★3722★

Wm. Wrigley Jr.
Top food companies in Standard & Poor's 500, 2001 ★540★

Woest; James
Top pay and benefits for the chief executive and top paid employees at Hope International University ★3340★

Wofford College
Division I NCAA colleges with that graduated more than 80% of their African American male athletes, 1990-91 to 1993-94 ★929★

Division I NCAA colleges with the highest graduation rates for female athletes, 1990-91 to 1993-94 ★931★

Division I NCAA colleges with the highest graduation rates for female basketball players, 1990-91 to 1993-94 ★932★

Division I NCAA colleges with the highest graduation rates for football players, 1990-91 to 1993-94 ★933★

Division I NCAA colleges with the highest graduation rates for male basketball players, 1990-91 to 1993-94 ★935★

U.S. colleges and universities least accepting of alternative lifestyles ★985★

U.S. colleges and universities with a large student body of conservative Republicans ★1016★

U.S. colleges and universities with the best financial aid programs ★1030★

Highest undergraduate tuition and fees at colleges and universities in South Carolina ★1554★

Average faculty salaries for institutions of higher education in South Carolina, 2000-01 ★3728★

Woglom; G.
Top full professor economists at elite liberal arts colleges, 1975-94 ★2175★

Wolf; Mary Alice
Top pay and benefits for the chief executive and top paid employees at Saint Joseph College in Connecticut ★3475★

Wolfe; D.A.
Most cited authors in the journal *Journal of Interpersonal Violence*, 1990 to 1995 ★1627★

Wolfe; Tom
Best U.S. works of journalism in the 20th century ★2769★

Wolff; K.
Most cited authors in dermatology journals, 1981 to 1996 ★1870★

Wolff; Mark
Top pay and benefits for the chief executive and top paid employees at Saint Thomas University in Florida ★3486★

Wolff; Nicole
All-America girls' high school basketball 3rd team, 2001 ★172★

Wolfgang; Marvin E.
Most cited authors in three criminal justice journals ★1633★

Most cited authors in three criminology journals ★1634★

Wolfram; Dietmar
Library and information science faculty with the most journal articles, 1993-1998 ★2711★